Congress and the Nation

VOLUME XI · 2001–2004

POLITICS AND POLICY IN THE 107TH AND 108TH CONGRESSES

D0002257

CQ PRESS

A Division of Congressional Quarterly Inc.
Washington, D.C.

CQ Press
1255 22nd Street, NW, Suite 400
Washington, DC 20037

Phone: 202-729-1900; toll-free, 1-866-427-7737
(1-866-4CQ-PRESS)

Web: www.cqpress.com

Cover design: Jeff Miles Hall, ION Graphic Design Works

Cover photo: Interior of the Rotunda of the U.S. Capitol with statue
of George Washington. *Andrew Prokos*

♾ The paper used in this publication exceeds the requirements of
the American National Standard for Information Sciences—
Permanence of Paper for Printed Library Materials,
ANSI Z39.48-1992.

Printed and bound in the United States of America

10   09   08   07   06   1   2   3   4   5

ISBN: 1-56802-850-4
ISSN: 1047-1324

Editors' Note

Congress and the Nation Vol. XI presents a record of major governmental developments during the first term of President George W. Bush, from 2001 through 2004. This four-year period—from his inauguration after the controversial 2000 election that left Republicans and Democrats bitterly divided through his reelection in 2004—was one of the most tumultuous in modern times.

The defining event of the period—an event certain to echo throughout U.S. domestic and foreign policy long after Bush leaves office—was the attack of September 11, 2001, by a group of nineteen men who commandeered four commercial jetliners and flew two into the World Trade Center towers in New York City, destroying them, and another into the Pentagon outside Washington, D.C., causing extensive damage. The fourth crashed in a rural area of Pennsylvania after the passengers, apparently aware of what had already happened on the East Coast, overpowered the hijackers. That airliner was thought to be headed for the U.S. Capitol. Nearly 3,000 persons died that day.

Sept. 11 changed entirely the complexion of the Bush administration, which launched, in the president's words, "a war on terror." The conflict was one of global proportions against a shadowy enemy driven by a reading of Islam that demonized the West, particularly the United States, and lay outside the traditional historic teachings of that religion. The response of the United States and other nations that experienced related terrorism proved complicated because, unlike in earlier wars, they had not been attacked by a "state," as a nation is traditionally understood. The nonstate nature of the enemy presented new challenges for the West.

In the immediate aftermath of the attacks on U.S. soil, bipartisanship characterized the support shown the president. Support for his policies carried into the new year, but the bipartisan atmosphere in Washington and the nation evaporated as the 2002 midterm elections approached. The president and his allies in Congress pursued an aggressive domestic and foreign policy agenda, much of it rooted in a conservative political ideology and a muscular approach to U.S. interests and options throughout the world. The Republican administration repeatedly cited the war on terror as justification for many of its most ambitious proposals, including U.S. military intervention abroad, a vast new homeland security department, the far-reaching USA PATRIOT Act (which critics argued unnecessarily jeopardized civil liberties), and expansive claims of executive privilege concerning the sharing of information with Congress and detention of individuals allegedly associated with terrorism. Democrats and a few Republicans, however, found their voice to criticize much of the administration's agenda. By the end of Bush's first term, the bitter and divisive political conditions rivaled those of the Vietnam war years, the Watergate scandal that drove President Richard Nixon from office, and the impeachment of President Bill Clinton in his last years in the White House.

The Sept. 11 attacks gave rise to two wars: one in Afghanistan—whose leaders tolerated and received support from al Qaeda's presence there—and the other in Iraq, ostensibly over the issue of weapons of mass destruction. The former received wide support because al Qaeda operated from Afghan territory and had established training camps there. The Iraq war was an entirely different matter, coloring Bush's presidency for the remainder of his first term and into his second. Bush ordered the United States to war—a "preventive" one of choice on the grounds that Iraqi president Saddam Hussein was developing and that Iraq probably already possessed weapons of mass destruction, including chemical and biological agents and nuclear devices. Critics noted that the war represented a major departure from past U.S. policy. That shift, and the Bush administration's assertion that the U.S. government essentially be the sole arbiter of when such a war should occur, strained relations with many long-standing U.S. allies, especially in Europe. The invasion of Iraq, which Congress had endorsed, quickly toppled Hussein's government, but produced an unstable nation plagued by an insurgency that adopted wide-scale indiscriminate killings of soldiers and civilians as a tactic.

The Bush administration based the invasion on its thesis that the United States had the power, justification, and responsibility to act preemptively against nations with weapons of mass destruction that could be used against Americans or U.S. interests or otherwise posed a threat to the country. Bush offered as another justification for the war the contention that Hussein might provide his alleged weapons to terrorists. Yet another justification relied on a view of the world, particularly the Middle East, that nations, once freed from the control of dictators, would embrace democracy and democratic institutions, in time producing stability and peace where neither had thrived before. Bush provided these shifting rationales as circumstances demanded—when it looked increasingly likely that no weapons would be found, and none were, and when Hussein was shown not to be linked to al Qaeda or its leader, Osama bin Laden.

Although the war, with its many justifications, initially garnered widespread support in the United States, skepticism grew as the conflict dragged on and as other nations continued to reject the Bush administration's aggressive foreign policy. The ongoing violence and instability in Iraq fueled this skepticism, as did the mounting evidence that the administration had carefully planned and well executed a war to oust Hussein, but had failed to plan for administering postwar Iraq. As doubts spread among Americans, Bush's approval ratings began to fall significantly. They reached a point near the end of his term at which Democrats, sensing that he might be vulnerable in the 2004 campaign, began to feel more comfortable criticizing his administration.

The increasingly unpopular war in Iraq represented only one source of the growing partisan divide of the period. In Congress, the Republicans forged ahead with a disciplined effort, primarily in the House, to push the GOP and White House agenda with little or no regard for participation by the Democrats. The party divisions in both chambers essentially mirrored the national political divide witnessed in the 2000 election returns. Unlike Republicans in the Senate, the Republicans in the House held a majority throughout Bush's first four years. Their disciplined leaders and cohesive rank and file excluded the Democrats from any meaningful participation in the legislative process. In defending their tactics, Republicans recalled that they had had little say during the decades that Democrats controlled the House. Regardless, the Republicans' approach produced results. In the House, they passed much of the GOP agenda, although sometimes only by arm-twisting and increasingly by using rarely seen tactics, such as late-night sessions. Some important votes occurred in the early hours of the day, and in one instance, the GOP leadership held open a roll call vote for hours while they rounded up enough votes for passage. These tactics contributed significantly to increasing partisan bitterness.

Matters were less auspicious for the Republicans in the Senate. In another remarkable event of the period, the 107th Congress convened with the Senate evenly split at 50–50. Vice President Dick Cheney, by virtue of his constitutional authority to break ties, gave Republicans control of the chamber. In June 2001, disaffected GOP senator James M. Jeffords of Vermont left the party to become an independent and to caucus with the Democrats. With a one-vote majority, Democrats took control of the Senate and all its committees. This development, as much as any, thwarted the disciplined effort in the House to push through the GOP agenda. Stalemate hampered much of the remainder of the 107th Congress, although some bills passed, such as the legislation that emerged in the aftermath of Sept. 11 and a bipartisan education bill.

Taking control of both chambers at the 2002 midterm elections, Republicans handed Bush some high-profile victories in its first session, but by the second session, with the 2004 elections approaching, they accomplished little. A notable exception was the sweeping overhaul of the nation's intelligence apparatus following an investigation into the Sept. 11 attacks.

One of the more interesting developments of the four-year period, and one with likely repercussions for years to come, was the evolution of the Republican Party from a traditional bastion of fiscal rectitude and advocate of limited federal government to almost the opposite. The party's apparent disregard of the combined effect of large tax cuts (often enacted with Democratic support) and vastly expanded government outlays epitomized this transformation. This outlook had sent the federal budget into deficit by fiscal 2002 after several years of surplus. Although much of the increased spending went to the military and for homeland defense, some kept afloat such programs as farm subsidies that budget hawks argued were unwise given the government's financial constraints. Passage of Bush's proposal for a prescription drug program for senior citizens, enacted at the end of 2003, highlighted the GOP's deviation from its traditional underpinnings. Projections predicted the program's ultimate cost ballooning into hundreds of billions of dollars. Conservative commentators scathingly debunked it as a huge entitlement antithetical to GOP principles.

Congress and the Nation Vol. XI records this period to help students, researchers, scholars, and others track its major events. In addition to discussing the successes and travails of President Bush, this volume focuses heavily on the legislative activities of the U.S. Congress and its members. In telling this story, the editors include the political, social, economic, electoral, and other significant trends that influenced the action of Congress's 535 members as well as the president. The chapters touch on earlier events as needed in addition to presenting detailed chronologies of congressional action in major areas.

Chapter 1, "Politics and National Issues," provides an overview of the period and its principal players. It features a legislative summary of each session of the 107th and 108th Congresses and discussion of the elections held during this period. The chapter forms a framework for the legislative chapters that follow. The concluding chapter, 16, focuses on the Bush presidency. These two chapters together outline the more detailed material in the other chapters.

Chapters 2 through 14, focusing on public policy, provide details on legislative issues, proposals, and bills; accounts of legislative and executive actions; lobbying activity; and key votes on selected issues. "Homeland Security Policy," chapter 3, is a new addition to this series. Chapter 15 examines Congress as an institution.

The book continues a series launched by Congressional Quarterly in 1965 with the publication of *Congress and the Nation Vol. I*, a 2,000-page reference covering national government and politics from 1945 through 1964. Each succeeding volume covers governmental action during a four-year presidential term: *Congress and the Nation Vol. II*, 1965–1968; *Congress and the Nation Vol. III*, 1969–1972; *Congress and the Nation Vol. IV*, 1973–1976; *Congress and the Nation Vol. V*, 1977–1980; *Congress and the Nation Vol. VI*, 1981–1984; *Congress and the Nation Vol. VII*, 1985–1988; *Congress and the Nation Vol. VIII*, 1989–1992; *Congress and the Nation Vol. IX*, 1993–1996; and *Congress and the Nation Vol. X*, 1997–2001. With the publication of this volume, librarians, historians, political scientists, journalists, and students have for research eleven volumes spanning more than half a century of Congressional Quarterly's reporting on national government, elections, and public policy.

HOW TO USE THIS BOOK

The **Summary Table of Contents** following this Editors' Note presents the overall organization of the volume. The detailed **Table of Contents** (p. xi) provides an outline of each chapter and is followed by a list of the many tables, figures, and boxed features in the book. To find a specific topic within a chapter, the reader should consult the **Index** *(p. 1085)*. Throughout the book, cross-references are provided to related subjects in other chapters (and to other volumes of *Congress and the Nation* for historical context). Such references speed research across an array of subjects and are particularly useful because Congress often legislates bills that cover a number of topics or that affect related topics.

The **Appendix** *(p. 765)* contains a variety of supplementary materials, including a glossary of congressional terms; an explanation of how a bill becomes law; key Senate and House votes (highlighted in boldface in the legislative chapters), with charts showing how each member voted; lists of committee and subcommittee chairs; biographical data on members of Congress between 2001 and 2005; profiles of cabinet members and other senior officials; controversial nominations; presidential vetoes; and major presidential speeches and messages to Congress as well as other important documents. In addition, the appendix includes extensive charts—including presidential, House, Senate, and gubernatorial election returns for the period—and tables record special elections and members who switched parties. The appendix also includes a complete list of public laws enacted during the four years.

This volume was prepared under the direction of editors at CQ Press, a division of Congressional Quarterly Inc. A group of veteran *Congress and the Nation* authors, many of whom covered Congress for Congressional Quarterly and other Washington news organizations, prepared and edited the chapters and appendix. The principal contributors were John Felton, Martha Gottron, David Hosansky, Ken Jost, Kerry Kern, Colleen McGuiness, Ann O'Connor, Julie Rovner, and David Tarr, who also served as volume editor for this edition. Special appreciation is due to two staff members of the Congressional Research Service at the Library of Congress: Judy Schneider reviewed, corrected, and expanded the glossary of congressional terms in the appendix, and Walter Oleszek reviewed and edited the explanation of the legislative process, also in the appendix.

At CQ Press, Tim Arnquist and January Layman-Wood provided invaluable research on committees, trends in government spending, and other issues, and Layman-Wood ably shepherded the manuscript through review and compilation before forwarding to the editing and production team. Sally A. Ryman effectively brought the material together during production. Indexing Partners LLC compiled the index. Doug Goldenberg-Hart was the sponsoring editor.

CQ Press editors also wish to express their thanks to the dedicated reporters and editors of the *CQ Weekly* and *CQ Almanac* for their assistance.

CQ Press Editors
March 2006

Summary Table of Contents

Contents

Tables, Figures, and Boxes

Congress and the Nation

CHAPTER 1

Politics and National Issues

Politics and National Issues

Uncertainty and insecurity were defining characteristics of U.S. politics during the first term of the presidency of George W. Bush. The uncertainty resulted largely from an economic recession that lasted just a few months, according to the statisticians, but lingered for years in the minds of millions of ordinary Americans. Insecurity suddenly became a factor in American life—for the first time in decades—following the Sept. 11, 2001, terrorist attacks that killed nearly 3,000 people on the East Coast, demonstrated the country's vulnerability, and led to massive U.S. military invasions of Afghanistan and Iraq.

Bush and Congress struggled to confront and even benefit from the uncertainty and insecurity, sometimes successfully, sometimes not. At least in the short term, Bush and his fellow Republicans on Capitol Hill gained the most politically from the events of the four tumultuous years: in 2004 Bush won a second term and the Republicans consolidated their control of Congress. Democrats again found themselves out of power in Washington and with no realistic strategy for regaining it anytime soon.

Even setting the Sept. 11 attacks aside, Bush's first term was destined to be a turbulent period because of the manner in which Bush entered office. The hotly disputed election of 2000—resolved only after the controversial intervention of the Supreme Court—gave Bush the presidency but not complete political legitimacy in the eyes of many Democrats. Bush's reported decision to govern as if he had a solid political mandate planted further seeds of political discord, seeds that quickly developed into some of the most bitter partisanship seen in Washington in decades. The politicians who governed the nation were deeply polarized at the beginning of Bush's term, briefly overcame that polarization in the wake of the Sept. 11 attacks, but then sank into even deeper polarization at the end of the term.

That polarization in the nation's capital was reflected in the nation as a whole, with about three-fifths of the voters split almost evenly between the two major parties. Perhaps more telling, the remaining two-fifths were not affiliated with either major party. Millions of other Americans simply opted out of the political process altogether.

With the electorate divided and the parties closely balanced in Congress, political leaders on both sides gave into

Sen. James M. Jeffords of Vermont holds a press conference in Burlington, Vt., on May 24, 2001, to announce that he is leaving the Republican Party to become an independent. Jeffords's move gave control of the Senate to the Democrats for the rest of the 107th Congress.
Source: AP/Wide World Photos/Stephan Savoia

the temptation to play up differences and avoid finding commonalities in hope of tipping the electorate their way. Although bipartisan majorities pulled together to support the president after the Sept. 11 attacks and on some specific domestic issues, they fell apart again and again over most domestic matters, particularly those involving questions on the role of government.

If the 2004 elections demonstrated anything, it was that partisanship likely would continue because leaders of both parties still saw more short-term benefit from confrontation than cooperation. Bush and Republicans held onto power by portraying Democrats as weak on moral values and national security matters; their goal of consolidating power for the future required sustaining that combative approach indefinitely. For their part, Democrats saw little reason to cooperate with a president who, they believed, was attempting to impose a right-wing agenda on a generally centrist country.

Ironically, this us-versus-them attitude by the leaders of both parties offered a degree of leverage, in some cases, to a political species long thought extinct in Washington: moderate Republicans. One moderate Republican, Vermont senator James Jeffords, threw Washington into upheaval and for a period gave Democrats control of the Senate by abandoning his party in mid-2001. A handful of other moderate Republicans helped put the brakes on some initiatives offered by Bush and the conservative House and Senate leaders. Whether these moderates would continue to exercise a similar degree of leverage was a major question at the outset of Bush's second term.

UNSETTLING CIRCUMSTANCES

The politics of Bush's first term played out against an extraordinary array of circumstances, as nearly a decade of economic prosperity and relative peace in the 1990s turned into a period of both domestic and international tumult.

By far the most unsettling events were the Sept. 11 terrorist attacks and the American response that followed, including the invasion of Afghanistan to hunt down Osama bin Laden and his extremist al Qaeda network that had perpetrated the attacks, the loosening of civil liberties safeguards in favor of national security concerns, and the March 2003 invasion of Iraq. By 2004 the trauma of the Sept. 11 attacks had been supplanted, at least in part, by new uncertainties about U.S. involvement in Iraq. Bush's rationale for invading Iraq and ousting its government—that Iraq was harboring illegal weapons of mass destruction and might give them to terrorists—was found to be faulty when U.S. inspectors could not find any of the weapons. At the end of Bush's first term, more than 130,000 U.S. service personnel remained in Iraq with the twin assignments of shoring up a new Iraqi government and fighting a fast-growing anti-U.S. insurgency.

Almost as unsettling as these events was the bumpy course of the national economy. The economy was already beginning to slump before Bush entered the White House, in large part because of the early-2000 bursting of a bubble in the high-technology industry, which had fueled much of the expansion of the 1990s. The economy tipped into mild recession after the terrorist attacks. Although the economy started to grow again later in 2001, relatively few new jobs were created over the next three years and thousands of workers who had been laid off remained out of work or underemployed.

Many workers viewed this economic expansion as a "jobless recovery"—a recovery on paper and perhaps on some companies' bottom lines but not one that was reflected in more jobs or pay raises. At Bush's urging, Congress enacted three major personal income tax cuts—in 2001, 2003, and 2004. Bush said the cuts would spur personal savings and business investment, and in the 2004 campaign he said that goal had been accomplished. Democrats insisted the tax cuts had little impact on economic growth and, instead, had merely rewarded Bush's wealthy constituency.

Starting with the bankruptcy in December 2001 of Enron—a giant energy company built largely on creative accounting—the nation also was rocked by a series of revelations of corruption at several of America's largest companies. WorldCom, Tyco, Adelphia, and dozens of other companies—including many of the country's largest insurance companies and mutual funds—were found to have engaged in deceptive accounting practices or even outright fraud. The scandals resulted in bankruptcies, criminal and civil charges against a lengthy list of corporate executives, and the loss of pensions and investment savings to thousands of Americans—many of whom had already lost retirement savings in the wake of the stock market bust of 1999–2000. Thousands of workers also lost their jobs when their companies failed. Congress and regulators responded in 2002 with tougher standards on business behavior, but by 2004 business groups were mounting campaigns to undo the new regulations.

The federal government had its own accounting problem during the Bush years. When Bush took office, the federal budget was showing a healthy surplus. But the recession, the three major tax cuts, and the substantial spending on the wars in Afghanistan and Iraq turned the surplus into the highest federal budget deficit (measured in dollars) in its history: $412 billion in fiscal 2004. Measured as a portion of the gross domestic product, however, the deficit for fiscal 2004 was 3.6 percent, historically, the mid-range for past federal budget deficits.

The country's trade deficit, however, reached historic highs measured both in dollars ($617 billion in 2004) and as a share of gross domestic product (5.3 percent). Worried politicians (including some Republicans) and economists (at times including even Federal Reserve Board chairman Alan Greenspan) warned of potential economic disaster if the country did not take action to bring its indebtedness under control. A notable feature of this deficit was that much of it was financed by foreigners, including the governments of China and Japan, whose long-term willingness to continue their lending was a matter of some speculation.

JOCKEYING FOR CONTROL

Few if any of these problems were anticipated when Bush entered office in January 2001. Instead attention was focused on whether the new president could claim enough legitimacy to govern effectively. Bush had lost the popular vote in November 2000 to the Democratic candidate, Vice President

Al Gore, but won the electoral vote after the Supreme Court ruled, five to four, against a recount of the disputed vote in Florida. The five-week-long constitutional crisis left many Americans with a bitter taste in their mouths, but once in office Bush forged ahead to carry out his campaign promises, particularly a massive reduction in individual income taxes.

The 107th Congress, which also took office in January 2001, was about as narrowly divided as a Congress could be. Republicans held only a nine-vote majority over the Democrats in the House of Representatives, and the Senate was tied fifty-fifty, with Republicans in nominal control because of Vice President Dick Cheney's status as presiding officer of the Senate with the power to cast tie-breaking votes. After eight years of chafing under Democratic president Bill Clinton (1993–2001) who had been able to block much of their legislative agenda, the Republicans seized their opportunity to pass the deepest tax cut enacted in two decades. Congress also began to work on Bush's other major domestic priority—an overhaul of federal education aid known as "No Child Left Behind." A compromise version of that measure, which conditioned continued federal aid to schools on their ability to improve all their students' reading and math scores, was completed at the end of the year with strong bipartisan support.

Republican control of the Senate lasted only six months, however. Objecting to the GOP's taxing and spending priorities, Jeffords of Vermont left the party in June to become an independent but caucusing with the Democrats, giving control of the Senate to the Democrats for the rest of the Congress. Suddenly Democrats, led by Tom Daschle of South Dakota, controlled the agenda in the Senate and could keep Republican priorities from reaching the floor. For the next three months—until the Sept. 11 attacks—Congress was largely in stalemate, as Senate Democrats rebuffed both their Republican colleagues and the Republican president. The Sept. 11 attacks gave Bush and his Republican allies the upper hand on some matters. Casting himself as a "wartime" president who needed united support, Bush easily won approval for measures he said were needed to fight terrorists. The new unity did not extend to all matters, however, as Senate Democrats continued to block many of Bush's domestic priorities, including an overhaul of federal energy policy and an expansion of the role of faith-based groups in providing federally funded social services.

In 2003 Republicans once again controlled both chambers of Congress, winning a few more seats in the House and regaining the Senate in the fall 2002 elections. In the Senate the lineup was fifty-one Republicans, forty-eight Democrats, and one independent, Jeffords, who usually voted with the Democrats. Much of the credit for the Republican victory was given to Bush, who campaigned nearly nonstop for GOP candidates in close races in the weeks running up to the Nov. 5 election. It was an extraordinary use of the political capital that he had accumulated after Sept. 11, and he won the enthusiastic loyalty of many Republicans on Capitol Hill. But Democrats were left deeply angry, not least because of a successful White House–engineered campaign to defeat Georgia senator Max Cleland (a highly-decorated, disabled Vietnam war veteran) by casting doubt on his patriotism. The 2002 campaign thus gave Democrats a grudge comparable to the one held by Republicans since the Jeffords defection a year earlier—setting the tone of partisan negativity that was to prevail during much of the remainder of Bush's first term.

When the 108th Congress convened in January 2003, Senate Republicans had a new leader: Bill Frist, of Tennessee, who was in only his second term. Frist had emerged quickly as a consensus candidate after the previous Republican leader, Trent Lott of Mississippi, was forced to step down because of impolitic remarks about civil rights. Frist brought a partisan edge to his leadership post, one that was matched point-for-point by Tom Daschle, the Democratic leader now back in the minority. As had many of their predecessors, both men regularly used Senate rules for partisan advantage: Frist controlling the flow of legislation to the floor, Daschle engineering filibusters to block some Republican legislative priorities and a select number of Bush's judicial appointments viewed by Democrats as too conservative.

The House remained under the firm control of Republicans, who appeared determined to keep Democrats powerless as the minority. To a degree not seen since the days of all-powerful Speakers in the late nineteenth and early twentieth centuries, the Republican leadership blocked nearly all significant Democratic amendments in committees and on the floor and even excluded Democrats from key conference committee negotiations. Speaker J. Dennis Hastert, of Illinois, had held his position unchallenged since 1999, but much of the real political power in the House was exercised by the controversial majority leader, Tom DeLay of Texas, who had built loyalty among his colleagues with contributions to their campaigns and a fierce determination to get his way, as signified by his nickname, "The Hammer." DeLay was plagued by several charges of ethical misbehavior and was even admonished by the Ethics Committee in 2004 for threatening retaliation against a fellow Republican unless he voted the way DeLay wanted on 2003 legislation adding prescription drug coverage to the Medicare program. Democrats attempted to paint DeLay as a corrupt, excessively partisan dictator—the same caricature they had successfully mounted in 1998 against then-Speaker Newt Gingrich, of Georgia. But DeLay lacked Gingrich's stature as the man who had put Republicans in charge of the House and was less useful to Democrats as a partisan foil.

PERVASIVE PARTISANSHIP

Except for a brief period after the Sept. 11 terrorist attacks, partisanship was the dominant fact of life on Capitol Hill during the first term of George W. Bush. In fact, the unity of purpose after Sept. 11—as the nation geared up for what Bush called a global war against terrorism—served to highlight the degree of partisanship on many other matters.

In the Senate, partisan disagreements about tax and spending priorities kept the annual budget resolution from coming to the floor in 2002. It was only the second time since the current budget law was enacted in 1974 that Congress had failed to complete action on its budget resolution. In 2004 Congress again failed to complete action on a budget resolution, this time because a handful of Senate Republican moderates insisted that any new tax cuts or entitlement spending be offset by revenue increases or spending cuts. In part because of the budget resolution disputes, the appropriations process was in disarray for much of the four years. In 2002 Congress was unable to clear eleven of the thirteen regular spending bills and had to package them into an omnibus measure that was not cleared until February 2003. Omnibus measures were also required in 2003 and 2004.

In the 108th Congress, passing legislation took second place to building "brand identity" that could be used in the tightly contested presidential and congressional elections. Republicans and Democrats used the machinery of Congress not so much to achieve legislative aims as to polish their images with voters and try to distinguish themselves from the competition.

For the Republicans the goal was to reinforce the message of the 2004 campaign: that the Republican Party was best able to keep America secure and would revive the economy by keeping taxes low and government unobtrusive. Republicans also blocked several Democratic initiatives that would have benefited labor, such as a hike in the minimum wage. While congressional Democrats often found themselves unable to shape the legislative agenda, they could block or deflect—Republicans would derisively say "obstruct"—GOP initiatives to make the point that Democrats would focus on lowering the deficit, would use more targeted tax cuts, and would more freely use government to protect consumers, workers, and the environment.

Democrats were able to block enactment of several presidential priorities, either because of narrow legislative disagreements or because neither party was willing to, or forced to, compromise. Among the most important of these measures were the president's proposal for overhauling federal energy policy (which failed primarily because of a dispute between Gulf State and Northeastern legislators over motor vehicle fuel additives); a long-pending rewrite of federal bankruptcy law (which died because of an unrelated controversy over abortion); and legislation that would cap noneconomic damages on medical malpractice suits. Bush may have gotten more mileage out of Congress's failure to pass the medical malpractice measure than he would have if it had been passed: on the campaign trail in 2004, he regularly blamed the Democrats for blocking the legislation, which he claimed would help reduce high health care costs.

Congress also was unable to reach compromise on reauthorizations of several major federal programs, including welfare programs, highway and mass transit laws, the Head Start program for low-income children, and vocational and technical education programs. As a result, across the board and across the country, federal programs were drifting into a policy limbo.

Delays in reauthorizations seldom threatened federal funding. Appropriators generally continued to allocate money for programs based on the policies in the expired authorizations, or Congress extended the expiring authorizations without altering policy. But the authorization impasse deprived Congress of a chance to apply meaningful oversight to important and expansive programs, and, in the opinion of critics, it led to piecemeal policymaking. Because so few renewal bills were passing through Congress, legislators were adding more and more policy riders to appropriations bills where they did not receive the same attention as they would if they had been submitted to the committee hearing and markup process that generally accompanied reauthorizations.

Despite the pervasive partisanship, Congress did pass several of the president's top priorities. These tended to be measures that either had broad popular support (for example, the two measures passed in 2001 and 2003 reducing individual tax cuts by $1.7 trillion over several years, and legislation providing prescription drug benefits for seniors under the Medicare program), or in which both sides were uncommonly willing to compromise (the "No Child Left Behind" education reform law).

The Medicare prescription drug bill (PL 108-173), passed in November 2003, illustrated both the perils of partisanship during the Bush years and what could be accomplished when both parties saw advantage in reaching consensus. Keeping a promise from his 2000 campaign, Bush put forth a proposal adding a limited prescription drug benefit to Medicare. The proposal faced strong opposition from the right, which viewed it as a major new federal program, and the left, which viewed it as failing to meet the needs of low-income senior citizens. To attract votes from both Democrats and Republicans, congressional leaders loaded the bill with special interest provisions, the most important of which were of direct benefit to the pharmaceutical industry. Only later did it become known that the Bush administration withheld from Congress an internal estimate that the bill was estimated to cost at least $536 billion over ten years—substantially more than the $400 billion price tag Congress was working with. In the end, members of both parties supported, with varying degrees of enthusiasm, a major piece of legislation that ran contrary to their basic philosophies: Republicans backed the largest new entitlement program since the underlying Medicare program was created in 1965, and Democrats backed new subsidies and other special provisions for the pharmaceutical industry.

Two other forces also trumped partisanship during Bush's first term in office. In 2002 legislators demonstrated that a closely divided Congress could pass even controversial legislation if there was a scandal strong enough to make inaction politically impossible. Democrats won GOP support for criminal penalties in accounting overhaul legislation largely because Republicans knew they could not oppose such an idea in the heat of the corporate corruption scandal. That same year supporters of campaign finance reform were able to push a bill to passage because many members of both parties had benefited from political donations by the bankrupt Enron Corporation, and they wanted to distance themselves from the scandal.

Legislators also were often able to reach agreement on spending bill "earmarks" that doled out federal spending to programs in individual members' districts. By one estimate, the fiscal 2004 omnibus appropriations bill contained nearly 8,000 so-called earmarks at a cost of almost $11 billion. Perhaps the most egregious example was the corporate tax bill passed just weeks before the 2004 elections. The measure, referred to as "Miss Piggy" by its chief House sponsor, made $137 billion in corporate tax cuts, including many tailored to fit specific industries, and even specific companies.

A SHIFT TO THE RIGHT?

Depending on one's viewpoint, the 2004 elections were either a solid mandate for the president and Republican Party or evidence that the country was still deeply divided, albeit perhaps leaning more toward the conservative side of the spectrum.

Guided by his political mentor, Karl Rove, Bush waged an extraordinarily focused campaign that put his accomplishments in the most positive light possible and that planted seeds of doubt in the voters' minds about the character of the Democratic candidate John Kerry of Massachusetts. Kerry was unable to shake off GOP charges that he had flip-flopped on the Iraq war and other issues, or that he had embellished his military record in the Vietnam war. Ultimately, Kerry was unable to persuade the voters that he, not George W. Bush, would be the stronger leader in the fight against terror.

Voter turnout was key to Bush's victory. With record numbers of voters going to the polls, Kerry and the Democrats turned out 8 million more Democratic votes in 2004 than did Al Gore in 2000. But Bush won 11.5 million more votes in 2004 than he had in 2000, giving him a 3 million vote lead over Kerry. Many analysts credited voter anger over gay marriage with turning out enough social conservative voters to give Bush the edge, particularly in the key state of Ohio, where Bush defeated Kerry with just 118,601 votes and clinched the electoral college victory.

Bush's victory was firmly rooted in the South, which he carried by some 6 million votes. The South was also kind to congressional Republicans, particularly in Texas, where a controversial redistricting plan engineered by Tom DeLay resulted in the turnover of five Democratic House seats to Republicans. The GOP also picked up all five Senate seats left open by retiring Democratic incumbents. The most stunning congressional victory for the GOP, however, came not in the South but in South Dakota, where voters turned out Senate Democratic leader Tom Daschle.

Much of the immediate commentary after the election focused on exit polling showing that "moral values" was a major factor in the turnout, and the prominence of the Christian right and other social conservatives in Washington political life appeared to be growing. But whether the election results reflected a permanent move of the electorate to the right remained to be seen. As political analyst Rhodes Cook observed, without the South, John Kerry would be president and Democrats would control both chambers of Congress. Whether the Republicans are able to solidify their hold on the White House and Congress in the 2006 and 2008 elections could well depend on events as unforeseen in 2004 as the Sept. 11 attacks were in 2000.

2001

The Legislative Year

Upheaval is the word that might best describe the first session of the 107th Congress that began in January 2001. The year opened with Republicans in control of the White House and both chambers of Congress—barely. George W. Bush, put in office by a 5–4 vote of the Supreme Court after a disputed election in 2000, had an uncertain mandate to govern. Republicans controlled the Senate by a single vote and the House by only a few votes more.

In the Senate, divided evenly between Democrats and Republicans, Vice President Dick Cheney, with his power to cast tie-breaking votes, became the most valuable player on Capitol Hill. But it only lasted for half a year. In late May the Capitol was stunned by the decision of Republican senator James M. Jeffords of Vermont to become an independent and vote with the Democratic caucus. Suddenly, mild-mannered Sen. Tom Daschle, Democrat of South Dakota, ascended to power as the majority leader, erasing from the agenda such GOP priorities as allowing faith-based groups to receive federal funding to run federal social programs and overhauling the bankruptcy code. Providing patients new rights in disagreements with their health plans and raising the minimum wage moved to the forefront. *(Jeffords's explanation text, p. 956)*

Just as Congress was adjusting to the newly divided government, its agenda was turned upside down once again, this time by the Sept. 11 terrorist attacks that brought down the two World Trade Center towers in New York City, devastated a wing of the Pentagon in suburban Washington, and killed nearly three thousand people. All the earlier debates suddenly seemed trivial, if not irrelevant.

After a day of frantic uncertainty and near paralysis, lawmakers regrouped, replacing debates over domestic issues with newly urgent debates on antiterrorism, a war in Afghanistan, and the need to bolster domestic security. Those tasks were further complicated when the economy slid into a mild recession and four years of budget surpluses slipped into deficits. Congress itself was threatened when anthrax spores arrived in the mail on Capitol Hill, shutting down offices and forcing aides to work from their bedrooms.

"This is a session of Congress without historical precedent," said congressional scholar Thomas Mann of the Brookings Institution. "Agendas changed as radically as I have ever seen them change."

NEWFOUND MANDATE

If 2001 was a year of upheaval for Congress it was also a year of uncertainty and upheaval for the American public. After the Sept. 11 attacks citizens looked to Washington to restore security. The federal government mattered again to Americans. How Congress was dealing with the attacks was

In a show of unity, House and Senate lawmakers from both parties gather for a vigil in the Capitol Rotunda on September 12, 2001, a day after the attacks on the World Trade Center and the Pentagon. *Source: Congressional Quarterly/Scott J. Ferrell*

reported on the six o'clock news and that in turn had a profound effect on lawmakers, who realized that constituents were carefully following their response to the attacks.

Suddenly, from a body whose only major action so far had been passage of President Bush's $1.4 trillion tax cut, legislation to combat terrorism poured forth. On Sept. 14, just three days after the attacks, Congress passed two measures, one authorizing the use of force against terrorists and the other appropriating $40 billion in emergency supplemental spending to help pay for the war on terror and to begin to clean up after the attacks. On Oct. 7 Bush and British prime minister Tony Blair announced the start of military operations against the Taliban regime in Afghanistan and against the al Qaeda terrorist network it harbored. *(Legislation details, p. 56, 234)*

Ten days after the Sept. 11 attacks Congress cleared a $15 billion bill to help airlines recover from the two days when all airports were closed as well as from the subsequent slump in air travel. With the White House putting top priority on building a global coalition to back its fight against terrorism, House GOP leaders dropped their objections to a bill releasing $582 million in back dues to the United Nations. The bill, which had been held up since February, cleared Sept. 24.

One of the most sweeping responses to the attacks cleared with little public debate. Despite misgivings over the possible impact on civil liberties, both chambers overwhelmingly agreed to give Attorney General John Ashcroft wide new authority to track, arrest, and prosecute suspected terrorists. The USA PATRIOT Act, whose implementation was highly controversial, included authority for the government to obtain nationwide search warrants and "roving" wiretaps," to conduct secret searches of suspects' property, and to detain immigrants indefinitely if they were viewed as national

CONGRESS IN 2001

The first session of the 107th Congress convened at noon on Jan. 3, 2001, and closed at 10:06 p.m. EST on Dec. 20, when the Senate adjourned *sine die*. The House had adjourned *sine die* at 5:08 p.m. the same day. The session stretched over 352 days. The Senate met on 173 days, for a total of 1,236 hours. The House met on 142 days, for a total of 922 hours.

There were 6,530 bills and resolutions introduced during the 2001 session, compared with 4,247 in 2000 and 6,593 in 1999. Congress cleared 136 bills in 2001 that were signed into public law, the lowest number since 1995, when 88 cleared bills were signed into law. President Bush did not issue any vetoes. *(Public laws, table, p. 14; presidential vetoes, p. 931)*

During 2001, the House took 507 recorded votes, 93 fewer than the 600 taken in 2000. The Senate took 380 recorded votes, 82 more than in 2000. (Totals do not include quorum calls.) *(Recorded votes table, p. 16)*

security threats. The measure also strengthened money-laundering laws. *(USA PATRIOT Act, p. 187)*

The legislation that took longest to pass was a measure strengthening security at the nation's airports and assigning responsibility for screening passengers and baggage to the federal government. The White House and House Republicans leaders opposed federalizing the airport security workforce but finally gave way in the face of public demand and unanimous support for it in the Senate. *(Aviation security, p. 198)*

The newfound spirit of cooperation following the attacks extended beyond anti-terrorist legislation to domestic legislation that before Sept. 11 was caught in partisan squabbles. Congress finished all thirteen regular spending bills, many without the policy battles of previous years. It came together to complete the first overhaul of federal aid to elementary and secondary school since the 1960s. Even the controversial fast-track trade legislation overcame its main hurdle of winning passage in the House and appeared likely to become law in 2002. *(Education bill, p. 540)*

REALITIES OF SIMPLE MATHEMATICS

The bills approved were all significant legislation. But if numbers were the basis for judging a legislative session, the first year of the 107th Congress won no awards for productivity. Excluding the naming of buildings and designations of special awareness days, Congress produced a third fewer laws than it had during the first year of President Bill Clinton's administration in 1993.

Beyond the terrorism-related legislation, the vast majority of the two parties' priorities remained unfulfilled. An over-

haul of campaign finance rules, a rewriting of federal bankruptcy law, a patients' bill of rights, a major farm bill, and public funding for programs operated by faith-based organizations had all withered. The crusade at the beginning of the year to eradicate "hanging chads" and reform the election process lost momentum even though memories of the confused 2000 presidential contest remained strong. Moreover, by year's end the two parties could not bridge their ideological divide to create a stimulus package to address a rapidly deteriorating economy.

Behind the stalemate was simple mathematics. With the Senate so closely divided between the two parties, neither side could amass the sixty votes needed to break a filibuster, which any senator could and frequently did use to block legislation. During the first part of the year the two parties could not even agree on rules to send legislation to conference, which blocked resolution of differences between Senate and House. Senate Democrats wanted equal representation on conference committees. Republicans, who with Cheney's vote controlled the chamber, wanted a one-set numeric edge. Nothing went to conference until Jeffords's switch broke the stalemate. In the end, Democrats won a one-seat majority. (Under Senate procedures, only the budget resolution and the tax package were exempt from the standoff.)

Stalemate continued elsewhere, however. Immediately after taking control, for example, Daschle muscled a patients' rights bill through the Senate, but the House later passed a substantially different version. As a result the legislation never emerged from conference. The two sides also fought vigorously over energy policy, an election overhaul, and an expansive farm bill. Campaign finance passed the Senate only to collapse in the House in wrangles over procedure.

The only two substantive pieces of domestic legislation, tax cuts and education, escaped stalemate in different ways. With Bush's ambitious tax plan, the administration successfully picked off enough centrist Democrats to support the bill. Senatorial procedures protected tax bills from attack by filibuster, removing the impediment that killed other legislation in the Senate during the year. With budget surpluses still a reality at the start of the year, Democrats had difficulty making a persuasive case that tax cuts would be harmful. Even House Democratic Leader Richard A. Gephardt of Missouri agreed that there would be a tax cut; the only issue was its magnitude.

Education traveled a different, less contentious path, buoyed to passage at year's end by an even broader bipartisan consensus than the tax bill had enjoyed. It was also a priority for Bush, but one from which he was willing to drop the most controversial element: distributing school vouchers. With that issue out of the picture, Democrats eagerly supported a bill that authorized substantially increased spending on education. (They would complain loudly in later years when Bush refused to request full funding for his own "No Child Left Behind" program.)

CONGRESSIONAL LEADERSHIP 2001–2005

107th Congress

Senate (until June 6, 2001)*

President Pro Tempore: Strom Thurmond, R-S.C.**
Majority Leader: Trent Lott, R-Miss.
Majority Whip: Don Nickles, R-Okla.
Republican Conference Chair: Rick Santorum, R-Pa.
Republican Conference Secretary: Kay Bailey Hutchison,
   R-Texas

Minority Leader: Tom Daschle, D-S.D.
Minority Whip: Harry Reid, D-Nev.
Democratic Conference Secretary: Barbara A. Mikulski,
   D-Md.

House

Speaker: J. Dennis Hastert, R-Ill.
Majority Leader: Dick Armey, R-Texas
Majority Whip: Tom DeLay, R-Texas
Chair of the Republican Conference: J.C. Watts,
   R-Okla.

Minority Leader: Richard A. Gephardt, D-Mo.
Minority Whip: David E. Bonior, D-Mich.
Chair of the Democratic Caucus: Martin Frost, Texas

108th Congress

Senate

President Pro Tempore: Ted Stevens, R-Alaska
Majority Leader: Bill Frist, R-Tenn.
Majority Whip: Mitch McConnell, R-Ky.
Republican Conference Chair: Rick Santorum, R-Pa.
Republican Conference Vice Chair: Kay Bailey Hutchison,
   R-Texas

Minority Leader: Tom Daschle, D-S.D.
Minority Whip: Harry Reid, D-Nev.
Democratic Conference Secretary: Barbara A. Mikulski,
   D-Md.

House

Speaker: J. Dennis Hastert, R-Ill.
Majority Leader: Tom DeLay, R-Texas
Majority Whip: Roy Blunt, R-Mo.
Chair of the Republican Conference: Deborah Pryce,
   R-Ohio

Minority Leader: Nancy Pelosi, D-Calif.
Minority Whip: Steny H. Hoyer, D-Md.,
Chair of the Democratic Caucus: Robert Menendez, N.J.

---

   * The Senate that convened at the beginning of 2001 was split 50–50 as a result of the 2000 general elections, with Republicans in control by virtue of Vice President Richard B. Cheney's tie-breaking vote as president of the Senate. On June 6, James M. Jeffords left the Republican Party to become an independent but caucusing with the Democrats. This switch gave control of the Senate to the Democrats. Daschle and the other Democratic leaders then became the majority, while Lott and the other Republican leaders became the minority. Republicans regained control of the Senate at the start of the 108th Congress in 2003 as a result of the 2002 general elections. (Jeffords switch, pp. 3, 8)

   ** Thurmond was succeeded by Robert C. Byrd, D-WVa., when party control of the Senate changed on June 6, 2001.

UNDER THE CLOAK OF PATRIOTISM

After Sept. 11 lawmakers were under strong pressure to stand by the president, even voting for measures they might otherwise find distasteful or contradictory to their political ideology. Democrats found themselves supporting measures to expand police authority even as civil liberties groups cautioned against it. Republicans grudgingly supported the Democratic plan to put the government, rather than the private sector, in charge of stepped-up passenger screening at the nation's airports.

Some political tactics were deemed outright inappropriate after Sept. 11. When Democrats slowed the process of reporting presidential nominations out of committee to the Senate floor, Republican leader Trent Lott of Mississippi responded by stalling action on appropriations bills. After the attacks Lott dropped the maneuver to avoid accusations of holding up funding for the government at a time of acute need. (In another sign that Congress was returning to its normal partisan stalemate, Lott tried the trick again in the last two days of the session, holding up the final spending bill to force a few more confirmations.)

Other issues wholly unrelated to the terror attacks received a boost from patriotic pressures. The House GOP urged passage of the fast-track trade bill as an American duty to support the president in a time of war, helping to carry the bill to passage in that chamber. But the appeal to patriotism did not always work. Those who wanted to open Alaska's Arctic National Wildlife Refuge to oil drilling argued that the United States more than ever needed to reduce dependency on foreign petroleum. Supporters of the farm bill called that legislation a way to ensure "food security." Neither bill cleared in the first session. *(Trade bill, p. 150; oil drilling, p. 417, 432)*

BUSH'S STYLE

The first session of the 107th Congress, in 2001, also revealed much about how Bush would work with Congress to achieve his legislative agenda. He typically began by outlining his desires in broad terms or principles, rather than offering detailed legislative language. Then after achieving what he considered to be the best outcome he could get, he declared victory, even when some of his original principles were scrapped or ideas ignored.

For example, Bush asked for a $1.6 trillion tax cut, settled for $290 billion less, and still was able too claim credit for the deepest tax cut in two decades. He asked for an education bill and signaled that everything was negotiable except annual testing in reading and math. By the time the final bill was assembled, annual testing was about all that remained of his original plan. Bush hailed the outcome as a "great symbol of what is possible in Washington when good people come together to do what's right."

The most sobering lesson of the first session, however, was that a narrowly divided Senate and House was not the answer for the bipartisan cooperation the public said it wanted from lawmakers. Leaders of both parties said the near tie in the 2000 elections was a mandate for cooperation. But the effect was just the opposite. With control of the House and Senate within reach for either side in 2002, the parties spent most of their energy trying to satisfy their political bases.

With the notable exception of the education bill, and much of the legislation that passed in response to the Sept. 11 attacks, rarely was there a discernible effort to build solid and unshakable support on both sides of the aisle. The story of 2001 was the persistent effort of both parties to peel away just enough votes from the other side to squeeze out a victory. Sometimes the strategy paid off; other times it failed or led only to fleeting victory. Either way, it was a strategy neither side was able to resist. And all signed pointed to even greater partisanship in the second session, as the elections approached and the memories of Sept. 11 receded.

The Political Year

There were no changes in the Senate in 2001 (with the exception of Jeffords switching his party designation from Republican to Independent). In the House, however, seven special elections were required to fill seats of members who died or resigned. Gubernatorial elections were also held in two states, New Jersey and Virginia.

House Special Elections

The first special election of the year was held to fill the seat left vacant by the resignation of E. G. "Bud" Shuster, Republican of Pennsylvania, the chair of the House Transportation and Infrastructure Committee. Shuster cited health reasons for his resignation, which was announced in February. He had won reelection to a fourteenth term in November,

less than a month after the House Ethics Committee had reprimanded him for violations of House rules, citing his ties to campaign donors and his business relationship with a former aide. The seat was won May 15 by Shuster's son Bill, a car dealership owner, amid charges that Shuster had deliberately timed his resignation to give an edge to his son. The younger Shuster defeated Democrat H. Scott Conklin by a margin of 52 percent to 44 percent. *(Shuster reprimand, Congress and the Nation Vol. X, p. 771; changes table, p. 877)*

Democrat Diane Watson, a former state senator and ambassador to Micronesia under Bill Clinton, was elected on June 5 to fill the California House seat left vacant by the death of Julian C. Dixon, who died in December 2000. Dixon was first elected in 1978. Watson defeated Republican Noel Irwin Hentschel with 75 percent of the vote in the heavily Democratic Los Angeles district.

On June 19 J. Randy Forbes, a Republican state senator, defeated a Democratic state senator, L. Louise Lucas, to win the Virginia House seat left empty with the death of Norman Sisisky, a popular moderate Democrat who was serving his tenth term in the House when he died unexpectedly some weeks after undergoing surgery for cancer. Forbes won 52 percent of the vote, and Republicans immediately hailed the victory as a harbinger for the 2002 mid-term elections. Of the seven special elections in 2001, this was the only one where there was a party change.

Another popular House member, Joe Moakley, Democrat of Massachusetts, died of leukemia on May 28. His seat was easily won by Stephen F. Lynch, a Democratic state senator, who defeated Republican state senator Jo Ann Sprague on Oct. 16. Lynch won 65 percent of the vote. In a separate election on Oct. 16, Republican Jeff Miller, a representative in the Florida legislature, won 66 percent of the vote to take the seat vacated by Republican Joe Scarborough, who resigned on Sept. 6 for personal reasons.

Republican Asa Hutchinson of Arkansas resigned his House seat in August after being confirmed as administrator of the Drug Enforcement Administration. The vacant seat was filled in a Nov. 20 special election by John Boozman, also a Republican. Boozman, an optometrist, won with 56 percent of the vote.

The last special election of the year was held on Dec. 18, to fill the seat left vacant by the death of South Carolina Republican Floyd Spence. The seat was won by Republican Joe Wilson, a state senator who stressed his ties to Spence. Wilson won 73 percent of the vote against Brent Weaver, a state banking regulator and former executive director of the state Democratic party.

Gubernatorial Races

In the two governor's races, Democrats won seats that had been held by Republicans. In New Jersey James E. McGreevey handily defeated Bret Schundler, former mayor of Jersey City. McGreevey replaced Donald T. diFrancesco, who had become acting governor after Christine Todd Whitman resigned the position to join the Bush administration as head of the Environmental Protection Agency. McGreevey had narrowly lost a direct challenge to Whitman in the 1997 gubernatorial election. Once viewed by many as a rising star in Democratic circles, McGreevey resigned the governorship in November 2004 after announcing earlier in the year that he was gay and had had an adulterous affair with a man. McGreevey was married with two children. McGreevey's tenure had also been marred after two Democratic fundraisers in the state were indicted on federal charges of extortion and tampering with witnesses.

In Virginia, venture capitalist Mark Warner became the first Democrat to sit in the governor's office since 1989. Warner beat former state attorney general Mark Earley to replace Republican James S. Gilmore, who was barred by state law from seeking another term. Warner won 50 percent of the vote to Earley's 48 percent.

2002

The Legislative Year

The war on terror and the impending invasion of Iraq dominated Congress in 2002 just as it dominated the nightly news. Driven by the specter that Iraq had weapons of mass destruction that its leader Saddam Hussein might use against the United States, Israel, or other countries or give to terrorist organizations such as al Qaeda, Congress authorized President George W. Bush to take military action against the country. The resolution encouraged Bush to seek the support of the United Nations first, but it authorized the United States to go to war against Iraq with or without U.N. approval.

Congress also spent much of the year debating and finally passing legislation to create a cabinet-level Department of Homeland Security. The new department, the biggest reorganization of the federal government since World War II, combined all or part of twenty-two agencies under one roof to coordinate counterterrorism efforts. *(Homeland security, p. 171)*

Underlying virtually every action taken by Congress was the political struggle for control of the Senate, where the change of just one seat in the November elections threatened to shift the majority from the Democrats to the Republicans. With fifty Democrats, forty-nine Republicans, and one independent, the margin of control was so close that nearly every issue before the Senate provoked a fight.

That struggle slowed the Senate even more than usual. Republicans sought to paint Majority Leader Tom Daschle, D-S.D., as an obstructionist and incompetent leader; Daschle resorted to stronger legislative tactics to keep the chamber's focus on Democratic priorities within his caucus. House Republicans pushed through several measures designed more to inoculate themselves from political attack and turn up the heat on Daschle than to be signed into law.

Bush, bolstered by strong public approval of his handling of the war on terrorism, accused Democrats of delaying passage of the homeland security bill—originally a Democratic initiative. The popular president also campaigned for GOP candidates in the crucial two weeks before the November election, a gamble that helped Republicans win back the Senate and extend their margin in the House.

WAR AND HOMELAND SECURITY

From the moment Bush entered the House chamber Jan. 29 to deliver his first official State of the Union address, it was clear that domestic issues would have a hard time competing with the war on terrorism and anything that could be linked to it. Bush spent the first half of his speech promising to continue the fight against al Qaeda and other terrorist groups, make Americans more secure at home, and keep "regimes that sponsor terror" from threatening the United States or its allies. In a phrase that marked a new focus on countries his administration saw as growing threats, Bush singled out Iraq, Iran, and North Korea as an "axis of evil" that was "arming to threaten the peace of the world."

With the nation in an economic slump, however, Bush also promised "economic security" for Americans. "My budget supports three great goals for America," he said. "We will win this war [against terrorism], we will protect our homeland, and we will revive our economy."

Protecting the homeland became the leitmotif of the second session. Congress did not actively begin debating the measure creating the Homeland Security Department until the middle of the year, and then it almost fell victim to a partisan standoff over personnel policy. But after Republicans swept the Nov. 5 elections, Senate moderates in both parties moved to give the GOP the votes necessary for Bush to win all the authority he had requested.

The other part of Bush's doctrine for preventing new attacks in the United States—preemptive strikes against nations that could use weapons of mass destruction or pass them on to terrorists—led to a divisive debate over whether to go to war with Iraq. The Bush administration initially argued that previous congressional and United Nations resolutions gave it all the authority it needed to invade if Iraqi leader Saddam Hussein continued to defy commitments he had made in April 1991, after the Persian Gulf War, to dismantle his nuclear, chemical, and biological weapons programs.

Many lawmakers on both sides of the aisle, envisioning a preemptive war that could last for years, were unwilling to buy that argument. On Sept. 4 Bush conceded, announcing

---

CONGRESS IN 2002

The second session of the 107th Congress convened at noon on Jan. 23, 2002, and closed at 2:23 p.m. on Nov. 22, when the House adjourned *sine die*. The Senate had adjourned *sine die* two days earlier, on Nov. 20 at 6:12 p.m. The session lasted 304 days. The Senate met on 149 days, for a total of 1,043 hours; the House met on 123 days, for a total of 772 hours.

A total of 4,269 bills and resolutions were introduced, compared with 6,530 in 2001 and 4,247 in 2000. Congress cleared 241 bills that were signed into public law, compared with 136 in 2001 and 410 in 2000. For the second year in a row, President Bush did not issue any vetoes. *(Public laws table, p. 14; presidential vetoes, p. 931)*

During 2002, the House took 483 recorded votes, 24 fewer than in 2001. The Senate took 253 recorded votes, 127 fewer than in 2000. (Totals do not include quorum calls.) *(Recorded votes, table, p. 17)*

Number of Public Laws Enacted, 1975–2004

Year	Public Laws	Year	Public Laws
1975	205	1990	410
1976	383	1991	243
1977	223	1992	347
1978	410	1993	210
1979	187	1994	255
1980	426	1995	88
1981	145	1996	245
1982	328	1997	153
1983	215	1998	241
1984	408	1999	170
1985	240	2000	410
1986	424	2001	136
1987	242	2002	241
1988	471	2003	198
1989	240	2004	300

that he would seek congressional approval before launching any military strikes against Iraq. The ensuing debate turned on such questions as whether Bush should be required to form an international coalition to share in the military action, whether he should be authorized to launch a preemptive strike, how broad the goals of the war should be, and how much oversight Congress should exercise.

After negotiating with congressional leaders of both parties, the Bush administration agreed to limit any military strikes to Iraq and to invoke the 1973 War Powers Act, which limited the president's ability to wage war without congressional oversight. Bush flatly refused, however, to agree to any language that would require him to get permission from other countries before launching military actions that he believed were necessary to protect U.S. security. The resolution giving the president broad authority to decide whether and when to go to war against Iraq passed easily in both chambers in mid-October, just weeks before the midterm elections, where foreign policy issues tended to favor GOP candidates. *(Iraq war, pp. 231, 238)*

OTHER ACCOMPLISHMENTS

In addition to passing the homeland security bill and the Iraq war resolution, Congress took several other steps in 2002 to shore up national security. Against the initial objections of the Bush administration, it created an independent commission to investigate the Sept. 11 attacks to locate the gaps that allowed the attacks to occur. Congress passed legislation to strengthen the security of the nation's seaports and oil and natural gas pipelines, gave airline pilots permission to carry guns in cockpits, and created a federal terrorism insurance program to protect commercial property and insurance companies in case of terrorist attacks.

On other fronts, lawmakers sought to calm the anger many Americans felt at corporate scandals such as the collapse of Enron Corp. and WorldCom Inc., both fueled by accounting fraud, that forced massive layoffs, devastated work-

ers' retirement savings, and added to the stock market turmoil that was playing havoc with the finances of millions of Americans. That public anger led to the passage of a corporate accountability bill tougher than many members of Congress thought possible, including new rules for accounting firms, new disclosure and conflict-of-interest rules for publicly traded firms, and stronger penalties for securities fraud.

The collapse of Enron led indirectly to passage of a major overhaul of the nation's campaign finance laws. The legislation had been stalled for seven years by Senate filibusters and other setbacks. But the Enron bankruptcy at the end of 2001 exposed the energy trader's network of political giving and influence and triggered a panic among both Democrats and Republicans who sought to distance themselves from uncomfortable questions about their campaign fundraising.

In other major action lawmakers granted fast-track trade negotiating authority to Bush, agreeing to take straight up-or-down votes on his trade agreements without the possibility of amendment. Congress had denied the authority to Bush's predecessor, Bill Clinton. Congress also passed a six-year farm bill that reversed a 1996 policy of limiting federal price supports. And lawmakers responded to the turmoil of the 2000 presidential election by creating new standards for federal elections and authorizing $3.9 billion in grants to the states over three years to meet those standards.

UNFINISHED BUSINESS

But the 107th Congress also left a long list of unfinished business, allowing some of the biggest domestic initiatives to fall victim to politics. For only the second time since the modern budget process had been put in place, Congress failed to pass a budget resolution. The resolution bogged down in the Senate where fiscally conservative Democrats said it placed too little emphasis on reducing the federal debt, while liberals complained that it did not promise enough for social programs. Partly because of that failure, Congress adjourned Nov. 22 without completing one of its fundamental tasks: It left all eleven of the fiscal 2003 nondefense appropriations bills unfinished, putting the job off to the next Congress.

Congress was also unable to agree on a means to jumpstart the lackluster economy. Carrying over an argument that had been raging since the end of the first session, Republicans wanted to pass broad tax relief for individuals and businesses, including acceleration of Bush's ten-year $1.4 trillion tax cut package enacted in 2001. Democrats wanted to extend unemployment benefits and spend more on infrastructure and homeland security. In the end lawmakers settled on a compromise that packaged a thirteen-week extension of jobless benefits with a few tax breaks to help businesses recover from the Sept. 11 terrorist attacks. Late in the year stimulus efforts faded altogether when Congress failed to pass a further unemployment benefits extension.

Divided over how to modify the 1996 welfare overhaul, which expired on Sept. 30, Congress left it to run on autopilot through annual appropriations. Lawmakers were unable to reauthorize the 1975 Individuals with Disabilities Education Act, also because of disagreements over how much the law should be rewritten. Differences over how much to spend on prescription drug coverage and whether it should be provided through Medicare or the private sector left that agenda item unfinished as well. Efforts to create a national energy policy stalled over such issues as how to restructure the electricity market and whether to allow oil and gas exploration in Alaska's Arctic National Wildlife Refuge.

President Bush failed to win congressional approval for his initiative to increase aid to faith-based social programs, a top priority left over from his presidential campaign. Democrats worried that the initiative would lead to subsidized religious discrimination. Like the previous two Congresses, the 107th was unable to agree on a patients' rights bill after a long-standing dispute over the right to sue managed-care plans proved fatal to the entire effort. And, for the third time in as many Congresses, members tried but failed to bring a bankruptcy overhaul bill to enactment.

DEPARTURES

Congress mourned the death of two liberal icons in 2002. Democratic Rep. Patsy T. Mink of Hawaii, first elected to the House in 1964 and nearing the end of her twelfth term, died in September of viral pneumonia after contracting chicken pox. In the Senate Democrat Paul Wellstone of Minnesota, an outspoken liberal firebrand who was just finishing his second term, was killed while campaigning for a third term when his twin-engine plane crashed in foul weather in northern Minnesota. *(Successors, pp. 16, 17; tables, p. 877)*

Congress also lost one its more legendary members to retirement in 2002. Strom Thurmond, Republican of South Carolina, retired at the end of the session just two weeks shy of his 100th birthday after having served forty-seven years in Congress.

Ethics transgressions led to the departure of two members of Congress in 2002. Democratic Sen. Robert G. Torricelli of New Jersey gave up a faltering reelection campaign after he was "severely admonished" by the Senate Ethics Committee for improperly accepting expensive gifts from a former campaign supporter. In the House James A. Traficant Jr., D-Ohio, was expelled after he was convicted of conspiracy to commit bribery and other charges and sentenced to eight years in jail. It was the first time since 1980 that a House member had been expelled.

The Political Year

It was not the tidal wave that swept the Republican Party into majorities in the House and Senate in 1994. But the Republicans carried the day Nov. 5, 2002, regaining control of the Senate, adding to their numbers in the House, and retaining their majority in the statehouses. It was the first time since 1934, when President Franklin D. Roosevelt won seats

in both the House and the Senate, that the president's party gained ground in both houses of Congress in a midterm election.

Although his name did not appear on any election ballot, President Bush was the big winner of the elections. The president had put his prestige on the line by campaigning nearly nonstop for GOP candidates in close races in the weeks running up to the election. The victories strengthened not only Bush's ability to control the legislative agenda but also his own political position going into the 2004 presidential election campaign.

Democrats, who had hoped to increase their majority in the Senate and possibly even win control of the House, were stunned by their losses—a net total of two in the Senate and six in the House. Political analysts widely agreed that the party and its candidates had failed because they offered no clear or convincing alternatives to Republican policies. One immediate consequence of the elections was the resignation of Democrat Richard A. Gephardt of Missouri as House minority leader. Gephardt said he was stepping down to prepare for a possible run for the Democratic presidential nomination, but others suggested he was trying to avoid a challenge to his leadership from disgruntled Democrats.

The Republican election victories were based on a combination of carefully chosen candidates, abundant campaign financing, and a strong get-out-the-vote drive. But the catalyst was the president himself. Bush appeared at sixty-seven fund-raising events throughout the country during the election period, raising more than $144 million for GOP candidates. During the final week of campaigning, Bush made seventeen stops in fifteen states on behalf of Republican Senate candidates in tight races.

Senate Races

The president's campaigning paid off. The Democrats lost Senate seats in Georgia, Minnesota, and Missouri and failed to win against vulnerable Republicans in Colorado and New Hampshire. Democrats picked up one Senate seat in Arkansas and held onto seats in South Dakota and Louisiana, where Bush had campaigned hard for the Republican challengers.

That put the party breakdown at the start of the 108th Congress at fifty-one Republicans, forty-eight Democrats, and one independent, James M. Jeffords of Vermont, whose switch from the Republican Party in May 2001 had given Democrats control of the Senate for most of Bush's first two years in office. The Nov. 5 elections restored control to the Republicans, but they still were far short of the sixty votes needed to end filibusters in the Senate. Minority Leader Daschle indicated that Senate Democrats would use whatever tactics they had to keep fighting for their priorities and blocking the Republican agenda.

The decision by Senate Democrats to block creation of the homeland security department in a dispute with Bush over personnel rules for the department's employees was widely seen as a key factor in the defeat of Democratic senators Max Cleland of Georgia and Jean Carnahan of Missouri. Bush appeared twice in Georgia to stump for Cleland's opponent, Rep. Saxby Chambliss. Chambliss was also aided by a negative ad campaign that accused Cleland—a triple amputee veteran of the Vietnam War—of being unpatriotic. Carnahan had been appointed to the Senate in 2000 for two years after her husband, Mel Carnahan, won the Senate election that year even though he had been killed in a plane crash three weeks before the election. The winner of the 2002 race, Jim Talent, was to complete the four years remaining in that term.

Republicans also won in another race where the Democratic candidate died just before the election. In Minnesota, Sen. Paul Wellstone was locked in a tight race with former St. Paul mayor Norm Coleman when Wellstone, his wife, daughter, and several campaign aides were killed in a plane crash less than two weeks before the election. Former vice president and senator Walter F. Mondale was enlisted to run in Wellstone's place, but Coleman won the election with barely more than 50 percent of the vote.

In New Jersey, former Democratic senator Frank J. Lautenberg handily won election after entering the race in early October to replace Sen. Robert Torricelli. Torricelli had suddenly withdrawn from the race on Sept. 30 after polls showed him losing to a Republican who constantly pummeled Torricelli on allegations that he had accepted improper campaign gifts and was thus not fit to hold public office. Torricelli, who had survived a criminal probe of his campaign finances and an admonishment from the Senate Ethics Committee for using "poor judgment," denied the allegations but apparently could not ignore the polling data.

One race that Bush did lose was in South Dakota. The president personally persuaded Representative John Thune to switch from a planned bid for governor to challenge Democrat Tim Johnson, who was seeking a second term. Johnson held on to his seat, barely. But Thune's campaign forced Senate Democratic leader Daschle to spend much of his campaign effort defending the seat of his home-state colleague—and in 2004 Thune would return to oust Daschle in a major victory for the GOP.

House Races

Reapportionment and redistricting were the key factors benefiting Republicans in the House. Because of population gains and losses tabulated by the 2000 census, twelve congressional seats were shifted to other states and the district lines in most states were redrawn. Republicans won most of the newly apportioned seats, and redistricting stabilized many of the Republican incumbents who had been elected by narrow margins in previous elections.

Thanks in large part to redistricting, Democrats and Republicans alike had great success in defending their incumbents. Only sixteen incumbents lost, and eight of those were

Recorded Vote Totals

Following are the recorded congressional vote totals between 1950 and 2004. The figures do not include quorum calls. The 95th Congress (1977–1979) took 2,696 recorded votes, the highest number for an entire Congress. The high for a single year was 1995, when 1,480 recorded votes were taken. That year was also the high mark for recorded votes in the House—867. The high for the Senate was 700 recorded votes in 1976.

Year	House	Senate	Total
1950	154	229	383
1951	109	202	311
1952	72	129	201
1953	71	89	160
1954	76	171	247
1955	76	87	163
1956	73	130	203
1957	100	107	207
1958	93	200	293
1959	87	215	302
1960	93	207	300
1961	116	204	320
1962	124	224	348
1963	119	229	348
1964	113	305	418
1965	201	258	459
1966	193	235	428
1967	245	315	560
1968	233	281	514
1969	177	245	422
1970	266	422	688
1971	320	423	743
1972	329	532	861
1973	541	594	1,135
1974	537	544	1,081
1975	612	602	1,214
1976	661	688	1,349
1977	706	635	1,341
1978	834	516	1,350
1979	672	497	1,169
1980	604	531	1,135
1981	353	483	836
1982	459	465	924
1983	498	371	869
1984	408	275	683
1985	439	381	820
1986	451	354	805
1987	488	420	908
1988	451	379	830
1989	368	312	680
1990	510	326	836
1991	428	280	708
1992	473	270	743
1993	597	395	992
1994	497	329	826
1995	867	613	1,480
1996	454	306	760
1997	633	298	931
1998	533	314	847
1999	609	374	983
2000	600	298	898
2001	507	380	887
2002	483	253	736
2003	675	459	1,134
2004	543	216	759

defeated by one of their House colleagues, half in primaries and half in the general election. Four other Democratic incumbents were denied renomination in their primary race. Only four incumbents were defeated by a nonincumbent on election day.

Republicans won three of the general election matchups between incumbents. The most lopsided was in Mississippi's third district, where Charles W. "Chip" Pickering Jr. defeated Democrat Ronnie Shows by nearly thirty percentage points. Republican John Shimkus bested Democrat David Phelps by ten percentage points in the Nineteenth District of Illinois. In Connecticut's Fifth District, ten-term Republican Nancy L. Johnson parlayed her seniority and superior fundraising into an eleven-point victory over Democrat Jim Maloney.

The one incumbent matchup won by a Democrat was in the seventeenth district of Pennsylvania, where Tim Holden edged Republican George W. Gekas, 51 percent to 49 percent.

Two of the four incumbents defeated by nonincumbents were Democrats Bill Luther of Minnesota and Karen L. Thurman of Florida. The two defeated Republicans were Felix J. Grucci Jr. of New York and Constance A. Morella of Maryland. Morella's departure left very few moderate Republicans in the House; two others, Benjamin A. Gilman of New York and Marge Roukema of New Jersey, announced their retirements earlier in the year and did not stand for reelection.

One of the newly elected members of the House was Katherine Harris, the former Republican secretary of state in Florida who was at the center of the ballot dispute in the 2000 presidential election.

State Races

Another person who figured prominently in the disputed presidential election of 2000 was Florida governor Jeb Bush. In 2002 he won election to a second term despite a concerted effort by Democrats to unseat him as payback for his role in the ballot dispute that ultimately gave his brother George the presidential election. Both former president Bill Clinton (1993–2001) and Gore campaigned in the state in 2002 for Tampa lawyer Bill McBride, who had defeated Janet Reno, attorney general in the Clinton administration, in the Democratic primary. But that was not enough to overcome the Bush brothers. The governor mounted the most expensive gubernatorial campaign in Florida history and, helped by strategically timed campaign appearances by the president, handily defeated McBride.

It was just one of several disappointments sustained by the Democrats who had predicted big gains in governorships, if for no other reason than because Republicans had so much more exposure. Of thirty-six seats up for election, Republicans held twenty-three. After all the votes were counted, however, Republicans had a net loss of only one governorship, from twenty-seven to twenty-six. Democrats had a net gain of three, picking up one Republican seat and two seats formerly held by independents.

Altogether twenty governorships changed party hands. Democrats won governorships in the politically key states of Illinois, Michigan, and Pennsylvania, as well as in Kansas, Oklahoma, and Wyoming. But Republicans picked up three Democratic seats in the South—Alabama, Georgia, and South Carolina. The biggest upset was in Georgia, where former state senator Sonny Perdue ousted Democratic incumbent Roy Barnes to become the state's first Republican governor since Reconstruction.

The gubernatorial elections were notable for the number of competitive women candidates. Four women were elected to governor's offices, breaking the previous single-year record of three set in 1990 and bringing the total number of sitting women governors to an all-time record of six.

Another sign that the Republicans had deepened their appeal came at the statehouse level. For the first time since 1954, Republicans held more legislative seats than did Democrats. After the elections, the GOP controlled the legislature in twenty-one states, up from seventeen. Democrats controlled seventeen, down one. Control was split in eleven states, and Nebraska was unicameral and nonpartisan.

Special Elections

There were also two special elections in the House in 2002. On Jan. 8 Republican John Sullivan defeated Democrat Doug Dodd to take the Oklahoma seat held by Steve Largent, who resigned to run for the governorship. Sullivan, a state representative, won 54 percent of the vote. Largent lost the governor's race in November.

The second election was held to fill the seat of Democrat Patsy T. Mink of Hawaii, who was elected to another term on Nov. 5 despite her death in September. Democrat Ed Case, a former state representative and a cousin to AOL-Time Warner Chairman Steve Case, won a special election to fill the remainder of Mink's 2001–2002 term, and in January he won a second special election to take Mink's seat in the 108th Congress.

2003

The Legislative Year

The opening session of the 108th Congress marked the first time in fifty years that Republicans had complete control of both the House and Senate and the White House. They used it to hand President Bush high-profile victories on top legislative priorities. By year's end Republicans had enacted the second major tax cut in three years, although it was only half as large as President Bush had requested. Against all odds, Republicans also enacted the biggest overhaul of Medicare since its creation—including a long-sought prescription drug benefit for seniors.

They cleared legislation outlawing a procedure called "partial birth" abortion by its critics, a goal that had been beyond the reach of social conservatives for many years. It was the first federal law barring an abortion procedure since the Supreme Court's 1973 decision in *Roe v. Wade* and was immediately challenged in three separate federal district courts. They authorized $15 billion over five years to fight the global spread of HIV/AIDS, a high-profile issue for Bush and an initiative Republicans hoped would appeal to swing voters in the 2004 presidential election. With an eye to those elections, they also gave quick approval to a series of bills with broad popular appeal: the "do not call" list to reduce annoying telemarketer phone calls; a follow-up "do not spam" bill to crack down on junk e-mail; and legislation to bolster the AMBER child-abduction alert system and outlaw "virtual" child pornography.

All this activity, however, was overshadowed by the U.S. invasion of Iraq in March. The military operation quickly led to the fall of Saddam Hussein's government and the eventual capture of Saddam himself. But the United States military remained in Iraq, trying to rebuild the country and help install a democratically elected government in the face of a building insurgency. Having authorized the president to launch the war in 2002, Congress was reduced to the role of bystander with little authority to do anything except pay the bills.

Lawmakers did that, approving $78.5 billion in fiscal 2003 supplemental spending for Iraq in April, little more than three weeks after getting Bush's request. In dollar terms, it was the largest supplemental spending bill ever—but not for long. In September Bush requested $87 billion in supplemental fiscal 2004 funds for military operations and reconstruction in Iraq and Afghanistan. By this time public confidence in Bush's handling of the war was beginning to slip. Attacks by insurgents were killing American soldiers nearly daily, a bomb blast at U.N. headquarters in Baghdad highlighted the lack of security, and so far none of the chemical, biological, or nuclear weapons of mass destruction that Bush claimed Saddam possessed had been discovered. Even Republicans were uneasy with the mounting cost of the war. But an effort by Democrats and some Republicans to require Iraq to repay some of the reconstruction costs ran into a veto threat and aggressive lobbying from the White House. In the end, Congress agreed to the supplemental funds, but GOP leaders in the Senate were so nervous about the possible outcome of a roll-call vote that they cleared the measure by voice vote.

Lawmakers had reason to be concerned about adding to the federal budget deficit. In May Congress cleared legislation increasing the statutory limit on the federal debt by $984 billion, the largest increase in history and more than double the $450 billion increase voted in 2002. Even at that, legislators expected the new ceiling to keep the government solvent only for a year or so.

DEFECTIONS AND REBELLIONS

On a few other key issues, there were enough Republican defections to deny Bush and the GOP leadership victory. Senate GOP leaders failed to break a Senate filibuster on a wide-ranging energy bill that was supposed to be one of their signature accomplishments. Moreover, the Republican-led Congress ended the year without finishing the annual appropriations bills—the same thing Republicans criticized Senate Democrats for doing when they ran the chamber in 2002. When Congress adjourned for the year only six of the thirteen regular fiscal 2004 spending bills had been enacted, leaving the rest to be bundled into a massive omnibus bill that was not cleared until January 2004.

Six of Bush's judicial nominations were held up by filibusters in the Senate. Democrats charged that Bush was nominating conservative extremists, and Republicans were unable

---

CONGRESS IN 2003

The first session of the 108th Congress began at noon on Jan. 7, 2003, and closed at 7:33 p.m. on Dec. 9, when the Senate adjourned *sine die*. The House had adjourned *sine die* at 9:40 p.m. on Dec. 8. The session lasted 337 days. The Senate met on 167 days for a total of 1,454 hours. The House met for 133 days for a total of 1,015 hours.

A total of 7,014 bills and resolutions were introduced compared with 4,269 in 2002 and 6,530 in 2001. Congress cleared 198 bills that were signed into public law, compared with 241 in 2002 and 136 in 2001. President Bush did not issue any vetoes. *(Public laws table, p. 14; presidential vetoes, p. 931)*

During 2003, the House took 675 recorded votes, 192 more than in 2002. The Senate took 459, 206 more than in 2002. (Totals do not include quorum calls.) *(Recorded votes, table, p. 17)*

to round up the votes to break the deadlock. On sixteen occasions Republican Bill Frist of Tennessee, the new Senate majority leader, failed to muster the sixty votes needed to invoke cloture and force a vote. It was the first time in more than twenty-five years that a filibuster was used to block a judicial nominee.

Some of Bush's second-tier priorities, such as limiting medical malpractice awards, redesigning the early childhood education program known as Head Start, and rewriting clean air standards, were sidetracked and left to an uncertain fate in the second session. In most cases, however, when one or both chambers balked on some other second-tier issues, such as efforts to privatize government jobs, relax media consolidation rules, and revise overtime labor regulations, Bush was able to get nearly all of the defeats reversed in the final bills, often with little or no compromise.

Even with those frustrations, however, Republicans ended the session convinced they were heading into a presidential election year with a solid record of accomplishments on the biggest issues of the day—the war on terror, the economy, and health care. "We set our sights high, and we exceeded expectations," Frist claimed.

RECORD-SETTING PARTISANSHIP

Even by the standards of the previous several years, partisanship in both the House and Senate was increasingly bitter in 2003.

When Senate Democrats blocked six of Bush's judicial nominees, Senate Republicans retaliated with a nearly forty-hour-long filibuster with the sole purpose of accusing the Democrats of obstructionism. Republicans shut all Democrats out of the House-Senate conference committee that wrote the energy bill, which eventually fell victim to a filibuster mounted by northeastern senators of both parties. Republicans also blocked all but two centrist Democrats from the conference committee that wrote the final Medicare bill. In retaliation, Senate Democrats blocked attempts to begin conference negotiations on two other bills. (*Energy bill, p. 425; Medicare bill, p. 496*)

House Republican leaders held open the vote on the Medicare conference report for nearly three hours until they could produce enough votes to win, leading some Democrats to charge that Republicans "stole" the vote (roll-call votes were supposed to last fifteen minutes). House Democrats forced a slew of procedural votes to castigate Republicans for not expanding the child tax credit for low-income families. In one bizarre episode House Ways and Means Committee Chair Bill Thomas, R-Calif., called Capitol Police to evict committee Democrats from a library after they had walked out of a markup—an action that many of his GOP colleagues said was over the line and ultimately led him to deliver an emotional apology on the House floor.

The signs of partisanship were not only anecdotal. Congressional Quarterly's analysis of the year's "party unity" votes—those that pitted a majority of one party against a majority of the other party—found that Congress was more polarized than it had been in the five decades that CQ had been tracking the annual voting patterns on Capitol Hill. The average House Republican voted with the party on 91 percent of the party unity votes, whereas the average Senate Republican did so on 94 percent of the votes. Democrats were a little less cohesive. Senate Democrats stuck together on 85 percent of the votes, while House Democrats did so on 87 percent of the votes. That was the highest unity score for the Democrats since 1960.

NEW LEADERSHIP

The 108th Congress began with a reshuffled House Republican leadership that soon proved itself muscular and skilled at consolidating power. J. Dennis Hastert of Illinois was entering his third term as Speaker, but Tom DeLay of Texas, the combative and fiercely ideological conservative, had just moved up from majority whip to majority leader after the retirement of fellow Texan Dick Armey (1985–2003). Roy Blunt of Missouri took DeLay's place as majority whip.

On the Democratic side, the leadership was starting with an almost entirely new slate. Nancy Pelosi of California was elected the new House minority leader after Richard A. Gephardt of Missouri gave up the post to run for president. While the aggressively liberal Pelosi reached out to moderates in her party, she made it clear she believed Democrats had nothing to gain from cooperating with Republicans on anything. The new minority whip, Steny H. Hoyer of Maryland, did not see eye-to-eye with Pelosi on all major issues—he had supported the war in Iraq, for example, while she opposed it—but he stood with her in urging Democrats to show a united front against the conservative agenda of the House Republicans.

In the Senate Bill Frist, an intense and smart former heart surgeon, was beginning his first year as majority leader, replacing Trent Lott of Mississippi. Lott had been forced to step aside after making racially charged remarks at a retirement celebration for Strom Thurmond, R-S.C. Frist's majority whip, Mitch McConnell of Kentucky, was new to the job as well. The top Senate Democratic leadership remained unchanged. Tom Daschle of South Dakota, a favorite target of the GOP, returned as minority leader, while Harry Reid of Nevada remained as minority whip.

The Political Year

The first session of the 108th Congress was a stable time institutionally. No lawmaker switched parties and the elected leadership of the House and Senate remained unchanged during the year. All 100 senators were sworn in on Jan. 7: fifty-one Republicans, forty-nine Democrats, and one independent. All served through year's end. In the House, where the party breakdown was 229 Republicans, 205 Democrats, and 1 independent, only two vacancies occurred during the year. One Republican resigned for personal reasons, another

Age Structure of Congress

Average ages of members at the beginning of each Congress.

Year	House	Senate	Total
1949	51.0	58.5	53.8
1951	52.0	56.6	53.0
1953	52.0	56.6	53.0
1955	51.4	57.2	52.2
1957	52.9	57.9	53.8
1959	51.7	57.1	52.7
1961	52.2	57.0	53.2
1963	51.7	56.8	52.7
1965	50.5	57.7	51.9
1967	50.8	57.7	52.1
1969	52.2	56.6	53.0
1971	51.9	56.4	52.7
1973	51.1	55.3	52.0
1975	49.8	55.5	50.9
1977	49.3	54.7	50.3
1979	48.8	52.7	49.5
1981	48.4	52.5	49.2
1983	45.5	53.4	47.0
1985	49.7	54.2	50.5
1987	50.7	54.4	52.5
1989	52.1	55.6	52.8
1991	52.8	57.2	53.6
1993	51.7	58.0	52.9
1995	50.9	58.4	52.2
1997	51.6	57.5	52.7
1999	52.6	58.3	53.7
2001	54.4	59.8	55.0
2003	53.9	59.5	54.9
2005	55.0	60.4	56.0

to become his state's governor. A third House resignation, announced in December, took effect early in 2004. *(Leadership, p. 10)*

Special Elections

Republican Larry Combest of Texas resigned from the House on May 31, citing personal reasons. He had announced his resignation in November 2002, soon after winning his tenth term. The June 3 special election to fill the seat, one of the most reliably Republican in the nation, was won by Republican land developer Randy Neugebauer of Lubbock by 587 votes—less than 1 percent of the vote cast—over accountant Mike Conaway, a partner of George W. Bush's in the 1980s oil business in Midland, Texas.

Republican Ernie Fletcher, who had represented east central Kentucky's Sixth District since 1999, resigned from the House on Dec. 8, the day before he was inaugurated as the state's governor.

Fletcher had won the governorship with 55 percent of the vote Nov. 4 against the state attorney general, Democrat Ben Chandler, to become the state's first Republican governor in thirty-two years. That was the longest period of any state in

the nation without a Republican chief executive, even though Kentucky had otherwise been part of the Southern shift to GOP dominance. The incumbent governor, Democrat Paul E. Patton, was barred by state term limits from seeking re-election. Chandler rebounded quickly from his loss in the gubernatorial race to run for and win Fletcher's seat in the House in a Feb. 17, 2004, special election.

In South Dakota, Republican Bill Janklow was convicted of second-degree manslaughter Dec. 8 as a result of a traffic accident and that evening announced his resignation from the House effective Jan. 20, 2004. Janklow had been elected to the House in November 2002. *(Details, p. 723)*

Gubernatorial Elections

There were four gubernatorial elections in 2003—three regularly scheduled ones, in Kentucky, Louisiana, and Mississippi, and a fourth in California, where voters elected Republican actor Arnold Schwarzenegger to succeed Democrat Gray Davis who was ousted in a recall election. The governorships in Kentucky and Mississippi also switched from the Democratic column to the Republican column, while Louisiana remained Democratic.

In California, lingering public anger over the state's energy crisis in 2000–2001, combined with distress over a $38 billion budget deficit, had risen to fever pitch in mid-2003 after Davis and Republican legislators deadlocked over the best way to reduce the deficit. A petition drive to place the recall question on the ballot succeeded in late July, and a special election was scheduled for Oct. 7, kicking off a scramble in both parties to win the right to succeed Davis if he lost the recall.

Schwarzenegger, perhaps best-known for his role in the *Terminator* movies, was a political neophyte, but once he entered the race in August he became the immediate front-runner. Davis lost the October recall election by a 55–44 percent margin. Schwarzenegger won the election to replace him with 48 percent of the vote—sixteen percentage points ahead of his closest rival, Democratic lieutenant governor Cruz Bustamante.

In Mississippi, Haley Barbour, an influential Republican lobbyist and former chair of the Republican National Committee, bested the incumbent governor, Democrat Ronnie Musgrove. Barbour won with 52 percent of the vote. In Kentucky, U.S. Representative Ernie Fletcher defeated the state attorney general, Democrat Ben Chandler, to become the first Republican governor in more than three decades. In Louisiana, Lieutenant Governor Kathy Blanco, a Democrat, won the right to replace two-term governor Murphy J. "Mike" Foster, a popular Republican who was barred by law from seeking a third term. Blanco defeated front-runner Bobby Jindal, a Republican, in a run-off election, collecting 52 percent of the vote. (In 2004 Jindal won a seat in Congress.)

2004

The Legislative Year

Intense election-year maneuvering, rifts between the House and the Senate, the deepening federal budget deficit, and the demands of the war in Iraq made the second session of the 108th Congress more notable for what it did not accomplish than for what it did do.

To be sure, lawmakers did enact some significant legislation. Congress cleared two tax bills, one a $146 billion multi-year extension of previously enacted middle-class breaks, the other a $137 billion tax cut mostly for manufacturers and multinationals but with plenty of other provisions to benefit most corporations. Congress managed to reduce discretionary domestic spending a bit, reauthorize the federal law governing the education of the disabled, and make it a federal crime to kill or injure a fetus during the commission of a crime, a long-sought victory for the president. In the final moments of the session, Congress also approved an overhaul of the nation's intelligence-gathering agencies, legislation that incorporated many, but not all, of the recommendations issued by an independent commission that investigated why the nation was unable to prevent the Sept. 11, 2001, terrorist attacks. *(Intelligence legislation, p. 263)*

But on many issues, partisanship overwhelmed consensus, and the president's wishes were frequently thwarted by a minority that complained about overreaching by the majority. As a result, Congress failed to reauthorize the nation's highway and mass transit statutes, the laws governing higher education and job training policies, the statutes governing Amtrak and space exploration, and the laws authorizing the Head Start early-childhood education program and the principal federal water projects program.

Some policy rewrites had stymied Congress for years. Amtrak had not been authorized since 1997; NASA not since 2000. Others were of more recent vintage. Parts of the authorizing legislation that overhauled the federal welfare program in 1996 expired in 2002 and had not yet been renewed. Renewal legislation stalled again in 2004, this time because of a dispute in the Senate over work rules and child-care funding.

In short, the results reflected a divisive election year where partisan tensions remained historically high and where substantive legislative wins were not the highest priority for President Bush or congressional leaders. For example, a bipartisan majority in the House passed a largely symbolic resolution endorsing his Iraq policy in March, on the first anniversary of the U.S.-led invasion of that country. The success of Republicans leaders to write the resolution in a way that ensured at least some Democratic support demonstrated that Bush's mantle as commander in chief would limit the ability of the Democrats to use the war as an election issue.

Some of Bush's high-profile losses may have been significant political victories. For example, a constitutional amendment to ban gay marriages died in the Senate after lawmakers failed to invoke cloture on the bill, and in the House after backers failed to win a two-thirds majority of those present and voting. But the votes could be interpreted as political sacrifices, allowing the Bush election campaign to mobilize socially conservative voters upset by court rulings in favor of gay marriage while expending little of the president's political capital on the doomed amendment.

Likewise, Senate Democrats' success in blocking a bill that would have limited punitive damages in medical malpractice litigation gave the president one of his major campaign themes. On the campaign trail Bush repeatedly blamed Democrats for preventing passage of the bill, which he said would end frivolous and wasteful lawsuits that were contributing to skyrocketing health care costs. Implicit in this message was criticism of the Democratic vice presidential contender, Sen. John Edwards, a former trial lawyer who had become a wealthy man representing claimants in malpractice suits.

The more solid margins in Congress as a result of the 2004 elections were expected to give a boost in the 109th Congress to some of Bush's priority proposals that had been stalled in the Senate, such as energy legislation and limits on medical malpractice suits. Some observers thought that Bush would be able to make a more convincing claim of public

---

CONGRESS IN 2004

The second session of the 108th Congress began at noon on Jan. 20, 2004, and closed at 8:38 p.m. on Dec. 7, when the House adjourned *sine die.* The Senate adjourned *sine die* at 10:54 p.m. on Dec. 8. The session lasted 324 days. The Senate met on 133 days for a total of 1,032 hours. The House met on 110 days for a total of 879 hours.

A total of 3,655 bills and resolutions were introduced, compared with 7,014 in 2003 and 4,269 in 2002. Congress cleared 300 bills that were signed into law, compared with 198 in 2003 and 241 in 2002. President George W. Bush did not veto any bills, making him the first president since John Quincy Adams (1825–1829) to finish an entire term of office without vetoing any legislation. *(Public laws table, p. 14)*

During 2004, the House took 543 recorded votes, 132 fewer than in 2003. The Senate took 216 recorded votes, 243 fewer than in 2003. (Totals do not include quorum calls.) *(Recorded votes, table, p. 17)*

support for his appointments of conservative judges. But it seemed likely that Democrats would do their best to continue to block nominations and legislation that was not to their liking.

The Political Year

George W. Bush won election on Nov. 2 to a second term as the nation's forty-third president, defeating Massachusetts senator John F. Kerry with 51 percent of the vote and 286 electoral votes, a small but decisive victory. It was a banner day for Republicans, who also added three seats to their majority in the House and picked up four seats in the Senate. One of those seats had belonged to Tom Daschle of South Dakota, the soft-spoken but partisan leader of the Senate Democrats whose defeat thrilled congressional Republicans nearly as much as Bush's victory.

Despite the GOP wins, political analysts cautioned that while the country might be leaning a little bit more Republican, it was still divided politically right down the middle. Commentators also observed that as a lame-duck president, Bush might have more trouble holding together a narrow Republican majority, particularly on issues such as overhauling Social Security and the tax code, areas where legislators were likely to encounter a great deal of resistance to change among their constituents.

The Presidential Election

The presidential election campaign of 2004 was the longest, most expensive, and perhaps most negative in recent memory. Yet most voters had apparently made up their minds before the campaign actually began, and the rallies, speeches, attack ads, position papers, innuendo, and allegations pumped out day after day for nearly ten months did relatively little to change their minds. From early February, when it became clear that John F. Kerry, the junior senator from Massachusetts, would win the Democratic nomination to challenge the incumbent Republican president, George W. Bush, until Election Day, the two candidates ran virtually neck-and-neck in the public opinion polls, with one pulling ahead for a few days or weeks only to drop back a few points before moving forward again.

Bush was judged to be vulnerable going into the campaign, with voters expressing deep doubts about his handling both of the economy and the war in Iraq. Kerry tried to take advantage of those doubts, challenging Bush for giving mammoth tax cuts to wealthy Americans while failing to provide jobs and health care for the middle class and for rushing the war in Iraq and diverting attention from the war on terrorism. But Bush kept Kerry on the defensive, skillfully portraying him as the epitome of a Massachusetts liberal and a "flip-flopper" on the issues. The Bush campaign also managed to raise questions about Kerry's Vietnam War record, in an effort to undermine the Democrat's credibility as a potential commander in chief.

Presidential Vote by Region

Unlike the 2000 election, President George W. Bush in 2004 won both the popular vote, which he lost four years earlier, and the Electoral College. He was the first presidential winner since 1988 to capture a majority of the popular vote because there was no significant third party candidate in the race. But his margin of victory of a little over 3 million votes was the smallest of any president to win reelection since Harry S. Truman in 1948. And Bush's margin in the Electoral College, thirty-five votes, was the smallest for any reelected president since Woodrow Wilson in 1916. Within the regions shown in the table only three states switched parties from 2000: Iowa and New Mexico went for President Bush in 2004 and New Hampshire went for John Kerry.

	2000				
	Popular vote			Electoral vote	
Region	Gore	Bush	Nader	Gore	Bush
East	56%	39%	4%	117*	9
Midwest	48	49	3	68	61
South	43	55	1	0	163
West	48	46	4	81	38
National	48	48	3	266*	271

	2004			
	Popular vote		Electoral vote	
Region	Kerry	Bush	Kerry	Bush
East	56%	43%	117	5
Midwest	48	51	58	66
South	42	57	0	168
West	50	49	77	47
National	48	51	252	286

* A Democratic elector from the District of Colombia withheld her electoral vote to protest lack of voting representation for the District in Congress.

On the campaign trail, voters often found it easier to see the difference in style between Bush and Kerry than the differences in policy. Bush was amiable and relaxed. Kerry often appeared distant and cool. Bush's penchant for simple, declarative statements helped voters see him as decisive and a strong leader. Kerry's tendency to overexplain himself, particularly early in the campaign, left voters uncertain what he had said and contributed to the Bush camp's charge that Kerry changed his position on the issues for political expediency.

In the end, the presidential campaign posed a choice that was shaped not so much by the candidates' stands on the economy or Iraq but by the uncertainties that had gripped the country since the terrorist attacks of Sept. 11, 2001: was it better in a time of tumult for voters to stick with a sitting president even though they disagreed with many of his policies? Or should the country take a chance on a candidate whose policies might be more agreeable but whose leadership was largely untested. On Election Day, Nov. 2, a majority of voters decided it was better not to change horses in the middle of the stream.

BUSH'S VULNERABILITY

As Congressional Quarterly reporter John Cochran observed, when it mattered most, Bush pushed hard to make the most of the hand he had been dealt. He had done that in 2000 in the presidential race against Democratic vice president Al Gore. Although Bush lost the popular vote in that election by more than half a million votes, he nonetheless won the presidency in the Electoral College, first by mounting an aggressive campaign to be certified the winner of the contested Florida vote and then by prevailing in the Supreme Court on the question of a recount. *(2000 election, Congress and the Nation Vol. X, p. 21)*

Despite lingering doubts about his legitimacy in the White House, Bush in his first five months in office was able to leverage his position as president, a huge budget surplus, and a narrow Republican majority in Congress to win the deep tax cut that became his signature legislative achievement. Three months later, a country traumatized by the Sept. 11 terrorist attacks turned to the president for leadership. Bush responded with a broadly defined war on terrorism that encompassed protecting the homeland, military operation in both Afghanistan and Iraq, and, toward the end of his first term, a mission to bring democracy to the Middle East.

Throughout his first term, Bush exerted extraordinary control over the agenda in Washington. He won enactment of two of the three biggest tax cuts in American history, brokered deals on his terms to revamp Medicare and federal education policy, and presided over the implementation of the so-called doctrine of preemption that led the nation to wage simultaneous wars in Afghanistan and Iraq.

But as the 2004 presidential campaign got under way, Bush was judged to be once again at a vulnerable point. His job approval ratings were plummeting as public concerns about the war in Iraq and the state of the economy mounted. A majority of Americans said the country was on the wrong track. Bumper stickers reading "Anybody but Bush" became popular.

DEMOCRATIC PRIMARY CAMPAIGN

The first question for Democrats was who the "anybody" would be. In addition to Kerry, eight other Democrats sought the nomination, including former Vermont governor Howard Dean; former House leader Richard A. Gephardt of Missouri; Joseph I. Lieberman, a senator from Connecticut and the Democratic vice presidential candidate in 2000; John R. Edwards, a successful trial lawyer and a first-term senator from North Carolina; and retired U.S. Army general Wesley Clark, the former head of NATO. The long shots in the race were Rep. Dennis J. Kucinich, a maverick politician from Ohio; former Illinois senator Carol Moseley-Braun, and the Rev. Al Sharpton, an outspoken Democratic activist from New York. Bob Graham, a senator and former governor of Florida, had dropped out of the race in October 2003.

Kerry entered the fray in the fall of 2003 as the early favorite of the Democratic establishment. But he quickly fell behind former Vermont governor Howard Dean who had announced his candidacy early in 2002 and spent the next year and a half using the Internet to raise a record $41 million and solicit supporters who were attracted to his anti-

Washington, antiwar message. In the months leading up to the first two major primary events—the Iowa caucuses on Jan. 19 and the New Hampshire primary on Jan. 27—Kerry's candidacy was nearly written off as dead. Kerry was said to be spending too much time tending to his disorganized and unfocused campaign organization instead of campaigning. His campaign financing had dried up, and he was having trouble raising more.

With the campaign all but lost, Kerry began to turn things around in mid-November 2003, replacing his campaign manager with longtime Democratic operative Mary Beth Cahill, mortgaging his Boston townhouse, and running a series of ads that portrayed the candidate as someone who understood and would deal with the problems of ordinary Americans. He also decided to focus his campaign almost entirely on the Iowa caucuses, abandoning for the time being New Hampshire, where he was badly trailing Dean. He also turned to fellow Vietnam veterans, who began turning out in force at his campaign rallies, praising Kerry's leadership and bravery during that war, and applauding wildly when Kerry challenged his Democratic rivals and President Bush to "bring it on!"

At the same time the Kerry campaign was gathering new energy the Dean campaign ran into trouble. Dean won endorsement in early December 2003 from former vice president Al Gore, the party's standard-bearer in 2000. But that strengthened the attacks on the frontrunner from the other Democratic candidates, his campaign began to run out of money, and the news media began to ask harder questions. One question that was particularly troublesome for Dean was why he had sealed more than half of his gubernatorial records for a decade after he left office. Dean also got into a negative war of attack ads with Gephardt in the week before the Iowa caucuses, which damaged both candidates. But even before then Dean made a series of intemperate comments that raised questions about his temperament and electability—doubts that were solidified by a notorious screaming rant after he came in third behind Kerry and Edwards in the Iowa caucuses.

A week later Kerry won New Hampshire, with Dean coming in second but still twelve percentage points behind. Kerry was unstoppable from that point on. Edwards and Clark on Feb. 3 each won a primary, but Kerry won the other five held that day and all but clinched the nomination. Dean focused his attention on winning the Wisconsin primary on Feb. 17, but after coming in third, behind Kerry and Edwards, he effectively ended his candidacy. Edwards, easily the most likable Democrat on the campaign stump with his boyish good looks and his insistence on running a positive campaign, slogged on for another two weeks but retired from the campaign after Kerry swept nine of ten primaries held on March 2. (The tenth was Vermont, which backed Dean, its former governor, even though he had pulled out of the race.)

Kerry named John Edwards as his choice for a running mate on July 6, ending a search that included Gephardt, Iowa governor Tom Vilsack, and Republican senator John McCain of Arizona, a close friend of Kerry's who ultimately campaigned for Bush against Kerry. In naming Edwards, Kerry reached for qualities that many Democrats feared the presidential candidate lacked: charisma, youthful energy, and an instinctively deft touch with ordinary people. Edwards also was a sharp contrast to the often dour Republican vice president, Dick Cheney, who assumed the role of the principal attack candidate in the Bush campaign.

Kerry and Edwards saw eye-to-eye on nearly every major issue despite differences of personality and style. Their records in the Senate were similar enough to suggest that they shared plenty of common ground and were unlikely to differ significantly on matters of policy in a Kerry administration. Democratic campaign strategists also hoped this similarity of views would help the ticket state clearly what Democrats stood for and what they would do with a governing majority—something the party had failed to do in either the 2000 presidential election or the midterm election in 2002, when the Republicans managed to widen their lead in the House and regain control, albeit narrow, in the Senate.

The two men already had domestic messages that were easy to mesh. When he announced that he had picked Edwards, Kerry embraced, word for word, his vanquished rival's pledge to bridge the "great divide" between the "two Americas, one of wealth and one of work." That blended neatly with Kerry's campaign speeches about the "middle-class squeeze": ordinary working people were suffering, Kerry said, while President Bush rewarded his wealthy supporters with tax breaks and other favors.

THE CAMPAIGN TRAIL

With polls showing that a majority of the states were already firmly in the Republican "red" column or the Democratic "blue" one, the campaigns concentrated their energies on a handful of "battleground" states, including Florida, Ohio, and Pennsylvania, where the presidential and vice presidential candidates each made multiple appearances. Bush often appeared at carefully scripted "town hall" meetings where the audiences consisted wholly of supporters who asked preplanned questions and applauded on cue. The TV news clips that followed such appearances usually showed a jovial and sincere President Bush, shirt-sleeves rolled up, giving an optimistic assessment of both the economy and the war in Iraq, while raising questions about Kerry's policy proposals and leadership capabilities. Vice President Cheney led a harsher assault on Kerry in a not-so-subtle effort to raise fears that the country would be vulnerable to terrorist attack if Kerry were elected—a message that was underscored by attack ads and surrogates speaking in behalf of the Republican candidates.

Kerry tried to keep his campaign focused on economic and domestic issues where the Democrats had a clear edge in the public opinion polls. But the dominant issue during much of the campaign was the war in Iraq and the underlying war on terrorism. It was the first time a foreign policy matter had been at the center of the nation's politics since the Vietnam War during the late 1960s and early 1970s. As with much of the year's campaign rhetoric, however, voters often found it difficult to discern the actual differences in the positions Bush and Kerry took. Kerry often was harshly critical of Bush's handling of Iraq and other foreign affairs matters, but his policy differences often were so subtle as to be indistinguishable to the average voter.

One of Kerry's chief problems was that the Bush campaign—and conservative groups supporting the president—had succeeded in defining him in negative terms before he was able to make his case as the Democratic nominee. As soon as Kerry's rivals dropped out, the Bush campaign began running negative television ads portraying him as weak and indecisive. Bush, Cheney, and campaign surrogates cited Kerry's votes during his twenty years in the Senate in such a way that Kerry appeared to have repeatedly shifted positions on controversial matters and had constantly voted for budget-busting spending programs and tax increases.

Perhaps even more damaging to Kerry were attacks challenging his service in the Vietnam War. Kerry served for fourth months in Vietnam as a navy lieutenant, where he was awarded the Silver Star, the Bronze Star, and three Purple Hearts. Upon his return home, Kerry became a prominent leader in the antiwar movement, and his heroism and then his opposition to the war had been the hallmarks of his political life. The first attacks, which surfaced in early February while Kerry was still focused on the primaries, focused on his antiwar activities. Kerry was charged with throwing away his medals, a charge he denied, and for impugning the honor of troops serving in Vietnam by describing the actions of some as "crimes."

The real damage came after the Democratic National Convention in July, when an group calling itself "Swift Boat Veterans for Truth" claimed in a series of ads that Kerry had lied about his dramatic rescue under fire of a fellow sailor and other elements of his navy career. Kerry was slow to respond to these ads, which ran in only a few markets but generated enormous controversy nationwide. By the time he did respond millions of voters had come to question the reputation he had carefully nurtured as a decisive, even heroic, military figure.

Questions also arose about Bush's Vietnam-era service but, ironically, appeared to cause less damage to the president. Bush had joined the Texas Air National Guard in 1968 just before he graduated from Yale and at the height of the Vietnam War. Bush trained as a fighter pilot and was honorably discharged from service in 1973. Over the course of his political career, however, critics had alleged that Bush's father, George H. W. Bush, had used political connections to get him the National Guard post. Questions also had been raised about a period of Bush's service when he transferred to an Alabama guard unit while working on a senatorial campaign but appeared not to have shown up for duty at least part of the time.

These questions arose again early in the 2004 campaign and were calmed after the White House released documents indicating that Bush had served during the disputed period but still leaving some questions unanswered. The controversy flared again in early September, when the CBS program "60 Minutes" reported that it had documents purportedly showing that Bush had shirked his Guard duty and subsequently lied about it. CBS later retracted that report, acknowledging that the documents it cited had been forgeries. The end result was that CBS was damaged more than Bush, who gained some sympathy because of what many supporters alleged was a partisan attack by the news media.

IRAQ

The Swift Boat attacks on Kerry came as Bush began to appear more vulnerable on Iraq, which had become the dominant issue of the campaign. By summer 2004 the United States had gotten bogged down fighting an increasingly strong insurgency throughout much of Iraq, in sharp contrast to Bush's cheerily optimistic prewar predictions that most U.S. forces would be back home by the end of 2003. Some critics were beginning to call the U.S. occupation of Iraq a "quagmire"—the term used to describe the later years of the Vietnam War.

This focus on Iraq ultimately became more of a problem for Kerry, the challenger, than for Bush the defender. Bush was able to use the conflict in Iraq to remind voters of his leadership in what he called the ongoing "war against terrorism" and to plant doubts in voters' minds about what kind of a leader Kerry would be. Kerry accused Bush and his administration of "incompetence" in Iraq but failed to articulate a clear alternative strategy.

Kerry criticized Bush for failing to plan for the postwar occupation of that country—a failure that had been documented in numerous academic studies and news accounts since shortly after the war. But on the fundamental question of whether Bush was justified in taking the nation to war in Iraq, Kerry waffled. In what he described as a major foreign speech, delivered in Seattle on May 27, Kerry suggested that Bush and his aides rushed into war without gaining adequate support from allies. "They looked to force before exhausting diplomacy," he said. "They bullied when they should have persuaded." Later in the campaign, Kerry defended his vote in October 2002 to authorize the war, and he offered a confusing, procedural explanation for his apparently conflicting votes in November 2003 on Bush's request for $87 billion to fund military operations and foreign aid in Iraq and Afghanistan. Bush used Kerry's convoluted explanation about voting for the $87 billion before he voted against it to great affect on the campaign trail; Bush's political adviser Karl Rove later referred to the Kerry statement as "the gift that kept on giving."

For his part, Bush repeatedly shifted his justification for the war to suit the circumstances. Early in the year, Bush stood by his contention that Iraq's leader Saddam Hussein had or was developing weapons of mass destruction and thus posed a threat to the United States and its allies. As more

and more evidence emerged that Iraq did not have those weapons, Bush fell back on vague terms that implied the same thing: Iraq had "weapons of mass destruction-related program activities" or simply the "capability" to produce those weapons, he said. Ultimately, Bush adopted a democracy and human rights rationale for the Iraq war, arguing that Saddam was a dictator whose removal laid the ground for democracy in Iraq and perhaps elsewhere in the Middle East.

NATIONAL NOMINATING CONVENTIONS

Gradually over the years since television became common in American homes, the national nominating conventions lost much of their interest for the public. With no decisions to be made about the nominees as a result of the growing importance of presidential primaries since the 1970s, virtually no controversy over the party platforms, and limited live coverage by the broadcast networks, the conventions were little more than rallying grounds for the faithful and launching pads for the fall campaigns. Still, both parties spent much time and money orchestrating speakers and speeches to present their candidate and their campaign messages in the most positive light possible.

For the Democrats, meeting at the Fleet Center in Kerry's home town of Boston July 26–29 the convention was an opportunity to showcase solid party support for their candidate. Party dignitaries speaking on Kerry's behalf included former presidents Jimmy Carter and Bill Clinton and former vice president Al Gore. Senators Edward M. Kennedy of Massachusetts, the elder statesman of Democratic liberalism, and Hillary Rodham Clinton of New York, a potential prospect for the Democratic nomination in 2008, spoke, as did Barack Obama, a candidate for the U.S. Senate from Illinois and a rising star in the Democratic Party. Obama, the son of a Kenyan father and a Kansan mother, gave the keynote address in which his eloquent call for a united and tolerant America was repeatedly interrupted by applauding delegates.

Democrats believed they scored a coup with the appearance of Ron Reagan, the son of former president and Republican icon Ronald Reagan, who had died in June after suffering from Alzheimer's disease for a number of years. The younger Reagan urged delegates to vote for candidates who would support embryonic stem cell research, which scientists believed held great promise for curing degenerative diseases such as juvenile diabetes, Parkinson's disease, and perhaps even Alzheimer's. President Bush had limited federal funding for such research. *(Reagan's Memorialization, p. 697)*

Kerry's speech on July 29 accepting the Democratic nomination, and the biographical film leading up to it, emphasized the senator's service in Vietnam in hopes that he could convince voters that he would be a strong commander in chief. "I defended this country as a young man," Kerry declared, "and I will defend it as president." Kerry also excoriated Bush for a litany of mistakes and misjudgments: "I will be a commander in chief who will never mislead us into war.

I will have a vice president who will not conduct secret meetings with polluters to rewrite our environmental laws. I will have a secretary of defense who will listen to the advice of the military leaders. And I will appoint an attorney general who upholds the Constitution of the United States."

The Republicans held their convention Aug. 30–Sept. 2 in New York City's Madison Square Garden, just four miles north of the World Trade Center site. The first night of the convention focused on the Sept. 11 attack on the trade center towers and on Bush's declaration of a new war on terrorism in response. One of the featured speakers was former New York mayor Rudolph Giuliani, a moderate Republican, whose stewardship of the city after the attacks was widely admired.

On Aug. 31 the emphasis turned to the party's themes of hope and optimism, with speeches by California governor Arnold Schwarzenegger, education secretary Rod Paige, and first lady Laura Bush all promising that with President Bush in the White House, the nation's best days still lay ahead. On Sept. 1, the gloves came off as Vice President Cheney and Democrat Zell Miller of Georgia laced into Kerry. Cheney said Kerry still did "not appear to understand how the world has changed" since the Sept. 11 attacks, while Miller accused him of being "more wrong, more weak, and more wobbly than any other national figure" on the "great issues of freedom and security." Miller, who in recent yeas had increasingly aligned himself with Senate Republicans, said that "George Bush wants to grab terrorists by the throat and let them get a better grip. From John Kerry, they get a 'yes-no-maybe' bowl of mush that can only encourage our enemies and confuse our friends."

Accepting the Republican nomination on Sept. 2, Bush promised to "build a safer world and a more hopeful America." He devoted the first half of his speech to a broad outline of his plans for a second term, including overhauling Social Security and Medicare, reducing the deficit, and making tax cuts permanent. He spoke of an "ownership society" and promised to transform fundamental government systems such as health coverage, pension plans, and worker training "so that all citizens are equipped, prepared—and thus truly free—to make your own choices and follow your own dreams." But the core of his message was that he was the candidate best suited to lead the country in time of great threat: "We have fought the terrorists across the Earth—not for pride, not for power, but because the lives of our citizens are at stake. We are staying on the offensive—striking terrorists abroad—so we do not have to face them here at home."

THE FALL CAMPAIGN

Bush and Kerry met in a series of three nationally televised debates in late September and early October that gave millions of Americans their best opportunity of the campaign season to weigh the presidential candidates and their policies in the closely fought election. For ninety minutes at a time, under two different and carefully controlled formats, Bush and Kerry clashed again and again over their differing approaches to leadership, to the Iraq war and the war on terror more broadly, and to a host of domestic issues from the economy and health care to stem cell research and gay marriage.

By most accounts, Kerry was the "winner," a judgment that was confirmed by public opinion polls. Before the first debate on Sept. 30, most polls showed President Bush in the lead by several percentage points; after the last debate, Kerry had pulled even with the president, and the two men remained roughly even, with Bush perhaps a bit ahead, for the rest of the campaign. Kerry, who appeared confident and focused, may have been aided in the first debate by the president, who frequently looked petulant and impatient as he waited for Kerry to finish his response. Bush seemed more comfortable in the second, town-hall-style debate, where the two candidates answered questions from the audience, and by the third debate, he was joking about his wife's admonition "to stand up straight and not scowl."

At the close of the last presidential debate on Oct. 13, Bush and Kerry were running neck and neck in the public opinion polls, and the issues had narrowed down to character and leadership, particularly as they concerned the war in Iraq. The Bush campaign impugned Kerry's ability to be a strong commander in chief, while Kerry questioned Bush's judgment and his refusal to take responsibility for the mistakes he had made. Each ticket claimed that it would do a better job of protecting the American homeland from terrorists and other threats.

In the final week, Kerry might have gained from news reports that the administration could not account for the whereabouts of 380 tons of powerful explosives that were missing from an Iraqi ammunition dump known as al Qaqaa. On Oct. 29 a videotape of al Qaeda terrorist leader Osama bin Laden was released by the al Jazeera news agency. Bin Laden made no direct threat against the United States on the tape but both Bush and Kerry interrupted their campaign schedules to declare separately that they were united in their determination to stand up to bin Laden.

It was unclear what effect, if any, the videotape had on voters, who seemed more concerned about a repeat of the voting disputes that characterized the 2000 presidential election. A *New York Times*/CBS News poll found that one-fifth of those polled had little or no confidence that the votes for president would be counted properly, three out of ten voters said they were worried that they might be prevented from casting a vote or that their vote would not be counted, and more than one-third said they thought deliberate efforts would be made to keep blacks from voting in some states.

Both campaigns enlisted thousands of poll watchers as well as attorneys at crucial polling places in Ohio, Florida, and other key states to ensure that duly registered voters were able to cast their ballots and to challenge (or, depending on party affiliation, come to the aid of) voters whose eligibility was questioned. Both camps also mounted the biggest and most aggressive get-out-the vote drives in presidential election history in the battleground states during the weekend before the vote and on Election Day itself. The two campaigns, the political parties, and outside groups, such as America Coming Together, a coalition of pro-Kerry organizations, spent at least $300 million on sophisticated efforts to target and turn out the vote.

ANOTHER LONG ELECTION NIGHT

Although Bush had a slight edge in public opinion polls going into Election Day, early exit polls suggested that Kerry was winning several key states. Data from the National Election Pool, a new vote projection system run by the TV networks, the Associated Press, and several major newspaper organizations were showing Kerry beating Bush in Ohio and Pennsylvania, and two out of three exit polls in Florida showed Kerry ahead there as well. By prior agreement, news agencies had promised not to project results based on exit poll data until after voting polls had closed across the country. But Kerry campaign workers with access to the data were jubilant. Bush operatives were in turn dismayed, then skeptical, and then certain that the exit polls were wrong. Rove later told reporters that he was sure something was wrong with the exit polls when he saw that they awarded Kerry South Carolina and Virginia, two states that had voted for Bush in 2000 and that both parties had conceded to Republicans early in the campaign.

As the actual vote count continued into the night, Bush increasingly looked like the winner. But Kerry was not willing to concede. Appearing in the middle of the night, at the Copley Plaza in Boston, Kerry's running mate, John Edwards, reminded supporters that "John Kerry and I made a promise to the American people that in this election every vote would count and every vote would be counted. Tonight we are keeping our word and we will fight for every vote. You deserve no less."

Shortly before 6:00 in the morning of Nov. 3, Andrew H. Card Jr., the White House chief of staff, announced to campaign workers in Washington that the White House was "convinced that President Bush has won reelection." By this time, the drama over the vote count had narrowed to Ohio, where Bush was running ahead of Kerry with about 150,000 provisional ballots still to be counted. After watching the count throughout the night, the Kerry campaign realized it would need to win virtually all of the provisional ballots to surpass Bush's 136,000 vote lead, which was highly unlikely. Although the outcome in Iowa and New Mexico was still uncertain, Ohio's twenty votes brought Bush's electoral vote total to 274, four more than the 270 he needed to win election. Kerry called Bush late in the morning of Nov. 3 to congratulate him on his reelection.

Kerry formally conceded later that afternoon. "I would not give up this fight if there was a chance that we would prevail," Kerry said to a gathering of his supporters in Boston's historic Fanueil Hall. "But it is now clear that even when all the provisional ballots are counted, which they will be, there won't be enough outstanding votes for us to be able to win

Ohio. And therefore we cannot win this election." The tired and disappointed Democrat then called on all Americans to join in "common effort without remorse or recrimination, without anger or rancor. America is in need of unity and longing for a larger measure of compassion."

"America has spoken," an obviously triumphant George Bush declared an hour or so later in a victory speech to his supporters at the Ronald Reagan Building in Washington. Bush promised to put forward an ambitious agenda, which included making income tax cuts enacted in 2001 permanent and rewriting the tax code, drawing up stricter educational standards, and overhauling Social Security to allow younger workers to maintain private accounts funded through payroll taxes. "Let me put it to you this way," a confident president said at a Nov. 4 news conference. "I earned capital in the campaign, political capital, and now I intend to spend it." Bush also said he intended to reach across party lines to win support for his agenda, but he made it clear he expected the Democrats to do most of the compromising.

THE VOTE

More than 122 million voters, about 60 percent of those registered, went to the polls on Nov. 2, the highest turnout since 1968. The 2004 vote total was 122.3 million. The turnout in 2000 was 105.4 million, slightly more than 54 percent of all registered voters. After all the votes were counted, Bush received 62 million popular votes with a winning margin of 3 million, and 286 Electoral College votes; Kerry won 59 million popular votes and 252 electoral votes. The total minor party vote was less than 1 percent of the total vote cast. It was the first election since 1988 in which a third party candidate had not figured prominently. Ralph Nader, who ran on the Green Party ticket in 2000 and who Democrats said had spoiled the election for Gore, was not a factor in 2004. He ran as in independent, did not appear on the ballot in several states, and won only 408,000 votes.

Despite the increased turnout, the state-by-state lineup barely changed. Only two states that had voted Democratic in 2004—Iowa and New Mexico—switched to vote for Bush in 2004 and then by less than a single percentage point. Only one state, New Hampshire, shifted out of the Republican "red" column into the Democratic "blue" column, and that shift reflected the absence of Nader as a factor.

Bush carried 54 percent of the white vote, about the same as he had in 2000. Despite preelection indications that the president might double his share of the black vote, nine out of ten African Americans cast their ballot for Kerry, who also held onto the majority of Hispanic votes. The gender gap narrowed somewhat in 2004, with fewer men supporting the Republican than in 2000 and fewer women supporting the Democratic candidate.

Democrats worked hard to register new voters under age thirty, and about 4.6 million turned out on Election Day. That was only a little over half of all young voters registered, but those who did vote were strongly for Kerry. Countering the youth vote, however, was sharply increased turnout among evangelicals, who supported Bush better than three to one. Karl Rove, the "architect" of Bush's winning campaign strategy, had long maintained that Bush had lost the popular vote in 2000 because 4 million evangelicals did not vote, perhaps, he said, because of reports about an old drunk driving charge against the president that came to light the week before the election, and perhaps because evangelicals were generally wary of politics and politicians. The evangelical vote turned out in force in 2004. Its influence was particularly acute in eleven states, including Ohio, that had ballot initiatives barring same-sex marriage. All eleven initiatives passed with 59 percent of the vote or more. Bush also won a majority of the Catholic vote; although a Roman Catholic, Kerry sparked opposition in the church by his positions on issues such as abortion and gay rights.

Exit polls showed Kerry drawing more votes than the president among those who rated the economy, health care, and education as the most important issues. He also was favored by three-fourths of those who thought the Iraq war was the most important problem. But voters who were more concerned about terrorism preferred Bush by an even wider margin. Bush was also the clear preference among voters who cited strong leadership, "clear stands on the issues," and honesty and trustworthiness as the most important qualities in a candidate.

The deciding factor, however, may have been that Republicans of every stripe—conservative, moderate, and liberal—voted more solidly for Bush than Democrats voted for Kerry—and more Republicans (37 percent of the total vote) than Democrats (36 percent) voted. Kerry won 89 percent of the Democrats voting and a slim majority of independent voters, but that was not enough to overcome the turnout and cohesiveness of Republicans who gave Bush 93 percent of their vote. Karl Rove summarized the situation succinctly the day after the election: "We had at the top of the ticket an inspiring individual who knew what he believed and did what he said. At the end of the day, people voted for him for two reasons. One is they thought he could do the job, and two, they had deep doubts about the other guy."

Much was made after the election of the effect of moral values on the outcome. The national exit polls showed that more than a fifth of all voters said "moral values" was their top concern, and three-quarters of the moral values voters said they voted for Bush. Commentators widely identified these voters as fundamentalists or social conservatives opposed to gay marriage and abortion rights. Yet a closer look seemed to show that "moral values" had a far broader meaning. More than three-fifths of those who expressed an opinion in the national exit poll said they supported either gay marriage or civil unions. And a postelection Zogby survey asking voters to identify the nation's most urgent moral problem found abortion and gay marriage far down the list. Leading the list were "greed and materialism" and "poverty and economic justice."

CAMPAIGN FINANCING

The 2004 elections were the most costly in history. Altogether spending on the races for the White House, Senate, and House of Representatives was estimated at about $3.9 billion, according to the Center for Responsive Politics, which tracked campaign financing. That was about one-third more than was spent in 2000.

The Bush campaign raised an all-time presidential record of $273 million from private contributors, but the Democrats also enjoyed record fund-raising, bringing in $249 million. Kerry was the first Democratic presidential candidate to decline public financing and its spending limits during the primary season. Bush declined public financing during the primary season in both 2000 and 2004. Both men received public financing—$75 million each—for the general election, which meant that both men had to stop taking private donations after the conventions.

Nearly as much money was raised and spent by nonparty political groups. Known as 527s for their section in the federal tax code, these independent groups spent nearly $550 million in the 2003–2004 election cycle. Most of this funding was devoted to the presidential election, where $266 million was spent on behalf of Kerry, $144 million on behalf of Bush. 527s emerged as a powerful force after the campaign finance reform law enacted in 2002 banned national party committees from collecting unlimited "soft money" from corporations, unions, and individuals. Democrats, who were hurt more by the soft money ban than Republicans, first realized the potential of 527s, when groups such as America Coming Together and MoveOn.org raised millions to finance voter-turnout operations aimed at targeting Democratic voters. Republicans initially challenged the legitimacy of the 527s, but after the Federal Election Commission refused to ban their activities, pro-Republican groups started to spring up. One of the more prominent was the Swift Boat Veterans for Truth, which pummeled Kerry in August with allegations that he had lied about his Vietnam service record.

By law 527s were to operate independently of the political campaigns and were barred from coordinating with them, although both campaigns charged that the other campaign had violated this restriction. Others expressed grave concern about the potential impact of unregulated and unaccountable organizations on political campaigns. The Senate authors of the 2002 campaign finance reform law, Republican John McCain of Arizona and Democrat Russ Feingold of Wisconsin, indicated that they would try to close the 527 loophole with new legislation, a move that Bush had endorsed. A federal lawsuit challenging 527s was still pending at year's end.

VOTING PROBLEMS

Although voters and election officials reported plenty of problems around the country, they did not come close to matching the dire predictions made beforehand. The largest voter turnout in U.S. history caused hours-long waits throughout the country and prompted judges to order voting hours extended in some polling places. Some unknown number of would-be voters chose not to wait. Voting machines broke down and polling places ran out of ballots. In the crucial state of Ohio, 638 voters cast ballots in one precinct but a computer recorded 3,893 extra votes for Bush (the error was corrected in the certified vote total for the state). Constituents in minority precincts reported receiving calls designed to lead them to vote in the wrong precinct on the wrong day. While many voters remained suspicious of the final vote tallies, particularly in Florida and Ohio, where the two campaigns had been warning of potential irregularities and fraud for weeks before the election, most voters were able to cast their ballot and have it counted without incident.

The biggest complication might have been posed by provisional ballots for people whose eligibility to vote was questioned at the polls, a new mandate Congress enacted in 2002 (PL 107-252). Lawsuits challenging various aspects of the balloting were not settled in many states until days before the election. In Ohio, the rules governing provisional ballots were still in contention on Election Day. Kerry's decision to concede the presidential race instead of contesting the results in Ohio cut off any additional litigation there. But in December Kerry asked for a statewide recount there. "It's critical that we investigate and understand any and every voting irregularity anywhere in our country, not because it would change the outcome of the election but because Americans have to believe that their votes are counted in our democracy," he said.

At least two investigations of election problems were planned. The Government Accountability Office, responding to a request from several Democratic lawmakers, said on Nov. 24 that it would investigate the accuracy of the vote and the methods used to count it, including the way election officials counted provisional ballots. The U.S. Election Assistance Commission, created by the election overhaul legislation passed in 2002, also said it would examine the voting results. It planned to report its findings in January 2005.

SENATE RACES

Senate Republicans won a net of four seats, to give them a total of fifty-five. That was not enough to guarantee that they could prevent filibusters, which required sixty votes, but it made the job a lot easier. When the 109th Congress began in 2005, Democrats would hold forty-four seats, the fewest for the party since Herbert Hoover was president in the late 1920s. The Senate's lone independent, James M. Jeffords, tended to vote with the Democrats.

The GOP swept all five seats left open by Democratic incumbents in the conservative South, clear evidence of the Republican rise to dominance in that region. Those gains gave Republicans twenty-two of the twenty-six seats in the South, leaving the Democrats with Arkansas's two senators and one senator each in Florida and Louisiana.

Women in Congress, 1947–2005

Congress		Senate	House
80th	(1947–1949)	1	7
81st	(1949–1951)	1	9
82nd	(1951–1953)	1	10
83rd	(1953–1955)	3	11
84th	(1955–1957)	1	15
85th	(1957–1959)	1	15
86th	(1959–1961)	2	17
87th	(1961–1963)	2	18
88th	(1963–1965)	2	12
89th	(1965–1967)	2	11
90th	(1967–1969)	1	11
91st	(1969–1971)	1	10
92nd	(1971–1973)	2	12
93rd	(1973–1975)	0	16
94th	(1975–1977)	0	19
95th	(1977–1979)	3	18
96th	(1979–1981)	1	16
97th	(1981–1983)	2	21
98th	(1983–1985)	2	22
99th	(1985–1987)	2	23
100th	(1987–1989)	2	23
101st	(1989–1991)	2	29
102nd	(1991–1993)	4	29
103rd	(1993–1995)	7	47
104th	(1995–1997)	9	49
105th	(1997–1999)	9	54
106th	(1999–2001)	9	56
107th	(2001–2003)	13	61
108th	(2003–2005)	14	60
109th	(2005–2007)	14	66

NOTE: House totals exclude nonvoting delegates. Totals are for an entire Congress and include women elected in general and special elections as well as those appointed to office. Totals for the 109th Congress are through September 2005.

The GOP also fended off strong Democratic takeover bids in Oklahoma, Kentucky, and Alaska. But the Republicans' most stunning victory in the Senate, both because of its political and legislative consequences, was the ouster of Tom Daschle, the Senate Democratic leader for the past ten years. Daschle, who lost to former House member John Thune by 4,500 votes, was the first Senate party floor leader to be defeated for reelection since Majority Leader Edward W. McFarland, an Arizona Democrat who held the job for only two years, was turned out by Republican Barry Goldwater in 1952.

The Republican takeovers included:

• Florida, where Republican Mel Martinez, Bush's former Housing and Urban Development secretary, narrowly defeated Democrat Betty Castor, a former state education commissioner, to succeed Democrat Bob Graham, who was retiring after three terms.

• Georgia, where, as expected, Republican House member Johnny Isakson easily defeated Denise L. Majette, a freshman House Democrat, to succeed maverick Zell Miller, who was retiring.

• Louisiana, where Rep. David Vitter became the first Republican ever elected to the Senate in the history of the state.

Vitter easily outdistanced his two opponents to succeed John B. Breaux. A Democratic centrist skilled in the art of senatorial compromise, Breaux was retiring after three terms in office.

• North Carolina, where Republican House member Richard M. Burr defeated Democrat Erskine Bowles, a former chief of staff to President Bill Clinton, to succeed John Edwards, the unsuccessful Democratic vice presidential candidate.

• South Carolina, where Democrat Inez Tenenbaum, the state superintendent of education, lost to Republican House member Jim DeMint by ten percentage points in the race for the seat of Democrat Ernest F. Hollings, who was retiring after thirty-eight years in the Senate.

The GOP did not lose a single incumbent, a sweep that had happened only twice before in the past thirty-five years: the party's banner years of 1980 and 1994. But Democrats' takeover wins in two open-seat races limited the damage to their party. In Colorado, Ken Salazar, the state attorney general, defeated Republican Peter Coors, a top executive in his family's brewing company, by a margin of 51–47 percent.

The Democratic party's fastest-rising star, Barack Obama, won the race for the Illinois Senate seat being vacated by Republican Peter G. Fitzgerald, who decided not to run for reelection. Obama, who won 70 percent of the vote to set a record for an Illinois Senate candidate, benefited from running against hard-line conservative Alan Keyes, a Maryland resident who was improbably recruited to run in Illinois.

The elections produced a more diverse Senate in the 109th Congress than it had been in the recent past. Salazar and Martinez would be the first Hispanics to serve in the Senate since Joseph M. Montoya, a New Mexico Democrat, was defeated for reelection in 1976. Obama would become only the third black senator since Reconstruction, and the first since another Illinois Democrat, Carol Moseley-Braun, was unseated in 1998.

HOUSE RACES

Republicans gained a net of three seats in the House of Representatives to give them a margin of thirty over the Democrats. The breakdown was 232 Republicans, 202 Democrats, and 1 independent.

Republican strategists attributed their win to their candidates' hard work and to voters' embrace of the Republican agenda. But a close look at the results showed that the GOP win was almost entirely the product of a sweeping redistricting plan that Texas Republicans enacted in 2003 with the goal of winning as many as seven Democratic seats in the state.

Republicans picked up five seats in Texas on Election Day by defeating four Democratic incumbents and successfully winning several newly created, Republican-leaning open seats. Including that of Rep. Ralph M. Hall, a veteran Democrat who switched to the Republican Party as a result of the remap, Republicans won six of the seven seats they wanted in

Blacks in Congress, 1947–2005

Congress		Senate	House
80th	(1947–1949)	0	2
81st	(1949–1951)	0	2
82nd	(1951–1953)	0	2
83rd	(1953–1955)	0	2
84th	(1955–1957)	0	3
85th	(1957–1959)	0	4
86th	(1959–1961)	0	4
87th	(1961–1963)	0	4
88th	(1963–1965)	0	5
89th	(1965–1967)	0	6
90th	(1967–1969)	1	5
91st	(1969–1971)	1	9
92nd	(1971–1973)	1	12
93rd	(1973–1975)	1	15
94th	(1975–1977)	1	16
95th	(1977–1979)	1	16
96th	(1979–1981)	0	16
97th	(1981–1983)	0	17
98th	(1983–1985)	0	20
99th	(1985–1987)	0	20
100th	(1987–1989)	0	22
101st	(1989–1991)	0	24
102nd	(1991–1993)	0	26
103rd	(1993–1995)	1	39
104th	(1995–1997)	1	38
105th	(1997–1999)	1	37
106th	(1999–2001)	0	37
107th	(2001–2003)	0	37
108th	(2003–2005)	0	37
109th	(2005–2007)	1	40

NOTE: House totals exclude nonvoting delegates. Totals are for an entire Congress and include blacks elected in general and special elections as well as those appointed to office. Totals for the 109th Congress are through September 2005.

the state. Those gains more than offset a small Democratic gain elsewhere.

Democrats conceded that the broad shift in the national mood they hoped for before the election never materialized. "I don't think there is any question that, to be candid, we did not get the wind, the uplift, that we had expected in this campaign," said Robert T. Matsui, chair of the Democratic Congressional Campaign Committee.

Outside of Texas, the overriding feature of the House elections was not change but stability. In addition to the four Texas Democratic incumbents that lost, only one other Democrat and two Republican incumbents lost their bid for reelection. Only twice since 1954 was the reelection rate higher, in 1988 and in 1998.

Two of the four defeated incumbents in Texas lost to Republican incumbents: Democrat Martin Frost lost to Republican Pete Sessions, while freshman Republican Randy Neugebauer defeated veteran Democrat Charles W. Stenholm, the ranking Democrat on the House Agriculture Committee. Two other Democrats lost to challengers: four-term lawmaker Nick Lampson lost to former county judge Ted Poe, while Max Sandlin lost to former state judge Louis Gohmert. The

Hispanics in Congress, 1947–2005

Congress		Senate	House
80th	(1947–1949)	1	1
81st	(1949–1951)	1	1
82nd	(1951–1953)	1	1
83rd	(1953–1955)	1	1
84th	(1955–1957)	1	1
85th	(1957–1959)	2	0
86th	(1959–1961)	2	0
87th	(1961–1963)	2	1
88th	(1963–1965)	1	3
89th	(1965–1967)	0	4
90th	(1967–1969)	0	4
91st	(1969–1971)	0	5
92nd	(1971–1973)	0	6
93rd	(1973–1975)	0	6
94th	(1975–1977)	0	6
95th	(1977–1979)	0	5
96th	(1979–1981)	0	6
97th	(1981–1983)	0	7
98th	(1983–1985)	0	10
99th	(1985–1987)	0	11
100th	(1987–1989)	0	11
101st	(1989–1991)	0	11
102nd	(1991–1993)	0	11
103rd	(1993–1995)	0	17
104th	(1995–1997)	0	17
105th	(1997–1999)	0	18
106th	(1999–2001)	0	18
107th	(2001–2003)	0	19
108th	(2003–2005)	0	24
109th	(2005–2007)	2	23

NOTE: House totals exclude nonvoting delegates. Totals are for an entire Congress and include Hispanics elected in general and special elections as well as those appointed to office. Totals for the 109th Congress are through September 2005.

only targeted Texas incumbent who survived the redistricting onslaught was seven-term lawmaker Chet Edwards, one of the most conservative House Democrats. He narrowly fended off his Republican challenger with 51 percent of the vote.

Elsewhere, Democratic businesswoman Melissa Bean took 52 percent of the vote in Illinois to unseat Republican Philip M. Crane, whose thirty-five-year tenure had made him dean of the House Republicans. In Georgia, Democratic county commissioner John Barrow defeated freshman Republican Max Burns. The one Democratic incumbent outside Texas to lose was Baron P. Hill of Indiana. He lost to Republican businessman Mike Sodrel by fewer than 2,000 votes.

Results in open-seat contests, usually the source of most partisan turnovers in each election cycle, further underscored the locked-in nature of most House seats in 2004. Only three of thirty-three open seats changed hands, with two going to the Democrats and one to Republicans. Democrat John Salazar's victory in Colorado helped make Nov. 2 a banner day for the Salazar family—his brother Ken won the Senate election to succeed retiring Republican Ben Nighthorse Campbell.

GUBERNATORIAL RACES

As in other recent election years, the greatest volatility was among governorships. Although the party lineup remained the same, twenty-eight Republicans to twenty-two Democrats, seven of the eleven states that held gubernatorial races in 2004 elected a new leader. The four governors who were reelected—all to a second term—were Republicans John Hoeven of North Dakota and Jim Douglas of Vermont and Democrats Michael F. Easley of North Carolina and Ruth Ann Minner of Delaware. The churning in 2004 was a continuation of the 2002 elections, when a record twenty-five of the thirty-six contests resulted in the election of new governors.

Of the seven departing governors, two were ousted in the primaries. In Missouri, Democrats nominated state auditor Claire McCaskill over incumbent governor Bob Holden. Despite running a strong general election campaign McGaskill lost to Republican Matt Blunt, Missouri's secretary of state and the son of House Majority Whip Roy Blunt of Missouri. The other governor ousted in a primary was Republican Olene S. Walker of Utah. The Republican nominee was John Huntsman Jr., a wealthy petrochemical businessman, who easily won election against Democrat Scott Metheson Jr., whose late father was once governor and whose brother Jim Matheson was reelected to the U.S. House on the same day.

Voters sent one incumbent in each party packing on Election Day. In New Hampshire, Republican governor Craig Benson was hurt by ethics questions that had forced the resignations of several high-ranking appointees. That created an opening for Democrat John Lynch, a first-time candidate who won by a margin of 51–49 percent. In Indiana, Republican Mitch Daniels—President Bush's former budget director and a rising star in the eyes of some Republican strategists—won by a comfortable 53 percent to 45 percent over Democratic governor Joseph E. Kernan.

Democrats took a second governorship held by Republicans when Montana rancher Brian Schweitzer defeated Bob Brown, the Republican secretary of state. Schweitzer replaced Judy Martz who did not run for reelection.

The outcome of one gubernatorial race remained in doubt for several weeks and was being challenged in court at the beginning of 2005. In Washington, state Democrat Christine Gregoire, the state attorney general, ran against former GOP state representative Dino Rossi to replace retiring Democrat Gary Locke. Although Gregoire was initially a strong favorite to win, Rossi closed the gap and after the election led the race by a handful of votes. A second machine count gave Rossi a lead of 42 votes out of 2.9 million ballots cast. That also triggered a state law allowing a hand count of the ballots, which Gregoire won by 129 votes. She was certified the winner in late December and sworn into office on Jan. 12, 2005. But Rossi and the Republican Party asked a state court to overturn the election and call for a revote. In June 2005 the court ruled against the GOP, sealing Gregoire's victory.

Democrats gained some ground in statehouses, where they raised the number of state legislatures they controlled by two, from seventeen to nineteen. Republicans controlled twenty, and control was split in ten states. Nebraska has a unicameral, nonpartisan legislature.

SPECIAL ELECTIONS

Democrats picked up two House seats in special elections in 2004 and held on to another vacant seat, to lower the Republican majority in the House. Going into the November elections, the line-up was 226 Republicans, 206 Democrats, and 1 Democratic-leaning independent. Two other Republican members also resigned late in the session, but no special elections were held to fill their seats.

In a special election in Kentucky on Feb. 17, Democrat Ben Chandler won the seat vacated by Republican Ernest Fletcher, who had been elected governor of Kentucky over a Democrat in November 2003. In South Dakota on June 1, Democrat Stephanie Herseth was elected to fill the seat left vacant by the retirement of Republican William J. Janklow, who had resigned after being convicted of second-degree manslaughter. Janklow had driven his car at high speed through a stop sign in South Dakota and collided with a motorcyclist, who died instantly. In North Carolina, veteran jurist G. K. Butterfield, a Democrat, was handily elected on July 20, to fill the vacancy created when fellow Democrat Frank W. Ballance Jr., announced his resignation, citing health reasons. Butterfield's arrival in the Capitol restored to thirty-seven the number of African American House members.

The two vacancies that were filled at the general election were created by the resignations of Doug Bereuter, Republican of Nebraska, who stepped down on Aug. 31 to become president of the Asia Society, and Porter J. Goss, Republican of Florida, who resigned Sept. 23 to become director of Central Intelligence. *(Table, p. 877)*

CHAPTER 2

Economic Policy

Economic Policy

The sense of prosperity and well-being that most Americans experienced during the 1990s gave way to feelings of uncertainty and anxiety in the early 2000s as the country contended with a series of shocks to its economy and national security.

Even as President George W. Bush was preparing to enter the White House in January 2001, the longest economic expansion in modern American history was drawing to a close. Then, in the space of a few short months, the country experienced the emotional and economic damage caused by the Sept. 11, 2001, terrorist attacks in New York and Washington, D.C., and the wrenching experience of sending young Americans to wage war in Afghanistan. The Sept. 11 attacks tipped the country into recession, causing widespread layoffs. A slump in the stock market devastated the retirement accounts of many workers and other small investors. Revelations of accounting fraud at several major corporations led to bankruptcies, further loss of jobs and retirement savings, and loss of investor confidence in the markets.

The recession, as measured by economists, was mild and ended quickly. But the erratic nature of the recovery—with fluctuating economic growth, sharp ups and downs in the stock market, and the persistent inability of the economy to generate jobs—left Americans feeling uncertain and uneasy about their economic well-being. The apprehension was all the more unsettling because the economic fundamentals were sound—except for the job market. Despite an upsurge in oil prices, inflation remained low in part because Americans were buying imported, low cost goods that once had been made in America. The Federal Reserve Board kept interest rates at their lowest levels in a generation. A boom in the housing market, fueled in important part by the low interest rates, allowed people to refinance their homes or buy bigger ones, pay off credit card and other debt, and still have money to spend. The housing market was so strong that some economists were warning, by the start of Bush's second term, that it might be experiencing a bubble that should it burst as did the technology bubble at the end of the 1990s would throw thousands of over-extended homeowners into financial trouble.

But this danger was not on the horizon in the early years of Bush's first term, and indeed, consumer spending—including housing and all its related requirements—drove the American economy—and much of the world economy, as record-high trade deficits reflected.

Throughout his first term, Bush framed key elements of his agenda as being necessary to promote economic growth: tax cuts would stimulate the economy and put people back to work. Reducing onerous environmental and business regulations would strengthen the ability of American business to compete with unregulated businesses abroad. Providing a domestic supply of energy by tapping into the nation's natural resources—even in wilderness areas—would protect Americans from disruption in foreign energy supplies.

Bush convinced Congress to adopt much of this agenda, particularly tax cuts, an always-popular platform with voters. Congress even added some tax cuts of its own that were specifically intended to stimulate consumer spending, the backbone of the economy. Most of the tax cuts Bush had proposed himself were geared toward promoting long-term savings and investment, especially by the wealthiest taxpayers, rather than providing immediate economic stimulus.

The president stuck with his agenda even after changing circumstances, such as the rising deficit and the need to finance wars after Sept. 11, raised questions about the prudence of a government policy based on spending and bor-

REFERENCES

Discussion of economic policy for the years 1945–1964 may be found in *Congress and the Nation Vol. I*, pp. 337–458; for the years 1965–1968, *Congress and the Nation Vol. II*, pp. 119–182, 253–305; for the years 1969–1972, *Congress and the Nation Vol. III*, pp. 53–145; for the years 1973–1976, *Congress and the Nation Vol. IV*, pp. 49–149; for the years 1977–1980, *Congress and the Nation Vol. V*, pp. 205–287; for the years 1981–1984, *Congress and the Nation Vol. VI*, pp. 27–120; for the years 1985–1988, *Congress and the Nation Vol. VII*, pp. 27–136; for the years 1989–1992, *Congress and the Nation Vol. VIII*, pp. 31–161; for the years 1993–1996, *Congress and the Nation Vol. IX*, pp. 31–148; for the years 1997–2001, *Congress and the Nation Vol. X*, pp. 33–170.

ECONOMIC LEADERSHIP

President George W. Bush was notable for the loyalty given to him by his staff and political appointees. It was thus not surprising that few top positions in the executive branch changed hands in his first term. The one exception was in the economic arena, where several of Bush's top appointees left government in mid-term. The most notable departure was Treasury secretary Paul H. O'Neill, who was forced out of his post, along with Lawrence B. Lindsey, director of the White House National Economic Council. Both men had become liabilities to the White House. Two informal but nevertheless key advisers to President Bush on economic issues remained on the job: Vice President Dick Cheney and Bush's chief political adviser Karl Rove. *(Bush key appointments, p. 919)*

Treasury Department

Bush's first Treasury secretary was Paul H. O'Neill, a former chairman and CEO of Alcoa, who was generally credited with turning around the fortunes of that company. A man who insisted on speaking his mind rather than cheerleading, O'Neill quickly ran into trouble with his boss early in 2001 when he publicly questioned the economic benefits of Bush's proposed tax cuts. O'Neill was criticized for gaffes that shook the markets, for not being around at crucial times, and for insulting important legislators and corporate executives.

With the president and Republican leaders in Congress planning to push more tax cuts in 2003 as the cure-all for both the slow economy and the budget deficit, the White House in December 2002 decided it was time for O'Neill to be replaced with someone who was better able to pitch the president's economic policies on Capitol Hill and to the public. The new Treasury secretary was John W. Snow, chairman of the railroad company CSX Corp.

One of Snow's toughest tasks was selling reluctant Republican legislators on the central feature of Bush's proposed 2003 tax cut—making dividend income tax free. Critics denounced that proposal as a favor for wealthy investors. Bush ended up with half the tax cut he wanted, largely as a result of congressional deficit concerns. A lower tax rate was set for

dividends and capital gains. Snow, a once outspoken deficit hawk, also found himself the leading spokesman for the White House view that deficits were tolerable because they amounted to only a small percentage of the economy. During the 2004 election campaign, Snow had the task of helping fend off Democratic attacks on Bush's fiscal policy and his dismal record on job creation. Snow was also the administration official called upon to calm fears that the declining dollar was destabilizing the economy.

Federal Reserve

When he became chairman of the Federal Reserve in 1987, Alan Greenspan was viewed as likely to stay above the political fray and focus on monetary policy, which, after all, was the Fed's job. His reputation for notoriously complex and equivocal public statements may have heightened those perceptions. But Greenspan defied expectations and frequently spoke out strongly on fiscal issues facing Congress. On occasion he stunned lawmakers by endorsing specific policy choices.

In 1993 Greenspan backed tax increases as part of the deficit-reduction package pushed by President Bill Clinton. In 2001, when enormous surpluses were expected over the next decade, he advocated cutting taxes to avoid a scenario in which the nation paid off its debt too quickly and was faced with the troubling prospect of investing excess tax revenue in the stock market. On both occasions, Greenspan's nod helped ensure enactment of contentious White House fiscal initiatives.

The terrorist attacks and the slumping economy in 2001 ensured that the nation would not have to worry for years to come about what to do with surplus revenue. As the value of the dollar relative to other currencies began to slide, raising the possibility of increased inflation and interest rates, Greenspan warned of the dangers of long-term deficits, and he called upon Congress to revive the pay-as-you-go rules that until 2002 required that tax cuts or extensions of entitlement programs be offset by revenue increases or other spending cuts.

Greenspan was first appointed to the chairmanship in 1987 by President Ronald Reagan. He was appointed to a sec-

rowing money at a record pace. A minority of Republicans argued that Congress needed to be more fiscally responsible by cutting spending, but the president made little effort to promote such a policy; in four years he did not veto a single appropriations (or any other) bill, and he rarely used a veto threat to force Congress to pare back spending. Democrats, on the other hand, called for rethinking the tax cuts, which they said were swelling the deficit and placing an unsustainable debt burden on future generations. Bush rejected this advice even more emphatically, insisting the tax cuts were necessary to promote economic expansion and to trim the size of the federal government.

What politicians on all sides of these arguments rarely acknowledged—except when it suited their purposes to do so—was that the government's taxation and spending policies played only a marginal role in shaping the overall economy. More important factors were interest rates and the collective judgments of consumers and investors about how to satisfy their own immediate personal interests. Presidents and other politicians in power liked to take credit for economic expansions, their critics liked to blame them for recessions, and voters tended to disregard this rhetoric and cast their ballots based on a variety of factors, the economy among them. None of the events in the four years of the first ond term by President George H. W. Bush and then to two more terms by President Bill Clinton. George W. Bush appointed Greenspan to a fifth term in 2004. He was required by law to leave the Fed in January 2006.

Office of Management and Budget

Bush's first director of the Office of Management and Budget (OMB) was Mitchell E. Daniels Jr., who had served in the Reagan administration and was a former executive with the pharmaceutical company Eli Lilly. President Bush called Daniels "the Blade" for his willingness to take on legislators for what he considered their excessive spending. Daniels once said that a more apt nickname might be "the Piñata," because "some folks think if they can knock my head off all the goodies in town will fall out."

When Daniels left OMB in mid-2003 to run, successfully, for governor of Indiana, his home state, Bush named his deputy White House chief of staff, Joshua B. Bolten, to the post. Bolten had a hand in most of Bush's early domestic issues, and his more temperate personality made him a welcome successor to Daniels to many on Capitol Hill. Bolten kept a relatively low profile in his first year until he engaged appropriators over a package of domestic spending add-ons. In the end, the White House agreed to a series of offsets and budgetary maneuvers that allowed Congress to extract more spending but that let Bush claim victory on his budgetary top line. In 2004 Bolten and the White House were even more successful, holding increases in discretionary domestic spending to less than 1 percent.

National Economic Council

The National Economic Council had been created in 1993 by President Bill Clinton. The council was to coordinate economic policy within the administration, as a counterpart to the National Security Council, which coordinated defense and foreign policy. Bush's first director was Larry B. Lindsey, who had been Bush's economic tutor during the 2000 presidential campaign and was a key architect of the 2001 tax cut. But Lindsey's overly optimistic economic forecasts and his po-

litical advice to the president made him seem out of touch with reality. Lindsey was said, for example, to have advised Bush to stop the corporate accountability legislation being considered in the Senate in 2002 even though the measure eventually passed unanimously. Lindsey was also criticized for publicly predicting that the cost of a war with Iraq could reach $200 billion, which was much higher than other administration officials were saying at the time but which turned out to be closer to actual spending.

Lindsey was forced out, along with O'Neill, and was replaced by Stephen Friedman, a former chairman of Goldman-Sachs. Friedman had also served as a vice chairman of the Concord Coalition, a group that opposed budget deficits, and some Republicans were concerned that he might oppose tax cuts. Those concerns were unfounded; Friedman supported Bush's economic policy for the two years he held the post, which he resigned late in 2004.

Council of Economic Advisers

The Council of Economic Advisers, the agency responsible for preparing the annual economic report of the president, had two chairs during Bush's first term. The first was R. Glenn Hubbard, widely credited as a chief architect of Bush's tax cut packages in 2001 and 2003. Hubbard was also the chief advocate in 2003 of eliminating taxes on stock dividends. Congress cut those dividends, along with capital gains, but did not end them. Hubbard left early in 2003 to become dean of Columbia University's School of Business.

He was succeeded by N. Gregory Mankiw, an economics professor on leave from Harvard and the author of two popular economic textbooks. Mankiw touched off a major controversy during a February 2004 news conference when he described outsourcing of American jobs to workers overseas as "just a new way of doing international trade." Although most economists would agree with Mankiw that the expansion of free trade in goods and services benefited all participating countries over the long run, Democrats immediately seized on Mankiw's remarks as confirming that Bush was insensitive to the plight of American workers.

Bush administration changed these facts of economic and political life.

Following is an overview of the U.S. economy during Bush's first term in office.

A LEAKING BUBBLE

A prime example of a politician being blamed for a downturn in the economy was the president's father, George H. W. Bush (1989–1993). Voters turned him out of office in 1992 after one term, largely because they did not believe he was paying enough attention to the economy, which was still feeling the lingering effects of a recession during 1990 and

1991. Unemployment in 1992 stood at 7.5 percent, the highest rate in nearly ten years, and the federal budget deficit was $290 billion, the highest ever recorded (measured in dollars). He was replaced by Democrat Bill Clinton, who entered the White House in 1993 just as the economic recovery was beginning. During the course of Clinton's presidency, unemployment fell to its lowest levels in thirty years, the budget deficit turned into a sizable and growing surplus, productivity growth rates quickened, real income increased, net worth increased even more, and inflation remained low.

The Clinton administration attributed the expansion to three mutually reinforcing factors that coincided in the

1990s: technological innovation, better business management, and federal fiscal discipline. The high-tech sector grew exponentially as businesses and consumers rushed to take advantage of the new opportunities created by innovations in computer hardware and software, telecommunications, and information processing technology.

At the same time, other sectors of the economy began to find ways to use the new technologies to streamline their operations and work more efficiently, thus producing more with less labor. The Clinton administration managed to prod and push a sometimes reluctant Congress into agreeing to tax and spending limits that put the budget deficit on a downward course. Declining federal budget deficits helped keep interest rates down and spurred private investment both at home and abroad, creating new markets, which in turn allowed for more growth.

No one expected the surging U.S. economy of the 1990s to last forever, and signs of the inevitable slowdown became obvious during the election year of 2000. Perhaps the most visible portent of trouble was the crash of high-technology stocks. Following a banner year on Wall Street in 1999, stocks of computer manufacturers, software developers, telecommunications firms, and especially Internet startup companies were hammered in 2000. In many cases, investors were simply correcting for their earlier overenthusiasm for stocks of companies that showed lots of promise but that had so far shown no signs of turning a profit. Many analysts said the collapse of high-tech stock prices also reflected a deeper concern that economic growth was on a downhill slide.

Whether it was self-fulfilling prophecy or not, final figures for 2000 showed that those concerns were justified. Real gross domestic product—the value of all the goods and services produced in the United States—grew at an overall rate of 4.2 percent for the year, but the economy slowed markedly in the second half, growing at a pace of just 1.4 percent in the fourth quarter. That was the worst quarterly growth since 1995, the last time the economy flirted with a recession.

2001: A Slowdown Begins

The slowdown continued into the first months of George W. Bush's presidency. Adjusted for inflation, growth in the April–June 2001 quarter was just 0.3 percent, which basically was no growth at all. Many analysts attributed at least some of the slowdown to an increase in energy prices, which had begun to rise late in 2000. Consumer and business confidence was further eroded by a brief but severe "energy crisis" in California that caused a series of one-day blackouts in the state and spawned unfounded fears of a broader energy crisis.

The first half of 2001 saw the emergence of the typical economic cycle of a downturn: retail sales weakened; profits declined, causing investors to pull back from the stock market, thereby reducing the amount of money available for business investment; and manufacturing companies in turn cut back on production in hopes of being able to sell off inventories.

Production cutbacks and faltering retail sales, of course, meant layoffs, which sapped consumer confidence even more. Early in the year some of the nation's best-known companies pared back employment, in some cases by tens of thousands of workers, both white- and blue-collar. Unemployment, which had reached a record low of 4.2 percent in 1999, climbed to 4.9 percent in August 2001. Most of the job loss came in the manufacturing sector; by the summer of 2001 fewer people worked in U.S. manufacturing plants than at any time since 1964.

In Washington, the new president confidently insisted that he had a cure for the slowdown: a $1.6 trillion tax cut plan he presented to Congress in late February, just five weeks after being sworn into office. Bush insisted that cutting taxes would stimulate the economy by encouraging investment and spending. Democrats and even Bush's own Treasury secretary, Paul H. O'Neill, said the president's plan would have little immediate impact because most of the cuts would not take full effect for several years. Congress addressed that concern by adding to Bush's plan an immediate "tax rebate" of up to $300 for individuals and $600 for couples. Congress approved a $1.4 trillion, ten-year tax cut on May 26, and Bush signed it into law (PL 107-16) on June 7. The rebate checks arrived in mailboxes during the late summer, but most analysts said the $39 billion worth of new spending would have only limited effect in the country's $10 trillion economy.

The Federal Reserve Board also moved to add stimulus to the economy. As 2001 began, the Fed initiated a series of cuts in its target for the federal funds interest rate (the rate financial institutions charge each other on overnight loans). During the course of the year, the Federal Reserve lowered the rate eleven times, bringing the federal funds rate from 6.5 percent at the end of 2000 to 1.75 percent on Dec. 11, 2001, its lowest point in forty years.

AFTERMATH OF 9/11

Then came Sept. 11. Confusion and fear of yet more attacks brought vast portions of the U.S. economy to a standstill in the hours immediately after Islamist terrorists affiliated with al Qaeda hijacked commercial airliners and flew them into the World Trade Center towers in New York City and into a wing of the Pentagon in suburban Washington. Although most economic activity was soon up and running again, the loss of life and destruction at the financial hub of the free world was devastating. More than thirty brokerage firms were headquartered in the World Trade Center, where nearly 3,000 people died; dozens of others were located in the surrounding area.

The U.S. stock markets, which had never opened on Sept. 11, remained closed for the week as financial firms and policy makers struggled to calm the world's fears and maintain confidence in the U.S. economy. Major central banks around the world pumped nearly $120 billion into their

A Look at the Economy, 1984–2004

Economic Growth...

Annual Percentage Change

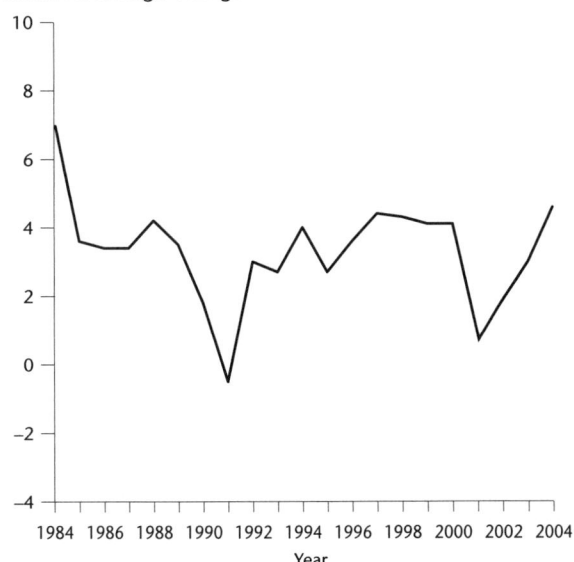

... declined during the 1990–1991 recession, but a prolonged recovery followed, lasting nine years from 1992 to 2000. Economic growth stalled in 2001 before picking up again in the second half of George W. Bush's term.

Growth: Annual changes in the gross domestic product (GDP).

SOURCE: Commerce Department, Bureau of Economic Analysis.

Inflation...

Annual Percentage Change

... before the 1990–1991 recession did not reach the historically high levels it did leading up to the recessions of the early 1980s. It has seen fairly consistent and tame increases since.

Inflation: Annual change in the consumer price index for all urban consumers, expressed as an annual average rate.

SOURCE: Labor Department, Bureau of Labor Statistics.

Unemployment...

Annual Percentage Average

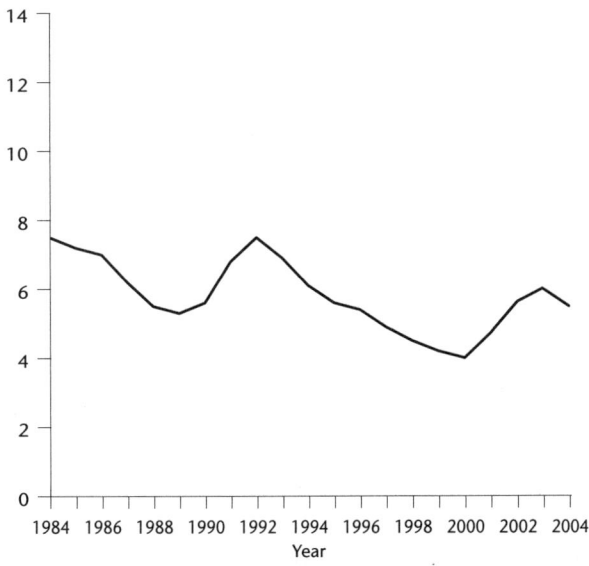

... surged after the 1990–1991 recession but then steadily declined until the early 2000s, when it experienced a slight uptick for three years before falling again.

Unemployment: Annual rate of unemployment for all civilian workers (does not include the military).

SOURCE: Labor Department, Bureau of Labor Statistics.

Interest Rates...

Annual Percentage Average

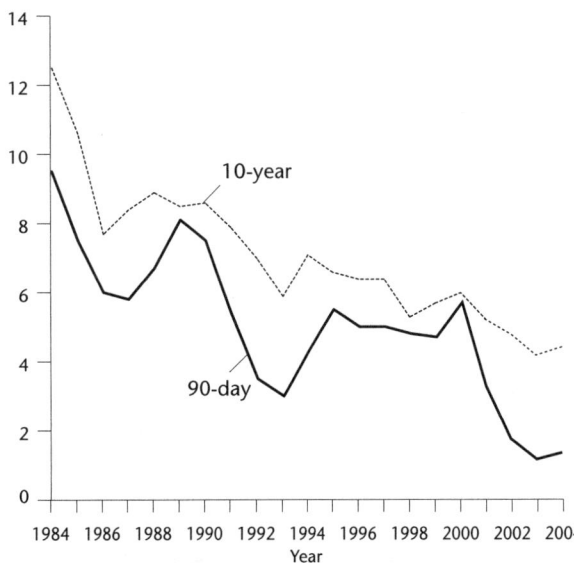

... on long- and short-term Treasury securities fell in 1993 to their lowest levels in almost twenty years, as the economy recovered slowly from the 1990–1991 recession. Since then rates remained stable or rose modestly until taking another downward turn in 2001–2003.

Interest rates: Annual average for new issues of 90-day Treasury bills and 10-year Treasury notes, adjusted for constant maturities.

SOURCE: Treasury Department.

financial systems in the days immediately after the attacks to ensure a normal flow of credit through world markets, and member banks were allowed to borrow liberally to prop themselves up against financial crisis.

Although these actions did a great deal to stabilize commercial dealings around the world, they did not prevent a loss of investor confidence. The reopening of U.S. stock markets on Sept. 17 ushered in the worst week on Wall Street since the Great Depression of the 1930s. Fifty companies posted profit warnings in a single day, Sept. 19. By the closing bell on Friday, Sept. 21, about $1.4 trillion in stock value had been wiped out. The Dow Jones Industrial Average fell 14.3 percent, the biggest weekly percentage drop since July 1933.

The tourism and travel industries also suffered immediate and direct losses as a result of the attacks. The federal government allowed only military flights for several days after the attacks; airports and airlines were allowed to reopen for business only after they put stepped-up security procedures in place. In the first ten days after the attacks, the airline and aviation industries laid off more than 100,000 workers. Several airlines said they were nearly broke, although no American airline had actually filed for bankruptcy protection by the end of the year. Tourism destinations like Las Vegas and Disney World were almost ghost towns, and hotels, restaurants, theaters, and night spots across the country reported slow times as people stayed close to home. Not surprisingly, New York City was especially hurt by the attacks. One preliminary estimate by the city's comptroller put the cost of the attacks at as much as $105 billion. That included property losses, loss of tax revenue, and loss of economic activity that would have occurred had it not been for the attacks, as well as the cost of cleanup. It did not cover the loss of life.

RECESSION CONFIRMED

Uncertainty about the future of the economy continued unabated in October as the United States invaded Afghanistan in an effort to wipe out al Qaeda operatives, including the fundamentalist group's leader, Osama bin Laden, and the Taliban regime that controlled the country and gave al Qaeda safe harbor. Americans also faced what appeared to be a new terrorist threat at home: anthrax contamination in the U.S. mails. Some 400,000 jobs were lost in October, the biggest monthly jump in unemployment since 1980.

On Nov. 26 the Business Cycle Dating Committee of the National Bureau of Economic Research, which dated the beginning and end of recessions, said that the U.S. economy had entered its tenth recession since World War II in March. Had it not been for the terrorist attacks, however, the decline in the economy might have been "too mild to qualify as a recession," the committee said. The official proclamation of a recession brought to a close an economic expansion that had begun exactly ten years earlier and was thus the longest expansion on record. The record had been held by the expansion in the 1960s, which lasted eight years and two months.

More bad news followed two days later, when the Bush administration acknowledged that it expected the federal budget to run a deficit for at least the next three years. Mitchell E. Daniels Jr., the director of the White House Office of Management and Budget, blamed the deficit on the recession, less optimistic projections about the growth of tax revenue, and increases required by the terrorist attacks and the invasion of Afghanistan. Democrats said they were not surprised by the return to deficit spending but maintained the primary cause was the president's tax cut, enacted in June.

Although Congress passed several measures to help the president in the fight against terrorism, it adjourned in 2001 without enacting the economic stimulus package that both parties had originally said was necessary to get the economy moving again. Signs that the economy was beginning to improve on its own dimmed some of the urgency for passing a stimulus measure. But it was partisan political bickering over who was to blame for causing the recession and how best to stimulate the economy that ground the debate to a standstill.

Republicans wanted to speed up at least some of the marginal individual tax rate reductions enacted earlier in the year and to give businesses relief from the corporate alternative minimum tax. Democrats demanded that a stimulus package expand eligibility for jobless benefits and subsidize 75 percent of the cost of temporarily continuing health insurance coverage for those who had lost their jobs. Republicans argued that tax cuts would increase consumer spending and business investment and thus would ensure a faster and longer-lasting economic recovery. Democrats said the GOP economic program was enriching the wealthy at the expense of the working class. At its core, this debate was over the fundamental philosophical issue that separated the two parties—the size and scope of the federal government. It was a debate that would arise again and again over the next three years and that would be a central feature of the 2004 presidential election race.

2002: Corporate Scandals, War Preparations

The economy grew in fits and starts in 2002, buffeted by a year-long slump on the stock market, corporate accounting scandals that sapped investor confidence, fears of more terrorist attacks, and preparations in Washington for an invasion of Iraq. Interest rates and inflation remained low, and consumer spending continued in the positive range, buoyed by a continuing boom in the housing market. Car sales also remained robust, as auto manufacturers and dealers retained the zero- or low-financing options they had introduced to lure car buyers back to the auto lots after the Sept. 11 attacks.

But corporate spending did not recover. In September, after the attacks, it fell at its fastest pace in nearly five years. The jobless rate stood at or near 6 percent for the entire year. By the end of 2002, corporate executives and business associations were warning that the picture was unlikely to change anytime soon. According to one industry survey, three-fifth of the nation's two hundred largest corporations were expecting to lay off more workers in 2003 and were planning no increases in capital spending.

SCANDALS AND BANKRUPTCIES

For much of the corporate world, the immediate uncertainties revolved around continuing low profits, the wallowing stock market, and troubles in several major industries. The long-troubled airline industry sustained two high-profile bankruptcies in 2002. U.S. Airways sought bankruptcy protection in August, while United Airlines filed for bankruptcy protection in December, after the federal government refused its request for a bailout. American, Delta, and several other major commercial carriers announced substantial layoffs. Meanwhile, the telecommunications and "dot.com" industries had still not recovered from the bursting of their stock market bubble at the turn of the century, and many manufacturing sectors were still trying to adjust to the new competitive pressures forced on them by globalization—the continuing expansion of trade and investment among and between countries.

Overhanging these troubles was a series of corporate accounting scandals that began with the collapse of the giant energy trader Enron Corporation in December 2001 amid allegations that top company executives, aided by the company's accountant Arthur Andersen, had used many questionable accounting practices to make its profits appear much larger than they were.

Allegations of accounting irregularities and outright fraud were reported over the next few months at several other leading firms. WorldCom, the country's second-largest telecommunications firm, disclosed in June 2002 that it had lowered its earnings statement by $4 billion. Weeks later WorldCom became the largest company in American history to declare bankruptcy, again amid allegations of corporate fraud and greed. By the end of July, at least fifteen major corporations and their accounting firms were under criminal and civil investigation for a variety of fraudulent or other irregular practices.

The revelations left the stock market reeling. Standard & Poor's 500 stock index, for example, lost 30 percent of its value between the first of May and the end of July. The scandals cost millions of investors, both large and small, billions in losses, and thousands of workers lost their jobs. Many people whose 401(k) retirement plans were invested in the stock market watched helplessly as their pension funds were reduced or even wiped out. Congress moved quickly to approve tough new accounting regulations, but confidence in the stock market was slow to return.

Repercussions from these corporate scandals continued into 2003 and 2004, as company executives were indicted and brought to trial for their alleged misdeeds. Dogged investigations by New York's attorney general, Eliot Spitzer, as well as by the Security and Exchange Commission turned up similar fraudulent and irregular practices in several financial industries, including mutual funds, insurance, investment banking, and two quasi-public mortgage giants, FannieMae and Freddie Mac. Congress took little action on any of these scandals, preferring instead to let federal and state regulators and the courts resolve the problems.

PREPARING FOR WAR

For many businesses and individuals, concerns about the nation's economic well-being were further unsettled by periodic warnings from the Justice Department about the possibility of another terrorist attack against the United States. Overshadowing those fears was the possibility that the United States would soon be engaged in a war with Iraq. Following his Jan. 29 State of the Union address, in which he identified Iraq as one of three countries in an "axis of evil," President Bush kept his administration focused on ousting Iraqi leader Saddam Hussein from power and using military force, if necessary, to disarm Iraq of the chemical and biological weapons the United States insisted Saddam was hiding. Weapons of mass destruction notwithstanding, Iraq was a major producer of oil; talk of war raised jitters about potential shortages with attendant increases in price.

Late in the year North Korea—another member of Bush's axis of evil (the third was Iran)—raised international tensions when it acknowledged to U.S. officials that it had begun a program to enrich uranium for the production of nuclear weapons. U.S. demands that North Korea halt its nuclear weapons program created the unsettling potential of yet another international standoff.

In testimony before Congress in mid-November, Federal Reserve Board chairman Alan Greenspan cited "heightened geopolitical risks" as a main factor slowing economic recovery. The Fed had already dropped its key interest rate target by another half a percentage point, to 1.3 percent, leaving little room for monetary policy to accomplish much more in the way of stimulus. By the end of the year, many public and private policy makers and analysts were openly concerned that the economy might fall back into recession.

2003: Jobs and Deficits

After two years of uneven growth, the U.S. economy showed signs of getting back on track toward the end of 2003. The economy grew at an annual rate of 3 percent, a full percentage point higher than in 2002. The Federal Reserve cut the key federal funds interest rate another quarter of a percentage point in June, to 1 percent. Inflation also remained low, while productivity grew at its fastest pace in twenty years. The value of the dollar declined against other currencies, stimulating growth in American exports. Investors started coming back to a rallying stock market, where the Dow Jones Industrial Average rose above 10,000 points on Dec. 11 for the first time in eighteen months.

Two disturbing trends raised questions about the durability of the recovery, however. Job creation remained stagnant throughout 2003, showing little sign of growing fast enough to bring down the unemployment rate, which stayed in the 6 percent range. And the federal budget deficit climbed to its highest dollar level ever—$378 billion at the end of fiscal 2003. The return of large budget deficits required Congress to enact a record increase of nearly $1 trillion in the legal limit on the national debt.

The hangover from the recession of 2001, lost revenue from massive tax cuts, and increased spending to finance the war on terrorism and the invasion, in March 2003, of Iraq conspired to push up the federal budget deficit. At $378 billion in fiscal 2003, the deficit's dollar amount was at an all-time high, but it remained within historical levels in relation to the overall economy, representing just 3.4 percent of the nation's nearly $11 trillion economy.

The Bush administration called that a manageable level, justifiable in the face of a slow economic recovery and the heightened need for spending on national security. Democrats, gearing up for the 2004 presidential elections, as well as some Republicans, disagreed, portraying the administration as fiscally reckless in pursuing tax cuts as the deficit spiraled out of control.

A JOBLESS RECOVERY

Fears of a lingering "jobless recovery" came true in 2003. By the end of August, the country had been in the longest hiring slump since 1939, when the government first began tracking employment. The jobless rate reached a high of 6.4 percent in June before falling back to 5.7 percent in December. Overall, about 8.4 million workers were counted as unemployed because they were actively looking for work. Another 1.5 million jobless workers wanted to work, according to the Bureau of Labor Statistics, but were discouraged and had not recently looked for a job. By the end of the year, with a net loss of 2.3 million jobs, Bush was in danger of becoming the first president since Herbert Hoover (1929–1933) to register a net job loss during a presidential term.

Several factors helped explain the dismal job growth picture. One was a pickup in the rate of productivity—the output a worker produced for each hour worked—largely because employers had figured out how to use technology more efficiently. For the year productivity was up about 5 percent over 2002. Overcapacity was another reason. Some companies had invested so much in plants and people during the boom years of the 1990s that they were still working off excess capacity in 2003. A third factor was trade expansion, as consumers turned away from higher-priced domestic goods to lower-priced imports for everything from clothing to computers and other electronic equipment.

But the most contentious factor was outsourcing or offshoring, as American workers complained that they were losing jobs to cheaper labor in China, India, and other foreign countries. Offshoring had started in the 1970s for many manufacturing sectors that found it more profitable to move their production facilities overseas. With the advent of high-speed computers and communications technology, information-based service industries had also began to outsource some of their operations, such as call centers and bookkeeping functions, to foreign countries. More recently companies had begun to move more high-skilled jobs to India, ranging from financial analysis and accounting to CAT scan readings and health insurance claims evaluation.

2003 TAX CUT

Bush continued to insist that tax cuts were the best way to deal with both the budget deficit and the slow pace of job creation. Tax cuts would stimulate economic growth that would give employers reason to take on new workers and that would produce the tax revenue to pay down the deficit so long as Congress held down federal spending.

In his State of the Union address in January, Bush called for $726 billion in tax cuts and tax credits. The centerpiece of the proposal was the elimination of most taxes on stock dividends paid to individuals, a proposal Democrats derided as "no millionaire left behind," a play on the Bush administration education initiative "no child left behind." Concerns about the fairness of the proposal along with its sheer size also made many congressional Republicans nervous, and Bush ultimately was forced to accept a tax cut that totaled $330 billion over ten years, along with another $20 billion in aid to the states. The key provisions of the bill, which was signed into law on May 28 (PL 108-27), reduced the tax rate on dividends and capital gains to 15 percent through 2008, accelerated some of the individual income tax cuts enacted in 2001, and increased the per-child tax credit in 2003 and 2004.

Another potential budget-buster was legislation passed at the end of 2003 overhauling the Medicare program and creating a prescription drug benefit for seniors, starting in 2006. The measure (PL 108-173) was a major victory for the president, not least because it robbed Democrats of a campaign issue on which they long campaigned. But the new program would almost certainly contribute to the federal budget deficit—it was estimated to cost $400 billion over ten years, and Congress passed it under rules that did not require the new entitlement to be offset by spending cuts or tax increases. Almost as soon as the measure passed, estimates of its cost climbed to at least $534 billion.

2004: The Economy, Taxes, and Presidential Politics

Despite the uncertainties of a close presidential election at home and a mounting insurgency in Iraq, the American economy turned in a sold performance in 2004. Annual economic growth stood at 4.4 percent for the year, the best rate since 1999. A record increase in world oil prices and a slide in the value of the dollar did not appear to affect consumer spending, business investment, and corporate profits, all of which remained strong.

Consumer spending, which accounted for two-thirds of economic activity, continued to underpin economic growth in 2004. U.S. households owned more than $14 trillion in real estate assets, almost twice as much as they held in stocks and mutual funds. That was the result largely of the biggest boom ever in housing prices, which had gone up nearly 7 percent a year for four straight years. The housing boom was showing signs of slowing by the end of the year, however, which could eventually have an effect on consumer spending. Although construction of new homes appeared to be continuing apace, houses were taking longer to sell, owners were running into price resistance, and more deals were falling through. The median price for an existing house fell back from a high of $191,000 in June to $187,000 in October.

One factor slowing the housing market might have been rising interest rates. Although inflation remained low in 2002, at an annual rate of 3.5 percent, the sudden spike in energy prices, coupled with two years of record high federal budget deficits and signs of slowing labor productivity, put upward pressure on prices. To keep inflation in check, the Federal Reserve, after steadily reducing interest rates from 2001 through June 2003, announced that it planned a gradual rate increase. Starting in June 2004, the Fed raised the federal funds rate on overnight loans five times, each time by a quarter of a percentage point. At the end of the year, the rate was 2.3 percent, still well below historical trends.

About 2.2 million jobs were added to the economy in 2004—enough to save Bush from becoming the first president in seventy years to preside over a net loss of jobs but still far short of the hopes of millions of American workers who were still out of work. The jobless rate, which had been hovering around 6 percent for two years, fell to around 5.5 percent in 2004, but the decline had as much to do with discouraged workers dropping out of the formal labor market as it did with new jobs being created.

The budget deficit reached a new record dollar high in fiscal 2004—$412 billion—and voices of protest grew louder among fiscal conservatives and Democrats, who warned that the debt was becoming unsustainable. Republican moderates in the Senate blocked passage of the annual budget resolution because it did not include pay-as-you-go rules, which required revenue increases or spending cuts to offset tax cuts or mandatory spending. Congress also managed to hold discretionary nondefense spending to a 1 percent increase over the previous year.

But spending on the military operations in Iraq and Afghanistan continued. By the end of 2004, the two operations had cost at least $201 billion that had not been previously budgeted. (*Congressional Research Service estimate, table, p. 355*)

In addition, election year pressures propelled two more tax cut packages through Congress in 2004. With solid support from both Democrats and Republicans, Congress in September cleared a ten-year $146 billion package of tax cut extensions, primarily for individuals and families, that did not contain any offsets. In October Congress approved a $137 billion package of corporate tax cuts filled with dozens of special interest provisions for companies large and small. The final bill was packed with so many goodies for so many states that even Democrats who had initially opposed the measure felt compelled to vote for it. The measure's authors said the costs would be offset by closing several loopholes; skeptics assumed that corporations and their lawyers would soon find new ones.

ECONOMY AND THE ELECTIONS

Deficits were not uppermost on voters' minds as they weighed whether to give President Bush a second term or to replace him with Massachusetts senator John Kerry. Kerry tried to keep his campaign focused on what he said were the shortcomings of Bush's economic policies—most notably the lack of job creation. Kerry argued that Bush's policies, led by the tax cuts, had benefited the wealthy at the expense of the middle class and the working poor. To reduce the deficit and pay for expanded health care coverage, Kerry said he would repeal the tax cuts enacted in 2001 and 2003 for all taxpayers earning more than $200,000 a year.

For his part, Bush emphasized the positive signs in the economy, defended his tax cut policies as the best way to stimulate the economy, and promised to cut the deficit in half in five years. Bush also managed to shift the focus of the campaign to issues of the two candidates' characters and their abilities to lead a country at war. In the end, the election turned not on the strength of the economy but on the strength of the nation's leader. National exit polls showed that voters most concerned about the economy and jobs preferred Kerry. But more voters wanted a strong leader who took clear stands on the issues, and they preferred Bush, who won with 51.4 percent of the vote.

NEW ECONOMIC THREAT?

By the end of the year, economists, commentators, and many policy makers were openly worrying that the high federal budget deficit, coupled with record U.S. trade deficits, was pushing the world economy toward instability. Preliminary figures put the 2004 trade deficit at $617.7 billion, compared with a deficit of $496.5 billion in 2003. The current account deficit—the combined balance on trade, international investment income, and other international financial transaction—was even higher, at an estimated $650 billion or so. Both the budget and the trade deficits were largely financed by foreign investors, including foreign governments. A steadily weakening dollar combined with an apparent slowing of foreign investments in American capital and financial assets toward the end of the year raised concerns that foreign lenders might be getting nervous about the ability of the United States to carry its massive debt.

The Bush administration downplayed those concerns, arguing that continued foreign willingness to finance the deficits was proof that foreigners saw investment in the United States as an opportunity rather than a great risk. The administration professed to supporting a strong dollar. But failure to prop up the dollar either by raising interest rates or intervening in foreign currency exchange markets indicated to analysts that the administration was willing to see the value of the dollar decline ever further.

Chronology of Action on Economic Policy: The Federal Budget

Introduction

The brief period of federal budget surpluses in the last years of the twentieth century ended almost as abruptly as it began. Washington was surprised in 1998 when the federal government posted its first budget surplus in nearly thirty years—the result largely of a booming economy and a roaring stock market that produced more taxpayers, higher incomes, and more taxable capital gains. Four years later the surplus had evaporated, a victim of economic recession, revenue lost to massive tax cuts, and increased spending to finance wars in Afghanistan and Iraq. By the end of fiscal 2004, the federal budget deficit had ballooned to $412 billion, a remarkable reversal from 2000, when the government ran a surplus of $236 billion.

Although the deficit's dollar amount at the end of 2004 was at an all-time high, it was well within historical levels in relation to the overall economy. The fiscal 2004 deficit represented just 3.6 percent of the nation's gross domestic product (GDP), the value of all the goods and services produced in the United States during the year—about $11 trillion. The Republican administration of President George W. Bush called the deficit manageable and said it was justified in the face of the slow economic recovery and the need for heightened spending on national security. *(Tables, pp. 45, 46)*

That stance was an unexpected role reversal. The last two Republican presidents to preside during an era of deficits, Ronald Reagan (1981–1989) and Bush's father, George H. W. Bush (1989–1993), paid at least public obeisance to the idea of balancing the budget, although in many of those twelve years the deficit as a percentage of gross domestic product was higher than in Bush's first four years. Also, in the early and mid-1990s it was congressional Republicans who called for a balanced-budget constitutional amendment to stop what they called the "tax and spend" Democrats, whom the GOP accused of driving the federal deficit to unacceptably high limits.

In the early 2000s Democrats took the mantle of fiscal responsibility, accusing the president and his party of jeopardizing the economic future of the country in pursuit of deeper and deeper tax cuts. But few Democrats talked about balanced budgets either, especially if that goal meant significant cuts in domestic spending programs.

Most politicians, as well as most economists, agreed that a short-term deficit was acceptable, even necessary, to smooth the economic rough edges caused by recession and war. They were more concerned about the long-term effects if the president and Congress proved unable to bring the deficit under control quickly. The first major wave of retirements from the baby boom generation, starting in 2008, was expected to increase Social Security and Medicare costs dramatically. The need for the government to borrow to finance those costs, added to an already large budget deficit, would stifle economic growth by raising interest rates, economists cautioned.

Declining revenues and the shift from federal budget surplus to deficit also sent the national debt soaring. Congress had to act three times, in 2002, 2003, and 2004, to raise the statutory ceiling on the total amount of debt the Treasury was allowed to have on its books at any one time. The debt limit

REFERENCES

Discussion of federal budget policy for the years 1945–1964 may be found in *Congress and the Nation Vol. I,* pp. 387–395; for the years 1965–1968, *Congress and the Nation Vol. II,* pp. 127–140; for the years 1969–1972, *Congress and the Nation Vol. III,* pp. 63–75; for the years 1973–1976, *Congress and the Nation Vol. IV,* pp. 57–81; for the years 1977–1980, *Congress and the Nation Vol. V,* pp. 211–230; for the years 1981–1984, *Congress and the Nation Vol. VI,* pp. 33–61; for the years 1985–1988 *Congress and the Nation Vol. VII,* pp. 33–74; for the years 1989–1992, *Congress and the Nation Vol. VIII,* pp. 37–86; for the years 1993–1996, *Congress and the Nation Vol. IX,* pp. 37–82.

The Federal Budget, Fiscal 1993–Fiscal 2004

(billions of dollars)

Year	Revenues	Outlays	On-budget	Social Security	Total[1] Surplus (Deficit)	Public Debt
1993	$1,154.4	$1,409.5	−$300.4	$46.8	−$255.1	$3,428.4
1994	1,258.6	1,461.9	−258.9	56.8	−203.2	3,433.1
1995	1,351.8	1,515.8	−226.4	60.4	−164.0	3,604.4
1996	1,453.1	1,560.5	−174.1	66.4	−107.5	3,734.1
1997	1,579.3	1,601.2	−103.3	81.3	−21.9	3,772.3
1998	1,721.8	1,652.6	−30.0	99.4	69.2	3,721.1
1999	1,827.5	1,703.0	1.9	124.7	124.4	3,632.4
2000	2,025.2	1,789.1	86.3	151.8	236.4	3,409.8
2001	1,991.2	1,863.0	−32.5	163.0	128.2	3,319.6
2002	1,853.2	2,011.0	−317.5	159.0	−157.8	3,540.4
2003	1,782.3	2,159.9	−538.4	155.6	−377.6	3,913.4
2004	1,880.1	2,292.2	−567.4	151.1	−412.1	4,295.5

1. Includes surplus (deficit) for the Postal Service.

SOURCE: Congressional Budget Office, *The Budget and Economic Outlook: Fiscal Years 2006–2015*, January, 2005.

went from $6 trillion in 2002 to $8.2 billion in 2004, and Congress was expected to face an additional increase in 2005. Failing to raise the debt limit could force the government to default on its obligations.

Voting to raise the debt ceiling was always a politically embarrassing task for lawmakers because it was a reminder of their inability to keep the nation's fiscal house in order. No Congress had ever failed to act when necessary, although the day of reckoning was often postponed as long as possible, forcing the Treasury to make unusual accounting maneuvers to avoid breaching the ceiling. In 2003, when Congress was forced to raise the ceiling by nearly $1 trillion, the House managed to approve the increase without taking an up-or-down vote. As a result, lawmakers avoided going on record on the always controversial issue.

HISTORICAL DEFICIT PATTERNS

Until the late 1960s the federal government had followed a fairly predictable cycle of deficits during times of war or economic crisis followed by surpluses during peacetime. The deficits that accompanied World War I and its immediate aftermath, for example, disappeared in 1920 and were followed by eleven years of surpluses during the "Roaring Twenties." As the Great Depression took hold President Franklin D. Roosevelt (1933–1945) sought to spur the economy and put people back to work through his version of Keynesian economics, which held that activist government intervention in the free market, including government spending, was the only sure route to economic prosperity and stability. Under Roosevelt Congress began a long-term expansion of the federal government. Yet even with the cost of World War II the federal ledger returned to surplus in 1947. Similarly, deficits

caused by the Korean War (1950–1953) turned to surpluses soon after the war ended.

The situation soon changed, however, giving way in 1961 to what would become a thirty-eight-year run of deficits, interrupted by one year of black ink: a $3.2 billion surplus in fiscal 1969. The end of the Vietnam War did not yield the "peace dividend" in the 1970s parallel to the postwar surpluses of the 1940 and 1950s. The difference, in large part, was the creation of entitlement programs such as Medicare and the expansion of others such as Social Security during Lyndon B. Johnson's presidency (1963–1969). Expenses for such programs increased so rapidly that the reduction in defense spending accompanying the U.S. pullout from Vietnam did not balance the federal ledger. (The U.S. formally withdrew in 1973.)

The annual deficit reached an all-time high of 6 percent of gross domestic product in fiscal 1983, after a massive tax cut and the cold war defense budget championed by President Ronald Reagan took hold. The highest deficit in terms of dollars before 2003 was $290 billion (4.7 percent of GDP), racked up in 1992. That deficit, and the tax increase imposed in an effort to control it, helped turn George H. W. Bush out of the White House after one term.

For the next several years, Republicans in Congress and Democratic president Bill Clinton (1993–2001) engaged in a titanic struggle over the budget and in 1997 agreed to a plan that called for a surplus beginning in 2002. They did not have to wait that long. A surging economy and stock market produced a wave of unexpected tax revenue that dwarfed the impact of the delicately negotiated deficit reduction package and produced a surplus of $69.2 billion in 1998. The federal balance sheets remained in the black through fiscal 2001, more than $400 billion was trimmed from the national debt, and budget surpluses were forecast for the foreseeable future.

RETURN OF DEFICITS

But in 2001 it all unraveled. In just one year the U.S. budget plunged from a $128 billion surplus, in fiscal 2001, to a $158 billion deficit, in fiscal 2002—a $285 billion swing. A recession of eight months' duration undermined revenue. President Bush and Congress further reduced the income stream with history-making tax cuts in 2001, then poured more money into defense and homeland security after the Sept. 11 terrorist attacks. *(Terrorist attacks, p. 229)*

Over the next three years a start-and-stop economic recovery continued to dampen federal revenues, while the Republican-led Congress in 2003 and 2004 enacted three more sizable tax cuts, drew up a new entitlement program giving seniors a prescription drug benefit at an estimated cost of $400 billion, and approved more than $200 billion for military operations and related costs in Afghanistan and Iraq, although the exact number was hidden in the complex and often opaque ledgers of military and intelligence budgets. By the end of fiscal 2004, the deficit had climbed to $412 billion. Both the tax cuts and the prescription drug benefit program

Deficit History, 1929–2004

(Fiscal years in billions of dollars)

Fiscal Year	Receipts	Outlays	Surplus or Deficit (−)	Surplus/deficit as % of GDP
1929	$3.9	$3.1	$0.7	—
1933	2.0	4.6	−2.6	−4.5%
1939	6.3	9.1	−2.8	−3.2
1940	6.5	9.5	−2.9	−3.0
1945	45.2	92.7	−47.6	−21.5
1950	39.4	42.6	−3.1	−1.1
1955	65.5	68.4	−3.0	−0.8
1960	92.5	92.2	0.3	−0.1
1965	116.8	118.2	−1.4	−0.2
1969	186.9	183.6	3.2	0.3
1970	192.8	195.6	−2.8	−0.3
1975	279.1	332.3	−53.2	−3.4
1980	517.1	590.9	−73.8	−2.7
1981	599.3	678.2	−79.0	−2.6
1982	617.8	745.8	−128.0	−4.0
1983	600.6	808.4	−207.8	−6.0
1984	666.5	851.9	−185.4	−4.8
1985	734.1	946.4	−212.3	−5.1
1986	769.2	990.4	−221.2	−5.0
1987	854.4	1,004.1	−149.7	−3.2
1988	909.3	1,064.5	−155.2	−3.1
1989	991.2	1,143.8	−152.6	−2.8
1990	1,032.0	1,253.1	−221.1	−3.9
1991	1,055.0	1,324.3	−269.3	−4.5
1992	1,091.3	1,381.6	−290.3	−4.7
1993	1,154.4	1,409.5	−255.1	−3.9
1994	1,258.6	1,461.9	−203.2	−2.9
1995	1,351.8	1,515.8	−164.0	−2.2
1996	1,453.1	1,560.5	−107.5	−1.4
1997	1,579.3	1,601.2	−21.9	−0.3
1998	1,721.8	1,652.6	69.2	0.8
1999	1,827.5	1,701.9	125.5	1.4
2000	2,025.2	1,789.1	236.1	2.4
2001	1,991.2	1,863.0	128.2	1.3
2002	1,853.2	2,011.0	−157.8	−1.5
2003	1,782.3	2,159.9	−377.6	−3.5
2004	1,880.2	2,292.2	−412.1	−3.6

SOURCE: Executive Office of the President, Office of Management and Budget, *Budget of the United States Government, Fiscal Year 2006, Historical Tables* (Washington, D.C.: Government Printing Office, 2005), Table 1.1.

GDP: Gross Domestic Product.

ensured a steady drawdown on federal revenues for years to come.

Initially the president and many legislators shrugged off the deficit, claiming it was justified by the recession and the war against terrorism. Even when the red ink more than doubled, from $158 billion in fiscal 2002 to $378 billion in fiscal 2003, calls for reducing it were muted. In part that may have been because there was little outside pressure to do much about the deficit. The business community, which mobilized on several fronts during the 1990s to persuade lawmakers to reduce the deficit, was noticeably quiet about its return. Voters did not seem particularly concerned, either. Asked whether they were more troubled about rising deficits or the lack of jobs, most said jobs, and for many voters nei-

ther issue was as important as winning the war against terrorism. In addition, a large part of the Republican Party's base was more focused on social issues, such as abortion and gay rights, than on government financial matters.

But gradually Republicans who saw the rising deficit as a looming economic problem and Democrats, who also saw it as a political vulnerability for Bush, began to make their voices heard. In 2002 the Senate was unable to pass the annual budget resolution setting tax and spending levels over Democratic objections that it did not contain enough debt reduction. The Senate failed again in 2004 to pass the budget resolution when a band of GOP moderates refused to support the conference report because Republican leaders had dropped language restoring so-called pay-as-you-go rules for tax cuts and new entitlement spending.

By 2003 the mounting red ink was also causing increased discomfort for fiscal conservatives in the Republican Party who feared their leaders were turning away from the party's long-held principles of small government and fiscal discipline. That discomfort was most apparent during debate in 2003 on creating a prescription drug benefit for seniors under Medicare. The measure, whose enactment was a top priority for Bush, was almost defeated, not once but twice, in the House when fiscal conservatives objected to adding a new entitlement. "I came to Washington to reform Great Society programs, not to ratify and enlarge them," said freshman Rep. Tom Feeney of Florida, referring to the name President Johnson gave to his programs of social welfare legislation in the mid-1960s.

"Republicans used to believe in fiscal responsibility, limited international entanglements, and limited government," Sen. Chuck Hagel of Nebraska wrote in November 2003. "We have come loose from our moorings. The Medicare reform bill is a good example of our lack of direction, purpose, and responsibility."

To appease the conservative wing of his party and his political base, President Bush in 2004 promised to cut the deficit in half in five years. Democrats questioned his credibility, noting that in the same budget he also asked for tax cut extensions, new tax breaks, and funding for space exploration of the moon and Mars.

CONTROLLING THE DEFICIT

With tax increases an impossibility in the Republican Party of Bush's years and defense spending likely to continue rising, the only area of the federal budget left to cut was domestic spending. Despite calls from Bush to hold the line on that spending, legislators—to no one's surprise—were unable to do so, raising domestic spending well above the rate of inflation in 2001, 2002, and 2003 even though Republicans were in firm control of Congress for much of the 2001 to 2005 period.

Controlling spending was difficult for several reasons. Many of the budgetary tools that Congress had used in the past to help maintain fiscal discipline—such as the pay-as-you-go rules—had been allowed to lapse. Republican leaders said they would support new rules requiring offsetting tax increases or spending cuts for new spending and entitlement programs but only if they did not apply to tax reductions.

Some fiscal conservatives blamed Bush for not exercising stronger leadership to hold down spending. They noted that Bush had not vetoed a single appropriations bill, even though many exceeded his budget requests. (Bush did not veto a bill of any type during the four years of his first term.) Others blamed Republican leaders, who often seemed no more prepared than Democratic leaders to say "no" to colleagues who wanted funding for local projects or expensive provisions for favored interests. Republicans wrote thousands of funding "earmarks" into spending bills. "There's no shame here. Earmarks have increased fourfold under Republicans," said Rep. Jeff Flake, a Republican from Arizona.

Increased spending was sometimes the inevitable result of mutually beneficial legislative dealmaking between House and Senate leaders or between Congress and the president. But as often as not it was also a result of individual members' unwillingness to refuse opportunities to please their constituents. Even many fiscal conservatives had trouble living up to their antideficit rhetoric. One conservative House member signed a December 2003 letter to House Speaker J. Dennis Hastert, R-Ill., berating the cost of the fiscal 2004 omnibus appropriations bill. Three days later the same member voted for the omnibus appropriations bill and her Web site touted her success in securing funding for a highway in her district.

By 2004 the political calculus had changed. With the fiscal deficit projected at more than $500 billion, and many of their chief legislative goals already achieved, Republicans of all stripes began to view the budget shortfall as an election-year liability. GOP moderates who previously had sought to reduce the deficit by calling for smaller tax cuts were now calling for spending restraint. With the White House and GOP leaders cracking the whip, Congress held discretionary, non-defense-related spending for fiscal 2005 to an increase of just 1 percent over comparable fiscal 2004 levels. It was the most fiscal restraint lawmakers had shown since the budget wars of fiscal 1995 and 1996.

But lawmakers still shied away from cutting into mandatory spending programs, such as Medicare, Medicaid, Social Security, and food stamps, in which persons who met eligibility requirements were entitled by law to receive benefits. Mandatory spending accounted for more than half of the $2 trillion federal budget and was the spending category that was likely to increase the most as the baby-boom generation reached retirement age.

Yet proposals for even minor cuts in mandatory spending tended to meet with immediate and intense opposition. In 2003, for example, House Budget Committee chairman Jim Nussle, R-Iowa, proposed a 1 percent cut in mandatory programs; within days, angry Republicans had forced him to scrap his plans. In 2004 Senate Budget chairman Don Nickles, R-Okla., proposed a reconciliation instruction in the budget resolution that would have forced $11 billion in Medicaid savings. It was stripped out on the Senate floor.

MORE RED INK?

As he prepared for his second term in office in late 2004 President Bush again pledged to cut the federal budget deficit in half in five years. Many observers, however, were skeptical that Bush would succeed or even that he meant it. They pointed to his continuing request to make tax cuts permanent, a move that analysts estimated would cost the government as much as $1.3 trillion over ten years. They also pointed to the United States' continuing military presence in Iraq and Afghanistan, and the start, in 2006, of the Medicare prescription drug benefit for seniors that was now expected to cost anywhere from $400 billion to twice that over ten years depending on whose estimates were used. (In addition, a devastating hurricane named Katrina in September 2005 hit several states on the Gulf of Mexico, especially Louisiana and Mississippi, and resulted in flooding of New Orleans that required the city to be evacuated. Cleanup and repair costs that the federal government would bear were expected to run into billions of dollars.)

Bush had also promised to propose an overhaul of the Social Security program to allow young workers to invest part of their payroll taxes in personal savings accounts. Analysts said the government would need to borrow as much as $2 trillion to cover the transition costs of such a change at the very time that the baby-boom generation was starting to retire and draw down the surplus in the Social Security trust funds.

There were only two ways those goals could be accomplished without significantly adding to the federal red ink. The economy had to grow for several years at rates faster than almost anyone, including administration officials, projected. Or legislators had to be willing to risk sacrificing their political lives to make unpopular spending and taxing choices. Few observers were willing to bet on either path.

2001–2002

In retrospect the budgeting and appropriations process in 2001 was the smoothest of any year in President George W. Bush's first term. Congress completed action on its annual budget resolution setting the parameters for tax and spending legislation on May 10 and finished all thirteen regular appropriations bills without resorting to catchall spending measures at the end of the year. In the following three years Congress was twice unable to adopt a budget resolution and had to use an omnibus appropriations package in each session.

Forecasts of big budget surpluses helped motivate Republicans to give their new president an early win on the centerpiece of his economic agenda: a huge cut in personal income taxes over ten years. To be sure, Senate moderates of both parties forced President Bush to accept a slightly smaller tax cut than he had proposed; nonetheless, the $1.4 trillion tax reduction allowed in the budget resolution and enacted in separate legislation late in May was the largest tax cut in more than twenty years. (*Tax reductions, p. 89*)

Setting spending limits and sticking to them turned out to be more difficult. In the end the White House agreed to add $6 billion to discretionary spending (the spending Congress had control over as opposed to entitlements, interest, and other payments the government was obligated by law to pay) in the budget resolution, and even more was added when Bush submitted a late request for defense spending. But appropriators in both parties and both chambers were still having trouble agreeing on spending levels and resolving controversial legislative riders that members sought to attach to the spending bills. Not a single one of the thirteen regular appropriations bills had passed by the time Congress left Washington for its annual August vacation.

That all changed in the aftermath of the terrorist attacks on New York and Washington. After Sept. 11, 2001, the White House and appropriators reached agreement on additional spending and disputes over legislative riders fell by the wayside. Congress did not adjourn until Dec. 20, but in the end all thirteen spending bills passed.

Congress in 2001 also passed an emergency supplemental after the terrorist attacks and a regular supplemental for fiscal 2001; such supplemental bills, considered toward the end of the fiscal year, were commonly used for expenses that were foreseen when the regular bills were written.

With the return of federal budget deficits as well as elections looming at the end of the year, the budgeting and appropriating process came close to grinding to a complete halt in 2002 when lawmakers were unable to agree among themselves or with the White House on discretionary spending levels. Congress failed to adopt a budget resolution for only the second time since the modern budget process was created in 1974. The breakdown came in the Senate where Democratic leaders decided not to bring the measure to the floor after a handful of Democrats said they would vote against it unless it did more to reduce the deficit.

The same stalemate over discretionary spending stymied action on the annual appropriations bills. Congress completed action only on the defense and military construction spending bills, leaving the other eleven to be completed at the beginning of the 108th Congress in 2003 when Republicans would have control over both chambers of Congress as a result of the 2002 elections. In the meantime, all departments and agencies covered by the unfinished bills were funded at fiscal 2002 levels under a string of five continuing resolutions. Congress did complete action in the middle of the year on a fiscal 2002 emergency supplemental spending bill to finance antiterrorism efforts abroad and security operations at home.

Congress in 2002 also was forced to raise the ceiling on the federal debt by $450 billion, to $6.4 trillion, to prevent the federal government from defaulting on its obligations. Republicans blamed the need to raise the debt limit on the terrorist attacks and the faltering economy; Democrats placed the blame on the tax cut and accused Republicans of being fiscally irresponsible.

Fiscal 2002 Budget Resolution

Adoption of the fiscal 2002 budget resolution, Congress's guide for the year's tax and spending decisions, was the bellwether test for President's Bush's budget agenda for his first year in office, including his bold request for $1.6 trillion in tax cuts. Although the GOP-controlled House was quick to endorse Bush's budget, the evenly divided Senate voted to limit the tax cuts to three-fourths of the amount the president wanted and allow discretionary spending to grow by at least $6.3 billion more than he sought. Nonetheless, the final budget resolution, adopted May 10, was a major victory for the president, setting the stage for the biggest federal tax cut in a generation while endorsing his pledge to restrain spending.

As adopted the budget resolution (H Con Res 83) called for $1.4 trillion in tax relief from 2001 through 2011, and $661.3 billion in fiscal 2002 discretionary spending—a 4 percent increase over fiscal 2001—with the understanding that more would be added later for defense after the new administration had reviewed Pentagon needs. The resolution allowed for additional tax cuts if the Congressional Budget Office (CBO) increased its estimate of the on-budget surplus.

The fiscal 2002 budget resolution was drafted without the usual aid of a full presidential budget from which to work. Although Bush submitted a budget outline on Feb. 28, the administration did not release a detailed budget until April 9. By that time both chambers had already adopted their initial versions of the budget resolution.

BACKGROUND

Although the budget resolution Congress votes on does not become law, it is an important planning tool for the law-

A BUDGET GLOSSARY

Appropriations. The process by which Congress provides budget authority, usually through the enactment of thirteen separate appropriations bills.

Budget authority. The authority for federal agencies to spend or otherwise obligate money, accomplished through enactment of appropriations bills.

Budget outlays. Money that is actually spent in a given fiscal year, as opposed to money that is appropriated for that year. One year's budget authority can result in outlays over several years, and the outlays in a any given year result from a mix of budget authority from that and other years.

Discretionary spending. Programs that Congress can finance as it chooses through appropriations (usually within the parameters set by authorization bills). With the exception of paying entitlement benefits to individuals and interest on the national debt (see mandatory spending), almost everything the government does is financed by discretionary spending. Examples include all federal agencies, Congress, the White House, the federal courts, the military, and activities from space exploration to child nutrition. About a third of all federal spending falls into this category.

Fiscal year. The budget year, which runs from October 1 of one year to September 30 of the next.

Mandatory spending. Spending on programs, made up mostly of entitlements, whose eligibility requirements are written into law. Anyone who meets those requirements is entitled to the money until Congress changes the law. Examples include Social Security, Medicare, Medicaid, unemployment benefits, food stamps, and federal pensions.

Another major category of mandatory spending is the interest paid to holders of federal government bonds. Social Security and interest payments are permanently appropriated. And although budget authority for some entitlements is provided through the appropriations process, appropriators have little or no control over the money. Mandatory spending accounts for about two-thirds of all federal spending.

Reconciliation. The process by which tax laws and spending programs are changed, or reconciled, to reach outlay and revenue targets set in the congressional budget resolution. Established by the 1974 Congressional Budget Act, it was first used in 1980.

Rescission. The cancellation of previously appropriated budget authority. This is a common way to save money that already has been appropriated. A rescissions bill must be passed by Congress and signed by the president (or enacted over his veto), just as an appropriations bill.

Revenues. Taxes, customs duties, some user fees, and most other receipts paid to the federal government. Some receipts and user fees show up as "negative outlays," however, and do not count as revenue.

Sequester. The cancellation of spending authority as a disciplinary measure to stop spending above the preset limits. Appropriations that exceed annual spending caps can trigger a sequester that would cut all appropriations by the amount of the excess. Similarly, tax cuts or new or expanded entitlement spending programs that are not offset under pay-as-you-go rules would trigger a sequester of nonexempt entitlement programs.

---

makers, setting parameters for appropriations and effectively limiting the scope of any tax cut. During the previous six years the budget resolution had been drafted largely as a political statement underscoring the GOP majority's commitment to tax cuts and spending constraints. Democratic president Bill Clinton vetoed a series of ambitious tax measures and, aided by appropriators from both parties, routinely demanded and won far more spending than the GOP budget resolution allowed. In 2000, for example, Congress simply included language in the foreign operations bill (PL 106-249) raising the caps on discretionary spending.

But with Republicans in control of the White House and both chambers of Congress at the outset of the 107th Congress, the dynamic changed. Republicans were under pressure to set a spending ceiling they could live with because they knew they could no longer blame the White House if it were broken. And the minority Democrats, no longer able to rely on a presidential veto, saw the budget resolution as their best hope for limiting tax cuts.

The budget resolution gave procedural protection to tax bills in the Senate, allowing them to be considered under special "reconciliation" rules that barred a filibuster, imposed a twenty-hour limit on debate, and restricted amendments. In the Senate, which was split 50–50 in the first months of the 107th Congress, Democrats knew that once a tax bill got such protection it would be all but impossible to stop. Using the budget resolution to limit the size of the tax cut that could be enacted was a key Democratic goal. (*Glossary of budget terms, above*)

HIGHLIGHTS

The final budget resolution contained the following highlights:

• **Tax cuts.** The House Ways and Means and Senate Finance committees were each instructed to report a reconciliation bill by May 18 that would reduce taxes by as much as $1.4 trillion through 2011. Of that amount $100 billion was intended as an economic stimulus in fiscal 2001 and 2002.

• **Discretionary spending.** The final budget provided for $661.3 billion, 4.2 percent above the $634.9 billion Bush said had been appropriated for fiscal 2001. In terms of regular appropriations the total was $6.3 billion more than Bush had sought; the president's budget included a $5.6 billion reserve fund for unforeseen emergencies that was not included in the budget resolution. A $5 billion emergency fund initially included in the conference report was dropped when House leaders could not agree on a method for allocating the money. The idea was to set aside money for the inevitable, if unpredictable, annual emergencies, thus restraining supplemental spending and making it more predictable.

• **Nondefense spending.** The overall discretionary spending limit included $336.2 billion for domestic and international programs. The CBO estimated that an additional $6.8 billion would be needed to continue those programs at existing service levels. The total was about $390 million more than the House or the president sought but $17.4 billion less than the Senate endorsed.

• **Defense spending.** Defense was allocated $325.1 billion, a 4.7 percent increase, as requested, pending completion of the administration's long-term review of defense needs and a supplemental request. The agreement also included $6.5 billion for a fiscal 2001 defense supplemental appropriation, a provision that was not contained in either the House or Senate budget resolution.

• **Agriculture.** One of the big winners, agriculture was allocated an additional $79 billion over ten years beyond existing programs. The conference agreement set aside $5.5 billion for support payments to farm producers before the end of fiscal 2001, $7.4 for a fiscal 2002 farm bailout, and $66.2 billion over ten years to pay for a new multiyear farm bill. *(Farm aid, pp. 449, 462)*

• **Medicare.** The agreement called for increasing Medicare spending by $313.7 billion over ten years. The total included a $300 billion reserve fund for Medicare reform and a prescription drug benefit, should they be enacted. The remaining $13.7 billion was earmarked to restore payments to Medicare home health care providers. *(Medicare changes, p. 496, prescription drug coverage, pp. 483, 496)*

• **Education.** The final budget did not include $294 billion over ten years that the Senate had added for education programs.

• **Surplus.** The budget projected a fiscal 2002 surplus of $218.6 billion, $47.7 billion of it on-budget and the remainder off-budget, almost entirely in the Social Security trust fund. The budget forecast a cumulative surplus of $3.4 trillion through fiscal 2011, $897 billion of it on-budget.

• **Debt reduction.** The publicly held debt was to be reduced by $2.4 trillion by fiscal 2011, leaving $818 billion.

BUSH BUDGET REQUEST

The vision President Bush laid out Feb. 28, 2001, in his $2 trillion fiscal 2002 budget was far from the sweeping reduction in federal power and the dramatic cuts in federal spending that his fellow Republicans had proposed when the party took over the Capitol six years earlier. Bush proposed holding discretionary spending—the funding Congress had power to allocate to various federal programs—to $660.6 billion, which he calculated as a 4 percent increase in budget authority. Defense and education were slated to get significant increases, which meant that most other departments would have to settle with less.

As promised during the presidential campaign, the central feature of Bush's budget request was a massive cut in personal income taxes, including across-the-board reductions in marginal tax rates, repeal of the estate tax, elimination of the "marriage penalty," an increase in the child tax credit, and wider benefits for charitable giving. The cost—$1.6 trillion over ten years—was revised from the $1.3 trillion Bush had promised in his 2000 election campaign.

The April 9 budget gave full details of Bush's domestic and foreign aid spending proposals, but the defense request—$310.5 billion—was essentially a place-holder, pending the results of a review of military strategy and resources that the Pentagon was conducting. The target completion date for the review was May 15—five days after Congress completed work on the fiscal 2002 budget resolution.

The administration said the budget's late release—two months after the usual deadline of early February—was necessary because it took that much time to rework the budget left by the Clinton administration. In a break from his predecessors, Clinton had not proposed a full fiscal 2002 budget as he left office. The document released Jan. 16 was described by the Clinton White House as a review of the last eight years, a set of baseline projections, and an economic outlook; it did not include any policy recommendations.

Although it might have been necessary, the delay nonetheless helped Bush win endorsement for the broad outlines of his tax and spending plans in the congressional budget resolution before legislators were faced with the details of the offsetting spending cuts that would be required to make those plans happen.

HOUSE ACTION

The House Budget Committee voted 23–19 along party lines March 21, 2001, to approve a budget resolution (H Con Res 83—H Rept 107-26) that generally followed Bush's broad budget proposals. The House resolution instructed the Ways and Means Committee to write four tax-cutting reconciliation bills with deadlines of May 2, May 23, June 20, and Sept. 11. It called for a fifth reconciliation measure—to be reported by the Ways and Means and Energy and Commerce committees by July 24—to alter Medicare, the federal health insurance program for the elderly and disabled, and to add a limited prescription drug benefit. Bush proposed spending $153 billion to that end in the next decade. Democrats complained that the resolution set unreasonable spending levels. But Republicans hung together and rejected all but a few of roughly three dozen Democratic amendments offered during the twelve-hour markup. The principal Democratic proposal was not a detailed alternative but a "framework" calling for a $713 billion tax cut; increases that at least kept pace with inflation in all categories of spending; and larger amounts, al-

President George W. Bush (followed by Senate Majority Leader Trent Lott, R-Miss.) leaves the House floor after his first address to Congress on February 27, 2001. In his speech, President Bush focused on the budget and lobbied for a $1.6 trillion tax cut. *Source: Congressional Quarterly/ Scott J. Ferrell*

though no figures were specified, for education, defense, agriculture, health research, transportation, veterans benefits, conservation, law enforcement, and other priorities. The Democratic framework was rejected by voice vote.

Indicative of the controversy surrounding the issue, the budget did not include Bush's assumption of new revenues from leases for oil drilling in the Arctic National Wildlife Refuge (ANWR). *(ANWR debate, pp. 412, 425, 432)*

The full House adopted the budget resolution March 28 on a party-line vote of 222–205. Three Democrats voted for the plan; only two Republicans voted no.

The House rejected four alternative budgets, all but one by significant margins. The one close vote came on an alternative offered by a group of fiscally conservative Democrats known as the Blue Dogs. The proposal called for a five-year budget that included more defense spending and a $180 billion tax cut through fiscal 2006. It was defeated 204–221 but drew the support of a dozen Republicans. The Democratic leadership's alternative, which called for a 7 percent spending increase in fiscal 2001 and $797 billion in tax cuts through 2011, was defeated 183–243.

A version offered by the Republican Study Committee, a group made up of the most fiscally conservative GOP members, called for cutting taxes by $2.3 trillion and spending controls to limit the growth in spending to 2.9 percent annually over the next ten years. It was defeated 81–341. The fourth version, offered by the Progressive Caucus, called for a $737 billion tax cut and higher levels of domestic spending. It was defeated 79–343.

SENATE ACTION

Senate Budget Committee Chair Pete V. Domenici, R-N.M., concluded that a markup by his panel would end in an 11–11 tie and thus fail to send the budget to the floor. The committee was evenly divided between the two parties under

a power-sharing arrangement worked out in January because the 2000 elections had produced an even 50–50 split between Republicans and Democrats. As a result, Republicans took advantage of special budget rules that allowed them to put measures directly before the Senate after April 1. The document Domenici readied for floor debate generally hewed to Bush's Feb. 28 budget outline. Like the House version, however, it did not count on any revenue from oil leasing in ANWR.

One week after Republicans pushed the president's version of the budget through the House, Bush's aspirations landed hard in the evenly divided Senate. When the horse-trading and compromises were over, the Senate voted 65–35 on April 6 to adopt a budget that limited the size of the tax cut to $1.2 trillion from 2002 through 2011. That was $440 billion less than Bush proposed. The Senate budget also called for as much as $85 billion in retroactive tax cuts for 2001, which Bush had not sought, bringing the total tax cuts in the budget to $1.3 trillion. The target for discretionary spending was at least $688 billion, 7 percent more than the level being sought in fiscal 2001, compared with the 4 percent growth that Bush wanted.

At the start of the Senate debate there was more action behind the scenes than there was on the Senate floor. Vice President Dick Cheney, White House Budget Director Mitchell E. Daniels Jr., and other White House officials descended on the Capitol to hunt for Democratic defections and to press Republican moderates to commit to Bush's plan. Only after White House negotiators and the GOP leadership gave up trying to find enough votes to preserve Bush's full tax cut was the Senate able to adopt the revised budget.

The key vote came on April 4 when three GOP moderates—James M. Jeffords of Vermont, Lincoln Chafee of Rhode Island, and Arlen Specter of Pennsylvania—broke from the fold to ensure adoption of an amendment reducing the tax cut by $448 billion, with the difference to be split between education spending and more debt reduction. The amendment, by Tom Harkin, D-Iowa, was adopted on a **key vote of 53–47 (R 4–46; D 49–1)** after Majority Leader Trent Lott, R-Miss., switched from a vote of "no" to a "yes" so that he could move to reconsider the vote later, a tactical maneuver often used by senators in the majority; he never did. *(2001 key votes, p. 801)*

Adoption of the amendment—ensuring that Bush would have to accept lower tax cuts if he wanted to get a bill through the chamber—appeared to stun the Senate. Democrats savored the moment. Minority Leader Tom Daschle of South Dakota went upstairs to the press gallery, as did several other Democratic senators, to tout the victory. Daschle predicted that more amendments to boost spending and reduce the tax cuts would be adopted. The next day senators engaged in a tit-for-tat battle over tax cuts, adopting some and defeating others. The net result was the restoration of $100 billion of the tax cuts removed by Harkin's amendment.

Bush put the best face on the outcome. "The fact that both houses of Congress have committed to finding significant relief is good for the American people and good for the economy," he said after the final vote.

Senate Republicans were able to claim one important procedural victory: the inclusion of reconciliation protection for tax cut legislation, without which their chances of writing a tax bill to their liking would have been markedly diminished. By a vote of 51–49 the Senate adopted a Domenici amendment to instruct the Finance Committee to report two reconciliation bills to the Senate that would reduce taxes by no more than Bush's goal of $1.6 billion. Zell Miller of Georgia, the sole Democrat to vote against the Harkin amendment, joined a united GOP bloc to form the majority. Democrats led by Robert C. Byrd of West Virginia had argued that reconciliation rules—written to make it easier to pass deficit-reduction bills in the Senate—should not be used to shield major tax cuts.

On April 3 Vice President Dick Cheney cast his first tie-breaking vote. It came on an amendment by Charles E. Grassley, R-Iowa, to reserve $300 billion over ten years to overhaul the Medicare program and create a Medicare prescription drug benefit. That was nearly double the amount Bush had proposed. The amendment was a response to a Democratic amendment that would have allocated $311 billion for that purpose but specified that the amendment could not be funded by surplus in the Medicare hospital trust fund, a move Republicans opposed. The Republican amendment, which also would have made the writing of a prescription drug plan optional, triumphed 51–50, with Cheney's vote providing the winning margin; the Democratic proposal failed on a 50–50 tie. *(Prescription drug plan, p. 496)*

CONFERENCE, FINAL ACTION

House and Senate conferees met only once. The real negotiations took place in meetings among GOP budget writers, the White House, and centrist Democrats. The White House bypassed Democratic leaders to concentrate on a handful of moderate but influential Senate Democrats such as John B. Breaux of Louisiana and Ben Nelson of Nebraska. Budget Committee Democrats were shut out. "We don't expect you to sign [the conference report], so we don't expect you to be needed," Domenici told them.

Bush, who had doggedly held to his position during the House and Senate debates, even stumping in members' districts to build support for his $1.6 trillion tax cut proposal, became more pragmatic when it was time to negotiate. "The dynamics have shifted in this debate," he said April 25. "We've come from the ideological to the practical, and I'm a practical man. I want to get it done."

The Republican conferees completed their work May 3. The House adopted the conference report (H Rept 107-60) on May 9 by a vote of 221–207. The Senate followed suit the next day 53–47. While Bush and his spokesman characterized the votes as "bipartisan" endorsements for the new administration's fiscal program, only six Democrats in the House and five in the Senate supported the final budget. Republicans lost only three GOP votes in the House and two in the Senate. The measure did not require the president's signature.

Fiscal 2002 Appropriations

With a fiscally conservative Republican in the Oval Office, the surplus-fueled spending surges of the late 1990s were expected to disappear. Instead the annual growth in spending continued to outpace both the president's budget and the congressional budget resolution—not to mention the long-since obsolete balanced budget caps set in 1997.

Although the need to respond to the Sept. 11, 2001, terrorist attacks accounted for much of the increase, Congress was poised even before then for a significant expansion in spending. With large budget surpluses projected and Bush focused on enacting his tax cut proposals, Congress passed a budget resolution (H Con Res 83) calling for a 4 percent increase in discretionary spending. In addition, the budget allowed Bush to pursue another $18.4 billion increase for defense spending after completing a preliminary review of the military requirements. That increase was in addition to—not at the expense of—domestic spending.

In all the GOP eventually endorsed spending $680 billion in the regular fiscal 2002 appropriations bills after Bush submitted his defense request, a 7 percent increase. It was a far cry from the first-year budget goals of previous Republican administrations. Bush's father, George H. W. Bush (1989–1993) proposed real dollar cuts in a number of domestic programs, and President Ronald Reagan (1981–1989) proposed eliminating some federal agencies entirely.

Nevertheless, appropriators in both parties chafed under the spending limits. Meanwhile, fiscal conservatives looked to Bush to follow through on a threat made earlier in the year to veto bills that broke the spending limits. Democrats wanted Bush to revise his own request upward. Otherwise, they said, they would stick to the budget resolution, forcing Bush either to accept bills with none of the big increases he wanted for defense and education or veto them because they did not spend enough.

Congress late in 2001 had not cleared a single fiscal 2002 spending bill by Sept. 11 when the terrorist attacks forced all sides to adjust their budget goals substantially. Republican leaders agreed to spend more on domestic programs to help minimize partisan bickering over the thirteen regular appropriations bills. Democrats agreed to the first installment of Bush's defense buildup without a complaint. Talk of a "lockbox" to protect surpluses in the Social Security and Medicare trust funds evaporated, and a balanced budget became a distant goal.

A major breakthrough came on Oct. 2 when top appropriators reached agreement with the White House to increase the fiscal 2002 discretionary spending limit by $6 billion, to $686 billion. Of that $4 billion went to education and $2 billion to emergency firefighting.

One by one the bills began to clear. Stubborn disputes over exports to Cuba, mining regulations, drinking water standards, and other issues were resolved or sidestepped. Three bills (Defense; Labor, Health and Human Services; and foreign operations) did not clear until Dec. 20, the last day of the session.

A series of eight continuing resolutions kept the government operating while the bills were being completed. When the books were closed on fiscal 2002, the Congressional Budget Office calculated total discretionary spending at $712 billion in budget authority—roughly 11 percent more than was appropriated in 2000, the last year of the Clinton administration—and $731 billion in outlays.

Following are highlights of the thirteen regulation appropriations bills.

DEFENSE

Congress cleared a $317.5 billion Defense Department spending bill for fiscal 2002 that postponed tough choices about the future shape of the military and funded nearly everything on the president's wish list—from cold war–style weapons to equipment for unconventional battles. As was customary, the measure closely followed the outlines of the annual defense authorization bill (PL 107-107). *(Defense authorization, p. 309)*

Still, the spending bill was dogged by controversy and delay, much of it tied to a separate fight between Congress and the Bush administration over allocating $20 million in emergency funding for counterterrorism and New York City's recovery from the Sept. 11 terrorist attacks on the World Trade Center. The defense bill was not cleared until Dec. 20, the final day of the session, making it the last of the thirteen regular appropriations bills sent to the White House. President Bush signed it into law (HR 3338—PL 107-117) on Jan. 10, 2002. *(Emergency spending, p. 317)*

The final bill was $1.9 billion less than Bush requested but about the same amount as approved by the House and Senate. The total was almost $19 billion more than the fiscal 2001 level, including fiscal 2001 supplemental spending.

The measure had an inauspicious start. Members of the House Defense Appropriations Subcommittee were meeting in the Capitol to begin work on the bill the morning of Sept. 11 when the session was abruptly canceled and the building evacuated shortly after terrorists crashed hijacked jetliners into the World Trade Center and the Pentagon.

Nearly a month later, on Oct. 9, the subcommittee tried again but again the session was canceled—this time to protest Bush's decision to limit the number of lawmakers who would be briefed on secret information about the administration's counterterrorism campaign. Leaks of information and published reports citing congressional sources infuriated Bush, who wanted to restrict the closed briefings. The White House eventually relented, allowing key members of defense, foreign policy, and intelligence oversight committees to receive the secret briefings.

The subcommittee finally met Oct. 10, quickly approving the bill by voice vote. The full committee approved the measure on Oct. 24 (H Rept 107-298), but Appropriations Committee chair C. W. Bill Young, R-Fla., delayed filing the measure with the House until appropriators decided what and how much in the emergency spending measure was to be included in the defense bill. Disputes over allocating the emergency funds and how much authority to grant the president delayed both measures for more than a month. Once those issues were resolved the House quickly and overwhelmingly passed a defense spending bill that made changes only at the margins of Bush's budget request. The vote was 406–20. *(Emergency supplemental, p. 318)*

In the Senate the Appropriations Committee added a provision that would allow the air force to dispose of forty-year-old refueling tankers and lease modified 767s from Boeing Co., a financial boon for the airline manufacturer hard hit by the downturn in the industry. Although some members challenged the leasing deal as a corporate bailout, the provision remained in the bill (HR 3338—S Rept 107-109) passed by the Senate Dec. 7 by voice vote. The provision faced more hurdles in the House-Senate conference as well as resistance from the Office of Management and Budget. But strong support from the Washington delegation, where Boeing had been headquartered and still had jet manufacturing plants, and from House Speaker J. Dennis Hastert, a Republican from Illinois where Boeing had recently moved its corporate headquarters, overcame the opposition, and the leasing arrangement stayed in the bill.

Once House-Senate conferees came to an agreement on allocation of the $20 million in the emergency supplemental both chambers moved quickly to clear the bill. The House adopted the conference report (H Rept 107-350) 408–6 on Dec. 20. The Senate cleared it a few hours later the same day on a vote of 94–2.

FOREIGN AID

Lawmakers cleared a $15.4 billion fiscal 2002 foreign operations spending bill on Dec. 20, the final day of the session. The measure, written well before the Sept. 11 terrorist attacks, emphasized long-standing foreign policy priorities, from antidrug aid to South America to combating AIDS overseas. The need to assist partners in the war on terrorism was addressed in separate emergency spending bills (PL 107-38, PL 107-117) or deferred to 2002. President Bush signed the foreign aid bill (HR 2506—PL 107-115) on Jan. 10, 2002. *(Homeland security, p. 171)*

Debate on the bill focused largely on perennial controversies, especially the link between international family planning assistance and abortion. This time the flashpoint was a decision by Bush shortly after taking office to reinstate Reagan-era abortion restrictions, known as the Mexico City policy, that prohibited aid to international family planning organizations that performed or promoted abortions even if they used their own funds to do so. President Bill Clinton had revoked the policy when he first entered the White House in 1993. An effort by Senate Democrats to drop the provision drew a veto threat; Democrats ultimately withdrew the provision but won increased federal aid for international family planning efforts. That angered conservative Republicans, who held off clearing the bill until the last moment. *(Mexico City policy, pp. 246, 247)*

Appropriators reduced aid for U.S. antidrug programs to Colombia, with lawmakers expressing growing skepticism that the aid was doing much to stop guerrilla warfare and drug trafficking in the country. Bush had requested $731 million for the Andean Counterdrug Initiative, but Senate Democrats reduced that amount to $547 million. The final bill included $625 million for the program. *(Drug program, p. 248)*

LABOR-HHS

Substantial increases for medical research and low-income school children paved the way for Congress to clear the spending bill (HR 3061) for the departments of Education, Health and Human Services (HHS), and Labor by wide margins. The House adopted the conference report on the measure (H Rept 107-342) 393–30 on Dec. 19; the Senate cleared the bill 90–7 on Dec. 20. The president signed it into law (PL 107-116) on Jan. 10, 2002.

Both chambers started unusually late on the biggest and most contentious of all spending bills; the fiscal 2002 measure did not begin to move through the Appropriations committees until October. But an agreement to provide generous funding increases for social programs helped the bill clear after some of the easiest negotiations in years.

Education and HHS were the big winners. Total spending for HHS increased by nearly 14 percent over fiscal 2001. Education spending grew by 15 percent. Overall, the bill appropriated $407.7 billion, most of it mandatory spending for programs such as Medicaid and unemployment benefits. Total discretionary funding, the portion under the control of appropriators, was $123.4 billion.

Appropriators got a late start on the spending measure because they were having trouble figuring out how to fit their domestic and defense priorities within limits set in the budget resolution (H Con Res 83); they also wanted to wait until they found out how much would be required under the separate overhaul of the 1965 Elementary and Secondary Education Act (ESEA) that was also moving through Congress. Both sides, however, wanted to avoid the extended fights over labor, education priorities, and abortion that had led to lengthy and unsatisfactory end-of-year negotiations in the past. *(Education overhaul, p. 540)*

In the House key appropriators from both parties agreed in June to push the White House for an extra $4 billion for education. They got the increase as part of an agreement with the administration finalized Oct. 2. Senate Democrats wanted substantially more, arguing that it was needed to help low-income schools comply with new testing requirements in the education overhaul bill, but they were unsuccessful.

A main stumbling block that prevented quick action by conferees was a Senate proposal to ease restrictions on insurance coverage for mental health care. The provision barred employers who offered mental health care coverage from putting tighter restrictions on it than on coverage they provided for physical illnesses—for example, by charging higher co-payments. The provision, which had been hotly contested in previous Congresses, was ultimately dropped at the insistence of House GOP conferees.

In other action the final bill agreed to provide $393 million to stockpile vaccines and drugs to limit damage from biological or chemical attacks. The spending bill also continued the 1995 ban on funding for research on embryos but declared that Bush's proposal to fund research on certain stem cell lines already extracted from embryos did not violate this policy.

TRANSPORTATION

Congress on Dec. 4 cleared a $59.6 billion fiscal 2002 spending bill for the Transportation Department and related agencies that provided a substantial increase in funding for highway, transit, and aviation programs. It also allowed Mexican trucks to operate nationwide, giving Bush an important victory and ending a long-running battle involving free trade, organized labor, and highway safety. The bill provided significant spending increases for the Coast Guard and included $1.3 billion for the new Transportation Security Administration created by a separate aviation security law. President Bush signed the appropriations bill (HR 2299—PL 107-87) on Dec. 18. *(Mexican trucking, p. 371; Transportation Security Administration, pp. 198, 200, 215)*

Most of the funding in the bill was beyond the control of appropriators. More than 70 percent of it was guaranteed under landmark highway and aviation funding laws enacted in 1998 and 2000, respectively. *(Congress and the Nation Vol. X, pp. 318, 331)*

The $15.3 billion in discretionary spending was a $1.3 billion decrease from fiscal 2001. By eliminating new funding for specific highway projects appropriators were able to provide modest discretionary increases for core transportation programs.

OTHER REGULAR SPENDING BILLS

The following nine regular fiscal 2002 spending bills were passed with relatively little controversy.

Agriculture

The $75.9 billion fiscal 2002 spending bill for the Agriculture Department and the Food and Drug Administration cleared Nov. 15, after lawmakers decided to drop contentious provisions so that Congress could concentrate on war-related issues after the Sept. 11 terrorist attacks. The president signed the bill (HR 2330—PL 107-76) on Nov. 28. Among the controversial issues dropped from the final bill was a House-passed provision that would help the elderly by allowing the re-importation of U.S.-made prescription drugs that were available abroad for less than they cost in the United States. Also dropped was a Senate-passed amendment that would have lifted sanctions on food and medicine exports to Cuba. The issue pitted state-farm lawmakers against Republican conservatives and Cuban-American representatives in Congress. In acknowledgment of the deepening recession Congress stepped up funding for nutrition programs, especially food stamps, which was $23 billion, $2.9 billion more than in fiscal 2001 and $1 billion more than the president requested. *(Drug reimports, p. 508; Cuba sanctions, p. 260)*

Commerce, Justice, and State

For the first time in nearly a decade, the annual spending bill for the departments of Commerce, Justice, and State and the federal judiciary was enacted free of controversy and comparatively early in the process. The fiscal 2002 bill, signed into law Nov. 28 (HR 2500—PL 107-77), provided $41.6 billion, a $1.9 billion increase over fiscal 2001 and $828 million more than President Bush had requested. Although most of the money approved after Sept. 11 to fight terrorism was enacted in a separate supplemental, the Commerce, Justice, State spending bill included $459 million for the FBI's terrorism program and another $251 million in grants to state and local governments for antiterrorism and terrorism prevention efforts.

Most provisions likely to provoke fights, such as a permanent change in immigration laws and a reduction in international peacekeeping funds, were dropped from the bill in conference. An attempt to require the FBI to hold records on background checks for gun purchases for at least ninety days failed in both chambers; that was a victory for Attorney General John Ashcroft who had proposed that such records be destroyed within twenty-four hours. The final bill did retain a controversial provision barring the use of funds to support creation of the International Criminal Court, but the White House had no intention of contributing to the court or its creation. *(Details, p. 256)*

District of Columbia

The $408 million fiscal 2002 District of Columbia appropriations bill cleared Dec. 7 with little of the rancorous debate that typically accompanied the measure. President Bush signed the bill, which also approved the city's $7.15 billion annual budget, on Dec. 21 (HR 2944—PL 107-96).

Energy-Water

The fiscal 2002 energy and water development spending bill provided $24.6 billion, a $2.1 billion increase over the president's request. President Bush signed the bill into law (HR 2311—PL 107-66) on Nov. 12.

A last-minute attempt to add money for nonproliferation programs to keep nuclear weapons out of the hands of terrorists was blocked, although appropriators promised to find another way to provide the money. The final bill included $804 million to detect, prevent, and counter the spread of nuclear weapons worldwide. That was $30 million more than requested but less than had been approved by either the House ($845 million) or the Senate ($881 million). An additional $226 million was subsequently appropriated as part of the fiscal 2002 defense spending bill. Proponents of the additional funding said it was necessary to keep nuclear weapons out of the hands of terrorists.

Interior

Putting aside most of their disputes over energy and public lands, lawmakers cleared the fiscal 2002 Interior Department spending bill with relative ease Oct. 17. The $19.1 billion bill provided $1 billion more than the president had requested, with increases going to a variety of accounts, including land conservation, energy research, and firefighting. President Bush had only minor objections and signed the bill (HR 2217—PL 107-63) on Nov. 5.

Debate in both chambers before Sept. 11 revolved around Democratic attempts to challenge administration environmental policies including drilling for oil and gas on national monument lands and in coastal waters, easing restrictions on hard-rock mining, and making it more difficult to add to the endangered species list. Meeting in October, after the terrorist attacks, conferees dropped several controversial provisions inserted by one chamber or another. But the final bill did include provisions barring new oil exploration in national monuments. Strong Democratic opposition from the outset ensured the death of administration proposals to allow drilling for oil and gas in the Arctic National Wildlife Refuge (ANWR). *(ANWR drilling, pp. 412, 425, 432)*

Legislative Branch

The fiscal 2002 legislative branch appropriations bill was cleared Nov. 1 after a last-minute decision to add $70 million for the Capitol Visitor Center, set to be built under the East Lawn and completed in 2005. The $3 billion spending measure was a 9 percent increase over the amount appropriated in fiscal 2001—essentially what Congress had asked President Bush to request. Bush signed the bill (HR 2647—PL 107-68) on Nov. 12.

Military Construction

Congress on Oct. 18 cleared a $10.5 billion fiscal 2002 military construction appropriations bill that exceeded President Bush's request by $529 million. Bush signed the bill into law (HR 2904—PL 107-64) on Nov. 5. The bill provided $1.6 billion, or 18 percent, more than Congress appropriated in fiscal 2001. It did not include funds for reconstructing the part of the Pentagon damaged in the Sept. 11 terrorist attacks; money for those repairs was included in the emergency supplemental spending bill (PL 107-38) enacted Sept. 18.

Treasury, Postal Service

Congress cleared a $32.8 billion fiscal 2002 spending bill for the Treasury Department and the Postal Service on Nov. 1. President Bush signed the measure (HR 2590—PL 107-67) on Nov. 12. The legislation also funded the Customs Service, the Secret Service, the Executive Office of the President, and the IRS among others agencies. The measure provided $2 billion more than the fiscal 2001 version. The U.S. Customs Service got an 18 percent increase over fiscal 2001, including nearly twice as much funding for its automated commercial service and additional funding to hire more agents along the U.S.-Canada border. The bill gave federal employees a 4.6 percent pay increase, equal to the amount for military personnel. A controversial House provision to bar the use of funds to enforce the U.S. ban on travel to Cuba was dropped in conference.

Veterans, Housing

Lawmakers cleared a $112.7 billion spending bill for the departments of Veterans Affairs and Housing and Urban Development late in the session after sidestepping lingering disputes over federal drinking water standards and grants to fight drug-related crime in public housing. The bill, which also funded the Environmental Protection Agency (EPA), the National Aeronautics and Space Administration, and a number of other independent agencies, was signed into law Nov. 26 (HR 2620—PL 107-73). The final version required the EPA to implement, without delay, drinking water standards drawn up by the administration of President Bill Clinton. That language effectively blocked the agency from easing standards set by the Clinton administration for arsenic levels in drinking water.

The bill exceeded President Bush's budget request by $2.1 billion and provided $4.4 billion more than the fiscal 2001 version. Despite budget constraints, lawmakers apparently could not curb their appetite for pork-barrel projects. The bill had a record 1,600 earmarks and included more than $1 billion for economic development, university research, and water and sewer construction projects not requested by the administration.

EMERGENCY SPENDING BILL

Within three days of the Sept. 11 terrorist attacks President Bush and Congress came together to provide $40 billion in emergency appropriations for what was widely described as a down payment on military action, national security, and reconstruction. The bill, which split the emergency spending evenly between fiscal 2001 and fiscal 2002, was signed into law (HR 2888—PL 107-38) on Sept. 18. But it took another three months for Congress and the White House to allocate all of the money. The Defense Department received the largest share, more than $17 billion. New York, Pennsylvania, and Virginia, the three states physically affected by the terrorist attacks, laid claim to more than $11 billion, leaving about $11 billion for agencies charged with protecting the home front from future attacks.

The White House distributed half the money on its own discretion; the remaining $20 billion was allocated under the fiscal 2002 defense appropriations bill (HR 3338—PL 107-117), signed Jan. 10, 2002. *(Defense bill, p. 316)*

Provisions:

Of the $20 billion distributed by the White House, $10 billion was available immediately and could be allocated as the president saw fit for emergency rescue and rebuilding efforts, security at airports and other transportation centers and at public buildings, investigating and prosecuting those responsible for the attacks, and supporting national security. The White House allocated $5.9 billion for defense and $4.1 billion to nondefense spending.

The remaining $10 billion became available fifteen days after Bush gave Congress his plan for allocating the money. The White House submitted the plan Oct. 17, with $8.1 billion going to defense.

The second $20 billion was available only after it was appropriated separately by Congress. This was the portion that was allocated as emergency supplemental spending under the defense appropriations bill. Congress allocated $3.5 billion for defense, less than half the $7.3 billion Bush had requested. The remaining $16.5 billion was divided almost evenly between disaster recovery ($8.2 billion) and homeland security ($8.3 billion), nearly double the president's request for that account.

Legislative Action

On Sept. 14, three days after the attacks, Congress cleared the $40 billion emergency spending package without a single dissenting vote. The House passed HR 2888 422–0, and the Senate cleared it by voice vote after passing an identical bill (S 1426) earlier in the day by a vote of 96–0.

The votes were an anticlimactic end to two days of behind-the-scenes arguments between senior administration officials and bipartisan congressional leadership over how much latitude Bush should have in allocating the money. With Washington still stunned by the attacks, GOP lawmakers at first seemed ready to write the president a blank check.

But leading Democrats on the appropriations committee refused to surrender so much authority to the White House. "There has to be consultation and there has to be reporting," Sen. Robert C. Byrd, D-W. Va., chair of the Senate Appropriations Committee, said. "We still have a Constitution." (By September, Democrats had regained control of the Senate when a disgruntled moderate Republican, James Jeffords, Vt., left the party to become an independent but voted with the Democrats to organize the chamber.) *(Details, p. 202)*

By the end of Sept. 12, leaders and appropriators from both parties were in agreement that some restrictions on Bush's spending discretion would be necessary. Aides said White House officials had pressed for such sweeping, unfettered presidential power over the emergency funds that Republicans and Democrats alike were drawn together to rebuff them. By the night of Sept. 13, the leadership and appropriators from both parties had reached an agreement that shared allocation of the funds between the president and Congress. Although officials from the White House Office of Management and Budget initially balked at the arrangement, they eventually backed down in the early morning hours of Sept. 14, clearing the way for Congress to pay the measure.

Allocation of Funds

Although Congress had unanimously agreed to allocate half of the emergency spending under normal appropriations procedures, they soon began to chafe under the $20 billion limit. Lawmakers called for increased security at the nation's borders, ports, and airports. New Yorkers demanded that Congress live up to its pledge to provide $20 billion for their recovery and rebuilding efforts. The arrival of anthrax-tainted mail on Capitol Hill highlighted the additional security weaknesses that lawmakers wanted to address. *(Anthrax mail, p. 712)*

When the clamor became too loud for Bush to ignore, he called top appropriators to the White House on Nov. 6 to announce that he would veto any bill that spent more than the $20 billion that had already been voted. Bush insisted that the $40 billion package provided all the cash the government needed or could spend in the next several months. Reassured by promises of another supplemental spending bill in the spring of 2002, most Republicans closed ranks behind the president.

New York Republicans, however, did not. The state's delegation waged a campaign to win $9.7 billion more and fulfill the pledge of at least $20 billion in recovery and rebuilding funds. After losing in the House Appropriations Committee, the New Yorkers threatened to undermine the $317 billion fiscal 2002 defense appropriations bill that was being used as the vehicle for allocating the remaining $20 billion in emergency spending unless they got a floor vote on their proposal.

The threat brought the White House back to the bargaining table. New York Republicans agreed to back off in exchange for more grants and loans directed to small businesses and unemployed workers. Democrats, who complained that

the emergency spending provisions were woefully inadequate, were incensed that GOP leaders brought the bill to the House floor under a rule that blocked three Democratic amendments to increase spending. Despite their objections, the House on Nov. 28 agreed 216–211 to debate the bill on the leadership's terms. Later in the day, the House passed the defense spending bill containing the emergency funding, 406–20. *(Details, p. 316)*

Bush's hard line on spending did not deter Senate Appropriations Committee Chairman Byrd from adding $15 billion more to the bill for homeland defense and recovery from the attacks. After three procedural votes proved Republicans would derail the entire defense spending bill to support the president, Democrats backed down, replacing the $35 billion measure with a $20 billion measure that sliced defense funds to $2 billion and redirecting the rest to provide $9.5 billion for disaster recovery and $8.5 billion for homeland security. The measure passed by voice vote on Dec. 7.

The final allocation, negotiated during the conference on the defense spending bill, raised the amount for defense to $3.5 billion, still less than half the amount Bush had requested. Disaster recovery was pegged at $8.2 billion and homeland security at $8.3 billion. The House adopted the conference report (H Rept 107-350) 408–6 on Dec. 20, the final day of the session. The Senate cleared the bill 94–2 later that day.

Fiscal 2001 Supplemental

Congress cleared a bill July 20 to provide $6.5 billion in additional fiscal 2001 spending, most of it for the Pentagon. Predictions of a dwindling surplus resulting from newly enacted tax cuts and a slowing economy helped foster a bipartisan commitment to fiscal restraint, leading to a package that hewed closely to President Bush's request. The bill was signed into law (HR 2216—PL 107-20) on July 24. *(Tax cuts, p. 89)*

Bush's request for a net $6.5 billion in supplemental spending was the leanest such proposal in the previous two decades. To stay within the limits permitted under the congressional budget resolution (H Con Res 83), Bush combined $7.1 billion in new discretionary spending with offsets and rescissions in prior appropriations totaling more than $600 million. The request was a marked shift from the pattern set by the Clinton administration and the Appropriations committees, which had found numerous ways in the late 1990s to exceed the limits set in the budget resolution.

Most of the request, a net $5.8 billion, was for defense-related spending, including replenishing operations and maintenance accounts tapped to finance peacekeeping operations in Kosovo. Nondefense items included $116 million to cover the cost of mailings related to the tax rebate mandated by the tax-cut bill (PL 107-16).

House and Senate appropriators stuck with Bush's bottom line, although each chamber emphasized different programs and proposed different sets of rescissions. The House passed its version of HR 2216 (H Rept 107-102) by a vote of 341–87 on June 20. The Senate passed an amended version (S Rept 107-33) by a vote of 98–1 on July 10.

The final bill, completed July 19 after a week of negotiations, was remarkably similar to Bush's original request. The net total for new discretionary budget authority was $6.5 million, with a net of $5.8 billion for defense. However, the overall total for new spending had grown to $8.3 billion, with $1.8 billion in rescissions, including a rescission of $527 million for procurement of the troubled V-22 Osprey aircraft.

The House adopted the conference report (H Rept 107-148) by a vote of 375–30 the morning of July 20. The Senate cleared the bill by voice vote a few hours later.

Fiscal 2003 Budget Resolution

Unable to reach any compromise on overall federal spending, Congress failed to produce a fiscal 2003 budget resolution. It was only the second time since the modern budget process was created in 1974 that the House and Senate had been unable to agree on a common set of numbers to guide their spending and tax decisions. (The first time was in 1998 during President Bill Clinton's second term.) The failure to adopt a budget resolution in 2002 signaled a breakdown in the budget process that would stop Congress from clearing any of the fiscal 2003 nondefense spending bills, forcing a lame-duck session and, ultimately, a continuing resolution to keep the government going into 2003. *(1998 budget resolution, Congress and the Nation Vol. X, p. 60)*

The chief sticking point was discretionary spending, the amount available for appropriators to allocate among the thirteen regular fiscal 2003 spending bills. GOP leaders steered a budget resolution (H Con Res 353) through the House in March that reflected President Bush's demand for a discretionary limit of $759 billion. In the Senate, Democrats pushed a budget plan (S Con Res 100) with a $768 billion limit through the Budget Committee, but they lacked the votes to prevail in the full Senate and never brought the measure to the floor. Although the two chambers were only $9 billion apart, it was enough to produce deadlock.

Appropriators in both chambers agreed that the $768 billion Senate figure was the minimum necessary to ensure that they could muster majorities for the thirteen regular appropriations bills, especially given the extra spending required for the war on terrorism and homeland security in the wake of the Sept. 11 attacks. But Bush held firm, warning on April 16 that he would veto domestic spending bills that exceeded his recommended limit, and House Republican leaders lined up staunchly behind the president.

Adding to the disarray, budget enforcement laws that had helped restrain spending increases and tax cuts since 1990 were set to expire on Sept. 30, and lawmakers were unwilling to extend them without a budget agreement. "We don't have budget numbers, we don't have enforcement mechanisms," lamented Senate Minority Leader Trent Lott, R-Miss., before the August recess. *(Budget enforcement rules, box, p. 60)*

BUSH BUDGET REQUEST

President Bush submitted a $2.2 trillion fiscal 2003 budget to Congress on Feb. 4, 2002, with domestic security and the war on terrorism as his top priorities. To make room for substantial increases in those areas the White House recommended freezing or cutting most domestic programs. Bush also called for $656 billion in tax cuts over ten years including making permanent the tax cuts enacted in 2001.

The president called on Congress to hold total discretionary spending to $747 billion. The Congressional Budget Office (CBO), Congress's official scorekeeper, did its own calculations in March, putting Bush's discretionary budget request at $759.1 billion. Both the White House and Congress agreed to use that number. CBO projected that if all Bush's proposals were enacted the government would run a deficit of $121 billion in fiscal 2003 and would return to surplus in fiscal 2005. (In fact, the deficit for fiscal 2003 reached $375 billion.)

Although Democrats and many Republicans were unhappy with the austerity of Bush's domestic budget, they were hemmed in by their support for the president's war efforts, their reluctance to push the country deeper into deficit, and the constraints imposed by a weak economy. At the ideological extremes, fiscal conservatives wanted to clamp down even harder on domestic spending while a handful of liberal Democrats favored delaying or repealing the 2001 tax cuts. Other Democrats and even some Republicans wanted to trade some of the defense spending sought by Bush for more spending on domestic programs such as highway construction, education, and job training. But the White House warned lawmakers not to try tapping the Pentagon or homeland security budgets to fund domestic priorities.

HOUSE ACTION

After rejecting numerous Democratic amendments Republicans on the House Budget Committee united March 13 to approve a budget resolution (H Con Res 353—H Rept 107-376) that closely tracked Bush's request. The vote was 23–17.

The resolution included a discretionary spending limit of $759 billion, a 7 percent increase over fiscal 2002. Of the total the military was slated to receive $392.7 billion, including a $10 billion contingency fund Bush wanted for antiterrorism efforts. The rest, $366.3 billion, was for nondefense spending, largely domestic programs.

The House resolution called for $28 billion in additional tax cuts over five years but did not instruct committees to prepare a reconciliation bill to make such changes. The Republicans made a few other adjustments to the budget, which allowed them to keep the overall total about $5 billion below the president's. Democrats praised Bush's conduct of the war on terrorism and pledged support for the defense budget but attacked the proposed cuts in domestic spending and charged that the Republicans were setting the country up for massive deficits. They presented no plan of their own, however, instead offering amendments to increase funding for various domestic programs in the GOP budget. Republicans cited that as further evidence that Democrats were not serious about reining in deficits.

The full House adopted the budget resolution March 20 by a vote of 221–209. Democrats were angry because the GOP-controlled Rules Committee allowed no floor amendments. But Republicans countered that the Democrats had offered no alternative of their own and should not be able to simply fire off amendments attacking the GOP plan.

SENATE ACTION

The Democratic-controlled Senate Budget Committee approved its budget resolution (S Con Res 100—S Rept 107-141) on a party-line vote of 12–10 on March 21. Signaling trouble ahead for the measure, however, at least two committee Democrats said they would not support the budget on the floor unless it was altered to provide more debt reduction. With only a one-vote margin in the Senate, Democratic leaders had to have every single Democratic vote if they wanted to pass the resolution. With little assurance that the resolution would pass, Senate Democratic leaders never brought the resolution to the floor.

The committee-approved resolution proposed a $768.1 billion limit on discretionary spending, $392.8 billion for defense and $375.3 billion for nondefense accounts. The plan included $9 billion more for domestic programs than the House version did.

The most substantive debate concerned the question of extending budget enforcement caps on appropriations. Although caps had been in place since 1990, the most recent version, set in the 1997 budget law (PL 105-33), was to expire Oct. 1. While the caps were routinely breached in times of surplus they had been useful in the past in enforcing deficit reduction. The committee rejected on an 11–11 tie an amendment by Russ D. Feingold, D-Wis., and Judd Gregg, R-N.H., to set new discretionary caps for the following five years. Senate proposals that exceeded the caps would have been subject to a point of order that took sixty votes to overcome. Feingold and Ernest F. Hollings of South Carolina were the two Democrats who said they could not support the committee version on the Senate floor. *(Budget rules, p. 60)*

House GOP leaders in May used a procedural motion (H Res 428) to hold House appropriators to the $749 billion discretionary limit set in the House-passed budget resolution. Senate appropriators operated as if their higher ceiling were in effect. The result was deadlock; Congress was unable to pass eleven of the thirteen regular appropriations bills before the 107th Congress adjourned. *(Details, below)*

Fiscal 2003 Appropriations

The appropriations process all but collapsed in 2002 with Congress leaving eleven of the thirteen regular spending bills unfinished and forwarding the problem to the 108th Congress that began in 2003. The only fiscal 2003 spending bills to become law were those for the Department of Defense (PL 107-248) and military construction (PL 107-249). Early in the year Congress also passed a defense supplemental for fiscal 2002. All nondefense programs were funded at fiscal 2002 levels under a series of five continuing resolutions, the last of which was good through Jan. 11, 2003.

The stalemate was the result of divisions between Democrats and Republicans and among Republicans themselves over how closely to stick to the limit set by President Bush for total discretionary spending—spending that was under Congress's control. Bush's fiscal 2003 budget called for a total of $759 billion in discretionary funds. That included a request for a $10 billion defense reserve fund, a blank check that appropriations refused to write. As a result, all parties eventually accepted $749 billion as the Bush request. *(Bush budget, p. 58)*

Within that total Bush sought a 13 percent increase for defense while essentially freezing nondefense spending at $366 billion. Appropriators in both parties on both sides of the Capitol made it clear they did not think that was enough to enable them to write thirteen bills that could garner the support needed to get through both chambers.

HOUSE VOTE ON SPENDING LIMIT

The prescription for trouble was written early in 2002 when the Senate failed to pass a fiscal 2003 budget resolution. The House had adopted a budget resolution (H Con Res 83) with a $749 billion discretionary total plus the $10 billion defense reserve. The Senate Budget Committee approved a discretionary limit of $768 billion with no defense reserve. But Senate Democratic leaders concluded they did not have enough votes to pass the resolution (S Con Res 100) and never brought the measure to the floor. Appropriators in both chambers said the Senate total was the minimum they needed. Despite threats from Bush saying he would veto spending bills that exceeded the House, total House appropriators began talking openly about producing spending bills with a total roughly equivalent to the Senate's more expensive bottom line.

House leaders soon came under pressure from the White House as well as from fiscal conservatives in their own ranks to hold the appropriators in check. To that end Republican leaders called on the House to cast another vote committing itself to living under the spending ceiling in its budget. Although the proposed language would have imposed no enforceable restraint on spending, appropriators were infuriated, arguing that they would be unable to win passage of domestic spending bills written under the ceiling.

BUDGET ENFORCEMENT RULES

Looming record federal budget deficits spurred unsuccessful moves in both the House and Senate to reimpose budget enforcement mechanisms on Congress that expired in 2002. The House in June 2004 soundly defeated an effort (HR 4663) to establish statutory "caps" on appropriations and a pay-as-you-go requirement for mandatory spending. In the Senate, insistence by a group of Democrats and moderate Republicans on the restoration of budget enforcement rules was enough to keep the annual budget resolution from being adopted in 2002 and 2004.

Statutory spending caps on discretionary appropriations and pay-as-you-go rules, also known as PAYGO rules, for new tax cuts and entitlement programs had been in place since 1990 (PL 101-508), when President George H. W. Bush and a Democratic-controlled Congress first enacted them as part of a package of tax increases and spending cuts (PL 101-508) designed to reduce a $152.5 billion budget deficit. (*Congress and the Nation Vol. VIII, pp. 44, 55, 56*

The statutory pay-as-you-go requirement was extended as part of the five-year, $500 billion deficit-cutting plan of 1993 (PL 103-66) and then extended again in 1997, as part of another five-year budget-balancing law (PL 105-33). The statutory requirement expired in 2002. (*1993 extension, Congress and the Nation Vol. IX, p. 44; 1997 extension, Congress and the Nation Vol. X, p. 50*)

The pay-as-you-go law theoretically triggered across-the-board spending reductions if tax cuts or new entitlement spending was not offset by revenue increases or entitlement cuts. The spending caps allowed budget points of order to be lodged against appropriations bills that exceeded the dollar targets. In the House, a simple majority can overcome a budget point of order, but in the Senate sixty votes are required, making the caps a more potent tool in that chamber.

In 1995, lawmakers writing the fiscal 1996 budget instituted a Senate pay-as-you-go rule. Unlike the statutory provision, the Senate rule did not have the force of law and could not trigger across-the-board spending cuts. But senators were able to raise points of order against legislation that violated the pay-as-you-go principle. Sixty votes were required to waive the rule. In following years, however, the Senate rule was significantly weakened.

Even when the rules were in place, Congress managed to avert PAYGO cuts each year simply by adopting language wiping the PAYGO scorecard clean. Even so, budget hawks said the rules had had a restraining effect on Congress. They warned that without the rules it would be easier for members to approve legislation that would worsen the deficit.

Senate Action in 2002

The first attempt to revive the rules came in the Senate in the spring of 2002, when Russ D. Feingold, D.-Wis., and Judd Gregg, R-N.H., offered an amendment to the fiscal 2003 budget resolution (S Con Res 100) that would have placed caps on discretionary spending for the next five years. After that amendment failed on an 11–11 tie vote, Feingold warned that he, and perhaps a few other Senate Democrats, probably would not support the budget resolution on the floor unless it contained tougher budget enforcement provisions. That was enough to kill floor action on the resolution in the Senate, which Democrats controlled by only a single vote. (*Budget resolution, p. 58*)

Feingold tried again, in June, offering an amendment to the fiscal 2003 defense authorization bill that would have extended statutory limits on discretionary spending for five years and pay-as-you-go rules. The amendment included a $768 billion cap in fiscal 2003. Although the amendment won support from some leading Senate Republicans, the White House lobbied strenuously against the amendment, insisting that Congress limit discretionary spending in fiscal 2003 to $759 billion. On June 20 the amendment fell on a 59–40 vote to waive a budget point of order; sixty votes were required to pass the waiver.

After months of maneuvering, the Senate agreed by voice vote Oct. 16 to a widely backed resolution (S Res 304) to restore Senate pay-as-you-go rules until April 15, 2003. The resolution also revived recently expired Senate points order against tax cuts or mandatory spending not provided for in a budget resolution.

Although popular, the resolution had been delayed for months by objections from Phil Gramm, R-Texas, who said the enforcement rules had done little to deter appropriators from spending more money but had been effective in blocking tax cuts. Gramm threatened a filibuster of the resolution but called it off after reaching agreement with the measure's proponents to extend the enforcement rules for six months, through April 15, rather than through Sept. 30, 2003, as originally proposed. The rules applied only to Senate procedures and could be changed by subsequent votes in the Senate.

In a vote that underscored the apparent futility of trying to impose meaningful spending caps, Congress cleared a separate bill shortly before adjourning that eased the $127 billion PAYGO deficit amassed in previously enacted legislation. The law also erased any PAYGO deficits for fiscal 2004–2006. The House passed the bill 366–19 on Nov. 14, and the Senate cleared it the next day by voice vote. President George W. Bush signed the bill (PL 107-312) Dec. 2.

Congress regularly passed such language before the end of a session, but the provision was usually buried in a must-pass bill. This year GOP appropriators, tired of being singled out by party leaders for failing to exercise fiscal discipline, decided to make the point that recent tax cuts and new mandatory spending in the 2002 farm bill and elsewhere dwarfed any discretionary spending they were seeking to add to the budget. The result was the separate roll call vote on a relatively routine measure.

Senate Action in 2004

With the budget deficit worsening, deficit hawks in both chambers tried, unsuccessfully, to impose some discipline on the budgeting process in 2004. During Senate debate on the fiscal 2005 budget resolution (S Con Res 95), four moderate Republicans joined Democrats in supporting an amendment by Feingold that would have reinstated pay-as-you-go language requiring that any new tax cuts or new entitlement spending be offset by accompanying tax increases or spending cuts or be subject to a point of order in the Senate, which could be waived only with the support of at least sixty senators. With conservatives in the House staunchly opposed to placing such restrictions on pending tax cut legislation, House-Senate negotiators were unable to find a compromise that satisfied the Senate GOP moderates, and the Senate never took up the final version of the resolution. *Fiscal 2005 budget resolution, p. 77)*

House Action in 2004

During House floor debate on the fiscal 2005 budget resolution, a group of conservative and moderate Republicans worried about the burgeoning budget deficit continued to press the Republican leadership for a commitment to schedule a floor vote on budget enforcement legislation. That bill (HR 3973), which would establish five-year statutory caps on discretionary spending and set pay-as-you-go budget rules for mandatory spending expansions, but not for tax cuts, moved through the Budget Committee on March 17 as part of a deal to secure votes for the budget resolution.

Leaders were initially reluctant to promise a vote on the bill, which had drawn concerns from the Appropriations and Rules committees. But as the group of rank-and-file Republicans continued to agitate, House Speaker J. Dennis Hastert, R-Ill., promised floor action on the bill before Memorial Day.

In the event, a similar bill (HR 4663) came to the House floor on June 24, where it was defeated 146–268 after eight hours of debate, shortly after midnight on June 25. Relatively little of the debate focused on the bill, however. Instead the discussion was dominated by a panoply of sweeping ideas on how to improve the budget process, many of which had been debated and rejected in previous years.

Not a single substantive amendment was adopted, and the votes on them seemed to demonstrate that many lawmakers were disinclined to grapple with such a complex topic. Many of them privately said the exercise was a waste of time. Ironically, the amendment that won the most votes, though nowhere near a majority, would have revived the pay-as-you-go rule in its original form to apply against tax cuts as well as mandatory spending. It was killed on a 179–233 vote.

The one group of legislators who appeared to take the debate seriously were Republicans on the Appropriations Committee, who opposed the budget enforcement rules. Chair C. W. Bill Young, R-Fla., said the attempt to write spending caps into the law represented an encroachment on Congress's power of the purse. Many rank-and-file Republicans voted with the appropriators, who were in the midst of trying to write their fiscal 2005 spending bills.

Balanced-Budget Amendment

One more effort to restrain budget deficits was made in late September, when the House Judiciary Committee began marking up a proposed constitutional amendment requiring that the federal budget be balanced. But the Republican-inspired amendment, intended largely for political gain, was abandoned after Democrats blasted the measure as hypocritical.

The proposed amendment would have required a three-fifths majority vote of both chambers to enact legislation that would result in a deficit (although it included an exemption for times of military conflict). A few GOP conservatives and leaders pushed the amendment in advance of the 2004 election in an attempt to force a controversial vote for the Democrats. But the attempt backfired at the beginning of the markup, when Democrats pointedly noted the huge tax cuts and record deficits that were piled up during President Bush's first term. "The gall and hypocrisy of this amendment is breathtaking," one Democrat on the panel said. Judiciary Committee Chair F. James Sensenbrenner Jr., R-Wis., recessed the markup and did not reconvene it.

The House last adopted a balanced-budget amendment in 1995, as part of the GOP majority's "Contract with America." Republican efforts to pass a balanced-budget amendment in the Senate failed in 1995, and again in both 1996 and 1997. The issue was mooted in 1998, when the government recorded its first budget surplus since 1969. *(Congress and the Nation, Vol. IX, pp. 62, 80; Congress and the Nation, Vol. X, p. 56)*

The key vote came May 22, 2002, on a procedural measure setting the rules for House floor debate on the fiscal 2002 supplemental appropriations bill (PL 107-206). Republican leaders had drafted the rule so that, if adopted, it would automatically attach the spending limit language to the widely popular spending bill; the only option that GOP appropriators had to avoid the spending limit was to defeat the rule. Such procedural matters are normally considered party loyalty votes, but in this case GOP leaders were stung by a handful of defections, with three Republican members of the House Appropriations Committee voting against the rule and three others voting "present" in protest. Several other GOP appropriators waited until late in the roll call to vote, forcing party leaders to work hard to head off other defections. But in the end the rule was adopted on the **key vote of 216–209 (R 214–3; D 1–205; I 1–1).** *(2002 key votes, p. 819)*

HOUSE, SENATE ON SEPARATE PATHS

Regrouping from that procedural vote House appropriators decided on a strategy that had proved successful in the recent past: moving several politically popular domestic spending bills to the end of the queue, underfunding them at the outset on the assumption that GOP leaders eventually would loosen the purse strings even if it meant breaking the discretionary spending limit. In July the House passed three domestic spending bills: for the Interior Department, legislative branch, and the Treasury Department and Postal Service.

But those were the only three domestic spending bills the House passed. Recognizing the familiar pattern, a small band of fiscal conservatives intervened in mid-July. They won a promise from Speaker J. Dennis Hastert, R-Ill., to move the biggest of the domestic bills—for the departments of Labor, Health and Human Services, and Education—to the front of the line after the August recess. When it became apparent in September that GOP leaders could not get the votes to pass that bill without spending more than the $130.9 billion in discretionary funds proposed by Bush, the appropriations process came to a halt in the House.

In the Senate, Appropriations Committee Chair Robert C. Byrd, D-W. Va., moved all thirteen bills through his panel by the end of July, with solid GOP support. The bills exceeded Bush's domestic spending request by about $13 billion, including some advance appropriations. The only domestic spending that made it through the full Senate, however, was for the legislative branch. Senate floor action on appropriations largely stopped after the August recess.

BUSH HOLDS LINE IN LAME-DUCK SESSION

House appropriators still hoped for a freer spending environment after the midterm elections. But Republican gains on Nov. 5 strengthened Bush's determination to hold firm.

With the president cautioning House leaders not to exceed his original limits, Hastert and other GOP leaders decided to put off action on the outstanding appropriations bills until January when the party would control both chambers of Congress.

To allow that to happen, the House voted 270–143 on Nov. 13 to pass a short-term spending bill (H J Res 124) that would keep domestic programs operating at 2002 levels until Jan. 11, 2003. The Senate cleared the continuing resolution 92–2 on Nov. 19, and Bush signed it Nov. 27 (PL 107-294).

The continuing resolution included language to extend expiring provisions of the landmark 1996 welfare overhaul law (PL 104-1993). It also contained a provision giving the secretary of the new Department of Homeland Security limited flexibility to transfer funds between agencies of the new cabinet department. That flexibility, strongly resisted by appropriators who feared their spending decisions would be rewritten by executive fiat, was limited to a total of $500 million and could not exceed 2 percent of any given account. The measure also provided $140 million in unspent appropriations as seed money for the new agency. *(Welfare reform, p. 525)*

DEFENSE APPROPRIATIONS

Congress on Oct. 16, 2002, cleared a fiscal 2003 spending bill for the Department of Defense that reflected wide agreement among lawmakers after the Sept. 11, 2001, attacks that no dollars should be spared in the war on terrorism and a looming showdown with Iraq. The $355.1 billion bill provided $37.5 billion more than Congress appropriated for fiscal 2002 ($20.7 billion more if supplemental spending were included). *(Fiscal 2002 bill, p. 326)*

Even so, the final bill was $1.6 billion less than Bush requested—excluding a $10 billion contingency request that appropriators did not fund. But it largely tracked administration plans to transform the military into a lighter, more agile force. As was customary, it closely followed the outlines of the annual defense authorization bill (PL 107-314). *(Defense authorization, p. 308)*

Lawmakers worked furiously to complete the spending bill before Congress recessed for the Nov. 5 midterm elections. With the war on terrorism, the growing possibility of an attack on Iraq, and political delays on legislation creating the Homeland Security Department, members were eager to show their commitment on defense. The significant increase in spending also reduced conflicts over priorities. Even Bush's request to spend $7.8 billion on a missile defense system, a highly contentious issue in previous years, drew little criticism. The final version of the bill gave Bush $7.4 billion for the program.

Lawmakers also accepted Defense Secretary Donald H. Rumsfeld's decision to cancel the army's Crusader mobile cannon, despite fierce opposition earlier in the year and the strong support for the $11 billion program from the GOP leadership in both chambers. The fate of the Crusader dominated much of the debate on the bill.

Appropriators did balk at the White House request for a $10 billion contingency fund for future expenses associated with the war on terrorism, saying it would amount to a blank check. They deferred action on the issue until the administration submitted a detailed request.

The final defense bill included $71.5 billion for weapons procurement, $57.8 billion for research and development, $114.8 billion for operations and maintenance, and $93.6 billion for personnel. The $37.5 billion increase over the fiscal 2002 spending bill represented by far the largest increase in defense spending since the Vietnam War.

The House passed its version of the bill (HR 5010—H Rept 107-532) 413–18 on June 27. The Senate passed an amended version (S Rept 107-213) 95–3 on Aug. 1. The House adopted the conference report (H Rept 107-732) 409–14 on Oct. 10, and the Senate cleared the bill 93–1 on Oct. 10. President Bush signed the bill Oct. 23 (PL 104-248).

MILITARY CONSTRUCTION

In addition to the Defense spending bill the only other regular fiscal 2003 spending bill passed in 2002 was for military construction, typically the least controversial of all the spending bills. The fiscal 2003 bill (HR 5011) provided $10.5 billion, including $5.6 billion for military construction, $4.2 billion for family housing, and $561 million for environmental cleanup and other projects related to base closings. The total was $835 million more than Bush had requested but $105 million below the fiscal 2002 level. Congress more than doubled the president's request for National Guard and reserve programs to $688 million.

The House passed HR 5011 (H Rept 107-533) 426–1 on June 27. The Senate passed its version of the measure by a vote of 96–3 on July 18. House and Senate conferees finished work on the bill Oct. 9. The House adopted the conference report (H Rept 107-731) by a vote of 419–0 on Oct. 10. The Senate cleared the bill by voice vote early on Oct. 11. President Bush signed it into law Oct. 23 (PL 107-249), along with the huge defense appropriations bill.

Fiscal 2002 Supplemental

Congress cleared a $28.9 billion fiscal 2002 supplemental spending bill devoted mainly to defense and homeland security in July 2002. In a test of strength over spending limits, President Bush used the threat of a veto to force House and Senate appropriators to give up what would have been an additional $2 billion in new spending. Bush signed the bill into law Aug. 2 (HR 4775—PL 107-206).

The bill contained $31.9 billion in new appropriations and $3 billion in rescissions and other offsets, producing the bottom line of $28.9 billion. About half the total, $14.4 billion, went to the Pentagon, including $11.9 billion for the Defense Emergency Response Fund to pay the incremental costs of the global war on terrorism, such as military operations, increased personnel, and additional intelligence gathering. Most of the remaining spending was devoted to homeland security ($6.7 billion), recovery assistance for

New York in the wake of the Sept. 11, 2001, attacks ($5.5 billion), and foreign assistance and embassy security ($2.1 billion). The bill also provided $1.1 billion in mandatory spending for veterans' compensation and pensions and $1 billion to avert an expected shortfall in the Pell Grants college loan program.

Final agreement was delayed for weeks as House and Senate conferees struggled to stay within the spending limits set by the administration. Bush had submitted a request in March for $27.1 billion in emergency funding to combat terrorism. Separately the administration had requested $1.3 billion for the Pell Grants program to assist needy students pay for college, for a total of $28.4 billion.

House appropriators initially planned to advance a $30 billion package, saying that was close enough to the request. But the White House Office of Management and Budget objected, and appropriators made changes—primarily an adjustment that Democrats derided as a gimmick—that brought the bill down to $28.8 billion. The House passed HR 4775 (H Rept 107-480) May 24 on a vote of 280–138. Despite threats that a larger bill would be vetoed, the Senate passed a version (S 2551—S Rept 107-156) on June 7 with a price tag of $31.5 billion, much of it in additional spending for homeland security. The vote on the Senate version of HR 4774 was 71–22.

Bipartisan negotiations produced a $30.4 billion compromise, but the White House declared the bill unacceptable and forced appropriators back to the drawing board. The final result was the $28.9 billion. The House adopted the conference report (H Rept 107-593) on July 23, and the Senate cleared the measure 92–7 the following day.

Of the total, $5.1 billion was designated as contingency emergency spending. The president was given thirty days to decide whether to use all or none of the money. On Aug. 13 Bush turned down the $5.1 billion, effectively cutting the bill's total to $23.8 billion. The biggest cuts were in homeland security, which was reduced to $4.4 billion.

Debt Ceiling Raised

To the immense relief of the Bush administration, the House, by the narrowest of margins, cleared a bill June 27, 2002, raising the legal limit on the federal debt by $450 billion, to $6.4 trillion. The vote was 215–214. President Bush signed the bill the following day (S 2578—PL 107-199), and the Treasury Department immediately announced plans to resume debt auctions.

The return of the federal budget deficits in 2002 had put Bush and congressional Republicans, who regularly castigated Democrats as big spenders, in the uncomfortable position of leading the drive for an increase in the debt ceiling. Treasury had said that the ceiling on accumulated debt had to be increased by June 28 to allow new government borrowing. Otherwise, the government risked defaulting on U.S. securities, halting the payment of Social Security and Medicare benefits, and interrupting government operations, including the war on terrorism. "If it hadn't been increased," Treasury secretary Paul H. O'Neill said afterward, "it would have put us in the position of defaulting on the full faith and credit of the U.S., or in the alternative, using potentially fraudulent accounting devices to paper over a lack of action by the Congress."

BACKGROUND

The statutory ceiling on the national debt covers federal debt held by the public in the form of treasury securities, savings bonds, and other notes as well as the government's obligations to the federal trust funds, primarily for Social Security and Medicare.

Because a default was unthinkable, Congress had never failed to raise the cap when it was necessary. But lawmakers often took the opportunity to score political points about deficit spending or to use must-pass debt limit bills to advance other legislation.

A debt ceiling increase was the vehicle used to advance the 1985 Gramm-Rudman-Hollings law (PL 99-177), which required across-the-board budget cuts if Congress failed to meet deficit-reduction targets. As part of the package Congress agreed to breach the $2 trillion mark, setting a new $2.1 trillion debt ceiling. *(Congress and the Nation Vol. VII, p. 44)*

In 1990 Congress passed a series of short-term increases in the debt ceiling while wrangling with President George H. W. Bush over the major deficit-reduction deal (PL 101-508) of his presidency. *(Congress and the Nation Vol. VIII, pp. 55, 56)*

In 1995 with the debt approaching the ceiling of $4.9 trillion, Republicans tried to use the issue to force President Bill Clinton to back a GOP deficit-reduction bill. The move failed, and Republicans took a beating in public opinion polls after the federal government was forced into a partial shutdown. *(Congress and the Nation Vol. IX, p. 76)*

The following year, with Treasury secretary Robert E. Rubin's options dwindling and Wall Street growing nervous, the debt ceiling was increased to $5.5 trillion, but not without a popular change in Social Security benefits and a provision to help small businesses challenge government regulation. Budget hawks were also rewarded with a controversial line-item veto measure (PL 104-130) that was linked to the debt-ceiling bill and that was later declared unconstitutional by the Supreme Court. *(Congress and the Nation Vol. IX, pp. 76–80; Vol. X, pp. 64–65)*

The last increase in the debt ceiling came during a rare time of peace in the budget wars when the GOP-controlled Congress and Clinton came together in 1997 to enact the landmark balanced-budget law (PL 105-33), including the $5.95 trillion ceiling. *(Congress and the Nation Vol. X, p. 48)*

DELAY IN HOUSE

Annual budget surpluses from fiscal 1998 through fiscal 2001 helped delay the need for yet another increase in the debt ceiling. But the accumulated national debt continued to grow as bonds piled up in the Social Security trust funds. The

return to deficits in fiscal 2002 meant the Treasury was also engaging in significant new public borrowing. The combination brought borrowing dangerously close to the legal limit.

O'Neill began asking Congress in December 2001 to increase the debt ceiling to $6.7 trillion. The administration repeated its request for a $750 billion increase throughout the spring of 2002.

But House Republicans wanted to avoid an up-or-down vote on a debt increase. GOP leaders repeatedly postponed floor action, hoping instead to attach the measure to the fiscal 2002 antiterrorism supplemental spending bill (HR 4775—PL 107-206), which would have allowed them to portray the debt increase as an unforeseen consequence of the Sept. 11 terrorist attacks.

For their part Democrats saw the must-pass debt increase as a chance to paint Republicans as fiscally irresponsible—with particular emphasis on Bush's $1.4 trillion, ten-year tax cut (PL 107-16) enacted in 2001, which Democrats said was a primary cause of the returned budget deficits. Senate Majority Leader Tom Daschle, D-S.D., would not acquiesce in attaching the debt increase to the supplemental. In the House, Minority Leader Richard A. Gephardt, D-Mo., offered the GOP little comfort. He said Republicans who voted for the Bush tax cut should bear the political burden now. "If you order the meal, you pay the bill," he said June 12.

The delays forced O'Neill to engage in the same kind of short-term accounting methods that Republicans had lambasted Rubin for in 1995 and 1996. For example, in late March Treasury reduced the number of bonds it normally auctioned in an attempt to stay under the debt ceiling until the influx of income tax receipts after April 15. In April O'Neill temporarily suspended investment in the Government Securities Investment Fund, or G-Fund, a kind of 401(k) program for federal employees. Treasury also redeemed some government assets in the Civil Service Retirement and Disability Trust fund, which funds the pensions of federal workers. In both cases the Treasury supplied IOUs to be replaced, with interest, when the debt crunch eased. That created enough borrowing authority to allow the government to meet the April federal payroll and pay Social Security, Medicare, Medicaid, and other mandatory government obligations.

The April 15 cash flow temporarily eased the situation, but officials warned they were running out of room to maneuver. On May 1 Treasury said that without congressional action the debt limit would be breached by late June, when payments to several trust funds, including Social Security, were due.

SENATE ACTION

With the House still hesitating, Senate leaders from both parties took the unusual step of advancing their own debt ceiling bill, a measure that by custom originates in the House. The measure (S 2578), introduced by Daschle, proposed to increase the debt ceiling by $450 billion, to $6.4 trillion. The Treasury estimated that the $450 billion increase would keep the government solvent at least until the middle of December and perhaps longer, depending primarily on how well the economy performed and generated tax receipts.

Minority Leader Trent Lott, R-Miss., snapped up what he said was a good offer. "He [Daschle] came up with a responsible number, a reasonable number," Lott said, "We both told our [members] this is not the kind of thing you play games with." With leaders of both parties backing the measure the Senate passed it on June 11 by a solid bipartisan margin of 68–29.

HOUSE ACTION

The Senate action and the lack of more politically palatable alternatives finally pushed the House to act. On June 27 House GOP leaders managed to clear the bill 215–214 with three Democrats voting in favor and six Republicans opposed. Democrats said they would support a short-term increase to provide time for a budget summit aimed at erasing the deficit, but that it was up to those who voted for the 2001 tax cut to provide the votes for a longer-term increase. Republicans argued that the economic recession and the Sept. 11 attacks were the principal reasons for having to raise the debt ceiling.

The bill came to the floor in a highly unusual manner. With almost no warning Republicans amended the rule on the fiscal 2003 military construction spending bill (HR 5011) to permit the House to consider the Senate-passed debt bill. The move provided minimal notice and minimal debate—just one hour.

Republican leaders had insisted for weeks that the debt ceiling increase would be attached to the fiscal 2002 supplemental spending bill, and even after the Senate passed its stand-alone bill, they stuck to that plan. But the supplemental was stalled in a slow-moving conference and the White House wanted quick action on the debt. With lawmakers preparing to leave for the July Fourth recess, Speaker J. Dennis Hastert, R-Ill., decided the night of June 26 to move to a quick vote the next day, clearing the Senate-passed debt ceiling increase.

2003–2004

The return of large budget deficits—spurred in part by the U.S. invasion of Iraq and subsequent reconstruction efforts there—cramped the appropriations process in 2003, but it did not prevent Congress from budgeting $350 billion for tax cuts over ten years and $400 billion for a Medicare prescription drug law. The annual budget resolution was adopted by both chambers, but only after the Senate cut President George W. Bush's tax relief request in half and then only with Vice President Dick Cheney casting a tie-breaking vote. *(Iraq, p. 231; Medicare, drugs, pp. 483, 496)*

As in 2002, progress on appropriations bills was slow in 2003 as lawmakers struggled to live within the budget. Action on the regular spending bills also was delayed by the need to complete action on an omnibus appropriations bill for fiscal 2003, left unfinished at the end of 2002, and to write three supplemental spending bills. Two of these totaled more than $160 billion for the military campaigns and reconstruction efforts in Iraq and Afghanistan; the third one, for just under $1 billion, was for emergency disaster relief. By the time Congress adjourned in December, only six of the thirteen regular spending bills had been approved; the remaining seven bills were packaged into an omnibus measure that was cleared in January 2004.

Election-year politics contributed to an already difficult budget process in 2004. The conference agreement on the fiscal 2005 congressional budget resolution stalled in June when a group of Senate GOP moderates refused to support it because it did not contain pay-as-you-go language that would offset spending increases or tax cuts with compensating tax increases or spending cuts. It was the second time in three years that Congress had been unable to pass its annual budget resolution.

Despite that failure, GOP leaders managed to hold nonsecurity-related spending for fiscal 2005 to the overall 1 percent increase that Bush had requested. But once again they required an omnibus spending bill to do so. Congress cleared just four regular fiscal 2005 appropriations bills before the presidential election on Nov. 2, 2004. Returning for a lame-duck session after the election, lawmakers bundled the remaining nine bills into a hastily written catchall package notable for the thousands of appropriations for narrow interests, known as earmarks, scattered throughout it. "Everyone's tired about a process that drags out until the end of the year and results in an omnibus that people don't have a chance to read and complain about," said a House Republican leadership aide.

Congress did not take up a supplemental in 2004 (although $25 billion in emergency funds for the wars in Iraq and Afghanistan was included in the regular defense spending bill, which cleared Congress in early August). In a move widely considered to be motivated by presidential politics, President Bush put off a larger request for funding for ongoing reconstruction efforts in Iraq and Afghanistan until 2005. In the last week before the election, news reports told of administration plans to seek about $70 billion in additional funding for Iraq.

The return of large budget deficits also forced Congress to approve huge increases in the legal limit on the national debt in both 2003 and 2004. Congress in 2003 cleared a bill increasing the statutory limit on the federal debt to $7.4 trillion, a record increase of $984 billion, just days before the federal government would default on its obligations. The new debt ceiling kept the government solvent only until November 2004, when Congress raised the debt ceiling for the third time in three years. The increase to $8.2 trillion was expected to keep the government going for about a year.

Fiscal 2004 Budget Resolution

The fiscal 2004 budget resolution, adopted in final form by both chambers April 11, 2003, was a crucial piece of legislation for President George W. Bush and congressional Republicans. The measure (H Con Res 95) laid the groundwork for a $350 billion, decade-long tax cut that cleared six weeks later, and it placed a $784.5 billion discretionary spending cap on the regular fiscal 2004 appropriations bills. The measure also approved $400 billion over ten years for a Medicare prescription drug program.

President Bush had asked for a $726 billion tax cut package, which he characterized as an economic stimulus. But opposition to the central feature of his proposal—an end to individual income taxes on dividends and capital gains that were also taxed at the corporate level—combined with concerns about rising budget deficits and the climbing costs of fighting wars in Iraq and Afghanistan led Congress to cut the package by more than half. Still, passage of the budget resolution and the subsequent tax reconciliation measure were clear victories for Bush, coming just two years after enactment of the president's $1.4 trillion tax cut (PL 107-16). *(2001 tax cut, p. 89, 2003; tax cut, p. 105)*

The discretionary spending limits, about $2 billion below Bush's request, were generally observed, although another $87.5 billion, enacted late in 2003 largely for emergency defense spending, did not count under the cap. The final budget resolution left a projected deficit of $385 billion in fiscal 2004 and did not project a return to surplus until 2012.

While the budget resolution itself was a set of congressional guidelines that did not become binding law, it was particularly important to GOP leaders in 2003 because of the protection it gave to subsequent legislation, in this case Bush's tax cuts. The resolution was the sole source of instructions that determined acceptable provisions for a reconciliation bill, which automatically qualified for special treatment in the Senate. Debate and amendments were limited, which meant the Republicans did not have to muster the sixty votes required under the cloture procedure to stop a filibuster.

They could prevail with a simple majority, which was crucial with their narrow fifty-one seat margin in the Senate.

In addition, without the total for discretionary spending set in the budget resolution the two chambers would not have a common number to work from when writing the fiscal 2004 appropriations bills. The Senate had failed to adopt a budget resolution in 2002 while under control of the Democrats, and Congress's inability to complete the fiscal 2003 spending bills until the start of the 108th Congress was blamed in part on the lack of a budget resolution. Republicans were eager to demonstrate that they could get the job done. They too failed, however, to complete action on the individual spending bills and ended up combining them into an omnibus spending package at the end of the year. *(Fiscal 2003 budget resolution, p. 67; fiscal 2004 spending bills, p. 69)*

HIGHLIGHTS

Following are the main components of the fiscal 2004 budget resolution (H Con Res 95):

- **Deficit.** The resolution projected a $385 billion deficit in fiscal 2004, declining gradually over the next seven years and returning to surplus in 2012. The cumulative deficit was projected at $1.4 trillion for fiscal 2004–2013. If Social Security trust funds were taken out of the calculation the ten-year deficit was $4 trillion.

- **Taxes.** The conference agreement assumed $1.2 trillion in tax cuts in fiscal 2003–2013 compared with $1.6 trillion proposed by Bush. Of the total, $550 billion could be achieved in 2003 using the filibuster-proof budget reconciliation process. However, that agreement was effectively modified by the Senate to allow only $350 billion under reconciliation.

- **Discretionary spending.** Of the $784.5 billion allowed for discretionary spending in fiscal 2004, $400.1 billion was for defense and $384.4 billion was for nondefense programs.

- **Medicare reserve.** The conference allowed $400 billion over ten years as a reserve to pay for a Medicare prescription drug benefit and Medicare modernization, should such legislation be enacted. *(Medicare changes, p. 496)*

- **Transportation.** The budget also permitted $280 billion in highway and mass transit spending over six years, roughly splitting the difference between the House and Senate figures. The purpose was to fund a major reauthorization of highway and mass transit programs due later in the year, but that legislation was left unfinished *(Highways, p. 387)*

- **Debt limit increase.** Under an arcane House rule, once the conference report on the budget was adopted the House was automatically deemed to have passed and sent to the Senate a bill to raise the statutory limit on the federal debt from $6.4 trillion to $7.4 trillion, the largest increase in history. *(Debt limit ceiling, p. 76)*

BUSH BUDGET REQUEST

The fiscal 2004 congressional budget process officially got under way Feb. 3, 2003, when President Bush submitted a $2.2 trillion budget request that called for substantial increases for defense and homeland security, a $400 billion overhaul of Medicare, and $1.5 trillion in tax cuts over eleven years. His proposals were projected to yield the largest deficits for fiscal 2003 and 2004, in dollar terms, in the nation's history.

Bush called for a limit of $782.2 billion on discretionary spending for fiscal 2004. The total did not include funds for the impending war in Iraq or for the ongoing costs of operations in Afghanistan, which were exceeding $1 billion a month. Bush subsequently requested $87 billion in fiscal 2004 for the two wars, all of it emergency spending. Early in the year Bush requested and Congress approved a $78.5 billion supplemental for fiscal 2003, primarily to pay for the war in Iraq and homeland defense. *(Fiscal 2003 and 2004 defense supplementals, pp. 75, 76)*

The Congressional Budget Office (CBO), Congress's official scorekeeper, issued its annual recalculation of the president's budget March 7 and estimated Bush's discretionary request at $786.6 billion. CBO said that was a 2.7 percent increase over the comparable fiscal 2003 bills. CBO numbers were used subsequently by both Congress and the White House and are used in this account as well.

The centerpiece of the budget request was Bush's call for a series of new tax cuts. The president's top tax priority was the $725.5 billion "economic stimulus package," which in addition to eliminating individual taxes on corporate dividends called for accelerating the phase-in of several tax cuts under the 2001 tax law, increasing the amount of individual income exempt from the alternative minimum tax, and increasing the amount that small businesses could deduct immediately for investment in new equipment. Other elements of the package extended through 2013 several tax provisions in the 2001 law that were scheduled to expire in 2010; provided new tax credits, deductions, and other tax incentives for specific purposes including charitable deductions, health care, and education; and put in place a package of tax administration changes designed to bring in $3.3 billion in additional revenue.

HOUSE COMMITTEE ACTION

The House and Senate Budget committees acted simultaneously on the fiscal 2004 resolution but headed in different ideological directions. The House Budget Committee approved its version of H Con Res 95 (H Rept 108-37) by a party-line vote of 24–19 early March 13 following a marathon markup that began the previous morning. Committee chair Jim Nussle, R-Iowa, had drafted an austere plan with an eye to preserving as much as possible of Bush's tax proposal while also satisfying House Republican pleas to reduce the gaping deficit. As approved by the committee the resolution called for $1.3 trillion in tax cuts over eleven years, with the $726 billion tax cut package protected as part of a reconciliation bill. It also contained instructions for a second reconciliation bill that would cut $467 billion over ten years from entitlement programs, including $200 billion from Medicare. Other entitlement programs affected included food stamps, school lunches, and health care benefits for federal employees. The only programs specifically protected from the cuts were Social Security and unemployment insurance.

The resolution also contained instructions that allowed a provision that would bring in revenue from opening portions of the Arctic National Wildlife Refuge (ANWR) to oil development. Opening ANWR to oil drilling was at the core of Bush's energy plan but supporters had been unable to muster the sixty votes required in the Senate to overcome a Democratic filibuster. By including ANWR in a reconciliation bill supporters would need only a simple majority to open the Alaskan reserve to oil and gas drilling. (*ANWR drilling, pp. 412, 425, 432*)

Finally, the resolution approved a $400 billion reserve for a Medicare prescription drug plan as part of a reconciliation bill that also would include $372 billion in mandatory spending cuts. Without the cuts the prescription drug plan would be limited to $27.7 billion.

Committee Democrats derided the GOP resolution, calling it reckless to cut taxes as the fiscal picture worsened and with the country on the brink of a war with Iraq. But they were having problems of their own in devising a palatable budget alternative given the bleak deficit forecasts.

HOUSE FLOOR ACTION

Nussle's proposed deep cuts in mandatory spending were so unpopular that he was forced to drop them from the bill even before it came to the floor. The revisions, adopted by voice vote as part of the rule for debate, specifically protected Medicare from across-the-board cuts and reduced the remaining cuts in mandatory spending to $265 billion over ten years. To compensate, the projected deficits were increased and a projected surplus was delayed until 2012 rather than 2010 as in the committee version.

Even with these changes, prospects for passage at times seemed bleak. Several moderates, concerned about advancing such large tax cuts while squeezing domestic spending, threatened to vote against the resolution. But GOP leaders urged queasy lawmakers to wait and see what would emerge from conference before voting "no."

In the end, Republicans heeded pleas from House Speaker J. Dennis Hastert, R-Ill., and Vice President Dick Cheney to avoid handing Bush an embarrassing defeat just as the war in Iraq was starting. Still, the final vote was touch-and-go for the leadership. After holding the vote open for several minutes beyond its scheduled fifteen minutes, Republicans finally edged ahead when two GOP members switched their votes from "nay" to "aye." The vote was quickly gaveled to a close and the resolution was passed on a **key vote of 215–212 (R 214–12; D 1–199; I 0–1).** (*2003 key votes, p. 837*)

SENATE COMMITTEE ACTION

The Senate Budget Committee approved its budget resolution (S Con Res 23–no written report) by a party-line vote of 12–11 on March 13. Drafted by the panel's new chair, Don

Nickles, R-Okla., the plan hewed closer to Bush's budget than did the House committee version because Nickles made less of an effort to offset the proposed tax cuts. The Senate version was more generous to the appropriators in the short term than the House version, it lacked the steep mandatory cuts proposed by Nussle, and it showed deficits until fiscal 2013. Like the House bill it offered protection for Bush's stimulus tax package but not for other tax cuts.

As approved by the committee, the Senate resolution also instructed the Energy and Natural Resources Committee to count future revenue from oil and gas drilling in ANWR, which offered de facto authority for drilling. And it approved a reserve fund of $400 billion over ten years for Medicare reform, but it did not offer the protection of a reconciliation bill; Senate Republicans objected to House plans to advance a prescription drug benefit through the reconciliation process.

SENATE FLOOR ACTION

The Senate adopted the budget resolution 56–44 on March 26, but only after Democrats forced two major changes. The first limited the tax cuts that could be protected by a reconciliation bill to $350 billion. The second excluded provisions relating to ANWR from reconciliation. Those decisions, if retained in the final budget, meant Republicans would have to muster sixty votes to get the proposals through the Senate. Centrists, led by John B. Breaux, D-La., struggled for more than a week to make sizable cuts in Bush's tax package. With support from two moderate Republicans Breaux pushed an amendment to shrink the total to $350 billion. That plan failed 38–62 after a handful of Democrats who opposed any tax cuts refused to support the amendment. That vote appeared to be a pivotal victory for Senate Republicans who were anxious to finish up work on the resolution. But Democrats delayed, insisting that they first needed to know how much fiscal 2003 supplemental spending Bush would seek for the war in Iraq. Over the weekend the White House announced that Bush was requesting $74.7 billion, a staggering sum and the largest supplemental request up to that point in history. At the same time, U.S. troops began running into fierce resistance in Iraq, bringing—along with American casualties—a sense that the war would take longer and be more costly than was initially expected.

Breaux tried again on March 25, reworking his amendment with nonbinding language that earmarked the money to be saved for Social Security. Several Democrats and a third Republican who voted against the first Breaux amendment announced they would support this new amendment. With a chance to deal a significant blow to Bush's fiscal agenda, Democrats flocked to the proposal, passing it on a **key vote of 51–48 (R 3–48; D 47–0; I 1–0.)** Earlier the Senate had dealt another blow to Bush when it voted March 19 to drop the provision that would have spared Republicans the need to get sixty votes to approve drilling in ANWR. The amendment was adopted on a **key vote of 52–48 (R 8–43; D 43–5; I 1–0).** (*ANWR details, p. 432; 2003 key votes, p. 837*)

FINAL ACTION

The chief challenge for House and Senate negotiators was finding a level of tax cuts large enough to satisfy House GOP conservatives and small enough for Senate moderates who continued to draw the line at $350 billion. Forced to abandon most of the mandatory spending cuts in their original budget, House leaders were loath to give in on taxes.

After intense negotiations, conferees agreed on an unusual procedure. The budget resolution would instruct the House and Senate tax committees to write bills cutting taxes by as much as $550 billion over eleven years. If the Senate bill exceeded $350 billion, however, it would be subject to a point of order on the floor that would require a sixty-vote majority to overcome. That effectively limited the initial Senate tax bill to $350 billion. The conference report on the tax bill would not be subject to the same point of order, which meant the final bill could cut as much as $550 billion.

On that basis House Republicans adopted the conference report (H Rept 108-71) April 11 without a single Democratic vote. The tally was 216–211. Then came the shock. Before the Senate voted, Charles E. Grassley, R-Iowa, chair of the tax-writing Senate Finance Committee, announced that he, Nickles, and Majority Leader Bill Frist, R-Tenn., had reached a deal with the moderates. "At the end of the day," Grassley said, "the tax cut side of the growth package will not exceed $350 billion." The Senate then adopted the conference report 51–50 with Cheney casting the decisive vote.

House leaders cried betrayal and alleged that Senate GOP leaders had reneged on a handshake agreement. Conservative members of the House GOP rank and file were furious. Many had voted for the conference report only on the understanding that they would at least have an opportunity to win a tax cut that exceeded $350 billion. Although the House version of the tax reconciliation bill (HR 2—PL 108-27) included a $550 billion tax cut, the Senate again prevailed, with the final bill providing an estimated $330 billion in tax cuts and refundable tax credits over eleven years. (*Tax cut, p. 105*)

Fiscal 2003, 2004 Appropriations

With majorities in both chambers of Congress and President George W. Bush in the White House Republicans controlled the appropriations process from start to finish for the first time since 1954. GOP leaders vowed to handle the fiscal 2003 bills smoothly, adhere to their tight budget, and avoid the end-of-session gridlock that occurred in 2002 when Democrats held the Senate. But partisan control was not enough to overcome a host of obstacles that slowed the bills and led to collapse just short of the finish line in December. Among these obstacles were tight spending limits; the need for additional money to fight the war in Iraq, which began in March; and, perhaps most important, internal divisions within the Republican caucus over high-profile policy riders attached to the fiscal 2004 spending bills.

Republican hopes were thwarted in part by the sheer volume of work confronting the appropriators. Before they could even begin work on the fiscal 2004 bills, they had to complete eleven fiscal 2003 measures left over from 2002. Those measures were quickly wrapped into an omnibus spending package for fiscal 2003 (H J Res 2—PL 108-7), which was passed in February.

The next order of business was passage of a budget resolution to guide their spending decisions. Work on H Con Res 95 was completed on April 11, but the final product left appropriators unhappy with the discretionary spending limit of $784.7 billion for fiscal 2004. Appropriators said that cap was uncomfortably tight. A later revision of the cap to $786 billion did little to ease the strains. (*Budget resolution, p. 67*)

As they worked on the regular spending bills, the appropriators also had to steer through Congress three supplemental spending bills requested by Bush. The first (PL 108-11), cleared April 12, was for $78.5 billion in fiscal 2003 spending, primarily to pay for military operations in Iraq and for homeland security. The second (PL 108-69), cleared July 31, appropriated nearly $1 billion in fiscal 2003 funds to replenish dwindling disaster aid accounts at the Federal Emergency Management Agency. The third (PL 108-106), cleared Nov. 3, provided $87.5 billion in fiscal 2004 funds for ongoing military and reconstruction costs in Iraq and Afghanistan. The two defense supplementals were the largest supplementals, in dollar terms, that Congress had ever enacted. (*Details, p. 75, 76*)

Despite GOP intentions, by the time fiscal 2004 began on Oct. 1 only three of the regular thirteen spending bills had been enacted—for defense, the legislative branch, and the new Department of Homeland Security. (Appropriations for Transportation and Treasury and their related agencies had been combined into a single spending bill to make way for a spending bill for Homeland Security without increasing the overall number of appropriations bills.) By Nov. 18 only three more had been cleared (energy and water, military construction, and the Interior Department), and appropriators decided it was time to wrap the remaining bills into an omnibus package.

The process allowed GOP leaders and the White House to prevail on virtually all of the issues that had stalled the bills—even on those provisions that had majority support in both chambers. Provisions dropped at White House insistence included a Senate attempt to stop the Labor Department from changing the rules for overtime pay, language backed by both chambers to block enforcement of the U.S. ban on travel to Cuba, and a House proposal to bar the administration from opening thousands of federal jobs to private contractors. A bipartisan provision to prevent media conglomerates from gaining greater control of the television market was substantially weakened. (*Details, overtime p. 574; Cuba p. 260; jobs p. 690; media 389*)

The conference agreement was completed on Nov. 25; the House adopted it on Dec. 8, but the Senate put off final action on the omnibus bill until 2004, clearing it on Jan. 22—just in time to begin the process again for fiscal 2005 spending.

FISCAL 2003 OMNIBUS APPROPRIATIONS

The first major order of business in the 108th Congress was completion of the eleven fiscal 2003 spending bills left unfinished at the end of 2002. The bills were wrapped into a single omnibus package that was cleared Feb. 13, 2003, and signed into law Feb. 20 (H J Res 2—PL 108-7). *(Background, 2002 action on spending bills, p. 59)*

The 3,000-page-plus bill provided $397.4 billion in discretionary spending, mainly for domestic programs. Of that amount $10 billion was for emergency defense and intelligence spending—$3.9 billion requested by President Bush for intelligence needs and $6.1 billion to replenish Pentagon accounts that had been tapped to finance antiterror operations in Afghanistan and elsewhere. The defense funds were added in conference at the urging of Vice President Dick Cheney, who played a significant role in negotiating the final bill. The package also appropriated $397.3 billion for mandatory programs and contained drought relief long sought by farmers and a reversal of scheduled Medicare budget cuts.

Congressional Republicans and the White House each claimed victory—Republicans for changing Bush's budget more to their liking and the White House for enforcing limits on domestic spending. Democrats, who complained of being shut out of the process, focused their criticism on homeland security, saying the GOP had provided too little funding even as the country was on increased alert for terrorist attacks.

Enactment marked the end of five months of stalemate and brinkmanship that left the fiscal 2003 appropriations near collapse at the end of the 107th Congress. Only two bills—for the Department of Defense (PL 107-248) and military construction (PL 107-249)—were enacted when lawmakers adjourned in November 2002.

Departments, agencies, and programs covered by the other eleven bills had their budgets frozen at the fiscal 2002 levels under a series of seven short-term continuing resolutions enacted in 2002. The last of them (PL 107-294) was good until Jan. 11, 2003. Three additional stopgap bills had to be enacted in January before the omnibus package was completed.

Lawmakers faced the same problem that had stumped them in 2002: a bottom line for domestic spending that was billions of dollars less than appropriators of both parties said they needed to cover all the programs and ensure adequate support for the bills. This time, however, appropriators and the White House were looking ahead to a new Congress and were determined to get the old business behind them.

Appropriators agreed reluctantly to Bush's demand that they limit total discretionary spending for fiscal 2003 to $750.5 billion. With $365.5 billion already allocated for defense and military construction, that left $385 billion for nondefense programs. Bush subsequently showed some flexibility, agreeing to add $825 million to fight fires in the West,

$1.5 billion to overhaul state and local election systems, and $2.2 billion to increase education spending. The final measure also included a 0.7 percent across-the-board cut in discretionary spending.

Legislative Action

Because the bills written in 2002 had died at the end of the 107th Congress, lawmakers used an unusual process to assemble and pass the omnibus package. On Jan. 8 the House passed by voice vote two continuing resolutions, the first (H J Res 1) to keep the government operating through the end of January, and the second (H J Res 2) essentially a shell. The Senate passed H J Res 2 69–29 on Jan. 23 after attaching its rewritten version of the eleven nondefense spending measures. The bill went straight to conference where the main issue was how to handle more than $11 billion added to the bill on the Senate floor. Once that was resolved the House adopted the conference report (H Rept 108-10) 338–83 on Feb. 13. The Senate cleared the bill that night on a 76–20 vote.

Highlights

An accurate total of the omnibus bill's cost was impossible to determine because it combined $397.4 billion in fiscal 2003 discretionary funds with $3.1 billion in mandatory drought relief, plus Highway Trust Fund spending that exceeded Bush's requests by $8.8 billion. It also included tens of billions of dollars in potential payments to doctors facing cuts in Medicare fees plus $2.2 billion in advanced fiscal 2004 appropriations for education, which drew strong protests from the White House.

Following are brief summaries of each of the eleven regular spending bills folded into the omnibus.

• **Agriculture.** Congress provided $74.4 billion for Agriculture Department farm, food, and nutrition programs. That was $1.3 billion more than the programs got in fiscal 2002 and $861 million more than President Bush requested. The omnibus package also contained $3.1 billion in emergency aid for farmers and ranchers hurt by drought, offset by cuts over ten years from a mandatory account for agriculture conservation programs. With the sagging economy expected to increase demand for food aid, the law included $41.9 billion for domestic food assistance programs, 10 percent more than was available in fiscal 2002. Food stamps accounted for most of the increase.

• **Commerce-Justice-State.** Funding for the departments of Commerce, Justice, and State and the federal judiciary remained essentially flat under the fiscal 2003 omnibus spending bill with increases over fiscal 2002 for programs related to homeland security offset by cutbacks in most other accounts. The measure provided $4.3 billion for the Federal Bureau of Investigation and $6.2 billion for the Immigration and Naturalization Service; both agencies had been folded into the new Department of Homeland Security. The bill also gave the Securities and Exchange Commission $716 million—a 46 percent increase over fiscal 2002—to hire new staff and beef up enforcement efforts. That action came in the wake of a string of corporate accounting scandals and the enactment of a law in 2002 giving the agency new responsibilities for policing corporate behavior. *(Corporate accounting law, p. 130)*

- **District of Columbia.** The District of Columbia received $512 million in federal funds under the fiscal 2003 omnibus. The total was 35 percent more than President Bush requested but $95 million less than was appropriated in fiscal 2002 when the District also received $200 million in emergency and supplemental funds for homeland security. For fiscal 2003 Congress added $50 million to modernize the city's sewer system, $10 million to help hospitals prepare for bioterrorism, and $10 million to create a unified communications system.

- **Energy-Water.** Energy and water development programs received $26.7 billion for fiscal 2003, $883 million more than Congress appropriated in fiscal 2002 and $515 million more than President Bush requested. As was typical—and despite the strained circumstances under which they were working—legislators added millions for projects that benefited their states and districts. Money was appropriated for fifty-five new construction starts for the Army Corps of Engineers; the president had proposed only one new project. Congress also raised the president's request for nuclear security from $8 billion to $8.1 billion, $410 million more than was appropriated in fiscal 2002.

- **Foreign Operations.** Congress appropriated $16.3 billion for foreign aid and other foreign operations—$242 million less than in fiscal 2002 and $148 million less than requested. Appropriators made room for new initiatives while reducing overall spending, in part by eliminating a program that provided fuel oil to North Korea in exchange for that country's promise to forgo a nuclear weapons program. The bill provided $876 million for AIDS prevention and control, including $248 million for the Global Fund to Fight HIV/AIDS, Tuberculosis and Malaria. The administration ultimately won its full request of $731 million to assist efforts in Colombia and neighboring countries to defeat drug traffickers and the left-wing guerrillas who protected them. Some members had wanted to cut back the drug program to free more funding for the global HIV/AIDS fund.

- **Interior.** Funding for the Department of the Interior and related agencies was $19.1 billion, nearly the same as the fiscal 2002 level and less than either chamber or the president had recommended. The final version also included several provisions that troubled environmentalists, including one that would greatly expand a pilot "forest stewardship" program under which timber companies could harvest lumber from national forests in exchange for clearing flammable underbrush and deadwood. Environmentalists said they feared the Bush administration would be too permissive in administering the program. Congress later in the year passed a "healthy forests" initiative along the lines of the pilot program. *(Details, p. 433)*

- **Labor-HHS-Education.** Congress approved $424.1 billion in fiscal 2003 spending for the departments of Labor, Health and Human Services, and Education. Of that amount $290.7 billion was mandatory spending for programs such as Social Security and Medicare. The fiercest fights over allocation of the discretionary funding concerned education, with Democrats and moderate Republicans charging that Bush was seriously underfunding the 2001 "No Child Left Behind" education law (PL 107-110) that he had championed. Legislators ultimately agreed to increase Title I grants for disadvantaged students to $11.8 billion, $1.4 billion more than in fiscal 2002 and $400 million above the request. Legislators also provided more money than Bush had requested for several other programs, including Head Start, special education, and heating assistance. *("No Child Left Behind" action, p. 540)*

- **Legislative Branch.** Lawmakers agreed to spend $3.4 billion in fiscal 2003 on the operation of Congress and its affiliated agencies—3 percent more than in fiscal 2002. The additional funding was mainly for raises to Capitol Police officers and a major upgrade of the Capitol power plant.

- **Transportation.** Fiscal 2003 spending for the Department of Transportation and related agencies was set at $64.6 billion, $8.6 billion more than the president had requested. Almost all of the increase over the president's request was to restore highway funding that the president had proposed cutting. Overall the bill represented a cut of nearly 3 percent from fiscal 2002 spending. The 1998 surface transportation law tied highway spending to gasoline tax revenues. Thus, when the Office of Management and Budget forecast declining gasoline tax revenues for fiscal 2003, Bush was also forced to cut his highway budget request. A more controversial increase over Bush's budget request was for the financially troubled National Railroad Passenger Corporation (Amtrak). Congress appropriated $1.1 billion for system, more than double Bush's request of $521 million. Congress did set various conditions that Amtrak had to meet to receive the funding. *(Amtrak legislation, pp. 379, 404)*

- **Treasury–Postal Service.** The omnibus spending bill provided $34.7 billion for the Treasury–Postal Service portion of the bill, roughly 2 percent more than the fiscal 2002 spending level. Gone from the omnibus were two provisions in the original bills that had drawn a veto threat from Bush. One proposed to bar enforcement of the ban on U.S. citizens traveling to Cuba that dated to the early days of Fidel Castro's communist regime in the 1960s. The other sought to block the administration from using numerical goals, targets, or quotas for "outsourcing" federal jobs to private-sector contractors. Conferees on the omnibus bill agreed to drop the Cuba provision altogether and to impose only limited conditions on the use of quotas for outsourcing federal jobs. *(Cuba travel, p. 299; federal jobs outsourcing, p. 690)*

- **VA-HUD.** Fiscal 2003 appropriations for the departments of Veterans Affairs and Housing and Urban Development (HUD) totaled $121.9 billion, $1.9 billion less than either the fiscal 2002 spending level or the president's request.

Appropriators rejected several major White House proposals, including a plan to start requiring some veterans to pay a deductible for health services, a call for a substantial reduction in funds for capital improvements to public housing, and an attempt to cut the budget for the Environmental Protection Agency by 6 percent. At the same time, Congress cut Bush's request for the Federal Emergency Management Agency by more than half, from $6.7 billion to $2.9 billion. Congress subsequently passed emergency funding to replenish FEMA's dwindling coffers. *(Disaster aid, pp. 73, 76, 81, 84)*

Congress also denied Bush's request to raise funding for the Corporation for National and Community Service (Americorps) by more than 50 percent. Conferees instead cut the budget by about $20 million, to $387 million. Bush had made Americorps a priority in his 2002 State of the Union address.

FISCAL 2004 DEFENSE APPROPRIATIONS

Driven by the grim reality of American soldiers fighting and dying on two fronts, in Iraq and Afghanistan, lawmakers dropped nearly all of their disagreements and approved the most expensive defense spending package in history. President Bush signed the $368.7 billion bill (HR 2658—PL 108-87) into law Sept. 30, 2003, just in time for the start of the new fiscal year on Oct. 1.

Even as they finished work on the regular defense spending bill, appropriators were beginning to discuss a supplemental fiscal 2004 request from Bush for $87 billion to pay for ongoing military operations in Iraq and Afghanistan. Those costs were not covered in the regular spending bill. *(Details of supplemental, p. 75)*

Partisan politics played almost no part in deliberation on the defense bill, and the measure moved quickly. The House passed its version of HR 2658 (H Rept 108-187) by a vote of 399–19 on July 8. The Senate passed a nearly identical version (S Rept 108-87) by a vote of 95–0 on July 17. Passage followed four days of debate in which Democrats raised questions and criticisms about the administration's handling of the war in Iraq. On Sept. 17, in the face of a deteriorating security situation in Iraq, House and Senate negotiators pushed the defense bill through conference in just twenty-five minutes. The House adopted the conference report (H Rept 108-283) 407–15 on Sept. 24 after just seven minutes of debate and with only two copies of the inch-thick text available for reading. The Senate acted almost as quickly the next day, clearing the bill 95–0. Sen. John McCain, R-Ariz., was the only senator to protest the speed with which the legislation moved.

The final bill included $115.9 billion for operations and maintenance, $74.7 billion for procurement, $65.2 billion for research and development, and $98.5 billion for military personnel. On specific items Congress agreed to $9.1 billion for ballistic missile defense programs, roughly equal to Bush's request and $1.4 billion above the fiscal 2003 level. Democrats remained concerned that work on the program

could destabilize efforts to control the spread of nuclear weapons, but they largely chose to ignore the issue, focusing their effort on nuclear research initiatives in other bills.

The final version also included large increases for Pentagon counterterrorism activities, including $4.5 billion for special operations forces and $1 billion for procurement and development of chemical and biological defenses. The bill dismantled a controversial Defense Department program, the Terrorism Information Awareness (TIA) system, that was supposed to screen tens of thousands of individuals for possible terrorist connections; most of TIA's functions were moved to an unspecified office. Critics had voiced privacy concerns about the program.

FISCAL 2004 ENERGY-WATER APPROPRIATIONS

Congress cleared a $27.3 billion fiscal 2004 energy and water spending bill Nov. 18, 2003 (HR 2754—Pl 108-137). The bill was stalled for most of the fall by conflicts over developing nuclear weapons and disposing of nuclear waste. Negotiators managed to strike a compromise just in time to keep the bill from being rolled into the year-end omnibus.

The bill increased funding for the Department of Energy and related agencies by $1.1 billion, or 4.3 percent, over fiscal 2003 and provided $382 million more than Bush requested. The final bill provided $6.3 billion for nuclear weapon activities of the Energy Department, including funding to study a nuclear version of the "bunker buster" used by U.S. bombers to destroy caves and bunkers in such places as Afghanistan. It also included $580 million for a controversial national nuclear waste disposal facility at Yucca Mountain, Nev. *(Yucca Mountain, p. 422, 439)*

The House passed HR 2754 (H Rept 108-212) 377–26 on July 18. The Senate passed its version of the bill (S Rept 108-105) 92–0 on Sept. 16. The House adopted the conference report (H Rept 108-357) 387–36 on Nov. 18, and the Senate cleared the bill later that day by voice vote. President Bush signed it into law Dec. 1.

FISCAL 2004 HOMELAND SECURITY APPROPRIATIONS

Congress cleared a $30.4 billion fiscal 2004 spending bill for the Department of Homeland Security (HR 2555—PL 108-90), the first devoted to the new department, on Sept. 24, 2003. Despite misgivings about management of the new department, Congress moved with uncommon speed to approve its funding. Bush got much of what he wanted, plus an additional $1 billion, to protect the nation's borders, ports, airports, and infrastructure from terrorism. Taken together, the twenty-two agencies that were merged to make up the department received a total of 2.2 percent, or $667 million, more than they received in fiscal 2003.

The biggest fight centered on the amount to provide "first responders": the police, fire, and emergency response crews that are first on the scene of an emergency. Senate Democrats pushed for $10 billion to $14 billion. The final bill provided $4.2 billion, just $600 million more than the $3.6 million the president had requested.

The law also included money for Project Bioshield, Bush's signature program to prepare for a bioterrorist attack, but the law made the funding discretionary rather than mandatory as Bush wanted. Lawmakers also required the new department to report back on at least two dozen ongoing security projects, including airline passenger profiling and aviation security technology. The requirements were indicative of lawmakers' desire to wrest back some of the wide-ranging management authority they gave the new department when it was created in 2002 (*Creation of department, p. 176; bioshield, p. 213*)

The House easily passed HR 2555 (H Rept 108-169) 425–2 on June 24. The Senate approved its version (S Rept 108-86) by a similarly lopsided vote of 93–1 on July 24 after four days of debate during which Democrats charged that the measure left the country "dangerously unprepared" for a future attack. Democrats were unable, however, to persuade the Senate to adopt any of a series of amendments that would have raised spending or rearranged priorities in the bill. The only success Democrats could claim was political: forcing Republicans to vote over and over against more funding for national security. The House adopted the conference report (H Rept 108-280) 417–8 on Sept. 24. The Senate cleared the bill by voice vote later in the day. President Bush signed the measure on Oct. 1.

FISCAL 2004 INTERIOR APPROPRIATIONS

Overall funding for the Interior Department and related agencies in fiscal 2004 was almost unchanged from the previous year. The fiscal 2004 spending bill (HR 2691—PL 108-108) included $19.7 billion in regular funds plus $400 million in emergency firefighting money. Without the emergency funds—which helped push the bill to enactment as wildfires devastated great swaths of California—the total was 2 percent below fiscal 2003 spending.

The measure moved relatively quickly through both chambers free of the contentious environmental riders that slowed Interior spending bills in the past. The House passed HR 2691 (H Rept 108-195) 268–152 on July 17, 2003. The Senate passed its version of the bill (S Rept 108-89) by voice vote on Sept. 23. The House adopted the conference report (H Rept 108-330) 216–205 on Oct. 30, and the Senate cleared the bill 87–2 on Nov. 3.

The main controversy involved cuts in funding for land acquisition. The final bill reduced the money available to buy property for federal parks, forests, and other natural preserves by 44 percent from the previous year. Another important dispute concerned lawsuits brought by American Indians alleging that the Interior Department had improperly accounted for timber, grazing, oil, and mineral lease royalties on land held in trust by the department since 1887. The final

version limited spending for the full accounting required by a U.S. district court to give Congress time to work out a possible solution to the problem. The final bill also limited, but did not ban, funding for studies on opening Forest Service and Interior jobs to competitive bidding by private contractors. Bush had threatened to veto the bill if it banned such funding.

FISCAL 2004 LEGISLATIVE BRANCH APPROPRIATIONS

Lawmakers on Sept. 24, 2003, cleared a $3.5 billion bill to pay for the operations of Congress and its affiliated agencies in fiscal 2004. The bill (HR 2657—PL 108-83) also carried a $938 million appropriation for fiscal 2003 emergency supplemental spending to combat wildfires in the West and pay for disaster relief, flood control projects, and an investigation of the space shuttle *Columbia* accident. Another $984 million in emergency fiscal 2003 disaster aid was enacted in a separate supplemental spending bill signed Aug. 8. Overall the fiscal 2004 spending bill for the legislative branch represented a 2.5 percent increase over the regular and supplemental appropriations for fiscal 2003. (*Disaster aid, pp. 76, 81, 84*)

The addition of the supplemental spending tied up action on the bill for several weeks. So did House-Senate disputes over funding for the underground visitors complex being constructed on the East Front of the Capitol and over a bid by Capitol Police for more money. Senate conferees ultimately persuaded their reluctant House counterparts to provide $49 million for the visitors center; that was the minimum the General Accounting Office said was needed to complete construction. The final bill cut spending for Capitol Police by 8 percent from fiscal 2003. That was far below the amount the Capitol Police wanted, but it still allowed an expansion of the force for the third time in as many years.

The House passed HR 2657 (H Rept 108-186) 394–26 on July 9. The Senate passed an amended version (S Rept 108-88) 85–7 on July 11. The House adopted the conference report (H Rept 108-279) 371–56 on Sept. 24, and the Senate cleared the bill by voice vote later in the day.

FISCAL 2004 MILITARY CONSTRUCTION APPROPRIATIONS

The military construction appropriations bill—usually one of the first to clear because of the funding it provided for local bases—was slowed in 2003 by tight budget constraints. The final bill (HR 2559—PL 108-132) provided $9.3 billion in fiscal 2004 for military construction, family housing, and costs associated with base realignments and closings, a full 13 percent below the fiscal 2003 spending level.

President Bush initially requested a 15 percent reduction, arguing that the Pentagon could afford to cut back on building runways, fitness centers, and educational facilities because of planned base closures. That did not sit well with lawmakers who counted on the funding to enhance local military bases, boost local construction companies, and earn voter support.

The House passed its bill (H Rept 108-173) 428–0 on June 26. The Senate passed its version (S Rept 108-82) 91–0 on July 11. After arguing for weeks over whose projects would get into the bill, House and Senate negotiators finally reached a compromise Nov. 4. The House adopted the conference report (H Rept 108-342) 417–5 on Nov. 5, and the Senate cleared the bill 98–0 on Nov, 12. President Bush signed it into law on Nov. 22.

An additional $525 million for military construction was included in the fiscal 2004 supplemental (PL 108-106) signed Nov. 6.

FISCAL 2004 OMNIBUS APPROPRIATIONS

With seven regular fiscal 2004 spending bills mired in disputes over policy and money, Congress turned to an omnibus spending package to fund much of the federal government. The measure (HR 2673—PL 108-199) provided $328.1 billion in new discretionary budget authority for eleven cabinet-level departments, the District of Columbia, and related agencies. Mandatory spending and disbursements from the highway and aviation trust funds brought the overall total to $820 billion.

While abiding by the Bush administration's ceiling of $786 billion in discretionary spending for all fiscal 2004 spending bills, including the six already passed, appropriators managed to squeeze about $4.6 billion in additional funding into the omnibus. In one of the last issues resolved in conference they agreed to pay for about $2.7 billion of the add-ons through a 0.6 percent cut in nondefense discretionary funding, even in the already enacted bills. They also cut $1.8 billion in unobligated funds, chiefly from the defense budget.

The decision to fashion an omnibus bill came shortly before Thanksgiving. The conference report on the Agriculture spending bill was used as the vehicle, and the early conference negotiations featured bipartisan talks among House and Senate appropriations subcommittee chairs and ranking minority members over the thousands of spending items in the unfinished bills. The appropriators thought they had reached a bipartisan, bicameral agreement until House Republican leaders intervened. Backed by liberally issued veto threats from the White House, they opened up several compromises drafted by the pragmatists who dominated the Appropriations committees in both chambers and rewrote the bill more to the president's liking.

At the urging of the Bush administration the conservative House leaders killed a Senate effort to block proposed rules limiting overtime pay for some white-collar workers, eliminated most congressional attempts to curb administration efforts to "outsource" federal jobs to private contractors, and watered down Senate language partially reversing Federal Communications Commission (FCC) rules to allow further concentration of television ownership. House GOP leaders and the White House also succeeded in adding language backed by the National Rifle Association that restricted federal oversight of sales by gun dealers. *(Outsourcing, p. 690; media concentration, p. 389)*

Democratic and some Republican conferees complained bitterly about their treatment at the hands of the top GOP negotiators and the White House, but the measure passed by wide margins in both chambers. The House adopted the conference report (H Rept 108-401) on Dec. 8 by a vote of 242–176. Senate Democrats were so irate at the tactics used to put the final bill together that they forced final action into the new year, but the Senate easily cleared the legislation Jan. 22, 2004, by a 65–28 vote.

Following are highlights from each of the seven bills melded into the omnibus measure.

Agriculture

The fiscal 2004 spending bill provided $80.6 billion for the Agriculture Department and related agencies—a $5.9 billion increase over fiscal 2003 spending. Most of the increase was for mandatory spending for food stamps and other nutrition programs. Of total spending in the bill only $16.9 billion was discretionary, which was $964 million less than in fiscal 2003 (not counting the across-the-board 0.6 percent cut included in the omnibus).

The main controversy as the bill moved through the House and Senate was over a program requiring country-of-origin labeling on agricultural products scheduled to begin Sept. 30, 2004. The final bill delayed the labeling for two years, except in the case of farm-raised and wild fish. Several other controversial provisions were dropped in conference, including a Senate proposal to ease travel to Cuba by farmers and medical suppliers selling their products and a House plan to allow limited reimportation of prescription drugs from Canada. *(Food labeling, p. 465; Cuba travel ban, p. 299; drug reimportation, p. 508)*

Commerce-Justice-State

The omnibus spending package provided $41 billion for the departments of Commerce, Justice, and State; the federal judiciary; and related agencies. The total was nearly in line with Bush's budget request and 1 percent above fiscal 2003 spending. The biggest dispute in the measure concerned provisions in both the House and Senate versions aimed at reversing a widely unpopular decision by the FCC to loosen the rules on media ownership. The White House adamantly opposed the language, and appropriators were forced to drop it in conference to avoid a veto. *(Media ownership, p. 389)*

The final bill also dropped House language that would have cut back provisions of the 2001 antiterror bill, known as the Patriot Act (PL 107-56). The provision reflected increasing congressional misgivings about the law and the Justice Department's use of its provisions in the war on terror. The final bill retained House language requiring federal officials to destroy records related to background checks of gun purchasers within twenty-four hours of their having been cleared to buy the weapons. *(USA PATRIOT Act, p. 187; new gun rules, p. 628)*

District of Columbia

The fiscal 2004 spending bill for the District of Columbia provided a $545 million federal payment, 7 percent above the fiscal 2003 level, to reimburse the District for costs associated with housing the federal government. Republicans' bid to make the District a proving ground for school vouchers dominated debate on the original spending bills and nearly sidetracked it in both chambers. The final version provided $14 million for federal vouchers to allow D.C. students to attend private schools, including those run by religious organizations. *(Vouchers, p. 549)*

Foreign Operations

Congress increased funding for foreign aid and export assistance to $17.3 billion for fiscal 2004—about 6 percent above the fiscal 2003 level. The total for foreign operations was 9 percent below the $18.9 billion that Bush requested, but the bill still included hefty startup funding for the president's two big initiatives: a five-year program to fight HIV/AIDS overseas, primarily in Africa and the Caribbean; and the Millennium Challenge Account, a new program to aid poor countries committed to democracy, human rights, and open-market economics. The perennial disagreement surround-ing Reagan-era restrictions on international family planning funds was a principal reason that the original bill did not clear and had to be incorporated into the omnibus spending bill. *(Family planning, p. 247; foreign aid, pp. 232, 257, 289)*

Labor-HHS-Education

The omnibus bill provided $471.8 billion for the departments of Labor, Health and Human Services (HHS), and Education. Mandatory programs in the bill, such as Medicare, Medicaid, and unemployment insurance compensation, were expected to cost $332 billion, a 14 percent increase over fiscal 2003. Less than one-third of the bill—$139.8 billion—was discretionary spending. That was $1.8 billion more than Bush requested and $7.5 billion more than fiscal 2003 spending. The bill provided large spending increases for education. Democrats said even more was needed to attract better teachers to poor schools and to help educate disabled children.

The most controversial issue, however, was the administration's proposed change in overtime rules. GOP leaders in the House narrowly beat back a Democratic amendment to block the new Labor Department rule during its consideration of the regular Labor-HHS-Education spending bill, but later in the year the House voted to instruct its conferees on the bill to accept the Senate-passed ban on the overtime rules. In the end, however, Republican leaders heeded a White House veto threat and stripped the language from the bill. *(Overtime rules, p. 574)*

Transportation-Treasury

The fiscal 2004 funding bill for the Transportation and Treasury departments and related agencies came close to reaching enactment on its own but it was added to the om-nibus spending bill after a final dispute with the White House over privatizing federal jobs dragged on too long. The omnibus bill provided $89.8 billion for Transportation and Treasury—a $3.3 billion increase over fiscal 2003 and $4 billion more than Bush originally requested. The overall increase came entirely in mandatory spending, largely for highway spending.

The original bill drew at least two veto threats. The first came on a House amendment to bar the administration from using funds in the bill to implement its proposal to privatize some federal jobs. The omnibus bill instead laid out a set of guidelines for the administration to follow, set some limits on jobs that could be privatized, and required an annual report to Congress. The second veto threat came on language endorsed by both chambers to relax the ban on travel to Cuba. The final bill dropped the language. *(Job privatization, p. 690; Cuba travel ban, p. 299)*

The omnibus bill did block, temporarily, final Treasury regulations on converting traditional pension plans to "cash-balance" plans. The cash-balance plans were said by some experts to be discriminatory against workers nearing retirement age. Treasury was also blocked from implementing rules that would permit banks to get into the real estate business.

VA-HUD

The omnibus spending bill provided $128.2 billion for the departments of Veterans Affairs and Housing and Urban Development. In response to veterans' groups that were pushing for more benefits, the amount included an additional $1.3 billion over Bush's request for veterans' health programs and discarded his proposal that some veterans pay new fees for health care. The omnibus legislation also provided $444 million for the national service program known as Americorps, a program that subsidized the expenses of young adults engaged in domestic public service. That was the biggest budget in the troubled agency's history. Americorps, a priority of the president, had been hampered for years by bad management, but the appointment of a new chief executive officer who promised to address the problems allowed Congress to give the president his full appropriation request.

FISCAL 2003 DEFENSE SUPPLEMENTAL APPROPRIATIONS

The fiscal 2003 defense supplemental (HR 1559—PL 108-11) appropriated $78.5 billion, mostly for ongoing military operations and construction. As signed the bill appropriated $62.4 billion for military spending. Conferees allocated $46.7 billion to specific accounts, with the remainder of that amount going to a fund the Pentagon could disburse on its own. Although Congress acted quickly on the request, passing the measure in less than a month, it was not willing to grant the administration the broad leeway it wanted in allocating the funds. Bush requested that the Pentagon be allowed to control virtually all of the military funds without congressional oversight. The bill also provided supplemental funds for airlines, foreign aid, homeland security, and public health. *(Military funds, p. 329)*

The House passed HR 1559 (H Rept 108-55) 414–12, on April 3, 2003. The Senate passed its version of the measure (S 762—S Rept 108-33) on April 7. After a short conference the Senate by voice vote on April 12 deemed HR 1559 cleared pending House action. The House adopted the conference report (H Rept 108-76) by voice vote on April 16. President Bush signed the measure into law later in the day.

FISCAL 2004 DEFENSE SUPPLEMENTAL APPROPRIATIONS

After a bitter struggle with the White House over whether Iraq should have to repay U.S. reconstruction aid, Congress in November 2003 agreed to spend almost $87 billion in fiscal 2004 for military and reconstruction efforts in Iraq and Afghanistan. Although both chambers were prepared to give Bush the amount he requested, the Senate with help from both parties adopted an amendment to make $10 billion of the Iraq reconstruction money a loan. The Senate eventually relented after the president personally lobbied against the loan approach in one-on-one and group meetings at the White House.

The final version gave Bush $65.1 million for the military and $21.8 billion for reconstruction and foreign aid. The $18.6 billion for Iraq reconstruction was a $1.7 billion cut in Bush's request. The bill created a job of inspector general to monitor the handling of the reconstruction money for Iraq but Bush limited the inspector general's power, blocking audits or investigations that would require access to intelligence matters.

The House passed the supplemental (HR 3289—H Rept 108-312) 303–125 on Oct. 17. The Senate passed its version of the measure (S 1689) 87–12 the same day. The House adopted the conference report (H Rept 108-337) 298–121 Oct. 31 and the Senate cleared the bill by voice vote on Nov. 3. The president signed the bill (PL 108-106) Nov. 6.

FISCAL 2003 DISASTER SUPPLEMENTAL APPROPRIATIONS

Congress cleared a fiscal 2003 supplemental spending bill in July 2003 that provided $984 million in emergency funds for the Federal Emergency Management Agency (FEMA). The money was needed to replenish dwindling disaster aid accounts. The disaster aid bill (HR 2859) supplied about half the $1.9 billion Bush requested; the remainder was provided later in the year as part of the fiscal 2004 legislative branch spending bill (PL 108-83). *(Details, p. 73)*

Bush sent his request for supplemental funds to Congress on July 7, asking for $1.6 billion for FEMA, $289 million to combat wildfires in the West, and $50 million for NASA's investigation into the Feb. 1 *Columbia* space shuttle disaster. *(Space shuttle, p. 695)*

Lawmakers were under particular pressure to provide the money for FEMA. They had deliberately cut almost $1 bil-

lion from the FEMA request in the fiscal 2003 omnibus appropriations package (PL 108-7) to free up money for spending elsewhere. But with the disaster aid fund running low and the hurricane season at hand, legislators were eager to ensure that the agency did not run out of money while Congress was on its August recess.

In an effort to speed action on the supplemental, the Senate attached it to its version of the fiscal 2004 legislative branch spending bill after adding $100 million for Ameri-Corps that funded expenses for youths working in domestic public service. Congress in the fiscal 2003 omnibus had also cut funding for that organization. The Senate then passed the legislative branch bill (S 1382–S Rept 108-88) by a vote of 85–7 on July 11.

The House Appropriations Committee approved $2 billion in supplemental spending as a stand-alone bill (HR 2859) by voice vote July 21. The committee added funding for several items not in the draft bill but it did not include funding for AmeriCorps. Although House Democrats had gotten the signatures of 244 House members supporting the additional $100 million for the program, House GOP leaders and appropriators were opposed to the Senate provision. They said the agency should not be rewarded for its vast management problems.

After House-Senate conference talks bogged down over the AmeriCorps issue, House appropriators, in consultation with Senate leaders, drafted a stripped down supplemental containing only a portion of the funding Bush requested for FEMA—a win for GOP leaders and conservatives looking to keep spending down. The House passed the bill by a vote of 352–60 and adjourned for its summer recess. That left the Senate little choice but to clear the bill without changes. It did so July 31 passing HR 2859 by voice vote. President Bush signed the bill into law Aug. 8 (PL 108-69).

Debt Limit Increase: 2003

Just days before a potential default on U.S. government obligations Congress sent President George W. Bush a bill to increase the statutory limit on the federal debt by nearly a trillion dollars, to $7.4 trillion. The $984 billion increase was the largest in history and more than double the $450 billion jump in the debt limit enacted in 2002. Lawmakers expected the new ceiling to keep the government solvent until sometime in the summer of 2004. Bush signed the measure into law May 27 (H J Res 51—PL 108-24). *(2004 action, p. 84)*

The previous limit of $6.4 trillion had been reached in February but the Treasury Department delayed breaching it through a series of accounting maneuvers including tapping into securities held in a retirement fund for civil servants. On May 15, however, Treasury announced that it was putting off its weekly offering of three-month and six-month Treasury bills "until further notice."

Four days later Treasury Secretary John W. Snow wrote lawmakers saying the department had run out of options and warned them to pass the debt limit extension by May 28 or risk a first-ever default that could imperil payment of Social Security checks and other obligations. "The Treasury has now taken all prudent and legal steps to avoid reaching the statutory debt limit," Snow wrote.

The debt ceiling applies to the sum of the public debt—including Treasury securities, savings bonds, and other government notes—and the government's obligations to federal trust funds, primarily Social Security and Medicare. Deputy Treasury secretary Kenneth Dam had written to congressional leaders in December 2002 informing them the debt could hit the existing $6.4 trillion ceiling by late February.

Although Congress had never failed to raise the limit when necessary, the debate typically gave the opposition party an opportunity to attack the fiscal policies of the majority. In this case Republicans were particularly uncomfortable increasing the debt at the same time they were trying to get a $350 billion tax cut measure through Congress. Democrats seized on the issue. "The president told us two years ago that the debt would be virtually eliminated by 2008 if we adopted his fiscal plan," said Kent Conrad of North Dakota, the ranking Democrat on the Senate Budget Committee. "Instead . . . the debt is soaring." *(Tax cuts, p. 89, 105)*

HOUSE ACTION

Under a special procedure known as the Gephardt rule after its author Richard A. Gephardt, D-Mo., the House was automatically deemed to have passed a debt limit increase when both chambers adopted the conference report on the fiscal 2004 budget resolution (H Con Res 95) on April 11. The bill (H J Res 51) generated under the rule contained a $984 billion increase, the amount required to keep the government afloat under the policies adopted in the budget resolution. *(Fiscal 2004 budget resolution, p. 67)*

Devised by the Democratic majority in 1979, the Gephardt rule was frequently derided by Republicans as a ruse to avoid direct responsibility for the nation's debt. Although the rule remained in place in the GOP-controlled 104th, 105th, and 106th Congresses, it was not used when the limit was raised in 1996 and 1997. The House GOP leadership repealed the provision in the 107th Congress but revived it at the start of the 108th after nearly failing to pass the 2002 debt limit bill. The House cleared that measure (PL 107-199) by a one-vote margin as the Treasury was approaching unprecedented default on U.S. obligations. An attempt by fiscally conservative Republicans to block the reinstatement of the Gephardt rule failed 55–113 during a GOP conference Jan. 6.

SENATE ACTION

The Senate cleared the debt limit bill May 23 by a vote of 53–44. Majority Leader Bill Frist, R-Tenn., orchestrated a one-day debate on the eve of the Memorial Day vacation after the House had already closed down for the recess. Senators, themselves eager to head home to their states, knew that making any changes in the resolution would send the measure back to the House for a vote. In practical terms that would mean missing the May 28 deadline for avoiding a government default because the House was already in recess. As a result, Democrats demanded roll-call votes on only five of twelve possible amendments and agreed to keep debate short.

All five amendments were turned back on near party-line votes. For the most part the amendments were designed for maximum political effect. The one that came closest to passing was an amendment to extend the temporary federal unemployment insurance program until Dec. 31 and provide twenty-six weeks of benefits for those whose benefits had lapsed. It was tabled (killed) on a 50–49 vote.

Fiscal 2005 Budget Resolution

For the second time in three years the House and Senate were unable to reach a compromise on a budget resolution to guide the year's taxing and spending decisions. The stumbling block was Senate-passed language restoring so-called pay-as-you-go, or PAYGO, rules requiring Congress to offset tax cuts and entitlement spending with spending cuts or increased revenue.

The possibility that Congress would be unable to adopt a budget resolution for fiscal 2005 was acknowledged from the start. Top Republicans warned that they might not be able to bridge disagreements between the party's moderates and conservatives over tax policy. In an election year, with the government anticipating record federal budget deficits, the stage was set for a particularly bumpy budget ride.

Senate GOP leaders signaled early on that President George W. Bush's most ambitious tax cut plans had no chance until he won a second term. Instead leaders sought to focus their efforts on extending a trio of popular tax breaks set to expire at the end of 2004: a $1,000 per child tax credit, an expanded 10 percent tax bracket, and tax relief for married couples. The leadership's plans were relatively modest and the political stakes clearly lower than in previous years. Yet several GOP moderates and deficit hawks signaled that the deepening deficit would make it difficult for them to support even that comparatively modest tax reduction.

The die was cast when four moderate GOP senators voted with all but one Democrat in support of an amendment to the resolution to require any new tax cuts or new entitlement spending program be offset by accompanying tax increases or spending cuts or face being struck down on a point of order that could be overcome only with the support of sixty or more senators.

House conservatives made it clear that they were adamantly opposed to placing any such restrictions on tax cuts in a compromise budget resolution. After weeks of tortured negotiations between House and Senate conferees GOP leaders in both chambers settled on a one-year budget deal that would exempt extensions for the three popular tax cuts from the pay-as-you-go rules. When the four Senate GOP moderates spurned that language as well, Senate GOP leaders decided not to bring the conference report to the floor where it faced certain defeat.

Ultimately the lack of a budget resolution had little practical effect on the GOP's election-year legislative activities. Both chambers managed to set an $821.9 billion appropriations cap by other means: the House by passing legislation deeming the conference report on the budget resolution to have been adopted, and the Senate by adding the spending cap to the defense appropriations bill, which was enacted in August (PL 108-287). The three tax cuts were extended in September without the benefit of a fast-track budget reconciliation bill. *(Tax cut extensions, p. 112)*

BUSH BUDGET REQUEST

In his annual budget request, sent to Congress on Feb. 2, Bush once again called for a cut in taxes, including making permanent the reductions enacted in 2001 and 2003. The budget called for the tightest lid on nondefense spending since fiscal 1996 when the newly installed Republican Congress managed to reduce spending by $22 billion below the last year of Democratic control. The budget projected a deficit of $521 billion in fiscal 2004, dropping to $364 billion in fiscal 2005. The actual fiscal 2004 deficit was $412 billion.

The request for appropriated spending in fiscal 2005— the approximately one-third of the budget that Congress allocates each year—included a 10 percent increase for homeland security and a 7 percent increase for defense but only a 0.5 percent increase for all other appropriated programs. It did not contain any funding for the occupation and rebuilding of postwar Iraq and Afghanistan; the White House said it would not request a supplemental to fund those operations until after the November elections.

Overall the president's budget called for total government outlays of $2.4 trillion in fiscal 2005, an increase of $81 billion, or 3.5 percent over fiscal 2004. Two-thirds of the increase was destined for mandatory spending programs such as Social Security, up $18 billion, and Medicare, up $24 billion.

The president proposed reinstating the statutory caps on appropriations that were in place (although often violated) from fiscal 1991 through fiscal 2002. For fiscal 2005 the cap on new budget authority would be $818 billion, a 3.9 percent increase over 2004. Subsequent caps would limit increases to about 3 percent. CBO put that number at $823 billion, the number that Congress used in its budget calculations.

Bush proposed $1.2 trillion in tax cuts over ten years, ending in 2014. The main proposal would remove the expiration dates from nearly all of the 2001 and 2003 tax cuts, at a cost of $936 billion. The tax cuts enacted in 2001 and 2003 were scheduled to begin expiring at the end of 2004 and to be gone at the end of 2010.

Those spending goals would be even more difficult to achieve than it appeared on the surface because Bush's budget was premised on adoption of several proposed user fees that Congress had previously rejected, including higher medical care fees for relatively affluent veterans and drug co-payments for veterans. Bush also proposed to terminate sixty-five programs and to trim another sixty-three, all at a savings of $12.8 billion. Many items on those lists, including earmarks inserted by lawmakers in previous years, had powerful backers on Capitol Hill.

Members of Congress in both parties criticized the proposal as soon as it was released. "It's not realistic, and unless Congress changes its habits of pork-barrel spending, it doesn't have a snowball's chance in Gila Bend, Arizona, of becoming reality," said Sen. John McCain, R-Ariz.

SENATE COMMITTEE ACTION

Acting before the House, the Senate Budget Committee approved a fiscal 2005 budget resolution (S Con Res 95) on March 4 on a party-line vote of 12–10. The plan would reduce the budget deficit faster and more deeply than Bush was proposing, mainly by curbing spending and generally ignoring his calls for tax cuts beyond those set to expire.

The Senate resolution called for $814 billion in discretionary appropriations in fiscal 2005. That was the same amount included in the fiscal 2004 resolution for fiscal 2005, and the committee was forced to adhere to it or risk being struck down on a point of order that would require sixty votes to waive.

The resolution allowed three reconciliation bills. One, for $81 billion, would facilitate the extension of three popular expiring tax cuts: to maintain the child tax credit at $1,000, to extend the 10 percent income tax bracket at current income levels, and to extend "marriage penalty" relief. It also assumed the reconciliation bill would accelerate repeal of the estate tax from 2010 to 2009. In proposing this reconciliation bill, Senate GOP leaders were conceding that they could not meet the White House goal of making the tax cuts of 2001 and 2003 permanent.

A second reconciliation bill would raise the $7.4 trillion ceiling on the national debt by $664 billion, and the third would trim $3.4 billion from mandatory programs over 2005–2009. The mandatory cuts, necessary to offset the extension of the child tax credit and marriage penalty relief, would include $11 billion in Medicaid payments and $3 billion in cuts in the earned-income tax credit for the working poor.

SENATE FLOOR ACTION

The Senate by a of 51–45 vote in the early morning of March 12 adopted S Con Res 95 after four days of debate and votes on dozens of amendments. Two days earlier the Senate dealt a blow to the Bush tax cut agenda by a **key vote of 51–48 (R 4–47; D 46–1; I 1–0)** to reinstate procedural hurdles to tax reductions and spending increases that helped to balance the budget in the late 1990s. But the Senate refused to swallow the tough spending medicine budget writers sought to help staunch the flow of red ink. *(2004 key votes, p. 854)*

The Senate overwhelmingly voted to restore $7 billion in proposed cuts to the president's defense budget request. And eight Republicans joined all but one Democrat in voting 53–43 to eliminate $14 billion in mandatory cuts for Medicaid and the earned-income tax credit. Those cuts were the kind of bitter pill Republicans of all stripes had claimed were necessary to get the deficit under control.

Democrat Russ D. Feingold of Wisconsin offered the amendment to reinstate the so-called pay-as-you-go rule; it would require any tax cut or new spending program proposed in the five-year window of the budget resolution to be offset or face a sixty-vote point of order in the Senate. GOP leaders opposed the amendment, but when the votes were counted four Republicans—Olympia J. Snow and Susan Collins of Maine, Lincoln Chafee of Rhode Island, and McCain of Arizona—had sided with the Democrats to approve the amendment. Feingold quickly said he would vote to override the reinstated rule to extend the three expiring tax cuts covered by the reconciliation instructions in the budget resolution.

HOUSE COMMITTEE ACTION

House Republicans remained unified, at least on the surface, as they pushed their version of the budget resolution (H Con Res 393—H Rept 108-441) through the House Budget Committee on a 24–19 party-line vote March 17. The measure set an $819 billion cap for the thirteen regular fiscal 2005 appropriations bills, provided for Bush's full defense request, and froze domestic spending unrelated to homeland security at the fiscal 2004 level. It provided for a five-year $138 billion tax cut under a reconciliation bill that would protect the tax cut from filibuster in the Senate. It also required five House committees to propose a combined $13.2 billion in savings over five years. In addition to extending the three popular tax breaks included in the Senate bill, the House version extended the tax cuts on capital gains and dividends enacted in 2003 as well as a tax break for small businesses. The House budget blueprint projected that the budget deficit would be cut in half by fiscal 2008, a year faster than the president's projection but a year later than the estimate in the plan adopted by the Senate.

Committee Republicans handily defeated more than two dozen amendments from Democrats hoping to reshape the budget's priorities. The bigger challenge for House GOP leaders, however, was a brief rebellion by moderates in the party who insisted that budget enforcement measures advance at the same time as the budget resolution. They delayed action on the budget resolution for a week until the committee approved by voice vote a separate bill (HR 3973) that would impose caps on annual appropriations and a pay-as-you-go requirement for new entitlement spending. The pay-as-you-go rule would not apply to tax cuts as they did during the 1990s.

HOUSE FLOOR ACTION

The House adopted its version of S Con Res 95 by a 215–212 vote on March 25. Ten Republicans voted against the plan and no Democrat supported it. Before passing the resolution the House rejected, by decisive margins, three alternative budget plans offered by Democrats and one put forward by GOP conservatives.

House GOP leaders had to work hard to keep rebellions by a few lawmakers from spreading to the party's rank and file. One of these arose on the pay-as-you-go legislation approved by the Budget Committee in March; leaders ultimately calmed the waters by promising to schedule a floor vote on the issue. A version of that measure (HR 4663) was soundly defeated when it came to the House floor in June. (House budget enforcement legislation, box, p. 60)

CONFERENCE ACTION

The main difference between the House and Senate versions of the budget resolution was the pay-as-you-go rule adopted by the Senate requiring that additional tax cuts as well as any increase in mandatory spending be offset with revenue increases or spending reduction. House Republican leaders, backed by the White House, made it clear that they were opposed to anything that would make tax cuts more difficult. "I'd rather not have a budget resolution than have PAYGO for taxes," House Majority Whip Roy Blunt of Missouri declared in late March.

The Republican rank and file were not in total agreement, however. House GOP leaders had to coax several members of their own party to switch their votes in order to avoid an embarrassing defeat on March 30 on a Democratic motion to instruct House conferees on the budget resolution to accept the Senate pay-as-you-go language. Although the motion was nonbinding, Republican leaders held the vote open for an extra twenty-three minutes until they managed a 209–209 tally, just enough to defeat the motion.

The House-Senate conference bogged down for weeks on the pay-as-you-go issue with the four Republicans remaining adamant that they would not support the resolution if it did not extend the budget enforcement rule to tax cuts. A Senate proposal to extend the rule for only three years was rejected by House leaders who said it could severely hamper Bush's tax cutting plans, assuming his reelection in the November presidential contest. The GOP Senate moderates rejected an offer by House Republicans that would have exempted from the pay-as-you-go rule tax cuts that advanced as part of reconciliation rules.

On May 19 exasperated House leaders opted for a strategy that dared the Senate moderates to block the budget resolution—and be responsible for handing the Democrats a victory. The leaders filed a conference report that significantly weakened the Senate language, reviving the pay-as-you-go rule for a single year, through April 15, 2005, and exempting the tax cuts contemplated in the fiscal 2005 budget reconciliation bill. The House adopted the conference report later in the day by a 216–213 vote, but the Senate moderates called the bluff, saying they could not support the conference report. Faced with the prospect of an embarrassing defeat,

Senate Majority Leader Bill Frist, R-Tenn., delayed a vote on the conference report until June at the earliest. Although occasional attempts were made to revive the budget resolution, it never came to a vote in the Senate.

HOUSE 'PLAN B'

As a fallback position, the GOP included language in the House rule for considering the conference report (H Res 649) that, when approved, "deemed" the budget resolution in force for the House as if it had been adopted by both chambers. The most significant effect of that was to set a discretionary spending cap for the Appropriations Committee to use in drafting its bills. The rule was adopted May 19 on a straight party-line vote of 220–204.

The conference report allowed for $821 billion in discretionary budget authority for the thirteen fiscal 2005 appropriations bills, some $2 billion less than President Bush had requested. The resolution included a 7 percent increase for defense, which could receive $421 billion, not counting the costs of the war and occupation of Iraq. Appropriations not associated with defense or homeland security would be all but frozen at fiscal 2004 levels. The final version of the budget resolution permitted GOP leaders to advance a reconciliation package containing $27.5 billion to cover a one-year extension of the expiring $1,000 child tax credit, the 10 percent income tax bracket, and tax relief for married couples.

Fiscal 2005 Appropriations

Lawmakers displayed fiscal restraint not shown since Congress cut domestic appropriations in fiscal 1995 and 1996 as they limited the increase in nonemergency discretionary appropriations unrelated to defense or homeland security to 1 percent. Yet Congress had to delay until after the national elections in November to accomplish the feat and for the third year in a row had to combine most of the thirteen regular appropriations bills into a vast catchall package.

After finishing just four fiscal 2005 spending bills before the election, lawmakers bundled the remaining nine bills into an omnibus package (HR 4818—PL 108-447) during their lame-duck session after the elections. Congress cleared the bill on Nov. 20, but it did not go to the president for two weeks because of a provision that would have lowered the privacy shield around individuals' income tax returns. The Senate adopted a resolution dropping the provision on Nov. 20, and the House followed on Dec. 6.

President George W. Bush signed HR 4818 into law on Dec. 8, just hours before a stopgap funding measure was set to expire. Agencies governed by the nine bills had been operating under three consecutive continuing resolutions since fiscal 2005 began on Oct. 1. The measures kept funding at fiscal 2004 levels until the appropriations process was completed.

Congress also approved three supplementals in 2004. The first appropriated $25 billion in supplemental spending for operations in Iraq and Afghanistan; it was included in the fiscal 2005 defense spending bill. In the wake of four devastating hurricanes, Congress also approved two disaster aid supplementals. One was a $2 billion stand-alone bill cleared early in September after Hurricane Charley swept through Florida in late August. The other was for $14.5 billion in hurricane relief and drought assistance; it was enacted as part of the fiscal 2005 military construction spending bill, which cleared in mid-October.

Following are summaries of the four regular spending bills that were passed individually, the omnibus measure, and the two disaster relief supplementals.

FISCAL 2005 DEFENSE APPROPRIATIONS

With lawmakers eager to make essential war funding available to the Pentagon before they adjourned for a six-week recess and the national party nominating conventions, Congress easily cleared the defense appropriations bill (HR 4613—PL 108-287) on July 22, making it the first of the fiscal 2005 spending measures to reach President Bush's desk.

The $417.5 billion bill included a record $391.4 billion for the core Pentagon budget—a 7 percent increase over fiscal 2004 and enough to fund most of Bush's robust defense agenda. The measure also provided $25 billion in emergency funding for war operations in Iraq and Afghanistan. Although Congress gave Bush the amount of emergency funding he requested, it did not give him the flexibility he wanted. The bill restricted how all but $2 billion of the money could be spent. With the $25 billion, Congress had appropriated a total of $203 billion since Sept. 11 for the wars in Iraq and Afghanistan and enhanced security at military facilities.

Although the administration advertised the $25 billion as a down payment on war operations in the initial months of fiscal 2005, Congress made the money available upon enactment. The provision proved prescient: just hours after the conference report was filed July 21, the Government Accountability Office estimated that the Pentagon would fall $12.3 billion short in fiscal 2004. Bush was expected to request more emergency funding for the war in fiscal 2005, but not until after the presidential election in November. In mid-2004, before a continuing insurgency intensified in Iraq, House Democrats estimated that between $40 billion and $55 billion in additional funding would be necessary. The White House said the situation in the Middle East was too unstable to project the cost. *(Iraq war, pp. 231, 238)*

Overall the administration fared well in the defense bill. Congress continued to fund most of the Pentagon's major weapon programs, including next-generation fighter aircraft and ships. The bill also provided $10 billion for missile defense, 2 percent less than Bush had requested but 11 percent above fiscal 2004 spending. That included full funding of Bush's effort to deploy a limited missile defense system in 2004, putting into place the initial elements of an antimissile shield first proposed by President Ronald Reagan in 1983.

The House passed HR 4613 (H Rept 108-553) on June 22 by a vote of 403–17. The Senate passed it 98–0 on June 24 after amending it to include its companion bill (S 2559—

S Rept 108-284). The House passed the conference report (H Rept 108-622) by a vote of 410–12 on July 22; the Senate cleared the bill later the same day 96–0. President George W. Bush signed it into law on Aug. 5. (*Defense funding details, p. 354*)

DISTRICT OF COLUMBIA

For the first time in almost a decade, the spending bill for the District of Columbia (HR 4850—PL 108-335) glided through Congress without the addition of controversial provisions that slowed or stalled the bill in past years. Fleeting attempts to add language that would have repealed the District's gun control law or banned gay marriage in the city were successfully warded off by the House and Senate Appropriations subcommittee chair responsible for the D.C. spending bill. The final version of the measure provided a $560 million federal payment to the District to compensate it for hosting the federal government. The bill also approved the city's $8.3 billion municipal budget. Both totals reflected both chambers' original versions of the bill.

The House passed HR 4850 (H Rept 108-610) July 20 by a vote of 371–54. The Senate passed HR 4850 by voice vote Sept. 22 after amending it to insert its version of the measure (S 2826—S Rept 108-354). The House adopted the conference report (H Rept 108-734) 377–36 on Oct. 6, and the Senate cleared the bill by voice vote later that day. President George W. Bush signed it into law on Oct. 18.

HOMELAND SECURITY

Although passage of the fiscal 2005 spending bill for the Department of Homeland Security frequently looked wobbly, Congress cleared a $33.1 billion bill (HR 4567—PL 108-334) Oct. 11. The total was $896 million more than Bush had requested and $2.8 billion more than was available in fiscal 2004.

But the money had a myriad of strings attached. In the absence of an authorization bill for the new department and firm guidelines on congressional oversight, appropriators stepped in with their own set of marching orders. Hundreds of millions of dollars for some of the department's highest-profile initiatives, such as the entry-exit program known as U.S. VISIT and the airline passenger screening program called Secure Flight, could not be spent until appropriators were satisfied that Homeland Security officials had met specific conditions.

The conference report required the department to submit more than forty studies, plans, and reports between the time the bill was enacted and 2006 on topics ranging from its hiring practices to its data-mining strategy. It also warned the department that incidents such as the hiring and spending freezes imposed at Immigration and Customs Enforcement in fiscal 2004 were not acceptable. Appropriators also created new programs, such as rail security initiatives and an office to manage geospatial mapping.

The final bill faced a veto threat over a provision to bar the department from privatizing approximately 1,100 immigration service jobs, but that threat was rendered moot when the department announced that it had decided to cancel the outsourcing initiative. Democrats, who supported the bill but were critical both of the department's performance and of the Republicans' unwillingness to spend more on homeland security, unsuccessfully tried to add $2 billion in conference to implement recommendations of the independent Sept. 11 commission, such as increases in funding for aviation transportation security, border patrols, and immigration inspection staff. (*Commission report, p. 275*)

The House passed HR 4567 (H Rept 108-541) 400–5 on June 18. The Senate passed its version (S 2537—S Rept 108-280) 93–0 on Sept. 14. The House adopted the conference report (H Rept 108-774) 368–0 on Oct. 9. The Senate cleared the bill by voice vote on Oct. 11, and President Bush signed it on Oct. 18.

MILITARY CONSTRUCTION

Congress easily approved $10 billion in fiscal 2005 funding for military construction. The amount was about $450 million more than President Bush requested and $162 million above the fiscal 2004 level including supplemental spending for that year. The bill (HR 4837—PL 108-324) also included $14.5 billion in fiscal 2005 emergency funding for disaster relief to help hurricane victims and farmers and ranchers affected by drought. (*Disaster aid, pp. 73, 76, 84*)

The final military construction bill included $5.5 billion for overall construction work and $4.1 billion for family housing projects. Members supplemented the president's request with nearly $500 million of their own projects. Reconciling the different earmarks in the House and Senate bills was a main issue in conference. A furor in the House over a budget-busting increase in spending on a program privatizing construction of some military family housing was ultimately quelled when the issue was dealt with in the defense authorization bill (HR 4200). (*Defense authorization, p. 346*)

The House passed HR 4837 (H Rept 108-607) 420–1 on July 22. The Senate passed its version of the bill (S Rept 108-309) 91–0 on Sept. 20. The House adopted the conference report (H Rept 108-773) Oct. 9 without dissent, and the Senate cleared the bill by voice vote Oct. 11. President Bush signed the bill on Oct. 13.

FISCAL 2005 OMNIBUS APPROPRIATIONS

The omnibus spending measure (HR 4818—PL 108-477), cleared on Nov. 20, contained $388.4 billion in discretionary spending, an increase of just 1 percent over comparable fiscal 2004 levels. Counting the four previously enacted bills (for defense, the District of Columbia, homeland security, and military construction), discretionary spending was held to $821.9 billion, the cap that the White House and GOP leaders had agreed to at the start of the year.

Unlike previous years, appropriators were unable to use gimmicks to evade limits and spend more, although the measure contained $393 million in emergency spending—and so not subject to the spending cap—that was provided with the administration's support. Actual discretionary spending for fiscal 2005 was likely to be much higher after tens of billions of dollars in emergency funds for disasters and operations in Iraq and Afghanistan were added in 2005.

From the start of the year, it was an open secret that election-year considerations would mean that most of the annual spending bills would be rolled into one massive bill, a process that allowed congressional leaders—and the president—to take the legislative shortcuts necessary to ensure that spending and policies could be shaped on their terms.

The House managed to pass all but one of the thirteen regular appropriations bills. The exception was the VA-HUD bill (HR 5041), which Majority Leader Tom DeLay, R-Texas, refused to bring up because of cuts it would have made at NASA, a major employer of his constituents. In the Senate Majority Leader Bill Frist declined to call up seven of the bills for floor debate and amendment.

The underlying vehicle for the omnibus was the foreign operations spending bill (HR 4818), which both chambers had passed in differing versions before the elections. Negotiations on the omnibus began after Bush's reelection that produced a gain of additional GOP seats in Congress, guaranteeing that his budget limits would be enforced. Senate appropriators had squeezed $8 billion into their bills above the House-passed levels, mostly using accounting maneuvers. About $6 billion worth of Senate increases were dropped, leaving difficult choices for negotiators. They ended up imposing a 0.8 percent across-the-board cut on all spending that was unrelated to defense or homeland security. The savings from that cut, combined with $1.9 billion in remaining accounting gimmicks, yielded about $5 billion to pump up popular programs for veterans' health care, education, and NASA.

Democrats derided the process that produced a 3,016-page bill that few members had an opportunity to see before voting on its contents. At the same time, however, the package contained thousands of hometown projects desired by lawmakers, ensuring that many Democrats would vote for the bill despite their criticism of the process.

That proved to be the case. The House passed the conference report on HR 4818 (H Rept 108-792) 344–51 on Nov. 20. The Senate passed it the same day 65–30.

The omnibus was not sent to the White House right away, however, because of an outcry over a clumsily drafted provision added by the House that permitted the leaders of the appropriations committees and their aides to look at individual tax returns as part of their oversight of the Internal Revenue Service. As soon as the Senate voted to clear HR 4818, it took up and passed by voice vote a resolution (H Con Res 528) striking the provision. The House adopted the resolution Dec. 6 on a vote of 381–0. That cleared the way for the omnibus to go to the president minus the offending provision. President Bush signed the bill into law Dec. 8, 2004.

Following are highlights of each of the nine spending bills wrapped into HR 4818.

Agriculture

The omnibus provided $86.2 billion for the Agriculture Department, the Food and Drug Administration (FDA), and related agencies, of which $17 billion was discretionary spending. That was virtually the same as in fiscal 2004 and 2 percent more than requested. Congress responded to the potential threats to food safety from disease and terrorism by increasing funding for food safety programs but cut back in other areas including conservation. Mandatory funding for the food stamp program increased 14 percent over fiscal 2004 to $35.2 billion. The bill also increased the allocation for the Women, Infants, and Children (WIC) program by 14 percent to $5.3 billion.

Among the contentious provisions stripped from the bill in conference were proposals to ease the importation of prescription drugs from Canada and boost the sale of medical supplies and farm goods to Cuba. Conferees also dropped a provision that would have weakened mandatory country-of-origin labeling of food products, scheduled to take effect in October 2006. *(Cuba, p. 299; labeling, p. 465)*

The bill included $27.1 billion for agriculture programs, a drop of about $5.8 billion or 18 percent from the fiscal 2004 level. Crop price supports that accounted for more than half the total were expected to decline by about 28 percent from fiscal 2004 because the market prices for many commodities had increased and fewer farmers needed to be reimbursed.

Commerce-Justice-State

HR 4818 provided $43.7 billion for the departments of Commerce, Justice, and State, the federal judiciary, and related agencies. The Justice Department was slated to receive $20.9 billion, 5 percent more than in fiscal 2004 and 4 percent more than Bush had requested. Most of the increase went to the FBI to fund counterterrorism and intelligence improvements. Perhaps the biggest change was in funding for the Small Business Administration. Its $580 million appropriation was 18.5 percent less than the 2005 level because of changes aimed at making the agency's popular small business and disaster-assistance loans self-sustaining.

Conferees abandoned language endorsed by the House that would have temporarily blocked new Bush administration regulations to limit the ability of Cuban Americans to send supplies to family members in Cuba. But conferees retained language to block disclosure of information collected by the Bureau of Alcohol, Tobacco, Firearms, and Explosives tracing the ownership history of firearms used in crimes. The language was a victory for gun manufacturers and the National Rifle Association, which sought to prevent such data from being used in future litigation.

Congress cut deeply into but did not eliminate funding, as Bush had requested, for the Community Oriented Policing Services (COPS) program, a signature initiative of the administration of President Bill Clinton that provided funds for hiring local law enforcement officers. Congress allocated

$10 million for the program, less than one-tenth of the $119 million provided in fiscal 2004.

Energy and Water

The fiscal 2005 energy and water development spending bill provided $29 billion to fund energy research, nuclear weapons programs, and civilian water projects. That total was about 2 percent more than Bush requested and about 5 percent more than the fiscal 2004 level. About 80 percent of the funding, or $23 billion, was for the Energy Department, with nearly 40 percent of that going to the National Nuclear Security Administration, which maintained U.S. nuclear weapons and sought to reduce the threat from weapons of mass destruction. Congress provided no funds to research a low-yield nuclear weapon designed to destroy underground bunkers or caves. The president had requested $27.6 million for the research. Opponents of the funding worried that the research might spark another nuclear arms race.

The issue that stalled the regular funding bill, however, was money for the nuclear waste repository at Nevada's Yucca Mountain. An annual battle, the issue was complicated this year by a White House proposal to use an off-budget trust fund to pay for most of the fiscal 2005 spending. When that move was thwarted, appropriators had to scramble to come up with extra money from other bills to keep the project going. Appropriators eventually agreed on $577 million for Yucca, roughly the same amount as in fiscal 2004. (*Yucca Mountain, p. 439*)

Foreign Operations

The fiscal 2005 spending bill for foreign operations, the underlying vehicle that carried the omnibus, was notable for the bipartisan cooperation it engendered. The $19.8 billion measure included $404 million in humanitarian aid for war-torn Sudan, including $75 million for African peacekeeping efforts in the Darfur region. The bill also included $2.3 billion in AIDS-related funding. Together with another $600 million from the Labor-HHS-Education spending bill, fiscal 2005 spending to fight HIV/AIDS totaled $2.9 billion. The allocation was $99 million more than Bush had requested and 21 percent more than Congress had provided in fiscal 2004. Much of the AIDS funding was slated for a five-year, $15 billion program that Bush initiated and Congress approved in 2003. Another $400 million was earmarked for the Global Fund to Fight HIV/AIDS, Tuberculosis, and Malaria.

Lawmakers cut back significantly on a Bush request for $2.5 billion for his Millennium Challenge Account, which provided aid to poor countries judged to be making progress on human rights, democratization, and free markets; the program was essentially a way to reward U.S. allies in the Middle East and the war on terror. The House and Senate initially cut the request roughly in half, but during the conference the White House weighed in, more money was unearthed, and the appropriation was raised to $1.5 billion. (*Millennium Challenge Account, p. 289*)

Interior

The omnibus provided $20 billion for the Department of the Interior and related programs. For the most part appropriators chose to use their limited funds to maintain existing programs run by the National Park Service, the Fish and Wildlife Service, and agencies serving American Indians while holding off on administration requests for new initiatives. The total in the bill was about $2 billion below fiscal 2004 spending and nearly 2 percent above Bush's request.

The final bill provided $2.5 billion for fighting wildfires— $250 million less than enacted for fiscal 2004 when wildfires devastated hundreds of thousands of acres of public lands, mostly in the West. It also included $500 million in emergency firefighting funds. The final bill also continued limited snowmobile access to Yellowstone National Park pending the outcome of a court battle over the Bush administration's decision to scrap a Clinton-era ban on all snowmobiles in the park. As expected, Senate Appropriations Committee Chair Ted Stevens, R-Alaska, prevailed in removing a House provision that would have stopped road building in Alaska's Tongass National Forest. Stevens viewed the roads as important to the state's economy.

Labor-HHS-Education

The fiscal 2005 spending bill for the departments of Labor, Health and Human Services, and Education provided $497.6 billion, including $143.3 billion in discretionary spending. The discretionary total represented an approximately 3 percent increase over fiscal 2004 funding. The final bill included $12.8 billion for Title I education programs for low-income school districts. That was a $500 million increase over fiscal 2004, but Democrats were quick to point out that the spending still fell $7.7 billion short of the amount authorized under the "No Child Left Behind" law enacted in 2001. The measure also provided $10.7 billion for special education grants to the states—a $607 million increase over 2004 but still far short of the amount authorized.

The National Institutes of Health were slated to receive a 3 percent increase to $28.6 billion. The Low-Income Home Energy Assistance Program was given $2.2 billion including $300 million in emergency funding to help poor families cope with the rising costs of natural gas and heating oil. Abstinence-only sex education programs received $100 million, $82 million less than the White House requested.

At the urging of House conservatives the final bill included language to permit health care providers to refuse to provide or fund abortions without jeopardizing their federal funding. But the final measure did not renew a provision in the fiscal 2004 omnibus spending law that would prevent an estimated 90,000 college students from losing their Pell grants. Under a veto threat conferees dropped language endorsed by floor votes in both chambers to block portions of new Labor Department rules that terminated the eligibility for overtime pay for some categories of workers. (*Abortion, pp. 479, 510; overtime, p. 574*)

Legislative Branch

In an election-year effort to demonstrate a capacity for fiscal restraint, Republicans held down spending increases in the bill that funded their own overhead expenses. The $3.7 billion fiscal 2005 spending bill for the legislative branch was just 1.4 percent higher than the fiscal 2004 bill. In addition, the bill was subject to the 0.8 percent across-the-board cut in discretionary funding.

Dissatisfaction with the way the Architect of the Capitol was managing construction of an underground visitors center in the Capitol Building helped lawmakers reach their goal. Instead of endorsing the architect's request for a 45 percent increase, Congress instead gave him a 12.5 percent cut. Congress also slashed funding for the Government Printing Office. Cuts in those two accounts allowed for modest increases for the House of Representatives and the Senate, the Capitol Police, and other agencies including the Library of Congress, the General Accountability Office, and the Congressional Budget Office.

Transportation-Treasury

The fiscal 2005 Transportation-Treasury spending bill provided $90.5 billion for the two departments, the White House, and several related agencies. The total was nearly the same as the amount enacted for fiscal 2004, but it was still $1.8 billion more than the president requested. The difference was due largely to a record $34.7 billion included by Congress for highways. The bill included $25.9 billion in discretionary funds, about 1 percent more than Bush requested but nearly 9 percent less than enacted for fiscal 2004.

Under a veto threat, conferees dropped language approved by both chambers to block or weaken an administration rule to expand the pool of federal jobs that could be contracted out to private firms. In the face of another veto threat, conferees dropped language to ease trade and travel sanctions on Cuba. Despite White House objections, the final version retained House language barring entry of Canadian and Mexican trucks on roads that did not comply with U.S. safety laws. Congress also rejected Bush's request to cut back sharply on funding for the ailing Amtrak passenger railroad. The bill included $1.2 billion for the railroad, about the same amount as in fiscal 2004 but 35 percent more than Bush requested. *(Mexican trucks, p. 371)*

Veterans, Housing, NASA, EPA

Controversies over spending and policy for NASA and housing programs slowed the fiscal 2005 bill to fund the departments of Veterans Affairs and Housing and Urban Development (HUD) as well as several independent agencies. That turned out to be a good thing for Bush and House Majority Leader Tom DeLay of Texas, who represented the space center in Houston. House appropriators had initially proposed to cut the president's request for NASA. But with Bush's reelection on November 2, the president and DeLay

were in a position to insist on more money for NASA. Conferees added a total of $822 million, or 5 percent more than in fiscal 2004, to begin pursuing Bush's goal of landing humans on the moon and Mars. Overall the final bill totaled $133.2 billion.

Conferees increased spending on the Veterans Health Administration by 5.5 percent. Spending for the Section 8 rent-voucher program was increased, but most other HUD programs suffered spending declines, including a $378 million cut in the community planning and development and housing programs. Other programs also suffered. The Environmental Protection Agency, the Corporation for National and Community Service, and the National Science Foundation all had their budgets cut.

Disaster Supplementals

Congress passed two supplementals in 2004 to provide disaster relief. *(Disaster aid, pp. 72, 73, 76, 81)*

After Hurricane Charley swept through Florida in late August, Congress quickly approved a stand-alone bill with $2 billion in emergency fiscal 2004 funds for the Federal Emergency Management Agency. Congress cleared the bill (HR 5005—PL 108-303) in a matter of hours Sept. 7, and President Bush signed it into law on Sept. 8.

The second bill, providing $14.5 billion in emergency disaster aid, was cleared as part of the fiscal 2005 military construction spending bill (HR 4837—PL108-324). Of the total, $11.6 billion was to help victims not only of Hurricane Charley but of hurricanes Frances, Ivan, and Jeanne. Florida, which was hit by all four hurricanes and was also a key battleground state in the presidential election, received the largest share of the funding. But funding also went to other battleground states, such as Pennsylvania and West Virginia, that were affected by the storms but to a much lesser extent. The remaining $2.8 billion was for ranchers and farmers whose livelihoods had suffered from drought and other natural disasters in 2003 and 2004.

Appropriators had first attached the emergency funding to the popular homeland security spending bill (HR 4567), but when it looked like that bill was going to bog down in disputes in the conference, they shifted the emergency funding to the conference agreement on the military construction bill (HR 4837), which both chambers adopted easily *(Details, p. 81)*

The emergency hurricane funding did not count against the fiscal 2005 budget cap, and the drought aid was offset by cuts to the Conservation Security Program created in the 2002 farm bill (PL 107-171). *(2002 farm bill, p. 449)*

Debt Limit Increase: 2004

Congress on Nov. 18, 2004, cleared a bill (S 2986) increasing the statutory limit on most federal government debt by $800 billion, or 11 percent, to $8.2 trillion. It was the third year in a row that Congress had to raise the debt ceiling to prevent the federal government from defaulting on its obligations. Altogether, the three actions raised the debt ceiling a total of $2.2 trillion. *(2002, 2003 action, pp. 63, 76).*

Legislators knew all year long that they would have to deal with the politically unpalatable issue of raising the debt limit. The vote was particularly embarrassing for Republicans who once campaigned on a platform of restraining federal spending and lowering the national debt. GOP House leaders had hoped to take advantage of the Gephardt rule, under which the House is deemed to have automatically passed an increase in debt ceiling once the budget resolution is adopted. But that option was not available with the budget resolution stalled in the Senate. House leaders next tried to put through an increase as part of the defense spending bill (HR 4613), which contained crucial funds for the war in Iraq and other military operations. Democrats were unable to stop them in the House, which passed the spending bill on June 22 with the debt limit increase attached. That maneuver again spared Republicans and Democrats from going on record on higher debt limit that reflected Congress's inability to control expenditures.

But when the defense bill moved to the Senate two days later, Democrats there made it clear that unless the debt limit increase was removed from the legislation, they would delay its passage as well members' July 4 recess. Senate Republicans quickly agreed to abandon the debt limit plan, allowing the $415 billion defense spending bill to pass 98–0 after a debate that lasted only a few hours.

Treasury secretary John W. Snow on Aug. 2 sent Congress a letter warning that the Treasury was likely to be able to finance government operations only through mid-November and asking the lawmakers to act on the issue before it recessed in October.

When it became apparent that a lame-suck session would be necessary after the November elections, GOP congressional leaders postponed a vote on the debt limit until after the campaign in which the Democratic contender, Sen. John Kerry of Massachusetts, had tried to make the record budget deficits under President George W. Bush a campaign theme. Democrats blamed the Bush tax cuts for the high deficits and the need to raise the debt ceiling. Republicans said the economic recession, the Sept. 11 attacks, and the wars in Afghanistan and Iraq were to blame.

With time for action fast running out, GOP leaders decided to move a stand-alone bill (S 2986) even though they had wanted to avoid such a vote. The Senate passed S 2986 increasing the debt limit by a vote of 52–44 on Nov. 17. The House cleared the bill 208–204 on Nov. 18, the day Treasury had set as the deadline for congressional action. Had the House failed to act then, Treasury would have been unable to pay interest on existing notes and bonds, redeem maturing securities, or borrow additional funds. President Bush signed the bill into law on Nov. 19.

Chronology of Action on Economic Policy: Tax Policy

Introduction

Years of frustration for the Republican congressional leadership and followers came to an end in June 2001 when President George W. Bush signed into law a measure that reduced individual income taxes by $1.4 trillion over ten years. It was the third-deepest tax cut Congress had ever enacted—and the first of four rounds of tax cuts during Bush's first term that together lowered taxes by about $2 trillion over ten years.

The tax cuts achieved a goal that Republicans had sought at least since drawing up the "Contract with America," their 1994 campaign tract that contained a list of tax cuts to aid families and senior citizens and promote economic growth. In 1995 Republican leaders pushed a measure containing many of the tax cuts through Congress but were unable to override a veto by Democratic president Bill Clinton (1993–2001).

That pattern repeated itself in 1998 when the government first began running a budget surplus, and again in 1999 when Republican legislation cutting taxes by $792 billion over ten years fell victim of Clinton's veto pen. Clinton maintained that the surplus should be used to restore Social Security and pay down the national debt, not for tax relief that primarily benefited wealthy taxpayers.

In 2000 the Republicans again pressed unsuccessfully for tax-relief legislation, but this time their effort was intended to bolster the presidential efforts of George W. Bush as their presidential candidate who was pushing a substantial cut in income tax rates on the campaign trail. After one of the failed override attempts House Majority Leader Dick Armey, R-Texas, told his GOP colleagues to take heart. "We've carried it as far as we can go this year," he said. "If we don't have it now, we'll have it within the first six months of the Bush presidency." As it turned out, they had it in five months.

2001 TAX CUT

Bush had made a $1 trillion-plus tax cut the focal point of his campaign to attract support from the more conservative elements of the Republican Party. Once he gained the nomi-

nation in 2000 the Texas governor continued to promote the tax cut as a core issue against the Democratic candidate, Vice President Al Gore, despite repeated polls showing that voters placed tax relief well behind other issues such as promoting education, saving Social Security, and providing prescription drug coverage for the elderly. In what would become a familiar criticism, Gore and the Democrats attacked Bush's plan as favoring the wealthy over the poor and the middle class. In what would become an equally familiar response, Bush doggedly promoted his plan as a needed reform to put money back into the hands of the taxpayers.

Bush shifted the primary rationale for the tax cut as the boom economy of the 1990s began to sour. In his first speech to a joint session of Congress after entering the White House in January 2001 the new president said a tax cut was needed to stimulate the economy. "To create economic growth and opportunity, we must put money back into the hands of the people who buy goods and create jobs," Bush said. Opponents disagreed. They said the tax cuts, many of which would

REFERENCES

Discussion of tax policy for the years 1945–1964 may be found in *Congress and the Nation Vol. I*, pp. 397–442; for the years 1965–1968, *Congress and the Nation Vol. II*, pp. 141–182; for the years 1969– 1972, *Congress and the Nation Vol. III*, pp. 77–96; for the years 1973–1976, *Congress and the Nation Vol. IV*, pp. 83–106; for the years 1977–1980, *Congress and the Nation Vol. V*, pp. 231–251; for the years 1981–1984, *Congress and the Nation Vol. VI*, pp. 63–82; for the years 1985–1988, *Congress and the Nation Vol. VII*, pp. 75–107; for the years 1989–1992, *Congress and the Nation Vol. VIII*, pp. 87–112; for the years 1993–1996, *Congress and the Nation Vol. IX*, pp. 83–107; for the years 1997–2001, *Congress and the Nation Vol. X*, pp. 87–119.

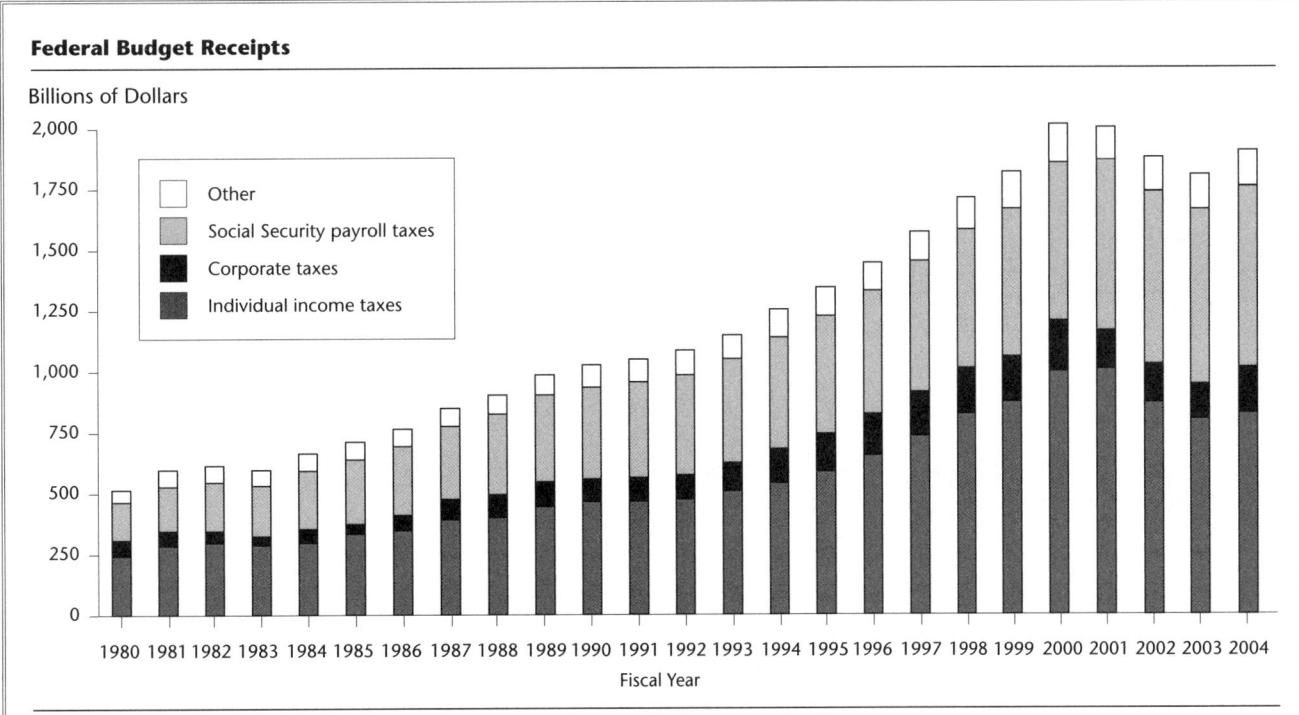

Federal Budget Receipts

Billions of Dollars

Legend:
- Other
- Social Security payroll taxes
- Corporate taxes
- Individual income taxes

Fiscal Year

SOURCE: Office of Management and Budget, *Historical Tables, Budget of the United States Government: Fiscal Year 2006* (Washington, D.C.: U.S. Government Printing Office, 2005), Table 2.1.

not take place for several years, would do almost nothing to stimulate the currently faltering economy and would instead have a long-term negative effect by forcing the government back into deficit spending, which in turn would ratchet up interest rates and weaken the economy.

The president had little trouble persuading the Republican-controlled House to adopt his plan. The momentum slowed in the Senate, where the balance of power was held by a small group of moderate Republicans and Democrats. In combinations that would differ depending on the circumstances, this band of moderates would retain their power over tax measures for Bush's entire first term.

Although most of the moderates favored the 2001 tax cut plan, moderate Democrats were determined to reduce the overall size of the proposed cuts so that Bush could not claim an unalloyed victory. The moderates in both parties settled on a ceiling of $1.4 trillion over ten years; that figure, which was about $300 billion less than Bush wanted, ultimately became the core of the bill that Bush signed into law on June 7.

The major features of the measure (PL 107-16) gradually reduced income tax rates across the board, eased the so-called marriage penalty, phased out the estate tax, and expanded the child tax credit. It also increased tax benefits for contributions to individual retirement accounts and pension plans and created or expanded various tax breaks for education. To keep the cost of the tax cut within limits permitted in the congressional budget resolution, several of the cuts

were not slated to take effect for several years, and all of them would lapse on Dec. 31, 2010, unless Congress acted to make the reductions permanent.

EXTENDING TAX RELIEF

Tax cuts gave way on the congressional agenda in 2002 to the fight against terrorism, beefing up both national security and homeland security, and corporate accounting scandals. House Republicans voted six times in 2002 to extend indefinitely all or some of the tax cuts enacted in 2001, but Republicans were never able to muster the sixty votes they needed in the Senate to waive that chamber's budget restrictions. Congress also agreed to a modest economic stimulus package that extended unemployment benefits and provided a pair of tax breaks aimed at helping businesses recover from the economic fallout surrounding the terrorist attacks of Sept. 11, 2001, and the decline in the stock market in early 2000 after revelations of corporate accounting fraud threw two major corporations into bankruptcy and tarnished the reputations of several others. The package was passed after the two parties had fought each other to a draw over a broader package of tax cuts and aid to laid-off workers.

After Republicans regained control of the Senate and added to their numbers in the House at the 2002 mid-term elections, tax cuts rose again to the top of the agenda. Congress quickly passed a measure in 2003 containing $330 billion in reductions and refundable tax credits over eleven years. The centerpiece was a new 15 percent rate on dividends and capital gains aimed at sparking economic growth by encouraging an "investor class," representing roughly half of U.S. households, to invest in stocks.

Bush and House Republicans had hoped for a tax cut nearly double that size as well as elimination of all taxes on dividends. But this time it was Republican moderates in the Senate who balked. Wary of the growing budget deficit, they said the $726 billion price tag was too high and, backed by Senate Democrats, refused to budge from the $330 billion figure. The Senate GOP leadership passed the conference report on the final bill only with a tie-breaking vote from Vice President Dick Cheney.

By 2004 election-year politics had changed the calculations on tax relief legislation. Bush called early in the year for Congress to make the 2001 and 2003 tax cuts permanent. With budget deficits projected to be at record highs, the GOP congressional leadership determined that was an unrealistic goal. Instead they focused on extending three popular tax breaks for families, all of which were set to expire. The Republican leaders reasoned that legislation that passed would help Republicans in the elections; if the legislation died, Republicans would blame the Democrats for voting against tax relief for the middle class. The White House tried to ensure this latter eventuality by demanding a more generous extension package with a vote closer to the election. But the Democrats, who had made tax relief for the middle class a focus of their campaign, decided to support the measure. Bush signed the $146 billion package into law just a month before the November election.

Corporations were the other tax beneficiary of election year politics when a bill to repeal a subsidy to U.S. exporters that had been ruled illegal by the World Trade Organization became a vehicle for tax breaks that benefited companies in nearly every state in the union. The final version replaced the subsidy with $137 billion in corporate tax cuts so strategically chosen that the bill passed with broad support from legislators in both parties. In contrast to every other major tax bill of his presidency, however, Bush shunned a celebratory signing ceremony. Already vulnerable to Democratic jibes that he was too cozy with industry, the president apparently wanted to avoid reinforcing that image.

PLUNGING TAX RECEIPTS

As he began his second term, Bush said he wanted to make the tax cuts of his first term permanent, overhaul the tax code from top to bottom, and cut the federal budget deficit in half at the same time. Whether he could accomplish those goals depended on many factors, one of which almost certainly was growth in federal tax revenues.

In fiscal 2000, the year before President Bush took office, federal tax receipts as a percentage of gross domestic product stood at 20.9 percent, and the government collected more than $2 trillion in revenue. By the end of fiscal 2004, federal receipts had fallen to 16.3 percent of GDP, their lowest levels since 1951. Revenue for the year totaled $1.9 trillion, slightly higher than it had been in fiscal 2003. Some of the loss of revenue was attributable to the tax cuts Congress enacted, but more of it was caused by the recession and slow recovery, which stunted growth and the incomes of the millionaires in the technology business that helped keep the U.S. Treasury flush with cash in the late 1990s.

Some analysts argued that economic growth, fueled by tax cuts, would serve as an engine to erase much of the gap between federal tax receipts and federal outlays. Indeed, that was one of the primary arguments Bush and his supporters made for enacting the tax cuts in the first place. Stephen Moore, president of the Free Enterprise Fund, a conservative lobbying group, had long argued that if the economy were to grow at a rate of 3.5 percent to 4 percent for five to ten years, the federal budget deficit would "largely go away," assuming spending remained level.

Even if the economy were to grow at such as sustained pace, something not even the Bush administration was predicting, federal spending was certain to accelerate, starting as early as 2008 when the baby-boom generation began retiring and collecting Social Security and Medicare benefits. Medicare, the health program for seniors, and Medicaid, a health program for low-income and indigent individuals, were projected to increase from 4.2 percent of GDP to 11.5 percent in 2030; outlays for Social Security were expected to rise to about 6 percent of GDP over the next three decades under current law, while Social Security taxes would remain at about 5 percent of GDP.

"We're raising about 16 percent of GDP in revenues and spending about 20 percent, and that's going up over time," said Alan Auerbach, a tax policy and public finance economist at the University of California at Berkeley, in early 2005. "There is no way, under the current configuration of taxes, that revenues will be sufficient to pay for a higher and rising level of spending."

2001–2002

A little less than five months after taking office, President George W. Bush delivered on the central feature of his campaign platform by signing into law a ten-year $1.4 trillion personal income tax relief bill—the biggest tax decrease since 1981. The new law gradually lowered income tax rates across the board, eased the so-called marriage penalty, phased out the estate tax, and expanded the child tax credit. At a formal signing ceremony in the White House East Room Bush hailed the law "as the first major achievement of a new era."

Perhaps just as pleased as Bush at the signing ceremony were most congressional Republicans, who had been repeatedly frustrated in their attempts to enact major tax relief legislation since the federal government began running a budget surplus in 1998. President Bill Clinton (1993–2001) consistently vetoed their bills, arguing that the surplus should be used to replenish Social Security and pay down the national debt, not for tax relief that primarily benefited the wealthy.

Enactment of the tax cut was an undeniable political victory for the new president who had entered the White House under the cloud of a disputed election and questions about his ability to lead. Even after making concessions to win the crucial support of a handful of moderate Democrats in the Senate, which was split fifty-fifty, Bush got most of what he sought.

One thing he did not get was permanent tax reduction. To keep the cost of the tax cut under the limit permitted in the congressional budget resolution, and thus avoid a point of order in the Senate that might have killed the legislation altogether, lawmakers added a "sunset" provision that specified that all the tax changes in the law would automatically expire on Dec. 31, 2010, unless Congress either made them permanent or extended them.

Bush and congressional Republicans immediately called for legislation to make the cuts permanent. But by the summer of 2001 the economic slowdown that had been obvious even as Congress was debating the tax bill began cutting into tax revenue. By late August the White House had lowered its surplus projections by nearly half. The terrorist attacks on the World Trade Center and the Pentagon in September 2001 tipped the economy into a mild recession and ratcheted up defense spending as the United States mounted a military operation against the Taliban regime in Afghanistan and the al Qaeda terrorist network that was operating there.

A bill to help stimulate the flagging economy through individual and business tax cuts bogged down at the end of the year under the weight of partisan differences. A stripped-down bill extending unemployment benefits for thirteen weeks and giving businesses a pair of tax breaks to help them recover from the downturn passed in March 2002. But House GOP plans to extend all or some of the tax cuts made in 2001 did not advance in the Senate. Congress also did not approve legislation restricting companies from reducing their taxes by moving their headquarters offshore.

Congress took tentative steps to eliminate a tax break for major U.S. export industries, labeled by the World Trade Organization as an illegal government subsidy. House Ways and Means Committee Chair Bill Thomas, R-Calif., introduced a bill that not only would repeal the tax break but also overhaul the foreign tax code. Facing strong opposition in his own committee, Thomas decided against holding a mark-up. But the issue would surface again in the 108th Congress where repeal of the illegal subsidy led to the largest number of changes in the corporate tax system since 1986, many of them benefiting narrow special interests. *(Corporate taxes, p. 115)*

2001 Personal Income Tax Cut

Handing President George W. Bush the biggest domestic policy victory of his first year in office, Congress May 26, 2001, cleared legislation aimed at cutting taxes by $1.4 trillion through fiscal 2011. To win broad support the tax benefits in the final package were focused more on low-income taxpayers than Bush had proposed and the total was somewhat less than he sought. The White House said the president's original proposal was worth $1.6 trillion, while the congressional Joint Committee on Taxation put the cost at $1.8 trillion.

By any measure, however, the package amounted to the deepest tax cut since the reductions President Ronald Reagan (1981–1989) pushed to enactment twenty years earlier in his first year in the White House. The central features of the 2001 law—a reduction in income tax rates, alleviation of the so-called marriage penalty, a phase-out of the estate tax, and expansion of the child tax credit—were the proposals at the heart of Bush's presidential campaign platform. Bush signed the measure into law June 7 (HR 1836—PL 107-16).

The measure was also a victory for congressional Republicans who had been frustrated repeatedly in their attempts to enact major tax relief legislation since the federal government began running a budget surplus in 1998. President Bill Clinton had consistently vetoed their bills, arguing that the surplus should be used to restore Social Security and pay down the national debt, not for tax relief that primarily benefited wealthy taxpayers. *(GOP tax cut efforts, Congress and the Nation Vol. X, p. 110)*

House Republicans began building momentum for Bush's proposal early in the year, passing four major elements of the package in quick succession. The first, a sweeping reduction in income tax rates (HR 3), was passed March 8 with no attempt to include Democrats in the writing of the legislation. Republicans then began courting Democrats, with some success, passing legislation to cut income taxes for married couples and people with children (HR 6) on March

Taxes and Other Revenues as Percentage of Gross Domestic Product, 1935–2004

Fiscal Year	Individual Income	Corporate Income	Social Insurance	Excise	Other	Total
1935	0.8	0.8	—	2.1	1.6	5.2
1940	0.9	1.2	1.8	2.0	0.7	6.8
1945	8.3	7.2	1.6	2.8	0.5	20.4
1950	5.8	3.8	1.6	2.8	0.5	14.4
1955	7.3	4.5	2.0	2.3	0.5	16.6
1960	7.9	4.2	2.8	2.3	0.8	17.9
1965	7.1	3.7	3.2	2.1	0.8	17.0
1970	8.9	3.2	4.4	1.6	0.9	19.0
1975	7.8	2.6	5.4	1.1	1.0	17.9
1980	9.0	2.4	5.8	0.9	1.0	19.0
1985	8.1	1.5	6.4	0.9	0.9	17.7
1986	7.9	1.4	6.4	0.7	0.9	17.4
1987	8.4	1.8	6.5	0.7	0.9	18.4
1988	8.0	1.9	6.7	0.7	0.9	18.2
1989	8.3	1.9	6.7	0.6	0.9	18.4
1990	8.1	1.6	6.6	0.6	1.0	18.0
1991	7.9	1.7	6.7	0.7	0.9	17.8
1992	7.6	1.6	6.6	0.7	0.9	17.5
1993	7.8	1.8	6.5	0.7	0.8	17.6
1994	7.8	2.0	6.6	0.8	0.8	18.1
1995	8.1	2.1	6.6	0.8	0.9	18.5
1996	8.5	2.2	6.6	0.7	0.8	18.9
1997	9.0	2.2	6.6	0.7	0.8	19.3
1998	9.6	2.2	6.6	0.7	0.9	20.0
1999	9.6	2.0	6.7	0.8	0.9	20.0
2000	10.3	2.1	6.7	0.7	0.9	20.9
2001	9.9	1.5	6.9	0.7	0.9	19.8
2002	8.3	1.4	6.7	0.6	0.8	17.8
2003	7.3	1.2	6.6	0.6	0.7	16.4
2004	7.0	1.6	6.3	0.6	0.7	16.3

NOTE: The Social Insurance category includes Social Security, Medicare, railroad and other retirement programs, and unemployment insurance. The Other category principally includes estate and gift taxes and customs duties.

SOURCE: Office of Management and Budget, *Historical Tables, Budget of the United States Government: Fiscal Year 2006* (Washington, D.C.: U.S. Government Printing Office, 2005), Table 2.3.

29, followed by the phase-out of the estate tax (HR 8) on April 4, and a package of tax incentives for retirement benefits (HR 10) on May 2.

The dynamic was far different in the Senate where half of the members were Republicans and half Democrats. Republican Charles E. Grassley of Iowa, who chaired the Finance Committee at the time, and ranking Democrat Max Baucus of Montana were slowed by the need to develop a bill that could win at least some bipartisan support. They also were waiting for Congress to complete the fiscal 2002 budget resolution (H Con Res 83), which was crucial in the Senate because it allowed the tax bill to move under special reconciliation rules that barred filibusters and limited amendments. It turned out, however, that at the insistence of Senate moderates in both parties the budget resolution also set a $1.4 trillion ceiling on the tax cuts. *(Budget resolution, p. 48)*

With the budget resolution in place and the Senate ready to act, the House repassed its income tax reduction measure as an official reconciliation bill (HR 1836) on May 16. The Senate then passed its own bill—similar to the comprehensive $1.4 trillion package that became law—on May 23. The House-Senate conference was completed two days later.

Reflecting the need to maintain the crucial support of moderate Democrats, and aware that their party was about to lose control of the Senate with the impending switch by James M. Jeffords of Vermont from Republican to independent, Republicans saw to it that the final package was negotiated by representatives of the White House and just four lawmakers: Grassley, Baucus, Thomas, and John B. Breaux, D-La., a leader of the Senate centrists. The House and Senate stayed in session into the Saturday of Memorial Day weekend to clear the bill. *(Jeffords switch, pp. 3, 8)*

HIGHLIGHTS

As enacted PL 107-16 included the following major provisions:

• **Income tax rates.** Replaced five existing tax brackets (15 percent, 28 percent, 31 percent, 36 percent, and 39.6 percent) with six brackets (10 percent, 15 percent, 25 percent, 28 percent, 33 percent, and 35 percent) by 2006.

- **Rebates.** Provided rebate checks of $300 for individuals, $500 for single parents, and $600 for married couples filing jointly to those who paid taxes in 2001. The rebate was added late in the process in hopes of stimulating the faltering economy.
- **Child tax credit.** Gradually doubled the child tax credit to $1,000 by 2010. Those with incomes above $10,000 could qualify for up to 10 percent of the credit as a tax refund from 2001 to 2004, and 15 percent thereafter.
- **Married couples.** Increased the standard deduction for married couples, and the amount of income subject to the 15 percent bracket, to double that of singles by 2005. Previously, under a quirk of the tax code known as the marriage penalty, many married couples, mostly those in which both people had similar incomes, had incurred more tax liability than they would have as two single filers.
- **Estate tax.** Gradually phased out taxes on estates, with a full repeal set for 2010. The tax on gifts made by a living donor did not change.
- **Education expenses.** Created or expanded a host of benefits for education programs, including increasing the limit on annual tax-free deposits in education savings accounts from $500 to $2,000.
- **Retirement savings.** Increased annual limits on contributions to individual retirement accounts—both traditional and Roth IRAs—and on 401(k)s and other retirement accounts starting in 2002. Low-income individuals could receive a tax credit for up to $2,000 annually for contributions to such plans.
- **AMT.** Increased the income threshold for taxpayers subject to the alternative minimum tax (AMT)—a parallel tax system intended to ensure that filers did not entirely wipe out their liability through deductions, exemptions, and credits.
- **Sunset.** Terminated all of the bill's provisions automatically on Dec. 31, 2010. The provision was needed to keep the cost of the bill within the limit set by the budget resolution.

At $875 billion, the cuts in income taxes accounted for 65 percent of the law's price tag. The increase in the child tax credit was expected to cost $172 billion (13 percent of the total); the estate tax cut, $138 billion (10 percent); the marriage penalty relief, $63 billion (5 percent); the retirement savings breaks, $50 billion (4 percent); and the education breaks, $29 billion (2 percent).

The only major item dropped from the final bill was a Senate provision to make permanent the research and development credit for businesses. It was one of the few provisions that would have benefited corporations, which had to change the quarterly schedules under which they paid taxes to help fund the measure. The bill did not extend a handful of other popular expiring provisions, which were subsequently added to an economic stimulus package enacted in March 2002.

BACKGROUND

Bush had made a ten-year tax cut package totaling $1.3 trillion through 2010 the centerpiece of his presidential campaign. The federal surplus, he argued, belonged to the taxpayers, and they should get part of it back. Even before he took office, however, evidence of a softening economy provided another rationale: Tax cuts were increasingly portrayed as a way to rejuvenate the economy. On Jan. 3 House Minority Leader Dick Gephardt, D-Mo., said that in the interests of strengthening the economy, House Democrats would be amenable to deeper tax cuts than they had supported in the last Congress, when they had fought the GOP on tax reduction at every turn. The outlook for Bush was further bolstered by expectations of bigger-than-ever increases in the federal surplus, despite signs that the economy was slowing.

Federal Reserve Board chairman Alan Greenspan weighed in Jan. 25 when he told the Senate Budget Committee that tax cuts enacted "sooner rather than later" could help ease a protracted economic slump. "Should current economic weakness spread beyond what now appears likely, having a tax cut in place may, in fact, do noticeable good," he said. Previously, Greenspan had urged that the surplus be used to reduce the debt and had tried to dampen the push for tax cuts or increased spending, although when pressed he had said tax reduction was the preferable of the two.

Bush worked to keep the bill focused on his priorities. "Some in Congress view this as an opportunity to load up the tax relief plan with their own visions," he said on the White House lawn Feb. 5. "I want the members of Congress and the American people to hear loud and clear: This is the right-size plan, it is the right approach, and I'm going to defend it mightily."

Two days later Bush delivered an equally clear message to corporate America, which was eager to broaden the package's focus beyond tax relief for individuals and Main Street businesses: your priorities will have to wait, the president told the nineteen executives he had invited to the White House. Corporations, including the U.S. Chamber of Commerce, the National Association of Manufacturers, the National Association of Wholesaler-Distributors, and the National Federation of Independent Business, responded by joining together to push for passage of the tax bill without corporate add-ons.

On Feb. 27 Bush addressed a joint session of Congress, offering a preliminary outline of his budget that put the cost of the tax cut package in fiscal 2002 through 2011 at $1.6 trillion, an amount he said was "just right." The central features, as in his campaign, included an across-the-board reduction in marginal income tax rates; steps to alleviate the marriage penalty; an increase in the child tax credit; a phase-out of the tax on estates, gifts, and trust funds; and expansion of the charitable deductions to those who did not itemize their deductions.

When Bush submitted the full details of his budget on April 9, he estimated the cost of the tax cut at slightly over

$1.6 trillion. (The Joint Committee on Taxation, Congress' official scorekeeper on tax issues, subsequently calculated the cost at $1.8 trillion.) By then, Congress was starting to weigh in. The Senate had approved a version of the budget resolution that set a $1.3 trillion limit on tax cuts—$1.2 trillion in 2002 through 2011, plus $85 billion for a retroactive tax cut for 2001, mostly in the form of refunds. While the House endorsed Bush's total, it had passed three pieces of the package that differed at least slightly—and sometimes substantially—from the president's proposals.

HOUSE ACTION ON SEPARATE BILLS

House Republicans spent March and early April passing the four main pieces of Bush's tax package, albeit with significant modifications. They had the majority required to pass the bills and no need to wait until the budget resolution was finished. Although some members complained about endorsing a huge tax cut before they saw the overall size of the budget, the crucial procedural protection offered by the budget resolution in the Senate was not relevant in the House, where floor debate was controlled by the GOP-run Rules Committee.

Income Tax Rate Reductions

With no pretense of seeking bipartisan support, House Republicans pushed through the Ways and Means Committee a $958 billion, ten-year reduction in income tax rates—the most expensive and controversial piece of the package—just two days after Bush's speech to Congress on Feb. 27. House passage came a week later.

The bill, similar to Bush's plan, proposed reducing the five existing income tax brackets to four (33 percent, 25 percent, 15 percent, and 10 percent) by 2006. The main difference was that it would phase in the new bottom rate more quickly by creating a 12 percent bracket retroactive to Jan. 1, and reducing it to 10 percent in 2006. Bush proposed starting the new rate at 14 percent in 2002, lowering it gradually to 10 percent in 2006. Making it retroactive was expected to mean a cut in 2001 of $180 for individual taxpayers, $360 for married couples filing jointly, and $300 for single parents. The bill also would repeal the existing limits on claiming the refundable child credit for taxpayers subject to the AMT.

The House passed the bill (HR 3—H Rept 107-7) March 8 on a **key vote of 230–198 (R 219–0; D 10–197; I 1–1.)** Ten Democrats joined a unified Republican bloc to support it. Fully one-quarter of House Democrats joined with the GOP in opposition to a Democratic substitute offered by ranking Ways and Means Committee member Charles B. Rangel, D-N.Y. Estimated to cost $585.5 billion through 2011, Rangel's plan would have created a new 12 percent tax bracket, expanded the earned income tax credit (EITC) for the working poor, and alleviated the marriage penalty. It was rejected 155–273. *(2001 key votes, p. 801)*

Passage of HR 3 was significant not only because it was the first vote on the new president's platform, but also because it was a vote in support of the central element of Bush's economic program. The vote also showed GOP House leaders that their caucus would unite behind the Bush tax cut despite divisions lurking just beneath the surface. The GOP leadership also learned that it could push through one of the most contentious bills of the year without even pretending to collaborate with Democrats and that at least a handful of Democrats would vote with the GOP anyway.

The vote further demonstrated to House GOP leaders that their main argument—that quick action was needed to boost the staggering economy—could triumph over the two most politically potent counterarguments. Liberals maintained that the Bush tax cut, especially the reductions in the personal income tax rates, were inappropriately skewed toward the rich. For their part conservatives argued that it was wrong to cut taxes before setting an overall budget framework that could balance the demands of what was, at the time, a robust federal surplus.

'Marriage Penalty' Tax Bill

The second piece of the package—a tax reduction for married couples and an increase in the child tax credit—had far broader appeal in Congress. Estimated to cost $399.2 billion through 2011, HR 6 also was the most substantial—and expensive—deviation from Bush's plans. Drafted by Ways and Means Chair Thomas, the bill called for cutting taxes for almost all married couples at a cost of $223.3 billion. It proposed making the standard deduction for married couples filing jointly double that of singles beginning in 2001, and the portion of a couple's income subject to the low, 15 percent tax bracket double that of singles by 2004.

The result would be a break not only for the mostly two-earner couples who suffered the penalty, but also for an almost equal number of couples whose tax liability declined as a result of their marriage. Those couples tended to have only one breadwinner or one spouse who earned much more than the other. The approach appealed to social conservatives who argued that couples with a stay-at-home spouse should get a tax break, too. By contrast, Bush's proposal, estimated to cost $111.8 billion, focused exclusively on those couples who paid more as a result of being married. It would have revived a provision enacted in Ronald Reagan's first year as president in 1981 (PL 97-34) but repealed five years later that allowed married couples to deduct up to $3,000 of the lower-earning spouse's income from their return.

Other provisions in the bill proposed changing the EITC to allow more low-income married couples to claim a greater refund even if they earned too little to be liable for income taxes. To answer criticism from both Democrats and Republicans that Bush's package would respond too slowly to the weakening economy, Thomas proposed making the initial $100 increase in the child tax credit retroactive to the start of 2001; Bush proposed making it effective in 2002.

The Ways and Means Committee approved the bill (HR 6—H Rept 107-29) 23–16 on March 22. In a reversal of the strategy used on the first tax bill, Thomas specifically included provisions aimed at attracting Democrats, designating extra help for the working poor and eschewing Bush's proposal to give wealthier parents and couples more of the package's proposed benefits. Still, Democrats were no more involved in writing the measure than they were in HR 3, and all Democrats present at the markup voted against the bill.

The breadth of support for a family tax cut was confirmed March 29 when sixty-four House Democrats joined a unified Republican bloc to pass the bill by a vote of 282–144. In 2000 fifty-one Democrats had supported a similar bill, which subsequently died when the House fell sixteen votes short of overriding Clinton's veto. (*Congress and the Nation Vol. X, p. 113*)

Estate Tax Repeal

The third tax bill passed by the House was a phase-out of taxes on estates, gifts, and trust funds at a cost estimated by the Joint Tax Committee at $185.6 billion through 2011. The bill called for gradually reducing the combined tax on gifts (assets given during a taxpayer's lifetime) and estates (assets transferred at death) until it disappeared in 2011. The existing top rate of 55 percent was to fall to 39 percent by 2010 and to zero thereafter. As under existing law the first $675,000 in assets, set to rise to $1 million in 2006, would be exempt from the tax. The measure was less expensive than the president's plan because the proposed phase-out was slower, and heirs who sold inherited property would be required to pay additional capital gains taxes on profits above $1.3 million. An estate tax repeal that would have cost $104 billion in the first ten years cleared in 2000 but was vetoed by Clinton. (*Congress and the Nation Vol. X, p. 115*)

The Ways and Means Committee approved the bill (HR 8—H Rept 107-37) by a vote of 24–14 on March 29. The House passed the measure April 4 by a solid majority of 274–154. The bill drew fewer "yes" votes than the 2000 version, in part because this time the president was ready to sign the bill, making the votes more consequential. The measure still had significant Democratic support—fifty-eight members from across the party's political spectrum voted for it compared with sixty-five in 2000. Three Republicans opposed it; none did in 2000.

The House voted 201–227 to reject the Democratic substitute, which would have increased the exemption limits to offer immediate relief to most of those who inherited family-owned farms and small businesses—the people that many members said were most deserving of estate tax relief.

Retirement Savings

The fourth tax bill—what sponsor Rob Portman, R-Ohio, called "the last big piece that can fit under the umbrella"— sought to increase the tax benefits of contributing to Individual Retirement Accounts (IRAs), 401(k)s, and other retirement accounts, and to make pensions more portable for the many workers who switched jobs. The product of a four-year partnership between Portman and Benjamin L. Cardin, D-Md., the bill was estimated to cost $51.7 billion in lost Treasury revenue through 2011. A nearly identical measure

had won 401 House votes in 2000 but had become entangled in a larger tax measure that stalled in the face of opposition from Clinton. (*Congress and the Nation Vol. X, p. 119*)

The Ways and Means Committee approved the bill (HR 10—H Rept 107-51, Part I) on April 25 by a vote of 35–6. The Education and the Workforce Committee approved the pension provisions over which it had jurisdiction by voice vote April 26 (H Rept 107-51, Part II). All but half a dozen Democrats on Ways and Means voted for the measure. Several more worried aloud that the bill would not do enough for the 70 million workers who did not have pension plans.

Richard E. Neal, D-Mass., proposed allowing workers with adjusted gross incomes up to $25,000 to claim a refundable credit on half their annual contributions to IRAs, 401(k)s, or other plans; those earning as much as $75,000 would have qualified for part of the credit. The cost was estimated at $35.5 billion over ten years. The amendment was defeated 15–24. Another Neal amendment, defeated 16–24, provided a tax credit for half the administrative and education expenses of businesses with 100 or fewer employees that start retirement plans and gave those same small businesses a tax credit worth 50 percent of their contributions to the retirement plans of lower-earning workers.

The House passed the bill by an overwhelming vote of 407–24 on May 2, after rejecting 207–233 a Democratic amendment to use tax credits to encourage lower-income workers and small businesses to start and contribute to pension plans.

ACTION ON RECONCILIATION BILL

With the completion of the budget resolution May 10 Congress had the go-ahead to move an official tax reconciliation bill. The House acted quickly, repassing the income tax rate reduction measure as a new bill (HR 1836) on May 16. The vote was 230–197.

Deputy Majority Whip Roy Blunt, R-Mo., said the bill was repassed to let the Senate know that a deep cut in the top rate was "critically important to the House." The day before the Senate Finance Committee had approved a top rate of 36 percent, compared with a 33 percent top rate in the House bill.

SENATE COMMITTEE ACTION

After weeks of negotiations the Senate Finance Committee on May 15 approved a $1.4 trillion comprehensive tax-reconciliation bill written by Grassley and Baucus with enough trade-offs to win the support of all ten of the panel's Republicans and four of its ten Democrats. The vote was 14–6. The bill had been unveiled on May 11, the day after the Senate adopted the final version of the budget resolution.

Grassley and Baucus followed the outlines of Bush's overall tax plan. But they rewrote the pieces, often in ways designed to keep the package's scope and cost within the confines of the budget resolution. They also crammed in several additional provisions, principally to secure the support of four key moderates on the panel: Republicans Jeffords of Vermont and Olympia J. Snowe of Maine, and Democrats Robert G. Torricelli of New Jersey and Blanche Lincoln of Arkansas.

They also wrote in several gimmicks that shaved the bill's official eleven-year cost and eased its consideration under the Senate's complex parliamentary rules. The most dramatic of these was a provision to "sunset," or repeal, the entire bill on Sept. 30, 2011. The provision was necessary because Senate budget rules disqualified provisions on a reconciliation bill that would reduce revenues for more than ten years. Without the sunset provision the bill would have been subject to a point of order when it reached the floor, requiring sixty votes to overcome—a threshold that tax cut proponents concluded they could not reach. Another provision, to delay the due date for certain quarterly corporate income tax payments by fifteen days, was added to shift revenue to years in which the surplus might not be sufficient to support that year's tax reductions without tapping the surplus in the Medicare Part A hospital trust fund.

Following are highlights of the bill:

• **Income tax rates.** Shifting the focus more to lower-income taxpayers the Senate proposed reducing the top rates by less than Bush or the House had proposed and making the new 10 percent rate retroactive to Jan. 1. The House and Bush had proposed phasing it in by 2006, though at different rates. By 2007 the upper rates under the Senate bill would be 36 percent, 33 percent, 28 percent, and 25 percent; the 15 percent rate would be unchanged.

• **Marriage penalty.** The less expensive Senate proposal increased the standard deduction for married couples and the portion of their income subject to the 15 percent bracket to double that of singles by 2005.

• **Child tax credit.** The credit was increased to $600 retroactively to Jan. 1, as under the House bill, but it would not reach $1,000 until 2011.

• **Estate tax.** Estate taxes were cut gradually until their repeal in 2011, as in the House bill, but the exemption would increase to $4 million in 2010. The gift tax would remain but at a lower rate. Like the House, the Senate included the proviso that heirs pay capital gains taxes on the profits that had accrued since the asset was originally purchased.

The biggest challenges came from Democrats. Minority Leader Tom Daschle of South Dakota, who was a member of the panel, joined Conrad and John D. Rockefeller IV of West Virginia in leveling a spate of withering criticism. Conrad called the bill "a monument to fiscal irresponsibility" because so many of its provisions would take effect in the second part of the decade when the baby-boomers neared retirement and the surplus projections on which the tax cut depended were the least reliable. Daschle described his vote in the House for Reagan's 1981 tax cut (PL 97-34) as "one of the greatest mistakes of my public career" and lamented that Congress was "faced with almost exactly the same circumstances and once again on the threshold of making that same mistake." But Democratic attempts to make changes in the measure were rejected.

SENATE FLOOR ACTION

With a dozen Democrats joining all of the Senate's Republicans in a sign that the Grassley-Baucus bill had captured the middle ground, the Senate passed an amended version of the committee bill May 23 that left most of the major compromises in place. The **key vote of 62–38 (R 50–0; D 12–38)** sent a clear signal that Congress was on the verge of enacting the deepest tax cuts in a generation and that Bush would score his first big legislative triumph, sooner than most observers had predicted. *(2001 key votes, p. 801)*

The 62–38 vote came in a chamber stunned by news that Jeffords was about to abandon the GOP to become an independent, turning control of the Senate over to the Democrats. The chamber had been divided 50–50 between the parties, but Jeffords said he would caucus with Democrats, giving them the necessary votes to take control. The impending change spurred Daschle to end a Democratic assault that had kept the bill on the floor for four days and two nights as amendment after amendment was offered and defeated.

The proposed income tax rate cut drew the sharpest attacks during the lengthy floor debate. Although Grassley and Baucus defended their compromise as the only one that could move through the Senate, many Democrats—and one prominent Republican, John McCain of Arizona—were skeptical. With McCain's help, Democrats nearly succeeded in cutting taxes further for low- and middle-income taxpayers. McCain called up an amendment to reduce the 39.6 percent rate by 1 percentage point and expand the portion of income taxed at the 15 percent rate. It failed on a 49–49 tie. Four Republicans joined McCain in backing the amendment, as did all but five Democrats. Democrats tried again the next day, making minor adjustments to the amendment so they could reintroduce it. That time it failed on a 50–50 tie.

Many of the failed Democratic amendments were attempts to limit the reduction in the top tax brackets and divert the funds to Medicare, education, or other social programs. Many of the proposals fell on points of order when the Senate failed to muster the sixty votes needed to override rules requiring that amendments be germane to the reconciliation bill. Among the more significant proposals rejected were amendments to cut temporarily the tax on gains on capital held more than one year from 20 percent to 15 percent; to create an expedited procedure for Congress to delay tax cuts if debt levels rose, or to increase discretionary spending if more debt were paid off than anticipated; to retain the estate tax but allow family-owned businesses and farms to escape it entirely and let couples exclude as much as $4 million from the tax; and to exempt individuals with adjusted gross incomes below $100,000 from the alternative minimum tax.

CONFERENCE

Although it took time for the political realities of the impending Democratic takeover of the Senate to set in, Republican conservatives ultimately swallowed their pride and agreed to a $1.4 trillion package of tax cuts that favored those of modest means far more than Bush and most Republicans advocated. Prodded by Bush and cognizant that their unilateral control of the Capitol was about to end, weary Republican leaders in both chambers agreed on the evening of May 25 to a deal with the ever-more-powerful centrist Senate Democrats.

The House adopted the conference report 240–154 on Saturday, May 26, and the Senate cleared it 58–33 the same day.

During the conference negotiations White House officials abandoned the administration's previous resistance to compromise and urged their Republican allies in Congress to quickly embrace any version of a tax cut deal that could become law. "The sooner the Congress completes its work, the sooner the American people will have their own money in their own pockets to save and invest as they see fit. Our economy cannot afford any further delays," Bush declared May 23.

In the end the compromise was a slightly altered version of the bill passed by the Senate. Conferees followed the Senate model of postponing some effective dates and lengthening some phase-ins to make room for priorities of both conservatives and moderates. They also included the language repealing the entire bill in 2010, allowing a somewhat deeper rate cut than the earlier Senate version while staying under the overall ceiling set by the budget resolution.

Although House Republicans made an effort in conference to cut tax rates by about $1 trillion—up from the $958 billion the House had supported and the Senate's $824 billion—Thomas had evidence from the outset that such a big increase could not survive in the Senate. He had been a frequent visitor to that chamber during the tax debate, spending more than half an hour talking with Baucus on the floor May 21 and many more hours in cloakroom meetings with the pivotal moderates. The proposals he and Majority Leader Dick Armey, R-Texas, pressed during much of the conference were designed at least as much to appeal to hesitant House conservatives as to make progress in the negotiations.

Fifteen Senate moderates, led by Breaux and Snowe, signed a letter threatening to oppose any conference report that did not "closely reflect the delicate compromise that was reached in the Senate."

The most expensive of Bush's proposals left out of the final bill—and the only major component directed explicitly at business—was the plan to make permanent the tax credit that companies could claim on as much as 20 percent of their research and experimentation expenses at a cost of $8 billion through 2011. The idea was popular in Congress. But the urgency of addressing it faded in the final round of negotiations, in part because the credit did not expire until 2004 and in part because its extension could be used as a vehicle or sweetener for some future tax package. As for the sunset provision, the administration said it was confident it would

never be realized because a future Congress and president would agree to extend the tax cuts. "To do anything other than that is to raise taxes on the American people," White House spokesman Ari Fleischer said May 31.

TAX LAW PROVISIONS

Following is a summary of the main provisions in the ten-year, $1.4 trillion tax package (PL 107-16) enacted June 7.

INDIVIDUAL INCOME TAX RATES

Before the bill's enactment individual income was taxed in five rate brackets: 15 percent, 28 percent, 31 percent, 36 percent, and 39.6 percent. The bill created a new 10 percent bracket, redefined the 15 percent bracket, and gradually reduced the four remaining marginal rates.

The bill also gradually repealed limits on the itemized deductions and personal exemptions that taxpayers could use to reduce their taxable income. Before enactment the amount of the deductions and exemptions was limited for taxpayers with income above certain thresholds.

• **10 percent bracket.** The bill created a new 10 percent bracket, retroactive to Jan. 1, 2001, for a portion of the taxable income previously taxed at 15 percent. In 2001 through 2007 the 10 percent rate applied to the first $6,000 of taxable income for individual taxpayers, $10,000 for single parents, and $12,000 for married couples filing joint returns. Beginning in 2008 the 10 percent bracket would apply to the first $7,000 of income for individuals, $10,000 for single parents, and $14,000 for married couples. Those amounts were to be indexed for inflation beginning in 2009.

• **Rebate.** In lieu of the 10 percent bracket in 2001 the bill provided a one-time refund of up to $300 for single taxpayers, $500 for single parents, and $600 for married couples. Taxpayers could not receive more than the actual amount of taxes they paid in 2000.

• **15 percent bracket.** The 15 percent tax bracket began where the new 10 percent bracket left off and ended at the same level as under previous law for a single person ($27,050) or a single parent ($36,250). For married couples filing jointly, the level was raised, as explained in the Marriage Penalty section (below).

• **Marginal rate cuts.** The bill gradually reduced the remaining four marginal rates. Cuts began July 1, 2001, when rates were reduced by 1 percentage point to 27 percent, 30 percent, 35 percent, and 38.6 percent. In 2004 the rates were slated to fall by an additional 1 percent, to 26 percent, 29 percent, 34 percent, and 37.6 percent. For 2006 the rates were set at 25 percent, 28 percent, 33 percent, and 35 percent.

• **Repeal of restrictions on itemized deductions and personal exemptions.** The limits on deductions and personal exemptions available to high-income taxpayers were to be gradually eliminated, beginning in 2006. They were scheduled to fall by one-third in 2006 and 2007 and two-thirds in 2008 and 2009, before being fully eliminated in 2010. Itemized deductions included state and local income and property taxes, unreimbursed medical expenses, charitable contributions, and certain other expenses. Taxpayers also were generally allowed to exempt a set amount from their taxes for each dependent, their spouse, and themselves. In 2001 the personal exemption was $2,900; after that, it was to be indexed annually for inflation.

Until 2006, itemized deductions would continue to be reduced by 3 percent of a taxpayer's adjusted gross income in excess of $132,950 ($66,475 per person for married couples filing separate returns), although the total could not be reduced by more than 80 percent. The personal exemption would continue to be phased out for individuals with adjusted gross incomes over $132,950 and for married couples filing jointly with incomes above $199,450.

Marriage Penalty

More than sixty provisions in the tax code treated single taxpayers differently from married couples filing jointly. When combined with other provisions in the code they created a "marriage penalty" for couples who paid more taxes than they would have as two single filers and a "marriage bonus" for others. Those in households where both spouses contributed significantly to the family income tended to have a marriage penalty. One-earner couples or those in which one spouse earned much more than the other tended to have a marriage bonus. The bill addressed the two major components of the marriage penalty, while giving additional tax relief to those who already enjoyed a marriage bonus.

• **Increased standard deduction.** The bill gradually increased the basic standard deduction for a married couple filing jointly to twice the deduction for an unmarried couple. The increase was phased in over a five-year period beginning in 2005 and would be fully effective by 2009. Before enactment the standard deduction for married couples filing jointly was 167 percent of that for a single individual.

• **Expansion of 15 percent bracket.** Beginning in 2005 the bill phased in over a four-year period an increase in the upper boundary of the 15 percent tax bracket for married couples filing jointly until the upper limit became double that for single taxpayers. Previously the 15 percent bracket covered taxable income up to $27,050 for individuals and $45,200 for couples. When the increase was fully phased in, up to $54,100 of a married couples' income would be taxed at 15 percent.

Expansion of earned-income tax credit

The bill made more married couples eligible for the EITC—a program designed to enhance tax refunds for certain low-income workers, including those who did not earn enough to owe income taxes. Before enactment, for example, the full credit was available to a filer with two or more children and an adjusted gross or earned income of $13,090 or less; a partial credit was available for a similar filer with income up to $32,121. Under the bill those limits were to increase to $16,090 and $35,121, respectively, by 2007. Income limits for individuals and those with one child were

similarly increased. Starting in 2009 the beginning and ending points would be adjusted annually for inflation. The bill also made several changes aimed at simplifying calculation of the credit.

Child and Family Tax Credits

Before enactment the child tax credit that was part of the 1997 tax reconciliation law (PL 105-34) provided a $500 tax credit for each child under age seventeen. The credit was available to individuals with modified adjusted gross incomes of up to $75,000 a year and couples making up to $110,000; it was phased out above these income levels and was not indexed for inflation. The credit was generally nonrefundable for taxpayers with fewer than three children, meaning they could not get the money in a check if they owed no taxes. However, for taxpayers with three or more qualifying children, the credit was refundable up to the amount that their Social Security and Medicare taxes exceeded their earned-income tax credit.

• **Child tax credit increase.** The child tax credit was doubled, to $1,000, over a ten-year period. It was scheduled to increase to $600 in 2001, to $700 in 2005, to $800 in 2009, and to $1,000 in 2010.

• **Refundability.** The child tax credit was made refundable for all families, no matter the number of children, for up to 10 percent of the taxpayer's earned income in excess of $10,000. This meant that those earning too little to be liable for income tax could qualify for the refundable child tax credit. The $10,000 earned-income floor was to be indexed for inflation beginning in 2002. Beginning in 2005 the credit would be available for up to 15 percent of earned income in excess of $10,000. Any refund that low-income taxpayers received because of the credit would not be counted as income when determining their eligibility for federal social programs or state or local programs financed with federal funds.

• **Adoption tax credit and exclusion.** Beginning in 2003 the adoption credit was increased to $10,000 per eligible child, up from $6,000 for special-needs children, and $5,000 for all other children. The new law also increased to $10,000, from $5,000 or $6,000, the amount that an employee could exclude from taxable income for expenses reimbursed through an employer adoption assistance program. In both cases, taxpayers adopting special-needs children did not have to actually incur adoption expenses to claim the credit, but those adopting other children did.

The beginning point of the income phase-out range for both the credit and the exclusion was increased from $75,000 to $150,000 of modified adjusted gross income, effective in 2003. In both cases, taxpayers with incomes greater than $190,000 were not eligible for any tax reduction for the adoption.

• **Dependent care tax credit.** Beginning in 2003 the tax credit to help offset the cost of child care or the care of physically or mentally disabled dependents was increased from 30 percent of costs to 35 percent. The amount of expenses that could be claimed increased from $2,400 to $3,000 for one dependent and from $4,800 to $6,000 for two or more. As a result, the maximum credit would be $1,050 for one dependent (up from $720) and $2,100 for two or more (up from $1,440). The income phase-out range began at $15,000 of adjusted gross income. Those with adjusted gross incomes over $43,000 would be eligible for a 20 percent credit.

• **Employer-provided child care.** The bill created a tax credit for companies that provide day care for their workers' children. Employers who construct, operate, or contract with a facility to provide child care would be eligible for a credit of up to 25 percent of expenses. Those who provided a child care resource or referral service were eligible for a credit of up to 10 percent of expenses. The total of the credits taken in one year could not exceed $150,000.

ALTERNATIVE MINIMUM TAX

Created in 1969 and bolstered over the years, the alternative minimum tax (AMT) was designed to ensure that wealthy individuals and corporations could not wipe out their entire tax liability by claiming a large number of deductions, exemptions, and credits. If a taxpayer's tax liability were greater under the AMT than under the regular system the person could not claim most tax breaks and was taxed on a larger portion of income. Because the system's income thresholds were not adjusted annually for inflation, as the rest of the tax system was, more and more upper-middle-income taxpayers were becoming subject to the AMT.

The limit on exemptions from the AMT for single taxpayers was increased by $2,000, to $35,750, and by $4,000 for married couples filing jointly, to $49,000. The provision took effect in 2001 and was scheduled to sunset at the end of 2004.

• **Allowing AMT taxpayers certain tax credits.** Under the bill the refundable child credit no longer was reduced by the amount of the taxpayer's AMT liability. Those subject to the AMT could claim the child credit, the adoption credit, and the new credit available to low- to moderate-income taxpayers for contributing to retirement savings.

EDUCATION INCENTIVES

The bill contained provisions to encourage taxpayers to set aside money for their children's education by utilizing tax-favored education savings accounts (ESAs) and state prepaid tuition programs. The measure also instituted a deduction for college tuition.

• **Education savings accounts.** The annual contribution limit to ESAs increased from $500 to $2,000 beginning in 2002. Contributions to ESAs were not tax-deductible, but distributions from these accounts would not be taxed if they were used to meet qualified education expenses.

Under prior law such distributions could be used only to pay for college expenses. The bill expanded the program to include qualified elementary and secondary school expenses—such as tuition, tutoring, books, and computers—for public or private schools.

Eligibility for the accounts was phased out for married couples with modified adjusted gross incomes higher than $190,000, up from $150,000 in prior law. Couples with incomes above $220,000, up from $160,000, were not eligible for the program. The thresholds were increased to make a married couple's limit double that of a single taxpayer.

A prohibition on claiming education tax credits known as HOPE credits and Lifetime Learning credits in the same year a taxpayer took tax-free distributions from an ESA was repealed. The distribution could not be used for the same education expenses for which the credit was claimed, however. Both the HOPE and Lifetime Learning credits were created by the 1997 tax law (PL 105-34). Under the HOPE program joint filers with adjusted gross incomes below $80,000 and individuals earning $40,000 or less could claim a tax credit of up to $1,500 for the cost of the first two years of college. Under the Lifetime Learning program such taxpayers could claim a credit of up to $1,000 to cover the cost of tuition and fees for the last two years of college, advanced degrees, or professional development classes.

• **Prepaid tuition programs.** Tax-exempt status was extended to prepaid tuition programs at private universities. Under prior law such benefits were available only for state tuition programs. Under the new law distributions from prepaid tuition programs could be excluded from a beneficiary's or contributor's gross income and taxpayers could claim the HOPE or Lifetime Learning credit and take tax-free distributions from the prepaid account in the same year. Most of the provisions were effective beginning in 2002, except the tax exclusion, which would not take effect until 2004.

• **Higher education expenses deduction.** From 2002 through 2005 taxpayers could claim an above-the-line deduction for tuition and other higher education expenses. Above-the-line deductions are available whether or not the taxpayer itemizes. Individuals with an adjusted gross income of up to $65,000 and married couples earning $130,000 could deduct up to $3,000 a year in 2002 and 2003. In 2004 and 2005 the deduction was set to increase to $4,000 a year for taxpayers in those income ranges. Taxpayers who earned between $65,000 and $80,000 could deduct up to $2,000 in education expenses. A taxpayer could not claim the deduction and the HOPE or Lifetime Learning credit for the same student. In addition, most distributions from ESAs or prepaid tuition plans would not be tax-free in years when the taxpayer claimed the deduction.

• **Employer-provided education assistance.** Beginning in 2002 the income tax exclusion for employer-provided educational assistance was expanded to cover both undergraduate and graduate education and was made permanent. The exclusion allowed employees to receive up to $5,250 annually for education expenses without having to include it in their taxable income. Prior to enactment, the exclusion covered undergraduate courses only and was set to expire at the end of 2001.

• **Student loan interest deduction.** Beginning in 2002 a sixty-month time limit on deducting interest on student loans was repealed and voluntary payments of interest were deductible. Individuals with modified adjusted gross incomes of $50,000 and married couples with incomes of $100,000 could qualify for the full deduction, which was limited to $2,500 a year. Individuals earning up to $65,000 and married couples earning up to $130,000 could qualify for a reduced deduction. Beginning in 2003 income ranges would be adjusted annually for inflation. Prior to enactment the deduction was phased out for individuals making between $40,000 and $55,000 and joint filers making between $60,000 and $75,000.

ESTATE AND GIFT TAXES

The bill phased out the estate and generation-skipping taxes over ten years and reduced the gift tax, but it required that heirs pay more capital gains taxes on inherited assets that are sold. (Generation-skipping taxes were levied on transfers to a beneficiary more than one generation away from the individual transferring the benefit.)

• **Declining rates.** In 2002 the top estate, gift, and generation-skipping tax rates were lowered from 55 percent to 50 percent, and the 5 percent surtax—added to the highest of the marginal tax rates—was repealed. From 2003 through 2007 the top rate was to decline by 1 percentage point each year until it reached 45 percent.

• **Estate, generation-skipping repeal.** All estate and generation-skipping taxes were to be repealed in 2010.

• **Gift tax.** The bill retained the gift tax and set the rate at the highest individual income tax rate (in 2010, that rate would be 35 percent).

• **Unified credit.** The point at which estate and generation-skipping taxes apply, known as the unified credit, was increased to $1 million in 2002, $1.5 million in 2004, $2 million in 2006, and $3.5 million in 2009. Beginning in 2004 the increase in the unified credit would apply only to transfers at death, leaving the unified credit for lifetime transfers (that is, for gifts) at $1 million. Under prior law the exemption from taxes under the unified credit was $675,000, with the amount scheduled to increase to $1 million by 2006.

• **State credit.** Taxpayers subject to federal estate taxes could claim a credit equal to the amount of inheritance taxes they paid to states. The bill reduced the credit by 25 percent in 2002, 50 percent in 2003, and 75 percent in 2004, and repealed it in 2005. However, taxpayers subject to such state levies would be able take the cost as a deduction on their federal taxes.

• **Capital gains basis.** The bill repealed the stepped-up basis under which the value of a property transferred to an heir was based on its fair-market value at the time of the deceased's death, not at the time the deceased acquired the property. Beginning in 2010 when the estate tax would be repealed the value of inherited assets would "carry over" from the deceased. Heirs would have to pay capital gains taxes on any increase in the value of the property from the time the asset was acquired by the deceased until it was sold by the heirs, generally resulting in a higher capital gain and higher tax liability for the heirs than under previous law.

The bill provided an exemption of $1.3 million in gain from the carry-over basis with an additional $3 million exemption for a surviving spouse, for a total of $4.3 million.

• **Conservation easements.** The bill expanded the estate tax rule for conservation easements, which generally allowed an executor to exclude from the taxable estate 40 percent of the value (up to $400,000 in 2001) of certain lands set aside for conservation purposes. Prior to enactment a qualified conservation easement had to be within ten miles of an urban national forest or within twenty-five miles of a metropolitan area, national park, or wilderness area. The bill repealed the mileage restrictions, effective in 2001.

PENSION AND RETIREMENT PROVISIONS

The bill increased the annual contribution limit for both traditional Individual Retirement Accounts (IRAs) and Roth IRAs. Contributions to a traditional IRA are tax deductible for some taxpayers, but amounts withdrawn are taxable. Contributions to Roth IRAs are not deductible, but withdrawals, including interest, are tax-free.

• **IRA contribution limits.** The limit on IRA contributions was increased to $5,000 a year, from the previous limit of $2,000 a year, phased in over seven years. The new limits: $3,000 in 2002, $4,000 in 2005, and $5,000 in 2008. Beginning in 2009 the amount would be indexed for inflation in $500 increments.

• **IRA catch-up contributions.** Taxpayers age fifty and older could make catch-up contributions to their IRAs, totaling $500 a year in 2002 through 2005 and an additional $1,000 in 2006 and each year thereafter. The catch-up contributions were in addition to the increased limits on all IRAs.

• **401(k) and other plans.** The amount that an individual could contribute annually to a 401(k) plan, a tax-sheltered annuity known as a 403(b), or a simplified employee pension (SEP) plan increased from $10,500 in 2001 to $11,000 in 2002. In 2003 and thereafter the limit was scheduled to increase in $1,000 annual increments until it reached $15,000 in 2006, with adjustments for inflation thereafter, in $500 increments.

• **SIMPLE plans.** The amount that an individual could contribute to a small-business (SIMPLE) retirement plan increased from $6,500 in 2001 to $7,000 in 2002, $8,000 in 2003, $9,000 in 2004, and $10,000 in 2005. Beginning in 2006 the $10,000 limit would be adjusted for inflation in $500 increments.

• **Section 457 plans.** The amount that could be contributed on a tax-deferred basis to a Section 457 plan—a type of pension plan offered by a state or local government or tax-exempt organization to its employees—increased from $8,500 in 2001 to $11,000 in 2002. It was then scheduled to increase in $1,000 increments each year until it reached $15,000 in 2006. The limit would be indexed for inflation in $500 increments beginning in 2007.

• **Catch-up contributions.** Individuals fifty and older could make catch-up contributions to a 401(k) plan, a tax-sheltered annuity, a SEP, or a Section 457 plan. They would be able to make additional contributions of up to $1,000 in 2002, $2,000 in 2003, $3,000 in 2004, $4,000 in 2005, and $5,000 in 2006. Contribution limits for SIMPLE small-business plans were 50 percent of the applicable catch-up provisions for other plans. Beginning in 2007 the limits would be indexed for inflation in $500 increments.

• **Compensation limitation.** The cap on total annual payments (from both employers and employees) to defined contribution plans, such as 401(k)s, was raised. Previously the cap was the lesser of $35,000 or 25 percent of an employee's compensation. Beginning in 2002 it was the lesser of $40,000 or 100 percent of compensation. Government and nonprofit workers who participated in 457(b) plans were to have their compensation limit increased from 33.3 percent to 100 percent.

In 2002 the bill increased from $170,000 to $200,000 the annual compensation of each participant that could be taken into account when plan managers determined contributions and benefits. The number would be indexed for inflation in increments of $5,000 beginning in 2003.

• **Defined benefit plans.** The annual benefit limit under a defined benefit plan—a traditional pension plan—was increased from $140,000 to $160,000 in 2002. The bill also lowered the age at which benefits were reduced, from before age sixty-five to before age sixty-two. Previously benefits were reduced if the recipient began receiving them before the Social Security retirement age—currently sixty-five—and increased if they began after the Social Security retirement age.

• **Top-heavy rules.** The definition of a "top-heavy" retirement plan—one that mostly benefits the highest-paid employees—was loosened to ensure that fewer companies faced the stricter vesting and contribution requirements placed on such plans. The bill redefined a "key" employee as an officer with compensation in excess of $130,000, instead of $70,000 as under prior law, and made several other changes to definitions, all effective in 2002.

• **Deduction limits.** The annual limit on the amount of tax-deductible contributions an employer could make to a profit-sharing or stock bonus plan increased from 15 percent of the taxable compensation of the plan's participants to 25 percent, beginning in 2002.

• **Roth 401(k) plans.** The bill provided for the establishment, beginning in 2006, of a qualified contribution program that allowed an employee to have all or a portion of his or her elective deferrals (that is, employee contributions to 401(k) and tax-sheltered annuities) treated as qualified contributions. Employee contributions to such a plan would receive the same tax treatment as contributions to a Roth IRA, meaning contributions would be in after-tax dollars but withdrawals after retirement were tax-free. The annual contribution limit for qualified-plus contributions would be the regular contribution limit for the plan (for example, $11,500 for 2001) minus contributions not allocated to the qualified-plus contribution program.

• **Retirement contribution tax credit.** Effective in 2002 through 2006 certain middle- and low-income taxpayers were eligible for a temporary, nonrefundable tax credit for contributions to eligible retirement plans.

Individuals with incomes up to $25,000 and married couples with incomes up to $50,000 were eligible for a credit of up to 50 percent on a maximum contribution of $2,000 to a 401(k) plan, a tax-sheltered annuity, a section 457 plan for government workers, a SIMPLE plan or a SEP, or a traditional or Roth IRA. The credit would be phased out for single taxpayers earning more than $15,000 and for married couples earning more than $30,000.

• **Credit for small businesses.** Beginning in 2002 small firms that set up a new defined benefit or defined contribution plan could claim a tax credit for up to 50 percent of the first $1,000 in administrative and retirement-education expenses incurred during the plan's first three years. Businesses that claimed the credit would not be allowed to also deduct the amount. A small business was defined as one that has no more than 100 employees who receive compensation in excess of $5,000. For the company to claim the credit, the retirement plan had to cover at least one employee who was not among the highest paid.

• **Hardship withdrawals from 401(k)s.** Before enactment, employees who withdrew money from their retirement account because of extreme financial hardship were prohibited in some cases from making any contributions to their account for a year after the payment was made. The bill directed the Treasury Department to immediately reduce that time to six months. It also clarified that all such withdrawals were not eligible to be treated as "rollovers," and were thus subject to tax beginning in 2002.

• **Retirement plans for domestic workers.** A 10 percent excise tax on certain retirement plan contributions not classified as a business or trade expense was lifted effective 2002, removing a disincentive to providing retirement plans for maids, nannies, gardeners, and other domestic workers.

• **Portability.** Employees moving from a job with one type of retirement plan—for example, a 401(k)—to a job with another kind—for instance, a government 457—could transfer their retirement savings to the new account, beginning in 2002. Under prior law savings often could be moved only to the same type of retirement account or to a traditional IRA. In addition, the Treasury secretary was given more leeway to waive rules requiring employees to "roll over" their savings to the new retirement plan within sixty days for the transfer to be tax-free.

• **Vesting.** Rules for pension plans were changed to require that workers be "vested"—or given the right to their employer's contribution to their pension accounts—within three years or in increments of 20 percent for each year beginning with an employee's second year of service. Once a worker is vested, the benefit cannot be taken away if he or she changes jobs. Prior law required vesting within five years or in increments of 20 percent beginning with the employee's third year of service.

• **Limits on defined benefit plan assets.** Employers generally were limited in the amount of contributions to a traditional pension plan that they could deduct if the plan were more than fully funded. In 2001 the level at which contributions could no longer be deducted was 160 percent of current liability. Under the bill, that level was increased to 165 percent in 2002 and 170 percent in 2003; it would be repealed in 2004. Employers still would be unable to claim deductions in excess of the plan's accrued liability minus the value of its assets.

• **Cash balance plans and other pension changes.** Within ninety days of enactment the Treasury secretary was required to issue regulations on the details that companies switching from a traditional defined benefit pension to another plan were required to include in notices to their employees. The bill required that companies issue such a notice "within a reasonable time," although it permitted Treasury to set a more specific deadline. The notice had to describe the benefit reduction caused by the proposed change in such a way that it could be understood by the average plan participant. Officials who failed to distribute such a notice could be fined $100 a day for each participant entitled to the notice, to a maximum of $500,000 a year. In cases of willful neglect, the switch to a new pension plan could be rejected under the Employee Retirement Income Security Act of 1974 (PL 93-406).

The issue came to the forefront after some companies, including IBM, came under public pressure for switching from a traditional pension to a so-called "cash-balance plan." The change put longtime workers at a disadvantage.

• **Repealing benefit limits for certain laborers.** Prior law limited the annual benefits that retirees could receive from multiemployer plans to no more than 100 percent of their average compensation over the three highest-paid years of their career. Such plans often are set up for construction workers and other laborers who work for many companies during their lifetime. Under the bill the limit was repealed in 2002. The change was strongly supported by many of the building-trades unions.

• **Employee Stock Ownership Plans (ESOPs).** Beginning in 2002, employers could deduct from their taxes dividends they paid to employees regardless of whether the employees took the dividend in cash or reinvested it in the company. Prior law allowed deductions only for cash dividends. The Treasury secretary was given the authority to disallow deductions in cases in which the chief purpose of the transaction appeared to be tax evasion.

• **Cashing out.** Under prior law when a worker with no more than $5,000 in vested retirement savings left a company the savings were automatically distributed to him in cash unless the employee elected to roll them over to another savings account. Under the bill employers would automatically transfer distributions of $1,000 to $5,000 to IRAs unless the worker requested the distribution in cash. The Labor secretary was required to issue regulations on this provision within three years.

MISCELLANEOUS PROVISIONS

• **Alaska Native settlement trusts.** Alaska Natives were allowed to transfer money or property to a trust for the purpose of promoting the health, education, and welfare of the beneficiaries and preserving their heritage and culture. Under the bill the trust would be taxed at the lowest personal income tax rate—10 percent.

• **Corporate estimated tax payments.** Payment of corporate quarterly estimated taxes, due Sept. 17, 2001, were deferred until Oct. 1, 2001. Corporations were required to pay only 80 percent of the quarterly estimated taxes due Sept. 15, 2004. The rest was due Oct. 1, 2004. The changes were included to shift federal revenue to years in which the budget surplus might not be sufficient to support that year's tax reductions without tapping into money set aside in the Medicare Part A hospital trust fund.

SUNSET PROVISION

All provisions of the law were due to expire after Dec. 31, 2010.

Economic Stimulus Bill

After fighting to an impasse over legislation to stimulate the economy in 2001, Republicans and Democrats agreed early in 2002 on a scaled-back measure built around unemployment benefits and limited business tax breaks. The bill cleared March 8 and was signed into law by President George W. Bush the following day (HR 3090—PL 107-147).

The measure, which was expected to cost $94 billion through 2007, gave an extra thirteen weeks of unemployment benefits to workers who had exhausted them and provided $43 billion worth of temporary business tax breaks, including an immediate 30 percent deduction of the cost of new equipment purchased through 2003. It also provided tax incentives for rebuilding lower Manhattan, devastated in the Sept. 11, 2001, attacks on the World Trade Center, and temporarily extended a package of narrow business tax provisions, most of which had expired at the end of 2001.

Enactment capped a long debate between and within the two parties over the best way to try to reinvigorate a flagging economy. Republicans promoted a broad package of tax relief for individuals and businesses, while Democrats focused on aid for the jobless and new spending on infrastructure and homeland security.

Even as those approaches were running aground in a bitterly divided Senate a consensus developed on a set of proposals that included extension of unemployment benefits, temporary tax relief for new investment, tax incentives for New York City, and tax relief for money-losing corporations.

Still, House Republicans and Senate Democrats focused for months on expanding the package to include party-defining proposals that had no chance of enactment. As the debate wore on, signs that the economy was recovering undercut the pressure for an economic stimulus.

Finally, with six months of benefits about to expire for workers unemployed since the Sept. 11, 2001, terrorist attacks, House Republicans persuaded their leadership to drop the gamesmanship in favor of a bill that could become law.

All sides declared victory though few found much to savor. "Bingo! Congress passes half a stimulus!" quipped Senate Minority Whip Don Nickles, R-Okla. On the other side of the Capitol, Rep. Jim McDermott, D-Wash., told his colleagues, "I urge everyone to vote for a bad compromise." Sen. John B. Breaux, D-La., who worked for months with other Senate centrists to broker a stimulus package deal, added: "We sort of filibustered our way through the recession, and the argument is not there for it anymore,"

HIGHLIGHTS

The following were the main elements of the new law:

• **Unemployment insurance.** Workers who had exhausted their twenty-six weeks of regular benefits in states that continued to experience unemployment rates of 4 percent or higher would receive an additional thirteen weeks of benefits. Estimated six-year cost: $13.1 billion. (*Unemployment benefit details, p. 573*)

• **Accelerated depreciation.** Businesses could receive an extra 30 percent first-year deduction for equipment purchased on or since Sept. 11, 2001. The provision was good for three years. The business lobby argued that depreciation schedules, which determine the pace at which companies can write off equipment purchases over time, needed updating to reflect the rapid pace of technological innovation. The high-tech community, in particular, lobbied aggressively for the provision. Estimated six-year cost: $59.5 billion.

• **Net operating loss carryback.** The period over which businesses could use net operating losses to offset past tax liability was temporarily extended from two to five years. The provision, meant to aid businesses that suffered losses during the recession, applied to losses in 2001 and 2002. Estimated six-year cost: $4.3 billion.

• **Expired tax breaks.** The bill extended, generally through Dec. 31, 2003, a set of narrow tax breaks, most of which had expired at the end of 2001. The provisions, orphaned for months by the political wrangling over the economic stimulus bill, included tax credits for employers who hired hard-to-place workers, credits for buying electric vehicles, and an extension through 2006 of a provision that allowed U.S. financial services firms or financing subsidiaries operating overseas to defer payment of U.S. taxes on income earned abroad. Estimated six-year cost: $12.8 billion.

• **New York City.** Tax incentives were granted to encourage investment and rebuilding in the area of lower Manhattan affected most directly by the Sept. 11 terrorist attacks. The bill included up to $2,400 in wage credits to firms affected by the attacks, a bonus 30 percent tax deduction for property investment in the area, an increase from $24,000 to $35,000 in deduction for small businesses that owned property in the area, and authorization for up to $17 billion in new or refinanced tax-exempt bonds to rebuild or rehabilitate property in the zone. Estimated six-year cost: $4.8 billion.

2001 ACTION

The Sept. 11 attacks—which destroyed the twin towers of the World Trade Center, closed the New York Stock Exchange for four days of trading, and sent shock waves through the economy—set off an intense debate over what Congress should do to stimulate a recovery. Lawmakers already had approved a $1.4 trillion, ten-year tax cut (PL 107-16) early in 2001. But the finding in November by the National Bureau of Economic Research that a recession had begun in March 2001, combined with the uncertainties growing out of Sept. 11, created new pressure for Congress to act. (*Tax cut, p. 89; terrorist attacks, pp. 229, 236*)

There was substantial agreement on the need to accelerate the rate at which business could write off capital purchases, extend the period during which firms could write off losses against past tax liability, and renew a package of temporary tax provisions. All sides also agreed on the need to extend unemployment insurance and provide $300 rebate checks for those working poor who had not received checks earlier in the year as part of President Bush's tax cut.

But there also were deep partisan differences. Republicans wanted to speed up some individual rate cuts enacted in the Bush tax law and to repeal the corporate alternative minimum tax (AMT), which prevented companies from using tax breaks to avoid any taxes. Democrats insisted that the bill expand eligibility for unemployment insurance, subsidize 75 percent of COBRA continuation health coverage premiums for those who had lost their jobs, and expand Medicaid to cover those ineligible for employer-sponsored COBRA plans. Created under the Consolidated Omnibus Budget Reconciliation Act of 1986 (PL 99-272), COBRA allowed the jobless to maintain coverage through former employers' plans if they paid up to 102 percent of the cost. The ultimate compromise contained none of those items.

An early version of HR 3090 (H Rept 107-251) squeaked through the Republican-controlled House in October 2001 by a vote of 216–214. The bill, estimated to cost $99.5 billion in 2002, consisted of individual and business tax cuts, including retroactive repeal of the corporate AMT, a 30 percent first-year deduction for new business equipment, accelerated depreciation for certain business purchases, and extension of the net operating loss carryback. It also would have reduced capital gains taxes, made the 25 percent tax rate in Bush's 2001 tax law effective in 2002, rather than in 2006, and sent $300 tax rebates ($600 for couples) to the working poor. Democrats tried but failed to delete the AMT repeal, add a one-year extension of unemployment benefits, and provide a 75 percent federal subsidy of COBRA premiums.

In the Senate Democrats pushed an equally partisan, $66.4 billion version of HR 3090 through the Finance Committee, but Republicans were able to block floor action. The bill included a thirteen-week extension of unemployment benefits, a 75 percent COBRA subsidy, a more limited set of business tax breaks, and rebate checks for the working poor, as well as $1.8 billion to rebuild New York City, help for Amtrak, and $6 billion in aid to farmers.

When efforts to produce a compromise failed, the House on Dec. 20 passed a new $89.8 billion stimulus bill (HR 3529) by a vote of 224–193 with nine Democrats and all but two Republicans voting in favor. The bill was built on the consensus provisions, including the thirteen-week extension of unemployment benefits, rebate checks, expansion of the net operating loss carryback, tax benefits for New York City, and renewal of expiring tax provisions. But it lost the support of most Democrats by including vouchers to cover 60 percent of the cost of premiums for COBRA or other health coverage, the immediate reduction of the 27 percent income tax rate to 25 percent, and AMT relief for corporations. The Senate did not take up the bill.

The highly partisan debate in 2001 was one of the first and deepest cracks in the united front Republicans and Democrats had put forth in the immediate wake of the Sept. 11 terrorist attacks. Yet even as they clung unyieldingly to their separate versions of the stimulus package, Republicans and Democrats alike sensed that the stimulus bill would have a minor influence at best on the economy. Many of the provisions would not take effect until the spring of 2002, when experts thought the economy might be well on its way to recovery anyway. Moreover, the government already had taken several steps that economists said should help, including interest rate cuts by the Federal Reserve, Bush's tax cut, and $40 billion in emergency spending enacted in the immediate wake of the terrorist attacks (PL 107-38). *(Emergency spending, p. 56)*

The only piece of the original stimulus bill to be enacted was a bill (HR 2884—PL 107-134) to provide tax relief to families of the victims of the Sept. 11 attacks, the subsequent anthrax mail attacks, and the 1995 Oklahoma City bombing. *(Anthrax scare, p. 712)*

2002 ACTION

Nonetheless, in the early weeks of 2002 Democrats and Republicans resumed what they all recognized as an exercise in futility. Senate Majority Leader Tom Daschle, D-S.D., brought a revised plan to the floor the week of Jan. 21 that included the thirteen-week extension of jobless worker benefits, the $300 rebate, a 30 percent first-year deduction for the cost of new business equipment, and a plan to send federal money to states to help them pay for Medicaid. GOP conservatives said the measure was far too limited, and many questioned whether it was worth the trouble. "At some point, you have to decide: Can we do this, and is it worth having?" said Minority Leader Trent Lott, R-Miss.

Daschle pulled the plug on the bill Feb. 6, after both sides fell short of the sixty votes needed to overcome procedural hurdles. Democrats failed 56–39 to invoke cloture, or limit debate, on their plan. Republicans failed 48–47 to move for-

ward on an $89 billion plan that mirrored the bill passed by the House in December 2001. At that point senators of both parties agreed to give up on an economic stimulus bill. Instead the Senate passed by voice vote a stripped-down bill (HR 622) containing only the thirteen-week extension of unemployment benefits.

Despite private pleas from Senate GOP leaders, the House voted 225–199 on Feb. 14 to send HR 622 back to the Senate after substituting a text nearly identical to the December House-passed stimulus measure. More than half of the fiscal 2002 cost of the $80.9 billion House bill was for business tax breaks.

Senate Republicans were not impressed. The same day they joined with Democrats to agree by voice vote to send HR 3090 back to the House—after stripping out the stimulus measure and substituting the text of HR 622, their unemployment extension.

After a weeklong congressional recess House GOP leaders decided their next move would be to advance a bill that combined a thirteen-week extension of unemployment benefits with a health care tax credit for the unemployed. They planned to bring up the bill under suspension of the rules, which required a two-thirds majority and allowed no amendments. The bill would fail, but not before it put Democrats, who vehemently opposed the tax credit approach for health insurance, in a bind.

But with workers who lost their jobs after Sept. 11 about to exhaust their six months of regular benefits, rank-and-file Republicans were losing patience. At a meeting March 6 House Republicans called on their leaders to put together a consensus bill that could pass the Senate. The tax cuts were narrowed to those with wide support. Gone were the individual cuts and corporate AMT repeal pushed by the Republicans. Gone, too, was the Democrats' plan to subsidize health care insurance for the unemployed. The House passed the bill March 7 on a 417–3 vote. The Senate cleared it the next day 85–9.

Permanent Tax Cuts

House Republicans passed a series of bills in the first half of 2002 aimed at making various pieces of President George W. Bush's signature 2001 tax law permanent. The offensive—dubbed the "flaming arrow strategy" by proponents—largely was ignored by the Democratic-controlled Senate, but it gave Republicans a chance to showcase their tax policies in an election year and to draw a clear distinction between themselves and most Democrats.

In an early test the House voted 235–218 on Feb. 6 to support a nonbinding resolution (H Con Res 312) stating that the tax cuts should not expire in 2010 as specified in the law. The House subsequently passed bills to make the tax cuts permanent by repealing the expiration date on the estate tax repeal, marriage tax breaks, pension incentives, and other provisions.

The expiration, or sunset, provision was the price Republicans and their newly elected president had paid to get Bush's $1.4 trillion, ten-year tax cut (PL 107-16) through Congress in May 2001. To keep costs within limits set in the fiscal 2002 budget resolution (H Con Res 83), and to satisfy Senate budget rules that disqualified provisions on a reconciliation bill that would reduce revenues for more than ten years, all provisions were set to expire Dec. 31, 2010. After that date, the tax code would revert to previous law.

Many Republicans hoped that in 2002 they could make the cuts permanent, a goal that Bush reaffirmed in his Jan. 29 State of the Union speech and assumed in his fiscal 2003 budget. But changed circumstances made that an uphill battle. The peace, prosperity, and budget surpluses of early 2001 had given way to the war on terrorism, a sagging economy, and a return to budget deficits.

Republicans said the economic effects of the Sept. 11, 2001, terrorist attacks and the downturn in the economy that began in mid-2000 were to blame for renewed deficits, and they argued that further tax relief would encourage spending and investment. Democratic leaders pointed to Bush's tax cuts as the chief culprit. Some, including Sen. Edward M. Kennedy, D-Mass., went further, calling for a delay or even a repeal of some of Bush's cuts.

REPEAL OF SUNSET PROVISION

On April 18 the House voted 229–198 to make Bush's tax cuts permanent. The vehicle was a Senate-passed bill (HR 586) aimed at expanding a tax credit for foster care payments. The House replaced those provisions with a proposal to repeal the sunset date for, among other provisions, the reductions in individual marginal rates, the repeal of the estate tax, the increase in the child tax credit, and the increase in the standard deduction for married couples. The Joint Committee on Taxation, Congress's final authority on the cost of tax bills, estimated the price tag at $372.8 billion for 2002 to 2012.

"This is a vote between the parties that is a philosophical difference," Thomas M. Davis III of Virginia, chair of the National Republican Congressional Committee, said April 18. "That's why we have campaigns: to fight over this." "Let me assure you that this vote is going to be the subject of a lot of campaigns for the House this fall," said Minority Leader Richard A. Gephardt, D-Mo. "We intend to raise this vote as the vote on whether or not you want to keep Social Security strong, or whether you don't care about Social Security." Nine Democrats backed the bill, as opposed to twenty-eight who had voted for the 2001 overhaul.

ESTATE TAX REPEAL

On June 6 the House endorsed a permanent repeal of the estate tax (HR 2143) on a bipartisan 256–171 vote. Joint Tax estimated the bill's cost in 2011–2012 at $80.7 billion.

Republicans viewed the estate tax repeal as the portion of the 2001 law most worth fighting for. Not only did it appeal to

their political base but it also had important Democratic support. While the repeal affected only a relatively small number of taxpayers—the majority of estates, those valued at less than $675,000, were exempt from taxation even before the 2001 law—Republicans successfully cast the debate as a fight to preserve family farms and family-controlled small businesses. That made the repeal attractive in farm states where several Democratic senators were in tight reelection races.

But the momentum behind the legislation collapsed a week later in the Senate. Phil Gramm, R-Texas, tried to waive budget rules in order to get a vote on a permanent repeal but failed on a 54–44 vote. While Gramm's supporters had a majority, they were short of the sixty votes required to waive the point of order. Majority Leader Tom Daschle, D-S.D., said the tally fulfilled a commitment he had made to allow a vote on the estate tax repeal in June and that he planned to let it stand as the Senate's final word on the tax cut permanency question for the year.

MARRIAGE TAX BREAKS

On June 13 the House voted 271–142 to pass legislation (HR 4019) to make the tax breaks for married couples permanent. Sixty Democrats voted for the bill, as did every Republican who voted.

The provisions in question gradually increased the standard deduction for married couples to twice that for individuals and changed the portion of their income subject to the 15 percent rate to double that of a single person. By 2008 a married couple would be able to earn $3,000 more than a single person and still qualify for the earned-income tax credit. Extending those provisions for two years, through 2012, would cost an additional $41.9 billion, according to the Joint Tax Committee.

PENSION INCENTIVES

On June 21 the House voted to remove the expiration date on tax incentives for pension and retirement contributions contained in the 2001 law. The vote on the bill (HR 4931) was 308–70.

The incentives included increased contribution limits for Individual Retirement Accounts and elective deferral plans such as 401(k)s; "catch-up" contributions for individuals age fifty and older; modifications to rollover rules for workers who moved their pension savings when changing jobs; faster vesting of pension plans; and modifications to pension security, enforcement and small-business regulations.

ADOPTION, HOLOCAUST SURVIVORS

On June 4 the House voted to make permanent two other popular pieces of the 2001 tax law. One of the bills (HR 4800) would have repealed the sunset on provisions that increased the adoption tax credit from $5,000 ($6,000 for children with special needs) to $10,000 and that doubled to $10,000 the amount an employer could deduct for employee-adoption assistance. The second (HR 4823) was to retain an income exclusion for Holocaust restitution payments. The bills passed on votes of 391–1 and 392–1, respectively, with deficit hawk Charles W. Stenholm, D-Texas, casting the only "nay" votes.

Corporate Inversions and Taxes

In the wake of a wave of corporate scandals many members of Congress were eager to show they were cracking down on corporate misbehavior. Several bills targeted U.S. companies that sought to minimize their U.S. tax bill by reincorporating in places such as Bermuda or the Cayman Islands where there was little or no taxation on businesses. Only one relatively weak provision was enacted, however: The law (PL 107-296) creating the Department of Homeland Security prohibited the awarding of some federal contracts to such companies. Stronger changes were included in the corporate tax bill passed in 2004. *(Corporate accounting scandal, pp. 123, 130; 2004 corporate tax bill, p. 115)*

The reincorporation practice was known as corporate inversion because the company first created an offshore subsidiary—often nothing more than a post office box—and then inverted its corporate structure by making the subsidiary the parent. The location of the company's actual operations remained unchanged with most employees still working in the United States.

Conservatives and some business trade groups, including the U.S. Chamber of Commerce, fought efforts to curb the practice, arguing that the best way to avoid corporate expatriation was to cut corporate taxes in the United States.

In June the Senate Finance Committee approved two bills (S 2119, S 2498) addressing the problem, but neither was brought to the floor. In July House Ways and Means Committee Chair Bill Thomas, R-Calif., introduced a bill to overhaul the tax treatment of income earned abroad (HR 5095) that sought to strip the advantages of registering a headquarters overseas. The bill was widely opposed and never put before the committee.

Democratic lawmakers found some success with a less direct approach: a push to deny federal contracts to companies that moved their headquarters offshore. On July 26 the House voted 318–110 to attach such a ban to the initial House homeland security bill (HR 5005).

On Sept. 5 Sen. Paul Wellstone, D-Minn., won voice vote adoption of a similar amendment to the Senate version of the homeland bill. But in final negotiations language was added allowing the Homeland Security Department secretary to waive the restriction. Three moderate Senate Republicans said they had assurances the waiver would be revisited in 2003. Stronger anti-inversion legislation was written in the fall but went no further. Thomas included a retroactive moratorium on offshore relocations in a draft investor tax cut package, but opposition from Republican leaders effectively scuttled the bill. Senate Finance Committee Chairman Max Baucus, D-Mont., proposed ending the tax breaks for inversions to help offset the cost of a small-business tax cut, but a lack of consensus doomed his package.

In November the Treasury Department proposed requiring companies to disclose the full costs and tax consequences of inversion transactions to shareholders.

Investor Tax Breaks

House Republican leaders were hoping in October 2002 to pass a pre-election package of tax breaks aimed at helping the 84 million Americans whose investments in stocks and mutual funds had suffered losses during the continuing decline in the stock market. The tax benefits would have relaxed retirement savings rules and increased the immediate write-off for stock market losses. But intraparty disputes over provisions that Ways and Means Committee Chair Bill Thomas, R-Calif., tried to add to the package prompted GOP leaders to put off further action until 2003.

Thomas had drafted the bills reluctantly under instructions from the top GOP leaders in the House but insisted that they go through his committee. The Ways and Means Committee approved two investor-friendly tax bills on party-line votes on Oct. 8. One (HR 1619—H Rept 107-734) would have raised to $8,250, from $3,000, the amount of capital losses taxpayers could deduct each year from ordinary income. The other (HR 5558—H Rept 107-733) would have increased the amount people could contribute tax-free to Individual Retirement Accounts, 401(k)s, and other retirement savings accounts, while gradually increasing to 70½ the age at which retirees were required to make annual withdrawals.

The leadership planned to combine the bills into a $65 billion, ten-year package and win passage before the midterm elections. The proposals had wide backing among Republicans. Democrats on the committee opposed the tax breaks, arguing that their combined cost would worsen the deficit and would benefit rich investors more than middle-income ones. But many Democrats supported some elements of the bills, particularly the retirement savings breaks.

But just before the measure was to go to the floor Thomas defied the leadership and inserted several controversial provisions, including small business tax cuts, a limited extension of unemployment benefits, and a proposal to retroactively penalize U.S. companies that relocated their headquarters to Bermuda or other offshore locations in order to reduce their federal income taxes. The provisions drew objections from rank-and-file Republicans, as well as the leadership, killing the tax package for the year.

Thomas's move was carefully calculated. With the White House ambivalent on new tax cuts and the Senate poised to kill the bill, he saw the effort as a waste of time and preferred laying down a marker for legislation to come in the 108th Congress, when more comprehensive solutions to corporate tax dodging and foreign tax disputes could be addressed.

2003–2004

The 108th Congress moved closer to giving President George W. Bush his long-stated wish to make the massive personal income tax cuts of 2001 permanent. It voted in 2003 to accelerate three of the most popular cuts and then voted a year later to effectively extend the accelerated cuts through 2010. In addition to speeding up the phase-in of lower income tax brackets, relief from the so-called marriage penalty, and increases in the child tax credit, the 2003 legislation also reduced personal income taxes on dividends and capital gains. Separate legislation approved in 2004 gave corporations the largest tax breaks they had received since 1986.

The tax cut bills, which totaled an estimated $476 billion in lost revenue over ten years, were enacted despite record deficits in the federal budget in 2003 and 2004. Democrats and some fiscal conservatives in the Republican Party complained that the tax cuts were irresponsible, especially at a time when the United States was engaged in military operations in Iraq and Afghanistan and faced untold expenses in fighting a global war on terror and providing homeland security. Democrats also argued that the personal tax relief measures gave too much benefit to the wealthy and not enough to the poor. But the measures also gave relief to the middle class, the group on which both parties were focusing election-year appeals. For many Democratic lawmakers principles about balancing the budget gave way to the politics of winning reelection.

The corporate tax bill was an even more blatant political exercise as members sought to attract votes and campaign contributions from business constituents. A measure intended to replace a yearly $45 billion business subsidy deemed illegal by the World Trade Organization ballooned into a $137 billion, ten-year measure filled with tax breaks for narrow interests from movies to restaurants to bows and arrows and for many individual companies. One investment firm dubbed the bill the "No Lobbyist Left Behind" act, a parody of Bush's education program "No Child Left Behind." Although Congress also voted to close some loopholes and curb some common tax avoidance practices in order to offset the costs of the tax breaks, many observers predicted that the new law would quickly create new loopholes and tax abuses. President Bush, who had signed the other tax cut bills into law amid great ceremony, signed this one in private, on the campaign trail, with none of the usual fanfare.

2003 Tax Cuts

Congress cleared a bill in May 2003 that provided the third-deepest tax cut in U.S. history and the second substantial reduction since President George W. Bush took office. Although lawmakers reduced and reworked Bush's initial request, the law still was seen as a major win for the president, who signed it at a White House ceremony May 28 (HR 2—PL 108-27).

Officially titled the Jobs and Growth Tax Relief Reconciliation Act of 2003, the measure reflected long-standing Republican tax priorities. It provided an estimated $330 billion in tax cuts over eleven years, largely by accelerating reductions in individual rates that were part of Bush's huge 2001 tax reduction, allowing faster write-offs for business investment, and lowering taxes on dividends and capital gains. To gain the support of key Senate moderates it also contained $20 billion in federal aid to help states cope with severe financial problems.

Bush originally proposed a far bigger tax cut package as part of his budget request for fiscal 2004. The Joint Committee on Taxation, Congress's tax scorekeeper, estimated the package would cost $725.7 billion over eleven years. The centerpiece of Bush's plan—and the most expensive element by far—was a $396 billion proposal to eliminate individual taxes on corporate dividends.

The initial fight in Congress over the size of the tax cut occurred as part of the debate on the fiscal 2004 budget resolution (H Con Res 95). The budget resolution determined the amount of any tax package that could go into a reconciliation bill, thereby granting special protection under Senate rules. Under those rules a reconciliation bill was not subject to a filibuster, which meant Republicans could pass it by a simple majority rather than assembling a sixty-vote margin needed under cloture rules to halt unlimited debate. Stopping a filibuster was always difficult in the Senate, but was a near impossibility in 2003 given the GOP's narrow control of the chamber in the 108th Congress. *(Fiscal 2004 budget resolution, p. 67)*

The House version of the budget allowed a reconciliation bill that included the full $726 billion stimulus plan, but Senate moderates succeeded in cutting that to $350 billion. House and Senate negotiators compromised on a $550 billion tax package, which the House accepted. But just before the Senate voted, Finance Committee Chair Charles E. Grassley, R-Iowa, announced a deal to get the support of two crucial moderate Republicans. "At the end of the day," he said, "the tax cut side of the growth package will not exceed $350 billion."

Enraged by what they considered betrayal by their Senate colleagues, House GOP leaders pressed ahead, passing a $550 billion tax-cutting reconciliation bill on May 9. Drafted by Ways and Means Committee Chair Bill Thomas, R-Calif., the measure abandoned Bush's call to end taxes on dividends in favor of a reduced tax rate for both dividends and capital gains.

To keep Senate moderates on board Grassley drafted a $350 billion reconciliation bill that included $20 billion in spending for states. To stay within the $350 billion limit he included a lengthy list of tax increases and other offsets that sparked quick opposition from business lobbyists. As passed by the Senate May 15 the bill called for reducing taxes on dividends in 2003 and eliminating them in 2004.

After Senate passage the White House stepped in to head off a lengthy and divisive conference with a call for lawmakers to send the bill to Bush by Memorial Day. House and Senate negotiators completed their work May 22. The House adopted the conference report early May 23, the Friday before the Memorial Day recess, with the help of just seven Democrats. A few hours later the deal squeaked through the Senate on Vice President Dick Cheney's tie-breaking vote.

The final tax bill included Thomas's alternative to Bush's dividend tax plan—a new 15 percent top rate on both dividends and capital gains that enjoyed the support of many business groups. The final compromise also dropped the Senate's revenue-raising offsets opposed by business lobbyists and House Republicans, substituting expiration dates as early as the end of 2004. Senate GOP moderates won $20 billion for state aid while preventing the net cost of the package from exceeding $350 billion.

Even after enactment the size of the tax cut was a matter of continuing controversy. Congress's Joint Committee on Taxation scored the cost at $350 billion, but Republicans already were arguing that many of the tax cuts should become permanent, prompting Democrats to charge that sunset provisions in the law were gimmicks to conceal the true impact on the deficit. The Center on Budget and Policy Priorities, a liberal think tank, argued that if the provisions were made permanent the eleven-year cost could grow to at least $670 billion and possibly more than $1 trillion.

HIGHLIGHTS

The following are highlights of the new tax law:

• **Dividends and capital gains.** A new, 15 percent tax rate for dividends and capital gains, beginning in 2003. For low-income taxpayers the rate was 5 percent, dropping to zero in 2008. The new rates were a dramatic change from prior law, which treated dividends as ordinary income with taxes as high as 38.6 percent; the top capital gains rate had been 20 percent. The changes were set to expire after 2008. The estimated eleven-year cost was $148.1 billion.

• **Individual tax rates.** Quicker reduction of individual income tax rates. The law revised the individual income tax brackets to 10, 15, 25, 28, 33, and 35 percent, beginning in 2003 and expiring after 2010. Under the 2001 tax law, those rates would not have been fully phased in until 2006. Without the new law, the 2003 rates would have been 10, 15, 27, 30, 35 and 38.6 percent.

• The new law also expanded the previous 10 percent tax bracket to cover the first $7,000 in taxable income for individuals (up from $6,000 under existing law) and the first $14,000 for couples (up from $12,000) in 2003 and 2004. Under the 2001 tax reduction those rates would not have started until 2008. The estimated cost of the changes in individual rates was $86.1 billion.

• **AMT.** An increase in the amount of income exempt under the alternative minimum tax (AMT), a tax system that prevented people from avoiding taxation through extensive use of deductions and other tax breaks. The law increased the exemption in 2003 and 2004 to $40,250 for single taxpayers (a $4,500 increase) and to $58,000 for joint filers (a $9,000 increase). Without the larger exemption the lower individual taxes that resulted from the 2001 tax law could have forced more people to pay the AMT. The estimated eleven-year cost was $17.8 billion.

• **Married couples.** Quicker increases in benefits for married couples filing jointly. The new law increased the standard deduction and broadened the 15 percent bracket for couples to twice those for singles in 2003 and 2004. The estimated eleven-year cost was $35.1 billion.

• **Child tax credit.** An increase in the per-child tax credit. In 2003 and 2004 the credit rose to $1,000 from $600 per year for each child under age seventeen. The estimated eleven-year cost was $32.5 billion.

• **Business tax cuts.** Increased deductions for small business investments in equipment. Under prior law businesses that purchased up to $200,000 in equipment could deduct up to $25,000 of the cost in the first year. The new law increased the first-year deduction in 2003 to $100,000 for businesses that bought up to $400,000 in equipment. In 2004 and 2005 the limits would be indexed for inflation; they would expire after 2005. The estimated eleven-year cost was $952 million.

• In addition, the law increased a first-year "bonus" deduction for certain business purchases to 50 percent from 30 percent under prior law. The bonus was only good for purchases made before Jan. 1, 2005. The estimated eleven-year cost was $9.2 billion.

• **State aid.** Temporary fiscal relief to the states. The law provided for $10 billion to be used for essential government services and $10 billion to help with Medicaid costs.

BACKGROUND

The 2003 bill was the third tax cut enacted since Bush came into office. The first and biggest of the three was the $1.4 trillion tax law (PL 107-16) enacted in June 2001. The central features were a reduction in individual income tax rates, benefits for married couples aimed at eliminating the so-called marriage penalty, a phase-out of the estate tax, and expansion of the child tax credit. To keep the bill's cost within limits set by the fiscal 2002 budget resolution, all the provisions were set to expire by the end of 2010. The tax cut was the second largest in U.S. history, exceeded only by President Ronald Reagan's 1981 tax package (PL 97-34), which cost $1.5 trillion in current dollars. *(Congress and the Nation, Vol. VI, p. 65; 2001 tax cut, p. 89)*

Unable to agree on a broad follow-up plan to stimulate the economy Congress in March 2002 cleared a $94 billion bill (PL 107-147) that combined a $13.1 billion extension of federal unemployment benefits with several tax cuts for businesses. The central feature was an accelerated depreciation provision that allowed businesses to deduct an extra 30 percent in the first year for equipment purchased after Sept. 11, 2001. *(Economic stimulus, p. 100)*

In January 2003 Bush began campaigning for a new round of tax cuts, this time focused on eliminating individual income taxes on corporate dividends. Under existing law corporate income was taxed twice: once under the corporate income tax and again when the money was received by an investor as dividends. Bush's plan intended not only to end the double taxation, but also to encourage companies to pay corporate taxes in the first place by limiting the tax-free status to dividends paid from after-tax corporate income.

Bush's stimulus plan was aimed primarily at cutting individual taxes to spur spending and investment. The benefits for business were mostly indirect. The plan's only direct business tax break was the relatively modest increase in write-offs for small businesses. A similar provision had been dropped during the negotiations that led to the 2001 law.

HOUSE ACTION

The House Ways and Means Committee approved its $550 billion tax-cut bill (HR 2—H Rept 108-94) by a vote of 24–15 on May 6. The committee bill replaced Bush's call for zero taxes on dividends with a reduction in taxes on both dividends and capital gains and added other tax cuts for business.

Despite a vigorous White House lobbying campaign, Thomas declared that Bush's dividend proposal could not be enacted. Democrats pointed to it as a bonanza for the wealthy; moderate Republicans worried about the effect on the deficit, and about unintended harm to local government bonds and to the tax treatment for investors in low-income housing and wind energy. The business community had never been enthusiastic about the plan, and many committee members wanted to make room in the bill for other tax cut priorities.

Thomas's proposal to reduce taxes on profits gained from selling stock and other assets appealed to a range of investors from Silicon Valley startups that seldom paid dividends to investors in stocks, real estate, and timber. The plan drew quick but reluctant support from the White House. "It's a big step in the right direction," said Treasury secretary John W. Snow.

Thomas also added two proposals not in Bush's budget. The first would allow businesses to deduct 50 percent in the first year for the cost of buying certain property put in service by Jan. 1, 2006. The 2002 law contained a 30 percent "bonus deduction" in the first year for equipment placed in service before Jan. 1, 2005. The second new provision would allow businesses to use a net operating loss to reduce taxes going back five years instead of two as under existing law. The estimated eleven-year costs were $21.5 billion and $14.6 billion, respectively.

The House passed Thomas's bill 222–203 on May 9.

The rule for floor debate allowed no amendments. Attempts by Democrats to send the bill back to committee with instructions for changes failed. Charles B. Rangel, D-N.Y., lost on a procedural vote when he tried to require that the bill be rewritten as a $177 billion tax package with smaller breaks for individuals and businesses, an extension of unemployment benefits, and grants to states to help with their budget crises. The House agreed 222–202 that the amendment was not germane. A Democratic attempt to instruct Ways and Means to add language stating that the provisions would not take effect until there was a balanced budget failed 202–218.

SENATE ACTION

The Senate Finance Committee approved its version of the bill (S 2) by a vote of 12–9 on May 8. To resolve a procedural snafu it moved the text to a new bill (S 1054), which included more special tax breaks and more offsets, and approved that measure by the same vote May 13.

The chief difference from the House-passed version was the Senate committee's treatment of dividends and capital gains. The Senate version provided for a partial exclusion from taxation of dividends that individuals received from both domestic and foreign corporations. The first $500 plus 10 percent of additional dividend income would be tax-free beginning in 2004. The extra amount would climb to 20 percent in 2008 through 2012. Capital gains were not covered. The estimated cost was $81.1 billion over ten years.

Many of the other tax cuts in the Senate bill were similar to those in the House bill, but the bill also called for $20 billion in assistance to states and more than $90 billion in offsetting tax increases needed to keep the package within the $350 billion limit. Many of the proposed offsets raised concerns in the business community and among Republicans. Business lobbyists reacted quickly to the specter of tax increases under Grassley's bill. The Tax Relief Coalition, a group made up of major trade associations and local chambers of commerce, broke with the White House to work against the Senate offsets.

The proposal for aid to the states was a placeholder with few details. Conservative Republicans, including House GOP leaders, said states had contributed to their own fiscal crises by not showing more restraint during the good times, but Grassley said the aid was necessary to win support from moderates such as Susan Collins, R-Maine, and Ben Nelson, D-Neb. The moderates, along with Democratic leaders, had been pushing hard for federal aid to help the states avoid deep cuts in human services.

The Senate narrowly passed the bill May 15, after substituting the amended text of S 1054. The vote was 51–49 with three Senate Democrats—Nelson of Nebraska, Evan Bayh of Indiana, and Zell Miller of Georgia—joining forty-eight Republicans to support the measure. Three Republicans—John McCain of Arizona, Lincoln Chafee of Rhode Island, and

Olympia J. Snowe of Maine—joined the remaining forty-five Democrats in opposing the bill.

Heavy White House lobbying of Senate moderates—including visits by Bush to stump for his proposal in Nebraska on May 12 and Indiana the following day—salvaged the president's zero tax plan for dividends. An amendment by Budget Committee Chair Don Nickles, R-Okla., to replace the committee's plan with a proposal to reduce individual income taxes on corporate dividends by 50 percent in 2003 and eliminate them in 2004 through 2006 was adopted 50–50 with Vice President Cheney breaking the tie. Nelson backed the amendment; Bayh did not. Although the Senate made several other changes to the committee bill, the provision on dividends was by far the most important.

FINAL ACTION

Spurred by the president to put aside their deepening differences and send him a bill by Memorial Day, House and Senate Republicans grudgingly closed ranks behind a $350 billion economic stimulus package that allowed Bush and each of the principal factions within the GOP to claim some measure of success. The key to the deal was language phasing in tax reductions and setting early expiration dates in order to preserve the cuts in the more expensive House bill under the $350 billion ceiling set by the more closely divided Senate.

In pushing for a rapid conclusion to the conference Bush agreed to live with the Senate's $350 billion ceiling on the bill's net cost and urged negotiators to work out their other differences. That initially appeared to be a defeat for Thomas and the House. But the House bill appeared a better bet for quick action because it enjoyed broad support both in Congress and among business lobbyists. The Senate bill, a product of Grassley's agreement with the moderates, had deeply divided the GOP and was opposed by business lobbyists because of its revenue-raising offsets.

Thomas argued that if the House accepted a smaller tax bill it should get a dominant role in determining the bill's content. In a surprising turnabout Bush agreed, abandoning the dividend exclusion and embracing Thomas's proposal for a combined capital gains and dividend tax reduction. The plan had strong support in the House where lawmakers concluded it would benefit investors in virtually all companies. Rural lawmakers liked it because it would save their constituents money on sales of livestock, timber, land, and small businesses, including hair salons and restaurants.

Grassley, who had believed that the final deal would include a limited version of Bush's dividend plan, reacted angrily. "I presume that a lot of my colleagues feel somewhat undercut by the White House just for the sake of getting something done this week," he told reporters. With the tax-writing chairs at odds, Cheney stepped in to broker a deal with pivotal GOP senator George V. Voinovich of Ohio to fit both the tax cuts and additional spending under the $350 billion ceiling by moving up the expiration date of the capital gains and dividend tax cut from 2009 to 2008, saving $29 billion.

The House adopted the conference report (H Rept 108-126) before dawn on May 23 by a **key vote of 231–200 (R 224–1; D 7–198; I 0–1).** The Senate cleared the bill later that morning when Cheney cast the deciding vote after the Senate deadlocked 50–50. *(2003 key votes, p. 837)*

Bush pronounced himself happy with the result, exhibiting no annoyance that the bottom line gave him about half of his original request. Bush had initially derided the $350 billion consensus forming in Congress as a "little bitty" amount inadequate to stimulate a sluggish economy. But he was ready to thank lawmakers for their work when he visited Capitol Hill on May 22 in advance of the final votes.

MAJOR PROVISIONS

The following are the principal provisions of the Jobs and Growth Tax Relief Reconciliation Act of 2003 (PL 108-27) signed May 8, 2003.

Dividends

Prior to enactment of the law stock dividends received by individuals were taxed as ordinary income at rates up to the existing top marginal rate of 38.6 percent. The new law treated these dividends as capital gains. Under the new law:

• **Tax rate.** Dividends received by individuals were taxed at the new capital gains rate of 15 percent. For low-income taxpayers in the 10 percent and 15 percent tax brackets (individuals earning $28,400 or less a year), the new tax rate on dividends was 5 percent through 2007 and zero in 2008. The new rates were retroactive to Jan. 1, 2003.

• **Sunset.** The dividend provisions were set to expire at the end of 2008, after which dividends would again be taxed at individual income tax rates.

• **Qualified dividends.** The new rates applied to stocks held for sixty days before dividends were issued. The rates applied to dividends received by individuals from domestic and qualified foreign corporations. A qualified foreign corporation had to be based in a country that had a tax treaty with the United States or had its stock traded on a U.S. stock exchange. Dividends from companies based in Barbados, which did have a tax treaty with the United States, were specifically excluded and did not qualify for the new rates.

• **Mutual fund distributions.** Only the dividends from stocks held by the mutual fund could be passed on to fund shareholders at the 15 percent rate. The rate did not apply to mutual fund distributions of income from other sources such as interest and short-term capital gains.

• **Real estate.** Dividends from real estate investment trusts, or REITs, were not eligible for the new rates, for the most part because REITs did not pay corporate income taxes and distributed nearly all of their income to shareholders.

Capital Gains

Prior to enactment capital gains on assets held for more than one year but less than five years were taxed at 20 percent. Individuals in the 10 percent and 15 percent tax brackets paid a 10 percent rate. Capital gains on assets held for more than five years were generally taxed at 18 percent (8 percent for low-income investors). Capital gains assets held for one year or less were considered short-term gains and taxed as regular income.

- **Tax rate.** The 20 percent and 18 percent rates on assets held more than one year were reduced to 15 percent for most investors. For those in the 10 percent and 15 percent tax brackets, the capital gains rate was reduced to 5 percent through 2007 and eliminated in 2008.

- **Sunset.** The new rates were due to expire at the end of 2008. Capital gains would return to the rates in effect under prior law starting in 2009.

- **Limits.** The new rates applied to gains realized from sales on or after May 6, 2003. Most assets, from stocks and bonds to real estate and mutual funds, were eligible for the new rates. Certain categories of assets, such as collectibles, which were taxed above 20 percent, would continue to be taxed at those higher rates. The law did not change the treatment of capital gains on stocks held less than a year.

Individual Income Taxes

The new law accelerated or extended key provisions of the 2001 tax law affecting income taxes paid by individuals and couples. Under the new law:

- **Top four brackets.** Reductions in the top marginal tax rate that had been scheduled to take place in 2004 and 2006 were fully implemented in 2003 and made retroactive to the beginning of the year. The four new top tax brackets were 25 percent, 28 percent, 33 percent and 35 percent. The rates still were scheduled to expire in 2010 as provided under the 2001 law.

- **10 percent bracket.** The 10 percent tax bracket—created in 2001 to cover the first $6,000 of individual income ($12,000 for married couples filing jointly)—was temporarily expanded. Under the 2001 law the amount of income taxed at 10 percent had been scheduled to increase to $7,000 for individuals ($14,000 for married couples filing jointly) in 2008 with adjustments for inflation annually after 2008. The new law put the increases expected in 2008 in place for two years beginning in 2003. In 2003 the 10 percent tax bracket applied to the first $7,000 of income for individuals ($14,000 for married couples). In 2004 the increased amounts were to be indexed for inflation. In 2005 the income amounts for the 10 percent tax bracket were scheduled to revert to prior law— $6,000 for individuals and $12,000 for married couples.

- **Married couples.** Provisions of the 2001 law intended to benefit married couples were temporarily accelerated. The 2003 tax law increased the basic standard deduction for married couples filing jointly to twice that of single filers for 2003 and 2004. In 2005 the deduction would revert to the level provided for in the 2001 law—174 percent of the standard deduction for single filers. The measure also increased the upper limit of the 15 percent tax bracket for married couples filing jointly to twice that of single filers for the tax

years 2003 and 2004. In 2005 the 15 percent tax bracket would revert to the size provided for in the 2001 law—180 percent of the upper limit for single individuals.

- **Child tax credit.** The per-child tax credit for qualifying children under age 17 was increased from $600 to $1,000 in 2003 and 2004. Under the 2001 law the tax credit would not have reached $1,000 until 2010. For 2003 the $400-per-child increase was paid in advance—similar to the "rebate checks" issued in 2001—using information provided on 2002 tax returns. The remaining $600 could be claimed on 2003 tax returns. In 2005 the credit would revert to $700, the level provided under the 2001 law.

- **Alternative minimum tax.** An expiring provision that increased the amount of income exempt from the alternative minimum tax was extended for two years.

Created in 1969 (PL 91-172) and modified through the years, the AMT was a parallel tax system designed to ensure that wealthy individuals could not wipe out their entire tax liability by claiming a large number of deductions, exemptions, and credits. Taxpayers subject to the AMT had to pay the amount they owed under the regular income tax schedule or the AMT, whichever was higher. Most taxpayers never had to calculate their taxes under the alternative system because their income was below a specified threshold. However, because the thresholds were not adjusted annually for inflation, more and more middle-income taxpayers were becoming subject to the AMT.

The 2001 tax law temporarily increased the amount of exempt income by $2,000 for single taxpayers and $4,000 for married couples filing jointly. The resulting thresholds— $35,750 for individuals and $49,000 for couples—were scheduled to expire at the end of 2004. The 2003 tax law temporarily increased the exemption for 2003 and 2004 to $40,250 for individual taxpayers and $58,000 for married couples. In 2005 the AMT exemption would revert to the levels provided for before the passage of the 2001 tax law: $33,750 for a single filer and $45,000 for married couples filing jointly.

Business Tax Breaks

- **Bonus depreciation.** The law temporarily increased the amount that a business could deduct in the first year for the cost of certain capital assets or property purchased after Sept. 11, 2001. Under a tax law enacted in 2002 (PL 107-147) companies could deduct an extra 30 percent of the cost of qualified capital assets or property that generally had a recovery period of twenty years or less. This depreciation "bonus," which applied to property purchased through the end of 2004, was in addition to regular annual depreciation deductions allowed under the modified accelerated cost recovery system. The new law increased the bonus deduction to 50 percent for property purchased after May 5, 2003, and before the end of 2004.

- **Small business expensing.** The new law temporarily increased the upfront deduction that a small business could take for newly purchased equipment. Under "Section 179" expensing rules, a small business could deduct up to $25,000 of the cost of business equipment the year it was purchased, instead of depreciating it over several years. The new law increased the deduction to $100,000 in 2003. Under prior law the full deduction was available for purchases of $200,000 or less and was reduced for every dollar above that amount. The new law raised the threshold at which the deduction was phased out to $400,000 for 2003. Both amounts were to be indexed for inflation in 2004 and 2005. Off-the-shelf computer software was added to the list of equipment that qualified for the deduction. As under prior law, the amount expensed could not exceed the business's taxable income for the year, but unused amounts could be carried forward to future tax years. Real estate and building structures did not qualify.

Aid to States

The new law provided $20 billion over two years beginning in 2003 in aid to the states. Half the money was earmarked for state-run Medicaid programs. The other $10 billion was for a general relief fund to be used by states for government services in 2003 and 2004.

Military Tax Breaks

After repeated false starts Congress cleared legislation in November 2003 providing tax breaks and related benefits for members of the military and their families. President George W. Bush signed the bill Nov. 11 (HR 3365—PL 108-121).

The core provisions—special tax treatment for travel expenses, death benefits, and capital gains from home sales—were not controversial, particularly at a time when military personnel were fighting and dying in Iraq. Still, the legislation bogged down for months over amendments to add tax breaks for a variety of special interests unrelated to the military and debate over whether to offset the cost of the package with revenue increases.

Following enactment of a $330 billion tax cut (PL 108-27) early in the year, Sen. Max Baucus of Montana, the senior Democrat on the Senate Finance Committee, was adamant that no additional tax cuts should be enacted during the year that would increase the budget deficit. Many House Republicans, however, objected to raising levies on some taxpayers to reduce them for others and had a particular problem with the offset the Senate chose: an exit tax on wealthy Americans who renounced their citizenship to avoid paying U.S. taxes. *(2003 tax cut, p. 105)*

In the end, the Senate got a revenue-neutral tax cut, but House Republicans did not have to swallow a tax increase to do so. The cost was covered by Customs user fees that were going to be renewed anyway.

HIGHLIGHTS

The following are the main provisions of the bill, which was expected to cost about $1.3 billion over eleven years. The entire cost was offset by the extension of Customs user fees through March 1, 2005.

• **Military death benefits.** The death gratuity paid to the survivors of military personnel killed in the line of duty was increased to $12,000, all of it tax-free. Under previous law the gratuity was $6,000, half of which was tax-free. The change was retroactive to Sept. 11, 2001.

• **Home sales.** Under existing law all taxpayers could exclude from taxes up to $250,000 ($500,000 for couples filing jointly) of the profits from selling their home. To qualify they had to have owned and occupied the residence for at least two of the five years prior to the sale. Any profits that were not excluded were subject to a capital gains tax of 20 percent (10 percent for those in the 10 percent or 15 percent tax brackets). The new law allowed members of the armed forces or foreign service who were on extended duty to spread the requirement over ten years. The change was effective for sales after May 6, 1997.

• **Travel expenses.** National Guard and reserve members were given an "above-the-line" tax deduction (subtracted from gross income before any itemized or standard deductions) for all overnight transportation, meals, and lodging expenses when they had to travel more than 100 miles from home to attend National Guard or reserve meetings. The deduction rate could not exceed that authorized for federal government employees.

• **Homeowners assistance.** The law made tax-free the aid provided by the Defense Department's Homeowners Assistance Program, which helped federal employees and members of the armed forces when their homes lost value because of military base realignment or closure.

• **Astronauts.** The new law waived income tax liability for two years for astronauts who died in the line of duty, made death benefits to the astronauts' families tax-free, and reduced their estate taxes. The bill applied retroactively to those who died on the *Columbia* space shuttle explosion. *(Columbia accident, p. 695)*

• **Other provisions.** The law also suspended tax filing deadlines for participants in "contingency operations"; allowed penalty-free withdrawals from education savings accounts for attendance at the United States Military, Naval, Air Force, Coast Guard, and Merchant Marine academies; and authorized the IRS to suspend tax-exempt status for any organization identified by the U.S. government as a terrorist organization.

LEGISLATIVE ACTION

The House passed a bill (HR 1307) by a vote of 422–0 on March 20, 2003, that outlined $835 million in tax benefits over eleven years for home sales, travel expenses, and death benefits for soldiers and their families. Ways and Means Committee Chair Bill Thomas, R-Calif., at first attempted to combine the provisions with a list of special-interest tax breaks, but he backed off under rank-and-file criticism.

The Senate upped the cost to $1.1 billion over ten years to accommodate more generous tax breaks for travel expenses pushed by John McCain, R-Ariz. Finance chair Charles E. Grassley, R-Iowa, added provisions to pay for the measure including an exit tax on wealthy Americans who renounced their citizenship, and the Senate passed the revised bill 97–0 on March 27.

Busy with other, more substantial legislation neither committee chair was willing to convene a formal conference to iron out the differences. Over the summer the provisions of HR 1307 became entangled with efforts to expand the child tax credit and enact other unrelated tax benefits. Finally, with pressure mounting from veterans' groups—including a series of press events and radio ads—and a rising death toll in Iraq, a bipartisan consensus formed in the House around a narrow bill (HR 3365), confined to the death benefit provision. The House passed that bill 413–0 after a cursory debate Oct. 29. *(Child tax credit, below)*

The Senate considered rubber-stamping the House bill, but under pressure from McCain senators agreed to add back the Senate's remaining military tax provisions. The only deviation from the previous Senate bill was to drop the controversial tax on expatriates and instead pay for the tax cuts with the extension of Customs user fees. The Senate passed the bill by voice vote Nov. 3. Despite the reluctance of some House Republicans to concede the need for offsetting revenue for the new tax breaks the House accepted the Senate's version of the bill on a 420–0 vote Nov. 5 and sent it to the president.

Child Tax Credit

As soon as Congress enacted the $350 billion tax reconciliation bill (PL 108-27) Democrats complained that millions of low-income families had been excluded from eligibility for the child tax credit. Although the House and Senate passed rival versions of a bill (HR 1308) in June aimed at helping those families, they never convened a conference in 2003 to resolve their differences. Ultimately HR 1308 became the underlying vehicle for a package of tax breaks enacted in 2004 that included the child tax credit. *(2003 tax cut, p. 105, 2004 tax cut, p. 112)*

The 2003 tax law increased what was then a $600-per-child tax credit to $1,000 for each child in 2003 and 2004. In 2005 that credit would revert to the 2001 tax law (PL 107-16), which provided for a credit of $700 in 2005, climbing back to $1,000 in 2010. *(2001 tax cut, p. 89)*

Unlike many tax credits the child credit was refundable, which meant it was available not only to those who paid taxes but also to families whose income was too low for them to owe taxes. In those cases the Treasury sent the family a check for the amount of the credit. A special formula limited a couple's total payment to 10 percent of their annual taxable income in excess of $10,500, up to a ceiling equal to the $1,000-per-child maximum. That meant, for example, that a family earning $15,000 per year was limited to a $450 payment and could not benefit from the increase in the credit. The Senate-passed version of the tax bill would have increased the special payout formula for low-income families to 15 percent at a cost of $3.5 billion, but that provision was dropped in the final hours of negotiation on the conference report.

A furor erupted almost immediately, triggered by a report from the liberal-leaning Center on Budget and Policy Priorities estimating that the omission meant 6.5 million low-income families would receive no benefit from the child credit increase. Democrats held a string of news conferences, mobilized advocacy groups, and threatened to disrupt legislative action until the problem was fixed.

Senate leaders acted quickly to quell the Democratic outcry. On June 5 the Senate called up HR 1308, a House-passed miscellaneous tax bill—the Constitution requires that revenue measures start in the House—and passed it by voice vote after deleting the House text and inserting a child tax credit proposal. The bill's $9.8 billion cost was to be offset by a seven-year extension of Customs user fees that were due to expire Sept. 30, including processing fees for air and sea passengers, commercial trucks, private aircraft, commercial vessels, and barges. Such revenue-raising offsets were anathema to House Republicans, but senators said there was no other way for them to pass tax cuts.

House Republicans resisted at first but soon decided to move a package that combined a fix in the refundability rules with other tax cuts. Despite a White House suggestion that House Republicans accept the Senate bill, they balked. The House passed HR 1308 on June 12 after expanding it into an $82 billion eleven-year tax cut bill that went well beyond the child tax credit and included no revenue-raising provisions to offset the cost. The vote was 224–201.

Most of the extra cost of the House bill resulted from a proposal to keep the child tax credit at $1,000 per child from fiscal 2003 through 2010 rather than letting it drop back to $700 in 2005.

By July national media attention had waned, taking pressure off GOP leaders to do anything more. House Democrats used the stalemate to highlight their position, calling seventeen procedural votes on motions to instruct the House conferees to accept the Senate language on the child tax credit. GOP opposition killed all but one of the motions. But with low-income families scheduled to get the increased payout formula anyway in 2005 under existing law, the issue seemed to lose its resonance, and no further action was taken on the measure in 2003.

Charitable Giving

Proposals to offer new tax incentives for charitable giving passed in both chambers in 2003, but significant differences prevented easy reconciliation. Those disagreements included how to pay for the proposed tax breaks and whether to place stiffer requirements on private foundations. The measures did not reach conference during the 108th Congress.

The centerpiece of both bills was a plan to create a charitable deduction for taxpayers who do not itemize deductions on their tax returns. Under the plan individuals would be allowed to deduct up to $250 in 2004 and 2005 once their annual contribution exceeded $250; joint filers could deduct $500 after the first $500 in contributions.

The Senate passed its bill (S 476—S Rept 108-11) in April after a bipartisan deal was reached to include $1.4 billion for Social Services block grants over two years. The bill's $13.2 billion eleven-year cost was to be offset by closing business tax loopholes. To get the bill to the floor, sponsor Rick Santorum, R-Pa., dropped plans to combine the tax proposals with controversial "charitable choice" provisions that would have expanded opportunities for faith-based groups to compete for federal grants.

The House passed a similar bill (HR 7—108-270) in September that included $12.7 billion in tax breaks over ten years aimed at spurring charitable contributions, but it contained neither the offsetting tax increases nor the proposed new social services spending. The bill did include a plan to force tax-exempt foundations to increase their charitable contributions.

The question whether to offset the costs of the new tax incentives was the chief difference between the two bills. House Republican leaders insisted that tax increases would not be considered. But senators warned that a conference report with a large net cost would be difficult to push through the Senate where deficit-conscious Democrats and moderate Republicans were taking a hard line against any additional tax cuts that were not accompanied by offsets. Congress already had cleared a $350 billion, eleven-year tax cut bill earlier in the session. Senators also expressed skepticism about the House proposal to tighten rules on foundations, while the White House objected to the social services funds in the Senate bill. *(Earlier tax cut, p. 105)*

The House and Senate did not attempt to negotiate a final bill. Senate Democrats blocked Republican efforts to go to conference as a way of protesting what they said was an unprecedented effort by the GOP majority to shut them out of conference negotiations in general, particularly on energy and Medicare legislation.

Estate Tax Repeal

For the third year in a row the House in 2003 passed a permanent repeal of the estate tax, but the Senate took no action and the measure died at the end of 2004. The House bill (HR 8) passed 264–163 on June 18 with support from 223 Republicans and 41 Democrats. The House passed a virtually identical bill in 2002 by a vote of 256–171, also with the help of forty-one Democrats. The Senate did not vote on that bill. Nor did Senate leaders bring up the House-passed bill in the 108th Congress; GOP tax aides said they had no

more than fifty-eight votes; sixty votes would have been required to overcome procedural hurdles to considering the bill.

Proponents of a repeal argued that the estate tax, a tax on assets transferred after death, was unfair because it was levied on income for which regular income taxes already had been paid. They also contended that family businesses often had to be sold to pay the estate tax, an assertion that opponents challenged. Opponents argued that few estates were large enough to fall under the tax and that assets subject to the tax often consisted largely of unrealized capital gains—accumulated wealth that had not been taxed. They also stressed the effect of a permanent repeal on the deficit.

A preliminary estimate from the Joint Committee on Taxation showed that the measure would cost $161.8 billion over the eleven-year period of 2003 through 2013, with almost all of the cost occurring in the years 2011 through 2013.

Lawmakers included a phase-out of the tax in the final version of the 2001 tax cut law (PL 107-16). But to keep the overall cost within limits set by the fiscal 2002 budget resolution the entire law was set to expire after 2010. As a result the estate tax would fall to zero for just one year in 2010 before reverting to the 2001 level with a top rate of 55 percent and the first $1 million exempt.

Tax Cut Extensions

In a major victory for President George W. Bush in the midst of a sharply contested presidential campaign Congress in 2004 easily cleared a measure (HR 1308—PL 108-311) extending three popular tax breaks, primarily for families and individuals. The measure, which contained no off-setting provisions to compensate for the lost revenue, was expected to cost $146 billion over ten years. Final action on the bill, just days before Congress was scheduled to adjourn for the campaign season, also cleared the way for passage of a long-stalled measure providing $137 billion in business tax cuts over ten years. *(Corporate tax bill, p. 115)*

As cleared on Sept. 23, 2004, HR 1308 extended the $1,000 per-child tax credit through 2009, the upper limit for the 10 percent income tax bracket through 2010, and tax breaks for married couples through 2008. It also extended for one year the existing income exemptions from the alternative minimum tax (AMT) and extended the business research and development tax credit through 2005.

Republicans had made extension of the personal income tax breaks a centerpiece of the party's election-year economic agenda. After passage they moved quickly to showcase their triumph on the campaign trail. "This legislation will give families and small businesses added certainty and keep us on the path to greater prosperity, and it brings us one step closer to making the tax relief permanent," Bush said the day the bill cleared.

Democrats also declared victory, vowing to support further extensions of tax cuts for the middle class while pressing for tax breaks for low-income families and higher taxes for the wealthy to help reduce the federal budget deficit. Democratic presidential contender Sen. John Kerry of Massachusetts supported the measure (although he was not in the Senate to vote for it), as did Senate Minority Leader Tom Daschle, D-S.D., who was in a tough and ultimately unsuccessful reelection campaign.

POLITICAL MANEUVERING

Debate surrounding the extension of the so-called middle-class tax cuts appeared to be spurred as much by election-year politicking as by a desire to help taxpayers.

The groundwork for the tax break extension was laid in 2001 when Congress passed legislation cutting taxes by $1.4 trillion (PL 107-16). The tax reductions in the 2001 bill were scheduled to phase in over several years, but a law enacted in 2003 (PL 108-27) accelerated some of the cuts—including those lowering tax rates, increasing the child tax credit, and eliminating the marriage penalty—to make them fully effective in 2003 and 2004. Without further action those cuts would have reverted in 2005 to the phased-in levels set in the 2001 law. (2001 law, p. 89; 2003 law, p. 105)

In his fiscal 2005 budget proposal Bush called on Congress to remove the expiration dates from nearly all of the 2001 and 2003 tax cuts. Republicans had long planned to make the tax cuts permanent, calculating that it would be politically difficult for Democrats to resist extending them.

In the House GOP leaders initially sought to put pressure on the Democrats by taking up and passing three measures (HR 4181, HR 4275, and HR 4359) to renew the expiring provisions permanently. The three bills, passed in late April and early May, won broad support from House Democrats as well as Republicans. A fourth measure, HR 4277, also passed in May, extended for one year the current exemptions on the alternative minimum tax (AMT). The AMT was enacted in 1969 to prevent wealthy Americans from using legitimate tax breaks to avoid paying income taxes altogether. But the trigger points for paying the AMT were never indexed to account for inflation. As a result, by the turn of the century many upper-middle-income taxpayers were also subject to the tax, an outcome never intended by Congress.

Several factors, however, made it unlikely that the four House bills would gain a hearing in the Senate. No budget resolution was in place to protect tax cuts that were not offset by other revenue increases from points of order in the Senate, and deficit concerns were mounting in both chambers and both parties. Another complicating factor was the need to proceed separately on a corporate tax bill aimed at lifting punitive tariffs imposed by the European Union on U.S. exports. By summer both chambers had passed versions of that measure, which contained billions in corporate tax breaks. (Budget resolution, p. 77; European Union tariffs, pp. 115, 147)

GOP leaders thus decided not to press for a Senate vote on the permanent tax cut extensions. Instead, at the urging of the White House, they put together a package extending the popular tax cuts that they hoped to rush through before Congress recessed for the Democratic National Convention in late July. Republicans saw the package as a strategy that could only benefit the GOP. If the measure were enacted Republicans would claim a legislative victory on Bush's top economic initiative. If the extensions were not enacted because of opposition from Democrats GOP candidates would cast blame on all congressional Democrats, including presidential candidate Kerry and his running mate, North Carolina senator John Edwards. Both men were focusing their campaign on attracting middle-class voters.

For their part Democratic leaders said they opposed any tax extensions that were not offset by other revenue increases. But shortly before the July recess Senate Finance Committee Chair Charles E. Grassley, R-Iowa, worked out a deal for a $75 billion, two-year extension of the popular tax breaks that had Daschle's backing and the tacit support of Kerry and Edwards.

The compromise, however, undercut the political strategy underlying the package; instead of forcing the Democrats into a tough vote it gave them a fairly easy choice that would allow both parties to claim victory for supporting popular tax cuts. So instead of settling for an easy win the White House decided to up the ante and insist on a five-year extension of the three expiring tax breaks. That strategy delayed the vote until September and gave the administration time to unify House and Senate Republicans in support of a longer extension of the expiring tax cuts that would be closer to the president's goal of making the cuts permanent.

END GAME

When lawmakers returned from their August recess Grassley temporarily held up action on HR 1308 while he sought assurances that GOP leaders would not abandon the stalled corporate tax overhaul once the middle-class tax relief bill was passed. During a Sept. 20 meeting Grassley, Senate Majority Leader Bill Frist of Tennessee, and House Ways and Means Committee Chair Bill Thomas, R-Calif., the chief author of the House corporate tax bill, reached agreement on an outline for completing the tax extension bill and for reducing the scope and cost of the corporate tax bill by moving several popular business tax breaks to the tax extension package. That shift would make it easier to offset other corporate tax breaks with revenue-raising provisions, a condition for any overhaul bill to win passage in the Senate, and was unlikely to jeopardize support for the tax extension bill.

With that agreement in place GOP leaders presented lawmakers with a package of tax relief measures that extended the three popular tax cuts for four to six years and continued the ATM exemptions for one year. To help guarantee bipartisan support, the package was expanded to incorporate some items on the Democratic wish list, including an acceleration of the refundable version of the child tax credit and a more generous version of that tax break for families of soldiers in combat. The underlying vehicle for the package was HR

1308, a bill to make low-income families eligible for a re-fundable child tax credit that had been passed by both chambers in differing versions in 2003.

In the House Democratic leaders continued to argue that the bill, by deepening the deficit, would do more harm than good to middle-class families in the long run. But they also made clear that rank-and-file members were free to support it if doing so would help their campaigns. As a result, Democrats backed the measure by a ratio of nearly two to one. The House adopted the conference report on the bill by a re-sounding vote including two of the most senior Democrats on the Ways and Means Committee, Charles B. Rangel of New York and Sander M. Levin of Michigan. The agreement on HR 1308 (H Rept 108-696) was approved Sept. 23 on a **key vote of 339–65 (R 213–0; D125–65; I 1–0.)**

GOP leaders argued that although the legislation would add to the deficit in the short term, it could spur economic growth and enhance tax revenue in the long run. Not a single House Republicans rejected that argument, not even the most fiscally conservative lawmakers who were annoyed at the expansion of the refundable child tax credit, which they characterized as an unbridled new entitlement similar to welfare.

In the Senate Democratic opposition collapsed altogether after Kerry, on the campaign trail in Pennsylvania, endorsed the package just before the vote as a means to help families "squeezed by the weak Bush economy." The only dissent came from a trio of deficit hawks who objected to the bill's $146 billion cost over ten years and the lack of offsets to pay for it. The Senate cleared HR 1308 on a **key vote of 92–3 (R 49–2; D 42–1; I 1–0).** *(2004 key votes, p. 854)*

PROVISIONS

As signed into law by President Bush on Oct. 4, 2004, HR 1308 temporarily extended several individual tax provisions included in the 2003 Jobs and Growth Tax Relief Reconciliation Act (PL 108-27) as well as several temporary business tax breaks that had expired or were about to expire. The Joint Committee on Taxation estimated that these provisions would reduce federal revenue by $145.9 billion over 2005–2014. The extensions of the individual tax cuts were estimated to cost $133 billion over the ten-year period, more than 90 percent of the total. The measure contained no revenue-raising offsets.

Individual Tax Cuts

• **Child tax credit.** The measure extended the $1,000 child tax credit for five years, through 2009. Under the 2001 tax law the increase in the child tax credit was scheduled to be fully implemented by 2010; therefore the credit was effectively extended through 2010. The measure accelerated the increase, currently scheduled for 2005, in the amount of earned income used to calculate the refundable child tax credit. Under the measure the amount would increase from 10 percent of earned income over $10,750 to 15 percent of earned income beginning in 2004.

• The agreement permitted members of the military to include combat pay, which currently was not included in taxable income, in their gross earnings to meet the income threshold for calculating the child tax credit. The measure also temporarily—from the date of enactment through 2005—permitted members of the military to include combat pay when determining eligibility for the Earned Income Tax Credit.

• **Marriage penalty.** The measure extended the existing marriage penalty tax provisions for four years, through 2008. Under the measure the basic standard deduction and the upper income limit for the 15 percent tax brackets for married couples filing jointly would remain twice that of single filers. Under the 2001 tax law both the increase in the basic standard deduction and the range of the 15 percent tax bracket to twice that of single taxpayers were scheduled to be fully implemented by 2009. Therefore HR 1308 effectively extended the marriage-penalty provisions through 2010.

• **10 percent tax bracket.** The measure extended through 2010 the expanded 10 percent tax bracket that applied to the first $7,000 of income for individuals and $14,000 for married couples filing jointly. Under the measure these amounts would be adjusted for inflation beginning in 2004.

• **AMT Income Exemption Limit.** The agreement extended for one year, through 2005, the increased alternative minimum tax (AMT) income limits included in the 2003 tax law of $40,250 for individual taxpayers and $58,000 for married couples.

Other Tax Extensions

The agreement extended—through the end of 2005 unless otherwise indicated—a number of temporary tax provisions primarily affecting businesses. The Joint Tax Committee estimated that these provisions would reduce federal revenue by $13 billion over ten years. Among the tax credits and deductions extended are the following:

• **Research and development credit.** Extended the current-law credit equal to 20 percent of a taxpayer's qualified research expenses, at an estimated ten-year cost of $7.6 billion.

• **Wind and biomass electricity facilities production credit.** Made a tax credit for the production of electricity from poultry waste, wind, and "closed-loop" biomass produced from plants grown specifically to produce electricity available for facilities placed in service after 2003 and before 2006. *(Details, pp. 425, 432)*

• **Liberty Zone Bonds.** Liberty Zone private activity bonds for New York City through 2009. The tax-exempt bonds were aimed at financing construction and rehabilitation of nonresidential property and residential rental property hard hit by the Sept. 11, 2001, terrorist attacks. It also extended the advance refunding of bonds through 2005.

• **Work Opportunity Credit.** Extended a credit of $2,400 to employers for employing certain individuals, including those receiving welfare benefits or food stamps.

• **Welfare-to-Work Credit.** Provided employers with a tax credit for wages paid during the first two years of employment to employees who are long-term family-assistance recipients.

- **Non-Refundable Personal Credits Against AMT.** Permitted individual taxpayers to offset regular and alternative minimum tax liability with personal nonrefundable credits.
- **Teacher Tax Deduction.** Provided an "above-the-line" tax deduction for teachers for the first $250 of "out-of-pocket" spending on student supplies.
- **Charitable Contribution of Computers.** Provided a tax credit for companies that donate computer technology and equipment to elementary and secondary schools.
- **Clean-Fuel Vehicle Deduction.** Extended the deduction for the purchase of clean-fuel (or hybrid/electric) vehicles.
- **Marginal Well Production.** Temporarily extended the current suspension of the 100 percent limit for marginal wells. Under existing law independent producers and royalty owners of oil and gas properties were allowed a depletion deduction equal to 100 percent of the net income from the property in any year but no more than 65 percent of the taxpayer's overall taxable income. Under existing law for marginal wells the 100 percent net income limitation did not apply for the tax years 1998 through 2003.
- **Business on Indian Reservations.** Extended the accelerated depreciation for business property on Indian reservations.

Corporate Tax Changes

A bill to repeal a subsidy to U.S. exporters that had triggered international sanctions turned in 2004 into the biggest corporate tax overhaul since 1986. The measure (HR 4520—PL 108-357), cynically referred to as "Miss Piggy" by its chief House sponsor, replaced the subsidy with $137 billion in corporate tax cuts over ten years, many of them targeted to narrow special interests. The bill also included a $10 billion buyout of tobacco farmers and curbs on tax shelters and other practices to offset the lost revenue.

The corporate tax cut bill—the fourth tax reduction enacted since President George W. Bush took office in 2001—was one of the major behind-the-scenes battles in the 108th Congress. Although both chambers passed the measure by wide margins, it took two years for tax writers to get the measure through a deeply divided Congress. In the Senate the measure got caught up in months of on-again, off-again debate on unrelated topics such as overtime pay and unemployment benefits. In the House Republicans quarreled among themselves over which companies should receive the breaks. In the end the tax writers succeeded by sweetening the pot with a rich patchwork of narrow-interest tax breaks too tempting for a majority of lawmakers to pass up in an election year.

The legislation grew out of the need for Congress to respond to a ruling by the World Trade Organization (WTO) that a U.S. tax break, known as the extraterritorial income exclusion (ETI), was illegal. The WTO authorized the Euro-

pean Union, beginning in March 2004, to impose up to $4 billion a year in trade sanctions against U.S. companies in retaliation for the $5 billion-a-year subsidy.

Lawmakers agreed on repealing the ETI, but Republicans were deeply divided over what should replace it. Some lawmakers wanted to compensate the biggest users of the export tax breaks; others wanted to reduce taxes on the global business of U.S. multinationals. Still others wanted to aid domestic manufacturers. Democrats in particular wanted any corporate tax incentives designed so they would keep jobs in the United States. By mid-2003 about 2.7 million jobs had been lost since President Bush took office, most of them in manufacturing. The White House refused to take a stance on how to replace the ETI.

At the same time, two other conditions helped make the measure a ripe target for corporate petitioners: pent-up demand and an open door to lobbyists. Since President Bush took office tax reductions were focused largely on individual taxpayers or small businesses that were treated as individuals in the tax law. Years of waiting by corporations eager for their turn, and promises that their time would come, only increased the pressure on legislators. With the White House refusing to take a stand and apply a brake, corporations could and did lobby strongly for their own special interests; in an election year their pleas were all the more irresistible to lawmakers who wanted to be seen as delivering to companies in their states and districts.

As a result, the final 650-page bill contained billions in targeted tax breaks that went far beyond what Treasury secretary John W. Snow described as the "core objective" of the legislation. The bill contained tax breaks for everything from horse and dog track gambling, railroads, and naval shipbuilders to Hollywood films, bows and arrows, and fishing tackle boxes. In what some observers considered a major irony, the bill that was meant in part to help American companies be more competitive in global markets even suspended duties on ceiling fans imported from China and sold through the Home Depot chain. A controversial $10 billion buyout for tobacco farmers, restoration of a federal income tax deduction for certain state sales taxes, and tax breaks for ethanol fuel ensured broad support for the measure.

Few legislators spoke favorably of the bill. Rep. Steny H. Hoyer of Maryland, the Democratic whip, referred to the House version of the measure as "an appalling orgy in self-indulgence." Budget watchdogs complained that rather than being revenue-neutral, the bill would actually increase the budget deficit by $80 billion because lawmakers used gimmickry to hide its true cost. The IRS warned that the centerpiece $77 billion tax break on manufacturing income would be impossible to administer and would encourage new tax abuses. A large contingent of Democrats said that the $43 billion in tax breaks on the overseas income of multinational corporations would have the perverse effect of encouraging more U.S. factories to move overseas. And in contrast to every other major tax bill of Bush's presidency, the White

House did not arrange a public signing for the bill. Bush signed it quietly on Oct. 22 while on the campaign trail.

HIGHLIGHTS OF THE BILL

HR 4250 repealed an export tax break worth $50 billion over ten years and replaced it with $137 billion in new tax cuts, offset by curbs on tax avoidance practices and budget accounting techniques. In effect the bill repealed a tax break for exporters and replaced it with tax deductions for all manufacturers, whether they export or not. Moreover, the deductions applied not just to traditional manufacturers but many others such as construction contractors, engineers, architects, software developers, film and energy producers, farmers and agricultural processors.

- **Export subsidies.** Exporters lost a $5 billion-a-year tax break, known as the extraterritorial income exclusion, which exempted from taxation as much as 30 percent of qualified foreign trade income. The subsidy was phased out between 2004 and 2007. Airplane makers, including Boeing Co., were allowed to claim the subsidy for the life of long-term sales contracts signed before Sept. 17, 2003.

- **Manufacturing income exclusion.** Companies, including partnerships and sole proprietorships, that paid tax through the individual income tax code, were allowed to exclude from taxation 9 percent of their profits on domestic manufacturing at an estimated ten-year cost of $77 billion. The exclusion was equivalent to a 32 percent tax rate on manufacturing activities, compared with the typical 35 percent corporate tax rate. The provision was fully phased in beginning in 2010. Although replaced the export subsidy, the phasing out of that provision and the phasing in of the new meant that some taxpayers could have the benefit of both between 2004 and the end of 2006.

- **International tax credits.** More than twenty new tax breaks, totaling $43 billion over ten years, went to U.S.-based multinational corporations for their overseas income, making it easier for companies to subtract taxes paid to foreign countries from their U.S. tax bills.

- **Narrow-interest provisions.** About $14 billion in tax breaks was sprinkled among a host of special interests, from fishermen to makers of bows and arrows.

- **Curbs on tax shelters.** Scores of tax shelters and tax avoidance practices totaling about $60 billion over ten years were prohibited to help offset revenue lost by the bill. One provision outlawed $27 billion in tax savings for financial institutions that claimed deductions through leasing arrangements for foreign and domestic municipal infrastructure.

- **Other revenue-raising provisions.** Almost $19 billion was raised by renewing Customs' users fees for ten years. An accounting change that would reclassify an ethanol tax break from an excise tax to an income tax was expected to raise $6 billion. About $50 billion was raised by repealing the ETI subsidy.

- **Tobacco growers buyout.** The measure created a $10.1 billion program to buy out tobacco growers and repeal the current federal tobacco support program, but the cost of the program was offset through contributions from tobacco companies. The measure did not provide for regulation of tobacco by the Food and Drug Administration, a bitter disappointment to health advocates who lobbied aggressively for the FDA power as part of the continuing campaign to combat cigarette smoking. (*Buyout, p. 386*)

BACKGROUND

The impetus for the legislation was the WTO ruling that the extraterritorial income exclusion was an export subsidy that violated international trade laws. The ETI was relatively new, but the dispute over U.S. export incentives was decades old. The General Agreement on Tariffs and Trade, predecessor to the WTO, had ruled in 1981 that an earlier tax incentive for U.S. exports—known as the Domestic International Sales Corporation provisions—violated international trade rules. In its place Congress passed legislation in 1984 (PL 98-369) allowing companies to set up offshore offices called Foreign Sales Corporations (FSCs) in places such as the Virgin Islands, Barbados, and Guam. Firms could exempt 15 percent to 30 percent of their earnings from exports sold through an FSC, as long as 50 percent of the product was made in the United States.

The EU complained that this, too, was an unfair subsidy because the tax breaks went exclusively to exporters, and in 1999 the WTO ruled in favor of the Europeans. To avert retaliatory sanctions Congress in 2000 substituted a new mechanism known as the extraterritorial income provision (PL 106-519). Like the FSC, the ETI allowed firms to exempt up to 30 percent of their export income from U.S. taxes. But in a change that Congress hoped would satisfy the world trade body, the exemption was also available for some foreign-source income that did not come from exports. (*Congress and the Nation Vol. X, p. 118*)

The change was not enough, however. In August 2001 the WTO ruled that the provision was a prohibited export subsidy. In August 2002 the WTO granted the EU permission to impose $4 billion in retaliatory tariffs on U.S.-manufactured goods shipped to Europe, starting in January 2004. In 2002 Ways and Means Committee Chair Bill Thomas, R-Calif., offered a bill that combined a repeal of the ETI with tax cuts tilted heavily toward multinationals, but Thomas's fellow committee members objected to his approach and the bill died.

ACTION IN 2003

In 2003 Thomas's opponents acted quickly, beating him out of the starting gate. In April Philip M. Crane of Illinois, the committee's senior Republican, worked with top panel Democrat Charles B. Rangel of New York to introduce a bill (HR 1769) to replace the ETI with a simple tax cut for manufacturers, effectively lowering their top tax rate from 35 percent to 31.5 percent. The plan was immediately popular as lawmakers of both parties rushed to support it. Nearly 150 House members signed on as cosponsors.

In July Thomas responded with a new version of his bill (HR 2896) that added $100 billion in domestic tax breaks, but he still failed to woo many to his side. One of Thomas's biggest problems was Speaker J. Dennis Hastert, R-Ill., who had given tacit approval to the Crane-Rangel bill. Hastert, like Crane, was eager to protect manufacturers headquartered in Illinois, including Caterpillar Inc. and Boeing Co. Both companies were big beneficiaries of the existing export tax break; they formed a coalition that included Microsoft Corp. to back the Crane-Rangel manufacturing tax cut.

In late September the EU increased the pressure on Congress to act. Lawmakers had assumed that a Jan. 1, 2004, EU deadline was flexible, as long as Congress demonstrated that it was working on the issue. But on Sept. 26 the EU warned that simply showing legislative progress would not help the United States avoid a trade war.

Thomas made more revisions and finally convinced Hastert that his bill had become as advantageous to Caterpillar as Crane-Rangel; Hastert gave his endorsement Oct. 2. The House Ways and Means Committee approved Thomas's revised bill in a strict party-line vote of 24–15 on Oct. 28. The bill included $140 billion in corporate tax cuts partially offset by $80 billion in revenue-raisers including the repeal of the export subsidy and curbs on tax shelters. But even as the committee voted it was clear that the same problem that had delayed action for months—a rebellion by Republicans who said the bill would do too little for domestic manufacturers—limited the bill's prospects for reaching the floor.

The Senate Finance Committee had approved a bipartisan bill (S 1637—S Rept 108-192) on Oct. 1. The bill promised about $101 billion over ten years in tax breaks for both domestic manufacturers and multinational companies; all of it was offset by revenue increases. Finance chair Charles E. Grassley, R-Iowa, pressed for floor action before Congress adjourned in November. But with a crowded calendar, Majority Leader Bill Frist, R-Tenn., decided to wait until House Republicans sorted out their disputes before moving ahead.

ACTION IN 2004

Beginning the week of March 1, 2004, the EU began imposing punitive sanctions on more than 1,600 U.S. products. The punitive tariffs began at 5 percent and were scheduled to increase by 1 percentage point each month, up to a ceiling of 17 percent, unless Congress repealed the offending export subsidy.

Senate Action

The Senate passed HR 1637 on May 11 by a vote of 92–5. The overwhelming vote in favor of the legislation belied more than two months of skirmishing between the two political parties. Side issues, unrelated to corporate tax policy, with hearty doses of procedural maneuvering, dominated weeks of on-again, off-again floor debate. In the end Democrats won a vote to block Labor Department rules limiting overtime pay eligibility—one of their election-year issues—

and lost on another: unemployment benefits for long-term jobless workers. *(Overtime pay, p. 574; jobless benefits, p. 573)*

There was little debate on the main tax provisions of the bill, which replaced the export tax break ruled out of order by the WTO with about $170 billion in new corporate tax cuts over ten years. Almost all the tax cuts were offset by provisions that would raise revenue.

Corporations and special interests were the big winners in the Senate bill. To build support for the measure on the floor, Grassley and Max Baucus, D-Mont., the ranking minority member on the Finance Committee, agreed to add billions more in corporate tax breaks to the breaks the Finance committee had already approved. In addition to the $65 billion break for manufacturing income, filmmakers, Oldsmobile dealers, and racetrack owners were among the beneficiaries. At the last minute the Senate also agreed to an amendment that would consider architectural and engineering firms, such as Halliburton, as manufacturers for purposes of claiming the new tax deduction on manufacturing profits provided in the Senate bill.

The bill also provided an array of tax breaks on the overseas income of multinational corporations (at a cost of $39 billion). It provided several tax breaks to promote energy production; many of these tax breaks had been included in the omnibus energy bill that stalled in 2003. The cost of the energy tax breaks was put at $18 billion. The bill also expanded and extended the tax credit for corporate research and development through 2005 ($10 billion), made permanent a tax break for employers that hired welfare recipients ($5 billion), and approved an assortment of targeted tax cuts at a cost of $20 billion.

To offset those costs the bill closed several tax shelters and loopholes that were regarded as abusive. The largest single revenue gain ($39 billion) came from closing down leasing schemes between finance companies and municipalities. Other revenue was raised by repealing the export tax break outlawed by the WTO, extending Customs user fees that were set to expire, and making several changes in the way energy tax breaks were treated.

House Action

Senate passage put the issue back with the House where Thomas rewrote the bill in June. Still faced with Republican holdouts demanding more for their districts, he decided to add completely unrelated items intended to attract support from Democrats and break the GOP opposition that was preventing the original committee bill from coming to the floor.

A $10 billion buyout for tobacco farmers, endorsed by the White House, and a $3.6 billion tax break for states with sales taxes but no income taxes—aimed at lawmakers in Florida, Texas, and Tennessee—did the trick. The Ways and Means Committee approved the revised bill (HR 4250—no written report) June 14 by a vote of 27–9 with three Democrats supporting the measure. The full House followed on June 17 by passing the bill 251–178. Forty-eight Democrats crossed party lines to support the measure.

Unlike Grassley and Baucus, Thomas could not make a wholesale appeal to Democrats by offsetting the new tax cuts with revenue-raisers. House GOP leaders would not accept many of the revenue-raisers in the Senate bill, which they considered tantamount to tax increases. So although Thomas added some revenue-raising provisions, they fell about $35 billion short of fully offsetting the $150 billion in tax breaks contained in the bill.

FINAL ACTION

Even before the start of the conference the House bill ran into problems in the Senate where there was a longstanding agreement that any bailout of tobacco families be paired with provisions giving the Food and Drug Administration (FDA) authority to regulate tobacco. In July the Senate took the unusual step of reopening its already passed bill and adding provisions that combined the tobacco buyout with FDA tobacco regulation.

House GOP leaders objected to the Senate's FDA provisions, but that was only one problem facing the bill. Negotiators had to reconcile the different special interest provisions that swelled the two versions. A final bill would not get through the Senate if it increased the deficit, but to appease House leaders its revenue-raising provisions had to be limited. Moreover, partisan wrangling between Democrats and Republicans in the Senate and between GOP leaders in the House and Grassley in the Senate kept the two versions of the bill from moving to conference.

Meanwhile, the White House was pressing tax writers to focus on finishing a separate bill (HR 1308—PL 108-311) to extend popular tax breaks for families. Thomas used that as an opportunity to take some of the pressure off the need to find offsetting revenue raisers for the corporate tax bill by winning agreement to shift $13 billion worth of popular tax breaks that were expiring or about to expire from the corporate tax bill to the popular tax extension bill where none of the tax cuts were offset. That bill cleared on Sept. 23. (*Tax cut extensions, p. 112*)

Thomas wrote the final legislation after conferring with House and Senate conferees from both parties to gain an understanding of what they needed to be able to vote for the final package. Thomas accepted the Senate position that the bill include enough curbs on tax abuses to offset the cost of the bill. He determined that he had to keep a tobacco buyout in the bill but gambled that he could still win Senate Democratic votes even if he jettisoned FDA regulation of tobacco products to get the measure through the House. To convince enough senators to back down on the FDA provisions Thomas packed the bill with lucrative provisions for certain states, including tax breaks for ethanol, timber, and shipping. Several tax provisions from the stymied energy overhaul were included.

Even Senate Minority Leader Tom Daschle, D-S. D., was forced to choose between his constituents and his party's

principles. Daschle was committed to linking the tobacco buyout with FDA regulation. But Thomas inserted four tax breaks targeted to South Dakota: provisions for ethanol producers, ranchers, and timber companies as well as the federal income tax deduction for state sales taxes. After some hesitation, Daschle, in a tough reelection fight, signed the conference report. His signature made it a foregone conclusion that the Senate would clear the legislation.

On Oct. 7, 2004, the day after agreement was reached on the conference report and only eight days after formal negotiations began, the House adopted the report on HR 4250 (H Rept 108-755) by a **key vote of 280–141 (R 207–16; D 73–124; I 0–1).** With the support of seventy-three Democrats, the vote on the measure was the most bipartisan endorsement of a tax bill during President Bush's first term. The Senate cleared the bill on Oct. 11 and immediately headed for the campaign trail. The **key vote was 69–17 (R 43–3; D 25–14; I 1–0.)** (*2004 key votes, p. 854*)

SUBSEQUENT EU ACTION

The EU said it would lift sanctions Jan. 1, 2005, when the phase-out of the export subsidy was scheduled to begin. However, the EU also said it planned to challenge one aspect of the new law, which would allow the Boeing Co. and other companies to continued receiving the export subsidy for the life of previously signed long-term contracts.

MAJOR PROVISIONS

The final version of HR 4520—PL 108-357, the American Jobs Creation Act, repealed the extraterritorial income exclusion (ETI) and provided approximately $137 billion in tax breaks for corporations over ten years. In addition to $49.2 billion in revenue raised by the repeal of the ETI, the measure also included $82 billion in additional revenue-raising provisions, thereby fully offsetting the cost of the tax cuts.

• **Repeal of extraterritorial income exclusion.** Like the House bill, the agreement phased out between 2005 and the end of 2006 the ETI exclusion that was ruled an illegal subsidy by the World Trade Organization. For transactions beginning in 2005, the agreement allowed taxpayers to claim 80 percent of their otherwise applicable ETI benefits, and 60 percent during 2006, after which the tax exclusion will be fully repealed. The Joint Committee on Taxation (JCT) estimated that the repeal would result in a net increase in federal revenue by $49.2 billion over ten years.

Business Tax Provisions

The measure provided $83.8 billion in tax incentives for businesses, including a tax deduction for domestic production, a two-year extension of increased expensing for small business, faster depreciation of leased property, and modifications to the tax treatment of small business S corporations.

• **Tax reduction for domestic production.** The agreement provided a 9 percent deduction from taxable income that was equal to a portion of the corporation's qualified domestic production activities, phased in over five years. For 2005 and 2006 the deduction would be 3 percent of income. For 2007 through 2009 the deduction would be 6 percent of income. In 2009 the deduction would be 9 percent.

Domestic production was defined as gross receipts derived from any sale, exchange, lease, rent, or license of property that was manufactured, produced, grown, or extracted in whole or in "significant part" within the United States. The agreement also specified that income derived from films would be considered domestic production if 50 percent or more of the total compensation relating to the production of the film was paid for services performed in the United States by actors, production personnel, directors, and producers. Domestic production would also include any sale, exchange, or other disposition, but not the transmission, of electricity, natural gas, or drinking water; construction activities performed in the United States; and engineering and architectural services performed in the United States for construction projects located in the United States. Domestic production would not include the sale of food or beverages prepared by the business at a retail establishment.

The tax deduction could be used in determining the alternative minimum tax. The provision would be effective beginning in 2005.

• **Two-year extension of increased expensing for small business.** The 2003 Jobs and Growth Tax Relief Reconciliation Act (PL 108-27) temporarily increased, from $25,000 to $100,000, the amount that a business could deduct for the purchase of certain equipment—instead of using depreciation schedules and deducting the cost of the equipment over a specified number of years—for the years 2003 through 2005. The law also increased the limit on the cost of qualifying property from $200,000 to $400,000 for property placed in service from 2003 through 2005. Both amounts were indexed for inflation beginning in 2004. The law also permitted off-the-shelf computer software to qualify for this deduction. Like the House bill, the agreement extended—for two years, through 2007—increased expensing and cost limits, including inflation indexing, on qualifying property in the 2003 tax agreement.

• **Shorter recovery period for depreciation of certain improvements and property.** Under current law a business could deduct the cost of purchasing certain equipment over a number of years through depreciation deductions. The amount that could be deducted each year was determined under the "modified accelerated cost recovery system," which specified how the costs for different types of property could be recovered. The recovery period for nonresidential real property and for improvements made on leased property was thirty-nine years. Like the House bill the agreement provided a fifteen-year recovery period for qualified leasehold-improvement property and qualified restaurant property placed in service before 2006. Under the measure, qualified restaurant property would mean any improvement to a building made more than three years after the date the build-

ing was first placed in service if more than half of the building's square footage is devoted to restaurant operations. Qualified leasehold improvements could qualify for an additional first-year depreciation deduction.

• **Chapter S Corporation modifications.** Under current law a Chapter S corporation was not subject to corporate taxation. Instead, shareholders included on their individual tax returns their share of the corporation's separately stated items of income, deduction, loss, and credit, and their share of nonseparately stated income or loss. A Chapter S corporation could have no more than seventy-five shareholders, all of whom had to be citizens or residents of the United States. Certain trusts, estates, and charities and qualified retirement plans also could hold stock in an Chapter S corporation. For purposes of the shareholder limitation a husband and wife were treated as one shareholder.

The measure provided that up to six generations of family members could elect to be treated as one shareholder for purposes of determining the number of shareholders in the corporation, effectively increasing the number of shareholders in Chapter S corporations. The agreement also increased the maximum number of eligible shareholders to 100 from 75. The measure allowed an individual retirement account (IRA), including a Roth IRA, to be a shareholder of a bank that was an Chapter S corporation.

The agreement also included a number of miscellaneous provisions related to the tax treatment of Chapter S corporations.

• **Tax credit for maintenance of railroad track.** Similar to the House bill the agreement provided a 50 percent business tax credit for qualified railroad-track-maintenance expenditures paid or incurred from 2005 through 2007.

• **Suspension of occupational taxes on alcohol producers.** The measure suspended the special occupational taxes on producers and marketers of alcoholic beverages for a three-year period—from July 2005 through June 2008.

• **Weather-related sale of livestock.** The measure extended to four years from two years the time in which a rancher could replace livestock sold due to weather-related conditions, such as drought or flood, without having to pay taxes on any gain realized from the original sale.

• **Small producer ethanol credit.** The new law allowed cooperatives to elect to "pass through" the small-ethanol-producer credit to its patrons.

• **Income averaging for fishermen.** The measure allowed fishermen, like farmers, to compute income by averaging it over the prior three-year period, and coordinated farmer and fisherman income averaging with the alternative minimum tax (AMT), so that the AMT would be calculated in each tax year as if income averaging had not been used.

• **Small refiners capital costs from complying with EPA sulfur regulations.** Small-business refiners were permitted to claim an immediate deduction for up to 75 percent of costs paid to comply with the Environmental Protection Agency's sulfur regulations.

• **Bows and arrows.** The excise tax on archery bows and arrows was simplified.

• **Fishing tackle boxes.** The excise tax was reduced to 3 percent.

• **Sonar devices.** The excise tax on sonar devices suitable for finding fish was repealed.

Corporate Tax Simplification Provisions

The new law included a number of modifications to the tax treatment of corporations and provisions related to tax simplification for U.S. businesses. The Joint Committee on Taxation estimated that these provisions would reduce federal revenue by $42.6 billion over ten years.

• **Modifications to interest expense allocation rule.** Under existing law in calculating the foreign-tax-credit limitation, interest expense was treated as attributable to all business activities regardless of the purpose for which interest was paid. Therefore interest allocation was made on the basis of assets rather than gross income. The new law agreement modified these allocation rules by providing a one-time election under which the taxable income of the domestic members of an affiliated group from sources outside the United States generally would be determined by allocating and apportioning domestic members' interest expense on a worldwide-group basis, that is, as if all members of the worldwide group were a single corporation. The provision would become effective in 2009.

• **Recharacterize overall domestic loss.** Under existing law the United States provided a credit for foreign income taxes paid or accrued. The foreign tax credit generally was limited to the U.S. tax liability on a corporation's foreign-source income in order to ensure that the credit mitigated the double taxation of foreign-source income without offsetting the U.S. tax on U.S.-source income. The new law applied a "re-sourcing" rule to U.S.-source income in cases in which a business's foreign-tax limitation had been reduced as a result of an overall domestic loss. Under the measure a portion of the company's U.S.-source income for each succeeding taxable year would be recharacterized as foreign-source income in an amount equal to the lesser of the amount of unrecharacterized overall domestic losses for years prior to the succeeding taxable year and 50 percent of the taxpayer's U.S.-source income for the succeeding taxable year.

The measure defined an overall domestic loss for this provision as any domestic loss to the extent that it offset foreign-source taxable income for the current taxable year, or for any preceding taxable year by reason of a loss carryback. An overall domestic loss would not include a loss for any taxable year unless the business elected the use of the foreign-tax credit for such taxable year. The provision would be effective beginning in 2007.

• **Reduction to two foreign-tax credit "baskets."** Under existing law the foreign-tax-credit limitation was applied separately to nine categories of income, or tax-credit "baskets." The foreign-tax-credit limitation had to be calculated separately for each basket. The new law reduced the number of categories of foreign-tax-credit limitations to two—passive income and general category income—and income previously allocated to the other categories was reallocated to one of the two categories, as appropriate. The provision would be effective beginning in 2007. Under the measure, taxes paid or accrued in a taxable year beginning before 2007 and carried to any subsequent year would be treated as if these provisions were in effect on the date those taxes were paid or accrued.

• **Repeal AMT limit on foreign tax credit.** Beginning in 2005 the measure repealed the current 90 percent limitation on the use of foreign tax credits against the corporate alternative minimum tax (AMT), allowing the foreign tax credit to potentially offset all tax liability.

• **Incentives to reinvest foreign earnings in the United States.** Under existing law income earned by a domestic partner corporation from foreign operations conducted by foreign corporate subsidiaries was generally subject to U.S. tax when the income was distributed as a dividend to the domestic corporation. The new law provided that certain dividends received by a U.S. corporation from controlled foreign corporations would be eligible for an 85 percent dividends-received tax deduction. The corporation would be able to use this deduction for dividends received either during the company's first taxable year after the date of enactment or during the firm's last taxable year beginning before the date of enactment. Dividends received after the election period would be taxed in the normal manner under existing law. The deduction would apply only to cash dividends and other cash amounts included in gross incomes as dividends and would be subject to a number of general limitations.

• **Foreign-tax-credit carryforward and carryback.** Under current law U.S. taxpayers could credit foreign taxes paid against U.S. tax on foreign-source income. The amount of foreign tax credits that could be claimed in a year was subject to a limitation that prevented taxpayers from using foreign tax credits to offset U.S. tax on U.S.-source income. The amount of creditable taxes paid or accrued in any taxable year that exceeded the foreign-tax-credit limitation was permitted to be "carried back" to two immediately preceding taxable years and "carried forward" five taxable years so that excess credits could be used in other tax years to offset taxes owed on foreign-source income. The new law extended the foreign-tax-credit carryforward period to ten years and limited the carryback period to one year.

• **Other simplification provisions.** The new law also made changes in the tax treatment of "look-through" rules applied to certain foreign dividends, the exclusion of certain foreign controlled assets, and the "look-through" treatment of sales of partnership interests. It also repealed certain foreign holding company and foreign investment company rules, and modified rules pertaining to certain aircraft leasing and shipping income.

Temporary State General Sales Tax Deduction

Under current law no itemized deduction was permitted against federal income-tax liability for state or local general sales taxes. The new law permitted taxpayers to deduct state and local general sales taxes in lieu of the itemized deduction provided under current law for state and local income taxes. Under the measure taxpayers would be able to deduct the total amount of general state and local sales taxes paid by accumulating the receipts showing the taxes paid, or a taxpayer could use tables created by the Treasury Department. The tables would be based on the average consumption by taxpayers, on a state-by-state basis, taking into account filing status, number of dependents, adjusted gross income, and rates of state and local general sales taxation. The measure was effective only for 2004 and 2005.

Tobacco Buyout

The measure repealed the current federal tobacco support program and provided incentives for tobacco farmers to quit the business or switch crops, ending a system that limited per-acre tobacco sales to protect prices for growers and others holding quotas. Tobacco quota holders would be paid $7 a pound on their basic quota allotment paid in equal installments over ten years. The measure also provided tobacco producers transition payments of $3 a pound based on their effective quota, paid in equal installments over ten years. Manufacturers and importers of tobacco products would pay a quarterly assessment into a newly formed Tobacco Trust Fund, which would be used for payments to quota holders and eligible producers as well as to pay for program losses incurred by the Agriculture Department. Funds from the Tobacco Trust Fund were expected to fully offset the costs of buyout. (*Tobacco buyout action, p. 386*)

Revenue-Raising Provisions

The agreement repealed the extraterritorial income exclusion, which was ruled illegal by the World Trade Organization. The repeal was expected to increase federal revenue by $49.2 billion over ten years. In addition, the measure included more than seventy-five other provisions, which would increase federal revenue by $82 billion over ten years. Some of the more significant ones are summarized here.

- **Repeal of extraterritorial income exclusion.** The measure phased out the ETI tax exclusion. For transactions prior to 2005 businesses would retain 100 percent of their ETI benefits. Beginning in 2005 taxpayers could claim 80 percent of their otherwise applicable ETI benefits for transactions during 2005, and 60 percent of the benefits during 2006, after which the tax exclusion would be fully repealed. The ETI exclusion would remain in effect for transactions in the ordinary course of a trade or business if those transactions were pursuant to a binding contract, or a purchase option, renewal, or replacement option included in a contract that was in effect by Sept. 27, 2003.

- **Extend Customs user fees.** The agreement extended customs-passenger, conveyance-processing, and merchandising fees through Sept. 30, 2014. These provisions were estimated by the Joint Committee on Taxation (JCT) to increase federal revenue by $18.6 billion over ten years.

- **Expatriated corporations.** The measure applied special tax rules to corporations that reincorporated overseas in what are known as "corporate inversion" transactions. The agreement denied the tax benefits of reincorporating overseas to companies where the inversion involved 80 percent or more of stock ownership.

- **Excise tax on stock compensation for officers of expatriated firms.** The measure also imposed a 15 percent excise tax on stock options and other stock-based compensation of certain corporate officers of expatriated corporations. The excise tax would increase to 20 percent beginning in 2009.

- **Expatriated individuals.** The measure clarified IRS rules for determining whether a U.S. citizen or long-term resident renounced his or her citizenship or residency to avoid paying taxes by providing for the use of an objective test with measurable standards. Those who failed the test would be taxed as U.S. citizens for the ten-year period following renouncement if they were present in the U.S. for more than thirty days in any year during that period.

- **Leasing arrangements by tax-exempt entities.** The agreement modified the recovery, or depreciation period, of certain property leased to a tax-exempt entity such as a municipality; altered the definition of the lease term for all property leased to a tax-exempt entity; and established rules to limit deductions associated with leases to tax-exempt entities if the leases did not satisfy specified criteria. These provisions were generally effective for leases entered into after March 12, 2004.

- **Other curbs on tax shelters.** The new law imposed several other curbs on abuse of tax shelters, including new limitations on the transfer and importation of built-in losses, new penalties for failing to disclose reportable transactions and other information about tax shelters to the IRS, expansion of the disallowance of interest deductions on convertible debt, and the disallowance of certain partnership losses.

- **Reduction of fuel-tax evasion.** The measure made several changes to reduce fuel-tax evasion. One of the most important revisions changed the taxation of aviation fuel so that the full rate of tax—21.9 cents per gallon—was imposed upon the removal of aviation fuel from a refinery or terminal, or upon entry into the United States. Under current law, unlike other fuels that generally were taxed upon removal from a terminal rack, aviation fuel was taxed upon the sale of the fuel by a producer or importer, and sales by a registered producer to another registered producer are exempt from tax, with the result that aviation fuel was not taxed until the fuel is used at the airport. Other provisions affected heavy vehicles and bulk transferers of taxable fuel, such as pipeline and tanker operators.

- **Permit private debt-collection companies to collect tax debts.** The measure permitted the IRS to use private debt-collection companies to locate and contact taxpayers owing outstanding tax liabilities of any type, and to arrange payment of those taxes by the taxpayers.

- **Donations of patents and other intellectual property.** The measure provided that if a taxpayer contributed a patent or other intellectual property, other than certain copyrights or inventory, to a charitable organization the taxpayer's initial charitable deduction would be limited to the lesser of the original value of the property or the fair market value of the property. In addition, the taxpayer would be permitted to deduct, as a charitable deduction, certain additional amounts in subsequent years based on a specified percentage, calculated on a sliding scale, of the qualified income received by the charitable organization with respect to the donated property.

• **Limit deduction for charitable contributions of vehicles.** The amount of a deduction for charitable contributions of vehicles was made dependent on the use of the vehicle by the organization receiving the donated vehicle. If the charity sold the donated vehicle the taxpayer's deduction could not exceed the proceeds from the sale. The measure imposed new substantiation requirements for deductions for which the claimed value was more than $500.

• **Tax on flu vaccine.** The measure added the vaccine against influenza to the list of vaccines that were taxable; the current rate was 75 cents a dose. Funds from the tax were deposited in the Vaccine Injury Compensation Trust Fund.

• **Close "SUV loophole."** The measure limited the ability of taxpayers to claim deductions under section 179 expensing for sport utility vehicles.

Chronology of Action on Economic Policy: Financial Regulation Policy

Introduction

Balance sheets, stock options, accounting standards, and other previously humdrum staples of business life suddenly became headline news during the first years of the twenty-first century as a series of financial scandals damaged the credibility of some of the country's major corporations and financial institutions. Revelations of misdeeds and wrongdoing began in late 2001 with the collapse of Enron Corporation, the giant Texas energy trading company. The Enron bankruptcy, at the time the largest bankruptcy in U.S. history, was quickly superseded by the bankruptcy in July 2002 of WorldCom, the country's second-largest telecommunications company. Several other large companies also declared bankruptcy, and senior executives at a dozen or so companies were arrested for criminal misconduct.

Subsequent investigations by New York attorney general Elliot Spitzer and the federal Securities and Exchange Commission (SEC) uncovered financial irregularities at brokerage firms, in the mutual funds and insurance industries, and at two huge, quasi-government mortgage lenders, Fannie Mae and Freddie Mac.

The corporate scandals undermined public confidence in both corporations and financial institutions. Millions of Americans began to doubt the wisdom of putting their life savings into the stock markets. Analysts said this drop in investor confidence in corporate culture contributed to the third consecutive year of declining stock values and slowed the nation's economic recovery from the mild recession of 2001.

The almost nonstop onslaught of news about misdeeds in corporate America during the first seven months of 2002 put enormous pressure on Congress, the Bush administration, and government regulators to take action to protect the public and investors. Enron's collapse was particularly embarrassing because the company had been an aggressive corporate contributor to candidates of both political parties, and its chairman, Kenneth L. Lay, was a long-time friend of President George W. Bush and a major financial supporter of his politi-

cal campaigns. In March Bush sent Congress a modest proposal for improving corporate governance, but by that point congressional and public opinion was demanding tougher action. In July the president signed legislation mandating the most important changes in federal regulation of corporate finances in decades. A key step was the creation of an independent board to oversee corporate accounting practices.

Once the corporate accounting law had been signed, however, Congress showed little appetite for dealing with the other financial problems uncovered in the mutual fund, insurance, and mortgage areas, preferring instead to let the industries, the regulators, and the courts work out the problems. As critics had predicted, legislators also seemed willing to pull back from some of the tough provisions in the 2002 law that tightened corporate accounting practices. The House passed legislation in 2004 that would have eased regulations on accounting for stock options, but the Senate put off action after regulators postponed the effective date of the new regulations.

REFERENCES

Discussion of financial regulation legislation for the years 1945–1964 may be found in *Congress and the Nation Vol. I*, pp. 337–386; for the years 1965–1968, *Congress and the Nation Vol. II*, pp. 253–279; for the years 1969–1972, *Congress and the Nation Vol. III*, pp. 135–145; for the years 1973–1976, *Congress and the Nation Vol. IV*, pp. 107–117; for the years 1977–1980, *Congress and the Nation Vol. V*, pp. 253–265; for the years 1981–1984, *Congress and the Nation Vol. VI*, pp. 83–93; for the years 1985–1988 *Congress and the Nation Vol. VII*, pp. 109–136; for the years 1989–1992, *Congress and the Nation Vol. VIII*, pp. 113–161; for the years 1993–1996, *Congress and the Nation Vol. IX*, pp. 109–148; for the years 1997–2001, *Congress and the Nation Vol. X*, pp. 120–144.

Congress took relatively little action on other financial regulation issues. An overhaul of the nation's bankruptcy laws failed in both the 107th and 108th Congresses, as it had in previous years. Legislators were able to clear a law on credit privacy, but mounting concerns over identity theft made it highly likely that Congress would be revisiting that issue as well as the bankruptcy overhaul legislation. In the aftermath of the terrorist attacks in 2001 Congress approved a measure temporarily capping the amounts commercial insurers could lose in the event of another terrorist attack. But legislation to extend the program failed to advance.

CORPORATE SCANDALS

The spate of corporate scandals in late 2001 and 2002 was unparalleled in modern American history. Five of the ten largest bankruptcies in U.S. history occurred in little more than a year. In addition to Enron and WorldCom, Global Crossing, another telecommunications company, headed to bankruptcy court, as did United Airlines, the second-largest U.S. air carrier, and insurance giant Conseco. Other household names that fell into bankruptcy during 2002 were the K-Mart discount retail chain and US Airways, the sixth-largest U.S. airline.

Three of the bankrupt companies—Enron, WorldCom, and Global Crossing—were among a dozen or so major corporations where senior executives were accused of issuing misleading financial reports, taking improper or illegal loans, or simply stealing from the corporate till. Allegations of corporate wrongdoing also plagued Adelphia, a major cable television provider; Tyco, an industrial conglomerate; and numerous other large firms. By the middle of the year Americans had become familiar with televised images of once high-flying corporate executives being led, handcuffed, from their homes following arrests.

No company suffered a worse fate than Arthur Andersen, the once-prestigious accounting giant that had certified the books for Enron, WorldCom, and several other troubled companies. The federal government filed an obstruction of justice charge against Arthur Andersen in April for its role in shredding documents at Enron and two months later won a guilty verdict against the company. Following its conviction, Andersen, which had already lost most of its accounting clients, closed its auditing practice and most of its U.S. offices. Several of Andersen's key components had been sold to rival accounting firms.

Numerous experts said the sensational reports about corporate and individual greed tended to obscure an important truth: company insiders would not have been able to get away with their misdeeds if investors and regulators had paid more attention to figures other than the short-term bottom line. During the stock market boom of the 1990s investors expected, even demanded, ever-rising values for their shares, and those values were largely based on reported revenues and net earnings. Few investors—whether individuals or giant institutions, such as pension funds—apparently bothered to scratch beneath the surface of quarterly and annual reports that tended to paint glowing pictures of corporate health. As a result, company insiders believed they would never be caught when they played with the books.

A succinct analysis of the problem came from the man who, perhaps more than anyone else, represented the U.S. financial establishment at the turn of the century— Federal Reserve Board chairman Alan Greenspan. Testifying before the Senate Banking Committee in July 2002 Greenspan diagnosed the problem facing corporate America as "infectious greed." Chief executive officers, he said, had created incentives for personal enrichment that "overcame the good judgment of too many corporate managers. It is not that humans have become any more greedy than in generations past. It is that the avenues to express greed have grown so enormously."

Following are snapshots of just a few of the corporate scandals that came to light between late 2001 and the end of 2002.

ENRON

The Enron Corporation was a Houston-based energy firm formed in 1985 from the merger of two natural gas pipeline companies. The innovative company grew quickly, becoming a trading company selling natural gas and electricity. By the late 1990s Enron was brokering deals for just about anything that could be sold in bulk, including coal, metals, wood pulp, and Internet services. Under Kenneth L. Lay, Enron's board chairman and, for most of the company's life, its chief executive officer as well, the company's reported revenues more than tripled between 1998 and 2000, from $31 billion to $100 billion. Its stock price rose accordingly, hitting $90 a share in August 2000 and closing that year at just over $88 a share. Lay touted Enron as the "world's leading energy company," and *Fortune* magazine consistently listed Enron as among the nation's "most admired companies."

By 2001 a few people were beginning to take a closer look at the company, and their findings were not all positive. In addition, California governor Gray Davis and other politicians were charging that the electricity shortages California was experiencing were caused primarily by Enron and other energy firms that were manipulating the markets by cutting supplies. Wall Street jitters about the company caused its stock to slide. By mid-August 2001 it stood at $45, half of what it had been a year earlier.

The public collapse of Enron began on October 16, 2001, when it reported a loss of $618 million for the third quarter of the year. Few details were offered, and the announcement raised many new questions about Enron's credibility. From then on the news from Enron was all bad. The company announced on Nov. 1 that the SEC had launched a formal investigation. On Nov. 8 Enron acknowledged that it was reducing its claimed earnings since 1997 by $586 million. On Nov. 19 it announced that it was unable to make payments on $690 million in outstanding debt. On Nov. 27 Standard and Poor's and Moody's, the credit rating services, cut Enron's rating to junk bond status. That move triggered contractual obligations for Enron to repay more than $3 billion in debt—money the company did not have.

After struggling unsuccessfully to line up emergency financing Enron announced on Dec. 2, 2001, that it was filing for bankruptcy protection. The next day Enron fired about 4,000 of the 7,500 employees at its Houston headquarters. Many of Enron's 21,000 employees lost the bulk of their retirement savings, which they had invested in Enron stock based on assurances by Lay and other executives that the company was sound. For nearly a month, between October and November, when Enron stock was plunging, Enron barred employees from selling the company shares in their retirement plans. Millions of other Americans also lost money on Enron through pension funds and mutual funds that had invested heavily in the company.

After Enron filed for bankruptcy it quickly became clear that the company had used questionable partnerships and other accounting gimmicks to disguise billions of dollars in debt and had claimed billions of dollars in revenues that did not exist. The revelations had continuing repercussions for the company, its top executives, and other companies that had participated in its fraudulent behavior.

As of the end of 2004, fifteen former Enron officials had pleaded guilty to civil or criminal charges and another six had been convicted. Of these the most important was Andrew S. Fastow, the former chief financial officer who was indicted in 2003 for allegedly developing the financial maneuvers that enhanced Enron's appearance of profitability. On Jan. 14, 2004, Fastow pleaded guilty to two charges of conspiracy to commit fraud. He agreed to a sentence of ten years in prison, forfeited $23.8 million in personal holdings, and was barred from ever again holding an executive office in a publicly traded company. Fastow's wife, an assistant treasurer at Enron, pleaded guilty to tax evasion; she was sentenced to one year in prison and one year of supervision after her release.

Jeffrey K. Skilling, Enron's former president who briefly served as chief executive before Enron's collapse, was charged with thirty-five financial misdeeds in February 2004. He pleaded not guilty to all of them.

In July 2004 Lay was charged with eleven counts of fraud and making false statements. He too pleaded not guilty and then held a press conference to declare his innocence, saying that only a "superman" could have kept track of everything at the giant firm. Later in the year the charges against Lay were split into two groups, meaning that he would face two separate trials: one dealing with four charges of fraud in his personal banking affairs and another dealing with seven charges of conspiracy and fraud in connection with his official acts at Enron. Those trials were not expected to take place until well into 2005 or later.

Enron was still undergoing reorganization in early 2005, but most of its viable businesses already had been sold off. Once the reorganization was complete, Enron's creditors, who had filed $67 billion in claims against the company,

were expected to receive between eighteen and twenty-two cents on the dollar. Enron's shareholders were to receive nothing for their stock, which was worthless.

In addition to Arthur Andersen, the Enron scandal affected at least three financial services firms. In July 2003 J.P. Morgan Chase and Citigroup settled federal charges against them in connection with hundreds of millions of dollars of loans to Enron under terms that disguised the debt or made the loans appear as revenue. In one case, for example, Enron borrowed $500 million from Citigroup and paid the money back a few days later—simply to allow it to book the $500 million as operating cash flow. The banks were not penalized in the settlement, but they were required to sign statements promising not to engage in similar transactions in the future.

In September 2003 Merrill Lynch & Company settled a federal case stemming from its participation in Enron deals during 1999; those deals allowed Enron to report inflated profits. Merrill Lynch pledged never again to engage in deals that might mislead investors, and it agreed to have an independent auditor approved by the Justice Department monitor some of its work related to complex financial transaction. Four Merrill Lynch investment bankers were convicted in November 2003 for their role in the fraudulent deals.

WORLDCOM

Enron's bankruptcy was exceeded a few months later by the collapse of WorldCom, a telecommunications firm created through an aggressive series of acquisitions by company founder Bernard J. Ebbers. The company declared bankruptcy in July 2002 after an SEC investigation discovered that the empire Ebbers had built was riddled with financial manipulations intended to bolster the appearance of profitability and thus WorldCom's share price. At the time of its bankruptcy WorldCom had accumulated debts of $42 billion. Subsequent investigations by the company showed that its earnings had been overstated by about $11 billion between 1999 and early 2002. In March 2004 the company restated its losses for the years 2000 through 2002, showing a total net loss for the period of $73.7 billion. Originally it reported a profit for this period.

As it moved through bankruptcy, WorldCom enjoyed one significant advantage over Enron: it had real assets and businesses that could form the basis for a revived company. WorldCom also appeared to have the advantage of a solid management team that took over after Ebbers, other top officials, and the board of directors were forced out. The new chairman and chief executive officer, Michael D. Cappellas, moved quickly to sell off unprofitable subsidiaries, laid off about 30,000 of the company's 85,000 employees, and focused on the company's core business, the long-distance carrier MCI, which Ebbers had acquired in 1999. As part of its emergence from bankruptcy in 2004 WorldCom changed its name to MCI.

Ebbers was indicted in March 2004 on three criminal counts of conspiracy, securities fraud, and filing false statements with the SEC. On the same day WorldCom's former chief financial officer Scott D. Sullivan entered a guilty plea to similar charges, strengthening the government's case against Ebbers, who was subsequently charged with six more counts of filing false statements. Sullivan also agreed to cooperate with federal investigators, and he testified against Ebbers at Ebbers's trial in early 2005. Ebbers, 63 at the time, took the stand in his own defense, claiming that he was unaware of the financial manipulations that were taking place at World-Com. The jurors apparently did not believe him. Ebbers was convicted on all nine counts in a decision announced March 15, 2005. On July 15 he was sentenced to twenty-five years in prison. Ebbers was expected to appeal his conviction.

Ebbers, other former WorldCom officials, and several investment banks that had financed the company also faced a shareholder class action suit, which was pending before a federal district court in New York at the end of 2004. The suit alleged that analysts at the banks had become concerned about WorldCom's financial health early in 2001 but had taken no action to make those concerns public. One of the banks, Citigroup, reached a settlement in the case in May 2004, agreeing to pay $2.6 billion to holders of WorldCom bonds and shares. The *Washington Post* estimated that investors in WorldCom's stocks and bonds had lost $175 billion.

WorldCom itself emerged from bankruptcy in a remarkably short period of time. The company's first major step toward regaining public confidence was its agreement to pay investors $750 million to settle civil fraud charges brought by the SEC. Another major step in rebuilding confidence was the company's acceptance of a radical restructuring of its corporate governance designed to ensure that the company's board of directors took an active role in monitoring the company instead of simply accepting management's claims about the financial health of the company.

TYCO INTERNATIONAL

Two former executives of Tyco International, an industrial conglomerate, were convicted in June 2005 of stealing hundreds of millions of dollars from the company. The two, Tyco's former chairman and chief executive L. Dennis Kozlowski and former chief financial officer Mark H. Swartz, had been indicted on twenty-two counts of grand larceny, falsifying business records, securities fraud, and conspiracy. Both were sentenced on Sept. 19, 2005, to between eight and a third and twenty-five years in prison. The indictments, in 2002, included stealing $170 million from the company and gaining about $430 million by secretly selling company shares, which had been artificially inflated.

The two also were ordered to pay a total of $134 million in restitution. In addition, Kozlowski was fined $70 million and Swartz $35 million.

Kozlowski had become something of a poster boy for corporate corruption. Previous reports, and evidence made public during the trial, showed that he dipped into corporate accounts to finance a lavish lifestyle. Public attention focused on a weeklong birthday party, costing at least $1 million, that Kozlowski held for his wife on the island of Sardinia in the Mediterranean, and the purchase, with company funds, of such items as a $6,000 shower curtain for his Manhattan apartment.

Tyco's troubles extended beyond the legal problems of its top managers. Its "lead director," Frank E. Walsh—a supposedly independent board member—pleaded guilty in December 2002 to securities fraud for soliciting a $20 million finder's fee for his role in arranging a business transaction involving Tyco. Walsh agreed to repay the $20 million, plus a $2.5 million fine. He was the first corporate director found guilty of a crime in the corporate scandals.

ADELPHIA COMMUNICATIONS CORP

Adelphia filed for bankruptcy protection in June 2002 following disclosure that the company's founder, John J. Rigas, and his two sons, Timothy and Michael, had defrauded the company of more than $1 billion in off-the-book loans. The publicly traded company was the sixth-largest cable television operator in the country. John and Timothy Rigas were convicted of several fraud charges in July 2004, but the jury deadlocked on the charges concerning Michael Rigas. He was awaiting retrial in October 2005.

Following the convictions, John Rigas was sentenced to fifteen years in prison and Timothy Rigas to twenty years. Both sentences were handed down in 2005. Before sentencing occurred, a settlement was reached in bankruptcy court that required the Rigas family to give up 95 percent of its assets, or more than $1.5 billion. The company in turn would pay $715 million to settle fraud charges against it.

In April 2005 Adelphia agreed to sell all its cable assets, including 5.2 million cable customers in thirty-one states, to two other major cable companies, Comcast Corp. and Time Warner Inc., for approximately $12.7 billion in cash and 16 percent of common stock in Time Warner Cable.

IMCLONE SYSTEMS AND MARTHA STEWART

In terms of public interest, the most closely watched corporate scandal involved Martha Stewart. One of the most recognized businesswomen in the United States, Stewart had built a media empire, called Martha Stewart Living Omnimedia, on a magazine and television show that offered advice to homemakers on cooking, gardening, and decorating. Many supporters said prosecutors had targeted Stewart simply because she was a famous woman; others said her prosecution showed that even someone as famous as Stewart could be brought to justice.

Stewart fell afoul of the law not because of her own business, but because of her sale of 4,000 shares in ImClone Systems on December 27, 2001—one day before the biotechnology company announced that its application for approval of a new cancer drug had been rejected by the Food and Drug Administration. Stewart insisted that her sale of the shares was based on a previous agreement with her broker relating to the value of the stock. Federal prosecutors disagreed, alleging that she had benefited from inside information received from her friend and ImClone's chief executive, Samuel Waksal. Stewart was charged with conspiracy, obstruction of justice, making false statements, and securities fraud. The latter charge, the most serious she faced, was dismissed, but she was convicted of the other charges on March 2, 2004.

On July 16 Stewart was sentenced to five months in prison, plus five months of home detention, two years of supervised probation, and a $30,000 fine. Although Stewart appealed her conviction, she voluntarily began serving her five-month sentence on Oct. 8, 2004, checking into a women's prison in Alderson, West Virginia.

INVESTMENT BANKS

Investigations in 2002 uncovered numerous other abuses in the securities industry, the most important of which appeared to be widespread conflicts of interests at some of Wall Street's biggest investment banks. Spitzer, New York's attorney general, the SEC, and other regulators found that banks had deceived investors by providing them with supposedly unbiased financial "research" that came from analysts who had financial relationships with the firms they were researching. During the 1990s some Wall Street analysts had gained fame and huge fortunes because of their ability to "pick" up-and-coming stocks ahead of time. Many of those favored companies, especially in the Internet and technology sectors, collapsed when the county's high-tech bubble burst in late 1999 and early 2000.

Congress included provisions in the corporate accountability bill to curb such conflicts of interests. In December 2002 Spitzer and the SEC reached what they called a "global settlement" with ten investment banks, settling charges that they had misled investors. Under the settlement the banks agreed to pay a total of $894 million in penalties and refunds to investors, $432.5 million to fund independent investment research for investors, and $80 million for programs to educate investors about how to judge the advice they received. The ten banks were Bear Sterns, Citigroup, Credit Suisse First Boston, Goldman Sachs, J.P. Morgan Chase, Lehman Brothers, Merrill Lynch, Morgan Stanley, Piper Jaffrey, and UBS Warburg.

MUTUAL FUNDS

The furor over the corporate accounting scandals had barely cooled when new revelations surfaced about improprieties in the mutual fund industry. Investigations by Spitzer, which were followed up by the SEC and other regulators, disclosed that several of the country's largest mutual funds had engaged in obscure practices that enriched a few investors, including managers at the funds, at the expense of the vast majority of shareholders.

By 2003 mutual funds had become the most popular form of long-term investment. According to some studies, more than 90 million Americans held shares in mutual funds, with most of it in pension-related investments. More than 8,000 funds held total assets of nearly $7 trillion—about half of it in stocks and the rest in bonds, money-market funds, and other types of investments. Americans assumed that their life savings were secure with mutual funds, which were obliged by law to operate solely in the interests of investors.

Those assumptions were challenged on Sept. 3, when Spitzer announced a $40 million settlement with Canary Capital Partners—a "hedge fund" that made investments based on speculation about future changes in share prices—and two related firms. Spitzer said the companies had engaged in two complex financial maneuvers known as "late trading" and "market timing" of shares in mutual funds. These practices cost the majority of investors only pennies apiece on each transaction but enriched the few—a version of stealing small amounts from large numbers of people in hopes that the losses would not be noticed.

Late trading involved the buying and selling of securities after the markets had closed for the day, but only if the closing prices of the securities had risen or fallen to a level enabling the trader to make money. Late trading was illegal in the United States, but an SEC survey conducted later in 2003 found that 25 percent of the nation's large brokerage firms allowed some clients to engage in the practice. Market timing was a legal practice in which investors bought and sold securities very rapidly to take advantage of fluctuations in market prices; most mutual funds, however, had rules prohibiting or severely restricting the practice. The SEC said its survey showed that nearly 70 percent of firms were aware that some customers engaged in market timing and 30 percent of firms admitted having helped those customers do it.

Both late trading and market timing could produce dramatic short-term profits. But when practiced at mutual funds these maneuvers damaged the overall financial picture of the funds, which were supposed to be havens for long-term investors.

Spitzer said his investigation had revealed evidence of "widespread illegal trading schemes" in the mutual fund industry. Based on the information gathered in the Canary Capital case, plus tips provided by whistle-blowers, Spitzer had already launched investigations into several large mutual funds. On Sept. 4 the SEC, which had primary federal authority for regulating the funds, sent letters demanding information from the country's largest funds and brokerage houses, then launched several investigations based on the responses.

The last three months of the year brought almost daily disclosures of illegal or improper dealings by some of the nation's biggest mutual funds; many others, however, apparently did not engage in the improper activities and were not named in investigations. Spitzer, the SEC, or in some cases both filed lawsuits that forced resignations of fund managers and led companies to change their operating policies. A few companies took action before charges were brought, apparently in hopes that preemptive action would lessen the bad publicity.

Putnam Investments, based in Boston, which had been the nation's fifth-largest mutual fund, suffered the biggest fall. It settled a suit with the SEC on Nov. 13 after its chairman was forced to resign and the company promised to institute the types of financial controls that it had previously claimed to have in place, including an independent board of directors. The SEC did not fine Putnam, but the company was nonetheless penalized by its investors, which pulled more than $20 billion—nearly 10 percent of the fund's primary holdings—out of Putnam in a few weeks.

Other mutual funds hit in the scandal included Morgan Stanley, the large investment bank, which agreed to pay a $50 million civil penalty to settle charges brought by the SEC; Charles Schwab, the nation's largest discount stockbroker; and Alliance Capital Management, one of the country's largest money managers, who agreed to pay its customers $250 million in restitution and reduce its fees by $70 million annually for five years.

In addition to late trading and market timing, investigators unearthed other common practices in the mutual fund industry that cost investors millions of dollars. Some funds were found to have charged investors fees and commissions without telling them or to have failed to give investors credit for volume discounts to which they were entitled. In December 2003 Merrill Lynch said it had engaged in the latter practice and would reimburse more than 20,000 customers of its mutual funds about $11 million that they should have received in volume discounts.

Battered by the surge of bad publicity about its practices the mutual fund industry produced a sudden battery of reforms in late October 2003. The industry's trade group, the Investment Company Institute, said it supported rules that would curb late trading and market timing. But the industry lobbied on Capitol Hill against proposed new legislation, saying it could clean up its own mess with the cooperation of the SEC. The House on Nov. 19 passed legislation (HR 2420) requiring mutual funds to tell investors about their fees and policies, and it established rules intended to make the board of directors of fund companies more independent from the managers. But the Senate took no action. Senate Banking Committee Chair Richard C. Shelby agreed that the industry and SEC should be given more time to work out new regulations.

INSURANCE COMPANIES

Late in 2004 New York attorney general Spitzer trained his sights on the insurance industry where he again uncovered a series of financial irregularities. Spitzer's first target was Marsh Inc., the world's largest insurance broker and a sub-

sidiary of the Marsh and McLennan Companies. Spitzer filed a lawsuit on Oct. 14 accusing Marsh of rigging prices and sending business to favored insurers in exchange for kickbacks. Spitzer said in a statement that his investigation would extend to many other companies because "virtually every line of insurance is implicated" in the kinds of practices he found at Marsh. Less that two weeks after Spitzer's lawsuit against Marsh was filed a major reshuffling took place at the company. Jeffrey W. Greenberg, chairman and chief executive of Marsh & McLennan, resigned on Oct. 25. Three weeks later five senior company officials left the board of directors.

Spitzer also filed suit Oct. 14 against two executives of American International Group (AIG) and one executive of Ace Ltd. AIG was already the subject of a long-running investigation by the SEC and major changes were anticipated at that company during 2005. Late in December the SEC also requested documents and other information from General Re, a reinsurance subsidiary of Berkshire Hathaway, the giant investment conglomerate run by Wall Street legend Warren Buffett. News reports suggested the SEC was expanding its investigation into several aspects of the insurance business.

FANNIE MAE AND FREDDIE MAC

Fannie Mae and Freddie Mac, the nation's two largest sources of money for home mortgages, came under intense scrutiny in 2003 and 2004 and for the first time in years were unable to rely for protection on their extensive Washington political connections. In June 2003 Freddie Mac ousted three top executives for failing to comply fully with an accounting audit and announced a $5 billion earnings restatement for the previous three years. The firings came just days after its regulator, the Office of Federal Housing Enterprise Oversight (OFHEO), in the Department of Housing and Urban Development, issued a rosy report about corporate governance at the two mortgage lending giants.

The scandal at Freddie Mac resulted in an investigation into Fannie Mae's accounting practices. In December 2004 its chief executive, Franklin D. Raines, and its chief financial officer, J. Timothy Howard, were forced to resign after the SEC required the company to correct its books in a way that reduced its claimed revenues by $9 billion over a three-and-a-half-year period. Fannie Mae had already agreed to make substantial changes in its accounting and management practices as a result of a report released by OFHEO in September. Among other things, OFHEO said Fannie Mae in 1998 had deliberately delayed booking expenses so Raines and other executives could get bonuses. Raines, who served as head of the White House Office of Management and Budget during the administration of President Bill Clinton, denied the charges.

2001–2002

Legislators had little on their financial regulation agenda when Congress convened in January 2001 other than to try again to pass legislation overhauling the nation's bankruptcy law, a long-sought goal of the business and financial communities. The terrorist attacks on Sept. 11, 2001, and a string of corporate accounting scandals that started coming to light in late 2001 changed the agenda completely. By the time the 107th Congress was finished at the end of 2002, legislators had still not been able to complete action on bankruptcy legislation. But they had provided a federal backstop to help the commercial insurance industry weather catastrophic losses in the event of future terrorist attacks. And, perhaps most important, Congress had passed landmark legislation regulating the accounting industry and cracking down on corporate fraud.

In other financial regulation action Congress passed legislation reducing fees charged by the Securities and Exchange Commission; the measure had been a top priority of Wall Street interests. But Congress failed to pass legislation that would have increased insurance coverage for bank depositors and make other changes in the federal deposit insurance system.

Bankruptcy Overhaul

For the third time in as many Congresses, legislation to overhaul federal bankruptcy law fell just short of the finish line. House and Senate conferees reached agreement on a bill (HR 333), but the conference report was scuttled in the closing days of the 107th Congress by a group of Republicans in the House opposed to abortion. They objected to a provision aimed at preventing antiabortion demonstrators from escaping court-ordered fines for their activities by declaring bankruptcy.

The measure, which would have made it harder for consumers to walk away from their debts, was a top priority for banks and credit card companies, which wanted to curb what they said was rampant abuse of the bankruptcy system. It was opposed by consumer advocates and bankruptcy attorneys who argued that it was a draconian assault on struggling debtors, especially when the economy was in recession. The bill would have forced more individuals filing for bankruptcy to use Chapter 13 of the bankruptcy code, which requires repayment of most debts, rather than Chapter 7, which allows individuals to escape remaining debts after liquidating their assets. The bill would have capped at $125,000 the amount of home equity a debtor could shield from creditors in bankruptcy proceedings for a house purchased within forty months of the bankruptcy filing.

BACKGROUND

The drive to rewrite the bankruptcy code began in response to a spike in consumer bankruptcy filings in the mid-

dle and late 1990s. The soaring numbers, which reached nearly 1.4 million in 1998, prompted complaints that many wealthier people were able to exploit the system to erase debts they could afford to pay. Opponents countered that the proposals to toughen bankruptcy requirements were an unwarranted attack on protections for the middle class, adding that they had little sympathy for credit card companies that flooded consumers with offers of easy credit.

Consumer filings dropped in 1999 and 2000, only to hit a new high of 1,452,030 in 2001. Experts said the increase stemmed from a combination of a souring economy and a market blitz by bankruptcy lawyers who warned debtors to file for protection before the law was changed.

Bankruptcy overhaul legislation had come close to enactment twice before. In both 1998 and 2000 the House and Senate completed negotiations on conference reports. The first one died in the Senate where Democrats were angry over the watering down of consumer protections. The second was pocket-vetoed by President Bill Clinton (1993–2001) who cited deletion of an earlier version of the provision aimed at anti-abortion protestors. He also criticized as too lenient a proposed $100,000 cap on the homestead exemption, applied only to homes held for two years or less before a bankruptcy filing. (*Congress and the Nation Vol. X, pp. 16, 142*)

LEGISLATIVE ACTION

When the 107th Congress began, bankruptcy reform seemed an odds-on favorite to be the first major legislative achievement of the session. With a new Republican president in the White House and a Republican majority in both chambers of Congress quick passage in 2001 seemed all but certain. The House and Senate easily passed separate bills in March (HR 333—H Rept 1073, Part I; S 420), but then power-sharing arguments in the Senate and the Sept. 11 terrorist attacks intervened and real negotiations on the measures did not get under way until 2002.

By mid-May 2002 negotiators had narrowed the differences to a single issue: a Senate provision aimed at preventing demonstrators—particularly protestors at abortion clinics—from filing for bankruptcy to avoid paying court-ordered fines and judgments. The dispute pitted the provision's Senate sponsor, Charles E. Schumer, D-N.Y., against abortion foe Rep. Henry J. Hyde, R.-Ill. For months the long-time adversaries refused to budge. But the pressure to advance the legislation, fueled by large campaign contributions from the financial services industry, finally forced them to reach a compromise in late July. (*Abortion debate, pp. 479, 510*)

GOP leaders were set to bring the conference report (H Rept 107-617) to the House floor before the August recess, but protests by a group of antiabortion Republicans led them to abandon their plans. The leadership tried again during the lame-duck session, but the opponents managed to defeat the rule for debate on the measure on a **key vote of 172–243 (R 124–87; D 48–155; I 0–1)**. *(2002 key votes, p. 819)*

On Nov. 15 the House passed the bill again after dropping the protest provision as well as language authorizing twenty-eight new bankruptcy judgeships. That maneuver killed any chance for passage. After the House vote Senate Minority Leader Tom Daschle, D-S.D., said the Senate would not pass the bill without the abortion provisions.

Lobbyists who had worked on the legislation for years only to see it collapse at the last minute said they were weary of the fight. Still, they said they would try again.

FARM PROTECTION

Although the broad bankruptcy overhaul bill collapsed, Congress did clear a temporary measure that extended bankruptcy protection for family farmers for six months, through June 30, 2003. The House passed the measure (HR 5472) by voice vote Oct. 1, and the Senate cleared it Nov. 20, also by voice vote. President George W. Bush signed it into law Dec. 19 (PL 107-377). *(Details, p. 456)*

SEC Fees

On the last day of the 2001 session lawmakers cleared a bill reducing fees charged by the Securities and Exchange Commission (SEC) on securities transactions. The legislation, which also increased the pay scale for SEC employees, was a top priority both for the agency and for Wall Street. President George W. Bush signed the measure into law on Jan. 16, 2002 (HR 1088—PL 107-123).

The new law was expected to reduce fees on stock transactions, the registration of securities, and merger and tender offers by $1.4 billion over the following decade. Supporters of the move noted that the volume of Wall Street trading had pushed revenue in the past several years to about six times the amount required to cover the SEC's annual expenses. For fiscal 2001, for example, the SEC was expected to receive $2.5 billion in total fees; the agency's expenditures were about $423 million. The leftover money went to Treasury and was treated as general tax revenue. Lawmakers said the collection amounted to an unfair tax because the costs were passed on to investors.

The SEC salary increase was aimed at creating pay parity between the agency's 3,000 employees and the better-paid employees at the three federal agencies charged with regulating banks: the Federal Reserve, the Comptroller of the Currency, and the Office of Thrift Supervision. The SEC had long complained that it was unable to keep professional personnel, especially lawyers, who often were lured away by Wall Street firms and other companies who needed experts in securities regulation and could pay higher salaries. The acting SEC chairman told the Senate Banking Committee in February 2001 that the agency had lost nearly a third of its accountants, attorneys, and examiners in the past two years.

Critics, including the White House, said the change would fragment the federal personnel system. Similar legislation foundered in the 106th Congress in part because House and Senate Republicans could not agree on the pay parity provisions. Key Senate Republicans insisted on including them while key House Republicans resisted, saying the higher salaries could open the door to overly aggressive securities regulation and enforcement.

MAJOR PROVISIONS

The following are the main provisions of PL 107-123:

• **SEC fee reductions.** Fees on securities transactions were reduced to $15 from $33.33 for each $1 million in securities bought or sold. Registration fees, paid by corporations and investment companies to register securities that they planned to sell, were reduced to $92 from $239 for each $1 million in securities. Fees on merger and tender offers were cut to $92 from $200 per $1 million in securities.

• **SEC pay parity.** The bill provided a demonstration program under which the SEC could increase the pay and benefits of any of its employees to levels comparable to those at the other federal bank regulatory agencies. The SEC was directed to consult with the Office of Personnel Management (OPM) in planning the new pay system and to submit a report to Congress and OPM before implementing the plan.

• **GAO study.** The General Accounting Office (GAO) was directed to prepare a study on the feasibility of allowing the SEC to collect fees to pay for its own operations without requiring the money to be appropriated, as it was under current law, and to set employee pay and benefit levels outside the federal civil service system.

LEGISLATIVE ACTION

The Senate acted first on the matter, passing its bill (S 143—S Rept 107-3) by voice vote on March 22. The House passed HR 1088 (H Rept 107-52, Part I) June 14 on a vote of 404–22. The bill had been held up for weeks while a turf battle over the pay parity issue was being resolved.

The bill stalled for another six months in the Senate where Democrats argued that not enough money was available under the fiscal 2002 budget resolution (H Con Res 83) to pay for both the SEC fee reductions and a separate patients' rights bill (S 1025). Several senators urged the House to take up the Senate bill and clear it for the president, but House leaders said that would violate the constitutional requirement that revenue bills start in their chamber. Finally, with pressure building to get the measure finished, the Senate cleared HR 1088 by voice vote Dec. 20. *(Budget resolution, p. 48; patients' rights, p. 475)*

Corporate Accounting and Governance

In a stark reversal of the deregulatory mood that had prevailed on Capitol Hill for several years, Congress cleared a landmark bill in 2002 to regulate the accounting industry and crack down on corporate fraud. The legislation came together in late July as a wave of corporate scandals battered the stock market and members scrambled to take action before the August recess. President George W. Bush signed the measure into law July 30 (HR 3763—PL 107-204).

The new law created an independent board, supervised by the Securities and Exchange Commission (SEC), to police the accounting industry with powers to set standards and to investigate and discipline violators. Accounting firms were generally barred from providing many lucrative consulting services to the companies whose books they audited. The law required that a company's audit committee—rather than company executives—assume responsibility for hiring and working with outside accounting firms. It also imposed new reporting and disclosure requirements on public companies and substantially increased criminal penalties for corporate fraud.

The impetus for the bill was a rash of corporate scandals that began with the collapse of the Houston-based Enron Corp. in December 2001. On Capitol Hill at least ten committees rushed to investigate the Enron collapse, at that time the largest bankruptcy in U.S. history. An overhaul of the accounting industry seemed all but certain.

The House passed an accounting regulation bill (HR 3763) in April 2002 that called for but would not have created a new public organization to oversee the auditing of publicly traded companies. The measure, sponsored by Financial Services Committee Chair Michael G. Oxley, R-Ohio, would have increased financial disclosure requirements and barred auditors from providing some consulting services to the companies they audited.

Many Democrats complained the bill lacked teeth, but by then the Enron scandal had receded from the headlines, subsumed by homeland security issues and a crisis in Israeli-Palestinian affairs. Conflicting congressional strategies and moves by the SEC to strengthen regulation on its own seemed to point toward stalemate.

The dynamic shifted dramatically in late June, however, when communications giant WorldCom Inc. disclosed that it had improperly accounted for $3.9 billion in expenses and Xerox Corp. revealed it had improperly accounted for $2 billion in revenue. The news jolted the stock markets, already suffering from a lack of investor confidence, and reinvigorated prospects for a much tougher bill (S 2673) in the Senate, sponsored by Paul S. Sarbanes, D-Md., chair of the Banking Committee.

When the Sarbanes bill passed the Senate July 15 without a single "nay" vote, the GOP-controlled House upped the ante, passing a separate measure (HR 5118) to increase criminal penalties for corporate fraud above even those in the broader Senate bill. With Bush and most members calling for final action before the August recess, the House and Senate quickly reached agreement, based largely on the Senate-passed bill.

The new law marked a shift away from the laissez-faire approach to business regulation of the previous several decades and toward more federal oversight of corporations, stock markets, and accounting firms. "The dramatic increase in huge audit failures has had an enormous psychological impact on investors and stock market levels," said Joel Seligman,

FUNDING AND LEADERSHIP AT THE SEC

Because the fiscal 2003 appropriations process broke down, the Securities and Exchange Commission had to wait to get extra funding to carry out its new responsibilities under the corporate accounting law. The agency ultimately got $716 million under the fiscal 2003 omnibus spending bill (PL 108-7) enacted in January 2003. That was less than the $776 million authorized under the accounting law but significantly more than the $567 million requested by President George W. Bush.

Meanwhile, Harvey L. Pitt abruptly resigned as SEC chairman Nov. 5, 2002. He was facing an internal SEC probe as well as the wrath of Sen. Paul S. Sarbanes, D-Md., and others over his handling of appointments to the oversight board. Sarbanes was a principal author of the corporate reform legislation. Pitt failed to tell the SEC commission before it confirmed William H. Webster III as chair that Webster had served as chair of the audit committee for financially troubled U.S. Technologies Inc. Webster, a former head of both the Central Intelligence Agency and the Federal Bureau of Investigation, later resigned. Earlier in the year Pitt had opened himself to ridicule when he tried, unsuccessfully, to get a provision in the corporate accounting bill to raise his pay and elevate his position to cabinet level. On Dec. 10, 2002, Bush picked William H. Donaldson to replace Pitt, subject to Senate confirmation. Donaldson, who co-founded the investment firm Donaldson, Lufkin & Jenrette, was a former chair and CEO of Aetna Inc., and a former chair of the New York Stock Exchange. However, Donaldson unexpectedly resigned at the end of June 2005 and was replaced by Christopher Cox, whom Bush appointed June 2. He was sworn into office Aug. 3, 2005. Cox was a former corporate lawyer and a House member who represented Orange County in California. (*Donaldson profile, presidential appointments, pp. 928–929*)

a securities law expert and dean of the Washington University School of Law in St. Louis. "What you are seeing at the moment is the clearest instance since the 1920s and 1930s that Congress is legislating precisely because they are concerned that investor confidence has been undermined."

HIGHLIGHTS

Following are the main components of the new accounting law:

• **Oversight board.** The law established a new, independent regulatory body—the Public Company Accounting Oversight Board—to police the auditing of publicly traded companies. The board, overseen by the SEC, was given authority to establish and enforce auditing standards and to investigate and discipline accountants or firms that violated the standards. Only two of the board's five members could be accountants. To ensure its independence, the board was to be funded by fees paid by public companies.

• **Auditor independence.** The law required that auditors be hired by and report to a company's audit committee. Accounting firms could not audit corporations whose top officials previously worked for the auditor and participated in the company's audit the previous year. Accounting firms were barred from performing eight specific services, including financial systems design, internal auditing, management consulting, and legal services, for public companies that they audited. Accounting firms had to rotate their lead audit partners at client corporations every five years.

• **Corporate responsibility.** Chief executive officers (CEOs) and chief financial officers (CFOs) were required to certify the accuracy of annual and quarterly financial reports. Willful violation could be punished by up to $5 million in fines and up to twenty years in prison. If the company was subsequently forced to restate its earnings, the CEO and CFO would have to pay back any bonuses or profits on company stock sales earned in the prior twelve months.

The SEC was directed to adopt new rules to prevent conflicts of interest by stock analysts and to place any civil penalties collected from corporate executives in a new fund that would be used to compensate victims who lost money because of the executives' violations of law.

• **Securities fraud.** The law established a new securities fraud penalty with a maximum prison sentence of up to twenty-five years and new criminal penalties of up to twenty years imprisonment for shareholder fraud and document shredding. It also gave corporate whistle-blowers federal protection against retaliation.

• **Accounting standards.** A majority of members of the Financial Accounting Standards Board (FASB), the private standards-setting body for accountants, could not have been affiliated with accounting firms in the previous two years.

• **SEC authorization.** The bill authorized $776 million for SEC operations in fiscal 2003, including $103 million to increase the salaries of SEC professionals and $98 million to hire 200 new employees.

BACKGROUND

Under federal law all corporations that sell stocks or bonds to the public are required to disclose detailed information about their financial condition. The financial statements are prepared by the company itself, in accordance with generally accepted accounting principles. They are then certified by independent outside auditors using random and systematic checks of company records and finances to verify the statements' accuracy.

Before enactment of the accounting bill the SEC had broad authority to regulate corporate accounting and the auditing of publicly traded companies, but it was limited by a lack of resources. As a result it tended to investigate and take enforcement action in only the most egregious cases.

The state boards of accountancy, which were responsible for licensing accountants to practice within their states, lacked the ability to investigate companies at a national level.

The most comprehensive supervision of accountants and auditors came from the industry's own trade association, the American Institute of Certified Public Accountants (AICPA), a voluntary organization funded entirely by the industry. While AICPA disciplined accountants, critics claimed that it generally resolved cases by issuing confidential letters to the parties involved rather than suspending or expelling the accountant from AICPA, which could disqualify the accountant from auditing some publicly traded companies.

The industry also had a peer review process under which accounting firms examined the audit work performed by other firms to determine whether it was done properly. That process was monitored by the Public Oversight Board, another body created and funded by the accounting industry. Since the board's creation in 1977 no major firm had ever failed a peer review, despite a series of accounting scandals, including the savings and loan crisis in the late 1980s.

SHOCK WAVES FROM ENRON

Just months before the energy giant Enron declared bankruptcy it had been widely regarded as one of the most innovative, fastest-growing, and best-managed businesses in the nation. The company also enjoyed close contacts with top Bush administration officials. But it turned out that the company's profitability was largely the result of creative accounting. Massive amounts of debt had been moved off Enron's books to special partnerships to prevent the losses from appearing on the company's financial statements. The shady bookkeeping was sanctioned by the company's auditor, Arthur Andersen LLP, which also earned millions of dollars in consulting fees from Enron. The accounting firm was later convicted of obstructing justice for shredding documents related to the Enron probe.

In response to the Enron scandal SEC chair Harvey L. Pitt in January called for a new private-sector body under the SEC to oversee and discipline auditors, replacing the supervisory functions performed by AICPA and the Public Oversight Board. The SEC also initiated numerous new reporting and disclosure rule-makings. Although Pitt promised to cooperate with Congress on legislation, he cautioned lawmakers not to go too far in mandating remedies.

As momentum for legislation built on Capitol Hill, President Bush sought to shape the debate, releasing a ten-point set of recommendations in March that relied heavily on SEC enforcement of existing laws. "Existing regulations should be clearer; penalties for wrongdoing should be tougher," he said March 7. Bush proposed blocking outside auditors from performing internal audits for the same client they audited and giving investors greater access to corporate financial data. He called for more rapid disclosure of stock transactions by corporate executives and said that CEOs should be required to vouch personally for corporate financial statements and surrender bonuses based on erroneous statements. One omission that drew immediate criticism from Democrats was any mention of additional funding for the beleaguered SEC.

Meanwhile many public companies began improving their financial reporting practices on their own in an effort to reduce investor wariness and demonstrate that they could police themselves. The trend included prominent companies such as General Electric, IBM Corp., and Intel Corp. Federal Reserve Board chair Alan Greenspan said market mechanisms were taking care of many issues that Congress was seeking to address through legislation.

HOUSE ACTION

The House Financial Services Committee approved Oxley's bill (HR 3763—H Rept 107-414) on April 16 by a vote of 49–12 with the support of sixteen Democrats.

The bill called for the SEC to develop and oversee the operations of a new regulatory body for the accounting industry with the organization's composition and powers left mainly to the SEC. It also called on the SEC to modify its own rules to prohibit accounting firms from performing two specific services—internal audits and designing financial information systems—for their audit clients.

The House passed the bill April 24 by a vote of 334–90. While ongoing criticism from Democrats spelled trouble ahead in the Senate, Oxley's immediate priority was to get a bill through the House. Democrats argued that Republicans had steered clear of a tougher measure because of their close ties to Wall Street.

As he had in committee, John J. LaFalce, D-N.Y., offered a substitute amendment aimed at strengthening the proposed new oversight board, including giving it subpoena powers, adding to the list of services that accounting firms would be barred from performing for their audit clients, and requiring greater accountability from corporate officers. The amendment was narrowly defeated on a near-party-line vote of 202–219.

In separate action the House Financial Services Committee gave voice vote approval April 11 to a bill (HR 3764—H Rept 107-415) to authorize $776 million for the SEC for fiscal 2003, 62 percent more than Bush requested.

SENATE ACTION

The Senate Banking, Housing, and Urban Affairs Committee approved Sarbanes's bill (S 2673—S Rept 107-205) on June 18 in a bipartisan vote of 17–4. The markup, which came after a last-minute deal that softened some provisions, ended a month-long standoff between Sarbanes and the panel's ranking Republican, Phil Gramm of Texas. The vote was a surprise to accounting industry lobbyists, who had fiercely opposed Sarbanes's approach.

The bill called for a new regulatory board under SEC oversight to monitor the accounting industry with powers to investigate and punish wrongdoing. It specified eight non-audit services or categories of service that auditors would not be able to provide to the companies they audited. The oversight board would be able to make exceptions on a company-by-company basis. CEOs and CFOs would have to certify company financial statements and lead audit partners could not be in charge of reviewing a single company's books for more than five consecutive years. Insider stock sales would be barred during "blackout" periods when employees were forbidden from selling shares from their retirement accounts.

The pace had quickened in late June as the revelations of shaky bookkeeping by WorldCom and Xerox reinvigorated Democrats and sent many Republicans rushing for cover. "The growing list of corporations under question makes clear that we aren't just talking about one or two isolated cases," Senate Majority Leader Tom Daschle, D-S.D., said pointedly, but "a deregulatory, permissive atmosphere that has relied too much on corporate America to police itself."

"The appearance and the potential for conflict is obvious," acknowledged Minority Leader Trent Lott, R-Miss. "Something's going to have to change."

The groundswell of support for the Sarbanes measure sent Bush rushing to get ahead of the debate. The president went to Wall Street on July 9 to chastise corporate executives and propose several legal and regulatory changes. Bush called for doubling prison sentences for mail and wire fraud and announced the creation of a corporate fraud task force to coordinate criminal investigations. "In the long run, there's no capitalism without conscience; there is no wealth without character," Bush said.

The Senate passed the Sarbanes bill July 15 by a vote of 97–0, then inserted the text into HR 3763 and sent it back to the House. As investors anxiously watched the markets and their dwindling retirement portfolios, the potential political fallout of failing to act had become obvious to all sides. Although Bush initially backed Oxley's approach, he signaled after the Senate vote that he would sign whatever bill Congress could get on his desk before the August recess.

During debate on the bill the Senate agreed to several amendments strengthening penalties for a variety of illegal activities. It rejected several others, including a proposal by John McCain, R-Ariz., to force businesses to report stock options as expenses for tax purposes. Democratic leaders prevented a vote on the amendment. Many companies, particularly high-tech ones, compensated their employees with stock options which they were not required to record as expenses for tax purposes. As a result, McCain and his supporters argued, shareholders were unaware of the real costs of compensation. Opponents of mandatory expensing of stock options countered that expensing would paint an unfair picture of a company's financial health, which could drive down stock prices. An attempt by Carl Levin, D-Mich., to require that the FASB review the treatment of stock options and adopt a rule governing that treatment was subsequently blocked by Gramm.

FINAL ACTION

Before going to conference House Republican leaders decided to seek some political cover by staking out a position on new and tougher criminal penalties for corporate fraud. The new bill (HR 5118), passed 392–28 on July 16, proposed to quadruple criminal penalties for mail and wire fraud to twenty years from five and to mandate criminal penalties for filing false statements with the SEC, among other provisions.

The conference report (H Rept 107-610), completed July 24, largely reflected the Senate bill and represented an ideological capitulation by congressional Republicans. Bush had outflanked members of his own party by calling on Congress to send him a bill before the August recess, leaving Republicans little choice but to abandon their traditional hands-off approach to securities market regulation. Moreover, Republicans were eager to put a halt to Democratic election-year attacks on the GOP as too cozy with business interests at a time when workers were losing their savings because of corporate fraud. A GOP pollster had warned Republicans that they would court disaster if they departed for a month-long vacation while the markets fell, without completing a bill.

While the Senate bill was the base text used by House and Senate negotiators, the increased penalties for corporate fraud also drew on the second House bill. House negotiators won some provisions, such as a requirement for real-time public disclosure of material changes in companies' financial conditions, as well as the requirement that civil penalties for securities law violations go into a fund for defrauded investors. Republicans also were able to rein in the independence of the new oversight board and place it more firmly under the aegis of the SEC than it would have been under the Senate-passed bill. New language in the conference report made it clear the SEC was empowered to require record-keeping by the board and to inspect the board's activities.

The House adopted the conference report in a nearly unanimous 423–3 vote on July 25, and the Senate cleared the bill 99–0 the same day.

PROVISIONS

As enacted PL 107-204 included the following major provisions overhauling regulation of the accounting industry and increasing corporate accountability:

Oversight Board

• **Board.** To protect the interests of investors, created a new, independent regulatory body, the Public Company Accounting Oversight Board, to oversee the auditing of publicly traded companies. Required the board to operate under Securities and Exchange Commission oversight and submit all of its rules, decisions, and sanctions to the SEC for approval. Allowed the SEC to censure or limit the board's activities, operations, and members for cause.

• **Membership.** Established the board of five full-time members with staggered terms of five years appointed by the SEC in consultation with the Federal Reserve chairman and the Treasury secretary. Allowed no more than two of the board members to have worked previously as certified public accountants. Required board members to serve full time and prohibited them from employment in any other business or professional activity during their terms. Limited board members to two terms.

• **Registration and inspection.** Required accounting firms that audit publicly traded companies to register with the oversight board. Required the board to conduct annual inspections of accounting firms that regularly audit more than 100 publicly traded companies, and to inspect other accounting firms at least once every three years. Made foreign public accounting firms that audit companies whose shares trade on U.S. exchanges subject to the new law.

• **Powers.** Gave the board authority to establish and enforce auditing standards and to investigate and discipline accountants or accounting firms that violate those standards. Empowered the board to require registered accounting firms to provide documents and testimony in the course of an investigation, and to ask other companies and individuals to provide documents and testimony, as well as request the SEC to issue subpoenas.

• **Penalties.** Authorized the board to suspend or bar individuals from being associated with registered accounting firms and suspend or revoke accounting firms' registration. Allowed it to levy civil penalties of not more than $100,000 for an individual or $2 million for a corporation. Made intentional, knowing, or reckless conduct punishable by a penalty of up to $750,000 for an individual and $15 million for a corporation.

• **Funding.** To ensure its independence, provided funding for the board through annual accounting fees assessed on publicly traded companies, with each company's assessment determined by its average annual market capitalization (the company's share price multiplied by the number of shares issued).

• **Auditing standards.** Required the board to establish or adopt standards for audits of public companies. Specified that the standards must require registered accounting firms to prepare and maintain audit work papers for seven years, including an evaluation of the internal financial controls of their public company clients.

Accounting Standards

• **Funding.** To ensure its independence, required the Financial Accounting Standards Board (FASB), which sets national accounting standards, to be funded by fees assessed on publicly traded companies.

• **Membership.** Required a majority of FASB's board be composed of individuals who have not been affiliated with accounting firms during their service or in the two years prior to their service.

• **Accounting system.** Directed FASB to conduct a study on the possible use of a "principles-based" accounting system, in which accounting guidelines are loosely drawn and based on principle, rather than the existing "rules-based" accounting system, which relies on specifically enumerated rules.

Auditor Independence

- **Audit committees.** Set out the following requirements:
  - Auditors must be hired by, and report to, a company's audit committee (or if there is no audit committee, the company's entire board of directors).
  - The audit committee must set compensation levels for outside accountants and be able to seek outside advice at company expense.
  - Accounting firms must report to audit committees regarding accounting policies and procedures, alternative treatments of financial information that the auditors have discussed with company management, if any, and material written communications between the auditors and company management.
  - Audit committees must set up a procedure for receiving complaints regarding the company's accounting and auditing, as well as confidential, anonymous information provided by company employees.
  - Each member of a corporation's audit committee must be "independent"—not part of the company's management and not receiving any compensation from the company for consulting or other services. Allowed the SEC to make exceptions.
  - Prohibited accounting firms from auditing a corporation if the chief executive officer, chief financial officer, controller, chief accounting officer, or any person serving in an equivalent position previously worked for the accounting firm and participated in the company audit during the previous year.
- **Nonaudit services.** Barred auditors from providing specified nonaudit services to the same publicly traded companies they audit. Barred services included bookkeeping or other services related to accounting records or financial statements; financial information systems design and implementation; appraisal or valuation services; actuarial services; internal audits; management or human resources; broker/dealer, investment adviser or investment banking services; legal and expert services; or other services the board decides are not permitted. Allowed the board to grant case-by-case exceptions to the banned services.

Allowed accounting firms to provide certain other nonaudit services, including tax services, to a corporation, if approved in advance by the audit committee. Specified that prior approval by the audit committee, or a designated subset of the audit committee, was not required if combined compensation for all such nonaudit services was 5 percent or less of the total compensation paid by the corporation to the auditor during the fiscal year, or if such services were not recognized as nonaudit services by the client at the time of engagement, or if such services are promptly brought to the audit committee's attention and approved by either the audit committee or one or more of its members before the completion of the audit.

- **Auditor rotation.** Required accounting firms to periodically rotate their lead audit partners, and the review partners, so that no one partner either leads an audit for a specific public company or reviews it for more than five years in a row.
- **GAO study.** Directed the Comptroller General to study the possible impact of requiring mandatory rotation of entire accounting firms on audits of publicly traded companies.

Corporate Responsibility

- **Executive responsibility.** Required corporate CEOs and CFOs and those persons performing similar functions at publicly traded companies—including U.S. companies that establish a shell headquarters abroad—to certify the accuracy of annual and quarterly company financial reports to the SEC. Required the executives to attest that they had reviewed the report and, based on their knowledge, vouch that it did not contain any untruths or misstatements of any significant facts and that the report represented an accurate description of the company's financial condition in all material respects. Required that they also verify that they have established, and are maintaining and periodically evaluating, internal controls so that they can become aware of any material changes in the company's financial condition.
- **Improper influence on audits.** Forbid company officers and directors from directly or indirectly fraudulently influencing, coercing, manipulating, or misleading the company's outside auditors.
- **CEO and CFO forfeitures.** If a company is later forced to restate its earnings because of material noncompliance or misconduct regarding financial reporting requirements, required the CEO and CFO to repay the company any bonuses or compensation based on incentives or stock, as well as any profits they earned from sales of company stock during the twelve months following the initial financial statement. Allowed the SEC to make exceptions.
- **Officer and director bars.** Allowed the SEC to ask a federal court to bar a person from serving as an officer or director of publicly traded companies if the person's conduct demonstrated "unfitness." (The previous standard was "substantial unfitness.")
- **Stock trading restrictions.** Prohibited corporate directors or executive officers from buying, selling, or transferring company stock during "blackout" periods of at least three consecutive business days when at least 50 percent of all participants and beneficiaries in the company-sponsored pension or 401(k) plan are barred from doing so. If an executive illegally conducts a stock transaction during blackout periods, allowed the company to go to court to recover any profits made from the transaction, subject to a two-year statute of limitations. Authorized shareholders to also go to court after waiting sixty days for the company to take action.

Specified that applicable blackout periods did not include regularly scheduled blackout periods that were part of the plan and disclosed to employees or that were imposed when participants or beneficiaries either begin or cease to be part of the plan as a result of a merger, acquisition, divestiture, or similar transaction that involved either the retirement plan or the plan sponsor.

(Plan administrators were generally required to notify participants and beneficiaries thirty days in advance of any blackout period—including the reasons for the blackout and when it was expected to begin and end—and issue a statement advising the participants or beneficiaries to review their individual investment decisions in light of the blackout period. The secretary of labor was authorized to fine plan administrators up to $100 per day per participant or beneficiary for failing or refusing to provide required notices.)

• **Attorney responsibility.** Required the SEC, within 180 days of enactment, to issue rules requiring attorneys who appear and practice before the commission on behalf of publicly traded companies to report material securities law violations, breaches of fiduciary duty, or similar violations to the company's chief legal counsel or its CEO. If those officers did not appropriately respond to the report, required the attorney to inform either the company's audit committee, another committee of independent directors, or the entire board of directors.

• **Fund for defrauded investors.** Required money collected through court-ordered disgorgements (refunds of money by defendants because of securities law violations), settlements involving disgorgements, or civil penalties must, at the SEC's discretion, be put into a fund to be paid to victims of the particular violation. Allowed the SEC also to accept gifts and bequests made to the United States for the fund.

Disclosure and Transparency Requirements

• **Off-balance-sheet disclosures.** Required corporations to include in their annual and quarterly financial reports to the SEC any information on off-balance-sheet transactions or partnerships that may have an effect on the company's financial condition. Prohibited a company's "pro forma" financial statements, such as preliminary reports or releases issued in advance of quarterly and annual SEC reports, from containing any untrue material statements or omitting material information that made the statement misleading, and required the company to depict the financial conditions and operations of the company under generally accepted accounting principles.

• **Special-purpose entities.** Directed the SEC to study filings by publicly traded companies to determine the extent to which off-balance-sheet transactions and special-purpose entities (complex business arrangements that can be used to transfer and hide debt) are used and whether generally accepted accounting rules provide for transparent disclosure to investors. Required the SEC to report to the president and the Senate Banking and the House Financial Services committees as to the number of off-balance-sheet transactions employed by publicly traded companies, the extent to which special-purpose entities were used as part of such transactions, and whether generally accepted accounting principles or SEC rules provided for transparent disclosure of off-balance-sheet transactions, and to issue SEC recommendations for improving the reporting of off-balance-sheet transactions.

• **Conflicts of interest.** Barred publicly traded companies from making loans to directors or officers. Allowed certain exceptions including home improvement and manufactured home loans; consumer credit; charge cards; and margin accounts for employees of securities brokers and dealers, so long as they were provided in the ordinary course of the company's consumer credit business and made available to the public on terms that are at least as favorable.

Specified that the prohibition did not apply to loans made or maintained by insured depository institutions if the loans were subject to prior restrictions on insider lending.

Required directors, officers, and owners of more than 10 percent of stock in a publicly traded company to file statements with the SEC indicating the amount of stock held and any changes in ownership before the end of the second business day that follows the day the relevant transaction occurred.

• **Internal controls.** Required annual company reports to the SEC to contain statements of management responsibility for establishing and maintaining internal controls and financial reporting procedures, along with an assessment of their effectiveness, and required the company's outside accounting firm to evaluate those statements and assessments.

• **Codes of ethics.** Required public companies to report to the SEC regarding whether they have codes of ethics for their senior financial officers. Required companies to immediately disclose any changes to or waivers of their codes of ethics.

• **Audit committee financial experts.** Required public companies to report to the SEC as to whether at least one member of the audit committee is a "financial expert," defined as someone who understands generally accepted accounting principles, including for estimates, accruals, and reserves; has experience in preparing or auditing financial statements at similar companies; and has experience with internal accounting controls as well as an understanding of the role of audit committees.

• **Enhanced SEC review.** Required the SEC to review public company filings at least once every three years, paying particular attention to companies that have restated their financial results, have especially volatile stock prices, have the largest market capitalizations, and "significantly affect" particular economic sectors.

• **Real-time disclosures.** Required publicly traded companies to plainly and publicly disclose "on a rapid and current basis" any material changes in their operations or financial conditions.

Securities Analysts

• **Conflicts of interest.** Required the SEC, or registered securities associations or national securities exchanges that the SEC designates, to adopt rules to prevent conflicts of interest by stock analysts.

Specified that the rules:

• Must limit the ability of investment bankers who underwrite stocks to supervise or affect the compensation of stock analysts who work for the same firm;

• Restrict advance approval of analyst reports by investment bankers;

• Prevent investment bankers from retaliating against affiliated stock analysts who issue unfavorable recommendations against stocks;

• Create structural and informational firewalls to separate the investment and research divisions of investment banks;

• Define periods surrounding initial public offerings of stock during which involved brokers and dealers should not publish or distribute research reports on the stock of the issuing company;

• Require a stock analyst, in preparing research reports and when making public appearances, to disclose the extent to which he owns the stock being discussed; whether the analyst or his employer has received any income from the company whose stock is being discussed; whether his employer has had any business dealings in the past year with the company; and whether the analyst's compensation was tied to investment banking revenues collected by his employer.

SEC Resources and Authority

• **Fiscal 2003 authorization.** Authorized $776 million for the SEC for fiscal 2003, $317.4 million more than the agency's fiscal 2002 appropriation. Of that amount, designated $102.7 million for commission salaries and benefits, $108.4 million for information technology, security, and recovery from the Sept. 11 terrorist attacks, and $98 million for hiring not fewer than 200 additional staff members.

• **Additional SEC authority.** Authorized the SEC to censure or bar from appearing or practicing before the commission any person whom it finds to be lacking in qualifications or integrity or to have engaged in improper or unethical conduct.

• **Penny stock bars.** Specified that courts have the authority to bar persons found to have engaged in misconduct from any offering of penny stocks, which are high-risk stocks that typically sell for less than one dollar a share, but allowed the SEC to grant exceptions.

Corporate Fraud

• **Document falsification and shredding.** Made punishable by a fine and/or up to twenty years in prison knowingly altering, falsifying, or destroying records, documents, or tangible objects with the intent to obstruct justice.

• **Audit records.** Required accountants to keep audit and review records for five years after the end of the fiscal period during which the audit or review occurred with violations punishable by a fine and/or up to ten years in prison.

• **Debts in bankruptcy.** Amended federal bankruptcy law so that debts resulting from judgments, orders, or settlements incurred because of securities law violations or common law fraud cannot be discharged in bankruptcy proceedings.

• **Statute of limitations.** Expanded the statute of limitations for civil lawsuits related to securities fraud to up to two years after discovery of the fraud or five years after the fraud occurred. (Previously the limit was one year after discovery of the fraud or three years after the fraud occurred. The longer period was backed by plaintiff lawyers.)

• **Whistle-blower protections.** Prohibited publicly traded companies and their agents from retaliating against whistle-blowers who provide information or otherwise assist in an investigation being conducted by the company, federal regulators or law enforcement, or members of Congress or congressional committees. Gave whistle-blowers who claim they suffered retaliation ninety days to file a complaint with the secretary of labor and allowed them to seek redress in federal court if there were no final decision in the dispute within 180 days.

• **Securities fraud felony.** Made a "scheme or artifice" to defraud shareholders or to obtain money or property in connection with securities fraud punishable by a fine and/or up to twenty-five years in prison.

White-Collar Crime

• **Mail and wire fraud.** Increased criminal penalties for mail and wire fraud to a maximum of twenty years in prison, up from five.

• **Pension law violations.** Made violations of the Employee Retirement Income Security Act of 1974 (PL 93-406) punishable by a fine of up to $100,000 and/or ten years in prison. (Previously the penalty was a fine of up to $5,000 and one year in prison.) Made corporations subject to a fine of up to $500,000. (Previously the penalty was a fine of up to $100,000.)

• **Certification of financial reports.** Required CEOs and CFOs to certify that SEC filings fully comply with legal requirements and that they fairly describe, in all material respects, the company's operations and financial condition. Made knowing violations punishable by a fine of up to $1 million and ten years in prison and willful violations punishable by a fine of up to $5 million and twenty years in prison.

• **Attempt and conspiracy.** Made attempting or conspiring to commit offenses under this section of the legislation crimes that carry punishments equal to those for committing the crime itself.

Corporate Fraud Accountability

• **Record tampering.** Made destroying or tampering with records, documents, or other objects, or attempting to do so, to obstruct or impede official proceedings subject to a fine and/or up to twenty years in prison.

• **Temporary freeze authority.** Allowed the SEC to petition a federal court to order that extraordinary payments by a public company under investigation to its officers, directors, employees, or other persons be held in escrow for up to ninety days.

• **Officer and director bars.** Empowered the SEC to prohibit persons, either temporarily or permanently, from serving as officers or directors of publicly traded companies upon a finding that they are unfit to do so.

• **Increased criminal penalties.** Made violations of the Securities and Exchange Act of 1934 punishable by a fine of up to $5 million and/or twenty years in prison. (Previously penalties were a $1 million fine and/or ten years in prison.) Made corporations subject to a fine of up to $25 million. (Previously the penalty was a fine of up to $2.5 million.)

• **Whistle-blower protections.** Specified that anyone who knowingly retaliates against a person who provides truthful information to a law enforcement officer shall be fined and/or imprisoned for up to ten years.

Terrorism Insurance

In November 2002, more than a year after terrorists crashed hijacked planes into the World Trade Center in New York City and the Pentagon outside Washington, D.C., Congress cleared legislation establishing a three-year federal terrorism insurance program. The program placed a cap on potential losses for commercial property and casualty insurers in the event of another cataclysmic terrorist attack. The aim was to encourage the insurance industry to provide commercial terrorism coverage at affordable rates in the wake of the Sept. 11, 2001, attacks, while giving it time to absorb the risks. The measure required the government to cover 90 percent of an insurance company's terrorism-related losses, once insured losses exceeded a specific trigger level. Total federal responsibility was capped at $100 billion a year. President George W. Bush signed the bill into law Nov. 26 (HR 3210—PL 107-297). *(Provisions and legislative action on HR 3210, pp. 203, 219)*

Enactment was a major victory for the commercial and real estate industries. The insurance industry said it would be able to cover all claims from Sept. 11 but might not be able to provide coverage for future terrorist acts. Concern quickly mounted that a lack of affordable terrorism insurance could severely disrupt the U.S. economy and further deepen the nation's economic problems. Commercial insurers, real estate investors, retailers, and others pressed Congress to act quickly.

Passage of the measure was also a victory for Bush who had made the legislation one of his top domestic priorities and who had personally lobbied for its passage. And it was a victory for Democrats, who successfully resisted the inclusion of a ban on punitive damages in terrorism cases. The dispute over punitive damages nearly sank the legislation. The House had included such a ban in the legislation it passed on Nov. 29, 2001. Many Senate Republicans insisted that such a ban be part of any terrorism insurance bill, demands that were backed by the White House. But such a ban

was anathema to many Senate Democrats, especially Majority Leader Tom Daschle of South Dakota. Daschle and other Democrats had long fought so-called tort-reform legislation that would limit or ban the punitive damages that could be awarded victims in medical malpractice and other types of injury suits.

The deadlock was finally broken in October 2002 when Bush unexpectedly struck a deal with Senate Democrats to drop the punitive damages provision and to consolidate in federal court civil lawsuits arising from terrorist acts. Punitive damages awarded in a lawsuit would not count as insured losses subject to government aid. Unhappy with the compromise, House Republicans continued to stall action on the final version of the bill until the president promised to push legislation in 2003 setting broad new limits on punitive damages.

Bank Insurance

A string of bank failures and a steady erosion of deposit insurance reserves spurred efforts in both chambers of Congress to increase insurance coverage for depositors and make other changes to the nation's deposit insurance system. The House passed a bill by an overwhelming majority in May, but a companion Senate measure never got out of the Banking Committee.

The bills (HR 3717, S 1945) proposed to merge the two existing federal deposit insurance funds, increase deposit insurance for individual accounts from $100,000 to $130,000 per account with future increases linked to inflation, and more than double coverage for individual retirement accounts. To add stability to the deposit insurance funds the Federal Deposit Insurance Corporation (FDIC) would be given authority to impose premiums on well-capitalized and well-managed banks that were not paying anything under the existing system.

Smaller banks wanted the increase in deposit insurance, hoping it would enable them to attract more depositors. But large banks, which were not as dependent on deposits as a source of lending capital, worried that increased coverage levels for depositors would lead to higher FDIC premiums for the banks.

BACKGROUND

The FDIC and the federal deposit insurance system were established in 1934 to stabilize the nation's banking system in the wake of a national run on banks and thrifts. Under the system the federal government guaranteed the funds of bank depositors in the event of a bank failure. Initially the FDIC insured deposits up to $2,500. Congress periodically increased the limit, most recently in 1980, when the previous $40,000 limit was raised to $100,000 per account (PL 96-221). *(Congress and the Nation Vol. V, p. 261)*

In the late 1980s and early 1990s Congress modified the deposit insurance system in response to the savings and loan crisis and bank failures. Among other things Congress eliminated the separate agency that had insured savings and loans (the Federal Savings and Loan Insurance Corporation) and established two distinct insurance funds under the FDIC—the Bank Insurance Fund (BIF), which insured commercial banks, and the Savings Association Insurance Fund (SAIF), which did the same for thrifts.

The two funds were required by law to maintain reserves equal to $1.25 for every $100 in insured deposits. If the BIF fell below that level premiums of up to twenty-three cents for every $100 of insured deposits would be automatically assessed on all banks—including well-capitalized low-risk institutions—until the funds climbed above the reserve ratio.

In reality both funds exceeded the legally required ratio; neither fund had dipped below it since 1996. The FDIC estimated that 92 percent of banks paid no premiums and that more than 900 institutions chartered since 1996 had never paid them. But the BIF ratio had been declining, both because of bank failures and because the uncertain stock market had led investors to shift funds into insured deposits.

Investment firms such as Merrill Lynch & Co. and Salomon Smith Barney were pouring money into insured bank deposit accounts. By spreading deposits among several of their affiliated banks they were able to tout aggregate FDIC protection as high as $1 million. According to the FDIC, the two firms had swept a total of $73 billion into BIF-insured accounts between March 2000 and September 2001, automatically sending the FDIC's reserve ratio to about 1.32 percent, uncomfortably close to the 1.25 percent trigger level. The investment firms were among the institutions that paid no premiums.

Commercial banks did not like the idea that they would be required to bear part of the burden if the reserve ratio fell much further. The FDIC argued that the system was too cyclical with most banks paying too little in a healthy economy, then facing drastic premium assessments in a sour one when they could least afford to pay them. Even opponents of premium increases wanted some adjustments to avoid a sudden assessment when reserves dipped too low.

The major elements of the bill would have:

• Raised the deposit insurance coverage from $100,000 to $130,000 per account and required increases indexed to inflation every five years.

• Increased coverage for certain types of retirement accounts, such as IRAs, 401(k)s, and Keogh plans from $100,000 to $260,000.

• Merged BIF and SAIF. There was widespread agreement among federal regulators and the private sector that there was no longer a need for two separate agencies since the ownership of banks and thrifts was now so commingled.

• Eliminated the statutory 1.25 reserve ratio and allowed the FDIC to establish an annual reserve that could range from $1.15 to $1.40 for every $100 of insured deposits. The FDIC would be authorized to impose risk-based premium assessments on all banks and thrifts whenever deposit insurance fund balances declined behold the threshold.

The House Financial Services Committee approved HR 3717 (HRept 107-467) by a vote of 52–2 on April 17. The bill breezed through the House 408–18 on May 22 under expedited procedures that barred amendments and required a two-thirds majority.

2003–2004

The 108th Congress enacted only one significant piece of financial regulation legislation—a measure that barred states from writing their own consumer credit reporting laws. The measure ensured that businesses would have to comply only with national privacy standards regarding consumer credit, rather than a mix of state laws, some of which might be tougher than the national standard.

Once again Congress was unable to complete action on legislation to overhaul the nation's bankruptcy system or to revise the federal deposit insurance system. Congress also failed to extend a federal terrorism insurance program enacted in 2002 despite a strong push from the insurance and real estate lobbies. Questionable practices in the mutual fund industry and at the mortgage finance giants Fannie Mae and Freddie Mac raised congressional concerns but did not compel Congress to take immediate action as had the corporate accounting scandals in 2002. The House passed legislation setting new regulations for the mutual fund industry, but with the Securities and Exchange Commission already taking steps to curb the abusive practices Senate Banking Committee Chair Richard C. Shelby, R-Ala., decided to delay further action. Partisan division and powerful lobbying by the two mortgage companies blocked action in both chambers on new regulations for Fannie Mae and Freddie Mac.

An effort to undo one of the regulations that was written in the wake of the corporate accounting standard was also left unfinished. In 2004 the House passed legislation blocking a new rule that would require companies to treat stock options as an expense on financials statements. But Shelby opposed the controversial legislation and refused to consider it.

Financial Privacy

In a victory for the financial services industry Congress in 2003 cleared legislation that blocked states from writing their own consumer credit reporting laws and ensured that businesses were covered by a single, nationwide privacy standard. The bill permanently extended portions of the Fair Credit Reporting Act that preempted state law and were scheduled to expire Jan. 1, 2004. President George W. Bush signed the bill into law (HR 2622—PL 108-159) on Dec. 4.

If Congress had not acted, states could have adopted tougher credit laws starting in 2004. Enactment nullified a California law set to take effect within months that would have allowed consumers to stop banks and other financial institutions from sharing their personal financial information with affiliated companies.

Business and financial groups made enactment a top priority and mounted an intensive lobbying effort. They argued that without national privacy standards they would have to comply with a patchwork of state regulations, which they said would result in higher interest rates for consumers, less access to credit, and less protection against identity theft.

Consumer groups, in contrast, urged Congress to let the provisions expire. They said that the law did not provide sufficient consumer protections—particularly on the sharing of information—and that states should be permitted to enact laws that better protect their citizens.

In the House Spencer Bachus, R-Ala., the sponsor of the bill, was able to mute consumer criticism and build bipartisan support for the measure by adding provisions, including "fraud alerts," to guard against the growing problem of identity theft. A Federal Trade Commission report said that 27.3 million Americans had been the victims of identity theft in the previous five years, leaving businesses on the hook for $48 billion and resulting in $5 billion in out-of-pocket expenses.

In the Senate, Banking Committee Chair Richard C. Shelby, R-Ala., struggled to reconcile his own strong support for more consumer privacy with pressure from the White House to advance bank-friendly legislation quickly. He ultimately threw his support behind the bill when it was expanded to include a version of one of his chief proposals—giving consumers more power to block solicitations from others parts of a financial conglomerate with which they were already doing business.

A final conflict was resolved during House-Senate negotiations when conferees agreed to block states from enacting identity theft statutes that were at odds with the bill. That was similar to language in the House bill and was a disappointment to consumer groups that had hoped to preserve a range of state powers to act in the area of identity theft.

BACKGROUND

The 1996 provisions permanently extended under the bill were enacted as part of the fiscal 1997 omnibus appropriations law (PL 104-208). They expanded the original Fair Credit Reporting Act (PL 91-508), which became law in 1970 in response to the rapid growth of the credit reporting industry. (*Congress and the Nation Vol. IX, p. 136*)

The 1996 provisions established specific procedures for credit bureaus to follow in checking and correcting disputed information in a consumer's file. They also extended the requirements to banks, retailers, and other businesses that furnished credit information to credit bureaus. They allowed the use of credit reports for "prescreening" activities that enabled companies to make unsolicited offers of credit or insurance to consumers. They also allowed affiliated companies to share with one another their customers' credit information, including credit applications and reports. The 1996 legislation generally preempted stronger state credit laws but set the exemption to expire on Jan. 1, 2004.

MAJOR PROVISIONS

As enacted PL 108-159 included the following major provisions:

• **Federal preemption.** Permanently extended provisions of the 1996 law that prevented states from enacting credit or credit reporting laws that conflicted with federal law.

- **One-call fraud alert.** Allowed consumers who believed they were victims of fraud to place a "fraud alert" in their credit report, good for ninety days, by calling a single national credit bureau that would pass the alert on to the others. Required creditors to take certain precautions before extending credit to consumers who had such alerts in their files. Allowed consumers, under some circumstances, to obtain alerts that were good for seven years.

- **Protecting consumer credit.** Allowed consumers to block adverse information caused by identity theft from being furnished to credit bureaus or from being given by one credit bureau to another party. As of December 2006 prohibited businesses that accepted credit or debit cards from printing on the receipts more than the last five digits of the card number.

- **Free credit reports.** Provided consumers the right to obtain a free copy of their credit reports once a year from each of the three national credit bureaus—Equifax, Experian, and TransUnion—through a centralized source. Required consumers to be notified when adverse or negative information had been furnished to a nationwide credit bureau. Required federal regulators to develop more stringent guidelines to ensure credit reports were accurate.

- **Marketing "opt out."** Allowed consumers to opt out of receiving solicitations from an affiliate based on consumer information supplied to a related company, good for five years and renewable for another five.

- **Credit scores.** Required credit bureaus to provide a consumer, upon request, information regarding the individual's most recent credit score—a numerical rating drawn from information in the credit report—at a reasonable fee. Required mortgage lenders to disclose credit scores to the borrower if the scores affected the loan.

LEGISLATIVE ACTION

Despite strong lobbying on both sides of the issue HR 2622 won broad support at every step of the legislative process. The House Financial Services Committee approved the bill (H Rept 108-263, Parts I and II) on July 24 with only three dissenting votes. The full House passed the bill 392–30 on Sept. 10. The Senate Banking Committee approved its version of the bill (S 1753—S Rept 108-166) by voice vote Sept. 23. The Senate passed HR 2622 by an overwhelming 95–2 vote Nov. 5 after substituting the text of its own bill. The House adopted the conference report (H Rept 108-396) by a vote of 379–49 on Nov. 21, and the Senate cleared the bill by voice vote the next day.

Bankruptcy Reform

A broad overhaul of the nation's bankruptcy laws (HR 975) failed to win congressional approval in 2004 for the fourth time in as many Congresses. The overhaul, which would have made it more difficult for some consumers to walk away from their debts, had considerable bipartisan support. But an amendment aimed at preventing abortion protestors from filing for bankruptcy to escape civil fines and judgments spelled the death knell for the reform bill, as it had in two previous Congresses. *(Background and previous action, p. 129)*

HR 975, like its predecessors in three previous Congresses, sought to impose a means test to steer more filers into repaying, rather than discharging, their debts. The new standard would apply to those seeking protection from creditors under Chapter 7 of the federal bankruptcy code, which allowed debtors to clear unpaid balances after liquidating their assets. Those with sufficient income to repay $10,000 or 25 percent of their debts over five years would be required to file instead under Chapter 13, which required repayment of most debts.

A homestead exemption would allow debtors to shield from creditors up to $125,000 of equity for homes bought within forty months of filing for bankruptcy. The bill also included provisions to make permanent Chapter 12 bankruptcy protection for family farmers and extend the coverage to family fishing businesses.

Lobbyists representing banks, credit card companies, retailers, and other businesses had beseeched Congress since 1997 to pass such legislation, arguing that it was needed to prevent abuses of the system by debtors who could afford to repay more of what they owed. On the other side, a coalition of consumer groups, unions, and other organizations opposed the legislation, saying it ignored practices by credit card companies that encouraged consumers to pile up high levels of debt, even in a weak economy. "All we do in this bill is sock it to people in desperate straits in many, many different ways," said Rep. Jerrold Nadler, D-N.Y. "This bill is a testament to the power of large financial institutions in our political system."

On March 19, 2003, the House handily passed a bankruptcy overhaul bill (HR 975) 315–113. But action stalled in the Senate where Republican leaders worried that the amendments, championed by Democrat Charles E. Schumer of New York, could be adopted in the closely divided Senate.

The Senate did, however, approve a measure extending bankruptcy protection to farmers (S 1920), and in January 2004 the House sought to force a conference with the Senate on the broader bankruptcy bill by combining the two measures. On Jan. 28 the House passed S 1920 on a 265–99 vote after incorporating the language of HR 975 by voice vote.

The House action was designed to make farm-state senators uncomfortable about standing in the way of the bankruptcy overhaul. Democrats blasted the move as a political ploy that could endanger the livelihood of farmers. Although he supported both bankruptcy measures, Senate Minority Leader Tom Daschle, D-S.D., gave no indication that he was willing to cut a deal to abandon or water down the abortion provision.

With the impasse over the Schumer amendment seemingly insurmountable, Congress quietly and without dissent agreed in October 2004 to extend the special federal bankruptcy protections for farmers through June 2005, a move signaling that the broader reform legislation had died for the fourth consecutive Congress.

The Senate passed the farm bankruptcy measure (S 2864) by voice vote Oct. 6; the House cleared it by voice vote Oct. 8. The president signed it into law (PL 108-369) on Oct. 25, 2004. The measure, which was retroactive to Jan. 1, 2004, allowed family farmers to restructure their debts without losing their land. *(Farm bankruptcy action, p. 465)*

Bank Insurance

The House passed a bill in April 2003 to streamline the federal bank insurance system and increase the limits on deposit insurance of individual consumers. But for the second year in a row the legislation ran aground in the Senate. Senate Banking Committee Chair Richard C. Shelby, R-Ala., opposed the increase in deposit insurance and refused to bring a companion bill before his committee. The House-passed bill (HR 522) died at the end of the 108th Congress.

The legislation was backed by small banks, which hoped a boost in individual deposit coverage would help them bring in more deposits and compete with better-funded big banks. Small banks depended more than their larger competitors on deposits as a source of lending capital. The Bush administration and the Federal Reserve opposed the bill, however, saying raising the insurance coverage would boost the government's risk without benefiting consumers.

HR 522 (H Rept 108-50) was virtually identical to one the House had passed in 2002. It proposed to merge the two existing federal deposit insurance funds; increase deposit insurance for individual accounts from $100,000 to $130,000 per account, with future increases linked to inflation, and more than double coverage for individual retirement accounts. *(2002 action, background, p. 138)*

The House Financial Services Committee approved the bill by voice vote March 13. The House passed the bill 411–11 on April 2. The strong vote was seen as support for raising the insurance limits on retirement accounts and for merging the two insurance funds.

Terrorism Insurance

Despite a strong push from the insurance and real estate lobbies, Congress did not complete action on legislation to extend a federal terrorism insurance program that was scheduled to expire at the end of 2005. The program, enacted in 2002, placed a cap on potential losses for commercial property and casualty insurers in the event of another cataclysmic terrorist attack similar to the one on Sept. 11, 2001, that killed nearly 3,000 people, destroyed the World Trade Center towers, and damaged the Pentagon. *(2002 action, p. 138)*

The 2002 legislation (HR 3210—PL 107-297) required the government to cover 90 percent of an insurance company's terrorism-related losses once insured losses exceeded a specific trigger level. Total federal responsibility was capped at $100 billion a year. The aim was to encourage the insurance industry to provide commercial terrorism coverage at affordable rates while giving it time to develop pricing and risk models for terrorism coverage that did not require the federal government to act as a backstop.

The industry, however, had not yet developed viable alternatives. It urged Congress to approve an extension because policies that extended beyond 2005 were already being negotiated. The House Financial Services Committee approved extending PL 107-297 through 2007, but no further action occurred. A Treasury Department report on the effectiveness of the program was due in June 2005.

Mutual Fund Regulation

Revelations in 2003 of a wave of trading abuses by mutual fund operators led the House in November to approve a set of new regulations for the industry. The Senate Banking Committee promised to look into the issue in 2004, but the panel decided to delay action when it became apparent that the Securities and Exchange Commission (SEC) was also taking steps to impose new curbs. Announcing in April that he would not introduce legislation, Banking Committee Chairman Richard C. Shelby R-Ala., said he would give the SEC "an opportunity to regulate and enforce as they should do."

For years mutual funds had been seen as a safe and reliable way to invest. They allowed individuals to pool small sums of money in a single fund and receive a diversified investment in stocks, bonds, and other securities held and managed by the fund. An estimated 95 million households, nearly half of all U.S. households, owned mutual funds to save for retirement, education, and other purposes.

Confidence in the industry sagged swiftly in September 2003 when New York attorney general Eliot Spitzer charged hedge fund Canary Capital Partners with buying shares of funds run by Bank of America after the 4 p.m. close of trade. Such "late trading" allowed the buyer to get the closing price while taking advantage of any breaking news that might increase the fund's price the next day. Regulators later determined that late trading was widespread, as was "market timing," the practice of executing quick buy or sell trades to take advantage of the fact that mutual fund prices often lagged behind changes in the value of the fund's holdings.

By November federal and state regulators had brought charges against other fund companies and their executives, alleging that insiders had skimmed millions from investors by executing quick in-and-out trades in mutual fund shares. The SEC followed up with actions against Putnam Investments and other firms.

On Nov. 19 the House passed HR 2420 by a 418–2 vote after expanding and strengthening the version that had been approved by the House Financial Services Committee in June (H Rept 108-351). Among other things, the measure barred mutual fund employees from engaging in any short-term trading of their own shares in the fund and prohibited any individual from managing both a mutual fund and a hedge fund at the same time. The bill also contained several provisions designed to force mutual funds to disclose fees to their investors and to strengthen the independence of fund boards.

Although the Senate Banking Committee held several hearings on mutual fund regulation, it decided to delay any further action when it became clear that the SEC was taking steps on its own to curb the abusive practices. Between September 2003 and May 2004 the SEC imposed $630 million in fines and penalties to settle allegations of abusive sales and trading practices. The agency also adopted or proposed more than a dozen regulations governing mutual funds, including some of those contained in the House-passed legislation.

Mortgage Finance Regulation

Legislation to overhaul regulation of Fannie Mae and Freddie Mac died at the end of 2004, the victim of partisan tensions and questions about how to effectively regulate the mortgage finance giants. Congress took up the issue after questions about accounting practices at the two companies began to surface in 2003. The Senate Banking, Housing, and Urban Affairs Committee approved a bill (S 1508) by a 12–9 April 1, 2004, but no further action was taken on it. A draft bill in the House was shelved in October 2003 after the White House objected to it.

BACKGROUND

Fannie Mae and Freddie Mac were the nation's largest and second-largest mortgage financing companies. Together they owned or guaranteed more than $3.6 trillion in home loans, nearly half of all outstanding home mortgages and an amount equal to about one-third of the value of the annual national economy. They were created by Congress—Fannie Mae in 1938 and Freddie Mac in 1970—to boost home ownership by buying mortgages from banks, savings and loans, and other lenders to free up money so those lenders could churn out new loans for home buyers.

The companies, whose roles changed as the economy changed, held some of those loans in their own portfolios, earning the interest and collecting the principal as the loans were repaid. However, Fannie and Freddie now pooled most of the loans they bought into assets known as mortgage-backed securities and sold those to Wall Street investors. Both operations spread the risk, which in turn kept mortgage interest rates down.

The growth of these two profitable enterprises coincided with a surge in U.S. home ownership to a record 68.6 percent at the end of 2003—and the maturing of what even their critics described as a successful housing finance system.

Fannie Mae and Freddie Mac were originally created as "government sponsored enterprises" and were changed to publicly traded companies (Fannie Mae in 1968; Freddie Mac in 1989). They still benefited, however, from one holdover from their days as quasi-governmental entities—they each had $2.3 billion lines of credit with the U.S. Treasury. The availability of that emergency cash led investors to believe the federal government would bail out either company in the event of a financial catastrophe. As a result, Wall Street lent to both companies at rates almost as low as those paid by the government on its own debt. Cheap loans allowed Fannie Mae and Freddie Max to purchase higher-yielding mortgages and profit from the difference, or "spread," between the two rates.

Critics had long warned that this perceived government guarantee allowed Fannie Mae and Freddie Mac to take on too much risk, more than investors would tolerate from companies that were not seen as affiliated with the government. Those concerns intensified in June 2003 when Freddie Mac ousted three top executives for failing to comply fully with an accounting audit and announced a $5 billion earnings restatement for the three previous three years. The firings came just days after its regulator, the Office of Federal Housing Enterprise Oversight (OFHEO), in the Department of Housing and Urban Development, issued a rosy report about corporate governance at the two mortgage lending giants. Congress set up OFHEO in 1992 as part of a larger effort to strengthen federal oversight of the two large government sponsored enterprises (PL 102-550). (*Congress and the Nation Vol. VIII, p. 153*)

The scandal at Freddie Mac resulted in an investigation into Fannie Mae's accounting practices; in September 2004 OFHEO released a scathing report accusing the company of accounting irregularities and earnings manipulations that misrepresented its financial well-being and may have helped enrich the companies top executives. As a result, Fannie Mae agreed to make major changes in its accounting and management practices. In December 2004 the Securities and Exchange Commission said its review had shown that Fannie Mae failed to account properly for its derivatives and used to hedge against swings in interest rates, and it told the company to restate its earnings. The order, which was expected to result in the company's lowering profits since 2001 by $9 billion, led to the ouster of Fannie Mae's two top executives.

Even before questions were raised about Fannie Mae and Freddie Mac, accounting irregularities were already a sensitive topic on Capitol Hill after bookkeeping scandals at Enron Corp., WorldCom Inc., and other publicly traded companies had rocked the stock market and angered investors and the general public. Congress had acted surprisingly quickly in 2002 to tighten oversight of corporate accounting. That accounting problems could threaten the financial viability of the two giant mortgage lenders was enough to get the attention of lawmakers and start a serious dialogue about how to better monitor and oversee the activities of the firms. It was not enough, however, for legislators, in an election year, to overcome partisan differences or strenuous lobbying by Fannie Mae and Freddie Mac.

LEGISLATIVE ACTION

In the House, Financial Services Committee Chair Michael G. Oxley, R-Ohio, spent weeks in 2003 working out a compromise aimed at balancing critics' desire for tougher regulation with the concern expressed by committee Democrats that a new law not restrict Fannie's and Freddie's role in facilitating home ownership by lower- and middle-class Americans. Oxley drafted a bill that would have shifted financial oversight of the two companies to a new regulatory agency to be created within the Treasury Department. But the White House objected, arguing that the measure did not give the regulator adequate authority to do its job. Oxley cancelled a markup scheduled for Oct. 8, and the committee took no formal action on the measure in the 108th Congress.

The Senate Banking Committee took a different tack, approving a bill that would have established a new safety and soundness regulator and allowed it to raise minimum capital requirements for the two enterprises. But the bill stalled in the face of strong lobbying from the two companies. Some lawmakers also objected to a provision that would allow the new regulator to appoint a receiver for the enterprises if they should end up in financial peril. Critics said that provision would undermine the long-held market perception that the federal government would bail out the firms if they were unable to meet their financial obligations.

Stock Option Expensing

The House easily passed legislation in July 2004 to block a proposed accounting rule that would require companies to treat stock options as an expense on financial statements. However, the Senate did not act on a companion bill and the legislation died at the end of the 108th Congress.

Stock options gave the holder the right to buy stock at some point in the future at a predetermined price. When stock prices rose the holders gained value because they could purchase the stock for less than it was worth in the market. Under the rule proposed by the Financial Accounting Standards Board (FASB) companies would be required to value employee stock options and deduct the amount from their earnings. The rule was set to take effect by the end of the year, but the FASB voted in October to delay implementation until June 15, 2005. The FASB, which set national accounting standards, was a technically independent agency that derived its authority from the Securities and Exchange Commission (SEC).

FASB had been trying to require companies to account for stock options as an expense for more than a decade, saying that such an accounting would give investors a more accurate picture of a company's financial condition. The board had little success, however, until the corporate accounting scandals at Enron Corp. and WorldCom, among others, impelled Congress to enact a tough corporate fraud law in 2002 that gave the FASB new political clout.

Start-up companies and high-tech firms opposed the rule because they relied heavily on options to compensate executives and other workers. If companies were required to account for options as an expense, as salaries and bonuses were treated, many companies would show losses instead of profits on their income statements. As a result, some companies, notably those in the technology industry, said the rule could force them to stop issuing stock options, which would harm their ability to recruit talented workers and hurt the competitiveness of U.S. companies in world markets.

In the House Financial Services Committee Chair Michael G. Oxley, R-Ohio, put off considering legislation throughout 2003. Oxley, whose name graced the corporate accounting bill passed in 2002, had long said that he thought expensing of stock options was inevitable at some point. But after considerable pressure from technology companies and colleagues from both sides of the aisle, Oxley relented. On June 15 the Financial Services Committee approved HR 3574 (H Rept 108-609, Part I) by a vote of 45–13. A month later, on July 20, the full House passed the measure 312–111.

As passed the House bill would have required companies to expense the stock options of their five most highly compensated individuals and estimate the value of those options assuming that the underlying stock would not rise or fall in price. The bill also would have prohibited the SEC from recognizing an expensing standard until an economic analysis was completed by the departments of Commerce and Labor.

In the Senate Richard C. Shelby, R. Ala., chair of the Banking, Housing, and Urban Affairs Committee, said he would not bring up legislation (S 1890) to block the FASB rule despite the measure's considerable support. Shelby and at least four other senators on the committee, including at least one Democrat, argued that politics should not interfere with the agency's independence and rule-making authority.

Chronology of Action on Economic Policy: Trade Policy

Introduction

Action on trade policy took a back seat to other economic issues during President George W. Bush's first term in office. But trade issues—especially the outsourcing of jobs to workers overseas—drew substantial attention as the political costs of globalization began to grow.

Globalization was the term applied to the expansion of trade and investment between nations bilaterally and among countries in multi-nation agreements. The concept arose in the late twentieth century from the convergence of several trends, including the collapse of communism in eastern Europe and the former Soviet Union between 1989 and 1991, the move toward capitalism in communist China (home to one-sixth of the world's population), the adoption of free market economic principles in many developing countries that had tried—and rejected—socialism, and creation of regional "free-trade" zones, particularly in Europe, North America, and South America. The mechanisms that encouraged globalization were the computer, the Internet, overnight air-freight deliveries, and other high-tech methods that allowed corporations and investors to move money, goods, and services around the world efficiently and seamlessly.

As the world's largest economy the United States was the most important engine for globalization. The country's decade-long economic expansion during the 1990s helped fuel growth and trade throughout the world. Washington was also a major factor in promoting international agreements to reduce barriers to trade. Among the principal achievements of Bill Clinton's presidency (1993–2001) were the North American Free-Trade Agreement (NAFTA), which eliminated most trade barriers among Canada, Mexico, and the United States; the completion of the Uruguay Round of the General Agreement on Tariffs and Trade, which reduced many tariffs and trade quotas worldwide and created the World Trade Organization (WTO) to monitor and enforce trade agreements; and the negotiation of a permanent trade agreement between the United States and China, which cleared the way for China to join the WTO.

Globalization had clear benefits, especially for corporations and consumers in industrialized countries. Companies had more markets in which to compete to sell their goods and services; consumers had more choices than ever before, and buyers enjoyed lower prices from the increased competition. Yet globalization was also controversial. Workers in the United States and other countries lamented the millions of industrial jobs lost to developing countries where pay and labor standards were lower. Environmentalists contended that weaker environmental regulations in developing countries resulted in more air and water pollution and the loss of irreplaceable natural resources. In addition, human rights groups and some religious leaders warned against multinational corporations that sought to maximize profits by shifting industrial production to wherever costs were lowest, regardless of the impact on workers and their families.

In the first years of the twenty-first century, as the U.S economy dropped from boom to bust and then began a slow and fitful recovery, more and more Americans saw globaliza-

REFERENCES

Discussion of trade action for the years 1945–1964 may be found in *Congress and the Nation Vol. I*, pp. 187–207; for the years 1965–1968, *Congress and the Nation Vol. II*, pp. 49–116; for the years 1969–1972, *Congress and the Nation Vol. III*, pp. 119–134; for the years 1973–1976, *Congress and the Nation Vol. IV*, pp. 125–137; for the years 1977–1980, *Congress and the Nation Vol. V*, pp. 267–276; for the years 1981–1984, *Congress and the Nation Vol. VI*, pp. 95–112; for the years 1985–1988, *Congress and the Nation Vol. VII*, pp. 139–166; for the years 1989–1992, *Congress and the Nation Vol. VIII*, pp. 165–200; for the years 1993–1996, *Congress and the Nation Vol. IX*, pp. 151–184; for the years 1997–2001, *Congress and the Nation Vol. X*, pp. 147–170.

Trade Balance

Billions of Dollars

NOTE: Trade includes the balance on trade in goods and services. The current account includes the balances on trade in goods and services, income, and net unilateral transfers such as private remittances.

SOURCE: Bureau of Economic Analysis, Department of Commerce, "U.S. International Transactions."

tion as a source of their misfortunes. Some companies found their products could no longer compete against cheaper imports. American workers complained that the cheaper imports were costing them their jobs. For many years American manufacturers had been moving some of their factory jobs to foreign countries where labor was cheaper. More recently American companies began moving service jobs overseas, particularly to India, which had an abundance of educated, English-speaking workers who could perform a range of tasks from staffing call centers to reading medical X-rays to preparing income tax returns—all for wages well below those for the same work performed in the United States. Economists said that productivity gains (a result largely of the same high technology that allowed globalization) were the main reason employers were slow to hire new workers after the mild recession of 2001. But many workers blamed job "outsourcing" for the "jobless recovery," and criticisms of the practice became a Democratic theme in the presidential elections of 2004.

FAST-TRACK LEGISLATION

The treatment of labor in trade agreements was a central element in the one significant trade debate during Bush's first term in office: restoring fast-track trade authority that allowed Congress to approve or reject, but not amend, trade agreements negotiated by the president and his representatives. With fast track in place U.S. negotiators and their counterparts from other countries could be reasonably certain

that Congress would not try to amend trade agreements after they were signed, thus forcing new rounds of negotiation. Bush lobbied hard for, and eventually won, the authority (which his administration called trade promotion authority). Yet congressional action stretched out over nearly eighteen months, the president had to accept an expanded program of aid for dislocated workers to win Democratic support, and even then victory was not ensured until the final votes were counted. The extended consideration of this high-priority request showed the ambivalence about globalization that permeated Congress, which in itself reflected the depth of controversy among workers throughout the U.S. economy.

The fast-track procedure had been in use since the late 1970s but lapsed in the 1990s. Congress last approved fast track in 1993, enabling President Clinton, an ardent promoter of free trade and globalization, to negotiate the final stages of the Uruguay Round. Clinton made a modest effort in 1995 to regain fast-track authority but was rebuffed by Republicans who had taken control of both chambers in the 1994 elections.

Clinton renewed his request for fast-track authority after his reelection in 1996 but this time encountered resistance from within his own party. Angered that the North American Free Trade Agreement that Clinton had pushed through Congress in 1993 appeared to result in the loss of U.S. industrial jobs to Mexico, many Democrats opposed giving the president unfettered authority to negotiate future trade agreements. Faced with the likelihood that only a small number of Democrats would support Clinton, House GOP leaders shelved the fast-track legislation without bringing it to a floor vote. The move marked one of the gravest defeats for any president on trade legislation in many years.

In 2001 House Democrats were again the main obstacle to renewing fast-track authority for the new Republican president, and for much the same reason—a concern that trade agreements could hurt American workers and undermine U.S. trade laws and environmental protections in the United States. They were joined by a small but significant group of Republicans, primarily from industrial districts where key constituents were facing pressure from foreign competitors. House Speaker J. Dennis Hastert, R-Ill., postponed a floor vote on the legislation three times after whip counts showed it would not pass. The measure finally came to the floor on December 6, 2001, where it passed by a single vote, 215–214, after the Republican leadership struck last-minute deals with a handful of Republicans from textile districts in the South.

In the narrowly divided Senate, which usually looked favorably on free trade, Democrats insisted that fast-track authority be paired with an expansion of assistance, including health insurance benefits to U.S. workers dislocated by foreign competition. Despite an explicit veto threat the Senate also adopted an amendment that would allow any part of a trade agreement that altered U.S. antidumping laws or other statutes providing remedies for unfair trade to be vetoed by a simple majority vote of the Senate. The amendment reflected a widespread congressional concern that in their zeal to liberalize trade U.S. negotiators would agree to deals that would deprive domestic producers of trade remedies under U.S. law. The amendment also would have violated the guiding principle of the fast-track procedure—that Congress could not amend trade agreements negotiated by the president.

The Senate version, passed in mid-May 2002, sparked significant opposition from House Republicans as well as from the White House. By mid-summer partisan maneuvering was threatening to kill the measure in conference. The November mid-term elections were approaching, labor unions were ramping up their anti-fast-track rhetoric, and leaders in both chambers were reluctant to force members to vote on the controversial measure. But with Bush insisting on quick action to aid the faltering economy and lawmakers eager to show voters that Congress was willing to act decisively, the House and Senate leaders of the conference committee met behind closed doors in late July. They worked out a compromise on a final bill that included expanded assistance for dislocated workers but dropped the Senate language that would have allowed Congress to alter language in trade agreements regarding trade remedies.

The Senate easily adopted the conference report, but it was still nip-and-tuck in the House even after a visit to the Capitol by the president. With the help of five pro-business Democrats who resisted pressure from their leadership and voted for the conference report after having opposed the initial House bill, the GOP leadership carried the day, winning adoption of the conference report 215–212.

Ironically, fast-track authority was probably not essential for approval of the five bilateral trade agreements that came before Congress in Bush's first term. A pact with Jordan was approved in September 2001, just two weeks after the terrorist attacks on the World Trade Center and the Pentagon. That agreement was the first to include requirements that neither country would lower its labor or environmental standards to promote trade. The Bush administration eased aside the last Republican objections to the agreement by emphasizing the importance of trade, especially with friendly countries in the Middle East, to the war against terrorism.

Pacts with Chile and Singapore were approved in 2003. Given the relatively modest volume of trade with these countries and their comparatively solid labor and environmental standards, the two bilateral agreements were relatively uncontroversial. Similarly, Congress easily approved trade agreements with Australia and Morocco in 2004. Some legislators from Western states warned that the pact with Australia could hurt American beef producers, but a desire to reward Australia for its support of the United States during the Iraq war outweighed that opposition.

Fast-track authority was likely to prove crucial, however, to a regional agreement the Bush administration negotiated with five Central American countries and the Dominican Republic in 2004. Many Democrats were opposed to the agreement with Costa Rica, El Salvador, Guatemala, Honduras, and Nicaragua because of concerns about labor stan-

dards. Republicans from states that produce sugar, citrus fruits, and textiles were also opposed to the agreement. Although there had been some talk of taking up the agreement during the lame-duck session after the November 2004 elections, consideration of the measure was put off until 2005.

THE UNITED STATES AND THE WTO

Protectionist sentiments spawned by workers' perceptions that they were losing jobs to foreigners were exacerbated by claims of a growing anti-U.S. bias in the World Trade Organization. Lawmakers cited trade disputes with the European Union over U.S. tax law that led to punitive tariffs on about 1,600 U.S. exports and WTO rulings against the United States on steel tariffs and cotton subsidies. In 2004 Congress used legislation repealing the disputed tax law as the underpinning for a massive rewrite (some said giveaway) of corporate tax laws. *(Corporate tax bill, p. 115)*

Although a committed free trader, Bush provoked the WTO ruling on steel tariffs after he imposed the tariffs in March 2002 in a move widely seen as a gambit to win the votes of steel workers in key electoral states such as Pennsylvania and West Virginia. The move backfired, however, after the WTO ruled that the tariffs were illegal. Bush had to decide between satisfying steel producers, who asked him to retain the tariffs despite the WTO ruling, and other manufacturers, including the big automakers, who complained that the tariffs, by raising the price of steel, were costing more jobs than they were creating. With the EU poised to begin WTO-sanctioned retaliatory tariffs on U.S. products, the Bush administration lifted the sanctions in late 2003.

Despite the occasional disputes with the WTO the United States was a central player in the organization, helping to create it in the 1990s and then providing critical leadership to hold it together when a round of global talks nearly collapsed in 2003.

The WTO was launched in 1995 in part to harmonize trade rules, but negotiations since then had exposed a deep rift between rich and poor nations. Led by the United States and Europe the wealthy countries had advocated free trade as a means of creating wealth and jobs throughout the world. The World Bank, for example, estimated in 2003 that if agreement were reached soon on agricultural and other trade issues, the resulting expansion would increase global incomes by $520 billion by 2015 and lift 144 million people in developing countries out of poverty. Developing countries argued, however, that many of the trade rules, especially those dealing with agriculture, were stacked against them and in some cases left poor countries even farther behind.

Such frustration had contributed to the collapse of WTO talks in 1999 in Seattle, Washington, which had been intended to begin a new round of negotiations. A global economic slowdown and the terrorist attacks in the United States on Sept. 11, 2001, renewed momentum for another round of trade talks, which began in November of that year in Doha, Qatar. The target date for these talks, which were to emphasize helping developing countries, including the least-developed countries, was Jan. 1, 2005.

But these talks came to an abrupt standstill in September 2003 when trade delegates from the developing countries walked out of a meeting in Cancun, Mexico, saying they would rather go away empty-handed than accept the modest compromises the United States and other developed nations were willing to offer on agriculture and other trade issues. Led by Brazil, China, and India, the delegates demanded larger cuts in the $300 billion in government subsidies paid to farmers annually in the United States and Europe. These subsidies resulted in overproduction of many crops that were then dumped on global markets, thereby depressing prices and hurting developing countries, especially those that relied on agricultural goods as their main trading commodities. At the same time many of these same developing countries were unwilling to reduce their own tariffs on agricultural imports, many of which were considerably higher than those imposed in the industrial countries.

U.S. Trade Representative Robert B. Zoellick, along with some other key figures, including Brazil's foreign minister, Celso Amorim, worked hard behind the scenes to break the deadlock. On Aug. 1, 2004, they announced that agreement had been reached on a preliminary framework calling for reductions in both agricultural subsidies and tariffs. Whether the WTO would reach a final agreement remained to be seen; none was expected until 2006 at the earliest. Even if the members of the WTO agreed to new trade rules along the lines contained in the preliminary framework, it was uncertain whether such an agreement could win congressional approval. Congress in 2002 passed farm legislation renewing many of the commodity price supports that would likely have to be cut under the preliminary trade agreement, and some lawmakers were already complaining that the 2004 agreement was selling out rural America.

THE UNITED STATES AND CHINA

The United States was also closely watching one of the WTO's newest members, China. The world's fastest-growing major economy, China was expected to overtake Japan as the world's second-largest economy by about 2020. Already China was moving alongside the United States as a major force in Asian economic life. For many years the United States had been the first- or second-largest export market for many Asian countries, but by the first years of the twenty-first century China was taking over the leading position. Most of the growth in exports by the majority of countries in the region since the 1997–1998 Asian financial crisis resulted from Chinese demand for raw materials and finished goods, not from American consumers.

Ever since a new U.S.-China trade agreement went into effect in 2001 as part of China's entry into the World Trade Organization, economics had replaced politics at the core of the relationship between the two countries. By 2004 China and the United States had become major trading partners; the United States was China's single biggest export market and China the fifth-largest export market for the United States. The balance of trade was decidedly in China's favor: a net of $124 billion in 2003, growing to $162 billion in 2004. In part because of that imbalance China also had become the second-largest holder of American dollars after Japan.

Largely because of the trade imbalance this expansion of trade was engendering some friction. Labor unions and manufacturers of consumer goods had complained for years that China's low-wage economy was competing unfairly, sending billions of dollars worth of clothing, electronic gadgets, and household goods to the United States at bargain prices that made American-made products uncompetitive. The Bush administration generally brushed aside such complaints, pointing to the benefits for American consumers of U.S. trade with China. In March 2004, however, at the outset of an election year, the administration filed the first formal trade complaint by any country against China since its entry into the WTO in 2001. The complaint alleged that China was using its tax code to give preferences to local makers of semiconductor chips at the expense of U.S chip manufacturers. After negotiations, China agreed to phase out the preferences. Later in the year China also agreed to crack down on counterfeiters who made illegal copies of American computer software, movies, and music and sold the counterfeits for hundreds of millions of dollars.

The Bush administration in 2003 and 2004 also pushed China to allow a revaluation of its currency, the yuan, which was linked to the value of the U.S. dollar. Economists said this yuan-dollar link meant that the Chinese currency traded at an artificially low value, perhaps by as much as 40 percent. That meant China's exports were cheaper than they would be if the currency was allowed to float on the free market. China resisted pressure from the United States and other trading partners on this score.

TRADE DEFICIT

The United States' net trade deficit with China was not the only trade imbalance it confronted. In 2004 the total U.S. trade deficit stood at a record high of $617.1 billion. Both exports and imports surged during the 1980s and 1990s, but since 2000 the trade deficit widened in dollar terms and as a percentage of gross domestic product (GDP). After averaging less than 2 percent of GDP in the 1980s and 1990s, the shortfall averaged 4 percent of the economy or more after 2000, reaching 5.3 percent of GDP in 2004.

The record trade deficits coincided with record federal budget deficits ($412 billion in 2004, or 3.6 percent of GDP) and a slide in the value of the dollar measured against other currencies. Long the strongest currency in the world, the dollar reached a peak relative to the euro, the yen, and other major currencies in April 2002 and then declined more or less steadily through the end of 2004 as analysts and investors grew increasingly wary of the rising U.S. trade and budget deficits, which were largely financed by foreign investors, including foreign governments.

In the short run the declining dollar was likely to help restore some balance in the U.S. trade deficit. Although foreign imports and vacations in Europe were more expensive for Americans, U.S. exports of goods and services were more competitive in foreign markets. Also, the domestic tourism industry, which had been devastated by the terrorist attacks, was likely to experience some renewal as foreigners took advantage of the weaker dollar to visit the United States. The declining dollar could also contribute to higher employment in the United States because some foreign manufacturers, such as foreign automakers, sought to cut their costs by expanding their production within U.S. borders rather than exporting the finished product.

The question concerning many observers was how far the dollar would fall and how fast. At one extreme were those analysts who worried that the dollar's realignment might happen too fast. They pictured scenarios in which a continuing slide would lead nervous foreign investors to cut their losses by selling off dollar assets. Under one scenario the results were higher interest and inflation rates and a slowdown in economic growth. Other scenarios envisioned worldwide recession or even depression.

At the other end of the spectrum were the analysts who thought the world economy could—and would—finance the U.S. deficits for many years while market forces helped realign the global currency and trade imbalances. One of these was Alan Greenspan, the chairman of the Federal Reserve Board, who argued that the process of globalization was the primary reason that America's twin deficits had not been a major drag on the world economy. So far, Greenspan said toward the end of 2004, the economic forces that were allowing the United States to run ever-larger deficits without substantial increases in interest rates or other interventions showed few signs of diminishing. But he cautioned that at some point investors were likely to turn away from dollar assets, if only to diversify their risks. And he warned that protectionism, signs of which were already evident in the United States and elsewhere, could undermine globalization and with it the global adjustment process.

2001–2002

In its most important action on trade issues during President George W. Bush's first term, Congress in 2002 gave the president power it had denied his predecessor, Bill Clinton: fast-track trade authority. Under this power the president could negotiate trade agreements with other nations that Congress could approve or disapprove but could not alter. Congress had allowed the authority to lapse in 1994 and refused Clinton's request in 1997 to renew it, which was widely seen as a stunning defeat for the president. Fast-track authority, which the Bush administration renamed trade promotion authority, was considered to be an important assurance to U.S. trading partners that a deal would not unravel once it reached Congress where parochial interests often outweighed broad national policies.

In other trade action during 2001–2002 the 107th Congress approved the first trade agreement that allowed one signatory to impose economic sanctions or other penalties if the other relaxed its environmental or labor laws to reap larger gains from trade. The controversial provisions, which were part of a trade deal with Jordan, nearly sunk the agreement in the Senate.

Congress also approved legislation extending normal trade relations to Vietnam, bringing to a close a quarter-century of prohibitively high tariffs against the United States' one-time enemy. The Export-Import Bank, which provided loans and grants to help make U.S. businesses more competitive against businesses subsidized by other countries, was extended through 2006. But Congress in the wake of the Sept. 11, 2001, terrorist attacks refused an industry effort to ease export controls on high-technology commercial items that could have military uses.

Fast-Track Trade Authority

After nearly eighteen months of debate and delays that ended in two weeks of frenzied deal-making, Congress granted President George W. Bush authority to negotiate international trade pacts without fear of last-minute changes from Congress. A rare appearance on Capitol Hill by the president and the support of a handful of Democrats helped get the legislation through a Congress often skeptical of free trade agreements. The bill cleared Aug. 1, 2002, and Bush signed it into law (HR 3009—PL 107-210) on Aug. 6, vowing to make quick use of it to accelerate trade talks with Chile, Singapore, and Morocco. The administration was also looking ahead to the next round of global trade talks and to negotiations on a free-trade zone for most of the Western Hemisphere.

Even with fast track, however, negotiations with other nations were expected to be difficult. Bush had lost the free-trade high ground when he had agreed to tariffs of up to 30 percent for certain steel imports and backed a farm bill (PL 107-171) that included increased export subsidies. Both actions were seen as a quest to win votes in Congress for fast-track extension and to better position himself for a 2004 reelection run in closely contested states. *(Steel imports, p. 151; farm bill, p. 149)*

Fast-track trade negotiating authority had lapsed in 1994. Bush's predecessor, President Bill Clinton (1993–2001), suffered one of the worst defeats of his presidency in 1998 when Democrats in Congress refused his request to renew the procedure. The new law renewed that power, which the Bush administration renamed trade promotion authority. The law required Congress to vote up or down on trade agreements within ninety days of receiving them from the president and barred all amendments. *(Congress and the Nation Vol. X, p. 153)*

The legislation renewing fast track also included a $12 billion expansion of the Trade Adjustment Assistance (TAA) program for workers dislocated as a result of trade deals. The TAA expansion was a priority of congressional Democrats who were under pressure from organized labor and other parts of their regular constituencies to resist giving the president a free hand to negotiate trade deals that they said threatened job losses by American workers and could undermine U.S. trade and environmental laws.

In other provisions the legislation also renewed an expired Andean trade preferences law that lowered tariffs on goods imported from Bolivia, Colombia, Ecuador, and Peru.

The trade bill had moved in fits and starts in the first session of the 107th Congress, passing the House by just one vote on Dec. 6, 2001. The Senate Finance Committee approved its own version Dec. 12, but Majority Leader Tom Daschle, D-S.D., put off floor action until 2002.

Democrats made substantial changes when the Senate took up its version of the bill (HR 3009) in May 2002, linking fast track to the large expansion of the three-decade-old program of trade adjustment assistance to displaced workers, as well as adding language allowing Congress to alter trade deals to protect U.S. antidumping laws.

Daschle hoped to use informal talks to reach a quick deal on a final bill, but House Ways and Means Committee Chair Bill Thomas, R-Calif., resisted. Meanwhile, Bush was insisting the bill be sent to him before Congress left for its August recess, and all sides agreed that the closer they got to the 2002 fall elections the less chance they would have for a compromise. A House-Senate conference finally convened in September with the daunting task of finding a deal that would hold the support of Senate Democrats, minimize the loss of GOP conservatives, and attract enough House Democrats to offset any defections.

Just when the goal seemed to slip out of reach Thomas and Senate Finance Committee Chair Max Baucus, D-Mont., struck a deal that allowed final action to send the bill to the president. The sudden turnaround was part of a spate of leg-

PRESIDENT BUSH, JOBS, AND STEEL TARIFFS

In an effort to deal with the unemployment problem in manufacturing—and gain political points at the same time—President George W. Bush decided to impose tariffs on steel imports in March 2002. But the move backfired, leading to an embarrassing reversal for the administration late in 2003.

Despite his support of free trade, the president approved tariffs of as much as 30 percent for three years on steel imports from Europe, Asia, and South America. He justified the duties as a step to help the ailing American steel industry recover from a surge of cheap, imported steel during the late 1990s. But the move was widely seen as a political gambit to win blue-collar votes in key election states such as Ohio, Pennsylvania, and West Virginia.

In July 2003 the World Trade Organization upheld complaints that the U.S. action was unwarranted and violated global trade rules. The European Union (EU) was authorized to impose $2.2 billion in retaliatory sanctions starting on Dec. 15 if the administration did not lift the steel tariffs. Seven other countries were authorized to impose additional sanctions.

The EU quickly let it be known that it would put tariffs on products that would raise prices for voters in key election states. The EU targeted citrus from Florida, textile mills in the South, and farm products from California and the Midwest with what *New York Times* reporter David E. Sanger described as "a precision that Karl Rove, the president's political adviser, must have grudgingly admired." Rove was said to have been the chief architect of the higher steel tariffs.

At home the president was caught between the steel-producing industry, which urged Bush to retain the tariffs, and steel-consuming manufacturers, such as automakers and appliance manufacturers, who said the higher steel prices that resulted from the tariffs were costing them more jobs than the steel industry was saving. Facing a possible trade war with the EU and other allies abroad, as well as political disaster at home, Bush on Dec. 4, 2003, repealed the tariffs, declaring that they had achieved their purpose. Steelmakers, he said, had consolidated, increased productivity, reduced costs, and become more competitive with foreign producers.

The early endorsement of Democratic presidential contender Richard A. Gephardt, a member of the House from Missouri, by the United Steelworkers of America may have influenced Bush's decision. The union represented many of the workers Bush hoped would support him in gratitude for imposing the tariffs.

---

islating before the August recess by lawmakers who were worried about looking passive at a time of reeling stock markets, unfolding tales of corporate fraud, and an unsteady economy.

HIGHLIGHTS

As signed into law PL 107-210 included the following main provisions:

• **Expedited procedures.** Authorized special trade promotion authority, formerly known as fast-track procedures, for congressional consideration of trade agreements reached before June 1, 2005, with an optional extension to June 1, 2007. Allowed Congress ninety days after receiving a trade agreement from the president to pass or reject an implementing bill but prohibited amendments to the agreement.

• **Consultations.** Required the U.S. trade representative (USTR) to consult with relevant congressional committees, as well as a newly created Congressional Oversight Group, before initialing any agreement. Provided that failure to consult with Congress would make the trade agreement ineligible for fast-track procedures, if both chambers agreed.

Required the president to report to Congress in advance of any proposals in trade negotiations that could mandate changes to U.S. trade remedy laws.

• **Unemployed worker benefits.** Extended for five years the Trade Adjustment Assistance program for workers who lost their jobs or had their wages reduced as a result of increased imports and a program of assistance to firms that faced layoffs because of foreign competition. Created a tax credit for laid-off workers equal to 65 percent of their health insurance costs. Extended benefits to secondary workers, such as employees of companies that supplied businesses affected by trade, and provided benefits to workers whose plants moved anywhere overseas. (Previously, benefits were available only to workers whose plants moved to Mexico or Canada under the North American Free Trade Agreement.)

• **Negotiating objectives.** Set a number of overall objectives for U.S. trade negotiators including more open, equitable, and reciprocal market access; agreement from trade partners not to weaken domestic labor or environmental laws in an effort to promote trade; and respect for worker rights and the rights of children consistent with International Labor Organization (ILO) core labor standards. Established a set of "principal trade negotiating objectives" that included preserving the ability of the United States to enforce its trade laws rigorously.

• **Andean trade.** Reinstated through 2006 the duty-free treatment of more than 6,000 products, including textiles, from the Andean countries of Bolivia, Colombia, Ecuador, and Peru.

• **African and Caribbean trade.** Increased the quantities of certain imported apparel eligible for duty-free treatment. Increased the cap for apparel made in the Caribbean from

U.S. TRADE REPRESENTATIVE

President George W. Bush's chief trade representative during his first term was Robert B. Zoellick, a pragmatic promoter of free trade known for his ability to put together deals. Those skills were greatly needed during Zoellick's tenure, as he completed negotiations on bringing China into the World Trade Organization, pushed fast-track authority for the president through a dubious Congress, and negotiated several bilateral and regional trade agreements with countries in the Middle East, Asia, and Latin America. Zoellick was also instrumental in launching a new round of multilateral trade talks known as the Doha Round, and then rescuing those talks from near-collapse.

When Secretary of State Condoleezza Rice chose Zoellick to be her deputy secretary of state in early 2005, at the start of Bush's second term, the president quickly picked Ohio representative Rob Portman to take the lead in advancing the administration's trade liberalization policies through Congress. Portman had not made trade his primary policy focus in Congress and was not well-known in global trade circles. But unlike Zoellick, whose sometimes acerbic style made for strained relations in Congress, Portman appeared to be well-liked on Capitol Hill. His nomination drew enthusiastic reactions from members of both parties as well as from many business and agricultural groups.

knit fabric made of U.S. yarn and clarified that T-shirts and other "knit-to-shape" items were included. Increased a cap on apparel made in sub-Saharan Africa from regional fabric and temporarily loosened some restrictions on apparel from Botswana and Namibia.

- **GSP.** Renewed tariff breaks for developing nations under the General System of Preferences (GSP), which extended duty-free treatment to thousands of products from more than 140 countries.

- **Customs Service.** Reauthorized the Customs budget with increased funding for border security.

BACKGROUND

The Constitution gave Congress the exclusive power to set tariffs and regulate foreign commerce, but since the 1930s lawmakers had delegated that authority to the president, who was seen as less vulnerable to pressure from individual industries, labor unions, and other narrow interests. The turning point was the 1930 Smoot-Hawley Act, which set extremely high tariffs that were considered partially responsible for the Great Depression. In 1934 President Franklin D. Roosevelt (1933–1945) pushed Congress to enact the first reciprocal trade agreements act, which gave the president authority to negotiate mutual tariff reductions with U.S. trading partners.

Congress renewed the authority repeatedly over the years, and successive presidents used the power to help reduce global tariff barriers.

Fast-track procedures to expedite Congress's approval of trade agreements were first enacted in the 1974 Trade Act (PL 93-618). *(Congress and the Nation Vol. IV, p. 131)*

The new procedures were first used by President Jimmy Carter (1977–1981) in the General Agreement on Tariffs and Trade (GATT) Tokyo Round Agreements, which were approved and implemented in the Trade Agreements Act of 1979 (PL 96-39). That act also renewed the procedures for another eight years, through Jan. 3, 1988. Fast track was reauthorized again under the 1988 omnibus trade bill (PL 100-418) through May 31, 1991, with a possible two-year extension, barring disapproval by either chamber. The extension was contingent on the president submitting progress reports to Congress on the negotiations. *(1979 bill, Congress and the Nation Vol. V, p. 270; 1988 legislation, Congress and the Nation Vol. VII, p. 148)*

In 1991 Congress defeated an attempt to disapprove the two-year extension. The White House lobbied heavily for the extension to enable President George H. W. Bush (1989–1993) to continue talks on GATT and begin talks on a U.S.-Mexico free-trade pact, which ultimately led to the North American Free Trade Agreement (NAFTA). *(1991 legislation, Congress and the Nation Vol. VIII, p. 189; NAFTA, Congress and the Nation Vol. IX, p. 155)*

In 1993, with Clinton in the White House, Congress extended fast-track authority through April 15, 1994 (PL 103-49), for the sole purpose of completing the GATT agreement, which included creation of the World Trade Organization. Clinton wanted the bill enacted before he attended a summit of industrial nations in Tokyo in July. The focus on GATT allowed him to avoid a fight with Congress over broader fast-track authority. *(Congress and the Nation Vol. IX, p. 161)*

Clinton tried but failed to get a long-term extension as part of the 1994 legislation (PL 103-465) implementing the GATT agreement. Republicans objected to Clinton's attempt to include labor and environmental requirements for trade talks. The following year, the House Ways and Means Committee approved a reauthorization good through Dec. 31, 1999, with a possible two-year extension, but the legislation advanced no further. Clinton wanted the renewal to facilitate talks with Chile, but he objected to provisions that would have barred trade negotiations from dealing with labor and environmental issues. *(Congress and the Nation Vol. IX, p. 178)*

In 1997 the Senate easily passed a bill acceptable to Clinton, but the House version was shelved after Clinton was unable to rally support from Democrats, who were under strong pressure from organized labor to defeat the measure. In 1998 the House defeated an attempt by Clinton to renew fast-track procedures. Opponents had turned the debate into a referendum on NAFTA, dooming the bill. The Senate Finance Committee approved a trade bill that included renewal of fast-track authority, but the full Senate never considered it. *(Congress and the Nation Vol. X, p. 153)*

Jordan and Vietnam completed trade agreements with the United States in 2000 without the use of fast-track procedures. But many countries expressed an unwillingness to negotiate a trade agreement without a guarantee that the deal would not subsequently be amended by Congress. *(Jordan, Vietnam pacts, pp. 159, 160)*

Renewing fast-track authority thus became a top priority for the Bush administration, particularly for negotiations on a Free Trade Area of the Americas and to reach new multilateral accords dealing with direct foreign investment, intellectual property, agriculture, and labor and environmental policies related to trade. (Additional pressure was raised when an agreement to begin formal negotiations in these areas was reached in November 2001 at the WTO ministerial meetings in Doha, Qatar.)

FAST-TRACK ACTION IN 2001

As in previous years the debate over fast track pitted free-traders, by and large Republicans, who wanted to smooth the passage of free-trade agreements through the congressional approval process, against a group of legislators who sought to ensure that trade agreements with less-developed countries would not weaken labor standards and environmental protection in the United States and its trading partners. The group was made up mainly of Democrats but included a small yet significant group of Republicans who represented primarily industrial districts, many of them electorally competitive.

House Action

Republican leaders in the House began their campaign for fast-track legislation in June when House Ways and Means Committee Chair Thomas introduced a straight renewal of fast track (HR 2149) that lacked any mention of labor or environmental protections. Republicans acknowledged that the measure was designed to gauge how many votes they would need to get outside their own party and how much compromise would be necessary. Although GOP leaders had pressed for a vote on the bill before the August recess, they postponed action when it became apparent that the measure would not pass.

The Sept. 11 terrorist attacks added a new impetus to the administration's push for trade authority, one that might have been carried too far. U.S. Trade Representative Robert B. Zoellick angered Democrats when he portrayed liberalized trade as a patriotic imperative and suggested that opposition was coming from legislators who were "held back for other rather narrow interests, reasons, some of them related to the understandable politics of where they get their money." Zoellick's remarks so irritated Charles B. Rangel, N.Y., the ranking Democrat on Ways and Means, that he blocked Republican plans for a markup of the fast-track legislation.

After a few days' delay to calm the situation Ways and Means Oct. 9 approved a revised version of the fast-track legislation (HR 3005—H Rept 107-249, Part I) on a vote that ran along party lines. Thomas acknowledged that the new bill was designed to hang onto Republican support while attracting just enough Democrats to win passage. The new bill stated that a "principal negotiating objective" for trade talks would be getting assurances that participating countries would effectively enforce their existing labor and environmental laws. The bill was silent on enforcement mechanisms but stated that labor and environmental provisions would be subject to the same "demonstrably effective" trade remedies used to enforce other parts of a trade pact. The details would be left to the negotiators.

Thomas's bill also sought to involve Congress more closely in trade negotiations by establishing a bipartisan oversight panel for each trade negotiation and requiring the president to consult with the group before, during, and after trade talks. If the president failed to involve Congress, lawmakers could disqualify the trade agreement from fast-track procedures by winning adoption of a disapproval resolution in both the House and Senate.

On Dec. 6, after months of wrangling, the House passed the fast-track bill by a **key vote of 215–214 (R 194–23; D 21–189; I 0–2)**. The balloting ran neck and neck and was held open while last-minute deals were struck with Republicans from the textile South. It was the fourth time since July that the House Speaker had scheduled a vote on the bill. *(2001 key votes, p. 801)*

The bill drew 194 Republicans, about thirty more than usual, largely because GOP leaders promised to take care of key interests such as agriculture, textiles, and steel, in future trade pacts. The leadership also argued that a defeat would undermine the president during a time of war. Republicans Jim DeMint of South Carolina and Robin Hayes of North Carolina changed their positions and supported the bill after party leaders pledged to try to change the sub-Saharan African and Caribbean Basin trade preference law (PL 106-200) enacted in 2000 to help protect textile dyeing and finishing industries in their districts. The promise also extended to the Andean nations trade bill (HR 3009), which had passed the House but was pending in the Senate. *(PL 106-200, p. 165; Andean trade pact, p. 154)*

The ranks of Democratic supporters, meanwhile, dwindled to twenty-one—about half the number that supported the failed 1997 effort to extend fast track under Clinton. Many members of the pro-trade New Democrat Coalition said they opposed the bill because it was out of date, focusing on manufacturing and agriculture rather than on issues such as antitrust and intellectual property. They were also concerned that the enforcement mechanisms for labor and environmental standards were not strong enough.

Other Democrats said they could not support the bill without first passing an economic stimulus measure (HR 3090) that GOP leaders were promising would include help for workers laid off after Sept. 11. Nor were Democrats satisfied with a separate bill (HR 3008), passed 420–3 earlier in the day, to expand Trade Adjustment Assistance designed to retrain and relocate workers displaced by trade actions. *(Stimulus bill, p. 100; trade adjustment assistance, p. 154)*

Senate Action

After waiting for the House vote the Senate Finance Committee met Dec. 12 to approve its version of the bill (HR 3005—S Rept 107-139). The 18–3 vote belied the undercurrent of dissatisfaction with the bill and with the manner in which it was handled.

Baucus and Charles E. Grassley, R-Iowa—at the time chairman and ranking member of the Finance Committee, respectively—presented a bill based on the House measure, with minor changes to make it more palatable to Democrats in the areas of labor, congressional review, and dumping. They made it clear they would reject all amendments, putting off for full House action contentious issues such as Democrats' demands for tougher labor and antidumping provisions.

RELATED TRADE ACTION IN 2001

Congress took action on two other trade bills in 2001 that were ultimately folded into the new trade law. The legislation concerned Trade Adjustment Assistance and an Andean trade pact.

Trade Adjustment Assistance

Both chambers acted on bills to reauthorize trade adjustment assistance. The program, enacted under the 1974 statute that created fast-track procedures, had expired Sept. 30, 2001. TAA included assistance for workers and firms; a third program was added in 1993 to cushion the effects of NAFTA.

Hoping to build momentum for the fast-track bill the House Ways and Means Committee on Oct. 5, 2001, approved a bill (HR 3008—H Rept 107-244) reauthorizing TAA for workers and firms with minor changes through September 2003. The House passed the bill Dec. 6 by a vote of 420–3 before voting on its separate fast-track bill.

The Senate Finance Committee on Dec. 4, 2001, approved a broader TAA bill (S 1209—S Rept 107-134). In addition to expanding the program and reauthorizing it through fiscal 2006, the bill would have subsidized 75 percent of the premium for COBRA health coverage for workers eligible for TAA assistance. COBRA allowed workers to continue coverage under their former employer's plan. But paying the employer's portion of the cost often was too expensive for people looking for new jobs. The subsidy, estimated to cost $3.3 billion through 2011, was the Republicans' chief complaint against the bill. The committee approved the bill by voice vote only after Grassley and Baucus agreed that it would be kept separate from fast track.

Andean Trade

The House Nov. 16 passed by voice vote a bill (HR 3009—H Rept 107-290) to extend and expand trade preferences for four Andean nations. The measure, strongly opposed by some Democrats, proposed extending through 2006 a 1991 law (PL 102-182) that provided duty-free treatment for some 6,000 products from Bolivia, Colombia, Ecuador, and Peru. The bill also called for ending tariffs on several goods previously exempt from the law, including tuna, petroleum products, footwear, and sugar. And it extended trade benefits for apparel covered under the 2000 African and Caribbean Basin trade law (PL 106-200).

Sponsors argued that the Andean law helped antidrug efforts by strengthening the economies of Andean nations, a major source of cocaine. Critics worried that it could hurt the domestic tuna and textile industries.

The Senate Finance Committee approved a revised version of the Andean trade bill (HR 3009—S Rept 107-126) on Nov. 29 that included fewer trade benefits for Andean textile exporters. The committee also adopted an amendment by John B. Breaux, D-La., to limit duty-free imports of canned tuna from Ecuador. According to the office of Bob Graham, D-Fla., since the Andean law was enacted, total two-way trade between the United States and the Andean region had more than doubled to $28.5 billion a year.

Authorization for the Andean trade preferences expired Dec. 4, 2001. On Feb. 14, 2002, Bush extended the duties for ninety days pending congressional renewal of the popular measure.

FAST-TRACK ACTION IN 2002

After eighteen days of debate and the adoption of several major amendments the Senate passed its trade legislation (HR 3009) the night of May 23. The **key vote was 66–30 (R 41–5; D 24–25; I 1–0)**. *(2002 key votes p. 819)*

The changes that allowed the bill to advance through the Senate, particularly the expansion of aid to dislocated workers, sparked significant opposition from House Republicans. Another change—an amendment allowing Congress to alter a trade pact in order to protect U.S. trade laws—brought a veto threat from the White House. The Senate made its revisions not to the House's fast-track bill, but to the separate, House-passed Andean trade bill.

Daschle began the Senate debate with an amendment that paired trade promotion authority with the worker assistance provisions from S 1209. Republicans argued that the worker provisions were too expansive and much too expensive, but they also were under strong White House pressure to win fast-track authority for the president. Daschle made it clear they would not get one without the other. While speakers marked time on the floor, senators from both parties and the White House engaged in lengthy negotiations over the worker assistance proposals. Finally, on May 9, Baucus and Grassley announced a deal that gave Democrats many, but not all, of their main goals. The following day, Baucus introduced the package as a substitute amendment that effectively became the underlying bill for the remainder of the debate. The Senate adopted the Baucus substitute by voice vote May 23 after voting 68–29 the previous day to limit further debate.

Despite an explicit veto threat from the White House, senators on May 14 voted to carve a wide exception from the core of the fast-track concept. Under the amendment—sponsored by Republican Policy Committee Chairman Larry E. Craig of Idaho and Democrat Mark Dayton of Minnesota—a simple Senate majority could remove any part of a trade agreement that altered U.S. antidumping or other trade remedy laws. The amendment was adopted by voice vote after a motion to table it was rejected by a filibuster-proof majority of 38–61. Sixteen Republicans, forty-four Democrats, and one independent voted to keep the proposal alive. The amendment was central to one of the most widespread congressional concerns about fast track: that in their enthusiasm to eliminate trade barriers U.S. negotiators would not fully protect domestic producers by agreeing to deals that would deprive workers of remedies under U.S. law.

In other action on the bill Democrats made several unsuccessful attempts to limit fast-track procedures to trade deals that included enforceable labor and environmental standards. Republicans also succeeded in blocking a Democratic amendment that would have made retired steelworkers eligible for one year of health insurance tax credits under TAA. A handful of GOP conservatives said they would rather see fast track die than provide such an unprecedented benefit. An attempt by George Allen, R-Va., to make low-interest government loans for mortgage payments available to displaced workers was tabled 50–49. Vice President Dick Cheney cast the tie-breaking vote, the third in his sixteen months in office.

House Conference Instructions

Before going to conference on HR 3009 the House agreed by the narrowest of margins to specify that the negotiations include the House-passed version of the fast-track bill (HR 3005), as well as specific House provisions on a number of other trade matters. None of these provisions were in HR 3009 as passed by the House.

The plan (H Res 450—H Rept 107-518) was drawn up by Ways and Means Committee Chair Thomas and adopted by a vote of 216–215 on June 26. Thirteen members who had voted in favor of the House bill in December defected. Many of the ten Democrats in the group favored liberalized international trade but opposed Thomas's strategy of going to conference with a package of provisions never fully voted on by the House.

In addition to including HR 3005 Thomas's resolution added the House-passed TAA bill (HR 3008) with new provisions related to health care benefits for displaced workers, provisions similar to those in the House version of a supplemental appropriations bill (HR 4775) to restrict certain textile imports from the Caribbean and Africa, language from a House-passed resolution (H Con Res 262) expressing congressional concern regarding WTO dispute panels and antidumping agreements, a House-passed Customs border security bill (HR 3129), and a measure to renew the General System of Preferences (HR 3010) not considered by the House.

House GOP leaders had to pull the resolution from the floor agenda June 20 because they lacked the votes for approval, but with appeals to party loyalty and free-trade philosophy they finally managed to eke out a one-vote victory for the controversial proposal.

FINAL ACTION

The conference opened July 23 with Republicans intent on reversing some of the concessions made in the Senate. Baucus, however, made it clear that any deal would have to include health insurance benefits for displaced workers. Republicans were loath to relent, fearful of setting a precedent for future health care legislation. The November elections were approaching, labor unions were elevating their anti-fast-track rhetoric, and leaders in both chambers were wary of forcing members to take such a controversial vote. The bill's prospects seemed increasingly dim, save for the possibility of a vote during a lame-duck session.

But with Bush insisting on quick action to aid the economy and lawmakers eager to convince voters that Congress was willing to act decisively, Thomas and Baucus held a lengthy meeting the evening of July 25 and reached agreement on a final bill. With victory still uncertain in the House Bush visited the Capitol the next day to make a personal plea for passage. Bush's persistence paid off. In a vote taken after 3 a.m. on Saturday, July 27, House leaders pulled out a victory on the conference report (H Rept 107-624). The **key vote was 215–212 (R 190–27; D 25–183; I 0–2)**. *(2002 key votes, p. 819)*

GOP leaders picked up five additional pro-business Democrats who resisted pressure from their party leadership. Free-trade Democrat Cal Dooley of California claimed credit for most of those votes. At Thomas's request Dooley had corralled twenty-five Democrats with ties to business and put them through back-to-back meetings with direct pitches from Baucus and Breaux, then U.S. Trade Representative Zoellick, chief White House lobbyist Nick Calio, and Commerce secretary Donald L. Evans. A handful of Republicans also got on board. With victory ensured, Republicans in districts with strong anti-fast-track constituencies, such as Robin Hayes of textile-rich North Carolina, were able to vote against the legislation.

The Senate, which was not due to leave for another week, cleared the bill on a drama-free 64–34 vote Aug. 1. President Bush signed the measure on Aug. 6, 2002 (PL 107-210).

KEY COMPROMISES

Following are the major compromises reached in conference on HR 3009:

• **Trade Adjustment Assistance.** The Senate prevailed on the $12 billion expansion of benefits to workers and firms injured by foreign competition. The program was extended through fiscal 2007, as the Senate wanted. The House would have extended it for two years, at an estimated cost of $500 million a year, through fiscal 2004. The program was expanded not only to suppliers of trade-affected firms, as endorsed by the House, but to other workers affected by NAFTA and workers whose factories moved abroad because of trade agreements or foreign competition. The bill increased job search and relocation allowances, established an alternate assistance program for older workers, and created a TAA program for farmers and ranchers.

• **Health insurance.** As part of the worker assistance package conferees agreed to a tax credit covering 65 percent of the cost of health care insurance under COBRA or certain state-based group plans. Democrats favored a subsidy covering 70 percent of premiums; Republicans wanted a tax credit for 60 percent of coverage. Thomas attempted to mold the provision into an individual private insurance policy tax credit, but Democrats would not budge.

• **Dayton-Craig.** The final bill did not include the Dayton-Craig amendment, which would have allowed the Senate to alter portions of trade agreements that could weaken antidumping or other U.S. trade remedy laws. That was the trade-off Baucus made to get House agreement to the TAA package. Instead Baucus included language elevating protection of those laws to the status of a principal negotiating objective and requiring the president to give Congress 180 days' advance notice before signing an agreement that would affect those laws. Daschle predicted a congressional mutiny if Bush started putting U.S. trade remedy laws on the table. "I would see the trade representative at the table negotiating something and we, in a very public way, admonish him to do something else," he said. "It would be very hard for him to negotiate with his trading partners with any authority or credibility if the Congress has taken a different point of view."

• **Andean trade.** In renewing and expanding trade benefits for Andean countries, the Caribbean, and Africa, the conference report closely followed the House version and provided less protection for the domestic textile industry than the Senate had wanted. It allowed trade preferences for Ecuadorian tuna but excluded canned tuna.

• **Labor and environment.** The final bill fell far short of Democratic demands that trade agreements eligible for fast track include enforceable labor and environmental provisions. Democrats had lost that fight in both chambers. Instead it included as official U.S. negotiating objectives ensuring that trade and environmental policies were mutually supportive and promoting respect for worker rights and the rights of children. Also, the president was required to review the impact of future trade agreements on U.S. employment.

MAJOR PROVISIONS

Trade Authority

• **Negotiating authority.** Renewed the president's authority to negotiate certain reductions in tariffs and nontariff barriers to trade, including unlimited authority to negotiate reciprocal duty elimination on a sector basis within the World Trade Organization forum. Specified that the authority covered trade agreements signed before June 1, 2005, with a possible extension to June 1, 2007.

• **Fast-track procedures.** Authorized special trade promotion authority, formerly known as fast-track procedures, for legislation to implement trade agreements entered into before July 1, 2005. Allowed Congress—once such legislation was introduced—ninety days to complete work, with the bill subject to up or down votes in each chamber with no amendments. Allowed trade promotion authority to be extended to cover agreements entered into before July 1, 2007, if the president requested it and neither chamber adopted a resolution of disapproval.

• **Notification and consultation.** Required the president to notify and consult with the House Ways and Means and Senate Finance committees, a new congressional oversight group, and other relevant congressional committees at least ninety calendar days before entering into negotiations. Required the president also to notify the House and Senate at least ninety days before signing a trade agreement governed by the bill.

• **Agriculture, textiles.** Required the president, before initiating negotiations on tariff reductions in agriculture and textiles, to assess whether U.S. tariffs on products bound by the Uruguay Round Agreements were lower than the tariffs set by the countries with which the president was negotiating, and whether the negotiation provided an opportunity to address any disparity.

• Required the president to consult with the House Ways and Means and Senate Finance committees, as well as the Agriculture committees in the case of agricultural products, concerning the results of this assessment, whether it would be appropriate for the United States to agree to further tariff reductions, and how all applicable negotiating objectives would be met.

• Included a new definition of import-sensitive agriculture to encompass products subject to tariff rate quotas, as well as products subject to the lowest tariff reductions in the Uruguay Round Agreement.

• **Congressional Oversight Group.** Created a new Congressional Oversight Group, composed of the chairs and ranking members of the House Ways and Means and Senate Finance committees, together with three additional members of those committees, and the chairs and ranking members of committees with jurisdiction over laws affected by specific trade agreements. Accredited the members as official advisers to U.S. delegations negotiating agreements. Authorized the U.S. Trade Representative to develop guidelines to facilitate useful and timely exchange of information, including regular briefings, access to pertinent documents, and coordination with Congress at all critical periods during negotiations, including at negotiation sites.

• **U.S. trade remedy laws.** Required the president at least 180 days before signing a trade agreement to transmit a report to the House Ways and Means and Senate Finance committees on proposals advanced in negotiations that could change U.S. trade remedy laws.

• **Changes in existing laws.** Required the president within sixty days of signing an agreement to submit to Congress a preliminary list of existing laws that would need to be changed to bring the United States into compliance with the accord.

• **Expedited procedures.** Allowed a total period for congressional consideration of ninety legislative days with no amendments allowed in committee or on the floor and the legislation subject only to up or down votes. Specified that procedures of the Trade Act of 1974 applied at the time the president formally submitted to Congress legislation to implement a trade agreement. Allowed House and the Senate committees of jurisdiction forty-five legislative days to report a bill following the day legislation is introduced. Required the House to vote on the bill within fifteen legislative days after it was reported or discharged from the committees. Required the Senate committees to act within fifteen days and the Senate to vote within another fifteen days.

• **Limitations on trade promotion authority.** Made an implementing bill ineligible for expedited treatment if both chambers agreed to a resolution of disapproval stating that the president had failed to meet requirements for notifying and consulting with Congress. Provided that any trade agreement or understanding with a foreign government that was not disclosed to Congress would have no effect under U.S. law.

• **Mock markups.** The absence of a time limit for the president to submit an implementing bill provided time for the committees of jurisdiction to conduct informal "mock markups" of the draft bill in consultation with the administration. The purpose was to allow Congress, the public, and the private sector to express opinions before the bill was formally submitted and changes are prohibited.

Negotiating Objectives

Established overall U.S. trade objectives, specified principal objectives to be pursued in trade talks, and added a list of priorities for the president, and by extension, U.S. trade negotiators.

• **Overall objectives.** Specified that overall U.S. trade objectives included:

• Obtaining more open, equitable, and reciprocal market access;

• Reducing or eliminating barriers and other trade distorting policies and practices;

• Further strengthening the system of international trading agreements and procedures, including dispute settlement;

• Fostering economic growth and full employment in the U.S. and global economies;

• Ensuring that trade and environmental policies are mutually supportive;

• Promoting respect for worker rights and the rights of children consistent with International Labor Organization core labor standards;

• Seeking provisions under which the parties strive to ensure that they do not weaken their labor and environmental protection laws to promote trade;

• Ensuring that small businesses have equal access to global markets;

• Reducing trade barriers that particularly affect small businesses;

• Promoting full compliance with ILO conventions aimed at eliminating the worst forms of child labor.

• **Principal negotiating objectives.** The principal objectives to be pursued in trade negotiations included:

• Reducing barriers to trade in services;

• Lowering barriers to foreign investment while ensuring that foreign investors are not accorded greater rights than U.S. investors in the United States;

• Preserving the ability of the United States to rigorously enforce its trade laws, including antidumping and countervailing duty laws;

• Eliminating government policies that unduly threaten sustainable development;

• Gaining market access for U.S. environmental technologies;

• Ensuring that labor, environmental, health, or safety policies and practices of parties to trade agreements do not arbitrarily or unjustifiably discriminate against U.S. exports or serve as disguised barriers to trade;

• Protecting intellectual property rights;

• Obtaining reciprocal market access for U.S. exports of agricultural commodities, textiles and apparel;

• Ensuring that trade protections apply to electronic commerce.

• Ensuring that trade negotiators respect a declaration adopted by the WTO in November 2001 that granted poor countries certain exemptions from intellectual property protections afforded to Western-produced pharmaceuticals, especially those related to treating HIV/AIDS.

• **Presidential priorities.** Presidential priorities included:

• Reporting to Congress under priorities set out for U.S. trade negotiators;

• Strengthening the ability of U.S. trading partners to promote respect for core labor standards and to set environmental and health standards;

• Reviewing the impact of future agreements on U.S. employment.

Trade Adjustment Assistance

• **Reauthorization.** Reauthorized through fiscal 2007 the Trade Adjustment Assistance program for workers who lost their jobs or had their wages reduced as a result of increased imports, at an estimated total cost of $12 billion over ten years. Reauthorized through fiscal 2007 the TAA program that provided technical assistance to firms making layoffs of workers due to foreign competition, at an estimated cost of $16 million.

- **Health insurance tax credit.** Established as part of the package for displaced workers a refundable tax credit to cover 65 percent of the cost of monthly health insurance premiums. Allowed the credit to be used to subsidize the cost of company-based (COBRA) or pooled health insurance policies, and for individual insurance in cases when a worker purchased such a policy one month before losing a job. Made the available tax credit good for twelve months and applicable to eligible TAA recipients and to Pension Benefit Guaranty Corporation (PBGC) pension recipients. Provided seed and support money for state high-risk pools and authorized National Emergency Grant funds to assist workers with health insurance costs on an interim basis.

- **Eligibility expansion.** Extended TAA eligibility for the first time to secondary workers who were suppliers to trade-affected businesses and to other "downstream" workers affected by trade with Mexico or Canada. Extended benefits to workers whose plants move anywhere overseas if the relocation resulted from a U.S. trade agreement. (Previously benefits were available only to workers whose plants moved to Mexico or Canada under NAFTA.)

- **Unified TAA programs.** Merged a third TAA program under NAFTA into the regular program for displaced workers.

- **Older workers.** Created a two-year pilot program for trade-affected workers age fifty or older who take a new job at lower pay. Provided wage insurance for part of the gap between old and new earnings for up to $10,000 over two years.

- **Farmers and ranchers.** Established a new TAA program to serve family farmers (with exceptions for some farmers receiving assistance under other laws) and ranchers. Directed the commerce secretary to study the feasibility of extending TAA benefits to fishermen.

- **Worker training.** Doubled the existing worker training budget to $220 million.

- **Income benefits.** Extended the maximum period during which a worker may receive trade adjustment allowances from fifty-two to seventy-eight weeks and provided an additional twenty-six weeks of income support for workers requiring remedial education, including English as a second language.

- **Cash benefits.** Increased the maximum job search allowance from $800 per worker to $1,250 per worker, and the maximum relocation allowance from $800 per worker to $1,250 per worker.

Customs Service

- **Customs authorization.** Authorized $1.4 million a year in fiscal 2003–2004 for noncommercial operations (functions related to individuals entering and exiting the United States), and $1.6 billion a year in fiscal 2003–2004 for commercial activities (import and export of goods by commercial entities).

- **U.S.-Canada border.** Earmarked $25 million for 285 new customs officers to serve at the U.S.-Canada border, and $90 million for antiterrorism and narcotics detection equipment for the U.S.-Mexico border, the U.S.-Canada border, and Florida and Gulf Coast seaports.

- **Textile trans-shipments.** Required the General Accounting Office (GAO) to audit the Customs Service's system for monitoring the illegal trans-shipment of textile and apparel products through third countries in order to claim preferential U.S. tariff treatment and recommend improvements. Authorized $10 million to enhance the Customs Service's textile trans-shipment enforcement operations.

- **Africa trade.** Authorized $1.3 million for the Customs Service to provide technical assistance to sub-Saharan African countries to develop and implement effective visa and anti-trans-shipment systems to prevent the illegal trans-shipment of textiles and other goods as required in the African Growth and Opportunity Act (PL 106-200).

- **World Trade Center.** Authorized funds to reestablish Customs Service operations, including a textile monitoring and enforcement center, formerly located at the World Trade Center in New York. (The Congressional Budget Office estimated the cost to replace the facilities at $100 million.)

Andean Trade

- **Reauthorization.** Reauthorized the 1991 Andean Trade Preferences Act (PL 102-182) through 2006, retroactive to Dec. 4, 2001, granting preferential treatment to more than 6,000 products made in Bolivia, Colombia, Ecuador, and Peru.

- **Expansion.** Added to the duty-free list Andean apparel made from U.S. fabric and a limited amount of Andean apparel made from Andean fabric, some kinds of packaged (noncanned) tuna caught from U.S. or Andean flagged vessels, as well as shoes, watches, petroleum products, and some leather items.

African and Caribbean Trade

Expanded the African and Caribbean Basin trade law of 2000 (PL 106-200) by raising caps for duty-free textile imports to the United States and by expanding the list of duty-free products.

- **African apparel.** Allowed more knit products to enter duty free from Africa, as long as they were made from U.S. or African yarn. Added African-made merino wool sweaters to the duty-free list. Added Botswana and Namibia to the list of nations permitted—for a two-year transition period—duty-free importation of knitted apparel made from third-country yarn.

- **Caribbean apparel.** Allowed Caribbean nations to export to the United States more knitted apparel duty free if the knits were made from U.S. yarn. Clarified the law that so-called knit-to-shape items, such as T-shirts, made in the Caribbean were duty-free.

Other Provisions

- **GSP.** Reauthorized the General System of Preferences through 2006, the fifth renewal of the program, which provided duty-free entry to the United States for more than

6,000 products from about 140 developing countries. (Nations qualifying for GSP must meet a set of conditions, such as abiding by U.S. intellectual property laws.) Denied eligibility to countries that engage in the worst forms of child labor, fail to conform to certain fundamental labor rights, or do not support U.S. efforts against terrorism.

- **USTR.** Reauthorized the office of the U.S. Trade Representative at $65 million over two years.
- **WTO dispute fund.** Created a $50 million fund to pay WTO fines.
- **ITC.** Reauthorized the U.S. International Trade Commission at $111 million over two years.

China Trade Status

In what would become the last in a series of debates that had taken place since 1980, the House decisively rejected an attempt in July 2001 to suspend normal trade relations with China for a year. The House rejected the resolution of disapproval (H J Res 50) by a vote of 169–259 on July 19. The Ways and Means Committee had reported the resolution unfavorably on July 12.

The action seemed almost anticlimactic. After a highly contentious debate in 2000, Congress had agreed to grant China permanent status as a normal U.S. trading partner once it had joined the World Trade Organization (WTO). China had not yet been admitted to the WTO, however, and that put the issue back on the congressional agenda. Because of the delay in the WTO's action, President George W. Bush granted yet another one-year waiver of a 1974 law restricting normal trade relations with certain communist countries. The waiver—and with it normal trade status—had been granted to Beijing each year since 1980.

Bush's action triggered what had become an annual debate in Congress on China's economic, military, labor, and human rights policies. The immediate focus was a resolution to disapprove the presidential waiver. Although Congress was never expected to agree to the resolution, the debate allowed lawmakers to address several contentious issues on the House floor. Topping the list was the collision of a Navy surveillance plane and a Chinese military jet over the South China Sea on April 1 and the subsequent ten-day detention of twenty-four U.S. crew members. The incarceration of several Chinese-born U.S. scholars, continued human rights abuses, and concerns regarding Chinese treatment of Taiwan also provoked controversy.

BACKGROUND

Chinese goods had entered the United States under reduced tariff rates since 1980 after President Jimmy Carter (1977–1981) reestablished trade ties with Beijing. Under the Jackson-Vanik amendment to the 1974 Trade Act (PL 93-618) the president had to renew the low tariffs annually. However, the WTO, established in 1995, required member nations to grant one another's products "permanent normal

trade relations status" unless they were willing to forgo the benefits of more open trade with a particular country. In November 1999 U.S. Trade Representative Charlene Barshefsky and Chinese premier Zhu Rongji reached an agreement to make deep cuts in tariffs, quotas, and other trade barriers on U.S. exports to China. In return, the United States agreed to support China's entry into the WTO.

To fulfill that agreement, President Bill Clinton (1993–2001) sought legislation from Congress to remove China permanently from the list of communist countries subject to Jackson-Vanik. With strong support from business leaders—particularly those in the high-tech and agriculture sectors—a skeptical House and a generally gridlocked Senate cleared a bill in 2000 (PL 106-286) that permanently applied the same low tariff rates to Chinese imports as those already applied to goods from all but a handful of countries. The new trade status was to take effect once China joined the WTO. *(Congress and the Nation Vol. X, pp. 160, 166)*

The need for one more annual waiver—because of the delay in China's WTO entry—seemed like a formality as the 107th Congress began in 2001. But the surveillance plane incident brought a wave of anger in Congress. Vote counters in both parties said the House might vote to disapprove of the waiver, although the Senate seemed likely to stand pat. By mid-summer, tensions over the incident had waned noticeably and the resolution instead became the vehicle for a lively debate over China's human rights record and foreign policy.

Meanwhile, Chinese and WTO negotiators managed to resolve differences—particularly over the degree to which China was allowed to subsidize its agricultural sector—and China was admitted into the WTO on Nov. 11.

U.S.–Jordan Trade Bill

With President George W. Bush's administration portraying trade as a key component in building a coalition against terrorism, Congress on Sept. 24, 2001, cleared long-delayed legislation implementing the 2000 U.S.-Jordan trade pact (HR 2603—PL 107-43). The pact was the first U.S. bilateral trade agreement to include labor and environmental requirements.

House Republicans and Senate Democrats guided the legislation, which authorized the necessary changes in U.S. tariff laws, through the House Ways and Means and Senate Finance committees July 26. GOP reluctance to endorse the pact because of the environmental and labor provisions was mostly alleviated by an exchange of letters on July 23 between U.S. Trade Representative Robert B. Zoellick and his Jordanian counterpart, Ambassador Marwan Muasher, in which both sides pledged to avoid the use of sanctions in enforcing provisions. Although they were wary of the letters, Democrats praised the pact as setting a precedent.

The House passed the bill easily July 31, but Sen. Phil Gramm, R-Texas, vowed to block it unless the labor and environmental provisions were dropped altogether. Gramm finally withdrew his objections after Sept. 11, but the hopes of free-trade advocates that the bill would smooth the way for enactment of a broader measure renewing expedited, or fast-track, treatment for trade agreements did not materialize. *(Fast-track legislation, p. 150)*

HIGHLIGHTS

The bill changed U.S. laws to conform to the trade agreement, which contained the following elements:

- **Tariffs.** The United States and Jordan agreed to eliminate tariffs on virtually all trade between the two countries over ten years.
- **Labor standards.** Both countries agreed to abide by core labor standards and pledged not to lower those standards to enhance trade.
- **Environmental protection.** The two countries agreed to eliminate tariffs on environmental goods and to avoid lowering environmental laws to promote trade.
- **Services.** Jordan agreed to give U.S. companies access to its services sector. Jordanian service companies already had full access to the U.S. market.

BACKGROUND

The U.S.-Jordan Free Trade Agreement was negotiated by the administration of President Bill Clinton (1993–2001) and signed Oct. 24, 2000. Although trade with Jordan was relatively small, totaling just $386 million in 2000, Democrats saw the pact as a major breakthrough because it was the first time bilateral commitments on workplace and environmental rules were included in the text of a U.S. bilateral trade agreement, making them enforceable by sanctions. Most Republicans opposed the provisions, arguing that trade pacts were not appropriate vehicles for addressing social policy issues.

Reluctant to set such a precedent, George W. Bush's administration refrained from submitting the pact to the 107th Congress for months. It did so only after the exchange of letters in which the two countries stated that given "the wide range of our bilateral ties and the spirit of collaboration that characterizes our relations," they would seek to resolve any differences about the agreement through means "that will help to secure compliance without recourse to traditional sanctions."

House GOP leaders hoped the bill would serve as a confidence-building measure to spur negotiations with centrist Democrats on Bush's top trade goal, renewal of fast-track negotiating authority. Fast track, which the new administration had renamed trade promotion authority, guaranteed that Congress would accept or reject trade agreements without altering them. Democrats wanted to require the inclusion of sanctions to enforce workplace and environmental commitments under such pacts; Republicans were equally determined that such issues not be subject to sanctions. House Ways and Means Committee Chair Bill Thomas, R-Calif., hoped the example of the Jordan pact would reassure both sides.

After the Sept. 11 terrorists attacks, administration officials pressed for quick enactment of the bill, arguing that trade was a key element in the campaign to build a global coalition against terrorism and stressing the importance of Jordan's King Abdullah as a Muslim ally in the effort.

LEGISLATIVE ACTION

Following the exchange of letters Thomas introduced the bill on July 24 and won voice vote approval in the committee two days later (HR 2603—H Rept 107-176, Part 1). The House passed the bill by voice vote July 31 under suspension of the rules, a procedure allowing no amendments.

The Senate Finance Committee approved a companion bill (S 643—S Rept 107-59) by voice vote July 26. It was the second try. Chair Max Baucus, D-Mont., had called a mark-up on July 17, hoping for quick action on the bill, but dissatisfied Republicans refused to stay long enough to give him a quorum.

Gramm's objections to the enforcement sanctions prevented further action until after Sept. 11, when the administration was finally able to persuade him to set aside his objections at least for the Jordan trade pact. The Senate then passed the House U.S.-Jordan trade bill (HR 2603) by voice vote Sept. 24, clearing the measure for Bush who signed it Sept. 28, 2001. Gramm and other Republicans insisted, however, the measure would not set a precedent for future negotiations or for a fast-track bill.

Vietnam Trade Status

Congress readily cleared legislation in October 2001 allowing the president to extend normal trade relations to Vietnam on an annual basis, thus implementing a U.S.-Vietnam bilateral trade agreement reached in 2000. Vietnam's National Assembly ratified the agreement on Nov. 28, 2001.

The legislation effectively approved a trade agreement brokered by the administration of President Bill Clinton (1993–2001) in July 2000. The approval was required under the Jackson-Vanik amendment to the 1974 Trade Act (PL 93-618) before the president could extend normal trade status to certain communist countries, including Vietnam. President George W. Bush signed the measure (H J Res 51—PL 107-52) on Oct. 16, 2001.

Although trade with Vietnam was minimal, the measure's easy enactment symbolized a new level of cordiality between the two former enemies. Since 1998 Vietnam had received narrower annual waivers, effectively making U.S. companies doing business there eligible for federal loans and guarantees. *(Congress and the Nation Vol. X, pp. 158, 167)*

BACKGROUND

The United States imposed a trade embargo on Vietnam during the Vietnam War in the 1960s, and most tariffs remained prohibitively high for a quarter century. But since the early 1990s the United States had taken several steps to improve relations with Vietnam.

Citing the progress made in accounting for prisoners of war and servicemen missing in action, President Clinton lifted the trade embargo in 1994. A liaison office was opened later that year and diplomatic relations were reestablished in 1995.

Normalizing U.S. trade with Vietnam was viewed as an important step in bringing that country fully into the world community. In July 2000 Clinton concluded an agreement with Vietnam to allow goods from that country to receive the same favorable tariff treatment as most of the United States' other trading partners. U.S. tariffs on Vietnamese goods would fall from an average of about 40 percent of value to about 3 percent of value. In return, Vietnam pledged to take several steps to open its markets for U.S. goods. The agreement did not cover textiles and apparel.

Bush submitted the agreement to Congress for approval on June 8.

Under the 1974 Jackson-Vanik amendment (PL-96-618) the president could waive provisions barring favorable tariff treatment for goods from a communist country; the waiver was good only for one year, and Congress had sixty days to block it using expedited rules. To qualify for a waiver a country had to have a trade agreement with the United States. (Jackson-Vanik amendment, Congress and the Nation Vol. IV, p. 131)

The U.S.-Vietnam bilateral trade agreement signed in 2000 was a three-year pact with automatic extensions after that unless either party renounced the agreement. Each extension required presidential determination that Vietnam was satisfactorily providing reciprocal trade treatment to U.S. exports. Vietnam agreed to take five major steps regarding U.S. goods, services, and investment: lower its own tariffs; eliminate nontariff barriers; protect U.S. intellectual property rights; open its markets to U.S. service and investment companies; and make its labor force available to U.S. manufacturing ventures.

Trade with Vietnam was not exceptionally valuable in economic terms. U.S. imports from Vietnam in 2000 totaled $822 million; U.S. exports came to $368 million.

LEGISLATIVE ACTION

The House Ways and Means Committee approved a one-year grant of nondiscriminatory trade treatment to products from Vietnam (H J Res 51—H Rept 107-198) by voice vote July 26. The full House passed the measure by voice vote Sept. 6. Immediately beforehand members voted 410–1 to pass a bill (HR 2833) that would prohibit nonhumanitarian aid to Vietnam unless the president certified to Congress that Hanoi had made substantial progress on human rights.

In separate action the House on July 26 rejected a measure (H J Res 55) that would have voided an executive order by Bush allowing companies doing business in Vietnam to qualify for federal aid, including import and export financing. Until normal trade ties were extended such as order was the principal way for the president to promote trade with Vietnam. The House defeated the joint resolution 91–324.

The Senate Finance Committee approved its version of the legislation allowing nondiscriminatory tariffs on Vietnamese goods (S J Res 16—S Rept 107-49) by voice vote July 17. The Senate took up the House-passed version of the measure Oct. 3, clearing it 88–12. Those voting against the measure objected to it either because they believed Vietnam's human rights record was not yet good enough to merit the reward of normal U.S. trade relations or because they wanted to signal displeasure with federal regulations that allowed imports of basa fish from the Mekong Delta to be labeled as catfish, thus harming the business of domestic catfish farmers.

The Senate took no action on H J Res 55.

High-Tech Export Controls

An industry-led effort to ease export controls on "dual-use" technologies—those with both military and commercial applications—failed once again after free-traders and national security conservatives in the 107th Congress were unable to reach a compromise.

The legislation would have reauthorized the 1979 Export Administration Act (PL 96-72), which expired in 1994. The law, which had been kept in place by short-term extensions and by executive order, allowed the executive branch to block the export of high-technology equipment that could be used to construct advanced weapons. (Congress and the Nation Vol. X, p. 166)

Lobbyists for the technology industry said the export control system was badly out of date and hurt U.S. businesses by blocking the export of devices that were readily available on world markets. But efforts to rewrite the law had collapsed repeatedly in disputes over whether the Commerce or the Defense department should play the main role in determining what exports to restrict. After the Sept. 11, 2001, terrorist attacks, passage of the legislation was further complicated by heightened concerns over national security.

BACKGROUND

Despite revolutionary advancements in technology the law regulating exports of duel-use technology had not been rewritten since it was enacted in 1979. That law established federal policy for licensing export of nearly 2,400 dual-use items, including high-performance computers and software. It also included penalties for companies and individuals who violated the act.

Congress had tried at different times since 1994 to update the cold war–era law but was unable to reconcile the demands of the high-tech industry, which wanted looser restrictions, especially on technologies that were available to mass-market consumers, and defense hawks, who feared that looser restrictions would allow U.S. technologies to reach hostile nations such as Iran, Iraq, and North Korea. After the last authorization of the Export Administration Act lapsed in 1994, President Bill Clinton (1993–2001) regulated exports of dual-use technology through executive orders and waivers. Interest in reauthorizing the act was revived after allegations in 1998 that China had improved its long-range missiles with technology gleaned from launching U.S. commercial satellites. A Senate bill would have reduced the number of products restricted for export abroad while raising the penalties for violations of export restrictions. But several Senate committee chairs blocked the legislation on both national security and jurisdictional grounds.

Instead a stopgap reauthorization (PL 106-508) was enacted in 2000, but it was due to expire in August 2001 and did not include the tougher penalties for export violations that sponsors said were needed.

During his election campaign George W. Bush endorsed the idea of a new export control system with tighter controls for "truly sensitive" technologies and lower barriers for those that were widely available.

LEGISLATIVE ACTION

With support from the Bush administration the Senate Banking Committee approved a bill (S 149—S Rept 107-10) on March 22, 2001, to reauthorize the export control law for at least three years. The legislation proposed an entirely new set of export controls, eliminating restrictions on the export of technologies that were mass-marketed or otherwise widely available, while significantly increasing penalties for those who knowingly violated the remaining controls.

Senate floor action on the bill was delayed for several months by Richard C. Shelby, R-Ala., chair of the Intelligence Committee. Shelby, along with the chairs of the Armed Services, Foreign Relations, and Commerce and Governmental Affairs committees, said the bill would compromise U.S. defense interests in pursuit of commercial goals. But after concluding that passage by a large majority was inevitable—the bill had the enthusiastic backing of both party leaderships as well as the Bush administration—a handful of defense hawks cut several deals on language they said would better protect national security. They then allowed the bill to come to a vote, although the changes they secured were not enough to win their support. The measure passed 85–14 on Sept. 6.

The House International Relations Committee approved a multiyear extension (HR 2581—H Rept 107-297, Part I) on Aug. 1, 2001. Approval came only after the committee adopted twenty-five amendments to tighten the regulation of dual-use exports and to bolster the Defense and State departments' roles in decisions about which technologies could be exported and to what countries. One committee Democrat said the altered House bill was "so overwhelmingly weighted" in favor of national security that it "strangulates the commercial enterprises."

In the wake of the terrorist attacks the House Armed Services Committee amended the bill with provisions to enhance the Pentagon's role in regulating exports. The committee approved its version of HR 2581 (H Rept 107-297, Part II) on March 6, 2002. Among other things, the Armed Services version would have reinstated a special list of items that were determined to be critical to U.S. military superiority. The list would have been controlled by the defense secretary, and items that were listed could not have been exported without Pentagon approval.

The dim prospects for reconciling this bill with the more business-friendly version passed by the Senate halted further action in the 107th Congress.

Export-Import Bank

Congress in 2002 agreed to reauthorize the Export-Import (Ex-Im) Bank of the United States through fiscal 2006 while calling for changes in the bank's "tied-aid" program. The Ex-Im Bank provided loans, credit guarantees, and credit insurance to help U.S. exporters compete with foreign companies that receive public financing. President George W. Bush signed the bill (S 1372—PL 107-189) into law June 14.

The law increased the total amount of bank loans, guarantees, and insurance that could be outstanding at any one time from $75 billion to $100 billion by 2006. It directed the bank to double the share of its financing used to boost exports of businesses with fewer than 100 employees, as well as those owned by women or by socially and economically disadvantaged individuals. Other provisions called for human rights impact assessments for any bank project over $10 million and authorized $80 million to upgrade the bank's technology.

The legislation won approval from House and Senate committees in 2001, but its journey from there to the president's desk was tortuous. Two Nebraska Republicans, Rep. Doug Bereuter and Sen. Chuck Hagel, led efforts to make the bank more independent. They were upset that the Treasury Department had blocked a bank grant aimed at helping a Nebraska-based company, Valmont Industries, sell farm equipment to China. The company lost a $5 million contract to a competitor.

Bereuter, chair of the House Financial Services subcommittee with jurisdiction over the bank, added language stating that the Treasury could not veto such tied-aid decisions, but conferees eventually agreed to a compromise that gave the president final say over the grants. Tied aid was provided on a long-term low-interest basis for public sector capital projects in developing countries. The purpose was to counter the aid that other countries used to help their businesses beat out direct U.S. competitors.

While Congress deliberated, the bank operated under a series of three short-term authorizations. The last one (PL 107-186) expired June 14, 2002. It was extended for four years in 1997. (*Congress and the Nation Vol. X, p. 156*)

LEGISLATIVE ACTION

The Senate passed the bill—which had been approved by the Banking, Housing, and Urban Affairs Committee in July 2001 (S Rept 107-52)—by voice vote March 14, 2002. It authorized the bank through fiscal 2006 and called for the bank to increase to18 percent from 10 percent the portion of its assistance used to finance exports by small businesses.

Rather than explicitly reining in the Treasury Department the committee included language in its report endorsing an agreement that had been reached between Treasury and the Ex-Im Bank on standards and procedures for making tied-aid grants. Banking Committee Chair Paul S. Sarbanes, D-Md., said his view of whether legislative change was needed would depend on whether the agreement was working. The report did state that if all of the procedures were followed, the case-by-case responsibility for deciding on tied aid would belong to the Ex-Im Bank.

The House passed the bill by voice vote May 1, after substituting the text of its own measure (HR 2871—H Rept 107-292). The bill directed Treasury and the Ex-Im Bank to jointly develop standards and procedures for the tied-aid grant program, which would be renamed the "Export Competitiveness Program and Fund." Bereuter included language in the bill stating that Treasury could not veto a specific tied-aid grant decision.

House and Senate conferees reached a final agreement May 24 after last-minute negotiations with the White House over the tied-aid fund. Treasury had warned that it would recommend a veto of any bill that took away its control over the tied-aid fund. After two days of talks with the White House, conferees agreed to make the president, not the Treasury, the final arbiter over the use of the fund. The House adopted the conference report (H Rept 107-487) by a vote of 344–78 on June 5. The Senate cleared the bill by voice vote without debate June 6.

Despite the amount of attention it received, the so-called tied-aid war chest was a relatively small part of the bank's work. Of the estimated $3.1 billion needed to implement the bill from fiscal 2002 through 2006 tied aid was expected to account for $128 million, or 4 percent.

Liberal Democrats and conservative Republicans opposed the conference report in the House, describing the Ex-Im Bank's work as a form of "corporate welfare" that could end up hurting rather than helping American workers. But sponsors were able to win the support of other Democrats by including language requiring the bank to consider the impact of a bank loan or grant on U.S. employment.

To assuage other lawmakers the final version of the bill required the bank to look at foreign nations' records on fighting terrorism in providing loans. It also prohibited the bank from extending loans to foreign companies found in violation of U.S. trade laws and required the bank to double, to 20 percent, its share of transactions with small businesses.

2003–2004

Having given President George W. Bush fast-track trade authority in 2002, legislators in the 108th Congress took a breather during 2003–2004, perhaps in anticipation of 2005 when fast-track renewal as well as continued membership in the World Trade Organization (WTO) would be up for debate. Lawmakers approved four bilateral trade agreements, with Chile and Singapore in 2003 and with Australia and Morocco in 2004, and they extended for three years a trade agreement with several African countries.

Although Congress approved those pacts with relative ease, lawmakers were already warning that a much more complex agreement the United States had negotiated with five Central American countries was likely to encounter stiff resistance when it reached Congress, expected sometime in 2005. Some members were expected to object to tariff reductions on textiles, sugar, and citrus products, while others were concerned that the Central American Free Trade Agreement with Costa Rica, El Salvador, Guatemala, Honduras, and Nicaragua did not provide strong enough protections to keep workers in those countries from being exploited to promote trade.

The trade legislation that caused the most anxiety during the 108th Congress was a generally routine measure to make technical corrections to tariffs and trade rules. Passage of the measure was delayed for months in the Senate as individual senators sought special treatment for trade interests of their constituents. The bill also was caught up in partisan disputes between Democrats and Republicans. Compromise was finally reached in the last days of the lame-duck session of 2004.

Two controversial matters that affected trade were debated in other contexts. The outsourcing of U.S. jobs to foreign countries such as India and China became a key issue during the presidential debate. And legislation to repeal a tax break for U.S. exporters that had led to trade sanctions authorized by the WTO and imposed by the European Union against U.S. companies became the vehicle for the biggest corporate tax overhaul since 1986. *(Corporate tax bill, p. 115)*

Chile, Singapore Trade Agreements

President George W. Bush signed bills in September 2003 implementing what supporters said were state-of-the-art trade agreements with Chile and Singapore. Approval of the agreements represented the first use of the renewed congressional fast-track procedures for trade bills (PL 107-210) enacted in 2002. *(Fast-track procedures, pp. 150, 151)*

The accords, several years in the making, included an end to tariffs on nearly all goods moving between the United States and the two countries. Duty-free treatment on the remaining goods was to be phased in over the next decade. The White House and congressional backers stressed that the pacts addressed such issues as intellectual property rights,

transparency of administrative procedures, and the fast-growing services sector. Multilateral trade talks had been bogged down by controversies over these and other issues.

The U.S.-Chile free-trade accord was the first such agreement with a South American country, while the U.S.-Singapore pact was the first with an East Asian nation.

Given the relatively modest volume of trade with these countries and their comparatively strong labor and environmental standards, the agreements did not generate the kind of pitched battles that had accompanied some recent trade legislation, including the fights in the 107th Congress over renewing fast-track procedures and approving a trade agreement with Jordan. House Democratic leaders supported both pacts but warned that their backing should not be viewed as unqualified support for all free-trade agreements. They vowed that they would block bilateral accords that had a greater potential impact on U.S. jobs or those with countries with weak labor standards.

The one exception to the general support concerned immigration. The agreements allowed 6,800 workers—5,400 from Singapore and 1,400 from Chile—to enter the United States each year using H-1B visas for skilled workers. The visas could be renewed indefinitely. Lawmakers from both parties questioned the fairness of such a provision at a time when many skilled Americans were out of work. Democrats made it clear that they did not view trade agreements considered under fast-track procedures as the appropriate place for changes in immigration law. The House Judiciary Committee won a number of changes in the immigration section before the bill was submitted to Congress, but several members still were not appeased.

Under the 2002 fast-track procedures—also known as trade promotion authority—lawmakers could not make changes once the trade agreements were introduced; the only option was to vote the measures up or down. Congressional input instead came through discussions and "mock markups" that took place before the administration formally sent the agreements to Congress.

U.S.-CHILE AGREEMENT

Trade talks with Chile began in late 1990. The Clinton administration in 1994 announced its interest in extending the North American Free Trade Agreement to include Chile although formal negotiations were never concluded. After that Canada and Mexico as well as the European Union and most of South America had concluded free-trade agreements with Chile. Formal U.S. talks with Chile accelerated in December 2000 and were completed in December 2002. The agreement was signed June 6, 2003. The Bush administration delayed submitting the compact to Congress for several months, signaling its disappointment with Chile's opposition to the war in Iraq. *(Iraq war, pp. 231, 238)*

Although total trade between the United States and Chile doubled in the 1990s, surpassing $9 billion in 2002, the U.S. market share in Chile dropped from 24 percent to 17 percent, largely, it was argued, because countries that had free-trade agreements with Chile were supplanting U.S. exporters. Most of Chile's exports to the United States already were duty-free under the Generalized System of Preferences, which provided entry to the United States without tariff for more than 6,000 products from about 140 developing nations.

The free-trade agreement made over 85 percent of bilateral trade between the two countries duty-free immediately, with most remaining tariffs eliminated within four years. After ten years, all trade in nonagricultural goods would take place without tariffs or quotas; for agricultural goods, the phase-out would take twelve years.

U.S.-SINGAPORE AGREEMENT

Comprehensive trade negotiations between the United States and Singapore began in the late 1990s. Formal talks accelerated in November 2000 and were completed in December 2002. The trade pact was signed May 6, 2003.

Singapore was the United States' eleventh-largest trading partner with total trade close to $40 billion in 2002. U.S. direct foreign investment in Singapore was $27.3 billion in 2001, mainly in high-tech manufacturing, finance, and petroleum. U.S. exports to Singapore included machinery and equipment, mineral fuels, chemicals, and foodstuffs. Singapore's primary exports were machinery and equipment, including electronics as well as consumer goods, chemicals, and mineral fuels.

The agreement focused on removing restrictions on trade in services because 99 percent of U.S.-Singapore trade in goods was tariff-free already. The two countries agreed to provide market access in almost all service sectors, including computer services, financial services, telecommunications, construction, express delivery, direct selling, adult education, energy, and tourism.

LEGISLATIVE ACTION

Bush sent the two implementing bills to Congress on July 15, 2003, after a period of informal consideration and comment by the relevant committees. The House Ways and Means Committee approved the Chile implementation bill 33–5 on July 17; the House Judiciary Committee had approved it by voice vote July 16 (HR 2738—H Rept 108-224, Parts I, II). The Senate Finance Committee approved the bill 21–0 on July 17, and the Judiciary Committee approved it 11–4 the same day. The two committees filed a joint report (S 1416—S Rept 108-116).

The House Ways and Means Committee approved the Singapore implementation bill 32–5 on July 17; the House Judiciary Committee had approved it by voice vote on July 16 (HR 2739—H Rept 108-225, Parts I, II). The Senate Finance Committee approved the bill 21–0 on July 17; the Senate Judiciary Committee approved it the same day 11–4.

Again the two committees filed a joint report (S 1417—S Rept 108-117).

The committees already had considered draft bills in June and July and held mock markups the week of July 7. That process produced some changes before President Bush formally submitted the implementation bills for approval.

Floor action was speedy and uncontroversial. The House on July 24 passed the Singapore agreement by a vote of 272–155 and the Chile agreement by a vote of 270–156. The Senate cleared both bills on July 31. The vote on the Singapore pact was 66–32; the Chile bill passed 65–32. President Bush signed both bills on Sept. 3, 2003 (Chile: HR 2738—PL 108-77; Singapore: HR 2739—PL 108-78).

Africa Trade Bill

Congress in June 2004 cleared a measure (HR 4103—PL 108-274) that extended for three years a provision of a 2000 law (PL 106-200) that allowed duty-free treatment of textiles imported from certain African countries, even if the clothing were made with fabric or yarns imported from the United States or other countries. That language was scheduled to expire on Sept. 30.

Backers of the legislation argued that extending the provision was critical to helping the fledgling African textile industry gain a share of the global apparel market before worldwide quotas were removed in January 2005 under a World Trade Organization Agreement on Textiles and Clothing. Supporters of the bill pointed out that since the 2000 law was enacted U.S. imports of African textiles had almost doubled in value, from $7.6 billion in 2001 to $13.2 billion in 2003.

HR 4103 also extended other provisions of the 2000 bill through 2015. Those provisions included technical assistance to certain African countries to help them improve their economies. *(2000 African trade initiative, Congress and the Nation Vol. X, p. 167)*

The House passed HR 4103 (H Rept 108-501) on June 14 by voice vote. The Senate passed the measure by voice vote on June 24, clearing it for President George W. Bush's signature. He signed the measure July 13, 2004.

Australia Trade Pact

The House and Senate in July 2004 voted overwhelmingly in favor of a U.S. free-trade agreement with Australia (HR 4759—PL 108-286). Although the measure had broad bipartisan support, the debate brought out a number of concerns about trade in agricultural products and the fast-track process under which such trade bills were considered by Congress.

Australia was the fifteenth-largest U.S. export market and one of the few large countries with which the United States ran a trade surplus: $6.7 billion in 2003 according to Commerce Department figures released in February 2004. Australia was also a key supporter of U.S. efforts in the war on terrorism and in Iraq.

The trade agreement negotiated by the Bush administration and the Australian government would eliminate duties on most manufactured goods shipped between the two countries, open up trade in services and electronic commerce, and strengthen intellectual property rights. Makers of autos and auto parts, construction equipment, paper, and wood products were among the U.S. industries that were likely to benefit most. A coalition of business groups that supported the trade accord estimated that the tariff reduction would increase exports to Australia by as much as $2.1 billion a year.

Free-trade advocates, however, were dismayed that the agreement did not open the U.S. sugar market and would only modestly improve access to U.S. markets for Australian beef and dairy products, which were among the principal U.S. imports from that country. At the same time legislators from beef- and dairy-producing states thought the agreement went too far. During informal consideration of the agreement in June the Senate Finance Committee narrowly adopted an amendment strengthening protection for the U.S. beef industry against increased Australian imports permitted under the trade agreement. The committee chair, Charles E. Grassley, R-Iowa, then persuaded the committee to reject the legislation by a 7–14 vote to register opposition to the amendment.

Had the committee passed the amended bill the amendment would not have been binding on the administration. Under the fast-track procedure for congressional review of trade agreements the House and Senate could not make changes to the agreement once the president had formally submitted the pact to Congress. The two chambers could only approve or reject the agreements. Thus any input from Congress had to come before the formal submission, during what was called a mock markup, and was only advisory. Still, adoption of the amendment demonstrated the strong concerns that some legislators from beef- and dairy-producing states had about making trade concessions in individual agreements absent a global framework for reducing agricultural trade barriers.

During formal consideration of the bill in July the amendment's author, Democrat Kent Conrad of North Dakota, complained that the administration had ignored the committee's vote on his amendment and warned that continued failures to take the concerns of legislators into account could put the future of the fast-track procedure in "deep danger." The legislation authorizing the fast-track procedures was scheduled to expire in 2005. Other lawmakers, however, praised the administration's consultations with Congress.

Formal congressional consideration of the trade agreement was straightforward. The House Ways and Means Committee approved the implementing legislation by voice vote on July 8, and the full House passed the measure on July 14 by a vote of 314–109. On the same day the House acted

the Senate Finance Committee approved companion legislation 17–4. The following day the Senate voted 80–16 to clear the trade deal and send it to the President George W. Bush. Bush signed it Aug. 3, 2004.

Morocco Trade Accord

Congress gave lopsided approval to a measure to implement a free-trade accord with Morocco, clearing the bill (HR 4842—PL 108-302) on July 22, 2004. Despite concerns of some lawmakers who blamed at least some of the American job losses on expanded trade, the measure was the third pro-trade measure to clear Congress in a month. *(Africa trade, Australia trade, p. 165)*

The U.S.-Morocco free-trade agreement eliminated tariffs on manufactured goods and updated protections for intellectual property rights. The agreement was also expected to give U.S. farmers and ranchers significantly expanded access to Moroccan markets.

Under a 2002 law (PL 107-210) that renewed fast-track consideration of trade deals Congress was prohibited from amending legislation to implement trade pacts negotiated by the administration and could vote only to accept or reject the accords.

The House Ways and Means Committee approved HR 4842 (H Rept 108-627) 26–0 on July 20. The Senate Finance Committee voted 21–0 in favor of its version of the measure (S 2677) the same day, and the Senate passed it 85–13 on July 21. After working out a few technical procedures between the chambers HR 4842 was given final approval by the House 323–99. President George W. Bush signed the implementing legislation on Aug. 17, 2004.

Miscellaneous Tariff and Trade Rules

After two years of stops and starts Congress cleared usually routine legislation to make miscellaneous changes to U.S. trade law. The legislation (HR 1047—PL108-429) excused companies from paying duties on hundreds of imported goods for which there was no domestic supplier, reimbursed companies that paid tariffs in the past on imports that should have been duty-free, and made several technical corrections to trade laws.

Under rules that governed the drafting of the normally routine measure, provisions had to be noncontroversial and have a minimal effect on the federal budget. Enacting the routine legislation had been a standard exercise for each Congress for more than two decades. But the 107th Congress failed to complete action on the measure before it adjourned, and similar legislation in the 108th Congress was stalled by controversy over trade provisions as well as unrelated issues.

PROVISIONS

In addition to making the routine adjustments in tariffs and trade rules HR 1047 repealed a 1916 law aimed at the "dumping" of foreign-made goods in the United States below market prices with the intent of injuring a U.S. industry. Repealing the law brought the United States into compliance with a World Trade Organization decision from 2000 that the 1916 antidumping law violated several major trade agreements. While the law had seldom been used, it served as a legal tool in a number of cases involving steel imports in the 1990s. U.S. trade partners, particularly Europe, had long sought its repeal.

The bill also extended normal trade relations to Laos and Armenia. It extended the Generalized System of Preferences to allow duty-free treatment for hand-knotted and hand-woven carpets to aid Afghanistan and Pakistan. It reversed an inadvertent increase in tariffs on handbags, luggage, and other items imported from the Andes region, and it allowed the president to impose emergency import restrictions on archaeological and ethnological materials from Iraq to prevent the sale of looted objects.

LEGISLATIVE ACTION

HR 1047 had its origins in the 107th Congress. Lawmakers had few substantive disagreements on the legislation but ran out of time and failed to clear a miscellaneous tariffs bill in 2002.

Similar legislation was introduced early in the 108th Congress and was expected to be completed quickly. The House passed HR 1047 (no written report) by a 415–11 vote on March 5, 2003. The Senate Finance Committee acted with similar dispatch on its version (S 671—no written report), approving it in February 2003. The measure was then delayed for a full year as senators from both parties blocked consideration to push for controversial changes in the legislation or to make political points on unrelated issues.

For example, Richard C. Shelby, R-Ala., chair of the Senate Banking Committee, held up action for months, insisting on a rewrite of a section of the 2002 fast-track trade law (PL 107-210) to help protect his state's sock industry from Caribbean imports. Despite his determination, Shelby was rebuffed and settled for a more modest change in sock packaging guidelines that would more clearly state the country of origin.

Then other senators blocked the bill over unrelated matters. Sen. Carl Levin, D-Mich., objected to acting on it to draw attention to Congress's refusal to renew special unemployment benefits. After those and other matters were resolved, the Senate passed HR 1047 by voice vote on March 4, 2004.

At that point the legislation became entangled in a broader partisan dispute. Democrats objected to conference negotiations on a number of bills including the tariff measure, saying they were not being afforded full participation in conferences. Conference action was delayed for months, and affected companies grew ever more frustrated by the impasse. Finally, in October, as the rush to leave town to campaign for the upcoming elections made it less likely that Republicans would attach controversial add-ons during negotiations, a conference was convened on Oct. 8 and a final bill negotiated within a matter of hours.

The House adopted the conference report on HR 1047 (H Rept 108-771) by voice vote later the same day and the Senate appeared poised to follow suit when Wisconsin's senators, Russ D. Feingold and Herb Kohl, objected to a provision added in conference to normalize trade relations with Laos. Their state had one of the nation's largest concentrations of Hmong immigrants, and they argued that Laos's human rights record toward its tribal Hmong people did not merit such an economic benefit.

That stalled the bill again and moved final consideration to the post-election lame-duck session. On Nov. 19 the Senate voted 88–5 to invoke cloture to limit debate on the bill, but even after that vote Feingold and others used some of the remaining debate time to underscore their opposition to the Laos provision. Feingold relented only when the Senate adopted by voice vote a resolution (S Res 475) calling on Laos to improve its human rights record. The Senate then adopted the conference report on HR 1047, clearing the measure for President George W. Bush who signed it Dec. 3, 2004.

CHAPTER 3

Homeland Security Policy

Homeland Security Policy

The hijacked airplanes that crashed into the World Trade Center, the Pentagon, and a field in Pennsylvania on Sept. 11, 2001, radically changed the landscape of American politics. Partisan differences and a host of domestic issues were abruptly shoved aside as President George W. Bush and congressional leaders scrambled to shore up the nation's defenses against further terrorist attacks at home and to launch attacks against potential enemies overseas. Before the year ended, Congress had agreed to fund antiterrorism activities, strengthen the hand of law enforcement agencies, and overhaul airport security procedures.

Within months, however, traditional political divisions returned. During the course of the first George W. Bush administration, Congress assented to a number of other homeland security measures, including the creation of a massive Homeland Security Department. But congressional leaders resisted White House demands to shift more power to the executive branch. In addition, state and regional delegations sparred over how to disperse antiterrorism funds, Democrats battled Republicans over security issues involving labor and industry, critics on both the right and the left raised concerns about the reach of law enforcement agencies, and powerful committee chairs resisted changes that would weaken their oversight.

In the immediate aftermath of the attacks that left nearly 3,000 people dead, shaken Democratic and Republican lawmakers came together to condemn the terrorists and promise quick action to protect the nation. After evacuating congressional office buildings in the hours after the attacks, they returned for a prayer vigil in the Capitol Rotunda on the evening of Sept. 11. Senators and representatives of both parties gathered on the steep marble steps of the Capitol and sang "God Bless America." House Minority Leader Richard A. Gephardt, D-Mo., pledged to cooperate so closely with his rival, Speaker J. Dennis Hastert, R-Ill., that there would be "no air and no light" between them. During the fall, lawmakers grew even more concerned about terrorist threats after several offices, including those of Senate Majority Leader Tom Daschle, D-S.D., received envelopes containing deadly amounts of anthrax.

Showing how quickly Congress could move in an emergency, lawmakers approved a $40 billion emergency appropriations measure just days after the Sept. 11 attacks. They followed that up in October with the USA PATRIOT Act, a historic broadening of law enforcement powers that passed despite some concerns over a possible infringement on civil liberties. The next month Congress agreed to federalize airport security, even though many Republicans found the notion of expanding the federal government to be anathema. Congress cleared bills to enhance border security, better guard the nation against bioterrorism attacks, and strengthen intelligence efforts, and it boosted funding for various antiterrorism programs.

But lawmakers could not reach agreements on a number of other homeland security issues. Proposals failed that would have increased funding for emergency personnel in high-risk areas, mandated inspections of air cargo, funded security procedures at ports, and tightened requirements for chemical plants and nuclear facilities. Committee chairs, engaging in turf battles, also tried to torpedo plans to centralize congressional oversight of homeland security—even though the fractionalization of congressional oversight had been faulted as part of the reason the government failed to adequately address the threat of terrorism before Sept. 11.

Throughout this period, congressional leaders asserted the power of their institution, even while generally deferring to the White House on matters of homeland security. As early as the first days following the attacks, appropriators resisted White House proposals for broad latitude over spending money to battle terrorists. Congress subsequently insisted on the right to confirm the director of homeland security and, despite White House qualms, created an independent commission to investigate the Sept. 11 attacks. During the 108th Congress, many on Capitol Hill raised worrisome questions about the performance of the new Homeland Security Department and pressed to repeal controversial provisions in the PATRIOT Act.

Despite the actions by Congress and the administration to secure the nation after Sept. 11, experts worried that more needed to be done to head off another terrorist attack. Thomas Kean, chair of the Sept. 11 commission, said that the commission had been repeatedly warned that "an attack of even greater magnitude is now possible and even probable—we do not have the luxury of time."

HOMELAND SECURITY LEADERSHIP

The Senate on Jan. 22, 2003, confirmed former Pennsylvania governor Tom Ridge as the first secretary of the new Homeland Security Department by a vote of 94–0. Although senators offered strong praise and no criticism of the nominee, they warned he was embarking on a high-profile job with little margin for error. Ridge, a Vietnam veteran who had been President George W. Bush's director of homeland security since October 2001, was sworn in Jan. 24 for what Sen. Arlen Specter, R-Pa., called "the toughest job in Washington today."

Members of the Senate Governmental Affairs Committee widely praised the former Pennsylvania governor (1995–2001) and seven-term House member (1983–1995) during a confirmation hearing Jan. 17. But it was clear that as Ridge's relationship evolved with the Senate committee that had primary oversight of the Department of Homeland Security, he would have to answer regularly for everything from bioterrorism preparedness to Coast Guard readiness to labor relations.

"America is undoubtedly safer and better prepared today than on Sept. 10, 2001," Ridge said in his opening statement at the hearing. But he added, "We are only at the beginning of what will be a long struggle to protect our nation from terrorism."

In a nod to the federal labor unions that had unsuccessfully fought Bush's demand for authority to fashion new labor rules for the department, Ridge—a former union member himself—promised lawmakers that he would "eagerly solicit and consider advice from employees, unions, professional associations, and other stakeholders."

Senators did not appear to hold him responsible for a dispute between the administration and Congress during the 107th Congress, when the White House resisted creating a top homeland security position that would be subject to Senate approval.

After Bush won reelection in 2004, Ridge announced he would step down. On Dec. 3, 2004, Bush announced his nomination of former New York police commissioner Bernard Kerik, who had won national praise after leading the New York City Police Department through the Sept. 11, 2001, terrorist attacks. But in a stinging embarrassment to the administration, Kerik withdrew his name from consideration one week later. He said he had discovered that a former housekeeper and nanny had a questionable immigration status. He also faced questions over possible conflicts of interest and past business dealings.

Bush on Jan. 11, 2005, nominated federal appeals court judge Michael Chertoff for the position. Chertoff had previ-

On January 22, 2003, the Senate confirmed former Pennsylvania governor Tom Ridge as the first secretary of the Department of Homeland Security. Ridge was installed as chief of the new agency in October 2001 by an executive order, but a Senate bill passed in 2002 created a cabinet-level department and gave the Senate authority to approve Ridge as secretary. *Source: Congressional Quarterly/Scott J. Ferrell*

ously served in the Bush administration as assistant attorney general in the Department of Justice's criminal division from 2001 to 2003. Democrats and Republicans alike praised him, although civil libertarians raised concerns about his roles in post-Sept. 11 detention policies and the writing of the 2001 antiterrorism law known as the USA PATRIOT Act.

The Senate approved Chertoff's nomination by a unanimous vote, 98–0, on Feb. 15, 2005. The nomination had been held up for a week while Sen. Carl Levin, D-Mich., demanded access to information about how the Justice Department had handled interrogation rules for terrorist suspects at Guantánamo Bay, Cuba. Justice officials said that Chertoff had nothing to do with the policies, and Levin let the vote go forward, despite his reservations.

CENTRALIZING HOMELAND SECURITY

One of the most pressing issues lawmakers faced was how to centralize responsibilities for homeland security and intelligence. Investigations into the attacks revealed a Byzantine structure of government agencies with often overlapping responsibilities. Federal Bureau of Investigation (FBI) agents

frequently failed to share information with their Central Intelligence Agency (CIA) counterparts; security agents at border crossings, airports, and ports operated under different guidelines and relied on different intelligence information.

The Bush administration, less than two weeks after the attacks, appointed Pennsylvania governor Tom Ridge to fill a new cabinet-level position: director of the Office of Homeland Security. But many on Capitol Hill wanted to change Ridge's post to make him subject to congressional confirmation. Influential lawmakers, including many Democrats, also pressed to consolidate diverse agencies with homeland security obligations, ranging from the Coast Guard to the Immigration and Naturalization Service, into a new executive department. After resisting the idea, Bush adopted it and helped steer landmark legislation through Congress to create the massive Department of Homeland Security (HR 5005—PL 107-296).

The legislation was generally viewed as a major victory for Bush and his Republican allies, especially because they overcame Democratic objections to exempting employees in the new department from some labor protections. The new department, however, stumbled several times in its first years. It faced ridicule for urging the public to buy duct tape and plastic sheeting to seal up doors and windows to defend against bioterrorist attacks, and it implemented a confusing color-coded terrorism alert system. By the end of Bush's first term, it was viewed by many as overly bureaucratic and in dire need of a shake-up. Lawmakers of both parties raised concerns, which were reflected in annual spending measures that required department officials to submit a multitude of reports to Congress.

Lawmakers turned to the nation's intelligence apparatus after hearing serious concerns about the gathering and dissemination of intelligence about terrorism activities. The Sept. 11 commission recommended establishing a cabinet-level national intelligence director within the White House who would control the budgets of all federal intelligence agencies. Although legislators passed a sweeping intelligence overhaul bill at the end of the 108th Congress that created a national intelligence director, it continued to give considerable authority to military intelligence agencies (S 2845—PL 108-458).

Members also found themselves sharply at odds over proposals to consolidate homeland security and intelligence oversight in Congress, as recommended by the Sept. 11 commission. Some sixty-one committees and subcommittees shared oversight of terrorism-related issues at the time the Department of Homeland Security was created. The House created a Select Committee on Homeland Security in the 108th Congress, but powerful chairs—including some who served on the committee—believed it should be disbanded because of overlap between their own panels and the new committee. Mired in jurisdictional disputes, the select committee failed to win passage of any major legislation.

Senators meanwhile weighed a plan to grant oversight of the Department of Homeland Security to the Senate Governmental Affairs Committee. But, as in the House, rival chairs assailed the idea and stripped away many of the committee's proposed powers.

By the end of the 108th Congress, oversight of homeland security issues remained dispersed among a number of com-mittees, and the outlook for consolidation under a single committee in each chamber appeared uncertain.

STRENGTHENING LAW ENFORCEMENT

Civil libertarians on both the right and left had long been wary of giving the government too much power. But with the FBI warning that more terrorist attacks could be imminent, Congress overwhelmingly cleared legislation less than two months after Sept. 11 to give the administration sweeping new authority to track, arrest, and prosecute suspected terrorists. The law, formally known as the USA PATRIOT Act (HR 3162—PL 107-56), enabled the government to obtain nationwide search warrants, conduct secret searches of suspects' property, and detain foreigners indefinitely if they were viewed as national security threats.

The Clinton administration, responding to the 1995 bombing of the federal building in Oklahoma City, had sought many of the same changes to surveillance law, including authority to conduct multiple "roving" wiretaps that could follow a person instead of having to get a separate court order for each phone line that was to be tapped. Conservative GOP lawmakers at the time were unwilling to give the government such powerful tools. But they were jolted into action by the events of Sept. 11.

By 2003, however, some lawmakers in both parties were having second thoughts about the law. Critics were particularly concerned that the law expanded the power of law enforcement authorities to conduct certain types of searches in secret and without much judicial oversight. House members in 2003 fired something of a shot across the bow of the administration, voting to add an amendment to the fiscal 2004 Commerce, Justice, and State appropriations bill to nullify a provision of the PATRIOT Act that allowed police to conduct searches and seize evidence without first notifying the subjects of the investigations. Even though the amendment did not survive conference, it indicated the depth of congressional unease and set the stage for possible battles during the 109th Congress, when many of the law's provisions were due to expire unless lawmakers renewed them.

ADDITIONAL MEASURES

Congress agreed to several additional measures aimed at boosting antiterrorism efforts. Among the most prominent, cleared in 2001, was a bill (S 1447—PL 107-71) that turned responsibility for airport security over to a new federal agency, the Transportation Security Administration, instead of private contractors. Republicans, with their traditional unease over expanding government, reluctantly bowed to public pressure at a time of great concern over flying safety, but they insisted on provisions that could return security to private contractors if certain conditions were met.

Republicans continued to voice their objections as the agency began operations. Critics included Rep. Harold Rogers, R-Ky., chair of the House Homeland Security Appropriations Subcommittee, who complained that the agency was overstaffed and had failed to complete background checks on all its employees, some of whom were found to have criminal records.

In 2002, with concerns mounting over bioterrorism, Congress cleared a bill to help federal, state, and local governments prepare for and respond to biological attacks and other public health emergencies (HR 3448—PL 107-188). The bill authorized increases in the nation's stockpiles of medicines and vaccines and mandated steps to safeguard food and water supplies. Lawmakers went further in 2004, signing off on Project Bioshield (S 15—PL 108-276), Bush's ten-year initiative to develop and stockpile vaccines and medications.

At the end of the 107th Congress, legislators passed a bill (HR 3210—PL 107-297), backed by the real estate and commercial insurance industries, that established a three-year federal terrorism insurance program. It placed a cap on potential losses for commercial property and casualty insurers in the event of a cataclysmic terrorist attack. Lawmakers hoped to encourage the insurance industry to provide commercial terrorism coverage at affordable prices, while giving it time to develop a market-based system for absorbing the risks.

Although the insurance industry counted the legislation as an important victory, it failed to persuade lawmakers in 2004 to extend the program beyond its expiration date of Dec. 31, 2005. Instead the issue was left to the 109th Congress.

PARTISAN AND REGIONAL DIVIDES

Despite such achievements, lawmakers found themselves too divided along regional or party lines to tackle a number of high-profile homeland security issues. As a result, experts worried that the nation remained vulnerable to another terrorist strike.

One of the most vexing issues proved to be funding for so-called first responders—the police and other emergency personnel who would be first on the scene after a catastrophe. Democrats pressed for much higher funding levels than the White House or congressional Republicans were willing to accept. The issue surfaced in several appropriations bills, including the fiscal 2004 Homeland Security appropriations bill (HR 2555—PL 108-90), which was the first devoted to the new department. Bush proposed $3.6 billion in that bill; Senate Democrats pressed for several times that amount but settled for $4.2 billion.

In addition to the overall funding levels, lawmakers could not agree on how to apportion the money, which was distributed in the form of grants by the Department of Homeland Security. The existing formula took population into account, but it also guaranteed that every state would get at least 0.75 percent of the total. As a result, states with low populations got more money per capita than high-density areas, which were considered the more likely terrorist targets. New York state, for example, received about $4.60 per capita in grants; Wyoming received $32.25.

This situation appeared to leave urban areas without important emergency personnel. In San Francisco, for example, the two nearest federally certified search-and-rescue teams were located miles outside the city in Menlo Park and Oakland.

Both Rep. Christopher Cox, R-Calif., chair of the House Select Committee on Homeland Security, and Sen. Susan Collins, R-Maine, chair of the Senate Governmental Affairs Committee, proposed legislation to channel more money to areas facing a higher threat of terrorism. But lawmakers failed to clear either bill. Instead they settled for nonbinding and vaguely worded "sense of Congress" language that homeland security grants should be distributed to enhance terrorism prevention and preparedness.

Congress also struggled to shore up transportation security. Experts warned that the nation's transportation system contained a number of vulnerabilities. For example, an estimated 22 percent of the nation's air cargo was carried on passenger airlines, but, unlike passenger luggage, it was not screened for explosives. Although the House and Senate advanced separate measures to require screening, cargo companies warned the extra red tape would be costly and slow the transport of goods. As part of a sweeping intelligence bill in 2004, lawmakers created trial projects for blast-resistant cargo holds.

The nation's ports appeared vulnerable as well, in part because only a small percentage of cargo containers were inspected. The 2002 Maritime Transportation Security Act (S 1214—PL 107-295) was supposed to address the issue, but the bill did not authorize any money to assess security at the country's major ports. In 2004 the Senate passed a bill to enhance port security—but only after removing a provision that would have allowed charging users fees at ports to pay for it.

Transportation systems aside, lawmakers struggled to balance security needs with the desire to promote freedom of commerce and movement of people. Chemical plants, nuclear power facilities, utilities, computer networks, and even sewage systems had increased security. Yet congressional legislation to mandate security upgrades for certain industries stalled, in part because of ideological differences over how much the government should regulate industry.

An interesting example was a debate over chemical plant security. Many Democrats, led by Sen. Jon Corzine of New Jersey, backed a bill to require all chemical facilities to conduct security studies and submit them to the Environmental Protection Agency for approval. They also wanted the facilities to study using chemicals that would be safer if they were released into the area. But Republicans wanted to take a lighter regulatory approach, requiring chemical plants only to keep their security plans on file, rather than submitting them for approval to the federal government. Neither plan passed.

Chronology of Action on Homeland Security

2001–2002

Homeland security, a secondary issue before the terrorist attacks on Sept. 11, 2001, erupted as the number-one legislative priority for the remainder of the 107th Congress. Just days after the attacks, lawmakers agreed to a $40 billion emergency appropriations measure to boost national security and recovery efforts. They followed up with a remarkable burst of action, passing several bills that dramatically reshaped the federal government and strengthened law enforcement procedures. While lawmakers generally backed President George W. Bush's priorities, they often put their own stamp on the laws by curbing the broad executive powers sought by the administration.

One of the most monumental legislative achievements during the 107th Congress was the creation of the massive Department of Homeland Security, which combined all or part of twenty-two federal agencies responsible for counterterrorism (HR 5005—PL 107-296). Bush initially resisted such a move, preferring to keep the Office of Homeland Security under White House control and retain the power to appoint its director by executive order rather than having to submit a nomination to the Senate for confirmation. But the White House changed course in 2002 amid public pressure.

The often heated debates over the legislation pitted Congress against the White House in a battle over the extent to which lawmakers would have oversight of homeland security activities, and Democrats against Republicans in a battle over the rights of employees in the new agency. So deadlocked were members that they did not agree to the legislation creating the new department until a lame-duck session after the 2002 elections, in which the GOP scored clear gains. Critics worried that the final deal gave the administration too much leeway over homeland security issues, particularly by creating a new personnel system for the department outside of civil service rules. Advocates, however, argued that strong measures were necessary to safeguard the country.

Another historic piece of legislation, formally titled the USA PATRIOT Act, greatly strengthened the authority of federal law enforcement agents to investigate and prosecute suspected terrorists (HR 3162—PL 107-56). Lawmakers on both the left and right raised concerns about the possible impacts on civil liberties, and some worried that the government was failing to impose important safeguards on federal agents. But at a time when the Federal Bureau of Investigation (FBI) was warning that subsequent terrorist attacks could be imminent, the administration, working with House and Senate leaders, ultimately got most of what it wanted by lopsided votes in both chambers. House Democrats furiously protested being excluded from much of the dealmaking, but a majority wound up supporting the measure.

Democrats scored a rare victory in the fall of 2001 when they successfully pressed for legislation that turned airport security over to a new federal agency instead of private contractors (S 1447—PL 107-71). House GOP leaders, with a traditional conservative mistrust of expanding the government, favored an alternative that would have given the administration the option of using federal or private contractors—an approach favored by the White House as well. But with the public demanding action to shore up aviation security and many Senate Republicans siding with Democrats, Congress cleared legislation creating the Transportation Security Administration shortly before the Thanksgiving holiday. Conservatives were able to win an important concession: airports could use private screeners after three years if certain conditions were met.

The pace scarcely slowed during 2002, although the White House and congressional Democrats and Republicans found themselves increasingly at odds with one another. Lawmakers cleared major bills shoring up border security and bioterrorism defenses and overcame differences over punitive damages in terrorism cases to create a three-year program to help insurers in the event of a terrorist strike.

Congress also, to the discomfort of the White House, created an independent commission to investigate the events of Sept. 11. Lawmakers worried that a joint investigation by the House and Senate Intelligence committees into the terrorist attacks was moving too slowly. They also were influenced by families of the victims of Sept. 11, who favored an independent inquiry.

But members failed to resolve differences on several other high-profile issues. Even as they passed a port security bill in

2002, they could not agree on a way to pay for the security upgrades. They also deadlocked, largely along partisan lines, over how to best safeguard industrial facilities from terrorist attacks. Democrats generally favored regulations to force the facilities to take certain safety steps; Republicans leaned toward a voluntary approach.

Homeland Security Department

Congress in 2002 cleared legislation (HR 5005—PL 107-296) authorizing the creation of a cabinet-level Department of Homeland Security, combining all or part of twenty-two federal agencies responsible for counterterrorism.

Enactment came after nearly a year of often bitter debate. While the administration and lawmakers had been in broad agreement over strengthening the government's homeland security capabilities, they had clashed over the scope of the new agency. In the end, the consolidation was the largest reorganization of the federal bureaucracy since defense and intelligence agencies were restructured in the late 1940s after the end of World War II and the beginning of the cold war between the Soviet Union and the western democracies.

President George W. Bush signed the bill into law Nov. 25, 2002.

BACKGROUND

On Sept. 20, 2001, less than two weeks after the attacks on the World Trade Center and the Pentagon, Bush used his speech to a joint session of Congress to announce the creation of a new cabinet-level post to centralize and coordinate the counterterrorism efforts of forty agencies and departments. Bush tapped Pennsylvania governor Tom Ridge, a Vietnam veteran and former House member (1983–1995), to head the Office of Homeland Security. "He will lead, oversee and coordinate a comprehensive national strategy to safeguard our country against terrorism and respond to any attacks that may come," Bush said in his speech. *(Bush text, p. 965)*

Ridge, who had received serious consideration for the 2000 Republican vice presidential nomination, resigned as Pennsylvania governor Oct. 5, 2001, and assumed his new duties Oct. 8. He worked out of a windowless office in the West Wing with a staff of fewer than twenty persons.

The idea of combining federal agencies responsible for counterterrorism and clarifying lines of authority had originated in the House and Senate after the attacks, and key lawmakers welcomed the president's decision. But they were not happy that Bush had installed Ridge in the cabinet by executive order rather than seeking congressional approval. Nearly unanimous sentiment existed in Congress to provide the homeland chief specific powers outlined in law to coordinate a multiagency system for protecting the United States. "In the strongest terms, we have to explain his authority as well as responsibility," which must be "bestowed by an act of Congress," said Sen. John McCain, R-Ariz., a member of the Senate Armed Services Committee.

The Bush administration initially resisted, arguing there was no need for Senate confirmation and that the job could be handled out of the White House Office of Homeland Security. The White House envisioned Ridge's job as similar to that of the national security adviser, a position dating from the administration of Dwight Eisenhower in the 1950s that owed its creation to congressional passage of the National Security Act of 1947 (PL 80-253) but did not require Senate approval.

But many lawmakers feared that without legislation giving Ridge statutory authority, the job would be merely advisory and the homeland chief would get caught in the turf wars among agencies. They also wanted Ridge to have authority over the $11 billion the government was set to spend on counterterrorism. Although the White House insisted that Ridge had all the authority he needed, lawmakers predicted that the collaborative effort among the agencies and departments in a time of crisis would give way to jurisdictional fights and conflicting priorities. At least a half-dozen bills were introduced in 2001 to codify Ridge's power by giving him budget authority over the more than forty agencies and departments involved in homeland security.

A muddled administration response to anthrax attacks on the Senate and U.S. postal offices in October 2001, along with contradictory assessments of the gravity of the anthrax threat, raised more questions about the authority of the homeland chief. Moreover, Ridge frustrated lawmakers by repeatedly declining to testify on the administration's plans. *(Anthrax attacks, p. 712)*

Amid rising congressional impatience, the Senate Governmental Affairs Committee in May 2002 approved a bill (S 2452), sponsored by Chair Joseph I. Lieberman, D-Conn., to create a cabinet-level homeland security department and give the Senate authority to approve its secretary.

BUSH ADMINISTRATION PLAN

In June 2002, facing increased congressional scrutiny of pre-Sept. 11 intelligence failures and declining public approval ratings, the Bush administration abruptly reversed course. In a June 6 announcement that caught official Washington and even some cabinet secretaries by surprise, Bush issued a proposal for the creation of a new homeland security department—a sprawling bureaucracy with at least 170,000 employees and a budget of $37.5 billion that would include the Federal Emergency Management Agency (FEMA), the Coast Guard, the Immigration and Naturalization Service (INS), Secret Service, Border Patrol, U.S. Customs Service, and the newly created Transportation Security Administration (TSA). The plan also called for "significant flexibility" in hiring, pay, and personnel management. The White House Office of Homeland Security would continue as a separate entity advising the president.

But the fifty-two-page draft plan submitted by the Bush administration lacked important details about handling so-called dual-purpose agencies such as the Coast Guard and

HOMELAND SECURITY BILL HIGHLIGHTS

Following are highlights of the law creating the Department of Homeland Security (HR 5005—PL 107-296). *(For a comprehensive list of provisions, see p. 183)*

Transferred agencies. The new department absorbed twenty-two existing federal agencies involved in border security, bioterrorism defenses, and disaster management. Major agencies shifted to the Department of Homeland Security included the Coast Guard, Transportation Security Administration (TSA), Federal Emergency Management Agency (FEMA), U.S. Customs Service, Secret Service, and the agricultural import and entry inspection functions of the Animal and Plant Health Inspection Service.

INS. The Immigration and Naturalization Service (INS) was abolished and split into two separate components—an immigration enforcement bureau and a citizenship bureau—both of which were placed within the new department.

Departmental structure. The legislation organized the department into four primary divisions:

• Border and Transportation Security, made up of various border control and transportation agencies, was to be responsible for setting U.S. visa policy and securing U.S. borders and transportation systems.

• Emergency Preparedness and Response, which combined FEMA and the functions of other agencies charged with preparing for and responding to terror attacks.

• Science and Technology, combining various science and technology programs. It was charged with developing countermeasures against terror threats involving weapons of mass destruction, including chemical, biological, radiological, and nuclear attacks.

• Information Analysis and Infrastructure Protection, charged with analyzing all intelligence information on possible terror attacks on the United States and evaluating critical U.S. infrastructure for vulnerabilities to terrorism.

Employee policies. The secretary of the new department was given broad authority to reorganize the transferred agencies and functions within the new bureaucracy and was allowed to create new personnel and pay grades outside of the civil service system. The measure set up a procedure for employee and union feedback on personnel and pay proposals, with a thirty-day review period and subsequent thirty-day negotiation period, after which the department could impose its new rules despite any employee objections. The authority was to expire after five years.

The president could strip employees of their union representation if the mission of their agency or division changed "materially" or if a majority of the employees within that union worked primarily with intelligence, counterintelligence, or investigations related to terrorism. The president was required to give advance notice of his intent to take such actions and submit a written explanation to Congress.

Liability limits. The law limited legal liability for certain antiterrorism products, including voiding pending lawsuits against drugmakers that made mercury-based vaccine additives. Some doctors suspected the additives caused autism in children. Republican leaders said the provision was needed to ensure that health professionals were not subject to lawsuits for administering vaccines to help prevent or treat bioterrorism threats.

The bill also extended through 2003 the federal Aviation War Risk Insurance program and the liability limits of commercial airlines whose aircraft were used in terror attacks.

Airport baggage screening. The law extended for one year, until Dec. 31, 2003, the deadline for airports to install explosive detection equipment to check airline passenger baggage for bombs. It also limited the legal liability of certain airport screening companies and allowed noncitizen U.S. nationals to work as airport passenger and baggage screeners.

Arming pilots. The TSA was required to establish a program under which trained commercial airline pilots would be allowed to carry guns aboard aircraft.

BATF. The Bureau of Alcohol, Tobacco and Firearms (BATF) was transferred from the Treasury Department to the Justice Department. The law required the bureau to establish a new explosives training center, and it set new federal restrictions on the possession and use of explosives.

Smallpox vaccinations. The Department of Health and Human Services (HHS) was authorized to administer the smallpox vaccine to segments of the population if it determined there was a public health threat posed by smallpox. The law protected drug companies and health professionals from legal liability for any adverse health reactions to the smallpox vaccine, provided for claims against the government for people who suffered such reactions, and gave liability protections to drug companies that made certain additives or components of other vaccines.

Charitable deduction. The legislation provided for the creation of tax-deductible charitable funds that could be used to compensate families of military personnel, Federal Bureau of Investigation (FBI) agents, intelligence agents, and other U.S. government representatives who died in the line of duty as a result of a terror attack.

Exemptions. Certain activities of the new department were exempted from several "good government" rules that generally applied to federal agencies, including the Freedom of Information Act (PL 104-231) and the Federal Advisory Committee Act (PL 92-463).

Corporate tax avoidance. The law prohibited the department from issuing contracts to companies that moved their headquarters overseas to avoid U.S. taxes, but waived the restriction if the contracts were necessary for national security, to prevent the loss of U.S. jobs, or to prevent additional government costs.

the U.S. Customs Service, which had both significant homeland security functions and core missions that had little to do with protecting the nation.

Although nearly every member of Congress supported the idea of coordinating the federal fight against terrorism, heated deliberations were almost inevitable given the stakes involved, the sweep of the plan, and the way it would allow the new department to rearrange functions, eliminate agencies, and transfer significant amounts of money between agencies without prior congressional approval.

House leaders decided to allow eleven committees with jurisdiction over the issue to mark up the Bush plan, which made it more permissible for members of both parties to air their criticisms. Though most party leaders endorsed creating the department as quickly as possible, some House Democrats voiced concern that Bush's plan was inadequate and potentially counterproductive because it might enlarge the bureaucracy without making the parts work together more smoothly. Democrats also contended that the proposal was not "budget neutral," as the White House claimed, but would require substantial revenues beyond the amounts the existing agencies already were spending.

Administration officials argued the department would not cost more if Congress gave the proposed secretary of homeland security significant leeway in management rules, including hiring and procurement. Bush asked for the right to cross-train workers and transfer some within the new department. The White House sought to ease concerns that such flexibility could erode federal employees' civil service protections and change their pay scales.

As the debate wore on and Senate Democrats resisted calls for flexibility, Bush characterized congressional dissent over his plan as the result of jurisdictional wars between lawmakers unable to put aside parochial concerns in the name of national security. But the crux of the dispute turned equally on how much power lawmakers were willing to cede to the executive branch. Administration insistence that the proposed department's unique missions and the threat of global terrorism justified broad exemptions from some laws and, by extension, congressional oversight rankled many powerful lawmakers. So did White House demands that the new department have the ability to transfer appropriated money within its constituent agencies, diluting the power of appropriators accustomed to controlling most aspects of federal spending. In the end, Republican gains in the midterm elections gave the administration the leverage it needed to prevail in the power struggle between the branches.

HOUSE COMMITTEE ACTION

The eleven House committees with jurisdiction over the president's plan held a frenzied series of markups the week of July 8 that produced some radically different versions of what a cabinet-level homeland security department should look like.

The panels were racing to meet a July 12 deadline imposed by House leaders, who had hopes of passing the bill before the anniversary of the Sept. 11 attacks. But the boldness with which the committees disagreed with the president, and the many ways in which they revised his plan, left tough choices for the newly created Select Committee on Homeland Security, which was charged with blending the recommendations into a single bill.

During the House markups:

• The administration backed down on a proposal to move all of the Agriculture Department's Animal and Plant Health Inspection Service to the new department after farm groups complained. Under a compromise worked out with the House Agriculture Committee, only functions involving import and border inspection would be transferred, while other functions would remain where they were.

• The Appropriations Committee rejected an administration request for broad control over the financing of the proposed department, especially authority to transfer within the department up to 5 percent of the money appropriated for individual programs, as well as 5 percent of unobligated balances available to agencies being relocated to the new department.

• The Energy and Commerce Committee rebuffed an administration plan to transfer health research from the Health and Human Services Department (HHS). Instead the panel voted to give the new department HHS's responsibility for overseeing the transfer of dangerous pathogens and toxins used in research laboratories.

• The Government Reform Committee agreed to administration requests to move the Coast Guard, FEMA, INS, and Secret Service to the new department, while backing down from a plan to defy the administration and shift all visa services from the State Department. Over the objections of most Republicans, the panel agreed to allow employees who moved to the new department to retain their collective bargaining agreements if their jobs were unchanged.

• The Select Intelligence Committee voted to create a separate intelligence agency within the new department that would be responsible for gathering information from other intelligence agencies, analyzing it, and disseminating it to state and local governments.

• The International Relations Committee backed the White House plan to have the State Department continue issuing visas but stipulated that the proposed new department would set policy.

• The Judiciary Committee defied the administration by opting to move only the law enforcement functions of the INS into the new department, instead of the entire agency. The committee's recommendation was nearly identical to an INS restructuring bill (HR 3231—H Rept 107-413) written by its chair, F. James Sensenbrenner Jr., R-Wis., and passed by the House 405-9, on April 25. The committee also bucked the White House by voting to transfer the Secret Service from the Treasury Department to the Justice Department, instead of to the new department. It also agreed to shift only a small portion of FEMA, leaving most of the agency independent.

• The Science Committee opted to block the proposed transfer of the National Institute of Standards and Technology's computer security division to the proposed department. In another departure from the administration plan, it called for creation of a corps of volunteers called NET Guard, to help communities recover from terrorist attacks on computer and communications systems.

• The Transportation and Infrastructure Committee rejected the administration's proposal to move the Coast Guard and FEMA into the new department. It also proposed that the TSA remain within the Transportation Department until it met deadlines to put security screeners and explosive detection systems in place at all airports.

Once the initial committees had their say, the nine-member Select Committee on Homeland Security ignored many of their departures and approved a bill (HR 5005—H Rept 107-609, Part 1) on July 19 that stuck close to the White House plan. After a daylong markup, the committee approved the measure, 5–4, along party lines. The bill was reported July 24.

The select panel did agree with the Judiciary Committee recommendation to split the INS and include only its enforcement and border protection services within the new department, instead of merging the entire agency intact.

And, anticipating major disagreements over the administration's personnel proposals, Majority Leader Dick Armey, R-Texas, who chaired the select committee, opted not to include them in the 216-page draft bill. Compromise language offered by panel member Rob Portman, R-Ohio, and accepted by voice vote at the markup, affirmed workers' bargaining rights but proposed to allow the secretary of the new department to exclude individuals who were involved in national security matters.

The panel tried to produce a compromise on appropriations by allowing for the new department to reprogram 2 percent of appropriated funds for up to two years, subject to fifteen days' advance notice. The select panel also asserted itself in the area of privacy, including language in the bill that would prohibit national identification cards. While there was no pending legislation to create such cards, the administration, in a homeland security strategy released July 16, called for uniform standards for state driver's licenses.

The functions of the TSA were the object of considerable attention. Armey included language in the draft to delay indefinitely the Dec. 31, 2002, deadline set by the 2001 aviation security law (S 1447—PL 107-71) for all airports to check screened baggage for explosives. Committee Democrats argued the language would relieve the agency and airports of having to implement key safety measures by a certain date. Eventually, the panel adopted, 6–3, a compromise by J.C. Watts Jr., R-Okla., to allow airports that could not meet existing deadlines to obtain a one-year waiver from the TSA.

The panel rejected, on a 5–4 party-line vote, language by Nancy Pelosi, D-Calif., that would have established the White House Office of Homeland Security in law and made its director subject to Senate confirmation. Republicans said

the language amounted to congressional micromanagement of the Executive Office of the President.

HOUSE FLOOR ACTION

The House passed HR 5005 by a vote of 295–132 on July 26, 2002, after Democrats unexpectedly won adoption of a proposal to bar the new department from contracting with any U.S. company, or its subsidiaries, that had its headquarters in an overseas tax haven.

The language was added on a "motion to recommit"—a procedural move to alter a bill on the verge of passage—offered by Rosa DeLauro, D-Conn. It gained support from some Republicans who were eager to make a political statement in the midst of a series of corporate scandals that began with the December 2001 collapse of Enron Corp., the giant energy-trading company. After 101 Republicans who initially opposed the motion switched their votes, the final tally for DeLauro's language was 318–110.

Much of the floor debate focused on federal personnel rules and whether worker protection language would diminish the president's powers. The House adopted 229–201 an amendment by Christopher Shays, R-Conn., that affirmed union members' rights but allowed the president to set aside collective bargaining agreements that could have an "adverse impact" on the new department's ability to keep the nation secure.

The Shays amendment was designed as an alternative to a proposal by Constance A. Morella, R-Md., that would have affirmed employees' rights to union representation unless their jobs were changed materially after they were transferred to the new department. Morella's amendment, which drew a veto threat from the White House, was rejected on a **key vote of 208–222 (R 5–214; D 202–7; I 1–1)**. *(2002 key votes, p. 819)*

The House rejected 118–309 another amendment strongly opposed by the White House that would have transferred the office that issued visas from the State Department to the new Homeland Security Department. The proposal was offered by Curt Weldon, R-Pa.

An amendment by James L. Oberstar, D-Minn., to drop the one-year extension for airports to install bomb-detecting equipment was rejected 211–217.

SENATE COMMITTEE ACTION

The Senate Governmental Affairs Committee had approved Lieberman's bill creating a cabinet-level homeland security department on May 22, 2002, and reported it June 24 (S 2452-S Rept 107-175). Then on July 25, at the end of a two-day markup, the panel approved a revised version (S 2452) by a vote of 12–5. Lawmakers were divided, mostly along party lines, over how much power to cede to the executive branch in the sweeping reorganization.

The new version came in the form of a comprehensive amendment by Lieberman.

INVESTIGATIONS OF ATTACKS ON SEPT. 11, 2001

Congress in 2002 reached an agreement with the White House to create an independent commission to investigate the Sept. 11, 2001, terrorist attacks on the World Trade Center in New York and on the Pentagon just outside Washington, D.C. Authorization for the commission was included in a fiscal 2003 intelligence bill (HR 4628—PL 107-306). *(For a complete report on the commission, its recommendations, the congressional investigation of 9/11, and congressional action on intelligence reorganization, see the Foreign Policy chapter, pp. 263, 274, 275)*

The failure of U.S. intelligence agencies to anticipate or prevent the Sept. 11 attacks had provoked an intense debate on examining what went wrong. Lawmakers at first rejected proposals to create an outside commission, deciding that Congress itself should conduct any inquiry. President George W. Bush also opposed the creation of an outside commission.

The House and Senate Intelligence committees on Feb. 14, 2002, launched an investigation into intelligence failures and activities before and after the attacks. But by summer the slow pace of the investigation prompted lawmakers to push for an independent commission. Families of Sept. 11 victims had also been persistently lobbying for an independent commission. Momentum intensified in September when hearings revealed several pieces of information that could have helped predict the attacks. By that point, most members of the Intelligence committees agreed on the need for an independent probe.

On Sept. 20 the White House dropped its opposition and sent a letter to House Speaker J. Dennis Hastert, R-Ill., advocating an independent inquiry as a follow-on to the congressional investigation. The Intelligence committees wrapped up their hearings in mid-October.

Eventually the pressure for an independent commission overcame lingering reservations, and Congress in November 2002 cleared HR 4628, authorizing creation of the commission.

Report of Joint House-Senate Panel

On Dec. 11, 2002, the House and Senate Intelligence committees released their recommendations and some of their findings, though their full report of more than 800 pages had yet to be declassified. As hinted during the committee hearings, the joint investigation found no instances where any U.S. agent had specific information related to the Sept. 11 attacks. But the report did find several missed opportunities that might have ultimately disrupted the terrorists' plot. It was harsh in its assessment of the intelligence agencies' preparedness to deal with terrorism, arguing that as terrorists prepared to launch the Sept. 11 attacks, U.S. agents still were operating under the cold war mentality of competing against a nation and not a transnational group of terrorists.

The two main recommendations were to create a cabinet-level director of national intelligence who would coordinate efforts among all the various agencies and to study the creation of a domestic intelligence agency, similar to Britain's MI5, to supplement the Federal Bureau of Investigation (FBI). The panel also urged more investment in technology at covert agencies and more funding for agencies to hire linguists.

The report also called for a review of federal classification procedures. The panels had complained repeatedly during the investigation about the slow pace at which documents were declassified, hinting that classification was being used to cover up errors.

9/11 Commission

The independent 9/11 commission created by Congress had a controversial start, when the two men appointed to lead it resigned before the investigation even began, citing potential conflicts. But their replacements—former New Jersey governor Tom Kean, nominated by Bush to chair the commission, and Rep. Lee Hamilton, D-Ind. (1965–1999), nominated by the Democrats to serve as vice chair—were soon in place and the investigation got underway. *(Commission members, p. 276)*

Formally known as the National Commission on Terrorist Attacks Upon the United States, the ten-member commission had a broad mandate to examine the government failings that allowed al Qaeda to launch its attacks on the World Trade Center and the Pentagon. Their investigation lasted twenty

The Bush administration turned up pressure on senators even before they finished work on the bill, threatening to veto the measure and contending it would not give the executive branch enough flexibility to manage the department in order to respond to terror threats. Lieberman said the bill gave the president 85 percent to 90 percent of what he had requested and vowed to continue to negotiate with the administration.

The biggest disagreement again focused on work rules for the new department. The Senate bill affirmed employees' rights to union representation unless their jobs were changed materially after the transfer to the new department. Democrats said they wanted to ensure that some 50,000 employees in the proposed department who were represented by federal worker unions would continue to enjoy collective bargaining months and took place against a backdrop of intense partisan divisions nationwide, but still the five Republican and five Democratic commissioners issued their final report unanimously.

The report, released July 22, 2004, as the presidential election campaign was getting underway, harshly criticized the executive branch and Congress for failing to understand the magnitude of the threat posed by terrorists. It raised serious questions about the performance of the nation's intelligence, law enforcement, and defense agencies. It spared neither Democrats nor Republicans. "Across the government, there were failures of imagination, policy, capabilities and management," the 567-page report stated. "Terrorism was not the overriding national security concern for the U.S. government under either the Clinton or the pre-9/11 Bush administration."

The report, which drew on more than 2.5 million pages of documents, 1,200 interviews, and numerous public hearings, opened an unusual window into the government's war on terror over the preceding years. It gave a detailed, even riveting, account of the terrorist plot that culminated with four nearly simultaneous hijackings, but it did not conclude whether the attacks could have been prevented.

"Since the plotters were flexible and resourceful, we cannot know whether any single step or series of steps would have defeated them," the commissioners wrote in the executive summary. "What we can say with confidence is that none of the measures adopted by the U.S. government, from 1998 to 2001, disturbed or even delayed the progress of the al Qaeda plot."

While not blaming individuals, the report provided sobering details about mistakes and bureaucratic inefficiencies that hamstrung virtually every government agency investigated. Among the most alarming details: the Central Intelligence Agency (CIA) and FBI failed to share crucial information; military and diplomatic plans to deal with al Qaeda were insufficient; border authorities overlooked false passports; aviation security officials failed to expand lists of people who should be excluded from flying; and immigration and aviation agencies were largely left outside of antiterrorism efforts.

The commissioners found considerable fault with intelligence agencies that tried to counter al Qaeda with tools and

tactics that were more appropriate for the cold war. Although the report cited the CIA for doing more than other agencies to attack al Qaeda before Sept. 11, it described the CIA's tactics, and those of other intelligence agencies, as hobbled by insufficient resources, internal rivalries, and competing priorities.

Looking at the nation's antiterrorism efforts since Sept. 11, the commission offered a mixed verdict. "Because of offensive actions against al Qaeda since 9/11, and defensive actions to improve homeland security, we believe we are safer today," the commissioners wrote in the executive summary. "But we are not safe." They especially praised the U.S. invasion that toppled the Taliban government in Afghanistan and ended that country's official sanctuary of al Qaeda leaders.

Intelligence Overhaul

The 9/11 commission's searing report, which was widely covered in the media and became a bestselling book, urged policy makers to restructure the nation's intelligence apparatus—or face an even more devastating attack. Its sweeping recommendations included the creation of a cabinet-level national intelligence director within the White House to improve coordination of antiterrorism efforts.

In addition to the criticism directed at executive agencies, the commission found fault with Congress. Lawmakers "responded slowly to the rise of transnational terrorism as a threat to national security" in the years before 2001, the report stated. It also warned that oversight of intelligence and counterterrorism issues was divided among too many committees and was "dysfunctional." Commissioners recommended that Congress give the House and Senate Select Intelligence panels authority over intelligence spending as well as policy and consolidate oversight of homeland security. Powerful committee chairs in both chambers, however, refused to yield substantial jurisdiction to a new committee. (Congressional oversight of intelligence, p. 274; homeland security committees, p. 222)

But the report did push hesitant lawmakers to enact legislation (S 2845—PL 108-458) after the 2004 elections that mandated the most comprehensive shake-up of the nation's intelligence community since the beginning of the cold war and contained a number of provisions designed to strengthen homeland security (Details, p. 263)

protections. They pointed to a Bush administration decision in January to end union representation for about 500 workers at several Justice Department agencies as justification for the language.

Republicans tried to carve out exemptions for the proposed department, citing the need to shift employees within constituent agencies to respond to various threats.

In considering amendments on this issue, the committee:

• Rejected 7–10 an attempt by ranking Republican Fred Thompson of Tennessee to strike language affirming union rights.

• Rejected 7–10 a Thompson amendment to give the new department's secretary broad discretion in hiring, firing, recruiting, and transferring employees.

• Adopted by voice vote a set of proposals by George V. Voinovich, R-Ohio, that, among other things, would give the proposed department and other federal agencies power to raise the salaries of experienced managers from $166,700 to $192,600 and give agencies expanded powers to offer early retirement buyouts to restructure the work force.

• Rejected on an 8–8 tie a Voinovich amendment to lift a 5,000-worker limit on the number of federal employees who could be involved in experimental personnel demonstration projects.

• Rejected on an 8–9 party-line vote an attempt by Thompson to give the proposed department so-called fast-track reorganization authority, which had existed government-wide from 1973 to 1984. The authority allowed a cabinet secretary to submit a plan to Congress and reorganize agencies within seventy-five days. Democrats said the new secretary would have sufficient flexibility under existing law to get the department established.

Lawmakers also debated an administration proposal that would allow it to redirect up to 5 percent of the funding appropriated for any agencies transferred to the new department. But an agreement between Lieberman, Senate Appropriations Committee Chair Robert C. Byrd, D-W.Va., and Appropriations Committee ranking Republican Ted Stevens of Alaska, who was also a member of Governmental Affairs, left Congress with authority over appropriated funds. The Governmental Affairs panel adopted by voice vote an amendment offered by Stevens and modified by Lieberman requiring that most funding and assets transferred to the department be used only for the purposes originally intended. The money could not be used to fund new positions created under the bill.

The panel agreed to additional barriers to reprogramming money, especially for the Coast Guard, which had a strong constituency and perennially was strapped for funds to meet its many responsibilities. The committee adopted 9–7 an amendment by Stevens and Susan Collins, R-Maine, to create a special status for the Coast Guard in the new department and prevent its assets from being diverted permanently from core missions, such as search and rescue, fisheries enforcement, and maritime navigation. The secretary of the new department would be permitted to assign the Coast Guard specific homeland security duties.

Moving closer to the administration's position on intelligence sharing, the committee:

• Adopted by voice vote an amendment by Carl Levin, D-Mich., to maintain the Central Intelligence Agency's counterterrorism center as the government's focal point for receiving and analyzing information about terror threats. The new department would review the threats and connect them to known vulnerabilities and could direct other agencies to address those threats. Lieberman had proposed establishing a terrorism directorate within the proposed department to serve as the focal point, but he acknowledged Levin's plan would avoid duplication.

• Rejected 8–8 an attempt by Thompson to put responsibility for information analysis and infrastructure protection under a single directorate in the new department.

• Adopted by voice vote an amendment by Robert F. Bennett, R-Utah, and Levin to exempt from Freedom of Information Act disclosure requirements some proprietary information that companies voluntarily provide to the department about infrastructure vulnerabilities. The amendment also narrowed the bill's definition of what constituted voluntary submission of information to ensure that applications for grants, permits, licenses, or other government benefits would remain subject to disclosure.

SENATE FLOOR ACTION

The Senate took up the bill Sept. 3, opening what would turn out to be weeks of futile floor debate and behind-the-scenes negotiations that focused primarily on the issue of employee rights in the new department. By the time the regular session ended to allow for the midterm elections, the chamber was so deadlocked that Senate Majority Leader Tom Daschle, D-S.D., pulled the bill from the floor. Democrats and Republicans vied over rival compromises on workers' rights, with neither side able to muster the sixty votes needed to head off a filibuster.

A majority of Republicans backed a substitute by Phil Gramm, R-Texas, and Zell Miller, D-Ga., that followed the president's original plans for the new department and included House language that would allow the government to remove employees from unions for national security reasons after giving notice in writing.

Democrats rallied around a proposal by centrists John B. Breaux, D-La., Ben Nelson, D-Neb., and Lincoln Chafee, R-R.I., to allow the president to remove employees from unions for national security reasons but permit the employees to appeal. The president would have to provide a detailed explanation for removing workers, and appeals would be lodged with the Federal Labor Relations Authority—an independent agency that administered labor-management relations programs for federal workers. The appeal would have to include "clear and convincing evidence" that the president's decision was not justified.

Republicans wanted a vote on the Gramm-Miller substitute; Democrats were intent on amending that proposal with the Breaux-Nelson-Chafee plan.

In back-to-back votes Sept. 26, the Senate rejected on a **key vote of 50–49 (R 1–48; D 48–1; I 1–0)** an attempt to invoke cloture, and thereby restrict debate, on the Democratic version of the bill offered by Lieberman—ten votes short of the necessary sixty-vote majority. An attempt to limit debate on the Gramm-Miller substitute failed 44–53. *(2002 key votes, p. 819)*

The Senate already had rejected two earlier attempts to cut off debate on the Lieberman plan, a step that would have sharply limited Republicans' ability to offer changes. On Sept. 19, the day Gramm and Miller unveiled their substitute amendment, senators rejected a Democratic cloture motion 50–49. A second attempt at cloture was rejected 49–49 on Sept. 25.

Through much of the Senate debate, Byrd conducted a lonely crusade against what he saw as administration pressure on Congress to rubber-stamp a sweeping government reorganization. His initial efforts to slow the process had forced Daschle to delay bringing the bill up until after the August recess.

Byrd slowed the debate with lengthy floor speeches critical of what he said was the administration's disregard for congressional oversight. "With the level of endorsement the Congress has given to this idea, you would think that the proposal for a new Homeland Security Department had been engraved in the stone tablets that were handed down to Moses at Mount Sinai," Byrd said in one animated floor speech. "But in reality, the idea was developed by four presidential staffers in the basement of the White House. For all we know, it could have been drafted on the back of a cocktail napkin."

On Sept. 24 the Senate rejected 28–70 an amendment by Byrd that would have required the administration to consult with Congress about the reorganization in three stages over thirteen months.

On at least two other occasions the Senate rejected attempts to extend Congress's reach into White House decision making.

Senators agreed by voice vote Sept. 17 to an amendment by Thompson to eliminate provisions that would have established the White House Office of Homeland Security by statute and required that its director be confirmed by the Senate. The Senate on Sept. 12 had rejected, 41–55, an attempt by Lieberman to kill Thompson's amendment. The Senate also rejected 48–49 on Sept. 12 an amendment by Ernest F. Hollings, D-S.C., to require that the secretary of the new department and the attorney general be made statutory members of the National Security Council.

For a time it seemed that the homeland security bill would become the vehicle for creating an independent commission to investigate intelligence failures leading up to the Sept. 11 attacks. On Sept. 24 the Senate adopted on a **key vote of 90–8 (R 41–8; D 48–0; I 1–0)** a Lieberman amendment to establish such a commission. But when it became clear that the homeland bill was bogged down in the fight over workers' rights, Lieberman and others switched their attention to the fiscal 2003 intelligence authorization bill (HR 4628—PL 107-306), which ultimately carried the 9/11 commission proposal to enactment. *(2002 key votes, p. 819)*

On other issues, the Senate:

• Adopted, by voice vote, a proposal by Barbara Boxer, D-Calif., and Robert C. Smith, R-N.H., to require the Transportation Department to deputize qualified pilots of commercial passenger and cargo planes to use lethal force in defense of their aircraft. Under the amendment, selected pilots would be allowed to carry guns in the cockpit after receiving training similar to that offered to federal law enforcement officers.

• Agreed by voice vote to an amendment by Paul Wellstone, D-Minn., to withhold homeland security department contracts from companies that reincorporated abroad to avoid U.S. taxes.

FINAL ACTION

The Republican gains in the 2002 midterm elections gave Bush the clout he needed to break the deadlock on the bill. "The single most important item of unfinished business on Capitol Hill is to create a unified Department of Homeland Security," Bush declared in his post-election press conference Nov. 7. "It's imperative that the Congress send me a bill that I can sign before the 107th Congress ends." *(2002 elections, p. 15)*

Bush directed Republican leaders to reconcile the House and Senate bills, and aides worked through the weekend to write the final legislation. The president also told GOP senators to keep amendments off the bill in order to push it quickly through the lame-duck session without the time-consuming process of a House-Senate conference.

Breaux, Nelson, and Chafee reluctantly agreed to allow the administration to create a new personnel system for the department outside of civil service rules. The compromise gave the president the power to remove workers from union representation on national security grounds.

The House passed the new language, introduced as HR 5710, by a vote of 299–121 on Nov. 13.

Senate leaders moved to expedite deliberations by cutting off floor debate and limiting amendments. Democrats made one final attempt to shape the legislation when Daschle tried to remove several special-interest provisions added by House GOP leaders at the last minute, including one to limit liability for pharmaceutical companies.

Republicans prevailed in the final showdown Nov. 19; moderates sided with the administration and defeated Daschle's amendment, 47–52. GOP leaders argued that the amendment would gut important provisions and kill the legislation for the year. Moderate Senate Republicans Collins, Chafee, and Olympia J. Snowe of Maine won assurances from House and Senate GOP leaders during the roll call vote that the provisions in dispute would be stripped early in the 108th Congress. The Senate then inserted the House-passed language into HR 5005 and passed the final measure by a vote of 90–9.

The final House vote clearing the bill was a formality, done by unanimous consent in pro forma session Nov. 22.

MAJOR PROVISIONS

As signed into law on Nov. 25, 2002, HR 5005 (PL 107-296) created the cabinet-level Department of Homeland Security. Following are the major provisions of the law:

Department Mission and Structure

Mission. The mission of the new Homeland Security Department was to prevent terrorist attacks within the United

States, reduce the nation's vulnerability to such acts, and make sure the country was prepared to deal with any disaster that resulted from an attack.

The department was not allowed to investigate or prosecute acts of terrorism. That function remained in the hands of federal agencies such as the Federal Bureau of Investigation (FBI) and local and state authorities. Otherwise, the law gave the secretary of homeland security wide-ranging powers, including making grants, agreeing to contracts, and making agreements with other federal agencies. The secretary also was directed to make sure all the disparate databases and computer systems throughout the department were integrated so that they could share information.

Structure. The new agency incorporated all or part of twenty-two federal agencies. It was divided into four substantive divisions: Information Analysis and Infrastructure Protection; Science and Technology; Border and Transportation Security; and Emergency Preparedness and Response. A fifth division was to handle management. Each was headed by an undersecretary and had several assistant secretaries.

Information Analysis and Infrastructure Protection

Mission. The division was responsible for receiving, analyzing, and assessing terrorism information from the Central Intelligence Agency (CIA), FBI, and other intelligence agencies, and issuing reports on the seriousness of the threat. It was directed to make a nationwide assessment of the nation's "critical infrastructure," much of which was privately owned, including power plants, water systems, railroads, highways, bridges, the Internet, telecommunications networks, financial networks, and the electrical grids. And it was responsible for sharing information on threats to the nation or its critical infrastructure with states, local governments, and private-sector entities as needed.

Personnel. Employees from the State Department, CIA, FBI, National Imagery and Mapping Agency, National Security Agency, and Defense Intelligence Agency could be assigned to this division to help with information analysis.

Agencies transferred. The following agencies were moved to this division (their previous agency or department is shown in parentheses):
- National Infrastructure Protection Center (FBI).
- National Communications System (Defense).
- Critical Infrastructure Assurance (Commerce).
- National Infrastructure Simulation and Analysis Center (Energy).
- Federal Computer Incident Response Center (General Services Administration—GSA).

FOIA protections. Private businesses that owned or managed anything deemed "critical infrastructure" voluntarily could submit information that revealed vulnerabilities, and that information could be kept secret and exempt from disclosure under the Freedom of Information Act (FOIA). This FOIA exemption also limited the liabilities of such companies from lawsuits that could arise if weaknesses in their security were revealed. Anyone who leaked this critical infrastructure information to the public or news media could be fined and sentenced to up to one year in prison.

Privacy officer. The secretary of homeland security was required to appoint a privacy officer to act as an in-house watchdog to make sure department policies and use of technology did not erode individual privacy. The privacy officer was required to make an annual report to Congress and enforce the provisions of the 1974 Privacy Act (PL 93-579), which barred the government from using personal, private information collected for one purpose for a totally different purpose. *(Congress and the Nation Vol. IV, p. 585)*

Net Guard. The undersecretary for information analysis and infrastructure protection was given authority to create a volunteer organization called Net Guard made up of technology experts or professionals who could help localities prepare for and defend against cyberattacks on critical information systems.

Information sharing. The law included a section called the Homeland Security Information Sharing Act, which encouraged the federal government to coordinate its terrorist intelligence gathering and to share information as needed with state and local governments. This information might need to be unclassified or edited in order to share it with some local or state law enforcement agents. The department was directed to develop information systems that allowed people with higher security clearance to access classified information while allowing other law enforcement officials access to unclassified information. These information systems were to pull from the National Law Enforcement Telecommunications System, the Regional Information Sharing System, and the Terrorist Threat Warning System of the FBI.

Cybersecurity. The law increased penalties for hackers or computer criminals who intentionally tried to injure or kill while carrying out cyberattacks. Sentences of up to life in prison were provided for cybercriminals who attempted to cause death through computer crimes.

Science and Technology

Mission. This was the research and development division, charged with improving law enforcement technologies and biological terrorism preparedness while establishing training centers for homeland security. It was to help develop, test, study, and approve products, equipment, or technologies that the department could use in the war against terrorism.

Advisory groups. Special committees were to be created to advise and consult with the department about antiterrorism technologies that could be used by federal, state, or local governments. They included a twenty-member Homeland Security Science and Technology Advisory Committee. The advisory committees were exempt from some federal open meeting rules.

Agencies transferred. The following agencies were moved to this division (their previous agency or department is shown in parentheses):

- Chemical, radiological, and biological preparedness division (Energy).
- National Bio-Weapons Defense Analysis Center, part of the Lawrence Livermore National Laboratory (Defense).
- Plum Island Animal Disease Center (Agriculture).

Smallpox. The Homeland Security Department was directed to coordinate a smallpox vaccination plan with the Department of Health and Human Services (HHS). The law limited federal liability for health problems that might arise from the smallpox vaccine.

Research centers. A Homeland Security Advanced Research Projects Agency was established and authorized at $500 million for fiscal 2003. The agency was intended to be similar to the Defense Advanced Research Project Agency (DARPA). The law also established a system of university-based homeland security research centers.

Border and Transportation Security

Mission. Border and Transportation Security, by far the largest division, was charged with protecting air, land, and sea transportation; protecting the nation's borders and territorial waters; and enforcing immigration and visa laws.

Agencies transferred. The following agencies were moved to this division (their previous agency or department is shown in parentheses):
- U.S. Customs Service (Treasury).
- U.S. Border Patrol (Justice).
- Transportation Security Administration (Transportation).
- Federal Protective Service, which provided security for federal buildings (GSA).
- Office of Domestic Preparedness (Justice).
- Federal Law Enforcement Training Center (Treasury).
- Immigration and Naturalization Service (Justice).

INS. The functions of the Immigration and Naturalization Service (INS) were transferred to the Homeland Security Department, and the INS was abolished. The law required that INS's immigration services and border security functions be organized into two separate bureaus in the department. The bureaus had to submit separate budget requests, accompanied by reorganization plans sent to the Judiciary and Appropriations committees of both chambers of Congress.

The law also allowed government buyouts for employees who chose to leave or retire under the INS restructuring. An employee who took a buyout and decided to return to the department within five years had to repay the government the bonus he or she received for leaving.

Bureau of Border Security. The new bureau was to enforce the nation's immigration laws, absorbing INS enforcement operations including the Border Patrol, inspections, investigations, intelligence, and detention and removal.

Customs Service. The Customs Service function of stopping contraband from entering the country was placed under the Border and Transportation Security Department.

Certain revenue collection and trade enforcement functions, however, remained under the Treasury Department.

Agricultural inspectors. The inspection functions of the Animal Plant and Health Inspection Service (APHIS) were transferred to the department, while quarantine duties remained in the Agriculture Department. APHIS inspectors were charged with identifying and preventing "agroterrorism"—intentional efforts to poison the food supply or introduce malicious viruses into produce or food products.

Transportation Security Administration. The law shifted the Transportation Security Administration (TSA) to the new department but specified that it was to remain a distinct entity within the Border and Transportation Security department for at least two years.

The law also extended the deadline for certain airports to install explosives detection systems for baggage until Dec. 31, 2003. The original law (PL 107-71) that created TSA set the deadline for Dec. 31, 2002. *(Aviation security, p. 198)*

Visas. The department was to be responsible for setting guidelines for visas for foreigners who wanted to visit the United States. State Department consular offices would still issue visas, but they had to follow rules set by Homeland Security. The secretary of homeland security was authorized to assign personnel to overseas consulates if he or she believed it was in the interests of homeland security. A special provision banned all "third party" screening for visas in Saudi Arabia and required that Homeland Security employees approve or reject Saudi visas. Every visa application rejected had to be put into an electronic database to better track the names of people denied visas.

Border fence. The law expressed the sense of Congress that finishing a fourteen-mile fence along the U.S.-Mexico border at San Diego should be a high priority.

Immigrant children. Authority to deal with children of illegal immigrants was transferred to the director of the Office of Refugee Resettlement at HHS, who was encouraged to keep the children's best interests in mind and attempt to reunite immigrant children with parents overseas. These children had to be protected from smugglers, traffickers, and other criminal elements. The law prohibited children from being released on their own recognizance if they were under eighteen.

Employee discipline. The secretary of homeland security and the attorney general were authorized to create within this division pilot projects to try out different ways of disciplining employees. Certain unions and managers were exempt from such pilot programs.

Immigration reports. The secretary of homeland security was required to submit reports to the president and Congress with detailed statistics about immigration applications and demographics of new immigrants.

Immigration office. The law gave the attorney general authority over the Executive Office for Immigration Review.

Emergency Preparedness and Response

Mission. The division was instructed to focus on preparing for and responding to terrorist attacks. Responsibilities included disaster aid as well as the stockpiling of treatments and vaccines for biological or chemical weapons attacks.

Agencies transferred. The following agencies were moved to this division (their previous agency or department is shown in parentheses):

- Federal Emergency Management Agency.
- Integrated Hazard Information System of the National Oceanic and Atmospheric Administration (Commerce). This system was to be renamed "Firesat" under the new department.
- National Domestic Preparedness Office (FBI).
- Office of Emergency Preparedness (HHS).
- National Stockpile of Vaccines (HHS).
- Nuclear Incident Response Team (Energy).

Public health. HHS was directed to work with Homeland Security on a national strategy for preparing public health workers to respond to a terrorist attack.

FEMA. The Federal Emergency Management Agency (FEMA) was designated as the emergency response agency for terrorist attacks but was still required to carry out its role of responding to other disasters such as hurricanes and floods.

Commercial technologies. To the maximum extent practicable, the department was directed to use off-the-shelf technologies—those readily available in the commercial market—in building information systems that shared intelligence. The department also was directed to buy many of its products or services from the private sector.

Other Agencies

In addition to the five divisions, several other agencies were transferred to or created in the new department.

Coast Guard. The commandant of the Coast Guard would report directly to the secretary of homeland security. The Coast Guard was to work closely with the under secretary of border and transportation security as well as maintain its existing independent identity as a military service. If there was a declaration of war or when the president so directed, the Coast Guard was to operate as an element of the Department of Defense, consistent with existing law. The Coast Guard remained a separate unit and had to continue its non-homeland-security duties, including search and rescue, marine safety, and environmental protection measures. The secretary of homeland security was not allowed to decrease the Coast Guard's work force in these non-homeland areas, except in emergencies.

The secretary, along with the commandant of the Coast Guard, was required within ninety days of enactment to submit a report on the deepwater program, a program to replace the Coast Guard's offshore ships and planes. The report was supposed to include ways to accelerate the deepwater overhaul from a twenty-year program to a ten-year program.

Bureau of Citizenship and Immigration Services. The immigration services of the INS were taken over by a new Bureau of Citizenship and Immigration Services under the deputy secretary of homeland security. The bureau was directed to develop pilot programs to eliminate the backlog of immigrant-related paperwork such as green cards.

Secret Service. The Secret Service and all its functions were transferred to the Homeland Security Department, but the Secret Service remained independent of the four directorates in the new department.

Office for State and Local Government Coordination. The law created a special office responsible for overseeing and coordinating department programs for and liaison with state and local governments.

Department Management

Undersecretary. An undersecretary of homeland security for management was to oversee budget, human resources, procurement, information technology, department grants, internal audits, building management, and security for employees and department facilities. The undersecretary was responsible for collecting immigration statistics from the Border and Transportation Security division. The undersecretary also was to oversee the chief information officer, chief financial officer, and chief human capital officer.

Human resources. The homeland security secretary was authorized to create and modify a unified human resources management system for all the agencies being merged. The system was to be "flexible" and "contemporary," but it had to maintain protections for whistle-blowers and union members. The law required collaboration with employees and unions for any changes to existing personnel rules. The authority to set new personnel rules was to expire five years after the law took effect Nov. 25, 2002.

Union rights. The president or the homeland security secretary was allowed to remove employees from unions or collective bargaining units if their jobs had "materially changed" or if the majority of employees within a collective bargaining unit had jobs that involved intelligence or investigative work.

Civil rights. The management division included a director of civil rights and civil liberties whose job was to assess all allegations of discrimination while enforcing civil rights rules in the department.

Employee rights. The department was not exempt from existing laws protecting whistle-blowers and had to provide equal employment protections required in other federal agencies.

Salary and benefits. The secretary of homeland security was required to submit a plan within ninety days of enactment that ensured there was no disparity in pay or benefits between the agencies that had been transferred into the department.

Inspector general. An inspector general's office within the department was to serve as the in-house investigator, but the secretary of homeland security had unusual authority to prohibit any inspector general's investigation if he or she thought it would not be in the interest of national security. This provision also allowed assistant inspectors general to carry guns and make arrests if necessary, if they had been given permission by the attorney general.

Contractors and Liability

The homeland security secretary had procurement power to fund research projects and approve pilot programs for new homeland security products or technologies. The secretary also could employ outside consultants or experts without having to follow certain government pay limitations.

Acquisition authority. The department had authority to make some purchases without going through a contracting process. "Micropurchases" for supplies and products of up to $7,500 were allowed for certain Homeland Security employees. The secretary had authority to sign contracts of up to $200,000 for purchases made inside the United States and up to $300,000 for purchases made outside the country without having to go through a competitive bidding process.

The secretary also could authorize purchases of commercial products up to $7.5 million under expedited procurement procedures. The normal limit was $5 million. The law also gave emergency acquisition authority to agency heads to make immediate purchases to help in recovery from a terrorist attack.

Unsolicited proposals. The Homeland Security Department was authorized to review unsolicited ideas for homeland security products or technologies in order to encourage innovation.

Antiterrorism technologies. The law allowed the secretary of homeland security to create a list of antiterrorism technologies or products that the department would buy.

Liability limits. Lawsuits were limited for the use of products that made the list. The law prohibited punitive damages—monetary awards for pain and suffering—against contractors whose homeland security products made the list. Lawsuits for economic damages—recovery of lost wages, salary, or property—were allowed, but plaintiffs had to prove that the contractor acted fraudulently or negligently.

The law allowed pain-and-suffering judgments against individuals or governments that sponsored terrorist acts.

Liability insurance. The law required Homeland Security contractors to carry the maximum amount of liability insurance available for their industry.

Miscellaneous Provisions

Homeland Security Council. The law established a Homeland Security Council within the Executive Office of the President to advise the president on homeland security matters. Members included the president, vice president, secretary of homeland security, attorney general, secretary of defense, and anyone else designated by the president. The council was to have a staff headed by an executive secretary appointed by the president.

BATF. The Bureau of Alcohol, Tobacco and Firearms (BATF) was transferred from the Treasury Department to the Justice Department. The law required the bureau to establish a new explosives training center. It also established new federal restrictions on the possession and use of explosives.

Airline liability. The law extended until the end of 2003 the federal Aviation War Risk Insurance program and the liability limits of commercial airlines whose aircraft were used in terror attacks.

Arming pilots. The TSA was required to develop a program under which trained commercial airline pilots would be allowed to carry guns aboard aircraft. Volunteer pilots could be deputized as federal flight deck officers and allowed to carry firearms after receiving training and achieving proficiency comparable to that for air marshals and meeting other TSA requirements.

Department transition. The department had one year from enactment to complete the merger of the twenty-two agencies. Sixty days after enactment, the president was required to submit a plan for transferring agencies into the department, identifying the funds and functions that would be transferred into Homeland Security.

Congressional committees. The law called on Congress to review its committee structure and possibly reorganize to handle the creation of the Homeland Security Department.

National ID program. The law specified that the Homeland Security Act should not be used as a justification to create a national identification program.

Advisory committees. The homeland security secretary was authorized to create advisory committees to consult with the department on various security matters. These committees were to terminate after two years.

Reorganization. The secretary was allowed to discontinue or reorganize divisions within the Homeland Security Department but was barred from eliminating agencies or units that were required to remain under the law.

Sale of property. The secretary was allowed to sell excess property that belonged to the department.

Budget request. The president was required to submit an annual homeland security budget proposal, starting with the 2004 budget. The law required the budget request, starting in fiscal 2005, to include future year projections for homeland security.

Limits on secretary's power. The secretary was prohibited from having any power over the military and was not given any war powers.

USA PATRIOT Act

Despite concerns about possible impacts on civil liberties, Congress overwhelmingly agreed to give the Bush administration sweeping new authority to track, arrest, and prosecute suspected terrorists after the Sept. 11, 2001, attacks on the World Trade Center and the Pentagon. Formally known as the USA PATRIOT Act, the bill was signed into law (HR 3162—PL 107-56) by President George W. Bush on Oct. 26, 2001.

When Attorney General John Ashcroft asked for the new law enforcement powers Sept. 19—calling on Congress to

PATRIOT ACT HIGHLIGHTS

Following are highlights of the USA PATRIOT Act (HR 3162—PL 107-56). *(For a comprehensive list of provisions, see p. 190)*

Search warrants. Created "one-stop shopping" for court orders for many law enforcement investigations, allowing one judge to issue a search warrant or approve surveillance that would be applicable across the country.

Electronic surveillance. Made it easier for investigators to track Internet communications using existing surveillance tools such as so-called pen register and trap-and-trace devices, which recorded the phone numbers of outgoing and incoming calls to a phone.

Secret searches. Allowed secret searches before suspects were served with search warrants. Investigators could withhold information about the searches for a "reasonable" time, though the bill did not define what that meant.

Grand jury disclosure. Allowed disclosure of information received during grand jury proceedings to law enforcement, intelligence, protective, immigration, or national defense or national security personnel.

Money laundering. Expanded the list of offenses eligible for prosecution under money laundering statutes and banned the undeclared movement of more than $10,000 across U.S. borders. U.S. banks were prohibited from offering correspondent accounts, used for wire transfers and currency exchanges to foreign "shell" banks that had no physical location.

---

clear a bill by the end of that week—Republicans and Democrats alike balked. The proposal included powers that the Justice Department had sought unsuccessfully for years.

But the Bush administration pushed hard, maintaining it needed the new powers immediately to guard against further terrorist attacks. And with the Federal Bureau of Investigation (FBI) warning that more attacks could be imminent, Congress ultimately agreed to much of what Ashcroft sought. This included authority for the government to obtain nationwide search warrants and "roving" wiretaps, to conduct secret searches of suspects' property, and to detain aliens (persons who were not citizens or nationals of the United States) indefinitely if they were viewed as national security threats. Congress also strengthened money-laundering laws and removed the statute of limitations on some terrorism crimes.

BACKGROUND

Within days of the terrorist attacks, Congress began to debate new antiterrorism legislation that would not have been seriously considered before Sept. 11. Next to authorizing the use of military force, many members believed that one of their most important tasks was to strengthen law en-

forcement powers without encroaching on civil liberties. They wondered whether existing laws were sufficient to stop terrorism in an age of digital technology, and whether law enforcement agencies had the needed resources to perform their assigned tasks.

The FBI and other agencies said they needed to use up-to-date technology to help infiltrate terrorist cells and head off future threats. In particular, they urged Congress to expand wiretapping and other surveillance authority to cover information transmitted via the Internet. Their prime suspect in the Sept. 11 attacks, Saudi dissident Osama bin Laden, and his associates were believed to have communicated via e-mail, messages embedded in computer files, and encryption software that scrambled electronic messages.

Some of the tools Ashcroft sought had been requested previously without success. In the wake of the 1995 bombing of the federal building in Oklahoma City, the Clinton administration sought many of the same changes to surveillance law, including authority to conduct so-called roving wiretaps—multiple wiretaps that could follow a person no matter what phone was being used instead of needing a separate court order to tap each phone line. But conservative GOP lawmakers were unwilling to give the government such powerful tools. The final 1996 antiterrorism law (PL 104-132) authorized the president to stop certain suspected terrorist groups from raising funds in the United States and gave the administration greater authority to turn people away at the border. *(Congress and the Nation Vol. IX, p. 727)*

Congressional deliberations on the 2001 antiterrorism package began in earnest Sept. 19 when the Justice Department sent a twenty-one-page draft proposal to Capitol Hill. "We need every tool available to us to curtail the potential of additional terrorist attacks," Ashcroft said after a meeting with congressional leaders.

The attorney general asked for roving wiretap authority. He also wanted the ability, for certain cases, to get a single search warrant in a nationwide investigation to proceed with searches and some electronic surveillance. Under existing law, authorities had to get a warrant or other permission from a judge in each jurisdiction where they were conducting an investigation.

Other Ashcroft priorities included giving the government the power to use surveillance equipment to track e-mail and Web travel; hold noncitizens indefinitely; use information obtained by foreign government wiretaps in U.S. criminal investigations even if the surveillance violated the rights of Americans; toughen penalties for terrorists; and define "terrorist" as anyone who "affords material support to an organization that the individual knows or should know is a terrorist organization," regardless of whether the support was related to terrorism.

Some lawmakers wasted little time in signaling that they were unwilling to go as far as Ashcroft wanted. Rep. Bob Barr, R-Ga., and four other members of the House Judiciary Committee sent a letter Sept. 21 to Chair F. James Sensenbrenner Jr., R-Wis., and ranking Democrat John Conyers Jr. of Michigan that divided Ashcroft's requests into four categories—from those they would readily approve to those that were "unacceptable as written." Included in the "unacceptable" category were requests for nationwide authority for e-mail search warrants and authorization for agents to seize terrorist suspects' assets before the suspects had been convicted of a crime.

The House and Senate Judiciary committees held one hearing each on the Ashcroft proposal, but no one who opposed the request testified for the record.

HOUSE COMMITTEE ACTION

After weeks of intense negotiations, Republicans and Democrats on the House Judiciary Committee reached a deal Oct. 2 on a streamlined version of the Ashcroft proposal. The committee approved the bill the next day by a vote of 36–0 and reported it Oct. 11 (HR 2975—H Rept 107-236, Part 1). The committee rejected Ashcroft's request to allow information obtained by foreign government wiretaps to be used against Americans even if the wiretap was unconstitutional. It also declined to give the attorney general the authority to detain noncitizens indefinitely or to conduct more secret searches.

The committee considered eighteen amendments during five and a half hours of deliberation, making mostly minor changes to the bill. The normally fractious committee cheered the final, unanimous vote. "This bill represents the essence of compromise," Sensenbrenner said. "The left is not completely happy with the bill, neither is the right. It certainly doesn't represent the Justice Department's wish list. I think it means we've got it just about right."

By voice vote, the committee approved an amendment by Barney Frank, D-Mass., to make it easier for people to sue the government when agencies leaked sensitive personal information about them. The change was meant to balance a provision that would expand how much personal information various government agencies could exchange about suspects.

The committee bill included a provision, opposed by the administration, to sunset many of the expanded surveillance and investigative powers in 2003 unless they were reauthorized by Congress. It would permit Foreign Intelligence Surveillance Act (FISA, PL 95-511) searches or surveillance as long as the "significant purpose" was gathering intelligence information, rather than evidence for a criminal case. Existing law required intelligence gathering to be a "primary purpose." The Bush administration wanted the requirement reduced to simply "a purpose." *(Congress and the Nation Vol. V, p. 720)*

The committee bill also made it easier for investigators to get court orders and track Internet communications; granted permanent legal resident status to immigrants who had already applied but whose sponsors died in the Sept. 11 attacks; created a deputy inspector general within the Justice Department to oversee the FBI and review alleged infringe-ments of civil rights or civil liberties; and permitted the Internal Revenue Service (IRS) to disclose tax information to the head of federal law enforcement agencies.

While the panel saw the action as a triumph for the committee system, the Bush administration began pressing the House leadership to ignore the committee's actions and instead bring some type of legislation to the floor that more closely resembled the administration's proposal.

SENATE DRAFT

Senate Judiciary Chair Patrick J. Leahy, D-Vt., began work on the bill in the Senate with a draft counterproposal to the Ashcroft plan. While Leahy's draft accommodated the Bush administration by authorizing greater surveillance on the Internet, it also proposed raising the legal threshold that authorities would have to meet to conduct such surveillance—something the law enforcement community had opposed. Leahy also left out many of the wiretap provisions requested by Ashcroft, and he expressed concern over a provision that would allow the indefinite detention of aliens.

Leahy, members of both parties, and representatives from the White House and Justice Department took part in sometimes heated negotiations with the goal of writing a bill that could pass the Senate with White House support. They reached a deal on Oct. 4.

The resulting bill was generally seen as a victory for the White House. It did not include a sunset provision. It allowed more secret searches if the government showed "reasonable cause to believe" that notifying the suspect of the search would produce an "adverse result," such as the destruction of evidence. And it included the same provision as the House bill to broaden FISA surveillance activities.

The bill also granted new tools to combat money laundering, such as additional record keeping requirements and restrictions on dealing with suspect foreign financiers.

But Ashcroft lost on a few points. The bill did not include provisions allowing the IRS to disclose tax information to federal law enforcement and intelligence agents, or allowing information obtained by foreign government wiretaps to be used against Americans even if the wiretap was unconstitutional. The bill restricted the attorney general's authority to detain noncitizens indefinitely.

SENATE FLOOR ACTION

The Senate passed the bill (S 1510) on Oct. 11, 2001, by a vote of 96–1 after less than three hours of actual debate. Russ D. Feingold, D-Wis., cast the only "nay" vote. The bill had never been considered by the Senate Judiciary Committee, and members were not given a report explaining its provisions.

Majority Leader Tom Daschle, D-S.D., told colleagues to avoid offering amendments so as to maintain the balance of the deal struck by the bipartisan leadership, top members of the Senate Judiciary Committee, and the Bush administration.

That angered Feingold. "What have we come to when we don't have committee or floor deliberation on an issue of this magnitude?" he asked. Feingold offered three amendments, all of which were overwhelmingly defeated after Daschle made his pitch. The amendments would have limited computer trespass provisions, limited roving surveillance to instances when it was ascertained that the surveillance target was present in the house or was using the phone that had been tapped, and ensured that the bill would not supercede certain state and federal privacy protections.

Arlen Specter, R-Pa., was one of the few senators to discuss the bill. He expressed concern that the lack of a legislative record could lead the Supreme Court to declare the bill unconstitutional if it became law. He noted the court "has invalidated acts of Congress where there was not a considered judgment" made by Congress.

HOUSE FLOOR ACTION

The House passed HR 2975 by a vote of 337–79 on Oct. 12, 2001, one day after the Senate acted. Though the bill number was the same as the committee-approved version, the committee's text had been replaced by a leadership measure that was far more to the administration's liking.

The move, which came after days of intense White House pressure, was aimed at heading off a difficult battle with the Senate and clearing the way for quick final negotiations to get a bill to the president's desk. Adding intensity to the debate was a message posted on the FBI's Web site Oct. 11 warning of possible new terrorist attacks within the United States and against U.S. interests overseas.

Speaker J. Dennis Hastert, R-Ill., closeted himself with Sensenbrenner and White House negotiators and staff for the entire day of Oct. 11, trying to move the House bill closer to the administration's position. Democrats, who had helped write the committee bill, no longer were included. After completing their discussions late that day, Hastert and Sensenbrenner introduced a new bill (HR 3108) containing their agreement. It was the text of the bill that was passed under the number HR 2975.

The leadership version of the bill included Ashcroft's request for more secret searches and lengthened the period of time that the wiretap provisions would be law. The 2003 expiration date set by the committee for many of the provisions was extended to 2006.

House leaders left out provisions to toughen laws prohibiting money laundering, a change significant enough to merit a warning from Daschle that a bill without such language would not become law. The House subsequently passed a separate money laundering bill (HR 3004—H Rept 107-250, Part 1) on Oct. 17 by a vote of 412–1.

The House bill also dropped a provision included in the Senate version to repeal a law that required federal prosecutors to obey the ethics laws of the state in which they practiced. The statute (PL 105-277) was known as the McDade law after former House member Joseph M. McDade, R-Pa. (1963–1999), who had been investigated by federal prosecutors for eight years before being acquitted at his bribery trial in 1996.

House leaders' decision to drop the Judiciary Committee bill and substitute their own enraged Democrats, who argued that the new measure lacked sufficient safeguards on the authority to be given to law enforcement. "The United States is not so threatened that we have to throw away our rights with no consideration," John D. Dingell, D-Mich., said of the late-night deal.

Sensenbrenner defended the new bill, arguing that there was a "clear and present danger" of more terrorist attacks that required Congress to act quickly. Hastert succeeded in persuading GOP colleagues to back the bill. The seventy-nine votes against the measure included those of just three Republicans: Ray LaHood of Illinois, C. L. "Butch" Otter of Idaho, and Ron Paul of Texas.

CONFERENCE, FINAL ACTION

Negotiators worked out the differences between the two bills behind closed doors and issued no report. The House leadership decided to put the agreement into yet another new bill (HR 3162), which passed the House and Senate and went to the president with no conference or committee reports. The House passed the bill Oct. 24, 2001, by a **key vote of 357–66 (R 211–3; D 145–62; I 1–1).** The Senate cleared it Oct. 25 by a **key vote of 98–1 (R 49–0; D 48–1; I 1–0).** *(2001 key votes, p. 801)*

On some of the more controversial issues, the final bill:

• Set an expiration date of 2005 for many but not all intelligence provisions, although the expiration would not apply to investigations already under way at that time.

• Allowed the government in certain cases to conduct searches without first notifying the suspects. Also grand jury information could be shared with law enforcement, intelligence, national security, and other agencies.

• Allowed use of FISA wiretaps for purposes other than foreign intelligence gathering as long as such intelligence remained a "significant purpose" of the operation.

• Allowed the attorney general to detain an alien for up to seven days before bringing deportation or criminal charges.

MAJOR PROVISIONS

As signed into law on Oct. 26, 2001, the antiterrorism law (HR 3162—PL 107-56), known formally as the USA PATRIOT Act:

Surveillance

Wiretap predicates. Added terrorism and computer fraud and abuse to the list of crimes that were "predicates" for obtaining a wiretap, which meant a court could give government agents permission to tap telephones when they were investigating such crimes. (Expiration date: Dec. 31, 2005.)

Information sharing. Allowed information received during grand jury proceedings to be disclosed to law enforcement, intelligence, protective, immigration, or national defense or national security personnel. Allowed any foreign intelligence information obtained by law enforcement officials during wiretaps, electronic surveillance, or a criminal investigation to be made available as well. (Expiration date for sharing foreign intelligence: Dec. 31, 2005.)

Defined "intelligence information" as any information that would help the United States protect against attacks, sabotage, and clandestine intelligence activities or that concerned foreign powers and related to national defense or foreign affairs.

Required a federal court be notified after any grand jury information was disclosed. Allowed grand jury information to be disclosed at the request of defendants when they argued that it included information that might be grounds for dismissal of the indictment against them.

Intelligence information collection. Clarified that authorities using wiretaps and other kinds of electronic surveillance to collect information for a foreign intelligence investigation were not bound by the procedures and restrictions that applied to authorities conducting the same kinds of surveillance for a criminal investigation.

Hiring translators. Authorized the Federal Bureau of Investigation (FBI) to hire additional translators.

'Roving' wiretaps. Permitted investigators working under the authority of the Federal Intelligence Surveillance Act (FISA) to use "roving" wiretaps when a court found that the actions of a suspect might thwart traditional wiretaps. In those cases, investigators were authorized to obtain a court order allowing them to tap whatever telephones a suspect might use, rather than getting a court order for each telephone. (Expiration date: Dec. 31, 2005.) FISA (PL 95-511) was the law authorizing wiretaps of suspected foreign criminals or spies.

Intelligence investigations. Allowed court orders for FISA investigations against people considered to be agents of a foreign power and who were not "U.S. persons" (generally a "U.S. person" was a U.S. citizen, a legal permanent resident, or a U.S. company) were good for 120 days, rather than the ninety days allowed previously. Allowed a court after that period to extend the order anywhere from ninety days to a year. Made search warrants in such cases good for ninety days rather than the forty-five days allowed previously. (Expiration date: Dec. 31, 2005.)

Additional FISA judges. Authorized an increase in the number of district court judges who approved FISA requests from seven to eleven and required that three of them live within twenty miles of the District of Columbia.

Voice mail seizure. Allowed the government to seize voice mail messages with a warrant. Permitted investigators to get one warrant that was good nationwide, rather than having to obtain a separate warrant for each jurisdiction. (Expiration date: Dec. 31, 2005.)

Credit card information. Allowed investigators to get subpoenas to obtain subscriber credit card or bank account numbers and other payment information from electronic communication providers, such as cable companies or Internet services.

Cable companies and the Internet. Allowed the government to conduct surveillance on Internet users without notice, even if they obtained their Internet access through a cable company rather than over telephone lines. (Previously, to protect the privacy of consumers, if the government sought information about a cable customer, the company had to notify the client of the request.) Expressly forbade revealing subscribers' cable viewing habits.

Emergency information disclosure. Permitted Internet service providers to show the government a subscriber's electronic communications when they believed there was a risk of immediate danger, death, or serious bodily injury. Allowed law enforcement agents with a court order or search warrant to force the providers to disclose such information. (Expiration date: Dec. 31, 2005.)

'Sneak and peek' searches. Allowed investigators to search suspects' property without notifying them immediately if the government thought prior notice of the search would have an "adverse result" on the investigation. Specified that the warrant could not be used to seize any property or electronic information, unless the court found reasonable necessity for the seizure. Required the individual be notified within a "reasonable period" after the search had taken place but did not define "reasonable." Permitted a court to allow investigators to keep the search secret longer if "good cause" was shown.

FISA wiretaps. Broadened the authority of the government to get court orders under FISA for using pen registers and trap-and-trace devices, which could be used to track telephone calls and Internet communications. Instead of showing that the person under surveillance was the "agent of a foreign power," investigators were required to show the information was "relevant" to an ongoing investigation aimed at protecting against international terrorism or clandestine intelligence activities. Specified that the government may not use this enhanced surveillance power against U.S. citizens if the investigation was triggered solely by activities protected by the First Amendment. For example, citizens could not be investigated simply based on what groups they associated with or things they had said. (Expiration date: Dec. 31, 2005.)

Business records. Permitted a court to issue a FISA order allowing investigators to obtain business records, but only in international terrorism or clandestine intelligence investigations. Specified that investigations of U.S. citizens could not be based solely on activities protected by the First Amendment. Broadened the type of business records that could be obtained with the FISA court order to include any books, records, papers, documents, or other items. Required the attorney general to report to Congress twice a year how many times such a court order had been requested and the outcome of each request. (Expiration date: Dec. 31, 2005.)

Internet communications tracking. Allowed pen registers and trap-and-trace devices, which record the phone numbers of incoming and outgoing telephone calls, to be used to track Internet communications. Allowed investigators to get one federal court order good throughout the country allowing them to use such devices but barring them from recording the content of the communications. Protected Internet service providers from liability in such cases. Required investigators who installed their own pen registers and trap-and-trace devices on a packet-switched data network to note who installed the device and anyone who had access to it, the date and time of installation and removal, the duration of any access to the information, what data were collected, and how the device was configured, including any modifications. Required this record to be provided to the court in secret within thirty days after the device was removed.

Computer hacking interception. Allowed law enforcement agents to intercept electronic communication if the owners of a computer system or network believed someone was attacking their system from the outside. Required that the agents' actions be part of an ongoing investigation and involve only communications to or from the suspects. (Expiration date: Dec. 31, 2005.) Allowed intelligence agents working under the authority of FISA to also intercept such communications.

Broadening intelligence authority. Allowed FISA investigations in those cases where obtaining foreign intelligence information was a "significant" purpose of the investigation. (Such surveillance previously was permitted only when obtaining foreign intelligence information was "the purpose" of the investigation.) (Expiration date: Dec. 31, 2005.)

Nationwide search warrant. Authorized nationwide federal search warrants good in any U.S. jurisdiction for terrorism investigations, instead of requiring a separate warrant in each jurisdiction.

Nationwide electronic search warrant. Allowed courts with jurisdiction over the crime under investigation to issue a nationwide federal search warrant, good anywhere in the country, for e-mail and other electronic information. (Expiration date: Dec. 31, 2005.)

Exports to Taliban. Allowed the president to unilaterally restrict exports of agricultural products, food, and medicine or medical devices to the Taliban or any part of Afghanistan controlled by the Taliban.

Internet service provider protection. Stated that the law did not impose any new technical obligation on Internet service providers in order to comply with its provisions. Authorized compensation for Internet service providers or anyone else who helped set up pen registers and trap-and-trace devices on computer networks.

Civil suits for disclosure of information. Allowed the United States to be sued in civil court if anyone unlawfully disclosed information obtained through the law's wiretap authority. Provided a minimum fine of $10,000 plus litigation costs if the court found the disclosure to have been unlawful. Barred jury trials for these cases. Provided that if the court found a government employee was guilty of unlawfully disclosing the information, the government had to investigate whether administrative action against the employee was also warranted. (Expiration date: Dec. 31, 2005.)

Liability protection. Specified that providers of wire or electronic communication services, a landlord, custodian, or anyone else who assisted with investigations could not be sued for providing information to law enforcement under this law.

Continuing investigations. Specified that investigations into offenses committed before the law's various surveillance provisions expired would be allowed to continue past their Dec. 31, 2005, expiration date.

Money Laundering

Special measure for risky institutions. Authorized the Treasury secretary to impose new "special measures" against foreign jurisdictions, foreign banks, transactions involving such jurisdictions or institutions, or one or more types of accounts that the secretary, after consulting with the secretary of state and the attorney general, determined were being used for money-laundering.

The special measures were: (1) requiring additional record-keeping or reporting for particular transactions; (2) requiring the identification of the real owners of the money in certain accounts at U.S. banks; (3) requiring the identification of customers of a foreign bank who wrote checks out of the bank's U.S. bank accounts; (4) requiring the identification of customers of a foreign bank who used one of its U.S. bank accounts for currency exchanges and other purposes; and (5) after consulting with the secretary of state, the attorney general, and the chair of the Federal Reserve Board, restricting or prohibiting the ability of certain foreign banks to open or maintain U.S. bank accounts. Barred the first four measures from being imposed for longer than 120 days without writing new regulations. Specified that measure five could be imposed only by regulation.

Due diligence requirements. Required foreign financial institutions that established, maintained, administered, or managed private bank accounts in the United States for non-U.S. citizens to ensure that the accounts were not being used for money-laundering. Required U.S. financial institutions doing business with foreign banks at risk of being used for money-laundering to watch for such transactions.

Prohibition on foreign 'shell banks.' Prohibited depository institutions, credit unions, and branches or agencies of foreign banks from establishing, maintaining, administering, or managing bank accounts in the United States for foreign banks that had no physical property.

Information sharing. Allowed regulators to help banks meet the law's new standards for oversight by giving them information about people engaged in or suspected of terrorist acts or money-laundering. Allowed banks to cooperate with each other in identifying and reporting people, entities, organizations, and countries suspected of terrorism or money-laundering.

Money-laundering predicates. Expanded the list of offenses covered by money-laundering laws to include foreign corruption offenses, such as export control violations, some customs and firearms offenses, and felony violations of the Foreign Agents Registration Act of 1938, which required agents of foreign governments to register with the Department of Justice.

Property confiscation rights. Permitted owners of property confiscated under money-laundering laws to present an "affirmative defense"—meaning they could go on the offensive against the government rather than simply defending themselves. (They could argue, for example, that there were mitigating circumstances that should exempt their property from confiscation.)

Federal jurisdiction. Gave U. S. district courts jurisdiction over foreigners engaged in money-laundering in the United States, over foreign banks opening U.S. bank accounts, and over foreigners who use, sell, or otherwise transfer assets that had been forfeited by order of a U.S. court. Allowed federal courts to issue a pretrial restraining order or take other action to keep forfeited property in the United States. Authorized federal courts to appoint a receiver to collect and take custody of assets forfeited because of criminal or civil money-laundering or forfeiture judgments.

Money-laundering crime. Made it a crime to use foreign banks for money-laundering.

'Payable-through' accounts. Specified that amounts deposited by foreign banks in an interbank "payable-through" account, a type of account they could hold at a U.S. bank, would be treated as having been deposited in the United States for purposes of forfeiture rules. Allowed the attorney general, in the interest of justice and in keeping with the U.S. national interest, to suspend a forfeiture proceeding.

Information response time. Required U.S. banks to reply within 120 hours to a request for information from a U.S. regulator who was checking on their compliance with money-laundering laws.

Foreign bank records. Required foreign banks that maintained their own accounts at U.S. banks to appoint agents to receive legal documents within the United States. Allowed the attorney general and the Treasury secretary to issue a summons or subpoena to any foreign bank for records, wherever located, from "correspondent accounts," another kind of account that foreign banks could maintain in the United States. Required U.S. banks to sever correspondent arrangements with foreign banks that did not answer or comply with such summons or subpoenas.

Foreign forfeiture. Allowed the government to seek a restraining order to keep people from moving or disposing of property outside the United States that was ordered forfeited or confiscated. Allowed U.S. courts to force a convicted criminal to return forfeited property located abroad. (Courts could order such property returned even if the owners had challenged the government's right to take it from them and were waiting for a ruling on their case.)

Broadened definition of financial institution. Added credit unions, futures commission merchants, commodity trading advisers, and commodity pool operators to the definition of financial institution for purposes of the Bank Secrecy Act (PL 91-508), a 1970 law that established transaction reporting requirements for financial institutions. Clarified that the term "federal functional regulator" included the Commodity Futures Trading Commission for purposes of the Bank Secrecy Act.

Corporate fugitive. Barred corporations from challenging forfeiture orders against them if their majority shareholder was a fugitive. Barred a fugitive from challenging a forfeiture claim on behalf of a corporation.

Anonymous funds transfers. Authorized the Treasury secretary to issue regulations concerning the maintenance of concentrated assets in accounts at U.S. depository institutions in order to prevent an institution's customers from anonymously directing funds into or through concentration accounts, a type of bank account that commingled funds from various sources.

Customer identification. Required the Treasury secretary to establish minimum standards that financial institutions had to meet in verifying the identities of customers. Required financial institutions to keep verification records and check the names of customers against lists of known or suspected terrorists.

Foreign customer identification. Required the Treasury secretary to report to Congress by April 2002 on the most effective way to verify the identities of foreigners opening accounts in U.S. financial institutions and assign them identification numbers that worked like the tax identification number given to U.S. citizens.

Money-laundering record. Required the Federal Reserve Board and the Federal Deposit Insurance Corporation, in ruling on bank mergers or similar applications, to look at how effectively banks or bank holding companies had combated money-laundering in the United States and in overseas branches. Applicable to applications submitted after Dec. 31, 2001.

Wire transfer origination. Required the Treasury secretary to take all reasonable steps to encourage foreign governments to require that wire transfers sent to the United States include the name of the person requesting the transfer.

Anonymous funds transfers. Increased civil and criminal penalties for people or institutions who tried to move money anonymously in and out of bank accounts in violation of the new monitoring standards.

Antimoney-laundering programs. Required financial institutions to establish antimoney-laundering programs, effective April 26, 2002.

Safe harbor. Allowed banks, when checking employment references, to share information with each other about employees who may have taken part in illegal activities. Barred banks from being sued for releasing such information as long as they did not do it with malicious intent.

Suspicious activity reports. Required the Treasury secretary to publish proposed regulations requiring broker-dealers to report suspicious transactions, with final regulations due by July 1, 2002.

IRS and bank secrecy. Required the Treasury secretary by April 2002 to report to Congress whether the responsibility for certain regulatory functions under the Bank Secrecy Act should be taken from the Internal Revenue Service (IRS) and given to another agency.

Information sharing. Allowed the government to use banking and financial information in intelligence activities aimed at fighting international terrorism.

Underground banking systems. The law clarified that the Bank Secrecy Act treated certain underground banking systems as financial institutions, and that record-keeping rules applied to them. Required the Treasury secretary to report to Congress by Oct. 26, 2002, on the need for additional legislation or regulatory controls addressing underground banking systems.

Loans and fighting terrorism. Allowed the Treasury secretary to instruct the U.S. executive director of the World Bank and other international financial institutions to support loans and other assistance for nations that the president determined were contributing to the fight against terrorism. Allowed the Treasury secretary to require audits of those financial institutions to ensure that the money was not paid to people engaged in terrorism or supporting it.

Financial crimes enforcement. Made the Financial Crimes Enforcement Network (FinCEN) a bureau within the Treasury Department and described the duties of the FinCEN's director. Required the Treasury secretary to establish operating procedures for the government-wide data access service and communications center that FinCEN maintained. Required the secretary to report by April 2002, and annually thereafter, on ways to improve the system for monitoring foreign bank and brokerage accounts owned by U.S. citizens. Required the secretary by July 2002 to work with FinCEN to establish a security network for financial institutions to file reports on suspicious transactions and provide them with information about transactions that deserved special scrutiny.

Increased penalties. Increased from $100,000 to $1 million the maximum civil and criminal penalties for a violation of the new investigation and special measures requirements.

Law enforcement. Allowed certain Federal Reserve personnel to act as law enforcement officers and carry firearms to protect and safeguard Federal Reserve employees and premises.

Reporting large transactions. Required any person who received more than $10,000 in one transaction or two or more related transactions in the course of his trade or business to file a report with FinCEN. People who did not report large transactions to FinCEN might have their money confiscated.

Required companies offering wire transfers to be licensed under state law or registered under federal law. Allowed funds transmitted illegally to be seized.

New smuggling crime. Made smuggling more than $10,000 into or out of the United States a violation of the Bank Secrecy Act.

Counterfeiting sentences increased. Increased the maximum sentences for various counterfeiting offenses and expanded the definition of counterfeiting to include making or acquiring an analog, digital, or electronic image of any "obligation or other security of the United States," such as U.S. currency. Increased the maximum sentences for various counterfeiting offenses involving foreign money and expanded the definition of counterfeiting to include making or acquiring an analog, digital, or electronic image of the currency of a foreign government.

Material support for terrorism. Expanded the legal definition of money-laundering to include providing material support or resources to terrorist organizations.

Reporting large transactions. Applied the financial crimes prohibitions to conduct committed abroad in cases where the tools or proceeds of the offense passed through or were in the United States.

Sunset provisions. Specified that the money-laundering provisions were to be terminated Oct. 1, 2005, if Congress enacted a joint resolution saying these provisions no longer had the force of law. Required any joint resolution to this effect to receive expedited congressional consideration.

Border Control

INS employees. Waived caps on the number of full-time employees at the Immigration and Naturalization Service (INS) and lifted the cap in the fiscal 2001 Commerce-Justice-State appropriations act (PL 106-553) on the amount of overtime the INS could pay its employees.

Northern border personnel. Authorized money to triple the number of Border Patrol agents, INS inspectors, and Customs Service personnel along the border with Canada.

Sharing of criminal background information. Required the FBI and the attorney general to provide information from the National Crime Information Center's Interstate Identification Index, the Wanted Persons File, and other sources, in order to help the INS and the State Department determine whether people applying for admission to the United States had criminal records.

Identification technology. Required the attorney general, working with the secretary of state and others, to develop a reliable technology standard for checking the identities of those seeking visas or trying to enter the United States.

Automated fingerprint system. Authorized $2 million for the attorney general, the FBI, and the INS to study whether the FBI's Integrated Automated Fingerprint Identification System could be used at U.S. ports of entry and at overseas consular posts.

Terrorist activity. Broadened the definition of "terrorist activity" for individuals seeking to enter the United States. Barred from the United States anyone who was a representative of a political or social group that publicly endorsed terrorist activity in the United States, and anyone who used a position of prominence within a country to endorse terrorist activities or encourage others to do so.

Authorized exclusions. Authorized the attorney general or the secretary of state to forbid entry to anyone they considered to be associated with a terrorist organization and who they determined would engage in activities that could endanger the welfare, safety, or security of the United States.

Terrorist activities. Added the use of explosives, firearms, and other dangerous devices to the definition of "terrorist activities." Broadened the definition of "a terrorist engaging in terrorist activity" to include those who had provided support to a group that they knew or should have known was engaged in terrorism, regardless of whether the support provided was for a terrorist purpose. Those were offenses that would keep someone out of the United States or lead to deportation.

Terrorist organization. Created a new definition of "terrorist organization" for use when determining whether to admit foreigners to the United States or deport those already here. Defined the term as a group of two or more individuals who the secretary of state determined was involved with terrorist activities. Made the provisions retroactive for any group that the secretary of state had previously listed as a terrorist organization.

Mandatory detention. Allowed the attorney general or the deputy attorney general to certify a foreigner as a terrorist if they had reasonable grounds to believe that the person was a terrorist or had committed a terrorist activity. Specified that those certified as terrorists had to be jailed.

Allowed the INS to detain suspected terrorists for seven days before bringing immigration or criminal charges against them but required foreigners not charged within seven days be released.

Allowed detainees to challenge the government's case against them, under a procedure called "habeas review." Required all habeas decisions to be based on the legal principles articulated by the U.S. Court of Appeals for the District of Columbia and the Supreme Court. Required all appeals of habeas decisions be heard by the U.S. Court of Appeals for the District of Columbia. Specified that aliens who were ordered deported but remained in U.S. detention were entitled to have their cases reviewed by the attorney general every six months. Allowed continued detention only upon a showing that "the release of the alien will endanger the national security of the United States or the safety of the community or any person."

Visa information sharing. Allowed the secretary of state to give foreign governments information in the State Department's computer database and other records on people seeking to enter the United States if that disclosure would help prevent, investigate, or punish acts of terrorism or trafficking in drugs, weapons, or people.

Entry-exit system. Authorized "such sums as may be necessary" to implement an automated entry-exit data system for the United States. The law included a "sense of Congress" resolution saying the attorney general should fully implement the entry-exit system as quickly as practicable, focusing in particular on the use of "biometric technology," such as fingerprint scanning devices, and the development of tamper-resistant documents.

Foreign students. Required the attorney general to implement a system to track foreign students in the United States and made $36.8 million available through Jan. 1, 2003, for the creation and implementation of the system.

Machine-readable passports. Required all countries that wanted to participate in the Visa Waiver Program to issue machine-readable passports by Oct. 1, 2003. (The deadline had been 2007.) Allowed the secretary of state to extend this deadline for a country that was making progress. (The Visa Waiver Program allowed citizens from a select group of mostly industrial countries to come into the United States for short visits for either business or pleasure without having to get a visa. The secretary of state had to perform annual audits of those countries allowed to participate in the program.)

Benefits for Aliens

Permanent residency status. Granted permanent residency status to aliens whose sponsors died in the Sept. 11, 2001, attacks. Allowed aliens who were disabled or lost their jobs as a direct result of the attacks to be declared permanent legal residents. Allowed their children and spouses to become permanent legal residents if they came to the United States no later than Sept. 11, 2003. Allowed the spouse or fiancé of a U.S. citizen killed in the Sept. 11 attacks eligibility for permanent resident status.

Disability extension. Allowed aliens who were legally in the country and were disabled in the Sept. 11 attacks to remain in the United States, along with their spouses and children, and get legal authorization to work for one year after the point when they were disabled. Allowed spouses and children of aliens who died in the terrorist attacks to get the same extension; they had to be admitted to the United States even if they required government assistance.

Extensions of deadlines. Provided a grace period for aliens who missed any filing deadlines because of the Sept. 11 attacks.

Waiver for some would-be immigrants. For aliens who were married to a citizen killed in the attacks, waived the requirement that they be married for two years before they were eligible for immigrant status. If a permanent resident killed in the attacks had filed papers to allow his or her spouse, child, or unmarried adult son or daughter to become a legal permanent resident, made those aliens eligible for the residency. In addition, if an alien spouse, child, or unmarried adult son or daughter of a permanent resident who died in the attacks was present in the United States on Sept. 11 but had not yet applied for permanent residence, the alien could petition for permanent residence.

Broadens definition of child. Lengthened the amount of time that aliens would be considered children for the purposes of immigration law if they filed petitions on or before Sept. 11.

Investigating Terrorism

Increased rewards. Specified there was no limit on the size of the rewards that the attorney general could offer to combat terrorism. Rewards of $250,000 or more needed the personal approval of the attorney general or president, as well as notice to Congress.

DNA database. Required persons convicted of terrorism to provide DNA for inclusion in the federal DNA database of convicted offenders.

Financial information. Allowed the FBI director or a designee no lower than deputy assistant director to request telephone, financial, or credit records if he or she certified that the information was relevant to an ongoing foreign counterintelligence investigation and that there were "specific, articulable" facts showing that the person targeted was the agent of a foreign power.

Secret Service jurisdiction. Gave the Secret Service concurrent jurisdiction with the Justice Department to investigate offenses involving computer fraud and related activity. Gave the Secret Service authority to investigate fraud at financial institutions.

Education records. Allowed a court to release student education records if the attorney general or the education secretary determined that the records would reasonably assist in investigating or preventing an act of terrorism.

Victims Compensation

Paperwork eased. Streamlined the Public Safety Officers Benefits Program application process for family members of law enforcement officers, firefighters, and emergency personnel who were killed or suffered serious injury in the terrorist attacks. Raised the total payment allowed under the program to $250,000, effective for any death or disability occurring on or after Jan. 1, 2001.

Victims of Crime fund. Authorized the Office for Victims of Crime to replenish the antiterrorism emergency reserve with as much as $50 million. Established a mechanism for replenishing the fund in future years and replaced the annual cap on the fund with a self-regulating system intended to keep the fund healthy. Allowed private gifts to the fund.

State programs. Increased the minimum amount authorized for the annual grant to state compensation programs. Clarified that compensation paid to a victim should not be used in means tests for federal benefit programs.

Governmental cooperation. Expanded the Department of Justice Regional Information Sharing Systems Program to facilitate information sharing among federal, state, and local law enforcement agencies to investigate and prosecute terrorist conspiracies and activities.

Changes in Criminal Law

Mass transit. Made it a federal crime to attack a mass transit system, punishable by a fine and as much as twenty years in prison. Increased the sentence to life if the vehicle was carrying a passenger at the time of the attack or if the attack killed someone.

Domestic terrorism. Defined "domestic terrorism" as activities that involved acts dangerous to human life that were a violation of federal or state laws and that appeared intended to intimidate or coerce a civilian population, change government policy, or affect the conduct of government by mass destruction, assassination, or kidnapping, and that occurred primarily within the United States.

Harboring terrorists. Made it a federal crime for individuals to harbor a person who they knew or should have known was engaged in or would engage in terrorist activities.

U.S. criminal jurisdiction. Extended U.S. jurisdiction to offenses committed by or against a U.S. national; U.S. diplomatic, consular, and military missions; and residences used by U.S. personnel assigned to such missions.

Material support for terrorism. Added three terrorism-related offenses to the list of those considered as providing material support to a terrorist. Explicitly prohibited providing terrorists with "expert advice or assistance," such as flight training, knowing or intending that it would be used to prepare for or carry out an act of terrorism.

U.S. forfeiture authority. Extended U.S. forfeiture authority to "all assets, foreign or domestic" owned or controlled by any person or group planning or carrying out an act of terrorism against the United States, its citizens, or residents or their property.

Material support for terrorists. Clarified that the provisions of the Trade Sanctions Reform and Export Enhancement Act of 2000 (PL 106-387) did not limit or otherwise affect the criminal prohibitions against providing material support to terrorists or designated terrorist organizations.

Crime of terrorism defined. Added the following as a list of offenses under the definition of "federal crime of terrorism": destruction of aircraft or aircraft facilities; violence at international airports; arson within special maritime and territorial jurisdiction; offenses involving biological or chemical weapons; kidnapping or assassination of members of Congress, the cabinet, or the Supreme Court; offenses involving nuclear materials or plastic explosives; arson and bombing of government property risking or causing death; arson and bombing of property used in interstate commerce; killing or attempted killing during an attack on a federal facility with a dangerous weapon; conspiracy to murder, kidnap, or maim persons abroad; offenses against the protection of computers; killing or attempted killing of officers and employees of the United States; murder or manslaughter of foreign officials, official guests, or internationally protected persons; hostage taking; destruction of communication lines, stations, or systems; injury to buildings or property within special maritime and territorial jurisdiction of the United States; destruction of an energy facility; presidential and presidential staff assassination and kidnapping; wrecking trains; terrorist attacks and other acts of violence against mass transportation systems; destruction of national defense materials, premises, or utilities; violence against maritime navigation; violence against maritime fixed platforms; certain homicides and other violence against United States nationals occurring outside the United States; use of weapons of mass destruction; acts of terrorism transcending national boundaries; harboring terrorists; providing material support to terrorists or terrorist organizations; torture; sabotage of nuclear facilities or fuel; aircraft piracy; assault on a flight crew with a dangerous weapon, explosive, or incendiary devices or endangerment of human life by means of weapons on aircraft.

No statute of limitations. Eliminated the statute of limitations for certain terrorism-related offenses if they resulted in or created a foreseeable risk of death or serious bodily injury to another person.

Increased prison terms. Raised the maximum prison terms to fifteen to twenty years—or to life imprisonment, if death resulted—for the following crimes: arson within the special maritime and territorial jurisdiction of the United States; destruction of an energy facility; destruction of national-defense materials; provision of material support to terrorists and terrorist organizations; sabotage of nuclear facilities or fuel; killings on aircraft; and destruction of interstate gas or hazardous liquid pipeline facility.

Conspiracy penalties. Added conspiracy provisions to the following criminal statutes: arson within special maritime and territorial jurisdiction of the United States; killings in federal facilities; destruction of communications lines, stations, or systems; destruction of property within special maritime and territorial jurisdiction of the United States; wrecking trains; material support to terrorists; torture; sabotage of nuclear facilities or fuel; interference with flight crews; carrying weapons or explosives on aircraft; and destruction of interstate gas or hazardous liquid pipeline facilities.

Supervised release. Authorized an extended period of supervised release for persons who had served their prison sentence for certain terrorism-related offenses that resulted in, or created a foreseeable risk of, death or serious bodily injury to another person.

Terrorism as racketeering. Included certain terrorism-related offenses within the definition of "racketeering activity," thereby allowing multiple acts of terrorism to be charged as a pattern of racketeering for purposes of the Racketeer Influenced and Corrupt Organizations (RICO) statute (PL 91-452), which could triple the damages imposed. Expanded the ability of prosecutors to prosecute members of established, ongoing terrorist organizations.

Computer hacking. Specified that the criminal statute prohibiting computer hacking included computers located outside the United States when used in a manner that affected the interstate commerce or communications of the United States.

Forensic laboratories. Required the attorney general to establish regional computer forensic laboratories and support existing computer forensic laboratories to help combat computer crime.

U.S. criminal jurisdiction. Expanded the biological weapons statute's definition of "for use as a weapon" to include all situations in which it could be proven that the defendant had any purpose not prophylactic, protective, or peaceful.

Intelligence Changes

Foreign intelligence management. Clarified the role of the Central Intelligence Agency (CIA) director in managing the collection, analysis, and dissemination of foreign intelligence gathered under FISA.

Revised definitions. Revised the definitions section of the National Security Act of 1947 (PL 80-253) to include international terrorism as a subset of "foreign intelligence," clarifying the CIA director's responsibility for collecting foreign intelligence related to international terrorism.

Information sharing. Required law enforcement agencies to notify intelligence agencies when a criminal investigation revealed information of intelligence value.

Miscellaneous

Civil rights oversight. Required the Justice Department's inspector general to designate one official to review information and receive complaints alleging abuses of civil rights and civil liberties by employees and officials of the Department of Justice.

Biometric identifier. Required the attorney general to report to Congress on the feasibility of using a "biometric identifier" system, with access to the FBI fingerprint database, at consular offices abroad and at points of entry into the United States. (Such devices scanned fingerprints or other physical characteristics to check an individual's identity.)

Charity telemarketing. Required any telemarketer soliciting for charity to disclose to people they called that they were telephoning to solicit charitable contributions, and make other disclosures that the Federal Trade Commission considered appropriate.

Hazardous materials background check. Allowed the Department of Transportation to check the background of any individual applying for a license to transport hazardous materials in interstate commerce.

Terrorism grants. Authorized a Justice Department program to provide grants to states to prepare for and respond to terrorist acts including acts involving weapons of mass destruction and biological, nuclear, radiological, incendiary, chemical, and explosive devices.

Infrastructure protection. Established a National Infrastructure Simulation and Analysis Center to address critical infrastructure protection and continuity through support for activities related to counterterrorism, threat assessment, and risk mitigation.

Property confiscation. Authorized the president to confiscate and vest properties of an enemy, defined as a country, person, or organization, when the United States was engaged in hostilities or had been the subject of an attack by that enemy. Classified information could be used to defend this determination to a judge and could be kept secret from the property owner.

Aviation Security

Two months after the Sept. 11, 2001, terrorist attacks, President George W. Bush went to Washington Reagan National Airport, just across the Potomac River from the Capitol, to sign sweeping aviation security legislation. The new law (S 1447—PL 107-71) turned responsibility for airport security over to the federal government instead of private contractors. Transportation secretary Norman Y. Mineta called it "a major milestone in the creation of a consistent, high-quality, nationwide aviation security force."

The bill's passage took place against a backdrop of extreme concern over flying safety. After the Sept. 11 attacks and the temporary grounding of all commercial flights, Bush authorized state governors to call up National Guard members to buttress airport security at federal expense. The Federal Aviation Administration (FAA) also took a number of interim steps, allowing only airports with tough new procedures to reopen.

The legislation, written largely in negotiations among lawmakers and with the White House, did not go through committee in either chamber. The Senate acted first, unanimously passing a bill Oct. 11 that called for full federalization of airport security. House GOP leaders, however, argued that federalizing the work force would not make flying safer. Instead, they worried it would simply expand the size and reach of government, which was anathema to conservatives, while increasing the rolls of labor unions that supported the Democratic Party. With a critical boost from Bush, the House Republican leadership won passage of a bill Nov. 1 that gave the president the choice of hiring government employees or private contract workers.

But in the post-Sept. 11 atmosphere, the public was less interested in ideological battles than in safety, and polls indicated that a majority wanted airport screeners to be federal workers. John McCain, R-Ariz., a leading sponsor of the Senate bill, criticized House leaders' concern over expanding union rolls. "The policemen and firemen that died at the World Trade Center were union members, and I think a lot of them voted for Republicans," McCain said.

House leaders also were undercut by White House signals that Bush was eager for any bill and would be willing to sign the Senate measure even though he preferred their version. After weeks of debate the House ultimately backed down on the key issue of federalization, clearing the way for enactment of the bill.

BACKGROUND

For years, some lawmakers and law enforcement experts had warned that airport security was inadequate, relying as it did largely on low-paid private contract workers who scanned hundreds of bags and passengers an hour. But the ability of hijackers to board the three jets used in the Sept. 11 attacks on the World Trade Center and the Pentagon, as well as a fourth jet that crashed in Pennsylvania, galvanized public and congressional opinion. The main questions became whether screeners should be federal employees or contract workers under federal supervision, and whether the operation should be put under the Transportation or Justice department.

For years, aviation security had been a three-level system: The FAA provided threat information, handled security policies and regulations, and evaluated the system's effectiveness. The nation's approximately 450 commercial airports were responsible for their buildings and grounds, including providing local law enforcement and protecting secure areas. The airlines were responsible for securing their aircraft and screening passengers, baggage, and freight.

Three laws governed this system. The first, enacted in 1974 (PL 93-366), required airports to have law enforcement authorities, prohibited weapons and explosives aboard aircraft, and required screening of passengers and baggage. *(Congress and the Nation Vol. IV, p. 582)*

Congress cleared two aviation safety bills in 1990, after Libyan terrorists in 1988 killed 270 people by use of an explosive device on Pan Am Flight 103 over Lockerbie, Scotland. One (PL 101-370) extended a program that allowed the FAA to fine airlines and pilots who violated air safety guidelines. The other (PL 101-604) strengthened federal aviation security measures by creating new safety-related positions in the Transportation Department, requiring new personnel standards for airport security employees, and accelerating the FAA's security research program. *(Congress and the Nation Vol. VIII, p. 420)*

Major airlines, which had resisted federalization in the past, supported the idea after the Sept. 11 hijackings. Democrats and some Republicans agreed, arguing that anything less than federalization would fail to reassure the public about airline safety. While Bush said the government should take responsibility for aviation security, he did not want the more than 20,000 people who actually checked baggage and passengers to be federal employees protected by civil service rules. The White House argued it would be too difficult to discipline or fire them.

Security companies and the Service Employees International Union, which represented many airport workers, lobbied against federalizing the jobs. The union representing government employees—the American Federation of Government Employees—supported the step.

SENATE FLOOR ACTION

The Senate passed its bill (S 1447) by a unanimous vote of 100–0 the evening of Oct. 11, 2001, after nearly two weeks of deadlock on the question of airport security workers. Under the bill, personnel who manned checkpoints at the largest 142 of the nation's 420 commercial passenger airports would be federal employees. Smaller airports could use a combination of federal employees and state or local law enforcement officers.

The measure also required airliners to be outfitted with cockpit doors that could be opened only by the flight deck crew, required federal air marshals on all domestic flights, and assessed airlines a per passenger fee of $2.50 per flight segment to pay for the new security system.

The Senate bill was modified by more than twenty amendments, all adopted by voice vote. The most significant, by Republicans Conrad Burns of Montana and Mike DeWine of Ohio, assigned oversight of airport security to the Justice Department, rather than the Transportation Department. Other amendments included proposals to allow, but not require, the FAA to let properly trained flight deck crew members carry firearms for self-defense, require the X-ray screening of all bags, create a deputy secretary for transportation security within the Transportation Department, and require existing airline and airport employees to undergo security checks.

Democrats tried to expand the bill to include financial help for laid-off aviation workers, but they gave up after failing to end debate on an amendment by Jean Carnahan, D-Mo., and Majority Leader Tom Daschle, D-S.D. The vote was 56–44, short of the sixty votes needed to invoke cloture. The amendment would have provided $1.9 billion to pay for an extra twenty weeks of unemployment benefits and twelve months of health insurance benefits for those laid off in the weeks following the Sept. 11 attacks. Republicans objected to adding the labor provisions, with Kay Bailey Hutchinson of Texas saying the legislation should focus on aviation security only.

Democrats' withdrawal of the Carnahan amendment automatically ended consideration of a proposal by Phil Gramm, R-Texas, to allow drilling for oil and gas in Alaska's Arctic National Wildlife Refuge. Gramm had offered his amendment in retaliation for the labor proposal.

Democrats also agreed not to pursue an amendment that would have added more than $3 billion to help Amtrak pay for better security, repair tunnels, and buy new equipment. Instead, Ernest F. Hollings, D-S.C., and Joseph R. Biden Jr., D-Del., introduced a bill (S 1530) to give Amtrak $3.2 billion in emergency spending and extend Amtrak's reauthorization to the end of fiscal 2003. The measure failed to make it to the Senate floor.

HOUSE FLOOR ACTION

With last-minute lobbying from Bush and the strong hand of Majority Whip Tom DeLay, R-Texas, House GOP leaders succeeded Nov. 1 in blocking the Senate bill and instead won passage of legislation (HR 3150) that gave Bush the option of having private or federal employees at airport checkpoints. The vote was 286–139. Before passage, the House rejected on a **key vote of 214–218 (R 8–211; D 205–6; I 1–1)** a Democratic substitute offered by James L. Oberstar, D-Minn., that contained the Senate language federalizing aviation security workers. *(2001 key votes, p. 801)*

As late as Oct. 28, White House chief of staff Andrew H. Card Jr. said publicly that Bush would probably sign the Senate bill if it were sent to him, albeit reluctantly. But under pressure from DeLay and other House GOP leaders, Bush pitched in to actively support the leadership bill, telephoning and meeting with undecided members.

The rule for floor debate allowed the leadership to add a manager's amendment that included provisions likely to win votes. One provision, aimed at protecting credit card companies from having to refund ticket costs, required air carriers to honor tickets of airlines that had flights disrupted by the terrorist attacks or that went bankrupt. Another limited liability from the Sept. 11 attacks for aircraft manufacturer Boeing Co.; jet engine manufacturers General Electric Co. and Pratt & Whitney; the Port Authority of New York and New Jersey, which built and operated the World Trade Center; and security companies that staffed the airport checkpoints through which the hijackers boarded.

The House voted 379–50 to remove one last-minute amendment that would have partially lifted a salary cap on the top executives of airlines applying for federal aid in the wake of the terrorist attacks.

As passed, the House bill created a Transportation Security Administration within the Transportation Department with responsibility for security issues. It "deputized" security workers as federal agents but allowed the president to decide whether to use federal employees or contract workers. Workers were subject to background checks and training and were prohibited from striking. HR 3150 directed the newly formed security agency to take steps to secure cockpit doors and allowed trained pilots to carry arms if they chose to do so. The bill also required airlines to collect up to $2.50 per one-way trip from passengers for the increased security.

CONFERENCE, FINAL ACTION

With the holidays approaching and continued public fears over air travel, House and Senate conferees agreed Nov. 15 that, within a year, baggage and passenger screening at all commercial airports would be in the hands of federal workers hired and supervised by the Transportation Department. The Senate adopted the conference report (H Rept 107-296) by voice vote Nov. 16, and the House cleared the bill later the same day by a 410–9 roll call.

The turning point came with the crash Nov. 12 of an American Airlines flight in Queens, New York. While the crash investigation pointed to an accident, rather than a terrorist attack, it convinced Senate Minority Leader Trent Lott, R-Miss., who was in New York that day, that prompt action was necessary. "There was a realization that a terrorist action could happen anywhere," a Senate GOP aide recounted later. Others quickly joined the call for action. "We need to act swiftly," Marianne McInerney, executive director of the National Business Travel Association, told the Senate Governmental Affairs Committee. "Passenger traffic is now down 28 percent, and security is still not under control."

By Nov. 14 Lott had presented a proposal to Hollings and DeLay that developed into the centerpiece of the final deal. Lott suggested placing federalized security workers at airports for four years, after which airport authorities could choose to replace them with private screeners. The House countered with a proposal to require federal screeners for two years, and the two sides agreed to split the difference with a one-year transition to a federal work force that would be kept in place for at least two more years.

Conferees included the liability limits sought by the House for the Port Authority of New York and New Jersey, and for the aircraft and engine manufacturers. But they left out the companies that screened passengers at airports where the hijackers boarded the planes.

While the final bill was viewed as a victory for the Senate, House Republicans pointed to the decision to place the new security agency in the Transportation Department rather than in the Justice Department. They also stressed that airports would be able to opt out of the federalization plan.

MAJOR PROVISIONS

As signed into law Nov. 19, 2001, major provisions of S 1447 (PL 107-71):

Passenger and Bag Screeners

Made the federal government directly responsible for airport passenger and baggage screening, relieving the airlines of this responsibility.

Federal work force. Required that within one year of enactment all airport screeners be federal employees, with airports subsequently allowed to opt out of the federal screening system and instead use private screeners.

Opt-out option. Permitted, once the system was totally federalized, up to five airports to resume use of private screeners in a two-year pilot program. Allowed other airports, at the end of that two-year period, to opt out and use nonfederal screeners if the Transportation Department found the airport's nonfederal screeners provided an equal or higher level of security.

Federal supervision. Required direct supervision by uniformed federal officers employed by a new Transportation Security Administration of all screening activities whether by federal employees, private contractors, or state or local law enforcement.

Contractor eligibility. Limited eligibility for private screeners at U.S. airports to U.S. companies, if available.

Baggage screening. Required that all checked baggage be screened by X-ray equipment or other means within sixty days of enactment. Required all checked baggage be screened using explosive-detection equipment by the end of December 2002.

Employment, Training, and Performance Standards

Citizenship requirement. Required all screeners, federal or private, be U.S. citizens and have a functional ability to speak, read, and write English.

Employee standards, pay. Required background and criminal history checks for all screeners. Authorized the Transportation Department to set pay levels.

Firing. Authorized federal supervisors to fire individual screeners for poor performance, regardless of whether the screener was a federal employee or a contract worker.

No strike provision. Allowed federal screeners to unionize but barred them from striking.

Passenger profiling. Allowed the Transportation Department to implement certain additional passenger and baggage screening procedures, including enhanced use of computer profiling, use of technologies to identify persons who might pose a danger to aircraft, and sharing of information with law enforcement and intelligence agencies to identify persons on passenger lists who might be a threat.

'Trusted passengers.' Authorized the Transportation Department to establish requirements for airlines to implement a "trusted passenger" screening program for the expedited screening of certain regular passengers.

Restricted area access. Required the Transportation Department to conduct background and criminal history checks on all personnel authorized to enter restricted areas of an airport.

Aircraft and Crew Security

Air marshals. Required air marshals on all "high risk" flights and required airlines to provide free seating for air marshals even if that meant bumping another passenger.

Cockpit security. Required cockpit doors to be fortified and locked during flights, and placed additional restrictions on access to an airliner's cockpit during flights.

Guns. Allowed pilots to have guns in the cockpit under certain circumstances and permitted law enforcement officers from other agencies to travel with guns to assist air marshals.

Crew communications. Authorized the Transportation Department to develop devices enabling cabin crews to discreetly notify the pilots of hijackings, and cameras or other devices allowing cockpit pilots to monitor activities in the aircraft cabin.

Transponders. Authorized development of means to prevent radar transponders from being turned off during a hijacking.

Cell phones. Required steps to ensure that emergency calls could be made by telephones in aircraft as well as in passenger trains.

Liability exemption. Exempted airline passengers and crews from legal liability for actions they might take in trying to thwart what they "reasonably believed" was a hijacking attempt, and exempted airline employees from liability for disclosing "suspicious" activities, if done in good faith.

Transportation Security Administration

Agency. Established a new Transportation Security Administration within the Transportation Department to be responsible for day-to-day security operations involving all modes of transportation, including civil aviation, rail, highway, and water transport. Established an undersecretary of transportation for security, to be appointed by the president and confirmed by the Senate.

Responsibilities. Specified the new agency was responsible for developing standards for hiring passenger and baggage screeners; performing background checks on screeners and persons with access to airport secure areas; training, testing, and directly supervising screeners; and administering the federal air marshal program.

Other Provisions

Passenger fees. Established a $2.50 per ticket fee each time a passenger boarded an aircraft, with a maximum fee of $5 per one-way trip, to help pay for the government's passenger screening costs.

Airline fees. Authorized the Transportation Department to collect funds from airlines, up to the amount each airline paid for security in calendar year 2000.

Authorization. Authorized $500 million for airlines to upgrade cockpit doors and make other cockpit security improvements and $1.5 billion to reimburse airports for the increased costs of security following the Sept. 11 attacks.

Airport improvement grants. Allowed all primary airports to use fiscal 2002 federal airport improvement grants for certain law enforcement expenses and general aviation airports to use airport grants for any expense.

Legal liability. Broadened liability limits enacted Sept. 22, 2001, as part of the Air Transportation Safety and System Stabilization Act (HR 2926—PL 107-42) to companies that built the airliners involved in the terrorist attacks, as well as to companies that built airliner components, such as engines, the owners and operators of airports involved, state port authorities, and anyone with a property interest in the World Trade Center. Specified those parties were liable for the resulting deaths and property damage only up to the limits of their insurance coverage; limited claims against New York City to its insurance coverage or $350 million, whichever was greater. *(Airline assistance, p. 377)*

Flying schools. Required background checks on all persons seeking flying lessons on certain aircraft or who sought training through flight simulators.

International flights. Required all U.S. and foreign airlines destined for the United States to electronically submit a detailed crew and passenger manifest to the U.S. Customs Service before landing.

Honoring other tickets. Required airlines for the eighteen months after the law's enactment to make a practicable effort to honor the tickets of other airlines that had filed for bankruptcy.

Aviation Security Revisions

The federal government's role in securing the nation's air transport system got a modest makeover in 2002 as Congress worked to refine the sweeping 2001 aviation security law. The changes were enacted as part of the law creating the new Department of Homeland Security (HR 5005—PL 107-296). *(Homeland security department, p. 176)*

The Transportation Security Administration (TSA), created under the 2001 law (S 1447—PL 107-71) to handle security operations for aviation and all other modes of transportation, was moved from the Transportation Department to the Department of Homeland Security, with the proviso that it remain a separate entity for at least two years. *(2001 aviation security law, p. 198)*

In addition, HR 5005 included provisions to arm and train airline pilots, give some airports an additional year to have machines in place to screen airline baggage for explosives, allow the TSA to hire legal residents of U.S. territories as airport screeners, and provide some liability protection for airlines. *(Liability protection, see airline assistance, p. 377)*

ARMING PILOTS

The 2001 aviation security law gave the Transportation Department discretion to begin arming some airline pilots, but the Bush administration chose not to implement the plan. Undersecretary John W. Magaw, the first director of the TSA, told the Senate Commerce, Science, and Transportation Committee on May 21, 2002, that pilots should not be armed. "Pilots need to concentrate on flying the plane," Magaw testified. "My feeling is you secure the cockpit, and if something does happen on that plane, they really have to be in control of the aircraft."

The airline industry lobbied against arming pilots out of concern over liability and the potential cost of weapons training. Commerce, Science, and Transportation Committee Chair Ernest F. Hollings, D-S.C., whose panel had jurisdiction over the issue in the Senate, initially opposed arming pilots, although he later agreed to give the program a chance.

The pilots, however, lobbied heavily to be able to carry firearms on flights, and congressional sentiment favored the pilots. "The government already has told us that if terrorists take control of one of our cockpits, they will send military aircraft to shoot down the airliner and all its crew and passengers," said Duane Woerth, president of the Air Line Pilots Association, which represented some 26,000 pilots. "We do not understand why these same government officials refuse to give pilots a last chance to prevent such a tragedy."

Magaw, who was unpopular with industry groups and members of Congress for a number of reasons, was removed July 18, 2002, and replaced by James M. Loy, a former commandant of the U.S. Coast Guard who had been second in command at the TSA. Loy quickly promised to review the policy of arming pilots.

The House Transportation and Infrastructure Subcommittee on Aviation produced a bipartisan compromise (HR 4635) to create a two-year demonstration program for arming a limited number of pilots. The full Transportation and Infrastructure Committee approved the bill by voice vote June 26 and reported it July 8 (H Rept 107-555, Part 1).

The House passed HR 4635 on July 10 by a vote of 310–113. Under the two-year demonstration program, at least 250 and up to 1,400 specially trained commercial airline pilots would be allowed to carry guns aboard aircraft.

On Sept. 5, the Senate agreed by voice vote to add similar language to the homeland security bill (HR 5005), although without the limits in the House bill. The provisions were included in the final version of the homeland bill.

The new law required the TSA to establish a program to deputize volunteer commercial airline pilots as federal "flight deck officers" and allow them to carry guns aboard the aircraft. Before they could bring guns aboard, the pilots had to achieve a level of training and proficiency comparable to that required of air marshals, and meet other TSA requirements. Preference was given to former military or law enforcement personnel. The law generally exempted the pilots and airlines from any liability that might result from defending a plane against terrorist acts.

BAGGAGE SCREENING

While the TSA met its Nov. 19, 2002, deadline for deploying federal screeners at 429 national airports, it was clear early on that it would not be able to meet the second deadline set in the 2001 law: to have machinery in place by Dec. 31, 2002, to screen all checked baggage for explosives.

Many airports had to make structural changes to accommodate the minivan-sized machines. Loy, who was winning excellent reviews from lawmakers for his common-sense approach to the job, testified Sept. 10 that the agency would find it "virtually impossible" to meet the deadline at some larger airports without inconveniencing passengers. In some cases, he said, engineering and installation problems could force travelers out to the curb as they waited in line at security checkpoints. Airports, particularly the Dallas–Fort Worth International Airport and McCarran International Airport in Las Vegas, lobbied heavily for some relief from the deadline.

The Senate passed a bill by voice vote Nov. 18 to provide leeway for up to forty airports. The Commerce, Science, and Transportation Committee had approved the measure by voice vote Sept. 19 and reported it Sept. 30 (S 2949—S Rept 107-293).

The proposal was the result of negotiations between the TSA, Hollings, and ranking committee Republican John McCain of Arizona—all of whom had acknowledged that the Dec. 31 deadline would be impossible to meet at some of the largest airports. The bill as introduced would have given airports six more months to meet the requirement, but an amendment by Kay Bailey Hutchison, R-Texas, adopted by voice vote of the committee, extended the deadline by one year. Hutchison said six months was not long enough for large airports with engineering challenges, such as Dallas-Fort Worth.

The bill also included a provision to remove the requirement in the 2001 law that airport screeners be U.S. citizens. Instead, it required only that they be U.S. nationals—noncitizens who owed permanent allegiance to the United States—a category that would include residents of a territory such as American Samoa.

The House version of the homeland security bill, passed July 26, included the one-year extension for airports.

As enacted, HR 5005 authorized the TSA director to grant the extension to Dec. 31, 2003, on a case-by-case basis. Until the machines were in place, the TSA had to use alterative methods, including hand searches, to ensure that 100 percent of the checked baggage was screened, and the TSA director had to report to Congress monthly on the airport's progress in meeting the extended deadline. It also included the U.S. nationals provisions.

Antiterrorism Appropriations

President George W. Bush and Congress needed just a few days after the Sept. 11, 2001, terrorist attacks before agreeing to a $40 billion emergency appropriations measure, widely described as a down payment on military action, national security, and reconstruction. Bush signed the bill into law (HR 2888—PL 107-38) on Sept. 18. But the terrorist attacks failed to fully dispel traditional political disputes over the spending of money, and it took another three months for Congress and the White House to finally allocate all of the money in the antiterrorism supplemental.

Appropriators also took other steps against terrorism. Most notably, the fiscal 2002 spending bill for the departments of Commerce, Justice, and State and the federal judiciary (HR 2500—PL 107-77) included $459 million for the antiterrorism program of the Federal Bureau of Investigation (FBI) and another $251 million in grants to state and local governments for antiterrorism and terrorism prevention efforts. Among the items were $12 million to strengthen the FBI's ability to guard against chemical, biological, and nuclear attacks on the United States, and $12 million for security related to the 2002 Winter Olympics in Salt Lake City.

But the antiterrorism supplemental was by far the major appropriation measure in the battle against terrorism. House and Senate leaders initially agreed to appropriate $20 billion to start repairing the damage and hunt down the attackers. But Bush doubled the price tag to $40 billion, assuring New York's congressional delegation that they would not be slighted at the expense of military action.

With Washington stunned by the attacks, lawmakers at first seemed ready to write a blank check, giving Bush broad latitude over how to spend the money. "We think the president needs that flexibility," said House Appropriations Committee Chair C. W. Bill Young, R-Fla., on Sept. 12. But other key members almost immediately spoke up for preserving the right of lawmakers to control spending, and by the end of Sept. 12 lawmakers and appropriators from both parties agreed that some restrictions were necessary.

Two days of behind-the-scenes negotiating between senior administration officials and bipartisan congressional leaders resulted in a hybrid bill. The White House got half of the $40 billion to distribute as it saw fit—$10 billion to spend immediately and another $10 billion to spend subject to notification. The remaining $20 billion would be appropriated later under the fiscal 2002 defense appropriations bill (HR 3338—PL 107-117), which was signed into law on Jan. 10, 2002. *(2002 defense appropriations, p. 316)*

On Sept. 14, 2001, Congress cleared the $40 billion package (HR 2888) without a single dissenting vote. The House passed the bill 422–0, and the Senate cleared it by voice vote after passing an identical bill (S 1426) earlier in the day by 96–0.

The president allocated the initial $10 billion, with $5.9 billion going to defense and $4.1 billion to nondefense spending.

But appropriators soon chafed under their $20 billion limit. Lawmakers called for increased security at the nation's borders, ports, and airports. New Yorkers demanded that Congress live up to its pledge to provide $20 billion for their recovery and rebuilding efforts. The arrival of anthrax-tainted mail on Capitol Hill highlighted additional security weaknesses that lawmakers wanted to address.

When the clamor became too loud for Bush to ignore, he called top appropriators to the White House on Nov. 6 to announce he would veto any bill that spent more than the $20 billion that had already been agreed to. Reassured by the promise of another supplemental spending bill in the spring, most Republicans closed ranks behind the president. New York Republicans pressed to win $9.7 billion more and fulfill the pledge of at least $20 billion, but they ultimately agreed to back off in exchange for more grants and loans directed to small business and unemployed workers.

LEGISLATIVE ACTION

The House Appropriations Committee gave voice vote approval on Nov. 14 to an emergency spending package (HR 3338—H Rept 107-298) that stayed within the $20 billion limit. The bill was reported Nov. 19. Largely following Bush's request, it consisted of:

• $7.3 billion for defense to prosecute the war in Afghanistan, rebuild the section of the Pentagon damaged on Sept. 11, and otherwise boost military readiness.

• $6.9 billion in disaster relief, including work at the World Trade Center site, and various grants and loans for New York

• $5.8 billion for homeland security, including airport security and bioterrorism response programs.

The committee defeated efforts by New York Republicans and by Democrats to add to the bill's bottom line.

The House passed the defense/emergency supplemental appropriations bill Nov. 28 by a vote of 406–20. Democrats continued to complain that the emergency spending provisions were woefully inadequate, and they sharply criticized Republicans for bringing the bill to the floor under a rule that blocked three Democratic amendments to increase spending.

The Senate Appropriations Committee on Dec. 4 approved by voice vote and reported its version of the supple-

mental package, along with the rest of the defense spending bill (S Rept 107-109). Essentially daring Bush to carry out his veto threat, Chair Robert C. Byrd, D-W.Va., added $15 billion for homeland defense and recovery from the attacks, bringing the total package to $35 billion.

When the Senate took up the bill Dec. 6, no one was certain of the outcome. But Byrd and his allies relented after losing three procedural votes. Democrats announced they would replace Byrd's $35 billion measure with a new $20 billion plan. Byrd, however, exacted a stern price. The rewritten bill, passed by voice vote on Dec. 7, sliced defense spending to $2 billion. It provided $9.5 billion of the remaining $20 billion for disaster recovery and $8.5 billion for homeland defense.

The final compromise, negotiated as part of the defense bill, provided $3.5 billion for defense, compared with $7.3 billion requested by Bush. It provided $8.2 billion for disaster recovery and $8.3 billion for homeland security.

The House adopted the conference report (H Rept 107-350), 408–6, on Dec. 20, the final day of the session. The Senate cleared the bill 94–2 later that day.

Terrorism Insurance

With a major push from the real estate and commercial insurance industries—and personal lobbying by President George W. Bush—Congress cleared a bill (HR 3210—PL 107-297) in 2002 establishing a three-year federal terrorism insurance program. The program placed a cap on potential losses for commercial property and casualty insurers in the event of a cataclysmic terrorist attack. Lawmakers hoped to encourage the insurance industry to provide commercial terrorism coverage at affordable prices in the wake of the Sept. 11, 2001, terrorist attacks, while giving insurers time to develop a market-based system for absorbing the risks.

Enactment was a major victory for Bush, who had made the legislation one of his top domestic priorities. It also was a win for congressional Democrats, who successfully resisted the inclusion of a ban on punitive damages in terrorism cases.

However, an effort to extend the program beyond its 2005 expiration date failed in the 108th Congress. *(Details, p. 219)*

BACKGROUND

Before Sept. 11, commercial insurance policies routinely included terrorism coverage. But the attacks sent shock waves through the commercial property and casualty insurance industry. Instantly, acts of terrorism went from a largely overlooked provision in policies to a very real risk that insurers said they had no idea how to price.

Insurers gave assurances that they were well capitalized and could pay the estimated $40 billion in claims stemming from Sept. 11. But, absent federal intervention, they said coverage for future acts of terrorism would be scarce or nonexistent. The large reinsurance companies, which insured the insurers, announced they would not continue covering terrorism insurance when policies came up for renewal, many of them on Jan. 1, 2003. That raised widespread fears that construction companies and other businesses would lose terrorism coverage, and thus their ability to obtain credit, with effects that could reverberate throughout the economy. Commercial insurers, real estate investors, retailers, and others pressed Congress to act.

Lawmakers scrambled to draft legislation that would encourage insurance companies to continue issuing terrorism coverage in the short term, while giving the market time to develop mechanisms to provide commercial coverage at reasonable prices in the future. The Senate Banking and House Financial Services committees unveiled sharply different plans for federal intervention at competing news conferences on Nov. 1, 2001.

The bipartisan Senate plan, negotiated with the White House, called for a direct federal subsidy to insurers in the event of a future terrorist attack that cost more than $10 billion in losses. The House bill, drafted without much Democratic input, took a different tack, calling for federal loans to cover losses above $1 billion, with the assistance paid back by the industry and policyholders.

HOUSE ACTION

The House Financial Services Committee approved a bill (HR 3210—H Rept 107-300, Part 1) by voice vote on Nov. 7, 2001, and reported it Nov. 19. Drafted by Chair Michael G. Oxley, R-Ohio, and Capital Markets Subcommittee Chair Richard H. Baker, R-La., it called for a one-year federal program, with a possible two-year extension.

Under the bill, the federal government would cover 90 percent of insured losses from future acts of terrorism, up to $100 billion, once the industry-wide losses exceeded $1 billion. Smaller insurance companies that suffered disproportionately large terrorist-related losses could receive federal aid once industry-wide losses exceeded $100 million. The first $20 billion in federal assistance would be recouped through direct assessments on insurance companies, and assistance between $20 billion and $100 billion would be repaid through surcharges on insurance policyholders. All lawsuits involving losses or injuries due to acts of terrorism would be considered in federal court rather than state courts. Punitive damage awards would be prohibited except against terrorists and conspirators, and noneconomic damages would be limited.

The bill was approved after a raucous, daylong markup. After ranking Democrat John J. LaFalce of New York complained that he had not been consulted in drafting the measure, Oxley and Baker eventually relented and agreed to negotiate changes to the bill before it reached the House floor.

On Nov. 16 the Ways and Means Committee gave voice vote approval to an amended version of the bill eliminating a provision that would have allowed commercial insurers to set aside long-term, tax-free reserves to prepare for paying future claims related to terrorism. Instead the committee called for a Treasury Department study. The panel reported the bill Nov. 19 (H Rept 107-300, Part 2).

The House passed the bill 227–193 on Nov. 29, after the Rules Committee had incorporated additional changes from the Judiciary Committee, which had not held a markup. At the behest of Judiciary Committee Chair F. James Sensenbrenner Jr., R-Wis., the new version included broad language requiring that all lawsuits related to terrorist acts—not just those involving insurers—be tried in federal court. The bill also banned punitive damages against any defendant and sharply limited rewards for other damages, such as pain and suffering.

Democrats sharply objected, and most voted against the bill. A Democratic substitute by LaFalce that would have increased the threshold for government loans and eliminated restrictions on lawsuits was rejected 197–222.

Although insurance lobbyists generally welcomed the legislation they worried that the repayment provisions would not give insurance companies enough incentive to keep covering acts of terrorism. The White House also expressed concern that the assessments could affect the economy negatively.

SENATE ACTION

The Senate Banking Committee's bill—negotiated with the Treasury Department and announced by Banking Chair Paul S. Sarbanes, D-Md., on Nov. 1, 2001—proposed a straight subsidy with no premiums or repayment requirements. Under the two-year plan, insurance companies would pay terrorism-related insurance claims up to an industry-wide total of $10 billion in one year. After that, the federal government would pay 90 percent of claims, up to $100 billion. Lawsuits involving losses or injuries resulting from terrorism acts would be considered in federal court; punitive damages would be barred.

Hardly had the bill been unveiled, however, than it was hastily pulled back. Majority Leader Tom Daschle, D-S.D., and others objected to the punitive damages ban. Further complicating matters, Commerce Committee Chair Ernest F. Hollings, D-S.C., claimed jurisdiction over the issue, promising to introduce a bill of his own.

Daschle tried to broker a deal among members of the two committees and the administration that he could take to the floor. But the punitive damages controversy proved too high a hurdle to overcome in the first session.

By the time Congress resumed work in 2002, the sense of urgency had receded. Plus, a string of corporate scandals, highlighted by the massive bankruptcy of Enron Corp. in December 2001, made members leery of taking action that could be seen as a handout to business. The bill remained stalled through the spring. Daschle refused to bring a version to the floor that included a ban on punitive damages, and Phil Gramm, R-Texas, and other Republicans refused to let him bring up a bill that did not.

But a retooled lobbying campaign led by real estate interests, along with the direct and sustained involvement of the president, turned the situation around.

Because most state regulators allowed insurers to eliminate terrorism coverage from their policies, the commercial real estate industry faced skyrocketing insurance rates and scarce terrorism coverage. Real estate lobbyists swung into action, redefining the bill as essential to keep commercial construction going and shore up the faltering economy. Bush touted the bill as critical to his efforts to jumpstart the economy, saying the lack of terrorism risk insurance had caused wary firms to forgo $15 billion in construction projects costing 300,000 jobs. While the numbers were disputed by consumer groups, business lobbyists worked to convince Democrats that a bill was needed.

On June 18, the Senate voted to invoke cloture on a terrorism insurance bill (S 2600) sponsored by Christopher J. Dodd, D-Conn. Under the bill, lawsuits involving losses or injuries caused by acts of terrorism would have to be considered in federal court. Punitive damages would not be covered by the federal program.

Democratic leaders enlisted the White House to win the cloture vote at the expense of GOP leaders, who wanted their rank and file to have the option of offering additional amendments. The vote for cloture was 65–31, five more than the required minimum; seventeen Republicans voted "yea."

The Senate then passed S 2600 by a **key vote of 84–14 (R 34–14; D 49–0; I 1–0)**. Subsequently, in order to go to conference, the Senate agreed July 25 to insert the text into HR 3210. *(2002 key votes, p. 819)*

The Senate-passed bill covered one year, with a possible extension for one more. The federal government would cover 80 percent of insured losses below $10 billion and 90 percent of total losses that exceeded $10 billion. Federal assistance would be capped at $100 billion. Each insurer would have to satisfy a deductible based on its market share before receiving assistance. The federal assistance would not have to be paid back.

During debate on the bill, the Senate also:

• Agreed 50–46 on June 13 to table (kill) an amendment by Mitch McConnell, R-Ky., that would have prohibited punitive damages unless a defendant was convicted of a criminal offense related to the plaintiff's injury.

• Agreed 70–24 on June 13 to table an amendment by Bill Nelson, D-Fla., that would have regulated terrorism insurance premiums.

• Adopted 81–3 on June 14 an amendment by George Allen, R-Va., to allow victims of terrorism to recover damages from the frozen assets of terrorists, terrorist organizations, or state sponsors of terrorist acts.

CONFERENCE, FINAL ACTION

House-Senate negotiations on a final bill did not begin in earnest until well after the August recess. The final agreement was struck Oct. 17, after many in Congress had left for the campaign trail, pushing final action into the lame-duck session after the November congressional elections. The House adopted the conference report (H Rept 107-779) by voice vote Nov. 14. The Senate cleared the bill 86–11 on Nov. 19.

Negotiations had sputtered until Oct. 16, when the White House, in a startling reversal, agreed to discard the provision on punitive damages. Ultimately, the administration decided it was better to back away from the provision than to end up with language that could undercut existing legal standards in states that either banned punitive damages or had caps on such awards.

Like both the House and Senate versions of the bill, the conference agreement required that civil lawsuits related to terrorism be consolidated in federal courts, a win for the "tort reform" movement, which argued that it would prevent venue-shopping by plaintiffs' attorneys in state courts. *(Tort reform, pp. 591, 608, 610)*

House GOP leaders, particularly Majority Whip Tom DeLay of Texas, were sufficiently irritated with the White House for cutting a bilateral deal with Daschle and his Senate Democratic allies that they kept Bush waiting until very near the end of the 107th Congress before agreeing to adopt the conference report. Many of them mulled whether to let the bill die in favor of trying again in the next Congress, when the GOP would control both chambers. But Bush relentlessly pushed Republican leaders to drop their opposition, promising to champion a conservative tort reform agenda in the 108th Congress to set broad new limits on civil litigation.

The bill faced one last obstacle. Gramm refused to allow a final vote until the Senate had passed a bill (HR 5005—PL 107-296) to create a cabinet-level Department of Homeland Security. That made the vote to clear the terrorism insurance bill the second to last Senate roll call vote of the 107th Congress.

MAJOR PROVISIONS

As signed into law Nov. 26, 2002, HR 3210 (PL 107-297):

Federal Safety Net

Required the federal government to pay 90 percent of claims arising from terrorist attacks once industry-wide insured losses exceeded a trigger level of $10 billion in 2003, $12.5 billion in 2004, and $15 billion in 2005. Capped losses covered by the program at $100 billion per year for the industry as a whole.

Allowed an individual company to qualify for aid before the industry-wide threshold was reached if its terrorism losses exceeded a certain percentage of the company's premiums. Set the threshold—essentially a deductible—at 7 percent in 2003, 10 percent in 2004, and 15 percent in 2005. (The company was responsible for 100 percent of losses up to those thresholds.)

Made government aid that was paid out after an insurance company met its deductible but before the larger industry-wide threshold was reached subject to repayment by commercial policyholders.

Specified that once the $100 billion cap was met no further federal funds would be provided and insurers that had covered their deductible for the year would not be required to cover any additional losses.

Terrorism Lawsuits

Required that all civil lawsuits arising from a terrorist attack be grouped together and considered in federal, rather than state, court. Specified that amounts awarded as punitive damages in such cases would not count as insured losses under the federal program.

Terrorism Coverage

Voided any state actions that exempted insurance companies from providing terrorism coverage. (As a result, upon enactment, all existing commercial property and casualty policies provided terrorism coverage. Insurers were expected to immediately send out notices of increased premiums for such coverage.)

Bioterrorism

Amid mounting concerns over bioterrorism, Congress in 2002 cleared a bill (HR 3448—PL 107-188) authorizing $4.2 billion in fiscal 2003 and additional amounts in future years to help federal, state, and local governments prepare for and respond to biological attacks and other public health emergencies.

The bill authorized increases in the nation's stockpiles of medicines and vaccines, expansion of facilities and labs run by the Centers for Disease Control and Prevention (CDC), tighter controls on biological agents, and steps to safeguard the nation's food and water supplies. It also reauthorized drug company user fees to speed Food and Drug Administration (FDA) review and approval of new drugs.

BACKGROUND

Lawmakers introduced bills in 2001 out of concern that the nation's public health system was unprepared to handle a major bioterror attack. Federal and local officials had trouble dealing with a handful of anthrax cases in Florida, New York, Connecticut, and Washington, D.C. A House and a Senate office building were temporarily closed after some lawmakers received tainted mail. Five people died following exposure to anthrax, most likely sent through the mail. *(Capitol anthrax attack, p. 712)*

Congress appropriated $2.5 billion for bioterrorism programs in fiscal 2002 without waiting for the separate authorization bill. The money, to buy more vaccines and antibiotics and to improve public health facilities, was provided as part of a supplemental spending package tied to the fiscal 2002 defense appropriations bill (HR 3338—PL 107-117).

But authorizers pressed ahead, saying their bill was necessary to provide clear guidance and legal certainty to federal and state governments. Lobbyists also warned that the authorization bill would be important for such matters as providing incentives for pharmaceutical companies researching new vaccines or drugs to treat toxins.

Edward M. Kennedy, D-Mass., chair of the Senate Health, Education, Labor, and Pensions Committee, and Bill Frist of Tennessee, ranking Republican on the Public Safety Subcommittee, introduced a bill in mid-November 2001, but they were unable to get it to the floor until immediately before adjournment. Frustrated by the slow pace in the Senate, the House passed a $2.9 billion bioterrorism bill (HR 3448) under suspension of the rules Dec. 12. The vote was 418–2. The measure was drafted by Billy Tauzin, chair of the House Energy and Commerce Committee, and John D. Dingell of Michigan, the panel's ranking Democrat.

The Senate passed the bill by voice vote Dec. 20, the last day of the session, after substituting the text of its own $3.2 billion measure (S 1765). Kennedy and Frist had spent more than a month working out the details. Kennedy originally wanted to invest $10 billion in preparations for bioterrorism but reduced his request to $3.2 billion in the interest of prompt floor action.

Both the House and Senate bills included provisions authorizing funds for the accelerated production of smallpox vaccine, as well as antibiotics and other medicines to combat bioterrorism. Both called for grants to states, local governments, and public health departments to prepare for health emergencies. Both authorized aid to hospitals, the CDC, public health networks, and food safety programs.

The House bill was somewhat narrower than the Senate version. One of the biggest differences was that it did not include a number of the Senate food import restrictions, which were opposed by the food industry. The Senate also included a provision, opposed by Dingell, to give drug companies a limited antitrust exemption so they could collaborate on drugs to prevent and fight a biological attack. Another controversial Senate provision gave companies accelerated approval of drugs by allowing them to use expedited research procedures with animals. Critics worried that such abbreviated research could compromise safety.

The House bill, unlike the Senate's, authorized funds to improve the safety of public water supplies.

CONFERENCE, FINAL ACTION

After weeks of quiet staff work, House and Senate conferees agreed on a final bill. The House adopted the conference report (H Rept 107-481) by a vote of 425–1 on May 22, and the Senate cleared the bill 98–0 the next day.

The biggest change agreed to in conference was the addition of FDA user fee provisions to allow the FDA to hire additional employees to review new pharmaceutical products. User fee supporters settled on the bill as the best way to renew the fees, created in 1992 (PL 102-571), before they expired Sept. 30. *(Congress and the Nation Vol. VIII, p. 603)*

Conferees dropped the Senate provision that would have given antitrust exemptions to drugmakers preparing to provide critical vaccines. They also dropped a Senate proposal that wastewater treatment plants be required to report to the Environmental Protection Agency (EPA) on safety plans and assessments of vulnerability to terrorism. Democrats tried but failed to include language codifying an FDA rule that required drugmakers to conduct separate pediatric safety tests for drugs prescribed for both adults and children. *(Pediatric drugs, p. 489)*

The final bill authorized $300 million per year in fiscal 2002 and 2003 to upgrade and expand CDC facilities. The House bill had included $300 million; the Senate included just under $120 million.

MAJOR PROVISIONS

As signed into law June 12, 2002, HR 3448 (PL 107-188):

Emergency Medical Stockpiles

Authorized $1.2 billion in fiscal 2002, and unspecified sums in succeeding years, for the Department of Health and Human Services (HHS) to expand stockpiles of vaccines, medicines, and other supplies. The total included $509 million to purchase additional smallpox vaccines.

State and Local Preparedness

Authorized $1.6 billion in fiscal 2003, and unspecified amounts in fiscal 2004 through 2006, for grants to states, local governments, and public and private health care facilities to improve planning and preparedness, increase laboratory capacity, train health care personnel, and develop new drugs, therapies, and vaccines. Set aside a total of $520 million for state grants to help hospitals and other health facilities prepare for biological attacks.

Biological Agents

Tightened controls on the possession and handling of dangerous biological agents and toxins. Directed HHS to establish a comprehensive national database on every individual who possessed, used, or transferred certain dangerous toxins or agents, such as anthrax and smallpox. Gave similar authority to the Agriculture Department to regulate agents that could threaten crops or farm animals.

Food Safety

Authorized $100 million in fiscal 2002, and unspecified sums in fiscal 2003 through 2006, to improve food safety efforts, particularly at ports of entry, with special emphasis on detecting the intentional adulteration of food. Authorized the FDA to hold food items for up to thirty days if there was credible evidence that they posed a serious health threat to humans or animals. Required food importers to provide the FDA with details about food shipments before they arrived at a U.S. port of entry and allowed entry of the food to be blocked if notice was not provided.

Drug Imports

Required foreign manufacturers to register annually before being allowed to import drugs and medical devices into the United States.

Drinking Water Safety

Authorized $160 million in fiscal 2002, and unspecified sums in succeeding years, to protect the safety of drinking water systems. Required drinking water systems across the country to provide the EPA with assessments of their vulnerability to terrorist attacks and to develop emergency plans to prepare for and respond to such attacks.

Prescription Drug User Fees

Reauthorized the FDA's user fee program for prescription drug manufacturers through fiscal 2007 and specified the fees should generate a total of $1.2 billion over five years. The funds were to be used by the FDA to review new drugs for safety and effectiveness and to enhance the safety review of drugs already on the market.

Border Security

Congress in 2002 cleared legislation (HR 3525—PL 107-173) designed to tighten U.S. border security and prevent terrorists from entering the country while also making it harder for aliens to overstay their visas without detection. The border bill was a response to the many weaknesses in the immigration system revealed by the Sept. 11, 2001, terrorist attacks. One of the suspected hijackers who died in the attacks, for example, had come into the United States as a student but never attended classes, a fact the school had not reported to the government.

Lawmakers took pains to stress that their goal was to catch terrorists, not to stem the flow of legal immigrants from Mexico and elsewhere. But provisions that would have made it easier for thousands of illegal immigrants to apply for legal residency were dropped from the bill.

LEGISLATIVE ACTION

The House passed HR 3525 by voice vote Dec. 19, 2001. Although it was introduced by Judiciary Committee Chair F. James Sensenbrenner Jr., R-Wis., it was not marked up by his committee.

The bill was expected to sail through the Senate in the first session. But Robert C. Byrd, D-W.Va., put a hold on the measure, saying it was so sweeping and would authorize so much new spending that members should have time to debate it and offer amendments.

In an effort to prod Senate action on border security, the House agreed 275–137 on March 12, 2002, to attach the provisions to a visa extension bill (HR 1885) and send the package to the Senate. That only seemed to complicate efforts. Byrd warned that he would continue to object to leadership attempts to bring up the bill under a unanimous consent agreement that allowed no amendments or debate.

However, pressure was building in the Senate to break the logjam. "The longer we wait to send this bill to the president . . . the longer it will take for our nation's border and visa procedures to be made more secure," sponsors warned in a letter to Majority Leader Tom Daschle, D-S.D.

Bowing to Byrd, Senate leaders brought HR 3525 to the floor April 18. Byrd won several changes, including a delay in the deadlines for some of the security requirements and more stringent penalties on schools that failed to adequately track their foreign students. The Senate then passed the amended bill 97–0.

After securing Senate agreement to drop one provision, the House accepted the Senate changes May 8, clearing the bill 411–0. The disputed provision would have permitted the attorney general to circumvent the normal bidding process in developing the computer database—called Chimera—that federal agents would use to screen visa applications. The Senate adopted a resolution May 8 striking the language.

MAJOR PROVISIONS

As signed into law May 14, 2002, HR 3525 (PL 107-173):

Border Controls

Additional inspectors. Authorized the Immigration and Naturalization Service (INS) to hire an additional 200 inspectors and 200 investigative personnel each year for five years, beginning in fiscal 2002.

Computer upgrades. Authorized $150 million for technology upgrades at INS inspection facilities. The money was for upgrading old computer systems and buying electronic scanners to check travel documents, such as visas and passports.

Salary increases. Authorized higher wages for INS border patrol agents and inspection assistants.

Training. Required INS officers to get ongoing training.

Visa System

Temporary visas. Prohibited the issuance of temporary visas for business or travel to citizens of countries judged to be state sponsors of terrorism, unless it was determined that the individual was not a security risk. Seven nations—Iran, Iraq, Syria, Libya, Cuba, North Korea, and Sudan—were classified as state sponsors of terrorism.

Student visas. Required schools that admitted foreign students to track the students' participation and notify the government of any who did not show up for classes. Schools that failed to comply with the reporting requirements would lose the right to accept foreign students.

Required universities and other institutions certified to receive foreign students to be reviewed every two years by the education secretary, the secretary of state, and the INS commissioner.

Chimera terrorist database. Mandated the establishment of a government-wide, electronic data-sharing system on persons with terrorist ties that could be used by federal officials to conduct more thorough background checks of people trying to enter the United States. The system, known as Chimera, was to include the names of suspected terrorists and other information from a wide variety of agencies, including the Federal Bureau of Investigation (FBI). The president was given responsibility for forming a nine-member federal commission to monitor the database and report annually to Congress.

Directed U.S. consular offices and embassies to form committees to watch for suspected terrorists and make sure their names were entered into the Chimera system.

Travel Documents and Manifests

Stolen passports. Required countries that participated in the Visa Waiver Program to inform U.S. officials about thefts of blank passports. The waiver program allowed citizens from a select group of mostly industrialized countries to enter the United States for short visits for business or pleasure without having to get a visa. The attorney general or the secretary of state could bar a country from the program for failing to report passport thefts.

High-tech visas. Required the State Department, beginning Oct. 26, 2003, to issue only machine-readable, tamper-resistant visas that included biometric identifiers, such as fingerprints. Biometric scanners to read these passports had to be installed at all U.S. ports of entry by that date.

Required all nations participating in the Visa Waiver Program to issue passports with the same high-tech features by that date.

Passenger manifests. Required all commercial airlines and vessels entering or leaving the United States to supply immigration officials with manifests listing all passengers and crew. By 2003 the manifests had to be in an electronic format. Airplanes or ships that failed to comply with the rule would be fined $1,000.

Port Security

Congress in 2002 cleared a port security bill (S 1214—PL 107-295) that for the first time required a comprehensive antiterrorism plan for the nation's 361 commercial seaports. It also expanded and formalized the preeminent role in port security assumed by the Coast Guard following the Sept. 11, 2001, terrorist attacks.

However, the new law's impact on the safety of U.S. maritime commerce seemed likely to be limited by a lack of money. Lawmakers could not agree on how to come up with an estimated $4 billion over six years to pay for the improvements and left the funding, instead, to the Bush administration and the next Congress.

BACKGROUND

Well before the Sept. 11 attacks, U.S. officials were concerned about the vulnerability of busy commercial seaports to terrorism. About 2 percent of the 6 million cargo containers entering the country each year were inspected; a month after the terrorist attacks, a suspected member of the terrorist organization al Qaeda was caught trying to travel from Italy to Canada in a container.

As Ernest F. Hollings, D-S.C., chair of the Senate Commerce, Science, and Transportation Committee, pointed out, sea and river ports handled about 95 percent of U.S. international trade, with large containers from ships loaded directly onto trucks and rail cars that immediately headed onto highways and rail systems. He called the lack of container inspections "a gaping hole in our national security that must be fixed."

Before Sept. 11, the Coast Guard, whose mission ranged from boating safety and drug interdiction to law enforcement and military activity, was planning to spend only about 14 percent of its resources on port safety and security. The lion's share of its $5.4 billion fiscal 2002 budget was to have gone to drug interdiction, fisheries enforcement, and search and rescue.

Immediately after the terrorist attacks, the Coast Guard reoriented its priorities to put 58 percent of its resources into port security and cut back on other missions. Cutters and smaller patrol boats that protected against poaching by foreign fishing trawlers in the days before the attacks were redeployed to guard key waterways, such as New York Harbor and the Los Angeles–Long Beach port complex. Reservists were summoned to duty in several harbors.

The Coast Guard also worked with local port police on a sea marshal program under which armed personnel boarded suspicious ships, interviewed crews, reviewed cargo manifests, and then escorted the ships into harbor. Special attention was paid to cruise ships or vessels carrying hazardous cargo, such as natural gas, and ships from the Middle East. In addition, the Coast Guard established a half-dozen intelligence centers to analyze happenings on the high seas that could compromise U.S. security.

SENATE ACTION

The Senate maritime security bill (S 1214), passed by voice vote on Dec. 20, 2001, had been drafted in July, before the terrorist attacks had made homeland security a top government priority. The aim was to establish a coordinated national policy to protect seaports from crime and terrorism.

Sponsored by Hollings, S 1214 was approved by his committee on Aug. 2 and reported Sept. 14 (S Rept 107-64). The bill:

• Required the Coast Guard to evaluate the vulnerability of the nation's fifty most important ports.

• Called for national and local committees to upgrade port security and coordinate federal, state, and local responses to security threats.

• Authorized $3.3 billion in loan guarantees and grants for improving port security infrastructure, as well as $1.1 billion over six years for additional Customs Service personnel, better training, and security improvements such as dockside cameras and guard dogs.

• Required vessels to provide electronic cargo manifest and crew information before arriving in a U.S. port.

• Called for an extension of tonnage duties through 2006 on cargo entering or leaving U.S. ports, with up to $59 million annually to be used to help pay for stepped-up security measures.

HOUSE ACTION

The House passed S 1214 by voice vote June 4, 2002, after substituting the text of its own bill (HR 3983—H Rept 107-405). The Transportation and Infrastructure Committee had approved the bill by voice vote March 20 and reported it April 11.

The measure, sponsored by committee chair Don Young, R-Alaska, authorized $83 million per year in grants for port security improvements in fiscal 2003 through 2005 and required the creation of a comprehensive maritime antiterrorism plan. The bill:

• Required the Coast Guard to conduct vulnerability assessments of U.S. ports and use the results to plan and implement national, state, and local security plans.

• Required the Coast Guard to evaluate security systems in certain foreign ports and to deny entry to vessels coming from foreign ports that did not maintain effective security.

• Authorized the transportation secretary to issue port security cards, which could only be denied if an individual was found to be a terrorist risk.

• Required the Transportation Security Administration to develop an antiterrorism identification and screening system for containerized cargo going into and out of the United States through a foreign port. The bill also required new standards for containers and locks.

• Authorized $4.2 billion for the Coast Guard in fiscal 2002. The House had passed this as a separate bill (HR 3507) on Dec. 20, 2001, but the Senate never acted on it.

• Established antiterrorism teams to patrol U.S. waters, authorize Coast Guard sea marshals to prevent or respond to terrorist threats in ports and aboard vessels, and continue a practice begun in late 2001 that required all captains of arriving vessels to give the Coast Guard ninety-six hours' notice before entering a twelve-mile "security zone." Commercial vessel operators would have to provide a manifest of passengers and crew members.

CONFERENCE, FINAL ACTION

Final agreement was delayed for months as Republicans objected to a proposal by Hollings for a user fee on cargo and passengers coming in and out of U.S. ports that would have raised an estimated $700 million a year. Senate Minority Leader Trent Lott, R-Miss., House Ways and Means Committee Chair Bill Thomas, R-Calif., and others attacked it as a new tax and an unnecessary burden on trade. Shipping companies and manufacturers lobbied heavily against it, and Thomas and Young insisted that port security funding should come from general revenue.

House and Senate conferees were able to reach a tentative deal in October only after Hollings relented and dropped the proposed fees. The final bill required the administration to submit a funding plan to address port security vulnerabilities within six months of enactment.

Hollings said that he proposed a new cargo fee and an extension of Customs Service tonnage duties because he doubted that Congress would be able to make room for port security programs in the fiscal 2003 budget.

Another barrier to Hollings's proposal was the constitutional requirement that all revenue bills originate in the House. Had the bill included the cargo tonnage duty, it would have been subject to a "blue slip" referring the entire measure to the Ways and Means Committee.

Conferees also faced a protracted, though less publicized, dispute over background checks for dockworkers. The Senate bill listed specific crimes for which workers could be denied security credentials, but the International Longshore and Warehouse Union objected. The House version did not list specific crimes. Conferees eventually agreed to leave it to the transportation secretary to decide who would receive credentials, which would be in the form of a transportation worker identity card.

The Senate adopted the conference report (H Rept 107-777) by a vote of 95–0 on Nov. 14, during the post-election lame-duck session. The House cleared the bill by voice vote the same day.

MAJOR PROVISIONS

As signed into law on Nov. 25, 2002, S 1214 (PL 107-295) included the following main provisions. Most tasks assigned to the Department of Transportation were expected to shift to the new Homeland Security Department, which was taking over responsibility for the Coast Guard.

Antiterrorism Planning

Required the Coast Guard to conduct vulnerability assessments of U.S. ports, vessels, and other shoreline facilities, such as nuclear power plants or chemical facilities, that were vulnerable to attack. The assessments were to be used to develop and implement local and national security plans as well as customized plans for specific facilities and vessels.

Response Teams

Directed the Coast Guard to establish maritime safety and security teams that could be deployed rapidly in the event of terrorist threats or criminal actions against vessels, ports, facilities, or cargo in U.S. waters.

Authorized armed Coast Guard personnel to act as "sea marshals," boarding incoming vessels to prevent or respond to acts of terrorism.

Antiterrorism Grants

Created a new grant program through fiscal 2008 to assist ports, as well as state and local governments, in upgrading port security.

Authorized $15 million a year through fiscal 2008 for research and development of technologies to help the Customs Service target suspicious cargo and detect explosives, chemical and biological agents, and nuclear materials.

Authorized $5.5 million a year to train maritime security workers.

Security Cards

Directed the Transportation Department to develop and issue a new, national transportation security card that would allow eligible port workers, merchant mariners, and truck drivers to work in "secure" areas of ports and other transportation facilities.

Foreign Port Assessments

Required the Coast Guard to assess security measures at certain foreign ports and authorized it to bar vessels from entering U.S. ports if they came from a foreign port that failed to meet security standards.

Container and Cargo Security

Required the Transportation Department to develop and maintain an antiterrorism cargo identification, tracking, and screening system for containerized cargo shipped through U.S. ports.

Authorized the Customs Service to require shippers to provide advance electronic information on cargo being shipped to or from the United States.

Intelligence

Authorized the Transportation Department to establish a maritime intelligence program to collect and analyze information concerning any vessel operating in U.S. waters in order to evaluate potential threats.

U.S. Territorial Limits

Extended the U.S. territorial sea from three miles offshore to twelve miles.

Tracking System

Required most commercial vessels, including passenger vessels, operating in U.S. waters to be equipped with transponders that identified the vessel and its location. Directed the Transportation Department to establish a long-range vessel tracking system using satellite technologies.

Coast Guard Authorization

Authorized a total of $6 billion for Coast Guard–related expenses in fiscal 2003, including $4.3 billion for the operation and maintenance of the Coast Guard. (It was the first time the Coast Guard had been authorized since 1998.)

INS Abolished

The Immigration and Naturalization Service (INS), long a target of congressional criticism, was abolished under the 2002 law that created the new Department of Homeland Security (HR 5005—PL 107-296). It was replaced with two separate bureaus in the new department—one to handle immigration services, the other to protect the borders and keep out illegal immigrants. (*Homeland Security Department, p. 176*)

Congress had sought for decades to reinvent the troubled agency, which was charged with the sometimes conflicting missions of tracking down and deporting those in the United States illegally, while assisting legal immigrants to work their way through the cumbersome process to become citizens. Complaints of mismanagement, ineffective border control, and a growing backlog of immigrant applications and petitions were common.

In the early 1990s Congress established the U.S. Commission on Immigration Reform to review and evaluate the immigration system. In 1997, the commission, chaired by former Rep. Barbara Jordan, D-Texas (1973–1979), recommended that the federal immigration system be fundamentally restructured, including the dismantling of the INS. The commission found that the INS suffered from conflicting priorities and mission overload, and that its service and enforcement missions were incompatible.

While the Clinton administration agreed with the commission's findings on INS management problems, it rejected the recommendation to abolish the agency. Instead, it proposed to restructure the INS by separating immigration and enforcement functions. However, the plan was never aggressively pursued.

Bills introduced in the 105th and 106th Congresses offered a variety of approaches for restructuring the INS, including dismantling the agency, but none went beyond the subcommittee level.

Congress substantially increased the INS budget—from $1.4 billion in fiscal 1992 to $5.6 billion in fiscal 2002—in hopes of improving the agency's performance. However, the problems continued, particularly in processing immigration applications, along with the agency's inability to stem the flow of undocumented workers and to track workers, students, and visitors once they arrived in the country.

House Judiciary Committee Chair F. James Sensenbrenner Jr., R-Wis., made overhauling the agency a priority in the 107th Congress, and he was joined by Attorney General John Ashcroft, who in 2001 announced an administration plan to restructure the agency. The House passed a bill to split the INS (HR 3231—H Rept 107-413) by a vote of 405–9 on April 25, 2002.

The Senate did not act on the separate INS restructuring bill because just as that chamber was preparing to enter the INS debate, the Bush administration decided to include immigration functions in the new Homeland Security Department.

Both the House bill and the administration proposal called for abolishing the INS and dividing it into separate bureaus to guard the borders and to handle immigration services. What they did not agree on was how the top of the new agency would be structured. The administration wanted a strong central figure to oversee immigration; Sensenbrenner wanted to give more authority to those in charge of the two bureaus.

Under the homeland security bill, it appeared there would be no strong, central immigration figure except the attorney general. INS immigration services were turned over to the Bureau of Citizenship and Immigration Services, which reported to the deputy secretary of homeland security. The bureau was directed to develop pilot programs to eliminate the backlog of immigrant-related paperwork such as green cards.

INS enforcement operations—including the Border Patrol, inspections, investigations, intelligence, and detention and removal—were absorbed by the Bureau of Border Security in the Border and Transportation Division.

Antiterrorism Treaties

Congress in 2002 sent President George W. Bush a bill to implement two international treaties aimed at cracking down on terrorists and their financial backers. The measure was signed into law June 25 (HR 3275—PL 107-197).

The bill updated U.S. law to comply with the International Convention for the Suppression of Terrorist Bombings (Treaty Doc 106-6) and the International Convention for the Suppression of the Financing of Terrorism (Treaty Doc 106-49). The Senate had approved the ratification of those accords Dec. 5, 2001.

The House Judiciary Committee reported HR 3275 (H Rept 107-307) on Nov. 29, 2001, and the House passed it Dec. 19 by a vote of 381–36. The Senate passed it 83–1 on June 14, 2002, after making several changes.

Under the revised bill, prosecutors could seek the death penalty for terrorist bombings, but only on the more limited grounds outlined in a law that prohibited the use of weapons of mass destruction. The original bill would have extended the death penalty to any individual guilty of violating the new statute. The amended bill also required prosecutors to show that a suspect knew he or she was helping to fund terrorists, a requirement lacking in the original House bill. The

House agreed to the changes by voice vote June 18, clearing the bill.

Nuclear, Chemical Industries

The Senate Environment and Public Works Committee in 2002, concerned about potential terrorist strikes, approved two Democratic-authored bills meant to protect two vulnerable industries: nuclear power and chemical manufacturing. Neither bill advanced further.

One measure (S 1602) required chemical companies to examine their plants for security flaws and then draft plans to respond to the flaws. Those that did not provide plans to the Environmental Protection Agency (EPA) and the White House Office of Homeland Security could be ordered to by the EPA or the Justice Department. S 1602 was reported (S Rept 107-342) on Nov. 15, 2002.

The other bill (S 1746) required more safeguards at nuclear facilities such as commercial power plants, spent fuel storage sites, and decommissioned reactor plants. As reported on Nov. 12, S 1746 (S Rept 107-335) required the Nuclear Regulatory Commission (NRC) to revise security plans for nuclear facilities in order to take into consideration threats "equivalent to the events of Sept. 11, 2001" and other potential assaults such as computer network attacks. Officials had to examine potential weaknesses in security, including standards affecting worker hiring and training, plant security plans, and emergency response plans. If an attack did occur, the bill required that stockpiles of potassium iodide tablets—which can lessen the health effects of massive releases of radiation—be distributed at public places, such as schools and hospitals, within fifty miles of each reactor.

The chemical industry opposed S 1602 because of its mandates and criminal penalties against those who did not adequately protect chemicals. The nuclear facility bill also drew criticism. Nuclear Regulatory Commissioner Edward McGaffigan Jr., who was appointed during the Clinton administration, expressed concerns that S 1746 was unnecessary and a burden for his agency.

The bills were written by Democratic senators worried about the security of industries that affected their states. The chemical plant bill was sponsored by Jon Corzine of New Jersey, and the nuclear measure by Majority Whip Harry Reid of Nevada—the location of Yucca Mountain, which had been designated the nation's permanent repository of high-level nuclear waste.

2003–2004

The pace of legislative action on homeland security measures slowed considerably in the 108th Congress after the dramatic legislative agreements of the previous Congress. Concerns over terrorist threats often took a backseat to partisan rivalries and parochial issues. In addition, lawmakers became wary of the growing power of the executive branch over antiterrorism initiatives, and they took several steps to reassert their influence.

The homeland security agenda was cast in the shadow of the war in Iraq and the recommendations of the independent Sept. 11 commission on revamping the nation's intelligence agencies. President George W. Bush viewed Iraq as the central front in the global struggle against terrorism and found himself on the defensive when an Iraqi insurgency began taking an unexpected toll on U.S. troops. While the administration believed the toppling of Iraqi leader Saddam Hussein was critical to protecting the United States from terrorists, others—including such influential lawmakers as Bob Graham of Florida, the ranking Democrat on the Senate Intelligence Committee—worried that the war instead would inflame anti-American sentiment and divert resources from the battle against al Qaeda, the terrorist network behind the Sept. 11, 2001, attacks. *(Iraq war, pp. 231, 238; Afghanistan war, pp. 230, 234)*

The Sept. 11 commission released its much-anticipated report in 2004. It faulted both the Clinton and Bush administrations, as well as Congress, for failing to take adequate steps against terrorism before the attacks. The commission report spurred legislators at the end of the 108th Congress to clear a massive restructuring of intelligence agencies (S 2845—PL 107-458). The law also contained a number of homeland security measures, including provisions to strengthen aviation security and disrupt financing for terrorism. *(Sept. 11 investigations, summary p. 180; details, p. 275; intelligence reorganization, p. 263)*

In terms of legislation that focused strictly on homeland security, the 108th Congress had a modest output. One of its major accomplishments was the passage of Project Bioshield, a White House–based initiative to develop vaccines and medications that would be vital in the event of a bioterrorism attack. The legislation was largely noncontroversial, but the bill became snagged for months because of a dispute over whether to make the program funding mandatory or to place it under the annual control of the appropriations process.

Congress had less success revamping the system by which homeland security grants were apportioned to states. Several influential lawmakers wanted to channel more money to urban areas such as New York that faced a high risk of a terrorist attack instead of continuing with a formula that gave every state a minimum percentage of the grants regardless of whether that state appeared to be a terrorist target. The Sept. 11 commission also proposed overhauling the formula. But legislation to revamp the formula stalled, partly because of regional divisions.

Lawmakers also clashed over plans to centralize congressional oversight of homeland security. Leaders in both the House and Senate took steps to create homeland security committees with considerable sway, a change that was recommended by the Sept. 11 commission. But in a series of jurisdictional turf battles, chairs of rival committees undermined the influence of the new panels.

Homeland security provoked several funding battles. Democrats pressed to appropriate more money for such items as emergency response teams and nonaviation transportation security than either the White House or GOP leaders were willing to accept. The appropriations bills also served as a battleground between Congress and the administration, as lawmakers refused to give the White House broad leeway over spending, and it tried to impose stricter accountability over the Homeland Security Department. During debate on the fiscal 2004 Commerce, Justice, and State appropriations bill (HR 2799), the House also voted to nullify a key provision of the controversial USA PATRIOT Act, a strong indication of mounting unease on both sides of the aisle over the law's impact on civil liberties. But the amendment was removed in conference negotiations.

Project Bioshield

After a tortuous year-long journey, legislation (S 15—PL 108-276) authorizing Project Bioshield, the Bush administration's ten-year initiative to develop and stockpile vaccines and medications to combat a bioterrorist attack, cleared Congress in 2004.

President George W. Bush originally announced the effort in his 2003 State of the Union Address. It was an attempt to encourage biotech and drug companies to develop antidotes to biological weapons, such as anthrax, smallpox, Ebola, and bubonic plague. Without a federal program, there was little market for such products and little incentive for companies to spend the time and money needed to develop them. Related legislation (HR 3448—PL 107-188) on a national stockpile of medicine and vaccines had been enacted in 2002. *(Details, pp. 477, 514)*

Members in both chambers generally agreed that shortcuts in regulatory procedures were justified in light of the potential catastrophe of a biological attack. The anthrax attacks in the fall of 2001 brought bioterrorism directly to Capitol Hill. The 2003 outbreak of severe acute respiratory syndrome (SARS) further reminded Congress that deadly afflictions were capable of spreading quickly. *(Anthrax attacks, p. 712)*

"There's probably nothing more important than this," said House Energy and Commerce Committee Chair Billy Tauzin, R-La. "We're not just talking about threats that could affect America. We're talking about threats that could eliminate human life on the globe."

Representatives Mike Pence, R-Ind.,
(with report), Carolyn B. Maloney,
D-N.Y., and Christopher Shays,
R-Conn., led a bipartisan group of
House members pushing for quick
action on the *9/11 Commission
Report* after its July 22, 2004, release.
*Source: Congressional
Quarterly/Scott J. Ferrell*

Bush said the government needed mandatory, open-ended funding to get the program started. The administration also asked for expedited review and procurement procedures to get research, development, and production going on high-priority drugs and vaccines; a permanent funding stream to guarantee companies a market for the new products; and the authority to allow emergency use of promising, but unapproved, drugs and treatments for bioterrorist attacks.

The House acted quickly, approving an authorization bill in July 2003, but Bush's proposal bogged down in the Senate over whether to provide guaranteed funding.

Robert C. Byrd of West Virginia, ranking Democrat on the Senate Appropriations Committee, blocked floor action on a Senate bill, saying that putting the funding outside the annual control of the appropriators would undermine Congress's ability to oversee the program.

In the meantime, with the legislation stalled, Congress nevertheless provided $890 million in discretionary funds for the initiative under the fiscal 2004 spending bill for the Department of Homeland Security (HR 2555—PL 108-90), which was signed Oct. 1, 2003. The money was part of a $5.6 billion advance appropriation available through fiscal 2013. But authorizing language was still necessary to set program parameters and future funding levels.

The impasse on the authorization was not broken until the spring of 2004, when Senate Budget Committee Chair Don Nickles, R-Okla., worked out a funding compromise with Byrd.

LEGISLATIVE ACTION

The Senate actually acted first, with the Health, Education, Labor, and Pensions (HELP) Committee voting 21–0 on March 19, 2003, to approve a bill (S 15) that reflected Bush's proposal. The original bill also included provisions to

compensate health and emergency workers who suffered complications from receiving smallpox vaccinations, but the committee could not agree on the terms and that part of the bill was dropped. The vaccine compensation subsequently cleared as a separate bill (HR 1770—PL 108-20). *(Smallpox, p. 515)*

S 15 was formally reported March 25 (no written report). But before floor debate could begin, Byrd put a hold on the bill because of his opposition to the mandatory funding.

Trying to find a middle ground the House Energy and Commerce Committee approved its version of the bill (HR 2122—H Rept 108-147, Part 1) by voice vote May 15 and reported it June 10, after reaching an agreement with House appropriators on a hybrid funding mechanism. The funding—$5.6 billion over ten years—was designated as discretionary, giving appropriators authority over the money. The appropriators agreed to provide the entire amount as a ten-year advance appropriation to be put into a special reserve fund that could be tapped once the White House agreed that a treatment should be added to the nation's stockpile.

"It's a guaranteed stream of funding, but [with] annual congressional oversight," said Harold Rogers, R-Ky., chair of the House Appropriations Subcommittee on Homeland Security and a member of the House Select Committee on Homeland Security.

The administration could tap $890 million of the money in fiscal 2004 and $3.4 billion through fiscal 2008. After that, it would gain more discretion over how much was spent and when. Congress could still block funds by passing legislation to rescind them, although such a prospect was unlikely. The money could be used for drugs, devices, and other products that could reasonably be expected to be delivered within five years; it could not be used for research and development, administrative costs, or procurement of vaccines under contracts entered into before the bill's enactment. It was an unusual assertion of congressional power over a national security matter. "We're trying to give [the White House] as much as we can without surrendering," Tauzin said.

Subsequently, two other committees took up the bill. The House Government Reform Committee agreed May 22 to minor modifications to the contracting language and reported it June 12 (H Rept 108-147, Part 2). The Homeland Security panel approved its version June 26 and reported it July 8 (H Rept 108-147, Part 3), after adding numerous new provisions, including language to authorize additional funding to hire more intelligence analysts at the Homeland Security Department. It also voted to reinforce existing requirements that other federal agencies forward all threat information to the department and allowed the government to use bioshield funds for an "in-house" government capability to develop countermeasures if private industry moved too slowly.

Biotech companies had hoped for liability protections, but they were disappointed. Tauzin said he would have "loved to put liability protections in here" but that such a controversial move could have doomed the bill.

The House passed the bill by a vote of 421–2 on July 16. Supporters hoped the overwhelming show of approval would dislodge the Senate bill.

Byrd said he would back the funding mechanism in the House-passed bill, but Senate Republicans initially stood firm in support of the Senate version. In mid-October, however, Senate HELP Committee Chair Judd Gregg, R-N.H., committee ranking Democrat Edward M. Kennedy of Massachusetts, and others reached a compromise to make funding for the Bioshield program discretionary but codify the appropriators' plan to guarantee $5.6 billion for the program over ten years. Like the House bill and the earlier Senate version, it included provisions to allow the government to relax federal acquisition procedures for medicines and vaccines in emergencies and to expedite the normal peer review process for grants, contracts, and cooperative agreements related to bioterrorism. The government also could rapidly distribute drugs it deemed appropriate for fighting bioterrorism, including those originally approved for other uses.

The dispute spilled over into the debate over the fiscal 2005 budget resolution, until Byrd and Nickles finally agreed in May 2004 to insert language into any conference agreement on the budget resolution that satisfied Byrd's concerns about usurping appropriators' prerogatives but also acknowledged the need for continuous funding.

Although no budget resolution was ever approved for fiscal 2005, the agreement did spring the Bioshield bill from its months-long limbo. The Senate passed S 15 on May 19 by a vote of 99–0. The House cleared the bill 414–2 on July 14.

MAJOR PROVISIONS

As signed into law on July 21, 2004, S 15 (PL 108-276):

Strategic Stockpile

Authorized $5.6 billion in fiscal 2004 through 2013 to purchase bioterrorism countermeasures for the Strategic National Stockpile. The stockpile, authorized in 2002 (HR 3448-PL 107-188), was a national repository of antibiotics, chemical antidotes, and other items that could be disbursed to state and local authorities in an emergency.

Of the $5.6 billion total, $890 million could be obligated in fiscal 2004, and $3.4 billion could be used in the first five years.

Research and Development

Allowed the Department of Health and Human Services (HHS) to use expedited procedures for approving grants for research and development of countermeasures for use against biological, chemical, nuclear, and radiological agents. The authority also could be used to respond to emergency health threats.

Allowed HHS to bypass the usual peer review process for awarding grants of less than $1.5 million.

Allowed HHS to waive competitive bidding rules when only a few companies provided goods and services needed for research and development.

Gave the National Institutes of Health flexibility to hire up to thirty people to respond to urgent research and development needs.

Emergency Use

Gave HHS the authority to distribute drugs and treatments not yet approved by the Food and Drug Administration in the event of a national emergency involving an actual or potential attack with biological, chemical, radiological, or nuclear agents. HHS could use the authority only if the Homeland Security or Defense departments determined there was a national emergency, or the potential for one.

Transportation Security

Efforts by the 108th Congress to improve the security of the nation's transportation system were only marginally successful. Bills to enhance rail and transit security were left unfinished. A bill to improve port security was passed by the Senate but died in the House. However, several aviation security–related provisions, after falling short through much of the first and second sessions, were folded into a major intelligence overhaul bill that lawmakers cleared at the end of the Congress (S 2845—PL 108-458).

AVIATION SECURITY

The 2001 aviation security law (S 1447—PL 107-71) that created the Transportation Security Administration (TSA) required the new agency to screen all cargo carried aboard passenger and cargo planes. But it did not specify how or when such guidelines should be in place. *(Aviation security, p. 198)*

The primary method used by the TSA was to require that only cargo from "known shippers" be transported on passenger planes, with all other cargo and mail weighing more than sixteen ounces diverted to all-cargo carriers. The known shipper program, which pre-dated the Sept. 11, 2001, terrorist attacks, defined acceptable shippers as those with an established reputation that were known in the industry. The TSA had strengthened the requirements but still relied on the system for security.

Senate Action

The Senate passed a bill (S 165) by voice vote May 8, 2003, to create a more rigorous cargo screening system, but the legislation went no further. Sponsored by Kay Bailey Hutchison, R-Texas, and Dianne Feinstein, D-Calif., it required the TSA to develop a strategic plan to ensure that all air cargo was "screened, inspected, or otherwise made secure." The bill would have increased TSA inspections of all air shipping facilities, established an industry-wide database of cargo shippers, created a security training program for air cargo handlers, required every all-cargo carrier to have a TSA-approved security plan for its entire operation, and permitted pilots of air cargo planes to participate in the federal flight deck officer program, which allowed certain passenger airline pilots to carry guns.

The Senate Commerce, Science, and Transportation Committee had approved the measure by voice vote March 13 and reported it (S Rept 108-38) April 24. Members agreed to a number of amendments by voice vote, including one that would have allowed pilots for all-cargo carriers to carry firearms in the cockpit and another that would have required a TSA report on defending passenger aircraft from shoulder-fired missiles.

The committee's report acknowledged the difficulties in creating a screening system, warning "any type of physical inspection or electronic screening would be extremely expensive and time consuming."

House Action

The House Transportation and Infrastructure Committee approved several changes in cargo security as part of a bill largely devoted to making technical changes to the 2001 aviation security law. The bill (HR 2144), by chair Don Young, R-Alaska, was approved by voice vote June 25, but it was never formally reported out of committee.

The bill included provisions to allow commercial cargo pilots to be armed and to require a joint TSA–Federal Aviation Administration (FAA) report evaluating blast-resistant cargo container technology. It also called for a pilot program to assess the capabilities of the private sector to inspect indirect air cargo carriers and screen air cargo. Additional provisions required that all airport workers be screened and that the General Accounting Office issue a report on the airline passenger database known as CAPPS II (Computer Assisted Passenger Pre-Screening System).

Versions of the provisions on arming cargo pilots and on CAPPS II were enacted in the FAA reauthorization (HR 2115—PL 108-176) signed into law Dec. 12, 2003.

APPROPRIATIONS BILLS

In 2003 Rep. Edward J. Markey, D-Mass., succeeded in adding language to the House version of the fiscal 2004 Homeland Security spending bill that required the TSA to find a way to screen all air cargo transported by commercial passenger jets. The amendment stated that none of the funds in the bill could be used to "approve, renew, or implement any aviation cargo security plan that permits the transporting of unscreened or uninspected cargo on passenger planes."

The House adopted Markey's amendment 278–146 on June 24. The House on Sept. 10 agreed 347–74 to a non-binding motion to instruct its conferees on the bill to seek the highest possible level of funding for homeland security, preparedness, and disaster response programs, and to insist on the Markey language.

But Senate Appropriations Chair Ted Stevens, R-Alaska, represented Anchorage, one of the largest cargo hubs in the country, and he made it clear he intended to change the language in conference. Instead of Markey's provision, the final bill (HR 2555—PL 108-90) designated $85 million for the TSA to develop new cargo screening technology and to improve its oversight of the known shipper program.

The following year the House Homeland Security Appropriations Subcommittee approved a $31.9 billion draft spending bill June 3. It included a funding increase of $546 million, or about 15 percent, for the Transportation Security Administration. Most of that increase was to be dedicated to doubling the number of inspections for air cargo that traveled in passenger airplanes.

With air cargo safety emerging as an issue in the 2004 presidential campaign, appropriators subsequently decided on $118 million for 100 additional air cargo inspectors and research into related technologies. The final bill (HR 4567-PL 108-334) required that the TSA triple the percentage of air cargo inspections on passenger jets. The measure also prohibited the department from implementing the controversial CAPPS II until a number of conditions were met.

INTELLIGENCE BILL

Lawmakers created a number of new programs and pilot projects intended to improve airport and airplane security as part of the sweeping intelligence bill (S 2845—PL 108-458) that cleared at the end of the 108th Congress. Many of the provisions were similar to those in a bill (HR 5121) approved by the House Transportation and Infrastructure Committee on Sept. 29, 2004. Unlike more contentious pieces of the intelligence bill, conferees came to agreement on the aviation security provisions relatively quickly. *(Intelligence bill details, p. 263)*

The House version (HR 10) mandated biometric technology standards for air travelers; turned over "no fly list" authority to the TSA; required explosives screening for carry-on baggage; and protected the anonymity of federal air marshals so they did not have to publicly identify themselves at airport security checks. The Senate version mandated consolidation of the no fly list; created pilot projects for blast-resistant airplane cargo holds; mandated explosives screening of carry-on baggage; and required development of a national transportation security strategy.

The conference agreement included programs for explosives detection for carry-on baggage, training for foreign air marshals, blast-resistant cargo and baggage holds, and more screening of airport workers. Lawmakers authorized $20 million for the TSA for research and development of biometric technology. In addition, the measure urged the president to pursue agreements to halt the proliferation of shoulder-fired missiles and directed the FAA to establish a system to approve antimissile technologies.

RAIL SECURITY

Rail security got additional attention from Congress after the March 11, 2004, terrorist bombings of commuter rail trains in Madrid, Spain, that killed nearly 200 people. Bills to enhance security on trains and buses won committee approval in both chambers but were stalled by turf battles and other problems.

The House Transportation and Infrastructure Committee on Sept. 29, 2004, gave voice vote approval to a bill (HR 5082) to authorize $3.5 billion over three years for rail and bus security. It required the departments of Transportation and Homeland Security to jointly assess major transit agencies for threats and weaknesses; the assessments would form the basis for security guidelines and strategies for improving public transportation agencies and making grant decisions. However, the measure, which was reported (H Rept 108-746) Oct. 6, ran afoul of GOP leaders because it gave control over transit security grants to the Transportation Department rather than to Homeland Security.

A Senate bill (S 2453) to authorize $5.2 billion over three years stalled as well after it won voice vote approval on May 6, 2004, and was reported (no written report) May 20 by the Senate Banking, Housing, and Urban Affairs Committee.

Another Senate bill (S 2273), which would have authorized about $1.2 billion for rail security through fiscal 2009, failed largely because the legislation included earmarks for Amtrak security. The Senate Commerce, Science, and Transportation Committee had reported S 2273 (S Rept 108-278) on May 21, and the Senate passed it by voice vote Oct. 1, but the House did not act on it. A House companion bill (HR 4604), by Transportation and Infrastructure Committee Chair Young, was not marked up.

PORT SECURITY

The Senate passed a bill (S 2279) by voice vote on Sept. 21, 2004, to enhance port security, but only after removing a provision that would have allowed the assessment of user fees on cargo and passenger vessels to pay for it.

S 2279 provided civil penalties for vessels that violated the 2002 port security law (S 1214—PL 107-295). It required the Homeland Security Department to submit a report to Congress on the progress made installing radiation detectors at seaports, as well as an assessment of how well foreign seaports were screening cargo. The bill also required that the department reevaluate its method for inspecting international cargo containers and assess the quality of security on cruise ships.

As introduced by Ernest F. Hollings, D-S.C., the bill had included the user fees provision. But the Senate Commerce, Science, and Transportation Committee voted 13–10 to drop that provision, before approving S 2279 by voice vote April 8. The panel reported the bill (S Rept 108-274) on May 20.

The House did not act on the bill.

Homeland Security Grants

Various bills to change how some homeland security grants were distributed among the states won approval in House and Senate committees in 2004 but failed to make it to the floor of either chamber. Instead lawmakers agreed in the conference report on S 2845 (PL 108-458), a sweeping intelligence overhaul bill, to nonbinding "sense of Congress" language that they must pass in the first session of the 109th Congress legislation to reform the system for distributing homeland security grants to enhance terrorism prevention and preparedness. But the report did not say how to achieve that goal.

A bill (HR 3266) by House Select Homeland Security Committee Chair Christopher Cox, R-Calif., would have used national intelligence estimates to determine which areas were most at risk of terrorist attacks and provide them with money for precautionary programs such as more police training, purchase of chemical suits, or beefed-up water plant security. Unlike existing law, Cox's proposal would not have guaranteed every state a minimum amount of money. Some localities, especially those in rural areas, would have received less money under Cox's formula.

The Select Homeland Security Committee approved the measure, 37–0, on March 17, 2004, and reported it (H Rept 108-460, Part 1) on April 2. But the legislation was referred to three other House committees as well, in part because other chairs were loath to cede jurisdiction over domestic security issues.

Indeed, House Transportation and Infrastructure Committee Chair Don Young, R-Alaska, had said that the Homeland panel should have no authority and should be disbanded at the end of the 108th Congress. During a June 2 markup Young's committee reversed the intent of core provisions of Cox's bill by adding a minimum funding guarantee. This would have done little to change existing Homeland Security Department formulas for "first responder" funding, guaranteeing every state at least 0.6 percent of available grant money, or about $18.7 million per year. It also broadened the focus to permit grant money to be spent on preparation for all forms of disasters—hurricanes, earthquakes and wildfires—in addition to terrorism. The panel reported HR 3266 (H Rept 108-460, Part 3) on June 21.

But the House Energy and Commerce Committee had sided with Cox's language and reported on June 14 a version (H Rept 108-460, Part 2) with no guaranteed minimum for each state.

The House Judiciary Committee approved Cox's bill, after amending it to guarantee each state a minimum share of the $3.4 billion pool. American Indian tribes would share in the allocations. The panel reported the bill (H Rept 108-460, Part 4) on June 21.

The committees did agree on one significant portion of the bill: a requirement that states meet a variety of benchmarks for terrorism preparedness before receiving money. The point was to make sure states and cities had firm plans for homeland security response, rather than spending the grant money on other law enforcement programs.

In addition to the committee turf battles, the dispute over homeland security grants to fire and police departments and other so-called first responders reflected some partisan divisions. It distinguished between urban areas, where the threat of terrorism was higher, and rural areas, where an attack was regarded as less likely. Those representing urban regions, more Democratic than not, said first-responder grants should be allocated by local threat levels. Those from rural regions, where Republicans predominated, said every state should be guaranteed a minimum share no matter the threat level.

Although Cox preferred a formula based on the threat level, he negotiated a deal with several Republicans to provide a small minimum for every state—about one-half of 1 percent—with the rest allocated on threat level.

He was ready to bring the grants bill to the House floor under an expedited procedure the week of July 19, but Democrats balked, saying they needed more time to negotiate.

Two Senate committees proposed bills to alter first-responder grant formulas, though neither was as expansive as Cox's. The Senate Governmental Affairs Committee on Feb. 10, 2004, reported a bill (S 1245-S Rept 108-225) to allocate funding based on risk while still providing minimum funding to each state. The Senate Environment and Public Works Committee on Feb. 25 reported a bill (S 930-S Rept 108-227) that would have based grants on the threat of terrorism while guaranteeing every state 0.75 percent of total grant funding. There was no further action on either bill.

USA PATRIOT Act

Less than two years after passing the USA PATRIOT Act, lawmakers in 2003 debated whether to expand or constrict the new powers they had given federal law enforcement authorities in the wake of the Sept. 11, 2001, terrorist attacks. Some members were anxious to give the government more tools for investigating suspected terrorists. Others were equally determined to roll back provisions of the law (HR 3162—PL 107-56) that they said chipped away at civil liberties. In the end, little changed. *(USA PATRIOT Act, 2001 action, p. 187)*

Congress did agree to enhance the FBI's ability to search business records for evidence of terrorist-related activity. But a Senate-passed bill to strengthen the hand of federal agents in monitoring foreigners suspected of terrorism died in the House. And lawmakers took no action on President George W. Bush's request for additional powers beyond those created under the 2001 law; at one point the House even voted to limit one of that statute's most contentious provisions.

FINANCIAL RECORDS

As part of the law authorizing intelligence programs for fiscal 2004 (HR 2417—PL 108-177), Congress expanded the FBI's access to financial records when investigating suspected terrorists.

The 1978 Financial Privacy Act (PL 95-630) allowed the FBI to demand financial records in terrorism cases from banks, credit unions, and other traditional financial institutions, without a court or grand jury order. The new provision broadened the definition of "financial institution" to include operations such as car dealerships, pawnbrokers, travel agencies, and casinos. *(Congress and the Nation Vol. V, p. 256)*

The expansion caused a last-minute uproar in the House, generating an unexpectedly large number of votes against the conference report. Members adopted it 264–163 on Nov. 20, 2003. The Senate cleared the bill by voice vote the next day. *(2004 intelligence authorization, p. 279)*

SURVEILLANCE POWERS

The Senate on May 8, 2003, passed a bill (S 113) 90–4 designed to make it easier for the government to use the Foreign Intelligence Surveillance Act (FISA) to investigate foreigners suspected of terrorism.

FISA, enacted in 1978 (PL 95-511), governed spying on suspected foreign agents. To get a search warrant or wiretap order under FISA, the government had to show probable cause that the suspect was a foreign power or an agent of one. During 2003 action, bill sponsors Jon Kyl, R-Ariz., and Charles E. Schumer, D-N.Y., proposed to eliminate that requirement, allowing the top-secret Foreign Intelligence Surveillance Court to authorize surveillance of non-U.S. citizens or permanent residents who were suspected of being involved in terrorist activities—whether or not they could be tied to a terrorist or foreign power. *(Congress and the Nation Vol. V, p. 720)*

Supporters said the bill would enable law enforcement to go after so-called lone wolf terrorists who might sympathize with terror groups but not be active agents. Critics warned the bill would open the door to potential violations of the Fourth Amendment to the Constitution, which protects citizens from "unreasonable" searches.

The Senate Judiciary Committee had approved the bill 19–0 on March 6, 2003. In return for a Democratic agreement to limit amendments, Kyl agreed to amend the bill so it would expire Dec. 31, 2005, the same date on which many provisions in the 2001 PATRIOT Act were due to expire. The committee reported the bill March 11 and filed its report (S Rept 108-40) on April 29.

The Senate adopted by voice vote May 8 an amendment by Russell D. Feingold, D-Wis., to require the Justice Department to report to the Senate Intelligence and Judiciary panels on how it was using the expanded powers. But it rejected 35–59 an amendment by Dianne Feinstein, D-Calif., that would have given judges the discretion to continue requiring law enforcement agencies to demonstrate that suspected terrorists had ties to foreign powers or organizations.

House Judiciary Chair F. James Sensenbrenner Jr., R-Wis., was cool to the FISA expansion, and the House did not take up the bill.

OTHER PROPOSALS

Other proposals either to limit or to expand PATRIOT Act provisions fell by the wayside, but one produced a key House vote that showed deep reservations about aspects of the USA PATRIOT Act.

Limiting Searches

During debate on the fiscal 2004 Commerce, Justice, and State appropriations bill (HR 2799) July 22, 2003, the House by a **key vote of 309–118 (R 113–114; D 195–4; I 1–0)** nullified for one year a provision of the PATRIOT Act that allowed police to conduct searches and seize evidence without first notifying the subjects of the investigations. But that broad bipartisan sentiment was never matched in the Senate, and the language to restrict such "sneak and peek" searches, offered by Rep. C.L. "Butch" Otter, R-Idaho, was abandoned when the appropriations measure was rolled into the omnibus spending package (HR 2673—PL 108-199). Otter was one of only three Republicans to vote against the PATRIOT Act in 2001. (*2003 key votes, p. 837; omnibus bill, p. 69*)

Bush Wish List

On Sept. 10, 2003, President Bush asked Congress for legislation to strengthen investigation and prosecution of terrorist suspects. He wanted to allow law enforcement officials to issue administrative subpoenas, which required no court approval, in the course of terrorism investigations; to make it more difficult for those arrested on suspicion of terrorism to win release before trial; and to allow federal prosecutors to seek the death penalty for all terrorists. Several bills were introduced, but Congress did not act on the request.

Privacy Protection

Lawmakers introduced a number of bills to scale back some of the powers given under the PATRIOT Act—for example, by curbing law enforcement's power to conduct searches without notifying suspects, by limiting "roving" wiretaps, or by exempting libraries and bookstores from certain searches. None of the bills moved forward.

DISTRICT COURT RULING

Lawmakers eager to reexamine several parts of the PATRIOT Act were cheered when U.S. District Judge Victor Marrero ruled Sept. 29, 2004, that a 1986 federal law (PL 99-508) allowing the FBI to issue "national security letters" for subscriber records and other information from telephone companies and Internet service providers was unconstitutional. (*Congress and the Nation Vol. VII, p. 744*)

The PATRIOT Act had relaxed the criteria for such letters, which did not require the approval of a judge. The language amending federal statutes on national security letters was not among the provisions in the 2001 law that were due to expire at the end of 2005.

Terrorism Insurance

Despite a major push by the insurance industry, legislation to extend a federal terrorism insurance program beyond its Dec. 31, 2005, expiration date died at the end of the 108th Congress. The House Financial Services Committee approved the measure, but the Senate Banking, Housing, and Urban Affairs Committee did not take up a companion bill.

The Terrorism Risk Insurance Act (HR 3210—PL 107-297) had been enacted in November 2002 to help stabilize the commercial property and casualty insurance markets in the wake of the 2001 terrorist attacks. The law authorized a three-year program, aimed at giving the private insurance market a transitional period in which to develop pricing and risk models. It required the government to cover 90 percent of terrorism-related losses, up to a cap of $100 billion, once insured losses reached trigger levels. Insurers were required to offer terrorism coverage in return for the government backstop. (*2002 action, p. 203*)

The aim was to give the private insurance market time to develop private market mechanisms for dealing with terrorism risk, but as of 2004 the industry had not developed an alternative. Critics said the program amounted to a federal subsidy for insurers and maintained that the industry would have to find ways to insure against terrorism if Congress did not extend it.

Insurers disagreed; with the law set to expire at the end of 2005, industry groups lobbied hard for Congress to extend the program. The extension had to be completed in 2004, they argued, because insurance policies that ran into 2006 already were being negotiated.

Both the House and Senate bills (HR 4634, S 2764) would have pushed the program's expiration date to Dec. 31, 2007. A key provision in the Senate version that was not in the House bill was a "soft landing" clause to allow policies written before the expiration date to keep the federal backstop until they expired.

The effort in the House bogged down in partisan bickering in June 2004, when GOP leaders halted work on a bipartisan bill and instead backed HR 4634, which had been introduced by Pete Sessions, R-Texas. Sessions was not a member of the House Financial Services Committee but was in a tight reelection race and stood to gain insurance industry contributions as a result. Angry committee Democrats responded by introducing their own two-year extension (HR 4772). The two sides reached a compromise when Republicans agreed to add group life insurance coverage, a key element of the Democratic bill, to the Sessions measure.

The Financial Services panel then approved HR 4634 by voice vote Sept. 29. Just before the preelection recess, Richard H. Baker, R-La., tried to add the language to the House intelligence overhaul bill (H 10) but was rebuffed by the Rules Committee. HR 4634 was reported (H Rept 108-780) on Nov. 18, but there was no further action on the bill.

In the Senate, Banking Chair Richard C. Shelby, R-Ala., resisted pressure from both sides of the aisle to take up the S 2764, saying he wanted to hold hearings in 2005. He was also awaiting a Treasury Department study on the program, due in mid-2005.

Detention Rules

President George W. Bush tried to sideline Congress in developing rules for detaining suspected terrorists by issuing executive orders, discouraging oversight, and asserting his constitutional authority as commander in chief of the armed forces. But in a decision on June 28, 2004, the Supreme Court pointedly reminded the administration that Congress was responsible under the Constitution for setting the legal ground rules for such incarcerations. *(Supreme Court decision, p. 632)*

The justices ruled that Bush could not hold U.S. citizens indefinitely without allowing them to contest their detentions. They also ruled that noncitizens held at the U.S. naval base at Guantánamo Bay, Cuba, could challenge their imprisonment in U.S. courts.

The administration's treatment of terrorist suspects had largely relied on an executive order Bush issued in November 2001 authorizing the Pentagon to detain noncitizens suspected of being terrorists. The administration issued similar directives with respect to U.S. citizens suspected of terrorism.

The June 28 rulings came in a trio of cases examining the government's right to detain terrorist suspects for indefinite periods. In one, the high court ruled 6–3 that foreigners held at Guantánamo Bay could contest their detentions in federal court. On another 6–3 vote the court held that Yaser Esam Hamdi, a U.S. citizen captured during fighting in Afghanistan in 2001, had the right to challenge his imprisonment before a "neutral decision-maker." In the third decision, the justices voted 5–4 on technical grounds to reverse a 2003 federal appellate court decision that Congress had not authorized Bush to put Jose Padilla, a U.S. citizen arrested at Chicago's O'Hare International Airport in 2002 on suspicion of terror-

ism, into indefinite military custody. But legal scholars said that the court's ruling in the Hamdi case was a strong signal that Padilla's challenge eventually would succeed as well.

The justices did not specify how the government should prosecute alleged enemy combatants or what would constitute meaningful "habeas corpus" review—the right to challenge imprisonment—for citizens such as Hamdi.

Many legal scholars said that the best way for the administration to avoid more setbacks was to work with Congress to devise procedures for detaining suspects. According to this line of thinking, creating statutory rules on detaining suspects would confer greater legal certainty and decrease the chances of overturning a policy on constitutional grounds.

The administration had been holding hundreds of noncitizens captured in Afghanistan and elsewhere at Guantánamo Bay since 2002 without charging them with crimes or putting them on trial.

In ruling that U.S. courts had jurisdiction over legal challenges by Guantánamo Bay detainees, a majority of the justices rejected the administration's claim that the base lay outside the jurisdiction of federal courts because Cuba retained "ultimate sovereignty." In his majority opinion, Justice John Paul Stevens wrote that the United States had "exclusive jurisdiction and control" over the base.

Rep. Adam B. Schiff, D-Calif., introduced legislation (HR 1290) in 2003 that would have authorized military tribunals and set specific rules for them, including granting public access and providing for Supreme Court review. There was no action on HR 1290, nor on another measure by Schiff (HR 1029) that would have authorized Bush to detain U.S. citizens as enemy combatants, subject to judicial review.

During July 8, 2004, action on a fiscal 2005 Commerce-Justice-State appropriations bill (HR 4754), the House rejected by voice vote an amendment by Brad Sherman, D-Calif., that would have barred the use of funds in the bill to detain for more than thirty days a U.S. citizen who had been apprehended on U.S. soil and classified as an enemy combatant.

Homeland Security Committees

The House and Senate took separate steps to consolidate power within a single committee in each chamber that would oversee homeland security activities. In both cases, however, influential chairs of other committees undercut the effort because they did not want to cede authority to a new panel. As a result, the House Select Committee on Homeland Security and the Senate Homeland Security and Governmental Affairs Committee faced uncertain prospects at the end of the 108th Congress.

Advocates of changes in the congressional committee system said it was crucial to centralize oversight for the nation's intelligence and counterintelligence efforts, as well as for the massive new Department of Homeland Security. The independent Sept. 11 commission recommended that Congress consolidate oversight for homeland security in a single committee in each chamber and revamp intelligence oversight either through a joint congressional committee or intelligence committees in each chamber that had both authorizing and appropriating powers. *(Commission report summary, box, p. 180; details, p. 275)*

Congressional oversight of terrorism was so fragmented that sixty-one committees and subcommittees, ranging from Agriculture to Finance, played some role when Congress debated the creation of the Department of Homeland Security in 2002.

The Appropriations committees avoided similar turf battles by creating new subcommittees for Homeland Security, chaired by Rep. Harold Rogers, R-Ky., and Sen. Thad Cochran, R-Miss. Those committees had no jurisdictional problems.

HOUSE SELECT COMMITTEE

At the beginning of the 108th Congress, the House created a Select Committee on Homeland Security to oversee the merger of twenty-two agencies into the 170,000-employee Homeland Security Department. Although its creation was only for the 108th Congress, House Speaker J. Dennis Hastert, R-Ill., said he was open to the possibility of making it permanent.

The creation of the committee culminated a year of ruminating over how the House and Senate should handle oversight of what would be one of the largest cabinet departments. In 2002 the House temporarily set up a similar homeland panel, chaired by Majority Leader Dick Armey of Texas (1985–2003), in his final months in Congress before retiring. The committee wrote the House version of the bill creating the Homeland Security Department but was disbanded once President George W. Bush signed the bill into law (HR 5005—PL 107-296).

The select committee, chaired by Christopher Cox, R-Calif., faced a difficult task from the outset. In addition to overseeing the development of the Homeland Security Department, the committee was charged with assessing whether the department was adequately protecting the homeland from terrorism as well as recommending rules changes for better oversight of homeland security agencies by the House. But many of the fifty members—twenty-seven Republicans and twenty-three Democrats—were chairs or ranking members on some of the panels that would have to surrender jurisdiction for the Homeland panel to work.

Cox envisioned his panel playing a coordinating role on homeland security, being a "one-stop shop" for the new department and avoiding jurisdictional conflict with other panels rather than asserting control. Programmatic details of the former Immigration and Naturalization Service, for instance, were to be left to the House Judiciary Committee. Overall security issues, however, were to be dealt with by the Homeland Security Committee.

Several committee chairs publicly criticized the new committee. "With all due respect, the select committee's work here is done," Joe L. Barton, R-Texas, chair of the House En-

ergy and Commerce Committee, said at a 2004 hearing of the Rules Subcommittee of the Homeland panel. "Frankly, the select committee has become an impediment to further progress."

Barton argued that his committee could handle matters such as nuclear security and public health threats, and such programs as Project Bioshield, a bioterrorism initiative. His comments were in line with those of other chairs.

The select committee held dozens of hearings, drawing top officials and experts in homeland security. But it marked up few bills. Cox proposed two major initiatives but failed to win House passage of either. One would have reauthorized the Homeland Security Department; the other would have overhauled the grant program for local emergency agencies.

The problems owed something to internal House politics. Cox twice canceled a markup of the authorization bill, designed to give his committee legislative authority over the Homeland Security Department's operations, because some of the Republican committee chairs on his panel would not show up. Several did not think it was necessary for the Homeland Security Committee to authorize a department that their own committees could adequately handle.

The measure was narrowly written to avoid jurisdictional disputes and instead focused on strengthening the department's intelligence operations and streamlining some management functions. Democrats wanted to force votes on high-profile domestic security issues and planned to offer as many as seventy amendments in such areas as aviation, port, rail, and chemical plant security. Cox's counter-strategy was to break the draft bill into nine separate pieces, making it harder for amendments to be germane, or relevant, to the underlying bill.

All the maneuvering came to naught, as the committee never marked it up.

Both Cox and ranking Democrat Jim Turner of Texas, despite their differences on the bills, lamented the breakdown in negotiations. "What you've seen in the past few days in our Homeland Security committee does reflect significant problems Congress has in oversight of homeland security," Turner said. "We had to adjourn the [markup] before it even began."

The dispute over homeland security grants to fire and police departments and other so-called first responders divided urban and rural legislators and broke down largely along party lines. *Homeland security grants, p. 217)*

SENATE COMMITTEE

The Sept. 11 commission report spurred the Senate to consider expanding the powers of its Governmental Affairs Committee, which had limited oversight of the Department of Homeland Security. But by the time the Senate passed its reorganization resolution, S Res 445, on Oct. 9, 2004, the committee's powers had been so eroded that Republican Susan Collins of Maine, who chaired the committee, and Joseph I. Lieberman of Connecticut, the committee's ranking Democrat, voted against the measure. It passed anyway, 79–6.

The reorganization plan had been put together by a twenty-two-member group headed by Republican Whip Mitch McConnell of Kentucky and his Democratic counterpart, Harry Reid of Nevada. But the measure, which would add to the standing rules of the Senate, reflected the great reluctance of powerful chairs and ranking committee Democrats to cede power, regardless of what the Sept. 11 commission suggested. The plan left jurisdiction for two of the largest agencies within the Homeland Security Department—the Transportation Security Administration (TSA) and the Coast Guard—in the hands of the Senate Commerce, Science, and Transportation Committee.

The measure went directly to the floor, where matters got far worse for the Governmental Affairs Committee. The first assault came Oct. 7, when Max Baucus, D-Mont., won voice vote adoption of an amendment to allow the Finance Committee, where he was the top Democrat, to keep jurisdiction over any commercial operations and functions previously exercised by the U.S. Customs Service. Next, the Senate ordered jurisdiction over the Secret Service and immigration policy to be returned to the Judiciary Committee, while the Commerce Committee easily repelled a bid by Collins, Lieberman, and John McCain, R-Ariz., to claim jurisdiction over TSA.

On Oct. 9 the Budget Committee piled on, winning a 50–35 vote to claim sole jurisdiction over the congressional budget process. The Governmental Affairs and Budget committees had shared jurisdiction, and it was no small irony that the Governmental Affairs panel wrote the 1974 law that established the modern congressional budget process and created the Budget Committee in the first place.

Collins and McCain suggested the entire debate was a waste of time. They protested that the new committee would have responsibility for oversight of the Homeland Security Department in name only since so many committees had preserved their jurisdiction.

"If we are not going to consolidate all the functions of the Department of Homeland Security under one authorizing committee . . . then let's not pretend that we are," said Collins, who would chair the Homeland Security and Governmental Affairs Committee in 2005.

Collins said at one point that the resolution, as amended, would leave a Homeland Security Committee with jurisdiction over less than 38 percent of the Department of Homeland Security's budget and just 8 percent of its personnel. And that was before the Judiciary Committee won back jurisdiction over the Secret Service.

The resentment felt by chairs and ranking members against the reorganization plan seemed to contribute to the votes, as slighted senators from panels such as Appropriations, Finance, Judiciary, and Commerce teamed up to help one another on amendments.

Senate leaders, including Majority Leader Bill Frist, R-Tenn., and Minority Leader Tom Daschle, D-S.D., opposed changes to the plan but did not twist arms to preserve their handiwork.

Senators also agreed in the resolution to raise the status of the Intelligence Committee. But, rejecting one of the main directives of the Sept. 11 commission, they did not give the Intelligence Committee budget authority, leaving that power instead with the Appropriations Committee. *(Congressional oversight of intelligence, p. 274)*

Homeland Security Department

A Navy installation in Northwest Washington was to become the Homeland Security Department's headquarters under legislation cleared in 2004. Homeland Security already occupied most of the buildings at the Navy's Nebraska Avenue facility and would become the official tenant by Jan. 1, 2005.

The measure (HR 4322—PL 108-268) directed the Homeland Security Department to pay for the Navy's relocation and cover its rent for a year in temporary offices. The Congressional Budget Office estimated that renovating the facility and moving the Navy offices out would cost about $100 million over five years.

The House Armed Services Committee approved the measure by voice vote on May 12, 2004. The House passed it by voice vote on June 14, and the Senate cleared it by voice vote on June 21. It was signed into law July 2.

Congress also in 2004 claimed a larger role in overseeing the financial practices of the Homeland Security Department. A new law (HR 4259—PL 108-330) brought Homeland Security under the purview of a 1990 law (PL 101-576) that required the president to appoint and the Senate to confirm a chief financial officer for all the other cabinet-level departments.

The measure included provisions sought by the House Select Homeland Security Committee, including the establishment of an office that would evaluate program budgeting and a delay until fiscal 2006 of a deadline for two internal audits.

The measure was reported by the House Government Reform Committee on June 9, 2004 (H Rept 108-533, Part 1). The House passed the measure on July 20 under suspension of the rules. The Senate cleared it by voice vote on Sept. 29, and President George W. Bush signed the legislation on Oct. 16.

Antiterrorism Appropriations

Lawmakers during the 108th Congress turned to annual spending and supplemental appropriations bills to weigh in on a variety of homeland security and antiterrorism issues.

FISCAL 2004 HOMELAND SECURITY

Congress cleared a $30.4 billion fiscal 2004 Homeland Security appropriations bill—the first devoted to the new department—on Sept. 24, 2003. President George W. Bush signed the measure into law Oct. 1 (HR 2555—PL 108-90), just in time for the start of the new fiscal year.

Despite misgivings about how the department was being run, Congress moved with uncommon speed to approve the funding. Bush got much of what he wanted, plus an additional billion dollars, to protect the nation's ports, airports, borders, and infrastructure from terrorists. Taken together, the twenty-two agencies that were merged to make up the department received an increase of 2.2 percent, or $667 million, over what they got in fiscal 2003.

The biggest fight centered on how much money to provide for "first responders"—the police, fire, and emergency response crews that would be first on the scene after a terrorist attack or other catastrophe. Senate Democrats pressed for $10 billion to $14 billion instead of the $3.6 billion Bush proposed. The final bill provided $4.2 billion.

In addition to first responders, the largest amounts of funding went to the Bureau of Customs and Border Protection ($5.8 billion), the Bureau of Immigration and Customs Enforcement ($3.7 billion), the Transportation Security Administration ($4.6 billion), and the Coast Guard ($6.8 billion).

Much of the $1 billion that lawmakers added to Bush's request was spread out over the bill in small increments. Agencies such as the Coast Guard, the Science and Technology Directorate, and the Information Analysis and Infrastructure Protection division all received significant increases for fiscal 2004.

The bill also included money for Project Bioshield, Bush's signature program to prepare for a bioterrorist attack, but made the funding discretionary instead of mandatory as Bush had wanted. Lawmakers also required the new department to report back on at least two dozen ongoing security projects, including airline passenger profiling and aviation security technology. The requirements were indicative of lawmakers' desire to wrest back some of the wide-ranging management authority they gave the new department when they created it in 2002. *(Bioterrorism, p. 206; Homeland Security Department, p. 176)*

Both chambers passed their versions of the bill by wide margins—425–2 in the House and 93–1 in the Senate—despite some concerns over how well the new agency was doing in such areas as aid to local police and fire departments and intelligence sharing. In the Senate, Democrats argued the bill would leave the country "dangerously unprepared" but were unable to persuade the chamber to adopt any of a series of amendments to breach the overall spending ceiling or to rearrange such priorities as directing more money to potentially vulnerable urban areas.

Conferees dropped several contentious provisions, such as a Senate attempt to limit the White House's ability to transfer employees within the department and a House provision requiring the full screening of all cargo on passenger jets. The House adopted the conference report (H Rept 108-280) 417–8 on Sept. 24, and the Senate cleared the bill by voice vote hours later.

FISCAL 2003 SUPPLEMENTAL

A $78.5 billion supplemental appropriations bill that Congress quickly passed in the spring of 2003 to pay for military operations in Iraq included important funding measures for homeland security. Bush signed the measure into law on April 16, 2003 (HR 1559—PL 108-11).

Although Bush got virtually all the funding he requested, Congress was not willing to grant the administration the broad leeway it wanted in allocating the money. Congress approved $3.9 billion for the Department of Homeland Security, about $400 million more than requested. The total included $2.2 billion for grants to state and local governments for first responders, which was $230 million more than requested. Other funding in the bill, including $497 million for the Federal Bureau of Investigation (FBI) and other Justice Department programs and $125 million for police and security at the Capitol, brought the total for homeland security to $5.1 billion.

The House Appropriations Committee approved the bill 59–0 on April 1, and the full House passed it two days later by a vote of 414–12. It largely matched Bush's request of $3.5 billion for the Department of Homeland Security. But the bill set aside $2.2 billion of the funds, $200 million more than Bush requested, for first responders including police, firefighters, and emergency medical workers. Although Democrats wanted significantly more for homeland security, they praised chair C. W. Bill Young, R-Fla., for dedicating $700 million of the fund for high-threat urban areas such as New York and Washington. That compared with $50 million requested by Bush. Rejecting Bush's request for a lump sum of $1.5 billion for other counterterrorism activities, the committee instead allocated the funds for specific purposes, including $428 million for Customs and border security, $390 million for the Transportation Security Administration, and $230 million for the Coast Guard.

The Senate Appropriations Committee also approved its version on April 1 by a 29–0 vote. It included $3.7 billion for homeland security, about $215 million more than requested, with Democrats pushing for more. Unlike the House version, the bill left most of the remaining homeland security funding in a single account to be allocated by the administration. The Senate passed the bill 93–0 on April 3 after adopting an amendment 65–32 by Arlen Specter, R-Pa., to increase funding for first responders by $200 million, bringing the total to $2.2 billion.

House and Senate negotiators quickly finished work, and the conference bill (H Rept 108-76) was cleared on April 12 without dissenting votes. Out of the $3.9 billion provided for the Department of Homeland Security, conferees put only $150 million—instead of the $1.5 billion requested—into a counterterrorism fund that the department could use as it chose. The rest was allocated to specific accounts.

FISCAL 2003 OMNIBUS BILL

The fiscal 2003 omnibus spending package, which comprised eleven spending bills left unfinished at the end of 2002, was signed into law Feb. 20, 2003 (H J Res 2—PL 108-7). *(Omnibus bill, p. 69)*

In the Energy and Water section, appropriators concerned about homeland security gave the National Nuclear

Security Administration $8.1 billion, a $410 million increase over fiscal 2002. That compared to Bush's request for $8 billion. Appropriators, overcoming the opposition of environmentalists, also extended portions of the Price-Anderson Act through Dec. 31, 2003. The 1957 law (PL 85-256) limited the liability of nuclear power plant owners in case of a catastrophic accident; the extension applied to new plants. *(Nuclear insurance, pp. 422, 440)*

The Transportation section appropriated $5.2 billion for the Transportation Security Administration but assumed that $2.7 billion would come from passenger fees. The total was $166 million less than requested, due primarily to a cap on staffing imposed by the conference agreement. The TSA was limited to 45,000 full-time employees in fiscal 2003, equal to a cap imposed in fiscal 2002. The administration had requested funds for almost 67,200 positions. The bill split TSA funding into four broad categories:

- 4.5 billion for aviation security, including passenger, baggage, and cargo screening; the stationing of law enforcement officers near screening checkpoints; and the reinforcement of cockpit doors. It was this spending that was to be partially offset through the collection of about $2.7 billion in screening fees paid by airline passengers.

- $245 million for maritime and land security activities, including port security grants, nuclear detection and monitoring systems, hazardous material trucking safety grants, intercity bus security, and Operation Safe Commerce—a public-private partnership to help ports track and protect cargo entering the country.

- $110 million for research and development activities, including next-generation explosives detection equipment, port security research and development, and research into other transportation security technologies.

- $309 million in a consolidated account for administration and other support.

The agreement also allowed the TSA to use state and local law enforcement officers—rather than federal officers, as previously required—at screening points in airports. The agency was required to reimburse state and local governments for the use of these personnel.

For the Coast Guard, the bill matched Bush's request for $6.1 billion in fiscal 2003, an increase of nearly 11 percent above the fiscal 2002 level. Most of the increase was for operations, including antidrug patrols and antiterrorism efforts. For years the Coast Guard had endured flat budgets and little money for modernizing its fleet, but the emphasis on homeland security raised the agency's profile and budget.

FISCAL 2004 DEFENSE

The Defense Department spending bill (HR 2658—PL 108-87), signed by Bush Sept. 30, 2003, included large increases for Pentagon counterterrorism activities and other programs to fight unconventional threats. It appropriated $4.5 billion for special operations forces—a 47 percent increase from fiscal 2003 spending—and $1 billion for procurement and development of chemical and biological defenses. *(2004 defense appropriations, p. 342)*

The bill dismantled a controversial Defense Department program, the Terrorism Information Awareness (TIA) system, that was supposed to screen thousands of individuals for possible terrorist connections. However, most of its functions were moved to an unspecified office. Critics had voiced privacy concerns about the program.

FISCAL 2005 OMNIBUS

Lawmakers combined nine spending bills into the fiscal 2005 omnibus appropriations bill. President Bush signed it into law on Dec. 8, 2004 (HR 4818—PL 108-447).

The Commerce-Justice-State section included $1 billion for counterintelligence and national security—more than twice the fiscal 2004 level and the amount requested by the administration. It provided for 1,194 new staff positions to improve intelligence and counterterrorism capabilities.

The bill also established a Directorate of Intelligence to strengthen the FBI's intelligence capacity and to ensure that intelligence was interwoven throughout the agency. The directorate would have "broad and clear" authority over intelligence-related functions including counterterrorism, counterintelligence, and criminal and cyber crime. Under the measure the directorate would ensure that intelligence was shared across these programs and would eliminate information "stove-piping" as well as allow the FBI to quickly adapt as threats changed.

The Treasury section included language to create an Office of Terrorism and Financial Intelligence within the Treasury Department, which would oversee terrorist financing, financial crimes, economic sanctions, financial intelligence, and security functions. The provision abolished the existing Office of the Undersecretary for Enforcement.

FISCAL 2005 HOMELAND SECURITY

The fiscal 2005 Homeland Security spending bill was signed into law (HR 4567—PL 108-334) on Oct. 18, 2004, after almost being derailed by unrelated provisions including disaster aid and dairy subsidies.

The problems fell away in a final weekend of activity. Top appropriators decided to use the military construction bill instead as a vehicle for emergency spending on drought aid for Midwestern farmers and hurricane aid for Florida. House and Senate conferees got enough votes to drop the dairy subsidies, which had been added by the Senate.

In the end the $33.1 billion bill provided $896 million, or 3 percent, more than the president requested and about 9 percent more than the fiscal 2004 law. Conferees dropped about $2 billion for programs such as explosives detection systems for airports, extra border patrols, and immigration inspection staff included in the Senate bill and offset by an extension of Customs user fees.

Under the bill, the department received increased funding for the entry-exit system for visitors to the United States (known as the US-VISIT program), the Coast Guard, and antimissile technologies for commercial aircraft.

In a continuing sign of legislative unease, the conference report required the department to submit more than forty studies, plans, and reports by 2006 on topics ranging from its hiring practices to its data-mining strategy. It also scolded the department's management, warning that incidents such as hiring and spending freezes at Immigration and Customs Enforcement in fiscal 2004 were not acceptable.

Appropriators moved to block several of the department's plans to shift components and create new programs such as rail security initiatives and an office to manage geospatial mapping.

The bill passed both chambers overwhelmingly: 400–5 in the House on June 18 and 93–0 in the Senate on Sept. 14.

But lawmakers clashed over spending provisions in conference. Democrats tried to attach $2 billion to implement recommendations of the independent Sept. 11 commission such as increases in funding for nonaviation transportation security, explosive-detection systems, communications, border patrols, and immigration inspection staff. Republicans rejected the add-ons.

The bill drew a White House veto threat over a provision banning the privatization of 1,100 immigration services jobs. The House had approved the provision, offered by Lucille Roybal-Allard, D-Calif., by a vote of 242-163 on June 18. Patrick J. Leahy, D-Vt., offered the provision in the Senate, where it was first approved as a perfecting amendment by a **key vote of 49–47 (R 5–46; D 43–1; I 1–0)** Sept. 8 and subsequently adopted by voice vote. The language was retained in the conference version. But the department put off the competitive-sourcing initiative, rendering the veto threat moot. *(2004 key votes, p. 854)*

The House adopted the conference report (H Rept 108-774) by a vote of 368-0 on Oct. 9, and the Senate cleared the bill by voice vote on Oct. 11.

CHAPTER 4

Foreign Policy

Foreign Policy

"On September 11, 2001, 19 men armed with knives, box-cutters, mace and pepper spray penetrated the defenses of the most powerful nation in the world. They inflicted unbearable trauma on our people, and turned the international order upside down."

Thomas H. Kean and Lee H. Hamilton
9/11 Commission Chairs, July 22, 2004

Those nineteen men hijacked four commercial airliners loaded with people and fuel and crashed them into the World Trade Center in New York, the Pentagon outside Washington, and a field in Pennsylvania. Nearly 3,000 people were killed that day and the nation was shaken to its very core. The international order was indeed turned upside down, as was the national agenda. Sept. 11 became the defining event of President George W. Bush's first term in office.

The White House and Congress would spend the ensuing days, weeks, months, and years grappling with obvious questions that would have complicated answers. How could a small band of terrorists have wreaked such havoc and horror on United States soil? How should the United States respond—and to whom? How could the United States prevent it from happening again?

In the immediate aftermath, partisan differences over foreign policy were put aside as lawmakers rallied around President Bush. Congress passed resolutions condemning the attacks and endorsing military strikes, and appropriated billions for recovery efforts and to prepare for armed conflict. The White House gained the upper hand on a number of foreign policy issues in which it had been locked in a standoff with Congress prior to the attacks.

In time, congressional support for Bush's war on terrorism went from backing retaliatory strikes to endorsing preemptive war. The decision to support war against Afghanistan for harboring the terrorist network responsible for Sept. 11 had come easily and quickly. War against the regime of Saddam Hussein in Iraq—primarily because of its alleged weapons of mass destruction programs—was a harder sell. But the Bush administration eventually made the sale.

It was this migration from patriotic support for a full response to an attack on the nation to the many strands of a new and muscular foreign policy that made the Bush administration one of the most controversial group of officials to hold office in modern history—strong leaders in the view of their supporters, dangerous in the eyes of their most vocal critics. The events of 2001 were to form a base on which the Bush administration articulated an aggressive stance in the world that reflected its officials' view of American interests first and foremost. Critics, especially in Europe, saw it as "unilateralist" approach to world affairs rather than the multilateral cooperation that had been the approach for half a century.

That led to a renunciation of treaties, a serious split with the United States' traditional allies in Europe, a constricted view of the United Nations' usefulness unless major changes were made in the organization's operations, and a sweeping view of how democratization would be accomplished worldwide and especially in the Middle East. Most significantly, Bush articulated his doctrine of preemptive military action against nations developing weapons of mass destruction. *(Bush presidency analysis, pp. 745, 748)*

PARTISANSHIP RETURNS

With control of Congress up for grabs in the 2002 elections and control of both Congress and the White House at stake two years later, the return of partisanship was inevitable. Particularly divisive was the question of how Sept. 11 should be investigated. Fearful that a probe could be

REFERENCES

Discussion of foreign policy for the years 1945–1964 may be found in *Congress and the Nation Vol. I,* pp. 91–232; for the years 1965–1968, *Congress and the Nation Vol. II,* pp. 49–116; for the years 1969–1972, *Congress and the Nation Vol. III,* pp. 853–948; for the years 1973–1976, *Congress and the Nation Vol. IV,* pp. 847–912; for the years 1977–1980, *Congress and the Nation Vol. V,* pp. 31–95; for the years 1981–1984, *Congress and the Nation Vol. VI,* pp. 123–197; for the years 1985–1988, *Congress and the Nation Vol. VII,* pp. 169–251; for the years 1989–1992, *Congress and the Nation Vol. VIII,* pp. 203–297; for the years 1993–1996, *Congress and the Nation Vol. IX,* pp. 187–250; for the years 1997–2001, *Congress and the Nation Vol. X,* pp. 173–231.

Outlays for International Affairs

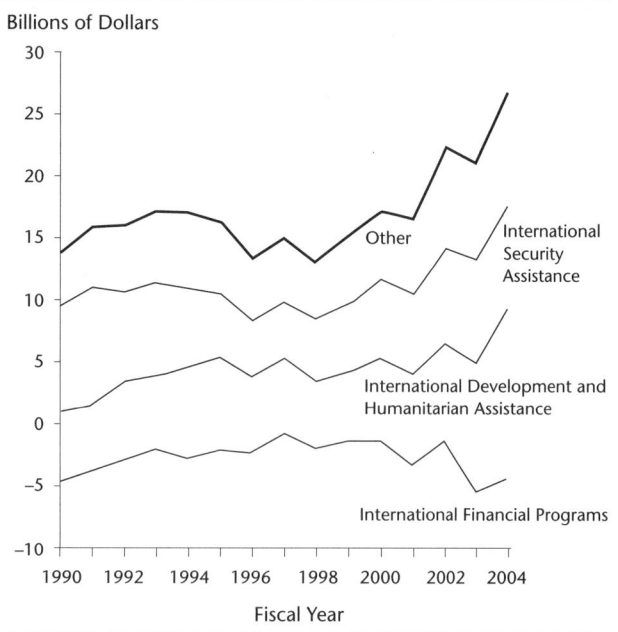

SOURCE: Office of Management and Budget, *Historical Tables, Budget of the United States Government: Fiscal Year 2006* (Washington, D.C.: U.S. Government Printing Office, 2005), Table 3.2.

politicized to Bush's disadvantage, the White House and its allies insisted on a narrow congressional inquiry. But advocates for a broader investigation—especially the families of victims of the Sept. 11 attacks—continued to push for a bipartisan independent commission. The slow pace of the congressional inquiry and the persistence of the 9/11 families kept the commission idea alive. The White House relented and a commission was created.

Recommendations growing out of the two inquiries laid the groundwork for major legislation overhauling the nation's intelligence community. Jurisdictional battles among agencies and their allies in Congress kept the measure's success in question until a final agreement was reached in the closing days of a lame-duck session. The independent commission's proposals for overhauling congressional oversight did not fare as well. Those turf battles were left for another day, if ever.

In the post-9/11 world, foreign aid—never a popular cause on Capitol Hill—found new life. Congress rewarded U.S. allies in the war on terrorism by increasing aid and waiving sanctions. At the administration's behest, lawmakers also gave their approval to major new aid initiatives.

9/11 RETALIATION: AFGHANISTAN

Just prior to Sept. 11 the congressional Democratic leadership had been hard at work to make a political issue of Bush's foreign policy, particularly his distaste for various international agreements. But Sept. 11 changed that, at least for the time being. Bitter fights over foreign policy issues and national security priorities that had roiled Congress only days

before were forgotten as the White House and members from both parties on Capitol Hill shared a single-minded focus on responding to the attacks and building a global coalition against terrorism.

On Sept. 14 Congress approved a resolution authorizing the use of force against the nations, organizations, or individuals responsible for the attacks and those who harbored such organizations or individuals. A $40 billion emergency appropriations bill to begin the recovery from the attacks and to launch a war on terrorism also passed.

The use-of-force resolution boosted Bush's efforts to rally international support against the terrorists. But the behind-the-scene discussions about the resolution's wording also revealed divisions over how to fight an unanticipated "war" that many acknowledged would be a long-term, if not permanent, campaign against a shadowy enemy.

One thing the majority of members did agree on was the need to protect congressional prerogatives. The Bush administration had initially proposed that Congress authorize not only retaliation for the Sept. 11 attacks but also the use of force "to deter and preempt any future acts of terrorism or aggression against the United States." Lawmakers opted instead for the narrowly drawn resolution that focused on retaliation for Sept. 11.

From day one, the primary suspect in the Sept. 11 attacks had been terrorist mastermind Osama bin Laden and his al Qaeda network. Bin Laden was a Saudi exile who was receiving sanctuary and support from a strict Islamic regime in Afghanistan known as the Taliban. He had been calling for attacks on Americans since the early 1990s. In a 1998 ABC-TV interview, he said that both military and civilians were considered targets and he warned that "if the present injustice continues . . . it will inevitably move the battle to American soil." His terrorist network was blamed for the 1998 bombings of American embassies in Tanzania and Kenya, as well as the 2000 bombing of the U.S. Navy destroyer *Cole* in the Yemeni port of Aden.

When Bush went to Capitol Hill on Sept. 20 to address the nation, he had bin Laden and Afghanistan directly in his sights. Bush issued an ultimatum to the Taliban government: turn over all al Qaeda leaders, close the terrorist training camps, and release all foreign nationals, including American citizens, unjustly detained in Afghanistan—or "share in their fate." The Taliban made no move to meet U.S. demands, and the war against Afghanistan began several weeks later.

WAR ON TERRORISM

The United States had broad international backing for the war in Afghanistan. Congress did its share in winning support for the war on terrorism.

One of the first steps lawmakers took was to authorize the release of another installment of U.S. dues owed the United Nations. The United States had begun paying back the nearly $1 billion it owed in 1999. A second payment was scheduled for 2001, but it became entangled with a proposal in the

House to ban U.S. participation in a new International Criminal Court. Quick action appeared unlikely despite a warning from U.N. Secretary-General Kofi Annan that U.S. effectiveness in the United Nations would soon be undermined if the debt were not paid. However, after the terrorist attacks and a pledge from the White House to back the court provision in other legislation, House GOP leaders dropped their objections to the dues payment.

In another move to build support Congress loosened existing sanctions on Pakistan, a country the White House hoped would be a frontline ally in the campaign in Afghanistan. The United States praised Pakistan for withstanding strong domestic opposition to provide the United States with military bases, overflight rights, and intelligence.

Congress was helpful in other areas as well. It cleared a long-delayed bill implementing a trade pact with Jordan. It lifted sanctions on Azerbaijan because of its support for the war on terrorism. Democrats dropped their opposition to the stalled nomination of John D. Negroponte to be U.S. representative to the United Nations.

PREEMPTIVE WAR: IRAQ

Although Congress had refused to give the White House an open-ended authorization to preempt terrorist acts in response to Sept. 11, the issue of preemptive action did not go away. A Bush doctrine of preemptive war evolved along with his case for ousting the regime of Saddam Hussein in Iraq.

There was no evidence that Saddam was involved in Sept. 11, but talk of regime change in Iraq had escalated after the attacks. As U.S. forces neared their goals in Afghanistan, hardliners pressured Bush to extend the war on terrorism to Iraq.

U.S. administrations had struggled for more than ten years with how to counter Saddam. In 1990 Iraq invaded neighboring Kuwait, claiming it was a renegade province, which resulted in 1991 in the Persian Gulf War, orchestrated and led largely by the United States. President George H. W. Bush narrowly won congressional authorization to wage that war, amid widespread Democratic opposition. Although successful—Kuwait was freed from Iraqi occupation and Saddam's regime was put under United Nations restrictions—Saddam remained in power and, in the opinion of important officials who came into office with Bush, a continuing threat to the United States and Middle East peace. (Persian Gulf War, Congress and the Nation Vol. VIII, p. 299)

After the war the elder Bush and then President Bill Clinton routinely faced crises as Saddam seemingly defied U.N. resolutions requiring him to dismantle his weapons of mass destruction and account for those in existence. Their administrations repeatedly had to mobilize U.S. forces to pressure Saddam to allow the inspections. U.N. inspectors were forced out for the last time in late 1998.

The hardliners in George W. Bush's administration and longtime supporters of military efforts to overthrow Saddam saw the post-9/11war on terrorism as a new opportunity to press their case. But Secretary of State Colin L. Powell disparaged arguments to oust Saddam and instead called for overhauling U.N. sanctions. Powell was intent on maintaining the diplomatic coalition for the ongoing campaign in Afghanistan. Key U.S. supporters of that war—from European allies to moderate Arab states to Russia—had said they would not support attacks on Baghdad.

Bush and his national security adviser, Condoleezza Rice, sought to bridge the differences within the administration's national security team by offering tough rhetoric on Iraq and calling for the return of weapons inspectors but putting off a military decision.

But Bush's position began to harden in 2002. In his State of the Union address he called Iraq, along with Iran and North Korea, the "axis of evil." He said that Iraq was continuing to flaunt its hostility toward America and to support terror, and that it was a regime with "something to hide from the civilized world." In a major policy speech at West Point in June, the president set out his new doctrine of striking first at terrorists and rogue states that had weapons of mass destruction.

Lawmakers from both parties were quick to embrace the broad outlines of Bush's strike-first doctrine, although some members raised concerns that Congress could lose what little influence it had on decisions about the use of military power abroad. But by the time Bush espoused his preemptive policy even some of the most prominent foreign affairs specialists in Congress seemed reconciled to the legislative branch's diminished role in decisions about the use of force.

Still, members of both parties insisted that they play some role. Lawmakers—who were both intimidated by Bush's popularity and largely supportive of his intention to topple Saddam—had been eager to maintain bipartisan support for the war on terrorism. But they were angered that the administration appeared to be moving toward military action that could involve a quarter million U.S. troops without consulting Capitol Hill. They wanted hearings and debate, and when that was over they wanted the president to win their blessing for preemptive action against Iraq.

Aggravating the war powers issues were divisions within the Republican ranks that surfaced when some prominent GOP figures publicly expressed their doubts about the administration's Iraq policy. In response, Bush's key allies and aides, with Vice President Dick Cheney as the point man, began to ramp up their defense of an attack on Iraq. Although there was widespread uncertainty about what weapons Iraq actually possessed, Cheney and others warned that Saddam had rebuilt much of the stockpile of chemical and biological weapons that U.N. inspectors destroyed after the 1991 Gulf War and that he was close to acquiring nuclear weapons.

Ultimately, Bush did go to Congress for its approval. In September 2002 he asked for a resolution authorizing whatever action was necessary to deal with the Iraqi threat. He got much of what he requested, despite the ambivalence of many members. Fears that Saddam was continuing to build up his arsenal of deadly weapons, that there might be another Sept. 11, and that they might look unpatriotic if they voted against the president just weeks before congressional elections spurred members to give wide bipartisan support to the resolution. With that vote, Congress essentially relegated itself to the sidelines. Administration officials moved ahead with their war plans, while lawmakers found themselves in the frustrating position of calling for briefings on Iraq and information on projected costs—all to little or no avail.

Debate over the war continued at the United Nations. Urged by many to get broad international support before acting, Bush had gone to the United Nations in September to press the Security Council to confront Saddam. Nearly two months later a unanimous Security Council approved a resolution that sent weapons inspectors back to Iraq and warned of "serious consequences" if Iraq failed to comply with its disarmament obligations.

But the administration felt the renewed inspections were not working and in 2003 called for a second resolution authorizing military action to disarm Iraq. That resolution was blocked in the Security Council. After a final ultimatum to Saddam to leave Iraq went unheeded, the United States, Great Britain, and a group of other mostly small nations went to war in Iraq on March 19, 2003. The Bush administration called it a "coalition of the willing"—at the outset, a group of thirty countries publicly supporting the war, plus fifteen others that were said to be privately backing the war.

Iraq's alleged weapons of mass destruction were not found, but the Bush administration insisted the war still was justified because of Saddam's presumed support of terrorism and his undeniable oppression of a large part of the Iraqi people.

INTELLIGENCE OVERHAUL

After Sept. 11, the country wanted to know how this could have happened. Figuring that out would not be easy, especially as the bipartisan unity that cloaked Washington in the early days after the attacks began to splinter.

Some in Congress wanted to create an independent commission, but others feared that could turn into an exercise in political finger-pointing. With the White House and top congressional leaders opposed to the idea, the House and Senate Intelligence committees launched a joint investigation. But their inquiry ran into problems, especially in trying to get information out of the intelligence agencies, and pressure for an outside commission mounted. The families of Sept. 11 victims made poignant pleas for a broad independent investigation that would give them the answers they were seeking.

The Bush administration finally agreed to an outside commission, but only after careful negotiations over power-sharing that would ensure the inquiry would not be politicized. Unlike the congressional probe, which was limited to exploring the intelligence agencies, the independent commission was given a broad mandate to look into almost anything it wanted ranging from the intelligence community to transportation security to immigration and border security. President Bush named Thomas H. Kean, a former Republican governor from New Jersey, to chair the commission. Democratic congressional leaders selected Lee H. Hamilton, a former Democratic representative from Indiana who had chaired both the Intelligence and the Foreign Affairs committees during his career in the House.

The commission ran into its own problems but managed to stay above the partisan battles swirling around it. It even got Congress to agree to extend the investigation, although that meant the commission's final report would be issued further into the 2004 presidential election season, something the White House had tried hard to avoid.

The 9/11 commission found a number of gaps in security and intelligence and missed opportunities that allowed the terrorists to prepare and carry out the attacks without being detected. The commission called for broad change in the executive branch and on Capitol Hill to safeguard the nation from further attacks.

There were significant obstacles in the way of such a sweeping overhaul. It would require juggling the jurisdictions of powerful agencies and congressional committees during a heated election year with only a few months left on the legislative calendar. But Congress was under tremendous pressure from commission members, 9/11 families, and—in the final stretch—the White House to get the job done. After marathon negotiations and several near-death experiences, a final bill emerged during a lame-duck session. Congress had managed to produce the most sweeping intelligence overhaul in the executive branch since World War II. But it did little with recommendations for changes in how it handled intelligence and homeland security.

FOREIGN AID RESURGENCE

Foreign aid, never wildly popular on Capitol Hill, hit a political nadir in the early 1990s. After the end of the cold war, it was derided as ineffective and wasteful. But, as with so much in Washington, Sept. 11 changed things. Members from all political quarters began to view foreign aid in a new light.

Their call for increasing aid was not limited to the basic calculation of helping and rewarding friends in the war on terrorism. The effort to boost assistance had been building before the terrorist attacks, as a coalition of religious conservatives and liberals called attention to the need to relieve third world debt and increase money to combat AIDS in Africa. At the same time, development experts and lawmakers proposed a new approach that would focus foreign aid on those nations working to solve their political and economic problems. As those efforts were gaining traction, Sept. 11 provided an impetus to spending more on foreign aid.

Congress gave its approval to a major Bush initiative—known as the Millennium Challenge Account—to target foreign aid to poor countries committed to democracy, human rights, and open-market economies. Also enacted was a new five-year global HIV/AIDS initiative. Bipartisan majorities, outraged over what they saw as genocide in the Darfur region of Sudan, stepped up relief funding for the humanitarian crisis in that region.

Chronology of Action on Foreign Policy

2001–2002

In the early months of the 107th Congress, the foreign policy agenda looked fairly typical. The usual bills were moving along, perennial issues were surfacing, familiar battles were being fought. But the terrorist attacks of Sept. 11, 2001, turned that agenda upside down. There was nothing typical or usual or familiar about what had happened to the United States and what was to come. In the aftermath of the attacks, Congress would sanction wars, authorize investigations, and take steps to win allies in the war against terrorism.

Three days after the attacks Congress authorized the president to use force against those responsible for Sept. 11 and any nation or entity that harbored them. And that meant the al Qaeda terrorist network of Osama bin Laden and the country of Afghanistan. When the Taliban-run Afghan government failed to heed President George W. Bush's ultimatum to turn over terrorist leaders, the United States in October launched airstrikes against Afghanistan and then sent in U.S. ground troops.

The Bush administration had hoped to win a more sweeping resolution supporting not only retaliation for Sept. 11 but also the use of force to deter or preempt future terrorist attacks. But Congress, ever mindful of its war powers after the extended conflict in Vietnam in the 1960s and early 1970s, kept the resolution focused on Sept. 11.

The debate, however, was not over. The following year Bush began building his case for a preemptive strike against Iraq, arguing that the regime of Saddam Hussein posed a threat to U.S. national security because of its attempts to acquire and develop weapons of mass destruction. He asked Congress to give him authority to use force if diplomacy failed to disarm Iraq. The idea of a preemptive strike against Iraq split the international community, with some of the United States' traditional allies bitterly opposed. Some members of Congress had deep misgivings too, but in the end a broad bipartisan majority gave the president the authority he sought. He would use it early in 2003.

The congressional response to Sept. 11 went beyond endorsing military action. Congress increased intelligence spending, particularly for new technologies, human spying, and better analysis. Members also wanted answers to the questions of how such an attack could have taken place on American soil and what changes were needed to prevent future attacks. Some called for an independent commission to investigate what went wrong, but the White House and congressional leadership were opposed to the idea. The House and Senate Intelligence committees launched their own joint investigation instead. But that investigation had its critics, as lawmakers became increasingly frustrated with its slow pace and the problems it was having extracting information from the intelligence community. The pressure for an independent commission intensified. The families of the Sept. 11 victims lobbied especially hard on Capitol Hill and in the White House for an outside investigation. Finally, the White House relented and an agreement for an independent commission was reached.

The independent investigation was to be a follow-on to the probe conducted by the Intelligence committees. The congressional investigation wrapped up in 2002 with a scathing critique of the intelligence community's preparedness to deal with terrorism. The committees called for a cabinet-level director of national intelligence and a study of whether a domestic intelligence agency should be created to take over the FBI's intelligence functions.

The effect of Sept. 11 could be seen in other moves by Congress as well. Members were eager to help the president rally international support for the war on terrorism. Less than two weeks after the attacks Congress sent the president legislation authorizing the release of another installment of the dues the United States owed the United Nations. The next month Congress allowed the president to waive key sanctions to reward Pakistan for its help in the war on terrorism. The following year Congress authorized the final payment of back dues to the United Nations at a time when Bush was pressing for a tough new Security Council resolution on Iraq.

Prior to Sept. 11, legislation had been enacted to tighten sanctions on Iran and Libya for their alleged support for terrorism and attempts to acquire weapons of mass destruction. Conference action on controversial sanctions legislation aimed at ending a civil war in Sudan was put aside after Sept. 11, but a compromise bill cleared in 2002.

FOREIGN POLICY LEADERSHIP

Secretary of State

Colin L. Powell was confirmed as secretary of state by voice vote on Jan. 20, 2001, just hours after President George W. Bush's inauguration. Powell had previously served as national security adviser to President Ronald Reagan and as chairman of the Joint Chiefs of Staff during the George H. W. Bush administration and for eight months of the Bill Clinton administration. Powell was enormously popular, and his confirmation hearing before the Senate Foreign Relations Committee was described by one senator as a "love-fest." During that hearing, Powell adroitly handled questions from committee chair Jesse Helms, R-N.C. In one exchange—a preview of a policy debate that would soon consume Washington— Powell challenged Helms's advocacy of efforts to overthrow Iraqi president Saddam Hussein, suggesting that maintaining and tightening United Nations sanctions would be a wiser course.

In the lead-up to the 2003 Iraq war Powell would win out over administration hardliners in arguing for the United States to go to the UN to seek international support. Powell continued as a counter-balance to conservatives during policy debates throughout President Bush's first term. Conservatives repeatedly criticized Powell for his reluctance to embrace and promote some Bush policies, such as those in Iraq and the Middle East, and his tolerance for State Department officials who went their own way. On Nov. 12, 2004—ten days after Bush won a second term—Powell announced his resignation. Bush nominated his national security advisor, Condoleezza Rice, to the position, much to the delight of conservatives who saw her term as an opportunity to replace independent-minded career bureaucrats at the State Department with people more in tune with Bush's views. *(Cabinet profiles, p. 919)*

CIA Director

George J. Tenet, who had become director of Central Intelligence in 1997 during the Clinton administration, remained until July 11, 2004, his seventh anniversary in that post. As the second-longest serving CIA chief (after Allen W. Dulles in the Eisenhower administration), Tenet presided over the agency during the Sept. 11, 2001, terrorist attacks on the United States and the launching of wars in Afghanistan and Iraq. Tenet submitted his resignation on June 3, just weeks before the anticipated release of a Senate Select Intelligence Committee report on pre-war intelligence on Iraq's weapons of mass destruction. The report was expected to castigate the CIA for out-dated information, sloppy analysis, and unreliable sources, and some on Capitol Hill linked the timing of Tenet's resignation to it. A second scathing assessment of the intelligence community—the report of the independent commission on the Sept. 11 attacks—was expected later that summer. Tenet's departure set the stage for a broad debate on restructuring the intelligence community. His deputy, John McLaughlin, became the acting CIA director after he stepped down. President Bush awarded Tenet the Presidential Medal of Freedom, the nation's highest civilian award, at a White House ceremony on Dec. 14, 2004. *(Intelligence reform, p. 263)*

In August 2004 Bush nominated Rep. Porter J. Goss, R-Fla., to be the new director. Republicans on Capitol Hill lauded the selection of Goss, who had been a CIA agent for a

9/11 Use-of-Force Resolution

In the aftermath of the Sept. 11, 2001, terrorist attacks on the United States, members of Congress rallied around President George W. Bush and overwhelmingly endorsed a resolution (S J Res 23—PL 107-40) authorizing the use of force to track down and punish those responsible. Within weeks the United States launched a military campaign against Afghanistan, where the Taliban regime was accused of harboring the alleged mastermind of the attacks, Osama bin Laden, and his al Qaeda terrorist network.

Nearly 3,000 people died in the Sept. 11 attacks. Two hijacked commercial airliners were crashed into the World Trade Center in New York City, another into the Pentagon outside Washington, and a fourth—believed to be headed toward the Capitol or the White House—in a field in Pennsylvania after passengers apparently fought their hijackers. *(Sept. 11 chronology, p. 236)*

Lawmakers pledged unqualified support for the effort to punish the attackers. Yet at the same time they struggled with an old debate over how much power Congress should cede to the president to initiate and conduct war. Earlier moments in history and prior legislative battles seemed an inadequate guide.

More than one lawmaker equated the shock of the attacks to the surprise Japanese bombing of Pearl Harbor, and some members called for Congress to declare war as it had on Dec. 8, 1941. But that was also the last time Congress had invoked its constitutional mandate to declare war. And, as many lawmakers pointed out, it also was not clear how a declaration of war would apply when the enemy was a small group of terrorists rather than a foreign nation.

S J Res 23 authorized the president to "use all necessary and appropriate force against those nations, organizations or persons he determines planned, authorized, committed or aided the terrorist attacks that occurred on September 11, 2001, or harbored such organizations or persons." *(Resolution text, p. 967)*

The Bush administration initially proposed that Congress support not only retaliation for the Sept. 11 attacks but also decade, a member of Congress since 1989, and chairman of the House Select Intelligence Committee since 1997. But Democrats warned that the selection of a politician instead of a career intelligence operative could lead to the politicization of intelligence, and, during Senate Intelligence Committee confirmation hearings, they grilled Goss on his votes and statements. Democrats provided all the dissenting votes when the full Senate approved the Goss nomination by a vote of 77–17 on Sept. 22, 2004. And they continued their criticism of the new director after Goss took several Capitol Hill staffers with him to the CIA and started shaking things up, moves that led to the resignations of several top officials in the CIA's clandestine services division.

U.N. Representative

John D. Negroponte, a veteran diplomat, was confirmed by the voice vote of the Senate on Sept. 14, 2001, to be U.S. permanent representative to the United Nations. Negroponte's confirmation had been delayed because of controversy over his tenure as U.S. ambassador to Honduras in the early 1980s. After the White House submitted Negroponte's nomination to the Senate in May, Senate Foreign Relations Committee Democrats had poured over hundreds of documents to trace what he had known about human rights violations by the Honduran military and whether embassy officials fully and accurately reported to Congress and the State Department on alleged ties between the Honduran military and death squads. But in the aftermath of the Sept. 11 terrorist attacks, members recognized the importance of having the U.S. representative in place at the United Nations instead of an interim figure and quickly moved the nomination through the Senate. Negroponte served in the U.N. post until June 22, 2004, when he left to become the first U.S. ambassador to post-war Iraq.

John C. Danforth, a former Republican U.S. senator from Missouri (1976–1995), was confirmed as Negroponte's successor by voice vote on June 24, 2004, ten days after President Bush submitted his nomination. The president had been eager to have Danforth in place at the U.N. prior to the June 30 U.S. turnover of political sovereignty to Iraq and before the United States was to help preside over the annual U.N. General Assembly session in September. In addition to his eighteen years in the Senate, Danforth's diverse career had included practicing law, serving as a Missouri prosecutor, and being ordained an Episcopal priest. At the behest of the Clinton administration, in 1999 he had conducted a probe of allegations of wrong-doing by the FBI during a raid at Waco, Texas, and since 2001 he had been serving as Bush's special envoy for peace in Sudan. Bush announced his plan to nominate Danforth for the U.N. post just days after Danforth had helped usher through agreements aimed at ending the twenty-one-year-old civil war in Sudan. But Danforth did not remain long. He resigned on Nov. 22, 2004, effective the following Jan. 20. The resignation surprised Washington observers who thought Danforth would be the U.S. representative for some period to come. To replace Danforth, Bush on March 7, 2005, picked John L. Bolton, a controversial State Department official. Democrats protested loudly and blocked his confirmation. Bush got around that by giving him an interim appointment. *(Bolton appointment, p. 927)*

"all necessary and appropriate force" to "deter and pre-empt any future acts of terrorism or aggression against the United States." But that went too far for many lawmakers, particularly Democrats, who feared that such an open-ended commitment could come back to haunt them, much as an earlier generation of lawmakers came to lament their support for the 1964 Gulf of Tonkin resolution (PL 88-408). That resolution was cited by the Johnson and Nixon administrations as congressional authorization for waging the Vietnam War. Congress repealed the resolution in 1970. *(Gulf of Tonkin resolution, Congress and the Nation Vol. I, p. 138; Vol. III, p. 911, p. 946)*

The White House welcomed passage of S J Res 23 though it was careful to cite the Constitution as the basis for the president's authority to act.

WAR POWERS

Since the Vietnam War, Congress and the White House had engaged in periodic battles over their respective responsibilities in initiating military hostilities. The debate was grounded in the divided powers provided under the Constitution, which gives the president the role of commander in chief while entrusting to Congress the power to declare war. But war had been declared only five times in the nation's history; every conflict since World War II had been fought without such a declaration, although in a few instances Congress had passed a policy resolution supporting a presidential decision to use force. The Persian Gulf resolution of 1991, in which Congress supported the use of force if needed to oust Iraqi invading forces from Kuwait, was regarded by many as the functional equivalent of a declaration of war. *(1991 resolution, Congress and the Nation Vol. VIII, p. 309)*

Congressional efforts to circumscribe the president's war-making powers peaked in the turbulent 1970s with the 1973 War Powers Resolution (PL 93-148). Enacted over President Richard M. Nixon's veto, the resolution stated that the president could commit U.S. armed forces to hostilities or imminent hostilities only if there was a declaration of war, specific statutory authority, or a national emergency created by an attack on the United States, its territories, or its armed forces.

SEPT. 11, 2001: A CHRONOLOGY

Following is a summary of events on Sept. 11, 2001, and the immediate aftermath. Nearly 3,000 people died in the attacks, including those on the planes: an estimated 2,759 at the World Trade Center, 189 at the Pentagon, and 44 on the plane that crashed in Pennsylvania. (Figures include the nineteen hijackers.)

Sept. 11, 2001

• 8:46 a.m.—American Airlines Flight 11, hijacked after take-off in Boston, crashed into the North Tower of the World Trade Center in New York City. The plane was carrying eighty-one passengers (including five hijackers), two pilots, and nine flight attendants.

• 9:03 a.m.—United Flight 175, also hijacked after a Boston take-off, crashed into the South Tower of the World Trade Center. Fifty-six passengers (including five hijackers), two pilots, and seven flight attendants were aboard.

• 9:25 a.m.—The Federal Aviation Administration shut down all U.S. airports.

• 9:45 a.m.—American Flight 77, hijacked from Washington's Dulles International Airport, crashed into the Pentagon. The plane carried fifty-eight passengers (including five hijackers), two pilots, and four flight attendants.

• 10:05 a.m.—The South Tower of the World Trade Center collapsed.

• 10:10 a.m.—One side of the Pentagon collapsed.

• 10:10 a.m.—United Flight 93, hijacked after take-off from Newark, N.J., crashed in rural Pennsylvania after passengers confronted hijackers. Thirty-seven passengers (including four hijackers), two pilots, and five flight attendants were aboard.

• 10:28 a.m.—The North Tower of the World Trade Center collapsed.

• 8:30 p.m.—President Bush spoke to the nation from the Oval Office after returning to Washington from Florida, via bases in Louisiana and Nebraska.

The Immediate Aftermath

• Sept. 14—Bush declared a national emergency and authorized the military to call up to 50,000 reservists to active duty.

• Sept. 17—The New York Stock Exchange reopened.

• Sept. 20—In an address to a joint session of Congress Bush said Afghanistan's Taliban government must turn over terrorist leaders or share their fate. He also announced creation of a Homeland Security office. *(Text, p. 965; Homeland Security office, p. 176)*

• Oct. 7—Bush announced that U.S. airstrikes had begun in Afghanistan.

• Oct. 19—U.S. ground troops were sent to Afghanistan after two weeks of bombing and airstrikes.

It required the president to consult with Congress "in every possible instance" before committing U.S. troops, report such a commitment to Congress within forty-eight hours, and terminate it within sixty to ninety days unless Congress authorized the action, extended the deadline, or was unable to meet because of an attack on the United States. *(PL 93-148, Congress and the Nation Vol. IV, p. 849)*

The practical effect in constraining the president was limited. No president from either party has acknowledged the constitutionality of the War Powers Resolution. Presidents typically have sought subsequent congressional support—but not prior authority—for decisions to use U.S. troops abroad. And in informing Congress about military actions, presidents usually have stated that their reports were "consistent with the War Powers Resolution." To say that a report was being filed "pursuant to" or "under" the resolution would have been interpreted as acknowledging the constitutionality of the act.

Congress, for its part, has been reluctant to act while U.S. forces are in harm's way or to do anything to undermine the president during a national crisis. Because members have been divided over the desirability and the constitutionality of the war powers act, Congress has neither repealed the law nor invoked the resolution to force changes in executive poli-

cies. In one instance, in 1983, Congress triggered the War Powers Resolution's clock for troop commitments, as part of a law authorizing U.S. participation in a multinational peacekeeping force in Lebanon. But in the compromise, reached after lengthy negotiations, Congress extended the deadline for withdrawal to eighteen months, and in return President Ronald Reagan signed a resolution invoking the War Powers Resolution while denying its constitutionality. *(Lebanon policy, Congress and the Nation Vol. VI, p. 156)*

A report issued in September 2001 by the Congressional Research Service found that presidents had submitted ninety reports consistent with the resolution. Only one of those reports—submitted by President Gerald Ford in 1975 when the United States rescued a U.S. freighter seized by Cambodian forces—cited the section that would have triggered the resolution's time limit, but that report was submitted after the military action had ended. *(Ford report, Congress and the Nation Vol. IV, p. 898)*

LEGISLATIVE ACTION

Senate Foreign Relations Committee Chair Joseph R. Biden Jr., D-Del., said S J Res 23 struck the right balance by giving both branches of government a say over military action. "We gave the president all the authority he needed, without giving up our constitutional right to decide whether force should be used," Biden said on the Senate floor Sept. 14.

Although some members favored giving the president more flexibility, a nearly unanimous Congress agreed to the resolution. The Senate on Sept. 14 passed S J Res 23 by a **key vote of 98–0 (R 47–0; D 50–0; I 1–0)**. The House cleared the measure by voice vote late the same evening, after approving an identical House resolution (H J Res 64) by a **key vote of 420–1 (R 214–0; D 204–1; I 2–0)**. The lone "no" vote in the House was cast by Barbara Lee, D-Calif. *(2001 key votes, p. 801*

The congressional response to the Sept. 11 attacks went beyond the use-of-force resolution. In the days and weeks after the attacks Congress cleared a series of high-priority bills aimed at helping the nation fight the war on terrorism, improve homeland security, and recover from the attacks. Among the bills was a long-stalled measure (S 248—PL 107-46) to release back dues to the United Nations, thereby removing a major obstacle to administration efforts to build a coalition to fight terrorism. Congress also agreed to waive key sanctions on Pakistan (S 1465—PL 107-57) and to lift restrictions on aid to Azerbaijan (HR 2506—PL 107-115) as a reward for their cooperation in the war on terror. The Senate finally cleared a long-delayed bill (HR 2603—PL 107-43) implementing a trade pact with Jordan. The Senate Foreign Relations Committee sought to lend a hand on the diplomatic front by approving the controversial nomination of John D. Negroponte to be the U.S. permanent representative to the United Nations. Plans to challenge the president's priorities during House and Senate consideration of the fiscal 2002 defense authorization bill (S 1438—PL 107-107) were dropped. Senate Democrats backed off plans to pursue, over White House objections, efforts to lift a ban on travel to Cuba. *(United Nations dues, p. 253; Pakistan sanctions, p. 255; U.S.-Jordan trade, p. 159; nominations, appendix p. 919; 2002 defense authorization, p. 308; Cuba policy, pp. 260, 299. See also Homeland Security chapter, p. 171)*

WAR IN AFGHANISTAN

The United States had helped bring the Taliban regime to power in Afghanistan through its support of an Islamic insurgency that in 1989 ended a decade-long occupation by the Soviet Union. In the anarchy and fighting among warlords that followed the Soviets' departure, a movement of former Afghan freedom fighters known as the Taliban rose to power and by the mid-1990s controlled much of the country. The Taliban rulers imposed an extreme form of Islam on the Afghan people and were accused of broad human rights violations and atrocities. The regime offered sanctuary to bin Laden and his network as well as other terrorist groups.

In 1998 President Clinton cited "convincing evidence" that Afghan bases had been involved in preparations for the bombings of two U.S. embassies in Africa. Clinton ordered retaliatory airstrikes against Afghanistan as well as a site in

Sudan said to be linked to bin Laden. *(Terrorism policy, Congress and the Nation Vol. X, p. 267)*

On Sept. 20, 2001, President Bush used a joint session of Congress to rally the nation and prime the American people for an attack on Afghanistan if it refused to turn over to U.S. authorities bin Laden and other members of al Qaeda. In his address Bush demanded that the Taliban immediately turn over al Qaeda leaders hiding in Afghanistan, close every terrorist training camp in their country, and give the United States full access to those camps. He warned that if the Taliban did not hand over the terrorists, they would share in their fate. "The hour is coming when America will act," Bush said. *(Text, p. 965)*

The Taliban did not meet Bush's demands and on Oct. 7 the president announced that the U.S. military had begun strikes against the al Qaeda terrorist training camps as well as Taliban military installations. Bush said that Great Britain had joined in the military operation—known as Operation Enduring Freedom—and that "[o]ther close friends, including Canada, Australia, Germany and France" had pledged forces as the operation unfolded. He also said that more than forty countries had provided overflight or landing rights and that many more had shared intelligence.

The military campaign initially consisted of airstrikes and special operations troops working with anti-Taliban forces. U.S. ground forces were sent in on Oct. 19. But the Pentagon largely left the task of ground operations to local allies, out of fear of incurring casualties such as those in 1993 that drove U.S. forces from Somalia. *(Somalia peacekeeping mission, Congress and the Nation Vol. IX, p. 191)*

The Taliban regime quickly collapsed, and its leaders were captured, killed, or fled into hiding. Terrorist bases were destroyed, but bin Laden managed to escape.

Until an Afghan army could take over, security was maintained by a U.N.-mandated International Security Assistance Force (ISAF) in Kabul and by U.S. forces outside the capital. As of late 2002, there were about 8,000 U.S. troops in and around Afghanistan, along with about 8,000 coalition troops.

Observers estimated that as much as $15 billion to $25 billion in international aid would be needed over the next decade to rebuild the war-torn country. The Bush administration hoped to shift responsibility for Afghanistan's future to other countries, arguing that the United States had already made its major contribution by ousting the Taliban regime. The United States provided $816 million in economic and military assistance to Afghanistan in fiscal 2002 and $817 million in fiscal 2003. Congress in 2002 cleared the Afghanistan Freedom Support Act (S 2712—PL 107-327), which authorized $2.5 billion over four years (fiscal 2002–2005) for economic, humanitarian, and political assistance, and the use of $300 million from resources in the Defense Department for military and security assistance to Afghanistan and certain other countries. The bill also expressed the sense of Congress that the ISAF should be expanded beyond Kabul and authorized a total of $1 billion over fiscal years 2003 and

2004 if that occurred. The Senate passed S 2712 (S Rept 107-278) by voice vote Nov. 14, 2002, and the House cleared the bill by voice vote the next day. It was signed into law Dec. 4.

Iraq Use-Of-Force Resolution

Congress in 2002 cleared a resolution (H J Res 114—PL 107-243) authorizing President George W. Bush to use military force against Iraq—with or without support from the United Nations. The resolution was adopted by wide bipartisan majorities in both chambers.

Since taking office, but especially since the Sept.11, 2001, terrorist attacks, Bush had pressed for action to disarm the regime of Iraqi president Saddam Hussein. Bush insisted that Iraq's attempts to acquire and develop weapons of mass destruction were a threat to U.S. national security that had to be addressed.

In making their case, the president and top administration officials argued that Saddam had established a track record of attacking and intimidating his neighbors and using whatever weapons he had in his possession, including chemical weapons. If Saddam were to acquire nuclear weapons, they warned, he would destabilize the entire Middle East, spurring an arms race with neighboring Iran, threatening Israel and the United States, and potentially passing on his weapons to terrorists.

They also said that the weapons inspections, required by the United Nations under a cease-fire agreement after U.S.-led forces defeated Saddam in the 1991 Persian Gulf War, had uncovered clear evidence that Saddam, contrary to international law, had attempted to develop nuclear weapons and massive arsenals of chemical and biological weapons. And they were convinced that his arms buildup had accelerated since 1998 when U.N. inspectors withdrew from Iraq after Saddam blocked their inspections of suspected weapons factories. (*Confrontations with Iraq, Congress and the Nation Vol. X, p. 197; 1991 Persian Gulf War, Congress and the Nation Vol. VIII, p. 299*)

In approving H J Res 114, Congress for the first time endorsed a possible preemptive strike against a sovereign nation. When the United States fought Iraq eleven years earlier, it was with broad international support. Even then, Congress set a high bar, demanding cost-sharing among allies and clear entry and exit strategies before authorizing the war.

This time, Bush asked Congress to look beyond the United States' tradition of never striking first and permit him to unleash the armed forces when he concluded that diplomacy had failed to disarm Iraq. The president made it clear that United Nations support would be sought but not required.

The resolution authorized the president to use U.S. forces "as he determines to be necessary and appropriate in order to (1) defend the national security of the United States against the continuing threat posed by Iraq and (2) enforce all United Nations Security Council resolutions regarding Iraq." The White House negotiated the final wording of the

resolution with House Minority Leader Richard A. Gephardt, D-Mo., after efforts to strike a bargain with Senate Democrats and Republicans bogged down. (*Text, p. 951*)

Bush hailed the outcome, describing it as a message to the world that "America speaks with one voice." But the votes in both chambers belied a deep ambivalence and substantial fears among lawmakers.

Members posed and sought answers to dozens of questions during three days of debate in the House and five in the Senate. Was war really necessary? If so, when would it begin, and how would it be executed and paid for? If the United States moved alone, was it willing to bear the responsibility of further destabilization in the Middle East region that could follow an invasion? Why Iraq, when there were other groups and nations that posed more serious threats to international security? What, precisely, was the connection between Iraq and the Sept. 11 attacks, a connection Bush said justified taking on Saddam? And what would happen to the unfinished war against terrorism in Afghanistan?

Bush's allies argued that waiting would only give Saddam more time to increase his arsenal. Also working in Bush's favor was the searing national memory of Sept. 11. Some lawmakers feared that if they failed to give Bush the power to act against Iraq, the nation would be vulnerable to further strikes. Others, despite their reservations, worried they would be labeled unpatriotic if they voted against a popular president in the final weeks before the 2002 congressional elections. In the end, many of those who had earlier questioned Bush's talk of war joined in an unexpectedly broad coalition behind the president.

CONGRESSIONAL ROLE

Talk of war with Iraq had escalated with almost dizzying speed. After Sept. 11 the goal of U.S. policy toward Iraq shifted from containment to regime change.

In late 2001 the House overwhelmingly adopted a nonbinding resolution (H J Res 75) demanding that Iraq allow U.N. inspectors to return to verify that Baghdad was not developing weapons of mass destruction. The vote was 392–12 on Dec. 20, 2001.

In his January 2002 State of the Union address, Bush singled out Iraq, along with Iran and North Korea, as composing an "axis of evil" in the world. He was more explicit in a June speech at West Point, where he described a new U.S. policy of preemptive attacks against countries suspected of developing weapons of mass destruction. That same month Gen. Tommy Franks, commander of U.S. forces in the Persian Gulf, briefed Bush on the basic blueprint for an invasion. In July Deputy Secretary of Defense Paul D. Wolfowitz met with officials in Turkey to discuss military cooperation during a potential invasion. In August Vice President Dick Cheney and other Bush allies publicly articulated a rationale for using force unilaterally to overthrow Saddam.

But other senior Republicans, including former national security adviser Brent Scowcroft and former secretary of state James A. Baker III, took exception, raising doubts about the wisdom of going it alone. And members of Congress were becoming increasingly insistent on the need for consultation. Senate Foreign Relations Committee hearings, which opened on July 31, reflected growing concern among some lawmakers that the administration was moving toward a major military confrontation with Iraq without a public discussion of the pros and cons of such an intervention—and without seeking congressional approval. Some top Republicans on Capitol Hill argued that it would be politically prudent to seek Congress's approval.

After initially insisting that Bush had all the legal justification he needed for military action, without further congressional or U.N. authority, the White House acceded. On Sept. 4 Bush invited eighteen leading lawmakers to the White House and informed them that he would seek congressional approval. But the president indicated that he wanted the approval granted quickly and without conditions. At the meeting, Bush handed each of the lawmakers a two-page letter calling for a broad expression of "congressional support for U.S. action to do whatever is necessary to deal with the threat posed by Saddam Hussein's regime." Senior officials were dispatched to Capitol Hill to brief members and to testify before the Armed Services, Intelligence, Foreign Relations, and International Relations panels.

On Sept. 12 Bush took his message to the United Nations where he stated his case for war against Iraq and warned that the United States was prepared to act with or without Security Council sanction. The administration pressed for the Security Council to adopt a new, no-nonsense arms inspection policy for Iraq and be prepared to use force if Saddam failed to disarm. If the Security Council fell short, Bush made clear, the United States would take unilateral action. (*Text, p. 949*)

Saddam raised the diplomatic stakes Sept. 16 by making a surprise offer to readmit U.N. weapons inspectors. Hans Blix, the U.N.'s chief weapons inspector, said the inspectors could be back in Baghdad within a month and would take at least four months before they could even tell the Security Council precisely which weapons systems needed to be dismantled. Administration officials said that timetable had to be shortened. They also dismissed Iraq's offer as a diplomatic gambit intended to buy time rather than a serious attempt to comply with Security Council resolutions.

Nonetheless, Saddam's offer slowed whatever diplomatic momentum Bush had gained after his Sept. 12 speech. But this setback only accelerated administration efforts to win congressional support for military action, with the White House pressing lawmakers to move forward the scheduled dates of hearings on Iraq and advance the consideration of a resolution.

NEGOTIATING A RESOLUTION

The precise language of the resolution was negotiated between congressional leaders and the White House before the measure ever reached the committee room or floor of either chamber. The outlines began to take shape Sept. 19 when the White House submitted a draft (S J Res 45).

Over the next ten days, White House negotiations focused largely on the Democratic-controlled Senate. The administration agreed to drop language authorizing forces to "restore international peace and security to the region"—which critics feared could justify wider military action. Negotiators included a reference to the 1973 War Powers Act (PL 93-148), absent from the original proposal, which required congressional notification before any military action or "as soon thereafter as may be feasible." And they added language putting the burden on Bush to certify that reliance on diplomacy "will not adequately protect" U.S. interests before going to war.

At that point, Republican leaders said they had made enough concessions. But Senate Majority Leader Tom Daschle, D-S.D., said Democrats still wanted more clarity about what Bush could do under the resolution and specific requirements to "explore other options" before taking unilateral action.

Frustrated, White House aides decided Oct. 1 to switch gears and try to cut a separate deal with House Minority Leader Gephardt. They also persuaded Henry J. Hyde, R-Ill., chair of the House International Relations Committee, to schedule a markup for the next day, increasing the pressure on Gephardt to reach a deal. Bush announced the resulting compromise in a Rose Garden ceremony Oct. 2, with dozens of lawmakers from both parties flanking him in a display of unified U.S. determination. Conspicuously absent from the gathering was Daschle.

Senate Democrats had been stunned by Gephardt's move, which left Daschle out in the cold. Some saw Gephardt as trying to improve his own chances as a presidential candidate in 2004 by ensuring that he did not look weak on national security. Gephardt denied that, insisting that Iraq was a problem that the United States needed to deal with diplomatically or, if necessary, militarily.

HOUSE ACTION

The House passed H J Res 114 on Oct. 10, 2002, by a **key vote of 296–133 (R 215–6; D 81–126; I 0–1).** The House International Relations Committee had reported the resolution (H Rept 107-721) on Oct. 7. (*2002 key votes, p. 819*)

Republicans said the compromise resolution supported Bush's policy of toppling Saddam without tying the president's hands. They also viewed it as offering little more than lip service to the United Nations. But Gephardt and many Democrats supported it because they said it would strengthen Secretary of State Colin L. Powell's effort to win U.N. Security Council support to confront Saddam over his weapons of mass destruction.

Many of those who voted for the resolution raised questions in their speeches that indicated ambivalence. But in the end the fear of not acting superseded most concerns. All challenges to the resolution in committee and during the floor debate were defeated.

On the floor, lawmakers on Oct. 10 rejected:

• 155–270 an amendment by John M. Spratt Jr., D-S.C., that would have required the president to seek a new U.N. resolution before taking military action. If the administration decided to proceed alone, the amendment required it to first seek congressional authorization.

• 77–355 an amendment by Barbara Lee, D-Calif., that would have urged the president to work through the United Nations and use peaceful means to resolve the weapons issue, including the return of weapons inspectors.

• 101–325 a motion by Dennis J. Kucinich, D-Ohio, to send the bill back to committee with instructions to insert language requiring the president, prior to using military force, to report to Congress as to the potential effects of war with Iraq on the U.S. economy, Iraqi citizens, and international stability.

SENATE ACTION

Ten hours after House passage, in the early morning hours of Oct. 11, the Senate cleared H J Res 114 by a **key vote of 77–23 (R 48–1; D 29–21; I 0–1)**. Until the very end of the debate, the Senate had considered S J Res 45, which was nearly identical to H J Res 114. *(2002 key votes, p. 819)*

Daschle backed the resolution after unveiling a list of conditions that he said should be met before undertaking a military campaign, top among them that the president be forthright about the threat and cost.

Robert C. Byrd, D-W.Va., mounted a quixotic, one-man campaign to persuade the Senate to flex its constitutional muscle and slow the march toward war. At the least, debate over a possible invasion of Iraq should not be conducted amid the passions of an election campaign, he said. But after several rounds of negotiations with Daschle, Byrd cut short his threat to filibuster the resolution. In any case, the chances that such a filibuster could have succeeded were quashed Oct. 10, when the Senate voted 75–25 to invoke cloture, and thereby limit debate, on an amendment offered by Joseph I. Lieberman, D-Conn., that made the Senate resolution's language virtually identical to the House's. The Senate adopted the Lieberman amendment by voice vote on Oct. 11 before taking up and passing H J Res 114.

In other action on S J Res 45, the Senate on Oct. 10 rejected:

• 31–66 a Byrd amendment to put a twelve-month limit on any congressional authorization of military action under the resolution, unless the president certified that an extension was necessary and Congress did not disapprove the extension.

• 14–86 a Byrd amendment that would have stated that the resolution would not "alter the constitutional authorities of the Congress to declare war."

• 24–75 an amendment by Carl Levin, D-Mich., that would have allowed the use of force only if it had been authorized under a proposed new U.N. Security Council resolution and only for the purpose of eliminating weapons of mass destruction in Iraq. It also would have required the president to certify to Congress that the United States had exhausted diplomatic and other peaceful means to obtain compliance by Iraq with the U.N. resolution.

• 30–70 an amendment by Richard J. Durbin, D-Ill., that would have authorized the use of force to meet "an imminent threat posed by Iraq's weapons of mass destruction," a higher threshold than the "continuing threat posed by Iraq" that was cited in the resolution.

FINAL PROVISIONS

Bush signed H J Res 114 into law on Oct. 16. The compromise gave him the latitude he wanted in deciding whether to go to war against Iraq. There was no provision for congressional review once hostilities began. It contained no expiration date and put no constraints on the military action Bush might order.

The resolution authorized the president to take military action both to defend against the "continuing threat posed by Iraq" and to enforce U.N. Security Council resolutions "regarding Iraq." The administration had released a list of sixteen such resolutions containing over fifty specific pronouncements, ranging from weapons inspections to repatriation of Kuwaiti prisoners and the return of Gulf War booty.

The resolution required the president to report to Congress prior to military action or no later than forty-eight hours after it began. Bush would have to certify that "diplomatic or other peaceful means" had failed and that any action he had ordered was "consistent" with the war on terrorism. The president would have to report on all military operations at least once every sixty days, as well as update Congress on the status of post-war planning. But there was no requirement that Congress approve his actions.

H J Res 114 offered a nod to the 1973 War Powers Resolution (PL 93-148), passed in response to years of war in Vietnam waged under the authority of the Gulf of Tonkin resolution (PL 88-408). The still-disputed 1973 law required Congress to declare war or issue a "specific statutory authorization"—which H J Res 114 explicitly stated that it was—at least sixty days into military conflict. *(PL 93-148, Congress and the Nation Vol. IV, p. 849; PL 88-408, Congress and the Nation Vol. I, p. 138; Vol. III, pp. 911, 946)*

U.N. ACTION

After nearly two months of arduous negotiations, the U.N. Security Council on Nov. 8, 2002, gave unanimous approval to Security Council Resolution 1441, which gave Iraq "a final opportunity" to comply with its disarmament obligations; required Iraq to declare within thirty days all of its programs for weapons of mass destruction; insisted that U.N. inspectors have unconditional and unrestricted access to any suspected weapons site; and warned Iraq that it would face "serious consequences" for failing to comply with these requirements.

Bush praised the U.N. action but added: "America will be making only one determination: Is Iraq meeting the terms of the Security Council resolution or not? The United States has agreed to discuss any material breach with the Security Council, but without jeopardizing our freedom of action to defend our country. If Iraq fails to fully comply, the United States and other nations will disarm Saddam Hussein."

U.N. weapons inspections resumed in Iraq on Nov. 27. But the United States soon insisted they were not working. On Feb. 5, 2003, Secretary of State Powell went before the United Nations and used satellite photos and communications intercepts to illustrate what he said were Iraq's attempts to conceal its weapons programs. He said Iraqi denials of supporting terrorism and of weapons of mass destruction were "all a web of lies." The next day, Bush announced his willingness to seek a second U.N. resolution, but he left no doubt where he was going: He said the United States would embrace such a resolution only if it sanctioned military action to disarm Iraq immediately.

The United States, Britain, and Spain introduced a new resolution, but France said it would veto it and Russia said it would probably do the same. Disagreement over Iraq had been particularly damaging to U.S. relations with France and Germany. Indeed, resentment became so high on Capitol Hill that House Administration Committee Chair Bob Ney, R-Ohio, ordered House restaurants to rename french fries "freedom fries."

The second resolution was withdrawn. Bush gave Saddam one final ultimatum: leave Iraq within forty-eight hours or there would be military conflict. U.N. weapons inspectors were pulled out of Iraq on March 18, 2003, and war was launched against Iraq the next day. The countries that joined with the United States in waging war—characterized by the Bush administration as the "coalition of the willing"—at the outset consisted of thirty that publicly supported it, along with fifteen nations that were supporting it privately. (Iraq war resolutions, p. 238; text, p. 951)

When no weapons of mass destruction were uncovered, the Senate Intelligence Committee in 2003 launched an inquiry into the intelligence leading up to the war. (Pre–Iraq war intelligence, p. 282)

2002 Intelligence Authorization

Congress in 2001 cleared a fiscal 2002 intelligence authorization bill (HR 2883—PL 107-108) aimed at responding to the failure of U.S. intelligence agencies to anticipate or prevent the Sept. 11 terrorist attacks on the World Trade Center and the Pentagon. The legislation increased the intelligence budget and put a greater emphasis on human spying and new technologies.

But one thing the bill did not include was authorization for a special commission to investigate the intelligence lapses.

Although the House version of the bill had provided for an outside commission to study existing impediments to better intelligence collection, conferees decided to let the two Intelligence committees conduct their own investigations unless President George W. Bush and congressional leaders decided otherwise. At that time neither Bush nor the leadership showed any interest in an outside panel. The White House shifted its position in 2002 and ultimately agreed to an independent commission. (2003 intelligence authorization, p. 243)

HR 2883 provided an increase of about 8 percent over the previous year's appropriations for national intelligence activities. Intelligence spending was classified, but the total in recent years was widely believed to be in the range of $30 billion. The measure covered the intelligence activities of the CIA, National Security Agency (NSA), Federal Bureau of Investigation, Defense Intelligence Agency, Coast Guard, the military services, and other agencies and offices in the Defense, State, Treasury, and Energy departments.

The increase in the intelligence budget inaugurated a five-year plan to accomplish four congressional objectives: improve human spying; upgrade the eavesdropping capabilities of the NSA, which collects intelligence from spy satellites and other sophisticated equipment; foster better analysis of intelligence data; and enhance research and development of new technologies. Revitalizing the NSA, which had been criticized for failing to keep pace with technological changes in signals intelligence such as fiber-optic communications, was a top priority, as was improving the agency's coordination with the CIA's human spies.

There had been widespread agreement after the Sept. 11 attacks that better coordination was needed among the intelligence agencies. Many lawmakers and intelligence officials wanted to expand the authority of the director of central intelligence, who had nominal oversight of all intelligence agencies but direct authority over only the CIA. But winning approval for such a move would not be easy, given the deep-seated jurisdictional rivalries among the various players—particularly between the CIA and the Pentagon, and between the Intelligence and Armed Services committees. In the mid-1990s when the Intelligence committees had attempted to expand the power of the CIA director, they were forced to scale back their proposals in the face of opposition from the Pentagon and its congressional allies. Defense Department officials argued that since they were the biggest consumers of intelligence, they ought to oversee the agencies. (Intelligence community overhaul, Congress and the Nation Vol. IX, p. 245)

LEGISLATIVE ACTION

The House passed HR 2883 by voice vote on Oct. 5, 2001. The House Intelligence Committee had reported the bill (H Rept 107-219) on Sept. 26.

The House bill would have increased intelligence spending by nearly 9 percent over the existing level and 2 percent over the president's pre-Sept. 11 request.

The committee-approved version of HR 2883 had called for a commission to examine why the intelligence agencies had failed to warn of the Sept. 11 attacks. The provision had triggered considerable debate inside the normally cordial and bipartisan Intelligence Committee, and the debate was far from over. During floor consideration on Oct. 5, the House adopted by voice vote an amendment, offered by House Intelligence Committee Chair Porter J. Goss, R-Fla., to refocus the proposed intelligence commission on impediments to current and future intelligence collection. But Democrats vowed to continue pushing for a panel that would look retroactively at what went wrong.

A proposal to scrap 1995 CIA guidelines on recruiting foreign agents had also sparked heated debate in the closed-door committee markup of HR 2883. During the mid-1990s, then-CIA director John M. Deutch had ordered the CIA to review all its contacts and operations to determine whether any involved links to human rights abuses. The agency subsequently developed guidelines that required field officers to obtain approval from headquarters before establishing a relationship with an individual who had engaged in disreputable activities. The CIA and some lawmakers maintained that the restrictions had not been a hindrance to obtaining information, but other lawmakers argued that the guidelines should be dropped to enable the agency to get better intelligence. In its report on HR 2883, the Intelligence Committee called for a new balance that recognized concerns about egregious human rights behavior but provided the flexibility to seize upon opportunities as they presented themselves. The Senate had approved a similar provision as part of its version of a Commerce-Justice-State appropriations bill (HR 2500).

The Senate passed HR 2883 by a vote of 100–0 on Nov. 8, after substituting the text of S 1428. The Senate Intelligence Committee had reported S 1428 (S Rept 107-63) on Sept. 14, and the Senate Armed Services Committee reported an amended version (S Rept 107-92) on Nov. 1.

S 1428 had been reworked in the aftermath of Sept. 11 to bring it in line with the version the House had passed. Aides said the Senate measure would fund intelligence activities at 7.7 percent above the existing level.

The legislation sought to increase funding for the analysis of raw intelligence data while at the same time adding money for research and development of new technologies, an area where Senate Intelligence Committee Chair Bob Graham, D-Fla., said funding often had been used to pay other bills. To help finance those increases, the bill reduced spending for two defense-related intelligence and reconnaissance programs. Although details were classified, Senate Armed Services members were troubled by the proposed reductions and urged conferees to restore the funding.

Most of the floor debate on the Senate bill focused on an amendment by Robert C. Smith, R-N.H., to make it easier for the Justice Department to deport illegal aliens suspected of terrorism by limiting the dissemination of classified information to the judge only. Democrats complained that the proposal would lead other nations to withhold details on U.S. citizens detained abroad. The Senate adopted an amendment by voice vote calling for the attorney general to study the issue.

FINAL ACTION

The House adopted the conference report on HR 2883 (H Rept 107-328) by voice vote Dec. 12, and the Senate cleared the bill by voice vote the following day. The bill was signed into law on Dec. 28.

The final bill's 8 percent increase in funding was a compromise between the 7.7 percent increase in the Senate bill and the 9 percent hike in the House version.

The conference committee deleted the House provision for an independent intelligence review commission. Graham said the conferees had agreed that if there was to be a commission, it should be done at the level of the president and congressional leadership. Opponents of the commission idea had warned it would be viewed as an exercise in political finger-pointing and would distract from the war on terrorism. Graham indicated that he and Goss were ready to have their committees conduct an examination of the current state of intelligence agencies as well as their performance prior to Sept. 11.

The conference bill also rescinded the 1995 CIA guidelines that restricted the recruitment of foreign intelligence agents who had human rights violations in their background and instructed the CIA to establish more flexible guidelines.

The bill made minor technical changes to the Foreign Intelligence Surveillance Act (PL 95-511), the main law used in obtaining wiretap information about suspected foreign criminals. Attorney General John Ashcroft had asked the Intelligence committees to consider broader revisions. More extensive provisions were included in the antiterrorism bill (HR 3162—PL 107-56). *(PL 95-511, Congress and the Nation Vol. V, p. 720; antiterrorism bill, p. 187)*

The attorney general was directed to review protections against the unauthorized disclosure of classified information. A provision that would have made most unauthorized and willful disclosures a felony had been removed from S 1428 before the Senate Intelligence Committee markup of the bill. The bill also required the attorney general to report on the state of proceedings to remove alien terrorists by the Immigration and Naturalization Service.

Other provisions of the bill strengthened protection for intelligence community whistle-blowers who disclosed information to Congress and added the U.S. Coast Guard as an element of the intelligence community.

The bill also required the president to report annually to Congress on the interdiction of aircraft used in illicit drug trafficking, including certifying the existence of appropriate procedures to protect against innocent loss of life. The provision was a response to the April 20, 2001, accidental shooting down by the Peruvian Air Force of a civilian aircraft carrying

U.S. missionaries. A CIA surveillance plane had mistakenly identified their aircraft as a suspected drug flight. A woman and her baby were killed. While assigning primary blame to human error, an Oct. 31 Senate Intelligence Committee report had echoed a State Department report in concluding that the CIA and the Peruvian Air Force had grown lax in enforcing safety procedures designed to prevent such accidents.

2003 Intelligence Authorization

Congress in 2002 cleared a fiscal 2003 intelligence authorization bill (HR 4628—PL 107-306) that provided for the creation of an independent commission to investigate the Sept. 11, 2001, terrorist attacks.

Agreement on a commission had not come easily. After opposing the idea of an independent probe since immediately after the attacks, the White House ultimately agreed to a power-sharing arrangement designed to ensure that neither party politicized the investigation. Support for an independent panel grew as members of the House and Senate Intelligence committees investigating Sept. 11-related failures became increasingly frustrated over their inability to get information from the intelligence agencies. The House included the establishment of a commission in its version of the intelligence bill, which it passed in July, while the Senate added it to a separate homeland security bill (HR 5005) in September. Agreement on the makeup and scope of the commission was finally reached after the November midterm elections.

The controversy surrounding the commission overshadowed the rest of the bill. HR 4628, however, did authorize a substantial increase in the intelligence community's budget. Although the amount authorized was classified, it was reported to be between $35 billion and $40 billion, about a 25 percent increase in funding over fiscal 2002 authorization levels.

The intelligence bill authorized the intelligence activities of the CIA, National Security Agency (NSA), Federal Bureau of Investigation, Defense Intelligence Agency, Coast Guard, the military services, and other agencies and offices in the Defense, State, Treasury, and Energy departments.

BACKGROUND

The failure of U.S. intelligence agencies to anticipate or prevent the Sept. 11 attacks on the World Trade Center in New York and on the Pentagon led to a debate in the fall of 2001 over the best way to examine what went wrong. Lawmakers working on the fiscal 2002 intelligence authorization bill (HR 2883—PL 107-108) ultimately rejected proposals to create an outside commission. They took the position that the president and top congressional leaders should be the ones to decide whether to have an outside commission and that in the meantime Congress should conduct its own inquiry.

On Feb. 14, 2002, the House and Senate Intelligence committees launched a joint investigation into intelligence fail-

ures and activities before and after the Sept. 11 attacks. The panels moved at their own pace for months, hiring staff, poring through gathered documents, and planning hearings. Members periodically voiced concerns that the panels were too close to the CIA to do a thorough job, or that the investigation was too narrowly focused on the intelligence agencies, or that the committees were slow-walking the probe. But most members seemed satisfied to let them proceed.

During the summer, however, lawmakers began to get impatient with the pace of the joint investigation, and support for an outside commission slowly grew. Public hearings originally expected in May or June slipped to summer and eventually to September. Some members began to accuse the CIA and other intelligence agencies of delaying the release of documents and information in hopes of running out the clock until the joint investigation expired in the spring of 2003.

Meanwhile, families of Sept. 11 victims persistently lobbied Congress and the White House to create an independent commission. Momentum intensified after joint hearings in September revealed several pieces of information that could have helped predict the attacks. At that point, most members of the Intelligence committees agreed that setting up an independent probe was the only way to get the necessary answers.

On Sept. 20 the White House switched course, sending a letter to House Speaker J. Dennis Hastert, R-Ill., advocating an independent inquiry as a follow-on to the congressional investigation. The Intelligence committees held their last hearing Oct. 17 and began writing their report. (*Congressional 9/11 probe, p. 245; independent 9/11 commission, p. 275*)

LEGISLATIVE ACTION

The House passed HR 4628 by voice vote on July 25, 2002. The House Select Intelligence Committee had reported the bill (H Rept 107-592) on July 18.

House passage came after an acrimonious debate over an amendment by Tim Roemer, D-Ind., to create a ten-member independent commission to examine intelligence failures leading up to Sept. 11. Lawmakers approved the proposal by a **key vote of 219–188 (R 25–183; D 193–4; I 1–1),** reflecting their growing impatience with the congressional probe. At the time, it was assumed that the provision would die in a House-Senate conference. (*2002 key votes, p. 819*)

In its original form, Roemer's amendment called for a commission that would look not only at intelligence failures but also at a broad array of other problem areas, including border and transportation security. But when GOP leaders said the bill went beyond the scope of the intelligence authorization bill and the jurisdiction of the Intelligence panels, Roemer redrafted his amendment to have the commission join the Intelligence committees in looking only at intelligence-related failures.

Most House Democrats supported the amendment, as did a group of moderate Northeast Republicans whose districts included families of Sept. 11 victims. They were joined by a band of conservatives who were unhappy with the performance of the CIA and other intelligence agencies, as well as with Congress's oversight of their work. Republicans on the House Intelligence Committee dismissed the vote as a politically motivated attempt to embarrass Bush, who had spoken out against the idea of an independent commission.

The controversy over the commission overshadowed debate on the details of the House bill, which lawmakers said would provide spy agencies with the largest single-year percentage increase in at least two decades.

The bill did not call for the broad legislative overhaul of intelligence gathering that many independent intelligence experts said was needed. The Intelligence committees were waiting for their joint inquiry into Sept. 11-related intelligence failures to end in February 2003 before trying such a politically daunting task. Instead the bill included a series of smaller steps to improve intelligence, such as authorizing a $10 million grant program for college instruction to address the lack of foreign language specialists. It also proposed curtailing the ability of foreign governments to make requests under the Freedom of Information Act (FOIA) to obtain documents from spy agencies.

The White House Office of Management and Budget issued a statement July 24 that largely was supportive of the legislation but repeated Bush's view that an investigation of the Sept. 11 attacks should be left to the House and Senate Intelligence panels.

The Senate passed HR 4628 by voice vote Sept. 25, after substituting the text of its own bill (S 2506). The Senate Intelligence Committee had reported S 2506 (S Rept 107-149) on May 13. The Senate Armed Services Committee reported an amended version (S Rept 107-208) on July 9.

The bill included provisions to hire more human spies, enable the NSA to improve equipment for eavesdropping on fiber-optic communications, and improve analysis of intelligence data. It also called for a commission to assess the future of intelligence research and development. Intelligence officials were concerned that the United States might be losing its cutting-edge capabilities in areas such as satellites and telecommunications.

There was no attempt to adopt an amendment calling for a Sept. 11 commission because the Senate had added the language the day before to the Homeland Security Department bill by a **key vote of 90–8 (R 41–8; D 48–0; I 1–0).** *(2003 key votes, p. 837)*

The Senate proposal—by Joseph I. Lieberman, D-Conn., and John McCain, R-Ariz.—was much stronger than the version that Roemer had added to the House intelligence bill. It called for a ten-member commission with broad authority to investigate all circumstances of the Sept. 11 attacks, including intelligence failures. The panel was to have subpoena powers and the power to investigate all branches of government. Although the Senate Governmental Affairs Committee, which Lieberman chaired, had approved the plan as a separate bill (S 1867—S Rept 107-150) on March 21 and re-

ported it May 14, the measure had languished for months before being revived in September. *(Homeland Security Department, p. 176)*

FINAL ACTION

The House adopted the conference report on HR 4628 (H Rept 107-789) on Nov. 15 by a vote of 366–3. The Senate cleared the bill later that day by voice vote. HR 4628 was signed into law Nov. 27.

Because there had been few differences between the two chambers' versions of the bill, the House-Senate conference had been expected to be swift and painless. Instead it was held up by a prolonged debate over the Sept. 11 commission. Negotiations dragged into the lame-duck session before a deal was finally reached.

Supporters pushed for a broad-ranging investigation that might last up to two years; White House officials insisted on having some control over the direction of the probe. Members thought they had a deal Oct. 10, but the plug was suddenly pulled because of White House objections.

Committee leaders had agreed to limit the investigation to post-Sept. 11 operations, as the White House wanted, and to employ extra safeguards to protect information about sources and methods used by intelligence agencies. Investigation into the administration's "response" to the attacks would be limited to the "immediate response." The president would name one cochair of the ten-member commission, which would have two years to finish its job.

White House officials refused to sign off on the deal, and House GOP leaders sided with them. At that point, lawmakers handed off the negotiations to family members of Sept. 11 victims, who spent the better part of a week talking with White House officials. The White House insisted on a presidentially appointed chair, rather than cochairs appointed by the two parties. It also insisted on limiting or dropping the notion of full subpoena powers.

The negotiations continued after the November elections, finally producing a deal that all sides accepted. The length of the probe was restricted to eighteen months, ensuring it would end well before the 2004 elections—a key White House demand. Senate Republicans agreed that one of their designees for the ten-member panel would be vetted by two strong backers of the probe, McCain and Richard C. Shelby, R-Ala. That selection, combined with the five appointments to be made by Democrats, would give commission proponents an effective majority and the votes needed to issue subpoenas.

In return, the president was allowed to pick the commission's chair, giving his designee substantial control over the direction and tone.

Lawmakers said compromises on the rest of the legislation had been worked out weeks before the bill was finally cleared. Conferees highlighted the need to improve information sharing and cross-community analysis; improve training, especially in language skills; ensure effective national imagery collection; and deal with enduring challenges such as improving NSA acquisition efforts, improving the depth and breadth of human intelligence, and rebuilding a robust research and development program.

Congressional 9/11 Probe

A joint House-Senate investigation into the activities of the nation's intelligence community before and after the Sept. 11, 2001, terrorist attacks on the United States concluded in late 2002 with a harsh assessment of the intelligence agencies' preparedness to deal with terrorism.

The House and Senate Intelligence committees' probe found no instances where any U.S. agent had specific information related to the Sept. 11 attacks. But their final report did find several missed chances in which the intelligence community either ignored suspicions about possible attacks or failed to comprehend the importance of information at hand. The report said that while terrorists prepared to launch the attacks on the World Trade Center and the Pentagon, U.S. agents still were operating under cold war rules as if they were competing against a nation, not a loose-knit transnational group of terrorists.

The Intelligence panels' two main recommendations were to create a cabinet-level director of national intelligence who would coordinate efforts among all the various agencies, and to study the creation of a domestic intelligence agency, similar to Britain's MI5, to take on the FBI's domestic intelligence functions.

The committees' investigation spanned most of 2002, and frustration over its slow pace finally spurred Congress to approve legislation (HR 4628—PL 107-306) creating an independent commission to investigate the Sept. 11 attacks. *(2003 intelligence authorization, p. 243; independent 9/11 commission, p. 275)*

BACKGROUND

The leaders of the two Intelligence committees—Rep. Porter J. Goss, R-Fla., and Sen. Bob Graham, D-Fla.—announced on Feb. 14, 2002, that their panels would conduct a joint inquiry into intelligence failures and the Sept. 11 terrorist attacks.

Congress in the past had formed panels of House and Senate members to conduct major investigations, such as the special committees that examined the Iran-contra Affair. But a joint investigation by two existing committees was unprecedented in congressional history. And, according to the nongovernmental research group National Security Archive, it had been a decade since the two panels had held a joint hearing. Informally, however, the two committees were as close as any two panels in Congress.

Goss and Graham spent part of their Feb. 14 press conference defending their choice of L. Britt Snider as the staff director of the joint inquiry. The hiring of Snider, who had worked for the Senate Intelligence Committee and for CIA

Director George J. Tenet at the agency's headquarters in Langley, Va., was praised by many in the intelligence community. But conservative critics feared he was too close to Tenet to lead an impartial probe of the intelligence agencies. Snider resigned as staff director in April after controversy erupted over his hiring of someone who had once failed a CIA polygraph test. He was replaced by Eleanor Hill, a former federal prosecutor, Pentagon inspector general, and Hill staffer.

During their investigation, the two Intelligence panels held nine public hearings and thirteen closed sessions. Staff members conducted or participated in hundreds of interviews, briefings, and discussions. And, according to the final report, staffers reviewed almost 500,000 pages of documents from the intelligence agencies and other sources.

As the investigation plodded along, concern mounted over whether the Intelligence committees would be able to get to the bottom of what went wrong on Sept. 11.

Some problems were simply inherent. The panels' jurisdiction was limited to intelligence gathering, hindering their ability to examine the shortcomings of the Immigration and Naturalization Service (INS), Federal Aviation Administration, and other government departments. In addition, because the committees were dependent on the intelligence community for classified information, critics said it could be difficult for them to operate at arm's length from the very agencies they were supposed to oversee. The committees also prided themselves on being nonpartisan, raising doubts about their tenacity in a highly charged election year.

But other problems were of the committees' own making, including the divisions over Snider and even over the very mission of the inquiry. In addition, critics complained that Goss and Graham were deliberately taking their time in conducting the inquiry. Goss was a former CIA agent, and his name frequently showed up on the short list of potential CIA directors, raising critics' questions about his impartiality. Goss in fact was appointed CIA director in 2004. *(Goss appointment, p. 927)*

In the face of such criticism the two committee chairs stepped up their probe and worked aggressively to make the case that they were the most qualified and best positioned to lead the investigation.

For months, many in Congress were content to let the committees take the lead. But disclosures that a month before the attacks President George W. Bush knew of Osama bin Laden's terrorist threats in the United States, and that FBI warnings were overlooked, opened a new line of questions and raised the political stakes. Frustrations mounted over the panels' inability to get information out of the intelligence agencies, and Congress ultimately decided on the probe by an independent commission. It was hoped that the commission's investigation would go further by delving into the presidential memos and briefings denied congressional investigators. Those White House documents were the largest gap in the Intelligence panels' report.

FINDINGS, RECOMMENDATIONS

The House and Senate Intelligence committees released their recommendations and some of their findings on Dec. 11, 2002. Each of the panels filed the declassified portions of their report on Dec. 20 and said the remaining portions would be submitted for declassification. The final report (H Rept 107-792, S Rept 107-351) was published in 2003. The 838-page report inadvertently omitted the panel's recommendations, which were released as a twenty-page errata print. *(Report executive summary text, p. 969)*

The final report included both factual findings and findings of systemic weaknesses that hindered the intelligence community's counterterrorism efforts before Sept. 11. From 1998 into the summer of 2001, the report said, the intelligence community had "received a modest, but relatively steady, stream of intelligence reporting that indicated the possibility of terrorist attacks within the United States." Nonetheless, the general view was that the attacks would most likely be against U.S. interests overseas. No action had been taken within the intelligence community even though there had been information at least since 1994 that terrorists were contemplating, among other things, using aircraft as weapons.

The panel found that the intelligence community "missed opportunities to disrupt the September 11th plot by denying entry to or detaining would-be hijackers; to at least try to unravel the plot through surveillance and other investigative work within the United States; and, finally, to generate a heightened state of alert and thus harden the homeland against attack."

The committee stressed the importance of addressing systemic weaknesses in order to minimize the possibility of another Sept. 11. The committee found that the intelligence community prior to Sept. 11 "was neither well organized nor equipped, and did not adequately adapt, to meet the challenge posed by global terrorists focused on targets within the domestic United States." The report faulted the intelligence community for a number of things, including not utilizing technology fully and effectively, not having sufficient analysis by experienced people, not being prepared to handle translations of foreign language intelligence, not sharing information, not developing human sources of intelligence, relying too much on foreign intelligence and law enforcement services, and not tracking and disrupting terrorist funding.

The panels' first recommendation was the creation of a cabinet-level position of director of national intelligence with the "full range of management, budgetary and personnel responsibilities needed to make the entire U.S. Intelligence Community operate as a coherent whole." It was a controversial proposal. The Defense Department's patrons in Congress consistently had fought the idea of creating an intelligence czar because it would mean wresting control of the bulk of covert operations from the Pentagon. Moreover, Tom Ridge, who had been designated as secretary of the new Department of Homeland Security, was lukewarm to the idea.

Senate Intelligence Chair Graham acknowledged that it would be tough to overcome institutional disdain for a new intelligence czar. But he argued that the lack of communication among agencies leading up to and following Sept. 11 highlighted the need for a single coordinator.

The report noted the FBI's "history of repeated shortcomings" in domestic intelligence and called on the FBI to take specific steps to strengthen its capability in this area. It also proposed consideration of whether the FBI should continue to be responsible for domestic intelligence or whether a new agency should be created.

The report called on the president to establish "clear, consistent, and current priorities" within the intelligence community. It urged more investment in technology at covert agencies and more funding for agencies to hire linguists.

The report also recommended that the president review federal classification procedures. Legislators complained repeatedly during the investigation about the slow pace at which documents were declassified, hinting that the agencies were using classification as a tool for covering up errors.

Aides said the final recommendations were approved by voice vote, with some dissensions, while the panels' findings were approved by a unanimous voice vote.

2002 Aid Appropriations

Congress in 2001 cleared legislation (HR 2506—PL 107-115) appropriating $15.4 billion for foreign aid and related programs in fiscal 2002. The measure, written well before the Sept. 11 terrorist attacks on the United States, emphasized long-standing foreign policy priorities. The need to assist partners in the post-Sept. 11 global coalition against terrorism was addressed in separate spending bills (HR 2888—PL 107-38; HR 3338—PL 107-117) or deferred to the second session. *(Antiterrorism supplemental, p. 56; 2002 defense appropriations, p. 316)*

Debate on the foreign operations spending bill focused largely on perennial controversies, especially antidrug aid to South America and the link between international family planning assistance and abortion. Appropriators reduced aid for U.S. antidrug programs in Colombia, with lawmakers expressing growing skepticism that the aid was doing much to help save that country from guerrilla warfare and drug trafficking. And final action on the bill was delayed until the end of the session by the abortion dispute, the same conflict that had held up the bill many times in the past.

This time, the flash point was President George W. Bush's decision shortly after taking office to reinstate Reagan-era abortion restrictions. Known as the "Mexico City policy"—for the city where it was first announced in 1984—the restrictions prohibited aid to nongovernmental international family planning organizations that performed or promoted abortions, even if they used their own funds to do so. The policy had been revoked by President Bill Clinton in 1993. During action on HR 2506, the Republican-controlled House backed Bush's decision, but the Democratic-controlled Senate voted

RESTRICTIONS ON FAMILY PLANNING ASSISTANCE

Following is a brief history of restrictions on international family planning assistance that became known as the "Mexico City policy" and the Kemp-Kasten amendment:

1984 At the second U.N. International Conference on Population in Mexico City the administration of President Ronald Regan announced a new policy of denying assistance to any foreign nongovernmental organization "which performs or actively promotes abortion as a method of family planning," even if it was done with the group's private funds. The directive became known as the Mexico City policy.

1985 Congress approved an amendment, offered by Rep. Jack Kemp, R-N.Y., and Sen. Bob Kasten, R-Wis., to a supplemental appropriations bill (PL 99-88) that said no U.S. funds could be given to any organization that supported or participated in the management of a program of coercive abortion or involuntary sterilization. The Kemp-Kasten amendment led to a total funding cutoff of the U.N. Population Fund (UNFPA), which operated in China, where the government was criticized for alleged coercive population control policies, including forced abortions. UNFPA (the acronym for its original name, the U.N. Fund for Population Activities) denied supporting abortion as a method of family planning. *(Population control, Congress and the Nation Vol. VII, p. 193)*

1989 Congress approved a foreign aid appropriations bill that mandated a contribution to UNFPA. The provision was one of several President George H. W. Bush cited in vetoing the bill. *(Population fund, Congress and the Nation Vol. VIII, p. 235)*

1991 Despite a veto threat from the White House, both the House and Senate approved a foreign aid authorization bill that would have dropped the Mexico City restrictions. But ultimately the House, whose members were reluctant to support a foreign aid bill during a domestic recession, rejected the conference report and the legislation died. *(1992–1993 aid authorization, Congress and the Nation Vol. VIII, p. 267)*

1993 In a memorandum to the director of the Agency for International Development, President Bill Clinton rescinded the Mexico City restrictions. Soon after, the administration ended the eight-year ban on aid to UNFPA, but Congress cut the request and placed conditions on the assistance (PL 103-87). *(U.N. Population Fund, Congress and the Nation Vol. IX, p. 209)*

1995 During consideration of the fiscal 1996 foreign operations funding bill (PL 104-99) the House voted to reinstate the Mexico City policy while the Senate rejected such a move. Conferees were deadlocked over the issue for months, until

early in 1996 when they agreed to reduce funding for international family planning programs by 35 percent from the previous year unless a separate bill authorizing those programs became law by July 1996. *(Congress and the Nation Vol. IX, p. 231)*

1996 Antiabortion lawmakers succeeded in delaying payment of fiscal 1997 family planning funds until July 1997 unless Congress voted separately to release them by the end of February 1997 (PL 104-208). Congress subsequently approved the early release (PL 105-3). *(PL 104-208, Congress and the Nation Vol. IX, p. 234; PL 105-3, Congress and the Nation Vol. X, p. 194)*

1997 Negotiators on the fiscal 1998 foreign aid spending bill (PL 105-118) deadlocked over a House provision to essentially reinstate the Mexico City policy. GOP leaders dropped the language but allowed spending for family planning organizations at the fiscal 1997 level, to be released at 8 percent a month. *(PL 105-118, Congress and the Nation Vol. X, p. 183)*

1998 Conferees on the fiscal 1999 foreign operations spending bill (PL 105-277) dropped a House provision reinstating the Mexico City policy, but the final bill did cut off funding for UNFPA. The House added the Mexico City restrictions to a State Department authorization bill, which Clinton vetoed. *(PL 105-277, Congress and the Nation Vol. X, p. 186; State Department authorization, Congress and the Nation Vol. X, p. 189)*

1999 Clinton agreed to a one-year deal on the fiscal 2000 foreign aid bill (PL 106-113) that barred aid to family planning groups that performed abortions—except in cases of rape, incest, or to save the life of the woman—or that lobbied to change abortion laws or government policies in other countries. The president could waive the restriction for up to $15 million, but under the law that waiver triggered a shift of $12.5 million in family planning aid to an account for child survival and disease prevention programs. The bill provided money for UNFPA under certain conditions. *(Congress and the Nation Vol. X, p. 210)*

2000 Republicans agreed to increase aid for family planning programs, but the fiscal 2001 foreign aid spending bill (PL 106-429) prevented spending the money until Feb. 15, 2001, a month after the inauguration of a new president. Republicans gambled that it would be George W. Bush. The bill provided money for UNFPA under certain conditions. *(Congress and the Nation Vol. X, p. 214)*

2001 President Bush reinstated the Mexico City policy by directive.

to overturn it, drawing a veto threat from the White House. Conferees compromised by dropping the Senate provision in return for increased funding for international family planning efforts, a decision that angered conservative Republicans and caused further delay. *(Mexico City Policy box, above)*

Lawmakers rebuffed a proposal by Bush to cut funding for the Export-Import (Ex-Im) Bank by 25 percent and voted instead to restore much of the money.

The annual foreign operations bill provided about two-thirds of total international affairs spending. Funding for

State Department operations was covered by the Commerce-Justice-State departments appropriations bill.

HOUSE ACTION

The House passed its $15.2 billion version of HR 2506 by a vote of 381–46 on July 24, 2001. The House Appropriations Committee had reported the bill (H Rept 107-142) on July 17.

The House managed to avoid much of the contentious debate of previous years, when Republicans regularly went to battle with the Clinton White House over foreign aid spending, especially for international family planning assistance. In contrast, the Bush administration found little to complain about in the House version of HR 2506.

At the strong urging of House Speaker J. Dennis Hastert, R-Ill., House appropriators had stopped short of making substantial cuts in funding for drug interdiction in Colombia and six neighboring countries, approving $675 million of Bush's $731 million request. Attempts to shift funds to other programs were resisted during committee consideration and on the floor. The bill did increase congressional oversight of the programs.

Hastert had made a personal crusade out of saving Colombia, South America's oldest democracy, from drug trafficking and guerrilla war. The Andean Counterdrug Initiative had begun as a joint effort between Hastert and Clinton, with an initial $1.3 billion in economic and military aid attached as supplemental funding to a fiscal 2001 military construction appropriations bill (PL 106-246) enacted in 2000. (*Colombia antidrug aid, Congress and the Nation Vol. X, p. 220*)

However, the standing of the Colombian government was deteriorating both in public opinion polls and on the battleground, and the poorly run drug interdiction program was drawing criticism from both sides of the aisle. Lawmakers worried that new weapons could intensify the Colombia conflict, while others warned that U.S. pilots could be killed or taken hostage, drawing the United States more deeply into the fighting that had sometimes been perceived as more a guerrilla war than a drug war.

Nonetheless, the House on July 24 turned back two Democratic attempts to reduce funding and shift money to global health programs. The amendments, by Barbara Lee of California and Jim McGovern of Massachusetts, were defeated by votes of 188–240 and 179–249, respectively. The House did agree by voice vote to an amendment by John Conyers Jr., D-Mich., to extend an existing law that limited to 800 the number of U.S. military personnel or civilian contractors allowed to participate in antidrug efforts in Colombia. The Appropriations Committee had dropped the requirement at the administration's request.

The House adopted by voice vote an amendment by Peter Hoekstra, R-Mich., to withhold $65 million in aid to Peru until the administration had safeguards to prevent a repeat of an incident in which the Peruvian Air Force, working with the CIA, accidentally shot down a light plane carrying U.S. missionaries. (*2002 intelligence authorization, p. 241*)

The House Foreign Operations Appropriations Subcommittee had restored about half of Bush's proposed cut to the Export-Import Bank, a priority of Subcommittee Chair Jim Kolbe, R-Ariz. The Ex-Im Bank financed overseas purchases of U.S. goods through low-interest direct loans, loan guarantees, and export credit insurance. Administration officials argued that businesses, particularly large exporters, should shoulder more of the burden when selling products overseas, but lawmakers from both parties had protested the proposed cuts. Bush requested $687 million, but the subcommittee recommended $805 million. That was reduced to $787 million when the full House reallocated some money in the bill during floor action.

SENATE ACTION

The Senate passed a $15.5 billion version of HR 2506 by a vote of 96–2 on Oct. 24. The Senate Appropriations Committee had reported the bill (S Rept 107-58) on Sept. 4.

Vermont Democrat Patrick J. Leahy, chair of the Senate Foreign Operations Appropriations Subcommittee, successfully managed to limit debate on the bill, arguing that the ongoing war on terrorism—as well as overall limits on spending—did not allow for extended deliberation on typically contentious concerns. Floor debate had already been delayed by Republicans protesting what they said was the Democrats' slow pace in confirming Bush's judicial nominees.

Leahy held off discussion of a provision he had authored in committee to overturn Bush's reinstatement of the Mexico City policy. And he beat back an attempt by Bob Graham, D-Fla., to increase the Andean antidrug money in the bill to the level requested by Bush. The Appropriations Committee had reduced the Andean aid by nearly one-fourth—from the $731 million requested to $567 million. And when the full Senate moved some money around in the bill that total was reduced even further—to $547 million. The bill also inserted several human rights conditions and required the administration to determine the safety of a herbicide sprayed on Colombia's coca crop.

Graham argued that failure to fully fund the program would lead to more cocaine on U.S. streets and put an unstable region at risk only a year after Congress had approved emergency funding for the region. But Leahy insisted that budget rules capped the bill's funding, and any additions would have to be offset by cuts in other programs. Graham's attempts to waive the budget rules failed, 27–72, on Oct. 24.

In other action that day, Sam Brownback, R-Kan., won voice vote adoption of an amendment to allow the president to waive restrictions on aid to Azerbaijan until Dec. 31, 2002, if he determined it was in the national interest. The administration said Azerbaijan was cooperating in the war against terrorism. The former Soviet republic of Azerbaijan and neighboring Armenia had been locked in a bitter dispute for more than a decade over the enclave of Nagorno-Karabakh.

Armenian Americans had considerable influence on Capitol Hill, and in 1992 Congress had barred direct U.S. government assistance to Azerbaijan until that nation lifted its war-related embargo on trade with Armenia (PL 102-511). But since then Congress had taken some steps to make it easier for energy companies and others to do business in the oil-rich Azerbaijan. An energy task force headed by Vice President Dick Cheney in 2001 pointed to Azerbaijan as a key source for oil and gas in the future. (Background, Congress and the Nation Vol. X, pp. 169, 185, 187)

The Appropriations Committee had recommended $806 million for the Ex-Im Bank, but that was reduced to $780 million during floor action.

CONFERENCE, FINAL ACTION

The House adopted the conference report on HR 2506 (H Rept 107-345) by a vote of 357–66 on Dec. 19, 2001. The Senate cleared the bill the next day by voice vote. President Bush signed it into law Jan. 10, 2002.

The bill's $15.4 billion total roughly split the difference between the earlier House and Senate versions. Compromise came quickly on all but the family planning provisions.

Senate Democrats were ready to relent on their bill's provision to overturn the Mexico City policy, but they insisted on getting a 50 percent increase in funds—a total of $37.5 million—for the United Nations Population Fund (UNFPA), which aided international family planning efforts. Angry GOP conservatives, led by Rep. Christopher H. Smith of New Jersey, threatened to block the conference report on the House floor. Conservatives were especially critical of UNFPA for undertaking family planning programs in China, where the government was accused of forcing women to undergo abortions as part of its population control programs. UNFPA denied that it supported abortion as a method of family planning.

Hoping to appease Smith and his allies and prevent their anger from affecting other bills, House Republican leaders kept postponing final consideration of the bill. In the end, they largely gave in to Senate demands. The final bill increased the U.S. contribution to UNFPA and dropped an annual provision that cut the U.S. contribution in direct proportion to the agency's activities in China.

MAJOR PROVISIONS

As signed into law, HR 2506 appropriated $15.4 billion for foreign aid and related programs in fiscal 2002. This included $578 million for export and investment assistance, $9.6 billion for bilateral economic assistance, $3.9 billion for military assistance, and $1.4 billion for multilateral assistance.

Major provisions of the bill:

Middle East

Provided $5.1 billion for Middle East assistance, including $2.8 billion in economic and military aid for Israel, $2 billion for Egypt, and $225 million for Jordan.

Andean Counterdrug Initiative

Provided $625 million for the next stage of the antidrug campaign in Colombia and neighboring countries. The bill also permitted the transfer of $35 million from International Narcotics Control and Law Enforcement funds.

The bill required the State Department to ensure that herbicides used in the aerial fumigation of coca did not pose health or safety risks to humans or the environment.

Conferees said they remained concerned about the prospects for U.S. involvement in Colombia's civil war and "strongly" expressed reservations and objections to any "mission creep" beyond the counterdrug effort.

The bill prohibited funding for the resumption of flights in support of Peru's air interdiction program until enhanced safeguards were in place.

Former Soviet Union

Appropriated $784 million for the republics of the former Soviet Union and $621 million for Eastern Europe and the Baltic states.

Azerbaijan

Allowed the president to waive restrictions on aid to Azerbaijan until Dec. 31, 2002, if he determined it was in the national interest.

HIV/AIDS Assistance

Provided $475 million to fight HIV/AIDS worldwide. Conferees also agreed to a $100 million contribution to the proposed global trust fund to fight AIDS, tuberculosis, and malaria, of which $40 million was to come from the $475 million. The global fund also received funding under the fiscal 2001 Labor-Health and Human Services-Education appropriations bill (HR 3061—PL 107-116) and the fiscal 2001 supplemental funding bill (HR 2216—PL 107-20).

Family Planning

Appropriated $447 million for international family planning programs.

The bill also provided $34 million to the United Nations Population Fund (UNFPA) but specified that none of it could be used for programs in China.

Export-Import Bank

Provided $779 million for the Export-Import Bank.

Debt Relief

Provided $229 million for international debt relief for poor countries.

2002 SUPPLEMENTAL

In July 2002 Congress cleared a $28.9 billion fiscal 2002 supplemental appropriations bill (HR 4775—PL 107-206).

President Bush subsequently declined to spend $5.1 billion that had been designated as contingency emergency spending.

As enacted, the bill's funding was primarily for defense and homeland security, but it did include $2.1 billion for foreign assistance and embassy security—$500 million more than requested but roughly equal to the House and Senate bills. This spending included $200 million for HIV/AIDS programs, $200 million for Israel, $50 million for the Palestinians, and $211 million for embassy construction and renovation in Afghanistan and Tajikistan.

The Senate version (S 2551—S Rept 107-156) had included a provision requiring the president to release by July 10 the $34 million appropriated in the regular 2002 foreign operations appropriations bill (HR 2506—PL 107-115) for U.N. family planning funds, if a White House commission found that U.N. workers did not aid or abet forced abortion or sterilization in China. A similar provision had been approved during House committee action and then dropped after GOP leaders warned that the provision could sink the entire bill. Conferees dropped the Senate language from the final bill (H Rept 107-593). On July 22—just two days before HR 4775 cleared—the Bush administration announced its decision to withhold the money. *(Details, 2003 aid appropriations, pp. 286, 287)*

The final bill restricted U.S. involvement with the new International Criminal Court, as had the House and Senate versions. *(International Criminal Court, p. 256)*

2003 Aid Appropriations

Both the Senate and House Appropriations committees in 2002 approved fiscal 2003 foreign operations spending bills, but neither reached the floor. The legislation initially was delayed by conflicts over abortion and then became ensnared in a broader spending dispute between Congress and the White House.

It was not until early in 2003 that a new Congress cleared an omnibus spending bill (H J Res 2—PL 108-7) with the foreign aid appropriations. In the meantime, a series of continuing resolutions in 2002 and 2003 had provided funding at the fiscal 2002 funding levels. *(PL 108-7, 2003 aid appropriations, p. 286)*

State Department Authorization

Congress in 2002 cleared a $13.8 billion fiscal 2003 State Department authorization bill (HR 1646—PL 107-228). HR 1646 authorized $8.6 billion for State Department and related operations, including efforts to enhance security at U.S. embassies and other diplomatic missions, and $5.2 billion for military aid and counterterrorism.

The bill had languished for months. It was sidetracked initially by more urgent priorities in the wake of the Sept. 11, 2001, terrorist attacks on the United States. Later it was stalled by disputes over such issues as GOP efforts to block U.S. co-

operation with a proposed International Criminal Court and whether to continue the State Department's certification that nations were complying with U.S. antidrug programs.

But by the fall of 2002 the situation had changed. With tension mounting over possible U.S. intervention in Iraq, members were eager to support the president's efforts. The turning point came Sept. 12, 2002, when President George W. Bush delivered a speech to the United Nations calling for a tough new U.N. Security Council resolution on Iraq. To bolster U.S. ties to the United Nations, the administration appealed for quick passage of the State Department authorization bill, which released $322 million in U.S. arrears to the United Nations and met Bush's pledge to rejoin the U.N. Education, Scientific and Cultural Organization (UNESCO). In less than three weeks, conferees resolved their differences, Congress cleared the bill, and Bush signed it into law. *(Iraq war, pp. 231, 238)*

The final bill also included several provisions to bolster ties with Russia, a permanent member of the U.N. Security Council whose support Bush needed for a strong new anti-Iraq resolution.

Disputes over the State Department authorization bill were nothing new. The legislation primarily authorized funding for State Department programs; multilateral aid administered by the department, such as international peacekeeping funds and refugee assistance; and U.S. information programs, such as Radio Free Asia and broadcasting to Cuba. (Most bilateral aid was authorized separately.) The programs had to be reauthorized every two years. But foreign affairs spending was not popular, and lawmakers typically avoided passing a separate State Department bill, instead attaching provisions to an appropriations bill. When HR 1646 stalled in 2001, for example, the need for a fiscal 2002 State Department authorization was waived under the Commerce-Justice-State appropriations bill (HR 2500—PL 107-77). The last time Congress had enacted a stand-alone bill was 1994.

HOUSE ACTION

The House passed HR 1646 on May 16, 2001, by a vote of 352–73. The House International Relations Committee had reported the bill (H Rept 107-57) on May 4.

The House bill authorized $8.2 billion for fiscal 2002 and such sums as were needed for fiscal 2003. Topping the list of issues that had threatened smooth passage of HR 1646 were abortion restrictions on international family planning aid and repayment of U.S. dues to the United Nations.

The debate over abortion-related restrictions on family planning aid went back to the Ronald Reagan administration's 1984 "Mexico City policy"—named for the city where it was first pronounced—which blocked U.S. aid to international family planning organizations that offered abortion counseling or lobbied nations to legalize abortion, even if they used their own money. The policy was rescinded in 1993 by President Bill Clinton but reinstated by Bush shortly after taking office in January 2001. The House International

Relations Committee voted 26–22 to amend HR 1646 to overturn Bush's decision, despite a warning from committee chair Henry J. Hyde, R-Ill., that the change could doom the bill. But the full House, where conservatives had more influence, reversed the committee decision by a vote of 218–210 on an amendment offered by Hyde May 16. On the vote, thirty-two Democrats crossed party lines to support the restrictions; thirty-three Republicans opposed them. *(Mexico City policy, box p. 247)*

Initially the bill authorized release of $826 million in back U.N. dues—$582 million in fiscal 2002 and $244 million in 2003. These were the second and third installments of a plan negotiated in December 2000, under which the United States agreed to pay a total of $926 million in back dues in exchange for a reduction in U.S. contributions and other organizational changes at the United Nations.

However, shortly before the House took up the bill, the United States lost its seat on the fifty-three-member U.N. Human Rights Commission. Loss of the seat in a secret ballot vote May 3 incensed lawmakers; the United States had been a member of the commission since its creation in 1946. Observers blamed the loss of the seat on the United States' mounting debt at the United Nations, plans to build a missile defense system, and its failure to ratify some international accords. House members retaliated by voting 252–165 on May 10 for a Hyde amendment to hold up the third installment of back dues until the United States regained its seat. The second installment was not affected, but after the bill stalled, it was authorized by separate legislation (S 248—PL 107-46). *(U.N. debt repayment, p. 253)*

Also not affected was the House International Relations Committee's decision, over opposition from conservative Republicans, to urge Bush to "take all necessary steps" to have the United States rejoin UNESCO. The United States withdrew from UNESCO in 1984 complaining of financial mismanagement and anti-Western bias. Supporters argued that UNESCO had changed substantially since then. Opponents acknowledged some of the changes but questioned devoting scarce budget resources to the agency. The House rejected, 193–225, on May 10 an amendment by Tom Tancredo, R-Colo., to remove the $67 million in the bill for the United States to rejoin.

Another issue concerned the proposed creation of an International Criminal Court to handle war crimes and other human rights violations. Opponents warned that such a court could expose U.S. troops to politically motivated accusations and trials. During May 10 action on HR 1646, the House adopted 282–137 an amendment by Majority Whip Tom DeLay, R-Texas, to bar any U.S. cooperation with the International Criminal Court. *(International Criminal Court, p. 256)*

Despite the opposition of Secretary of State Colin L. Powell, the House on May 16 adopted 216–210 an amendment to cut off military education and training funds for Lebanon, unless that country used its army to oust Hezbollah guerril-las from its southern border with Israel. Guerrillas in that area regularly launched rocket attacks on Israel. The amendment, offered by Tom Lantos, D-Calif., also called for the administration to develop a plan for cutting off $35 million in economic assistance if Lebanon did not comply within six months. Opponents said the amendment would further destabilize the Middle East.

SENATE ACTION

The Senate Foreign Relations Committee reported an $18.4 billion fiscal 2002–2003 State Department authorization bill (S 1401—S Rept 107-60) on Sept. 4, 2001, but that bill never reached the Senate floor. S 1401 provided for the release of the second installment of U.N. dues payments, and the administration had hoped it would be finished before Bush attended the opening of the General Assembly in September. But Chair Joseph R. Biden Jr., D-Del., said at the time his panel approved the bill in August that a crowded Senate calendar and significant differences between the House and Senate versions of the bill made that unlikely. Ultimately, the events of Sept. 11 sidelined the authorization legislation for months.

The Senate passed HR 1646 by voice vote on May 1, 2002, after substituting the text of a foreign military assistance bill (S 1803). The Senate Foreign Relations Committee had reported S 1803 (S Rept 107-122) on Dec. 11, 2001, and the full Senate had passed it by voice vote on Dec. 20.

Biden argued that the military assistance part of the House bill provided enough common ground for the two versions to be reconciled in conference. The pre-conference work on the State Department bill gained momentum after the United States in April 2002 was elected to return to the U.N. Human Rights Commission for the period 2003–2005.

The House agreed to a conference on Sept. 12—the same day Bush called for U.N. approval of a new resolution on Iraq—by a vote of 382–0.

CONFERENCE, FINAL ACTION

With Congress focused on a request by Bush for sweeping war powers against Iraq, House and Senate conferees met Sept. 18, 2002, and quickly agreed on a compromise State Department bill.

The House adopted the conference report on HR 1646 (H Rept 107-671) by voice vote Sept. 25, and the Senate agreed by voice vote the next day. The president signed it into law Sept. 30.

A major obstacle to House-Senate agreement on the bill had been removed when Rep. DeLay attached his International Criminal Court amendment to a popular fiscal 2002 supplemental spending bill (HR 4775—PL 107-206) that cleared in July. Senate Democrats had vowed to oppose any final version of the State Department authorization that included DeLay's language.

In addition to releasing the $322 million to the United Nations, the final bill modified conditions set in U.S. law for paying the arrears, bringing them close to an agreement that had been reached with the United Nations in 2000. To avoid future arrears, Congress also recommended that the United States should move toward paying its dues at the beginning of the U.N. budget cycle in January, rather than the beginning of the United States' fiscal year in October.

Final negotiations bogged down briefly over an attempt by House International Relations Committee Chair Hyde to include a bill (HR 3969) on U.S. government broadcasting and international exchange programs in the final conference report. HR 3969 (H Rept 107-493) had been reported by Hyde's committee on June 5, 2002, and passed by voice vote of the House on July 22. The bill sought to shake up the nation's "public diplomacy" bureaucracy and authorize an additional $255 million for international outreach and media programs, including expanded efforts to improve the U.S. image in the Arab world. But Biden objected to Hyde's plans to alter the role of the board charged with overseeing U.S. government broadcasters. Unable to resolve the dispute, conferees left the provisions out of HR 1646.

The bill suspended the State Department's annual drug certification program for two years. Under a 1986 law (PL 99-570), the president was required to draw up and send to Congress an annual list of countries that were major sources or conduits for illicit drugs and then determine which ones were not fully assisting U.S. antidrug efforts. Unless the president waived punishment, such countries could lose part of their U.S. aid, as well as trade benefits. The countries contended that the process was humiliating, and they questioned how the United States, as the largest consumer of illegal drugs, could challenge their antidrug efforts. Secretary of State Powell requested the moratorium, saying the grading process insulted allies such as Mexico and hurt U.S. antidrug operations. The Senate bill had called for a three-year suspension; the House bill would have left the existing process in place. *(PL 99-570, Congress and the Nation Vol. VII, p. 723)*

Conferees adopted a Senate initiative to forgive certain Russian debts in exchange for investments in nonproliferation programs. Russia had assumed the Soviet Union's debt and owed roughly $2.7 billion to the United States. The measure also revived a State Department program to relocate Russian scientists to the United States in an effort to prevent them from taking jobs with U.S. enemies, such as Iraq. From 1992 through its expiration in 1996, the program (PL 102-509) allowed up to 750 highly skilled scientists and their families to emigrate from the former Soviet Union to the United States without meeting the normal requirement that they first be recruited by a U.S. employer. The conference agreement extended the program for four years and increased to 950 the number of scientists who could be admitted. *(PL 102-509, Congress and the Nation Vol. VIII, p. 794)*

Conferees scaled back a House amendment that would have punished Lebanon for not adequately controlling Hezbollah guerrillas operating on its border with Israel.

The conference agreement included a provision that effectively recognized Jerusalem as the capital of Israel. Among other things, it urged the president to immediately begin the process of relocation of the U.S. embassy in Israel from Tel Aviv to Jerusalem as called for in a 1995 law (PL 104-45). President Bush sidestepped the issue by declaring the provision in question "advisory" rather than "mandatory" when he signed the bill into law. The U.S. government had long declined to endorse anyone's claims to sovereignty over disputed Jerusalem, leaving the resolution of the matter to Israeli-Palestinian negotiations. *(PL 104-45, Congress and the Nation Vol. IX, p. 249)*

MAJOR PROVISIONS

As signed into law, HR 1646 authorized a total of $13.8 billion for fiscal 2003—$8.6 billion for State Department and related operations and $5.2 billion for military aid and counterterrorism.

Major provisions of the bill:

U.N. Debt Repayment

Authorized $322 million in back payments to the United Nations—$244 million for the fiscal 2003 payment, plus $78 million in U.S. dues that had accumulated since Congress began considering the legislation in 2001.

The bill modified conditions set in U.S. law for paying the arrears and expressed the sense of Congress that the United States should move toward paying its U.N. dues in January, instead of October, to coincide with the U.N. budget cycle. *(U.N. debt repayment, p. 253)*

Embassy Security

Authorized $555 million for embassy security, construction, and maintenance, and raised from $900 million to $1 billion per year the additional embassy security funding authorized under the fiscal 2000 omnibus appropriations act (PL 106-113). *(PL 106-113, Congress and the Nation Vol. X, p. 217)*

International Broadcasting

Authorized $486 million, including funding for Radio Free Asia, broadcasts to Cuba, and Voice of America services to the Middle East.

International Organizations, Peacekeeping

Authorized $891 million for assessed contributions to international organizations in fiscal 2003, much of it for the United Nations. In addition, the law authorized $726 million for assessed U.S. contributions to the United Nations and regional organizations for international peacekeeping activities in fiscal 2003.

Foreign Military Sales, Training

Authorized $4.1 billion for foreign military sales programs, particularly military funding for Israel and Egypt.

The bill also authorized $85 million for International Military Education and Training.

Drug Certification

Suspended for two years the State Department's annual drug certification program.

Russia

Forgave certain Russian debts in exchange for investments in nonproliferation programs. Up to 10 percent of the funds saved by Russia because of any debt relief was to be used to promote independent media and the rule of law in Russia.

The bill also revived and extended for four years a State Department program to relocate Russian scientists and their families in the United States without meeting the normal requirement that they first be recruited by a U.S. employer. The number of scientists who could be admitted was increased from a total of 750 set in the original program to 950.

Taiwan

Authorized the sale of four *Kidd*-class Navy destroyers to Taiwan. It also boosted Taipei's standing in the pecking order of U.S. military sales, raising it to the status of a "major non-NATO ally."

Lebanon

Authorized $25 million in military training funds to Lebanon but held another $10 million in escrow until Lebanon asserted its authority over Hezbollah guerrillas operating along Lebanon's southern border with Israel.

Israel

Expressed Congress's commitment to relocating the U.S. embassy in Israel to Jerusalem and urged the president to immediately begin the process of relocation called for in a 1995 law (PL 104-45). The bill also prohibited the use of funds to operate a U.S. consulate or diplomatic facility in Jerusalem that was not under the supervision of the U.S. ambassador and prohibited the publication of any government document that listed countries and their capitals and did not identify Jerusalem as the capital of Israel. It also permitted Americans born in Jerusalem to list Israel as their place of birth on a passport or birth certificate. (President Bush declared that he would consider this section of the law to be "advisory.")

Palestinians

Required the president to report every six months on whether the Palestine Liberation Organization (PLO) and Palestinian Authority were abiding by commitments to renounce violence and assume responsibility over all PLO personnel. Failure of the Palestinians to comply could result in U.S. sanctions.

International Criminal Court

Barred any of the funds appropriated for the regular budget of the United Nations from being used for the International Criminal Court.

U.N. Debt Repayment

The 107th Congress moved to bolster U.S. ties with the United Nations by agreeing to complete the United States' repayment of back U.N. dues. Congress cleared a bill in 2001 to release the second installment (S 248—PL 107-46) and in 2002 authorized payment of the third and final installment as part of the 2003 State Department authorization bill (HR 1646—PL 107-228).

After the Sept. 11, 2001, terrorist attacks on the United States, Bush administration officials had pressed for quick action, arguing that failure to pay the debt was an obstacle to rallying diplomatic support for the war on terrorism. The bill authorizing the second installment cleared a little less than two weeks after the attacks. Approval of the final payment came a year later as tension mounted over possible U.S. intervention in Iraq and Congress was eager to support the president's efforts to win U.N. Security Council support for a tough new resolution on Iraq.

BACKGROUND

During the previous decade, concern over some U.N. programs, dissatisfaction with U.S. financial contribution levels, and partisan politicking had frayed relations between the United States and the United Nations.

Arrears had mounted over several decades for a variety of reasons. The United States had fallen behind almost $300 million in contributions to the U.N.'s regular budget because Congress, in a series of bills, ordered the administration to withhold the money. The United States also owed almost $1 billion for peacekeeping operations in Somalia, Bosnia, and other places. The Clinton administration had disputed about $250 million of that, in part because a 1994 law (PL 103-236) blocked the United States from paying more than 25 percent of the peacekeeping budget, even though other U.N. members had never agreed to reduce the U.S. share below about 31 percent. *(PL 103-236, Congress and the Nation Vol. IX, p. 212)*

The fiscal 2000 omnibus appropriations law (PL 106-113) contained what was known as the Helms-Biden agreement, after Foreign Relations Chair Jesse Helms, R-N.C., and ranking Democrat Joseph R. Biden Jr. of Delaware. The agreement authorized $926 million in back payments. The total consisted of $819 million ($100 million in fiscal 1998 funds, $475 million in fiscal 1999, and $244 million in fiscal 2000), plus $107 million owed by the United Nations for U.S. peacekeeping that would be used instead to reduce U.S. arrears. *(PL 106-113, Congress and the Nation Vol. X, p. 219)*

The first $100 million was released in December 1999. But to receive the remaining money, the United Nations had to agree to a number of conditions, including a reduction in the U.S. share of the regular U.N. budget from 25 percent to 22 percent and a cut in the U.S. portion of the peacekeeping budget from 31 percent to 25 percent. Release of the second and third installments required authorizing legislation confirming that the United Nations had met the conditions.

In December 2000 Richard C. Holbrooke, the Clinton administration's representative to the United Nations, negotiated an agreement that came close enough to the Helms-Biden plan to receive endorsement from both senators. The United States agreed to repay $926 million in exchange for permanent reduction in U.S. payments to 22 percent of the regular budget and 28 percent of the peacekeeping budget, declining to about 26 percent by 2004.

SECOND INSTALLMENT

The Senate passed S 248 by a vote of 99–0 on Feb. 7, 2001. The Senate Foreign Relations Committee had reported the bill earlier that day (no written report).

House International Relations Committee Chair Henry J. Hyde, R-Ill., originally opposed taking up the stand-alone bill, arguing that it should be considered together with a bill (HR 1794) by Majority Whip Tom DeLay, R-Texas, to bar U.S. participation in a proposed International Criminal Court. The House included the U.N. repayment, as well as DeLay's proposal, in the fiscal 2002–2003 State Department authorization bill (HR 1646) it passed May 16. That bill initially authorized the release of both the second and third installments. However, two weeks before House passage, the United States was removed from the U.N. Commission on Human Rights. An angry House responded on May 10 by adopting, 252–165, an amendment conditioning the third installment on the United States regaining its seat. *(2003 State Department authorization, p. 250; International Criminal Court, p. 256)*

The administration hoped to have the debt payment in hand by September, when President George W. Bush was due to attend the opening of the General Assembly. U.N. Secretary-General Kofi Annan warned July 31 that unless the debts were repaid they would soon undermine U.S. effectiveness in the United Nations. But quick Senate action on HR 1646 appeared unlikely, and Hyde did not want to move the U.N. payment without DeLay's court provision.

With the Sept. 11 attacks, however, Washington put a premium on international cooperation against terrorism. After receiving assurance from the administration that it would support legislation barring cooperation with the International Criminal Court, the House cleared S 248 by voice vote Sept. 24 with only twenty minutes of debate.

As signed into law Oct. 5, 2001, the measure:

• Authorized the release of $582 million as a second installment of back payments of U.S. dues to the United Nations.

• Modified conditions for releasing the money set in existing law to bring them in line with the agreement struck with the United Nations in December 2000. S 248 increased the cap on U.S. contributions to the U.N. peacekeeping budget from 25 percent to 28.2 percent.

THIRD INSTALLMENT

The third installment of back dues ended up in the State Department authorization bill after all. By the time HR 1646 cleared on Sept. 26, 2002, the United States had been voted back onto the Human Rights Commission for the 2003–2005 term, so that issue was off the table. Moreover, it was in the United States' interests to pay the debt and be in good standing at the United Nations if it hoped to win backing for the Iraq resolution.

As signed into law on Sept. 30, 2002, the measure:

• Released $322 million in back payments to the United Nations—$244 million for the fiscal 2003 payments, plus $78 million in U.S. dues that had accumulated since Congress began considering the legislation in 2001.

• Modified conditions set in U.S. law for releasing the money to bring them close to the agreement struck with the United Nations in December 2000. The bill provided for the cap on U.S. contributions to the U.N. peacekeeping budget to drop from 28.2 percent in fiscal 2001 to 27.4 percent in fiscal 2004. The cap of 25 percent set in PL 106-113 was to be restored after 2004. The United Nations had been calculating the U.S. share at 30 percent, which contributed to the buildup of U.S. arrears. U.S. payments to the U.N. general budget were set at 22 percent of the total.

• Expressed the sense of Congress that the United States should move toward paying its U.N. dues in January, rather than October, to coincide with the U.N. budget cycle. The fact that the United States was perpetually behind was a major factor in the arrears.

Iran-Libya Sanctions

Congress in 2001 cleared a five-year extension of sanctions on foreign businesses that invested in the energy industries of Iran or Libya (HR 1954—PL 107-24). The sanctions, which also were tightened under the new law, were aimed at punishing Iran and Libya for their alleged support for terrorism and their efforts to acquire nuclear, chemical, and biological weapons.

Business groups and European governments successfully blocked the implementation of the original 1996 Iran-Libya sanctions act (PL 104-172), which was set to expire Aug. 5, 2001. They hoped that with a new Republican administration in office, the law would not be renewed. President George W. Bush and Vice President Dick Cheney had signaled their opposition to the law in the past, and Iran and Libya had taken some steps toward rapprochement with the United States. *(PL 104-172, Congress and the Nation Vol. IX, p. 239)*

But strong lobbying by pro-Israel groups—aided by mixed views within the administration—enabled supporters to pass the five-year extension with relative ease. The final bill also lowered the threshold for the level of investment in Libya that would trigger sanctions.

Although Bush had called for a two-year extension along with a comprehensive review, he signed the bill into law.

BACKGROUND

U.S. sanctions on Iran dated to the 1979 seizure of the U.S. embassy in Tehran. Economic sanctions were first imposed in 1984 after the Reagan administration determined that Iran had been involved in the bombing of a U.S. Marine barracks in Beirut the year before. In 1995 President Bill Clinton issued a series of executive orders that effectively prohibited the export of U.S. goods and services to Iran, banned the re-export of certain U.S. goods and technology to Iran from third countries, and prohibited any U.S. investment in or financing of Iran-related ventures. Clinton's actions were triggered by Iran's growing efforts to get nuclear expertise and its ties to groups accused of carrying out terrorist attacks in Israel.

Sanctions on Libya were initially a response to the 1988 bombing of Pan Am Flight 103 over Lockerbie, Scotland, which killed 270 people, including 189 Americans. U.S. and British authorities in 1991 had charged two mid-level Libyan intelligence agents in connection with the bombing, but at the time Libya had refused to turn them over for trial.

The 1996 Iran-Libya sanctions law was passed after Iran decided to open its petroleum and gas markets to foreign investment in the mid-1990s. It required the president to impose at least two out of a list of six possible sanctions on foreign firms that invested more than $20 million a year in Iran's energy sector, or $40 million a year in Libya's. Sanctioned firms could be denied access to Export-Import Bank credits, U.S. military exports, U.S. bank loans, or U.S. government contracts. The president could waive the sanctions if he determined that doing so was in the national interest.

Because of strong opposition from business groups, especially within the European Union (EU), the sanctions were never imposed. The EU argued that the sanctions were an attempt by the United States to apply U.S. law internationally and threatened to take the matter to the World Trade Organization. Clinton waived sanctions several times in return for increased cooperation in fighting terrorism and arms and technology trade with those nations.

With energy prices at historically high levels, and with Cheney, who had opposed sanctions during his years as an oil industry executive, in charge of drafting the administration's energy plan, opponents of an extension hoped to limit, if not end, the sanctions.

Moreover, Iran and Libya had taken some steps since 1996 to improve their relations with the United States. Iran had twice elected a moderate cleric, Mohammad Khatami, as president, and Iranian and U.S. officials had taken some tentative steps toward rapprochement. Libya, meanwhile, turned over the intelligence agents believed to have carried out the Pan Am Flight 103 bombing. One of those suspects was sentenced to life in prison Jan. 31, 2001.

LEGISLATIVE ACTION

The House passed the sanctions bill, 409–6, on July 26, 2001. The House International Relations Committee had reported HR 1954 (H Rept 107-107, Part I) on June 22, and the House Ways and Means Committee reported its version (Part II) on July 16. House debate was delayed for a week while the two committees argued over which version would come to the floor. The final bill largely reflected the International Relations bill, which provided for a five-year extension instead of the two-year extension favored by Ways and Means. A Ways and Means Committee proposal for a presidential report on the effectiveness of the sanctions survived, although the final version did include the committee's provision for an expedited vote on removing the sanctions if the report was critical.

The Senate passed its bill (S 1218) by a vote of 96–2 on July 25. The Senate Banking, Housing, and Urban Affairs Committee had reported the bill (no written report), which was identical to the House International Relations Committee version, on July 23. Following House passage of HR 1954, the Senate took up that bill and cleared it by voice vote July 27. Bush signed it Aug. 3.

MAJOR PROVISIONS

As signed into law, HR 1954:

• Extended the 1996 Iran-Libya sanctions act until Aug. 5, 2006.

• Lowered the threshold for investment in Libya from $40 million to $20 million—the same as for companies investing in Iran.

• Closed a loophole that allowed companies with oil contracts in Libya or Iran that existed before the 1996 law went into effect to amend those contracts without being subject to sanctions.

• Required the president to submit a report on the effectiveness of sanctions no earlier than twenty-four months and no later than thirty months after enactment of HR 1954.

Pakistan Sanctions

Congress in 2001 cleared legislation (S 1465—PL 107-57) allowing the president to waive key sanctions on Pakistan for two years. The Bush administration had urged Congress to pass the legislation to reward Pakistan for its cooperation in the war against terrorism.

President George W. Bush had moved quickly after the Sept. 11, 2001, terrorist attacks to aid Pakistan, including lifting sanctions related to the country's 1998 nuclear weapons test. He also provided $100 million in aid—$50 million each in fiscal 2001 and 2002. To provide additional assistance, however, Bush needed congressional authority.

S 1465 provided that authority, though it required the president to certify that such aid "would facilitate the transition to democratic rule" before sanctions could be waived in fiscal 2003.

(Authority to waive the sanctions subsequently was extended through fiscal 2004 by the fiscal 2004 Iraq supplemental appropriations bill (HR 3289—PL 108-106) and through 2006 by the intelligence overhaul bill (S 2845—PL 108-458).)

BACKGROUND

Pakistan had been subject to a variety of U.S. sanctions since the 1980s. Under a 1985 amendment (PL 99-83) to the Foreign Assistance Act (PL 87-195), economic and military aid to Pakistan was cut off automatically unless the president certified, before the start of each fiscal year, that Pakistan "does not possess a nuclear explosive device" and that the aid would "reduce significantly" the risk that Pakistan would acquire such weapons. *(Pakistan aid, Congress and the Nation Vol. VII, p. 225)*

During the 1980s, Presidents Ronald Reagan and George H. W. Bush provided the certification despite some serious reservations about Pakistan's nuclear potential. At the time, Pakistan was viewed as a strategic ally in the drive to expel the Soviet Union from neighboring Afghanistan. But in 1990, with reports that Pakistan had developed the ability to launch a nuclear strike, Bush declined to renew the certification and aid was suspended. By then the Soviets had withdrawn from Afghanistan.

Pakistan's test of a nuclear weapon in May 1998, following a similar test by India, triggered sanctions against both countries under 1994 amendments (PL 103-236) to the 1968 Arms Export Control Act (PL 90-629). *(PL 103-236, Congress and the Nation Vol. IX, p. 212)*

But President Bill Clinton soon lifted most of those sanctions, and the fiscal 2000 defense appropriations bill (PL 106-79) gave him further authority to waive the nuclear sanctions. *(PL 106-79, Congress and the Nation Vol. X, pp. 223, 283)*

Pakistan's failure to make payments on its debts to the United States, and the 1999 overthrow of Pakistan's democratically elected government by Gen. Pervez Musharraf, who later became president, triggered new layers of sanctions under various provisions of the Foreign Assistance Act. The act allowed the president to waive sanctions under certain conditions but limited the amount of aid that could be provided to $50 million a year.

After the Sept. 11 attacks the Bush administration, led by Secretary of State Colin L. Powell, concentrated on assembling an international coalition to combat terrorism. Powell praised Musharaff for facing down strong domestic opposition to provide the United States with military bases, overflight rights, and intelligence to counter terrorist leader Osama bin Laden's al Qaeda network and Afghanistan's Taliban government. *(Afghanistan war, pp. 230, 234)*

On Sept. 22 Bush issued an executive order lifting the nuclear weapons sanctions in return for Pakistan's cooperation as a frontline ally in the campaign in Afghanistan. That allowed him to release $50 million in aid; he released another $50 million Oct. 17, after the start of the new fiscal year.

LEGISLATIVE ACTION

The Senate passed S 1465 by voice vote Oct. 4, 2001. The Senate Foreign Relations Committee had reported the bill (no written report) earlier that day.

The pace slowed slightly when the bill reached the House, where it ran into opposition from lawmakers who favored warm ties with India and from appropriators concerned about Congress losing its oversight in a key area of foreign policy. The appropriators expressed particular concern about waiving prodemocracy sanctions in fiscal 2003, when Pakistan was scheduled to hold elections. They had regularly included a provision in the annual foreign operations spending bill that barred aid to military-led governments that had deposed civilian rulers. The Senate bill scaled back this requirement by asking instead that the president certify that aid to Pakistan would facilitate its transition to democracy.

But when the House took up the bill, Secretary of State Powell was in Islamabad meeting with Musharraf, and few House members were willing to buck the administration. The House cleared S 1465 by voice vote Oct. 16. Bush signed it Oct. 27.

MAJOR PROVISIONS

As signed into law, S 1465:

• Gave the president authority to waive all sanctions against Pakistan in fiscal 2002. The president could waive the sanctions in fiscal 2003 if he certified to Congress that doing so would ease Pakistan's transition to democracy and assist U.S. actions against international terrorism. He would have to notify Congress five days in advance of such a waiver.

• Allowed the president in fiscal 2003 to waive additional sanctions imposed on Pakistan for violating the Missile Control Technology Regime by acquiring arms from China.

• Ended prohibitions on loans and economic assistance placed on Pakistan because of its default on loans.

• Eased restrictions on U.S. shipments of excess weaponry to nations able to assist in antiterrorism efforts.

International Criminal Court

Congress in 2002 cleared legislation (HR 4775—PL 107-206) barring U.S. cooperation with the newly formed International Criminal Court. Opponents of the court, which had been created to handle war crimes, genocide, and other major human rights violations, feared that it could expose U.S. troops to politically motivated accusations and trials.

The Bush administration's decision in 2002 to revoke the United States' signature to the treaty creating the court gave court opponents the go-ahead to attach their proposal to HR 4775, a must-pass fiscal 2002 supplemental spending bill. Known as the American Service Members' Protection Act, the amendment prohibited U.S. participation in or cooperation with the court, restricted—with some exceptions—military aid to nations that ratified the treaty creating the court, and granted the president sweeping authority to use military force to retrieve U.S. or allied personnel detained by the court. The amendment also restricted U.S. participation in certain peacekeeping operations unless there were guarantees that they would be outside the court's jurisdiction. The president could waive the restrictions under certain conditions.

BACKGROUND

Despite intense opposition from the Pentagon and key congressional leaders, the United States had signed the 1998 treaty creating the court on Dec. 31, 2000. Though President Bill Clinton's decision to sign it heartened human rights activists, Clinton himself said that the treaty had "significant flaws" and that he would not submit it to the Senate for approval or recommend that his successor, George W. Bush, do so. He said that the United States had signed the accord to indicate support for international accountability and bringing to justice perpetrators of crimes against humanity, and also to remain involved in the court's formation. Treaty supporters said signing it would enable the United States to exercise particular influence in the period before the treaty entered into force.

The treaty went into effect on July 1, 2002, after sixty states had ratified it. But two months earlier, on May 6, the Bush administration renounced the treaty, echoing opponents' views that the court could entangle U.S. service members.

LEGISLATIVE ACTION

House Majority Whip Tom DeLay, R-Texas, first attached the amendment barring cooperation with the court to a fiscal 2002–2003 State Department authorization bill (HR 1646). His amendment was adopted by a vote of 282–137 on May 10, 2001. But that bill stalled, in part because Senate Democrats, angered by the provision, vowed to oppose any final version of the State Department bill that included DeLay's language. *(State Department authorization, p. 250)*

Faced with that prospect, DeLay saw little chance of his measure becoming law—until the White House renounced the treaty. The administration's announcement—and a strong statement assailing the court by Defense Secretary Donald H. Rumsfeld—gave DeLay the green light to move quickly on his provision and attach it to other, more viable legislation. After conferring with the White House, DeLay offered his provision as an amendment to the supplemental spending bill. The amendment was adopted by a vote of 38–18 in the House Appropriations Committee.

HR 4775 was a popular bill, and Senate Democrats opposed to DeLay's provision acknowledged that they would

be unable to stop it. Indeed, the full Senate adopted a nearly identical amendment, offered by John W. Warner, R-Va., by a vote of 75–19 on June 6, 2002. The Senate provision, which added language authorizing cooperation in international efforts to bring to justice certain individuals such as terrorist leader Osama bin Laden, was the version enacted into law on Aug. 2.

The court controversy surfaced during debate on other bills as well. For example, the Senate on Sept. 10, 2001, during consideration of the fiscal 2002 Commerce-Justice-State appropriations bill (HR 2500—PL 107–77), adopted by voice vote an amendment offered by Larry E. Craig, R-Idaho, to prohibit U.S. money from going to the creation of the court. Conferees included Craig's amendment in the final bill. The Senate on Dec. 7, 2001, by a vote of 78–21, attached an amendment similar to DeLay's to the 2002 defense appropriations bill (HR 3338—PL 107–117). That provision, sponsored by Jesse Helms, R-N.C., was dropped in conference, but the final bill did include a provision preventing Pentagon funds from being used to support the court. During consideration of the fiscal 2003 defense authorization bill (HR 4546—PL 107–314), the House on May 10, 2002, adopted, 264–152, an amendment by Ron Paul, R-Texas, expressing the sense of the House that no funds authorized by the bill could be used to cooperate with the court. Conferees dropped the provision, saying it was no longer necessary because of the enactment of HR 4775. The State Department authorization that was the original vehicle for DeLay's proposal (HR 1646—PL 107-228) included language to prevent funds appropriated for the regular budget of the United Nations from being used for the court.

HIV/AIDS Assistance

Both the House and Senate passed legislation (HR 2069) aimed at increasing U.S. support for overseas HIV/AIDS programs, but the bill died at the end of the 107th Congress when negotiators for the two chambers failed to reach agreement on a compromise version. Differences over money and the scope of the bill had proved insurmountable.

After years of relative apathy, there was widespread agreement in Washington that more had to be done to control the spread of AIDS, particularly in sub-Saharan Africa. According to the United Nations, more than 25.3 million adults and children in that region were infected with the disease, making up more than 70 percent of the worldwide total. An estimated 17 million Africans had died from AIDS, including 2.4 million in 2000. There already were 6.5 million orphans as a result of the AIDS epidemic, a number that was expected to grow to more than 15 million by 2010.

In response, Congress in 2000 increased bilateral spending on the disease and pledged to contribute to multilateral efforts to fight its spread. *(PL 106-264, Congress and the Nation Vol. X, p. 230)*

Although the United States was already the largest single donor to anti-AIDS efforts in Africa, contributions from governments of wealthy countries fell far short of what United Nations officials said was needed. In early 2001 U.N. Secretary-General Kofi Annan called for a global fund to halt and reverse the spread of HIV/AIDS and the greater incidence of tuberculosis and malaria in those who suffered from the disease. The concept for an international funding mechanism had its roots in a G8 summit meeting the previous year. A U.N. General Assembly special session on HIV/AIDS endorsed the concept in mid-2001, and the Global Fund to Fight AIDS, Tuberculosis, and Malaria was established in January 2002.

U.N. officials said the global fund would need $7 billion to $10 billion a year, about half for prevention and half for treatment, including care for orphans. About $2 billion was projected to come from the African nations themselves and the rest from wealthy countries and private donors such as a foundation supported by Microsoft cofounder Bill Gates.

The House passed HR 2069 by voice vote Dec.11, 2001. The House version would have authorized $1.4 billion in fiscal 2002 to target AIDS, including $750 million for a global fund or other multilateral efforts to combat AIDS, $560 million for bilateral programs operated primarily by the U.S. Agency for International Development, and $50 million for a pilot program to help African nations buy medicines to treat AIDS. The House International Relations Committee had reported HR 2069 (H Rept 107-137) on July 12.

The Senate passed HR 2069 by voice vote July 12, 2002, after substituting the text of a bill (S 2525—S Rept 107-206) reported by the Senate Foreign Relations Committee July 3. The Senate version would have authorized $4.7 billion in fiscal 2003–2004, including $2.2 billion for the global fund. The total also included $1.7 billion for bilateral programs and $500 million in fiscal 2003 for international activities administered by the Department of Health and Human Services (HHS), primarily the Centers for Disease Control and Prevention. The Senate bill also called for more debt relief for AIDS-afflicted countries and included authorization for additional funds for vaccine programs and programs to treat tuberculosis and malaria.

House and Senate negotiators came close to a compromise authorizing $4 billion for international AIDS programs over two years, with a $2 billion cap on money for the new global fund. Senate provisions on debt relief and HHS programs would have been dropped because of objections from several House chairs who said they intruded on their committees' jurisdictions. But the compromise stalled because two Senate Republicans anonymously placed holds on the bill and House leaders were skeptical about trying to push such an expensive measure through in the last hours of the session.

The following year, however, Congress was able to overcome partisan and bicameral differences and pass a $15 billion, five-year authorization bill (HR 1298—PL 108-25). *(HIV/AIDS assistance, pp. 257, 296)*

Congress in 2001 approved an additional $100 million for international HIV/AIDS assistance as part of a fiscal 2001 supplemental appropriations bill (HR 2216—PL 107-20). The fiscal 2002 foreign operations appropriations bill (HR 2506—PL 107-115) provided $475 million for HIV/AIDS treatment and prevention, as well as $100 million for a proposed global trust fund to fight AIDS, tuberculosis, and malaria ($40 million of which was to come from the $475 million). A fiscal 2002 supplemental appropriations bill (HR 4775—PL 107-206) included $200 million for HIV/AIDS programs. The fiscal 2003 foreign operations spending bill (H J Res 2—PL 108-7) provided more than $800 million for assistance to prevent and treat HIV/AIDS, as well as tuberculosis and malaria. HIV/AIDS funds were included in other appropriations as well. *(2002 aid appropriations, p. 246; 2003 aid appropriations, p. 286)*

Sudan Sanctions

Congress in 2002 cleared legislation (HR 5531—PL 107-245) aimed at helping end a two-decade civil war in the African nation of Sudan. A coalition of religious conservatives and African American lawmakers had pushed the issue onto the congressional agenda.

HR 5531 called for sanctions against Sudan if the Khartoum government did not take part in peace talks. It also authorized aid to democratic groups outside the government's control.

The United States was already taking many of the steps outlined in the bill under numerous existing sanctions against Sudan, such as those enacted because of its state sponsorship of terrorism. Moreover, HR 5531 was far less stringent than legislation (HR 2052) the House had passed the previous year. But HR 2052 had contained a controversial provision to prevent companies from raising capital in the United States if they played a role in Sudan's expanding oil and gas industries. Wall Street and the White House opposed the provision, and conference action on that bill was blocked in the Senate.

After a yearlong standoff, a compromise was reached in the form of HR 5531.

BACKGROUND

War between Sudan's northern Muslim government and people in the south—most of whom practiced Christianity or folk religions—had raged since the early 1980s, causing widespread famine, killing an estimated 2 million people, and displacing an estimated 4 million others. The Sudanese government had been accused of blocking humanitarian aid and food shipments, bombing villages, and allowing slavery.

Terrorist mastermind Osama bin Laden reportedly had been based in Sudan from 1991 to 1996, and Khartoum was regularly identified as a state sponsor of terrorism. In the wake of the 1998 bombings of two U.S. embassies in Africa, the United States launched retaliatory air strikes against several targets, including a site in Khartoum. *(Terrorism policy, Congress and the Nation Vol. X, p. 267)*

In 2000 both chambers of Congress passed legislation focusing on Sudan's human rights abuses. But Congress ran out of time before it could reconcile the House bill, which called for a significant tightening of sanctions, and the Senate bill, which did not.

In 2001 the new Bush administration condemned human rights violations in Sudan, though it opposed sanctions. Responding to members of Congress, President George W. Bush in September named former senator John Danforth, R-Mo. (1976–1995), an Episcopal priest, as a special envoy to try to bring peace to Sudan. Danforth later became U.S. representative to the United Nations. *(Foreign policy leadership, p. 234)*

Another conflict in Sudan, this time in the western region of Darfur, would capture the attention of lawmakers in the 108th Congress. *(Sudan relief assistance, p. 298)*

LEGISLATIVE ACTION

The House had passed HR 2052 by a vote of 422–2 on June 13, 2001. The House International Relations Committee had reported the bill (H Rept 107-92, Part I) on June 8. The committee bill included a provision—opposed by the Bush administration—to block businesses that operated in Sudan from trading securities in U.S. capital markets unless they disclosed to the Securities and Exchange Commission details of those activities in reports that were to be made public. And when the bill reached the floor, the House adopted by voice vote an amendment by Spencer Bachus, R-Ala., that barred foreign companies from raising capital in the United States or listing their securities on U.S. markets if they participated in Sudan's oil or gas industry.

The Senate passed its version (S 180) by voice vote July 19. The Senate Foreign Relations Committee had reported the bill (no written report) on July 16. The Senate bill contained neither of the controversial House provisions.

House leaders delayed going to conference on the bill in the wake of the Sept. 11 terrorist attacks. Though the State Department had regularly labeled Khartoum a state sponsor of terrorism, Sudan was cooperating in the effort to build an antiterrorism coalition. Late in the session, however, the House leadership relented. The House agreed by voice vote Nov. 15 to pass S 180, after inserting the text of its own bill, and to appoint conferees.

But the prospect that a compromise bill might include the ban on foreign companies participating in Sudan's oil and gas industries drew sharp opposition from Wall Street, the White House, and Republican leaders in the Senate. They feared that enactment of the controversial provision would lead to a rash of attempts to politicize U.S. capital markets,

damaging their business credibility and driving investors to overseas exchanges. The White House also wanted to maintain links with Khartoum, which it had cited as a useful source of intelligence in the war on terrorism. Phil Gramm of Texas, ranking Republican on the Senate Banking Committee, blocked appointment of conferees on the bill.

Nearly a year later, House sponsor Tom Trancredo, R-Colo., finally conceded, and he and Sen. Sam Brownback, R-Kan., reached a compromise that could be endorsed by both chambers. But the two warned that if this bill did not bring the warring parties to the peace table, they would push for the United States to abandon peace talks and instead move to recognize southern Sudan as independent from the north.

The House passed HR 5531 by a vote of 359–8 on Oct. 7, 2002, and the Senate cleared it by voice vote the next day. The president signed it Oct. 21.

MAJOR PROVISIONS

As signed into law, HR 5531:

• Condemned human rights violations in Sudan.

• Authorized $100 million for each of fiscal years 2003, 2004, and 2005 to aid areas outside the Sudanese government's control to prepare the population for peace and democratic governance.

• Called for sanctions if the president determined that the Khartoum government had not engaged in good faith negotiations to achieve a permanent peace agreement or was not in compliance with such an agreement. Sanctions would include requiring U.S. officials to push for a cut off of loans from international financial institutions and to support an arms embargo on Sudan at the United Nations.

Middle East Resolutions

As violence in the Middle East escalated, both the House and Senate in 2002 passed strong, but nonbinding, resolutions voicing their support for Israel. The resolutions passed with overwhelming majorities on May 2, just days before Israeli prime minister Ariel Sharon was scheduled to visit the White House.

Both resolutions stated Congress's solidarity with Israel and commitment to Israel's right to self-defense. Both demanded that the Palestinian Authority dismantle the terrorist infrastructure in the Palestinian areas. But the House resolution (H Res 392), sponsored by House Majority Whip Tom DeLay, R-Texas, and Tom Lantos, D-Calif., went much further, condemning Palestinian Authority president Yasser Arafat and other members of the Palestinian leadership for their "ongoing support of terror."

DeLay had become Israel's most outspoken ally on Capitol Hill. Like that of many conservatives, DeLay's support for Israel was grounded in his devout religious beliefs, which supported Israel's biblical claim to the West Bank. Standing with Israel also gave him the opportunity to make the Republican

Party more attractive to Jewish voters and their campaign contributions. Capturing some of that support from the Democrats would be a major coup for DeLay, a savvy political strategist and one of the GOP's top fund-raisers.

The White House's handling of the resolutions was a case study of mixed signals and frantic last-minute appeals that reflected both the administration's rapidly shifting Middle East policy and its recognition of Israel's clout in Congress. Until a week before passage, the White House seemed paralyzed, largely resisting entreaties from both the State Department and Congress to weigh in, either for or against the resolutions. As the administration procrastinated, DeLay came under growing pressure from rank-and-file Republicans to move forward with the resolution. The pressure on Capitol Hill reflected increasing concern among conservative Republicans that the administration—and Secretary of State Colin L. Powell in particular—was wavering in its support for Israel.

But before DeLay could bring his resolution to the floor, President George W. Bush's national security adviser, Condoleezza Rice, asked that the resolution be shelved. Her request came after Bush met with Saudi crown prince Abdullah at the president's Texas ranch April 25, when the two leaders agreed to cooperate in forcing Israelis and Palestinians to the negotiating table. At the time, Bush was also in the midst of persuading Sharon to lift Israel's siege of Arafat at his headquarters in Ramallah.

Against that delicate diplomatic backdrop, DeLay bowed to Rice's appeal. However, the resolution did not stay shelved for long. At a May 1 meeting with leaders from both parties, Bush unexpectedly gave Senate Majority Leader Tom Daschle, D-S.D., the green light to move ahead with the less strident Senate resolution (S Res 247), which had been sponsored by Joseph I. Lieberman, D-Conn., and Gordon H. Smith, R-Ore. Informed of Bush's reversal, DeLay demanded—and won—White House support for moving his resolution.

The White House, however, continued to haggle with DeLay over the strong language of his resolution until shortly before it was taken up by the House. They worked to find compromise wording that conservatives could support and administration diplomats said would be the least inflammatory to Arab states. Ultimately, the administration succeeded in winning only minor changes. Among them were the excision of language that said Palestinian officials had "coordinated" acts of terrorism and that Arafat had direct control over an organization designated by the United States as a terrorist group. The changes were aimed at removing suggestions that Arafat himself was a terrorist. Bush had publicly declared that he would not negotiate with terrorists.

On May 2, the House adopted H Res 392 by a vote of 352–21, with twenty-nine members voting "present." That same day the Senate adopted the text of S 247 as an amendment to an unrelated trade bill (HR 3009) by a vote of 94–2. In a surprise announcement only hours after the resolutions were adopted, Secretary Powell proposed a peace conference.

Other bills aimed at cutting many U.S. ties to the Palestinian Authority were also introduced in the 107th Congress, but none advanced.

Cuba Sanctions

After the previous Congress approved some easing of the trade embargo against Cuba, supporters pushed for further changes in U.S. policy toward Cuba in the 107th Congress. But their efforts to loosen restrictions on trade with and travel to Cuba proved unsuccessful.

BACKGROUND

The United States had imposed a unilateral embargo in 1962, in an attempt to topple Cuban leader Fidel Castro and his communist regime. For decades the embargo proved ineffective, thanks to the assistance given Cuba by its communist allies. When the fall of communism in the Soviet Union and Eastern Europe had a devastating effect on Cuba's economy, the United States attempted to take advantage of the situation by twice tightening the embargo, once in 1992 (PL 102-484) and again in 1996 (PL 104-114). But still Castro remained in power, and pressure to resume some trade with Cuba began to grow. *(PL 102-484, Congress and the Nation Vol. VIII, p. 295; PL 104-114, Vol. IX, p. 237)*

In 1999 President Bill Clinton took several steps, albeit small ones, to increase contacts with Cuba. The following year farm-state lawmakers succeeded in adding language to the fiscal 2001 Agriculture appropriations bill (PL 106-387) lifting food and medicine sanctions on Cuba, a change bitterly opposed by conservative Republicans and Cuban American legislators who wanted to keep the sanctions in place. The price for the provision was agreement to bar public or private financing of Cuban agricultural purchases and to codify travel restrictions, previously implemented by executive order, that prevented most Americans from traveling to Cuba. *(PL 106-387, Congress and the Nation, Vol. X, p. 223)*

RENEWED ATTEMPTS

Much of the compromise language in PL 106-387 was set to expire after a year, opening the door for another round of debate for fiscal 2002. Byron L. Dorgan, D-N.D., promised to renew his efforts to loosen further the sanctions on food and medicine exports to Cuba. But by the time the fiscal 2002 Agriculture funding bill (HR 2330—PL 107-76) reached the Senate floor in October 2001, Democrats had decided Congress did not need the distraction of a debate on Cuba policy while it was considering war-time emergencies in the wake of the Sept. 11 terrorist attacks.

Cuba policy emerged as an issue during consideration of the fiscal 2002 Treasury–Postal Service appropriations bill (HR 2590—PL 107-67). By a vote of 240–186, the House on July 25, 2001, adopted a Jeff Flake, R-Ariz., amendment to lift restrictions on travel to Cuba. Under existing law, U.S. citizens could travel to Cuba only if they obtained a special license from the Treasury Department—which generally limited access to journalists, academics, government officials, and people on humanitarian missions. The Bush White House strongly opposed any weakening of the sanctions and subsequently threatened to veto the bill if the controversial language remained. In other action on the bill, the House rejected, 201–227, a broader amendment by Charles B. Rangel, D-N.Y., that effectively would have repealed the Cuba trade embargo. When the Senate took up its version (S 1398) the week after the Sept. 11 attacks, Dorgan again backed away from his plan to offer a Cuba travel amendment. HR 2590 stalled for a time in conference, in part because of the Cuba travel language, which Dorgan championed, but in the end conferees dropped the provision.

Flake and Rangel tried again in 2002. During consideration of the fiscal 2003 Treasury funding bill (HR 5120), the House on July 23 voted 262–167 for a Flake amendment to block the use of federal money to enforce the ban on travel to Cuba. Seventy-three Republicans broke with the White House to support it. GOP leaders had mounted a vigorous campaign to derail the amendment. Select Intelligence Committee Chair Porter J. Goss, R-Fla., had offered an alternative that would have tied any lifting of the ban to a presidential certification that Cuba did not have and was not developing biological weapons, providing such technology to terrorists, or providing aid to terrorists. Those who favored lifting the ban said Goss's alternative was little more than an attempt to use the terrorism issue to undercut Flake, and defeated it, 182–247.

In other action on HR 5120, the House adopted, 251-177, a second Flake amendment to allow Cuban Americans to send more money to their families back home by blocking enforcement of the $1,200 annual limit on such remittances. Another Rangel bid to lift the embargo altogether was rejected 204–226.

The Senate Appropriations Committee version of the Treasury funding bill (S 2740—S Rept 107-212) included a provision to lift the travel ban as well. In the face of a White House threat, conferees dropped the travel ban provision, along with the other House-approved amendment, in the final bill, which cleared in early 2003 (H J Res 2—PL 108-7).

Conferees on a 2002 farm bill (HR 2646—PL 107-171) dropped a Senate provision that would have repealed the statutory restrictions against private financing of agricultural sales to Cuba, despite the House having voted 273–143 on April 23, 2002, to instruct conferees to agree to the Senate provision.

Peace Corps

The Senate in 2002 passed two different bills to reauthorize the Peace Corps, but the House took no action on either one.

By voice vote Oct. 16, 2002, the Senate passed S 2667 authorizing a five-year funding increase and raising the Peace Corps's budget to $560 million in fiscal 2006. The Senate Foreign Relations Committee had reported the bill Oct. 10 (no written report). S 2667's funding level was $72 million more than the Bush administration had requested for its five-year plan. In his State of the Union address, President George W. Bush had urged the service organization to double the number of volunteers—to 14,000—by 2007.

After the House refused to consider S 2667, the Senate passed by voice vote Nov. 20 a bill (S 12) that held funding to Bush's target. But the Senate acted after the House essentially had wrapped up its legislative work for the year. So, both S 2667 and S 12 died at the end of the Congress. Funding for the Peace Corps was continued through appropriations bills.

Zimbabwe Aid

Congress in 2001 cleared legislation (S 494—PL 107-99) aimed at coaxing the southern African nation of Zimbabwe to undertake land reforms and halt government abuses.

The bill came in response to reports that for nearly two years, groups of armed black "war veterans" had tried to force white farmers off their land in Zimbabwe. Scores of farmers had been killed, while Zimbabwean president Robert Mugabe had been accused of supporting the attacks to divert attention from his authoritarian government's corruption and mismanagement. Many of the purported veterans were far too young to have fought against the white-ruled government of the former Rhodesia in the 1970s.

S 494 required Zimbabwe to strengthen its land-use laws and create conditions for a fair presidential election in March 2002. Once the president certified to the appropriate congressional committees that Zimbabwe had made those changes, the bill offered in return forgiveness of some of Zimbabwe's debt to the United States and support in international financial institutions for aid and debt relief for Zimbabwe. The bill also authorized $26 million in fiscal 2002 to support land reform and democratic institutions.

S 494 was reported (no written report) by the Senate Foreign Relations Committee on July 16, 2001, and passed by voice vote of the full Senate on Aug. 1. The House International Relations Committee reported an amended version (H Rept 107-312, Part I) on Dec. 4, and the House passed it, 396–11, later that day. The Senate agreed to the House amendment by voice vote Dec. 11, clearing the bill. The president signed it Dec. 21.

Radio Free Afghanistan

Congress in 2002 cleared legislation (HR 2998—PL 107-148) to establish Radio Free Afghanistan, a U.S-sponsored broadcasting service similar to Radio Free Europe. The bill authorized $17 million in fiscal 2002—$8 million for broadcast operations and $9 million for capital improvements—to establish a service that would provide eight hours of daily broadcasts.

In 2001 the State Department had objected to the legislation, arguing that it had other options. During the war in Afghanistan, the United States had increased broadcasts to the Central Asian nation through the existing Voice of America. But lawmakers contended that broadcasts beyond the Voice of America were key to winning the war against terrorism. *(Afghanistan war, pp. 230, 234)*

By a vote of 405–2 on Nov. 7, 2001, the House had passed its initial version of HR 2998, which authorized $27.5 million in fiscal 2002 and 2003 and provided for twelve hours of daily broadcasts. The Senate Foreign Relations Committee on Dec. 14 reported a bill (S 1779—S Rept 107-125) that reduced both the cost and broadcasting hours of the new service. The full Senate by voice vote on Feb. 7, 2002, passed HR 2998, after substituting the text of S 1779. The House agreed to the Senate amendment by a vote of 421–2 on Feb. 12, clearing the bill. The president signed it into law March 11.

Child Protection Treaty

The Senate in 2002 approved the ratification of two optional protocols—Treaty Doc 106-37(A) and Treaty Doc 106-37(B)—to the Convention on the Rights of the Child. The first protocol to the international treaty prohibited using children as soldiers and the second sought to combat child pornography, child prostitution, and child slavery.

More than 300,000 boys and girls were being used in government or rebel forces in armed conflicts throughout the world and an estimated one million were being trafficked for coerced sexual exploitation or labor, according to a State Department press release on Dec. 23, 2002, the day the United States formally ratified the protocols. The United States had signed the protocols on July 5, 2000, and submitted them to the Senate July 25. The Senate Foreign Relations Committee reported the protocols (Ex. Rept. 107-4) on June 12, 2002, after adding various understandings, conditions, and other statements. The Senate gave its advice and consent to the ratification of the two protocols by voice vote June 18.

'Microenterprise' Aid

Legislation to reauthorize and revise a loan program for small businesses in developing countries (HR 4073) was scuttled in 2002 in retribution against a House Republican for his role in derailing an unrelated bill.

The measure would have authorized $175 million in fiscal 2003 and $200 million in fiscal 2004 for small loans—sometimes less than $100—to entrepreneurs in developing countries. Legislation setting up the loan program for an initial two-year period had been enacted in 2000 (PL 106-309). *(PL 106-309, Congress and the Nation Vol. X, p. 230)*

The House International Relations Committee reported HR 4073 (H Rept 107–453) on May 10, 2002, and the House passed it by voice vote June 4. The Senate Foreign Relations Committee reported its amended version (no written report) on Oct. 8, and the Senate passed it by voice vote Nov. 13. The House was set to clear the bill, but then it was pulled to retaliate against its sponsor, Rep. Christopher H. Smith, R-N.J., after he embarrassed GOP leaders by leading a revolt against an unrelated bankruptcy bill (HR 333) over abortion provisions. *(Bankruptcy bill, pp. 129, 141)*

Illegal Diamond Trade

The House in 2001 overwhelmingly passed legislation (HR 2722) aimed at restricting trade in illegal diamonds, but the Senate did not act on the measure and it died at the end of the 107th Congress.

The diamonds—known as conflict or blood diamonds—came from regions in Sierra Leone, Liberia, and the Congo where rebel, and sometimes government, militias forced civilians to mine the gems under threat of death or mutilation and used the profits to finance their operations.

For nearly two years, legislation aimed at restricting trade in illegal diamonds had met with limited success. That changed following the Sept. 11, 2001, terrorist attacks on the United States, with reports that the al Qaeda terrorist network had used the illegal diamond trade to launder money. One of the main challenges in writing the legislation was to devise an approach to block the illegal diamonds while not thwarting trade in clean diamonds, especially since the United States was the world's largest consumer of diamonds. House members moved quickly to negotiate with the Bush administration on legislation that would allow but not require the president to restrict imports of conflict diamonds, with the strictest rules applying to polished, set diamonds.

The House passed HR 2722 by a vote of 408–6 on Nov. 28, 2001. There had been no committee action.

2003–2004

A measure to overhaul the nation's intelligence system was one of the signature pieces of legislation in the 108th Congress. Enactment of the bill had been far from a sure thing, but Congress got the job done in the closing days of a post-election session.

The legislation grew out of investigations by Congress and an independent commission into the Sept. 11, 2001, terrorist attacks on the United States. Both probes put substantial blame for the intelligence failures leading up to Sept. 11 on fragmentation and inadequate sharing of information within the intelligence community.

The commission's investigation, a follow-on to a more limited probe by the Intelligence committees in the previous Congress, led to recommendations for sweeping changes in how both the executive branch and Congress handled intelligence matters. When the commission issued its final report in July 2004, lawmakers were well aware of the obstacles they would face in legislating such broad change. These included chairs who wanted to protect legislative jurisdictions, executive agencies reluctant to give up any authority, a tight legislative calendar, a bitterly partisan election year, and lack of real consensus on complex policy questions with far-reaching consequences for national security.

But the pressure was on, especially from the 9/11 commission members and the families of victims of the terrorist attacks. With eleventh-hour lobbying by the White House and some final tweaking of language, Congress managed to clear the bill. Key among its provisions was the creation of the position of director of national intelligence. The new director would have broad authority over budgeting for the entire intelligence community, but the Pentagon still retained control over its intelligence agencies' spending and operations. This question of how authority would be divided up had been the major stumbling block during consideration of the bill.

Not surprisingly, Congress was far more willing to overhaul the executive branch than it was to tackle the 9/11 commission's recommendations for changes in congressional oversight. The commission had labeled oversight of intelligence "dysfunctional" and recommended specific structural changes in the committee system. By the end of the 108th Congress, the Senate had made a few modest changes while the House had made none at all.

The Senate Intelligence Committee launched a probe into another intelligence failure—the prewar assessments that Iraq was attempting to acquire and develop weapons of mass destruction. The alleged weapons had been the Bush administration's initial justification for going to war in Iraq, but no weapons were ever found. In its report, the committee put the blame for the faulty intelligence on the CIA. But, in a dissenting view, Democrats claimed that intelligence analysts had been subject to political pressure from the administration. At the Democrats' insistence, a second phase was added to the inquiry to allow for an examination of the administration's use of the intelligence. That phase had not been completed by the end of the 108th Congress.

Both chambers adopted resolutions on the Iraq War within days of its start in March 2003, and the House adopted another resolution on the war's one-year anniversary. The debates surrounding passage of those resolutions reflected partisan divisions over the war and President George W. Bush's leadership, particularly in the House.

The 108th Congress agreed to authorize two foreign aid initiatives proposed by the Bush administration. The new Millennium Challenge Account was aimed at providing increased assistance to developing countries that were making progress on human rights, democratization, and free markets. Also approved was a multibillion-dollar, five-year program to combat the international spread of HIV/AIDS.

A particularly compelling issue for Congress was the plight of people living in the war-torn Darfur region of Sudan. Bipartisan majorities in both chambers adopted a series of resolutions that condemned the Sudanese government and the militia groups it supported for attacks against civilians and that denounced the violence as "genocide." Additional humanitarian and refugee aid was provided as well. The previous Congress had approved sanctions against Sudan as a tool to pressure the Sudanese government to end a civil war in the country.

Legislation requiring sanctions against Syria was finally enacted. The Bush administration previously had opposed sanctions but dropped its objections this time because Syria was not fighting terrorism or assisting in the Middle East peace process. The president could waive the sanctions on national security grounds.

Intelligence System Overhaul

Congress in late 2004 cleared legislation (S 2845—PL 108-458) mandating the most comprehensive overhaul of the nation's intelligence community since the end of World War II and the start of the cold war.

S 2845 was enacted in response to the terrorist attacks of Sept. 11, 2001. Both Congress and an independent commission conducted inquiries into how the United States could have been so unprepared for terrorist attacks that killed nearly 3,000 people and what could be done to protect the country against future attacks. Their investigations found much to criticize, but a central failure they identified was the intelligence community's fragmentation and poor information sharing. Although the CIA director was the titular head of all intelligence agencies, he had neither budgetary nor operational control over much of the intelligence community. Most of the intelligence budget was under the Pentagon's

INTELLIGENCE COMMUNITY

As of 2004, the U.S. intelligence community consisted of fifteen federal agencies, offices, and elements of organizations within the executive branch. They included:

Independent Agency

Central Intelligence Agency (CIA)

Defense Department

Defense Intelligence Agency (DIA)
National Security Agency (NSA)
National Geospatial-Intelligence Agency (NGA)
National Reconnaissance Office (NRO)
Army, Navy, Air Force, and Marine Corps intelligence organizations

Other Executive Departments

Department of State/Bureau of Intelligence and Research (INR)
Department of Justice/Federal Bureau of Investigation (FBI)
Department of Homeland Security/Directorate of Information Analysis and Infrastructure Protection
Department of Homeland Security/U.S. Coast Guard Intelligence
Department of Energy (DOE)/Office of Intelligence (IN)
Department of Treasury/Office of Terrorism and Financial Intelligence (INF)

March 31, 2005, Report of the Commission on the Intelligence Capabilities of the United States Regarding Weapons of Mass Destruction, Appendix C.

control. (*Congressional 9/11 inquiry, p. 245; Independent 9/11 commission, p. 275*)

Congress included in S 2845 key provisions aimed at unifying efforts within the intelligence community. The bill created a new cabinet-level position of director of national intelligence with exclusive authority to develop and determine the budgetary levels for national intelligence programs, although the Pentagon retained control over the flow of money to and the daily operations of its intelligence agencies. The bill codified a new center to analyze and integrate U.S. intelligence related to terrorism and counterterrorism and to plan—but not direct—counterterrorism operations. S 2845 also codified a new council designed to promote the sharing of information across agency lines.

Other provisions of the bill dealt with immigration and border security, FBI law enforcement, terrorist money laundering, civil liberties, and transportation security.

Enactment of S 2845 had been far from a sure thing. Following the July 2004 release of the 9/11 commission's report,

Congress had found itself under considerable pressure to act on its recommendations. Commission members, along with families of victims of the Sept. 11 attacks, kept up the pressure for a bill during the August congressional recess and all fall. They held news conferences and met with members to argue passionately for changes in intelligence, border and aviation security, Middle East policy, and other areas they said were critical in preventing another attack.

But the legislation followed an erratic path. For starters, the House and Senate in October passed bills that differed substantially on key issues, including budget authority, intelligence budget secrecy, immigration and law enforcement, and information-sharing. The legislation stalled in negotiations before the Nov. 2 election, then appeared to be moving toward a successful conference agreement in a lame-duck session, only to stall once again as the 108th Congress lurched toward final adjournment. Only after aggressive lobbying by the White House and some delicate final negotiations did a compromise bill emerge from Congress.

S 2845 did not address the 9/11 commission's proposals for overhauling how Congress handled intelligence matters. The commission had labeled congressional oversight of intelligence and counterterrorism "dysfunctional." But by the end of the 108th Congress, only the Senate had approved a few modest changes (S Res 445). (*Congressional oversight of intelligence, p. 274*)

BACKGROUND

Proposals to create a cabinet-level intelligence czar had been circulating since the end of the cold war in the early 1990s. Over the years, commission after commission, often headed by well-known public figures, had recommended consolidation in intelligence agency management. It started when the CIA was only two years old. In 1949 former president Herbert Hoover headed a panel that studied the effectiveness of the fledgling spy shop, which was still considered a work in progress at the time.

More recently, the chairs of the House and Senate Intelligence committees in 1992 proposed creation of a director of national intelligence who would have budget control over Defense intelligence agencies. That idea collapsed under pressure from then-Defense Secretary Dick Cheney and other Pentagon officials. Congress adopted more modest changes instead. (*Congress and the Nation Vol. VIII, p. 284*)

The 9/11 commission was the latest, and maybe the most powerful, to suggest an overhaul. While many in Congress embraced the report, lawmakers trying to distill the report into legislative language consistently knocked heads with Pentagon advocates, especially key members of the Armed Services and Appropriations committees, who wanted to tone down some of the commission's ideas.

Under the existing system, about 85 percent of the total intelligence budget went to the Pentagon for the operations of such agencies as the National Security Agency, Defense Intelligence Agency, National Reconnaissance Office, and

National Geospatial-Intelligence Agency. Pentagon leaders worked quietly for months in 2004—in open hearings, classified briefings, and one-on-one lobbying—to reduce the role the proposed director of national intelligence would be able to play in controlling those agencies.

Beginning with a series of rare hearings held during the August recess, Pentagon officials warned against an intelligence director with too much authority. The Pentagon's primary case for keeping operational and significant budgetary control over its agencies rested on a simple principle: The ability to act quickly was essential to accomplishing battlefield goals. The military argued that critical intelligence for troops in battle zones should not have to be sifted through another layer of bureaucracy such as a national intelligence director before it could be acted on in the field. The Pentagon also made a practical argument for its playing a key role in shaping the intelligence legislation: the military was the biggest consumer of intelligence. Furthermore, they argued that it did not make sense to shift power away from the Defense Department when the 9/11 commission found no fault with military intelligence. The commission's fixes, they said, did not address real problems and might even do more harm than good.

Defense Secretary Donald H. Rumsfeld, at an Aug. 17 hearing, said national intelligence and tactical intelligence often overlapped, indicating that the legislation should require an intelligence director to coordinate with the Department of Defense. At that same hearing, Gen. Richard B. Myers, chairman of the Joint Chiefs of Staff, said that the capture of Iraqi leader Saddam Hussein, which involved a flurry of shared intelligence from high-level national intelligence officials as well as battlefield intelligence units, illustrated in vivid detail why the Pentagon wanted to keep as much control as possible.

President George W. Bush on Aug. 27 issued a series of executive orders to implement some of the 9/11 commission's recommendations. The orders strengthened the powers of the CIA director, established a National Counterterrorism Center, set up a board to safeguard civil liberties, and outlined steps a new Information Systems Council and the CIA director should take to promote information sharing.

But White House officials said they would need legislation to give those changes any real teeth. And that would mean navigating a minefield of entrenched bureaucracies and congressional jurisdictional struggles.

SENATE ACTION

The Senate passed S 2845 on Oct. 6, 2004, by a **key vote of 96–2 (R 51–0; D 44–2; I 1–0).** The Senate Governmental Affairs Committee had reported an identical bill (S 2840—S Rept 108-359) on Sept. 27. *(2004 key votes, p. 854)*

The Senate had jumped out in front on the reform issue, responding with a sense of urgency initially absent in the House and the executive branch. On July 22, the day the 9/11 commission released its report, groups of lawmakers in both

the House and Senate said they planned to unveil legislation in September. Later that day the Senate's leaders went a step further, announcing the creation of a working group to assess the commission's proposals for congressional reform. And Senate Majority Leader Bill Frist, R-Tenn., and Minority Leader Tom Daschle, D-S.D., took to the floor that evening to announce that the Governmental Affairs Committee would coordinate an effort to evaluate the report's proposals and would aim to propose legislation by Oct. 1, the targeted adjournment date. The leaders of Governmental Affairs—Chair Susan Collins, R-Maine, and ranking Democrat Joseph I. Lieberman of Connecticut—said on July 23 they were prepared to go into a lame-duck session after Election Day if necessary to get the legislation passed.

That their task would not be an easy one was soon apparent. On Aug. 22 Senate Intelligence Committee Chair Pat Roberts, R-Kan., set off the first legislative fireworks with a far-reaching proposal to subdivide the CIA into four directorates and reassign the Pentagon's intelligence agencies among the four. Another senior Republican senator, John W. Warner of Virginia, took the opposite approach, warning that he would use his chairmanship of Senate Armed Services to fight any diminution in the authority of military intelligence agencies.

On Sept. 15 Collins and Lieberman unveiled a draft bill that called for a national intelligence director with significant budget authority. Under their plan, the new chief would be in charge of the CIA, several agencies that were then under the Defense Department, and part of the Homeland Security Department. The bill did not touch tactical intelligence under the armed services. The next day the White House sent Congress its proposed legislation, calling for a new national spymaster with budgetary powers similar to those outlined in the Collins-Lieberman bill but with weaker operational authority. The White House subsequently endorsed the Senate bill.

The Senate Governmental Affairs Committee approved the Collins-Lieberman draft bill unanimously on Sept. 22, and the 191-page measure was introduced as an original bill the next day. The panel's ten-hour markup over two days offered a glimpse of what was to come on the Senate floor. While some senators who oversaw the Pentagon tried to carve up the powers of an intelligence czar, others pushed for a much more powerful director with day-to-day operational control of both civilian and military intelligence organizations. Most of the two groups' amendments were either rejected or modified before being adopted.

The battle continued on the Senate floor. Intelligence Committee Chair Roberts joined with two former Intelligence chairs—Arlen Specter, R-Pa., and Richard C. Shelby, R-Ala.—to attempt to make the case for an intelligence director with unprecedented powers to fight the war on terrorism. But the idea never had a chance. An amendment offered by Specter, which would have given the new national intelligence director day-to-day operational control over the entire fifteen-agency intelligence system was tabled (killed) on a 78–19 vote Sept. 28. Rising in opposition to Specter's amendment, Warner argued that three of the intelligence agencies—the National Security Agency, the National Geospatial-Intelligence Agency, and the National Reconnaissance Office—were vital to soldiers in the field and had to remain under Pentagon control.

Roberts acknowledged that they were bumping up against a long history of inertia when it came to shaking up the intelligence structure. He noted that twenty-four commissions or study groups over the previous fifty years had called for changes in intelligence management but that each time the Pentagon had managed to persuade policy makers to maintain its hold over military intelligence. "They've done it twenty-four times. This is twenty-five," he said.

"They" were the Pentagon and its biggest supporters on Capitol Hill, including a group known as the "Big Four"—Warner, Armed Services Committee ranking Democrat Carl Levin of Michigan, Appropriations Committee Chair Ted Stevens, R-Alaska, and Daniel K. Inouye of Hawaii, the ranking Democrat on the Defense Appropriations Subcommittee.

Still, the Senate debate rarely became partisan or heated. Collins and Lieberman quietly cajoled and compromised with some of the most senior senators in the chamber. When S 2845 came to the floor, the chamber faced as many as 300 amendments. But as Collins and Lieberman each worked their party caucuses, most amendments were withdrawn, ruled out of order, or tabled. Many were adopted on a voice vote but only after being rewritten to Collins's and Lieberman's liking.

The two negotiated deals to address concerns over the extent of power a national intelligence director would have over certain military intelligence programs. They reached agreement with Levin on a revised amendment, adopted by voice vote, to limit the authority of the director to transfer individual military personnel, while allowing the money and the billet slots for those individuals' jobs to be moved among intelligence agencies. Levin's original amendment would have denied the director authority to transfer active duty military personnel within the national intelligence system. Collins and Lieberman also negotiated middle ground with Warner over which military intelligence programs would fall under the "national intelligence program" to be run by the intelligence director. The Senate adopted by voice vote a Warner amendment that was reworked to give both the national intelligence director and the Pentagon a say in joint military intelligence programs. Previously, the bill gave only the national intelligence director authority over such programs.

The Senate on Oct. 4 tabled 55–37 a Stevens amendment to delete language requiring the public disclosure of the grand total spent on intelligence. The next day the Senate voted 85–10 to invoke cloture to limit debate on the bill.

By the time the last roll call came in the Senate on Oct. 6, leaders from both sides of the aisle were liberally using the terms "bipartisan" and "historic" to describe the final version of the legislation.

HOUSE ACTION

The House passed its version (HR 10) on Oct. 8, 2004, by a vote of 282–134. The House on Oct. 16 passed S 2845 by voice vote, after inserting the text of HR 10.

The House bill had been reported on Oct. 4 by the Intelligence Committee (H Rept 108-724, Part I), Armed Services Committee (Part II), and Financial Services Committee (Part III). The next day HR 10 was reported by the Government Reform Committee (Part IV) and Judiciary Committee (Part V). The Judiciary Committee filed a supplemental report (Part VI) on Nov. 16. The bill was discharged from eight other committees.

The House Republican leadership's initial response to the 9/11 commission's report was muted compared to the Senate's reaction. At a news conference shortly after the one the commission held on July 22, House Speaker J. Dennis Hastert, R-Ill., did not bring up the recommendations. When asked about them, he responded: "We're not going to rush through anything." The next day, however, Hastert and House Majority Leader Tom DeLay, R-Texas, announced that House committees would hold hearings in August and produce legislative recommendations in September, for consideration before adjournment. But no committee was designated to take the lead and no clear plan of action for producing legislation was put forth. Nine committees held hearings in August.

On Sept. 15 DeLay rebuffed Democratic criticism that the House was not moving as efficiently as the Senate. "We're going to make sure we do the job right," he said. "We're not going to let either the calendar or politics get in the way." Earlier in the month the majority leader had insisted that the House would not consider any bill that simply mirrored the commission's recommendations. This was disheartening news for sponsors of a bipartisan bill (Republican Christopher Shays of Connecticut and Democrat Carolyn B. Maloney of New York) and of a Democratic measure (Minority Leader Nancy Pelosi of California and Intelligence Committee ranking Democrat Jane Harman of California) that would have implemented many of the commission's proposals.

HR 10, an omnibus-style bill written by House leaders and committee chairs, was introduced on Sept. 24. HR 10 had plenty in common with the Senate's bill, including a national intelligence director, information-sharing guidelines, and a national counterterrorism center. However, it also contained hundreds of pages of language aimed at bolstering a range of homeland security programs, as well as a series of controversial immigration and law enforcement provisions that were not in the Senate bill.

The leaders of the 9/11 commission, Republican Thomas H. Kean and Democrat Lee H. Hamilton, said the House bill had provisions that were "highly controversial. We respectfully submit that they can harm our purpose." But the five committees that almost simultaneously marked up HR 10 managed to push back nearly every Democratic amendment that would have substantially changed the omnibus bill to bring it in line with Collins-Lieberman.

When the bill reached the House floor, Democrats, along with a handful of moderate Republicans such as Shays, used their time to complain that HR 10 was too bogged down with poison pill provisions that would doom it in conference with the Senate. House Republicans gave opponents one big chance to amend the bill with a substitute amendment by Robert Menendez, D-N.J., which was nearly identical to the Collins-Lieberman bill. The Rules Committee had ruled a bipartisan Shays-Maloney amendment that would have substituted the Senate version for the House bill out of order, while moving to the floor the one by Menendez, a member of the Democratic leadership team. HR 10 opponents decried that maneuver because it gave members a stark choice between a Democratic bill and a Republican bill with no bipartisan alternative.

Not surprisingly, on Oct. 8 the Menendez amendment failed on a 203–213 vote that included eight Republican defectors. It was clear that the vast majority of House Republicans would rally behind their leadership's bill.

In other action, the House first adopted, then rejected on a second vote, an amendment by Christopher H. Smith, R-N.J., that would have stripped from the bill language that increased the burden of proof on asylum seekers claiming torture or abuse in their home country. Smith said that under that provision refugees who faced danger in returning to their native countries could be forcibly deported without a hearing. Shortly after Smith prevailed on a 212–203 vote, Judiciary Chair F. James Sensenbrenner Jr., R-Wis., called for a second vote. And in that vote, the House defeated the Smith amendment, 203–210.

KEY DIFFERENCES

After both chambers passed their respective intelligence overhaul bills, it was obvious that a difficult conference loomed ahead.

A key difference was over what kind of budget authority the new national intelligence director would have. The Senate bill created a separate appropriations account in the Treasury Department, from which the director could draw and disperse to individual agencies. It also created a new comptroller for the director's office who would have direct control over executing and setting the budget. That included tracking how and when the money was spent after it was appropriated.

The House bill provided for no separate comptroller and left much of the accounting to the Pentagon's comptroller when it came to the military's intelligence agencies.

The Senate bill also gave the director the power to set the budgets of every program in the intelligence community outside of joint military and tactical intelligence programs, which were purely military functions. The House, by contrast, authorized the director only to "manage and oversee" development of the budget via the current heads of intelligence agencies. That language did not represent a major departure from the status quo. Indeed, the House bill was peppered with words such as "guidance" and "concurrence" when describing the budgetary powers of an intelligence director. Critics charged that more powerful cabinet heads or military chiefs could overrule this new executive during budgetary disputes. But backers of the House bill said that was exactly what was needed to ensure that the military's access to intelligence remained unbroken.

The two chambers also disagreed on whether to limit the director's ability to transfer funds among agencies. The Senate bill granted virtually unlimited authority to move money around while the House bill capped such moves at $100 million.

The Senate bill would have made the grand total spent on intelligence public, but House Republicans, joined by the White House, opposed such openness. The 9/11 commission and those lawmakers backing the idea of budget declassification said that a public top line was necessary if the intelligence director was to have a unified budget under his or her control. There was also a political angle to the proposal as well. If the total was known to the public, the intelligence director would have political leverage year after year in arguing for more money. But opponents said publishing the top line would disclose vital information to terrorists.

Stricter deportation rules, more permissive surveillance laws, and tougher sentencing and imprisonment guidelines for terrorist suspects had been top priorities of House Republicans ever since the antiterrorism law known as the PATRIOT Act (HR 3162—PL 107-56) was enacted six weeks after the Sept. 11 terrorist attacks. But when the provisions found their way into HR 10, critics immediately took notice. Civil libertarians raised concerns, and Democrats in both chambers criticized the provisions as obstacles to a quick conference. The leaders of the 9/11 commission also weighed in, noting that their report made no mention of such changes in criminal law. *(PATRIOT Act, p. 187)*

Realizing that the term "connecting the dots" had become a mantra for antiterrorist intelligence analysis, Senate sponsors included in their bill a provision requiring creation of a database that would link all intelligence agencies and improve information sharing. The House bill included no such mandate, and critics said that such an interconnected, interagency database could pose security risks. The House bill required the president to establish guidelines for information sharing, but it did not require a larger strategy for intelligence and homeland security information sharing.

CONFERENCE ACTION

The House agreed to the conference report (H Rept 108-796) by a **key vote of 336–75 (R 152–67; D 183–8; I 1–0)** on

Dec. 7, 2004. The Senate cleared the bill the next day by a vote of 89–2. S 2845 was signed into law Dec. 17. *(2004 key votes, p. 854)*

The House and Senate versions of the intelligence overhaul had had a host of sharp differences. Much the same could have been said about the conferees the two chambers appointed to work out a compromise.

Among the Senate's thirteen negotiators were S 2845 sponsors Collins and Lieberman, as well as several Intelligence Committee members, including Chair Roberts, who had supported an even stronger version of intelligence overhaul than the one passed. Missing were the powerful critics—Warner and Stevens—who had fought to curb the powers that a new intelligence director would have over military agencies.

By contrast, the House sent eight lawmakers, including five Republicans who staunchly supported the House GOP version of the bill. Anchoring the House conferees was Armed Services Chair Duncan Hunter, R-Calif., a blunt-spoken supporter of the Pentagon who said the Senate bill was downright "dangerous" because it gave a civilian intelligence chief certain authorities over military functions. Another conferee, Judiciary Chair Sensenbrenner, was the author of the law enforcement provisions in the House bill. A third House negotiator, Peter Hoekstra, R-Mich., who had recently been appointed chair of the Intelligence Committee, had helped kill the Menendez floor amendment.

The White House initially appeared reluctant to get deeply involved in the conference, despite earlier statements of administration support for the Senate version. On Oct. 18 the administration sent conference leaders Collins and Hoekstra a ten-page letter that laid out the parameters of a possible compromise and singled out provisions from both House and Senate versions of the bill for praise and criticism. This was followed up by calls from White House Chief of Staff Andrew H. Card Jr., urging the conference committee to complete their work before Election Day. On the highest-profile issue, the administration sided with the Senate in backing broad budget authority for an intelligence director. The White House preferred the House plan for a national terrorism center and several law enforcement and terrorist tracking provisions. It also sided with House Republicans in opposing the declassification of the top line of the intelligence budget.

Complicating things was an Oct. 21 letter the chair of the Joint Chiefs of Staff, sent to Hunter, placing the Pentagon firmly behind the House provision that allowed the military's combat support agencies to maintain authority over their intelligence budgets. Gen. Myers's letter was a rare departure from the administration line on national security, but it reflected concerns of Pentagon leaders, as well as House and Senate Armed Services Committee members, that a national intelligence director could have too much control over the intelligence used by military forces in Iraq and Afghanistan.

This rare fracturing among Republicans—with House and Senate Republicans, the White House, and the administration's top general reading from different scripts—produced a deepening stalemate over the bills. Conferees were unable to complete their work before the Nov. 2 election, and the fate of the intelligence overhaul legislation was left to a lame-duck session.

Some members feared that with the election over the political momentum created by the 9/11 commission report might be lost. But negotiators persisted and differences narrowed. Conferees in one room worked on intelligence provisions, as conferees in another room dealt with immigration issues. Finally an agreement was reached, but the bill stalled again when some House Republicans objected to several compromises that a majority of the conferees had backed. The major sticking points were:

• The House-Senate conference agreement had granted a director of national intelligence the power to set budget levels for Pentagon intelligence agencies. It also had allowed the director to manage the collection, analysis, and dissemination of intelligence throughout the fifteen-agency intelligence community. Opponents said such powers would disrupt the military chain of command and potentially interfere with the real-time flow of intelligence between commanders and battlefield troops.

• The agreement had called on states to submit plans to the Transportation Department to meet national driver's license standards, but House opponents preferred more extensive language that prescribed a list of identification criteria for issuing licenses. Some House conservatives also wanted language that would prohibit states from giving driver's licenses to illegal immigrants.

• Some House conservatives also objected to the conference agreement's elimination of House language that would make it harder for refugees to claim asylum. They insisted that the language was needed to prevent would-be terrorists from being granted legal residence in the United States.

Leading the opposition was Hunter, who insisted on shielding the existing military chain of command from the powers of a new national intelligence director. The Armed Services chair was able to muster a coalition of allies who took advantage of the White House's less-than-forceful support for a strong intelligence director. Hunter's stance had been bolstered at a Nov. 17 House Armed Services Committee hearing in which he asked all four military service chiefs whether they agreed with Gen. Myers's concerns about handing over budgetary powers for the Pentagon's intelligence agencies to a national intelligence director—and they did.

Also aiding Hunter were Sensenbrenner and other conservatives who wanted to keep the immigration provisions in the final bill. Democrats in both chambers, as well as some prominent Hispanic Republicans, objected because they thought the provisions went beyond preventing terrorism to affect the nation's growing Hispanic population. Critics said the provisions could be perceived as a major crackdown on Hispanic immigrants.

In a Nov. 20 caucus of House Republicans, Hunter was able to persuade a majority of his colleagues that the conference agreement would endanger U.S. troops on the battlefield—including his own son, a marine who had served in Iraq. Although there were enough Democrats ready to vote "aye" to guarantee the bill would pass in the House, Speaker Hastert was loath to fracture his membership with a divisive vote or to rely on Democrats. When it became clear that the arguments in the caucus meeting were not leading toward consensus, Hastert called off an expected floor vote on the conference report.

The bill's delay ignited a political uproar, with Republican senators, such as Roberts, calling Hunter's arguments about the flow of intelligence to the troops a "canard." Other supporters of a strong national intelligence director accused Hunter of protecting both the Pentagon and the turf of his own committee. Family members of Sept. 11 victims charged that lawmakers who opposed the bill had "put America in peril" and would have "blood on their hands" if there was another terrorist attack on U.S. soil.

Embarrassed by the legislative breakdown, the White House, with the support of Defense Secretary Rumsfeld, said it would make a renewed push to get the bill passed. President Bush spoke out publicly in support of the bill, while he and Vice President Cheney lobbied Hunter, Sensenbrenner, and others in private to let the compromise version go forward. And the nation's top general got on board, too. After saying at a Nov. 23 news conference that he stood by his earlier letter to Hunter, Gen. Myers on Dec. 2 said his concerns about the intelligence bill had been accommodated. Some House Armed Services members viewed Myers's comments as part of a coordinated White House effort to pull the rug from under Hunter's opposition to the bill.

In the meantime, key lawmakers continued to work behind the scenes to resolve the impasse and find language that would mollify opponents. On Dec. 5 Collins and Lieberman proposed alternative wording and the following day Hunter agreed to vote for language promising that the powers of the new director of national intelligence would not "abrogate" the military chain of command. "That means when somebody is in a shooting battle, they get the information when they need it," Hunter said. "In my estimation it builds a fence around the chain of command." Collins said she was willing to add the language to appease Hunter because she thought it would not impede the powers of the intelligence director.

Sensenbrenner, the only House conferee not to sign the agreement, did not win the immigration provisions he sought, but House leaders and the White House committed to pursuing immigration legislation early in the next Congress.

And so, just two weeks after its prospects seemed moribund, S 2845 cleared Congress with bipartisan, lopsided majorities. With the exception of those conservatives who had wanted the strong immigration controls, all sides—House defense hawks, Senate conferees, the White House, and the families of people who died on Sept. 11—came away more or less satisfied with the final bill.

MAJOR PROVISIONS

Following are major provisions of S 2845, as signed into law:

Director of National Intelligence

The law created the position of director of national intelligence (DNI) to serve as head of the U.S. intelligence community. The DNI was to act as principal adviser to the president, the National Security Council, and the Homeland Security Council on intelligence matters.

Role of the director. The director, who was to be appointed by the president and confirmed by the Senate, was charged with ensuring that all federal departments and agencies, the Joint Chiefs of Staff, and relevant committees of Congress would have access to the intelligence they needed to carry out their missions. The DNI was to have access to all national intelligence acquired by any federal department or agency, unless the president or existing law provided otherwise.

Other responsibilities included monitoring the implementation of intelligence operations—though the DNI was not directly in charge of the CIA's clandestine operations—and creating governmentwide priorities and standards for collecting and analyzing intelligence. The director also was to oversee the coordination of relations with the intelligence or security services of foreign governments and international organizations.

The DNI could not serve simultaneously as CIA director.

Budget authority. The director was supposed to "develop and determine" the annual budget for the National Intelligence Program, which included the CIA and parts of the National Security Agency, National Reconnaissance Office, and National Geospatial Intelligence Agency. It did not include Joint Military Intelligence Programs or Tactical Intelligence and Related Activities, both of which were purely military intelligence functions. DNI could participate in creation of those budgets.

However, the DNI could not abrogate the military chain of command, meaning the intelligence chief could not use his budgetary powers to override decisions by military leaders.

The DNI had the power to tell the intelligence agency comptrollers how to allocate money but lacked day-to-day power over budgetary operations at the agencies.

The DNI had the authority to "reprogram," or move around, funds within the intelligence community. But such moves were limited to $150 million or 5 percent of an agency budget, whichever was less, and required approval from the director of the Office of Management and Budget. The transfers could not terminate any program.

Personnel. The law authorized 500 new personnel billets to staff the new DNI office. The DNI could detail up to 150 personnel within the intelligence community to the office for up to two years, and could transfer personnel among intelligence agencies for up to two years.

Office of the Director of National Intelligence. The law established the office and specified that it include a principal deputy director of national intelligence, a general counsel, a civil liberties protection officer, a director of science and technology, a national counterintelligence executive, and up to four deputy directors appointed by the DNI. Only one of the deputy directors could be an active military officer.

Information Sharing

The law required the DNI to establish a far-reaching system within the intelligence community to share information from agency to agency, which had been one of the problems with intelligence leading up to the Sept. 11 terrorist attacks.

Governmentwide standards. The DNI was given responsibility for establishing uniform procedures, technology standards, and policies for information sharing, and for purchasing whatever equipment and technology was necessary to build a technology architecture that aided information sharing.

Protecting sources. The DNI also was expected to create across-the-board standards for keeping secret the sources and methods that spies were using to collect sensitive information.

Improving Analysis and Coordination

National Intelligence Council. The council, appointed by the DNI, was to be composed of senior analysts within the intelligence community and experts from the private sector. It would be responsible for creating the National Intelligence Estimates similar to the report used to justify the invasion of Iraq. The DNI was allowed to hire private sector contractors to provide help in crafting those intelligence estimates.

National Counterterrorism Center. The center, within the Office of the DNI, would be the primary government organization for analyzing and integrating intelligence on international terrorism and counterterrorism. It was authorized to conduct strategic planning for big-picture intelligence goals, but it was not allowed to assign responsibilities or direct intelligence operations for individual intelligence agencies.

The center would absorb the existing Terrorist Threat Integration Center, which was created by executive order. The center's director would work for the DNI, after being appointed by the president and confirmed by the Senate.

National Counterproliferation Center. The center, to be created by the president, would serve as the primary organization within the government for analyzing and integrating all intelligence related to the proliferation of weapons of mass destruction.

The president was allowed to waive any portion of this section if he believed it was in the interest of national security. This section also authorized creation of specialized intelligence centers to focus on specific threats, such as bioterrorism, or geographic areas, such as North Korea.

'Red teaming.' The DNI was directed to set up a group responsible for producing alternative, or competitive, analysis of intelligence. This so-called "red team" analysis was a common tool used to poke holes in intelligence assumptions and test conclusions of the regular analysts. It was put into the law in the wake of the faulty intelligence used to declare that Iraq had weapons of mass destruction.

The DNI was required to appoint a special officer who would conduct investigations into whether intelligence analysis lacked objectivity or had been compromised by politics.

Differences in analytic judgment of intelligence were supposed to be fully considered and brought to the attention of policy makers.

Civil Liberties

Office of the DNI. The law created a Civil Liberties Protection Officer within the Office of the DNI charged with ensuring that the civil liberties and privacy of U.S. citizens were protected when intelligence activities and policies were being carried out.

Oversight board. A new Privacy and Civil Liberties Oversight Board was created within the Executive Office of the President. It was to review executive-branch policies and regulations on terrorism to see that there was "adequate supervision" of the executive branch's use of a particular governmental power to ensure protection of privacy and civil liberties. The powers of the board were weakened in conference, leaving it without subpoena powers. Also, the law allowed the DNI to withhold information from the oversight board if it was in the interest of national security.

CIA. The law reiterated that the CIA lacked the power to conduct any police, subpoena, or law enforcement operations inside the United States.

Other Intelligence Changes

Education and training. The DNI was directed to develop new education and linguistic training requirements for the intelligence community in an effort to improve the spy agencies' abilities to penetrate terrorist cells and interpret intercepted communications. A new intelligence-community scholarship program would offer scholarships to college students interested in going into the intelligence field.

'Open source' intelligence. The law required the DNI to ensure that the intelligence community was making adequate use of "open source" intelligence—meaning publicly available, unclassified information that might contain clues or insights into national security threats. It recommended that a special center be created for this purpose.

Reserve Corps. The DNI was also authorized to establish a National Intelligence Reserve Corps of former or retired intelligence employees who could be called on to work at intelligence agencies during a national emergency.

CIA changes. The CIA director was given 180 days from enactment to submit to the DNI and congressional Intelligence committees a strategy for improving intelligence analysis and human intelligence.

The CIA was directed to develop a more effective foreign language program and to hire people with "diverse" backgrounds, a move aimed at getting more agents with Arab or Middle-Eastern backgrounds into the clandestine services.

The law abolished several top-level CIA positions, including assistant directors of central intelligence for collection, analysis and production, and administration.

Defense-CIA coordination. The CIA and Department of Defense, often depicted as competitive and turf-conscious on intelligence matters, were required to develop new procedures to improve coordination between military and civilian intelligence operations. The procedures were to include language guaranteeing that top officials at the CIA and Defense knew exactly what intelligence activities the other was pursuing.

The law also required creation of an "information-sharing environment"—a virtual, multi-agency information-sharing system designed to share intelligence data, not only within the federal government but also with state and local law enforcement authorities. To create the system, the law authorized $20 million in fiscal 2005 and 2006.

FBI changes. The FBI, which shouldered much of the blame for pre-Sept. 11 intelligence failures, was required to create a new "national intelligence workforce" intended to establish a career track within the agency for domestic intelligence work. The provision addressed concerns that career success at the FBI had hinged more on being a top criminal agent than on being a collector or analyst of intelligence. The FBI's existing Office of Intelligence was elevated to a "Directorate of Intelligence" as part of this effort.

The law also created a Reserve Service of former or retired FBI employees who could be called on to help the FBI during a national emergency, as determined by the FBI director. The mandatory FBI retirement age was raised from sixty to sixty-five.

Security clearances. The law attempted to break up the backlog in processing security clearances by requiring the president to select a single department or agency to be responsible for oversight of all such clearances. Agencies also were required to accept security clearances from other agencies to reduce repetitive clearances. The law set a goal of processing 90 percent of security clearance applications within sixty days. At that time waits were often more than a year.

The law also called on the president-elect, shortly after a presidential election, to submit to the agency in charge of clearances all the names of candidates being considered for national security positions so the clearances could be processed quickly.

Transportation Security

The secretary of homeland security was required to develop a national strategy for transportation security that set threat priorities and laid out a damage-recovery plan in case of another attack. The Transportation Security Administration (TSA) had been criticized for focusing to too great an extent on "fighting the last war," meaning concentrating on airplane security alone.

Biometric technology. The law required the Homeland Security Department to begin deploying a biometric screening system at airports. Such systems obtained biological information through methods such as retinal or iris scanning, fingerprints, or face recognition to identify individual travelers. Within two years, the TSA was to integrate that system with the biometric identification systems used by the Justice and State departments. The TSA was required to establish national technology requirements for this system by March 31, 2005, along with a list of products and vendors that met the standards. The law authorized $20 million for the TSA for research and development of advance biometric technologies for use in aviation security.

Advanced passenger screening. The law directed the TSA to test a new airline passenger screening system that ran names through "no fly" lists and an integrated terrorist watch list, and to establish a procedure that allowed passengers to dispute their inclusion on the list. This was in response to the problem of mistaken identities in which people were blocked from flying because their names were similar to that of someone on the no-fly list.

Employee screening. Employees—whether they worked for the airport, airlines, or security services—would also have to undergo screening, filling what critics said had been a hole in airport security.

Baggage screening. Within ninety days of enactment, the TSA had to submit a plan to Congress for screening all passengers and their carry-on bags for explosives. The law authorized $250 million for research and development of devices to detect biological, radiological, and nuclear materials at airport checkpoints and another $150 million to test experimental weapons-detection technologies at five airports in fiscal 2005 and 2006.

In addition, the law authorized $400 million a year—up from $250 million—for airport security improvement projects.

Air marshals. The law directed the TSA to come up with rules to make it easier for armed air marshals to protect their anonymity. Air marshals had complained that because of a strict business dress code, their cover was easily blown on airplanes. The law also required the Homeland Security Department to train air marshals in foreign countries so they could travel on foreign airliners bound for U.S. airspace.

Other aviation security measures. The law directed the TSA to revise the list of prohibited items on airplanes to include butane lighters, a reaction to the "shoe bomber" incident in 2001.

The Federal Aviation Administration was required to come up with improved pilot licensing standards to reduce the chance of fraud.

The law urged the president to pursue diplomatic dialogue with foreign governments to limit the easy availability of shoulder-fired missiles that could threaten airplanes on takeoff and landing.

The law authorized $900 million in fiscal 2005 through 2007 to improve cargo security on airplanes. It also authorized $2 million for a test program to evaluate blast-resistant cargo containers for airplanes.

Maritime security. The law required the secretary of homeland security to implement a program for screening passengers and crew members on cruise ships against terrorist databases. Such a rule would lead to creation of the maritime equivalent of no-fly lists. However, the secretary could waive the requirements if they were deemed impractical.

Border Security and Immigration

This section of the law addressed the concerns of the Sept. 11 commission that immigration rules and border security were partially to blame for allowing terrorists to enter and move around the country freely even though some were here on expired visas.

Border agents and Customs. The Homeland Security Department was authorized to add 2,000 full-time border patrol agents every year between fiscal 2006 and 2010. It was allowed to hire 800 new immigration investigators and provide 40,000 new beds for detention facilities that housed illegal aliens during that time. To patrol the northern border, the law authorized the use of unmanned airplanes and other technologies such as video sensors. The law also expanded the presence of U.S. immigration officers in foreign airports, increasing the number of foreign "pre-inspection" stations from twenty-five to fifty.

Visa requirements. The law required that all visa applicants be interviewed in person by U.S. consular officials. It created a new visa and passport security program to investigate how terrorists used fraudulent documents and which countries facilitated such actions. The State Department was required to report to Congress by May 31, 2005, on the feasibility of giving border agents access to real-time, constantly updated information on stolen passports. The measure also required creation of a Visa and Passport Security Program at the State Department.

Illegal immigrant treatment. The law created a Human Smuggling and Trafficking Center aimed at halting terrorist entries into the United States and cracking down on human smuggling. It allowed deportation of anyone who had received military-style training from a terrorist organization. It also forbade entry into the United States by any foreign national who had committed torture or other atrocities abroad. If such individuals were already in the country, they could be deported. The law also prohibited judicial review of visa revocations, taking away an appeals process for people whose visas had been revoked.

Consular officers. The secretary of state was authorized to add 150 new consular officers per year between fiscal 2006

and 2009 for consulates around the world. Most aliens applying for nonimmigrant visas had to be interviewed in person by a consular official, not a foreign national. Consular officers were to receive training to better detect fraudulent documents that terrorists might use to acquire visas.

Fraudulent travel documents. The law called on the president to lead efforts to draw up international agreements to better track terrorist travel and crack down on use of stolen or falsified passports and visas, and to help establish an international system for "real time" verification of visas and passports.

Immigration security. The secretary of homeland security was put in charge of the "immigration security initiative," which placed U.S. immigration officers at foreign airports. The measure authorized $105 million over three years to carry out the program.

Driver's license standards. The Homeland Security and Transportation departments were required to develop federal standards for the types of documents that states could accept in issuing driver's licenses. In what some critics called a "loophole," the law stated that such federal regulations could not infringe on a state's power to decide who was eligible for a driver's license.

Birth certificates. The Health and Human Services Department had to establish federal standards for state-issued birth certificates, although the department was not allowed to require that all states adhere to a specific design for birth certificates.

Social Security numbers. The Social Security Administration had to create minimum standards for verifying documents used by people who wanted either an original or replacement Social Security card. The law also limited people to three replacement cards in a year or ten for their entire life. The provision created an interagency task force composed of Social Security and Homeland Security officials that was responsible for combating Social Security card fraud. States were prohibited from displaying Social Security numbers on driver's licenses, which used to be standard practice in many states.

Terrorist travel information. The Homeland Security Department was required to set up a program to oversee dissemination of terrorist travel intelligence to all federal authorities involved in transportation security.

Identification standards. States were required to certify to the Transportation Department that they were meeting minimum federal standards for issuing driver's licenses, birth certificates, and other identification documents. The departments of Transportation and Homeland Security had to write such standards within eighteen months of enactment. The measure was aimed at getting a national standard for IDs used to board airplanes.

Terrorism Prevention

'Lone wolf' terrorist. This portion of the law amended the Foreign Intelligence Surveillance Act (PL 95-511) to allow the FBI to conduct surveillance on a single terrorist who might not be connected to any foreign power or agent of a foreign power. Prior law allowed surveillance on U.S. soil of people suspected of spying for a foreign power, but critics said that prevented monitoring of a potential terrorist who was working as a "lone wolf." This provision also required amending the 2001 PATRIOT Act (PL 107-56).

Pretrial imprisonment. Terrorist suspects had to be denied bail and held in jail until trial, unless they could prove they were not flight risks or dangers to society.

Material support to terrorists. The law made it a crime to provide material support—meaning money, lodging, advice, training, or any other aid—in helping to carry out an act of terrorism. The provision expired at the end of 2006.

Terrorist hoaxes. The law also made it a crime for anyone to convey false or misleading information about a terrorist attack or possible terrorist attack. If convicted, the suspect could be sentenced to five years in prison. If the hoax caused bodily harm or death to anyone, the suspect could be sentenced to twenty years to life in prison.

Weapons of mass destruction. The law specified that it was a crime to use the mail or any postal-like service to carry out an attack with a weapon of mass destruction.

Biological and radiological weapons. Criminal penalties were expanded for production, possession, and use of radiological explosive devices, or "dirty bombs," and the variola virus, which was the carrier of smallpox.

Grand jury information. Existing law permitted sharing of grand jury information with state and local governments to help enforce federal laws. The new law expanded that authority to allow the sharing of grand jury information with foreign governments to help U.S. law enforcement. The law allowed sharing of foreign intelligence with foreign governments but only after the Justice Department and the DNI submitted guidelines for such information sharing.

Criminal background checks. Private employers were allowed to ask the Justice Department to conduct criminal background checks on private security officers, but the employer had to have written consent from the employee to do the investigation.

Financial Provisions

Financial Crimes Network. The law authorized $35.5 million in fiscal 2005 to boost the Treasury Department's Financial Crimes Enforcement Network, with most of the money going to a program designed to securely receive and analyze data from financial institutions. The law also extended provisions in the Money Laundering and Financial Crimes Strategy Act (PL 105-310) and required the Treasury Department to submit to Congress a national strategy for combating money laundering. This section also made terrorist-financing provisions in the PATRIOT Act permanent. All the provisions were geared toward better tracking of terrorist financial networks.

Currency engraving. The Bureau of Engraving and Printing was authorized to print currency and other sensitive documents for foreign governments. This was designed to allow the bureau to test anticounterfeiting measures that could be used in future upgrades in U.S. currency, while also helping developing nations that were U.S. allies to upgrade their currency systems. The printing of money for foreign countries had to be consistent with U.S. foreign policy.

Financial market emergencies. The law expanded the authority of the Securities and Exchange Commission to take emergency actions to halt trading and close financial markets in case of a national emergency. Under the new law, the SEC could extend emergency orders for up to thirty business days, up from ten days in existing law.

Bank examiner rules. Senior federal bank examiners were barred from accepting employment at a bank they had investigated for at least one year after leaving the Federal Deposit Insurance Corporation.

Reports to Congress. Within 270 days after enactment of the law, the Treasury Department was required to submit a report on the effectiveness of U.S. efforts to stop terrorist financing. The department was also required to work more closely with the International Monetary Fund to battle global terrorist financing.

Foreign Policy Provisions

The Sept. 11 commission had recommended significant outreach efforts to improve diplomatic relations throughout the world, and the law had several provisions aimed at accomplishing this goal.

Terrorist sanctuaries. A "sense of Congress" provision stated that the United States should be aggressive in identifying terrorist sanctuaries and countries that sheltered terrorists. It recommended that the United States help countries that unknowingly harbored terrorists to come up with strategies for eliminating the conditions that created the terrorist sanctuaries.

Export Administration Act. The law amended the Export Administration Act of 1979 (PL 96-72) to ensure that regulations relating to state sponsors of terrorism also applied to all terrorist sanctuaries.

Pakistan. The law declared that a stable Pakistan was critical to the stability of the region and the United States should help Pakistan fully control its territorial borders. The law waived existing restrictions on foreign assistance to Pakistan through fiscal 2006.

Afghanistan. This provision reiterated U.S. support for democracy in Afghanistan, backed efforts to slow down the narcotics trade, and called for the president to create a long-term strategy for Afghanistan. It authorized "such sums as may be necessary" for assistance to Afghanistan in fiscal 2005 and 2006. The law created the position of a "coordinator for assistance" to Afghanistan and called for the Afghan government, with U.S. assistance, to disarm Afghan warlords.

Saudi diplomacy. The law expressed a sense of Congress that Saudi Arabia should remain a key ally but that the Saudi government had not done a good job preventing financial support from being provided to terrorists in Saudi Arabia. The president was required to submit to Congress within 180 days of enactment a new strategy for collaborating with Saudi Arabia, including intelligence cooperation. A similar report outlining a long-term strategy for dealing with Pakistan also had to be submitted within 180 days.

'Moral leadership.' In a section dealing with efforts to combat Islamic terrorism, the law acknowledged the U.S. reputation in the Islamic world had suffered and stated that the United States should offer an example of "moral leadership" to the world by treating people humanely and respecting Muslim traditions.

Using media in diplomacy. The law called on the State Department to promote a free press in the Muslim world. The measure authorized the secretary of state to make grants to the National Endowment for Democracy to fund a private sector group to manage a "media network" of individuals and government officials that would help develop free and independent media in the Islamic world. No specific amount of money was authorized.

Muslim outreach. A pilot program was created to provide scholarship grants to American-sponsored schools in Muslim countries. The State Department was directed to establish an "International Youth Opportunity Fund" to improve public education in predominantly Muslim countries, but no specific amount of money was authorized. The law authorized continued funding—with no specific dollar figure—for the Middle East Partnership Initiative, a program designed to promote the rule of law in the Middle East.

Human rights. The law reiterated U.S. support of the U.N. Human Rights Commission and called on the president and State Department to establish training courses in multilateral diplomacy for Foreign Service officers.

Free trade. The measure declared that the United States would work toward creating a "Middle East Free Trade Zone" by 2013 and would use economic policies and free trade to combat the conditions that lead to terrorism.

Homeland Security

This section began with a sense-of-Congress statement that the Department of Homeland Security needed to develop a unified "incident command system" so there was a national communications and response plan in case of another major terrorist attack.

Capital region aid. The law authorized mutual aid between local governments and regional authorities in the Washington area. The aid could be used by regional or local authorities to share emergency services or resources in responding to a terrorist attack.

Emergency communications. The law had several provisions aimed at improving emergency-communications systems. It called on Congress to pass a law to set aside certain radio spectrum and analog television spectrum for emergency responders. It also required the Department of Homeland Security to work with the Commerce Department to es-

tablish a program to enhance public safety communications and authorized $118 million over five years for the program.

First-responder funding. The law did not change the formula for distributing first-responder grants, although both the House and Senate versions called for a greater emphasis on high-threat areas while guaranteeing a minimum to all states. Instead, the law stated a sense of Congress that the 109th Congress should overhaul the formula, with no specific recommendation for how to do so.

Alert system. The law authorized a pilot study to see whether the Homeland Security Department could develop a homeland security warning system similar to the AMBER Alert system commonly used to disseminate information about missing children.

Counternarcotics office. The duties of the counternarcotics office were expanded to allow the director to serve on the Joint Terrorism Task Force to facilitate the investigations of connections between terrorism and narcotics trafficking.

Geospatial Management. The law created an Office of Geospatial Management in the Department of Homeland Security to coordinate mapping, satellite analysis, and other geographic technologies in an effort to improve terrorism intelligence.

Civil liberties. The law required the department's inspector general to designate a senior staff member to handle civil rights and civil liberties cases for the department. The official would review complaints and initiate investigations when there were allegations of violations of civil rights or civil liberties. However, this section did not contain any new civil liberties protections and did not give any subpoena powers to civil liberties offices of Homeland Security or the DNI.

Miscellaneous Provisions

Financial disclosure. The Office of Government Ethics was required to submit a report to Congress on conflict of interest rules regarding financial disclosure reporting for government officials.

Plane tickets on bankrupt airlines. The law extended for an additional year—through Nov. 19, 2005—a provision in existing law that required airlines to honor tickets on other airlines that had suspended service or gone out of business.

FBI computers. The law required the FBI to maintain state-of-the-art information-technology systems and to report annually to the House and Senate Judiciary committees on the progress of those systems.

Congressional Oversight of Intelligence

The independent commission that investigated the Sept. 11, 2001, terrorist attacks called on Congress to change the way the nation handled intelligence. Writing legislation to reorganize the intelligence community was a major challenge, but perhaps the most difficult task the 9/11 commission laid down for Congress was to overhaul its own structure and processes.

Labeling congressional oversight of intelligence and counterterrorism "dysfunctional," the commission proposed specific steps Congress should take. It called for either creating a joint House-Senate panel on intelligence or empowering the Intelligence committees with both authorizing and appropriating powers. The commission recommended that Congress create permanent standing committees on homeland security. Its proposals also included ending existing term limits for the House and Senate Intelligence committees, which were six and eight years, respectively, so that the panels would not lose valuable expertise. *(Independent 9/11 commission, p. 275)*

The commission's recommendations roiled the power structure on Capitol Hill. The proposals would have required shuffling committee jurisdictions, taking authority away from committees and giving it to others. Powerful committee chairs and ranking Democrats were reluctant to cede their panels' authority. And so, although it had managed to produce broad intelligence overhaul legislation (S 2845—PL 108-458) for the executive branch, the 108th Congress eschewed significant changes on its own turf. *(Intelligence system overhaul, p. 263)*

SENATE

Senate leaders assigned to a twenty-two-member bipartisan working group the job of drafting proposals to implement the commission's proposals. The group's recommendations were introduced as S Res 445. The Senate Rules and Administration Committee reported the resolution (no written report) on Oct. 5, 2004, and the full Senate adopted an amended version on Oct. 9 by a vote of 79–6. The end result fell well short of what the 9/11 commission had recommended.

S Res 445 raised the status of the Intelligence Committee to category "A" to give panel members more time to focus on intelligence issues. Under existing rules, senators could serve on no more than two "A" panels. The resolution also ended the term limit on Intelligence members; gave the majority and minority leaders power to appoint all panel members, including the chair and vice chair; and reduced the size of the committee from seventeen to fifteen members.

But the Senate rejected the idea of consolidating authorization and appropriation powers in the Intelligence Committee. An amendment by John McCain, R-Ariz., to give appropriating authority to the Intelligence panel was defeated, 23–74, on Oct. 7. The Senate instead left that power with the Appropriations Committee and opted to create a new Appropriations subcommittee to handle the intelligence budget. S Res 445 also established a subcommittee on oversight in the Intelligence Committee. The Intelligence Committee was denied on-demand sequential referral, meaning it would not get automatic jurisdiction of all legislation that included intelligence-related material.

The 9/11 commission's proposal for a restructuring of homeland security oversight made little headway either. *(Details, homeland security chapter, p. 171)*

HOUSE

The House took no action in 2004 on the 9/11 commission's oversight recommendations. But opposition to certain proposals was voiced.

House Majority Leader Tom DeLay, R-Texas, and Majority Whip Roy Blunt, R-Mo., were clear in their opposition to giving an authorizing committee any appropriations powers. They also said they were against ending term limits for Intelligence panel members.

And House appropriators did not like the idea of a subcommittee just for intelligence funding, as the Senate had approved. They thought such a move would require the Defense and Military Construction panels to merge, resulting in military housing and other construction areas being given short shrift.

Independent 9/11 Commission

The independent commission created to investigate the Sept. 11, 2001, terrorist attacks on the United States completed its probe in 2004 and called for an overhaul of the nation's spy agencies and of Congress's oversight of the intelligence community.

In its unanimous final report, released July 22, 2004, the bipartisan commission—known formally as the National Commission on Terrorist Attacks Upon the United States—gave a detailed account of the attacks. It said the nation had been unprepared and recommended a series of steps that should be taken within the executive branch and Congress to prevent future attacks. Key recommendations included the creation of a new position of national intelligence director, establishment of a National Counterterrorism Center, and a committee restructuring to fix Congress's "dysfunctional" oversight of intelligence and counterterrorism.

The urgency conveyed in the report's recommendations, combined with visits to Capitol Hill by the commission's leaders and families of Sept. 11 victims, jolted lawmakers into action. Despite formidable institutional barriers to the kind of change the commission called for, major reform legislation (S 2845—PL 108-458) was cleared in the closing days of the 108th Congress. *(Intelligence reform, p. 263)*

The 9/11 commission had had to overcome a series of obstacles as well, including winning a controversial two-month extension of its work (S 2136—PL 108-207) that put the release of its final report in the midst of the presidential nominating season.

BACKGROUND

In the aftermath of the 2001 terrorist attacks, the Bush White House had consistently opposed creation of an independent commission to look into the failures that led to Sept. 11. The administration, fearful that the investigation would be politicized, pushed instead for a probe by Congress. A joint inquiry by the House and Senate Intelligence

9/11 COMMISSION MEMBERS

The independent 9/11 commission created in 2002 got off to a rocky start. The two men appointed as chair and vice chair resigned before the investigation even began.

During the Nov. 27, 2002, White House signing ceremony for the authorizing legislation (HR 4628—PL 107-306), President George W. Bush announced his selection of former secretary of state Henry A. Kissinger, who had served in the Nixon and Ford administrations, to chair the new commission. Democratic congressional leaders later that day tapped former Senate majority leader George J. Mitchell, D-Maine (Senate, 1980–1995; majority leader, 1989–1995) as vice chair. But both men soon withdrew in the face of arguments from family members of Sept. 11 victims that the two would be hampered by potential conflicts of interests at their full-time jobs. Mitchell dropped out on Dec. 11, Kissinger on Dec. 13.

On Dec. 16 Bush named former New Jersey governor Thomas H. Kean (1982–1990) to take the job of chair. Democrats chose as vice chair former representative Lee H. Hamil-

ton, D-Ind. (1965–1999), who during his House career had chaired both the Intelligence Committee (1985–1987) and the International Relations Committee (1993–1995).

Other Democrats named to the commission were Max Cleland, a U.S. senator from Georgia (1997–2003); Tim Roemer, a U.S. representative from Indiana (1991–2003); Richard Ben-Veniste, a former Watergate prosecutor and Senate Whitewater Committee counsel; and Jamie S. Gorelick, former Clinton administration deputy attorney general. Cleland, who was defeated for reelection in the November 2002 election, left the commission in December 2003 to become a member of the Export-Import Bank board and was replaced by former Nebraska senator Bob Kerrey (1989–2001).

Republican commissioners included Slade Gorton, a former U.S. senator from Washington (1981–1987, 1989–2001); James R. Thompson, a former governor of Illinois (1977-1991); John F. Lehman, former Reagan administration secretary of the Navy; and Fred F. Fielding, former Nixon White House deputy counsel and Reagan White House counsel.

committees was launched, but as the investigating committees became increasingly frustrated in their efforts to get information out of the intelligence agencies calls for an outside commission grew louder. The White House, under great pressure from the Sept. 11 victims' families, eventually relented, but it insisted on a power-sharing arrangement designed to prevent either party from turning the investigation into a political vehicle. *(Sept. 11 chronology, p. 236; Congressional 9/11 probe, p. 245)*

An intelligence authorization bill (HR 4628—PL 107-306) enacted in late 2002 contained a section authorizing a commission to "make a full and complete accounting" of the circumstances surrounding the attacks, as well as the country's preparedness for and its immediate response to the attacks. The commission was also charged with making recommendations for corrective measures. Its work was to build on the Intelligence committees' probe. *(2003 intelligence authorization, p. 243)*

The commission was given a broad purview. Its investigation of "relevant facts and circumstances" could include everything from "any relevant legislation, Executive order, regulation, plan, policy, practice, or procedure" to "intelligence agencies; law enforcement agencies; diplomacy; immigration, nonimmigrant visas, and border control; the flow of assets to terrorist organizations; commercial aviation; the role of congressional oversight and resource allocation; and other areas of the public and private sectors determined relevant by the Commission for its inquiry."

To ensure that the ten-member commission would be bipartisan, President George W. Bush was to pick the chair and

the Democratic congressional leadership was to choose the vice chair. Selection of the remaining members was allocated among the House and Senate Republican and Democratic leaders. The law stipulated that no more than five members of the commission could be from the same political party.

INVESTIGATION

Given its daunting mandate and the potential political fallout from its investigation, the commission's path was not always smooth.

The process of selecting commission members faltered initially, when the first choices for chair and vice chair backed out, after some questioned whether they might have conflicts of interest. But the eventual choices to lead the commission—former New Jersey governor Thomas H. Kean, a Republican, and former representative Lee H. Hamilton of Indiana (1965–1999), a Democrat—were widely hailed as nonpartisan, independent voices. *(Commission members, p. 276)*

The commission was hampered initially in getting security clearances for all its members. And once the investigation got underway, investigators complained that the administration was not delivering requested documents or providing enough witnesses. Indeed, in the fall of 2003 the commission issued a series of subpoenas—to the Federal Aviation Administration, the Defense Department, and the City of New York—after citing inadequate cooperation. In the end, the issues were resolved without litigation.

The commission also tangled with the White House over access to the top-secret Presidential Daily Briefs (PDBs), classified documents that only the president and a handful of advisers saw. In November 2003 a deal was struck that let some commission members look at edited sections of some PDBs, provided they did it inside the White House. But other members criticized the compromise as too limited. Ultimately, according to the commission, a four-person review team saw all the PDB items requested and prepared a detailed report and briefing for the other commission members.

By early January 2004, commission members were expressing concern that they would have to curtail their probe in order to meet their original deadline. Under carefully negotiated language in the authorization measure, the commission was to submit its final report to the president and Congress no later than eighteen months after enactment of the authorizing legislation. That meant the report was due May 27, 2004. But on Jan. 27, 2004, the commission asked for more time. It said it needed an extension of at least two months to wrap up its investigation. Members said they already had had to cancel some public hearings, and they had wrangled repeatedly with the Bush administration over access to materials, which had slowed their progress. Plus, they were still negotiating to get Bush, Vice President Dick Cheney, and national security adviser Condoleezza Rice to testify.

The two-month extension idea was said to be the result of a bipartisan consensus of the commission's staff and members, who maintained that it was the minimum amount of time needed to complete their interviews, write the report, and declassify it. But an additional two months would have the panel revealing its findings in July—around the time of the 2004 presidential nominating conventions and far too close to the November elections for the White House's taste. Not surprisingly, the proposal set off political fireworks. With the president's aides advising the commission to stick to its original deadline, some GOP leaders echoed the White House line. Other Republicans proposed that the panel's deadline be extended for six months, which would have pushed the publication of its findings safely beyond Election Day. Some Democrats opposed a six-month extension, saying the commission should be given the two months it requested so the president could be held accountable at the November polls for any failures. Other Democrats wondered whether Bush was simply trying to run down the clock, forcing an end to an investigation he never particularly supported.

In the end, Bush went along with the two-month extension proposal after his administration concluded that a longer one would subject the president to charges of buying time past Election Day. The Senate Intelligence Committee on Feb. 26, 2004, reported legislation (S 2136—no written report) extending the commission's deadline until July 26, which also was the opening day of the Democratic National Convention. The Senate approved the bill by voice vote on Feb. 27.

But then the proposal was blocked by Speaker J. Dennis Hastert, R-Ill., who said he would not ask the House to vote on it. Democrats charged that Hastert was trying to protect Bush by forcing the probe to wrap up before the campaign season's peak. The Speaker denied any political motivation and said he wanted the panel to finish by the original deadline so Congress might act on its recommendations in 2004. But he relented when Senate backers of the extension held a stopgap highway bill (HR 3850—PL 108-202) hostage as leverage. The House cleared S 2136 by voice vote March 3, and the president signed it into law (PL 108-207) March 16.

Partisan fighting flared later in March when the commission held a hearing on counterterrorism policy. There were moments in which the participants seemed interested in rising above the toxic party wars that pervaded Washington at that time. The first day of testimony included the secretaries of defense and state for the Clinton and Bush administrations, discussing common enemies and shared culpability. But the brawling began the next day, when former Bush administration counterterrorism adviser Richard A. Clarke testified that the White House largely ignored the al Qaeda threat before the attacks and fixated on Iraq instead. Even the commissioners took on a partisan edge, as the Democratic commissioners showered Clarke with praise while Republicans grilled him. His book *Against All Enemies,* arrived in bookstores only two days before his testimony, which drew Republican charges of opportunistic timing. The administration spent much of the week attempting to discredit Clarke, while Democrats defended him and urged the White House to halt its campaign against him. Democrat Tom Daschle of South Dakota, the Senate minority leader, accused the White House of waging a "character attack" on Clarke.

The White House insisted that Clarke had strongly supported the president throughout his time at the National Security Council (NSC) and that the proof of that support could be found in secret testimony Clarke gave in July 2002 to the joint House and Senate Intelligence committees' inquiry into the Sept. 11 attacks. Senate Majority Leader Bill Frist, R-Tenn., on March 26 said that he wanted to declassify Clarke's testimony and compare it with his testimony before the commission to see if he had lied under oath to Congress. John D. Rockefeller IV of West Virginia, the ranking Democrat on the Senate Intelligence Committee, countered that if anyone thought Clarke had perjured himself, the matter should be referred immediately to the Justice Department.

In the meantime, House Intelligence Committee Chair Porter J. Goss, R-Fla., had already shipped Clarke's testimony to the executive branch for a declassification review. It was sent first to the NSC on March 24—the day Clarke appeared before the commission—and then to the CIA on March 26. Goss's action set off a firestorm in his own committee, with the panel's top Democrat, Jane Harman of California, charging that it gave the impression that sensitive material was being "selectively declassified for political reasons, rather than national security or the public interest." Harman backed away from her initial suggestion that Goss might have violated committee rules by not consulting with her—a charge Goss staunchly disputed—but Democrats said the chair's action had strained party-line divisions on the traditionally nonpartisan panel.

Both Democrats and Republicans said they wanted Clarke's testimony declassified, but the two sides had radically different ideas of what the testimony would reveal. Democrats said it would prove that Clarke was consistent all along while Republicans insisted that it would show how he had changed his tune in an effort to boost sales of his book.

The White House on March 30 finally agreed to allow national security adviser Rice to testify in public before the commission. She had previously met with the commission in private. The White House for months had resisted the commission's request for public testimony, arguing that it would be a violation of the principle of separation of powers to compel Rice to disclose her communications with the president. But the president relented after receiving written assurances from the 9/11 commission and congressional leaders that her appearance would not be viewed as a precedent for future requests for public testimony by White House officials.

The response to Rice's testimony divided along partisan lines. Her performance won rave reviews from GOP lawmakers, who said she was right to say there was no "silver bullet" that might have thwarted the attacks. For many Democrats, however, Rice's statements left a tangle of unanswered questions. Foremost among them was whether the Bush administration—at its highest levels—was aware in the spring and summer of 2001 that al Qaeda cells within the United States were planning to strike the U.S. homeland. At the center of the debate was an Aug. 6, 2001, Presidential Daily Briefing entitled, as Rice revealed in her testimony, "Bin Laden Determined to Attack Inside the United States." Rice insisted that the memo was "historical information based on old reporting," rather than an explicit warning. The commission's leaders, who had wrangled with the White House for months to get limited access to the memo, promptly called on the White House to declassify the PDB, which the White House just as promptly agreed to do. Ultimately, the commission was given everything in the Aug. 6 PDB pertaining to al Qaeda and the threat of attacks on the United States.

The administration also on March 30 announced that the president and vice president would meet in one joint private session with all ten commission members. That meeting, which lasted more than three hours, took place on April 29. The commission had met privately with former president Bill Clinton and former vice president Al Gore earlier in April.

Over the course of its investigation, the 9/11 commission worked with a cumulative budget of $15 million and more than eighty staff members. It interviewed more than 1,200 people in ten countries, reviewed more than 2.5 million pages of documents, and held nineteen days of public hearings at which more than 160 witnesses testified.

FINDINGS

The commission found that Islamist extremists had given "plenty of warning" that they intended to kill large numbers of Americans indiscriminately. "The 9/11 attacks were a shock, but they should not have come as a surprise, " the report stated, recounting the growing threat of Islamist terrorism from the first attack on the World Trade Center in 1993 to the attack on the USS *Cole* in 2000. In the spring and summer of 2001, there was a stream of warnings that al Qaeda was planning something big, according to the report, but because the specific threat information pointed overseas, precautions were taken abroad and not at home. *(Report summary text, p. 969)*

The report gave a detailed accounting of the Sept. 11 attacks, from the terrorists' preparations to the attacks themselves and the U.S. response. The commission acknowledged it had the advantage of hindsight and said it did not want to be unjust to those who had "made choices in conditions of uncertainty and in circumstances over which they often had little control." Still, the commission concluded that "there were specific points of vulnerability in the plot and opportunities to disrupt it," but nothing the government had done from 1998 to 2001 had disturbed or delayed the hijackers' plot. This it attributed to failures of imagination, policy, capabilities, and management.

Because of a lack of imagination—said to be the most important failure—officials did not understand that the threat posed by Osama bin Laden and al Qaeda was something radically new and different from the terrorism the United States had experienced up to that time. Because of a lack of imagination, the intelligence community had never analyzed how an aircraft could be used as a weapon, let alone figured out what to look for and how to defend against it.

Since the growing threat from al Qaeda was not understood, terrorism was not the overriding national security concern for either the Clinton or Bush administrations and policies commensurate with the threat were not developed. Prior to Sept. 11, a U.S. invasion of Afghanistan was said to be practically inconceivable.

The commission found fault in the capabilities of the CIA, Defense Department, and NORAD (North American Aerospace Defense Command) but said that the most serious weaknesses in agency capabilities were in domestic agencies, including the FBI, Immigration and Naturalization Service, Federal Aviation Administration, and others.

The commission found both operational and institutional management problems. Information was not shared among agencies, particularly across the divide between foreign policy and domestic policy agencies, and duties were not clearly assigned. The commission also faulted top managers for how they set priorities and allocated resources.

In addition to these general findings, the final report cited specific problems in diplomacy, military options, the intelligence community, the FBI, border and immigration controls, aviation security, tracking al Qaeda funding, homeland defense, and emergency response.

The commission also found that Congress, like the executive branch, had been slow to respond to the new transnational threat of terrorism. It said that Congress's attention had been "episodic" and that terrorism had been a second- or third-order priority for the committees responsible for national security. It criticized Congress for neglecting its oversight function and splintering it across committee lines, and said the legislative branch needed to restructure itself in order to give intelligence agencies oversight, support, and leadership.

RECOMMENDATIONS

Although the commission said that it believed the country was safer today because of steps taken since Sept. 11, it added: "But we are not safe."

The commission made a number of recommendations for what could be done to make the United States safer and more secure. Those recommendations were divided into two parts: a global strategy and government reorganization.

The global strategy recommendations focused on what needed to be done: attack terrorists and their organizations, prevent the continued growth of Islamist terrorism, and protect against and prepare for terrorist attacks.

The commission then recommended steps to carry out that global strategy. It said it could be done by restructuring the government with the clear purpose of building unity of effort. It focused on unifying strategic intelligence and operational planning, placing the intelligence community under one director, establishing an information-sharing system that transcended traditional governmental boundaries, unifying and strengthening congressional oversight, and strengthening the FBI and homeland defenders.

Key among its specific recommendations were:

• Establish the position of National Intelligence Director to oversee the entire intelligence community and its budget and serve as chief intelligence adviser to the president. The CIA director at that time served as titular head of all intelligence agencies but controlled less than one-fifth of the budget.

• Form a National Counterterrorism Center to integrate strategic intelligence from all sources into joint operational planning. The center would assign the responsibility for carrying out operations to the appropriate agencies.

• Establish either a joint House-Senate congressional panel on intelligence, like the old Joint Committee on Atomic Energy, or a single intelligence committee in each chamber that would have both authorizing and appropriating powers. The second option would have radically changed the decades-old tradition of the Intelligence committees authorizing the budget before letting the Armed Services and Appropriations panels have the final say on how the funding would be allocated among the intelligence agencies.

• Abolish existing term limits for the House and Senate Intelligence committees, which were six and eight years, respectively. The idea was to avoid having committee members step down just as they began to acquire expertise in intelligence issues.

• Consolidate intelligence spending into a single annual appropriations bill and make the total amount public while keeping specific programs secret. The classified budget was estimated to be about $40 billion, with at least 80 percent going to Pentagon intelligence agencies. At that time there was no separate intelligence appropriations measure, which meant that Defense Appropriations Subcommittee members had the last word on spending decisions.

• Create permanent homeland security committees in both chambers. The Senate had no homeland security committee, while the House panel had been unable to carve out authority on any issue that challenged other committees' turf. Jurisdiction over homeland security was so diffuse, the report said, that officials testifying on the issue had to appear before more than eighty committees and subcommittees.

• Speed up the transition process between administrations so Congress could confirm officials responsible for national security within a month of a new president's inauguration. This proposal was aimed at minimizing as much as possible disruptions in national security policy making.

RALLYING SUPPORT

The 9/11 commission closed its doors a month after releasing its final report. But commission members did not consider their job to be over. Kean and Hamilton said that the ten commissioners would continue to work to educate the country about their report and to monitor the implementation of their recommendations. They joined together to form the 9/11 Public Discourse Project, an organization that was to pursue those goals over the following year.

Their job became easier when the final report made the bestseller list. To ensure that the report was widely available and affordable, the commission had chosen W.W. Norton & Company to publish a $10 paperback edition. The report was also made available on the commission's website.

Several staff monographs with more detailed treatment of subjects investigated by the commission were subsequently released. These included reports on al Qaeda financing and on immigration, border security, and terrorist travel, released in August 2004, and one on the four Sept. 11 flights and civil aviation security, released in January 2005.

2004 Intelligence Authorization

Congress in 2003 cleared a fiscal 2004 intelligence authorization bill (HR 2417—PL 108-177) that addressed areas that critics had cited since the Sept. 11, 2001, terrorist attacks as intelligence shortcomings—including failures in information sharing, human intelligence, and intelligence analysis. But lawmakers continued to emphasize the need for a far-reaching intelligence overhaul.

The intelligence budget was classified, but it was estimated to total around $40 billion. The fiscal 2003 version (HR 4628—PL 107-306) reportedly authorized between $35 billion and $40 billion, and members of the Intelligence committees said the fiscal 2004 measure included a slight increase. *(2003 intelligence authorization, p. 243)*

HR 2417 authorized the intelligence activities of the CIA, National Security Agency (NSA), Federal Bureau of Investigation (FBI), Defense Intelligence Agency, Coast Guard, the military services, and other agencies and offices in the Defense, State, Treasury, Energy, Justice, and Homeland Security departments. Money for their programs was appropriated in classified sections of several appropriations bills, with the Pentagon receiving the lion's share.

Some members pointed to the fact that spending on covert military operations had risen considerably and called for more oversight. Military activities, including clandestine operations preceding a conflict, fell outside the definition of covert action under the 1991 intelligence law (PL 102-88) that required a presidential finding and "timely" notification to congressional committees of covert operations. *(PL 102-88, Congress and the Nation Vol. VIII, p. 280)*

LEGISLATIVE ACTION

The House passed HR 2417 by a vote of 410–9 on June 27, 2003. The House Intelligence Committee had reported the bill (H Rept 108-163) on June 18.

In its report, the House panel called for "fundamental structural and management changes within the intelligence community." The greatest needs identified in the committee report included recruiting more spies and managing them more effectively, paying greater attention to intelligence analysts, and training more officers in foreign languages. During floor action, Sherwood Boehlert, R-N.Y., vice chair of two Intelligence subcommittees, warned the CIA to act, in particular on improving intelligence officers' language training, "or else."

The full House adopted by a vote of 418–0 on June 26 an Alcee L. Hastings, D-Fla., amendment to require the CIA director to create a pilot project aimed at improving intelligence agencies' recruitment of minorities and women, and by voice vote on June 25 a Jane Harman, D-Calif., amendment to require the CIA director to report on how well federal watch-list databases, instituted after the Sept. 11 attacks, had helped identify known or suspected terrorists. On June 26 the House rejected by a vote of 76–347 a Dennis J. Kucinich, D-Ohio, amendment to require an audit of prewar contacts between Vice President Dick Cheney and the CIA concerning Iraq's weapons of mass destruction, and by a vote of 185–239 a Barbara Lee, D-Calif., amendment to require a study on how much prewar intelligence the Pentagon and U.S. intelligence agencies shared with U.N. weapons inspectors.

The Senate passed HR 2417 by voice vote and without debate on July 31, after substituting the text of its own measure (S 1025). The Senate Intelligence Committee had reported S 1025 (S Rept 108-44) on May 8, and the Senate Armed Services had reported the bill (S Rept 108-80) on June 26.

After reporting the bill, the Senate Intelligence panel issued a statement saying the measure urged a renewed focus on analysis in addition to intelligence gathering. Committee aides said most of the changes were based on recommendations that came out of findings by the joint congressional inquiry that examined intelligence failures preceding the Sept. 11 attacks. *(Congressional 9/11 probe, p. 245)*

FINAL ACTION

The House adopted the conference report (H Rept 108-381) on Nov. 20 by a vote of 264–163, and the Senate cleared the bill by voice vote the following day. HR 2417 was signed into law on Dec. 13.

The Intelligence committees had put off conference negotiations until late fall while they focused on other business, including inquiries into prewar intelligence on Iraq. As the conference report neared completion in November, a last-minute wrangle had broken out over an expansion of the FBI's search powers under the 1978 Financial Privacy Act (PL 95-630). That law allowed the FBI to demand financial records in terrorism cases from banks, credit unions, and other traditional financial institutions without a court or grand jury order. HR 2417 broadened the definition of "financial institution" to include such entities as car dealerships, pawnbrokers, travel agencies, and casinos.

The FBI provision had been in both chambers' versions of the bill, but it was not until the conference report neared final agreement that some lawmakers openly expressed concern over it. Five Democrats and one Republican on the Senate Judiciary Committee wrote a letter Nov. 18 to the leaders of the Senate Intelligence panel warning that the FBI could use the broader definition to seize financial records that traditionally had been protected under financial privacy laws. In the conference, Democrat Richard J. Durbin of Illinois, a member of both the Senate Judiciary and Intelligence panels, proposed a "sunset" clause for the provision that would have required Congress to explicitly renew it after one year. Durbin lost on a party-line vote of House and Senate conferees. But the unusual number of "no" votes on the conference report in the House—fifteen Republicans, 147 Democrats, and one independent—reflected uneasiness over the provision.

The final bill authorized money to promote improved information sharing of raw intelligence among agencies and called for a single, governmentwide terrorist watch list under the auspices of the new Terrorist Screening Center, whose creation was announced by the Bush administration on Sept. 16. It also directed the CIA to provide a "lessons learned" report on the Iraq war to Congress no later than a year after the bill's enactment.

The bill required the establishment of a new Office of Intelligence and Analysis in the Treasury Department to coordinate foreign intelligence-gathering on financial flows to terrorist groups. The conference report described the existing coordination between Treasury and intelligence agencies as "uneven and disjointed."

The bill reauthorized funds for intelligence and intelligence-related activities used to support Colombia's antidrug efforts and banned U.S. troops and contractors from taking part in combat there. And it extended tort liability protection to certain CIA and NSA personnel if they acted to protect an individual from violence or prevent the escape of an individual suspected of a violent act against such personnel.

2005 Intelligence Authorization

Congress in 2004 cleared the fiscal 2005 intelligence authorization bill (HR 4548—PL 108-487) but only after reaching agreement on separate legislation to overhaul the intelligence community.

HR 4548 had been sidetracked for more than a month while Congress completed action on the intelligence reform bill (S 2845—PL 108-458) during a lame-duck session. Both chambers had passed versions of HR 4548, but the House held off naming conferees, primarily because the motion to instruct them would have opened the House floor to debate, thereby giving Democrats a chance to criticize Republicans for not passing the intelligence overhaul bill before Congress left for the Thanksgiving break. *(Intelligence reform, p. 263)*

Although most of the bill was classified, HR 4548 was estimated to authorize about $40 billion for the intelligence activities of the CIA, National Security Agency (NSA), Federal Bureau of Investigation (FBI), Defense Intelligence Agency, Coast Guard, the military services, and other agencies and offices in the Defense, State, Treasury, Energy, Justice, and Homeland Security departments.

The bill continued the Intelligence committees' post-Sept. 11 emphasis on the need for greater foreign language training and information-sharing among the intelligence agencies.

LEGISLATIVE ACTION

The House passed HR 4548 on June 23, 2004, by a vote of 360–61. The House Intelligence Committee had reported the bill (H Rept 108-558) on June 21.

The bitterly partisan battle that preceded House passage was a marked contrast to House action on the often routine intelligence authorization bill in recent years. Only nine House members had voted against the annual authorization bill the previous year, and the four previous bills had been passed by voice vote.

But the long era of bipartisanship ended during consideration of HR 4548. Final passage came after the House rejected, on a party-line vote of 197–224, a Democratic motion to send the bill back to the Intelligence Committee. Democrats said the GOP-written bill authorized less than one-third of the money needed for counterterrorism. And they complained that they were not allowed to offer an amendment to increase the funding. Republicans countered that Democrats were resorting to election-year grandstanding.

The partisanship had begun in the Intelligence Committee, when Democrats voted against the measure after five of their amendments were rejected. A showdown had been guaranteed after the Rules Committee voted to restrict amendments to the bill on the floor and refused to consider most Democratic amendments.

Intelligence Chairman Porter J. Goss, R-Fla., said the measure would authorize a record amount of intelligence spending, 16 percent more than President George W. Bush had requested. The bill increased funding for human intelligence activities—spies in the field—and created a chief information officer to improve coordination among intelligence agencies. Goss said the House bill mostly tracked legislation (S 2386) approved unanimously by the Senate Intelligence Committee.

The Senate, by voice votes on Oct. 11, first passed S 2386 and then HR 4548, after substituting the text of its bill. The Senate Intelligence Committee had reported S 2386 (S Rept 108-258) on May 5, and the Senate Armed Services Committee had reported it (S Rept 108-300) on July 8.

The authorization bill had languished in the Senate all summer and into the fall, while the Senate focused its attention on legislation to reform the intelligence community. The Senate passed S 2386 less than a week after completing its reform bill.

During floor action on S 2386, the Senate by voice vote rejected an Intelligence Committee decision to abolish the panel's eight-year term limit for its members. Both Democrats and Republicans on the panel had argued that it took years to develop expertise in intelligence issues and that term limits discouraged that development. The Senate subsequently abolished the term limits in its response to recommendations made by the 9/11 commission for changes in congressional oversight (S Res 445). *(Congressional oversight of intelligence, p. 274)*

Senators also struck from the bill a provision that would have allowed Defense Intelligence Agency (DIA) personnel to conceal their identities when gathering intelligence on U.S. citizens. Under a thirty-year-old law (PL 93-579), federal agents had to identify themselves when collecting information stateside. The CIA was prohibited from domestic spying in all circumstances, but other intelligence agencies could gather information inside the United States as long as they disclosed to their sources who they were.

The Senate included in its bill a provision to allow surveillance of a foreign terrorist suspect even if the agency did not have evidence linking that person to a state or terrorist group. There was no comparable "lone wolf" provision in the House version, although the House did include one in its intelligence overhaul bill.

FINAL ACTION

The House adopted HR 4548's conference report (H Rept 108-798) on Dec. 7, and the Senate cleared the bill the next day, both by voice vote. President Bush signed it into law Dec. 23.

The portion of the bill made public included a requirement that the newly created director of national intelligence conduct an intelligence assessment to identify countries or regions that were sanctuaries for terrorists.

The final bill also included provisions that would increase funding levels for language studies and mandate that senior intelligence officials have certain language skills. This emphasis came after criticism that the intelligence community did not have enough translators of Middle Eastern languages before the Sept. 11, 2001, terrorist attacks.

The bill created a chief information officer for the intelligence community. This technology chief was to manage large-scale information-sharing projects for agencies within the intelligence community and direct research and development initiatives. The idea behind the position was for spy agencies to be more aggressive in developing technologies that would reduce the "stove-piping" that prevented agencies from sharing intelligence.

The bill reauthorized funds for intelligence and intelligence-related activities used to support Colombia's antidrug efforts and banned U.S. troops and contractors from taking part in combat there.

The Senate's "lone wolf" provision was dropped, but a similar provision had been included in the final intelligence overhaul bill.

Pre–Iraq War Intelligence

The Senate Intelligence Committee in 2004 produced Congress's first detailed report on the intelligence on Iraq's alleged weapons of mass destruction that President George W. Bush used in justifying war against Iraq. The 511-page report (S Rept 108-301) painted a damning picture of the CIA, charging that it not only relied on flawed and outdated intelligence on Iraq's weapons but also failed to correct those flaws or even inform policy makers just how shaky their key judgments were.

The report charged that the CIA failed to share information with other intelligence agencies, which might have led to exaggerated findings in the October 2002 National Intelligence Estimate (NIE)—the community-wide assessment on Iraq's banned weapons handed to Congress just days before it voted to authorize the use of force against Iraq. As a result of those failings, the report said, "most of the major key judgments in the [October 2002 NIE] either overstated, or were not supported by, the underlying intelligence reporting." *(Iraq use-of-force resolution, p. 238)*

The committee's unanimous approval of the report seemed on the surface to exonerate Bush, placing blame for the war's flawed underpinnings squarely on the CIA and its outgoing director, George J. Tenet. But the sharp partisan divisions that had marked the Iraq intelligence inquiry since it began in June 2003 quickly resurfaced with the report's release on July 9, 2004, leaving the issue of Bush's culpability unresolved.

In a separate section of dissenting views, Democrats insisted that intelligence analysts had been subject to political pressure, while Republicans countered that the only pressure analysts faced was normal and even desirable.

The report's scope also was disputed. Democrats charged that the report left out the most important story: whether policy makers exaggerated and manipulated intelligence to make the political case for war. And for all its detail on the CIA's intelligence failures, the report offered no specific recommendations for fixing the intelligence community's shortcomings—in sharp contrast to the 2002 report by the joint congressional inquiry on the Sept. 11, 2001, terrorist attacks, which was also highly critical of the intelligence agencies. *(Congressional 9/11 probe, p. 245)*

BACKGROUND

The report capped an exhaustive thirteen-month effort by the Senate Intelligence Committee and its staff, which undertook the probe as evidence from Iraq indicated that no weapons of mass destruction would be found.

From the start, however, the Senate panel was riven by partisan divisions over the scope of the probe. Democrats sought a broad investigation that would examine how policy makers used and characterized the intelligence they were receiving. Initially, Republicans sought to keep the probe confined to the closed-door sessions of the Intelligence Committee. They also eschewed the word "investigation" with its implications of subpoena powers and other potent tools.

Republicans continued to insist that the review look only at the quality of prewar intelligence, not its political use. In contrast, Democrats wanted to revisit the prewar statements of Bush, Vice President Dick Cheney, and national security adviser Condoleezza Rice, who said that Iraqi leader Saddam Hussein had nuclear weapons, or would have them soon. Those officials also suggested that Saddam had active ties with al Qaeda.

Tensions on the Senate panel came to a boiling point in November 2003, when Intelligence Committee Chair Pat Roberts, R-Kan., halted all official committee business after a strategy memo from the office of Committee Vice Chair John D. Rockefeller IV, D-W.Va., was leaked to the news media. Although Rockefeller insisted that he had not signed off on the memo, Roberts and other Republicans were infuriated by its proposals, which included a suggestion that Democrats exploit the probe's limited scope for political gain.

In February 2004 Roberts and Rockefeller announced that they had struck a deal. At the Democrats' insistence, there would be a second phase, in which the committee's inquiry would be broadened to include an examination of the administration's use of intelligence, as well as a probe of two Pentagon offices that provided intelligence to the White House on possible Iraq–al Qaeda ties.

FINDINGS

The Senate Intelligence Committee came to 117 conclusions after the first phase of its probe into pre–Iraq War intelligence. The major ones included:

• The key judgments in the October 2002 National Intelligence Estimate on Iraq's weapons of mass destruction overstated or contradicted intelligence reporting—a consequence of poor information-sharing, weak analysis, and inadequate human intelligence gathering.

• Analysts could not always get important information about their sources—or determine whether they were credible. The intelligence agencies in general relied too much on third-party reporting, thereby opening up the chance for manipulation.

• The allegation that Iraq attempted to buy uranium from the African state of Niger, which was referred to by President Bush in his 2003 State of the Union address but was later revealed to be false, inspired fifteen separate conclusions. The report placed the primary blame for the controversy on CIA Director Tenet, instead of Bush or his top White House officials.

The CIA had dispatched former ambassador Joseph C. Wilson IV to Africa in 2002 to investigate reports that Iraq had attempted to buy uranium. In July 2003, after Wilson had published an op-ed piece in the *New York Times* saying his trip had produced no such evidence, a leak disclosed that his wife, Valerie Plame, was an undercover CIA operative specializing in weapons of mass destruction and had had a hand in getting him the Africa assignment. Wilson charged that the leak, which subsequently became the subject of a Justice Department investigation, was part of a White House campaign to discredit the conclusions from his trip. (The Justice Department turned over the investigation to a special counsel, Patrick J. Fitzgerald, the U.S. attorney in Chicago. He originally set out to determine who leaked Plame's identity to reporters and whether federal laws prohibiting revealing the name of an undercover CIA operative were broken. Instead his investigation led in October 2005 to a broad indictment of I. Lewis "Scooter" Libby, Vice President Dick Cheney's chief of staff, for lying to federal investigators in the probe and obstructing justice. Libby resigned his position with Cheney. At the end of October President Bush's political adviser, Karl Rove, widely considered the most important member of the White House staff, was said to be under investigation.)

The Intelligence Committee's report concluded that the CIA should have told Vice President Cheney that it had sent Wilson to investigate the alleged uranium deal. It also maintained that the agency should have briefed Cheney on Wilson's failure to find any evidence of such a sale.

• The CIA and the Defense Intelligence Agency incorrectly assumed that aluminum tubes Iraq was trying to procure were for nuclear purposes. The CIA clung to that assumption despite objections from the Energy and State departments, the report said.

POSTSCRIPT

Preparation of a preliminary report from the second phase of the inquiry was underway as the 108th Congress came to a close. But Roberts said he would honor a request by Tenet to come before the panel in closed session before the report was released, to address any charges of a systemic intelligence failure.

The CIA took the unusual step of posting a detailed defense of the October 2002 NIE on its Web site Nov. 28, 2004. The CIA was careful not to further aggravate tensions by singling out lawmakers for criticism or policy makers for any misuse of the intelligence estimate. Instead, the agency addressed what it called "myths" about the NIE. Among other things, it argued that the NIE contained a sufficient amount of caveats and dissenting views to account for the failure to find any illegal weapons in Iraq to date.

Iraq War Resolutions

Both chambers of Congress adopted resolutions (H Con Res 104, S Res 95) on the Iraq War within days of its start in 2003, and the House adopted another resolution (H Res 557) on its one-year anniversary in 2004. Agreeing on the language in those resolutions proved particularly controversial in the House.

2003 RESOLUTIONS

Only days after the war began in 2003, House members bickered over the proper wording of a resolution (H Con Res 104) expressing support for U.S. forces and the president. Democrats opposed language praising President George W. Bush's leadership as too broad. After both sides agreed to wording that referred to Bush indirectly, H Con Res 104 was adopted by a vote of 392–11 (twenty-two others voted "present") on March 21, 2003. The Senate had passed its resolution (S Res 95) commending U.S. forces and the president by a 99–0 vote the day before. Both resolutions praised the president "as commander-in-chief," without specifically naming Bush, wording that mollified Democrats by limiting praise to the president's war leadership without endorsing Bush's diplomatic skills.

2004 RESOLUTION

After a highly partisan debate, the House in 2004 adopted a Republican-drafted resolution (H Res 557) marking the first anniversary of the Iraq War. But instead of a noncontroversial resolution celebrating a military victory and commending the troops, House Republican leaders were determined to use the resolution to endorse Bush's foreign policy leadership. H Res 557 did commend the U.S. and coalition troops in Iraq, but the key language, drafted without the help of Democrats on the International Relations Committee, declared that "the United States and the world have been made safer with the removal of Saddam Hussein and his regime."

Opponents of the Bush policy, GOP leaders suggested, might have preferred appeasement of America's enemies. "What would you have us do? Wait until Saddam proved that he had nuclear weapons by detonating one in New York City? Wait like we waited for al Qaeda to prove that they re-

PRESIDENTIAL COMMISSION ON PREWAR INTELLIGENCE

The failure of U.S. arms inspectors to find weapons of mass destruction in Iraq—President George W. Bush's stated reason for going to war in 2003 to oust the regime of Iraqi leader Saddam Hussein—prompted calls for a broad-based independent inquiry into what had gone wrong in prewar intelligence. Bush resisted the idea for months, content to let Congress look into the matter. But when it became apparent that the issue would not go away, the president in early 2004 appointed a commission to examine the intelligence failures that preceded the war.

The commission in a 2005 report concluded that the intelligence community had been "dead wrong in almost all of its prewar judgments about Iraq's weapons of mass destruction" and called for "dramatic change" to prevent future failures. Most of the commission's seventy-four recommendations could be accomplished through executive actions or internal rule changes at the intelligence agencies and would require only minor changes in the broad overhaul of the intelligence community that had been enacted (S 2845—PL 108-458) a few months earlier. Like the report of the 9/11 commission, the recommendations also called for stronger and more efficient congressional oversight of intelligence agencies. *(Intelligence system overhaul, p. 263; independent 9/11 commission, p. 275; congressional oversight of intelligence, p. 274)*

Pressure for Commission

For months the strategy of the White House and its GOP allies in Congress for keeping a lid on the Iraq intelligence controversy had seemed simple and effective enough.

The House and Senate Intelligence committees kept the focus of their closed-door hearings on the intelligence agencies rather than the White House while Republicans rebuffed calls for an independent probe. They argued that the chance of finding illegal weapons programs in Iraq remained strong and the panels were doing a sufficient job of looking into how and why prewar intelligence estimates of Iraq's banned weapons failed to match up with the postwar facts.

But that changed in early 2004 as Democrats in Congress and in the race for the presidency found their voice on the once politically risky issue of Bush's stewardship of foreign affairs. To be sure, the conflict in Iraq had been simmering on Democratic back burners for some time. But it began to

smoke after David Kay, Bush's outgoing chief arms inspector, told Congress on Jan. 28 that prewar intelligence on Iraq's weapons of mass destruction was "all wrong" and that the alleged weapons probably did not exist.

Democratic focus on the issue turned aggressive—and unambiguously political—after CIA Director George J. Tenet stated on Feb. 5 that he had never advised the administration that Iraq posed an "imminent" threat to the United States.

"That's not what the Bush White House told the American people," said Sen. John Kerry of Massachusetts, the frontrunner in the race for the Democratic presidential nomination. "They said Iraq posed a 'mortal threat,' an 'urgent threat,' an 'immediate threat,' a 'serious threat,' and, yes, an 'imminent threat' to the people of the United States. Americans should be able to trust what the president tells them is true—especially when it comes to the life and death decisions of war and peace."

Also troubling for the White House was the decision by some Republicans, including Sens. Chuck Hagel of Nebraska and John McCain of Arizona, to back a new probe after Kay's testimony.

Against this backdrop the Bush administration made the major tactical switch to name a commission and keep Congress—despite its friendly Republican majority—from taking matters into its own hands. On Feb. 2 the White House announced that it would no longer oppose an independent investigation into prewar intelligence on Iraq.

Commission Members

The Commission on the Intelligence Capabilities of the United States Regarding Weapons of Mass Destruction was established by executive order on Feb. 6. Bush named a politically heterogeneous group, ranging from liberal Democrats to conservative Republicans, to the commission.

Charles S. Robb, a former Democratic governor (1982–1986) and U.S. senator (1989–2001) of Virginia, and retired judge Laurence H. Silberman, a conservative who served as deputy attorney general in the administrations of presidents Richard M. Nixon and Gerald R. Ford, were appointed to cochair the commission.

Other members included Richard C. Levin, president of Yale University; Sen. McCain; Henry S. Rowen, a senior fel-

ally meant business on Sept. 11, 2001?" House Majority Leader Tom DeLay, R-Texas, asked opponents of H Res 557.

Predictably, House Democrats offered a different analysis of how the president's policy had played out. They wanted to focus on the loss of lives of U.S. soldiers to show the price Americans were paying, the shortages of body armor and armored vehicles to demonstrate the administration's lack of

preparation, and the $1-billion-per-week cost of the occupation and the administration's failure to enlist other nations to share that burden.

But when the March 17, 2004, floor debate was over, the GOP majority had prevailed on the contents of the resolution. After defeating a Democratic bid to block the resolution on a procedural vote, 228–195, the House adopted low at the Hoover Institution and a Defense Department official in the George H. W. Bush administration; Walter B. Slocombe, a Defense Department official in the administrations of presidents Jimmy Carter and Bill Clinton and an adviser in 2003 to the Coalition Provisional Authority in Baghdad; William O. Studeman, a retired admiral who had served as deputy director of the CIA and director of the National Security Agency; Charles M. Vest, former president of Massachusetts Institute of Technology and a member of the President's Council of Advisors on Science and Technology in the Clinton and Bush administrations; and Patricia Wald, a former federal judge and a judge of the international criminal tribunal for the former Yugoslavia at the Hague, Netherlands.

Lloyd Cutler, a former White House counsel in the Carter and Clinton administrations, was named to assist as a counsel to the commission.

Commission Report

The commission issued its 600-page report on March 31, 2005.

On the basis of assessments from the intelligence community, the commission noted, the United States had asserted that Saddam had reconstituted his nuclear weapons program, had biological weapons and mobile biological weapons production facilities, and had stockpiled and was producing chemical weapons, but none of these allegations could be confirmed. The commission called this "one of the most public—and damaging—intelligence failures in recent American history."

The commission attributed the failure to several factors. It said that there were analytical shortcomings because analysts were "too wedded to their assumptions about Saddam's intentions." It found that the intelligence agencies had failed to collect enough information to analyze and "much of what they did collect was either worthless or misleading." And, it said, the intelligence community had failed to communicate to policy makers "just how little good intelligence it had—or how much its assessments were driven by assumptions and inferences rather than concrete evidence."

The commission report went on to say that these shortcomings reflected the intelligence community's struggle in the post–cold war era to confront an environment in which the single threat of the Soviet Union has been replaced by broad, diffuse, and hidden threats. The commission said the intelligence community had to be transformed to meet these new challenges. Instead of focusing on current intelligence and tactical requirements, the community also needed to develop strategic capabilities and long-term plans to identify threats and penetrate targets. Instead of the existing "fragmented, loosely managed, and poorly coordinated" community, intelligence agencies should be integrated to coordinate the allocation and direction of their resources. The community needed to be more flexible so it could respond to shifting threats and technological changes.

The commission found that the new director of national intelligence (DNI), a position created by the intelligence overhaul legislation, had been given "broad responsibilities, but only ambiguous authorities." The report recommended that the president give more power to the DNI and that someone else should prepare and deliver the president's daily intelligence briefing so the DNI could focus on longer-term strategic goals for intelligence. It also called for a reorganization within the FBI to combine counterintelligence and counterterrorism resources into one office. The commission called on policy makers to demand more from the intelligence community by asking tough questions about the intelligence they were provided.

Most of the report's recommendations on congressional oversight mirrored what the 9/11 commission had suggested. For example, it called on the Intelligence committees to get rid of term limits for members, something the Senate Intelligence Committee had already done, while the House had not. The report suggested creation of Intelligence Appropriations subcommittees, which also had been a recommendation of the 9/11 commission.

In an attempt to head off criticism, the commission emphasized that it had not been authorized to investigate how policy makers used the intelligence they were given. But the criticism came, nonetheless. "It apparently fails to review an equally important aspect of our national security policy-making process—how policy makers use the intelligence they are provided," said Senate Minority Leader Harry Reid, R-Nev. "I believe it is essential that we hold both the intelligence agencies and senior policymakers accountable for their actions."

H Res 557 by a **key vote of 327–93 (R 222–2; D 105–90; I 0–1)**. *(2004 key votes, p. 854)*

The five-hour debate on the anniversary resolution demonstrated that partisan divisions had only deepened with the failure to find weapons of mass destruction in Iraq. With the presidential campaign heating up, some House Democrats did not feel an obligation to blunt their criticism while the shooting continued. "Iraq was not an imminent threat to America. . . . The only mushroom cloud resulting from the war in Iraq is that represented by the Bush administration's barrage of deception and lies," said Democrat Robert Wexler of Florida.

But in the end the resolution divided Democrats as well as making them angry. Some said they backed the resolution to support U.S. troops, not because they accepted the conclusion that the war had made the world safer.

2003 Aid Appropriations

Congress in early 2003 approved $16.3 billion in foreign operations appropriations as part of a fiscal 2003 omnibus spending package (H J Res 2—PL 108-7).

Both the Senate and House Appropriations committees had approved versions of the funding bill in 2002, but the legislation never reached the floor of either chamber. The foreign operations funding bill initially was delayed by conflicts over abortion and then was caught up along with ten other appropriations bills in a dispute between Congress and the White House over total fiscal 2003 nondefense spending. Agreement on a final bill was not reached until early in the 108th Congress. A series of ten short-term resolutions—seven in 2002 and three in 2003—continued funding for the programs covered by the eleven bills at fiscal 2002 levels. *(Fiscal 2003 appropriations bills, pp. 59, 69)*

Final action on the fiscal 2003 foreign operations portion of the omnibus package was relatively trouble-free. Floor fights had been expected in 2002 over two perennial controversies—aid for international family planning programs and support for counterdrug activities in Colombia and neighboring countries—but when the new Congress convened in January 2003, the focus was on wrapping up the spending bills and moving on.

Family planning aid was settled with relatively little pain. H J Res 2 left in place the so-called Mexico City restrictions, which barred U.S. funding to any international nongovernmental organization that performed or supported abortion in a foreign country, even if it did so with its own funds. The bill also continued an existing prohibition—known as the Kemp-Kasten amendment—on funding any organization or program that supported or participated in the management of a program of coercive abortion or involuntary sterilization. Legislation approved by the Senate Appropriations Committee in 2002 would have overturned the Mexico City policy and revised the Kemp-Kasten amendment. H J Res 2 also provided funds for the U.N. Population Fund (known as UNFPA, the acronym for its original name, the U.N. Fund for Population Activities) but barred disbursement unless the president certified that the fund did not support or participate in the management of a program of coercive abortion or involuntary sterilization. President George W. Bush's administration had blocked disbursement of fiscal 2002 funds to the UNFPA. *(Restrictions on family planning assistance, box p. 247)*

The administration ultimately won its full request for assistance to efforts in Colombia and its neighboring countries to defeat drug traffickers and the left-wing guerrillas who protected them. The Senate Appropriations Committee bill would have cut the funding and earmarked much of it.

The foreign operations bill provided about two-thirds of total international affairs spending, including most U.S. foreign aid expenditures.

2002 COMMITTEE BILLS

The Senate Appropriations Committee reported a $16.4 billion foreign aid bill (S 2779—S Rept 107-219) on July 24, 2002.

While the Senate Foreign Operations Appropriations Subcommittee and the full Senate Appropriations Committee considered the bill, the Bush White House was weighing its decision on whether to release the $34 million Congress had appropriated the previous year for the UNFPA. In a clear signal of its frustration with the president, the committee approved $50 million for the U.N. agency in fiscal 2003—Bush had requested only $25 million to be held in reserve for the group.

On July 22 the Bush administration decided not to release the fiscal 2002 money. A carefully written compromise in the fiscal 2002 foreign operations law (HR 2506—PL 107-115) permitted but did not require the United States to contribute to the agency. The administration cited the Kemp-Kasten amendment and said contributions to the U.N. family planning agency could end up aiding forced abortions as part of China's one-child family planning program. U.N. officials insisted that they worked only in regions of China where such policies had been lifted. *(2002 aid appropriations, p. 246)*

S 2779 would have revised the Kemp-Kasten amendment to bar funds only to organizations or programs that "directly participate" in coercive abortion or involuntary programs. It also would have rolled back one of Bush's first acts in office: his reinstatement of the Mexico City policy.

The Senate bill called for $637 million for the Andean Counterdrug Initiative, $94 million less than Bush requested.

The House Appropriations Committee reported a $16.6 billion version (HR 5410—H Rept 107-663) on Sept. 19, 2002. The House bill included an additional $350 million requested by Bush for international HIV/AIDS programs and for aid to Israel and the Palestinians. That extra money originally had been included in a fiscal 2002 supplemental spending law (HR 4775—PL 107-206), but Bush objected to its designation as "emergency spending" and refused to use it.

Both the House Foreign Operations Appropriations Subcommittee and the full House Appropriations Committee decided for the most part to sidestep the contentious issue of overseas family planning aid. Subcommittee Chair Jim Kolbe, R-Ariz., attempted a compromise on UNFPA aid by designating $25 million for the organization but adding a new condition barring release of any of the funding if the U.N. agency provided aid to China's State Planned-Birth Commission or its regional affiliates.

Unlike its Senate counterpart, the House panel agreed to fully fund Bush's request of $731 million for the Andean Counterdrug Initiative and did not try to allocate funds for specific purposes.

The committee adopted an amendment to limit assistance to any potential Palestinian state until the administration could certify that the new government was dedicated to peace with Israel and to democracy.

2003 FINAL BILL

To permit swift action on the unfinished spending bills, House and Senate appropriators agreed in January 2003 to live within overall spending limits requested by Bush. They allocated $16.3 billion in discretionary funds for the foreign operations bill, less than either committee had approved in 2002.

House Republican leaders came up with an unusual strategy for wrapping up the stalled bills. On Jan. 8, 2003, the House by voice votes adopted two continuing resolutions: H J Res 1 was another stopgap spending bill and H J Res 2 was to become a vehicle to which the Senate would attach the eleven revised spending bills. After Senate passage, the resolution would go straight to conference—meaning the full House would never get a chance to amend the package, only to vote it up or down.

The Senate passed the revised H J Res 2 by a vote of 69–29 on Jan. 23. Because the Senate had not reorganized its committees in the new Congress, the measure had not gone through the Appropriations Committee.

During floor action on Jan. 22, the Senate agreed, 48–46, to table (kill) an attempt by Bill Nelson, D-Fla., to add $600 million in famine relief for Africa if the president agreed to declare the situation an emergency. The next day, however, the Senate agreed by voice vote to a Nelson amendment to provide $500 million for African famine relief.

House and Senate conferees finalized the omnibus bill and filed their report Feb. 13. The House adopted the conference report (H Rept 108-10) 338–83 later the same day, and the Senate cleared the bill that night 76–20. Kolbe said the foreign operations section was one of the least difficult to resolve. President Bush signed it Feb. 20.

MAJOR PROVISIONS

As signed into law, H J Res 2 appropriated $16.3 billion for foreign aid and related programs in fiscal 2003. This included $373 million for export and investment assistance, $10.2 billion for bilateral economic assistance, $4.3 billion for military assistance, and $1.5 billion for multilateral assistance. (These totals and the numbers below do not reflect a 0.65 percent across-the-board cut in discretionary spending approved as part of the omnibus bill.)

Major provisions of the bill:

Middle East

Appropriated $2.7 billion in military and economic assistance for Israel and $1.9 billion for Egypt.

The measure continued existing aid programs for Palestinians in the West Bank and Gaza but prohibited funding to support a Palestinian state unless the secretary of state determined that the entity was governed by a democratically elected leadership that was taking steps to counter terrorism and demonstrating a commitment to peaceful coexistence with Israel.

Andean Counterdrug Initiative

Appropriated $700 million and authorized the transfer of another $31 million to assist efforts in Colombia and neighboring countries to defeat drug traffickers and the guerrillas who protected them. The bill specified that the combined authority to fight guerrillas and drug traffickers would cease if the secretary of state found that the Colombian military was not actively trying to restore government authority and human rights in areas that had been controlled by guerrillas. The bill retained the existing cap on the number of U.S. personnel in Colombia and a prohibition against U.S. forces participating in combat operations.

HIV/AIDS Assistance

Provided not less than $800 million to prevent and treat HIV/AIDS. That total included $591.5 million from the Child Survival and Health Programs Fund, $38.5 million from other foreign aid accounts, and an estimated $170 million to be allocated for HIV/AIDS from funding in the bill for U.N. agencies and the Global Fund to Fight AIDS, Tuberculosis, and Malaria. The foreign operations portion of the bill appropriated $250 million in all for the Global ATM Fund. (Additional funds were provided in the Labor-Health and Human Services-Education section of the omnibus bill.)

Family Planning

Provided $446.5 million for international family planning assistance. The total included $34 million for the United Nations Population Fund (UNFPA), but the bill barred disbursement of the money unless the president certified that the fund did not support or participate in the management of a program of coercive abortion or involuntary sterilization.

Export-Import Bank

Provided $568 million for the Export-Import Bank.

2003 SUPPLEMENTAL

In April 2003 Congress cleared a fiscal 2003 supplemental appropriations bill (HR 1559—PL 108-11) that provided an additional $78.5 billion. The money was primarily for military operations in Iraq and for homeland security, but the bill also included a requested $7.5 billion for bilateral economic and military assistance for U.S. allies in the war against terrorism. *(2003 defense supplemental, p. 329)*

Recipients of the additional aid included Israel, Egypt, Jordan, Pakistan, Turkey, Afghanistan, and the Philippines. The total included $2.5 billion for a new Iraq Relief and Reconstruction Fund. Although the State Department traditionally oversaw reconstruction aid, the White House wanted the Pentagon to control postwar reconstruction in Iraq. Both chambers went on record opposing such a shift but the White House persisted. In the end lawmakers agreed to let the president disburse the reconstruction funds through the department of his choosing but insisted on congressional oversight.

The House passed its version of HR 1559 by a vote of 414–12 on April 3, 2003. The House Appropriations Committee had reported the bill (H Rept 108-55) the day before.

The House bill recommended $7.4 billion in foreign assistance. The main change made on the floor was the inclusion of language to bar companies organized under the laws of France, Germany, Russia, and Syria from getting U.S. funds to provide goods or services for postwar reconstruction in Iraq. The amendment, adopted by voice vote, was offered by Mark Kennedy, R-Minn. Deputy Secretary of State Richard L. Armitage had written a letter urging Congress to reject such an amendment, saying it would jeopardize efforts to build support in the United Nations and would force the United States to pay a disproportionate share of costs associated with the Iraq War.

The House rejected 110–315 a Randy "Duke" Cunningham, R-Calif., amendment to delete $1 billion in the bill for assistance to Turkey. Cunningham, whose amendment also had been rejected in committee, said Turkey's refusal to allow U.S. forces to operate from its soil had "cost the lives of American soldiers" in the war against Iraq. But Armitage and national security adviser Condoleezza Rice sent letters to Congress praising the nearly sixty-year strategic partnership between the two countries and the importance of nurturing the relationship.

An attempt to reduce aid to Turkey and redirect it to the National Guard, offered by Peter A. DeFazio, D-Ore., was rejected 113–312. A Jim McGovern, D-Mass., proposal to cut Andean counterdrug assistance and add money for first responders was defeated 209–216.

The Senate passed its bill (S 762) by a vote of 93–0 on April 3 and then passed HR 1559 by voice vote April 7, after inserting the text of S 762. The Senate Appropriations Committee had reported S 762 (S Rept 108-33) on April 1.

The Senate committee bill recommended $7.6 billion for foreign aid. During floor action on S 762, the Senate adopted, 67–26, a proposal by Herb Kohl, D-Wis., to add $600 million for food assistance to Iraq under the PL 480 program. John Ensign, R-Nev., offered an amendment to bar companies organized under the laws of France or Germany from winning U.S.-funded contracts for postwar reconstruction in Iraq. But, bending to pressure from the White House and Senate colleagues, he withdrew it before a vote.

The conference report (H Rept 108-76) cleared on April 12 and the bill was signed into law April 16. The conference committee split the difference between the two chambers and settled on $7.5 billion in bilateral aid.

Conferees designated the $2.5 billion included for the Iraq Relief and Reconstruction Fund as bilateral economic assistance under the 1961 Foreign Assistance Act. While pointing out that such funds were customarily administered by the State Department and the U.S. Agency for International Development, conferees allowed the president to assign the money to other departments, including Defense. The conference report stated that food, water, electricity, and other direct relief should be the top priority and required five days advance notification of spending from the fund. The president also was required to report quarterly to Congress on reconstruction activities in Iraq. The House provision excluding companies in France, Germany, Russia, and Syria from reconstruction projects was dropped.

The final bill included $369 million for PL 480 food aid to Iraq.

2004 Aid Appropriations

Congress in early 2004 approved $17.3 billion in foreign operations appropriations as part of a fiscal 2004 omnibus spending package (HR 2673—PL 108-199).

The total for foreign operations was 9 percent below the $18.9 billion that President George W. Bush had requested, but the bill still included hefty startup funding for the president's two big initiatives: a five-year program to fight HIV/AIDS overseas, primarily in Africa and the Caribbean, and the Millennium Challenge Account (MCA), a new program to aid poor countries committed to democracy, human rights, and open-market economies. *(Millennium Challenge Account, box p. 289)*

Appropriators had hoped to clear the foreign operations measure as a stand-alone bill in 2003, but unfinished business—writing an authorization for the MCA after the State Department authorization bill (HR 1950) stalled, meeting a White House demand that they find more money for the MCA, and resolving a perennial dispute over Reagan-era restrictions on family planning funds—pushed the bill into negotiations on the omnibus package. *(State Department authorization, pp. 250, 294)*

The final bill included $1.7 billion for the first year of the program to combat global HIV/AIDS, tuberculosis, and malaria. Combined with $754 million in the Labor-Health and Human Services (HHS)-Education section of the omnibus, it brought total funding for the effort in fiscal 2004 to $2.4 billion. Bush had called in his State of the Union address for a $15 billion, five-year initiative against the pandemic ravaging Africa and the Caribbean, and in May 2003 he signed a bill (HR 1298—PL 108-25) authorizing $3 billion a year in fiscal 2004 through 2008. In his budget, however, Bush requested a total of $2 billion for fiscal 2004, $1.4 billion of it through the foreign operations bill. The White House argued that stricken countries could not absorb $3 billion so quickly, but a number of lawmakers said the initiative was being short-changed. *(HIV/AIDS assistance, pp. 257, 296)*

Bush's MCA proposal encountered a rougher time. Although the president had requested $1.3 billion for this ini-

MILLENNIUM CHALLENGE ACCOUNT

Congress in 2004 authorized and funded the "Millennium Challenge Account," a new approach to foreign aid proposed by President George W. Bush to reward developing countries that were moving toward democratization and market-based economies.

Under the initiative increased aid would be made available to countries that respected human rights, fought corruption, spent a sufficient amount of money on health and education, and opened their markets.

Background

Bush announced his proposal for the Millennium Challenge Account in a March 14, 2002, speech at the Inter-American Development Bank in Washington. He said that the United States supported the international development goals adopted at the September 2000 United Nations Millennium Summit. At that meeting world leaders agreed on specific targets for improving the human condition by 2015.

Bush said the United States would increase development assistance to $5 billion a year by fiscal 2006. The money—which amounted to a 50 percent increase in core assistance to developing countries over three years—was to go into the new Millennium Challenge Account (MCA). In return Bush said the United States would expect developing nations to adopt reforms and policies that would make development effective and lasting. Countries would be rewarded for rooting out corruption, respecting human rights, and adhering to the rule of law; investing in better health care, better schools, and broader immunization; and having more open markets and sustainable budget policies.

Bush reaffirmed his commitment to the initiative in an address on March 22, 2002, at the International Conference on Financing for Development in Monterrey, Mexico. The conference pulled together world leaders, finance and foreign ministers, heads of international organizations and financial institutions, and business and civic leaders to address the challenges that lay ahead in alleviating poverty and achieving sustainable economic growth.

Legislative Action

During consideration of its State Department authorization bill (HR 1950), the House in 2003 agreed to Bush's full request of $1.3 billion in fiscal 2004, $3 billion in fiscal 2005, and $5 billion in fiscal 2006 for the MCA. The Senate bill (S 925) would have included $1 billion in fiscal 2004, $2.3 billion in fiscal 2005, and $5 billion in fiscal 2006.

The administration wanted the MCA to be run by a new, independent agency, but during consideration of S 925 the Senate Foreign Relations Committee voted to have it run by the State Department so as not to undercut Secretary of State Colin L. Powell's authority. The White House threatened to veto the bill if it contained the committee plan. A substitute bill approved on the Senate floor included a compromise plan to create a separate organization but have it report to Powell and be under Powell's direct authority and foreign policy guidance. S 925 was pulled from the floor when Democrats attempted to attach unrelated amendments. No stand-alone State Department authorization cleared in the 108th Congress. *(State Department authorization, p. 250)*

Ultimately, authorization for the new account was included in the foreign operations appropriations section of the fiscal 2004 omnibus spending package (HR 2673—PL 108-199). HR 2673 provided $1 billion for the Millennium Challenge Account, $300 million less than Bush had requested. Lawmakers saw the bill's other new program, an AIDS initiative, as more urgent in the short term and shifted part of the money there. The bill also included language authorizing the program and a new government corporation, the Millennium Challenge Corporation, to administer it. The corporation was to be managed by a chief executive officer appointed by the president and confirmed by the Senate. A board of directors, chaired by the secretary of state, would oversee the corporation. *(2004 aid appropriations, p. 288)*

tiative to target foreign aid, conferees initially agreed on only $650 million. The White House pressured GOP leaders, who came up with another $350 million in the omnibus to provide a total of $1 billion.

The White House had threatened to veto the bill if it retained a Senate provision that would have overturned the so-called Mexico City policy, which barred aid to international family planning organizations that performed or promoted abortions, even if they used their own funds to do so. House conferees insisted on the provision's removal, but as a trade-off conferees agreed to resume funding for the U.N. Population Fund (still known by the acronym UNFPA for its previous name, the U.N. Fund for Population Activities). In 2002 Bush had canceled UNFPA funding after allegations arose that its programs in China violated a provision in a 1985 law (PL 99-88) that barred appropriations to any organization that supported or participated in the management of a program of coerced abortions or involuntary sterilization. HR 2673 provided that the $34 million Bush withheld in 2002 would go to UNFPA in fiscal 2004, and another $25 million withheld in fiscal 2003 would fund a new program to combat trafficking in women and children. *(Restrictions on family planning assistance, p. 247; 2003 aid appropriations, p. 286)*

Overall, the foreign operations bill typically provided funds for bilateral economic and military assistance, contributions to international financial aid organizations, and as-

During the 108th Congress, the Senate Foreign Relations Committee, chaired by Richard G. Lugar, R-Ind., right, tangled with the Bush administration over leadership of the Millennium Challenge Account. The MCA, a foreign policy initiative to provide aid to developing countries, ties foreign aid from the United States to measurable progress toward democratization and a market-based economy by each nation. *Source: AP Wide World Photos/Dennis Cook*

sistance to exporters. Fiscal 2004 funds for reconstruction in Iraq and Afghanistan were provided separately through a supplemental spending bill (HR 3289—PL 108-106). *(Supplemental, p. 291)*

HOUSE ACTION

The House passed a $17.2 billion foreign operations spending bill (HR 2800) by a vote of 370–50 on July 24, 2003. The House Appropriations Committee had reported the bill (H Rept 108-222) July 21.

The House rejected Democratic attempts to move money from other programs to the AIDS initiative, just as the full Appropriations Committee had done during markup of HR 2800. Jim Kolbe, R-Ariz., chair of the House Appropriations Subcommittee on Foreign Operations, said the $2 billion in the bill would be sufficient for the first-year startup, while Democrats argued that it was disingenuous to clear a $3 billion-a-year authorization and not provide full funding. During floor debate July 24, the House:

• Rejected 192–228 a Carolyn Cheeks Kilpatrick, D-Mich, amendment to provide an additional $300 million to fight AIDS by reducing funds for the MCA.

• Rejected 195–226 a Jim McGovern, D-Mass., amendment to add $75 million for AIDS, offset by cuts in foreign

military financing and in the fund to combat Andean drug trafficking.

SENATE ACTION

The Senate approved an $18.4 billion version of HR 2800 by voice vote on Oct. 30. The Senate Appropriations Committee had reported an $18.1 billion spending bill (S 1426—S Rept 108-106) on July 17.

The full Senate agreed to a Mike DeWine, R-Ohio, amendment to boost funding for AIDS programs by $289 million, after Republicans resolved an intraparty skirmish over where the money would come from. A plan to offset the AIDS funding increase with unspent defense money from fiscal 2003 settled the matter, and the DeWine amendment was adopted 89–1 on Oct. 30.

After that the Republican majority held together to defeat a series of Democratic attempts to boost AIDS funding further. The Senate on Oct. 30:

• Rejected 42–50 on a budget point of order a proposal by Richard J. Durbin, D-Ill., to add another $589.7 million for AIDS to reach the $3 billion authorization level.

• Rejected 41–51 a Jeff Bingaman, D-N.M., amendment to boost the appropriation for AIDS by another $200 million, offset by a corresponding cut in MCA funding, which would have brought the MCA money down to the House-approved level of $800 million.

The Senate also rejected 45–47 a Dianne Feinstein, D-Calif., amendment to increase flexibility in the spending of AIDS funding. Feinstein proposed loosening the bill's requirement that at least one-third of AIDS prevention money go toward abstinence programs.

CONFERENCE, FINAL ACTION

The House adopted the conference report (H Rept 108-401) on the omnibus appropriations bill on Dec. 8, 2003, by a vote of 242–176. But the Senate did not clear the bill until Jan. 22, 2004, when it adopted the report by a vote of 65–28. Bush signed it into law the next day.

Conferees went with the higher Senate figure of $1.7 billion for the AIDS programs, which, when combined with money elsewhere in the bill, brought the total to $2.4 billion. The White House initially insisted that $2 billion was the most that could be used in the first year, but Kolbe said administration officials accepted a larger figure when they saw Congress was determined to spend more.

Conferees initially agreed on $650 million for the new MCA, half what Bush requested. But under continuing White House pressure, the appropriators finally agreed to another $350 million as part of a package of last-minute additions to the omnibus that required a 0.59 percent across-the-board cut in nondefense discretionary spending.

At the insistence of House conferees, the Senate's Mexico City provision, which had drawn the veto threat, was omitted from the final bill. As they had in previous years, the appropriators agreed instead to increase family planning funds. In this case, they agreed to resume the UNFPA funding. (Conferees also dropped a Senate provision in the Commerce-Justice-State portion of the omnibus funding bill that would have blocked the State Department from implementing an Aug. 29, 2003, Bush directive broadening the Mexico City policy to include family planning aid administered by the State Department. Previously the policy had applied only to programs administered by the U.S. Agency for International Development.)

MAJOR PROVISIONS

As signed into law, HR 2673 appropriated $17.3 billion for foreign aid and related programs in fiscal 2004. This included $11.2 billion for bilateral economic assistance, $4.5 billion for military assistance, and $1.7 billion for multilateral assistance. (These totals and the numbers below do not reflect a 0.59 percent across-the-board cut in discretionary accounts. Virtually the entire foreign operations portion of the omnibus bill was discretionary spending, with the exception of $44 million in mandatory spending for the Foreign Service Retirement and Disability Fund.)

Conferees said there was no subsidy appropriation for the Export-Import Bank of the United States because of the bank's "extraordinarily high level of carryover balances," which totaled about $575 million.

Major provisions of the bill:

Millennium Challenge Account

Appropriated $1 billion for a new initiative to target foreign aid to poor countries committed to democracy, human rights, and open-market economies. The bill also contained language authorizing the MCA and creating a Millennium Challenge Corporation to administer the program, including developing specific eligibility criteria and selecting countries to receive funds.

HIV/AIDS Assistance

Provided $1.7 billion to prevent and treat HIV/AIDS, tuberculosis, and malaria (another $754 million was included in the Labor-Health and Human Services-Education appropriations section of the omnibus bill). The $1.7 billion included:

• $491 million to launch Bush's new five-year global HIV/AIDS initiative, providing money for staffing and for new and expanded programs in twelve African countries, plus Haiti, Guyana, and another country yet to be selected.

• $517 million in the Child Survival and Health Programs Fund to aid communities, including children orphaned by AIDS.

• $185 million in the Child Survival and Health fund to fight infectious diseases including tuberculosis and malaria.

• $400 million for the Global Fund to Fight AIDS, Tuberculosis, and Malaria.

• $54 million in economic and military aid and regional accounts.

Middle East

Appropriated $2.7 billion in military and economic assistance for Israel, $1.9 billion for Egypt, and $456 million for Jordan.

Andean Counterdrug Initiative

Appropriated $731 million.

Family Planning

Allocated $34 million in fiscal 2004 for the United Nations Population Fund (UNFPA), the amount the administration had withheld in fiscal 2002 funding (PL 107-115). The bill also allocated $25 million of the withheld fiscal 2003 funds (PL 108-7) for a new program to combat trafficking in women and children. None of the bill's UNFPA funds could be used for a country program in China, nor could the money be made available unless UNFPA kept it in a separate account and did not fund abortions.

2004 SUPPLEMENTAL

In November 2003 Congress cleared an $87.5 billion supplemental appropriations bill (HR 3289—PL 108-106) for fiscal 2004. It was the largest supplemental spending bill in U.S. history, breaking the record that had been set less than seven months earlier by a fiscal 2003 supplemental. *(2003 supplemental, p. 394)*

Although the bulk of the money, $65.1 billion, was for military operations in Iraq and Afghanistan, the bill also appropriated $21.8 billion for reconstruction, primarily in Iraq, and for foreign assistance. This amount included $18.4 billion for relief and reconstruction in Iraq; $210 million for Jordan, Liberia, and Sudan; and $1.2 billion to rebuild Afghanistan.

HR 3289 cleared after a bitter dispute with the White House over whether Iraq should be required to repay the reconstruction aid. During a series of hearings, Democrats and Republicans in both chambers had questioned why the United States should foot the bill almost singlehandedly to rebuild a country that had the second-largest oil reserves in the world. The answer, said Ambassador L. Paul Bremer III, the chief U.S. administrator in Iraq, was that Iraq already was burdened with $200 billion in debt to other nations and could not afford any more. Many lawmakers were not convinced. The White House and Republican leaders were able to block loan amendments in the House, but the Senate defied President Bush and passed an amendment. Congress ultimately agreed to provide all the reconstruction money as grants, but it took a veto threat from Bush and aggressive lobbying by the president and other administration officials to get the Republicans to back down.

The House passed its version of HR 3289 by a vote of 303–125 on Oct. 17, 2003. The House Appropriations Committee had reported the bill (H Rept 108-312) on Oct. 14.

During committee consideration, Zach Wamp, R-Tenn., had intended to offer an amendment that would have turned half the Iraq reconstruction money into loans, but a call from Bremer and a White House meeting with Bush and Secretary of State Colin L. Powell persuaded him to drop the idea. When the bill reached the floor GOP leaders used their tight control over proceedings to fend off a similar amendment from Mike Pence, R-Ind. Several Republicans spoke in favor of the Pence amendment, which appeared to have enough support to win approval. But because it included directives to the administration on how the money could be spent, it was ruled out of order as legislating on an appropriations bill.

Later, Democrats David R. Obey of Wisconsin and Tom Lantos of California offered a version of the loan amendment stripped down to two sentences so it could not be ruled out of order. But after Majority Leader Tom DeLay, R-Texas, spoke strongly against the proposal, any possible Republican support for it evaporated, and it was defeated on Oct. 16 by a **key vote of 200–226 (R 18–208; D 181–18; I 1–0).** *(2003 key votes, p. 837)*

In other action the House adopted 248–179 an amendment by Brad Sherman, D-Calif., to require normal bidding procedures for all government contracts relating to Iraq's oil infrastructure, even in emergencies. The amendment was a broadside against the administration for giving a no-bid contract for oil work in Iraq to Halliburton Co., which Dick Cheney had headed before becoming vice president.

The House rejected by a vote of 209–216 an Obey proposal to transfer $3.6 billion in Iraq reconstruction funds to quality-of-life enhancements for U.S. service members, and by a vote of 156–267 an attempt by Ron Kind, D-Wis., to cut the Iraq construction funds in half.

The Senate on Oct. 17 passed its bill (S 1689) by a vote of 87–12 and then passed HR 3289 by voice vote, after substituting the text of S 1689. The Senate Appropriations Committee had filed its report on S 1689 (S Rept 108–160) Oct. 2.

Although similar proposals had been defeated during committee consideration, when the bill reached the floor an unlikely bipartisan coalition handed a stinging defeat to Bush and Senate GOP leaders by converting half the Iraq reconstruction funds to loans. Under the amendment, offered by Democrat Evan Bayh of Indiana, $10.3 billion in reconstruction money would be offered as a grant and another $10 billion would be a loan that would be converted to a grant only if other countries forgave 90 percent of Iraq's prewar debt. The amendment was adopted by a **key vote of 51–47 (R 8–43; D 42–4; I 1–0)** on Oct. 16. *(2003 key votes, p. 837)*

In other action, the Senate adopted by voice vote an amendment by Democrats Byron L. Dorgan of North Dakota and Ron Wyden of Oregon to cut $1.9 billion in projects from the Iraq assistance package, similar to reductions made by House appropriators. The Senate rejected by a vote of 38–59 a Robert C. Byrd, D-W.Va., amendment to eliminate $15.2 billion of the Iraq reconstruction money and use the remaining $5.1 billion to train and equip Iraqi security forces.

The Senate tabled (killed) a number of amendments, including:

- 56–43 a Richard J. Durbin, D-Ill., amendment to reduce the Iraq reconstruction money by $879.7 million and use it instead to fight global HIV/AIDS;
- 55–44 a Tom Daschle, D-S.D., amendment that would have required the president to certify that future appropriations beyond the amount in the bill would be equal to or exceeded by international contributions;
- 52–47 a Mary L. Landrieu, D-La., amendment that would have required Iraq to use its oil revenues to finance reconstruction;
- 57–42 a Joseph R. Biden Jr., D-Del., amendment to offset Iraqi reconstruction costs by reducing income tax cuts under the 2001 tax law (HR 1836—PL 107-16) for the wealthiest 1 percent of Americans; and
- 67–32 a Jon Corzine, D-N.J., amendment to establish an independent commission to investigate the use of intelligence leading up to the Iraq war.

The House agreed to the conference report on HR 3289 (H Rept 108-337) by a vote of 298–121 on Oct. 31, and the Senate cleared the bill by voice vote Nov. 3. It was signed into law Nov. 6.

Bending to White House pressure, conferees dropped the controversial loan provision. Also dropped was the House no-bid contract prohibition.

Conferees agreed to $18.6 billion for Iraq reconstruction, as proposed by the House, instead of the $20.3 billion requested by Bush and the $18.4 billion recommended by the Senate. Of that total, $210 million was to be used for other countries. Among the items dropped from Bush's request were $40,000 for garbage trucks, $100 million for housing projects, and $400 million to build prisons.

The final bill provided the $1.2 billion for aid to Afghanistan the House recommended, up from the $800 million Bush requested and the Senate approved.

2005 Aid Appropriations

Congress in 2004 approved $19.8 billion in foreign operations appropriations as part of a fiscal 2005 omnibus spending package (HR 4818—PL 108-447).

HR 4818 continued President George W. Bush's policy of expanding foreign aid, though at a slower rate than he wanted. The total, which was subject to a further 0.8 percent across-the-board cut in the omnibus, was 13 percent more than was appropriated for foreign operations in fiscal 2004, not counting supplemental spending, but it was still 7 percent below the $21.4 billion that Bush had requested.

The foreign operations bill in the past had often sparked disputes on issues ranging from abortion to United Nations dues to money for combating HIV/AIDS. But in 2004, an election year, the bill stood out for the bipartisan cooperation it engendered. The bill sailed through both chambers with little opposition and was selected as the vehicle for a year-end package that bundled together nine appropriations bills. Congress cleared the omnibus bill during a lame-duck session. In the interim, agencies governed by the nine bills had been funded by three consecutive continuing resolutions enacted since fiscal 2005 began Oct. 1, 2004. *(Fiscal 2005 appropriations bills, p. 80)*

The omnibus funding package contained the most money Congress had ever appropriated to fight HIV/AIDS around the world. Responding to Bush's call for increased funding to combat the global pandemic, the final bill provided a total of $2.9 billion in AIDS-related funding: $2.3 billion from the foreign operations portion of the bill and another $600 million from Labor-Health and Human Services-Education appropriations. The allocation was $99 million more than the president's request. Much of the AIDS money would go to a five-year, $15 billion international relief program that Bush outlined in his 2003 State of the Union address and that Congress established that year (HR 1298—PL 108-25). *(HIV/AIDS assistance, pp. 257, 296)*

Appropriators also managed to find more money for another of Bush's aid programs, the Millennium Challenge Account (MCA), but still not nearly as much as Bush wanted. The president had asked for $2.5 billion for the program, which provided assistance to poor countries that were judged to be making progress on human rights, democratization, and free markets. Until the conference on HR 4818, appropriators had been planning to provide no more than half the president's request. But with a push from the White House appropriators boosted the MCA funding up to $1.5 billion. Justifying an amount that still fell $1 billion short of Bush's request, appropriators maintained—as they had the previous year—that the fledgling program could not absorb the sums requested in the budget. But they insisted they were still on track to meet the president's original goal of $9.3 billion by fiscal 2006. *(Millennium Challenge Account, box p. 289)*

The bill met the White House requests to boost economic and military aid for U.S. allies such as Israel, Poland, Pakistan, and Afghanistan. And it provided $404 million for relief efforts in Sudan, where government-backed Arab Muslim militias were waging a campaign of ethnic cleansing against black African Muslims in the Darfur region. That came on top of $95 million in emergency relief for Darfur that had been attached to the fiscal 2005 defense spending bill (HR 4613—PL 108-287).

HOUSE ACTION

The House passed a $19.4 billion version of HR 4818 on July 15, 2004, by a vote of 365–41. The House Appropriations Committee had reported the measure (H Rept 108-599) on July 13.

When House appropriators crafted the bill, a major objective had been to reward U.S. allies in the war on terrorism. But when the bill reached the House floor, debates broke out over two longtime Middle Eastern allies that many lawmakers considered to be less than steadfast: Egypt and Saudi Arabia.

Tom Lantos of California, the top Democrat on the International Relations Committee, led a bipartisan group of lawmakers who sought to convert $570 million of the bill's $1.3 billion in military aid for Egypt into economic assistance. He said the money would be better spent on desperately needed economic and social programs for that country. But the proposal also tapped an undercurrent of anger among lawmakers who contended that Egypt had not assisted U.S. military operations in Iraq and Afghanistan, or done enough to combat the spread of radical Islam and anti-Americanism.

In a letter to Congress before the vote, Secretary of State Colin L. Powell said military aid to Egypt was a cornerstone of the 1978 Camp David Accords between Egypt and Israel and a vital part of the administration's effort to combat terrorism. Lantos derided Powell's arguments as "phony," but the letter lent clout to a move by appropriators to derail the proposal. In the end, Lantos's amendment was soundly rejected 131–287.

The administration was less successful at beating back a largely symbolic amendment to prohibit any assistance in the bill for Saudi Arabia, a nation many lawmakers believed had shielded Islamic terrorists. The amendment, sponsored by New York Democrat Anthony Weiner, was adopted 217–191, and the conclusion of the vote was greeted by a round of applause on the House floor. Weiner said the language would remove $25,000 in funding for Saudi military education and training and make Saudi Arabia ineligible to receive discounts to purchase such training.

The House bill fully funded Bush's program to combat AIDS and met the White House requests to boost economic and military aid for U.S. allies in the war on terrorism. But the House bill provided just half the money Bush called for in his MCA request.

SENATE ACTION

The Senate passed a $19.7 billion version of HR 4818 by voice vote Sept. 23 after substituting the text of its own bill (S 2812). The Senate Appropriations Committee had reported S 2812 (S Rept 108-346) on Sept. 16.

The deteriorating situation in the Darfur region of western Sudan dominated discussion on the measure for weeks. The crisis was one of the few issues to unite Republicans and Democrats in the supercharged campaign season. Secretary of State Powell in September asked Congress to boost aid to help stop the violence. The Senate bill provided the Bush administration with access to $300 million to supply aid to refugees and help outfit peacekeeping troops in Darfur. Senate appropriators had come up with $225 million, and the full Senate adopted by voice vote an amendment by Jon Corzine, D-N.J., and Mike DeWine, R-Ohio, to provide an additional $75 million in emergency funding for support of an African Union peacekeeping force. *(Background, Sudan relief assistance, p. 298)*

The Senate bill provided $1.1 billion of Bush's $2.5 billion request for MCA and $2.4 billion for HIV/AIDS assistance, $220 million more than requested.

The Senate-passed bill included language added in committee that gave the Egyptian government less say in how U.S. funds to promote democratization in that nation could be spent. The amendment's sponsor, Kansas Republican Sam Brownback, said Egypt was the only nation with such a veto.

CONFERENCE, FINAL ACTION

The House adopted the conference report on HR 4818 (H Rept 108-792) by a vote of 344–51 on Nov. 20, and the Senate cleared the bill later that day by a vote of 65–30. The measure was signed into law Dec. 8.

Conferees settled on $2.3 billion for global AIDS programs, splitting the difference between the House and Senate bills' allocations. Of that total, $338 million was to go to the Global Fund to Fight AIDS, Tuberculosis, and Malaria.

Using some of the $3.1 billion that was saved through the 0.8 percent across-the-board cut in the omnibus bill, conferees were able to boost funds for the MCA to $1.5 billion from the expected $1.2 billion.

Conferees included increased funding for the war-torn Sudan.

MAJOR PROVISIONS

As signed into law, HR 4818 appropriated $19.8 billion for foreign aid and related programs in fiscal 2005.

Major provisions of the bill:

Millennium Challenge Account

Appropriated $1.5 billion for the Millennium Challenge Account.

HIV/AIDS Assistance

Provided $2.3 billion to prevent and treat HIV/AIDS and the related diseases of tuberculosis and malaria (another $600 million was included in the Labor-Health and Human Services-Education appropriations section of the omnibus bill). The $2.3 billion included:

• $858 million for bilateral programs funded through the bill's Child Survival and Health Programs Fund; and

• $1.4 billion for President Bush's Global HIV/AIDS Initiative.

Middle East

Appropriated $2.6 billion in military and economic assistance for Israel, $1.8 billion for Egypt, and $456 million for Jordan.

The final bill included language to reduce Egypt's control over funds to promote democracy in that country.

War on Terrorism Allies

Boosted military and economic aid to reward U.S. allies in the war on terrorism. These additions included: a $73 million increase in Israel's foreign military financing grants, $400 million for Afghanistan to train its new army, $300 million to Pakistan for a new program aimed at capturing

al Qaeda forces on its border with Afghanistan, and $66 million in military assistance for Poland, a 230 percent increase.

Andean Counterdrug Initiative

Appropriated $731 million.

Family Planning

Included $441 million for international population-planning assistance, subject to the Mexico City policy restrictions. The bill allocated $34 million in fiscal 2005 for the United Nations Population Fund (UNFPA), specifically prohibited any U.S. funds from being used in China, and continued the existing Kemp-Kasten amendment restrictions. *(Restrictions on family planning assistance, p. 247)*

Sudan

Provided $404 million for humanitarian relief in Sudan, including $75 million in emergency funding for African Union peacekeeping efforts in the Darfur region.

State Department Authorization

The House in 2003 passed a bill (HR 1950) to reauthorize the State Department and some foreign assistance programs, but Senate Republican leaders pulled a companion bill (S 925) from the floor after Democrats tried to attach an unrelated proposal to raise the minimum wage. The Senate Foreign Relations Committee reported another bill (S 2144) in 2004, but that bill never reached the floor, reportedly because the leadership expected a replay of 2003. There was no further action on any of the bills in the 108th Congress.

All of the bills also contained provisions to reauthorize the Peace Corps and launch a new Bush administration initiative, the Millennium Challenge Account, to aid poor countries that demonstrated a commitment to democratic government and free market economies. *(Millennium Challenge Account, p. 298)*

HR 1950 had called for spending $45.3 billion through fiscal 2007, including $21.3 billion in fiscal 2004 and $18 billion in 2005 (the 2005 figure did not include foreign military sales). S 925 would have authorized $27 billion in fiscal 2004 and S 2144 would have authorized $29 billion in fiscal 2005.

Foreign affairs legislation was not popular on Capitol Hill. Congress had cleared a stand-alone State Department authorization bill (HR 1646—PL 107-228) in 2002, but that was the only time it had done so since 1994. Foreign aid legislation had had an even tougher time. Congress had not completed a separate foreign aid authorization bill since 1985. Members found it easier to continue funding for the various programs in appropriations bills instead. Richard G. Lugar, R-Ind., who chaired the Senate Foreign Relations Committee in 1985 and resumed its chairmanship in January 2003, had hoped to recover the ground his panel had lost to the Appropriations Committee over the years. But when the State Department legislation stalled in the 108th Congress, the appropriators took the reins once again. *(2002 State Department authorization, p. 250)*

Even before the minimum wage amendment doomed the legislation, both of the 2003 House and Senate authorization bills had faced veto threats over abortion language. The House eliminated the problem by agreeing to excise a provision added by the International Relations Committee that would have given the U.N. Population Fund $50 million per year in fiscal 2004 and 2005. Critics claimed the fund played a role in coerced abortions in China; supporters disagreed.

S 925 had included language to overturn the so-called Mexico City policy, which dated to the Reagan administration and barred U.S. aid to overseas organizations that performed abortions or promoted abortion rights, even if they used their own money to do so. The White House said President George W. Bush would veto a bill containing such a provision. One of Bush's first acts after taking office in 2001 was to restore the policy, which had been rescinded by President Bill Clinton. *(Mexico City policy, p. 247)*

HOUSE ACTION

The House passed HR 1950 by a vote of 382–42 on July 16, 2003. The House International Relations Committee had reported the bill (H Rept 108-105, Part I) on May 16 and had filed a supplemental report (Part II) on June 12. The Armed Services Committee had reported the bill (Part III) on June 30, and the Energy and Commerce Committee reported it (Part IV) on July 11.

After a heated debate, the House on July 15 adopted 216–211 a Christopher H. Smith, R-N.J., amendment that struck the bill's $100 million authorization for the U.N. Population Fund (also known as UNFPA). The committee bill would have allowed the money to be used if the administration certified that UNFPA did not directly support or participate in coercive abortions or sterilization—a less restrictive requirement than the so-called "Kemp-Kasten" language regularly inserted into the annual foreign operations appropriations bill. First enacted in 1985, the Kemp-Kasten provision (PL 99-88) barred U.S. funding for any organization that "supports or participates in the management" of a program of coercive abortion or involuntary sterilization. The Bush administration had withheld money appropriated for UNFPA in the fiscal 2002 foreign operations bill (HR 2506—PL 107-115) on the grounds that the organization was in violation of Kemp-Kasten. *(Details, 2003 aid appropriations, p. 286)*

The House on July 16 adopted 368–52 a Henry J. Hyde, R-Ill., amendment authorizing $9.3 billion over three years for the Millennium Challenge Account and $1.7 billion over four years for the Peace Corps. Those authorizations had not been in the original committee bill.

Provisions in the International Relations Committee version that dealt with global warming and commercial satellites were deleted when the bill was sent to the committees with jurisdiction in those areas.

SENATE ACTION

The Senate began debate on S 925 on July 9, 2003, but Majority Leader Bill Frist, R-Tenn., pulled the measure July 11 after Edward M. Kennedy, D-Mass., went to the floor intending to offer an amendment to increase the minimum wage, the first hike in seven years, and a second amendment strengthening federal hate-crimes laws. No further action was taken on S 925.

The Senate Foreign Relations Committee had reported S 925 (S Rept 108-39) on April 24. Chairman Lugar had tried to keep the committee bill clean of foreign aid provisions in hopes of being able to pass a separate foreign aid authorization bill. He gambled that White House support for a Millennium Challenge Account authorization would carry the separate bill through. But when the bill reached the floor Lugar shifted his strategy and offered a substitute that also included language from two other bills reported by his committee May 29. The first (S 1160—S Rept 108-55) authorized the Millennium Challenge Account and the second (S 1161—S Rept 108-56) authorized foreign aid programs. The changes were adopted by voice vote July 10.

Despite a blunt veto threat, the Senate on July 9 adopted by voice vote an amendment by Barbara Boxer, D-Calif., to repeal the Mexico City policy. Earlier the Senate had rejected 43–53 an attempt to table (kill) the amendment.

The Senate Foreign Relations Committee tried again in 2004, reporting S 2144 (S Rept 108-248) March 18. The bill's totals matched the president's request for fiscal 2005—$10.9 billion for State and $18.3 billion in foreign aid. But the panel made several adjustments, cutting funds for the Millennium Challenge Account to $2 billion from the requested $2.5 billion and trimming the Peace Corps budget request by $50 million, to $351 million. Despite the committee's unanimous support, the bill never reached the floor. GOP aides said Frist did not schedule floor time because he expected a repeat of the previous year's minimum wage fight.

Syria Sanctions

Congress in 2003 cleared legislation (HR 1828—PL 108-175) requiring the president to impose sanctions on Syria unless he concluded that doing so would not be in the United States' national security interests.

For two years congressional sentiment had been building to punish Syria for allowing terrorists to cross its border into Iraq, for continuing its military occupation of neighboring Lebanon, and for allegedly possessing weapons of mass destruction. But the White House had opposed sanctions, persuading lawmakers in the 107th Congress to drop an earlier version of the legislation to allow Secretary of State Colin L. Powell and other advocates of diplomacy to take the lead in dealing with Syria.

By the fall of 2003, however, the Bush administration dropped its objections, citing Syria's failure to act against terrorism or assist in the Middle East peace process. Pro-Israel groups, such as the American-Israel Public Affairs Committee, lobbied hard for passage of the bill.

The Commerce Department estimated that Syria imported $269.4 million of U.S. goods in 2002.

LEGISLATIVE ACTION

The House passed HR 1828 on Oct. 15, 2003, by a vote of 398–4. The House International Relations Committee had reported the bill (H Rept 108-314) that same day.

The committee had marked up the bill on Oct. 8, only days after Israel conducted an airstrike against an alleged Palestinian terrorist base outside Damascus in response to a suicide bombing in the northern city of Haifa that killed nineteen Israelis. The Bush administration had refused to criticize the raid, warning Damascus it was on the "wrong side" of the war against terror. The White House said on the day of the markup that the administration was "not opposed to this bill."

At the same time, however, George W. Bush signaled a more nuanced approach, appointing veteran diplomat Margaret Scobey to be the next U.S. ambassador to Syria. The appointment surprised supporters of the legislation, who said they feared it would dilute the bill's hard-line message to Syria. Scobey was subsequently confirmed Dec. 9.

The Senate passed the sanctions bill 89–4 on Nov. 11, after adopting by voice vote a Richard G. Lugar, R-Ind., amendment giving the president authority to waive any of the bill's sanctions if he determined it was "in the national security interests" to do so. This was a less stringent standard than under the House bill, which would have required the president to cite "vital national security interests" before waiving sanctions and would not have allowed him to waive sanctions on the export of arms or so-called dual-use products that have both commercial and military uses.

The House accepted the Senate's amendment, voting 408–8 on Nov. 20 to clear the bill. The president signed it Dec. 12.

MAJOR PROVISIONS

As signed into law, HR 1828:

• Banned exports to Syria of weapons and dual-use items (commercial products that also have military use).

• Required the president to impose at least two of the following sanctions: bar U.S. exports to Syria except food and medicine; prohibit U.S. investment in Syria; restrict Syrian diplomats to a twenty-five-mile radius of Washington or New York; ban Syrian aircraft from U.S. airspace; reduce diplomatic contacts with Damascus; and freeze Syrian government assets in the United States.

• Gave the president authority to waive the sanctions if he determined it was in the interest of national security to do so but he had to report to Congress on the reasons.

• Kept Syria on the State Department's list of state sponsors of terrorism, demanded the withdrawal of Syrian troops from Lebanon, condemned Syria's chemical and biological weapons programs, and held Damascus responsible for terrorism against U.S. troops in Iraq. The bill stated that the United States would not provide any assistance to Syria and would oppose multilateral aid until Syria withdrew its armed forces from Lebanon, halted the development and deployment of weapons of mass destruction and medium- and long-range ballistic missiles, and complied with various U.N. resolutions.

HIV/AIDS Assistance

Congress in 2003 cleared a $15 billion, five-year authorization bill (HR 1298—PL 108-25) to combat the international spread of HIV/AIDS. Despite partisan and bicameral disagreements over the most effective strategies to use, Congress bowed to White House pressure and approved the legislation.

Lawmakers had come close to passing a multibillion-dollar AIDS authorization bill (HR 2069) in the waning days of the 107th Congress but were unable to reach final agreement. They returned in January 2003 determined to finish the job. They got an early boost from President George W. Bush, who called for the program in his State of the Union address. *(Background and 107th action, HIV/AIDS assistance, p. 257)*

But the momentum dissipated quickly as fights over the details consumed the better part of four months. The central disputes included how much to focus on abstinence and monogamy as opposed to other approaches, such as distributing condoms, and how much of the money should go to the Geneva-based Global Fund to Fight AIDS, Tuberculosis and Malaria.

As the debate went on Bush publicly urged quicker action. "In the three months since I announced the emergency plan," Bush said from the White House April 29, "an estimated 760,000 people have died from AIDS, 1.2 million people have been infected, more than 175,000 babies have been born with the virus. Time is not on our side."

Congress got the message and cleared the legislation within weeks. The final bill set aside one-third of U.S. funds for abstinence programs and about $200 million a year was expected to be distributed through the Global Fund.

Enactment did not put an end to the funding issue. Although the new law authorized up to $3 billion a year for programs to fight AIDS overseas, appropriators included only $2.4 billion in the fiscal 2004 omnibus appropriations package (HR 2673—PL 108-199), which cleared in early 2004. Congress came much closer in the fiscal 2005 omnibus appropriations bill (HR 4818—PL 108-447), which provided a total of $2.9 billion in AIDS-related funding. *(2004 aid appropriations, p. 288; 2005 aid appropriations, p. 292)*

HOUSE ACTION

The House moved quickly after Bush's April 29 statement, passing HR 1298 by a vote of 375–41 on May 1. The House

International Relations Committee had reported the bill (H Rept 108-60) on April 7.

During committee action, conservatives had watched aghast as Democrats took advantage of GOP absences and defections to protect provisions that gave condom distribution programs the same priority as abstinence and monogamy advocacy, and to limit protections for faith-based groups. But once HR 1298 reached the floor, Republicans were able to bring it more in line with the desires of social conservatives. They revived a pair of amendments that had failed in committee, though Democrats said they were surprised to see that the provisions had been toned down.

During the May 1 debate, the House:

• Adopted 220–197 an amendment by Joe Pitts, R-Pa., to require that at least 33 percent of AIDS prevention funds be used for abstinence and monogamy education programs. Pitts's original amendment would have required that such programs be emphasized and condoms be allowed only as a backup.

• Adopted by voice vote a Christopher H. Smith, R-N.J., amendment to clarify that faith-based groups not be required to distribute condoms or use other approaches they found offensive in order to participate in the program. The floor amendment was worded to require that groups show a moral or religious objection to certain programs to receive the exemption. Democrats argued that the existing bill provided such protections, but Smith said the language was vague.

SENATE ACTION

The Senate passed HR 1298 by voice vote on May 16.

At the time of House passage, the Senate Foreign Relations Committee was still negotiating the terms of its own AIDS bill (S 1009). The main issue holding up the bill was disagreement over U.S. contributions to the Global Fund. But committee chair Richard G. Lugar, R-Ind., agreed to set the bill aside after Bush asked him May 13 to simply pass the House version unchanged so the president could have a global AIDS bill in hand at the G8 summit of industrialized nations in Evian, France, in June.

In the end, Democrats allowed the measure to pass with only one minor change—a bipartisan amendment adopted by voice vote that recommended debt relief for nations hit hardest by AIDS. But during the debate Majority Leader Bill Frist of Tennessee and other Republican senators incurred the minority party's wrath as they fended off most Democratic amendments. Republicans argued that defeating the amendments meant quicker enactment and quicker disbursement of funds.

During the May 15–16 debate, the Senate:

• Rejected 48–52 a Richard J. Durbin, D-Ill., amendment to authorize at least $500 million for the Global Fund in fiscal 2004.

• Rejected 48–52 on a procedural motion a proposal by Byron L. Dorgan, D-N.D., to provide emergency funding for food aid to HIV/AIDS-affected populations in sub-Saharan Africa.

• Rejected 45–52 a Dianne Feinstein, D-Calif., amendment to strike the requirement that 33 percent of AIDS prevention money be devoted to abstinence programs.

• Rejected 42–54 an Edward M. Kennedy, D-Mass., amendment to require that AIDS drugs purchased using funds in the bill be obtained at the lowest possible price consistent with assured quality.

• Rejected 45–50 an amendment by Barbara Boxer, D-Calif., to require a specific plan to assist those caring for children orphaned after losing their parents to AIDS.

• Rejected 44–51 a Christopher J. Dodd, D-Conn., amendment to expand the AIDS programs to Caribbean nations.

FINAL BILL

The House cleared HR 1298 by voice vote May 21, and the president signed it into law May 27.

The new law authorized $3 billion a year in fiscal years 2004 through 2008. Other provisions of the bill:

Global Fund

Allowed but did not require the administration to contribute up to $1 billion to the Global Fund to Fight AIDS, Tuberculosis, and Malaria in fiscal 2004.

If the salary of any single fund employee exceeded that of the vice president of the United States, the administration would be required to cut the following year's donation by an amount equal to the difference between the employee's and the vice president's salary.

Prevention Programs

Encouraged recipients of U.S. funds to follow the ABC plan—"A" for abstinence, "B" for be faithful, and "C" for condom distribution. However, one-third of U.S. funds had to be directed toward abstinence programs.

Faith-based Groups

Allowed faith-based groups to forgo certain programs to which they might object, such as condom distribution, and still receive federal dollars to participate in other programs.

AIDS Coordinator

Created within the State Department a new position, known as the HIV/AIDS Response Coordinator, to oversee and coordinate all international AIDS programs. The position was subject to Senate confirmation.

Vaccine Funds

Authorized U.S. contributions to international organizations seeking vaccines for AIDS and malaria.

Tuberculosis and Malaria

Authorized unspecified funding to help combat the spread of tuberculosis and malaria, with special attention to a program known as Directly Observed Treatment Short-Course, a World Health Organization–recommended strategy for treating tuberculosis.

Health Professional Relocation

Authorized a program to investigate the feasibility of moving U.S. health care professionals to areas hardest hit by AIDS and authorized the administration to create incentives to encourage individuals to participate in the program.

Families and Orphans

Authorized new programs to provide care for orphans and survivors of AIDS victims.

Sudan Relief Assistance

Congress in 2004 found a number of avenues to express its outrage over the deteriorating situation in the Darfur region of western Sudan, where Arab Muslim militias backed by the Sudanese government were waging a violent campaign against the black African Muslim population. Republicans and Democrats were united in their belief that Congress needed to take the lead to help alleviate suffering in the region.

The conflict in Darfur had broken out in early 2003 when rebel groups took up arms against government forces to protest an agreement on the distribution of economic resources. The Sudanese government attempted to crush the rebels and their supporters by arming Arab militias and deploying its own militia. Since then more than one million black African villagers had been uprooted and tens of thousands had died.

The conflict in Darfur was separate from the north-south civil war that had torn Sudan for several decades. Congress had approved sanctions (HR 5531—PL 107-245) in 2002 designed to bring the Sudanese government to the negotiating table to end that war. *(Sudan sanctions, p. 258)*

But it was Darfur that captured Congress's attention in 2004.

RESOLUTIONS

In May both chambers adopted resolutions condemning the Sudanese government and the militia groups it supported for attacks against civilians in Darfur and demanding an immediate stop to the attacks. The resolutions called for, among other things, targeted sanctions on Sudan's government, a war crimes investigation, a U.N. Security Council resolution addressing Darfur, and full access to the region for aid groups. The Senate passed S Con Res 99 by voice vote May 6, and the House passed H Con Res 403 by a vote of 360–1 on May 17.

In July the House and the Senate denounced the violence in Darfur as "genocide" in separate resolutions. The House passed H Con Res 467 by a vote of 422–0 on July 22, and the Senate passed S Con Res 133 by voice vote that same day.

Secretary of State Colin L. Powell also used the term "genocide" to describe the ethnic cleansing in Darfur when he testified Sept. 9 before the Senate Foreign Relations Committee.

In September, lawmakers urged President George W. Bush to step up diplomatic pressure on the Sudanese government. The Senate adopted by voice vote Sept. 15 a resolution (S Con Res 137) that called on the secretary of state to push for Sudan's immediate suspension from the U.N. Commission on Human Rights. The House adopted the resolution by voice vote Sept. 22. Sudan had been a member of the commission since 2002.

ASSISTANCE

Congress stepped up aid to the region as well. Lawmakers added $95 million in emergency relief for Darfur to the fiscal 2005 defense spending bill (HR 4613—PL 108-287). But an attempt by Sen. Joseph R. Biden Jr, D-Del., to add $118 million more in Darfur aid was tabled (killed) by a vote of 53–45 on June 24.

The aid had been added to the defense spending bill because it offered a quicker avenue to get relief funding into law. That measure cleared in July. But over the next two months it became clear that more funds were needed. Powell urged Congress to boost aid in his Sept. 9 testimony. *(2005 defense appropriations, p. 354)*

At that same hearing, Senate Foreign Relations Committee Chair Richard G. Lugar, R-Ind., announced the introduction of legislation (S 2781) to authorize an additional $300 million in fiscal 2005 humanitarian aid for Sudan. The Senate passed S 2781 by voice vote Sept. 23, and the House passed an amended version by voice vote Nov. 19. The Senate cleared the bill by voice vote Dec. 7. As signed into law Dec. 23, S 2781 (PL 108-497) authorized $200 million for humanitarian assistance in the Darfur region and eastern Chad, mainly for aid groups working in the region. Another $100 million was slated for Sudan on the conclusion of a comprehensive peace agreement that applied to all regions of Sudan, including Darfur. Sudan and the rebels in the south did agree at the United Nations Nov. 19—the same day the House cleared S 2781—to halt their hostilities by the end of the year, and a north-south peace agreement was signed on Jan. 9, 2005. But that agreement did not cover Darfur.

The Senate gave the administration access to $300 million for relief efforts, as part of the fiscal 2005 foreign operations bill (HR 4818). The Senate Appropriations Committee had come up with an extra $225 million for relief efforts, and an additional $75 million in emergency aid was added on the floor Sept. 23, when the Senate adopted by voice vote an amendment offered by Jon Corzine, D-N.J., and Mike DeWine, R-Ohio. The House version of the spending bill, which had passed in July, had no money for Darfur, but it did provide $311 million for refuges in southern Sudan, with the stipulation that no money could be provided to the Sudanese government until it halted support for the Arab militias terrorizing Darfur.

The conference version of HR 4818, which was signed into law (PL 108-447) in December, provided $404 million for humanitarian and refugee assistance for Sudan. The final bill included language similar to that in the House-passed bill, providing $311 million in assistance if the Sudanese government took steps to improve security and humanitarian aid in Darfur. No more than $45 million could be used outside the Darfur region without proper notification of Congress. In addition, the bill provided $93 million in emergency funding: $75 million for African Union peacekeeping operations in Darfur and $18 million for humanitarian assistance.

Middle East Resolutions

Both the House and Senate in June 2004 adopted resolutions (H Con Res 460, S Res 393) expressing support for U.S. policy in the Middle East.

In an April 14, 2004, letter to Israeli prime minister Ariel Sharon, President George W. Bush had voiced his approval of Israeli plans to unilaterally withdraw from the Gaza, maintain some Israeli settlements in the West Bank, and effectively reject Palestinian refugees' "right of return" to what is now Israel. Bush said the United States remained committed to the Middle East "road map" to peace and the vision of two states living side by side in peace and security.

Refugees and final borders had long been considered so-called final status issues, to be negotiated by both sides in a comprehensive peace settlement. Bush's position appeared to upend the decades-long U.S. role of unbiased broker in such a settlement and infuriated the Arab Middle East and Muslims worldwide. Sharon's own right-wing Likud Party rejected his plan, and Bush seemed to back off after King Abdullah of Jordan visited the White House in May to stress the importance of a negotiated settlement.

The House and Senate resolutions noted, among other things, Bush's letter to Sharon. H Con Res 460, adopted June 23 by a vote of 407–9, "strongly" endorsed the principles Bush articulated in the letter. S Res 393, adopted June 24 by a vote of 95–3, endorsed U.S. policy in the Middle East and reaffirmed its commitment to the Middle East road map and the two-state vision. Both resolutions expressed support for working with others in the international community to build up Palestinian institutions so they will be capable and willing to fight terrorism, dismantle terrorist organizations, and protect Israel's security in the areas from which it withdraws.

Cuba Sanctions

Repeated attempts to ease U.S. sanctions against Cuba proved unsuccessful in the 108th Congress. The debate was especially heated in 2004, a presidential election year, because of the voting clout of Cuban Americans in the battleground state of Florida.

Advocates for change in U.S. policy won some easing of the decades-long embargo against Cuba in 2000 and had chalked up some significant floor victories since then, but none of their provisions made it out of conference. *(Cuba Sanctions, Background, p. 260)*

TRANSPORTATION-TREASURY BILL

Restrictions on travel to Cuba that were written into law (PL 106-387) in 2000 were a perennial target. During action on the fiscal 2004 Transportation and Treasury departments appropriations bill (HR 2989), the House on Sept. 9, 2003, voted 227–188 to lift the ban on most travel to Cuba. Despite a White House veto threat, fifty-three Republicans voted for the amendment offered by Jeff Flake, R-Ariz., and Jim McGovern, D-Mass., while twenty-two Democrats voted against it. It was the fourth consecutive year the House had voted to lift the ban. And, for the first time ever, the Senate voted to lift the ban as well. By a **key vote of 36–59 (R 30–19; D 6–39; I 0–1)** on Oct. 23, the Senate rejected an attempt to table (kill) an amendment by Byron L. Dorgan, D-N.D., to ease the ban. Dorgan's amendment was then added to the bill by voice vote. The last time the Senate had voted on the issue, in 1999, only forty-three senators supported ending the travel ban. *(2003 key votes, p. 837; 1999 vote, Congress and the Nation Vol. X, p. 210)*

In addition to the travel amendment, the House also adopted, 222–196, an amendment by Bill Delahunt, D-Mass., to bar use of funds in the bill to enforce restrictions on money people in the United States could send to families in Cuba for their personal upkeep. And it adopted 246–173 a proposal by Jim Davis, D-Fla., to rescind a recent administration decision to halt certain educational trips to Cuba known as "people to people" exchanges.

All the Cuba-related provisions were dropped from the final bill during the conference on an omnibus fiscal 2004 spending package (HR 2673—PL 108-199) that cleared in early 2004.

Later in 2004 the Senate Appropriations Committee added language to its fiscal 2005 Transportation-Treasury appropriations bill (S 2806) to lift the ban on travel to Cuba, but Flake did not offer a similar amendment to the House version (HR 5025) as he had in past years. "Neither party can see past Florida when trying to decide what to do about Cuba," the Arizona Republican said, referring to the election battle over Florida's twenty-seven electoral votes. "Our efforts will resume when the electoral smoke clears." Florida, home to a powerful anti–Fidel Castro constituency, was the pivotal battleground in the 2000 election and was expected to be a major factor in 2004.

Other House members, however, moved forward with their amendments to HR 5025 during floor action in September. By voice vote, the House adopted a Barbara Lee, D-Calif., amendment to lift a recently issued rule that sharply restricted educational trips to Cuba. Also adopted by voice vote was a Maxine Waters, D-Calif., amendment to remove impediments to private commercial sales of agricultural commodities, medicine, or medical supplies to Cuba. And by a vote of 225–174 the House adopted a Davis amendment to roll back a recent rule that made it more difficult for Cuban Americans to visit relatives on the island. Under that rule, Cuban Americans could visit Cuba to see immediate family only once every three years.

Under threat of a veto, all the Cuba-related provisions were dropped in conference on the fiscal 2005 omnibus funding package (HR 4818—PL 108-447).

AGRICULTURE BILL

The Senate in 2003 and again in 2004 attempted to make it easier for farmers and medical suppliers to sell their products in Cuba during action on the annual Agriculture Department funding bills. Legislation to allow the sale of agricultural and medical supplies to Cuba had been enacted in 2000 (PL 106-387), but farm-state lawmakers complained that the Bush administration was not approving the necessary licenses.

During committee action on its fiscal 2004 Agriculture funding bill (S 1427), the Senate Appropriations Committee approved a provision, offered by Dorgan and Republican Larry E. Craig of Idaho, that would have enabled farmers and medical suppliers to travel to Cuba to sell their goods without obtaining travel licenses from the State Department. Despite a White House veto threat, there was no effort to remove it on the floor. The provision was dropped in conference on the fiscal 2004 omnibus appropriations bill.

Dorgan and Craig tried again the next year, but the outcome was the same. Their proposal was popular with Midwest farmers eager to build sales to Cuba but anathema to many Cuban Americans. Given that it was an election year and President George W. Bush was trying to keep the politically active Cuban American community in Florida solidly behind him, it was a tough sell. The amendment was included in the Senate committee's fiscal 2005 Agriculture funding bill (S 2803), but conferees yielded to White House pressure and dropped it in conference on the end-of-the-year omnibus appropriations package.

COMMERCE-JUSTICE-STATE BILL

During action in July 2004 on its fiscal 2005 spending bill for the Commerce, Justice, and State departments (HR 4754) the House adopted 221–194 a Flake amendment to temporarily block new administration regulations that limited the ability of Cuban Americans to send supplies to family members in Cuba and limited personal baggage carried by travelers to the island nation. Bush had issued the new regulations after a presidential commission in May said that gift parcels to Cuba lessened the need for that country's communist government to ensure basic supplies for its population and raised revenue for the government. The rules restricted the kind of goods that could be included in parcels bound for Cuba by excluding seeds, clothing, fishing equipment, and veterinary medicines, and limiting the number of parcels to one a month for every household rather than one per person. Flake's amendment was dropped in the conference on the fiscal 2005 omnibus spending bill.

North Korea Aid

Congress in 2004 cleared bipartisan legislation (HR 4011—PL 108-333) designed to increase pressure on the communist regime in North Korea to improve its human rights policies.

The measure authorized $24 million a year for fiscal years 2005 through 2008 to provide humanitarian relief and support a variety of human rights and democracy initiatives. The bulk of that annual authorization, $20 million, was to go to organizations that assisted and protected North Korean refugees. The findings section of HR 4011 noted that perhaps hundreds of thousands of North Koreans had fled their country because of "the threat of starvation, the risk of persecution, and the lack of freedom and opportunity."

The legislation also clarified the eligibility of North Koreans for U.S. refugee programs and endorsed increased humanitarian assistance inside North Korea while also seeking greater transparency and monitoring of that aid.

The House International Relations Committee reported HR 4011 (H Rept 108-478, Part I) on May 4, 2004, and the House passed it by voice vote July 21. The Senate passed an amended version by voice vote Sept. 28, and the House concurred on Oct. 4, clearing the bill. It was signed into law Oct. 18.

The legislation produced a harsh response from North Korea. A spokesman for the foreign ministry issued a statement Oct. 4, declaring that the bill "has deprived North Korea of any justification to deal with the U.S., to say nothing of the reason for holding the six-party talks for settling the nuclear issue."

CHAPTER 5

Defense Policy

Defense Policy

After eight years with Democrat Bill Clinton as president, the defense community had high expectations when Republican George W. Bush moved into the White House in 2001.

The military and its Capitol Hill supporters had always been suspicious and sometimes hostile to President Clinton. From his youthful avoidance of military service, to his unsuccessful attempt to allow gays to openly serve in the military, to his slim defense budgets, and his deployments of U.S. forces on humanitarian and peacekeeping missions, they found much to criticize. In the later stages of Clinton's tenure, Congress routinely had added billions of dollars for defense—largely for items requested by the services but dropped by the Clinton White House.

Bush, on the other hand, was the son of former president George H. W. Bush, the commander in chief during the Persian Gulf War in 1991. Moreover, his running mate, Dick Cheney, had served as secretary of defense in the senior Bush's administration. Although some Democrats and media reports raised questions about George W. Bush's National Guard service in the Vietnam era, allegations that he had not fulfilled his obligations to the Guard were never proven. In a campaign speech at The Citadel, he said: "I will renew the bond of trust between the American president and the American military." And the military believed that he would.

During the presidential campaign, Bush and Cheney assailed Clinton and his vice president, Al Gore, who was the Democratic nominee in 2000, arguing that the military had been underfunded and used too freely. Bush vowed to boost defense spending, to transform the military into a more mobile and high-tech force, and to install a national missile defense system.

Dramatic increases in defense spending were coming, of course, but for very different reasons than anticipated. On Sept. 11, 2001, nineteen hijackers crashed planes into the World Trade Center in New York City, the Pentagon outside Washington, and a field in Pennsylvania. Nearly three thousand people died that day. The targets of the terrorists were not random—they had chosen symbols of America's financial and military might. Although no one knew for sure, many thought the plane that crashed in Pennsylvania as passengers fought back had been headed toward the White House or the U.S. Capitol.

The response from the White House and Congress was sweeping and multi-faceted, affecting government agencies and economic sectors across the spectrum. But none was more important than the military response. The country had been stripped of its sense of security, its vulnerability exposed. The most powerful nation in the world had been struck by a small group of men, armed with little more than box cutters and fully fueled planes as weapons, who managed to inflict enormous physical and psychological damage.

A war on terrorism was declared and military retaliation began within weeks of the Sept. 11 attacks. The United States determined that terrorist leader Osama bin Laden and his al Qaeda network were behind the attacks. Bin Laden was no stranger. His network had been blamed for terrorist attacks on two U.S. embassies in Africa in 1998 and on the U.S. Navy destroyer *Cole* in a port in Yemen in 2000. The terrorists had been given safe haven in Afghanistan, and Bush ordered the Taliban regime that ruled that country to turn them over or "share in their fate." When they failed to comply with U.S. demands, Bush, with the backing of Congress, sent U.S. forces into Afghanistan to oust the Taliban and root out the terrorists.

But the president called for a broader response than the retaliatory war in Afghanistan. He wanted to prevent terrorist attacks from happening in the first place, and for that he

REFERENCES

Discussion of defense policy for the years 1945–1964 may be found in *Congress and the Nation Vol. I*, pp. 237–334; for the years 1965–1968, *Congress and the Nation Vol. II*, pp. 827–890; for the years 1969–1972, *Congress and the Nation Vol. III*, pp. 191–252; for the years 1973–1976, *Congress and the Nation Vol. IV*, pp. 153–197; for the years 1977–1980, *Congress and the Nation Vol. V*, pp. 125–176; for the years 1981–1984, *Congress and the Nation Vol. VI*, pp. 201–257; for the years 1985–1988, *Congress and the Nation Vol. VII*, pp. 273–340; for the years 1989–1992, *Congress and the Nation Vol. VIII*, pp. 335–412; for the years 1993–1996, *Congress and the Nation Vol. IX*, pp. 253–323; for the years 1997–2001, *Congress and the Nation Vol. X*, pp. 235–311.

Outlays for National Defense

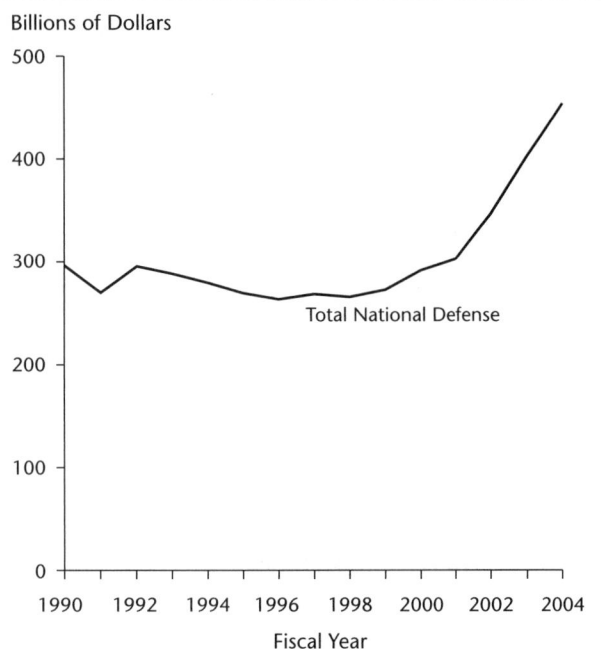

SOURCE: Office of Management and Budget, *Historical Tables, Budget of the United States Government: Fiscal Year 2006* (Washington, D.C.: U.S. Government Printing Office, 2005), Table 3.2.

espoused a doctrine of preemptive action. If the United States perceived a threat, it would strike first, Bush vowed. "If we wait for threats to fully materialize, we will have waited too long," Bush declared in a June 2001 policy speech to graduating officers at West Point. "The war on terror will not be won on the defensive. We must take the battle to the enemy, disrupt his plans, and confront the worst threats before they emerge."

The president specifically stressed the need for an American military that could "strike at a moment's notice in any dark corner of the world," using "preemptive action, when necessary, to defend our liberty and to defend our lives."

Lawmakers from both parties were quick to embrace the broad outlines of Bush's strike-first doctrine. But some Democrats were troubled by indications that Bush intended to apply the doctrine much more widely. In his West Point speech Bush seemed to allude to the rogue nations that made up what he called the "axis of evil"—Iraq, North Korea, and Iran. "Containment is not possible when unbalanced dictators with weapons of mass destruction can deliver those weapons on missiles or secretly provide them to terrorist allies," Bush said.

The United States put the preemption doctrine into practice in early 2003 when it went to war to remove Iraqi leader Saddam Hussein and end his alleged programs to develop weapons of mass destruction. Congress gave the president immediate and continuing support, even when the war proved to be far more difficult than the White House and

most military leaders had anticipated. Administration supporters of the war had predicted for months that the conflict would be swift and that the United States and the coalition it had assembled would prevail.

In a dramatic gesture that later backfired, Bush flew onto the aircraft carrier U.S.S. *Abraham Lincoln* in the co-pilot's seat of a navy S-3B Viking jet on May 1, 2003, just six weeks after the war began, and declared that "major combat operations" were over. He landed with a huge banner saying "Mission Accomplished" as a backdrop. Although the navy later took responsibility for the banner idea, both Bush's message and the carrier image that was widely published came back to haunt the White House as the war dragged on and U.S. casualties grew in number far beyond the initial toll of dead and wounded between March and May.

Instead, the U.S.-led invasion left more than 100,000 American soldiers occupying Iraq and fighting an increasingly dangerous and stubborn insurgency. American soldiers and the vehicles they traveled in were especially vulnerable to the enemy's roadside bombs. The Iraqi soldiers and police recruited by the Americans became easy targets of the insurgents. By October 2005 U.S. military deaths in Iraq had reached a symbolically important number of 2,000.

With lawmakers from both parties anxious to demonstrate their support for troops in war zones, the Bush administration's requests for funding were politically sacrosanct in Congress. Indeed, members approved additional spending to protect the troops, increase benefits, and help military families back home.

And despite the escalating war costs, the regular defense budget did not suffer. Both the administration's transformation plans and most of the conventional weapons in the pipeline continued to be funded. Given the mounting federal budget deficit, no one was certain how long that would last. But certainly during the 107th and 108th Congresses, the guns-or-butter tradeoff did not seem to apply.

TRANSFORMING THE MILITARY

The pressure to transform America's post–cold war military from a conventional weapons giant into a more agile force raised difficult questions for the Pentagon about where and how to spend its money. The administration's first defense budget outlined the promises by Bush and Defense Secretary Donald H. Rumsfeld to transform the military, but it did not identify specific programs it would fund—nor those it would cut.

Bush had made it clear that he wanted to consider radically reshaping U.S. strategy in ways that might eliminate or sharply reduce multibillion dollar programs for traditional weapons. And Rumsfeld had pressed the military to make conventional combat units more mobile and agile by using networks of sensors, computers, robot weapons, and precision-guided munitions that could supplant some of the seventy-ton tanks, $5 billion aircraft carriers, and fighter planes that were the centerpieces of the existing force. He pushed for another round of base closings—never a popular issue on Capitol Hill—as one of many efficiencies needed to squeeze funds out of existing budgets to pay for developing transformational forces.

Rumsfeld cited Sept.11 to buttress his more fundamental argument that the military must change. The attacks highlighted the country's susceptibility to the catastrophic damage that could be caused by a wide range of nontraditional attacks, he said. "Because of the end of the cold war, and because of the [Persian] Gulf War which told people not to compete with armies, navies and air forces, countries do look for asymmetrical ways they can threaten the United States and Western countries," Rumsfeld said soon after the attacks. "We have to recognize the magnitude of the threat and the extent to which people are willing to give their lives, as these pilots of these airplanes did, and impose damage on us."

The debate about transformation was not over whether the new technology was desirable but rather how quickly U.S. forces should incorporate those changes and at what cost to existing programs that had strong political backing. But the hard choices were put off after Sept. 11. The terrorist attacks altered the politics of the defense debate by making far more money available for defense than had seemed remotely possible only a day before. Despite all the dire predictions, only two major conventional weapons were canceled during the 107th and 108th Congresses: the $11 billion Crusader cannon program and the $39 billion Comanche attack helicopter program.

There had been an outcry on Capitol Hill when the Crusader was canceled but barely a word of protest when the Comanche program was killed. What had changed since then, according to lawmakers, defense analysts, and industry executives, was a procurement "train wreck" bearing down on the Pentagon: not enough money existed to pay for all of the new weapons systems scheduled to roll off the assembly line. Among the programs were the $72 billion F/A-22 Raptor fighter, the $200 billion F-35 Joint Strike Fighter, the $82 billion *Virginia*-class attack submarine, the $92 billion Future Combat System, and the $48 billion V-22 Osprey tiltrotor aircraft. The missile defense program had consumed $82 billion through fiscal 2004 and another $10 billion was authorized for the next year. Congress rejected a $20 billion plan to lease aerial refueling tankers, but it gave the Air Force the go-ahead to contract to buy them instead.

Other costs were spiraling as well.

WAGING WAR

By the end of 2004 nearly $179 billion had been allocated for the wars in Afghanistan and Iraq—$54 billion for military operations and occupation in Afghanistan and $125 billion in Iraq. Those figures did not include the costs for reconstruction.

The human costs were climbing as well. As of Nov. 10, 2005, there had been 203 U.S. military deaths in Afghanistan, 123 of those killed in action. In Iraq, there had been 2,047

U.S. military deaths as of that date, 1,599 killed in action. Of those killed in action in Iraq, 1,490 deaths had occurred since May 1, 2003, when President Bush had declared that major combat operations were over. Of the 15,568 wounded in action in Iraq, about half returned to duty within three days. The vast majority—15,026—occurred after Bush's declaration. Soldiers from other countries and countless Iraqis had been killed and injured as well.

The United States had gone to war in Afghanistan in early October 2001 with broad international support. The Taliban regime had been defeated quickly and the terrorist camps closed, although bin Laden and some Taliban leaders escaped. U.S and United Nations forces were left to maintain security until an Afghan army could be trained to take over.

The U.S. decision to go to war in Iraq divided the international community. Although the Bush administration touted its coalition members as partners in the war, the burden largely fell on the United States. Saddam Hussein's regime was quickly toppled after the war began in March 2003, but the coalition military forces soon found themselves fighting an insurgency for which their leaders had not planned, with woefully inadequate equipment.

The army that had dashed up the Euphrates Valley in Iraq in sixteen days to capture Baghdad was invincible in its speed and overwhelming firepower. But when its mission slowed to occupation—patrolling city streets and plodding through crowded neighborhoods—the army became vulnerable to insurgents. After finding it did not have enough foot soldiers to patrol restive cities and towns, the Pentagon shuffled troop rotations, called up more National Guard and reserve units, kept badly needed soldiers from leaving the service, and shifted some from South Korea, in the process reducing the number of ground forces in that troubled peninsula. Many of the soldiers scheduled to return home from Iraq after a year or more of fighting were told to stay put, and deployments in some cases stretched as long as fifteen months, taxing soldiers mentally and physically. At the same time, recruiting and retention rates made army officials nervous, as the casualty lists from Iraq grew. Long months of active duty made service less attractive in the reserves, which by early 2005 provided 40 percent of U.S. forces in Iraq.

Equipment problems were equally frustrating. Vehicles that had raced largely unscathed across the desert were later targeted by crude roadside bombs in Iraq's cities and towns, their crews hunted by snipers. The blasts, which tore through the army's thin-skinned Humvees and trucks, were responsible for about half the U.S. deaths by early 2005. Soldiers found themselves scavenging rusty steel plates from dumps to fortify their vehicles, calling it "hillbilly armor." And the Pentagon ran up billions of dollars in maintenance bills as its equipment began to wear out under Iraq's harsh desert conditions.

Morale was further damaged when inspectors searching for Saddam's weapons of mass destruction came up emptyhanded, and by stories and pictures of prisoner abuse at the

U.S. military's Abu Ghraib prison near Baghdad that shocked the world.

Lawmakers gave the Bush administration nearly all the funds it requested to wage the wars, although usually not the flexibility the Pentagon wanted in spending the money. Nearly all the funding for the wars was provided in a series of emergency supplemental appropriations bills, which had the advantage of not being counted as part of the defense spending baseline and therefore not encroaching on the regular defense budget.

But not everyone in Congress was pleased with the use of supplementals, several of which contained record-breaking amounts. Democrats accused the White House of trying to hide the true costs of the war by funding it in a piece-meal fashion. In addition, because emergency supplemental spending bills traditionally went only to the Appropriations panels and not the Armed Services committees, some authorizers worried that they were being cut out of debate on a substantial part of the Pentagon's budget and being side-stepped by the Pentagon when they sought to carry out their oversight role.

Members of Congress found other ways to assist the military forces and their families back home, ranging from increasing benefits to adding money for more armored Humvees. Mindful of the strains facing National Guard and military reserve units from near-constant service since the Sept. 11 attacks, Congress mandated the largest increase in active-duty troop levels in decades. It expanded access for reservists to the military's health care system. Lawmakers approved pay raises for members of the armed forces as well as hikes in imminent danger pay and family separation allowances. They eliminated a statutory cap on spending for a popular program to encourage private construction of military family housing.

SHIELDING THE NATION

As Congress and the White House focused on the war on terrorism and Iraq, the most politically contentious military issue for nearly two decades—missile defense—was all but taken off the table. After dividing Republicans and Democrats since the Reagan administration in the 1980s, the question of whether to build a national missile defense system or a more limited system or any system at all appeared to have been settled.

Late in his presidency Clinton had put off the decision of whether to deploy a missile defense system. Citing technical problems and diplomatic opposition, Clinton said he would defer the decision to his successor.

No one doubted what that decision would be after Bush was elected president. In his first year Bush asked for—and got—a huge increase in funding for the system, and by the end of his first term there were missile interceptors in silos in Alaska and California.

The missile defense debate had quickly gone from "whether" to "how"; there were several reasons for that.

Bush's determination had much to do with it. On the campaign trail, he had pledged to field a missile defense "at the earliest possible date." His position had the full support of Defense Secretary Rumsfeld. A veteran cold warrior, Rumsfeld had led a commission in 1998 that forecast missile threats from North Korea and Iran within five years.

Bush managed to remove a key obstacle in his way: the 1972 Anti-Ballistic Missile (ABM) Treaty with Russia, which prohibited a national missile defense system and certain tests the administration wanted to conduct. Opponents of missile defense argued that withdrawal from the treaty would harm U.S. relations with Russia, anger European allies, and possibly lead to an arms race in Asia. But in late 2001 Bush gave Russia the required six months' notice of U.S. withdrawal. "The cold war is long gone. Today, we leave behind one of its last vestiges," he said.

The Sept. 11 terrorist attacks dramatically altered the missile defense debate. Critics insisted that the attacks vindicated their belief that the country faced far more probable threats than missiles, but antimissile proponents contended that the attacks showed there were groups eager to inflict massive, indiscriminate destruction on vulnerable U.S. cities. Ultimately the attacks strengthened Bush's resolve and melted that of his opponents. In the wake of the attacks, Democrats dropped plans to challenge Bush's funding request.

Pentagon officials also linked missile defense to their goal of transformation. They argued that the technology would thwart a threat that conventional forces could not stop.

Although the decision to deploy a missile defense seemed settled, there were still occasional clashes on the issue.

The Pentagon's decision in 2002 to provide Congress with far less information on the program than it had in the past did not go over well on Capitol Hill. Critics said Rumsfeld was trying to shield the system from the tough technical scrutiny to which other major weapons programs were subject. Congress eventually insisted that the Pentagon provide the same information as in the past—and then it added a few more requirements.

Questions also were raised about the missile shield program bypassing much of the routine testing and oversight that nearly every other military weapon system received. Advocates of missile defense, mostly Republicans, justified the special treatment by pointing to the unprecedented nature of the threat. They argued that rogue states and possibly even terrorist groups were developing nuclear capabilities rapidly, and traditional Pentagon acquisition methods needed to be pushed aside in the name of survival. Democrats, having all but given up on killing missile defense, pushed back on the issue of testing and oversight. They said abbreviating the testing regime was shortsighted, and they had significant nonpartisan support backing them up. Taxpayer groups, the

Government Accountability Office (GAO), and even the Pentagon's own testing agency supported the proposition that no one really knew if the "interceptors" going into the ground would intercept anything. But Senate Democrats' attempts in 2004 to require more independent testing of the first phase of the system were rejected.

As the debate over missile defense subsided, some lawmakers turned their attention to the administration's increased emphasis after Sept. 11 on the U.S. nuclear arsenal. Of particular concern was Bush's request for funding to study a nuclear weapon that could burrow deep underground to destroy an enemy bunker. After going back and forth on it for several years, Congress in 2004 handed the White House a defeat when it refused to fund research on the nuclear "bunker buster."

Chronology of Action on Defense

2001–2002

The return of a Republican to the White House in 2001 inspired high hopes in the defense community. After slim budgets under Democratic president Bill Clinton (1992–2001), defense advocates were looking forward to far more robust military spending with George W. Bush as commander in chief.

For that reason Bush's decision to review military strategy before seeking extra money shocked and angered the defense community and its supporters on Capitol Hill. The White House managed to calm its critics, at least for the time being, with hints of spending to come once the review was completed. But the amended budget Bush submitted later in 2001 was still far short of expectations and prompted another round of criticism.

By the time Bush submitted the next year's budget, however, everything had changed. In the aftermath of the Sept. 11, 2001, terrorist attacks, the United States was fighting a retaliatory war in Afghanistan and was developing plans for a broader war on terrorism at home and abroad. In 2002 Bush requested and got the largest increase in defense spending since the Vietnam War more than three decades earlier, reflecting wide agreement that no dollars should be spared on defense after Sept. 11.

During his presidential campaign Bush promised to deploy a missile defense system; this resolve only intensified after the terrorist attacks. Democrats shelved their efforts to cut funding, and Congress agreed to increase missile defense spending by more than $3 billion over the previous year. To ensure that he would have a free hand to test the system and begin initial deployment in Alaska, Bush in late 2001 gave notice to Russia that the United States would withdraw from the 1972 Anti-Ballistic Missile (ABM) Treaty in six months. The ABM treaty stood in the way of some of the tests that were planned as well as Bush's ultimate goal of a national missile defense system.

Another top priority for the Bush administration was the transformation of the military into a lighter, agile, high-tech force, but how that modernization would translate into line items in the budget was uncertain. Some in the military were hopeful that the increased defense budgets would permit the military services to continue buying big-ticket conventional

weapons while also taking steps toward transformation. No weapons were canceled in Bush's first year, but the main reasons were time constraints and the Sept. 11 attacks, and not a willingness to grant the military all it sought. The next year one of those conventional weapons—the forty-ton Crusader mobile howitzer—proved impossible to reconcile with the army's drive to field lighter, more easily deployable forces. The Pentagon canceled the $11 billion program and Congress went along.

But Congress did not go along with everything. The House balked when the president called for a new round of military base closings in 2003. Few issues were more politically difficult for members because of the economic repercussions and voter anger that a local base closing could trigger. Although House members were unable to get the Senate to oppose the president's proposal, they did win a two-year reprieve, postponing the base closing process until 2005.

Over administration objections Congress took steps to expand the pensions of disabled veterans. Under a law that dated back to 1891 veterans could not receive their full disability payments and regular pensions at the same time. The law required that their pensions be reduced dollar-for-dollar to offset their disability payments; many in Congress thought that was wrong. The administration insisted that veterans were well-compensated and threatened to veto any bill that repealed the ban on so-called concurrent receipts. Congress and the White House eventually agreed to a compromise that allowed the most disabled of combat veterans to receive full benefits.

Congress attempted to halt administration plans to study the feasibility of a nuclear weapon that could burrow deep into the ground to attack enemy bunkers. Members refused to repeal a law that barred research and development of certain small nuclear weapons and prohibited funds for the project until the secretary of defense reported to Congress on the proposed weapon.

2002 Defense Authorization

Congress in 2001 cleared a $343.3 billion fiscal 2002 defense authorization. The total authorized by the final bill

(S 1438—PL 107-107) was roughly equal to the amount President George W. Bush had sought.

Despite much talk of reshaping the post–cold war military to deal with emerging threats such as terrorism, wholesale changes were put off. S 1438 largely tracked the proposals Bush made prior to the Sept. 11 terrorist attacks and closely resembled previous years' bills.

Final action on the bill was delayed by a month-long stalemate over the president's request for a new round of military base closings in 2003. House negotiators adamantly opposed another round, while members of the Senate favored the plan. Facing the threat of a presidential veto, House conferees ultimately relented but insisted that the next round be put off until 2005.

A comprehensive review of the nation's military by Defense Secretary Donald H. Rumsfeld had delayed Bush's detailed budget proposal until June 2001. Potential changes that emerged quickly from the strategic study—base closings, weapons cuts, and shifts in spending from conventional tanks and ships to high-tech weapons—drew criticism from the uniformed services and some members of Congress.

The House and Senate Armed Services committees began shaping their versions of the defense budget to reflect the political leadership and meet the demands of their rank-and-file members. In the GOP-controlled House, the committee ignored Bush's politically explosive request for more base closings. Meanwhile the Democratic majority on the Senate Armed Services Committee took aim at Bush's request to increase spending to develop a missile defense system and begin construction at an Alaska site that would violate the 1972 Anti-Ballistic Missile (ABM) Treaty with the former Soviet Union (and subsequently with Russia). Defense hawks wanted more money for defense but were thwarted by Bush's $1.4 trillion tax cut (HR 1836—PL 107-16) and a national economic slowdown that began shortly before Bush took office.

The Sept. 11 terrorist attacks and subsequent war in Afghanistan quashed most of the partisan fights over the defense budget. A handful of Democrats in the Senate and House abandoned their plans to press for cuts in missile defense spending, a tacit acknowledgment that they would lose a fight with the Bush administration over a system that the Pentagon could tout as an essential protection for a nation under siege.

But the issue of base closings did not go away. Proponents, particularly those in the Senate, argued that closing unnecessary installations would free up dollars for the war on terrorism. Opponents said it was premature to proceed while the military was still figuring out its needs to combat terrorism. The impasse was finally ended when House and Senate negotiators agreed to put off the next round of closings for another two years.

The final bill authorized Bush's request for a military pay raise ranging from 5 percent to 10 percent, depending on rank. Congress added money to Bush's budget request to let the Air National Guard continue operating the B-1 bomber for a year while studies were conducted; to begin converting four rather than two Trident submarines to carry long-range cruise missiles; and to buy more Blackhawk helicopters than requested. S 1438 also repealed a requirement for a referendum on the future of a navy bombing range in Puerto Rico.

DEFENSE BUDGET

In April 2001 Bush submitted a $310.5 billion budget for Defense Department military programs. Once atomic energy defense programs and other defense-related activities were added, Bush's proposed national defense budget totaled $325.1 billion.

The $310.5 billion was considered a place-holder with the final number expected to increase by early summer. The administration was waiting for Rumsfeld to finish his review before sending Congress a full defense budget request.

Bush had made it clear that he wanted to consider radically reshaping U.S. strategy in ways that might eliminate or sharply cut back multibillion dollar programs for traditional weapons, such as fighter jets and tanks. The savings—plus the additional funds that were expected—were to underwrite new weapons relying on stealth, precision-guidance, and far-flung sensor networks.

The fiscal 2002 budget resolution (H Con Res 83), adopted in May, put the temporary ceiling for national defense at $325.1 billion. After months of delay, and with Rumsfeld's study still evolving, Bush on June 27 requested an additional $18.4 billion, bringing the total defense request up to about $343.5 billion. Most of the money was earmarked for pay, medical care, facilities, and other routine operating expenses. Republicans for years had contended that the Clinton administration was underfunding these sections of the budget, and Rumsfeld insisted that the shortfalls were worse than he anticipated.

Many pro-military lawmakers complained that the request fell far short of the increases recommended by a number of senior military leaders and private defense specialists. They were particularly unhappy that very little of the money would go to replace aging weapons or to modernize U.S. forces with new technologies that would make them more lethal and more agile, as Bush and Rumsfeld repeatedly had promised. Pro-defense Democrats complained that Bush's tax cut had cut so deeply into projected budget surpluses that it was hamstringing efforts to bolster the Pentagon. But the Sept. 11 attacks, the campaign against terrorism, and the sudden war-footing significantly altered the budget dynamic, and the hard choices on where to spend money were postponed. Rumsfeld said the administration's new defense strategy would be reflected in the fiscal 2003 budget. (Tax cuts, pp. 89, 105)

Several lawmakers also balked at the administration's call for a new round of base closings and Rumsfeld's plans to retire some B-1 bombers. The president's proposed hike in spending on a missile defense system, a 56 percent increase over the fiscal 2001 level, was sharply criticized by several Democrats.

HOUSE COMMITTEE ACTION

The House Armed Services Committee reported its $343 billion version of the defense bill (HR 2586—H Rept 107-194) on Sept. 4, 2001. The committee had approved the bill on Aug. 1 but put off reporting it until the House reconvened in September in order to hedge against the possibility that Congress might decide in the fall to cut billions of dollars from Bush's defense request to balance the books. Waiting until September not only would make it easier for the panel to rewrite the measure before it reached the floor, but also would give authorizers some control over defense allocations. Otherwise, House and Senate appropriators—not the authorizers—would be the ones making adjustments for changing fiscal conditions.

The committee made only minor changes in Bush's proposal for spending the money, amid members' complaints that Bush's tax cut and the economic slowdown had created a budget squeeze. Specifically, lawmakers said the four services' list of "unfunded priorities"—which added up to more than $32 billion—would remain largely unfunded.

The Armed Services Committee defeated a Democratic move to block administration plans to deploy antimissile rockets at a military base in Alaska. But on some other contentious issues, the committee challenged Bush administration proposals. One provision in the committee bill prevented the navy from closing a training range on the Puerto Rican island of Vieques, as Bush had promised, without a replacement. Another blocked the retirement of some B-1 bombers assigned to the Air National Guard until several reports related to the plan were submitted to Congress. In addition, although the White House had made it clear it wanted a new round of military base closings, the committee took no action.

The committee trimmed $135 million for consultants from Bush's $8.3 billion missile defense request. In a rare break with the panel's long tradition of bipartisanship, Democrats attempted to shift nearly $1 billion more from the missile defense request to other projects, but the amendment was rejected on a party-line vote. The Democrats' proposal was seen as both an attempt to get more money for some widely supported programs and another gambit in the unfolding, largely partisan war over Bush's greatly broadened and accelerated antimissile effort. Nearly 60 percent of the proposed cut would have come from the plan to install five test missiles in launch silos with their maintenance and communications equipment at Fort Greely in eastern Alaska. The Pentagon considered the base a test site; critics said it was a back-door effort to deploy weapons in violation of the ABM Treaty. Administration officials acknowledged that the missiles would provide a rudimentary defense against an attack.

The committee also voted to delay the retirement of thirty-three B-1 bombers at bases in Georgia, Kansas, and Idaho, pending a military review. The bill added $100 million for their continued operation.

On the issue of Vieques, the committee included a provision to prohibit closing the Puerto Rico bombing range until the Pentagon found a single replacement site. The navy had used the range since 1941. It was the only site where navy and marine forces could simultaneously practice coordinated attacks with aircraft, marine amphibious landing units, and naval gunfire, all using live ammunition. But long-simmering resentment over what residents claimed was high-handed treatment by the navy crystallized into a demand for an end to live-fire training after a bomb killed a civilian range employee in April 1999. The training was halted, and the Clinton administration worked out an agreement with Puerto Rican governor Pedro Rossello that called for a referendum on the island of Vieques to determine whether the navy would stay or go. If residents voted the navy out, the service would have to leave in 2003.

The navy's decision to resume live-fire training after a year's suspension set off protests. In one well-publicized incident in April 2001, Rep. Luis V. Gutierrez, D-Ill., was arrested, along with more than 160 others, including entertainment and political figures, for entering the navy property to protest. With Rossello's successor, Gov. Sila Maria Calderon, pushing for the training operations to end immediately, the Bush administration in June 2001 announced that the navy would stop using the bombing range by 2003. The House Armed Services Committee went along with Bush's proposal to repeal a provision in the fiscal 2001 defense authorization bill (PL 106-398) that had required the referendum on the firing range's future. (PL 106-398, Congress and the Nation Vol. X, p. 290)

The committee rejected Bush's assumption that $190 million would be saved by narrowing the application of the Davis-Bacon Act, which linked wage rates on federal construction projects to prevailing local wages. Under existing law, projects costing less than $2,000 were exempt from Davis-Bacon; the administration proposed raising that threshold to $1 million. Repealing Davis-Bacon had long been a goal of Republicans, who argued that the law made the government pay union wages that were higher than the prevailing wages in a local area. Organized labor adamantly opposed such a change.

The committee also rejected the administration's projection of $140 million in savings from contracting out some of the work done by government-operated depots.

The committee agreed to an amendment making it easier for federal employees to compete successfully with private companies for Defense Department work.

HOUSE FLOOR ACTION

The House passed HR 2586 on Sept. 25 by a vote of 398–17. In preparation for conference the House subsequently took up the Senate-passed bill (S 1438), substituted the text of HR 2586, and passed S 1438 by voice vote on Oct. 17.

The Sept. 11 terrorist attacks, and the push for bipartisanship in their aftermath overwhelmed several efforts to challenge the president's defense priorities.

Before the attacks, Armed Services Committee Democrats John M. Spratt Jr. of South Carolina and Ike Skelton of

Missouri had planned to offer an amendment that would have cut an additional $920 million from the antimissile program. But House Democrats abandoned those plans, agreeing instead with Republicans on a $265 million reduction in addition to the $135 million already cut in committee. The House adopted by voice vote Sept. 25 an amendment offered by Armed Services Committee Chair Bob Stump, R-Ariz., to cut the $400 million from Bush's request and add $400 million to the budget to beef up intelligence and antiterrorism programs.

The only real fight came on the perennially contentious effort, pursued by administrations of both parties, to contract out to private companies some of the work performed by federal employees. The language adopted in committee to enable federal employees to compete with private companies for Pentagon work was reversed as part of an amendment offered by Stump and adopted by voice vote Sept. 25. The new provision gave the Pentagon more leeway to contract out government jobs. A procedural move by Minority Whip David E. Bonior, D-Mich., to reinstate the committee language was rejected Sept. 25 on a 197–221 vote that broke nearly along party lines.

In other action that day the House adopted 242–173 a proposal by James A. Traficant Jr., D-Ohio, to allow military personnel to be assigned to border patrol and customs duties, at the request of the attorney general and the Treasury secretary. Reprising what had become an annual battle, the House rejected 199–217 an amendment by Loretta Sanchez, D-Calif., to allow female service members or their dependents overseas to obtain privately funded abortions in military hospitals. Sanchez's amendment had been defeated in committee as well.

SENATE COMMITTEE ACTION

The Senate Armed Services Committee reported its defense authorization (S 1416—S Rept 107-62) on Sept. 12. The bill had been approved Sept. 7 and therefore did not reflect reaction to the Sept. 11 terrorist attacks.

Committee approval—on a party-line vote of 13–12—came after a divisive fight in which the majority Democrats prevailed in limiting Bush's missile defense program. Underscoring the depth of partisan feeling on the issue, the senior Democrat and Republican on the committee for the first time in decades held separate news conferences on the bill.

The bill cut $1.3 billion from Bush's $8.3 billion request for missile defense and prohibited any antimissile tests that violated the ABM Treaty unless Congress voted to allow the test or the United States and Russia agreed to change the treaty so it would not be violated. Attempts by John W. Warner, ranking Republican on the committee, to restore $1 billion of the funding and to eliminate the curbs on testing failed on party-line votes. Defense Secretary Rumsfeld warned that if the provisions remained in the bill he would recommend a presidential veto.

The other changes made to Bush's defense budget request were minor in comparison to the action on missile defense.

The committee added funds to increase the housing allowance for service personnel living off base, to accelerate the conversion of submarines so they could carry conventionally armed cruise missiles, to increase to thirty-five from twenty-five the number of Blackhawk-type helicopters authorized, to upgrade B-52 and B-2 bombers, and to temporarily keep in service thirty-three B-1 bombers that the administration wanted to retire.

The bill cut the administration's request for funds for continued development and production of the V-22 Osprey tilt-rotor aircraft, the troubled plane that was being redesigned after two crashes in 2000 resulted in twenty-three deaths. The Osprey, which took off and landed like a helicopter but tilted its engines to fly like a plane, could travel faster, farther, and more quietly with a larger payload than existing helicopters. Marine leaders, who had been lobbying vigorously for the plane for years, planned to use the revolutionary aircraft as a troop carrier and insisted that it was vital to their future. The Osprey program was expected to cost $40 billion, including development and a total of 458 planes over several decades—360 for the marines, 50 for the air force, and 48 for the navy. Among the Osprey's strongest supporters on Capitol Hill were lawmakers—many of them influential—from Texas and Pennsylvania, where the aircraft was largely manufactured by the Boeing Co. and Bell Helicopter Textron.

The Armed Services panel also trimmed funding to continue development of the Joint Strike Fighter, three versions of which were planned to replace 1970s-era jets.

The Armed Services Committee went along with the president's proposal for another round of base closings in 2003 and agreed to a pay raise of at least 5 percent for all military personnel.

SENATE FLOOR ACTION

The Senate passed S 1438, a later version of the fiscal 2002 defense authorization bill, on Oct. 2 by a vote of 99–0. The terrorist attacks and the push for bipartisanship tamped down many potential fights.

Like their House counterparts Senate Democrats abandoned any concerted effort to limit Bush's missile defense program. Days after the attacks Democrats dropped their efforts to limit tests that would violate the ABM Treaty. On Sept. 21 the Senate adopted by voice vote an amendment, offered by Senate Armed Services Chair Carl Levin, D-Mich., and committee ranking Republican Warner, that restored $1.3 billion to the bill. The amendment allowed Bush to use the money either to replace the $1.3 billion Levin's committee cut from the missile defense request or to pay for antiterrorist efforts.

That left base closings as the most contentious issue during nearly two weeks of floor debate. Opponents of base closings contended that the Sept. 11 terrorist attacks undermined the argument for eliminating facilities because the Pentagon was not even close to deciding what new organizations or deployments would be needed in a stepped-up war against terrorism. Opponents also argued that, with the softening economy, localities should not be confronted with the threat of losing a major source of jobs. Supporters of further closings countered that the terrorist attacks made it imperative that the Pentagon shed unneeded bases to free up money to improve other installations.

The Senate on Sept. 25 tabled (killed) an amendment by Jim Bunning, R-Ky., to strip the authority for base closings from the bill by a **key vote of 53–47 (R 21–28; D 31--19; I 1–0)**. *(2001 key votes, p. 801)*

The Senate rejected an attempt by Phil Gramm, R-Texas, to scrap a provision in the bill that allowed private companies to compete with federal prison work programs to sell office furniture and other goods and services to the Pentagon. Under existing law the Defense Department, like other federal agencies, was required to purchase items and services from federal prison work programs, if available. For years, industry, small business, and organized labor had tried to break what they said was an unfair monopoly, and this time the Senate agreed, voting 74–24 on Sept. 25 to table a proposal by Warner to drop the provision. A week later, the Senate adopted by voice vote an amendment by Gramm and Craig Thomas, R-Wyo., that made minor changes in the provision.

The Senate adopted a variety of noncontroversial amendments. Among them was one by Warner, approved by voice vote, to clear the way for rebuilding the Pentagon, which was badly damaged on Sept. 11. Warner proposed repealing a cap of $1.1 billion on spending to renovate the Pentagon that had been included in the fiscal 1997 defense authorization bill (PL 104-201) to control the cost of a reconstruction project slated to run through 2012. The first phase of that work was nearly complete when a hijacked airliner crashed into the newly renovated section of the building.

Also adopted by voice vote was an amendment by Russ D. Feingold, D-Wis., to require a report to Congress on technical problems with the V-22 Osprey aircraft.

CONFERENCE ACTION

On Dec. 13, 2001, the House adopted the conference report (H Rept 107-333) by a vote of 382–40, and the Senate cleared it by a vote of 96–2.

Final agreement had come after a month-long impasse over base closings. In a Nov. 15 letter to Congress Rumsfeld had raised the specter of a presidential veto if the final bill did not include a base-closing provision. All the living Defense secretaries, except Vice President Dick Cheney, lent their support to another round of base closings in 2003. What finally spurred the authorizers to compromise on a new round in 2005, however, was the push to complete legislation in the closing weeks of the session—and their fear of being marginalized in the defense debate as the defense appropriations bill (HR 3338) brought their bill forward. *(2002 defense appropriations, p. 316)*

While the final bill did not embody the wide-ranging changes Rumsfeld had talked about early in the year, it took

some modest steps to transform the military to deal with unconventional threats such as terrorism.

Congress strongly backed the notion of equipping long-range weapons with high-tech sensors that would enable them to locate and attack ground targets. Congress added money to modify B-2 bombers and to buy or modify remotely piloted airplanes. In the report accompanying the bill House and Senate conferees ordered the Pentagon to produce a long-range plan to modernize its fleet of reconnaissance planes, many of which were modified versions of aging Boeing jetliners.

In a nod to Bush's work on a global coalition against terrorism, and as the United States and Russia moved toward reducing their respective nuclear arsenals, the bill repealed a provision of law (PL 105-85) prohibiting any reduction in long-range missile and bomber forces until the 1993 U.S.-Russia Strategic Arms Reduction Talks (START II) treaty took effect. The lower house of the Russian parliament, the Duma, had agreed to the treaty in 2000, but with conditions—including continued adherence to the ABM Treaty—that made it uncertain whether or when the pact would go into effect. *(START II background, Congress and the Nation Vol. IX, pp. 292, 320)*

As in the House version, the final bill rejected Bush's assumption that the Pentagon could save $190 million by increasing the Davis-Bacon threshold and $140 million by shifting some scheduled overhauls of aircraft and other equipment from government-operated depots to private contractors. To make up the savings the bill cut $330 million across the board from Bush's operations and maintenance budget.

MAJOR PROVISIONS

As signed into law on Dec. 28, 2001, S 1438 authorized $343.3 billion in defense spending in fiscal 2002, roughly equal to the president's request.

Military Personnel

Authorized $82.3 billion for military personnel.

Authorized for fiscal 2002 the requested active-duty force of 1,387,400, an increase of 5,158 over the previous fiscal year's authorized ceiling.

Authorized an average pay increase of 4.6 percent for military personnel, equal to what Bush sought.

Authorized $17.6 billion for defense health programs, about the same as Bush requested but $6 billion more than the previous fiscal year. The fiscal 2001 authorization bill (PL 106-398) had expanded the military's health care system, ensuring lifetime care for Medicare-eligible military retirees and their families, beginning in 2002. *(2001 defense authorization, Congress and the Nation Vol. X, p. 290)*

Operations and Maintenance

Authorized $123.9 billion.

DEFENSE LEADERSHIP

Secretary of Defense

Just hours after President George W. Bush's inauguration on Jan. 20, 2001, Donald H. Rumsfeld was confirmed as secretary of defense by voice vote of the Senate. It was not a first for Rumsfeld, who was secretary from 1975 to 1977 during the administration of President Gerald R. Ford. *(Bush nominations, p. 919)*

Rumsfeld had won widespread praise for his managerial experience, familiarity with key defense issues, and personal stature. In addition to his previous tour at the Pentagon, his credentials included service as a member of the House (1963–1969), NATO ambassador under President Richard M. Nixon, White House chief of staff for President Ford, and chair of a congressionally mandated bipartisan commission on missile defense in 1998. Rumsfeld also had been the chief executive officer of two corporations. *(Antimissile deployment, Congress and the Nation Vol. X, p. 266)*

With Rumsfeld's high-profile role on the missile defense issue and Bush's support for deployment of such a system, the topic was a focal point of Rumsfeld's six-hour confirmation hearing before the Senate Armed Services Committee on Jan. 11. The nominee stressed the importance of protecting the United States and its allies from at least a small number of missiles. He told the committee that the new administration would pursue Russian agreement to deploy a missile defense, which would require changes in the 1972 Anti-Ballistic Missile (ABM) Treaty, but he made it clear that he considered the treaty to be "ancient history."

Despite calls from some quarters for Rumsfeld's resignation in the wake of a 2004 scandal over the abuse of Iraqi prisoners by U.S. military personnel, Rumsfeld continued to have the president's support and was asked to stay on as secretary of defense in Bush's second term. *(Abu Ghraib prison scandal, pp. 359, 360)*

Deputy Secretary of Defense

President Bush nominated veteran national security official Paul Wolfowitz to serve as deputy secretary of defense—the No. 2 job at the Pentagon. He was confirmed by voice vote of the Senate on Feb. 28, 2001.

Wolfowitz's public service included the post of deputy assistant secretary of defense for regional programs during the administration of Jimmy Carter, top policy posts at the State Department and appointment as ambassador to Indonesia during the administration of Ronald Reagan, and the post of undersecretary of defense for policy—the No. 3 job in the department—under President George H. W. Bush. He also served on the 1998 Ballistic Missile Defense Commission chaired by Rumsfeld. He was dean of the School of Advanced International Studies at Johns Hopkins University at the time of his 2001 appointment.

Wolfowitz was part of a group of prominent "neoconservatives" in the George W. Bush administration who promoted a strategic vision of American global leadership. Others included Vice President Dick Cheney and Rumsfeld. In his role at the Pentagon, Wolfowitz became one of the chief architects of the war in Iraq.

Because of that role Bush's decision early in his second administration to nominate Wolfowitz to succeed James D. Wolfensohn as head of the World Bank was controversial. Nonetheless, the board of the World Bank unanimously confirmed his nomination March 31, 2005.

Joint Chiefs Chairman

Gen. Richard B. Myers won voice vote approval from the Senate on Sept. 14, 2001, to succeed Gen. Henry H. Shelton as chairman of the Joint Chiefs of Staff. Myers assumed the post on Oct. 1, the day after Shelton retired.

Myers, a career air force officer, had been serving as the vice chairman of the Joint Chiefs of Staff since March 2000. Prior positions included that of commander in chief of the North American Aerospace Defense Command and U.S. Space Command, and commander of the Air Force Space Command and the Pacific Air Forces.

Facilities

Authorized $10.5 billion for military construction and family housing.

Repealed a $1.1 billion cap in existing law (PL 104-201) on Pentagon renovations, as had the Senate bill.

Missile Defense

Authorized $8.3 billion for development of a missile defense system, the full amount requested by Bush for the cornerstone of his plans for a future military force. The amount was a $3 billion increase over fiscal 2001. An announcement by Bush in December 2001 that the United States would abandon the ABM Treaty cleared the way for construction of a site in Alaska. *(Missile defense, p. 331)*

Missiles

Added $15 million to the $50 million requested for the Tomahawk missile program to accelerate work on a new, less costly version that could hover over a battlefield until a target location was radioed to the missile.

Repealed restrictions on retiring strategic weapons, as had the Senate bill. The House would have repealed the restrictions only as they affected the MX missile. As in the Senate bill the final measure added $12 million for equipment to be used in retiring the MX.

Ground Forces

Authorized the $511 million requested for the army to develop a futuristic combat vehicle, intended to be as lethal as a 70-ton M-1 tank but less than one-third the weight. A C-130 cargo plane could transport the vehicle.

Authorized the $663 million requested to buy off-the-shelf armored cars for combat units. Congress added $35 million to accelerate work on versions of the armored car and a commercial truck with hybrid-electric propulsion. Theoretically such systems would reduce the amount of fuel required by a combat unit, cutting the amount of supplies that would have to be hauled to the front line and making combat units more agile.

Aviation Forces

Authorized $2.7 billion, as requested by Bush, for thirteen F-22 Raptors, the air force's next generation fighter plane, with an additional $865 million for research and development.

Authorized $1.5 billion, close to the administration's request, for development of the Joint Strike Fighter, an aircraft to be used by the air force, navy, and Marine Corps.

Authorized $3.1 billion for forty-eight F/A-18 E/F aircraft, the navy's upgrade of the existing F/A-18 C/D.

Authorized the air force to proceed with the retirement of thirty-three B-1 bombers after providing Congress with a report on the consolidation. The bill fulfilled Bush's request for $96 million for B-1 modifications and $195 million for research and development. It also added $100 million for the Air National Guard B-1 fleet until the retirement of the thirty-three aircraft was completed.

Added $63 million to modify B-2 bombers to enable them to strike newly discovered targets with so-called smart bombs.

Added $33 million to the $233 million Bush requested to buy or modify various remotely piloted airplanes with target detection equipment.

Added $30 million to increase the number of Marine Corps Harrier jets equipped with an Israeli-designed pod that carried night-vision television designed to hunt for ground targets and a laser to direct smart bombs. Northrop Grumman Corp. built the system.

Naval Forces

Authorized $594 million for the navy's next generation surface combat ship, the DD-21.

Authorized $1.6 billion, as requested, to purchase the fourth boat in the *Virginia*-class of attack submarines to replace the *Los Angeles*-class subs, which were being retired.

Added $178 million for the navy to modify four Trident submarines to carry 154 Tomahawk cruise missiles each; at the time the subs were carrying twenty-four nuclear-armed ballistic missiles. Bush had sought $116 million to begin modification of just two submarines.

Authorized $3 billion, as requested, for three *Arleigh Burke*-class Aegis guided-missile destroyers, the DDG-51.

Included $594 million of the $644 million requested to build a new class of destroyers designed to attack ground targets with precision-guided cannon shells and missiles. The cut reflected the navy's decision to reorganize the program, which would delay the service's choice between two competing teams of shipbuilders.

Added $11 million to the $20 million requested for the navy to begin work on a new smaller warship intended to operate close to shore. To protect existing boats, $7.5 million was authorized to equip the ships with night-vision television cameras capable of detecting small, missile-launching boats. Another $5 million was authorized to modify computer-operated anti-aircraft guns designed to shoot down approaching cruise missiles.

Provided $104 million in loan guarantees for commercial shipbuilders, $100 million more than Bush sought.

Air Transport

Authorized $1.3 billion for eleven V-22 Ospreys for the Marine Corps—$70 million and one aircraft less than Bush requested; $447 million for V-22 navy research and development—$100 million less than requested; and the $102 million Bush sought for special operations command of V-22 component development. The bill also required a report to Congress on technical problems with the aircraft.

Base Closings

Authorized another round of base closings, but not until 2005, using the same process as in the 1991 and 1996 rounds. An independent commission, chosen by the president and Congress, would review the Pentagon's proposed shutdown and realignment list and pick the bases to close. Congress would have to accept or reject the list in toto.

Antiterrorim

Authorized $6 billion for Defense Department programs to combat terrorism.

Nuclear Weapons

Authorized $14.4 billion for defense-related activities carried out primarily by the Energy Department.

Other Provisions

Cancelled a controversial local referendum on the future of the navy bombing range on the Puerto Rican island of Vieques, putting the future of the facility in the hands of the navy. Before closing the range the navy was required to find a qualified replacement site or sites. The Bush administration had announced on June 14, 2001, that the navy would stop using the range by 2003.

MILITARY BASE CLOSINGS: A VOLATILE ISSUE

President George W. Bush's 2001 request for congressional approval of another round of military base closings in 2003 produced a heated debate on Capitol Hill. The Senate went along with the president's request, but House members adamantly opposed further closings. In the end, House-Senate negotiators included a base closing provision in their version of the fiscal 2002 defense authorization bill (S 1438—PL 107-107), but the new round was delayed until 2005.

Base closure was always a volatile issue.

With the strong support of senior military officers, Bush insisted that billions of dollars to modernize and train the services were being wasted maintaining unneeded bases. The Pentagon said it had 20 to 25 percent more capacity than it needed and would save $3 billion a year by disposing of some of it.

But many members of Congress had long opposed the closings of bases, which usually were major contributors to local economies. For decades that opposition had been compounded by the suspicion that presidents used political criteria to decide which bases to close and which to keep open. Moreover, since the Sept. 11, 2001, terrorist attacks base-closing opponents had argued that giving up any installations was premature until the Pentagon identified its needs in light of the emphasis on homeland defense and counterterrorism operations abroad.

Base-Closing Process

The base-closing process was designed to prevent—or at least minimize—congressional or other political interference.

To circumvent lawmakers' efforts to block closure of individual bases, Congress in 1988 passed a law (PL 100-526) creating an independent commission to make recommendations on base closings. The Pentagon and Congress had to accept or reject the report of the Commission on Base Realignment and Closure (BRAC) in its entirety. *(Congress and the Nation Vol. VII, p. 335)*

Congress refined the process in 1990 with another law (PL 101-510) that charged the Defense Department with drawing up an initial list of bases for consideration by the commission. The commission's list of recommended closings would have to be accepted or rejected in its entirety by the president and Congress. The procedure was to be used for the next three Congresses. *(Congress and the Nation Vol. VIII, p. 353; Vol. IX, pp. 288, 319)*

But the process suffered a severe political blow during the 1995 round. The commission recommended closing two maintenance depots—one in California and one in Texas. As an alternative to shutting the depots in the two politically powerful states, President Bill Clinton proposed having private contractors take over maintenance work at the sites. The decision enraged many Republicans, who charged that Clinton could not be trusted to respect the apolitical nature of the process.

Clinton's actions were the main reason that lawmakers did not agree until 2001 to schedule another round of closings.

Cost Effectiveness

The four rounds of base closings—in 1988, 1991, 1993, and 1995—resulted in the decision to close, reduce the size of, or otherwise change domestic military bases. Many of those actions were minor, and some reversed decisions made in earlier rounds. According to the General Accounting Office (GAO) in 2001, the four rounds had closed 451 facilities of varying size.

The Pentagon had estimated that those four rounds would yield net savings of $15.5 billion by the end of fiscal 2001 and annual savings of $6.1 billion each year thereafter. Savings began to exceed costs in 1998.

Base closing critics contended that the savings figure was an estimate that the Defense Department could not justify in detail. The only clear impact on the Pentagon's budget, they argued, was the billions of dollars it cost not only to move units from a base that was being closed to another site, but also to build the needed facilities at the new location.

But the GAO, the Congressional Budget Office, and various Pentagon accounting agencies concurred that although the department's estimate of net savings contained some uncertain assumptions, the closures had saved plenty of money.

The Defense Department's "accounting systems, like all accounting systems, are not oriented to identifying and tracking savings," the GAO said in a July 2001 report. The congressional watchdog agency (which was renamed the Government Accountability Office in mid-2004) also pointed out that the Pentagon's estimate of the cost of base closings did not include $1.2 billion in federal grants to communities affected by the closings. "Nevertheless, we and others have consistently expressed the view that these factors are not significant enough to outweigh the fact that substantial savings are being generated from the closure process," the report said.

Using the Pentagon's data the GAO calculated that through fiscal 2001 base closings cost $22.2 billion, with most of that expense going to operating costs ($7.7 billion), construction of new facilities ($6.7 billion), and environmental cleanup at the sites being closed ($7 billion).

On the other hand, the GAO estimated the amount the Pentagon did not have to spend—and, thus, saved—totaled $37.7 billion. In 1998 the Defense Department estimated that the four rounds of base closings had eliminated 71,000 federal civilian jobs and 39,800 military positions.

Meanwhile, communities found uses for the facilities. Austin, Texas, for example, turned the Bergstrom Air Force Base into an international airport. Lowry Air Force Base on the outskirts of Denver became the site of new housing, parkland, schools, and businesses.

Authorized $820 million for the military's drug interdiction efforts.

Repealed a provision of the fiscal 1998 defense authorization bill (PL 105-85) that banned any reduction in the long-range missile and bomber forces until the 1993 U.S-Russia START II arms reduction treaty took effect.

Included a Senate provision allowing private contractors to compete with federal prison work programs to sell office furniture and other goods and services to the Defense Department.

2002 Defense Appropriations

Congress in 2001 cleared a $317.5 billion fiscal 2002 Defense Department appropriations bill. The spending bill (HR 3338—PL 107-117) had been dogged by controversy and delay, much of it tied to a separate fight between Congress and the Bush administration over emergency funding for counterterrorism and for New York City's recovery from the Sept. 11 terrorist attacks. HR 3338 did not clear until the final day of the session, making it the last of the thirteen regular appropriations measures sent to the White House.

HR 3338 appropriated $1.9 billion less than President George W. Bush requested. But when combined with funds in other appropriations bills—including $10.5 billion in the military construction appropriations bill (HR 2904—PL 107-64) and $14.5 billion in the energy and water development appropriations bill (HR 2311—PL 107-66)—HR 3338 brought regular fiscal 2002 defense spending to about $343.3 billion, close to Bush's $343.5 billion request. In addition, HR 3338 allocated $3.5 billion in emergency defense funding that had been included in an antiterrorism emergency supplemental bill (HR 2888—PL 107-38). *(2002 military construction, p. 319; antiterrorism supplemental, p. 319)*

As was customary, HR 3338 closely followed the outlines of the annual defense authorization bill (S 1438—PL 107-107). Both bills postponed tough choices about the future shape of the military and funded most of the administration's requests—from cold war–style weapons to equipment for unconventional battles.

The House passed a defense bill that for the most part only made changes at the margins to Bush's defense budget. In the Senate lawmakers added a controversial provision allowing the air force to dispose of forty-year-old refueling tankers and lease replacements from the Boeing Co., a financial boon for the airline manufacturer hard hit by the downturn in the industry. Some critics derided the deal as a corporate bailout.*(Boeing tanker controversy, p. 348)*

House and Senate negotiators spent the final weeks of the session trying to resolve disagreements with the administration over the leasing deal, as well as differences over shipbuilding. Controversy remained even after Congress cleared HR 3338, as some opponents of the leasing deal—estimated to cost $20 billion over ten years—vowed not to let the issue rest.

HOUSE ACTION

The House passed its version of HR 3338 on Nov. 28, 2001, by a vote of 406–20. The House Appropriations Committee had reported the $317.5 billion funding bill (H Rept 107-298) on Nov. 19.

The measure had an inauspicious start. Members of the House Defense Appropriations Subcommittee were meeting in the Capitol to begin work on the bill the morning of Sept. 11 when the session was suddenly canceled and the building evacuated shortly after terrorists crashed jetliners into the World Trade Center and the Pentagon.

Nearly a month later, on Oct. 9, the subcommittee tried again, but that session was canceled as well—this time to protest Bush's decision to limit the number of lawmakers who would be briefed on secret information about the administration's counterterrorism campaign. Leaks of information and published reports citing congressional sources infuriated Bush, who tried to restrict the closed sessions. The White House eventually relented, allowing key members of defense, foreign policy, and intelligence oversight committees to be briefed in closed meetings.

The subcommittee finally met and approved the bill on Oct. 10. Panel members provided no details, reflecting the secretive atmosphere following the dispute with the White House.

When the full House Appropriations Committee met to consider the defense measure, the terrorist attacks and the subsequent war in Afghanistan loomed large. The committee added nearly $1.7 billion for extra antiterrorism efforts by the Pentagon and CIA, including money to protect against cyberterror attacks on computers and to develop and stockpile vaccines and antibiotics to respond to the potential threat of biological warfare. The $1.7 billion increase was mostly offset by across-the-board cuts of more than $1.5 billion that the committee ordered the Defense Department to absorb by reducing the payroll at headquarters, hiring fewer consultants, and cutting back on the use of government credit cards for small purchases. *(Sept. 11 terrorist attacks, p. 229; war in Afghanistan, pp. 230, 234)*

The committee made relatively minor changes to the amounts requested for hundreds of procurement and research programs. However, there were a few significant initiatives. Among them was an add-on of $340 million to test the feasibility of using modified Boeing 767 jetliners to replace hundreds of aging midair refueling tankers and various types of large electronic eavesdropping and radar planes. The plan was promoted by Air Force Chief of Staff Gen. John Jumper and Defense Appropriations Subcommittee member Norm Dicks, D-Wash., a tireless advocate for Boeing, his state's economic linchpin. The committee also added $820 million for a fourth Aegis destroyer—the administration requested three—and $463 million to accelerate the conversion of four submarines, two more than requested, to carry Tomahawk cruise missiles.

The full Appropriations Committee approved the defense measure on Oct. 24, but committee chair C. W. Bill Young,

R-Fla., delayed filing the measure until appropriators decided what and how much to include in a supplemental spending package that was to be attached to the defense bill.

More than a month later, the House overwhelmingly passed HR 3338. Paired with the defense funding bill was a $20 billion emergency spending package, with $7.3 billion to pay for the war in Afghanistan, rebuild the section of the Pentagon damaged Sept. 11, and otherwise boost military readiness. With many of the legislative fights already played out on the defense authorization bill, much of the floor debate focused on the emergency spending. Democrats, who complained that the emergency spending provisions were woefully inadequate, were incensed that GOP leaders brought the bill to the floor under a rule that blocked three Democratic amendments to increase spending. Despite their objections, the House agreed 216–211 to debate the bill on the leadership's terms.

SENATE ACTION

The Senate passed its version of HR 3338 on Dec. 7 by voice vote. The Senate Appropriations Committee had reported the $317 billion bill (S Rept 107-109) on Dec. 4.

The measure largely tracked Bush's request, but the Appropriations Committee angered the administration by slashing $600 million from the $2.8 billion requested for operations in Bosnia and Kosovo. The committee argued that the Defense Department had hundreds of millions of dollars left in its Balkans operations account and the number of troops in the region had declined steadily.

Far more contentious was the committee's decision to allow the air force to lease 100 Boeing 767s for the crucial mission of refueling aircraft in midair. Under the Senate plan the air force would be able to dispose of 136 smaller Boeing tankers that had become very expensive to maintain after four decades of hard use. Proponents of the plan argued that the 767s would be cheaper to operate than the aging tankers and that the leasing arrangement would reduce the initial cost of the program. Critics feared that the relatively low short-term cost would mask a higher price tag in the long run. Office of Management and Budget (OMB) Director Mitchell E. Daniels Jr. strongly opposed a proposal to lease the planes for twenty years, arguing that it would cost more than buying the aircraft.

Another controversial issue during floor debate was a proposed International Criminal Court. The court was supposed to handle war crimes and other human rights violations, but U.S. military leaders and many lawmakers contended that it would expose U.S. troops to politically motivated accusations and trials. The Senate on Dec. 7 adopted 78–21 an amendment by Jesse Helms, R-N.C., to bar U.S. cooperation with the court. The amendment also restricted U.S. participation in U.N. peacekeeping operations unless U.S. troops were exempted from prosecution by the court, and it barred U.S. military aid to countries unless they signed agreements to shield U.S. troops from being handed over to the court. A counter amendment by Christopher J. Dodd, D-Conn., that would have permitted significant U.S. cooperation with the court to try war criminals was rejected 48–51. (*International Criminal Court, p. 256*)

By voice vote the Senate adopted dozens of minor amendments, including seventy-three that earmarked a total of $438 million for specific projects. Only two of the seventy-three involved more than $10 million. One of those, an amendment offered by Richard G. Lugar, R-Ind., restored $46 million that the Appropriations Committee had cut from the administration's $403 million request for the so-called Nunn-Lugar program. Named for its sponsors, former senator Sam Nunn, D-Ga. (1972–1997), and Lugar, the program was intended to help former Soviet republics dispose of nuclear, chemical, and biological weapons.

Like the House-passed bill the Senate version included the $20 billion supplemental appropriations package. Of that total, $2 billion was to go to defense.

CONFERENCE ACTION

The House adopted the conference report on HR 3338 (H Rept 107—107-350) on Dec. 20, 2001, by a vote of 408–6. The Senate agreed to it later that day 94–2.

Agreement on leasing Boeing 767s for use as refueling tankers cleared the way for House and Senate conferees to sign off on the bill. Boeing's decision months earlier to move its corporate headquarters from Seattle to Chicago had gained the aircraft builder a powerful patron—House Speaker J. Dennis Hastert, R-Ill. Washington's congressional delegation had remained loyal to Boeing, which maintained jet plants in the Puget Sound region of Washington, and members lobbied aggressively to get the $20 billion, ten-year deal in the defense bill. The idea faced hurdles, including resistance from OMB, but several meetings and the support of Hastert sealed the deal.

Conferees accepted the president's request for three Aegis destroyers, dropping the House-approved funding for a fourth ship. Supporters of the extra ship had argued that it was needed to keep the two shipbuilding yards in Mississippi and Maine busy because of delays in designing a new class of destroyers.

The conference committee provided funding for procurement of nine V-22 Ospreys for the Marine Corps and two of the aircraft for the Special Operations Forces. Despite two crashes involving the V-22 that killed twenty-three people in 2000, the Pentagon and Congress continued to buy more of the controversial tilt-rotor aircraft.

Conferees dropped the controversial Senate amendment on the International Criminal Court but did bar any of the bill's funds from going to assist or support the court.

MAJOR PROVISIONS

As signed into law Jan. 10, 2002, HR 3338—PL 107-117 appropriated $317.5 billion for Defense Department spending in fiscal 2002.

The final bill also allocated $20 billion in emergency supplemental spending, including $3.5 billion for defense. Bush had requested $7.3 billion for defense. *(Antiterrorism supplemental, below)*

Major provisions of HR 3338:

Military Personnel

Appropriated $82 billion for military personnel.

Included a 4.6 percent pay increase for military personnel, which was specified in the fiscal 2002 defense authorization bill, as well as targeted pay raises for a variety of enlisted personnel and officer grades.

Set a ceiling on the number of active-duty personnel in fiscal 2002 at 1,387,400, as requested.

Operations and Maintenance

Appropriated $105 billion.

Missile Defense

Appropriated $7.8 billion of the $8.3 billion requested by Bush to develop and field missile defenses. The Pentagon was required to overhaul development of the Spaced-Based Infra-Red System (SBIRS)-Low program, a fleet of satellites carrying infrared telescopes to detect attacking missiles and help steer intercepting rockets. Arguing that the program was plagued with delays, technical shortcomings, and cost overruns, the conferees provided $250 million of the $385 million requested.

The bill also provided $100 million to pay the contract termination costs for a navy antimissile program that the Pentagon had decided to cancel. *(Navy program canceled, box p. 331)*

The bill met the president's request for $3.2 billion for ground-based midcourse defense programs. The total included $786 million in advanced funding for the Pacific missile defense test bed, including upgrades and construction at Fort Greely, Alaska.

Ground Forces

Appropriated $448 million, as the president requested, to continue developing the forty-ton Crusader mobile cannon, which was supposed to be operational by 2008. *(Crusader program cancelled, box p. 321)*

Aviation Forces

Authorized the air force to lease new, modified 767s from Boeing at an estimated cost of $20 billion over ten years. The 100 leased planes were to replace the existing fleet of forty-year-old refueling tankers. No funds were provided.

Appropriated $2.6 billion for thirteen F-22 Raptors, the air force's next generation fighter plane that was designed to replace the F-16, plus $882 million for research and development.

Appropriated $1.5 billion for development of the Joint Strike Fighter, about the amount sought by the administration. Three versions of the fighter were slated to replace several 1970s-vintage planes used by the navy, air force, and Marine Corps. The Pentagon had selected Lockheed Martin to build the plane.

Appropriated $3 billion for forty-eight of the F/A-18 E/F fighter jet, the navy's upgrade of the existing F/A-18 C/D.

Appropriated $155 million, as requested, to improve the capability of the B-2 stealth bomber, plus an additional $63 million for a data link to allow the planes to exchange targeting data with other U.S. aircraft, ships, and ground units. The House had proposed cutting the funds by $80 million.

Provided $250 million more than requested for remotely piloted drone aircraft, or unmanned aerial vehicles (UAVs), reflecting widespread consensus among House and Senate negotiators over the development of UAVs for reconnaissance. In Afghanistan, the drones were being equipped successfully with laser-guided missiles for combat.

Naval Forces

Appropriated $3 billion for three *Arleigh Burke*-class Aegis guided-missile destroyers, the DDG-51, as requested, and added $125 million in advanced funding for a fourth ship.

Appropriated $324 million to allow the navy to convert four Trident submarines, rather than the two requested, to carry dozens of Tomahawk cruise missiles each.

Appropriated $1.6 billion, as requested, to buy the fourth boat in the *Virginia*-class of new attack submarines to replace the retiring *Los Angeles*-class submarines.

Air and Sea Transport

Trimmed $36 million from the $2.9 billion requested for fifteen additional C-17 wide-body, long-range cargo jets, but added $143 million as a first installment toward buying more of the Boeing-built planes than the 134 already purchased or included in budget plans.

Provided $1 billion for procurement of nine V-22 Ospreys for the Marine Corps and two of the tilt-rotor aircraft for the Special Operations Forces.

Appropriated $267 million to continue work on a helicopter carrier and $371 million for a supply ship.

Antiterrorism

Appropriated $881 million for a new account devoted to activities to counter terrorism and other nonconventional threats.

Other Provisions

Appropriated $403 million for the Nunn-Lugar program to help former Soviet states dismantle nuclear, chemical, and biological weapons.

Barred the use of any of the bill's funds to support or assist the International Criminal Court and its activities.

2001–2002 Supplemental Appropriations

Congress approved a series of supplemental appropriations bills for fiscal 2001 and 2002 that included additional money for defense.

2001 SUPPLEMENTAL

Congress appropriated a net $5.8 billion for defense as part of a $6.5 billion fiscal 2001 supplemental spending bill (HR 2216—PL 107-20) that was signed into law July 24, 2001. The defense-related spending included money to replenish accounts that had been tapped to finance overseas operations in Kosovo. (*Fiscal 2001 supplemental appropriations, p. 57*)

The final bill appropriated $6.9 billion for defense, offset partially by $1.1 billion in rescissions in prior defense appropriations. The appropriations included $3 billion to replenish general operation and maintenance accounts; $1.6 billion for health programs; $515 million for military personnel; $573 million for procurement; $493 million for research, development, testing, and evaluation; $297 million for shipbuilding and conversion programs; and $277 million for nuclear weapons programs. Among the rescissions was $527 million for procurement of the troubled V-22 Osprey aircraft.

The versions passed by the House (HR 2216—H Rept 107-102) and the Senate (S 1077—S Rept 107-33) resulted in a conference package (H Rept 107-148) that closely tracked President George W. Bush's request for a net $6.5 billion in supplemental spending.

The final bill included Senate language barring the use of funds in the bill to retire any B-1 bombers. The Pentagon had planned to consolidate its B-1 force in South Dakota and Texas as part of an effort to save $165 million by shrinking the number of bombers—a move ardently opposed by lawmakers in the states that would lose planes: Georgia, Kansas, and Idaho.

ANTITERRORISM SUPPLEMENTAL

Congress approved $17.5 billion for defense as part of a $40 billion emergency appropriations package (HR 2888—PL 107-38) that was signed into law Sept. 18, 2001, just a week after the Sept. 11 terrorist attacks. The money in the antiterrorism supplemental was split evenly between fiscal 2001 and fiscal 2002.

When Democrats and some Republicans resisted giving the White House a free hand in dispensing the $40 billion, a compromise was reached allowing the White House to allocate half the money and Congress to allocate the other half through the fiscal 2002 defense appropriations bill (HR 3338—PL 107-117).

Of the first $10 billion, which was made available to the president immediately, $5.9 billion went to defense. The second $10 billion was to become available fifteen days after the president submitted his allocation plan to Congress. His plan, calling for $8.1 billion of the $10 billion to go to defense, was submitted Oct. 17.

The $20 billion allocated by Congress in HR 3338 included $3.5 billion for defense. Bush had requested $7.3 billion for defense. The House had included that amount in its version of HR 3338, but the Senate approved only $2 billion

after a bruising battle over an attempt by Senate Appropriations Committee Chair Robert C. Byrd, D-W.Va., to add another $15 billion to the package. Byrd's $35 billion package would have allocated $7.4 billion for defense, but when Byrd lost, so did the Pentagon.

2002 SUPPLEMENTAL

Congress appropriated $14.4 billion for defense as part of a $28.9 billion fiscal 2002 supplemental spending bill (HR 4775—PL 107-206) that was signed into law Aug. 2, 2002. Included in the defense total was $11.9 billion for the Defense Emergency Response Fund to pay the incremental costs of the global war on terrorism, such as military operations, increased personnel, and additional intelligence gathering. (*Fiscal 2002 supplemental appropriations, p. 63*)

President George W. Bush had requested $14 billion for defense. The House included that amount in its bill (HR 4775—H Rept 107-480), plus $1.8 billion in unrequested money for a contingency fund to help pay for the war in Afghanistan. The Senate approved Bush's request in its version (S 2551—S Rept 107-156), and conferees settled on $14.4 billion in the final bill (H Rept 107-593).

HR 4775 restricted U.S. involvement with the International Criminal Court, as had the House and Senate versions. (*International Criminal Court, p. 256*)

Conferees used their report to strongly object to the way in which the Pentagon had canceled the Crusader cannon program. They said the proposal should have been in the president's initial budget in order to give Congress sufficient time to hold hearings and scrutinize the decision. The administration had requested money for the Crusader mobile artillery system in its fiscal 2003 budget, but Defense Secretary Donald H. Rumsfeld then announced on May 8, 2002, that he would cancel the weapon; a budget amendment to immediately terminate the program was submitted on May 29. (*Crusader program cancelled, p. 321*)

2002 Military Construction

Congress in 2001 cleared a $10.5 billion fiscal 2002 military construction appropriations bill (HR 2904—PL 107-64).

HR 2904 appropriated nearly $529 million more than President George W. Bush requested and $1.6 billion more than Congress approved for military construction the previous fiscal year in regular and supplemental appropriations bills.

Typically one of the most popular appropriations measures in Congress, the annual military construction bill included money for almost every state and was usually the first measure to be acted on. The bill paid the costs of building military bases around the world, housing military personnel and their families, closing unneeded military bases, and providing the U.S. share of NATO's infrastructure fund.

HR 2904's funds for family housing totaled $4.1 billion— $438 million more than the fiscal 2001 level. Clearing up the backlog of dilapidated military housing at home and abroad was a top objective for appropriators, who said housing conditions were making it more difficult for the armed forces to retain skilled personnel. Bush had toured bases early in 2001, promising to devote an additional $400 million to military housing in fiscal 2002.

The bill added about $100 million to Bush's $532 million request to complete the shutdown of military bases already designated for closure. Senators argued that the extra money was necessary to ensure that environmental cleanup at the shuttered bases would be adequately funded.

HR 2904 did not include funds for reconstructing the part of the Pentagon damaged in the Sept. 11 terrorist attacks; money for those repairs was included in the emergency supplemental spending bill (HR 2888—PL 107-38) enacted a week after the attacks. *(Antiterrorism supplemental, p. 319)*

LEGISLATIVE ACTION

The House passed a $10.5 billion military construction bill on Sept. 21, 2001, by a vote of 401–0. The House Appropriations Committee had reported HR 2904 (H Rept 107-207) the previous day.

During floor action House appropriators stressed that the fiscal 2003 version would have to focus on better defending the Pentagon and other military buildings. Military Construction Appropriations Subcommittee Chair David L. Hobson, R-Ohio, said the Pentagon should have more of the protective windows and sprinkler systems that had been installed in the section of the building struck by a hijacked plane on Sept. 11. Those changes were credited with helping to save lives. Hobson also said soldiers should be provided with safe, adequate housing as the military prepared for its unconventional war against terrorism.

The Senate passed HR 2904 by a vote of 97–0 on Sept. 26, after substituting the text of its own $10.5 billion bill (S 1460). The Senate Appropriations Committee had reported S 1460 (S Rept 107-68) on Sept. 25.

CONFERENCE ACTION

The House adopted the conference report on HR 2904 (H Rept 107-246) by a vote of 409–1 on Oct. 17. The Senate cleared the bill by a vote of 96–1 the next day.

One main difference between the House and Senate versions was the amount allocated for completing the shutdown of military bases already designated for closure. Bush had requested $532 million. The House approved $553 million, but the Senate wanted to appropriate $682 million. Supporters in the Senate had argued that base closure programs had been underfunded and questioned whether $682 million would be sufficient to meet the costs of the accompanying environmental cleanups. Conferees agreed on $633 million, as Senate negotiators again stressed the importance of adequate funding. "This is certainly something that we should consider before we embark on any future rounds of base clo-

sures," said Dianne Feinstein, D-Calif., chair of the Senate Military Construction Appropriations Subcommittee. HR 2904 included no money for new base closings because lawmakers put off a new round until 2005 as part of the fiscal 2002 defense authorization (S 1438—PL 107-107). *(2002 defense authorization, p. 316)*

MAJOR PROVISIONS

As signed into law on Nov. 5, 2001, HR 2904:

Military construction. Appropriated $5.8 billion—$572 million more than requested—for projects such as barracks and training facilities. Most of the funds were destined for local companies that contracted to build structures on military bases.

In addition to the $5.8 billion for general construction, the bill appropriated $163 million, as requested, for the U.S. share of NATO construction.

Family housing. Appropriated $4.1 billion—$29 million more than requested—to operate and maintain existing housing units and for new construction and improvements.

Base closings. Appropriated $633 million—$101 million more than requested—for base closure projects, including funding for environmental restoration and for the Homeowners Assistance Fund, which helped personnel affected by the closure of military bases.

2003 Defense Authorization

Congress in 2002 cleared a $392.9 billion fiscal 2003 defense authorization bill (HR 4546—PL 107-314). The total was $3.5 billion less than President George W. Bush's request, but $43 billion more than was ultimately authorized the previous year, making it the largest increase in defense spending since the Vietnam War in the 1960s.

With U.S. troops seeking to root out al Qaeda terrorists in Afghanistan and shipping off to the Persian Gulf region for an anticipated war in Iraq, lawmakers were not disposed to make many major changes to Bush's proposal. The political pressures of the coming midterm elections also contributed to an atmosphere that left many members unwilling to take on a wartime president.

Several major issues nevertheless arose during congressional debate on the bill.

One controversy was over the fate of the Crusader, a forty-ton cannon that the Pentagon decided to cancel. Critics said the weapon was a throwback to the cold war and had no place in a modern military focused on rapid deployment. Despite fierce opposition from some on Capitol Hill, especially members from Oklahoma, where the gun was to be built, the Bush administration prevailed. *(Crusader program canceled, p. 321)*

Also controversial was Bush's request for a $10 billion contingency fund to spend as needed for the war on terrorism. The Senate went along with the idea, but the House did not because members thought it amounted to a blank check.

CRUSADER PROGRAM CANCELED

In 2002 the Bush administration announced that it was canceling the army's Crusader mobile cannon, an $11 billion program derided by critics as an example of weaponry designed to counter a long-gone Soviet threat.

The decision to cancel the Crusader was a follow-on to George W. Bush's promises during the 2000 campaign that, as president, he would create the "military of the next century," scrapping the congressionally popular conventional weapons designed for the cold war to make room for high-technology weapons suited to an agile, lightweight force. Time constraints for the new administration and the Sept. 11, 2001, terrorist attacks made it difficult for Bush to follow through on that promise in his first year.

In 2002, however, Defense Secretary Donald H. Rumsfeld took the initial step when he announced on May 8 that he would cancel the Crusader, a self-propelled cannon being developed as the heir to the Paladin howitzer. The army insisted the new cannon was necessary because the Paladin lacked the range of enemy artillery, while the Crusader was designed to lob heavy shells up to twenty-four miles. The first Crusader was expected to be operational by 2008, and the army wanted 482 in all at an estimated price tag of $11 billion.

Rumsfeld said the forty-ton cannon was too heavy for rapid deployment to distant conflicts. The charge was not a new one. With just such concerns of its own, the army in 1999, five years after development of the Crusader began, demanded that the system be made lighter to fit with its transformation to a more agile force. United Defense LP, the weapon's manufacturer, responded by reducing the weight of the cannon and its resupply vehicle to around forty tons each. Nonetheless, the weapons's size continued to haunt it.

In announcing the cancellation Rumsfeld said the priority of transforming the military into a lighter, more mobile force and the budget realities of a government fighting to climb out of the red combined to make the Crusader expendable. Although the administration had requested $476 million for the Crusader in its fiscal 2003 budget, Rumsfeld submitted a budget amendment on May 29 to immediately terminate the program.

The decision drew quick opposition from several lawmakers, including two Oklahoma Republicans—Senate Minority Whip Don Nickles and House Republican Conference Chair J.C. Watts Jr., in whose district the big gun was to be built. The politically well-connected United Defense launched a lobbying campaign as well.

But Bush and senior Pentagon officials were determined to eliminate the program, and the White House threatened to veto the entire fiscal 2003 defense authorization bill (HR 4546—PL 107-314) if Congress spared the Crusader. Under this pressure Congress went along with Bush.

The last time the Pentagon had canceled a major weapons system was 1991, when Defense Secretary Dick Cheney eliminated the navy's A-12 attack plane because of production delays and cost overruns. (*Congress and the Nation Vol. VIII, p. 379*)

The fund was included in the final bill, but the money was never appropriated.

The biggest fight, however, was over a proposal by both chambers to change a 111-year-old law that barred veterans from receiving full disability compensation while still receiving full pension benefits. The dispute pitted the Bush administration against a bipartisan, bicameral group of lawmakers and delayed final action on the bill until the post-election lame-duck session in November. Veterans' organizations had lobbied for years to eliminate the ban on "concurrent receipts." The White House strongly opposed such a change, saying it could add as much as $58 billion to defense spending over ten years. Pentagon officials also argued that military veterans were well compensated, drawing full pensions that were indexed for inflation and included lifetime health care and other benefits. A compromise was finally reached to give certain severely disabled veterans full benefits.

By the time agreement on the final bill was reached, the fiscal 2003 defense appropriations bill—the bill that actually provided most of the money—had become law (HR 5010—PL 107-248). Still, without the authorization, many programs would have died. Among the items in jeopardy were $10.4 billion in military building programs, a pay raise aimed at encouraging mid-level officers to stay in the armed forces, and the authorization to end work on the Crusader. Authorizers also worried that if they failed to complete work on the bill, future decisions on defense programs might be shifted from the authorizers to the Appropriations committees, ceding even more power to the spending panels.

HOUSE COMMITTEE ACTION

The House Armed Services Committee reported a $383.4 billion version of HR 4546 (H Rept 107-436) on May 3, 2002. A supplemental report (Part II) was filed May 6.

The panel went along with much of Bush's budget proposal, but it balked at the request for the $10 billion, no-strings-attached contingency fund for the war on terrorism. The committee asked Bush to submit more details. In the meantime, the committee agreed to use $3.7 billion of the $10 billion to pay for ongoing military operations in Afghanistan and homeland security activities.

To keep within the discretionary spending cap set in the House budget resolution, the committee shifted the $3.7 billion (later revised to $3.1 billion) worth of programs to a separate bill (HR 4547). That created room in the main bill for members' priorities. The committee subsequently added language to allocate much of the rest of the $10 billion to specific projects and reported HR 4547 (H Rept 107-603) July 23. The full House passed HR 4547 on July 24 by a vote of 413–3 and the next day the text of the bill was incorporated into HR 4546.

The committee added $21 million to Bush's $7.8 billion missile defense request. It included the $476 million originally requested for the Crusader cannon and directed the Pentagon not to halt the program until it had completed a study of the alternatives. The committee proposed that the most severely disabled military retirees, those whose disabilities were 60 percent or more combat-related, be allowed to receive both their full retirement pay and their full disability payments by 2007.

Several conservative Democrats joined Republicans in rejecting Democratic-sponsored amendments aimed at restricting nuclear weapons programs. In a "nuclear posture review," made public in January 2002, the administration said it was considering putting some decommissioned warheads in reserve and indicated that it wanted to reduce the time needed to resume nuclear tests. Republicans argued that the Democratic proposals would limit a president's future options. *(Nuclear weapons, p. 362)*

The committee endorsed two changes in response to a Pentagon request for eight exemptions from environmental laws to facilitate training exercises, allowing limited waivers from the Endangered Species Act and the Migratory Bird Treaty Act. Pentagon officials, with the backing of several Armed Services Committee members, argued that it was increasingly difficult for military units to conduct realistic training because of the combination of environmental laws and restrictions imposed by urban development. *(Environmental laws, p. 440)*

In other action the committee rejected an attempt to cancel the next round of military base closings slated for 2005.

HOUSE FLOOR ACTION

The House passed HR 4546 on May 10 by a **key vote of 359–58 (R 212–1; D 146–56; I 1–1)**, after GOP leaders easily turned back a number of Democratic challenges. *(2002 key votes, p. 819)*

Democrats continued to express concern that the administration was reversing a decades-old bipartisan goal of reducing both the number of nuclear weapons and U.S. reliance on them. But the House on May 9 rejected 172–243 an amendment by Edward J. Markey, D-Mass., to prohibit research on a nuclear "bunker-buster" that would destroy command posts and chemical weapons plants buried deep underground. The program was the centerpiece of the administration's new vision for nuclear weapons. The House then adopted 362–53 an amendment by Curt Weldon, R-Pa., to allow research and development but bar the construction of a prototype nuclear bunker-buster. The fiscal 1994 de-

fense authorization bill (PL 103-160) had prohibited the Pentagon from researching or developing new low-yield nuclear weapons, which it defined as those that produced an explosion equivalent to 5,000 tons (5 kilotons) or less of TNT—about one-third the explosive power of the bombs that the United States dropped on Hiroshima and Nagasaki in World War II. The intent was to ban the use of such weapons. Weldon's amendment would have repealed that section of PL 103-160.

In action on missile defense, the House on May 9 rejected 159–253 an amendment by John F. Tierney, D-Mass., to prohibit development of "space based" missile defense programs. Tierney said his amendment was intended to block deployment of antimissile weapons in space, but Republicans complained that it was so broadly worded that missile detection and communications satellites used by ground-based antimissile systems would be undermined. The House on May 10 rejected 193–223 a motion by John M. Spratt Jr., D-S.C., to recommit the bill to committee with instructions to add language banning the use of funds to develop or deploy nuclear-tipped antimissile interceptors.

Reprising similar votes from recent years, the House rejected 202–215 an amendment offered by Loretta Sanchez, D-Calif., to allow female service members and dependents stationed overseas to obtain abortions at local U.S. military hospitals, provided they paid for the procedure. The amendment had been defeated during committee action as well.

SENATE COMMITTEE ACTION

The Senate Armed Services Committee reported a $393.4 billion authorization bill (S 2514—S Rept 107-151) on May 15.

In a break with the House, the Senate panel included the $10 billion war reserve fund without dipping into it.

The panel, on a party-line vote, reduced Bush's request for missile defense by $814 million and shifted $690 million to the navy's shipbuilding account. Committee chair Carl Levin, D-Mich., said national security was being "shortchanged by the focus on missile defense."

The bill added $1.1 billion in all to Bush's $8.2 billion shipbuilding request. That included $229 million added to the $244 million requested for components for a nuclear powered aircraft carrier. The ship, which was to be built at Newport News Shipbuilding and Drydock Co. in Virginia, had been slated for the fiscal 2006 budget, but limited budgets forced the navy to slow that schedule. The Senate committee's increase, which matched the House amount, was designed to put the carrier back on schedule for funding in fiscal 2006.

S 2514 prohibited spending $15 million that Bush requested to develop the nuclear bunker-buster and required a report from the secretary of defense on the proposed weapon.

The bill included funds for the Crusader, but Levin left open the possibility that the funding might be dropped after the committee received details from the Pentagon on its decision to cancel the weapon.

SENATE FLOOR ACTION

The Senate on June 27 first passed a $393.3 billion version of S 2514 by a vote of 97–2 and then incorporated the text into HR 4546 and passed it by voice vote.

Passage came after Bush persuaded the Democratic-controlled Senate to endorse his $7.8 billion request for missile defense. Faced with a presidential veto threat issued June 19, Democrats agreed June 26 to authorize the requested amount, but to specify that the president could use $814 million of it for missile defense or to fight terrorism at home and abroad. John W. Warner of Virginia, the Armed Services Committee's ranking Republican, offered the amendment giving Bush discretion over the $814 million. Levin insisted on adding language to stipulate that counterterrorism was the higher priority. Republicans resisted for nearly two days. In the end they took the money and let the Democrats have the rhetoric, but only after administration lawyers assured them that the compromise language would give Bush a free hand on missile defense. Both the Levin and Warner amendments were adopted by voice vote.

In further action on missile defense, the Senate:

• Adopted by voice vote June 26 an amendment by Dianne Feinstein, D-Calif., and Ted Stevens, R-Alaska, to bar development or deployment of nuclear-armed missile defense interceptors.

• Adopted by voice vote June 27 an amendment by Armed Services Strategic Forces Subcommittee Chair Jack Reed, D-R.I., to require the Pentagon to send Congress a report in both a classified and unclassified form within 120 days of a missile defense test. In early June the Pentagon had stated that it would reduce greatly the amount of information released about future tests of the ground-based interceptor missile slated for deployment in Alaska. Critics charged that Secretary of Defense Donald H. Rumsfeld was trying to shield the program from tough technical scrutiny by exempting it from some of the detailed oversight applied to other major weapons programs.

The Senate approved an amendment by Levin that gave Rumsfeld a nearly free hand to kill the Crusader cannon. The amendment, adopted on June 19 by a vote of 96–3, shifted the $476 million designated for the cannon to the army's Future Combat System, a new generation of lightweight tanks, troop carriers, long-range artillery, and other equipment. The amendment also required that the army complete a comparative analysis of the Crusader and three alternatives and report to Rumsfeld within thirty days of the bill's enactment. Rumsfeld was then to submit the report to Congress along with his plans for the funds. Thirty days after that Rumsfeld would be free to reprogram the $476 million to accelerate other artillery programs and pay a cancellation fee to United Defense LP. The Armed Services Committee had approved an earlier version of the amendment on June 13 after

receiving additional information from the Pentagon about the program. The amendment was revised on the floor when the Senate agreed to drop language requiring that the House and Senate Armed Services and Appropriations committees approve Rumsfeld's proposal on how to spend the Crusader funds.

Brushing aside a fresh veto threat, the Senate June 19 adopted by voice vote an amendment to repeal over five years the law under which veterans' pensions were reduced dollar-for-dollar to offset their disability payments.

In other action the Senate adopted 93–0 on June 24 a Robert C. Smith, R-N.H., amendment to prohibit any military superior from requiring or pressuring female service members stationed in Saudi Arabia to wear an abaya, the traditional religious garment that enshrouded a woman from head to toe. The Pentagon had required female personnel in Saudi Arabia to wear the garment when leaving their base on grounds that it would respect local customs and protect the Americans against being singled out by terrorists.

The Senate adopted 52–40 on June 21 an amendment by Patty Murray, D-Wash., to allow female service members or dependents stationed abroad to obtain abortions in local U.S. military hospitals, provided they paid for the procedure.

Senators agreed 50–49 on June 25 to table (kill) an amendment by Edward M. Kennedy, D-Mass., to require the Pentagon to conduct public-private competitions for many contracts that it routinely awarded to private companies.

CONFERENCE ACTION

The House adopted the conference report on HR 4546 (H Rept 107-772) on Nov. 12 by voice vote. The Senate agreed to it by voice vote the next day, clearing the bill for the president.

Conferees had hoped to finish before Congress adjourned in mid-October, but the dispute with the White House over veterans' benefits delayed final action until after the November elections. Administration officials had threatened to veto any bill that repealed the existing ban in an 1891 law on so-called concurrent receipts. Under that law, retirees' disability payments had to be deducted from their pensions. The law had reflected Congress's displeasure that some veterans of the Mexican War (1846–1848) were collecting payments for disabilities resulting from that conflict while they were also receiving a retirement pension or still on active duty. The policy enshrined in that law was the administration's fundamental position in 2002: The liberal package of pay and fringe benefits available to retirees was intended to compensate them in full for the stresses of military service—including the risk of severe injury. In the administration's view, a disability payment was intended as an economic safety net for veterans who did not qualify for retirement but whose earning potential was impaired by disability. And because the disability payment was tax-free, there was some monetary incentive for retirees to give up some of their taxable pension in return for the tax-free payment.

After a decade of measures that always ended on the budget-cutting floor, Congress in 2002 began moving on the concurrent receipts issue in earnest in 2002, catching the administration off guard. The Senate bill would have eliminated the ban outright over five years, affecting about 700,000 retirees. The House bill would have phased it out over five years for about 90,000 of the most severely disabled retirees. Many lawmakers and lobbyists bet that Bush would not veto the bill over the provision, given veterans' political clout and the fact that 90 percent of the House and 83 percent of the Senate had cosponsored legislation to liberalize the restriction. But the subject was too hot to handle before the election.

Following the election the administration and Congress compromised. The deal, largely engineered by Warner, was expected to cost $2 billion over ten years. It extended full retirement and disability benefits to any retiree disabled as a result of enemy fire and to retirees classified as at least 60 percent disabled because of injuries suffered in combat, training, or other hazardous duty. Warner termed the deal "Purple Heart Plus Others." Veterans groups vowed to push in the 108th Congress for complete repeal.

The final bill provided $7.8 billion for missile defense and prohibited the use of any fiscal 2003 funds for nuclear-armed interceptors for a missile defense system. The Senate bill had contained an outright ban; the House bill had no similar provision. Conferees rejected both Rumsfeld's insistence that Congress accept less detailed reporting on the missile defense program and the Senate bill's requirement of detailed reports on four high-profile antimissile weapons. Instead they incorporated into the final bill the House position that the administration should continue its current reporting practices on missile defense, plus a few new requirements. *(Missile defense details, p. 362)*

Conferees dropped House language that would have repealed a section of the fiscal 1994 defense authorization bill (PL 103-160) in order to allow research and development of a prototype nuclear bunker-busting weapon. The conference bill barred the use of funds in HR 4546 for a bunker-buster until after the secretary of defense submitted a report to the congressional defense committees on the proposed weapon.

Conferees agreed to redirect the $476 million requested for the Crusader to the army's Future Combat System.

They also agreed to include the $10 billion that Bush requested as an unallocated contingency fund to cover future operations in the war against terrorism. But the authorizers' action was irrelevant because the companion defense appropriations bill, which was signed into law Oct. 23, did not include the $10 billion. Neither the House nor Senate Appropriations committee would give the administration that much money without congressional oversight or control. *(2003 defense appropriations, p. 326)*

One of the most contentious weapons issues in the bill was a controversial effort by the air force and Boeing Co. to set up a program to lease Boeing 767 jetliners for use as midair refueling tankers at an estimated cost of $18 billion to $20 billion. The leasing plan had been authorized in the previous year's defense appropriations bill (HR 3338—PL 107-117), but no funds had been provided. HR 4546 prohibited any agreement unless it was authorized and funded by law or the secretary of the air force made a formal "reprogramming" request to the Senate and House Armed Services and Appropriations committees asking that he be allowed to begin leasing the planes with funds Congress had appropriated for other Pentagon programs. In its statement on the bill, the White House said it would construe that provision as requiring that the secretary make the request before signing the lease—but not that he needed to wait for congressional approval. *(2002 defense appropriations, p. 316)*

Conferees dropped a House provision that would have made it harder to close military installations when a new round of closures began in 2005. It required a unanimous vote by the nine-member commission before additional facilities could be added to the secretary of defense's proposed list of bases slated for closure. Existing law required seven members to vote for an addition. Instead, the final bill simply included a House requirement that two of the commission members visit a base before it could be added to the list.

The bill added $920 million to Bush's shipbuilding requests. Defense hawks had decried the Pentagon budget as too small to sustain the fleet for the long term at its existing size of about 300 ships. However, the increase did not add any new ships to the five in the administration's request. Most of the increase went to pay for cost increases in ships funded in earlier years ($488 million), refueling a nuclear-powered submarine that otherwise would have been mothballed despite being fit for years of additional service ($200 million), and buying components for the next aircraft carrier so construction could be started sooner than the administration planned ($229 million).

Conferees accepted a deal worked out by Levin that gave the Pentagon a temporary reprieve from the Migratory Bird Treaty Act while the Interior Department worked out a long-term solution. The House bill would have amended the act to exempt training activities. House Republicans were forced to abandon efforts to loosen the Endangered Species Act.

The final bill dropped the Senate amendment that would have allowed privately funded abortions for U.S. military personnel at overseas military facilities. A House amendment setting a cap of 500 U.S. troops in Colombia also was not included. There was an existing cap of 400 on the number of U.S. military personnel who could operate in Colombia.

MAJOR PROVISIONS

As signed into law on Dec. 2, 2002, HR 4546 authorized $392.9 billion in defense spending in fiscal 2003, about $3.5 billion less than requested.

Major provisions of HR 4546:

Military Personnel

Authorized $93.8 billion for military personnel.

Authorized for fiscal 2003 an active-duty force of 1,389,700, as requested—an increase of 2,300 above the previous fiscal year's ceiling.

Authorized a minimum 4.1 percent pay increase, as requested, for military personnel, with higher raises for mid-grade and senior noncommissioned officers and mid-grade officers.

Operations and Maintenance

Authorized $129.8 billion.

Facilities

Authorized $10.4 billion for military construction and family housing, about $1.5 billion more than requested. The increases were made in military construction accounts rather than housing.

Missile Defense

Authorized $7.8 billion for development of a missile defense system, about the same amount as requested. The money included funds for an initial deployment of the system in Alaska.

Gave the president the option of redirecting up to $814 million of the $7.8 billion to the war on terrorism.

Prohibited the use of any fiscal 2003 funds for research, development, testing, evaluation, procurement, or deployment of nuclear-armed interceptors for a missile defense system.

Ground Forces

Redirected the $476 million requested for the Crusader cannon to the army's Future Combat System and stipulated that by fiscal 2008 the army should be provided with an alternative non-line-of-sight cannon. The bill added $293 million to aid the army in developing a cannon that made use of Crusader technology. (Crusader program canceled, p. 321)

Authorized $915 million, as requested, to continue developing the Comanche scout helicopter, a missile-armed reconnaissance helicopter with a "stealthy" design intended to shield it from radar and infrared detectors. But in their report the conferees made clear their unhappiness with the army's management of the program. The bill required detailed quarterly reports to Congress on Comanche's status.

The Comanche program began in 1983 as an effort to replace some 5,000 Vietnam-era helicopters, and in 1991 a joint team of Boeing and the Sikorsky division of United Technologies had won the contract. Because of a series of budget cuts, cost increases, and delays, the helicopter's budget and schedule had been changed six times. As of 2002, the program was budgeted at $48 billion, with the aim of fielding 1,213 helicopters, starting in 2009, at an average cost of $38 million apiece.

The Comanche program ultimately was canceled in 2004. (2005 defense appropriations, p. 354)

Aviation Forces

Authorized $4.1 billion, as requested, for twenty-three F-22 Raptors, the air force's next-generation fighter plane, with an additional $627 million for research and development.

Authorized $3.5 billion, roughly the same amount as requested, for the Joint Strike Fighter, the multipurpose aircraft to be used by the air force, navy, and Marine Corps.

Authorized $3.4 billion for forty-eight F/A-18 E/F aircraft, the navy's upgrade of the existing F/A-18 C/D.

Authorized nearly $1 billion for drone airplanes (unmanned aerial vehicles) similar to those being used in Afghanistan.

Prohibited any agreement to lease Boeing 767 jetliners for use as midair refueling tankers unless it was authorized and funded or the secretary of the air force made a formal reprogramming request to the Senate and House Armed Services and Appropriations committees asking that he be allowed to begin leasing the planes with money appropriated for other programs.

Naval Forces

Authorized $969 million for the navy's next generation surface combat ship, the DD(X)—formerly known as the DD-21.

Authorized $2.4 billion, as requested, for two *Arleigh Burke*-class Aegis guided-missile destroyers, the DDG-51.

Authorized $1.6 billion, as the administration sought, to purchase the fifth boat in the *Virginia*-class of attack submarines to replace the *Los Angeles*-class subs, which were being retired.

Authorized $4 million to begin designing a so-called littoral combat ship. Although the funds had not been requested, the navy planned to buy the ships for missions in littoral seas—shallow, island-strewn waters near coastlines where some navy officials believed future conflicts most likely would occur. While providing funds to accelerate their purchase, the bill also required close review of the navy's rationale for the new ship.

Base Closings

Required that two members of the base closing commission visit a site before it could be added to the secretary of defense's proposed list of base closings.

Antiterrorism

Authorized $7.3 billion, as requested, for Defense Department programs to combat terrorism.

Nuclear Weapons

Authorized $16.5 billion for defense-related activities carried out primarily by the Energy Department.

Barred use of any Energy Department funds in the bill for the Robust Nuclear Earth Penetrator program—commonly known as the bunker-buster program—until thirty days after the secretary of defense submitted a report to the Senate and House Armed Services committees on the proposed weapon. The report was to cover the need for such a weapon, its targets, and how its capability compared with that of conventional weapons.

Veterans' Benefits

Changed existing law to allow veterans to receive both their full military pension and their full disability payment—if the disability resulted from a combat wound for which they earned a Purple Heart or their disability rating was at least 60 percent as a result of "combat-related" disability.

Contingency Fund

Authorized $10 billion as a contingency fund for future war on terrorism costs, as requested.

Other Provisions

Authorized a temporary exemption from the Migratory Bird Treaty Act (PL 93-300) for the incidental killing of migratory birds during authorized military readiness activities. The bill directed the secretary of the interior to prescribe regulations within one year of enactment to exempt such activities. The bill also required the secretary of defense, in consultation with the secretary of the interior, to identify measures to minimize the adverse impact of training activities on migratory birds.

Eliminated or modified requirements for twenty-two periodic reports to Congress mandated by earlier legislation, most of which covered narrow subjects or had been overtaken by events. At the same time it required new reports on some major weapons programs such as the one on the army's Comanche helicopter. It also included provisions designed to improve scrutiny of some programs by top-level Pentagon agencies, particularly those that viewed programs from a "joint," or multiservice, perspective. The Pentagon grudgingly accepted the reporting provisions in the bill.

2003 Defense Appropriations

Congress in 2002 cleared a $355.1 billion fiscal 2003 Defense Department appropriations bill (HR 5010—PL 107-248). The measure reflected substantial agreement among lawmakers after the Sept. 11, 2001, terrorist attacks that no dollars should be spared on defense.

HR 5010 provided $11.6 billion less than President George W. Bush requested, but $10 billion of the difference was due to Congress's deferral of the president's request for a lump-sum contingency fund to pay for future operations against terrorism. Aside from that money the defense bill made only modest changes to Bush's budget and largely tracked administration plans to transform the military into a lighter, more agile force. As was customary, it closely followed the outlines of the annual defense authorization bill (HR 4546—PL 107-314).

The defense bill and the companion military construction bill (HR 5011—PL 107-249) were the only two fiscal 2003 appropriations measures to clear before Congress recessed for the Nov. 5 midterm elections. With the war on terrorism, the growing possibility of an attack on Iraq, and political delays to legislation creating a new Department of Homeland Security, members were eager to show their commitment on defense. The significant increase in spending also reduced conflicts over priorities. Even the missile defense system, a highly contentious issue in previous years, drew little criticism.

Lawmakers also accepted Defense Secretary Donald H. Rumsfeld's decision to cancel the army's Crusader mobile cannon, despite fierce opposition earlier in the year and strong support for the $11 billion program from members of the GOP leadership in both chambers. (*Crusader program canceled, p. 321*)

Appropriators did balk at the White House request for the $10 billion contingency fund, saying it would amount to a blank check. They deferred action on the issue until the administration submitted a detailed request.

Total defense appropriations for fiscal 2003 amounted to about $381.3 billion, when HR 5010's Defense Department funds were combined with defense-related funds in other appropriations bills. The latter included $10.5 billion in the military construction appropriations bill and $15.7 billion for the Energy Department's atomic energy defense activities in the fiscal 2003 omnibus appropriations bill (HJ Res 2—PL 108-7).

HOUSE ACTION

The House passed a $354.7 billion version of HR 5010 on June 27, 2002, by a vote of 413–18. The House Appropriations Committee had reported the bill (H Rept 107-532) on June 25.

The House bill appropriated $7.4 billion for antimissile defense. During the floor debate GOP leaders easily turned back an effort to hamstring Bush's plans. By a vote of 112–314, members rejected an amendment that would have eliminated $122 million earmarked for construction of five antimissile interceptor launch silos at Fort Greely in Alaska.

Critics of the missile defense system, including the amendment's sponsor, John F. Tierney, D-Mass., argued that the administration was rushing work on the silos so it could claim by the 2004 election that a missile defense had been deployed. They also contended that interceptor missiles had not been adequately tested. The silos were part of an expanded network of test facilities scattered around the eastern Pacific for more realistic testing of missile defense. The administration said the test interceptors in the five Fort Greely silos could provide a rudimentary defense against a missile fired from North Korea.

The House went along with Rumsfeld's request to eliminate funding for the Crusader cannon and redistribute the $476 million initially requested for the project to other accounts. But the Appropriations Committee had stressed in its report that it was acting "with some degree of trepidation" and directed the army to build a replacement cannon that incorporated many of the technologies developed for the Crusader. The committee had shifted $280 million, as requested, to develop lightweight rocket launchers, highly accurate rockets and cannon shells, and other artillery upgrades. But it devoted the remaining $196 million specifically to accelerating development of a new long-range mobile artillery piece using Crusader-based technologies. Appropriators added $173 million to the effort to ensure the development of a vehicle and munitions suitable for the new technology and mission.

The bill included $915 million, as requested, to continue development of the army's Comanche scout helicopter, but the Appropriations Committee's report excoriated the service for repeated delays and cost increases that had plagued the program. The appropriators said that their support for the program was in jeopardy unless the army could show marked progress over the next few years, adding that the army should start considering cheaper alternatives. *(Details, 2003 defense authorization, p. 320)*

The committee took more drastic steps on two army projects to develop "smart" weapons. Appropriators said the projects were taking too long and costing too much, on top of which the weapons were not performing as promised. Funds for one of the projects were denied, and deep cuts were made in the other.

The House bill included the $4.6 billion requested to buy twenty-three F-22s. However, the committee expressed concern over Lockheed Martin's rapid production schedule, given the aircraft's history of cost overruns and technical problems. The committee report specified that before ordering more than sixteen of the planes, Pentagon officials would have to certify to Congress that the advantages of faster production outweighed the risk of extensive modifications if problems were discovered later.

House appropriators included $250 million in unrequested funds for improvements to the CVN-77, the navy's next nuclear aircraft carrier that would serve as a transition ship from the *Nimitz*-class of nuclear carriers to the next generation, designated the CVNX. The navy had dropped plans to incorporate a new type of radar in the CVN-77 that would have given a commander a more comprehensive view of the ship's surroundings. Criticizing that decision as shortsighted, the appropriators added the funds to install the modern radar.

SENATE ACTION

The Senate passed a $355.4 billion defense bill 95–3 on Aug. 1. The Senate Appropriations Committee had reported the bill (S Rept 107-213) on July 18.

The bill totaled $1.4 billion less than Bush requested, not counting the contingency fund. Senate appropriators trimmed the $1.4 billion from the defense bill in order to add funds to the military construction and Energy Department appropriations bills.

The Senate measure honored most of the administration's major Pentagon initiatives, including the decision to cancel the Crusader. Instead of dividing the Crusader money among specific programs as Rumsfeld proposed, Senate appropriators added it to the budget for the Future Combat System, the army's program to deploy a new class of light combat vehicles and artillery beginning in 2008. And, like the House, the Senate added $173 million to accelerate work on a lightweight replacement cannon that capitalized on the labor and technologies that had been dedicated to the heavy cannon.

The Senate included $7.8 billion for missile defense programs but appropriated only $6.9 billion of it outright, giving Bush discretion to use the remaining $814 million either for missile defense or counterterrorism costs.

The Senate bill added $586 million to the $2.7 billion requested for C-17 wide-body cargo jets, which would allow the air force to continue to buy the planes at a rate of fifteen per year instead of the twelve the air force requested for fiscal 2003. The measure also added $229 million to the $244 million requested for components for use in the new CVNX aircraft carrier. Bush had proposed delaying the start of construction of the carrier from 2006 to 2007, and the added funds eliminated half of the delay.

The usually quick action on the defense spending bill took longer than expected because John McCain, R-Ariz., balked at a plan to lease Boeing jets to replace the air force's forty-year-old refueling tankers. Enacted as part of the fiscal 2002 defense spending bill (HR 3338—PL 107-117), the $20 billion deal allowed the air force to lease 100 new, modified 767 jets from Boeing to replace the service's fleet of tankers. McCain assailed the deal as a bailout for the troubled company, saying it ultimately would cost $6 billion more than proponents claimed. During the floor debate McCain challenged what amounted to an offshoot of the leasing deal—a provision to appropriate $31 million toward the $400 million cost of a six-year lease on four of the Boeing aircraft for use in shuttling senior Pentagon officials around the world. The Senate then agreed by voice vote to his amendment to require "full and open" competition for the leasing of the four planes. McCain eventually dropped another amendment that would have required approval by the defense authorizers of all leasing deals. *(2002 defense appropriations, p. 316)*

Among other amendments adopted by voice vote was one by Richard G. Lugar, R-Ind., to allow the president to waive certain congressionally mandated restrictions on providing money to help Russia dispose of its huge stockpiles of lethal chemical weapons left over from the cold war. Bush sought the waiver to free his hands in allocating funds under the so-called Nunn-Lugar program, created in the 1990s to help former Soviet republics dispose of nuclear, chemical, and biological weapons and their delivery systems. The bill included $417 million, as requested, to continue the Nunn-Lugar program.

CONFERENCE ACTION

The House adopted the conference report on HR 5010 (H Rept 107-732) on Oct. 10 by a vote of 409–14. The Senate agreed to it 93–1 on Oct. 16, clearing the bill.

Conferees accepted the administration's decision to cancel development of the Crusader. They earmarked funds for a replacement cannon and added funds for new artillery programs. They also strongly endorsed the army's plan to field six brigades equipped with lightweight armored cars, called Strykers. The provision came in response to reports that top Pentagon officials might reduce the number of such units to save money. The brigades were an interim step in the transformation of the army to a lighter, more mobile force.

Conferees approved $9 billion for navy shipbuilding, an increase of $842 million over Bush's request. The extra funds largely were to cover cost overruns on ships funded in earlier years, but the bill also included money to start work on the CVNX aircraft carrier earlier than the administration planned and unrequested money to upgrade the electronic warfare system for the CVN-77.

The conference bill included funding for twenty-three F-22 fighters but, like the House bill, limited the purchase to sixteen planes unless top Pentagon officials justified to Congress the need for faster production. The bill also provided for forty-six navy F/A-18E/F fighters—two more than requested—and for fifteen additional C-17 cargo jets instead of the twelve requested.

To make room for their own initiatives funded in the bill, conferees agreed to cut more than $2 billion from Bush's request, targeting spending that they insisted would not affect defense readiness. The cuts reflected a reduction in air patrols over U.S. territory and lower-than-anticipated spending for a new health care benefit for military retirees. They were also aimed at forcing the Pentagon to reduce the amount spent on consultants and to enforce greater discipline in the use of government credit cards.

MAJOR PROVISIONS

As signed into law Oct. 23, 2002, HR 5010 appropriated $355.1 billion for fiscal 2003 military spending.

Major provisions of HR 5010:

Military Personnel

Appropriated $93.6 billion for military personnel.

Included a 4.1 percent pay raise for military personnel, equal to the president's request, with targeted pay increases of up to 6.5 percent for senior personnel.

Set a ceiling on the number of active duty personnel in fiscal 2003 at 1,389,700, as requested.

Operations and Maintenance

Appropriated $114.8 billion.

Missile Defense

Appropriated $7.4 billion for the program to develop and build an antimissile system, about $43 million less than requested.

Of that total $2.6 billion was slated to be used to develop ground-launched interceptor missiles that could be deployed at five launch silos to be built in Alaska as part of a test range.

Ground Forces

Earmarked $369 million to develop a replacement cannon for the Crusader cannon, which the Pentagon had canceled. Combined with changes in other artillery-related programs either proposed by the administration or initiated by Congress, that brought the total for new artillery programs to $591 million—an increase of $115 million over the administration's original request.

Appropriated the $812 million requested to continue buying lightweight armored cars called Strykers and developing a version equipped with a large cannon. The bill added $60 million to accelerate the purchase of other equipment that would be used by the six brigades the army planned to equip with Strykers.

Appropriated $915 million, as requested, to continue developing the army's missile-armed Comanche helicopter, a joint production of Boeing and the Sikorsky division of United Technologies. The bill also included $270 million to buy nineteen Sikorsky Blackhawk helicopters—an increase of seven aircraft and $117 million over the Bush request. The House had called for four extra Blackhawks, while the Senate called for nine. Some of the choppers would go to army reserve units.

Aviation Forces

Appropriated $4.1 billion, as requested, for twenty-three additional F-22 Raptor fighters, an aircraft intended to replace the F-15 and F-16 and designed to have both air-to-air and air-to-ground fighter capabilities. However, only sixteen planes could be purchased unless top Pentagon officials justified to Congress the need for faster production. The bill also appropriated $809 million for research and development on the aircraft.

Appropriated $3.5 billion, as requested, to develop the multi-role F-35 Joint Strike Fighter, which was slated to replace several 1970s-vintage warplanes.

Appropriated $3.2 billion to buy forty-six F/A-18E/F fighter planes, the navy's upgrade of the F/A-18 C/D—two planes and $120 million more than requested.

Appropriated $765 million, as requested, for Joint Direct Attack Munition (JDAM) satellite-guided air-to-surface "smart" bombs. This was more than triple the amount requested the previous year.

Appropriated $131 million, $26 million more than requested, to accelerate production of the Predator drone aircraft, which was being used to spot targets in Afghanistan.

Naval Forces

Appropriated $2.3 billion, as requested, for two DDG-51 *Arleigh Burke*-class Aegis guided-missile destroyers.

Appropriated $1.5 billion, as requested, to buy the fourth in the *Virginia*-class of new attack submarines to replace the retiring *Los Angeles*-class submarines.

Appropriated $825 million to replace ballistic nuclear missiles with long-range conventional Tomahawk cruise missiles on four submarines.

Appropriated $404 million—$160 more than requested—to begin work on the first ship in the new CVNX class of aircraft carriers. The administration would have delayed the start of construction on the ship by one year, to 2007. The bill also added $90 million to upgrade the electronic warfare system for the CVN-77, the navy's next nuclear aircraft carrier that would serve as a transition to the CVNX.

Appropriated $311 million to pay for shifting several shipbuilding contracts among shipyards in Maine, Louisiana, and Mississippi. The navy said the complicated swap would save time and money over the long run.

Air and Sea Transport

Appropriated $4.2 billion to purchase fifteen additional C-17 wide-body cargo jets—three planes and $586 million more than requested.

Appropriated the requested $243 million to continue building a $1.5 billion helicopter carrier, designated an LHD, designed to carry 1,700 marines plus the helicopters and landing craft to haul them ashore.

Other Provisions

Appropriated $417 million for the Nunn-Lugar program to assist in the dismantling of nuclear, chemical, and biological weapons and their delivery systems in the former Soviet Union. The bill allowed the president to waive an existing prohibition against the use of Nunn-Lugar funds for a chemical weapons destruction facility in Russia, provided he certified to Congress that the waiver was necessary and in the national security interests of the United States, and that he had a plan for Russia to fully disclose details of its chemical weapons stockpile.

Appropriated $150 million for breast cancer research and $85 million for prostate cancer research.

2003 Defense Supplemental

In 2003 Congress approved another $62.4 billion for military spending in fiscal 2003 as part of a $78.5 billion supplemental appropriations bill (HR 1559—PL 108-11). The bill was primarily to pay for military operations in Iraq and for homeland security, but it also contained international aid,

including relief and reconstruction assistance for Iraq, and aid for the troubled U.S. airline industry. *(2003 supplemental appropriations for international aid, p. 287)*

President George W. Bush had submitted a $74.7 billion supplemental request for fiscal 2003 on March 25, 2003, just five days after the start of the U.S. invasion of Iraq. Members of Congress, eager to send Bush a bill before their spring recess, finished their work in less than three weeks. They gave the president the entire $62.4 billion he requested for defense, but not the leeway he wanted to allocate the money. Bush had asked that $59.9 billion be put in a Defense Emergency Response Fund that the Pentagon could tap without congressional guidance or approval, but lawmakers of both parties considered the request a threat to their jealously guarded power of the purse. Congress eventually allowed $11 billion in defense appropriations to be left to the administration's discretion.

LEGISLATIVE ACTION

The House had passed a $77.9 billion version of HR 1559 on April 3 by a vote of 414–12. The House Appropriations Committee had reported it (H Rept 108-55) the day before.

The House version allocated all but $25.4 billion of the $62.4 billion in the bill for defense. In its report, the Appropriations Committee said the need for flexibility "does not obviate the need for Congress to be fully involved . . . in establishing the terms and conditions under which the appropriated funds are to be used."

The Senate approved its $77.9 billion supplemental bill (S 762) on April 3 by a vote of 93–0. The Senate Appropriations Committee had reported S 762 (S Rept 108-33) on April 1. The Senate subsequently inserted the text of S 762 into HR 1559 and passed that bill by voice vote on April 7.

The Senate version left even less money to the discretion of the administration—$11 billion. Senate appropriators had put the rest of the war-fighting money in specific operations and maintenance accounts, organized differently than those in the House version.

House and Senate negotiators worked quickly, filing a conference report (H Rept 108-76) on April 12. The House adopted the conference report by voice vote that same day. The bill was then automatically cleared because the Senate had agreed by voice vote a day earlier to deem the conference report adopted when it was received from the House.

MAJOR PROVISIONS

As signed into law April 16, HR 1559 appropriated $62.4 billion for military spending. Conferees allocated $46.7 billion of that to specific accounts. The other $15.7 billion was appropriated for a new Iraq Freedom Fund that the Pentagon could disburse, although further restrictions reduced to about $11 billion the amount that the Pentagon could spend as it chose.

Specific appropriations included:

- $13.4 billion for military personnel. Conferees included a Senate-passed provision increasing combat pay from $150 to $225 a month and the family separation allowance from $100 to $250 a month, retroactive to Oct. 1, 2002.
  - $31.2 billion for operations and maintenance.
  - $1.8 billion for classified programs.
  - Up to $1.4 billion in payments to Pakistan, Jordan, and other nations that cooperated in the fight against terrorism.
  - $1.3 billion for procurement.
  - $1.1 billion for fuel costs.
  - $502 million for military health programs.
  - $489 million for a new Natural Resources Risk Remediation Fund to pay for putting out fires and repairing damage to Iraqi oil facilities. The bill also allowed foreign contributions to the fund.

In addition to the $62.4 billion, the bill included $203 million for military construction.

2003 Military Construction

Congress in 2002 cleared a $10.5 billion fiscal 2003 military construction appropriations bill (HR 5011—PL 107-249).

HR 5011 provided $835 million more than President George W. Bush requested, but the total was still $105 million below the amount appropriated in the previous year's regular and supplemental appropriations bills.

HR 5011 and the defense appropriations bill (HR 5010—PL 107-248) were the only two fiscal 2003 appropriations measures to clear before the 107th Congress adjourned. The general dispute over fiscal 2003 spending levels that left the domestic appropriations bills stranded had little impact on the military construction measure. Typically the least controversial of the thirteen regular appropriations bills, it paid for building and repairing barracks, family housing, and other facilities as well as for the costs associated with base closings. Ninety-seven of 495 major bases had been closed since 1988.

The final bill included $1.2 billion for new construction and modernization of the nation's 12,819 barracks spaces, nearly half of which were at least thirty years old. Recognizing that the all-volunteer force meant more service members with families, Congress provided $2.9 billion for existing family housing and $1.3 billion for new housing. The Defense Department had estimated that 180,000 of the 300,000 family housing units it operated were substandard, and the cost of improvements or replacements would be more than $16 billion.

Congress more than doubled the president's request for National Guard and reserve programs to $688 million.

LEGISLATIVE ACTION

The House passed its $10.1 billion version of HR 5011 by a vote of 426–1 on June 27, 2002, after less than an hour of debate. The House Appropriations Committee had reported the bill (H Rept 107-533) on June 25.

The House bill added more than $1 billion to Bush's original request. The president initially requested $9 billion for military construction, $1.7 billion less than was appropriated for fiscal 2002. At the same time he sought a significant increase in defense spending—$48 billion more than appropriated in the previous year. Criticizing the president's priorities, the House Appropriations Committee shifted $594 million from an account Bush proposed for the war on terrorism in the Defense budget to the military construction bill. The committee said that because the $594 million was intended for construction to improve security at U.S. facilities, it belonged in the military construction bill and not the regular defense appropriations bill. The appropriators also added $541 million from other accounts.

The Senate passed HR 5011 by a vote of 96–3 on July 18 after inserting the text of its $10.6 billion military construction funding bill (S 2709). The Senate Appropriations Committee had reported S 2709 (S Rept 107-202) on July 3.

By the time the Senate panel approved the bill on June 27 the White House had revised its request to include not only the original $9 billion but also the $594 million for increased security protection and another $122 million. The revision had not been sent to the Hill in time to be incorporated into the House version. The Senate bill was still $900 million more costly than Bush's request, a fact that drew sharp criticism from the White House.

CONFERENCE ACTION

The House adopted the conference report on HR 5011 (H Rept 107-731) by a vote of 419–0 on Oct. 10. The Senate cleared the bill by voice vote Oct. 11.

Although the bill's $10.5 billion bottom line represented a victory over initial White House proposals, appropriators still felt shortchanged. The total was closer to the Senate's $10.6 billion, but the House had agreed by voice vote Sept. 10 to instruct its conferees to insist on the higher of the House or Senate funding levels for most items.

One exception was the funding for military base closing costs. Senate appropriators had approved $645 million, $100 million more than the administration request and the House version. The extra money was earmarked for cleanup costs. But conferees opted for just $16 million more.

MAJOR PROVISIONS

As signed into law on Oct. 23, 2002, HR 5011:

Military construction. Appropriated $5.6 billion—$860 million more than requested—for projects such as barracks and training facilities.

The bill also included $167 million—$1 million less than requested—for the U.S. share of NATO infrastructure projects.

Family housing. Appropriated $4.2 billion—$40 million less than requested—for family housing. That total included $2.9 billion to maintain existing housing and $1.3 billion to construct new housing.

Base closings. Appropriated $561 million—$16 million more than requested—for environmental cleanup and other projects related to base closings.

Missile Defense

President George W. Bush came into office advocating a robust missile defense system; despite protests from his critics, he made considerable progress toward that goal during the 107th Congress. He won dramatic increases in funding for missile defense, made plans to build test facilities in Alaska that could be used as a rudimentary antimissile system, and took action to void a thirty-year-old arms control pact that stood in the way.

The administration had made clear for months that its missile defense testing program would soon conflict with the restrictions of the 1972 Anti-Ballistic Missile (ABM) Treaty, a pact that the United States had signed with the Soviet Union and had continued to observe with Russia after the break-up of the Soviet Union. Some antimissile tests were put off because of the treaty, but the Bush administration clearly would not allow the treaty to impede its plans indefinitely.

Bush made it official on Dec. 13, 2001, when he announced his decision to withdraw from the treaty, effective six months from that date. "The cold war is long gone. Today, we leave behind one of its last vestiges," he said.

Congressional Democrats fumed at Bush's move, which they said would harm U.S. relations with Russia, anger European allies, and potentially lead to an arms race in Asia—all while the United States was seeking to lead an international coalition against terrorism. But they acknowledged that there was little they could do about it in the short term. Russian president Vladimir V. Putin called the U.S. withdrawal "mistaken," but seemed mollified by the prospect of nuclear arms reductions.

PUSH FOR SYSTEM

Ever since President Ronald Reagan proposed his Strategic Defense Initiative in 1983, Republicans had longed for a system that would make the United States invulnerable to a missile attack.

Reagan's ambitious plan to explore both land-based and space-based systems, which critics derided as "Star Wars," was never realized. President George H. W. Bush narrowed the focus of his antimissile program to a defense against limited missile attacks. Republican efforts to turn missile defense into a political issue met with public indifference in the post–cold war era, allowing President Bill Clinton to leave development of the antimissile program on the back burner for most of his two terms from 1993 to 2001. *(Antimissile defense chronology, Congress and the Nation Vol. X, p. 307)*

Several events in the late 1990s, however, sped up development of a system, setting the stage for George W. Bush's decision.

NAVY PROGRAM CANCELED

A navy antimissile program was terminated in late 2001 because of ballooning costs.

Under the Nunn-McCurdy provision of the fiscal 1983 defense authorization bill (PL 97-252), if the per-unit cost of any weapon grew by 25 percent or more over the last estimate, the Pentagon had to drop it unless the secretary of defense certified that it was essential to national security and there was no cheaper alternative.

The navy's short-range antimissile program, intended to protect ships at sea and in port, failed the test. The system's price tag had grown by 65 percent and on Dec. 14, 2001, the Pentagon announced that it had axed the program, terminating a multibillion dollar deal with defense contractor Raytheon. The fiscal 2002 defense appropriations bill (HR 3338—PL 107-117), which was in conference at the time, provided $100 million to pay contract termination costs.

In 1998 a panel of experts led by Donald H. Rumsfeld—who would become Bush's secretary of defense—warned that Iran and North Korea could have missiles within five years that would be capable of reaching the U.S. mainland. North Korea tested a medium-range missile over the Pacific Ocean that year. The following year Congress cleared and Clinton signed legislation (PL 106-38) declaring U.S. intentions to deploy a national missile defense as soon as technologically feasible. Citing technical problems and diplomatic opposition, Clinton ultimately left that decision to his successor. *(PL 106-38, Congress and the Nation Vol. X, p. 306)*

During the 2000 presidential campaign Bush had made clear that developing a system that would protect all fifty states from at least a limited number of ballistic warheads was one of his top national security priorities. Opposition from Russia, European allies, China, and congressional Democrats failed to sway Bush to change his mind.

The Sept. 11, 2001, terrorist attacks made it easier for the president to argue his case, with Bush portraying missile defense as another element of his overall plan to protect the nation from missile attacks by rogue states or terrorist groups.

But the ABM Treaty appeared to be a roadblock to his plans. For the Bush administration to continue its plans to test and deploy a missile defense system, the treaty would have to be revised, replaced, or terminated.

ABM TREATY

For almost three decades the ABM Treaty had framed the strategic nuclear balance of power between the United States and the Soviet Union, and then Russia.

Under the pact signed on May 26, 1972, each nation was allowed two antimissile defense sites (later reduced to one) to protect a limited area but not the entire country. The underlying strategy was "mutually assured destruction"—neither side would launch a first strike because it could not protect itself from retaliation. *(Background, Congress and the Nation Vol. III, p. 895)*

Another fundamental goal was to prevent what was known as a "breakout" potential. The treaty's limits were intended to make it difficult for either side suddenly to seize the upper hand by quickly deploying a much more robust defense than the pact allowed and undermining the other country's ability to deter an attack.

Limits on the number of antimissile interceptors could be easily circumvented because the missiles were small and could be covertly built and stockpiled. Some antimissile missiles might be almost indistinguishable from antiaircraft missiles, which the treaty did not limit. The pact instead limited the number and location of the radars needed to detect an approaching missile and steer an interceptor into it. The treaty required that all radars and antimissile launchers at each country's permitted site be located within a circle 300 kilometers (186 miles) in diameter. Because of the curvature of the earth, radars in that small an area could provide coverage for only a small portion of either country. Because the radars were huge and took years to build, either side would have ample warning if the other embarked on expanding the geographic scope of its antimissile defense.

The treaty also aimed to inhibit rapid breakout by banning the development or deployment of mobile sensors or antimissile launchers that were part of a defense against long-range missiles, including those based on planes, ships, or space satellites. Thus the pact would have barred the so-called Space-Based Infra-Red System (SBIRS)-Low program, a network of orbiting telescopes designed to detect attacking missiles with real warheads rather than decoys and help steer intercepting rockets.

It also prohibited the use of interceptor missiles launched from ships or air-borne lasers designed to destroy ballistic missiles soon after they were launched and before they could deploy decoys.

The treaty required the parties to discuss the status under the treaty of any new types of sensors and weapons that could be used against long-range strategic missiles. Treaty critics contended this would give Russia a veto over the testing and deployment of such promising technologies as space-based lasers.

Either party to the treaty could withdraw six months after giving formal notice.

TESTING PROGRAMS

Pentagon officials had telegraphed Bush's decision for months, with Rumsfeld warning in October 2001 that the missile defense testing program "was going to bump up against the treaty." That month Rumsfeld deferred tests that he said could have violated the treaty; the action came shortly before Bush was to meet with Putin to discuss revisions to the accord, among other issues.

The deferred tests would have involved use of an Aegis radar aboard a warship to track a long-range missile; its purpose was to assess the feasibility of modifying the navy's fleet of ships to supplement other antimissile weapons.

Pentagon officials had concluded that plans to build an additional testing facility in Alaska also could violate the accord. The testing range was to include five missile silos on Kodiak Island and a command center and five missile silos at Fort Greely on the Alaskan mainland, connected to an upgraded radar at Shemya Island. While additional testing facilities of this type might have been allowed under the treaty, Pentagon officials had said that they might deploy the system on an emergency basis by 2004, which would have been a violation of the accord.

Democrats and arms control groups argued that those steps were unnecessary given the immaturity of missile defense technology. They said the administration intentionally scheduled the tests to force a showdown over the treaty. "There is a lot more fanfare, a lot more interest in bumping up against the treaty than in trying to help find a system that works," said Sen. Jack Reed, D-R.I.

Russia had been insisting that the treaty be preserved because it undergirded mutual deterrence between the two nuclear powers. A more extensive U.S. missile defense than the limited one allowed by the treaty would give the United States an intolerable degree of psychological leverage over Russia, according to some observers. And many thought the pact was at least as important to Moscow symbolically as it was militarily. With Russia's economy shaky and large parts of its military establishment in decay, its strategic nuclear force was one of its few claims to superpower status. The ABM Treaty and the other strategic arms agreements embodied the country's status as an equal of the United States.

But some speculated that to the extent that Bush accorded Putin standing as a valued partner in the war on terrorism, it might be easier for Russia to accept a new strategic framework that would supplant the ABM Treaty, particularly if it required the United States to make the same kind of deep cuts in its nuclear force that Russia soon would have to make for budgetary reasons. Stuck with an aging arsenal it could not afford to replace, Russia had long sought mutual reductions. At that time the United States had more than 7,000 long-range nuclear warheads and Russia had more than 6,000. Russia had pressed for years to cut that number to about 1,500, but the Pentagon had resisted a reduction that large. During the 2000 presidential campaign Bush had promised significant—but unspecified—nuclear arms reductions.

The search for a new U.S.-Russian agreement—either a substantial revision of the ABM Treaty or a replacement for it—was to have been a focal point of a Bush-Putin summit meeting in November 2001. No agreement on the ABM Treaty emerged from that meeting, but both sides did agree to cut their nuclear arsenals. Bush said that he had informed Putin that the United States would reduce its deployed nuclear warheads to a level between 1,700 and 2,200 over the next decade. Putin said that Russia would "try to respond in kind."

BUSH ANNOUNCEMENT

The failure of the two leaders to reach an agreement on the ABM pact set the stage for Bush's December announcement that the United States would withdraw from the treaty.

"We know that the terrorists, and some of those who support them, seek the ability to deliver death and destruction to our doorstep via missile," Bush said Dec. 13. "And we must have the freedom and the flexibility to develop effective defenses against those attacks."

Although angered by the decision, congressional Democrats knew it would be politically difficult to challenge Bush, who was riding a wave of popularity as the commander in chief of the successful military operation in Afghanistan.

Moreover, although the legal record was not crystal clear, it appeared that Bush had the constitutional authority to withdraw the United States from the ABM pact without seeking congressional approval. "In practice, U.S. treaties have been terminated in a variety of ways," said David M. Ackerman, a legislative attorney with the Congressional Research Service of the Library of Congress. "Most commonly the president takes the initiative." In 1979 congressional conservatives had been unsuccessful in getting the courts to prevent President Jimmy Carter from unilaterally terminating the 1955 mutual defense treaty with Taiwan. *(Court case, Congress and the Nation Vol. V, p. 101)*

Although the response from Russia on the ABM Treaty was muted, senior Bush administration officials indicated they would be willing to yield to Moscow's demands that proposed cuts in both countries' nuclear arsenals be codified, with appropriate verification and enforcement mechanisms. Following up on Bush's November pledge to reduce its nuclear warheads, Putin had announced Dec. 14 that he would cut his arsenal to between 1,500 and 2,200 warheads. The United States and Russia signed an arms reduction treaty in May 2002, which was approved by the Senate in 2003. *(Arms reduction treaty, p. 363)*

European allies, reluctant to criticize Bush as they participated in the global anti-terrorism campaign, also muted their criticism.

LEGISLATIVE ACTION

The Sept. 11 terrorist attacks and the subsequent boost for defense programs spared Bush's $8.3 billion request for the missile defense system from any congressional cuts or significant changes in 2001. Democrats had planned to add a provision to the fiscal 2002 defense authorization bill (S 1438—PL 107-107) to keep testing of the program within the bounds of the ABM Treaty, but those initiatives were dropped after the attacks. That left intact administration plans to install the five

test missiles at Fort Greely. The final version of the bill provided the full amount sought by Bush, a $3 billion increase over the previous fiscal year's total. *(2002 defense authorization, p. 308)*

Congress cut about $500 million from Bush's request in the fiscal 2002 defense appropriations bill (HR 3338—PL 107-117). Appropriators were especially critical of the SBIRS-Low program, which had been plagued by delays, technical problems, and cost overruns. HR 3338 directed the Pentagon to overhaul it. The bill also included funds to terminate a navy antimissile program that had far exceeded its budget. *(2002 defense appropriations, p. 316; Navy program canceled, p. 331)*

In 2002 Congress authorized the requested $7.8 billion for antimissile defense, including funds for the initial deployment in Alaska, as part of the fiscal 2003 defense authorization bill (HR 4546—PL 107-314). The bill barred use of any of the funds for work on a nuclear-armed interceptor. No missile defense programs in development at that time used nuclear warheads, but some Pentagon officials had raised the possibility. *(2003 defense authorization, p. 320)*

The most contentious topic in the conference on HR 4546 was congressional oversight of the missile defense program. At issue was how much detail the Pentagon should be required to give Congress about the projected costs, progress, and performance of the system. Rumsfeld was insisting that Congress should accept less detailed information on the program as it became more fluid in its long-range goals and timetables. He wanted authority for the Pentagon to shift funds from one program to another and make other changes without going through the often lengthy reprogramming process of informing Congress and receiving its approval.

A number of lawmakers were uneasy with the administration's approach. The stakes were exceedingly high for liberal critics, who stood to lose access to the type of information that had provided them with some of their most potent ammunition against the program. Even some centrist members who backed missile defense were troubled, insisting that Congress needed more information simply to do its job. The Senate bill would have required highly detailed reports on four high-profile antimissile weapons. There was no such requirement in the House version, but in its report accompanying the measure the House Armed Services Committee directed the Pentagon to continue providing Congress with the data it had been receiving before Rumsfeld's changes. Rumsfeld said the president would veto the bill if it included the Senate's requirements. Conferees settled on language that basically incorporated the House requirement into law along with some additional reporting requirements.

The 2003 defense appropriations bill (HR 5010—PL 107-248) included $7.4 billion for missile defense. An attempt by House critics to cut funding for the Alaska deployment was rejected during the floor debate. *(2003 defense appropriations, p. 326)*

Defense Review

In a congressionally mandated Pentagon review issued just three weeks after the Sept. 11, 2001, terrorist attacks on the United States, Secretary of Defense Donald H. Rumsfeld called for giving U.S. forces an edge in combating adversaries who could exploit technology to threaten U.S. interests at home and aboard.

To move toward the Bush administration's goal of transforming America's post–cold war military from a conventional weapons giant into a more agile force, the Quadrennial Defense Review (QDR), released Oct. 1, 2001, recommended larger investment in space satellites, robot planes, and precision-guided weapons for the military. However, while the QDR outlined broad themes and called for a handful of specific steps, it provided no details about the cost of the reshaped strategy or existing Pentagon programs that should be canceled or cut back to pay for the changes.

Although the review had been under way for several months and was largely completed before Sept. 11, Rumsfeld said in a written preface that those assaults confirmed the review's conclusions, including "its emphasis on homeland defense, on surprise, [and] on preparing for asymmetric threats."

The review cited as the Pentagon's top priority the defense of U.S. territory, which included the controversial Reagan-era missile defense system and protection of critical domestic infrastructure against terrorist attack. The review said the Pentagon would consider designating a high-ranking commander in chief for military forces involved in homeand defense.

More than twenty advisory panels had participated in the quadrennial assessment of defense capabilities.

TWO-WAR STRATEGY

In the 1990s Pentagon planning focused on keeping U.S. forces ready to win two major regional wars simultaneously. In 1997 the previous quadrennial review added to the "two-war" standard a requirement that U.S. forces be ready to conduct less demanding peacekeeping and humanitarian missions. *(Defense assessments, Congress and the Nation Vol. X, p. 263)*

Maintaining the combat readiness of forces to meet the two-war strategy took priority over all other considerations. To fulfill that requirement service members were transferred among units on short notice, funds that were earmarked to repair facilities were diverted to pay training costs, and budgets to develop new technologies were short-changed, according to Republican critics of President Bill Clinton's policies. Moreover, Republicans accused the Clinton administration of wasting the combat capability of the armed forces on missions the GOP dismissed as peripheral to U.S. security interests.

There was speculation that Rumsfeld would drop the two-war goal in his defense assessment, but the secretary opted instead for a more complex change. The previous policy had been interpreted as a requirement that U.S. forces be massive enough to not only defeat two enemies on the battlefield but also to occupy both rivals' capitals and change their political regimes. Rumsfeld's standard still required the services to win two major wars at the same time. In fact, the new policy expanded the range of missions that U.S. forces had to fulfill simultaneously, requiring that they also be able to protect the United States as well as conduct several smaller peacekeeping and humanitarian missions. However, the new standard significantly reduced the size of the force needed by requiring that only one of the two enemy capitals be occupied.

FEW SPECIFICS

Those awaiting a detailed outline of the Pentagon's budget priorities were disappointed by the report's lack of specifics.

Senate Armed Services Committee Chair Carl Levin, D-Mich., said the document "seems to me to be full of decisions deferred . . . rather than the comprehensive road map to the force of the future envisioned by Congress."

"It has nice words and goals, but it doesn't really glue things together," said Ike Skelton of Missouri, ranking Democrat on the House Armed Services Committee. "It's not that helpful."

Aides to Rumsfeld argued that critics were overlooking administration initiatives to deal with nontraditional threats. Pentagon officials cited the increase of more than 50 percent in spending for the missile defense system as an example of transformation. They argued that the technology would thwart a potential threat that conventional forces could not stop—a small number of ballistic missiles that could strike the United States. Rumsfeld also had made some changes in the Pentagon's budget process designed to foster more realistic long-range plans that would place a higher priority on developing high-tech forces for the future while maintaining the current force.

While not calling for any change in the military's size, the review did suggest redeploying some units so forces could more quickly be deployed to distant trouble spots. These steps included stationing more navy ships in the western Pacific and developing high-speed transport ships for marine units. It also called for deploying in Europe by 2007 a newly organized army brigade equipped with lightweight combat vehicles.

The report said a new Pentagon office, reporting directly to Rumsfeld, would be created to encourage the services to transform themselves with new organizations and new technologies to make units more lethal and agile.

One of the initiatives endorsed by the review was an increase in the size and complexity of large-scale war games, using actual combat forces to try out new ways of organizing and equipping units.

The nearest thing to a budgetary commitment was the review's call for spending 3 percent of the defense budget on basic research, compared with a roughly 2.7 percent share in President Bush's $343.3 billion budget for fiscal 2002.

Nuclear Posture Review

President George W. Bush's plans to restructure the U.S. nuclear arsenal to counter new threats to national security led to debate in the 107th Congress over whether his proposals would expand the use of nuclear weapons or merely continue existing policies.

The debate was begun by the administration's "Nuclear Posture Review," a congressionally required report laying out the direction for U.S. nuclear forces over the next five to ten years.

In the review, which was submitted to Congress at the end of 2001, the administration indicated that it wanted to be ready to resume nuclear testing within as little as eighteen months if the president decided it was necessary. The United States had adhered to a self-imposed moratorium on testing since the administration of Bush's father nearly a decade earlier. Despite the Senate's rejection of the Comprehensive Test Ban Treaty in late 1999, few in Congress believed that underground testing should resume anytime soon. *(Nuclear test ban, Congress and the Nation Vol. VIII, p. 392; nuclear test ban extension, Congress and the Nation Vol. IX, box p. 293; test ban treaty, Congress and the Nation Vol. X, p. 310)*

The administration also said that as it reduced the U.S. nuclear arsenal, a significant number of demobilized nuclear warheads would be maintained in a ready-for-deployment condition as part of a "responsive force" if some future buildup were warranted. During negotiations with Russian president Vladimir V. Putin in 2001, President Bush had announced that the United States would reduce its nuclear arsenal from about 6,000 warheads to between 1,700 and 2,250 in the next decade, a move that had been welcomed by arms-control advocates and many in Congress.

UNCLASSIFIED CONCLUSIONS

In an unclassified section of the Nuclear Posture Review released Jan. 9, 2002, the administration concluded that:

• The United States should no longer "plan, size or sustain" its nuclear forces as though Russia presented a smaller version of the threat posed by the former Soviet Union. Instead, planning should shift from the threat-based approach of the cold war to an approach based more on capabilities.

• A strategic posture that relied solely on offensive nuclear forces was inappropriate for deterring terrorism and other potential threats to the United States.

• The United States' offensive strike capability should go beyond the cold war triad of intercontinental ballistic missiles, submarine-launched ballistic missiles, and long-range nuclear-armed bombers.

• The United States should develop and deploy both active and passive defenses such as missile defense systems.

• Spending on aging buildings and other infrastructure at nuclear weapons laboratories and factories should be increased.

• Although the existing policy banning underground weapons tests should remain in place, plans should be made to resume testing quickly if the president decided such tests were needed.

CLASSIFIED PORTION

Subsequent leaks of the classified portion of the Pentagon's Nuclear Posture Review forced into the open the debate over the uses of nuclear weapons at a time when the cold war standoff largely had given way to potential conflicts with a half-dozen smaller powers and the threat of terrorism.

The Pentagon report suggested that nuclear weapons could be used to prevent—or retaliate against—attacks from terrorists and countries, such as Iraq or North Korea, armed with chemical or biological weapons. In particular the review called for developing miniaturized nuclear warheads that could penetrate underground military facilities while minimizing radiation and other dangers to civilian populations.

The report claimed there were more than 10,000 underground military facilities in more than seventy countries, with 1,400 such facilities deemed of special importance because they housed weapons of mass destruction, ballistic missiles, or top-level military command stations.

Defending the new strategy, President Bush told reporters March 13, "We've got to have all options on the table, because we want to make it very clear to nations that you will not threaten the United States or use weapons of mass destruction against us or our allies or friends."

Many congressional Democrats, however, said the Pentagon's plan to broaden the potential use of nuclear weapons while developing a new line of "low-yield" weapons would endanger longstanding U.S. efforts to halt nuclear development in other regions. But Republicans said the Pentagon was simply trying to provide the president with the maximum number of options in a potential conflict.

In a July 2001 report to Congress that had been requested in the fiscal 2001 defense authorization bill (PL 106-398), the Defense Department noted that conventional explosives often were ineffective or counterproductive in attacking underground targets and that even a successful conventional attack could endanger nearby civilians by spreading chemical or biological agents to nearby areas. Small nuclear weapons, on the other hand, had a "unique ability" not only to destroy the bunker, but also to neutralize the chemical and biological weapons stored there, the report said.

But the administration's proposal for a bunker-buster ran counter to a provision in the fiscal 1994 defense authorization bill (PL 103-160) that prohibited the Pentagon from researching or developing new low-yield nuclear weapons, defined as those that produce an explosion equivalent to 5,000 tons (five kilotons) or fewer of TNT. An attempt to repeal that provision was rejected during action on the fiscal 2003 defense authorization bill (HR 4546—PL 107-314). HR 4546 barred funding for the bunker-buster program until after the secretary of defense submitted a report to the congressional defense committees on the proposed weapon. *(Nuclear weapons research, p. 362)*

NATO Expansion

Congress in 2002 passed legislation (HR 3167—PL 107-187) declaring its support for expansion of the North Atlantic Treaty Organization (NATO). The bill cleared in May as President George W. Bush prepared for a NATO summit that was expected to begin considering which of ten countries that had applied for membership should be admitted to the alliance.

Although HR 3167 did not specifically designate which countries should join NATO, it did authorize $55.5 million in military aid for the seven countries that lawmakers and outside experts thought were most likely to be offered membership: Estonia, Latvia, Lithuania, Slovakia, Slovenia, Bulgaria, and Romania. (Albania, Croatia, and Macedonia were the other three countries hoping to join.)

At a November 2002 summit those seven were invited to accession talks with NATO, and they formally joined in 2004. The Senate in 2003 approved a modification of the 1949 treaty forming the alliance to include the new members. *(108th Congress action, NATO expansion, p. 365)*

Some members of Congress had been concerned that U.S. support for the inclusion of the former Soviet-controlled Baltic states of Estonia, Lithuania, and Latvia might harm U.S.-Russian relations, particularly attempts to reach a deal on missile defense. Those countries bordered Russia, had substantial Russian minorities, and were ruled by the former Soviet Union for half a century.

But in June 2001 Bush made clear his position that Russian concerns should not influence NATO's decision. And after the Sept. 11, 2001, terrorist attacks on the United States, Russian leader Vladimir V. Putin indicated that Russia was less concerned about such expansion, particularly if its own relations with NATO were strengthened. At the May 2002 summit NATO created a new role for Russia, giving it a place at the table for discussions of common issues such as peacekeeping, terrorism, arms control, and missile defense.

NATO was last expanded in 1999, when the Czech Republic, Hungary, and Poland joined. *(NATO expansion, Congress and the Nation Vol. X, p. 272)*

LEGISLATIVE ACTION

The House passed HR 3167 by a vote of 372–46 on Nov. 7, 2001. The House International Relations Committee had reported the bill (H Rept 107-266) on Nov. 5.

The Senate approved HR 3167 by a vote of 85–6 on May 17, 2002, clearing the bill for the president. The Senate Foreign Relations Committee had reported HR 3167 (no written report) on Dec. 12, 2001, but John W. Warner of Virginia, ranking Republican on the Senate Armed Services Committee, blocked floor action on the bill for months.

Warner, who had also opposed the 1999 expansion of NATO, argued that adding new members only diluted the alliance's effectiveness and cohesion. But Richard G. Lugar, R-Ind., a senior member of the Foreign Relations Committee, insisted that NATO needed to be expanded as part of a broader strategy to shift it from a defensive alliance to an organization dedicated to countering terrorism and the proliferation of weapons of mass destruction. Warner relented and allowed the bill to move forward after Secretary of State Colin L. Powell and Defense Secretary Donald H. Rumsfeld wrote a letter to congressional leaders urging Senate action.

MAJOR PROVISIONS

As signed into law on June 10, 2002, HR 3167:

Endorsed the vision of President Bush and former president Bill Clinton to expand the NATO alliance.

Authorized foreign military financing on a grant basis to the following: Estonia ($6.5 million); Latvia ($7 million); Lithuania ($7.5 million); Slovakia ($8.5 million); Slovenia ($4.5 million); Bulgaria ($10 million); and Romania ($11.5 million).

Nonproliferation Funds

Funding for Energy Department nonproliferation programs was the main issue during conference action on the fiscal 2002 energy and water development appropriations bill (HR 2311—PL 107-66). Democrats had wanted more money for programs to detect, prevent, and counter the spread of nuclear materials worldwide, but the $804 million in the final bill, although $30 million more than requested, was still less than in either the House version ($845 million) or the Senate bill ($881 million).

House conferees had rejected a proposal by Chet Edwards, D-Texas, to shift $131 million from weapons programs to nonproliferation efforts in the former Soviet Union. Edwards and others cited concerns that al Qaeda leader Osama bin Laden and other terrorists might try to acquire nuclear weapons from Russia or elsewhere. Several House Democrats voted against the conference report (H Rept 107-258), which cleared Nov. 1, 2001, specifically because of the failure to increase nonproliferation funding.

An additional $226 million was subsequently allocated by the fiscal 2002 defense spending bill (HR 3338—PL 107-117) from the emergency funds provided in the aftermath of the Sept. 11 terrorist attacks (HR 2888—PL 107-38).

2003–2004

The 108th Congress, like the preceding one, gave President George W. Bush much of what he wanted for defense. The president's military spending requests had gone all but unchallenged after the nation suffered the Sept. 11, 2001, terrorist attacks and fought a retaliatory war in Afghanistan. That situation continued as the United States in 2003 launched a broader, more complicated, more deadly war in Iraq. Lawmakers were not going to deny their commander in chief or the armed forces he sent into battle the resources that were needed.

Ongoing military operations in Afghanistan and the war in Iraq were funded mostly by a series of supplemental spending bills. Despite complaints from Democrats that this piecemeal approach was keeping Congress in the dark about the true costs of the war, the legislators gave the White House the money it wanted. The measure covering the initial costs of the Iraq war was at the time the largest supplemental appropriations ever enacted, but that record was broken less than seven months later by a second war supplemental. Congress, however, refused to give the Pentagon the latitude it wanted in spending and transferring the money, and instead allocated much of it.

Members were generous as well when it came to regular Pentagon spending, which continued to grow each fiscal year. Although many experts acknowledged that more big-ticket weapons were in development than the military would be able to afford, the Pentagon continued to back most of them, and so did Congress. One notable exception during the 108th Congress was the decision by Defense Secretary Donald H. Rumsfeld to cancel the army's Comanche helicopter, a multibillion dollar program plagued by cost increases and delays, and more recently by questions about its effectiveness on the battlefield.

Congress remained supportive of the administration's goal of transforming the military into a lighter, agile, high-tech force. It did not, however, give the Pentagon a blank check, and by 2004 members were taking a closer look at several of the transformation programs and making some cuts in spending.

Lawmakers were particularly attentive to the needs of the men and women in uniform, approving pay raises and increasing benefits for service members and their families. Mindful of the burdens placed on members of the National Guard and reserve forces called to active duty to serve in Afghanistan and Iraq, they gave those without employer-provided health insurance access to the Defense Department's health care system. For veterans who had retired with disabilities, Congress continued to expand the pool of persons who could receive both full disability compensation and retirement benefits.

Congress also wanted to increase the number of men and women in uniform. Over Pentagon objections, lawmakers authorized the largest increase in troop levels in decades.

Members of the 108th Congress grappled with some particularly contentious issues. Efforts to stop or at least postpone another round of base closings in 2005 were defeated. House attempts to impose more rigid "Buy American" requirements for Pentagon procurement were blocked. Members were told to start over on a controversial plan for the air force to acquire aerial refueling tankers.

Administration plans to study the feasibility of a nuclear "bunker buster" that would burrow deep into the ground to destroy enemy bunkers suffered a setback. The 108th Congress at first agreed to let the Energy Department proceed with its study but then refused to fund it.

Congress continued to back Bush's plans for missile defense and fully funded deployment of the first antimissile interceptors in 2004.

2004 Defense Authorization

Congress in 2003 cleared a $401.3 billion fiscal 2004 defense authorization bill (HR 1588—PL 108-136). President George W. Bush had requested $400.5 billion.

There was no significant challenge to the overall funding level, a fact members of both parties attributed to a hawkish national mood after the Sept. 11, 2001, terrorist attacks.

Still, the bill had been stalled for months in one of the longest House-Senate defense conferences in memory. But, in a departure from most defense debates, the battles were mainly over policy questions, not weapons systems. Among the central issues were "Buy American" protections for U.S. suppliers, new work rules for civilian Pentagon employees, and the acquisition of airborne tankers from the Boeing Co. The focus on policy was the result of both a consensus on spending for most weapons and a new House Armed Services Committee chair—Duncan Hunter, R-Calif.—who was eager to put his stamp on the bill.

Congress approved most of the money that Defense Secretary Donald H. Rumsfeld requested to transform U.S. forces into new high-tech units that relied more on speed, stealth, and precision than on massed firepower and heavy armor. At the same time, though, it provided funding for some of the old-fashioned weapons systems Rumsfeld was hoping to replace, such as the seventy-ton M1 Abrams tank and the twenty-five-ton Bradley fighting vehicle.

Rumsfeld also got broad leeway to hire, fire, and transfer civilian Pentagon employees and link their pay raises to performance—another major element of his transformation strategy. Democrats had fought vigorously against the changes, saying federal workers, most of whom belonged to unions, would lose civil service protections, and that the bill's employee protections were inadequate.

Conferees agreed on a plan to buy eighty Boeing 767 aerial refueling tanker planes and lease another twenty instead of the Pentagon's original plan of leasing all 100 for six years before buying them. Critics argued that the original plan was a sweetheart deal for Boeing that would cost much more than buying 100 new tankers. Just a week after HR 1588 was enacted, the Pentagon put the plan on hold after two Boeing executives were fired for unethical conduct in connection with the tanker deal. (*Boeing tanker deal investigation, p. 348*)

The brightest sparks were generated by debate over the Buy American language. Rumsfeld had asked Congress for greater leeway in waiving existing Buy American requirements for defense procurement. The Senate had agreed to give him some of the flexibility he wanted, but the House had gone in the opposite direction, adding more restrictions. The final bill encouraged the Pentagon to purchase products from domestic suppliers, but it did not include House provisions aimed at blocking purchases of certain defense-related materials from foreign suppliers.

HR 1588 authorized a range of improved benefits for troops, including a 4.1 percent pay raise, and expanded the number of disabled veterans who could receive their full retirement and disability benefits at the same time. The bill also gave the military more flexibility in complying with environmental laws that the Pentagon said hindered training operations by limiting areas open to use.

HOUSE COMMITTEE ACTION

The House Armed Services Committee reported its $400.5 billion version of HR 1588 on May 16, 2003, and filed a supplemental report on May 21 (H Rept 108-106, Parts I and II).

Committee members spent two days in often partisan battles on hot-button issues, but the lopsided 58–2 vote to approve the bill reflected the panel's customary bipartisan consensus on most facets of the defense budget. In one key respect the consensus was broader than ever: for the first time in years, there was no significant debate on Bush's missile defense program. The bill authorized $9.1 billion, the amount Bush requested.

The committee adopted a modified version of Rumsfeld's civilian personnel proposal that had been approved by the House Government Reform Committee May 7. The Government Reform panel, which had principal jurisdiction over federal civilian workforce issues, added several employee safeguards, including the creation of an independent board to hear employees' appeals of adverse personnel actions. Democrats and labor unions dismissed those amendments, warning that the proposed changes would open the door to political and personal favoritism, which the civil service system was designed to prevent. Republicans insisted that the personnel system's rigidity rewarded mediocrity and stifled initiative. But even some committee Republicans acknowledged discomfort with the sweeping authority Rumsfeld was seeking and the short time lawmakers had to digest it.

The committee rejected Rumsfeld's request for authority to allow general staff officers to serve longer before being forced to retire. Rumsfeld said the changes would promote

faster transformation of the military, but opponents said it was unclear how the changes would work and why they were needed in the first place.

In response to Rumsfeld's request for more flexibility to waive Buy American requirements, the House bill went in the opposite direction. Rumsfeld argued that the waivers were justified to promote the standardization of equipment among U.S. and allied forces, to help U.S. forces meet emergency needs, and to save the Pentagon millions of dollars. Pentagon officials also pointed out that U.S. companies relied increasingly on foreign sources for both raw materials and components, and that strict adherence to domestic-content laws could require a U.S. contractor to raise its prices or turn down the job altogether. But the House committee bill, reflecting Hunter's staunch support for protecting the nation's industrial base, authorized $100 million for a fund to develop U.S. suppliers for key materials and components. It also proposed to expand the list of items the Pentagon was required to purchase from domestic suppliers and limited the defense secretary's existing authority to waive the requirement.

The committee approved a bipartisan compromise on a White House request to repeal a provision of the fiscal 1994 Defense Authorization Act (PL 103-160) that prohibited research and development that could lead to production of a nuclear weapon with an explosive yield of 5 kilotons or less. The compromise allowed research on small weapons but prohibited construction of prototypes. The bill included a requested $15 million to research a nuclear weapon—known as the Robust Nuclear Earth Penetrator or "bunker buster"— to destroy hardened and deeply buried targets, and an additional $6 million to study other novel nuclear weapons.

The committee added $727 million to the administration's budget to continue M-1 and Bradley upgrade programs that the Pentagon wanted to terminate so the money could be used for transformational programs.

Under threat of a presidential veto, the committee agreed to remove from the bill language that would have blocked the next round of base closings in 2005. But the committee did stipulate that the commission deciding which bases to close would have to preserve enough domestic bases to accommodate a somewhat larger active-duty force than existed at the time. (*Background, military base closings, p. 315*)

The panel rejected attempts to strike language in the bill aimed at giving the military leeway in complying with the Endangered Species Act of 1973 (PL 93-205) and the Marine Mammal Protection Act of 1972 (PL 92-522). The Pentagon asked Congress for limited exemptions from those two laws, as well as several others, including the Clean Air Act Amendments of 1990 (PL 101-549), the Resource Conservation and Recovery Act of 1976 (PL 94-580), and the Comprehensive Environmental Response, Compensation, and Liability Act of 1980 (PL 96-510), also known as the superfund law. The Defense Department owned or controlled 25 million acres of land, much of it wilderness that provided habitat to an estimated 300 endangered and threatened species. Military leaders had been trying to convince Congress that while they sought to be good stewards of their lands, they needed some leeway to provide realistic training such as beach assaults, tank battles, or bombing runs.

HOUSE FLOOR ACTION

The House passed the $400.5 billion bill on May 22 by a vote of 361–68.

During the May 22 floor debate, the House rejected 199–226 an amendment by Ellen O. Tauscher, D-Calif., to transfer $21 million in research funds for nuclear weapons, including the bunker-buster bomb, into research on non-nuclear methods for destroying hardened and deeply buried targets. Her amendment was defeated during committee consideration as well. During a visit to Capitol Hill the day before the floor vote, Rumsfeld insisted the plan was merely to study whether nuclear weapons might be useful for specific missions. But most Democrats maintained that the administration's legislative proposals, combined with its January 2002 nuclear strategy statement, portended a decision to base U.S. strategy increasingly on the possible use of nuclear weapons. In the 2002 statement the Pentagon said it was considering putting some decommissioned nuclear warheads in reserve and indicated that it wanted to reduce the time it would take to resume nuclear tests if a decision was made to do so. *(Nuclear posture review, p. 335)*

Democrats were blocked by the rule for floor debate from offering an amendment to require that any new civilian personnel system respect certain employee rights, including the rights to unionize and to appeal adverse personnel actions. The only option the GOP-written rule gave Democrats was to offer an amendment to eliminate the civilian personnel provisions—which the Democrats turned down as politically hopeless. As a result, the only House vote on the civilian personnel issue came at the end of debate on a Democratic motion to recommit the bill to committee with instructions to add the language. The motion was defeated on a near party-line vote of 204–224.

As part of an en bloc amendment adopted by voice vote, the House agreed to require that Pentagon purchases subject to the Buy American Act have at least 65 percent domestic content instead of 50 percent as required by existing law.

The House rejected 201–227 a Loretta Sanchez, D-Calif., amendment to allow servicewomen and female military dependents stationed overseas to obtain abortions in U.S. military medical facilities if they paid for the procedure themselves.

SENATE COMMITTEE ACTION

The Senate Armed Services Committee had reported its $400.5 billion version of the bill (S 1050—S Rept 108-46) on May 13.

The committee deferred action on Rumsfeld's civilian personnel proposal; members of both parties said they had not had enough time to study it.

The defense secretary had more success in winning committee approval of the combat-oriented elements of his transformation plan. Like the House panel the committee approved the fiscal 2004 budget requests for such projects as a new family of lightweight army combat vehicles and a new type of navy destroyer designed to operate with a smaller crew.

The administration's proposals for new types of low-yield nuclear weapons were the most controversial issue. The committee approved the repeal of the 1993 provision prohibiting research on developing low-yield nuclear weapons. The committee also approved the $15 million requested to continue studying the feasibility of modifying existing nuclear bombs to attack underground targets, although it stipulated that it was not giving the go-ahead for testing or fielding a new weapon. But S 1050 did require the Energy Department to upgrade its nuclear test site in Nevada so an underground test could be conducted within eighteen months if a president decided to order one. Although the U.S. government had voluntarily observed a moratorium on nuclear testing since 1992, the Senate had refused to ratify the Comprehensive Test Ban Treaty in 1999, opening the way for resumed testing. *(Test ban treaty, Congress and the Nation Vol. X, p. 310)*

Other provisions of the bill authorized the $9.1 billion requested for missile defense and gave the Pentagon the leeway it requested for dealing with the requirements of the Endangered Species Act. The bill barred the air force from signing an agreement to lease Boeing refueling tankers until the service conducted a formal assessment of other ways to deal with its aging fleet of tankers.

SENATE FLOOR ACTION

The Senate passed S 1050 by a vote of 98–1 on May 22. It passed HR 1588 by voice vote on June 4, after inserting the text of S 1050.

Democrats were rebuffed in their attempt to limit the bill's nuclear weapons provisions during debate May 21, but they claimed a victory of sorts for drawing public attention to the administration's nuclear policy and requiring congressional approval before new weapons could be developed. The Senate voted 51–43 to table (kill) a Dianne Feinstein, D-Calif., amendment to strike the language repealing the 1993 provision that banned research and development of low-yield nuclear weapons. But the Senate adopted 59–38 an amendment by Armed Services Chair John W. Warner, R-Va., requiring the administration to obtain specific congressional authorization before beginning development of a low-yield weapon. Warner's amendment modified a proposal by Jack Reed, D-R.I., that would have allowed basic research on such weapons but prohibited design and development. The Senate then adopted the revised Reed amendment 96–0. The Senate tabled 56–41 a Byron L. Dorgan, D-N.D., amendment to block the $15 million requested for the bunker buster, but it adopted by voice vote amendments by Bill Nelson, D-Fla., to require congressional authorization before any nuclear earth penetrator weapon was manufactured and to require the Pentagon to study the use of nonnuclear explosives for that purpose.

The Senate adopted by voice vote a Jeff Bingaman, D-N.M., amendment requiring congressional authorization before beginning the design or development of a space-based antimissile interceptor missile. An amendment by Reed, also adopted by voice vote, required more detailed Pentagon reports about the performance specifications and planned test programs for antimissile weapons.

The Senate on May 22 rejected 48–51 an amendment by Patty Murray, D-Wash., to ease abortion restrictions at U.S. military hospitals overseas. Members voted 85–10 on May 20 to, among other things, allow National Guard and reservists to enroll with their immediate families in Tricare, the military health care plan for active-duty members. The amendment had been proposed by Minority Leader Tom Daschle, D-S.D., and modified by a Lindsey Graham, R-S.C., amendment.

In an unusual procedure, the Senate allowed votes on several more amendments June 4 when it took up HR 1588. The Senate rejected 42–53 a proposal by Dorgan and Trent Lott, R-Miss., to cancel the 2005 round of base closings.

The Senate adopted by voice vote a proposal by Minority Whip Harry Reid, D-Nev., to repeal a provision in an 1891 law that barred veterans with service-related disabilities from receiving both full retirement pay and full disability compensation, known as "concurrent receipts." Congressional estimates placed the ten-year cost at up to $58 billion. In 2002, after a long standoff, the fiscal 2003 defense authorization bill (HR 4546—PL 107-314) included a provision that allowed a small pool of retirees injured during battle to collect both their pensions and their disability payments. *(2003 defense authorization, p. 320)*

CONFERENCE ACTION

The House on Nov. 7 adopted the conference report on HR 1588 (H Rept 108-354) by a vote of 362–40. The Senate cleared the bill on Nov. 12 by a vote of 95–3.

The bill had been tied up in conference for months as negotiations between Hunter and Warner dragged on with no progress. Eventually, however, House Majority Leader Tom DeLay, R-Texas, gave Hunter an ultimatum: clear the defense bill within forty-eight hours—in time for Veterans' Day—or the leaders would break out the popular concurrent receipt provision and send it to the floor as stand-alone legislation. Hunter promptly compromised on several divisive issues.

The House language to restrict the foreign content of weapons attracted a flurry of opposition not only from the administration, but from most of the defense industry, the nation's closest allies, and perhaps most important, Warner and Sen. John McCain, R-Ariz. But Hunter stood firm. He had been arguing for years that U.S. forces could not rely on foreign manufacturers for critical combat equipment, and his commitment to preserving a strong U.S. defense industry coincided with the more parochial concerns of lawmakers whose companies back home faced foreign competition for defense contracts. Rumsfeld's deputy, Paul D. Wolfowitz, and Hunter appeared to work out a compromise, but Warner opposed it and a meeting of top officials at the White House ultimately rejected it.

Rancor over the Buy American issue carried through the conference negotiations, until Hunter backed down and settled for a provision directing the secretary of defense to establish a program to encourage contractors to purchase machine tools manufactured in the United States. Hunter said the provision would "provide a resurgence" of the U.S. machine tool industry; at the time, most high-end tools came from Germany and Japan.

Hunter, as well as the chairs of the House and Senate Defense Appropriations subcommittees, backed the air force plan to spend $17 billion to lease 100 refueling tankers from Boeing for six years and an additional $4 billion to buy the planes at the end of the lease. Defense Department officials agreed with critics of the plan that it would be cheaper to simply buy 100 new tankers. But since federal budgeting rules required the armed services to pay the full cost of major purchases up front, air force officials maintained the service could not afford to buy the new planes. A lease, they argued, would allow the service to spread the cost over many years, thus consuming a smaller amount of the annual air force budget in any one year. Warner at first offered a compromise that called for the air force to lease twenty-five planes and buy seventy-five, but the Pentagon objected. Warner subsequently proposed that twenty planes be leased and eighty purchased. The Pentagon and Hunter ultimately went along with Warner, and the compromise was incorporated into the conference report, despite objections from House Speaker J. Dennis Hastert, R-Ill., whose state was home to Boeing's corporate headquarters.

Conferees compromised on Rumsfeld's personnel plans, accepting a flexible, merit-based hiring and promotion system while preserving some collective bargaining rights and whistle-blower and other civil service protections. But many Democrats remained strongly critical of the changes.

Conferees accepted the Senate proposal to authorize access to Tricare for National Guard and reserve members who did not have access to employer-provided insurance. They also agreed to phase in concurrent receipt of disability benefits and full retirement pay for some veterans, despite Democrats' objections that the legislation would exclude two-thirds of all disabled veterans.

Before concluding, conferees waded into one last policy matter that focused on the strains facing the National Guard and military reserve units from near-constant service since Sept. 11, 2001. Hunter and fifty other House members wrote Rumsfeld in October 2003, asking the Pentagon to greatly increase the number of active-duty soldiers under arms. The Pentagon and Warner disagreed, saying it would be several years before large numbers of new troops would be ready for the battlefield. The conference report contained a modest increase of 2,400 army soldiers.

MAJOR PROVISIONS

As signed into law Nov. 24, 2003, HR 1588 authorized $401.3 billion for defense spending in fiscal 2004, slightly over Bush's request for $400.5 billion.

Major provisions of HR 1588:

Military Personnel

Authorized $98.9 billion for military personnel.

Authorized for fiscal 2004 an active-duty force of 1,390,500—2,400 more than requested for fiscal 2004 and 800 more than authorized for fiscal 2003.

Authorized an across-the-board 4.1 percent pay raise for military personnel increases in imminent danger pay from $150 per month to $225 per month, and a boost to the family separation allowance from $100 to $250 per month through Dec. 31, 2004.

Authorized access to Tricare, the Defense Department's health care system, for National Guard and reserve members who lacked access to employer-provided health insurance.

Civilian Personnel

Revised personnel rules for the Pentagon's civilian workforce, including relaxing restrictions on the hiring and firing of personnel and allowing pay and promotion to be more directly linked to performance.

Operations and Maintenance

Authorized $114.9 billion.

Facilities

Authorized $9.3 billion for military construction and family housing.

Missile Defense

Authorized $9.1 billion as requested for ballistic missile defense. The total included funding for the initial deployment of a national missile defense system based in Alaska.

Ground Forces

Authorized the requested $1.7 billion to develop a new family of army combat vehicles that would weigh less than twenty tons and would eventually supplant the seventy-ton M1 Abrams tank and the twenty-five-ton Bradley fighting vehicle.

Authorized $458 million in unrequested funds to upgrade the M1 and Bradley.

Aviation Forces

Authorized the air force to buy up to eighty Boeing 767 aerial refueling tanker plans and to lease up to twenty more, with deliveries starting in 2009.

Authorized $4.4 billion for development of the Joint Strike Fighter, a multi-role fighter aircraft to be used by the air force, navy, and Marine Corps.

Authorized $3.5 billion for the F/A-22 Raptor, the air force's next-generation, premier fighter intended to replace the F-15 and F-16. The bill also authorized $936 million for research and development for the plane.

Authorized $3 billion for forty-two next-generation F/A-18 E/Fs, the navy's upgrade of the F/A-18 C/D aircraft.

Naval Forces

Authorized $1 billion, as requested, for the navy's next-generation surface combat ship, the DD(X).

Authorized $3.2 billion for three DDG-51 *Arleigh Burke*-class Aegis guided-missile destroyers.

Authorized $1.5 billion for procurement of the sixth boat in the *Virginia*-class of new attack submarines.

Nuclear Weapons

Authorized $17.3 billion for defense-related activities carried out primarily by the Energy Department.

Allowed research on low-yield nuclear weapons by repealing a provision of the fiscal 1994 Defense Authorization Act (PL 103-160) that had barred research and development that could lead to production of a nuclear weapon with an explosive yield of five kilotons or less. But HR 1588 stated that nothing in the repeal should be construed as authorizing the testing, acquisition, or deployment of such a weapon.

The bill included $15 million for research on an earth-penetrating nuclear weapon to destroy hardened and deeply buried targets, along with $6 million for other advanced initiatives. The bill barred the energy secretary from beginning the engineering development phase of the so-called Robust Nuclear Earth Penetrator weapon unless specifically authorized by Congress.

Veterans' Benefits

Authorized military retirees considered to be at least 50 percent disabled under Department of Veterans Affairs guidelines to receive their full retirement and disability benefits at the same time. This concurrent receipt was to be phased in over the next ten years. For certain veterans with combat-related disability, concurrent receipt began in January 2004. The estimated ten-year cost was $22 billion. *(Earlier provision, 2003 defense authorization, p. 320).*

Buy American Issue

Encouraged the Pentagon to purchase products from domestic suppliers. The bill directed the defense secretary to establish an incentive program for contractors to purchase American-made machine tools.

Other Provisions

Barred the interior secretary from designating areas on military training ranges as "critical habitat" under the Endangered Species Act of 1973 (PL 93-205) if the area already was subject to a Defense Department natural resources management plan. HR 1588 also gave the military more leeway under the Marine Mammal Protection Act of 1972 (PL 92-522) to conduct activities that might disturb whales and other sea mammals.

Required that the Defense Department conduct open competitions for contracts related to the reconstruction of Iraq's oil industry, and required that noncompetitive contracts for work on Iraq's infrastructure be made public. The existing contract to manage Iraq's oil industry had been awarded on a sole-source basis to Halliburton Co., formerly headed by Vice President Dick Cheney.

2004 Defense Appropriations

Congress in 2003 cleared a $368.7 billion fiscal 2004 defense appropriations bill (HR 2658—PL 108-87). The legislation was the most expensive defense spending package in history, although it was still $3.6 billion less than President George W. Bush requested.

Driven by the grim reality of soldiers serving and dying in Iraq and Afghanistan, lawmakers put partisan politics aside for the most part and moved quickly on the legislation. Total spending was virtually the same in the House and Senate versions. At Bush's urging, negotiators made swift work of the conference report after returning from the August recess, and the two chambers adopted it with little debate.

But the rapid action did not erase all differences. Defense hawks warned that the amount appropriated for procurement—$74.7 billion—was woefully inadequate. Democrats, meanwhile, complained that the administration was giving Congress no estimates of the costs of the Iraq war, instead funding it piecemeal through supplementals.

In a sign of concern over the battering that military equipment was taking with increased operations around the world, HR 2658 contained $115.9 billion for operations and maintenance, $1.2 billion more than the fiscal 2003 level.

The bill provided $9.1 billion for ballistic missile defense programs, roughly equal to Bush's request. Democrats remained concerned that work on the program could destabilize efforts to control the spread of nuclear weapons, but they largely chose to ignore the issue, focusing their effort on nuclear research initiatives in other legislation. *(Nuclear weapons research, p. 362)*

Most of the main programs for the air force, navy, and army were funded at or near the administration requests. The bill also included an average 4.1 percent raise for military personnel, as requested.

Early in their work on HR 2658, GOP appropriators had agreed to a White House proposal to cut about $3 billion from Bush's original defense request and shift it to domestic spending to reduce the fiscal pressure on those bills. That left discretionary allocations of $368.7 billion for the defense bill in the House and $368.6 billion in the Senate. While the ap-

propriators were looking ahead to a fiscal 2004 supplemental spending bill to restore some of that $3 billion, they also wanted an immediate way to get more funds in HR 2658. Their answer was to rescind $3.5 billion in unused funds from the Iraq Freedom Fund, allowing them to spend that much more in the fiscal 2004 bill. The money had been appropriated in the fiscal 2003 supplemental spending law (HR 1559—PL 108-11) enacted in April 2003. The White House criticized the move as limiting the flexibility needed by the president and the Pentagon to plan war efforts. But Senate Appropriations Committee Chair Ted Stevens, R-Alaska, said there was nothing financially questionable about the transaction, noting that HR 1559 had provided about $6 billion that probably would not be spent by the end of the fiscal year. *(2003 supplemental, p. 329; 2004 supplemental, p. 344)*

In addition to HR 2658's military spending, other components of the defense budget approved in 2003 included $16.4 billion for atomic energy defense activities in the fiscal 2004 energy-water appropriations bill (HR 2754—PL 108-137) and $9.3 billion for military construction and family housing in the fiscal 2004 military construction appropriations bill (HR 2559—PL 108-132).

HOUSE ACTION

The House passed its $369.2 billion version of HR 2658 by a vote of 399–19 on July 8, 2003. The House Appropriations Committee had reported the bill (H Rept 108-187) on July 2.

The Appropriations Committee had approved the bill after less than a half hour of debate. Committee members made clear their disappointment at the loss of the $3 billion to the domestic spending bills, and as a quick remedy, the panel approved a rescission of $2 billion from the fiscal 2003 supplemental.

The committee rejected the navy's request for multiyear contract authority to purchase seven *Virginia*-class submarines over five years and instead approved funding for one in fiscal 2004. The panel expressed concern that the multiyear plan could end up absorbing too much of the navy's budget.

The committee added $458 million in unrequested funds to upgrade Bradley armored troop carriers and M1 Abrams tanks, a reflection of House support for traditional army weapons systems. These were the kind of heavy fighting vehicles that Defense Secretary Donald H. Rumsfeld was seeking to replace as part of his "transformation" initiative aimed at creating lighter, more mobile forces. However, the panel also included $990 million for the Stryker, a lightweight armored vehicle, and $1.7 billion for the Future Combat System, a family of lightweight fighting vehicles and robots armed with precision-guided weapons.

During floor action the only amendment voted on was a proposal by John Hostettler, R-Ind., to block the use of funds in the bill to carry out the round of military base closures set to begin in 2005. It was rejected 57–358. The amendment was a last-ditch effort by closure opponents who had failed to block the base closing during action on the fiscal 2004 defense authorization bill (HR 1588—PL 108-136). *(2004 defense authorization, p. 337)*

Several Democrats offered amendments but withdrew them after being assured their concerns would be addressed in conference.

SENATE ACTION

The Senate passed a $369.1 billion version of HR 2658 by a vote of 95–0 on July 17. The Senate Appropriations Committee had reported its version (S 1382—S Rept 108-87) on July 9.

The only dust-up during committee action came when Larry E. Craig, R-Idaho, tried to require the air force to send sixteen C-130 cargo planes to Air National Guard units after it completed the planned procurement of forty C-130s through 2015. Craig had become increasingly vocal about the poor quality of C-130s provided to Guard units and in protest had blocked the usually routine Senate votes on the promotions of more than 200 officers. Craig's amendment was defeated, but several members said they sympathized with his complaints and would push for enhanced planes for the Guard.

Unlike its House counterpart, the Senate panel agreed to allow multiyear purchasing of *Virginia*-class submarines. But citing potential cost overruns, the panel proposed to limit the navy to five new submarines instead of seven in fiscal 2004 through 2008.

S 1382 included an extra $61.9 million for Bradley vehicles for the National Guard. But the Appropriations Committee diverted other resources to the army's Stryker brigades—faster, lighter units based on the new armored vehicle.

The Senate panel rescinded $3.2 billion from the 2003 supplemental.

The Senate agreed to substitute the text of S 1382, when it took up HR 2658. During four days of floor debate Democrats raised questions and criticisms about the administration's handling of the war in Iraq. Working together, Appropriations Chair Stevens and Daniel K. Inouye of Hawaii, the ranking Democrat on the Defense Appropriations Subcommittee, turned back most of those amendments. But questions remained, particularly about future costs of the operation in Iraq.

Amendments rejected included proposals by:

• Richard J. Durbin, D-Ill., to block disbursement of $50 million until the president submitted a report on the role played by executive branch policy makers in the development and use of intelligence relating to the Iraq war. His amendment was tabled (killed), 62–34.

• Jon Corzine, D-N.J., to create an independent commission to study the administration's development and use of intelligence leading up to the Iraq war. The proposal was tabled 51–45.

• Byron L. Dorgan, D-N.D., to require the administration to send a fiscal 2004 budget amendment to Congress outlining expected costs of continued operations in Iraq. It was tabled 53–41.

• Barbara Boxer, D-Calif., to require monthly administration reports on the cost of military actions in Iraq. The amendment was tabled 50–45.

• Edward M. Kennedy, D-Mass., to require an administration report on strategies for Iraqi reconstruction and schedules for seeking international assistance in Iraq. His proposal was tabled 52–43.

• Jeff Bingaman, D-N.M., to require a full accounting of enemy combatants taken prisoner during either the war on terrorism or the wars in Iraq and Afghanistan. Human rights activists argued that the prisoners should either be formally charged or be released. The amendment was tabled 52–42.

• Robert C. Byrd of West Virginia, the ranking Democrat on the Appropriations Committee, to shift $1.1 billion to programs covered by other spending bills to halt the global spread of AIDS. The amendment was tabled 71–24.

• Byrd, to set limits on how long reservists could be deployed in a single year. It was tabled 64–31.

CONFERENCE ACTION

The House adopted the conference report by a vote of 407–15 on Sept. 24. The Senate cleared it the next day by a vote of 95–0.

With a speed born of the deteriorating security situation in Iraq, House and Senate negotiators had pushed the defense bill through conference in just twenty-five minutes. Their report was filed a week later, and twenty-seven minutes after that it was called up on the floor without going through the Rules Committee and then passed after seven minutes of debate. The Senate acted almost as quickly.

The final bill changed little from the nearly identical House and Senate versions. Conference negotiations centered on the question of how many *Virginia*-class submarines to buy and whether to grant multiyear procurement authority to the navy. Conferees bowed to the Senate, fully funding the sub at $2.3 billion in fiscal 2004 and approving multiyear procurement authority for five boats through fiscal 2008.

But the conferees stated in their report that they did not agree lightly to the multiyear procurement. The appropriators had allowed such procurement in the past when the navy had accepted a fully tested and proven system and a production capability had been fully established. In this case the lead ship had not been fully tested and was not scheduled to be delivered to the navy until late 2004. The conferees said they were deviating from traditional policy with the expectation that multiyear procurement would serve to stabilize the program and reduce the overall costs to the government. They promised to reconsider the multiyear authority if this was not the case. They also criticized the navy for concluding contracts to buy two submarines in fiscal 2007 when only one had been approved by Congress.

Conferees decided to continue the Defense Department's Terrorism Information Awareness (TIA) system, while dismantling its existing structure. The critics had voiced privacy concerns about the program, which was supposed to screen thousands of individuals for possible terrorist connections. The intelligence-gathering program had attracted criticism on Capitol Hill when lawmakers learned of a government-funded research project to create an online futures market designed to predict the likelihood of violence in the Middle East. Sponsored by the Pentagon's Defense Advanced Research Projects Agency (DARPA), the project was quickly scrapped after it came under fire from lawmakers in both parties. Conferees agreed to strip DARPA of all funding for TIA and move it to an unidentified agency. Addressing a persistent complaint by congressional critics, Stevens said the program would "only be used for foreign activities."

The conferees kept $418 million in unrequested funds in the bill for improvements to the Bradley fighting vehicle and the M1 tank. Rep. Jerry Lewis, R-Calif., chair of the House Defense Appropriations Subcommittee, said the older weapons performed well in Iraq and argued that it was important to keep making improvements to them.

Conferees agreed to $9.1 billion for missile defense, about $200 million more than in either the House or Senate version.

MAJOR PROVISIONS

As signed into law on Sept. 30, 2003, HR 2658 appropriated $368.7 billion for fiscal 2004 military spending.

Major provisions of HR 2658:

Military Personnel

Appropriated $98.5 billion for military personnel.

Included an average 4.1 percent pay increase for military personnel in fiscal 2004, equal to Bush's request.

Included $128 million for increases in family separation allowances and imminent-danger pay for troops in Iraq and Afghanistan.

Set a ceiling on the number of active-duty personnel in fiscal 2004 at 1,388,100, as requested.

Operations and Maintenance

Appropriated $115.9 billion.

Missile Defense

Appropriated $9.1 billion for ballistic missile defense programs, roughly equal to Bush's request.

Ground Forces

Appropriated $1.7 billion, as requested, for the Future Combat System, a family of lightweight fighting vehicles and robots armed with precision-guided weapons.

Appropriated $990 million for Stryker vehicles, $35 million more than requested.

Appropriated $418 million in unrequested funds for improvements to the Bradley fighting vehicle and the M1 Abrams tank.

Aviation Forces

Appropriated $3.6 billion—$80 million less than requested—to purchase twenty-two F-22 Raptor fighters, the air force's next-generation, premier fighter designed to have both air-to-air and air-to-ground fighter capabilities and intended to replace the F-15 and F-16.

Appropriated $4.3 billion—$43 million less than requested—for continued development and testing of the multi-role Joint Strike Fighter planned for the air force, navy, and Marine Corps.

Appropriated $3 billion, as requested, for forty-two next-generation F/A-18 E/Fs, the upgrade of the existing F/A-18 C/D, which was the navy's and Marine Corps' primary strike aircraft.

Appropriated $1.4 billion for procurement and continued development of unmanned vehicles, or drones. The vehicles had proven particularly useful in identifying and tracking enemy targets in Afghanistan and Iraq and conducting missions considered too dangerous for manned aircraft.

Naval Forces

Appropriated $2.3 billion for the *Virginia*-class of new attack submarines. The bill allowed multiyear contracting authority to buy a total of five boats through 2008, instead of seven over five years as the navy had wanted.

Appropriated $3.2 billion, as requested, for three DDG-51 *Arleigh Burke*-class Aegis guided-missile destroyers.

Antiterrorism

Appropriated $4.5 billion for special operations forces—a 47 percent increase from fiscal 2003 spending—and $1 billion for procurement and development of chemical and biological defenses.

Dismantled a controversial Defense Department intelligence-gathering program, the Terrorism Information Awareness system, but most of its functions were moved to an unspecified office.

Rescission

Rescinded $3.5 billion from the fiscal 2003 supplemental spending law (HR 1559—PL 108-11).

2004 Iraq Supplemental

Just weeks after clearing the regular fiscal 2004 defense bill (HR 2658—PL 108-87), Congress cleared an $87.5 billion fiscal 2004 supplemental appropriations bill (HR 3289—PL 108-106) to pay for the ongoing military and reconstruction costs in Iraq and Afghanistan. The bulk of the supplemental, $65.1 billion, was for military operations.

Lawmakers had planned all along to pay for the cost of the wars through a supplemental, but the price tag had taken members by surprise. It was the largest supplemental spending bill in U.S. history, breaking the record that had just been set by a $78.5 billion fiscal 2003 supplemental bill (HR 1559—PL 108-11) that covered the initial costs of the war in Iraq. *(2003 defense supplemental, p. 329)*

For some lawmakers in both parties the president's request for an $87 billion war supplemental seemed to confirm suspicions that the mission in Iraq was not going as well as the administration had predicted. The government of Iraqi leader Saddam Hussein had fallen in April 2003, and Bush had declared major combat operations over May 1. Yet U.S. soldiers were dying in a near-daily series of attacks by insurgents in Iraq. Questions also were being raised about the accuracy of prewar intelligence, particularly administration claims that Saddam was hiding weapons of mass destruction, none of which had been found. *(Pre-Iraq war intelligence, p. 282)*

LEGISLATIVE ACTION

The money for military operations was never in doubt—nobody was ready to cut off funding for troops who were putting their lives on the line—but questions were raised about the reconstruction money, in particular whether Iraq should be required to pay some of it back. Only after a veto threat and aggressive lobbying by the White House did Congress agree to provide all of the reconstruction money as grants. *(2004 aid appropriations, p. 288)*

Bush announced his $87 billion request in a televised address to the nation Sept. 7, 2003. The House passed its $86.9 billion version of HR 3289 (H Rept 108-312) by a vote of 303–125 on Oct. 17. The Senate passed an $86.4 billion version (S 1689—S Rept 108-160) by a vote of 87–12 that same day, and then inserted the text into HR 3289 and passed that bill by voice vote. The House agreed to the conference report (H Rept 108-337) by a vote of 298–121 on Oct. 31. The Senate cleared the bill by voice vote Nov. 3.

MAJOR PROVISIONS

As signed into law Nov. 6, HR 3289:

Appropriated $65.1 billion for military operations in Iraq and Afghanistan, including military construction costs related to the global war on terrorism. An additional $135 million was inserted to pay for reconstructing military facilities damaged by Hurricane Isabel, which struck the East Coast of the United States in September.

Appropriated $18.4 billion for relief and reconstruction in Iraq, plus $210 million for Jordan, Liberia, and Sudan.

Appropriated $1.2 billion for reconstruction in Afghanistan.

Appropriated an unrequested $500 million for disaster relief activities related to California wildfires and Hurricane Isabel.

Expanded Tricare, the health care program for the military, to extend coverage for one year to National Guard members, reservists, and their families who lacked medical insurance, were unemployed, or did not have access to employer-provided insurance. The expansion, approved

over White House opposition, was expected to cost about $400 million and affect about one-fifth of National Guard and reserve members.

Established an inspector general to monitor the Coalition Provisional Authority's handling of Iraq reconstruction money. When Bush signed the bill, he limited the inspector general's power, blocking audits or investigations that would require access to intelligence matters, among other things.

Allowed the Pentagon to transfer $3 billion between accounts, rather than the $5 billion the administration had sought.

2004 Military Construction

Congress in 2003 cleared a $9.3 billion fiscal 2004 military construction appropriations bill (HR 2559—PL 108-132).

The military construction bill—usually one of the first spending bills to clear due to the inclusion of millions of dollars for members' districts—was slowed in 2003 by tight budget constraints. President George W. Bush initially had proposed $9.1 billion for the bill, a 15 percent reduction from the previous year's regular and supplemental appropriations total. The White House argued that the Pentagon could afford to cut back construction of runways, fitness centers, and educational facilities because of planned base closures. That did not sit well with lawmakers, who counted on earmarks to enhance domestic military bases, boost local construction industries, and burnish their reputations. The budget squeeze led to weeks of bickering between House and Senate negotiators over which chamber's programs would ultimately make it into the conference bill.

Conferees finally reconciled Pentagon and legislative priorities into the $9.3 billion package, partly by reducing spending on overseas bases to accommodate domestic projects. The final bill was 13 percent below the fiscal 2003 total.

An additional $525 million for military construction had been included in the fiscal 2004 Iraq supplemental appropriations bill (HR 3289—PL 108-106) that cleared a few weeks earlier. *(2004 Iraq supplemental, p. 344)*

LEGISLATIVE ACTION

The House passed a $9.2 billion version of HR 2559 on June 26, 2003, by a vote of 428–0. The House Appropriations Committee had reported the bill (H Rept 108-173) on June 23.

The only suspense came when Democrats announced that David R. Obey of Wisconsin, the Appropriations Committee's ranking Democrat, would offer an amendment to add $958 million to the bill, to be offset by a one-year reduction in a recently enacted tax cut (HR 2—PL 108-27) for taxpayers with annual incomes above $1 million. Obey's amendment had been defeated during subcommittee and full committee consideration. When the bill reached the floor, the House voted 220–200, along strict party lines, to preclude the Obey amendment on procedural grounds.

The Senate passed HR 2559 by a vote of 91–0 on July 11 after inserting the text of its own $9.2 billion bill (S 1357). The Senate Appropriations Committee had reported S 1357 (S Rept 108-82) on June 26.

The Senate version established a congressional panel to study U.S. overseas bases and report to Congress within a year on a possible reconfiguration. Kay Bailey Hutchison, R-Texas, the Military Construction Appropriations Subcommittee chair, said Congress was waiting for the Pentagon to offer more concrete details on its plans to restructure forces based abroad. Pentagon plans included moving U.S. forces out of Western Europe and to smaller bases in Africa, Eastern Europe, and the Caucasus that could be staging areas to deploy troops more quickly to the Middle East, Africa, and other unstable areas. The Defense Department also said U.S. forces in South Korea would draw back from the North Korean border and out of Seoul.

CONFERENCE ACTION

The House adopted the conference report on HR 2559 (H Rept 108-342) on Nov. 5 by a vote of 417–5. The Senate cleared the bill on Nov. 12, 98–0.

The chief impediment to quick agreement was the different rosters of projects in the two bills. The final bill roughly split the projects between the two chambers, although House members complained that the Senate got the bigger half.

House negotiators had accused the Senate of trying to shortchange foreign bases to free up money for home-state spending. But Hutchison argued against meeting the president's request for $1 billion for overseas military construction projects, saying it made little sense to spend on facilities in Germany and South Korea if the Pentagon was planning to shift forces out of those places. The final bill provided $698 million for overseas military construction.

Conferees also included—over the objections of the Office of Management and Budget—the Senate provision establishing a commission to study the overseas military force structure.

MAJOR PROVISIONS

As signed into law on Nov. 22, 2003, HR 2559:

Military construction. Appropriated $4.9 billion for military construction—$370 million more than requested.

The bill also included $161 million—$8 million less than requested—for the U.S. share of NATO infrastructure projects.

Family housing. Appropriated $3.8 billion for family housing—$164 million less than requested.

Base closings. Appropriated $370 million, as requested, for environmental cleanup and other projects related to base closings.

Commission. Established a commission to review the overseas military force structure and report to Congress by Dec. 31, 2004.

2005 Defense Authorization

Congress in 2004 cleared a $445.6 billion fiscal 2005 defense authorization bill (HR 4200—PL 108-375). President George W. Bush had requested $448.1 billion.

The defense authorization debate had been a lengthy affair. As a result, for the third year in a row, the authorization was enacted after appropriators had completed the companion spending bill (HR 4613—PL 108-287), thus reducing the authorizers' influence on military funding. But the authorizers retained their say on matters of policy, weighing in on the future of a troubled refueling plane program, base closures, troop levels, and military pay and benefits. They also detailed how the military should spend $25 billion in emergency funds for ongoing military operations in Iraq and Afghanistan.

The refueling tanker issue had been the most difficult one for House-Senate conferees. HR 4200 required the air force to start over on a deal to replace its aging fleet of refueling tanker aircraft. Members had been battling over the proposed deal since December 2001, when a proposal to lease the aircraft from Boeing Co. was initially approved by the Senate Defense Appropriations Subcommittee. HR 4200 barred the air force from leasing the aircraft and appeared to require competitive bids for any new tanker deal, although Boeing's congressional allies disputed that. (*Air force tanker deal, box p. 348*)

The final bill did not include House language to delay for two years the round of base closings planned for 2005. The White House had threatened to veto the bill if it contained such a provision. Also dropped was a Buy American provision in the House bill to restrict the ability of the Pentagon and its contractors to buy from any source around the world.

Congress mandated the largest increase in troop levels in decades. HR 4200 boosted the size of the army by 20,000 and the Marine Corps by 3,000. The increases did not affect force levels in Iraq.

The bill also made numerous improvements to benefits for military personnel, retirees, and their families. Besides a 3.5 percent pay raise, the law authorized larger benefits for survivors of deceased military personnel, concurrent receipt of full pensions and full disability payments in 2005 for veterans considered 100 percent disabled, and expanded access for reservists to the military's health system. The bill eliminated a statutory cap on spending for a popular program to encourage private construction of military housing. At least 50,000 families had to wait for improved homes until Congress addressed the cap. An attempt to raise the cap failed during consideration of the fiscal 2005 military construction appropriations bill (HR 4837—PL 108-324) because doing so would have pushed the bill over its spending allocation. (*Background, 2005 military construction, p. 353*)

HR 4200 authorized $10 billion for missile defense systems, including interceptors being installed in Alaska and California as part of the first national antimissile shield. (*Missile defense, p. 362*)

HOUSE COMMITTEE ACTION

The House Armed Services Committee reported a $447.2 billion version of HR 4200 (H Rept 108-491) on May 14, 2004.

The committee bill closely followed the president's funding request but differed from the administration and the Senate committee version on several key points. For example, the bill increased the size of the military by 39,000 troops, delayed the planned 2005 round of base closings, and dictated how the president should spend his $25 billion war request. All were certain to draw protests from the White House, but, nonetheless, the bill was approved by a 60–0 vote.

During markup Democrats unsuccessfully targeted Bush's request for $27.6 million to study development of a nuclear bomb that would burrow deep into the earth to destroy underground enemy bunkers. Supporters stressed that the program was only a study of a Robust Nuclear Earth Penetrator, or nuclear "bunker buster." But critics said any research toward a new nuclear weapon would damage U.S. counterproliferation efforts and encourage nuclear activity by other countries. They also said the $485 million that the Energy Department planned to spend on the program between fiscal 2005 and 2009 suggested the administration was conducting more than a study.

Committee Democrats also attempted to cut or redirect missile defense spending, again unsuccessfully.

But the issue of base closings transcended partisan divisions, as the committee voted to delay the planned 2005 closure round until 2007. The White House claimed that closing unneeded facilities could save the Pentagon $6.5 billion a year, and in the past the president had threatened to veto bills that would stop base closures. Still, House proponents were hopeful that a delay would be more likely to survive politically than past attempts to kill the closures altogether. (Background, military base closings, box p. 315)

Bush on May 12 sent Congress his official request for a $25 billion emergency fund for operations in Iraq and Afghanistan. The president sought nearly unlimited control over the funds despite recent disclosures that the White House took advantage of flexibility granted in previous supplementals to use at least $178 million appropriated to fight terrorism and recover from the Sept. 11 attacks for projects to prepare for the war in Iraq. This time the administration requested $20 billion for operations and maintenance for the military and $5 billion for activities it did not specify. The proposal also would have permitted Defense Secretary Donald H. Rumsfeld to "transfer the funds provided herein to any appropriation or fund" within the Pentagon budget.

But the House Armed Services Committee included instructions to divide up the $25 million, including $16.2 billion for operations and maintenance, $5.3 billion for personnel, and $2.4 billion for Humvees, body armor, unmanned aerial vehicles, and more.

The committee bill authorized $95 million for development and advanced procurement of Boeing KC-767 refueling tankers.

The committee expressed concern about the army's Future Combat System (FCS), a planned $92 billion network of new-technology weapons, sensors, and vehicles that formed part of the lighter, faster, and deadlier army envisioned by Rumsfeld. The panel recommended $3 billion for FCS, $245 million less than requested, but it limited the authorization to $2.2 billion until the army reported to the committee on the program's progress. The committee in its report said it supported the army's transformation goals and capabilities that FCS promised, but that it was "greatly concerned about the army's ability to deliver these capabilities within cost and schedule estimates. The army has never managed a program of the size and complexity of FCS."

Armed Services Committee Chair Duncan Hunter, R-Calif., a vocal proponent of offering protection to the U.S. defense industry through "Buy American" laws, took aim at "offsets"—the practice of foreign governments conditioning their purchases of U.S.-built weapons on investments by U.S. companies in their countries. Hunter wrote into the House bill a provision to block the Pentagon from trading with foreign companies whose governments required a defined level of offsets when buying U.S. goods.

HOUSE FLOOR ACTION

The House approved its $447.2 billion version of HR 4200 on May 20 by a vote of 391–34.

During debate that day the House soundly rejected 162–259 an amendment to delete the bill's language delaying the next round of base closures for two years, leaving it as scheduled for 2005. Among those voting in support of the delay—even after the language drew an explicit veto threat from the White House—were 103 Republicans, 47 percent of the caucus, a rare instance of parochial political considerations triumphing over House GOP loyalty to the president.

Lawmakers on May 19 adopted 231–191 an amendment by Virgil H. Goode Jr., R-Va., that allowed members of the armed services to assist the Homeland Security Department with border protection. Democrats opposed the amendment, arguing it would unnecessarily strain the military.

An amendment by Hunter to condemn prisoner abuse at Iraq's Abu Ghraib prison was adopted 416–4 on May 19, but only after Democrats argued the proposal would be better if it called for a full investigation into the charges. Henry A. Waxman, D-Calif., on May 20 offered a motion to recommit the bill so that language to authorize such an investigation could be added. The motion failed 202–224. The House also voted 308–114 to urge the Pentagon to raze the Abu Ghraib prison. Opponents said the Iraqi people, and not the Pentagon, should decide the prison's fate. (Wartime prisoner abuse, p. 359)

By 290–132 the House adopted an amendment to authorize a Pentagon training program for the Taiwanese military.

Democrats unsuccessfully sought to shift $36.6 million from research programs on nuclear weapons, including the $27.6 million for the bunker buster, to improving intelligence

AIR FORCE TANKER DEAL

An air force plan to replace its aging fleet of refueling tanker aircraft with Boeing aircraft proved to be the most difficult issue to resolve during the conference on the fiscal 2005 defense authorization bill (HR 4200—PL 108-375). Even after conferees thought they had everything settled and the final bill cleared, lawmakers were still arguing over what the conference agreement meant.

This was not much of a surprise—members had been battling over the issue for four years. Critics derided it as a sweetheart deal for Boeing. Supporters saw it as a fair deal that would also assist an important member of the aviation industry in the post-Sept. 11 downturn.

Deal's Origin

The tanker saga began in December 2001, when the Defense Appropriations Subcommittee marked up the fiscal 2002 defense spending bill (HR 3338—PL 107-117). That legislation allowed the air force to negotiate to lease 100 Boeing 767 passenger jets that had been modified to become KC-767 tankers. The estimated price tag at the time was $20 billion over ten years.

Before that action, the air force had not requested replacements for its fleet of more than 500 KC-135 tankers, many of which were built during the administration of President Dwight D. Eisenhower in the 1950s. The air force had said those planes would not need replacing for years.

But three months before the appropriations markup, the Sept. 11, 2001, terrorist attacks sent the commercial aviation market into a nosedive. Also, Boeing had lost the $245 billion Joint Strike Fighter competition to Lockheed Martin Corp. Ted Stevens of Alaska, then ranking Republican on the Senate Appropriations Committee and its Defense Subcommittee, said he wrote the leasing provision for the 767s into law out of concern for the military's increasing refueling requirements in the war on terrorism. Aides said he was supported by Democratic senators, including Daniel K. Inouye of Hawaii, then the Defense Subcommittee chair, and Patty Murray of Washington, where Boeing was then based (its headquarters were later moved to Illinois) and where it continued to build 767s.

The original idea apparently was Boeing's. The company had pitched it to the air force in February 2001. After the provision became law, the air force became an advocate for the lease proposal, discussing for the first time what was termed a serious corrosion problem in the tankers and urging their rapid replacement. By leasing the planes, rather than buying them, more planes could be obtained sooner because fewer dollars were required up front, the air force, Boeing, and their congressional allies all said.

Criticism Mounts

Almost immediately Sen. John McCain, R-Ariz., began to criticize the deal as "corporate welfare" and "war profiteering." His voice was amplified by taxpayer groups and a host of government agencies that advised on federal spending.

In the three years after Stevens's provision became law, criticisms were leveled by the Congressional Budget Office, the Congressional Research Service, the Pentagon's Program Analysis and Evaluation Office, the Office of Management and Budget, the Pentagon's Inspector General, the Defense Science Board, and the Government Accountability Office. They said either that the planes were not needed as quickly as the air force maintained because the corrosion problem had been overstated, or that leasing them would cost billions more than buying them. Some critics made both arguments.

The Defense Department did not conduct its own formal evaluation of alternatives to the Boeing deal. The Pentagon document that established the need for the planes was written to suit the Boeing KC-767, McCain argued. An early version of the document even had the plane's name in the title.

Proponents of the deal continued to argue that the planes would be needed sooner rather than later and that leasing them was the only way to get them quickly enough.

Deal Setbacks

In the fall of 2003 the House Armed Services Committee and the two Defense Appropriations subcommittees—three of the four congressional committees that had to approve the tanker deal—had done so. Only the Senate Armed Services Committee was balking. The fiscal 2004 defense authoriza-

capabilities and conventional "bunker busters" to deal with deeply buried targets. They argued that the money would be wasted because many potential targets were in urban areas where the United States would never use a nuclear weapon. But Republicans countered that the United States needed to pursue all weapons programs if it was to maintain a credible deterrence for its enemies. The amendment by Ellen O. Tauscher, D-Calif., was rejected 204–214.

The House also rejected 202–221 an amendment by Susan A. Davis, D-Calif., to allow female service members stationed overseas to obtain abortions at military hospitals as long as they paid for them.

SENATE COMMITTEE ACTION

The Senate Armed Services Committee reported its $422.2 billion version of the 2005 defense authorization bill (S 2400—S Rept 108-260) on May 11. Because the committee had completed its work on the bill before Bush sent his formal request for war funding, it did not address the $25 billion request for Iraq and Afghanistan operations.

tion law (HR 1588—PL 108-136) approved a lease of no more than twenty tankers and purchase of no more than eighty.

On Nov. 24, 2003, President Bush signed that bill into law. Later that same day, Boeing revealed it had fired two of its top executives, chief financial officer Mike Sears and a missile-defense executive, Darleen Druyun. Druyun, a former principal deputy assistant secretary for air force acquisition and management, had secretly negotiated with Sears for her job with Boeing while overseeing the tanker program and other Boeing initiatives, the company said. A month later, Boeing's chief executive, Phil Condit, stepped down. Almost immediately, Defense Secretary Donald H. Rumsfeld suspended the tanker program.

The drumbeat of criticism continued into 2004, including a Pentagon advisory board statement that the KC-135 corrosion problem was not as bad as the air force had argued and a Pentagon inspector general report that said the proposal did not satisfy the military requirement for refueling planes, did not protect taxpayers with complete auditing standards, and used "questionable" pricing assumptions. In May, Rumsfeld deferred action on the program until November, while further studies were conducted of the refueling requirements and the best way to meet them.

On Oct. 1 Druyun was sentenced to nine months in jail after admitting that, while serving as a senior air force official, she accepted a higher than justified price for the tankers, part of more than $4 billion in favors she did for Boeing to repay the company for deciding to hire her and two of her relatives.

A New Approach

The plan to lease twenty and buy eighty of the Boeing planes had an estimated price tag of $23.5 billion. But the 100 planes might have been just the start of a program several times larger because there were 544 KC-135 tankers that would some day need to be replaced.

In 2004 the two chambers' fiscal 2005 defense authorization bills took contrasting approaches to the program. The House bill (HR 4200) would have authorized $98.5 million to start it. Similarly, the fiscal 2005 defense appropriations act (HR 4613—PL 108-287) provided $100 million. The House authorizers ordered the Pentagon to sign a contract by March 2005. In a nod to the problems the inspector general found in the first contract, the House bill set up a blue ribbon panel to oversee the acquisition.

The Senate bill (S 2400), by contrast, prescribed numerous stipulations for any future deal. Their net effect was to bar a lease and to establish extensive independent oversight of any new contract.

In the final hours of the House-Senate conference on HR 4200, the tug of war between conferees over the tanker issue was coming to a close, and the House was running out of rope.

The resulting conference report made fundamental changes in the program. The measure authorized $95 million to start the program but did not allow any planes to be leased. To ensure that a competition occurred, the bill barred the air force from acquiring tankers under the authority of Stevens's fiscal 2002 provision, which empowered the air force to negotiate with Boeing alone. HR 4200 also required a competition for a $5.7 billion maintenance contract that, under the previous plan, would have been given to Boeing without competition.

Disagreements Continue

The new law appeared to require competitive bids for any new tanker deal, although Boeing's congressional allies disputed that interpretation.

On Oct. 8 Rep. Norm Dicks, a Democrat from Washington, suggested in a House floor colloquy with House Armed Services Chair Duncan Hunter, R-Calif., that they had won in conference. "The most important point," Dicks said, "is we don't have to go back and have yet another procurement because if we did that, it would take years and years before we would start getting tankers."

As if in response to the Dicks-Hunter exchange, Senate Armed Services Chair John W. Warner, R-Va., inserted in the Oct. 9 Congressional Record a written exchange with McCain. Not surprisingly, they also claimed victory. In direct contrast to Dicks's contention, McCain insisted that the bill said "the air force cannot acquire, by lease or purchase, Boeing 767s without full and open competition."

And so the debate continued. But, at a minimum, a new contract had to be drawn up.

S 2400 largely mirrored the president's defense authorization request, with a few small exceptions.

The Senate committee bill included several provisions intended to benefit military personnel, including a 3.5 percent pay raise and an increase of more than $400 million in the president's allocation for reservists' health benefits.

Further evidence that lawmakers were focused on helping the troops, especially those in harm's way, was the committee's addition of $603.2 million to the president's request for protective gear and clothing and $925 million for heavily armored Humvees and other vehicle protection.

Unlike the House bill S 2400 did not require the armed forces to expand, but it did authorize Rumsfeld to increase the size of the army by 30,000 by 2009 if he decided that was necessary.

S 2400 granted Bush's request for $10.2 billion for missile defense and fully funded his $27.6 million request to study the feasibility of developing a nuclear bunker buster.

Also intact in the Senate bill was the $4.6 billion requested to continue development of the Joint Strike Fighter warplane. The bill provided funds for twenty-two F/A-22 Raptor fighters, two less than Bush requested.

The committee fully funded the requested $3.2 billion for the army's Future Combat System.

It also authorized seven new warships, including three *Arleigh Burke*-class destroyers and a *Virginia*-class submarine. The panel provided $1.5 billion to continue development of the next-generation DD(X) destroyer, and added $150 million as a down payment on an amphibious assault ship called LHA(R). The first of that type of vessel was expected to cost at least $3.1 billion. The administration had not requested funding for the amphibious ship, which would be built in Pascagoula, Miss., but the navy asked Congress to fund the project if money was available. The committee did not propose making a similar down payment on an additional *Arleigh Burke*-class destroyer that Maine lawmakers wanted to build.

SENATE FLOOR ACTION

The Senate passed a $447.2 billion version of S 2400 on June 23 by a 97–0 vote. The Senate then passed HR 4200 by voice vote after substituting the text of its bill.

Senate passage came after weeks of debate on a range of complex and often politically charged issues.

The bill first came to the floor May 17, but initial deliberations soon bogged down, primarily because members of the Armed Services Committee, who generally managed debate on the defense bill, were distracted by hearings and briefings on prison abuses in Iraq. After a week of largely desultory debate, Senate Majority Leader Bill Frist, R-Tenn., set the bill aside temporarily to take up other legislation. *(Prisoner abuse findings, p. 360)*

Debate on the bill resumed in early June for several days until senators left Washington, many bound for France to commemorate the sixtieth anniversary of the Normandy invasion in World War II. The bill was further delayed when the leadership put aside regular congressional business to manage the highly ritualized proceedings of a state funeral for former president Ronald Reagan, who died on June 5.

The debate finally resumed on June 14 and intensified late in that week. Majority Leader Bill Frist, R-Tenn., threatened on June 16 to limit debate in an effort to complete work on the measure, but late the next day he called off the threat, citing the progress that had been made. Democrats said he did not have the sixty votes needed to invoke cloture.

During the sixteen days of debate on S 2400, the Senate considered 195 amendments. Democrats lost four votes on missile defense amendments, three of which required independent testing of the proposed missile shield the president planned to deploy in Alaska and California starting in the fall of 2004. Democrats also failed by close margins to create a law against "war profiteering," to bar contractors from interrogating prisoners, and to ban research into a new generation of nuclear weapons.

During the debate, the Senate approved several non-defense matters, including increasing fines for broadcast indecency and expanding federal hate crime laws to cover sexual orientation, gender, and disability. *(Broadcast indecency, p. 394; hate crimes, p. 628)*

Senate action on amendments included:

Base closings. The Senate on May 18 rejected by a **key vote of 47–49 (R 21–29; D 26–19; I 0–1)** an amendment by Trent Lott, R-Miss., to limit the next base closure round that was scheduled for 2005 to U.S. overseas facilities and put off consideration of domestic military bases until 2007. *(2004 key votes, p. 854)*

War-related issues. The Senate on June 2 adopted 95–0 an amendment by Senate Armed Services Committee Chair John Warner, R-Va., to authorize the $25 billion for military operations in Iraq and Afghanistan.

The Senate on June 16 rejected 54–43 an amendment by Christopher J. Dodd, D-Conn., to bar contractors from interrogating detainees at U.S. military facilities. The military and intelligence agencies had hired companies to help interrogate detainees in Iraq, Afghanistan, and Guantánamo Bay, Cuba. Dodd's proposal would have given the president ninety days to replace the contractors with Defense Department personnel, but Warner and other Republicans said the Defense Department needed a longer transition period to hire and train enough U.S. military personnel to perform the interrogations.

Earlier that day the Senate by voice vote adopted a Richard J. Durbin, D-Ill., amendment to require the Pentagon to draft new antitorture regulations and report violations to Congress.

The treatment of prisoners at U.S. military facilities came up again during debate on June 23, when Patrick J. Leahy, D-Vt., offered an amendment to establish in law the presumption that detainees whose Geneva Convention status was unclear were entitled to its protections and to require the Pentagon to provide Congress numerous reports on prisoner issues. A second Leahy proposal would have modified that amendment to require the Justice Department to give lawmakers all of its documents pertaining to prisoners' treatment since President Bush took office.

Leahy prevailed on the amendment that included the Geneva Convention provision and Pentagon reporting requirements. It was adopted by voice vote after a motion to table, or kill, the proposal failed 45–50. But the amendment requiring the release of Justice Department documents was defeated 46–50. Opponents argued that a wholesale release of such information could put American soldiers in peril. The reporting requirement got far less attention than the demand for Justice Department documents, but backers considered it significant.

The Senate on June 16 had defeated 46–52 another Leahy amendment that would have created a new criminal penalty for "war profiteering" by contractors abroad. An alternative amendment by Warner adopted 97–0 extended the jurisdiction of U.S. courts over such alleged crimes overseas, but rather than creating a new criminal statute it referred to existing ones.

Missile defense. The Senate on June 17 rejected 42–57 an amendment by Barbara Boxer, D-Calif., to require the Pentagon's testing director—not contractors or officials with the Missile Defense Agency—to oversee tests of the system and certify that it was ready before deployment.

The Senate took up a second missile defense amendment that day as well. This one, offered by Jack Reed, D-R.I., was similar to Boxer's in that it called for the independent testing office to run the exercises, but it did not make deployment contingent on such testing. Reed's amendment was adopted by voice vote, but only after it was modified by a Warner amendment, adopted 55–44, that required the defense secretary to set the criteria for tests after consulting with the Pentagon's testing director. Warner's provision also required the Pentagon to conduct a test according to those criteria by October 2005 and to apply them to future tests.

Another Reed amendment was rejected 45–53 on June 23. This one conditioned $550.5 million of the Missile Defense Agency's request for ground-based midcourse interceptors on certification by the director of operational test and evaluation that the system was effective and suitable for combat.

A day earlier the Senate rejected 44–56 a Carl Levin, D-Mich., amendment to shift $515.5 million from the ground-based midcourse interceptors to nonproliferation programs and other homeland security and antiterrorism activities.

Nuclear research. The Senate on June 15 defeated 42–55 an amendment by Democrats Edward M. Kennedy of Massachusetts and Dianne Feinstein of California to eliminate $36.6 million for the Energy Department's study of the Robust Nuclear Earth Penetrator, or bunker buster, and its Advanced Concepts Initiative that included research into a "low yield" nuclear weapon. Opponents of the nuclear studies said they were unnecessary because conventional weapons could accomplish the same mission and because such programs would make counterproliferation diplomacy more difficult. Supporters argued that there was no evidence that nuclear proliferation was affected by U.S. research and that it would be imprudent to forgo any option to get at deeply buried targets. *(Nuclear weapons research, p. 362)*

Military benefits. On June 2 the Senate adopted 70–25 an amendment by Minority Leader Tom Daschle, D-S.D., and Lindsey Graham, R-S.C., to give members of the National Guard and reserves access to the military's Tricare health system regardless of whether they were deployed. Reservists at that time were covered only while on active duty and for a limited period afterward. The amendment required them to pay 28 percent of the cost.

The Senate vote on the health care amendment defied the Pentagon and Warner, who argued that the cost of the proposal, an estimated $14.2 billion over the next decade, was too large and that the new benefit would take away an incentive for soldiers to join the regular forces. But Daschle and Graham said recruiting and retaining reservists could be increasingly difficult without improved benefits. By the end of 2004 about 40 percent of the U.S. forces serving in Iraq would be members of the Guard or reserve. Many of them had been deployed for longer than they had expected, often with salaries and benefits less generous than those they received in their civilian jobs.

The Senate on June 23 rejected an amendment by Jon Corzine of New Jersey to bring down the age at which reservists could receive retirement benefits. The vote of 49–49 fell short of the sixty votes required to overcome a budgetary point of order. Later that day senators also rejected an amendment by Daschle to boost benefits for veterans at an average annual cost of $30 billion. Under a similar point of order the vote was 49–48.

The Senate accepted by voice vote June 23 a Mary L. Landrieu, D-La., amendment to halt the drop in annuities to the widowed spouses of service members once they turned sixty-two. The provision, as well as a similar one in the House version, would have authorized the spending of billions of dollars over the next decade.

Troop levels. Republican senators defied their president when they joined with Democrats on June 17 to vote 93–4 to increase the number of soldiers from 482,400 to 502,400 in fiscal 2005. Rumsfeld had appealed to lawmakers not to lock the Pentagon into a higher number, instead asking that the military be given flexibility to adjust troop levels. Rumsfeld was concerned that the cost of the added soldiers would divert funds needed to modernize weapons. He also said the answer was retraining people in the army, not adding more.

But with conflicts in Iraq and Afghanistan, volunteer soldiers being required to stay longer than they signed on for, and troops being diverted from Korea to bolster the force in Iraq, senators were not receptive to Rumsfeld's pitch. Although the added troops would not be of immediate assistance in Iraq, many senators believed the United States was in the global war on terrorism for the long haul and would need a bigger military to wage it.

Buy American. In contrast to the more protectionist approach of the House bill, the Senate adopted 54–46 on June 22 an amendment by John McCain, R-Ariz., allowing the defense secretary to waive Buy American laws for a handful of close U.S. allies, broadening the secretary's existing waiver authority.

Technology sales. Also on June 22 the Senate adopted by voice vote a Warner amendment to make it easier to sell unclassified military technologies to the United Kingdom and Australia by waiving State Department rules that required U.S. companies to get licenses for such exports. Warner's amendment had proliferation safeguards, including a presidential certification that the exemption was in the national interest.

Under the 1976 Arms Export Control Act (PL 94-329), U.S. companies had to obtain a license from the State Department to export military equipment, services, and data controlled by the International Traffic in Arms Regulations

(ITAR). State processed 56,000 applications for licenses in fiscal 2003. The median time it took to obtain a license, if the State Department acted on its own, was twelve days. If the department had to consult other agencies, the median time rose to seven weeks. Although licenses were taking less time to process than in prior years, the wait was still too long to suit U.S. defense industry trade groups, overseas companies, and foreign governments. (*Military aid, Congress and the Nation Vol. IV, p. 873*)

Because of those concerns President Bill Clinton's administration had proposed an ITAR waiver in 2000 for U.S. companies trading in unclassified products with counterparts from Britain and Australia. In response Henry J. Hyde, R-Ill., chair of the House International Relations Committee, won enactment of the Security Assistance Act of 2000 (PL 106-280), which restricted the conditions under which the president could exempt shipments from the licensing requirement. Nations were required to sign binding agreements to adopt export controls at least comparable to those of the United States. In 2001 and 2002 the Bush administration took up the cause of ITAR waivers, seeking to negotiate agreements with Britain and Australia that would meet the law's requirements. But the new administration realized it could not alter the rules the way it wanted to without getting Congress to change the law. Initial attempts to do that had failed. (*Military aid authorization, Congress and the Nation Vol. X, p. 229*)

Tanker deal. Rumsfeld on May 25 put off a decision on the acquisition of air force refueling tankers for at least six months until two studies had been completed on the requirement for the planes and the best way to meet it. The Senate adopted by voice vote on June 22 a McCain amendment to codify Rumsfeld's pledge to complete the studies before signing any contract.

McCain's amendment also required that any tanker contract be reviewed by the Pentagon inspector general and the General Accounting Office and that it meet Office of Management and Budget (OMB) scoring rules for leases. A Senate Republican aide said the OMB provision could mean the air force would have to pay up front for the planes it leased—negating the reason to lease rather than purchase the aircraft, which was to pay less at the outset.

Other amendments. On May 19 the Senate rejected 49–50 an amendment by Frank R. Lautenberg, D-N.J., to revise a 1977 law (PL 95-223) that prohibited U.S. firms from doing business with states that sponsored terrorism. The amendment language was designed to block companies from maneuvering around the law by using foreign subsidiaries to conduct business with countries such as Iran.

On June 3 the Senate rejected 48–48 an amendment by Maria Cantwell, D-Wash., to delete the bill's language permitting on-site burial of nuclear waste then in holding tanks at the Savannah River Site in South Carolina, instead of requiring shipment to a planned nuclear waste repository at Yucca Mountain in Nevada. The vote came after a lengthy debate on how to dispose of some of the radioactive byprod-

ucts of the cold war–era nuclear arsenal. (*Nuclear waste disposal, pp. 422, 439*)

CONFERENCE ACTION

The House agreed to the HR 4200's conference report (H Rept 108-767) on Oct. 9 by a vote of 359–14. The Senate cleared the bill later that day by voice vote.

Although staff-level negotiations and some meetings of members had been going on for three months, the conference on HR 4200 did not officially convene until late September. Congressional recesses, national party conventions, the Abu Ghraib prison scandal, and a proposed reorganization of the intelligence community had diverted members' attention. But once conferees sat down, they completed the bill relatively quickly.

The differences between the two chambers were negligible on many issues. Both versions authorized $447.2 billion, including $25 billion for the operations in Iraq and Afghanistan. There were few disagreements between the House and Senate on major weapons programs. And both bills increased the number of soldiers in uniform in fiscal 2005, with relatively small differences.

But despite their broad agreement on the shape of the measure, conferees had to resolve several difficult conflicts between the two versions. Their job was complicated because Congress wanted to complete its work so members could return home to campaign before the November elections.

President Bush had vowed to veto the bill if it included the House provision postponing the 2005 round of base closings until 2007. The provision had strong bipartisan backing in the House, but the Senate had defeated, albeit narrowly, a proposal to put off domestic base closings for two years. As painful as they knew it would be for members who represented areas where bases might face cuts or closure, conferees went along with Bush and allowed the process to go forward.

Buy American provisions in the House bill also posed problems for conferees. The House version banned trade with countries that required U.S. defense firms to invest in their economies in exchange for their purchases from the U.S. companies. But the Senate bill went in the opposite direction by giving the defense secretary greater flexibility to waive certain Buy American restrictions. Conferees dropped both bills' provisions.

Disagreement over how to procure air force refueling planes proved the most difficult conflict for conferees to resolve. Conferees eventually decided the air force should begin again. The compromise barred the leasing of aircraft, as the original plan had called for, and appeared to inject competition into what had been an exclusive deal with Boeing.

Conferees dropped Warner's amendment to provide an ITAR exemption for unclassified defense exports to qualified British and Australian purchasers. In its place, the bill ordered the administration to write regulations that would expedite the process of licensing unclassified materials for Britain and Australia, but not eliminate the need for licenses. Dropping the Senate-passed waiver was a victory for Hyde and Hunter, who opposed Warner's provision, saying they would rather keep U.S. defense technology at home and risk angering allies than have dangerous weapons show up on the global arms market. The wrangling over the arms export issue among Republican conferees underscored a larger debate over two increasingly important and sometimes conflicting imperatives: the need to cooperate with allies in building weapons vs. the need to minimize the risk that such cooperation might make it easier for terrorists to obtain ever more lethal arms.

MAJOR PROVISIONS

As signed into law on Oct. 28, 2004, HR 4200 authorized $445.6 billion for defense spending in fiscal 2005, about $2.5 billion less than requested. That total included $25 billion in emergency funds.

Major provisions of HR 4200:

War Funds

Authorized $25 billion in emergency funds for the operations in Iraq and Afghanistan. The bill detailed how the money would be spent but allowed the defense secretary to transfer $1.5 billion of that money between accounts. Congress was to be notified of each transfer.

Military Personnel

Authorized $106.5 billion for military personnel.

Authorized for fiscal 2005 an active-duty force of 1,406,00—23,000 more than requested for fiscal 2005 and 15,500 more than authorized for fiscal 2004. Specifically, the bill required the army to grow to 502,400 troops in 2005, from the existing level of 482,400, and allowed it to increase to 512,400 by 2009. The Marine Corps was required to increase to 178,000 in 2005, up from 175,000, and was allowed to grow to 184,000 by 2009.

Authorized a 3.5 percent across-the-board pay raise.

Authorized greater access to Tricare, the Defense Department's health care system, for National Guard and reserve members. For every ninety days of consecutive service on active duty, a reservist would be eligible for a year of Tricare while not on active duty. Under previous law, reservists were allowed access to the health care network only for brief periods while not serving on active duty.

Operations and Maintenance

Authorized $121.5 billion.

Facilities

Authorized $10 billion for military construction and family housing.

Eliminated a cap on a military housing privatization program. Spending on the initiative had been capped at $850 million by law (PL 104-106) in 1996, a ceiling that would be reached within weeks of the conference agreement. If the cap had survived, at least 50,000 military families would have had to wait for new or renovated homes. The Congressional Budget Office said eliminating the cap would cost $6 billion over the next five years.

Missile Defense

Authorized $10 billion for missile defense systems.

Ground Forces

Authorized $2.9 billion for research and development of the army's Future Combat System.

Authorized $905 million for Stryker lightweight armored vehicles.

Authorized an additional $572 million to produce armored Humvees—a vehicle being used in the conflicts in Iraq and Afghanistan—at the required rate of 450 per month. The bill also authorized an additional $100 million for kits to provide additional armor for wheeled vehicles to protect them from antipersonnel projectiles, also known as improvised explosive devices (IEDs), which were often used by insurgents in Iraq.

Aviation Forces

Authorized $95 million for the air force to launch a new program to procure as many as 100 aerial refueling tankers. The bill barred any lease of Boeing KC-767A tanker aircraft, as had been envisioned in the original plan. The bill required competitive bids for a nearly $6 billion maintenance package, but members disagreed as to whether the Boeing Co. would have to compete for the contract to build the planes. A new contract would have to be drawn up no matter what was ultimately decided.

Authorized $4.3 billion for development of the Joint Strike Fighter, a multi-role fighter aircraft slated for use by the air force, navy, and Marine Corps.

Authorized $4.1 billion for twenty-four of the air force's F/A-22 Raptor fighter planes. The bill also authorized $555 million for research and development of the plane.

Authorized $3 billion for the navy's F/A-18 E/Fs.

Naval Forces

Authorized $1.5 billion to continue development and begin construction of the Navy's next-generation surface combat ship, the DD(X).

Authorized $3.5 billion for procurement of three DDG-51 *Arleigh Burke*-class Aegis guided-missile destroyers.

Authorized $2.3 billion for procurement of a *Virginia*-class attack submarine.

Authorized the requested $236 million for amphibious assault ship procurement, plus an extra $150 million to accelerate procurement of the first LHA(R) amphibious assault ship.

Nuclear Weapons

Authorized $17.6 billion for defense-related atomic energy activities carried out primarily by the Energy Department.

Authorized $27.6 million for research on the Robust Nuclear Earth Penetrator, or bunker-buster, and $9 million for other advanced initiatives.

Reclassified high-level nuclear waste left over from bomb manufacturing during the cold war as incidental waste to allow South Carolina to bury waste from the military's Savannah River site on location rather than requiring shipment to a planned permanent repository at Yucca Mountain in Nevada.

Moved a program to help ailing former atomic weapons workers from the Energy Department to the Labor Department and designated it as mandatory spending. The Energy Department had experienced significant delays in processing claims for compensation from thousands of people.

Veterans' Benefits

Authorized increased benefits for survivors of deceased military personnel.

Allowed military retirees who were considered 100 percent disabled to receive both their full pensions and disability benefits as of Jan. 1, 2005, instead of having them phased in as had been required under existing law.

2005 Defense Appropriations

Congress in 2004 cleared a $417.5 billion fiscal 2005 defense appropriations bill (HR 4613—PL 108-287).

HR 4613 funded most of President George W. Bush's robust defense agenda, providing all but about $1.5 billion sought by the administration. The bill included a record $391.2 billion for the Pentagon's core budget and an emergency $25 billion war appropriation to pay for operations in Iraq and Afghanistan. Although the administration said the $25 billion was for the initial months of fiscal 2005, Congress made the money available upon enactment. That decision appeared farsighted in light of a Government Accountability Office estimate, issued the day before HR 4613 cleared, that the Pentagon faced a $12.3 billion shortfall in war funds in the final months of fiscal 2004.

With 140,000 U.S. soldiers in Iraq and with the United States under the constant threat of another major terrorist attack, GOP leaders easily met their goal of sending the defense measure to Bush before Congress adjourned for a six-week summer recess and the national party presidential nominating conventions. HR 4613 cleared more than two months before the companion defense authorization bill (HR 4200—PL 108-375). *(2005 defense authorization, p. 346)*

Overall the administration fared well in HR 4613. Congress continued to fund most of the Pentagon's major weapons programs, including next-generation fighter aircraft and ships. HR 4613 also provided $10 billion for missile defense efforts, 2 percent less than Bush had sought but 11 percent above the previous year's funding. The total included full funding of Bush's effort to deploy a limited missile defense system in 2004, putting into place the first elements of an antimissile shield proposed by President Ronald Reagan in 1983.

But the defense spending measure was not a full success for the Bush administration. Appropriators refused to give the president the nearly unlimited authority he sought to spend the $25 billion war fund, restricting all but $2 billion of the money to specific accounts. In addition, one of Defense Secretary Donald H. Rumsfeld's top priorities, "transformation" programs to remake the military into a leaner, more technologically oriented force, did not fare well.

The administration's $3.2 billion request for the Future Combat System, the centerpiece of the army's modernization effort, was reduced by about 8 percent, as it had been in HR 4200. The conference report expressed concerns about the initiative, divided the money among specific accounts, and mandated a report on its future. A few hours after the conference report was filed, army Chief of Staff Gen. Peter J. Schoomaker told the House Armed Services Committee that the futuristic program linking vehicles, weapons, and sensors was being restructured and that fielding it would take two years longer than planned.

Another major element of the transformation agenda fared worse. The space-based radar program, an air force system of nine satellites that was to provide near-continuous global radar imagery and tracking of moving targets, received less than a quarter ($75 million) of the amount Bush had sought ($328 million). The program was estimated to ultimately cost $34 billion. Senators agreed to a House plan to restructure it, calling the program unaffordable and unlikely to yield promised results. Congress also cut $300 million, or 39 percent, from Bush's $775 million request for the air force's transformational communications satellites, a program aimed at providing U.S. war fighters with global access to secure, high-bandwidth links. The price tag for this program had doubled since early 2003 to $12 billion, according to Senate appropriators.

The cuts in transformation programs reflected concerns in Congress that the Pentagon had more big-ticket weapons programs in its development pipeline than were affordable. But in an election year appropriators were reluctant to make deeper, broader cuts.

In addition to HR 4613's military spending, other components of the defense budget approved in 2004 included $16.6 billion for atomic energy defense activities in the energy-water appropriations portion of the fiscal 2005 omnibus funding bill (HR 4818—PL 108-447) and $10 billion for military construction and family housing in the fiscal 2005 military construction appropriations bill (HR 4837—PL 108-324).

HOUSE ACTION

The House passed its $417.7 billion version of HR 4613 on June 22, 2004, by a vote of 403–17. The House Appropriations Committee had reported a $416.9 billion version (H Rept 108-553) on June 18. Another $780 million in nondefense emergency funding was added during floor debate.

The House passed its defense spending bill on a quick and bipartisan basis, even though it was considered under an open rule that allowed any member to offer amendments.

MILITARY COSTS: AFGHANISTAN, IRAQ, DOMESTIC FACILITIES

The following chart shows Congressional Research Service (CRS) estimates of appropriations for combat, ongoing military operations, and occupation in Afghanistan and Iraq. It also includes funding for enhanced security in the United States for defense installations and for Pentagon reconstruc-

tion. It covers regular and supplemental appropriations measures enacted from 2001 through 2004. CRS based its calculations on Defense Department information and congressional committee reports.

	(in billions of dollars)		
	Afghanistan	Iraq	Enhanced Security, Other Expenses
Fiscal 2001 Antiterrorism Supplemental (HR 2888—PL 107-38); Fiscal 2002 Defense Appropriations (HR 3338—PL 107-117)	$11.9	—	$4.6
Fiscal 2002 Emergency Supplemental (HR 4775—PL 107-206)	$12.5	—	$ 1.5
Fiscal 2003 Defense Appropriations (HR 5010—PL 107-248)*	$ 3.0	—	$ 4.1
Fiscal 2003 Omnibus Appropriations (H J Res 2—PL 108-7)	$10.0	—	—
Fiscal 2003 Emergency Supplemental (HR 1559—PL 108-11)	$ 5.1	$ 48.5	$ 5.5
Fiscal 2004 Supplemental (HR 3289—PL 108-106), Fiscal 2004 Transfers*	$ 7.8	$ 54.7	$ 7.1
Fiscal 2005 Defense Appropriations (HR 4613—PL 108-287)*	$ 3.5	$ 21.5	—
TOTAL:	$53.8	$124.8	$22.7

Source: "The Cost of Operations in Iraq, Afghanistan, and Enhanced Security," by Amy Belasco (Congressional Research Service Report for Congress, No. RS21644, updated March 14, 2005).
*Denotes CRS estimate.
Totals may not add due to rounding. Includes $14 billion in intelligence funding.

The bill gave the White House nearly all the money it sought but made adjustments to specific programs.

Bush's request for the $25 billion war fund was a central issue during committee deliberations on the bill. An expected showdown over its size was averted after David R. Obey of Wisconsin, the top Democrat on the Appropriations panel, decided not to offer an amendment to add another $50 billion to the amount. Democrats argued that the fund should reflect the true costs of war operations in 2005, which, by nearly all estimates, would be at least double the $25 billion requested. But Obey backed down in the face of

strong opposition from Republicans and some Democrats, who backed Bush's plan to wait until early in 2005 to seek additional war funding. The bill, however, granted little of the flexibility Bush had sought to spend and transfer the $25 billion. Instead, it divided that money into twenty-two specific accounts and it allowed just $2 billion to be transferred.

The measure included another $2.2 billion to replenish armored combat vehicles, helicopters, trucks, and ammunition in Iraq and Afghanistan.

Although Bush was opposed to permanent increases in force size, the House bill added $200 million to begin paying for the 13,000 additional army soldiers and marines called for in the House-passed version of the defense authorization bill.

HR 4613 continued production of major systems, including the *Virginia*-class submarine and the F/A-18 fighter jet.

Missile defense, a top Bush priority, received $9.7 billion, down from the $10.2 billion requested. But the bill fully funded Bush's efforts to deploy the first antimissile interceptors in Alaska and California, the initial elements of a national missile shield.

The bill provided $1.2 billion more than Bush's $68 billion request for research and development. It did not terminate any major weapons systems in the Pentagon's development pipeline, though it did endorse the army's decision to cancel the RAH-66 Comanche attack helicopter and transfer its funding to other aircraft programs. The army had announced that it was canceling the $39 billion Comanche program—on which $7 billion had already been spent—on Feb. 23, 2004. The program had been plagued by delays and cost increases. The decision to terminate the Comanche also reflected battlefield lessons. Army officials said the downing of nine U.S. military helicopters in Iraq had led them to reevaluate the program as doubts also grew that the Comanche could perform its reconnaissance mission against an enemy armed with shoulder-fired missiles and relatively cheap rocket-propelled grenades. Each helicopter costs $53 million.

Congress's subdued response to the Comanche program cancellation reflected members' awareness that there was not enough money to pay for all the weapons being developed. Still, the Comanche money was going to be spent on other programs, and not saved.

The House restricted $1.4 billion of the $4.4 billion appropriated for the F-35 Joint Strike Fighter aircraft, pending reports on schedule and cost changes to the aircraft, which was 2,400 pounds over its target development weight. The bill cut $221 million from Bush's $1.4 billion request for the navy's new DD(X) destroyer, warning that the program's development was too ambitious and that construction of the first ship should be delayed. The House bill reduced funding for the air force's Space-Based Radar from the requested $328 million to $75 million and called for the program to be restructured.

HR 4613 weighed in on the Pentagon plan to acquire 100 tanker refueling aircraft from Boeing. The bill reaffirmed language in the House defense authorization measure (HR 4200) ordering the Pentagon to sign a contract for the Boeing tankers by March 2005 and included $100 million to initiate the effort.

SENATE ACTION

The Senate passed its $416.3 billion version of HR 4613 on June 24 by a vote of 98–0 after substituting the text of its bill (S 2559). The Senate Appropriations Committee had reported S 2559 (S Rept 108-284) on June 22.

The Senate's final vote capped a dizzying three days of legislative action on the annual defense bills. On June 22 Senate appropriators approved S 2559 in two markups that did not see a single amendment proposed. The following day, the Senate completed weeks of debate and passed its fiscal defense authorization bill (S 2400), setting the stage for floor debate on the appropriations measure. Angry Democrats initially threatened to delay action on the funding bill because of a GOP plan to use it as a vehicle for increasing the government's borrowing limit. But Senate Appropriations Committee Chair Ted Stevens, R-Alaska, helped cut a deal to abandon the plan once it became clear that the debt limit controversy was going to imperil his speedy timetable for S 2559.

And speedy it was. While the Senate spent sixteen days debating 195 amendments to the defense authorization bill, Stevens zipped through the appropriations measure in an afternoon. Most of the forty-three proposed amendments were earmarks that had been agreed to in advance and were adopted by voice vote. There were only three roll call votes, including 89–9 an amendment by Robert C. Byrd of West Virginia, the top Democrat on the Appropriations Committee, to express the sense of the Senate that future requests for military funding, including war operations, be included in Bush's regular budget. The administration preferred to pay for war costs incrementally using emergency supplemental spending requests, and had irritated lawmakers by refusing to provide estimates of future war costs. Byrd complained that the administration had ignored similar language in the fiscal 2004 defense appropriations law (HR 2658—PL 208-87).

The Senate bill provided the $25 billion Bush requested for Iraq and Afghanistan operations but placed it in the Iraq Freedom Fund, a contingency emergency reserve established by appropriations in a fiscal 2003 supplemental spending law (HR 1559—PL 108-11). The money could be transferred to established appropriations accounts once the president designated it emergency funding. Any transfers would require five days' advance notice to Congress, and the administration had to provide quarterly reports on the use of the money. The committee report accompanying the Senate bill said that approach "provides necessary financial flexibility and ensures proper congressional oversight."

Like the House bill S 2559 funded most of Bush's requests for personnel, procurement, and operations. But the Senate bill called for an even greater increase in the size of the military than the House bill had, providing $605 million for 20,000 additional army soldiers. And, in contrast to the House version, it added money to Bush's requests for missile defense—$100 million for risk reduction. While the House bill would have delayed construction of the first DD(X) destroyer, the Senate bill added $99 million to begin procurement of a second destroyer.

The Senate bill did not address the air force's refueling tanker deal. Stevens said he believed appropriators should steer clear of the issue.

CONFERENCE ACTION

Senators were so eager to wrap up their work that they acted ahead of the House, adopting the conference report on

HR 4613 (H Rept 108-622) by a vote of 96–0 on July 22, pending adoption by the other chamber. That came a little more than an hour later, when the House adopted it by a vote of 410–12, clearing the bill for the president.

Conferees had moved quickly on the bill, ensuring that the bill would clear before Congress adjourned for six weeks on July 23. GOP leaders had put the legislation on the fast track because it contained the $25 billion emergency war fund.

Conferees did not provide Bush with the nearly unlimited authority he had sought to spend and transfer money from the war fund, but they did fund most of Bush's defense agenda. The bill added money to Bush's request to replace equipment and munitions used in Iraq and Afghanistan and to deploy more armored vehicles. It also fully funded Bush's plan to deploy the first elements of a national missile defense system.

Language in the House version of the defense bill to force the Pentagon to sign a contract to buy refueling tanker aircraft from Boeing Co. was not included in the final report. The bill did include $100 million to establish a fund so the air force could begin replacing its aging refueling aircraft once a plan was finalized.

The House agreed to drop language to delay procurement of the navy's first DD(X), which was to be built at the Ingalls shipyard in Mississippi, home state of Thad Cochran, the No. 2 Republican on the Senate Appropriations Committee.

House conferees also agreed to a Senate provision advocated by Maine Republicans Olympia J. Snowe and Susan Collins to add funds for advance procurement to build a second DD(X) at the Bath Iron Works in their home state, Ingalls's only rival in the destroyer trade.

The conference report sidestepped a major debate in Congress about whether to require the Pentagon to increase the size of the armed forces. Strong support existed in both the Senate and House for a permanent increase in the size of the military, which many lawmakers believed had been stretched too thin by the Iraq war. But Rumsfeld opposed a mandated increase, arguing that the Pentagon already was using emergency powers to temporarily increase force levels. Appropriations aides in both chambers said the conference report was carefully worded to avoid endorsing a permanent increase in force structure. But $1.3 billion was included in the $25 billion war fund to pay for war-related personnel expenses, providing funding if the final version of the defense authorization bill required a permanent troop level increase, which it did.

Conferees went along with the House decision to slash funding for the air force's space-based radar, while ordering the program to be restructured.

As a fast-moving, must-pass bill, the defense measure also became an ideal vehicle to carry emergency spending provisions sought by lawmakers. The bill included more than $1.3 billion of such add-ons, but designating them as "emergency" funding allowed lawmakers to get around spending limits placed on appropriations bills.

MAJOR PROVISIONS

As signed into law on Aug. 5, 2004, HR 4613 appropriated $417.5 billion. Of that, $416.2 billion was for fiscal 2005 military spending and $1.3 billion was for non-defense emergency spending.

Major provisions of HR 4613:

War Funds

Appropriated $25 billion in emergency funding for military operations in Iraq and Afghanistan. The bill restricted how all but $2 billion of the money could be spent and limited transfer authority.

Military Personnel

Appropriated $103.7 billion for military personnel.

Included the requested 3.5 percent military pay raise.

Set a ceiling on the number of active-duty personnel in fiscal 2005 at 1,383,000, as requested.

Operations and Maintenance

Appropriated $121.1 billion.

Missile Defense

Appropriated $10 billion for missile defense, $200 million less than requested, but the total included the full $4.6 billion requested to deploy the first antimissile interceptors in 2004.

Ground Forces

Appropriated $2.9 billion for the army's Future Combat System—$268 million less than requested—and ordered a report on the program.

Appropriated an additional $625 million to purchase and field another brigade of Stryker armored vehicles.

Aviation Forces

Appropriated $3.6 billion—$30 million less than requested—to procure twenty-four F/A-22 Raptor fighter jets and another $523 million to begin advanced procurement of additional aircraft.

Appropriated $4.4 billion—$100 million less than requested—for the multiservice F-35 Joint Strike Fighter and mandated a new cost estimate.

Appropriated the requested $2.9 billion for forty-two F/A-18 fighter jets.

Naval Forces

Appropriated the requested $2.5 billion for one *Virginia*-class submarine and advance procurement of future vessels.

Appropriated $3.4 billion, as requested, for three DDG-51 *Arleigh Burke*-class Aegis guided-missile destroyers.

Appropriated $1.2 billion for development of the DD(X) destroyer, about $200 million less than requested, and $306 million to begin advance procurement of two of the destroyers at different shipyards.

Emergency Add-ons

Appropriated the following as emergency funding: $665 million for the State Department to set up a new U.S. diplomatic mission in Iraq; $500 million to help suppress fires in Western states; $95 million in humanitarian assistance for refugees in Sudan's western Darfur region; $50 million ($25 million each) to help pay for security at the national party conventions in Boston and New York; and $26 million to help federal courts pay for more public defenders in death-penalty cases. *(Sudan relief assistance, p. 298)*

2005 Military Construction

Congress in 2004 cleared a $10 billion fiscal 2005 military construction appropriations bill (HR 4837—PL 108-324). The bill, one of only four fiscal 2005 appropriations bills to clear during the regular session, also provided $14.5 billion in emergency hurricane and drought relief.

HR 4837 appropriated about $450 million more than President George W. Bush requested for military construction in fiscal 2005 and about $162 million more than was appropriated in fiscal 2004's regular and supplemental spending bills.

The annual measure paid for building and repairing barracks, family housing, and other facilities, as well as ongoing costs from base closings. The opportunity to earmark millions of dollars for projects in congressional districts across the country made the bill a perennial favorite in Congress, and HR 4837 was no exception. The White House said there were eighty projects in the original House bill and seventy-five in the Senate version that were not requested by the Pentagon.

The only major issue during debate on HR 4837 concerned a spending cap on a popular program that encouraged private construction of military family housing. The Pentagon expected to hit the cap in November 2004, which would have left at least 50,000 families in several states waiting for better homes. House and Senate appropriators wanted to lift the cap but were unable to because the bill then would have exceeded its discretionary spending allocation. The issue was resolved when conferees on the fiscal 2005 defense authorization bill (HR 4200—PL 108-375)—which included military construction accounts—eliminated any restriction on spending for the program. Once HR 4200 cleared conferees on the military construction bill quickly completed their work. *(2005 defense authorization, p. 346)*

LEGISLATIVE ACTION

The House passed HR 4837 on July 22, 2004, by a vote of 420–1. The House Appropriations Committee had reported the bill (H Rept 108-607) on July 15.

During House action on the $10 billion funding bill, all other military construction programs took a back seat to the program that privatized some military family housing.

Congress began the program and capped its spending at $850 million in the fiscal 1996 defense authorization bill (PL 104-106), enacted in 1996. Under the program, developers and property managers built or renovated homes using mostly their own money, then managed and maintained the properties. The Pentagon paid the rents, using allowances in the personnel accounts ordinarily used to build on-base housing or pay families' off-base rents. Privatizing the projects, advocates said, resulted in homes built years sooner for millions of dollars less than would have been required by spending limited family housing funds the old way.

Republicans and Democrats agreed that the arrangement worked, and House Appropriations Chair C. W. Bill Young, R-Fla., called it "one of the best programs we've ever done." Despite that support, Congress had been unable to lift its own spending cap. In 2003 the Congressional Budget Office (CBO) ruled that any increase in the spending ceiling should be scored up front—in the first budget year—according to the long-term obligation the projects represented, not their initial costs. The budget office then scored an attempt in the fiscal 2004 defense authorization bill (HR 1588—PL 108-136) to raise the cap by $50 million as having a full cost of eight times that amount. The CBO scoring meant that lifting the cap by any significant amount would require lawmakers to find several billion dollars, virtually impossible in an era of tight discretionary spending limits. The attempt in 2003 to raise the cap in the defense bill failed.

House appropriators included a provision in HR 4837 raising the cap by $500 million, but CBO said the increase did not represent the true long-term cost of $1.2 billion, which it said should be carried on the books in fiscal 2005. Doing so, however, would have put the grand total for the bill well above the $10 billion set by GOP leaders—meaning the overall discretionary spending total for fiscal 2005 probably would have been breached. The committee report accompanying HR 4837 acknowledged "the importance of fiscal discipline" but said "CBO's approach is unmerited and exaggerates the financial risk to the federal government."

The issue provoked a furor that split the House into atypical camps. On one side were Budget Committee Chair Jim Nussle, R-Iowa, and the GOP leadership. In the other corner were President Bush, Defense Secretary Donald H. Rumsfeld, senior members from both parties on the Appropriations and Armed Services committees—and almost every House Democrat.

Despite the formidable ranks arrayed against him, Nussle played the House rules adroitly. The rule governing debate on the bill had been written, with the leadership's blessing, to make the housing cap provision vulnerable to removal on a point of order, the offense being legislation on an appropriations bill. The rule was adopted 212–211 on July 21. That same day Nussle, who had taken a beating from his critics, responded by introducing a stand-alone bill (HR 4879) to eliminate the cap. The leadership allowed him to bring it to the floor for a debate, and it quickly passed 423–0 even as his opponents on the spending bill derided this legislation as an inadequate "fig leaf." The next day, as expected, Nussle made his point of order, and the cap hike provision in HR 4837 fell. A motion by David R. Obey of Wisconsin, the top Appropriations panel Democrat, to recommit HR 4837 so the committee could add language increasing the cap to $1.3 billion was rejected 201–217.

The Senate passed HR 4837 by a vote of 91–0 on Sept. 20 after substituting the text of its $10 billion funding bill (S 2674). The Senate Appropriations Committee had reported S 2674 (S Rept 108-309) on July 15.

Senate appropriators also wanted to lift the cap on the housing program, but they made no attempt to do so in their funding bill. Kay Bailey Hutchison, R-Texas, chair of the Senate Appropriations Military Construction Subcommittee, said appropriators wanted to defer to Armed Services Committee members to set the policy, which they were to attempt to do in the conference on the fiscal 2005 defense authorization bill (HR 4200).

But if it was not settled during the authorization conference, Hutchison said the issue would be taken up during the appropriations conference. A manager's amendment adopted by voice vote on Sept. 15 during a brief Senate debate on the measure required the Pentagon to report to Congress on the impact of not lifting the cap. The report provision—unimportant in itself—was a way to ensure that the cap issue could be in play during the conference on HR 4837. Without it, the cap would be outside the scope of the military construction conference because neither version would have addressed the subject.

CONFERENCE ACTION

The House adopted the conference report on HR 4837 (H Rept 108-773) by a vote of 374–0 on Oct. 9. The Senate cleared the bill by voice vote Oct. 11.

Both chambers had divided their $10 billion spending packages identically at the level of major subcategories. But beneath those aggregates, there were numerous differences on individual earmarks. Members had supplemented the president's request with nearly $500 million worth of their own projects and reconciling them was a main issue in conference.

One issue that was not on the table was the cap on the family housing privatization program, thanks to conferees on HR 4200. Military construction conferees had been keeping one eye on the defense authorization conference in hopes that it would lift the cap and they could avoid taking up the issue. The conference version of HR 4200 did include a provision eliminating the cap, which CBO said would cost $6 billion over the next five years.

Senate and House conferees had already reconciled differences between their two bills when some House members decided they wanted to use the measure as a vehicle for hurricane relief funding and possibly other spending. An additional $14.5 billion in emergency aid, primarily for victims of hurricanes in the Southeast and drought in the Midwest, was added. (*Disaster relief appropriations, pp. 72, 73, 76, 81, 84*)

MAJOR PROVISIONS

As signed into law Oct. 13, 2004, HR 4837:

Military construction. Appropriated $5.5 billion for military construction—$636 million more than requested.

The bill also included $161 million—$5 million less than requested—for the U.S. share of NATO infrastructure projects.

Family housing. Appropriated $4.1 billion for family housing—$119 million less than requested.

Base closings. Appropriated $246 million, as requested, for environmental cleanup and other projects related to base closings.

Hurricane, Drought aid. Appropriated $14.5 billion in emergency aid, including $11.6 billion in assistance to victims of hurricanes in the Southeast and $2.8 billion to help farmers and ranchers in the drought-stricken Midwest.

Wartime Prisoner Abuse

Members of Congress expressed their outrage and disgust in 2004 when photos became public showing U.S. soldiers abusing Iraqi prisoners at the U.S. military's Abu Ghraib prison near Baghdad. The startling pictures showed some detainees stripped naked, covered with hoods, and threatened with electrocution.

Secretary of Defense Donald H. Rumsfeld and other top Pentagon officials were summoned to back-to-back hearings by the House and Senate Armed Services committees. Democrats called for Rumsfeld's ouster. Both the House and Senate adopted nonbinding resolutions (H Res 627, S Res 356) condemning the abuse and urging an investigation. Lawmakers expressed their outrage again in the fiscal 2005 defense authorization bill (HR 4200—PL 108-375) and set criteria for a new Pentagon policy that would ensure the humane treatment of prisoners.

Nevertheless, Congress left the investigations to the Pentagon and backed away from demands for detailed information about detainee operations and policies in Iraq, Afghanistan, and Guantanamo Bay, Cuba. Two high-level Pentagon reports were issued in August 2004.

BACKGROUND

The photos had been taken in October–December 2003. The military announced in a one-paragraph news release in January 2004 that an investigation into "reported incidents of detainee abuse at a Coalition Forces detention facility" was under way. The investigation was completed in March, but the report was classified as secret and not released outside the Pentagon.

On April 28 CBS News broadcast a story on the Abu Ghraib abuses after delaying the report for two weeks at the request of Joint Chiefs of Staff Chairman Gen. Richard B. Myers. On April 30 a detailed story was posted on the *New*

PRISONER ABUSE FINDINGS

The findings of two Pentagon investigations into the prisoner abuse scandal at the U.S. military's Abu Ghraib prison in Iraq were released on successive days in August 2004.

Schlesinger Panel

This four-member committee was appointed by Defense Secretary Donald H. Rumsfeld in May 2004. Chaired by James R. Schlesinger, who served as defense secretary from 1973 to 1975 during the administrations of Presidents Richard M. Nixon and Gerald R. Ford, the committee investigated Defense Department detention operations worldwide. The panel issued its report on Aug. 24. The Schlesinger investigation:

- Cited 300 allegations of prisoner abuse by U.S. military forces in Iraq, Afghanistan, and Guantánamo Bay, Cuba. As of Aug. 24, 155 investigations had been completed and abuse had been found in sixty-six cases. Five detainees died as a result of abuse by U.S. personnel during interrogations, and twenty-three other detainee deaths were under investigation.
- Concluded that abuses of prisoners by U.S. personnel were "widespread" and not the work of a few rogue guards. But the panel found no evidence that the abuses were part of an interrogation policy condoned by senior military or civilian authorities to gain intelligence information. Schlesinger noted that none of the prisoners in televised photos of abuse from the Abu Ghraib prison in Iraq were intelligence targets.
- Placed blame for the prisoner abuses on military leadership failures at all levels of command, including Rumsfeld and the Joint Chiefs of Staff, but did not call for any resignations.
- Blamed military leaders for failing to plan for the outbreak of a major insurgency in Iraq and for not providing more military police when it became clear large numbers of prisoners would have to be guarded. Noted there was one guard for every seventy-five prisoners at Abu Ghraib, compared with one guard per prisoner at Guantánamo Bay.
- Faulted Lt. Gen. Ricardo Sanchez, the former top U.S. commander in Iraq, for failing to correct leadership problems at Abu Ghraib after he became aware of them.
- Concluded that a breakdown in discipline by noncommissioned officers at Abu Ghraib would have been avoided with proper training and oversight.
- Noted that the panel did not receive full cooperation from the CIA and said that agency's role in the abuse of prisoners needed to be investigated further.
- Recommended that the United States explicitly define and document its policies for treatment of detainees and interrogation techniques and make sure all personnel clearly understand the policies.
- Called for clearer guidelines for military intelligence and CIA personnel in Defense Department detention facilities.
- Called for new procedures so "bad news" could be reported up the chain of command to Pentagon leaders more quickly.
- Called for more resources and specialists in detention and interrogation operations.

Fay-Jones Report

For this internal army investigation, a team of twenty-eight investigators led by Maj. Gen. George R. Fay and Lt. Gen. Anthony R. Jones, and overseen by Gen. Paul Kern, investigated reports of prisoner abuses by U.S. personnel at Abu Ghraib. A summary of their 9,000-page report, which was largely classified, was released on Aug. 25. The Fay-Jones investigation:

- Found forty-four alleged instances of abuse at Abu Ghraib "ranging from inhumane to sadistic," including one prisoner who died. The abuses were committed or witnessed by forty-eight people. Most of the forty-eight implicated were soldiers in the military intelligence brigade.
- Found that CIA personnel hid the presence of at least eight detainees at Abu Ghraib from Red Cross delegations in violation of Defense Department rules. Found indications that CIA personnel used interrogation techniques that violated Defense Department guidelines, adding to confusion about what techniques were permissible.
- Attributed abuses at Abu Ghraib to individual misconduct, a lack of discipline, and a lack of leadership. Faulted Sanchez and other "senior-level officers" for failing to monitor operations at the prison and take corrective actions when concerns were raised by the International Committee of the Red Cross.
- Faulted Sanchez for issuing conflicting and confusing rules on the interrogation of prisoners.
- Faulted senior officers for failing to provide clear, consistent guidelines for treatment of prisoners and concluded that confusion about what interrogation techniques were authorized contributed to some of the abuses.
- Referred the commander of the military intelligence brigade at Abu Ghraib and four other officers for discipline.

Yorker magazine's website. The photos shocked the world as they flashed across television screens and the Internet.

President George W. Bush maintained that he had not been told about the report or the pictures either, but he clearly sensed the scope of the political damage. His aides, who almost never leaked internal disputes to the press, quickly spread word that the president had scolded Rumsfeld on May 5 for not alerting him that the photos and report existed. Bush appeared on Arab television networks to try to convince international viewers that the images did not represent the principles Americans stood for. And on May 6, during an appearance with Jordan's King Abdullah II, Bush offered a public apology.

Lawmakers were outraged not only by the abuses but also by the administration's failure to warn them of the enormity of the case and its devastating international implications. Many said the Pentagon should have told them in March when the internal military report had documented the abuses instead of keeping the case from them until it broke in the news media. According to the Defense Department, a small group of lawmakers was informed a few hours before the CBS broadcast, but they did not see the pictures until the program ran.

LEGISLATIVE ACTION

The House passed H Res 627 by a vote of 365–50 on May 6 after somehow managing to turn bipartisan outrage into another partisan battle. The resolution condemned the abuses and urged the secretary of the army to conduct a thorough investigation. Democrats thought it should also call for congressional investigations, but Republicans did not and proceeded to act on H Res 627. Minority Whip Steny H. Hoyer, D-Md., said the Republicans should have reached out to Democrats and that the number of opposing votes "should have been zero." Republicans were soon accusing Democrats of politicizing the crisis.

The Senate passed its resolution on May 10 by a vote of 92–0. Unlike the House resolution, S Res 356 called for an investigation by both the Senate and the executive branch.

In the months that followed three House committees—Armed Services, International Relations, and Judiciary—shot down resolutions of inquiry requesting that the Bush administration provide Congress with documents about its policies affecting the treatment of detainees in Iraq and elsewhere. Senate Judiciary Committee Democrats sought unsuccessfully in June to get their GOP colleagues to subpoena the Justice Department for detainee-related documents.

The Senate Armed Services Committee was more aggressive in its pursuit of reports of prisoner abuses than the House Armed Services Committee, which showed little appetite for such inquiries. Duncan Hunter, R-Calif., chair of the House panel, criticized his Senate counterpart, John W. Warner, R-Va., for continuing his hearings on the issue. Hunter complained that Warner was taking U.S. commanders away from the battlefield to testify "so the Senate can

Sen. John W. Warner, R-Va., stands with a stack of classified documents related to the Abu Ghraib prison scandal during a news conference on Capitol Hill on Aug. 25, 2004. As chair of the Senate Armed Services Committee, Warner oversaw hearings on reported abuses of war detainees. *Source: AP Wide World Photos/Evan Vucci*

have a lot of publicity." Warner's aides countered that top generals who testified were in Washington anyway. But even Warner stressed the limitations of his panel's hearings, calling them an "inquiry" rather than an investigation and saying the job of investigating the abuses should be left to the Defense Department.

The only binding legislation on the abuses was buried deep within the fiscal 2005 defense authorization law (HR 4200—PL 108-375). In addition to sense-of-Congress language expressing outrage and a desire to see a thorough investigation, HR 4200 set minimum criteria for a new policy to be drafted by the defense secretary that would ensure humane treatment of detainees, and it required the secretary to certify the proper training of those who handled or interrogated detainees.

HR 4200 also required regular reports to Congress on the development and implementation of the new policies, on any criminal investigations arising from detentions, and "aggregate data" on foreign national detainees in U.S. custody. A Senate provision to require the Pentagon to turn over specific details on the number of detainees at specific locations was dropped in conference.

REPORTS ISSUED

An independent panel, appointed by Rumsfeld and chaired by former defense secretary James R. Schlesinger, found that the abuses extended well beyond Abu Ghraib and were not the work of a small number of rogue soldiers. The report, released on Aug. 24, 2004, confirmed sixty-six charges of detainee abuse in Iraq, Afghanistan, and Guantanamo Bay, Cuba. The panel blamed prisoner abuses on military leadership failures at all levels of command, all the way up to Rumsfeld and the Joint Chiefs of Staff, but it found no evidence that the Abu Ghraib abuses were part of a high-level policy to gain intelligence from prisoners.

A second investigation, led by army Maj. Gen. George R. Fay and Lt. Gen. Anthony R. Jones, released a summary of its largely classified report on Aug. 25. This investigation, which focused on charges of abuse at Abu Ghraib, found forty-four alleged instances of abuse at the prison that were committed or witnessed by forty-eight people, mostly soldiers in the military intelligence brigade.

Both reports were highly critical of Lt. Gen. Ricardo Sanchez, the three-star general who had been the top U.S. commander in Iraq, for allowing chaos to reign at the prison. But neither recommended disciplinary action against senior military officials.

The two Pentagon reports were more than many critics of the military had expected, especially in light of an army inspector general's report earlier in the summer that called abuses at Abu Ghraib "aberrations." The candid nature of the reports was greeted with approval on Capitol Hill, though lawmakers cautioned that it would take time to digest and analyze the findings. (*Prisoner abuse findings, p. 360*)

Missile Defense

After years of acrimony the debate on missile defense in the 108th Congress was almost muted, as lawmakers gave President George W. Bush much of his request to pursue the initial deployment of a national missile defense system. (*Background, missile defense, p. 331*)

Bush requested $9.1 billion for fiscal 2004, and both the defense authorization bill (HR 1588—PL 108-136) and the defense appropriations bill (HR 2658—PL 108-87) gave it to him. (*2004 defense authorization, p. 337; 2004 defense appropriations, p. 354*)

He requested $10.2 billion for fiscal 2005 and got $10 billion in both the defense authorization bill (HR 4200—

PL 108-375) and the defense appropriations bill (HR 4613—PL 108-287). Both measures fully funded the president's $4.6 billion request for deployment of the first antimissile interceptors in 2004. Senate Democrats' attempts during debate on HR 4200 to press for independent testing of that first phase of the system were rejected. (*2005 defense authorization, p. 346; 2005 defense appropriations, p. 354*)

On July 22, 2004, an antimissile interceptor was lowered into its silo at Fort Greely, Alaska, the first of forty interceptors slated for deployment by 2009 in Alaska, California, and a third undetermined location. Some observers speculated that the third site would be in Eastern Europe to defend against a potential Iranian missile attack, although former Soviet states in Central Asia also were thought to be candidates. The Pentagon's Missile Defense Agency would not confirm or deny any possible non-U.S. sites. The first interceptor at Vandenberg Air Force Base in California was placed in its underground silo on Dec. 10, 2004.

Nuclear Weapons Research

Congress in 2004 rejected a major White House priority by providing no funding to study a possible Robust Nuclear Earth Penetrator, a nuclear weapon that would penetrate enemy bunkers deep underground.

President George W. Bush had requested $27.6 million in fiscal 2005 for research on the so-called nuclear bunker-buster. Congress authorized the spending in the defense authorization bill (HR 4200—PL 108-375) but provided no funding for it in the energy and water development appropriations bill (HR 4818—PL 108-447).

Many lawmakers had raised concerns about the program, saying that a U.S. foray into nuclear weapons development could spark another nuclear arms race. The administration maintained that it was only conducting a study, not building a weapon. But concerns were heightened in 2004 when longer-term budget projections indicated spending $485 million for the study over five years. Putting an end to the program had backing in both parties.

EARLIER ACTION

Ever since the Sept. 11, 2001, terrorist attacks, the Bush administration had increased its emphasis on the importance of nuclear weapons to the U.S. arsenal, seeking to reverse almost a decade of post–cold war policies that cut back funding for the nation's nuclear weapons infrastructure. (*Nuclear Posture Review, p. 335*)

But in 2002 Congress refused to repeal a provision in a 1993 law (PL 103-160) that had prohibited research and development on small tactical nuclear weapons with an explosive force equivalent to 5,000 tons (5 kilotons) or less of TNT—about one-third the explosive power of the bombs that the United States dropped on Hiroshima and Nagasaki in World War II. Legislators included in the fiscal 2003 defense authorization bill (HR 4546—PL 107-314) a provision barring use of the bill's funds for the bunker-buster until after the secretary of defense submitted a report to the defense committees on the proposed weapon. *(2003 defense authorization, p. 320)*

In 2003, however, the administration scored a major victory when it persuaded a divided Congress to repeal the 1993 provision. Congress also authorized the $15 million requested for research on the bunker buster in the fiscal 2004 defense authorization (HR 1588—PL 108-136), although the measure did bar development of the weapon unless Congress specifically authorized it. The energy and water bill (HR 2754—PL 108-137) that year appropriated only half of the amount Bush wanted—$7.5 billion—for the research. *(2004 defense authorization, p. 337)*

2004 ACTION

In 2004 the White House hoped to build on the previous year's victory by increasing funding. But after winning its request for $27.6 billion for bunker-buster research in the defense authorization bill, the administration's luck changed when it came to actually getting the money. *(2005 defense authorization, p. 346)*

The most potent critic of the administration's plan was a plain-spoken Republican from Ohio: David L. Hobson, chair of the House Energy and Water Development Appropriations Subcommittee. In that position, he had the power to challenge Bush's nuclear ambitions. And Hobson was deeply skeptical about tapping scarce discretionary money to boost spending on new weapons that he believed should serve only as a deterrent and never be used. He also pointed to Bush's own call for greater international efforts to reduce nuclear weapons.

"With all the proliferation threats we now face with countries like Iran, Pakistan, and North Korea, are we really sending the right signals to those countries and the rest of the world when we embark on nuclear weapons initiatives?" Hobson asked Defense Secretary Donald H. Rumsfeld at a Feb. 12, 2004, defense appropriations hearing.

In the end, Hobson's view prevailed and the money was left out of the energy and water funding bill.

Bryan Wilkes, spokesman for the National Nuclear Security Administration, said that the agency's request was "carefully calibrated" and that he was disappointed that Congress would not back it. "These are certainly programs and issues that have been misunderstood by members of Congress," he said, such as the perception that the administration was pursuing development of a new bunker-busting bomb. What the agency actually intended to do, he said, was to research reinforcing the outer shell of a bomb that was already in the U.S. nuclear arsenal.

Democratic Rep. Ellen O. Tauscher of California, who lost a close vote on an amendment to kill the earth-penetrating weapons program during debate on the fiscal 2004 defense authorization, hailed the outcome on the energy and water bill. "The administration is using the war on terrorism as a flimsy excuse to find new uses for existing nuclear weapons and new nuclear weapons—weapons that the Pentagon hasn't even officially asked for," Tauscher said. "Until our war-fighters have a military requirement for a new nuclear weapon or have exhausted conventional alternatives, Congress should not support the development of such a weapon."

Arms Reduction Treaty

The Senate in 2003 approved ratification of an arms control agreement between the United States and Russia (Treaty Doc 107-8). The Strategic Offensive Reductions Treaty (SORT), also known as the Moscow Treaty, required the two countries to reduce their nuclear stockpiles to between 1,700 and 2,200 each by 2012.

President George W. Bush and Russian president Vladimir V. Putin had signed the pact at a meeting in Moscow on May 24, 2002. The treaty entered into force on June 1, 2003, following the Senate's approval of the pact in March 2003 and the Russian parliament's in May.

COMMITTEE ACTION

The Senate Foreign Relations Committee reported Treaty Doc 107-8 (Exec Rept 108-1) on Feb. 20, 2003.

During July 2002 hearings, committee members had expressed concerns over Russia's implementation of the accord and how to help the Kremlin with the costs of dismantling or storing the nuclear warheads it was required to remove from submarines, bombers, and missiles. They also questioned Secretary of State Colin L. Powell and Defense Secretary Donald H. Rumsfeld about the agreement's failure to address the issue of short-range tactical nuclear weapons and Bush's decision to retain thousands of surplus long-range weapons in storage rather than destroy them.

Rumsfeld sought to dispel congressional concerns that the treaty had no independent means of verification, relying instead on satellites, and that many of the weapons were housed in the same locations as those covered under the earlier START I arms reduction treaty. Rumsfeld said Russian objections had prevented verification measures from being included in the new treaty, but he said the administration would continue to press for such measures in follow-up negotiations. He expressed confidence that such verification controls would be in place before START I expired in 2009.

But one problem in verifying the accord was the new counting method the administration insisted upon to tally the weapons cuts. Under previous agreements the United States and Russia disabled the missiles, bombers, and submarines carrying nuclear warheads. Then they totaled the number of weapons those systems were capable of carrying—cuts that were easy to verify. The Moscow Treaty, however, called for verifying the status of the individual warheads carried by those delivery systems, a much more difficult task. Rumsfeld said the Pentagon sought the new counting method so it could retain the intercontinental ballistic missiles (ICBMs) and use them to deliver conventional weapons.

Rumsfeld also defended the administration's decision to retain many of the banned weapons in a strategic reserve

NUCLEAR ARMS CONTROL AGREEMENTS

Following is a chronology of major nuclear arms control agreements between or including the United States and the Soviet Union/Russia, from the 1963 test ban treaty through the signing of the Moscow Treaty in 2002.

• October 1963: The Limited Test Ban Treaty, in which the United States, Britain, and the Soviet Union agreed to prohibit all atmospheric, underwater, or space testing of nuclear devices, went into effect. Other nations signed the treaty as well. *(Congress and the Nation Vol. I, p. 134)*

• November 1969: The United States and the Soviet Union began Strategic Arms Limitation Talks (SALT). *(Congress and the Nation Vol. III, p. 201)*

• March 1970: The Nuclear Nonproliferation Treaty, aimed at preventing the spread of nuclear weapons, went into effect. *(Congress and the Nation Vol. III, p. 201)*

• May 1972: President Richard M. Nixon and Soviet leader Leonid I. Brezhnev signed the Anti-Ballistic Missile (ABM) Treaty, which prohibited the deployment of a national missile defense system, and a five-year interim agreement limiting offensive nuclear weapons. *(Congress and the Nation Vol. III, p. 894)*

• July 1974: Nixon and Brezhnev signed a treaty to limit underground nuclear weapons tests, but the treaty did not enter into force until December 1990 after additional verification provisions had been negotiated. The two sides said in 1976 that they would observe the treaty's threshold for banned tests. *(Congress and the Nation Vol. IV, p. 881; Vol. VIII, p. 366)*

• June 1979: President Jimmy Carter and Brezhnev signed the SALT II pact to limit offensive nuclear weapons. Though it was never ratified, the two sides agreed to observe it. *(Congress and the Nation Vol. V, p. 193)*

• December 1987: President Ronald Reagan and Soviet leader Mikhail S. Gorbachev signed a treaty eliminating intermediate-range nuclear-force missiles. *(Congress and the Nation Vol. VII, p. 332)*

• July 1991: President George H. W. Bush and Gorbachev signed the Strategic Arms Reduction Talks (START) treaty cutting U.S. and Soviet nuclear arsenals to 6,000 aerial bombs and missile warheads each. *(Congress and the Nation Vol. VIII, p. 388)*

• October 1991: Gorbachev announced a test moratorium. A test ban was enacted in the United States in October 1992. *(Congress and the Nation Vol. VIII, p. 392)*

• January 1993: Bush and Russian president Boris Yeltsin signed a new Strategic Arms Reduction Talks (START II) treaty to reduce U.S. nuclear warheads to 3,500 and Russian nuclear warheads to 3,000 by 2003. A 1997 protocol extended the deadline to 2007. The treaty never entered into force. *(Congress and the Nation Vol. IX, pp. 292, 320)*

• May 1995: Nations agreed to extend indefinitely the twenty-five-year-old Nuclear Nonproliferation Treaty.

• September 1996: The Comprehensive Test Ban Treaty was approved by the U.N. General Assembly. President Bill Clinton was the first to sign the treaty, but the Senate rejected it in October 1999. *(Congress and the Nation Vol. IX, p. 322; Vol. X, p. 310)*

• March 1997: Clinton and Yeltsin agreed on guidelines for START III negotiations that included a limit of 2,000–2,500 deployed strategic weapons by 2007.

• December 2001: President George W. Bush gave Moscow the required six months' notice that the United States was withdrawing from the ABM Treaty in order to proceed with advanced testing for a national missile defense system. *(Missile defense, p. 362)*

• May 2002: Bush and Russian president Vladimir V. Putin signed the Strategic Offensive Reductions Treaty (SORT) limiting their stockpiles of nuclear warheads to 1,700–2,200 each by 2012. The United States insisted on retaining flexibility to store rather than destroy weapons. *(Arms reduction treaty, p. 363)*

rather than destroy them. He said such a reserve was needed because the United States, unlike Russia, no longer had factories producing new nuclear weapons. He added that the United States needed both a large deployed nuclear force and a large reserve of warheads to deter countries such as China from aspiring to match the U.S. nuclear arsenal.

Senate Foreign Relations Committee Chair Joseph R. Biden Jr., D-Del., and one of the panel's senior Republicans, Richard G. Lugar of Indiana, urged Rumsfeld to estimate Russia's cost for dismantling its surplus weapons and how the United States might help Moscow pay the expense. Lugar and former Senate Armed Services Committee chair Sam Nunn, D-Ga. (1972–1997), were the architects of a series of

programs aimed at dismantling Russia's cold war arsenal of nuclear, chemical, and biological weapons and the missiles, submarines, and bombers that could deliver them. Collectively, the programs were known as "Nunn-Lugar." Nunn-Lugar was first authorized in 1991 (PL 102-228). *(Aid to Former USSR, Congress and the Nation Vol. VIII, p. 260)*

FLOOR ACTION

The Senate adopted the resolution agreeing to ratification by a vote of 95–0 on March 6, 2003.

During two days of debate Senate Democrats tried and failed several times to strengthen the three-page treaty, which they said was a vague and toothless international agreement.

In the end, however, rather than oppose a disarmament plan, they joined Republicans in approving the agreement. Still, Democrats said they would send multiple letters to the White House, urging the president to consider everything from enhanced verification regimes to taking U.S. nuclear missiles off high-alert status.

Democrats won one concession. Lugar, by then the chair of the Foreign Relations Committee, agreed to co-sign a letter by Democrat Richard J. Durbin of Illinois requesting administration reports on efforts to strengthen disarmament verification programs.

While the treaty called for reductions in the nuclear stockpiles of each nation, it set out no protocols for disarmament. During the treaty debate, Democrats said they were worried that disarmament was required only until the last day the treaty was in effect, meaning nations could begin restocking their weapons one day later. Worse, they argued, was the decision to allow both countries to forgo destruction of the nuclear warheads and store them instead.

"It almost represents a treaty for the sake of a treaty," Sen. John Kerry, D-Mass., said during debate March 6. "It's as flimsy a treaty as the United States has ever considered."

But for all their criticism, Democrats ultimately forced votes on only two amendments. At one point, senators had been told to expect up to ten.

Kerry offered an amendment that would have required U.S. intelligence agencies to report to the Senate on their ability to verify Russian disarmament programs. It failed 45–50.

Democrat Carl Levin of Michigan offered an amendment that would have required the administration to give Congress sixty days' notice if it decided to make changes to or withdraw from the treaty. It was rejected 44–50.

NATO Expansion

The Senate in 2003 approved a modification of the 1949 North Atlantic Treaty to expand the alliance to include seven Eastern European countries: Bulgaria, Estonia, Latvia, Lithuania, Romania, Slovakia, and Slovenia (Treaty Doc 108-4).

The seven states had been invited in 2002 to begin accession talks with the North Atlantic Treaty Organization (NATO). Protocols, or amendments, to the NATO treaty expanding the alliance to include those states had been signed by representatives of NATO states on March 26, 2003. The next step was for each of the nineteen member countries to approve the expansion. President George W. Bush submitted the protocols to the Senate on April 10. *(107th Congress action, NATO expansion, p. 336)*

The ratification process was completed by early 2004 and the seven states formally joined NATO on March 29, 2004, bringing NATO's membership to twenty-six nations and advancing the borders of the alliance all the way to Russia. It was the fifth and largest expansion in NATO's history. *(NATO members, box above)*

NATO MEMBERS, 1949–2004

Twelve nations founded the North Atlantic Treaty Organization (NATO) in 1949. By March 2004, NATO had been enlarged five times and there were twenty-six member states. They are listed below with the dates they joined the alliance.

1949: Belgium, Canada, Denmark, France, Iceland, Italy, Luxembourg, the Netherlands, Norway, Portugal, the United Kingdom, and the United States.

1952: Greece and Turkey.

1955: Germany (German reunification in 1990 brought the territory of the former German Democratic Republic under NATO).

1982: Spain.

1999: Czech Republic, Hungary, and Poland.

2004: Bulgaria, Estonia, Latvia, Lithuania, Romania, Slovakia, and Slovenia.

COMMITTEE ACTION

The Senate Foreign Relations Committee reported Treaty Doc 108-4 (Exec Rept 108-6) on April 30. In a brisk business meeting that day, the panel unanimously approved amending the NATO treaty to extend membership to the seven states.

NATO's proponents said the alliance had no choice but to restructure itself to tackle the challenges of the post-Sept. 11 world.

One reason NATO expansion enjoyed such broad support on the Hill was that all seven of the new candidates for membership—in contrast to France, Germany, and Belgium—had backed the U.S. effort in Iraq. They also had assisted in stabilization efforts in Afghanistan, as Secretary of State Colin L. Powell noted in his April 29 testimony before the Foreign Relations Committee.

"We shouldn't expect Slovakia to show up as a world-class force, but they can perform 'niche' capabilities," said Powell. He also cited other contributions, such as Romania's "Carpathian Hawks" battalion in Afghanistan, Czech and Slovak biological and chemical weapons specialists in Kuwait, and Bulgaria's decision to let the United States use its air base in Burgas during the Iraq war.

FLOOR ACTION

The Senate approved Treaty Doc 108-4 by a vote of 96–0 on May 8.

Although support for expansion was unchallenged, several senators had voiced doubts about the unwieldiness of NATO's consensus-based decision-making procedures.

The absence of a NATO provision to suspend or expel members who might violate basic NATO principles, including democratic government and the rule of law, also had provoked some criticism.

During the May 7 floor debate on NATO expansion, Pat Roberts, R-Kan., Carl Levin, D-Mich., John W. Warner, R-Va., and Jeff Sessions, R-Ala., offered a nonbinding "sense of the Senate" amendment that called on President Bush to bring up these issues for discussion by the North Atlantic Council within the next eighteen months. Bush would then have up to sixty days to report back to Congress. The amendment was adopted by voice vote.

"As we expand NATO, there is a greater likelihood . . . that some day, some country is not going to live up to NATO's requirements," Levin warned. But he added that the amendment would ask only that the issue be raised, not resolved one way or another.

Also during the debate, Sen. Richard J. Durbin, D-Ill., cautioned that the United States must be prepared to accept divisions within the alliance from time to time. He cited the divide between the United States and European public opinion over the Iraq war. "It would be the height of irony if the organization originally formed to confront totalitarian government would disintegrate because of the lack of tolerance for disagreement with U.S. policy," Durbin cautioned.

Although the House had no role in approving the treaty protocols, it had lent its support for the NATO expansion on March 30, 2004, when it approved 422–2 a resolution (H Res 558) welcoming "with enthusiasm" the accession of the seven states to NATO.

Military Draft

Rampant rumors that either Congress or the White House was going to reinstate the military draft found their way to the House floor Oct. 5, 2004, when the Republican leadership brought up a Democratic bill (HR 163) to require all citizens between eighteen and twenty-six to perform some type of national defense service. The House rejected HR 163 by the lopsided vote of 2–402.

The sponsor, Charles B. Rangel of New York, had introduced the measure in early 2003 largely to make a political point about the unfairness of an all-volunteer armed services whose ranks skewed toward the lower and middle classes.

By late 2004 Republicans essentially decided to call Rangel's bluff—putting HR 163 on the floor calendar without any hearings, with little notice, and under suspension of the rules, the place on the calendar reserved for the least controversial bills.

Those GOP tactics turned Rangel into an opponent of his own bill. He called the tactics a "prostitution of the legislative process." The resulting floor debate was often testy, and often about anything but the draft. Most of the forty minutes devoted to the bill was spent on partisan posturing and arguing about presidential politics.

The consideration of Rangel's bill was a sign that rumors about resurrecting the draft had hit the political boiling point. E-mail campaigns and left-wing Web sites had disseminated "Draft Alert" messages. An organization called Mothers United to Stop the Draft had been founded.

Administration officials consistently denied such claims. President George W. Bush weighed in during a campaign appearance in Iowa on Oct. 4, saying: "We will not have a draft so long as I am president of the United States."

The real draft, as opposed to the Internet-inspired legend, ended in 1973, replaced by an all-volunteer military supplemented by National Guard and reserve personnel. The Selective Service System still existed in case the draft ever needed to be resumed. *(Selective Service, Congress and the Nation Vol. III, p. 225)*

CHAPTER 6

Transportation, Commerce, and Communications

Transportation, Commerce, and Communications

Congress from 2001 to 2005 produced a limited record of action on transportation and communications issues. A few high-profile pieces of legislation were cleared and signed into law. But on most matters the lawmakers shuffled back and forth without reaching final decisions, even though Republicans controlled the White House and both houses of Congress during more than half the time.

In part, the inaction reflected the contentiousness of many issues with deeply entrenched commercial and consumer interests on all sides. It also reflected uncertainty about how to proceed, particularly in the rapidly evolving telecommunications field, as well as the relatively low level of importance that these issues commanded during the period after the Sept. 11, 2001, terrorists attack on the United States and the launching of a preemptive war in Iraq in 2003.

A major disappointment to almost everyone was Congress's inability to finish a surface transportation bill, largely because of substantial differences between the White House and lawmakers—principally Republicans—over the costs of highways and other transit programs. The failure was a tough blow to many legislators who craved new financing for roads and mass transit in their states and districts to tout to voters. But not surprisingly, Congress once again could not devise a formula to save or dismantle the national passenger railway system, Amtrak. Except for a few high-population corridors, such as in the Northeast, Amtrak's financial future looked bleak. However, because its lines ran through dozens of states and congressional districts, it had a built-in constituency in Congress that, at the minimum, tilted against ending the experiment in long-haul passenger trains.

Lawmakers resolved a long dispute over a buyout of tobacco farmers who had been buffeted by legal actions against cigarette makers as well as other changes in the economies of growing tobacco. The buyout was expected to cost about $10 billion over a decade. Criticism of the legislation arose from what it did not include: authority for the Food and Drug Administration to regulate tobacco as a public health issue. Advocates believed that the highly controversial regulatory power would come only if wedded to the buyout legislation, but it was blocked in the face of unswerving opposition in the House.

Another important piece of legislation that made its way to the president was an extensive reauthorization of the Federal Aviation Administration and related agencies. Like surface transportation, aviation authorization was important to many areas of the nation—and their senators and representatives—because of funding for aviation operations, airport improvements, and other issues such as increasing flights from some airports. Congress in 2001 swiftly approved legislation providing up to $15 billion to stabilize the airline industry in the wake of the 2001 terrorist attacks that devastated the air travel business.

The contentious issue of Mexican trucks on U.S. highways was resolved in late 2001. The vehicles were allowed to operate throughout the country under requirements to ensure safety. The action was vigorously opposed by organized labor.

In telecommunications policy, Congress had a more mixed record during the four-year period.

A ban on taxing activity on the Internet, dating from 1998, was continued in both the 107th and 108th Congresses, reflecting a stalemate between revenue-strapped state and local governments and the high-tech industry and Internet

REFERENCES

Discussion of transportation, commerce, and communications policy for the years 1945–1964 may be found in *Congress and the Nation Vol. I,* pp. 517–562, 1159–1185; for the years 1965–1968, *Congress and the Nation Vol. II,* pp. 227–251, 281–305, 779–823; for the years 1969–1972, *Congress and the Nation Vol. III,* pp. 147–187, 659–700; for the years 1973–1976, *Congress and the Nation Vol. IV,* pp. 146–147, 433–451, 505–555; for the years 1977–1980, *Congress and the Nation Vol. V,* pp. 291–362; for the years 1981–1984, *Congress and the Nation Vol. VI,* pp. 261–286, 289–329; for the years 1985–1988, *Congress and the Nation Vol. VII,* pp. 357–413; for the years 1989–1992, *Congress and the Nation Vol. VIII,* pp. 415–464; for the years 1993–1996, *Congress and the Nation Vol. IX,* pp. 327–398; for the years 1997–2001, *Congress and the Nation Vol. X,* pp. 318–338.

Outlays for Transportation

Billions of Dollars

SOURCE: Office of Management and Budget, *Historical Tables, Budget of the United States Government: Fiscal Year 2006* (Washington, D.C.: U.S. Government Printing Office, 2005), Table 3.2.

users. Congress also could not reconfigure telecommunications policy to deal with Internet service over telephone lines, one of the most heavily lobbied issues of the period. Another high-profile issue involved alleged indecency broadcasting on television and, to a lesser extent, on radio. Efforts to increase fines for broadcasting programming considered indecent, in spite of wide support, became ensnared in controversies over unrelated legislation.

With a speed seldom seen in the deliberative halls of Congress, legislators zipped through a bill that endorsed a program set up by the Federal Trade Commission—the "do not call" registry—that allowed persons to block telemarketing calls to their home phones. Congress also acted to allow continued satellite transmission of programming to areas of the country poorly served by conventional methods of sending signals. Disputes between satellite companies and local over-the-air stations threatened to halt satellite broadcasting in many areas, raising the possibility of TV screens going black in households nationwide, which members of Congress knew they would have heard about promptly.

The volatile issue of media ownership plagued the 107th and 108th Congresses. Rulings by the Federal Communications Commission (FCC) to allow media companies to own stations that reached a larger portion of the audience than previously allowed drew vocal criticism from consumer advocates and—unexpectedly—an unusual coalition of liberals and conservatives in and out of Congress. Congress in the end rolled back the upper limit of holdings that the FCC ruling would have allowed, but other parts of the agency's rules were struck down in court decisions.

Chronology of Action on Transportation, Commerce, and Communications

2001–2002

Legislative action in the 107th Congress was relatively light on transportation and communication issues. The two main proposals that were enacted involved Mexican trucks in the United States and assistance to the nation's airlines after the Sept. 11, 2001, terrorist attacks on the World Trade Center in New York City and the Pentagon outside Washington, D.C.

Congress acted within two weeks of the attacks to stabilize the airline industry, which was shut down for two days after the attacks and then crippled by the reluctance of Americans to travel on planes. Even before the attacks the airline industry was in deep economic trouble as a result of the recession that began in 2000. The legislation was designed as a lifeline to help preserve the nation's air transport system, which was in danger of failing altogether.

The Mexican trucks controversy was one of numerous issues that grew out of the 1993 North American Free Trade Agreement, which was intended to wipe out trade barriers among Mexico, the United States, and Canada. Organized labor resisted the part that allowed Mexican trucks on U.S. roads, citing safety concerns and fears of job losses by Americans. In the end, in action that was widely considered a victory for business over labor, Congress did allow Mexican trucks in, albeit under carefully crafted safety requirements.

Other issues received less attention. Congress extended an earlier prohibition on activity on the Internet, in effect postponing a full debate on the issue.

Mexican Trucks on U.S. Roads

A dispute over Mexican trucks on U.S. roads was resolved late in 2001. The vehicles were permitted to operate throughout the country under a set of requirements designed to ensure highway safety. Action came on the $59.6 billion fiscal 2002 transportation spending bill (HR 2299—PL 107-87).

In spite of the requirements, organized labor objected loudly to the legislation. It feared loss of jobs and argued that the Mexican trucking business would compromise highway safety. The final agreement was widely seen as a victory for the George W. Bush administration and business interests.

BACKGROUND

The 1993 North American Free Trade Agreement (NAFTA) was approved over fierce opposition from organized labor, environmentalists, and others. The pact was designed to phase out tariffs and trade barriers among the United States, Canada, and Mexico. (NAFTA, Congress and the Nation Vol. IX, p. 155)

One provision of NAFTA required that the United States and Mexico allow trucks to operate freely in each other's country. Initially, this was to occur by 1995 but was later changed to January 2000. President Bill Clinton decided to confine Mexican trucks to a twenty-mile commercial zone along the border, but a NAFTA commission ruled in February 2001 that the restriction violated the trade agreement. President Bush issued rules to allow the trucks into the country starting Jan. 1, 2002. This action set off a fight in Congress between those who argued that an open border would increase international trade and those who said Mexico's lack of regulations covering hours of service, insurance, and licensing for truck drivers would unleash dangerous vehicles on the U.S. highways.

The 2001 fight was not the first time Congress confronted the truck issue. In 1995 the Senate Commerce, Science, and Transportation Committee reported a bill to prevent Mexican tractor-trailers longer than fifty-three feet to cross the border. No further action was taken on that measure. (Earlier action, Congress and the Nation Vol. IX, p. 367)

LEGISLATIVE ACTION

The truck issue was one of the most controversial riders to a major appropriations bill, and it delayed consideration of the transportation spending measure for four months. The skirmishing began in the House Appropriations Committee

COMMERCE, TRANSPORTATION, SMALL BUSINESS LEADERSHIP

President George W. Bush named Donald L. Evans of Texas to head the Department of Commerce. Evans won broad praise at his confirmation hearings with senators of both parties commending his background in business and as chair of the governing board of the University of Texas college system. The Senate confirmed his nomination by voice vote on Jan. 20, 2001.

Evans was chair and chief executive officer of Tom Brown Inc., a large firm in the oil and gas business, where he had worked since 1975 as a "roughneck" on oil rigs and later in the executive suites. Perhaps more pertinent to his appointment was a long association with Bush. He had raised funds for Bush's Texas gubernatorial campaigns and then raised about $100 million for his 2000 presidential race.

Fund-raising was not at issue in his hearings, however. Trade was, with Democrats focusing on their continuing criticism of trade practices they claimed were costing American jobs. Evans acknowledged he was an advocate of free trade but added that it "must never be a one-way street."

He also said he would continue a policy of Bush's predecessor, Bill Clinton, to have agency employees, not political appointees, arrange trade trips to ensure that they are not linked to fund-raising. He endorsed continued research into global climate change, from which the Bush administration later was to disassociate itself, and efforts to nurture the growth of high-tech industry.

Evans stayed on through most of Bush's first term. He submitted his resignation on Nov. 9, 2004, immediately following the election, as part of a wider cabinet shakeup. He was succeeded by Carlos M. Gutierrez, the Cuban-born head of the Kellogg cereal company.

The secretary of transportation position went to Norman Y. Mineta, the only Democrat in Bush's cabinet. He was confirmed unanimously, 100–0, on Jan. 24, 2001. A widely respected former member of the House from 1975 to 1995, Mineta had served as commerce secretary in the Clinton administration.

Other than his political affiliation, Mineta was a natural selection for the job. Transportation policy is one of the more bipartisan areas in the government and a subject Mineta learned thoroughly during his years in Congress and for a short time after leaving when he served as a vice president at Lockheed Martin Corp. working on the development of "smart" transportation technologies. (Clinton had tried to interest Mineta in the transportation secretary's job when he won the White House.) Mineta had represented the California Bay Area with its heavy concentration of high-technology companies, which showed in his interest in using technology to improve the nation's transportation system.

The four years proved more challenging than he expected. The Sept. 11, 2001, terrorists attacks threw the airline industry, already suffering economic woes, into turmoil and threatened the existence of some carriers. The department had been facing issues of an antiquated air traffic control system and travel congestion. Airline mergers and cost cutting contributed to consumer complaints. The 107th and 108th Congresses were unable to pass a reauthorization of the basic surface transportation that was a central part of the department's mission. The dispute, largely between Republicans in Congress and Bush in the White House, boiled down to cost: Members, including Democrats, wanted to authorize highway and mass transit spending significantly larger than the administration was willing to accept.

The appointment of Michael K. Powell as chair of the Federal Communications Commission (FCC) subsequently would be seen as one of Bush's more controversial ones. Powell, who was the son of Secretary of State Colin Powell, had served three years on the five-member commission and was considered a reliable if occasionally independent conservative. He also had worked in the antitrust division of the Justice Department.

Powell was well known for his enthusiasm for the operation of the market in consumer and business decisions. One critic said he was "enamored by the philosophy of the marketplace." During his tenure he became an outspoken advocate of telecommunications deregulation, including allowing media companies to grow in size through acquisitions. This view, which was reflected in an important set of new rules promulgated by the FCC, set off a firestorm of controversy led by critics who said it would put control of the nation's television and other media in the hands of a few giant corporations, thereby stifling diversity and local control of broadcasting. An unlikely coalition of conservatives and liberals, in and out of Congress, forced a retreat on the rules. In addition, a federal court said the FCC had not fully justified its decision on the rules. The end result was a stinging rebuke to Powell's approach on the commission. Powell stayed through the four years of Bush's term but announced he would step down from the post in early 2005.

Bush on March 17, 2005, named Kevin J. Martin as FCC chair. Martin was best known for his strong advocacy for more stringent penalties against broadcasters for indecency on the airwaves.

Bush's nominee to head the SBA was Hector V. Barreto, who was confirmed by the Senate by voice vote on July 26, 2001. Barreto was serving as vice chair of the board for the U.S. Hispanic Chamber of Commerce and was involved in small business enterprises in his home town of Kansas City, Missouri.

when Martin Olav Sabo of Minnesota, the ranking Democrat on the Transportation Appropriations Subcommittee, proposed an amendment to prohibit Mexican trucks beyond the twenty-mile zone unless they passed safety reviews similar to those for domestic trucks. Republicans, holding the majority on the committee, approved a substitute amendment that allowed Mexican trucks to operate in the United States for an eighteen-month provisional period while they were monitored for safety. The June 20, 2001, vote on the amendment, which was sponsored by Transportation Appropriations Subcommittee Chair Harold Rogers, R-Ky., was 37–27.

When HR 2299 reached the House floor, opponents fared better. Sabo proposed to bar the use of funds in the bill to process applications by Mexico-domiciled motor carriers to operate beyond the border zone. His amendment was adopted on June 26 by 285–143, with 82 Republicans joining 201 Democrats and two independents in support. The administration strongly opposed the amendment.

The Senate Appropriations Committee on July 12 approved, as part of a companion measure (S 1178—S Rept 107-38), a compromise engineered by Patty Murray, D-Wash., and Richard C. Shelby, R-Ala., the chair and ranking member of the Transportation Appropriations Subcommittee, respectively. The amendment would lift the truck ban but add nearly two dozen safety requirements. Mexican trucks were required to cross the border only at operating inspection facilities. The full opening of the border would be delayed until the Transportation Department published final rules covering safety regulations and confirmed that new inspectors were fully trained. Mexican firms would be required to provide sufficient information on the safety records of their companies and drivers to permit U.S. monitoring and show that they understood U.S. safety standards. Mexican truck companies would need U.S. insurance and two safety audits within eighteen months before receiving a permanent operating certificate for travel in the states.

The Senate passed HR 2299 by voice vote on August 1 but only after breaking a nine-day filibuster, 100–0, by border-state senators opposed to the restrictions on Mexican trucks.

Conferees had to work out compromises on the truck and other issues. The final bill cleared on Dec. 4 and was signed into law until on Dec. 18.

The legislation allowed the president to open the Southwest border to long-haul Mexican trucks in accordance with NAFTA requirements. A total of $140 million was provided for border inspection stations and staff. The legislation barred the trucks until the Transportation Department certified that opening the border would not threaten highway safety, a process that was expected to take about six months.

Under the deal, Mexican trucking companies that wanted to operate within the United States had to have their equipment, insurance, and driving records inspected and certified by the Transportation Department. The trucks could enter the United States only at border crossings with inspectors to carry out safety checks. At least half of all Mexican truck drivers had to have their licenses checked upon entering the country, including all those with hazardous cargo. Each truck had to be physically inspected every ninety days, similar to a boarder inspection system used in California.

Teamsters president James P. Hoffa scorned the agreement. Other union officials claimed satisfaction with the safety requirements but said that they did not assuage fears that low-wage Mexican drivers would cost U.S. jobs and depress wages.

Broadband Access

A major effort to reconfigure telecommunications policy rules that govern high-speed broadband service came to naught in the 107th Congress. The House in 2002 passed legislation (HR 1542) to deregulate the market for broadband Internet service over telephone lines, but it stalled in the Senate. Key senators were skeptical of allowing the regional Bell companies—the principal beneficiaries of the bill—the untrammeled freedom provided by HR 1542.

Sponsored by Energy and Commerce Committee Chair Billy Tauzin, R-La., and ranking Democrat John D. Dingell of Michigan, it sought to ease restrictions in the 1996 Telecommunications Act (PL 104-104) designed to promote local phone competition. (*1996 law, Congress and the Nation Vol. IX, p. 387*)

The House bill allowed the Bells—Verizon Communications, BellSouth Corp., SBC Communications Inc., and Qwest Communications International Inc.—to offer advanced data services over long distances without first having to meet requirements in the 1996 law that they open their local systems to competition. The Bell companies were the progeny of the once-dominant long-distance carrier AT&T Corp. after its breakup over antitrust issues. But the Bells themselves had grown into huge companies with significant economic clout in the highly competitive telecommunications business. (The Bells had become so large that early in 2005 SBC proposed to buy AT&T Corp., a merger that was subsequently approved. SBC said that the AT&T names would be retained. Qwest also was reported to be in talks with MCI, another large telecommunications company, about a merger. However, an even larger Bell, Verizon, made a bid for MCI and eventually prevailed.) The Bells said the legislation was necessary to make their services competitive with cable companies, which were not covered by the 1996 requirements, and to speed deployment of broadband services over enhanced telephone lines, known as digital subscriber lines (DSL).

Opponents initially included AT&T, which offered broadband services through its cable TV before they were sold to Comcast Inc., and small Bell competitors known as competitive local exchange carriers (CLECs). They argued the bill would remove all incentives for the Bells to open their local systems and would create a new Bell monopoly leading to higher prices for consumers and weaker oversight by the Federal Communications Commission (FCC). Lobbying on the legislation spilled over from Capitol Hill into the media and generated new interest groups, such as Voices for Choices, and millions of dollars in ad campaigns. The Bells enlisted support from disparate groups, such as the Communications Workers of America, the National Black Chamber of Commerce, and the Grange, representing the interests of underserved urban areas and rural communities that wanted access to broadband services.

BACKGROUND

The Tauzin-Dingell bill addressed issues that had increasingly roiled the telecommunications industry.

To promote competition and expand service to consumers, the 1996 Telecommunications Act offered a trade-off: If the regional Bell telephone companies would open their local telephone systems to competition, they would be allowed to provide long-distance services within their service territories. The law also required the local telephone companies to lease individual parts of their local network to competitors at below-retail prices. The role of the Bells was crucial because only they owned the electronic switching equipment and extensive network of lines that reached most American consumers. Without access to this long-established network, new companies would be effectively barred from the business because of the prohibitive costs of building entirely new networks. But the Bells always chafed at the requirement, as they saw it, of having to sell access to their customers to competitors at cut rates so the competitors could try to take away their customers.

In addition, at the time of the 1996 law's enactment the evolution of communications technology was not fully appreciated. In particular, during the following decade the unregulated cable companies began voice communications delivery over the Internet into a growing number of American homes that subscribed to cable, thereby entirely bypassing the Bells' networks. Furthermore, in the following years the cell phone market rapidly expanded. This development offered customers long-distance as well as local connections, adding another significant factor to the competitive landscape. However, a number of the largest cell phone companies were subsidiaries of the Bells.

The 1996 law modified the 1982 court order that broke up the AT&T telephone monopoly into seven regional Bells, later consolidated into four. AT&T was allowed to continue as a long-distance carrier, and the Bells were expressly prohibited from entering that market. *(1982 action, Congress and the Nation Vol. VI, p. 270)*

The Bells resisted opening their networks from the outset. But the growth of the Internet and cable companies became an even more daunting threat as the speed of cable connections continued to increase. (Cable companies controlled about 70 percent of the residential broadband market by 2002.) In 1999 the FCC ruled that the 1996 line-sharing requirements applied to equipment and lines used for DSL broadband services, thereby allowing competitors such as CLECs to use the Bells' local lines to offer limited DSL connections.

The Bells themselves began to offer limited DSL services but initially did not treat it as a major business. Only with the expansion of cable, and the clear potential of cable lines to carry vast amounts of material at high speeds, did the Bells begin to rethink their views of delivering not only voice but also other types of content. The Bells complained that the telephone competition requirements of the 1996 law unduly impeded them, creating economic disincentives to upgrading their lines and equipment to further deploy broadband DSL services. (The original DSL technology, over standard copper lines used for telephones, had inherent limitations. One of the most important required a user to be within a mile or two of a telephone switching office to use DSL. To overcome this problem the Bells were faced with running fiber-optic lines into neighborhoods to hook up with the copper lines into homes, which was an expensive undertaking.) The Bells argued that the regulations were intended for voice traffic and that the 1996 law did not anticipate the swift introductions of high-speed data services.

Congress had to decide what role, if any, the government should play in regulating telecommunications.

The majority of the House and FCC chair Michael K. Powell favored lifting the 1996 restrictions and allowing the Bells to compete head-to-head with cable. But less sympathy for the Bells existed in the Senate, where Ernest F. Hollings, D-S.C., who headed the Commerce Committee, and a number of other senior members of both parties were wary of tinkering with the 1996 law, which many of them had spend long months negotiating. Some remained angry that the Bells mounted court challenges to provisions in the act after participating in negotiations leading to its passage.

LEGISLATIVE ACTION

The Tauzin-Dingell bill sailed through rough waters from the spring of 2001 to the end of the year, when House leaders decided the issue was too controversial to bring to the floor in that session of Congress.

The bill made its way out of the Energy and Commerce Telecommunications and the Internet Subcommittee on April 26 by a slim 19–14 margin after a long and contentious markup that revealed significant differences over whether the legislation would alter the competitive balance in a telecommunications market being buffeted by an economic slowdown. Critics were particularly concerned that the bill would allow the Bells to squeeze out small, independent Internet service providers. The measure survived a major challenge when the subcommittee defeated, 14–19, an amendment by Steve Largent, R-Okla., to kill language that critics said would remove safeguards ensuring that competitors had access to the Bells' local networks.

The full Energy and Commerce Committee approved HR 1542 by a narrower than expected 32–23 vote on May 9. The measure was formally reported (H Rept 107-83, Part I) on May 24. The most contentious amendment, which was defeated when the committee deadlocked 27–27, would require the Bells to share with CLECs and other competitors any new high-speed fiber-optic lines they built to deploy DSL services beyond the restricted one to two miles of standard copper-wire DSL. Bill supporters labeled this a killer amendment, arguing that fiber-optic line sharing would eliminate any incentive for the Bells to build out systems and provide high-speed Internet services in new markets and locations. Supporters of the amendment, sponsored by Bill Luther, D-Minn., and Heather A. Wilson, R-N.M., said it would keep the Bells in check and ensure that residential customers had a choice of high-speed Internet providers.

In other action, the committee rejected, 18–36, a Thomas M. Davis III, R-Va., amendment to define broadband service as any transmission rate to the subscriber of 1,500 kilobits per second or higher. HR 1542 would set the lower speed of 384 kilobits per second as the threshold. Davis argued that his provision would ensure that the Bells offered the best service available when they built new systems. Opponents said it would force the Bells to deploy more expensive service that would shut out some small businesses and lower-income individuals. The panel also rejected, 17–37, a Largent, Bart Stupak, D-Mich., and Ted Strickland, D-Ohio, amendment to require the Bells to deploy broadband networks to underserved areas 150,000 feet or closer to the companies' central offices within three years of enactment. Instead, the committee adopted, by voice vote, an amendment by Bobby L. Rush, D-Ill., and Tom Sawyer, D-Ohio, to require the Bells to offer high-speed service to underserved areas within 15,000 feet of their central offices within five years. The amendment also would require the Bells to report to the FCC regularly on their progress in upgrading their central switching facilities.

Energy and Commerce rejected an amendment by Anna G. Eshoo, D-Calif, by 18–28, that would codify FCC rules requiring the Bells or their affiliates to regularly report the quality of their service. Opponents said that such a requirement ran counter to the bill's deregulatory intent and that the FCC had already indicated it would revisit the rules. Two Davis amendments, offered en bloc, were rejected by voice vote. They would allow the FCC to impose fines of up to $25 million on Bells repeatedly found to have engaged in anticompetitive activities in the broadband market. Opponents argued that the amendments singled out the Bells and raised constitutional issues.

The committee adopted several amendments aimed at ensuring fairness in the broadband market, including one by Cliff Stearns, R-Fla., stipulating that the bill would not affect existing contracts allowing telecommunications companies to connect with each others' systems.

Tauzin said he planned to ask the House Rules Committee to merge HR 1542 with a related measure (HR 1765) sponsored by Fred Upton, R-Mich., chair of the Telecommunications and the Internet Subcommittee. HR 1765 would significantly increase penalties for violations of the Telecommunications Act and tracked requests by FCC chair Powell that Congress increase the fines the agency could levy on phone companies that violated local competition rules. The bill proposed to increase maximum penalties from $120,000 to $1 million per violation and cap monetary fines at $10 million for repeated offenses. It would increase the amount of time the FCC had to take action against violators from one to two years.

Also controversial was the tension between the Commerce and Judiciary committees during consideration of HR 1542. Tauzin insisted that the bill was only about telecommunications issues. The Judiciary Committee saw it differently and obtained a limited referral of the bill to examine antitrust issues. Committee chair F. James Sensenbrenner Jr., R-Wis., won voice vote approval of an amendment to require the Bells to seek antitrust approval from the Department of Justice before they could enter the long-distance market. That would give the department regulation over the Bells, requiring the attorney general to approve requests to offer long-distance broadband services. The department would determine whether the companies had opened their local facilities to competitors as required by the 1996 law. Existing law gave this power to the FCC; the Justice Department's role was advisory. The Sensenbrenner amendment also would overturn a 2000 decision by the 7th U.S. Court of Appeals in *Goldwasser v. Ameritech* that a Bell's refusal to allow a competitor to connect to its local network would not constitute an antitrust violation. The amendment affirmed that antitrust laws could apply to the Bells—a distinction that would subject them to increased fines and possible divestiture. Supporters of HR 1542 on the Judiciary Committee argued that the proposal exceeded the scope of the panel's jurisdiction because it would give the Justice Department new regulatory powers (to block the Bells' entry into the long-distance market). They also contended that it would carve out new functions for the department without ensuring that the agency had the necessary expertise or resources.

Staff aides and others said that Sensenbrenner had had to exert significant pressure on committee members to accept his amendment. The division in the committee was reflected in its subsequent action by voice vote June 13 to report HR 1542 unfavorably. The bill was formally reported (H Rept 107-83, Part II) on June 18.

Lawmakers' ambivalence was further demonstrated when the Judiciary Committee rejected, 15–19, a stand-alone bill (HR 2120) that largely mirrored Sensenbrenner's amendment. The bill would have been used as backup if the chair's language had been ruled out of order.

That was as far as HR 1542 got in 2001. House leaders scheduled a vote for Dec. 14 but at the last minute pulled it back until the next session. Lawmakers expressed discomfort about holding what was expected to be a close vote on one of the most heavily lobbied bills of the session. Members also resisted being forced to choose between the Bells and the long-distance companies.

The House passed HR 1542 on Feb. 27, 2002, by 273–157. Most of the debate focused on the extent to which the regional Bell telephone companies should be forced to open their lines to rival telecommunications companies, generally smaller firms that supporters said would provide needed competition to the near-monopoly held by the Bells. The major challenge to the bill was language offered by Chris Cannon, R-Utah, and John Conyers Jr., D-Mich., that would have retained the access rules for Bell competitors that were mandated in the 1996 telecommunications law. It was effectively rejected on Feb. 27 via a procedural motion on a **key vote of 173–256 (R 62–157; D 109–99; I 2–0)**. *(2002 key votes, p. 819)*

The House added language to the bill, by voice vote after a lengthy series of parliamentary maneuvers, to provide separate rules for fiber-optic and copper lines. Bells using fiber-optic lines to provide broadband Internet services would be required to carry competitor's broadband services at "just and reasonable" rates and terms set by the FCC, a change from the existing requirement that competitors be allowed access to Bell lines at discounted rates. Competitors could still lease copper lines for DSL service at a discount, but technology limited service to customers who were no more than a mile or two of a Bell switching station.

An amendment by Upton and Gene Green, D-Texas, was adopted 421–7 on Feb. 27. It would increase FCC penalties on phone companies that violated requirements of the 1996 act; increase the maximum fine per violation from $120,000 to $1 million per day, with a cap for continuing violations rising from $1.2 million to $10 million; and for repeat offenders, doubled the penalty per violation to $2 million a day, with a cap of $20 million. The amendment also doubled, from one year to two, the statute of limitations for the FCC to bring enforcement actions against phone companies.

The rule for floor debate (H Res 350), approved by voice vote Feb. 27, automatically made a change that had been negotiated by the Energy and Commerce and Judiciary panels. The language required Bells that planned to transmit high-speed data services across long-distance boundaries—but had not gained FCC approval to provide long-distance voice services in those areas—to notify the Justice Department at least thirty days before starting the data transmissions. The rule also clarified that the 1996 law did not override or diminish federal antitrust laws, thereby overturning *Goldwasser v. Ameritech.*

After James M. Jeffords of Vermont left the Republican Party in June 2001, the Senate majority tipped to the Democrats. Hollings, a staunch foe of the Bells, became head of the Commerce, Science, and Transportation Committee, thus seriously dimming the prospects for HR 1542. He held several hearings on telecommunications competition but did not allow the bill to advance. To the surprise of many ob-

servers, the committee's ranking Republican, John McCain of Arizona, once a proponent of even more sweeping deregulation, branded the Tauzin-Dingell bill a special interest piece of legislation.

John B. Breaux, D-La., and Don Nickles, R-Okla., offered what was seen as a milder version of Tauzin-Dingell. The bill, S 2430, would give the FCC four months to come up with rules that ensured "regulatory parity" between all broadband providers—DSL, cable TV, and satellite. The Bells thus would be given some relief offered by HR 1542, but the requirements of the 1996 law relating to voice services would be explicitly maintained. The FCC would have exclusive jurisdiction over broadband.

Hollings offered a bill (S 2448) calling for loans and grants to encourage broadband deployment, especially in rural and underserved areas. Money collected from the 3 percent federal telephone excise tax would finance the program, establish wireless technology pilot projects, and fund research. Another Hollings bill (S 1364) would split each of the Bells into separate retail and wholesale companies to spur more local telephone competition.

S 2430, S 2448, and S 1364 were referred to the Senate Commerce, Science, and Transportation Committee and saw no further action.

Internet Taxation

Congress continued to be vexed about taxing activity on the Internet. In the end, legislators in 2001, in action on HR 1552, only extended a moratorium on Internet taxes that dated from 1998 when the issue first became a fiercely lobbied technology issue. The moratorium was further extended in 2004. *(108th Congress action, p. 400)*

The controversy pitted revenue-strapped state and local governments against the high-tech industry and Internet users who wanted to keep the new communications media free of what they claimed would be crippling taxation. Business interests were more divided, with some saying that tax-free Internet purchases were harming the business of brick-and-mortar stores while others with both traditional stores and Internet Web sites were more circumspect.

BACKGROUND

The controversy circled around separate but related issues. Both involved whether the Internet would remain free of taxation or become a source of government revenue support as had long been the case with the sale of goods in stores and the use of communications media such as the telephone. Within that framework, one question was whether to tax the sale of goods made over the Internet. A second question was whether to tax access to the Internet itself. The latter was an increasingly contentious matter as Internet providers began developing reliable voice communication technology that would compete directly with traditional telephone service, which was taxed.

The nation's approximately 7,500 state and local governments, allied with the National Governors Association (NGA), said the growth of e-commerce was siphoning customers from regular businesses and eroding tax revenues. The concern was compounded by the economic downturn that came in 2000. Many retailers agreed, saying that the Internet should not continue to operate as a tax-free zone.

But the same downturn had badly battered the high-tech industry, which feared any effort to limit the growth and use of the Internet. It argued that new taxes could crush the Internet economy when expansion was needed.

Collecting taxes on sales conducted over the Internet was difficult. Transactions could occur across several states, with a purchaser in one state linking to a computer in a second state that linked to a retailer in a third state. Moreover, in a 1992 case, *Quill Corp. v. North Dakota*, the U.S. Supreme Court ruled that states could not force vendors to collect sales taxes unless the purchaser lived in a state where the company had a physical presence, such as a retail store. (*Court ruling, Congress and the Nation Vol. VIII, p. 850*)

Nineteen states had passed laws based on a model developed by the NGA to create a simplified system for collecting taxes from "remote sellers" located in any of the member states. The nation's governors wanted congressional endorsement for such a compact but were vigorously opposed by the high-tech industry.

Unable to find a solution acceptable to all sides, Congress in 1998 put the sales tax issue aside and cleared a three-year moratorium (PL 105-277) that applied to all new taxes specifically imposed on Internet access and commerce. The moratorium was scheduled to expire Oct. 21, 2001. (*Congress and the Nation Vol. X, p 327.*)

LEGISLATIVE ACTION

The House Judiciary Commercial Law Subcommittee by voice vote Aug. 2, 2001, approved a five-year extension of the moratorium. HR 1552 would permanently ban Internet access charges and do away with a loophole in existing law that allowed eleven states to continue charging fees that were enacted before 1998. But the full Judiciary Committee, wary of basic changes, adopted 19–15 on Oct. 10 a Spencer Bachus, R-Ala., amendment to extend the ban two years and drop the effort to close the loophole. Another Bachus amendment, stating that Congress should approve a sales tax compact once twenty-five states had agreed to join, was ruled out of order. The committee approved HR 1522 on Oct. 10 by voice vote and formally reported it (H Rept 107-240) on Oct. 16. The bill passed the House by voice vote under suspension of the rules Oct. 16.

The Senate cleared HR 1552 on Nov. 15, nearly four weeks after the moratorium had expired. The delay came as senators tried to resolve the state sales tax issue, to no avail. Michael B. Enzi, R-Wyo., tried to strengthen the states' hands by offering an amendment to encourage the formation of a compact if twenty states agreed. A John McCain, R-Ariz., mo-

tion to table (kill) the Enzi amendment was agreed to 57–43 on Nov. 15. Opponents argued that the amendment was so loosely worded that it could lead to taxes being levied every time a person accessed content on the Internet. They also questioned whether endorsing the compact essentially would allow twenty like-minded states to reverse any Supreme Court decision.

Several local government organizations that had opposed the two-year extension changed their position and endorsed it. The U.S. Conference of Mayors, National Conference of State Legislatures, National Association of Counties, and National League of Cities said a simple two-year extension would allow for more negotiations on sales taxes. The administration had recommended a simple extension.

The bill was signed into law on Nov. 28 (PL 107-75).

Airline Assistance

Within two weeks of the Sept. 11, 2001, terrorists attacks in New York City and just outside Washington, D.C., legislation (HR 2926) was enacted providing $15 billion to help stabilize the nation's airline industry. (*Sept. 11 attacks, p. 230*)

The legislation provided $5 billion cash and up to $10 billion in loan guarantees. It also limited liability for United and American airlines, whose planes were used in the attacks, and set up a Justice Department system through which victims of the crashes and their families could receive compensation. It classified the spending as mandatory, making it essentially an entitlement. The bill did not include $3 billion the administration had sought for airline and airport security improvements but affirmed Congress's intent to act quickly on the request. (*Aviation security, p. 198*)

BACKGROUND

Even before the terrorist attacks, the U.S. airline industry was suffering major financial losses from the economic slowdown that began in 2000, which reduced business and leisure travel. The attacks greatly magnified airline losses, threatening the stability and even the viability of the U.S. aviation system, which in normal conditions constituted about 10 percent of the nation's gross national product.

U.S. airlines were expected to lose almost $5 billion through the end of 2001 after the government shut down all airline travel for two days. Continuing losses were predicted as Americans avoided air travel and the airlines faced increased costs for security.

Most airlines reduced their flight schedules. An industry spokesperson said total layoffs could exceed 100,000 and put several weak airlines in danger of bankruptcy unless the financial aid came quickly.

LEGISLATIVE ACTION

The aviation assistance bill, HR 2926, bypassed the normal committee process and was brought directly to the House and Senate floors. The House passed the legislation

Federal Aviation Administration head Jane Garvey, left, and Department of Transportation secretary Norman Y. Mineta and deputy secretary Michael Jackson testify September 20, 2001, at a Senate hearing on aviation security in the wake of the 9/11 attacks. *Source: Congressional Quarterly/Scott J. Ferrell*

356–64 on Sept. 21, 2001, and the Senate cleared it by voice vote the same day. Earlier on Sept. 21 the Senate had passed an identical companion measure (S 1450) by 96–1. Although the bill moved quickly, the road was not entirely smooth. An initial effort to pass an emergency aid bill in the early morning hours of Sept. 15 was blocked by members asking for more time to consider the legislation. Some members said the measure set a bad precedent, encouraging other industries affected by the attacks to seek aid.

The package that became law was negotiated by a handful of senior members from both chambers and Office of Management and Budget director Mitchell E. Daniels Jr. They wanted to limit the bill to financial aid for airlines but faced pressure from Republicans to include liability protection for the carriers. Democrats sought unsuccessfully to include protection for airline workers who were likely to lose their jobs.

A deal reached Sept. 10 collapsed the next day after some lawmakers had second thoughts about protecting the airlines from liability. The administration originally proposed giving $5 billion to the airlines but without loan guarantees. The

administration offered a compromise proposal that included a board to oversee the loan guarantees and ensure that the loans did not go to airlines that were financially insolvent.

Lawmakers were emphatic that the bill not be considered a bailout for an industry that was suffering financially long before the terrorist attacks.

Congress acted in 2002 to extend, though 2003, the war-risk insurance program, which provided federal insurance to commercial aircraft that fly overseas into high-risk areas for foreign policy and national security needs, such as ferrying troops and equipment to war zones, when commercial insurance was not available or prohibitively expensive. The program's revolving fund was financed by premiums paid by airlines that receive coverage under the program. The extension was enacted as part of the law that created the Department of Homeland Security (HR 5005—PL 107-296). The law also extended through 2003 a $100 million limit on an airline's liability for injuries suffered as a result of terrorist attacks. *(Homeland Security Department creation, p. 176)*

MAJOR PROVISIONS

As enacted, HR 2926 (PL 107-42) contained the following major provisions.

Cash assistance. Made available immediate cash assistance of $5 billion to compensate for losses stemming from the Sept. 11, 2001, attacks. Of the total, allotted $4.5 billion for passenger airlines and the rest for cargo carriers.

Required carriers, to receive cash aid, to provide proof of their losses to the Transportation Department and General Accounting Office (GAO). Based payments on the lesser of either actual losses or a pro rata share based on a carrier's percentage of industry-wide mileage multiplied by its seats or cargo tonnage.

Loan guarantees. Provided up to $10 billion in loan guarantees or other credit assistance to passenger airlines and created a four-member Air Transportation Stabilization Board to review and approve applications. The board was composed of the secretaries of transportation and the Treasury, the Federal Reserve chair, and the comptroller general of the GAO. Required airlines to agree to freeze compensation for top executives for two years to be eligible.

Airline liability. Limited liability for United and American airlines for deaths and property damage to the limits of their insurance. Required all lawsuits against the two airlines to go through one court—the U.S. District Court for the Southern District of New York.

Victim compensation. Allowed persons injured in the attacks and the families of those killed, including people on the hijacked aircrafts and on the ground, to seek compensation through one of two mechanisms: lawsuits filed in federal court or a new Justice Department compensation program to be administered by a special master appointed by the attorney general. Required the special master to determine compensation for levels of claimants within 120 days of the time a claim was filed. Specified that claimants did not have to prove negligence of any party. Specified that upon filing a claim individuals waived their right to seek any compensation through lawsuits in a federal court.

Future liability. Allowed the Transportation Department to limit the liability of U.S. airlines in any terrorist attacks within the following six months to $100 million, with the federal government assuming responsibility for the rest.

Aircraft insurance. Allowed the Transportation Department, for the following six months, to use funds from the federal aviation war-risk insurance program to reimburse U.S. airlines for higher insurance premiums resulting from the attacks. (After Sept. 11, many insurance companies notified airlines of huge premium increases.)

Airline taxes. Waived interest penalties on airlines for failing to pay certain aviation taxes on time, including employment taxes and fuel and ticket excise taxes.

Internet Royalties

Congress in 2002 cleared legislation limiting the royalties of small Internet music broadcasters. The bill (HR 5469) codified a two-year agreement between the recording industry and small Webcasters on the royalty rates that the Webcasters would pay to performers and record companies. The deal applied only to Webcasters with gross revenues of $500,000 or less in 2003 and $1.3 million or less in 2004.

By voice vote the Senate passed the bill Nov. 14 and the House cleared it Nov. 15. It was signed into law on Dec. 4 (PL 107-321). The House initially passed the bill by voice vote Oct. 7. However, Jesse Helms, R-N.C., held up action in the Senate after receiving complaints from noncommercial and religious radio Webcasters that they had not been included.

Small Webcasters argued that a new royalty schedule proposed in June by the Library of Congress would have put them out of business. The library was responsible for overseeing copyright matters such as payment rates for the use of musical performances.

The final version delayed imposition of any new royalties for six months. It allowed Webcasters to pay royalties based on their expenses or revenue, which they said would mean less out-of-pocket expenses for them. It also provided a potentially lower-cost option for tax-exempt, noncommercial Webcasters.

Spectrum Auction

Congress in 2002 with little dissent delayed indefinitely a Federal Communications Commission (FCC) auction of part of the airwaves used by television broadcasters. President George W. Bush signed the bill into law June 19 (HR 4560—PL 107-195).

The delay was enacted at the behest of a number of wireless telecommunications firms that argued the FCC should not auction the electromagnetic spectrum in the 700 megahertz band without a comprehensive spectrum management plan in place. The companies also cited the struggling econ-

omy and signs that television broadcasters were unwilling to vacate that part of the airwaves before a 2007 deadline.

BACKGROUND

To prepare for a transition from analog to digital television, the FCC in 1997 allocated television stations an additional bank of electromagnetic spectrum in which to begin broadcasting a digital signal. Stations were expected to continue analog broadcasts while they made the transition. Congress codified many of the FCC's deadlines for this transition in the 1997 Balanced Budget Act (PL 105-33), including a requirement that all stations broadcast digital signals by the end of 2006. Broadcasters then would be required to discontinue their analog broadcasts and return that spectrum to the FCC for reassignment to other users. *(1997 action, Congress and the Nation Vol. X, p. 325)*

To count the revenue within the five years covered by the bill, however, the law required that the returned analog spectrum be auctioned off for other uses by Sept. 30, 2002, more than four years before the return deadline. The law required that television spectrum in the upper 700 megahertz band, corresponding to TV channels 60 to 69, be allocated between public safety services and commercial uses, with the commercial auctions to begin after Jan. 1, 2001.

In 1999 Congress advanced the timetable for auctioning the channels in the 60 to 69 spectrum, requiring that the proceeds from this auction be deposited in the U.S. Treasury no later than Sept. 30, 2000. The anticipated revenue was to offset part of the costs of the fiscal 2000 omnibus appropriations act. The FCC repeatedly postponed the auction.

LEGISLATIVE ACTION

The House passed HR 4560 by voice vote May 7, 2002, shortly after the Energy and Commerce Committee had given its approval, also by voice vote. The bill was formally reported (H Rept 107-443) on May 7. The legislation postponed all auctions of the 700 megahertz band indefinitely.

The Senate by voice vote on June 18 passed the bill, amended to allow the FCC to auction a slice of the 700 megahertz band. The change was negotiated with Sen. Ted Stevens, R-Alaska, who was concerned that smaller, rural wireless telecommunications carriers, including some in his home state, would not have enough spectrum to offer advanced services in rural areas. The House cleared the amended bill by voice vote the same day.

The final bill postponed the scheduled auction, except for two blocks of the lower 700 megahertz band, which had to be auctioned no later than Sept. 17. The FCC was then left to reschedule auctions for the upper 700 megahertz band.

Amtrak

As so often previously, Congress could find no common ground to resolve the problems of the National Rail Passenger Corporation, better known as Amtrak. The railroad was left to survive on emergency cash infusions when legislation to reauthorize the corporation died in the face of continued disagreement about the purpose and future of the system. *(108th Congress action, p. 404)*

The Transportation Department gave Amtrak a $100 million loan in June 2002 to avert a shutdown of the perennially troubled railroad, and Congress provided $205 million in supplemental funding (PL 107-206) a month later. *(Supplemental, p. 63)*

Proponents said Amtrak needed more money, at least $1.2 billion, to keep it running through fiscal 2003. Meanwhile, the railroad suffered several summertime accidents in 2002 that injured more than one hundred passengers and damaged or destroyed thirteen passenger cars.

BACKGROUND

Amtrak was created by the Rail Passenger Service Act of 1970 (PL 91-518) to relieve privately owned railroads of their money-losing passenger lines, thereby allowing them to focus on money-making freight cargo. *(1970 act, Congress and the Nation Vol. III, p. 161)*

But passenger railroading proved no more profitable under government control with federal grants and loan guarantees than it had been in private hands. Congress added to Amtrak's problems by requiring service on unprofitable routes (few representatives or senators wanted to see rail service disappear from areas they represented) and by imposing labor rules that deterred layoffs and private contracting. Lawmakers in the 1980s also reduced capital grants, which saddled the railroad with aging and expensive equipment and left it poorly positioned against aggressive airline competition.

The ambivalence in Congress mirrored the uncertainty among politicians and policy planners about the role of rail passenger carriers in national transportation policy. The heyday of passenger trains ended decades earlier as airlines, autos, and modern highways proliferated after the 1940s. But supporters of Amtrak said it was an important part of the national transportation grid even though its share of passenger traffic had drastically shrunk (the system carried under 1 percent of intercity traffic by 2002) and should be encouraged as part of a balanced policy. They argued that Amtrak could be run profitably but that profitability alone was not the only justification for its existence. Opponents argued that Amtrak was an egregious misuse of public funds when many alternate forms of transit were available, even to rural communities. Opponents, however, often conceded that rail transit made sense in densely populated corridors such as the Northeast corridor from Boston to Washington, D.C., although even then they favored turning those routes over to private ownership.

Nevertheless, the numbers continued to bode ill for Amtrak. It nearly crashed in 1994 as its operating deficit approached $200 million and management announced plans to slash service. Management said its goal was to survive without operating subsidies by fiscal 2002 but that it would continue to rely on federal support for capital. After Republi-

cans took control of Congress in 1995, some key GOP allies moved into important committee positions, easing the worries of railroad supporters, who feared that long-standing Republican opposition to Amtrak subsidies would spell the end of the line. But by early 1997, the General Accounting Office (GAO) reported Amtrak was going deeper into debt, losing $1.6 billion in 1995 and 1996, despite streamlining its operations and dropping some routes. *(Earlier action, Congress and the Nation Vol. IX, p. 369; Congress and the Nation Vol. X, p. 320)*

Amtrak lost another $1.1 billion in fiscal 2001 and continued to hemorrhage millions of dollars a day. A report by the GAO in 2002 said Amtrak had not carried out much of a network growth strategy announced two years earlier. It had started three of twelve planned new routes, one of which was canceled when it did not attract expected freight business.

LEGISLATIVE ACTION

Amtrak legislation never got beyond committee action in the 107th Congress. The Senate Commerce, Science, and Transportation Committee by 20–3 on April 18, 2002, approved a five-year passenger rail measure (S 1991), which was formally reported (H Rept 107-157) on May 29. It authorized $1.4 billion in fiscal 2003 for security and tunnel safety improvements, $7.8 billion over five years for high-speed rail projects, and $13.3 billion over five years for Amtrak. The bill also authorized $35 billion for loans and loan guarantees under the Railroad Rehabilitation and Infrastructure Financing program, which was created but not funded under the 1998 surface transportation law (PL 105-178). In addition, the bill repealed the requirement in the 1997 Amtrak Reform and Accountability Act that the carrier be operationally self-sufficient by the end of 2002.

Before approving S 1991, the committee adopted by voice vote an amendment requiring that 50 percent of the rail security funds be spend outside the Northeast corridor, which runs between Washington, D.C., and Boston. Other provisions included labor protections and requirements that Amtrak continue to operate as a national system, that it implement new financial planning and accounting methods, and that it put any net revenues from nonpassenger operations into maintaining sufficient working capital to prevent major service disruptions.

The committee rejected two amendments offered by ranking Republican John McCain of Arizona: to establish an Amtrak Control Board to monitor the rail company's finances, approve Amtrak's budgets, and provide management assistance (5–18), and to require Amtrak to have the transportation secretary's approval before taking on new debt (10–13). The panel by voice vote adopted two McCain amendments: to require that new high-speed rail projects funded under the bill be subject to a competitive bidding process, and to allow states to put up some of the funds for high-speed rail projects (the underlying bill required a 100 percent federal share). The committee also adopted, by voice vote, a Gordon H. Smith,

R-Ore., amendment to clarify that the bill would not preclude Amtrak from maintaining non-high-speed service in certain parts of the country; a Smith amendment to add Portland, Oregon, to the list of high-speed rail priority locations; a John D. Rockefeller IV, D-W.Va., amendment to make non-railroad entities eligible for loans and loan guarantees under the bill; a Ron Wyden, D-Ore., amendment to require the Transportation Department to hire an independent consultant to examine Amtrak route and service planning decisions; a Wyden amendment to apply executive branch conflict of interest standards to Amtrak board members and Amtrak officers; and a Bill Nelson, D-Fla., amendment to designate the Tampa-to-Orlando corridor as a priority for high-speed rail service.

In the House, the Transportation and Infrastructure Railroads Subcommittee on May 8 by voice vote approved a pair of bills: a $1.9 billion Amtrak reauthorization bill (HR 4545) for fiscal 2003 and legislation (HR 2950) to authorize $59 billion over ten years to build high-speed rail lines in several areas of the country. The reauthorization bill included $1.2 billion requested by the railroad for operations, capital improvements, and retirement payments and $775 million for security and repairs to tunnels in New York, Baltimore, and Washington, D.C. In return, it required greater supervision of Amtrak by the Transportation Department, congressional committees, and GAO. The high-speed bill reflected the findings of the Amtrak Reform Council and other experts that the future of passenger rail in the United States lay in swift routes over limited distances up to 300 miles where trains could compete on service and price with airlines. The bill also allowed states to issue tax-exempt and tax-credit bonds for high-speed rail lines—up to $2.4 billion worth of bonds each year through 2012. States that issued the bonds would be required to pay for some rail improvements such as eliminating grade crossings and rehabilitating or building stations. The bill also included $35 billion for the Railroad Rehabilitation and Infrastructure Financing program.

Subcommittee chair Don Young, R-Alaska, withdrew both bills from full committee consideration because of a dispute among House Republicans, the Association of American Railroads, and unions representing construction and railroad workers. The unions wanted to ensure that members got a majority of potential jobs from the bond program and that the new employees were covered by federal railroad labor laws. Republican lawmakers and the railroad association balked and the bills went no further.

2003–2004

The 108th Congress turned in a more productive record than its predecessor on transportation and commerce issues but still left many matters for the future, especially in telecommunications.

Lawmakers reauthorized the Federal Aviation Administration and grant programs that members eagerly sought to expand air travel activities in their states. The legislation was one of several bills on which the Republicans and Democrats clashed over White House efforts to turn over federal jobs to private contractors. Faced with a filibuster in the Senate, the privatizing issue was put aside to get the airport bill through.

Congress was not successful, however, in moving legislation for ground transportation or the nation's rail passenger system, Amtrak. Both chambers began 2003 fully expecting to pass a six-year highway and transit bill worth billions of dollars to states and districts but wound up in a deadlock with the administration over the costs of the legislation. Similarly, members once again did not pass any fundamental restructuring of Amtrak, in large part because nobody had yet figured out what to do with it.

Legislators had more success with the long-stalled tobacco buyout proposal. They approved a ten-year, $10 billion buyout program for tobacco farmers but refused to add provisions giving the Food and Drug Administration (FDA) regulatory authority for tobacco. Health advocates were unhappy with that decision because they saw linking the two as perhaps the only way to get the FDA the authority to deal with the health issues of cigarette smoking. The regulatory authority was approved by the Senate but was dropped in the face of unrelenting opposition from House Republican leaders.

Media ownership was another highly controversial issue during the 108th Congress. It, too, was rooted in differing opinions of regulatory activity. The Republican majority on the Federal Communications Commission (FCC), led by Chair Michael K. Powell, issued new rules that allowed media companies to expand. In the case of television, they were allowed to buy additional stations that in total allowed them to reach up to 45 percent of the nation's viewers. The rules also allowed more cross-ownership of TV and radio stations and newspapers in the same community.

The new rules produced a huge and unexpected backlash of an improbable coalition of liberals and conservatives who said the rules would allow a few giant media companies to control most of the nation's mass communication system. This, they argued, would all but smother broadcasting diversity and local control of programming. In response, Congress changed the rules applicable to the TV audience issue to make the cutoff for national audience saturation 39 percent; under previous rules it was 35 percent. Congress did not try to change the other parts of the new FCC rules, but court decisions struck them down. Those decisions, confirmed in early 2005, left the cross-ownership issues unsettled.

In other actions, Congress swiftly endorsed a Federal Trade Commission (FTC) program allowing Americans to block telemarketing calls to their home phones. A court decision had threatened to overturn the FTC program. But otherwise, Congress considered but was unable to act on many telecommunications issues, including broadcasting indecency penalties, gambling on the Internet, intellectual property protection, online piracy, spyware controls, and allocation of broadcast spectrum to public safety agencies.

FAA Reauthorization

After struggling over the contentious issue of privatizing the nation's air traffic control system, Congress ducked the issue and approved an extensive reauthorization of the Federal Aviation Administration (FAA) and related agencies through fiscal 2007. President George W. Bush signed the legislation into law Dec. 21, 2003 (HR 2115—PL 108-176). The last reauthorization (PL 106-181), enacted in 2000, had expired on Sept. 30. (2000 law, Congress and the Nation Vol. X, p. 331)

Opponents of privatization, who had threatened a filibuster in the Senate, eventually were appeased by a promise that the FAA would not turn over air traffic control functions to contractors in fiscal 2004. Labor unions and their Democratic allies in Congress vowed to seek a ban on privatization written into law in the future.

HR 2115 authorized $62 billion over four years for FAA programs and operations. It allowed additional flights into Ronald Reagan Washington National Airport, where the number of takeoffs and landings was restricted because of congestion and noise. The airport was located in Northern Virginia, just outside Washington, D.C., and was heavily used by members of Congress. The bill permitted cargo pilots to carry handguns. The measure also extended war-risk insurance for the first time to aircraft manufacturers and airline vendors.

BACKGROUND

The two principal issues during debate on the legislation were privatization and the expansion of slots at Reagan National Airport.

The issue of turning air traffic control over to private contractors was first raised by the Bush administration in early 2001 as part of a general push to outsource federal jobs, but it went nowhere after the Sept. 11, 2001, terrorist attacks in New York and outside Washington. In June 2002 Bush issued an executive order designating air traffic control as a commercial instead of an inherently governmental function, which meant the FAA could privatize the jobs at its discretion. The government already contracted out air traffic control at 219 small airports, with several dozen more eligible for the program. Air traffic controllers fought further privatization with arguments about safety, reaching a receptive audience in Congress.

The administration had no immediate plans to privatize control towers. Air traffic controllers had been put in a category of commercial jobs that would not be contracted out. But the threat energized labor groups such as the Transportation Trades Department of the AFL-CIO and the National Air Traffic Controllers Association.

Many Democrats were determined to insert language in law explicitly prohibiting privatization. The Bush administration was equally determined to retain its flexibility, and the White House threatened to veto any bill that restricted its ability to privatize portions of the air traffic control system.

Reagan National was one of the last airports in which the number of takeoffs and landings during the day was strictly controlled to reduce congestion. Operations late at night were banned to reduce noise over nearby residential areas. Slot controls at New York's Kennedy International and La-Guardia airports and Chicago's O'Hare International Airport were being phased out.

Those decisions were made after a lengthy debate as part of the 2000 FAA reauthorization. The 2000 law authorized twelve new slots, called slot exemptions, for long-distance flights at National. It also authorized twelve more slots for shorter flights provided they went to new entrant carriers to fly to small and medium-size communities.

Del. Eleanor Holmes Norton, D-D.C., and other Washington-area lawmakers opposed the change, arguing that additional flights would increase congestion, pollution, and noise as well as siphon business from nearby Dulles International Airport, which was designed to handle transcontinental and intercontinental flights.

But expansion was backed by powerful legislators who had airlines in their states and districts that stood to benefit from increased access to Reagan National. House Transportation and Infrastructure Chair Don Young, R-Alaska, favored more slots on behalf of Alaska Airlines, while Aviation Subcommittee Chair John L. Mica, R-Fla., was helping Florida-based AirTran Airways. Senate Commerce Chair John McCain, R-Ariz., looked out for the interests of Phoenix-based America West. Added slots were advocated by Sens. John Ensign, R-Nev., and Maria Cantwell, D-Wash. Las Vegas McCarran International Airport and Seattle-Tacoma International Airport both stood to get additional flights from the expansion.

The airlines engaged in a stiff lobbying battle. United Airlines, for example, worried that adding more takeoff and landing slots at Reagan National would give that airport an unfair advantage over Dulles, where United was the dominant carrier. US Airways had traditionally dominated Reagan National and feared that expansion would erode its market share.

A number of smaller carriers lobbied for access to the airport or for an increase in the flights they already had. America West Airlines and Alaska Airlines—the eighth- and ninth-largest carriers, respectively—had won access to Reagan National in the past decade and now wanted a larger share of the market.

LEGISLATIVE ACTION

The House Transportation and Infrastructure Committee by voice vote May 21, 2003, approved a four-year reauthorization bill, after adopting a compromise on the expansion of slots at Reagan National Airport. The total included $14.8 billion for the Airport Improvement Program, $31.3 billion for FAA operations, and $12.3 billion for facilities and equipment. The committee formally reported HR 215 (H Rept 108-143) on June 6.

The panel had approved by voice vote a Mica amendment to increase the number of new slot exemptions by twelve for long-haul flights and eight for short-haul flights. Norton said it was an acceptable compromise for the time being, but the opponents hoped it would be dropped in conference.

The committee-approved bill also prohibited the FAA from privatizing air traffic controllers but did not extend the prohibition to technicians, specialists, and support staff.

The House passed the $58.9 billion, four-year bill June 11 by a vote of 418–8. Despite a White House veto threat, lawmakers did not remove the privatization provisions. Young said he would stand against the administration with the support of an overwhelming House majority. The House adopted a manager's amendment that dropped a requirement that six of the slots for service to small airports go only to new entrants, thereby allowing airlines already serving National to provide that service. It also allowed seventy-six-seat regional jets to qualify for commuter slots at Reagan National. The rule (H Res 265) for floor consideration of HR 2115 prevented Norton and James P. Moran, D-Va., from offering an amendment to delete the slot expansion provisions.

The Senate Commerce, Science, and Transportation Committee approved a three-year bill (S 824) by voice vote May 1. It was formally reported (S Rept 108-41) the next day. Introduced by Chair John McCain and ranking Democrat Ernest F. Hollings of South Carolina, the measure authorized $44 billion for fiscal 2004 through fiscal 2006. Of the total, $23.2 billion would go toward FAA operations and $10.5 billion toward the Airport Improvement Program.

The committee approved, 12–11, an amendment by Ensign and Cantwell to increase by twelve the number of slots at Reagan National available for takeoff to destinations beyond 1,250 miles and to increase the number of long-haul flights per hour to three from two. The panel adopted, 12–10, an amendment by Barbara Boxer, D-Calif., to require certification of safety and security training for flight attendants. The proposal was opposed by the airline industry as a potentially costly mandate. S 824 included a provision not in the House version to allow commercial cargo pilots to carry handguns.

The Senate passed HR 2115 June 12 by a 94–0 vote after substituting the text of S 824. The Senate version would prohibit the FAA from privatizing either air traffic control personnel or support staff. The anti-privatization language was drafted by Frank R. Lautenberg, D-N.J., in conjunction with the National Air Traffic Controllers Association. It was adopted 56–41 on June 12. Casting the debate as security versus cost-cutting, Lautenberg made direct comparisons between air traffic control privatization and the fight over federalizing baggage screeners that roiled Congress in the wake of Sept. 11. McCain and Trent Lott, R-Miss., who chaired the Aviation Subcommittee, opposed the amendment, arguing that some functions, such as weather services, could be performed ably by private employees.

The provisions to expand slots at Reagan National Airport were stripped out of the bill as part of a compromise amendment adopted by voice vote to avoid a showdown on the issue.

First Conference Report

House and Senate conferees reached agreement on a bill July 24, and the conference report (H Rept 108-240) was filed in the House the next day.

While most of the dealmaking was bipartisan, Democrats said they were cut out of the talks on privatizing air traffic control jobs. The GOP conferees agreed to allow immediate privatization of air traffic controllers at sixty-nine airports that operated under visual flight rules or limited instrument rules. All support jobs could be privatized immediately, and controllers at all other airports could be privatized after Oct. 1, 2007.

Lawmakers who had backed the prohibitions passed by both chambers were furious. This left Republican backers of the legislation trying unsuccessfully for weeks to gather enough votes to make it worthwhile to bring the conference report up for adoption in either chamber.

Because a conference report cannot be amended on the floor, the only solution seemed to be to send it back to the conference committee. Republican leaders did not want to do that, however, until they were sure they had a deal that could get the bill through both chambers while avoiding a veto. Finally, on Oct. 28, Republican leaders offered a resolution (H Res 377) to recommit the bill to the conference committee, and the House adopted it 407–0.

Conference/Final Action

GOP leaders filed a new conference report (H Rept 108-334) in the House on Oct. 29.

Those who had opposed the privatization provisions in the first report wanted conferees to restore the ban passed by both chambers. What they got back instead was legislation with no privatization language at all. By its silence, the measure allowed the Bush administration to contract out airport control towers and jobs across the country.

Democrats were livid and nearly brought the House to a halt Oct. 30 with procedural delays. When the final vote was held in the evening, the revised conference report was adopted 211–207, with eleven Republicans voting against the measure. Republican leaders marshaled support from airports and business groups, most of which were eager for infrastructure grants to continue without interruption or for provisions such as the slot expansion at Reagan National to be enacted.

But in the Senate, Lautenberg and others threatened to filibuster the conference report. On Nov. 17 an attempt by the leadership to invoke cloture, thereby limiting the debate, failed on a **key vote of 45–43 (R 42–3; D 3–39; I 0–1)**, well short of the sixty votes required to prevail. *(2003 key votes, p. 837)*

The ensuing negotiations finally resulted in a letter from FAA administrator Marion C. Blakey stating that no employees "directly related to our air traffic control system" would be privatized during fiscal 2004. Minutes after the letter was received on Nov. 21, the Senate cleared the conference report by voice vote.

MAJOR PROVISIONS

As enacted, HR 2115 (PL 108-176) contained the following major provisions.

Authorization

Airport improvement program. Authorized $14.2 billion over four years for the program, which provided grants to local airports for airport development, safety and security improvements, and noise abatement. Funding was set to increase by $100 million per year, starting from $3.4 billion in fiscal 2004 and reaching $3.7 billion in fiscal 2007.

FAA operations. Authorized $31.3 billion over four years, increasing from $7.6 billion in fiscal 2004 to $8.1 billion in fiscal 2007.

FAA facilities and equipment. Authorized $12.3 billion over four years for FAA purchases to modernize facilities and equipment.

FAA research and development. Authorized $1.4 billion over four years for research, engineering, and development programs.

Funding guarantee. Extended provisions of the 2000 reauthorization that ensured that all the revenues and interest credited to the Airport and Airway Trust Fund each year were spent on aviation programs.

Aviation Security

Grants. Authorized $500 million annually to be given to airports for various security improvements.

Reimbursement. Required the federal government to reimburse airlines for the cost of screening airline catering companies and to reimburse airports for the costs of checking documents at security checkpoints.

General aviation. Authorized $100 million to reimburse general aviation businesses for costs resulting from new security restrictions imposed after the Sept. 11, 2001, terrorist attacks. Eligible businesses included general aviation entities at and around the Washington, D.C., area and certain other general aviation companies nationwide.

Arming cargo pilots. Authorized commercial cargo pilots to carry handguns or Tasers (a nonlethal type of gun) and to defend their planes with lethal force, following the same protocols and training requirements as passenger airline pilots.

Self-defense. Required airlines to provide a basic security training program to help airline pilots and flight attendants prepare for potential threats. Required the Homeland Security Department to develop an advanced self-defense training program but made the training voluntary.

Background checks. Required the Homeland Security Department to conduct background checks of all foreign citizens seeking flight training on large aircraft at U.S. flight schools.

Air charters. Required the Homeland Security Department to establish passenger screening and other security protocols for flights by large charter aircraft. Exempted air charters that transported U.S. military personnel.

Passenger screening. Prohibited the Transportation Security Administration (TSA), an agency of the Homeland Security Department, from fully implementing its Computer Assisted Passenger Prescreening System 2 program, or CAPPS2, until the Homeland Security Department certified to Congress that the system was accurate and would not be abused. The system used a variety of indicators to determine whether a passenger should be more carefully scrutinized.

License revocation. Required the FAA to revoke an individual pilot's license if the Homeland Security Department notified it that the pilot was a security risk, but provided a right to appeal if a pilot were a U.S. citizen.

Funding Issues and Grants

Passenger fees. Streamlined procedures under which airports could apply to the FAA for approval to impose passenger facility charges (PFCs) and clarified that passengers on military charter flights were not required to pay such fees. (The 2000 FAA reauthorization [PL 106-181] allowed airports to impose a surcharge of $4 or $4.50 on each paying passenger boarding an aircraft at the airport if the money generated were used for projects to improve air safety or security, increase airline competition, reduce congestion, or reduce noise.)

Aviation scholarships. Authorized $10 million per year for the FAA to offer scholarships to individuals engaged in aviation-related studies and $10 million per year for the National Aeronautics and Space Administration to offer scholarships to individuals studying aerospace-related fields.

Aviation data. Authorized about $4 million per year for the Transportation Department's Bureau of Transportation Statistics to collect and analyze aviation data.

Airport Grants

Airport security. Allowed Airport Improvement Program (AIP) grants, typically construction grants for structural improvements, to be used for aviation security projects only if they were paid for from AIP discretionary allocations, not AIP entitlement funding, which typically was earmarked for specific purposes such as general aviation or cargo service.

Cargo entitlements. Increased AIP entitlements for airports with cargo service to 3.5 percent from 3 percent of total AIP funds.

Land development. Created a prototype program at ten privately owned public-use airports under which states or localities could use an airport's AIP entitlement funding to purchase land development rights to ensure that the property would continue to be used as an airport.

Airport Projects

Environmental reviews. Required the Transportation Department, acting through the FAA, to coordinate multiagency environmental reviews of proposed airport capacity, safety, or security projects, so that the reviews could be done concurrently. Authorized $4.2 million per year through fiscal 2007 for the FAA to coordinate and facilitate these reviews.

Small and Underserved Airports

Essential Air Service program. Increased to $77 million the annual authorization for the Essential Air Service (EAS) program, which subsidized airline service to remote cities and rural areas, and continued the existing $50 million per year mandatory appropriation for EAS subsidies.

Alternative programs. Allowed communities to opt out of the EAS program and instead use the funds to develop their own transportation services, including air taxi services and surface transportation alternatives.

Small Community Air Service Program. Reauthorized the Small Community Air Service Development Pilot Program at $35 million a year for five years. (Congress created the program in the 2000 law to aid small commercial airports that had infrequent service and high fares.)

Miscellaneous Provisions

Reagan National Airport. Allowed Ronald Reagan Washington National Airport to add twenty flights a day, with twelve of those for destinations beyond 1,250 miles from the airport, the previous limit for flights from the airport. Changed the definition of commuter aircraft at National to allow regional jets with up to seventy-six seats to use the airport's commuter aircraft slots.

War-risk insurance. Extended the Transportation Department's authority to offer war-risk insurance to airlines until March 30, 2008, and expanded the program to cover U.S. aircraft manufacturers in some instances.

Flight cancellations. Extended for an additional nine months the requirement that airlines honor the tickets of passengers from other airlines whose flights were canceled because of bankruptcy.

Country of manufacture. Required U.S. airlines to include on the safety information placard in the seat-back pocket of airliners a notice stating where the plane was manufactured.

Air cargo transfers in Alaska. Allowed foreign air carriers to carry cargo between an airport in Alaska and any other point in the United States, provided two or more air carriers were involved and the cargo originated at, or was being transported to, destinations overseas. Under previous law, all cargo shipped between any two points in the United States generally had to be carried by U.S. airlines.

Flight attendant certification. Established a certification program for flight attendants and required that flight attendants be certified to work.

Air carrier ownership. Clarified that to qualify as a U.S. airline for the purposes of domestic flights and other activities, a carrier had to be under the "actual control" of U.S. citizens.

Whistle-blowers. Provided whistle-blower protection to employees of FAA contractors.

Tobacco Growers Buyout

A multibillion, ten-year buyout for tobacco farmers was enacted as part of a corporate tax overhaul in 2004 (HR 4520—PL 108-357). The legislation did not include a Senate proposal to give the Food and Drug Administration (FDA) authority to regulate tobacco, a power long sought by public health advocates. *(Background, Congress and the Nation Vol. X, p. 322)*

The cost of the program was estimated at $10 billion, which was to come from a Tobacco Trust Fund set up in the legislation and funded by manufacturers and importers of tobacco products.

The buyout became a powerful political issue for tobacco farmers in North Carolina and other states who pressed their representatives to abolish the federal quota system and reimburse farmers for their losses. The seventy-year-old tobacco program included acreage allotments and marketing quotas designed to keep supplies in line with demand at market prices. Farmers in recent years had grown to dislike the quotas, saying they made it harder to compete with foreign tobacco farmers who did not have the same constraints.

LEGISLATIVE ACTION

Tobacco-state members found a vehicle to fix their constituents' problem when House Ways and Means Chair Bill Thomas, R-Calif., needed southern votes for a time-sensitive corporate tax bill. Thomas included the buyout in HR 4520, which the House passed 251–178 on June 17, 2004. The Senate by then had already passed its version of the tax bill (S 1637) but, before going to conference with the House, reopened the measure to insert its own tobacco provisions. The amendment combined a tobacco buyout advocated by Mitch McConnell, R-Ky., with FDA regulation of tobacco products championed by Mike DeWine, R-Ohio, and Edward M. Kennedy, D-Mass. A number of senators opposed a buyout for tobacco growers unless it was paired with increased federal regulation of tobacco products. The amendment was adopted by a 78–15 vote on July 15. *(Corporate tax bill, p. 115)*

The amendment also dismantled the tobacco quota system and authorized $12 billion over ten years to give farmers

and quota holders time to switch crops and get out of the business. The buyout was to be financed by assessments on tobacco companies. The amendment also would

• Authorize the FDA to regulated levels of tar, nicotine, and other components of tobacco products. Give Congress authority to veto any effort to ban cigarettes.

• Require tobacco companies to disclose all harmful and potentially harmful ingredients in their products to the secretary of Health and Human Services (HHS). Require HHS to publish the information for each brand in an easily available and understood format.

• Require warnings to take up at least 20 percent of tobacco labels, which were to be placed on the front or back of the pack, not the side.

• Prohibit the use of terms on tobacco products such as "light" and "low-tar" unless approved by the FDA.

• Ban flavored cigarettes, not including menthol brands.

• Require magazine advertisements for tobacco products to be in black and white.

• Require tobacco manufacturers to pay for regulation through a user fee.

In conference, the Senate provisions to give the FDA authority to regulate tobacco as a public health issue were dropped in the face of unswerving opposition in the House. It was a bitter disappointment to advocates who believed that such power would be approved by Congress only through tying it to other tobacco legislation acceptable to producers.

Support for FDA regulation had been increasing over the years as the health costs of smoking became more indisputable. Perhaps significant for future efforts, one major tobacco company had broken ranks with others in the business to support regulation. That company, Philip Morris USA, was the nation's largest cigarette company with about one-half the market. Earlier, the company had spent millions of dollars lobbying successfully against regulation. But as pressure grew for regulation, Philip Morris decided carefully drafted regulatory powers—which it helped write for the Senate provisions—would be beneficial for its business by providing more consistency and predictability. But other cigarette producers, who continued to fight regulation, worried that regulation would restrict their growth to the benefit of the dominant Philip Morris company.

The House adopted the conference report (H Rept 108-755) on Oct. 7 by 280–141. The Senate cleared the bill by 69–17 on Oct. 11. President George W. Bush signed the legislation Oct. 22.

MAJOR PROVISIONS

As enacted, the tax bill (HR 4520—PL 108-357) contained the following tobacco provisions:

• Repealed the existing federal tobacco support program and provided incentives for tobacco farmers to quit the business or switch crops, ending a system that limited per acre tobacco sales to protect prices for growers and others holding quotas.

• Repealed the federal tobacco support program, including marketing quotas and non-recourse marketing loans. In place of the repealed program, provided tobacco quota holders $7 per pound on their basic quota allotment paid in equal installments over ten years.

• Provided tobacco producers transition payments of $3 per pound based on their effective quota, paid in equal installments over ten years.

• Required manufacturers and importers of tobacco products to pay a quarterly assessment into a newly formed Tobacco Trust Fund to be used for payments to quota holders and eligible producers and to pay for program losses incurred by the Agriculture Department.

Surface Transportation Authorization

Six-year reauthorization legislation (HR 3550, S 1072) for federal highway, public transportation, and road safety programs was left stranded in a Senate-House conference in 2004 when members could not agree on how to distribute money to state highway programs. The programs had been running on a series of temporary extensions since the last authorization expired Sept. 30, 2003. Unable to get a new authorization, Congress extended the program to May 31, 2005 (HR 5183—PL 108-310).

The reauthorization legislation was designed as the successor to the 1998 Transportation Equity Act for the 21st Century (PL 105-178), known as TEA-21. It authorized spending on highway and transit projects through fiscal 2003. *(1998 law, Congress and the Nation Vol. X, p. 318)*

The program was popular with members of Congress because it funneled millions of dollars into states and districts for highly visible transportation projects. Both chambers passed bills to reauthorize the program by veto-proof margins in 2004, defying White House threats of a veto over costs. The votes occurred early enough in 2004 to permit ironing out Senate-House differences and getting a final vote. Conference committee meetings on the differing bills were held in the summer and fall, but agreement eluded the members. Some observers said the massive legislation was too much and too controversial to complete in the crowded weeks leading up to the national election and the brief postelection sessions. A few Republicans said Democrats obstructed a final agreement because they did not want to give President George W. Bush a multibillion spending bill he and other GOP candidates could tout to voters before the November elections. Democrats dismissed the charges as nonsense.

Congress began 2003 committed to enacting a six-year highway and transit bill. But the lawmakers quickly found themselves on a collision course with the administration over money and put off the tough decisions to the second session. The overall cost was the biggest obstacle in early consideration of the legislation. The growing fuel tax revenues that financed TEA-21 had trailed off, leaving Congress the choice of authorizing a more modest expansion of highway projects than many members wanted or raising taxes, a solution unacceptable to the White House and many congressional Republicans.

The Bush administration's answer was to hold down spending. The administration proposed continuing to link highway funding with revenue from fuel taxes, then supplementing it with $1 billion in general revenue for the Highway Trust Fund. In addition, all revenue from the tax on gasohol—a cleaner-burning blend of gasoline and corn-based ethanol—would go to the trust fund. Under existing law, 2.5 cents per gallon of the tax went to general revenues in the Treasury.

A bipartisan majority of lawmakers wanted to spend significantly more. Key senators sought $311 billion over six years; House counterparts wanted $375 billion. But no agreement was reached on how to raise the additional money. Proposals included increasing the federal gasoline tax and floating construction bonds. The administration threatened to veto any attempt to pay for the bill by increasing taxes.

Another divisive issue that was to prove fatal in reconciling the legislation was the distribution of highway funds among the states. TEA-21 guaranteed that each state would receive federal highway spending equal to at least 90.5 percent of the federal highway taxes paid by its citizens. The donor states—those that paid more than they got back—were pressing for a better deal. Both the House and Senate bills promised to increase the guarantee to 95 percent. But lawmakers from the donee states that benefited under the existing system were not eager for a change.

Environmental controversies added to the problems. Environmentalists were angered by a number of changes proposed in the Senate bill; the House bill did not yet have an environmental section. The Senate bill called for a new, more streamlined process for handling environmental reviews for transportation projects, with the Transportation Department designated in statute as the lead federal agency. It also encouraged different agencies to conduct their reviews on a project at the same time, instead of sequentially.

S 1072 also called for fewer demonstrations under the 1990 Clean Air Act Amendments (PL 101-549) to show that a highway plan conformed to an area's efforts for reaching clean air standards. Under the law, an area that did not comply with air quality standards had to have a plan to do so, and federal agencies could not finance projects in those areas without a demonstration that the project fit into the compliance plan. The bill proposed to require such demonstrations every four years, instead of every three. Also, the bill allowed the use of publicly owned land in parks, recreation areas, refuges, and historic sites for transportation projects if it would have "de minimus impacts" on the area. *(Clean Air Act, Congress and the Nation Vol. VIII, p. 473)*

LEGISLATIVE ACTION

Senate jurisdiction over surface transportation was divided among several committees. The Environment and Public Works Committee approved a bill containing core highway and environmental provisions, and the Commerce,

Science, and Transportation Committee approved the safety-related portions. Neither the Banking, Housing, and Urban Affairs panel, which handled mass transit, nor the Finance Committee, which was responsible for any tax changes, acted in 2003.

With pressure mounting to get the reauthorization moving, the Environment and Public Works Committee approved a $221.7 billion bill (S 1072) by a vote of 17–2 on Nov. 12, 2003. The measure was formally reported (S Rept 108-222) on Jan. 9, 2004. When all the pieces of the bill were assembled, the total was expected to reach $311 billion.

However, the committee put off decisions on a handful of contentious issues, including the formula for determining how much transportation money each state would get. S 1072 proposed to guarantee each state a return of 95 percent of its contributions and each donee 10 percent growth in returns over the life of the bill, but it gave no details.

The Senate Commerce, Science, and Transportation Committee, which was responsible for safety programs, gave voice vote approval June 26 to a piece of a larger bill that would reauthorize the National Highway Traffic Safety Administration (NHTSA) and several other transit safety programs. The provisions were reported Nov. 25, 2003, as S 1978 (S Rept 108-215). The bill included a requirement—opposed by manufacturers of sport-utility vehicles and other large passenger vehicles—for the NHTSA to establish rollover crashworthiness standards.

In the House, Don Young, R-Alaska, chair of the Transportation and Infrastructure Committee, introduced legislation (HR 3550) that provided a $375 billion, six-year authorization. He hoped it would be paid for with an increase in the 18.4 cents per gallon gasoline tax, even through that approach was strongly opposed by both the administration and the House GOP leadership. As a result, Young waited until the end of the year to even introduce HR 3550 and then left it to the Ways and Means Committee to figure out how to pay for it. Young's bill included a guarantee that each state would get a return on its highway taxes of at least 95 percent by 2009. Young proposed to allocate $298.7 billion for highways, $69.2 billion for mass transit, and the rest to safety programs.

No further action occurred in either chamber in 2003.

The Senate by 76–21 on Feb. 12, 2004, passed S 1072, which was assembled from legislation written by the Environmental and Public Works Committee, the Finance Committee, the Banking, Housing, and Urban Affairs Committee, and the Commerce, Science, and Transportation Committee. The six-year measure provided $318.9 billion in contract authority with an obligational limit of $297 billion. Consideration of the bill had proceeded after the Senate voted 75–11 on Feb. 2 to invoke cloture (and thus limit debate).

The day before the Senate passed S 1072, the White House issued a statement warning that if the bill were sent to Bush, his advisers would recommend a veto because the total exceeded the president's desired budget limit and because the bill included Amtrak provisions, which the administration

said belonged in a separate measure. Backers said that the funding level was inextricably linked to the state allocation of highway money developed by the Environment and Public Works Committee. As long as there was enough money, even a small decline in a state's percentage could still translate into an increase in highway dollars. In addition, they said, the $318.9 billion would allow significant funding increases for programs not based on formula allocations to the states.

Not all senators saw their states as winners. Eight states that were paying less into the trust fund than they got in aid were slated to become donor states in 2009—Connecticut, Iowa, Kansas, Nebraska, New Hampshire, New York, Pennsylvania, and Wisconsin. And some senators objected to the bill's overall cost.

During floor consideration on Feb. 12, the Senate rejected a Kay Bailey Hutchison, R-Texas, amendment to allocate $9.25 billion to increase formula highway funding so that all states would be guaranteed a 91 percent return in fiscal 2005, rising to 95 percent by 2009, by 17–78, and a Jon Kyl, R-Ariz., amendment to reduce the total cost of the bill to $256 billion to match the administration's request, by 20–78.

The House bill (HR 3550) combined provisions drafted by three committees. First, the House Transportation and Infrastructure Committee, which wrote the core of the measure, approved a scaled-back version of Young's proposal by voice vote March 24. It was formally reported (H Rept 108-452, Part I) on March 29. The measure provided $283.2 billion in contract authority over six years with an obligational limit of $275 billion. (As a small protest, the panel also gave voice vote approval to a bill—HR 3994—that reflected Young's original $375 billion proposal.) HR 3550 also included a provision aimed at forcing Congress to revisit highway funding levels in 2005.

The bill contained the so-called reopener provision that would cut off funding for highway programs in fiscal 2006, unless a new law was enacted that authorized enough funding to allow each state to receive at least 95 percent of the money it contributed to the Highway Trust Fund by fiscal 2009. The provision was important in retaining the support of committee members from donor states. The bill also earmarked $11 billion for members' high-priority projects—all 2,838 of them.

"Equity" in distributing highway money was the most contentious issue during House Transportation and Infrastructure markup. John L. Mica, R-Fla., offered, and then withdrew, an amendment on behalf of the donor states that would enlarge the pool of money distributed by formula to include the $11 billion in earmarked projects and $6.6 billion in the bill for "projects of regional and national significance," a category that included large projects at key interstate bottlenecks. The effect would be to reduce each state's formula allocation by the amount it received in earmarked projects, instead of using them to supplement the formula funds.

Second, the Ways and Means Committee gave voice vote approval March 17 to a bill (HR 3971—H Rept 108-444) that was estimated to increase revenue for highway programs by $17.7 billion in fiscal 2004 through 2009. The measure, sponsored by Chair Bill Thomas, R-Calif., would increase trust fund revenue by shifting the cost of ethanol subsidies to the general Treasury, by cracking down on fuel tax evasion, and through other, smaller tax adjustments.

Third, the Science Committee on Feb. 4 approved a bill (HR 3551—H Rept 108-662, Part I) authorizing surface transportation research and development grants for fiscal 2004 through 2009.

The House passed the $283.2 billion HR 3550 on April 2 by 357–65. In warning of a veto, the Office of Management and Budget cited the bill's cost and reiterated the administration's insistence that the bill be paid for out of the Highway Fund without increasing taxes or issuing bonds and without dipping into the general fund.

Before bringing the bill to the floor, Young and his committee added hundreds of pages of last-minute changes, including fresh earmarks, changes in the environmental review process for road projects, and billions of dollars in tax breaks that had been approved by the Ways and Means Committee but had little to do with highways. The tax proposals included a two-year extension of a law that allowed small businesses to deduct up to $100,000 for business equipment in the year it was purchased. The bill also proposed to exempt more small companies from the corporate alternative minimum tax. The changes were made part of the rule (H Res 593—H Rept 108-456) for floor debate that passed April 1.

The House rejected, 170–254, on April 2 a Johnny Jackson, R-Ga., amendment to shift $17.7 billion into the pool of money distributed by formula to the states.

House and Senate conferees then faced two big challenges: agreeing on a figure for total spending, and satisfying the competing demands of donor states, which pay more in highway taxes than they get in assistance, and the donee states, which receive more dollars than they pay.

Republican conferees backed spending of $299 billion, which House Ways and Means Chair Thomas said the White House could support. The package included a change in the ethanol fuel credit that would shift money from the government's general fund to the Highway Trust Fund. To offset the lost revenue, the bill included provisions—eventually included in the corporate tax bill (PL 108-357) cleared in October—to close loopholes and crack down on fuel fraud. (*Corporate tax bill, p. 115*)

But negotiators could not find a formula for dividing the money that satisfied both the donor and donee states. House leaders had enough conferees prepared to sign onto the compromise, but Senate Environment and Public Works Chair James M. Inhofe, R-Okla., could not gather enough support in the Senate to overcome objections that Western states and public transit programs were shortchanged. Also, Inhofe had alienated Senate Democrats by vowing to push a bill through conference without their support if necessary.

On Sept. 30, 2004, Congress cleared an eight-month extension (HR 5183) of existing surface transportation programs. On Sept. 30 the House passed the bill 409–8, and the

Senate followed suit, by voice vote, completing congressional action. The president signed the measure the same day.

Media Ownership

Media ownership continued to plague lawmakers throughout the 108th Congress.

The Federal Communications Commission (FCC) in a June 2, 2003, ruling relaxed federal regulations that restricted media company expansion. The FCC, led by Chair Michael K. Powell, who strongly supported more deregulation of the industry, voted 3–2 to allow a single company to own broadcast television stations that collectively reached up to 45 percent of the nation's viewers. That was up from 35 percent under the 1996 Telecommunications Act (PL 104-104). The FCC also lifted a twenty-eight-year-old cross-ownership ban that had prohibited one company from owning television stations and newspapers in the same market, and it changed the methods by which radio markets were defined. The FCC's actions relaxed limits on owning multiple broadcast outlets in local markets. (*1996 law, Congress and the Nation Vol. IX, p. 387*)

The backlash was immediate and furious, taking many lawmakers by surprise. Liberal and conservative groups and individuals joined together to oppose the changes, arguing that they would allow a handful of giant media companies to gain control of most of the nation's mass communications system while smothering diversity in broadcasting and local control of programming. However, in 2004 a federal court ruling blocking the FCC changes kept the issue unsettled. All of the other parts of the FCC rules changes remained contentious, and even the one issue—national ownership—supposedly settled in 2003 was not accepted by FCC critics as the final word. In the end, the White House and GOP leaders agreed to permanently reset the ownership cap at 39 percent.

LEGISLATIVE ACTION

Even before the FCC published the text of its June ruling, the Senate Commerce, Science, and Transportation Committee gave voice vote approval June 19, 2003, to a bill (S 1046) to restore the 35 percent ownership cap. The bill, formally reported (S Rept 108-141) on Sept. 3, was introduced in May by Ted Stevens, R-Alaska, the second-ranking Republican on the committee, and Ernest F. Hollings, D-S.C., the ranking Democrat, as word of the ruling began to leak out. The bill initially was backed by the National Broadcasters Association, which represented smaller station owners and stations affiliated with TV networks.

But large and small broadcasters united against the bill after the Commerce Committee amended it to reverse other parts of the FCC decision. The amendments sought to nullify the FCC's plans to allow more consolidation in the radio business and to drop the ban on newspaper cross-ownership.

Meanwhile, in the House Richard M. Burr, R-N.C., vice chair of the Energy and Commerce Committee, and ranking committee Democrat John D. Dingell, Mich., introduced their own bill to restore the 35 percent limit. But in the House the Commerce Committee Chair, Billy Tauzin, R-La., as well as House Speaker J. Dennis Hastert, R-Ill., and Majority Leader Tom DeLay, R-Texas, backed the FCC changes and the White House's opposition to rolling back the new rules. Tauzin said the FCC decisions could be viewed by courts as not going far enough. DeLay was more emphatic: "This is a private property rights issues. This is a freedom of speech issue. We should be unregulating instead of regulating people's right to own property and business."

With Tauzin adamant, House and Senate lawmakers looked to the Commerce-Justice-State appropriations bill (HR 2799), which funded the FCC, to attach the media ownership provision. The House Appropriations Committee added language July 16, 2003, barring the FCC from spending any of its fiscal 2004 funding to administer licenses that would result in one company owning television stations that reached more than 35 percent of the national audience. The amendment, offered by David R. Obey, D-Wis., was adopted 40–25.

When the bill was sent to the House floor, members brushed aside a White House veto threat and the entreaties of top GOP leaders and passed the measure 400–21 July 23, a margin that was widely interpreted as a vote of approval for the lower ownership limit. To keep the issue focused on the media ownership controversy, opponents of the FCC's action agreed to remove language that would have reversed the other parts of the FCC decision, especially the cross-ownership provision. The House rejected a Maurice D. Hinchey, D-N.Y., amendment to add cross-ownership language, 175–254 on July 22.

The Senate Appropriations Committee added identical language in adopting by voice vote Sept. 4 an amendment offered by committee chair Ted Stevens, R-Alaska, to its version of the bill (S 1585) in an effort to take the issue away from conferees. But then the Senate went further. On Sept. 16 senators on a **key vote of 55–40 (R 12–38; D 42–2; I 1–0)** approved a joint resolution (S J Res 17) to reverse the FCC's rulings. The resolution was permitted under the 1996 Congressional Review Act (PL 104-121) that allowed Congress to overturn new federal regulations with a simple majority vote of both houses and the president's signature. Although a rarely used device, it did give Congress the potential for much greater control over regulations adopted by the federal bureaucracy. The only time it had been used successfully was in 2001 when a Republican Congress repealed workplace ergonomics regulations put in place at the end of the Clinton administration. (*Ergonomics rules, p. 565; 2003 key votes, p. 600*)

In this case, the vote was symbolic because the House was not going to consider S J Res 17 and the president would not have signed the resolution even if it did get through that chamber. But it did demonstrate the intensity of feeling in the Senate and laid the groundwork for a later compromise.

During consideration of the fiscal 2004 Commerce, Justice, and State appropriations bill (HR 2799—H Rept 108-

221), the House Appropriations Committee, over the objection of GOP leaders, adopted 40–25 an amendment by ranking Democrat Obey to bar the FCC from using funding in the bill to administer licenses that would result in one company owning television stations that would reach more than 35 percent of the national audience.

The vote was a rebuke to Majority Leader Tom DeLay, R-Texas, and Energy and Commerce chair Billy Tauzin, R-La., both of whom vowed to fight any attempt to reverse the FCC decision. But they could not hold back members of both parties who said the FCC changes would give a handful of corporate giants too much control over the nation's media. On July 22 the White House threatened a veto if the provision remained in the bill.

The committee rejected by voice vote an Anne M. Northup, R-Ky., amendment to block the FCC from carrying out another part of the June 2 ruling, which would allow a single company to own a newspaper and TV station in the same market.

Although GOP leaders opposed the FCC provisions, they made no attempt to strip them from the bill once it became apparent that they would be rebuffed on the floor.

The Senate Appropriations Committee, during consideration of the Senate version of the bill (S 1585—S Rept 108-144), by voice vote adopted a Stevens amendment that mirrored the House language prohibiting the FCC from increasing the media ownership cap for a single company to 45 percent of the national viewing audience. The committee action came a day after the U.S. Court of Appeals for the Third District, in Philadelphia, issued a stay blocking the new FCC rules from taking effect on schedule Sept. 4 so the court could review the changes.

The Commerce, Justice, and State spending bill was folded into an omnibus spending package (HR 2573). Conferees agreed to a ceiling of 39 percent of the population, which was well under the 45 percent favored by the FCC but enough to allow ABC and NBC to buy new stations and take Fox and CBS, both over the 35 percent limit, off the hook from divestiture requirements. The new limit became permanent law (PL 108-199), enacted on Jan. 23, 2004. The FCC thus could not increase the limit without an act of Congress.

Dispute over media ownership blocked final passage of legislation regarding decency standards for the media. During consideration of S 2056, the Senate Commerce, Science, and Transportation Committee adopted, 13–10, a Byron L. Dorgan, D-N.D., amendment to impose a yearlong moratorium on the FCC's plan to relax media ownership rules to allow the Government Accountability Office to study the issue. The House rule (H Res 554) providing for floor consideration of HR 3717 prevented Democrats from offering a media ownership amendment. The House passed HR 3717 by 391–22 on March 11.

Senate GOP leaders held up the legislation because they opposed the media ownership provision and sought to avoid a protracted floor fight with Democats. However, Dorgan succeeded in getting media ownership language included in the fiscal 2005 defense authorization bill (S 2400) before it went to conference. Conferees subsequently dropped the provision. The 108th Congress adjourned without final action on indecency penalties or other aspects of media ownership.

COURT RULING

The U.S. Court of Appeals for the Third District on June 24, 2004, had ruled that the FCC's action in promulgating the rules "falls far short of its obligation to justify its decisions to retain, repeal, or modify its media ownership regulations with reasoned analysis." The decision did not overturn the rules on their merits but said that the FCC had not sufficiently justified its actions. Supporters of the rules changes hoped the federal government would appeal the circuit court's decision to the U.S. Supreme Court, but on Jan. 27, 2005, the Justice Department said it would not do so. Although the action did not alter the 39 percent rule that Congress had legislated, it did leave the rest of the cross-ownership rules in limbo. The FCC could present new justification for its actions, could write entirely new rules, or do nothing. The commission was expected to reexamine the matter in 2005, although under a new chair, as Powell had announced his intention to step down.

'Do Not Call' Registry

With speed seldom seen in Congress, both chambers in 2003 rushed through legislation (HR 3161) to validate the Federal Trade Commission (FTC) "do not call" registry that was intended to halt unwanted telemarketing calls into private homes.

Even before Congress acted, deluged with complaints about sales call to home phones, often interrupting family evenings, the FTC created a database that allowed people to register telephone numbers they wanted off-limits to telemarketers. Violators could be fined $11,000 per call. The program generated widespread interest. By the end of the year, the registry contained more than 55 million phone numbers.

Telemarketing companies, faced with a major impediment to their livelihood, took the FTC to court to block enforcement of the no-call service, which was scheduled to take effect Oct. 1, 2003. They argued that the barriers were an infringement on free speech and would eliminate millions of telemarketing jobs. On Sept. 23 U.S. District Court Judge Lee R. West in Oklahoma ruled that the FTC did not have the authority to begin enforcing its registry.

The public outcry was swift and loud, and it was clearly heard in the halls of Congress. The opportunity to block unwanted sales calls was hugely popular across the country. On Sept. 24 Rep. Billy Tauzin, R-La., chair of the House Energy and Commerce Committee, met with aides at noon and ordered them to draft legislation explicitly authorizing the FTC to launch the registry. From there on it was a fast train to enactment.

Tauzin at first encountered difficulty in getting HR 3161 to the House floor as leaders were reluctant to add it to a continuing funding resolution. He then turned to the news media, holding a 3 p.m. press conference at which he attacked the Oklahoma court ruling. That in turn launched a deluge of statements and press releases from other House members expressing outrage at the decision. By 5:30 p.m. House leaders agreed to take up the legislation the following day. On Sept. 25 the House on a **key vote of 412–8 (R 219–5; D 192–3; I 1–0)** passed the bill before lunchtime. The Senate cleared the bill by a 95–0 vote later the same day. *(2003 key votes, p. 837)*

Before President George W. Bush signed the bill into law Sept. 29 (PL 108-82), a federal judge in Denver, Colorado, put the registry on hold, ruing that it violated the free speech rights of telemarketers because it exempted charitable organizations. Judge Edward W. Nottingham blocked the FTC plan to begin enforcement on Oct. 1. A federal appeals court ruled Oct. 7 that the FTC could begin enforcing the list while the case was argued.

On Feb. 17, 2004, the U.S. Court of Appeals for the Tenth Circuit, where several cases had been consolidated, upheld the constitutionality of the law. The U.S. Supreme Court on Oct. 4, 2004, upheld the decision by declining to review the lower court ruling.

Telemarketers argued the registry violated First Amendment free speech rights. They also contended that similar restrictions were not placed on charitable groups or political calls. The appeals court in its ruling said the "registry is a valid commercial speech regulation because it directly advances the government's important interests in safeguarding personal privacy and reducing the danger of telemarketing abuse without burdening an excessive amount of speech." The judges said the registry "offers consumers a tool with which they can protect their homes against intrusions that Congress has determined to be particularly invasive."

Internet Gambling

Efforts to clamp down on Internet gambling did not succeed despite considerable agreement that this new means of wagering posed significant dangers for many individuals, especially persons addicted to gambling. The House passed a bill (HR 2143) in 2003 to prohibit credit card companies and other financial institutions from accepting online bets. In a controversial move, however, the bill exempted state-regulated gambling interests. The Senate Banking, Housing, and Urban Affairs Committee approved a similar bill (S 627) without the exemption, but the legislation never came to the floor for a vote.

The issue was further complicated when the World Trade Organization (WTO) in March 2004 ruled that any U.S. prohibitions on Internet gambling violated international trade rules designed to open markets between nations. The WTO agreed with a complaint made by the Caribbean nations of

Antigua and Barbuda in June 2003 that U.S. law against Internet gambling would harm Caribbean countries' ability to sell one of their leading exports, Internet betting. American trade officials were dismayed. Robert B. Zoellick, the chief U.S. trade negotiator, called the decision "outrageous" and promised it would be appealed.

BACKGROUND

Opponents of gambling had been trying to curtail the growing online versions for years, arguing that unregulated, off-shore, and sometimes fraudulent Web casinos hurt American consumers. Some critics also linked online casinos to money laundering and said they were a potential source of cash for terrorists. A study by a New York investment firm, Bear Stearns Companies Inc., found as many as 1,800 Internet gambling sites with projected revenues of $4.2 billion in 2003.

Internet gambling was considered illegal under the 1961 Interstate Wire Act (PL 87-216), which prohibited use of the telephone in betting. But restricting the industry was difficult because almost all online casinos were outside the United States and beyond the reach of U.S. law. As a result, lawmakers sought to strangle the industry financially by blocking Internet wagers.

The main dispute was over whether to include state-regulated gambling operations. HR 2143 allowed states to regulate Internet gambling within their own borders as long as the Web gambling sites were not accessible to people outside the state, an exemption supported by a coalition of gambling and sports interests including lottery, horse racing, and jai alai. Conventional forms of gambling such as casino wagering, slot machines, horse racing, and state-run lotteries were legal in many states, with each state determining allowable types of gambling and regulating the activity.

LEGISLATIVE ACTION

The House Financial Services Committee approved HR 2143 by voice vote May 20, 2003. The committee formally reported the legislation (H Rept 108-133, Part I) on June 2 and reported a supplemental report (H Rept 108-133, Part II) on June 3. The bill prohibited credit card companies and other financial institutions from processing transactions from Internet casinos with the exception of those authorized or licensed by a state. By voice vote March 13 the committee had approved a scaled-back version of the legislation (HR 21—H Rept 108-51, Part I), which included civil remedies, criminal penalties, and regulatory enforcement authority. These provisions allowed the Judiciary Committee (H Rept 108-51, Part II) to share jurisdiction. It deleted the state exemption by 16–15 on May 14. Judiciary Committee Chair F. James Sensenbrenner Jr., R-Wis., and others argued that the exemption would allow states to sanction online gambling and override any federal restriction.

By leaving out virtually all references to criminal penalties, HR 2143, sponsored by Spencer Bachus, R-Ala., denied

the Judiciary Committee shared jurisdiction with the Financial Services Committee. The House passed the bill by a substantial margin, 319–104, on June 10, just after rejecting a Sensenbrenner amendment, 186–237, to remove the state exemption. Whether that exemption amounted to an expansion of states' rights to regulate gambling was the subject of heated debate. However, the issue did not divide along usual party or ideological lines. A coalition sympathetic to the needs of legalized gambling, including Republicans, horse racing interests, sports leagues, and lottery advocates, said the exemption was needed to prevent the federal government from preempting states' traditional authority to regulate all forms of wagering. Several Democrats, including those from states with significant horse racing industries, also backed the exemption language.

Opposed was a loose collection of members who disdained gambling altogether and wanted a strict bill without any exemption for state-regulated ventures. Some Democrats who sided with this view found themselves in rare company with the Traditional Values Coalition, a religious group that also opposed the exemption.

The Senate Banking, Housing, and Urban Affairs Committee easily approved a companion bill (S 627) by 21–0 on July 31. The measure was formally reported (S Rept 108-173) on Oct. 27. S 627 included provisions to prohibit Internet gambling businesses from knowingly accepting bets placed with credit cards, as well as to make it illegal for credit card companies knowingly to process such transactions. Violators would be subject to fines and prison terms of up to five years. The bill also proposed a new Office of Electronic Oversight in the Justice Department to coordinate U.S. efforts to end the presence of casinos on the Internet.

The panel adopted by voice vote an amendment offered by Chair Richard C. Shelby, R-Ala., explicitly barring exceptions for state-licensed online gaming operations and instead providing more narrow exemptions for American Indian gaming operations and some state-sanctioned wagering on horse and dog races. Shelby argued, "Gambling can be highly addictive, and we have all seen the devastation that pathological gambling can visit on addicts and their families."

The American Gaming Association, representing the casino industry, saw the situation differently and vowed to fight the changes. The organization said it did not oppose HR 2143 because "it preserves states' rights, maintains parity among all forms of gaming, and does not criminalize legal gaming activities."

The legislation went no further in 2003 and remained stuck in 2004, complicated by the WTO's position on Internet gambling under international trade rules.

Junk E-Mail Restrictions

Internet users were provided some hope of relief from the stream of junk e-mail that flooded into mail boxes every day. Congress cleared legislation (S 877) in 2003 to halt the exponential grow of fraudulent, pornographic, and misleading junk e-mail, usually dismissively called spam.

Spam in the Internet world was most commonly understood to mean usually unsolicited commercial messages sent as mass mailings to a large number of recipients. The practice had become so prevalent that even legitimate offers from a sender piled up in e-mail inboxes and raised the cost of doing business. Moreover, increasing amounts of the spam were illegal or shady offers or for pornographic purposes.

Public demand for spam controls increased dramatically as use of the Internet began to grow rapidly in the 1990s. By some estimates, spam accounted for 50 percent of the world's e-mail traffic. It cost business and consumers billions of dollars in lost space on computer servers, clogged networks, reduced productivity, new filter purchases, and damage from viruses embedded in spam e-mails.

President George W. Bush signed the bill into law Dec. 16 (PL 108-187), capping a year of debate in Congress and the technology industry over how to stop unsolicited e-mail. The final bill was not as strict as the more ardent anti-spam advocates wanted but still was more restrictive and punitive than legislation the marketing industry helped write earlier in the year. The new law did not ban spam but gave consumers the right to opt out of unsolicited e-mail messages and outlawed some of the most common tools used by spammers to reach mass audiences. It also provided a "do not spam" registry similar to the "do not call" list put in place by the Federal Trade Commission to halt unwanted phone calls from telemarketers. ("Do not call" registry, p. 391)

Nevertheless, lawmakers and technology experts were under no illusion that the law would halt all spam but hoped it would at least halt the most fraudulent junk e-mailers. Skeptics said it would just create a planning guide for e-mail marketers. More important, they noted the central weakness in regulating junk e-mail: The Internet by its nature is decentralized, with spammers constantly changing online addresses and often working from locations beyond the reach of U.S. laws. This proved to be the case as of early 2005 when groups that monitored spam reported ever larger amounts of junk e-mail circulating over the Internet.

Anti-spam legislation had been under consideration in Congress for several years but gained no traction until the Direct Marketing Association changed its earlier position opposing federal regulation of unsolicited e-mail. Even the marketers had concluded that legitimate businesses were being hurt by the huge volumes of spam clogging the Internet. In addition, major technology companies and online giants, including American Online and Microsoft Corp., backed legislation.

LEGISLATIVE ACTION

The Senate Commerce, Science, and Transportation Committee approved a version of S 877 by voice vote June 19. The bill, formally reported (S Report 108-102) on July 16, was sponsored by Ron Wyden, D-Ore., and Conrad Burns,

R-Mont. It would outlaw the sending of any unsolicited e-mail if the consumer had asked to be taken off the mailing list. It would require marketers to include a valid return e-mail address and physical address in their solicitations and would bar techniques such as harvesting and dictionary attacks. It included language to empower the FTC and states and individual Internet service providers the right to sue spammers. It also provided for fines of up to $1 million but allowed courts to award three times that amount in lawsuits.

Before approving S 877, the committee gave voice vote approval to a Byron L. Dorgan, D-N.D., substitute amendment to call for the FTC to study the potential creation of a "do not spam" registry and to send Congress a report within six months of completing the implementation of the "do not call" registry.

The Senate passed S 877 by 97–0 on Oct. 22, reflecting the growing pressure on Congress to act. Provisions strengthening the penalties and plans for a "do not spam" registry, which were adopted by voice vote, were proposed by Judiciary Committee Chair Orrin G. Hatch, R-Utah, and were based on a separate bill (S 1293) that his committee had approved Sept. 25. The amendment added five felony offenses, with penalties of three to five years for repeat offenders and people using spam to commit other felonies.

The Senate also adopted by voice vote a Charles E. Schumer, D-N.Y., amendment to strengthen the "do not spam" provisions, instructing the FTC to send Congress within six months of the bill's enactment a plan and timetable for setting up a registry.

Meanwhile, House legislation was stalled by differences between Sensenbrenner and Energy and Commerce Committee Chair Billy Tauzin, R-La., who backed a more industry-friendly bill (HR 2214), and a coalition fighting for much stricter controls on spammers (HR 2515) proposed by Heather A. Wilson, R-N.M., and Gene Green, D-Texas. The two groups were divided over fundamental issues such as how to define spam and who should enforce anti-spam rules. Wilson and Green wanted to allow users to opt out of all future "commercial e-mail," while Sensenbrenner and Tauzin used the term "unsolicited commercial e-mail," which left open more possibilities. For example, a request for information from a Web site could be considered as establishing a customer relationship and therefore any follow-up e-mail pitches might not be "unsolicited" under this definition. HR 2214 would limit the amount of money state attorneys general could recover from a spammer in prosecuting a case and gave more enforcement power to the FTC. HR 2515 would give more power to state attorneys general.

As Congress moved toward adjournment, the two sides worked out a last-minute agreement in a meeting that included the key House figures and Burns, Wyden, Senate Commerce Committee Chair John McCain, R-Ariz., and others who had worked on the legislation. Included in the bill was the stronger definition of spam as all commercial e-mail except for messages having to do with existing transactions between the recipient and the sender. The measure would allow attorneys general to sue spammers who willfully violated the new rules or used fraudulent business practices in sending junk e-mail, but damages would be capped at $2 million—and $6 million for repeat offenders. The compromise was inserted as an amendment, and the House passed S 877 under suspension of the rules, 392–5, on Nov. 22.

A late addition in the House was a provision to allow wireless phone users to block all commercial e-mail messages. While wireless spam had not yet become an issue for most cell phone users in the United State, it was a major problem in Europe and Asia where mobile phone users relied more heavily on their wireless devices for e-mail. That was expected to change as more Americans used text capabilities of wireless devices such as the popular BlackBerrys and the increasingly sophisticated cell phones with keypads and Web browsers.

The Senate made further changes to the bill Nov. 25, and the House cleared it Dec. 8.

MAJOR PROVISIONS

As enacted, S 877 (PL 108-187) included the following major provisions.

Labeling. In an effort to reveal the identity of elusive spammers, required all commercial e-mail to include a subject line showing that it was a commercial message, a valid return e-mail address, and a physical address where recipients could reach the sender. Specifically prohibited false header information and deceptive subject lines as well as commercial e-mail with sexually explicit material unless it included a warning in the subject line.

Opt-out option. Required commercial e-mailers to include within the body of the e-mail an address or link where the recipient could contact them to opt out of future communications, which had to be honored within ten days.

Prohibited practices. Outlawed some of the technological tools used by spammers to generate thousands, and sometimes millions, of e-mail messages each day, including harvesting e-mail addresses from Web sites using automated software and dictionary attacks, a form of mass e-mailing in which the spammer tries millions of permutations of names and numbers, hoping to find valid e-mail addresses. Made it illegal to use another person's computer or e-mail account to send commercial e-mail.

'Do Not Spam' registry. Authorized, but did not require, the Federal Trade Commission to develop plans for a national "do not spam" registry similar to the FTC's "do not call" telemarketing registry. (A spam registry would allow individuals to register their e-mail addresses and prohibit commercial entities from sending unsolicited e-mail to those locations.) Required a plan for the registry to be submitted to Congress for review within six months.

Penalties and enforcement. Established criminal penalties for using another person's computer or e-mail account

to send commercial e-mails, with fines and prison terms of up to five years.

Specified that violators of labeling and other requirements could be fined $250 per e-mail up to a maximum of $2 million with fines tripled to $6 million for repeat offenders.

Preempted about three dozen state laws, including more restrictive state anti-spam laws such as one approved by California in 2003.

Gave both state and federal officials authority to prosecute violators but did not allow individuals to sue junk e-mailers.

Broadcasting Indecency Penalties

Efforts (HR 3717, S 2056) to increase fines for broadcast indecency were not successful despite having widespread congressional support. The issue became entangled with legislation to limit media consolidation as well as with mustpass bills on defense (HR 2400). *(Media ownership, p. 389)*

BACKGROUND

Congress had wrestled for decades with the complex issue of defining and controlling indecent content carried over the nation's increasingly complex telecommunications system. The legislators had enough problems with the issue when content was limited to traditional over-the-air television and radio broadcasting. The rapid growth of cable and then satellite delivery followed by the flowering of the Internet in the1990s compounded the challenge. The complexity from this mix of content delivery pushed more members of Congress as well as many outside observers and critics to believe that policing content, especially that available to children, was the responsibility of consumers, perhaps aided by new technology, such as the television V-chip, that automatically blocked certain broadcast content.

One event, however, pushed the indecency controversy back as a high-profile issue for many citizens and for lawmakers. Before millions of viewers during the National Football League's Super Bowl halftime show on Feb. 1, 2004, singer Janet Jackson's top came undone, fully exposing her naked breast. The incident, which her singing partner, Justin Timberlake, called a "wardrobe malfunction," infuriated members of Congress, who called it brazen and offensive. The incident ignited a new push in the halls of Capitol Hill to increase penalties for content that could be considered indecent.

The government's term for indecent displays dated originally from 1973. The U.S. Supreme Court never offered a concrete definition of indecency, but the operating definition of the Federal Communications Commission (FCC) was based on court decisions—so-called case law—and was refined since the high court upheld it in a 1978 case, *Federal Communications Commission v. Pacifica Foundation.* Justices in that case ruled that the FCC could ban material that was indecent even if not obscene. The FCC's long-running defin-

INDECENCY RULINGS

Efforts by Congress, federal regulators, and the courts to prevent broadcasting of indecent material spanned three decades.

1973. Radio station WBAI in New York airs George Carlin's "Seven Dirty Words" monologue, prompting a listener complaint to the Federal Communications Commission (FCC). The agency issues a declaratory order against the station for violating indecency standards.

1978. The U.S. Supreme Court, responding to an appeal of the FCC order in *Federal Communications Commission v. Pacifica Foundation,* upholds the FCC's authority to regulate a radio broadcast that was indecent but not obscene. *(FCC v. Pacifica Foundation, Congress and the Nation Vol. V, p. 774)*

1995. The FCC establishes a "safe harbor" for indecent broadcasting between 10 p.m. and 6 a.m. after the U.S. Circuit Court of Appeals for the District of Columbia finds that an attempt by Congress to limit indecency on the airwaves twenty-four hours a day (PL 100-459) was unconstitutional.

1996. Congress makes a first attempt at blocking children from gaining access to pornographic material on the Internet, including language in the 1996 Telecommunications Act (PL 104-104) barring the online transmission of "patently offensive" communications. The Supreme Court declares that language unconstitutional the following year. *(1996 law, Congress and the Nation Vol. IX, p. 387)*

2003. The Supreme Court upholds a 2000 law (PL 106-554) requiring libraries and schools that accept federal grants for computer equipment and discounted Internet access to install filtering software on their computer terminals to shield children from online pornography. *(2000 law, Congress and the Nation Vol. X, p. 81)*

2004. The FCC rules that fines can be handed out for each "utterance" of indecent content in a given program. The commission also rules that use of the "f-word" constitutes a violation.

---

ition was "language or material that, in context, depicts or describes, in terms patently offensive as measured by contemporary community standards for the broadcast medium, sexual or excretory activities or organs." *(1978 case, Congress and the Nation Vol. V, p. 774)*

The FCC tried to elaborate on its indecency standard over the years, including a lengthy 2001 policy statement listing the reasoning behind several fines it imposed. The agency also refined its definition of indecency. In March 2004 the FCC found the passing use of the "f-word" by the rock singer Bono during his acceptance speech at NBC's "Golden Globe Awards Show" in 2003 constituted a violation. That overturned an earlier ruling by the FCC's enforcement bureau and resonated in media corporate offices. Executives and producers alike said they were increasingly unsure what content would pass muster in the future. Many persons in the broadcast industry said they remained confused by the rules. The absence of a clear standard for indecency and the FCC's increased willingness to use its powers after the Super Bowl incident led some broadcasters to censor material that might be deemed objectionable. NBC, for example, extracted a scene from its series "ER" in which an elderly woman's breast was shown, and radio stations pulled some songs that used potentially offensive words.

The Jackson incident plus a series of offensive remarks by high-profile radio shock jocks forced policy makers to consider how the FCC standard could be used to police offensive content, both on the airwaves and the Internet. But in attempting to apply the indecency standard to the modern media, lawmakers faced the question of whether the government's longstanding criterion for indecent fare still held up in an era when Americans got their entertainment via high-speed Internet networks, satellite signals, cable TV, and in increasingly uninhibited movie depictions of sex and violence. The new array of delivering images and sound from—essentially—any part of the world made it much more difficult to define a single community standard.

Though indecent material was constitutionally protected speech, the Supreme Court in a landmark 1978 decision, *Federal Communications Commission v. Pacifica Foundation,* ruled that material that did conform to the FCC's definition of community standards could be regulated at certain times of the day on public airwaves because broadcast media had a unique and pervasive presence in American life. The case was prompted by complaints about a New York radio station's decision to air comedian George Carlin's "Seven Dirty Words" monologue, a sendup of the government's attempts to police language on the public airwaves. *(1978 case, Congress and the Nation Vol. V, p. 774)*

Unlike the Internet, where precedent for regulating content was legally murky, the government possessed clear regulatory authority in the broadcasting world. Congress, the FCC, and the Supreme Court agreed that broadcasters had a public-interest obligation to weed out indecent fare because the spectrum they used to transmit programming was a scarce commodity. The FCC issued highly prized licenses allowing the use of the spectrum but expected compliance with certain standards in return. The airing of indecent material was restricted to the hours of 10 p.m. to 6 a.m., when children were presumed unlikely to be viewing or listening. Under existing law, indecency violations could be punished with fines of up to $32,500 on broadcasters. It was this level of fines that gave rise to the congressional action in 2004 that did not pass.

OBSCENE OR INDECENT: AN OVERVIEW

In the last several decades of the twentieth century, increasing amounts of material on television, radio, and the Internet were considered offensive by large numbers of people. Some of it was judged obscene, and some was found to be indecent. The U.S. Supreme Court ruled that obscenity was not a form of protected speech and thus could be banned in public settings although not in the privacy of one's home. The Court held that indecent material was protected by the First Amendment but could be restricted when doing so served a compelling interest, such as protecting children.

Obscenity Not Protected by the First Amendment

The Supreme Court created a three-part test, known as the Miller test, to determine whether a work or act is obscene. The Miller test asks

(1) Whether the "average person applying contemporary community standards" would find that the work, taken as a whole, appeals to the prurient interest.

(2) Whether the work depicts or describes, in a patently offensive way, sexual conduct specifically defined by the applicable state law.

(3) Whether the work, taken as a whole, lacks serious literary, artistic, political, or scientific value.

Indecency Protected by the First Amendment

The Supreme Court said that "the normal definition of 'indecent' merely refers to nonconformance with accepted standards of morality." In the context of broadcast regulation, indecency was defined as material that "depicts or describes, in terms patently offensive as measured by contemporary community standards, sexual or excretory activities or organs."

Indecent material protected by the First Amendment may be restricted by the government only "to promote a compelling interest" and only by "the least restrictive means to further the articulated interest," the Court ruled.

LEGISLATIVE ACTION

The House Energy and Commerce Subcommittee on Telecommunications and the Internet approved HR 3717, sponsored by Fred Upton, R-Mich., by voice vote Feb. 12, 2004. The bill proposed a tenfold increase in the maximum fine for on-air vulgarity. The full committee March 3 by 49–1 approved an expanded version of the bill, which was formally reported (H Rept 108-434) on March 9. The panel had given voice vote approval to a package of amendments. The legis-

lation would increase maximum FCC fines against broadcasters to $500,000 per indecency violation and increase maximum fines on individual performers from $11,000 to $500,000 with no cap for a continuing violation. It also would direct the FCC to take into account a violator's ability to pay fines, based on market size and location and whether the violator was a company or an individual. Furthermore, the FCC would be directed to take into account factors such as whether the program was live or recorded, whether the indecent incident was scripted or unscripted, whether a time delay to block objectionable material was used, whether a station that did not produce the programming was given adequate opportunity to review it or had reason to know of its content, what the size of the audience was, and whether the incident was part of a children's television program. The committee version of HR 3717 also would trigger an immediate FCC license revocation hearing for broadcasters that had three or more indecency violations in a licensing term.

The only amendment that inspired any serious dissension was the proposal by Christopher Cox, R-Calif., and Cliff Stearns, R-Fla., to make it easier for the FCC to fine individual artists and performers for their own indecent actions. The FCC had the power to fine individuals, but only through a cumbersome process. An attempt to strike the amendment on the grounds that it would place unconstitutional restrictions on speech failed by voice vote.

The Senate Commerce, Science, and Transportation Committee approved S 2056 by 23–0 on March 9. The bill was formally reported (S Rept 108-253) on April 5. The panel had adopted a Byron L. Dorgan, D-N.D., amendment to relax media ownership rules, 13–10; a Ted Stevens, R-Alaska, amendment to require the FCC to consider revoking the licensing of broadcasters after three violations of indecency rules, 11–10; a Stevens amendment to increase the maximum penalty for broadcasters from $275,000 in the underlying bill to $375,000 for a second violation and $500,000 for any additional violation, by voice vote; a George Allen, R-Va., amendment to allow the FCC to apply the same fines to individual performers, by voice vote; a John Ensign, R-Nev., amendment to direct the FCC to look at a broadcaster's ability to pay indecency fines based on factors such as revenues and market size when determining the amount of the penalty, by voice vote; and an Ernest F. Hollings, D-S.C., amendment to require the FCC to study whether consumers were taking advantage of v-chip technology to block violent content on television, by voice vote. Congress mandated the technology in the 1996 Telecommunications Act (PL 104-104), but critics said it was not widely used and was ineffective. The committee also rejected, 11–12, a John B. Breaux, D-La., amendment to give the FCC the power to regulate expanded basic cable content the same way it regulated over-the-air broadcasts. *(1996 act, Congress and the Nation Vol. IX, p. 387)*

The House passed HR 3717 on March 11, 391–22. Action in the Senate was held up by the media ownership issue. On June 22 by 99–1, the Senate adopted a Sam Brownback,

R-Kan., amendment to the fiscal 2005 defense authorization bill (HR 2400). It was a scaled-back version of the broadcast indecency legislation, which omitted the media ownership provision. However, the Senate accepted language limiting the FCC's power to allow greater media consolidation. Brownback tried to keep the issues apart, mainly because his legislation enjoyed a solid consensus and the media consolidation was highly controversial. He acquiesced, nevertheless, believing the media provisions would be dropped by conferees. Instead both nondefense subjects were taken out of S 2400 in conference. Conferees decided they were too contentious and wanted to keep the defense bill unencumbered.

HOUSE AND SENATE BILLS COMPARED

The House-passed HR 3717 would allow the FCC to fine broadcasters up to $500,000 per indecency violation, up from $27,500. The maximum penalty on artists and performers would rise to $500,000 from $11,000, and the FCC would be able to fine artists without initial warnings. The Senate bill included penalties on broadcasters of up to $275,000 for each incident, with a doubling of fines for "aggravated behavior," and maximum of $3 million within a twenty-four-hour period.

Both measures included greater authority for the FCC to revoke licenses for repeat offenses. Those licenses were worth billions of dollars in some cases. The "three strikes" provision in both bills required that the FCC begin license revocation hearings—the first step in the process of removing a broadcaster's license—after the third offense.

The House bill provided for a "shot clock," or deadline, of 270 days for the FCC to resolve outstanding indecency complaints. Lawmakers on both sides of the aisle criticized the FCC for its backlog of complaints.

Both measures included protections for small affiliates. Lawmakers wanted to ensure the FCC would not put small stations out of business with massive fines, particularly, they said, when the stations' network parents often pressured them to air syndicated programming. The FCC would be directed under both bills to consider a company's size and ability to pay when assessing fines.

The Senate bill addressed the issue of media ownership. It also called for the FCC to study the effectiveness of the v-chip, a device in televisions that allowed consumers to block unwanted programming based on its ratings. If the FCC found the system was not working as intended, it would have to issue rules to regulate violent TV content in the same way indecency or profane materials were regulated.

Digital Satellite Television

In 2004 provisions were tucked into a fiscal 2005 omnibus spending bill (HR 4818—PL 108-447) that ensured continued satellite television signals would be available to viewers in areas poorly served by conventional TV broadcasts, mainly rural areas of the country. Key parts of the 1999

Satellite Home Viewer Improvement Act (PL 106-113) that allowed this service were set to expire at the end of 2004, possibly denying thousands of viewers—perhaps as many as two million, by some estimates—television access to football, sitcoms, or reality shows. This was the central motivating factor behind extending the law, because no elected member of Congress wanted to face constituent wrath if the TV went dead.

But the consensus behind the extension was mired throughout the 108th Congress, with controversies over satellite providers taking viewers—and advertising revenue—from local broadcast stations. The 1999 law allowed satellite television companies—such as DirectTV and EchoStar Communication's DISH Network—to deliver local broadcast stations across the country, effectively matching the services provided by cable television systems and providing the first significant competition to cable. *(1999 act, Congress and the Nation Vol. X, p. 338)*

The key dispute was whether to let satellite companies start selling digital network programming in areas where the local affiliates of the major networks—CBS, NBC, ABC, and Fox—did not broadcast digitally. Consumer groups and electronics manufacturers were frustrated with the slow advance of digital broadcasting, and they charged that local stations were dragging their feet in switching from existing analog signals to digital. They argued that satellite digital signals would push local stations to offer digital broadcasts, which can be transmitted over the air and received by regular roof antennas. Broadcasters, however, opposed the change, saying it would drain prime-time viewers from network affiliates.

The House Energy and Commerce Subcommittee on Telecommunications and the Internet approved a draft bill on April 28, 2004, by voice vote. The subcommittee voice vote had approved an amendment by Chair Fred Upton, R-Mich., to prevent consumers from signing up for satellite broadcasts of network channels in other markets when the satellite provider offered those network station locally. The panel also approved, by voice vote, an Edward J. Markey, D-Mass., amendment to extend to satellite companies many of the consumer privacy rules that had been in place for digital cable providers for years. Companies would be barred from disclosing such things as a customer's viewing habits. The draft did not include language to allow satellite providers to offer out-of-market digital programming.

By voice vote June 3, the full committee approved the bill (HR 4501), which had been formally reported (H Rept 108-634) on July 22. The measure reflected a bipartisan and bicameral consensus on many of the key issues. It included provisions to require satellite providers to offer all of an area's local analog programming on a single home satellite dish within a year. It also granted satellite companies the authority to provide subscribers "frequently viewed" programming from a neighboring area.

The House Judiciary Subcommittee on the Courts, the Internet, and Intellectual Property approved its own draft measure by voice vote May 6. The full committee, by voice vote, approved the bill (HR 4518) on July 7 and formally reported it (H Rept 108-660) on Sept. 7. HR 4518 tracked closely with HR 4501, but it included new language proposing a temporary 12 percent increase in the royalties that satellite companies paid to holders of program copyrights. The increase was intended to account for inflation in the five years since Congress had last addressed the issue. The existing rate was 15 cents per month for each distant network signal beamed to a consumer. The new rate was to go into effect in 2005 and 2006, when a panel appointed by the Librarian of Congress was to complete an arbitration process to set a fair-market value for the content. In the meantime, the rate would get a cost-of-living increase every year, starting in 2007. Some lawmakers feared satellite carriers could pass on the royalty increases to consumers in the form of higher subscription rates. Others said the legislation did not go far enough in requiring satellite companies to pay fair-market rates.

The Senate Judiciary Committee approved its satellite TV reauthorization bill (S 2013) on June 17, after adopting a substitute amendment to a skeletal proposal that was introduced by Chair Orrin G. Hatch, R-Utah. The measure fell in line with the House on most matters but did not provide for the immediate 12 percent increase in royalties that was included in HR 4518. The Hatch-sponsored proposal called for a copyright arbitration panel selected by the Librarian of Congress to set a fair-market royalty rate by June 1, 2005, for the network programming that a satellite provider retransmitted.

The Senate Commerce, Science, and Transportation Committee by voice vote July 22 approved S 2644 and formally reported the bill (S Rept 108-427) on Dec. 7. The legislation included a provision granting satellite providers limited authority to offer out-of-market digital programming to some consumers, in lieu of broadcasters who had not completed their transition to digital programming. Broadcasters opposed the provision, saying it would introduce new competition in their markets for prime-time viewers. Supporters said it would force broadcasters to speed up their federally mandated transition to digital broadcasting.

Provision sponsor John Ensign, R-Nev., offered a substitute amendment, adopted by voice vote, that scaled back his original language to address concerns of broadcasters. The bill gave the FCC two years to develop a model to predict which consumers could not receive digital broadcasts. Satellite companies could not offer digital network programming until the FCC completed its model. Satellite companies also would be required to cease digital network transmissions once customers could get them from local broadcasters. Aside from the digital programming provision, S 2644 included nearly identical language to HR 4501.

The House passed HR 4518 by voice vote under suspension of the rule Oct.6, after combining it with HR 4501.The manager's amendment dropped the 12 percent increase in

royalties, instead allowing for private negotiations between the parties to settle on a new rate.

Final action in the Senate was stalled because of disagreements over whether to include the digital programming provisions opposed by broadcasters. After a series of last-ditch talks in the lame-duck session, negotiators agreed to phase in the authority for satellite providers. That cleared the way for the digital satellite TV provisions to become part of the omnibus appropriations measure, which was signed into law Dec. 8.

MAJOR PROVISIONS

As enacted, the omnibus spending bill (HR 4520—PL 108-357) contained the following satellite TV provisions.

Distant network signals. Extended through Dec. 31, 2009, the statutory license that allowed satellite operators to retransmit a broadcast television signal from a distant market. However, satellite subscribers could not sign up for distant channels once their satellite provider offered local network affiliate channels, know as "local into local" service. That was intended to protect small local broadcasters from prime-time competition from large distant network affiliates.

Significanly viewed channels. Allowed satellite operators to carry "significantly viewed" out-of-market stations, provided they first offered local-into-local service to their customers. Significantly viewed stations are stations outside a consumer's designated market area that can nonetheless be received easily over the air. Under existing law, cable operators had similar authority to transmit such stations, and the FCC determined whether stations met certain criteria to be "significantly viewed."

Single-dish requirement. Required all satellite companies to transmit all local analog broadcast channels on a single satellite dish within eighteen months of enactment. The provision was intended to block a practice used by EchoStar Communications Corp. that separated programming on two dishes. The second dish often was used for religious or Spanish-language programming.

Royalty payments. Under existing law, the license that allowed satellite companies to retransmit network signals and superstations required the carriers to pay royalty fee to compensate the studios and stations that produced the programming. Under the new law, the rates could be set through voluntary negotiations instead of by a government panel. It required the Librarian of Congress to initiate, by Jan. 2, 2005, voluntary negotiation proceedings for the purpose of determining the royalty fee to be paid by satellite carriers.

Digital television signals. Broadcasters were in the process of converting from analog to digital broadcast signals, and many had not completed their transition. Under the new law, satellite providers would be allowed to broadcast a distant digital signal from another market to certain customers who were not able to receive digital signals from their local broadcasters. Satellite providers had to phase in the new digital offerings over a 2½-year period. The FCC was charged with developing a predictive model to determine which consumers would be eligible for the digital signal.

Intellectual Property

Congress considered legislation (HR 4077, S 2237, S 1933, S 3021) to increase protection for intellectual property but was able to complete action on only one measure (HR 3632).

HR 3632. HR 3632, signed into law (PL 108-482) on Dec. 23, 2004, would make it more difficult for counterfeiters to peddle fake goods by restricting the buying and selling of authentication devices that mark copyrighted works as genuine, such as holograms and special inks. The bill, sponsored by Lamar Smith, R-Texas, also applied to the gear used to attach the devices to products such as compact discs and software, packaging, or packaging inserts.

The legislation was intended to halt the theft of authentication devices by counterfeiters, who then attach them to fake goods to increase the value of the products. It also made it illegal to alter or falsify the version, edition, or authorized-user information for a piece of software. Because no state or federal laws currently prohibited trafficking in genuine authentication devices, Smith said prosecutors had been reluctant to seize such components or prosecute cases of theft.

The bill also included another intellectual property measure offered by Smith that stiffened penalties for knowingly submitting false contact data to domain name registrars when purchasing a Web address. The legislation increased the sentences for federal crimes committed in connection with domain name registration fraud. Those sentences would be doubled or increased by seven years, whichever was less.

The House Judiciary Committee approved HR 3632 by voice vote on June 23. The bill was formally reported (H Rept 108-600) on July 13. The House passed the measure by voice vote under suspension of the rules Sept. 21. The Senate passed the bill by voice vote Dec. 8, completing congressional action.

HR 4077. HR 4077 would authorize $15 million for enforcement of Internet piracy law and made it easier for prosecutors to prove criminal copyright infringement. The bill also created stiff penalties for unauthorized reproduction of works before their official release and outlawed use of camcorders in movie theaters. The bill legalized technologies that could filter sexually explicit or graphic content on DVDs. Existing copyright law required prosecutors to show that an individual had willfully distributed copyrighted works with a retail value of at least $1,000. The bill changed the standard to reckless disregard by a user in uploading one thousand or more works or material with a total value of at least $10,000.

The House Judiciary Committee approved HR 4077 by voice vote on Sept. 8, 2004, and reported it (H Rept 108-700) on Sept. 24. The House passed the bill by voice vote under suspension of the rules Sept. 28. The Senate took no action on the measure.

S 2237. S 2237 would allow the Justice Department to file civil charges against anyone sharing or distributing copyrighted songs and movies online.

The Senate Judiciary Committee approved S 2237 by voice vote on April 29, 2004, and reported it (no written report) the same day. The Senate passed the bill by voice vote June 25. The House took no action on the measure.

S 1933. S 1933 would tighten enforcement of copyright laws and expanded requirements for reporting crimes involving obscenity and sexual exploitation of minors. It was intended to help the recording industry by expanding an antitrust exemption in a 1998 law that allowed record companies and music publishers to negotiate royalties associated with new technologies.

The Senate Judiciary Committee approved S 1933 by voice vote on May 20, 2004, and reported it (no written report) the same day. It saw no further congressional action.

S 3021. S 3021, which dealt with patents, online piracy, music royalties, and obscenity, got caught up by a controversial rider offered by John McCain, R-Ariz., to establish national safety regulations for boxing. The Senate passed S 275, which would create a U.S. Boxing Commission to oversee the sport, establish national standards for safety, and protect boxers from unscrupulous promoters, by voice vote on March 31. The House, however, was little interested in attaching the language to S 3021.

The Senate passed S 3021 by voice vote Nov. 20, 2004. The bill died upon adjournment.

Online Piracy

Congress hardly got started on a controversial proposal (S 2560) targeting online piracy. Eagerly sought by the entertainment industry seeking to shut down Internet file-sharing services, the bill would hold companies liable if they "intentionally induce" customers to infringe copyrights. Electronics manufacturers, software makers, Internet service providers, and consumer groups complained that the legislation was too broad and might prohibit products with legitimate uses and discourage innovation. The House and Senate passed narrower bills (S 1932, S 2237, HR 4077), but none was enacted.

In April 2003 a federal judge in Los Angeles ruled that two major file-sharing companies—Streamcast Networks Inc. and Grokster—could not be held liable for the songs, movies, and other copyright works swapped online by their users. The entertainment companies said the practice was costing them billions of dollars in lost revenue each year. But the court said the file-sharing companies were not liable because, among other things, they did not have central servers pointing users to copyrighted material. The Ninth Circuit Court of Appeals upheld the ruling in August 2004.

S 2560, sponsored by Senate Judiciary Committee Chair Orrin G. Hatch, R-Utah, would make it illegal for any company to facilitate or intentionally induce infringement by computer users. Opponents said the bill could undermine two decades of copyright protections emanating from a 1984 U.S. Supreme Court ruling that legalized VCRs (video cassette recorders) and underpinned innovation in technology. Hatch tried for months to find a compromise that would satisfy both the entertainment industry and bill opponents. But even with the help of the Library of Congress, which was asked to weigh in with its own middle-of-the-road proposal, he could not strike a deal. S 2560 was referred to Senate Judiciary Committee and saw no further action.

The Senate did pass S 2237, sponsored by Patrick J. Leahy, D-Vt., by voice vote June 25, 2004. The legislation would give prosecutors the right to file civil suits against online pirates, sparing them the negative publicity associated with bringing criminal charges against college students and others who used Internet file-sharing systems. It also would authorize $2 million for the Justice Department to bring federal prosecutors up to speed on the nuances of digital copyright law.

The Senate Judiciary Committee had approved the measure (no written report) by voice vote April 29. Public-interest groups said the bill amounted to a handout to the entertainment industry.

S 1932, sponsored by John Cornyn, R-Texas, was aimed at cracking down on the distribution—either in physical form or via the Internet—of copies of movies or songs before they were officially released or fully marketed. The bill, also passed by the Senate by voice vote June 25, would make it a federal crime to use a camcorder or other recording device in a movie theater. The motion picture industry said more than 90 percent of the pirated movies online originated from camcorders. S 1932 also would authorize $5 million per year in fiscal years 2005 through 2009 for the Justice Department to prosecute violations of intellectual property rights.

The House passed HR 4077 by voice vote Sept. 28, 2004. The measure, sponsored by Lamar Smith, R-Texas, would give the Justice Department new enforcement tools by lowering the bar prosecutors had to meet to prove criminal copyright infringement in the online world.

Supporters said existing law made it too difficult for prosecutors, forcing them to show "willful" reproduction or distribution of copyrighted works worth at least $1,000. Proving files were distributed over the Internet and determining their value was difficult. HR 4077 sought to ease those standards by making it a criminal offense to upload and make available with "reckless disregard of the risk of further infringement" one thousand or more copyrighted works. Offenders could get as many as five years in prison.

The House Judiciary Committee had approved the bill Sept. 8, after adding language to legalize devices designed to filter objectionable content from DVD home movies. Several Hollywood studios had sued the most prominent maker of the technology, ClearPlay, claiming that altering the movie content amounted to copyright infringement. The panel had formally reported the measure (H Rept 108-700) on Sept. 24.

Backers of legislation to curtail online piracy tried to bundle them into an end-of-session omnibus, but disputes over the movie-filtering language and whether too much power was being given to federal prosecutors to combat piracy combined to sink the plan.

Internet Taxation

Congress continued to bicker over taxation of access to the Internet but could do no more than extend (S 150—PL 108-435) an existing moratorium.

The measure revived a moratorium that was enacted originally in 1998 (PL 105-277) and extended in 2001 (PL 107-75). The moratorium was meant to ensure that the Internet could continue to serve as an economic engine by barring taxes that would apply uniquely to it. The moratorium prohibited taxes on access service, taxes that treated products sold online differently from those sold in stores, and taxes that resulted in a single purchase being taxed more than once, such as by two states. The Bush administration joined the technology industry and online retailers in supporting a permanent moratorium. *(2001 action and background, p. 376)*

For years, lobbyists for state and local governments had argued that a permanent ban on Internet access taxes should be linked with provisions to help states collect sales taxes on products sold over the Internet. While states were not prohibited from levying sales taxes on Internet purchases by their citizens, a 1992 U.S. Supreme Court ruling (*Quill Corp. v. North Dakota*) barred them from requiring out-of-state retailers to collect the taxes. States were also thwarted by the complexity of tracking Internet transactions. *(1992 ruling, Congress and the Nation Vol. VIII, p. 850)*

The House Judiciary Committee approved its version of the bill (HR 49) by voice vote July 16, 2003. Members expressed the view that a ban on taxation of Internet connections would stimulate deployment of high-speed Internet connections nationwide. The panel gave voice vote approval to a Melvin Watt, D-N.C., amendment to make it clear that all forms of technology used to connect to the Internet would be exempt from any access taxes. Watt said the bill, as originally written, could create a loophole for states to tax newer and faster forms of broadcast Internet access such as digital subscriber line, cable modem, wireless or satellite connections. Bill cosponsor Chris Cannon, R-Utah, said allowing any state to tax Internet access would undercut efforts to bridge the gap that left lower-income households with less access than others. The bill was formally reported (H Rept 108-234) on July 24.

The House passed the measure, under suspension of the rules, by voice vote Sept. 17. In addition to making the three-part moratorium permanent, it provided for the immediate elimination of a "grandfather" exemption that allowed ten states to maintain Internet access taxes that had been imposed before the 1998 moratorium. The states—Hawaii, New Hampshire, New Mexico, North Dakota, Ohio, South Dakota, Tennessee, Texas, Washington, and Wisconsin—stood to lose between $80 million and $120 million a year in tax revenue if they lost their exemption, according to the Congressional Budget Office.

The Senate Commerce, Science, and Transportation Committee approved S 150 by voice vote July 31, 2003. Like HR 49, it proposed to make the three-part moratorium permanent and end the grandfather clause, although it would wait three years before eliminating the exemptions. When S 150 was brought to the Senate floor, state and local governments protested that it would cost them billions of dollars in tax revenue, and the measure was pulled Nov. 7.

After months of stalemate, Senate proponents of a permanent ban gave up. The Senate passed the revised S 150 by 93–3 on April 29. The measure reflected the terms of a compromise, intended in part to win support from lawmakers who wanted to protect states and localities, brokered by John McCain, R-Ariz. It would

• Extend the moratorium on Internet access taxes for four years, instead of permanently, as the House preferred. The four years dated from Nov. 1, 2003.

• Exempt the nine states that taxed dial-up service before 1998 for the duration of the bill and exempt states that taxed digital subscriber lines (DSL) services for two years. The House bill would require states that charged any form of Internet taxes to stop collecting those taxes immediately.

• Specify that the tax moratorium would not affect states' authority to tax Internet voice calls. The House bill made no mention of Internet phone services. House sponsors said it was unnecessary because the legislation was meant to keep only Internet access tax-free, not voice applications.

In a crucial vote, the Senate on April 29 agreed, 64–34, to invoke cloture and thus end debate on McCain's amendment. Before final passage of the bill, a Dianne Feinstein, D-Calif., amendment to allow a four-year extension for states that tax DSL connections was tabled (killed) by 59–37 on April 29.

House Judiciary Committee Chair F. James Sensenbrenner Jr., R-Wis., and backers of HR 49 held out for the permanent tax ban. But as the lame-duck session drew to a close, Sensenbrenner yielded, accepting the temporary ban in exchange for a provision shortening his home state's exemption from the moratorium to two years from four. Sen. Kay Bailey Hutchison, R-Texas, requested an exemption that would allow municipalities in her state to keep collecting franchising and right-of-way fees on telecommunications infrastructure. The Senate agreed to both requests, modifying S 150 though a concurrent resolution (S Con Res 46) adopted by voice vote Nov. 17. The House adopted the resolution Nov. 19 by voice vote and went on to clear S 150, by voice vote under suspension of the rules. The bill was signed into law on Dec. 3.

First-Responders' Spectrum

Congressional efforts to give more frequencies on the broadcast spectrum to public safety agencies had broad con-

gressional support, but the issue proved too contentious for enactment.

The call for Congress to improve the ability of emergency responders to radio one another was among the less-noticed recommendations of the National Commission on Terrorist Attacks Upon the United States (Sept. 11 commission). The independent, bipartisan commission found that poor communications at the site of the World Trade Center attacks in New York City may have cost firefighters and police officers their lives. *(Sept. 11 commission, p. 275)*

Sen. John McCain, R-Ariz., and Rep. Jane Harman, D-Calif., introduced bills (S 2774, HR 1425) that would require television broadcasters to stop using any frequencies reserved for, but not claimed by, public safety personnel. The portion of the spectrum in question, in the 700 megahertz band, was particularly valuable to first-responders because it could penetrate walls and travel long distances. It also could be used to develop more advanced, broadband-based communications systems

The proposal had widespread support. However, McCain, who was chair of the Senate Commerce, Science, and Transportation Committee, saw a chance to recover even more spectrum, generating billions of dollars for the Treasury and giving new technologies, such as wireless broadband, a coveted slice of the airways. The committee approved S 2820 by voice vote Sept. 22, after adopting a Conrad Burns, R-Mont., amendment that reduced the portion of the spectrum broadcasters would have to vacate.

As introduced, S 2820 would require all analog broadcasters to stop using their frequencies by 2009 as they moved to a different part of the radio spectrum to offer broadcasts in a new digital format. As amended, it required that stations return the frequencies by Jan. 1, 2008, but it allowed the Federal Communications Commission (FCC) to exempt certain broadcasters to avoid "consumer disruptions" for viewers whose television sets could only receive the older type of analog programming. McCain criticized the National Broadcasters Association (NBA) for backing Burns's approach, which would force only some stations off the air. The NBA said Burns's plan would turn off about seventy-five stations, while McCain's would apply to 1,700.

The committee rejected, 9–13, a McCain amendment to let broadcasters comply with the Burns proposal through 2008, while mandating the stricter 2009 deadline in his original language. FCC chair Michael K. Powell said broadcasters could delay the transition for decades unless Congress forced their hands.

The committee-approved S 2820 also would create a trust fund using the proceeds from auctions of the returned frequencies—which experts estimated were worth $30 billion to $40 billion—to help viewers with sets that could not process digital signals. The bill would let the Commerce Department spend as much as $1 billion to buy set-top converters for affected viewers. It also would authorize $117 million over five years for the Homeland Security Department

SAFECOM office, which was responsible for overseeing public safety communications infrastructure improvements.

After seeing S 2830 watered down, McCain offered an amendment to the intelligence overhaul legislation (S 2845). The amendment, similar to the language in the original version of his bill, sought a complete handover of analog spectrum by broadcasters. Burns challenged the proposal, and McCain agreed to a compromise under which broadcasters would have to relinquish only public safety channels and only when specifically asked to do so by local first-responders. The Senate adopted the amendment by voice vote in September. But the House did not include a similar provision in its intelligence bill, and it was omitted in the conference report. *(Intelligence overhaul, p. 263)*

Spyware Controls

Both houses of Congress considered legislation (HR 2929, HR 4661, S 2145) attempting to deal with spyware—computer programs that surreptitiously access personal computer hard drives to gather personal information for third parties. The bills, however, died upon adjournment.

HR 2929. The House Energy and Commerce Committee on June 24, 2004, by voice vote approved a revised version of a bill (HR 2929) introduced by Mary Bono, R-Calif. The legislation was formally reported (H Rept 108-619) on July 20. The Commerce, Trade, and Consumer Protection Subcommittee had approved the measure by voice vote June 17.

In an effort to target the specific behaviors associated with spyware, the bill included a list of off-limits practices, such as redirecting a user's browser to another Web site without permission; delivering advertisements that a computer user could not close without turning off the machine or shutting down all browser windows; collecting personally identifiable information, such as Social Security or bank account numbers, by tracking a user's keystrokes; tying up or damaging the system's resources; and inducing a user to download or execute a program by misrepresenting its identity or purpose.

The distributor of any program capable of "information collection" would have to get the user's permission before the program could be installed or executed. Information collection programs were defined as those that gathered personally identifiable information, tracked a user's Web browsing habits, and sent such information to a third party. The bill provided guidelines for those notices companies would have to give users, suggesting language such as: "This program will collect and transmit information about you and your computer use and will collect information about Web pages you access and use that information to display advertising to your computer. Do you accept?" The company would have to provide readily accessible information about the program and its purpose to assist users in determining whether to grant consent.

Under the bill, the Federal Trade Commission (FTC) was charged with enforcing the measure with fine of up to $3 million for violators. The legislation would preempt state laws on spyware.

The committee adopted by voice vote a Cliff Stearns, R-Fla., amendment that added liability protections for several industries, including Internet service providers and network security providers. The bill also exempted law enforcement officers in the performance of their duties.

The House passed HR 2929 by 399–1 under suspension of the rules on Oct. 5.

HR 4661. The House Judiciary Committee by voice vote Sept. 8 passed HR 4661, which was sponsored by Robert W. Goodlatte, R-Va. The bill would make it illegal to hack into a computer to obtain sensitive information, such as credit card numbers, Social Security numbers, or passwords, or to cause damage to the computer. Offenders would be subject to fines and up to two years in prison. Those who used their access to another's machine in furtherance of another federal crime, such as credit card fraud, could get up to five years in prison.

The panel adopted by voice vote a Goodlatte amendment to authorize $10 million over four years for the Justice Department to prosecute cases involving spyware and "phishing"—the use of fraudulent e-mail and Internet schemes to lure consumers into disclosing sensitive financial information. An attempt by Robert C. Scott, D-Va., to remove a provision that would prevent victims of spyware from bringing civil suits under state laws was rejected by voice vote.

The House passed HR 4661 by 415–0 under suspension of the rules on Oct. 7.

S 2145. The Senate Commerce, Science, and Transportation Committee approved S 2145 by voice vote Sept. 22. The bill, sponsored by Conrad Burns, R-Mont., was formally reported (S Rept 108-424) on Dec. 7. The original measure closely tracked HR 2929, but a Burns substitute amendment, adopted by voice vote, changed the overall approach to address the concerns of software makers.

The committee-approved bill would make it illegal to install software on a user's computer without permission but did not include specific technical guidelines on how software makers should get that authorization. It also sought to regulate "adware"—programs that launch Internet pop-up ads. Serving up such ads would be illegal when users were not visiting a Web site affiliated with the software company or to launch ads "in a manner or at a time such that a reasonable user would not understand that the software is responsible for delivering the advertisements."

The bill included liability protections for legitimate companies, including Internet service providers who unknowingly transmitted spyware programs over the Web to users, and network security providers, who often rely on software utilities that operate in the background to secure computers. Enforcement was given primarily to the FTC, though the Agriculture Department, the Federal Deposit Insurance Corporation, and other agencies would have some authority. No new penalties specific to spyware were mentioned.

The panel also adopted by voice vote a George Allen, R-Va., amendment to institute criminal penalties for spyware providers. The amendment, similar to HR 4661, would make it illegal to gain unauthorized access to a computer to obtain sensitive information, such as credit cared numbers, Social Security numbers, or passwords, or to cause damage to the computer. The penalties were the same as under HR 4661.

Telecommunications, Emergency 911 Calls

Congress in 2004 cleared a telecommunications package (HR 5419) that was intended to resolve an accounting problem at the federal agency that financed Internet connections in schools and libraries, staving off a potential increase in the "universal service" fees consumers paid on their phone bills. The measure also authorized state grants to upgrade emergency 911 services and established a trust fund to streamline the transfer of broadcast frequencies from government agencies to the private sector.

The only obstacle the legislation faced was a debate over whether it would be the vehicle for an unrelated bill (S 275) on boxing safety, sponsored by John McCain, R-Ariz. McCain tried to add the boxing language to several bills that were moving as the session's end neared, but House Republicans balked. *(Intellectual property, p. 399)*

LEGISLATIVE ACTION

The Senate Commerce, Science, and Transportation Committee approved its enhanced 911 (E-911) legislation (S 1250) by voice vote on July 17, 2003. Formally reported Aug. 26 (S Rept 108-130), the bill saw no further action.

The House Energy and Commerce Committee approved its version (HR 2898) by voice vote on Nov. 1, 2003. The bill was formally reported (H Rept 108-311) on Oct. 14.

The main difference between S 1250 and HR 2898 was the amount to be authorized for grants to states for E-911 upgrades. The Senate measure would authorize $500 million a year for five years, while the House bill called for $100 million a year over the same timeframe.

The House Energy and Commerce Committee approved a spectrum relocation bill (HR 1320) by voice vote April 30, 2003. The bill was formally reported (H Rept 108-137) and was passed by the House by 498–10 under suspension of the rules on June 11. Proponents said the legislation would make it easier to free up spectrum for next-generation wireless services, providing a boost to the beleaguered telecommunications industry.

The Senate Commerce, Science, and Transportation Committee approved HR 1320 by voice vote June 26. The panel included in the bill, which was formally reported (S Rept 108-168) on Oct. 17, an amendment that threatened to kill it. The John E. Sununu, R-N.H., amendment would

guarantee spectrum to a terrestrial communications company, Northpoint Technology, without a traditional auction. Critics said the amendment was the result of a politically connected company peddling its influence. No further action was taken on the bill until late in 2004, when it was rolled into the telecommunications package, with the Northpoint provision stripped out.

The last piece of the telecom package was the E-Rate language. Without the provisions, the Universal Service Administrative Co. might have to increase the fees it charged telecom companies to raise money. Industry experts said that could result in an increase on phone bills of as much as $12 a month. Against that backdrop, lawmakers were eager to enact an E-Rate fix before adjourning.

Fred Upton, R-Mich., combined the E-Rate with the E-911 and spectrum bills in a package (HR 5419) that was introduced as Congress was rushing to finish its business for the year. The House passed HR 5419 on Nov. 19 by voice vote, and the Senate followed suit on Dec. 8, completing congressional action. The president signed the bill into law (PL 108-494) on Dec. 23.

MAJOR PROVISIONS

As enacted, HR 5419 (PL 108-494) contained the following major provisions:

E-Rate funding. Exempted the E-Rate program from the Anti-Deficiency Act, which barred federal agencies from committing to expenditures without having the cash on hand to meet all their obligations.

Congress created the E-Rate program under the 1996 Telecommunications Act (PL104-104) to subsidize Internet connections for school districts, libraries, and rural health centers. It was funded by a portion of the universal service fee, which was paid by the nation's telephone companies. *(1996 law, Congress and the Nation Vol. IX, p. 387)*

The Universal Service Administrative Co., which administered the program, typically sent letters of commitment before collecting all funds needed to meet the obligations, because it took schools many months to send back invoices. Without the exemption, the Federal Communications Commission (FCC) would have had to prohibit the practice, forcing a freeze in new E-Rate funding commitments.

Spectrum relocations. Aimed to provide a clear, predictable mechanism for compensating federal agencies that had to vacate radio frequencies that were being sold to wireless communications companies.

The law established the Spectrum Relocation Fund, a federal trust fund, to compensate federal agencies. It required the FCC to notify the Commerce Department's National Telecommunications and Information Administration at least six months in advance of an auction of frequency licenses. The office was then responsible for helping any federal agency affected by the auction to find a suitable new frequency and to estimate the cost of such a move.

Under the new law, bidding in the auction could not close until it equaled at least 110 percent of the estimated cost. The money would go into the newly created spectrum fund, which the affected agency could draw upon as it shifted over to a different frequency. Previously, companies negotiated individually to reimburse agencies.

E-911 services. Provided for the creation of a joint program—under the Commerce Department's assistant secretary for communications and information and the administrator of the National Highway Traffic Safety Administration—to coordinate implementation of enhanced 911 upgrades across the country. E-911 systems enabled public safety operators to pinpoint the location of callers who were using cell phones

The law authorized grants of up to $250 million per year in fiscal 2005 through 2009 to help states upgrade 911 emergency services. States could use the grants to improve emergency communications planning, make infrastructure and equipment upgrades, and hire and train new personnel. The federal share of each project was limited to 50 percent.

Amtrak

Lacking a consensus on whether Amtrak should be run as a business or a public service, Congress put off a debate on reauthorizing the passenger rail service. The inaction once again postponed decisions on what to do with the rail company's organizational structure. *(107th Congress action, p. 379)*

Congress in 2003 appropriated $1.2 billion for Amtrak as part of the Transportation-Treasury section of the fiscal 2004 omnibus spending package (PL 108-199). President George W. Bush had requested $900 million. Amtrak said it needed $1.8 billion. Congress in 2004 appropriated $1.2 billion in the fiscal 2005 Transportation-Treasury appropriations measure (PL 108-447), which was $317 million more than the House or Bush wanted. It also directed the railroad and the Transportation Department to agree on a schedule for Amtrak and to repay a $100 million federal loan that had been deferred for a number of years. If Amtrak and the department did not reach a deal in sixty days, the loan would come due.

The best chance for an Amtrak reauthorization came early in 2004 when some members considered trying to attach an Amtrak overhaul to the surface transportation reauthorization bill (HR 3550). House Republican leaders nixed the idea, which probably would have drawn a presidential veto threat. As in the past, the central problem was whether Amtrak, a government-owned corporation, should be treated as a public service entity operating with the aid of federal subsidies or as a moneymaking business that did not require public aid. Amtrak critics, including the Bush administration, wanted the passenger rail service privatized.

A White House plan, introduced by John McCain, R-Ariz., sought to break Amtrak into three operating companies, which eventually could be privatized. It handed much of the cost and responsibility for operating and maintaining rail lines to the states and discontinued direct federal subsidies used to fund Amtrak since its creation. A competing measure by Republicans Kay Bailey Hutchison of Texas, Trent Lott of Mississippi, Conrad Burns of Montana, and Olympia J. Snowe of Maine generally retained Amtrak's structure, authorizing the service at $60 billion over six years, $48 billion of which would come from issuing tax-exempt bonds. Both bills met with lukewarm interest in the 108th Congress.

The last Amtrak authorization was enacted in 1997 (PL 105-134) and expired in 2002. *(1997 law, Congress and the Nation Vol. X, p. 320)*

Coast Guard Reauthorization

After setting aside a dispute over the security of foreign ships that had bogged down the measure since 2003, Congress cleared legislation (HR 2443) in 2004 to reauthorize the Coast Guard and expand the service to help it meet its new homeland security duties. The bill was signed into law Aug. 9 (PL 108-293).

The $8.2 billion fiscal 2005 reauthorization measure provided for a personnel level of 45,500 and included $1.1 billion for the Coast Guard's twenty-year program to replace its deteriorating ships and aircraft, known as Deepwater. The bill extended training bonuses and housing-related privileges to the Coast Guard as a way to encourage enlistment and bring the service in line with benefits given to other military branches. It also allowed Coast Guard personnel to carry firearms, make arrests, and hold vessels whose owners owed civil penalties for maritime security law violations.

The House originally passed the bill (H Rept 108-233) by voice vote Nov. 5, 2003. It would authorize $7.1 billion for fiscal 2005 but did not cover fiscal 2005. The measure stalled over a provision that required the Coast Guard to approve security plans for foreign vessels entering U.S. ports. The Bush administration opposed it because of the extra cost it required. The Senate version did not include the proposal, and conferees agreed to drop the provision.

Economic Development Reauthorization

Congress in 2004 cleared legislation (S 1134) to reauthorize the Economic Development Administration through 2008 in a victory for an agency that conservatives had long sought to eliminate. The agency, founded in 1965 as part of President Lyndon B. Johnson's Great Society programs, won fans in Congress by responding to criticism with internal overhauls that resulted in successful projects. S 1134 authorized the Commerce Department agency to spend $2.3 billion plus $33 million for one year of administrative expenses. The agency estimated that the authorization would fund projects creating more than 623,000 jobs.

The money would be spent on grants for projects in economically distressed areas, generally defined as those where the two-year average unemployment rate was 1 percentage point greater than the national average or where per capita income was less than 80 percent of the national average.

The Senate Environment and Public Works Committee approved S 1134 by voice vote June 23, 2004. The bill was formally reported (S Rept 108-382) on Oct. 1. The full Senate passed S 1134 by voice vote Oct. 6. The House passed the measure 388–31 under suspension of the rules the next day, completing congressional action.

President George W. Bush signed S 1134 into law (PL 108-373) on Oct. 27.

CHAPTER 7

Energy and Environment

Energy and Environment

Energy issues during President George W. Bush's first term enjoyed a high profile but suffered from competing interests and controversial proposals that blocked final action on most legislative proposals. For environmentalists, this was good news because most thought the administration's agenda to be fundamentally flawed. For energy companies, the outcome was disappointing because they believed that long-sought legislation would finally pass with Republican control of the White House for four years and Congress for more than two years.

In fact, the period resembled the eight preceding years when a Democratic president, Bill Clinton, and a Republican Congress fought to a near standstill on much the same agenda of issues that had divided the nation for years. The deep divisions in Congress and in the nation over competing interests and values doomed far-reaching changes in energy policy. President Bush put forth an agenda rooted in expanding energy sources and lifting or easing environmental restrictions that producers said thwarted finding and using oil, gas, and other energy resources.

Environmental legislation as understood by the environmental lobby was never a major part of the Bush administration's agenda. The proposals it did put forth were denounced by environmentalists as efforts to roll back laws already on the books. Moreover, the administration opposed action on certain issues, particularly global warming, that environmentalists advocated.

The deadlock mirrored the ambivalence of many Americans about energy and environmental policy that was reflected in an unambiguous desire for clean air and water while being able to light and heat homes comfortably and fill up large and often fuel-inefficient vehicles at the gas station. In the end environmental advocates were better positioned than producers to leverage this ambivalence in a closely divided Congress to stop significant changes in policy. In spite of this, some bills did pass and a comprehensive energy package nearly was finished, which gave energy companies hope of success in the next Congress.

ENERGY TAKES THE SPOTLIGHT

The Bush administration made no secret that its top priority on energy and environmental issues would be developing new energy resources and, as it deemed necessary, cutting back or even repealing laws and regulations that obstructed that goal. To this end, Bush quickly established the National Energy Policy Development Group, headed by Vice President Dick Cheney, to prepare a national energy plan. Throughout its life, and even after, this group was shrouded in secrecy and controversy. Environmentalists and many Democrats charged that it was composed largely of representatives from energy companies, with little if any input from advocates of greater energy conservation. *(Cheney group challenges, p. 714)*

The legislative plan that grew out of the work of Cheney's group reflected, as expected, an emphasis on finding and exploiting new oil and gas resources, although some recommendations also were made to lower energy demand. Unfortunately for the administration, the ideas that made their way into legislation were too many and too sweeping to produce a consensus in Congress. The legislators spent the better part of four years trying to find enough common ground to pass a bill, and in late 2004 came tantalizingly close to success. A complete bill had been passed by both chambers in the 108th Congress and differences reconciled in conference. Ironically,

REFERENCES

Discussion of environmental and energy policy for the years 1945–1964 may be found in *Congress and the Nation Vol. I,* pp. 771–1095; for the years 1965–1968, *Congress and the Nation Vol. II,* pp. 463–528; for the years 1969–1972, *Congress and the Nation Vol. III,* pp. 745–849; for the years 1973–1976, *Congress and the Nation Vol. IV,* pp. 201–320; for the years 1977–1980, *Congress and the Nation Vol. V,* pp. 451–530, 533–597; for the years 1981–1984, *Congress and the Nation Vol. VI,* pp. 333–400, 403–482; for the years 1985–1988, *Congress and the Nation Vol. VII,* pp. 417–495; for the years 1989–1992, *Congress and the Nation Vol. VIII,* pp. 467–532; for the years 1993–1996, *Congress and the Nation Vol. IX,* pp. 401–476; for the years 1997–2001, *Congress and the Nation Vol. X,* pp. 341–414.

Outlays for Natural Resources and Environment

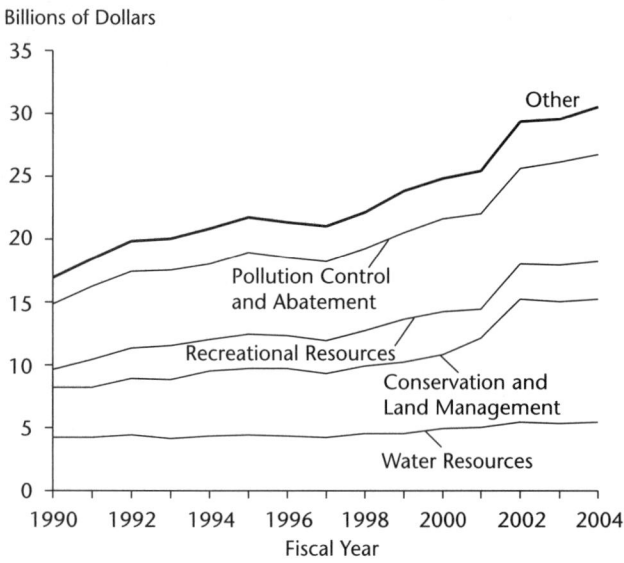

Billions of Dollars

SOURCE: Office of Management and Budget, *Historical Tables, Budget of the United States Government: Fiscal Year 2006* (Washington, D.C.: U.S. Government Printing Office, 2005), Table 3.2.

the measure fell victim to a dispute largely between Republicans from different states over a fuel additive that was known to pollute groundwater sources. States where the substance was made, including Texas, insisted on a liability waiver for producers, while states with significant groundwater contamination said that was unacceptable.

The dispute, however, masked the far-reaching differences that made the energy legislation so controversial throughout the period. The most prominent issue—allowing oil and gas exploration in Alaska's Artic National Wildlife Refuge, a fragile area in the northeast area of the state adjacent to Canada—was so controversial that eventually advocates of drilling there simply abandoned efforts to get it in the bill.

There were other hot button issues also. One was a controversial plan by a government regulatory agency to redesign national wholesale electricity markets and power transmission networks. A related proposal to repeal a 1930s New Deal law was expected to result in more consolidation in the power industry. Another section required more use of renewable energy sources, which power companies argued was uneconomical. The use of ethanol in gasoline was vigorously supported by Midwest farm-state members because the product came from corn but opposed by coastal states because its use was likely to cause higher gas prices. The regional differences seen in the ethanol debate were mirrored in many parts of the bill because benefits to certain states were seen as likely to be costly to consumers in other states.

In addition to the many policy controversies, the Republicans pushing the legislation made matters more difficult for

themselves by largely excluding Democrats from participating in the writing of the provisions, thus giving the Democrats no vested interest in helping pass the measure.

However, not all parts of the energy bill were lost on its death. When it became clear late in 2004 that the omnibus bill was doomed, a number of tax provisions were rolled into other measures that were certain to reach the president's desk. These provisions, which were to cost billions of dollars over their lifetimes, largely benefited power generation and extractive industries through lower tax rates and credits and other subsidies.

NUCLEAR WASTE

The Bush administration and Congress pushed ahead on a long-term solution to the vexing problem of handling and disposing of radioactive waste from nuclear plants that would remain lethal for thousands of years. As expected, the administration officially designated Yucca Mountain in Nevada as the repository, and Congress endorsed the decision in spite of vehement opposition from Nevada officials of every political stripe.

A secondary issue emerged in 2004 when Congress allowed the Energy Department to seal nuclear waste from some, but not all, weapons plants in permanent containers that would remain at the site rather than being transported to Nevada. The decision was condemned by environmentalists who argued that the canisters could rupture and leach radioactive waste into the ground.

ENVIRONMENTAL ISSUES

Little serious attention was paid to environmental initiatives, reflecting the preference of the White House and congressional Republicans to focus on energy issues. However, Congress did approve late in 2003 an administration proposal that the White House said would reduce the risk of wildfires by thinning and removing debris on as much as 20 million acres of national forests. The so-called "Healthy Forests" initiative had considerable bipartisan support in Congress, although some environmentalists said it could allow increased logging that would harm forests.

Bush's other major proposal in this area involved air pollution, but it went nowhere in the face of vigorous opposition from environmentalists. Bush sought to alter rules that regulated air pollution, a plan vigorously endorsed by the power industry and condemned by environmentalists. With the controversial proposal blocked in Congress, the administration moved ahead with regulatory changes to essentially accomplish much of the purpose of the legislation. Democrats lost on a Senate vote in 2002 to delay the regulatory changes, a vote seen largely as a symbolic protest over all of the administration's environmental record.

The most controversial issue, however, was one on which nothing actually happened: global warming. The administration came into office vehemently opposed to the 1997 international climate treaty signed in Kyoto, Japan. The Kyoto treaty required signatories to significantly reduce greenhouse gases but exempted a number of the world's developing nations. Controversial from the start, particularly in the business community that saw the requirements as a major threat to economic activity, the treaty stood little change of approval by the Senate in any event. But the Bush administration made it official policy by renouncing the agreement, to the consternation of environmentalists, many scientists, and much of the rest of the world including the nations that had signed onto the pact.

As a result, Congress was largely on the sidelines in the continuing debate over whether gas emissions, especially from burning fossil fuel, were creating atmospheric changes that could in time threaten the ecological balance of the world. Some hearings were held, and Sen. John McCain, R-Ariz., who differed with his party's view of the issue, forced a Senate vote in 2003 that would have required a reduction in carbon dioxide and other greenhouse gas emissions. Although he lost, the vote of 43–55 was closer than many observers expected in light of the widespread agreement in the chamber and outside that the Kyoto treaty had fundamental flaws.

In one instance, however, the Bush administration suffered an unexpected setback when, in early 2001, it sought to delay tough new regulations proposed by the Clinton administration to reduce levels of arsenic in drinking water. The proposal was condemned by environmentalists and proved highly unpopular with the general public. The House, generally a bastion of support for Bush proposals during the presi-

Outlays for Energy

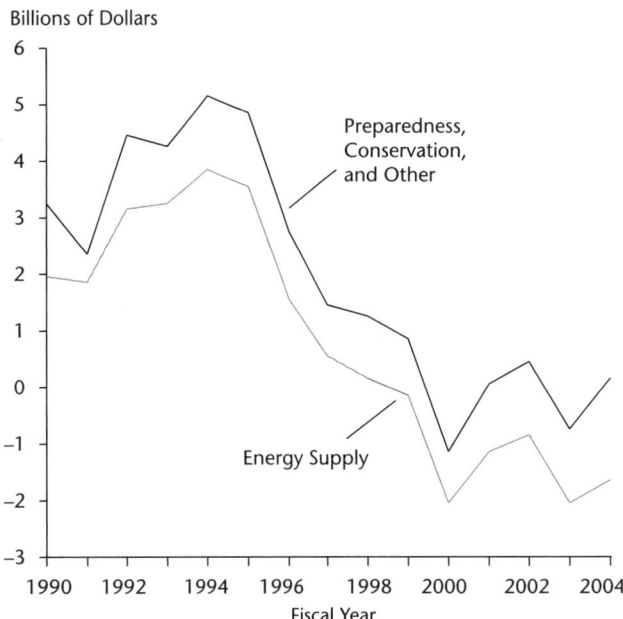

SOURCE: Office of Management and Budget, *Historical Tables, Budget of the United States Government: Fiscal Year 2006* (Washington, D.C.: U.S. Government Printing Office, 2005), Table 3.2.

dent's term, voted to prohibit the administration from weakening the Clinton administration standards. After that, the Bush administration backed away and allowed the tougher standards to take effect in 2006.

Chronology of Action on Energy and Environment

2001–2002

President George W. Bush's energy program became a prominent part of his policy agenda in the early months of his administration. With a Republican majority in Congress and the active support of energy producers long frustrated by roadblocks to finding new oil and gas resources, Bush made energy legislation one of his important legislative goals.

Events were to conspire against him in the 107th Congress. Initially, the GOP controlled the House and had a 50–50 split in the Senate, which gave the party control through the tie-breaking vote of Vice President Dick Cheney. But in the spring a Republican moderate, James M. Jeffords of Vermont, left the party to become an independent after clashing with the White House and prominent GOP leaders over, among other things, the direction of the party. He then caucused with the Democrats, giving them the necessary votes to take control of the Senate and its agenda. Even without this change, however, some observers thought that other GOP moderates would not fully support the Bush energy agenda.

Far worse, however, were the Sept. 11, 2001, terrorist attacks in New York and Washington, which fundamentally changed the direction of the 107th Congress. Defense and security became the top priorities for both parties, pushing lesser issues and most contentious proposals to the side.

The energy proposal was certainly contentious, and no part of it more so than the part that allowed drilling for petroleum on Alaska's Artic National Wildlife Refuge. This was a flashpoint between energy companies and environmentalists on which there was little if any room for compromise. Although the most prominent, it was only one of numerous issues that made enactment of energy legislation a long shot from the beginning.

The session was not without some final action, however. Perhaps most important was passage of legislation to provide more funding to clean up and redevelop polluted industrial sites, usually referred to as brownfields. In addition, a bill was enacted to improve the safety and security of the na-

tion's nearly 2 million miles of pipelines. This issue took on increased visibility after the 2001 terrorist attacks when new concerns arose about potential terrorist strikes on the nation's infrastructure including pipes that carried oil and natural gas.

Another issue that moved ahead, although less smoothly, was settling on a permanent storage location for high-level radioactive waste that had been accumulating from the nation's nuclear power plants. A decision was made that the location would be Yucca Mountain in a desolate area of Nevada even though that location was opposed by virtually every elected official in the state. However, a related issue of extending liability insurance to the nuclear industry under a law known as the Price-Anderson Act languished until the 108th Congress.

To nobody's surprise, environmental issues did not play a significant role in the activities of the 107th Congress.

Energy Policy

The deep divisions in Congress, and in the nation, over competing interests and values doomed far-reaching changes in U.S. energy policy. Having recaptured the White House for Republicans, President George W. Bush set an energy agenda that favored increased energy sources and fewer environmental restrictions that frustrated producers. This policy view was reflected in major energy legislation that lawmakers worked on but were unable to complete in either the 107th or 108th Congresses. (2003–2004 action, p. 425)

BACKGROUND

Escalating gasoline prices and an electricity shortage that produced rolling blackouts in California pushed energy issues onto the national agenda at the start of 2001. Not since the 1970s had Americans shown as much concern that the country had a serious energy problem. Historically, major energy disruptions had spawned significant changes in pub-

Vice President Dick Cheney addresses the Nuclear Energy Institute's annual conference in Washington, D.C., on May 22, 2001. Cheney chaired the Bush administration's National Energy Policy Development Group, which was charged with creating a national energy strategy. *Source: AP Wide World Photos/Doug Mills*

lic policy. The 1975 Energy Policy and Conservation Act (PL 94-163) followed the Arab oil embargo of that period. The 1979 oil shortage following the fall of the Shah of Iran helped President Jimmy Carter persuade Congress to enact conservation and emergency rationing programs as well as other energy development legislation. *(Congress and the Nation Vol. V, p. 451)*

High oil prices after Iraq invaded Kuwait in August 1990, which led to the Persian Gulf War a year later, helped drive the 1992 energy bill (PL 102-486), the last major piece of comprehensive energy legislation to be signed into law. *(Congress and the Nation Vol. VIII, pp. 469, 500)*

Even before the new energy events captured public attention, Bush had pledged during his presidential campaign to develop a comprehensive national energy policy. Shortly after entering office, he established the National Energy Policy Development Group charged with putting together a national strategy. Chaired by Vice President Dick Cheney, the group issued more than 100 recommendations in May 2001. Warning of "the most serious energy shortage since the oil embargoes of the 1970s," the task force emphasized increased production, while also offering some proposals to reduce energy demand. On June 28 Bush sent Congress a plan for comprehensive energy legislation that filled in some of the details of the Cheney report.

Republicans hoped to push that plan, or something close to it, to enactment. But falling gasoline prices and stabilization of electricity supplies on the West Coast reduced the sense of urgency, and old disputes stymied progress on the bill. Republicans argued that increasing domestic production of oil and gas was a national security issue. With 56 percent of the nation's oil coming from imports, they warned, a future reduction of supplies from the Middle East could trigger another conflict in the Persian Gulf.

Democrats generally maintained that expanded energy independence lay in conservation, not more drilling for petroleum. They stressed renewable energy sources and vowed to fight to keep oil companies out of such environmentally sensitive areas such as Alaska's Artic National Wildlife Refuge (ANWR). Democrats cast their GOP opponents as champions of large oil, gas, and coal companies. The intense rhetoric and emotions overshadowed the fact that the two parties had broad agreement on many of the issues, including tax incentives for energy production and conservation, research on cleaner-burning coal, pipeline safety, and fuel assistance for low-income people.

Drilling in the Alaska Refuge

The Arctic refuge was both a real and a symbolic issue for the debate between the parties on energy, as well as a potent fund-raising issue for both sides. Bush proposed exploration and drilling on a coastal plain that covered 1.5 million acres of the 19-million-acre refuge in the northeastern corner of the state. The U.S. Geological Survey estimated that the area harbored 5.7 billion to 16 billion barrels of oil.

The issue had divided lawmakers and pitted environmentalists against oil companies and Alaskan officials for more than forty years. The refuge was set aside in 1960, after years of fighting between oil companies and environmentalists. In 1980 Congress passed a law (PL 96-487) that put most of the refuge off-limits but left it up to future Congresses to decide the fate of the coastal plain. *(Congress and the Nation Vol. V, p. 577)*

The Interior Department sought to open the land for drilling in 1987, during the administration of President Ronald Reagan, provoking an outcry from environmentalists and a rebuff from Congress. In 1991, after the Persian Gulf War, a provision to allow drilling was included in an energy

Map of Alaska detailing the Arctic National Wildlife Refuge (ANWR). In addition to debating petroleum drilling in ANWR, the 107th and 108th Congresses also considered a federal loan guarantee for a proposed natural gas pipeline from Alaska to the lower 48 states (see 2003–2004 Senate Committee Action, p. 428). Source: CQ Weekly.

bill but was dropped after a filibuster. (Congress and the Nation Vol. VII, p. 476; Congress and the Nation Vol. VIII, p. 512)

When Republicans took control of Congress in 1995, they tried to open ANWR to exploration as part of a budget reconciliation bill. President Bill Clinton cited that provision when he vetoed the bill. (Congress and the Nation Vol. IX, p. 472)

The stakes were high for all sides. For Alaska residents, drilling in the federal refuge meant money. With neither sales nor income taxes, the state received two-thirds of its revenue from oil royalties. Much of the remaining royalties went into a permanent fund that paid each eligible Alaskan man, woman, and child an annual dividend that approached $1,900 in 2001. Under existing law, Alaska stood to receive 90 percent of the royalties and other revenue from development of ANWR: $200 million to $2.5 billion annually, according to the Congressional Research Service.

For Bush and many Republicans, developing the swath of treeless wilderness along the Barents Sea was the linchpin of a strategy they said was essential to wean the United States from its dependence on foreign oil. Proponents of drilling also said new computer-based exploration technologies significantly improved the probability of hitting oil while minimizing environmental disruptions.

Democrats and environmental lobbyists said the coastal plain was tantamount to sacred ground, serving as an important birthing place for caribou, a feeding ground for snow geese, and a den site for polar bears. Opening the area permanently would alter it, they argued, no matter how carefully it was done. In the fragile permafrost, a lone tractor passing in winter could damage the landscape for decades.

Critics also said it would take about ten years to begin piping oil from the refuge.

Environmentalists claimed public opinion was on their side. An Associated Press poll released on Feb. 1, 2001, found that 53 percent of those polled opposed opening the refuge to oil exploration, compared with 33 percent in favor. The rest were undecided. (2003 action, p. 425)

Fuel Economy Standards

The dispute over fuel standards had a long history as well. Under existing corporate average fuel economy (CAFE) standards, each manufacturer's fleet of passenger cars had to average at least 27.5 miles per gallon (mpg), while light truck fleets—minivans, pickups, and the popular sport utility vehicles (SUVs)—had to meet a 20.7 mpg standard. Automakers lobbied aggressively against an increase, saying it would force them to produce fewer of the vehicles American consumers were purchasing and more of those that were in lower demand. Instead, they urged Congress to provide tax incentives for technology that would improve fuel efficiency. The Cheney task force called for about $4 billion in tax credits for buyers of hybrid gas/electric or fuel cell cars.

The CAFE standards had been introduced in 1975 and had remained virtually unchanged since 1985. Between 1995 and 1999, House Majority Whip Tom DeLay, R-Texas, led a group of Republicans who inserted language in the annual transportation appropriations bill to block even a study of new standards on the assumption that a study would lead to tougher restrictions. In 2000, under pressure from the Senate, House negotiators accepted provisions in the fiscal 2001 transportation spending law (PL 106-346) that required a study by the National Academy of Sciences to evaluate the effectiveness and impact of CAFE standards. (Congress and the Nation Vol. X, p. 333)

The National Academy of Sciences issued its report July 31, 2001. While making no specific recommendations about increasing CAFE standards, it said higher fuel economy could be achieved "without degradation of safety." The White House supported "increasing automobile fuel economy" but asked Congress to leave the Transportation Department free to determine how best to accomplish that. The fiscal 2002 transportation law (PL 107-87) did not seek to block new standards.

HOUSE ACTION

Most of the energy legislation action during 2001 occurred in the House. Republicans passed a comprehensive bill in August over the objections of environmentalists and many Democrats who complained that the measure tilted too far toward industry. But the legislation stalled in the Senate over the insistence of some Republicans that portions of ANWR be opened to oil and natural gas drilling.

The House package largely reflected recommendations for a national energy strategy from the Cheney task force but did not address electricity deregulation, which sponsors considered too complex and divisive, or extend the Price-Anderson Act that gave liability protection for nuclear power plants, considered too controversial. The bill included $33.5 billion in tax incentives for energy producers and consumers. *(Nuclear liability, pp. 422, 440)*

Aggressive lobbying by the Bush administration, some labor unions, and the oil, gas, and coal industries helped get the measure through the House. Democrats were unsuccessful in removing language that would open ANWR to drilling or in adding a provision to raise fuel economy standards for SUVs and other light trucks. The fuel standards issue caused alarm among Democrats in the blue-collar Midwest who feared it might lead to job losses in the auto industry.

Four House committees approved major pieces of the GOP energy plan in July: Energy and Commerce, Ways and Means, Resources, and Science. As part of their sales strategy, Cheney and members of Bush's cabinet joined congressional Republicans in town hall meetings across the country during the week to stress what they said was a balanced approach on energy.

Energy and Commerce Committee

The Energy and Commerce Committee approved the bill (HR 2587—H Rept 107-162, Pts. 1, 2) by a vote of 50–5 in July without substantial changes to the draft produced by the Energy and Commerce Subcommittee. The most heavily debated provision in the bill remained intact: a requirement that SUVs and other light trucks save at least 5 billion gallons of gasoline by 2010. Other provisions included a National Academy of Sciences study of alternatives to the existing CAFE standards; a joint study by the Environmental Protection Agency (EPA) and Energy Department of federal, state, and local pollution requirements for motor fuels that could lead to regional or national specifications; off-budget protection for the $10 billion Nuclear Waste Fund established in 1982 that was funded with fees from utilities to finance construction of a storage site for spent nuclear fuel; accelerated programs for producing electric power using "clean coal" methods; tax credits for emission reductions and efficiency improvements in existing coal-fired electric power plants; a requirement that the EPA develop a rule for switching to reformulated gasoline in summertime to help combat ozone depletion; mandatory efficiency requirements for federal buildings to reduce energy consumption by 35 percent; expanded grants to states for weatherizing homes to make them more energy-efficient; and authorization for $3.4 billion a year through fiscal 2005 for home heating aid to low-income residents.

Resources Committee

The House Resources Committee approved a bill in July (HR 2436–H Rept 107-106, Pt. 1) to open up more federal lands to oil and gas exploration. The approval vote was 26–17. The key ANWR provision opened the coastal plain to oil and gas leasing; an attempt to strike the section was defeated 19–30. The bill also included provisions to expedite reviews of barriers to additional onshore oil and gas leases; require government officials to explain in detail the reasons for denying oil and gas leases; provide financial incentives for offshore drilling in the central and western Gulf of Mexico; require a study of whether new pipelines could be laid in existing rights-of-way across federal lands; require a federal inventory of the coal, geothermal, wind, and solar power potential on all federal lands except parks and wilderness areas; provide greater flexibility for oil companies to pay federal royalties with oil rather than cash; and expedite federal action on geothermal energy leases.

House Ways and Means Committee

The Ways and Means Committee in July approved $33.5 billion in energy tax breaks through 2011. The bill (HR 2511—H Rept 107-157), which was approved 24–17, combined tax incentives for energy conservation favored by members of both parties in Congress with tax benefits for oil and gas producers to encourage exploration and distribution. Of the total, almost $12.6 billion in tax breaks were devoted to conservation, $13 billion to improving the reliability of the nation's energy supply, and $8 billion to energy producers. The main elements were the following: $3.3 billion in tax credits for investing in or producing electricity with "clean coal" technology; $2.8 billion to extend a tax credit for companies producing fuel from nontraditional sources, including shale, tar sands, and biomass; $2.1 billion in tax credits for purchasers of fuel cell, hybrid, and other low-emission vehicles; $1.6 billion to provide a 20 percent credit of up to $2,000 for energy-efficient home improvements; $992 million to phase out the 4.3-cents-per-gallon excise tax on diesel fuel used in trains and barges that operate in inland waterways; $958 million to allow businesses to deduct oil and gas exploration expenses; $292 million in credits for appliance manufacturers for energy-efficient refrigerators and clothes washers; and $125 million in tax credits to homeowners who purchased solar energy systems and heaters.

Science Committee

The House Science Committee approved the last piece of the package by voice vote in July. The bill (HR 2460—H Rept 107-177) proposed authorizing $6 billion in fiscal 2002 for an array of programs on renewable energy, conservation, and nuclear power. The authorizations included $200 million for grants to develop commercial applications for alternative-fuel vehicles; $2.1 billion over three years for energy conservation; $490 million over three years for global climate change programs; $1.7 billion over three years for renewable energy; $690 million over three years for nuclear energy; $2.5 billion over ten years for coal technology; $742 million over three years for oil and gas research and development; $655 million in fiscal 2002–2003 for a magnetic fusion burning plasma experiment and a fusion energy sciences program; and $276.3 million for fiscal 2002 and declining amounts through fiscal 2006 for the Spallation Neutron Source project at Oak Ridge National Laboratory in Tennessee.

House Floor Action

The House passed the GOP energy plan—assembled into a single package (HR 4) by the leadership—by a vote of 240–189 on the first day of August. Aggressive lobbying by the administration, labor unions, and the oil, gas, and coal industries helped keep Bush's plan intact through the acrimonious daylong debate. Lawmakers rejected a significant increase in fuel economy standards for SUVs and other light trucks as well as an attempt to block oil and gas exploration in ANWR. In the end, the Bush administration was pleased. "A lot of the pundits said we'll never get an energy bill out of the Congress, and we had, I thought, a surprisingly strong vote over here last night for a good, sound, solid, comprehensive, long-term energy plan," said Cheney.

In addition to lobbying undecided House members, Cheney and other Republicans turned to the International Brotherhood of Teamsters and other unions to help them argue that increased oil, gas, and coal production on public lands would create jobs. Opponents of higher CAFE standards enlisted the United Auto Workers to reinforce their contention that requiring more fuel efficiency from popular SUVs would hurt sales by the auto industry and cost jobs. Environmental groups also lobbied intensively, particularly to prevent oil exploration in ANWR, a fight they thought they could win in the House.

The House-passed bill contained no substantive changes from the package of legislation that emerged from the Energy and Commerce, Ways and Means, Resources, and Science committees in July. As part of the rule for floor debate, however, the House adopted an amendment by Jim Gibbons, R-Nev., to strike language that would have taken the $10 billion Nuclear Waste Fund off budget and made it a dedicated funding source for a future nuclear waste repository. The administration had joined House appropriators in objecting to the provision.

The most important vote on the legislation came, as expected, on the ANWR issue. The House rejected on a **key vote of 206–223 (R 34–186; D 171–36; I 1–1)** an attempt to drop language in the bill opening portions of the Alaska reserve to drilling. *(2001 key votes, p. 801)*

Drilling proponents focused the debate on the potential economic benefits. The Teamsters ran a series of radio advertisements saying that opening the refuge to oil and gas exploration would create as many as 750,000 jobs, a figure environmentalists immediately disputed as overblown. The House also rejected 160–269 an amendment to increase combined CAFE standards for cars and light trucks, including SUVs, to 26 mpg for model years 2005 and 2006, and 27.5 mpg, the same as for cars, in model year 2007 and beyond.

As passed by the House on Aug. 1, 2001, HR 4 opened 1.5 million acres of coastal plain in Alaska's ANWR to oil and gas exploration; required fuel economy standards for SUVs and other light trucks between the 2004 and 2010 model years that would save 5 billion gallons of gasoline compared with 2002 standards; provided incentives for more offshore oil and gas drilling and authorized increased funding for renewable energy research and clean coal programs; and provided $33.5 billion over ten years in tax credits and deductions to encourage energy production and conservation and encourage other energy-related activities.

SENATE ACTION

In the Senate Alaska Republican Frank Murkowski, chair of the Energy and Natural Resources Committee, predicted in mid-May 2001 that he would have a bill on the floor within a month. Murkowski had introduced a bill (S 388) that emphasized domestic oil and gas production, but GOP plans were thwarted when the Senate shifted to Democratic control in June. *(Senate control, pp. 3, 8)*

House passage of HR 4 raised hopes among supporters that the Senate would act quickly. Initial efforts by the Energy and Natural Resources Committee were sidetracked by the Sept. 11, 2001, terrorist attacks. Then, when it became clear that a majority on the panel supported drilling in ANWR, Majority Leader Tom Daschle, D-S.D., canceled further markups. In December Senate Democrats introduced their comprehensive bill (S 1766), which included a ban on drilling in ANWR and focused on renewable energy and conservation. Daschle promised a floor debate by mid-February 2002.

Comprehensive energy legislation remained high on the congressional agenda in the second session of the 107th Congress, but in the end lawmakers remained far apart on fundamental energy issues. The huge bill collapsed of its own weight with the House focused on increasing energy production, reflecting the White House's plan, and the Senate under Democratic control giving emphasis to energy conservation.

Senate Floor Action

The Senate passed its version of energy legislation on April 25 (S 517) after six weeks of debate and voting, including two key votes, and then substituted it for the House language in HR 4. A number of Republicans voted for the legislation to get the bill to conference where they hoped House provisions on energy production—especially the ANWR provisions—would prevail.

Before that could happen, however, the Senate had to work through a litany of highly contentious issues under the shadow of the fall national elections. One Republican senator, Olympia J. Snowe, Maine, caught the flavor when she said: "There's no sense of urgency. We're all consumed with the political aspects of the debate instead of the policy."

Renewable fuels. One issue involved the conflicting views of environmentalists who wanted to push the nation toward using renewable energy and electricity companies that argued renewables were an impractical source of energy for the foreseeable future. Less than 3 percent of the nation's electricity came from renewables, excluding hydropower. The Senate bill contained provisions requiring utilities to generate at least 10 percent of their electricity from renewable sources, such as wind and sun, by 2020. The language was intended to replace existing law that required utilities to buy power from renewable energy sources when it was available. Utilities said this law forced them to pay too much for power.

The requirement stayed in the bill after a series of weakening amendments were defeated, mostly by substantial margins, suggesting that the Senate was generally comfortable with the concept of pushing use of renewable energy.

Fuel efficiency standards. Existing CAFE standards had long been a flash point between environmentalists and many interest groups, especially vehicle manufacturers and labor unions that believed tougher fuel standards would harm auto and truck sales and cost jobs. While the White House professed support for better fuel efficiency, it wanted Congress to leave the Department of Transportation unencumbered to determine how best to do it.

This issue was joined when the Senate on March 13 by a **key vote of 62–38 (R 43–6; D 19–31; I 0–1)** approved an amendment by Carl Levin (D-Mich.) and Christopher S. Bond (R-Mo.) to require the National Highway Safety Administration to increase mileage standards for light trucks, including SUVs, within fifteen months and for cars within two years. If the agency did not act in that time, or if it set standards lawmakers did not like, Congress could step in. The effect of the amendment was to freeze congressional action for two years. The White House and auto makers lobbied aggressively for this approach, which reflected the constituencies of the two sponsoring senators from states where auto manufacturing was important. *(2002 key votes, p. 819)*

Electricity. The Senate bill repealed the 1935 Public Utility Holding Company Act (PUHCA), which restricted the territory and businesses in which utilities could operate, as well as the 1978 law that required utilities to buy power from renewable energy sources when it was available. The bill substituted other, less stringent requirements.

Ethanol. The Senate bill included a provision requiring smog-prone states such as California and New York to discontinue use of methyl-tertiary-butyl-ether (MTBE), a petroleum-based additive that adds oxygen to fuel and reduces air pollution in engines. MTBE had been found to contaminate groundwater and already was banned in a number of states. Instead, the states would be required to use ethanol, alcohol distilled mainly from corn, as an additive. This requirement was ardently supported by Midwest state senators and their farm constituency and opposed by California, New York, and other state senators who feared higher gasoline prices. After sharp debate, the Senate killed an attempt to allow states to get expedited thirty-day wavers from the federal government when ethanol supplies were low to avoid gas price spikes. *(MTBE background, Congress and the Nation Vol. X, p. 390)*

ANWR drilling. The Senate rejected the centerpiece of President Bush's energy plan: oil and gas exploration in the Alaska wildlife refuge. The Democratic leadership forced a vote April 18, 2002, on whether to invoke cloture, thereby limiting debate, on a pending proposal by an Alaska senator to allow ANWR drilling. The cloture motion was defeated on a **key vote of 46–54 (R 41–8; D 5–45; I 0–1)**. The outcome showed that Republicans could not muster even a majority, let alone the sixty votes needed to approve cloture. The vote left many senators resigned to stalemate over energy policy, reflecting the public's ambivalence on the subject. *(2002 key votes, p. 819)*

Major Senate Provisions

The Senate bill reflected the Democratic view that conservation and renewable energy should be at least as important as developing new energy sources, the Bush administration's preference.

Its bill included provisions to encourage fuel efficiency and greater use of energy sources, such as the wind and sun, that are permanent. It rejected drilling in the Alaska wildlife refuge and called for $15.2 billion in tax incentives, split nearly evenly between boosting production and promoting conservation. It also called for easing electricity regulations, strengthening the ability of federal regulars to review utility mergers, and requiring increased use of ethanol in gasoline.

CONFERENCE, FINAL ACTION

Conference negotiations to meld the two approaches began in June, but the differences in detail and philosophy were too vast. They could not even agree on a slimmed-down bill that included nuclear liability protections and pipeline safety, two mostly noncontroversial issues. Both passed separately after the omnibus bill died. The House's Energy and Commerce Committee Chair, Billy Tauzin, R-La., pushed relentlessly for a bill in 2002. He set a Sept. 30 deadline for a deal and laid out a detailed week-by-week schedule to get there. The effort was to come to naught. The stakes were too high.

On ANWR, Republicans proposed possible compromises including setting aside additional areas as refuge wilderness that would be off-limits to developments. But the Democrats remained adamant about any drilling in ANWR, essentially dooming compromise and putting the controversy on the shelf for debate another day.

Revamping the way electricity was regulated and marketed was one of the original catalysts for the energy legislation, but it became one of the biggest obstacles to an agreement. The House energy bill had no electricity deregulations provisions comparable to those in the Senate version. House conferees worked from an existing bill by Joe L. Barton, R-Texas, chair of the House Subcommittee on Energy and Air Quality. Barton's plan called for repealing PUHCA and adding incentives for utilities in all parts of the nation to join regional transmission networks, which were independent

ENVIRONMENT, ENERGY LEADERSHIP

President George W. Bush's nominees for key energy and environmental leadership posts were caught up in the controversies that engulfed the administration's attempts to alter policy in these contentious subjects after eight years of a Democrat in the White House. The turmoil continued throughout the president's term and reflected the deep divisions in the nation and in Congress over environmental and energy policy.

Department of Energy. For energy secretary, Bush selected former senator Spencer Abraham, a Michigan Republican who had lost his reelection bid in 2000. Abraham, a lawyer, also had been a vice presidential aide and chair of the Michigan Republican Party. His one term in the Senate helped ease the confirmation road where senators often show deference to former colleagues. He was confirmed by voice vote on Jan. 20, 2001. *(Background, cabinet profiles, p. 923)*

His major weakness, in the opinion of some observers, was his lack of experience on energy matters. He was also criticized for sponsoring legislation as a senator to abolish the Energy Department. In confirmation hearings Abraham told senators that the changing U.S. energy situation and improvement in the department's management structure led him to change his mind about abolishing it. Abraham said he would seek an energy policy "that includes increasing domestic production of energy in an environmentally responsible manner, increasing our use of renewable energy, decreasing our re-

liance on imported oil and developing new technologies that conserve fossil fuels and reduce energy-related pollution."

His nomination came at a difficult time with the price of oil and natural gas moving upward rapidly and California in the midst of a crisis over electricity availability and cost. His term also coincided with the administration's inability to get major energy legislation through Congress, which had been one of President Bush's top agenda goals. In addition, related administration proposals—especially involving air pollution regulations and global warming—were so controversial that they diminished the department's overall record even though other agencies were involved in these policies.

Environmental Protection Agency. The job of EPA administrator, a cabinet-rank position, went to Christine Todd Whitman, a moderate Republican who had served as New Jersey governor from 1993 to 2001. The EPA administrator position was widely seen as one of the more thankless in the government's bureaucratic hierarchy. This agency chief is charged with enforcing a variety of environmental laws, many of which dated from earlier decades when support for cleaning up air and water pollution, protecting endangered species, reversing land contamination, and similar activities had wider public and congressional support. In recent years under prodding from business interests, and especially after Republicans took control of the House in 1995, the EPA came under increasing fire from conservatives for heavy-handed

---

operations that managed electricity transmission within a geographical area. The Senate bill had no provisions on regional organizations.

Negotiators focused on at least four key issues: how much authority the Federal Energy Regulatory Commission (FERC) should have in reviewing utility company mergers; whether all utilities that benefited from improvements in electricity grids, such as those in the Midwest and Northeast, should be required to pay for costs; how to address a controversial FERC proposal that aimed to create a seamless national grid for transmitting electricity; and the extent to which utilities should be required to use more renewable fuels in electricity generation.

The issues divided lawmakers by regional as well as partisan lines, dramatically showing the difficulty of enacting complex legislation where interests and needs varied widely. Westerners and southerners wanted to kill the FERC rule, which they feared could hurt their consumers. The rule, known as "standard market design," sought to eliminate state control over power transmission lines and establish uniform regulations for trading electricity around the country. The goal was to carry forward the creation of competitive markets for electricity that began in the early 1990s.

State regulators and public power companies, which were exempt from FERC oversight, saw the rule as a power grab to expand the commission's control over utilities. Tauzin proposed changes that would allow the rule to become final only after FERC had met a set of conditions, including a showing that prices would decline. Democrats, however, were opposed to a provision that revoked FERC's authority to review power industry mergers. If PUHCA were repealed, analysts expected a large number of mergers in the industry.

Other issues, including renewable resources, ethanol, and climate change, all produced similar controversies. The climate change issues reflected the provisions establishing a greenhouse gas registry and establishing a White House Office of Climate Change Response to develop and implement a plan to reduce global warming. In October 2002, with elections only weeks away, legislators gave up on a comprehensive energy bill.

Brownfields Cleanup

Legislation to increase funding for the cleanup and redevelopment of polluted industrial sites known as brownfields was approved shortly before Congress adjourned in 2001.

regulation, poor science, and unwillingness to balance economic costs against environmental goals.

Whitman had built an often-praised record of environmental policy and actions in New Jersey including fighting urban sprawl and preserving open spaces. She was approved without dissent by the Environment and Public Works Committee and confirmed by a 99–0 vote of the Senate on Jan. 31, 2001. However, in the increasingly conservative GOP, Whitman, who supported many women's rights issues, was sometimes seen as lacking the influence of higher-profile conservatives in the administration. She and the agency became caught between bitterly opposed environmental groups on the one hand and corporate interests, particularly energy producers, and the White House on the other. Although she denied it, many reports circulated that she was routinely overruled by the administration on policy issues. She departed on June 27, 2003; her relatively short two-year term reflected the underlying difficulties.

Bush nominated Utah governor Michael O. Leavitt to succeed Whitman. Leavitt was confirmed by the Senate on Oct. 28, 2003, by an 88–8 vote. Although he won praise from many quarters, not all environmentalists were enthused and some used the confirmation process to denounce the Bush administration's environmental policies. A typical comment was from Carl Pope, Sierra Club executive director, who said Leavitt's Utah record "suggests that he will be a good fit for the Bush administration but a disappointing choice for Americans concerned with environmental protection."

Department of the Interior. For his Interior secretary, Bush selected westerner Gale A. Norton, who had served as Colorado attorney general from 1991 to 1999. Norton, a lawyer practicing in Denver, also had worked in the Interior and Agriculture departments and run unsuccessfully in 1996 for the Republican Senate nomination in Colorado. Norton's nomination was a lightening rod for criticism from environmentalists, with her critics focusing on her past statements and record. (Background, cabinet profiles, p. 924)

The criticism of Norton began in the two days of Senate confirmation hearings. Brent Blackwelder, president of Friends of the Earth, an environmental lobbying group, was typical in his comments: "[President] Bush deliberately made a very provocative choice in [Norton's] nomination." Environmental groups were reported to have spent almost a million dollars on an ad campaign to defeat her nomination. The effort was to no avail. The Senate voted 75–24 on Jan. 30 to confirm her, with Democrats dividing almost evenly, 25–24, in favor. She was sworn in Jan. 31, 2001. But the vote did little to calm the controversies. Environmentalists remained critical of her and department (and Bush administration) policies throughout the four years, while business interests, energy producers, and land owners commended her actions.

The bill was signed into law by President George W. Bush on Jan. 11, 2002 (HR 2869—PL 107-118). The law also extended liability protection for small businesses and landowners under the 1980 Superfund program that was created to identify and clean up land and waters contaminated by toxic wastes, especially chemicals. A companion bill, however, died in 2002. (Details, p. 421)

Brownfields legislation was one of President Bush's top environmental priorities; with substantial support in both the House and Senate, passage had seemed ensured. But the bill ran into several obstacles including disagreements over the proper role of the Environmental Protection Agency (EPA), concern about wages for workers at the cleanup sites, and a packed congressional workload in the months following the Sept. 11, 2001, terrorists attacks in New York City and the Washington, D.C., area. The bill finally cleared Dec. 20 after dealmaking and administration pressure.

The bill combined two measures: S 350, passed by the Senate in April, and HR 1831, passed by the House in May. The Senate bill provided grants to states to study and clean up contaminated urban brownfields sites. The House bill provided protection from liability under the Superfund hazardous waste law to small businesses and others responsible for small amounts of contamination. The final bill also guaranteed that workers on brownfields projects would receive the prevailing wage in the area, usually the union wage.

BACKGROUND

Toxic wastes sites were recognized, beginning in the 1970s, as intolerable threats to public health. Congress in 1980 enacted the Superfund law (PL 96-510) based on the principle that those responsible for the damage, rather than the government, should pay the cleanup costs. (Superfund background, Congress and the Nation Vol. X, pp. 352, 396)

Brownfields were sites that were not hazardous enough to come under Superfund criteria but that had been certified by a state environmental agency as containing or potentially containing a hazardous substance. For years, brownfields restoration was caught in debates about revising the Superfund program itself.

A key feature of the Superfund act made any party that contributed to the pollution of a site liable for the cost of the cleanup. That meant a single business could be forced to pay for the entire cost, even if others contributed to the pollution, unless earlier polluters could be located and brought in to share costs.

While approximately half of the identified sites had been successfully decontaminated and redeveloped, the program was plagued by lawsuits as polluters tried to find others to share their liability. Repeated efforts to overhaul the system foundered over issues such as the proper roles for state and federal government, although there were some piecemeal changes. The most recent was language in the fiscal 2000 Omnibus Appropriations Act (PL 106-113) that exempted businesses that recycle paper, glass, plastic, metals, textiles, and rubber from certain Superfund liability.

Cleanup of the more lightly polluted brownfields sites was not specifically authorized under the Superfund law, but the EPA created a grant program in 1995. States took the lead, but the problem was huge with an estimated 450,000 potential brownfields sites nationwide. Cleanup efforts also were slowed by the lack of liability protection for companies developing previously contaminated sites. State governments urged Congress to authorize an EPA brownfields program with its own set of liability standards and funding for cleanup efforts. The initiative had broad support in Congress and within the Bush administration, but some lawmakers feared that breaking it out as separate legislation would undercut momentum for a broader Superfund rewrite.

LEGISLATIVE ACTION

The Senate Energy and Natural Resources Committee approved S 350 (S Rept 107-2) on March 12 by a vote of 15–3. Introduced by Lincoln Chafee, R-R.I., it was similar to a bill that had received the support of sixty-seven senators, the National Governors Association, and the administration of President Bill Clinton during the 106th Congress. Despite the approval, members expressed concern that the EPA could reevaluate and reopen a site it had previously declared clean.

The Senate passed the bill 99–0 in April after Environment and Public Works Chair Robert C. Smith, R-N.H., had worked with colleagues to produce a substitute amendment to assuage the concerns of opponents. Bush issued a statement supporting the bill. As passed the Senate bill authorized more than $1 billion over five years in federal grants for cleanups, provided some liability protections for landowners and developers, and gave states the lead role in cleanup decisions. The bill limited the EPA's ability to seek additional cleanup once a state certified a site as restored and allowed the agency to step in only when a potential release of contaminants posed an "imminent and substantial danger" to public health or the environment. It also gave preference to cleanup sites where contamination affected minority groups and children.

The House took a different approach, concentrating on Superfund liability protection rather than on funding specific projects. The Energy and Commerce Committee gave voice vote approval in May to a bill (HR 1831—H Rept 107-70, Pt. 1). The Transportation and Infrastructure Committee endorsed the bill by voice vote May 16 also (H Rept 107-70, Pt. 2). Neither committee amended the legislation.

The bill focused on limiting the liability of small businesses. It included an exemption for businesses responsible for dumping less than 110 pounds of liquid waste or 200 pounds of solid waste prior to April 1, 2001. If a company met these requirements it did not have to pay for the cleanup; however, the burden of proof fell on the company. Small businesses, defined as having fewer than 100 employees, were exempt. The measure also codified the EPA's practice of reducing fines for companies that could not afford the cost of cleanup.

The House passed the bill 419–0 later that month. After months of negotiations, the House in December passed a bill (HR 2869) containing the core provisions of S 350 and HR 1831. The Senate cleared the measure later that day, sending the bill to the president; both chambers acted by voice vote.

Haggling over the scope of federal oversight had stalled competing drafts of brownfields legislation in the House, with the GOP holding out for a version that offered the states more authority in the cleanup process. EPA Administrator Christine Todd Whitman warned in June that without a strong guarantee of federal oversight similar to that in the Senate bill the measure was likely to die. Under pressure from the White House and the House GOP leadership, Republicans on the Energy and Commerce Committee agreed to accept the Senate language in return for support for the House liability reform bill. The compromise was introduced on Sept. 10 and scheduled for House floor action the next day. With the Sept. 11 terrorist attacks, the measure was rescheduled for the week of Sept. 24.

By then, however, a new issue emerged that further delayed consideration. In September House Democrats, along with Sen. James M. Jeffords, I-Vt., requested that the EPA clarify that provisions of the Davis-Bacon law (PL 88-349) would be used to determine the wages paid to workers involved in cleanups in all states At the time, nineteen states would not have met the requirement that workers be paid the prevailing wages in the area, usually the higher rates required under union contracts. HR 2869 did not address the issue and the EPA refused to provide the requested clarification.

In December the House managers agreed to rewrite the language so that the wage requirements would apply to all cleanups. Though conservatives—often unsympathetic to unions and the higher business costs resulting from union wage levels—were unhappy, they went along with the revision at the urging of House Speaker J. Dennis Hastert, R-Ill. With this language in place, the bill cleared in the closing hours of the session. In signing the measure on Jan. 11, 2002, Bush said it would "protect innocent small business owners and employees from unfair lawsuits, and focus our efforts instead on actually cleaning up contaminated sites."

MAJOR PROVISIONS

As signed, PL 107-118 contained the following major provisions:

Brownfields grants. Provided a total of $1.3 billion for fiscal years 2002 through 2006: $150 million a year for grants to states to assess sites for cleanup and $50 million a year for grants to clean up the sites. Provided an additional $50 million for cleaning up sites contaminated with petroleum.

EPA limitations. Limited the EPA's authority to reevaluate and reopen a site that had been declared clean. Allowed the EPA to take additional actions if a state requested federal help, if contamination had migrated or would migrate across state lines or onto federal property, if a release of toxins posed a danger to public health or the environment, or if new information concerning contamination levels emerged. Prohibited the EPA from designating a moderately polluted waste site as a Superfund site if the state or another party was actively engaged in cleaning it up but allowed the agency to take action after one year if the state was not making reasonable progress on the cleanup or a cleanup agreement had not been reached.

Jurisdiction. Required that funds be available for sites where there was a threat to minority communities or public health. Gave state governments jurisdiction over projects within its borders and EPA jurisdiction when a site crossed state lines or state-federal property lines. Allowed the EPA to take over a brownfields cleanup if there were a significant risk to public health or the environment, particularly when the state was unaware of the source of the contamination.

State lists. Required states to maintain and annually update public lists with the name and location of waste sites at which cleanup activities had been completed under state response programs, as well as sites where future response actions were planned.

Superfund liability exemptions. Exempted from liability under the Superfund hazardous waste law businesses that were responsible for less than 110 pounds of liquid waste or 200 pounds of solid waste. Exempted small businesses with fewer than 100 employees from lawsuits by companies responsible for a majority of the waste matter. Exempted owners of residential property and small businesses who dispose household garbage in a site previously designated to fall under the Superfund program.

Davis-Bacon compliance. Specified that federal wage laws, including the 1931 Davis-Bacon Act (PL 88-349) requiring that workers be paid the wages prevailing in the area, apply to workers participating in cleanup programs, including work done by the states.

2002 COMPANION LEGISLATION DIES

The House passed a bill in June 2002 (HR 2941—H Rept 107-448) designed to allow communities to use federal programs to clean up contaminated brownfields sites, but the Senate did not act. The bill was seen as a complement to the 2001 law (PL 107-118) that established a separate brownfields program.

HR 2941 formally authorized the Housing and Urban Development Department (HUD) brownfields redevelop-ment grant program and eased requirements that discouraged smaller communities from applying for grants. It would have increased access to capital for smaller communities that historically had been unable to get HUD assistance. Specifically, it proposed to eliminate a HUD requirement that local governments obtain Community Development Block Grant Section 108 loan guarantees before they could receive HUD brownfields grants. Small cities, in particular, had trouble getting the loan guarantees.

Arsenic Standards

The administration of George W. Bush suffered an embarrassing environmental defeat early in the president's term when the House rejected a plan to delay strict standards for arsenic in drinking water that had been proposed by President Bill Clinton. The proposed delay, announced by Environmental Protection Agency (EPA) Administrator Christine Todd Whitman in the spring, became a rallying cry for environmental lobbyists already sharply criticizing Bush for policies they believed favored industry.

Arsenic, which occurs naturally in soil and water, can be released in dangerous quantities by some industrial processes. Studies had linked long-term exposure to arsenic in drinking water to cancer of the bladder, lungs, skin, kidney, liver, and prostate. Regulators in the Clinton administration proposed lowering the allowable standard from fifty parts per billion—the level that had been permitted for decades—to ten parts per billion. The lower standard had been recommended by the European Union (EU) and the World Health Organization. Five years earlier Congress had directed the administration to study the health risks associated with arsenic as part of its safe drinking water amendments (PL 104-182).

Mining and chemical companies opposed the more stringent Clinton regulations, arguing that science did not support such a tough policy. The regulation also was opposed by officials from many of the 3,000 towns that would have to update their water systems.

When Whitman insisted that the regulation be put on hold, she said the EPA should take the time to ensure that the policy, which was not slated to take effect until 2006, was founded in science, though she herself supported the more stringent standard. Environmentalists pounced on her announcement as a sign that the White House was abandoning the policy and, as many lobbyists put it, trying to allow more cancer-causing chemicals in the public's water.

The Bush administration had delayed or reversed several orders and regulations that Clinton had issued in the waning days of his term, but none of those actions resonated as did the arsenic decision. Amid a flood of news stories and negative polls, it was clear that the new administration had overstepped national opinion on this issue.

On July 27, 2001, House Democrats succeeded in attaching an amendment to the fiscal 2002 appropriations bill for the departments of Veterans Affairs and Housing and Urban

Development (HR 2620) to prohibit the EPA from weakening the Clinton standards for arsenic in drinking water. The amendment, offered by Minority Whip David E. Bonior, D-Mich., was adopted on a key vote of **218–189 (R 19–182; D 198–6; I 1–1).** *(2001 key votes, p. 801)*

The vote was one of the relatively few times during Bush's four years that the House had rejected a White House plan. The administration did not admit defeat, but it retreated in the following months. At the EPA's request, the National Academy of Sciences studied the issue. Its report, completed in September, found that arsenic in drinking water was more harmful to humans than previous studies had indicated. The report suggested that the government consider arsenic limits even more restrictive than those proposed by Clinton. Following this report, Whitman announced on Oct. 31 that the EPA would, after all, adopt the Clinton standard.

Nuclear Liability Insurance

The House in 2001 passed a fifteen-year extension of a law limiting the liability of nuclear power plants. Senate leaders, however, refused to take up the bill. Senate Majority Whip Harry Reid, D-Nev., strongly opposed the measure out of concern that it might lead to more high-level nuclear waste, which the government was planning to store in Nevada's Yucca Mountain, an action vigorously opposed by Reid and virtually every other Nevada official. (Congress in 2004 extended the law for two years.) *(2004 action, p. 440)*

The bill (HR 2983) sought to extend the 1954 Price-Anderson Act through 2017. The act permanently limited the liability of owners of existing nuclear reactors in case of a catastrophic accident. But the law was set to expire in August 2002, and without an extension, reactors built after that would not be covered. Congressional debate centered on whether the government should continue to shield the nuclear power industry from liability. The Price-Anderson Act, which was part of the seminal Atomic Energy Act (PL 83-703), was designed to protect an industry in its infancy and help it to compete better with coal-fired and hydro power plants. *(Congress and the Nation Vol. I, pp. 932, 935)*

Under Price-Anderson protections, last reauthorized in 1988 (PL 100-408), the entire industry's liability was capped at $9.4 billion. If an accident occurred, the federal government would be responsible for damages above the cap. Each operator was required to carry as much commercial insurance as it could get for its facility (about $200 million for each reactor, per incident, through the Hartford, Conn., American Nuclear Insurers) and contribute an additional $88 million to an insurance pool. *(Congress and the Nation Vol. VII, p. 479)*

The law had never been tested. Damages from the nuclear power industry's worst accident, at Pennsylvania's Three Mile Island in 1979, did not exceed that year's cap. Companies such as Exelon Nuclear, General Electric, Westinghouse Electric, and General Atomics, which were eager to develop new types of nuclear reactors, lobbied hard for a renewal. Utility companies said that without the liability cap insurers might refuse to provide coverage, jeopardizing the nuclear power industry. Some also expressed concern that if the law lapsed, the congressional climate could shift so that one day the industry might lose its protection.

Environmentalists, on the other hand, argued that Congress should avoid extending legal protection for nuclear producers, especially in light of the increased fear of disasters after the Sept. 11, 2001, terrorist attacks. Some public interest groups and environmental lobbyists said the measure was a potential giveaway of federal taxpayer dollars to a dangerous industry. Rep. Edward J. Markey, D-Mass., a leading critic of the nuclear industry, argued that it should have to compete on its own without a federal subsidy. The Bush administration supported the extension as part of its comprehensive energy plan.

HOUSE ACTION

The House Energy and Commerce Committee approved the bill (H Rept 107-299, Pt. 1) by voice vote in October, after ranking Democrat John D. Dingell of Michigan reached a deal with Republicans requiring more accountability from Department of Energy contractors.

The bill had started in the Energy and Air Quality Subcommittee, where Chair Joe L. Barton, R-Texas, won voice vote approval for it in early October. But full committee consideration was delayed while Chair Billy Tauzin, R-La., sought a compromise with Dingell. Dingell wanted to require accountability from negligent contractors at Energy Department nuclear facilities, who under Price-Anderson were shielded from liability. Dingell said that without the change, the bill was "an enticement and incentive to misconduct." The Tauzin-Dingell compromise, adopted by voice vote, stripped liability protection for contractors who engaged in "intentional misconduct" and allowed the attorney general to recover all profits derived from the contract.

The House passed the bill by voice vote in late November under suspension of the rules, a procedure that allows no amendments and is generally reserved for legislation with broad support.

Nuclear Waste Site

Congress in 2002 endorsed a decision by President George W. Bush to make Yucca Mountain in Nevada the permanent repository for high-level radioactive waste from the nation's nuclear power plants. The action was the latest in a long saga extending back twenty years that pitted nuclear power advocates against environmentalists and many state officials. The congressional decision came with the approval of a joint resolution that overrode a veto of the project by the governor of Nevada (PL 107-200).

BACKGROUND

Disposing of nuclear waste was a major impediment for the nuclear power industry because it remained lethally radioactive for thousands of years. The Nuclear Waste Policy Act of 1983 (PL 97-425) set a timetable for the Energy Department to begin disposing of used nuclear fuel in a safe geological repository by Jan. 31, 1998, and prescribed a process for selecting a site. It also established a Nuclear Waste Fund with fees from utilities to finance construction of a permanent storage site. In 1986 the Energy Department issued environmental assessments for five potential geological disposal sites, including Nevada's Yucca Mountain. *(Congress and the Nation Vol. VI, p. 361)*

In 1987, however, Congress changed its mind and directed the government to focus exclusively on Yucca Mountain, to the consternation of the Nevada delegation and the relief of members from other states that might have been selected. Yucca Mountain was a desolate volcanic ridge in the desert 100 miles northwest of Las Vegas. *(Congress and the Nation Vol. VII, p. 483)*

The 1987 law (PL 100-203) also authorized construction of a temporary storage site, an interim solution backed by the nuclear power companies. But the Energy Department was not allowed to select a short-term site until it had recommended the construction of the permanent Yucca Mountain site. No short-term site was ever named, and the federal government defaulted on its obligation to begin removing used nuclear fuel from reactor sites by Jan. 31, 1998.

In 1998 and 1999 the Energy Department issued a series of reports concluding that Yucca Mountain could be used as the permanent site with no adverse impact on public health or safety. The reports also provided a design for the storage site. In 2001 the department issued a study concluding that the proposed repository could meet the EPA's radiation protection standard. *(1990s action, Congress and the Nation Vol. X, pp. 361, 407)*

While the scientific studies were being conducted, high-level radioactive waste was accumulating, stored in 131 above-ground facilities composed of temporary concrete-encased pools in thirty-nine states. Nearly 161 million people in the United States lived within seventy-five miles of those sites.

The Yucca Mountain site was expected to store that waste, along with future waste projected at 2,000 tons per year, in specially designed containers buried 1,000 feet underground. Advocates of the site said the waste could be safely stored there for 10,000 years, although opponents questioned the validity of those estimates.

Opposition came largely from the Nevada delegation of both parties and from environmentalists concerned about possible threats to human health and environmental integrity. They cited studies that raised questions about the project, including a report by the Nuclear Waste Technical Review Board (created to provide an independent assessment of the project) that questioned the technical basis for the Energy Department's safety estimates. Opponents worried that nuclear wastes eventually could seep into groundwater or that containers could be ruptured by earthquakes. They also raised concerns over transporting the waste through forty-three states and within one mile of 50 million Americans.

Supporters countered that twenty years of scientific studies established the unique suitability and safety of the site and pointed to the Energy Department's flawless safety record in shipping defense-related waste to a site in New Mexico. Backers of Yucca Mountain also said opening the site was an important step in renewing the nuclear power industry. But even these advocates acknowledged that using the Nevada site would not mean new power plants would be constructed. No nuclear power plant had been built since a partial meltdown at Pennsylvania's Three Mile Island facility in 1979. After that event, new regulations made nuclear power plant construction uneconomical.

Energy Secretary Spencer Abraham on Jan. 10 notified Nevada's governor, Republican Kenny Ginn, that he would recommend Yucca Mountain officially be designated as the permanent waste repository. President Bush on Feb. 15 formally accepted Abraham's recommendation. Under the 1987 law, Nevada's governor and legislature had sixty calendar days to disapprove of the official decision to designate Yucca Mountain as the repository. Congress had another ninety days to overturn the veto by passing a resolution by majority vote in both chambers. Guinn on April 9 vetoed the decision, as expected.

LEGISLATIVE ACTION

In the House, where the vote was never in doubt, the H J Res 87 passed 306–117 on May 8. The Energy and Commerce Committee had approved the measure (H Rept 107-425) in late April.

The Senate action was not so swift, but the outcome the same. After months of maneuvering and debate, the Senate on July 9 voted 60–39 to proceed to debate on the resolution, which then was adopted by voice vote. The Energy and Natural Resources Committee had approved the measure (S J Res 34—S Rept 107-159) by voice vote in June. President Bush signed the resolution on July 23. The Energy Department planned to seek a license from the Nuclear Regulatory Commission (NRC) in 2004 to begin moving nuclear waste into the repository by 2010.

The decision by the federal executive and legislative branches meant that the controversy would proceed next to the judicial system. Nevada state officials and environmentalists had several lawsuits pending in federal court and promised to file more. Meanwhile, states had an estimated 77,000 tons of nuclear waste waiting to be transported and buried in tunnels hundreds of feet below the Nevada desert.

Pipeline Safety

Legislation to improve the safety and security of the nation's 1.8 million miles of pipelines was approved by Congress in 2002 and signed into law by President George W. Bush at the end of the year (HR 3609—PL 107-355). The bill required that half of all interstate oil and gas pipelines be inspected within five years and that all get an initial inspection within a decade. Reinspection would occur every seven years. The legislation increased civil penalties to $100,000 from $25,000 per incident for a pipeline operator who violated safety requirements. The maximum penalty for a series of violations was raised to $1 million from $500,000.

The legislation authorized up to $189.7 million for the Transportation Department for pipeline safety and security. It also provided for an interagency study of streamlining environmental reviews of pipeline repairs and included whistle-blower protections for pipeline employees who reported safety violations. The bill established a five-year, $100 million research program to be run by the Transportation and Energy departments, along with others, that would look for ways to improve pipeline safety.

BACKGROUND

Safety advocates had been urging changes in the wake of a number of pipeline accidents in recent years. This concern took on new momentum after the Sept. 11, 2001, terrorist attacks that destroyed the World Trade Center buildings in New York City and significantly damaged the Pentagon on the outskirts of Washington, D.C. *(Terrorist attacks, p. 230)*

Pipeline accidents during the previous decade had resulted in hundreds of deaths, thousands of injuries, and millions of dollars in damages to property. Accidents usually were attributed to aging pipes and the expansion of suburbs into previously rural areas, which brought residents closer to oil and gas pipelines. After the 2001 terrorist attacks, concern grew over pipeline safety as part of the general review of the nation's infrastructure exposure to hostile attacks.

Federal regulation of pipeline safety was the responsibility of the Office of Pipeline Safety within the Department of Transportation. The office had been criticized for failing to address safety concerns or implement congressional mandates, such as regular inspections.

LEGISLATIVE ACTION

The legislation was one of the least controversial parts of energy proposals before Congress with Senate-House differences focused largely on the amount of increase in fines and differing opinions on actions to improve pipeline safety. The Senate had passed a safety bill (S 235) early in 2001 by a 98–0 vote, but no further action occurred. The main focus of action then became the House bill (HR 3609), which was reported by two committees: Transportation and Infrastructure and Energy and Commerce (H Rept 107-605, Pts. 1, 2). The House passed a compromise version in July by an overwhelming margin of 423–4.

Rather than taking the legislation to conference, House members decided to resolve differences as part of negotiations on the omnibus energy bill (HR 4). Pipeline safety provisions had already been added to the Senate version of the energy bill. But that legislation proved too controversial for the 107th Congress to handle. When it became clear that energy legislation was going to die with adjournment, energy conferees extracted pipeline safety provisions, and the Senate passed HR 3609 in September after it was amended to reflect primarily the House's approach to the subject. Then both chambers cleared the legislation by voice vote. It was signed by President Bush on Dec. 17, 2002.

2003–2004

The 108th Congress proved almost as frustrating for the Bush administration on energy and environmental policy as did its immediate predecessor. Once again a major energy bill was the centerpiece of the administration's agenda, and once again the issue of drilling in the Artic National Wildlife Refuge in Alaska was the central controversy. Essentially, nothing had changed in the view of either side—the energy companies and their Republican supporters or the environmentalists with their Democratic backers. But in the 2002 elections Republicans regained narrow but firm control of the Senate and maintained their safe majority in the House. This increased their hopes of passing energy legislation, but in the end passage came only tantalizingly close for the GOP.

The energy bill, without the Alaskan drilling provisions, made its way through conference and was ready for a final vote. Ironically, the final obstacle to enactment came from Rep. Tom DeLay, a Texas Republican who was that party's majority leader in the House. The issue was granting a liability waiver to producers of a fuel additive, methyl-tertiary-butyl-ether (MTBE), that had been found to contaminate ground water in a number of states. The substance was produced largely in Gulf Coast states, including DeLay's district. He insisted on the waiver, which was unacceptable to a number of states' senators who filibustered the conference report. Although MTBE was the cause of the bill's death, there were many other issues, including tax breaks for producers and high-efficiency cars as well as efforts to make far-reaching changes in the nation's electricity generation and distribution structures.

However, the 108th Congress accomplished more than the previous Congress in the energy and environment fields. A number of the tax breaks in the failed energy bill were placed in other legislation and passed. A major bill on thinning forests to maintain their health was approved, following a period of intense and highly destructive forest fires in the West. Additional funding was approved to carry forward the Yucca Mountain nuclear disposal site. Also new federal funds were provided for a huge California water project that had long been stalled.

Environmentalists were pleased that no serious effort was made to rewrite the Endangered Species Act, which many Republicans had threatened in response to long-standing complaints from property owners and developers. However, additional exemptions to the act's requirements were made to military sites after defense officials said the law's requirements were hampering training. Stalemate continued on the debate over global warming, although new reports suggested the problem was a real and dangerous one for society to face.

Energy Policy

An overhaul of national energy policy came close to approval in the 108th Congress but once again eluded lawmakers as it had in the 107th Congress. A vast omnibus bill was approved by both chambers and even made its way through conference and final House action. But Republican leaders, who wrote the final bill in secret, could not break a Senate filibuster supported by some members of their party.

The bill was laden with controversy, none more contentious than that which pitted advocates of more production of energy supplies against groups that argued for increased emphasis on conservation. But there were many other sections that focused on regional interests, raised fears of water pollution from a chemical fuel additive, and showed deep philosophical differences over deregulation of electricity generation and delivery.

Most of the action occurred in 2003, but the final burial did not occur until late in the following year, even though certain tax provisions did become law in another piece of legislation. The omnibus energy bill was based largely on a national energy policy that President George W. Bush had announced in 2001. The $31.1 billion omnibus bill (HR 6) that Congress acted on in 2003 contained generous tax subsidies for energy producers, particularly the oil, gas, coal, nuclear, and ethanol industries. It proposed an overhaul of the nation's electricity laws aimed at attracting private investment for power plants and transmission lines and at better coordinating the use of power grids to prevent blackouts.

With Republicans in control of the White House and, once again, of both chambers of Congress, the administration and party leaders began 2003 confident that the legislation, one of Bush's top domestic priorities, could be enacted. Congress had failed to complete a similar energy bill in 2002 after conference negotiations collapsed, but the Senate was under Democratic control then. *(2001–2002 action, p. 412)*

The House moved swiftly in 2003, passing a bill on April 11 that closely tracked the business-friendly recommendations of a 2001 White House energy task force led by Vice President Dick Cheney. But problems in the Senate foreshadowed the bill's demise in that chamber later in the year. In March the Senate struck at the core of Bush's energy plan by dropping language from its version of the fiscal 2004 budget resolution (S Con Res 23) that would have required only a simple majority to approve drilling for oil and gas in Alaska's Arctic National Wildlife Refuge (ANWR). Without such a change any proposal to open ANWR required sixty votes to break a Democratic filibuster that was certain to occur. *(Budget resolution, p. 67)*

Four months later, unable to resolve a bitter partisan deadlock over several features of their energy bill, Senate leaders agreed, as a way to get to conference with the House, to scrap the attempt and substitute language from the energy bill that Senate Democrats had written in 2002.

The legislation gained momentum during the August recess when a massive power blackout affected 50 million Americans and Canadians. Images of New York City plunged

In their opposition to oil drilling in Alaska's Artic National Wildlife Refuge (ANWR), Democrats, including Sen. Debbie Stabenow of Michigan, emphasized conservation and renewable energy sources over increased petroleum drilling. Republicans argued that increasing domestic production of oil and gas was a matter of national security. *Source: Congressional Quarterly/Scott J. Ferrell*

into darkness underscored problems with the nation's power grids. Sen. Pete V. Domenici, R-N.M., who chaired the House-Senate conference on the bill, and Billy Tauzin, R-La., the lead House negotiator, convened negotiations in early September with the hope of delivering a bill to Bush by Thanksgiving. In a move that enraged Democrats, GOP leaders negotiated the bill's major provisions in private.

Republicans turned out to be anything but unified, and the conference negotiations dragged on for ten weeks. The measure was stalled by regional disagreements over federal electricity regulation and requirements for the use of ethanol—a corn-based additive for gasoline—and later by disputes over the bill's tax package, which was negotiated separately by Congress's two lead tax writers, Sen. Charles E. Grassley, R-Iowa, and Rep. Bill Thomas, R-Calif.

Intervention by Cheney, Senate Majority Leader Bill Frist, R-Tenn., and House Speaker J. Dennis Hastert, R-Ill., finally settled the disputes, and the Republican conferees approved a final bill by Nov. 17. The House adopted the conference report the following day.

But the bill still faced obstacles in the Senate. Mindful that he needed sixty votes to ward off a filibuster, Domenici had included a generous mandate to more than double the production of ethanol to win support from Democrats in the Midwest, including Minority Leader Tom Daschle of South Dakota. Republican leaders also agreed to drop a House ANWR drilling provision from the bill. It was not enough. Opponents complained that the bill focused only on energy production and did not address rising consumption. Fiscal conservatives said its $25.7 billion tax package was excessive. Lawmakers from the Northeast were upset that a plan to give the Federal Energy Regulatory Commission (FERC) more control over power transmission lines would be delayed until 2007.

However, the issue that most galvanized opposition to the bill was a liability waiver for producers of methyl-tertiary-butyl-ether (MTBE), a fuel additive that, like ethanol, made gasoline burn more cleanly but that had been found to contaminate groundwater. *(MTBE background, Congress and the Nation Vol. X, p. 390)*

MTBE was produced largely in Gulf Coast states, and Tauzin and House Majority Leader Tom DeLay, R-Texas, insisted on the liability waiver. Other lawmakers, especially from the Northeast, feared the waiver would leave their taxpayers with the bill for cleaning up MTBE contamination. In the end, a half-dozen Republican senators, all but one from the Northeast, voted to support a filibuster led by New York Democrat Charles E. Schumer. Last-minute intervention by Bush failed to persuade DeLay to drop the MTBE waiver. Two votes short of invoking cloture, Frist announced that the bill would be put off until early 2004.

HOUSE COMMITTEE ACTION

The House energy bill was assembled from legislation approved by four separate committees.

• The Energy and Commerce Committee April 3, 2003, approved an omnibus bill (HR 1644—H Rept 108-65) by a vote of 36–17 that included provisions on oil, gas, and coal production; alternative fuels; conservation; and electricity regulation.

• The Ways and Means Committee April 3 approved $18.7 billion in energy tax breaks (HR 1531—H Rept 108-67) by a vote of 24–12. The tax package was scaled back considerably from the $33.5 billion proposed in the 2001 House bill. The bill emphasized incentives for traditional oil and gas production and for maintaining the existing electricity infrastructure, although it allocated more than a third of the tax benefits, or $6.7 billion, for alternative fuels and conservation.

• The Science Committee April 2 gave voice vote approval to a $31.7 billion energy research and development bill (HR 238—H Rept 108-128). The bill included $1.8 billion for Bush's hydrogen research initiative, which had the goal of developing a hydrogen-fueled vehicle by 2020.

• The Resources Committee April 2 voted 32–14 to approve provisions that would encourage energy development on public lands and allow oil and gas exploration in ANWR. An attempt by Edward J. Markey, D-Mass., to delete the ANWR provision was rejected 17–27.

When combined, the provisions resulted in a bill that was quite similar to the measure the House had passed in 2001, with an emphasis on greater domestic energy production including drilling in ANWR. The main difference was the inclusion this time of a controversial section on electricity deregulation. *(2001 action, p. 425)*

Energy and Commerce Chair Tauzin and Joe L. Barton, R-Texas, chair of the panel's Subcommittee on Air Quality, negotiated behind the scenes with FERC Chair Patrick Wood III to fashion a compromise on state and federal regulation of electricity markets and transmission.

Investor-owned utility groups, such as the Edison Electric Institute, wanted Congress to open all electricity markets to free competition and favored a plan by FERC to create a nationwide structure for wholesale electricity markets with regional networks that would coordinate power supplies and ensure reliability. EEI said it would attract investment, expand electricity transmission capacity, and ultimately bring down prices for all consumers.

But states that regulated electricity as a monopoly argued that local power companies should be rewarded for their high capital investments with protection for their markets. Small independent utilities, rural cooperatives, and municipal power companies that were not major players in interstate power transmission also opposed being put under FERC control. Under the compromise, FERC would be allowed to go ahead with plans to create the "Standard Market Design." But states would retain the authority to regulate retail electricity systems, such as cooperatives, whose customers had been guaranteed reliable supplies of power at fixed prices.

The new language mollified Charlie Norwood, R-Ga., a leader in efforts to block the FERC rule altogether, although he said he would like the bill to state explicitly that FERC had no power to regulate the retail sale of electricity, traditionally the role of state authorities.

HOUSE FLOOR ACTION

The House passed the package, which had been introduced as a new bill (HR 6), by a vote of 247–175 on April 11. Republicans headed off several Democratic attempts to remove some of the bill's most controversial provisions. During the floor debate the House rejected 193–237 an attempt by John D. Dingell of Michigan, ranking Democrat on the Energy and Commerce Committee, to replace the electricity deregulation provisions with a substitute that would have expanded FERC's antifraud powers and retained regulations that limited a utility company's market power and ability to manipulate prices. The House adopted 226–202 an amendment by Heather A. Wilson, R-N.M., to limit the surface area of oil company operations in ANWR to 2,000 acres. The amendment applied to surface covered by "production and support facilities, including airstrips and any acres covered by gravel berms or piers for support of pipelines." It did not mention road networks. It also rejected 197–228 another attempt by Markey to eliminate the ANWR authorization from the bill, and 162–268 an amendment by Sherwood Boehlert, R-N.Y., to require that by 2010 cars and light trucks consume 5 percent less gasoline than allowed under average fuel economy standards for 2004.

SENATE COMMITTEE ACTION

The Senate Energy and Natural Resources Committee approved its energy bill 13–10 on April 30 (S 1005—S Rept 108-43). The measure was then introduced as a new bill (S 14). The tax component, a $15.7 billion package of energy tax credits, was approved 18–2 by the Finance Committee on April 2, 2003 (S 597, S 1149—S Rept 108-54).

Democrats were largely shut out of writing the measure, as they had been in the House. Mary L. Landrieu of Louisiana, who won approval of a pair of amendments important to her state, was the only committee Democrat who voted for the Senate bill. Domenici got the bill through five days of markups held over the course of a month partly by avoiding contentious issues, such as ethanol and MTBE, and calling for party unity on others. The biggest differences between the Senate and House bills were over ANWR and electricity deregulation. Domenici left ANWR provisions out of his bill because he did not have the sixty votes needed to prevent a filibuster when the measure reached the floor.

On electricity Domenici cut through concerns from southern and western senators about a FERC usurpation of state authority over regional electricity markets by offering a provision requiring the commission to rewrite its Standard Market Design rule and delaying any orders related to the rule until July 1, 2005.

Domenici had scheduled time to debate a bipartisan amendment by Jim Talent, R-Mo., that would have doubled the mandate for use of renewable fuel to 5 billion gallons per year by 2012 to meet Clean Air Act requirements. But the amendment also included a four-year ban on the use of MTBE. Many Democrats expressed concern that the MTBE ban would drive up gas prices in states forced to use other fuel additives to meet requirements of the Clean Air Act. Because ethanol, which was produced mostly in the Midwest, was the most likely alternative, the coastal states had the most to lose. Dianne Feinstein, D-Calif., was waiting with more than forty amendments to block Talent's proposal. "She did that last year, and she'll do it again on the floor," a staff member said. Talent's amendment was dropped.

The committee rejected 11–12 a proposal by Jeff Binga-man, D-N.M., to include a renewable-fuels standard to require utilities to generate 10 percent of their electricity using wind, solar, or other alternative power sources by 2020. His amendment included a credit trading system that industries could use instead of having to pay government fees for missing the targets. It provided more time for utilities to meet the targets than had a similar provision in the 2002 bill. Republicans said the shift to renewables should be left to the free market.

The committee adopted without objection an amendment by freshman Lisa Murkowski, R-Alaska, to authorize a federal loan guarantee for a proposed Alaska natural gas pipeline of as much as $18 billion or 80 percent of the pipeline's estimated costs.

SENATE FLOOR ACTION

The Senate passed HR 6 by a vote of 84–14 on July 31 after substituting the text of its 2002 bill. The vote concluded an extraordinary turnabout after Minority Leader Daschle went to the floor and told Frist he should revive the Democrats' bill that had passed 88–11 the previous year if Republicans were serious about wanting to deliver energy legislation to the White House. Domenici said he had floated that very idea to Frist a week before but nobody pursued it. But when it came up on the floor Frist told Daschle: "If we have the opportunity to take that bill up as suggested by the Democratic leader, let's do it. Let's pass it today, and then we can move on." They left the floor to negotiate.

Frist, who had already given up on completing the Senate bill before the August recess as he had promised, seemed relieved at the outcome. The Senate had been debating and amending the Republican bill intermittently since May 6. Republicans made no secret that the move was simply the fastest way to get to conference, where they planned to completely rewrite the bill.

Before setting the Republican energy bill aside, senators voted on a host of amendments that demonstrated sentiment in the chamber on various energy issues. The Senate:

• Adopted 67–29 an amendment by Frist to require gasoline refineries to use 5 billion gallons of ethanol or other alternative renewable fuels annually by 2012 and phase out the use of MTBE. Before adopting Frist's amendment, the Senate rejected repeated attempts by Democrats from California and New York to create various exemptions from the ethanol requirement based on geography, a state demonstrating its ability to comply with the Clean Air Act, or evidence that the requirement would cause a precipitous rise in the cost of gasoline.

• Narrowly rejected 48–50 an attempt by Ron Wyden, D-Ore., to strike a package of loan guarantees for new nuclear power plants, combined with an Energy Department program to buy electricity from those plants. The nuclear power financing was a top priority for Domenici.

• Rejected 32–65 an attempt by Richard J. Durbin, D-Ill., to require an increase in corporate average fuel economy (CAFE) standards. Pre-2006 model year passenger cars would have to average twenty-five miles per gallon (mpg), rising to forty mpg by model year 2015. Nonpassenger vehicles would have to increase from an average of seventeen mpg for pre-2006 models to twenty-seven and one-half mpg for model year 2015 vehicles.

• Rejected 48–50 an amendment by Maria Cantwell, D-Wash., to revise the Federal Power Act to deem a long list of power trading practices as neither just nor reasonable under rate-setting rules, and to direct FERC to bar power sales by any company found to knowingly manipulate markets. Cantwell argued that killing PUHCA without substituting other regulation was a mistake, especially in light of revelations about energy market manipulations by Enron Corp. "We repeal the only consumer protection law that has been on the books since 1935, and in place put some language that basically . . . doesn't have any teeth in it," she said.

• Tabled (killed) 54–44 an amendment by Bingaman that would have allowed FERC to issue orders related to its Standard Market Design before July 1, 2005, while prohibiting the commission from establishing the actual rule before that time.

CONFERENCE, FINAL ACTION

Domenici and Tauzin opened the conference on the bill almost as soon as Congress returned from an August recess, with promises to have it on Bush's desk by Thanksgiving. Domenici made it clear he intended to use his bill (S 14) as a starting point in negotiations, rather than the Senate-passed Democratic bill. He said he and Tauzin would avoid "weeks of squabbling" in formal conference meetings by negotiating and writing the bill themselves, releasing it section by section to other conferees for their comment and amendment. Thomas and Grassley held parallel talks on the tax provisions.

By negotiating much of the bill behind closed doors, Domenici and Tauzin infuriated Democrats and put themselves in the position of needing rock-solid support from Republican conferees to guarantee a conference majority. That was risky in the Senate, where Republican conferees outnumbered Democrats by just one vote, seven to six. The need for every GOP vote in conference gave huge leverage to individual Republican conferees.

Domenici also had to consider the Senate as a whole, constructing a bill that could get the sixty votes needed to stop a filibuster. Further complicating the task, some of the most difficult issues in conference—the electricity, MTBE, and ethanol provisions, for example—were not partisan but regional.

The major issues in conference included:

Electricity markets. The Aug. 14, 2003, blackout gave new urgency to the electricity section of the bill, but regional differences held up a final agreement. Sens. Rick Santorum,

R-Pa., and Edward M. Kennedy, D-Mass., along with other lawmakers from the Northeast and Midwest hit by the blackout wanted FERC to immediately implement its Standard Market Design rules for selling electricity on the wholesale market. FERC also wanted authority to force local utilities to join regional networks that would coordinate power supplies and enforce reliability rules.

But Sens. Trent Lott, R-Miss., and Richard C. Shelby, R-Ala., along with other lawmakers from the Southeast and Pacific Northwest where electricity was relatively abundant and cheap, said the plan would usurp local authority and force their constituents to pay higher rates to subsidize regions that had not adequately invested in power infrastructure. Lott said the fact that his state had lower rates helped it attract new industry. "That gives us a distinct advantage, and we ain't giving it up," he said. To get the bill to conference, Domenici had promised Lott and Shelby that he would support a three-year delay of FERC's proposed rule. But Lott wanted the bill to make clear that FERC could not require state power companies to participate in regional transmission organizations.

In the end, the bill directed FERC to reconsider its proposed Standard Market Design rule and prohibited the rule from taking effect before 2007. It encouraged, but did not require, local power companies to join the RTOs. It also guaranteed utilities that they could protect consumers who had been guaranteed reliable supplies at fixed prices.

Transmission lines. Another holdup was Lott's insistence that new power companies be directly assessed for the cost of building or upgrading the power lines they used, a practice known as participant funding. Lott said it was unfair for local customers to pay the cost for electric companies that were building plants along the Gulf Coast to sell to customers in the North. Critics said the proposal would help incumbent utilities ward off competition and discourage the construction of new power plants, but much of Lott's plan was incorporated in the conference report.

The National Governors Association fought a proposal in the House bill to give FERC broad authority to override states on the construction of new interstate power lines. If state regulators did not approve an application to build or modify an electric line in an "interstate congestion area" within a year FERC could step in and issue the permit. The governors and their allies argued that the provision would create a "national zoning board" that could override legitimate decisions for holding up permits, such as public safety or environmental concerns.

However, conferees retained the provision.

MTBE. One of the biggest stumbling blocks in conference concerned MTBE, an ethanol competitor as well as a groundwater pollutant. The dispute pitted Daschle, Grassley, and other lawmakers from ethanol-producing states against Tauzin, DeLay, and others from the Gulf states where MTBE was produced. More than half the nation's MTBE producers had operations in DeLay's home state, Texas, and the industry was a major source of his campaign contributions.

Tauzin and DeLay wanted to allow the states to decide whether to outlaw MTBE, and they demanded a broad liability waiver to protect producers of the additive. Grassley and Daschle demanded a federally mandated phaseout of MTBE and opposed a liability waiver. The waiver also was strongly opposed by senators from the Northeast, who feared their states could be forced to pay for the cost of cleaning up sites contaminated by MTBE. New York's Schumer escalated the dispute on Oct. 8 by threatening to filibuster the conference report if it included the liability waiver.

DeLay and Tauzin won a liability waiver in the final bill. The measure banned the use of MTBE, but not until 2015; however, states could continue to ban it sooner. The conference agreement also eliminated the requirement in existing law that set a minimum oxygen content for gasoline sold in high pollution areas.

Ethanol. Conferees remained hung up for weeks over the ethanol provisions. The dispute involved not only whether to mandate increased use of ethanol but also how to structure ethanol tax subsidies. That, in turn, linked the debate to highway funding. The issue pitted the oil industry against agribusiness, states against the federal government, and the Midwest against both coasts. *(2002 action, p. 417)*

Midwesterner Daschle insisted that the bill require refiners to more than double their use of ethanol within seven years to 5 billion gallons a year. That was one year faster than a timetable passed by the Senate and four years faster than a mandate in the House energy bill. "I will oppose this legislation if ethanol isn't written as we think it ought to be, as the Senate passed it," Daschle threatened. Coastal-state lawmakers strongly objected. "Forcing states to use ethanol they do not need and forcing states to pay for ethanol they do not use amounts to a transfer of wealth from all states to the Midwest corn states," Feinstein said during Senate debate on the bill. House Republicans backed a broad exemption that would allow states to opt out if the mandate would cause them economic harm. The final bill required 5 billion gallons a year by 2012, three years faster than the House plan.

Meanwhile, Grassley also was fighting for a change in the tax on gasohol, a blend of ethanol and gasoline. Gasohol was taxed at 5.2-cents-a-gallon less than gasoline to offset the greater expense of producing the cleaner burning fuel. Grassley and Daschle wanted to eliminate that differential, which would increase revenue to the Highway Trust Fund, and instead give gasohol blenders a tax credit based on the volume of ethanol they used.

The proposal had strong support from proponents of highway funding. Daschle gathered signatures of twenty-nine senators, including sixteen Republicans, on a letter to Domenici and Tauzin that insisted that it be included in the conference report. Don Young, R-Alaska, chair of the House Transportation and Infrastructure Committee, agreed.

ETHANOL CAUSED REGIONAL DISPUTES

One big obstacle to completing the 2004 omnibus energy bill was ethanol—how it was used, taxed, and subsidized. The heart of the debate was neither energy policy nor environmental protection but money—who would make it and who stood to lose it.

Ethanol was a grain alcohol distilled almost entirely from the sugars in corn grown in the Midwest. When added to gasoline—10 percent was the most common blend—the mixture was called gasohol, and the ethanol raised the oxygen level to help the fuel burn more completely. In an automotive engine, that meant lower emissions of carbon monoxide and the volatile organic compounds that form ozone.

The small ethanol industry in the Midwest received a major boost with amendments to the 1990 Clean Air Act (PL 101–549) that required urban areas across the country to add oxygen to their motor fuels because their air quality exceeded national standards for carbon monoxide and ozone. Urban areas in the Midwest turned to ethanol produced in the region; those on the coasts began using methyl-tertiary-butyl-ether (MTBE), an oxygenate made from petroleum products that was cheaper and easier to transport because ethanol could not be shipped through petroleum pipelines. Use of MTBE in the 1990s was more than double that of ethanol. When the additive was found to be a source of water pollution, however, some states began to ban its use.

The main problem with ethanol, even in the Midwest, was that it cost more than gasoline to produce. Even some environmentalists, who otherwise supported using ethanol because it reduced emissions and came from a sustainable energy source, worried that the production process might consume more energy and produce more pollution than was saved by ethanol use. Congress's solution to the price problem was to subsidize ethanol to make it competitive. Rather than the excise tax paid on gasoline of 18.4 cents per gallon, Congress set the gasohol tax at 13.2 cents—a 5.2 cent exemption that those who blended the fuel collected right away.

In addition, small ethanol producers could qualify for an income tax credit of 10 cents a gallon for pure ethanol. At least twenty states in the Midwest had also enacted their own subsidies. The result was a steady growth in ethanol use from about 660 million gallons in 1996 to 1.1 billion gallons in 2002 and the construction of more ethanol plants. An estimated 10 percent of the nation's 10-billion-bushel corn crop was being used for ethanol, a particularly important factor with corn prices low.

Unpopular Subsidies

Critics of the ethanol subsidy said that instead of helping farmers it really helped the corporations that distilled the grain alcohol, including the largest, Illinois-based Archer Daniels Midland Co., which owned a third of all ethanol production capacity. The subsidies also were unpopular with state highway officials and road builders. Not only was there a lower federal tax for gasohol, but 2.5 cents per gallon of that tax went to the U.S. Treasury as a regular tax revenue rather than to the Highway Trust Fund to build roads. As a result, gasohol contributed about half as much as gasoline did to the trust fund.

For some time there had been talk of doing away with ethanol subsidies. Republican Bill Archer of Texas (1971–2001), former chair of the House Ways and Means Committee, wanted to get rid of the subsidies in the late 1990s. House and Senate committees looking for a way to increase highway spending in a new surface transportation bill considered redirecting at least some of the money to the Highway Trust Fund. (Congress in 2004 did pass some tax provisions favorable to ethanol.) *(Ethanol tax breaks, p. 432)*

Still, the existing arrangement might have continued undisturbed except for the discovery in 1995 that MTBE was contaminating groundwater in many parts of the country where it had been in use. The choice for states where MTBE was being used was either to switch to ethanol or persuade Congress and the administration to lift the oxygen-additive requirements of the Clean Air Act. Some states who wanted to relax the rules argued that more advanced engines and gasoline blends could produce lower emissions without using an oxygen additive.

California, in particular, argued that ethanol produced in the Midwest would be exorbitantly expensive on the West Coast. The state's lobbying for a temporary waiver of the Clean Air requirements energized the ethanol industry and corn growers who launched a lobbying campaign to require the use of ethanol. However, Congress deadlocked over the liability protection for MTBE groundwater pollution, blocking enactment of the omnibus energy legislation in 2004. *(Energy policy, pp. 412, 425)*

But Thomas refused, saying the provision belonged in the surface transportation reauthorization bill that would be written in 2004. A senior House Republican said Thomas said privately he needed to keep the ethanol tax changes in his pocket to use as a bargaining chip to fight off proposals for a 5-cent increase in the gasoline tax in 2004.

The dispute between Grassley and Thomas grew into such a problem for the conference that Cheney intervened on Nov. 5 to broker a deal. The compromise included both the ethanol excise tax credit and the 5.2-cents-per-gallon tax exemption, giving blenders a choice until the surface transportation bill was enacted.

ANWR. Domenici and Tauzin released a draft of the bill on Sept. 22 that allowed oil and gas drilling in ANWR, and they announced they would fight to include it in the final legislation. But Domenici made it clear that his commitment was strictly rhetorical as long as he lacked the sixty votes to overcome a filibuster. The provision was not in the final bill.

Tax subsidies. The Grassley-Thomas fight over gasohol was one of many disputes between the two tax writers that held up the conference report for weeks. Both sides agreed to a tax package costing about $16 billion over ten years. But Thomas wanted to narrow or delay Senate proposals for tax subsidies for technology to produce cleaner-burning coal, a new generation of automobiles powered by electricity, and clean fuels such as hydrogen and natural gas, and a Senate proposal for tradable tax credits for tax-exempt utilities that used renewable fuels. Grassley argued behind the scenes that Thomas was pushing tax breaks for oil companies important to his district. Grassley and other senior senators sharply criticized tax breaks in the bill for operators of wells that contained viscous, or heavy, oil, a common commodity in Thomas' district.

Another dispute concerned the Senate provision to provide tax incentives for the proposed $20 billion Alaska natural gas pipeline. The tax breaks, which would kick in if the market price of natural gas declined below a benchmark, were opposed by House leaders and the administration.

As the weeks dragged on, Frist and Hastert periodically intervened to try to loosen the gridlock, freeing up individual provisions. Failure to get the bill out of conference would have been a major embarrassment for the two leaders. "If we don't pass an energy bill this year, ultimately it will be the fault of Republicans, not Democrats," said Tauzin's spokesperson, Ken Johnson. "We'll have no one to blame but ourselves."

By November, a worried White House stepped up pressure for a settlement. "Resolve your differences," Bush told lawmakers during an Oct. 30 speech in Ohio. "Understand that if you're interested in people finding a job, we need an energy policy." Energy Secretary Spencer Abraham was dispatched to Capitol Hill, and Cheney consulted with Frist, Hastert, Grassley, and Thomas. On Nov. 5, Cheney stepped in to resolve the seemingly intractable dispute between Grassley and Thomas over the formula for taxing gasohol.

But the two tax writers continued to squabble over other provisions with no end in sight. Finally, with Thanksgiving approaching and most other issues close to resolution, Frist and Hastert dispatched aides to take control of the final tax negotiations and cut deals on the remaining sticking points. "It's done," Domenici said afterward. "They took over these four or five issues. If it's got some things in it that are not perfect, then I'm sorry, but it's done." After ten weeks of wrangling and cajoling, the conference report (H Rept 108-375) was filed on Nov. 18.

The House adopted the conference report Nov. 18 by a vote of 246–180. But an attempt by Frist to invoke cloture and end a filibuster of the bill in the Senate failed Nov. 21 on **a key vote of 57–40 (R 44–7; D 13–32; I 0–1).** Frist switched his vote to "no" in a procedural move that allowed him to offer a motion to reconsider, meaning GOP leaders needed to change only two votes to win cloture. *(2003 key votes, p. 837)*

During the House debate Democrats attacked the bill as a giveaway to the oil, coal, gas, and nuclear industries that would weaken environmental and consumer protections. "This ... is the worst bill to come before Congress in a generation," said Markey, a twenty-seven-year House veteran. But 46 House Democrats joined 200 Republicans in support of the measure, more than offsetting 25 Republican defections.

All eyes, however, were already on the Senate, where Schumer was making good on his filibuster threat. Domenici had banked on the ethanol provisions to secure the support of Daschle and other midwesterners, and the bill was filled with scores of other provisions to win over individual senators. The strategy helped. Daschle handled the issue gingerly, saying he "reluctantly" supported the bill and voted to end debate even as a majority of Democrats voted to sustain a filibuster. In all, thirteen Democrats, mostly from oil-producing states or the Farm Belt, voted in favor of limiting debate and forcing a final vote on the bill.

But in the end it was not enough to offset a determined band of six GOP senators: five from the Northeast, plus John McCain of Arizona, who criticized the billions of dollars in proposed subsidies to the oil, gas, coal, nuclear, and ethanol industries and dozens of smaller interests.

For the northeasterners—Judd Gregg and John E. Sununu of New Hampshire, Olympia J. Snowe and Susan Collins of Maine, and Lincoln Chafee of Rhode Island—the breaking point was the MTBE waiver. Gregg and Sununu were particularly outraged that the waiver was retroactive to Sept. 5, which would wipe out a lawsuit their state had filed Oct. 6 against twenty-two oil companies over MTBE contamination. The U.S. Conference of Mayors had estimated that it would cost $29 billion overall to clean up water systems and homes contaminated by MTBE.

Despite three days of lobbying by the leadership, not one senator agreed to switch sides. Domenici, who at first defended the MTBE waiver, decided it had to go. "At the end, the president personally tried to get the House to support the MTBE removal," Domenici said later. "He made the call at our request to DeLay."

But DeLay refused to back down. "We don't see any reason to give way to the trial lawyers just because a minority in the Senate wants to filibuster the bill," said DeLay spokesperson Stuart Roy.

Had the cloture motion succeeded, opponents had a backup plan. Gregg said he had lined up several lawmakers who voted for cloture to support a budgetary point of order against the legislation because its cost would violate the fiscal 2004 budget resolution. "We actually had a lot more than six

[Republican votes]," Gregg said. "They were fortunate that they lost the cloture motion, and I explained that to [Frist] and he understood. If they had won the cloture motion we would have killed the bill on a point of order."

Energy Tax Provisions

With the failure of Congress to complete the omnibus energy bill, HR 6, lawmakers began an urgent search for other vehicles to which they could attach important energy tax provisions that were included in the larger bill. They settled on two pieces of legislation that were certain to pass: a family tax bill (HR 1308) and a corporate tax bill (HR 4520). *(Omnibus energy bill, p. 425)*

FAMILY TAX BILL

The first vehicle used to enact energy-related pieces stuck in HR 6 was a bill (HR 1308) extending individual income tax credits for five years. This high-profile legislation also was seen as all but guaranteed to clear Congress before adjournment.

Energy provisions were added in conference at the urging of Sen. Charles Grassley (R-Iowa), who also was head of the conference committee and chair of the Senate Finance Committee. One provision extended for a year the tax credit for electricity produced from wind, biomass, and poultry waste. (This extension was subsequently mooted by the addition and expansion of the credit in the corporate tax bill.) Other provisions extended accelerated depreciation of business property on Native American reservations (which affected mineral rights), continued suspension through 2005 of a limitation on percentage depletion for oil and gas from marginal wells, and postponed through 2005 a phaseout of deductions for qualified clean-fuel vehicles and electric vehicles and related property.

President George W. Bush signed HR 1308 on Oct. 4, 2004 (PL 108-311).

CORPORATE TAX BILL

HR 4520 was legislation to end an international trade dispute between the United States and the European Union that grew out of a ruling by the World Trade Organization that provisions in the U.S. tax code were an illegal subsidy for American companies under world trade rules. As a result, European countries were authorized to increase tariffs on an array of U.S. goods, creating significant domestic pressure for repeal of the U.S. tax subsidy provisions. Some members of Congress decided HR 4520 was a good vehicle for the energy tax riders.

Provisions added to HR 4520 benefited energy companies through two general business provisions. Industries engaged in resource extraction were to get a lower income tax rate, and oil companies benefited from a lower tax rate on foreign earnings for multinational companies.

Midwestern members also saw that ethanol got favorable treatment in the bill. Ethanol is a corn-based fuel additive that is important to the Midwest region. Provisions extended existing alcohol fuels income tax credits through 2010, repealed a long-standing excise tax subsidy for ethanol-blended fuels, expanded the small ethanol producer tax credit, and established a new tax credit for biodiesel fuel through 2006. Other tax incentives were included for the oil and gas industry, electric utilities, nuclear energy, coal producers, petroleum refiners, and brownfields demonstration projects.

The largest energy tax break involved a production tax credit that encouraged electric generation from renewable energy sources. The tax credit already in the law applied to a variety of production such as wind, poultry waste, and others. The provisions extended the tax advantages to additional forms of renewable energy generation including municipal solid waste (including landfill gas), geothermal, solar, and others. These changes were estimated to cost the government about $2.3 billion in revenues over their life.

President Bush signed HR 4520 on Oct. 22, 2004 (PL 108-357).

ANWR Drilling Ban

Controversy continued to swirl around proposals to drill for petroleum in a section of Alaska that environmentalists said was too fragile for exploration. The major vote on the issue came when the Senate removed language in the fiscal 2004 budget resolution intended to give procedural protection to legislation authorizing oil drilling in part of Alaska's Arctic National Wildlife Refuge (ANWR). *(Budget resolution, p. 67)*

President George W. Bush's energy plan, first released in 2001, focused largely on increasing domestic production of oil, gas, and coal to reduce the nation's dependence on foreign oil. A main element of Bush's plan was oil drilling in ANWR, a remote area on Alaska's northeastern coast. But efforts in the 107th Congress to authorize drilling were blocked in the Senate by environmentalists who argued that it would harm wildlife in the refuge. Supporters of the plan countered that it would provide a new source of energy and create hundreds of thousands of jobs.

After an attempt to break a Democratic filibuster mustered just forty-six votes in 2002, Republican leaders tried a new approach in the 108th Congress. They sought to sidestep a filibuster by including a provision in the Senate version of the budget resolution (S Con Res 23) to provide de facto authority for oil drilling in ANWR by assuming that federal royalties from energy leases in the refuge would produce $2.1 billion in fiscal 2004 revenue. Revenue and spending provisions in the budget resolution are protected from filibusters. *(2001–2002 action, p. 412)*

GOP leaders then set about winning the simple majority needed to keep the language from being stripped from the resolution. They targeted four senators they thought might be wavering: Arkansas Democrats Mark Pryor and Blanche Lincoln, and Republicans Gordon H. Smith of Oregon and Norm Coleman of Minnesota. But all four ultimately voted against allowing ANWR drilling.

On March 19, 2003, the Senate in a **key vote of 52–48 (R 8–43; D 43–5; I 1–0)** adopted an amendment by Barbara Boxer, D-Calif., stripping the ANWR language from the budget resolution. *(2003 key votes, p. 837)*

The vote was a major setback for the White House and Alaska Republican Ted Stevens, chair of the Appropriations Committee and a leading supporter of ANWR drilling. "People who vote against this today are voting against me, and I will not forget it," Stevens said.

GOP leaders, at the urging of the White House, continued to press for ANWR drilling. The House included a provision that would authorize drilling when it passed its version of the omnibus energy bill (HR 6) in April. That language was included in an early House-Senate conference committee draft of the legislation, but the move was mostly symbolic. As expected, House and Senate leaders agreed to remove the language from the final energy bill after failing to secure the sixty votes needed to shut down a promised Democratic filibuster in the Senate. The energy bill ultimately was stalled by a filibuster over a liability waiver for a fuel additive. *(Energy bill, pp. 412, 425)*

New Mexico Republican Pete V. Domenici, chair of the Energy and Natural Resources Committee, said the March vote was the Republicans' best chance to pass ANWR. "We lost it and we could have won it," Domenici said.

Forest Thinning, Clearing

Congress reached agreement in late 2003 on legislation designed to reduce the risk of wildfires by thinning and removing debris on up to 20 million acres of national forest. The measure, signed into law on Dec. 3 (HR 1904—PL 108-148), was based on a "Healthy Forests" initiative promoted by President George W. Bush, although it was modified substantially to win bipartisan support in Congress. The legislation relaxed environmental requirements and provided an accelerated judicial review process for forest-thinning projects aimed at protecting communities, drinking-water supplies, and critical habitat. *(1990s action, Congress and the Nation Vol. X, p. 368)*

Bush made the forests initiative one of two principal environmental goals, visiting several national forests in August to pressure Congress to act. His other environmental initiative, air pollution legislation dubbed Clear Skies, went nowhere during 2003. *(Clear Skies, p. 437)*

BACKGROUND

Bush announced his Healthy Forests initiative in August 2002. Wildfires had been particularly serious in 2000 and

2002, and there was widespread agreement that excessive vegetation such as undergrowth, dead trees, and debris left after logging fueled them. To encourage the removal of this growth, Bush proposed to limit and expedite environmental and judicial reviews for forest-thinning projects.

Supporters of Bush's approach argued that rigorous environmental reviews required under the 1969 National Environmental Policy Act (PL 91-190), including the analysis of alternative approaches, delayed efforts to remove the undergrowth and contributed to wildfires. The U.S. Forest Service and the Bureau of Land Management (BLM) typically analyzed three to five alternatives to each forest-thinning project, including the option of inaction, a process that could take several years.

Most Democrats agreed that some clearing and thinning was necessary, but they wanted to concentrate on areas near human habitation while allowing nature to take its course in remote regions. Without such restrictions, they argued, timber companies would concentrate on deeper forest areas with larger and more profitable trees. Environmental groups contended that delays because of environmental rules were exaggerated; some claimed that a main objective of the legislation was to give timber companies easier access to federal land.

A General Accounting Office study released May 14, requested by the Senate Energy and Natural Resources Committee's top Democrat, Jeff Bingaman of New Mexico, found that 24 percent of all wildfire prevention projects were appealed on environmental or judicial grounds in fiscal 2001 and 2002. When calculating the percentage of "appealable" projects, which were those that were not categorically excluded from the requirement to prepare an environmental impact statement, the percentage appealed jumped to 59 percent. The study found that 79 percent of appeals were processed within ninety days.

Bush's wildfire prevention legislation was endorsed by a House committee in 2002. In the Senate, Republicans Pete V. Domenici of New Mexico and Larry E. Craig of Idaho sought to add key parts of the initiative to the fiscal 2003 Interior appropriations bill but eventually gave up in the face of a Democratic filibuster.

One of the more controversial pieces of Bush's plan, so-called stewardship contracting, was enacted in February 2003 as part of the fiscal 2003 omnibus appropriations package (PL 108-7), which included the Interior bill. It gave commercial logging companies increased opportunities to log on federal lands for ten years in exchange for removing excess vegetation and carrying out other activities aimed at preventing wildfires. HR 1904 was designed to implement the remainder of the president's plan by removing environmental and judicial obstacles to such projects.

In the previous five years, Interior appropriations had risen by one-third, largely because of firefighting demands. Congress appropriated $1 billion to battle wildfires in fiscal 2000 and $2 billion in fiscal 2003.

HOUSE ACTION

Three House committees approved pieces of Bush's proposal without amendment. The Resources Committee approved the measure 32–17 on April 30; the Agriculture Committee acted by voice vote May 8 (H Rept 108-96, Pt. 1); and the Judiciary Committee approved the judicial review provisions 18–13 on May 14 (H Rept 108-96, Pt. 2).

The resulting bill proposed that the Forest Service and BLM carry out thinning and removal of debris on up to 20 million acres of federal land. Priority would be given to projects that protected communities and watersheds but without specific boundaries. Agencies would be allowed to skip the study and development of alternative approaches required under the 1969 law before approving a forest-thinning project. Preliminary court injunctions against such projects would be limited to forty-five days, subject to renewal once the court had reviewed them. The House bill also contained language ordering the courts to give weight to recommendations from the secretaries of agriculture and interior.

In addition, the bill called for an accelerated program of assessments on up to 1,000 acres of forest at a high risk for bark beetle infestation that would allow agencies to proceed without stringent environmental analysis. Democrats and environmentalists claimed that the clause could permit "clear cutting" swaths of forest.

The House passed the bill May 20 by a vote of 256–170 with support from forty-two Democrats. Democrats were permitted to offer just one amendment, which was rejected 184–239. Offered by George Miller, D-Calif., the amendment would have stricken the insect research provision, restored full judicial and environmental reviews, and required that funding be concentrated on projects nearer to communities and watersheds.

SENATE ACTION

The Senate was deeply divided between Republicans who favored the White House's aggressive approach and Democrats and GOP moderates who supported thinning near houses and communities but opposed it in deeper parts of forests where the oldest and largest trees grow. The Senate Agriculture Committee approved the bill by voice vote with only a few changes after a brief session on July 24 (HR 1904—S Rept 108-121). But with no consensus in the Senate, the bill's future was uncertain. Neither the Agriculture bill nor alternatives offered by several other senators were thought to have the sixty votes necessary to overcome a filibuster. Both sides considered the Interior appropriations bill as a possible opportunity to debate changes in forest policy in the face of an otherwise busy Senate floor schedule, but that approach ran the same risk of a filibuster. Senators from western states bemoaned the fact that Congress repeatedly appropriated more money to fight wildfires and clean up afterward but seemed incapable of doing anything beforehand to prevent future fires.

A bipartisan group of senators, with White House participation, determined to break the stalemate worked out a compromise bill over six weeks that proponents thought could win a filibuster-proof majority. Pushed to action by wildfires in California that burned more than 750,000 acres, the Senate on Oct. 30 passed the revised measure, 80–14, with help from thirty Democrats. "The California wildfires have affected this debate in a dramatic fashion," said Ron Wyden, D-Ore.

The following compromises helped win votes from Democrats and GOP moderates:

Environmental reviews. The measure was less sweeping than the House version in proposing to limit environmental restrictions on forest-thinning projects. Instead of allowing an agency to review only the proposed project, as the House recommended, the Senate bill called for reviews of the proposed project, one alternative, and the effects of doing no thinning.

Judicial review. Under the Senate bill, preliminary court injunctions would be limited to sixty days, subject to renewal once the court had reviewed them, rather than forty-five days as in the House bill.

Priorities. The Senate bill stipulated that at least 50 percent of the money for forest thinning be spent in wildland-urban interface zones, defined as areas within a half-mile of communities thought to be at risk for wildfires. It also required that the Forest Service and BLM "fully maintain, or contribute toward the restoration" of old-growth trees. Neither provision was in the House bill.

CONFERENCE, FINAL ACTION

The central issues in conference, as throughout the year, were where to allow expedited forest thinning and how much to relax environmental restrictions. Environmentalists and their Democratic allies generally opposed the House bill, saying it was designed to help the timber industry. When an agreement was reached, the final bill incorporated much of the Senate compromise by focusing on the "wildland-urban interface" around inhabited areas and concentrating 50 percent of the funds there. However, the agreement expanded the definition to cover areas within 1.5 miles of at-risk communities, instead of 0.5 miles as recommended by the Senate. The final bill also kept the Senate requirement that federal agencies "fully maintain or contribute toward the restoration" of old-growth trees.

In a compromise on environmental reviews, the final bill required a single review for projects within 1.5 miles of a community that did not have its own plan. Beyond 1.5 miles, the conference report allowed additional reviews. The final bill also limited preliminary court injunctions against thinning projects to sixty days, subject to renewal once the court had reviewed them. However, it also kept House language aimed at discouraging appeals of lawsuits intended to stall forest-thinning projects by requiring those filing appeals to submit "specific written comments" during the public comment period on the project. Republicans said the provision would force litigants to work out their problems in earlier stages of the project's development.

The bill authorized $760 million a year for thinning, about twice as much as had been appropriated in recent years. House and Senate conferees reached agreement on Nov. 20. The House adopted the conference report (H Rept 108-386) on Nov. 21 by a vote of 286–140, and the Senate cleared the bill by voice vote later the same day.

MAJOR PROVISIONS

President Bush signed PL 108-148 on Dec. 3, 2003. The law contained the following provisions:

Forest-Thinning Projects

The law authorized the U.S. Forest Service and the BLM to carry out "hazardous fuel reduction projects" in "wildland-urban interface areas," defined as zones within 1.5 miles of at-risk communities that did not already have a plan of their own.

Reducing fuel. The law directed the BLM and the U.S. Forest Service to conduct "hazardous fuel reduction projects" on up to 20 million acres of federal land by thinning trees and reducing underbrush to reduce the severity of wildfires and the risk to inhabited areas. Depending on the site's ecology and the project's cost, the agencies could use fire and "various mechanical methods such as crushing, tractor and hand piling, thinning (to produce commercial or precommercial products), and pruning" to reduce forest fuel. The Forest Service and BLM were directed to track the number of acres burned in large wildfires and the degree of severity.

Priority areas. Priority for fuel reduction projects was given to wildland-urban interfaces, defined as land within a mile and a half of the boundary of a community at risk of wildfire, unless the community had its own wildfire protection plan; municipal watersheds that could be threatened by wildfire; forests that had been damaged by weather conditions or insect infestation; and forests where endangered species were at risk from wildfire.

Thinning projects were not to be carried out on federal lands that were part of the National Wilderness Preservation System, lands that were declared Wilderness Study Areas, or lands where the removal of vegetation was prohibited by federal law.

Funding authorization. The law authorized $760 million for forest-thinning projects, approximately twice as much as had been allocated in recent years. Half of whatever amount Congress appropriated had to be spent in the wildland-urban interface areas.

Old-growth trees. The BLM and the Forest Service were required to fully maintain and contribute toward the restoration of stands of the oldest, largest trees in a forest. In addition, the law required that the agencies update old-growth protection standards that were more than ten years old. The law encouraged the agencies to focus their thinning efforts on small-diameter trees and to try to retain all larger trees, which are the most resistant to fire.

Environmental analysis. The law directed the Forest Service and BLM to conduct environmental reviews of forest-thinning projects in accordance with the 1969 National Environmental Policy Act (NEPA; PL 91-190), but it limited the number of reviews. Under NEPA all federal agencies were required to consider the environmental impact of any action they proposed to take or pay for an environmental impact statement if such an action or project was thought to have a significant impact on the environment, with an analysis of reasonable alternatives including doing nothing.

In the case of fuel reduction projects, the new law limited the scope of environmental impact statements based on the project's distance from a community:

• If a project were within a wildland-urban interface, the agencies were required to conduct an environmental review of the proposed project only and no alternatives.

• If the project were more than 1.5 miles from a community's boundary but within an area described by the community's own wildfire protection plan—for example, it might include a wildland-urban interface of three miles from the town limits—the agencies were required to review the project and one alternative.

• For projects beyond those limits, an agency's environmental review had to consider the proposed project, one alternative project, and the consequences of not taking any action.

Administrative appeals. To be eligible to appeal a forest-thinning project to the agency involved, citizens had to have submitted specific written comments on the proposed action to the agency during the public comment period.

Judicial review. To expedite judicial proceedings, anyone challenging a hazardous fuel reduction project covered by the law first had to exhaust the administrative appeals processes provided by the BLM or Forest Service. A suit could be brought only in the federal district where the forest thinning project was to be carried out. Congress encouraged courts to expedite the consideration of any lawsuits against forest fuel reduction projects "to the maximum extent practicable." This applied to the determination of jurisdiction and consideration of the merits of the case. Any preliminary injunction against a forest-thinning project could not last longer than sixty days, although the injunction was subject to renewal by the court. A court could renew the injunction an unlimited number of times.

If there were a request to renew an injunction, the agency and plaintiff were required to provide an update on the status of the authorized project, including the conditions of the forest lands at issue and the extent to which the risk of disease, insect infestation, or wildfire had increased since the temporary restraining order or preliminary injunction was granted. Courts reviewing challenges to thinning projects were required to weigh the long- and short-term effects to the surrounding ecosystem if the project was halted. In doing this, the courts were required to consider the impact of halting or proceeding with the project.

Forest monitoring. The BLM and Forest Service regional offices were required to monitor the results of the fuel reduction projects and report every five years on whether the projects were meeting the goals and whether changes were needed. The two agencies were allowed to collect monitoring data by entering into agreements with, or providing grants to, small businesses and other organizations.

Insect Infestations

Studies and research. The law required the Forest Service and the U.S. Geological Survey to research forest-damaging insects and associated diseases. It authorized those agencies to conduct studies on federal lands if they determined that the lands were at risk for insect infestation. Such research was defined as including timber harvesting, thinning, prescribed burning, pruning, and any combination of these activities.

Insect infestation research on forest tracts of 1,000 acres or less was exempt from the environmental review requirements of NEPA. Exemptions could not be given for a tract that was adjacent to another tract already exempted. No more than 250,000 total acres could be exempted from NEPA for insect infestation research.

Research projects were prohibited in the National Wilderness Preservation System, lands that were declared Wilderness Study Areas, or lands where the removal of vegetation was prohibited by federal law. The law required peer review of research projects, including use of nonfederal experts, before they began. In addition, the agency involved had to have given public notice and accepted public comment. The law authorized such sums as might be necessary for fiscal 2004 through fiscal 2008.

Watershed Forestry

Cost-sharing. The law authorized the agriculture secretary to establish a watershed forestry cost-sharing program to be administered by the Forest Service and implemented by state foresters or equivalent officials. Communities, nonprofit groups, and nonindustrial private forest landowners would be eligible for funding for projects to protect watershed health. The grant could not be greater than 75 percent of the total cost of the project.

The law authorized $15 million annually from fiscal 2004 through fiscal 2008. At least 75 percent of the money was to be allocated to the cost-sharing program; the remainder could be for technical assistance, education, or planning.

Tribal assistance. The law established a parallel program for Native American tribes and authorized $2.5 million annually from fiscal 2004 through fiscal 2008. It mandated that 75 percent of those funds go to the watershed forestry program, with the remaining 25 percent for technical assistance.

Priorities. In considering how to distribute the funds, the agriculture secretary was expected to take into account a number of issues, including each state's acreage of agricul-

tural land, nonindustrial private forest land, and highly erodible land; the number of nonindustrial private owners; and water quality cost savings that could be achieved through forest watershed management.

Forest Conservation

Healthy Forests Reserve. The law directed the Forest Service, in coordination with the BLM and the Commerce Department, to establish a Healthy Forest Reserves Program for restoring and enhancing forest ecosystems to promote the recovery of threatened and endangered species and improve biodiversity. The owners of the lands could enroll in a ten-year cost-sharing agreement or give the government a thirty-year easement or a ninety-nine-year easement to their property in return for federal compensation. Enrolled lands were subject to a restoration plan to be developed jointly by the landowner and the Forest Service to restore and enhance habitat. Total enrollment in the program was limited to 2 million acres.

The Forest Service was required to provide landowners with technical assistance to comply with the terms of the restoration plans. To carry out the program, the law authorized $25 million in fiscal 2004 and such sums as might be necessary for fiscal 2005 through fiscal 2008.

Forest inventory and monitoring. The agriculture secretary was directed to establish a monitoring program for forest stands, with an emphasis on hardwood forests in the National Forest System and on private forest land with willing owners. A forest stand was defined as an area that was relatively uniform in species composition or age. The program would attempt to identify and assess environmental threats, including insects, diseases, invasive species, fires, and weather-related risks. It also would address loss or degradation of forests and forest stands and quantify the rate at which carbon from the atmosphere was absorbed.

The agriculture secretary was required to develop an early warning system for environmental threats so that forest managers could isolate and treat a threat before it became uncontrollable. For this purpose, the agreement authorized $5 million annually from fiscal 2004 through fiscal 2008.

Biomass

Grants. The law authorized the secretaries of agriculture or interior to make grants to individuals who owned or operated facilities that used biomass as a raw material to produce electricity, heat, transportation fuels, or substitutes for petroleum-based products. Biomass is organic material such as wood, plant waste, manure, or garbage. The law authorized grants to community-based and small-business enterprises created to make use of biomass.

The law authorized a total of $50 million for biomass grants and assistance.

Forest technology. The law authorized the Forest Service to carry out a program to accelerate adoption of biomass technology. It also modified an existing biomass-use research program to authorize grants to develop new forest-thinning systems and equipment that would be more efficient and inexpensive. Appropriated funds for the program could be used to train forestry managers and community leaders in the use of such techniques and equipment.

Clean Air

Legislation to alter the rules used to control air pollution drew the usual contentious debate in the 108th Congress but was not a sufficiently high-priority agenda item and was not approved. President George W. Bush in 2002 put forth a plan, which he called "Clear Skies," that would have made important changes in treatment of pollutants and was enthusiastically endorsed by the power industry. Elements of the proposals were so controversial that the legislation had little chance of passing in the closely divided Senate. As a result, the administration moved aggressively to implement parts of the "Clear Skies" plan through regulatory action. The outcome of those action, which faced legal challenge, remained uncertain.

In the Senate a key vote was taken to delay implementation of one aspect of the regulatory action rules promulgated by the Bush administration that involved power plant pollution. The effort to delay the rules changes was defeated.

BUSH PROPOSAL

The Bush administration's "Clear Skies" plan was promoted by the White House as a way to reduce air pollution. Bills introduced in both chambers were vehemently opposed by environmentalists. The legislation proposed to phase in limits for sulfur dioxide and nitrogen oxides, which contribute to acid rain, as well as mercury, which is toxic to humans in concentrated amounts and can impair children's development. The White House said the plan would cut emissions of the three pollutants by 70 percent over fifteen years.

Environmentalists and most Democrats opposed the legislation because it did not address a fourth pollutant—carbon dioxide emissions—that many scientists said was the main cause of global warming. Instead the administration proposed a voluntary program to reduce "greenhouse gas intensity," a measurement linked to the rate of economic output, by 18 percent by 2012. The administration proposal was based on a "cap and trade" program under which power plants that produced more than their allotted share of pollutants could buy credits from companies that reduced their emission levels below the federal standards.

The Senate bill (S 485) introduced by Sen. James M. Inhofe, R-Okla., and the House bill (HR 999) introduced by Rep. Joe L. Barton, R-Texas, mirrored the Bush initiative. The two members headed the committees with jurisdiction over the issue. On Nov. 10 Inhofe offered a revision that eased the proposed limit on allowable mercury emissions from twenty-six tons per year to thirty-four tons. At the time

coal-burning power plants in the United States were emitting an estimated forty-eight tons of mercury each year. Businesses, backed by many Republicans, said Bush's original caps were too strict. The new number was based on revised administration estimates of the amount of mercury that would be removed annually through "co-benefit" reduction; that is, as a side effect of removing sulfur dioxide and nitrogen oxides from power plant emissions without additional effort or equipment.

With legislation stymied, the Bush administration in late 2003 announced plans to implement the president's proposals through regulation. On Dec. 15 the Environmental Protection Agency (EPA) said it was seeking comment on two alternatives for reducing mercury emissions: by requiring power plants to install specific pollution controls, reducing emissions by 29 percent by the end of 2007, or by setting a mandatory declining cap and allowing emissions trading, which the EPA said would reduce emissions by nearly 70 percent by 2018. Two days later, the EPA issued a proposed rule for reducing emissions of sulfur dioxide and nitrogen oxides in twenty-nine eastern states and the District of Columbia.

SENATE ACTION

In a vote that was considered a symbolic effort by Democrats to highlight their criticism of Bush administration environmental policies, the Senate in 2003 defeated an amendment to authorize a National Academy of Sciences study of new rules that would reinterpret the "New Source Review" (NSR) section of the Clean Air Act (PL 101-549) and delay implementation of those rules for six months. The NSR program required power plants and other industrial facilities, such as refineries and chemical plants, to install modern pollution control technology whenever major modifications were made to facilities that affected air pollution. The administration's plan allowed power plants and factories greater leeway to make changes under "routine maintenance," which would not require federal review or new pollution control equipment.

An amendment to the fiscal 2003 omnibus bill (H J Res 2— PL 108-7), offered by John Edwards, D-N.C., would have delayed the proposed pollution control regulations for six months. It also would have required a National Academy of Sciences study "to determine the effects of the final rule on air pollution and human health." *(Omnibus bill, p. 70)*

Critics, including northeastern Republican senators who would prove pivotal on a number of environmental issues throughout the year, said the rule would allow power plants to pollute more, costing states more for environmental cleanup. The administration disputed that contention and said power plants were discouraged from performing routine maintenance because of the burdensome regulations.

The coal-burning factories and power plants targeted by the pollution controls were concentrated in the Midwest and parts of the South, but their emissions often were carried by easterly winds to the Northeast and fell to the ground in the form of acid rain. In the end, all five northeastern Republicans and independent James M. Jeffords of Vermont voted for the amendment. But the administration pulled a handful of southern Democrats to its side: the four senators from Louisiana and Arkansas, plus Zell Miller of Georgia. The Edwards amendment was rejected Jan. 22, 2003, on a **key vote of 46–50 (R 6–45; D 39–5; I 1–0).** *(2003 key votes, p. 837)*

The regional breakdown of New England Republicans opposing the president and some southern Democrats backing him was an indication of Senate sentiment on environmental issues in 2003 and 2004. It would be echoed throughout the 108th Congress on omnibus energy legislation (HR 6) and on a global warming bill (S 139) to regulate carbon dioxide emissions. *(Omnibus energy bill, p. 425; global environment, p. 442)*

Before the Edwards amendment was defeated, the Senate adopted 51–45 an alternative offered by Inhofe calling for the same study but allowing the new rules to take effect in March. The report was due in March 2005.

Corps of Engineers Projects

The House voted overwhelmingly in fall 2003 to authorize about $4 billion for beach, harbor, and flood control projects carried out by the Army Corps of Engineers. The bill (HR 2557) contained a widely supported, bipartisan agreement to modify Corps procedures for approving water projects, including instituting an external peer review process for costly projects. The Senate Environment and Public Works Committee was preoccupied with work on a multiyear highway bill and put off action on the water projects bill until 2004. A Senate version (S 2773) was reported but did not reach the floor for a vote.

The water resources bill, the biennial vehicle for authorizing Army Corps of Engineers water projects, usually had broad support, especially in the House, because it allowed members to bring infrastructure projects home to their districts. That same spending, however, made it a target for deficit hawks and for critics of the corps, who pushed for stricter procedures for approving projects. A series of reports and newspaper articles, including a 2000 Defense Department study and a 2001 report from the National Academy of Sciences, raised questions about the data and methods used by the corps and increased the pressure in Congress to make changes.

Efforts to produce a water bill in the 107th Congress failed because lawmakers were unable to agree on how to address these problems. Some members wanted to revise the standards used by the corps for selecting projects, require more environmental mitigation, and make the most expensive projects subject to an independent review. Others preferred to keep the status quo. The previous authorization bill had been enacted in 2000 (PL 106-541). *(Congress and the Nation Vol. X, p. 372)*

With the bill stalled in the Senate, some House members, led by Don Young, R-Alaska, chair of the Transportation and Infrastructure Committee, tried unsuccessfully to attach similar provisions to the fiscal 2004 energy and water spending measure (HR 2754) in conference.

HOUSE ACTION

After agreeing to compromise language on independent reviews, the House Transportation and Infrastructure Committee approved a bill by voice vote on July 23, 2003 (H Rept 108-265). Under the compromise, an independent panel would review all the corps' information and conclusions on any project that exceeded $50 million, including economic and environmental assumptions and projections, project evaluation data, economic and environmental analyses, engineering analyses, the formulation of alternative plans, and models used in evaluating economic or environmental impacts. The review would be undertaken concurrently with the corps' study of a proposed project. The compromise also required the corps to include in its project planning more detail on environmental mitigation activities. In addition, addressing earlier Democratic objections, sponsors modified the bill's provisions that would have streamlined environmental reviews.

The House passed the bill Sept. 24 by a vote of 412–8. In a statement of policy issued that day, the White House supported the idea of peer review but criticized the bill's lack of "fiscal discipline," saying the administration would support the new projects in the bill if they were offset by stopping work on projects that were not cost effective.

The House bill included the following principal components:

• Required an independent peer review for projects costing $50 million or more, a threshold that was expected to cover about 30 percent of Corps projects. The review panels were to be established by the National Academy of Sciences, a similar independent scientific technical advisory organization, or an experienced nonprofit organization that had no conflicts of interest on the project. The reviews would be nonbinding, and the corps' chief of engineers could exempt projects that were not controversial and would have no negative environmental impact.

• Directed to the corps to coordinate and streamline the environmental review process to avoid project delays. The committee report accompanying the bill said that under the existing system other federal agencies often did not raise objections until a project study was nearly complete, leading to needless delay.

• Made permanent the corps' authority to retain and use recreation user fees collected at corps recreation areas.

• Provided authorization for hundreds of individual projects.

SENATE ACTION

In the Senate, S 2773, approved by the Environment and Public Works Committee in June 2004, subjected a broader range of projects to the review process than were covered in the House bill. This approach was vigorously pressed by environmental advocates, but port authorities and other government entities hoping to expedite corps activities feared the extra scrutiny would slow down projects and drive up costs. The more aggressive approach to review increased the controversy over the legislation, which was never brought to the floor for a Senate vote.

California Water Projects

Congress in 2004 agreed to provide new federal funds for the huge California Federal Bay-Delta (CalFed) project, authorizing $389 million for the project over the following six fiscal years plus $15 million for restoration of the Salton Sea in southern California and $6 million for other water projects. Members of the California congressional delegation had been trying for nearly five years to get more federal funding for CalFed. The program was first authorized as a federal-state project in 1996 (PL 104-208). The federal portion of the program expired in 2000, but competing interests among farmers, environmental groups, and others within and outside the state kept compromise elusive until election-year momentum brought the parties together.

The program was designed to improve water quality and storage in the San Francisco Bay and Sacramento-San Joaquin River Delta region, which supplied water to the fertile farming fields of California's Central Valley. The bill provided funding mainly to increase water storage, but additional money was included to improve water supplies and to stabilize aging levees and restore ecosystems statewide.

Over time, the bill's price tag has shrunk significantly. In the 107th Congress, Sen. Dianne Feinstein, D-Calif., sought $2.4 billion for the program. The bill she introduced in 2004 authorized $880 million, and that was cut below $400 million by the Energy and Natural Resources Committee in April.

An impasse over the extent of latitude to give the Interior Department almost crippled the bill. The House wanted to permit the department to approve water storage projects subject to a congressional veto within 120 days. But after negotiations involving California Republican governor Arnold Schwarzenegger, House members accepted Senate language that directed Interior to simply be "involved" in any delayed project.

The House passed HR 2828 (H Rept 108-573, Pt. 1) by voice vote July 9. The Senate passed the bill, amended, by voice vote on Sept. 15, and the House cleared it on Oct. 6 by voice vote. President George W. Bush signed it into law on Oct. 25 (PL 108-361).

Energy, Water Funds; Nuclear Waste Site

A funding shortfall for the Yucca Mountain nuclear waste dump in Nevada threatened the fiscal 2005 energy and water development appropriations bill, but senior legislators freed up additional money for the project in the waning hours of the November 2004 lame-duck session. With an agreement reached, the bill was rolled into the fiscal year 2005 omnibus spending package (HR 4818) that cleared Nov. 20. *(Omnibus appropriations, p. 80; 2002 Yucca Mountain action, p. 439)*

The final $29 billion bill funded much of the Energy Department as well as popular water projects. The total, which did not include a 0.8 percent across-the-board cut, was 2 percent more than President George W. Bush requested and 5 percent more than the amount appropriated for fiscal 2004. Most of the funds, $23 billion, was for the Energy Department, including $6.5 billion for nuclear weapons programs. No money was provided for research into a nuclear "bunker buster," a weapon to penetrate underground enemy strongholds that the Bush administration was eager to develop. Bush asked for $27.6 million for the project.

But it was the dispute over Yucca Mountain, located 100 miles northwest of Las Vegas, that nearly caused appropriators to give up and settle for an extension of fiscal 2004 funding levels before reaching a last-minute compromise. Yucca Mountain was approved in 2002 as the national disposal site for high-level radioactive waste. The administration had requested $880 million for Yucca Mountain in fiscal 2005 as the project neared a construction phase. But the White House plan called for drawing $749 million of that from an off-budget trust fund financed by nuclear utilities, a proposal that even supporters of the project acknowledged would have difficulty passing Congress.

Opponents, including longtime foe Sen. Harry Reid of Nevada, the Democratic whip in that chamber, vowed to block such extensive use of the trust fund, contending it would reduce congressional oversight of future spending on Yucca Mountain. Unable to authorize the trust fund proposal, David L. Hobson, R-Ohio, chair of the House Energy and Water Appropriations Subcommittee, could provide only $131 million for the nuclear waste repository in his panel's bill (HR 4614), which passed the House in June.

Hobson's Senate counterpart, Pete V. Domenici, R-N.M., floated a proposal to pay for the project in fiscal 2005 with a surcharge on nuclear utilities. Conservatives and utilities companies opposed that idea, calling it a tax that would be passed on to consumers. Domenici's panel never approved a bill.

With time running out on the 108th Congress, staff discussions shifted to whether a short-term or long-term extension of 2004 energy and water funding would be better. But the congressional chiefs at the helm of the Appropriations committees—Sen. Ted Stevens, R-Alaska, and Rep. C. W. Bill Young, R-Fla.—were not willing to let the bill die, not least because it would provide $4.7 billion for water projects through the Army Corps of Engineers. They freed up $800 million in additional funding for the bill, mostly by cutting other domestic spending measures, to provide funding for Yucca and increase spending for pet nuclear and defense projects of Domenici and Hobson.

The House passed HR 4614 (H Rept 108-554) on a 370–16 vote on June 25. It was later incorporated into the omnibus appropriations legislation (HR 4814), which was cleared in November.

In a policy statement, conferees inserted language in the omnibus bill's report expressing the intent of Congress that the Federal Energy Regulatory Commission (FERC) would have exclusive jurisdiction over approval and location of thirty liquefied natural gas (LNG) terminals that were proposed for both U.S. coasts and the Gulf of Mexico. Although the language was nonbinding, it expressed a congressional sense that federal regulation should supersede state control of these facilities, some of which were controversial because they would be built near population centers. The terminals to bring in LNG were seen as essential to offset gas supply shortages in the nation. In March FERC asserted jurisdiction over the projects under the Natural Gas Act of 1938. The California Public Utility Commission, however, challenged the FERC ruling. That agency argued that FERC could not preempt the state's environmental requirements. The specific dispute involved a planned LNG facility near the heavily populated Long Beach.

LNG is frozen and condensed natural gas that is transported as a liquid on container ships from regions such as the Caribbean, which have an abundance of natural gas. At the close of 2004, there were four LNG storage sites in the United States—in Georgia, Louisiana, Maryland, and Massachusetts—where the material can be heated back to its normal size and transported through standard natural gas pipelines. Another ten LNG terminals had received approval from government agencies and many more were on the drawing boards or before the agencies for approval.

Nuclear Liability Insurance

Unable in the 107th Congress to get a long-term extension for the existing nuclear liability program for commercial nuclear reactors, lawmakers settled late in 2004 for a two-year reauthorization of the program for government contractors at nuclear weapons sites. (*2001 action, p. 442*)

The program, known as Price-Anderson after the original sponsors of the law, provided nuclear liability insurance for the Department of Energy nuclear weapons facilities. The extension, through the end of 2006, was tucked into the fiscal 2005 defense authorization bill (HR 4200) that President George W. Bush signed on Oct. 28 (PL 108-375). (*Authorization bill, p. 346*)

Price-Anderson limited the nuclear accident liability of Energy Department contractors. The department was required to indemnify against all nuclear-damage payments experienced by companies, universities, and other organizations that run department nuclear facilities under contract. (Similar indemnification authority for commercial nuclear reactors expired at the end of 2003 and had not been extended by the end of the 108th Congress in 2004. However, existing commercial reactors had continuing coverage under grandfather provisions and were not affected by the lapse. But new commercial reactors would not be covered unless the law was extended, one of many obstacles to development of new facilities.)

Endangered Species Act

Congress continued to wrestle with the contentious disputes of the thirty-year-old Endangered Species Act (ESA) but made no sweeping changes to the law. It granted, however, various exemptions from the ESA's requirements to the Defense Department, which had argued that military training was being compromised by restraints on the use of some Defense-owned lands. The bills that dealt with ESA overhaul were in the House, where criticism of the law and sentiment for extensive revision was strong among many Republicans. No legislation was brought forth in the Senate, where criticism of the law was less pronounced.

In related action, Congress in both the 107th and 108th Congress considered proposals to exempt certain Defense Department locations from ESA and other environmental requirements. (*Details, pp. 322, 325, 326, 337, 342, 441*)

BACKGROUND

In the three decades since President Richard Nixon in 1973 signed the legislation establishing ESA (PL 93-205), the law became increasingly controversial, particularly with landowners and developers whose property use was curtailed by the presence of threatened species of animals and plants. It was not that way at the beginning. Not only did Congress approve the law by overwhelming margins, but Nixon, a staunch GOP president, endorsed the legislation and even asked Congress for tougher laws to build on existing statutes. (*Congress and the Nation Vol. IV, p. 289*)

The Endangered Species Preservation Act of 1966 (PL 89-669), the first comprehensive law, authorized the interior secretary to protect certain native fish and wildlife species and to purchase lands for a "National Wildlife Refuge System" where habitats of endangered species would be preserved. (*Congress and the Nation Vol. II, pp. 481, 484*)

The law was strengthened by the Endangered Species Conservation Act of 1969 (PL 91-135), which restricted importation of endangered species, extended protection to more native species and certain foreign species, and established penalties for violations of the act. (*Congress and the Nation Vol. III, p 755*)

The first endangered species list, published in March 1967, included seventy-two native species. By the end of 1976, 609 species were listed as endangered, among them grizzly bears, butterflies, bats, crocodiles, and trout. But over time the list expanded into hundreds more, many of which were increasingly seen by the critics as obscure exotic species that, if fully protected, extracted a huge economic cost in development. Critics were particularly fond of pointing to such species as the snail darter, the kangaroo rat, and the Delhi fly.

A second major reason the law became so controversial was its use by environmental advocates as a tactic to stop development in which a species became a secondary player in the struggle between pro- and antidevelopment groups. (*Background on controversies, Congress and the Nation Vol. IX, pp. 416, 458*)

In the wake of the growing controversy, the ESA had not been renewed since it technically expired in 1992. The law, however, remained in effect because of annual appropriations measures. The most outspoken critics of the law, primarily developers and landowners who were restrained or blocked in their freedom to gain economic benefit from their land, saw new hope for change when Republicans gained control of Congress in 1995. Environmentalists feared the opposite but were reassured in their opposition to change by the presence of a Democratic president, Bill Clinton, in the White House through the remainder of the decade. *(Reauthorization attempts, Congress and the Nation Vol. X, pp. 349, 385)*

That dynamic changed with Republican control of the White House beginning in 2001 and of both houses of Congress in 2003. Still, efforts to revamp the entire law came up short.

ESA REVISIONS

The primary action occurred in 2004 in the House Resources Committee, whose chair, Richard W. Pombo, a California rancher, made revising ESA a top priority. Pombo and other revision advocates acknowledged that getting major changes through the Senate was unlikely in the 108th Congress. As a result, they pushed legislation in two House bills designed to draw bipartisan support and make changes they said would be at the margins of ESA practices, even though they candidly acknowledged that their long-term goal was a rewrite of the ESA law to make it more favorable to landowners. The changes were aimed at the U.S. Fish and Wildlife Service (for land and river species) and the National Marine Fisheries Services (for marine species).

The committee in July approved two bills, largely along party lines, aimed at the use of scientific review in making endangered species decisions and another dealing with the definition of habitat. Both were endorsed by groups such as the National Association of Home Builders and criticized by an array of environmental groups.

The first (HR 1662—H Rept 108-785) required the agencies to use more field study data and encouraged federal agencies to consider input from affected landowners and states. It also required that most decisions be reviewed by a panel of three scientists knowledgeable about the issue and species. Both agencies made hundreds of decisions each year about endangered species. The changes required a peer review for each decision.

The second bill (HR 2933—H Rept 108-786), the more controversial of the two, altered the definition of "critical habitat" for endangered species to reduce the land area protected under the law. The bill limited the amount of land that could be set aside to areas a species uses for such "essential behavioral patterns" as breeding, feeding, and sheltering. Existing law allowed protection of habitat "essential to the conservation of the species." The language meant that agencies needed to determine that land was critical to a species' survival, not just the conservation and recovery of a species. The bill also required the agencies to consider the economic costs when they examined critical habitat for protection. Once reported, the bills received no further action during the congressional session.

Defense and Environmental Issues

A number of environmental issues involving military installations and nuclear sites were considered by Congress between 2001 and 2005. The issues involved the cost and adequacy of environmental cleanup on military sites and whether additional exemptions from environmental laws were needed to allow adequate military training operations. A related issue was whether radioactive wastes at former nuclear production plants could be reclassified to permit permanent storage at the sites rather than moving the material to the planned permanent facility at Yucca Mountain.

ENDANGERED SPECIES ACT EXEMPTION

Congress in 2003 approved an exemption from certain requirements of the Endangered Species Act (ESA) and the Marine Mammal Protection Act. The exemptions, urged by defense officials and President George W. Bush, were put into the fiscal 2004 defense authorization bill (HR 1588—PL 108-136), enacted late in that year. Military officials argued that environmental requirements were interfering with military training and readiness activities. *(Details, pp. 322, 325, 326, 337, 342; Endangered species overhaul, p. 440)*

The changes in PL 108-136 blocked new designations of critical habitat for species on the existing lists on military installations where an "Integrated Resources Management Plan" had been put together with state fish and wildlife officials so long as such a plan benefited the species "for which critical habitat is proposed for designation."

This was one of numerous efforts by the military to ease environmental law requirements that defense officials said were compromising their ability to train personnel and conduct military operations on the land. The Defense Department owned more than 25 million acres of public land, much of it remote and inaccessible, that was seen as especially valuable habitat for fish and wildlife. Environmentalists and their mostly Democratic supporters in Congress resisted these exemptions as unnecessary encroachments on the purposes of ESA and other environmental laws.

BASE CLEANUPS

A number of other defense bills approved during 2003 and 2004 addressed cleanup of environmental contamination at both closed and active military bases. The defense authorization, military construction, and appropriations bills for fiscal 2004 and 2005 all included funding for base cleanups, whether the bases were active or retired. Most of these also required reports on the impact of the Clean Air Act, Solid Waste Disposal Act, and the Comprehensive Environmental Response, Compensation, and Liability Act (CERCLA) on military installations, but none provided exemptions to these laws sought by armed services officials.

They also required studies of the danger to human health from exposure to perchlorate (used in munitions propellants). There was growing concern about groundwater contamination from perchlorate. *(Details, chapter 5, p. 303)*

NUCLEAR WASTE

Much of the controversy about disposal of nuclear waste surrounded the plan to move radioactive material to Yucca Mountain in Nevada where it would be stored permanently. But a prominent related issue emerged over whether to provide the Energy Department with authority to classify certain high-level radioactive wastes at former nuclear weapons sites in a way that would permit long-term storage on-site. This proposal affected sites in Washington, Idaho, and South Carolina where wastes were currently stored in underground tanks. Energy Department officials proposed sealing these tanks with a special cement. However, the Nuclear Waste Policy Act required all such wastes to be removed from the tanks and placed in a centralized geologic repository, which was to be Yucca Mountain. Energy officials asked that the requirement be changed for plants in these states to lower costs and speed closure of the tanks. *(2002 action, p. 442; 2004 action, p. 439)*

The request was highly controversial among affected state officials, many members of Congress, and environmentalists, primarily from the concern that the tanks might someday begin leaking wastes that would go into the soil and groundwater. Some of the tanks were known to have leaked already.

The reclassification debate was mainly in the Senate where Sen. Lindsey Graham, R-S.C., won approval of a provision allowing energy officials to reclassify high-level nuclear waste as a low-level waste in tanks at the Savannah River former nuclear weapons production facility in his state. The provision was added to the fiscal 2005 defense authorization bill (HR 4200—PL 108-375). The Senate in June 2004 voted against removing the authority from the legislation. In conference on that legislation, conferees added similar language for the Idaho National Environmental and Engineering Laboratory. But the option was not made available for Washington state's Hanford nuclear reservation. That state's Democratic senator, Maria Cantwell, tried unsuccessfully to get Lindsey's amendment stricken from the authorization bill, arguing that its inclusion set a bad national precedent and could allow contamination of river and water supplies near Hanford. Some of the Hanford tanks were known to have leaked into the Columbia River.

Global Environment

Controversy continued to swirl around concerns by environmentalists and many nations over global warming that most scientists believe resulted from accumulating greenhouse gases. Congress and President George W. Bush, however, rejected proposals to curtail and roll back carbon diox-ide emissions that were produced by burning fossil fuels. Global warming is the theory that emissions of gases such as carbon dioxide trap heat in the atmosphere, cause the temperature to rise. Most—but not all—scientists believe this creates the potential for climatic catastrophe, such as the melting of the polar ice caps.

One major issue was the landmark international treaty on global warming negotiated in Kyoto, Japan, in 1997. The Kyoto treaty required signatories to substantially reduce their greenhouse gas emissions. For the United States the reduction would have been 7 percent below 1990 levels by 2012. However, the treaty ran into huge opposition in the United States from business and members of Congress who said it would constrict economic growth and was flawed in many respects, especially its unequal application to developing nations. President Bill Clinton signed the treaty with misgivings but never submitted it to the Senate for ratification because of vocal opposition. *(Background, Congress and the Nation Vol. X, p. 354)*

Bush came to the White House in 2001 vowing unalterable opposition to the treaty. On March 27, 2001, the new administration announced that the United States would not pursue its implementation. His opposition was expected and reflected a broad sentiment in Congress that the Kyoto treaty was flawed and fundamentally unfair to the United States. The Senate in July 1997 on a 95–0 vote adopted a nonbinding resolution stating that the administration should sign a global warming treaty only if it included commitments from developing countries. Kyoto exempted such large developing nations as India and China from mandatory emission restrictions. In the following years Congress inserted provisions in numerous appropriations bills prohibiting any spending on activity related to Kyoto if the treaty had not been ratified.

LEGISLATIVE ACTION

The basic dynamics of the issue changed little throughout Bush's entire first term, but a few members of Congress continued to push for action on global warming. Democrats briefly succeeded in adding language to a bill stating that the United States should take a leadership role in fighting global climate change, particularly by helping negotiate and eventually signing any future versions of the Kyoto treaty. This occurred in the House International Relations Committee in May 2003 when it was preparing the foreign relations authorization bill (HR 1950). However, the language did not stay in long. A short time later, in July, the Energy and Commerce Committee, which had jurisdiction over the issue, voted 28–17 to remove the provision from the bill. The vote was along party lines. *(HR 1950, p. 289)*

One member who continued to take global warming concerns seriously was Sen. John McCain, R-Ariz., who made no secret that he differed with his party and the Bush administration over the issue. As chair of the Senate Commerce

Committee he was able to extended hearings on the issue although no legislation resulted.

The only major vote on the issue came late in 2003 when the Senate rejected a proposal to reduce carbon dioxide and other greenhouse gas emissions to 2000 levels by 2010. The vote on Oct. 30 was 43–55 against the proposal, a closer margin than many observers expected in light of previous sharp criticism of Kyoto. The rejected proposal was a substitute for the contents of a bill (S 139) sponsored by McCain that required emissions to reach 1990 levels by 2016. McCain and cosponsor Joseph I. Lieberman, D-Conn., who offered the substitute, had little expectation their proposals would be approved. "The purpose of the vote was to get the Senate on record," McCain said. "We will prevail over time because this issue is not going to go away. We want to get everyone on record so they can explain [their votes] to their constituents," he said. But the vote demonstrated the difficulty of legislating on the subject. A number of votes against the proposals came from Democrats generally sympathetic to environmental issues, including senators from coastal areas and states with large power plants.

As the 108th Congress neared the end in 2004 McCain in one of his last acts as head of the Commerce Committee heard testimony on a major new global warming report. It was the Arctic Climate Impact Assessment issued by the Arctic Council, made up of the United States and several other Arctic nations: Canada, Finland, Iceland, Norway, Denmark, Russia, and Sweden, all of whom had ratified the Kyoto treaty. The report was the work of about 300 scientists over four years. It predicted that at least half of the summer sea ice in the Arctic would melt by the end of the century along with much of the Greenland ice sheet as the climate of the region warmed by 7 to 13 degrees.

Ocean Policy

New attention was focused on oceanic issues during George W. Bush's first term, but major legislation was not enacted. Meanwhile, the Law of the Sea treaty remained in limbo in the face of conservative criticism. Congress did, however, receive new comprehensive reports on oceanic issues from a commission set up under legislation enacted in 2000 and from a private organization.

COMMISSION ON OCEAN POLICY

Although no major legislation passed, two smaller bills were approved. One bill, S 1218, which was incorporated into the final omnibus fiscal 2005 appropriations bill (HR 4818), set up a national interagency program to coordinate research efforts on the role of oceans in human health. It authorized $67 million over four years for study and planning and $9 million over three years for the Commerce Department to expand public knowledge. A second bill (S 3014—PL 108-456), which Bush signed on Dec. 10, 2004, reautho-

rized and expanded programs to research the growth of algae and so-called red tides. The bill authorized $998.5 million for fiscal 2005–2008 for this purpose.

However, broader bills that were based on recommendations in the major studies remained unenacted. One, S 2647, would have established the National Oceanic and Atmospheric Administration (NOAA) as the principal federal agency on ocean and atmospheric matters and expanded and better defined its functions. NOAA was a Commerce Department agency established by executive order in 1970 and never given a statutory mandate from Congress. The bill called for developing a twenty-year integrated research plan for exploration and monitoring the oceans and atmosphere, including climate change, and called for a fifteen-member science advisory board to assist the NOAA administrator. The bill was approved by the Senate Commerce Committee but went no further. In the House, an Oceans Caucus existed, headed by two Republicans and two Democrats, with members all from states with coastal borders. This group introduced legislation that gave statutory recognition to NOAA and defined its functions and structure to focus on management of ecological systems and expand the importance of marine and atmospheric education and ocean exploration. It also set up a permanent Ocean and Great Lakes Conservation Trust Fund and established a national oceans council in the executive office of the president. No action was taken on the proposal. Another bill (HR 4546) in the House also formally established NOAA as a Commerce Department agency and specified its functions in line with the major reports.

The reports received by Congress called for far-reaching policy changes to reduce or halt deterioration of the nation's coasts and waters. The U.S. Commission on Ocean Policy, established in 2000, issued its final report on Sept. 20, 2004. The most recent comprehensive review of U.S. ocean policy was done in 1966. Since that time the oceans and coasts around the United States changed significantly, according to the report. The authors noted that "more than 37 million people, 19 million homes, and countless businesses have been added to coastal areas. Marine transportation and coastal recreation and tourism have become two of the top drivers of the national economy. These developments, however, come with costs, and we are only now discovering the extent of those costs in terms of depleted resources, lost habitat, and polluted waters." The report made 212 recommendations, called for "ecosystem-based management" to halt decline of the nation's oceans and coasts, a new governance framework, more investment in marine science, and a new stewardship ethic.

The 2000 law required the president within ninety days to submit proposals that would implement or respond to commission recommendations. On Dec. 17, 2004, Bush formed a Committee on Ocean Policy to coordinate action of federal agencies on the issues and named as head James Connaughton, chair of the White House Council on Environ-

444 CH. 7 ENERGY AND ENVIRONMENT

mental Quality. Earlier, in 2003, the Pew Oceans Commission made a similar report following a three-year study.

LAW OF THE SEA TREATY

The UN Convention on the Law of the Sea was signed by 117 nations on Dec. 10, 1982. The United States, the United Kingdom, and nearly thirty other nations did not sign because of disagreements over seabed mining of minerals; these nations feared the terms would restrict commercial development. The treaty in its entirety was intended as an international set of rules to govern use of the seas, including codification of international law on territorial waters, sea lanes, and ocean resources.

The treaty went into effect in 1994. The seabed terms specified that minerals on and below the ocean floor outside of a nation's territorial jurisdiction were "the common heritage of mankind" that were to be governed by international rather than national authority. Amendments to the treaty in 1994 satisfied the United States, which then submitted it to the Senate for approval. A major section of the treaty extended a nation's territorial waters to twelve miles from three miles. Also, coastal nations were granted exclusive rights to fish for up to 200 miles, which had been a contentious issue between nations in which commercial fishing was an important economic activity.

Once the changes were made, most U.S. groups interested in the oceans urged Senate ratification. This included the Bush administration. The Senate Foreign Relations Committee approved the treaty (Treaty Doc 103-39) in early 2004. But conservative critics quickly emerged to attack the document. Some said the agreement did little to advance environmental protection or deal with environmental terrorism. Others said the treaty was an attack on U.S. sovereignty and the nation's position as the world's principal economic and military power. Foreign Relations Committee Chair Richard Lugar, R-Ind., responded that "vague and sometimes fantastical" concerns were being made "primarily by those who oppose virtually any multilateral agreement." The treaty had been bottled up in Lugar's committee for years when it was chaired by conservative Jessie Helms, R-N.C.

Agricultural Policy

Agricultural Policy

Agricultural issues during the first term of President George W. Bush were overshadowed by national security and foreign policy concerns following the terrorist attacks on New York City and the Pentagon outside Washington, D.C. But American farmers had much to worry about as they were hit by natural disasters, including drought, floods, and hurricanes, and by a failed experiment enacted in 1996 to change the nation's basic agriculture policy. Congress responded to these events in different ways, but all were intended to prop up sagging farm income.

The principal vehicle of assistance was a rewriting of the primary farm law, which was scheduled to expire in 2002, to take account of changed realities since the law was last revised in 1996. In that year, Republicans—who had recently regained control of Congress—sought to move farmers away from the farm policy of subsidies that stretched back to New Deal days a half century earlier. Instead, the GOP wanted to encourage farmers to base production decisions on market forces, not government supports. But the plan was undermined by a series of international financial crises, particularly in Asia, that dramatically undercut commodity prices. Congress in response passed a series of emergency farm aid packages between 1998 and 2001 but still faced the question of whether the 1996 law would work in the agricultural world of the twenty-first century.

The decision, in the 2002 omnibus farm bill, the major agricultural legislation of the period, was not only to reestablish farm subsidies abolished in 1996 but also to retain a fixed payment scheme that was put in place at that time to wean farmers off subsidies. The upshot was a sweeping farm program of aid that was projected to cost upward of $750 billion over ten years. Although much of the spending would occur in any event for nutritional programs, primarily food stamps, about $74 billion of the amount was expected to be new outlays, compared with existing law, as a result of the 2002 legislation.

The 107th Congress also came to the aid of farmers by approving additional mandatory agricultural spending. In 2001 lawmakers provided $5.5 billion in extra funds, the fourth time in as many years that the regular farm subsidies had been supplemented. The need for the extra aid was viewed as additional evidence that the 1996 law had not

Outlays for Agriculture

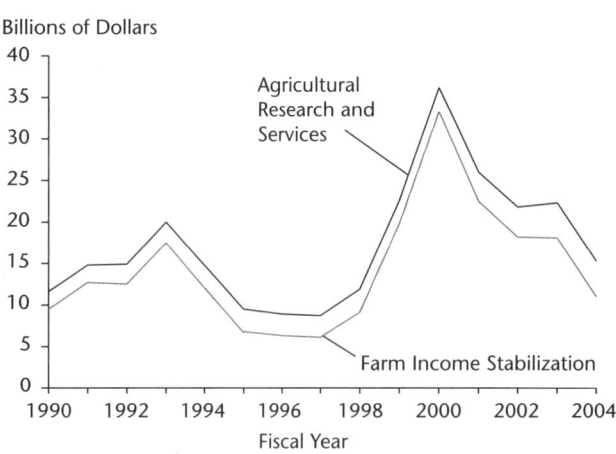

SOURCE: Office of Management and Budget, *Historical Tables, Budget of the United States Government: Fiscal Year 2006* (Washington, D.C.: U.S. Government Printing Office, 2005), Table 3.2.

worked as planned to wean farmers off subsidies. The 108th Congress also provided additional financial help for disaster-ridden farmers hard hit by drought, flooding, and hurricanes. The lawmakers extended a bankruptcy law provision designed to protect farmers against loss of their holdings

REFERENCES

Discussion of agricultural policy for the years 1945–1964 may be found in *Congress and the Nation Vol. I*, pp. 665–767; for the years 1965–1968, *Congress and the Nation Vol. II*, pp. 555–597; for the years 1969–1972, *Congress and the Nation Vol. III*, pp. 331–352; for the years 1973–1976, *Congress and the Nation Vol. IV*, pp. 717–740; for the years 1977–1980, *Congress and the Nation Vol. V*, pp. 365–395; for the years 1981–1984, *Congress and the Nation Vol. VI*, pp. 485–516; for the years 1985–1988, *Congress and the Nation Vol. VII*, pp. 499–539; for the years 1989–1992, *Congress and the Nation Vol. VIII*, pp. 535–557; for the years 1993–1996, *Congress and the Nation Vol. IX*, pp. 479–505; for the years 1997–2001, *Congress and the Nation Vol. X*, pp. 417–431.

when natural or financial troubles threatened agricultural prices.

Consumers were helped by legislation passed during the period. Congress in the omnibus farm bill provided for food labeling by country of origin, a requirement vigorously fought by the food processing industry. Lobbyists for the industry managed to get the requirement delayed two years but were unsuccessful in having it repealed. Consumers also benefited from a new requirement, approved in 2004, that food substances known to cause common, and often serious, allergies be clearly labeled on food containers. And a report of a single cow in Washington State found to have mad cow disease prompted lawmakers to increase funding for Agriculture Department divisions charged with food safety inspection.

Chronology of Action on Agriculture

2001–2002

Congress during 2001 and 2002 wrestled with the economic consequences of an attempt six years earlier to change fundamentally the way American agriculture operated. That attempt, farmers contended, was a failure that pushed many growers toward bankruptcy and sometimes—particularly for family farms—into it. The troubles of agriculture were compounded by a series of natural disasters including drought in some places, too much rain in others, and an unprecedented series of hurricanes that hit the southeastern part of the United States.

Legislators in the 107th Congress sought to provide disaster relief but were faced with the major task of renewing the basic national farm law that had been approved in 1996. That law, the "Freedom to Farm" act, sought to wean farmers from government subsidies and encourage them to rely on market forces in deciding which crops to grow and sell. But commodity prices collapsed following a number of international financial crises, particularly in Asia, requiring farmers to return to Congress for help several times between 1998 and 2001. As a result, Congress reversed the 1996 experiment when it turned to renewing the omnibus farm law in 2001. Besides providing subsidy increases for major crops such as wheat and corn, the law added support for a number of other crops. In the end, the legislation was estimated to cost nearly $441 billion over its six-year life.

Omnibus Farm Bill

Congress in 2002 cleared a sprawling multi-year farm bill (HR 2646) that reversed an effort just six years old to change the way American agriculture functioned. The legislation overturned a central tenet of the 1996 "Freedom to Farm" act (PL 104-127) by reestablishing farm subsides that had been abolished in the earlier law while at the same time renewing fixed annual payments that had been instituted as a way to wean farmers off the subsidies. President George W. Bush signed the bill into law May 13, 2002 (PL 107-171).

At the time of enactment, the total cost of all programs under the bill was estimated at $440.8 billion over six years, $45.1 billion more than the cost of continuing existing law.

Over ten years the cost was estimated at $746.9 billion, a $73.5 billion increase over existing law. The numbers were based on estimated costs of the programs in April 2001. Unlike funds provided in most authorization bills, the amounts in the farm bill were mandatory spending, not subject to annual appropriations.

Besides providing large subsidy increases for the major row crops—wheat, corn, oats, rice, cotton, and soybeans—HR 2646 added support for dry peas, lentils, and chickpeas; created a new national dairy program; and revamped the peanut subsidy program. Spending rose for conservation, rural development, and research, with a new focus on energy development. It also set tighter limits on annual federal payments to farmers, reinstated food stamps for legal immigrants, and began a country-of-origin labeling program for meat, fish, fruit, vegetables, and peanuts. The labeling program, however, subsequently was delayed until 2006 after intense lobbying from industry opponents. *(Food labeling, p. 465)*

A large part of the cost—$535.1 billion over ten years—was for nutrition programs, mainly food stamps, although most of that would have been spent under existing law. The increases under the new law were mainly for farm programs.

Backers of the 1996 act hoped it would encourage farmers to base their production decisions on the market forces instead of on government supports. But a wave of financial crises around the world, particularly in Asia, caused commodity prices to collapse. Instead of being weaned off government support, farmers returned to Congress for a series of emergency farm aid packages totaling $30.5 billion between 1998 and 2001.

When work on a replacement farm bill began in 2001, significant interest was expressed from the Bush administration and key congressional Democrats in reducing the emphasis on support for growers of traditional crops—programs that provided disproportionate benefits to huge "factory farms." Instead, they proposed to spend more on conservation programs that helped small farmers who agreed to set aside or otherwise preserve land.

But the push for more conservation spending could not withstand a drive by many farm-state lawmakers to expand

AGRICULTURE LEADERSHIP

President George W. Bush picked a California lawyer, Ann M. Veneman, as his first secretary of agriculture. She was confirmed by the Senate Jan. 20, 2001, by voice vote and became the first woman to head the agriculture department. Veneman had served as deputy agriculture secretary from 1991 to 1993 and was secretary of the California Department of Food and Agriculture from 1995 to 1999.

In cordial Senate confirmation hearings, she pledged to help farmers and ranchers through difficult times, end trade barriers to U.S. farm products, and work on new marketing opportunities for farmers. But she came into office amidst declining farm income and a new farm law that sought to push American agriculture toward market-based decisions and away from government subsidies. Her background in California, where agriculture was less dominated by subsidies than in the Midwest, was an additional burden on her acceptance as the chief representative for farmers and ranchers in all regions. Her tenure was buffeted by a scare over mad cow disease, a series of natural disasters including drought and excessive rainfall, and enactment of a major farm bill that reversed the law on market-based decisions. On Nov. 15, 2004, Veneman announced her intention to resign her post. She left office on Jan. 20, 2005.

To succeed her, Bush chose Mike Johanns, who was serving as governor of Nebraska. The Senate confirmed him by voice vote Jan. 20, 2005.

traditional commodity-based support programs for row crops. Election-year pressures played a major role, especially in the Senate, where party control was up for grabs in 2002 and the most vulnerable incumbents were from farm states. The two-year debate showed the deep philosophical and regional fault lines in agriculture policy. The traditional crop subsidies generally benefited the large, often corporate, farms and were defended by representatives and senators from the large farming states. Their opponents wanted to move agriculture policy in a way that benefited farmers of any size and to put a new emphasis on conservation initiatives to anyone in the farming business. As a result, the close-knit coalition of farm-state legislators were set against a growing group of urban and suburban members.

Although HR 2646 increased conservation spending by nearly 80 percent, the total—$38.5 billion over ten years—still paled by comparison to the $124.8 billion provided for commodity support programs. Supporters hoped the increased subsidies would end the need for emergency appropriations to supplement farm income.

LEGISLATIVE ACTION

Farm-state lawmakers wanted a new, multi-year farm bill passed in 2001. Although the 1996 law was not due to expire until Oct. 1, 2002, they were anxious to lay claim to $73.5 billion in new spending for farm programs that had been set aside under the fiscal 2002 budget resolution. With the federal budget surplus vanishing, they feared the money might not be available if they waited. But regional and party differences foiled plans for quick action. By the end of 2001 the House had passed a ten-year farm bill while the Senate was deadlocked over a bigger, five-year bill. *(2002 budget resolution, p. 48)*

The House passed its version of the bill Oct. 5, 2001, agreeing to $73.5 billion in new spending for agriculture programs over ten years, most of it to maintain and expand subsidies for growers of row crops. Members narrowly defeated an amendment that embraced the idea of de-emphasizing traditional crop subsidies in favor of conservation initiatives available to every farmer.

In the Senate, Agriculture Committee Chair Tom Harkin, D-Iowa, set out to write a bill that would restructure farm policy to emphasize conservation payments that would benefit small farmers. He succeeded in increasing funding for conservation but to win support for the bill he agreed to add even more money to revive and expand the commodity-based support policies of the past.

The legislation that emerged from the House and Senate was based on the same general principles: fixed federal payments to farmers; new countercyclical aid tied to a guaranteed per bushel target price; marketing loans for grains, cotton, and oilseeds; and planting flexibility with no supply controls. The Senate bill, however, put more benefits into loan deficiency payments linked to prices while the House bill put more money into the fixed payments. The Senate bill was front-loaded so that more of the money would be spent in the first five years.

The White House objected to the House bill but it disliked the costlier Senate bill even more. The White House Office of Management and Budget (OMB) said the price supports in both measures would encourage overproduction, increase government support in a time of declining revenue, and risk violating the restrictions on agriculture subsidies in global trade agreements.

The administration favored putting more money into conservation programs and de-emphasizing commodity price supports but it remained aloof from the bill-writing process. After the terrorist attacks on Sept. 11, 2001, the White House's main goal for the farm bill was to postpone a vote in the Senate, thereby delaying the conference until 2002 when it could focus on the issue. Barring that, officials favored a late entry, a proposal by Republicans Pat Roberts of Kansas and Thad Cochran of Mississippi that focused on farm savings accounts—instead of target-price payments—that would be matched by government funds when prices

MAJOR FARM LAWS

Direct federal involvement in the farm economy dated to the Great Depression of the 1930s. Hoping to bring temporary relief to suffering farmers, Congress cleared and President Franklin D. Roosevelt signed the first-ever farm bill, the Agricultural Adjustment Act of 1933 (PL 73-10). *(Congress and the Nation Vol. I, pp. 665, 683)*

The stopgap measure, which sought to stabilize the market by propping up prices and holding down production, quickly became permanent. The Agricultural Act of 1949 revised the system by giving the secretary of agriculture more flexibility in setting price-support levels. The overhaul represented a middle-ground position in the debate that Congress would revisit repeatedly in the following decades between advocates of government management of farm programs and supporters of a free market for agricultural products.

The government added yet another benefit in the 1960s: income support for farmers in the form of direct payments. Thereafter federal programs grew to become an increasingly large part of farmers' incomes.

Major revisions to the farm law included the following.

• The Agricultural Act of 1970 (PL 91-524) maintained crop and price controls but added a "set-aside" program that paid farmers for taking portions of their land out of production. *(Congress and the Nation Vol. III, p. 336)*

• The Agriculture and Consumer Protection Act of 1973 (PL 93-86) replaced the old support prices for major commodities—cotton, wheat, rice, corn, and other feed grains—with "target prices" that reimbursed farmers when the market dropped sharply. *(Congress and the Nation Vol. IV, p. 719)*

• The 1981 farm bill (PL 97-98) maintained price supports and added a new support program for sugar. *(Congress and the Nation Vol. VI, p. 487)*

• The 1985 farm bill (PL 99-198) provided massive income-support payments to farmers struggling in the midst of a devastating farm depression, at a cost of $69.4 billion over five years. *(Congress and the Nation Vol. VII, p. 501)*

• The 1990 farm bill (PL 101-624) sought to reduce the cost of federal farm programs. It froze farm price support and income-support rates at existing levels and began the "triple base acreage" program, which made 15 percent of farmland ineligible for crop subsidy payments but still allowed farmers to cultivate the land and sell its products. *(Congress and the Nation Vol. VIII, p. 537)*

• The 1993 budget reconciliation bill (PL 103-66) contained another round of cuts, totaling $3.2 billion, to agriculture programs. The largest savings—$586 million over five years—came from limiting the agriculture secretary's ability to threaten increased price-support payments as a bargaining chip in trade negotiations. Other savings came from reducing fraud and abuse in the crop insurance system; decreasing participation in the Conservation Reserve Program; and reducing the size of payments to farmers who agreed not to plant certain subsidized grain crops. *(Congress and the Nation Vol. IX, p. 485)*

The 1996 farm law (PL 104-127), written by Republicans after they took control of Congress in 1995, was a major departure from past farm policy and was grounded in the belief that agriculture programs should be deregulated. It aimed to end farmers' dependence on government subsidies and move them to the free market while at the same time freeing them from government mandates on what they planted. It retained marketing loans but eliminated other farm subsidies. Instead it provided fixed, declining payments—known as AMTA payments, after the provision that created them, the Agricultural Market Transition Act—to help farmers adapt to the new system. *(Congress and the Nation Vol. X, p. 494)*

But the law did not work as intended. When crop prices fell from record highs in the mid-1990s, the fixed payments proved insufficient to protect farmers from the devastating dips. So each year after the 1996 law's enactment, Congress and the White House propped up farmers and the agriculture economy by providing ad hoc "disaster" payments, ultimately totaling $30.5 billion over five years.

Those emergency packages made clear that the system enacted in 1996 had not curbed production enough to keep prices from falling when supply exceeded demand. As the 107th Congress prepared to write a new multi-year farm law, farm-state lawmakers were determined to address needs that had been demonstrated since 1996, including a countercyclical income-support component that would kick in when prices plummeted.

were down. Although that proposal failed, Senate Republicans held firm to block three attempts in December to bring the underlying bill to a vote in 2001. *(Terrorist attacks, pp. 230, 234)*

HOUSE COMMITTEE ACTION

The House Agriculture Committee took the first step July 27, 2001, approving by voice vote a bill to make $167 billion available over ten years for farm programs. The measure (HR 2646) included increases of $45 billion in subsidies for growers of the nation's principal crops—corn, wheat, soybeans, rice, and cotton—$16.3 billion for conservation and $3.7 billion for food and nutrition assistance. HR 2646 was formally reported (H Rept 107-191, Part I) by House Agriculture on Aug. 2; a supplemental report (H Rept 107-191, Part II) was filed by the committee on Aug. 31. The House International Relations Committee reported the measure (H Rept 107-191, Part III) on Sept. 10.

President George W. Bush addresses the Farm Journal Convention in Washington, D.C., on November 28, 2001, in the midst of congressional debate on the 2002 omnibus farm bill. President Bush called for "generous but affordable" legislation that would give farmers a safety net without leading to overproduction of crops. *Source: AP Wide World Photos/ Doug Mills*

Agriculture Committee Chair Larry Combest, R-Texas, and ranking Democrat Charles W. Stenholm of Texas had managed to garner crucial support from committee members, mostly Democrats, who were seeking to bolster spending on conservation and nutrition programs. Revised estimates from the Congressional Budget Office (CBO) of the long-term cost of the commodity programs, which comprised the bulk of the bill, allowed Combest and Stenholm to redirect $3.7 billion that had been set aside for farmer support in an earlier draft, moving $1.3 billion to conservation and $1.4 billion to food stamps and other nutrition aid.

The new estimates allowed bigger allocations to virtually every section of the bill, including a higher fixed-payment rate and higher target prices for soybean farmers. The authors also resurrected subsidy programs for honey, mohair, and wool that had been dropped under the 1996 law and included a new, $350 million-a-year program for peanut farmers similar to the one in place for grain and cotton farmers.

The bill proposed to revive sugar-marketing allotments, limiting domestic production for U.S. processors of sugarcane and sugar beets, although the U.S. Department of Agri-culture (USDA) could lift them if imports grew too high. That provision was an attempt to address the concerns of domestic sugar refiners, who complained that imports of low-cost "stuffed molasses"—a mixture of molasses, sugar, and water that was allowed to enter the United States duty-free—constituted unfair competition for their products.

Lawmakers who wanted to steer agriculture funding away from commodity subsidies and toward new conservation and research initiatives held off, recognizing that they did not have the votes in the farm-state-dominated panel. Collin D. Peterson, D-Minn., offered, but later withdrew, an amendment to overhaul and scale-back crop subsidies to make room in the bill for more conservation funding. Ron Kind, D-Wis., also offered and later withdrew an amendment he said would provide $5 billion a year for conservation, compared with $3.7 billion in HR 2646. Kind and others were interested in, among other things, increasing the amount of acreage eligible for the Conservation Reserve Program.

After more than three hours of debate July 27, the panel rejected by voice vote an amendment by John Thune, R-S.D., to require country-of-origin labeling on beef, lamb, pork, farm-raised fish, and perishable commodities. Lawmakers representing both ranchers and catfish farmers, who were feeling increasingly threatened by a surge in imported fish from Vietnam, argued that U.S. consumers had a right to know where their food came from. Opponents said the labeling would be burdensome to U.S. producers and would provoke retaliation by foreign governments.

The panel gave voice vote approval to amendments by

• Marion Berry, D-Ark., to double to $150,000 the limit on payments that farmers could receive under the commodity loan program.

• Richard W. Pombo, R-Calif., to allow a program that developed overseas markets for commodities, funded at $67 million under the bill, to focus on value-added products.

• Bob Etheridge, D-N.C., to make tobacco eligible for the Market Access Program.

• Saxby Chambliss, R-Ga., to phase out "last resort" loans to farmers.

• Ernie Fletcher, R-Ky., to classify horses for the first time as livestock qualifying for benefits under the farm bill.

HOUSE FLOOR ACTION

The House passed the farm bill by a vote of 291–120 on Oct. 5, 2001, agreeing to spend $167 billion on agriculture programs over ten years, most of it to maintain and expand subsidies for growers of row crops. By that point, however, the federal budget surplus was diminishing rapidly, the White House was urging the House not to pass the bill, and Congress's priorities had been transformed by the Sept. 11 attacks.

Farm-state lawmakers had scrambled to complete the committee bill before the August recess, hoping to bring it to the floor their first week back in September. By the time they returned, both CBO and OMB had revised their fiscal projections to show a sharply reduced budget surplus. The new numbers touched off concerns about whether the huge agriculture increases farm-state lawmakers had envisioned would be possible. Critics of farm spending, as well as Democratic leaders, said the debate should be put off until Bush produced a new budget that provided for more farm spending. GOP leaders worried the bill would give Democrats a vehicle to accuse Republicans of fiscal recklessness.

In the end, the lawmakers concluded that a delay would make matters worse, not only for the farm bill but also for Bush's top trade priority: revival of presidential fast-track trade authority. Combest already had yanked his support from the fast-track bill (HR 2149) to signal displeasure over a Bush administration decision on the treatment of U.S. farm subsidies under world trade rules. Other farm-state members indicated that their support for fast track might be contingent upon passing a generous farm bill. *(Fast track, p. 150)*

But plans to bring the bill to the floor the week of Sept. 10 were shelved after the Sept. 11 attacks. Then, on Sept. 19, the administration came out against the approach embodied in the House bill, calling for "fundamental, far-reaching changes" in farm policy and urging a shift in emphasis from commodity supports to conservation programs.

On Oct. 3, as the House was about to open its debate, the White House issued a statement strongly opposing HR 2646. The OMB statement said the legislation "misses the opportunity to modernize the nation's farm programs through market-oriented tools, innovative environmental programs, including extending benefits to working lands, and aid programs that are consistent with our trade agenda." It advised that "the administration does not support HR 2646 and urges the House of Representatives to defer action." Combest, Stenholm, and other bill supporters said they felt sandbagged by the White House, which had offered little guidance on Bush's views until shortly before the vote.

Conservation. The most important House decision came the night of Oct. 4 when members rejected by a **key vote of 200–226 (R 54–161; D 145–64; I 1–1),** a Kind amendment to shift spending away from crop subsidies and into conservation programs. The proposal was much closer to the approach administration officials and leaders of the Senate Agriculture Committee said they preferred. *(2001 key votes, p. 801)*

Kind had allied with two leading environmentalists among House Republicans, Sherwood Boehlert of New York and Wayne T. Gilchrest of Maryland, as well as with John D. Dingell, D-Mich. The four proposed reducing the bill's ten-year increase in commodity subsidies by $19 billion and dedicating the money instead to conservation programs, such as paying farmers to idle environmentally sensitive land and protecting wildlife and wetlands.

Combest and other Agriculture Committee members contended that amendment supporters—members from urban and suburban districts, lawmakers interested in preserving wildlife for hunting and fishing, and members with constituencies that did not produce the crops that got the lion's share of federal payments—were tinkering with a farm policy they did not understand and putting farmers at risk. Combest said that he would pull the measure from the House floor if the amendment were adopted. The amendment drew the support of 25 percent of the Republicans and 69 percent of the Democrats.

Dairy. Lawmakers from the Upper Midwest thwarted attempts from the Northeast and South to resurrect, if not expand, a regional milk pricing system that could benefit those areas. The coalition had been trying all year to preserve the Northeast Dairy Compact, which allowed six New England states to band together to set a higher price for fluid milk than the federal price floor. Created under the 1996 farm law, the program expired Sept. 30.

Opponents, who viewed the compacts as cartels that rewarded overproduction and depressed dairy prices, prevailed on parliamentary grounds. Judiciary Committee chairman F. James Sensenbrenner Jr., R-Wis., whose state's dairy farmers stood to lose the most from such compacts, argued successfully that because dairy compacts involve interstate commerce and the Constitution, they should be considered by his committee and not be debated as part of the farm bill.

The House on Oct. 4 rejected 194–224 an amendment by leading compact proponent Bernard Sanders, I-Vt., to create a national dairy policy that would allow any state to receive a premium above the federally set price floor for its fluid milk.

Sugar. The House rejected 177–239 an amendment by Democrat George Miller of California and Republican Dan Miller of Florida to phase out the existing sugar program, reduce sugar loan rates, and increase the penalty that producers had to pay if they forfeited their sugar to the federal government. The amendment reflected long-standing complaints by urban and suburban lawmakers that sugar price supports drove up the cost of their constituents' cereal, soda, and candy purchases.

The House also adopted a number of amendments not related to specific commodities, including proposals to

- Shift $1 billion from fixed commodity payments into rural development programs. Offered by Eva Clayton, D-N.C., it was adopted 235–183 on Oct. 4.
- Require country-of-origin information on perishable agricultural products. Offered by Mary Bono, R-Calif., it was adopted 296–121 on Oct. 4.
- Prevent labeling a type of fish imported from Vietnam as "catfish." Offered by Charles W. "Chip" Pickering Jr., R-Miss., the amendment was adopted by voice vote on Oct. 4.

SENATE COMMITTEE ACTION

After promising to produce a five-year bill that would restructure federal farm policy, Senate Agriculture Committee Chair Harkin ended up producing legislation that differed little from the House bill, except that it was slightly bigger. It combined traditional congressional support for commodity programs with greater incentives for land conservation and energy production and help for economic development in rural areas.

The Senate Agriculture Committee approved the five-year, roughly $90 billion bill (S 1731) by voice vote on Nov. 15, 2001, after a markup that spanned two weeks. Aides projected at the time that if the measure were extended over ten years, it would cost a total of $174 billion. The bill was formally reported (S Rept 107-117) on Dec. 7.

Agriculture secretary Ann M. Veneman had telephoned members of the Agriculture Committee the week of Oct. 22 asking that the bill be postponed.

Harkin called the bill a "broad and balanced" approach to farm policy. But he acknowledged having to make numerous concessions, such as moving money from his pet conservation proposal to commodities subsidies, to win the votes of committee Democrats.

He retreated from his earlier pledge to cut payments to big grain and cotton farmers, and he added money for rice and peanuts to placate Southern Democrats Blanche Lincoln of Arkansas and Zell Miller of Georgia. The inclusion of a national dairy support program favored by Patrick J. Leahy, D-Vt., added $3 billion over ten years to the bill's cost. The commodities program, initially structured to cost $11 billion less than the House version over a ten-year period, had grown by the end of the markup process to $1.5 billion more than the House measure over five years.

The Senate committee began debating the bill Oct. 31, approving a $50 million agricultural credit section designed to help beginning farmers and ranchers obtain loans.

From Nov. 6 to Nov. 8 members adopted additional provisions dealing with energy, forestry, trade, research and rural development, including provisions to authorize funding for energy programs ($600 million), forestry programs ($250 million), international agricultural trade ($2.1 billion), food security research ($610 million), and rural development ($2.3 billion).

Commodities. The panel demonstrated its preference for commodity programs Nov. 8, rejecting 7–13 an amendment by ranking Republican Richard G. Lugar of Indiana that would have increased annual funding for the Agricultural Research and Extension program from $120 million to $360 million over four years.

On Nov. 15, the panel approved 12–9 a contentious commodities section that would increase loan rates slightly, continue AMTA payments, and create a countercyclical program to reimburse farmers when crop prices fell below government target levels. Soybeans and oilseeds were added to the program for the first time.

Lugar, who had pushed an $82 billion, five-year alternative (S 1571) that would phase out subsidies and emphasize water and land conservation, withdrew his measure after the committee tabled it. That same day, the Bush administration, which had spoken favorably of Lugar's plan, issued a statement supporting another alternative, sponsored by Roberts

and Cochran. The proposal, which the committee rejected 9–11, would simplify complex funding formulas, allow for countercyclical payments, and set up farm "savings accounts" to help eligible farmers save money for lean years with federal matching funds.

Competition. The committee dealt Harkin's bill a major setback Nov. 13, rejecting 9–12 a proposal intended to curb unfair or deceptive practices by agribusinesses. Harkin said the provision was necessary because of the trend away from competition in agriculture, where he said the top four firms that slaughtered steers and heifers accounted for 81 percent of the market, up from 36 percent in 1980.

Nutrition. The panel agreed by voice vote on nutrition provisions that would authorize increased spending on food stamps and restore benefits to legal immigrants. If stretched out over ten years, the nutrition programs were projected to cost $6.2 billion. Lugar failed, by a vote of 12–9, to win approval of an alternative plan that would have cost $10 billion over ten years.

Conservation. The cornerstone of Harkin's bill was the conservation section, approved by voice vote, that increased funds for conservation on land in production while expanding government support for programs that remove crop and grazing land from production. It included a new Conservation Security Program that would give incentive payments to farmers and ranchers who voluntarily adopted conservation measures. It increased funding for the Environmental Quality Incentives Program by $200 million a year, to $1.3 billion.

SENATE FLOOR ACTION: 2001

After a grueling, two-week debate that descended into filibuster and rank partisanship and that saw three failed attempts in seven days to move toward final passage, Senate majority leader Tom Daschle, D-S.D., pulled the farm bill Dec. 19, 2001. Democrats accused Republicans, who backed the White House view that the bill should be postponed, of stalling. Republicans argued that Democrats had written sloppy, bad policy.

Eleventh-hour changes to the Agriculture Committee-approved measure had allowed Democratic leaders to cut the cost and bring the bill to the floor in late November. The changes included revising the dairy proposal, which required fluid milk processors and the federal government to contribute to a fund whenever farm milk prices fell below a federal target price. The money would be paid to milk producers in monthly increments. The committee bill had routed the money through new regional boards; under the revised bill, the money would be administered through the existing federal milk marketing orders, thus taking them off-budget and bringing the bill within budget limits. Also, under the revisions, states with their own milk marketing programs, such as California, could opt out.

Democrats survived one key challenge Dec. 11, when the Senate voted 51–47 to table an amendment by Michael D. Crapo, R-Idaho, to delete the dairy provisions. Eliminating the provisions would have cost the bill the crucial votes of senators from the Northeast.

Bill supporters also rejected proposals to

• Shift $6.3 billion from commodities to nutrition programs. The Lugar amendment was tabled (killed) by 70–30 on Dec. 12.

• Cut out the federal sugar program and shift funds to nutrition programs. The Judd Gregg, R-N.H., amendment was tabled (killed) by 71–29 on Dec. 12.

• Allow the use of the term "catfish" on imported Vietnamese fish. The John McCain, R-Ariz., amendment was tabled (killed) 68–27 on Dec. 18.

• Allow the administration to block food and medicine sales to Cuba. The Robert C. Smith, R-N.H., amendment was tabled (killed) by 61–33 on Dec. 18.

• Create individual retirement account-type farm savings accounts to be matched by government funds, instead of using target price-based payments. The Roberts and Cochran amendment was tabled (killed) by 55–40 by Dec. 18.

• Replace the text of the bill with provisions similar to the House bill. The Tim Hutchinson, R-Ark., amendment was tabled (killed) by 59–38 on Dec. 19.

Democratic attempts to invoke cloture, thereby limiting debate and moving to a vote on the bill, were rejected Dec. 13 (53–45), Dec. 18 (54–43), and Dec. 19 (54–43). Sixty votes were required to prevail. Daschle warned Republicans that they risked cutting the farm funding allotment by "25, 30, 40 billion [dollars.] . . . It is clearly an open question how much in resources will be available for agriculture next year," he said after the Senate failed for the third time to invoke cloture.

Democrats nonetheless vowed to regroup and bring the same bill back at their first opportunity in 2002.

Senate Floor Action: 2002

After six days of floor debate and amendments, the Senate passed its version of HR 2646 by a **key vote of 58–40 (R 9–38; D 48–2; I 1–0)** on Feb. 13, 2002. The biggest change was a controversial amendment to reduce the total federal payments that individual farmers could receive each year. *(2002 key votes, p. 819)*

The White House lobbied the Senate to reject the bill, and all but nine Republicans voted against it. Lugar, ranking Republican on the Agriculture Committee, complained that the measure would go "in the wrong direction" by continuing a system that awarded two-thirds of the subsidies to 4 percent of all farmers.

At the time of the Senate vote, the Congressional Budget Office said the bill would increase spending by $73.5 billion over ten years, the amount allowed in the fiscal 2002 budget resolution, which continued to govern the bill. Total spending over ten years, including nutrition and rural development programs, was estimated at $578.5 billion in the Senate and House versions. Over five years, however, the Senate bill was expected to cost $45 billion in new spending, $9 billion more than the House bill. Harkin said the bill was front-loaded because farmers needed the help immediately, but the higher five-year cost was also the result of election-year pressures in the Senate for more spending, particularly for row crops.

In all major areas of the bill—conservation, rural development, trade, research, and energy—the Senate plan was more expensive. Another $2.4 billion in emergency agriculture assistance was added Feb. 12 after Max Baucus, D-Mont., succeeded on a 69–30 vote in exempting the package from budget restrictions. The assistance included $1.8 billion for crop losses and $500 million for livestock producers.

Payment limit. Senators stunned the agriculture community Feb. 7 by agreeing to sharply reduce the total federal subsidies that any one farmer or farm operation could receive. In place of the existing $460,000 annual cap, the Senate endorsed a limit of $225,000 for individuals and $275,000 for couples. The change, contained in an amendment by Byron L. Dorgan, D-N.D., and Charles E. Grassley, R-Iowa, was adopted by voice vote after an attempt by Lincoln to table (kill) it failed 31–66 on Feb. 7.

The Agriculture Committee had voted to increase the cap to $500,000. Harkin had tried to reduce it but compromised on the limit to get the bill out of his committee. The House bill proposed raising the limit to $550,000 per farm.

To make the limits even stricter, the amendment required counting commodity certificates, which were issued by the Agriculture Department and were the equivalent of cash. Exclusion of the certificates under existing law allowed some farmers to greatly exceed the cap. The amendment also proposed to eliminate the "three entity rule," which allowed a farmer to receive full benefits for the first farm and up to half the amount for two additional farms, effectively doubling the overall cap.

The stricter payment limits were backed by Midwestern senators who represented regions with small farms and by many members from urban areas who opposed government payments to large agribusinesses. An environmental group had drawn public attention to the issue in 2001 by posting a list on its Web site of every federal farm subsidy recipient between 1996 and 2000. Drawn from Agriculture Department data, the list showed that the top 10 percent of 2.4 million recipients of federal crop subsidies received two-thirds of all payments.

But senators from the South and West who represented regions with large farms adamantly opposed the lower cap, saying it did not take into account the high operating costs for their regional commodities. Hutchinson called it "nothing less than war on Southern farmers."

Meat-packing industry. Another controversial Senate provision sought to prohibit meatpackers from owning or controlling livestock for more than fourteen days before slaughter, with exceptions for farmer cooperatives and small packers. The provision—inserted by a group of Midwestern senators led by Grassley and Tim Johnson, D-S.D.—was aimed at halting consolidation in the meat-packing industry.

Critics said a handful of corporations, such as ConAgra Foods and Smithfield Foods Inc., had gained a stranglehold on beef and pork processing and prices.

The proposal was pushed mainly by lawmakers from the Great Plains who represented small livestock operations that had been getting squeezed out of the market. It was strongly opposed by lawmakers from the South and West, including House Agriculture Committee Chair Combest, who represented large cattle and hog operations.

Harkin and Grassley amended the bill on the floor to clarify that the ban would not affect marketing arrangements when the packer did not exercise operational, managerial, or supervisory control over the livestock or the farming operation that produced the livestock. A motion by Larry E. Craig, R-Idaho, to table (kill) the amendment failed 46–53 on Feb. 12.

Dairy program. In addition to continuing the existing milk price support program, the Senate bill proposed a new, three-year, $2 billion program to provide countercyclical payments to dairy farmers. For the Northeastern states, the payments would kick in when prices fell below a target price; for other states, payments would occur when milk prices fell below the five-year average for that quarter. The program was a priority for the six Northeastern states that had been part of the Northeast Dairy Compact, a regional system that had allowed members to set prices for their dairy farmers above federally guaranteed levels. The compact had expired Sept. 30, 2001, and efforts to reauthorize it had been blocked by members from Western and Midwestern states with large dairy operations.

An attempt by Pete V. Domenici, R-N.M., to substitute flat, direct fixed payments to dairy producers was tabled by a vote of 56–42 on Feb. 13.

In other floor action, the Senate

• **Food stamps.** Adopted 96–1 on Feb. 7 an amendment by Richard J. Durbin, D-Ill., to restore food stamp benefits to legal immigrants that were eliminated in the 1996 welfare law (PL 104-193). The amendment followed Bush administration policy but it included a provision by Phil Gramm, R-Texas, to end benefits if an immigrant lost legal status for at least twelve months. *(Welfare law, Congress and the Nation Vol. IX, p. 578)*

• **Bankruptcy.** Adopted 93–0 on Feb. 7 an amendment by Jean Carnahan, D-Mo., to make permanent Chapter 12 of the bankruptcy code, which covered farmers. The provision had expired Sept. 30.

• **Farm Savings Accounts.** A small, $18 million test program was all that remained in the bill of the national farm savings accounts plan proposed by Roberts and backed by the White House. An amendment by Harkin that would create a $510 million, four-year program in ten states was rejected 17–80 on Feb. 12. Harkin proposed the idea during a larger partisan fight over nutrition spending, a move that Roberts called "disingenuous." The Senate chair argued that he had given Republicans a chance to support the plan.

• **Water rights.** Westerners opposed an attempt to require farmers and ranchers to lease or sell water rights to the federal government if they took part in a new conservation program. Harry Reid, D-Nev., modified the plan to make it a test program in seven states, with the states having discretion on how to resolve water conservation problems. That did not satisfy critics such as Crapo, who offered an amendment to remove the language. His motion was tabled 55–45 on Feb. 12.

On other amendments, the Senate

• Rejected 11–85 on Feb. 7 a proposal by Lugar to replace the commodity subsidy programs with annual payments of $7,000 per eligible farmer.

• Rejected 44–52 on Feb. 6 an amendment by Paul Wellstone, D-Minn., to maintain a cap on the amount of cost-share aid that new or expanding large-scale animal feeding operations could receive under the Environmental Quality Incentives Program.

• Adopted 82–14 on Feb. 6 a Harkin amendment to give farmers with beef and pork production contracts the same rights as poultry producers to discuss contracts with bankers, lawyers, or federal and state officials.

CONFERENCE/FINAL ACTION

House and Senate conferees took nearly two months to agree on a final bill. The House adopted the conference report (H Rept 107-424) by a vote of 280–141 on May 2, 2002. The Senate cleared the bill 64–35 on May 8. "I've never voted for a farm bill conference report. I will vote for this one. That's how good I feel about this farm legislation," said Senate majority leader Daschle, who helped iron out the final details.

His enthusiasm was not shared by many in the House, who argued during the final debate that the new bill was a throwback to New Deal-era government support policies. Two House conferees, Cal Dooley, D-Calif., and John A. Boehner, R-Ohio, refused to sign the final report. "It represents the most sweeping non-military expansion of the federal government since the Great Society and will create more problems than it will solve," they said in a joint statement.

Combest argued that the conference report was "the best compromise that we are likely to see. In addition to desperately needed help for farmers, it contains the largest single increase in conservation funding in history, significant gains for food stamp and nutrition funding, more resources for agricultural research, increased incentives for renewable fuels production, and a strengthened commitment to our rural communities. And it is all accomplished within limits of the budget."

Revising the Senate Bill

Senate negotiators had come into the conference in an awkward position. House and Senate aides had already begun poring over the competing versions of the bill when the Congressional Budget Office found it had underestimated the ten-year cost of the Senate version by $6.1 billion. Instead of matching the ten-year funding increase of $73.5 billion in the House-passed bill—the figure that the administration and congressional leaders had agreed to—the Senate version was calculated to boost spending by $79.6 billion.

"I am not trying to blame the Senate," said Combest, "but if one has an extra $6.1 billion, one can make a lot more of the competing interests satisfied." Combest had publicly questioned how the Senate had managed to propose higher spending for every major section of the bill and still stay within the $73.5 billion limit.

Harkin said the mistake occurred because CBO had missed a major change made in the original Senate bill (S 1628) and contained in subsequent rewrites. Traditionally, direct commodity payments to farmers were calculated on 85 percent of their eligible acreage but the Senate bill provided that they be based on 100 percent of a farmer's acreage. "It is a disappointment that CBO has made an error of this magnitude," Harkin said.

The revised estimate meant that Harkin had to negotiate cuts with senators who had voted for the bill because of its largess. A suggestion by Combest that the Senate simply drop all its extra provisions, including the dairy program, garnered no support. Instead senators dug deeply into proposed conservation and nutrition programs as well as smaller items, such as a farmers' credit plan, to preserve the funding increases for the commodity subsidies that were key to winning Senate support.

The House agreed March 19 to let the Senate use the modified numbers as a starting point for negotiations.

Splitting Their Differences

The main differences during negotiations were between populist Senate Democrats, whose bill was designed to help small farmers and livestock producers, and House members from both parties who wanted a more traditional farm bill. In many areas, they split the difference. Even the six-year term of the final bill was a compromise between the Senate's five-year bill and the ten-year House measure.

Payment limits. The final bill drew loud criticism in the House from members who wanted sharp limits on federal payments to farmers. Although the original House-passed bill would have increased the annual limit to $550,000, the House subsequently voted 265–158 on April 18 to instruct its conferees to agree to the Senate position in favor of a $275,000 limit. The final compromise was a $360,000 limit; conferees dropped Senate proposals to count commodity certificates under the cap and to eliminate the three-entity rule.

"They carved out exceptions that would basically blow the lid off of any limitation," complained Wisconsin Democrat Kind, who with Nick Smith, R-Mich., tried to send the conference report back to the drawing board with instructions to adopt the $275,000 payment cap and divert more money to conservation, nutrition, rural development, and energy programs, but the motion failed 172–251 on May 2.

Commodity supports. Commodity support programs were increased by $47.8 billion over ten years. The Senate had proposed raising loan price supports used to help farmers get bank financing. House conferees argued that a farmer would have to produce to get the higher loan rates, leading to overproduction. Instead, they pushed for fixed cash payments. The agreement contained higher loan rates during the first two years of the bill, and then a decline.

Meat-packing plants, Country of origin. Conferees dropped the Senate ban on meatpackers owning cattle, hogs, or sheep within fourteen days of their slaughter. Midwestern lawmakers did win inclusion of another provision they sought: a requirement that meat, fish, fruit, and vegetables be labeled with their country of origin, a provision largely directed at meat from Canada. Conferees agreed to a voluntary labeling provision that would become mandatory after two years.

Dairy. The final bill reauthorized the milk price support program, as both chambers had recommended and created a new, three-and-a-half-year national dairy program to give farmers additional help when dairy prices dropped below a fixed level. The cost was estimated at $1.3 billion through Sept. 30, 2005. The Senate's separate program for the Northwest was not included.

Dooley, whose state of California was the nation's largest dairy state, argued that the provisions would effectively increase consumer prices for the types of milk products made in California, such as powdered milk and butter, by at least twenty cents. "That's a huge impact in the market prices because of an effort to hand out money to dairy farmers across the country," Dooley said. But the dairy program was needed to secure the votes of Northeastern lawmakers.

Conservation. The final bill provided $17.1 billion in new spending for conservation programs, compared with $21.5 billion in the Senate bill and $15.8 billion passed by the House. Harkin expressed particular satisfaction that the bill provided $2 billion for his proposed Conservation Security Program, which would pay farmers and ranchers for land, water and wildlife conservation efforts. Harkin had originally sought $3.2 billion. Environmental groups were critical of Senate negotiators for backing away from the Senate's higher total for conservation.

Part of the increase in conservation funding went to the Environmental Quality Incentives Program to help large hog producers comply with new Environmental Protection Agency rules. Rep. Tom Latham, R-Iowa, contended that this funding to large operators was "a reward for not taking care of the environment." He voted against the bill.

Bankruptcy. The conference agreement extended Chapter 12 of the bankruptcy code to Dec. 31, 2002. A provision to make Chapter 12 permanent had been included in a separate bankruptcy overhaul bill but that measure was stalled in conference. Chapter 12 had expired Oct. 1, 2001. The Senate farm bill would have re-enacted Chapter 12 with no expiration date. Although the House version had no comparable provision, the

House voted 424–3 on April 10 to instruct conferees to accept the Senate provision. (The farm bankruptcy law was extended in the 108th Congress.) *(Bankruptcy, p. 466)*

In separate action, the House on April 16 passed a bill to restore Chapter 12 for eight months, retroactive to Oct. 1, 2001. The vote was 407–3. The Senate cleared the bill by voice vote April 23, and Bush signed it May 7 (PL 107-170).

Disaster funds. The final bill did not include the $2.4 billion in disaster assistance proposed by the Senate. It did include a Senate plan to give $94 million in assistance to apple producers.

Cuba. Conferees dropped a Senate provision that would have repealed statutory restrictions against private financing of agricultural sales to Cuba, thereby allowing U.S. banks to finance such exports. The House-passed bill did not address the issue, but the House voted 273–143 on April 23 to instruct conferees to agree to the Senate provision.

MAJOR PROVISIONS

As enacted, HR 2646 (PL 107-171) contained the following major provisions.

Commodity Programs

The bill reauthorized through 2008 many provisions of existing law related to core commodity programs, including fixed payments and marketing loans, while making some modifications to those programs. It created a new countercyclical program to assist farmers affected by low market prices, thereby establishing a system of payments similar to the "safety net" structure that was abolished by the 1996 farm law (PL 104-127). The bill also reauthorized and made changes to the programs for sugar, peanuts, and fruits and vegetables, and created a new national dairy program.

Fixed payments. The bill extended through 2008 fixed payments created under the 1996 law. The payments, which were not tied to specific crops or market prices, were originally intended to wean farmers away from crop subsidies. The bill added soybeans and other oilseeds to the program.

Market loans. The bill reauthorized marketing assistance loans and loan deficiency payments to producers of major program crops and soybeans. Marketing assistance loans allowed producers to borrow money from the government using their crops as collateral. If the crop sold for less than the loan rate, producers were allowed to repay their loans at the lower rate. Loan deficiency payments were direct federal payments to producers for the difference between the going rate for their crop and the marketing assistance loan rate.

Countercyclical payments. A new subsidy was created for producers of major program crops and soybeans, with payments based on fluctuations in market prices to counter downturns in the farm economy. The payments would be triggered whenever a crop's effective price fell below a target price defined in the bill.

Peanuts. The Depression-era peanut quota system, which limited the amount farmers produced to maintain high mar-

ket prices, was scrapped. Instead, peanuts were treated similarly to major program crops, with fixed and countercyclical payments and marketing loans. Quota holders were to be compensated at 11 cents per pound per year for five years during the transition from the old program.

Sugar. The bill repealed a 1-cent-per-pound penalty in the 1996 bill that was imposed on sugar producers when they forfeited sugar that was used as collateral against government loans.

Dairy. The new law created a three-and-one-half year national dairy program, retroactive to Dec. 1, 2001, to give farmers additional financial aid when prices dropped below a target price. Monthly payments were to equal 45 percent of the difference between $16.94 per hundredweight and the Boston Class I price. Producers were eligible for payments on up to 2.4 million pounds of production annually. The U.S. Department of Agriculture was to report to Congress on the program's effectiveness one year after the bill's enactment.

Other commodities. The bill reinstated wool and mohair subsidies that were deleted in 1996 and added honey and crops such as small chickpeas, lentils, and dry peas. Also, $94 million was included in direct aid for apple growers, and the federal government was to spend $200 million annually to purchase other fruits and vegetables and other specialty crops.

Payment limits. The annual cap on total federal payments to farmers was lowered from $460,000 to $360,000. The limit for fixed payments was $40,000 per person, the cap for marketing loan gains and loan deficiency payments was $75,000 per person, and the limit for new countercyclical payments was $65,000 per person. The bill continued the use of generic certificates and the three-entity rule, under which some producers could receive higher total federal benefits than the cap would otherwise allow. Congress also mandated a system to track benefits going to farmers or corporations.

Trade compliance. The Uruguay Round Agreement on agriculture set a ceiling of $19.1 billion per year on domestic farm support programs that were considered most likely to distort production and trade. The farm bill stated that the secretary of agriculture would adjust expenditures if necessary to avoid exceeding the limit and report to Congress.

Conservation Programs

The bill reauthorized existing conservation programs and created two new ones: the Conservation Security Program and the Grassland Reserve Program.

Conservation Security Program. Under the new program, farmers would receive payments for employing soil, water, or wildlife habitat conservation methods on working lands. Land enrolled in the Conservation Reserve Program, the Wetlands Reserve Program, or the Grassland Reserve Program, as well as land that had been idle for four of the last six years, would not be eligible for enrollment in this program, which was expected to cost $2 billion over ten years.

Conservation Reserve Program. Under this voluntary program, farmers received annual rental payments in return for removing highly erodible land from production for ten years and devoting it to conservation uses. The program was reauthorized at an estimated cost of $1.5 billion over ten years. The law increased the enrollment cap from 36.4 million acres to 39.2 million acres and expanded a wetlands pilot project to 1 million acres in all states.

Wetlands Reserve Program. Under the Wetlands Reserve Program, farmers agreed to preserve wetlands in exchange for annual or lump-sum payments from the Agriculture Department, as well as cost-sharing payments, to restore an area to the original wetland condition. The $1.5 billion, ten-year cost allowed for the amount of eligible acres to increase to 2.3 million.

Environmental Quality Incentives Program. The program, created under the 1996 law, provided technical assistance and cost-sharing and incentive payments to encourage livestock producers and farmers to manage the use of nutrients and manure so as to improve water quality. The bill increased annual payments to $1.3 billion in a series of steps, totaling $9 billion over ten years. Sixty percent of the funds would go to livestock producers and 40 percent to crop producers. The increase was a major factor in the $17.1 billion overall increase for conservation in the bill.

Grassland Reserve Program. The aim of the new program was to enroll up to two million acres of virgin and improved pastureland under ten-, fifteen-, or twenty-year contracts. The ten-year cost was $254 million.

Other conservation programs. The bill authorized the Farmland Protection Program (at a cost of $985 million over ten years); the Wildlife Habitat Incentives Program ($700 million over ten years); the Water Conservation Program ($600 million over ten years); the Small Watershed Rehabilitation Program ($275 million over ten years); and a $200 million, ten-year plan to help conserve desert terminal lakes. The Farmland Protection Program, which paid farmers near urban areas to keep their land in production, included a plan by the Dracut Land Trust in Massachusetts to protect from development the farm operated by American Airlines captain John Ogonowski, the pilot of Flight 11 that was hijacked Sept. 11 and crashed into the World Trade Center. The Water Conservation Program sets aside $50 million for producers in the Klamath Basin region in the Northwest.

Trade

Market Access Program. Funding for the program—which provided financial assistance to U.S. producers and exporters for promotional activities abroad—was increased to $200 million annually by 2006.

Food for Progress. The program provided commodities on credit or on a grant basis to developing countries and emerging democracies. It also was intended to help U.S. producers by removing surpluses from the domestic market. The law reauthorized the program at a cost of $308 million over ten years and increased the cap on the amount of funds spent to transport the commodities.

Other trade provisions. Other programs that were reauthorized included the Food for Peace program, adding conflict prevention as a program objective; Technical Assistance for Specialty Crops, which provided exporter assistance to address barriers against U.S. specialty crops; and the Foreign Market Development Cooperator Program, which promoted value-added products such as wheat flour and soybean oil. The George McGovern-Robert Dole International Food for Education and Child Nutrition Program, a maternal, infant, and child nutrition program, also was extended. The bill also authorized the establishment of a program to provide live lambs on an emergency food relief basis to Afghanistan. The Farmers from Africa and Caribbean Basin Program was added to the Farmer-to-Farmer program with a $10 million authorization to establish and administer bilateral exchange programs to provide technical assistance to farmers in Africa and the Caribbean Basin.

Nutrition

Food stamps. The $6.4 billion nutrition program modified previous law by allowing states to provide transitional food stamp benefits for five months to families leaving welfare for work under Temporary Assistance for Needy Families.

The bill also restored food stamp benefits to legal permanent residents who had lived in the country for five years, effective April 2003, recently arrived children, the disabled, and refugees. The 1996 welfare overhaul law (PL 104-193) revoked the eligibility of most legal immigrants to receive food stamps. In 1998 the benefits were restored to children and the elderly who arrived in the country before 1996.

The law included new procedures to simplify and streamline the food stamp program to align it with other public assistance programs and to improve the quality control system. States with a high or significantly improved performance in the food stamp program would be eligible for bonuses from a $48-million-per-year fund beginning in fiscal 2003. The bill also consolidated nutrition assistance funding for Puerto Rico and American Samoa, set aside $5 million a year beginning in fiscal 2002 for community food project grants, and authorized $140 million a year in commodities purchases for the Emergency Food Assistance Program, which provided commodities to food banks and soup kitchens.

Commodity distribution. The new law reauthorized the distribution of surplus commodities to special nutrition projects and the Commodity Supplemental Food Program, and it set aside $60 million for emergency food aid.

Child nutrition and related programs. The law encouraged institutions participating in the school lunch program and the school breakfast program to include in their food purchases locally produced foods. A pilot program would make available to students in twenty-five elementary or secondary schools in each of four states and on one American Indian reservation free fresh and dried fruits and fresh vegetables throughout the school day.

Funding was increased for the Women, Infants, and Children Farmers' Market Nutrition Program and for the Seniors Farmers' Market Nutrition Program.

The Congressional Hunger Fellows Program was created to encourage the pursuit of careers in humanitarian service.

Credit

Farm ownership loans. Beginning farmers and ranchers were given greater access to USDA farm credit programs through loan guarantees. The loan repayment program for beginning farmers and ranchers was increased to fifteen years. Under a pilot program, beginning farmers or ranchers in at least five states were to get loan guarantees to help purchase farms on a land contract basis.

Emergency loans. The measure authorized loans in response to emergency quarantines imposed by the USDA under plant protection or animal quarantine laws as well as natural disasters.

Farm credit. The secretary of agriculture was authorized to provide unused funds allocated for socially disadvantaged farmers and ranchers within a state to other states that had pending loan applications for socially disadvantaged farmers and ranchers.

The secretary was authorized to make an operating loan to a borrower who had received debt forgiveness on not more than one occasion that directly and primarily resulted from a natural disaster as designated by the president.

Rural Development

Miscellaneous grants. The law authorized $30 million per year for water or wastewater disposal grants; $15 million for rural business opportunity grants; $30 million a year for the Community Water Assistance program to maintain water quality in rural communities, particularly in emergencies; $10 million per year for grants to nonprofit organizations to finance the construction, refurbishing and servicing of individually owned household well water systems in rural areas for low- to moderate-income individuals; $60 million in grants and loans for water and waste facilities for American Indian tribes; grants for water systems for rural and native villages in Alaska; rural cooperative development grants; and $10 million per year in grants for rural tribal college and university facilities and the development of day care facilities in rural areas.

Value-added agricultural products market development. The law expanded the eligibility for grants under this program, with $40 million authorized each year. Five percent of the funds were to be used for the Agriculture Marketing Resource Center.

Renewable energy systems. The law allowed low-interest (4 percent) loans, loan guarantees and grants to be used by producers for energy systems and improvements, including wind systems and anaerobic digesters.

Rural electronic commerce. The law created a new rural electronic commerce extension program to help small businesses and microenterprises in rural areas. It authorized

$360 million over six years for grants to eligible regional development centers and land grant colleges to develop business strategies and provide training.

Rural telework. Nonprofit or educational institutions or American Indian tribes were eligible to apply for grants of up to $2 million to use telecommunications to perform work functions at rural work centers located outside an employer's place of business.

Historic barn preservation. The law called for preservation of barns that were at least fifty years old and were eligible for listing on national, state, or local registers or inventories of historic structures.

Delta regional authority. The bill included $7 million per year for grants to develop state-of-the-art technology in animal nutrition and value-added manufacturing to promote economic development.

Northern Great Plains Regional Authority. The bill provided $30 million per year for grants to the authority—which included Iowa, Minnesota, Nebraska, North Dakota and South Dakota—for transportation improvements, telecommunications networking, job training, business development, aid to distressed areas, and other economic development programs.

Rural Business Investment Program. The program provided $280 million in guarantees for rural business investment companies to provide equity investment for businesses. The six-year cost of the program was $100 million.

Rural Strategic Investment Program. Under the law, regional investment boards could receive up to $3 million for economic development. The six-year cost was $100 million.

Rural broadband access. The Rural Electrification Act of 1936 was amended to provide funds to allow rural consumers to receive high-speed broadband service at a six-year cost of $100 million, as well as to allow for expansion of 911 telephone service.

SEARCH grants. The law authorized $51 million per year for grants to small communities for environmental projects.

Rural television loan guarantees. The law authorized $80 million over six years for loan guarantees to ensure that local television broadcast signals reached rural residents in unserved or underserved areas. Unused funds could be used to expand broadband access.

Rural development backlogs. The law authorized $360 million over six years to speed processing of applications for water and wastewater programs.

Farm worker training. A program to train farm workers in new technologies required for higher-value crops was authorized for $10 million per year.

Rural Firefighters and Emergency Personnel Grant Program. The law authorized $50 million over six years to train rural firefighters and emergency personnel.

Research

Agriculture Extensions. The law continued numerous programs totaling $1.3 billion over six years, including policy research centers; the Human Nutrition Intervention and

Health Promotion Program; the pilot research program to combine medical and agricultural research; the Nutrition Education Program; an animal health and disease research program; an increase from $15 million to $25 million a year for grants to upgrade agricultural and food sciences facilities at land-grant colleges; national research and training virtual centers; Hispanic-serving institutions; competitive grants for international agricultural science and education programs; university research; supplemental and alternative crops; aquaculture research facilities; rangeland research; a national genetics resources program; a nutrient management research and extension initiative; an agricultural telecommunications program; an assistive technology program for farmers with disabilities; partnerships for high-value agricultural product quality research; bio-based products; integrated research; an education and extension competitive grants program; the Equity in Educational Land-grant Status Act of 1994; 1994 institution research grants; an endowment for 1994 institutions; precision agriculture; the Thomas Jefferson initiative for crop diversification; research regarding diseases of wheat, triticale, and barley caused by *Fusarium graminearum* or by *Tilletia indica;* the Office of Pest Management Policy; National Agricultural Research, the Extension, Education, and Economics Advisory Board; grants for research on production and marketing of alcohols and industrial hydrocarbons from agricultural commodities and forest products; agricultural experiment stations research facilities; and competitive, special and facilities research grants for the National Research Initiative.

Initiative for Future Agriculture and Food Systems. The program, which studied future food production, environmental quality and natural resources management, farm income and rural economic, business and community development, received a funding increase from $120 million a year to $200 million.

Bovine Johne's Disease Control Program. The USDA was authorized to conduct research, testing and evaluation of programs for management of Johne's disease in livestock.

Biosecurity. In addition to the usual agricultural research, extension and education funding, the bill gave special authorization for such sums as necessary for biosecurity planning and response.

Forestry

Forest Land Enhancement Program. New funding totaling $100 million was committed for a new cost-share program to assist private non-industrial forest landowners in adopting sustainable forest management practices.

Enhanced community fire protection. The bill authorized $35 million per year to coordinate efforts to prevent and fight wildland fires.

Energy

Federal procurement of biobased products. The bill authorized $6 million for a new program under which federal agencies would purchase biobased products—industrial products, other than food and feeds, made from renewable plant and animal material.

Biodiesel fuel education. The bill created a grant program to educate government and private fuel consumers about the benefits of biodiesel fuel use, at a cost of $5 million.

Renewable energy system and energy efficiency improvements. The bill established a loan guarantee and grant program to assist farmers in purchasing renewable energy systems and making energy efficiency improvements, at a cost of $115 million.

Biomass Research and Development Act of 2000. The act was reauthorized and funded through 2007, at a cost of $75 million.

Bio-energy program. The bill authorized $204 million over six years to allow the secretary of agriculture to continue making payments to bio-energy producers who purchased agricultural commodities for the purpose of expanding production of biodiesel and fuel grade ethanol.

Miscellaneous

Country-of-origin labeling. The bill required the USDA to provide guidelines for voluntary labeling of meat, fruits, vegetables, fish, and peanuts by Sept. 30, 2002. The program was to become mandatory in two years. For a commodity to be labeled a U.S.A. product, it had to be born, raised, and processed in the United States. Commodities that were ingredients in processed products would not fall under the labeling requirement. In separate action in the 108th Congress, the mandatory date for the program was delayed two years. *(Food labeling, p. 465)*

Crop insurance. The Adjusted Gross Revenue pilot crop insurance program offered coverage for crops for which traditional crop insurance was not available. It was initially offered in five states and then expanded to seventeen states. The new law required that at least eight counties in California and at least eight counties in Pennsylvania be added to the pilot program in 2003.

Disaster assistance. Eligibility and aid were expanded in several areas under the bill, including $94 million for apple producers for the loss of markets during the 2000 crop year; livestock producers affected by shortages of feed or sudden increases in production costs; and $10 million for onion farmers in New York's Orange County who suffered losses during one or more of the 1996 through 2000 crop years.

Orchard assistance. Farmers with commercial orchards who suffered more than a 15 percent loss as a result of a natural disaster were to be reimbursed 75 percent of the cost of replanting trees.

Animal welfare. The law prohibited interstate movement of animals for animal fighting.

Animal health protection. Under the bill, the secretary of agriculture could prohibit or restrict entry of any animal or related material if necessary to prevent spread of any livestock pest or disease. The secretary also could prohibit or restrict exports to prevent the spread of disease from or within the United States. The secretary's authority extended to holding, seizing, treating, or destroying any animal or limiting the interstate movement of animals and acting to detect, control or eradicate any pest or disease of livestock. Owners would be paid based on fair market value of destroyed animals and related material.

Livestock. Growers with swine production contracts would be provided the same statutory protections as livestock sellers and poultry growers under the law. Also, livestock and poultry producers could discuss contracts with state and federal agencies and other individuals having a fiduciary or familial relationship, notwithstanding a confidentiality provision in any contract between a producer and a processor for the sale of livestock or poultry.

Specialty crops. The secretary of agriculture was authorized to use not less than $50 million each fiscal year to purchase fresh fruits and vegetables for distribution to schools and service institutions. The bill included $10 million for a cranberry acreage reserve program, which involved purchasing permanent easements on wetlands or on buffer strips adjacent to wetlands that were environmentally sensitive and had been or were currently used for cranberry cultivation. Another $10 million per year cost-share pilot program was established to create demonstration projects intended to increase fruit and vegetable consumption and to promote healthful eating. The bill also provided $94 million of Commodity Credit Corporation (CCC) funds for 2002 to pay apple producers who suffered market losses during the 2000 crop year, with eligible crops not to exceed five million pounds. CCC funds totaling $10 million also were to be used to assist onion producers in Orange County, N.Y., who suffered losses between 1996 and 2000. A program to promote the expansion of farmers markets was included.

Organic products. A National Organic Certification Cost Share Program was created to help producers and handlers get certification under the National Organic Program. Also, farmers who produced and marketed solely 100 percent organic products and did not produce any non-organic products were exempt from assessments under commodity promotion laws.

Assistant secretary of agriculture for civil rights. The bill created an office to ensure USDA's compliance with civil rights laws.

Socially disadvantaged farmers and ranchers. The bill provided assistance for socially disadvantaged farmers and ranchers, including an Indian tribal community college, an Alaska native cooperative college, West Virginia State College, and a Hispanic-serving institution. The law also required the secretary of agriculture to report on participation rates of socially disadvantaged farmers and ranchers by race, ethnicity, and gender.

Catfish and ginseng. The law stated that only fish classified within the family Ictaluridae could be labeled or advertised as "catfish." Also, "ginseng" could be considered a common name only for any herb or herbal ingredient derived from a plant classified within the genus *Panax*.

Food safety. The bill provided for the establishment of a fifteen-member Food Safety Commission to recommend how to improve food safety.

Irradiation. The term "pasteurization" was redefined to include other processes besides heat treatment for eliminating microbial pathogens, potentially allowing foods treated with irradiation, high pressure, or ultraviolet light to be labeled as pasteurized. The secretary of health and human services was to issue a final rule to regulate labeling of irradiated foods.

Biotechnology education. A public education program about the safety of foods produced using biotechnology was established.

Downed livestock. The secretary of agriculture was to investigate and report to Congress on nonambulatory animals—livestock too sick or injured to stand—and enforce new regulations.

Commercial fisheries failure. Emergency disaster relief was made available to the commercial fishery industry in the Northeast.

Plant protection. Criminal penalties were increased for anyone who knowingly destroyed records, moved pests in commerce or committed multiple violations of the Plant Protection Act.

Family farmer bankruptcy. Chapter 12 bankruptcy provisions were extended to Dec. 31, 2002.

Farm Aid Package

Congress approved a farm aid package in 2001 (HR 2213) that provided $5.5 billion in additional mandatory agriculture spending for that fiscal year. It was the fourth time in as many years that lawmakers supplemented the subsidies already being received by farmers. President George W. Bush signed the bill into law (PL 107-25) on Aug. 13.

The total was equal to the amount requested by the administration and set aside under the fiscal 2002 budget resolution. The bill provided the money by changing the rules for mandatory spending, a move unrelated to the appropriations process; the supplemental payments had to be made by Sept. 30, the end of the fiscal year.

The bill provided

• $4.6 billion to be distributed among farmers eligible for federal payments under the Agricultural Marketing Transition Act (AMTA)—the primary mechanism, created by the 1996 "Freedom to Farm" act (PL 104-127), for distributing annual support payments to producers of the nation's principal crops (wheat, corn, rice, and cotton). *(1996 law, Congress and the Nation Vol. X, p. 494)*

• $169 million for producers of specialty crops, mostly fruits and vegetables, distributed through grants to states.

• Additional funding for producers of soybeans and other oilseeds ($423 million); tobacco ($129 million); cottonseed ($85 million); peanuts ($52 million); and wool and mohair ($17 million).

- Language stating that federal block grants for specialty crops were not gratuitous payments, ensuring that grapegrowers received compensation for the impact of Pierce's Disease, and increasing the loan deficiency payment limit to $150,000.

BACKGROUND

The farm aid bill was viewed as further evidence that the 1996 law had fallen short of its main objective. The 1996 overhaul instituted a system of fixed but declining subsidies intended to wean farmers from payments that surged and subsided based on the weather and crop prices. But the farm economy had sagged soon after the law was enacted; between 1998 and 2000 alone Congress stepped in with a combined $25 billion in aid. The fiscal 2001 farm aid bill was viewed as a precursor to a rewrite of the 1996 law, which was due to expire Sept. 30, 2002. (Omnibus farm bill, p. 449)

Anticipating the demand both for short-term aid and for money to pay for a new farm bill, the fiscal 2002 budget resolution (H Con Res 83) set aside $79.1 billion in emergency agricultural assistance for fiscal years 2001 through 2011. Of the total, $5.5 billion was allocated for fiscal 2001, $7.4 billion for fiscal 2002, and the remaining $66.2 billion for fiscal 2003 through 2011. One of the main issues in debating the short-term aid bill was whether to dip into the money intended for future years, thereby reducing the amount that would be available for the farm bill rewrite.

HOUSE ACTION

The House Agriculture Committee approved $5.5 billion in extra help for farmers after narrowly resisting a Republican attempt to increase the total by $1 billion. The panel approved the bill (HR 2213) on June 20 by a lopsided vote of 31–14, but the vote to stay within the $5.5 billion was a narrow 24–23. HR 2213 was formally reported (H Rept 107-111) on June 26.

The draft bill brought to the markup by committee chair Larry Combest, R-Texas, would have allowed $6.5 billion in spending. The $5.5 billion set aside for fiscal 2001 would have been used to give farmers who received AMTA payments the same amount they got in 1999. The additional $1 billion—taken from the money set aside for fiscal 2002—would have gone to other producers.

The Bush administration opposed Combest's plan. Office of Management and Budget (OMB) director Mitchell E. Daniels Jr. June 14 said he would recommend that Bush not sign the legislation if it cost more than $5.5 billion.

But it fell to the committee's senior Democrat, Charles W. Stenholm of Texas, and the second ranking Republican, John A. Boehner of Ohio, to write the key amendment and orchestrate its adoption. Their alternative called for $4.6 billion in AMTA payments, about 85 percent of the 2000 total, and $900 million for other farmers. To keep the package within the $5.5 billion limit, the amendment required that any additional spending be offset with prorated cuts in the rest of the bill.

Stenholm's majority—seven Republicans and seventeen Democrats—included fiscal conservatives from both parties who worried about the precedent of dipping into fiscal 2002 funds set aside for the new farm bill. It also included Democrats who viewed the existing distribution of farm assistance as inequitable, and Republicans whose farm constituents grew crops other than the row crops that had benefited most from recent emergency farm aid packages.

Taking Combest's side were nineteen Republicans and four Democrats, generally those whose House districts were home to the grain and cotton farms that had received the lion's share of the recent aid. Combest argued that farmers were counting on receiving AMTA payments at the 1999 level, as they had in 2000, and that the extra $1 billion would be spent soon regardless. Stenholm and Boehner argued that once the committee consented to spending even one cent more than allotted for fiscal 2001, the floodgates would open in both the House and the Senate.

After the committee adopted the substitute, which limited the bill to programs that could be implemented and paid for by Sept. 30, proposals to add more funds quickly disappeared or were pared back. The panel did adopt, by voice vote, an amendment by Marion Berry, D-Ark., to double to $150,000 the limit on Agriculture Department payments triggered when prices fell below a certain level but only for crops sold in fiscal 2001.

The House passed the $5.5 billion bill by voice vote June 26. "In my opinion, this amount is not sufficient to meet the needs of our producers," Combest said during the floor debate. "But today, the important point is to move this process along."

Combest and other Republicans said they would focus—as commodity lobbyists and farmer groups already had begun to do—on boosting the total in the Senate bill. "I intend to work with the other body to ensure that the cuts made last week are restored," said Frank D. Lucas, R-Okla., whose district was in the heart of wheat country.

Stenholm said such a move would be irresponsible. "I cannot disagree with those who say that $5.5 billion is inadequate," he said, but "this is all we can afford at the moment."

SENATE ACTION

Picking a multibillion-dollar fight with Bush, the Senate Agriculture Committee approved a $7.4 billion farm aid bill (S 1246) by voice vote July 25 (no written report). "The truth is that the farm and ranch families across the nation are in need," committee chair Tom Harkin, D-Iowa, said at the markup. "Some of these just can't wait another year, and they need this money right now."

Led by Richard G. Lugar of Indiana, the ranking GOP member on the panel, Republicans tried to limit the package to $5.5 billion, arguing that spending the extra money would shrink the amount available for the farm bill rewrite. OMB director Daniels again warned he would counsel Bush not to sign a bill that exceeded $5.5 billion for 2001.

The action was a partisan role reversal from the situation in the House where Democrats had spearheaded the effort to hold down the bill's price tag. Senate Democrats argued that the extra funding would help compensate farmers who had not benefited from the existing subsidy structure. The committee bill included $5.5 billion for those farmers, plus another $1.2 billion for growers of oilseeds and "specialty crops" including tobacco, peanuts, and sugar, and $542 million for conservation programs. Harkin viewed conservation spending as a means to equalize federal farm support, because all producers could qualify for the benefits. The House bill had no conservation money.

After a week of wrangling, the Senate on Aug. 3 cleared the House-passed version of the bill by voice vote. The action came after the leaders of the Democratic majority—faced with the impending August recess and an explicit veto threat from Bush—found themselves unable to muster sufficient support for the $7.4 billion committee bill.

Democrats abandoned their campaign for Harkin's more generous package Aug. 3 after they lost on a **key vote of 49–48 (R 2–46; D 46–2; I 1–0)** an attempt to invoke cloture, thereby limiting debate on their bill. Sixty votes were required. *(2001 key votes, p. 801)*

With senators ready to head to the airport for the recess, Lugar was able to get a vote on the House bill. His victory reversed a decision made in the first key vote of the debate July 31, when the Senate voted 52–48 to table (kill) a Lugar amendment that would have reduced the cost of Harkin's bill to $5.5 billion.

Additional Farm Aid

Farm-state senators tried repeatedly in 2002 but without success to pass emergency legislation to aid farmers and ranchers stricken by drought that year and the year before. Their attempts stretched from an early effort to get emergency money into the 2002 farm bill to an end-of-session bid to pass a separate farm aid measure. The Bush administration and many Republicans argued that any aid should come out of the 2002 farm bill (HR 2646—PL 107-171) enacted in May or that it should be offset by spending cuts. *(Farm bill, p. 449)*

In February, the Senate added $2.4 billion to its version of the six-year farm bill to aid farmers and ranchers who suffered weather-related disasters in 2001. The assistance included $1.8 billion for crop losses and $500 million for livestock producers. It was approved by voice vote Feb. 12 after Max Baucus, D-Mont., succeeded 69–30 in exempting the amendment from budget restrictions.

But the provision was dropped in conference after it drew a veto threat from the White House. A major rationale for the large agriculture subsidies in the underlying farm bill was that they would eliminate the need for annual emergency aid for farmers.

Just before the August recess, Senate Agriculture Committee chairman Tom Harkin, D-Iowa, scheduled a markup for a disaster aid bill (S 2801—S Rept 107-223) introduced by Baucus but postponed it because members could not agree on how to pay for the assistance. Harkin, Majority Leader Tom Daschle of South Dakota, and other Senate Democrats wanted the aid treated as emergency spending that would not count against allocations for the fiscal 2003 agriculture appropriations bill; committee Republicans called for offsets.

Ignoring the administration's opposition, the Senate voted overwhelmingly Sept. 10 to attach nearly $6 billion in drought assistance to the fiscal 2003 Interior spending bill (HR 5093). The amendment, by Daschle, was adopted by voice vote after he won a procedural motion 79–16. Eager to help drought-stricken farmers and to protect themselves politically, thirty-one Republicans joined Democrats to support the amendment.

The measure, based on the Baucus bill, would have provided emergency support to farmers and ranchers who had lost income because of weather-related disasters in 2001 and 2002. While the Congressional Budget Office estimated the cost at $5.9 billion, others said it could cost much more because of the severity of the drought,.

House majority leader Dick Armey, R-Texas, said the drought aid clearly was aimed at improving the re-election prospects of Democrats such as Sen. Tim Johnson, Daschle's colleague from South Dakota, who was in a close race with Republican representative John Thune. "Anybody who does not recognize that is walking through life with blinders on," Armey told reporters. "Well, if I just did it to help Democrats," Daschle responded, "I guess I am puzzled why so many Republicans would help us."

GOP lawmakers said they expected money in the Daschle amendment to be reduced in conference. Senate Republican Policy Committee Chair Larry E. Craig of Idaho voted for the amendment to show concern for his state's farmers, but he predicted that farm aid in the final bill would be reduced to around $3 billion. "This amendment is a budget buster," he said. "That's why this amount will never become law." The issue became moot, however, because the Senate never completed the Interior bill.

Baucus made a last-ditch effort Nov. 19, seeking to bring up a Daschle bill (S 3099) that was similar to the Interior amendment but Minority Leader Trent Lott, R-Miss., objected, saying the cost was unclear.

Although President George W. Bush consistently had said the farm bill he signed in May included more than enough entitlement spending to deal with weather conditions and bad crops, the administration abruptly changed course a few weeks before the election. On Sept. 19 agriculture secretary Ann M. Veneman appeared at a press conference with Thune and other farm-state Republicans to announce plans to spend $752 million to aid Midwestern livestock producers whose herds had been ravaged by heat and drought. The money was drawn from excess customs fees, money that usually went to child nutrition programs and commodity purchases.

2003–2004

The 108th Congress, which was focused on the aftermath of the Sept. 11, 2001, terrorist attacks, did not have an extensive agriculture agenda. But the lawmakers did pass a number of bills including several to help protect consumers.

One ongoing battle was resolved, at least for the time being, in favor of consumers when Congress delayed but did not repeal an existing requirement that food products be labeled by the country of origin. The requirement originated in the 2002 omnibus farm bill but was opposed by many agricultural producers. The program was made voluntary until 2006 but would become mandatory at that time. To protect consumers who are at risk from food allergens, Congress required food manufacturers to clearly label common substances known to cause allergic reactions in humans. Legislators also sought to improve food safety inspections by increasing funding for several Agriculture Department agencies. The extra money was approved after a cow in Washington State was discovered to have mad cow disease.

Farmers received assistance from Congress by extension of a provision in bankruptcy law aimed at protecting family farms from being lost to creditors. In addition, Congress approved significant financial aid to farmers hard hit by a continuing array of drought and other natural disasters.

Food Labeling

In action on annual agriculture appropriations legislation, Congress postponed but did not repeal a controversial provision on food labeling that was included in major farm legislation enacted in 2002. The requirement that major food products, including meat, fish, and vegetables, show the country of origin had divided U.S. agricultural producers.

BACKGROUND

The food labeling requirement was a relatively small part of the sweeping 2002 farm bill (PL 107–171). The measure reestablished subsidy payments that had been abolished only six years earlier and included many other contentious provisions. *(Farm bill, p. 449)*

The Department of Agriculture had to provide guidelines for voluntary labeling of meat, fruits, vegetables, fish, and peanuts by Sept. 30, 2002. The program was to become mandatory in two years. To be labeled a U.S.A. product, a commodity had to be born, raised, and processed in the United States.

The requirement was controversial from the start. Consumer advocates and other supporters of labeling said the requirement would better inform Americans about where their food was produced. Some farm groups also said labeling would help protect them from imports. Midwestern farmers favored the labels to help domestic beef producers distinguish their products from Canadian imports.

Opponents, particularly large meat-packing companies and many retailers, said the labeling would be a costly undertaking that would push up the price of food. J. Patrick Boyle, president and chief executive officer of the American Meat Institute, said, "Country-of-origin labeling is one of the most costly and cumbersome pieces of legislation ever introduced." In addition, members of Congress from the southwest said ranchers often mixed Mexican and American meat.

LEGISLATIVE ACTION

Efforts to delay and repeal the requirement were centered in the House and championed by Rep. Henry Bonilla, R-Texas, who was chair of the Agriculture Appropriations Subcommittee. Bonilla was positioned to place obstacles in the way of labeling through the annual agriculture appropriations bill.

During subcommittee consideration of the fiscal 2004 agriculture funding, Bonilla offered language, which was part of a manager's amendment that was adopted by voice vote, to bar funding indefinitely for country-of-origin labeling of meat. The provision did not apply to labeling of fruit, vegetables, or fish. The full House by 193–208 on July 14, 2003, rejected an attempt by Denny Rehberg, R-Mont., and Darlene Hooley, D-Ore., to restore the funding for country-of-origin labeling for meat and meat products. The same day, the White House issued a statement backing Bonilla's approach on country-of-origin labeling. "This is not a food safety issue, but a marketing issue and should be treated as such," the statement said.

The Senate adopted a nonbinding sense of the Senate amendment offered by Minority Leader Tom Daschle, D-S.D., that the country-of-origin labeling law should be fully funded. Daschle's language was agreed to by voice vote after a Robert F. Bennett, R-Utah, motion to table (kill) it fell, 36–58, on Nov. 6. The conference report on the omnibus appropriations bill (HR 2673—H Rept 108-401), which included agriculture funding, cleared Congress on Jan. 22, 2004, after the Democrats gave up efforts to filibuster over the country-of-origin labeling provision and other matters. Labeling was the most contentious issue during final negotiations on the agriculture spending provisions. Conferees' agreement to block enforcement for two years was a victory for the administration as well as for grocery stores, meatpackers, and processors. An exclusion of wild fish was sought by Senate Appropriations Committee Chair Ted Stevens, R, whose home state of Alaska wanted to label its catch. In addition, the fish exemption was supported by Republican senator Thad Cochran of Mississippi, which was a major producer of farm-raised catfish.

Bonilla and his allies resumed the fight against the country-of-origin labeling language in the 108th Congress in an effort to repeal the provision entirely. The House added language to the fiscal 2005 agriculture appropriations bill (HR 4766) to make the program voluntary. The Senate, during consideration of its companion measure (S 2803), rejected an attempt to move up the start date for mandatory country-of-origin labels on meat, fruit, vegetables, and other food products. The two measures subsequently were rolled into an omnibus funding bill (HR 4818). Conferees dropped the labeling language. *(Omnibus appropriations bill, p. 80)*

Food Safety

A sick Holstein cow in rural Washington State prompted Congress in 2004 to provide additional funds for food safety programs. As a result, several agencies charged with inspecting and monitoring the nation's food supply received increased appropriations. The funding increases came through fiscal 2005 agricultural appropriations legislation (HR 4766, S 2803), which was eventually rolled into an omnibus measure (HR 4818—PL 108-447) signed into law Dec. 8, 2004. *(Omnibus spending bill, p. 80)*

The first U.S. case of bovine spongiform encephalopathy, commonly called mad cow disease, arose in December 2003 and prompted the Bush administration to seek more funding for agencies that monitor the food supply. By coincidence, just two days before the omnibus measure cleared Congress Nov. 20, the Agriculture Department announced it was investigating a possible second case of an infected cow, although that later turned out to be a false alarm.

Humans cannot contract mad cow disease but consuming contaminated beef is thought to cause an incurable ailment, Creutzfeld-Jacob Disease, that destroys the brain.

The government insisted that the infected cow in Washington did not enter the food supply, but the discovery led a number of countries—including Australia, Japan, Mexico, and South Korea—to halt U.S. beef imports. The National Cattlemen's Beef Association said the mad cow scare cost the industry at least $2 billion in lost exports in the first half of 2004.

In response, Congress increased food safety spending in the agriculture bill for several agencies.

• For the Food and Drug Administration (FDA), which regulates animal feed, the bill increased funding by 5 percent, to $1.5 billion, over fiscal 2004 amounts.

• For the Agriculture Department Animal and Plant Health Inspection Service, which tests animals for the disease, the bill increased funding by 14 percent, to $820 million, over fiscal 2004.

• For the Agriculture Department Food Safety and Inspection Service, which monitors the safety of the food supply, the bill increased funding by 6 percent, to $824 million, over fiscal 2004.

Specific legislation to require that meat be tested for mad cow disease was not acted on. HR 3705 was introduced Jan. 20, 2004, by Rep. George Miller, D-Calif., and sent to the Agriculture Committee. The bill mandated that all cows in the United States slaughtered for human consumption be screened by the Animal and Plant Health Inspection Service. Funding for the work would come from fees paid by companies involved in the slaughtering, canning, salting, packing, and rendering of beef. But these industries, and the Agriculture Department, showed little interest in the bill. Lobbyists for the American Meat Industry said the legislation would be costly and significantly cut into profits. Miller was not on the Agriculture Committee, whose members generally were allied with the meat-packing industry.

Farm Bankruptcy

Congress in 2004 cleared legislation (S 2864–PL 108-369) that extended a program allowing family farmers to restructure their debts without losing their lands. The extension was required when a larger rewrite of federal bankruptcy law (HR 975, S 1920) became entangled in partisan disputes and died upon adjournment. The law had been extended in the 107th Congress as part of the omnibus farm bill and was made retroactive to Oct. 1, 2001, when it had expired. *(2001 extensions, p. 457; bankruptcy bill, pp. 129, 141)*

The farm bankruptcy bill extended Chapter 12 of the federal bankruptcy code that allowed family farmers to restructure debt without the consent of creditors. In addition, persons using Chapter 12 who could make rental payments did not have to surrender their farms or ranches to creditors. Under Chapter 12 a farmer had to show a breakdown of income and assets as well as living expenses including farming expenses such as feed and fertilizer. The information then was used to determine the amount a farmer has available to repay creditors.

The existing protection for farmers had expired on Jan. 1, 2004. S 2864 extended it for eighteen months, until July 1, 2005. Chapter 12, the only temporary chapter in the federal bankruptcy code, was written to aid family farmers during the Great Depression in the 1930s.

When it became clear that the larger bankruptcy bill was not going to be enacted, Republican Charles Grassley of Iowa, a major farm state, introduced S 2864. Earlier, Senate Republicans had hoped inclusion of the noncontroversial farm bankruptcy bill in the large bill, which was highly contentious, would force Democrats to negotiate a final version of that measure. They particularly targeted Senate minority leader Tom Daschle, D-S.D., who represented a state with many troubled farms and who faced a difficult reelection effort in 2004. (Daschle lost his seat as a result of the November elections.)

The Senate passed S 2864 by voice vote on Oct. 6, and the House cleared it Oct. 8. President George W. Bush signed the measure on Oct. 25.

Farm Disaster Assistance

Congress in 2003 and 2004 sought to provide financial aid to farmers who had been hit by drought and other natural disasters but, as in the past, ran up against finding the necessary money to pay for the assistance. Two major relief packages were funded from a new conservation program enacted in 2002, over the vocal opposition of a number of senators.

An omnibus appropriations bill (H J Res 2–PL 108-7), cleared on Feb. 20, 2003, provided $3.1 billion in drought relief for farmers. The measure included eleven appropriations bills for fiscal 2003 that had not cleared at the end of the 107th Congress. One of those was the regular agriculture appropriations bill in which the funding was carried. *(Fiscal 2003 omnibus, p. 69)*

The fiscal 2005 military construction appropriations bill (HR 4837—PL 108-324), cleared on Oct. 11, 2004, provided $14.4 billion that included $11.6 billion to help victims of four major hurricanes that hit the United States in 2004 and $2.8 billion for farmers and ranchers hurt by drought, freezes, floods, and other natural disasters during the previous year.

The bill provided a variety of assistance not only to farmers and ranchers who had suffered drought conditions but also to many others such as Florida growers whose crops were damaged by the hurricanes. The bill included $9 million for the "reseeding, rehabilitation, and restoration of oyster reefs" in Alabama, Florida, Louisiana, and Mississippi. Democratic senator Daniel K. Inouye of Hawaii saw that the package included $7.2 million in assistance for sugar plantations on the islands of Maui and Kauai that had sustained damage from high winds and rain in 2004.

Providing disaster relief for farmers was one thing; finding the money to pay for it under tight budget restrictions and White House skepticism was another. Legislators turned to a new program, the Conservation Security Program, enacted as part of the 2002 farm bill (PL 107-171) under the sponsorship of Democrat Tom Harkin of Iowa. The entitlement program authorized payments of as much as $45,000 per farm annually to improve conservation of soil, water, energy, and other natural resources. *(Farm bill, p. 449)*

Legislators found money to pay for the disaster relief by capping amounts available for use in the new conservation program, over the strenuous objections of Harkin and other farm-state senators. Appropriators provided that the conservation program cuts would have no budgetary effect until fiscal 2008, but Harkin was unmoved. "The farm bill [conservation program] had a major conservation initiative," Harkin said. "The president and his administration keep talking about it, but the president's people are up here gutting the program."

Harkin and other farm-state Democrats had long pushed for funding to help farmers employ sound conservation practices. Soil erosion and water runoff from farms are serious problems that can reduce production and damage natural resources. Farmers were able to use money under the program to comply with Clean Air Act and Clean Water mandates.

House appropriators, however, did not like the program because they said it usurped their authority by making funding for many activities mandatory instead of discretionary, which put control of programs more under their decisions.

Harkin succeeded in delaying action on HR 4837 and relented only after the Senate by voice vote Oct. 11 adopted a nonbinding resolution (S Res 465) urging conferees on one of the unfinished spending measures to restore the cuts.

Food Allergen Labeling, Animal Drugs

Congress in 2004 passed legislation requiring food manufacturers to clearly identify ingredients associated with food allergies and use the familiar names of the eight most common allergens when labeling products. The largely noncontroversial bill (S 741) passed the Senate (S Rept 108-226) March 8 and the House (H Rept 108-608) July 20 on voice votes. President George W. Bush signed it into law Aug. 2 (PL 108-282).

The legislation was designed to make labels more informative for people who are allergic to certain ingredients. Products often can contain derivatives of those foods, but the ingredient lists do not make those relationships clear. "Now consumers won't have to wonder what is in a labeled food product," said Rep. Rosa DeLauro, D-Conn. "They can protect themselves from exposure to potentially deadly allergens just by reading the label at the store or in the kitchen."

The most common allergens were milk, eggs, fish, crustaceans, tree nuts, wheat, peanuts, and soybeans. These eight ingredients accounted for 90 percent of all food allergies, which affected about seven million Americans. Food allergies also appeared to be on the rise in some cases; peanut allergies, in particular, were increasing among children.

An estimated 150 people died each year from food-related allergic reactions and thirty thousand required emergency room treatment.

The legislation allowed manufacturers to choose from two label formats similar to those required for the disclosure of nutritional information. It also required the Food and Drug Administration (FDA) to develop a rule for voluntary "gluten-free" labeling. Gluten, a protein left behind after starch is washed away from wheat flour dough, causes severe stomach problems in about 1.5 million Americans. In addition, the bill required the FDA to inspect food manufacturing facilities for cross-contamination of foods with allergens during processing.

"The supermarket industry commends Congress for approving a plain-language allergen labeling bill," said Tim Hammonds, president and chief executive officer of the Food Marketing Institute. "This measure will provide vital information for the millions of Americans who are allergic to certain foods."

S 741 also allowed some veterinary drugs to be marketed before they receive full approval by the Food and Drug Administration. That provision created incentives for pharmaceutical companies to develop drugs for rare diseases and to treat so-called minor animal species such as sheep, goats, and game birds. It defined minor species as all animals except cattle, horses, chicken, turkeys, dogs and cats; and rare diseases as those that occur infrequently, in only a few species, in limited geographical areas, or in only a small number of animals annually.

The animal provisions were needed, supporters say, because many pharmaceutical companies shy away from manufacturing drugs for minor species because of the small market shares, low profit margins, and high capital investment involved. They added that it was often difficult for researchers to design and conduct studies to determine safety and effectiveness because the animal populations are small and conditions of animal management may vary widely.

The conditional approval would let drugmakers recoup some development costs through marketing prior to full FDA approval.

CHAPTER 9

Health and Human Services

Health and Human Services

Although national defense and foreign affairs dominated President George W. Bush's first term, some of the most pitched ideological battles on the domestic agenda came over the issues of health and human services.

Still, President Bush managed to accomplish a surprisingly large number of items on his domestic to-do list, including a major overhaul of the Medicare program that added a first-ever outpatient prescription drug benefit to the program and took the first tentative steps aimed at reining in the massive entitlement's spiraling costs.

That law, however, proved highly divisive and sidestepped what had become one of the biggest health issues of the new century: the rising cost of prescription drugs. Other efforts to hold down drug spending, most notably by opening U.S. borders to drugs from Canada and other developed countries, proved unsuccessful.

Several legislative accomplishments were not among those the president promised on the campaign trail in 2000 but rather those necessitated by the terrorist attacks of Sept. 11, 2001, and the anthrax attacks on Capitol Hill and elsewhere a month later. The 107th Congress passed a sweeping bill aimed at preventing and detecting bioterrorism, while its successor approved measures to provide compensation to first-responders and others injured by the vaccine to prevent smallpox, and to create incentives for drug and biotechnology firms to create tests and treatments for potential bioterror weapons.

Many more high-profile measures fell by the wayside. Leading that list was a "Patients' Bill of Rights," which Congress had been struggling with for half a decade. Both the Senate and House passed bills that were not that different in 2001, but the ideological split over where aggrieved patients should be able to sue and for how much proved too hard to bridge, and the Sept. 11 attacks focused attention elsewhere.

Bush also failed to prevail on another medicolegal front: capping damages in medical malpractice lawsuits. The House repeatedly passed bills to limit awards for "pain and suffering," which backers of the measure said could hold down medical malpractice insurance premiums. But the Senate just as steadfastly refused to go along.

The Senate also refused to go along with House-passed efforts to ban human cloning, as the two chambers sparred over bioethical questions involving human embryos and the promise of stem cell research.

But abortion opponents realized the most legislative success since the 1980s when Ronald Reagan was president. After an eight-year struggle Congress passed the first-ever abortion procedure ban, outlawing a little-used procedure abortion foes called "partial-birth" abortion. Three separate federal judges, however, promptly halted the law's enforcement, calling it an unconstitutional infringement on women's rights. Another abortion restriction that Bush signed made it easier for health care entities like hospitals or insurance plans to refuse to provide or refer for abortions. Social conservatives also won passage of a law that made it a federal crime to injure or kill a fetus during commission of a federal violent crime on a pregnant woman.

MEDICARE OVERHAUL

The 108th Congress proved an old adage wrong: major changes to popular entitlement programs do not have to be broadly bipartisan in order to become law. With scant support from Democrats, President Bush and GOP leaders in the House and Senate managed to push through their vision of changes to Medicare, albeit with the help of a historic

REFERENCES

Discussion of health policy for the years 1945–1964 may be found in *Congress and the Nation Vol. I*, pp. 1122–1194; for the years 1965–1968, *Congress and the Nation Vol. II* pp. 665–707; for the years 1969–1972, *Congress and the Nation Vol. III*, pp. 551–580; for the years 1973–1976, *Congress and the Nation Vol. IV*, pp. 323–375; for the years 1977–1980, *Congress and the Nation Vol. V*, pp. 601–653; for the years 1981–1984, *Congress and the Nation Vol. VI*, pp. 521–556; for the years 1985–1988, *Congress and the Nation Vol. VII*, pp. 547–606; for the years 1989–1992, *Congress and the Nation Vol. VIII*, pp. 561–610; for the years 1993–1996, *Congress and the Nation Vol. IX*, pp. 513–569; for the years 1997–2001, *Congress and the Nation Vol. X*, pp. 429–485.

Mandatory Outlays for Medicaid and Medicare

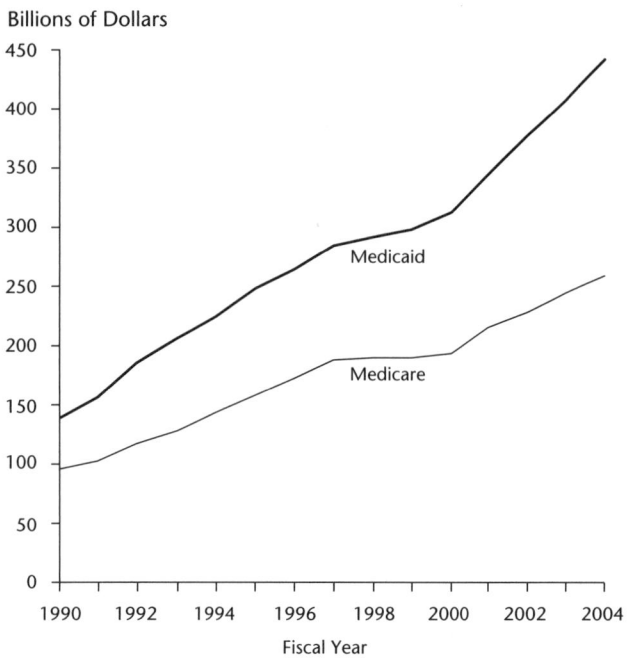

Billions of Dollars

SOURCE: Office of Management and Budget, *Historical Tables, Budget of the United States Government: Fiscal Year 2006* (Washington, D.C.: U.S. Government Printing Office, 2005), Table 8.5.

dead-of-night roll call in the House that was held open for three hours to round up the necessary votes.

The centerpiece of the bill was the first-ever outpatient prescription drug benefit for the then nearly forty-year-old program. Medicare's 41 million elderly and disabled beneficiaries had been clamoring for drugs to be added to the program's benefit menu for more than a generation. But Republicans did not want to simply tack on the new benefit; they wanted to use it to leverage more private participation in the program on the theory that the private sector could do a more effective job holding down rising costs than the federal bureaucracy.

Writers of the legislation managed to cobble together a bill from the center out. For Democrats and liberal Republicans, they included substantial aid for Medicare beneficiaries with low incomes. For conservatives, many of whom were wary about adding at least $400 billion over ten years to an entitlement program whose future was already shaky, even more sweeteners were added. Not only did the program keep the drug benefit private, it included a small step toward requiring wealthier beneficiaries to pay higher premiums and created a demonstration program to allow Medicare to compete head-to-head with private health plans providing comprehensive care. To garner the final conservative votes needed to pass the bill, sponsors also included authorization of new "Health Savings Accounts" for the non-Medicare

population. The accounts were intended to make consumers more responsible for the cost of their own health care in an effort to slow medical inflation.

Despite a promise by House leaders, however, the bill did not include language opening the United States to lower-cost prescription drugs from Canada and elsewhere. Such "reimportation" was widely popular and a bill allowing it had passed the House by a surprisingly strong margin in 2003. But it was vehemently opposed by the drug industry, which stood to lose big profits, and the Food and Drug Administration, which was concerned about potential safety problems.

Even with the last-minute support of the influential senior group AARP, the new Medicare law was met with mixed reviews from seniors who were confused by its complexity and disappointed with its relatively modest size. Still, efforts in 2004 to more directly address drug prices, by allowing reimportation or giving Medicare officials authority to negotiate directly with drugmakers for lower prices instead of having private plans do it, proved unsuccessful.

BIOTERRORIST THREAT

If the Sept. 11, 2001, attacks showed how vulnerable the nation's air traffic system was to terrorist infiltration, the shipment of anthrax spores through the mail a month later showed the nation was even more vulnerable to a bioterrorist attack.

The 107th Congress was quick to react to the anthrax incidents, which hit perilously close to home, closing down one of the Senate's three office buildings for months. By the end of 2001 Congress as part of an emergency spending bill had provided $1.1 billion to state and local public health departments and first-responders to prepare for not just biological but also chemical and radiological attacks.

The formal authorization took somewhat longer—until May 2002. But the bill cut a broad swath. It directed funds to help public health agencies improve communications, add laboratory facilities, and train personnel to detect and respond to bioterrorist incidents. It also provided $1.2 billion for a national pharmaceutical stockpile to organize antibiotics and other medications in ready-to-deploy packs. And it required federal registration for those handling potentially dangerous biological agents and toxins, and called for stepped up security for the nation's food and water supply.

Preparations for a potential bioterror attack, however, hit a snag in early 2003 when federal officials sought to vaccinate half a million health workers and first-responders against smallpox. Many of those targeted to receive the vaccine resisted because the vaccine had the potential to cause serious injury or death in a small percentage of patients. The 108th Congress responded in 2003 by passing a bill to compensate health and emergency workers who suffered adverse effects from the vaccine

A year later Congress addressed another bioterror conundrum: how to encourage drug and biotechnology firms to develop tests and treatments for germs unlikely to appear except in an attack. The answer was Project Bioshield, which provided a guaranteed federal market for the products and funding of $5.6 billion over ten years.

PATIENTS' BILL OF RIGHTS

While the Medicare bill represented a major victory for Bush and congressional Republicans, many more health priorities were not realized. Topping the list was a "patients' bill of rights" to provide patients in managed health care plans with federally guaranteed ways to redress grievances. Bush had signed a bill providing patients with a limited right to sue in Texas when he was governor and hoped to forge a similar compromise on the federal level where lawmakers had been sparring over the issue since 1996. The House passed a bill acceptable to the administration in 2001 after Bush cut a deal with a key Republican who had been pushing the issue since the late 1980s. But Senate Democrats, who took over the chamber in June after the defection of former Republican senator James Jeffords of Vermont, made the bill their first order of business. Their version included a much broader right to sue than the president said he would accept.

In the end the bill failed for several reasons. One was clearly the Sept. 11, 2001, terrorist attacks, which dramatically changed congressional and administration priorities. Another was the fact that the seemingly small differences between the House and Senate bills actually represented an ideological divide that would have been difficult to bridge in any case. Finally, as health inflation was again reaching double digits after a nearly decade-long reprieve, the need to control costs was starting to gain a higher priority than giving patients legal protections.

MALPRACTICE LIMITS

Ideological divisions between the parties also helped doom efforts to impose federal standards for medical malpractice lawsuits. Since Republicans took control in 1995, the House had passed a bill in each Congress to limit noneconomic damages—those for "pain and suffering"—to $250,000. That was the amount in a 1975 California law many doctors had credited with slowing malpractice insurance premiums in that state. (Consumer advocates said it was actually a separate insurance rate regulation law passed several years later that ended that state's insurance crisis). The Senate, however, more heavily tilted toward trial lawyers, steadfastly resisted.

Unlike President Bill Clinton, who opposed the bill when in office, President Bush made it a priority, calling "frivolous" lawsuits a major driver of not only doctors' malpractice premiums but also of health care costs in general. And the elevation to Senate majority leader of Bill Frist, R-Tenn., that chamber's only physician, was seen as finally giving the bill the boost backers had wanted. But even with Frist's strong support the Senate remained unwilling to go along, and the simmering dispute went unsettled.

CLONING BAN

Congress also failed to pass a bill pushed by the president to ban the cloning of human embryos, either to produce a baby or to derive embryonic stem cells for scientific research. At issue was not so-called "reproductive" cloning—an effort to produce a live baby. That was universally abhorrent to lawmakers who wanted it banned. The split, however, came over the propriety of cloning embryos for their stem cells. Many abortion opponents said that creating embryos, only to kill them after several days, was tantamount to murder. But others, including some leading abortion foes like Sen. Orrin Hatch, R-Utah, said the potential promise of stem cell research to provide treatments for such intractable ailments as diabetes, Parkinson's disease, or spinal cord injuries, outweighed the destruction of the embryos.

The House in both the 107th and 108th Congresses passed the full cloning ban supported by the president. But not only did the Senate refuse to go along, it also appeared there might have been a majority in that chamber to roll back embryonic stem cell research funding restrictions that Bush had imposed by executive order in August 2001. In the end the two sides fought to a draw with no bill to ban cloning and no relaxation of the research funding restrictions.

ABORTION

While abortion opponents failed in their efforts to ban all forms of human cloning, that was a rare defeat in Bush's first term. The president made clear his support for the antiabortion cause in his first business day in office, using the anniversary of the landmark Supreme Court decision *Roe v. Wade*, to reimpose abortion restrictions Clinton had removed.

The president's strong support helped propel several bills into law, most notably the "Partial Birth Abortion Ban Act," which he signed Nov. 5, 2003. It was the first-ever ban of a specific abortion procedure. Clinton had twice vetoed similar bills and the Supreme Court in 2000 struck down a substantially similar Nebraska law.

An omnibus spending bill that cleared at the very end of the 108th Congress included House language to make it easier for health care "entities" like hospitals or health plans to refuse to provide abortions or make referrals for the procedure. Backers said the measure was needed to protect Catholic and other religious-based health facilities, but opponents said existing "conscience clause" laws allowing individuals to opt out of performing procedures they objected to were sufficient.

The president also signed legislation making it a federal crime to harm or kill a fetus while committing a violent federal crime against a pregnant woman. The law was named for Laci Peterson—who was murdered while eight months pregnant—and her unborn son Conner, despite the fact that her murder was not a federal crime and would not have been covered by the law. But the law did give legal status to a fetus for the first time, which abortion-right supporters contended was its true purpose—to lay the groundwork for an overturn of the federal right to the procedure. Backers of the bill countered that it was not an attack on abortion rights but rather a recognition that an attack on a pregnant woman could harm two victims.

HUMAN SERVICES

Bush was less successful on the human services front than on health care issues. Neither of his two top priorities—a reauthorization of the 1996 welfare act and legislation to allow broader federal funding of faith-based social service providers—made it to his desk.

The 1996 welfare overhaul (PL 104-193) ended more than sixty years of guaranteed government aid and instituted a five-year limit on assistance. Most lawmakers credited the landmark law with reducing welfare caseloads by half, but some critics said it was really the robust economy of the 1990s that drove the sharp decline, and others said those who left the program simply had joined the growing ranks of the working poor and were still struggling.

The House passed reauthorization bills in both the 107th and 108th Congresses that reflected GOP desires to beef up the bill's work requirements. But Senate Democrats and some moderate Republicans wanted more funding for child care and restoration of benefits to legal immigrants, which the 1996 law largely ended. The impasse proved unbridgeable, and the program was kept running by a series of short-term extensions.

And, as it had with so many of Bush's priorities, the House passed a bill aimed at making federal money available for nine new categories of faith-based social services. The measure also would have created tax incentives for private charitable donations. But Democrats opposed a core provi-

sion that would have allowed faith-based groups participating in the program to use religion as a basis for hiring.

In the Senate, advocates of faith-based programs never managed to get beyond the basic dilemma of how to increase faith-based charities' access to federal funds enough to address unmet social needs but not so much as to violate the constitutional separation of church and state. The Senate Finance Committee approved a scaled-back version of the bill in 2002 but the measure never reached the floor, and died at the end of the Congress.

VETERANS' BENEFITS

Veterans' groups scored a series of victories in the 107th and 108th Congresses as more attention to the nation's military forces resulted in more attention to those who had completed military service.

A key victory was the loosening of a law dating back more than a century that barred "concurrent receipt," or the practice of collecting both full retirement and disability benefits simultaneously. A 2002 compromise resulted in allowing dual benefits for veterans whose disability resulted from combat wounds that earned them a Purple Heart, or who were at least 60 percent disabled as a result of combat-related injuries. In 2003 another bill was approved that allowed dual benefits to all retirees who were at least 50 percent disabled as a result of service-related injuries; it also set up a commission to study whether a redefinition of eligibility was needed.

The 108th Congress also boosted funding for veterans' health care, expanded benefits to spouses of deceased veterans and to some children of veterans, and made it easier for veterans whose military service prevented them from repaying debts to obtain civil relief.

Chronology of Action on Health

2001–2002

Before Sept. 11, 2001, by far the biggest health issue for the 107th Congress was the continuing debate over a "patients' bill of rights." That was an effort to extend to consumers more power to challenge medical decisions made by their health insurers in general, and the more restrictive health maintenance organizations (HMOs) in particular. While the terrorist attacks effectively swept that issue off the agenda, in fact, it more than likely would have foundered anyway. The relatively small differences between the House- and Senate-passed bills were probably politically impossible to overcome.

In the wake of not only the Sept. 11 attacks but an outbreak of anthrax from spores sent through the mail the following month, Congress turned its major health attention toward preventing, detecting, and dealing with acts of bioterrorism. While early steps to address the possibility of bioterrorism had been taken by Congress and the Clinton administration as early as 1998, the events of 2001 led to a major effort that cleared in 2002.

Ethical issues in health care also took center stage in the 107th Congress, with debates over the use of embryonic stem cells in research and how to ban human cloning. Neither was fully resolved. Congress also continued its periodic and emotional debate over abortion.

Patients' Rights

Legislation to give patients new rights in dealing with their managed-care plans died quietly when the 107th Congress adjourned in 2002. Neither chamber formally appointed conferees to resolve differences over legislation (HR 2563) that had set off heated battles between Senate Democrats and House Republicans in 2001. Informal efforts to find a compromise between a Senate-passed patients' rights bill and the House version, favored by the White House, foundered over the same issue that had sunk previous patients' rights bills: whether and how to cap the liability of health plans that denied treatment to a patient.

The House-passed bill would have capped damages at $1.5 million and sharply limited opportunities for punitive damages. The Senate version, far more friendly to plaintiffs, would have allowed up to $5 million in punitive damages in federal court and no federal limits in state courts.

Democrats claimed the two sides could not reach a deal because the administration was catering to the insurance industry. Republicans accused Democrats of being too closely aligned with trial lawyers and said their proposal would dramatically increase the cost of health insurance.

In fact, given the narrow partisan divide in Congress, the impending midterm elections, and the fact that voters were focused on other issues such as national security and the sagging economy, there was little incentive for either side to make dramatic concessions.

Democrats recognized that the health care environment had changed since the late 1990s when they began championing patients' rights legislation in earnest. Their chief argument then was that health plans, particularly health maintenance organizations, or HMOs, were unfairly denying patients the care they needed. *(Congress and the Nation Vol. X, pp. 454, 466)*

In the intervening years, patients had gained some leverage. Responding to complaints from workers and their employers, managed-care plans had loosened some of the restrictions that had tamped down health care spending. State courts began entertaining novel new challenges by patients that cracked the liability shield of insurers. Patients began choosing preferred provider organizations and other types of networks that offered discounts without the sharp restrictions on choices of doctors, hospitals, and other providers that closed-network HMOs imposed. Given these gains, many Democrats felt little need to compromise on liability, which was important to their supporters, particularly plaintiffs' attorneys.

Republicans concluded that the political sting had dissipated from the patients' rights debate and that voters were more concerned about other issues, particularly in the wake of the Sept. 11 terrorist attacks. As a result, they too saw no need to compromise. Conservatives also were concerned that the rising costs of health care would be exacerbated by the liability provisions and coverage requirements in the patients' rights legislation.

Outlays for Health

Billions of Dollars

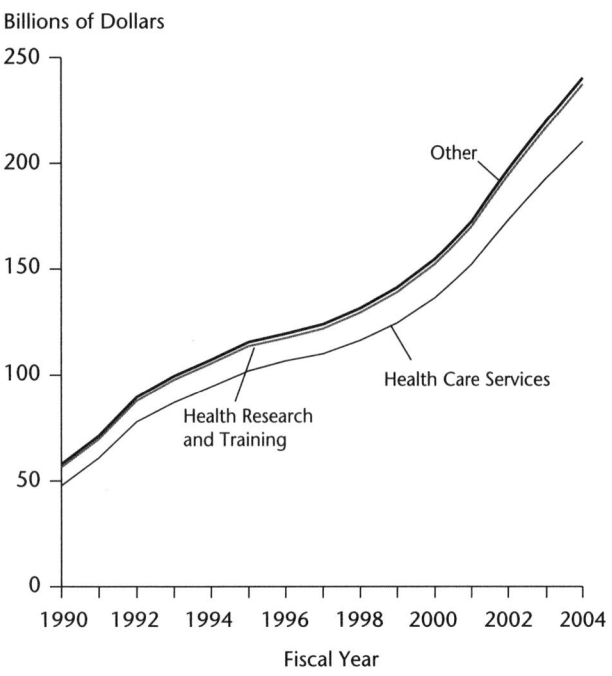

SOURCE: Office of Management and Budget, *Historical Tables, Budget of the United States Government: Fiscal Year 2006* (Washington, D.C.: U.S. Government Printing Office, 2005), Table 3.2.

A June 20, 2002, decision by the Supreme Court also may have factored into the lack of progress. In *Rush Prudential HMO, Inc. v. Moran*, the court affirmed that states had the right to pass laws giving patients an external review when their insurers denied them coverage of a treatment. Creating such independent reviews was key to both versions of the patients' rights bill. If the court had struck down the Illinois law at the center of the case, Congress might have felt compelled to act; instead, the ruling reduced the urgency for a federal law. *(Supreme Court decision, p. 675)*

LEGISLATIVE ACTION

Democrats made the patients' rights bill the first order of business when they took control of the Senate in June 2001, after the surprise defection of Sen. Jim Jeffords, I-Vt., from the Republican party. A bipartisan bill (S 1052)—sponsored by John McCain, R-Ariz., Edward M. Kennedy, D-Mass., and John Edwards, D-N.C.—passed on a **key vote of 59–36 (R 9–35; D 50–0; I 0–1)** on June 29, with universal backing from Democrats and the support of nine Republicans, three of whom were up for reelection. *(2001 key votes p. 801; Jeffords defection, pp. 3, 8)*

The Senate bill would have allowed millions of Americans for the first time to sue their health plans in federal court when they believed they had been injured by the plan's coverage decision. Plaintiffs could have collected punitive damages of up to $5 million and unlimited economic and non-

economic damages. Patients challenging their plan's medical decisions could have sued in state court, where damages would be determined by state laws. Before passing the bill, the Senate added language to shield employers from most lawsuits over denied care, and to limit attorney fees and "class action" lawsuits.

The House seemed poised to pass a similar bill, but the day before the vote one of the main sponsors, Charlie Norwood, R-Ga., suddenly abandoned his Democratic allies and struck a separate deal with President George W. Bush on a more industry-friendly bill (HR 2563) that passed by a vote of 226–203 on Aug. 2. The most important vote on the issue, however, occurred earlier the same day when Norwood struck a deal with the White House on a measure the president could support. Previously, Norwood had allied himself with Greg Ganske, R-Iowa, as well as John Dingell, D-Mich., who was a leading House advocate of a strong rights bill. Republicans had been especially embarrassed because Norwood was a dentist and Ganske a surgeon. Their original version of HR 2563 expanded an individual's ability to sue health plans in federal courts and allowed plaintiffs to collect civil damages of up to $5 million and unlimited economic and noneconomic damages.

But Norwood independently came up with a softer version more acceptable to the White House, infuriating both Ganske and Dingell. His alternative was adopted by a **key vote of 218–213 (R 214–6; D 3–206; I 1–1)**. *(2001 key votes, p. 801)*

The Norwood substitute was criticized by all sides—conservatives, moderates, and most Democrats. Even many who voted for it said they did so only to get a bill to conference. But the measure succeeded well in one regard: it gave cover to many Republicans who were under pressure to support patients' rights legislation of some kind while also supporting their party's president.

The substitute measure proposed capping punitive and compensatory damages at $1.5 million each in state or federal courts, with punitive damages available only in the rare instance when a plan ignored the recommendation of an external review panel. The House bill also would have banned patients from using the Racketeer Influenced and Corrupt Organizations (RICO) law (PL 91-452) against insurers.

In a new protection for insurers, a patient who lost an appeal to an external reviewer would have to overcome a "rebuttable presumption" that the insurer had been correct in denying care. The patient would have to provide clear and convincing evidence that this was false. Patients would not have been given the same presumption.

Additionally, patients would have had to prove that a denial was "the" proximate cause of an injury—not just "a" cause, potentially among many others.

Lawmakers struggled behind the scenes in 2002 to find a compromise that could blend the two approaches. For months, the cosponsors of the Senate-passed bill—McCain, Kennedy, and Edwards—worked quietly with the Bush administration in an effort to reconcile their bill and the House

HEALTH AND HUMAN SERVICES LEADERSHIP

When filling the post of secretary of the vast Department of Health and Human Services, President George W. Bush turned to GOP governors with whom he had served while governor of Texas.

Tommy Thompson, elected to four terms as Wisconsin's governor, was confirmed by the Senate on Jan. 24, 2001, as the department's nineteenth secretary.

Thompson had made his mark as a welfare reformer, initiating programs in his state that served as a model for sweeping federal legislation that became law in 1996. He came to Washington primarily to oversee reauthorization of that law, although that did not happen during his four-year tenure. Instead, Thompson helped transform the agency after the Sept. 11, 2001, terrorist attacks, creating a state-of-the-art command post outside his office and successfully pushing through Congress a series of bills to better prepare the nation for any future attack. Thompson also became active in international health issues, including becoming chair of the board of the Global Fund to fight AIDS, Tuberculosis, and Malaria. *(Background, cabinet profiles, p. 923)*

Thompson stepped down after the 2004 elections and was replaced by another former governor who had served with Bush—Utah's Michael Leavitt. Leavitt, whom Bush had already brought to Washington to head the Environmental Protection Agency in 2003, was approved by the Senate for his new post Jan. 26, 2005.

For surgeon general, Bush turned to the nationally unknown Richard Carmona, a former nurse, paramedic, swat team member, and emergency physician. The colorful Carmona, who once conducted a cliffside rescue that inspired a television movie, was approved by the Senate July 23, 2002, to become the nation's seventeenth surgeon general. He was the second Hispanic to hold the post, following Antonia Novello, who had served in the administration of Bush's father, President George H. W. Bush.

---

proposal that Bush favored. However, they could not resolve differences over liability caps. Democrats insisted on giving patients broad rights to sue their health insurers when a denial of coverage resulted in harm. Republicans insisted on caps on damages and limits to any lawsuits.

Giving up on the informal negotiations, Senate majority leader Tom Daschle, D-S.D., moved to appoint conferees on Aug. 1, but Republicans objected, saying they had not been given sufficient notice. As the congressional midterm elections and the final days of the session approached, the debate collapsed in partisan bickering over liability.

Bioterrorism Preparedness

In response partly to the Sept. 11, 2001, terrorist attacks and even more to attacks using anthrax spores sent through the mail the following month, Congress in 2002 cleared legislation (HR 3448—PL 107-188) authorizing $4.2 billion in fiscal 2003 and additional amounts in future years to help federal, state, and local governments prepare for and respond to biological attacks and other public health emergencies.

The bill authorized increases in the nation's stockpiles of medicines and vaccines, expansion of facilities and labs run by the Centers for Disease Control and Prevention (CDC), tighter controls on biological agents, and steps to safeguard the nation's food and water supply.

The bill also carried an unrelated measure—reauthorizing drug company "user fees," first authorized in 1992. The fees enabled the Food and Drug Administration (FDA) to hire more workers to review drug approval applications, and had succeeded in reducing approval times.

Some critics complained that the fees made the drug industry the FDA's "client," an inappropriate relationship for a regulatory agency. But supporters, including Sen. Edward M. Kennedy, D-Mass., said the bill balanced speedy approval of life-saving drugs with new money and authority to conduct ongoing safety studies of drugs once they landed on pharmacy shelves.

BACKGROUND

The legislation was introduced in 2001 out of concern that the nation's public health system was unprepared to handle a major bioterror attack. Federal and local officials had trouble dealing with a handful of anthrax cases in Florida, New York, and Washington D.C. Five people died after exposure to the spores.

Congress had appropriated $2.5 billion for the bioterrorism programs in fiscal 2002, without waiting for the separate authorization bill, but authorizers pressed ahead, saying their bill was necessary to provide clear guidance and legal certainty to federal and state governments. *(Earlier legislation, Congress and the Nation Vol. X, p. 481)*

LEGISLATIVE ACTION

The House passed a $2.9 billion version of the authorization bill Dec. 12, 2001. The vote was 418–2 for the measure, whose fast-track consideration barred amendments. The measure was jointly authored by Reps. Billy Tauzin, R-La., and John D. Dingell, D-Mich., the chair and ranking member, respectively, of the House Energy and Commerce Committee.

The Senate followed Dec. 20, passing by voice vote a $3.2 billion version whose details had been worked out between

Kennedy, the Senate Health, Education, Labor and Pensions Committee chair, and Bill Frist, R-Tenn., ranking Republican on the panel's Public Safety Subcommittee. But Senate passage came on the final day of the first session of the 107th Congress, leaving no time in 2001 to resolve differences between the two chambers' measures.

Both versions authorized funds to develop and produce anthrax vaccines, antibiotics, and other medicines to combat bioterrorism. Both authorized grants to states, local governments, and public health departments to prepare for health emergencies, bioterror-related or naturally occurring. Both also authorized aid to hospitals, the CDC, public health networks, and food safety programs.

The House bill, but not the Senate version, also authorized funds to improve the safety of public water supplies. The Senate bill had more detailed food safety inspection requirements. It also included a provision—opposed by Dingell—to give drug companies a limited antitrust exemption so they could collaborate on drugs to prevent and fight a biological attack. Another controversial Senate provision would have given companies accelerated approval of drugs by allowing them to use expedited research procedures with animals. Critics worried that such abbreviated research could compromise safety.

It took House and Senate conferees until the spring of 2002 to work out their differences. The conference report (H Rept 107-481)—including not only the bioterrorism provisions but also the reauthorization of the drug user fee program—was filed on May 21. The House adopted the report, 425–1, on May 22 and the Senate cleared the bill, 98–0, the next day.

The compromise bill included changes sought by both sides. At the House's insistence, conferees dropped the Senate's provision to give antitrust exemptions to drugmakers preparing to provide critical vaccines. Also dropped was a Senate proposal that wastewater treatment plants be required to report to the Environmental Protection Agency (EPA) on safety plans and assessments of vulnerability to terrorism. Tauzin cited objections from House Transportation and Infrastructure Committee Chair Don Young, R-Alaska, whose panel had jurisdiction over water safety issues.

But Kennedy forced the House to drop a proposal to create a user fee system for medical device makers. Medical device user fees were cleared in a separate bill (HR 5651—PL 107-250) later in 2002. *(Details, p. 482)*

MAJOR PROVISIONS

As signed into law June 12, 2002, HR 3448 (PL 107-188):

Emergency Medical Stockpiles

Authorized $1.2 billion in fiscal 2002, and unspecified sums in succeeding years, for the Department of Health and Human Services (HHS) to expand stockpiles of vaccines, medicines, and other supplies. The total included $509 million to purchase additional doses of smallpox vaccine.

State and Local Preparedness

Authorized $1.6 billion in fiscal 2003, and unspecified amounts in fiscal 2004 through fiscal 2006, for grants to states, local governments, and public and private health care facilities to improve planning and preparedness, increase laboratory capacity, train health care personnel, and develop new drugs, therapies, and vaccines. A total of $520 million was set aside for state grants to help hospitals and other health facilities prepare for biological attacks.

Biological Agents

Tightened controls on the possession and handling of dangerous biological agents and toxins. HHS was directed to establish a comprehensive national database on every individual who possessed, used, or transferred certain dangerous toxins or agents, such as anthrax or smallpox. Anyone who possessed these agents was required to register with HHS, report any transfer of the agents, and submit to screening and inspections. The Agriculture Department was given similar authority to regulate agents that could threaten crops or farm animals.

Food Safety

Authorized $100 million in fiscal 2002, and unspecified sums in fiscal 2003 through fiscal 2006, to improve food safety efforts, particularly at ports of entry, with special emphasis on detecting the intentional adulteration of food. The Food and Drug Administration (FDA) could hold food items for up to thirty days if there was credible evidence that they posed a serious health threat to humans or animals. All facilities that manufactured, processed, packed, or held food for consumption in the United States were required to register with the FDA. Food importers were required to provide the FDA with details about food shipments before they arrived at a port of entry. If notice was not provided, the food could not enter the United States. The FDA could ban importers who repeatedly violated U.S. food safety regulations.

Drug Imports

Required foreign manufacturers to register annually before being allowed to import drugs and medical devices into the United States.

Drinking Water Safety

Authorized $160 million in fiscal 2002, and unspecified sums in succeeding years, to protect the safety of drinking water systems. Drinking water systems across the country were required to provide the EPA with assessments of their vulnerability to terrorist attacks and to develop emergency plans to prepare for and respond to such attacks. In response to concerns over security at the EPA, the law exempted the assessments from release under the Freedom of Information Act, required the agency to take steps to secure and limit access to the documents, and set criminal penalties for anyone who disclosed the contents.

Prescription Drug User Fees

Reauthorized the FDA's user fee program for prescription drug manufacturers through fiscal 2007 and specified the fees should generate a total of $1.2 billion over five years. The funds were to be used by the FDA to review new drugs for safety and effectiveness, and, for the first time, to enhance the safety review of drugs already on the market.

Abortion

A strongly antiabortion House—bolstered by a strongly antiabortion president for the first time in nearly a decade—continued its efforts to place restrictions on the contested procedure. But a more abortion-rights leaning Senate managed to thwart most of the changes proposed in the 107th Congress.

The most far-reaching changes came from President George W. Bush himself without congressional action. On his first business day in office, Jan. 22, 2001, Bush reinstated the "Mexico City" policy that barred U.S. aid to international organizations that "perform or promote" abortion. In August of that year, Bush tried to settle an abortion-related fight over federal funding of research on stem cells derived from days-old human embryos left over in fertility clinics. Most abortion opponents contended that destroying embryos to remove the stem cells was tantamount to murder. But scientists—and even some who opposed abortion—said the potential benefits, including possible cures for such ailments as diabetes or Parkinson's disease, outweighed the moral questions, particularly for embryos that were to be discarded in any case. The president sought a middle ground, announcing a policy Aug. 9 that would allow funding for stem cell lines already in existence as of 9 p.m. that night but not for lines created in the future. The compromise pleased few; research backers claimed there were not enough fundable lines available while foes said it authorized state-sponsored destruction of embryos.

The only congressional action that resulted in a new law was passage of the relatively noncontroversial "Born Alive Infant Protection Act," which made it a crime to kill an infant fully outside a pregnant woman, even if that infant was accidentally born during an abortion procedure. Abortion-rights supporters backed the measure in order to put to rest rumors of accidentally-born fetuses being left to die.

Groundwork was laid for passage in the 108th Congress of a new version of the "Partial-Birth Abortion Ban Act," which had been the subject of several veto showdowns with President Bill Clinton. (*Congress and the Nation Vol. X, p. 472*)

The House also passed a bill to make it a crime to injure or kill a fetus during the commission of a federally-designated violent crime against a pregnant woman. The legislation was enacted in the next Congress as well. (*Fetal protection, pp. 481, 513*)

INFANT PROTECTION BILL

Legislation guaranteeing legal protection to babies born alive at any stage of development was signed into law Aug. 5, 2002 (HR 2175—PL 107-207). The House passed the bill by voice vote March 12 under expedited procedures; the Senate cleared it by voice vote July 18. The measure had White House support and was relatively noncontroversial, especially because many states already had such laws.

The bill established in statute that fetuses "born alive" are human beings legally alive and entitled to the same constitutional protections as other individuals. A fetus "born alive" was defined as one that had been expelled from the woman and was breathing or had a beating heart, a pulsating umbilical cord, or muscle movement. Backers said the bill was needed to protect infants who survived late-term abortions.

The House Judiciary Committee, which had approved the bill by 25–2 on July 24, 2001, and reported it Aug. 2 (H Rept 107-186), said that it did not intend to mandate medical treatment for infants in cases where doctors did not advise it. The bill also stated that it was not intended to grant any more rights than were already recognized for a fetus. That provision convinced Democrats that the measure would do nothing more than duplicate state laws. "This legislation is, I believe, unnecessary but harmless," said Jerrold Nadler, D-N.Y. There are "no such things as born-alive abortions," he said.

A similar bill passed the House in 2000 but was never acted on by the Senate. The Senate had voted 98–0 to add a similar bill to patients' rights legislation (S 1050) in 2001.

PARTIAL BIRTH BAN

Two years after the Supreme Court struck down a Nebraska law banning a procedure abortion opponents called "partial birth" abortion, federal lawmakers returned with a revised version of a federal ban they said could pass constitutional muster. The House passed a bill (HR 4965) in 2002, but there was no further action in the 107th Congress.

Earlier versions of the legislation had passed the House and Senate in the 104th and 105th Congresses but were vetoed by President Bill Clinton. The House overrode the veto each time but the Senate fell short. (*Congress and the Nation Vol. IX, p. 563; Congress and the Nation Vol. X, p. 455*)

The House and Senate in the 106th Congress also passed a ban but never sent it to President Clinton, after the Supreme Court in 2000 ruled in *Stenberg v. Carhart* that a substantially similar Nebraska law violated a woman's constitutional right to an abortion. (*Congress and the Nation Vol. X, p. 473*)

Each version of the bill sought to ban a specific procedure, known medically as "intact dilation and extraction," or D&X, and called "partial birth abortion" in the legislation. The bill defined the procedure as one in which a doctor "intentionally vaginally delivers a living fetus . . . for the purpose of performing an overt act that the [doctor] knows will kill the partially delivered living fetus."

The bill would have allowed the procedure only when it was necessary to save a woman's life. Those who performed the procedure for other reasons—including risks to a woman's health that were short of life-threatening—would have faced fines and up to two years in prison. The woman would not have been criminally liable.

In the 2000 Nebraska case, the Court found that state's law wanting on two counts. First, the Court said, the definition of the procedure was so vague that it could have banned not just the rarely used D&X procedure but also the far more common "dilation and evacuation" procedure, or D&E. The Court majority also cited the Nebraska law's lack of an exception allowing use of the procedure to protect a pregnant woman's health in addition to her life. President Clinton based his vetoes on the lack of a health exception.

The bill introduced in 2002 (HR 4965) sought to address both of those issues. It tightened the definition of the procedure to be banned. But rather than add a health exception—which abortion foes pointed out had been interpreted to include mental health, and thus would have allowed the procedure for any woman upset about being pregnant—bill sponsors tried a new tactic. They included fifteen pages of congressional "findings" holding that no exception was needed because the procedure "is never medically necessary" to protect a pregnant woman's health.

The House Judiciary Committee approved the bill on a 20-8 party-line vote July 17, 2002, and reported it July 23 (H Rept 107-604). The Constitution Subcommittee had approved it, 8–3, on July 11.

Republicans on the full committee turned back six Democratic amendments to limit the scope of the bill—including two that would have provided some kind of exception for cases where the procedure was necessary for the woman's health.

The House passed the bill July 24 by a vote of 274–151 with one member voting "present." The leadership brought the bill to the floor under a closed rule that barred amendments. Democrats had hoped to offer a number of amendments to add some type of health exception. Instead, they tried to recommit the bill to the Judiciary Committee with instructions to include such an exception. The motion failed, 187–241.

The Senate, under Democratic control, never took up the House-passed bill in 2002.

ABORTION SERVICES REFUSAL

The House on Sept. 25, 2002, passed a bill (HR 4691) to let hospitals, insurance plans, and other health care providers refuse to perform abortions or to refer women elsewhere for such services without losing Medicaid funds or other federal money. The vote for the "Abortion Non-Discrimination Act" was 229–189, with thirty-seven Democrats voting in favor and twenty-four Republicans voting against the bill.

Because the legislation had been bottled up in the House Energy and Commerce Committee, Majority Leader Dick Armey, R-Texas, moved it directly to the House floor for a vote. The bill's sponsor, Energy and Commerce Health Subcommittee Chair Michael Bilirakis, R-Fla., said the bill was intended to clarify "conscience clause" language already written into the Public Health Service Act (PL 78-410) that explicitly protected doctors who refused to perform abortions from being penalized by the federal government or any state or local government that received federal money. The bill would have rewritten the section of the law to say that "health care entities" covered by the conscience clause should include "other health professionals, a hospital, a provider-sponsored organization, a health maintenance organization, a health insurance plan, and any other kind of health care facility, organization, or plan."

Supporters said the change was needed to counter state court interpretations that excluded hospitals from the conscience clause language. They cited a 1997 Alaska Supreme Court ruling that a hospital in that state had to allow doctors to perform abortions there because it was the only hospital in the area, making it a quasi-public facility.

Opponents said the bill would greatly expand existing law and weaken a woman's legal right to an abortion by limiting its availability. They said it would not allow exemptions in cases of rape or incest or to save the life of the woman, and would allow hospitals and insurers to stop physicians and others from providing abortions or even referring women to others for abortion services.

Catholic hospital groups and secular medical chains lobbied for the bill to guarantee not only that they could continue to receive federal funding while refusing to perform abortions, but also that they would not face sanctions under state law or regulations.

The rule for floor debate allowed no amendments. An attempt by Sherrod Brown of Ohio, ranking Democrat on the Health Subcommittee, to send the bill back to committee failed on a vote of 191–230. *(2004 action, p. 512)*

PARENTAL INVOLVEMENT

The House voted 260–161 on April 17, 2002, to pass a bill (HR 476) that would make it a crime to circumvent state parental consent or notification laws by knowingly taking a minor across state lines for an abortion. Violators would have faced fines of up to $100,000 and a year in prison. The measure included an exception from prosecution if the abortion was necessary to save the life of the minor; the minor could not be prosecuted under the bill.

The House had passed similar bills in the 105th and 106th Congresses, but the Senate did not act on them. The Senate failed to act in the 107th Congress as well. *(Congress and the Nation Vol. X, pp. 456, 474)*

The bill was designed to buttress laws in states that required pregnant girls to notify or get one or both parents' permission before obtaining an abortion. More than half the states required notification of or consent by a parent before a minor could have an abortion. Most of the state laws also allowed a minor to get permission from a judge instead.

But opponents argued that the bill might not encourage parental involvement. "This bill is not going to encourage teens to talk to their parents," said Lynn Woolsey, D-Calif. Rather, she said, the measure could prompt teenagers to "seek unsafe, illegal abortions."

The rule governing the April 17 debate did not allow floor amendments, but Democrats tried to send the bill back to the House Judiciary Committee for additional language that would exempt siblings, grandparents, or clergy who transported a minor across state lines for an abortion. The motion, by Sheila Jackson Lee, D-Texas, was rejected, 173–246.

The House Judiciary Committee had approved the bill on a 19–6 party-line vote March 20, 2002, and reported it April 11(H Rept 107-397). Republicans easily fended off Democratic amendments, including a proposal to exempt grandparents and adult siblings. Democrats also tried but failed to add an exemption for girls who become pregnant as a result of sex with a parent or guardian.

ABORTION AND BANKRUPTCY

A fight over abortion played a key role in blocking a seemingly unrelated bill in 2002—one to revise the nation's bankruptcy laws (HR 333). The dispute prevented the third Congress in a row from completing action on a sweeping bill that would have made it harder for consumers to walk away from their debts. *(Bankruptcy bill, p. 129)*

At issue was a Senate provision aimed at preventing demonstrators—particularly protesters at abortion clinics—from filing for bankruptcy to avoid paying court-ordered fines and judgments. The dispute pitted Senate sponsor Charles E. Schumer, D-N.Y., against abortion foe Rep. Henry J. Hyde, R-Ill.

For months, the longtime adversaries refused to budge. But the pressure to advance the bill, fueled by large campaign contributions from the financial services industry, which badly wanted the bill, finally forced them to reach a compromise in late July 2002.

Hyde agreed to bar debtors from filing for bankruptcy to escape fines for "intentional, knowing or reckless actions" that interfered with or caused violence against people who provided "lawful goods or services." Schumer agreed that the bill would make clear that the restriction was not intended to cover activities protected by the First Amendment, including peaceful picketing, prayer, or other similar types of demonstrations.

GOP leaders were set to bring the conference report to the House floor before the August recess, but protests by a group of antiabortion Republicans led them to abandon their plans. The leadership tried again on Nov. 14 during the lame-duck session, but opponents managed to defeat the rule for debate on the conference report by a **key vote of 172–243 (R 124–87; D 48–155; I 0–1).** *(2002 key votes, p. 819)*

The next day the House passed the bill again, 244–116, after dropping the protest provision as well as language authorizing new bankruptcy judgeships, but that version doomed the measure's chances in the Senate.

ABORTION AND FOREIGN AID

Abortion, as usual, remained one of the flashpoints in the annual debate over foreign aid in both 2001 and 2002. At issue were two separate policies. One was the so-called "Mexico City" language that from 1984 to 1993 prohibited aid to international family planning organizations that performed or promoted abortions, even if they used their own funds to do so. The other was funding for the United Nations Population Fund (UNFPA), which had long come under fire from antiabortion forces in the United States because of its controversial funding of population programs in China, whose population policies sometimes coerced abortions. *(2002 aid appropriations, p. 246; 2003 aid appropriations, p. 286)*

President George W. Bush himself kicked off the annual fight over the Mexico City language by formally restoring it by executive order on Jan. 22, 2001, his first weekday in office (and, not coincidentally, the anniversary of the Supreme Court's *Roe v. Wade* ruling). President Bill Clinton had used the same anniversary, eight years earlier, to rescind the policy.

As in past years, the Senate included language to overturn the policy in its version of the fiscal 2002 foreign aid appropriations bill (HR 2506—S Rept 107-58). The House did not.

Senate conferees ultimately agreed to drop their Mexico City language, in exchange for House conferees' agreement to boost by 50 percent funding for UNFPA, to $34 million. That angered House GOP conservatives, who threatened to block the conference report on the House floor but ultimately relented.

The fight, however, dragged into 2002, when conservatives urged Bush not to spend the UNFPA money due to charges the organization was funding programs in China that involved forced abortions. UNFPA officials had long maintained that they funded only programs in parts of the country where no abortions were forced or coerced. Even though a State Department-appointed investigatory committee found no evidence that "UNFPA has knowingly supported or participated in the management of a program of coercive abortion or involuntary sterilization," Bush decided in July to withhold the money anyway—infuriating the Senate conferees who had negotiated the increase the previous year.

The debate continued through the year, and the fiscal 2003 bill was not completed by the end of calendar 2002.

Fetal Protection

A bill to make it a federal crime to harm or kill a fetus while committing a federal violent offense against a pregnant woman passed the House in 2001 but stalled in the Senate. The bill (HR 503) would have given federal legal status to a fetus for the first time.

Bill sponsor Lindsey Graham, R-S.C., said the legislation would send a strong signal: "If you attack a pregnant woman, you get prosecuted not once but twice."

Democratic opponents said the bill was a back-door attempt to undermine the landmark 1973 *Roe v. Wade* Supreme Court decision, which legalized abortion nationwide. In that ruling, the Court had concluded that "the unborn have never been recognized in the law as persons in the whole sense." Democrats tried unsuccessfully to substitute language that would have increased penalties for attacking a pregnant woman but would not have recognized the fetus as a separate human being.

The House had passed a similar bill in 1999, but the Senate did not act on it. That version had been presented as a crime-fighting bill although it was drafted with the help of antiabortion groups. According to the National Right to Life Committee, twenty-four states already had such statutes on the books. *(Congress and the Nation Vol. X, p. 474)*

In fact, for all the work on the bill, it would have applied only in very limited circumstances: making it a federal crime to harm or kill a fetus while committing any one of sixty-eight existing federal offenses or a crime under military law. Most violent offenses were prosecuted under state statutes.

With the GOP initially controlling both chambers and the White House, enactment seemed likely. But action in the Senate stalled after Democrats took control of that chamber in June 2001.

A bill was enacted in the 108th Congress. *(2004 action, p. 513)*

LEGISLATIVE ACTION

After extensive debate the House Judiciary Committee approved HR 503, formally known as the "Unborn Victims of Violence Act," March 28 on a 15–9 party-line vote and reported it April 20 (H Rept 107-42, Part 1). The panel's Constitution subcommittee had given approval by voice vote March 21.

Subcommittee Chair Steve Chabot, R-Ohio, said the bill would help close "an unfortunate gap in the law" that allowed offenders who attacked pregnant women in federal crimes to escape punishment for harm done to the fetus. He rejected Democrats' argument that the aim was to erode abortion rights established with *Roe v. Wade*. "The bill simply does not apply to abortion," Chabot said.

Jerrold Nadler, D-N.Y., disagreed. "We should have no illusions about the purpose of this bill—that it is yet another battle of a war of symbols in the abortion debate, in which opponents of a woman's right to choose attempt to portray fetuses . . . as children," he said. The bill "clearly recognizes the fetus as the victim of violence," a premise that he said was "at odds with the holdings of the Supreme Court and the Constitution."

Democrats offered a substitute amendment, defeated 13–20, to increase penalties for attacking a pregnant woman and causing harm to her pregnancy but without recognizing the fetus as a crime victim.

The House passed the bill April 26 by a vote of 252–172, with the support of fifty-three Democrats. The vote in 1999 had been 254–172, with fifty-six Democrats in favor. The Bush administration issued a statement endorsing the bill and strongly opposing the Democratic substitute.

The highly charged floor debate focused on the question of when life begins. Democrats and abortion rights advocates insisted the bill was an unconstitutional assault on abortion rights. Supporters insisted the measure was aimed at punishing crime. They cited the case of Glendale Black of Wisconsin, who beat his wife when she was nine months pregnant. She survived the attack but lost the pregnancy; Black was prosecuted only for assaulting his wife.

The Democratic alternative—to create a federal crime for an attack on a pregnant woman that kills or damages the fetus—was rejected, 196–229.

Medical Device User Fees

Congress in 2002 cleared a bill (HR 5651—PL 107-250) creating new user fees for manufacturers of medical devices, modeled on a similar fee paid by drug companies. The legislation was a top priority for the industry, which agreed to pay the fees in return for getting swifter reviews of their products by the Food and Drug Administration (FDA).

The bill authorized the FDA to collect $150 million over five years to defray the cost of hiring new regulators to speed up its device review process. The user fee applied to companies making a broad variety of products including breast implants, defibrillators, and respirators. The bill set time goals for the FDA and allowed device manufacturers to hire independent contractors to conduct some safety inspections of their factories. The measure codified an agreement that the Bush administration had struck with the medical device industry in May 2002.

BACKGROUND

The bill was a victory for industry groups that had lobbied for years to get a dedicated funding source for FDA reviews in hopes of getting their products to market more quickly. They complained that the average FDA review time in 2001 for premarket approval applications was 411 days, more than twice the 180-day statutory requirement. The industry did not get all it wanted, however. A proposal to allow private contractors to review and recommend approval for many new medical devices was scaled back. Instead, the bill allowed private contractors to assume some of the FDA's duties to inspect manufacturing facilities.

The medical device user fee program was based on the one already in place for drugmakers. Created in 1992, the drug user fee was reauthorized in 2002 as part of a law (HR 3448—PL 107-188) funding efforts to battle bioterrorism. Manufacturers had hoped to tack the medical device fee onto the bill as well, but Democrats resisted, saying the proposal was too broad. Critics also contended that the shift to user fees risked turning the FDA into a captive of the industries it was regulating. *(Bioterrorism preparedness, p. 477)*

LEGISLATIVE ACTION

After the proposal was dropped from the bioterrorism bill, the House passed a stand-alone medical device user fee bill (HR 3580) on Oct. 9, 2002, by a vote of 406–3. The House Energy and Commerce Committee had approved the bill by voice vote Oct. 2 and reported it Oct. 7 (H Rept 107-728).

The measure contained most of the provisions that ultimately were enacted into law. Like the final bill, it did not set an exact amount for individual fees but provided a total to be collected each year. It set a benchmark premarket application fee of $139,000 in fiscal 2003. In addition, the bill called for the FDA to receive an extra $15 million per year in appropriations. Companies with less than $10 million in sales would pay reduced fees or be exempted altogether. The user fees would expire after fiscal 2005 if the agency had not received $45 million in matching federal money over three years.

Although the bill got overwhelming support in the House, some Senate Democrats who supported the measure, particularly Edward M. Kennedy, D-Mass., chair of the Senate Health, Education, Labor, and Pensions Committee, still had safety concerns about third-party plant inspections and about sterilization and reuse of disposable items such as catheters and syringes.

Rather than passing a separate Senate bill and reconciling the two versions in conference, a group of senior House and Senate lawmakers negotiated a bipartisan compromise that was introduced as a clean bill (HR 5651) on Oct. 16. The House passed it by voice vote several hours later, and the Senate cleared it by voice vote the next day.

At Kennedy's urging, the original House bill was amended to specify that the FDA would conduct every third inspection of a domestic medical device factory, allowing independent contractors to do other reviews.

The bill also was revised to expand the number of companies exempted from some user fees. It waived fees for first-time applications for firms with annual sales under $30 million, instead of the $10 million in the original bill. The Advanced Medical Technology Association, which led negotiations with the White House on the user fee plan, wanted to limit the threshold to $10 million. The group feared that if more companies were exempted, total user fee revenue could fall short and trigger automatic fee increases on those that did pay. The rival Medical Device Manufacturers Association sought a waiver for up to $100 million in sales but agreed to $30 million.

The bill required Congress to appropriate an additional $60 million in general funds over four years or see the user fee program expire.

MAJOR PROVISIONS

As signed into law Oct. 26, 2002, HR 5651 (PL 107-250):

User Fees

Authorized the Food and Drug Administration (FDA) to collect $150 million in user fees from the medical device industry—$25 million in fiscal 2003, $27 million in fiscal 2004, $30 million in fiscal 2005, $33 million in fiscal 2006, and $35 million in fiscal 2007.

Set the initial benchmark fee for premarket applications at $154,000 in fiscal 2003.

Required the FDA to use the fees to meet performance goals and speed up its review and approval process.

Small-business Waivers

Waived fees for first-time applications from companies with annual sales under $30 million.

Federal Spending

Called for Congress to provide an additional $15 million per year for the program from general funds. Provided that the user fees would expire if lawmakers did not appropriate $60 million through fiscal 2006.

Third-party Inspections

Allowed device manufacturers to hire independent contractors to conduct safety inspections of their factories. Required the contractors to be approved by the FDA, and required the agency to perform every third inspection of domestic facilities.

Postmarket Studies

Authorized $3 million in fiscal 2003 and $6 million in fiscal 2004 to expand FDA studies of the safety of new products after they reached the market.

Reprocessed Medical Devices

Established new regulations governing the sterilization and reuse of catheters and other products that previously were approved only for single use. Required such products to be clearly labeled so patients would know they were safe and effective according to FDA standards.

Medicare Drug Benefit

Congress in 2002 debated but could not agree on legislation to add a prescription drug benefit to Medicare, the federal health insurance program for elderly and disabled Americans. Republicans passed a prescription drug bill in the House, but partisan differences doomed each of four proposals considered in the narrowly divided Senate.

Although election-year politics and partisan bickering contributed to the deadlock, members of both parties said the philosophical differences were so great that agreement would have been difficult under the best of conditions.

Republicans insisted that any prescription drug coverage should conform to the demands of the marketplace, with private insurers setting the premiums, deductibles, and coverage terms within guidelines. Democrats said the government should design and manage a guaranteed benefit that would be uniform across the nation, available to all seniors,

Sen. John B. Breaux, D-La., and Sen. Bill Frist, R-Tenn., at a news conference on February 15, 2001, after introducing legislation to add a prescription drug benefit to Medicare. After foundering in the Senate in 2002, the drug benefit made it through the newly Republican-controlled 108th Congress and was signed into law on December 8, 2003, as part of the largest overhaul of Medicare in its thirty-eight year history. *Source: Congressional Quarterly/Scott J. Ferrell*

and embedded in the traditional Medicare fee-for-service program. Democrats favored broad coverage despite the cost, while Republicans were willing to have beneficiaries pick up the full tab for some of their drug expenses.

"That's the fundamental divide, and it's pretty hard to mask over that divide," said Senate majority leader Tom Daschle, D-S.D.

The GOP House-passed bill (HR 4954), which would have cost $350 billion over ten years, would have allowed Medicare beneficiaries to buy new private insurance policies for prescription drugs. House Democrats offered a far more generous plan costing $800 billion over ten years. It would have given the federal government the authority to determine premium rates and the details of coverage for all enrollees.

The Senate initially debated three prescription drug proposals: a government-run plan backed by Democrats; a "tripartisan" approach proposed by moderates that included both private and public sector coverage options; and a more modest GOP plan that would have given beneficiaries access to discount drug cards and offered coverage on a sliding income scale for people with extremely high annual drug costs.

When none of the plans were adopted—all failed to get the sixty votes needed to overcome objections that they exceeded Senate spending limits—a small group of Democrats and moderate Republicans offered a scaled-back alternative aimed at helping poor seniors and those with high annual drug bills. But that, too, failed to win sixty votes. Finally, the Senate passed the underlying bill (S 812), which would have

made it harder for big drug companies to block approval of cheaper generic drugs, but the measure died in the House.

Lawmakers from both parties vowed in their reelection campaigns to resolve the issue in the 108th Congress. A drug coverage plan was enacted in 2003 as part of a sweeping Medicare bill. *(Medicare overhaul, p. 496)*

MAJOR ISSUES

All of the comprehensive bills proposed a voluntary prescription drug benefit for Medicare beneficiaries under a new "Part D" of the program. The following were some of the major issues that differentiated the bills:

Government, private sector roles. Republican plans relied completely or in part on private insurers to design and provide new drug-only insurance policies. To encourage insurers to offer such policies, they included government subsidies and other financial incentives, in effect absorbing part of the risk. The overall plan was to be administered through a new Medicare office.

Under the Democrats' plans, prescription drug coverage would have been designed and administered by Medicare, which would have contracted with private sources such as pharmacy benefit managers and health plans. The government was to bear most of the risk.

Coverage. Under the GOP approach, benefits could have differed from one region to another but there would have been a minimum or "standard" level. Democrats favored a uniform benefit set by the government and available to all enrollees.

The potential cost to the enrollee varied considerably among plans. Republicans proposed an annual deductible, plus monthly premiums that would have been set by the insurer and would have varied by region. After the deductible was met, a percentage of costs was to be covered by insurance up to a limit of about $2,000. Beyond that, the beneficiary would have to bear all of the cost until his or her out-of-pocket expenses reached an upper threshold of nearly $4,000, after which the government and the insurer were to pay all of the costs.

The Democrats generally favored full coverage with no gap, although enrollees might have had to choose from a list of covered drugs.

Low-income beneficiaries. All of the plans included subsidies for low-income beneficiaries, although coverage differed, ranging from 135 percent of the federal poverty level to 170 percent.

BACKGROUND

Beginning with a proposal for a prescription drug benefit offered by President Bill Clinton in 1999, the two parties had been arguing over how such a benefit should be delivered, what the government role should be, and how much it should cost.

Democrats made the addition of such a benefit to Medicare one of their top legislative priorities. They argued that use of prescription drugs was an increasingly important part of health care treatment and that seniors should receive drug coverage as part of their Medicare benefits. Medicare did not pay for outpatient prescription drugs unless a senior joined a managed-care plan that offered benefits. The addition of a drug benefit would be one of the most expensive expansions of the program since it was created in 1965.

Recognizing the public interest in a drug benefit, House Republicans presented their own plan in 2000. It relied on the private insurance market to develop coverage and proposed federal subsidies to help insurers cover the costs. The bill squeaked through the House, 217–214, far short of the votes needed to override Clinton's promised veto. But the Health Insurance Association of America (HIAA), a key industry trade group, surprised its longtime GOP allies by opposing the plan as unworkable. Industry officials said such policies would not be profitable, given the fact that the purchasers would tend to be seniors with particularly high drug bills. (Congress and the Nation Vol. X, p. 465)

There was little action on the issue in 2001 as lawmakers focused on other priorities including President George W. Bush's tax cut plan, a massive overhaul of education law, and the aftermath of the Sept. 11 terrorist attacks in New York and Washington.

In 2002, hoping to inoculate their party from Democratic criticisms on the issue during an election year, House GOP leaders worked again to introduce a prescription drug bill. The legislation that the House ultimately passed in June was based on the bill that Republicans had written two years earlier. This time, with more money in the bill for them, the insurers were on board. "There is now a much better chance that our members will offer the benefit," HIAA President Donald A. Young, told House Ways and Means Chair Bill Thomas, R-Calif., in a letter June 18.

A separate issue that complicated the debate in 2002 involved reimbursements for Medicare providers, who argued their payments had been cut too deeply under the 1997 Balanced Budget Act (PL 105-33). The House bill included $30 billion over ten years, which helped win over some wavering Republicans but also cut into the total funds available for the prescription drug benefit. (Congress and the Nation Vol. X, p. 432)

HOUSE COMMITTEE ACTION

The House Republican bill (HR 4954), introduced June 18, 2002, was considered by two committees—House Ways and Means and House Energy and Commerce.

Coverage limits were dictated in part by GOP leaders' decision to stay within the parameters of the House-passed fiscal 2003 budget resolution (H Con Res 353), which allowed $350 billion for the bill over ten years. To do that, they proposed to cover 80 percent of an enrollee's prescription costs from $251 to $1,000, then 50 percent of the next $1,000. The enrollee would pay all of the costs between $2,001 and a "catastrophic cap" of $4,500. Beyond that, the federal govern-

ment and insurers would pick up the entire cost. The gap in coverage, dubbed the "doughnut hole," was an easy mark for Democratic critics.

The bill was more generous than the Republicans' 2000 plan, which would have covered 30 percent of pharmaceutical costs between $1,250 and $1,350, rising to 90 percent once a beneficiary's annual bill reached $6,000 or more.

Premiums would have varied by region; sponsors estimated that they would have averaged $34 per month. To encourage private insurers to offer policies even in areas where it might not otherwise be profitable, the bill called for federal subsidies of 65 percent or more of the cost of providing coverage.

In addition to the prescription drug provisions, GOP drafters included more than $30 billion to increase payments to Medicare health care providers. Doctors, hospitals, and others were threatening to leave the program unless they got more money, and sympathetic lawmakers, particularly those from rural areas, made their support for the drug plan contingent upon getting help for their local providers.

The bill also included policy changes that proponents said would contain Medicare spending and help ensure that the program could handle the coming wave of baby-boomers. Those provisions were key for many Republicans, including Thomas, a cosponsor of the measure.

Ways and Means Committee. After a bitterly partisan, thirteen-hour markup, the House Ways and Means Committee approved HR 4954 in the early morning hours of June 19. The vote was 22–16 along mostly party lines. The panel reported the bill on June 26 (H Rept 107-539, Part 1).

The measure had the backing of the health insurance industry and key health provider groups but drew criticisms from some consumer and seniors' lobbying groups.

At the insistence of some Republicans, the cap on out-of-pocket expenses was reduced to $3,800.

Democrats had no luck in changing the bill. More than a dozen Democratic amendments were rejected, including a substitute offered by Charles B. Rangel of New York. The Democrats' $800 billion, ten-year plan called for a more generous benefit to seniors through the existing government-run, fee-for-service Medicare program rather than requiring beneficiaries to buy separate drug-only policies from private insurers. Enrollees would have paid a $25 monthly premium and a $100 annual deductible. Medicare would have picked up 80 percent of drug costs until the enrollee had paid $2,000, then cover 100 percent of costs after that.

Health Subcommittee Chair Nancy L. Johnson, R-Conn., who introduced the GOP bill, called the Democrats' plan "breathtakingly irresponsible." Pete Stark of California, the ranking Democrat on the subcommittee, responded that the Democratic alternative was more costly because a meaningful drug benefit "doesn't come on the cheap. It's a matter of priorities."

Energy and Commerce Committee. One day after the Ways and Means markup began, the House Energy and

Commerce Committee started its own marathon session. Chair Billy Tauzin, R-La., broke the proposed legislation into thirteen narrower bills, allowing him to rule many of the proposed Democratic amendments out of order. All of the Democratic amendments that were offered were rejected. The markup continued past midnight and finally concluded at about 8:30 a.m. on the morning of June 21 when the committee voted, 30–23, to approve a bill that reunited the separate pieces. The bill was reported June 26 (HR 4988—H Rept 107-542, Part 1).

The only major area of bipartisan agreement came on a $34.5 billion package of increased payments to Medicare providers. The entire bill would have cost $341 billion over ten years, according to the Congressional Budget Office (CBO).

The key showdown occurred early on when the committee rejected, 23–30, the $800 billion Democratic substitute for the drug benefit provisions. The amendment was offered by ranking Democrat John D. Dingell of Michigan.

Republicans rejected, 31–24, a Democratic proposal to set a $35 premium in law that would rise annually in proportion to the growth in per capita Medicare drug costs. Other defeated Democratic amendments included proposals to close the coverage gap, which in the Energy and Commerce version would have hit an upper limit of $3,700 before Medicare picked up the full cost; give the secretary of the Department of Health and Human Services (HHS) the authority to negotiate price discounts with drug manufacturers; and guarantee enrollees the lowest prescription drug price available.

HOUSE FLOOR ACTION

The House passed HR 4954 on a near-party line **key vote of 221–208 (R 212–8; D 8–199; I 1–1)** that concluded at about 2:30 a.m. on June 28. Passage followed an extraordinary day of lobbying by Speaker J. Dennis Hastert, R-Ill., the White House, and health industry trade groups. In the end eight Republicans strayed from the fold to vote against the bill while an equal number of Democrats voted for it. *(2002 key votes, p. 819)*

Before the bill came to the floor, the GOP-controlled Rules Committee made several changes to the version approved by the Ways and Means Committee. The bill proposed a $3,700 ceiling on out-of-pocket costs, as approved by the Energy and Commerce Committee, rather than the $3,800 in the Ways and Means version. It increased the subsidy for insurers from 65 percent of the cost of providing coverage to 67 percent. It also dropped a Ways and Means provision that would have established a copayment for home health care.

Republican leaders faced dissension within their own ranks right up to the opening moments of the debate. Action was delayed for hours June 27 as the leadership lobbied more than three dozen members who had either expressed concerns about the measure or said they intended to vote against it. Several industry groups, including the Pharmaceutical Research and Manufacturers of America, were called in to help

get members on board. White House aides visited members' offices, and Republican leaders granted favors. At one point, Hastert threatened to hold the House in session into the weekend, delaying the start of the Fourth of July recess if necessary, to ensure action on the bill.

To maintain control and force Democrats into an up-or-down vote, the Rules Committee had approved a closed rule for debate that barred amendments. The 218–213 vote to adopt the rule gave GOP leaders confidence they had enough support to pass the bill.

As the floor debate dragged into the early morning of June 28, Democrats accused Republicans of designing the bill to please their allies in the drug and insurance industry rather than to give seniors the prescription drug coverage they needed. They said the bill was the first step toward privatization of Medicare and pointed to criticism from groups such as Consumers Union, Families USA, and the seniors' group AARP. In a June 18 letter to Thomas, AARP Executive Director and Chief Executive Officer William D. Novelli had said the bill's "large coverage gap is a strong disincentive to enrollment."

The Democrats were particularly angry that Republicans refused to let them offer their plan as a substitute. They were allowed only a motion to recommit, which failed by a vote of 204–223.

Republicans accused Democrats of designing a drug bill more for political gain than to help seniors and said it would break the federal budget. "Democrats care only about outbidding Republicans in an attempt to score political points for the election," said Michael Bilirakis, R-Fla., chair of the Energy and Commerce Health Subcommittee.

Among Republicans who voted against the bill were Jo Ann Emerson of Missouri and Gil Gutknecht of Minnesota, who led an effort to lower drug costs by allowing the wholesale importation of U.S. drugs from Canada, where they were cheaper, and tightening patent laws to make it harder for manufacturers of brand-name drugs to impede low-cost generic competition.

SENATE ACTION

Across the Capitol, Senate majority leader Daschle called the House-passed measure "a terrible bill" and said House Republicans were "so far to the right on this issue that it is a challenge to see how we can reconcile our differences." In hopes of spurring a compromise, he gave the Senate Finance Committee a deadline of July 15 to report a bill for floor consideration.

With several factions competing for support, the committee missed the deadline. Some Finance members, including ranking Republican Charles E. Grassley of Iowa, later complained that the panel could have produced a bill if given more time, but Daschle said the committee had had its chance.

Daschle began floor consideration of legislation (S 812) on July 15. The bill was intended to lower prices by making it difficult for brand-name drugmakers to extend their patents. The measure served as the vehicle for the larger prescription drug debate. Because the Senate had not adopted a fiscal 2003 budget resolution, any proposal had to be within the $300 billion approved for a Medicare plan in the fiscal 2002 budget resolution (H Con Res 83). Anything costing more was subject to a point of order that required sixty votes to overcome, a hurdle that ultimately proved too high for all of the proposals.

Three major prescription drug plans were offered as amendments to S 812, along with a scaled-back compromise.

Democratic plan. Most Democrats, including Daschle, supported a bill (S 2625) sponsored by Bob Graham of Florida, Zell Miller of Georgia, and Edward M. Kennedy of Massachusetts. The bill called for a uniform benefit available to all Medicare beneficiaries with a $25 monthly premium, plus copayments of $10 for each generic drug and $40 for each brand-name drug on a list of approved drugs. There would be no deductible, and the beneficiary's out-of-pocket costs would be capped at $4,000 a year. The plan would be run by HHS, which would contract with private sources such as pharmacy benefit managers and health plans. CBO said the bill would cost $594 billion over ten years.

Republicans found it too expensive and government-driven. An attempt to waive the budget limits got the support of all fifty Democrats, plus Peter G. Fitzgerald, R-Ill., and James M. Jeffords, I-Vt. But the 52–47 vote was short of the sixty needed, and the amendment fell July 23.

Tripartisan plan. A second proposal, known as the tripartisan plan, was sponsored by Republican Grassley, Democrat John B. Breaux of Louisiana, and independent Jeffords. It offered three different options for coverage: the traditional fee-for-service Medicare program, a Medicare managed-care plan, or a stand-alone drug policy to be offered by private insurers. It included a $24 monthly premium, a $250 deductible, and a 50 percent cost share for expenses of between $251 and $3,450. Insurers could alter the premiums, benefits, and copayments if they got approval from the government. A special Medicare Competitive Agency would be established in HHS to administer the plan. The bill was estimated to cost $370 billion over ten years.

That proposal, too, failed to get the necessary sixty votes. It had the backing of forty-five Republicans, Jeffords, and Louisiana Democrats Breaux and Mary L. Landrieu. It fell, 48–51, on July 23.

Discount card. A third alternative, by Chuck Hagel, R-Neb., would have provided a discount card to help low-income seniors buy drugs at reduced prices, along with financial help to seniors who had extremely high annual drug costs. The estimated cost was $150 billion over eight years.

Democrats said the benefits were too limited. Hagel failed, 51–48, to overcome a point of order on July 24. He was backed by forty-seven Republicans and four Democrats.

Graham-Smith compromise. Finally, in a last-ditch effort, Graham and Republican Gordon H. Smith of Oregon offered a scaled-back proposal to provide prescription drug coverage to Medicare recipients with incomes of less than 200 percent of the federal poverty level. It also would have provided catastrophic coverage for those with drug costs above $3,300 per year for an annual payment of $25.

Some members hoped that the fear of leaving for the August recess empty-handed would push the Senate to overcome its differences, and the Graham-Smith compromise seemed to offer the best hope for a deal. But like the other plans, it needed sixty votes to overcome a budget point of order because its cost exceeded the $300 billion limit. The **key vote of 49–50 (R 4–44; D 45–5; I 0–1)** on July 31 was well short of the required sixty votes. *(2002 key votes, p. 819)*

"I think a lot of people are concerned about leaving out so much of the middle . . . people are legitimately concerned about backlash from a large group of seniors," said Breaux, about the Graham-Smith compromise.

After two weeks of debate over the prescription drug proposals, the Senate on July 31 passed the underlying generic drug bill, 78–21, with twenty-eight Republicans in favor. CBO estimated that the bill would reduce total spending on prescription drugs by $60 billion, or 1.3 percent, over ten years; S 812 later died in the House.

Medicare 'Givebacks'

Despite high hopes and considerable lobbying, doctors, hospitals, and other Medicare providers failed to persuade Congress in 2002 to enact a third rollback of payment cuts enacted in 1997 as part of a drive to reduce the deficit. The proposal had wide support in Congress, but it was packaged with prescription drug legislation that died at the end of the session.

The House included $30 billion for Medicare providers over ten years as part of a $350 billion bill to add prescription drug coverage to Medicare (HR 4954). The bill passed in June, but partisan conflicts doomed the legislation in the Senate. *(Medicare drug benefit, p. 483)*

For five years, providers who cared for Medicare's nearly 40 million recipients had complained that the 1997 Balanced Budget Act (PL 105-33) cut their reimbursements too deeply. Twice, in 1999 and 2000, Congress increased payments to providers in what came to be known as "giveback" legislation.

Congress in 1999 included a $16 billion, five-year package of givebacks in an omnibus appropriations law (PL 106-113). Medicare providers won a second installment in 2000, receiving about $35 billion over five years as part of another omnibus spending bill (PL 106-554). *(Congress and the Nation Vol. X, p. 461)*

The providers, including physicians, hospitals, nursing homes, and home health agencies, began pushing early in 2002 for a third giveback bill. The American Medical Association led the fight because a glitch in the Medicare funding formula was promising a second straight year of payment reductions without congressional action. The $30 billion included in the House prescription drug bill (HR 4954) helped win votes for that measure, particularly among lawmakers from rural areas. It also raised providers' hopes that Congress would hear their concerns.

While there was bipartisan support in the Senate for more provider funds, no givebacks were included in the various versions of the Medicare prescription drug benefit that were offered on the Senate floor in July. All those proposals failed.

Generic Drugs

With the debate over creating a prescription drug benefit for seniors stalled in Congress, Senate Democrats looked for ways to attack the high price of prescription drugs for Americans of all ages. In July 2002 the Senate passed a bill (S 812) to tighten patent laws in order to make generic drugs more readily available, and to allow the so-called reimportation of U.S.-made drugs from Canada, where they often were less expensive. The bill had significant Republican support—its lead cosponsor was Sen. John McCain, R-Ariz.—but while Democrats hailed its passage as a major victory for their party, their hopes of also using it as a vehicle to carry wide-ranging Medicare prescription drug legislation fizzled.

House Republicans never took up the Senate bill. They preferred to keep the focus on the fact that they had passed a Medicare prescription drug benefit (HR 4954) in June and the Democratic-controlled Senate had not, a point they hoped would resonate with voters in the midterm elections.

On Oct. 21, two weeks before the 2002 congressional elections, President George W. Bush unveiled his own plan to get more generic drugs on the market—a proposal less objectionable to the brand-name drug industry, but at the same time a message to voters that he and congressional Republicans cared about lowering drug prices.

BACKGROUND

The focus of the debate on generic drugs was a 1984 law (PL 98-417) known as the Hatch-Waxman act for its original sponsors, Sen. Orrin G. Hatch, R-Utah, and Rep. Henry A. Waxman, D-Calif. Although the law was designed to speed generic versions of brand-name drugs to market, critics said that goal had often been thwarted over the years as loopholes in the law had been found and exploited. (*Congress and the Nation Vol. VI, p. 547*)

Lobbyists for the drug industry and their allies on Capitol Hill replied that the Hatch-Waxman act was working as Congress intended and that abuses were rare. They noted that, since the bill's enactment, the generic industry's share of the overall market had jumped from less than 20 percent to almost 50 percent. Drugmakers also pointed to the cost of developing new lifesaving drugs—$800 million on average to get a new drug to market, they said—and warned that further limits on their ability to protect their patents would reduce their incentive for research and development.

Dr. Gregory J. Glover, who testified on behalf of the Pharmaceutical Research and Manufacturers of America (PhRMA) at a Senate hearing in May 2002, called Hatch-Waxman "one of the most successful pieces of consumer legislation in history." He told the Senate Health, Education, Labor, and Pensions Committee, "What is a loophole in the eyes of the generics is a fundamental procedure that protects the intellectual property rights of the innovators."

But Democrats and many Republicans said that pharmaceutical companies had abused the law to unfairly extend the life of their patents, blocking competition and keeping drug prices high. A report issued by the Federal Trade Commission (FTC) on July 30 detailed abuses and recommended legislative action to modify two provisions of the law that the FTC said provided particular opportunities for drugmakers to keep generic drugs off the market.

Under Hatch-Waxman, a brand-name drugmaker facing a patent challenge could file suit to stop the generic from entering the market, automatically blocking the Food and Drug Administration (FDA) from approving the generic for thirty months while the legal issues were resolved. The pharmaceutical company could then list additional patents for variants on the drug, providing new grounds to file suit and getting multiple thirty-month stays—often resulting in years of protection.

At the May hearing, Sen. Charles E. Schumer, D-N.Y., the lead cosponsor of the bill with McCain, cited the example of the pain medication Ultram, whose manufacturer, Johnson & Johnson, won a new patent by developing a new dosing schedule: taking one-fourth of a pill, and slowly building to a full dose. He said the new patent allowed the company to extend its exclusive right to the drug.

The FTC report recommended a single thirty-month stay.

The second provision of Hatch-Waxman singled out by the FTC gave a generic that successfully challenged a brand-name drug 180 days of exclusive access to the market before other generic competitors could begin selling their products. In some cases, brand-name companies had turned what was meant as an incentive into another barrier. A company, for example, could make a deal with the generic to put off actually bringing the product to market, which could delay the start of the 180-day period and hold off other generics. The FTC recommended that drugmakers and producers of generics be required to disclose such deals.

LEGISLATIVE ACTION

The Senate Health, Education, Labor, and Pensions Committee approved the Schumer-McCain bill (S 812), by a vote of 16–5 on July 11. In an indication of the issue's political appeal, half the committee's ten Republicans voted for the bill; all five were facing reelection in the fall. S 812 was reported that same day (no written report).

As introduced, the bill would have eliminated the automatic thirty-month delay in FDA approval of generic drugs when the brand company filed suit. A substitute version, adopted by voice vote in the committee, allowed for a single thirty-month stay per application from a generic producer under limited circumstances.

The amended bill also allowed generic drugmakers to seek a declaratory judgment in federal civil court to challenge brand-name patents listed in the so-called Orange Book, the FDA's registry of pharmaceutical products, formulations, and applications that were protected from competition. Under existing law, the FDA simply listed the patents without evaluating them; only the listing company could remove them from the list.

The declaratory judgment language was the subject of the most intense debate, with some Republicans charging it would lead to a proliferation of lawsuits.

The committee adopted a separate amendment by voice vote to clarify that the generic cause-of-action language would not authorize award of damages and would be allowed only in challenges to patents within thirty days of approval of a brand-name application.

The Senate passed the bill, 78–21, on July 31 after two and a half weeks of debate, much of it spent trying to add various Medicare prescription drug amendments. All attempts to amend the bill with a prescription drug plan failed. John B. Breaux, D-La., was the only Democrat to vote against the bill; twenty-eight Republicans voted for it.

Byron Dorgan, D-N.D., won voice vote approval for his amendment to allow pharmacists and wholesalers to import FDA-approved, U.S.-manufactured drugs from Canada. He said consumers could save as much as $38 billion a year.

The amendment was a narrower version of a law (PL 106-387) enacted in 2000 that sought to allow reimports from all major industrialized countries. Department of Health and Human Service (HHS) secretaries in both the Clinton and Bush administrations had chosen not to implement the law, citing concerns about the safety of drugs purchased outside the United States. Dorgan and his cosponsors, including Maine Republicans Susan Collins and Olympia J. Snowe, said that narrowing the bill to Canada should ease any worries over the safety of the drugs. But the provision, even if it had become law, was unlikely ever to have been implemented, because the Senate also voted 99–0 for the same language requiring safety and cost-saving certification that had prompted the HHS secretaries to reject the earlier reimportation provision. *(Congress and the Nation Vol. X, p. 483)*

Other amendments adopted on the floor included an additional $9 billion in Medicaid and social services funding to help states cope with rising Medicaid costs.

The Senate on July 18 voted 56–43 to allow states to use their volume purchasing power to buy lower-priced drugs for uninsured people who did not qualify for Medicaid.

On July 30 the Senate voted 57–42 to table (kill) an amendment by Mitch McConnell, R-Ky., that would have put caps on punitive damages and attorneys' fees in medical malpractice cases.

But that was as far as the measure advanced. House Republican leaders had no interest in taking up the Senate bill or a companion House measure. "We want to keep the pressure on the Senate to do a drug benefit," explained John Feehery, a spokesman for Speaker J. Dennis Hastert, R-Ill.

Minority Leader Richard A. Gephardt, D-Mo., and McCain circulated a "discharge petition" in an attempt to force the House version (HR 1862) to the floor for a vote, but they were able to gather only 150 signatures of the 218 they needed.

Hastert's office described the discharge effort as "another desperate attempt to change the subject away from another major House accomplishment—passage of a fair, fiscally responsible, and comprehensive plan to strengthen Medicare with prescription drug coverage."

On Oct. 21 President Bush surprised Capitol Hill by issuing a plan to make regulatory changes affecting the Hatch-Waxman act. The changes included allowing only one thirty-month automatic stay when a brand name challenged a generic's attempt to enter the market and imposing penalties for "frivolous" patents—such as those to change a pill's bottle or its color—that were listed in the FDA's Orange Book. Administration officials said the president's plan would save consumers $35 billion over the coming decade. The Congressional Budget Office had estimated that the Senate-passed plan would save $60 billion over the same period.

The drug industry, a longtime ally and potent fundraiser for Bush and the Republican Party, stood to lose billions with the Bush plan, but the industry perceived it as far less onerous than the Senate bill. Jeff Trewhitt, a spokesman for PhRMA, called Bush's proposal "an important development that needs to be weighed very carefully."

HIGHLIGHTS

Following are the main components of S 812, as passed by the Senate:

Thirty-month stay. A brand-name pharmaceutical company would get only one thirty-month stay against FDA approval of a generic drug whose entry into the market was being challenged by the brand-name company.

'Rolling' 180-day exclusivity. A generic company that won a patent challenge would have exclusive access to the market for 180 days. However, if it did not bring its product to market because it had reached a financial settlement with the brand company or for other reasons, the 180-day exclusivity would pass automatically to the next generic applicant in line.

Timely suit. A brand-name company would have to bring a suit within forty-five days of being challenged by a generic. Otherwise, it would forfeit its right to sue on that patent against that generic drugmaker.

Drug reimportation. Licensed pharmacists and wholesalers would be allowed to import FDA-approved, U.S.-manufactured drugs from Canada under strict safety procedures.

Pediatric Drug Exclusivity

Congress in 2001 agreed to renew a program giving pharmaceutical companies an extra six months of exclusive rights to name-brand drugs if they agreed to test the drug for use by children. The program, begun in 1997, was aimed at encouraging companies to provide consumers with information on the appropriate usage of adult drugs by children. The bill, signed into law (S 1789—PL 107-109) by President George W. Bush on Jan. 4, 2002, extended the program through fiscal 2007. It had been set to expire at the end of 2001.

Supporters of the five-year extension said the law had worked, encouraging the development of information on proper dosages for children, as well as the side effects of many drugs. Critics, such as Rep. Henry A. Waxman, D-Calif., however, argued that granting six months of additional patent protection for brand-name drugs gave a windfall to drug companies while delaying the availability to consumers of cheaper generic drugs. They said drug companies could increase their profits by billions of dollars while spending no more than a few million dollars on the tests.

The bill was endorsed by the brand-name drug industry group Pharmaceutical Research and Manufacturers of America, as well as by many patient and children's health groups. However, the final bill was a rebuff to Bristol-Myers Squibb Co., which had lobbied vigorously to win three years' protection from competition for Glucophage, a popular diabetes drug.

BACKGROUND

The six-month extension of patent exclusivity was originally enacted as part of the 1997 Food and Drug Administration Modernization Act (PL 105-115). *(Congress and the Nation Vol. X, p. 444)*

President Bill Clinton had wanted drug companies to be required to test their drugs for use by children. Instead, the bill authorized the six months of extra patent protection as an incentive. During that period, no other company could market a generic alternative to the medicine. The Clinton administration later issued a companion regulation, called the "pediatric rule," which enabled the Food and Drug Administration (FDA) to order drugmakers to test new products on children in certain cases.

The goal of both the pediatric exclusivity law and the pediatric rule was to provide information on the safety and efficacy of treating children with medicines initially designed for adult use. For many major medications, there was no information on potential side effects, the proper dosage, or method of administration for children. The law authorized the Department of Health and Human Services (HHS) to develop a list of drugs on which additional research would be beneficial. To receive the extension, drug manufacturers had to submit their product for review by Jan. 1, 2002. The HHS secretary gave good marks to the program in early 2001 in a report required under the 1997 law.

LEGISLATIVE ACTION

The Senate Health, Education, Labor, and Pensions Committee approved a version of the bill by voice vote Aug. 1 and reported it Oct. 4 (S 838—S Rept 107-79). Senators generally agreed to withhold amendments until the measure came to the floor. Hillary Rodham Clinton, D-N.Y., offered an amendment to limit the patent protection to drugs with an-

nual sales below $800 million but withdrew it following a request from Christopher J. Dodd, D-Mass., who sponsored the bill with Mike DeWine, R-Ohio.

The Senate passed the bill by voice vote without debate Oct. 18.

A companion bill (HR 2887) introduced in the House by James C. Greenwood, R-Pa., ran into greater opposition. The Energy and Commerce Subcommittee on Health approved the measure, 24–5, on Oct. 4, after five hours of debate. Democrats attacked the bill as a boon to drug manufacturers and offered many amendments to scale it back—all of them unsuccessful.

The full House Energy and Commerce Committee approved the bill by a vote of 41–6 on Oct. 11 and reported it Nov. 9 (H Rept 107-277). Democrats again tried to limit the benefits to the drug companies, charging that the fact that the program was working was not reason enough to continue it. "Giving the drug industry the key to the federal treasury would also work," said Rep. Sherrod Brown, D-Ohio. "Does that mean it's a good idea?"

The House passed the bill, 338–86, on Nov. 15 under suspension of the rules, a procedure that limited debate and barred amendments. Supporters tried to counter Democratic arguments that the bill would line the pockets of drug companies by stressing that most of the medications that had been granted exclusivity were not "top sellers."

A compromise measure negotiated by the bills' sponsors was introduced as a clean bill (S 1789) on Dec. 8. The Senate passed it by voice vote Dec. 12, and the House cleared it Dec. 18, also by voice vote.

The final bill closed a loophole that had been used by Bristol-Myers and several other drugmakers to seek extended protection from low-cost competitors. Bristol-Myers said that because it now marketed Glucophage to treat teenagers under new labeling approved by the FDA, it should get three years of patent protection under a law (PL 98-417) that rewarded companies for discovering new uses for drugs. The company argued that without the protection, it would lose $1.7 billion in profits annually.

But generic drugmakers countered that approving Glucophage for teenagers did not constitute a new use. The FDA had given tentative approval to a low-cost competitor, pending resolution of the patent issue by Congress. Waxman said that Congress never intended to allow drugmakers to delay competition "simply by changing the label."

MAJOR PROVISIONS

As signed into law Jan. 4, 2002, S 1789 (PL 107-109):

Exclusivity

Reauthorized through Oct. 1, 2007, provisions that gave drug companies an extra six months of market exclusivity for a brand-name drug if the company tested the drug for use on children at the request of the Food and Drug Administration (FDA). During the six-month period, the company could market the drug without competition from generic alternatives.

Pediatric Health

Established two new offices—the Foundation for Pediatric Research at the National Institutes of Health (NIH) and the Office of Pediatric Therapeutics within the FDA—charged with overseeing activities dealing with pediatric health and medicine for their respective agencies.

NIH Testing

Authorized $200 million in fiscal 2002 and such sums as necessary through fiscal 2007 for pediatric testing of medicines that were not protected by patents. If a drug company declined an FDA request to study a patented drug for pediatric use, the NIH was authorized to fund a study.

Labeling

Amended labeling requirements, mandating the inclusion of pediatric testing results. The new law shortened the period for negotiation between companies and the FDA concerning labeling information, and established an appeals process for drug companies. If a drug was found to be unsuitable for children, the company was required to label the product accordingly.

Studies

Required the comptroller general to report to Congress by 2006 on the program's effectiveness in ensuring that medicines used by children were tested and properly labeled, and on its economic impact on pharmaceutical companies, medical insurance programs, and consumers.

Required the General Accounting Office (GAO) to conduct a study on the extent to which children of ethnic and racial minorities were included in studies and report its findings no later than Jan. 10, 2003.

Community, Rural Health Programs

Congress reauthorized funding through fiscal 2006 for community health centers, the National Health Service Corps, telehealth, and rural health care programs in a bill signed into law by President George W. Bush on Oct. 26, 2002 (S 1533—PL 107-251).

The bill was part of a plan by Bush to increase funding sufficiently to ensure a doubling by 2006 of the more than 11 million patients being served by community health centers. Approximately 40 percent of the patients seeking treatment at such centers were uninsured; one-third of those were children. It was one of the few steps taken by the 107th Congress to address the surge in the ranks of the uninsured, which jumped almost 15 percent to 41.2 million in 2001, according to the Census Bureau.

As reported by the Senate Health, Education, Labor, and Pensions Committee (S Rept 107-83) on Oct. 11, 2001, and passed by voice vote of the Senate April 16, 2002, the bill authorized $1.4 billion for community health centers in fiscal 2002 and unspecified sums through fiscal 2006. The House on Oct. 1 passed by voice vote a similar bill (HR 3450) for fiscal 2003 through 2006. The final bill—which the House passed, 392–5, on Oct. 16 and the Senate cleared by voice vote Oct. 17—was a compromise between the two.

As signed into law, S 1533:

• Authorized $1.3 billion in fiscal 2002 and unspecified amounts through fiscal 2006 for community health centers.

• Reauthorized the National Health Service Corps, allotting $146 million in scholarship and loan repayment incentives in fiscal 2002 and "such sums as may be necessary" through 2006 as incentives to health profession students who agreed to serve as primary care clinicians in underserved areas in exchange for the educational support. The health service corps had placed more than 22,000 health care providers in rural communities, urban centers, and other areas with a shortage of physicians and other health professionals during the previous thirty years.

• Authorized $40 million in fiscal 2002 and unspecified funds in future years for grants to improve the quality of rural health care services. Created a new grant program to promote the use of telecommunications technology to give patients and health care providers in rural areas access to high-quality health care services and information.

• Authorized a new Healthy Communities Access Program to help communities and groups of health care providers develop coordinated health care services for the uninsured. Made both private and public organizations eligible for grants under the program, of which no more than thirty-five could be awarded each year through fiscal 2006. Authorized $50 million over five years for state grants to innovative programs that addressed the needs of areas with limited access to dental care.

Medical Malpractice Limits

As they had in each Congress since taking control in 1995, House Republicans in 2002 passed a sweeping bill to limit damage awards and plaintiff attorneys' fees in medical malpractice lawsuits. But the Senate had already rejected a more limited plan, making it clear the legislation would not be enacted in the 107th Congress.

The Senate proposal would have capped punitive damages in medical malpractice cases at twice the compensatory damages, limited attorneys' fees, and required lawsuits to be filed within two years of the discovery of an injury. It failed July 30, 2002, when offered as a floor amendment to an unrelated generic drug bill (S 812). Six Republicans joined all fifty Democrats and James M. Jeffords, I-Vt., to kill the proposal, 57–42.

The House bill (HR 4600), passed Sept. 26, mirrored a proposal offered by President George W. Bush. It included a $250,000 cap on noneconomic damages, restrictions on attorneys' fees, strict limits on punitive damages, and protection for drug and medical device manufacturers whose products were approved by the Food and Drug Administration (FDA).

The American Medical Association (AMA), which had made overhauling liability laws its top legislative priority, endorsed the House bill. "As medical liability insurance becomes unaffordable or unavailable, physicians are forced to limit services, leave their practices, or relocate—seriously impeding patient access to health care," said AMA president-elect Dr. Donald J. Palmisano.

Both Democrats and Republicans agreed on the need to address the soaring cost of malpractice insurance; premiums had increased by nearly 50 percent in a number of states over the previous two years. But the two sides had sharply conflicting views on the causes and proper remedies.

Republicans, joined by doctors and insurance companies, blamed rising jury awards for the huge premium increases. Democrats, backed by trial lawyers and consumer groups, pointed to the insurance industry as the culprit, saying insurers were using a handful of cases to justify rate increases so they could recoup stock and bond market losses and make up for bad business decisions in the 1990s. Some suggested ending the industry's partial exemption from antitrust laws.

BACKGROUND

The problem of malpractice costs began to grow in the 1970s, when a number of private insurers stopped offering coverage, saying the costs were prohibitive. With congressional Democrats deflecting efforts to curb malpractice insurance lawsuits, the states took the lead. Several states passed laws limiting damages, most of them modeled on California's 1975 Medical Injury Compensation Reform Act (MICRA). Doctors who hoped to stave off rising rates in the future banded together to create physician-owned insurance companies.

A decade later, when premiums once again started to rise, state legislatures passed more laws. California addressed the issue again with comprehensive insurance regulations through an initiative known as "Proposition 103," which affected a wide range of industries including health care.

All told, more than three dozen states had passed damage caps, although some had been repealed or ruled unconstitutional. According to the National Council of State Legislatures, all states had some sort of limits on tort litigation, such as a requirement that defendants pay only the share of damages for which they were responsible, limits on attorneys' fees, provisions to allow periodic payments of awards, or caps on some awards.

LEGISLATIVE ACTION

HR 4600 was considered by two committees: House Judiciary and House Energy and Commerce. The Judiciary Committee went first, approving the bill by voice vote Sept. 10, 2002, and reporting it Sept. 25 (H Rept 107-693, Part 1).

Reversing the parties' traditional roles on states' rights, Republicans defeated a series of Democratic amendments aimed at protecting state laws and otherwise limiting the scope of the bill. "We need to do something about this national problem, and we need a national law," argued F. James Sensenbrenner Jr., R-Wis., chair of the committee. Jerrold Nadler, D-N.Y., meanwhile, charged that the bill's central provision, capping awards for noneconomic damages, would "gut" state statutes that set higher limits.

The panel rejected by voice vote several amendments by Robert C. Scott, D-Va., including proposals to limit the bill to cases in federal courts; drop the time limit on filing medical malpractice suits; strike the limits on noneconomic damages and the requirement that liability be shared by lawsuit defendants based on their percentage share of fault; strike the limit on punitive damages; strike the limits on lawyers' contingency fees; and drop a provision that would override state court rulings that defendants could not reduce damages by showing that a plaintiff had been compensated by an insurer. The closest Democrats came was a 14–14 vote rejecting a bid by Nadler to index damage awards to inflation.

The Energy and Commerce Committee approved the bill on Sept. 18 by a vote of 27–22 and reported it Sept. 25 (H Rept 107-693, Part 2). Democrats Jane Harman of California and Ralph M. Hall of Texas crossed party lines to vote for the bill. Republicans Lee Terry of Nebraska and Robert L. Ehrlich Jr. of Maryland voted against it.

Committee Republicans defeated a series of Democratic amendments aimed at reducing the scope of the bill or allowing higher damage awards. The only amendment that survived during committee action was a symbolic sense of Congress provision written by Republican Charlie Norwood of Georgia, stating that a health insurer should be liable for damages when a patient is harmed by a decision as to what care is medically necessary or appropriate.

The House passed the bill Sept. 26 on a largely party-line vote of 217–203, with each side accusing the other of supporting positions that would put the nation's health care system at risk. Only fourteen Democrats voted for the legislation; fifteen Republicans voted against it. The bill was considered under a closed rule for debate that barred all amendments.

Before passing the bill the House rejected, 193–225, a motion by John Conyers Jr., D-Mich., to send it back to committee with instructions to include language stating that none of the provisions would preempt state laws on the liability of health maintenance organizations.

HIGHLIGHTS

The House-passed bill applied to any health care lawsuit brought in federal or state court or subject to an alternative dispute resolution system. HR 4600 would have:

Economic damages. Allowed full economic damages—defined as "objectively verifiable monetary losses" incurred as a result of an injury, such as past and future medical expenses, loss of past and future earnings, the cost of obtaining domestic services, loss of employment, and loss of business or employment opportunities.

Noneconomic damages. Limited noneconomic damages to $250,000, regardless of the number of defendants or the number of separate claims resulting from the same incident. The bill defined noneconomic damages as damages for physical and emotional pain, suffering, inconvenience, physical impairment, mental anguish, disfigurement, loss of enjoyment of life, loss of society and companionship, loss of consortium, hedonic damages, injury to reputation, and all other noneconomic losses. The jury would not have been informed of the damage cap.

Punitive damages. Limited punitive damages that could be awarded in a health care lawsuit to two times economic damages, or $250,000, whichever was greater. Punitive damages were defined in the bill as those awarded "for the purpose of punishment or deterrence." Again, the jury would not have been informed of the cap.

A plaintiff would have been able to file for punitive damages only after the court had found a "substantial probability" that he or she would prevail in the claim. Punitive damages could have been awarded only if it was proven "by clear and convincing evidence" that the defendant acted with malicious intent to injure, or that the defendant "deliberately failed to avoid unnecessary injury" that it knew the plaintiff was "substantially certain" to suffer. Punitive damages could not have been awarded if there were no compensatory damages.

Joint and several liability. Prohibited the use of joint and several liability, under which plaintiffs could have recovered all or part of the damages from any one or all of the defendants found responsible for the injury. Instead, each defendant would have been liable for his or her share of the damages, as determined by the judge or jury.

FDA-approved medical products. Shielded drug manufacturers and makers of medical devices from punitive damages if their products were approved by the FDA or were generally considered safe. The exemption would not have applied if the manufacturer had knowingly withheld information from the FDA.

Statute of limitations. Required that a health care lawsuit be filed within three years of the date of the injury, or one year after the plaintiff discovered—or should have discovered—the injury, whichever occurred first. The deadline could have been extended if there was proof of fraud or intentional concealment.

Attorneys' fees. Capped attorney "contingent fees"—a predetermined percentage of any amount awarded by the court to the client. The total of all contingent fees for representing all plaintiffs in a health care lawsuit could not have exceeded 40 percent of the first $50,000 recovered, 33.3 percent of the next $50,000, 25 percent of the next $500,000, and 15 percent of any amount over $600,000.

State laws. Preempted state laws that conflicted with the application of any provision in the bill. However, the bill would not have preempted any state statutory limit on the amount of compensatory, punitive, or total damages awarded in a health care lawsuit, whether the state total was higher or lower than the caps provided for in the bill. The provisions dealing with caps on awards would have applied only to those states that had no set statutory limits on damage awards in health care lawsuits.

Human Cloning Ban

The House voted July 31, 2001, to ban all cloning of human embryos, whether for reproductive purposes or for biomedical research. It was the first time either chamber had gone on record on what was one of the most rapidly growing areas of the life sciences. The Bush administration backed the bill (HR 2505); the biotechnology industry lobbied strongly against it. However, the measure got no further when the Senate did not take up the bill.

Under HR 2505, sponsored by Dave Weldon, R-Fla., researchers who cloned human embryos would face up to ten years in prison and at least $1 million in fines. The bill also would have prohibited the importation of a cloned human embryo or any product derived from one. The proposed ban was aimed at a process known as somatic cell nuclear transfer, which involved stripping an egg of its DNA, implanting genetic material from another egg, and then inducing the egg to develop.

Human cloning was one of the most passionate science issues facing the 107th Congress, requiring lawmakers to consider whether a days-old embryo deserved the same moral status as a person. There was general agreement that cloning a human was morally objectionable and should be outlawed. But many Democrats and medical researchers urged lawmakers to distinguish between cloning intended to produce a complete human being, and "therapeutic" cloning to create stem cells that researchers hoped could one day be used to treat or cure life-threatening diseases like Parkinson's, diabetes, or Alzheimer's.

The questions gained added urgency when Advanced Cell Technology, based in Worcester, Mass., and the Jones Institute for Reproductive Medicine in Norfolk, Va., announced plans to clone human embryos to harvest stem cells for research purposes.

Although the cloning bill did not address the question directly, the debate was closely linked to the question of whether to allow federal funding for research on embryonic stem cells—primordial cells in embryos capable of evolving into any kind of human tissue. Scientists were excited about the cells' potential. But extracting them involved destroying the embryo, an act that abortion foes equated with murder. Stem cell research proponents pointed out that without cloning, realizing stem cells' potential as treatments might be limited, because the cells would have to be derived from the patient himself or herself in order to prevent tissue rejection.

BACKGROUND

In 1996 scientists in Scotland used the somatic cell process to successfully clone the first mammal—a sheep named Dolly. Shortly afterward, President Bill Clinton issued a ban

Senators Sam Brownback, R-Kan., Orrin G. Hatch, R-Utah, Gordon H. Smith, R-Ore., and Bill Frist, R-Tenn., testify at a Senate hearing on stem cell research on July 18, 2001. On July 31, 2001, the House passed a bill to ban all cloning of human embryos, but the bill died in the Senate as lawmakers clashed on whether or not to include "therapeutic" cloning, or stem cell research, in the ban. *Source: Congressional Quarterly/Scott J. Ferrell*

on the use of federal funding to clone humans using the technique. Clinton also asked the National Bioethics Advisory Commission to address the ethical and legal issues related to human cloning. In June 1997 the commission recommended that the moratorium on federal funding for human cloning be continued, and that legislation be enacted to prohibit anyone from attempting to create a child using this cloning process. The panel cited the harm such cloning might have on family relationships, identity, and religious beliefs. The commission also recommended that any legislation include a sunset clause to ensure that Congress reviewed the issue to determine whether the ban should continue.

In 1997 the House Science Committee approved a bill similar to Weldon's proposal, but it never reached the floor. The next year the Senate debated a similar bill offered by Bill Frist, R-Tenn., and Christopher S. Bond, R-Mo. In a pattern that would continue, they had some unlikely opponents: abortion foes, such as Sens. Strom Thurmond, R-S.C., and Connie Mack, R-Fla. (Senate, 1989–2001), argued that the bill was too broad, citing personal and family experiences with serious diseases. The Frist-Bond proposal died after Dianne Feinstein, D-Calif., objected to bringing it up, and proponents of the bill failed to muster the sixty votes needed to overcome her objections. *(Congress and the Nation Vol. X, p. 459)*

LEGISLATIVE ACTION

The House Judiciary Crime Subcommittee approved Weldon's bill by voice vote July 19, 2001, but the conflicting views on the issue were evident. Chair Lamar Smith, R-Texas, urged quick action, warning that there were "a growing number of groups that claim they can and will" clone human beings. His strategy was bolstered by White House support of the bill. On the other side, ranking sub-

committee member Robert C. Scott, D-Va., cited a letter from the American Society for Reproductive Medicine stating that anticloning legislation would outlaw promising scientific techniques "before we could even explore [their] potential good," The group also said a complete cloning ban would cause "the burgeoning biotech industry [to] suffer" because foreign competitors had no such restrictions. The full Judiciary Committee approved HR 2505 on July 24 by an 18–11 party-line vote and reported it July 27 (H Rept 107-170). Democrats had offered several amendments aimed at weakening the bill, all of which were rejected on party-line votes.

The House passed the bill July 31 by a 265–162 vote. "The House spoke very, very loudly today that this is morally and ethically inappropriate," Weldon said after the vote. "It clearly sends a message that there is a place we don't want to go and that is the manufacture of scientific embryos for research."

The House rejected on a **key vote of 178–249 (R 25–194; D 153–53; I 0–2)** a substitute amendment offered by James C. Greenwood, R-Pa., that would have outlawed human cloning for the purpose of creating a child but allowed it for medical research. Opponents termed his amendment unworkable, saying it would be impossible to track what became of all cloned embryos. *(2001 key votes, p. 801)*

The four hours of often emotional floor debate again suggested that members' views on human cloning did not break precisely along the same lines as they did on abortion. On passage, sixty-three Democrats joined with two independents and 200 Republicans to support the bill.

Many opponents expressed discomfort with the idea of having to assimilate complicated technical information and impose new regulations on a still-developing field. "I think the Senate will look at this with a lot more deliberation and avoid a rush to judgment," said Henry A. Waxman, D-Calif., who supported Greenwood's substitute. "This came so quickly to the House floor, and is so new and complicated, that many members don't understand the differences between what the Weldon bill and the Greenwood bill would do," he said.

In the Senate, Majority Leader Tom Daschle, D-S.D.—who supported a ban on cloning for reproductive but not for medical research purposes—promised a floor debate in 2002. But when Advanced Cell Technology announced Nov. 25, 2001, that it had successfully cloned a human embryo,

Sam Brownback, R-Kan., who had introduced a companion bill to Weldon's, pressed for a six-month interim moratorium. Senate GOP leaders decided to offer the moratorium as part of a complex ploy to derail a Democratic economic stimulus bill. Minority Leader Trent Lott, R-Miss., paired it with a separate proposal to allow oil drilling in part of Alaska's Arctic National Wildlife Refuge in an amendment that drew so much opposition that Lott himself voted against bringing it up. His motion to cut off debate was rejected, 1–94, on Dec. 3. Despite Daschle's promise, he and Brownback were not able to agree on terms for a debate in 2002 and the legislation died at the end of the Congress.

2003–2004

The 108th Congress proved that major changes to the politically sensitive Medicare program did not have to be made with overwhelming bipartisan majorities. Indeed, the Medicare Modernization Act, the most sweeping overhaul of the program since its inception in 1965, came with the support of only a handful of Democrats in both the House and Senate.

The achievement, however, was anything but easy. President George W. Bush and Republican congressional leaders had to navigate their fragile compromise between fiscal conservatives in their own party, who disapproved of adding an expensive new prescription drug benefit to the program, and the drug industry, which supported drug coverage but feared government price controls. The GOP also had to court the support of senior groups like the AARP, which insisted that the benefit help those with low incomes and prevent employers from dropping existing drug coverage for retirees, as well as providers such as doctors and hospitals, who wanted higher Medicare payments.

Passage of the bill in 2003, however, did not end the debate. Democrats spent much of 2004 trying to foment opposition to the program, which they said helped the drug and insurance industries more than Medicare's beneficiaries. At the same time, bipartisan coalitions in the House and Senate tried—albeit unsuccessfully—to force votes on measures to allow lower-cost prescription drugs to be imported from Canada and other developed countries, and to repeal a provision of the Medicare bill that barred the government from negotiating directly with drug companies for lower prices.

While Medicare took center stage, the 108th Congress also continued to build on earlier efforts to protect the nation from a potential bioterrorist attack. It passed bills to compensate those who suffered adverse reactions to the smallpox vaccine, and to create an incentive system to accelerate research into vaccines, diagnostic tests, and treatments for the germs most likely to be used in a bioterror attack.

Medicare Overhaul, Drug Benefit

After years of debate, Congress succeeded in passing a sweeping overhaul of Medicare in 2003, making the most significant structural changes to the federal health program for the elderly and disabled in its thirty-eight-year history. The bill (HR 1—PL 108-173) provided beneficiaries for the first time with outpatient prescription drug coverage, expanded the role played by private insurers, and created tax-free health savings accounts for unreimbursed medical expenses. President George W. Bush had made its passage his top domestic priority for the year.

Efforts to add drug coverage to Medicare failed in the 106th and 107th Congresses after Republican-written bills passed the GOP-controlled House but died in the Senate. The effort in the 108th was different, in part because Republicans were in control of both chambers. Also neither party wanted to face voters empty-handed in the 2004 campaign after running on the drug coverage issue for years. Republicans were determined to give Bush a victory, while Democrats feared being labeled obstructionists on an issue they had long championed. *(2002 action, p. 483)*

The fiscal 2004 budget resolution (H Con Res 95) gave lawmakers another incentive. It allowed Congress to commit $400 billion over ten years for a Medicare prescription drug benefit and Medicare "modernization." With rising deficit projections, lawmakers saw the opportunity as fleeting. "Chances are very slim that we'll have as much as $400 billion to spend in future years," noted Max Baucus of Montana, ranking Democrat on the Senate Finance Committee. *(Budget resolution, p. 67)*

The new law allowed Medicare beneficiaries to get prescription drug coverage, beginning in 2006, either through privately-provided, stand-alone drug insurance plans (for those who preferred to remain in the traditional fee-for-service Medicare program); through health maintenance organizations (HMOs), which had long been available to Medicare beneficiaries; or through less restrictive private managed care networks, similar to preferred provider organizations (PPOs). Medical benefits could vary between fee-for-service and private plans, but companies offering drug coverage would have to offer benefits of at least equal value. The law also included billions of dollars in fee increases for hospitals, physicians, and other providers in rural areas—money that helped attract bipartisan support for the overhaul.

In the eighteen months before the program was to begin, beneficiaries could enroll in a prescription drug "discount card" program that officials estimated would save them 15 percent to 25 percent on their drug costs.

The law required seniors to pay deductibles and monthly premiums for the new drug benefit. The coverage would initially stop once their drug costs had risen above a $2,250 threshold, but it would kick back in for catastrophic costs after the beneficiary spent $3,600 on drugs out of his or her own pocket. The coverage gap, dubbed the "doughnut hole" during the debate, attracted sharp criticism from Democrats in both chambers, who called for a more continuous benefit.

The two chambers passed their respective versions of the bill within hours of each other on June 27, 2003—the House by a single vote, the Senate with considerably more bipartisan support. The House-Senate conference on the bill was largely a Republicans-only affair. Conference chair Bill Thomas, R-Calif., head of the House Ways and Means Committee, included only two Democrats—Baucus and Sen. John B. Breaux of Louisiana—in the private talks held mostly in

Thomas's office in the Capitol. Thomas defended the exclusion of other Democratic conferees on the grounds that they would be less willing to compromise.

Negotiations continued through the fall, periodically appearing on the verge of collapse. But with Bush calling publicly for Congress to "finish the job," Republican leaders completed the bill in late November and drove it through both chambers to enactment.

The final bill reflected Republicans' willingness to scale back some long-running efforts to boost private market competition and add accompanying cost controls to Medicare. Republicans believed it allowed them to go into the 2004 elections having coopted one of the Democrats' signature issues. While Democrats worried that the changes could undermine Medicare's traditional fee-for-service system, many decided to take what they could get, mindful that such a substantial increase in a domestic program was rare in a time of war and deepening budget deficits.

Each side also saw the law as a potential first step toward its longer-term goals. Republicans looked for the private sector to play a growing role, with market forces reducing costs and offering more choices. Democrats hoped that creating a drug benefit then would allow them to expand it later to make it more generous.

BACKGROUND

Policy makers had grappled for almost as long as Medicare had existed with how to provide a prescription drug benefit for those who needed it most—the approximately 10 million seniors who did not have drug coverage—without altering Medicare's core principle of equal treatment for all seniors.

Many fiscal conservatives favored targeting drug benefits to the neediest, an approach they hoped would be less likely to turn into a broad new federal mandate that would grow over time. But the idea was unacceptable to most lawmakers. Liberal Democrats, in particular, feared it would erode support for Medicare from the middle-class and better-off voters who financed the system through payroll taxes. "Medicare is not a welfare program," insisted Ways and Means Committee member Benjamin L. Cardin of Maryland, a relatively conservative Democrat. "If basic benefits are denied based on income, you're compromising the philosophy of Medicare."

But providing full coverage to each of the 40 million Medicare beneficiaries would cost too much, far exceeding the $400 billion over ten years that was available to lawmakers in 2003. The Congressional Budget Office estimated that Medicare beneficiaries would spend a total of $1.8 trillion on prescription drugs between 2004 and 2013.

In the end, Congress agreed to provide the same basic drug benefit to all seniors but make it less costly by providing relatively generous benefits to those with lower drug costs—in an effort to increase the proportion who would sign up for the voluntary benefit—and then no coverage at all except to those with catastrophic costs. The result was the controversial coverage gap, or doughnut hole.

Maintaining parity in coverage was further complicated by the fact that the Bush administration and its congressional allies wanted not only to add drug coverage but to do it as part of moving more beneficiaries into privately managed health plans. Bush and many Republicans saw private plans as a way to inject competition into seniors' health care, which they believed would result in more cost-effective services and reduced expense to the government.

Most Democrats did not oppose the option of private plans in Medicare, but they insisted that seniors get the same drug coverage regardless of whether they stayed in traditional fee-for-service Medicare or moved to a private plan.

Congress ultimately agreed on a core set of benefits that all plans would have to offer if they wanted to participate in the program. Beyond that, Republicans were confident that private plans would offer better deals and more choices to attract consumers. Democrats were more concerned with getting as much coverage as possible as part of the standard benefits.

Lawmakers from more rural areas fought for another kind of parity—parity in access to the programs Congress was designing. Even though private HMOs had been offering coverage to Medicare beneficiaries since the early 1980s, there were few or no plans in rural areas, where payments were lower and provider networks more difficult to negotiate. The fallback provision was one answer, guaranteeing that the government would offer benefits in a region if private plans did not. The law also provided extra aid for rural hospitals, doctors, and other providers, who had long decried their lower payments compared to providers in urban and suburban areas.

As the bill moved through Congress, other interests had to be balanced as well to maintain support for the legislation. Provisions for physicians, teaching hospitals, home health care services, oncologists, and many others made their way into the bill. Lawmakers' willingness to accept coverage gaps and other steps to limit costs enabled them to add billions of dollars for subsidies to providers, as well as incentives to attract insurers to the program and to dissuade employers from stopping drug coverage for their retirees once the federal program was in place.

SENATE COMMITTEE ACTION

The first formal action came when the Senate Finance Committee voted 16–5 on June 12, 2003, to approve a Medicare drug bill (S 1) written by Chair Charles E. Grassley, R-Iowa, and Baucus, the ranking Democrat. S 1 was reported the next day (no written report).

It was the first time the panel had approved a Medicare bill in five years. The strong bipartisan vote reflected growing momentum behind the legislation.

Adding to the bill's momentum, Edward M. Kennedy, D-Mass., a staunch defender of health care entitlement programs, called the bill a major breakthrough. "This is not the bill we would have written but to finally get something moving is a major step forward," he said. Kennedy said Democrats would work to improve it.

But tensions also were evident with opposition from both conservatives and liberals. Voting against the bill were Republicans Don Nickles of Oklahoma and Trent Lott of Mississippi, and Democrats John D. Rockefeller IV of West Virginia, Bob Graham of Florida, and John Kerry of Massachusetts.

The sharpest criticism from Democrats centered on the gap in drug coverage. Under the Senate measure, seniors would pay a monthly premium that would average $35 and a $275 annual deductible. Medicare would pick up half the senior's drug costs from $276 to $4,500, then stop until the beneficiary had paid $3,700 in out-of-pocket expenses. Medicare would then step back in to cover 90 percent of remaining costs.

Conservatives, meanwhile, said the bill did not do enough to foster market-based competition to contain costs and offer seniors more choices. Jon Kyl, R-Ariz., offered an amendment to require more competition in the system by allowing plans to bid on a purely competitive basis, removing the links in the bill between payments for the traditional fee-for-service program and the private plans. Kyl agreed to withdraw his proposal when Grassley said he would work with him on the issue before the measure passed the Senate.

In considering dozens of amendments during the day-long markup, the committee:

• Rejected, 8–13, an attempt by Nickles, who criticized the bill's cost, to strip out language by Graham to allow states to restore coverage to legal immigrant children and pregnant women under the State Children's Health Insurance Program. Graham's amendment aimed to restore some of the public benefits to legal immigrants that were cut off in the 1996 welfare overhaul (PL 104-193). *(Congress and the Nation Vol. IX, p. 578)*

• Rejected, 7–14, an attempt by Minority Leader Tom Daschle, D-S.D., to ensure that monthly Medicare premiums for seniors, which could vary widely across regions, would not rise more than 5 percent above the national average.

• Rejected, 7–14, a Rockefeller amendment to offer all seniors a government-run drug plan. Under the bill, such a plan would be provided only as a "fallback" if two plans did not enter a geographic area.

SENATE FLOOR ACTION

The Senate passed the bill on a **key vote of 76–21 (R 40–10; D 35–11; I 1–0)** on June 27, 2003. *(2003 key votes, p. 837)*

Passage came after approval of a carefully negotiated amendment that split $12 billion in previously unallocated funding between Republican and Democratic priorities. The proposal, offered by Grassley and Baucus, authorized two demonstration programs that would begin in 2009 and last

five years. Half the $12 billion would be used to provide extra subsidies to help private insurance companies attract seniors to their Medicare plans. The amendment would eliminate a requirement that government payments to the private networks be linked to, or capped by, payments for the traditional government-run Medicare program. The other $6 billion would be used to enhance preventive and chronic care benefits for seniors who remained in the traditional government-run Medicare program.

"Republicans say that the private sector can do a better job of providing health care for seniors, and we say [traditional] Medicare can," said Kennedy. "This amendment tests both." Baucus said the amendment was critical to getting the bill through the closely divided chamber. It was adopted, 71–26.

Before adopting the compromise, the Senate on June 26 rejected, 39–59, an alternative by Byron L. Dorgan, D-N.D., that would have devoted all $12 billion to reduce the monthly premium for seniors. Democrats offered twenty-three amendments during the debate aimed at providing more generous benefits in the bill. All were rejected. Many sought to close the gap in drug coverage for seniors with expenses between $4,500 and $5,813. Democrats described the gap as an arbitrary and confusing threshold, particularly when those with high drug costs were among the nation's poorest and sickest seniors.

Republicans and Democratic supporters defended the gap, saying that filling it would cost more than the $400 billion available under the budget resolution and be a drain on future generations who would have to foot the bill.

With those arguments, bill supporters on June 25 defeated, 39–56, a Democratic substitute by Richard J. Durbin of Illinois that would have offered more generous drug coverage, partly by using the program's nationwide purchasing power to negotiate lower drug prices. The substitute also would have eliminated the coverage gap, although it would have terminated the program in 2010 to stay within the constraints of the budget resolution.

Senators, however, did agree to some changes. They adopted, 94–1, on June 19 an amendment by Judd Gregg, R-N.H., and Charles E. Schumer, D-N.Y., to bring cheaper generic drugs to market more quickly by making it harder for the makers of name-brand drugs to extend patents.

The Senate also voted 62–28 on June 20 for an amendment by Dorgan to authorize the secretary of the Department of Health and Human Services (HHS) to create regulations that would allow pharmacists and wholesalers to import prescription drugs from Canada. But it was essentially negated by a second-degree amendment by Thad Cochran, R-Miss., to require HHS to certify that importing the drugs from Canada would not pose a health risk and would save consumers money. Two successive HHS secretaries had refused to make such a certification in 2001.

The Senate bill was nearly derailed at the end of the debate when Nickles and Dianne Feinstein, D-Calif., proposed that wealthy seniors pay a greater share of the premiums for outpatient coverage under Medicare Part B. Democrats did not have the votes to defeat the amendment, but Kennedy bitterly opposed it and threatened to hold the bill hostage unless it was defeated.

To Feinstein and other supporters, the amendment was an effort to solidify Medicare's finances. But to Kennedy, who believed means testing would violate Medicare's principle of treating all seniors equally, the amendment threatened to unravel a carefully balanced bipartisan compromise.

Because Democrats could not defeat the Feinstein-Nickles amendment with a roll call vote—an attempt to table (kill) it failed on a 38–59 vote—senators resolved the dispute by holding a voice vote instead. Democrats prevailed by shouting their "no" votes at the top of their lungs.

HOUSE COMMITTEE ACTION

Two House committees—Ways and Means, and Energy and Commerce—shared jurisdiction over the legislation and marked it up in mid-June. Republicans defeated repeated Democratic efforts to reshape the plan.

Much of the substantive debate concerned the federal role in a revamped Medicare system. Democrats wanted to add a government fallback option as a safety net if private plans did not offer drug coverage in a particular area of the country. Unlike the Senate measure, the House bill had no such plan. Instead it offered higher payments to private plans in the hope of attracting them to underserved markets.

Democrats also criticized a provision in the House bill—absent in the Senate version—requiring that Medicare compete directly with private plans starting in 2010. Republicans softened the provision in the face of sharp criticism, phasing it in over five years and adding protections to ensure that seniors who chose to remain in fee-for-service plans would not have their premiums skyrocket during the first five years. But Democrats still opposed the concept as a move to privatize the Medicare system.

Ways and Means

The Ways and Means Committee approved the Medicare drug bill by a vote of 25–15 on June 17 and reported it July 15 (HR 2473—H Rept 108-178, Part 2).

In a sometimes vitriolic debate, committee Democrats charged that the bill would gut Medicare's traditional system and force seniors to depend on private health plans. Republicans branded Democrats as irresponsible big spenders.

During the markup, the committee:

• Rejected, 14–26, a substitute offered by Pete Stark, D-Calif., to create a prescription drug benefit for all seniors with a premium of $25 per month, a $100 yearly deductible, and a $2,000 out-of-pocket limit each year. Medicare would pay 80 percent of beneficiaries' costs. The proposal would have more than doubled the ten-year cost of the bill.

• Rejected, 15–23, an amendment by Cardin to provide a government-run fallback plan available to all beneficiaries.

• Rejected, 14–23, an amendment by Jim McDermott, D-Wash., to strike the competitive bidding language.

• Adopted, 39–0, a proposal by Jim Nussle, R-Iowa, to increase Medicare reimbursements for rural health providers.

Energy and Commerce

The Energy and Commerce Committee finished its work on HR 2473 late June 19, approving it by a vote of 29–20 at the conclusion of a three-day markup. The panel reported the bill June 25 (H Rept 108-178, Part 1).

Chair Billy Tauzin, R-La., frequently reminded his colleagues during the sometimes acrimonious sessions to keep the debate polite and not personal. He angrily cut off Democrat Sherrod Brown of Ohio twice when Brown implied that Republicans' motive for overhauling the program was driven by drug industry campaign contributions.

During the markup, the committee:

• Rejected on a 25–29 party-line vote an attempt by Brown to strike the language requiring traditional Medicare fee-for-service plans to compete with private health plans.

• Rejected, 22–28, an amendment by Ted Strickland, D-Ohio, to set initial premiums for all participating prescription drug plans at $35 per month in 2006, indexed each year for inflation. Strickland said it would eliminate a potential disparity in premiums between rural and urban areas.

• Rejected, 23–30, a proposal by Lois Capps, D-Calif., to require HHS to offer a nationwide prescription drug plan. Capps argued that the GOP-drafted bill provided no guarantee that seniors in rural areas would be able to obtain coverage. She said all the bill did was to offer "sweeteners and enticements" to lure providers into rural areas.

• Rejected, 24–30, a proposal by Gene Green, D-Texas, to count employer and Medigap spending toward the cost threshold at which catastrophic coverage would begin, thereby closing the coverage gap more quickly.

HOUSE FLOOR ACTION

The House passed its Medicare bill, 216–215, in a dramatic 2:33 a.m. vote June 27 that was held open for fifty minutes while GOP leaders scrambled frantically to find a majority.

Republican leaders worked the well of the floor, going after conservatives such as Scott Garrett, a New Jersey freshman, who eventually decided to back the bill. At about 2:30 a.m., a tearful Jo Ann Emerson, R-Mo., and C. L. "Butch" Otter, R-Idaho, were persuaded to change their votes from "no" to "yes," giving the Republicans the necessary margin to declare victory. In return for switching, Emerson won the promise of a floor vote on a drug importation bill (HR 2427) that she backed. That bill subsequently passed but was not included in the final Medicare package (*Prescription drug imports, p. 508*)

Vice President Dick Cheney had come to the Capitol to court votes, and Republican supporters were assigned undecided members to lobby. At an early afternoon rally GOP leaders pledged to pass the bill that day even though their whip counts suggested they did not yet have the votes.

To bolster support for the bill among free-market conservatives, Republican leaders at the last moment expanded medical savings account legislation (HR 2351-H Rept 108-177) that had been approved by the Ways and Means Committee the previous week. They renumbered the measure HR 2596 and wrote a rule for debate that automatically added it to the Medicare drug bill, itself renumbered HR 1, upon passage. HR 2596, which was approved June 26 by a 237–191 vote, provided for two types of tax-preferred savings accounts to cover unreimbursed health care expenses, Health Savings Accounts (HSAs) and Health Savings Security Accounts (HSSAs). This move boosted HR 1's total price tag well above the $400 billion over ten years allocated in the budget resolution. There was no equivalent provision in the Senate bill.

GOP leaders also included language to permit the importation of drugs from Canada, under limited conditions. And they adopted Senate-passed language to limit brand-name drug manufacturers' ability to extend patents and speed the approval process for generic drugs.

Collin C. Peterson, D-Minn., said he and other conservative Democrats, as well as lawmakers from both parties representing rural areas, would vote for the bill because it contained $28 billion for hospitals, physicians, and other providers in rural areas, the largest such package the House had passed.

The House defeated, 175–255, a Democratic alternative that would have created a more generous drug benefit. The proposal, offered by Ways and Means ranking Democrat Charles B. Rangel of New York and Energy and Commerce ranking Democrat John D. Dingell of Michigan, would have required a $25 monthly premium, a $100 yearly deductible, and 20 percent coinsurance until a senior hit $2,000 in annual drug expenses. After that point, all costs would be covered. It would have cost $800 billion over ten years.

CONFERENCE ACTION

Conference negotiations were conducted among Republicans. With the exception of Breaux and Baucus, Democrats played no role. To keep up the pressure, Senate majority leader Bill Frist, R-Tenn., set an Oct. 17 deadline for producing a conference report.

The negotiations involved not only what the conferees could agree on but what they thought they could sell in their respective chambers. In addition there were dozens of second-tier issues and requests for help from individual groups. Each of these had to be worked out in detail, adding to the time-consuming task.

Finally, on Nov. 15, Frist and House Speaker J. Dennis Hastert, R-Ill., announced they had arrived at an agreement in principle with the top negotiators on the bill. The deal gained a huge boost when the senior advocacy group AARP endorsed it—a development that weakened Democratic opposition and attracted enough Democratic votes to offset defections by conservative Republicans. The conservatives said

the final legislation would not inject enough market competition into the program and would not require Congress to control costs should government spending on a drug benefit surge.

The conference report (H Rept 108-391) was filed in the House on Nov. 21.

Conferees in late September and early October had settled on several positions at odds with the Bush administration. Negotiators agreed on a plan that would not limit the number of private health insurance plans that could offer coverage to seniors in any region of the country. They also agreed to provide drug coverage under Medicare—not Medicaid—for beneficiaries who qualified for both programs. The White House preferred to keep that coverage under Medicaid.

Negotiators went with the Senate position and agreed to provide government-run prescription drug coverage to beneficiaries if private plans did not step in to do so.

They leaned toward the House in designing the drug benefit to favor seniors whose drug costs were $2,250 or less. After meeting a $250 deductible seniors would have to pay 25 percent of drug costs between $251 and $2,250. Once beneficiaries reached $5,100 in spending, or $3,600 in out-of-pocket costs, catastrophic coverage would begin.

GOP leaders struck a deal with Baucus and Breaux to create a pilot program in which Medicare's traditional fee-for-service program and private health plans would compete on price. The deal infuriated conservatives, who felt it did not go far enough to promote competition, as well as Democrats, who believed it would open the door to a gradual undermining of traditional Medicare.

Conferees also agreed on tax-free subsidies to encourage employers not to drop existing drug coverage for their retirees and they offered more assistance for low-income seniors. They wooed some fiscal conservatives by preserving the House language creating health savings accounts to allow Americans to save for unreimbursed medical expenses, although they dropped the more expensive Health Savings Security Accounts.

The bill included approximately $25 billion in additional funds for doctors, hospitals, and other rural providers. Grassley—who fought for the bill's big increases in payments to rural hospitals and other providers—hailed the measure as the "best thing rural America has ever seen."

FINAL ACTION

The House adopted the conference report on a **key vote of 220–215 (R 204–25; D 16–189; I 0–1)** in a dramatic vote near dawn Nov. 22. The Senate cleared the bill, 54–44, on Nov. 25, sending it to the president for his signature. *(2003 key votes, p. 837)*

The vote put House Republicans' vaunted whip operation to the test. During a meeting of the House Republican caucus on the evening of Nov. 21, GOP leaders won several members' support by promising to reevaluate a new system for reimbursing oncologists for cancer drugs. They reminded members that the $400 billion set aside for the effort was not likely to be available again. And they emphasized that failure to act by year's end would push overhaul efforts into an election year, when they would be sidetracked by campaign politics.

Democrats remained largely united against the bill, and their leadership kept up pressure on the rank and file to force Republicans to pass the bill without any help. Conservative "Blue Dog" Democrats, led by Baron P. Hill, D-Ind., teamed up with GOP conservatives to push separate legislation (HR 3549) that included the rural funding provisions of the Medicare bill as a stand-alone package.

Republican leaders did not begin the balloting until 3 a.m. An hour later, the electronic scoreboard in the House chamber showed Republicans losing, 216–218. Hastert and Majority Leader Tom DeLay, R-Texas, scanned a sheet of individuals who voted "no" and began lobbying on the floor. With the GOP's top domestic priority on the line, Republican leaders took the unprecedented step of holding the vote open for two hours and fifty-three minutes—believed to be the longest recorded tally since electronic voting began in 1973—while party leaders and Bush, working the phones, confronted renegade members of the caucus.

Finally, at 5:51 a.m., Otter switched his vote from "no" to "yes." So did Republican Trent Franks of Arizona. Their decisions put the "yes" votes at 218 and transferred victory from the Democrats to the Republicans. Democrat David Wu of Oregon then voted yes. Republicans whooped; Democrats booed. Over the din, Democratic whip Steny H. Hoyer of Maryland went to the microphone in the well and accused the Republicans of playing unfair, to no avail.

Several days later Nick Smith, R-Mich., created a stir when he wrote in a newspaper column that someone had offered $100,000 in financial support to his son Brad's congressional campaign in exchange for a "yes" vote on the bill. Smith, who voted "no" despite heavy pressure from GOP leaders, later recanted, saying his statements were "technically incorrect." He said offers to help his son's campaign to succeed him in the House did not involve money and came from outside Congress, but Democrats seized on the story as evidence of Republican heavy-handedness.

In the Senate, Democrats made two attempts to delay action, both of which failed. Kennedy failed in an attempt to filibuster the bill when the Senate voted 70–29 on Nov. 24 to invoke cloture and shut off debate. Daschle raised a budget point of order against the bill on the grounds that the competition and health savings account provisions violated various terms of the fiscal 2004 budget resolution. The Senate voted 61–39 to waive all budget points of order against the bill, with eleven Democrats joining the Republican majority. The Senate then cleared the bill with relative ease the next day.

At a bill signing ceremony Dec. 8 Bush hailed the legislation as "the greatest advance in health care coverage for America's seniors since the founding of Medicare."

But the victory was only a respite in the decades-long battle between the parties over the future of Medicare. Democrats said the law did far more for the insurance and drug in-

dustries than for seniors, and already were pressing to shift more of the benefits to beneficiaries. The law also did nothing to stop the rising costs of pharmaceuticals or to dampen public support for importing drugs from Canada and other countries. Meanwhile, estimates of the program's cost were rising.

"I don't know of any analyst, left, right or center, who thinks this $400 billion number is real," Robert E. Moffit of the Heritage Foundation said even before the bill was signed. "It's not a ceiling, it's a floor; and it's probably going to get a lot bigger."

MAJOR PROVISIONS

As signed into law Dec. 8, 2003, HR 1 (PL 108-173) contained the following major provisions:

Prescription Drug Benefit

Options for coverage. Seniors would be able to receive a prescription drug benefit through insurance plans that offered drug-only coverage or through "Medicare Advantage" plans that would provide both drug coverage and coverage for other health services such as hospital stays and doctors' visits. Medicare Advantage plans would be offered on a local basis and on a regional basis. Medicare Advantage plans would replace the "Medicare+Choice" program, in which managed care plans provided coverage to Medicare beneficiaries.

Temporary drug cards. Starting June 1, 2004, beneficiaries could enroll in a "Medicare-endorsed" prescription drug card program, which Department of Health and Human Services (HHS) officials estimated would save them 15 percent to 25 percent on their drug costs until the drug benefit began on Jan. 1, 2006.

Beneficiaries would be able to choose from at least two cards offered by different drug manufacturers, retailers, insurers, or some other private groups. A beneficiary enrolled in one card in 2004 could change that selection in 2005. Beneficiaries could have as many nongovernment drug discount cards as they wished. The cards would not exist after Dec. 31, 2005.

Drug card subsidy. Beneficiaries whose incomes were less than 135 percent of the calculated poverty level ($10,874 in 2002 for a married couple over the age of sixty-five) would receive a subsidy of $600 in each of 2004 and 2005 to help them pay for prescription drugs, in addition to a drug card. Beneficiaries with incomes between 100 percent and 135 percent of the poverty level would have to pay 10 percent of the cost of each prescription. Those whose incomes were less than 100 percent of the poverty level would pay 5 percent of the cost of each prescription.

A card sponsor could charge an annual enrollment fee of up to $30, and the government would pay the fee for individuals whose incomes were less than 135 percent of the poverty level.

Enrollment. The drug benefit, known as Medicare Part D, would begin Jan. 1, 2006, and would be optional for Medicare beneficiaries.

A six-month initial enrollment period would begin Nov. 15, 2005, for beneficiaries. Those who tried to enroll after that period would incur a financial penalty: Their monthly premiums would be increased by either an amount the HHS secretary determined was actuarially sound, or 1 percent for each month the individual did not have coverage after the end of the initial enrollment period, whichever was greater.

The HHS secretary would establish enrollment periods for special circumstances, such as involuntary loss of prescription coverage under a group health plan.

The HHS secretary was also required to disseminate comparative information to beneficiaries during subsequent annual open enrollment periods.

Design of benefit. Beneficiaries were required to meet a $250 yearly deductible before benefits would begin. From that point on for the rest of the year, the government would pay 75 percent of drug costs up to $2,250.

Beyond that point, government coverage would not resume until a beneficiary had spent a total of $3,600 out of pocket. (The formula meant the beneficiary had purchased $5,100 worth of drugs by the time the coverage began again: $250 for the deductible, $500 as copayment on the next $2,000 plus $1,500 for the government's other 75 percent, and another $2,850 unmatched by the government to reach $3,600). After that, the government would pick up 95 percent of remaining drug costs, known as catastrophic coverage, for the rest of the year. Money that beneficiaries spent on drugs not included on a plan's list of approved medicines would not count toward the $3,600.

Insurers had to adhere to the $250 deductible and the $3,600 level for the commencement of catastrophic drug coverage but otherwise could adjust cost-sharing and other elements of the benefit as long as it was actuarially equivalent to the standard Medicare drug benefit. Once beneficiaries selected a plan they were required to remain in the plan for a year.

Only the beneficiaries' own spending, money paid by a family member, federal subsidies, or money from a state pharmaceutical assistance program could count toward the $3,600 out-of-pocket expenses cap. Money paid by a former employer on behalf of a retiree would not count toward the $3,600 level.

Beginning in 2007 the amount of the deductible, the $2,250 limit, and $3,600 cap would be indexed annually to the percentage increase in the average per-capita expenditure for prescription drugs for Medicare beneficiaries.

Premiums. Beneficiaries would pay an estimated premium of $35 a month in 2006, which could be deducted directly from a beneficiary's Social Security check, through an electronic funds transfer, or through other means as defined by the HHS secretary. Premiums could change from year to year.

Covered drugs. Prescription drugs, biological products, and insulin, including medical supplies associated with the injection of insulin as defined by the HHS secretary, would

be covered. Drugs that were excluded from Medicaid coverage, such as those that aid in weight loss or gain, could be excluded from coverage. Drugs that were paid for under Medicare Part A and B were excluded, as were drugs that did not meet Medicare's definition of medically necessary or were not prescribed by a physician.

Every participating insurance plan would have a preapproved list, or formulary, of drugs eligible for coverage.

Functional equivalence. The HHS secretary was prohibited from publishing regulations or any other guidance saying that there was a "functional equivalence" between two medicines. But the secretary was not prohibited from deeming a particular drug to be identical to another drug if the two products were pharmaceutically equivalent and bioequivalent as determined by the commissioner of the Food and Drug Administration.

Pharmacies and formularies. Insurers would have to accept any pharmacies willing to agree to the plan's terms and conditions and were required to have enough pharmacies in their network—other than mail order or Internet—so that beneficiaries had convenient access to drugs.

Plans would be required to have a committee review how well their preapproved list of covered drugs worked. The committee would have to have at least one practicing physician and one practicing pharmacist who had expertise in the care of elderly or disabled persons and were free of any conflicts of interest. The majority of members on the committee had to be physicians or pharmacists. Therapeutic categories and classes of drugs could be changed once a year. But the HHS secretary could permit other changes to take into account new therapeutic uses and newly approved covered drugs.

Beneficiaries would be able to appeal to obtain coverage for a drug not on the formulary if the beneficiary's prescribing physician determined that the covered drugs would not be as effective for the individual or had adverse effects.

A plan could change its list of drugs at any time. "Appropriate notice" had to be provided to enrollees, pharmacists, pharmacies, and physicians before a drug was removed from a formulary or its tier status was changed.

Electronic prescription program. The HHS secretary was required to set standards that would allow prescription information and a patient's medical history to be transmitted electronically. Information to be transmitted included items such as drugs covered under a plan's formulary, information on the drug being prescribed and other drugs listed in the patient's medical history, and information on the availability of lower-cost, therapeutically appropriate alternative drugs.

Fallback coverage. Beneficiaries would be guaranteed access to at least one prescription drug plan and one integrated plan—such as a health maintenance organization or a preferred provider organization—from which to choose coverage. Two prescription drug plans had to be available if no integrated plan was available.

If no private plans bid to offer coverage in a region, the government would provide a drug plan for beneficiaries. It could not have just one fallback plan that covered the entire nation.

Low-Income Beneficiaries

Medicaid beneficiaries. Low-income beneficiaries who qualified for both Medicare and Medicaid, known as "dual eligibles," were eligible for the Medicare drug benefit and qualified for a full premium subsidy for the lowest-cost plan. Dual eligibles with incomes up to 100 percent of the poverty level would have no deductible and no coverage gaps. But they would be required to make payments of $1 for each generic drug purchase and $3 for each brand-name prescription until they met the $3,600 out-of-pocket threshold. They would have no copayment requirements after they reached that threshold.

Dual eligibles with incomes above 100 percent of poverty would qualify for a full-premium subsidy for the lowest-cost plan and would have no deductible or coverage gap. But they would be required to make payments of $2 for each generic drug purchase and $5 for each brand-name prescription until they met the $3,600 out-of-pocket threshold. They would have no copayment requirements after they hit that threshold.

The deductible amounts would increase each year beginning in 2007 by the annual percentage increase in per capita beneficiary expenditures for Part D covered drugs. The cost-sharing amounts would increase by the increase in the Consumer Price Index. State Medicaid programs and the Social Security Administration would determine which individuals could qualify.

Medicaid funds. In 2006 states would have to return to the federal government 90 percent of what they would have spent on drug coverage for dual eligibles; a 10 percent savings for states compared with previous law. This return, known as a "clawback," would be reduced annually over ten years until it reached 75 percent, resulting in an annual 25 percent savings for states.

Non-Medicaid, low-income beneficiaries. Low-income beneficiaries who were not dual eligibles could also receive some financial help. Those beneficiaries with incomes below 135 percent of poverty and who had no more than $6,000 in assets as an individual and $9,000 as a couple would not have to meet a deductible but were required to make copayments of $2 for generics and $5 for brand-name drugs. They would not have any cost-sharing once they reached the annual $3,600 threshold.

Enrollees with incomes below 150 percent of poverty who had assets of no more than $10,000 per individual and $20,000 for a couple would pay a $50 annual deductible and 15 percent cost-sharing for purchases up to the annual $3,600 threshold. Above that level, they would make copayments that were the greater of either 5 percent of the drug purchase or $2 per generic prescription and $5 per brand-name prescription. Those copayment amounts would be indexed to grow annually according to the growth in Medicare per capita drug spending. State Medicaid programs and the Social Security Administration would determine which individuals could qualify.

Private Insurers

Bidding process. Bids to provide prescription drug plans and Medicare Advantage plans had to include a variety of items, such as information on the prescription drugs to be provided and the size of the service area. The HHS secretary had the authority to negotiate the terms and conditions of the plans. The HHS secretary could not interfere with the negotiations between drug manufacturers and pharmacies and prescription drug sponsors, nor could the secretary require a particular formulary or institute a price structure for the reimbursement of Medicare-covered drugs.

Payments to insurers. In 2006 the HHS secretary would determine Medicare Advantage payment rates by comparing health plan bids to a benchmark amount set specifically for local plans and for regional plans. For local Medicare Advantage plans, payment would be based on county payment rates for the service area. Regional plans were paid their bids. Bids were used in proportion to the private plan national market share and a statutory formula to determine a benchmark. If a plan bid below the benchmark, 75 percent of the savings would go to beneficiaries while 25 percent would be returned to the government.

For both prescription drug plans and Medicare Advantage plans, Medicare would cover 74 percent of the insurance plans' cost for basic drug coverage. For beneficiaries whose drug costs exceeded $3,600, the government would provide 80 percent "reinsurance" of allowable costs.

Medicare also would help cover insurers' costs using target levels, known as "risk corridors," based on a variety of factors such as total amounts paid to the plan and administrative expenses assumed in the plan's bid. For example in 2006 and 2007 the government would cover 75 percent of insurers' costs that were between 2.5 percent and 5 percent above the target level. Anything above 5 percent would be covered by the government at 80 percent.

If the cost for a plan fell below the target, the insurer was required to share those savings with beneficiaries and the government. It had to return in some form 75 percent of the savings to beneficiaries and 25 percent to the government if costs fell between 2.5 percent and 5 percent below the target level. For savings of more than 5 percent below the target, the insurer had to share 80 percent with beneficiaries, with 20 percent going to the government.

From 2008 to 2011 plans would receive less help from the government if their costs exceeded the target level.

Negotiated pricing. Insurers would negotiate discounts with manufacturers and suppliers of covered drugs. Each plan had to disclose to the HHS secretary details of any price concessions. Drug discounts would not be applicable to Medicaid's "best price" provisions.

Incentive fund. From Jan. 1, 2007, through Dec. 31, 2013, approximately $10 billion would be available to provide incentives for health plans to enter each region or to stay in hard-to-serve regions. The HHS secretary was allowed to use the money to respond to market conditions. But if the money was used for two consecutive years, the secretary was required to report to Congress on the underlying market conditions. Beginning in 2008 annual reports would be required to monitor the amount of money spent and evaluate the quality of plans that received fund money.

Payments for Medicare Advantage plans. In 2004 Medicare Advantage plans would be paid the higher of four different amounts: a minimum, or floor, rate set by the Centers for Medicare and Medicaid Service; a blend of local and national payment rates; a rate reflecting a minimum increase from the previous year's rate; or 100 percent of payments made for persons enrolled in traditional Medicare programs.

For 2005 and beyond, the minimum percentage increase would be the greater of a 2 percent increase over the previous year's payment rate or the previous year's payment increased by the percentage of the national per capita Medicare Advantage growth.

Size of Medicare Advantage regions. The HHS secretary would establish ten to fifty regions across the nation. Plans wishing to participate in this program would be required to serve an entire region, and the plans would be allowed to serve more than one region. There would be no limit on the number of plans per region.

The HHS secretary was required to publish a list of Medicare Advantage regions by Jan. 1, 2005. To the extent possible, each region was to include at least one state, was not to divide states across regions, and was to include multi-state metropolitan statistical areas in a single region.

To the extent possible, Medicare Advantage regions would be the same as regions for prescription drug plans.

Beneficiary rebate. Medicare Advantage plans had to provide an enrollee with a monthly rebate equal to 75 percent of any average per capita savings. To ensure that beneficiaries' savings were uniform, the benchmark and the bid would be adjusted on a state or regional basis. The government would retain 25 percent of the average per capita savings.

Separately the HHS secretary could waive or modify requirements that hindered the ability of employers, labor organizations, or trustees of a fund to offer a Medicare Advantage plan. The Medicare Advantage plan could also restrict enrollment to individuals who were beneficiaries and participants of such a plan.

Competition with traditional Medicare. Beginning in 2010, private insurance companies would compete against Medicare on price in six metropolitan statistical areas for six years. To qualify as a demonstration area, a metropolitan statistical area had to have at least 25 percent of eligible Medicare beneficiaries enrolled in a local coordinated Medicare Advantage plan and at least two local coordinated Medicare Advantage plans offered by different organizations. The HHS secretary would select the demonstration areas.

Bids from private plans and rates for traditional fee-for-service Medicare would be averaged to create a benchmark for competitive bidding. At the end of the demonstration, the HHS secretary was to submit a report to Congress that included an evaluation of the demonstration's financial effect on Medicare, changes in access to physicians and other health care providers, and beneficiary satisfaction under the demonstration project and under Medicare's fee-for-service program. Congress then would have to decide whether to expand the demonstration project.

Other Drug Coverage Options

Retiree drug coverage. Employers who provided retiree drug coverage would receive a government subsidy equal to 28 percent of those costs above $250 but not greater than $5,000 per retiree. That amount would be adjusted annually by the percentage increase in Medicare per capita prescription drug costs. Employers would not have to pay taxes on subsidy payments.

Qualified retiree plans would have flexibility on plan design, formularies, and networks.

Employers would be able to provide premium subsidies and cost-sharing assistance for retirees who enrolled in a Medicare drug plan and integrated plans.

Medigap. No new supplemental Medigap plans with drug coverage would be sold, issued, or renewed after Jan. 1, 2006, for beneficiaries who enrolled in the Medicare drug benefit. Beneficiaries who enrolled in the drug benefit could still buy Medigap policies that covered costs other than those for prescription drugs.

Medigap would also feature two new benefit packages that would provide partial coverage of Part A and Part B beneficiary cost-sharing.

Providers

Hospitals. For fiscal 2004 the rate of change in payments to hospitals was to match the rate of change in the price for a "market basket" of certain goods used by hospitals.

For fiscal 2005, 2006, and 2007, hospitals would have to furnish information on quality to the Centers for Medicare and Medicaid Services or face a reduction in payments.

Teaching hospitals would receive an additional $400 million in payments over the next decade. A redistribution of unused resident positions would increase both direct and indirect graduate medical education spending by an anticipated $800 million from fiscal 2004 through fiscal 2013.

Low-volume hospitals with fewer than 800 discharges a year that were twenty-five road miles away from a similar hospital, could qualify for up to a 25 percent increase in Medicare payments.

Payments to outpatient hospitals for covered drugs were expected to increase by $700 million from fiscal 2004 through fiscal 2008.

For eighteen months from the date of enactment, physicians would not be able to refer Medicare patients to new specialty hospitals in which they had an investment interest. Existing hospitals or those under construction as of Nov. 18, 2003, were not included. Specialty hospitals were also prohibited from increasing the number of physician investors as of Nov. 18, 2003, or expanding the number of illnesses they treated.

By March 2005, the Medicare Payment Advisory Commission, or MedPAC, would complete a study on the effects of a physician having an ownership interest in an entire hospital, as opposed to an interest in only a specialty department.

A one-time geographic reclassification process to increase hospitals' wage index values for three years was expected to increase hospital payments by $900 million from 2004 through 2008. The HHS secretary would establish a wage index appeals process by Jan. 1, 2004. Hospitals wishing to be reclassified would have to submit an appeal to the Medicare Geographic Classification Review Board by Feb. 15, 2004. Reclassifications would be effective for a three-year period beginning April 1, 2004.

If a Medicare Advantage plan was unable to reach an agreement on payments with a hospital that was essential to service beneficiaries in a particular region, the HHS secretary could use money from a special fund to help cover the difference in payment between what Medicare Part A would pay the hospital and how much the hospital charged. To qualify, the hospital would have to demonstrate why its costs exceeded the Medicare Part A payment rate. Beginning in 2006, $25 million would be available for such payments, increasing each year by the growth in the hospital market basket percentage.

Physicians. The law blocked a 4.5 percent cut in Medicare payments in 2004 and an additional cut in 2005. Instead, doctors would receive at least a 1.5 percent increase in 2004 and 2005. In calendar years 2004 and 2005 Alaskan physicians would receive higher practice cost payments.

Beginning in 2004 the HHS secretary was required to make adjustments in practice expenses for physicians who administered certain drugs in their offices, including chemotherapy administrations. The HHS secretary was also required to "promptly evaluate" existing drug administration codes for physicians' services to ensure accurate reporting and billing for those services.

An additional payment would be made for drug administration services furnished from April 1, 2004, through Dec. 31, 2005. The payment for 2004 was 32 percent; for 2005 it was 3 percent.

MedPAC was required to review the payment changes as they affected payments for items and services furnished by other specialists. The report on oncologists' payments was due by Jan. 1, 2006, and the report on other specialists was due Jan. 1, 2007.

Dentists, podiatrists, and optometrists would be able to privately contract with Medicare beneficiaries.

The formula for calculating the sustainable growth rate, which was a factor in determining how much Medicare paid physicians, would be modified. Beginning with 2003, the gross domestic product, which was used in the calculation, would be based on the annual average change over the preceding ten years.

Laboratories. Payment rates to laboratories would be frozen for five years.

Home health care. For the last quarter of 2003 and the first quarter of 2004 payments to home health agencies would be increased by the rate of change in the price of a market basket of items used in that industry. For the remainder of 2004, 2005, and 2006, the payment would be the rate of change in that market basket minus 0.8 of a percentage point.

Durable medical equipment. Rates for most durable medical equipment, such as walkers, crutches, and bedpans, and services surrounding them would be frozen from fiscal 2004 to 2008. For 2005, payments for certain items, including oxygen and oxygen equipment, would be reduced to the price paid by the Federal Employee Health Benefits Program.

Competitive bidding in the ten largest metropolitan statistical areas would begin in 2007, with a goal of reaching eighty such areas in 2009. The HHS secretary could exempt items and services for which competitive bidding would not be likely to result in significant savings.

The HHS secretary was required to establish and implement quality standards for suppliers of durable medical equipment items, such as orthotics and prosthetic devices.

The HHS secretary was required to report to Congress by July 1, 2009, on savings, reductions in cost-sharing, access to items and services, and beneficiary satisfaction under competitive bidding.

Changes in antikickback statute. Remuneration in the form of a contract, lease, grant, loan, or other agreement between a public or a nonprofit private health center and an individual or entity providing goods or services to the center would not be a violation of the antikickback statute if such an agreement would contribute to the ability of the health center to maintain or increase the availability or quality of services provided to a medically underserved population. The HHS secretary would be required to establish standards to evaluate such arrangements.

AIDS patients at skilled nursing facilities. The per-diem payments to skilled nursing facilities that treated AIDS patients would rise 128 percent. The increase could change, however, after the HHS secretary reviewed each center to determine the level of costs incurred to care for patients.

Therapy caps. Caps on the amount of outpatient therapy individuals could receive were suspended until Dec. 31, 2005.

The HHS secretary was to report to Congress by March 31, 2004, on alternatives to a single annual dollar cap on outpatient therapy and differences in how therapies were used and delivered from region to region. The General Accounting Office was to report to Congress by Oct. 1, 2004, on conditions or diseases that might justify waiving the application of therapy caps.

Ambulatory surgical centers. Starting April 1, 2004, the payment update for these centers—facilities where Medicare patients went for outpatient procedures such as cataract removal or colonoscopies—would be based on the government's Consumer Price Index for all urban consumers, estimated as of March 31, 2003, minus 3 percentage points. For the last quarter of calendar year 2005 and each of the calendar years 2006 through 2009, the update would be zero.

Medicaid disproportionate share. Hospitals that served a large number of uninsured patients and Medicaid patients, known as disproportionate share hospitals, would receive more federal money to compensate them for that care. In fiscal 2004, payments would be set at 116 percent of fiscal 2003 allotments and would not be subject to the 12 percent cap on state allotments for medical assistance payments. States would receive the same amount for subsequent fiscal years unless the HHS secretary determined that the amount states would have received before enactment of the Medicare drug law would equal or no longer exceed the fiscal 2004 payments. If that was the case, states' payments would rise by the same rate of increase in the Consumer Price Index for the previous fiscal year.

As a condition of receiving such payments, each state would have to submit to the HHS secretary an annual report for the previous fiscal year identifying disproportionate share hospitals that received a payment and how much they received.

Rural Package

Hospitals. In fiscal 2004 hospitals in rural and small urban areas would receive a permanent 1.6 percent increase to Medicare's base rate, or the payment hospitals received for each discharged patient. Higher payments would be made to rural and small urban hospitals that had a disproportionate share of low-income patients. Hospitals in low-wage areas would receive more money to help them compete with other hospitals for workers. The Medicare payments would help the hospitals in low-wage areas pay higher wage rates.

Inpatient, outpatient, and covered skilled nursing facility services provided by a critical access hospital would be reimbursed at 101 percent of reasonable costs of services furnished to Medicare beneficiaries. Critical access hospitals could operate up to twenty-five beds. A requirement that only fifteen of the twenty-five beds be used for acute care at any time would be dropped.

On or after Jan. 1, 2005, Medicare reimbursement of on-call emergency room providers would be expanded to include physician assistants, nurse practitioners, and clinical nurse specialists as well as emergency room physicians.

Physicians. Physicians serving in rural areas that had a low number of physicians available to serve beneficiaries would receive an additional 5 percent in Medicare payments from 2005 to 2007.

Ambulance services. Payments would be based on the ambulance service's fee blended with either the national fee schedule amount or a combined rate of the national fee schedule and a regional fee schedule, whichever resulted in the larger payment.

Payments for ground ambulance services would be increased by one-quarter of the per-mile payment rate otherwise established for trips longer than fifty miles occurring on or after July 1, 2004, and before Jan. 1, 2009.

For low-density rural ambulance areas the HHS secretary would provide a percentage increase in the base rate of the fee schedule for ground ambulance services furnished on or after July 1, 2004, and before Jan. 1, 2010. Qualified rural areas were those in which the lowest population densities collectively represented a total of 25 percent of the population in the general area.

In addition, payments for ground ambulance services originating in a rural area would be increased by 2 percent (on top of increases for payments for long trips and for low density areas) for services furnished on or after July 1, 2004, through Dec. 31, 2007. The fee schedule for ambulances in other areas (after the long trip adjustment) would increase by 1 percent.

Home health care. Rural home health care providers would receive a 5 percent bonus from April 2004 to April 2005.

Drug Importation

Certification. Prescription drugs could be imported from Canada, but only if the HHS secretary certified the safety of the drugs and that the practice saved consumers money.

The HHS secretary, in consultation with appropriate government agencies, was to study problems related to the implementation of existing drug importation law, including safety concerns and anticounterfeiting technologies that could be used to help ensure the safety of imported drugs.

HHS and other agencies were required to conduct a study and report on drug pricing practices of countries that were members of the Organization for Economic Cooperation and Development. The study also had to evaluate how the reduction or elimination of price controls and similar practices could lower prices for U.S. consumers.

Generic Drugs

Patent protections. Brand-name pharmaceutical manufacturers would receive only one thirty-month stay of their patent protection while applications for generic versions of their drug were considered, but only if the brand-name patent application was submitted before that of the generic drug.

Qualifications. Multiple companies could qualify for the 180-day market exclusivity as long as they filed all of their applications on the first day of eligibility.

Judgments. Generic drug companies would have an improved ability to obtain declaratory judgments against brand-name drugmakers in court and move a generic version to the market more quickly.

Medicare Parts A and B

Income relating. Beginning in 2007, Part B Medicare premiums would be subsidized on the following income schedule:

Singles' salaries	Couples' salaries	Premium subsidies
Under $80,000	Under $160,000	75%
$80,000 to $100,000	$160,000 to $200,000	65%
$100,000 to $150,000	$200,000 to $300,000	50%
$150,000 to $200,000	$300,000 to $400,000	35%
Over $200,000	Over $400,000	20%

Average wholesale price. Beginning in 2004 payment for many drugs under Medicare Part B would be reduced from 95 percent to 85 percent of the average wholesale price. Certain categories of drugs and drug products would continue to be paid at 95 percent of the average wholesale price, including blood products and clotting factors.

Payments for some drugs under Medicare Part B could be further reduced to 80 percent of the average wholesale price in 2004, depending on data collected by the General Accounting Office and the HHS Office of Inspector General. Beginning in 2005, payment for these drugs would be either the average sales price plus 6 percent or through competitive acquisition programs.

Preventative care. Beginning on Jan. 1, 2005, new beneficiaries would be allowed to receive a physical within six months of joining Medicare Part B. Screening and preventative services included mammographies, pelvic exams, bone mass measurement, and screening for prostate cancer, glaucoma, and diabetes.

As of Jan. 1, 2005, all Medicare beneficiaries would qualify for coverage of cardiovascular screening blood tests. Diabetes screening tests would be covered for individuals at risk of diabetes. Screening and diagnostic mammographies and intravenous immune globulin for treatment in the home of primary immune deficiency disease would also be covered.

Medicare Part B deductible. The Medicare Part B deductible would remain at $100 through 2004 and would be $110 in 2005. In subsequent years, the deductible would be increased by the same percentage as the Part B premium increase, rounded to the nearest dollar.

Chiropractic services. The HHS secretary would establish a two-year demonstration program at four sites to evaluate the feasibility and desirability of covering additional chiropractic services under Medicare. The projects could not be implemented before Oct. 1, 2004.

Undocumented immigrants. Medicare would spend $250 million per year in additional funding in fiscal years 2005 through 2008 for emergency health services for undocumented immigrants. For each of the fiscal years 2005 through 2008, the HHS secretary was required to distribute $83 million of the $250 million among eligible providers in the six states with the highest number of apprehended undocumented immigrants.

Research. The Agency for Healthcare Research and Quality would receive $50 million for fiscal 2004 to address the scientific information needs and priorities identified by the Medicare, Medicaid, and State Children's Health Insurance Programs.

The law also authorized $3 million for fiscal years 2005 and 2006 for the agency and the HHS secretary to establish a "Citizens' Health Care Working Group," which would submit a report to Congress and the president on issues such as the cost of health care and the role of evidence-based medicine and technology in improving quality and lowering costs.

Beneficiary Services

Medicare contractors. Medicare contractors had to respond within forty-five days of receiving a written inquiry. Contractors also were required to have a toll-free telephone number that beneficiaries, providers, and suppliers could call to obtain information regarding billing, coding, claims, coverage, and other Medicare information. Contractors also were required to identify the person supplying information and to monitor the accuracy, consistency, and timeliness of the information provided.

The HHS secretary could seek competitive bids for Medicare claims processing services at least every five years.

Medicare ombudsman. The HHS secretary was required to appoint a beneficiary ombudsman no later than one year after enactment. The ombudsman would receive complaints, grievances, and requests for information from beneficiaries and provide assistance.

Medicare appeals. When claims were denied, Medicare had to provide a written notice explaining why and notifying a beneficiary of his or her right to appeal. The notice also had to tell the beneficiary how to appeal the decision.

Administrative agency. A new Center for Beneficiary Services was established to administer Medicare Advantage, the prescription drug benefit, and beneficiary information activities.

Regulatory and Contractor Reform

Regulatory relief. New material could not be added to final rules governing Medicare until the public was allowed to comment. New regulations and policies could not be applied retroactively. Providers could not be sanctioned if they followed written, erroneous guidance from the government or its agents.

Appeals. Medicare administrative law judges were transferred from the Social Security Administration to the Department of Health and Human Services to ensure their independence.

Expedited review. The law expedited access to judicial review for legal issues that could not be resolved administratively and required expedited review of certain provider agreement determinations.

Cost Containment

Legislative requirement. The president was required to submit legislation to Congress to curtail Medicare spending if general revenue contributions to the program were projected to pay more than 45 percent of total Medicare expenditures for two consecutive years. The House and Senate were required to follow specific guidelines for consideration of such legislation.

Beginning in 2005, the Medicare Board of Trustees' annual reports to Congress had to include new information on Medicare spending. The information had to include projections of growth in general revenue Medicare spending as a percentage of the total Medicare outlays for seven, ten, fifty, and seventy-five years after the current fiscal year.

Health Savings Accounts

Paying for high deductibles. Beginning Jan. 1, 2004, individuals under age sixty-five who had high deductible insurance policies could establish tax-free savings accounts, called Health Savings Accounts (HSAs). No contributions could be made once an individual qualified for Medicare.

For individual coverage the plan had to have an annual deductible of at least $1,000 for self-only coverage and $2,000 for family coverage. Out-of-pocket expenses could be no more than $5,000 for individual coverage and $10,000 for family coverage.

The maximum aggregate annual contribution that could be made to an HSA was the lesser of 100 percent of the annual deductible under the high deductible health plan or the maximum deductible permitted under an Archer Medical Savings Account high deductible health plan under existing law, as adjusted for inflation. For 2004 the amount of the maximum high deductible was estimated to be $2,600 in the case of self-only coverage and $5,150 in the case of family coverage.

An employer could contribute to an individual's HSA. Individuals age fifty-five and older could make contributions beyond the standard limit. Those increases were $500 in 2004, $600 in 2005, $700 in 2006, $800 in 2007, $900 in 2008, and $1,000 in 2009 and thereafter.

Contributions to HSAs would be tax-free, as would distributions from the account if the funds were used for health care needs not covered by the insurance policies. Eligible expenses included Medicare Part A and Part B premiums, Medicare health maintenance organization premiums, and the employees' share of premiums for employer-sponsored retiree health insurance. Premiums for Medicare supplemental insurance known as Medigap were not included.

These accounts would be owned by the individual and would follow that person from job to job and into retirement. When the person died, HSA ownership could be transferred to the person's spouse on a tax-free basis.

Prescription Drug Imports

In response to public concern about the rising cost of prescription drugs, the House voted by a surprisingly strong margin in 2003 to allow the importation of drugs from twenty-five industrial countries. To answer safety concerns, the bill (HR 2427) required that both the drugs and the facilities that manufactured them be approved by the Food and Drug Administration (FDA). But the Bush administration, the drug industry, and a bipartisan majority in the Senate strenuously opposed the legislation, arguing that it could permit counterfeit, ineffective, or adulterated medicines into the country and endanger consumers.

The issue was ultimately finessed in the Medicare prescription drug bill that was signed into law Dec. 8, 2003 (HR 1—PL 108-173). That measure allowed importation from Canada—but only if the secretary of the Department of Health and Human Services (HHS) first certified that the practice was safe and would save consumers money. HHS secretary Tommy G. Thompson said as early as 2001 he could not guarantee the safety of imported drugs. The Medicare law also called for a study on safety and trade issues surrounding drug importation. *(Medicare overhaul, p. 496)*

The fact that the House voted on the bill at all was due to the determination of Jo Ann Emerson, R-Mo., who led the fight in that chamber for drug importation. With the Medicare prescription drug bill on the verge of defeat on the House floor in June, Emerson withheld her support until her party's leaders promised an up-or-down vote on the reimportation measure, which was written by Gil Gutknecht, R-Minn.

BACKGROUND

Allowing pharmacists, drug wholesalers, and consumers in the United States to purchase drugs from foreign wholesalers or pharmacies had become a hot issue because the same drugs often were available much less expensively abroad. Under existing law—the 1987 Prescription Drug Marketing Act (PL 100-293)—only drug manufacturers could legally import prescription drugs into the United States, although individuals bringing in a small amount for personal use usually were not stopped or prosecuted. *(Congress and the Nation Vol. VII, p. 601)*

Previous efforts to change the law had been limited by language—inserted by opponents of drug imports—requiring that the HHS secretary certify that drugs could be imported safely and would save consumers money before the change would be allowed to take effect. HHS secretaries in both the Clinton and Bush administrations, from 1993 onward, had concluded that it was bureaucratically impossible to meet such a requirement. A provision in the fiscal 2001 Agriculture appropriations law (PL 106-387) allowing drug importation from Canada was not implemented for that reason.

In the meantime state and local governments and even citizens had begun taking matters into their own hands, openly debating ways to allow employees to import drugs from Canada, sponsoring Web sites to allow such purchases, and arranging seniors' bus trips to Canada to buy drugs. A Kaiser Family Foundation-Harvard School of Public Health survey of 2,043 adults in August found 63 percent of respondents approved allowing consumers to buy drugs from abroad despite concerns that the practice could allow unsafe or counterfeit medications to enter the market.

The House version of the fiscal 2004 Agriculture spending bill (HR 2673) would have barred the FDA from enforcing the ban on prescription drug imports, but the proposal was dropped in conference. The White House strongly opposed the provision and warned Nov. 5, 2003, that it would "threaten public health and result in unsafe, unapproved, and counterfeit drugs being imported into the United States."

LEGISLATIVE ACTION

The House gave an unexpectedly strong endorsement to HR 2427, passing it by a **key vote of 243–186 (R 87–141; D 155–45; I 1–0)**, on July 25, 2003, despite furious lobbying against it by the usually influential drug industry. *(2003 key votes, p. 837)*

One of the most remarkable aspects of the debate was the extent to which it scrambled the otherwise stark partisan divide in the House. Liberal Democrats, such as John D. Dingell of Michigan and Robert Menendez of New Jersey, the party's conference chair, aligned with the FDA and the pharmaceutical companies against the bill. They argued it would bring unsafe drugs into the country. Dingell had led efforts to pass the 1987 law that outlawed most drug imports in the first place.

Conservative Republicans such as Dan Burton of Indiana and Jeff Flake of Arizona abandoned some of their traditional allies to support the measure, saying it was not fair for American taxpayers to finance drug research and then have to pay more than consumers in other countries to buy those drugs.

Gutknecht displayed a chart comparing the cost of drugs purchased at U.S. pharmacies compared with the cost at the Munich Airport in Germany. Sixty tablets of Tamoxifen, a drug used to treat breast cancer, cost $360 in the United States and $60 in Germany. The cost of 100 tablets of Coumadin, a

blood thinner, was $89.95 in the United States and $21 in Germany.

Opponents said the bill would not only expose consumers to unsafe drugs but also hurt research and development of life-saving cures. "I think we're taking huge risks for little or no gain," said Anna G. Eshoo, D-Calif.

Proponents said the lobbying may have helped bring support to their side. "Largely, people just got fed up with the whole lobbying effort," said Gutknecht. "For all the money [drugmakers] spent, it probably did more harm than good."

House GOP leaders had agreed with Emerson that, if the bill passed, it would be adopted as the chamber's formal position on drug importation in conference negotiations on the Medicare prescription drug bill.

However, House Republican leaders opposed the measure as did a bipartisan majority in the Senate. Just hours after the House vote, fifty-three senators sent a letter to the Medicare conferees asking that existing law remain unchanged. Signers included members from across the political spectrum such as conservative GOP Conference chair Rick Santorum of Pennsylvania and liberal Democrats Edward M. Kennedy of Massachusetts and Patty Murray of Washington. GOP Senate conferees Orrin G. Hatch of Utah, Jon Kyl of Arizona, and Don Nickles of Oklahoma also signed the letter.

The House import language was ultimately jettisoned from the final Medicare measure, replaced with language allowing imports only from Canada but again giving the HHS secretary veto authority and calling for a study, due after the 2004 elections.

Even though the drug import language was dropped from the Medicare bill, the separate House bill remained alive and viable in 2004. Bipartisan efforts to force a Senate vote on the bill, however, even with strong public support in an election year, were successfully parried by Senate majority leader Bill Frist, R-Tenn. The measure died at the end of the 108th Congress.

HIGHLIGHTS

As passed by the House, HR 2427:

• Required the FDA to design and implement a system to allow individuals, pharmacists, and wholesalers in the United States to import FDA-approved prescription drugs manufactured in FDA-approved facilities. The FDA would have to implement the program within 180 days of enactment.

• Allowed importation of drugs only from the European Union, Australia, Canada, Iceland, Israel, Japan, Lichtenstein, New Zealand, Norway, Switzerland, and South Africa.

• Required all prescription drugs sold in the United States, whether produced domestically or imported, to use counterfeit-resistant packaging. Any drugs without such packaging would be considered misbranded. Wholesalers would be required to test each pharmaceutical shipment, unless the packaging used counterfeit-resistant technology.

• Prohibited importation of pharmaceutical narcotics.

Abortion

The 108th Congress was, by nearly any measure, one of the most successful ever for opponents of abortion. Legislation passed by the House in earlier Congresses—to outlaw a specific procedure opponents called "partial-birth" abortions and to deny federal funds to states or localities that compelled health entities to perform or refer for abortion—also passed the Senate and were signed into law by President George W. Bush. Abortion foes also held off efforts to loosen restrictions added earlier in the Bush presidency.

Legislation making it a separate federal crime to injure or kill a fetus during an attack on a pregnant woman was enacted as well. (*Fetal protection, p. 513*)

PARTIAL-BIRTH ABORTION BAN

After an eight-year crusade, social conservatives won enactment Nov. 5, 2003, of a law banning a procedure they called "partial birth" abortion (S 3—PL 108-105). It was the first federal statute to restrict an abortion procedure since the Supreme Court legalized abortions in its landmark 1973 *Roe v. Wade* decision.

Within hours after Bush signed the bill, however, the struggle over the legislation moved to the courts. By the end of the year, federal district judges in New York, San Francisco, and Nebraska had halted enforcement of the new law, and the Justice Department had mounted a defense of it.

Getting the bill enacted was a top Republican priority. The House and Senate easily passed versions early in the year, but threats from Senate opponents slowed the start of a conference to resolve a single difference between the bills. Once the ten-member conference opened it took only a few hours to reach agreement. The final bill, cleared Oct. 21, was identical to the House-passed version and omitted language added on the Senate floor reaffirming the *Roe v. Wade* decision.

Supporters had been trying since 1995 to get the ban enacted. Twice, in 1996 and 1997, bills outlawing the procedure reached the White House but were vetoed by President Bill Clinton.

The 2003 law banned the procedure in all instances except when a pregnant woman's life was endangered "by a physical disorder, physical illness, or physical injury." Doctors who performed the procedure were subject to fines and up to two years in prison. Husbands, and parents of a girl under eighteen, could sue doctors for damages in civil court. The law did not allow an exception for cases in which a woman's health was in jeopardy. Instead it relied on more than a dozen pages of congressional "findings" that such a procedure was never medically necessary.

Critics said the findings were not enough to respond to one of the Supreme Court's main objections in striking down a similar Nebraska law in 2000. In *Stenberg v. Carhart,* the high court said the Nebraska law did not include an exception for cases where the banned procedure was needed to protect a woman's health. The high court specifically re-buffed the state's arguments that a health exception was not needed because "safe alternatives" to the partial-birth abortion procedure were available. The court also said the definition of the banned procedure was so broad it could include dilation and evacuation, one of the most commonly performed abortion procedures.

Bill supporters, led by Sen. Rick Santorum, R-Pa., and Rep. Steve Chabot, R-Ohio, insisted they had rewritten the measure to survive a constitutional challenge, in part by adding the findings. "We have, without question, clarified that record to make sure that the court knows that there is no medical evidence out there that this procedure is ever necessary to protect the health of a mother," Santorum said.

In addition, the sponsors had refined their definition of the procedure as one in which "the person performing the abortion deliberately and intentionally vaginally delivers a living fetus until, in the case of a headfirst presentation, the entire fetal head is outside the body of the mother, or, in the case of breech presentation, any part of the fetal trunk past the navel is outside the body of the mother for the purpose of performing an overt act that the person knows will kill the partially delivered living fetus."

Supporters said the description of the fetus's location in relation to the woman's body specifically ruled out dilation and evacuation.

Bill opponents argued there were times when a partial-birth abortion was needed to protect a woman's future fertility. They said it also might be the best technique in cases where a fetus had an abnormal fluid accumulation in the brain, causing swelling, or the fetus's brain had formed outside its body. They added that the Supreme Court rarely gave any deference to congressional findings when considering the constitutionality of a law.

Opponents swiftly challenged the constitutionality of the law. At year's end the lawsuits had resulted in three injunctions halting enforcement against most of the doctors who performed abortions in the United States.

In New York a temporary restraining order was issued in response to a challenge mounted by the American Civil Liberties Union on behalf of the National Abortion Federation (NAF). The injunction was effective nationwide for members of the federation, which represented doctors who performed abortions.

In a separate ruling on a petition filed by Planned Parenthood Federation of America, a district judge in San Francisco issued a temporary restraining order against the law. The injunction blocked enforcement in Planned Parenthood-affiliated clinics nationwide.

A third and far more limited temporary restraining order issued by a district judge in Nebraska applied to four doctors named in a lawsuit brought by the Center for Reproductive Rights. One of those doctors, Leroy Carhart, had been the named plaintiff in the 2000 Supreme Court case.

In 2004, judges in all three cases found for the plaintiffs, ruling that the law, as in the 2000 Supreme Court case, unconstitutionally left out required exceptions for a woman's health and was so broad as to encompass other abortion procedures. The Bush administration appealed the cases.

Background

Abortion foes had tried in the four previous Congresses to enact the ban. In all cases the legislation would have made it a federal crime, punishable by fines and up to two years in prison, for a doctor to perform the procedure unless it was deemed necessary to save a pregnant woman's life.

104th Congress. In 1995 both chambers approved measures to outlaw the procedure. It was the first time either chamber had voted to criminalize an abortion procedure and reflected the newfound strength of abortion opponents resulting from the Republican takeover of the 104th Congress.

The House passed its bill, 288–139, on Nov. 1, 1995. The Senate amended the bill to strengthen the exception if a woman's life was in danger and passed it, 54–44, on Dec. 7. On March 27, 1996, the House voted 286–129 to accept the Senate version, clearing the bill for the president. On April 10 Clinton followed through on his pledge to veto the bill, citing its failure to allow the procedure to be used to protect the woman's health. The House provided the two-thirds majority needed to override the veto in a 285–137 vote Sept. 19, but the Senate on Sept. 26 voted 57–41 to override, nine votes short of the sixty-six needed. *(Congress and the Nation Vol. IX, p. 563)*

105th Congress. The process was repeated in the 105th Congress. The House passed a bill, 295–136, on March 20, 1997. The Senate passed its version, 64–36, on May 20 after tweaking some of the language in an effort to broaden support. The House agreed to the Senate version, 296–132, on Oct. 8, clearing it for Clinton who vetoed the bill two days later. Although support for the bill had grown in both chambers since the previous Congress, it was not enough to override the veto. The House voted 296–132 to override on July 23, 1998. But the Senate again sustained the veto; the vote on Sept. 18 was 64–36, three votes short. *(Congress and the Nation Vol. X, p. 455)*

106th Congress. This time the Senate went first, passing a bill, 63–34, on Oct. 21, 1999. The House passed a similar measure, 287–141, on April 5, 2000. But after the Supreme Court struck down the Nebraska law, supporters dropped the effort while they struggled to figure out how to get around the court's objections. *(Congress and the Nation Vol. X, p. 473)*

107th Congress. On July 24, 2002, the House revived the bill, passing it by a vote of 274–151, with the congressional "findings" declaring the health exception never medically necessary. But with Democrats in control of the Senate, that chamber never took up the measure. *(2002 action, p. 479)*

Supreme Court Rulings

With *Roe v. Wade*, the Supreme Court established that a woman had a constitutional right to decide to terminate a pregnancy. While states could not bar a woman from having an abortion, the Court said they could regulate and even ban abortions performed after a fetus was viable "except where it is necessary, in appropriate medical judgment, for the preservation of the life or health of the mother." In the accompanying case *Doe v. Bolton*, the Court held that the term "health" was to be interpreted broadly, "in the light of all factors—physical, emotional, psychological, familial, and the woman's age—relevant to the well-being of the patient. All these factors may relate to health." That led abortion opponents to resist all health exceptions, arguing that they essentially rendered restrictions moot.

In *Planned Parenthood of Southeastern Pennsylvania v. Casey,* the Supreme Court in 1992 gave states the authority to regulate abortions done before a fetus was viable, but it said such regulations could not place an "undue burden" on a woman's ability to terminate a pregnancy.

The Nebraska law struck down in 2000 was found unconstitutional on both grounds: It did not allow an exception for the health of the woman, and by providing such a broad definition of abortion, the court found, it placed an "undue burden" on her ability to have an abortion.

Senate Action

Santorum introduced the 2003 bill (S 3) on Feb. 14. It went directly to the Senate floor where it passed, 64–33, on March 13. Sixteen Democrats voted for the legislation, an increase of two from 1999. The thirty-three senators voting "no" consisted of twenty-nine Democrats, three Republicans, and James M. Jeffords, I-Vt.

Some of the amendments that posed the most difficult questions for members were dismissed easily or on procedural grounds. During the debate, the Senate:

• Rejected a proposal by Patty Murray, D-Wash., to require group health insurance plans to offer some coverage for prescription contraception, such as birth control pills. It also blocked hospitals from receiving federal funds for health-related programs if they did not provide sexual assault victims with information about emergency contraception, high doses of regular birth-control pills that were highly effective in preventing pregnancy if taken soon after unprotected intercourse. It also gave states the option to expand the States' Children's Health Insurance Program to include low-income pregnant women.

Rather than risk defeat in an up-or-down vote, GOP leaders challenged Murray's amendment on procedural grounds. Her attempt to waive the point of order against the amendment required sixty votes to succeed. It was rejected, 49–47, on March 11.

• Adopted, 52–46, on March 12 an amendment by Democrats Tom Harkin of Iowa and Barbara Boxer of California reaffirming *Roe v. Wade*.

While the language was nonbinding, Harkin and abortion-rights advocates said the vote was a rare chance to put members on record with their fundamental beliefs on abortion. "I want to make sure with all of this going on that we send a strong signal to the women of this country that *Roe v. Wade* is appropriate, it was a good decision, and it is not going to be overturned," Harkin said.

The vote showed no new support among Republicans other than newly appointed Alaska senator Lisa Murkowski, who joined eight others in her caucus to vote in support of the *Roe* language. The other GOP "yes" votes came from Ben Nighthorse Campbell of Colorado, Lincoln Chafee of Rhode Island, Susan Collins of Maine, Kay Bailey Hutchison of Texas, Olympia J. Snowe of Maine, Arlen Specter of Pennsylvania, Ted Stevens of Alaska, and John W. Warner of Virginia.

Five Democrats—John B. Breaux of Louisiana, Zell Miller of Georgia, Ben Nelson of Nebraska, Mark Pryor of Arkansas, and Harry Reid of Nevada—voted "no."

• Rejected a substitute amendment by Richard J. Durbin, D-Ill., to ban the procedure when done after viability, as determined by a doctor. Durbin's proposal included an exception if one doctor certified—and another concurred— that the pregnancy posed a risk of "grievous injury" to the woman's physical health. The amendment was tabled (killed), 60–38, on March 12.

• Rejected, 35–60, on March 12 an amendment by Dianne Feinstein, D-Calif., to ban all post-viability abortions unless a doctor determined that the abortion was necessary to protect the life or health of the woman. A doctor who performed a post-viability abortion on a woman whose health or life was not at risk could be fined up to $100,000.

Opponents of the two amendments said they would not cover the majority of partial-birth abortions done before a fetus was viable. They said the proposals were political cover for senators who wanted to vote against the underlying bill but also wanted to tell constituents they voted to curtail the controversial procedure.

House Action

After a contentious debate, the House Judiciary Committee approved its version of the bill (HR 760) by a vote of 19–11 on March 26. The panel's Constitution Subcommittee had approved it, 8–4, the previous day. Committee Democrats offered six amendments, all of which were defeated in party-line votes. The bill was formally reported April 3 (H Rept 108-58).

The House passed the bill, 282–139, on June 4 and inserted the provisions into S 3 in preparation for conference with the Senate.

Republican leaders allowed one amendment—a proposal by Democratic whip Steny H. Hoyer of Maryland and Republican James C. Greenwood of Pennsylvania that was similar to Feinstein's proposal in the Senate. It would have outlawed abortions conducted after a fetus was viable outside the womb, but it would have provided exceptions for both the health and the life of a pregnant woman.

Abortion foes said the Hoyer-Greenwood alternative amounted to a "phony ban" because it would leave the deter-

mination of viability up to doctors performing the procedure and could allow post-viability abortions even when it was the woman's mental health that was threatened. The amendment was rejected, 133–287.

Conference, Final Action

In contrast to the quick legislative action in each chamber, it took months for lawmakers to officially reconcile the House- and Senate-passed bills, even though the only difference was the Senate provision reaffirming *Roe v. Wade.* Senate Democrats, led by Boxer, delayed the process by insisting that the Senate debate the motion to go to conference. Boxer and Harkin continued to insist on more floor time to debate the conference report, once it was completed in late September.

Conferees finally filed the report (H Rept 108-288) the evening of Sept. 30. During a brief meeting of the conferees that day, negotiators had voted along party lines to reject an attempt by Rep. Jerrold Nadler, D-N.Y., to add a health exception to the bill. They also had rejected Feinstein's substitute that would have banned all post-viability abortions, with an exception to save the life or health of the woman and no criminal penalties for offenders.

The House acted quickly, adopting the report by a **key vote of 281–142 (R 218–4; D 63–137; I 0–1)** on Oct. 2. The Senate cleared the bill on a **key vote of 64–34 (R 47–3; D 17–30; I 0–1)** on Oct. 21. *(2003 key votes, p. 837)*

Abortion foes insisted that the ban was narrowly focused. "All this bill would do is ban this one procedure," insisted Senate Judiciary Chair Orrin G. Hatch, R-Utah. "We are not talking about the entire framework of abortion rights here but just one procedure."

Opponents of the bill were not convinced. "Let's be very clear: This is an attack on *Roe*," Feinstein said. "I've watched the Senate on a march to eliminate a woman's right to abortions for a long, long time. Bit by bit, what's happening is a pushing back of the clock to the way abortion was thirty years ago."

ABORTION SERVICES REFUSAL

The fiscal 2005 omnibus appropriations bill (HR 4818— PL 108-447) included language significantly expanding so-called "conscience clauses" under federal law that shielded physicians and other health care providers from being required to perform abortions if it violated their personal beliefs. That language was similar to that of the "Abortion Non-Discrimination Act," which passed the House in the 107th Congress but was never considered by the Senate. *(2002 action, p. 480)*

In the month following the bill's signing, the National Family Planning and Reproductive Health Association and the State of California filed separate lawsuits seeking to block enforcement of the law. They contended that it conflicted with other laws that required women to be informed of all their options, including abortion, when faced with an unintended pregnancy.

The language stipulated that "health care entities" covered by the conscience clause should include not just doctors and individual health professionals but also "a hospital, a provider-sponsored organization, a health maintenance organization, a health insurance plan, and any other kind of health care facility, organization, or plan." In order to be included in a spending bill, the measure worked by denying federal aid to states or localities that compelled health care entities to provide, fund, or refer for abortion services.

Supporters said the change was needed to counter state court interpretations that excluded hospitals from the conscience clause language. They cited a 1997 Alaska Supreme Court ruling that a hospital in that state had to allow doctors to perform abortions there because it was the only hospital in the area, making it a quasi-public facility.

Opponents said the bill would greatly expand existing law and weaken a woman's legal right to an abortion by limiting its availability. They said it would not allow exemptions in cases of rape or incest or to save the life of the woman and would allow hospitals and insurers to stop physicians and others from providing abortions or even referring women to others for abortion services.

Legislative Action

On July 14, 2004, the House Appropriations Committee added the language by Dave Weldon, R-Fla., to its version of the Labor-HHS-Education spending bill (HR 5006, which later was incorporated into the omnibus legislation). It was not challenged when the measure was debated by the full House. Many lawmakers expected the language to be stripped from the bill by conferees during negotiations with the Senate, where a majority of members had generally supported abortion rights.

But the language survived at the insistence of House conservatives, whose leverage was strengthened by election day results suggesting social conservatives played a pivotal role in the outcome of races nationwide.

Senate Democrats led by Barbara Boxer, D-Calif., contemplated delaying action on the omnibus to protest the inclusion of the provision. They backed off after Republican leaders promised a later vote on repeal legislation. Such a vote was expected to be largely symbolic, however, because it was unlikely to also pass the House.

The House voted 344–51 to adopt the conference report on the omnibus bill (HR 4818—H Report 108-792) on Nov. 20; the Senate cleared the bill, 65–30, that same day. President Bush signed the omnibus bill Dec. 8.

INTERNATIONAL ABORTIONS,
FAMILY PLANNING

In contrast to much of the previous decade, fights over international family planning programs and overseas abortions were relatively low-key in the 108th Congress, having largely been settled in the first two years of Bush's presidency.

The fiscal 2003 omnibus spending bill (H J Res 2—PL 108-7), which did not become law until Feb. 20, 2003, provided $446 million for international family planning assistance and left in place the so-called "Mexico City" policy, which barred U.S. funding to any private, nongovernmental, or multilateral organization that performed or supported abortion in a foreign country, even with its own, non-U.S. funds.

The bill also included $34 million for the United Nations Population Fund (UNFPA) but barred disbursement unless the president certified that the fund did not support or participate in the management of a program of coercive abortion or involuntary sterilization. Bush had requested $25 million and asked that it be held in reserve. In July 2002 the Bush administration had blocked disbursement of a $34 million fiscal 2002 appropriation for UNFPA as part of a dispute over whether the organization was funding a program in a province in China that was still practicing coercive policies. The UNFPA said it was not, and a State Department fact-finding mission found no evidence to the contrary. *(2003 aid appropriations, p. 286)*

An effort by the Senate to strip the Mexico City restrictions failed in the fiscal 2004 foreign operations funding bill, which ultimately became part of yet another year-end omnibus spending measure (HR 2673—PL 108-199). At the insistence of House conferees, the Senate's Mexico City provision, which had drawn a veto threat from Bush, was omitted from the final bill. *(2004 aid appropriations, p. 288)*

Also, as in previous years, the appropriators agreed instead to increase funding for family planning. In this case they agreed to resume funding for UNFPA at $34 million, the amount the administration withheld in 2002. Another $25 million withheld in 2003 was to fund a new program to combat trafficking in women and children. President Bush, however, again declined to distribute those funds.

The fiscal 2005 bill (HR 4818—PL 108-447) was also part of an omnibus bill. It included $441 million for international population-planning assistance, again subject to the Mexico City restrictions. The measure allocated $34 million for UNFPA, but again allowed the president to withhold the funds if he determined the agency was participating in coercive family planning activities. *(2005 aid appropriations, p. 292)*

Fetal Protection

After a long-fought battle, legislation to create a separate federal offense for harming or killing a fetus while committing a violent federal crime against a pregnant woman was enacted in 2004. President George W. Bush signed the bill (HR 1997—PL 108-212) into law April 1. The law gave legal status to a fetus for the first time, and abortion-rights supporters contended its true purpose was to lay the groundwork for an overturn of the federal right to an abortion. Backers of the bill denied that was its intent.

The legislation provided penalties for harming during the commission of a federal crime an embryo or fetus at any stage after implantation in the womb. Defendants could be charged with a separate offense regardless of whether they intended to harm the embryo or fetus—or even knew the woman was pregnant. The legislation included exemptions for people who gave medical treatment to pregnant women as well as for those who performed an abortion with the consent of the woman or someone legally authorized to act on her behalf. A pregnant woman who harmed her own embryo or fetus would also be exempt.

The key portion of the bill, however, was its definition of the phrase "unborn child," as "a member of the species homo sapiens, at any stage of development, who is carried in the womb."

The House passed similar bills in 1999 and 2001, but the measures were blocked in the Senate. The legislation gained fresh momentum with the discoveries in April 2003 of the bodies of Laci Peterson, a Modesto, Calif., woman, and her unborn son, whom the family named Conner. Sponsors renamed the bill—originally the Unborn Victims of Violence Act—"Laci and Conner's Law," even though the bill would not have applied to that murder because it was not a federal crime. Peterson's husband, Scott, was subsequently convicted of double murder in the case under an existing California state law. *(2001 action, p. 481)*

Crimes the law did cover included those committed against federal workers while carrying out their duties, on Indian reservations, military bases, national parks, or other federal lands or facilities.

LEGISLATIVE ACTION

The House Judiciary Constitution Subcommittee approved HR 1997 by a vote of 6–3 on July 15, 2003, after a short but politically charged debate. The subcommittee rejected by voice vote an amendment by Robert C. Scott, D-Va., that called for stiffer sentences for existing federal crimes that caused injury or death to a pregnant woman, taking into account harm done to the fetus, without expressly recognizing the fetus as an individual under the law. The full Judiciary Committee approved the bill Jan. 21, 2004, by a vote of 20–13 and reported it Feb. 11 (H Rept 108-420, Part 1).

Abortion rights advocates opposed the measure, arguing that giving separate legal recognition to a fetus could undermine the reproductive freedom guaranteed by the Supreme Court's 1973 landmark ruling in *Roe v. Wade*, which legalized abortion.

"The court clearly said 'the unborn have never been recognized in the whole sense,' and concluded that 'person,' as used in the Fourteenth Amendment of the Constitution, does not include the unborn," Rep. Jerrold Nadler, D-N.Y., said during the markup. "The rhetoric used by proponents of this bill—urging that the law must 'recognize' the fetus as a victim—is a direct assault on that holding in *Roe*."

Supporters of the bill countered that it was not an attack on abortion rights; rather, they said, the legislation simply recognized that attacks on pregnant women could result in harm to two victims. "This particular bill stands on its own," said Rep. Steve Chabot, R-Ohio, chair of the Constitution Subcommittee. "I don't think it's particularly productive to get into a debate on 'is it related to abortion or not related to abortion?'"

The House passed the bill—for the third time—on Feb. 26, 2004, by a vote of 254–163. Before passage, members defeated, 186–229, a Democratic substitute offered by Zoe Lofgren of California that called for additional penalties for those convicted of federal violent crimes against pregnant women that resulted in harm to their fetus but did not include language defining an "unborn child."

The Senate took up the House-passed bill—for the first time—and passed it March 25, clearing it for President Bush. The **key vote was 61–38 (R 48–2; D 13–35; I 0–1)**. *(2004 key votes, p. 854)*

Senate Democrats led by Dianne Feinstein of California narrowly failed in an effort to substitute an amendment that would have allowed prosecutors to pursue multiple charges against defendants who harmed pregnant women and affected their pregnancies but would not have established a separate legal status for fetuses. The proposal was defeated, 49–50.

Republican Mike DeWine of Ohio said Feinstein's amendment "creates a legal fiction" in that it did not explicitly recognize that a crime against a pregnant woman could result in two victims.

The Bush administration also weighed in, releasing a statement of administration policy the day of the Senate debate opposing Feinstein's language.

Senators also defeated an amendment offered by Patty Murray, D-Wash., to expand the Family and Medical Leave Act (PL 103-3) to allow workers to take emergency leave to deal with incidents of domestic or sexual violence, and to extend unemployment benefits to people who lost their jobs as a result of domestic violence or sexual assault. The amendment, which required a sixty-vote waiver of budget rules to pass, fell on a 46–53 vote.

Project Bioshield

Congress in 2004 approved legislation authorizing Project Bioshield, President George W. Bush's ten-year initiative to develop and stockpile vaccines and medications to combat a bioterrorist attack (S 15—PL 108-276). *(PL 108-276 details, p. 213)*

The president's proposal sought to encourage biotech and drug companies to develop new vaccines and other measures to counter biological terrorist agents such as smallpox, anthrax, and botulism toxin, as well as other pathogens such as Ebola and plague. Little incentive existed for companies to develop these products without a federal program.

Lawmakers generally agreed that flexibility in regulatory procedures was justified in light of the potential catastrophe of a biological attack. The 2001 anthrax attacks had brought bioterrorism directly to Capitol Hill. *(Anthrax attacks, p. 712)*

The House in July 2003 approved a $5.6 billion authorization over ten years for a reserve fund that the White House could tap for the effort (HR 2122). But the measure bogged down in the Senate in controversy over providing guaranteed funding, which the Bush administration said was needed to get the program started. The administration also asked for expedited review and procurement procedures to get research, development, and production going on high-priority drugs and vaccines; a permanent funding stream to guarantee companies a market for the new products; and the authority to allow emergency use of promising, but unapproved, drugs and treatments for bioterrorist attacks. A funding compromise was not worked out until the following spring. The Senate approved the compromise May 19, 2004; after a couple more false starts, the House cleared the bill July 14.

HIGHLIGHTS

As signed into law July 21, 2004, S 15 (PL 108-276) included the following major provisions:

Research and development. Accelerated procedures for approving grants to companies for research and development on bioterrorism countermeasures, including allowing the administration to bypass competitive bidding rules in certain circumstances.

Procurement. Authorized the secretary of the Department of Health and Human Services (HHS) to contract to purchase specific drugs, vaccines, medical equipment, or other bioterrorism countermeasures, thereby guaranteeing a market once the item was developed. The provision built on legislation (HR 3448—PL 107-188) enacted in the 107th Congress to create a strategic national stockpile repository of antibiotics, chemical antidotes, antitoxins, and other items. *(2002 action, p. 477)*

Emergency use. Allowed HHS to use a drug or device that had not yet been approved by the Food and Drug Administration if an emergency were declared.

Smallpox Vaccine Compensation

Congress cleared legislation (HR 1770—PL 108-20) in 2003 to compensate health and emergency workers who suffered adverse effects from smallpox vaccines. Enactment came after top lawmakers and the White House reached a compromise on the compensation levels.

The smallpox vaccination program became a high-profile priority for President George W. Bush after he announced plans in December 2002 to vaccinate 500,000 nurses, firefighters, police, and other "first-responders" against bioterrorism threats. But uncertainty about how health and emergency workers would be compensated if they got sick after receiving the vaccine hampered the effort. Because the only available vaccine used a live virus, it carried a significant risk of complications and a small risk of serious injury or death. As a result only about 31,300 volunteers had stepped forward to be vaccinated as of April 4, 2003. Nurses, police officers, and firefighters cited the lack of a compensation fund as a major reason for the low vaccination rate.

The compromise bill addressed many of the concerns raised by Democratic lawmakers—most notably Sen. Edward M. Kennedy, D-Mass.—as well as by first-responders. Lobbying by those groups led to the defeat of an earlier Republican bill in the House while a similar measure stalled in the Senate.

"I am confident that we have crafted a compensation package that gives health care workers and first-responders the confidence they need to proceed with vaccinations," said Sen. Judd Gregg, R-N.H., who had authored the original Senate bill. That measure, which had White House backing, would have capped lifetime lost-wage payments at $50,000, an amount Democrats called inadequate.

The fiscal 2003 supplemental defense spending bill (HR 1559—PL 108-11) set aside $42 million for the compensation.

LEGISLATIVE ACTION

The administration's willingness to compromise came after several attempts to place stricter limits on compensation had failed.

The Senate Health, Education, Labor, and Pensions Committee dropped provisions on vaccine compensation from a bill (S 15) that it approved March 19, 2003, after Gregg and Kennedy failed to reach agreement. Gregg, who chaired the committee, proposed a $262,000 lump sum for survivors of individuals who died or were permanently disabled as a result of smallpox inoculations. The amount was derived from a formula used to calculate federal benefits for police officers and firefighters who died in the line of duty. Gregg also proposed payments equal to two-thirds of lost wages after an employee missed five days of work, up to a total of $50,000. Workers would have had to be inoculated within 120 days of the bill's enactment in order to be covered.

Kennedy, the panel's ranking Democrat, scuttled the measure by preparing seventy-four amendments to challenge the caps on compensation and the timetables for vaccination. First-responders "are being put at risk for the protection of all of us," Kennedy said. "We just want to make sure we're going to have people participating."

The panel instead approved a less controversial section of the bill related to "Project Bioshield," a Bush initiative to encourage the development of next-generation drugs and vaccines to combat a bioterrorist attack. *(Project Bioshield, p. 213)*

Gregg tried again April 2. This time, he got a slightly revised smallpox compensation bill (S 719) through the committee on a party-line vote of 11–10. The panel rejected amendments by Kennedy to eliminate the caps on lost wages, extend compensation to those disfigured by the vaccine, and designate the fund as mandatory spending. "It is not fair to workers, and it is not enough to protect our nation," Kennedy said.

"This is not a health issue. This is a national security issue. We are at war," Gregg said. "The passage of this legislation is vital to the safety of the American people."

Committee members said the need for a fund had grown even more urgent since the deaths of two health care workers and a National Guardsman days after they received the inoculation. Those deaths were caused by heart attacks, not a known side effect of the vaccine. The Centers for Disease Control and Prevention recommended that individuals with heart problems avoid the vaccine until they investigated the link. At least ten states had suspended their smallpox vaccination programs in the wake of the deaths.

Across Capitol Hill, an attempt by House Republicans to speed a compensation bill (HR 1463) through that chamber without a committee markup backfired March 31. The House rejected the measure, 184–206, with twenty-one Republicans joining 185 Democrats in opposing it.

The bill, sponsored by Richard M. Burr, R-N.C., included the $262,000 lump sum to survivors but was more generous than Gregg's version when it came to lost wages. Individuals who missed more than five days of work because of complications from the vaccine would be reimbursed two-thirds of their salaries, up to a $262,000 lifetime limit. If workers had dependents, the rate would rise to 75 percent of their salary.

After an earlier version of the bill stalled in the Rules Committee, Burr and Republican leaders decided that by voting under suspension of the rules, which allowed no amendments, they could force Democrats to vote with them or go on the record against a compensation program.

But interest groups such as the American Nurses Association made a late push against the bill, saying it would not provide enough money. The International Association of Fire Fighters, the American Federation of State, County and Municipal Employees, and the Service Employees International Union announced their opposition as well. "We can do better than this bill, and we will," Lois Capps, D-Calif., a registered nurse who helped lead the opposition to Burr's bill, said before the vote.

Lawmakers and the administration reached agreement on a revised bill late April 10. Aides said the deal addressed many of the concerns raised by Democrats who had particularly opposed a cap on lost-wage payments.

The House passed the bill by voice vote April 11 and the Senate cleared it later the same day, also by voice vote.

HIGHLIGHTS

As signed into law April 30, 2003, HR 1770 (PL 108-20) contained the following major provisions:

Permanent disability. Made individuals who were permanently disabled by complications from the vaccine eligible for annual payments of 66 percent of their wages—75 percent if the person had a spouse or dependents—up to $50,000 per year with no lifetime limit.

Lost wages. Provided that workers who missed work would be reimbursed for 66 percent of their lost wages up to $50,000 annually with a lifetime cap of $262,000.

Death benefit. Made the spouse of a person who died eligible for a lump sum payment of $262,000. Allowed a family with children to choose the $262,000 or yearly payments of 75 percent of the deceased worker's salary until the youngest child turned eighteen.

Lawsuits. Allowed a worker who was unsatisfied with an award to sue under the 1946 Federal Tort Claims Act, although the law provided immunity to hospitals and health care workers who administered the vaccine.

Tobacco Regulation

A plan in the Senate to combine increased regulation of tobacco products with a government buyout for tobacco farmers collapsed in 2004 in a dispute over whether and how big a role to give the Food and Drug Administration (FDA). The tobacco buyout went ahead (HR 4520-PL 108-357); the FDA regulation did not, to the consternation of public health advocates in and out of Congress. *(Buyout details, p. 386)*

Republican senator Mitch McConnell of Kentucky introduced a bill (S 1490) in July 2003 to end the seventy-year-old tobacco subsidy program, which used a system of acreage allotments and marketing quotas to keep supplies in line with demand at market prices. Farmers complained that the quotas had hurt them in recent years by limiting how much they could grow and by setting prices that restricted their ability to compete with lower-priced tobacco from foreign growers. McConnell proposed to end the subsidies and give the farmers a series of fixed payments designed to ease them out of the tobacco business over six years. Meanwhile, Judd Gregg, R-N.H., chair of the Senate Health, Education, Labor, and Pensions (HELP) Committee, and Mike DeWine, R-Ohio, were drafting regulatory legislation that they hoped to put together with McConnell's bill. They proposed to grant the FDA regulatory control over the marketing of tobacco products to minors and over the use of hazardous materials in cigarettes, cigars, chewing tobacco, and snuff.

McConnell said he did not believe the Senate would pass buyout legislation unless it was paired with FDA regulation of tobacco. Similarly, the FDA regulation measure did not have enough votes to pass without the tobacco bill.

However, negotiations over Gregg's bill in the HELP Committee came to naught because of disagreements over how much authority to give the FDA. The draft bill would have given Congress, not the FDA, sole discretion to determine whether nicotine levels in cigarettes could be reduced to zero. It was generally believed that if the FDA were to gain regulatory control over tobacco, it would be compelled under the 1938 Food, Drug, and Cosmetic Act to ban nicotine.

Public health advocates, both lawmakers and lobbyists, worried that the language would weaken the FDA's ability to control what cigarette companies made and sold. On the other side, South Carolina Republican Lindsey Graham, a HELP Committee member, said he could not support Gregg's draft because he feared the regulation would "basically drive the industry into the ground." House Republicans also generally opposed FDA regulation of tobacco, with or without the buyout. In 2004, however, House Ways and Means Committee Chair Bill Thomas included the buyout in a time-sensitive corporate tax bill (HR 4520) for which he needed southern votes. That bill passed the House easily on June 17. *(Corporate taxes, p. 115)*

The Senate backed the buyout, adding it to the Senate version of the tax bill, but insisted that it be paired with FDA regulation of tobacco products.

The Senate FDA amendment, put together by DeWine and HELP ranking Democrat Edward Kennedy of Massachusetts, would have authorized the FDA to regulate the levels of tar, nicotine, and other components of tobacco products. Congress, however, would have retained veto power over any effort to ban cigarettes or prohibit nicotine as an ingredient. It also would have required tobacco companies to disclose harmful and potentially harmful ingredients to the Department of Health and Human Services; required that warnings take up at least 30 percent of tobacco labels and that those labels be placed on the front or back of the pack, not the sides; required that magazine ads for tobacco products be in black and white only; and required tobacco manufacturers to pay for regulation through a user fee.

House conferees on the corporate tax bill, however, jettisoned the Senate FDA amendment from the bill, although they left the buyout intact. Despite support for the proposed tobacco regulation from cigarette-maker Philip Morris, a division of the Altria Group Inc., smaller tobacco companies vehemently opposed the Senate provision, and they had the backing of House majority leader Tom DeLay, R-Texas.

Food Allergens Labeling

Congress in 2004 passed a bill (S 741—PL 108-282) requiring food manufacturers to clearly identify ingredients associated with food allergies and use the familiar names of the eight most common allergens when labeling their products. *(PL 108-282 details, p. 467)*

The bill required manufacturers by 2006 to provide plain English labeling of foods containing milk, wheat, soybeans, peanuts, tree nuts, fish, shellfish, or eggs. Those accounted for an estimated 90 percent of all food allergies but were sometimes listed on labels by scientific names, such as albumin for eggs or casein for milk. The bill also required the Food and Drug Administration to develop a definition of the term "gluten-free," to help those with celiac disease, an autoimmune disorder that required patients to avoid most grains, including wheat, rye, and barley.

The Senate passed S 741 (S Rept 108-226) by voice vote March 8, 2004, as part of a measure to create incentives for drug companies to develop drugs for rare diseases in animals and to treat so-called "minor" species of animals such as

sheep, goats, and game birds. The House passed the bill (H Rept 108-608) by voice vote July 20. President George W. Bush signed it into law Aug. 2.

Medical Malpractice Limits

For the fifth consecutive Congress, the House approved legislation to limit damages in medical malpractice lawsuits only to see it die in the Senate. The House passed a bill in 2003 and another one in 2004.

President George W. Bush made damage award limits a signature part of his health agenda, blaming skyrocketing insurance premiums and frivolous lawsuits for both running up the nation's health care bill and driving physicians to stop performing high-risk procedures or stop practicing medicine entirely.

Democrats, trial lawyers, and consumer groups, however, argued that damage limits punished those who had already proven their case and blamed rising premiums on malpractice insurers rather than large jury payouts.

Republicans had tried without much success since the mid-1990s to curb medical malpractice lawsuits, but a confluence of events gave them new hope in 2003. Among the factors were public concern over rising health care costs, highly publicized walkouts by doctors in several states protesting increases in malpractice insurance premiums, and the fact that the Senate's only doctor, Republican Bill Frist of Tennessee, had just taken over as majority leader. *(2002 action, p. 491)*

The House Judiciary and House Energy and Commerce committees sent a bill (HR 5) to the floor in 2003 patterned on a 1975 California law that doctors in that state credited with arresting their rising premiums. Consumer groups said a separate insurance regulation initiative had more to do with California's relatively low rates than its $250,000 cap on noneconomic damages (those for "pain and suffering"). Still, with the strong backing of the American Medical Association, the House passed the bill for the seventh time since Republicans took control of the chamber in 1995. And it tried again the next year (HR 4280).

While the Senate voted on the measure three times in 2003 and 2004, it remained nearly a dozen votes short of the sixty needed to break a threatened filibuster. The Senate also proved a graveyard for other GOP efforts to overhaul tort law—dooming bills to shift more class action suits from state to federal court and to establish a fund to pay claims for asbestos exposure. *(Class action lawsuits, p. 591; asbestos compensation, p. 611)*

LEGISLATIVE ACTION

The fast-moving House medical malpractice bill (HR 5) survived back-to-back markups in the House Judiciary and Energy and Commerce committees largely intact.

The Judiciary Committee rejected Democratic amendments to increase or index the caps, to strip provisions limiting attorneys' fees, and to lengthen the statute of limitations before approving the measure by a vote of 15–13 on March 5, 2003.

The Energy and Commerce Committee approved the bill by voice vote a day later. The committee defeated amendments similar to those offered at Judiciary, as well as efforts to drop from the bill a provision protecting health insurance companies, as well as drugmakers and medical device makers from punitive damages in most cases. Republicans rejected, 22–25, an attempt by Frank Pallone Jr., D-N.J., to strip the provisions.

HR 5 was formally reported by the two committees on March 11 (H Rept 108-32, Parts 1 and 2).

The House passed the bill, 229–196, on March 13 under a closed rule with no amendments allowed. Angry Democrats—who had sought to offer twenty-nine amendments, including a comprehensive substitute to limit frivolous lawsuits but not damages—failed in an effort to recommit the bill to the Judiciary Committee. That vote was 191–234.

Frist tried to bring up the companion Senate bill (S 11) on July 7, 2003, without committee consideration, but GOP supporters lacked the votes to force their way past Democratic objections and formally take up the bill. A cloture vote July 9 failed by a vote of 49–48, eleven short of the sixty votes required.

Frist did not give up, however. In 2004 Senate GOP leaders sought to recast the issue as a matter of health for women and children. A new bill (S 2061) would have shielded obstetrician/gynecologists and nurse midwives from damage awards greater than $250,000 and limited attorney fees. A cloture vote on that measure failed on a **key vote of 48–45 (R 47–3; D 1–41; I 0–1)** on Feb. 24. *(2004 key votes, p. 854)*

Frist tried again in April, this time adding protections for emergency room and trauma center personnel in addition to obstetrician/gynecologists. Cloture on that measure (S 2207) also failed, 49–48, on April 7.

The House actually passed its bill for a second time May 12, 2004, as part of its actions to commemorate "Cover the Uninsured Week." The vote on the same bill with a different number (HR 4280) was 229–197. The Senate, however, failed to take any further action in the 108th Congress.

MAJOR PROVISIONS

As approved by the House in 2003, HR 5 included the following major provisions:

Noneconomic damages. For states that did not impose their own caps, limited noneconomic damages (those for pain and suffering) to $250,000, regardless of the number of parties against whom the lawsuit was brought or the number of separate claims or actions brought with respect to the same incident. Specified that the jury would not be informed of the cap and any award in excess of $250,000 would be reduced.

Punitive damages. Limited the amount of punitive damages—those intended to punish the defendant for wrongdoing—to twice the economic damages or $250,000, whichever was greater. Prohibited a jury from awarding punitive damages in a case in which no economic damages were awarded.

Liability limitations. Shielded drug companies and medical device manufacturers and distributors from punitive damages related to a product that was approved by the Food and Drug Administration (FDA). Specified that doctors and other health care providers who prescribed a product approved by the FDA would not be liable in a class action suit against the manufacturer, distributor, or seller of the product.

Attorneys' fees. Capped the amount an attorney could charge in "contingent fees"—a predetermined percentage of any amount awarded by the court to the client. Specified that the total of all contingent fees for representing all plaintiffs in a health care lawsuit could not exceed 40 percent of the first $50,000 recovered; 33.3 percent of the next $50,000; 25 percent of the next $500,000; and 15 percent of any amount over $600,000.

Statute of limitations. Required that the suit be filed within three years of the date of the injury, or one year after the plaintiff discovered or should have discovered the injury through the use of "reasonable diligence," whichever occurred first.

Human Cloning Ban

For the second consecutive Congress, the House in 2003 passed a bill to make it illegal to clone a human embryo for any reason. But, as in the previous Congress, the effort stalled in the Senate with lawmakers divided over whether to allow cloning for medical research purposes.

The House bill (HR 534) made it a crime to knowingly perform, attempt to perform, or participate in an attempt to perform human cloning. It also made it illegal to ship, receive, or import a cloned human embryo or any product derived from a cloned human embryo. Criminal penalties of up to ten years in prison and civil penalties of no less than $1 million were provided for violating the prohibitions.

The bill specifically banned a procedure known as "somatic cell nuclear transfer," in which the nucleus of an egg cell was replaced with the nucleus of an adult cell that would not multiply in its original state. The new nucleus was then manipulated into multiplying, creating an embryo containing stem cells that could evolve into different types of human tissue. If implanted into a woman's womb, the embryo could develop into a baby that would be genetically identical to the person who provided the adult cell nucleus.

Researchers, however, wanted to use cloning not to make babies but to harvest those embryonic stem cells in the hope they could ultimately be used to treat or cure a wide variety of ailments, from Parkinson's disease to diabetes to spinal cord injuries.

The procedure was controversial because extracting the stem cells required that the embryo be destroyed—an act abortion opponents equated with murder. Other opponents of the practice worried that cloning could prompt scientists to genetically manipulate embryos to produce desired traits, and that poor women might be enticed—or coerced—into participating in cloning experiments by donating their eggs for the procedure.

The bill mirrored a measure that passed the House in 2001 but died in the Senate. The issue was resurrected early in the 108th Congress following unverified reports in December 2002 that a Bahamian company affiliated with a sect known as the Raelians had cloned a human baby. *(2001–2002 action, p. 493)*

President George W. Bush called for a ban on human cloning in his 2003 State of the Union address. The day before the House vote in February 2003 Bush issued a statement strongly supporting the bill, which was sponsored by Reps. Dave Weldon, R-Fla., and Bart Stupak, D-Mich. "The administration unequivocally is opposed to the cloning of human beings either for reproduction or for research," the statement said. "The moral and ethical issues posed by human cloning are profound and cannot be ignored in the quest for scientific discovery."

But, as in 2002, the companion Senate measure (S 245), sponsored by Sam Brownback, R-Kan., did not have the sixty votes needed to overcome a filibuster. Research advocates in the chamber, including Arlen Specter, R-Pa., Orrin Hatch, R-Utah, and Dianne Feinstein, D-Calif., wanted to ban cloning for the purposes of starting a pregnancy while allowing use of somatic cell nuclear transfer for the purpose of creating embryonic stem cells.

LEGISLATIVE ACTION

The House Judiciary Committee approved HR 534 by a vote of 19–12 on Feb. 12, 2003, after defeating several Democratic amendments to continue the ban on cloning for reproductive purposes but to allow it for stem cell research. The panel reported the bill on Feb. 25 (H Rept 108-18).

The House passed the bill, 241–155, on Feb. 27.

For the second time in two years, Rep. James C. Greenwood, R-Pa., unsuccessfully offered an amendment that would have permitted cloning for medical research but banned it for purposes of starting a pregnancy. It was rejected, 174–231.

Bill sponsor Weldon criticized Greenwood's alternative, saying it would force the government to keep track of cloned embryos to make sure all were destroyed for their stem cells and none would be implanted in a surrogate mother. "If this isn't a slippery slope that is steep and fast, I don't know what is," Weldon said. "It will open a Pandora's box of frightening possibilities."

Opponents of the Weldon bill, however, argued that it would unfairly restrict the promise of stem cell research. Rep. Zoe Lofgren, D-Calif., said the measure represented "an unprecedented intrusion into science by the political process."

Chronology of Action on Human Services

2001–2002

The 107th Congress experienced mostly frustration on the human services front. One of President George W. Bush's top domestic priorities, providing federal funding for faith-based social service providers, passed the Republican-led House but stalled in the Senate after Democrats took over following the defection of Vermont's James Jeffords from the Republican party. Similarly, efforts to reauthorize the landmark 1996 welfare overhaul law passed the House but foundered in the Senate where a bipartisan group of lawmakers tried to boost funding for child care and restore benefits for legal immigrants. *(Jeffords' action, pp. 3, 8)*

Faith-Based Charities

Seeking a quick victory for one of President George W. Bush's signature social policy initiatives, the House passed a bill (HR 7) in 2001 aimed at making federal money available for nine new categories of faith-based social services. The measure also would have created tax incentives for private charitable donations. But Senate Democrats were hostile to a core provision that would have allowed faith-based groups participating in the program to use religion as a basis for hiring. The Senate Finance Committee approved a scaled-back version of the bill in 2002, but the measure never reached the floor and died at the end of the 107th Congress.

In the absence of congressional action, however, Bush ordered cabinet departments to carry out many of the provisions by executive order.

BACKGROUND

The basic charitable choice provisions of the House bill—allowing religious groups to deliver federal services on an equal basis with other organizations without playing down their religious mission or hiring people who did not share their faith—were not new. They were an expansion of provisions in the 1996 welfare overhaul (PL 104-193) that allowed religious groups to provide federally funded family assistance services, foster care, and adoption assistance without removing religious icons or giving up their exemption under the 1964 Civil Rights Act to use religious beliefs in their hiring and firing decisions. The groups could not discriminate against beneficiaries, however. Subsequent laws added several more services that such groups could provide. *(Congress and the Nation Vol. IX, pp. 571, 578)*

What ignited controversy over the House bill was the proposed expansion of charitable choice to virtually the entire range of social services including crime prevention, housing grants, job training, and programs for older Americans.

Many Democrats and moderate Republicans worried about allowing religious groups to discriminate in hiring with federal funds. They also worried that the bill would supersede state and local antidiscrimination laws, particularly those that protected the hiring of gays and lesbians and provided domestic partner benefits. Some religious leaders, meanwhile, worried that federal funding would subject them to ever-increasing levels of bureaucratic scrutiny, restricting their freedom to operate their faith-based social services as they chose.

REFERENCES

Discussion of human services policy for the years 1945–1964 may be found in *Congress and the Nation Vol. I,* pp. 1225–1331; for the years 1965–1968, *Congress and the Nation Vol. II,* pp. 745–778; for the years 1969–1972, *Congress and the Nation Vol. III,* pp. 605–633; for the years 1973–1976, *Congress and the Nation Vol. IV,* pp. 403–432; for the years 1977–1980, *Congress and the Nation Vol. V,* pp. 679–712; for the years 1981–1984, *Congress and the Nation Vol. VI,* pp. 581–612; for the years 1985–1988, *Congress and the Nation Vol. VII,* p. 607–632; for the years 1989–1992, *Congress and the Nation Vol. VIII,* pp. 611–624; for the years 1993–1996, *Congress and the Nation Vol. IX,* pp. 571–596; for the years 1997–2001, *Congress and the Nation Vol. X,* pp. 486–496.

Outlays for Income Security

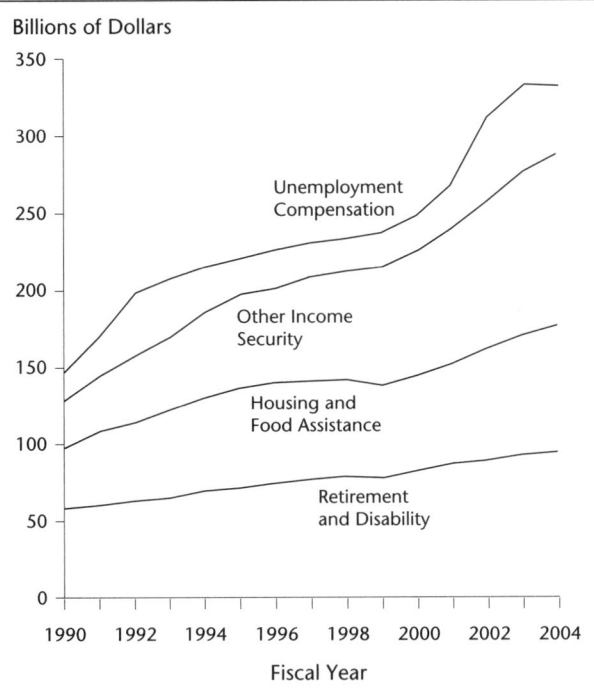

Billions of Dollars

SOURCE: Office of Management and Budget, *Historical Tables, Budget of the United States Government: Fiscal Year 2006* (Washington, D.C.: U.S. Government Printing Office, 2005), Table 3.2.

LEGISLATIVE ACTION

Pressed by the Bush administration to act quickly, the House passed HR 7 on July 19, 2001, by a vote of 233–198. The bill had been approved by the House Judiciary Committee on June 28 by a vote of 20–5 and by the House Ways and Means Committee on July 11 by a vote of 23–16. HR 7 was reported by Judiciary on July 12 and by Ways on Means on July 16 (H Rept 107-138, Parts 1 and 2).

But the floor win for Bush in the House was tempered by the fact that GOP leaders had to pull the measure from the floor a day earlier to put down a rebellion by Republican moderates. Despite the delay, the leadership lost only four Republican votes while gaining the votes of fifteen Democrats and one independent.

The moderates' uprising was short-lived and easily quelled, but it generated a spate of headlines about discrimination that discomfited the White House. Led by Mark Foley of Florida, the GOP moderates threatened to send the bill back to the Judiciary Committee with instructions to drop the preemption of state and local bias laws and require federally funded groups to comply with the ban on hiring discrimination in the 1964 Civil Rights Act. In return for abandoning the motion to recommit, they extracted a pledge from House GOP Conference chair J. C. Watts Jr. of Oklahoma that any House-Senate conference on the bill would "more clearly address" their concerns.

In the Senate, however, advocates of faith-based programs never managed to get beyond the basic dilemma of how to increase faith-based charities' access to federal funds enough to address unmet social needs but not so much as to violate the constitutional separation of church and state.

Bush's prospects turned on a bipartisan compromise developed by Sens. Joseph I. Lieberman, D-Conn., and Rick Santorum, R-Pa. Like the House-passed bill, the Lieberman-Santorum plan (S 1924) would have increased tax breaks for charitable donations and required equal treatment for faith-based organizations competing to deliver a range of federally funded social services. But, unlike the House bill, the Lieberman-Santorum plan did not seek to exempt religious groups from state and local antidiscrimination laws outside the scope of federal law or allow federal agencies to offer indirect aid to religious groups, such as vouchers needy families could take to religious groups to pay for drug treatment or day care.

Many Senate Democrats still objected, fearing the bill would leave the door open for groups to practice hiring discrimination while using federal funds. The Senate Finance Committee instead approved only the tax portion of HR 7 by voice vote June 18, 2002. The bill was formally reported on July 16 (S Rept 107-211). Lieberman and Santorum hoped to add their charitable choice provisions on the Senate floor, but the bill never made it that far.

With Senate action stalled, Bush announced Dec. 12, 2002, that key provisions of the legislation would be implemented by executive order. He directed all federal agencies to maintain what he called "a level playing field for faith-based organizations" when awarding social service grants and specified that groups could retain their religious identity while carrying out federally funded programs. He called specifically on the Federal Emergency Management Agency, the Housing and Urban Development Department, and the Health and Human Services Department to revise policies to give equal consideration to religious organizations. The White House also issued a guidebook explaining what faith-based organizations needed to do to qualify for government grants, including the proper uses of federal money.

Welfare Law Reauthorization

A strong push by President George W. Bush and passage of a bill by the House were not enough to break the logjam over rewriting the 1996 welfare overhaul in the 107th Congress. Lawmakers agreed instead to extend major provisions of the 1996 law, which expired in 2002, until early 2003, and embark on a full reauthorization in the 108th Congress. *(108th Congress action, p. 525)*

Bush had made updating the welfare law a centerpiece of his social agenda for 2002. The debate in Congress lacked the stark ideological divides of 1996 when the choice was whether to end sixty years of welfare as an open-ended entitlement. But, while most members no longer questioned the idea of welfare as temporary aid, there were sharp disputes over the details.

Bush and most congressional Republicans said the 1996 law largely had been successful with welfare caseloads falling by more than half since enactment. "History tells us we were right, absolutely right in what we did in taking people out of a life of dependence," said Rep. E. Clay Shaw Jr., R-Fla., the main author of the 1996 measure. Republicans generally wanted to maintain the basic spending levels while nudging additional recipients into the workforce.

Most Democrats and some moderate Republicans argued that any increase in work requirements had to be tied to a significant increase in aid, particularly for decent child care. They also stressed the importance of training and counseling to enable recipients to stay in the workforce.

The issue that polarized lawmakers, however, was whether to restore welfare benefits for legal immigrants. Pressure to revive those benefits, which were cut under the 1996 law, came from state officials, influential senators, and Hispanic voters whose support was being courted intensely for the midterm congressional elections in November. But House conservatives insisted that the 1996 law discouraged welfare dependency among immigrants and ensured that those who sponsored new arrivals would take responsibility for their care.

Bush opened the debate over the welfare law Feb. 26, 2002, proposing that recipients be required to work a full forty-hour week rather than the thirty hours required under the 1996 law and that states have 70 percent of their welfare recipients in jobs or actively seeking work by 2007, compared with 50 percent under existing law. In a nod to conservatives, he also proposed new, federally funded programs to promote marriage and encourage teenagers to abstain from sex.

The House welfare bill (HR 4737), passed in May, closely tracked the administration's proposal, including the work and caseload requirements and $250 million to promote marriage and teen sexual abstinence. Conservatives agreed to add $1 billion over five years to mandatory spending for child-care grants.

The Senate Finance Committee approved an alternative version of the bill that would have maintained the thirty-hour workweek for recipients, made it easier for them to take college classes or get vocational training, increased mandatory child-care subsidies by $5.5 billion over five years, and allowed states to use federal money to provide cash benefits to legal immigrants. Though the plan had the support of some moderate Republicans, Majority Leader Tom Daschle, D-S.D., opposed it and vowed to seek more child-care funding on the Senate floor.

At one point, it seemed a deal might be possible in the lame-duck session after the fall elections. But Republicans set that idea aside after their victory at the polls in November. With no agreement in sight, cash-strapped state officials pressed Congress for a three-year extension of the 1996 law

to guarantee continued funding. The law was set to expire Sept. 30, 2002.

Congress opted instead for short-term extensions. The first stopgap appropriations bill (H J Res 111—PL 107-229), enacted Sept. 30, kept welfare programs running through Dec. 31. The final continuing resolution of the year (H J Res 124—PL 107-294) extended those programs until Jan. 11, 2003.

BACKGROUND

The 1996 welfare overhaul law (PL 104-193) ended a six-decade-old guarantee of cash benefits to all eligible low-income mothers and children and replaced it with a block grant program aimed at moving those on welfare into the workforce. The new Temporary Assistance for Needy Families (TANF) program took the place of the Aid to Families with Dependent Children (AFDC), providing fixed block grants for programs designed and operated by the states. The law authorized $16.5 billion per year for TANF block grants through fiscal 2002. (Congress and the Nation Vol. IX, p. 578)

States had broad discretion in deciding how to use the funds—including providing cash assistance, child care, education, job training, and transportation—and in determining who would be eligible for various TANF-funded benefits and services.

However, the law did set certain criteria. To receive federal welfare funds, states were required to spend at least 75 percent of what they spent on AFDC and similar programs in fiscal 1994. States were barred from using federal welfare funds to aid most legal immigrants unless they had been in the United States for at least five years. The states could use their own funds to provide benefits to recent immigrants but fewer than half did.

The law also required that 50 percent of the families receiving assistance under TANF engage in some kind of work-related activity for at least thirty hours each week. No family could receive federally funded assistance for more than five years. Families that received aid entirely from state funds were not subject to the federal five-year limit. About twenty states had time limits shorter than five years, but states often provided exceptions for some groups of families that met certain criteria.

HOUSE ACTION

The House Education and the Workforce Committee kicked off formal consideration, approving its version of the bill (HR 4092) by a party-line vote of 25–20 on May 2, 2002. The bill was reported May 10 (H Rept 107-452, Part 1). The measure included the forty-hour-per-week work requirement, with at least twenty-four hours at a work site, and mandated that states increase the portion of welfare recipients who worked from 50 percent to 70 percent by 2007.

In response to complaints from Democratic committee members that the GOP bill demanded more work from welfare clients without helping them pay for child care and other expenses, the panel agreed to authorize $2.3 billion for discretionary child-care programs in fiscal 2003, a $200 million increase over the original proposal. The amendment, by Michael N. Castle, R-Del., was adopted, 25–21.

The bill also included a proposal for "super waivers" to allow states to combine two or more block grants in a demonstration project in areas such as employment, adult literacy, and child care. Other provisions included a denial of cash assistance to those who failed to show up to work for more than two consecutive months and up to $200 million in federal funds for programs to promote marriage.

The House Ways and Means Committee approved its version of the bill (HR 4090) also on May 2, the same day the Education and Workforce panel acted. The party-line vote was 23–16. The bill was reported May 14 (H Rept 107-460, Part 1).

The committee proposed to hold mandatory spending on child-care grants to $2.7 billion annually through fiscal 2005. (Ways and Means had jurisdiction over the mandatory grants, while Education and the Workforce had oversight over discretionary programs.)

Like the Education and the Workforce Committee version, the Ways and Means bill required that 70 percent of welfare recipients be working by fiscal 2007 and that they work forty hours per week. Other provisions increased from 30 percent to 50 percent the portion of TANF funds that states could transfer to their child-care block grants and authorized $300 million annually for programs to promote stable marriages, including premarital education, counseling and research into keeping families together.

An attempt by Pete Stark, D-Calif., to boost the funds by $11.3 billion over five years failed, 13–22. Committee Chair Bill Thomas, R-Calif., said he would support adding $2 billion over five years when the bill was prepared formally for the House floor in the Rules Committee.

The House passed a new bill (HR 4737) May 16 incorporating the work of the two committees. The **key vote was 229–197 (R 214–4; D 14–192; I 1–1).** *(2002 key votes, p. 819)*

The measure would have increased annual mandatory child-care grants from $2.7 billion to $2.9 billion, a total increase of $1 billion over five years. It would have authorized $2.3 billion in discretionary spending on child care in fiscal 2003, an increase of $200 million. An additional $200 million would have been authorized for each succeeding year, reaching a total of $3.1 billion in fiscal 2007. States would have been allowed to shift up to 50 percent of their welfare grants to child care each year, up from 30 percent.

Other provisions included authorizing up to $300 million a year in federal and matching state grants for marriage-promotion programs and $50 million a year for initiatives aimed at encouraging teenagers to abstain from sex.

Democrats said the measure demanded more of low-income parents without helping them get adequate education and training, or paying for care for their children while they worked. A Democratic substitute, offered by Benjamin L. Cardin, D-Md., would have increased mandatory spending on child care by $11 billion over five years, maintained the thirty-hour-per-week work requirement, allowed legal immigrants to receive benefits, and increased TANF funding annually to keep up with inflation. It was rejected, 198–222.

The bill reached the floor after a last-minute debate within the GOP caucus over the super-waiver proposals. Thomas and other backers of the idea hoped it would allow states to provide creative services for welfare families, such as putting food stamp coupons and welfare payments on the same debit cards or designing a single application for housing and job-training aid. But appropriators and authorizers complained that the provision would allow states to flout restrictions that Congress had placed on grant programs. The leadership revised the bill slightly to clarify that states could not get waivers for congressional restrictions on funding, especially bans on moving funds from one account to another.

SENATE ACTION

Senate Finance Committee Chair Max Baucus, D-Mont., pushed a more bipartisan version of HR 4737—a necessity if the measure was to have a chance of passing in the narrowly divided chamber. The Finance Committee approved the bill June 26 by a vote of 13–8 with the help of three Republicans—Orrin Hatch of Utah, Frank H. Murkowski of Alaska, and Olympia J. Snowe of Maine. However, Baucus lost the vote of Daschle, who served on the committee and cast the one Democratic "no" vote.

The bill, which was reported July 25 (S Rept 107-221), retained the existing requirement that adults on welfare work thirty hours per week. It called for extending health care coverage to some legal immigrants. And it included an additional $5.5 billion in mandatory child-care spending over five years—significantly more than the $1 billion, five-year increase called for in the House-passed bill. (The committee had jurisdiction over the mandatory funds.)

Some Senate Democrats wanted to add as much as $11.3 billion over five years for child care, arguing that low-income parents needed significantly more help in paying for day care as they worked their way off welfare. Daschle and others planned a fight on the issue later in the summer when the bill was expected to reach the floor. "If we are serious about moving people from assistance to self-sufficiency, we need to give them the tools to do so," Daschle said.

During the markup, the committee also approved, 12–9, an amendment by Bob Graham, D-Fla., to give states the option of allowing some legal immigrants, including children and pregnant women, to receive health insurance coverage under Medicaid and the State Children's Health Insurance Program (SCHIP). Graham said his amendment, expected to cost $660 million over five years, would help bring health care to 176,000 people, including many children.

Republicans winced at the price tag. Jon Kyl, R-Ariz., noted that legal immigrants entering the United States had to have a local sponsor who pledged to provide financial backing if needed, including medical expenses. "We don't need to provide an incentive for people to immigrate here who are a burden on society," he said.

The Senate Health, Education, Labor, and Pensions (HELP) Committee gave voice vote approval to a separate bill (S 2758) on Sept. 4. It called for a $1 billion increase in discretionary child-care subsidies in fiscal 2003, bringing the total authorization for that year to $3.1 billion. The Senate was expected to merge the bill with the Finance Committee version of HR 4737.

S 2758, sponsored by Christopher J. Dodd, D-Conn., required that states set aside 10 percent of the grant money to improve the quality of child care and 5 percent to increase payment for child-care providers. HELP Committee Chair Edward M. Kennedy, D-Mass., said only one in seven day care centers provided a level of quality that promoted healthy development and that the annual turnover rate for child-care workers was more than 30 percent. Senate Democrats and a few Republicans said many eligible families were denied subsidies because the program did not have enough money.

The committee rejected by voice vote a substitute offered by ranking Republican Judd Gregg of New Hampshire that would have added $1 billion in discretionary money over five years.

There was no further action in the Senate on either bill.

2003–2004

Republicans began the 108th Congress in 2003 eager to move early on portions of the Bush administration domestic agenda. Topping their list was a rewrite of the 1996 welfare law that had been left hanging at the end of the 107th Congress, and a reauthorization of the popular Head Start early childhood education and nutrition program. But neither bill was able to get through both the House and Senate and to the president's desk despite full GOP control of the Congress.

Welfare Law Reauthorization

The House passed a bill (HR 4) in February 2003 that reflected President George W. Bush's proposals for tougher work requirements for the welfare program initially passed in 1996. But the change of control that put the Senate in GOP hands in 2003 was not enough to win support for Bush's plans in that chamber.

With the two chambers at odds, lawmakers on Sept. 30, 2003, cleared a short-term extension (HR 3146—PL 108-89) to keep programs such as cash assistance and child-care grants operating through March 31, 2004. It was the fifth extension since the 1996 law expired Sept. 30, 2002. The Senate Finance Committee managed to report a bill in September 2003. But when Senate floor action stalled in March 2004, Congress was again forced to temporarily extend the old law, first through June 2004 (S 2231—PL 108-210) and again through March 2005 (HR 5149—PL 108-308).

The 1996 welfare overhaul (PL 104-193) had ended more than sixty years of guaranteed government aid and instituted a five-year limit on assistance. It required that states have at least 50 percent of their welfare recipients employed and that recipients work at least thirty hours a week. Parents with children younger than six years old had to work twenty hours a week. The law also provided a total of $13.9 billion for mandatory child-care grants over six years. *(Congress and the Nation Vol. IX, pp. 571, 578)*

Most lawmakers credited the landmark law with reducing welfare caseloads by half, but some critics said it was really the robust economy of the 1990s that drove the sharp decline and others said those who left the program simply had joined the growing ranks of the working poor and were still struggling.

The House-passed reauthorization bill reflected Bush's proposal to increase the work requirement to forty hours a week by 2008. It proposed reducing the amount of time that vocational education could be counted as a work activity and it called for $1 billion in additional mandatory funding for child-care grants and $200 million per year for programs to promote marriage.

Senate Finance Chair Charles E. Grassley, R-Iowa, brought HR 4 before his committee in September 2003, after leaving it on the back burner while he tackled Bush's tax cut bill (HR 2—PL 108-27) and Medicare prescription drug legislation (HR1—PL 108-173). To win over moderates, he altered the work requirement to thirty-four hours a week and twenty-four hours for parents of children under age six. He also promised Olympia J. Snowe, R-Maine, that she could offer an amendment to increase child-care funding during floor debate. Those changes were enough to move the bill out of committee.

The administration argued that sufficient funding was already flowing to the states. Health and Human Services secretary Tommy G. Thompson announced Sept. 23 that forty-one states and the District of Columbia would share $200 million in bonuses for meeting goals established under the 1996 law. But Democrats said states were cutting their child-care budgets in the wake of deficits and that the House bill would place unfunded mandates upon the local governments.

Both versions of the bill proposed to reauthorize the Temporary Assistance for Needy Families (TANF) block grant program though fiscal 2008 at the existing level of $16.5 billion a year. Families would still be limited to a maximum of five years of benefits, and states would still be required to spend at least 75 percent of their 1994 contribution to their welfare program to receive TANF funds.

Both bills also continued the existing prohibition on using federal TANF funds to aid most legal immigrants until they had been in the United States for at least five years.

HOUSE ACTION

The House passed the administration-backed bill, sponsored by Deborah Pryce, R-Ohio, by a vote of 230–192 on Feb. 13, 2003. House Republicans were so eager to move HR 4 that they brought it to the floor without any committee markups. GOP leaders said the arguments on both sides had been well vetted because more than twenty hearings had been held on the issue in the 107th Congress. They said they wanted to give the Senate enough time to pass a measure and allow a House-Senate conference.

Changes to the welfare law proposed in the bill included:

Work requirements. By 2008 recipients had to work, or engage in work-related activities, for forty hours per week, up from thirty. Of the total, twenty-four hours had to be spent in "direct work activities." The remaining sixteen hours could be used for education, drug treatment efforts, and other activities. Recipients with children under the age of six had the work requirements increased from twenty hours per week to twenty-four. Also by 2008 states had to increase the percentage of families engaged in work or work-related activities to 70 percent, up from 50 percent.

Child care. The bill recommended $2.9 billion a year over five years for mandatory child-care grants, a $200 million a year increase. It also proposed to increase the discretionary authorization for child-care funding by $200 million per year, reaching $3.1 billion by fiscal 2008.

Vocational education. The amount of time that vocational education could be counted as a work activity was reduced from twelve months to no more than four months over a two-year period.

Marriage counseling. The bill authorized $100 million per year over five years for matching grants to the states to "promote and support healthy, married two-parent families," and $100 million a year for research and other assistance. The plan was a priority for the administration.

Employment credit. The 1996 law allowed a state to reduce the 50 percent work requirement by the same percentage that it reduced its average monthly welfare caseload below fiscal 1995 levels. The White House said 58 percent of adults on welfare still had not found jobs, in large part because the caseload reduction credit created a loophole. The House bill altered the credit to reward job retention and increased earnings by those finding jobs, and cut the funding in half.

Democrats criticized the bill, saying it would hurt cash-strapped state governments and recipients competing for jobs at a time unemployment rates were touching eight-year highs. They argued that the House should be providing more money and greater access to education and job-training programs to help lead recipients out of poverty.

Republicans responded that the only way to lead the nation's 2 million welfare families out of poverty was through employment, even during an economic slump. "Democrats still don't trust people to make this vital transition to independence themselves," said Majority Leader Tom DeLay, R-Texas. "They just don't get the downside to dependency."

Before passing the bill, the House rejected Democratic substitutes by Dennis J. Kucinich of Ohio and Benjamin L. Cardin of Maryland to continue the existing thirty-hour-per-week work requirement, increase child-care funding, and make other changes. The amendments were rejected by votes of 124–300 and 197–225, respectively.

SENATE ACTION

The Senate Finance Committee approved a revised version of HR 4 on a straight party-line vote of 9–8 on Sept. 10 and reported it Oct. 3 (S Rept 108-162).

With just a one-seat GOP advantage on the committee, Grassley had to walk a fine line to get all nine Republicans on board. He included more-stringent work requirements for recipients in accordance with Bush administration wishes. But he also mollified holdout Republicans who wanted to preserve child-care assistance and job training programs that they said were working well in their states.

He sidestepped a dispute over expanded child-care spending by leaving it for floor debate. That prevented fiscal conservatives on the committee from objecting to billions of dollars in increased government spending. But Grassley promised Snowe that she could offer an amendment on the

floor to increase child-care funding by an additional $5 billion to $6 billion over five years.

That was approximately the level recommended in a 2002 welfare reauthorization bill that the committee approved when it was under Democratic control. Snowe and Orrin G. Hatch of Utah supported that bill—which is why Grassley had to tread so carefully to get his bill approved in 2003.

Democrats and Snowe said the amount in the House bill was inadequate to cover rising child-care costs, particularly at a time when many states were grappling with budget crises and cutting back some social services.

But some Republicans objected. "It's important to not just create a direct entitlement that anybody who wants child care, gets child care," said Rick Santorum, R-Pa. "Making people struggle a bit is not necessarily the worst thing."

Major provisions of the committee-approved bill included:

Work requirements. The number of hours welfare recipients were required to work would increase from thirty hours a week to thirty-four with at least twenty-four hours in core work activities. The remaining ten hours could include activities such as job searches, substance abuse programs, and education and training. An amendment offered by Snowe to allow postsecondary education and vocational training to count as work activities was adopted by voice vote. Recipients with children under age six would be required to work twenty-four hours per week. States would also be required to have at least 70 percent of recipients in jobs by 2008.

Marriage promotion. The bill provided $100 million a year in matching grants for marriage promotion and $100 million a year for research and other assistance. Democrats and civil liberties groups complained that the programs would infringe on private decisions and could induce people to stay in abusive relationships. "Marriage is a personal, private choice," said Baucus. "It's not something the government should interfere with." Republicans noted that children fared better when raised in a two-parent household, and that the program was voluntary and included measures to address domestic violence. "Marriage is the best institution for taking care of children," Santorum said.

Child care. The measure called for increasing mandatory child-care spending by $1 billion over five years.

During the markup the committee rejected, 10–10, a substitute offered by Baucus that consisted of the committee's 2002 bill.

The committee also rejected, 9–11, an amendment by Jeff Bingaman, D-N.M., to increase the mandatory funding authorization for child care by $11.2 billion over five years, offset by an extension of Customs user fees.

The bill finally reached the Senate floor March 29, 2004. But four days of sharp partisan debate later both sides decided to walk away with nothing—choosing instead to blame one another in an election year for jeopardizing efforts to improve one of the most fundamental transformations of social policy since the Great Society of the 1960s.

Republican leaders suspended debate April 1 after their motion to invoke cloture on the measure—which would have blocked Democratic amendments on a series of workplace and labor issues—failed by a vote of 51–47, nine votes short of the sixty needed.

Democrats had wanted to offer amendments to raise the federal minimum wage from $5.15 to $7.00 per hour; to overturn controversial Bush administration changes to overtime rules; and extend unemployment benefits.

Grassley thought Snowe's amendment—to boost additional funding for child care from the House bill's $1 billion to $6 billion over five years—would be adopted and serve as a sweetener to win Senate approval for the bill. He was half-right; Republicans and Democrats embraced it, but then refused to budge on whether to hold votes on the labor-related issues.

The White House came out against Snowe's proposal. The administration argued that because welfare caseloads had been cut by more than half since 1996 states had sufficient child-care funds. But Snowe's amendment gave senators from both parties a chance to make a statement in favor of children and families in an election year. The amendment was adopted on a **key vote of 78–20 (R 31–19; D 46–1; I 1–0)** on March 30. Grassley and Senate majority leader Bill Frist, R-Tenn., joined Snowe and twenty-eight other Republicans in breaking with the president to support the amendment. *(2004 key votes, p. 854)*

Head Start

A Bush administration plan to restructure Head Start ran into stiff opposition in 2003, slowing action on a bill to reauthorize the popular education, nutrition, and social service program for low-income preschoolers. House Republicans managed to pass a scaled-back version of the White House proposal by a single vote in July. A more bipartisan Senate bill won committee approval in October, but the measure never made it to the Senate floor and the effort died with the end of the Congress.

Members of both parties had reasons to back a new authorization—Republicans hoped to change the program's focus, Democrats wanted to expand its scope and reach—but bridging the partisan divide proved too difficult.

President George W. Bush called in February 2003 for Congress to reshape the $6.7 billion program. He proposed giving all fifty states the option of taking more control over Head Start and coordinating it with their other early childhood programs. He also said he wanted to move federal responsibility for Head Start from the Department of Health and Human Services (HHS) to the Department of Education to increase the emphasis on school readiness and improve coordination with other education programs.

Anticipating stiff resistance to the administration's plan, House Republicans in May introduced a five-year reauthorization bill (HR 2210) that dropped the idea of transferring the program to the Education Department. The concept of state control was reduced to a pilot program that would allow eight states to integrate their own preschool programs with Head Start. The bill also proposed that Head Start centers operated by church groups be allowed to hire staff on the basis of religious preferences, part of Bush's larger faith-based initiative, which had mostly stalled in Congress. *(Faith-based charities, p. 520)*

Democrats such as George Miller of California, ranking member on the House Education and the Workforce Committee, argued that the GOP approach would ultimately result in turning Head Start over to the states, gutting what was arguably the most popular legacy of President Lyndon B. Johnson's War on Poverty. Backed by early childhood education advocates, opponents launched an aggressive grassroots campaign to win support from moderate Republican members. Although sponsor Michael N. Castle, R-Del., rewrote the House bill twice in an effort to mollify GOP moderates, he still was able to muster only a bare majority for it when it reached the floor.

In the Senate, Judd Gregg, R-N.H., chair of the Health, Education, Labor, and Pensions (HELP) Committee, left the state pilot project out of his five-year draft bill because of opposition from key GOP committee members. The Senate bill (S 1940) also omitted the faith-based hiring provision. But Gregg did push another administration proposal for expanded assessment and testing of children in the program, mirroring education accountability measures that Bush spearheaded as governor of Texas.

Castle acknowledged that the state pilot project faced long odds. "Obviously, there is a lot of resistance to the state demonstration program," he said. "I'm a political realist. I'm not going to beat my head against the wall forever."

BACKGROUND

Established in 1965 as part of the War on Poverty (PL 89-253), Head Start was based on the premise that early intervention with disadvantaged children and their parents would improve their chances for academic success and family self-sufficiency. In addition to early childhood education, Head Start services included nutrition, health, and parent training. The program was federally funded but operated by local private and public agencies. *(Congress and the Nation Vol. II, p. 760)*

The last Head Start authorization, in 1998 (PL 105-285), was set to expire Sept. 30, 2003. The 1998 law stressed improving the quality of instruction, requiring that by Sept. 30 at least half of all Head Start teachers have an associate or bachelor's degree in early childhood education or a related field. It dedicated substantial funding to quality improvements, including better training. *(Congress and the Nation Vol. X, p. 491)*

Bush was not the first president to try to restructure Head Start. In 1978 President Jimmy Carter sought to transfer the program from HHS to the newly proposed Department of Education. The Reagan administration that followed Carter tried to transform Head Start into a block grant program. Both attempts failed because of staunch opposition from

Congress, backed by staff at Head Start centers and parents of children enrolled in the Great Society program.

While acknowledging Head Start's popularity, Bush and congressional Republicans argued that change was needed. They said that while the more than 900,000 children enrolled in Head Start were learning, they lagged behind their peers in math and literacy skills when they started elementary school. "Children in Head Start are learning—but they aren't learning as much as they deserve to be learning," said House Education and the Workforce Chair John A. Boehner, R-Ohio.

The White House argued that states were in the best position to coordinate early childhood education programs and tailor them to the curriculum that children faced when they entered elementary school. Bush's proposal to give states more control tracked with the administration's broader effort to transfer authority to the states for a variety of programs in areas such as Medicaid and welfare.

Democrats argued that Bush's plan amounted to a block grant that would remove federal control over the quality of the program and allow states to come up with a patchwork of standards that could weaken Head Start's role in helping disadvantaged three- and four-year-olds. They also worried that the new emphasis on literacy skills would come at the expense of health and nutrition programs. Democrats argued that the emphasis should be on expanding Head Start, which was serving only 60 percent of eligible children. They noted that its program for the children of migrant and seasonal workers served only 19 percent of eligible preschoolers.

The lead advocacy group fighting Bush's proposal was the Washington-based National Head Start Association, a private group that represented the staff and parents of children in the program. It established a Web site and mobilized vocal groups of parents and children for protests in local communities and on Capitol Hill.

HOUSE ACTION

A House Education and the Workforce subcommittee approved HR 2210 by a vote of 11–9 on June 12, 2003. The measure authorized $6.9 billion in fiscal 2004 and unspecified sums through 2008. Castle had been forced to rewrite the measure before the Education Reform Subcommittee markup in the face of criticism that it would turn Head Start into a block grant without federal standards.

Castle's original proposal would have allowed states generally to participate in a demonstration program that integrated state and federal early childhood education programs. The revised bill limited to eight the number of states that could take part in a five-year pilot program. Participating states could not make any budget cuts in their early childhood programs. A state's spending on Head Start or other prekindergarten programs would have to equal at least half of its federal Head Start funding.

The changes did not placate Democrats. Miller said the states would not have to abide by federal teacher quality standards or by a federal requirement that teachers assess children three times every year to evaluate their progress. Democrats also were upset over the provision to allow Head Start centers operated by faith-based groups to hire staff on the basis of religious preferences.

The Education and the Workforce Committee approved the bill on a 27–20 party-line vote June 19 after defeating several Democratic attempts to increase funding and expand eligibility for Head Start. HR 2210 was reported June 26 (H Rept 108-184).

The degree of polarization in Congress over Head Start became clear July 25 when House GOP leaders pulled out all the stops and still managed to pass the bill by only one vote. The **key vote was 217–216 (R 217–12; D 0–203; I 0–1).** *(2003 key votes, p. 837)*

To help ensure victory Majority Leader Tom DeLay, R-Texas, dispatched an aide to get John Sullivan, R-Okla., who was under doctor's orders for bed rest after a July 23 car accident damaged his eyesight. Sullivan, clad in a T-shirt, athletic shorts, sandals, and dark sunglasses, was pushed in a wheelchair by an aide into the chamber shortly before 1 a.m. and was helped to stand so he could vote. With twelve Republicans voting against the measure and no Democratic support, Republicans had to leave the vote open for ten minutes before they could claim victory.

All Democrats voted against the bill with the exception of two who were absent—Richard A. Gephardt of Missouri, who was seeking the Democratic nomination for president, and Ed Pastor of Arizona. Democrats repeated their argument that the program needed more money, not a remake. "It doesn't matter if you call it a block grant, a pilot program, a demonstration program, or an experiment—the bottom line is that it begins to dismantle Head Start," said Miller.

Castle had made more revisions before bringing the bill to the floor. In addition to the $6.9 billion for fiscal 2004, the bill specifically authorized $7 billion in fiscal 2005, $7.1 billion in fiscal 2006, $7.2 billion in fiscal 2007, and $7.4 billion in fiscal 2008. To participate in the eight-state demonstration program, a state would have been required to have school readiness standards in place in fiscal 2003. It would have had to fund all existing local Head Start centers for five years instead of three and ensure that all comprehensive health and nutrition services being provided at the time by Head Start would continue. The changes were made as part of the rule for floor debate.

An amendment by Rep. Lynn Woolsey, D-Calif., to remove the language that allowed hiring on the basis of religion was defeated, 199–231.

A broader Democratic substitute offered by Miller that would have removed the faith-based language and dropped the eight-state demonstration project was also rejected, 200–229.

Bill supporters had to argue their case alone because there was no significant outside lobbying effort for the measure. Connecticut governor John G. Rowland, a moderate Republican, was the only governor to say publicly that his state would apply for the pilot program.

Opposition to the bill was highly organized. Local chapters of the National Head Start Association bombarded undecided lawmakers' offices with calls and e-mail. The Head Start organization was joined by various other family advocacy and education groups. Democrat Donald M. Payne of New Jersey said he had never received as much constituent feedback as he did on this bill.

Catholic Charities USA, which served 20,000 children through Head Start, opposed the bill because of concern that state programs could make public schools the preferred providers for early-childhood education. The United Way of America, with extensive business backing, said Head Start's comprehensive services would not be guaranteed under the bill. The American Civil Liberties Union opposed the bill because of the hiring provisions.

SENATE ACTION

The Senate HELP Committee approved a five-year authorization bill, 21–0, on Oct. 29, 2003, and reported it Nov. 24 (S 1940—S Rept 108-208). Approval came only after a last-minute deal that eliminated language linking Head Start test results to funding levels. At least forty child advocacy groups had written to lawmakers warning that many schools would be unable to meet the new "outcome standards" in the bill and Democrats threatened to offer numerous amendments.

The standards would have required preschool students to master the alphabet, recognize numbers, and be able to measure lengths, weights, and time, among other things. Instead the revised bill directed the National Academy of Sciences to review the proposed outcome standards and make final recommendations.

The amended bill also authorized $7.2 billion for Head Start in fiscal 2005, $7.6 billion in fiscal 2006, and $8 billion in fiscal 2007.

Democrats still expressed concern over a requirement for "the regular assessment" of children, which they feared meant testing for three- and four-year-olds. HHS already had started a nationwide test to gauge basic literacy and math skills among four-year-olds in Head Start. Some Democrats wanted the bill to keep the HHS test as a pilot project.

Gregg ruled out the state pilot project after Republicans on his panel said they opposed it. Instead he accepted an idea from Lamar Alexander, R-Tenn., to establish 200 "centers of excellence" to help states coordinate their early childhood programs with local Head Start centers without actually taking over the federal programs.

Nevertheless, Senate Democrats blocked the bill from reaching the floor in the remainder of the 108th Congress. They were concerned that, if it were allowed to pass, Republicans in charge of the Senate-House conference committee would include the pilot project in the final bill, leaving Democrats powerless to stop it.

Chronology of Action on Veterans Affairs

2001–2002

After years of debate, lawmakers agreed in the 107th Congress to change a law that dated back more than a century and allow greater retirement benefits for some disabled veterans. Congress also cleared bills to create or expand a series of veterans' benefits and to set up emergency preparedness centers at Department of Veterans Affairs (VA) hospitals. But action on a veterans' health care package was left for the 108th Congress after lawmakers failed to reach agreement.

Disabled Retirees' Benefits

Congress in 2002 agreed to loosen restrictions on the retirement benefits of some disabled veterans, as part of the fiscal 2003 defense authorization bill (HR 4546-PL 107-314).

Veterans' groups had been fighting for years to overturn a law barring what was known as "concurrent receipt" of full retirement and disability benefits. Under the law, which had been on the books since 1891, any disability pay was deducted dollar-for-dollar from a veteran's retirement pay.

The Pentagon contended the military retirees with disabilities who qualified for pensions already received generous benefits, indexed for inflation, as well as lifetime health care. They said disability payments were intended to compensate veterans who left the military after a few years' service and did not qualify for full military pensions.

The debate had simmered for years, with Rep. Michael Bilirakis, R-Fla., and a small contingent of House allies pushing for the dual benefits with little success, regardless of which party was in control of Congress. The Senate, meanwhile, made it a standard practice to include concurrent receipt of benefits in the annual defense authorization bill, only to see House negotiators strike the provision in conference.

That began to change in 2002 when Congress agreed in HR 4546 to allow dual benefits for veterans whose disability resulted from combat wounds that earned them a Purple Heart or who were at least 60 percent disabled as a result of combat-related injuries. Controversy surrounding that decision delayed final action on the defense bill until after the November congressional elections. (*2003 defense authorization, p. 320*)

Veterans' Benefits

Congress cleared a veterans' benefits package (S 2237—PL 107-330) in 2002 that reflected a compromise between the House and Senate Veterans' Affairs committees on S 2237 and a series of veterans' bills that the House had passed earlier in the 107th Congress.

Among its main provisions, the compromise bill:

• Extended Department of Veterans Affairs (VA) health care eligibility to the surviving spouse of a veteran when the spouse remarried after age fifty-five.

• Expanded eligibility for special compensation for women veterans with service-related loss of breast tissue, including by mastectomy or radiation treatment.

• Shielded National Guard personnel from certain actions, such as evictions and foreclosures, if they were called up by a governor for a national emergency. Prior law protected only active-duty military.

• Expanded benefits for veterans with hearing loss.

• Permitted veterans to retain Veterans' Mortgage Life Insurance beyond age seventy.

REFERENCES

Discussion of veterans' programs for the years 1945–1964 may be found in *Congress and the Nation Vol. I*, pp. 1335–1373; for the years 1965–1968, *Congress and the Nation Vol. II*, pp. 453–460; for the years 1969–1972, *Congress and the Nation Vol. III*, pp. 537–548; for the years 1973–1976, *Congress and the Nation Vol. IV*, pp. 158–181; for the years 1977–1980, *Congress and the Nation Vol. V*, pp. 177–191; for the years 1981–1984, *Congress and the Nation Vol. VI*, pp. 613–625; for the years 1985–1988, *Congress and the Nation Vol. VII*, p. 633–644; for the years 1989–1992, *Congress and the Nation Vol. VIII*, pp. 625–637; for the years 1993–1996, *Congress and the Nation Vol. IX*, pp. 597–603; for the years 1997–2001, *Congress and the Nation Vol. X*, pp. 497–503.

Outlays for Veterans Benefits and Services

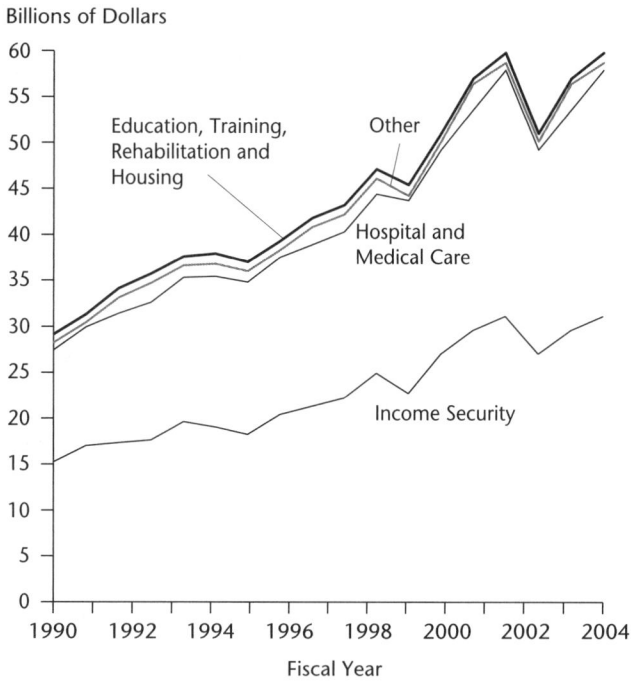

Billions of Dollars

SOURCE: Office of Management and Budget, *Historical Tables, Budget of the United States Government: Fiscal Year 2006* (Washington, D.C.: U.S. Government Printing Office, 2005), Table 3.2.

• Increased the annual benefit for Medal of Honor recipients from $600 to $1,000.

• Authorized the creation of a Battle of the Bulge memorial at Arlington National Cemetery.

Sen. Bill Nelson, D-Fla., temporarily slowed work on the bill in November 2002 to protest the deletion of a provision that would have made it illegal for companies to offer lump-sum cash payments in exchange for a veteran's monthly benefits checks. The lump-sum payments were smaller than the lifelong value of the benefits.

The Senate Committee on Veterans' Affairs reported S 2237 (S Rept 107-234) on Aug. 1, 2002, and the full Senate passed it by voice vote Sept. 26. The House passed the bill by voice vote Nov. 15, after inserting the compromise measure. The Senate cleared the bill by voice vote Nov. 18, and President George W. Bush signed it Dec. 6.

Emergency Preparedness

Congress in 2002 cleared a bill (HR 3253—PL 107-287) to authorize $100 million over five years to set up four centers where Department of Veterans Affairs (VA) doctors could plan the appropriate response to various kinds of terrorist attacks. Bill sponsors said VA doctors were uniquely qualified for this work because the health problems affecting veterans often were caused by the same kinds of toxins or the type of violence that could occur in terrorist attacks.

The four centers were to conduct research and develop detection, diagnosis, prevention, and treatment methods for chemical and biological agents, as well as serve as clearinghouses for information going to other health care providers. The VA also was directed to develop education and training programs on medical response to terrorist activities.

The bill gave the VA what Rep. James P. Moran, D-Va., said was "a formal role in the national disaster medical system" and authorized VA hospitals to treat first-responders, military forces responding to domestic attacks, and members of the public who were victims of a terrorist attack.

Implementation had to be delayed, however, until appropriators provided funds for the program, a step both Veterans' Affairs committee members and appropriators said would occur when the 108th Congress convened.

The bill was lobbed back and forth between the House and Senate beginning in May 2002. The House Veterans' Affairs Committee reported HR 3253 (H Rept 107-471) on May 16 and the full House passed it by voice vote May 20. The Senate passed an amended version by voice vote Aug. 1. The House agreed, with an amendment, by voice vote on Sept. 17. The Senate amended the bill again, passing what would be the final compromise version by voice vote Oct. 15 and the House cleared it the next day, also by voice vote. The bill was signed by President George W. Bush on Nov. 7.

Health Benefits

Veterans' health benefits legislation was approved by the House in 2002 but stalled in the Senate.

The House Veterans' Affairs Committee reported its veterans' health care bill on July 22, 2002, and the full House passed it by voice vote later that day (HR 3645—H Rept 107-600). The Senate Veterans' Affairs Committee approved its version (S 2043—S Rept 107-231) on June 6, but the bill went no further.

One of the major stumbling blocks was a House proposal to overhaul the procurement system of the Department of Veterans Affairs (VA) to institute national buying guidelines, instead of allowing each facility to negotiate its own pur-

chase deals. Senators argued that the plan was too ambitious and said it would be best to give the VA time to come up with its own more limited overhaul.

The Senate also objected to House proposals to require more oversight of research and educational companies that operated at VA facilities.

2003–2004

Veterans' groups and their supporters in Congress scored a number of successes in the 108th Congress. They won broader access to full benefits for disabled military retirees, got a significant boost in federal funding for veterans' health care, won tax benefits for service members and veterans, and got other changes in veterans' health care and benefits. "This probably reflects one of the most productive years we've had in terms of veterans' affairs," Bob Filner, D-Calif., a member of the House Veterans' Affairs Committee, said in 2003.

Disabled Retirees' Benefits

Lawmakers in 2003 agreed as part of the fiscal 2004 defense authorization bill (HR 1588—PL 108-136) to further liberalize benefits for some disabled veterans.

Members had begun in the previous Congress to loosen a law dating back more than a century that barred disabled veterans from receiving both full retirement and disability benefits—a practice known as "concurrent receipt." Legislation enacted in 2002 (HR 4546-PL 107-314) allowed full benefits for veterans whose disability resulted from combat wounds that earned them a Purple Heart or who were at least 60 percent disabled as a result of combat-related injuries. *(Background, 2002 action, p. 530)*

Emboldened by their success in 2002, veterans' and military organizations pushed to expand the provisions to all disabled retirees. Democrats jumped on the issue, arguing that Republicans should not be willing to send troops to war if they were not prepared to give them full benefits. Republicans said that expanding concurrent receipt to all retirees could cost up to $58 billion over ten years, breaking the budget.

In 2003 the Senate again included language in its version of the fiscal 2004 defense authorization bill to allow veterans with service-related disabilities to receive both benefits. By September House Democrats had 203 of the 218 signatures needed on a discharge petition to force floor action on a bill (HR 303) that offered the full dual benefit. In the end, House GOP leaders offered a plan to allow full dual benefits for retirees who were considered at least 50 percent disabled as a result of service-related injuries and to form a commission to study whether a redefinition of eligibility was necessary. The Senate quickly latched onto the proposal, which was included in the final version of the defense bill. *(2004 defense authorization, p. 337)*

For veterans with combat-related injuries, the program was to begin in January 2004. For other eligible veterans, it would be phased in over ten years. The estimated ten-year cost was $22 billion. The final bill also called for a commission to study whether a redefinition of eligibility was necessary.

Health Benefits

President George W. Bush signed a veterans' health benefits bill (S 1156—PL 108-170) into law Dec. 6, 2003.

As enacted, S 1156:

- Allowed the secretary of the Department of Veterans Affairs (VA) to enter into agreements with Medicare and Medicaid to expand health care options for veterans.

- Extended for five years the VA's authority to provide enrolled veterans with a range of noninstitutional extended care services.

- Allowed chiropractors to work in VA facilities.

- Increased the funds authorized for mental health services related to the treatment of posttraumatic stress disorder and substance abuse.

- Guaranteed health service to veterans who participated in chemical and biological tests between 1962 and 1973 regardless of whether they could prove their illnesses were related to the testing.

- Authorized $277 million for VA medical construction projects.

The Senate Veterans' Affairs Committee reported the bill (S Rept 108-193) on Nov. 10, 2003, and the full Senate passed it by voice vote Nov. 19. The House cleared it, 423–2, on Nov. 21.

Miscellaneous Benefits

Congress increased miscellaneous veterans' benefits as part of legislation (HR 2297—PL 108-183) signed by President George W. Bush Dec. 16, 2003.

As enacted, HR 2297:

- Allowed spouses of deceased veterans who remarried after age fifty-seven to receive certain benefits.

- Expanded grants to disabled veterans for house and car purchases.

- Provided increased benefits to children with spina bifida born to veterans who served in the demilitarized zone between North and South Korea between October 1967 and May 1975.

- Provided increased compensation to members of the Philippine Scouts and Philippine Commonwealth Army who served during World War II and became U.S. citizens or permanent residents.

The House Veterans' Affairs Committee reported the bill (H Rept 108-211) on July 15, 2003 and the full House passed it by a vote of 399–0 on Oct. 8. The Senate passed an amended version by voice vote Nov. 19 and the House cleared it by voice vote Nov. 20.

Civil Relief

President George W. Bush on Dec. 19, 2003, signed legislation (HR 100—PL 108-189) to clarify and update provisions of the Soldiers' and Sailors' Civil Relief Act of 1940. The act had last been revised in 1991 (PL 102-12).

Under the act, a service member whose military service limited his ability to repay a debt incurred before he entered the military could get the interest rate on the debt reduced to 6 percent. The new law required that any additional interest above 6 percent be forgiven and that monthly payments be reduced to reflect the new rate.

Under the prior law, eviction proceedings against a service member could be delayed for at least ninety days for a lease of less than $1,200 per month. That was doubled to $2,400 per month to reflect the increase in rental costs, with future increases tied to inflation. A new provision allowed service members who were being relocated or deployed for more than ninety days to terminate housing leases. *(Congress and the Nation Vol. VIII, p. 634)*

Other provisions gave those on active duty an automatic ninety-day stay of civil court proceedings and prevented cancellation of life insurance policies.

The House Veterans' Affairs Committee reported the bill (H Rept 108-81) April 30, 2003, and the full House passed it by a vote of 425–0 on May 7. The Senate passed it by voice vote Nov. 21, after substituting the text of a similar bill that had been reported by its Veterans' Affairs Committee Nov. 17 (S 1136—S Rept 108-197). Changes included the increase to $2,400 per month for eviction proceedings. The House accepted the amendments by voice vote Dec. 8, clearing the bill for the president.

CHAPTER 10

Education Policy

Education Policy

President George W. Bush made overhauling education the centerpiece of his 2000 presidential campaign and a top legislative priority of his new administration upon taking office in 2001. The focus of his proposal was accountability. He called for states to design and administer annual tests to measure student performance as a condition for receiving federal education money. Schools that repeatedly fell short of state-set standards would be subject to sanctions, such as being forced to divert a share of their federal funds to vouchers to pay for private schooling or tutoring for needy children.

A reauthorization of the Elementary and Secondary Education Act, known as No Child Left Behind (NCLB), became law in 2002. It contained the bulk of President Bush's education overhaul proposals, with the exception of his plan for government vouchers to use for private school tuition. Enactment followed bitter debate in Congress over the extent to which the federal government should go in influencing public school policy, which is determined primarily by the state and local governments that provide most education funding.

Two years after enactment the assessment of NCLB was mixed. Bush, at an appearance at a Knoxville, Tennessee, grade school, maintained that "as a result of strong accountability measures and good teachers and more funding, the results are positive." Acting deputy secretary of education Eugene Hickok, on the PBS program "Newshour," was more circumspect. He said, "[I]t's way too soon to say that this law has been fully implemented and had the impact we think it will have." (He did, however, go on to state that the school the president visited had shown improvement in test scores.) Meanwhile, Democrats claimed, among other things, that the program was significantly underfunded; did not allow for differences between schools, such as urban and rural, in the accountability process; and made finding qualified teachers too difficult.

In a move widely perceived as an effort to head off a campaign issue, the administration in 2004 announced changes to some NCLB standards. Most students with serious disabilities were allowed to be tested separately from the other students. Also, the testing requirements for limited English proficiency students were relaxed, making it easier for states to meet the law's targets. And schools in rural districts were given more leeway in deeming teachers highly qualified, as defined by NCLB.

SUGGESTIONS FOR CHANGE

The National Conference of State Legislators (NCSL) on Feb. 23, 2005, issued a report suggesting ways to improve implementation of No Child Left Behind. The report was based on the results of a ten-month study and was prepared by a special task force. NCSL sought improvements to the legislation through congressional and administrative action.

NCSL maintained that the goals of the legislation, improving the overall quality of education and narrowing the gaps in achievement, were not set at the federal level, but stemmed from work that was being done by the states. However, instead of freeing the states to pursue their educational goals, NCLB came to be seen as imposing restrictions that curtailed innovation and experimentation. New York state senator Steve Saland, co-chair of the task force, said, "[T]he federal government's role has become excessively intrusive in the day-to-day operations of public education. States that were once pioneers are now captive of a one-size-fits-all educational accountability system." A key recommendation, as

REFERENCES

Discussion of education policy for the years 1945–1964 may be found in *Congress and the Nation Vol. I*, pp. 1195–1215; for the years 1965–1968, *Congress and the Nation Vol. II*, pp. 709–733; for the years 1969–1972, *Congress and the Nation Vol. III*, pp. 581–604; for the years 1973–1976, *Congress and the Nation Vol. IV*, pp. 377–402; for the years 1977–1980, *Congress and the Nation Vol. V*, pp. 655–677; for the years 1981–1984, *Congress and the Nation Vol. VI*, pp. 555–580; for the years 1985–1988, *Congress and the Nation Vol. VII*, pp. 647–663; for the years 1989–1992, *Congress and the Nation Vol. VIII*, pp. 641–660; for the years 1993–1996, *Congress and the Nation Vol. IX*, pp. 607–634; for the years 1997–2001, *Congress and the Nation Vol. X*, pp. 507–549.

Outlays for Education

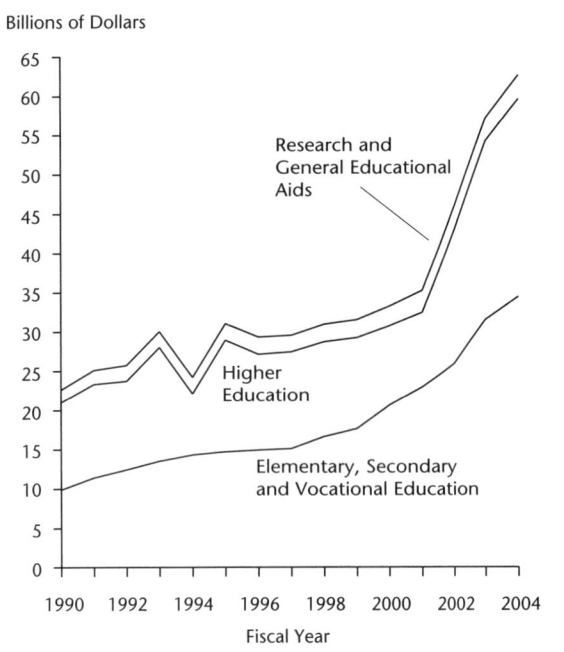

Billions of Dollars

Research and
General Educational
Aids

Higher
Education

Elementary, Secondary
and Vocational Education

Fiscal Year

SOURCE: Office of Management and Budget, *Historical Tables, Budget of the United States Government: Fiscal Year 2006* (Washington, D.C.: U.S. Government Printing Office, 2005), Table 3.2

cited in the executive summary of the report, was that "Congress should create a revitalized state-federal partnership that acknowledges diversity among states and shifts focus from processes and requirements to outcomes and results."

Of particular concern was NCLB's adequate yearly progress (AYP) provisions, which hold schools accountable for student performance as reflected in an objective measure of achievement, such as standardized testing. NCSL cited what it saw as methodological flaws in the requirements: "NCLB mandates that schools be evaluated by comparing successive groups of students against a static, arbitrary standard, not by tracking the progress of the same group of students over time. The AYP requirements constitute a 'static' evaluation model because they hold all schools, regardless of demographic factors and prior achievement levels, to the same benchmark. Standardized tests are far from perfect measures of student achievement and function better in combination with other measures, such as student portfolios." The report recommended that states be provided "much greater flexibility in meeting the objectives of the adequate yearly progress provisions"; be given "the option of adding or substituting a 'student growth' approach to testing and accountability, rather than the 'successive group' approach prescribed by NCLB"; and be allowed "to use multiple measures rather than relying exclusively on standardized tests to evaluate performance." Task force co-chair Steve Kel-

ley, a Minnesota State senator, remarked: "To say that only one measurement can be used to judge every school's effectiveness is not practical."

The report also called "counterintuitive and counterproductive" the law's requirement that students in a failing school be allowed to transfer to other schools before the school gets a chance to improve. Furthermore, the transfer option is not feasible in many urban and rural school districts.

Although NCSL applauded the fact that NCLB covered students with disabilities and limited English proficiency, the challenge to reach the required standards of achievement in accordance with the timetable set by the law seemed insurmountable. In addition, the task force pointed out a couple of contradictions: "NCLB requires students with disabilities to be tested by grade level, while [the Individuals with Disabilities Act] mandates that students be taught according to ability"; and "NCLB's definition of 'highly qualified' special education teachers conflicts with state certification practices."

In a similar vein, the task force expressed concerns with the often-special circumstances faced by urban and rural schools, which largely are not addressed by the law. For example, the heterogeneity of urban schools can make teaching more difficult, and the geographic isolation of rural schools can make offering supplemental educational services harder. The report recommended that states be allowed to deviate from the law to address "the unique conditions of urban and rural communities." These schools also have trouble attracting the kind of teacher required by the law—teachers who can prove content knowledge for every subject they teach. The task force recommended that states be permitted "to allow teachers who are teaching multiple subjects to be considered highly qualified based on a single means of evaluation" and "to establish conditions under which exceptions could be granted to the highly qualified teacher provisions."

Finally, the report highlighted the states' desire for a substantial increase in federal funding to cover "the costs of complying with the administrative processes of the law" and "a separate set of costs . . . to reach the law's standards of proficiency." Furthermore, the NCLS was concerned that the government, in effect, was coercing states to comply with No Child Left Behind and thus was violating "the spirit of a state-federal partnership to improve education." States were told that if they did not participate, they would forfeit Title I funds, which provide support for students qualifying for free or reduced-price school lunches, and "other formula and categorical funds for such programs as after school, drug free school, and literacy."

While education groups responded well to the report, the Bush administration was less impressed. U.S. Assistant Secretary for Elementary and Secondary Education Ray Simon said the report "could be interpreted as wanting to reverse the progress we've made. . . . Children must be challenged to reach their full potential, not told to settle for someone else's lowered expectations. No Child Left Behind is bringing new hope and new opportunity to families throughout America, and we will not reverse course."

THE FUTURE OF NCLB

Congress remained divided over how far the federal government should go in influencing school policy. Democrats believed the bipartisan collaboration seen during negotiations on No Child Left Behind had evaporated. In both the House and Senate, they complained that the Bush administration shortchanged funding in the law and had not provided enough flexibility for school districts to make the law work. For that reason, they were reluctant to cut any new deals with the administration. At the same time, conservatives wanted to limit further federal involvement in education policy, recalling the Republican revolution of the mid-1990s that preached the virtues of smaller government and advocated abolishing the Department of Education.

Andrew Rotherham, director of education policy at the Progressive Policy Institute and former Clinton administration domestic policy adviser, said members of Congress were most concerned about ensuring that NCLB was implemented properly and less inclined to expand its reach.

In early 2005 many of the nation's governors began reasserting themselves by attempting to raise standards in an area that NCLB did not specifically address—high schools. The governors, convinced that academic progress would translate into economic growth, weighed in just as the divided 109th Congress began contemplating another Bush initiative to expand the law to students through the eleventh grade.

Chronology of Action on Education

2001–2002

President George W. Bush wanted to use reauthorization of the Elementary and Secondary Education Act, the main source of federal aid to schools, as an opportunity to link the aid more directly to student and school performance. The resulting enactment, known as No Child Left Behind, emphasized annual testing of students. Rewards would be given to the best states and schools and penalties for the worst, along with annual report cards on the schools—the basis of a new accountability system.

Elementary and Secondary Education Act

In the most ambitious overhaul of the 1965 Elementary and Secondary Education Act (ESEA), Congress in 2001 cleared legislation (HR 1)—signed into law (PL 107-110) in early 2002—that for the first time tied federal education aid to improvements in students' test scores. The bill, dubbed the No Child Left Behind Act, required annual student testing and school improvements aimed at helping disadvantaged children catch up with their peers. It created consequences for schools with chronically low student test scores and offered children in those schools alternatives such as private tutoring and other services partly at public expense. The six-year bill authorized $26.3 billion for assistance to elementary and secondary schools in fiscal 2002, an increase of $8 billion over fiscal 2001.

BACKGROUND

Enacted in 1965 as one of President Lyndon B. Johnson's Great Society antipoverty programs, the Elementary and Secondary Education Act (PL 89-10) provided grants for several K–12 programs, most of them aimed at students from poor communities or at risk of failing their lessons or dropping out of school. *(1965 law, Congress and the Nation Vol. II, p. 720)*

Over the years other social issues became entangled in the debate on the education law. In 1988 the rewrite was almost killed over a bid to outlaw pornographic phone services. In the 1994 reauthorization President Bill Clinton sought to steer extra money to needy schools and stave off Republican calls to abolish the Education Department, while lawmakers battled over gun control and school prayer. *(1988 action, Congress and the Nation Vol. VII, p. 655; 1994 action, Congress and the Nation Vol. IX, p. 609)*

The next attempt to reauthorize the law, at the end of 1999, foundered on the upcoming presidential elections. In poll after poll voters said education was their top concern, but views on how to improve education varied widely. Finding little incentive for compromise, lawmakers used the issue largely to make political points. Republicans and Democrats were already far apart on what defined good education policy—less federal intervention for Republicans, school construction and other new programs for Democrats. In 1999 and 2000, House Republicans passed party-line bills, only to have them stopped in the more evenly divided Senate. As a stopgap solution, lawmakers funded ESEA programs for one year through the fiscal 2001 Labor, Health and Human Services, and Education appropriations law (PL 106-554). *(1999–2000 action, Congress and the Nation Vol. X, p. 531)*

HOUSE ACTION

The House Education and the Workforce Committee approved its five-year bill (HR 1—H Rept 107-63) on May 9, 2001, by a vote of 41–7. The bill was a delicate compromise worked out by John A. Boehner, R-Ohio, and George Miller, D-Calif. The deal, approved by voice vote May 2, assured Democratic support but left GOP conservatives complaining that their priorities were slipping away and that President Bush was not fighting for his principles. All but six Republicans supported the bill, though some said they did so only to give Bush a needed win.

The bill required states to set education standards and test all students in third through eighth grades annually in reading and math to measure progress in meeting the goals. Poor parents of children in failing schools could use federal money for additional tutoring through public or private programs, and local districts would get unprecedented flexibility in spending federal aid.

To get Democrats' support, Boehner agreed to a significant increase in authorized funding for education, including

EDUCATION LEADERSHIP

Houston, Texas, school superintendent Rod Paige was confirmed as secretary of education by voice vote Jan. 20, 2001. He would serve throughout President George W. Bush's entire first term.

Succeeding Paige was Margaret Spellings, who won Senate confirmation by voice vote on Jan. 20, 2005. She had been Bush's education adviser when he was governor of Texas and was the top domestic policy adviser in the Bush White House. (Background, cabinet profiles, p. 922)

a doubling of Title I aid to poor schools over five years. Total ESEA funding would grow from $18.6 billion to $22.8 billion. Title I funding would rise from $8.6 billion in fiscal 2001 to $17.2 billion in fiscal 2006.

Boehner also toned down a GOP proposal—known as "Straight A's"—that would let states spend federal funds for virtually any education purpose as long as they got better academic results. The compromise was to let school districts use up to 50 percent of federal funds for other educational purposes but otherwise leave the existing programs intact. Boehner also dropped a charitable choice provision in the Bush proposal that would have allowed faith-based after-school programs to receive federal funds without abandoning their religious content.

The one major conservative proposal Boehner left in the bill—to give poor parents of students at failing schools the option of using federal funds to help pay for private school tuition—turned out to be the easiest to knock out. Five Republicans joined all twenty-two Democrats to strip vouchers from the measure.

More than two dozen conservative groups, including the Family Research Council, Focus on the Family, the Eagle Forum, and the Traditional Values Coalition, announced they would not support the measure.

Boehner had to put the markup on hold May 3 to talk conservatives out of offering a Straight A's amendment, which Democrats said would blow apart the compromise.

Though the annual testing requirement remained in the bill, committee members on both sides were wary. In a close call, Betty McCollum, D-Minn., offered an amendment to strip out the testing, gaining enough support to indicate she might have a strong chance of winning. To prevent a crippling blow to Bush's education plan, Miller persuaded Mc-Collum not to ask for a roll-call vote, and Boehner declared the amendment defeated on a voice vote.

Democrats repeatedly pushed to dedicate and increase funding for individual programs (the opposite of the Straight A's approach), scoring some successes. In one case, the panel voted 35–5 to approve an amendment by Dale E. Kildee,

D-Mich., Carolyn McCarthy, D-N.Y., and Mark Souder, R-Ind., to maintain drug-abuse prevention and after-school programs as separate programs instead of consolidating them into a single block grant.

Bush said he would support a House floor amendment to restore vouchers, though his congressional liaisons made it clear he would declare victory even if the House bill remained as it was.

The House overwhelmingly passed the five-year, $22.8 billion ESEA reauthorization May 23 by 384–45. Although unhappy GOP conservatives and skeptical liberal Democrats were looking for reasons to bolt, in the end, only thirty-four Republicans, ten Democrats, and one independent voted against the package. Moderate Republicans aligned with most Democrats to rebuff a series of challenges, leaving the bill in the same basic form as when it emerged from the committee. That was the key to its success: in each instance, the bipartisan compromise remained intact, losing a few lawmakers from both ends of the political spectrum, but keeping everyone else in the fold.

The biggest challenge was an attempt by Peter Hoekstra, R-Mich., and Barney Frank, D-Mass., to strike the annual testing. Though it drew heavy support from conservative Republicans and liberal Democrats, the amendment was rejected, on a **key vote of 173–255 (R 52–166; D 119–89; I 2–0)**, on May 22. Hoekstra and Frank blamed their defeat on heavy lobbying by White House officials, including Chief of Staff Andrew H. Card Jr. and presidential adviser Karl Rove, to discourage conservative support for the amendment. (2001 key votes, p. 801)

Although conservative groups such as the Christian Coalition warned that Bush's state-based testing proposal could lead to national tests, the White House and its allies in the business community saw testing as the centerpiece of Bush's proposal. While only fifty-two Republicans and two independents voted to strike the testing, the amendment drew the support of 119 Democrats, including Minority Leader Richard A. Gephardt of Missouri, Minority Whip David E. Bonior of Michigan, and David R. Obey of Wisconsin, ranking member on the Appropriations Committee.

The biggest potential threat to the bill's bipartisan support was defused before it ever came to the floor. Bush persuaded Jim DeMint, R-S.C., not to offer an amendment that would have established a Straight A's demonstration program in seven states and twenty-five school districts. Although Senate Democrats had accepted similar language, their House colleagues said they would abandon their support for the bill if it were approved.

Republicans came close to losing Democratic support when they pushed through an amendment to allow two districts in each state to spend funds from four major programs however they chose. It was a provision many Democrats considered to be Straight A's under another name. The proposal, by Pat Tiberi, R-Ohio, and Michael N. Castle, R-Del., squeaked through 217–209 on May 22. The four programs were teacher quality, the Innovative Programs block grant, Safe and Drug Free Schools, and technology grants.

Majority Leader Dick Armey, R-Texas, on May 23 failed in two attempts to revive school vouchers. The first, to restore Bush's proposal to give vouchers to children in failing schools, was defeated 155–273. The second, which called for setting up five voucher demonstration projects, was defeated 186–241.

Conservative Republicans won some small victories, including a rider by Charlie Norwood, R-Ga., to allow school districts to suspend or expel special education students who brought weapons to school. It was adopted 246–181 on May 23. Under existing law, schools could suspend or expel a student with disabilities, but the school district had to continue providing education services to the student at home or in an alternative setting. Under the amendment, the services would not have to continue unless the state required such treatment of children without disabilities.

Van Hilleary, R-Tenn., won voice vote approval for a proposal to cut off federal funds to school districts that refused to let the Boy Scouts of America use their school facilities. The amendment was aimed at several school districts that were boycotting the Boy Scouts for excluding homosexuals as members and leaders.

Democrats suffered several defeats, including an attempt by Major R. Owens, D-N.Y., to send the bill back to committee to add money to renovate schools and to reduce class size by hiring more teachers, which was rejected 207–223 on May 23.

SENATE ACTION

The Senate Health, Education, Labor, and Pensions Committee had approved a seven-year reauthorization bill (S 1—S Rept 107-7) by 20–0 on March 8.

Crafted while Republicans still held the majority in the Senate, the bill included Bush's provisions to test students each year in grades three through eight in reading and math and launch a new reading program. But committee Democrats persuaded Republicans to steer extra federal money to the neediest schools and give states an additional year (four years instead of three) to begin the new tests. The bill included $400 million to help states develop the new exams.

Despite the bipartisan spirit, sharp differences emerged between Democrats and Republicans over how much leeway to give states in spending federal money and how many federal education programs should be consolidated. Democrats chafed at their inability to add more money to the bill and said their support might not come so easily on the Senate floor if the funding was not increased.

Christopher J. Dodd, D-Conn., lost, 10–10, on an amendment to increase Title I funding by $3.8 billion a year, giving it enough money to serve all eligible low-income children by fiscal 2008. Democrats said the $8.6 billion for Title I in fiscal 2001 was only enough to reach about a third of eligible low-income children. The committee's bill already included a major increase, boosting the authorization to $15 billion in fiscal 2002. Dodd's amendment would have increased that to $37.7 billion in fiscal 2008. Committee Republicans, who had agreed to the $15 billion figure in negotiations with Democrats when the bill was being drafted, refused to go any higher without a commitment to more state and local flexibility.

Democrats also lost party-line votes in the evenly divided committee on proposals to increase funding to hire more teachers and renovate schools. The committee defeated, 10–10, amendments by:

• Patty Murray, D-Wash., to authorize $2.6 billion for schools to reduce class sizes.

• Edward M. Kennedy, D-Mass., to reserve $1.5 billion for teacher training. The bill instead called for $3 billion for class-size reduction and teacher training.

• Tom Harkin, D-Iowa, to authorize $1.6 billion for school renovation.

Conservatives expressed disappointment that the bill contained neither vouchers nor a charter states proposal that would let some states use federal education money for any purpose as long as they achieved better results.

Judd Gregg, R-N.H., offered, then withdrew, an amendment that mirrored Bush's campaign-trail proposal for private school vouchers. The money would go to children in low-performing public schools, but Democrats said it would only remove aid from schools that needed the most help. Bill Frist, R-Tenn., offered and withdrew an amendment similar to Bush's block grant proposal that would give states greater latitude in spending funds in exchange for improving performance. Both Frist and Gregg promised their amendments would resurface on the Senate floor.

After six weeks of floor debate, the Senate passed HR 1 on June 14 by an overwhelming vote of 91–8, after substituting the amended version of its own bill. The Senate-passed HR 1 would authorize $33 billion for ESEA programs in fiscal 2002, compared with the $22.8 billion in the House-passed legislation. It provided for a demonstration program negotiated with the administration and included in the manager's amendment to the bill to give seven states and twenty-five school districts broad powers to spend federal funds as long as test scores improved.

The Senate added $8.8 billion in mandatory spending for fiscal 2002 ($181 billion over ten years) for programs under the 1975 Individuals with Disabilities Education Act (IDEA, PL 94-142). The amendment, by Harkin and Chuck Hagel, R-Neb., was adopted by voice vote May 3. It required full funding of IDEA within six years. The program, which was being funded at $16.3 billion, would get an additional $2.5 billion a year until it covered 40 percent of state and local special education costs, the goal set in the 1995 law. *(IDEA, Congress and the Nation Vol. IV, p. 389; IDEA reauthorization, p. 547)*

Also on May 3 the Senate agreed to authorize a $132 billion increase over ten years to make sure Title I aid to poor schools reached all eligible children. The amendment, by Dodd and Susan Collins, R-Maine, was adopted 79–21.

An attempt by Larry E. Craig, R-Idaho, to limit the funding increase to schools that were improving their test scores was rejected May 8 by a vote of 27–73.

Mary L. Landrieu, D-La., subsequently added a requirement that Congress target any new Title I funds specifically to school districts with the highest concentrations of poor children. The vote, on June 11, was 57–36. Landrieu said she wanted to highlight the fact that Title I money often did not reach the poor schools it was supposed to help. Use of old formulas allowed the funds to continue to flow to districts that were no longer poor.

Bush and his conservative Senate allies were again rebuffed on the issue of private school vouchers. Democrats beat back an attempt by Gregg to create a demonstration program that would allow public school students in three states and ten school districts to use federal money for transportation to other public schools, such as charters, or tuition at a private school. The amendment was rejected 41–58 on June 12.

The Senate did adopt by voice vote an amendment by Gregg and Thomas R. Carper, D-Del., to authorize $125 million in grants to help communities that allowed children in underperforming schools to attend better public schools.

Attempts to delay or defer the testing provisions also were defeated. An amendment by Jean Carnahan, D-Mo., to defer testing if the federal government did not provide the full authorized funding was rejected 43–55 on June 7. Paul Wellstone, D-Minn., lost a similar bid to defer testing until Congress provided a $24.7 billion maximum for the bulk of Title I programs for poor students. The amendment was rejected 23–71 on June 7.

The Senate on May 3 did adopt 93–7 a proposal by James M. Jeffords, R-Vt., to allow states to suspend testing if Congress did not appropriate at least $370 million in fiscal 2002, rising to $430 million in fiscal 2008, to offset the costs.

The Senate rejected two amendments by Dodd that Republicans said were deal-breakers. The first, to require states to even out the financing disparities between rich and poor school districts, was rejected, 42–58, on June 12. The second, to exempt after-school programs from a block grant demonstration program, was rejected 47–51 on June 13.

Conservatives logged some victories. The Senate adopted an amendment by Jeff Sessions, R-Ala., to allow schools to expel disabled students for bad behavior. The proposal initially failed on a 50–50 tie vote, but a procedural lapse gave it new life. No one tabled the motion to reconsider the vote, a common practice. The Senate then agreed 51–47 to reconsider the amendment and adopted it by voice vote June 14. Harkin argued that Sessions' amendment, which was similar to language in the House bill, would "turn the clock back and segregate these kids." Harkin's alternative, which would have allowed schools to expel students only if their behavior was not related to their disability, was rejected on June 14 by 36–64.

The Senate also fought over, and ultimately approved, an amendment by Jesse Helms, R-N.C., to cut off federal aid to districts that refused to let the Boy Scouts use school facilities because of the group's refusal to admit gays. It was adopted, 51–49, on June 14. However, the Senate adopted by voice vote an amendment by Robert C. Byrd, D-W.Va., to specify that the Helms proposal applied to "patriotic societies," including the Boys and Girls Clubs of America and Little League Baseball Inc. Byrd said the original language was so broad that it could have shielded hate groups as well. Barbara Boxer, D-Calif., then succeeded in adding language that would give the groups equal access to school facilities regardless of their policies toward homosexuals—without threatening the loss of federal funds if school districts violated the policy. Her amendment was adopted 52–47 on June 14.

FINAL ACTION

Nearly five months after they began work, House and Senate conferees agreed to a final version of the ESEA reauthorization bill Dec. 11. The House adopted the conference report (H Rept 107-334) 381–41 on Dec. 13. The Senate cleared the bill 87–10 on Dec. 18.

House Republicans kept all plans to make special education funding mandatory out of the final conference report. Democrats struggled to retain the plan, hoping it would free up more discretionary spending for ESEA programs, particularly Title I. Kennedy and Miller were especially eager to carve out the extra money after appropriators agreed to limit the actual increase for education in fiscal 2002 to $3.5 billion, instead of the $10 billion increase they were urging.

The final bill authorized $13.5 billion in fiscal 2002 for grants for disadvantaged children, more than double the fiscal 2001 appropriation. The bill authorized increasing amounts for each of the succeeding five years, reaching $25 billion in fiscal 2006.

Conferees agreed to require that states design and administer annual tests within four years or lose a small portion of federal money. To verify the results, states also were required to give a national independent test to a sample of children. States had to set a standard test score for proficiency and get all children to that level in twelve years. Schools that consistently failed to reach state goals would lose some federal money and much of their autonomy.

House GOP leaders, long proponents of states' rights and local control, wanted to give school districts the flexibility to shift up to half their federal education money among education programs of their choosing. The Senate, concerned about local governments diluting the intent of federal programs, such as bilingual education, opted for a demonstration project that would limit flexibility to seven states and a handful of school districts. Negotiators agreed to combine elements of both approaches: all states and school districts could shift small portions of their federal grant money from one program to another, though money directed to the poorest children could not be diverted. A pilot program would let seven states and up to 150 local districts shift more of their federal money among programs as long as test scores improved.

Conferees agreed to allow the Education Department to continue to issue grants for programs designed to prevent hate crimes. Some Republicans had argued to end federal aid to programs that taught children about hate crimes, amid

Sen. Edward M. Kennedy, D-Mass., oversees Senate education legislation as the new floor manager after Democrats took control of the Senate in May 2001. The No Child Left Behind Act, signed into law January 8, 2002, featured requirements for annual student testing in math and reading as well as increased aid to disadvantaged children. *Source: Congressional Quarterly/Scott J. Ferrell*

concerns that government money was used to portray some religious groups as bigots.

MAJOR PROVISIONS

The following are major provisions of HR 1, signed into law (PL 107-110) on Jan. 8, 2002.

Testing, Accountability

The bill made states responsible for administering annual standardized tests, collecting and reporting test scores by schools and overseeing the corrective actions required for schools that fail to make annual progress in meeting state standards. Previous law did not require annual testing.

Annual reading and math tests. By the 2005–2006 school year, states were required to begin administering annual, statewide reading and math tests for grades three through eight. States could select and design their own tests, which had to be in line with state academic standards.

Science tests. By the 2007–2008 school year, states were required to begin giving annual statewide science tests to one grade within each of the three levels of a K–12 education: elementary, middle and high school.

National Assessment of Educational Progress (NAEP). States were required to give a sample of fourth and eighth graders the NAEP in reading and math every other year. The tests, often called the nation's report card, would be a benchmark for verifying the results on state-administered tests.

Funding. The law authorized $400 million for fiscal 2002 to help states pay for developing and administering their annual tests. The federal government would pay the cost of giving the NAEP tests; $69 million was authorized for fiscal 2002. States could delay or interrupt for one year their annual testing schedules for each year that Congress failed to appropriate the testing funds. No federal rewards or sanctions would be based on test results.

Report cards. Test results would be reported by race, income, disability status, and other categories with an aim toward identifying and helping any groups of children who were falling behind. Beginning with the 2002–2003 school year, states and school districts were required to provide annual report cards with a range of information, including scores broken down by subgroups. Existing report cards had to be changed to comply with the law.

Academic progress. States could set their own definition for academic proficiency, but they had to reach the goal for all students within twelve years. States could not set the minimum bar for proficiency below the performance of the lowest-achieving student group or schools at the time of enactment. States were to pace themselves by raising the bar for students incrementally.

Safe harbor. The law provided a safe harbor for schools in which particular groups of students had not technically made annual progress under the law. As long as schools could show that those students were making significant progress toward proficiency, the schools would not be deemed to be failing under the law.

Other measures of achievement. States were also required to find another way of measuring school progress besides the math and reading test scores. For high schools, that measurement had to include graduation rates.

Two years of failure. Schools that failed to make progress for two consecutive years would get technical assistance. The neediest children at those schools would be given the choice of attending another better-performing public school. The school district would have to use up to 5 percent of its administrative funds under the Title I program for disadvantaged students to provide transportation for students who chose schools in other districts.

Three years of failure. Schools that failed to make progress for three straight years would have to expand school choice options by offering parents supplemental educational services, including private tutoring. The district would have to use up to 5 percent of its Title I money to pay for that option. The district could use an additional 10 percent of its Title I money to pay for public school transportation costs or supplemental services.

Four years of failure. Schools that failed to make adequate progress for four consecutive years would be subject to corrective actions by the district. Such actions could include replacing certain staff members or adopting a new curriculum.

Five years of failure. Schools that failed to make adequate progress for five consecutive years would be "reconstituted."

They could be turned over to state control, or closed and re-opened as a charter school—a public school that operates with public money but is free of many of the rules for traditional public schools.

Already failing schools. Schools identified as failures under previous law had to begin giving students the option of attending another public school in the fall of 2002.

Disadvantaged Children

The law authorized $13.5 billion in fiscal 2002 for the largest program within ESEA (Title I), which focuses federal money on the poorest districts and neediest children, including funds for teachers, lessons, and special programs. Rules and funds for testing and reading programs also fall under this section. The law defined "disadvantaged children" to include those who are American Indian; are from poor families; speak little or no English; are disabled, neglected, or abused; or are from migrant-worker families.

Targeting funds. The law made minor changes to formulas used to compute grants for all school districts. For instance, Puerto Rico would receive money to place its schools more on par with states. States with smaller populations received an increase in the minimum amounts they could receive. States that strive to distribute their own funds more equally throughout the state instead of using property tax-based formulas would also receive targeted aid. For the first time, Congress appropriated money for that aid: $1 billion for targeted grants and $793 million for education finance incentive grants.

Teacher Training and Development

The law consolidated the class-size reduction and Eisenhower professional development programs into a single teacher quality program, authorized to receive $3.6 billion for fiscal 2002. The funds could be used to hire new teachers to limit class sizes, train special education teachers or principals, and create incentives to schools and districts that improve their teacher workforce.

'Highly qualified' teachers. All states were required to employ only "highly qualified" teachers by the end of the 2005–2006 school year. The law defined highly qualified teachers as those who have been certified or licensed by a state and have demonstrated through a test or other means that they are highly competent in the subjects they teach. Highly qualified teachers could take alternative routes to certification, including mid-career training that does not require a graduate degree in education.

Teachers' aides. Within three years, all paraprofessionals, or aides, hired with federal funds had to have completed at least two years of college, have an associate's or higher degree, or have reached a high-quality standard that has been locally established.

Liability protection. The law protected educators from legal liability for undertaking "reasonable actions" to maintain order and discipline in the classroom. Educators were

protected as long as their actions did not include the commission of a crime.

Troops to Teachers. The law continued the Troops to Teachers program, which encouraged retired military personnel to become teachers.

National Writing Project. The law continued the main federal program aimed at improving writing, which trained educators to teach writing more effectively at 164 sites in the fifty states, the District of Columbia, and Puerto Rico.

Math and science education. Authorized to receive $450 million in fiscal 2002, the new program aimed to encourage states, colleges, districts, and schools to form partnerships to improve student performance in math and science.

Teaching of traditional American history. This new grant program was aimed at teaching American history in a course separate from general social studies curricula. Congress did not authorize a specific amount for the grants program.

Reading

Reading First. This new program, authorized to receive $900 million in fiscal 2002, was intended to help states and districts create reading programs for children in kindergarten through third grade. States could use up to 20 percent of the money to train teachers, among other options.

Early Reading First. This new program, authorized to receive $75 million in fiscal 2002, was aimed at helping children ages three to five prepare to read. Roughly thirty thousand preschoolers nationwide were expected to benefit, including children in impoverished areas.

Even Start. The law authorized $260 million for the program, aimed at helping young children as well as their parents develop better reading skills. The program was named after retired representative William F. Goodling, R-Pa. (1975–2000), former chair of the House Education and the Workforce Committee.

School Technology

Several education technology programs were consolidated into a single technology grant program, authorized to receive $1 billion in fiscal 2002. Programs allowed under the law ranged from helping poor and rural students get computer access to training more teachers. Districts were required to use at least 25 percent of the money to help teachers become proficient in technology unless they could show that they already provided such training.

Ready-to-learn television. The law continued the 1994 public television Ready to Learn program, a daily commercial-free broadcast of educational shows such as "Clifford the Big Red Dog" and "Reading Between the Lions."

Bilingual Education

The law consolidated several bilingual education programs into one, authorized to receive $750 million in fiscal 2002. Students with limited English skills had to be tested in reading and language arts in English after they attended school in the United States for three consecutive years. Some children could receive a two-year waiver, on a case-by-case basis. The new law ended a requirement that 75 percent of federal bilingual education funds be spent on programs that use a child's native language for instruction.

School Safety

The program, authorized to receive $650 million in fiscal 2002, helped states and districts improve safety and reduce drug use in schools. Activities receiving money had to be based on scientific research.

Hate crimes. The Education Department was to continue to issue grants for programs designed to prevent hate crimes.

21st Century Community Learning Centers. The program, authorized to receive $1.25 billion in fiscal 2002, paid for activities before and after school. Under the new law, in addition to school districts, other community groups, including faith-based groups, could receive the funds.

Gun-free schools. The law included several changes to the existing requirement that students who brought guns to school be expelled for one year. The punishment was made to apply to anyone caught with a gun at school, whether or not he was the one who brought it. It also clarified that the term "school" meant the entire school campus, any setting under the control and supervision of the local school district. It also required that all modifications of the terms of a student's expulsion be put in writing.

Environmental tobacco smoke. The law banned the use of tobacco in government facilities that house programs for children, including schools, kindergartens, and day care facilities.

Flexibility

The law allowed school districts and states to transfer certain federal funds to a variety of programs that paid for their most-pressing needs, such as hiring more teachers or buying new books, in exchange for meeting certain performance goals.

Innovative Education Program strategies. The program, authorized to receive $450 million for fiscal 2002, provided block grants to states for innovative approaches to helping students learn. However, states had to send at least 85 percent of the money to districts. The law added school repair and other projects to the list of items on which the money could be spent.

Transferability. Districts were allowed to transfer up to 50 percent of the money to several major education programs. However, funds could be transferred into, but not out of, the Title I program for poor and otherwise disadvantaged children. States could transfer up to 50 percent of state activity funds to several major education programs.

Flexibility demonstration. A new demonstration project would give some school districts and states even more flexi-

bility in spending federal dollars. The law allowed 150 districts to consolidate all of their funding under major education programs in exchange for an annual Education Department review of their student performance. Money for Title I was excluded. Seven states could consolidate all their administration and state activity funds for major education programs. Title I money was included.

Other Provisions

Boy Scouts. No school or district could deny the Boy Scouts, or any other group listed as a "patriotic society," the same access to schools for after-school meetings as other outside groups.

Public charter schools. The program, authorized to receive $300 million in fiscal 2002, helped states and local districts support charter schools. Support included money for buildings and research.

Fund for the Improvement of Education. The law authorized $550 million in fiscal 2002 for projects and programs deemed to be nationally significant by the education secretary. The wide range of programs included those for character education, Reading is Fundamental book distributions to poor children, activities for gifted and talented students, foreign language lessons, physical education, arts education, and economics education. Congress also earmarked dozens of local projects in this program.

Rural education. The law authorized $300 million in 2002 for two programs. The first gave small, rural districts more latitude in spending federal money; the second provided flexible grants to rural districts with at least 20 percent of students living in poverty.

Indian education. By 2004, schools funded by the Bureau of Indian Affairs had to be accredited or be in the process of obtaining accreditation by an approved agency, state, or tribal.

Impact aid. The law made minor changes to the method of distributing funds to school districts that lost tax money because they were on federal land, such as military bases and American Indian reservations. The law authorized $150 million in fiscal 2002 for school construction. The entire impact aid program was reauthorized in a separate law (PL 106-398) in 2000. *(2000 law, Congress and the Nation Vol. X, p. 535)*

School prayer. The Education Department was directed to provide guidance to states, districts, and the public on constitutionally protected prayer in public schools. The guide had to be revised every two years. All school districts had to prove that their local policies did not restrict such prayer or lose federal aid.

Military recruitment. Schools that received federal education funds had to provide military recruiters the same access to students allowed for college and job recruiters.

2003–2004

Lawmakers struggled during the 108th Congress to reauthorize the Individuals with Disabilities Education Act, which guaranteed special needs children a free public education and provided federal funding to states and school districts. A major matter of contention was a proposal to change discipline policies by allowing schools to treat disabled students in the same manner they would their nondisabled peers for any violation of school rules, without determining whether the offense was the result of a disability. The final bill mandated stronger certification standards for special education teachers and denied funding to states if their local school districts did not comply with bill provisions.

A controversial proposal to create a private school voucher program in Washington, D.C., was enacted into law. Republicans had long sought to implement voucher programs. Proponents said vouchers would give underprivileged children the same educational opportunities as their wealthier counterparts. Opponents argued that public money should be used solely to fund public schools.

IDEA Reauthorization

HR 1350, reauthorizing for five years the Individuals with Disabilities Education Act (IDEA), the main federal education program for the nation's more than six million disabled students, became law (PL 108-446) in 2004.

IDEA, originally enacted in 1975 (PL 94-142) and last rewritten in 1997 (PL 105-97), was as much a civil rights law as an education package. Its primary aim was to guarantee that special needs children be able to obtain a free, "appropriate" public education in the "least restrictive environment." *(1975 law, Congress and the Nation Vol. IV, p. 389; 1997 law, Congress and the Nation Vol. X, p. 515)*

Each child receiving services under IDEA had to have an individualized education program (IEP) spelling out the specific special education and related services that were to be provided. A parent was required to participate with the team that planned and oversaw the implementation of the IEP.

Program funding had been a perennial sticking point in IDEA reauthorization. The original law authorized the federal government to reimburse states for as much as 40 percent of the average additional per pupil cost of educating every child with a disability. But Congress never came close to meeting that level. In fiscal 2004, for example, it provided $10.1 billion, covering just 19 percent of costs. School administrators complained that the federal contribution put local districts in a bind because the costs of educating special needs children were much higher than for nondisabled students. Supporters of mandatory funding contended that making the law an entitlement program was the only way to guarantee that Congress would reach 40 percent in an era of increasing budget deficits. The mandatory designation also would free the program from the funding pressures of the annual appropriations process.

HOUSE ACTION

The Education Reform Subcommittee of the House Education and the Workforce Committee approved HR 1350 by voice vote April 2, 2003. The subcommittee chairman, Michael N. Castle, R-Del., decided against including a pilot program that would allow disabled students to use vouchers to attend private schools at state expense. The voucher program, a pet issue of GOP conservatives, was offered in a separate bill (HR 1373) that saw no action.

During markup, the subcommittee rejected 9–11 a Lynn Woolsey, D-Calif., amendment to make the funding mandatory and reach the 40 percent funding level within six years. Adopted by voice vote was an amendment by Woolsey and Jim DeMint, R-S.C., to allow parents to use IDEA funds in the setting of their choice until their child reached kindergarten. Existing law allowed such an option for parents of children under three. The amendment would provide parents with basic protections under IDEA regardless of where they sent their child to preschool. Also adopted by voice vote were several modifications by Castle, including postponing the elimination of short-term benchmarks in IEPs until the 2005–2006 school year. By that time all districts were required to use new report cards under the overhaul of the Elementary and Secondary Education Act (HR 1—PL 107-110), known as No Child Left Behind (NCLB). *(Education act, p. 540)*

The House Committee on Education and the Workforce approved HR 1350 by 29–19 on April 10. The bill was formally reported (H Rept 108-77) on April 29.

The full committee rejected another attempt by Woolsey to make the funding mandatory and set authorization levels to reach 40 percent in six years. The party-line vote was 22–26. The panel adopted by voice vote a Jon Porter, R-Nev., amendment to continue the program's discretionary funding but authorize an additional $2.2 billion for fiscal 2004 and $2.5 billion for fiscal 2005, allowing an increase to 21 percent of the per pupil cost by 2004. The committee rejected 22–26 a John F. Tierney, D-Mass., amendment to restore the requirement that, before removing a special education student from the classroom for more than ten days, the school hold a hearing to determine whether the action was related to the child's disability. Democrats argued the amendment would ensure the schools did not expel an epileptic child for accidentally hitting another student during a seizure or punish a child with Tourette's syndrome from involuntarily shouting out in class. By voice vote the panel did adopt an amendment by Max Burns, R-Ga., to prohibit school officials from requiring parents to medicate their children before school.

The House passed HR 1350 by 251–171 on April 30. Democrats complained of being shut out of the debate, citing House Republican leaders' refusal to allow a floor vote on converting the program's discretionary funding into an entitlement program. The rule for floor debate (H Res 206), which limited the amendments, was adopted 211–195.

Before final passage on April 30, the House adopted 413–0 a David Vitter, R-La., amendment to mandate that the General Accounting Office (GAO) review of IDEA include recommendations to reduce paperwork requirements for teachers. The amendment also required a GAO report on the review every two years. The House rejected 182–240 an amendment by DeMint to allow states to use federal funds to set up programs for disabled children to attend private schools. Also rejected by a 176–247 vote was a Marilyn Musgrave, R-Colo., amendment to allow school districts to give the parents of disabled children in private schools up to $1,400 to be used for the children's education needs. Tom Tancredo, R-Colo., offered an amendment to define "special learning disability" as a disorder resulting from a medically detectable and diagnosable psychological condition relying on physical and scientific evidence. It was rejected 54–367.

Many districts complained that they had to spend heavily to defend themselves against questionable lawsuits by parents of special education students. Disability advocates argued that they were forced to file such claims only when educators failed to carry out requirements under the law. The House-passed bill allowed governors to set the attorneys' fees in their states for IDEA cases in which the parents prevailed. Parents would have one year to file complaints.

The bill allowed ten states to set up demonstration projects aimed at reducing paperwork. It also limited the frequency with which IEPs would be required to once every three years.

HR 1350 applied standards in NCLB to special education teachers in middle and high school. It also prevented children from being mislabeled special education students when they had a problem with only one skill, such as reading. (*Education law, p. 540*)

The bill authorized an additional $2.2 billion for fiscal 2004 and another $2.5 billion in fiscal 2005. In addition it set a course to reach the 40 percent funding level within seven years. But the measure did not set specific authorization levels beyond 2005.

SENATE ACTION

The Senate passed HR 1350 95–3 on May 13, 2004, after substituting the text of S 1248, which had been reported from the Senate Committee on Health, Education, Labor, and Pensions (S Rept 108-185) on Nov. 3, 2003.

During floor consideration of S 1248, Tom Harkin, D-Iowa, and Chuck Hagel, R-Neb., offered an amendment to provide mandatory $2.2 billion increases over the next six years to reach the 40 percent threshold. (The Senate approved a similar amendment in 2001 during consideration

of the Elementary and Secondary Education Act, but it was dropped in conference.) Because the amendment did not propose offsetting cuts to compensate for the mandatory funding it would require, the language was subject to a budgetary point of order that required sixty votes to overcome. The 56–41 vote on the amendment, which took place on May 12, 2004, fell four votes short.

Instead, the Senate on May 12 adopted 96–1 a Judd Gregg, R-N.H., amendment to authorize discretionary funding to reach the 40 percent mark by 2011, a provision similar to the funding mechanism in the House-passed bill. The Gregg amendment authorized $12.4 billion for IDEA grants in fiscal 2005.

IDEA allowed schools to remove special education students from classrooms for as long as forty-five days only for serious offenses, such as possession of a gun. The Senate-passed version would add serious bodily injury to the suspension list. Parents who disputed a discipline decision could obtain an appeal hearing within twenty days of a request. The bill did not change the existing law requirement that school officials consider whether a disciplinary infraction was a result of a child's disability.

The Senate May 12 by voice vote approved a Gregg amendment to allow school districts to recover attorneys' fees when parents filed a frivolous lawsuit alleging that their disabled child received inadequate schooling. The amendment clarified that the parents would not be responsible for the cost. The Senate-passed bill gave parents a two-year limit for filing complaints after an incident in which a school allegedly failed to uphold the law.

On May 13 the Senate adopted by voice vote a Rick Santorum, R-Pa., amendment to permit as many as fifteen states to obtain waivers from the Education Department to create demonstration projects to reduce the paperwork they were required to file. To ease parents' concerns Santorum's amendment mandated that states could not waive civil rights protections in their quest to reduce recordkeeping. The bill allowed issuance of IEPs to be made less frequently only for those students between the ages of eighteen and twenty-one.

Under NCLB, all public school teachers have to be certified by their states as "highly qualified" in the subject areas that they teach. Many special education teachers worried that they would have to be certified in many different categories even though they could serve in only an advisory role to the regular classroom teacher in that subject.

The bill clarified that special education teachers working in middle and high schools would not need certification in every subject they teach, as long as they provided only a consulting role to the regular classroom teacher. As more disabled students were placed back in regular classroom settings, a special education teacher could play a greater consulting role by adjusting the curriculum to the student's individual needs and ensuring that the appropriate accommodation were available for the child in the classroom. The bill also provided an exemption to special education teachers who teach primarily children with a significant cognitive disability such as mental retardation or autism.

FINAL ACTION

Senate Democrats delayed sending the IDEA reauthorization bill to conference until fall, so that President Bush would not be handed a legislative accomplishment before the election. Conferees agreed on a compromise just before the end of the November lame-duck session.

The final bill maintained the existing requirement that administrators must consider disabilities when disciplining special education students, dropping a House provision that would have treated disabled students the same as nondisabled peers for any violation of school policy. The bill allowed the Education Department to issue waivers to as many as fifteen states to reduce paperwork requirements. In addition, fifteen states would be allowed to develop a three-year IEP for students. Short-term objectives would be provided only for children with the most significant disabilities. It also mandated stronger certification standards for special education teachers by the end of the 2005–2006 school year and denied funding to states if their local school districts did not comply with bill provisions.

The measure authorized $12.4 billion to help state pay for special education programs in fiscal 2005, with the amount increasing until it reached $26.1 billion in fiscal 2001. The amount appropriated for fiscal 2005 (HR 4818—PL 108-447) was $10.7 billion.

The House adopted the conference report (H Rept 108-779) on HR 1350 by a 397–3 vote Nov. 19, 2004. The Senate adopted the report by voice vote the same day, completing congressional action. The bill was signed into law on Dec. 3.

D.C. School Vouchers

Congress in 2003 created the nation's first federally funded private school voucher program. The action came in the form of an amendment to the fiscal 2004 District of Columbia appropriations bill (HR 2765) to authorize subsidies for low-income students in D.C. to attend private schools. The bill subsequently became part of an omnibus spending package (HR 2673—PL 108-199).

House and Senate negotiators on HR 2673 approved $14 million for federal vouchers to allow D.C. students to attend private schools, including those run by religious organizations. Students whose parents earned up to 185 percent of the poverty level would be eligible for vouchers of up to $7,500 annually, with priority going to children in poorly performing schools. If the number of eligible applicants exceeded the available vouchers, a lottery would be held to select the recipients. The bill included a provision authorizing the program for five years. The measure also provided $26 million in extra funding evenly divided between public schools and charter schools.

President Bush and GOP congressional leaders said vouchers were an educational lifeline for underprivileged children, particularly minorities, in failing schools. Bush initially asked for voucher funding for several cities, but Republican leaders dropped that plan, prompting critics to accuse lawmakers of conducting experiments in the District that they would not try in their home states. Critics, including teacher unions and school administrators, also argued that taxpayer fund should go only to public schools and that private schools that would benefit from the vouchers would not be held to the same requirements.

Congress in 1998 cleared legislation providing for a D.C. voucher program, but President Bill Clinton vetoed the bill. (*Congress and the Nation Vol. X, p. 528*)

HOUSE ACTION

The House D.C. Appropriations Subcommittee on July 9, 2003, by voice vote approved a draft bill laying out fiscal 2004 District spending. In an initial vote of confidence for the voucher plan, the bill included $10 million in federal subsidies for private school tuition. It did not contain extra money for public or charter schools, however. Authorization for the vouchers was included in a separate bill (HR 2556) that the House Government Reform Committee approved 22–21 on July 10.

The House Appropriations Committee approved HR 2765 (H Rept 108-214) by voice vote July 15 and formally reported the measure two days later. The panel rejected 24–32 a Chaka Fattah, D-Pa., amendment to switch the $10 million for vouchers to an existing city schools program. Also failing to gain approval was a Fattah amendment to hold up funding for the voucher program until the Education Department certified that 90 percent of public school students in the city were being taught by a "highly qualified" teacher as defined by the overhaul of the Elementary and Secondary Education Act (PL 107-110) and that educational materials in the District were comparable to those in top schools around the metropolitan region. (*Education act, p. 540*)

The full House took up HR 2765 on Sept. 5, but GOP leaders abruptly interrupted floor action after barely prevailing on a pair of voucher-related amendments. In both cases, they kept the voting open for several minutes after voting time expired to round up enough voucher supporters to keep the plan alive.

The first of the amendments, sponsored by Thomas M. Davis III, R-Va., added a section authorizing the voucher program. It was adopted on a **key vote of 205–203 (R 201–14; D 4-188; I 0-1).** The second, by Del. Eleanor Holmes Norton, D-D.C., stripped out the $10 million in funding for the program. It failed on a 203–203 tie. (*2003 key votes, p. 837*)

With Democrats ready to use a seldom-invoked parliamentary procedure to obtain a second vote on the Davis amendment, Republicans postponed further voting to avoid losing a second cliffhanger. When the House returned to the bill on Sept. 9, the Davis amendment was reconsidered. The leadership prevailed 209–208, but only by holding the vote open for an extra twenty-five minutes to retrieve John Linder, R-Ga., from a party for his sixty-first birthday to cast the tie-breaking vote.

The House passed HR 2765 on Sept. 9 by 210–206.

SENATE ACTION

The Senate Appropriations Committee had approved its version of the bill (S 1583—S Rept 108-142) on July 17, 2003, by 22–7, pending any amendments that might subsequently be adopted. Chair Ted Stevens, R-Alaska, suspended the markup before the bill was finished, after it appeared that a proposal by Richard J. Durbin, D-Ill, to strip the voucher program might prevail. The panel did not complete the bill until Sept. 4, after Republicans won support from Dianne Feinstein, D-Calif., to keep the voucher program.

The committee agreed to authorize the D.C. vouchers as well as to appropriate money for them. It allocated $13 million apiece for vouchers, public schools, and charter schools and $1 million for administrative costs, brining the total to $40 million. The committee adopted, 16–12, an amendment by Feinstein and D.C. Appropriations Subcommittee Chair Mike DeWine, R-Ohio, to increase the D.C. mayor's role in designing the program and to require voucher recipients to take achievement tests comparable to those given in public schools.

Following a seven-week stalemate over school vouchers, GOP leaders agreed to drop the provisions. The Senate passed the bill by voice vote Nov. 18. By then it was clear that the measure would be part of negotiations on an omnibus bill, where Republicans could restore the voucher plan.

The Senate had begun debating the bill on Sept. 24, with Republicans hoping to reach a compromise on vouchers that could win over enough moderates to overcome a filibuster. DeWine negotiated behind the scenes with his panel's ranking Democratic, Mary L. Landrieu of Louisiana, and with Thomas R. Carper, D-Del. The Democrats proposed, among other things, to limit vouchers to students in failing schools, require that recipients be evaluated using the same tests as students who continued in public schools, and ensure that those teaching voucher recipients would have college degrees. DeWine said the two sides got close to an agreement, but he could not guarantee that the changes would get through conference. The talks subsequently stalled.

The Senate considered the bill again Sept. 29–30, but Republicans still lacked the votes to invoke cloture, and Majority Leader Bill Frist, R-Tenn., decided to pull the measure from the floor. During debate Sept. 25 Feinstein won voice vote approval for her proposal to tighten accountability and testing requirements in the voucher program.

Higher Education Act

President George W. Bush on Oct. 25, 2004, signed into law (HR 5185—PL 108-366) a one-year extension of the Higher Education Act, providing about $70 billion in grants and loans for college tuition.

The extension would provide lawmakers additional time to complete a rewrite of the education law, which was last updated in 1998 (PL 105-244). *(Congress and the Nation Vol. X, p. 509)*

House Education and the Workforce Committee Chair John A. Boehner, R-Ohio, introduced HR 5185. The House agreed by voice vote on Oct. 6 to suspend the rules and pass the measure. The Senate passed HR 5185, also by voice vote, without amendment on Oct. 9, thus clearing the bill.

Boehner had sponsored another reauthorization measure (HR 4283), which was stalled by opposition from traditional public and private colleges and universities. They objected to changing the rules in ways that favored for-profit institutions, saying it was not in the public interest to subsidize these companies with federal aid so they could expand their facilities and course offerings.

College Loan Subsidies

Congress in 2004 cleared legislation (HR 5186) to eliminate for one year a federally backed college loan subsidy that allowed some lenders to earn unusually large profits. The bill was signed into law (PL 108-409) on Oct. 30.

HR 5186 suspended, through the end of fiscal 2005, language first enacted in 1980 as part of the Higher Education Act reauthorization (PL 96-374) that provided a subsidy to lenders who sold tax-exempt bonds to finance the loans they made to people in college. The subsidy effectively guaranteed those lenders a 9.5 percent return on the federally backed loans they extended, which constituted a huge markup, given that the current market rate for such loans was about 3.5 percent. *(Congress and the Nation Vol. V, p. 672)*

The House Oct. 7, 2004, agreed 414–0 to a John A. Boehner, R-Ohio, motion to suspend the rules and pass HR 5186. Lawmakers said they hoped to permanently eliminate the subsidy in the 109th Congress through a long-term reauthorization of the Higher Education Act.

The Senate Oct. 9 by voice vote passed the bill without amendment, clearing the measure.

Though Democrats did not oppose the measure, they complained that the Bush administration did not act quickly enough to end the subsidy. Democrats added that the Republican-written legislation left an exemption for lenders who "recycle" payments on existing loans to create new ones that still would qualify for the higher return. Nonprofit leaders succeeded in lobbying Congress not to restrict this recycling because, they said, they passed on the subsidy to their borrowers through programs such as loan forgiveness and lower interest rates.

Edward M. Kennedy of Massachusetts, the top Democrat on the Senate Health, Education, Labor, and Pensions Committee, supported the legislation, but he vowed to push for additional changes. He said the student loan program would remain flawed until older borrowers were required to refinance their student loans at current market rates.

Republicans countered that Democrats had held up a GOP reauthorization bill (HR 4283) of the Higher Education Act, which included provisions to end the subsidy. They said recycled loans amounted to a small proportion and were mostly used by nonprofit lenders who turned profits from the subsidy into additional aid for students. *(Higher Education Act, p. 550)*

Students and their families do not bear the cost of the subsidy; taxpayers do. The White House said the cost to the Treasury could exceed $4.9 billion over ten years.

Reps. Dale E. Kildee, D-Mich., and Chris Van Hollen, D-Md., sponsored a bill (HR 5113) to end the subsidy entirely and apply the saving to boosting the maximum amount of Pell grants for low-income college students. HR 5113 died upon adjournment.

Tuition for D.C. Students

Legislation (HR 4012), cleared in 2004, would extend for two years a program providing tuition aid to District of Columbia students who wanted to attend public colleges elsewhere in the country. The bill was signed into law (PL 108-457) on Dec. 17.

Since 1999 the District of Columbia Tuition Assistance Grant program (PL 106-98) helped make up the difference between in-state and out-of-state tuition costs for District students attending public colleges outside the city. (Unlike each of the fifty states, the District had no state-subsidized university system.) Students paid the equivalent of in-state tuition and the grants made up the difference, up to $10,000 per year. *(Grant program, Congress and the Nation Vol. X, p. 547)*

In addition to public colleges and universities, the program provided for students to attend private schools in the Washington metropolitan area and private historically black colleges and universities nationwide. Students also could receive grants of up to $2,500 a year to attend Washington area schools or black colleges. The program had provided roughly $63 million in tuition assistance to more than sixty-five hundred students.

The House Committee on Government Reform reported HR 4012 (H Rept 108-527) on June 8, 2004. The House agreed by voice vote July 14 to a Thomas M. Davis III, R-Va., motion to suspend the rules and pass the bill.

The Senate Governmental Affairs Committee reported HR 4012 (no written report) on July 22. The panel reported a Senate version of the measure (S 2347—S Rept 108-349) on Sept. 20. The committee had adopted an amendment to S 2347 by Sen. George V. Voinovich, R-Ohio, limiting the reauthorization to five years instead of making it permanent. The change made the two bills identical.

During floor consideration of HR 4012, the Senate on Nov. 24 adopted an amendment, proposed by Mitch McConnell, R-Ky., for Voinovich, to reduce the extension to two years. The Senate passed the bill by voice vote the same day. The House on Dec. 6 agreed by voice vote to a Davis motion to suspend the rules and accept the Senate changes, thus clearing the bill.

The fiscal 2005 appropriations bill for the District of Columbia (HR 4850—PL 108-335) included $25.6 million for the tuition grants.

School Lunch Programs

Congress in 2004 cleared legislation (S 2507) reauthorizing the school lunch programs and other federal meal plans. The bill was signed into law (PL 108-265) on June 30.

The House Education and the Workforce Committee on March 10, 2004, voted 42–0 to approve HR 3873 and formally reported it (H Rept 108-445) on March 23. The panel had defeated 18–25 an amendment by Tim Ryan, D-Ohio, to allow the agriculture secretary to set nutritional standards for all foods sold on school campuses. Under existing law, the secretary could regulate only food sold in school cafeterias. The secretary's authority had been limited since 1983, when PepsiCo Inc. successfully sued to overturn a regulation prohibiting sale of foods with "minimum nutritional value" in schools during the school day. Such foods were defined as those providing less than 5 percent of the daily requirement of eight nutrients. Republicans said the amendment would have infringed on the rights of parents and school officials.

HR 3873 also required schools to develop "wellness policies" setting standards for nutrition education and physical activity and to establish guidelines for food sold on campus. According to the Center for Disease Control and Prevention, since 1980 the overweight population doubled among youths ages six to eleven and tripled in adolescents ages twelve to nineteen.

The House on March 24 agreed to a John A. Boehner, R-Ohio, motion to suspend the rules and pass the bill. The vote was 419–5.

The Senate passed its version (S 2507) by voice vote June 23. The legislation had been reported (H Rept 108-279) from the Senate Agriculture, Nutrition, and Forestry on June 7. The House passed S 2507, without amendment, by voice vote June 24, clearing the measure.

Vocational Education

A House committee and a Senate panel in 2004 reported legislation to rewrite the nation's main vocational education program to emphasize training in order that students could meet the demands of a high-tech workplace.

The House Committee on Education and the Workforce formally reported HR 4496 (H Rept 108-659) on Sept. 7. The measure, sponsored by Michael B. Enzi, R-Wyo., reauthorized and renewed the Carl D. Perkins Vocational and Technical Education Act of 1998 (PL 105-332), which provided state grants for career and technical education. The grants made available vocational education courses for many low-income students, from those in high school to adults who were changing careers. *(Congress and the Nation Vol. X, p. 513)*

The Senate Committee on Health, Education, Labor, and Pensions formally reported S 2686 (S Rept 108-382) on Oct. 4. Unlike the House bill, S 2686 did not merge the Perkins state grant program with the Technical Prep program, which provided specialized math and science training to make it easier for high school students to transfer to a vocational school or a community college. Some lawmakers complained that the Tech-Prep program was implemented poorly and duplicated more traditional vocational education programs.

The bills went no further in the campaign-shortened legislative year.

CHAPTER 11

Housing and Urban Aid

Housing and Urban Aid

When Republicans gained the majority in both the House and Senate in 1995, they proposed to eliminate the Department of Housing and Urban Development (HUD). That plan never came to fruition, and talk of phasing out the department was not picked up by the George W. Bush administration. However, generally speaking, housing policy and urban aid issues were not a top priority for President Bush. Meanwhile, reflecting past trends, too little money was available to fund HUD as richly as its advocates wanted. Tightening the purse strings further, following the Sept. 11, 2001, terrorist attacks, the administration, according to HUD secretary Mel Martinez, sought to perform "a strong balancing act" between spending on regular programs and homeland security. Reflected in the debate to allocate funding was the continuing struggle between the competing ideologies of Republicans and Democrats.

Although housing and urban aid issues were not on the front burner, the administration did have some goals for setting housing policy. One goal was to increase homeownership, particularly amongst minorities. To that end, the president in 2003 signed into law the American Dream Downpayment Act, which would help first-time, low- and moderate-income home buyers afford down payments and closing costs. According to Sen. Wayne Allard, R-Colo., the bill's sponsor, "only 47 percent of African-American and Hispanic families own their homes, as compared to 75 percent of white families." The purpose of the legislation was to close that gap. However, while the act authorized $200 million a year in grants to states, the fiscal 2004 appropriations fell far short of that mark. The National Low-Income Housing Coalition (NLIHC) lauded the Bush administration for seeking to close the gap between minority and non-minority homeownership. At the same time, the group was concerned that the emphasis on homeownership came at the expense of those who lived in rental housing. NLIHC claimed that the administration proposed inadequate funding, for example, for Section 8 vouchers.

Another stated goal of the administration was "ending the most chronic forms of homelessness for those living with a mental illness, addiction, or disability." The administration estimated there were between 100,000 and 200,000 people without a home for long periods of time or on many occa-sions. Bush called for consolidating several federal housing programs and transferring the Federal Emergency Management Agency's Emergency Food and Shelter Program (EFSP) to HUD. As described by the United Way of America, EFSP "meets the needs of hungry and homeless people and those at risk of becoming homeless due to emergency and/or economic downturn by allocating federal funds to supplement the work of local agencies providing food, shelter, and utility assistance." United Way claimed that "[a]dvocates for poor and homeless people" objected to moving EFSP to HUD, "as it would dramatically alter the identity and efficacy of a program that has remained fast, efficient, and effective for 20 years." The National Alliance to End Homelessness said the administration did not provide adequate funding to reduce chronic homelessness and maintain housing for former homeless people who had already made the transition. Congress did not act to transfer EFSP to HUD.

The administration approached housing policy with an eye toward weeding out what it considered ineffective and duplicative programs. As a result, it proposed eliminating funding for the HOPE IV program in the fiscal 2004 budget. The program was supposed to demolish dilapidated public housing projects and replace them with affordable housing. Despite its widely acknowledged inefficiencies, the program

REFERENCES

Discussion of housing and urban aid action for the years 1945–1964 may be found in *Congress and the Nation Vol. I*, pp. 459–515; for the years 1965–1968, *Congress and the Nation Vol. II*, pp. 183–226; for the years 1969–1972, *Congress and the Nation Vol. III*, pp. 635–657; for the years 1973–1976, *Congress and the Nation Vol. IV*, pp. 471–502; for the years 1977–1980, *Congress and the Nation Vol. V*, pp. 429–448; for the years 1981–1984, *Congress and the Nation Vol. VI*, pp. 629–639; for the years 1985–1988, *Congress and the Nation Vol. VII*, pp. 667–684; for the years 1989–1992, *Congress and the Nation Vol. VIII*, pp. 663–700; for the years 1993–1996, *Congress and the Nation Vol. IX*, pp. 637–650; for the years 1997–2001, *Congress and the Nation Vol. X*, pp. 553–567.

Outlays for Community and Regional Development

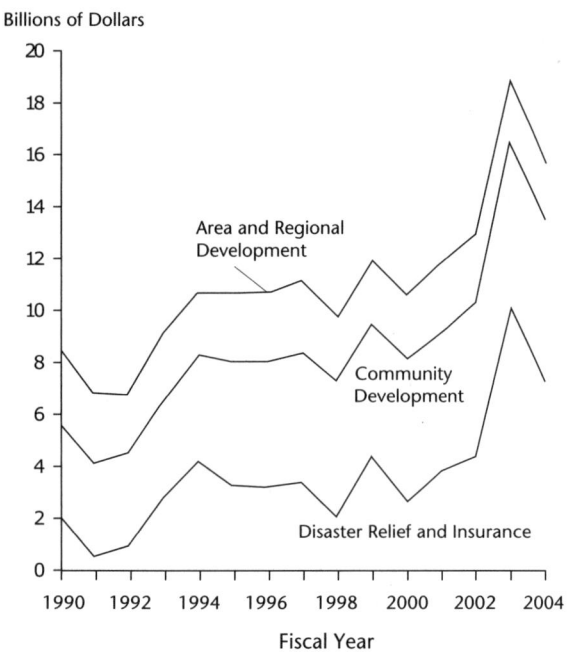

Billions of Dollars

SOURCE: Office of Management and Budget, *Historical Tables, Budget of the United States Government: Fiscal Year 2006* (Washington, D.C.: U.S. Government Printing Office, 2005), Table 3.2.

was popular with local officials. The administration failed in its effort to eliminate the program, but funding was dramatically cut back. HOPE IV had received $574 million in fiscal 2003. Its appropriation dropped to $150 million in fiscal 2004; $144 million in fiscal 2005. Members said the funding, while reduced, kept the program alive and sent a signal to the White House that they did not want it scrapped.

Democrats in Congress fought proposed cuts in housing programs throughout Bush's first term. They faced a new challenge in 2004 from, they believed, the National Aeronautics and Space Administration (NASA). Democrats charged that low-income and affordable housing programs were being tapped to pay for the president's proposed moon and Mars missions. Of the fiscal 2005 HUD appropriations, Barney Frank of Massachusetts, ranking Democrat on the House Financial Services Committee, said, "It's bad. It's not the disaster that the administration wanted, but it's part of a slow and steady decline in affordable housing." For the administration, Frank said, "HUD is a piggy bank to fund other

priorities." The administration was helped in its effort to secure a large increase for NASA, covered by the same legislation that funded HUD, by House minority leader Tom DeLay, R-Texas. Many of DeLay's constituents were employees of the Johnson Space Center in Houston, Texas. Administration officials denied that cuts in the housing agency were related to NASA's budget.

Some lawmakers urged Congress to exercise greater control over mortgage financing giants Federal National Mortgage Association (Fannie Mae) and Federal Home Loan Mortgage Corporation (Freddie Mac). Fannie Mae and Freddie Mac were created by Congress as government-sponsored enterprises (GSEs). They played a special role in the housing market—financing about 46 percent of all the home loans issued in the United States. Even though they became publicly traded companies seeking the highest returns for their investors, they benefited from one holdover from their days as quasi-governmental entities: they each had a line of credit with the U.S. Treasury. The availability of that emergency cash allowed investors to believe the federal government would bail out either company in the event of a financial crisis. Critics warned that this perceived guarantee allowed Fannie Mae and Freddie Mac to take on too much risk. Others, however, cited regulators who said they saw no immediate risk of financial disaster on the horizon. They rejected the argument that the taxpayers would be on the hook if either giant suffered a serious crisis as well as the idea that such a circumstance would jeopardize the housing finance system. Furthermore, they worried that the wrong kind of regulator could undermine the ability of the companies to expand ownership among the poor and middle class.

In a letter dated June 28, 2004, seventy-six Democratic House members urged President Bush to work with Congress on legislation regarding housing-related GSEs. They expressed their concern with the administration's public criticisms of GSEs and with what they saw as a negative image of GSEs being fostered by the White House. During a Senate Banking Committee hearing on April 7, 2005, Treasury secretary John Snow said, "The risks undertaken by the GSEs, if not properly managed, may pose a threat to . . . [the] solvency [of Fannie Mae and Freddie Mac], the stability of the other financial institutions and the strength of our economy." The administration had failed to back congressional efforts to increase oversight of the lending institutions, saying the legislation did not go far enough. The disagreement over how to set limits on the mortgage lenders was ongoing.

Chronology of Action on Housing and Urban Aid

2001–2002

Rent-to-Own Contracts

The House by 215–201 on Sept. 18, 2002, passed HR 1701, stipulating that states would lose their ability to cap the interest rates on rent-to-own contracts. The House Financial Services Committee approved the bill by 29–9 on June 27, 2002, and formally reported it (H Rept 107-590, Part I) on July 18. The House Judiciary Committee, which shared jurisdiction, reported the measure (H Rept 107-590, Part II) on Sept. 9.

During debate in Financial Services Republicans argued that a need existed for a single national standard while Democrats urged flexibility to let states handle the issue as they saw fit. Rep. Melvin Watt, D-N.C., said that rent-to-own agreements on furniture, appliances, and other high-ticket items were "inherently intrastate transactions" on which the panel was "trying to impose an interstate system." He said, "There is no federal interest here."

Bill sponsor Walter B. Jones, R-N.C., called the committee-approved measure "a win for both consumers and business." He offered an amendment, approved by the panel, to prohibit merchants from imposing a balloon payment or special fee to acquire ownership of an item at the end of a rent-to-own agreement and to prohibit merchants from charging more than one late fee per delinquent payment. The amendment also prohibited merchants from requiring customers to waive legal claims as part of the agreement or entering a customer's property without permission. It blocked states from characterizing rent-to-own agreements as credit transactions.

Consumer groups said that distinction was crucial because businesses engaged in credit transactions could be required to meet state usury regulations and finance charge limits. In a letter, consumer groups said that the bill's sole purpose was to "preempt strong laws in Minnesota, New Jersey, North Carolina, Wisconsin, and Vermont." Bill cosponsor Jim Maloney, D-Conn., however, said the legislation would not preempt state laws.

During floor debate the House on Sept. 18 rejected a John J. LaFalce, D-N.Y., amendment to limit the cost of a product bought through a rent-to-own contract to twice its cash price. The vote was 184–232. At least half of every periodic payment made by a consumer would go toward ownership of the product. The formula for determining a product's cash price would be derived by the Federal Reserve and would be based on the approximate standard retail price adjusted by special costs related to rent-to-own transactions. The same day, the House also rejected by a 157–255 vote a Maxine Waters, D-Calif., amendment to prohibit merchants from making consumers liable for loss, damage, or destruction of property in rent-to-own contracts except in cases of intentional or negligent conduct.

Before the vote on passage Waters offered a motion to recommit the bill to the House Financial Services Committee with instructions to strike provisions that would preempt more stringent state laws on rent-to-own contracts, including those that would treat such agreements as credit transactions subject to Truth in Lending Act requirements. The motion was rejected 190–227 on Sept. 18.

Brownfields

The House June 4, 2002, by voice vote agreed to suspend the rules and pass HR 2941, which would make it easier for communities to clean up contaminated industrial sites through a Department of Housing and Urban Development (HUD) program. The bill, reported (H Rept 107-448) from the House Financial Services Committee on May 8, would eliminate a requirement that neighborhoods secure a Community Development Block Grant Section 108 loan guarantee to obtain HUD grants to clean up the sites, known as brownfields. It also would authorize the HUD program through 2007 at "such sums as necessary" each year.

The United States had approximately 500,000 brownfield sites. The urban industrial and commercial sites are contaminated, but not polluted enough to qualify for coverage under the superfund hazardous waste cleanup program. As a result, Congress has been seeking to remove liability and other obstacles to restoration of those areas. Earlier in 2002, lawmakers cleared a measure (HR 2869—PL 107-118) to provide liability protection for those who buy brownfield sites. The law also modified and expanded the EPA cleanup program. *(Brownfields details, p. 481)*

HR 2941 required HUD to consider what other federal money a community has received and whether it had been used to encourage private developers to clean up and redevelop brownfields. It also expanded HUD's definition of brownfields to include mine-scarred lands.

The Congressional Budget Office estimated the measure's cost at $96 million over five years.

Low-Income Home Ownership

The House Financial Services Committee on July 10, 2002, by voice vote approved legislation (HR 3995) to aid some municipal workers seeking to become homeowners and create a new voucher program for low-income renters. The bill authorized funds for a laundry list of federal housing laws. It also established a program to help teachers, police, and firefighters to make down payments on homes in the communities in which they work.

HR 3995 was formally reported (H Rept 107-640, Part II) on Sept. 17. (The bill had been jointly reported from the House Judiciary Committee (H Rept 107-640, Part I) on Sept. 4.)

On a 33–28 vote June 20, following an emotional partisan debate, Financial Affairs adopted an amendment by Bernard Sanders, I-Vt., Barbara Lee, D-Calif., and Steve Israel, D-N.Y., to establish a national trust fund for the construction and rehabilitation of affordable housing. Knowing that Republican leaders—who opposed the use of Federal Housing Administration revenue for that purpose—were seeking to reverse the vote, Sanders offered an amendment July 10 to make rental housing construction subject to annual appropriations. It was rejected 34–35. By voice vote the panel then adopted a compromise amendment striking Sanders's original proposal and replacing it with language to provide matching funds for states and cities that have their own trust funds for affordable housing.

The most heated debate came when Lee sought to reauthorize through fiscal 2005 a program designed to fight drugs in housing projects. Before her amendment was rejected, Democrats defended the program while Republicans countered that it had been a source of waste, fraud, and abuse.

2003–2004

First-Time Home Buyers

President George W. Bush on Dec. 16, 2003, signed into law S 811 (PL 108-186), dubbed the American Dream Downpayment Act, which would assist some first-time, low- and moderate-income home buyers with down payments and closing costs.

S 811, introduced by Sen. Wayne Allard, R-Colo., authorized $200 million annually, which translated to an average of $5,000 to an estimated forty thousand home buyers. The allocation formula for the grants was established so that states and other jurisdictions could receive funding according to the proportion of low-income people in an area. The legislation also allowed up to 20 percent of the grants to be used for assistance in rehabilitating units to make housing safer.

The funds would be distributed to state and local governments through HOME Investment Partnerships, a Department of Housing and Urban Development program.

The House, under suspension of the rules, passed its version of the bill (HR 1276) by voice vote on Oct. 1, 2003. The measure, introduced by Rep. Katherine Harris, R-Fla., had been reported from the House Financial Services Committee (H Rept 108-164) on June 19. The Senate passed S 811 by voice vote Nov. 24. The House followed suit Dec. 8, completing congressional action.

Small Housing Authorities

The House by voice vote May 5, 2004, agreed to suspend the rules and pass HR 27, to exempt certain small public housing agencies from having to prepare an annual public housing agency plan required under the Quality Housing and Work Responsibility Act of 1998 (PL 105-276). The House Financial Services Committee reported the bill (H Rept 108-458) on April 2. *(Congress and the Nation Vol. X, p. 555)*

Public housing authorities were required to submit a five-year plan as well as an annual plan to the Department of Housing and Urban Development (HUD). The annual plan would spell out updates and changes to the five-year plan. According to bill sponsor Rep. Doug Bereuter, R-Neb., the annual plan included information about "[h]ousing needs of the families in the jurisdiction; strategies to meet these needs; statement of financial resources; and [public housing authority] policies governing eligibility, selection, and admissions."

Bereuter added that, although HUD had streamlined the plan's requirements, the public housing authorities were in need of regulatory relief. Furthermore, he said that small public housing authorities, often financially strapped, had to hire consultants to assist in preparing annual plans because they do not have the necessary computer software to prepare them.

Under HR 27 a small public housing authority would be exempt from submitting an annual plan if it administers fewer than one hundred dwelling units and Section 8 vouchers; has not been designated a trouble agency by HUD; and continues to provide housing residents with, as Bereuter said, "an adequate and comparable opportunity for participation and notice regarding the establishment of goals, objectives and policies" of the housing authority.

Advocates of retaining the annual plan believed that it helped housing authorities to engage public housing tenants and could anticipate the development of serious problems. Proponents of HR 27 said that the legislation would preserve the rights of tenants and their representative organizations, so their voices still would be heard.

Mortgage Regulation

Draft legislation to strengthen oversight of the mortgage lending giants Federal National Mortgage Association (Fannie Mae) and Federal Home Loan Mortgage Corporation (Freddie Mac) stalled in the House Financial Services Committee in 2003. The White House had come out against the bill, saying the measure would not go far enough to protect the financial health of the two companies and guard against a threat to taxpayers.

Fannie Mae and Freddie Mac were the nation's largest and second-largest mortgage financing companies, respectively. Together they owned or guaranteed almost half of the nation's $7.2 trillion in home mortgages. They were created by Congress—Fannie Mae in 1938 and Freddie Mac in 1970—to boost homeownership. They served as a secondary market, buying mortgages from financial institutions and freeing up money for those lenders to issue more loans. Both companies had long been public corporations, but they still enjoyed lines of credit with the U.S. Treasury—a relationship that would have continued under the Financial Services bill. Partly because of this line of credit, they benefited from a market perception that they were implicitly backed by the government, an assumption that enabled them to borrow at rates almost as low as those paid by the U.S. Treasury. In 1970 both were allowed to issue mortgage-backed securities, bundling pools of home loans and selling them on the market. *(Congress and the Nation Vol. III, p. 648)*

Rep. Richard H. Baker, R-La., chair of the Financial Services Subcommittee on Capital Markets, Insurance, and Government-Sponsored Enterprises, had introduced similar bills three times with little success. An accounting scandal at Freddie Mac in June 2003 got lawmakers' attention. Freddie Mac had ousted three top executives for failing to fully comply with an accounting audit, then quickly announced plans to restate its earnings for the previous three years. Critics said the growth of the two companies and their implicit government guarantee were a formula for disaster. The risk was that taxpayers would be left to pay the bill in the event of a financial crisis.

Financial Services Committee chair Michael G. Oxley, R-Ohio, had spent weeks working out a compromise in an effort to balance critics' desire for tougher regulation with the concern expressed by committee Democrats that a new law not restrict Fannie's and Freddie's role in facilitating homeownership by lower- and middle-class Americans.

Oxley finally produced a draft bill that shifted financial oversight of the two companies to a new regulatory agency to be created in the Treasury Department. The existing regulator within the Department of Housing and Urban Development would continue to approve the companies' entrance into new lines of business. Treasury would have a consulting role.

The administration, however, wanted to give Treasury the power to reject new activities by the lenders.

Ranking committee Democrat Barney Frank of Massachusetts and other Democrats disagreed. Giving the Treasury Department the power to say "no" to new activities, they said, would hand the Treasury power to impair the mortgage financiers' ability to help low- and middle-income Americans purchase homes. Some also feared that the administration would use the new Treasury regulatory agency to advance the interests of banks by cracking down on competition from the two big lenders.

Oxley scrapped a planned Oct. 8 markup, sending the legislation back to the drawing boards.

Labor and Pension Policy

Labor and Pension Policy

The two Congresses that met during President George W. Bush's first term from 2001 to 2005 studied a variety of issues facing the troubled American pension system but made no fundamental changes. Legislative activity during the period pleased business interests, which won approval for several matters they considered important, but was seen by organized labor with profound disappointment. Labor was able, with help from moderate Republicans including members in competitive election areas, to obtain several extensions of unemployment compensation payments to soften the burden of workers who lost jobs after the Sept. 11, 2001, terrorist attacks and the economic recession that began in 2000. The unemployment benefits were the high-water mark for unions during Bush's term, except for one bill on which labor and business agreed. Other important actions all favored business or were at best a stalemate for labor. Separately, federal employee unions fought an ongoing battle with the Bush administration in opposition to outsourcing government jobs and exempting many employees in a new Homeland Security Department from longstanding labor protection coverage. *(Homeland Security Department creation, p. 176)*

The difficulties of organized labor reflected the ascendancy of Republicans during the period and the relative weakness of their Democratic allies in Congress. Also, the attention of Congress was focused more intently on the aftermath of the 2001 terrorist attacks, including homeland security, and the war in Iraq that began in 2003. In addition to these concerns, the Republican agenda in Washington was focused on lowering business and personal income taxes. There was relatively little interest in labor and pension issues except for a few items of much concern to businesses.

RAILROAD WORKER PENSIONS

The single main exception involved a special case of railroad worker pensions. Retired rail workers received pensions from a system outside of the Social Security program that covered most Americans. Created in 1936, during the Great Depression, the railroad retirement program in recent years faced funding shortages to meet expected payments to retirees. Railroad unions and companies came together on

changes in the funding apparatus for the system that they said would provide bigger returns and relieve or eliminate long-range shortfalls for pension payments.

The changes, which allowed investing retirement trust fund money in stocks and bonds, was in some ways a reflection of the coming debate over revisions in the much broader Social Security system. A special commission appointed by President Bush delivered a report that, in effect, endorsed the administration's already decided opinion that Social Security recipients should be allowed to invest some of their taxes in private accounts that would be invested in the stock market. However, the president did not put forth a Social Security program during the four years.

PROBUSINESS CONGRESS

One of the most notable business achievements came early in the 107th Congress when Republicans quickly—Democrats charged in the dark of night—applied an obscure and seldom-used law from 1996 that allowed Congress to overturn major regulations by a simple majority vote in both

REFERENCES

Discussion of labor and pension policy for the years 1945–1964 may be found in *Congress and the Nation Vol. I,* pp. 565–657, 1220–1272, 1289–1320; for the years 1965–1968, *Congress and the Nation Vol. II,* pp. 601–622, 734–743, 745–778; for the years 1969–1972, *Congress and the Nation Vol. III,* pp. 605–621, 703–742; for the years 1973–1976, *Congress and the Nation Vol. IV,* pp. 403–432, 681–713; for the years 1977–1980, *Congress and the Nation Vol. V,* pp. 231–251, 399–425; for the years 1981–1984, *Congress and the Nation Vol. VI,* pp. 643–672; for the years 1985–1988, *Congress and the Nation Vol. VII,* pp. 687–709; for the years 1989–1992, *Congress and the Nation Vol. VIII,* pp. 703–738; for the years 1993–1996, *Congress and the Nation Vol. IX,* pp. 653–675; for the years 1997–2001, *Congress and the Nation Vol. X,* pp. 571–585.

Outlays for Social Security

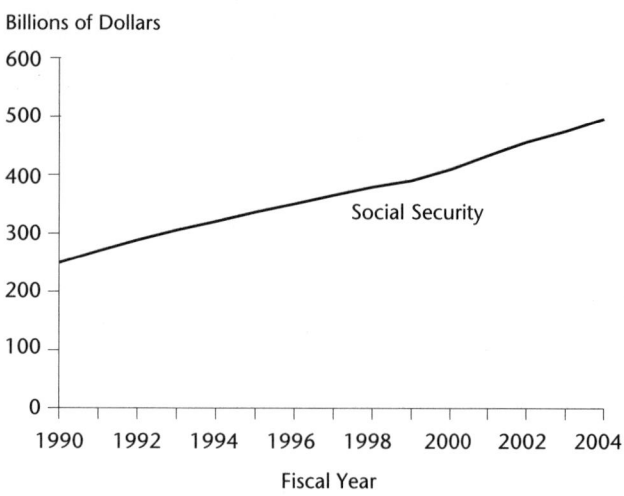

Billions of Dollars

SOURCE: Office of Management and Budget, *Historical Tables, Budget of the United States Government: Fiscal Year 2006* (Washington, D.C.: U.S. Government Printing Office, 2005), Table 3.2.

chambers. At issue in 2001 was a set of Clinton administration regulators from the Labor Department designed to reduce repetitive motion injuries. Businesses of all types were adamantly and vociferously opposed to the so-called ergo-nomics rules, which they said would cost billions of dollars to implement.

Another big win for business was enactment of regulations from the Bush administration that allowed employers to reclassify thousands of workers as professional or managerial employees who were not eligible for overtime pay. Unions vigorously opposed the changes, charging that they would deny millions of ordinary workers substantial amounts of income. Business also succeeded in the 108th Congress in changing the way companies calculated the value of their regular pension trust funds to avoid making significantly larger contributions to meet legal funding standards. However, the changes were only temporary, for two years.

Organized labor faced mostly defeats during Bush's first term. No increase in the minimum wage—a high priority—was enacted. Efforts to shore up protection against workers losing pensions when companies went bankrupt—as occurred when the energy giant Enron collapsed in scandal—were not completed. Nor was Congress able to enact any long-range changes in pension law that protected workers as well as the government agency that backed up—and often had to take over—private pension plans that companies shed when they ran into economic decline or went out of business. Although the issue was studied, serious action was put off to future congresses.

Chronology of Action on Labor and Pension Policy

2001–2002

Although Democrats had control of the Senate for most of the 107th Congress, after disaffected Vermont senator James Jeffords left the Republican Party in early 2001, the power switch was of only limited help to organized labor. Soon after convening, before Democrats took over in June, Republicans swished through a bill repealing regulations from the Clinton administration in 2000 that were aimed at reducing repetitive motion injuries. Republicans and their business allies said the rules would cost billions of dollars to implement. The repeal was a stinging blow to unions, which had lobbied for the regulations for years. *(Party switch, pp. 3, 8)*

The action set the tone for labor law activities in Congress for the two years and foretold an even more stringent pro-business attitude that followed in the 108th Congress after Republicans won control of both chambers by narrow but comfortable margins. Nevertheless both parties did come together to extend unemployment benefits that had run out for many workers in the face of a mild economic recession. Almost all Democrats and a sizeable number of Republicans in competitive districts where labor unions were stronger backed the extension. Still, the Republican leadership was lukewarm about the extensions, contributing to their expiration on Dec. 28, 2002. This allowed Democrats to gleefully blast Republicans for insensitivity to working persons in the middle of the holiday season. An additional extension was rushed through at the beginning of 2003 at the urging of President George W. Bush.

On one issue, however, the parties and business and organized labor came together—railroad worker pensions. Congress cleared legislation with unusual bipartisan support that allowed restructuring the federal railroad pension system to allow some of the funds to be invested in stock and bonds to earn higher returns. The move was thought necessary because the pension funds were running significantly short of funding to pay the expected claims of railroad retirees.

However, in another area of pension legislation Congress simply ground to a halt. In the wake of devastating business scandals and bankruptcies, particularly the nearly total collapse of energy giant Enron in 2001, Congress considered giving new protection to employee retirement savings. In spite of pressure from worried employees, organized labor, and many experts, Congress could not accomplish anything during President Bush's first four years in office. As a result the issue of pension safety was put off until after 2004 when Congress was expected to consider extensive changes to pension and retirement laws.

Ergonomics Rules

The Republican majority in Washington after the 2000 elections moved quickly to repeal regulators on repetitive motion injuries issued in the final days of the Clinton administration. The ergonomics rules had taken effect on Jan. 16, 2000, with enforcement scheduled to begin on Oct. 14. But working swiftly and quietly, Republicans used a little-known legislative device to overturn the regulations, and President George W. Bush signed the bill (S J Res 6—PL 107-5) on March 20. A subsequent measure calling for narrow, clearly defined regulations stalled in committee later in the 107th Congress.

Congressional Republicans, backed by a united business community, persuaded a handful of centrist Democrats in both the House and Senate to join them in passing legislation to repeal the rules. They were aided by an untested law known as the Congressional Review Act (CRA). Enacted in 1996 (PL 104-121), the CRA allowed lawmakers to erase major rules by a simple majority in each chamber. Democrats said they felt ambushed by the GOP maneuver, developed behind the scenes by Republican senator Don Nickles of Oklahoma and lobbyists for the business community. "I'm still trying to figure out what the hell happened," said one Democratic aide after the Senate vote.

The regulations, issued by the Occupational Safety and Health Administration (OSHA), required employers to educate workers about ways to prevent injuries from repetitive motion such as typing, sorting, or lifting heavy loads. If a worker reported an injury, the employer would have had to reconfigure the workplace to prevent recurrences. Workers who reported injuries lasting seven days or longer would have been eligible for compensation of up to 90 percent of their salary for as long as ninety days if they were unable to work.

The business community was unified to an almost unprecedented degree on the need to overturn the ergonomics rules. Business groups argued that they would cost U.S. companies more than $100 billion annually. Democrats were particularly upset over the use of the CRA because it barred the administration from writing a substitute regulation in "substantially the same form." Bills (S 598, HR 1241) to order the secretary of labor to issue narrower, clearly defined ergonomics regulations never got out of committee.

BACKGROUND

Since the administration of President George Bush (1989–1993), OSHA had been working on regulations to limit injuries or disabilities from performing repetitive tasks. Earlier attempts by the administration of President Bill Clinton

(1993–2001) to finalize the rules were blocked by the GOP majority in Congress.

In 2000 the GOP tried to include language in the fiscal 2001 appropriations bill for the departments of Labor, Health and Human Services (HHS), and Education to bar OSHA from finalizing the rules. The White House offered to accept language allowing OSHA to publish the final rules but delaying enforcement until June 2001, after a new president was in office, but GOP leaders rejected the deal. When the spending bill stalled for several weeks, OSHA published the final rules, effectively taking the issue off the table but fanning partisan flames. Republicans and business groups argued that the administration had overstepped its authority, a claim that became the basis for using the CRA to overturn the ergonomics rule.

The CRA required that agencies submit reports on rules to Congress, delayed the implementation of major rules, and created special parliamentary procedures to allow Congress to block executive action. If Congress wanted to block a rule, it had sixty legislative days from the time it received the report to pass a joint resolution of disapproval. Key to the fate of President Clinton's ergonomics rules was a provision specifying that, when a rule was submitted near the end of a Congress or after it adjourned, the sixty-day clock began ticking again on the fifteenth day of the new session. Under most circumstances, the president could be expected to veto a resolution that dealt with overruling actions of the executive branch. However, in 2001, a change of administrations brought in a Republican president who was ready to counteract the rulemaking of the previous Democratic administration.

LEGISLATIVE ACTION

The Senate passed S J Res 6 by a **key vote of 56–44 (R 50–0; D 6–44)** on March 6, 2001, with the help of six centrist Democrats. Careful planning by Nickles, Michael B. Enzi, R-Wyo., and others had given Democrats and their labor allies only four days to mobilize, which proved insufficient to counter the antiregulation campaign. The House followed suit on March 7, clearing the measure by a **key vote of 223–206 (R 206–13; D 16–192; I 1–1)**. The sixteen Democrats who supported the resolution more than made up for the thirteen Republicans who sided with organized labor. President Bush signed the measure (PL 107-5) on March 20, 2001. *(2001 key votes, p. 801)*

Rail Workers' Pensions

In an unusual joint victory for labor and management, Congress cleared a bill in 2001 restructuring the federal railroad pension system to allow part of the funds to be invested in stocks and bonds. By earning higher returns in the private market, the railroads and the railway workers' unions hoped to cover the shortfall between what was being held in the pension fund and the potential claims of railroad retirees.

The bill allowed a new board of railroad company and union representatives to invest $15.3 billion from a federal railroad retirement fund in stocks and bonds rather than in Treasury securities. It also decreased payroll taxes on employers, increased benefits, lowered the retirement age for longtime railroad workers, and increased benefits for survivors.

However, Congress had to overcome two significant problems first. Under budget rules, transferring the trust fund money to the new board counted as $15.3 billion in federal spending—essentially busting the budget for fiscal 2002. Similar concerns prompted Senate GOP leaders to kill a House-passed version of the bill in the 106th Congress. The solution was to include language exempting the bill from the rule. Also, while the plan originally was portrayed as a test, albeit on a small scale, for administration interest in partially privatizing Social Security, Bush officials were opposed to the government itself investing in the stock market for fear that decisions on buying and selling securities would become politicized. As a result the bill put the investment decisions in the hands of a private board.

BACKGROUND

Enactment of the railroad retirement bill ended a three-year odyssey that began with historical foes—rail management and labor—coming together to negotiate an agreement. Both had a major incentive to cooperate: the existing Railroad Retirement System was $40 billion shy of the amount required to meet its obligations to more than 900,000 current and future beneficiaries, a shortfall that required a new financing mechanism.

The system was created in 1936 to help an industry that was vital to the nation's economy and important to ending the Great Depression. Payroll taxes paid by railroads and their workers were held in a federal trust fund that invested in government securities. Benefits were paid in two tiers: the first, financed by a 15.3 percent payroll tax (with half paid by railroads and half by employees), provided benefits similar to those of Social Security, which rail workers did not receive. The second, funded by an additional 21 percent payroll tax (16.1 percent from the railroads and 4.9 percent from workers) was based on an earnings formula.

Because the federal railroad retirement system was the only private industry pension plan established by statute and administered by the federal government, any changes required legislative action. The last major overhaul of the system occurred in 1981 (PL 97-35) and 1983 (PL 98-76). The legislation in those years made numerous changes to the system including raising Tier 2 tax rates for both employers and employees and for the first time subjecting Tier 2 retirement benefits to federal income tax. They also raised from sixty to sixty-two the age at which workers with thirty years of service could receive a full annuity. (*Congress and the Nation Vol. VI, pp. 648, 666*)

Congress in 1974 overrode a veto of legislation by President Gerald R. Ford that made numerous changes in the retirement program and provided additional funding to counteract an increasingly large deficit in the system's trust fund. (*Congress and the Nation Vol. IV, p. 698*)

In 1998 in response to congressional hearings on the railroad retirement system—particularly the need to increase benefits for the widows of railroad workers—rail labor and management initiated discussions on comprehensive restructuring of the system. In 2000 the House passed a bill that embodied an agreement reached between railroads and a majority of rail labor to reform the Tier 2 program. But the Senate never acted on the measure, and efforts to add it to a year-end appropriations bill stalled because of concerns over the cost. (*Congress and the Nation Vol. X, p. 580*)

HOUSE ACTION

The House Transportation Committee approved the bill (HR 1140—H Rept 107-82, Pt. 1) by voice vote on May 16, after the panel's Subcommittee on Railroads endorsed it by voice vote May 9. The bill also was referred to the Ways and Means Committee, which did not take it up. The House passed the bill in an overwhelming vote, 384–33, on July 31 after GOP leaders inserted language that eliminated the main budgetary hurdle. The new language declared that the transfer was not an outlay but a budget-neutral "means of financing" government operations, akin to buying Treasury bonds with surplus revenue. Transportation Committee Chair Don Young, R-Alaska, argued that the existing rules required only a "fictional outlay."

But Sam Johnson, R-Texas, and other opponents maintained that it might be necessary to tap into the Social Security and Medicare trust funds to support the new system if bad investments were made. They argued that a fail-safe measure in the bill—potential payroll tax increases to cover a shortfall in funds—would be insufficient to cover big losses in the market. Also, the nature of the board that would make the investment decisions was changed. Originally, members would have been appointed by the Railroad Retirement Board to represent the interests of labor and management. As passed, the bill required a board made up of three members chosen by labor, three chosen by management, and a seventh chosen by the other six. The White House had called for leaving investment decisions in the hands of beneficiaries, not the government.

SENATE ACTION

Although the bill enjoyed broad bipartisan support in the Senate, it became ensnared in procedural and political maneuvering. Sens. Don Nickles, R-Okla., and Phil Gramm, R-Texas, opposed the bill, arguing that it would drain the federal fund and inevitably lead to a taxpayer bailout. As the Democrats controlled the Senate by the time the bill came to the floor, Senate majority leader Tom Daschle, D-S.D., found another vehicle, a House-passed bill (HR 10) that had been set aside because most of its provisions were enacted as part of Bush's tax bill (PL 107-16). When Daschle tried to call up the moribund bill on Nov. 29, he was opposed by a small group of Republican conservatives, who described the railroad retirement plan as a boondoggle, and from GOP leaders, who insisted the Senate should concentrate exclusively on the fiscal 2002 appropriations bills and an economic stimulus package (HR 3090). The Senate voted 96–4 to prevent a filibuster.

With lobbyists for the railroads and their workers lining the ropes outside the chamber to urge a "yes" vote, several GOP senators said their desire to block the Democrats from setting the agenda was exceeded by their support for the bill. "The Democrats have the votes, they're in charge, so we have to take it as it comes," said Chuck Hagel, R-Neb. Besides, he said, "it's still the same good bill that it was."

Minority Leader Trent Lott, R-Miss., then tried to slow the bill by offering an amendment consisting of major energy legislation and a six-month moratorium on human cloning. He gambled that enough senators would support one or the other to hand him an impressive majority but the strategy backfired. With whip counts coming up short, GOP leaders gave up, losing a vote to limit debate on the amendment, 1–94. Daschle promptly won cloture on the railroad bill on a 81–15 vote.

Senate Republicans conceded that the combination of energy and cloning, along with the broad support enjoyed by the railroad measure and Democrats' unity behind Daschle, ultimately derailed the amendment. A number of other GOP amendments were defeated, including a proposal by Pete V. Domenici, R-N.M., to strike the House language specifying that the $15.3 billion transfer from the trust fund should not be considered an outlay under budget rules. The amendment failed 40–59 despite the support of Budget Chair Kent Conrad, D-N.D. "Directed scoring is a bad idea," Conrad said. "We ought to report accurately to our colleagues the true cost." Before passing the bill, the Senate agreed by voice vote to substitute the railroad pension provisions. The Senate then passed the measure by a vote of 90–9 on Dec. 5.

FINAL ACTION

The House cleared HR 10 by a 369–33 vote on Dec. 11. President George W. Bush signed the measure (PL 107-90) on Dec. 21, 2001.

MAJOR PROVISIONS

As enacted PL 107-90 contained the following major provisions:

Investments. Created a National Railroad Retirement Investment Trust, through which Tier 2 assets, previously invested only in Treasury securities, could be invested in private securities. Enactment required a one-time transfer of $15.3 billion in Tier 2 assets held by the Treasury to the new trust.

Investment board. Created a seven-member independent board of trustees—three chosen by labor, three by management, and one chosen by the other six—to manage and oversee investment of the assets.

Employer taxes. Reduced the Tier 2 payroll tax on railroad employers to 14.2 percent by 2003 and adjusted it thereafter to reflect the earnings performance of the investment fund.

Surviving spouse. Doubled the Tier 2 benefits paid to surviving spouses.

Eligibility. Lowered to sixty from sixty-two the age at which rail workers with thirty years of service were eligible for full Tier 1 benefits.

Vesting. Reduced to five years from ten years the time that railroad employees had to work before being vested.

Social Security Changes

A bipartisan commission on Social Security, appointed by President George W. Bush in May 2001, released its recommendations for overhauling the system Dec. 11. The sixteen-member commission offered three options, all centered on Bush's proposal to allow workers to invest some Social Security contributions in private markets through personal savings accounts, potentially earning greater returns. The panel was cochaired by former senator Daniel Patrick Moynihan (D-N.Y., 1977–2001) and Richard Parsons, chief executive-designate of AOL-Time Warner.

The 141-page report made clear that personal retirement accounts alone would not solve Social Security's financial problems, as more workers retired during the following fifty years and fewer were left to pay into the system. The panel acknowledged that some combination of benefit reductions and tax increases would be needed to keep the program solvent, and that Congress would still have to find approximately $2 trillion over the next seventy-five years to cover startup costs for the accounts and the program's remaining cash deficits.

But the report said personal savings accounts would allow Americans to "build substantial wealth" in a way they had not been able to do through the 12.4 percent annual payroll tax contributed to Social Security. Even after the startup costs to the government, the options would still be less costly than the $3.4 trillion in deficits Social Security would run if nothing was done, the panel argued. "I think we have given [lawmakers] some options that they will find sensible, as we do," Parsons said.

When Bush announced the commission's creation at a Rose Garden ceremony on May 2, he said the threat to Social Security had been apparent for decades. "We can postpone action no longer. Social Security is a challenge now; if we fail to act, it will become a crisis. We must save Social Security and we now have the opportunity to do so."

But the commission's report generated only modest interest, and there were no plans for immediate action. A number of factors contributed to the tepid reception. The White House had not made Social Security a high-profile issue, and top Bush advisers had warned groups supporting the overhaul not to expect legislative action until after the 2002 elections. The Sept. 11, 2001, terrorist attacks in New York and Washington, D.C., focused attention elsewhere. The on-budget surplus that might have taken some of the pain out of a Social Security overhaul had vanished, at least in the short term. The stock market's dismal performance since 2000 also gave Democrats ammunition to argue that putting Social Security funds into the market was a bad idea.

Democrats and labor groups lambasted the report. Senate Democratic Policy Committee Chair Byron L. Dorgan, D-N.D., charged that the panel was "handpicked to arrive at a preconceived conclusion" that personal savings accounts must be included in any Social Security overhaul. "The commission's options will not seriously be pursued by Congress or anyone else who reviews them thoroughly," he said. But the critics did not offer their solutions—a fact that allowed supporters of private savings accounts to claim the high ground in the debate. "This is a bit like sitting on the Titanic and saying, 'Well, I don't like that lifeboat,'" said Michael D. Tanner, director of the libertarian Cato Institute's Project on Social Security Privatization. "Well, that's fine, but you've got to find a lifeboat you do like."

RECOMMENDATIONS

The Commission to Strengthen Social Security recommended three ways to add private savings accounts to Social Security:

Option 1

- Allow workers to invest 2 percent of their Social Security payroll taxes in personal retirement accounts.
- Make no other changes to Social Security, meaning this option would not address the financing problems expected as the number of retirees grows.
- Cost $3.4 trillion over seventy-five years to make up for Social Security's expected cash shortfall, plus $1 trillion in startup costs for the retirement accounts.

Option 2

- Allow workers to invest 4 percent of their payroll taxes, up to $1,000 a year, in personal retirement accounts.
- Slow future benefit increases by linking them to inflation rather than growth in personal wages.
- Increase benefits to widows, and guarantee that low-income workers (disproportionately women) retire with an income of at least 120 percent of the federal poverty level.
- Cost $2 trillion over seventy-five years to cover startup costs of the retirement accounts and any deficits not eliminated by the benefit changes.

Option 3

- Allow workers to redirect 2.5 percent of their payroll taxes, up to $1,000 a year, into personal retirement accounts if they also contribute 1 percent of their annual earnings to the accounts.

- Slow future benefit increases by adjusting them to reflect the fact that most people are expected to live longer.
- Dedicate new tax revenues to shoring up Social Security's finances. No specific sources were recommended.
- Increase benefits to widows, and guarantee that low-income workers (disproportionately women) retire with an income of at least 100 percent of the federal poverty level.
- Cost $2.25 trillion over seventy-five years to cover startup costs of the retirement accounts and any cash deficits not eliminated by the benefit changes.

Pension Security

Legislation to protect employee retirement savings from corporate misdeeds died in the Senate at the end of the 107th Congress in 2002 because of an end-of-session disagreement over whether to attach nonpension items such as business tax breaks. The issue of pension safety, which arose in response to the collapse of Enron Corp. and WorldCom, brought out fundamental differences between the political parties over whether the government should impose specific restrictions to safeguard pension plans or give employees choices that would allow them to protect their private retirement funds.

The bankruptcy of energy giant Enron at the end of 2001 and the resulting evaporation of its employees' retirement savings prompted the Bush administration in February 2002 to propose legislation to safeguard 401(k) retirement plans. President George W. Bush's proposal, combined with intense interest on Capitol Hill, appeared to guarantee that Congress would seek to remedy flaws in the pension system illustrated by the Enron debacle. *(Enron collapse, pp. 123, 124)*

BACKGROUND

In previous generations most workers who were eligible for company-provided retirement savings—particularly those represented by unions—were covered by defined-benefit plans. Under those plans the company contributes annually to a pension trust fund and the employee is guaranteed a set yearly benefit after retiring. A trustee or fiduciary appointed by the employer decides how to invest the funds in the pension plan. Under the 1974 Employee Retirement Income Security Act (PL 93-406), known as ERISA, the fiduciary is required to act solely in the best interests of those covered by the plan. *(Congress and the Nation Vol. IV, p. 690)*

Along with a decline in union membership, the number of workers in such plans fell from 30 million in 1983 to 22.3 million in 2000. Increasing numbers of workers instead participated in defined-contribution plans, such as 401(k) retirement savings accounts, first authorized by Congress in 1978 (PL 95-600). Under these plans employees make pretax contributions to their own retirement accounts. Employers often match a portion of those savings by contributing either cash or company stock. Money in the accounts is taxed on withdrawal but continues to grow tax free while held in employee accounts—assuming dividends are reinvested and the market value of securities or bonds increases. Employees are responsible for deciding how to invest the funds, usually by choosing from a range of alternatives selected by the employer or the fiduciary. Mutual funds are often on lists of choices but company stock of an employee may be one of the options. The value of the retirement benefit depends on the balance in the account: the sum of all contributions, plus interest, dividends, and capital gains or losses. The Pension Benefit Guaranty Corporation (PBGC), established by ERISA, insures only defined-benefit plans, not defined-contribution plans. Companies originally were given broad leeway to run their 401(k) programs in the hope of encouraging more of them to participate.

ENRON COLLAPSE SPURS ACTION

The drive to assert more control over defined-contribution plans began in early 2002 after revelations that thousands of employees at Enron had lost much of their retirement nest eggs because Enron's contributions to its 401(k) plans were almost entirely in the form of company stock, which became worthless. Workers at WorldCom, which was driven toward insolvency in June by nearly $4 billion in accounting wrongdoing, also had invested heavily in company stock.

Bush presented a plan on Feb. 1 that required firms to give their employees more flexibility in selling company stock held in their 401(k) plans while allowing businesses to provide independent investment advice to their workers. It also barred executives from selling company stock during so-called blackout periods when employees were blocked from doing so.

The speed with which the administration produced the 401(k) overhaul proposal, just three weeks after assembling a cabinet-level task force, demonstrated the political potency of the issue. "Employees who have worked hard and saved all their lives should not have to risk losing everything if their company fails," Bush said in his State of the Union address on Jan. 29. (*Text, p. 936*)

The next step was up to Congress, where the labor and tax-writing committees had long battled for control of the pension issue and Democrats and Republicans were at odds over solutions. The labor panels had jurisdiction over ERISA, which governs pension plans and contains civil and criminal penalties for breaches of a pension plan manager's fiduciary duties. The House Ways and Means and Senate Finance committees had jurisdiction over the Internal Revenue Code, which contains the qualification requirements pension plans must meet to receive tax benefits; the tax code also contains the penalty excise taxes often used to keep companies in line.

HOUSE COMMITTEE ACTION

The House Ways and Means Committee moved first, approving a bill (HR 3669—H Rept 107-382, Pt. 1) on March 14, 2002, that required companies that provide their stock as a matching contribution in employee 401(k) accounts to allow the workers to begin selling those shares after they had participated in the plan for three years. Chairman Bill Thomas, R-Calif., decided to go ahead with the markup despite an agreement worked out by House GOP leaders with the Ways and Means, Education and the Workforce, Energy and Commerce, and Financial Services committees to work toward a common pension bill, to be assembled by the House Rules Committee. The markup was preceded by a series of explosive closed-door meetings between Thomas and John A. Boehner, R-Ohio, chairman of the Education and the Workforce Committee, concerning whose panel would have primary control over the process.

The Ways and Means bill proposed penalty excise taxes for employers who failed to provide quarterly "education notices" to participants in 401(k) programs, including information on the merits of diversifying investments. Excise taxes would also apply if employers failed to provide thirty days' notice before implementing a blackout period in which workers were barred from trading in their accounts.

Under the bill's diversification requirements, workers immediately would be able to begin selling the company stock that they had bought in their 401(k) plans. They could sell the employer's matching contribution after three years, and other employer contributions after five years. The percentage of company stock that employees could sell would be phased in gradually to prevent a large-scale sell-off. Workers could use a portion of their salary through tax-free payroll deductions to purchase professional investment advice.

The committee approved a Thomas amendment that exempted employee stock options or stock purchase plans from payroll taxes. The IRS had not imposed such taxes in the past but the Treasury Department issued proposed rules in November 2001 to begin applying them in January 2003.

The House Education and the Workforce Committee approved its bill (HR 3762—H Rept 107-383, Pt. 1) on March 20 by a mostly partisan vote of 28–19. The bill placed no limits on the amount of its own stock that a company could provide in its 401(k) plan. Employees would be free to sell those shares after being in the plan for three years. Quarterly account statements would have to include information on the benefits of diversifying. Employees could receive investment advice from the same financial service providers that managed their 401(k) plans as long as the firm disclosed fees and any potential conflicts of interest. Employers would be responsible for workers' savings during blackout periods.

HOUSE FLOOR ACTION

The House passed HR 3762 on April 11 by a vote of 255–163. In a deal worked out by Majority Leader Dick Armey, R-Texas, the bill consisted largely of Boehner's bill, plus certain provisions from the Ways and Means version. Democrats struggled to decide whether to break with their party to support the GOP bill or risk having to defend a vote against "pension reform" in an election year. Despite an intense effort by Democratic leaders, who condemned the bill as favoring employers over employees, forty-six Democrats joined 208 Republicans to support it.

The resulting bill contained provisions to:

Diversification. Allow workers to sell company-issued matching stock after holding the shares for three years. Companies would have the option of allowing sale of the matching stock after the employee had been in the plan for three years. In order to prevent a market-disrupting sell-off, employees could sell the employer-contributed stock already in their plans before the bill took effect in 20 percent increments over a five-year period, beginning in 2003.

Blackout periods. Give thirty-day advance notice to plan participants before any blackout period of more than three days. Employers could not sell any company stock during a blackout period.

Investment advice. As in the Boehner bill, employees could get advice from financial service providers who managed their 401(k) plans as long as the advisers disclosed fees and potential conflicts of interest. Employees also could use a portion of their salaries through a pretax payroll deduction to purchase professional investment advice, as under the Thomas bill.

The House rejected 187–232 a Democratic substitute offered by George Miller of California, ranking member on the Education and the Workforce Committee. The proposal allowed workers to sell company-issued stock in their 401(k) plans after participating in the plan for three years. Employees could sell company stock already in their 401(k) plans one year after enactment. Employers that offered company stock as an investment option in their 401(k) plans would have to provide independent investment advice to employees. Like the bill, the amendment required a thirty-day advance notice of a blackout period but it applied the notice to a blackout of any length, not just to those lasting more than three days. The substitute also required equal representation of employees and employers on 401(k) boards.

SENATE COMMITTEE ACTION

Partisan tensions were more pronounced in the Senate. In the Health, Education, Labor, and Pension Committee, Chair Edward M. Kennedy, D-Mass., pushed a sweeping measure (S 1992—S Rept 107-226) that limited the amount of company stock workers could acquire in their 401(k) plans. The bill passed on an 11–10 party-line vote on March 21.

Under S 1992 those companies that did not offer traditional defined-benefit pension plans could offer their stock either as a matching 401(k) contribution or as an investment option for employees but not both. Employees would be allowed to sell company stock in their 401(k) plans after three years of service. Employees could receive investment advice from third parties not connected with the retirement plan. Company executives would be held liable for knowingly tak-

ing or concealing actions that harmed the interests of 401(k) plan participants. Kennedy's bill would have allowed employees to serve on company boards that oversee pension plans. Workers also could file suit against company executives alleging malfeasance to recover 401(k) losses.

Republicans immediately pronounced the Kennedy bill dead on arrival. They were critical particularly of the proposal to limit employee investments in company stock. Democrats argued that some degree of diversification should be required in a retirement plan that provided no guaranteed pension benefit upon retirement.

Finance Committee Chair Max Baucus, D-Mont., and ranking committee Republican Charles E. Grassley of Iowa took a different approach, pushing a measure that more closely resembled the House measure. The Finance Committee approved the Baucus bill (S 1971—S Rept 107-242) by voice vote July 11 after the chair agreed not to offer it as an amendment to the accounting regulation bill (S 2673) that was before the Senate. In return, Majority Leader Tom Daschle, D-S.D., promised to put pension legislation on the floor in September and urged Baucus and Kennedy to come up with a compromise in the interim.

Under the Finance Committee bill employees would be allowed to sell company stock offered as matching contributions after three years of service. This provision addressed former Enron employees' complaints that the company prohibited them from selling such shares until they reached age fifty, leaving them helpless when the stock became valueless when the company collapsed. Companies would be required to notify employees thirty days before a blackout period. They also would have to notify employees promptly after an executive sold company stock. Similar to the Kennedy bill, the measure allowed a company to hire a financial firm to provide employee investment advice only if it did not administer the company's 401(k) plan.

Baucus incorporated eight amendments, including a proposal by John Kerry, D-Mass., to allow workers fifty-five years or older immediately to divest company stock out of a 401(k) plan. In an effort to rein in various corporate perks that had come under scrutiny in the recent scandals, the bill proposed that deferred compensation held by executives in offshore trusts be taxed. Company loans to executives would be treated as compensation that could be taxed unless the official put up collateral, arranged for a fixed payment schedule or signed a promissory note. Bonuses and commissions that totaled $1 million or more annually would be subject to withholding taxes at the top tax rate of 38.6 percent, rather than the supplemental wage rate of 27 percent.

Baucus also included an amendment that he sponsored requiring a chief executive officer to sign a company's federal tax return under penalty of perjury. "I think this is ridiculous," said Don Nickles, R-Okla. "There is not a CEO in the country that prepares a tax return." Baucus said CEOs would have to have a "woeful, willful, and almost intentional knowledge" of wrongdoing to be convicted.

SENATE FLOOR ACTION

Congress returned from its August recess with a full agenda, limited time, and the political pressures of the impending midterm election. Appropriations bills, homeland security, and a potential war with Iraq were the dominant priorities, leaving little time for fractious disputes that could eat up valuable floor time. With that in mind, Daschle sought to broker a compromise on a narrow pension bill, which he planned to bring to the floor the week of Sept. 23. The most substantive provision in the compromise bill was a requirement that employees be allowed to sell matching contributions of company stock in their 401(k) plans after holding them for three years. The bill did not contain controversial provisions to limit the amount of company stock that could be held in 401(k) plans, a restriction that would be similar to an existing 10 percent cap on holdings of company stock in traditional pension fund assets.

Unions, fearful that the bill was being eviscerated, backed a Kennedy floor amendment that would have required employees to be represented on trustee boards that managed 401(k) plans. Unions said employee members would keep coworkers informed about any problems in retirement plans. But such an amendment was almost certain to trigger a GOP filibuster. "We think this is a stalking horse for something unions have always wanted: seats on corporate boards," said Grassley. "That isn't going to happen." When it became apparent to Daschle that the threat of this amendment along with others on a variety of unrelated stalled legislation would make the project too unwieldy, he pulled the bill from floor consideration.

BLACKOUT PERIODS

Although the pension bills died at the end of the Congress, lawmakers did set new requirements for pension plan blackout periods as part of the corporate accountability law (PL 107-204) that President Bush signed on July 30, 2002. The law required companies to notify workers thirty days before a blackout period of three days or more that restricted employees' ability to sell stock in their 401(k) accounts. Employers were required to tell workers why they could not access their 401(k) accounts, as well as the stop and start dates of the blackout. The law also prohibited senior executives from selling company stock during such blackout periods. (*Corporate accountability action, p. 130*)

Unemployment Benefits

Congress agreed in March 2002 to extend federal unemployment benefits for thirteen weeks, in part because payments were about to run out for workers who had been laid off after the Sept. 11, 2001, terrorist attacks. However, an attempt at the end of the session to continue the extension into 2003 collapsed, leaving an estimated 2.1 million jobless workers without benefits in the new year and postponing the problem to the 108th Congress. (*2004 action, p. 573*)

Jobless workers typically could apply to states to receive up to twenty-six weeks of unemployment insurance. Reacting to the economic downturn and the plight of those who lost their jobs after the attacks, Congress began working in late 2001 on a broad economic stimulus bill that included an additional thirteen weeks of federally provided unemployment benefits. But partisan disputes over the rest of the package doomed the bill. Lawmakers finally gave up and settled for a scaled-back measure consisting of the unemployment benefits and several business tax breaks. The bill cleared March 8 and was signed into law the following day (HR 3090—PL 107-147). The unemployment benefits were scheduled to expire Dec. 28. Both chambers passed bills during the November lame-duck session aimed at avoiding the cutoff, but differences over the length of the extension and unrelated provisions on Medicare physician payments scuttled the effort.

The House passed a bill (HR 5063) by voice vote on Nov. 14 that called for a five-week extension of benefits at an estimated cost of $900 million. But the bill also contained provisions added by Ways and Means Committee Chair Bill Thomas, R-Calif., to block a 4.4 percent cut in the Medicare reimbursement rate for physicians that was scheduled to take effect Feb. 1, 2003. (*Medicare reimbursements, p. 487*)

Hours later the Senate passed a bill (HR 3529) by voice vote that provided for another thirteen-week extension. The Senate bill did not contain the Medicare rider because the top Republican and Democrat on the Senate Finance Committee insisted that doctors receive no additional funds unless other Medicare providers did. The other providers also were scheduled for reimbursement cuts. Thomas refused to budge and House leaders insisted that anything more than a five-week extension could deplete too much of the $29 billion in the federal unemployment trust funds. They said they would reassess the nation's unemployment situation in January.

Seven senators, including the unlikely duo of Hillary Rodham Clinton, D-N.Y., and GOP whip Don Nickles of Oklahoma, sought a compromise and wrote to President George W. Bush on Nov. 19, urging him to endorse the Senate bill. "Too many of these Americans have worked hard, played by the rules, and paid into the unemployment trust fund," the senators wrote. "Yet, as the holiday season approaches, they are facing an end to their critically needed benefits."

The letter was signed by Clinton, Majority Leader Tom Daschle, D-S.D.; Gordon H. Smith, R-Ore.; Maria Cantwell, D-Wash.; Arlen Specter, R-Pa.; Paul S. Sarbanes, D-Md.; and Edward M. Kennedy, D-Mass.

The White House declined to enter the fray. Nickles on Nov. 19 offered a nine-week extension and made a pitch to Thomas, according to a Senate GOP aide. But the House held to its all-or-nothing stance. "The House has already acted," said an aide to Speaker J. Dennis Hastert, R-Ill. Democrats made the most of the bill's collapse. "I have to say, this is a story right out of Charles Dickens," said Daschle, referring to the prospect of benefits ending three days after Christmas.

2003–2004

In the 2002 off-year elections Republicans regained a narrow but firm control of both the House and Senate. With continued control of the White House, business interests dominated congressional action on labor issues. Unions and their Democratic allies lost major battles—including the attempt to boost the minimum wage—but won a limited extension of unemployment benefits.

Labor's worst loss was failure to block changes in overtime pay regulations that business had ardently sought for years. The Bush administration's Labor Department promulgated rules that reclassified thousands of workers—the exact number was a hotly disputed contention between unions and the administration—in a way that allowed companies to exclude them from time-and-a-half pay when they worked more than forty hours a week. Labor supporters were able to block a proposal that would have allowed business to offer employees compensatory time off in lieu of the extra pay. Although business interests would have welcomed the change, their lobbyists never worked hard for approval.

One issue that did bring together Republicans and many Democrats was legislation that gave business some reprieve from what they claimed were crushing pension funding requirements. The legislation that passed allowed business to use an index calculation to determine the value of their pension funds. This approach replaced a previously used calculation based on conservative interest rates from Treasury bonds. The latter meant business interests were facing significantly increased contributions to their pension plans in order to conform to legal requirements. President George W. Bush signed the changes into law just days before thousands of businesses would have had to ante up millions of dollars in additional contributions. However, the changes in calculations were to be in effect for just two years.

Unemployment Benefits

In a continuing saga of sparring between parties over federal help for unemployed workers in the face of an economic downturn, Congress early in 2003 extended through the year a benefits extension that the Republican leadership had expired at the end of 2002. The action extended a program that allowed jobless people to receive thirteen weeks of federal aid after they had exhausted their regular twenty-six weeks of state unemployment assistance. Democrats and some Republicans, who said that the program should be renewed because the economic recovery had not been spread evenly across the country, agitated throughout 2004 for a further extension. While the House did pass an extension in February 2004, the bill went no further.

2003 LEGISLATION ACTION

The first law enacted in the 108th Congress was an extension of the thirteen weeks of federal unemployment benefits.

Congress cleared the bill on the second day of the new session; President George W. Bush signed it into law hours later (S 23—PL 108-1). The bipartisan measure, drafted by Sens. Don Nickles, R-Okla., and Hillary Rodham Clinton, D-N.Y., was effective through May 31. It was retroactive to Dec. 28, 2002, when the original program expired, allowing an estimated 750,000 workers whose benefits were cut off on that date to receive the remainder of their thirteen weeks. Jobless workers in high unemployment states were eligible for an additional thirteen weeks of federal aid, for a total of twenty-six weeks of benefits. However, because of the strict requirements only a handful of states qualified at the time as high unemployment states.

The thirteen-week extension had been established initially in March 2002 (PL 107-147) at a time when workers who had been unemployed since the Sept. 11, 2001, terrorist attacks were about to exhaust their regular six months of state benefits. The temporary program was good until Dec. 28 but with relatively high unemployment—the average rate for 2002 was 5.8 percent—Congress hoped to continue it. (2002 action, p. 572)

Both the House and Senate passed bills in November 2002 but the leadership could not agree on the length of the extension or whether to include unrelated provisions on Medicare physician payments. The White House rebuffed pleas from senators of both parties to broker a compromise, and Democrats took to the airwaves to bash Republicans for playing scrooge to unemployed workers. Bush subsequently broke his silence, using his weekly radio address Dec. 14 to demand that the 108th Congress make an extension of unemployment benefits its first order of business.

The Senate passed the new bill by voice vote Jan. 7; the House cleared it the next day, 416–4. It was essentially the same measure the Senate had passed the previous November.

SECOND EXTENSION

In late May 2003 Congress extended the program through Dec. 31, brushing aside some Republican uneasiness with the notion that Congress was essentially creating a new entitlement. The House passed the bill 409–19 on May 22, and the Senate cleared it by voice vote the following day. Bush signed it into law May 28 (HR 2185—PL 108-26).

Democrats pressured the GOP leadership to move yet another extension at the end of the year. Their bills (HR 1652, S 1708) proposed to double, to twenty-six weeks, the duration of federal benefits for those who exhausted state benefits, with even longer-lasting federal help in states with high unemployment rates. Republicans from the Northwest, the region with the highest unemployment, also lobbied for action. They were rebuffed by Republican leaders who noted that the unemployment rate was declining and argued that the economic recovery was strong enough to bring the program to an end.

House minority leader Nancy Pelosi of California addresses a rally on May 17, 2003, calling for an extension of federal unemployment benefits to jobless workers. As the economic recovery failed to reach millions of Americans in 2003, Congress voted twice to extend benefits by thirteen weeks. *Source: Congressional Quarterly/ Scott J. Ferrell*

2004 LEGISLATIVE ACTION

Although Democrats agitated all year for an extension of unemployment benefits, Republican leaders in both chambers managed to sidetrack the efforts without allowing up-or-down floor votes. In early February the House added a six-month extension to a reauthorization bill for the Community Services Block Grant program (HR 3030). Thirty-nine Republicans crossed the aisle to support the amendment, which was approved by a **key vote of 227–179 (R 39–179; D 187–0; I 1–0)**. Every Democrat on the floor supported the amendment. *(2004 key votes, p. 854)*

HR 3030 was then passed by voice vote. The Senate passed its version of the bill later in February but the measure went no further. Other Senate attempts to extend benefits were blocked by procedural maneuvering even though roll calls showed a majority favored the extension.

Most Republicans who supported the amendment were from states that had lost manufacturing jobs; others were moderates or the holders of politically competitive seats. The vote was an embarrassing loss for the Republican leadership and demonstrated the sympathy in the House for extending jobless benefits. It also showed the political sensitivity of the issue as the national elections approached.

Overtime Rules Changes

Changes in overtime pay regulations advocated by business interests and opposed by organized labor forced the 108th Congress to take several contentious votes. Republicans, however, were able to block all Democratic efforts to stop the Bush administration's Labor Department from changing the rules. The dispute reflected battles waged over decades between business seeking the lowest cost of labor possible and unions seeking to advance the wages and benefits of its members. Business argued that existing rules were outdated for the twenty-first century, while labor said the changes could remove as many as 6 million mostly white-collar workers from benefits of time-and-a-half pay for work beyond the normal workweek.

The underlying provisions of law were enacted in the Fair Labor Standards Act, which established the basic forty-hour workweek at regular pay and provided time-and-a-half over that. The Bush administration, which claimed labor's estimate of 6 million affected workers was wildly exaggerated, issued new rules effective Aug. 23, 2004, that reclassified many white-collar workers as executives, administrators, or professionals who would not qualify for overtime. In 2003, in drafting an earlier version of the changes, the Labor Department estimated that 644,000 workers eligible for overtime pay would no longer qualify. The administration also claimed the changes would make an estimated 1.3 million low-income workers eligible for overtime for the first time.

The odds of labor and its Democratic allies in Congress blocking the changes were slim, especially after the Republicans gained a firm control of both chambers in the 2002 elections. Nevertheless, Democrats were able to persuade a handful of moderate Republicans sympathetic to organized labor to join them in voting against the changes. This coalition managed to approve several proposals to block the changes but Republican leaders saw that all were dropped from final bills. The votes, however, embarrassed Republican candidates, including the national ticket in the 2004 elections, as Democrats and labor portrayed the GOP as captive of business interests with little concern for the livelihood of workers.

LEGISLATIVE ACTION

In 2003 the Senate voted to include language blocking the change in the fiscal 2004 Labor, Health and Human Services (HHS), and Education spending bill. The amendment, by Tom Harkin, D-Iowa, was adopted by a **key vote of 54–45 (R 6–44; D 47–1; I 1–0)** on Sept. 10 with the help of six Republicans. The Bush administration threatened to veto the bill if the amendment was included in the final version. The House narrowly defeated a similar proposal. The House amendment, by David R. Obey of Wisconsin, ranking Democrat on the Appropriations Committee, was rejected by a **key vote of 210–213 (R 14–210; D 195–3; I 1–0)** on July 10. Although House leaders strongly opposed the amendment, the House subsequently adopted a nonbinding resolution to instruct conferees on the Labor, HHS, and Education bill to agree to the provision. The motion was adopted 221–203 on Oct. 2. *(2003 key votes, p. 837)*

The dispute became the central issue in conference negotiations on the appropriations bill. Arlen Specter, R-Pa., chair of the Senate Labor-HHS Appropriations Subcommittee, battled for weeks to include the provision, which also had the support of Senate Appropriations Chair Ted Stevens of Alaska. Once the Labor, HHS, and Education bill was incorporated into negotiations on a multibill omnibus, however, the stakes for holding out grew higher. Specter, bowing to a White House threat to veto the entire bill if the language remained, removed the provision from the conference bill before the final House and Senate votes.

The drama was repeated in the second session in 2004 but the outcome was the same. On Sept. 9, 2004, the House easily adopted an Obey amendment to the fiscal 2005 Labor, HHS, and Education appropriations bill. This time the vote was 223–193. The Republican leadership was reportedly willing to let the vote occur because it was confident the amendment would be dropped later and would give moderate GOP members an opportunity to show prolabor sympathies. Twenty-two mostly moderate Republicans did just that.

In the Senate a similar amendment, again offered by Iowa's Harkin, was adopted by a **key vote of 52–47 (R 5–46; D 46–1; I 1–0).** The six Republicans who crossed party lines were Lisa Murkowski of Alaska, Ben Nighthorse Campbell of Colorado, Lincoln Chafee of Rhode Island, Olympia J. Snowe of Maine, and Specter of Pennsylvania. The lone Democrat to oppose the amendment was Zell Miller of Georgia. The amendment was added to a corporate tax cut bill, a high priority for Republicans. *(2003 key votes, p. 837)*

The Senate Appropriations Committee later added the Harkin amendment to its version of the Labor, HHS, and Education spending bill. But in the end, with the White House continuing to promise a veto, all the prohibitions against enforcing the rules changes were dropped in confer-

ence or in later action when spending bills were wrapped into a single omnibus package after the 2004 election.

Compensatory Time

House Republican leaders in April 2003 pushed legislation to allow private-sector employers to grant time off instead of extra pay for overtime work. The House Education and the Workforce Committee approved the measure (HR 1119—H Rept 108-127) on April 9 on a 27–22 party-line vote. Republicans argued the bill was a worker-friendly measure that would give employees the option to spend more time with their families. Democrats said it could lead to forced overtime without adequate compensation.

Under the bill, sponsored by Judy Biggert, R-Ill., employers could offer workers one-and-one-half hours of compensatory time per hour of overtime worked. The Fair Labor Standards Act of 1938 required that most workers be paid at least one-and-a-half times their base pay for more than forty hours of work per week. The bill exempted company executives, professionals, and workers covered under collective bargaining agreements from the overtime mandate. Public-sector employers already had a comp time option.

Under the bill, employers could decide whether to offer the compensatory time option, when to offer it, and to whom. They could deny time off if it would "unduly disrupt" business operations. They could also "cash out" employees' compensatory time accounts at overtime pay rates, provided they gave thirty days' notice. Employees could not be forced to take compensatory time instead of pay under the bill. They would have to agree in writing to accept time off in lieu of overtime pay.

The committee rejected 21–26 an amendment by Robert E. Andrews, D-N.J., to reverse a proposed rule change announced by the Labor Department on March 31 that would redefine who was eligible for overtime and who was exempt. Andrews said such a change should be made only by Congress, not by administrative action. *(Overtime changes, p. 574)*

Organized labor launched an extensive grassroots campaign against the bill, targeting Republican lawmakers in districts with significant union membership. Business lobbyists backed the bill but did not lobby aggressively for it. With such lack of support, House leaders pulled the measure from the floor schedule on June 4, a day before it was to come up for debate. The House had passed similar legislation in 1997 but it died by filibuster in the Senate. *(Congress and the Nation Vol. X, p. 576)*

Minimum Wage

Republicans in the 108th Congress blocked Democrats from getting a floor vote in either chamber on an increase in the minimum wage. The unsuccessful effort was one of several Democrats pushed in the Congress to picture Republicans as unfriendly to workers. Organized labor used the votes to attack GOP candidates in the 2004 national elections.

Democrats proposed increasing the minimum wage to $7 an hour over two years. It had remained at $5.15 an hour since 1997. They argued that because the wage has not kept up with inflation, millions more Americans qualify as "working poor." *(1999–2000 action, Congress and the Nation Vol. X, p. 579)*

Republicans countered that raising the minimum wage would increase unemployment because businesses forced to raise salaries would shed workers. They also maintained that few workers actually earn the minimum wage for long; the proportion of hourly workers at or below the minimum wage had fallen from 13.4 percent in 1979 to 2.9 percent in 2003, according to the Bureau of Labor Statistics. The influential U.S. Chamber of Congress lobbied all year against increasing the wage.

Sen. Edward M. Kennedy of Massachusetts and other Democrats tried to attach a minimum wage increase to two separate measures—a welfare reauthorization bill (HR 4) and a class action lawsuit overhaul (S 2062). Republican leaders attempted to limit debate and block the amendments by invoking cloture; when that failed they withdrew the underlying legislation rather than allow a vote on the minimum wage. They also did not allow a stand-alone minimum wage bill (S 2370) to come up on the floor.

In the House, Republicans used their control over committees and floor rules to prevent any proposed minimum wage increase from reaching the floor. Republicans discussed an alternative proposal raising the minimum wage to a lesser amount—Democratic aides put the figure at $6.25—but it was never offered as stand-alone legislation or as an amendment.

Corporate Pension Contributions

A variety of businesses facing huge pension funding contributions pressured Congress in early 2004 to pass legislation allowing employers relief from existing pension requirements. Without the new legislation, many companies with defined-benefit plans—which pay retirees a set amount, usually based on years of service and earnings—faced a substantial increase in pension contributions as early as April 15, 2004.

Many of these companies were having difficulty meeting funding requirements for their plans because low interest rates on thirty-year Treasury bonds in recent years prevented earnings on the funds from meeting targets. The lobbying was so intense that even a number of liberal Democrats, not normally sympathetic to business' pleas, voted for the legislation. President George W. Bush's signature on a two-year extension came only days before the deadline for new corporate pension contributions. The temporary fix allowed companies to calculate their assets based on the yield of a blend of corporate bonds, rather than on the much lower yield of Treasury bonds. The more their assets were worth, the less

they would have to contribute to their pension plans to cover expected liabilities.

BACKGROUND

Companies typically invest their pension funds in a mix of stocks, bonds, and other instruments. During the heady days of the stock market boom in the 1990s, many companies did not need to make contributions to their plans because soaring stock prices fattened their holdings. But the market decline and the low interest rates that followed the 2001 recession dramatically altered corporate pension balance sheets; by 2002, a number of major companies were facing the need to make big contributions just as they were battling operating losses.

The situation was compounded by the Treasury Department's decision in 2001 to stop issuing thirty-year bonds, which led to a fall in rates on the long-term securities. The low yields required companies to assume an especially low rate of return when calculating their pension fund assets. When assets fell below 90 percent of liabilities, companies were required to cover the shortfall through additional contributions.

"The improper funding burdens caused by continued use of the obsolete thirty-year Treasury bond has made the sponsorship of defined-benefit plans much more difficult," said James Klein, president of the American Benefits Council, which represented companies. "Without immediate correction, plans will continue to terminate or freeze benefits, putting millions of American retirees and workers in peril."

Congress gave the companies a respite in 2002, with a law—added to the bill extending unemployment benefits (PL 107-147)—that allowed them to assume a return on plan investments equal to 120 percent of the four-year average interest rate on thirty-year Treasury bonds. The fix was good for two years, after which companies would have to go back to using a return of 105 percent. That meant putting aside billions of extra dollars to cover their pension obligations.

Many members of Congress agreed with unions and employers that making it easier for corporations to fund their pension plans would help dissuade companies from terminating their plans and turning over the obligations to the Pension Benefit Guaranty Corporation (PBGC), the government agency that insures pensions. The agency insured the pensions of 44 million Americans and was funded by more than $800 million a year in corporate assessments. However, if enough companies terminated their plans, the PBGC's $30 billion plus in assets might be depleted, forcing taxpayers to pick up the tab.

But many lawmakers also wanted to make the relief temporary to keep up pressure for a broad overhaul of pension law. Otherwise, they feared the problem of underfunded pension plans would grow, creating an even greater threat to the PBGC. The PBGC reported a record deficit of $11.2 billion in its program for single employer plans in fiscal 2003, three times larger than any previously recorded. It said the plans suffered a net loss of $7.6 billion in fiscal 2003 alone, with pension terminations and declining interest rates as the chief causes.

The agency also calculated that pensions run by financially troubled companies were underfunded by $85.5 billion at the end of fiscal 2003, up from $35.4 billion a year before. "The continued erosion of PBGC's financial condition underscores the need for comprehensive reforms to put pension plans on a path to better funding" Executive Director Steven Kandarian said in the year-end statement. "While the PBGC has sufficient assets to pay benefits to workers and retirees for a number of years, the growing gap between our assets and liabilities puts at risk the agency's ability to continue to protect pensions in the future."

LEGISLATIVE ACTION

HR 3108 was sponsored by John A. Boehner, R-Ohio, chair of the Education and the Workforce Committee. Although referred to committee, it was brought directly to the House floor in October, a reflection of the urgency of pension funding relief. The House on Oct. 8, 2003, passed HR 3108 by a vote of 397–2.

The Senate Health, Education, Labor, and Pensions Committee gave voice vote approval Oct. 29 to a bill (S 2005—S Rept 108-221) that proposed replacing the thirty-year bond rate with a composite corporate bond rate for three years. The bill, sponsored by chair Judd Gregg, R-N.H., was projected to save companies $30.5 billion in 2004 through 2006. It also called for a blue-ribbon panel charged with finding ways to combat pension underfunding.

The Senate, however, passed its version of HR 3108 by a wide bipartisan margin of 86–9 on Jan. 28, 2004, brushing aside White House objections. At issue for the Bush administration were Senate provisions that allowed airlines, steelmakers, and possibly other financially struggling firms to substantially reduce their pension fund contributions. Such relief was in addition to the reduced corporate pension contributions that HR 3108 allowed during 2004 and 2005.

The Senate's expansive view of the legislation made a conference compromise difficult. But House Republicans including Boehner, the bill's primary sponsor, and Sam Johnson of Texas, chair of the House Employer-Employee Relations Subcommittee, sided with the White House in opposing special relief for some companies. On April 1, 2004, Boehner made a last attempt at a compromise, offering relief for the most severely underfunded multi-employer plans. When Democrats demanded more, Republicans moved on and approved a conference report (H Rept 108-457) that reduced company pension contributions by $80 billion over two years and provided very limited additional relief.

The conference report was adopted by the House on April 2 by a vote of 336–69. Boehner acknowledged before the conference committee vote and on the House floor that the legislation lacked as much multi-employer relief as many members would prefer. "We need to get this bill finished, and we need to get it finished today," he said April 2.

In the Senate Edward M. Kennedy, D-Mass., continued to insist that any pension funding bill include relief for multi-employer plans. The White House threatened a veto if the bill allowed employers to avoid fully funding the plans. The final bill included only a small amount of relief for multi-employer plans, and the administration backed away from the veto threat.

Pressure to enact the measure was enormous. Republicans and Democrats were hearing from companies back home that they desperately needed Congress to act fast. Minority Leader Tom Daschle of South Dakota also opposed the bill but decided not to press his Democratic colleagues to resist it. Business-friendly Democrats already were getting anxious about the lack of action on a corporate tax overhaul bill and it appeared that Daschle would fail to hold the forty-one Democratic votes he would need to block action on the pension bill. *(Corporate tax bill, p. 115)*

With companies lobbying desperately for the bill, including airlines and steelmakers that would win special funding waivers, many Democrats decided they had no choice but to support it. "A lot of people need this bill passed," said Sen. Max Baucus of Montana, who voted for the bill on the floor despite opposing it in conference. Baucus was among those legislators who got an earful from airlines concerned that partisan sniping might sink the legislation. Even stalwart liberal Democrats such as Barbara Boxer of California and Hillary Rodham Clinton of New York voted to clear the bill.

As a result the Senate voted 78–19 on April 8 to adopt the conference report on the bill, clearing it for the president. The vote represented a victory for about 30,000 companies, such as Exxon Mobil Corp. and Dana Corp., that would be able to reduce pension contributions by $80 billion over two years, beginning with payments due the week of April 12.

MAJOR PROVISIONS

President Bush signed the measure (PL 108-218) on April 10. The law contained the following provisions:

Single-employer Pension Funding Relief

Temporarily replaced the current interest rate that employers used to determine their defined benefit pension contributions—the thirty-year Treasury bond interest rate. Required the Treasury Department to establish a new interest rate based on a blend of corporate bond index rates, which would assume a higher rate of return on pension investments, thereby providing an estimated $80 billion in relief to companies over two years. Provided the new formula would expire at the end of 2005.

Additional Pension Funding Relief

Granted an extra layer of relief to airlines and steel companies with chronically underfunded pension plans. Allowed these companies to reduce by 80 percent special "deficit reduction contributions" they are required to make, providing an additional $1.6 billion in pension funding relief.

Multi-employer Pension Funding Relief

Provided pension funding relief to about 4 percent of multi-employer pension plans, which used a method different from that used by single-employer plans to calculate their contributions. Specified that to be eligible a plan must have had a net investment loss of 10 percent or larger for 2002, and the plan's actuary must certify that the plan is expected to have a funding deficiency in 2004, 2005, or 2006. Prevented qualifying plans from increasing benefits during the deferral period, unless the benefit increase was already negotiated under an existing collective bargaining agreement or if contributions to the plan exceed the annual charges attributable to the benefit change.

Greyhound Lines

Permitted Greyhound Lines to use an alternate mortality table when calculating its pension contributions. (The provision permitted Greyhound to use a mortality table that more closely reflected the ages of the beneficiaries in its plan. Under existing law, pension contributions were determined using mortality tables based on the life expectancy of a retiring fifty-year-old. But Greyhound's average pension recipient was seventy because it closed its plan to new entrants in 1983. Greyhound received a ten-year exemption from the contribution rules in 1997 but that began to phase out at the end of 2003.)

BROADER BILLS STALL

The House Ways and Means Committee on July 18, 2003, approved a broad pension and retirement savings bill (HR 1776) that included a new formula for funding defined-benefit plans. But the measure—sponsored by Rob Portman, R-Ohio, and Benjamin L. Cardin, D-Md.—fell victim to a partisan brawl between Chair Bill Thomas, R-Calif., and committee Democrats, and it never reached the House floor. The bill was approved on a Republicans-only voice vote, after Democrats walked out of the markup. Thomas summoned Capitol Police to remove protesting Democrats from a committee library. Although he later offered a tearful apology on the House floor, another markup was never scheduled.

Among its many provisions, the broader bill would have replaced the thirty-year bond with a conservative blend of long-term corporate bonds as the benchmark for calculating defined-benefit plan assets. Other provisions of the bill included accelerating to 2004 increases in the limits on annual tax-free contributions to individual retirement accounts (IRAs) and 401(k) accounts that were scheduled to take effect in 2008 and 2006 respectively; gradually increasing the age at which retirees were required to make annual

withdrawals from retirement accounts from seventy and one-half to seventy-five years; and expanding and extending a tax credit aimed at encouraging low- and middle-income taxpayers to save for retirement.

The Senate Finance Committee gave voice vote approval on Sept. 17 to a draft bill that combined short-term relief with a longer-term pension overhaul. The bill proposed to phase in funding rules starting in 2007 that would force companies with older workers who were close to retirement to assume lower rates of return on their pension investments. That would make it difficult to fund pensions without cutting back on benefits, holding down other expenses such as wages, cutting profits, or some combination of all three. "We did not find this an easy thing to do," said Chair Charles E. Grassley, R-Iowa. Earlier in the year, Grassley had criticized a similar White House plan.

The bill did give companies some of what they wanted— permission to use the rate on an index of high-quality corporate bonds instead of the thirty-year bond rate for three years when calculating pension assets. The bill also included special breaks for airlines, steelmakers, and other companies that ran into financial trouble during the 2001 recession and its lackluster aftermath. Companies whose plans were fully funded in 2000 would be treated as if they were fully funded from 2004 through 2006. That would exempt businesses, such as United Airlines, from requirements that called for larger pension contributions when assets fell below 90 percent of liabilities. Similar provisions applied to bus operator Greyhound Lines Inc.

The White House opposed the provisions on the grounds they would significantly weaken funding requirements for the pension funds. The Senate bill also proposed to raise $1 billion over ten years by blocking executives from sheltering deferred benefit payments from taxes by using offshore trusts. The bill also would allow workers to sell company stock put into their 401(k) plans as matching contributions once they had been employed at the company for three years.

With the session nearing an end the House passed a separate bill, HR 3521, on Nov. 20 that included pension provisions similar to HR 3108. In addition, for pension plans established and maintained by commercial passenger airlines, contributions would be slashed for 2004 and 2005 to 20 percent of the levels required by the existing formula. The White House opposed the airline provisions, arguing that relieving troubled companies of pension obligations could end up shifting the problem to the PBGC, potentially harming taxpayers. Some lawmakers also winced at giving a special break to one industry. The Senate did not act on the bill.

CHAPTER 13

Law and Justice

Law and Law Enforcement

President George W. Bush's first term began with a fierce partisan battle over the nomination of Republican senator John Ashcroft of Missouri to be attorney general, and it ended with equally spirited fights over such issues as gay marriage and tort laws. In between, however, Democrats and Republicans in Congress came together to pass several significant pieces of legislation. Their achievements included new laws that toughened penalties for those convicted of crimes against juveniles and gave federal and state prison inmates access to sophisticated genetic testing.

Bush took the oath of office against a backdrop of Democratic anger over his disputed victory in the presidential race and bitterness over how GOP lawmakers had treated President Bill Clinton during his second term. The nomination of Ashcroft, who ultimately won confirmation despite liberal unease over his unyielding opposition to abortion and gun control, aggravated partisan tensions. Senate Democrats and Republicans, striving for an upper hand in a chamber that was closely divided between the parties, also clashed fiercely over procedures to handle Bush's nominees to the federal bench.

During the 107th Congress, the terrorist attacks of Sept. 11, 2001, served to ease—but not eliminate—partisan differences. Lawmakers temporarily focused on shoring up the nation's defenses, passing such landmark laws as the USA Patriot Act, which strengthened the hand of law enforcement agencies. *(Homeland security, p. 171)*

They also reasserted congressional control of the Justice Department by reauthorizing it for the first time in a generation. However, Republicans and Democrats continued to square off over politically sensitive issues, including judicial nominees and class action lawsuits.

With the Republicans controlling both chambers in the 108th Congress, conservatives won enactment of legislation that toughened penalties on those who committed crimes against children, despite concerns by some that the new law went too far. Democrats and Republicans also joined forces to clear measures on DNA (deoxyribonucleic acid) testing of convicted criminals—an important issue at a time when DNA tests had demonstrated the innocence of some death row inmates—and granted new rights to crime victims. They worked together to expand visas for foreign technology

workers and attempted, unsuccessfully, to find common ground on such issues as establishing a fund for claims related to asbestos exposure and moving most class action lawsuits to federal courts.

But the 108th Congress was marked by fiercer partisan debates. Lawmakers broke largely along party lines as they clashed over gay marriage, the power of federal courts, gun control, and tort laws. Perhaps the most dramatic showdowns took place over judicial nominees, with Democrats mounting an unprecedented series of filibusters against several of Bush's more conservative choices. As adjournment neared, the parties seemed as divided as ever over legal and judicial issues, with Republicans going so far as to float a plan that would put an end to filibusters of judicial nominees.

BIPARTISAN SUCCESSES

The major legislative achievement of the 107th Congress was the first full-fledged reauthorization of the Justice Department in twenty years. Lawmakers hoped the legislation, signed into law in 2002, would be a tool for reasserting congressional oversight of the department after years of scant attention. The department's operations had been authorized on a year-to-year basis as part of the annual appropriations

REFERENCES

Discussion of law enforcement policy for the years 1945–1964 may be found in *Congress and the Nation Vol. I,* pp. 1671–1676; for the years 1965–1968, *Congress and the Nation Vol. II,* pp. 309–334; for the years 1969–1972, *Congress and the Nation Vol. III,* pp. 255–286; for the years 1973–1976, *Congress and the Nation Vol. IV,* pp. 559–618; for the years 1977–1980, *Congress and the Nation Vol. V,* pp. 715–753; for the years 1981–1984, *Congress and the Nation Vol. VI,* pp. 675–709; for the years 1985–1988, *Congress and the Nation Vol. VII,* pp. 713–784; for the years 1989–1992, *Congress and the Nation Vol. VIII,* pp. 741–799; for the years 1993–1996, *Congress and the Nation Vol. IX,* pp. 679–758; for the years 1997–2001, *Congress and the Nation Vol. X,* pp. 589–683.

Outlays for Law Enforcement

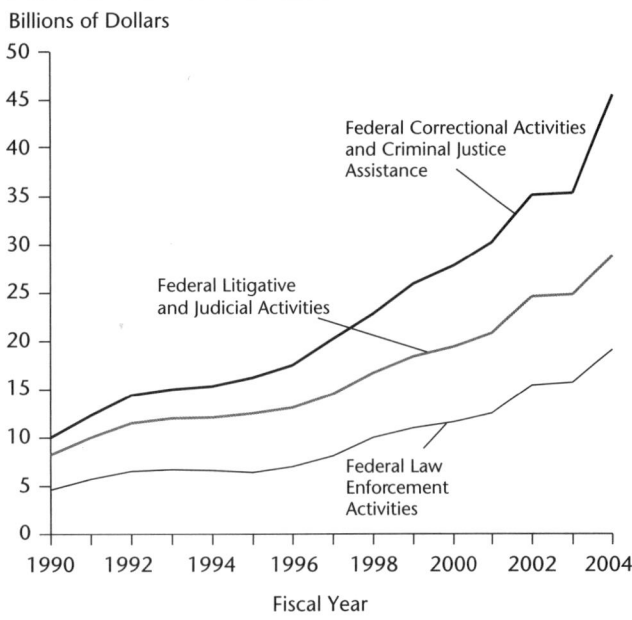

Billions of Dollars

SOURCE: Office of Management and Budget, *Historical Tables, Budget of the United States Government: Fiscal Year 2006* (Washington, D.C.: U.S. Government Printing Office, 2005), Table 3.2.

process, which did not allow the House and Senate Judiciary Committees to review long-term policy goals.

The new reauthorization came at a time when the department was taking on increased responsibilities as part of the war on terrorism. Members of both parties on the House and Senate Judiciary Committees were concerned about lapses in internal security at the department, perceived mismanagement at a number of Justice agencies, and disagreements with Justice officials over the reach of Congress's oversight powers.

The bill authorized fiscal 2002 and fiscal 2003 funding, and it required the department to submit regular reports to Congress. It incorporated provisions from a number of other measures that dealt with a range of issues, from drug treatment programs to patent and trademark law. Lawmakers established a Violence Against Women Office, with a director appointed by the president and confirmed by the Senate.

Conference negotiators, after resolving minor differences on the core Justice Department provisions, focused on a number of add-ons, such as the authorization of eight new permanent district court judgeships, grants to states for jail-based substance abuse programs, juvenile crime prevention grants and the consolidation of five juvenile justice programs, and a modification to U.S. trademark laws.

At the beginning of the 108th Congress, legislators cleared a sweeping child crimes measure. The law bolstered the nationwide AMBER (America's Missing: Broadcast Emergency Response) child-abduction alert system, outlawed "virtual" child pornography, mandated life sentences for twice-convicted child sex offenders, opened the door for electronic

surveillance to investigate child pornography, dropped the statute of limitations on crimes involving sexual abuse or kidnapping of children, and limited the ability of federal judges to depart from sentencing guidelines.

House Judiciary Committee Chair F. James Sensenbrenner Jr., R-Wis., pushed the package through to enactment despite pressure to drop the other provisions in favor of getting a stand-alone AMBER alert bill into law quickly. He had failed in 2002 to win Senate support for a similar bill. But in the 108th Congress, he successfully used a Senate-passed measure on computer-generated child pornography, which was an important issue for Senate Judiciary Committee Chair Orrin G. Hatch, R-Utah, as the vehicle for his broader measure. The added publicity from a Utah kidnapping case made the bill unstoppable.

The child pornography provisions were the latest attempt by lawmakers to apply obscenity and indecency standards to new technological media. They were a response to a 2002 U.S. Supreme Court ruling that struck down as "overbroad and unconstitutional" virtual pornography provisions enacted in 1996.

Much of the debate over the child crimes bill in conference centered on House language limiting federal judges' ability to hand down sentences lighter than those in federal sentencing guidelines. Democrats favored a study by the sentencing commission instead. Conferees compromised by narrowing the House provisions so they would apply only to cases involving sex crimes and crimes against children.

In 2004 legislators broke a five-year logjam by clearing a bipartisan proposal to give federal and state prison inmates access to sophisticated genetic testing that could prove their innocence. The legislation capped lengthy debates over proposals to give death row inmates access to post-conviction DNA tests and to ensure that defendants in capital cases had adequate legal representation. Supporters finally found success with a comprehensive bill that included provisions that appealed to diverse constituencies in Congress. It no longer focused exclusively on death row inmates. It included new criminal justice grants for states to ensure adequate legal representation for defendants in capital cases, as well as provisions supported by the Bush administration to speed the processing of biological evidence collected from rapes and other crimes.

The measure provided a bridge for lawmakers with opposing views about the death penalty. Many capital punishment supporters viewed the bill as a way to make the justice system closer to foolproof. "We will lose the death penalty unless it is applied in a very judicious way," said Arlen Specter, R-Pa. Opponents of capital punishment, while still seeking a federal moratorium on the death penalty, said the bill would reduce the chances of an innocent person being put to death.

Although Republican opponents kept the bill off the Senate floor in the 107th Congress, supporters were bolstered by a series of events that focused attention on the death penalty. The Supreme Court had issued two rulings in June 2002 that restricted the use of the death penalty, and some inmates were released from death row after DNA testing refuted their convictions.

Republican opponents of the bill still worried that the grants to states could end up putting opponents of the death penalty in charge of the systems put in place to defend those accused of capital offenses and that the legal standard for allowing new trials after post-conviction DNA testing was too low. But proponents made several changes to meet their objections, clarifying who could direct state programs and raising the standard for new trials.

SAME-SEX MARRIAGE

The issue of gay marriage came to the fore in 2003, temporarily shouldering aside abortion as the top focus of social conservatives. A sharply divided Supreme Court threw out state anti-sodomy statutes early in the year, which was followed by a Massachusetts Supreme Court ruling that gay couples must be allowed to wed under the Massachusetts constitution.

The rulings ignited a firestorm of criticism in conservative circles against the courts. Conservatives worried that allowing homosexuals to wed would cheapen the institution of marriage to such an extent that heterosexuals would abandon it in droves, threatening the fabric of American society. The only solution, they said, was to add an amendment to the U.S. Constitution defining marriage as "a union of a man and a woman."

Few Democrats supported gay marriage, but they accused amendment supporters of being intolerant and divisive. Although many Republicans supported an amendment, others worried about making changes to the Constitution or argued that Congress's role was to ensure that states retain their prerogative to define marriage.

Even more than many legislative issues in the presidential election year of 2004, the debate over gay marriage appeared to be driven by political calculations. Senate Republicans, although clearly lacking the two-thirds majority necessary to pass a constitutional amendment, pushed the issue to the top of the crowded congressional agenda in the weeks before the Democratic National Convention in Boston. Senators defeated the measure when they rejected a motion to invoke cloture on it, or cut off debate.

House leaders subsequently brought the amendment to the floor, bypassing the Judiciary Committee and its chair, Sensenbrenner, who opposed same-sex marriage but also had reservations about amending the Constitution. The House vote was well short of the two-thirds majority of lawmakers present and voting necessary to adopt the measure. Though House Republican leaders predicted the result well before the vote, the occasion allowed them to again criticize "activist" judges, who conservatives contended were unilaterally rewriting the Constitution from the bench.

THE ROLE OF THE COURTS

Perhaps no judicial issue proved more divisive in 2001–2004 than the handling of nominees for federal judgeships.

Although no Supreme Court vacancy occurred during the four years, Bush and his Republican allies in the Senate made a priority of reshaping the federal judiciary in a more conservative vein. Democrats and liberal advocacy groups, still smarting over the way Republicans stalled Clinton nominees, were intent on setting boundaries for that effort.

In the 107th Congress, the Democratic-controlled Senate Judiciary Committee rejected two nominees to the Court of Appeals for the Fifth Circuit, in New Orleans—Charles W. Pickering Sr. and Priscilla Owen. It declined to consider some others, such as Miguel A. Estrada, who was nominated to the D.C. Court of Appeals. Although the Senate confirmed a total of one hundred of the president's selections for federal judgeships in 2001–2002, a frustrated Bush said the confirmation system was "poisoned and polarized." He proposed new rules, which were not considered, that would eliminate the Senate's authority to reject nominees in committee and required floor votes on every nomination.

The battle over judicial nominees escalated in the 108th Congress. Bush renominated Pickering and Owen—the first time a president resubmitted the name of a rejected nominee. Democrats, now in the minority, turned to the filibuster to block Bush's most controversial choices. Although senators had hesitated to use filibusters against judicial nominees, and no appellate court nominee had ever been successfully filibustered in the past, Democrats used the tactic effectively against ten of Bush's nominees. The president retaliated by using his power to make recess appointments to temporarily install Pickering to the Fifth Circuit Court and William H. Pryor Jr. to the Eleventh Circuit. Democrats then stalled action on all the nominees until Bush pledged to refrain from additional recess appointments.

Despite the successful Democratic tactics, most of Bush's nominees won confirmation. By the end of his first administration, Bush had filled 203 lifetime seats on the federal trial and circuit appeals courts, or 24 percent of the total.

Nominations aside, congressional Republicans tried to curb what they regarded as the judicial system's activist tendencies. The House passed a pair of bills in 2004 that would limit federal court oversight of a 1996 law that gave states the option of not recognizing same-sex marriages and stripped federal courts of jurisdiction over constitutional challenges to the wording of the Pledge of Allegiance. Republicans also sought to break up the Circuit Court of Appeals for the Ninth, which was viewed as especially liberal. But the Senate declined to take up any of the measures.

CURBING LAWSUITS

In both the 107th and 108th Congresses, Republicans advanced plans that would restrict various types of lawsuits. But the measures did not become law.

The House in 2002 passed a bill to limit class action suits, but it died in the face of Democratic opposition in the Senate and the reluctance by many members to be seen as protecting businesses in the midst of a series of corporate scandals. The bill would give jurisdiction over most class action

William H. Pryor Jr., meets with his Senate sponsor, Richard Shelby, R-Ala., prior to his hearing before the Senate Judiciary Committee on June 11, 2003. The battle over judicial nominees heated up in the 108th Congress, as Senate Democrats used the filibuster to stymie Bush's efforts to appoint more conservative judges to the bench. The president swung back, installing two of his rejected nominees, Pryor and Charles W. Pickering Sr., as recess appointments. *Source: AP Wide World Photos/Dennis Cook*

lawsuits to federal district courts and establish a "bill of rights" for plaintiffs in federal class action lawsuits.

In 2003 the House passed another measure to limit class action suits. The Senate Judiciary Committee approved the bill after Democrats narrowed its scope. Although still controversial, the measure appeared to have the backing of enough Democrats to ensure its passage. But procedural maneuvers by Senate majority leader Bill Frist, R-Tenn., alienated members of both parties, and an attempt to cut off debate fell sixteen short of the necessary sixty votes.

Republicans also took aim at medical malpractice lawsuits. Arguing that out-of-control medical malpractice awards were forcing some doctors to leave markets and jeopardizing patient care, House Republicans won passage of bills in both the 107th and 108th Congresses to cap noneconomic and punitive damages.

Democrats, however, favored an approach that would seek to reduce malpractice costs without limiting damage awards. They pointed to insurers, not jury awards, as the cul-

prit behind rising rates, and they also warned that capping awards would deny proper compensation to the victims of medical malpractice. In the 108th Congress, Senate Republican leaders pressed ahead with their effort to cap damages. They failed to overcome a filibuster, even after breaking up medical malpractice legislation into small segments.

OTHER LEGISLATION

With gun control advocates wielding limited clout in the Capitol, lawmakers spent comparatively little time debating firearms measures. The House in 2003 passed a bill to make it harder to file civil lawsuits against firearms manufacturers and gun dealers. But the measure subsequently was rejected in the Senate after it was amended to include several gun control provisions, including a continuation of an expiring 1994 law that banned semiautomatic assault weapons. Congress ultimately failed to extend the popular ban on assault weapons, which was a major setback for gun control advocates.

In the 108th Congress, the Senate debated establishing a fund that would pay no-fault claims related to asbestos exposure. But it could not get past the conflicting demands of lawmakers, corporations, insurers, union officials, and trial lawyers. The Senate Judiciary Committee approved a bill in 2003 with a $108 billion fund, but the compromises required to get it out of committee dampened hopes of moving it further. Senate majority leader Frist introduced a new version of the bill in 2004, but he could not win Senate passage. The plan died despite an unusual attempt at mediation and negotiations between Frist and Minority Leader Tom Daschle, D-S.D.

On immigration, both chambers in the 107th Congress passed versions of legislation to extend a program, known as 245(i) after its section in immigration law, that permitted some immigrants to apply for U.S. residency even if they were in the country illegally. But the measure fell victim to powerful enemies and plain bad luck: The House was poised to clear the bill Sept. 11, 2001, but the terrorist attacks intervened. Proponents failed to get it back on the agenda.

In the 108th Congress, lawmakers added provisions to the omnibus spending measure that aimed to settle a pair of long-running disputes over immigration policy. The provisions, which involved visas for foreign workers known as H-1B and L-1, not only expanded by about one-third the number of visas available for foreign technology workers but also cracked down on the use of imported temporary workers.

Chronology of Action on Law Enforcement

2001–2002

Lawmakers got off to a rocky start on law and justice issues, as President George W. Bush's nomination of John Ashcroft as attorney general sparked an intense partisan battle. Liberal groups criticized his staunchly conservative views, and the Senate vote to confirm him was the narrowest margin of victory for any attorney general nominee in recent times. The two parties also squared off over procedures for reviewing judicial nominees.

But the terrorist attacks of Sept. 11, 2001, tamped down partisan rhetoric somewhat for the rest of the 107th Congress. Lawmakers reached consensus to pass the first reauthorization of the Justice Department in a generation, thereby reasserting congressional oversight of the department. The new law contained significant juvenile crime provisions, authorizing juvenile crime prevention grants and consolidating five juvenile justice programs.

Congress also made some headway on proposals to ban "virtual" child pornography and to ensure that inmates on death row had access to DNA (deoxyribonucleic acid) testing that could prove their innocence. However, it failed to clear the measures. On immigration, Congress came close to clearing legislation to extend the 245(i) program, which permitted some immigrants to apply for U.S. residency even if they were in the country illegally. But the House had scheduled final action on the bill Sept. 11, 2001, and the terrorist attacks intervened. Proponents were never able to get it back on track.

On other issues, lawmakers divided along predictable fault lines. The House passed a bill to limit class action suits, but the measure ultimately fell to Democratic opposition and the reluctance by many members to protect businesses in the midst of a series of corporate scandals. The House, on a mostly party-line vote, also passed legislation to limit medical malpractice damages and plaintiff attorneys' fees, but the Senate rejected a less-sweeping version. Similarly, House members passed a bill to toughen penalties for crimes against juveniles, but many of its provisions proved too much for the Senate.

Some of the most intense partisan battles broke out over Bush's judicial nominees. Democrats declined to act on several nominations, and the Judiciary Committee rejected two

outright on party-line votes. Bush proposed changing Senate rules to require floor votes on every nominee.

Justice Department Reauthorization

For the first time in twenty years, Congress in 2002 cleared legislation reauthorizing the Department of Justice. Lawmakers hoped the bill, signed into law Nov. 2 (HR 2215—PL 107-273), would be a tool for reasserting congressional oversight of the department after years of scant attention.

The bill authorized $17.6 billion for the department in fiscal 2002 and $20.5 billion in fiscal 2003. It required Justice to submit regular reports to Congress and incorporated provisions from a number of other bills ranging from drug treatment programs to patent and trademark law.

BACKGROUND

The last full-fledged Justice Department reauthorization had been enacted in 1979 (PL 96-132), with extensions in 1980 and 1981. Since then, the department's operations had been authorized on a year-to-year basis as part of the annual appropriations bill for the Commerce, Justice, and State Departments, a method that did not allow for review of long-term policy goals by the House and Senate Judiciary Committees. *(1979 action, Congress and the Nation Vol. V, p. 733; 1981 action, Congress and the Nation Vol. VI, p. 677)*

For years, controversial riders had doomed efforts to reauthorize the Justice Department. In 1998, for example, a similar reauthorization easily won House passage, but the Senate Judiciary Committee did not act on it until September, and disputes over wiretapping provisions and other language in the measure stalled action in that body. In other years, fights over gun control provisions slowed the bill's progress in the Senate.

The new reauthorization came at a time when the department was taking on increased responsibilities as part of the war on terrorism. The House and Senate Judiciary Committees were concerned over lapses in internal security at the department, perceived mismanagement at a number of Justice

JUSTICE DEPARTMENT LEADERSHIP

After five weeks of impassioned and polarizing debate, the Senate on Feb. 1, 2001, confirmed the nomination of former Republican senator John Ashcroft of Missouri to be attorney general. The 58–42 vote broke largely along party lines, with eight Democrats joining all fifty Republicans to support the nominee. The Judiciary Committee had confirmed him on a 10–8 vote on Jan. 30 with just one Democrat—Russell D. Feingold of Wisconsin—joining all nine Republicans in support.

The Missourian emerged as the most controversial pick for President George W. Bush's cabinet. He had been among the most conservative members of the Senate before losing his reelection bid, and his conservative ideology drew fire from liberal groups. A devoutly religious man, Ashcroft had sponsored legislation that would outlaw all abortions except to save the life of the woman. During his single term in the Senate (1995–2001), he opposed adding new restrictions to gun show purchases and expanding the federal definition of hate crimes to cover acts motivated by the victim's sexual identity. Many questioned whether he would be able to enforce laws he had opposed, such as those intended to protect abortion clinics from violence.

"In the case of Senator Ashcroft, his thirty-year record of intense opposition on so many critical issues involving civil rights, women's rights, gun control, and nominations speak volumes and demonstrate—clearly and convincingly—that he is the wrong person to be attorney general of the United States," said Sen. Edward M. Kennedy, D-Mass.

Opponents also said Ashcroft's 1998 interview with a neo-Confederate magazine and a 1999 appearance at Bob Jones University showed an insensitivity to racial issues that would handicap an attorney general. While outside groups concentrated their fire on Ashcroft's conservative positions, many Senate Democrats were most angered over his aggressive tactics in opposing President Bill Clinton's nominations, particularly that of Ronnie L. White to be a federal judge in Missouri.

Ashcroft repeatedly pledged to uphold the nation's laws. Conservative groups mobilized to support the nomination, and Republican senators angrily defended him, saying his record was being distorted. "A sophisticated group came together and created a caricature of who John is," said Jeff Sessions, R-Ala. "Now they want us to vote against" that caricature.

In the end, Ashcroft won with fewer votes than any successful cabinet nominee in decades. His was the most contested nomination for attorney general since the battle over Edwin Meese III in 1984–1985. (*Meese appointment, Congress and the Nation Vol. VII, p. 1043*)

Ashcroft announced his resignation after Bush won reelection in 2004. The nomination of his successor, White House counsel Alberto Gonzales, sparked almost as much controversy as the Ashcroft nomination. Many Democrats objected to the role Gonzales played in crafting Bush administration policies on the treatment of prisoners. The Senate confirmed him on Feb. 3, 2005, by a vote of 60–36.

On May 24, 2001, Theodore Olson won Senate confirmation as solicitor general on a 51–47 vote, despite accusations that he gave misleading testimony about his role in efforts to smear President Clinton. Ben Nelson of Nebraska and Zell Miller of Georgia were the only Democrats to vote for the nomination, which was supported by all Republicans who were present.

The nomination came to the floor after Majority Leader Trent Lott, R-Miss., exercised his option under the Senate's power-sharing agreement to discharge nominations that got a tie vote in committee. The Judiciary Committee had split 9–9 on May 17 over whether to send Olson's nomination to the floor.

Democrats said Olson's testimony before the Judiciary Committee was evasive, primarily about the extent of his involvement in a project by the conservative magazine the *American Spectator* to uncover damaging information about then-president Clinton and first lady Hillary Rodham Clinton.

Olson, a lawyer in private practice, had argued the Supreme Court case, *Bush v. Gore*, that resolved the presidential election and made his client, George W. Bush, president.

Olson stepped down in July 2004. Bush named Paul D. Clement acting solicitor general.

Other Bush nominees were less controversial. On Aug. 2, 2001, Robert S. Mueller III won Senate confirmation to a ten-year term as director of the Federal Bureau of Investigation (FBI) by a vote of 98–0. That followed a 19–0 endorsement by the Judiciary Committee earlier that day. Mueller, who had been U.S. attorney in San Francisco, had a reputation as a tough manager—a quality many in Congress felt was needed at a time when the nation's top law enforcement agency faced a series of embarrassments from losing documents in the Timothy J. McVeigh case to the discovery of a high-ranking double agent within the bureau. Mueller replaced Louis J. Freeh.

The Senate on Aug. 1, 2001, voted 98–1 to confirm the nomination of Rep. Asa Hutchinson, R-Ark., to head the Drug Enforcement Administration (DEA). Hutchinson subsequently moved over to the Department of Homeland Security to oversee border and transportation issues, and the Senate, on July 31, 2003, confirmed the nomination of Karen P. Tandy to succeed him at DEA.

On July 31, 2001, the Senate confirmed, by voice vote, the nomination of James W. Ziglar to be commissioner of the Immigration and Naturalization Service. Ziglar was the Senate sergeant at arms for the preceding two years and was popular on both sides of the aisle for his strong management skills.

agencies, and disagreements with Justice officials over the reach of Congress's oversight powers. Senate Judiciary Committee Chair Patrick J. Leahy, D-Vt., and his House counterpart, F. James Sensenbrenner Jr., R-Wis., complained in particular about Justice's failure to respond to their inquiries about the implementation of a sweeping anti-terrorism law enacted in 2001 (PL 107-56), known as the USA Patriot Act. *(2001 law, p. 187)*

In addition, lawmakers were concerned about a series of blunders at the Federal Bureau of Investigation (FBI), including the discovery in 2001 that top special agent Robert Hanssen had been spying for Russia for more than a decade. That news followed revelations that hundreds of documents the FBI had agreed to give to attorneys for Oklahoma City bomber Timothy J. McVeigh never had been turned over. Lawmakers in 2002 were angered by reports of evidence and opportunities missed in the months before the Sept. 11, 2001, terrorist attacks.

Even before HR 2215 began to move, at least three bipartisan pairs of senators proposed solutions to management issues at the FBI. Leahy and Charles E. Grassley, R-Iowa, focused on removing restrictions that require the Justice Department's inspector general to get permission from the attorney general or the deputy attorney general to do any investigations of the FBI or the Drug Enforcement Agency. Richard J. Durbin, D-Ill., and Arlen Specter, R-Pa., introduced a bill (S 1065) to establish a separate and fully independent inspector general for the FBI. And Charles E. Schumer, D-N.Y., and Orrin G. Hatch, R-Utah, proposed a blue-ribbon commission to do a strategic review of the agency.

LEGISLATIVE ACTION

With members of both parties in accord, the House Judiciary Committee on June 20, 2001, gave voice vote approval to HR 2215 after adopting a Sensenbrenner amendment to create a deputy inspector general at the Justice Department to be responsible solely for investigating the FBI. The legislation also called for a review of some of the restrictions that limited the ability of the Justice Department inspector general to investigate the FBI. HR 2215 was formally reported (H Rept 107-125) on July 10.

Another significant part of the Justice Department authorization changed the way the department was allowed to move money between accounts during a fiscal year. Reprogramming requests allow a department or agency to shift money between accounts with the permission of a few members of Congress. Sensenbrenner said during the markup that the House and Senate Judiciary Committees had been left out of the reprogramming process while appropriators reviewed budget changes. The bill required that the Justice Department notify the authorizing committee of those requests.

Most Justice programs were authorized at the level requested by the administration, but the legislation included a $10 million increase for the inspector general, in part to pay for the new deputy.

Sensenbrenner said the billions of dollars of grants given out annually by the Justice Department's Office of Justice Programs needed greater oversight. The bill required extensive reports to Congress from grant operators, including sworn statements from recipients about how they used the money they received.

The bill also made permanent an office within the Justice Department to deal with violence against women. The current office devoted to the issue exists only at the discretion of the attorney general. And, at the urging of Judiciary Committee member Bob Barr, R-Ga., the bill would require that the Justice Department provide a detailed report on the FBI's "Carnivore" program, a highly secretive e-mail surveillance project.

The House passed HR 2215 by voice vote under suspension of the rules July 23 after minimum debate.

In one of its final legislative acts of the first session, the Senate passed HR 2215 by voice vote the night of Dec. 20, 2001, after having adopted a Leahy substitute amendment. The Senate-passed bill was similar to the House-passed version in that it authorized Justice Department operations for fiscal 2002, generally at the levels requested by the president. It also aimed to improve congressional oversight of the department by, among other things, requiring it to submit regular reports to Congress on its operations. And it created a Violence Against Women Office in the department.

But the Senate version also contained provisions that threatened to snag the bill in conference. It authorized several new programs, including one for drug abuse prevention and treatment. It also created twelve new federal judgeships in California, Illinois, North Carolina, Ohio, and Texas.

CONFERENCE AND FINAL ACTION

With minor differences on the core Justice Department provisions easily resolved, conference negotiations centered on the Senate add-ons. In the end, Senate Democrats largely prevailed. The conference report (H Rept 107-685) was filed Sept. 25, 2002, and the House adopted it by a vote of 400–4 the next day. Final Senate action was held up briefly by Republicans who were angry over Leahy's handling of Bush's judicial nominations or upset over unrelated bills being folded into the conference report. The Senate cleared HR 2215 by voice vote Oct. 3, but only after the leadership won a 93–5 vote to invoke cloture, thus limiting the debate.

Some of the provisions that negotiators attached to the bill built on the core mission of reasserting Congress's power to oversee the department. Others, such as language on patents and trademarks, had no easy connection to the original measure. The following were among the main conference decisions.

Judgeships. Like the Senate-passed bill, the final version authorized eight new permanent district court judgeships— five in California, two in Texas, and one in North Carolina. In addition, four temporary judgeships were made permanent—two in Illinois and one each in New York and Virginia.

The bill also created seven new temporary judgeships—one each in Alabama, Arizona, California, Florida, New Mexico, North Carolina, and Texas—and extended the temporary judgeship in Ohio for five years.

Drug abuse. The Senate also won inclusion of a number of provisions from a bill (S 304), approved by the Senate Judiciary Committee in 2001, authorizing grants to states for jail-based substance abuse programs. The House bill had no comparable provisions, and House Energy and Commerce Committee Chair Billy Tauzin, R-La., and ranking Democrat John D. Dingell of Michigan had said the issue should be handled as part of their committee's work in 2004 to reauthorize the Substance Abuse and Mental Health Services Administration.

Juvenile justice. The agreement incorporated, with some modifications, provisions of two bills passed by the House in 2001. HR 863, formally reported (H Rept 107-46) by the House Judiciary Committee on April 20 and passed by the full House by voice vote under suspension of the rules Oct. 16, authorized juvenile crime prevention grants to the states for three years. HR 1900, formally reported (H Rept 107-203) by the House Education and the Workforce Committee on Sept. 10 and passed by the full House by voice vote under suspension of the rules Sept. 20, reauthorized the Juvenile Justice and Delinquency Prevention Act. It consolidated under one umbrella five juvenile justice programs including boot camps, mentoring services, and child abuse treatment services. *(Juvenile crimes, p. 590)*

Trademark and patents. The conference agreement incorporated provisions from a bill (HR 741) modifying U.S. trademark laws to allow companies to take advantage of the international trademark treaty known as the Madrid Protocol. The House Judiciary Committee formally reported HR 741 (H Rept 107-19) on March 13, 2001, and the full House passed it by voice vote under suspension of the rules the next day. It got stuck in the Senate, however. Conferees also attached a bill (S 1754) reauthorizing the Patent and Trademark Office from fiscal 2003 through 2008, authorizing the office to receive appropriations in amounts equal to the fees it collected each year, and directing the office to develop a user-friendly electronic system for filing and processing patent and trademark applications. The Senate Judiciary Committee formally reported S 1754 (no written report) on June 20, 2002, and the full Senate passed an amended version by voice vote on June 26. Also included was language from a bill (S 487 amending the 1976 Copyright Act [PL 94-553]) to allow teachers to send digitized books, music and movies over the Internet without first getting permission. The Senate Judiciary Committee formally reported S 487 (S Rept 107-31) on June 5, 2001, and the full Senate passed it by voice vote two days later. The House Judiciary Committee reported a revised version (H Rept 107-687) Sept. 25, 2002. *(Copyright law, Congress and the Nation Vol. IV, p. 612)*

FBI. Many of the provisions aimed at boosting security and oversight at the bureau and improving its computer systems were drawn from an FBI overhaul bill (S 1974), which had been reported (no written report) by the Senate Judiciary Committee on April 25, 2002. Leahy subsequently filed a report (S Rept 107-148) on May 10. S 1974 included statutory authority for an FBI police force to protect buildings and personnel. The FBI also was directed to submit a plan to Congress for implementing the Webster Commission's recommendations on FBI internal security functions in the wake of the Hanssen espionage case.

Other provisions required the attorney general and FBI director to submit a report to Congress on the use of the Carnivore system; authorized "danger pay" for FBI agents in hazardous duty locations outside the United States; and required the FBI director to report to Congress on the bureau's information management and technology programs, including recommendations for any legislation needed to enhance their effectiveness. The bill authorized an additional $2 million in fiscal 2003 for the FBI to hire fourteen full-time employees for the bureau's Office of Professional Responsibility.

Violence Against Women Act. Like both the House and Senate versions, the final bill established a Violence Against Women Office, with a director appointed by the president and confirmed by the Senate. The director was authorized to award all grants and contracts under the office and was responsible for generally carrying out the responsibilities of the Violence Against Women Act (PL 106-386).

In other provisions, the new law

Boys and Girls Clubs. Authorized grants to the Boys and Girls Clubs of America to help establish twelve hundred additional clubs with the goal of having four thousand Boys and Girls Clubs in operation by 2007.

Disaster litigation. Incorporated the text of a bill (HR 860), to streamline and consolidate the process by which multidistrict litigation governing disasters was adjudicated. The House Judiciary Committee had formally reported HR 860 (H Rept 107-14) on March 12, 2001, and the full House passed it by voice vote under suspension of the rules on March 14.

Judicial Improvements Act. Included provisions from a bill (HR 3892) to reorganize and clarify existing mechanisms for filing complaints against federal judges. The changes were intended to provide more guidance to circuit chief judges when evaluating complaints, while providing individuals with more information on the status of their cases and making the process more user-friendly. HR 3892 was formally reported (H Rept 107-459) by House Judiciary on May 14, 2002, and passed by voice vote under suspension of the rules by the full House on July 22. It was reported by the Senate Judiciary Committee (no written report) on July 31.

HR 2215 included the following authorizations.

Justice Department operations. $17.6 billion in fiscal 2002 for Justice Department operations and $20.5 billion in fiscal 2003. The bill also required the president to submit a Justice Department authorization request for fiscal 2004 and fiscal 2005 when he submitted his fiscal 2004 budget.

Immigration and Naturalization Service. $4.1 billion—$3.3 billion of it for the border patrol.

Prisons. $4.6 billion for the federal prison system.

FBI. $4.3 billion for the detection, investigation, and prosecution of federal crimes. The bill included a number of requirements aimed at improving security at the agency.

Inspector General. $66 million for the Office of the Inspector General, with specific authority to investigate all allegations of criminal or administrative misconduct by Justice Department employees, including FBI personnel. This codified a rule issued by Attorney General John Ashcroft in July 2001 expanding the inspector general's jurisdiction over the FBI. The bill authorized $2 million to hire twenty-five full-time employees to conduct an increased number of audits, inspections, and investigations of alleged misconduct by FBI employees. It also required a report to Congress on whether an inspector general should be established for the FBI.

U.S. Attorneys. $1.6 billion for the ninety-four U.S. attorneys and their offices and the Executive Office of U.S. Attorneys. At least $10 million was to be used to augment the investigation and prosecution of intellectual property crimes. Also, two hundred assistant U.S. attorneys from the six litigating divisions were to be transferred from the main FBI headquarters in Washington, D.C., to various field offices around the country.

Immigration

With the backing of the White House, both chambers passed versions of legislation (HR 1885) to extend a program that permitted some immigrants to apply for U.S. residency even if they were in the country illegally. But the measure fell victim to powerful enemies and plain bad luck: The House was poised to clear the bill Sept. 11, 2001, but the terrorist attacks intervened. Congress did clear a bill (HR 3525) that sought to enhance the border security of the United States.

The program—known as 245(i) after its section in immigration law—allowed immigrants who were eligible for residency, but who had overstayed their visa or were otherwise in the country illegally, to pay a $1,000 fine and complete their residency application in the United States. The applicant also had to be sponsored by an employer or a family member who was a legal resident or U.S. citizen. Without the program, immigrants had to return to their home countries and apply there to become U.S. residents. But because of their illegal status while in the United States, they could be barred from returning for up to ten years.

The 245(i) program expired April 30, 2001. Many applicants missed the deadline, however, because the Immigration and Naturalization Service (INS) was slow to draft rules for the process.

The House easily passed a four-month extension, but the proposal stalled in the Senate, where many wanted to give the program a longer life span. The Senate subsequently passed an extension through April 2002. That version came up against the forces of Sept. 11.

The White House supported attaching the extension to the fiscal 2002 Commerce-Justice-State (CJS) spending bill (HR 2500). S 1215 (S Rept 107-42) contained a permanent extension of 245(i) that was opposed by House conservatives. House Judiciary Chair F. James Sensenbrenner Jr., R-Wis., said the 245(i) bill should go through regular order and asked his Republican colleagues to drop it from the CJS conference report, which they reluctantly did.

BACKGROUND

The issue of extending the 245(i) program was part of a broader debate about revising U.S. immigration laws, particularly toward Mexico. As governor of Texas and then as president, George W. Bush took a particular interest in promoting closer relations with Mexico. He also was at the forefront of Republican efforts to court the increasingly powerful Hispanic electorate, for whom immigration was a big concern.

Bush's first official trip abroad was to Mexico, where he met with President Vicente Fox in February 2001. The two announced plans to conduct negotiations on migration policy, with the goal of having a deal by the time Fox came to Washington, D.C., in early September for the Bush administration's first state visit. However, the administration's plan remained vague. Reports said only that it would likely include some kind of temporary guest-worker program as well as a process that would allow some of the millions of illegal immigrants in the United State to become legal residents.

When Fox came to Washington on Sept. 5, he presented a surprise timetable that called for a U.S-Mexico agreement by the end of the year. The White House at first played down the idea, but Bush said Sept. 6 that he understood why Fox felt such urgency on immigration and pledged to try to accommodate his schedule. Despite significant opposition from within his own party, it looked likely that Bush would push through a major rewrite of immigration laws.

Then came Sept. 11, which abruptly refocused the immigration debate on issues of border security and visas. Any overhaul of immigration policy was put on hold. Some wrote off the liberalization move entirely. Bush was careful, however, to distinguish between "people who come to our country to visit, to study or to work" and those "who come to hurt the American people." And he and congressional leaders of both parties took pains to assure pro-immigrant groups that a larger move toward liberalizing immigration laws would not be abandoned.

The most immediate immigration issue for Congress was the 245(i) extension. The program was created in 1994 as a three-year trial, and it expired at the end of 1997. Under a compromise worked out between the Clinton administration—which supported a permanent extension—and congressional Republicans, the provisions were renewed for four months, through April 30, 2001, as part of a fiscal 2001 omnibus appropriations bill (PL 106-554). On the final days of the extension, huge lineups surrounded immigration offices as thousands sought to file their applications before the deadline. *(Immigration relief, Congress and the Nation Vol. V, p. 672)*

On May 1, 2001, Bush sent a letter to congressional leaders seeking a temporary extension of the program. He noted that up to 200,000 of the 500,000 estimated eligible immigrants did not file applications by the April 30 deadline, in part, because INS regulations were not issued until late March. Bush did not say how long an extension he wanted, but a senior administration official said that a six- to twelve-month time frame was discussed when Bush met with Fox.

Bush's backing for an extension of the program was difficult for GOP conservatives, who previously opposed any such move. But the opponents of 245(i) agreed to consider a brief extension because the INS had not issued regulations for the previous extension quickly enough.

LEGISLATIVE ACTION

The four-month extension (HR 1885) sailed through the House on May 21, 2001, under suspension of the rules on a vote of 336–43. The bill, sponsored by George W. Gekas, R-Pa., was limited to applicants who had been in the United States by Dec. 21, 2000. The family or employment relationship that qualified them for visa status had to have existed before the law expired April 30.

But Judiciary Chair Orrin G. Hatch of Utah and other Senate Republicans argued that four months would not be enough time to get all the applications processed by INS, an agency that had a reputation for inefficiency. "It would be better to try and do it right" than push the House bill through, Hatch said. Many Democrats wanted to extend the program for a year, and White House spokesman Ari Fleischer said Bush was siding with the Senate. House Judiciary Chair Sensenbrenner, however, warned that such a tack could cause House support to dissipate.

On July 26, the Senate Judiciary Committee gave voice vote approval to a bill (S 778—no written report) that would extend the program through April 30, 2002. The committee adopted, by voice vote, an amendment by Jon Kyl, R-Ariz., to make 245(i) available only to those who had been in the United States since Dec. 21, 2000, and had established family or job ties at the time the bill was enacted. Kyl argued that, the way the original bill was worded, anyone who established their eligibility by April 2002 would be able to use it.

The Senate passed HR 1885 by voice vote Sept. 6, after substituting the text of S 778.

Six months after it was pulled from the House floor during the evacuation of the Capitol, HR 1885 began moving again. The House under suspension of the rules March 12, 2002, voted 275–137 to adopt H Res 365. The resolution provided for House acceptance of the Senate changes to HR 1885 and with the addition of the text of a separate bill (HR 3525) to tighten border security.

The House had passed HR 3525 on Dec. 19 by voice vote under suspension of the rules. House leaders hoped that combining it with the 245(i) extension would act as a sweetener to move the Senate to act on the border security bill. HR 3525 would extend the program until Nov. 30, 2002. To qualify, immigrants would have to show they have a job offer in the United States or a close relative who was either a U.S. citizen or a legal resident. They must have met those qualifications by Aug. 15, 2001.

The extension was opposed by some conservatives who argued that it rewarded people for breaking the law. Supporters, however, said the program helped keep families together.

Instead of taking up the combined measure, the Senate passed the HR 3525 as a stand-alone bill April 18, 2002, by 97–0. The House agreed 411–0 on May 8 under suspension of the rules to accept the Senate changes, completing congressional action. Bush signed HR 3525 (PL 107-173) into law on May 14.

HR 1885, meanwhile, stalled. Sen. Robert C. Byrd, D-W.Va., successfully blocked attempts to bring it up, including a plan to add it to the Senate companion Commerce-Justice-State appropriations bill (S 2778). He said the program rewarded lawbreakers.

Juvenile Crime

The House in 2001 passed a pair of bills (HR 863, HR 1900) on juvenile crime, one of which focused on penalties and the other on prevention. The Senate did not act on either of the measures. However, a measure that Congress cleared in 2002 to reauthorize the Department of Justice (HR 2215—PL 107-373) included key provisions from the juvenile crime bills. *(Justice reauthorization, p. 585)*

HR 863 would authorize $1.5 billion over three years for juvenile justice grants to state and local governments. HR 1900 would consolidate five juvenile justice and delinquency preventing programs into a single block grant to be used by states for activities designed to prevent and reduce juvenile crime.

PENALTIES

The House Judiciary Committee Crime Subcommittee approved HR 863—sponsored by subcommittee chair Lamar Smith, R-Texas—by voice vote March 21.

Smith and ranking Democrat Robert C. Scott of Virginia worked to keep the $1.5 billion measure free of amendments that could bog it down. They were determined to avoid the kind of controversial amendments that had sunk a nearly identical bill in 1999. Then, intense reaction following the massacre at Columbine High School in Colorado, where two teenagers killed themselves after gunning down twelve other students and a teacher, spawned days of floor debate and resulted in provisions to toughen penalties for many juvenile crimes and—in the Senate version—impose some gun control measures. *(1999 action, Congress and the Nation Vol. X, p. 633)*

In the 2001 bill, the only requirement on states seeking the grant money was that they allow local jurisdictions to develop and implement a program of graduated sanctions for juvenile offenders. Smith said the point of graduated sanctions was to "break the cycle of delinquency," which can allow a young offender to commit a series of ever-more-serious offenses without consequence until he or she commits a crime that results in a jail sentence.

Asa Hutchinson, R-Ark., and Mark Green, R-Wis., won voice vote approval for an amendment to add "restorative justice" programs to the list of approved uses for the money. Restorative justice programs let juveniles work out restitution agreements with their victims.

The full Judiciary Committee approved HR 863 by voice vote March 28 and formally reported it (H Rept 107-46) April 20. Ranking Democrat John Conyers Jr. of Michigan argued that "preventing juvenile crime is about thwarting easy access to guns," but he was blocked by committee rules from offering gun control amendments. The committee approved, by voice vote, a manager's amendment by Smith that broadened the kinds of programs that could be funded under the bill.

The House passed the bill by voice vote Oct. 16. Supporters succeeded in having the measure brought to the floor under suspension of the rules, which barred Conyers and others from offering amendments.

As passed, the bill contained provisions to

Authorization. Authorize $500 million in each of fiscal years 2002 through 2004 for grants to state and local governments for juvenile justice programs—twice the amount appropriated for juvenile justice block grants for fiscal 2001. The grants could be used for a wide range of activities including developing graduated sanctions; building corrections facilities; hiring additional juvenile court judges, officers, and prosecutors; training police officers to prevent and control juvenile crime; and establishing juvenile drug and gun courts.

Eligibility. Require states and localities receiving grants to establish a graduated sanctions plan for juvenile offenders. Graduated sanctions punish an offender in some way for each offense he or she commits. Although the punishment usually increases in severity along with the crime, the bill would not require harsher penalties at each stage.

It was not clear that it would be so easy to ward off amendments in the Senate. Dianne Feinstein, D-Calif., a leader in the gun control movement, said she considered the juvenile justice bill a fair target for gun control amendments.

PREVENTION

HR 1900 would reauthorize the 1974 Juvenile Justice and Delinquency Prevention Act (PL 93-415) through fiscal 2006. *(1974 law, Congress and the Nation Vol. IV, p. 581)*

The bill, cosponsored by James C. Greenwood, R-Pa., and Scott began in the Education and the Workforce Committee. It won voice vote approval in the Select Education Subcommittee on June 21, 2001, and the full committee approved the bill by a vote of 41–2 on Aug. 1. HR 1900 was formally reported (H Rept 107-203) Sept. 10.

The House passed the bill by voice vote under suspension of the rules Sept. 20. As passed, it would

Authorization. Consolidate five federal juvenile justice programs—dealing with mentoring, state challenge activities, boot camps, victims of child abuse and neglect, and gang prevention—into a single block grant, authorized for fiscal years 2002 through 2006. Grants would go to states based on the size of their juvenile population and their crime statistics. Recipients of the funds could include community-based organizations, law enforcement agencies, school districts, local governments, and social service providers.

Eligibility. Continue existing conditions for states receiving the grants, including requirements that juveniles be held separate from adults in jails and lock-ups. But the bill would double the time—from twenty-four to forty-eight hours—that youths in rural areas could be incarcerated with adults before making an initial court appearance.

Class Action Suits

The House in 2002 passed a bill (HR 2341) to limit class action suits but the measure went no further, halted by Democratic opposition in the Senate and reluctance by many members to be seen as protecting businesses in the midst of a series of corporate scandals. The legislation would give jurisdiction over most class action lawsuits to federal district courts and established a "bill of rights" for plaintiffs in federal class action lawsuits.

Even before House passage, Senate Judiciary Committee Chair Patrick J. Leahy, D-Vt., made clear that the issue was not on his to-do list for the rest of the 107th Congress. Democrats, who controlled the Senate, generally favored leaving the civil litigation system unchanged, arguing that it offered an appropriate means for aggrieved consumers to band together to fight well-financed companies. Their view was bolstered by Enron Corp.'s December 2001 bankruptcy filing, which prompted class action lawsuits by thousands of employees who lost their life savings because they were invested in what became worthless company stock.

BACKGROUND

Class action suits were filed by large groups of people who alleged that similar harm was caused them by a company or industry for the same reason. They allowed people who were financially unable to sue on their own to pool their resources and create an "affected class." Attorneys for such plaintiffs preferred being heard in state courts because the rules there often were considered friendlier to plaintiffs, and jury awards tended to be larger.

Under existing law, the only class action cases heard in federal court were those in which every plaintiff stood to receive at least $75,000 and in which the defendant and the lead plaintiff lived in different states.

Republicans, who controlled the House, had long sought to protect businesses from the cost of fighting class action suits in state courts. Businesses said that existing law allowed attorneys in class action suits to shop nationwide for the venue they determined would be most sympathetic to their case and that it inappropriately allowed state courts to make decisions that could affect hundreds or thousands of people across the country.

Business groups, such as the National Association of Manufacturers and National Federation of Independent Business, supported the effort to curb class action suits. Trial lawyers and consumer groups, however, opposed HR 2341.

The House passed a similar bill in the 106th Congress, but it died in the Senate in the face of a filibuster threat.

LEGISLATIVE ACTION

The Judiciary Committee approved HR 2341 by 16–10 on March 7, 2001, after Republicans easily fended off several Democratic amendments. It was formally reported (H Rept 107-370) March 12. Republican Robert W. Goodlatte and Democrat Rick Boucher, both of Virginia, sponsored the measure.

The committee
• Rejected 9–16 a proposal by Jerrold Nadler, D-N.Y., to require that more class action settlements be made public.
• Rejected 11–17 an amendment by Adam B. Schiff, D-Calif., to allow suits filed by private citizens and authorized by state attorneys general "on behalf of the public interest" to be heard in state courts.
• Rejected 9–15 an amendment by Melvin Watt, D-N.C., specifically designed to scuttle the bill.

With the last-minute endorsement of the Bush administration, the bill won a solid 233–190 majority on the House floor on March 13. The vote went largely along party lines; only seventeen Democrats voted for the bill, and five Republicans voted against it.

Under the plan, class action cases could be heard in federal court if the expected total jury award was at least $2 million, there were at least one hundred members in the affected class, and any of them lived in a state or country different from that of the defendant. However, this would not apply if a substantial majority of the plaintiffs and defendants were from one state, the claims primarily involved the laws of the state where the action was originally filed, or the primary defendants were state governments or state officials.

All plaintiffs in a class action would have to be given easy-to-understand settlement explanations. Supporters said that in some instances the complex legal jargon used to inform claimants that they had "won" a case masked the fact that they would not receive actual cash awards.

Again, a series of Democratic amendments were easily defeated. The House on March 13
• Rejected 191–234 a proposal by Barney Frank, D-Mass., to specify that suits not certified as class actions subject to a federal court's jurisdiction could then be tried in state court. The case would not later be subject to removal to federal court unless it met the existing party diversity standards.

• Rejected 202–223 a proposal by John Conyers Jr., D-Mich., to prevent a company from moving a case from state to federal court by incorporating a new company abroad and acquiring the original company.
• Rejected 174–251 an attempt by Maxine Waters, D-Calif., to require that anyone who withheld or shredded documents that were required to be handed over through a discovery motion in a class action lawsuit be found to have admitted to the facts of that motion.
• Rejected 194–231 an attempt by Zoe Lofgren, D-Calif., to strike a provision in the bill that would exclude civil suits brought on behalf of the general public by local prosecutors from being deemed class actions.
• Rejected 177–248 a proposal by Sheila Jackson-Lee, D-Texas, to block a party in a class action suit from moving the case's venue to federal court if that party destroyed, falsified, or altered material evidence.
• Rejected 191–235 a motion to send the bill back to the House Judiciary Committee with instructions to add language blocking defendants who knowingly committed a terrorist act from moving a class action suit to federal court.

'Virtual' Child Pornography

Both chambers in 2002 passed bills (HR 4623, S 2520) to ban "virtual" child pornography, but they were not able to agree on a final version before the 107th Congress adjourned.

The legislation was a response to a U.S. Supreme Court ruling in April that the original law addressing the issue (PL 104-208) was overly broad and thus unconstitutional. That 1996 law prohibited any image that "is, or appears to be, of a minor engaging in sexually explicit conduct." The ban included images that were simulated by computer technology or that used adults who looked like children. The high court found in *Ashcroft v. Free Speech Coalition* that extending the reach of child pornography laws to computer-generated and other images involving no real children would also prohibit visual depictions, such as films, art, or medical manuals, that had redeeming social value. *(Court ruling, p. 699)*

HR 4623 proposed to bar any computer-generated image that was "nearly indistinguishable . . . from that of a minor engaging in sexually explicit conduct." The bill's sponsor, Lamar Smith, R-Texas, and other supporters said they believed the new version would pass constitutional muster because it was more narrowly drawn than the law it would replace. They also argued that it would prevent child pornographers from using a familiar legal argument—that there was no proof that the distributed images showed real children.

Critics, however, said HR 4623 was no more constitutional than the 1996 law. Robert C. Scott, D-Va., said it tried to do "exactly what the Supreme Court said you cannot do."

The House Judiciary Committee approved the bill by 22–3 on June 19, 2002, and formally reported it (H Rept 107-526) on June 24. The House passed the measure by 413–8 under suspension of the rules on June 25.

S 2520, which the Senate passed by voice vote Nov. 14, began as an effort by Judiciary Committee ranking Republican Orrin G. Hatch of Utah and panel chair Patrick J. Leahy, D-Vt., to write a law more likely to withstand constitutional scrutiny. But before the Judiciary Committee approved the bill (no written report) by voice vote Nov. 14, it adopted two amendments by Hatch that brought the measure closer to its House counterpart. Critics said the resulting bill was constitutionally weaker and indicated that Congress was increasingly seeking to test the bounds of the U.S. Constitution in this area.

As introduced, the Hatch-Leahy bill would make it a crime to pander, or solicit, material that "conveys the impression that the material is, or contains, an obscene visual depiction of a minor engaging in sexually explicit conduct." One of the amendments would expand the definition of a minor to include "a computer or computer-generated image that is virtually indistinguishable from an actual minor." The other amendment would expand the pandering portion of the bill to include "purported material" that conveys the impression that a minor is engaging in obscene sexual behavior.

The high court consistently had maintained that pornography was protected speech unless it was ruled to be obscene. But it also had held that pornography involving minors could be banned, regardless of whether it was obscene, because of the compelling interest in protecting children.

Child Protection

The House in 2002 passed an omnibus bill (HR 5422) to combat crimes against children, but many of the provisions were too sweeping for the Senate, which did not consider it. The package, assembled by Judiciary Committee Chair F. James Sensenbrenner Jr., R-Wis., would build on a popular proposal aimed at speeding up the development of a federal alert system for abducted children, known as the AMBER (America's Missing: Broadcast Emergency Response) Plan.

Some pieces of the package had already passed in the House as separate bills but were stalled in the Senate. They provided for lifetime supervision of sex offenders (HR 4679), new prohibitions on sex tourism (HR 4477), a two-strikes-and-you're-out policy for sex offenses against children (HR 2146), and wiretapping in child sex crime investigations (HR 1877).

AMBER PLAN

The centerpiece of the package was a bill (HR 5422) to provide national coordination and assistance to states and localities that participated in the AMBER Plan, a partnership between law enforcement agencies and broadcasters that was credited with having saved thirty abducted children.

The system—named after Amber Hagerman, a nine-year-old girl abducted and killed in Arlington, Texas, in 1996—used the Emergency Alert System, similar to what was used to broadcast severe weather emergencies, to issue an alert when a child was abducted, including descriptions of the abducted child, the suspected abductor, and any vehicle involved. Twenty-four states had developed statewide plans, with many states linking together through regional systems. But the system was still a patchwork, with large areas not covered. Communication across state and local systems often was not possible.

The House Judiciary Committee approved HR 5422 by voice vote Oct. 2, 2002, and formally reported it (H Rept 107-723, Part I) Oct. 7. The House passed it Oct. 8 by 390–24 under suspension of the rules.

The Senate had passed its own version of the bill (S 2896, no written report), sponsored by Kay Bailey Hutchison, R-Texas—by voice vote Sept. 10, 2002. President George W. Bush supported the bill and urged House GOP leaders to finish it in time for an Oct. 1 conference on missing, exploited, and runaway children. At that conference, Bush announced that he was directing the attorney general to establish an AMBER alert coordinator in the Justice Department to serve as a nationwide point of contact for state and local officials and to establish national standards for the plans.

The House plan would establish a national coordinator within the Justice Department to work with state and local officials to develop the AMBER alert network. The coordinator would

• Work to eliminate gaps in the network, including gaps in areas of interstate travel; help states to develop more AMBER plans; and support efforts to ensure regional coordination.

• Notify and consult with the Federal Bureau of Investigation (FBI), the Transportation Department, and the Federal Communications Commission (FCC) about each alert issued for an abducted child through the AMBER network.

• Work with the Transportation Department, the FCC, and state and local broadcasters and law enforcement agencies to establish voluntary minimum standards for broadcasting alerts throughout the AMBER network.

HR 5422 also would establish a matching grant program within the Transportation Department and authorize $20 million in fiscal 2003 to help states develop electronic message boards and other forms of communication along highways to spread the word about abducted children. It would create a matching grant program within the Justice Department, authorized at $5 million in fiscal 2003, to help states support the AMBER alert network, including education and training, law enforcement programs, and equipment. In addition, it would increase a grant to the National Center for Missing and Exploited Children from $10 million to $20 million per year in fiscal 2003 and 2004.

LIFETIME CONSEQUENCES FOR SEX OFFENDERS

HR 4679 would permit judges to order lifetime supervision of sex offenders who had completed their sentences. It would apply to those convicted of sexual abuse, sexual exploitation, and other abuse of children; transportation for illegal sexual activity; and sex trafficking of children by force, fraud, or coercion. It would also apply to those convicted of coercion and enticement, the use of interstate facilities to transmit information about a minor, and kidnapping of a minor under the age of eighteen. Under existing law, federal judges could order up to five years of post-incarceration supervision of sex offenders.

The House Judiciary Committee approved HR 4679 by voice vote June 19, 2002, and formally reported it (H Rept 107-527) June 24. The House passed the bill 409–3 under suspension of the rules June 25.

SEX TOURISM PROHIBITION

HR 4477 would make it easier to prosecute those who travel to another country to have sex with a minor, regardless of whether the person originally intended to do so.

The bill would make it a crime, punishable by up to fifteen years in prison, to travel into the United States for the purpose of engaging in any illicit sexual conduct. It also would make it a crime for a U.S. citizen or permanent resident traveling abroad to engage or attempt to engage in illicit sexual conduct, even if the individual did not travel with the intent of engaging in these acts. As a result, prosecutors would no longer have to prove intent for those traveling in foreign countries. Violation would be punishable by fines and up to fifteen years in prison.

In addition, the bill would

• Make it an offense, punishable by up to fifteen years in prison, to arrange, induce, procure, or facilitate the travel of a person knowing that the individual was traveling in interstate or foreign commerce for the purpose of engaging in illicit sexual conduct.

• Define an illicit sexual act as a sexual act that would be illegal under certain statutes if it occurred in the special maritime and territorial jurisdiction of the United States or as any commercial sex act with a person under the age of eighteen.

• Specify that only those who knew or should have known that they were engaging in sexual activity with a minor under the age of eighteen could be charged. Defendants would have to prove by a "preponderance of the evidence" that they reasonably believed the person was at least eighteen years old.

• Make it an offense, punishable by up to fifteen years in prison, to attempt or conspire to violate these provisions.

The House Judiciary Committee approved HR 4477 by voice vote June 19, 2002, and formally reported it (H Rept 107-525) June 24. The House passed the measure by a vote of 418–8 on June 26 under suspension of the rules.

TWO STRIKES AND YOU'RE OUT

HR 2146 provided for a mandatory sentence of life in prison for anyone convicted a second time of a sexual offense against a child. Specifically, it called for a life sentence,

unless the death penalty was imposed, against an individual convicted of a federal sex offense against a child under the age of seventeen if the perpetrator had been convicted of a previous federal or state sexual offense against a child. If the prior offense was under state law, it would have to have been an offense under federal law had the crime taken place in a federal jurisdiction.

The measure would apply to second convictions for seven specific crimes—aggravated sexual abuse, sexual abuse, sexual abuse of a minor or ward, abusive sexual contact, sexual abuse resulting in death, the selling or buying of children, and transporting a minor in interstate or foreign commerce for the purposes of prostitution or for illegal sexual purposes under a state law.

The House Judiciary Committee approved HR 2146 by voice vote March 6, 2002, and formally reported it (H Rept 107-373) March 12. The House passed the bill by a vote of 382–34 on March 14.

WIRETAPPING IN CHILD SEX CRIMES

HR 1877 would authorize the use of wiretaps and other electronic surveillance in investigating crimes of child pornography, the buying and selling of children for sexual exploitation, inducing or coercing someone to cross state lines to engage in illegal sexual activities, and transporting minors for illegal sexual activity.

The House Judiciary Committee approved the bill 20–4 on April 24, 2002, and formally reported it (H Rept 107-468) May 16. The House passed HR 1877 by 396–11 under suspension of the rules May 21.

OTHER PROVISIONS

The omnibus package also contained provisions to increase penalties for sex crimes against children. The bill would make murder involving child abuse, child assault, or torture a first-degree murder charge. It increased maximum penalties for sexual exploitation of a child; for shipping, receiving, or distributing by any means, including by computer, child pornography, or any visual depictions of minors engaged in sexually explicit conduct; for transporting a minor for prostitution and traveling in interstate or foreign commerce to have sex with minors; and for forced sex trafficking of minors.

HR 5422 also would direct the U.S. Sentencing Commission to increase the minimum sentencing for kidnapping and increase the sentencing range for kidnappers who sexually exploited the victim. It provided for a mandatory minimum sentence of twenty years for the kidnapping of a person under the age of eighteen. The measure would repeal a provision in the existing sentencing guidelines that decreased the minimum sentencing levels if the victim was released within twenty-four hours.

The bill also would

• Abolish the statute of limitations for the prosecution of child abduction and felony sex offenses against minors, meaning a perpetrator could be prosecuted for the crime regardless of how much time had passed since it occurred. The provision would not apply to military cases.

• Deny pretrial release for anyone charged with rape or kidnapping of a minor.

• Require federal, state, and local law enforcement agencies to report each case of a missing person under the age of twenty-one, up from age eighteen under existing law, to the National Crime Information Center of the Department of Justice.

• Require the Justice Department to report to Congress on the number of times since 1993 that the department had inspected the records of producers of pornographic material to ensure that minors were not being used in such productions, including the number of prosecutions resulting from the inspection.

DNA Testing

Legislation (S 486) aimed at ensuring that the innocent were not mistakenly executed was reported (S Rept 107-315) by the Senate Judiciary Committee on Oct. 16, 2002, but it went no further.

Committee Chair Patrick J. Leahy, D-Vt., had been able to get his panel's voice vote approval of S 486 on July 18. The 12–7 vote—which included "ayes" from two Republicans, Sam Brownback of Kansas and Arlen Specter of Pennsylvania—marked a major success for Leahy and a new high for the legislation, which had been stuck in the Judiciary Committee for two years.

S 486 sought to ensure that those on death row had adequate legal representation and access to new, sophisticated DNA (deoxyribonucleic acid) tests that could prove their innocence. But opponents argued that the bill would infringe on states' rights, and they questioned the measure's underlying premise that the system for applying the death penalty was flawed.

The bill would require DNA testing in federal cases in which the tests have the "scientific potential" to produce new evidence supporting an inmate's claim of innocence. It also would bar the destruction of biological evidence in federal criminal cases while defendants are incarcerated, unless they are notified first.

States that accepted federal funds for DNA programs would face similar requirements for their own cases.

The committee action came amid mounting debate over the death penalty. In June 2002, the U.S. Supreme Court ruled 72–2 in *Ring v. Arizona* that a jury—not a judge—must determine whether a capital defendant is sent to death row. In a separate decision, the high court barred executions of the mentally retarded (*Atkins v. Virginia*, 2002). States were scrutinizing the system as well. Illinois, for example, imposed a moratorium on executions after thirteen innocent inmates were released from death row. *(Court rulings, p. 646)*

Leahy struck a fragile last-minute deal with two of his bill's opponents, Republicans Jeff Sessions of Alabama and Mike DeWine of Ohio. The deal eased the measure's path through the committee, but it did not allay all of their concerns about the grant program that would be established by the legislation.

States would use the grants to improve their defense of indigents in capital cases. States that accepted the money would have to create or improve a system that was "effective" in providing competent legal representation in capital cases. The effectiveness of the programs could be enforced through civil suits in federal court. If states did not accept the grants, the funding would go to groups that provided legal services in capital cases. Under the deal, those groups could not use the money for political activities.

The committee's ranking Republican, Orrin G. Hatch of Utah, said the language represented a "Hobson's choice" for states, which could accept grants and run the risk of being sued or allow grant money to go to private capital defender organizations. Hatch instead favored legislation to authorize post-conviction DNA testing when a federal defendant could show the DNA test would establish his or her "actual innocence."

Judicial Nominations

The partisan fight over President George W. Bush's selections for federal judgeships became one of the harshest battles of the 107th Congress. The Senate confirmed one hundred presidential nominees to the U.S. Court of Appeals and federal district court. The Judiciary Committee rejected two of his picks in high-profile battles, and an additional twenty-eight nominees did not get votes in the committee.

The most intense debates broke out over two nominees to the Fifth Circuit Court of Appeals in New Orleans, Charles W. Pickering Sr. and Priscilla Owen, both of whom were rejected in committee; a nominee to the Fourth Circuit Court of Appeals in Richmond, Dennis Shedd, who was narrowly approved by the Senate; and a nominee to the D.C. Circuit Court of Appeals, Miguel A. Estrada, who was not considered.

Bush's 77 percent success rate was lower than that of the previous two presidents during their first two years in office. Bill Clinton won confirmation of 90 percent of his nominees while working with a Senate run by fellow Democrats in 1993–1994; George Bush had a 95 percent success rate in 1989–1990 with a Democratic Senate.

When the 107th Congress adjourned, there were thirty-four vacancies on the federal trial courts (5 percent of the total authorized judgeships) and twenty-five vacancies (14 percent) on the appeals courts.

BACKGROUND

Senate Republicans made a priority of helping Bush reshape the federal judiciary in a more conservative vein. The Democratic majority and its allies in liberal advocacy groups were intent on setting boundaries for that effort. Both parties viewed the fight—which focused on a handful of appellate court seats and on the pace of Senate action on Bush's nominees—as a dress rehearsal for a showdown over the next U.S. Supreme Court nominee.

The power to choose judges for lifetime appointments is one of the most significant prerogatives of the president, allowing him to direct judicial philosophy—and therefore the interpretation of federal law—long after he has left office. But under the U.S. Constitution, the Senate must give its "advice and consent."

As the 107th Congress began, Democrats were smarting over the difficulties that Clinton had encountered in getting his judges through a Republican-controlled Senate, which significantly undercut his efforts to shape the judiciary. The atmosphere around appointments developed an unusually partisan tinge, with Republicans accusing Clinton of choosing liberal activists and Clinton accusing Republicans of delaying women and minority candidates.

Virtually none of Clinton's nominees was rejected. Instead, Senate Republicans prevented them from being voted on, in committee or on the Senate floor. Vital to their success was the "blue slip"—literally, a blue slip of paper that senators used to register their position on a judicial candidate from their state. Senate Judiciary Chair Orrin G. Hatch, R-Utah, almost always refused to hold a hearing on a nominee unless he had received a positive blue slip back from both home state senators.

This blocked Clinton from getting judges on the bench but spared senators from casting many votes. During the eight years of the Clinton presidency, only one judicial nomination, that of Ronnie L. White of Missouri, was rejected. The Senate rejected his nomination to be a district court judge in 1999 on a party-line 45–54 vote.

Clinton had particular problems winning confirmation of appellate court judges. The Senate approved sixty-five of his nominees to the courts of appeal, a success rate of 61 percent. By contrast, President Ronald Reagan won approval of eighty-three appeals court judges and enjoyed a success rate of 87 percent. The Clinton administration blamed Republicans for obstructionist tactics, but some observers said the president failed to put enough of a focus on the nomination process.

After eight years of a Democratic administration, Republican appointees still dominated the appellate courts. Of the twelve circuit courts, three had a majority of Democratic appointees, seven were dominated by Republicans, and two were evenly split.

At the end of Clinton's presidency, forty nominations were left pending. Democrats feared that dozens of vacancies would go to conservative judges selected by Bush. (*Congress and the Nation Vol. X, p. 677*)

The judicial approval process increasingly had drawn the attention of interest groups since the Democratic-controlled Senate rejected conservative Supreme Court nominee Robert H. Bork 42–58 in 1987. Both Democrats and Republicans had come to view the fight over federal judges as another powerful way to mobilize their base on election day. It drew a clear connection between the ideological balance of the courts and the balance of power on such hot-button issues as abortion and gun control.

At the same time, senators and interest groups turned more of their focus to the lower courts, particularly the Court of Appeals. With the Supreme Court hearing a smaller share of the cases filed each term, the appeals courts often had the final word on controversial issues.

Consequently, the scrutiny of those nominees and the resulting partisan battles had grown more frequent and more intense. Moreover, membership on the Supreme Court had been unusually stable. The court's makeup had not changed since Stephen G. Breyer was confirmed as a justice in 1994.

The standoff eroded the president's authority to shape the federal judiciary, leaving a sometimes understaffed bench when some vacancies had gone unfilled for years. At the same time, the concerted effort by parties to link judicial nominations to political ends threatened to undermine the public's confidence in the independence and integrity of the courts, warned scholars who study judicial selection.

EARLY SKIRMISHES

The first signs of tension emerged in March 2001, when Republicans still controlled the Senate chamber. Bush withdrew sixty-two executive and judicial nominations that Clinton had sent to the Senate in his final days as president. Among the most controversial of these withdrawn nominations was that of Richmond, Virginia, attorney Roger Gregory to the U.S. Court of Appeals for the Fourth Circuit. Clinton at the end of 2000 had used a recess appointment to install him to the court for one year. Gregory became the first minority judge on the Fourth Circuit, which had the largest African American population of all the circuit courts. Though Bush officially withdrew the nomination for a lifetime judgeship, Gregory's supporters, including Republican senator John Warner of Virginia, were still hopeful that he would get the job.

Just one month later, senators began fighting over the procedure for reviewing judicial nominations. At issue was the tradition under which senators registered their position on a judicial candidate from their state using a blue slip of paper. At a closed-door Judiciary Committee meeting on April 24, Hatch told the panel he intended to enforce a policy under which only one senator's approval could be enough to allow a nomination from his or her state to proceed. Democrats declared Hatch's announcement an unfair change in policy since the days when a single senator could use the blue slip to sink Clinton's picks.

More than an hour of debate did not resolve the issue. Democrats issued a sharp warning to Republicans, even departing from Senate etiquette by threatening to filibuster Bush's nominations. "There is absolute unanimity within our caucus that we will respect the same blue-slip approach to nominations that the Republicans insisted upon over the last several years," said Senate minority leader Tom Daschle, D-S.D. If a Senate Democrat had not "signed off" on the nominee, Daschle added, "there will not be a confirmation vote. . . . We'll extend debate, and we can guarantee that they will not reach cloture."

But Hatch warned, "They want an absolute right to veto a presidential nomination, and I'm not going to give it to them."

Democrats effectively had the clout to enforce a blue slip policy. That was because the eighteen-member Judiciary Committee was evenly divided between members of the two parties, and Democrats could prevent the committee from reaching a quorum, and thereby doing business, merely by refusing to show up. They could also block a vote by endlessly debating a nomination.

Tensions also flared over a letter that White House counsel Alberto R. Gonzales sent to the American Bar Association (ABA) saying the group no longer would be asked to evaluate the professional abilities of judicial candidates. For almost fifty years, the ABA provided presidents with confidential reviews of potential nominees, but Republicans, who decried the political positions espoused by the ABA, objected to giving the group a unique role in the nomination process.

Despite the early skirmishing, Democrats generally praised the White House for working with them on its first batch of nominations. On May 9 Bush announced eleven nominees to the courts of appeal—a group that, while generally conservative, included two judges supported by Clinton, three women, one Hispanic, and two African Americans, including Gregory. Democrats were pleased that the administration postponed several controversial nominations, particularly that of conservative representative Christopher Cox, R-Calif., to the U.S. Court of Appeals for the Ninth Circuit.

A DEMOCRATIC MAJORITY

The decision of James Jeffords of Vermont to leave the Republican Party and throw his support to the Democrats, effective June 5, 2001, greatly complicated Bush's ambition to solidify a conservative bent on the federal judiciary. The new Judiciary Committee Chair, Patrick J. Leahy of Vermont, quickly reinstated the blue slip system that required the White House to get approval from both home-state senators for each judicial nomination. Democrats also said the committee would not act on a nomination until it has received the report of the ABA on each candidate.

Republicans unsuccessfully sought new rules in an organizing resolution that would commit the Senate to a floor vote on all Supreme Court nominees. Daschle pledged only that all high court nominees would get a floor vote regardless of their vote in the Judiciary Committee.

Partisan tensions, the mid-year Senate reorganization, and the requirement for ABA reports meant that Democrats moved slowly on Bush's nominations. By the end of 2001,

the Senate had confirmed just twenty-eight of the sixty-six judicial nominations. Democrats noted that was one more than the number of judges seated in 1993, Clinton's first year in office, when the Democrats also controlled the Senate. But Bush's first-year confirmation rate was just 42 percent, whereas Clinton won confirmation of 84 percent of his first-year nominees.

Senate Democrats worried that Bush nominees had strong conservative backgrounds, which left the liberal interest community up in arms. Angered Republicans maintained that the Democratic Senate majority was deliberately stalling to prevent Bush from putting his stamp on the judiciary. Presidential spokesman Ari Fleischer, noting that there would be ninety-eight vacancies in the federal judiciary when the Senate returned for the second session, told reporters Dec. 21 that "the president deserves to have his team in place, particularly during a time of war." Democrats, however, said that all twenty-eight of the judicial confirmations in 2001 happened since they took control of the Senate in June and that several judges were confirmed after the Sept. 11, 2001, attacks.

BATTLE OVER PICKERING

The Judiciary Committee rejected the nomination of Judge Charles W. Pickering Sr. to the U.S. Court of Appeals for the Fifth Circuit March 14, 2002. In three roll-call votes, the committee defeated, by the same party-line 9–10 tally, motions to report the nomination favorably to the Senate, to report the nomination without recommendation, and to report the nomination unfavorably. This was the first major battle over a Bush nominee and, according to the Congressional Research Service, just the ninth time since 1977 that the Judiciary Committee had voted down a judicial nomination. Usually, if nominees ran into trouble, they did not get a committee hearing or a vote, or they withdrew their name.

A federal district judge in Mississippi and father of Rep. Charles W. "Chip" Pickering Jr., R-Miss., the nominee stirred controversy because of his long and evolving record as a Mississippi political figure and his penchant for using the bench as a vehicle for expressing his views. The ABA gave Pickering its top rating of "well qualified" for a promotion. But liberal interest groups, such as People for the American Way and the NAACP (National Organization for the Advancement of Colored People), painted a picture of someone who was once supportive of his home state's segregationist policies and whose sensitivity to the concerns of racial minorities had not grown sufficiently since. They criticized Pickering for a legal article he wrote in 1959 suggesting ways to strengthen Mississippi's law against interracial marriages, for several decisions he had written as a federal trial court judge that they said showed he was not committed to enforcing civil rights and employment laws, and for his work in 1976 on a Republican Party platform plank that called for a constitutional amendment banning abortion.

Conservative groups, including the Family Research Council and the Free Congress Foundation, pointed to

Pickering's work toward racial reconciliation and to his support from Mississippi black leaders. Republicans, led by Minority Leader Trent Lott, R-Miss., said Pickering had shown great courage when, as a county attorney in 1967, he helped the Federal Bureau of Investigation (FBI) investigate and prosecute the Ku Klux Klan. They also said his decisions typically were upheld on appeal and his rate of reversal was lower than the national average for a district court judge.

Hatch tried to convince one committee Democrat to vote with Republicans to send Pickering's nomination to the full Senate without a recommendation, a parliamentary maneuver that would allow the nomination to come to a vote on the floor. At least two Democrats not on the committee—Zell Miller of Georgia and Ernest F. Hollings of South Carolina—had said they would vote for Pickering, so it appeared Pickering could win confirmation if the full Senate voted on him.

But the committee Democrats refused to budge. They criticized the White House for declining to consult with them before nominating Pickering, and they said they hoped the confrontation—and Pickering's defeat—would encourage the Bush administration to seek more input from Democrats into judicial nominations.

Republicans said Pickering was caught up in a not-so-subtle campaign by Democrats to convince the White House not to nominate a strong conservative to the Supreme Court, should any of the current justices step down during his administration. Bush said in a statement after the vote that he was "deeply disappointed." The committee action, he said, "was unfortunate for democracy and unfortunate for America."

For the vote, the Judiciary Committee had to move to a larger hearing room in the Dirksen Senate Office Building to accommodate the huge demand for seats. As it was, there was standing room only, at least at the start of the four-and-a-half hour meeting. The crowd included representatives of dozens of interest groups both for and against Pickering's nomination, including the liberal Alliance for Justice and the conservative Free Congress Foundation.

Leahy allowed everyone on the committee to speak as long as he wanted, and most went on record to explain their decisions. But the vote had been a foregone conclusion.

"The issue is whether Judge Pickering's record justifies this promotion to a court that is just one step below the Supreme Court," Leahy said. "Appellate judges in the circuit courts write opinions that eventually can become law affecting all of us, no matter where we live. I have concluded that the judge's record does not justify this promotion."

Republicans said Pickering was well qualified. They accused Democrats of blocking his nomination for ideological and political reasons. "Opposition to Judge Pickering boils down to a real desire to keep conservatives off the court as much as possible," said Jon Kyl, R-Ariz.

During the committee meeting and after, Democrats and Republicans alike referred to GOP obstructionist tactics during the Clinton years. "I think that this is payback," said Lott. "The problem with payback is, when does it ever end?"

An emotional Lott took to the floor after the vote, saying Pickering was a personal friend and he took the vote as a slap against him and his state. The following day, he said he would block the nomination of Jonathan S. Adelstein, an aide to Daschle, to a Democratic seat on the Federal Communications Commission. He said the move was not retaliation for Pickering's defeat, but he warned that the Pickering vote could cause widespread problems in the Senate.

A SECOND REJECTION

The Judiciary Committee rejected a second Bush nominee Sept. 5, 2002, also on a party-line vote of 9–10. The jurist, Priscilla Owen, had been nominated to the U.S. Circuit Court of Appeals for the Fifth Circuit.

During the panel's July 23 hearing on Owen, Democrats argued that her rulings as a justice on the Texas Supreme Court showed an anti-abortion and probusiness bias. They also said that she too often contorted facts and legal precedent to support her views.

Owen's supporters maintained she was a fair jurist and brilliant legal scholar. Owen said all her opinions during her seven years on Texas's highest court had been based on the law and precedent. "The picture that some special interest groups have painted of me is wrong," Owen said. "If I am confirmed, I will do my utmost to apply the statutes you have written as you have written them—not as I would have written them or others might want me to interpret them."

Owen's case was the first in which abortion became a central issue. Advocacy groups on both sides mobilized, putting pressure on senators and the White House. Owen, portrayed by Democrats as one of the most conservative of Bush's appellate nominees, drew criticism for her opinions in the case of minors who wanted to waive a requirement under Texas law that they notify a parent before getting an abortion. Under the statute, minors can get a waiver when they appear "sufficiently well informed" to obtain an abortion, when notification is not in their best interests, or when they would face abuse as a result of telling a parent.

Two years before, the Texas Supreme Court struggled to define the criteria and ruled in favor of the minors in a series of cases. But in dissenting opinions, Owens wrote that the standards her fellow jurists had used were not strict enough. She said minors should have to demonstrate they are fully aware of the "philosophic, social, moral and religious arguments" surrounding abortion.

In her testimony before the Senate Judiciary Committee, Owen said she wrote her opinion based on Supreme Court precedent and the legislative intent behind the parental consent law. But key Democrats on the closely divided panel appeared skeptical. "You've looked in other places, it seems to me, to find a rationale not to do what the Texas law calls for," said Dianne Feinstein of California, who was initially pinpointed as one of a handful of possible swing votes. Hatch, the committee's top Republican, said the personal views of judicial nominees should not play a role in their confirmation.

But Democrat Charles E. Schumer of New York said ideology should remain a factor. He said, "Judges bring their experiences, their biases and their ideology to the table."

BUSH PROPOSAL

Bush on Oct. 30, 2002, proposed new rules for the Senate on how to handle judicial nominations, saying the existing system was "poisoned and polarized." But his solution would eliminate the Senate's authority to reject nominees in committee, requiring floor votes on every nomination.

Under the Bush plan, judges would notify the White House of their retirement a year in advance. The president would submit nominations to the Senate within six months of receiving notice of a vacancy. The Senate Judiciary Committee then would hold a hearing within ninety days of receiving a nomination. No matter how the committee voted, the full Senate would agree to hold a vote on each nominee within 180 days of receiving his or her nomination. The new rules would prevent senators from exercising their prerogative to refuse to hold floor votes on certain nominations.

"The current state of affairs is not merely another round of political wrangling," Bush said. "It is a disturbing failure to meet our responsibilities under the Constitution."

Republicans were particularly outraged when Leahy, earlier in October, postponed a scheduled vote on appellate nominee Dennis Shedd, tapped for the Fourth U.S. Circuit Court of Appeals. The move angered Lott and Strom Thurmond, R-S.C., who had championed Shedd's nomination.

Bush's complaint echoed those made by Clinton, who accused Senate Republicans of politicizing the selection process and delaying votes on his nominees. Democrats said Bush's proposal was purely political. "The timing and handling of this unilateral White House proposal, a week before the elections, and after ignoring all previous invitations to consult with the Senate, cannot help but raise questions about its purpose," Leahy said. But GOP lawmakers, including Hatch, maintained that the Bush plan was a legitimate effort to improve the system.

Democrats complained that the nomination and confirmation process had been slowed by the Bush administration's decision to break with precedent and no longer ask the ABA to review candidates before submitting nominations to the Senate. The Judiciary Committee still factored the ABA review into its decision, but that process did not begin until the nominations arrived at the committee.

On Nov. 19, the Senate approved the final nominee of the 107th Congress, confirming Shedd by a vote of 55–44 despite the opposition of liberal advocacy groups. The vote was widely seen as an act of senatorial courtesy to the retiring Thurmond, who had employed Shedd as a top aide. Shedd had been one of Bush's first eleven judicial nomina-

tions May 9, 2001. Of those eleven, five had been confirmed; five did not receive consideration; and one, Owen, was defeated in committee.

Despite such numbers Democrats argued that they moved much faster on Bush nominees than Republicans did during the latter part of the Clinton administration, noting the fifty-nine vacancies on the federal bench at the end of the 107th Congress, compared with the 110 when Democrats took control of the Judiciary Committee in June 2001. But Senate minority leader Lott countered that the Senate did an "extremely poor job and a very unfair job in the way we handled judicial nominations."

Among the nominations that never came up for a vote was that of Miguel Estrada, nominated to the influential Circuit Court of Appeals for the District of Columbia. He had been a partner in the law firm that represented Bush before the Supreme Court during the disputed 2000 election.

During a hearing Sept. 26, 2002, Judiciary panel Democrats noted that one of Estrada's supervisors when he was an assistant to the solicitor general in the Clinton administration had said that he lacked the judgment necessary to serve on the appellate bench. A Hispanic group maintained that his pro bono work on anti-loitering statutes caused "grave concerns" about how well he represented the Hispanic community. Estrada's supporters hailed him as a rising star and one of the nation's most impressive young lawyers.

Flag Desecration

In what had become a routine vote, House members in 2001 passed a joint resolution (H J Res 36) to amend the U.S. Constitution and prohibit flag desecration. The Senate did not take up the measure.

Three times in the preceding six years—1995, 1997, and 1999—the House passed the amendment with a two-thirds majority, seeking to override a U.S. Supreme Court decision that protected flag burning as a form of political speech. The Senate had twice come within a few votes of passing the measure, in 1995 and 2000. But in the 107th Congress, Senate Judiciary Committee Chair Patrick J. Leahy, D-Vt., whose panel had jurisdiction, opposed the measure and declined to take it up. *(1995 action, Congress and the Nation Vol. IX, p. 754; 1997, 1999, and 2000 action, Congress and the Nation Vol. X, pp. 610, 666)*

Amending the Constitution requires a two-thirds vote in the House and Senate and ratification by three-quarters of the states.

The House Judiciary Committee approved the bill June 20, 2001, on a party-line vote of 15–11. The panel defeated 9–13 an attempt by Melvin Watt, D-N.C., to specify that the proposed amendment could not interfere with First Amendment rights. Robert C. Scott, D-Va., also offered an amendment, defeated by voice vote, which would replace "desecration" with "burning." H J Res 36 was formally reported (H Rept 107-115) on June 27.

The House on July 17 passed the measure 298–125. Earlier the same day, the full House rejected, 100–324, the Watt amendment.

For supporters of a ban, the flag is "more than just a piece of cloth," Randy "Duke" Cunningham, R-Calif., said on the House floor. Destroying a flag "represents a desecration of those [American] values, those ideas and those thoughts." Opponents argued that the proposed amendment would violate one of the freedoms the flag symbolizes—freedom of speech. "If a jerk burns a flag, America is not threatened," said Gary L. Ackerman, D-N.Y. "Even a despicable lowlife malcontent has the right to disagree."

Background Checks

During consideration of the fiscal 2002 Commerce, Justice, and State annual appropriations bill (HR 2500—PL 107-77), members tussled over a decision by Attorney General John Ashcroft to dramatically shorten the time the Federal Bureau of Investigation (FBI) was permitted to hold records of background checks on gun buyers.

To buy a gun through a federally licensed dealer, purchasers had to have their names run through the National Instant Check System to determine whether they had a felony conviction or other records that would prevent the gun purchase. Under President Bill Clinton, the FBI had held the records for up to 180 days to do audits of the system. Ashcroft said he wanted to destroy the records within twenty-four hours of their creation, a position the National Rifle Association had advocated for years.

On the House floor, Rep. James P. Moran, D-Va., offered an amendment to require that the records be retained for ninety days. He said a study of the system showed that more than five thousand people were able to get around the background check and purchase weapons, something that probably would have gone unnoticed if the records were not available for review. The amendment was rejected, 161–268, on July 18, 2001.

Hate Crimes

Although Democrats considered it a priority, legislation (S 625, HR 1343) to broaden the federal definition of hate crimes failed to get a floor vote in either chamber. Democratic leaders pulled a hate crimes bill from the Senate floor in 2002 after sponsors were unable to muster the votes needed to limit debate. In the House, supporters tried but could not get enough signatures on a discharge petition to bring a similar bill directly to the floor.

The bills would expand hate crime laws to cover offenses committed because of a victim's gender, sexual orientation, or disability. Existing law (PL 90-284), enacted in 1968, allowed federal prosecution of crimes based on race, color, religion, or national origin. It could be used only under six specified situations of federal involvement, including crimes committed against victims while they voted or were on federal property. *(1968 law, Congress and the Nation Vol. II, p. 378)*

S 625, sponsored by Edward M. Kennedy, D-Mass., was approved by the Senate Judiciary Committee by voice vote July 16, 2001. A report (S Rept 10-147) was filed on May 9, 2002. The full Senate took up the measure the next month. Opponents drafted several amendments—many related only loosely, if at all, to the underlying bill—and threatened a protracted debate on the legislation.

To stave off the amendments, Majority Leader Tom Daschle, D-S.D., filed a motion to invoke cloture, or limit the debate. Republicans lobbied a handful of bill supporters in their own caucus, arguing it was too early to stop debate and that cloture would block legitimate amendments. The bill's proponents campaigned, too, but were unable to get the sixty votes needed to limit debate. The cloture motion failed 54–43 on June 11. Republican opponents persuaded two GOP cosponsors, John Ensign of Nevada and Arlen Specter of Pennsylvania, to vote with them against limiting debate. Four GOP senators—all cosponsors of the bill—voted for cloture: Gordon H. Smith of Oregon, Lincoln Chafee of Rhode Island, and Susan Collins and Olympia J. Snowe, both of Maine.

Proponents of similar legislation in the House (HR 1343) made a last-ditch effort to force the bill to the floor with a discharge petition. They had 208 cosponsors when the 107th Congress adjourned, still short of the 218 needed to prevail. The House bill was sponsored by John Conyers Jr., D-Mich.

Prison Labor

The House Judiciary Committee on April 24, 2002, gave voice vote approval to a bill (HR 1577) that would phase out a mandate that government agencies, whenever possible, buy goods made by prison labor. The bill was formally reported (H Rept 107-583) on July 16. It did not go any further.

Business groups had fought for years to change the rule that gives prison workshops first dibs on large federal contracts for everything from office chairs to uniforms. HR 1577 would gradually eliminate, over five years, the mandate that agencies generally do business with the Federal Prison Industries (FPI) program. Inmates still would be paid far less than workers on the outside, but businesses said they could compete for lucrative government contracts if only given the chance.

The panel voted 5–22 to reject an amendment offered by Rep. Darrell Issa, R-Calif., that would continue the preference for prisons when 80 percent of the inmates are less than two years away from being released or entering a pre-release program.

Under current law, federal agencies that wanted to buy at least $2,500 worth of goods first had to check whether the Federal Prison Industries made the products they wanted. If not, the agency was allowed to buy from a private company.

But if FPI did make the product, the agency had to buy the prison-made version.

A great deal of money was at stake: FPI, which did business as UNICOR, recorded $583.5 million in sales in 2001. The program had been in effect for sixty-eight years.

One reason for the bill's approval was the ascension of a supporter, F. James Sensenbrenner Jr., R-Wis., to the Judiciary chairmanship. His predecessor, Republican Henry J. Hyde of Illinois, opposed the bill and blocked it from consideration during his six years as Judiciary Committee Chair. *(Earlier action, Congress and the Nation Vol. X, p. 652)*

The legislation split Republicans between those such as Sensenbrenner, who said private industry needs to be able to compete for federal contracts, and those such as Hyde, who said FPI provides valuable job training for inmates and should be protected. More than three hundred businesses and business groups, including the U.S. Chamber of Commerce and the National Federation of Independent Businesses, lobbied for the bill. So did organized labor, which believed the current law cost their workers jobs.

Concealed Weapons

The Senate Judiciary Committee gave voice vote approval on Nov. 14, 2002, to legislation (S 2480) that would exempt off-duty and retired law enforcement officials from bans on carrying concealed weapons. It was formally reported (S Rept 107-345) on Nov. 19. The bill did not advance further.

Twelve of the nineteen members of the committee signed on as cosponsors to the bill. Supporters included Chair Patrick J. Leahy, D-Vt., and ranking Republican Orrin G. Hatch of Utah. But committee member Edward M. Kennedy, D-Mass., called the bill "a giant step in the wrong direction." Kennedy failed on a 9–9 vote to amend the bill to limit the kinds of weapons that retired and off-duty officers could conceal and carry.

The committee adopted by voice vote a substitute amendment that Leahy and Hatch offered that responded to some of Kennedy's concerns. The amendment was designed to clarify that the bill would apply only to firearms, not to other weapons, such as bombs.

Retired police officers would be required to have fifteen years of experience to carry concealed firearms. They also would have to meet the same training and qualification standards required of active-duty officers.

Gun Liability

Two House committees in 2002 approved legislation (HR 2037) that would shield gun manufacturers, sellers, and trade organizations from some liability lawsuits. The full House did not take up the measure. *(108th Congress action, p. 614)*

Supporters said the measure was necessary to protect the gun industry from frivolous lawsuits filed by municipalities. But opponents said it was a sop to the gun lobby.

Moving first, the Energy and Commerce Committee approved the bill Sept. 25 on a 30–16 vote. A number of Democratic gun rights supporters crossed party lines to back the measure, including ranking Democrat John D. Dingell of Michigan and cosponsor Chris John of Louisiana.

"The problem of frivolous lawsuits by municipalities against lawful firearms manufacturers is a serious one, and the legislation before us today presents us with a sensible solution," Dingell said.

The House bill would require the Commerce Department to maintain a voluntary list of manufacturers or sellers of firearms or ammunition engaged in interstate or foreign commerce. Those on the list acting in compliance with federal and state firearms laws would be protected from lawsuits stemming from third-party gun violence.

An amendment by Henry A. Waxman, D-Calif., that would allow lawsuits in cases in which gun or ammunition dealers sell to a member or suspected member of a terrorist organization, or to someone likely to supply to a member or suspected member of a terrorist organization, was defeated 15–37.

On Oct. 2, the Judiciary Committee approved the measure 18–7. Members adopted 18–5 a substitute offered by Judiciary Committee Chair F. James Sensenbrenner Jr., R-Wis. He struck the text of the bill approved by Energy and Commerce and inserted slightly modified language from two other measures (HR 123, HR 1966). The legislation's intent was unchanged, but the new language put the measure into the Judiciary Committee's jurisdiction.

Although House GOP leaders intended to take up the bill the week of Oct. 7, a series of sniper shootings in the greater Washington, D.C., area prompted them to delay consideration. Bill sponsor Cliff Stearns, R-Fla., said the decision was made in the ongoing public concern about the shootings.

HR 2037 was formally reported from Energy and Commerce (H Rept 107-727, Part I) on Oct. 7 and from Judiciary (H Rept 107-727, Part II) on Oct. 8.

COPS Reauthorization

The Senate Judiciary Committee approved legislation (S 924, no written report) by voice vote April 11, 2002, to reauthorize the Community Oriented Policing Services (COPS) program for six years, but the measure did not advance further.

When Congress created the program in 1994, it was pitched as a six-year effort to put 100,000 police officers on the nation's streets. The Clinton-era program expired in 2000, and it had handed out enough federal dollars to hire an estimated 114,000 new officers. But it proved so popular with communities—with the lawmakers who get to hand out the money back home—that Congress continued to fund it. *(1994 action, Congress and the Nation Vol. IX, p. 683)*

President George W. Bush's proposed fiscal 2003 budget asked Congress to slash the program by more than $400 million. Since the program's inception, more than $7 billion in grants had been awarded to law enforcement agencies, and Justice Department officials said COPS had met its goals.

But Senate Democrats said the program was needed more than ever, and they proposed reauthorizing the program formally for another six years at $1.2 billion a year. The Senate bill's sponsor, Delaware Democrat Joseph R. Biden Jr., credited the program with reducing crime rates by encouraging community policing, which teams police officers with community members to combat crime.

The money that S 924 would make available could be used to help communities keep officers once the three-year grants expire. The money also could be used to pay overtime and cover training costs.

Senate Judiciary Committee member Jon Kyl, R-Ariz., said he opposed extending the program. When he voted as a House member in 1994 to support the legislation (PL 103-322) creating the COPS program, he said he did so with the understanding that the program would be temporary. Sen. Richard J. Durbin, D-Ill., suggested that lawmakers who opposed reauthorizing the bill were doing so simply because they opposed President Bill Clinton, who pushed the COPS program.

2003–2004

Although sharply divided along party lines, Congress cleared several significant bills in the area of law and justice. House Judiciary Committee Chair F. James Sensenbrenner Jr., R-Wis., successfully pushed through sweeping child crimes legislation that toughened penalties for those convicted of crimes against juveniles and bolstered the nation's nationwide child-abduction alert system. Lawmakers also found common ground in clearing a landmark bill to give federal and state prison inmates access to sophisticated genetic testing. The measure contained provisions from another, bipartisan measure conferring rights on crime victims.

Members tried to bridge the partisan divide on other legislation but came up short. A GOP-backed measure that had some Democratic support would move most class action suits to federal courts, but it ultimately stalled in the face of procedural quarrels and partisan differences. Another GOP-backed measure to establish a fund for claims related to asbestos exposure could not overcome disagreements among interest groups, even though Majority Leader Bill Frist, R-Tenn., and Minority Leader Tom Daschle, D-S.D., tried to negotiate a compromise.

Lawmakers found themselves more deeply divided over a number of politically charged bills dealing with social issues. Among the most hotly debated was a proposed constitutional amendment to ban gay marriage—an issue that took center stage after a pair of court decisions affirming gay rights. Democrats in both chambers amassed enough votes to prevent backers from reaching the two-thirds threshold required for a constitutional amendment. Members also clashed over gun rights, with gun control advocates sinking a measure that would limit liability for the gun industry but coming up short in an effort to renew a ban on assault weapons.

Perhaps the harshest partisan battles were waged over President George W. Bush's judicial nominees. In a significant escalation of the years-long fight over reshaping the federal judiciary, Senate Democrats successfully filibustered ten appellate court nominees—an unprecedented tactic that infuriated Republicans and provoked proposals to do away with filibusters against judicial nominees. Bush retaliated by using his recess appointment authority to temporarily install two of them to the bench.

The federal judiciary figured in a series of bills pushed by conservatives to curb the power of judges. The House passed two measures that would prevent federal courts from having jurisdiction over certain provisions of a 1996 law that defined marriage as a heterosexual union and having jurisdiction over constitutional challenges to the wording of the Pledge of Allegiance. A third bill would break up the U.S. Court of Appeals for the Ninth Circuit, widely viewed as one of the nation's more liberal courts. The Senate declined to take up the measures.

In their ongoing campaign to overhaul the nation's tort system, House conservatives won passage of a bill to cap noneconomic and punitive damages in medical malpractice lawsuits. But Senate Republican leaders failed repeatedly to overcome a Democratic filibuster. Conservatives also could not win support in the Senate for a bill that would toughen sanctions on lawyers who filed "meritless" civil lawsuits.

On immigration, lawmakers were successful in adding provisions from a stalled immigration measure to an omnibus spending bill. The provisions not only would expand by about one-third the number of visas available for foreign technology workers but also would crack down on the use of imported temporary workers.

Child Protection

Moving with unusual speed, Congress in 2003 cleared a sweeping child crimes measure (S 151). The legislation bolstered the nationwide child-abduction alert system, outlawed "virtual" child pornography, mandated life sentences for twice-convicted child sex offenders, opened the door for electronic surveillance to investigate child pornography, dropped the statute of limitations on crimes involving sexual abuse or kidnapping of children, and limited the ability of federal judges to depart from sentencing guidelines. President George W. Bush signed the bill into law (PL 108-21) April 30, 2003.

House Judiciary Committee Chair F. James Sensenbrenner Jr., R-Wis., pushed the package through to enactment despite pressure—particularly following the March rescue of kidnapped Utah teenager Elizabeth Smart—to drop the other provisions in favor of getting a stand-alone AMBER (America's Missing: Broadcast Emergency Response) alert bill into law quickly. Sensenbrenner had failed in 2002 to win Senate support for a similar bill that combined AMBER provisions with other House-passed measures aimed at combating sex crimes against children. This time, he successfully used a Senate-passed bill on computer-generated child pornography—an important issue for Senate Judiciary Committee Chair Orrin G. Hatch, R-Utah—as the vehicle for his broader measure. The added publicity from the Smart case made the bill unstoppable. *(2002 action, p. 593)*

The only issue that slowed final action was a dispute over sentencing provisions that capped the number of judges who could serve on the U.S. Sentencing Commission and required the attorney general to report on judges who were too lenient. Sen. Edward M. Kennedy, D-Mass., argued the provisions would undermine the sentencing commission, but he ultimately dropped his objection.

SENATE ACTION

The Senate by 84–0 on Feb. 24, 2003, passed S 151, which outlawed virtual pornography. The Judiciary Committee had approved the measure, sponsored by Hatch, by voice vote Jan. 30, and a report (S Rept 108-2) was filed Feb. 11. The report stated that the legislation was "not designed to challenge [the 2002 U.S. Supreme Court decision] in any way" but "to work within the limitations established by that decision."

The provisions struck down by the Court, enacted as part of the fiscal 1997 omnibus spending law (PL 104-208), prohibited individuals from creating, possessing, or distributing child pornography, including visual depiction that "is, or appears to be, of a minor engaging in sexually explicit conduct." Ruling in *Ashcroft v. Free Speech Coalition*, the Court found that the definition of child pornography was "overbroad and unconstitutional" because it could apply to material that was neither obscene nor an example of pornography that used real children. *(Earlier action, Congress and the Nation Vol. IX, p. 739; 2002 decision, p. 699)*

The committee pointed to two changes in the new language intended to make the proposal constitutional. First, the children portrayed in the sexually explicit depictions to be outlawed had to appear "virtually indistinguishable from actual minors," meaning they looked "just like actual children to an ordinary observer." Second, the bill included an affirmative defense that would absolve the defendant of liability if he could show that no actual children were used in creating the images in question.

Some backers expressed concern that the measure still might be vulnerable to legal challenges. "It is important that we do all we can to end the victimization of real children by child pornographers, but it is also important that we pass a law that will withstand First Amendment scrutiny," said co-sponsor Patrick J. Leahy, D-Vt. Hatch said he was confident the measure would survive a court challenge.

In separate action on Jan. 21, 2003, the Senate by 92–0 passed a bill (S 121) to establish a national AMBER alert coordinator at the Department of Justice, which would set minimum standards for participants in the system. The measure also authorized $20 million in fiscal 2004 for grants to states to set up AMBER alert systems.

HOUSE ACTION

Despite increasing pressure to take up the Senate's standalone AMBER alert bill, the House Judiciary Committee approved Sensenbrenner's omnibus child crimes package (HR 1104) by a vote of 18–2 on March 18, 2003. It was formally reported (H Rept 108-47, Part I) on March 24. The Subcommittee on Crime, Terrorism, and Homeland Security had approved the measure by voice vote March 11.

Sensenbrenner was counting on the popularity of the AMBER provisions to propel the rest of the package through the Senate. Several of the other proposals had languished there for years, including one to establish a mandatory life sentence for twice-convicted child sex offenders and another to expand the list of crimes that justified wiretaps and electronic surveillance.

In addition to requiring the Justice Department to establish a national coordinator for the AMBER system, the bill authorized $25 million in fiscal 2004 to help piece together the patchwork of alert systems around the country. The rest of the bill was nearly identical to the measure Sensenbrenner had shepherded through the House in 2002, including the wiretap and two-strikes-and-you're-out provisions and language to allow lifetime supervision of sex offenders and to make it easier to prosecute those who traveled abroad to have sex with a minor. The bill proposed to eliminate the statute of limitations for child abduction and sex crimes, bar accused rapists and child kidnappers from being released before their trials, and make murder involving child abuse and child torture first-degree murder in federal cases.

The measure included one new provision, sought by the Bush administration, to make it easier for law enforcement to go after parents suspected of trying to kidnap their children and take them to another country.

Critics worried that the non–AMBER provisions were unduly harsh and overbroad prescriptions for combating crimes against children.

During markup, the committee rejected an attempt to strip all but the AMBER provisions from the bill. The amendment by Sheila Jackson-Lee, D-Texas, fell on a 5–17 vote. The panel adopted an amendment by voice vote to remove statutory rape from the bill's scope. The amendment also added two other crimes to the bill: raping a child while in production of child pornography and the enticement or coercion of a minor to engage in prostitution.

The House passed HR 1104 by 410–14 on March 27 after the leadership blocked Democrats from forcing a vote on the Senate's stand-alone AMBER legislation.

To help ensure Hatch's support, Sensenbrenner and House leaders arranged to pair the measure with Hatch's virtual child pornography bill, then request a conference with the Senate. The maneuver avoided the prospect of having to negotiate Sensenbrenner's bill in conference with the stand-alone Senate AMBER bill.

During floor debate, the House on March 27 adopted 406–15 a Lamar Smith, R-Texas, amendment adding provisions on virtual child pornography that were similar to those in the Senate-passed bill; adopted by voice vote a Mike Pence, R-Ind., amendment making it a crime to deliberately use a seemingly innocuous Internet domain name, such as www.whitehouse.com, that led Web surfers to a site with adult content; and adopted 357–58 a Tom Feeney, R-Fla., amendment reducing the ability of courts to hand down sentences that were lighter than those in federal sentencing guidelines.

CONFERENCE AND FINAL ACTION

House and Senate negotiators reached agreement on the bill April 9. The House adopted the conference report (H Rept 108-66) by 400–25, on April 10, and the Senate cleared the bill 98–0 later the same day.

Senators Leahy and Joseph R. Biden Jr., D-Del., persuaded GOP conferees to incorporate provisions on topics ranging from an Internet "tip line" for reporting child exploitation to boosting the liability of building owners for illegal drug use on their property.

In the end, the provisions related to the AMBER system occupied a small part of the conference report. Nevertheless, the Smart family, which had publicly deplored Sensenbrenner's tactics, sent an open letter to Congress on April 9 urging swift passage of the omnibus bill, saying it would "make an immediate difference in safely rescuing those who are abducted and in preventing crimes against children."

Much of the debate in conference centered on the House amendment limiting federal judges' ability to hand down sentences lighter than those in federal sentencing guidelines. Democrats, including Biden and Kennedy, pleaded with their GOP counterparts to drop the provisions in favor of a study by the sentencing commission.

The conferees adopted an amendment by Hatch, Sensenbrenner, and Sen. Lindsey Graham, R-S.C., that narrowed the provisions so they would apply only to cases involving sex crimes and crimes against children. The compromise also called on the U.S. Sentencing Commission to review the use of lighter-than-recommended sentences by all judges—not just those in sex and child crime cases—and to amend the sentencing guidelines to reduce the number of lighter sentences. It capped at three the number of judges who could serve on the seven-member sentencing commission, which opponents said would limit the voice of judges in deciding such issues.

The most serious challenge to the conference report came from Kennedy, who objected to the federal sentencing guideline provisions. After the House voted to adopt the conference report, Kennedy threatened to raise a point of order against it on the Senate floor, arguing that some provisions fell outside the scope of the conference. He brandished a letter from Chief Justice William H. Rehnquist that said the sentencing provisions "would do serious harm to the basic structure of the sentencing guideline system and would seriously impair the ability of courts to impose just and responsible sentences."

In the end, however, Kennedy not only dropped his threat, but also voted to adopt the conference report.

The following were highlights of S 151 (PL 108-21).

AMBER Alert. The law required the Justice Department to establish a national coordinator for the AMBER (America's Missing: Broadcast Emergency Response) alert network and make federal grants available to states that implemented the system. The AMBER system was a network of local, state, and regional programs that broadcast bulletins about missing children on local television and radio stations. It was named after Amber Hagerman, a nine-year-old Texas girl who was kidnapped and murdered in 1996. The new law authorized $20 million in fiscal 2004 for grants to states for developing local AMBER systems and $20 million per year in fiscal 2004 and 2005 for the National Center for Missing and Exploited Children.

'Virtual' pornography. The law made it illegal to create, distribute, or possess computer-generated or "virtual" child pornography. The definition of child pornography included visual depictions such as "a digital image, computer image or computer-generated image that is, or is indistinguishable from, that of a minor engaging in sexually explicit conduct." It narrowed the definition of pandering child pornography so that it would not apply to someone who simply possessed such material, and it made it a felony to use real or virtual child pornography to persuade minors to engage in sex or to produce more child pornography. The measure allowed both producers and possessors of child pornography to assert an affirmative defense that no actual children were used in making it.

Lifetime supervision. Judges were permitted to order lifetime supervision for sex offenders who had completed their prison sentences. The previous maximum was five years.

Life sentences. Anyone convicted for a second time of a sexual offense against a child faced a mandatory life sentence.

Stiffer penalties. The law increased penalties for kidnapping and other sexual crimes against children. For example, it increased the maximum penalty for sexual exploitation of a child from twenty years to thirty years, and from thirty years to fifty years for a second sex offense conviction. The maximum sentence for transporting a minor for prostitution rose from fifteen to thirty years, and the maximum penalty for shipping, receiving, or distributing child pornography increased from fifteen to twenty years (from thirty to forty years for those with a prior conviction). The law made murder involving child abuse or assault a first-degree murder charge.

Sex tourism. The law lowered the bar for prosecuting individuals who had sex with minors in foreign countries by allowing the government to prosecute such cases without having to prove the defendant traveled abroad with that intent. The crime was punishable by fines and up to thirty years in prison. The law also made it a crime to travel across state lines to engage in illicit sexual conduct.

Sentencing guidelines. The new law limited judges' discretion to hand down sentences lighter than those in federal sentencing guidelines for crimes against children or for sex crimes. It made it easier for appeals courts to review lower court sentences that were less than what was contained in the sentencing guidelines and limited the number of judges who could serve on the U.S. Sentencing Commission to three, the minimum number under previous law.

Electronic surveillance. Federal law enforcement officials could seek authority to use wiretapping and electronic surveillance for an expanded list of crimes that included sex trafficking of children, transmitting of child pornography, transporting children for illegal sexual activity, and buying or selling children.

False IDs. The law made it a crime to use authentication features, such as holograms or watermarks, to make false identification cards.

Controlled substances. It became a crime for property owners and managers to knowingly allow property to be used for making, using, or distributing controlled substances.

DNA Testing

Congress in 2004 cleared a bipartisan proposal (HR 5107) to give federal and state prison inmates access to sophisticated genetic testing that could prove their innocence. The bill was signed into law (PL 108-405) on Oct. 30.

The legislation capped five years of work on proposals to give death row inmates access to post-conviction DNA (deoxyribonucleic acid) tests and to ensure that defendants in capital cases had adequate legal representation. Supporters finally found success with a comprehensive bill that included provisions that appealed to diverse constituencies in Congress. It no longer focused exclusively on death row inmates but included new criminal justice grants for states to ensure adequate legal representation for defendants in capital cases, as well as provisions supported by the Bush administration to speed the processing of biological evidence collected from rapes and other crimes.

BACKGROUND

The legislation was the result of lengthy negotiations that went back to 2000, when Sen. Patrick J. Leahy, D-Vt., introduced a bill he called the Innocence Protection Act. Bill Delahunt, D-Mass., and Ray LaHood, R-Ill., introduced a companion bill in the House, which focused primarily on ensuring that death row inmates had adequate legal representation and access to new, sophisticated DNA tests that could prove their innocence. For the remainder of the 106th Congress and much of the 107th Congress, Delahunt and LaHood slowly built support in the House. In the Senate, the Judiciary Committee, chaired at the time by Leahy, approved his bill 12–7 in July 2002. *(2002 action, p. 595)*

Although Republican opponents kept the legislation off the Senate floor, supporters were bolstered by a series of events that focused attention on the death penalty. The U.S. Supreme Court had issued two rulings in June 2002 that restricted the use of the death penalty, reversing a trend of expanding the use of capital punishment. The Court ruled that a jury, not a judge, had to determine whether a capital defendant was sent to death row. The justices also barred executions of the mentally retarded. *(Court cases, p. 646)*

States were scrutinizing the system as well. In Illinois, thirteen inmates were released from death row by DNA testing that refuted their convictions. GOP governor George Ryan subsequently began a process that ended up commuting the sentences of all the state's 167 death row inmates by mid-January 2003.

Republican opponents blocked the Leahy bill because of concerns that the criminal justice grants to states could end up putting opponents of the death penalty in charge of the systems established to defend those accused of capital offenses. They also worried that the legal standard for allowing new trials after post-conviction DNA testing was too low.

Early in the 108th Congress, supporters of the Delahunt-LaHood legislation turned a corner when House Judiciary Committee Chair F. James Sensenbrenner Jr., R-Wis., decided to assemble a variety of DNA testing and similar bills into one comprehensive package. Sensenbrenner directed committee staff to begin working with Delahunt and LaHood on a way to include their language. When Bush announced a plan in March 2003 to speed up the analysis of biological evidence and eliminate a backlog of untested samples, Sensenbrenner saw the proposal as a natural fit for the package.

HR 5107 provided a bridge for lawmakers with opposing views about the death penalty. Many capital punishment supporters viewed the bill as a way to make the justice system closer to foolproof. "We will lose the death penalty unless it is applied in a very judicious way," said Arlen Specter, R-Pa. Opponents of capital punishment, while still seeking a federal moratorium on the death penalty, said the bill would reduce the chances of an innocent person being put to death.

2003 LEGISLATIVE ACTION

The House Judiciary Committee approved a version of the legislation (HR 3214) by a vote of 28–1 on Oct. 8, 2003. It was formally reported (H Rept 108-321, Part I) on Oct. 16. After Majority Leader Tom DeLay, R-Texas, signed off on the bill Nov. 5, the House passed the measure under suspension of the rules by 357–67, a testament to the broad support for the package.

During the debate, lawmakers pointed out that DNA and other evidence had been used to exonerate 111 death row inmates since 1976, when the Supreme Court allowed the reinstatement of the death penalty. Sensenbrenner said the emphasis on improving capital defense and post-conviction DNA testing ultimately might help preserve the death penalty.

Overall, the bill would authorize more than $1 billion over five years to expand and improve forensic laboratories, test stored biological evidence such as that collected in "rape kits," and improve law enforcement's use of sophisticated DNA tests that could help pinpoint criminals or exclude potential suspects. Much of the legislation—including the provisions aimed at speeding testing of backlogged evidence—had broad, bipartisan support.

The five-year bill authorized programs for fiscal 2005 through 2009. It included provisions to

Test federal inmates. Authorize post-conviction DNA testing for federal prisoners if a negative test match could raise "a reasonable probability" that the inmate did not commit the offense for which he or she was jailed. An inmate would qualify for a new trial if post-conviction DNA test results and other evidence established "by a preponderance of the evidence that a new trial would result in an acquittal."

Test state inmates. Authorize $25 million over five years to defray the costs and encourage states to provide DNA testing to state prison inmates.

Reduce DNA testing backlog. Authorize $755 million over five years to accelerate the processing of stored biological samples that might help solve crimes. Bush had requested $1 billion over five years to reduce the backlog of DNA samples sitting untested in the nation's crime laboratories.

Support research and training. Authorize state grants to train law enforcement officials in DNA collection and analysis, and to expand and improve crime laboratories.

Target capital cases. Authorize $500 million over five years for grants to states to improve the prosecution of capital cases and to build systems in which indigent defendants in capital cases would have access to competent legal representation. The grants would be structured so that, if states accepted a prosecution improvement grant, they also would have to accept money and develop a system to give defendants access to competent legal representation.

The Senate Judiciary Committee did not hold hearings on HR 3214 in 2003, and the legislation was not put on its agenda for that year. While the bill had the support of most committee members, a handful of Republicans, led by Jon Kyl of Arizona and Jeff Sessions of Alabama, vowed to fight it with amendments in committee and on the floor.

Their concerns stemmed mainly from the section offering $100 million per year for grants to states to improve the quality of legal representation in death penalty cases. To get a grant, a state would have to create an "effective" system for providing competent legal representation to indigent defendants. Specifically, the state would have to assign the job of selecting and appointing the attorneys to "(a) a public defender program that relies on staff attorneys, members of the private bar, or both, to provide representation in capital cases, or (b) an entity ... composed of individuals with demonstrated knowledge and expertise in capital representation."

The opponents expressed concern that public prosecutors would be barred from developing the program and that, as a result, the top jobs would end up being filled by passionate opponents of the death penalty. Kyl introduced an alternative proposal (S 1828) that did not include the "competent counsel" provisions.

Fiscal conservatives also worried about the bill's price tag, which the Congressional Budget Office put at $1.85 billion over five years.

2004 LEGISLATIVE ACTION

Prospects for the legislation appeared all but dead for much of the year. But proponents gradually broke down opposition by making concessions to conservative critics, and lawmakers ultimately cleared a revamped HR 5107.

The Senate Judiciary Committee approved S 1700 (no written report) on Sept. 21, 2004, by a vote of 11–7. Kyl, Sessions, and John Cornyn, R-Texas, vigorously fought the measure in committee, offering nearly two dozen weakening amendments during a markup that ran from July to September and was repeatedly interrupted when the panel could not

hold its quorum. But a coalition of bill supporters helped beat back the efforts.

The committee's approval appeared to be the high-water mark for the bill because a handful of GOP conservatives continued their objections, saying the measure would encourage a rash of unfounded requests for post-conviction DNA testing of crime evidence, such as from inmates who initially pleaded guilty or in cases in which the evidence could have been tested in an earlier trial. They also worried the measure would impose an overly liberal standard for new trials as a result of post-conviction DNA testing. Conservatives were particularly concerned about a section of the legislation known as the Innocence Protection Act, which would create separate state grants to improve the quality of legal representation for indigent capital defendants and to aid prosecutors. They argued that cash-starved states would leap at the federal dollars and, eager to qualify for the grants, put staunch death penalty foes in charge of their capital representation programs.

On Sept. 22, by voice vote, the House Judiciary Committee approved HR 5107, which combined the text of the DNA measure with a modified version of a separate proposal (S 2329) that would confer eight specific rights on crime victims. The gambit, by Sensenbrenner, was an attempt to allow the DNA legislation to hitch a ride on the popular victims' rights bill. HR 5107 was formally reported (H Rept 107-711) on Sept. 30. *(Victims' rights, p. 616)*

During the week of Oct. 4, bill backers once again made changes to the legislation, this time in a bid to secure support from the Department of Justice and appease Senate conservatives who were blocking S 1700. The efforts resulted in House passage of HR 5107 by a vote of 393–14 on Oct. 6. The revamped version would authorize $755 million over five years to speed the processing of unanalyzed biological crime evidence. It also included popular provisions to authorize grants designed to defray the cost to states of post-conviction DNA testing, promote using forensic technology to identify missing persons, and train first-responders in handling biological crime evidence. Much of the grant funding would be contingent upon states preserving biological crime evidence for post-conviction DNA testing.

In the manager's amendment, Sensenbrenner tried to win over critics by raising the standard for obtaining a new trial based on the outcomes of post-conviction DNA testing. The underlying bill would allow retrials to be ordered if the test results and other evidence established by a preponderance of the evidence that a new trial would result in an acquittal. The amendment raised the threshold to instances in which there was "compelling evidence that a new trial would result in an acquittal."

The new version also changed the point at which information could be entered into state and national databases of DNA profiles. The initial bill would prohibit the entry of information about people who had been arrested but not indicted—which was allowed in three states. The final bill would allow those states to continue that practice.

The time frame during which federal inmates could secure post-conviction testing of biological crime evidence also was changed. The bill initially imposed no time limit. The House-passed version would encourage defendants to apply for testing within five years of their convictions, during which time there would be a presumption in their favor. Afterward, the burden of proof would shift to defendants. Motions for new tests would be granted if a judge found that an applicant was not competent at trial, if there was newly discovered DNA evidence, or if denying the application for new tests would result in "manifest injustice."

Opponents still complained that the latest round of changes was not enough to block inmates from manipulating the court system and filing motions for DNA tests even when they were guilty.

Kyl, Hatch, and Leahy reopened negotiations over the time limit under which convicts could easily obtain DNA tests. They reached a deal to tighten it to three years after conviction. Also under discussion was the issue of capital defense grants. Sessions, in particular, was concerned that capital defender programs would be placed under staunch death row opponents. Under the final compromise, language was added clarifying that, with the exception of current prosecutors, anyone with "demonstrated knowledge and expertise in capital cases" could direct the programs.

On Oct. 9, the Senate passed HR 5107 on a voice vote, completing congressional action. Afterward, senators took the unusual step of demanding that the House adopt an enrolling resolution (H Con Res 519)—usually used to correct typographical errors in bills—to include the final changes such as the three-year time limit for convicts to easily obtain DNA tests. Had the House not done so, the Senate would have nullified its action on HR 5107.

MAJOR PROVISIONS

As enacted, HR 5107 (PL 108-405) contained the following major provisions.

Post-conviction DNA tests. Courts would presume that federal inmates had a right to DNA tests of crime evidence within three years of their convictions and five years of enactment. DNA testing could be ordered in cases in which an inmate asserted under penalty of perjury that he was innocent and when the test might produce new material evidence supporting the claim, raising a reasonable probability that the inmate did not commit the crime at issue.

Time limits on post-conviction tests. Applications for DNA tests filed more than five years after enactment and three years after conviction would be presumed by the courts not to be timely. That presumption could be rebutted by inmates who showed good cause for the delay. New tests might be ordered if a court found that an applicant was not competent at trial, if new DNA evidence was discovered, or if a

court found that denying the application for a new test would result in manifest injustice.

Burden of proof for new trials. Courts could grant new trials or resentencings in cases in which test results might exonerate a convict, if the test results and other compelling evidence showed that a new trial would result in an acquittal.

Destruction of DNA evidence. The government would be barred from destroying DNA evidence in federal criminal cases while a defendant remained incarcerated, with some exceptions, such as when a defendant waived his or her right to testing.

Victims' rights. Victims of federal crimes would be granted specific rights including the right to be reasonably protected from the accused; the right to reasonable, accurate, and timely notice of certain proceedings and events; the right not to be excluded from certain proceedings; the right to be reasonably heard at certain proceedings and to consult with government attorneys on the case; the right to full and timely restitution; the right to proceedings free from unreasonable delay; and the right to be treated with fairness and respect for the victim's dignity and privacy.

Grants to states. An existing grant program that aimed to help states and localities speed up the processing of biological crime scene evidence, including samples collected as part of rape investigations, would be reauthorized and expanded. The bill would authorize $151 million annually for the following five years for such purposes and disburse the money by formula.

Capital defense and prosecution grants. Annual grants to states totaling $5 million would be authorized through 2009 to help defray the cost of post-conviction DNA tests. Annual grants totaling $30 million would be authorized through 2009 for sexual assault forensic exams to help first-responders and medical personnel process and preserve DNA samples and evidence. Annual grants totaling $75 million would be authorized to improve the representation of defendants in capital cases and improve the representation of the public in state capital cases.

Class Action Suits

Legislation aimed at moving most class action suits to federal courts passed in the House (HR 1115), but fell victim to partisan bitterness in the Senate (S 274, S 1751, S 2062). The issue had been a top item on the Republican tort reform agenda for the 108th Congress. *(107th Congress action, p. 591)*

Both the House and Senate versions of the class action overhaul took aim at what supporters characterized as "venue shopping" by trial lawyers—filing cases in state courts that had a reputation for delivering big-dollar judgments. Opponents, however, said the legislation would clog federal court dockets and make it even harder for wronged individuals to seek redress.

The legislation was the focus of intense lobbying, with corporations pushing hard for action aimed at trial lawyers who doggedly resisted new rules for civil litigation. Neither side would concede any ground to the other.

The bills provided for class action cases to be sent to federal courts if at least $5 million was at stake and most of the plaintiffs were from different states than the defendant. They also contained a "consumer class action bill of rights" to protect plaintiffs from being exploited by attorneys. The chief difference was that the House bill included the right to immediate appeal of a judge's decision on whether to certify a group of plaintiffs as a class. The House bill also applied retroactively to class action cases that were begun but not certified by the enactment date.

Under existing law, class action suits could be heard in federal courts only if each plaintiff stood to receive at least $75,000 and all the plaintiffs lived in different states from all the defendants. The result was that most class action cases were heard in state courts, and the standards used to determine whether a suit qualified as a class action varied from state to state.

2003 LEGISLATIVE ACTION

The Senate Judiciary Committee approved S 274 on April 11, 2003, after adopting two amendments by Dianne Feinstein, D-Calif., that narrowed the scope of the measure. The vote to approve the bill was 12–7. It was formally reported (S Rept 108-123) on July 31.

As amended by Feinstein, the bill allowed for state class actions to be sent to federal courts when at least $5 million was at stake and less than two-thirds of the plaintiffs in the case lived in the same state as the defendant. Charles E. Grassley, R-Iowa, the bill's sponsor, originally proposed that suits involving $2 million be eligible for removal to federal court. Feinstein's changes were adopted 11–8.

A second amendment, by Feinstein and Arlen Specter, R-Pa., struck provisions in the original bill that would allow two kinds of lawsuits other than class actions to be pushed into federal court. The amendment, adopted by voice vote, dropped "private attorney general" cases—cases brought by a named plaintiff, other than the state attorney general, who claimed to act in the interests of the general public. It also dropped non-class action cases involving one hundred or more plaintiffs, known as "mass tort" cases. Feinstein, whose backing was viewed as crucial to getting the sixty votes needed to overcome a filibuster on the floor, said she would not support the bill if it contained the private attorney general provision. California was the only state that allowed such suits.

The committee rejected a number of Democratic amendments, including proposals to exclude suits related to civil rights, gun violence, consumer protection, environmental protection, and tobacco products.

The House Judiciary Committee on May 21, 2003, voted mostly along party lines to approve a bill (HR 1115) sponsored by Republican Robert W. Goodlatte and Democrat Rick Boucher, both of Virginia. The vote was 20–14. The bill was formally reported (H Rept 108-144) on June 6.

Under the bill, class action cases could be moved to federal court if the expected damages totaled at least $2 million and the action involved at least one hundred class members, any of whom lived in states that were different from that of the defendant. Unlike S 274, the House bill applied the new rules to class action cases that had been filed, but in which a class had not yet been certified. Lamar Smith, R-Texas, said the language was needed to avoid a rush to the courts in advance of enactment.

During the markup, the committee rejected by voice vote an attempt by California Democrats Linda T. Sanchez and Zoe Lofgren to drop the provision allowing cases brought by a named plaintiff on behalf of unnamed parties or the general public to be certified as class actions in federal court. The panel also rejected by voice vote an attempt by Robert C. Scott, D-Va., to remove a provision allowing cases involving one hundred or more plaintiffs to be moved to federal court.

The House passed HR 1115 by a vote of 253–170 on June 12 following an angry debate in which Republicans lambasted trial lawyers and Democrats accused Republicans of shilling for big corporations.

The House on June 12 agreed by voice vote to an amendment by Judiciary Committee chairman F. James Sensenbrenner Jr., R-Wis., raising the threshold for federal jurisdiction from $2 million to $5 million. The amendment also provided that if less than one-third of the plaintiffs and the defendant were citizens of the same state, the case would automatically be eligible for federal court jurisdiction; if more than two-thirds of the plaintiffs and the defendant were citizens of the same state, the case would remain in state court.

The House also rejected, 170–255, on June 12 a Democratic substitute offered by John Conyers Jr. of Michigan and Max Sandlin of Texas. It would establish a multidistrict litigation panel that could consolidate class actions in state courts for pretrial proceedings. The same day, the House rejected 186–234 an amendment by Sanchez and Lofgren to strike the private attorney general language.

Unable to get agreement to bring up the committee-approved bill, Senate majority leader Bill Frist, R-Tenn., decided to put a new version of the legislation (S 1751) to a test vote in October 2003. S 1751 resembled the committee-approved bill, except for compromise language that allowed for many "mass action" cases to be removed from state courts. An effort to invoke cloture (end debate) on taking up S 1751 failed Oct. 22 on a **key vote of 59–39 (R 50–1; D 8–38; I 1–0)**—one vote short of the sixty needed. *(2003 key votes, p. 837)*

Sensing the nearness of victory, Frist made it clear in a floor speech several hours later that he would not let the legislation die. Supporters predicted they would win passage in 2004. The compromise bill (S 2062) differed in several respects from earlier ones, and it left out a controversial provision that would bar "bounties," or disproportionate payments to the plaintiff that represented the class.

The legislation enjoyed support from sixty-two senators, including eleven Democrats—more than enough to overcome a filibuster. But Frist's procedural moves alienated some Republicans and many of the bill's leading Democratic backers, who wanted the opportunity to attach amendments to one of the last authorization bills expected to move in this Congress. When the two sides failed to agree on how many unrelated amendments to allow, Frist used his prerogative as majority leader to fill up the bill's "amendment tree," which effectively shut off amendments from other senators. That gave him complete control over which provisions were introduced, but the move angered Democrats and Republicans alike.

Frist's last hope was a motion to invoke cloture and limit the debate to amendments germane to civil litigation. But on July 8, 2004, his cloture motion on S 2062 failed on a **key vote of 44–43 (R 42–3; D 2–39; I 0–1)**—sixteen short of the sixty votes required to shut off debate. Ten of the twelve Democratic supporters of the bill stuck with their party leader on this test of wills, and three Republicans who wanted to amend the bill with their election-year priorities also voted against cloture. Frist then pulled the bill from the floor. *(2004 key votes, p. 854)*

'Meritless' Lawsuits

During "tort reform week" in 2004, designed to highlight problems in the civil justice system, the House took up four bills that were intended to toughen sanctions on lawyers who filed "meritless" civil lawsuits and to help shield certain groups, such as volunteer fire departments, from lawsuits. But one of the measures failed and none of the remaining three was taken up by the Senate. Of the four, the measure to toughen sanctions on lawyers sparked considerable controversy

Packaging similar bills with one overarching theme had become a routine in the House in 2004. Republicans organized weeks in May and June dedicated to legislation on job creation, health insurance, bureaucratic red tape, and life-long learning. Those bills were often recycled versions of measures that had already passed.

On Sept. 14, the House passed a pair of tort bills. HR 1787, formally reported (H Rept 108-680) from the House Judiciary Committee on Sept. 13, was designed to help shield volunteer fire departments, and it would limit the liability of companies and full-time fire departments that donate surplus equipment, ranging from hoses to fire trucks. The measure, which passed 397–3 under suspension of the rules, would not protect manufacturers of the equipment. HR 1084, formally reported (H Rept 108-679) from House Judiciary on Sept. 13, would provide liability protection to nonprofit volunteer pilots who flew public benefit missions, such as transporting patients or donated organs. It passed 385–12 under suspension of the rules.

HR 3369, to shield nonprofit groups that organize sports leagues, lacked the two-thirds majority needed under an expedited procedure that limits debate and bars amendments. It failed, 217–176 on Sept. 14. Democratic floor manager Robert C. Scott, D-Va., spoke against the measure, saying its overly broad language might unintentionally block a wider array of lawsuits in civil rights, labor or environmental cases. The House Judiciary Committee approved HR 3369 by 14–7 on Sept. 8 and formally reported it (H Rept 108-681) on Sept. 13.

The most broadly written measure (HR 4571)—intended to toughen sanctions on lawyers who filed meritless civil lawsuits—generated significant opposition and passed by a vote of 229–174 Sept. 14. In pushing the bill, lawmakers found a way to anger federal judges.

The bill would revise a federal rule governing civil trials to mandate sanctions against attorneys who file "frivolous" claims. Such sanctions were imposed at the discretion of a judge. HR 4571 would reverse changes in civil procedure rules adopted by the courts in 1993 and not rejected at the time by Congress. It would eliminate a rule that allowed attorneys to avoid sanctions by quickly withdrawing meritless claims. The language of Rule 11 of the Federal Rules of Civil Procedure would revert to how it stood from 1983 to 1993. New provisions also would suspend for a year lawyers who filed three meritless claims in any single judicial district during the course of their career.

Federal judges were put off by the decision to bypass the usual process for amending the rules of civil procedure. Normally, proposed changes would first go through a lengthy review process by committees of judges and lawyers. Leonidas Ralph Mecham, secretary of the federal judiciary's policy arm, the Judicial Conference of the United States, wrote House Judiciary Committee chairman F. James Sensenbrenner Jr., R-Wis., in July that the changes would "frustrate the purpose and intent" of the 1934 Rules Enabling Act, which established the review process. But bill sponsor Lamar Smith, R-Texas, said, "If we waited for the Judicial Conference to go through the cumbersome process, it might never have happened."

The bill was heralded by Republicans and business groups, such as the U.S. Chamber of Commerce, as a way to stem what they charged was a tide of frivolous lawsuits used to force defendants into lucrative settlements. Democrats and the Judicial Conference said the bill was unnecessary and might result in more litigation, not less. Before the 1993 rules changes, legal experts said, the mandatory sanctions provision sparked lawsuits among parties trading charges of meritless claims. Democrats also criticized provisions that would extend mandatory sanctions to state courts in cases involving interstate commerce and alter the venues where defendants can bring personal injury claims. They called these provisions impositions on states' rights.

Personal injury plaintiffs would have to file suits where they live, where they are injured, or where a corporation's principal business was located. Democrats objected that limitation might prevent litigation against foreign companies, an assertion Republicans said was untrue. The House Sept. 14 rejected 196–211 a motion to send HR 4571 back to the Judiciary Committee and amend it to address those concerns.

The House also rejected 177–226 on Sept. 14 an amendment by Jim Turner, D-Texas, that would strike the entire text of the bill and insert new language. Turner's proposal would not automatically suspend an attorney who filed three meritless lawsuits in one court. It would keep the safe harbor provision allowing attorneys to quickly withdraw meritless claims. And it was not as strict in limiting where personal injury plaintiffs may file suit.

The House Judiciary Committee had approved HR 4571 by 18–10 on Sept. 8 and formally reported it (H Rept 108-682) on Sept. 13. The panel approved language designed to protect volunteer fire departments and pilots by voice vote with little debate, and it approved language protecting sports leagues by a vote of 14–7. GOP supporters said the provisions were needed to ensure that people are willing to participate in voluntary and nonprofit community activities, but Judiciary Committee Democrats questioned whether action was needed.

Asbestos Fund

Efforts in the Senate to establish a fund that would pay no-fault claims related to asbestos exposure could not get past the conflicting demands of lawmakers, corporations, insurers, union officials, and trial lawyers. The Senate Judiciary Committee approved a bill (S 1125) in 2003 proposing a $108 billion fund, but the compromises required to get it out of committee dampened hopes of moving it further. Senate majority leader Bill Frist, R-Tenn., introduced a new version of the bill (S 2290) in 2004, but he could not win Senate passage. An unusual attempt at mediation also failed.

BACKGROUND

Industrial companies and commercial property and casualty insurers had been lobbying Congress for years for legislation to shield them from legal liability related to asbestos, a substance linked to lung cancer and other illnesses that was used for decades as a fire-retardant in products ranging from vehicle brakes to office buildings, homes, and schools.

While the hazards of asbestos exposure had long been known, a series of lawsuits beginning in the 1970s showed that industrial manufacturers covered up the health risks for years. Plaintiffs who had been exposed to the substance filed a bevy of claims against thousands of U.S. corporations. The total cost of past and future asbestos-related claims was estimated at as much as $275 billion. The RAND Institute for Civil Justice estimated that more than 600,000 plaintiffs had filed claims against 6,000 companies alleging injuries caused by asbestos.

Businesses and insurers wanted a way to pay a finite amount of money into a no-fault fund in exchange for ending their civil liabilities and escaping the uncertainties of the tort system. For their part, labor unions and their Democratic allies wanted a law that would provide enough money to be fair to workers sickened by asbestos exposure while enabling them to avoid the arduous process of pursuing their claims through the courts.

Trial lawyers, another important Democratic constituency, opposed any plan that would take asbestos claims out of court. Conservative lawmakers, meanwhile, worried that taxpayers would have to bail out the fund if it ran out of money before paying all claims.

Senate Judiciary Committee Chair Orrin G. Hatch, R-Utah, began 2003 determined to strike the balance necessary to get a bill through the Senate. He urged defendant companies, insurers, and union officials to agree on a single measure. When no consensus materialized, Hatch introduced S 1125 in May to establish a $108 billion fund, financed largely through twenty-seven years of periodically declining contributions from businesses and insurers, to pay no-fault claims arising from physical injuries linked to asbestos. The bill proposed creating a special court to handle the claims.

Hatch maneuvered the measure through a series of four markup sessions, brokering crucial compromises with Democrats on issues ranging from medical criteria to a contingent flow of money for the fund. But the compromises garnered the vote of only one committee Democrat, Dianne Feinstein of California—and even she reserved judgment on whether to vote for the bill on the Senate floor.

It was difficult for lawmakers to assess the adequacy of the bill because no one could be certain how many people would lay claim to the fund or how much money each claimant would be eligible to receive. The Congressional Budget Office (CBO) in October 2003, after analyzing the Hatch measure, concluded that the fund it proposed creating would pay $136 billion in claims. CBO director Douglas Holtz-Eakin, in a March 24 letter to Hatch, said a revised analysis showed that the fund would have to pay out $123 billion.

Critics assailed the accuracy of both estimates, which were based in part on numbers CBO received from the Asbestos Study Group, a coalition of defendant companies that were pushing for the bill. One asbestos litigation expert, Mark A. Peterson, estimated that more than $200 billion would be needed to pay all of the claims that would be made upon the fund.

In an April 8 letter to lawmakers, Holtz-Eakin underscored the difficulty of guessing at future asbestos claims. "Uncertainty over the number, timing and types of compensation claims that the fund would face is substantial, and even small changes in the rate of inflation could easily change the lifetime costs of the fund by $10 billion," he said.

2003 ACTION

The Senate Judiciary Committee approved S 1125 by a vote of 10–8 after a daylong markup July 10, 2003. That narrow vote turned out to be the zenith for the legislation, which was formally reported (S Rept 108-118) July 30.

The tally was the culmination of a process that began June 19 and spanned four sessions, two of which lasted late into the night. The central issues were what medical criteria to use in determining claims, how much to pay each claimant, and how to provide for the possibility that the fund could run out of money before all claims were paid.

The following were the main modifications to the bill approved by the committee.

Payments to claimants. Feinstein and Hatch devised a compromise on claims payment amounts that struck a middle ground between Hatch's initial numbers and much higher claims amounts proposed by Democrats Patrick J. Leahy of Vermont and Edward M. Kennedy of Massachusetts.

The compromise, which varied the payments depending on which of ten medical categories the claims covered, was adopted on a bipartisan 14–3 vote. The proposed awards ranged from medical monitoring expenses for claimants who were exposed to asbestos but did not become sick to $1 million for victims of mesothelioma, a rare cancer that had been firmly linked to asbestos. Claimants with lung cancer would be eligible for $25,000 to $1 million depending on the stage of the cancer, with nonsmokers getting significantly more than smokers.

Feinstein's fellow Democrats on the committee said the claim amounts were still too low to be fair to victims of asbestos exposure, a view echoed by labor officials.

Contributions. The original bill called for $90 billion in mandatory contributions to the fund, split evenly between defendant companies and insurers. An additional $4 billion was to be funneled in from existing bankruptcy trusts, and the remaining $14 billion was to come from other companies that would voluntarily buy into the fund to gain immunity from future liability. Democrats worried about the uncertainty of the voluntary contributions, and even Hatch admitted to being unsure of whether they would yield $14 billion.

Hatch brokered a deal on an amendment by Leahy to strike the $14 billion in voluntary contributions in favor of $14 billion in new mandatory contributions: $7 billion from defendant companies and $7 billion from insurers. The committee adopted the amendment by voice vote July 10.

The amendment was a deal-breaker for insurance lobbyists, who immediately stopped supporting Hatch's bill and began working to kill it. The lobbyists already objected to paying half the $90 billion, saying it was unfair to ask a few dozen insurance companies to bear the same financial burden as hundreds of defendant businesses. Insurers said they would not support legislation that required them to pay more than $45 billion altogether.

Backstopping the fund. On June 26, Hatch agreed to a Democratic amendment by Feinstein and Herb Kohl of Wisconsin to allow the fund administrator to delay or decrease the periodic reductions in contributions from businesses and insurers if doing so was necessary to keep the fund solvent. The amendment, adopted by voice vote, also allowed the administrator to ask for $2 billion per year in voluntary

contributions from businesses and insurers beginning in the twenty-eighth year. Companies that chose not to contribute further would once again be subject to lawsuits in federal—though not state—courts.

Sunset. Before approving the bill, the committee voted 15–4 to automatically abolish the compensation system if, in any particular year, the fund administrator could not certify that at least 95 percent of claims were being paid. Claimants then would once again be able to seek redress in the courts.

The amendment, by Joseph R. Biden Jr., D-Del., was anathema to businesses and insurers, and it emerged as the biggest obstacle to lining up private sector support for the committee-reported bill.

Both the Feinstein and Biden amendments meant businesses could pay millions of dollars into the fund for several years to escape liability and still suddenly find themselves back in court if the fund was overwhelmed by claims.

The committee also replaced Hatch's initial proposal for a new court with the Federal Court of Claims to hear cases and distribute funds. It included a provision to ban the manufacture, distribution, or importation of products to which asbestos had been deliberately added. Although asbestos use in the United States had been sharply reduced, it was still legal for manufacturers to use the substance. The panel strengthened administrators' ability to enforce contributions to the fund by permitting punitive damages for willful failure to pay. And it extended the statute of limitations for filing a claim from two years to four from the date the individual became aware of the asbestos-related injury.

2004 ACTION

Frist, who called the asbestos issue a "personal priority," introduced S 2290 on April 7, 2004. The measure, co-sponsored by Hatch, called for a fund of as much as $124 billion, established through contributions from businesses and insurers. In return, the companies would be shielded from lawsuits. Senate Republicans on April 22 failed to muster enough votes to overcome a Democratic filibuster. The vote to limit debate on a motion to proceed to formal consideration of the measure failed 50–47—ten votes short of the sixty needed.

Frist's bill stripped many of the Democratic amendments approved during the Judiciary markup. Democrats and their labor allies labeled Frist's measure unworkable, saying it was too small to adequately compensate claimants. The AFL-CIO said a fund of $153 billion would be needed. For their part, the Bush administration and fiscal conservatives in Congress questioned whether taxpayers would have to bail out the fund if it was depleted before all claims were paid. The White House also worried about language in the bill that would make the Labor Department, instead of special masters at the U.S. Court of Federal Claims, responsible for processing claims.

Setting back the bill's chances, the Congressional Budget Office released a cost estimate on April 20 suggesting that the trust fund would collect $118 billion from businesses and insurers over twenty-six years and face claims of $140 billion over the next fifty years.

After losing the vote to overcome a filibuster, Frist pulled the bill and took the unusual step of agreeing with Minority Leader Tom Daschle, D-S.D., to enlist Edward R. Becker, a former chief judge of the U.S. Court of Appeals for the Third Circuit, to mediate negotiations among key stakeholders beginning on April 26. But Becker decided to end talks on May 6 after making little progress.

Hopes for a bill briefly revived when Daschle on June 24 proposed to Frist that Congress establish a $141 billion trust fund. Frist and Daschle ultimately narrowed their differences on the size of the fund to around $136 billion. That was still too low for the AFL-CIO, which insisted that $149 billion was the minimum needed to adequately compensate claimants. Even if lawmakers could agree to the size of the fund, two major sticking points remained: how to treat claims already in the courts, and how much money businesses and insurers would contribute in the fund's early years.

Gay Marriage

Both the Senate and House in 2004 rejected a proposed constitutional amendment (S J Res 40, H J Res 106) to ban gay marriage, although the measure was a major priority for social conservatives.

BACKGROUND

The focus on gay marriage was touched off by a pair of 2003 court decisions. In June, a sharply divided U.S. Supreme Court ruled in *Lawrence v. Texas* that homosexuals had a constitutional right to engage in consensual relations. The ruling threw out state anti-sodomy statutes. In November, the Massachusetts Supreme Judicial Court drew national headlines with a ruling that gay couples must be allowed to wed under the Massachusetts constitution. The closely divided state court ruled that marriages, not civil unions, were the only way to grant gay couples equal rights. (*U.S. Supreme Court ruling, p. 673*)

The rulings ignited a firestorm of criticism in conservative circles against the courts. Conservatives worried that gay marriage threatened the very fabric of American society, and they said the only way to safeguard the institution of marriage was to define it in the U.S. Constitution as "a union of a man and a woman."

For social conservatives, perhaps no issue was more important. Even their long-standing crusade against abortion rights took a backseat to keeping marriage the sole province of heterosexual couples. They worried that allowing gays to wed would cheapen the institution to such an extent that heterosexuals would abandon it in droves. They also worried that, sooner or later, the Supreme Court would rule that a 1996 law (PL 104-199), known as the Defense of Marriage

Act, was unconstitutional. (*1996 law, Congress and the Nation Vol. IX, p. 746*)

But Democrats accused amendment supporters as being intolerant and divisive.

In February 2004, after months of careful hedging, President George W. Bush, who had no formal role in the process, endorsed a constitutional amendment banning gay marriage. Even more than many legislative issues in a presidential election year, the debate over gay marriage appeared to be driven by political calculations. Although polls indicated that most Americans, including the middle-class suburbanites and swing voters that both parties coveted, had qualms about gay marriage, the issue ranked far lower as a concern than the war in Iraq or the economy. But it was a meaningful issue to conservative Christians—an increasingly significant GOP constituency.

Republican leaders pushed the issue to the top of the crowded congressional agenda in the weeks before the Democratic National Convention in Boston. But even before the Senate debate began, it was clear that backers were far short of the two-thirds majority needed for a constitutional amendment. The House voted on the issue in September, even though the amendment had already been rejected in the Senate.

The issue appeared to resonate on election day. Voters in eleven states cast ballots Nov. 2 to rewrite their state constitutions to forbid weddings of same-sex couples. Dozens of states had already enacted laws or changed their constitutions to bar gay marriage.

SENATE ACTION

The Senate rejected a motion to invoke cloture (thus end debate) on the gay marriage constitutional amendment (S J Res 40) on July 14, 2004, by a **key vote of 48–50 (R 45–6; D 3–43; I 0–1)**. Backers were twelve short of the number (sixty) needed to move the measure forward on the Senate floor, and nineteen away from the two-thirds majority (sixty-seven) needed to advance a constitutional amendment. (*2004 key votes, p. 854*)

For months leading up to the vote, Sen. Wayne Allard, R-Colo., and other supporters of the so-called Family Marriage Amendment struggled over the wording of the proposal as they tried to gain votes. Many Republicans opposed such an amendment altogether; others thought Congress's role was to ensure that states retain their prerogative to define marriage.

In the end, Senate Republican leaders decided to bring the proposed constitutional amendment directly to the floor, bypassing the Judiciary Committee, where it might have been rejected. But Senate majority leader Bill Frist, R-Tenn., failed to muster his caucus behind a single proposal.

Allard's resolution proposed a two-sentence addition to the U.S. Constitution. The first sentence would define marriage as "the union of a man and a woman." The second would mandate that "neither this Constitution, nor the constitution of any State, shall be construed to require that marriage or the legal incidents thereof be conferred upon any union other than the union of a man and a woman." The second sentence was aimed at ensuring that state legislatures—but not state courts—could create other constructs, such as civil unions or domestic partnerships.

Under the Constitution, the resolution would require the approval of two-thirds of those present and voting in both the House and Senate, followed by ratification by three-quarters (thirty-eight) of the states.

During the Senate debate, supporters of Allard's resolution were careful to cast themselves as defenders of marriage and, by extension, children and families, not as against gay rights. Allard and his allies argued that unless the Constitution was amended, "activist" judges would hijack the democratic process and legalize gay marriage everywhere. Opponents of the constitutional amendment said that despite the fears of conservatives, the 1996 marriage law remained in effect. They also argued that the question of who can marry whom should be left to the states, where it traditionally resided.

Democrats said they would not block an up-or-down vote on Allard's resolution, and on July 9 Senate minority whip Harry Reid, D-Nev., said his caucus was "ready to rock and roll." But when the Senate resumed debate July 12, Rick Santorum of Pennsylvania, the Senate Republican conference chair and a main driver of the gay marriage debate, announced that Republicans wanted to allow a vote on an amendment to the resolution, by Gordon H. Smith, R-Ore., that would remove the second sentence. John Cornyn, R-Texas, estimated that the shortened resolution would pick up ten votes. Smith, a gay rights supporter who has publicly agonized over his opposition to same-sex marriage, said the shorter version would steer clear of civil unions and partnerships.

Democrats were confident that as many as twelve GOP senators would vote against the Allard resolution. But they were not willing to risk a vote on the one-sentence version. Senate minority leader Tom Daschle, D-S.D., said that allowing for any changes to Allard's resolution on the floor would be tantamount to "making the Senate a constitutional convention." Frist then engineered the July 14 procedural vote.

Despite the final tally, proponents of amending the Constitution said they were sanguine about their prospects. They viewed the July 14 vote as just the beginning of a process that they likened to the lengthy struggle for passage of the 1964 civil rights law (PL 88-352). (*1964 law, Congress and the Nation Vol. I, p. 1635*)

HOUSE ACTION

House leaders brought H J Res 106 to the floor Sept. 30, 2004, bypassing the Judiciary Committee and its Chair, F. James Sensenbrenner Jr., R-Wis., who opposed same-sex marriage but also had reservations about amending the Constitution to achieve that end.

The House fell well short of the two-thirds majority of lawmakers present and voting necessary to adopt the measure. The Sept. 30 decision came on a **key vote of 227–186 (R 191–27; D 36–158; I 0–1)**. (*2004 key votes, p. 854*)

Though House Republican leaders predicted the result well before the vote, the occasion allowed them to again criticize "activist" judges, who conservatives contend are unilaterally rewriting the Constitution from the bench. Marilyn Musgrave, R-Colo., the author of the proposed amendment, argued that a federal constitutional amendment to bar gay marriage was essential to preserve the will of the people against the courts. But during floor debate on the proposal, Democrats accused the Republican majority of using the Constitution to divide the electorate and obscure other prominent issues, such as the war in Iraq. Democrats also charged the amendment would, for the first time, write discrimination into the Constitution.

The House proposal, like the Senate version, would define marriage in the Constitution as "solely . . . the union of a man and a woman." It also would forbid federal and state judges from ruling that gay marriage is a constitutional right. Although H J Res 106 failed, the House had passed a bill (HR 3313—H Rept 108-614) by 233–194 on July 22, 2004, designed to bar federal courts from hearing challenges to a provision of the 1996 law that gives states the option of not recognizing same-sex marriages performed in other states. The Senate took no action. (*Court restrictions, p. 618*)

Gun Liability

A bill (HR 1036) to make it harder to file civil lawsuits against firearms manufacturers and gun dealers sailed through the House in 2003, handing the gun lobby a victory. But the Senate rejected a companion measure (S 1805) after it was amended to include several gun control provisions, including extending a ten-year-old prohibition on certain types of assault weapons. (*Assault weapons ban, p. 615*)

BACKGROUND

Supporters said action was urgently needed to protect manufacturers from lawsuits intended to force them into bankruptcy. The aim of the legislation was to block certain civil lawsuits against manufacturers, distributors, dealers, and importers of firearms and ammunition—principally those aimed at assessing liability for gun violence against the makers and sellers of weapons. Trade groups also were protected under the legislation. Although such lawsuits generally failed, defendants had to spend large sums on legal expenses.

The restrictions would not apply to lawsuits alleging a breach of contract or suits brought against any manufacturer or seller who "knowingly and willfully violated" a state or federal law in selling or marketing a weapon and, therefore, contributed to gun violence. The legislation also would not apply to civil lawsuits brought as a result of "physical injuries or property damage resulting directly from a defect in design or manufacture of the product, when used as intended."

Critics said the legislation would unfairly shut the courtroom door to victims of gun violence. They called it a sop to the gun lobby and said the firearms industry had a responsibility to ensure its products were not misused.

The White House expressed strong support for the legislation. "The manufacturer or seller of a legal, nondefective product should not be held liable for the criminal or unlawful misuse of that product by others," the administration said in a policy statement issued the day of the House vote.

Proponents also appealed to lawmakers' institutional pride, arguing that gun control advocates had turned to the courts because they had failed in the political arena. As a result, they said, the courts—not Congress—were deciding firearms policies.

The measures were in part a response to lawsuits filed by municipalities, including an unsuccessful one by the city of New Orleans. The U.S. Supreme Court declined in 2001 to review a Louisiana Supreme Court decision upholding a state law barring New Orleans from suing gunmakers for the costs of gun violence. Louisiana was among more than thirty states that restricted lawsuits against gun manufacturers.

The House Judiciary Committee approved a virtually identical bill in 2002, essentially on party lines. The measure never made it to the floor because Republican leaders thought it was too politically risky following a series of sniper attacks in the Washington, D.C., area. *(107th Congress action, p. 601)*

LEGISLATIVE ACTION

The House Judiciary Committee approved HR 1036 by 21–11 on April 3, 2003. It formally reported the bill (H Rept 108-59) on April 7. The House passed the measure April 9 on a vote of 285–140.

Supporters turned back a series of Democratic amendments designed to narrow the scope of the bill. The House on April 9 rejected 148–278 an attempt by Robert C. Scott, D-Va., to eliminate a provision that would bar a civil suit against a person who transferred a firearm unless the person had already been convicted of the crime. It rejected on April 9 by 134–289 an amendment by Linda T. Sanchez, D-Calif., that would allow lawsuits against a seller or manufacturer who transferred guns or ammunition to a drug addict. The House also rejected by 144–280 on April 9 an amendment by Martin T. Meehan, D-Mass., that would permit individuals to recover damages in cases against negligent manufacturers, sellers, or trade organizations.

The Senate in 2003 did not consider either the House-passed bill or the companion measure (S 1805), sponsored by Larry E. Craig, R-Idaho. Supporters, chiefly the National Rifle Association, set out to win commitments from at least sixty senators, which was the threshold needed to shut off a filibuster.

Senate Republicans orchestrated the defeat of S 1805, which they had once embraced. After it was amended to include several gun control provisions, the Senate rejected the measure March 2, 2004, by a vote of 8–90.

The measure had appeared likely to win Senate passage with relative ease and was being pushed by the Bush administration. But gun control advocates, leveraging a bit of election-year momentum, succeeded in adding a trio of amendments embodying the heart of their legislative agenda, which had been moribund since the collapse of a gun control and juvenile justice package four years before.

On Feb. 26, senators voted 70–27 on a Barbara Boxer, D-Calif., amendment to require the sale of child safety locks or a storage box with every handgun. On March 2, senators adopted 53–46 a Jack Reed, D-R.I., and John McCain, R-Ariz., amendment to require criminal background checks before any firearms sale at most gun shows. Gun control advocates were able to build support for the amendment by capitalizing on heightened concerns about terrorists acquiring firearms. The same day, the Senate voted 52–47 to add language offered by Dianne Feinstein, D-Calif., extending for an additional ten years the ban on semiautomatic assault weapons that had been enacted (PL 103-322) in 1994. That ban was scheduled to expire Sept. 13. *(1994 action, Congress and the Nation Vol. IX, p. 683)*

Bill supporters easily turned back four other amendments designed to expand exemptions in the gun liability measure, including a proposal to protect any lawsuits stemming from the October 2002 sniper attacks in the Washington, D.C., area. Nevertheless, the National Rifle Association—whose principal agent in the Senate was Craig, an NRA board member—directed its allies in the Senate to turn against the measure. Most gun control advocates did as well, concluding that their victories had little chance of survival in conference negotiations.

Assault Weapons Ban

Congress in 2004 allowed a popular ten-year ban on assault weapons (PL 103-322) to expire. The Senate voted to extend the ban for another ten years, but the House did not take up the issue. *(Weapons ban, Congress and the Nation Vol. IX, p. 683)*

The expiration of the assault weapons ban represented a major blow to the gun control movement, in part because, on the surface, reauthorizing the law appeared to be a simple task. White House officials repeatedly said President George W. Bush supported reauthorizing the existing ban, which outlawed the manufacture, sale, or possession of large-capacity ammunition clips and nineteen specific semiautomatic guns. In addition, polls indicated that as many as 77 percent of Americans wanted the law reauthorized.

Reauthorizing the law would be a mostly symbolic victory, because even supporters privately acknowledged that gunmakers had found a way around much of the ban. But the fact that gun control advocates lost spoke volumes about the degree to which gun control had eroded as a political issue since the early 1990s, when it was a focus for many Democrats. Since then, Democrats believed that the issue may have been a factor in the GOP takeover of Congress in 1994, and it might have cost presidential nominee Al Gore votes in swing states in the 2000 election.

Ban supporters met insurmountable resistance in the House, where Majority Leader Tom DeLay, R-Texas, repeatedly ruled out putting reauthorizing legislation (HR 3831) on the floor. DeLay maintained that there were not enough votes to pass the bill and said he was unwilling to waste floor time on a proposal that was doomed to fail.

Facing opposition from House GOP leaders, law supporters set their sights on the Senate. Dianne Feinstein, D-Calif., the architect of the 1994 assault weapons ban and a leading proponent of its renewal, worked to build support for a stand-alone bill (S 2498) that would reauthorize the statute for ten years.

But Feinstein and other Senate ban backers, including Democrat Charles E. Schumer of New York, said their best shot was in getting the language added to some fast-moving or must-pass legislation, such as one of the thirteen annual appropriations bills. In February they got their chance, when the Senate began considering the NRA-backed gun liability legislation (S 1805). *(Gun liability, p. 614)*

On March 2, 2004, the Senate adopted Feinstein's assault weapons ban as an amendment to S 1805 by a **key vote of 52–47 (R 10–41; D 41–6; I 1–0).** The chamber dealt other setbacks to the gun rights lobby with a 53–46 vote March 2 on a John McCain, R-Ariz., amendment to add language cracking down on sales at gun shows and a 70–27 vote Feb. 26 on a Barbara Boxer, D-Calif., amendment to require child safety locks on handguns. *(2004 key votes, p. 854)*

The votes were a short-term victory for gun control advocates, who forced firearms supporters to decide whether the liability bill was worth the added language. In the end, gun rights proponents calculated that the cost was too high, and the underlying bill was defeated 8–90.

In July, Feinstein said she would not try again to add the assault weapons language to other legislation. Some moderate Republicans who voted with her March 2 were unwilling to repeatedly cast votes in favor of renewing the law, Democratic aides said.

Concealed Weapons

Congress in 2004 cleared a bill (HR 218) that would allow off-duty and retired law enforcement officers to carry concealed weapons.

House Judiciary Committee Chair F. James Sensenbrenner Jr., R-Wis., dropped his long-standing objections to moving such a measure and allowed HR 218 to advance. The panel approved the measure 23–9 on June 16, 2004. It was formally reported (H Rept 108-560) on June 22.

The House bill had wide bipartisan support. However, it had languished for more than a year because Sensenbren-

ner contended local officials should decide who carried concealed weapons in their communities. Sensenbrenner yielded at the urging of Republican leaders after bill sponsor Randy "Duke" Cunningham, R-Calif., backed off a threat to force the bill to the House floor by gathering the required 218 House members' signatures on a discharge petition.

During the markup, the panel adopted 21–7 a Sensenbrenner amendment that would require officers to carry proof that they had qualified for the waiver within the previous year. Also adopted by voice vote was an amendment by Robert C. Scott, D-Va., to exclude law enforcement officers under the influence of alcohol or other intoxicating or hallucinatory drugs.

Committee Democrats joined Sensenbrenner in making states' rights arguments. But the panel rejected a substitute amendment by ranking Democrat John Conyers Jr. of Michigan that would allow states to opt out of the waiver.

The House passed HR 218 by voice vote under suspension of the rules June 23. The Senate passed the bill by voice vote July 7, completing congressional action. The president signed the measure into law (PL 108-277) on July 22.

The Senate Judiciary Committee had approved a companion measure (S 253) March 6, 2003, on an 18–1 vote. Edward M. Kennedy, D-Mass., cast the sole "nay" vote. Sponsored by Ben Nighthorse Campbell, R-Colo., the measure would establish an exemption from state and local laws banning concealed weapons. A written report (S Rept 108-29) was filed on March 26.

Victims' Rights

Advocates of a proposal (S J Res 1) to confer specific rights on victims of crime abandoned their long-standing plan to amend the U.S. Constitution when it became clear they lacked the necessary support in both chambers. Instead, they supported legislation that would mandate the rights by statute. The stand-alone bill (S 2329) stalled in the House, but the language eventually became law as part of other legislation (HR 5107—PL 108-405). *(DNA testing, p. 595)*

BACKGROUND

Most lawmakers supported the goal of a victims' rights constitutional amendment, but they disagreed over the approach.

Critics argued that even the most well-written and well-intentioned amendment can have unintended consequences when made part of the Constitution and later interpreted in the nation's courtrooms. They worried that, in this case, an amendment could infringe on existing constitutional protections for defendants, and they warned that, while a statute would be relatively easy to change, it could take years to amend the Constitution again to fix any flaws.

In the Senate, Dianne Feinstein, D-Calif., Jon Kyl, R-Ariz., and other supporters insisted that nothing less than an amendment to the Constitution, which granted rights to criminal defendants, would be strong enough to survive legal challenges. They said that judges and prosecutors had not always heeded federal laws in this area and that state laws and constitutions did not establish a uniform standard for protecting victims and their families.

Amendment supporters pointed to the Oklahoma City bombing case. In 1996, federal district judge Richard Matsch barred from the courtroom victims who wanted to testify about the impact of the 1995 attack, saying their testimony could be tainted by watching the proceedings. Two separate appeals to the U.S. Court of Appeals for the Tenth Circuit were rejected.

A 1990 law (PL 101-647) guaranteed victims a number of rights, including the right to be notified of and present at all court proceedings involving the offense, the right to confer with the prosecution, and the right to information about any conviction, sentencing, and imprisonment of the offender. A subsequent law enacted in 1994 (PL 103-322) expanded the opportunities for victims and their families to participate in the sentencing phase of certain criminal cases. *(1990 law, Congress and the Nation Vol. VIII, p. 764; 1994 law, Congress and the Nation Vol. IX, p. 683)*

In response to the Oklahoma City bombing trial, Congress in 1997 passed a law (PL 105-6) that said victims could not be excluded from a federal criminal trial solely because they intended to make a statement from the witness box describing how the crime affected them or their families. Matsch reversed himself and allowed the victims to watch the trial, but he also allowed defense lawyers to question the victims and to ensure that their testimony had not been influenced by what they had seen in the courtroom. *(1997 law, Congress and the Nation Vol. X, p. 609)*

Feinstein and Kyl said the Oklahoma City bombing victims' rights were not adequately protected by the process. Critics said that, in the end, most of the bombing victims said they had been treated fairly.

General agreement exists that if a victims' rights amendment cleared Congress, ratification by three-quarters (thirty-eight) of the states as required by the Constitution would not be a problem. Already, thirty-three states had amended their own constitutions to include similar language, and every state had some statutory protection of victims.

A similar measure made it to the Senate floor during the 106th Congress, where it died after a week of debate in which critics said the amendment was too long and complicated. The new version in the 108th Congress was significantly shorter than previous versions backed by Feinstein and Kyl. *(Earlier action, Congress and the Nation Vol. X, p. 668)*

2003 ACTION

In 2003 victims' rights advocates focused on amending the Constitution. The Senate Judiciary Committee, 10–8, approved the proposed amendment (S J Res 1) on Sept. 4 to enumerate specific rights for victims of crime. It was the latest step in a seven-year campaign by Feinstein and Kyl. It also was the high point for the legislation. A report (S Rept 108-191) was filed Nov. 7.

The proposed amendment would give victims or their representatives the right to be heard at public parole, plea, sentencing, and other proceedings. Judicial officials would have to take victims' safety into account when deciding the fate of defendants. Victims also would have the right to "reasonable and timely notice" of public proceedings and of defendant releases or escapes. The resolution specified that the amendment could not be used as grounds for a new trial or claims for damages.

The committee rejected 7–10 a substitute by the ranking Democrat, Patrick J. Leahy of Vermont, that would put into statute several rights for victims, including protection from suspects, consultation before detention hearings, and consultation on plea agreements. It also would establish victim-related grant programs.

Richard J. Durbin, D-Ill., argued that writing victims' rights into the Constitution could unfairly tip the balance, jeopardizing the accused's constitutional rights to counsel, due process, and a speedy trial, as well as the prohibition against self-incrimination, unreasonable search and seizure, and cruel and unusual punishment. As a solution, Durbin suggested rewriting the amendment to include language that clarified that the rights of the accused were not diminished by the rights of the victim. His proposed change was defeated 6–11 in a committee session July 31.

Despite the committee's approval, supporters acknowledged they would have difficulty winning enough support in the Senate to meet the Constitution's requirement that an amendment receive the support of two-thirds of those present and voting. In the House, Judiciary Committee Chair F. James Sensenbrenner Jr., R-Wis., was reluctant to amend the Constitution for any reason.

2004 ACTION

The victims' rights advocates finally yielded to political reality during the week of April 19, 2004. Faced with almost certain Senate defeat of S J Res 1, Kyl and Feinstein embraced a statutory approach. By 96–1 on April 22, the Senate passed a bill (S 2329) intended to confer eight specific rights upon victims of federal crimes.

Kyl and Feinstein decided to settle for the legislation just before the Senate was to take up their constitutional amendment. The debate was timed to coincide with Crime Victims' Rights Week.

Supporters of the constitutional approach said they wanted to acknowledge victims' rights during the 108th Congress, even if that meant embracing the alternative approach advanced by critics of the amendment. If the legislation was later viewed as providing inadequate protection, the case for a constitutional amendment would be stronger, the victims' rights proponents concluded.

The bill passed by the Senate sought to guarantee victims or their representatives the right to be heard at public court proceedings when a defendant is brought before a judge for sentencing, release, or discussion of a plea bargain. It also would require judicial officials to take victims' safety into account when deciding the fate of defendants.

While the proposed constitutional amendment would apply to victims of violent crime in federal and state courts, the bill would apply only in the federal courts. Because most crimes were tried in state courts, the bill would extend rights to as few as 1 percent of the victims who would be protected by the proposed constitutional amendment.

But supporters of the legislation noted that the bill would apply to victims of all federal crimes, not just violent ones. It would also authorize spending $16.3 million in fiscal 2005 and $26.5 million annually in fiscal 2006 through 2009 to improve victim notification and encourage states to protect victims' rights.

The bill still did not advance quickly in the House. Sensenbrenner tried to capitalize on its popularity to build support for separate legislation (S 1700, HR 3214) that would make it easier for federal inmates to seek post-conviction DNA (deoxyribonucleic acid) tests that could help exonerate them.

Sensenbrenner ultimately added a modified version of the Senate-passed victims' rights bill to a version of the DNA measure. The House passed the newly combined legislation (HR 5107—H Rept 108-711) on Oct. 6 by a vote of 393–14. The Senate cleared it by voice vote Oct. 9. *(DNA testing, p. 595)*

President George W. Bush signed it into law Oct. 30, 2004.

Court Restrictions

Amid growing conservative criticism of federal judges who were perceived as overly liberal, three bills (HR 3313, HR 2028, S 878) were considered that sought to restrict the jurisdiction of federal courts or otherwise rein in federal judges.

House Republican leaders, who chafed at what they said were "activist" judges legislating from the bench, were eager to exercise Congress's constitutional power to define federal court jurisdiction and draw appellate court maps. But that campaign did not draw much support from Democrats.

SAME-SEX MARRIAGE

On July 22, 2004, the House voted mostly along party lines 233–194 to bolster a 1996 law defining marriage as a heterosexual union. The bill (HR 3313) would prevent all federal courts—including the U.S. Supreme Court—from having jurisdiction over a provision in the 1996 law (PL 104-199), known as the Defense of Marriage Act, that gave states the option of not recognizing same-sex marriages performed in other states. The House Judiciary Committee had approved HR 3313 by 21–13 on July 14, 2004, and formally reported it (H Rept 108-614) on July 19. *(1996 law, Congress and the Nation Vol. IX, p. 746)*

House Republicans defended the bill as an urgent necessity, particularly after the Senate refused just one week earlier to limit debate and vote on a motion to take up the proposed constitutional amendment to bar same-sex marriage (S J Res 40, H J Res 56). GOP lawmakers said HR 3313, sponsored by John Hostettler, R-Ind., would ensure that states remain the final arbiter over laws concerning marriage. *(Gay marriage, p. 613)*

Congress had cleared the 1996 law after three gay couples sued in Hawaii for the right to marry. The law, which had not been challenged in federal courts, defined a spouse as "a person of the opposite sex who is a husband or a wife." In addition to allowing states to refuse to recognize same-sex marriages, it precluded gay couples from seeking spousal benefits under Social Security or other federal programs.

Conservatives feared that the law could be undermined by a Massachusetts Supreme Judicial Court's ruling in 2003 that held same-sex marriage legal under that state's constitution. On July 20, a lesbian couple married in Massachusetts filed suit in U.S. District Court in Tampa after Florida did not recognize their marriage license.

But Democrats decried HR 3313 as a back-door attempt to amend the U.S. Constitution. They also said the bill would undermine the federal judiciary by stripping courts' ability to rule on the 1996 law's constitutionality. Under the bill, each state court would determine the constitutionality of the federal 1996 law. Republicans argued it would ensure that same-sex couples have access to judicial review. However, opponents said it was a recipe for chaos because states could wind up interpreting the Constitution in conflicting ways.

The bill attracted the support of twenty-seven Democrats; seventeen Republicans voted against it. Among the opponents of the legislation was former representative Bob Barr (R-Ga., 1995–2003), chief sponsor of the 1996 law, who said the bill would set a "dangerous precedent for future Congresses" that could find it tempting to insert similar language in other bills.

The debate on the House floor had the flavor of a constitutional law school class, as each side lectured the other on historical precedents.

Bill supporters said Article III of the Constitution gave Congress authority to regulate federal court jurisdiction. They cited a series of recently enacted laws that limited judicial review on issues ranging from the construction of the World War II memorial to fighting forest fires. In recent decades, Republicans had unsuccessfully pushed similar proposals to limit federal court jurisdiction over abortion, recitation of the Pledge of Allegiance, and school prayer.

But Democratic opponents contended that such measures amounted to unprecedented attempts at "court stripping" that would undermine the separation of powers. Congress had rarely, if ever, passed laws that would bar all federal courts from reviewing the constitutionality of a statute, according to many constitutional scholars. And with so few precedents, the constitutionality of such a measure remained an open question, the Congressional Research Service concluded. Opponents also said the bill would be an infringement on gay and lesbian couples' right to equal protection under the Constitution.

As amended by the Judiciary Committee, HR 3313 would apply only to the provision in the 1996 law giving states the option of not recognizing same-sex marriages performed in other states. Definitions of "marriage" and "spouse" under the act could still be challenged in federal courts.

The bill was not considered in the Senate, where some staunch supporters of the constitutional amendment were reluctant to limit the jurisdiction of federal courts.

PLEDGE OF ALLEGIANCE

On Sept. 23, 2004, the House passed 247–173 a bill (HR 2028) that would strip federal courts of jurisdiction over constitutional challenges to the wording of the Pledge of Allegiance. Thirty-four Democrats joined the majority and six Republicans voted with the minority.

The measure was written in response to a 2002 ruling by the U.S. Court of Appeals for the Ninth Circuit that the phrase "under God" in the pledge was an unconstitutional establishment of religion. The Supreme Court reversed the Ninth Circuit in June on a technicality, not on constitutional grounds. Social conservatives were concerned that the high court had left the pledge open to more constitutional challenges.

Congress had added "under God" to the pledge in 1954 (PL 83-396). *(Congress and the Nation Vol. I, p. 1669)*

The House Judiciary Committee had voted along party lines 17–10 to approve the measure Sept. 15. Under the bill, sponsored by Todd Akin, R-Mo., and formally reported (H Rept 108-691) on Sept. 21, no federal court could hear cases pertaining to the "interpretation" or "validity under the Constitution" of the pledge. State courts could still hear such cases, but their decisions could not be appealed to the Supreme Court. Democrats called the bill an unconstitutional attempt to "close the courthouse doors" to religious minorities.

On the floor, House Democrats bitterly opposed what they described as an ideologically driven attempt to punish federal judges for decisions that displeased social conservatives. By voice vote Sept. 23, the House adopted an amendment by F. James Sensenbrenner Jr., R-Wis., that would allow the local courts of Washington, D.C., which were creations of Congress, to hear constitutional challenges to the pledge.

An amendment by Melvin Watt, D-N.C., to preserve appellate jurisdiction for the Supreme Court was rejected 202–217 on Sept. 23. Sheila Jackson-Lee, D-Texas, offered another amendment that would permit federal courts to hear constitutional challenges to the pledge that alleged coercion or mandatory recitation. The House rejected it by voice vote on Sept. 23.

The House, during consideration of the fiscal 2004 Commerce, Justice, and State appropriations bill (HR 2799), had adopted 307–119 on July 22, 2003, a John Hostettler, R-Ind., amendment to bar the Justice Department from enforcing the Ninth Circuit ruling regarding the Pledge of Allegiance. The language, however, was dropped in conference.

NINTH CIRCUIT COURT OF APPEALS

A closely divided House during consideration of S 878 on Oct. 5, 2004, adopted an amendment by 205–194 that would carve the U.S. Court of Appeals for the Ninth Circuit into three separate appellate jurisdictions. The bill would create dozens of additional court judgeships. The Ninth Circuit, which sprawled over nine states, was seen as the most liberal appellate court in the country, and conservatives were often angered by its decisions—especially by the ruling that the phrase "under God" in the Pledge of Allegiance was an unconstitutional establishment of religion.

Idaho Republican Mike Simpson, who offered the amendment, insisted that he wanted to split up the Ninth Circuit not because of its decisions, but because its sheer size made it too unwieldy to be efficient. His proposal would leave California, Guam, Hawaii, and the Northern Mariana Islands in the Ninth Circuit. It would create a Twelfth Circuit encompassing Arizona, Idaho, Montana, and Nevada, and a Thirteenth Circuit made up of Alaska, Oregon, and Washington.

The vote on the amendment was so close, with several California Republicans weighing in against the measure, that GOP leaders held the vote open. Simpson and House Judiciary Committee Chair Sensenbrenner persuaded thirteen Republicans, including ten from California, to switch from "no" to "yes" to give conservatives a victory. The House passed the underlying bill by voice vote on Oct 5.

Some California Republicans who ultimately backed the plan said they initially were concerned that a reduced Ninth Circuit would be even more liberal without the seven states targeted for removal. According to some of those lawmakers, Sensenbrenner persuaded them to switch by reminding them that the underlying bill provided for several new judgeships for the Ninth Circuit, which could serve to tilt it toward the right.

Sen. Dianne Feinstein, D-Calif., announced that she would block the measure in the Senate because of the Ninth Circuit provisions. Feinstein cited objections from Ninth Circuit judges, lawyers, and California's Republican governor, Arnold Schwarzenegger. She argued that Simpson's plan would mean added government expenses and a higher caseload for the new Ninth Circuit than for either of the other two. Even without Simpson's amendment, the legislation was imperiled because the House Judiciary Committee stripped dozens of federal bankruptcy judgeships.

The Senate Judiciary Committee approved S 878 on May 15, 2003. The full Senate passed the bill by voice vote May 22. The House Judiciary Committee approved S 878 by voice vote Sept. 9, 2004, and formally reported it (H Rept 108-708) on Sept. 29. The House passed the bill by voice vote Oct. 5.

Flag Desecration

The House in 2003 passed a constitutional amendment (H J Res 4) to give Congress the authority to ban desecration of the U.S. flag, and the Senate Judiciary Committee also gave approval to an identical measure (S J Res 4) in 2004. The full Senate did not take up the joint resolution.

The proposed House amendment, introduced by Randy "Duke" Cunningham, R-Calif., was an attempt to overturn a 1989 U.S. Supreme Court ruling in *Texas v. Johnson* that state laws against flag burning violate the First Amendment. Congress responded to the ruling with a 1989 law banning flag desecration (PL 101-131), but the high court rejected it on the same grounds in 1990 (*United States v. Eichman*). *(1989 and 1990 rulings, Congress and the Nation Vol. VIII, p. 836; 1989 law, Congress and the Nation Vol. VIII, p. 760)*

Since then, supporters had fought passionately for a constitutional amendment to give Congress the authority to ban any kind of flag desecration. The House provided the two-thirds majority needed to pass such a resolution in 1995, 1997, 1999, 2001, and again in 2003. Similar efforts in the Senate failed in 1989, 1990, 1995, and 2000. *(1995 action, Congress and the Nation Vol. IX, p. 754; 1997, 1999, and 2000 action, Congress and the Nation Vol. X, pp. 610, 666; 2001 action, p. 599)*

The House voted 300–125 on June 3, 2003, to pass a resolution proposing the constitutional amendment (H J Res 4), after rejecting a substitute by Melvin Watt, D-N.C., that would allow Congress to bar the physical desecration of the flag but only if it was consistent with the First Amendment. Watt's substitute was rejected 129–296 on June 3. The House Judiciary Committee had approved H J Res 4 by 18–13 on May 21 and formally reported it (H Rept 108-131) on June 2.

H J Res 4 would add a single phrase to the Constitution: "The Congress shall have the power to prohibit the physical desecration of the flag of the United States."

Amendment supporters argued that, before the 1989 ruling, desecrating the flag was widely believed to be illegal. Supporters, mostly Republicans, also said that flag desecration was tantamount to obscenity and should not receive constitutional protection.

Opponents insisted that flag desecration was an exercise of free speech guaranteed by the U.S. Constitution. Critics also argued that the proposed amendment would open the door to demands for constitutional protections for other icons, including the cross and the Bible.

The Judiciary Subcommittee on the Constitution, Civil Rights, and Property Rights approved S J Res 4 on June 2, 2004, by a party-line vote of 5–4, and the full committee approved it 11–7 on July 20. A report (S Rept 108-334) was filed Aug. 25. Supporters said the proposal would be an appropriate way to honor the flag and ensure that a symbol of freedom was not desecrated in any way. Opponents, however, worried that the proposed amendment would undermine some of the nation's founding principles, including the First Amendment's guarantee of a right to free expression.

Majority Leader Bill Frist, R-Tenn., never brought S J Res 4 to the floor because supporters lacked the two-thirds majority needed for passage.

Gang Violence

In a rare show of bipartisanship on a significant piece of legislation, the Senate Judiciary Committee approved a bill (S 1735) in 2004 that would increase federal law enforcement's role in cracking down on gang violence. The bill did not advance further.

Four Democrats joined all but one of the committee's Republicans in voting 13–6 in favor of the measure June 24, 2004 (no written report), which would make it a federal crime to participate in a "criminal street gang."

The bill would define a criminal street gang as three or more people who cooperated to commit two or more "gang crimes," ranging from murder to money laundering. It also would criminalize the recruitment of minors and authorize $650 million for gang prevention and suppression programs.

The American Civil Liberties Union criticized the bill's provisions expanding the federal death penalty and transferring more youths into the adult criminal justice system.

The committee rejected 7–12 a substitute measure by Democrats that would provide more money for witness protection programs and allow rural communities and smaller jurisdictions to apply for grants to combat gangs. The substitute would not expand the federal death penalty or the prosecution of juveniles as adults.

Also rejected, 8–11, was an amendment by Edward M. Kennedy, D-Mass., to increase the bill's witness protection funding from $12 million to $60 million a year. An amendment by Richard J. Durbin, D-Ill., rejected 6–13, would strip a provision that would place the burden of proof onto juvenile defendants regarding shifting them between the adult and juvenile criminal justice systems.

Dianne Feinstein, D-Calif, cosponsored the bill, and three Democrats—Joseph R. Biden Jr. of Delaware, Herb Kohl of Wisconsin, and Charles E. Schumer of New York—joined her in voting for it. Jeff Sessions of Alabama was the sole Judiciary Committee Republican to oppose the bill. He said he believed prosecutors had enough tools to fight gangs and balked at the bill's high price tag.

Drug Penalties

A House Judiciary subcommittee approved a bill (HR 4547) in 2004 that would increase mandatory minimums and constrain judges' sentencing discretion as a way to toughen penalties for selling drugs to minors or near treatment centers. But the bill did not advance further.

The bill came after a U.S. Supreme Court decision ruled in June that a central component of Washington State's sentencing guidelines—the ability of judges to base sentences on factors not considered by a jury—was unconstitutional.

This ruling left judges nationwide issuing contradictory interpretations. *(Blakely v. Washington, p. 655)*

The legislation was approved Sept. 23, 2004, by voice vote by the Judiciary Subcommittee on Crime, Terrorism, and Homeland Security after the panel adopted a substitute amendment, also by voice vote. The bill would make it easier to penalize traffickers for attempting or conspiring to sell drugs to persons younger than eighteen or selling drugs in protected zones, such as within one thousand feet of schools and colleges. It would expand the list of those zones, where drug crimes carried higher penalties, to include day-care facilities and public libraries.

Under the bill, sponsored by Judiciary Committee Chair F. James Sensenbrenner Jr., R-Wis., it would be a crime punishable by at least five years in prison to distribute drugs within one thousand feet of a drug treatment facility or to anyone undergoing treatment. The bill also would increase the length of mandatory minimum sentences and expand the types of offenses that qualified. Those changes drew strong opposition from Democrats, the American Bar Association, civil rights groups, and the federal judiciary's policy arm, the Judicial Conference of the United States.

The measure also incorporated provisions of another bill (HR 881) that would undo changes to federal guidelines that sought to allow shorter sentences for low-level drug offenders compared with major traffickers. Republicans argued that those smaller players made drug trafficking possible. But ranking Democrat Robert C. Scott of Virginia said that would mean sorority sisters with prior felony offenses who shared drugs at college would receive the same penalties as drug kingpins who sold to students. Scott urged the Judiciary Committee to delay further consideration of the bill pending clarification from the Supreme Court about the validity of federal sentencing guidelines.

The substitute bill stripped provisions that would increase mandatory minimums for defendants younger than twenty-one charged with distribution and apply them equally to incompetent persons and minors. The subcommittee deleted, as requested by the Judicial Conference, a section in the original bill that would require federal rules of civil procedure regarding plea agreements to be consistent with sentencing guidelines.

D.C. Gun Control

Legislation that would repeal the District of Columbia's municipal gun control laws—some of the toughest in the nation—was decisively passed by the House on Sept. 29, 2004. The Senate disregarded the bill (HR 3193), but the vote nonetheless illustrated how skittish Democrats had become about gun control in an election year.

The vote on the measure was 250–171. Fifty-two mostly Southern and rural Democrats broke with the majority of their caucus to support an end to restrictions on gun ownership in the nation's capital, including thirteen who voted against a similar measure in 1999.

The bill would lift a ban on private ownership of handguns and their ammunition, and it would allow Washington, D.C., residents to legally own semiautomatic weapons not prohibited by federal law. Residents would be allowed to keep firearms in their homes and businesses and would no longer be required to keep weapons unloaded and disassembled or with the trigger locked. The legislation went to the House floor without a markup by any committee.

Advocates of HR 3193 said the city's strict gun laws had done little to stem violence and instead left residents defenseless in their own homes. The bill's sponsor, Mark Souder, R-Ind., also suggested the current regulations were unconstitutional encroachments on residents' Second Amendment right to bear arms.

Opponents said the bill was ill conceived while Washington was on high alert against a possible terrorist attack and had seen a recent surge in juvenile shooting deaths. Overall, the District's murder rate had declined 38 percent in the past decade, to 248 homicides in 2003.

The District's nonvoting delegate, Democrat Eleanor Holmes Norton, called the bill "an insult to American principles of self-government and home rule."

Republicans addressed one Democratic complaint by adding language that would limit possession to residents' homes and property. Democrats argued the original text of the bill would allow fully loaded assault rifles to be carried in public.

The vote was an almost exact reversal of an amendment to a 1999 juvenile justice bill that would lift D.C.'s firearms ban. That measure, which was rejected 175–250, came only two months after the shootings at a Columbine, Colorado, high school. Vice President Al Gore's subsequent defeat in the 2000 presidential election convinced many Democrats that supporting gun control may have cost them votes in tight races.

Visa Waiver Program

The Senate in 2004 cleared legislation (HR 4417—PL 108-299) to give the government and twenty-seven friendly nations an extra year to issue new, high-tech passports.

In its final act before adjourning for a six-week summer recess, the Senate passed the bill July 22 by voice vote, clearing it for the president. The House had passed the measure by voice vote under suspension of the rules June 14. President George W. Bush signed the bill Aug. 9.

The twenty-seven countries, mostly in Western Europe, were part of a waiver program that allowed their residents and U.S. citizens to temporarily visit without first obtaining visas.

Congress passed a law (PL 107-173) after the Sept. 11, 2001, terrorist attacks requiring the United States and its visa waiver partners to issue more secure passports. The new passports had to be readable by computers and include a "biometric identifier" such as a digital photo. The law set an Oct. 26, 2004, deadline for the new documents.

The departments of State and Homeland Security asked Congress for a two-year extension of the deadline, saying neither the United States nor the other countries were prepared to issue the passports.

The House passed the bill allowing a one-year extension on June 14. A spokesperson for Sen. Saxby Chambliss, R-Ga., who had sponsored a bill (S 2324) giving the agencies a two-year extension, said he was prepared to extend the deadline another year in 2005.

The State Department said it probably would not meet the October 2005 deadline.

Identity Theft

Hoping to crack down on one of the fastest-growing crimes in the country, Congress in 2004 cleared a bill (HR 1731) to establish tougher criminal penalties for identity theft and make it easier for prosecutors to go after the perpetrators. It was signed into law (PL 108-275) on July 15.

Lawmakers were concerned about the growing problem of stolen identities, which affected ten million Americans in 2003. The Federal Trade Commission estimated that in 2002 businesses and financial institutions lost $47.6 billion from identity theft, while the cost to consumers was $5 billion. Identity thieves were increasingly using the personal information of others to open credit card accounts, take out loans, and conceal their true identities from law enforcement.

Several provisions designed to deter identity theft were part of the financial services law (PL 108-159) that President George W. Bush signed in 2003. The financial services law required that no more than the last five digits of credit and debit card numbers appear on restaurant and store sales receipts. It also allowed consumers to receive one free credit report each year and to place fraud alerts on their credit reports. *(Financial services, p. 140)*

HR 1731 went much further. It established penalties for "aggravated identity theft," which it defined as identity theft committed in conjunction with felonies, including bank, wire, or mail fraud. Those convicted of such a crime could expect a mandatory sentence of two additional years beyond the penalty for the underlying crime, while those who stole identities in conjunction with a terrorist act would receive a mandatory five extra years in prison. The bill also targeted corporate insiders by directing the U.S. Sentencing Commission to amend its guidelines to appropriately punish identity theft offenses involving the abuse of a position.

The House Judiciary Committee approved HR 1731 by voice vote May 12, 2004, after expanding its scope to cover fraud involving federal benefits, such as Social Security, Medicare, and veterans' and disability payments. The provision allowed prosecutors to aggregate all individual amounts of federal benefits stolen using fraudulent identities to ensure that such cases qualify for enhanced penalties.

The amendment, by bill sponsor John Carter, R-Texas, also would permit prosecutors to aggregate all individual amounts of federal benefits stolen using fraudulent identi-

ties—to ensure that such cases qualify for enhanced penalties. And it would direct the U.S. Sentencing Commission to amend its guidelines to punish insider offenses that involve an "abuse of position." The panel adopted the amendment by voice vote. HR 1731 was formally reported (H Rept 108-528) on June 8.

HR 1731 received overwhelming bipartisan support on June 23 in the House, which passed the measure by voice vote under suspension of the rules. Opposition to the bill came mainly from foes of mandatory minimum prison sentences. "The bill imposes unnecessary and unproductive restrictions on the ability of the sentencing commission and judges in individual cases to ensure a rational and just system of sentencing as a whole," said Robert C. Scott, D-Va.

But Democrat Adam B. Schiff of California, who cosponsored the measure, said "the plague of identity theft" was one instance in which mandatory minimums were justified. Because identity theft and the resulting crime were merged for the purposes of sentencing, Schiff said, prosecutors would otherwise have little incentive to pursue such cases.

The Senate passed HR 1731 by voice vote June 25, completing congressional action. Senators on March 19, 2003. had passed a similar measure (S 153) imposing tougher penalties on identity theft crimes.

Immigration Policy

Lawmakers added immigration provisions to the omnibus spending measure (HR 4818—PL 108-447) that aimed to settle a pair of long-running disputes over immigration policy. The provisions would not only expand by about one-third the number of visas available for foreign technology workers but also crack down on the use of imported temporary workers.

The language involved visas for foreign workers known as H-1B and L-1, both of which had come under increased scrutiny as businesses outsourced jobs to foreign workers. The H-1B visa was available to foreign workers in "specialty" occupations, most often in high-tech fields. Congress capped the number of such workers who could enter the country at sixty-five thousand per year and required that they be paid the same as U.S. citizens in comparable jobs, or the prevailing industry wage. Businesses, however, said the H-1B visa program was too limited. The number of available visas for fiscal 2005 was exhausted Oct. 1—the first day of the fiscal year.

The L-1 visa was supposed to be used by companies to transfer foreign executives to U.S. locations. Unlike the H-1B, Congress did not limit the number of L-1 visas. Critics of the program said this led to instances in which companies used the system to circumvent the H-1B cap by bringing in foreign workers who are then hired out to third parties as temporary workers.

The provision in the omnibus essentially merged two pieces of legislation that did not advance in the 108th Congress. Organized labor and groups opposed to increased immigration had lobbied against the provision.

S 1635, sponsored by Sen. Saxby Chambliss, R-Ga., revised the eligibility for the L-1 visa. It required that L-1 workers be supervised by the companies sponsoring them, and attempted to prohibit companies from hiring out their L-1 workers to a third party. S 1635 was approved by the Senate Judiciary Committee Sept. 30, 2004, and reported (no written report) Oct 4.

HR 4166, sponsored by Rep. Lamar Smith, R-Texas, allowed an exemption to the H-1B cap for foreign workers who earned advanced degrees from U.S. universities. Both Smith's bill and the omnibus provision—at Smith's insistence—capped the exception at twenty thousand graduates per year. Groups opposed to the provision said Congress should not act to bring in more foreign labor at a time when thousands of American technology workers are jobless.

Lawmakers turned to the omnibus after stand-alone legislation stalled.

Judicial Nominations

The acrimony over judicial nominations reached new heights in the 108th Congress. President George W. Bush enjoyed considerable success. By the end of his first term, he had filled 203 lifetime seats on the federal trial and circuit appeals courts, or 24 percent of the total.

But such statistics belied the intense partisanship and rancor over the makeup of the courts, which rose to new levels in 2003 when Democrats mounted the first coordinated filibusters against judicial nominations in more than a quarter-century. By the end of the 108th Congress, they used this maneuver to block ten of Bush's picks from taking appeals court seats. Bush retaliated, using his power to make recess appointments to place two of the nominees on the bench for temporary terms.

CHALLENGE TO DEMOCRATS

With the Senate under Republican control, the 108th Congress opened with Bush resubmitting thirty judicial nominations that were not confirmed by the Democratic-controlled Senate in the 107th Congress. In a challenge to Democrats, Bush renominated Priscilla Owen and Charles W. Pickering Sr. to seats on the U.S. Court of Appeals for the Fifth Circuit, both of whom had been rejected by the Judiciary Committee when the Democrats ran it. It was the first time any president had renominated a rejected federal court candidate. (*107th Congress action, p. 595*)

The president and GOP senators pushed hard to advance those and other nominees. The Judiciary Committee moved with unusual speed, even at times overriding the concerns of Democrats from the nominees' home states, who had traditionally been given great deference in the process. But Democrats made clear from the outset that they would not hesitate to block nominees whose jurisprudence they considered out of the mainstream.

Partisan conflicts first emerged Jan. 30, when Miguel A. Estrada became the first Bush nominee to be endorsed in 2003 by the Senate Judiciary Committee. The Democratic-controlled Senate in 2002 had declined to consider his nomination to the powerful D.C. Circuit Court of Appeals.

But the party-line committee vote 10–9, which came one day after a heated, twelve-hour hearing on three other appellate court nominees, clearly signaled that Republicans and Democrats were refusing to give any ground in the ongoing fight to shape the federal judiciary.

Democratic opposition to Estrada hinged on what Judiciary panel Democrats called his lack of experience and scant information about the nominee's views. Unlike other appellate nominees pending in the Senate, Estrada had not amassed a dossier of court opinions that could show his legal philosophy. The Bush administration resisted Democratic requests to release internal memos related to Estrada's work as a deputy in the solicitor general's office under President Bill Clinton, and Estrada had been in private practice since 1997.

The influential D.C. Circuit appeals court was split evenly between judges appointed by Democratic and Republican presidents. There were four vacancies on the twelve-member panel, which has an important role in considering the appeals of rulings of federal regulatory decisions.

ESTRADA FILIBUSTER

In February 2003, Republicans tried four times to schedule a vote on Estrada's nomination; Democrats objected to every attempt. Democrats said they needed more information from the administration about Estrada's tenure in the solicitor general's office for the deadlock to be broken. But the administration refused, contending that releasing the documents could jeopardize decision making in that office.

For weeks, the nomination was the main business on the Senate floor as Republican leaders weighed how to go forward. No lower court nomination in history had been blocked by a filibuster, and the stakes for both parties were enormous.

Many in the GOP caucus said they were reluctant to vote on—and risk losing—a motion to invoke cloture and cut off debate. They feared it would firmly establish a sixty-vote threshold for confirming people to the federal district and appeals courts. Senate Democrats also were uneasy. Moderates in the caucus posed the biggest obstacle: They were reluctant to try a move that could come back and haunt them the next time the White House was in Democratic hands. "It is as broad as it is long," said Ben Nelson, D-Neb. "Sooner or later, you're on the other side of it."

Democratic leaders told members that the caucus had to stay united and fight Estrada's nomination or risk a potentially more treacherous precedent. If Estrada was confirmed despite what Democrats characterized as a paucity of information about his views, the Bush administration might grow emboldened and send the Senate other appeals court candidates with similar backgrounds. By Feb. 11, Democrats had secured more than the necessary forty-one votes to continue the filibuster.

But Republicans waited until March to schedule a cloture vote. Republicans believed that the longer the debate wound on, the greater the chance some Democrats would relent. They also felt the battle would cost Democrats politically. On the Senate floor and in numerous news conferences, Republican senators repeatedly accused Democrats of holding up a highly qualified Hispanic judicial nominee who emigrated from Honduras as a teenager. If confirmed, Estrada would have been the first Hispanic on the influential D.C. Circuit.

The nomination stalled on March 6, 2003, when senators by a **key vote of 55–44 (R 51–0; D 4–43; I 0–1)** refused to invoke cloture and thereby limit debate on Estrada. A successful cloture vote would have required sixty votes. *(2003 key votes, p. 837)*

On March 13, Republicans again sought to invoke cloture and failed on a similar vote, 55–42. At the same time, Republicans sought to engage the Democrats on additional fronts, trying to schedule floor debates on other controversial nominees. Majority Leader Bill Frist, R-Tenn., on March 11 made a series of requests to get five other nominees considered on the Senate floor. Democrats initially rejected each request, though Ninth Circuit nominee Jay S. Bybee ultimately was confirmed 74–19 after a brief debate March 13.

Five more attempts were made to invoke cloture in the Estrada debate. All failed: 55–45 on March 18, 55–44 on April 2, 52–39 on May 5, 54–43 on May 8, and 55–43 on July 30.

The filibuster of Estrada signaled a momentous escalation in the battle over judicial nominees. It was the first successful use of a filibuster against a judicial nominee since 1968, when U.S. Supreme Court justice Abe Fortas was blocked from becoming chief justice. The tactic had never been used to scuttle a nomination to a lower court. In a few cases, the Senate had voted to shut off potentially lengthy debates on nominees to the appeals court.

Some Republicans tried unsuccessfully in 2000 to mount a filibuster against two of Clinton's lower court nominees—Richard A. Paez and Marsha L. Berzon, whose nominations to the Ninth Circuit were held up for years. At the time, some in the Republican caucus, including Orrin G. Hatch of Utah and then-majority leader Trent Lott of Mississippi, warned that a filibuster would set a dangerous precedent. Ultimately, enough Republicans backed off from the strategy, and cloture votes on Paez and Berzon succeeded by lopsided margins.

Democrats believed it was important to demonstrate that Bush nominees would undergo tough scrutiny. "The goal here isn't to block [everyone] by filibuster," said Russell D. Feingold, D-Wis. "The purpose of it is to demonstrate once or twice that senators are a part of this process."

But not all Democrats were united behind the strategy of blocking a vote on Estrada. At least three moderates—John B. Breaux of Louisiana, Zell Miller of Georgia, and Nelson—said they would vote to shut off debate on Estrada. They worried that filibustering a lower court nominee would set a dangerous precedent.

ADDITIONAL FILIBUSTERS

Emboldened, the Democrats on May 1, 2003, blocked a confirmation vote on Texas judge Priscilla Owen, who was nominated to the U.S. Circuit Court of Appeals for the Fifth Circuit in New Orleans. The Judiciary Committee in 2002, controlled by Democrats, had rejected her nomination, but Republicans tried to advance her the next year. An effort to invoke cloture, or limit debate, on Owen's nomination failed on a 52–44 vote, with two Democrats joining Republicans in voting in favor of cutting off debate. Three additional failed cloture attempts were made in the Owen case: 52–45 on May 8, 53–43 on July 29, and 53–42 on Nov. 14.

During the rest of the 108th Congress, Democrats filibustered an additional eight nominees. In some cases, they defeated multiple cloture attempts. The eight nominees were William H. Pryor Jr., Eleventh Circuit (53–44, July 31, 2003, and 51–43 on Nov. 6); Charles W. Pickering Sr., Fifth Circuit (54–43 on Oct. 30, 2003); Carolyn Kuhl, Ninth Circuit (53–43 on Nov. 14, 2003); Janice Rogers Brown, D.C. Circuit (53–43 on Nov. 14, 2003); William G. Myers III, Ninth Circuit (53–44 on July 20, 2004); Richard A. Griffin, Sixth Circuit (54–44 on July 22, 2004); David W. McKeague, Sixth Circuit (53–44 on July 22, 2004); and Henry W. Saad, Sixth Circuit (52–46 on July 22, 2004). Two of these nominees—Pryor and Pickering—made it to the bench through recess appointments by Bush.

The nominees were filibustered for various reasons. Bush's picks for the Sixth Circuit, for example, were blocked because the two Democratic senators from Michigan, the biggest state in that circuit, said they had not been adequately consulted on the president's choices. Democrats filibustered the nomination of Interior Department solicitor Myers from a seat on the Ninth Circuit because of his environmental views. They were concerned about Brown and Kuhl because of their views on abortion rights and civil rights. They also vowed to block an additional nominee, Defense Department general counsel William James Haynes II for a seat on the Fourth Circuit, because of his role in developing administration policy on the handling of enemy combatants and detainees in military custody.

The filibusters sparked furious accusations by Republicans and conservative special interest groups that Democratic senators were unfairly blocking nominees solely because the candidates' ideology did not conform to a liberal agenda. Democrats countered they were only taking on nominees they viewed as far outside the mainstream. Democrats also noted that many judicial selection experts said Bush's nominees were further to the right than Clinton's were to the left.

At times, the atmosphere in the Senate turned unusually tense and other legislation appeared to be getting pushed aside. In the week before the 2004 August recess, GOP leaders used almost daily cloture votes on stalled nominees to try to back up their argument that Democrats were obstructing highly qualified judicial candidates. Debate became particularly heated during discussion of Pryor when Democrats denounced a series of ads that accused them of anti–Catholic bias.

Some GOP senators worried that the filibusters could set a dangerous precedent for blocking presidential nominees. "This is really a ratcheting up, a changing of the ground rules of huge proportions that's leading us into a serious crisis," said Jeff Sessions, R-Ala., whose own bid for the U.S. District Court was rejected by the Senate Judiciary Committee in 1986.

Although the U.S. Constitution specifically enumerated that a supermajority is needed in four separate instances, such as ratifying treaties, the document—in Article II, Section 2—did not lay out a specific vote threshold for the confirmation of federal judges.

SEARCHING FOR SOLUTIONS

The rancor over judicial nominations had members of both parties searching for a way to streamline the confirmation process. In a rare move, every freshman senator, led by Judiciary Republican John Cornyn of Texas and Democrat Mark Pryor of Arkansas, signed a letter in 2003 to the White House saying they wanted to find "a bipartisan solution that will protect the integrity and independence of our nation's courts, ensure fairness for judicial nominees and leave the bitterness of the past behind us."

Sen. Charles E. Schumer, D-N.Y., advanced a plan that would allow bipartisan commissions to help select potential nominees. Less than a dozen states, including California, had such nominating panels in place.

Along more confrontational lines, some Republicans pushed for lawsuits or floor challenges. There was even talk of a strategy, sometimes referred to as the "nuclear option," under which a bare majority of senators would vote to bar filibusters of judicial nominees. The tactic would likely invite retaliation from Democrats who threatened to shut down Senate actions if the rights of the minority were so curtailed.

Frist proposed a plan (S Res 138) that would ultimately forbid the use of a sixty-vote Senate filibuster on executive branch nominees, essentially surrendering to the White House a traditional chamber prerogative. Under his proposal, motions to invoke cloture on presidential nominations would be subject to declining majority votes. The first motion would, as under current rules, require sixty votes to prevail. A second motion would need fifty-seven votes, and a third would require fifty-four. The fourth cloture motion could be approved with fifty-one.

"We have entered upon a new era, damaging to the Senate as an institution, where a majority will be denied its right to consent to a nomination because a minority will filibuster to hold that nomination hostage," Frist said on the floor. "The need to reform the filibuster on nominations is obvious, and it is now urgent."

Democrats said a move was not necessary. "It ain't broke," Minority Leader Tom Daschle of South Dakota said of the judicial nomination system. He and other Democrats pointed out that the Senate had confirmed most of Bush's nominations, including several controversial ones. Daschle stressed that his caucus was picking its battles when it comes to judicial nominees. "I don't want to abuse the practice of filibusters," Daschle said. "When we do decide to filibuster, we want to be very careful with those with whom we have made that decision."

In fact, with Bush winning confirmation of most of his judicial nominees, the rate of vacant federal judgeships dropped to its lowest level in more than a decade. And some observers said they preferred the occasional filibuster to the situation during the Clinton administration, when many nominees never received a vote.

"Right now in terms of advice and consent—and this is a very unorthodox thing to say now—it's a nice shining moment for democracy, to see it out in the open, to see it being discussed, to have the Democrats holding filibusters on nominees but not holding up the works entirely," said Sheldon Goldman, a political science professor at the University of Massachusetts at Amherst and the author of a book on the judicial selection process. "This is government at its best, where people see what's going on; where, if you're opposed to a nominee, you've got to justify it."

BUSH VICTORIES

Despite the high-profile filibusters, Republicans had a number of wins. One of the first controversial nominees to be confirmed was Jeffrey S. Sutton to the Sixth Circuit by a vote of 52–41 on April 29, 2003. Sutton had drawn considerable criticism for his work as a lawyer in private practice and as the Ohio state solicitor general. He was heavily opposed by groups that represent people with disabilities because of work he did in which he challenged the 1990 Americans with Disabilities Act (PL 101-336). Sutton once argued before the Supreme Court that it is unconstitutional to allow disabled state employees to sue their employers under the law. *(1990 law, Congress and the Nation Vol. VIII, p. 743)*

But Democrats did not mount a filibuster against Sutton—in part because he had support from some in their caucus. For instance, Democrat Dianne Feinstein of California voted for Sutton when he was considered by the Judiciary Committee. Also, unlike Owen, Sutton did not draw the ire of the powerful abortion rights lobby, and he won praise from Democrats for openly responding to questions at a twelve-hour confirmation hearing Jan. 29.

One of the most controversial nominees to win Senate approval was Arkansas attorney J. Leon Holmes, named to the U.S. District Court for the Eastern District of Arkansas. He was confirmed on July 6, 2004, by a 51–46 vote that did not break along strict partisan lines. Six Democrats voted for him, but five Republicans opposed the nomination, including Kay Bailey Hutchison of Texas, vice chair of the Senate Republican Conference.

Opponents said they were troubled by a comment on abortion and rape that Holmes made in a 1980 letter to the editor of an Illinois newspaper. In the letter, Holmes argued that rape victims should not necessarily be allowed to obtain abortions because "conceptions from rape occur with approximately the same frequency as snowfall in Miami." Holmes later apologized for the remark. Hatch angrily defended Holmes from criticism that his statement evinced an appalling disregard for the many rape victims who become pregnant. "I believe all of us have made statements in the past that we wish we could apologize for," Hatch said.

RECESS APPOINTMENTS

At the beginning of 2004, Bush used his powers to bypass the Senate and temporarily install two of his contested appeals court nominees. He appointed Pickering to the Fifth Circuit appeals court on Jan. 16 and Pryor to the Eleventh Circuit on Feb. 20. Both candidates' nominations had been blocked in the Senate by Democratic filibusters. Both appointments were made while the Senate was in recess, a presidential prerogative under the Constitution.

The two nominees had come under sharp fire from liberal interest groups over their ideology, and Bush's tactic infuriated Democrats. On March 26, Daschle promised to block floor action on all of Bush's nominees. He kept his caucus united by depicting Bush as intent on bypassing the Senate and its constitutional power to offer advice and consent on his nominees.

After a seven-week stalemate, Bush on May 18 yielded to Democratic demands that he refrain from making further recess appointments through the November elections. In return, Democrats agreed to allow Senate floor votes on twenty-five mostly noncontroversial nominees—including five appellate court nominees—before June 25.

The agreement did not cover nominations that Democrats had filibustered that were still pending in the Senate. It also did not include two other appellate court nominations that Democrats had signaled they intended to hold up.

Obesity Lawsuits

The House passed a bill (HR 339) in 2004 that would shield the food industry from lawsuits filed by customers claiming the food they ate made them obese. The Senate did not act on the legislation.

The bill, by Ric Keller, R-Fla., was written in response to lawsuits brought against McDonald's and other fast food giants in the preceding few years claiming the companies' high-calorie offerings were to blame for the plaintiffs' obesity. Plaintiffs were helped in some cases by the same lawyers who successfully battled the tobacco industry. One lawsuit filed against McDonald's Corp. in August 2002 claimed that the

chain should be legally responsible for the weight gain and related health problems of two children. It was later dismissed.

The House measure, dubbed "the cheeseburger bill," sought to block civil lawsuits against food manufacturers, sellers, or trade associations in federal or state court when a claim was based on an individual's weight gain, obesity, or any weight-related health condition. Plaintiffs still could file suit for breach of contract or warranty, or when a food manufacturer or seller "knowingly and willfully" violated a federal or state law regarding the manufacturing or marketing of a product.

The Judiciary Committee approved the measure by voice vote Jan. 29, 2004, and formally reported it (H Rept 108-432) March 5. The House passed HR 339 by 276–139 March 10.

Supporters said Americans needed to take personal responsibility for their weight problems by eating better and exercising more. They also pointed to the risk that lawsuits posed to the food industry's estimated 12 million workers. Liability lawsuits, they said, could force companies to incur millions of dollars in expenses, even if the cases were later deemed frivolous

Critics—only a handful of whom spoke during the floor debate—argued that the bill was unnecessary because truly frivolous claims would be tossed out of court and the lawyers who brought them could be sanctioned; the original obesity lawsuit against McDonald's had been dismissed in 2003. The opponents of the bill, mostly Democrats, also said the House would be better off considering proposals aimed at America's weight problem.

The House on March 10 rejected a series of amendments designed to limit the scope of the bill.

• By Melvin Watt, D-N.C., to apply the legislation only to civil liability lawsuits brought in federal courts, by a vote of 158–261.

• By Robert C. Scott, D-Va., to permit lawsuits brought by state agencies to enforce consumer protection laws, such as those against mislabeling or other deceptive trade practice, by a vote of 177–241.

• By Gary L. Ackerman, D-N.Y., to allow lawsuits against meat slaughtering and packing facilities in cases in which they had processed downed animals—livestock too sick to walk—by a vote of 141–276.

• By Nick Lampson, D-Texas, to permit lawsuits filed on behalf of children under eight years old, by voice vote.

Social Security Privacy

Companies and government agencies would have more difficulty selling or publicly displaying Social Security numbers under a bill (HR 2971) approved in 2004 by the House Ways and Means Committee. The plan did not advance further.

The panel approved the measure July 21, 2004, by voice vote, after adopting a substitute amendment offered by

Chair Bill Thomas, R-Calif., by a vote of 33–0. HR 2971 was formally reported (H Rept 108-685, Part I) Sept. 14.

Members said the bill was vital to efforts to combat identity theft, which often started with a stolen Social Security number.

The Government Accountability Office said in a January report that information resellers, consumer reporting agencies, and some health care organizations routinely obtained Social Security numbers from customers and relied on them to determine customers' identities and accumulate information about them. Several states—including California—had adopted laws to restrict such use.

The bill would bar displaying Social Security numbers on checks issued for payment or on a driver's license or other forms of identification issued by state motor vehicle departments. It also would toughen verification requirements for issuing Social Security numbers to newborn children and for replacement Social Security cards. Prisoners would be barred from working in jobs that give them access to the numbers.

The substitute would limit the number of replacement cards that could be issued to most individuals to three per year and ten over a lifetime. It also outlined exemptions sought by the Social Security Subcommittee to the ban on selling, buying, and displaying Social Security numbers.

The biggest threat to the legislation was the limited time left in the session. The House Energy and Commerce and Financial Services panels shared jurisdiction over some provisions, and neither panel scheduled consideration of the measure after the summer recess.

Thomas insisted on a roll-call vote to remind the other committees how popular the bill was. "The concern is that we aren't the only committee of jurisdiction," he said after the markup.

Video Voyeurism

Lawmakers in 2004, worried that the proliferation of affordable, high-resolution digital cameras was spurring "video voyeurism," made it a federal crime to videotape or photograph people in various stages of undress. The legislation (S 1301) targeted anyone using the cameras to spy on people who are unclothed or undressing on federal property.

S 1301 took aim at a problem lawmakers said was growing because technological advances made digital cameras smaller and cheaper. In addition to buying cell phones with cameras, consumers could easily purchase hard-to-detect video cameras. Such devices had been used to secretly videotape people in dressing rooms and in showers aboard Navy warships. The bill would make it a crime to videotape, photograph, film, or otherwise electronically record naked or undergarment-clad genitals or breasts without consent when the targeted person had a reasonable expectation of privacy.

Violators could be fined as much as $100,000 or sent to prison for as long as a year, or both. The legislation would apply only in federal jurisdictions, such as military bases or national parks, but supporters said they expected the bill to serve as a model for states seeking to enact similar laws.

The Senate Judiciary Committee on July 24, 2003, gave voice vote approval to S 1301 (no written report). Republican senator Mike DeWine introduced it in response to an incident in his home state of Ohio in which a woman discovered someone was using a video camera to record under her dress. The Senate passed the bill by voice vote Sept. 25.

The House Judiciary Committee approved an amended version of the bill May 12, 2004, and formally reported it (H Rept 108-540) May 20. The full House passed it Sept. 21 by voice vote under suspension of the rules. The Senate accepted the House changes Dec. 7, completing congressional action. President George W. Bush signed the bill (PL 108-4965) Dec. 23, 2004.

Copyright Judges

Disputes about how to distribute copyright royalties would be handled by a new panel of three judges under a measure (HR 1417—PL 108-419) cleared by Congress in 2004.

The legislation replaced a system under which ad hoc copyright arbitration royalty panels, known as CARPs, were appointed by the librarian of Congress to settle disputes over royalty rates and distributions related to the commercial use of copyrighted works, such as music. Widespread agreement existed that this system, established in 1993 (PL 103-198), was inefficient, arbitrary, and unnecessarily expensive. Participants also complained that arbitrators lacked relevant expertise and could be influenced by either side. *(1993 law, Congress and the Nation Vol. IX, p. 714)*

Under HR 1417, judges would be attorneys with at least seven years of experience and with varied specialties, including adjudication, economics, and copyright law. They would serve six-year terms and could be removed by the librarian of Congress.

The House Judiciary Committee reported HR 1417 (H Rept 108-408) on Jan. 30, 2004, and the House passed it on March 3, 406–0 under suspension of the rules. The Senate Judiciary Committee by voice vote approved the bill (no written report) by voice vote Sept. 21 with a substitute amendment that included minor changes. The Senate passed the amended measure Oct. 6 by voice vote. The House Nov. 17 by voice vote under suspension of the rules accepted the Senate changes, completing congressional action. President George W. Bush signed the bill (PL 108-419) Nov. 30, 2004.

Counterfeiters

Congress in 2004 cleared legislation (HR 3632) designed to protect intellectual property from counterfeiters, as well as to crack down on Internet domain name fraud. It was signed into law (PL 198-482) on Dec. 23.

The bill would make it more difficult for counterfeiters to peddle fake goods by restricting the buying and selling of authentication devices, such as holograms and special inks, that counterfeiters attached to fake goods to increase their value. It also would make it illegal to alter or falsify the version, edition, or authorized-user information for a piece of software.

Because no state or federal law prohibited trafficking in authentication devices, the bill's sponsor, Lamar Smith, R-Texas, said prosecutors had been reluctant to seize such components or prosecute such cases.

The measure also would stiffen penalties for knowingly submitting false contact data to domain name registrars when signing up for a World Wide Web site. The legislation would increase the sentences for federal crimes committed in connection with domain name registration fraud. Sentences would be doubled or increased by seven years, whichever was less.

At a March 31 markup of HR 3632, the Subcommittee on Courts, the Internet, and Intellectual Property voted to exclude digital authentication from the bill's scope in response to concerns from Internet service providers that did not want to be held accountable for the trafficking of such devices over their networks.

The House Judiciary Committee on June 23, 2004, approved the measure by voice vote and on July 13 formally reported (H Rept 108-600) it. The panel adopted, by voice vote, an amendment by Smith that would protect "gray marketers" who reimported goods into the United States from abroad.

The House passed the measure by voice vote Sept. 21 under suspension of the rules.

Similar provisions had been included in a more comprehensive package of intellectual property provisions (S 3021) that the Senate passed on Nov. 20, 2004—but only with the addition of what proved to be a poison pill: a proposal by Sen. John McCain, R-Ariz., to begin the federal regulation of boxing. Once House members served notice that they would not touch any bill with the boxing language, the Senate agreed to act on the limited bill already endorsed by the House. The Senate passed HR 3632 by voice vote Dec. 8, completing congressional action.

Antitrust Legislation

Lawmakers in 2004 cleared legislation (HR 1086) to partially shield developers of technical standards from running afoul of federal antitrust laws. The bill, signed into law (PL 108-237) on June 22, was designed to encourage the development of voluntary technical standards by nonprofit organizations such as the American Society of Mechanical Engineers and the National Fire Protection Association.

The House Judiciary Committee approved HR 1086 by voice vote May 7, 2003, and formally reported it (H Rept 108-125, Part I) May 22. A supplemental report (H Rept 108-125, Part II) was filed by the Judiciary Committee June 4. The full House passed the bill by voice vote under suspension of the rules on June 10. The Senate passed an amended version April 2, 2004. Senators increased penalties and maximum prison terms for antitrust violations and expanded a Justice Department program that offered reduced charges to the first party in an antitrust case that cooperated with the government.

The House by voice vote under suspension of the rules on June 2 accepted the Senate changes, completing congressional action.

Gun Control

During consideration of the fiscal 2004 Commerce, Justice, and State appropriations bill (HR 2799), the House Appropriations Committee adopted, 31–30, an amendment by Todd Tiahrt, R-Kansas, to relax Bureau of Alcohol, Tobacco, Firearms, and Explosives oversight of gun retailers. The amendment would effectively bar the agency from requesting transaction records from retailers unless the request was part of a criminal investigation. Tiahrt said his language had been vetted by the National Rifle Association. The provision, however, was not included in the conference report for the fiscal 2003 omnibus spending bill (HR 2673—PL 108-199), into which HR 2799 was incorporated.

Conferees did retain House language requiring federal officials to destroy records related to background checks of gun purchasers within twenty-four hours of their having been cleared to buy weapons. The conference report also prohibited public disclosure of Bureau of Alcohol, Tobacco, Firearms, and Explosives records on gun dealers, and it banned the promulgation of any requirement that gun dealers take inventory of their stock.

The final version included a provision that would block disclosure of information collected by the Bureau of Alcohol, Tobacco, Firearms, and Explosives tracing the history of firearms used in crimes. The information, which revealed the sellers and dealers of such guns, could not be disclosed to "anyone other than a federal, state or local law enforcement agency or prosecutor . . . for use in a bona fide criminal investigation."

The provision was in response to a ruling by a federal judge that New York City could access federal trace information as part of a case against firearms manufacturer Beretta USA Corp. Preventing that data from being used in future litigation was of considerable importance to both gun manufacturers and the National Rifle Association.

Hate Crimes

During consideration of the fiscal 2005 defense authorization bill (S 2400), the Senate in 2004 adopted an amendment that would expand federal hate crime laws to cover sexual orientation, gender, and disability. The amendment, by Edward

M. Kennedy, D-Mass., and Gordon H. Smith, R-Ore., was adopted 65–33 on June 15. But it was stripped out in conference negotiations between the House and Senate. *(107th Congress action, p. 600)*

Current federal hate crimes law imposed stricter sentences in cases in which people were attacked because of their race, color, religion, or national origin than similar crimes committed without evidence of bias. The amendment would represent the first protection for gays and lesbians in federal civil rights law, according to a Senate Democratic aide.

Few lawmakers were willing to criticize the proposed hate crimes expansion. But GOP leaders had thwarted similar efforts, arguing that all violent crimes should be punished and that special federal categories should not be created for some of them.

For example, the Senate in 1999 added a hate crimes amendment to the fiscal 2000 Commerce, Justice, and State appropriations bill (PL 106-113) by voice vote with no debate, but it was quickly dropped during conference. In 2000, Kennedy offered an amendment to a fiscal 2001 defense authorization bill (PL 106-398) and won adoption of the language on a 57–42 vote. But the proposal again was stripped out of the defense bill in conference. *(Defense authorization, Congress and the Nation Vol. X, p. 290)*

The Supreme Court

The U.S. Supreme Court paved the way for George W. Bush to become president by cinching his narrow electoral college majority in December 2000. Four years later, however, the Court gave the president a muted but unmistakable rebuke by rejecting the administration's aggressive legal tactics in the post–Sept. 11, 2001, war on terror.

In between those high-profile rulings, the Court continued to chart a generally conservative course, but with some dramatic exceptions. For example, it handed down two closely divided decisions in 2003 upholding racial preferences in college admissions and striking down laws banning gay sex.

The Court also distressed legal conservatives by upholding a new campaign finance law limiting the use of unregulated soft money in federal campaigns. And it threw state and federal prosecutors and judges into disarray by declaring the most common type of sentencing guidelines systems to be unconstitutional.

Balanced against those rulings, conservatives counted victories in decisions that upheld private school vouchers in the face of a church-state separation challenge and somewhat protected state governments against suits before federal courts or agencies. The Court also rejected constitutional challenges to popular anticrime measures enhancing penalties for repeat offenders and requiring sex offenders to register with authorities after release from prison.

The Court also adopted a new limit on capital punishment by prohibiting the execution of mentally retarded offenders. And it shifted course somewhat on federalism issues in 2003 and 2004 with decisions backing federal courts' jurisdiction over private suits to enforce federal laws or constitutional provisions.

By August 2004, the Court had gone a near record ten years without a change in membership—the longest period without a vacancy since 1811–1823 when there were only seven justices. In November 2004, however, the likelihood of a retirement loomed following the disclosure that Chief Justice William H. Rehnquist was being treated for thyroid cancer.

Based on the limited information made public, many medical experts speculated that Rehnquist was suffering from an aggressive form of the disease. Rehnquist's office said that he was continuing to work from home. But he was absent for the Court's arguments in November and December 2004 and announced that he would vote in the November cases only if the remaining eight justices were deadlocked. (Rehnquist was still the sitting chief justice when he died Sept. 3, 2005. John Roberts, confirmed 78–22 on Sept. 29, 2005, succeeded him in the post.)

Rehnquist led a sometimes-fragile conservative majority that included four other justices appointed by Republican presidents: Sandra Day O'Connor, Antonin Scalia, Anthony M. Kennedy, and Clarence Thomas. The five justices typically voted together in backing law enforcement in criminal law cases, states on federalism issues, and religious organizations on church-state questions. But O'Connor or Kennedy (or both) broke with the others in a number of cases, including the affirmative action and gay rights decisions. (O'Connor on July 1, 2005, announced her intention to retire, upon confirmation of a successor. Samuel Alito was confirmed 58–42 on Jan. 31, 2006.)

Separately, Scalia and Thomas cast pivotal votes in the line of cases that limited the power of judges instead of juries to determine factual issues used to determine sentencing in guideline schemes or under death penalty statutes. The two justices—typically viewed as the Court's strongest conserva-

REFERENCES

Discussion of the Supreme Court for the years 1945–1964 may be found in *Congress and the Nation Vol. I*, pp. 1441–1454; for the years 1965–1968, *Congress and the Nation Vol. II*, pp. 335–340; for the years 1969–1972, *Congress and the Nation Vol. III*, pp. 289–327; for the years 1973–1976, *Congress and the Nation Vol. IV*, pp. 619–659; for the years 1977–1980, *Congress and the Nation Vol. V*, pp. 755–791; for the years 1981–1984, *Congress and the Nation Vol. VI*, pp. 711–768; for the years 1985–1988, *Congress and the Nation Vol. VII*, pp. 785–840; for the years 1989–1992, *Congress and the Nation Vol. VIII*, pp. 801–851; for the years 1993–1996, *Congress and the Nation Vol. IX*, pp. 759–799; for the years 1997–2001, *Congress and the Nation Vol. X*, pp. 684–729.

tives—also joined in a significant but somewhat overlooked decision in 2004 that made it more difficult for prosecutors to use prior statements from witnesses who are unavailable to testify at trial.

The Court's liberal-leaning bloc was made up of Justices John Paul Stevens and David H. Souter, both named by GOP presidents, and Ruth Bader Ginsburg and Stephen G. Breyer, both appointed by Democrat Bill Clinton. They typically were more inclined than the conservatives to back civil rights plaintiffs, to favor procedural protections for suspects and criminal defendants, to uphold federal power over the states, and to limit government aid to religious institutions.

Statistically, the Court's output continued to be much lower than in previous decades. The Court issued on average fewer than seventy-five signed decisions per year: the seventy-one signed decisions for the 2002–2003 term represented the smallest number since the 1953–1954 term. The Court's docket reached a record 9,406 cases in the 2002–2003 term but fell by more than 500 cases in the 2003–2004 term, mostly because of a drop in so-called *in forma pauperis* or indigent cases.

ELECTION LAW

The Court safeguarded Bush's claim to the White House by upholding in 2000 his narrow popular vote margin in Florida and, with it, the state's twenty-five electoral votes needed to best his Democratic challenger, Vice President Al Gore. After Gore invoked state law to ask for a recount, Florida's Supreme Court ordered a statewide retabulation. Bush, in response, asked the U.S. Supreme Court to block it. In a 5–4 ruling split along conservative-liberal lines, the Court on Dec. 12, 2000, effectively barred the recount. *("Bush v. Gore," Congress and the Nation Vol. X, p. 686)*

The majority in *Bush v. Gore* found an equal protection violation in the state high court's failure to set clear standards for the recount, while the liberal dissenters said the state courts should have been given time to develop uniform rules. Despite the political import, the legal impact of the ruling was unclear. The unsigned opinion included a passage specifying that the ruling dealt only with "the present circumstances, for the problem of equal protection in election processes generally presents many complexities."

Almost three years later, the Court again split 5–4 in a major election-related case when it upheld all major provisions of the Bipartisan Campaign Reform Act—commonly called the McCain-Feingold Act after its principal Senate sponsors, John McCain, R-Ariz., and Russell D. Feingold, D-Wis. The law restricted the raising of unlimited soft money for federal campaigns and limited the ability of corporations and labor unions to run election-time issue advertising on radio or television. The act was challenged as an infringement of political speech by an array of entities that included the National Republican Committee, Republican and Democratic state party committees, and interest groups ranging from the Chamber of Commerce and the AFL-CIO to the American Civil Liberties Union and the National Rifle Association.

In an unusual opinion jointly authored by Stevens and O'Connor, the Court in *McConnell v. Federal Election Commission* (2003) upheld the soft money ban as a valid attempt by Congress to prevent "undue influence" by campaign donors. The ruling also upheld the provision requiring that labor unions and corporations pay for election-time issue advertising only through separate political action committees (PACs), not from union or corporate treasuries. O'Connor cast the pivotal vote to uphold the law, while her four conservative colleagues dissented.

In two other campaign finance cases, the Court in 2001 upheld a provision of the post-Watergate Federal Election Campaign Act Amendments limiting the amount of money that a political party can spend in coordination with a candidate for Congress. Two years later, it also upheld a Federal Election Commission regulation subjecting nonprofit advocacy groups to the same rule as profit-making corporations barring campaign expenditures except through separate PACs.

The Court issued an anticlimactic ruling on the issue of political gerrymandering, the long-dishonored practice of drawing congressional or district lines for partisan effect. The Court in 1986 had ruled that partisan gerrymanders were subject to constitutional challenge but had never dealt with the issue again until it agreed to hear a challenge by Pennsylvania Democrats to a congressional map drawn by the state's Republicans in 2002 aimed at ensuring a GOP majority in the state's delegation.

By a 5–4 vote, the Court in *Vieth v. Jubelirer* rejected the challenge. Four of the justices said they wanted to overrule the 1986 decision and bar any challenges to partisan gerrymanders. Scalia said there were "no judicially discernible and manageable standards" on the issue. But Kennedy, providing the fifth vote, said he was not ready to preclude any challenge to partisan redistricting. The four dissenters criticized the ruling but did not agree among themselves on a standard to use in such cases.

In another important redistricting case, the Court gave states subject to the federal Voting Rights Act discretion to move blacks out of majority-minority districts if they offset the reduced voting strength with gains in minority groups' political influence elsewhere. The ruling upheld a Democratic-written legislative districting that moved blacks out of some so-called supermajority-minority districts to increase Democratic voting strength in adjoining districts. In an earlier case, the Court made it slightly harder to overturn racial redistricting by holding that challengers had to show that an alternative plan would produce significantly more racial balance while also promoting any legitimate government interests.

The Court in 2001 also dealt the congressional term limits movement another setback by barring so-called informed voter provisions requiring congressional candidates' position

TERRORISM CASES

For two years after the Sept. 11, 2001, attacks, the U.S. Supreme Court stayed on the sideline while President George W. Bush and Congress went to war against terrorism. The government aggressively rounded up hundreds of persons of Arab descent on immigration or other charges and used secret proceedings to deport many of them. At Bush's behest, Congress passed a tough law—called the USA Patriot Act—aimed at giving the government new power to go after terrorists at home and abroad. And the president launched invasions of Afghanistan in 2001 and then Iraq in 2003.

The administration's policies raised significant legal issues—notably, in the treatment of hundreds of people held as prisoners. The administration transported more than six hundred of them to the U.S. Naval Base at Guantanamo Bay, Cuba, where they were held effectively incommunicado, without access to relatives, lawyers, or the courts. In addition, the administration held two U.S. citizens as "enemy combatants" in a naval brig in Charleston, S.C—again, without access to family or lawyers.

The Court passed up several opportunities to take on terrorism-related issues, including challenges to the post–Sept. 11 roundups of immigrants. But the justices finally agreed to hear three detention cases in late 2003 and early 2004. The Court's decisions, issued in late June 2004, rejected the administration's claims for a virtually free hand to detain suspected enemy combatants. Instead, the Court ruled, detainees must have some opportunity to challenge their confinement in federal courts or before some impartial tribunal.

The three cases arose as separate habeas corpus petitions filed on behalf of the two U.S. citizens, Yaser Hamdi and José Padilla, and a consolidated habeas corpus case on behalf of a number of Australian, British, and Kuwaiti citizens held at Guantanamo. Hamdi had been captured in Afghanistan but later was determined to be a U.S. citizen. Padilla was detained in May 2002 as he arrived at the Chicago airport from an overseas flight. Officials claimed he was plotting to plant a radioactive bomb in Washington, D.C., or some other U.S. city. Federal appeals courts rejected the Guantanamo detainees' petitions and Hamdi's. But the federal appeals court in New York ruled in Padilla's case that the president had no statutory or constitutional authority to detain a U.S. citizen as an enemy combatant.

In a fractured ruling, the Court held in *Hamdi v. Rumsfeld* that the president has the power to detain a U.S. citizen cap-

tured on the battlefield as an enemy combatant. The vote was 5–4. In a plurality opinion for four justices, Sandra Day O'Connor based the president's authority on a broadly worded resolution passed by Congress authorizing use of "all necessary and appropriate force" against any nations, organizations, or persons that had carried out the terrorist attacks or "harbored" those who had.

By a 6–3 vote, however, the Court held that the government had to notify Hamdi of the charges against him and give him an opportunity to contest the charges before some independent tribunal. "[D]ue process demands that a citizen held in the United States as an enemy combatant be given a meaningful opportunity to contest the factual basis for the detention before a neutral decisionmaker," O'Connor wrote. David H. Souter and Ruth Bader Ginsburg joined in the vote to produce a majority result but disagreed that the president had any authority to hold Hamdi.

Significantly, only one justice—Clarence Thomas—agreed with the administration's position that Hamdi could be held on the basis of limited evidence and denied any review of his detention. The other two dissenters from the final order—John Paul Stevens and Antonin Scalia—said that a citizen suspected of being an enemy combatant had to be tried in regular criminal courts unless the right of habeas corpus had been suspended.

In Padilla's case, the Court did not reach the merits but instead by a 5–4 vote ordered the petition dismissed on the ground that it should have been filed in federal court in South Carolina, not New York. Padilla's lawyers refiled the petition in South Carolina shortly after. (Padilla was indicted on Nov. 22, 2005, for conspiring to murder, kidnap, and maim people overseas. None of the original allegations was part of the indictment. The Supreme Court on Jan. 3, 2006, granted the administration's request to transfer Padilla from military to civilian custody.)

In the Guantanamo case, the Court held on a 6–3 vote that the detainees could bring habeas corpus challenges in a federal court even if the base was outside the court's jurisdiction. The ruling in *Rasul v. Bush* did not specify what further proceedings must be held. The administration began convening limited military tribunals at Guantanamo, but lawyers for the detainees challenged the procedures as inadequate.

on the issue to be listed on the ballot (*Cook v. Gralike*). Six years earlier, the Court had ruled that states could not impose service limits on members of Congress except by amending the Constitution.

CRIMINAL LAW

The Court's conservative majority on criminal law issues fractured somewhat in high-visibility decisions that barred

execution of mentally retarded offenders and upset state sentencing guideline schemes. In a major civil liberties ruling, the justices also invalidated state anti-sodomy laws—statutes enforced almost exclusively against gay men. In most areas, though, the Court backed law enforcement, including in closely watched challenges to popular laws prescribing long sentences for three-time offenders and requiring sex offenders to register with authorities after their release from prison.

The ruling to block the death penalty for mentally retarded offenders as a "cruel and unusual" punishment under the Eighth Amendment reversed a 1989 decision in a Texas case that found no "national consensus" against the practice. In the new decision, *Atkins v. Virginia* (2002), Stevens said a national consensus had formed on the issue given that thirty-one states—eighteen with capital punishment and thirteen others—did not allow execution of mentally retarded offenders. O'Connor and Kennedy joined the liberals in the 6–3 decision.

Several other rulings in capital cases indicated somewhat greater concern among the justices about administration of the death penalty. Twice, the Court overturned death penalties in Texas cases because of defective instructions on the use of mental retardation as a mitigating factor in capital sentencing hearings. In another Texas case, the Court overturned a death sentence after sharply criticizing prosecutors for concealing evidence that discredited the government's witnesses. And in one other Texas case, the Court gave a black death row inmate a new hearing on his claim that African Americans had been improperly excluded as potential jurors.

The sentencing procedure decisions built on a 2000 ruling, *Apprendi v. New Jersey,* that a defendant is entitled to a jury trial and proof beyond a reasonable doubt on any fact needed to increase a sentence beyond the statutory maximum. In 2002 the Court extended the rule to capital cases by holding that only a jury, not a judge, can determine factual issues needed to make a defendant eligible for the death penalty *(Ring v. Arizona).* The ruling affected capital murder laws in nine states, though two years later the Court softened the impact by holding that the decision would not be applied retroactively.

In a broader decision, the Court in 2004 extended *Apprendi* to state sentencing guideline systems that allowed judges to make factual findings used to increase a sentence above the normal—not just the maximum—statutory range. The 5–4 ruling in *Blakely v. Washington* matched the unusual lineup in *Apprendi,* with Scalia and Thomas joining three liberal justices in the majority and Breyer siding with three conservatives in dissent. The decision promptly cast doubt on the federal sentencing guidelines, which Breyer had helped write before joining the high court.

The Court took up two federal cases at the start of the 2004–2005 term that would resolve the issue. In a bifurcated decision, the Court in January 2005 ruled by the same 5–4 vote that the federal scheme also violated defendants' jury trial rights but by a different 5–4 vote cured the problem by declaring the federal guidelines to be advisory instead of mandatory as Congress had provided. Ginsburg joined the four dissenters from the previous rulings to partly salvage the guidelines *(United States v. Booker).*

The constitutionality of three-strikes laws reached the Court in companion cases challenging a California statute that prescribed a life sentence with no parole before twenty-five years for someone convicted for a third time of a broadly

---

---

defined "serious" or "violent" felony. The defendants had received life sentences after convictions for shoplifting $150 worth of videotapes in one case and $1,200 worth of golf clubs in the others. By a 5–4 vote, however, the Court said the sentences were not so "grossly disproportionate" as to amount to cruel and unusual punishment *(Ewing v. California, Lockyer v. Andrade).*

The Court in 2003 also rejected constitutional challenges to so-called Megan's laws enacted in virtually all the states requiring persons convicted of sex offenses to register with local law enforcement authorities *(Smith v. Doe, Connecticut Department of Public Safety v. Doe).* The Court also reaffirmed that sex offenders can be civilly committed after expiration of criminal sentences but ruled in 2002 that commitment was permitted only if the government proved a sex offender would have "serious difficulty" controlling his or her behavior if released. The next year the Court struck down a California law that allowed prosecutors to bring a child molestation case after the original statute of limitations had expired.

In a significant trial procedure ruling, the Court in 2004 barred prosecutors from using an out-of-court statement from an unavailable witness unless the defense had had an opportunity for cross-examination. The ruling in *Crawford v. Washington* overturned a 1980 decision that allowed judges to admit such statements if found "reliable." In another defense victory, the Court in 2002 ruled that an indigent

U.S. Supreme Court Caseload

	2000–2001	2001–2002	2002–2003	2003–2004
Number of cases on docket	8,965	9,176	9,406	8,883
Cases decided summarily	124	70	63	50
Cases argued and decided	89	90	87	93
Cases disposed of by signed opinion	83	85	79	89
Number of signed opinions	77	76	71	73

SOURCE: Harold W. Stanley and Richard G. Niemi, *Vital Statistics on American Politics, 2005–2006* (Washington, D.C.: CQ Press, 2006), 288–289.

defendant could not be given a suspended jail sentence without being afforded a court-appointed lawyer.

The Court generally continued to give police a wide berth in search and seizure cases. By a 5–4 vote, the Court in 2001 said police could make a custodial arrest in a traffic case even if the charge carried only a fine and no jail time. In another 5–4 ruling, the Court in 2004 upheld a state law making it a crime for someone to refuse to give police identification when stopped on the basis of reasonable suspicion. In separate highway checkpoint cases, the Court said police could establish roadblocks to try to find witnesses in a criminal investigation, but not to check vehicles for illegal drugs.

In search cases, the Court in 2004 ruled that police executing a search warrant could forcibly enter a home shortly after announcing their presence if they feared destruction of evidence. For the same reason, the Court had earlier said that police could prevent a resident from entering his or her home while the officers moved to obtain a search warrant. The Court also slightly broadened police discretion to search drivers or passengers after automobile stops and upheld warrantless searches of probationers based on reasonable suspicion of criminal activity.

By contrast, the Court in 2001 ruled that police need a search warrant to use an infrared sensing device to detect heat patterns inside a home. Conservatives Scalia and Thomas joined three liberal justices in the 5–4 decision to limit the high-tech technique used to spot indoor marijuana cultivation.

The justices were closely divided in police interrogation cases. In one 5–4 decision, the Court in 2004 limited a common police tactic of questioning a suspect without *Miranda* warnings and then using the information in a second session after advising the suspect of his or her rights. In the pivotal opinion, Kennedy said that the results of the second interrogation were inadmissible unless police took special steps to cure the initial failure to give warnings. On the same day, however, Kennedy joined a 5–4 majority to allow the use of physical evidence uncovered as a result of a *Miranda*-violative interrogation. Also in 2004, the Court declined to establish special protections for interviewing a juvenile suspect when not in custody.

The Court rejected efforts in several cases to strengthen procedural protections for defendants who plead guilty. In one unanimous decision, the Court limited a defendant's ability to withdraw a guilty plea because of the judge's failure to give a complete advisory of his or her rights. Two years earlier, the Court ruled unanimously that prosecutors do not have to disclose information casting doubt on the credibility of government witnesses during plea bargaining.

Finally, the Court ventured into the debate over medical marijuana by ruling that federal drug laws take precedence over state measures to legalize the practice for seriously ill patients. The 8–0 ruling in *United States v. Oakland Cannabis Buyers' Cooperative* (2001) blocked a California-based "cannabis dispensary" from using "medical necessity" as a defense to federal enforcement actions aimed at shutting it down.

INDIVIDUAL RIGHTS

The Court ended its 2002–2003 term with dramatic rulings on successive days reaffirming the use of racial preferences in college and university admissions and striking down state anti-sodomy laws. Civil rights advocates won several other victories during Bush's first term in rulings favoring plaintiffs in job discrimination suits. But the Court also somewhat narrowed protections under the federal Americans with Disabilities Act (ADA) and issued two rulings significantly narrowing civil rights suits against local governments.

The justices used two companion cases from the University of Michigan's undergraduate college and its law school to revisit the issue of affirmative action in higher education for the first time since its famous *Bakke* decision in 1978. As in *Bakke*, the Court gave colleges and universities a green light to give limited preference to disadvantaged racial or ethnic minorities in the admissions process.

O'Connor's opinion for a 5–4 majority in the law school case, *Grutter v. Bollinger*, held that racial diversity on campuses was a "compelling" government interest that justified racial preferences as long as applicants received "individualized" consideration instead of "mechanical, predetermined diversity bonuses." In *Gratz v. Bollinger*, however, O'Connor and Breyer joined the four conservatives in rejecting the college's application process, which awarded minority applicants a fixed bonus often effectively guaranteeing admission.

The rulings represented a partial setback for the Bush administration, which had urged the Court to reject both admissions systems. But Bush cautiously praised the decision for recognizing "the value of diversity" while requiring universities to consider "race-neutral alternatives." In her opinion in the law school case, O'Connor concluded by saying, "We expect that twenty-five years from now, the use of racial preferences will no longer be necessary to further the interest approved today."

Among other civil rights rulings, the Court in 2002 upheld the power of the Equal Employment Opportunity Commission to seek punitive damages against employers even if the complaining employee had signed an arbitration agreement barring such penalties. The Court also allowed larger "front pay" awards to job discrimination plaintiffs rehired after winning a court judgment. Another ruling made it somewhat easier for plaintiffs to win so-called mixed motive cases when evidence exists of neutral as well as racially motivated reasons for an adverse employment action.

The Court barred private civil rights suits against state or local governments for federally financed programs unless plaintiffs showed evidence of discriminatory intent. The 5–4 ruling in *Alexander v. Sandoval* (2001) held that Title VI of the Civil Rights Act of 1964 did not permit private suits for "disparate racial impact." In another ruling, the Court in 2002 appeared to broadly bar punitive damages in private suits against local governments for any civil rights violations in federally financed programs. The ruling in *Barnes v. Gorman* dealt specifically with a local government's failure to accommodate persons with disabilities as required by the ADA, but Scalia's opinion applied to any federal law imposing requirements on local governments under the Constitution's Spending Clause.

In other cases, the Court significantly eased burdens on employers under the ADA. In one ruling, the Court in 2002 held that employees qualify for protection under the act only if they have an impairment limiting daily life apart from work. Later that term, the Court allowed employers to dismiss or refuse to hire a worker because of a safety-endangering disability. Both rulings were unanimous.

Disability rights advocates lost one ruling but won another in suits against state governments under the ADA. The federalism decisions blocked suits by state employees under one section of the ADA but allowed a suit under another section for failing to make courthouses barrier-free. And disability rights advocates won a high-profile ruling in an unusual setting: professional golf. The Court in 2001 said that the PGA Tour's rule banning use of carts violated the rights of golfer Casey Martin, who had a disability limiting his ability to walk.

The ruling to bar state anti-sodomy laws represented a major victory for gay rights advocates, erasing a 1986 precedent upholding such statutes. The 6–3 decision in *Lawrence v. Texas* (2003) struck down a Texas law specifically banning sodomy by persons of the same sex, but Kennedy's opinion also applied to laws in other states prohibiting such practices by heterosexuals or homosexuals. Some thirteen states had anti-sodomy laws on the books, but they were rarely enforced—almost exclusively against gay men.

The issue reached the Court in a case brought by two Houston-area men arrested by police responding to a neighbor's complaint about an alleged disturbance. In his opinion, Kennedy said the Due Process Clause gave the men "the full right to engage in their conduct without the intervention of the government." He stressed that the decision involved private, consensual conduct between adults and did not involve "formal recognition" of the relationship—a tacit reference to the looming issue of gay marriage. In a sharp dissent, Scalia said the majority had "signed onto the so-called homosexual agenda."

In other privacy-related issues, the Court in 2001 barred a city hospital's policy of giving police the results of drug tests administered to pregnant women but the next year upheld a local school board's policy of random drug testing for any high school students participating in extracurricular activities. The 5–4 decision extended an earlier decision allowing random drug testing for high school athletes. In the same year, the Court barred individual damage suits against school board officials for violating the federal law guaranteeing privacy of educational records.

Immigration rights advocates scored two significant victories in 2001. In *Zadvydas v. Davis,* the Court barred the government from indefinitely holding criminal aliens for deportation when no country was willing to accept them. On the same day the Court ruled that criminal aliens can use habeas corpus to challenge their deportation despite recently enacted provisions aimed at restricting judicial review. Two years later, though, the Court ruled that criminal aliens can be detained pending deportation without an individual hearing to determine whether they posed a flight risk or danger to society.

Finally, the Court issued a mixed ruling in a case testing the ability of foreigners to file damage suits in U.S. courts under a 1789 law, the Alien Tort Statute, for human rights violations committed overseas. The unanimous decision in *Sosa v. Alvarez-Machain* (2004) barred a suit by a Mexican national against a former Mexican police officer for kidnapping him and bringing him to the United States to stand trial. Justices divided, however, on how far to extend the ruling. Six justices said federal courts could allow suits for violations of well-recognized international norms, while three others sided with business groups and the Bush administration in voting to preclude virtually all such cases.

FIRST AMENDMENT

The Court gave the Bush administration and social conservatives a major victory by upholding the use of vouchers at church-affiliated schools. It sidestepped a dispute over the "under God" phrase in the Pledge of Allegiance, but the action cheered religious groups—and most Americans—by throwing out a lower court ruling that would bar mandatory recitation of the phrase in public schools. In other First Amendment cases the Court issued mixed rulings on laws aimed at limiting children's access to sexually explicit materials on the Internet while extending free-speech protections in some other areas.

The school voucher ruling, *Zelman v. Simmons-Harris* (2002), rejected an Establishment Clause challenge to a Cleveland program that gave low-income families up to $2,250 toward tuition at private schools of their choice. The vast majority of families used the vouchers to attend parochial schools. In a 5–4 decision, however, the Court held that the program did not violate the constitutional ban against establishment of religion. Rehnquist said the program was "entirely neutral with respect to religion" because eligibility was not based on religion and families exercised "genuine choice" among secular or religious schools.

The Bush administration had argued in support of the program. Education secretary Rod Paige said afterward that the ruling would usher in "a new birth of freedom" for parents and children. But education groups and church-state separation organizations echoed the warnings from dissenting justices that the decision would invite religious divisiveness.

Somewhat surprisingly, the Court ruled two years later that states may deny college scholarships to students preparing for the ministry. Writing for the majority in the 7–2 ruling, Rehnquist said Washington State's restriction was justified because of its "antiestablishment interests."

In another high-profile dispute, the Court used a legal technicality to duck a definitive decision on the constitutionality of the "under God" phrase in the Pledge of Allegiance. Eugene Newdow, the noncustodial father of an elementary school–aged daughter, had challenged the policy of a Sacramento-area school district requiring recitation of the pledge at the beginning of each school day. The federal appeals court for California ruled for Newdow—touching off a national firestorm of criticism. After hearing arguments the Supreme Court in 2004 ruled that Newdow had no legal standing to bring the case and threw out the appeals court decision.

In one other religious dispute the Court in 2001 held that local school boards cannot bar Christian clubs from using school facilities for meetings after the end of the school day. By a 6–3 vote, the Court said the policy of a local New York school board amounted to "viewpoint discrimination" prohibited by the First Amendment's Free Speech Clause.

The Court's most closely watched free speech disputes involved a different subject: Internet pornography. Three rulings produced mixed results for Congress's efforts to limit children's access to sexually explicit materials on the Internet.

Despite two tries the Court failed to make a final decision on the constitutionality of the Children's Online Protection Act, a narrower version of an earlier law that the Court had struck down in 1997. The new law made it a crime to disseminate sexual material "harmful to minors" on the World Wide Web for commercial purposes but exempted Web publishers that used credit card or age verification procedures to block youngsters' access. A federal appeals court ruled the law unconstitutional because it used local instead of national standards in determining harm to minors. The Court in 2002 threw out that decision and sent the case back for a ruling on other aspects of the law.

In a broader decision the federal appeals court again ruled the law unconstitutional and the Court again took up the government's effort to uphold it. In a fractured ruling,

the Court in 2004 extended the injunction blocking the law from taking effect but again failed to reach a final decision. Writing for the 5–4 majority, Kennedy said the government had failed to prove that the law was the "least restrictive" alternative to limiting children's access to Internet porn. He specifically pointed to software filters as less restrictive and possibly more effective. The ruling gave the government an opportunity to address the issue before the appeals court, but most experts said the government seemed unlikely to succeed.

The government prevailed in another Internet-related case, however. By a 6–3 vote the Court upheld a law passed by Congress requiring libraries to install software filters on computers to prevent youngsters from accessing sexually explicit materials. But the Court in 2002 struck down another law aimed at banning "virtual" child pornography—computer-generated images appearing to depict minors in sexual activities. For the majority, Kennedy said the law "prohibits speech that records no crime and creates no victims by its production."

The Court threw out two other federal laws on free speech grounds. By a 5–4 vote the Court in 2001 struck down a law banning federally funded legal aid lawyers from challenging state or federal welfare programs. In the same year, the Court blocked state or federal provisions making journalists civilly liable for publicizing the contents of illegally intercepted phone conversations when they relate to public issues. But the justices in 2003 rejected a First Amendment challenge to a law—heavily lobbied by the motion picture and recording industries—that extended by twenty years the term on most existing and future copyrights.

In cases involving state or local laws the Court threw out an ordinance adopted by a small village in Ohio that required a permit for door-to-door political solicitation or religious proselytizing. But it upheld a Virginia law that made cross burning a crime, with the proviso that prosecutors had to prove the action was intended as a threat and not as symbolic speech.

FEDERALISM

The Rehnquist Court gave state governments some additional protections against federal powers but appeared to call a halt to the trend with several decisions that rejected states' claims to immunity from federal courts' jurisdiction. In the most important of the cases, the Court allowed private damage suits against state governments for denying workers' rights to family or medical leave or for failing to make courthouses accessible to persons with disabilities.

Three of the pro-states' rights decisions reflected the same split as in comparable, earlier rulings between a five-vote conservative bloc and four liberal dissenters. O'Connor broke ranks with the conservatives in several of the later rulings supporting federal powers. And Rehnquist himself—regarded as the major architect of the new federalism jurisprudence—startled observers by writing the 6–3 decision that permitted suits against state governments under the federal Family and Medical Leave Act.

In the most important victory for state governments the Court in 2001 ruled 5–4 that states were immune from suits for claimed violations of the employment provisions of the Americans with Disabilities Act. For the majority Rehnquist said that Congress had failed to establish a "pattern of unconstitutional discrimination" by state governments against persons with disabilities and that the remedy imposed on state governments was "not congruent and proportional" to the violations.

In the same year the Court barred private damage actions against state or local government officials for policies with discriminatory effects but no intentional discrimination. Dissenters said the 5–4 ruling disregarded prior rulings and congressional intent. A year later, the Court ruled in another 5–4 decision that state governments were also immune from private citizen complaints in quasi-judicial proceedings before federal administrative agencies.

By narrowly construing the federal Clean Water Act, the Court in 2001 also barred federal jurisdiction over isolated ponds or wetlands. The 5–4 ruling allowed a local government consortium to fill several ponds to build a solid waste disposal facility. The U.S. Army Corps of Engineers had claimed jurisdiction over the ponds because they served as a habitat for migratory birds. In another statutory ruling, the Court in 2002 gave states a procedural victory by denying plaintiffs with related state and federal claims an extended deadline for filing a suit against a state governmental defendant.

The first turnaround from decisions extending states' immunity from damage suits came in 2003 in a case filed by a former Nevada state employee charging his agency with violating the federal law requiring both private and public employers to grant workers up to twelve weeks' unpaid family or medical leave under certain circumstances. For the majority Rehnquist said the federal law was a proper exercise of Congress's enforcement powers under Section 5 of the Fourteenth Amendment. In contrast to the evidence before Congress in connection with the disabilities measure Rehnquist said that "the States' record of unconstitutional participation in, and fostering of, gender-based discrimination in the administration of leave benefits was weighty enough to justify the enactment of prophylactic section 5 legislation." O'Connor also joined in the 6–3 decision; conservatives Scalia, Kennedy, and Thomas dissented.

A year later O'Connor again provided a pivotal vote in a 5–4 decision holding that states could be sued for failing to make courthouses accessible as required by the ADA's provisions in Title II barring discrimination against persons with disabilities in government programs and services. For the majority, Stevens said that Congress had been given substantial evidence that "many individuals . . . were being excluded from courthouses and court proceedings by reason of their disabilities." Rehnquist, speaking for the four dissenters, disagreed.

In another 2004 decision, the Court unanimously held that state officials are not entitled to sovereign immunity from claims arising under federal court-approved consent decrees even when those decrees contain requirements that go beyond federal law. Plaintiffs in a suit against a Texas agency over health services for indigents had gone to federal court to enforce the decree. Texas officials had argued that under the Eleventh Amendment a federal judge could enforce only those provisions specifically needed to comply with federal law.

In the same year, the Court also ruled that states could be sued in federal court over the constitutionality of state tax credits used to pay tuition at religious schools. Arizona officials had argued that the federal Tax Injunction Act prohibited federal court suits over state tax matters. In a 5–4 decision, however, the Court said the law did not "bar all lower-court interference with state tax systems." For the dissenters, Kennedy said the ruling treated state courts as "second-rate constitutional arbiters."

State governments suffered other, lesser procedural setbacks during the period. In 2002 the Court ruled unanimously that a state cannot claim Eleventh Amendment immunity from federal jurisdiction after voluntarily removing a case from state to federal court. In another unanimous ruling the Court held in 2003 that a state law immunizing tax officials from private suit did not necessarily block such suits in another state. And in 2004 the Court held 7–2 that the Eleventh Amendment did not block a federal bankruptcy court from discharging or forgiving a student loan debt owed to a state government entity.

For their part, local governments won no major dispensations from the new federalism decisions. The Court in 2003 ruled unanimously that private citizens could sue local governments under the Civil War–era False Claims Act for defrauding the federal government. Three years earlier the Court had barred such suits against state governments. In another setback for local governments, the Court in 2004 unanimously held that Congress had constitutional power to make bribery of local officials a federal crime even if the offense did not involve a federally financed program or activity.

BUSINESS CASES

Business groups won several significant victories on civil justice issues, including a ruling to set loosely defined limits on punitive damage awards. They also won some battles over federal or state regulations but failed in an effort to require cost-benefit analysis on federal air pollution controls.

After more than a decade of inconclusive rulings the Court in 2003 specified loose numerical guidelines for judging the constitutionality of punitive damage awards. In an opinion rejecting a $145 million penalty in a bad-faith insurance case, the Court said that punitive damages should rarely be more than ten times the amount of compensatory damages and that a one-to-one ratio might be the limit in cases with a "substantial" compensatory award.

The 6–3 ruling in *State Farm Mutual Automobile Insurance Co. v. Campbell* also limited the ability of state courts to punish business defendants for conduct in other states. Two years earlier the Court had also helped business defendants by ruling that federal appeals courts must make an independent determination of the constitutionality of punitive damage awards.

Health maintenance organizations (HMOs) won a major victory in 2004 with a ruling on federal preemption grounds that patients cannot sue HMOs in state courts for refusing to pay for doctor-recommended care or medications. Earlier, however, the Court had upheld state laws requiring HMOs to provide patients second opinions on benefit denials and to admit any physicians willing to abide by a network's terms, including fee schedules.

Among other civil justice cases, business groups won a ruling in 2001 generally allowing employers to require employees and job applicants to use arbitration instead of litigation for any employment-related disputes. And the Court in 2004 ruled that employers can favor older workers over younger workers without violating the federal age discrimination law.

Property rights advocates came up short in three efforts to win compensation for landowners adversely affected by land-use regulations. In the most important decision the Court in 2002 ruled that governments ordinarily do not have to pay a landowner for limiting the use of property under a temporary moratorium imposed while crafting permanent regulations.

In environmental cases the Court rebuffed an industry-backed challenge to national air-quality standards established under the federal Clean Air Act. The Court unanimously in 2001 ruled that the act did not allow the Environmental Protection Agency (EPA) to consider costs of compliance in setting standards. It also rejected an industry claim that the law amounted to an unconstitutional delegation of congressional power to the agency.

The Court also backed federal regulation in a 2004 ruling that upheld the EPA's authority to override an Alaska agency's decision to allow a major polluter to use less expensive emission controls. In the same year, though, the Court ruled that an effort by a Southern California agency to impose tighter emission requirements on automobiles was preempted by federal law.

Supreme Court Decisions
November 2000–June 2004

Business Law

ANTITRUST

Verizon Communications, Inc. v. Law Offices of Curtis V. Trinko, LLP (540 U.S. 398), decided by a 9–0 vote, Jan. 13, 2004; Scalia wrote the opinion.

A local telephone company's failure to share its network with competitors, as required by the Telecommunications Act of 1996, is not a violation of antitrust laws. The ruling protected the large regional telephone companies from antitrust claims by rival carriers seeking to dislodge their monopoly holds on local markets.

U.S. Postal Service v. Flamingo Industries (USA) Ltd. (540 U.S. 736), decided by a 9–0 vote, Feb. 25, 2004; Kennedy wrote the opinion.

The Court held unanimously that, even though the Postal Reorganization Act made the United States Postal Service subject to suit, it has immunity from antitrust suits brought under the Sherman Act because it is a part of the U.S. government and not a separate "person," under federal antitrust laws. The ruling barred an antitrust suit by a California corporation, Flamingo Industries, that claimed the Postal Service had unfairly terminated its contract to produce mail sacks to suppress competition and create a monopoly in mail sack production.

F. Hoffmann-La Roche Ltd. v. Empagran S.A. (542 U.S. 155), decided by an 8–0 vote, June 14, 2004; Breyer wrote the opinion; O'Connor did not participate.

Foreign companies or consumers cannot use U.S. antitrust laws to sue foreign manufacturers for price-fixing practices if they base their claims solely on the effects on commerce outside the United States.

Intel Corporation v. Advanced Micro Devices, Inc. (542 U.S. 241), decided by a 7–1 vote, June 21, 2004; Ginsburg wrote the opinion; Breyer dissented; O'Connor did not participate.

Federal courts may grant discovery to a company that files an antitrust complaint against a rival concern with the European agency that enforces competition laws. The ruling was a partial victory for Advanced Micro Devices in its effort to obtain information from the Intel Corporation, a larger rival in the microprocessing industry.

BANKING

Beneficial National Bank v. Anderson (539 U.S. 1), decided by a 7–2 vote, June 2, 2003; Stevens wrote the opinion; Scalia and Thomas dissented.

National banks can have state court suits charging them with illegal interest rates transferred to federal court. The Court held that the suit belonged in federal court because the National Bank Act completely preempts state suits against national banks for excessive interest.

BANKRUPTCY

Archer v. Warner (538 U.S. 314), decided by a 7–2 vote, March 31, 2003; Breyer wrote the opinion; Thomas and Stevens dissented.

A North Carolina couple was allowed to try to collect a debt from another couple who had agreed to settle a civil fraud suit against them but later filed for bankruptcy without paying the full settlement. The petitioners claimed that the remaining debt was not covered by the bankruptcy because of an exception in the law for debts "obtained by . . . actual fraud." The Court held that the fraud exception could apply, as the settlement agreement does not bar the petitioners from showing that the settlement debt arose out of "false pretenses, a false representation, or actual fraud" and is consequently nondischargeable.

Kontrick v. Ryan (540 U.S. 443), decided by a 9–0 vote, Jan. 14, 2004; Ginsburg wrote the opinion.

A debtor in a bankruptcy liquidation cannot strike a creditor's late-filed objection to discharging a debt if the debtor does not raise the timeliness issue until after a ruling on the merits. The ruling resolved a split among lower federal courts

639

over how to apply the Federal Rule of Bankruptcy Procedure 4004, which requires a creditor to file any objection to discharging a debt within sixty days of the first meeting of creditors. The Court held that Rule 4004 is a "claim-processing rule" that does not determine which cases bankruptcy courts are competent to adjudicate.

Lamie v. United States Trustee (540 U.S. 526), decided by a 9–0 vote, Jan. 26, 2004; Kennedy wrote the opinion.

A debtor's attorney acting in a liquidation bankruptcy proceeding is not eligible for court-awarded fees unless he or she is hired by the trustee for the bankrupt estate.

Till v. SCS Credit Corp. (541 U.S. 465), decided by a 5–4 vote, May 17, 2004; Stevens wrote the plurality opinion; Thomas concurred in the judgment; Scalia, Rehnquist, O'Connor, and Kennedy dissented.

A bankruptcy judge may allow a debtor who has defaulted on a loan to make payments to a creditor at a lower interest rate than the creditor could have obtained had it foreclosed on the loan.

CLASS ACTIONS

Devlin v. Scardelletti (536 U.S. 1), decided by a 6–3 vote, June 10, 2002; O'Connor wrote the opinion; Scalia, Kennedy, and Thomas dissented.

Someone who unsuccessfully objected to the fairness of a proposed class action settlement can appeal the decision even if he or she was not a named party or an intervener in the action.

COPYRIGHT

New York Times Co. v. Tasini (533 U.S. 483), decided by a 7–2 vote, June 25, 2001; Ginsburg wrote the opinion; Stevens and Breyer dissented.

Federal copyright law does not allow newspaper or magazine publishers to include freelance articles in digital databases without obtaining the authors' permission. The ruling backed a copyright infringement suit brought by six freelance authors against three major news organizations (the New York Times Co., Tribune Co., and AOL Time Warner) and two electronic publishers (LEXIS/NEXIS and University Microfilms International). The news organizations licensed the electronic publishers to include their publications on digital databases that computer users could search by individual article. The Court agreed with the authors' contention that the news organizations and the electronic publishers both infringed their copyrights.

Eldred v. Ashcroft, Attorney General (537 U.S. 186), decided by a 7–2 vote, Jan. 15, 2003; Ginsburg wrote the opinion; Stevens and Breyer dissented.

The Court upheld a major revision of federal copyright law that Congress passed in 1998, extending by twenty years the term of future and existing copyrights. The ruling rejected a constitutional challenge to the Sonny Bono Copyright Term Extension Act, which lengthened copyright terms to seventy years from the death of the author or artist for individual works or ninety-five years after creation for copyrights held by a corporation.

A group of small businesses and publishers that specialize in distribution of "public domain" works—ones whose copyrights have expired—contended that the extension of existing copyrights went beyond Congress's authority under the Copyright Clause to grant authors "exclusive rights" for "limited times." The Court ruled that Congress had constitutional authority to extend the term of existing copyrights.

INSURANCE

Kentucky Association of Health Plans, Inc. v. Miller, Kentucky Commissioner of Insurance (538 U.S. 329), decided by a 9–0 vote, April 2, 2003; Scalia wrote the opinion.

States may require health maintenance organizations to admit any health care provider who agrees to abide by the network's terms and conditions, including its fee schedules. The ruling rejected arguments by the managed care industry that "any willing provider" laws that a number of states have enacted were preempted by the federal law regulating employer-provided health benefits.

INTERNATIONAL TRADE

United States v. Mead Corp. (533 U.S. 218), decided by an 8–1 vote, June 18, 2001; Souter wrote the opinion; Scalia dissented.

Judges are not required to defer to individual tariff rulings by U.S. Customs Service officials. The ruling—a significant administrative law decision—held that an individual tariff ruling is not entitled to the deference required under the Supreme Court's 1984 decision *Chevron U.S.A. v. Natural Resources Defense Council, Inc.* but may be "eligible to claim respect according to its persuasiveness."

MARITIME LAW

Norfolk Shipbuilding & Drydock Corp. v. Garris (532 U.S. 811), decided by a 9–0 vote, June 4, 2001; Scalia wrote the opinion.

Federal courts have jurisdiction under maritime law for wrongful-death suits based on negligence. The Court in 1970 had first recognized federal maritime jurisdiction over wrongful-death suits based on unseaworthiness. This ruling stated that there was "no rational basis for distinguishing negligence from seaworthiness."

PATENTS

TrafFix Devices, Inc. v. Marketing Displays, Inc. (532 U.S. 23), decided by a 9–0 vote, March 20, 2001; Kennedy wrote the opinion.

The Court made it harder for the manufacturer of a product with an expired patent to prevent competitors from copying the product by claiming infringement of its design or "trade dress" protection.

J. E. M. Ag Supply v. Pioneer Hi-Bred International, Inc. (534 U.S. 124), decided by a 6–2 vote, Dec. 10, 2001; Thomas wrote the opinion; Breyer and Stevens dissented; O'Connor did not participate.

Sexually reproduced plants and their seeds can be patented under the general federal patent law. The Court agreed that the more specific federal laws protecting bioengineered plants did not preclude coverage under the general federal patent law.

Festo Corp. v. Shoketsu Kinzoku Kogyo Kabushiki Co. Ltd. (535 U.S. 722), decided by a 9–0 vote, May 28, 2002; Kennedy wrote the opinion.

A patent holder is not completely barred from pursuing an infringement claim because of amendments made during the patent application process. The ruling reversed a decision—intensely controversial among patent attorneys—issued by the Court of Appeals for the Federal Circuit, which has exclusive jurisdiction over patent case appeals.

The case relied on the "doctrine of equivalents," which allows an infringement claim even if a challenged device is not identical to a patented invention. The Federal Circuit ruled that the amendment of the patent during the application process—the "prosecution history" of the patent—operated as a complete bar, or "estoppel," to the infringement claim. The Court held that the Federal Circuit went too far in completely barring infringement claims based on prosecution history estoppel. A patent holder who narrows a claim to obtain a patent may still pursue an infringement claim, if the narrowing amendment did not "relinquish equivalents unforeseeable at the time of the amendment and beyond a fair interpretation of what was surrendered." The patent holder bears the burden of proof on the issue.

SECURITIES LAW

The Wharf (Holdings) Ltd. v. United International Holdings, Inc. (532 U.S. 588), decided by a 9–0 vote, May 21, 2001; Breyer wrote the opinion.

A securities issuer's secret intention not to honor an option to buy stock violated the broad antifraud provision of the federal securities law known as Rule 10b–5. The ruling also upheld a $125 million jury award in connection with the company's refusal to honor the contract.

Securities and Exchange Commission v. Zandford (535 U.S. 813), decided by a 9–0 vote, June 3, 2002; Stevens wrote the opinion.

The antifraud provisions of federal securities law can be applied to brokers who sell their customers' stock for personal gain. The ruling reinstated a civil complaint by the Securities and Exchange Commission against a former Maryland stockbroker for allegedly milking more than $400,000 from an account established by an elderly investor for the benefit of his mentally retarded daughter.

Securities and Exchange Commission v. Edwards (540 U.S. 389), decided by a 9–0 vote, Jan. 13, 2004; O'Connor wrote the opinion.

A moneymaking scheme offering a contractual entitlement to a fixed, not a variable, return is an investment contract subject to regulation under federal securities laws. The Court held that an agreement offering a fixed rate of return can be an investment contract and thus a "security" subject to federal securities laws.

TAXATION

Gitlitz v. Commissioner of Internal Revenue (531 U.S. 206), decided by an 8–1 vote, Jan. 9, 2001; Thomas wrote the opinion; Breyer dissented.

Shareholders in certain insolvent small businesses can reduce their federal income tax by treating a discharge of debt as income to allow past losses to be claimed as deductions.

Young v. United States (535 U.S. 43), decided by a 9–0 vote, March 4, 2001; Scalia wrote the opinion.

The Court limited federal taxpayers' ability to use back-to-back bankruptcy filings to nullify recent tax liabilities. The ruling rejected an effort to use a New Hampshire couple's 1997 bankruptcy filing to "discharge" a tax liability on their 1992 federal income tax return due in October 1993. The federal bankruptcy law included a provision—a "three-year lookback period"—that allowed an individual to discharge any tax liabilities due more than three years prior to a bankruptcy filing. The Court held that the three-year lookback period is tolled while a prior bankruptcy petition is pending.

United States v. Cleveland Indians Baseball Co. (532 U.S. 200), decided by a 9–0 vote, April 17, 2001; Ginsburg wrote the opinion.

Back wages are subject to Social Security, Medicare, and unemployment taxes by reference to the year when the wages are paid, not when the wages were earned. The ruling backed the Internal Revenue Service in a dispute with the Cleveland Indians management and a group of eight players who received back pay in 1994 to settle free agency-related claims for the years 1986 and 1987.

United Dominion Industries, Inc. v. United States (532 U.S. 822), decided by an 8–1 vote, June 4, 2001; Souter wrote the opinion; Stevens dissented.

Affiliated corporations must claim product liability expenses for federal income tax purposes on a consolidated basis instead of company by company. The ruling favored a corporate taxpayer in a dispute with the government over the proper way to calculate product liability losses used as deductions on previous years' returns.

United States v. Craft (535 U.S. 274), decided by a 6–3 vote, April 17, 2002; O'Connor wrote the opinion; Thomas, Stevens, and Scalia dissented.

The federal government can enforce a tax lien against marital property held jointly by a husband and wife even if it is trying to collect taxes owed by only one of the spouses. The ruling cleared the way for the Internal Revenue Service to try to collect part of $482,446 in unpaid income taxes owed by a Michigan man, Don Craft, from the proceeds of the sale of a piece of real property once owned jointly by Craft and his wife, Sandra. The Crafts owned the property in a "tenancy of the entirety"—a form of joint ownership in which a husband and wife each are deemed to have indivisible ownership of the "entire" property. Both spouses have the right to use the property, but neither spouse can unilaterally sell or mortgage his or her interest.

United States v. Fior D'Italia, Inc. (536 U.S. 238), decided by a 6–3 vote, June 17, 2002; Breyer wrote the opinion; Souter, Scalia, and Thomas dissented.

The Internal Revenue Service (IRS) can estimate the amount of Social Security taxes that restaurants owe for tips paid to waiters and other employees. Social Security taxes—technically known as Federal Insurance Contribution Act or FICA taxes—are levied on employees and employers, but tip income often goes un- or underreported by employees. In an effort to improve collection of the tax from employers, the IRS began assessing restaurants for taxes calculated by using credit card receipts to estimate the total amount of tips paid to employees. The Court ruled the IRS method was legal but acknowledged that the practice raised policy issues that Congress could consider.

Boeing Co. v. United States (537 U.S. 437), decided by a 7–2 vote, March 4, 2003; Stevens wrote the opinion; Thomas and Scalia dissented.

The Court sided with the government and against a major aircraft manufacturer in a $419 million dispute over how to allocate research and development costs for products sold through a tax-favored foreign sales subsidiary. The ruling upheld a Treasury Department regulation in effect from 1979 through 1987 on the allocation of R&D costs between a U.S. corporation and separate subsidiaries created under federal law intended to encourage exports.

United States v. Galletti (541 U.S. 114), decided by a 9–0 vote, March 23, 2004; Thomas wrote the opinion.

The proper assessment of a tax against a partnership suffices to extend the time for collecting the tax from its general partners even if they were not separately assessed for the tax. The ruling upheld the effort by the Internal Revenue Service (IRS) to collect about $400,000 in unpaid federal employment taxes for the years 1992 through 1995 from partners of a California business. The IRS assessed the taxes against the partnership within the three-year period allowed by law, thereby extending the statute of limitations for collection to ten years. The partnership never paid the levy, and the two general partners later filed for bankruptcy. The Supreme Court held the government did not have to assess the partners separately to take advantage of the extended time for collecting the unpaid taxes as long as the partnership had been properly assessed within the three-year period.

TRADEMARK LAW

Moseley v. V Secret Catalogue, Inc. (537 U.S. 418), decided by a 9–0 vote, March 4, 2003; Stevens wrote the opinion.

The Court established a somewhat strict requirement for owners of famous trademarks to win legal protection against businesses for "dilution" of the value of the mark under a recently enacted federal law. The ruling—the Court's first interpretation of the Federal Trademark Dilution Act—held that the owner of a famous trademark must show evidence of actual dilution, not merely the likelihood of dilution, to invoke the law.

Dastar Corp. v. Twentieth Century Fox Film Corp. (539 U.S. 23), decided by an 8–0 vote, June 2, 2003; Scalia wrote the opinion; Breyer did not participate.

Uncredited copying of an uncopyrighted work does not amount to a violation of federal trademark law known as "reverse passing off." The ruling rejected an effort by Twentieth Century Fox Film Corp. and two other entertainment companies to win damages from a video production company, Dastar Corp., for Dastar's use of once copyrighted material in a series of videos about World War II. The Court ruled that Dastar had not violated trademark law by using the uncopyrighted material without credit.

Courts and Procedure

APPEALS

Becker v. Montgomery, Attorney General of Ohio (532 U.S. 757), decided by a 9–0 vote, May 29, 2001; Ginsburg wrote the opinion.

Failure to sign a notice of appeal does not require dismissal of the appeal if the appellant or the appellant's attorney promptly corrects the omission after learning of it. The ruling reinstated an appeal by an Ohio inmate, Dale Becker, of a lower court decision dismissing a prison condition suit contesting his exposure to secondhand cigarette smoke. Becker typed his name on a government-printed notice of appeal. The Sixth U.S. Circuit Court of Appeals dismissed the appeal, saying that the Federal Rules of Civil Procedure required a handwritten signature. The Court ordered the appeal reinstated, citing another provision of the rules allowing the omission of a signature to be corrected.

ARBITRATION

Green Tree Financial Corp.-Alabama v. Randolph (531 U.S. 79), decided by a 5–4 vote, Dec. 11, 2000; Rehnquist wrote the opinion; Ginsburg, Stevens, Souter, and Breyer dissented.

A consumer arbitration agreement can be enforced even if it includes no provision about the costs of the arbitration.

The ruling turned aside a suit by an Alabama woman protesting a financing agreement that included a standard provision requiring binding arbitration to settle any disputes. It said nothing about how much the arbitration would cost or who would pay.

Howsam v. Dean Witter Reynolds, Inc. (537 U.S. 79), decided by an 8–0 vote, Dec. 10, 2002; Breyer wrote the opinion; O'Connor did not participate.

An arbitrator instead of a court should interpret the six-year time limit provision in the Code of Arbitration Procedure rules adopted by the National Association of Securities Dealers, a self-regulatory organization.

PacifiCare Health Systems, Inc. v. Book (538 U.S. 401), decided by an 8–0 vote, April 7, 2003; Scalia wrote the opinion; Thomas did not participate.

The Court sidestepped a decision on whether an arbitrator can award triple damages under the Racketeer Influenced and Corrupt Organizations (RICO) Act, the federal anti-racketeering law, if the arbitration agreement prohibits "punitive" or "exemplary" damages. The Court held that the request to block the arbitration was premature because it was unclear whether an arbitrator could award triple damages on the RICO counts. Prior Supreme Court rulings suggested, without explicitly ruling, that RICO's triple damage provision was compensatory, not punitive. On that basis, "the application of the disputed language to RICO claims is, to say the least, in doubt."

Citizens Bank v. Alafabco, Inc. (539 U.S. 52), decided by a 9–0 vote, June 2, 2003; per curiam opinion.

The Alabama Supreme Court was wrong when it refused to enforce an arbitration clause in a dispute between an Alabama bank and a local construction company over a debt-restructuring plan. The bank invoked the arbitration clause and cited the Federal Arbitration Act, which provides for the enforcement of arbitration clauses in any contract "evidencing a transaction involving commerce." The Alabama Supreme Court refused to order arbitration, saying the debt-restructuring agreement had too little connection to interstate commerce to come under the act.

The Court said the Alabama justices misapplied precedents interpreting the federal law. The debt-restructuring agreement satisfied the "involving commerce" test, the Court said, because of the construction company's interstate operations as well as "the broad impact of commercial lending on the national economy."

Green Tree Financial Corp. v. Bazzle (539 U.S. 444), decided by a 5–4 vote, June 23, 2003; Breyer wrote the main opinion; Rehnquist, O'Connor, Kennedy, and Thomas dissented.

A badly fractured Court failed to decide whether consumer disputes subject to binding arbitration can be converted into class action suits. The ruling sent back to an arbitrator a dispute stemming from separate complaints by customers of Green Tree Financial Corp. charging that the company had failed to inform them of their rights to name their own lawyers and insurance agents.

ATTORNEY FEES

Buckhannon Board and Care Home, Inc. v. West Virginia Department of Health and Human Resources (532 U.S. 598), decided by a 5–4 vote, May 29, 2001; Rehnquist wrote the opinion; Ginsburg, Stevens, Souter, and Breyer dissented.

Federal attorney fee statutes allow an award of fees only for winning a judgment or court-approved settlement, not a legislative or other voluntary change of the opposing party's conduct. The ruling—a setback for civil rights and environmental plaintiffs, among others—rejected the "catalyst theory" for awarding attorney fees for changes adopted in response to litigation but without formal court action.

Gisbrecht v. Barnhart (535 U.S. 789), decided by an 8–1 vote, May 28, 2002; Ginsburg wrote the opinion; Scalia dissented.

Judges can use contingency fee agreements to determine fee awards for lawyers who successfully represent Social Security benefits claimants in courts, but they can also review fees for reasonableness. The ruling largely upheld the prevailing practice whereby lawyers representing Social Security claimants had clients sign agreements calling for a fee equal to 25 percent of any past-due benefits recovered.

Scarborough v. Principi, Secretary of Veterans Affairs (541 U.S. 401), decided by a 7–2 vote, May 3, 2004; Ginsburg wrote the opinion; Thomas and Scalia dissented.

An applicant for attorney's fees awards against the government can supply a missing element of the application after the deadline if the request was filed within the thirty-day deadline after the end of the case. The ruling resolved a split between federal appeals courts on how to deal with technical defects in applications for attorney's fees awards under the federal Equal Justice to Access Act of 1980.

CLASS ACTIONS

Dow Chemical Company v. Stephenson (539 U.S. 111), decided by a 4–4 vote, June 9, 2003; Stevens did not participate.

Two Vietnam veterans with recently discovered illnesses were allowed to continue their efforts to collect damages from the manufacturers of the chemical herbicide Agent Orange despite an earlier class action settlement by the companies.

The ruling sent the case of one veteran back to lower federal courts to decide whether it had been improperly removed from state court and allowed the other veteran to pursue his claim on the basis of a deadlocked, 4–4 vote. The action left the legal issue in the case unresolved: Under what circumstances can someone who was not involved in a class action attack a settlement of the case by claiming that he or she was not adequately represented at the time?

DISMISSALS

Semtek International, Inc. v. Lockheed Martin Corp. (531 U.S. 497), decided by a 9–0 vote, Feb. 27, 2001; Scalia wrote the opinion.

In a technical but procedurally significant ruling, the Court ruled that a federal court's dismissal of a civil suit without adjudication of the substantive issues does not necessarily bar a state court from hearing a claim arising from the same dispute.

DIVERSITY OF CITIZENSHIP

Grupo Dataflux v. Atlas Global Group, L.P. (541 U.S. 567), decided by a 5–4 vote, May 17, 2004; Scalia wrote the opinion; Ginsburg, Stevens, Souter, and Breyer dissented.

A pretrial change in party citizenship does not create diversity jurisdiction in a state lawsuit brought in federal court when the parties were not diverse at the time the suit was filed. Diversity of citizenship jurisdiction requires "complete diversity"—none of the parties on one side of the case can be of the same citizenship as parties on the opposite side. The Court strictly enforced the rule that diversity of citizenship must be established at the time a suit is filed.

FEDERAL COURTS

Holmes Group, Inc. v. Vornado Air Circulation Systems, Inc. (535 U.S. 826), decided by 9–0 and 7–2 votes, June 3, 2002; Scalia wrote the opinion; Ginsburg and O'Connor concurred in the result but disagreed with the legal holding.

The federal appeals court established to handle appeals in patent cases has jurisdiction only in cases in which the patent issue is raised by the plaintiff, not by the defendant.

JP Morgan Chase Bank v. Traffic Stream (BVI) Infrastructure Ltd. (536 U.S. 88), decided by a 9–0 vote, June 10, 2002; Souter wrote the opinion.

Federal courts can exercise jurisdiction over corporations organized under the laws of the British Virgin Islands even though they are not "subjects or citizens" of the United Kingdom under British law.

Roell v. Withrow (538 U.S. 580), decided by a 5–4 vote, April 29, 2003; Souter wrote the opinion; Thomas, Stevens, Scalia, and Kennedy dissented.

A federal magistrate can hear a case even without written consent from both parties as long as they voluntarily appear after being informed of their right to a trial before a regular federal judge. The Federal Magistrate Act of 1979 expanded the power of magistrate judges to conduct any civil judicial proceedings, including a jury trial, after referral by a district court judge and "upon the consent of the parties." The Court held that a party's consent to proceeding before a federal magistrate judge need not be in writing but can be inferred from a party's conduct during litigation.

Nguyen v. United States (539 U.S. 69), decided by a 5–4 vote, June 9, 2003; Stevens wrote the opinion; Rehnquist, Scalia, Ginsburg, and Breyer dissented.

A territorial judge has no authority to sit on a federal appeals court panel. The federal judicial code permits an appeals court to designate "one or more district judges within the circuit" to sit on the court of appeals "whenever the business of that court so requires." A territorial judge, however, does not have life tenure and the salary protections enjoyed by other federal district court judges.

FOREIGN IMMUNITY

Dole Food Company v. Patrickson (538 U.S. 468), decided by a 7–2 vote, April 22, 2003; Kennedy wrote the opinion; Breyer and O'Connor dissented in part.

A foreign corporation cannot claim protection under the Foreign Sovereign Immunities Act as an "instrumentality" of a foreign government unless the foreign state owns a majority of that corporation's shares, not a majority of shares of a parent corporation.

The ruling in a legally and factually complex case blocked an Israeli corporation from removing to federal court a suit by farm workers from several Latin American countries for alleged injuries from exposure to an agricultural pesticide. The Foreign Sovereign Immunities Act of 1976 (FSIA) grants legal protections, including the right to remove a case to federal court, to "any entity . . . a majority of whose shares or other ownership interest is owned by a foreign state or political subdivision thereof." The Court held that the Israeli companies could not claim protection under the FSIA because as indirect subsidiaries they were not instrumentalities of the Israeli government.

RECUSALS

Sao Paulo State of the Federative Republic of Brazil v. American Tobacco Co. (535 U.S. 229), decided by a 9–0 vote, April 1, 2002; per curiam opinion.

A judge need not step out of a case unless a reasonable person would question his or her impartiality after knowing all the circumstances of the judge's connection to the issue or case. Citing a 1988 precedent, the Court in an unsigned opinion said recusal is not required in Barbier's case, as "we think it self-evident that a reasonable person would not believe he had any interest or bias."

REMOVAL

Syngenta Crop Protection, Inc. v. Henson (537 U.S. 28), decided by a 9–0 vote, Nov. 5, 2002; Rehnquist wrote the opinion.

A federal court that had approved settlement of an insecticide exposure suit was wrong to order the removal of a similar tort suit from a Louisiana state court. The ruling represented a setback for business interests, which often preferred federal to state courts in personal injury litigation.

The Court ruled that the state court suit should not have been removed because it did not involve federal law claims.

Breuer v. Jim's Concrete of Brevard, Inc. (538 U.S. 691), decided by a 9–0 vote, May 19, 2003; Souter wrote the opinion.

An employer can remove an employee's suit for alleged violations of federal wage and hour laws from state to federal court.

STATE COURTS

Raygor v. Regents of the University of Minnesota (534 U.S. 533), decided by a 6–3 vote, Feb. 27, 2002; O'Connor wrote the opinion; Stevens, Souter, and Breyer dissented.

A federal law easing time limits for plaintiffs with related state and federal claims cannot be used to extend the deadline for filing a suit against a state governmental defendant. The ruling narrowed a federal law that extended the deadline or statute of limitations for filing a state court suit in cases in which a federal court dismissed the federal parts of a suit raising both federal and state claims. In those cases, the 1990 federal law provided for extending the state deadline—or "tolling" the statute of limitations—for the period the case was in federal court.

STATUTES OF LIMITATION

Jinks v. Richland County, South Carolina (538 U.S. 456), decided by a 9–0 vote, April 22, 2003; Scalia wrote the opinion.

A federal law easing time limits for plaintiffs with related state and federal claims can be used to extend the deadline for filing a suit against a local government. The Court held that the law did not infringe state sovereignty when used to extend the time for filing a suit against a local government.

Criminal Law and Procedure

APPEALS

United States v. Cotton (535 U.S. 625), decided by a 9–0 vote, May 20, 2002; Rehnquist wrote the opinion.

A defective indictment is normally not the kind of legal error that deprives a court of the power to hear a case even if the defendant does not raise it. The ruling had the effect of limiting federal defendants' ability to take advantage of two recent Court rulings on sentencing procedures. The rulings—*Jones v. United States* (527 U.S. 373, 1999), and *Apprendi v. New Jersey* (530 U.S. 466, 2000)—required that any facts needed to increase a sentence beyond the statutory maximum be included in an indictment and found by a jury. The Court held that a defective indictment does not amount to a jurisdictional error.

ARRESTS

Atwater v. City of Lago Vista (532 U.S. 318), decided by a 5–4 vote, April 24, 2001; Souter wrote the opinion; O'Connor, Stevens, Ginsburg, and Breyer dissented.

Police can arrest a suspect for a minor offense without a warrant even if the maximum penalty is a fine and no jail time. The Court held that the Fourth Amendment does not prohibit a full custodial arrest for a minor offense.

CAPITAL PUNISHMENT

Shafer v. South Carolina (532 U.S. 36), decided by a 7–2 vote, March 20, 2001; Ginsburg wrote the opinion; Thomas and Scalia dissented.

The Court strengthened a prior ruling requiring judges in some capital cases to tell jurors that a defendant would be ineligible for parole if given a life sentence instead of the death penalty. The ruling rebuffed for a second time South Carolina's efforts to prevent jurors from being told that state law made a defendant sentenced to life imprisonment in a capital case ineligible for parole.

Penry v. Johnson, Director, Texas Department of Criminal Justice, Institutional Division (532 U.S. 782), decided by a 6–3 vote, June 4, 2001; O'Connor wrote the opinion; Thomas, Rehnquist, and Scalia dissented.

The Court for a second time overturned the death sentence of a mentally retarded Texas man because jurors were not properly informed that they could consider his retardation and past abuse as mitigating evidence.

The ruling required Texas courts to reopen sentence proceedings against Johnny Paul Penry, who was convicted and sentenced to death in 1980 for the rape-murder of a Texas woman the previous year. The Court in 1989 reversed Penry's death sentence, rejecting Penry's plea to completely ban the execution of mentally retarded defendants but holding that Texas law at the time did not allow a jury to consider mental retardation as a mitigating factor in deciding whether to impose death or a lesser penalty. The law required capital juries to answer yes to three "special issues" before imposing a death sentence: whether the killing was "deliberate"; whether the defendant was likely to commit criminal acts in the future; and, if provoked by the victim, whether the killing was "unreasonable."

The judge in Penry's retrial in 1990 gave the same three-part instruction used in the first trial and a supplemental instruction that said if jurors considered a life sentence "appropriate" because of mitigating evidence, they could answer "no" to any of the three special-issue questions. Penry's lawyers contended that the revised directions still gave jurors no effective vehicle to consider mitigating evidence. The Court held that the revised jury instructions did not comply with the prior ruling.

Kelly v. South Carolina (534 U.S. 246), decided by a 5–4 vote, Jan. 9, 2002; Souter wrote the opinion; Rehnquist, Scalia, Kennedy, and Thomas dissented.

The Court reversed a South Carolina inmate's death sentence because the jury was not told that he would be ineligible for parole under state law if sentenced to life imprisonment. The ruling—the third such reversal in a South Carolina capital case since 1994—ordered a new sentence for William Arthur Kelly for his 1996 murder conviction because the trial judge refused Kelly's lawyer's request to instruct the jury that Kelly would be ineligible for parole if sentenced to life in prison.

Atkins v. Virginia (536 U.S. 304), decided by a 6–3 vote, June 20, 2002; Stevens wrote the opinion; Scalia, Rehnquist, and Thomas dissented.

The execution of a mentally retarded offender is forbidden by the Eighth Amendment's prohibition against "cruel and unusual" punishment. The ruling extended nationwide a ban already on the books in eighteen of the thirty-eight death penalty states. Overturning its 1989 decision in *Penry v. Lynaugh*, 492 U.S. 302, the Court voted to categorically bar execution of someone who was mentally retarded.

Ring v. Arizona (536 U.S. 584), decided by a 7–2 vote, June 24, 2002; Ginsburg wrote the opinion; O'Connor and Rehnquist dissented.

Only a jury, not a judge, can make a factual determination needed to impose a death sentence on a defendant. The ruling, in an Arizona case, effectively invalidated death penalty systems there and in four other states—Colorado, Idaho, Montana, and Nebraska.

Sattazahn v. Pennsylvania (537 U.S. 101), decided by a 5–4 vote, Jan. 14, 2003; Scalia wrote the opinion; Ginsburg, Stevens, Souter, and Breyer dissented.

A defendant can be sentenced to death in a retrial following reversal of a conviction even if the first trial ended in a sentence to life imprisonment. The Court ruled there was no constitutional bar to seeking the death penalty in this retrial, as neither the jury deadlock nor the judge's imposition of a life sentence in the first trial amounted to an "acquittal" of capital murder so as to trigger double jeopardy protections.

Nelson v. Campbell, Commissioner, Alabama Department of Corrections (541 U.S. 637), decided by a 9–0 vote, May 24, 2004; O'Connor wrote the opinion.

An Alabama death row inmate can use a federal civil rights suit to challenge as cruel and unusual punishment the state's plan to surgically open one of his veins to prepare him for execution by lethal injection. The limited ruling reinstated a suit by a convicted murderer, David Nelson, brought under 42 U.S.C. §1983, the federal statute providing a civil remedy for any person deprived of a right under the U.S. Constitution. Nelson, whose veins were collapsed because of past drug use, claimed that the state's plan to use a "cut down" procedure to access his veins for lethal injection amounted to cruel and unusual punishment under the Eighth Amendment.

The Court ruled that Nelson could use section 1983 to challenge the procedure as a condition of his confinement, but it stopped short of holding that method-of-execution claims could be brought under the statute.

Beard, Secretary, Pennsylvania Department of Corrections v. Banks (542 U.S. 406), decided by a 5–4 vote, June 24, 2004; Thomas wrote the opinion; Stevens, Souter, Ginsburg, and Breyer dissented.

A new rule invalidating capital sentencing guidelines that require juries to disregard mitigating factors not found unanimously does not apply retroactively to death penalty cases decided before the rule took effect.

The ruling upheld the death sentence of a Pennsylvania man, George Banks, who challenged his 1983 conviction and sentence on the ground that the jury relied on capital sentencing schemes that required them to disregard any mitigating factors other than those on which they unanimously agreed. These sentencing guidelines, Banks argued, had been rendered invalid by the Supreme Court's opinion in *Mills v. Maryland* (1988), which it reaffirmed in *McKoy v. North Carolina* (1990).

The Court held that *Mills* did amount to a new constitutional rule but did not meet either of the criteria to be applied retroactively.

Tennard v. Dretke, Director, Texas Department of Criminal Justice, Correctional Institutions Division (542 U.S. 386), decided by a 6–3 vote, June 24, 2004; O'Connor wrote the opinion; Rehnquist, Scalia, and Thomas dissented.

A Texas death row inmate was allowed to seek to overturn his sentence on the ground that the jury was not properly instructed that it could consider his mental retardation as a mitigating factor.

CONFRONTATION

Crawford v. Washington (541 U.S. 36), decided by a 9–0 vote, March 8, 2004; Scalia wrote the opinion.

Prosecutors cannot introduce an unavailable witness's testimonial statement against a defendant at trial, regardless of the statement's reliability, unless the defendant has prior opportunity for cross-examination. The Court held that use of such a statement was barred by the Sixth Amendment's

Confrontation Clause, which was intended as a ban against testimonial hearsay.

CRIMINAL OFFENSES

Cleveland v. United States (531 U.S. 12), decided by a 9–0 vote, Nov. 7, 2000; Ginsburg wrote the opinion.

The Court limited the ability of federal prosecutors to use antifraud statutes to charge an individual for making false statements to obtain a state license.

United States v. Jimenez Recio (537 U.S. 270), decided by an 8–1 vote, Jan. 21, 2003; Breyer wrote the opinion; Stevens dissented.

A defendant can be convicted of criminal conspiracy even if he or she joins the conspiracy after the government has prevented possible completion of the planned offense.

Virginia v. Black (538 U.S. 343), decided by 6–3 and 7–2 votes, April 7, 2003; O'Connor wrote the opinion; Souter, Kennedy, and Ginsburg disagreed on the main issue; Scalia and Thomas disagreed on the secondary issue.

States can make it a crime to burn a cross with an intent to intimidate as long as prosecutors prove that the action was meant as a threat and not solely as symbolic speech. The fractured ruling gave a green light to states to criminalize a practice targeted through the twentieth century at African Americans and some other minority groups.

The Court rejected arguments that any law banning cross burning violated the First Amendment's protection for freedom of speech. In the specific case, however, the Court held Virginia's former cross-burning statute unconstitutional because it allowed juries to convict someone without specific proof of an intent to intimidate. The ruling set aside the convictions of three men obtained under the 1952 statute, which had been re-enacted in a different form by the time of the Court's decision.

Sabri v. United States (541 U.S. 600), decided by a 9–0 vote, May 17, 2004; Souter wrote the opinion.

Congress acted within its authority under the Constitution's Necessary and Proper Clause by making it a federal crime to bribe local government officials, even in matters not directly involving federal funds. The ruling upheld the indictment of a Minneapolis real estate developer who was charged with offering bribes to a city council member in violation of 18 U.S.C. §666(a)(2), which proscribes bribery of state and local officials of entities that receive at least $10,000 in federal funds.

COMPETENCY

Sell v. United States (539 U.S. 166), decided by a 6–3 vote, June 16, 2003; Breyer wrote the opinion; Scalia, O'Connor, and Thomas dissented.

The Court ruled that the government may forcibly administer antipsychotic drugs to mentally ill criminal defen-

dants to render them competent to stand trial, but only if strict conditions are met. The involuntary administration of antipsychotic drugs to nondangerous defendants was allowable only if the treatment was "medically appropriate" and "substantially unlikely to have side effects that may undermine the fairness of the trial." In addition, a court asked to order involuntary use of antipsychotics must find that any alternative, less intrusive treatments are "unlikely to achieve substantially the same results."

DETAINERS

Alabama v. Bozeman (533 U.S. 146), decided by a 9–0 vote, June 11, 2001; Breyer wrote the opinion.

A prisoner transferred under an interstate agreement from one state to another for prosecution on a pending charge cannot be returned to the original state before trial without dismissal of the case. The Interstate Agreement on Detainers provides that the receiving state must try the defendant within 120 days. It also provides that if the defendant is not tried before he or she is returned to the "sending state"—in this case the federal government—any charge "shall not be of any further force or effect" and must be dismissed "with prejudice."

DOUBLE JEOPARDY

Seling, Superintendent, Special Commitment Center v. Young (531 U.S. 250), decided by an 8–1 vote, Jan. 17, 2001; O'Connor wrote the opinion; Stevens dissented.

Sexual offenders held after expiration of their prison sentences under civil commitment proceedings cannot challenge their confinement as a violation of the constitutional prohibitions against double jeopardy or retroactive punishment.

DRUGS

United States v. Oakland Cannabis Buyers' Cooperative (532 U.S. 483), decided by an 8–0 vote, May 14, 2001; Thomas wrote the opinion; Breyer did not participate.

Federal law prevents states from legalizing the manufacture or distribution of marijuana for medical purposes. The ruling cleared the way for federal enforcement actions against cannabis medical dispensaries established in California following voter approval of a 1996 initiative that sought to legalize the possession or cultivation of marijuana for medical purposes.

EVIDENCE

Illinois v. Fisher (540 U.S. 544), decided by a 9–0 vote, Feb. 23, 2004; per curiam opinion.

Police failure to preserve potentially useful evidence in a criminal case does not constitute a denial of due process of law unless a defendant can show the police acted in bad faith. The Court had previously held that due process is violated whenever the state destroys material exculpatory evidence but that only a showing of bad faith will support finding a violation when the evidence is merely "potentially useful." The effect of such a rule, the unsigned opinion concluded, is to "limit the extent of the police obligation to preserve evidence to reasonable grounds and confine it to that class of cases where the interests of justice most clearly require it."

EX POST FACTO LAWS

Rogers v. Tennessee (532 U.S. 451), decided by a 5–4 vote, May 14, 2001; O'Connor wrote the opinion; Scalia, Stevens, Thomas, and Breyer dissented.

Tennessee courts did not violate a murder defendant's due process rights by abolishing a common-law "year and a day" rule, which provided that no defendant could be convicted of murder unless the victim died within a year and a day of the act, and retroactively applying the new ruling to his case. The Court held that the due process rights had not been violated because the Tennessee court's abolition of the outdated rule was not unpredictable.

Stogner v. California (539 U.S. 607), decided by a 5–4 vote, June 26, 2003; Breyer wrote the opinion; Kennedy, Rehnquist, Scalia, and Thomas dissented.

In a setback for cases against sexual molestation of children, the Court ruled that a law extending the time period for prosecuting a crime cannot be used to revive charges against a defendant after the expiration of the previous deadline.

When the Court agreed to hear the case, the George W. Bush administration filed a friend-of-the-court brief noting that after the Sept. 11, 2001, terrorist attacks, Congress passed a comparable law retroactively extending the statute of limitations for terrorist offenses. The Court ruled the retroactive extension of the statute of limitations violated the Ex Post Facto Clause.

FIREARMS

United States v. Bean (537 U.S. 71), decided by a 9–0 vote, Dec. 10, 2002; Thomas wrote the opinion.

Federal courts have no authority to release convicted felons from federal restrictions on possessing firearms or ammunition. Federal law establishes that convicted felons subject to firearms disabilities may petition the Bureau of Al-

cohol, Tobacco, and Firearms for a lifting of the restrictions, but Congress since 1992 has prohibited the use of any appropriated funds for processing such applications.

FORFEITURE

Dusenbery v. United States (534 U.S. 161), decided by a 5–4 vote, Jan. 8, 2002; Rehnquist wrote the opinion; Ginsburg, Stevens, Souter, and Breyer dissented.

The government does not have to guarantee actual notice to prison inmates before forfeiting property seized in connection with their offenses. The Court held that due process requirements were satisfied if the government's effort was "reasonably calculated" to "apprise a party of the pendency of the action."

GUILTY PLEAS

United States v. Vonn (535 U.S. 55), decided by an 8–1 vote, March 4, 2002; Souter wrote the opinion; Stevens dissented.

A defendant who fails to object to a legal error at a guilty plea hearing can set aside the plea only by satisfying the "plain error" rule and showing that the error affected his or her substantial rights. The Court also held that an appeals court could consult "the whole record" and not just the guilty plea hearing itself in making that determination.

Iowa v. Tovar (541 U.S. 77), decided by a 9–0 vote, March 8, 2004; Ginsburg wrote the opinion.

The Sixth Amendment does not require a trial judge to warn a defendant of the specific dangers and disadvantages of self-representation in entering a plea of guilty.

United States v. Dominguez Benitez (542 U.S. 74), decided by a 9–0 vote, June 14, 2004; Souter wrote the opinion.

A defendant who fails to object to incomplete warnings before entering a guilty plea in federal court cannot withdraw the plea without showing a reasonable probability that but for the error he would not have pleaded guilty.

HABEAS CORPUS

Artuz, Superintendent, Green Haven Correctional Facility v. Bennett (531 U.S. 4), decided by a 9–0 vote, Nov. 7, 2000; Scalia wrote the opinion.

The Court somewhat relaxed the one-year time limit on filing federal habeas corpus petitions for inmates with pending applications for post-conviction relief in state courts. The statute of limitations provision of the Antiterrorism and Effective Death Penalty Act of 1996 sets a one-year deadline for habeas corpus petitions after all state remedies have been exhausted but does not count the time when a "properly filed" application for post-conviction relief is pending. The Court held that an inmate's application is properly filed "when its delivery and acceptance are in compliance with the applicable laws and rules governing filings," even if it contains claims that the inmate is procedurally barred from raising.

Fiore v. White, Warden (531 U.S. 225), decided by a 9–0 vote, Jan. 9, 2001; per curiam opinion.

The Court threw out on state law grounds a Pennsylvania man's conviction for operating a hazardous waste facility without a permit because he had a state permit for the facility.

Duncan, Superintendent, Great Meadow Correctional Facility v. Walker (533 U.S. 167), (2001), decided by a 7–2 vote, June 18, 2001; O'Connor wrote the opinion; Breyer and Ginsburg dissented.

The Court refused to extend the one-year time limit for filing a federal habeas corpus petition for any time when an earlier petition was pending without a conclusive ruling. The ruling strictly interpreted a provision of the Antiterrorism and Effective Death Penalty Act of 1996 that "tolled" a one-year statute of limitations for bringing a federal habeas corpus petition—that is, extended the time period—for any time "during which a properly filed application for State post-conviction or other collateral review" was pending. The Court held that the provision gave inmates additional time only for the period when they had state post-conviction proceedings pending.

Tyler v. Cain, Warden (533 U.S. 656), decided by a 5–4 vote, June 28, 2001; Thomas wrote the opinion; Breyer, Stevens, Souter, and Ginsburg dissented.

A state inmate cannot use a new constitutional ruling by the U.S. Supreme Court to justify filing a second federal habeas corpus petition unless the Court has held the ruling to be retroactive. The ruling strictly interpreted a procedural hurdle in the Antiterrorism and Effective Death Penalty Act of 1996, which generally limited state prison inmates' ability to file successive habeas corpus petitions after an initial petition was rejected.

Lee v. Kemna (534 U.S. 362), decided by a 6–3 vote, Jan. 22, 2002; Ginsburg wrote the opinion; Kennedy, Scalia, and Thomas dissented.

The Court revived a Missouri inmate's federal habeas corpus petition seeking to overturn a murder conviction because the trial judge refused to grant a continuance after his defense witnesses vanished hours before their scheduled testimony.

Bell v. Cone (535 U.S. 685), decided by an 8–1 vote, May 28, 2002; Rehnquist wrote the opinion; Stevens dissented.

The Court rejected a Tennessee inmate's effort to set aside his death sentence on the ground of ineffective assistance of counsel during the penalty phase of his murder trial. The ruling relied on the recently enacted provision of the Antiterrorism and Effective Death Penalty Act of 1996 that barred federal courts from granting habeas corpus relief unless a state court decision was "contrary to, or involved an unreasonable application of, clearly established federal law."

Carey v. Saffold (536 U.S. 214), decided by a 5–4 vote, June 17, 2002; Breyer wrote the opinion; Kennedy, Rehnquist, Scalia, and Thomas dissented.

The Court broadened somewhat the time period for state inmates to file federal habeas corpus petitions after unsuccessful post-conviction challenges in state courts. The ruling involved a provision of the Antiterrorism and Effective Death Penalty Act of 1996 that set a one-year statute of limitations for an inmate to file a federal habeas corpus after a state conviction becomes final. The law specified that the statute of limitations is "tolled"—or held up—while any post-conviction challenge is "pending" in state court. The Court held that the one-year deadline ordinarily does not include the time between a state court's ruling on a prisoner's post-conviction petition and an inmate's appeal.

Horn v. Banks (536 U.S. 266), decided by a 9–0 vote, June 17, 2002; per curiam opinion.

A federal appeals court made a mistake in granting a Pennsylvania death row inmate's federal habeas corpus petition without first deciding whether the inmate could take advantage of a constitutional ruling handed down after his original conviction. The petitioner claimed that the jury form used in his trial violated standards the Court laid down in a 1988 decision, *Mills v. Maryland*, 486 U.S. 367. The Court agreed and sent the case back for further proceedings.

Stewart v. Smith (536 U.S. 856), decided by a 9–0 vote, June 28, 2002; per curiam opinion.

An Arizona death row inmate lost an effort to have federal courts review his claim that he received inadequate legal representation during the sentencing phase of his 1982 kidnapping and murder trial. In rejecting the federal habeas corpus petition, Smith was free to try to show why he should still be allowed to raise the issue in state courts.

Early, Warden v. Packer (537 U.S. 3), decided by a 9–0 vote, Nov. 4, 2002; per curiam opinion.

A federal appeals court exceeded its authority under federal habeas corpus law in ordering a new trial for a California prison inmate who claimed that the judge coerced the jury into convicting him of murder. The ruling reinstated the second-degree murder conviction.

Woodford, Warden v. Visciotti (537 U.S. 19), decided by a 9–0 vote, Nov. 4, 2002; per curiam opinion.

A federal appeals court was wrong to order a new sentencing hearing for a California death row inmate who claimed ineffective assistance of counsel during the penalty phase of his capital murder trial. The Court said that the Ninth U.S. Circuit Court of Appeals exceeded the limited review of state court decisions under the federal habeas corpus law, the Antiterrorism and Effective Death Penalty Act of 1996.

Miller-El v. Cockrell, Director, Texas Department of Criminal Justice, Institutional Division (537 U.S. 322), decided by an 8–1 vote, Feb. 25, 2003; Kennedy wrote the opinion; Thomas dissented.

A Texas death row inmate won a new chance to overturn his sentence on the ground of racial discrimination in the selection of the jury that convicted him of capital murder in a 1986 trial. The ruling held that a federal appeals court misapplied provisions of the 1996 federal habeas corpus overhaul law by denying the African American inmate a "certificate of appealability" to review his claim. The Court held that an inmate need make only a "substantial showing of the denial of a constitutional right" to appeal a lower federal court's dismissal of a habeas corpus petition.

Woodford, Warden v. Garceau (538 U.S. 202), decided by a 6–3 vote, March 25, 2003; Thomas wrote the opinion; Souter, Ginsburg, and Breyer dissented.

A federal habeas corpus petition is subject to the restrictive provisions of a 1996 law if the inmate filed the application for relief after the law's effective date even if he or she had presented other filings earlier. The ruling slightly broadened the effect of the Antiterrorism and Effective Death Penalty Act of 1996, which made it harder for state inmates to use federal habeas corpus to set aside their convictions or sentences.

Price, Warden v. Vincent (538 U.S. 634), decided by a 9–0 vote, May 19, 2003; Rehnquist wrote the opinion.

A Michigan inmate seeking to overturn a first-degree murder conviction on double jeopardy grounds was not entitled to federal habeas corpus relief because the state court decision rejecting his plea was not clearly wrong. The Court held that the case had not met the strict statutory standard for setting aside a state court judgment.

Yarborough, Warden v. Gentry (540 U.S. 1), decided by a 9–0 vote, Oct. 20, 2003; per curiam decision.

A federal appeals court made a mistake in granting a California man's request for a new trial based on finding his defense lawyer's closing argument constitutionally inadequate.

Mitchell, Warden v. Esparza (540 U.S. 12), decided by a 9–0 vote, Nov. 3, 2003; per curiam decision.

A federal appeals court was wrong to order a new trial for an Ohio death row inmate who was convicted as the lone gunman in an armed robbery murder but not specifically charged as the "principal offender" under the state's capital murder statute.

Castro v. United States (540 U.S. 375), decided by a 9–0 vote, Dec. 15, 2003; Breyer wrote the opinion.

A court may not treat a prisoner's effort to set aside a conviction as a request for habeas corpus relief without first warning the defendant that any additional habeas petitions

may not be allowed and giving the prisoner the opportunity to withdraw or amend the motion.

Banks v. Dretke, Director, Texas Department of Criminal Justice, Correctional Institutions Division (540 U.S. 668), decided by a 7–2 vote, Feb. 24, 2004; Ginsburg wrote the opinion; Thomas and Scalia dissented.

The Court overturned a Texas inmate's death sentence by ruling that prosecutors had wrongfully concealed evidence that the defendant's attorneys could have used to discredit two of the witnesses against him.

Banks, who had no prior criminal record, had been only ten minutes away from a scheduled execution on March 12, 2003, when the Court granted his request to stay the death sentence.

Baldwin v. Reese (541 U.S. 27), decided by an 8–1 vote, March 2, 2004; Breyer wrote the opinion; Stevens dissented.

A state prisoner does not fairly present a claim to a state court for federal habeas corpus purposes if that court must read beyond the inmate's petition or brief to identify his or her federal constitutional claim.

Middleton, Warden v. McNeil (541 U.S. 433), decided by a 9–0 vote, May 3, 2004; per curiam opinion.

A federal appeals court made a mistake in throwing out a California woman's second-degree murder conviction because of an erroneous jury instruction that undercut her claim of self-defense for killing her husband.

Pliler, Warden v. Ford (542 U.S. 225), decided by a 7–2 vote, June 21, 2004; Thomas wrote the opinion; Ginsburg and Breyer dissented.

Federal district court judges are not required to advise prison inmates filing habeas corpus petitions how to comply with a one-year deadline when raising claims that first need to be considered in state courts. The complex, somewhat fractured decision set aside a decision by the Ninth U.S. Circuit Court of Appeals and returned the case for a ruling whether the defendant was entitled to more time because he was misled by a magistrate judge's ruling.

The ruling skirted the broader issue posed by the "stay and abeyance procedure" adopted by the Ninth Circuit to deal with the deadline problem in "mixed" habeas petitions with both exhausted and unexhausted claims. Under this procedure, federal district courts were allowed to "stay" a habeas corpus petition and hold it in "abeyance" while the petitioner went to state court with unexhausted claims.

INTERROGATION

Texas v. Cobb (532 U.S. 162), decided by a 5–4 vote, April 2, 2001; Rehnquist wrote the opinion; Breyer, Stevens, Souter, and Ginsburg dissented.

The Court gave police additional leeway to interrogate a criminal defendant without a lawyer present as long as the questioning concerns a charge that is not the same as one already filed in court.

Kaupp v. Texas (538 U.S. 626), decided by a 9–0 vote, May 5, 2003; per curiam opinion.

Texas courts were wrong to allow the use of a confession by a teenaged suspect in a rape-murder case because he was arrested without probable cause and was not shown to have consented to the interrogation. The Court said the confession "must be suppressed" because it resulted from an illegal arrest. The ruling set aside the petitioner's murder conviction and fifty-five-year prison sentence.

Fellers v. United States (540 U.S. 519), decided by a 9–0 vote, Jan. 26, 2004; O'Connor wrote the opinion.

The Court reaffirmed the rule against interrogating a criminal defendant after indictment without a lawyer present. The Court ruled that police had violated the Sixth Amendment by deliberately eliciting information from the petitioner after indictment, outside the presence of counsel, and in the absence of any waiver of his rights. On that basis, the Court sent the case back to the appeals court to decide an issue left open in its previous cases: whether a Sixth Amendment violation requires suppression of later incriminating statements, even if the defendant voluntarily waives the right to counsel.

Yarborough, Warden v. Alvarado (541 U.S. 652), decided by a 5–4 vote, June 1, 2004; Kennedy wrote the opinion; Breyer, Stevens, Souter, and Ginsburg dissented.

State courts did not have to consider a teenaged suspect's age and inexperience with law enforcement in determining whether police needed to give him *Miranda* warnings before interviewing him regarding a murder case.

Missouri v. Seibert (542 U.S. 600), decided by a 5–4 vote, June 28, 2004; Souter wrote the plurality opinion; Kennedy concurred in the judgment; O'Connor, Rehnquist, Scalia, and Thomas dissented.

A suspect's confession obtained on the basis of statements made in an initial interrogation in which police deliberately withheld *Miranda* warnings cannot be used in court unless special steps are taken to cure the failure. The ruling curtailed the use of a two-step interrogation technique said to be increasingly common among police.

The Court issued the decision on the same day as a second, *Miranda*-related ruling, *United States v. Patane.* In that case, the Court voted to permit introduction of a gun found on the basis of a statement made by a suspect without *Miranda* warnings.

United States v. Patane (542 U.S. 630), decided by a 5–4 vote, June 28, 2004; Thomas wrote the plurality opinion; Kennedy and O'Connor concurred in the judgment; Souter, Stevens, Ginsburg, and Breyer dissented.

The Fifth Amendment does not require suppression of physical evidence derived from voluntary statements made at the time of arrest by a suspect who has not been advised of his *Miranda* rights. The ruling upheld the conviction of a man for possession of a firearm following previous felony convictions. Police attempted to advise him of his rights as prescribed by *Miranda v. Arizona* (1966), but he interrupted the officers before they finished, saying that he already knew his rights. He then acquiesced to questioning and told the officers that he had a gun.

The Court ruled the evidence admissible, holding that *Miranda* was a "prophylactic employed to protect against violations of the Self-Incrimination Clause" and that the constitutional protection provided by the rule was not implicated by a suspect's voluntary statements. On that basis, the fruits of such statements were not tainted and could be used against a suspect at trial.

JURY TRIAL

Schriro, Arizona Department of Corrections v. Summerlin (542 U.S. 348), decided by a 5–4 vote, June 24, 2004; Scalia wrote the opinion; Breyer, Ginsburg, Stevens, Souter, and Ginsburg dissented.

A criminal defendant's newly recognized Sixth Amendment right to have a jury determine the aggravating factors leading to a death sentence does not apply retroactively in a case already final on direct review.

PLEA BARGAINING

United States v. Ruiz (536 U.S. 622), decided by a 9–0 vote, June 24, 2002; Breyer wrote the opinion.

Prosecutors do not have to give defendants information that could cast doubt on the credibility of government witnesses during the plea bargaining process.

POSTCONVICTION PROCEDURES

Clay v. United States (537 U.S. 522), decided by a 9–0 vote, March 4, 2003; Ginsburg wrote the opinion.

The one-year time period for a federal prisoner to file a petition for post-conviction relief begins to run when the Supreme Court upholds the conviction or when the time for seeking review with the Court expires. The ruling settled a conflict among federal appeals courts by adopting a somewhat relaxed rule recommended by the government as well as the defendant in the case.

Massaro v. United States (538 U.S. 500), decided by a 9–0 vote, April 23, 2003; Kennedy wrote the opinion.

A defendant may raise a claim of ineffective assistance of counsel in a post-conviction proceeding even if the claim was not raised on direct appeal. In contrast to the normal rule requiring defendants to raise legal challenges on direct appeal, the Court said that ineffective-assistance claims would be litigated most efficiently in a separate proceeding.

Bunkley v. Florida (538 U.S. 835), decided by a 6–3 vote, May 27, 2003; per curiam opinion; Rehnquist, Kennedy, and Thomas dissented.

The Florida Supreme Court was told to reconsider whether a defendant carrying a three-inch knife was improperly convicted of burglary with a dangerous weapon because of a later judicial ruling defining a statutory exception for "common" pocketknives.

PRISONS AND JAILS

Shaw v. Murphy (532 U.S. 223), decided by a 9–0 vote, April 18, 2001; Thomas wrote the opinion.

Prison officials can prevent prisoners from providing legal assistance to other inmates. The Court wrote that it declined "to cloak the provision of legal assistance with any First Amendment protection above and beyond the protection normally accorded prisoners' speech."

Booth v. Churner (532 U.S. 731), decided by a 9–0 vote, May 29, 2001; Souter wrote the opinion.

Prisoners contesting conditions or treatment must exhaust administrative remedies before filing a federal court suit, even if they are seeking relief that cannot be granted through the administrative process. The ruling strictly construed a provision of the Prison Litigation Reform Act of 1995, which requires a prisoner to exhaust "such administrative remedies as are available" before suing over prison conditions.

Porter v. Nussle (534 U.S. 516), decided by a 9–0 vote, Feb. 26, 2002; Ginsburg wrote the opinion.

Prisoners must exhaust administrative grievance procedures before filing any federal suit challenging conditions of their confinement, including allegations of individual mistreatment or abuse.

Overton, Director, Michigan Department of Corrections v. Bazzetta (539 U.S. 126), decided by a 9–0 vote, June 16, 2003; Kennedy wrote the opinion.

The Court upheld restrictions adopted by the State of Michigan on visitation rights for prisoners that barred visits by an inmate's nieces or nephews or an inmate's own children if parental rights have been terminated.

The ruling rejected a class action suit filed by Michigan inmates challenging visitation restrictions, aimed at reducing the overall volume of visitors, that were adopted in 1995 in response to prison overcrowding. The Court held that the visitation restrictions were constitutional because they were rationally connected to legitimate prison interests.

RIGHT TO COUNSEL

Glover v. United States (531 U.S. 198), decided by a 9–0 vote, Jan. 9, 2001; Kennedy wrote the opinion.

Any increase in a defendant's sentence constitutes prejudice for purposes of determining whether a defendant was hurt by ineffective assistance of counsel.

Mickens v. Taylor (535 U.S. 162), decided by a 5–4 vote, March 27, 2002; Scalia wrote the opinion; Breyer, Stevens, Souter, and Ginsburg dissented.

A defendant cannot set aside a conviction because of a conflict of interest on the part of defense counsel unless the conflict is shown to have adversely affected the lawyer's performance at trial.

Alabama v. Shelton (535 U.S. 654), decided by a 5–4 vote, May 20, 2002; Ginsburg wrote the opinion; Scalia, Rehnquist, Kennedy, and Thomas dissented.

An indigent criminal defendant must be provided a court-appointed lawyer before being given a suspended jail sentence. The ruling extended previous right to counsel decisions that covered all felony cases and any misdemeanor cases that resulted in imprisonment.

Wiggins v. Smith, Warden (539 U.S. 510), decided by a 7–2 vote, June 26, 2003; O'Connor wrote the opinion; Scalia and Thomas dissented.

The Court threw out a Maryland man's death sentence because his two public defenders failed to uncover a long history of physical and sexual abuse that could have been used as mitigating evidence in his trial. The decision appeared to ease somewhat the hurdles that death row inmates face in using federal habeas corpus to overturn state court death sentences on grounds of ineffective assistance by counsel.

Holland, Warden v. Jackson (542 U.S. 649), decided by a 5–4 vote, June 28, 2004; per curiam opinion; Stevens, Souter, Ginsburg, and Breyer dissented.

The Court ruled that a federal appeals court misapplied the U.S. Supreme Court standard for ineffective assistance of counsel set forth in *Strickland v. Washington* (1984) in reversing a Tennessee man's 1987 murder conviction on grounds of ineffective assistance of counsel.

SEARCH AND SEIZURE

City of Indianapolis v. Edmond (531 U.S. 32), decided by a 6–3 vote, Nov. 28, 2000; O'Connor wrote the opinion; Rehnquist, Scalia, and Thomas dissented.

A highway checkpoint program primarily aimed at discovering illegal drugs violates the Fourth Amendment's prohibition against unreasonable seizures. The ruling invalidated a highway checkpoint program instituted by the city of Indianapolis in 1998 under which police stopped motorists, checked for license and registration, and used drug-sniffing dogs during the stop to look for illegal narcotics.

Illinois v. McArthur (531 U.S. 326), decided by an 8–1 vote, Feb. 20, 2001; Breyer wrote the opinion; Stevens dissented.

Police can prevent a drug suspect from reentering his home and possibly destroying drugs inside the house if they have probable cause and are acting without undue delay to obtain a search warrant.

SEARCH AND SEIZURE

The right of the people to be secure in their person, houses, papers and effects, against unreasonable searches and seizures, shall not be violated, and no warrants shall issue but upon probable cause, supported by oath or affirmation and particularly describing the place to be searched, and the persons or things to be seized.

Fourth Amendment, U.S. Constitution

Arkansas v. Sullivan (532 U.S. 769), decided by a 9–0 vote, May 29, 2001; per curiam opinion.

The Arkansas Supreme Court was wrong to suppress drugs found in an automobile search because it deemed the motorist's arrest for a routine traffic offense to have been a pretext. The Court said the Arkansas tribunal's decision was "flatly contrary" to an earlier ruling, *Whren v. United States* (1996), that a police officer's subjective intent is irrelevant to judging the legality of a search. The Court also rejected the Arkansas court's ruling that it was free to interpret the U.S. Constitution more broadly than the justices were.

Florida v. Thomas (532 U.S. 774), decided by a 9–0 vote, June 4, 2001; Rehnquist wrote the opinion.

The Court failed to decide whether police can search a car after arresting a driver who has already left the vehicle.

Under a 1981 Court ruling, *New York v. Belton,* police can search a car incident to a lawful arrest. But the Florida Supreme Court ruled that *Belton* did not apply because the defendant had already gotten out of his car when officers placed him under arrest. The Court agreed to hear the state's appeal to decide whether to extend its prior ruling but ruled that it had no jurisdiction to hear the case because the state court's ruling was not final.

Kyllo v. United States (533 U.S. 27), decided by a 5–4 vote, June 11, 2001; Scalia wrote the opinion; Stevens, Rehnquist, O'Connor, and Kennedy dissented.

Police need a search warrant before using a high-tech infrared sensing device to detect heat patterns inside a home. The ruling sustained a Fourth Amendment challenge brought by an Oregon man, Danny Kyllo, who was charged with manufacturing marijuana after federal law enforcement officers used a "thermal imaging device" pointed at his house from a car parked on the street to locate an indoor marijuana-growing operation in his home.

United States v. Knights (534 U.S.), decided by a 9–0 vote, Dec. 10, 2001; Rehnquist wrote the opinion.

Police do not need a warrant to search someone on probation if they have reasonable suspicion of criminal activity and the individual has agreed to submit to a search as a condition of probation.

United States v. Arvizu (534 U.S. 266), decided by a 9–0 vote, Jan. 15, 2002; Rehnquist wrote the opinion.

Lower courts should consider all factors in determining whether law enforcement agents had reasonable grounds for an automobile stop or search.

United States v. Drayton (536 U.S. 194), decided by a 6–3 vote, June 17, 2002; Kennedy wrote the opinion; Souter, Stevens, and Ginsburg dissented.

Police looking for drugs or weapons can ask bus passengers for permission to search their persons or belongings without first informing them of their right not to cooperate.

The ruling reinstated federal cocaine distribution charges against two men who were arrested following a search while they were traveling on an intercity bus en route to Detroit. Three plainclothes police officers boarded the bus during a scheduled stop as part of a routine drug and weapons interdiction effort. The Court ruled that the officers' action did not amount to a seizure of the bus passengers and that Drayton and Brown had voluntarily consented to be searched.

Kirk v. Louisiana (536 U.S. 635), decided by a 9–0 vote, June 24, 2002; per curiam opinion.

A Louisiana man won a new chance to suppress drugs found on his person during a warrantless arrest inside his apartment because state courts did not determine whether police had "exigent circumstances" to justify their actions.

United States v. Banks (540 U.S. 31), decided by a 9–0 vote, Dec. 2, 2003; Souter wrote the opinion.

Police officers conducting a lawful search can forcibly enter a residence fifteen to twenty seconds after knocking if they have reasonable grounds to believe that delay would allow destruction of evidence. The Court held that the officers' wait satisfied the Fourth Amendment's requirement of reasonableness.

Maryland v. Pringle (540 U.S. 366), decided by a 9–0 vote, Dec. 15, 2003; Rehnquist wrote the opinion.

Police officers can arrest all the occupants of a car if illegal drugs are found anywhere in the vehicle, even if none of the passengers admits ownership of the substances.

Illinois v. Lidster (540 U.S. 419), decided by a 6–3 vote, Jan. 13, 2004; Breyer wrote the opinion; Stevens, Souter, and Ginsburg dissented in part.

Police can arrest a motorist based on evidence obtained at a highway checkpoint if the main purpose of the stop is to elicit information about a crime in all likelihood committed by someone else.

United States v. Flores-Montano (541 U.S. 149), decided by a 9–0 vote, March 30, 2004; Rehnquist wrote the opinion.

Government agents trying to stop drug smuggling at the border can dismantle and search a vehicle's fuel tank without reasonable suspicion that the owner is transporting any illegal substances.

Thornton v. United States (541 U.S. 615), decided by a 7–2 vote, May 24, 2004; Rehnquist wrote the opinion; Stevens and Souter dissented.

Police can search the entire passenger compartment of an automobile after arresting the driver or other occupant even if police first encounter the person arrested outside the vehicle.

The Court extended its ruling in *New York v. Belton* (1981), which said that police could search the passenger compartment of a car after arresting an occupant of the vehicle to protect an officer's safety and to preserve evidence for trial. The 1981 law also permitted automobile searches conducted after an individual is arrested while outside the vehicle.

Hiibel v. Sixth Judicial District Court of Nevada, Humboldt County (542 U.S. 177), decided by a 5–4 vote, June 21, 2004; Kennedy wrote the opinion; Breyer, Stevens, Souter, and Ginsburg dissented.

A state law authorizing police to demand identification from an individual stopped under reasonable suspicion of being involved in a crime is valid under the Fourth and Fifth Amendments. The ruling upheld Nevada's "stop and identify" statute, which empowered police to stop an individual who they reasonably suspect "has committed, is committing or is about to commit a crime."

SELECTIVE PROSECUTION

United States v. Bass (536 U.S. 862), decided by a 9–0 vote, June 28, 2002; per curiam opinion.

A Michigan murder defendant claiming racial discrimination in the federal government's selection of death penalty cases presented too little evidence for a court order to examine prosecutors' files to gather evidence to support his claim.

SELF-INCRIMINATION

Ohio v. Reiner (532 U.S. 17), decided by a 9–0 vote, March 19, 2001; per curiam opinion.

A witness who denies any involvement in a crime may nonetheless invoke the Fifth Amendment's privilege against self-incrimination in refusing to answer questions about the incident.

SENTENCING

Lopez v. Davis, Warden (531 U.S. 230), decided by a 6–3 vote, Jan. 10, 2001; Ginsburg wrote the opinion; Stevens, Rehnquist, and Kennedy dissented.

The federal Bureau of Prisons may bar drug offenders convicted of using a firearm in connection with their crime from winning reduced sentences by completing a drug treatment program. The ruling upheld a regulation issued by the Bureau of Prisons in 1997 under a federal law passed in 1990 requiring the bureau to provide drug abuse treatment programs.

Buford v. United States (532 U.S. 59), decided by a 9–0 vote, March 20, 2001; Breyer wrote the opinion.

Federal appeals courts should defer to trial judges' rulings in interpreting the career offender provision in the federal Sentencing Guidelines that allows for a stiffer sentence based on a defendant's prior criminal convictions. The career offender provision requires at least two prior convictions for violent felonies and stipulates that any "related" counts be treated as a single conviction.

Daniels v. United States (532 U.S. 374), decided by a 5–4 vote, April 25, 2001; O'Connor wrote the opinion; Souter, Stevens, Ginsburg, and Breyer dissented.

A federal prisoner may not use the post-conviction procedure for correcting sentences to attack the constitutionality of prior state convictions used to enhance the sentence.

Previously, the Court ruled in a 1994 decision, *Custis v. United States,* that federal prisoners could not use federal habeas corpus to challenge prior convictions used to increase sentences. The Court held that—with limited exceptions— federal defendants cannot challenge the validity of prior state convictions through federal post-conviction remedies.

Lackawanna County District Attorney v. Coss (532 U.S. 394), decided by a 5–4 vote, April 25, 2001; O'Connor wrote the opinion; Souter, Stevens, Ginsburg, and Breyer dissented.

A state prisoner cannot use federal habeas corpus to challenge the validity of prior state convictions used to enhance a sentence for a new offense. The Court said the ruling was based on the same grounds as the decision issued the same day, *Daniels v. United States,* that limited the ability of federal defendants to challenge prior convictions used to increase sentences.

Harris v. United States (536 U.S. 545), decided by a 5–4 vote, June 24, 2002; Kennedy wrote the plurality opinion; Thomas, Stevens, Souter, and Ginsburg dissented.

Judges may make factual determinations needed to raise a defendant's minimum sentence for an offense as long as the facts are sentencing factors rather than elements of the crime.

The Court ruled that judges may increase a minimum sentence on the basis of sentencing factors neither included in the indictment nor proven at trial. The ruling upheld judges' roles in handing out graduated mandatory minimum sentences.

Ewing v. California (538 U.S. 11), decided by a 5–4 vote, March 5, 2003; O'Connor wrote the plurality opinion; Scalia and Thomas concurred in the judgment; Breyer, Stevens, Souter, and Ginsburg dissented.

A sentence of twenty-five years to life imprisonment for grand theft imposed on a defendant with four prior felony convictions did not amount to cruel and unusual punishment under the Eighth Amendment.

The ruling rejected a constitutional attack on California's controversial "three-strikes law," the most severe of laws enacted in many states in the 1990s imposing increased prison terms on repeat offenders—so-called recidivists. The law provided that a defendant with two prior "serious" or "violent" felony convictions be given an indeterminate sentence of life imprisonment upon a third conviction for a qualifying felony. A prisoner serving a life sentence under the law was ineligible for parole until having served twenty-five years.

Lockyer, Attorney General of California v. Andrade (538 U.S. 63), decided by a 5–4 vote, March 5, 2003; O'Connor wrote the opinion; Souter, Stevens, Ginsburg, and Breyer dissented.

The Court rejected a federal habeas corpus challenge to a life prison sentence imposed under California's "three-strikes" law on a repeat offender after he was convicted of stealing about $160 worth of videotapes. The ruling rejected a claim that the defendant's life sentence for two counts of petty theft amounted to cruel and unusual punishment under the Eighth Amendment.

Dretke, Director, Texas Department of Criminal Justice, Correctional Institutions Division v. Haley (541 U.S. 386), decided by a 6–3 vote, May 3, 2004; O'Connor wrote the opinion; Stevens, Kennedy, and Souter dissented.

Having agreed to hear this case to decide whether to expand the innocence rule to noncapital sentences, the Court sidestepped a decision on whether to allow use of federal habeas corpus petitions to correct sentences in noncapital cases resulting from constitutional defects not previously raised in state courts.

The ruling permitted a Texas man to use an alternate legal claim to try to throw out a sixteen-year sentence as a three-time loser that was belatedly discovered to be erroneous under state law. Texas law allows an enhanced prison term as a habitual offender for a defendant upon a third felony conviction if the second prior felony was committed after the first prior conviction became final. The ruling went beyond a previous Supreme Court decision, *Sawyer v. Whitley* (1992), which had allowed an innocence claim to excuse a procedural default in death penalty cases.

Blakely v. Washington (542 U.S. 296), decided by a 5–4 vote, June 24, 2004; Scalia wrote the opinion; O'Connor, Rehnquist, Kennedy, and Breyer dissented.

Any facts necessary to raise a defendant's sentence above the standard statutory maximum for the offense, other than a prior conviction, must be found by a jury, not by a judge alone. The ruling cast doubt on sentencing procedures in many states as well as the Federal Sentencing Guidelines.

SEXUAL OFFENDERS

Kansas v. Crane (534 U.S. 407), decided by a 7–2 vote, Jan. 22, 2002; Breyer wrote the opinion; Scalia and Thomas dissented.

A sexual offender cannot be civilly committed to a mental hospital after finishing his or her criminal sentence unless the state shows the person has "serious difficulty" controlling his or her behavior.

The ruling sent back to Kansas courts an effort by a twice-convicted sex offender to set aside a civil commitment order issued after he completed a sentence for aggravated sexual battery. The Kansas Sexually Violent Predator Act of 1994 permitted civil detention of a person convicted of any of several specified sexual offenses if the state showed beyond a reasonable doubt that the offender suffered from a "mental abnormality" or "personality disorder" that made it likely that he or she would engage in repeated acts of sexual violence. The law was ruled unconstitutional by the Kansas Supreme Court but reinstated by the U.S. Supreme Court in a 1997 decision, *Kansas v. Hendricks* (521 U.S. 346).

McKune v. Lile (536 U.S. 24), decided by a 5–4 vote, June 10, 2002; Kennedy wrote the plurality opinion; Stevens, Souter, Ginsburg, and Breyer dissented.

Sex offenders can be denied prison privileges for refusing to participate in treatment programs that require them to admit all past sex-related offenses, including any that had not resulted in convictions or charges. The ruling rejected a claim by a Kansas man that his loss of privileges for refusing to acknowledge past offenses violated his Fifth Amendment freedom against self-incrimination.

Connecticut Department of Public Safety v. Doe (538 U.S. 1), decided by a 9–0 vote, March 5, 2003; Rehnquist wrote the opinion.

A convicted sex offender subject to a mandatory registration law has no constitutional right to a hearing to prove that he is not currently dangerous to be exempted from the law.

The ruling rejected a limited constitutional challenge to Connecticut's sex offender registry law under the procedural requirements of the Constitution's Due Process Clause. The statute required convicted sex offenders to register with law enforcement authorities and provide current information about their residence and employment. An unidentified sex offender challenged the Connecticut law on the ground that it failed to provide a hearing for him to show that he was not dangerous and should be exempted from the requirement. The Court rejected the due process claim and ruled that the law could go into effect but noted that the law could still be challenged as a violation of "substantive due process."

Smith v. Doe (538 U.S. 84), decided by a 6–3 vote, March 5, 2003; Kennedy wrote the opinion; Stevens, Ginsburg, and Breyer dissented.

A state law requiring previously convicted sex offenders to register with law enforcement authorities and provide current information about their residence and employment does not amount to retroactive punishment in violation of the Constitution's Ex Post Facto Clause because it was not punitive in intent or effect.

The ruling rejected a constitutional challenge by two unidentified sex offenders to a 1994 Alaska law that is comparable to ones enacted by Congress and in all fifty states and the District of Columbia. The so-called Megan's laws generally required convicted sex offenders to register with law enforcement authorities and provide current contact information; the states made much of the information available to the public, often, as in Alaska's case, on the Internet. The laws were named after a New Jersey girl, Megan Kanka, who was sexually assaulted and murdered by a neighbor who, unbeknownst to her family, was a convicted sex offender.

Election Law

CAMPAIGN FINANCE

Federal Election Commission v. Colorado Republican Federal Campaign Committee (533 U.S. 431), decided by a 5–4 vote, June 25, 2001; Souter wrote the opinion; Thomas, Rehnquist, Scalia, and Kennedy dissented.

A federal law limiting the amount of money that a political party can spend in coordination with a candidate for Congress does not violate the party's First Amendment freedom of speech.

The ruling upheld one of the provisions of the Watergate-era campaign finance law against a constitutional challenge pressed by the Republican Party in connection with a 1986 Senate race in Colorado. The law limited contributions by a national or state party committee to a Senate candidate to either $20,000, later adjusted for inflation, or two cents multiplied by the state's voting-age population, whichever was greater. The law further defined as a contribution any "expenditures" made in cooperation with or at the request of a candidate or his or her campaign. The Court ruled the party expenditure provision was constitutional because it served to minimize circumvention of the law's limits on campaign contributions by individuals.

Federal Election Commission v. Beaumont (539 U.S. 146), decided by a 7–2 vote, June 16, 2003; Souter wrote the opinion; Thomas and Scalia dissented.

Nonprofit advocacy corporations can be prohibited from making campaign contributions to federal candidates except through separate political action committees.

The ruling rejected a challenge by a state antiabortion organization, North Carolina Right for Life, Inc. (NCRL), to a broad application of the long-standing ban on direct corporate contributions to federal candidates. The ban, first enacted in 1907, was later amended to allow a corporation to establish and solicit contributions for a "separate segregated fund" for political purposes—a political action committee. NCRL filed a federal court suit in North Carolina contesting the application of the law to nonprofit advocacy groups, relying in part on the U.S. Supreme Court's decision in *Federal Election Commission v. Massachusetts Citizens for Life, Inc.,* 479 U.S. 238 (1986), which allowed corporations to make unlimited independent expenditures in connection with federal elections.

The Court held that the ban on direct campaign contributions by nonprofit corporate advocacy groups did not violate the First Amendment's protections for political speech.

McConnell, United States Senator v. Federal Election Commission (540 U.S. 93), decided by a 5–4 vote on major issues, Dec. 10, 2003; Stevens and O'Connor wrote the main opinion; Rehnquist and Breyer wrote opinions for the Court on secondary issues; Rehnquist, Scalia, Kennedy, and Thomas wrote opinions dissenting on the major issues.

The Court largely upheld the constitutionality of a major overhaul of federal campaign finance law that sharply restricted the raising of unlimited soft money—funds contributed to political parties ostensibly for general party-building purposes instead of for specific campaigns—and limited the ability of corporations and labor unions to run election-time issue advertising on radio or television.

The ruling, issued over strong dissents from four conservative justices, kept intact all but two minor provisions of the Bipartisan Campaign Reform Act of 2002, more commonly known as the McCain-Feingold Act, after its principal Senate sponsors (Sens. John McCain, R-Ariz., and Russell D. Feingold, D-Wis.). The act was designed to close two major gaps in federal law setting limits on contributions and expenditures for presidential or congressional campaigns.

The ruling was the Court's most extensive treatment of campaign finance issues since its landmark decision *Buckley v. Valeo* (1976), which upheld the post-Watergate Federal Election Campaign Amendments of 1974. In that ruling, the Court upheld limits on campaign contributions but struck down on First Amendment grounds limits on campaign expenditures.

CONGRESSIONAL ELECTIONS

Cook v. Gralike (531 U.S. 510), decided by a 9–0 vote, Feb. 28, 2001; Stevens wrote the opinion.

A Missouri initiative aimed at penalizing congressional candidates for failing to support term limits went beyond the state's constitutional authority to regulate elections for Congress.

The ruling, invalidating a 1996 initiative approved by Missouri voters as an amendment to the state constitution, represented the Court's second blow to the flagging term limits movement. In 1995 the Court ruled in *U.S. Term Limits, Inc. v. Thornton* that states had no power to prescribe service limits for members of Congress except by amending the

U.S. Constitution. In response, several states passed "informed voter provisions" aimed at showing a congressional candidate's position on term limits on the ballot. The Missouri initiative specified that members of Congress be instructed to support a term limits amendment and that lawmakers who failed to follow the instruction be identified on the ballot as having "disregarded voters' instructions on term limits."

The Court said the amendment could not be justified under the states' power to regulate congressional elections under the Elections Clause or under the powers reserved to the states by the Tenth Amendment.

ELECTORAL COLLEGE

Bush v. Palm Beach County Canvassing Board (531 U.S. 70), decided by a 9–0 vote, Dec. 4, 2000; per curiam opinion.

The Court gave Republican presidential candidate George W. Bush a boost in his fight with Democrat Al Gore for Florida's twenty-five electoral votes but failed to resolve the legal issue in the dispute.

The ruling set aside the Florida Supreme Court's decision extending the deadline to certify the popular vote winner in the Nov. 7 voting—as Gore had urged and Bush had opposed. Bush had a small margin over Gore in unofficial totals, but Gore wanted to extend the time for the state's elections canvassing board to certify the winner to allow for manual recounts of ballots in several counties. The Florida Supreme Court extended the deadline from Nov. 14 to Nov. 26. Bush challenged that decision before the U.S. Supreme Court, saying it violated provisions of the U.S. Constitution and federal election law regarding selection of states' presidential electors. In particular, Bush claimed the altered timetable amounted to a court-ordered change in law that infringed the legislature's prerogatives to determine the procedures for choosing presidential electors under Article II of the Constitution. He also argued that the change was contrary to an 1887 law, the Electoral Vote Count Act, which gave legal protection to a state's certification of electors if made at least six days prior to the prescribed date for electors to cast their votes.

The Court set aside the Florida court's ruling because of what it called "considerable uncertainty about the precise grounds for the decisions." Specifically, the Court said it was "unclear as to the extent to which the Florida Supreme Court saw the Florida Constitution as circumscribing the legislature's authority." The Court also said it was "unclear as to the consideration" that the Florida court gave to the federal statute. The ruling sent the case back to the Florida Supreme Court for further proceedings. The dispute returned to the Court after the Florida high court acted in a separate legal proceeding to require a statewide recount level.

Bush v. Gore (531 U.S. 98), decided by a 5–4 vote, Dec. 12, 2000; per curiam opinion; Stevens, Souter, Ginsburg, and Breyer dissented.

The Court halted a state court-ordered recount of the presidential vote in Florida, saying that the use of varying standards for counting previously untabulated votes violated due process and equal protection requirements.

The ruling effectively clinched the 2000 presidential election for Republican Bush over Democrat Gore by blocking Gore's effort to overcome Bush's certified 930–vote margin in Florida's popular vote. Either candidate needed the state's twenty-five electoral votes to have a majority in the electoral college. Gore filed an election contest suit under Florida law and asked for a recount of punch-card ballots that had not been read as valid votes during the initial machine counts. A lower state court judge rejected Gore's request, but the Florida Supreme Court, by a 4–3 vote, ruled in his favor and ordered a recount to begin on Dec. 9.

Bush's lawyers asked the U.S. Supreme Court to stay the order, saying the recount violated federal constitutional and statutory provisions regarding the selection of presidential electors. Bush also argued that the lower court judge's decision to allow county election boards to set their own standards in counting the previously uncounted ballots violated the Due Process and Equal Protection clauses of the Fourteenth Amendment. The Supreme Court stayed the ordered recount on Dec. 9 and scheduled oral arguments for Monday, Dec. 11.

In a 5–4 decision issued late the next day, the Court held that the recount did not satisfy "rudimentary requirements of equal treatment and fundamental fairness" and could not be completed before the Dec. 12 date prescribed under federal law for states to complete selection of presidential electors.

JUDICIAL ELECTIONS

Republican Party of Minnesota v. White (536 U.S. 765), decided by a 5–4 vote, June 27, 2002; Scalia wrote the opinion; Ginsburg, Stevens, Souter, and Breyer dissented.

State judicial ethics rules prohibiting incumbent judges or judicial candidates from announcing positions on legal or political issues while campaigning violate the First Amendment's Freedom of Speech Clause because it improperly advances the state's interest in the impartiality of the judiciary.

The ruling invalidated a canon of the Minnesota Code of Judicial Conduct—known as the Announce Clause—comparable to provisions in a majority of the thirty-one states with contested elections for some or all state court judges. The provision, drawn from the American Bar Association's Model Code of Judicial Conduct, provided that a candidate for judicial offices, including an incumbent judge, shall not "announce his or her view on disputed legal or political issues."

REAPPORTIONMENT AND REDISTRICTING

Sinkfield v. Kelley (531 U.S. 28), decided by a 9–0 vote, Nov. 27, 2000; per curiam opinion.

Voters cannot challenge a legislative redistricting plan as an illegal racial gerrymander unless they show that they were assigned to a particular district because of their race. The ruling threw out a suit challenging an Alabama legislative redistricting plan brought by white voters who lived in majority-white districts adjacent to newly created majority-black districts.

Hunt, Governor of North Carolina v. Cromartie (532 U.S. 234), decided by a 5–4 vote, April 18, 2001; Breyer wrote the opinion; Thomas, Rehnquist, Scalia, and Kennedy dissented.

Plaintiffs challenging a redistricting plan on racial grounds must show that the legislature had other ways to achieve legitimate political objectives that would have resulted in significantly greater racial balance than the plan being attacked. The ruling—the Court's fourth decision in a decade-long dispute—upheld a North Carolina congressional redistricting scheme that included a heavily African American district embracing parts of three widely separated cities in the center of the state.

Branch v. Smith (538 U.S. 254), decided by a 7–2 vote, March 31, 2003; Scalia wrote the opinion; O'Connor and Thomas dissented in part.

The Court upheld a federal court's decision to reject a congressional redistricting plan drawn up by a Mississippi state court because it had not been precleared as required by the federal Voting Rights Act. It went on also to approve the federal court's decision to draw up its own districting scheme instead of requiring at-large elections in the state. The ruling upheld a plan, favored by Republicans and opposed by Democrats, that became necessary when Mississippi lost one seat in the House of Representatives as a result of the 2000 census.

Georgia v. Ashcroft, Attorney General (539 U.S. 461), decided by a 5–4 vote, June 26, 2003; O'Connor wrote the opinion; Souter, Stevens, Ginsburg, and Breyer dissented.

States subject to the federal Voting Rights Act have flexibility to reduce the number of blacks in legislative districts the majority of whose voters are members of minorities if they offset the reduced voting strength with gains in minority groups' political influence elsewhere.

The ruling tentatively backed a redistricting plan for the state senate in Georgia, one of the states subject to the Voting Rights Act because of past discrimination. The plan was backed by Democrats and opposed by Republicans and the George W. Bush administration. The Democratic-written plan, adopted in 2001, spread black voters from overwhelmingly black districts into adjoining districts, with the expressed hope that the increased black population in those "influence" or "coalition" districts would help elect Democratic candidates.

Vieth v. Jubelirer, President of the Pennsylvania Senate (541 U.S. 267), decided by a 5–4 vote, April 28, 2004; Scalia wrote the plurality opinion; Kennedy concurred in the judgment; Stevens, Souter, Ginsburg, and Breyer dissented.

The Court rejected a challenge by Democratic voters to Pennsylvania's Republican-drawn congressional redistricting and came one vote short of completely barring constitutional challenges to partisan gerrymanders in federal courts.

The ruling left in place a new map of House districts that helped Republicans gain a 12–7 majority of Pennsylvania's congressional delegation in the 2002 elections. Democratic voters challenged the plan in federal court, claiming that population variations between some of the districts violated the "one-person, one-vote" standard. They also said the overall plan amounted to an unconstitutional partisan gerrymander under the Supreme Court's 1986 decision *Davis v. Bandemer*.

The Supreme Court upheld the redistricting plan by a 5–4 vote, with four of the justices saying they would overturn the earlier decision and rule all challenges to partisan gerrymanders "nonjusticiable" or beyond courts' authority to decide.

Environmental Law

AIR POLLUTION

Whitman, Administrator of Environmental Protection Agency v. American Trucking Associations, Inc. (531 U.S. 457), decided by a 9–0 vote, Feb. 27, 2001; Scalia wrote the opinion.

The Environmental Protection Agency (EPA) may not consider compliance costs in setting national air-quality standards under the Clean Air Act. The ruling in this complex regulatory case also rejected a challenge that the EPA had improperly exercised legislative authority in 1997 in revising air standards for smog and soot.

The decision represented a double-barreled defeat for industry groups and a significant victory for environmental organizations and the EPA itself. But the Court also ruled that the agency exceeded its statutory authority in one part of the regulations that tightened standards and deadlines for "nonattainment areas" that had not complied with existing smog standards.

Alaska Department of Environmental Conservation v. Environmental Protection Agency (540 U.S. 461), decided by a 5–4 vote, Jan. 21, 2004; Ginsburg wrote the opinion; Kennedy, Rehnquist, Scalia, and Thomas dissented.

The Environmental Protection Agency (EPA) can override a state agency's decision on what air pollution control technology to require for new factories or power plants. The ruling, upholding the EPA's authority under a major provision of the Clean Air Act, sustained the federal agency's decision to block a permit for a new electricity-generating plant at a major mining operation in Alaska's Arctic Circle region.

Engine Manufacturers Association v. South Coast Air Quality Management District (541 U.S. 246), decided by an 8–1 vote, April 28, 2004; Scalia wrote the opinion; Souter dissented.

The federal Clean Air Act preempts local regulations prohibiting the purchase of private fleet vehicles in Southern California that fail to meet emission requirements stricter than federal standards.

The ruling overturned the decisions of two lower federal courts upholding the Fleet Rules, which were established by the South Coast Air Quality Management District, the California subdivision responsible for air pollution control in the Los Angeles metropolitan area. The Fleet Rules prohibited public and private fleet vehicle operators from purchasing or leasing vehicles that failed to meet the rigorous emission specifications promulgated by the California Air Resources Board.

The ruling sent the case back to lower courts to determine which parts of the rules were and which were not preempted.

ENVIRONMENTAL IMPACT STATEMENTS

Department of Transportation v. Public Citizen (541 U.S. 752), decided by a 9–0 vote, June 7, 2004; Thomas wrote the opinion.

U.S. agency rules governing the cross-border operations of Mexican trucks, made pursuant to a presidential foreign-affairs action, are exempt from federal environmental-review requirements.

The ruling upheld the operating rules for Mexican trucks established in March 2002 by the Federal Motor Carrier Safety Administration, an arm of the U.S. Department of Transportation. The Court ruled that the agency did not have to consider the environmental effects of allowing Mexican trucks to enter the United States because it had no power to prevent the cross-border operations.

PUBLIC LANDS

Norton, Secretary of the Interior v. Southern Utah Wilderness Alliance (542 U.S. 55), decided by a 9–0 vote, June 14, 2004; Scalia wrote the opinion.

Federal courts have no authority to order the federal Bureau of Land Management (BLM) to bar off-road vehicles from areas being studied for wilderness protections.

The ruling effectively threw out a suit by wilderness protection groups contesting BLM's failure to bar off-road vehicles (ORVs) from about 3.3 million acres of public lands in southern Utah that had been designated as "wilderness study areas" under the Federal Land Policy and Management Act of 1976. The law required BLM, an agency within the U.S. Interior Department, to manage wilderness study areas "in a manner so as not to impair the suitability of such areas for preservation as wilderness."

Southern Utah Wilderness Alliance and other wilderness protection groups filed a federal court suit in 1999 under the Administrative Procedure Act seeking to force BLM to prohibit use of off-road vehicles. The Court held that the Administrative Procedure Act could not be used to require BLM to protect wilderness study areas from off-road vehicle use.

WATER POLLUTION

South Florida Water Management District v. Miccosukee Tribe of Indians (541 U.S. 95), decided by an 8–1 vote, March 23, 2004; O'Connor wrote the opinion; Scalia dissented.

Pumping stations that convey pollutants from one body of water to another are subject to the permit requirements of the Clean Water Act even if they are not the source of the pollution.

The limited ruling in a case involving the pumping of water from residential and agricultural areas in South Florida into the Everglades left unresolved larger questions that could also affect water transfers in the West. Specifically, the Court told the federal appeals court that heard the case to consider the George W. Bush administration's argument that all navigable waters in the United States should be viewed as a unitary whole and that no permit is required for transfers between different bodies of water.

WETLANDS

Solid Waste Agency of Northern Cook County v. United States Army Corps of Engineers (531 U.S. 159), decided by a 5–4 vote, Jan. 9, 2001; Rehnquist wrote the opinion; Stevens, Souter, Ginsburg, and Breyer dissented.

In a major setback for wetland protection advocates, the Court ruled that the Army Corps of Engineers has no authority under the Clean Water Act to regulate isolated ponds or wetlands that are not navigable or adjacent to navigable waterways.

Borden Ranch Partnership v. U.S. Army Corps of Engineers (537 U.S. 99), decided by a 4–4 vote, Dec. 16, 2002; per curiam opinion; Kennedy did not participate.

A deadlocked Court upheld a $500,000 fine levied by the U.S. Army Corps of Engineers for violation of provisions of the Clean Water Act that require a person to obtain a permit before filling or dredging a waterway.

A California developer was charged with 358 violations between 1993 and 1997 for "deep ripping"—a process involving heavy bulldozers dragging five-foot-long plow shanks through soil to allow water to penetrate deep enough for plants with long roots—about two acres of wetlands on a Central Valley ranch while converting pasture to vineyards and orchards.

Federal Government

CENSUS

Utah v. Evans (536 U.S. 452), decided by a 5–4 vote, June 20, 2002; Breyer wrote the opinion; O'Connor, Scalia, Kennedy, and Thomas dissented.

The Census Bureau can use a statistical technique called "hot-deck imputation" to fill in gaps in the decennial population count that determines the number of seats each state has in the House of Representatives. The ruling rejected a statutory and constitutional challenge to the 2000 census filed by the State of Utah in an effort to gain an additional House seat at the expense of the State of North Carolina.

FEDERAL EMPLOYEES

Postal Service v. Gregory (534 U.S. 1), decided by a 9–0 vote, Nov. 13, 2001; O'Connor wrote the opinion.

The agency that reviews disciplinary actions against federal employees may consider prior infractions by a worker even if the employee is still challenging the charges. The ruling rejected an argument by a fired U.S. Postal Service worker that the Merit Systems Protection Board could not consider pending charges in deciding whether to uphold a disciplinary action. The Court held that the board had "broad discretion" in determining how to review prior disciplinary actions. The ruling sent the case back to the appeals court because one of the prior charges had been set aside in arbitration while the appeal was proceeding.

FEDERAL JUDGES

United States v. Hatter, Judge, United States District Court for the Central District of California (532 U.S. 557), decided by 7–0 and 5–2 votes, May 21, 2001; Breyer wrote the opinion; Scalia and Thomas dissented in part; Stevens and O'Connor did not participate.

The Court upheld Congress's decision in 1982 to extend the Medicare tax to sitting federal judges but ruled the imposition of Social Security taxes one year later violated judges' constitutional protection against reductions in pay while in office.

The decision split the difference in a suit by sixteen federal judges who claimed that the imposition of the Medicare and Social Security taxes on judges along with other federal employees violated the Constitution's Compensation Clause, which guarantees federal judges a "compensation, which shall not be diminished during their continuance in office." The Court ruled that the Social Security levy amounted to an improper reduction in sitting judges' pay but upheld the imposition of the Medicare tax.

As an initial matter, the Court overruled an old ruling, *Evans v. Gore* (1920), that had barred the imposition of a newly enacted federal income tax on sitting judges. On that basis, the Court said the extension of the Medicare tax to sitting judges was constitutional.

FEDERAL REGULATION

Buckman Co. v. Plaintiffs' Legal Committee (531 U.S. 341), decided by a 9–0 vote, Feb. 21, 2001; Rehnquist wrote the opinion; Stevens and Thomas dissented.

Federal law preempts state courts from hearing claims based on alleged fraud against the Food and Drug Administration in obtaining approval to market medical devices. The ruling threw out a class action suit brought in federal court under a state law claim by more than five thousand people for injuries allegedly resulting from the use of a bone screw in orthopedic operations.

Lorillard Tobacco Co. v. Reilly, Attorney General of Massachusetts (533 U.S. 525), decided by a 5–4 vote, June 28, 2001; O'Connor wrote the opinion; Stevens, Souter, Ginsburg, and Breyer dissented.

The federal cigarette labeling law precludes state and local governments from regulating for health reasons the content or location of cigarette advertising. The decision also held that Massachusetts's regulations for cigarette, smokeless tobacco, and cigar advertising violated the First Amendment.

The ruling invalidated all but a minor part of sweeping restrictions that the Massachusetts attorney general imposed on tobacco advertising in 1999. The regulations—issued under the attorney general's authority to define "unfair or deceptive" trade practices—prohibited any outdoor advertising for tobacco products within one thousand feet of a school or playground. They also prohibited any in-store displays less than five feet from the floor in stores located within one thousand feet of a school or playground. And they prohibited self-service displays of cigarettes or other tobacco products in any retail establishment.

National Cable & Telecommunications Association, Inc. v. Gulf Power Co. (534 U.S. 327), decided by 6–2 and 8–0 votes, Jan. 16, 2002; Kennedy wrote the opinion; Thomas and Souter dissented in part; O'Connor did not participate.

The Federal Communications Commission (FCC) can regulate the rates utility companies charge cable systems for attaching equipment to their poles even if the devices are used for Internet access or wireless communications instead of cable TV. The ruling—a victory for the cable industry—upheld the FCC's broad interpretation of provisions of the 1978 Pole Attachment Act, which gave the agency power to set "just and reasonable" rates for telephone or electric utilities to charge cable systems for pole attachments.

Wisconsin Department of Health and Family Services v. Blumer (534 U.S. 473), decided by a 6–3 vote, Feb. 20, 2002; Ginsburg wrote the opinion; Stevens, O'Connor, and Scalia dissented.

States are free to adopt an "income-first" method that makes it harder for some elderly nursing home residents to qualify for financial assistance under the joint state-federal Medicaid program for low-income persons.

The ruling upheld an interpretation of the Medicare Catastrophic Coverage Act of 1988 adopted by a majority of states over an alternative "resources-first" method. Before the law, couples had to reduce their assets for one of the spouses to qualify for nursing home benefits under Medicaid. Under the law, a spouse living at home (the "community spouse") could reserve a certain amount of income and assets needed to meet minimum monthly maintenance needs.

In the "income-first" method, states considered some of the income of the "institutionalized spouse" as earnings available to the community spouse seeking to raise the minimum monthly allowance. In the "resources-first" method, the institutionalized spouse's income was not considered as available to the community spouse. Instead, additional assets—"resources"—could be protected to produce income needed to meet the community spouse's needs.

New York v. Federal Energy Regulatory Commission (535 U.S. 1), decided by 9–0 and 6–3 votes, March 4, 2002; Stevens wrote the opinion; Thomas, Scalia, and Kennedy dissented in part.

The Court upheld an order by the Federal Energy Regulatory Commission (FERC) requiring some but not all electric utilities to transmit competitors' electricity over its lines on the same terms that the utility applies to its own transmissions. The ruling backed the FERC's procompetitive "open access" policy against a challenge by state utility regulators while also rejecting an effort by a leading electricity wholesaler to force the agency to go further.

Department of Housing and Urban Development v. Rucker (535 U.S. 125), decided by an 8–0 vote, March 26, 2002; Rehnquist wrote the opinion; Breyer did not participate.

Local public housing agencies may evict a tenant for any drug activity on or off the premises by any family member or guest even if the tenant did not know about the offense. The ruling upheld a "zero tolerance" policy for drug offenses in public housing that stemmed from a provision of the Anti-Drug Abuse Act of 1988.

Verizon Communications Inc. v. Federal Communications Commission (535 U.S. 467), decided by 7–1 and 6–2 votes, May 13, 2002; Souter wrote the opinion; Breyer dissented, joined by Scalia on one issue; O'Connor did not participate.

In a massive opinion, the Court upheld Federal Communications Commission (FCC) regulations aimed at promoting local telephone competition by allowing new entrants to share on somewhat favorable terms existing network equipment of the former monopoly companies.

The ruling rejected challenges by the four regional Bell companies—BellSouth, SBC Communications, QWest, and Verizon—to rules that the FCC adopted under the procompetitive Telecommunications Act of 1996, which required the incumbent carriers to lease network equipment on request to new entrants at rates to be determined under methodologies to be established by the FCC.

Verizon Maryland Inc. v. Public Service Commission of Maryland (535 U.S. 635), decided by an 8–0 vote, May 20, 2002; Scalia wrote the opinion; O'Connor did not participate.

State utility commissions can be sued in federal court to determine whether they are correctly applying federal law governing interconnection agreements between established local telephone companies and competing carriers.

City of Columbus v. Ours Garage; Wrecker Service, Inc. (536 U.S. 424), decided by a 7–2 vote, June 20, 2002; Ginsburg wrote the opinion; Scalia and O'Connor dissented.

Local governments can impose safety regulations on tow truck operators. The ruling rejected an argument by a Columbus, Ohio, tow truck company that a federal trucking deregulation act—the Interstate Commerce Commission Termination Act (1995)—allowed state governments but not municipalities to impose safety regulations. The Court held the law "spares from preemption" both local and state safety regulations.

Yellow Transportation, Inc. v. Michigan (537 U.S. 36), decided by a 9–0 vote, Nov. 5, 2002; O'Connor wrote the opinion.

The Court barred states from raising motor carrier registration fees in effect prior to enactment of a 1991 law aimed at simplifying registration for interstate trucking firms. The ruling involved a provision of the Intermodal Surface Transportation Efficiency Act of 1991 that directed the former Interstate Commerce Commission to adopt a uniform registration system capping state fees at $10 and limiting any state to the fee it "collected or charged as of November 15, 1991." The Court held that states may not charge motor registration fees in excess of those charged or collected under reciprocity agreements in effect when the law was passed.

Sprietsma v. Mercury Marine (537 U.S. 51), decided by a 9–0 vote, Dec. 3, 2002; Stevens wrote the opinion.

Manufacturers of recreational boats may be sued in state courts for failing to install safety devices not required under federal law.

The ruling reinstated a product liability suit in Illinois state court by an Illinois man for the death of his wife in a boating accident in 1995 when she was struck by the propeller of a rented ski boat after having fallen overboard. The Federal Boat Safety Act of 1971 authorized the Coast Guard to adopt safety standards for recreational boats. The agency had considered but not adopted a regulation to require propeller guards. The manufacturer of the boat sought to dismiss the suit on grounds that it was preempted under federal law.

The Court held that the federal act did not preempt state court suits, either expressly or impliedly. "[T]he Coast Guard's decision not to require propeller guards does not convey an 'authoritative' message of a federal policy against propeller guards."

Pierce County v. Guillen (537 U.S. 129), decided by a 9–0 vote, Jan. 14, 2003; Thomas wrote the opinion.

The Court upheld but narrowed a federal law limiting the ability of automobile accident victims to use as evidence in court information gathered by state and local governments under a federal highway safety program.

Federal Communications Commission v. NextWave Personal Communications, Inc. (537 U.S. 293), decided by an 8–1 vote, Jan. 27, 2003; Scalia wrote the decision; Breyer dissented.

The Federal Communications Commission cannot revoke the wireless communication licenses that a telecommunications company won in an auction because the company later filed for bankruptcy.

Pharmaceutical Research and Manufacturers of America v. Walsh, Acting Commissioner, Maine Department of Human Services (538 U.S. 644), decided by a 6–3 vote, May 19, 2003; Stevens wrote the main opinion; O'Connor, Rehnquist, and Kennedy dissented in part.

Drug manufacturers failed to bar Maine's prescription drug rebate plan for the state's residents but were given a second chance to show that the plan was preempted by the federal Medicaid statute.

The ruling in a closely watched case removed one legal cloud over an innovative program that Maine enacted in 2000 to lower prescription drug costs, while appearing to shift the issue of Medicaid preemption to the George W. Bush administration. The program—known as Maine Rx—was aimed at giving uninsured residents a discount on prescription drugs through a program of state payments to pharmacists from a fund financed by rebates from participating drug manufacturers. Manufacturers that did not participate in the program were to be disfavored in providing prescription drugs under the state's Medicaid program for the indigent.

In a fractured decision, the Court rejected the drug manufacturers' interstate commerce argument and turned aside the Medicaid preemption argument at this stage of the litigation. The decision sent the case back to lower federal courts for further proceedings, while also anticipating an administrative ruling on Maine's program by the secretary of health and human services.

Entergy Louisiana, Inc. v. Louisiana Public Service Commission (539 U.S. 39), decided by a 9–0 vote, June 2, 2003; Thomas wrote the opinion.

A state public utility commission cannot reevaluate discretionary cost allocations between affiliated energy companies made pursuant to a rate filing approved by the Federal Energy Regulatory Commission.

American Insurance Association v. Garamendi, Insurance Commissioner, State of California (539 U.S. 396), decided by a 5–4 vote, June 23, 2003; Souter wrote the opinion; Ginsburg, Stevens, Scalia, and Thomas dissented.

The Court struck down a California law whose purpose was to help Holocaust survivors recover proceeds from unpaid insurance policies, saying that the law interfered with presidential efforts to resolve the same issue through voluntary negotiations with European insurers.

The ruling relied on federal preemption to invalidate a 1999 California statute, the Holocaust Victim Insurance Relief Act, that required any insurer doing business in the state to disclose information about all policies sold in Europe be-

tween 1920 and 1945. The law was a response to efforts by Holocaust survivors to force European insurers to pay the proceeds of insurance policies of family members who perished in German death camps during World War II.

Nixon, Attorney General of Missouri v. Missouri Municipal League (541 U.S. 125), decided by an 8–1 vote, March 24, 2004; Souter wrote the opinion; Stevens dissented.

States may prohibit municipalities or municipally owned utilities from offering telecommunications services despite a provision in federal law generally preempting any state or local laws that limit entry into cable, telephone, or other telecommunications businesses. The Court held that the federal law did not preempt a state or local government's power to limit the ability of political subdivisions to offer telecommunications services.

Household Credit Services, Inc. v. Pfennig (541 U.S. 232), decided by a 9–0 vote, April 21, 2004; Thomas wrote the opinion.

Banks and credit card companies do not have to list fees for exceeding a cardholder's credit limit as a "finance charge" in monthly billing statements but can instead include the fee along with miscellaneous charges.

FEDERAL TORT CLAIMS ACT

Central Green Co. v. United States (531 U.S. 425), decided by a 9–0 vote, Feb. 21, 2001; Stevens wrote the opinion.

The federal government may sometimes be forced to pay for property damage from water from federal flood control projects. The ruling reinstated a claim by the owner of a California pistachio orchard for damages resulting from leaking water from the Madera Canal in the San Joaquin Valley. The canal is part of the Central Valley Project, a federal water project for flood control, irrigation, and other purposes.

FREEDOM OF INFORMATION

Department of Interior v. Klamath Water Users Protective Association (532 U.S. 1), decided by a 9–0 vote, March 5, 2001; Souter wrote the opinion.

Documents exchanged between Indian tribes and the U.S. Interior Department in connection with legal proceedings are not exempt from the Freedom of Information Act (FOIA) under the exception for intra-agency memorandums.

The ruling upheld an effort by a private association of water users in Oregon to use the FOIA to obtain documents that the Klamath Indians filed with the Interior Department in connection with a water rights dispute. The Court agreed that the FOIA required disclosure of the documents.

National Archives and Records Administration v. Favish (541 U.S. 157), decided by a 9–0 vote, March 30, 2004; Kennedy wrote the opinion.

Death-scene photographs compiled by a federal law enforcement agency are exempt on privacy grounds from disclosure under the Freedom of Information Act unless the individual requesting the materials shows likely government misconduct.

The ruling overturned a federal appeals court decision granting a request by a California attorney, Allan Favish, for photographs of deputy White House counsel Vincent Foster taken when his body was discovered in a park outside Washington, D.C., in 1993. Skeptical of the government's finding that Foster committed suicide, Favish asked for eleven photographs from the Office of Independent Counsel under the Freedom of Information Act (FOIA). The Court held that the privacy interests of Foster's family were protected under Exemption 7(C) of FOIA and that those interests carried greater weight than Favish's reasons for obtaining the photographs.

GOVERNMENT CONTRACTS

Franconia Associates v. United States (536 U.S. 129), decided by a 9–0 vote, June 10, 2002; Ginsburg wrote the opinion.

Property owners in a program aimed at promoting low-cost housing in rural areas did not wait too long to sue the federal government for changing the terms of participating in the program.

The ruling reinstated claims by developers who took advantage of a Farmers Home Administration program offering low-interest mortgage loans in exchange for commitments to devote the properties to low- and middle-income housing for the life of the loans. Initially, the program allowed developers to pay off the mortgages at any time. Congress eliminated the prepayment option in 1988 because the number of developers exercising that right was limiting the effectiveness of the program. A number of property owners filed a claim against the government in 1997 for alleged repudiation of contract. The U.S. Court of Appeals for the Federal Circuit ordered the claim dismissed because of the general rule setting a six-year time limit for bringing a claim against the federal government for breach of contract.

The Court held the time period for bringing any claim would not begin until the government rejected an offer of prepayment.

National Park Hospitality Association v. Department of the Interior (538 U.S. 803), decided by a 7–2 vote, May 27, 2003; Thomas wrote the opinion; Breyer and O'Connor dissented.

The Court declined to decide whether the National Park Service must follow a general federal law regulating government contracting dispute procedures in disagreements with Park Service concessionaires, saying the issue was not ripe for review.

MINERAL RIGHTS

BedRoc Ltd. v. United States (541 U.S. 176), decided by a 6–3 vote, March 31, 2004; Rehnquist wrote the plurality opinion; Stevens, Souter, and Ginsburg dissented.

Sand and gravel are not valuable minerals reserved to the United States in land grants issued to Nevada settlers under the Pittman Underground Water Act of 1919, which was aimed at encouraging agricultural development in the state. The ruling settled ownership rights for plentiful minerals that were commercially worthless in sparsely populated Nevada but became more valuable with the expansion of Las Vegas beginning after World War II.

NATIVE AMERICANS

C&L Enterprises, Inc. v. Citizen Band Potawatomi Indian Tribe of Oklahoma (532 U.S. 411), decided by a 9–0 vote, April 30, 2001; Ginsburg wrote the opinion.

Indian tribes are subject to suit in state courts to enforce arbitration awards if they agree to arbitrate disputes arising from commercial contracts for work performed outside reservations.

The ruling reinstated a suit by an Oklahoma contractor who claimed the Potawatomi Tribe backed out of a contract to install a new roof on a building owned by the tribe. The contract—proposed by the tribe—included provisions requiring that disputes be submitted to private arbitration and that the contract be governed "by the law of the place where the Project is located." The Court held that the tribe had waived its sovereign immunity by agreeing to the arbitration clause contained in the contract.

Atkinson Trading Co. v. Shirley (532 U.S. 645), decided by a 9–0 vote, May 29, 2001; Rehnquist wrote the opinion.

The Navajo Nation was barred from imposing a hotel occupancy tax on a popular tourist site owned by non–Indians on nontribal land within the boundaries of the Navajo reservation. The Court said the tribe could not impose the tax because it failed to meet the conditions established in *Montana v. United States* (1981) for exercising authority over nonmembers on non–Indian land.

Idaho v. United States (533 U.S. 262), decided by a 5–4 vote, June 18, 2001; Souter wrote the opinion; Rehnquist, O'Connor, Scalia, and Thomas dissented.

The Court backed the claim by the Coeur d'Alene Indian tribe over that of the State of Idaho to submerged lands under parts of Lake Coeur d'Alene and the St. Joe River. The ruling resolved an issue dating to the time of Idaho's admission as a state in 1890 that became current after state officials moved to open parts of the lake and river lying within the tribe's reservation to recreational fishing and boating. The Court ruled that the government held title to the lands in trust for the Coeur d'Alene tribe.

Nevada v. Hicks (533 U.S. 353), decided by 9–0 and 6–3 votes, June 25, 2001; Scalia wrote the opinion; O'Connor, Stevens, and Breyer disagreed with the legal holding.

Tribal courts have no authority to hear a tribe member's private damage suit against state officials for executing a search warrant for a crime committed off the reservation. The Court held that the tribal court had no jurisdiction over the trespass and abuse of process claims because the tribes "lacked legislative authority to restrict, condition, or otherwise regulate the ability of state officials to investigate off-reservation violations of state law."

Chickasaw Nation v. United States (534 U.S. 84 (2001), decided by a 7–2 vote, Nov. 27, 2001; Breyer wrote the opinion; O'Connor and Souter dissented.

Indian tribes must pay federal taxes on gambling operations, including lotteries, even though states are exempt from such levies. The ruling rejected an effort by the Chickasaw and Choctaw Nations to win an exemption from the federal levies under what justices on both sides of the case agreed was a poorly drafted provision of the Indian Gaming Regulatory Act of 1988. The 1988 law gave Indian tribes the same exemption enjoyed by states from federal laws concerning "the reporting and withholding of taxes" on gaming operations but included in a listing of those laws a provision relating to the imposition of taxes. The Court concluded that the cross-reference in the act to the provision imposing gambling-related taxes was "simply a drafting mistake."

United States v. Navajo Nation (537 U.S. 488), decided by a 6–3 vote, March 4, 2003; Ginsburg wrote the opinion; Souter, Stevens, and O'Connor dissented.

The Court blocked the Navajo Nation from pursuing a $600 million breach of trust claim against the government for allegedly mishandling coal lease negotiations with a private company during the 1980s. The ruling rejected a suit brought by the Navajo under the Indian Mineral Leasing Act in connection with 1987 amendments to an agreement originally signed in 1964 allowing the Peabody Coal Co. to mine on the tribe's reservation. The act allows tribes to lease land for mining purposes "with the approval of" the secretary of the interior. The Court held that Interior secretary Donald Hodel (1985–1989) had not committed a breach of trust under the mineral leasing law.

United States v. White Mountain Apache Tribe (537 U.S. 465), decided by a 5–4 vote, March 4, 2003; Souter wrote the opinion; Thomas, Rehnquist, Scalia, and Kennedy dissented.

The White Mountain Apache Tribe was allowed to proceed with a $14 million claim against the federal government for allowing the historic Fort Apache military reservation to fall into disrepair. The ruling stemmed from the tribe's effort to require the government to pay the estimated $14 million cost of rehabilitating buildings on the seven thousand-acre site in accordance with standards for historic preservation. The tribe filed a claim against the government under a 1960 law that stipulated the property would be "held by the United States in trust" for the tribe. The Court ruled that the government could be held liable for failing to maintain the property.

Inyo County v. Paiute-Shoshone Indians (538 U.S. 701), decided by a 9–0 vote, May 19, 2003; Ginsburg wrote the opinion.

An Indian tribe cannot use federal civil rights law to assert a sovereign immunity claim to try to block execution of a search warrant in a local or state law enforcement investigation.

The ruling cleared the way for Inyo County, California, to obtain, as part of a welfare fraud investigation, the payroll records of members of a Paiute-Shoshone tribe who worked for a tribally owned casino. The tribe filed suit to block execution of a search warrant to obtain the records under the federal civil rights law known as "section 1983" (542 U.S.C. §1983), which provides that any "citizen" or "other person" may obtain legal relief—money damages or an injunction—from any "person" who "under color of" state law deprives them of federally protected rights. The Court said the tribe did not qualify as a "person" for purposes of invoking section 1983 to assert a sovereign immunity claim. The ruling sent the case back to lower federal courts for the tribe to argue its alternative claim that federal common law barred execution of the search warrants.

United States v. Lara (541 U.S. 193), decided by a 7–2 vote, April 19, 2004; Breyer wrote the opinion; Souter and Scalia dissented.

Congress has the constitutional power to pass legislation authorizing Indian tribes to exercise criminal jurisdiction over Indians who are members of other tribes. The Court held that Congress had properly authorized tribes to prosecute nonmember Indians under inherent tribal authority rather than as a delegation of federal power.

PRISONERS OF WAR

Hamdi v. Rumsfeld, Secretary of Defense (542 U.S. 507), decided by a 6–3 vote, June 28, 2004; O'Connor wrote the plurality opinion; Souter and Ginsburg concurred in the judgment; Scalia and Stevens dissented; Thomas dissented.

The government has statutory authority to detain a U.S. citizen captured on the battlefield in Afghanistan as an enemy combatant, but it must notify him of the charges against him and give him an opportunity to contest the charges before a neutral decision maker.

The ruling—rejecting part of the Bush administration's post–Sept. 11, 2001, legal strategy against suspected terrorists—reinstated a federal habeas corpus petition filed by Yaser Esam Hamdi. Born in Louisiana, Hamdi moved with his family to Saudi Arabia as a child and went to Afghanistan sometime before the 2001 attacks on the United States. A week later, Congress passed the Authorization for Use of Military Force resolution, which empowered the president to "use all necessary and appropriate force against those nations, organizations, or persons he determines planned, authorized, committed, or aided the terrorist attacks" or "harbored such organizations or persons." Under that resolution, President George W. Bush directed U.S. forces into Afghanistan to subdue al Qaeda and oust the Taliban regime, which had supported the group.

Hamdi was seized by forces of the U.S.-aligned Northern Alliance and turned over to U.S. authorities. Held as an enemy combatant, Hamdi was first taken to Guantanamo Bay Naval Base in Cuba. After authorities recognized that Hamdi was a U.S. citizen, he was transported to a naval brig in the United States. Hamdi's father filed a habeas corpus petition, saying that the government was illegally holding his son without charges or access to counsel. In later statements, Hamdi's father said his son had gone to Afghanistan to do relief work less than two months before Sept. 11 and could not have received military training during his short time there.

The Fourth U.S. Circuit Court of Appeals ruled that, because Hamdi was captured in a combat zone, no factual inquiry or evidentiary hearing was necessary or proper. Hamdi appealed that decision to the U.S. Supreme Court, which upheld the president's authority to detain Hamdi but ruled that he was entitled to notice and an opportunity to defend himself before some neutral decision maker.

Rasul v. Bush, President of the United States (542 U.S. 466), decided by a 6–3 vote, June 28, 2004; Stevens wrote the opinion; Scalia, Rehnquist, and Thomas dissented.

Foreign nationals captured during the Afghanistan war and held at Guantanamo Bay Naval Base can bring habeas corpus petitions in federal court to challenge the legality of their detentions.

The ruling—a setback to the George W. Bush administration's aggressive legal stance in the war against terrorism—cleared the way for nearly six hundred aliens held for more than two years at the U.S. naval base in Cuba to go into federal court to argue for their release. The aliens, apparently all Muslim and representing various countries in the Middle East and elsewhere, were captured during the U.S.-led war to oust Afghanistan's Taliban government because of its sheltering of the terrorist group al Qaeda. The administration classified the aliens as unlawful enemy combatants and transported them to the Guantanamo Bay base.

The administration denied the detainees access to lawyers or family members. Relatives representing two groups of aliens—sixteen Kuwaitis in one case and two Britons and two Australians in another—filed habeas corpus petitions in federal district court in Washington, D.C., to challenge the legality of the detentions. In each case the aliens claimed they were not involved in hostile actions against the United States. The federal habeas corpus statute—28 U.S.C. §2241—gives federal courts "within their respective jurisdictions" the authority to hear applications for habeas corpus by any person who claims to be held "in custody in violation of the Constitution or laws or treaties of the United States."

The Court ruled that federal courts have jurisdiction to consider the legality of the detention of foreign nationals captured abroad and incarcerated at Guantanamo Bay. The Court said that a subsequent Court decision—*Braden v. 30th Judicial Circuit Court of Kentucky* (1973)—allows a federal court to hear a habeas petition filed by someone incarcerated outside the court's jurisdiction and concluded that it was "clear" that federal courts had jurisdiction to hear the aliens' challenges.

Rumsfeld, Secretary of Defense v. Padilla (542 U.S. 426), decided by a 5–4 vote, June 28, 2004; Rehnquist wrote the opinion; Stevens, Souter, Ginsburg, and Breyer dissented.

A U.S. citizen challenging his detention as an enemy combatant in a naval brig in Charleston, South Carolina, should have filed his habeas corpus petition with a federal court there instead of in New York.

The ruling delayed but did not end a challenge by José Padilla to his detention after being arrested in Chicago on May 8, 2002, on a material witness warrant in connection with a suspected conspiracy to plant a radioactive bomb somewhere in the United States. Padilla was then transferred to a jail in New York City. After Padilla's court-appointed lawyer moved to set aside the warrant, President George W. Bush issued an order classifying Padilla as an enemy combatant, saying that he was "closely associated" with the al Qaeda terrorist group, had prepared for acts of international terrorism against the United States, and represented "a continuing, present and grave danger" to U.S. national security. Under the order Padilla was transferred, without prior notice to his lawyer, to the Consolidated Naval Brig in Charleston. Two days later, the lawyer filed a habeas corpus petition in federal district court in New York City, naming Defense secretary Donald Rumsfeld as defendant.

Padilla was held in solitary confinement and without access to family, nonmilitary personnel, or counsel for nearly two years while the habeas corpus petition proceeded. The district court sustained its jurisdiction over the case and upheld the president's authority to detain Padilla as an enemy combatant but ordered that he be given access to a lawyer. On appeal, the Second U.S. Circuit Court of Appeals also upheld the New York court's jurisdiction over the case but ruled that the president had no authority to order a U.S. citizen held as an enemy combatant under statute or under his powers as commander in chief.

The Court decided that Padilla should have filed the habeas corpus petition in South Carolina, not New York, against the commander of the naval brig, not the secretary of defense. Because of this, the case would have to be refiled in a federal district court in South Carolina.

SEPARATION OF POWERS

Cheney, Vice President of the United States v. United States District Court for the District of Columbia (542 U.S. 367), decided by a 7–2 vote, June 24, 2004; Kennedy wrote the opinion; Ginsburg and Souter dissented.

The Court blocked two advocacy groups from getting court-supervised discovery into the operations of an energy task force headed by Vice President Dick Cheney in the first year of the George W. Bush administration.

The interim ruling in the politically charged case ordered a federal appeals court to give further consideration to the administration's separation-of-powers argument for resisting court-ordered discovery about the "structure and membership" of the National Energy Policy Development Group. President Bush established the task force in 2001 and named Cheney to head it.

Two interest groups filed separate suits in federal court in Washington, D.C., and California seeking information about the task force's operations. They argued that the task force was subject to open-meeting and disclosure requirements of the Federal Advisory Committee Act, which applies to any advisory committee "established or utilized by the President" unless it is "composed wholly of full-time, or permanent part-time, officers or employees of the Federal Government."

After the cases were consolidated in Washington, a federal district court issued an order allowing the two groups discovery, subject to specific claims of executive privilege that Cheney might raise. The vice president filed a motion seeking either an interim appeal or a judicial order—a writ of mandamus—to vacate or set aside the lower court's ruling. The appeals court refused to consider the interim appeal or to issue the writ of mandamus.

The U.S. Supreme Court sent the case back to the appeals court after holding that Cheney did not have to assert executive privilege first for the court to consider his separation-of-powers argument for opposing discovery.

SOCIAL SECURITY

Barnhart v. Walton (535 U.S. 212), decided by a 9–0 vote, March 27, 2002; Breyer wrote the opinion.

The Court upheld two regulations by the Social Security Administration making it somewhat difficult to meet the minimum time period required to qualify for disability benefits. The ruling upheld regulations the agency issued to determine eligibility for disability insurance benefits or for payment of supplemental security income to individuals with disabilities. The Court ruled that both regulations were "permissible" interpretations of "ambiguous" language in the act.

Washington State Department of Social and Health Services v. Guardianship Estate of Keffeler (537 U.S. 371), decided by a 9–0 vote, Feb. 25, 2003; Souter wrote the opinion.

States may use disability or supplemental income benefits due to children under Social Security to reimburse costs of foster care for the children. The ruling rejected a class action suit brought on behalf of foster care children in the State of Washington against the state's Department of Social and Health Services for using benefits due foster care children under two Social Security programs—Old Age, Survivors, and Disability Insurance and Supplemental Security Income.

Barnhart, Commissioner of Social Security v. Thomas (540 U.S. 20), decided by a 9–0 vote, Nov. 12, 2003; Scalia wrote the opinion.

The Social Security Administration may deny disability benefits to someone even if the only job he or she can perform no longer exists in significant numbers in the national economy.

First Amendment

CHURCH AND STATE

Good News Club v. Milford Central School (533 U.S. 98), decided by a 6–3 vote, June 11, 2001; Thomas wrote the opinion; Souter, Stevens, and Ginsburg dissented.

A local school district violated the free speech rights of a Christian club for elementary school students by prohibiting it from using school facilities for weekly meetings after the school day. The Court held that denying permission for use of school facilities amounted to unconstitutional viewpoint discrimination.

Zelman v. Simmons-Harris (536 U.S. 639), decided by a 5–4 vote, June 27, 2002; Rehnquist wrote the opinion; Souter, Stevens, Ginsburg, and Breyer dissented.

A government program providing vouchers for private school tuition does not violate the Establishment Clause if it allows a neutral choice between using the grants at religious or nonreligious schools. The landmark ruling upheld a Cleveland program established in 1995 that provided up to $2,250 for families with children from kindergarten through eighth grade to use for tuition at participating private or public schools in other districts. The Court ruled the program was constitutional because it was "entirely neutral with respect to religion."

Locke, Governor of Washington v. Davey (540 U.S. 712), decided by a 7–2 vote, Feb. 25, 2004; Rehnquist wrote the opinion; Scalia and Thomas dissented.

States can refuse to provide college scholarships to students pursuing a degree in theology for purposes of entering the ministry.

The ruling in the closely watched case rejected a religious freedom challenge by a Washington State student who was ruled ineligible for a state-provided scholarship because he was majoring in pastoral ministries. The Court ruled that excluding students pursuing a degree in devotional theology from a state scholarship does not violate the free exercise of religion or other constitutional protections, as the exclusion for theology students was not motivated by "animus towards religion" but was justified by the state's "antiestablishment interests."

Elk Grove Unified School District v. Newdow (542 U.S. 1), decided by an 8–0 vote on result and a 5–3 vote on legal issue, June 14, 2004; Stevens wrote the opinion; Rehnquist,

RELIGION, SPEECH, AND PRESS

Congress shall make no law respecting an establishment of religion, or prohibiting the free exercise thereof; or abridging the freedom of speech, or of the press; or the right of the people peaceably to assemble, and to petition the Government for a redress of grievances.

First Amendment, U.S. Constitution

O'Connor, and Thomas concurred in the judgment; Scalia did not participate.

The Court effectively threw out a suit aimed at striking the phrase "under God" from the Pledge of Allegiance, saying an atheist father lacked legal standing to challenge recitation of the pledge in his daughter's school because the mother had been awarded the sole right to make all decisions about their daughter's education under a state court custody decision.

The Court's decision ended the politically volatile case without a ruling on whether a school district violates the Constitution's prohibition against establishment of religion by prescribing recitation of the pledge at the beginning of each school day.

COMMERCIAL SPEECH

United States v. United Foods, Inc. (533 U.S. 405), decided by a 6–3 vote, June 25, 2001; Kennedy wrote the opinion; Breyer, O'Connor, and Ginsburg dissented.

A federal program requiring mushroom growers to pay for promotional advertising violated the First Amendment rights of producers opposed to the advertising.

The ruling sustained a challenge by United Foods, a large Tennessee-based agricultural concern, to a program operated by the U.S. Department of Agriculture under the 1990 Mushroom Promotion, Research, and Consumer Information Act, which authorized an assessment on mushroom growers to pay for promotional advertising. The Court agreed that the mushroom advertising program violated the free speech rights of growers opposed to it.

Thompson v. Western States Medical Center (535 U.S. 357), decided by a 5–4 vote, April 29, 2002; O'Connor wrote the opinion; Breyer, Rehnquist, Stevens, and Ginsburg dissented.

The Court ruled unconstitutional a federal law limiting advertising by pharmacists engaged in the legal practice of "compounding" drugs—combining, mixing, or altering prescription drugs to create medications tailored to an individual patient's needs. The ruling struck down major provisions of the Food and Drug Administration Modernization Act, which permitted drug compounding under restrictions aimed at preventing potential health risks or circumventing the Food

and Drug Administration's regular drug approval procedures. The Court held the law was an unconstitutional restriction on commercial speech because the government could have achieved its objective by non–speech-related restrictions.

FREEDOM OF SPEECH

City News and Novelty, Inc. v. City of Waukesha (531 U.S. 278), decided by a 9–0 vote, Jan. 17, 2001; Ginsburg wrote the opinion.

The Court dismissed as moot—or legally over—an effort by a former adult bookstore operator to require courts to rule promptly on a local government's refusal to grant a license to such stores. The Court agreed to hear the case to settle an issue left unresolved in prior decisions: whether an adult bookstore operator is constitutionally entitled to a prompt decision in any court challenge to a denial of a business license. The Court said the case was moot because the company had notified the city that it had withdrawn its application for a renewal.

Legal Services Corp. v. Velazquez (531 U.S. 533), decided by a 5–4 vote, Feb. 28, 2001; Kennedy wrote the opinion; Scalia, Rehnquist, O'Connor, and Thomas dissented.

The Court struck down on free speech grounds a federal law that prohibited federally funded legal aid offices from challenging existing provisions of state or federal welfare laws. The ruling invalidated a provision Congress enacted in 1996 in authorizing funds for the Legal Services Corporation, the quasi-governmental organization that funnels money to state and local legal aid offices. The Court ruled that the law violated the First Amendment.

Bartnicki v. Vopper (532 U.S. 514), decided by a 6–3 vote, May 21, 2001; Stevens wrote the opinion; Rehnquist, Scalia, and Thomas dissented.

The First Amendment bars a civil suit against an individual for publicizing contents of an illegally intercepted telephone conversation if the person was not involved in the interception and if the conversation relates to matters of public interest.

Thomas v. Chicago Park District (534 U.S. 316), decided by a 9–0 vote, Jan. 15, 2002; Scalia wrote the opinion.

Public park boards can deny applications for large-scale events such as parades or rallies under a content-neutral permit system without first going to court. The ruling rejected a challenge by a marijuana legalization group to a park permit ordinance administered by the Chicago Park District that required a permit for an event with more than fifty persons.

Ashcroft v. American Civil Liberties Union (535 U.S. 564), decided by an 8–1 vote, May 13, 2002; Thomas wrote the plurality opinion; Stevens dissented.

The Court partially upheld the Child Online Protection Act, which aimed at limiting children's access to sexually explicit material on the Internet by approving the use of community standards to determine what is "harmful to minors" under the law. The ruling sent the case back to a federal appeals court to resolve other constitutional challenges to the law.

City of Los Angeles v. Alameda Books, Inc. (535 U.S. 425), decided by a 5–4 vote, May 13, 2002; O'Connor wrote the plurality opinion; Souter, Stevens, Ginsburg, and Breyer dissented.

The Court upheld a Los Angeles ordinance prohibiting the operation of adult bookstores and video arcades under the same roof.

Illinois ex rel. Madigan, Attorney General of Illinois v. Telemarketing Associates, Inc. (538 U.S. 600), decided by a 9–0 vote, May 5, 2003; Ginsburg wrote the opinion.

States can bring fraud prosecutions against professional fund-raisers working for charitable organizations for intentionally misleading potential donors without violating the First Amendment's protection of free speech.

Virginia v. Hicks (539 U.S. 113), decided by a 9–0 vote, June 16, 2003; Scalia wrote the opinion.

The Court reinstated a local housing authority's no-trespassing policy that had been struck down by the Virginia Supreme Court on First Amendment grounds as unconstitutionally overbroad. Although limited, the decision was hailed by housing authorities as an aid to efforts to control drug dealing and other crime in public housing projects. The decision returned the case to the Virginia Supreme Court.

United States v. American Library Association, Inc. (539 U.S. 194), decided by a 6–3 vote, June 23, 2003; Rehnquist wrote the main opinion; Stevens, Souter, and Ginsburg dissented.

The Court upheld but softened a recently enacted federal law requiring public libraries to install software filters on computers to prevent juveniles from viewing sexually explicit materials on the Internet.

The ruling rejected a First Amendment challenge to the Children's Internet Protection Act brought by the American Library Association along with some public libraries, library patrons, and Web site publishers. Congress passed the law in 2000 after legislators took up complaints from parents and antipornography groups that youngsters were using public library computers to access sexually explicit Internet sites.

The law stipulated that to receive federal assistance for Internet access, public libraries had to install computer software that "blocks or filters Internet access" to obscenity, child pornography, or "visual depictions" that were "harmful to minors." The law allowed a library to "disable" the filter "to enable access for bona fide research or other lawful purposes."

The Court ruled that the law was a valid exercise of Congress's spending powers and did not impose unconstitu-tional conditions on public libraries. Two of the justices in the majority minimized the impact of the law by interpreting it to require libraries to allow unfiltered access to any adult on request.

INTERNET

Ashcroft, Attorney General v. American Civil Liberties Union (542 U.S. 656), decided by a 5–4 vote, June 29, 2004; Kennedy wrote the opinion; Breyer, Rehnquist, O'Connor, and Scalia dissented.

The Court extended a ban on enforcing a law aimed at limiting children's access to sexually explicit materials on the Internet, saying that it may violate constitutional protections for freedom of speech.

The ruling upheld, pending further lower court proceedings, a preliminary injunction against enforcement of the Child Online Protection Act, which made it a crime for commercial publishers to post on the World Wide Web sexually explicit material "harmful to minors" unless they used age verification systems, such as use of a credit card.

OBSCENITY AND INDECENCY

Ashcroft v. Free Speech Coalition (535 U.S. 234), decided by 7–2 and 6–3 votes, April 16, 2002; Kennedy wrote the opinion; O'Connor dissented in part; Rehnquist and Scalia dissented.

The Court struck down a federal law aimed at outlawing "virtual" child pornography by prohibiting material that appeared to depict children in sexually explicit activity even if real children were not used.

The ruling upheld a federal appeals court decision that the 1996 Child Pornography Prevention Act violated the First Amendment's freedom of speech provision. Congress passed the law to extend the existing ban on child pornography to cover lifelike, computer-generated images of children. The Court ruled that the "virtual" child porn and the pandering provisions of the law were unconstitutionally overbroad.

City of Littleton v. Z. J. Gifts D-4, L.L.C. (541 U.S. 774), decided by a 9–0 vote, June 7, 2004; Breyer wrote the opinion.

A local ordinance regulating licenses for adult businesses must ensure a prompt judicial decision, not just review, on any refusal to issue a license, but the requirement can be met by ordinary rules of judicial review. The mixed ruling reinstated an ordinance adopted by the city of Littleton, Colorado, that set out various requirements for the issuance of a business license to any adult book, novelty, or video store.

SOLICITATION

Watchtower Bible & Tract Society of New York, Inc. v. Village of Stratton (536 U.S. 150), decided by an 8–1 vote, June 17, 2002; Stevens wrote the opinion; Rehnquist dissented.

A local ordinance requiring a permit for any door-to-door solicitation violated the free speech rights of persons engaged in religious proselytism, handbill distribution, or anonymous political speech.

The ruling struck down an ordinance adopted by the tiny village of Stratton, Ohio, in 1998 and challenged by a society of Jehovah's Witnesses, who view religious proselytizing as an integral part of their faith. The ordinance prohibited "canvassers" from "going in or upon" private residential property without first having obtained a "solicitation permit" from the mayor. The Court said the ordinance was unconstitutional because it was too broad and not narrowly tailored to the village's stated interests of protecting residents' privacy and preventing fraud or other crime.

Immigration Law

ASYLUM

Immigration and Naturalization Service v. Orlando Ventura (537 U.S. 12), decided by a 9–0 vote, Nov. 4, 2002; per curiam opinion.

A federal appeals court was wrong to decide itself, instead of sending to an immigration court, the government's effort to deny asylum to a Guatemalan immigrant because of changed conditions in his native country.

CITIZENSHIP

Nguyen v. Immigration and Naturalization Service (539 U.S. 69), decided by a 5–4 vote, June 11, 2001; Kennedy wrote the opinion; O'Connor, Souter, Ginsburg, and Breyer dissented.

Congress can make it harder for a child born out of wedlock overseas to a citizen-father to become a U.S. citizen than for a child in similar circumstances born to a citizen-mother.

Under a provision of the Immigration and Nationality Act—§1409—a child born out of wedlock overseas to a citizen-mother becomes a U.S. citizen at birth if the mother had been physically present in the United States for at least one year before the birth. A child born to a citizen-father, however, could become a U.S. citizen only if additional requirements were met. The Court ruled the act constitutional, saying that it substantially related to two governmental interests: establishing parentage and ensuring the potential for a relationship between father and child.

DEPORTATION

Calcano-Martinez v. Immigration and Naturalization Service (533 U.S. 348), decided by a 5–4 vote, June 25, 2001; Stevens wrote the opinion; Scalia, Rehnquist, O'Connor, and Thomas dissented.

Federal courts of appeals cannot hear a challenge by a legal immigrant facing deportation because of prior criminal convictions. The immigrant can challenge removal, however, with a habeas corpus petition in federal district court.

The ruling—interpreting a provision of the Illegal Immigration Reform and Immigrant Responsibility Act of 1996—

was a companion to a longer decision in another case the same day, *Immigration and Naturalization Service v. St. Cyr.* The provision at issue barred federal courts of appeals from exercising "jurisdiction to review any final order of removal against any alien" subject to deportation because of convictions for specified criminal offenses.

Immigration and Naturalization Service v. St. Cyr (533 U.S. 289), decided by a 5–4 vote, June 25, 2001; Stevens wrote the opinion; Scalia, Rehnquist, O'Connor, and Thomas dissented.

Legal immigrants subject to deportation because of guilty pleas in criminal cases can use federal habeas corpus proceedings to challenge their removal from the United States. The ruling—which also barred retroactive application of a provision broadening the category of criminals subject to deportation—significantly narrowed sections of two 1996 laws aimed at restricting judicial review of immigration cases.

Zadvydas v. Davis (533 U.S. 678), decided by a 5–4 vote, June 28, 2001; Breyer wrote the opinion; Kennedy, Rehnquist, Scalia, and Thomas dissented.

The government cannot indefinitely detain a deportable alien if it cannot find a country to which to send the individual. Instead, the alien is normally entitled to release six months after a final removal order. The ruling represented a major victory for immigrant rights groups and possibly affected as many as three thousand aliens in detention at the time of the decision.

Demore v. Kim (538 U.S. 510), decided by a 5–4 vote, April 29, 2003; Rehnquist wrote the opinion; Souter, Stevens, Ginsburg, and Breyer dissented.

Immigrants previously convicted of certain crimes can be detained during deportation proceedings without an individual hearing to show that they are neither a flight risk nor a danger to the community.

Individual Rights

AFFIRMATIVE ACTION

Adarand Constructors, Inc. v. Mineta (534 U.S. 103), decided by a 9–0 vote, Nov. 27, 2001; per curiam opinion.

The Court dismissed without a ruling a challenge by a white Colorado contractor to a federal program aimed at helping minority-owned companies get a bigger share of federal highway construction projects.

Gratz v. Bollinger (539 U.S. 244), decided by a 6–3 vote, June 23, 2003; Rehnquist wrote the opinion; Stevens, Souter, and Ginsburg dissented.

The Court ruled that the admissions program at the University of Michigan's main undergraduate college was unconstitutional because it awarded a fixed numerical bonus to all applicants from disadvantaged minority groups.

The decision was a limited victory for affirmative action opponents, offset by the Court's decision the same day upholding more individualized use of race in admissions policies at the university's law school (*Grutter v. Bollinger*). In contrast to the law school admissions policies, the undergraduate program used a numerical system with a maximum of 150 points and automatically awarded 20 points to African American, Hispanic, and Native American applicants. A score of 100 points qualified for admission.

The Court ruled that the program violated the Equal Protection Clause of the Fourteenth Amendment because its use of race was "not narrowly tailored to achieve the interest in educational diversity that [university officials] claim justifies their program." The automatic distribution of 20 points had the effect of making race the decisive factor "for virtually every minimally qualified underrepresented minority applicant."

Grutter v. Bollinger (539 U.S. 306), decided by a 5–4 vote, June 23, 2003; O'Connor wrote the opinion; Rehnquist, Scalia, Kennedy, and Thomas dissented.

The Court narrowly but decisively upheld the use of race-conscious admissions policies at public colleges and universities to promote what it held to be a "compelling interest" in racial diversity on campuses.

The ruling—a major victory for supporters of affirmative action—rejected a challenge by an unsuccessful white applicant to admissions policies at the University of Michigan Law School. In a companion decision the same day in *Gratz v. Bollinger,* however, the Court ruled that the admissions policies at the university's main undergraduate college were unconstitutional.

The Court said the law school's admissions policies satisfied constitutional standards because they were "narrowly tailored" to achieve the goal of attaining a diverse student body. On that basis, the admissions program satisfied the "strict scrutiny" standard that any government use of race must meet. The Court also suggested that race-conscious admissions policies should not be permanent, as colleges and universities should include "sunset provisions" and "periodic reviews" to determine whether racial preferences are still needed to achieve student body diversity.

DAMAGE SUITS

Brentwood Academy v. Tennessee Secondary School Athletic Association (531 U.S. 288), decided by a 5–4 vote, Feb. 20, 2001; Souter wrote the opinion; Thomas, Rehnquist, Scalia, and Kennedy dissented.

A nominally private association that regulates high school athletics in Tennessee was held to be a "state actor" subject to constitutional limitations because of its "pervasive entwinement" with public officials.

Alexander, Director, Alabama Department of Public Safety v. Sandoval (532 U.S. 275), decided by a 5–4 vote, April 24, 2001; Scalia wrote the opinion; Stevens, Souter, Ginsburg, and Breyer dissented.

A private individual cannot sue state or local government officials to enforce federal civil rights regulations that prohibit federally financed programs from adopting policies with discriminatory effects but no intentional discrimination. The ruling—a sharp setback for civil rights advocates—rejected a class action suit by a Spanish-speaking Alabama woman over a decision by the Alabama Department of Public Safety to offer driver's license examinations only in English.

Saucier v. Katz (533 U.S. 194), decided by votes of 6–3 and 8–1, June 18, 2001; Kennedy wrote the opinion; Ginsburg, Stevens, and Breyer disagreed with the legal holding but concurred with the result; Souter agreed with the legal holding but dissented from the result.

The Court made it easier for police officers to avoid trials in damage suits charging them with use of excessive force. The Court held that an officer who uses unreasonable force is entitled to qualified immunity as long as a reasonable officer would have made the same error under the same circumstances.

TRW Inc. v. Andrews (534 U.S. 19 (2001), decided by a 9–0 vote, Nov. 12, 2001; Ginsburg wrote the opinion.

Someone injured by a credit reporting company's mistake has two years from the time of the error to file suit under federal law even if he or she does not learn of the mistake until later.

Correctional Services Corp. v. Malesko (534 U.S. 61 (2001), decided by a 5–4 vote, Nov. 27, 2001; Rehnquist wrote the opinion; Stevens, Souter, Ginsburg, and Breyer dissented.

Federal inmates in prisons operated by private companies cannot sue the companies for violations of constitutional rights. The ruling rejected a damage suit by a man with a heart condition who suffered a heart attack after he was required by a guard to climb stairs to the fifth floor of a halfway house where he was serving his sentence instead of being allowed to use an elevator. He sued under the Supreme Court's 1971 ruling, *Bivens v. Six Unknown Fed. Narcotics Agents,* which allowed federal employees to be held liable for constitutional violations. In a sharply divided decision, the Court refused to extend *Bivens* to allow constitutional claims against private companies.

Owasso Independent School District No. I011 v. Falvo (534 U.S. 426), decided by a 9–0 vote, Feb. 19, 2002; Kennedy wrote the opinion.

Teachers may use students to grade each other's assignments and tests without violating the federal law guaranteeing privacy of educational records. The ruling rejected a suit brought by an Oklahoma woman under the federal Family Educational Rights and Privacy Act of 1974, arguing that the "peer grading" practice subjected her learning-disabled son to embarrassment and derision from his classmates.

Christopher v. Harbury (536 U.S. 403), decided by a 9–0 vote, June 20, 2002; Souter wrote the opinion.

The Court threw out major parts of a lawsuit filed by the American widow of a Guatemalan rebel against U.S. foreign policy officials for allegedly misleading her about her husband's execution during his country's civil war.

Gonzaga University v. Doe (536 U.S. 273), decided by a 7–2 vote, June 20, 2002; Rehnquist wrote the opinion; Stevens and Ginsburg dissented.

Students or parents cannot use the general federal civil rights statute to sue schools or universities for damages for violating the federal law guaranteeing privacy of educational records. The Court held that the Family Educational Rights and Privacy Act of 1974 did not create a personal right enforceable through private damage suits.

Hope v. Pelzer (536 U.S. 730), decided by a 6–3 vote, June 27, 2002; Stevens wrote the opinion; Thomas, Rehnquist, and Scalia dissented.

Alabama prison guards had fair warning as early as 1995 that they could be held liable for administering cruel and unusual punishment to inmates by handcuffing them to a "hitching post" or restraining bar.

The ruling reinstated a federal civil rights suit by an Alabama inmate charging three prison guards with violating the Eighth Amendment's prohibition against cruel and unusual punishment for having used the hitching post to discipline him on two occasions. The Court held the guards were not entitled to qualified immunity and ordered the suit reinstated.

City of Cuyahoga Falls, Ohio v. Buckeye Community Hope Foundation (538 U.S. 188), decided by a 9–0 vote, March 25, 2003; O'Connor wrote the opinion.

A predominantly white suburb of Akron, Ohio, won dismissal of a civil rights damage suit filed by a nonprofit corporation for a delay in the construction of a low-income apartment complex.

The ruling barred a suit by the nonprofit Buckeye Community Hope Foundation that claimed equal protection and due process violations in connection with a 1996 referendum aimed at blocking construction of a low-income housing complex in the city of Cuyahoga Falls. The foundation claimed that the referendum was racially motivated in violation of the Equal Protection Clause and that it amounted to an arbitrary deprivation of a property right in violation of the Due Process Clause. The Court ruled that the foundation could not proceed with the suit, as it did not present sufficient evidence of discriminatory intent on the part of city officials to sustain an equal protection claim.

City of Los Angeles v. David (538 U.S. 715), decided by a 9–0 vote, May 19, 2003; per curiam opinion.

A federal appeals court was wrong to require the city of Los Angeles to provide a hearing within five days to any motorist seeking to recover impoundment fees for an automobile towed for parking violations.

Chavez v. Martinez (538 U.S. 760), decided by separate 6–3 and 5–3 votes, May 27, 2003; Thomas wrote the main opinion; Souter wrote an opinion for the Court on a second issue; Stevens, Kennedy, and Ginsburg dissented on the first issue; Thomas, Rehnquist, and Scalia disagreed on the second issue.

Police are not automatically liable for damages for failing to warn suspects of their *Miranda* rights but might be held liable for a due process violation if interrogation amounts to outrageous conduct.

Doe v. Chao, Secretary of Labor (540 U.S. 614), decided by a 6–3 vote, Feb. 24, 2004; Souter wrote the opinion; Ginsburg, Stevens, and Breyer dissented.

An individual must show damages to qualify for a minimum statutory award of $1,000 for a governmental violation of the federal Privacy Act of 1974. The ruling denied monetary compensation to "John Doe," who, along with six other black lung claimants, sued the U.S. Department of Labor for violating the Privacy Act by disclosing their Social Security numbers to a group of claimants, their employers, and lawyers involved in the cases.

Groh v. Ramirez (540 U.S. 551), decided by a 5–4 vote, Feb. 24, 2004; Stevens wrote the opinion; Thomas, Rehnquist, Scalia, and Kennedy dissented.

A warrant that fails to describe the place to be searched violates the Fourth Amendment, and a police officer executing a search with such a warrant is not entitled to qualified immunity in a civil damage suit.

Muhammad v. Close (540 U.S. 749), decided by a 9–0 vote, Feb. 25, 2004; per curiam opinion.

A prisoner asserting a federal civil rights claim attacking only the conditions of his confinement need not first assert an available habeas corpus claim challenging the validity of his conviction or the duration of his sentence.

The ruling overturned a federal appeals court's application of the "habeas exhaustion rule" in *Heck v. Humphrey* (1994) to a suit filed under the federal civil rights statute—42 U.S.C. §1983—by a Michigan inmate against a prison official for retaliation for prior lawsuits and grievances. The Court said that the habeas exhaustion rule does not apply categorically to all suits challenging prison disciplinary proceedings.

DISABILITY RIGHTS

PGA TOUR, Inc. v. Martin (532 U.S. 661), decided by a 7–2 vote, May 29, 2001; Stevens wrote the opinion; Scalia and Thomas dissented.

The PGA Tour, a nonprofit entity, violated the federal Americans with Disabilities Act (ADA) by denying a disabled professional golfer the right to use a cart during tournament play. The Court held that the ADA applied to PGA tournaments and that use of a cart was a reasonable accommodation of Martin's disability because it would not "fundamentally alter the nature" of the game.

Toyota Motor Manufacturing, Kentucky, Inc., v. Williams (534 U.S. 184), decided by a 9–0 vote, Jan. 8, 2002; O'Connor wrote the opinion.

A physical ailment qualifies as a disability under federal civil rights law only if it severely restricts an individual from carrying out activities that are central to daily life. The Court's ruling significantly narrowed the federal Americans with Disabilities Act.

US Airways, Inc. v. Barnett (535 U.S. 391), decided by a 5–4 vote, April 29, 2002; Breyer wrote the opinion; Scalia and Thomas dissented; Souter and Ginsburg dissented.

Employers do not ordinarily have to bend a seniority system to accommodate an employee's disability, but a disabled worker can show in an individual case that an exception to seniority rules would not be an undue hardship for the employer. The Court ruled that seniority systems generally but not always take precedence over the right of an employee with a disability to accommodation under the law.

Chevron U.S.A., Inc. v. Echazabal (536 U.S. 73), decided by a 9–0 vote, June 10, 2002; Souter wrote the opinion.

An employer can dismiss or refuse to hire an individual if the worker has a disability that would pose a direct threat to his or her health on the job. The ruling upheld a regulation issued by the Equal Employment Opportunity Commission interpreting the business necessity defense under the federal Americans with Disabilities Act.

Barnes v. Gorman (536 U.S. 181), decided by 9–0 and 6–3 votes, June 17, 2002; Scalia wrote the opinion; Stevens, Ginsburg, and Breyer concurred in the result but disagreed with the legal holding.

Local governments are not subject to punitive damages for failing to accommodate persons with disabilities as required by federal law. The Court said that punitive damages were not "appropriate" relief under the two disability rights laws—the Americans with Disabilities Act of 1990 and the Rehabilitation Act of 1973—because both acts specified that remedies would be the same as allowed under Title VI of the Civil Rights Act of 1964.

Clackamas Gastroenterology Associates, P.C. v. Wells (538 U.S. 440), decided by a 7–2 vote, April 22, 2003; Stevens wrote the opinion; Ginsburg and Breyer dissented.

Shareholders of a professional corporation are not counted as employees for purposes of determining the cor-

poration's coverage under the federal disabilities rights law if they independently manage the corporation's affairs instead of being subject to its control. The ruling adopted a multi-part, case-by-case test for determining whether shareholders of a professional corporation count as employees in determining whether the corporation has fifteen or more employees—the threshold for being subject to the Americans with Disabilities Act.

Raytheon Co. v. Hernandez (540 U.S. 44), decided by a 7–0 vote, Dec. 2, 2003; Thomas wrote the opinion; Souter and Breyer did not participate.

An employer's neutral, no-rehire policy may not serve as the basis for a so-called disparate treatment or intentional discrimination claim under the federal law prohibiting discrimination against persons with disabilities.

Tennessee v. Lane (541 U.S. 509), decided by a 5–4 vote, May 17, 2004; Stevens wrote the opinion; Rehnquist, Scalia, Kennedy, and Thomas dissented.

States can be sued for monetary damages for violating the federal Americans with Disabilities Act of 1990 (ADA) by failing to make courthouses accessible to persons with disabilities. The narrowly divided ruling cleared the way for two private suits against the State of Tennessee by wheelchair-using paraplegics who claimed that they were denied access to court services because of the lack of elevators in courthouses in a number of counties.

While the suits were pending, the Supreme Court ruled in *Board of Trustees of the University of Alabama v. Garrett* (2001) that states were immune from damage suits under the ADA's Title I provisions prohibiting employment discrimination against persons with disabilities. The Court left open the issue of damage suits under Title II. The Court ruled that Congress acted within its authority to enforce the Fourteenth Amendment in providing for damage suits against states for denying persons with disabilities access to court services.

DRUG TESTING

Ferguson v. City of Charleston (532 U.S. 67), decided by a 6–3 vote, March 21, 2001; Stevens wrote the opinion; Scalia, Rehnquist, and Thomas dissented.

Doctors and hospitals cannot give police the results of drug tests on patients without their consent if the policy is adopted for law enforcement purposes.

The ruling stemmed from a discontinued policy at the Medical University of South Carolina Hospital in Charleston of testing pregnant women for drug use and turning the information over to law enforcement authorities for possible prosecution. Ten women who tested positive for drug use, including two who were eventually prosecuted, filed a federal court suit against hospital officials, seeking damages for violations of their Fourth Amendment rights against unreasonable searches. The Court ruled that the drug-testing policy was not justified under the special needs doctrine, which can be used in some circumstances to justify a search policy serving non–law enforcement needs.

Board of Education of Independent School District No. 92 of Pottawatomie County v. Earls (536 U.S. 822), decided by a 5–4 vote, June 27, 2002; Thomas wrote the opinion; Ginsburg, Stevens, O'Connor, and Souter dissented.

Schools can require students to agree to random drug testing to participate in extracurricular activities.

The ruling upheld a drug-testing policy adopted by the Tecumseh, Oklahoma, school district in 1998. The policy formally required middle or high school students to consent to drug tests to participate in any extracurricular activity but in practice was applied only to students in competitive activities, such as athletics, band, choir, and academic team. The Court upheld drug testing for high school athletes in a 1995 decision, *Vernonia School District 47J v. Acton* (515 U.S. 646).

The Court held the policy was a reasonable means of detecting and preventing drug use and did not violate the Fourth Amendment's prohibition against unreasonable searches. The Court said that the drug tests—requiring collection and analysis of urine samples—do not involve a "significant" invasion of students' privacy and that the policy "effectively serves the School District's interest in protecting the safety and health of its students."

GAY RIGHTS

Lawrence v. Texas (539 U.S. 558), decided by a 6–3 vote, June 26, 2003; Kennedy wrote the opinion; Scalia, Rehnquist, and Thomas dissented.

In a historic victory for gay rights advocates, the U.S. Supreme Court outlawed, on privacy grounds, laws banning private consensual sexual conduct between persons of the same sex. The ruling appeared to invalidate anti-sodomy laws on the books in Texas and twelve other states and gave gay rights advocates a potentially powerful precedent to use in challenging other forms of discrimination against homosexuals.

The decision overturned the 1998 convictions of two Houston men, John Lawrence and Tyron Garner, for violating a Texas law that banned "deviate sexual intercourse"—defined as oral or anal sex—between persons of the same sex.

In a decision on the final day of the term, the Court overturned Lawrence's and Garner's convictions and also overruled the 1986 Supreme Court decision in *Bowers v. Hardwick,* 478 U.S. 186, permitting anti-sodomy laws. The decision included a forceful declaration of sexual liberty for homosexuals. "The petitioners are entitled to respect for their private lives. The State cannot demean their existence or control their destiny by making their private sexual conduct a crime. Their right to liberty under the Due Process Clause gives them the full right to engage in their conduct without the intervention of the government."

HOUSING DISCRIMINATION

Meyer v. Holley (537 U.S. 280), decided by a 9–0 vote, Jan. 22, 2003; Breyer wrote the opinion.

The owners and officers of real estate firms are ordinarily not individually liable for housing discrimination violations committed by the company's employees or agents. The Court ruled that housing discrimination suits are governed by general principles of corporate law that shield individual owners and officers from so-called vicarious liability for wrongs committed by employees or agents.

JOB DISCRIMINATION

Clark County School District v. Breeden (532 U.S. 268), decided by a 9–0 vote, April 23, 2001; per curiam opinion.

The Court blocked a civil rights suit by a Nevada woman who claimed she was transferred from a position with the Clark County School District in Nevada in retaliation for complaining about alleged sexual harassment.

The Court ruled the suit should have been dismissed, as the complained of interchange amounted to "an isolated incident" that did not amount to sexual harassment. It also said that Breeden's transfer was not retaliatory because it occurred before her supervisor learned she had filed suit.

Pollard v. E.I. du Pont de Nemours & Co. (532 U.S. 843), decided by an 8–0 vote, June 4, 2001; Thomas wrote the opinion; O'Connor did not participate.

Federal job discrimination law sets no limit on "front pay awards"—compensation for pay lost between judgment and a person's reinstatement to a previous job or in place of reinstatement.

Title VII of the Civil Rights Act originally provided for back pay and attorney's fees and was later amended to permit front pay awards. Congress in 1991 added provisions for compensatory damages for other economic losses and emotional suffering and punitive damages but set a $300,000 limit on those damages. The Court held that front pay awards were not subject to the cap on damages contained in the 1991 law.

Equal Employment Opportunity Commission v. Waffle House, Inc. (534 U.S. 279), decided by a 6–3 vote, Jan. 15, 2002; Stevens wrote the opinion; Thomas, Rehnquist, and Scalia dissented.

The Equal Employment Opportunity Commission (EEOC) can seek compensatory and punitive damages from employers in individual job discrimination cases even if the employee has agreed to arbitrate any work-related disputes. The ruling—a significant victory for civil rights groups—held that an arbitration agreement does not limit the EEOC's ability to seek damages in a suit against the employer.

Swierkiewicz v. Sorema N.A. (534 U.S. 506), decided by a 9–0 vote, Feb. 26, 2002; Thomas wrote the opinion.

A plaintiff in a federal employment discrimination case does not have to include specific facts to support his claim in his initial suit.

Edelman v. Lynchburg College (535 U.S. 106), decided by a 9–0 vote, March 19, 2002; Souter wrote the opinion.

The Court upheld an Equal Employment Opportunity Commission regulation that allowed a job discrimination complainant to put the complaint under oath after the three hundred–day deadline for bringing the charge. The Court upheld the regulation allowing an otherwise timely filer to verify a charge after the time for filing has expired and said the filing deadline and verification requirement were independent of each other.

National Railroad Passenger Corporation v. Morgan (536 U.S. 101), decided by a 5–4 vote, June 10, 2002; Thomas wrote the opinion; O'Connor, Rehnquist, Scalia, and Kennedy dissented.

In a mixed ruling, the Court strictly interpreted the time limit for filing job discrimination complaints based on specific incidents but broadened the ability of plaintiffs to include past conduct as evidence in "hostile work environment cases."

Desert Palace, Inc. v. Costa (539 U.S. 90), decided by a 9–0 vote, June 9, 2003; Thomas wrote the opinion.

The Court held that a plaintiff in a federal job discrimination suit need not present direct evidence of employment discrimination to be entitled to a favorable jury instruction in so-called mixed motive cases as long as the plaintiff presents sufficient evidence for a jury to conclude that illegal bias was a motivating factor.

General Dynamics Land Systems, Inc. v. Cline (540 U.S. 581), decided by a 6–3 vote, Feb. 24, 2004; Souter wrote the opinion; Thomas, Scalia, and Kennedy dissented.

Employers can adopt practices or policies that favor older workers over younger ones without violating the federal Age Discrimination in Employment Act of 1967.

The ruling barred a "reverse age discrimination" suit by employees of a division of General Dynamics attacking the company's decision in 1997 to eliminate future retirement health benefits for all employees who had not yet reached the age of fifty. The Court held that the law does not prohibit discrimination in favor of older workers.

Jones v. R. R. Donnelley & Sons Co. (541 U.S. 369), decided by a 9–0 vote, May 3, 2004; Stevens wrote the opinion.

Racially hostile work environment claims brought under a 1991 federal civil rights law are governed by a catchall federal four-year statute of limitations instead of the typically shorter time periods prescribed by state law.

The ruling settled a dispute between federal courts of appeals over the time period governing suits brought in federal court under the Civil Rights Act of 1991, which amended a Reconstruction-era law to explicitly allow claims for on-the-job racial harassment or mistreatment. Separately, Congress in 1990 passed a general law that prescribed a four-year statute of limitations for any cause of action "arising under" a federal law passed after 1990. The Court held that the suit arose under the 1991 act and was thus governed by the four-year statute of limitations.

SEXUAL HARASSMENT

Pennsylvania State Police v. Suders (542 U.S. 129), decided by an 8–1 vote, June 14, 2004; Ginsburg wrote the opinion; Thomas dissented.

The Court gave employers a limited defense in suits by former employees claiming they were effectively forced to resign because of sexual harassment. The Court held that a "constructive discharge" may be—but is not always—a tangible employment action so as to deprive an employer of the affirmative defenses available in suits for sexual harassment by a supervisor.

International Law

FOREIGN SOVEREIGN IMMUNITY

Republic of Austria v. Altmann (541 U.S. 677), decided by a 6–3 vote, June 7, 2004; Stevens wrote the opinion; Kennedy, Rehnquist, and Thomas dissented.

The Court retroactively applied a 1976 law narrowing foreign governments' immunity in U.S. courts to allow a suit by a Jewish refugee to recover from the Austrian Gallery $130 million worth of paintings allegedly confiscated by the Nazis.

The ruling broadened the application of the Foreign Sovereign Immunities Act, a 1976 statute aimed at codifying foreign governments' protection from suits in U.S. courts. The law generally granted foreign governments immunity, but with a number of exceptions—including one in cases alleging illegal expropriation of property. The U.S. Supreme Court held that the act applies to conduct prior to its enactment.

Labor Law

ARBITRATION

Circuit City Stores, Inc. v. Adams (532 U.S. 105), decided by a 5–4 vote, March 21, 2001; Kennedy wrote the opinion; Souter, Stevens, Ginsburg, and Breyer dissented.

Employers in most industries can require workers and job applicants to agree to resolve any employment-related disputes through arbitration instead of litigation in court. Basing its ruling on a broad interpretation of the Federal Arbitration Act, the Court held that only transportation workers were exempt and that the law therefore required enforcement of arbitration agreements for other workers.

Eastern Associated Coal Corp. v. United Mine Workers (531 U.S. 57), decided by a 9–0 vote, Nov. 28, 2000; Breyer wrote the opinion.

A labor arbitrator's decision ordering the reinstatement of a truck driver fired after testing positive twice for drug use was not contrary to public policy and was enforceable in court.

Major League Baseball Players Association v. Garvey (532 U.S. 504), decided by an 8–1 vote, May 14, 2001; per curiam opinion; Stevens dissented.

Baseball player Steve Garvey failed to overturn a labor arbitrator's decision denying damages for alleged collusion between baseball clubs in preventing him from getting a contract for the 1988 and 1989 seasons.

FAMILY AND MEDICAL LEAVE

Ragsdale v. Wolverine World Wide, Inc. (535 U.S. 81), decided by a 5–4 vote, March 19, 2002; Kennedy wrote the opinion; O'Connor, Souter, Ginsburg, and Breyer dissented.

The Court invalidated a U.S. Labor Department regulation broadening employers' obligations to allow their workers unpaid family or medical leave if they fail to notify the workers of their right to time off under federal law.

The ruling threw out a regulation the secretary of labor issued to implement the Family and Medical Leave Act of 1993. The Court held the regulation was contrary to the act and beyond the secretary of labor's authority to issue.

ILLEGAL ALIENS

Hoffman Plastic Compounds, Inc. v. National Labor Relations Board (535 U.S. 137), decided by a 5–4 vote, March 27, 2002; Rehnquist wrote the opinion; Breyer, Stevens, Souter, and Ginsburg dissented.

The National Labor Relations Board cannot award back pay to illegal aliens as a remedy for employers' violations of federal labor law. In a ruling sharply criticized by immigrant rights' groups, the Court rejected the back pay award because it would "condone" and "encourage" immigration law violations.

JOB SAFETY

Chao v. Mallard Bay Drilling, Inc. (534 U.S. 235), decided by an 8–0 vote, Jan. 9, 2002; Stevens wrote the opinion; Scalia did not participate.

The federal Occupational Safety and Health Administration has authority to regulate working conditions on vessels such as oil and gas barges if they are not inspected by the Coast Guard.

LABOR-MANAGEMENT RELATIONS

National Labor Relations Board v. Kentucky River Community Care, Inc. (532 U.S. 706), decided by 9–0 and 5–4 votes, May 29, 2001; Scalia wrote the opinion; Stevens, Souter, Ginsburg, and Breyer dissented.

Nurses may be deemed to be supervisors and denied collective bargaining and other rights under federal labor law. The decision rejected a ruling by the National Labor Relations Board that six nurses employed at a mental health facility should be included in a bargaining unit for a union representation election.

PENSIONS AND BENEFITS

Egelhoff v. Egelhoff (532 U.S. 141), decided by a 7–2 vote, March 21, 2001; Thomas wrote the opinion; Breyer and Stevens dissented.

The Court held that the federal Employee Retirement Income and Security Act, which governs employer-provided pensions and benefits, preempts state statutes that nullify the designation of a divorced spouse as the beneficiary.

Great-West Life & Annuity Insurance Co. v. Knudson (534 U.S. 204), decided by a 5–4 vote, Jan. 8, 2002; Scalia wrote the opinion; Ginsburg, Stevens, Souter, and Breyer dissented.

Health benefit plans cannot sue an employee in federal court to recover money for medical expenses that the worker received from a third party through a court suit or settlement.

Barnhart v. Sigmon Coal Co., Inc. (534 U.S. 438), decided by a 6–3 vote, Feb. 19, 2002; Thomas wrote the opinion; Stevens, O'Connor, and Breyer dissented.

Coal companies do not have to pay lifetime health benefits for miners who retired from some other firms that went out of business and were taken over by other concerns.

The ruling narrowed the scope of the Coal Industry Retiree Health Benefit Act, a 1992 law aimed at guaranteeing health benefits for retired miners. The law required that benefits be provided by the company that had last employed the miners if it was still in business. The Court held that the law did not allow the commissioner of Social Security to assign retired miners to the successor companies of out-of-business coal operators.

Rush Prudential HMO, Inc. v. Moran (536 U.S. 355), decided by a 5–4 vote, June 20, 2002; Souter wrote the opinion; Thomas, Rehnquist, Scalia, and Kennedy dissented.

States may require health maintenance organizations to allow patients covered by employer-provided health plans to seek an independent second opinion after benefits are denied for a requested medical treatment or procedure. The ruling upheld an Illinois statute—comparable to laws in forty-two states and the District of Columbia—that the health insurance industry challenged as preempted by the Employee Retirement Income Security Act, which regulates employer-provided benefits.

Barnhart, Commissioner of Social Security v. Peabody Coal Co. (537 U.S. 149), decided by a 6–3 vote, Jan. 15, 2003; Souter wrote the opinion; Scalia, O'Connor, and Thomas dissented.

Coal companies can be required to pay retirement benefits for miners under a federal pension rescue plan even if the government did not meet the deadline for assigning responsibility for the retired workers to individual companies.

The ruling rejected arguments by several coal companies that could have nullified actions taken by the Social Security commissioner in carrying out provisions of the Coal Industry Retiree Health Benefit Act of 1992, which sought to ensure pension benefits for retired coal miners or their families by establishing an industrywide fund financed in part by premiums paid by individual companies. The Court ruled that the initial assignments of responsibility for retired coal miners' benefits were valid even though late.

Black & Decker Disability Plan v. Nord (538 U.S. 822), decided by a 9–0 vote, May 27, 2003; Ginsburg wrote the opinion.

Employer-provided health benefit plans do not have to give special weight to medical opinions from employees' physicians. The Court held that health plans governed by the federal Employee Retirement Income Security Act need not follow a treating physician preference rule.

Raymond B. Yates, M.D., P.C. Profit Sharing Plan v. Hendon (541 U.S. 1), decided by a 9–0 vote, March 2, 2004; Ginsburg wrote the opinion.

The working owner of a business with a profit-sharing pension plan covered by the Employee Retirement Income Security Act of 1974 is entitled to the same legal protections as employees under the plan.

Central Laborers' Pension Fund v. Heinz (541 U.S. 739), decided by a 9–0 vote, June 7, 2004; Souter wrote the opinion.

The federal law regulating pensions and benefits bars a pension plan from expanding the categories of post-retirement employment that trigger suspension of early retirement benefits already accrued under the plan. The ruling resolved a conflict between federal appeals courts on an interpretation of the anti-cutback rule of the federal Employee Retirement Income and Security Act of 1974, which provides that a retiree's "accrued benefit" may not be decreased by an amendment to the plan.

PROTECTED ACTIVITIES

BE&K Construction Co. v. National Labor Relations Board (536 U.S. 516), decided by a 9–0 vote, June 24, 2002; O'Connor wrote the opinion.

The Court limited the ability of the National Labor Relations Board to punish employers for filing unsuccessful lawsuits against unions for retaliatory motives.

SEAMAN SUITS

Lewis v. Lewis & Clark Marine, Inc. (531 U.S. 438), decided by a 9–0 vote, Feb. 21, 2001; O'Connor wrote the opinion.

State courts can adjudicate most seaman suits for personal injuries despite a long-standing federal law—the Judiciary Act of 1789—that allows ship owners to bring an action in federal court to limit their liability.

Property Law

LAND USE REGULATION

Tahoe-Sierra Preservation Council, Inc. v. Tahoe Regional Planning Agency (535 U.S. 302), decided by a 6–3 vote, April 23, 2002; Stevens wrote the opinion; Rehnquist, Scalia, and Thomas dissented.

The government ordinarily does not have to compensate an owner for a temporary moratorium restricting use of property while developing a long-term land use plan. In a setback for property rights advocates, the Court ruled that an automatic rule requiring compensation for development moratoria would unduly hamper governments in devising land use plans.

LAWYER TRUST ACCOUNTS

Brown v. Legal Foundation of Washington (538 U.S. 216), decided by a 5–4 vote, March 26, 2003; Stevens wrote the opinion; Scalia, Rehnquist, Kennedy, and Thomas dissented.

Use of interest from lawyers' short-term trust accounts to help fund legal aid for the poor does not amount to an unconstitutional taking of the clients' property.

The ruling upheld a legal aid financing scheme used in all fifty states and the District of Columbia. The IOLTA plans—an acronym for "interest on lawyers' trust accounts"—pooled funds held for short time periods by lawyers or in some states real estate professionals. The interest that the pooled accounts earned was funneled to support organizations that provided legal services for the poor. The Court ruled that the program did not violate clients' rights.

TAKINGS

Palazzolo v. Rhode Island (533 U.S. 606), decided by a 5–4 vote, June 28, 2001; Kennedy wrote the opinion; Ginsburg, Stevens, Souter, and Breyer dissented.

A Rhode Island man won a procedural victory in his effort to obtain compensation for the state's blocking him from developing coastal wetlands property, but the Court also limited his potential recovery.

The ruling—claimed as a victory by property rights advocates—came in a constitutional takings claim brought over failed efforts to win a permit to develop eighteen acres of primarily wetlands in the coastal town of Westerly. The Court held that Palazzolo's claim was not barred because of the timing of his acquisition of the property but rejected his argument that the state had denied him any economic use of the property and instead allowed him to seek compensation only under a more limited legal theory.

State and Local Governments

BORDER DISPUTES

New Hampshire v. Maine (532 U.S. 742), decided by an 8–0 vote, May 29, 2001; Ginsburg wrote the opinion; Souter did not participate.

New Hampshire was blocked in a financially significant border dispute with Maine from claiming ownership of the island site of the Portsmouth Naval Shipyard under a doctrine known as "judicial estoppel."

The ruling fortified Maine's claim to Seavey Island, which lies in Portsmouth Harbor on the border between Maine and New Hampshire, and to tax revenues from civilian workers employed at the shipyard on the island.

Virginia v. Maryland (540 U.S. 56), decided by a 7–2 vote, Dec. 9, 2003; Rehnquist wrote the opinion; Kennedy and Stevens dissented.

The citizens and local governments of Virginia may withdraw water from the Potomac River and construct improvements along the Virginia shore of the river without regulatory interference from Maryland.

The ruling affirmed the decision of the Court-appointed special master, who struck down a 1933 permitting system requiring Virginia governmental entities and citizens to seek permits from Maryland to construct improvements and withdraw water from the river. Maryland claimed that it was entitled to regulate Virginia's rights of waterway construction and water withdrawal pursuant to the results of a binding arbitration conducted in 1879 that placed the boundary between the two states at the low-water mark on the Virginia shore of the Potomac. The Court held that the 1879 arbitration precluded Maryland from regulating Virginia's use of the river.

COMMERCE CLAUSE

Hillside Dairy Inc. v. Lyons, Secretary, California Department of Food and Agriculture (539 U.S. 59), decided by an 8–1 vote, June 9, 2003; Stevens wrote the opinion; Thomas dissented in part.

The Court reinstated a complaint by Arizona and Nevada milk producers against a California law requiring them to pay into a fund used to support prices and stabilize income for California dairy farmers.

The ruling stemmed from a challenge by the out-of-state producers to changes that California adopted in its milk pricing and pooling regulations in 1997. The out-of-state dairy farmers, who were ineligible for payments from the pool, filed federal court suits claiming that the regulation violated the negative (or dormant) Commerce Clause by improperly interfering with interstate commerce. They also said the scheme abridged their federal rights as citizens under the Privileges and Immunities Clause.

The Court held that the federal law did not immunize California's milk pricing and pooling scheme from a legal challenge for interfering with interstate commerce.

FALSE CLAIMS ACT

Cook County v. United States ex rel. Chandler (538 U.S. 119), decided by a 9–0 vote, March 10, 2003; Souter wrote the opinion.

Local governments can be sued under the federal False Claims Act for defrauding the federal government. The ruling rejected an effort by Cook County, Illinois—which includes Chicago—to dismiss a whistle-blower's suit alleging that false statements were filed to obtain a $5 million federal grant for drug abuse research.

GOVERNMENT CONTRACTS

Lujan, Labor Commissioner of California v. G & G Fire Sprinklers, Inc. decided by a 9–0 vote, April 17, 2001; Rehnquist wrote the opinion.

State government contractors are not entitled to a hearing before having payments withheld as long as state law allows an in-court remedy for breach of contract. The ruling rejected a due process claim by a fire sprinkler company that was cited by the California Division of Labor Standards Enforcement for violating the state's prevailing wage law on three public works projects.

IMMUNITY

Board of Trustees of the University of Alabama v. Garrett (531 U.S. 356), decided by a 5–4 vote, Feb. 21, 2001; Rehnquist wrote the opinion; Breyer, Stevens, Souter, and Ginsburg dissented.

States cannot be required to pay damages in private suits for violating the federal law that prohibits discrimination in employment against persons with disabilities.

The ruling—another in a series of Rehnquist Court decisions protecting states' rights in federalism disputes—rejected damage suits in federal court brought by two former Alabama state employees under the federal Americans with Disabilities Act (ADA). The Court held that allowing private damage suits against state governments under the ADA would go beyond Congress's power to enforce constitutional rights under the Fourteenth Amendment.

Lapides v. Board of Regents of University System of Georgia (535 U.S. 613), decided by a 9–0 vote, May 13, 2002; Breyer wrote the opinion.

A state cannot claim Eleventh Amendment immunity from federal court jurisdiction after it voluntarily removes a case from a state to a federal court.

Federal Maritime Commission v. South Carolina State Ports Authority (535 U.S. 743), decided by a 5–4 vote, May 28, 2002; Thomas wrote the opinion; Breyer, Stevens, Souter, and Ginsburg dissented.

In another decision favoring the states on federalism issues, the Court ruled that states are immune from private citizen complaints in quasi-judicial proceedings before federal administrative agencies.

Frew v. Hawkins (540 U.S. 431), decided by a 9–0 vote, Jan. 14, 2003; Kennedy wrote the opinion.

State officials are not entitled to sovereign immunity from claims arising under consent decrees designed to protect federal interests, even when such decrees contain requirements that go beyond federal law. The ruling reinstated the enforcement of a 1996 consent decree in a class action suit that required Texas state health officials to improve services for indigent children under the state-federal Medicaid program.

Franchise Tax Board of California v. Hyatt (538 U.S. 488), decided by a 9–0 vote, April 23, 2003; O'Connor wrote the opinion.

States do not have to recognize laws of another state that give its tax-collecting agencies immunity from private damage suits.

The ruling cleared the way for a onetime California resident to pursue a suit against the state's Franchise Tax Board for an allegedly abusive tax investigation in his newly adopted State of Nevada. The Court held that the Nevada court could entertain the suit against the California tax board despite California's law protecting tax-collecting agencies from suit. "The Constitution does not confer sovereign immunity on States in the courts of sister States," O'Connor wrote.

Nevada Department of Human Resources v. Hibbs (538 U.S. 721), decided by a 6–3 vote, May 27, 2003; Rehnquist wrote the opinion; Kennedy, Scalia, and Thomas dissented.

State employees can sue state governments for monetary damages for violating the federal law guaranteeing unpaid leave to care for an ailing family member.

The ruling—a turnaround from previous decisions extending states' immunity from damage suits—cleared the way for a Nevada man's suit against a state agency for a claimed violation of the Family and Medical Leave Act, which required private or government employers to allow employees to take up to twelve weeks' unpaid leave annually when needed to care for a spouse, child, or parent with a "serious health condition."

Tennessee Student Assistance Corporation v. Hood (541 U.S. 440), decided by a 7–2 vote, May 17, 2004; Rehnquist wrote the opinion; Thomas and Scalia dissented.

A federal bankruptcy court can discharge or forgive a student loan debt owed to a state government entity without violating the state's immunity from private suits under the Eleventh Amendment.

Hibbs, Director, Arizona Department of Revenue v. Winn (542 U.S. 88), decided by a 5–4 vote, June 14, 2004; Ginsburg wrote the opinion; Kennedy, Rehnquist, Scalia, and Thomas dissented.

The law generally prohibiting federal court suits that interfere with state tax collections does not bar a constitutional challenge to a state tax credit to pay tuition for students at religious schools.

The ruling allowed Arizona taxpayers to proceed in federal court with a constitutional challenge to a 1997 law allowing a $500 tax credit for donations to nonprofit organizations providing scholarships for tuition at private elementary and secondary schools. The Court upheld the Arizona residents' right to challenge the state's use of tax revenue for funding of religious schools.

TAXATION

Director of Revenue of Missouri v. CoBank ACB (531 U.S. 316), decided by a 9–0 vote, Feb. 20, 2001; Thomas wrote the opinion.

Federally chartered banks for farm cooperatives are subject to state income taxation. The ruling rejected an effort by CoBank, part of the national Farm Credit System, for tax refunds from the State of Missouri.

Fitzgerald, Treasurer of Iowa v. Racing Association of Central Iowa (539 U.S. 103), decided by a 9–0 vote, June 9, 2003; Breyer wrote the opinion.

An Iowa law taxing revenues from slot machines at racetracks at a higher rate than revenues from slot machines on excursion riverboats is constitutional.

The ruling reversed a decision by the Iowa Supreme Court that the 1994 state law establishing the rate differentials violated the Equal Protection Clause. The Court said the law satisfied the rational basis test for judging laws that do not discriminate on a suspect basis.

WATER RIGHTS

Kansas v. Colorado (533 U.S. 1), decided by 9–0 and 6–3 votes, June 11, 2001; Stevens wrote the opinion; O'Connor, Scalia, and Thomas dissented in part.

The State of Colorado was required to pay the State of Kansas prejudgment interest for improper diversion of water from the Arkansas River—but for a substantially shorter period of time than Kansas had urged.

The multipart ruling came in a fifteen-year legal battle touched off by Kansas's accusation that Colorado was violating the terms of a 1949 compact governing the allocation of the waters of the Arkansas River, which rises in Colorado and flows through Kansas, Oklahoma, and then Arkansas before joining the Mississippi River.

A fractured Court majority settled on 1986—the date of the filing of Kansas's complaint—as the date to begin calculating interest instead of 1950, when Kansas claimed the improper diversions had begun.

Tort Law

ALIEN TORT STATUTE

Sosa v. Alvarez-Machain (542 U.S. 692), decided by a 9–0 vote, June 29, 2004; Souter wrote the opinion.

A Mexican doctor who was kidnapped to stand trial in the United States but later acquitted was barred from bringing suit in federal court against a former Mexican police officer or the U.S. government for their parts in the abduction.

The ruling—in a case with significant implications for multinational corporations as well as international human rights advocates—upheld the dismissals of separate suits brought by the doctor under the Alien Tort Statute and the Federal Tort Claims Act. The Court ordered the dismissal of both claims with a compromise ruling that limited but did not completely eliminate federal court jurisdiction over personal injury suits by aliens for events outside the United States. The decision also virtually barred use of the Federal Tort Claims Act for actions committed in foreign countries.

ASBESTOS

Norfolk & Western Railway Co. v. Ayers (538 U.S. 135), decided by a 5–4 vote, March 10, 2003; Ginsburg wrote the opinion; Kennedy, Rehnquist, O'Connor, and Breyer dissented in part.

Railroad workers suffering asbestosis as a result of workplace exposure to asbestos can recover damages for mental anguish resulting from fear of developing cancer.

The ruling—a major setback for defendants in the growing number of asbestos-related suits—upheld awards by a West Virginia jury totaling about $4.9 million in favor of six plaintiffs who had been exposed to asbestos while working at various times for the Norfolk & Western Railway Co.

HEALTH CARE

Aetna Health Inc. v. Davila (542 U.S. 200), decided by a 9–0 vote, June 21, 2004; Thomas wrote the opinion.

Patients covered by employer-provided health plans cannot sue health maintenance organizations in state court for refusing to pay for doctor-recommended medical care.

In a victory for managed care insurers, the Court ruled that the suits originally filed in Texas courts by two patients under a "patients' rights" law comparable to statutes in eight other states were preempted by the Employee Retirement Income Security Act of 1974.

PUNITIVE DAMAGES

Cooper Industries, Inc. v. Leatherman Tool Group, Inc. (532 U.S. 424), decided by an 8–1 vote, May 14, 2001; Stevens wrote the opinion; Ginsburg dissented.

Federal appellate courts should exercise independent review over the constitutionality of punitive damage awards. The ruling reinstated an effort by an Oregon-based tool manufacturer to reduce a $4.5 million punitive damage award won in an unfair competition suit by a rival company, contending that appeals courts should use a "de novo" standard for reviewing punitive damage awards—in effect, make an independent decision—instead of applying the more deferential "abuse of discretion" standard. The Court agreed that the broader standard of review should be applied.

State Farm Mutual Automobile Insurance Co. v. Campbell (538 U.S. 408), decided by a 6–3 vote, April 7, 2003; Kennedy wrote the opinion; Scalia, Thomas, and Ginsburg dissented.

The Court threw out as "excessive" a $145 million punitive damage award against a major insurance company for bad faith in mishandling an automobile accident claim against one of its policyholders. Without setting a fixed ratio, the Court suggested that punitive damages should rarely if ever be as much as ten times the amount of a compensatory damage award.

In a significant victory for insurance and business groups, the Court held that the punitive damage award violated the Due Process Clause of the Fourteenth Amendment, mainly because it punished the insurance company for conduct outside the state and unrelated to the case.

RACKETEERING

Cedric Kushner Promotions, Ltd. v. King (533 U.S. 158), decided by a 9–0 vote, June 11, 2001; Breyer wrote the opinion.

The sole shareholder of a closely held corporation may be subject to suit under the federal antiracketeering law for using the company to conduct a "pattern" of racketeering activity.

The ruling reinstated a suit by boxing promoter Cedric Kushner against a rival promoter, Don King, brought under the federal Racketeer Influenced and Corrupt Organizations Act (commonly known as RICO). The law allows a civil damage suit against any "person" employed by an "enterprise" who conducts its business through the commission of two or more specified crimes—which are defined as a "pattern of racketeering activity." The Court held that King was sufficiently distinct from the corporation to be subject to suit under the RICO.

Scheidler v. National Organization for Women, Inc. (537 U.S. 393), decided by an 8–1 vote, Feb. 26, 2003; Rehnquist wrote the opinion; Stevens dissented.

The Court threw out a $250,000 damage award and nationwide injunction issued against antiabortion protesters, saying that their campaign of abortion clinic blockades did not constitute "extortion" under the federal antiracketeering law.

The ruling came in a class action suit filed by the National Organization for Women on behalf of abortion clinics nationwide under the federal Racketeer Influenced and Corrupt Organizations Act (known as RICO). The defendants included various antiabortion activists and groups. The suit charged that the groups' campaign of blockades at abortion clinics amounted to "extortion" under the federal Hobbs Act that could form the basis for a civil damage racketeering suit. The Hobbs Act defines extortion to mean "the obtaining of property from another . . . by wrongful use of actual or threatened force, violence or fear. . . ."

The Court held that the antiabortion protesters' actions did not constitute extortion because they did not obtain "property" from the clinics. Without the Hobbs Act violations, there was no basis for the racketeering suit. On that basis, the Court declined to rule on a second issue in the case: whether a private party could obtain a nationwide injunction in a RICO action.

WARSAW CONVENTION

Olympic Airways v. Husain (540 U.S. 644), decided by a 6–2 vote, Feb. 24, 2004; Thomas wrote the opinion; Scalia and O'Connor dissented; Breyer did not participate.

An airline is liable for the death of a passenger under the Warsaw Convention if the conduct of its employees constitutes a link in a chain of causes leading to the passenger's death.

The ruling upheld a wrongful death judgment against the Greek airline Olympic Airways for its role in precipitating the fatal asthma attack of a passenger onboard a December 1997 flight from Cairo to San Francisco by refusing to act on repeated requests to have the passenger moved away from the airline's smoking section.

CHAPTER 14

General Government

General Government

George W. Bush was the first president with a masters of business administration, and he brought his generally probusiness outlook to the White House. The administration, for example, sought to outsource federal services in an effort to cut costs and reduce the federal workforce. It also looked to protect business interests by limiting federal regulations.

PRIVATIZATION

The Bush administration had limited success in gaining more management control and flexibility over federal personnel. In its first year the administration identified more than 800,000 federal jobs it considered essentially commercial in nature; almost half of the entire civilian workforce thus was targeted for outsourcing. In May 2003 the Office of Management and Budget issued regulations designed to streamline and accelerate the competition between government workers and private companies to provide federal services.

The push for more outsourcing of federal services and jobs endeared Bush to Republicans who had a fundamental distrust of the bureaucracy, and in a broader context of government itself. Republicans were outspoken proponents of limiting governmental functions and calling in private contractors to, for example, mow the lawn at a Social Security field office or integrate agency computer systems. Meanwhile, Bush was at odds with the powerful federal employee unions and members of Congress who vociferously protected their turf when it came to federal jobs or programs in their districts. Democrats challenged claims that outsourcing would be cheaper than retaining federal jobs. They maintained that they were concerned not only about people losing their jobs, but also about people losing their jobs unfairly, based on unproven assumptions about cost savings. Although the administration never spelled out an ultimate goal that would flow from the concept of outsourcing, Bush critics charged that it would lead logically to a federal workforce that performed only duties that were inherently governmental—meaning to make policy if it is a federal agency, fly planes if it is the Air Force, and protect the homeland if it is the Department of Homeland Security.

House Government Reform Committee Chair Thomas M. Davis III, R-Va., said that Congress and the administration should get beyond the ideological divisions over privatizing government functions and focus on reforming the process. The federal government, he said, should spend more on employee training to give workers the expertise to compete with the innovations of the private sector. But critics of Bush's plans argued that too much outsourcing would demoralize the federal workforce. They strongly believed that some functions should remain under the federal government, and argued that sensitive security and safety functions should be performed by government employees rather than contractors.

REGULATORY REFORM

President Ronald Reagan by executive order in 1981 created the Office of Information and Regulatory Affairs (OIRA) within the Office of Management and Budget as a way to control federal rulemaking. Business leaders had complained for years that federal agencies promulgated regulations with little regard for the cost of implementing them and that rules often were out of proportion to their public benefit or unfairly restricted business options, such as use of land. On the other side, environmental, consumer, and other groups argued that making government regulations on the basis of cost-effectiveness would be unwise public policy that could endanger public health and natural resources.

REFERENCES

Discussion of general government action for the years 1945–1964 may be found in *Congress and the Nation Vol. I*, pp. 1455–1516; for the years 1965–1968, *Congress and the Nation Vol. II*, pp. 655–660; for the years 1969–1972, *Congress and the Nation Vol. III*, pp. 435–468; for the years 1973–1976, *Congress and the Nation Vol. IV*, pp. 795–826; for the years 1977–1980, *Congress and the Nation Vol. V*, pp. 817–870; for the years 1981–1984, *Congress and the Nation Vol. VI*, pp. 771–793; for the years 1985–1988, *Congress and the Nation Vol. VII*, pp. 843–867; for the years 1989–1992, *Congress and the Nation Vol. VIII*, pp. 855–909; for the years 1993–1996, *Congress and the Nation Vol. IX*, pp. 803–858; for the years 1997–2001, *Congress and the Nation Vol. X*, pp. 733–754.

Outlays for Science, Space, and General Government

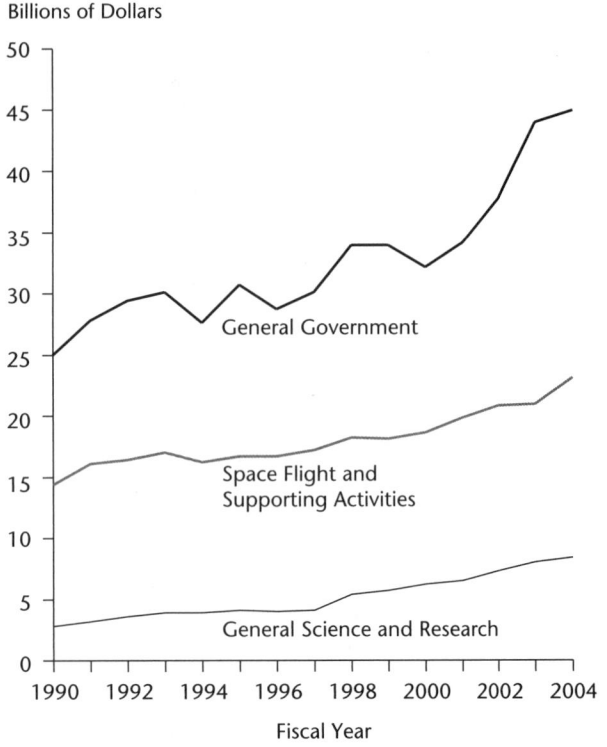

Billions of Dollars

SOURCE: Office of Management and Budget, *Historical Tables, Budget of the United States Government: Fiscal Year 2006* (Washington, D.C.: U.S. Government Printing Office, 2005), Table 3.2.

Not since the Reagan administration was OIRA so active as it was under the Bush administration. OIRA rejected most proposed regulations, saying they were too far-reaching, too costly, or unsupported by adequate analysis. Supporters said OIRA simply was imposing order and reasoned analysis on a regulatory machine that had spiraled out of control. Opponents said OIRA was achieving the administration's political goals by stalemating regulations. Furthermore, some public interest groups said they worried that OIRA could be trying to assume duties that agencies were required by law to perform. Consumer activists said only agencies with the required resources and knowledge should be writing regulations.

During consideration of the fiscal 2001 Treasury and General Government appropriations bill (PL 106-554), business and industry groups had a big hand in writing a little-noticed rider, which took effect on Oct. 1, 2002. OIRA was directed to oversee the process by which federal agencies were required to draft guidelines to ensure the accuracy of data on which they based regulations. Once the guidelines were established, anyone could challenge government statistics underlying a range of federal rules.

Government regulations frequently were challenged in court, and the cases sometimes lasted for years. Conservatives argued that the new policy allowed business groups and others to question the data underlying regulations, thereby placing a barricade that required rigorous examination and defense of rules. In anticipation of implementation of the policy, business groups began poring over regulations to see which could be vulnerable. They analyzed environmental, health, and worker safety rules for what they considered flaws. The National Federation of Independent Business, for example, developed a computer program designed to estimate the cost of federal regulations for small businesses.

Trade groups and consumer advocates both saw the new policy as the beginning of an era in which organizations that could hire scientists and other experts to back up their assertions would have a huge advantage over those that could not. Consumer and environmental lobbyists worried that the policy could add months or years to the process of issuing new and needed federal regulations, even though the stated goal of more accurate and balanced data was worthy.

One unresolved issue was whether data quality questions could be raised while a rule was being written. The concern was that the regulatory process could stall if early intervention were allowed. If challenges were permitted, agency officials could be in a bind, particularly if they have a congressional or court-ordered deadline to meet for fashioning a rule. Under existing law, agencies were not supposed to delay rules unreasonably. Furthermore, with many agencies feeling the budget squeeze, some officials were concerned that the added burden of defending data could slow them down.

Another point of contention about the guidelines was whether they would be legally enforceable. Agencies and departments were to follow the guidelines when practical; they were not legally binding regulations. Also, guidelines for each agency varied—some limited the amount of time after a piece of information was published that groups could question the data and some specified that the challenger be someone who was directly affected by the information. Each agency determined how a challenge must be presented and who in its department would hear appeals. Resolution of such arcane differences could have a big impact on the outcome.

Chronology of Action on General Government

2001–2002

Postal Service Overhaul

Reviews released in 2001 by the U.S. Postal Service and the General Accounting Office concluded that financial problems at the Postal Service were coming more rapidly than previously expected. The 107th Congress, however, took no action to overhaul the nation's postal system. *(108th Congress action, p. 691)*

Electronic payment systems and e-mail provided consumers with quick and inexpensive alternatives to traditional mail, and the rapid growth of these modes of communication posed a threat to the cornerstone of the U.S. mail system—universal service in every part of the country. The mail service's debt was expected in fiscal 2002 to hit the statutory cap of $15 billion set in a 1989 law (PL 101-227). That prospect prompted renewed pressure to find cost-cutting measures within the postal system and to pass legislation that would allow the Postal Service to implement them.

Reps. John M. McHugh, R-N.Y., and Danny K. Davis, D-Ill., cosponsored legislation to give the Postal Service more flexibility in setting rates by allowing it to change prices without explicit permission of the Postal Rate Commission. The 170-page draft bill would allow the Postal Service to make a profit pegged to the rate of inflation that could be reinvested, as opposed to the existing process that essentially tied rate making to the cost of service.

Rep. Philip M. Crane, R-Ill., introduced a bill (HR 5702) to privatize the Postal Service. It was referred to the House Government Reform Committee and died upon adjournment.

The Postal Service was a quasi-independent agency providing a public service widely considered to be essential. It had a monopoly on first-class mail. Because of a patchwork of laws that governed its operation, it was required to break even but could not make a profit. To meet rising costs, it either had to raise postal rates, cut costs, or develop new products and services.

However, its cost-cutting plans were hindered by laws put in place to protect local post offices. Congress had made closing post offices so cumbersome that the Postal Service declared a voluntary moratorium on the practice to focus internal attention on other possible remedies, even though twenty-six thousand of the nation's thirty-eight thousand post offices—more than two-thirds—lost money each year.

In March 2001 the Postal Service announced a plan to temporarily stop construction on eight hundred post office projects that included new buildings and expansions of existing ones. The move was expected to conserve about $1 billion. Lawmakers representing areas of growing population objected to the plan.

On Dec. 11, 2002, the Bush administration announced the establishment of the Presidential Commission on the U.S. Postal Service. The nine-member commission was to "identify the operational, structural, and financial challenges facing the Postal Service; examine potential solutions; and recommend legislative and administrative steps to ensure the long-term viability of postal service in the United States." A report was due by July 31, 2003.

White House Accounts Consolidation

During consideration of the fiscal 2002 Treasury and Postal Service appropriations legislation (HR 2590), the House by voice vote on July 25, 2001, adopted a Rep. Ernest Istook, R-Okla., amendment to merge ten of eighteen accounts that the White House wanted consolidated. The House Appropriations Committee (H Rept 107-152) had rejected a proposal to consolidate all eighteen, on a 31–31 tie vote. The issue helped create a logjam to final action on HR 2590. Senate opponents, led by Byron L. Dorgan, D-N.D., succeeded in dropping the White House plan in conference, despite personal intervention by Vice President Dick Cheney.

Republicans said the change was needed to give the executive branch more budgeting flexibility; Democrats said it would hinder congressional oversight.

The White House pursued the same proposal in 2002, but it proved to be a nonstarter. Congressional aides said that administration recalcitrance on numerous issues—from Office of Homeland Security director Tom Ridge's refusal to testify before Congress to noncompliance with congressional requests for documents related to the bankrupt Enron Corp.—

PAPERWORK REDUCTION

The General Accounting Office (GAO), in a 2001 report, said that fiscal 2000 federal paperwork increased by a net of nearly 180 million "burden hours." That was the second largest yearly gain since 1995, when a law (PL 104-13) designed to reduce federal paperwork was enacted. *(1995 law, Congress and the Nation Vol. IX, p. 840)*

A burden hour is supposed to measure the time it takes to collect data and fill out federal forms, surveys, and reports. Although the measurement has been used for half a century, GAO said that the burden hour's relationship to the real burden "is unclear."

According to the GAO, the Internal Revenue Service (IRS) was responsible for 83 percent of the paperwork load, followed at a great distance by the Departments of Labor, Transportation, and Health and Human Services and the Environmental Protection Agency. While some agencies reduced their paperwork burdens in fiscal 2000—the Federal Trade Commission and the Departments of Defense and Transportation—the IRS's estimate for fiscal 2000 increased by 240 million burden hours over fiscal 1999. The difference was attributed to changes in tax forms 1040 and 1040A.

Under PL 104-13, the Office of Management and Budget is supposed to keep the flurry of forms in check.

strengthened the case for continuing detailed congressional oversight of White House accounts.

Presidential Records

The House Government Reform Committee by voice vote Oct. 9, 2002, approved a bill (HR 4187) to countermand President George W. Bush's decision to put a protective cloak over the papers of his predecessors. HR 4287, sponsored by Rep. Steve Horn, R-Calif., was formally reported (H Rept 107-790) on Nov. 22. Under the bill an incoming president would have six months to review records slated for release, and executive privilege claims would be subject to review by Congress and the national archivist.

Bush on Nov. 1, 2001, had signed an executive order restricting release of presidential records. Under the order, past presidents may prevent release of records that include conversations with their advisers and lawyers.

Bush's apparent aim was to halt release of sixty-eight thousand pages of papers from the administration of Ronald Reagan, who served from 1981 to 1989. The president's father, George Bush, was Reagan's vice president. Furthermore, Reagan aides included such George W. Bush administration figures as Secretary of State Colin L. Powell and Office of Management and Budget director Mitchell E. Daniels Jr.

GOP lawmakers who wanted access to Clinton administration documents were furious about Bush's action. They questioned whether he had undermined the 1978 Presidential Records Act (PL 95-591), which made most papers of outgoing presidents public property. The law was an effort to broaden a 1974 law (PL 93-526) designed to prevent the destruction of former president Richard M. Nixon's tapes and papers. *(1978 law, Congress and the Nation Vol. V, p. 830; 1974 law, Congress and the Nation Vol. IV, p. 952)*

Bush on Dec. 12, 2001, instructed Attorney General John Ashcroft not to hand over White House papers subpoenaed by lawmakers, invoking executive privilege for the first time. The papers dealt with why President Bill Clinton's attorney general, Janet Reno, declined to investigate alleged campaign finance abuses and how the Federal Bureau of Investigation bungled an organized crime case in the 1960s.

The White House said that the executive order created a step-by-step process for the release of presidential papers and was not intended to undermine public access to information. HR 4187 saw no further congressional action, falling victim to the administration's objections and scant support from rank-and-file Republicans.

Vice Presidential Residence

Congress in 2002 directed the Navy to pay the electricity bills for the vice presidential residence, located on the grounds of the Naval Observatory in Northwest Washington, D.C. Action came on the fiscal 2003 Transportation and Postal Service appropriations measure (HR 2590—PL 107-67).

The Navy and the Office of the Vice President had been sharing the cost for the past three years. However, costs had more than doubled after Al Gore moved out and Dick Cheney moved in. The administration wanted the Navy to assume full responsibility to insulate Cheney from "the fluctuating and unpredictable nature of utility costs."

Democrats lambasted the request as hypocritical, citing a widely quoted Cheney comment that energy consumption should be a matter of individual responsibility. They also said that the electricity bills were evidence that Cheney, who had taken the lead in shaping President George W. Bush's energy policy, was insufficiently attuned to the need for conservation.

The House Appropriations Committee July 17 rejected 29–33 an amendment by ranking committee Democrat David R. Obey of Wisconsin to delete the cost-shifting language and to drop a second administration proposal to permit donations of food, drinks, flowers, tents, and other supplies for use in the vice president's official entertaining. A similar exception to the government gratuities rule applied to the White House.

On the House floor, a July 25 attempt by Jay Inslee, D-Wash., to bar the Navy from paying the electricity bills at the vice president's mansion was defeated, 141–285. The same day, the House rejected 151–274 a Maurice D. Hinchey, D-N.Y., amendment to strike the provision on donated food and drinks.

Senate appropriators decided against joining the campaign to compel the vice president's office to pay the entire electricity bill for the vice presidential residence.

D.C. Partners' Benefits

In a victory for home-rule advocates, the fiscal 2002 District of Columbia appropriations bill (HR 2944—PL 107-96) permitted the city for the first time to use local, though not federal, money to implement a 1992 D.C. law that allowed city employee health plans to provide benefits to unmarried and same-sex domestic partners.

On Sept. 25, 2001, before passing HR 2944, the House rejected by a 194–226 vote a Dave Weldon, R-Fla., amendment to reverse the House Appropriations Committee language providing for domestic partner benefits. The version of the measure (S 1543) adopted by the Senate Appropriations Committee Oct. 1 also allowed D.C. to use local funds to pay health benefits to unmarried domestic partners.

Printing Office Dispute

Congress in 2002 ordered the Bush administration to comply with a federal law (PL 90-62) requiring that government documents go through the Government Printing Office (GPO). The stipulation initially was inserted in the Senate version of the fiscal 2003 legislative branch appropriations legislation (S 2720) and then was included in a series of stop-gap budget laws.

Office of Management and Budget (OMB) director Mitchell E. Daniels Jr. on May 3, 2002, had issued a memorandum ordering federal agencies to use private printers if they could do the jobs faster and more cheaply. The policy was supposed to take effect on Sept. 1, 2002.

GPO subcontracted 84 percent of its work to private printers. But the OMB memorandum said GPO premiums and fees were costing agencies an extra $50 million to $70 million a year. Senate appropriators, however, said in the report accompanying S 2720 (S Rept 107-209) that the memorandum showed the proposed change could increase the government's costs by as much as $335 million in the first year.

President George W. Bush said he did not think Congress ought to be dictating where the executive branch takes its printing jobs. He said that Congress's language "violates the constitutional principles of separation of powers and therefore is not binding on the executive branch."

In an agreement between GPO and OMB announced June 6, 2003, federal agencies would be able to choose among approved private sector printers that agreed to offer their services to the government at their lowest rates.

Dollar Redesign

House appropriators in 2002 moved to squelch a proposed "liberty dollar" with an abridged version of the Con-

stitution printed on the back. Language in the fiscal 2003 Treasury and Postal Service appropriations bill (HR 5120) would ban a redesign of the buck.

Students of Liberty Middle School in Ashland, Va., lobbied members of Congress with their idea for the $1 bill redesign, which was conceived after the Sept. 11, 2001, terrorist attacks.

Operators of coin-operated games and vending machines argued that the makeover would force their industry to spend $240 million to update machines to handle the new money. Congressional appropriators called the proposal an unfunded mandate on business.

And, if the idea had gained traction, Rep. Doug Bereuter, R-Neb., said, it "might be impossible" to agree on how to abbreviate the wording.

Rep. Ernest Istook, R-Okla., said the main reason for the redesign of the $100, $20, $10, and $5 bills was to incorporate features to foil counterfeiters, such as off-center portraits, fine threads, and holograms. Istook and Sen. Ben Nighthorse Campbell, R-Colo., said criminals had little use for $1 bills, except to bleach them to make bigger bills.

Istook said the main support for a new bill came from coin collectors and currency design contractors.

By way of compromise, Sen. George Allen, R-Va., suggested putting the Constitution on the back of the $2 bill. Featured on the front is Thomas Jefferson, drafter of the Declaration of Independence and third president of the United States. Rep. Jim Kolbe, R-Ariz., said the $2 bill needed a facelift to match other redesigned bills.

Istook suggested another place to exhibit the Constitution: a postage stamp. Allen replied, "I don't think it'll fit unless it's a real big one."

NSF Reauthorization

Congress in 2002 cleared legislation (HR 4664) to reauthorize the National Science Foundation (NSF) for fiscal years 2003 through 2007.

As enacted, HR 4664 provided $5.5 billion for fiscal 2003, including $4.2 billion for research and related activities, $1 billion for education and human resources, $172 million for major research equipment and facilities construction, $191 million for salaries and expenses, $3.5 million for the Office of the National Science Board, and $7.7 million for the Office of Inspector General; $6.4 billion for fiscal 2004, including $4.8 billion for research and related activities, $1.2 billion for education and human resources, $211 million for major research equipment and facilities construction, $210 million for salaries and expenses, $3.9 million for the Office of the National Science Board, and $8.5 million for the Office of Inspector General; $7.4 billion for fiscal 2005, including $5.5 billion for research and related activities, $1.3 billion for education and human resources, $259 million for major research equipment and facilities construction, $231 million for salaries and expenses, $4.3 million for the Office of the National Science Board, and $9.3 million for the Office of Inspector General; $8.5 billion for fiscal 2006; and $9.8 billion for fiscal 2007.

The NSF director was called upon to carry out the foundation's research and education programs, including those pertaining to information technology; nanoscale science and engineering; plant genome research; innovative partnerships; mathematics and science education partnerships; the awarding of grants to institutions of higher education to provide scholarships, stipends, and programs to recruit and train mathematics and science teachers; science, mathematics, engineering, and technology talent expansion; secondary school reform initiatives designed to promote scientific and technological literacy; an experimental program to stimulate competitive research; a comprehensive program to advance the goals of the 1980 Science and Engineering Opportunities Act (PL 96-516); and astronomical research and instrumentation. *(Congress and the Nation Vol. V, p. 855)*

The House Science Committee reported HR 4664 (H Rept 107-488) on June 4, 2002. Before passing the bill 397–25 on June 5, the House rejected 165–259 a Lynn Woolsey, D-Calif., amendment to authorize $35 million to establish a biosafety research program that would study the impact on biological systems of new variations of plant and other species. The Senate passed an amended version of the measure by voice vote on Nov. 14. The House agreed to the Senate changes the next day, completing congressional action.

The president signed the bill into law (PL 107-368) on Dec. 19.

World War II Memorial

Congress in 2001 cleared legislation (HR 1696) to speed up construction of a proposed World War II memorial on the National Mall in Washington, D.C. The bill was signed into law (PL 107-11) on May 28.

Congressional action was prompted by a National Capital Planning Commission move to reconsider its approval of the memorial. The commission, which was facing a legal challenge to its earlier votes, had agreed unanimously May 3, 2001, to hold two more days of hearings in June and review its approval of the memorial. The National Coalition to Save Our Mall fought the proposed site at the east end of the Reflecting Pool, saying it would ruin the scenic and symbolic open space between the Lincoln Memorial and the Washington Monument.

Memorial backer and House Armed Services Committee Chair Bob Stump, R-Ariz., persuaded House Resources Committee Chair James V. Hansen, R-Utah, to waive his panel's jurisdiction over HR 1696, which would end any further review of the memorial, even those issues pending in court. The memorial had been in the planning stage for eight years.

The House passed the bill on May 15 by 400–15 under suspension of the rules. The measure would require that ground be broken "expeditiously." It also would make bind-

ing all previous decisions on the 7.4-acre memorial and exempt them from further administrative or judicial review. The Senate on May 21 passed an amended HR 1696 by voice vote. The House, by voice vote under suspension of the rules on May 22, cleared the bill.

A Senate version of the legislation (S 580) had been referred to the Senate Governmental Affairs Committee.

The National World War II Memorial opened to the public on April 29, 2004. Operated by the National Park Service, the memorial is located on 17th Street, between Constitution and Independence Avenues.

African American Museum

Congress in 2001 cleared legislation (HR 3442) to establish the National Museum of African American History and Culture Plan for Action Presidential Commission to develop a procedure for the establishment and maintenance of the National Museum of African American History and Culture in Washington, D.C.

Bill sponsor John Lewis, D-Ga., a civil rights pioneer, had been trying since 1988 to get a museum of African American history on the National Mall. HR 3442 authorized the Smithsonian Institution to renovate its Arts and Industries Building for an African American museum. The measure stipulated no overall price tag, but Lewis expected that two-thirds of the cost would be raised privately.

The House passed HR 3442 on Dec. 11 by voice vote under suspension of the rules. The Senate passed the bill by voice vote Dec. 17, completing congressional action. The president signed the legislation into law (PL 107-106) on Dec. 28.

The Smithsonian had first agreed to the plan in 1991 and the Senate passed an authorizing bill, but Rep. Gus Savage (D-Ill., 1981–1993) demanded a larger museum and blocked the measure. The House passed similar legislation in 1993, but Sen. Jesse Helms (R-N.C., 1973–2003) bottled it up in the Senate Rules Committee, complaining of its potential cost. *(Congress and the Nation Vol. IX, p. 825)*

Adams Memorial

Congress in 2001 cleared legislation (HR 1668) honoring John Adams, the second president of the United States, and his family. Adams's wife, Abigail, was an abolitionist and early advocate of women's rights, and his son, John Quincy Adams, was the nation's sixth president.

Rep. Mark Souder, R-Ind., said that a popular book about Adams by historian David McCullough renewed interest in a man who was one of the driving forces behind the Declaration of Independence.

The House passed the bill by voice vote under suspension of the rules June 25, 2001. The Senate Energy and Natural Resources Committee reported the measure (S Rept 107-77) on Oct. 1. The Senate passed HR 1668 on Oct. 17 by voice vote. It was signed into law (PL 107-62) on Nov. 5.

Tribal Casino

During conference committee negotiations, Congress in 2001 included a provision in the fiscal 2002 Interior appropriations bill (HR 2217—PL 107-63) that could open the way for the Wyandotte tribe of Oklahoma to build a casino next to the Huron Indian Cemetery in Kansas City, Kansas.

The language was sought by the tribe and by former representative Louis A. Bafalis (R-Fla., 1973–1983), who was a lobbyist for North American Sports Management Inc., a promoter of the casino project. The provision would allow the interior secretary to create a reservation for the tribe and permit a casino.

Sen. Sam Brownback, R-Kan., offered an amendment to the fiscal 2002 Labor, Health and Human Services, and Education appropriations measure (HR 3061—PL 107-116) nullifying the Interior bill language regarding the Indian casino. The amendment was adopted by voice vote on Nov. 1, 2001. However, it was stripped from the bill in conference.

The Wyandotte said the land in dispute is an ancestral burial ground, and they claimed the right to a reservation there under an 1855 treaty. Brownback said the tribe's proposal was opposed by local and state officials as well as four Kansas tribes.

Indian Tribe Compensation

The House and Senate in 2002 passed legislation (S 434) to provide equitable compensation to the Yankton Sioux Tribe of South Dakota and the Santee Sioux Tribe of Nebraska for land flooded along the Missouri River because of dam construction in 1944. The bill died upon adjournment.

S 434 (S Rept 107-214) was formally reported by the Senate Indian Affairs Committee on July 22, 2002. Two days later, the full Senate passed the bill by voice vote.

On Oct. 1, the House Committee on Resources reported S 434 (H Rept 107-706) and the full House agreed to suspend the rules and pass the bill, 357–37. Differences between the Senate- and House-passed versions were not reconciled before Congress adjourned.

The House panel had reported a companion measure (HR 2408—H Rept 107-689) on Sept. 25.

2003–2004

Federal Job Privatization

White House plans to contract out federal jobs to private workers made headway in the 108th Congress.

FISCAL 2003 OMNIBUS APPROPRIATIONS

The Treasury-Postal Service section of the fiscal 2003 omnibus appropriations bill (H J Res 2—PL 108-7) allowed quotas for contracting out federal jobs if they were "based on considered research and sound analysis of past activities and [were] consistent with the stated mission of the executive agency." However, the conference report (H Rept 108-10) expressed opposition to "arbitrary" quotas and required that the government report to the House and Senate Appropriations Committees on any quotas that were used. The Bush administration had warned of a possible veto if a provision blocking the outsourcing language were not dropped from the legislation.

FISCAL 2004 APPROPRIATIONS BILLS

During consideration of the fiscal 2004 Transportation-Treasury funding bill (HR 2989), the House on a **key vote of 220–198 (R 26–195; D 193–3; I 1–0)** on Sept. 9, 2003, adopted a Chris Van Hollen, D-Md., amendment to bar the Office of Management and Budget (OMB) from enforcing a May 29, 2003, directive to federal agencies to make 15 percent of their jobs available for private sector competition by the end of September 2003. In a statement of administration policy, OMB warned that the provision would trigger a veto and said "prohibiting funding for public-private competitions is akin to mandating a monopoly regardless of the impact on services to citizens and added costs to taxpayers." *(2003 key votes, p. 837)*

The Senate avoided a second confrontation with President George W. Bush over HR 2989 when it rejected, 47–48 on Oct. 23, a Barbara A. Mikulski, D-Md., amendment to prohibit OMB from implementing its directive on opening some government jobs to private contractors. Instead, the Senate by 95–1 on Oct. 23 adopted a Craig Thomas, R-Wyo., and George V. Voinovich, R-Ohio, amendment to require reports to Congress on the status of competitive bidding, allow federal employees whose jobs had been outsourced to appeal the decision, remove the requirement that federal jobs be assessed for outsourcing every five years, and prohibit contracting out if the purpose was to move those jobs overseas.

House and Senate negotiators reached agreement on a compromise Transportation-Treasury bill, adopting language on federal job privatization that they assumed the White House would accept. However, the administration objected to the outsourcing language, and House GOP leaders prevented appropriators from filing their conference report. Instead, HR 2989 was made part of the conference on the fiscal 2004 omnibus spending bill (HR 2673—H Rept 108-401).

The initial conference report on the Transportation-Treasury bill included language similar to a provision in the Defense (HR 2658—PL 108-87) and Interior (HR 2691—PL 108-108) appropriations legislation that allowed outsourcing of government jobs only if a private contractor could do the job for 10 percent or $10 million less, whichever was lower. The omnibus limited the provision to programs covered by the Defense and Interior Departments. For employees of agencies covered by the Transportation-Treasury bill, the provision became just one of many options to be considered during an outsourcing review. At the administration's insistence, the omnibus also dropped language that would establish an appeals process for workers whose positions were to be privatized.

Two significant provisions survived from the original conference deal: federal jobs would no longer automatically be considered for privatization every five years, and positions could not be privatized if those jobs would be sent overseas.

The final Interior spending bill also limited but did not ban funding for studies on opening Forest Service, Interior Department, and Energy Department jobs to bidding by private contractors. Bush had threatened to veto HR 2691 if it banned such funding. Conferees placed caps on the money each could spend to study outsourcing—$5 million for the Forest Service, $2.5 million for Interior, and $500,000 for Energy.

FAA REAUTHORIZATION

Privatization also became an issue during consideration of a bill (HR 2115—PL 108-176) to reauthorize the Federal Aviation Administration (FAA). In June 2002 Bush issued an executive order designating air traffic control as a commercial instead of an "inherently governmental function," which meant the FAA could privatize the jobs at its discretion. The government already contracted out air traffic control at 219 small airports, with several dozen more eligible for the program. Air traffic controllers fought further privatization, and their arguments about safety had a receptive audience in Congress.

The version of HR 2115 approved by the House Transportation and Infrastructure Committee prohibited the FAA from privatizing air traffic controllers, but did not extend the prohibition to technicians, specialists, and support staff. Despite a White House veto threat, the full House did not remove the privatization provisions from the bill.

The Senate on June 12, 2003, adopted 56–41 anti-privatization language drafted by Frank R. Lautenberg, D-N.J., in conjunction with the National Air Traffic Controllers Association. Lautenberg cast the debate in terms of security versus cost cutting.

During conference negotiations, Democrats said they were cut out of the talks on privatizing air traffic control jobs. The GOP conferees agreed to allow immediate privatization of air traffic controllers at sixty-nine airports that operated under visual flight rules or limited instrument rules. All support jobs could be privatized immediately, and controllers at all other airports could be privatized after Oct. 1, 2007.

Lawmakers who backed the prohibitions passed by both chambers were furious. Republicans tried unsuccessfully for weeks to gather enough votes to make it worthwhile to bring the conference report (H Rept 108-240) up for adoption in either chamber. Because a conference report cannot be amended on the floor, the only solution seemed to be to send it back to the conference committee.

Those who had opposed the privatization provisions in the first report wanted conferees to restore the ban passed by both houses. What they got instead in a new conference report (H Rept 108-334) was no privatization language at all. By its silence, the measure thus allowed the administration to contract out airport control towers and jobs across the country.

Democrats were livid and nearly brought the House to a halt with procedural delays. But the revised report was adopted 211–207 on Oct. 30. Republican leaders marshaled support from airports and business groups, most of which were eager for infrastructure grants to continue without interruption or for other provisions of the bill. In the Senate, a motion to invoke cloture (limit debate) put forth by the GOP leadership failed 45–43 (sixty votes were required) on Nov. 17. The ensuing negotiations ended with a letter from the FAA administrator stating that no jobs "directly related to our air traffic control system" would be privatized during fiscal 2004. The Senate thus cleared the measure by voice vote on Nov. 21.

FISCAL 2005 HOMELAND SECURITY APPROPRIATIONS

In December 2003, the Homeland Security Department set in motion a competition that could have led to the privatization of more than eleven hundred immigration service jobs. The struggle between the employees of the department's Citizenship and Immigration Services bureau and the companies that might bid for their jobs subsequently spilled over into debate on the fiscal 2005 Homeland Security funding measure (HR 4567).

On June 18, 2004, during floor consideration of HR 4567, the House adopted 242–163 a Lucille Roybal-Allard, D-Calif., amendment to prevent Homeland Security from carrying out its plans to contract out the jobs. Some of the Republicans who supported the amendment had immigration services workers as constituents; others represented districts where labor unions were a potent force. The Office of Management and Budget warned the Senate against following the House's lead, saying President George W. Bush's advisers would recommend a veto if the spending bill restricted the administration's competitive sourcing efforts, which it said would save $1 billion over time.

Sen. Patrick J. Leahy, D-Vt., offered an amendment that mirrored the House language. Leahy argued that the work, which included citizenship application processing, was too sensitive to be left to the private sector. The Senate on Sept. 8 adopted the amendment on a **key vote of 49–47 (R 5–46; D 43–1; I 1–0)**. The Senate action was a rebuff to the president. *(2003 key votes, p. 837)*

With the support of Arlen Specter of Pennsylvania, one of the most pro-labor Republicans in the Senate, the provision was retained in the conference agreement on the bill completed Oct. 8 (H Rept 108-774). However, Homeland Security secretary Tom Ridge had a letter delivered to the conferees announcing that he was canceling the jobs competition on his own authority. The veto threat therefore became moot, and the bill was signed into law (PL 108-334) on Oct. 18.

GAO Workers Pay Guidelines

Congress in 2004 cleared legislation (HR 2751) to require General Accounting Office (GAO) employees to meet minimum performance standards to earn a pay raise. The bill also renamed the investigative agency the Government Accountability Office.

HR 2751, sponsored by Rep. Jo Ann Davis, R-Va., granted GAO managers more discretion to distribute bonuses and benefits in an effort to recruit and retain top-flight workers. It made permanent the agency's authority to offer early retirement to its workers. Higher relocation benefits and increased vacation pay for new GAO workers also were made available.

The Congressional Budget Office estimated the new rules would cost $40 million through fiscal 2013. Danny K. Davis of Illinois, ranking Democrat on the Government Reform Subcommittee on Civil Service and Agency Organization, said the bill would create a demonstration project that could spread to the rest of the federal workforce.

The House Government Reform Committee reported HR 2751 (H Rept 108-380) on Nov. 19, 2003. The full House passed the bill 382–43 on Feb. 25, 2004. The Senate passed the measure by voice vote June 24, completing congressional action. The president signed HR 2751 (PL 108-271) on July 7.

The Senate had passed a companion measure (S 1522—S Rept 108-216) by voice vote Nov. 24, 2003.

Postal Service Overhaul

Despite bipartisan support in three congressional committees, legislation (HR 4341, S 2468) to overhaul the U.S. Postal Service operations did not reach the floor in either chamber and died upon adjournment of the 108th Congress. Postal Service reform made no progress in the 107th Congress. *(Earlier action, p. 685)*

HR 4341 was approved 40–0 on May 12, 2004, by the House Government Reform Committee (formally reported Sept. 8, H Rept 108-672, Part I) and by voice vote Sept. 15 by the House Judiciary Committee (formally reported Sept. 23,

H Rept 108-672, Part II). S 2468 was approved 17–0 on June 2, 2004, by the Senate Governmental Affairs Committee and was formally reported (S Rept 108-318) on Aug. 25.

Both bills aimed to make the 730,000-employee Postal Service operate more like a business. They would give postal officials flexibility to adjust rates on products that must compete with FedEx Corp. and United Parcel Service Inc. (UPS) and would allow the Postal Service to enter into profitable agreements with large customers. Under such work sharing agreements, private mailers would get rate discounts in exchange for performing some functions, such as bar coding and sorting mail, that typically were done by Postal Service workers.

HR 4341 and S 2468 proposed creating a Postal Regulatory Commission that would be a strong oversight board with subpoena powers and called for postage rates on letters, periodicals, and advertising mail to be regulated so that annual rate shifts do not exceed changes in inflation.

The Senate panel had voted 9–8 to adopt a Joseph I. Lieberman, D-Conn., amendment to limit to four years the period during which the Postal Service could give "excessive discounts" to private mailers who entered into work sharing agreements. The amendment brought the Senate version of the bill closer to the House language. The committee adopted by voice vote a John E. Sununu, R-N.H., amendment to direct the Treasury Department to consult with the Postal Service and an independent accounting firm to develop recommendations for the service's accounting practices with regard to its competitive products. Also adopted by voice vote was a Richard J. Durbin, D-Ill., amendment to require the General Accounting Office to issue a study on the possibility of offering rate incentives for mailers who used recycled paper.

In drafting the bills, proponents brought together most of the major stakeholders, including unions, private mailers, consumer groups, and Postal Service competitors such as UPS, which had worked against earlier reform efforts. However, the Treasury Department opposed a provision in both bills that would transfer to Treasury the liability for pension benefits of military retirees who later worked for the Postal Service, which tallied about $27 billion. A 2003 law (PL 108-18) shifted that burden from Treasury to the Postal Service, which is considered off-budget; that is, its finances are kept separate from the budget. The Bush administration wanted the liability to remain there.

The last restructuring of the Postal Service took place in 1970 (PL 91-375). (Congress and the Nation Vol. III, p. 441)

Presidential Succession

A bill (HR 2319) to include the secretary of homeland security in the line of presidential succession was introduced on June 4, 2003, by House Homeland Security Committee Chair Christopher Cox, R-Calif. The measure was referred to the House Judiciary Subcommittee on the Constitution and saw no further congressional action.

The bill would place the homeland security secretary eighth in line of succession, after the attorney general. It also would prohibit congressional leaders elected after a disaster from supplanting a cabinet member who had assumed the presidency.

D.C. City Budget

Congress in 2004 cleared HR 3797 (PL 108-386) to enact legislation that had been passed by the District of Columbia's City Council and signed by the mayor. The bill authorized and set requirements for various functions for the city's government that, in the past, were covered in the annual D.C. appropriations measure cleared by Congress. Lately, some contentious issues—such as school vouchers—kept that legislation from becoming law in a timely manner. HR 3797 was not intended to address such issues, which would remain part of the appropriations process. (D.C. school vouchers, p. 549)

HR 3797 required that the District's school board give the mayor a budget reconciliation plan for a specific allotment of money. It also changed the fiscal year for the school system to July 1 through June 30 and gave the City Council fifty-six days to review the mayor's budget, six days longer than under existing law. The bill, dubbed the "first annual" District authorization bill, also allowed D.C. to offer its employees flex time.

The House Committee on Government Reform reported HR 3797 (H Rept 108-551, Part I) on June 17, 2004. The House passed the bill on June 21 by voice vote under suspension of the rules. The Senate passed the measure Oct. 11 by voice vote, completing congressional action. It was signed into law on Oct. 30.

In related action, the Senate by voice vote on Dec. 9, 2003, passed S 1267, which would split D.C.'s local budget from the federal appropriations process. The measure died upon adjournment.

Under the bill, Congress would retain authority to prohibit the use of local, as well as federal, funds for certain activities. However, the District's budget, which is approved as part of the annual D.C. appropriations measure, would be controlled principally by local officials.

Furthermore, S 1267 called for the D.C. City Council to submit a plan for use of its own funds. Congress would have thirty days to intervene by clearing a joint resolution, which requires the president's signature. The bill also would make permanent the position of the District's chief financial officer.

Federal funds would continue to be provided through the annual funding measure. And Congress would maintain its ability to restrict the use of local funds.

Before passing the bill, the Senate adopted a Carl Levin, D-Mich., amendment to S 1267 by voice vote Dec. 9. It required the city to begin using meters in its cabs, although the D.C. mayor would be able to opt out. The Senate Governmental Affairs Committee had reported the bill (S Rept 108-212) on Nov. 25.

National Flood Insurance

Congress in 2004 cleared legislation (S 2338) that sought to reduce the number of repeat claims filed under the national flood insurance program. The Bunning-Bereuter-Blumenauer Flood Insurance Reform Act of 2004 extended the program through Sept. 30, 2008.

Congress created the federal flood insurance program in 1968 (PL 90-448). Such insurance was funded through homeowner premiums, although it was backed by the federal government. When the program has extensive losses, it can tap the Treasury's line of credit. Repetitive loss properties cost about $200 million annually. They made up about 1 percent of insured properties, but were expected to account for between 25 and 30 percent of the claims paid. *(1968 act, Congress and the Nation Vol. II, p. 968)*

As enacted S 2338 required people living in flood-prone areas to lessen their risk of flooding or pay higher premiums. The bill established a pilot program, set to expire on Sept. 30, 2009, to reduce severe repetitive loss properties, which are defined as any property with four or more federal flood claims each exceeding $5,000 and the cumulative amount exceeding $20,000 or with two or more claims that cumulatively exceed the value of the property. According to this definition, approximately sixty-two thousand properties would qualify as severe repetitive loss properties, according to the Federal Emergency Management Agency. Severe repetitive loss property owners would be charged a higher rate, closer to the actuarial, risk-based rate, for flood insurance if two conditions were met. First, the property fit the definition of a severe repetitive loss property. Second, the owner refused a mitigation measure from a state or locality, such as elevation of the property or a buyout. If both conditions were fulfilled, the rate would be increased by 50 percent. An additional 50 percent increase would be imposed for each claim exceeding $1,500.

The House Financial Services Committee had reported HR 253—sponsored by Rep. Doug Bereuter, R-Neb., and cosponsored by Rep. Earl Blumenauer, D-Ore.—on Sept. 5, 2003 (H Rept 108-266). The full House passed the bill 352–67 on Nov. 20. The Senate Banking, Housing, and Urban Affairs Committee reported S 2338 (S Rept 108-262) on May 13, 2004. The Senate passed the measure, sponsored by Sen. Jim Bunning, R-Ky., by voice vote June 15. The House by voice vote agreed to suspend the rules and pass S 2338 on June 21. The president signed the bill into law (PL 108-264) on June 30.

In related action, Congress in 2003 had cleared a bill (S 1768) to extend the national flood insurance program for three months—until March 31, 2004. The Senate passed S 1768 by voice vote Oct. 27, 2003. The House passed an amended version by voice vote on Nov. 21. The Senate accepted the House changes on Nov. 24, completing congressional action. The president signed the measure, dubbed the National Flood Insurance Program Reauthorization Act of 2004, into law (PL 108-171) on Dec. 6.

NOAA Reorganization

Members with authority over oceans policy generally agreed that the National Oceanic and Atmospheric Administration (NOAA) needed to be restructured so that it would have a stronger voice in the federal bureaucracy. While lawmakers in the 108th Congress began to seriously consider the problem, no NOAA reorganization legislation was enacted.

HR 4546, approved by the House Science Subcommittee on Environment, Technology, and Standards on Sept. 29, 2004, would create a deputy assistant secretary for science and technology and reorganize the agency within its current home, the Department of Commerce.

HR 4368 would move NOAA from Commerce to the Department of the Interior. The House Resources Subcommittee on Fisheries Conservation, Wildlife, and Oceans on Sept. 30, 2004, held a hearing on the measure.

S 2647, approved by the Senate Commerce, Science, and Transportation Committee on Sept. 22, 2004, would give the NOAA administrator independent authority over the agency's budget and operations, taking those responsibilities away from the Commerce Department. Commerce would retain authority over the agency's policy direction. The bill was formally reported (S Rept 108-407) on Nov. 10.

HR 4607, the Bush administration-backed version of the legislation, would codify the agency's responsibilities but leave much of NOAA's current structure in place. Administration officials argued against transferring the agency to Interior. The House Science Subcommittee on Environment, Technology, and Standards held hearings on the bill July 15, 2004.

NOAA was created by President Richard M. Nixon in 1970, bringing together several science agencies—such as the Weather Bureau and the Bureau of Commercial Fisheries—that had existed since the late nineteenth century. Because the agency was created by executive order and not by Congress, it was never authorized as one entity. Over the years, the agency developed from a hodgepodge of federal laws. But ocean policy extended beyond NOAA, touching several different departments and agencies, such as Commerce, Interior, the Environmental Protection Agency, and the Department of Defense. *(NOAA establishment, Congress and the Nation Vol. III, p. 757)*

In 2000, President Bill Clinton signed the Oceans Act (PL 106-256) designed to create a more comprehensive oceans policy. That law created the U.S. Commission on Oceans Policy, which compiled research and recommendations for Congress, the administration, and states on ways to reduce coastal pollution and overfishing. *(2000 act, Congress and the Nation Vol. X, p. 392)*

The commission's final report, issued Sept. 20, 2004, said that "a stronger, more effective, science-based and service-oriented ocean agency is needed, one that works with others to achieve better management of oceans and coasts through an ecosystem-based approach." The commission also wanted

On February 12, 2003, NASA administrator Sean O'Keefe appears before a joint congressional hearing looking into the *Columbia* shuttle disaster. The report released by the board investigating the accident would later determine that a "broken safety culture" at NASA was ultimately to blame for the tragedy. *Source: Congressional Quarterly/Scott J. Ferrell*

Congress to pay more attention. It urged lawmakers to increase funding for drinking water and wastewater infrastructure, better protect coral ecosystems, and support initiatives to improve ocean technology, research, and education. The report also recommended that Congress work to restructure regional fisheries councils, which were often vulnerable to political manipulation and conflicts of interest.

NASA Reauthorization

The Senate Commerce, Science, and Transportation Committee by voice vote Sept. 22, 2004, approved S 2541, a five-year, $87 billion National Aeronautics and Space Administration (NASA) reauthorization bill that reflected President George W. Bush's new plans for human space exploration. The measure was formally reported (S Rept 108-418) on Nov. 19, but saw no further action.

Bush announced plans on Jan. 14, 2004, to shift NASA's long-term focus from the space shuttle and the international space station to the creation of a new manned space vehicle that would allow astronauts to return to the moon as early as 2015 and to explore Mars by 2030. Bush said the venture would cost $12 billion over five years, about $11 billion of it to be reallocated from other NASA programs.

The Senate committee-approved S 2541 mirrored Bush's proposal, including plans to retire the space shuttle upon completion of the space station in 2010 and to have a new space vehicle operational by 2014. The bill included $744 million in earmarks.

Lawmakers, however, were slow to rally behind Bush's plan and the Senate measure. Many were critical of the projected four-year gap in the ability to launch payloads and people into space. They also questioned whether the space

station would be completed in 2010 when the shuttle would be retired. And some worried about protecting workers who would be laid off in their districts.

Retiring the shuttle was, in part, a monetary concern. If assembling the space station went beyond 2010 and no major overhaul or replacement had been done of the shuttle fleet, NASA would not be in compliance with recommendations by the panel that investigated the *Columbia* accident. It recommended that NASA re-inspect and certify as safe its shuttle fleet if the vehicles were to fly beyond 2010—a costly venture. (Columbia *disaster, p. 695*)

During markup of S 2541, the Senate panel gave voice vote approval to a Bill Nelson, D-Fla., amendment aimed at protecting the jobs of workers who largely depend on the shuttle program for their employment. It would require NASA to find them other related jobs within the agency. Nelson, whose state includes the Kennedy Space Center and its launch pads at Cape Canaveral, was concerned about the loss of skilled workers at NASA who would be redirected toward other functions. Critics saw the amendment as micromanagement.

Although the reauthorization bill was stymied, the fiscal 2005 omnibus appropriations measure (HR 4818—PL 108-447) boosted NASA's budget to $16.2 billion—just $44 million shy of what Bush requested. The bill also gave NASA "unrestrained" authority to transfer money within its accounts, which was a rare exception for any agency.

NASA Workforce Pay, Perks

Congress in 2004 cleared legislation (S 610) to allow the National Aeronautics and Space Administration (NASA) to offer scholarships, bonuses, and higher salaries to attract and retain its top scientists.

COLUMBIA DISASTER

The space shuttle *Columbia* disintegrated as it reentered Earth's atmosphere on Feb. 1, 2003. The Columbia Accident Investigation Board, chaired by retired Adm. Harold W. Gehman Jr., issued a 248-page report on Aug. 26, 2003.

The cause of the disaster was foam insulation that had come dislodged during liftoff, hitting and then shifting a joint in the left wing. The gap widened further during reentry, leading to the accident. All seven astronauts on board were killed.

The report concluded that a "broken safety culture" at the National Aeronautics and Space Administration was at the root of the catastrophe. The report warned that the shuttle's days were numbered. It said that the vehicle would require a costly upgrade after 2010, and it called for development "as soon as possible" of a multibillion-dollar replacement vehicle for astronauts.

The board's report listed twenty-nine recommendations to return the space shuttle to flight and guard against accidents. Among the recommendations were the following.

• Initiate a program to eliminate debris shedding from the external tank thermal protection system during launch.

• Increase the shuttle's ability to sustain minor debris damage. Develop a plan to closely inspect and determine the structural integrity of critical shuttle shielding.

• Upgrade imaging capacities to provide at least three useful views of the shuttle during liftoff and initial ascent.

• Establish a capability to obtain and downlink high-resolution images of critical sections of the shuttle's exterior and of the external tank after it separates during launch.

• Use spy satellites to take images of the shuttle during every mission.

• Reorganize the shuttle program management structure. Establish a technical engineering authority to operate independently and without consideration of schedule concerns or program costs.

• Expand training of mission managers to include safety contingencies beyond launch and ascent.

• Develop a means to inspect all shuttle wiring.

• Conduct a vehicle recertification of materials, components, systems, and subsystems for all shuttles that fly beyond 2010.

The space shuttle *Challenger* exploded during launch in 1986. *(Space program review, Congress and the Nation Vol. VII, p. 850)*

S 610 allowed NASA to pay bonuses to highly skilled workers and designate "critical employees" to be paid as much as the vice president of the United States. The bill established a NASA scholarship program to help recruit top candidates in science and technology. The measure also allowed NASA to pay moving and recruitment bonuses to attract employees and gave employees big bonuses if they might otherwise leave the agency.

A similar bill (HR 1085) was approved 21–14 on July 22, 2003, by the House Science Committee. The measure, sponsored by committee chair Sherwood Boehlert, R-N.Y., was formally reported (H Rept 108-244, Part I) on Aug. 4, 2003. Democrats opposed language in HR 1085 that expanded NASA's authority to make changes to civil service personnel rules. They also wanted assurances that bonuses and pay raises would not go to political appointees. S 610 addressed those concerns and won Democratic support.

The Senate Governmental Affairs Committee reported S 610 (S Rept 108-113) on July 28, 2003. The full Senate passed the bill, by voice vote, on Nov. 24. During House floor consideration, Rep. Jeff Flake, R-Ariz., offered an amendment to balance new spending authority for NASA with offsetting cuts elsewhere in the agency's budget. Boehlert and House Government Reform Committee Chair Thomas M. Davis III, R-Va., assured Flake that pay raises and bonuses would come from within NASA's existing budget, and Flake withdrew his

amendment. The House passed S 610 by voice vote on Jan. 28, 2004. The president signed the bill into law (PL 108-201) on Feb. 24.

The Congressional Budget Office estimated that the bill would cost $80 million over five years, but aides to the bill's sponsors said it did not explicitly authorize new spending. Unions representing government employees sought increased funding for NASA during the appropriations process because without more money the agency would have to let workers go if others were to be paid more.

The incentives bill was intended to address concerns about the agency's aging workforce. Almost a quarter of NASA's employees would be eligible for retirement in five years. For every three scientists over sixty years old, there was only one under thirty. And the pipeline of new talent was drying up. The number of undergraduate and doctoral degrees awarded in aerospace science and engineering declined about 20 percent in the previous ten years.

Competition with private companies also did not help. NASA was ranked as the best federal employer by the Partnership for Public Service, a nonprofit group that encourages young people to work for the government. But steering graduates away from lucrative jobs in the aerospace industry proved difficult.

In addition, NASA's workforce was a source of concern before and after the February 2003 loss of the space shuttle

Columbia. A September 2001 General Accounting Office (GAO) report said personnel factors such as the loss of experienced workers posed a safety risk for the space program. In a January 2003 report, the GAO said that "NASA's shuttle workforce had declined significantly in recent years, to the point of reducing NASA's ability to safely support the shuttle program." Boehlert said, "Events of the past year [following the *Columbia* disaster] have highlighted NASA's need to attract and retain that best workforce imaginable, and yet NASA is on the brink of losing the talent it already has." *(Columbia disaster, box, p. 695)*

Space Tourism

Congress in 2004 cleared legislation (HR 5382) to promote the development of the emerging commercial human space flight industry. The president signed the bill into law (PL 108-492) on Dec. 23.

Under HR 5382, sponsored by House Science Subcommittee on Space and Aeronautics chairman Dana Rohrabacher, R-Calif., the Federal Aviation Administration (FAA) would enforce passenger safety rules on private spacecraft, but only by prohibiting technologies already proven to have resulted in a fatality or near-fatality. FAA would have full regulatory authority over safety starting in 2012.

The House passed HR 5382 by 269–120 under suspension of the rules Nov. 20. The Senate passed the measure by voice vote Dec. 8, completing congressional action.

A Senate companion bill (S 1260) was reported from the Commerce, Science, and Transportation Committee (S Rept 108-111) on July 24, 2003.

Another Rohrabacher-sponsored bill, HR 3752, gave the FAA regulatory authority over space tourism and streamlined FAA regulations for issuing experimental permits to companies that wanted to test new flight vehicles. The House Science Committee reported the measure (H Rept 108-429) on March 1, 2004, and the full House passed it 402–1 on March 4.

In related action, Congress in 2004 also cleared HR 5245, to extend the liability indemnification regime for the commercial space transportation industry. By voice vote, the House passed the bill on Oct. 8, 2004; the Senate, on Nov. 16. It was signed into law (PL 108-428) on Nov. 30.

Nanotechnology Research

In an effort to bolster the U.S. role in the emerging field of nanotechnology, Congress in 2003 authorized $3.7 billion for research and development (R&D). The bill (S 189), signed into law (PL 108-153) on Dec. 3, also strengthened coordination of nanotechnology research.

Nanotechnology involved the design and manufacture of extremely small electronic circuits and mechanical devises built at the molecular level of matter. A nanometer is one-billionth of a meter, about 100,000 times smaller than a strand of human hair.

While most lawmakers knew too little about nanotechnology to consider it a pressing priority, supporters said the science and the tiny devices it made possible could spur tremendous advances over the next twenty years in fields such as computing, medicine, and energy. According to the National Science Foundation, the market in products using nanocomponents could reach $1 trillion annually by 2015.

In urging passage, supporters also pointed to formidable competition from researchers in Europe and Asia. The European Union had budgeted $1.2 billion for nanotechnology in 2003 and 2004, and Japan was expected to invest $180 million in fiscal 2003.

The bill's authorization, for fiscal years 2005 through 2008, covered five of the sixteen agencies that make up the National Nanotechnology Initiative, a federal program that coordinated multi-agency efforts in the field. The five agencies were the Energy Department, the Environmental Protection Agency, the National Aeronautics and Space Administration, the National Institute of Standards and Technology, and the National Science Foundation. They were expected to distribute funds to colleges, universities, and research centers.

S 189 established a National Nanotechnology Program to set goals and priorities for research programs, invest in federal R&D, and strengthen overall coordination. It also established two centers. The Center for Nanomaterials Manufacturing was to conduct research on new manufacturing technologies and develop the means of transferring those technologies to U.S. industry. The American Nanotechnology Preparedness Center was to coordinate and disseminate studies on the potential impact of nanotechnology on society.

Appropriations for nanotechnology research had gone from $255 million in fiscal 1999 to $774 million in fiscal 2003. Supporters of S 189 said a multi-year authorization would encourage long-term planning.

LEGISLATIVE ACTION

The House passed its three-year, $2.4 billion bill (HR 766) by a 405–19 vote on May 7, 2003. The measure authorized $713 million in fiscal 2004, $784.5 million in 2005, and $864 million in 2006 for nanotechnology research and development programs at the five agencies and provided a formal structure for coordinating research across the agencies.

The House Science Committee had approved the legislation by voice vote May 1. The committee agreed on a 22–19 party-line vote to an amendment by committee chair Sherwood Boehlert, R-N.Y., offered at the request of the White House, to give the administration more flexibility in overseeing the program than the original bill provided. The amendment also added $226 million for nanotechnology research funded by the Energy Department.

The panel rejected by voice vote an amendment by Brad Sherman, D-Calif., and Chris Bell, D-Texas, to set aside at least 5 percent of the funds in the bill for research on societal and ethical implications of nanotechnology. Almost a dozen other amendments, clarifying provisions of the bill, were adopted by voice vote.

HR 766 was formally reported (H Rept 108-89) by the House Science Committee on May 6.

During floor consideration, the House on May 7 by voice vote adopted an Eddie Bernice Johnson, D-Texas, amendment to ensure that public input and outreach were integrated into nanotechnology research on societal and ethical concerns through the covening of public panels and educational events. The House on May 7 rejected two Bell amendments: by 209–214, to require the bill's program activities to include toxicological and environmental impact studies; and by 207–217, to require research and development on the potential of nanotechnology to produce or facilitate production of clean, inexpensive energy.

The Senate passed S 189 by voice vote Nov. 18, 2003. Before passage, the Senate adopted by voice vote an amendment by sponsors Ron Wyden, D-Ore., and George Allen, R-Va., to authorize a total of $3.7 billion in fiscal 2005 through 2008.

As approved by the Senate Commerce, Science, and Transportation Committee, the bill would have authorized $4.7 billion for fiscal 2004 through 2008. However, by the time the bill cleared, fiscal 2004 was under way. The committee approved S 189 by voice vote June 19 and formally reported it (S Rept 108-147) on Sept. 15.

The House on Nov. 20 by voice vote under suspension of the rules passed S 189, completing congressional action.

Nickel Redesign

Congress in 2003 cleared legislation (HR 258) to allow the Treasury secretary, in consultation with an advisory committee, to redesign the nickel. The redesign of the reverse (tails) side of the coin, which would be temporary, would depict one big event of Thomas Jefferson's tenure as the third president of the United States—such as engineering the Louisiana Purchase of 1803 or commissioning the Meriwether Lewis and William Clark expedition across North America. A profile of Jefferson, featured on the obverse (heads) side of the nickel, would remain unchanged.

The U.S. Mint considered permanently changing the coin, scotching the depiction of Monticello, Jefferson's Virginia home, in favor of something new. The Virginia congressional delegation and the Thomas Jefferson Foundation, which owns Monticello, objected. As cleared, HR 258 would return Monticello to the reverse of the nickel after 2005.

The House Financial Services Committee reported the bill (H Rept 108-20) on Feb. 26, 2003. Later that same day, the full House agreed under suspension of the rules to pass the measure, 412–5. The Senate passed H 258 by voice vote April 11, completing congressional action. The president signed the bill (PL 108-15) on April 23.

Two Senate bills (S 471 and S 474), to ensure continuity for the design of the nickel, were introduced and referred to committee. Both died upon adjournment.

Dollar Coin Redesign

The House Financial Services Committee June 24, 2004, reported a bill (HR 3916—H Rept 108-568) to replace the image of Sacagawea, the American Indian woman who served as a guide to the explorers Meriwether Lewis and William Clark, on the obverse (heads) side of the $1 coin with the likenesses of all the U.S. presidents. The Statue of Liberty would replace the eagle on the reverse (tails) side.

The measure, dubbed the Presidential $1 Coin Act of 2004, was modeled after the 1997 law that ordered the redesign of the quarter (PL 105-124), under which fifty individual coins were to be minted. Under HR 3916, four different $1 coins would be minted each year—starting with George Washington, John Adams, Thomas Jefferson, and James Madison in 2006—with the presidents appearing in their order of service. Presidents who served successive terms would get one coin; those who served nonsequential terms would get a separate coin for each term. As a result, Franklin D. Roosevelt, who was elected four times, would be on only one coin, while Grover Cleveland—the only president to serve nonsuccessive terms—would get two coins. Once all the presidents had been featured, production of the Sacagawea dollar would resume. (*1997 law, Congress and the Nation Vol. X, p. 129*)

HR 3916 also would authorize the minting of $10 bullion coins, to be marketed to collectors, with images of all the first ladies.

The purpose of the bill was to help continue interest in coin collecting while generating funds for the U.S. Treasury. When the government mints a new coin to replace one taken from circulation by a collector, it raises revenue for the federal coffers through the process of seigniorage—essentially the difference between the face value of a coin and the cost of the metal to make it. The state quarters, for example, raised an estimated $4 billion in revenue.

The vending machine industry and public transportation agencies supported the bill. Dollar coins work better in vending machines, and coins last much longer than bills. Because many vending machines are configured for the existing size and weight of the $1 coin, the industry would oppose changing it, despite complaints among consumers and merchants that the dollar coin is too close in size and feel to the quarter. Some groups have advocated phasing out the dollar bill in favor of the dollar coin. Bill sponsor Michael N. Castle, R-Del., rejected that idea.

Reagan Memorialization

Following the June 5, 2004, death of Ronald Reagan, Republicans drew up plans to memorialize the fortieth president of the United States on U.S. currency. However, no legislation advanced beyond subcommittee consideration.

Any change in who is memorialized on U.S. currency is serious business. In the case of Reagan, Democrats were not excited about branding coins or notes with the image of a president who provoked their ire. And they were unenthusiastic about any GOP effort to memorialize Reagan that involved removing a famous Democrat from the currency.

HR 4528, sponsored by Rep. J. D. Hayworth, R-Ariz., would substitute Reagan for Alexander Hamilton, the nation's first secretary of the Treasury, on the $10 bill. GOP lawmakers said the plan would be less contentious than attempting to displace a former president. The bill was referred to the House Financial Services Subcommittee on Domestic and International Monetary Policy, Trade, and Technology and saw no further action.

HR 3633, sponsored by Rep. Mark Souder, R-Ind., would put Reagan on the dime, replacing Democratic president Franklin D. Roosevelt. However, Souder announced in June 2004 that he would not pursue the legislation, citing objections from former first lady Nancy Reagan to a displacement of Roosevelt, after whom Reagan patterned himself. The bill was referred to the House Financial Services Subcommittee on Domestic and International Monetary Policy, Trade, and Technology and saw no further action.

HR 4525, sponsored by Rep. Jeff Miller, R-Fla., would put Reagan on the half-dollar coin, replacing President John F. Kennedy, another Democratic icon. The bill was referred to the House Financial Services Subcommittee on Domestic and International Monetary Policy, Trade, and Technology and saw no further action.

Rep. Dana Rohrabacher, R-Calif., wanted Reagan's image on the $20 bill, replacing President Andrew Jackson. However, Jackson hailed from Tennessee, home state of Senate majority leader Bill Frist.

Sen. Trent Lott, R-Miss., suggested the minting of a $1 gold coin, which he referred to as "the Ronnie."

Constitution Holiday

Robert C. Byrd of West Virginia, dean of the Senate Democrats, in 2004 introduced legislation (S 2808) to make the date of the 1787 signing of the U.S. Constitution—Sept. 17—a national holiday. The bill was referred to the Senate Judiciary Committee and died upon adjournment.

Byrd had more luck with the fiscal 2005 omnibus appropriations bill (HR 4818—PL 108-447), which included a provision to spread his message that the Constitution is something everyone should know about and understand. On Sept. 17, 2005, every employee of a federal agency could expect to see training and education materials about the document dropped on their desks. Also on that day, schoolchildren across the country would get a lesson on the work of the founders.

Furthermore, HR 4818 officially designated the anniversary—known as Citizenship Day—as Constitution Day and Citizenship Day.

Vietnam Memorial Visitors Center

Congress in 2003 cleared legislation (HR 1442) to authorize a visitors center at the Vietnam Veterans Memorial in Washington, D.C., and prohibit new construction on the National Mall.

The visitors center, to be paid for by private contributions to the Vietnam Veterans' Memorial Fund, would be mostly underground. The bill required the government to operate and maintain the center. Designed by architect William Lecky, it would display photos and artifacts left at the memorial over the last two decades.

Opponents said that the war could not be defined within a single exhibit and that the center would distract from the original intent of the memorial. Supporters said the center would be a valuable educational tool.

HR 1442 also prohibited new statues, monuments, or memorials in the area from the Capitol to the Lincoln Memorial and from the White House to the Jefferson Memorial. While opponents of growth on the National Mall cheered that provision, Senate and House aides agreed it could be waived if a future Congress wanted new construction.

The Senate Energy and Natural Resources Committee approved S 1076 by voice vote June 25, 2003, and formally reported it (S Rept 108-98) on July 11. The panel by voice vote June 5 had adopted an amendment, sponsored by Jeff Bingaman, D-N.M., and Craig Thomas, R-Wyo., to designate part of the National Mall as "The Reserve" and prohibit building of additional monuments there. The amendment was added to a similar bill in 2002, which died on the Senate floor because of objections from then-senator Phil Gramm (R-Texas, 1985–2002), who wanted to ensure that land was available for memorials to President Ronald Reagan or some future president. During floor consideration of S 1076, with Gramm retired from Congress, no senators voiced objections. The Senate passed the bill by voice vote July 17.

The House Resources Committee approved HR 1442 on Sept. 24 and formally reported it (H Rept 108-295) on Oct. 2. The House passed the bill by voice vote under suspension of the rules Oct. 15. The House version did not contain the Senate's prohibition on further monument building.

The Senate passed an amended HR 1442 by voice vote Nov. 5. The next day the House accepted the changes, completing congressional action. The president signed the legislation into law (PL 108-126) on Nov. 17.

In related action, Congress in 2003 included in the fiscal 2004 appropriations bill for the Interior Department and related agencies (HR 2691—PL 108-108) provisions to stop funding altogether for a proposed underground visitors center for the Washington Monument and to tighten restrictions on commercial advertising on the National Mall.

Kennedy Center Reauthorization

Congress in 2004 cleared legislation (HR 5294) to reauthorize maintenance and construction programs at the John F. Kennedy Center for the Performing Arts in Washington, D.C., and to tighten oversight of its plaza expansion project.

The center is the capital city's main memorial to the thirty-fifth president of the United States. It was named for him after his Nov. 22, 1963, assassination.

HR 5294 authorized $17 million in fiscal 2004 and $18 million in fiscal 2005, 2006, and 2007 for maintenance, repair, and security work. The bill also created a project management team to oversee a ten-year plan to revamp the center's eight-acre plaza and add two buildings. A 2003 law (PL 107-224) authorized as much as $400 million for the project.

The measure required that any proposed modifications to the plaza project be approved by the project team, and the Kennedy Center board would have to consult with the team regarding its efforts to construct new buildings on the plaza. The bill did not, however, diminish the board's existing authority to construct buildings on the plaza with nonfederal funds.

The legislation also required a periodic Government Accountability Office review of the center's capital projects.

The House passed HR 5294 by voice vote Oct. 8, 2004. The Senate followed suit Oct. 11, completing congressional action. The bill was signed into law (PL 108-410) on Oct. 30.

A companion measure (S 1757) had been reported (S Rept 108-174) by the Senate Environment and Public Works Committee on Oct. 28, 2003. The Senate passed an amended version by voice vote on Oct. 31.

Another version of the legislation (HR 3198) had been reported (H Rept 108-319) by the House Transportation Committee on Oct. 15, 2003. By voice vote Nov. 17, the House passed the bill under suspension of the rules.

African American Museum

Congress in 2003 cleared legislation (HR 3491—PL 108-184) to authorize the building of the National Museum of African American History and Culture as part of the Smithsonian Institution.

The idea for such a museum was first proposed in 1915 by the Committee of Colored Citizens, a group of black Civil War veterans. While the Smithsonian has been on record in support of the museum since 1991, squabbles over where to put it caused a series of delays. Real estate on the National Mall in Washington, D.C., is scarce and highly prized, and any space selected had to meet strict security guidelines.

HR 3491, sponsored by Rep. John Lewis, D-Ga., required the Smithsonian's Board of Regents to choose from among four locations: the Banneker Overlook site on the city's southwestern waterfront; the Smithsonian's Arts and Industries Building; the area bounded by Constitution Avenue, Madison Drive, and Fourteenth and Fifteenth Streets N.W.; and land at the foot of the Fourteenth Street Bridge in the District of Columbia.

The board would be advised by the museum director and a nineteen-member National Museum of African American History and Culture Council, which would be responsible for the museum's funding and exhibits as well as working with educational institutions and other museums. HR 3491 authorized $32 million in fiscal 2004 for the council's work.

The council would be required to consider the findings of a presidential commission established in 2001 (PL 107-106). *(Presidential commission, p. 688)*

HR 3491 was passed by the House by 409–9 under suspension of the rules Nov. 19, 2003. The Senate passed the measure without amendment by voice vote Nov. 20. It was signed into law on Dec. 16.

The Senate by voice vote June 23, 2003, had passed a companion bill (S 1157).

Museum and Library Services Reauthorization

Congress in 2003 cleared a bill (HR 13) to provide a significant increase in federal funds to museums and libraries. The president signed the legislation into law (PL 108-81) on Sept. 25.

HR 13 authorized $232 million for libraries and $38.6 million for museums for fiscal 2004 and unspecified sums for fiscal 2005 through 2009. The programs had been funded at $150 million and $28.7 million, respectively. The bill also doubled to $680,000 the minimum amount states receive in library services and technology grants.

The House Committee on Education and the Workforce reported HR 13 (H Rept 108-16) on Feb. 25, 2003. The House passed the bill 416–2 on March 6. The Senate Committee on Health, Education, Labor, and Pensions reported a companion measure (S 888—S Rept 108-83) on June 26. The Senate passed HR 13, after substituting the language of S 888, by voice vote Aug. 1. The House, by voice vote under suspension of the rules Sept. 16, agreed to the Senate changes, thus completing congressional action.

Nuclear Bomb Sites

The Senate on Nov. 24, 2003, by voice vote passed S 452, which designated as national parks sites where nuclear bombs were tested in Nevada and from which nuclear forces were commanded in Colorado. The Senate Energy and Natural Resources Committee reported the bill (S Rept 108-134) on Aug. 26.

The bill, sponsored by Majority Whip Harry Reid, D-Nev., authorized $300,000 for the interior secretary to conduct a study on sites with cold war significance that could be added to the national park system or be commemorated in some other way. The measure recommended inclusion of the Nevada test site where atmospheric nuclear tests were conducted and defense installations at Cheyenne Mountain, Colorado, leaving open the possibility for more locations. It also directed the interior secretary to publish an interpretive handbook on the cold war within four years.

The National Park Service already operated one cold war commemorative, the Minuteman Missile National Historic Site in South Dakota, complete with a missile launch control center and missile silo.

A House companion bill (HR 114), sponsored by Rep. Joel Hefley, R-Colo., was referred to the House Resources Subcommittee on National Parks, Recreation, and Public Lands for consideration.

Woodson Home

Congress in 2003 cleared legislation (HR 1012) to memorialize Carter G. Woodson—known as the father of black history—by making his Washington, D.C., home part of the National Park Service.

An author and historian, Woodson established the Negro History Week in 1926, which later became Black History Month. He also founded the Association for the Study of African-American Life and History and established the organization's headquarters in his home.

The House on May 14, 2003, agreed by voice vote to suspend the rules and pass HR 1012. The Senate Energy and Natural Resources reported the measure (S Rept 108-138) on Aug. 26. An amended version passed the Senate by voice vote Nov. 24. The House agreed to the Senate changes Dec. 8, completing congressional action. The president signed the bill into law (PL 108-192) on Dec. 19.

U.S. Olympic Committee

The Senate on Sept. 23, 2003, by voice vote passed a bill (S 1404) to overhaul the U.S. Olympic Committee (USOC). The Senate Commerce, Science, and Transportation Committee had reported S 1404 (S Rept 108-114) on July 28. Two similar House measures (HR 3144, HR 3825) underwent subcommittee consideration.

The legislation, which sought to revamp the Ted Stevens Olympics and Amateur Sports Act (PL 105-277), was a response to financial scandals and the departure of three USOC presidents in two years. The troubles at the USOC were so pronounced that John Hancock Financial Services, a major sponsor, raised the possibility of ending its support after contributing an estimated $100 million over ten years. The company's chairman accused the USOC of mishandling its money and complained that only 75 percent of its resources had been allocated to athletes. The USOC, meanwhile, initiated its own review of the organization's leadership structure.

As passed by the Senate, S 1404 slashed the size of the USOC from 124 members to nine elected directors—five of whom would be independent, two would be nominated by the

Athletes Advisory Council, and two would be nominated by the National Governing Bodies Council. The board of directors would be responsible for establishing audit, compensation, ethics, and nominating and governance committees. The chief executive officer of the USOC would be barred from being a member of the board. The ethics committee would be charged with establishing an ethics policy for the USOC, based on best corporate and government practice. An assembly of all USOC stakeholders would meet annually and would have ultimate authority to decide matters related to the Olympic Games. Biennial reports, including annual financial statements, would be prepared for the president and Congress.

Indian Gaming Revenue

The Senate Indian Affairs Committee voted July 14, 2004, to approve a measure (S 1529) to restrict the money that states could collect from Indian casino operations. S 1529, which was formally reported (S Rept 108-380) on Sept. 28, saw no further congressional action.

Bill sponsor Ben Nighthorse Campbell, R-Colo., was committee chair as well as a Northern Cheyenne tribal chief. He said that his bill to amend the 1988 Indian Gambling Regulatory Act (PL 100-497), which set the rules for Indian casinos, would protect cash-starved states from viewing tribal gambling as a cash cow. The legislation would allow states only to share money left after tribes pay for their government programs and operations or in exchange for providing tribes with economic benefits. (1988 act, Congress and the Nation Vol. VII, p. 864)

S 1529 was seen as a severe blow to many state governments that had come to rely on Indian gambling proceeds. For example, in 2003, the state and local governments of Arizona collected $43 million from Indian casinos; California, $132 million; Connecticut, $396 million; New Mexico, $37 million; New York, $39 million; and Wisconsin, $32 million.

Critics expressed concern about a provision in the bill that would let tribes operate some types of electronic games without state regulation. Business for Indian casinos increased with the introduction of electronic bingo and pull tabs, machines that look almost identical to slot machines but are regulated differently.

Bingo is classified as a Class II game, while slot machines and electronic games of chance are considered Class III games. The 1988 law required tribes to enter tribal-state compacts approved by the interior secretary to run Class III games, under a provision designed to ensure that tribal casinos are regulated similarly to commercial casinos. The compacts generally included agreements that required tribes to distribute some of their revenue to the states. Indian casinos operating Class II games did not have to enter such agreements and were solely regulated by the National Indian Gaming Commission.

At issue was whether electronic bingo and pull tab games should be operated as Class II games, as S 1529 would allow.

Court rulings were inconclusive on the issue. Critics said the bill could lead to the proliferation of these games without proper regulation, a concern shared by the Justice Department. Defenders said that the bill would strengthen oversight of Class II games by creating new responsibilities for the National Indian Gaming Commission, including regulation and record-keeping requirements.

Tribal Labor

The House on Sept. 9, 2004, rejected 185–227 a J. D. Hayworth, R-Ariz., amendment to the fiscal 2005 Labor, Heath and Human Services, and Education appropriations bill (HR 5006) to prohibit the National Labor Relations Board from exercising jurisdiction over tribal business. The impetus for the amendment came from a May 28, 2004, board ruling that gave the agency authority to settle a labor dispute at the San Manuel Indian Bingo and Casino near Highland, California.

Hayworth argued that the tribes had always had sovereignty over enterprises on tribal land and that the federal agency had discretionary authority only when the business was outside tribal land. The issue was to take on greater importance as American Indian tribes looked to expand their casino operations off tribal lands and into areas with large populations. Tribal casinos typically were not unionized, and organized labor had launched an aggressive outreach to organize those employees.

By offering the amendment, Hayworth sought to force Democrats to pick between two of their most loyal constituencies—tribal governments and unions.

A separate Hayworth-sponsored bill, HR 4680, would amend the National Labor Relations Act to ensure that Indian tribes and any organizations owned, controlled, or operated by Indian tribes were not considered employers for purposes of the act. The measure was referred to the House Education and the Workforce Subcommittee on Employer-Employee Relations and saw no further congressional action.

Indian Housing

Congress in 2004 cleared a bill (HR 4471) to clarify the loan guarantee authority under the Native American Housing Assistance and Self-Determination Act of 1996 (PL 104-330).

HR 4471, the Homeownership Opportunities for Native Americans Act of 2004, made a home loan program for Indian reservations more attractive to investors by guaranteeing government repayment of 95 percent of the principal in the event of a default.

The bill was sponsored by Rep. Rick Renzi, R-Ariz., whose district included much of the Navajo reservation. In May 2004 Renzi organized a House Financial Services Subcommittee on Housing field hearing in Arizona and arranged a tour of the Navajo reservation. Subcommittee chair Bob Ney, R-Ohio, ranking member Maxine Waters, D-Calif., and Jim Matheson, D-Utah, whose district also included part of the Navajo Nation, attended the subcommittee's first ever hearing on tribal lands.

They described the housing as some of the worst they had seen. Almost 40 percent of Native American homes were considered substandard, compared with a national average of 6 percent, according to the subcommittee's staff.

The House Financial Services Committee reported HR 4471 (H Rept 108-550) on June 17, 2004. The full House agreed to suspend the rules and pass the bill by voice vote on June 21. The Senate passed the bill unchanged, by voice vote Oct. 11, completing congressional action. The president signed the bill (PL 108-393) on Oct. 30.

The Senate had passed a companion measure (S 2571) by voice vote Oct. 11, 2004.

Apology to Indians

The Senate Indian Affairs Committee on June 23, 2004, gave voice vote approval to a resolution of apology to American Indians on behalf of the United States. S J Res 37 was formally reported (S Rept 108-310) on July 15.

The joint resolution, sponsored by Sen. Sam Brownback, R-Kan., expressed regret to "all native peoples for the many instances of violence, maltreatment, and neglect inflicted on native peoples by citizens of the United States." The resolution urged the president to acknowledge the wrongdoings against American Indians throughout history. But it specified that nothing in the resolution could be construed as authorizing or settling any claim against the United States.

The National Congress of American Indians, an advocacy group representing more than 250 tribal governments, expressed concern that the resolution was inadequate without compensation.

A companion measure (H J Res 98) was introduced in the House by Rep. Jo Ann Davis, R-Va.

Cowlitz Indian Settlement

Congress in 2004 cleared a bill (HR 2489) to provide for the distribution of funds awarded by the Indian Claims Commission Docket No. 128 to the Cowlitz Indian Tribe of Washington State.

HR 2489 set aside 20 percent of the funds from the settlement for a tribal elderly assistance program, with the remainder distributed among eight other areas. They include an education, vocational, and cultural training program; a housing assistance program; economic development, tribal, and cultural centers; natural resources; cultural resources; health needs; and a tribal administration program.

The House Resources Committee reported the bill (H Rept 108-368) on Nov. 17, 2003. The House on March 23, 2004, agreed 404–0 to suspend the rules and pass HR 2489. The Senate passed the measure without amendment by voice vote April 20. The president signed the legislation into law (PL 108-222) on April 30.

Inside Congress

Inside Congress

Since 1997, at the start of each new Congress, Reps. Ray LaHood, R-Ill., and Charles W. Stenholm, D-Texas, organized a bipartisan "civility" retreat at a resort outside Washington, D.C., in an attempt to build better relations between the parties. In 2003, at the start of the 108th Congress, the gathering was held at the Greenbriar resort in West Virginia. However, only about one quarter of the House membership attended the retreat, the worst attendance ever. Because members—from the leadership on down—expressed so little interest in continuing the event, LaHood and Stenholm decided against scheduling a retreat for the beginning of the 109th Congress.

The breakdown in civility in Congress had several causes. In the House, the long period of near-partisan parity made the minority party—the Democrats—an ever-present threat to the ruling Republicans. The close division encouraged the two parties to sharpen their differences rather than seek consensus in hopes of galvanizing enough like-minded voters to win a clear governing majority. The House also had become faster-paced and more impersonal. Lawmakers found increasing difficulty developing genuine friendships that could help bridge partisan divisions. Members return to their districts regularly, and when in the Capitol fewer socialized with colleagues. And members less frequently learned about bills directly from each other, often sending their aides to do the talking.

Of fundamental importance was the practice over the previous three decades of drawing the vast majority of House districts with lines that made them politically safe for one party or another. These polarized districts elected members who often were disinclined to work with the other side. The resulting standoff, with neither side giving quarter to the other, was politically expedient for both.

Unlike the House, where most members labor in relative obscurity, senators wielded considerable power and some measure of cross-party dialogue was essential for getting business done. However, the Senate stalled repeatedly as Democrats and Republicans squabbled over legislation. Leading the closely divided—and at the beginning of the 107th Congress, evenly divided—and polarized chamber was a daunting task.

CONGRESSIONAL LEADERSHIP

The style and manner of the congressional leaders during the four years from 2001 to 2005 were a response to the divided nature of both the Senate and House.

As majority leader for most of the 107th Congress, Tom Daschle, D-S.D., faced a list of obstacles: a razor-thin majority, issues that divided not only the two parties but also his own caucus, and a Republican minority that wanted to keep his list of accomplishments as short as possible. Daschle, who had been known as the "nice guy" with a soft-spoken, consensus-building style and extraordinary patience, began using more aggressive parliamentary maneuvers. He said he was merely being practical. His critics, mostly Republicans, called the tactics heavy-handed. His supporters and advisers viewed Daschle as learning the skills and techniques necessary to run the Senate. They also said he had little choice but to switch gears once he became the GOP's top political target, as well as the focus of some unusually vicious attacks by outside conservative groups. The National Conservative Campaign Fund, for example, sent out a fund-raising letter that ran Daschle's picture next to American Taliban fighter John Walker Lindh and asked, "Who Is More Dangerous to America?"

REFERENCES

Discussion of congressional affairs for the years 1945–1964 may be found in *Congress and the Nation Vol. I*, pp. 1407–1431; for the years 1965–1968, *Congress and the Nation Vol. II*, pp. 893–924; for the years 1969–1972, *Congress and the Nation Vol. III*, pp. 353–433; for the years 1973–1976, *Congress and the Nation Vol. IV*, pp. 743–794; for the years 1977–1980, *Congress and the Nation Vol. V*, pp. 873–953; for the years 1981–1984, *Congress and the Nation Vol. VI*, pp. 797–840; for the years 1985–1988, *Congress and the Nation Vol. VII*, pp. 871–910; for the years 1989–1992, *Congress and the Nation Vol. VIII*, pp. 913–988; for the years 1993–1996, *Congress and the Nation Vol. IX*, pp. 861–925; for the years 1997–2001, *Congress and the Nation Vol. X*, pp. 757–794.

The GOP regained the majority in the Senate in the 2002 elections. Bill Frist, R-Tenn., became majority leader in the aftermath of a controversy surrounding a statement that expected leader Trent Lott, R-Miss., made, reopening old wounds of racism and segregation. Frist sought to coax the independent, closely divided Senate into producing on issues, to show that Republican-led government can work. Meanwhile, he had an obligation to try to move the president's congressional agenda and to satisfy the House of Representatives, which was generally more conservative and where leaders were more eager to confront than work with Democrats.

House Republicans acknowledged Frist's difficulties, but some of them questioned whether he did enough to force GOP legislation forward or, when he could not, to put the onus on Democrats. Some lobbyists and aides said privately that Frist could have closed the deal on some legislation if he had been savvier or more forceful. They said he could be reticent to press his points hard with colleagues or twist arms when necessary. They said he gave too much latitude to committee chairmen, making the Senate harder to govern.

Senate Democrats said Frist reached out to them at times, but then poisoned the atmosphere by accusing them of obstruction, excluding them from conference negotiations, and abandoning Senate positions in negotiations with the House. In addition, Frist angered many Democrats when he traveled to South Dakota in May 2004 to campaign personally against Democratic minority leader Daschle, a highly unusual step for a Senate leader. Even some Republican senators said privately that it unnecessarily heightened the tension in the Senate. (Daschle would lose his reelection bid.)

J. Dennis Hastert, R-Ill., was unexpectedly elevated to House Speaker after GOP setbacks in the 1998 midterm elections forced Newt Gingrich, R-Ga., from the post. Coming to the job with a reputation as a "regular order" type lawmaker, Hastert as Speaker grew steadily bolder, occasionally railing against Republicans in the Senate as well as the Bush administration for choosing pragmatic compromises with Democrats instead of standing behind more conservative GOP principles. Democrats complained that Hastert's partisan approach too often prevented them from even offering alternatives to major legislation. At the very least, Hastert condoned the pressure tactics and partisan warfare waged by Tom DeLay, R-Texas—majority whip, then majority leader—with whom he had few public disagreements. And Hastert publicly endorsed the concept of win at all costs, even if it meant holding a roll-call vote open for three hours—as he did with the Medicare reform bill (HR 1) in November 2003—to secure a victory. Although this event was the most widely publicized, there were numerous other instances of long-open roll calls and late night (often into the early morning) sessions to secure victory on legislation the GOP thought essential.

When Richard A. Gephardt, D-Mo., stepped down as minority leader after presiding over a dwindling number of House Democrats, Nancy Pelosi, D-Calif., became in 2003 the first female ever to lead a political party in Congress. Her tenure was marked by a quest for an agenda that ignored faction-making policies, but rallied all her troops behind the common goal of ousting the House Republican majority. Her bid to unify her caucus in support of the mainstream Democratic themes of "prosperity, opportunity and security" had much success. The caucus was more unified under Pelosi than at any time in years. To form an agenda around which her party would rally, Pelosi named voices from across her caucus's ideological spectrum, and both junior and senior members, to shape the message. She sought to protect the Democrats' fragile unity by not asking members to adhere to issues that divided them—such as proposals to extend or expand some taxes. Beyond the legislative agenda, she sought to energize members by promoting a "minority bill of rights," a list of changes she believed should be instituted to protect the interests of the out-of-power caucus from the sorts of abuses Democrats said they saw at the hands of the GOP.

ETHICS CHARGES STAND-DOWN

An odd consequence of the partisanship in the House was an apparent temporary halt in the swapping of ethical charges against members. However, a rules change affecting the House Committee on Standards of Official Conduct (ethics committee) beginning in 2005 would serve to benefit the GOP.

In the face of persistent suggestions that policing of House ethics rules had been broken—and, in particular, that lawmakers had a tacit understanding not to call out violations on each other—the leaders of the House ethics committee on March 11, 2004, sent a five-page letter to all House members saying there was no "ethics truce" and it was "regrettable" if lawmakers refrained from filing complaints out of fear of retaliation.

The letter said the committee, in fact, had been busy since 1997, when a spate of seemingly politically motivated ethics charges forced a short-term moratorium on filing complaints and a revision of ethics rules and committee procedures. Among the changes was the elimination of a provision allowing outside groups to file complaints with the committee. From then on, investigations could be prompted only by a member complaint or initiated by the committee itself.

The Republicans in late 2004, when considering rules changes for the 109th Congress, did attempt to protect one of their own—Minority Leader DeLay—from fallout from a possible future ethics problem. Besides being admonished by the ethics committee twice in one year, DeLay was linked to targets of an ongoing investigation in Texas into campaign financing abuses. His fellow Republicans feared he would be indicted and, thus, according to existing rules, would be forced to step down from his leadership post. The rules change would allow an indicted member to remain as party leader or committee chairman. However, in 2005, the Republicans decided against adopting the new rule, upon DeLay's request.

Despite the rules retreat, House GOP leaders did make changes that were expected to tilt the ethics process in the Republicans' favor. On Feb. 2, 2005, Doc Hastings, R-Wash., was appointed to replace Joel Hefley, R-Colo., as House ethics committee chair. Hefley, who had earned a reputation for being independent-minded, also was removed from the committee. Two new members were put on the committee: Lamar Smith, R-Texas, and Tom Cole, R-Okla. Both members had made donations (Smith, $10,000; Cole, $5,000) to the DeLay Legal Expense Trust, according to the watchdog group Public Citizen.

More important, a majority vote now would be required for an ethics investigation to go forward. Under the old rule, if the evenly divided ethics committee deadlocked, a probe would automatically ensue. Under the new rule, if a tie vote were not broken within forty-five days of the filing of a complaint, the case would be dropped. The expectation was that fewer investigations would take place and that any GOP leader in trouble would not find his political survival in the House at stake.

Chronology of Action on Congress: Members and Procedures

2001–2002

One Republican, increasingly uncomfortable with his party and his president, decided to change his political affiliation and, in doing so, ended six years of GOP reign in the Senate. Republican James M. Jeffords of Vermont put the Democrats back in power in the 107th Congress when he became an independent.

Democrats in the House broke ground in the 108th Congress when they chose a woman, Nancy Pelosi of California, as minority leader. Furthermore, Robert Menendez of New Jersey, when he was elected Democratic Caucus chair, became the highest-ranking Hispanic member in the history of Congress.

Organization: 107th Congress

A scorecard was needed to keep track of the changing fortunes of Republicans and Democrats in the Senate. The House was relatively calm, although a number of turnovers in committee chairmanships were mandated by term limits.

SENATE

The even split of fifty Republicans and fifty Democrats that resulted from the 2000 elections posed a special problem for the Senate at the opening of the 107th Congress in 2001. Having recognized the potential for deadlock, Senate leaders Tom Daschle, D-S.D., and Trent Lott, R-Miss., negotiated a power-sharing arrangement, which was unprecedented in Senate history.

Between Jan. 3 and Jan. 20, President Clinton was still in office, so the tie-breaking vote in the Senate belonged to Democratic vice president Al Gore. For seventeen days, Daschle was majority leader and Lott served as minority leader. When Republicans George W. Bush and Dick Cheney were sworn into office at noon on Jan. 20, Lott regained the title of majority leader, which he held in the previous Congress, and Daschle went back to his job leading the minority.

At the close of business June 5, 2001, Vermont Republican James M. Jeffords became an independent and began caucusing with the Democrats—putting them in charge of the Senate and throwing the GOP into the minority.

Majority Leadership

Republicans elected their leaders for the 107th Congress on Dec. 5, 2000.

Trent Lott of Mississippi and Don Nickles of Oklahoma were reelected, without opposition, as majority leader and majority whip, respectively. (Lott and Nickles did not take these titles until Bush became president. They would revert to minority leader and minority whip, respectively, after Jeffords' defection from the GOP.) Larry E. Craig of Idaho and Pete V. Domenici of New Mexico vied for Republican Policy Committee chair. Craig retained the post. Rick Santorum of Pennsylvania defeated Christopher S. Bond of Missouri for the Republican Conference chairmanship. Santorum succeeded Connie Mack of Florida, who retired from Congress. Kay Bailey Hutchison continued as secretary of the Senate Republican Conference, and Bill Frist of Tennessee was chosen to succeed Mitch McConnell of Kentucky as chair of the National Republican Senatorial Campaign Committee.

Minority Leadership

Facing no opposition, Tom Daschle of South Dakota was reelected minority leader and Harry Reid of Nevada was reelected minority whip. (When Congress convened, Daschle and Reid were majority leader and majority whip, respectively. They became part of the minority leadership when Bush was sworn in as president and then reverted to their majority posts when Jeffords became an independent and made the Democrats the ruling party.) Barbara A. Mikulski of Maryland also was returned as secretary of the Democratic Conference.

Committees

The power-sharing arrangement gave the two parties equal representation on committees. If a committee were tied on a bill or nomination, the full Senate could vote to bring the matter to the floor, where the vice president could cast the deciding vote if necessary. The deal was announced Jan. 5, 2001, and given voice vote approval by the Senate the same day. The arrangement left Republicans as chairmen to reflect the impending tie-breaking vote of the GOP vice president.

After Jeffords left the Republican Party, the Senate had to fashion a new organizing resolution to replace the power-sharing agreement. The talks, which involved setting new committee ratios and allocating staff and office space, stalled for weeks over Republicans' demands that they be guaranteed floor debate on any Bush Supreme Court nominee, even if it had been rejected by the Judiciary Committee. When Republicans dropped that demand, the new organizing resolution (S Res 120) was adopted easily by voice vote June 29. It gave Democrats one extra seat on Senate committees.

The new committee chair—all Democrats, except Jeffords—and those whom they replaced (all Republicans), who became the ranking members (unless otherwise noted), were Agriculture, Nutrition, and Forestry, Tom Harkin of Iowa, replacing Richard G. Lugar of Indiana; Appropriations, Robert C. Byrd of West Virginia, replacing Ted Stevens of Alaska; Armed Services, Carl Levin of Michigan, replacing John W. Warner of Virginia; Banking, Housing, and Urban Affairs, Paul S. Sarbanes of Maryland, replacing Phil Gramm of Texas; Budget, Kent Conrad of North Dakota, replacing Pete V. Domenici of New Mexico; Commerce, Science, and Transportation, Ernest F. Hollings of South Dakota, replacing John McCain of Arizona; Energy and Natural Resources, Jeff Bingaman of New Mexico, replacing Frank H. Murkowski of Alaska; Environment and Public Works, Jeffords, replacing Robert C. Smith of New Hampshire; Finance, Max Baucus of Montana, replacing Charles E. Grassley of Iowa; Foreign Relations, Joseph R. Biden Jr. of Delaware, replacing Jesse Helms of North Carolina; Governmental Affairs, Joseph I. Lieberman of Connecticut, replacing Fred Thompson of Tennessee; Health, Education, Labor, and Pensions, Edward M. Kennedy of Massachusetts, replacing Jeffords (Judd Gregg of New Hampshire would become the new ranking member); Judiciary, Patrick J. Leahy of Vermont, replacing Orrin G. Hatch of Utah; Rules, Christopher J. Dodd of Connecticut, replacing Mitch McConnell of Kentucky; Small Business, John Kerry of Massachusetts, replacing Christopher S. Bond of Missouri; Veterans' Affairs, John D. Rockefeller IV of West Virginia, replacing Arlen Specter of Pennsylvania; Special Committee on Aging, John B. Breaux of Louisiana, replacing Larry E. Craig of Idaho; Select Committee on Ethics, Harry Reid of Nevada, replacing Pat Roberts of Kansas; Indian Affairs, Daniel K. Inouye of Hawaii, replacing Ben Nighthorse Campbell of Colorado; and Select Intelligence, Bob Graham of Florida, replacing Richard C. Shelby of Alabama. *(Committee chair rosters, p. 891)*

Rules

In addition to providing for the equal division of the parties on committees, leaving Republicans as panel chairs, and allowing the full Senate to vote on a motion to place on the floor calendar legislation that was stalled by a deadlocked committee vote, the Senate rules adopted by voice vote Jan. 5, 2001, stipulated that Republicans and Democrats were to be provided equal staff and office space. Furthermore, senators were prohibited from filing cloture motions on bills as a way to block amendments from being considered. Also, leaders of each party pledged not to "fill the amendment tree" to block the other party from offering amendments.

The Senate Republican Conference on June 25, 2002, sought to clear up the vagueness of a rule, approved in 1995 and effective in 1997, that limited GOP senators' terms as committee chairs. The new rule, written by Sen. Robert F. Bennett, R-Utah, and approved 32–14, allowed Republicans to serve up to twelve years in the top slot on a committee: six years as ranking member plus six years as chair. However, it placed top priority on the time served as chair. Therefore, once a Republican had served six years as chair he had to relinquish the top slot regardless of whether he had served any time as ranking member. *(1995 action, Congress and the Nation Vol. IX, p. 886)*

Democrats did not impose any term limits on their chairs in either the Senate or the House.

HOUSE

Changes in House rules made six years earlier began to be felt in 2001; thirteen chairmanships changed hands. The leadership, otherwise, remained largely the same for the Republicans as well as the Democrats.

Majority Leadership

J. Dennis Hastert, R-Ill., was reelected as House Speaker on a 222–207 vote Jan. 3, 2001. Reelected by Republicans were Dick Armey of Texas as majority leader; Tom DeLay of Texas, majority whip; J. C. Watts Jr. of Oklahoma, House Republican Conference chair; Christopher Cox of California, Republican Policy Committee chair; and Thomas M. Davis III of Virginia, National Republican Congressional Committee chair.

Minority Leadership

Democrats reelected Richard A. Gephardt of Missouri as minority leader. David E. Bonior of Michigan was chosen to continue as minority whip. He resigned the post Jan. 15, 2002, to concentrate on his race for governor. Bonior was succeeded by Nancy Pelosi of California, who had been elected to fill the vacancy on Oct. 10, 2001. Martin Frost of Texas was reelected Democratic Caucus chair.

Committees

The House in 2001 saw thirteen new committee chairs installed, a changing of the guard that resulted largely from

WHITE HOUSE CAPITOL OFFICE

In January 2001 Republican House leaders gave aides to Vice President Cheney the use of room H-208, the former Ways and Means Committee room, located in the Capitol just off the floor.

Rep. Marcy Kaptur, D-Ohio, during a June 27, 2001, Legislative Branch Appropriations subcommittee hearing on the budget of the architect of the Capitol, raised an objection to the arrangement. The room "belongs to the House," Kaptur said. "We have enough incursions by the executive branch on our authority. Now they want our office space, too."

Kaptur acknowledged that, constitutionally, the vice president, as president of the Senate, is entitled to offices on the Senate side—but not on the House side.

term limits Republicans had imposed on their committee chairs when they gained the majority in 1995. Members of the GOP Steering Committee nominated the new chairs after a six-hour meeting Jan. 4, and the entire Republican conference confirmed them several hours later. The new chairs—who, unless otherwise noted, took over after term limits ended the tenures of sitting chairs—were Armed Services, Bob Stump of Arizona, succeeding Floyd D. Spence of South Carolina; Budget, Jim Nussle of Iowa, succeeding John R. Kasich of Ohio, who retired from Congress; Education and the Workforce, John A. Boehner of Ohio, succeeding Bill Goodling of Pennsylvania, who retired from Congress; Energy and Commerce, Billy Tauzin of Louisiana, succeeding Thomas J. Bliley Jr. of Virginia, who retired from Congress; Financial Services, Michael G. Oxley of Ohio, succeeding Jim Leach of Iowa, who gave up the chairmanship of the defunct Banking and Financial Services Committee; International Relations, Henry J. Hyde of Illinois, succeeding Benjamin A. Gilman of New York; Judiciary, F. James Sensenbrenner Jr. of Wisconsin, succeeding Hyde; Resources, James V. Hansen of Utah, succeeding Don Young of Alaska; Science, Sherwood Boehlert of New York, succeeding Sensenbrenner; Small Business, Donald Manzullo of Illinois, succeeding James M. Talent of Missouri; Standards of Official Conduct, Joel Hefley of Colorado, succeeding Lamar Smith of Texas; Transportation and Infrastructure, Don Young, succeeding Bud Shuster of Pennsylvania, who would retire from Congress in February 2001; Veterans' Affairs, Christopher H. Smith of New Jersey, succeeding Bob Stump of Arizona; and Ways and Means, Bill Thomas of California, succeeding Bill Archer of Texas.

The ranking member slots, held by Democrats, changed on five committees. George Miller of California succeeded William L. Clay of Missouri on Education and the Workplace; Tom Lantos of California replaced Sam Gejdenson of Connecticut, International Relations; Nick J. Rahall II of

West Virginia succeeded Miller, Resources; Martin Frost of Texas replaced Joe Moakley of Massachusetts, Rules; and Nancy Pelosi of California succeeded Julian C. Dixon of California, Select Intelligence.

Rules

A package of new rules, adopted 215–206 on Jan. 3, 2001, included a committee realignment that shifted jurisdiction over securities and insurance from the Commerce Committee to a new Finance Services Committee. The Commerce Committee became Energy and Commerce; Financial Services replaced the Banking and Financial Services Committee; and House Oversight became House Administration.

The new rules expanded the Select Committee on Intelligence from sixteen to eighteen members, giving each party one additional seat. The rules also required that appropriations bills with unauthorized spending include details on when the program was last authorized and for how much.

One rule included in the original slate of proposed changes, to resurrect the practice of allowing proxy votes in committee when members could not be present, was dropped.

In November 2001, Republican leaders decided to make the thirteen appropriations subcommittee chairs subject to approval by the Steering Committee. For decades, the Appropriations Committee chairs and their subcommittee chiefs, forming the so-called college of cardinals, had driven the deals to send large amounts of federal largess to members' districts to pay for bridges, roads, farm supports, and other pet projects. The process went on almost without questioning from higher-ups. But in the 107th Congress, as lawmakers grappled with a rising budget deficit and expensive demands to improve homeland security, Republican appropriators increasingly clashed with their party leaders. The rule change essentially forced the cardinals to re-interview for their chairmanships before the start of the 108th Congress.

Contingency Plans

After the Sept. 11, 2001, terrorist attacks, lawmakers began considering steps to ensure Congress's continuity in case tragedy struck on Capitol Hill. (*2003–2004 action, p. 719*)

The situation was less urgent for the Senate because governors can appoint new senators to fill vacancies. However, the only mechanism for succession in the House was to hold special elections in each district with a vacant seat. Without a faster method, according to those who studied the issue, a terrorist attack while Congress was in session could make it impossible for the House to assemble a quorum for months.

Three proposals to solve the problem initially emerged. First, two former House Speakers—New Gingrich, R-Ga., and Thomas S. Foley, D-Wash.—wrote a March 17, 2002, opinion piece for the *Washington Post* proposing a change in House rules, by a simple majority vote, to allow members to name interim successors, who would serve until a special election. Gingrich and Foley also called for a constitutional amendment to guard against legal challenges. Second, Rep.

Crews testing for the presence of anthrax operate October 23, 2001, from an outdoor command post in the shadow of the Capitol. Although no one on Capitol Hill got sick, nearly 1,200 people were treated for possible exposure to anthrax, and Congress was effectively shut down for a week. *Source: Congressional Quarterly/Scott J. Ferrell*

Brian Baird, D-Wash., introduced a resolution (H J Res 67) proposing a constitutional amendment to allow a governor to name a temporary successor to a dead or incapacitated House member from his state. The replacement would leave after ninety days, or as soon as a special election had been conducted. The provisions would apply only when one quarter or more of all House members had been killed or incapacitated. Third, addressing the issue of partisan balance, Sen. Arlen Specter, R-Pa., introduced a resolution (S J Res 30) proposing a constitutional amendment to require governors to appoint interim House members of the same party as the members they would replace. The provisions would apply only when half the House seats were considered vacant. Both H J Res 67 and S J Res 30 saw subcommittee consideration but went no further.

A bipartisan House working group, headed by the chairs of the GOP Policy Committee and the Democratic Caucus, began meeting in May 2002. It had been formed after 218 House members, led by Baird, asked for a bipartisan forum to debate how to fill House seats in the event of a disaster with mass casualties. The group appeared to favor addressing the issue through legislation or a rules change, instead of a constitutional amendment.

Reps. Martin Frost, D-Texas, and Christopher Cox, R-Calif., in a compromise move, offered H Res 559, to encourage states to expedite special elections if disaster struck. The full House passed the measure, 414–0 on Oct. 2, 2002.

In related action, House and Senate leaders changed a long-standing rule that allowed only the House Speaker or Senate pro tempore to convene their respective chambers. Other lawmakers—their identities were not made public—were appointed to do the job in case either leader was killed.

Also, Rep. Jim Langevin, D-R.I., on Dec. 13, 2001, introduced HR 3481, which called for a study of the feasibility of building an advanced telecommunications system, equipped with electronic voting and video-teleconferencing capabilities, that would allow all legislative activities to continue in the event of an emergency that warranted evacuation of the Capitol. Skeptics worried that lawmakers would overuse the system for everyday votes and meetings, tarnishing the process of legislative debate and compromise envisioned by the founders. Others said such concerns were exaggerated. Widespread agreement existed that the use of the system should be restricted to emergency situations, though how such an emergency would be declared remained undetermined. One option was to create statutory guidelines that outline when an "electronic Congress" could convene; another was to leave the decision to the discretion of House and Senate leaders. Opponents of the plan said arranging for Congress to meet physically at a location away from the Capitol, or even outside Washington, D.C., would be preferable. A critic called the e-Congress proposal unconstitutional because it would not require Congress to assemble physically.

Lobbying Senators

Lawmakers prefer to work with lobbyists who share their goals, but the Senate Select Committee on Ethics in 2002 warned that the practice could be carried too far.

In an Aug. 1 letter, Ethics Committee Chair Harry Reid, D-Nev., and Vice Chair Pat Roberts, R-Kan., warned senators that a research project by conservative activists to identify Democratic lobbyists should not be used to deny access to those lobbyists.

While the letter did not mention any senator by name, Democrats said it was meant as a warning to Republican Conference chair Rick Santorum of Pennsylvania. Santorum reportedly met with members of Americans for Tax Reform about its research project, which identified business group lobbyists who used to work for congressional

ANTHRAX AND RICIN

A small white envelope hand-addressed to Senate majority leader Tom Daschle, D-S.D., brought the threat of bioterrorism home to Congress on Oct. 15, 2001. A letter, written in clunky, black letters, said: "You can not stop us. We have this anthrax. You die now. Are you afraid? Death to America. Death to Israel. Allah is great." As an aide opened the letter, a puff of fine, white dust escaped into the air of Daschle's personal office in the Hart Senate Office Building.

Twenty-two congressional aides and six Capitol police officers were exposed. By the end of the week, more than thirty-nine hundred lawmakers, aides, reporters, lobbyists, and others received nasal swabs and a few days' supply of the antibiotic Cipro as a precaution. Ultimately, nearly twelve hundred people who were treated at the Capitol, including seventy Senate aides, were put on sixty-day courses of Cipro to prevent anthrax infections. As an extra precaution, forty-eight of the aides later received an extra forty days of Cipro and an experimental anthrax vaccine.

Congress's initial reaction to the anthrax exposure was confused. On Oct. 17 House Speaker J. Dennis Hastert, R-Ill., and Minority Leader Richard A. Gephardt, D-Mo., announced that the House would wrap up its legislative business for the week that afternoon—a day ahead of schedule. They maintained that the move was not a surrender to terrorism, but a prudent response to a genuine concern. The same day, Daschle and Minority Leader Trent Lott, R-Miss., proposed a pro forma session for the rest of the week, meaning no legislative business would be conducted. The idea was roundly shouted down by senators of both parties. Senators said the House had jumped the gun; House members said senators were most interested in scoring political points.

Lawmakers returned Oct. 23, but all offices remained off-limits as agents from an array of federal law enforcement agencies searched for additional bacteria. The leadership sought temporary spaces where lawmakers could work. A flurry of floor action allowed Congress to project an air of cautious normalcy. However, behind the scenes, it was anything but business as usual. Dozens of committee hearings were canceled for lack of meeting space. And an array of

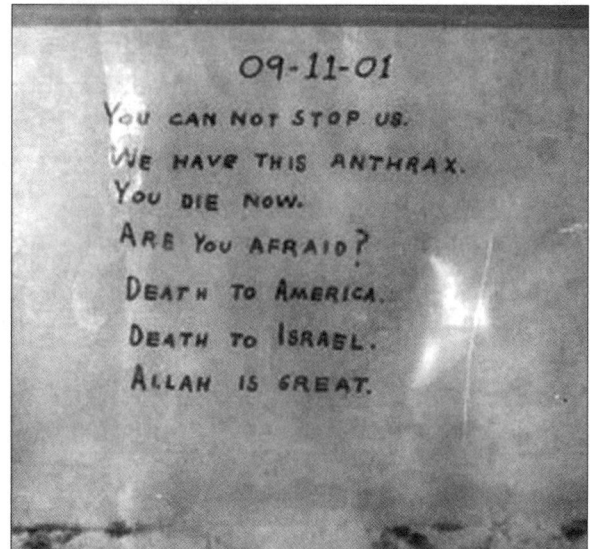

This threatening letter addressed to Senate majority leader Tom Daschle and opened on October 15, 2001, contained anthrax spores and contributed to a climate of fear as the nation, still reeling from the attacks of Sept. 11, experienced a wave of mysterious anthrax mailings. *Source: AP Wide World Photos/FBI*

legislation stalled because the necessary paperwork could not be retrieved from quarantined offices.

The Russell building reopened Oct. 24, allowing thirty-six senators back in their suites. The next day, the House reopened its Cannon and Rayburn buildings, where 310 members work. On Oct. 26, the Dirksen building was reopened, except for the mailroom, which had handled the Daschle letter and where anthrax spores had been found Oct. 17.

The Federal Bureau of Investigation announced Nov. 16 that it had discovered a letter addressed to Sen. Patrick J. Leahy, D-Vt., that appeared to contain anthrax. That same day, National Guardsmen began taking security positions around the Capitol complex. Ultimately, 110 guardsmen were stationed in rotating positions in three daily shifts. The guardsmen carried 9 mm handguns and were deputized by

Democrats or had given money to Democrats. The organization said the report was aimed at business groups, not members of Congress, and was intended to notify the groups that they were not well represented by hiring lobbyists who had worked against their interests.

Reid and Roberts warned that any senator who used the list to deny access to lobbyists would be in violation of Senate rules. Under Rule 43 of the Standing Rules of the Senate, the decision to help lobbyists "may not be made on the basis of contributions or services, or promises of contributions or services, to the Member's political campaigns or to other

organizations in which the Member has a political, personal, or financial interest." Therefore, "any effort to deny access to those discussions to those who do not share a Member's party affiliation, have not made political contributions, or have made political contributions to those not in the Member's party, would appear to violate Senate Rule 43," the committee warned.

Santorum and other top Senate Republicans said the point of the research was not to blacklist anyone, but to ensure that Republicans can seek out like-minded political allies to work on common goals.

the District of Columbia's Metropolitan Police Department to have the power to make arrests in Washington, D.C.

During the week of Nov. 19, officials found trace amounts of anthrax in the mailrooms of Christopher J. Dodd, D-Conn., and Edward M. Kennedy, D-Mass., whose offices in the Russell building were on the same mail delivery route as that of Leahy. Law enforcement officials said the small quantities of spores found in the offices could not have sickened any senators, their aides, or visitors to the building. No one in the Russell building was tested or treated for anthrax exposure.

The same week, the offices of four members (Mike Pence, R-Ind.; Rush D. Holt, D-N.J.; John Baldacci, D-Maine; and Elijah E. Cummings, D-Md.) in the Longworth House Office Building where traces of anthrax were found were undergoing decontamination and testing.

The Hart building was declared safe on Jan. 15, 2002. The tenants of the four Longworth suites tainted by anthrax began moving back in on Jan. 18. The rest of the building had been reopened Nov. 5, 2001.

Nearly six months after the anthrax-filled letter was unsealed there, Daschle's office reopened April 3, 2002. The anthrax was so widespread in his two-story suite that it was completely gutted. Lighting, carpeting, and the interior walls were stripped out, although the contents of the file cabinets were saved. The mailroom of the office of Russell Feingold, D-Wis., which was connected by a door to the Daschle suite, also had to be renovated.

In the aftermath of the anthrax-filled letters that were sent to Daschle and Leahy, the U.S. Postal Service sent all congressional mail to private companies to be irradiated as a safety precaution before it reached Capitol Hill. The process was intended to kill dangerous microbes, but it left the mail looking burned and slightly brittle. Between Jan. 22 and Feb. 4, 2002, about seventy-three Senate staffers from all three Senate office buildings complained of headaches, skin rashes, dry mouth, and eye irritation after handling irradiated mail. While a direct link was not made between the mail and the health complaints, officials from the Sergeant at Arms' Office, the Postal Service, the Capitol physician's office, and the Environmental Protection Agency told senators Feb. 6 that the mail would be treated with lower radiation levels, and it would be aired out before delivery.

RICIN

Ricin was discovered in the Dirksen office of Senate majority leader Bill Frist, R-Tenn., on Feb. 2, 2004. Aided by technological advances and the confidence that came with Capitol Hill experience with anthrax, congressional offices and federal agencies sprang into action with new and improved procedures. The scare in Frist's office resulted in the closing of all three Senate office buildings, but the Hart and Russell buildings were reopened within three days and Dirksen reopened a week after the discovery.

Daschle was annoyed to learn that the Bush administration had not informed Senate leaders that a letter containing ricin and addressed to the White House was intercepted in November 2003. Capitol Police said they knew about the earlier incident but decided they could not brief lawmakers on every potential threat to Congress.

Ricin, made from the waste left over from processing castor beans, is deadly when people are exposed to it in certain ways and in certain amounts. But as a powder—the form in which it was found in Frist's office—it does not become airborne nearly as easily as anthrax. Experts agree that ricin can kill in amounts as small as the head of a pin. But because it is not easily inhaled and is even less likely to be injected (the most deadly form of exposure), the main concern on Capitol Hill was that someone would get ricin on his hands and then accidentally ingest it. Swallowing ricin would be much less dangerous than inhaling a similar amount. Ricin is easily neutralized. Any danger of accidental ingestion could be averted by using a bleach solution to clean any surface that could have been exposed to the toxin.

The House sergeant at arms Bill Livingood and Chief Administrative Officer Jay Eagen announced Feb. 13 that all congressional mail would be opened at an off-site facility, in the name of safety. According to congressional aides, the new process would add at least three days to delivery schedules in the House and one day in the Senate.

Ethics Probes

In the most high-profile cases, ethics transgressions led one representative to be expelled from Congress and one senator to abandon his reelection bid.

REP. JAMES A. TRAFICANT JR.

On July 24, 2002, on a 420–1 vote, Rep. James A. Traficant Jr., D-Ohio, was expelled from the House of Representatives. On April 11, a federal court jury in Cleveland, Ohio, had found Traficant guilty of conspiracy to commit bribery, seeking and accepting illegal gratuities, racketeering, obstruction of justice, and filing false federal income tax returns. He was sentenced on July 30 to an eight-year prison term.

Traficant had pled not guilty to the charges on May 11, 2001. The forty-one-page indictment contained ten criminal counts and detailed activities dating back to 1987. Among the counts, federal prosecutors charged that, over a period of nine years, Traficant handed out political favors to the Asphalt Specialist Company in Ohio in exchange for free

GAO VERSUS CHENEY

A federal lawsuit filed by the General Accounting Office (GAO) against Vice President Dick Cheney to force him to release records from an energy task force meeting he headed in 2001 was dismissed on Dec. 9, 2002. As a result, the investigative and auditing arm of Congress suffered a setback that could hinder its ability to enforce even routine requests for information from the White House.

The legal battle arose after congressional Democrats accused the Bush administration of relying heavily on advice from big business to draft national energy policy. They asked the administration to release documents related to private meetings of Cheney's National Energy Policy Development Group. When the administration refused, Reps. John D. Dingell, D-Mich., and Henry A. Waxman, D-Calif., asked the GAO to look into the task force. They did not try to use committee subpoenas to get the information, because the House GOP majority almost certainly would have blocked them.

Comptroller General David M. Walker, who headed the GAO, took up the cause and repeatedly demanded information from the White House about the task force. When Cheney refused, the GAO filed a lawsuit Feb. 22, 2002, seeking to compel the vice president to provide the names of everyone who participated in the task force meetings. It was the first time the GAO had sued the executive branch to disclose documents.

The White House insisted its deliberations and consultations with federal employees and outsiders were private matters, protected by the U.S. Constitution. The case was assigned to U.S. District Judge John D. Bates, a former member of Independent Counsel Kenneth W. Starr's legal team, who had been named to the federal bench by President George W. Bush.

Cheney's lawyer, Paul D. Clement, asked Bates to dismiss the case, saying the GAO lacked the standing to sue the vice president and that Congress had other ways of obtaining the information, such as issuing subpoenas. The GAO argued that a dismissal of the case would cripple its ability to investigate federal programs. Such a move would "essentially put the GAO out of business" because it would encourage other federal agencies to deny requests for information, said attorney Carter G. Phillips.

Bates dismissed the case, echoing the administration argument that the GAO lacked standing to compel the disclosure of the task force records. In addition, he said the court could not get involved in the separation of powers struggle that would result if the congressional office was allowed to force Cheney to release the records. "Such an excursion by the judiciary would be unprecedented and would fly in the face of the restricted role of the federal courts under the Constitution," Bates wrote. He went on to say that the GAO was only "an agent of Congress" and noted that no subpoena for the information had been issued by the House, the Senate, or any congressional committee.

Waxman called the court ruling "convoluted and bizarre" and urged the GAO to appeal the decision. He said Bates appeared to ignore a 1983 U.S. Supreme Court ruling, in *Bowsher v. Merck & Co.*, that a pharmaceutical company had to give the GAO records of its business with federal agencies even though the accounting office was only responding to the request of individual members. *(1983 case, Congress and the Nation Vol. VI, p. 768)*

On Feb. 7, 2003, Walker announced that the GAO would not appeal the decision because such an appeal would require an "investment of significant time and resources over several years." In addition, because Bates did not rule on the merits of the GAO's argument, "it has no effect on GAO's statutory audit rights or on the obligation of agencies to provide GAO with information," he said. Waxman called the decision not to appeal Bates's ruling "a tremendous setback for open government."

Private organizations had better luck forcing the Bush administration to turn over some of the task force documents. In February 2001, U.S. District Judge Gladys Kessler ordered the Energy Department to turn over thousands of pages of records related to the task force that had been requested by the Natural Resources Defense Council, an environmental group. The lawsuit forced the department to release eleven thousand pages of documents, though critics said the administration deleted important information from them.

---

construction services on his Greenford, Ohio, farm. Prosecutors also charged that Traficant helped Ohio businessman Arthur David Sugar obtain a reduced sentence for his son, who had been convicted of drunk driving. In exchange, Sugar, his son, and Sugar's Honey Creek Contracting Company Inc. provided free work on Traficant's farm. Traficant also was charged with obstructing justice by asking a Youngstown-area attorney hired as an administrative counsel to destroy evidence and provide false testimony to a fed-

eral grand jury. Traficant was convicted on all ten counts. *(Earlier action, Congress and the Nation Vol. X, p. 774)*

While no House rules require an ethics investigation when a member is indicted, a probe is automatically triggered when a member is convicted of a felony. A subcommittee of the House Committee on Standards of Official Conduct examined ten ethics counts that were based on the criminal proceedings, heard three days of testimony, and deliberated for five hours. On July 18, 2002, the panel decided that Traficant had violated House rules, finding him guilty on nine of ten ethics counts. Later that same day, the full committee recommended his expulsion.

Traficant on July 24 offered a rambling, forty-five-minute defense, in which he maintained that he was the victim of a government vendetta. Traficant had spent his nearly nine terms in office railing against federal conspiracies, unproven cover-ups, China's influence on the U.S. government, and the Internal Revenue Service. He became only the fifth House member ever expelled and only the second since the Civil War.

Traficant ran for reelection in 2002 from his prison cell as an independent. He received 15 percent of the vote.

SEN. ROBERT G. TORRICELLI

The Senate Ethics Committee on July 30, 2002, "severely admonished" Sen. Robert G. Torricelli, D-N.J., for improperly accepting expensive gifts from a former campaign supporter. Amid plummeting poll ratings, Torricelli dropped his reelection bid on Sept. 30.

The U.S. Attorney's Office for the Southern Division of New York investigated whether Torricelli had accepted thousands of dollars in unreported gifts. David Chang, who pleaded guilty in 2000 to making $53,700 in illegal contributions to Torricelli's 1996 election campaign and subsequently was sentenced to eighteen months in jail, alleged that he gave Torricelli cash, suits, a Rolex watch, and an expensive television set. Federal law and congressional gift rules barred lawmakers from accepting gifts worth $50 or more, though gifts from personal friends were exempt if they were not given in return for official favors. Chang, a New Jersey businessman, was once among Torricelli's closest political supporters, and Torricelli had called him a "friend" of several years.

U.S. Attorney Mary Jo White announced January 3, 2002, that no charges would be filed against Torricelli and that the criminal investigation had been closed. Prosecutors lacked sufficient credible evidence for an indictment, but they forwarded their files to the Senate Ethics Committee. The chair Harry Reid, D-Nev., recused himself from the probe, after news reports revealed that he had contributed $500 to the New Jersey senator's legal defense fund in 2001.

After six months of closed-door staff work, the panel invited Torricelli to meet with committee lawyers to answer questions under oath, which he did. Chang offered to testify from prison, but was rebuffed. On July 30, after hearing from no other witnesses, six Ethics members (three from each party) issued a letter citing Torricelli for violating Senate rules. The panel concluded that Torricelli's relationship with Chang "created at last the appearance of impropriety," and it ordered Torricelli to pay Chang the fair-market cost of the items he accepted. The full Senate was not required to act. On the Senate floor, Torricelli apologized to the Senate and to his constituents.

After Torricelli abandoned his reelection campaign, the Democrats successfully petitioned the New Jersey Supreme Court to order the distribution of ballots using the name of their replacement candidate—Frank R. Lautenberg, who had served in the Senate from 1982 to 2001—notwithstanding a state law that set a deadline of fifty-one days before an election for replacing candidates. The U.S. Supreme Court declined to reconsider that decision, and Lautenberg went on to win in the November 2002 election.

REP. EARL F. HILLIARD

The House Committee on Standards of Official Conduct issued a "letter of reproval" to Rep. Earl F. Hilliard, D-Ala., on June 20, 2001, following a nineteen-month investigation into misuse of campaign funds. The letter represented the lowest level of punishment that can be issued. It was part of a negotiated settlement in which Hilliard agreed to admit to violating House rules. *(Background, Congress and the Nation Vol. X, pp. 765, 772)*

The committee found that Hilliard had diverted campaign money to pay for, among other things, campaign aides who were doing work for businesses connected to Hilliard's family. The panel rebuked Hilliard for "serious official misconduct that brought discredit to the House."

The committee voted unanimously to issue the letter, but its report showed that more severe punishment had been considered. It said the "imposition of a sanction greater than a letter of reproval could be supported by many factors, including the demonstrated systematic and deliberate conversion of campaign funds by Representative Hilliard to personal use and . . . the lack of complete cooperation and candor by" Hilliard and his attorney. Panel members, however, concluded that Hilliard's admission under the settlement and the public release of the investigative report provided adequate punishment.

Hilliard denied receiving "monetary gains" but did not dispute the committee's report.

REP. STEVE BUYER

Charges that Rep. Steve Buyer, R-Ind., had used his office to lend support to Republican operatives during the 2000 ballot recount in Florida following the disputed presidential election between George W. Bush and Al Gore were dismissed on Aug. 1, 2001. House Committee on Standards of Official Conduct Chair Joel Hefley, R-Colo., and ranking member Howard L. Berman, D-Calif., sent a letter to Buyer informing him that the panel had found the allegations to be baseless.

Rep. Peter Deutsch, D-Fla., had asked for an investigation on July 16, the day after the *New York Times* published a story saying that in November 2000 Buyer had asked the Pentagon for contact information for service men and women whose absentee ballots had been disqualified. The newspaper said the information was used to put the voters in touch with Florida Republicans organizing a public relations campaign to persuade counties to reconsider rejected ballots. Buyer said he requested the information because his Armed Services Military Personnel Subcommittee was investigating reports of problems with military ballots. He said he sent only surveys and knew nothing about information going to the Republican Party in Florida.

REP. GARY A. CONDIT

On July 20, 2001, Rep. Bob Barr, R-Ga., in a seven-page formal complaint to the House Committee on Standards of Official Conduct requested that an investigation be made into whether Rep. Gary A. Condit, D-Calif., impeded a police probe into the disappearance of intern Chandra Levy. The complaint accused Condit of obstructing justice and other "improper conduct that brings discredit" to the House.

Condit lost his March 2002 Democratic primary. He first came to Congress in 1989.

Levy, one of Condit's constituents from Modesto, California, worked at the Bureau of Prisons in Washington, D.C. She disappeared in early May 2001 and was the focus of a highly publicized police search. Condit originally said he and Levy were just friends, but according to published reports, he later told police that they had an affair. Police never named Condit a suspect in the case.

Levy's body was found in Rock Creek Park in Washington, D.C., on May 22, 2002. The D.C. medical examiner subsequently ruled her death a homicide. On Dec. 16, 2002, Condit filed a lawsuit against *Vanity Fair* writer, Court-TV host, and crime book author Dominick Dunne for slander and sought $11 million in damages. On Dec. 19, 2003, Condit filed a lawsuit against the *National Enquirer, Star,* and *Globe* tabloids and their parent companies, seeking $209 million in damages. The suit, which charged that the magazines knowingly printed false information about Condit, was settled in 2004. The details of the settlement were confidential.

As of early 2006, Levy's murderer had not been found.

Capitol Visitors Center

A new visitor center was designed to be a 580,000-square-foot subterranean complex, three quarters the size of the Capitol, to be built under the East Front. The center was first conceived in the 1970s as a way to improve the comfort and education of tourists, and for years lawmakers hoped that private donations would pay for most of the cost. But a consensus had formed that the government should pay for the bulk of the project—as much as 85 percent—because of the desire to implement the center's other benefit: creating a single Capitol entrance for anyone who is not a lawmaker, aide, journalist, or lobbyist. *(108th Congress action, p. 725)*

Security concerns expedited planning for the visitors center, but some lobbyists, whose livelihoods depend on easy public access to lawmakers, were afraid the security push would force them to file in through the same door as bus-

loads of tourists. They wanted credentials similar to those given staff members and the press.

House Administration Committee Chair Bob Ney, R-Ohio, wanted to create a "frequent visitor's pass" to allow lobbyists, state officials, and others to bypass lines of visitors. But Sens. Jon Corzine, D-N.J., and Russell D. Feingold, D-Wis., promoted a resolution (S Res 188) to bar Congress from letting lobbyists skirt lines and use doors set aside for staff and journalists. Corzine argued that an elderly American who "spends her own money to come to Washington to protect her Social Security benefits" should have the same access to the Capitol as corporate lobbyists. The American League of Lobbyists strongly opposed the resolution, which died upon adjournment.

When funding was first provided, in 1999 (PL 105-275), the center was expected to cost $265 million. Congress appropriated another $70 million (PL 107-68) after the Sept. 11, 2001, attacks for the House and Senate "shell" spaces on each side of the center.

Commemorative Meeting

Congress on Sept. 6, 2002, held a "special meeting" to honor the victims and survivors of the Sept. 11, 2001, terrorist attacks. Lawmakers met at Federal Hall in Manhattan, where members first convened in 1789. It is about a half-mile from Ground Zero. Vice President Dick Cheney also attended, in his capacity as president of the Senate.

Democratic representative Charles B. Rangel and other New York lawmakers read the text of a resolution (H Con Res 448), adopted by voice vote in the House and Senate on July 26, 2002, that called for the special meeting "in remembrance of the victims and the heroes of Sept. 11, 2001, and in recognition of the courage and spirit of the City of New York." The meeting, however, was not devoid of detractors. Sen. Robert C. Byrd, D-W.Va., pointedly stayed away from the event, saying that Congress had far more important legislative business to attend to in Washington.

When the hour-long session ended, members joined New York City mayor Michael Bloomberg and other dignitaries at a Wall Street hotel for chateaubriand on a bundle of truffled greens and white asparagus. Most costs for the ceremonies were paid through a $1 million grant to New York City by the Annenberg Foundation.

The special meeting marked only the second time that Congress gathered outside of Washington, D.C., since moving to the Capitol in 1800. The other time was in 1987, when lawmakers traveled to Constitution Hall in Philadelphia, Pennsylvania, for a session in honor of the bicentennial of the U.S. Constitution. *(Bicentennial observance, Congress and the Nation Vol. VII, p. 889)*

2003–2004

Republicans won back the majority in the Senate, putting the entire Congress and the White House in GOP hands.

Organization: 108th Congress

Senate Republicans and House Democrats saw an almost complete turnover in their leaderships, while the House GOP leadership endured its own shifts with the retirement of the majority leader. Only the Senate Democratic leadership remained stable.

SENATE

The Senate unexpectedly got a new Republican leader. Democrats stuck with their old hands.

Majority Leadership

Trent Lott of Mississippi, who had served as Senate Republican leader since 1996, was set to be reelected majority leader for the 108th Congress without opposition. Then, in a birthday speech for Sen. Strom Thurmond, R-S.C., on Dec. 5, 2002, Lott suggested that the nation would have been better off if Thurmond had succeeded in his segregationist presidential campaign of 1948. Pummeled by embarrassed Republicans and outraged Democrats, Lott on Dec. 20 removed himself as a candidate for the Republican leader post. Bill Frist of Tennessee on Dec. 23 was chosen by acclamation to fill the vacancy. Mitch McConnell of Kentucky was elected majority whip, replacing Don Nickles of Oklahoma, who was leaving the No. 2 leadership job because of self-imposed GOP term limits. Rick Santorum of Pennsylvania remained as chair of the Senate Republican Conference, the third-ranking leadership post, while Jon Kyl of Arizona was set to take over as chair of the Republican Policy Committee, replacing the term-limited Larry E. Craig of Idaho. George Allen of Virginia became chair of the National Republican Senatorial Committee. He succeeded Frist, who did not seek reelection as chair. Frist, McConnell, Santorum, Kyl, and Allen all ran unopposed.

Minority Leadership

Tom Daschle of South Dakota ran unopposed for a fifth term as Senate Democratic leader. Harry Reid of Nevada won a third term as minority whip. He was unopposed for the post. Barbara A. Mikulski of Maryland was unopposed for a third term as Democratic Conference secretary.

Committees

New GOP chairs took over from Democrats (unless otherwise noted). At Agriculture, Nutrition, and Forestry, Thad Cochran of Missouri succeeded Tom Harkin of Iowa; Appropriations, Ted Stevens of Alaska took over from Robert C. Byrd of West Virginia; Armed Services, John W. Warner of Virginia replaced Carl Levin of Michigan; Banking, Housing, and Urban Affairs, Richard Shelby of Alabama succeeded Paul S. Sarbanes of Maryland; Budget, Don Nickles of Oklahoma replaced Kent Conrad of North Dakota; Commerce, Science, and Transportation, John McCain of Arizona took over from Ernest F. Hollings of South Carolina; Energy and Natural Resources, Pete V. Domenici of New Mexico succeeded Jeff Bingaman of New Mexico; Environment and Public Works, James M. Inhofe of Ohio replaced James M. Jeffords of Vermont, an independent; Finance, Charles E. Grassley of Iowa succeeded Max Baucus of Montana; Foreign Relations, Richard G. Lugar of Indiana took over from Joseph R. Biden Jr. of Delaware; Governmental Affairs, Susan Collins of Maine replaced Joseph I. Lieberman of Connecticut; Health, Education, Labor, and Pensions, Judd Gregg of New Hampshire succeeded Edward M. Kennedy of Massachusetts; Indian Affairs, Ben Nighthorse Campbell of Colorado took over from Daniel K. Inouye of Hawaii; Judiciary, Orrin G. Hatch of Utah replaced Patrick J. Leahy of Vermont; Rules and Administration, Trent Lott of Mississippi succeeded Christopher J. Dodd of Connecticut; Select Ethics, George V. Voinovitch of Ohio took over from Harry Reid of Nevada; Select Intelligence, Pat Roberts of Kansas succeeded Bob Graham of Florida; Small Business and Entrepreneurship, Olympia J. Snowe of Maine replaced John Kerry of Massachusetts; Special Aging, Larry E. Craig of Idaho took over from John B. Breaux of Louisiana; and Veterans' Affairs, Arlen Specter of Pennsylvania succeeded John D. Rockefeller IV of West Virginia.

Likewise, the committees got new Democratic (unless otherwise noted) ranking members, who succeeded Republicans. Harkin succeeded Lugar as the ranking member on Agriculture, Nutrition, and Forestry; Byrd replaced Stevens on Appropriations; Levin took over from Warner on Armed Services; Sarbanes replaced Phil Gramm of Texas on Banking, Housing, and Urban Affairs; Conrad succeeded Domenici on Budget; Hollings took over from McCain on Commerce, Science, and Transportation; Bingaman replaced Frank H. Murkowski of Alaska on Energy and Natural Resources; Jeffords, an independent, succeeded Robert C. Smith of New Hampshire on Environment and Public Works; Baucus took over from Grassley on Finance; Biden succeeded Jesse Helms of North Carolina on Foreign Relations; Lieberman succeeded Fred Thompson of Tennessee on Governmental Affairs; Kennedy took over from Gregg on Health, Education, Labor, and Pensions; Inouye succeeded Murkowski on Indian Affairs; Leahy succeeded Hatch on Judiciary; Dodd replaced Mitch McConnell of Kentucky on Rules and Administration; Reid succeeded Roberts on Select Ethics; Rockefeller took over from Shelby on Select Intelligence; Kerry succeeded Bond on Small Business and Entrepreneurship; Breaux replaced Craig on Special Aging; and Graham succeeded Specter on Veterans' Affairs.

The Senate on Oct. 9, 2004, adopted S Res 445 by 79–6, which enhanced the power of committees responsible for intelligence and homeland security programs and would take effect at the beginning of the 109th Congress. The resolution raised the status of the Intelligence Committee, ended the eight-year term limit on Intelligence members, gave the majority and minority leaders power to appoint all panel members, and reduced the size of the panel from seventeen to fifteen members. The resolution created a new Appropriations subcommittee to handle the intelligence budget. And it gave jurisdiction over some functions of the Department of Homeland Security to the Governmental Affairs Committee, which was renamed the Homeland Security and Governmental Affairs Committee.

HOUSE

Both the Republicans and Democrats saw a shakeup in their leadership.

Majority Leadership

J. Dennis Hastert of Illinois was elected 228–202 on Jan. 7, 2003, to a third term as Speaker. Tom DeLay of Texas moved up from the No. 3 position of majority whip to the No. 2 position of majority leader, succeeding Dick Armey of Texas, who retired from Congress. DeLay protégé Roy Blunt of Missouri was elected to succeed him as majority whip. Hastert, DeLay, and Blunt all ran unopposed. Deborah Pryce of Ohio was elected chair of the House Republican Conference. Succeeding J. C. Watts Jr. of Oklahoma, she received 133 votes, besting J. D. Hayworth of Arizona (61 votes) and Jim Ryum of Kansas (28 votes). Christopher Cox of California continued as chair of the Republican Policy Committee. Thomas M. Davis III of Virginia did not seek reelection as National Republican Congressional Committee chair. The post was won by Thomas M. Reynolds of New York with 119 votes versus 90 votes for Jerry Weller of Illinois.

Minority Leadership

Richard A. Gephardt of Missouri gave up his position as minority leader after Democrats failed to gain the majority for the fourth time since he became House Democratic leader. Nancy Pelosi of California, who had been the Democratic whip, moved into Gephardt's slot. She became the first woman to lead a political party in Congress. Pelosi won the top job with 177 votes; Harold E. Ford Jr. of Tennessee got 29 votes. Steny H. Hoyer of Maryland was elected without opposition to take Pelosi's place as Democratic whip. Robert Menendez of New Jersey became the highest-ranking Hispanic lawmaker in congressional history when he was elected chair of the Democratic Caucus, defeating Rosa DeLauro of Connecticut, 104–103. Menendez replaced Martin Frost of Texas, who was barred by party rules from seeking another term.

Committees

Few changes were seen in committee chairs or ranking members. Republicans Robert W. Goodlatte of Virginia succeeded Larry Combest of Texas, who retired from Congress, as head of Agriculture; Duncan Hunter of California took over from Bob Stump of Arizona, who retired from Congress; Tom Davis of Virginia succeeded Dan Burton of Indiana at Government Reform; and Richard W. Pombo of California succeeded James V. Hansen of Utah, who retired from Congress, on the top seat of Resources. Democrats Barney Frank of Massachusetts replaced John J. LaFalce of New York as ranking member of Financial Services; John B. Larson of Connecticut succeeded Steny H. Hoyer of Maryland on House Oversight; Bart Gordon of Tennessee took over from Ralph M. Hall of Texas on Science; Jane Harman of California succeeded Nancy Pelosi of California on Select Intelligence; and Allan B. Mollohan of West Virginia replaced Howard L. Berman of California on Standards of Official Conduct.

Christopher Cox, R-Calif., and Jim Turner, D-Texas, served as chair and ranking minority member, respectively, on the newly created Select Committee on Homeland Security.

Rules

The rules package (H Res 5) was adopted on a party-line vote of 221–203 on Jan. 7, 2003. Some of the rules changes were a response to the rules put in place in 1995, which had proved impractical in some instances. The new rules repealed the eight-year term limit for the Speaker, for instance, in recognition that a lame duck Speaker's powers could be sharply curtailed. A change also was made in the limit on gifts that would allow lobbyists to cater meals in the House, which could benefit both the Republican and Democratic leadership.

Before the rules package reached the floor, House ethics committee chair Hefley persuaded leaders to tighten a rule that would permit charitable groups to pay for members to attend their celebrity golf tournaments or similar fundraising functions. The leadership initially would allow members to accept travel and lodging reimbursements from all 501(c) tax-exempt organizations, such as labor and business groups.

The new rules also allowed House members to earn as much as $22,500 as doctors and dentists.

Democrats complained that some changes were designed to stifle dissent. For example, getting consideration of nonbinding floor motions to instruct conferees, which are often used by the minority to advance their arguments on legislation, would now take longer. Also under the new rules, chairs could postpone committee votes.

On April 11, 2003, Hefley and ranking member Mollohan issued a memorandum detailing the ethics committee's interpretation of the new rules. The memo required House officers to ensure that no lobbyist was covertly covering the costs of travel and lodging for members at a charity event. It expressly forbid members from accepting travel or lodging from a charity "if those expenditures would be paid using donations that were earmarked, either formally or informally, for payment of expenses of congressional participants." The guidelines also limited the time members could spend at charity functions, to one or two nights. Furthermore, members and staff who accepted transportation or lodging to such events could bring a spouse or dependent, but not both. Lawmakers also were obligated to ascertain that the main purpose of such events was to raise money for charity. The committee suggested that "at least half of the fee paid" by attendees be tax deductible. On the issue of free food, the panel reminded lawmakers and their staffs that such a gift "must be refused entirely if the person offering it has a direct interest in the particular legislation or other official business on which staff is working at the time."

Filibuster Change

The Senate Rules and Administration Committee by voice vote June 24, 2003, approved S Res 138, which sought to weaken the filibuster to make it all but impossible for the minority party to prevent floor votes on confirmations. The measure was reported (no written report) on June 26 and saw no further action.

Traditionally, a filibuster involved one or more senators gaining control of the floor and talking for hours and using other tactics to halt the proceedings, often in an attempt to get senators to agree to make changes in pending legislation, kill a bill, or derail a presidential nomination. In recent times, the mere threat of a filibuster usually was enough to get Senate leaders to alter their plans or to move to invoke cloture (end debate). Although Senate rules do not describe a filibuster, Rule XXII of the Standing Rules of the Senate created a procedure for ending one. Typically, the Senate's majority party leadership submits a petition for cloture to end a filibuster—actual or threatened. Two legislative days later, the motion to invoke cloture must be voted on. If three-fifths of the membership, or sixty senators when there are no vacancies, vote for cloture, further debate on the issue at hand would be limited to thirty hours, amendments must be germane, and no tactics could be used to prevent an up-or-down vote after that time.

The proposal, offered by Senate majority leader Bill Frist, R-Tenn., would amend Rule XXII as it applied to nominations for either judgeships or executive branch posts. On successive motions to invoke cloture—and thereby limit debate—on a nomination, the number of votes necessary for approval would gradually decline. The first motion would require sixty votes to prevail, the same as under existing procedures. A second motion would require fifty-seven votes; a third, fifty-four. If all those efforts failed, cloture could be invoked on the fourth attempt with only fifty-one votes, a simple majority and the same number needed for confirmation if all senators voted.

Frist and his allies argued that the Constitution's framers never envisioned that confirmation would take anything more than a simple majority vote. While the Constitution requires a supermajority in several instances, such as ratifying treaties, it does not lay out a specific threshold for the confirmation of federal judges. The Constitution tells the Senate to give its "advice and consent" on nominations. Because breaking a filibuster requires the support of three-fifths of all senators, Frist argued that Democrats were trying to establish another, unconstitutionally high standard for confirmations. Democrats cited the Constitution's mandate to justify their decision to filibuster nominees they viewed as unfit for the federal bench.

Frist lacked the votes to beat a Democratic filibuster of the resolution on the floor. Under an extreme scenario, Republicans could have invoked the constitutional right of a majority of senators to determine the rules of the Senate—with the help of a ruling from the chair—forcing the filibuster resolution through the chamber on a simple majority vote. The risk was that it would have inflamed Democrats and possibly locked up the floor for weeks or months, stalling top GOP legislative priorities. Frist contemplated forcing a vote during an extraordinary around-the-clock debate on the president's judicial nominees, orchestrated by Republicans to highlight the Democratic filibusters. But he ultimately backed away, saying he did not want the vote to be lost in the noise of that debate.

Congressional Caucuses

Reps. Michael E. Capuano, D-Mass., and Vito J. Fossella, R-N.Y., on Jan. 15, 2003, announced formation of the Congressional Caucus on Korea. Officially created to "provide a formal structure" for Congress to address issues on the Korean peninsula, Capuano and Fossella said it was intended to strengthen the U.S. relationship with South Korea while working to promote democracy in North Korea.

In a similar move, Rep. Zoe Lofgren, D-Calif., announced the creation of a U.S.-Philippine Caucus.

Contingency Plans

In post–Sept. 11, 2001, a concern arose that many House and Senate seats could be vacant or held by incapacitated members for an extended period after a catastrophe—just when prompt action by Congress on emergency response plans could be needed. While the Seventeenth Amendment allows states to appoint senators to fill a vacancy caused by death or departure from office, no provision in the Constitution covered widespread and severe injury. *(107th Congress action, p. 710)*

The House Administration Committee Nov. 19, 2003, approved HR 2844 (H Rept 108-404, Part I) to require states to hold special elections within forty-five days after the Speaker of the House declared more than one hundred vacancies in that chamber. The bill, offered by Rules Chair David Dreier, R-Calif., and Judiciary Chair F. James Sensenbrenner Jr., R-Wis., was approved 4–3. Initially, the measure would have given states a twenty-one-day window to hold the elections. House Administration Chair Bob Ney, R-Ohio, said the change was made at the prompting of state officials to give parties more time to recruit candidates and election planners more time to print ballots and test election systems.

Support for the bill by top House Republicans deflated backing for a constitutional amendment to allow for the appointment of House members in emergency situations. The Continuity of Government Commission, a joint project of the Brookings Institution and the American Enterprise Institute, which reported its recommendations to Congress on June 4, 2003, supported amending the Constitution to allow for faster replacement of House members, arguing that it was the only way to ensure that the government could operate in an emergency. Backers of HR 2844, however, were among many House members who took pride in being elected "by the people," not appointed by the state, and thus opposed a constitutional amendment.

The House April 22, 2004, by 306–97 passed HR 2844. The vote tally belied the level of dissatisfaction with the measure, especially among House Democrats. Many of them said they would prefer amending the Constitution to permit the appointment of replacement House members after disasters, at least until the states could hold special elections. But the sponsors replied that any procedure allowing for an appointed House member would undo one of the central tenets of the founders: that one chamber of the national legislature should be "the people's house," its members unalterably subject to a popular vote. Democrats also complained that, as happened far too often in their view, they were essentially left out of the legislative deliberations that climaxed in the floor debate—a slight all the more offensive on a matter of institutional, not political, importance.

Other proposals to allow the appointment of congressional replacements were introduced by Democrats John B. Larson of Connecticut (H J Res 89), Brian Baird of Washington (H J Res 77), and Zoe Lofgren of California (H J Res 90) and Republican Dana Rohrabacher of California (H J Res 92). All died upon adjournment of the 108th Congress.

The House Judiciary Committee on May 5 voted adversely to report out H J Res 83, calling for a constitutional amendment that would have each member, upon election, choose two potential successors who could be appointed by the representative's home-state governor in the event that a majority of House members were killed or left unable to serve by a catastrophe. The 17–12 vote on the measure, sponsored by Baird, fell along party lines. Democrats complained that the bill had not been given a fair and sufficient hearing. The joint resolution was formally reported May 19 (H Rept 108-503).

Committee chairman Sensenbrenner said he opposed the bill partly because the founders explicitly rejected the idea of appointing lawmakers to the House. The committee rejected two motions by Rep. Zoe Lofgren, D-Calif., to delay the committee markup for at least two weeks so lawmakers could hold additional hearings.

The House on June 2 by 63–353 rejected H J Res 83. Many lawmakers, especially Republicans, said they opposed appointing members under any circumstances, and others balked at the idea of amending the Constitution. But bill sponsor Baird argued that his measure would not override HR 2844 but would fill a gap in leadership, while states scrambled to hold special elections. Before the final vote, Lofgren offered a motion to recommit the joint resolution to the House Judiciary Committee, hoping for further discussion and hearings on the topic. The motion was rejected 194–221 on June 2.

The Senate Judiciary Subcommittee on the Constitution, Civil Rights, and Property Rights by voice vote May 13, 2004, approved a proposed constitutional amendment (S J Res 23) that addressed the possibility of mass incapacitation caused by an attack on Capitol Hill. The bill, sponsored by panel Chair John Cornyn, R-Texas, would permit each chamber to set terms for replacing members by passing enabling legislation. The action would be required if one-fourth of either chamber were killed or incapacitated. Constitutional amendments require support from two-thirds of the House and Senate and three-fourths of the states must ratify any proposed change to the Constitution.

Cornyn also introduced S 2031, which would allow states to decide how to replace senators if a majority were incapacitated. He said his bill was not intended to counter HR 2844. Because it did not call for appointing new members, that measure did not require a constitutional amendment.

At the beginning of the 108th Congress, lawmakers made rules changes regarding continuity. Both chambers were allowed to convene outside Washington, D.C. In the House, the Speaker could declare an emergency recess at any time. The Speaker regularly filed a secret list of temporary successors in case of his incapacitation. A group of members also went to a secure location whenever the president addressed a joint session of Congress.

Corrections Office

During consideration of the fiscal 2004 legislative branch appropriations bill (HR 2657), House and Senate negotiators on Sept. 17, 2003, agreed to eliminate funding for the House Corrections Calendar Office.

The Corrections Calendar was created in 1995 to expedite noncontroversial measures that would repeal ambiguous, arbitrary, or obsolete federal laws and regulations. In its first two years of existence, twenty-two such bills were considered in the House. The Corrections Office was established in 1997.

It had been funded each year at $791,000 or more, for a total of $5 million since it was created. Only eight corrections bills had been considered on the House floor in that time.

The Corrections Office did not occupy a physical space on Capitol Hill. The two dozen aides on its payroll had full-time jobs in the offices of Democratic and Republican leaders. Beginning in fiscal 2004, House leaders paid for the aides out of their office budgets. HR 2657 would have provided additional funding for those budgets.

Ethics Probes

The actions of one of the most powerful members of the House came under scrutiny by the ethics committee.

REP. TOM DELAY

House majority leader Tom DeLay, R-Texas, two times in one week in 2004 was admonished by the House Committee on Standards of Official Conduct for exceeding the bounds of acceptable behavior in promoting his political and legislative agenda. In 1999, the ethics committee had found that then-majority whip DeLay had improperly threatened to retaliate against a trade association for hiring a Democrat as its president. *(1999 action, Congress and the Nation Vol. X, p. 773)*

On March 17, 2004, the ethics committee voted to create a subcommittee to formally investigate claims by Republican Nick Smith that "members and groups" offered financial help for the campaign of Brad Smith, his son and would-be successor in the Seventh District of south-central Michigan, if he changed his mind and backed a bill to add prescription drug coverage to Medicare (HR 1—PL 108-173). In the early hours of Nov. 22, 2003, Republican leaders had held open the vote on the measure for almost three hours in an effort to persuade enough members to switch their votes in favor of the measure. In a column posted on his congressional Web site the day after the vote—and published by a newspaper in his district the next week—Smith maintained that he was told that members or groups would be "working against Brad" if Smith voted against the bill. However, he stuck to his "nay" vote. Smith subsequently recanted, saying members made no explicit promise of financial support for his son in return for a "yea" vote. He also never said publicly which lawmakers sought to influence him. *(Medicare overhaul, p. 496)*

On Sept. 30, the full ethics panel admonished DeLay for using tactics that probably violated House rules in pursuing Smith's vote on the Medicare bill. However, the panel found no evidence of any bribe and admonished Smith for making that claim. It admonished DeLay for promising to endorse Brad Smith in return for Nick Smith's vote, and it admonished Rep. Candice S. Miller, R-Mich., for threatening to retaliate against the Smiths if the representative did not vote the leadership's way.

The committee also noted the unusually intense and personal efforts by Bush administration officials, led by Health and Human Services secretary Tommy G. Thompson, to win the Medicare vote. It recommended that House rules be changed to ban cabinet-level officials from the House floor during debate, except those who once served in the House. The report concluded that the extended, late-night vote and intense lobbying "contributed to an environment in which the usual traditions of civil discourse and decorum amongst members were not always followed."

Rep. Chris Bell, D-Texas, on June 15, 2004, filed an eighteen-page complaint with the ethics committee, charging that DeLay had solicited campaign donations from Westar Energy Inc., the largest electricity provider in Kansas, in return for favorable consideration of the company's views in writing the energy overhaul bill (HR 6); had pressured Federal Aviation Administration officials to help find Democratic Texas lawmakers who had left the state in 2003 in a bid to prevent the congressional redistricting plan being pushed by DeLay; and had participated in a scheme to subvert state law by funneling corporate contributions to Texas state House candidates in 2002. Bell's complaint, which was accompanied by 187 pages of exhibits that included internal e-mails, financial disclosure statements, House committee testimony, and newspaper stories, opened a formal congressional inquiry into DeLay's activities. DeLay denied the charges, saying Bell was simply bitter because he had lost his primary.

On Oct. 6, a unanimous ethics committee said DeLay "went beyond the bounds of acceptable conduct" by appearing to link political donations to legislative favors in one instance in 2002 and by improperly contacting a federal agency for help in a political endeavor in 2003. The panel warned DeLay that it had identified a clear pattern of misbehavior by him and would be on the lookout for additional infractions. It also faulted Bell for including innuendo, speculation, and unwarranted conclusions in his complaint against DeLay and for promoting it publicly with "excessive or inflammatory language or exaggerated charges in press releases and other public statements."

Besides the two congressional cases, DeLay was associated with an ongoing case in Texas. The county district attorney in Austin, Ronnie Earle, in 2003 began an investigation into the alleged use of corporate contributions in state legislative campaigns, which was against state law, in 2002 by the Texas Association of Business and Texans for a Republican Majority Political Action Committee (TRMPAC), a campaign organization created by DeLay. The inquiry centered on efforts by DeLay, the Texas business group, and state House Speaker Tom Craddick to gain GOP control of the state House in the 2002 elections. Their success led to the redrawing of the state's congressional map in 2003 in hopes of gaining seven new seats for the Republicans in November 2004. *(Redistricting, p. 30)*

DeLay's PAC raised almost $1.5 million in 2002—about $600,000 from corporations, mostly through their Washington lobbyists. The PAC contributed to twenty-one state legislative candidates. State law prohibited the spending of corporate or union money directly on campaigns, although a political committee could use such money to cover

DOWNLOADED DEMOCRATIC FILES

Senate sergeant at arms William Pickle on March 12, 2004, sent to the Justice Department for further review his report concluding that two Republican Senate Judiciary Committee aides had downloaded thousands of mainly Democratic files from the panel's computer system. The attorney general was free to decide whether and how to respond to the report. He could assign career Justice Department prosecutors to the case, direct a U.S. attorney to investigate, appoint a special counsel, or ignore the matter altogether.

According to the report, which was released publicly March 4, Jason Lundell and Manuel Miranda systematically gained access to and made copies of 4,670 files, most of which belonged to Democratic staff, in the committee computer system between November 2001 and the spring of 2003. The contents of several Democratic memos outlining the party's strategies for derailing some of President Bush's more contentious nominees for federal appeals judgeships were reported by the *Wall Street Journal* and the *Washington Times.* The Coalition for a Fair Judiciary, which supported Bush's picks for the courts, posted several of the memos on its Web site.

The report cited a "significant lack of security" in the Judiciary Committee's computer system as making the expropria-

tion of the materials easy to do and hard to detect. It said that Lundell did most of the work at the keyboard searching the computer, with Miranda directing his junior partner on what to look for and where to focus his efforts. Through their attorneys, both Lundell and Miranda denied wrongdoing. Miranda did wage a public relations offensive, excoriating Democrats for what he viewed as improper collusion with interest groups to thwart Bush's efforts to shape the courts. He said he was free to access files left unsecured on the committee computer system. Furthermore, he suggested that Judiciary Committee Chair Orrin G. Hatch, R-Utah, may have been complicit in the accessing of the files. Through a spokesman, Hatch declined to comment on Miranda's remark.

The investigation began in November 2003. When Pickle made his report to the Judiciary Committee in March 2004, the panel initially responded with rare bipartisan resolve. But the determination to stay united while getting to the bottom of the affair vanished, once again supplanted by the sort of partisan acrimony that characterized so much of the committee's work. Although the committee members appeared to agree that the panel should ask the attorney general to open a criminal probe, the matter of the letter to be sent to the Justice Department then arose. The panel Democrats wanted to

---

administrative costs. DeLay's fund-raising director, Jim Ellis, and TRMPAC lawyer Terry Scarborough said none of the PAC's corporate contributions was spent illegally.

One matter under investigation was whether the PAC, in effect, illegally laundered its contributions through the Republican National Committee (RNC) in the fall of 2003. The PAC donated $190,000 to an arm of the RNC that helped state legislative candidates, and soon thereafter that RNC committee wrote checks totaling $190,000 to seven candidates for the Texas Legislature.

On Sept. 21, a Travis County, Texas, grand jury handed up a thirty-two-count indictment resulting from a nearly two-year investigation by the Austin district attorney into the campaign financing activities of TRMPAC. Ellis, DeLay's political aide, head of DeLay's Americans for a Republican Majority Political Action Committee (ARMPAC), and a TRMPAC officer, was charged with one count of money laundering. John Colyandro, the executive director of TRMPAC in 2002, was charged with one count of money laundering and thirteen counts of illegally accepting corporate political contributions. Warren Robold, a TRMPAC fund-raiser, was charged with nine counts each of soliciting and accepting illegal corporate political contributions.

The grand jury alleged that Ellis, Colyandro, and Robold took part in a scheme to solicit $190,000 in corporate dona-

tions to TRMPAC, which were generally barred by state law, and funnel them to seven Texas House candidates using an arm of the RNC as a conduit. Eight companies were charged with making the illegal donations: Alliance for Quality Nursing Home Care Corp.; Bacardi USA Inc.; Cracker Barrel Old Country Store, a subsidiary of CBRL Group Inc.; Diversified Collection Services Inc.; Questerra Corp., a subsidiary of MeadWestvaco Corp.; Sears Roebuck and Co.; Westar Energy Inc.; and Williams Companies Inc. DeLay was never subpoenaed in the case, and his name was not mentioned in the indictment.

Although DeLay was not identified as a target in Earle's inquiry, House Republicans voted in a closed session Nov. 17 to propose that the chamber's rules be changed at the beginning of the 109th Congress to allow the majority leader to continue in that post were he indicted. They sought to change an eleven-year-old caucus rule that had required party leaders or committee chairmen to relinquish those jobs if charged with a felony. The new rule, however, would require that a leader convicted of a felony be removed immediately. Congressional watchdog groups assailed the GOP plan.

In an unexpected turnaround, DeLay on Jan. 3, 2005, asked the rank-and-file Republicans not to make the rule change that would permit an indicted member to continue serving in a leadership post. However, they did vote to remake several specific requests that the Republicans, and especially Hatch, were opposed to including. Hatch, who preferred a simple referral to Justice, prevailed by default when the committee could not agree. Separately, three Democratic and three Republican committee members sent a letter to Attorney General John Ashcroft asking him to appoint a prosecutor to look into the matter. The letter included the Democrats' suggestion of a special counsel, as well as a request that whoever was chosen could not be removed from the case except in extreme circumstances.

Unlike a federal prosecutor, Pickle did not have the power to compel people to cooperate in testifying and handing over evidence. Because of these limitations, Pickle could not determine how the published documents were transmitted outside the Senate. None of the media outlets or advocacy groups names in the report cooperated fully with the investigation. Pickle said the Senate anti-leaking rules for committees put in place in 1992 may have been violated. (The rules, adopted in the aftermath of Supreme Court justice Clarence Thomas's confirmation fight, barred disclosure of "secret or confidential business or proceedings of the Senate, including the business and proceedings of committees and offices of the Senate." Senators who violate the rules can be expelled. Aides

are subject to dismissal and prosecution outside Congress.) Pickle also summarized several federal and District of Columbia laws that could have been broken.

The report made several recommendations for securing Judiciary Committee computers.

- System administrators should receive additional training, with an emphasis on security policies.
- All staff members should receive training to ensure that they use their own computers in a secure manner.
- A security audit of the committee's computer network should be undertaken.
- Ethics training for new employees should be considered.

The report also made suggestions for improving computer security Senate-wide.

- A technical skills assessment and certification program should be developed for current system administrators, and new administrators should have to meet minimal qualification standards developed by the sergeant at arms and the Committee on Rules and Administration. System administrators also should be required to receive continuing technical education.
- Ethics and professional responsibility training should be mandatory for all new employees.

quire a majority vote on the ethics committee for an investigation to go forward. In the past, if a tie vote of the panel, which is evenly split between Republicans and Democrats, remained unchanged for forty-five days, a probe would be triggered.

REP. JIM MCDERMOTT

Rep. Jim McDermott, D-Wash., on Oct. 22, 2004, was ordered by District Judge Thomas F. Hogan in federal court in Washington, D.C., to pay $60,000 and lawyer fees to Rep. John A. Boehner, R-Ohio, for disclosing the contents of a 1996 telephone conversation in which House Speaker Newt Gingrich, R-Ga. (1979–1999), was discussing with Boehner ethical allegations the Speaker was facing. According to Boehner's chief of staff, the representative spent $545,000 in campaign funds in legal fees.

"The Court finds that [McDermott's] conduct was malicious in that he intentionally disclosed the tape to the national media in an attempt to politically harm the participants through an invasion of their privacy," Hogan wrote in his decision. "[McDermott's] argument that he was acting in the public interest by exposing official misconduct is unsupported by the evidence."

Hogan had ruled Aug. 20 that McDermott, while he was the top Democrat on the House Committee on Standards of

Official Conduct, broke a 1986 federal wiretapping law (PL 99-508) by knowingly accepting a tape of the call—recorded illegally by a Florida couple, who had intercepted it on a radio scanner—and giving copies to two newspapers. *(1986 law, Congress and the Nation Vol. VII, p. 744)*

Boehner sued McDermott in 1997. He sought $10,000 in punitive damages and hundreds of thousands of dollars in legal fees amassed in the fight. McDermott maintained that he had a First Amendment right to disclose the tape. But Hogan, who took that view in dismissing the case in 1998, rejected that argument in light of appeals court victories subsequently won by Boehner. *(Earlier action, Congress and the Nation Vol. X, pp. 765, 774)*

The court's 2004 award did not close the case. McDermott appealed, and on Nov. 16 Rep. David L. Hobson, R-Ohio, filed a complaint with the ethics committee, alleging that McDermott has violated House rules when he disclosed the intercepted phone conversation. Two days later the panel announced that it had established an investigative subcommittee to look into the matter.

REP. BILL JANKLOW

Rep. Bill Janklow, R-S.D., was convicted Dec. 8, 2003, of second-degree manslaughter in the death of a motorcyclist in a high-speed crash Aug. 16. He also was convicted of reckless driving, running a stop sign, and speeding. Shortly after hearing the verdict, Janklow announced his resignation from the House, effective Jan. 20, 2004.

Janklow faced possible penalties of as much as ten years in prison and a fine of up to $10,000. On Jan. 22, 2004, he was sentenced to one hundred days in jail, fined $5,750, and ordered to pay $50 a day for his incarceration. He was eligible after thirty days in jail to leave each day for up to ten hours to do court-appointed community service. After serving his time, Janklow would be on probation for three years and would not be allowed to drive in that period.

At trial, Janklow's defense was that, as a diabetic, he was suffering from low blood sugar and so was inattentive at the time of the crash. The prosecution emphasized Janklow's long record of speeding.

A special election was held June 1, 2004, to fill the vacancy left by Janklow's resignation from the House. Democrat Stephanie Herseth was sworn in June 3.

SEN. RICHARD C. SHELBY

The Senate Ethics Committee in 2004 began an investigation into whether Sen. Richard C. Shelby, R-Ala., while he was vice chair of the Select Intelligence Committee, leaked classified information to reporters in 2002. The matter had been referred to the committee by the Justice Department.

The Federal Bureau of Investigation was investigating whether Shelby illegally, or at least inappropriately, disclosed the content of National Security Agency (NSA) intercepts that were discussed during closed-door testimony before the House and Senate Intelligence committees in June 2002. The two panels were conducting a joint investigation into intelligence activities before the Sept. 11, 2001, terrorist attacks, and Shelby had accused intelligence agencies of delaying the release of documents and other relevant information. Shelby's office released a statement Aug. 6, 2004, denying any wrongdoing by the senator, whose term on the Intelligence Committee expired in January 2003.

The Justice Department probe focused on Shelby after news reports in June 2002 disclosed that the NSA had intercepted two messages Sept. 10, 2001, that said an event was planned, but the communications were not translated until Sept. 12. A report aired by Cable News Network (CNN) said that the messages were: "Tomorrow is zero hour" and "the match begins tomorrow."

That information apparently came from the closed-door testimony of Gen. Michael Hayden, NSA director, that was delivered to the Intelligence Committee the same day as the CNN report. Vice President Dick Cheney complained about the leak of the information, and Intelligence Committee leaders called on the Justice Department to find the source.

If panel members decide there was enough evidence to move forward on the probe of Shelby, an outside counsel would be used to investigate the matter and report the findings back to the committee. Shelby would be given time to respond to any charge against him made to the Ethics Com-

mittee, according to Senate ethics guidelines. No official schedule for the investigation by the committee had been set by end of 2004.

REP. KAREN MCCARTHY

The House Office of Standards of Official Conduct on Nov. 18, 2004, said that Rep. Karen McCarthy, D-Mo., had violated House rules prohibiting the personal use of campaign funds except for "bona fide campaign or political purposes." She was ordered to reimburse her campaign committee for thousands of dollars she spent on a trip to the Grammy Awards ceremony in New York in 2003. The ethics committee did not initiate formal disciplinary proceedings because McCarthy was just days away from retiring from Congress.

McCarthy argued that she had spent the money legally because many of her Kansas City constituents were recording artists. That explanation did not seem to hold up, however, and she had several tense exchanges with the Missouri news media.

The ethics committee said that McCarthy's trip could have been legitimately paid for at least in part by campaign funds, but she failed to respond to repeated requests for information about the events.

The panel did not say how much McCarthy should repay, but press reports put the price tag for her four-day stay at the Waldorf-Astoria Hotel at $2,916.

In 2003, McCarthy admitted to having a drinking problem and took a month-long hiatus at a rehabilitation center.

REP. JOHN CONYERS JR.

The House Committee on Standards of Official Conduct in 2004 started informal inquiries into whether Rep. John Conyers Jr., D-Mich., violated House rules by using his Detroit district office to conduct campaign activities. The outcome would determine whether the panel opened a full investigation.

Allegations had been made that Conyers and his top aides had ordered, in violation of federal law, congressional staffers to work on political campaigns in Michigan, on the local and statewide levels, on government time in 2002 and 2003. One of those campaigns was the 2002 state Senate bid of Monica Ann Conyers, Conyers's wife. House staffers are not precluded from working on campaigns, but they can do so only on their own time and without the use of government resources.

Conyers's attorney said that the representative was cooperating with the ethics committee and that documents supplied to the panel would show his innocence.

No further developments in the case were made public before the 108th Congress adjourned.

REP. CURT WELDON

Rep. Curt Weldon, R-Pa., became the target of an ethics investigation beginning in 2004. The House Committee on Standards of Official Conduct sought to determine whether

Weldon, in violation of House rules, had used his office to help a company that employed his daughter.

Weldon reportedly was an aggressive advocate for Itera International Energy Corp., which sought to develop a gas field in western Siberia. The company was under suspicion of taking part in questionable business deals. Weldon appealed to top Bush political adviser Karl Rove and Secretary of Energy Spencer Abraham on behalf of Itera. Meanwhile, Solutions North America, a company owned by his daughter, Karen, and Charles P. Sexton Jr., a political ally of Weldon's, was awarded a $500,000 contract by Itera for public relations work. Officials at Itera claimed that competitors were the source of the allegations of unethical practices.

Weldon also promoted Saratov Aviation, a Russian company that was developing an experimental aircraft, and sought visas for Serbian brothers Dragomir and Bogoljub Karic, who had links to former Yugoslav president Slobodan Milosevic. Saratov Aviation and a family foundation connected to the Karic brothers both had hired Solutions North America. The company was to earn an estimated $1 million from the contracts.

The House committee was supplied documents that Weldon's lawyer said proved the member was not guilty of any ethical breaches in the matter.

The case was ongoing as of early 2005.

Capitol Visitors Center

Building of the Capitol Visitors Center was marked by slow progress and rising costs.

On April 21, 2003, the architect of the Capitol, Alan M. Hantman, announced that he had awarded a $144.2 million contract to Manhattan Construction Corp. of Tulsa, Oklahoma, to complete Sequence 2 of the center. The contract was about 20 percent higher than the $120 million Hantman initially estimated the second construction phase would cost.

For fiscal 2004, another $38.5 million for security enhancements was approved, bringing the total estimate, before the contract for Sequence 2, to $373.5 million. The appropriators set five conditions for release of the funds. The architect of the Capitol would have to provide monthly financial reports; eliminate a separate $18 million contingency account that Rep. David R. Obey, R-Wis., in an April 9, 2003, letter to the architect, equated to a slush fund; notify the committee of cost overruns or any change in the status of the project; submit a reprogramming request to the committee if a cost increase was in excess of either $500,000 or 10 percent of a specific element's estimated cost; and undergo audits of his monthly reports by the General Accounting Office. *(Earlier action, p. 716)*

While the center originally was scheduled to be completely by the 2005 presidential inaugural, center officials blamed bad weather and a limited number of contractors for what could be an almost year-and-a-half delay in completion. Furthermore, by the end of 2004, the project was expected to go as much as $100 million over budget.

Senate Commission on Art

With the help of a group of Senate spouses—including Catherine Stevens, wife of Appropriations Committee Chair Ted Stevens, R-Alaska—Sen. Ben Nighthorse Campbell, R-Colo., helped establish the Senate Commission on Art with $500,000 in seed money to buy back pieces of antiquity that were filched from the Senate over the last two centuries. The funds were approved as part of the fiscal 2004 legislative branch appropriations conference report (HR 2657—H Rept 108-279), which cleared Congress on Sept. 24, 2003. Under the bill, the commission could accept monetary donations from private parties to be used for buying back pieces of Senate history. Under prior law, donated property, but not financial gifts, could be accepted.

On June 27, 2003, the Senate adopted a resolution (S Res 178) to bar anyone from taking furniture or artwork for personal use. Pilfering Senate property had become common practice.

Northern Mariana Islands Representation

Had HR 5135 become law, nonvoting representation in the House would have increased by one, to six. The more than seventy-eight thousand people who live on the Northern Mariana Islands, who have been U.S. citizens since 1986, would have sent a nonvoting delegate to the House beginning in 2007. The string of fourteen islands is in the middle of the Pacific Ocean, nearer to Japan than Hawaii.

The House Resources Committee approved HR 5135 on Sept. 29, 2004, and formally reported it (H Rept 108-761) on Oct. 7. The bill, sponsored by Rep. Richard W. Pombo, R-Calif., died upon adjournment.

The Northern Mariana Islands played a major role in U.S. history. The *Enola Gay* and *Bock's Car,* the B-29 bombers that dropped atomic bombs on Hiroshima and Nagasaki in August 1945, took off from and returned to an airstrip on the island of Tinian. After the war, the islands remained under U.S. control and won the right of self-government in 1976. Ten years later, the island's residents were granted U.S. citizenship.

Critics of prior efforts to grant representation to the islands complained that its labor laws were unfair. Intervening efforts to improve the situation lessened opposition.

American Samoa, the District of Columbia, Guam, Puerto Rico, and the U.S. Virgin Islands each sends a nonvoting delegate to the House. The addition of a delegate representing the Northern Mariana Islands was expected to cost as much as $1.1 million a year.

Chronology of Action on Congress: Election Issues

2001–2002

The debacle of the 2000 presidential contest was an impetus for Congress to address problems in the U.S. electoral system. Democrats sought to protect Americans' right to vote, while Republicans looked to curtail voter fraud.

After years of debate, members successfully fashioned a broad overhaul of the nation's campaign finance laws.

Election Overhaul

Nearly two years after the closest and most hotly debated presidential election in modern U.S. history, Congress in 2002 cleared a bill (HR 3295—PL 107-252) that for the first time set nationwide standards for the conduct of elections and authorized federal aid to help states meet those standards. The new law was known as the Help America Vote Act of 2002.

BACKGROUND

Since the nation's founding, the states have run and paid for all elections, with minimal federal involvement. At the same time, the Constitution gives Congress wide authority to regulate the election of federal candidates. As a practical matter, that means Congress can regulate the conduct of all elections because states are unlikely to maintain separate voting systems for federal candidates.

Under Article I, Section 4, each state sets the "time, place and manner" of House and Senate elections, but Congress may "by law make or alter such regulations" at any time. In 1842, Congress used its authority under this section to require that states elect their congressional delegations from single-member districts. In February 2001, the U.S. Supreme Court reaffirmed Congress's power over congressional elections in *Cook v. Gralike*, striking down a Missouri law requiring that ballots label those candidates opposed to term limits. The high court stressed that any authority states have over congressional elections is delegated by Congress. *(Court case, pp. 631, 656)*

Congress also has the power to force changes in state laws by attaching conditions to federal money, such as when it used highway dollars to get states to set speed limits on interstates. That power, upheld by the courts, is rooted in the taxing and spending authority granted Congress by Article I, Section 8, of the Constitution.

In addition, the Fourteenth Amendment guarantees all citizens equal protection under the law, and the Fifteenth Amendment forbids states to deny anyone the right to vote on the basis of race. If evidence exists that minority votes or others are being treated unfairly, Congress has the power to step in.

The Fourteenth Amendment's guarantee of equal protection formed the basis for the Supreme Court's ruling in *Bush v. Gore*, which stopped the recounts of Florida's presidential ballots in 2000 and effectively handed the presidency to Republican candidate George W. Bush. In the 5–4 decision, the majority said the recounts should be halted because standards for determining voter intent on partially punched ballots varied by county and therefore violated constitutional rights to equal protection. Some legal experts said the case seemed at least to provide an opening for requiring some internal uniformity in the way states and counties run elections. But the Court took pains to limit its ruling to the standoff in Florida, writing that "the problem of equal protection in election processes generally presents many complexities." That qualifier muddied the waters for many lawmakers, analysts, and scholars. Some legal experts said they doubted the ruling gave Congress any more power than the authority it already had to regulate elections. *(2000 presidential election, Congress and the Nation Vol. X, p. 20)*

Many federal lawmakers, along with state and local officials, argued against creating federal election mandates. The tradition of local control is long, the costs varied, and the bureaucracies entrenched, some said, that Congress would have trouble making changes even if it tried. Some preferred to offer federal money with strings attached, making grants contingent on states meeting standards for accuracy, accessibility, and accountability while maintaining the long tradition of local control. Some state and county officials called for federal guidelines in setting standards and identifying the best practices in election administration. They also wanted federal money to help pay for new equipment and training election workers. But ultimately, state and local officials said they knew best what kinds of equipment and procedures worked for their constituents. A number of ad hoc groups outside of Congress also warned against edicts from Washington. Two of the most prominent—a study group of state and local election officials and a national task force led by former presidents Jimmy Carter and Gerald R. Ford—urged states to adopt uniform statewide standards for counting votes. They also said the federal government should get more involved in helping to set standards for elections and in paying for the upgrade of voting equipment, although both groups opposed federal mandates.

A 2001 George Washington University study estimated the total cost of replacing all punch-card and lever machines at $600 million. The machines served about 88 percent of voters. The Massachusetts Institute of Technology and the California Institute of Technology released a report in July 2001 saying that between four million and six million people nationwide were unable to or were prevented from casting votes, or had their votes invalidated in the 2000 presidential election. Faulty equipment was partly to blame, the report said.

HR 2275, sponsored by Vernon J. Ehlers, R-Mich., and James A. Barcia, D-Mich., aimed to improve the accuracy and security of voting machines nationwide. The bill established a commission in association with the National Institute of Standards and Technology that would include state and local election officials to develop voluntary technical standards for voting machines and systems. The measure also established a research program to improve electronic voting systems, voter privacy, fraud prevention, and access for people with disabilities. HR 2275 was reported (H Rept 107-263) from the House Committee on Science on Oct. 31, 2001. The measure died upon adjournment.

S 379, sponsored by Charles E. Schumer, D-N.Y., authorized $2.5 billion over five years for improving voting equipment and election methods. The bill was backed by Republicans Sam Brownback of Kansas and John McCain of Arizona. S 379 was referred to the Senate Committee on Rules and Administration, but saw no further action.

HOUSE ACTION

House Administration Committee Chair Bob Ney, R-Ohio, and ranking member Steny H. Hoyer, D-Md., offered a bipartisan election overhaul bill (HR 3295), which the panel approved 8–0 on Nov. 15, 2001. The measure was formally reported (H Rept 107-329, Part I) on Dec. 10.

As introduced, HR 3295 created a new set of national standards, while giving states broad latitude to carry them out. States had until November 2002 to set a procedure for

voters to cast provisional ballots. A total of $2.7 billion was authorized to help states overhaul their voting systems, including $400 million to replace punch-card machines. By 2004, states were required to have statewide registration systems accessible by local jurisdictions, have accurate voter registration records, and adopt a uniform definition of a valid vote on each type of equipment used in the state. To reduce the number of invalidated ballots, states were required to set rules allowing voters to correct errors in the polling place. The bill established a federal commission that could develop standards, but not issue regulations. The commission also could assist states in counting votes and monitoring error rates and voter turnout, notifying the Justice Department when states failed to comply with the minimum standards.

The House panel by voice vote adopted a Mark Steven Kirk, R-Ill., amendment to allow polling places on military installations for people who live on the bases and were registered locally. The military commander would set the opening and closing times of the polling stations. The committee rejected, 3–5, an amendment to require states to equip polling places so that voters who are blind or disabled could cast secret ballots.

The full House passed HR 3295 on Dec. 12 by 362–63. No amendments were allowed, but the rule for floor consideration (H Res 311) included a manager's amendment that made several changes.

• Jurisdictions receiving money for replacing punch cards were required to "consider the use of new technology by individuals with disabilities," including blindness.

• States receiving federal aid had to report to the new election commission how the money was spent.

• Votes cast by military personnel and citizens overseas had to be reported separately.

• The bill did not provide that official election materials be mailed for half the cost of first-class mail.

SENATE ACTION

Senate Rules and Administration Committee Chair Christopher J. Dodd, D-Conn., and ranking member Mitch McConnell, R-Ky., offered separate bills that illustrated the split in Congress over the question of federal mandates. Dodd's bill (S 565) called for national standards for voting machines, access to polling places and the upkeep of voter rolls, and offered federal money to help states meet the new standards. It required that voting systems be designed to notify voters when they made a mistake that would invalidate their ballots, such as voting twice for a single office, and give them a chance to fix their errors. States were required to mail sample ballots and voting instructions ten days before election day and offer provisional ballots, allowing voters whose registration was in doubt to cast a vote that would be counted later if they were found to be on the rolls. McConnell's bill (S 953) offered money to states as an incentive to improve their voting systems. The grants—$2.5 billion over five years—were contingent on states adopting provisional balloting and meeting standards for accuracy, accessibility, and accountability. A new Election Administration Commission would set the standards.

At McConnell's urging, Republicans boycotted a Rules Committee markup of Dodd's bill on Aug. 2, 2001, leaving Democrats to approve the legislation, 10–0. McConnell had demanded that the committee agree beforehand to send his bill to the Senate floor for a vote. Dodd refused, though he said McConnell could offer his bill as a substitute in committee. Meanwhile, the two Democratic cosponsors of McConnell's measure—Schumer and Robert G. Torricelli of New Jersey—switched their allegiance and backed Dodd's bill. The bitter breakdown stalled talks in the Senate for months.

A bipartisan group of senators offered a compromise on a package of election changes, which were inserted in S 565. The bill won Democrat-only approval in the Rules and Administration Committee in November. The compromise called for creating national standards, to take effect in 2006, that were more explicit than those laid out in the House legislation. States would have to allow voters to verify their ballots and correct errors before their votes were counted. States also would have to provide voters who are disabled or blind with the same voting accessibility and privacy as others. States with large numbers of non-English speakers would have to provide ballots in other languages. States also would have to provide provisional ballots, post detailed explanations about voting procedures in all polling places, and ensure that election returns met new standards aimed at limiting mechanical errors in voting equipment. The legislation would authorize $3.5 billion in grants over five years to help states meet the new federal mandates, including $100 million to help make polling places more accessible to voters who are disabled or blind. A federal commission would be created to administer the new federal requirements, as well as to approve grants to states. The Justice Department would monitor compliance with the national standards and could sue states that failed to comply. To receive federal funding, states would have to provide the Justice Department with a plan to identify, deter, and investigate election fraud. Voters who registered by mail would be required to present valid identification (ID) when voting for the first time in their new jurisdiction. Those who voted by mail would be required to submit their ballot with a copy of a photo ID card or other verification of their name and address.

On Feb. 14, 2002, the Senate

• Rejected 44–50 a Richard J. Durbin, D-Ill., amendment to require states to allow all voters, including those using punch-card voting machines, to verify their votes and correct any errors. The bill required states that used other voting technologies to permit such verification, but sponsors argued that because nearly one-third of Americans used punch-card machines, Durbin's proposal would be too burdensome.

• Rejected 31–63 a Harry Reid, D-Nev., and Arlen Specter, R-Pa., amendment to restore voting rights to felons who served their full sentences.

• Rejected 46–49 a Joseph I. Lieberman, D-Conn., amendment to allow federal employees to take time off to serve as nonpartisan poll workers in federal elections.

• Rejected 40–55 a Conrad Burns, R-Mont., amendment to allow states to purge the rolls of people who failed to vote in federal elections for four consecutive years.

• Agreed by voice vote to add language specifying that six states would retain exemptions from the National Voter Registration Act of 1993 (PL 103-31), which required states to allow citizens to register to vote when they applied for a driver's license. Idaho, Minnesota, New Hampshire, North Dakota, Wisconsin, and Wyoming either did not require voter registration or allowed same-day registration at polling stations. (*'Motor voter,' Congress and the Nation Vol. IX, p. 807*)

The debate subsequently bogged down in a dispute over how to curb fraud at the polls without disenfranchising voters. Schumer and Ron Wyden, D-Ore., argued that the requirement would disenfranchise poor and disabled people. They proposed that new voters be allowed to vouch for their identities with a signature, which would be matched against records on file with state or local election officials. Republicans said that would invite additional fraud. An attempt by Christopher S. Bond, R-Mo., to table (kill) Schumer's amendment failed 46–51 on Feb. 27. Republicans responded by saying they would stop any additional work on the bill unless the amendment was withdrawn. Two unsuccessful attempts were made to invoke cloture and thus limit debate: on March 1, 49–39 (sixty votes are required), and on March 4, 51–44.

Off-the-floor negotiations produced a plan, adopted by unanimous consent March 22, that allowed the Senate to finish work on the bill. Democrats had agreed, at least for the time being, to give up trying to scale back the antifraud provision. That left the question of what to do about Oregon and Washington, which already had vote-by-mail systems in place. Oregon relied exclusively on mail-in ballots, and the system accounted for about two-thirds of Washington's turnout in 2000. The solution was to allow voters in those two states who registered by mail to submit their driver's license number or the last four digits of their Social Security number, then mark their ballots with that same number as a means of proving their identity. In other states, voters who registered by mail would have to prove their identities at the polls with a driver's license, utility bill, canceled government check, or some other proof of residence and identity.

Upon resuming floor consideration, the Senate on April 11 adopted 56–43 a Pat Roberts, R-Kan., amendment to drop a requirement that election officials notify provisional ballot voters within thirty days as to whether their vote was counted and rejected 48–42 a Hillary Rodham Clinton, D-N.Y., amendment to require the government to set a "residual vote error rate" but allow a waiver for areas with historically high rates of intentional undervoting. The Senate then passed S 565, on a **key vote of 99–1 (R 48–1; D 50–0; I 1–0)**, on April 11, then inserted the language into HR 3295 and passed that bill by voice vote. (*2002 key votes, p. 819*)

FINAL ACTION

House and Senate negotiators reached an agreement on the bill Oct. 4. Bond's insistence on the antifraud provisions and the support he got from other Republicans were among the factors that delayed completion of the conference.

The House adopted the conference report (H Rept 107-730) 357–48 on Oct. 10. The Senate cleared HR 3295 on Oct. 16 by 92–2. The two "nay" votes were cast by Clinton and Schumer, who said the antifraud provisions would still discriminate against millions of New Yorkers who did not have driver's licenses.

To fund the measure, lawmakers included $400 million in the fiscal 2002 supplemental appropriations law (PL 107-206), but it was part of $5.1 billion in emergency funds that President Bush chose not to spend. Hopes that money would be provided in the fiscal 2003 Treasury-Postal Service spending bill collapsed when Congress adjourned without completing any of the domestic appropriations bills. *(Fiscal 2002 supplemental appropriations, p. 63)*

PROVISIONS

The following are the main provisions of the election overhaul law (HR 3295—PL 107-252) signed Oct. 29, 2002.

Buyout of Outdated Voting Machines

Machine replacement. Authorized $325 million for one-time payments to help states replace punch-card and lever voting machines. A state could get $4,000 for each polling precinct that used a punch-card or lever machine in the 2000 election.

Administering elections. Sought to improve the administration of elections by authorizing $325 million in payments to states, to be distributed on the basis of the state's voting-age population. The grants could be used to train election officials and poll workers.

Election Commission

Establishment. Created a four-member Election Assistance Commission, its members nominated by the president and subject to Senate confirmation.

Authority. Stipulated that the commission was to serve as a clearinghouse of information on voting equipment; set voluntary guidelines to help states comply with the new election standards; make the annual grant payments to the states; provide for the testing and certification of voting system hardware and software; conduct studies on subjects such as military and overseas voting, voters who register by mail, and the impact of the use of Social Security numbers in elections; and establish the Help America Vote College Program to encourage college students to serve as poll workers or assistants.

Limitation on authority. Did not extend authority to the commission to issue any rules or regulations, except as permitted under the National Voter Registration Act of 1993 (PL 103-31).

Grants

Authorized $3 billion over three years—$1.4 billion in fiscal 2003, $1 billion in fiscal 2004, and $600 million in fiscal 2005—for a grant program administered by the commission to help states meet election requirements, train poll workers, provide voter education, and administer elections.

Authorized $100 million over three years to make polling places physically accessible to voters with disabilities.

Authorized $20 million in fiscal 2003 for research on improving voting equipment and technology.

Authorized $10 million in fiscal 2003 for a pilot program to test improvements to voting equipment and technology.

Authorized $30 million over three years to establish the new Election Assistance Commission.

Authorized $30 million over three years for state protection and advocacy programs.

Authorized $5 million in fiscal 2003 to establish the Help America Vote College Program to encourage college students to serve as poll workers or assistants.

Authorized $5 million in fiscal 2003 to establish the Help America Vote Foundation to recruit secondary school students to serve as poll workers or assistants.

Authorized $200,000 in fiscal 2003 to conduct mock elections for students and parents.

Election Standards

Correcting voting errors. Stipulated that voters had to be able to check for and correct errors on their ballots in a private and independent way. Effective in 2006.

Provisional voting. Required that a voter whose eligibility was questioned had to be able to cast a provisional ballot, which would be counted if state or local election officials later determined that he or she was eligible to vote. Voters who cast provisional ballots had to sign an affidavit stating their belief that they were registered in that jurisdiction and eligible to vote in that election. They could check a "free access system," such as a toll-free telephone number or a World Wide Web site, to determine whether their votes were counted. Effective by 2004.

Voting extensions. Stipulated that, if a federal or state court ordered a polling place to remain open beyond the closing time set by state law, all votes cast after the normal closing time had to be provisional, and those ballots had to be separated from other provisional ballots.

Statewide voter registration list. Required each state to have a uniform, centralized, and computerized statewide voter registration list. A unique identification number had to be assigned to each registered voter. Each state had to design a system to make sure its list was accurate and updated regularly. Consistent with the National Voter Registration Act of 1993, voters who did not respond to a notice in the mail and then failed to vote in two consecutive general elections in federal election years could be removed from the list, but they could not be removed solely for not voting. Effective in 2004, with a possible waiver until 2006.

Access for voters with disabilities. Required each precinct to have at least one voting machine that allowed voters with disabilities to vote in a private and independent manner. Effective in 2006. In addition, any new voting system purchased with federal funds starting in 2007 had to be accessible to people with disabilities.

Voting definition. Required states to adopt a "uniform and nondiscriminatory" definition of what constituted a legal vote and what would be counted as a vote for each type of voting machine used in the state. Effective in 2006.

Error rate. Stipulated that each state had to have a voting system with an error rate that did not exceed the rate established by the Federal Election Commission's Office of Election Administration. The job of setting the rate was to be transferred to the new Election Assistance Commission. Effective in 2006.

Multilingual accessibility. Instructed states to continue to provide alternative language accessibility pursuant to Section 203 of the 1965 Voting Rights Act (PL 89-110). *(1965 law, Congress and the Nation Vol. II, p. 356)*

Antifraud Protections

Voter registration. Required individuals to provide a driver's license number when registering to vote. People without a driver's license could provide the last four digits of their Social Security number. Those possessing neither a driver's license nor a Social Security number would be assigned a unique identifier. Effective in 2004, with a possible waiver until 2006.

Voter identification. Required first-time voters who registered by mail to provide proof of identity at some point in the process—when they registered or when they voted in person or by mail. They could provide a current, valid photo identification or a copy of a bank statement, paycheck, utility bill, or other government document that showed their name and address. If they could not produce any of those documents, they could cast provisional ballots that would be counted only if officials later verified they were eligible to vote. Effective in 2003.

Enforcement

By the states. Stipulated that states receiving funds under the bill had to establish an administrative procedure for resolving grievances. Anyone who believed the new election standards had been violated, or were about to be violated, could file a complaint and request a hearing. The state had to make a decision within ninety days, either by providing a remedy or dismissing the complaint. If the state failed to meet the deadline, an alternative dispute resolution procedure had to be available to resolve the complaint within sixty days.

By the United States. Authorized the Justice Department to file a civil action in federal court to seek relief, including an injunction or restraining order, against any state or jurisdiction that did not apply the new requirements in a uniform and nondiscriminatory manner. Individuals did not have a right to sue. States that did not accept funds under the bill had to either establish a grievance procedure or submit a compliance plan with the Justice Department.

Military and Overseas Voting

State regulation. Required each state to designate a single office to provide information to members of the armed forces about registration and absentee voting in that state. States had to report to the Election Assistance Commission the number of military and overseas applications they received and the number of ballots that were received too early. If they rejected registration applications from military and overseas voters, they had to give those voters a reason that the applications were rejected.

Federal regulation. Required the Defense Department to guarantee, to the maximum extent possible, that military voting assistance officers had the time and resources they needed to help military personnel vote. The Pentagon also had to make certain, to the maximum extent possible, that all military ballots had postmarks or other official proof of the mailing date to ensure that no such ballots arrived after election day.

Campaign Finance

After numerous filibusters, years of debate, and hundreds of votes, Congress in 2002 cleared a major rewrite (HR 2356—PL 107-155) of the nation's campaign finance laws, the first in three decades. But the new law only moved the battle over regulating campaign funding into a new phase: The two sides would fight on in the courts.

BACKGROUND

The House and Senate had debated since 1980 whether to revamp the campaign finance system, which had not changed significantly since 1974 (PL 93-433), in the wake of the Watergate scandal that drove President Richard M. Nixon from office. Both parties repeatedly promised an overhaul but made little effort to deliver it. *(1974 law, Congress and the Nation Vol. IV, p. 991; Watergate, Congress and the Nation Vol. IV, p. 931)*

Momentum for an overhaul had been building at least since the 1994 elections, when the parties took in a record-breaking $102 million in soft money. Soft money—called "non-federal funds" by the Federal Election Commission (FEC) because it fell outside the reach of federal limits on direct-to-candidate contributions—was supposed to go to "party-building" activities, such as voter mobilization and registration. The U.S. Supreme Court opened the door for broader use of soft money with a June 1996 ruling that parties could spend an unlimited amount to promote their positions on issues as long as they did not coordinate the activity directly with candidates. In 1996, a bipartisan bill including voluntary spending limits and a ban on contributions from

Sen. John McCain, R-Ariz., Rep. Christopher Shays, R-Conn., and Rep. Martin Meehan, D-Mass., before discussion on campaign finance reform on January 30, 2001. The landmark campaign finance reform law, whose key provisions include limits on "soft money" and broadcast political advertising, was eventually signed into law on March 27, 2002, but immediately faced court challenges from a diverse coalition of critics. *Source: AP Wide World Photos/Susan Walsh*

political action committees (PACs) was stopped by a Senate filibuster. The House defeated both a GOP bill to impose new limits on contributions and a Democratic alternative. *(Court ruling, Congress and the Nation Vol. IX, box, p. 915; 1996 action, Congress and the Nation Vol. IX, p. 914))*

After the 1996 elections, questionable fund-raising practices by both parties focused public attention on the widening loophole in existing law. In 1997, Sens. John McCain, R-Ariz., and Russell D. Feingold, D-Wis., introduced a measure that included a ban on soft money, free or discounted television advertising, and postage for candidates who adhered to voluntary spending limits, as well as new restrictions intended to draw a clearer line between spending to promote candidates and spending to promote issues. Christopher Shays, D-Conn., and Martin T. Meehan, D-Mass., introduced a companion bill in the House. The Shays-Meehan legislation passed the House in 1998, but died upon adjournment. Another Shays-Meehan measure met the same fate in the 106th Congress, having passed in 1999. *(1997–1998 action, Congress and the Nation Vol. X, p. 776; 1999 action, Congress and the Nation Vol. X, p. 788)*

In the 2000 election, the two major parties combined spent $495 million in soft money.

SENATE ACTION

In 2000, McCain made campaign finance reform the foundation of his run for the Republican presidential nomination, boosting him and the cause to national prominence. Riding on the momentum of his failed bid, McCain managed to build enough support for a campaign finance bill (S 27), cosponsored by Feingold, to force the Senate's first wide-open debate on the issue in years. At a Republican cau-

cus retreat on Jan. 4, 2001, Thad Cochran of Mississippi announced that he had decided to support campaign finance reform legislation. He was the first old-style conservative to sign on, and his support gave McCain and Feingold the sixty votes needed to make their bill filibuster-proof. Cochran's move was an embarrassment to Senate majority leader Trent Lott, R-Miss., who was struggling to consolidate his power in the evenly divided Senate and who had long maneuvered to keep campaign finance legislation off the floor. Lott subsequently agreed to clear the calendar of all other business for two weeks.

The floor fight was expected to be tough. McCain and Feingold warned supporters that Sen. Mitch McConnell, R-Ky., and other opponents would seek to weigh the bill down with so many amendments that everyone could find a reason to oppose it. Meanwhile, the White House signaled that President Bush might sign a campaign finance bill. Opponents of the bill thus could not count on him for a veto if the legislation cleared Congress.

Generally, opponents argued that the bill would infringe on free speech rights and undercut the political parties by diverting contributions to outside groups operating independently of the parties and the candidates. Supporters argued that the legislation would end the corrupting influence of big-money contributions on the political system.

S 27 sought to ban soft money in federal elections in most instances. However, the Senate March 29 by voice vote adopted a Carl Levin, D-Mich., amendment to allow local and state party committees to spend soft money on get-out-the-vote and voter registration drives in federal elections under certain conditions. Most important, the effort could not mention a federal candidate. Also, no donor could give more than $10,000 per year. The Levin amendment represented a key compromise, particularly for Democrats concerned that the ban on soft money would put them at a disadvantage.

Republicans demanded that the bill's limits on hard money contributions be increased. Many Democrats balked, as Republicans typically had the edge in raising hard money. Fred Thompson, R-Tenn., and Dianne Feinstein, D-Calif., offered a compromise amendment to increase the limit on individual hard money contributions to Senate candidates from $1,000 per election to $2,000 and to index it to inflation. Furthermore, the amendment would increase aggregate contribution limits for individuals from $25,000 per year to $37,500. Limits on individual contributions to national parties would increase from $20,000 per year to $25,000 and would be indexed to inflation. The amendment was adopted on March 28 by 84–16, with all the "nay" votes coming from Democrats.

By a 70–30 vote, the Senate March 20 adopted the so-called millionaires amendment, offered by Pete V. Domenici, R-N.M. The amendment raised the hard money contribution limits for candidates facing wealthy opponents who poured their own money into their campaigns. It increased limits on contributions from both individuals and PACs, using a sliding scale based on state voting-age population and how much personal money a wealthy, self-financing candidate spent.

In an effort to cut more money out of politics by reducing the cost of campaigning, Robert G. Torricelli, D-N.J., offered an amendment to require broadcasters to offer cheap airtime to candidates and political parties. Candidates and parties would be guaranteed an advertising rate not to exceed the lowest rate offered in the preceding year. Broadcasters could not preempt the ads for higher-paying advertisers. The Senate adopted the amendment 69–31 on March 21.

Charles E. Schumer, D-N.Y., offered an amendment intended as insurance against a pending U.S. Supreme Court case, *Federal Election Commission v. Colorado Republican Federal Campaign Committee*, that many feared would open a new loophole in campaign finance law. A lower-court decision eliminated limits on the money that political parties could spend in coordination with candidates to help them pay for television advertising and other expenses. If the Court upheld the lower-court ruling, Schumer's amendment would guarantee the low broadcast ad rates to parties only if they agreed voluntarily to abide by coordinated spending limits. The amendment was adopted on March 28, 52–48. In a 5–4 ruling June 25, the Court struck down the earlier court's ruling, upholding the limits on coordinated spending.

In another preemptive move, an Arlen Specter, R-Pa., amendment provided an alternative definition of "electioneering communications," for use if the courts struck down the original language. Adopted 82–17 on March 29, the amendment said the restriction on issue ads would apply to any advertising that supported or attacked a candidate, "re-gardless of whether the communication expressly advocates a vote for or against a candidate and which also is suggestive of no plausible meaning other than an exhortation to vote for or against a specific candidate."

With the help of Republicans, who hoped to undercut the bill's support on final passage, the Senate adopted an amendment, offered by Paul Wellstone, D-Minn., to broaden S 27's restrictions on issue advertising to cover nonprofits, such as the National Rifle Association and the Sierra Club. As the bill was originally written, the restrictions applied only to for-profit corporations and labor unions. The courts had long said that the Constitution demands a delicate balance between free speech and the government's need to combat the corrupting influence of campaign cash. The U.S. Supreme Court in the 1986 case *Federal Election Commission v. Massachusetts Citizens for Life* said the Constitution protects the ability of outside advocacy groups to run issue-related ads. McCain and Feingold fought Wellstone's amendment, arguing that it appeared unconstitutional. *(1986 case, Congress and the Nation Vol. VII, p. 816)*

On a unanimous 99–0 vote March 22, the Senate adopted a Don Nickles, R-Okla., amendment to strike language in the bill that would have codified a court decision requiring unions to let nonmembers opt out of having their fees used for political purposes.

All of the amendments deemed poison pills by the bill's backers were rejected. Bill Frist, R-Tenn., offered an amendment to make the legislation "non-severable," meaning that it would stand or fall as a whole in the courts. The issue took on significance with the adoption of the Wellstone amendment broadening the bill's issue ad restrictions. The original language included a "severability clause," explicitly stating that the rest of the legislation would stand if the courts struck down any of its provisions. Such a clause does not necessarily protect a law; a court still could throw out the entire legislation if it found one part questionable. The Senate voted 57–43 on March 29 to table (kill) the Frist amendment.

The Senate also tabled, 69–31 on March 21, an Orrin G. Hatch, R-Utah, amendment to require unions and corporations to get the permission of dues-paying members or shareholders before spending money for political purposes. Supporters called it "paycheck protection" and argued that it would give union members a greater voice regarding which candidate their unions support. Bush had expressed his support of such a measure in a statement of campaign finance "principles" released before the debate. Opponents, however, said the Hatch amendment was a GOP effort to make it difficult for organized labor, which often leaned Democratic, to exert influence over elections.

A main threat to McCain-Feingold was an alternative offered by Chuck Hagel, R-Neb. The plan had three parts. The first would cap soft money contributions to national parties at $60,000 per year, instead of banning them. The second would raise hard money contribution limits for individuals and PACs. Individuals could give $3,000 per election to candidates and $60,000 per year to parties. PACs could give $7,500 per election to candidates and $30,000 per year to parties. The third part would require greater disclosure of who was funding political advertising, as well as more frequent disclosure of the contributions to candidates and political parties. Hagel presented the three parts of his plan as separate amendments, and McCain moved to table each in turn. The amendment to increase hard money limits was tabled 52–47 on March 27. The cap on soft money was tabled 60–40 on March 27. The Senate, however, rejected 0–100, on March 27, McCain's motion to table the increased disclosure requirements, the least controversial part of Hegel's plan. The amendment then was adopted by voice vote.

The Senate passed S 27 on a **key vote of 59–41 (R 12–38; D 47–3),** on April 2. *(2001 key votes, p. 801)*

HOUSE ACTION

Sponsors of the House companion measure (HR 2356)—Shays and Meehan—set about rewriting their legislation with two challenges in mind. First, they had to hold together an increasingly restless coalition of supporters to get the bill through the House. In the past, members had voted for campaign finance legislation knowing it would die in the Senate. Second, Shays and Meehan wanted to keep the measure close enough to the Senate-passed version to avoid a conference committee, where opponents would get another chance to kill or rewrite it.

House Republican leaders, who opposed HR 2356, introduced an alternative (HR 2360) aimed at exploiting new reservations about the soft money ban, particularly among members of the Congressional Black Caucus.

The House Administration Committee voted 5–3 on June 28, 2001, to report the Shays-Meehan bill (H Rept 107-131, Part I) with an unfavorable recommendation. The same day, with the same vote, the committee approved HR 2360 (H Rept 107-132), which was similar to Senator Hegel's plan. Both measures were formally reported July 10. HR 2360, sponsored by panel chair Bob Ney, R-Ohio, capped soft money contributions to national parties at $75,000 per year, instead of banning them, while keeping existing limits on individual hard money contributions to candidates. Parties could not spend soft money on anything but "generic" party activities, such as get-out-the-vote efforts and voter registration, that did not mention specific federal candidates. HR 2360 did not restrict the ability of unions, for-profit corporations, and nonprofits to directly fund broadcast ads. But groups running television or radio ads that mentioned federal candidates, reached their electorate, and aired within 120 days of a primary or general election would have to disclose within twenty-four hours the names of their officers and the amount spent on the ad. The same stipulation would apply to groups that spent more than $50,000 for "targeted mass communication" in broadcast or print.

Shays and Meehan asked the House Rules Committee to bundle fourteen proposed changes to their bill, mostly aimed at bringing it into line with the Senate version, into a single manager's amendment. The Rules Committee said no, requiring instead that each of the changes be voted on separately on the floor. Shays, Meehan, and their supporters accused the GOP leadership of trying to bring down the bill with a complicated, obstacle-strewn rule. Republicans countered that Democrats were looking for a face-saving way to scuttle the bill because they did not have the votes to pass it.

Speaker J. Dennis Hastert, R-Ill., offered to compromise on the rule, but conservatives in his caucus demanded that the original rule go forward. The rule was rejected on a **key vote of 203–228 (R 201–19; D 1–208)** on July 12. It was the first time that Hastert lost a vote on a rule, which is typically seen as a matter of party loyalty from which members have little room to deviate. With the defeat, campaign finance dropped from the House agenda. Hastert said he had no intention of bringing it up again. *(2001 key votes, p. 801)*

Upon defeat of the rule, Shays and Meehan began collecting signatures on a discharge petition to force the bill back to the floor under rules more to their liking. By Sept. 11, 2001, they were just nine names short of the 218 they needed. The terrorist attacks put the effort on hold for more than three months. Then, in December, four more lawmakers signed the petition, making it appear to the bill sponsors that victory was possible. That same month, the Enron Corporation collapsed, becoming the biggest corporate bankruptcy in U.S. history. The bankruptcy exposed the energy trader's network of political giving and influence and triggered a panic among both Democrats and Republicans who had benefited from the company's largess. Many lawmakers faced uncomfortable questions about their campaign fund-raising and were looking to distance themselves from the debacle. One day after Congress reconvened in January 2002, the last of the needed signatures was collected for the discharge petition.

On the House floor, Shays and Meehan succeeded in defending a revised version of their bill against two GOP-sponsored substitutes. One of the substitutes was the version of Shays-Meehan that passed the House in 1999. It was now out of sync with the Senate-passed version—missing, for example, the provision raising contribution limits for candidates facing wealthy opponents—and would have forced a conference. The House rejected the substitute amendment, offered by Ney, 53–377 on Feb. 13. The other substitute, offered by Majority Leader Dick Armey, R-Texas, banned all soft money at the national, state, and local levels. It also prohibited corporations, unions, and tax-exempt groups from using soft money for voter registration and get-out-the-vote activities. The amendment was rejected 179–249 on Feb. 13.

The House on Feb. 13 adopted 240–191 the revised Shays-Meehan bill offered as a substitute. The sponsors then beat back all efforts to derail the legislation.

A Charles W. "Chip" Pickering Jr., R-Miss., amendment was rejected 209–219 on Feb. 13. It exempted communications about gun rights from the advertising restrictions in the bill. Several Republicans said the proposal was aimed at winning the votes of Southern Democrats and creating political havoc in the midterm elections for those who did not support the measure.

Also rejected was a Roger Wicker, R-Mass., amendment to ban non-U.S. citizens, including permanent legal residents, from donating to campaigns. The House had accepted a similar amendment in 1999. Amendment supporters charged that the existing system gave "enemies of the state access to our political system." Hispanic and other minority lawmakers said that assertion was a slur against immigrants. The Feb. 13 vote was 160–268.

Also on Feb. 13, the House turned back amendments to lift the bill's advertising restrictions when the content related to civil rights (185–237); to advocacy for veterans, military personnel, senior citizens, and families (200–228); and to advocacy for workers, farmers, and family issues (191–237).

Bill supporters offered three amendments that sought to win votes and align the measure with the Senate-passed legislation. The first, by Zach Wamp, R-Tenn., doubled hard money limits for candidates from $1,000 to $2,000 per election. It was adopted 218–211 on Feb. 13. The second, by Shelley Moore Capito, R-W.Va., raised the limit still further for candidates facing wealthy opponents who pumped large amounts of their own money into their campaigns. It was adopted by voice vote on Feb. 13. The third, by Gene Green, D-Texas, stripped out a Senate provision to guarantee cheap television ad rates to candidates and political parties close to election day. Supporters feared the provision would jeopardize the bill in the House. It was adopted 327–101 on Feb. 13.

Before the House passed HR 2356, on a **key vote of 240–189 (R 41–176; D 198–12; I 1–1)** on Feb. 14 (in the session that began Feb. 13), Ney offered a substitute, cosponsored with Albert R. Wynn, D-Md., to cap, not ban, soft money. The amendment was rejected, 181–248. *(2002 key votes, p. 819)*

FINAL ACTION

Senator McConnell managed to delay action on the bill for more than a month. He forced bill supporters to prove that they had the sixty votes required to overcome a filibuster, which they did in a 68–32 vote March 20. The Senate then cleared HR 2356 the same day on a **key vote of 60–40 (R 11–38; D 48–2; I 1–0)**. *(2002 key votes, p. 819)*

Although President George W. Bush signed the measure March 27 (PL 107-155) he described it as "flawed" and pointedly avoided the traditional signing ceremony that would have brought the bill's sponsors, including his rival, Arizona's Republican senator John McCain, to the White House.

Immediately after the bill became law, McConnell and a diverse coalition of groups sued to overturn it, saying it trampled on the rights of Americans to speak out and participate freely in the political process. A provision called for "expedited judicial review" put the measure on a fast track to the U.S. Supreme Court, with hearings before a special three-judge panel in U.S. District Court in Washington, D.C., held in December. Meanwhile, the four principal sponsors of the campaign finance legislation challenged the Federal Election Commission regulations implementing the statute. Shays and Meehan sued in U.S. District Court in October 2002 to overturn the FEC's new soft money rules. The rules, approved in July, narrowed the definition of solicitation, which the sponsors said would permit parties to set up "sham" entities that would be able to raise and spend soft money on the parties' behalf. Restricted by Senate ethics rules from joining a lawsuit as a plaintiff, McCain and Feingold promised to lead a legislative challenge in the 108th Congress by filing a resolution under the Congressional Review Act (PL 104-121), which provided a process for Congress to overturn agency rulemaking. *(Court action, box, p. 000; PL 104-121, Congress and the Nation Vol. IX, p. 842)*

MAJOR PROVISIONS

The following are the main provisions of the campaign finance reform law (HR 2356–PL 107-155) signed March 27, 2002.

- **Soft money.** National party committees could not accept or spend soft money. State and local party committees could spend soft money on voter registration and mobilization in federal elections only under certain conditions: The effort must not mention a federal candidate. No donor could give more than $10,000 per year. Soft money could not be raised by federal candidates or national parties, and it could not go to broadcast advertising, except for ads that mentioned only state or local candidates. State and local parties must spend soft money in a mix with hard money. Party committees could not collaborate with each other to raise the money, and they could not transfer it to national parties, candidate committees, or any other organization.

- **Hard money.** The limit on individual contributions to House and Senate candidates was $2,000 per election, double the old limit, and it was indexed to grow with inflation. The aggregate contribution limit for individuals was $95,000 per two-year election cycle—$37,500 to candidates and $57,500 to parties and political action committees (PACs). To give the two-year maximum, at least $20,000 must go to national parties. Individuals could give $10,000 per year to state party committees.

- **Broadcast advertising.** Labor unions, for-profit corporations, and nonprofits could not fund broadcast advertising directly if the ad referred to a federal candidate, reached at least fifty thousand people within the candidate's electorate, and ran within sixty days of a general election or thirty days before a primary. Such ads could be paid for only through a PAC and with regulated hard money contributions.

- **Independent and coordinated expenditures.** Independent expenditures of $1,000 or more made on a candidate's behalf within twenty days of an election must be reported to the Federal Election Commission within twenty-four hours. Further out from elections, independent expenditures of

$10,000 or more made on a candidate's behalf must be reported within forty-eight hours. When spending to help a candidate, political parties must choose in each election whether to work independently or in concert with the candidate. They could not do both in the same election. Coordinated expenditures were limited; independent expenditures were not. Any money spent by a person, other than a candidate, in concert with a political party would be treated as a contribution to the party. The FEC must issue new rules regulating coordination between candidates or parties and outside groups. The law specified that the new regulations should not require evidence of formal coordination or agreements between outside groups and candidates or parties to establish that election activity was "coordinated."

• **Self-financed candidates.** The law raised the limits on hard money contributions to House and Senate candidates who faced wealthy, self-financed opponents. It also increased the limits on the amount political parties could spend in concert with those candidates.

• **Fund-raising by candidates.** Federal candidates and officeholders could not raise or spend soft money for federal election activities. The prohibition applied to political action committees associated with federal candidates, known as leadership PACs. The law made an exception for federal officeholders who were running for state office, as long as the money was not spent on advertising or other activities that mentioned federal candidates.

• **Fund-raising for nonprofits.** Candidates and officeholders could help nonprofits raise money for voter registration and mobilization, soliciting individual contributions of up to $20,000 per year. Candidates and officeholders were prohibited from soliciting such contributions from labor unions and corporations. They could solicit general contributions for nonprofits from any source, including corporations and labor unions, if the nonprofit's principal purpose was not voter registration or get-out-the-vote activities and the solicitation did not specify how the money would be spent.

2003–2004

Congress and the courts had to deal with challenges to the 2002 enactment of campaign finance reform. The provisions of the new law generally were upheld. A special target was the so-called 527 political groups, which played an aggressive role in the 2004 presidential race.

FEC and 527s

The Federal Election Commission (FEC) on May 13, 2004, rejected a proposal to strictly regulate 527 political organizations. Candidates for president and Congress, as well as national party organizations, were barred from accepting large, unregulated donations under the campaign finance overhaul (PL 107-155) enacted in 2002. But groups organized under Section 527 of the Internal Revenue Code received such soft money contributions, and they could continue as a result of the FEC ruling. *(Campaign finance, p. 730)*

Democrats, who in the past relied more on soft money as part of their campaign funding than did Republicans, were the main beneficiaries of 527 activities in 2004. Republicans, as usual more successful than Democrats at raising the strictly limited and regulated hard money donations from individuals and political action committee, joined with campaign watchdog groups to urge the FEC to clamp down on the 527s, portraying them as shadow party organizations created to evade the legal restrictions on soft money.

The rejected proposal, offered by Republican Michael E. Toner and Democrat Scott E. Thomas, would have required many of the 527 organizations to register with the FEC as political committees, which would have then subjected them to the law's strict hard money contribution limits. The authors argued that prompt intervention was needed to ensure that the campaign finance laws were properly administered and to prevent abuses.

Opponents countered that the commission was rushing through a complex rule-making process late in an election cycle. The FEC announced it was considering regulations only in March 2004. Furthermore, opponents said that neither Congress, when it debated the new campaign finance law, nor the Supreme Court, when it upheld the law in December 2003, authorized the FEC to regulate 527s. *(Court ruling, box, p. 737; see also pp. 631, 656)*

Rep. John L. Mica, R-Fla., who voted against campaign finance reform, berated the FEC for refusing to restrict the 527s. Rep. John B. Larson, D-Conn., who supported the legislation, praised the FEC for stepping carefully and said the new law could be difficult to interpret. Many Democrats wrote the FEC telling the commission to lay off the 527s. Larson said if the commissioners were looking to restrict the organizations, they also ought to examine the activities of another sort of outside group, 501(c)s, which he said were dominated by the GOP and were less transparent.

On Sept. 18, 2004, a federal judge in Washington, D.C., said the six-member FEC, instead of faithfully implementing the 2002 campaign finance law, undermined it with regulations that flouted the intent of Congress and would foster corruption. In response, the sponsors of the law announced the introduction of legislation (HR 5127 and S 2828) to crack down on fund-raising by independent partisan groups and to refashion the FEC. They proposed a three-member agency: two commissioners from different parties and a strong chairman, with broad administrative powers, appointed to a ten-year term. The purpose was to start afresh with a new agency that would enforce the law and not collude with the political parties and candidates to open loopholes.

Working against the plan, however, was that no matter the number of commissioners or their powers, it would still fall to the president to nominate them and the members of the Senate to confirm. Because those are the very players whose campaigns the FEC regulates, the temptation to stack the deck by nominating the pliant and the partisan would continue to be enormous. Critics of the reconfiguration plan said that one party, in practice, would enjoy a two-to-one edge. The prospect frightened lawmakers on both sides. The current commission, evenly split between the parties, does lead inevitably to gridlock but ensures that neither party can run roughshod over the other.

Sen. John McCain, R-Ariz., and Rep. Martin T. Meehan, D-Mass., sponsored legislation (S 1913 and HR 3617, respectively) to overhaul the presidential financing system to encourage candidates to accept public financing instead of declining the money to avoid spending limits. McCain and Rep. Christopher Shays, R-Conn., sponsored bills (S 1388 and HR 2709, respectively) to replace the Federal Election Commission with a new agency they said would be a more effective enforcer of federal campaign finance rules. All these measures were referred to committee and died upon adjournment.

The campaign finance law in its "Stand by Your Ad" provision required candidates for federal office to take credit personally and prominently for each ad they air on television or radio. Sens. Ron Wyden, D-Ore., and Lindsey Graham, R-S.C., introduced a bill (S 2392) to expand the law to cover campaign ads on the Internet and recorded telephone calls from candidates, which were exempt. Ads by outside groups were not affected by the law. S 2392 was referred to the Senate Committee on Rules and Administration and saw no further action.

Delaying Elections

House Administration Committee chairman Bob Ney, R-Ohio, and Senate Rules and Administration Committee chairman Trent Lott, R-Miss., shot down suggestions that members consider procedures for postponing the November

CAMPAIGN FINANCE RULINGS

The U.S. Supreme Court on Dec. 10, 2003, ruled 5–4 in *McConnell v. Federal Election Commission* to uphold the major provisions of the campaign finance reform measure (PL 107-155) enacted in 2002. The law imposed a ban on soft money to the national political parties and restrictions on political ads by outside groups. *(Campaign finance, p. 730)*

The law—known as McCain-Feingold after its Senate sponsors, Republican John McCain of Arizona and Democrat Russell D. Feingold of Wisconsin—was the first major rewrite of campaign finance laws in a generation. Two sometimes competing interests were at stake: on one side was the government's interest in safeguarding campaigns from corruption or the appearance of corruption. On the other was the public's right to speak out and participate freely in the political process.

Opponents of the law, led by Sen. Mitch McConnell, R-Ky., were the American Civil Liberties Union and a group of eleven sets of plaintiffs, including the National Rifle Association, the AFL-CIO, and the Republican National Committee. Their challenge was a First Amendment case in which they argued that the soft money ban and the restrictions on ads were an unprecedented infringement on political speech.

Supporters said the law was simply meant to refine campaign finance regulations to end "massive circumvention" of campaign finance rules that the Court had long upheld. They said the political parties, candidates, and outside groups had made a mockery of the previous law when they flooded the system with soft money, the large unregulated contributions from corporations, labor unions, and wealthy individuals.

Under a provision of the law calling for expedited judicial review, the case was bound from the start for the Supreme Court. The fight's first round was before a special three-judge panel in Washington, D.C., which on May 2, 2003, issued a fractured and confusing ruling. The judges agreed May 19 to set their ruling aside, leaving the law in place until the Supreme Court ruled. Chief Justice William H. Rehnquist refused to lift that stay.

The majority opinion in *McConnell*, written by Justices John Paul Stevens and Sandra Day O'Connor, spoke of the need to show "proper deference to Congress' ability to weigh competing constitutional interests in an area in which it enjoys particular experience" and to provide Congress "sufficient room to anticipate and respond to concerns about circumvention of regulations designed to protect the political process's integrity." The majority also strongly said Congress did not need to show a risk of direct quid pro quo corruption to regulate money in politics. The integrity of the process—and the public's faith in democratic institutions—could be undermined by donations meant to curry favor with lawmakers indirectly, such as soft money to political parties, the Court said. Dissenting justices called the decision a clear defeat for the First Amendment.

In upholding the ban on national parties' use of soft money, the majority also preserved restrictions on state parties, which in general were not allowed to spend soft money on federal election activities. It also upheld the law's restrictions on labor unions, for-profit corporations, and nonprofit groups directly funding campaign advertising close to election day, as well as the law's broadened definition of which ads could be regulated. The latter provisions were aimed at stopping such groups from using soft money to finance what supporters of the law argued were thinly veiled campaign ads, circumventing a long-standing ban on corporations and unions giving directly to candidates.

The Court also ruled on challenges to lesser provisions of the law, striking down unanimously a ban on anyone younger than eighteen contributing to campaigns. The provision was meant to keep donors from funneling money through their children to circumvent limits on individual contributions. Also struck down was language requiring political parties, when spending money in behalf of a candidate, to choose between making those expenditures in coordination with the candidate or making them independently.

The Court declined to rule on two important provisions because justices said the plaintiffs did not have standing to challenge them. The provisions were the "millionaires amendment," which set higher contribution limits for candidates facing wealthy opponents who bankrolled their own campaigns, and one that increased limits on regulated hard money contributions that went directly to candidates.

In an earlier action, the Supreme Court on June 16, 2003, decided 7–2 to uphold restrictions on political contributions from advocacy groups. In *Federal Election Commission v. Beaumont*, the Court upheld the constitutionality of requiring nonprofit corporations to form political action committees to contribute to federal candidates, just as for-profit corporations and labor unions must do.

In the case, North Carolina Right to Life had sued for the right to give directly to candidates, arguing that advocacy groups, as purveyors of ideas, should not be treated the same as for-profit corporations. But the decision in *Beaumont* stressed a long history of restrictions on corporate giving and said in a footnote that corporate contributions were "furthest from the core of political expression," because corporations' First Amendment protections are derived largely from their individual members.

2004 elections in the event of a terrorist attack. DeForest B. Soaries Jr., chair of the Election Assistance Commission, sent a letter to Homeland Security secretary Tom Ridge noting that, unlike New York, which postponed primary balloting under way on Sept. 11, 2001, the federal government "has no agency that has the statutory authority to cancel and reschedule a federal election." However, after the letter became public, Soaries quickly backpedaled, saying July 13, 2004, that "there are no circumstances that could justify the postponement or cancellation" of a U.S. presidential election.

Under the Constitution, Congress sets the date for presidential elections and would have to craft procedures for a postponement.

Chronology of Action on Congress: Pay and Benefits

2001–2002

Public hand-wringing over allowing themselves a pay raise was a thing of the past for members of the 107th Congress.

Congressional Pay

House and Senate lawmakers in 2001 and 2002 did not turn away their annual pay raise. Under a 1989 law (PL 101-194), members receive an annual pay increase—based largely on the increase for civil servants—unless they vote to prevent it. *(Congress and the Nation Vol. VIII, p. 965)*

The appropriations bill covering the Treasury Department, Postal Service, White House, general government overhead, and other federal agencies and programs was the customary venue for members who want to block the annual, automatic congressional pay raise. The last time that happened was in 1998. *(Congress and the Nation Vol. X, p. 791)*

During consideration of the fiscal 2002 Treasury, Postal Service spending bill (HR 2590—PL 107-67), House Republican and Democratic leaders in 2001 agreed not to make a political issue of the annual pay increase. The House 293–129 on July 25 agreed to a John Linder, R-Ga., motion to order the previous question (thus ending debate and the possibility of amendment) on adoption of the rule (H Res 206) to provide for floor consideration of HR 2590. The effect was to avoid a vote on a Jim Matheson, D-Utah, and Doug Ose, R-Calif., amendment to deny members of Congress the cost-of-living adjustment (COLA). The Senate also did not seek to jettison the pay hike. As a result, most member salaries were boosted by 3.4 percent, to $150,000, in 2002. (Congressional leaders earn more.)

During consideration of the fiscal 2003 Treasury, Postal Service appropriations measure (HR 5120), the House by 258–156 on July 18, 2002, agreed to a Linder motion to order the previous question on the rule (H Res 488) governing floor debate on the bill. The effect was to block Matheson, as in 2001, from offering an amendment to disallow the automatic pay increase. Matheson's effort had a going-through-the-motions feel, however, as he did not seek House Rules Committee permission to offer an anti-COLA amendment on the floor and he limited his speech on the issue to one minute.

While the Senate Appropriations Committee considered its version of the Treasury-Postal bill (S 2740), the measure never reached the floor. Accounts covered by the legislation were kept alive through a series of stopgap bills.

Given that lawmakers in 2002 did not act to deny themselves a pay raise, their salaries increased to $154,700 in 2003. Senators also got the pay boost.

In related action, Rep. Bob Riley, R-Ariz., in 2001 introduced a bill (HR 241), called the Congressional Pay Integrity and Accountability Act, to eliminate the automatic pay adjustment for members of Congress. The measure was referred to the House Subcommittee on the Civil Service and Agency Organization on Feb. 13. It saw no further action in the 107th Congress.

Daily Expense Allowance

House Speaker J. Dennis Hastert, R-Ill., and Minority Leader Richard A. Gephardt, D-Mo., in 2001 went on record in opposition to a House Administration Committee proposal to provide House members with a $165 per day expense allowance. Upon taking control of the House in 1995 the GOP privatized—and thus trimmed subsidies to—some services, including restaurants, barbershops, and beauty salons in the Capitol complex. Nevertheless members still had a number of good perks.

• Free outpatient medical care at the National Naval Medical Center in Bethesda, Maryland, and the Walter Reed Army Hospital in Washington, D.C.

• Routine medical care from the Capitol's attending physician at a cost of $324 per member (in 2001).

• Use of the House gym in the Rayburn office building for $100 per year.

• A $3,000 per year automatic tax deduction for housing, meals, and other living expenses in Washington. No receipts were required.

• Free parking at the Capitol complex and at all three Washington-area airports.

• Frequent-flier miles accrued while on government travel could be kept for personal use.

• Members could receive diplomatic passports from the State Department upon request, which allowed them to avoid customs checks while traveling overseas.

2003–2004

Members of the 108th Congress quietly upped their annual salaries. Public and press criticism was absent, despite the rising costs of the ongoing war with Iraq and record budget deficits.

Congressional Pay

Republicans and Democrats in both 2003 and 2004 agreed to allow the annual pay raise for Congress to go forward.

The House GOP leadership in 2003, during consideration of a newly created Transportation-Treasury spending bill (HR 2989), arranged to use a procedural motion offered by Thomas M. Reynolds, R-N.Y., to squelch opponents of a congressional pay raise. The House voted 240–173 on Sept. 4 to, in effect, prevent any changes in the leadership's terms for debating the bill, which were written to prevent an up-or-down vote on an amendment to block the pay raise. A nearly equal number of lawmakers from each party voted in support of such a vote. That was slightly better than opponents of the raise fared in 2002 and 2001. *(Earlier action, p. 739)*

During consideration of HR 2989, the Senate on Oct. 23 agreed 60–34 to a Ted Stevens, R-Alaska, motion to table (kill) a Russ Feingold, D-Wis., amendment to bar a cost-of-living adjustment for members of Congress.

Congress subsequently did not use the Treasury-Postal Service appropriations section of the fiscal 2003 omnibus spending bill (H J Res 2—PL 108-7) to block a pay raise for members. Without such a provision, the increase was automatic and brought pay for most members to $158,100 as of Jan. 1, 2004. (Leaders earn more.)

The House on Sept. 14, 2004, agreed 235–170 to a Reynolds motion to order the previous question, and block amendments, on a rule (H Res 770) governing debate on the fiscal 2005 Transportation-Treasury appropriations bill (HR 5025). As a result, the members did not have to consider spurning their annual pay raise. Only Rep. Jim Matheson, D-Utah, spoke out against the pay increase on the floor.

The Senate also did not fight salary adjustment.

The Transportation-Treasury bill was folded into an omnibus bill (HR 4818—PL 108-447). As of 2005, most members earned $162,100.

Committee Mailings

House Resources Committee Chair Richard W. Pombo, R-Calif., sought a substantial increase in funding for his committee to send out mailings, including mass mailings to advertise committee field hearings.

Pombo asked for $500,000 in postage for the 108th Congress. The House Administration Committee allocated just $100,000, but, according to Rep. Brad Sherman, D-Calif., that amount was more than any panel had asked for in the 108th or any other Congress.

Congressional Pay History

Year	Annual Salary[1]
1789–March 3, 1817	$1,500
1817–1856	$2,000
1856–1865[2]	$3,000
1865–1871	$5,000
1871–1873	$7,500
1874–1907	$5,000
1907–1925	$7,500
1925–1932	$10,000
1932–1933	$9,000
1933–February 1934	$8,500
February–July 1934	$9,000
1935–1947	$10,000
1947–1955	$12,500
1955–1965	$22,500
1965–1969	$30,000
1969–1975	$42,500
1975–1977[3]	$44,600
1977–1979	$57,500
1979–1982	$60,662.50 per year[4]
December 1982–1983	$69,800 (House)
July 1983	$69,800 (Senate)
1984	$72,600
1985–1986	$75,100
January 1987	$77,400
February 1987–1990	$89,500
1990	$96,600 (House)
1990	$98,400 (Senate)
January 1991	$125,100 (House)
	$101,900 (Senate)
1992	$129,500
1993–1998	$133,600
1998–2000	$136,700
2000	$141,300
2001	$145,100
2002	$150,000
2003	$154,700
2004	$158,100
2005	$162,100
2006	$165,200

[1] From 1789 to 1856 members of Congress were paid on a per diem basis while Congress was in session, except for the period December 1815 to March 1817, when they received $1,500 a year. First established at $6 a day in 1789 ($7 for senators from March 4, 1795, to March 3, 1796), the per diem was raised to $8 in 1818 and remained there until 1856 when members were placed on annual salaries. For this table the per diem rates have been converted to per annum rates based on a hypothetically possible 250-day session.

[2] In 1857 Congress provided for a pay at the rate of $250 per month while in session, or a maximum of $3,000 annually.

[3] Between 1976 and 1983 the salary actually paid to members was less than that to which they were entitled under the annual comparability pay procedure (PL 94-82). On several occasions Congress did not appropriate funds to pay any or some of the new salary increases mandated by PL 94-82. The salaries in the table are the salaries actually paid to members.

[4] Percentage increases in congressional salaries generally are rounded to the nearest $100. The 1979 increase was not rounded because of specific language in the enacting legislation.

NOTE: The top six leaders of Congress—the Speaker of the House, the Senate president pro tempore, and the majority and minority leaders of both chambers—receive additional pay. Highest paid is the House Speaker, whose salary was $212,100 in 2006. Salaries for the majority and minority leaders in the Senate and House and the Senate president pro tempore were $183,500 in 2006.

Source: Paul E. Dwyer, Congressional Research Service

Pombo used some of the money to send mass mailings to residents in districts represented by Republicans who could face tough reelection bids. Democrats objected to the mailings. Sherman accused Pombo of using official committee expenses to protect targeted Republicans. Republicans questioned the Democrats' motives, disputed their facts, and countered that a mailing also went to a Democratic district.

Sherman wanted to cap committee spending on postage at $25,000 a year with an amendment to the fiscal 2005 legislative branch spending bill (HR 4755). Republicans turned back the effort July 8, 2004, voting 223–194 for a rule (H Res 707) that did not allow the amendment.

Hill Employees' Student Loan Perk

At an April 8, 2004, Senate Legislative Branch Appropriations Committee hearing, Richard J. Durbin, D-Ill., suggested that more uniform standards would improve a student loan forgiveness program for Senate employees.

The fiscal 2002 legislative branch appropriations bill (HR 2647—PL 107-68) established the program, conceived by Durbin and Appropriations Chair Ted Stevens, R-Alaska, giving individual senators wide latitude to use their office accounts to pay as much as $500 per month per employee to cover student loan costs. The perk was intended to recruit and retain employees who agreed to stay on the job at least one year.

At issue was that, in the Senate, the size of the benefit varied greatly from individual to individual and from office to office. A similar program in the executive branch gave essentially all employees of a given agency identical benefits.

CHAPTER 16

The Bush Presidency

The Bush Presidency

To a degree rare in American history, the presidency of George W. Bush was shaped by a single event on a single day: the terrorist attacks on Sept. 11, 2001, that killed nearly 3,000 people in the eastern United States. All previous presidents had been forced to alter their agendas in response to events and forces beyond their control, but Bush found himself revising nearly every aspect of his presidency in the wake of the Sept. 11 attacks. The most damaging and traumatic case of terrorism on American soil gave Bush what he called a "mission" for his presidency, enhanced his stature as a leader, briefly made him the most popular president in a half-century, and provided the impetus for two large-scale military occupations of foreign countries, both of which were still under way at the end of Bush's first term.

When he entered office in January 2001, Bush did not plan any special focus on terrorism, nor was he prepared to send tens of thousands of U.S. soldiers into both Afghanistan and Iraq. Instead, according to his own statements, he planned to concentrate on domestic matters, starting with a round of large tax cuts he said were needed to revive the economy and stimulate long-term investment. Bush also had an agenda of social programs, notably the imposition of new federal standards on education that, he said, would revitalize the nation's public schools. The new president's major national security initiative was to be an acceleration of a long-planned system intended to protect the nation from missile attacks by unfriendly nations, such as North Korea.

Bush got a head start toward all three of those priorities in the early months of his presidency but still struggled to gain political traction in Washington where the environment was much more partisan than anything he had dealt with previously as governor of Texas. After Sept. 11, combating terrorism became the central focus—critics said fixation—of his first term. Bush declared himself a "war president" and gave top spending priority to activities his aides described as the "global war on terror." A handful of other important things were accomplished in Washington during the post–Sept. 11 portion of Bush's term, but many priorities fell by the wayside as money and attention were diverted from domestic to military priorities.

Even had the Sept. 11 attacks not occurred Bush might have proven to be a somewhat different president than many voters had expected after the divisive 2000 election. In the 2000 campaign, Bush called himself a "uniter, not a divider" and left voters with the impression that he represented the moderate wing of the Republican Party. Bush turned out to be one of the most divisive figures in modern American politics, matching or exceeding in that category even his impeached predecessor, Bill Clinton (1993–2001). A poll sponsored by the *Economist* magazine just before the November 2004 election found that 90 percent of Republicans approved of Bush's performance as president while only 10 percent of Democrats did so. Such polls—confirmed by the results of the election—showed that any unity Bush had fostered in the wake of the Sept. 11 attacks had all but evaporated three years later. The nation (or at least that part of the nation that voted) was split 50–50 in 2000 and remained almost as evenly divided at the end of Bush's first term.

One reason for this continuing division was the conservative ideology that Bush sought to impose on what was, for all practical purposes, a generally centrist nation. In calling himself a "compassionate conservative" in 2000, Bush led many voters to believe he would follow a centrist path and eschew the hard-right agenda of former House Speaker Newt Gingrich and fellow Republican leaders who had taken control of the House of Representatives in 1994. Aside from Bush's self-description, the principal evidence for this expectation was that his father, President George H. W. Bush (1989–1993), generally was a throwback to the moderate Republicanism of post–World War II era.

The younger Bush enthusiastically embraced a traditional Republican agenda of tax cuts and reducing government regulations affecting business. Not since Herbert Hoover had the nation "had a president who has been more closely allied with business and more sympathetic to large and powerful corporations," Alan Brinkley, a Columbia University historian who specialized in the American presidency told the *Washington Post* in 2004.

However, Bush added an overlay of social issues—advanced primarily by religious conservatives—that did not quite fit the middle-of-the-road image he had emphasized as a candidate. Prominent among these were his embrace of restrictions on abortions in certain cases and his "faith-based initiative" to give federal funds to religious groups engaged

DICK CHENEY: THE ULTIMATE INSIDER

In retrospect, George W. Bush's choice of Dick Cheney as his vice presidential running mate in 2000 should not have come as a surprise. Cheney had served more than a decade in Congress and nearly as long in the executive branch, first as a White House staff aide and then as secretary of defense under Bush's father, George H. W. Bush. Cheney thus added government experience and Washington gravitas to a ticket headed by a capital outsider who had held public office for only six years. The politically conservative Cheney also had excellent credentials with the Republican base of support, and he apparently did not harbor any presidential ambitions. A low-key man who did not seek out the limelight, Cheney seemed a sound choice to take on a substantive role as vice president.

Once in office, Cheney did just that. He skillfully used his insider's knowledge of Washington and its ways to help shape the president's program and advance it on Capitol Hill. Within the White House, he became a leading proponent—and eventually a vocal defender—of the administration's "war on terror" and the invasion of Iraq. Supporters and critics alike called Cheney the most influential vice president in recent times and, by some accounts, perhaps in all of American history.

Background

Richard Bruce Cheney was born in Lincoln, Nebraska, on Jan. 30, 1941, and grew up in Casper, Wyoming. He attended Yale University and Casper College before earning a political science B.A. in 1965 and an M.A. in 1966, both from the University of Wyoming. Cheney finished political science Ph.D. course work at the University of Wisconsin, but did not complete his thesis. Cheney did not serve in the military.

In 1964 Cheney married his high school girlfriend, Lynne Vincent Cheney, an author and political commentator. The couple had two children, Elizabeth, an attorney, and Mary, who was described as one of Cheney's closest confidants and a key campaign aide. Openly gay, Mary was likely the source of one difference of opinion between her father and Bush on a sensitive campaign issue. Largely to appease his conservative base, Bush ultimately announced his support for a constitutional amendment that defined marriage as the union of a man and a woman and left it to individual states to determine whether and what legal arrangements outside of marriage should be accorded to gay couples; Cheney did not support a constitutional amendment banning gay marriage, preferring to leave the matter to the individual states to resolve.

Cheney went to Washington in 1968, as a congressional fellow in the office of Wisconsin Republican William A. Steiger. In 1969 he served as special assistant to the director of the Office of Economic Opportunity, at that time Donald H. Rumsfeld. He became a White House staff assistant in 1971 and later that year was named assistant director of the Cost of Living Council. He became vice president of Bradley, Woods & Co. in 1973, but returned to public life in 1974

when he was named deputy assistant to President Gerald R. Ford and then became the youngest White House chief of staff in history.

Two years later, at age thirty-seven, Cheney suffered the first of four heart attacks. The last one occurred in 2001, shortly after he took office. Cheney subsequently had a cardiac defibrillator implanted in his chest; as of 2004 it had never discharged.

Political Highlights

In 1977, after Ford left office, Cheney moved back to Wyoming, where he ran successfully for the state's at-large House seat in 1978 against Democratic attorney Bill Bagley, winning 59 percent of the vote. Cheney won election five more times, never with less than two-thirds of the vote. In the House, Cheney served six years as chairman of the Republican Policy Committee, two years as Republican Conference chair, and two months as the minority whip before resigning in March 1989 to become secretary of defense under the first President Bush. Cheney holds the distinction of being the only whip never to lose a vote—no votes in which the whip was active were taken during his brief time in the job.

As secretary of defense, Cheney directed U.S. military operations in Panama in December 1989 and in Iraq in January 1991. In both operations, the targets were dictators who were deemed to have overstepped their bounds. In Operation Just Cause U.S. forces were sent to capture dictator Manuel Noriega, who had been indicted in the United States on narcotics charges in 1988 and who had annulled the results of a presidential election won by the opposition leader. Noriega was taken to Florida and later convicted on drug charges.

Operation Desert Storm was launched after Iraq's dictator Saddam Hussein invaded the small, oil-producing country of Kuwait in August 1990 and proclaimed Kuwait to be Iraq's "nineteenth province." The United States assembled an international military alliance that defeated the Iraqi army in three days.

At the end of Bush's presidency in January 1993, Cheney went to the American Enterprise Institute, a conservative think tank in Washington, as a senior fellow. In 1995, he was named chair and chief executive officer of Halliburton Co, the giant oil services company headquartered in Texas. He remained in that post until 2000 when George W. Bush asked him to head the search for a vice presidential candidate and then surprised most pundits by choosing Cheney as his running mate. Cheney became a wealthy man while working for Halliburton; in 2004 he was thought to be worth between $30 million and $100 million, most of it amassed during his years with the Texas firm.

Relations with Congress

As vice president, Cheney generally received high marks from his Republican congressional colleagues for his policy knowledge and negotiating skills. Cheney spent more time on

Capitol Hill than many previous vice presidents. He joined Senate Republicans on many Tuesdays at their weekly luncheon, and, in a break with precedent, he maintained an office near the floor of the House as well as the ceremonial office the vice president had in his official capacity as president of the Senate.

During his House service, Cheney compiled a voting record that grew more conservative over time, reflecting the views of his Wyoming constituents. By the end of his House career, he was earning perfect voting scores from the American Conservative Union, and he rarely strayed from the votes cast by the working coalition of Republicans and southern Democrats.

But he also had a reputation as a good mediator, open to hearing all sides of an issue and always searching for constructive solutions. He still displayed those same qualities as vice president, according to Republican legislators, and that made him a trusted negotiator when they needed someone to settle disputes between the two chambers or among different GOP factions.

Cheney played key roles in negotiating the compromises that allowed passage of the administration's tax cut measures. In 2003, for example, Hill Republicans gave Cheney much of the credit for brokering the final talks that led to the enactment of the $350 billion tax cut package (PL 108-27). Cheney was also instrumental in the outcome of that bill for another reason: it required his tie-breaking vote in the Senate to clear the measure. In his first term as vice president, Cheney cast six tie-breaking votes.

And the vice president was often sent to Capitol Hill to persuade wavering Republicans to put aside their concerns and support the president's position. Cheney was called upon, for example, to convince several House conservatives to support the largest expansion of the Medicare entitlement since its creation, the prescription drug law (PL 108-173) that was enacted by the thinnest of margins in November 2003.

Cheney's efforts did not always pay off, however. He put in long hours in 2003 trying to mediate disputes between key House and Senate Republicans over legislation to carry out the energy policy he helped formulate (HR 6), only to have it stall out in the Senate.

Protecting Executive Power

Cheney's close ties to Congress did not prevent him from seeking opportunities to champion the power of the presidency, and by extension, the executive branch. Early in his vice presidency, Cheney touched off a sharp controversy when he refused to name the participants in the energy policy task force he ran in 2001. The task force, said to be composed largely of oil industry executives and lobbyists, drafted the Bush administration's energy policy, which emphasized energy production and called for reducing environmental regulations that hindered energy companies. A suit brought by the General Accounting Office (GAO) to force Cheney to reveal the names of task force participants was dismissed by a federal judge in 2002. In 2004 the Supreme Court ruled in Cheney's favor in a separate lawsuit by private groups trying to gain access to the energy task force records—but only after a protracted legal battle that strengthened the administration's reputation for secrecy, and the disclosure of a duck-hunting trip that he took with Supreme Court justice Antonin Scalia that raised questions about the court's impartiality.

On at least two other significant occasions, Cheney worked to prevent a close examination of executive branch actions. In the spring of 2004, as congressional hearings into the abuse of Iraqi prisoners picked up speed, it was Cheney who encouraged a conservative revolt in hopes of tamping down the controversy over who was responsible for the abuses. After Defense Secretary Rumsfeld faced tough questions from the Senate Armed Services Committee in May, the vice president declared that Rumsfeld's critics should "get off his case," touching off a conservative backlash that made it more difficult for lawmakers from both parties to sustain an aggressive investigation.

Cheney and Bush also fought to prevent the creation of the independent commission that investigated the Sept. 11, 2001, terrorist attack on the World Trade Center and the Pentagon. Both men eventually capitulated and even agreed to testify before the commission, although not publicly.

A chief proponent of the invasion of Iraq in 2003, Cheney expressed no doubt that Iraqi dictator Saddam Hussein had stockpiled quantities of biological and chemical weapons and was trying to build nuclear weapons. Even after no weapons of mass destruction were found, Cheney was slow to back down from his allegations. He also continued to talk of a conspiratorial relationship between Iraq and the al Qaeda terrorist leader Osama bin Laden long after the independent commission concluded there was none of significance.

Cheney's controversial role in the politics of Iraq was made more so by his former stewardship of Halliburton, the Texas oil services company, subsidiaries of which won several lucrative no-bid reconstruction contracts in Iraq. Democratic insinuations that Cheney used his position to help his former employer infuriated the vice president. It reportedly was a comment about the Cheney-Halliburton relationship that triggered Cheney's insulting, and widely publicized, directive about a sexual act to Vermont Democratic senator Patrick J. Leahy during a gathering in the Senate chamber for the senators' official photograph.

That comment combined with Cheney's dogged insistence that the administration was pursuing the right course in Iraq, even as U.S.-led forces were unable to quell a growing insurgency there, cost the vice president some popularity in the public opinion polls in mid-2004 and even spawned some short-lived speculation that Bush might dump Cheney from the 2004 ticket. Bush showed no inclination to switch running mates, however, and the Republican ticket won reelection with 51 percent of the popular vote.

in social work. A devout "born-again" Christian, Bush did not hesitate to cast many of his decisions and policies in religious terms—a tendency that inspired his supporters and deepened the angst of his critics.

Yet another aspect of Bush's presidency that might have come as a surprise to some Americans voters was his approach to following through on a campaign promise to "restore" (his word) the power and prestige of the presidency in the wake of the scandals of the Clinton years. In many ways, the Bush administration was the most focused and single-minded in decades. Cabinet officers were given little leeway on policy or personnel matters; the White House enforced a "one-message-each-day" policy on the entire administration; and senior officials, starting with the president, appeared obsessed with keeping secrets, even from congressional leaders.

This corporate governing style of the Bush team was in part a reaction to the relatively relaxed attitude of the Clinton administration but it also stemmed from the backgrounds of the president and many of his aides. Bush was the first president in history to have earned a masters of business administration (although his subsequent business ventures were far from successful); four of his original cabinet members had been chief executive officers of large corporations; and many top officials had broad experience in senior government positions, notably Vice President Dick Cheney, Secretary of State Colin Powell, and Defense Secretary Donald H. Rumsfeld. The White House attempt to mandate uniformity did not always work, however: Powell and Rumsfeld (and their respective departments) bickered as openly as any top officials in recent decades, and Treasury Secretary Paul O'Neill was shoved aside in 2002 after he questioned the fiscal cost of continued large-scale tax cuts.

The rejection of Clinton's governing style was not the only way in which Bush and his aides sought to stake out a course dramatically different from that of the Clinton years. Indeed, many of Bush's policies appeared crafted specifically because they were in contrast to those of Clinton's. Washington learned a new acronym summarizing the Bush approach: ABC, or Anything But Clinton. This approach was most noticeable in some areas of foreign policy, particularly Bush's refusal to follow Clinton's lead on Middle East peace talks. In important aspects of domestic affairs, notably environmental and energy polices, Bush and his aides also seemed determined to move in directions diametrically at odds with those of the Clinton years.

The sharp right-hand turn did not apply to all areas of policy making by the Bush team. Breaking with prevalent views in his own Democratic Party, Clinton had been an enthusiastic promoter of international free trade agreements and the general expansion of global commerce that had come to be known as "globalization." Bush adopted a nearly identical approach that included an uphill effort to negotiate a broad free-trade agreement covering all of the Western Hemisphere except Cuba. Bush also followed a path similar to Clinton's in dealing with China: an initial period of hard-line rhetoric against Beijing followed by a reconciliation based on mutual interest between the current dominant superpower and the country that appeared to be emerging as the superpower of the future.

Bush Foreign Policy

When Bush entered office, few could have imagined that his presidency would become dominated by international affairs. Aside from promising a strong military and calling for a nationwide system to defend the country against ballistic missile attacks, Bush generally had steered away from foreign policy matters during his 2000 presidential campaign. His most noteworthy foreign policy position, as a candidate, had been a stated disdain for what he called "nation-building"— the large-scale peacekeeping operations to which President Clinton committed thousands of U.S. troops in Haiti, Bosnia, and Kosovo. Bush clearly expected to spend most of his presidency dealing with domestic matters on which his conservative approach would be a marked contrast to Clinton's.

Indeed, most of the early months of Bush's presidency were dominated by domestic affairs, notably the economy. International controversies did arise, however, some as a result of Bush's own actions and some because of events beyond his control. In the former category were three steps taken by the new administration that provoked broad concerns, especially in Europe, that Washington suddenly was reverting to a "unilateralist" approach to world affairs, as opposed to the multilateral cooperation that had been the hallmark of the Clinton years and had been the stated—if not always the practiced—premise of U.S. policy making for more than a half-century.

Two of these unilateral steps by Bush involved United Nations treaties. In March 2001, the new administration said it would withdraw the U.S. signature from the Kyoto Protocol, an international treaty negotiated late in 1997 committing the United States and other industrialized countries to curbing their emissions of carbon dioxide and other so-called "greenhouse gases" said, by most scientists, to be largely responsible for a perceived change in the global climate. As a candidate, Bush had opposed the Kyoto treaty, and the Senate already had gone on record against it as well. Even so, the administration's formal renunciation of the treaty generated widespread dismay in Europe, where concern about the effects of climate change was more widespread than in the United States. President Bush also retreated from a promise candidate Bush had made to seek federal regulations on emissions of carbon dioxide.

The administration's second step, of a similar nature, was to reject as unworkable an internationally supported agreement to add enforcement clauses to the 1972 Biological Weapons Convention. That treaty had banned the production and stockpiling of biological weapons, but it contained no procedure for the United Nations Security Council to enforce the ban. After nearly six years of negotiations, diplo-

President George W. Bush meets with the National Security Council on Sept. 12, 2001, to discuss the previous day's terrorist attacks. Gathered around the president from left to right are CIA director George Tenet, Secretary of Defense Donald Rumsfeld, Secretary of State Colin Powell, Vice President Dick Cheney, Joint Chiefs of Staff chair Gen. Henry Shelton, and National Security Advisor Condoleezza Rice. *Source: AP Wide World Photos/Doug Mills*

mats in late 2000 and early 2001 reached agreement on a plan to add such an enforcement mechanism. The new Bush administration used its diplomatic clout to kill the agreement and thus end any prospect for putting teeth in the biological weapons treaty.

The administration's third significant move of a unilateral nature was its stated determination to pull out of the 1972 Anti-Ballistic Missile (ABM) treaty, under which the United States and the Soviet Union (later Russia) had agreed never to build nationwide missile defense systems. Advocates of arms control treaties considered the ABM treaty the cornerstone of diplomatic efforts to slow what had been a nuclear weapons race between Washington and Moscow, and they expressed fears that revoking the treaty could spur a new race to build the next generation of nuclear weapons. Bush and his aides said the treaty was outdated and stood in the way of what they insisted was a more effective approach: building a defensive system to protect Americans against enemy missiles (North Korea was considered the most likely country to try to attack the United States with missiles).

An example of how external events suddenly could upset a president's agenda came just a little over two months after Bush took office. On April 1, 2001, a Chinese jet fighter collided with a U.S. surveillance plane over the South China Sea, killing the Chinese pilot and forcing the American plane to make an emergency landing on China's Hainan Island. China held the twenty-four-member U.S. crew for eleven tense days, during which the two sides engaged in public recriminations while conducting diplomacy behind the scenes.

It was Bush's first real foreign crisis, and its successful conclusion—with the crew members returned safely—appeared to indicate that the new president could be a diplomat when circumstances required.

SEPT. 11, 2001

The drama of the spy plane episode in China faded into insignificance just five months later with the events of a beautiful late-summer morning. Armed only with knives and a deep religious fervor, nineteen young men from Saudi Arabia and other Arab countries demonstrated that wide oceans and the world's strongest military were not enough to insulate the United States from the cares of the world. The men hijacked four commercial airliners on the East Coast and flew two of them into the World Trade Center towers in New York City and a third into the Pentagon, just outside Washington, D.C. The fourth plane crashed in a field in southwestern Pennsylvania after passengers resisted the hijackers; that plane apparently was to have been used for an attack against the U.S. Capitol building or the White House. Altogether, nearly 3,000 people died as a result of the attacks, most of them workers at the World Trade Center buildings. The attacks stunned the nation as had few events in recent history, among them the assassination of President John F. Kennedy in 1963 and the Japanese attack on Pearl Harbor in 1941.

Administration officials quickly concluded that the coordinated attacks had been sponsored by al Qaeda, a terrorist network of Islamist extremists headed by Saudi Arabian exile Osama bin Laden, which had carried out the simultaneous

Standing in the rubble of the World Trade Center, President Bush puts his arm around a rescue worker on Sept. 14, 2001. Bush's promise that ". . . the people who knocked down these buildings will hear all of us soon" would become reality when a U.S.-led coalition invaded Afghanistan on October 7, 2001. *Source: AP Wide World Photos/ Doug Mills*

bombings of U.S. embassies in Kenya and Tanzania three years earlier. Bush told aides the Sept. 11 attacks had given him a "mission" for his presidency, and he explained that mission to the nation with a determined address to a joint session of Congress nine days later: The United States would use all resources available to it for a relentless war against all terrorist groups of "global reach." Bush insisted that the United States had no quarrel with Arabs or Muslims in general, only with those who used terrorism to attack civilians.

The first front in the "global war" against terrorism was opened a little more than a month later when thousands of troops from the United States, Britain, and a handful of other countries invaded Afghanistan, where al Qaeda had based its operations in collaboration with the Islamist regime known as the Taliban. The invasion had wide international support, based in large part on sympathy for the United States in the wake of the Sept. 11 attacks. Chief in importance among those siding with Washington was Pervez Musharraf, the

military leader of Pakistan, which previously had been the chief international supporter of the Taliban.

The massive invasion quickly overwhelmed the Taliban and al Qaeda fighters, and by late November 2001 a collection of U.S.-backed Afghan warlords, known as the Northern Alliance, was able to march into Kabul, the capital. Although the invasion succeeded in driving the Taliban from power and dispersing the several thousand al Qaeda fighters who had been operating in Afghanistan, it failed to result in the capture of bin Laden; he was presumed to have escaped into the rugged mountain region on the Pakistan side of the border with Afghanistan. Bush was thus thwarted in what he had described as an aim of capturing bin Laden "dead or alive." Bin Laden was to remain at large through the rest of Bush's first term, although several top and mid-level aides were captured by U.S. or Pakistani authorities.

The task of putting Afghanistan back together again would prove more difficult than capturing a poorly defended Kabul. After a quarter-century of war, the country was devastated economically and physically and most of its territory was controlled by warlords. A UN-sponsored conclave in Bonn, Germany, in December 2001, led to the appointment of an interim government headed by Hamid Karzai, a moderate leader of the largest ethnic group, the Pashtuns. Bush and other Western leaders promised billions of dollars in aid to rebuild Afghanistan, but the promises arrived more quickly than did the money. Three years later only a minority of Afghan citizens had seen significant improvement in their daily lives. Karzai eventually won Afghanistan's first-ever presidential election, in October 2004, but continuing violence in much of the country forced repeated postponements of elections for a parliament.

THE NEXT STAGE: IRAQ

The war in Afghanistan had barely been concluded, in November 2001, when Bush signaled what was to become the next front in his war against terrorism. At a White House news conference, the president warned that Iraq, and its longtime leader, Saddam Hussein posed a danger to the world. Iraq in the past had developed biological and chemical weapons and had tried to build nuclear weapons, Bush said, and the country supported terrorists. Iraq thus posed a "threat" to the United States and its allies, Bush warned. Unknown to the public at the time, Pentagon officials had already begun planning an invasion of Iraq; their plans envisioned a quick victory over Iraq's army, with power transferred to a group of Iraqi exiles who had been lobbying in Washington for action against Saddam.

In the summer of 2002, Vice President Cheney and other officials began making the public case for military action against Iraq. Saddam, they said, was rapidly expanding his arsenal of biological and chemical weapons and had resumed his quest for nuclear weapons—all in violation of numerous resolutions adopted by the United Nations Security Council since the 1991 Persian Gulf War. In making these statements, administration officials cited what they said was irrefutable intelligence information.

Along with preparing for a war and explaining why Iraq was the specific target, the Bush administration in 2002 formulated an intellectual argument placing action against Iraq within a broader policy framework. In a speech to West Point academy graduates on June 1, and then in a document called a "National Security Strategy" made public on Sept. 20, Bush articulated an idealistic view of the United States as the most important force for good in the world. Bush said the United States would do whatever was necessary to combat terrorism, protect the peace, and promote democracy on a global scale. The strategy's most-quoted, and most controversial, passages justified preemptive action against threats to U.S. national security. "The greater the threat, the greater the risk of inaction—and the more compelling the case for taking anticipatory action to defend ourselves even if uncertainty remains as to the time and place of the enemy's attack," the strategy said. "To forestall or prevent such hostile acts by our adversaries, the United States will, if necessary, act preemptively." Such language was intended to be, and was widely interpreted as, providing legal, moral, and political justification for the impending war against Iraq.

Implicitly acknowledging that such a war could be successful only with some support from other nations, Bush also sought to portray the menace of Iraq as a global challenge. On Sept. 12, 2002—a date chosen because it fell one year and one day after the terrorist attacks against the United States— Bush went before the United Nations General Assembly with a demand for united action by the world against Iraq. Bush also won congressional passage in October of a broadly worded joint resolution (PL 107-243) authorizing the president to take military action in Iraq. Careful diplomacy by Secretary of State Powell then led to a unanimous vote in the UN Security Council, on No. 8, 2002, insisting that Iraq allow resumption of UN weapons inspections, which Baghdad had halted nearly four years earlier. In many respects, the UN vote was the foremost diplomatic achievement by the Bush administration because it demonstrated a remarkable unity of purpose by countries with widely varying interests.

Subsequent events showed, however, that Powell's diplomacy had fostered only an illusion of unity at the United Nations. UN weapons inspectors did begin returning to Iraq in late 2002 and made slow progress inspecting sites where Saddam's technicians were presumed to be building and storing weapons of mass destruction. That progress was too slow and halting for the Bush administration, however, which insisted Saddam's government would never give up its weapons unless forced to do so. In one of the most dramatic moments in recent diplomatic history, Powell went before the Security Council on Feb. 5, 2003, and presented satellite photographs, electronic intercepts of telephone conversations, and other evidence that he said proved that Iraq possessed weapons of mass destruction, was building more of them, and was hiding them from the UN inspectors.

Despite its high drama, Powell's presentation failed to sway a half-dozen world leaders—notably French president Jacques Chirac, German chancellor Gerhard Schroeder, and Russian president Vladimir Putin—whose support would be necessary for a follow-up Security Council resolution explicitly authorizing military action against Iraq. Most officials in the Bush administration had never really wanted to return to the Security Council for such authority, arguing that the United States already had the legal and moral authority to protect its own interests. But Bush's key ally in any invasion of Iraq, British prime minister Tony Blair, desperately wanted the UN's imprimatur for a war in Iraq, the prospect of which was opposed by a majority of his citizens.

That a war was approaching was undeniable. For months the Pentagon had been training troops for battle in desert conditions, building or upgrading command centers in the Persian Gulf region, and shipping thousands of tons of equipment and supplies to the region. The visible nature of these war preparations heightened deep anxiety worldwide, particularly among Europeans, few of whom shared Bush's view that Iraq posed an immediate threat. These sharply differing views about the necessity of a war strained relations between the United States and Europe to a greater degree than any other time since World War II. Antiwar protesters marched by the tens of thousands in European capitals early in 2003, harshly denouncing Bush and the European leaders who were supporting him. In addition to Blair, those leaders included Italian prime minister Silvio Berlusconi, Spanish prime minister Jose Maria Aznar, and the leaders of several formerly communist countries in Eastern Europe that recently had, or were about to, join the U.S.-led NATO alliance. Defense Secretary Rumsfeld described this European cleavage in graphic terms as an argument between "old Europe" (meaning France and Germany, in particular) and "new Europe" (meaning such newly democratic countries as the Czech Republic and Poland). This remark further inflamed passions in Europe, in part because it appeared symbolic of a widespread view within the Bush administration that Europe was so divided, and so weak militarily, that the U.S.-European alliance had lost much of its usefulness for Washington.

Despite the international controversy, Bush pushed ahead with his plans for the Iraq war, giving Saddam one last chance—on March 17, 2003—to avoid a conflict by giving up power and leaving his country. Saddam spurned the offer, and on March 19 the United States, with support from Britain and a handful of other countries, launched what was to become a massive invasion of Iraq, primarily from the south across the border with Kuwait, and from naval ships in the Persian Gulf. Irregular Iraqi forces put up unexpectedly fierce resistance at several points, but Saddam's regular armies proved no match for the combined weight of the 150,000-some invading troops and overwhelming U.S. and British airpower. The symbolic collapse of the Iraqi regime came on April 9, 2003, when U.S. Marines helped Iraqi citizens pull down a statue of Saddam in central Baghdad.

Saddam himself went into hiding, as did most of his senior aides. U.S. soldiers found him eight months later, hiding in a hole in the ground near the Tigris River, north of Baghdad.

Nearly every major aspect of the war to oust Saddam went according to the Pentagon's well-laid plans. Virtually nothing that happened in Iraq after the war followed the outlines of Pentagon plans, however. First to go was the plan to install a new government in Baghdad headed by the Pentagon's favored Iraqi exiles, whose sudden appearance on the scene generated broad opposition in Iraq. Instead, a Pentagon-appointed administration led by U.S. and British officials ran civilian affairs in Iraq for a full year, until nominal authority was transferred, in late June 2004, to an "interim" Iraqi government chosen in secretive bargaining sessions among Iraq's leading ethnic, political, and religious factions. That government in turn was to be replaced early in 2005 by a "transitional" government responsible to a temporary parliament chosen in Iraq's first-ever free elections.

All of these political arrangements for Iraq's future were burdened by legacies of the past, in particular conflicts among the country's three major groups: Sunni Muslims, who had long dominated the country despite constituting only about 20 percent of the population; Shiite Muslims, long Iraq's underclass even though they represented a majority of nearly 60 percent of the population; and Kurds, who since the 1991 Persian Gulf War had become accustomed to substantial autonomy in their northern provinces. Fashioning a workable political arrangement among these and other groups was certain to be among the foremost challenges faced by Iraq for years to come.

A more immediate challenge—one that forced yet another change in the Bush administration's plans for Iraq—was providing security. The Pentagon originally had planned to withdraw most U.S. troops from Iraq by the end of 2003 but an upsurge of violence in the months after the war forced the administration to maintain a massive U.S. presence all through 2004 and 2005 and into 2006. The violence took many forms, including car bombs, roadside bombs, assassinations of key Iraqi figures, and kidnappings of foreigners. By 2004 it was clear that most of the violence was caused by loyalists to Saddam's ousted regime, plus criminals and extreme Islamists who hoped the U.S. presence in Iraq would inspire a region-wide holy war against the West. Among the latter were an undetermined number of Muslims from elsewhere in the Middle East. The vast majority of those killed in the violence were Iraqis, both civilians and recruits for a new army and police force that were being trained by the United States. But dozens of U.S. service personnel also lost their lives each month as a result of the violence. Only 115 U.S. troops had died in combat during the three-week war in 2003 but by the end of 2004 another 918 troops died in combat or as the result of bombings, shootings, and other violence by insurgents. Thousands of Iraqi civilians also died in violence during and after the war; an exact figure was impossible to determine because no one kept accurate counts.

The Bush administration made every effort to portray its military occupation of Iraq in the most benign terms possible, insisting that keeping an average of 150,000 foreign troops there was necessary to provide security and foster stability so democracy could flourish. These efforts were substantially undermined in the spring of 2004 when U.S. news organizations published photographs showing American guards abusing and sexually humiliating Iraqi detainees at the notorious Abu Ghraib prison near Baghdad. Numerous official and unofficial investigations showed that the abuse fit into a pattern of maltreatment of prisoners held by the U.S. military and intelligence services in Afghanistan, Iraq, the U.S. naval base at Guantanamo Bay, Cuba, and elsewhere. Even so, the Bush administration insisted the publicized abuses represented isolated incidents, in violation of official policy.

Also embarrassing the administration was its failure to locate in Iraq the vast arsenals of weapons of mass destruction that Bush had insisted posed a grave and imminent threat to the United States and its allies. After the 2003 war, a CIA-led team of more than 1,000 experts combed through Iraqi military installations, but found none of the weapons. A final report issued in 2004 by the head of the inspections team concluded that Iraq had destroyed all of its biological and chemical weapons after the 1991 Persian Gulf War and had made no serious effort to rebuild them. Likewise, the report said, Iraq had done virtually nothing to revive its program to develop nuclear weapons after that work was dismantled in the early 1990s by UN weapons inspectors. A parallel report by the Senate Intelligence Committee pointed to numerous flaws in U.S. intelligence-gathering about Iraq's alleged weapons, but the Republican-led panel said it found no evidence that the White House had put undue pressure on the intelligence agencies.

Despite the evidence undercutting his rationale for the war in Iraq, Bush continued to tell voters on the campaign trail in 2004 that Iraq had wanted to build these weapons, thereby justifying his decision to go to war. Bush and his aides also pointedly refused to be drawn into a discussion of whether the demonstrably faulty intelligence about Iraq's weapons would make it more difficult to justify a preemptive war against some other perceived threat in the future—as had been promised in the September 2002 National Security Strategy.

EUROPE AND RUSSIA

The transatlantic diplomatic dispute over Iraq early in 2003 exposed to public view a line of thinking in the Bush administration that Europe no longer was the vital center of U.S. interest that it had been for most of the previous two centuries. No one in the Bush administration argued that Europe was unimportant; instead, key officials, especially at the top echelons of the Pentagon, insisted that the United States should focus greater effort on confronting new challenges to U.S. national security, including terrorism, the potential acquisition of nuclear weapons by Iran and North

Korea, guaranteeing Middle Eastern energy sources, the rise of China, and other matters.

In this context, the administration appeared to adopt an approach of ignoring, to the extent possible, France, Germany, and other European countries whose leaders took stands at odds with U.S. policy on such matters as Iraq. By contrast, Bush and his aides heaped praise on those leaders, such as Britain's Blair and Spain's Aznar, who supported the Iraq war. The one leader who escaped being categorized in this fashion by the Bush administration was Russian president Putin. After their first meeting, in Slovenia in June 2001, Bush declared that he had looked into Putin's "soul" and discovered a man who was determined to move his country into a democratic future. After the September 2001 terrorist attacks, Bush had a practical reason to be grateful to Putin: the Russian leader prevailed on several former Soviet republics in Central Asia to allow U.S. overflights, and even military bases, for the invasion of Afghanistan. Putin's subsequent actions that generated controversy internationally—limiting the growth of democratic institutions in Russia, continuing a brutal war against separatist forces in the region of Chechnya, and opposing the Iraq war—brought only the mildest of protests from Washington.

OTHER 'AXIS OF EVIL' COUNTRIES

As part of his campaign to convince the American people of the necessity of war in Iraq, Bush had highlighted his January 2002 State of the Union address by characterizing Iraq as one of three countries constituting an "axis of evil." Also on the list were Iran and North Korea. Bush said both countries were trying to develop nuclear weapons—in violation of their UN treaty commitments—and were repressing the rights of their people, although in markedly different ways.

Of the two, there was widespread agreement in the United States that North Korea posed by far the greater danger. This was because North Korea was presumed to have already built one or two nuclear weapons, was attempting to build long-range missiles capable of carrying nuclear weapons as far as portions of the western United States, and was led by the erratic Kim Jong Il, who used bluster and threats to get his way. The Bush administration refused to deal directly with North Korea and instead arranged, starting in 2003, a series of six-party talks in which North Korea was confronted by China, Japan, Russia, South Korea, and the United States. Despite the heavy-duty diplomatic firepower brought to bear, these talks had made little or no headway by the end of 2004. In fact, most observers agreed that North Korea had become even more dangerous during Bush's term, having kicked out UN weapons inspectors in late 2002 and then begun reprocessing plutonium from spent nuclear fuel rods—a step that experts said could give Pyongyang enough material for several more nuclear weapons.

The Bush administration also accused Iran of working to develop nuclear weapons, but the evidence for the accusation was more ambiguous than in the case of North Korea. By 2003 the International Atomic Energy Agency had determined that Iran had withheld information about its nuclear activities, in violation of its treaty commitments, but inspections by the agency found no hard evidence that Iran actually was trying to produce weapons. European diplomats in 2003 and 2004 attempted to negotiate a solution under which Iran would give up any ambitions for nuclear weapons in exchange for economic incentives. While deeply skeptical of this diplomacy, the Bush administration reluctantly went along with it for the time being because it had no obviously workable alternative to offer. At the end of Bush's term, the prospects for a successful agreement were limited.

The Bush years did see one success in the world's long and often-frustrated campaign to persuade countries to give up the quest for weapons of mass destruction. That success came in an unlikely place: Libya, which in previous decades had topped the U.S. list of "rogue" nations. Libyan leader Muammar Qadaffi early in 2003 initiated diplomatic contacts with Britain and the United States that led eventually to his agreement to turn over to Washington and the United Nations all of Libya's limited work to develop chemical and nuclear weapons. Bush insisted the Iraq war had stimulated Qadaffi to act, out of fear that he might be next on Washington's target list. However, most diplomatic observers said Qadaffi took this unexpected step for other reasons, including a desire to reopen Libya to foreign investment, which had been foreclosed for years by international sanctions.

CHINA

The diplomatic fracas over the downing of a U.S. spy plane in China in April 2001 had gotten relations between the Bush administration and Beijing off on a wrong foot, but both sides recovered quickly. By the end of Bush's first term, relations between the two countries were generally as positive as at any point since they resumed diplomacy nearly three decades earlier.

Bush and his Chinese counterpart, Jiang Zemin, met repeatedly and appeared to develop a good working relationship; the same appeared to be developing after 2003, when Hu Jintao began the elongated process of taking over Jiang's top leadership posts. Just as important, the United States and China were developing a normal diplomatic discourse—rather than shouting across the Pacific—to resolve the inevitable disagreements. For the most part this held true even on contentious trade issues, a field where China had gained the upper hand by virtue of its multi-billion-dollar surplus in exports to the United States.

One potentially serious disagreement still unresolved as Bush entered his second term was China's claim to Taiwan. Bush in 2001 had made explicit what had been an implicit U.S. policy of protecting Taiwan against an armed invasion by China. The chance that Bush, or any future president, would be called upon to honor that promise ebbed and flowed with the level of rhetoric between Beijing's new leaders and Taiwan's pro-independence president.

ELSEWHERE IN THE WORLD

Bush's war against terrorism—which he defined broadly to include the war in Iraq and the aftermath there—tended to push to the side nearly all other foreign policy concerns of the United States. But other matters did intrude, forcing the administration and occasionally Congress to divert attention elsewhere.

At the top of this list of what had become second-tier matters was the perennial conflict between Israel and the Palestinians. Bush entered office just weeks after former president Clinton had failed in the second of two major, last-minute efforts to secure a long-term peace agreement. The failure of Clinton's first effort, at a Camp David summit in July 2000, had led to a violent Palestinian uprising, called an intifada, that continued all through Bush's first term and cost the lives of about 3,000 Palestinians and 1,000 Israelis.

Wary of being dragged into the morass that Clinton had entered, Bush adopted a hands-off approach to the Israeli-Palestinian dispute. Bush made two major exceptions to this approach, however. In June 2002, he accepted an appeal by Israeli prime minister Ariel Sharon for a new hardline approach of isolating Palestinian leader Yaseer Arafat, who Sharon accused of fomenting terrorism against Israel. Bush called on Palestinians to elect new leadership and made clear that the United States would have no further direct dealings with Arafat.

After the end of the Iraq war, Bush in April 2003 formally published a document called a "road map" to Middle East peace, which had been negotiated the previous summer by diplomats from the United States, the European Union, Russia, and the United Nations (the so-called "quartet"). The road map called on both Israel and the Palestinians to make concessions, in a series of stages, with the goal of a final peace agreement and creation of a Palestinian state by 2005. In June 2003 Bush met at the Red Sea resort town of Aqaba, Jordan, with Sharon and Mahmoud Abbas, whom Arafat had appointed—under U.S. pressure—as Palestinian prime minister. Bush promised to "ride herd" on the two sides until they reached a peace agreement. But renewed violence and political upheavals in the Palestinian community quickly ended any hopes for rapid progress, and just months after making his pledge, Bush turned his attention elsewhere.

Yet another potential opportunity for peace emerged in late 2004, when Arafat died after a brief illness and the more moderate Abbas seemed poised to take over the Palestinian leadership. Bush again promised help, but said it was now up to the Israelis and Palestinians to take the lead in resolving their decades-old conflict.

Another long-term, and even deadlier, conflict appeared to be approaching its end, in part because of active international diplomacy by the Bush administration. This was a civil war between the government of Sudan (dominated by Muslims of Arab heritage) and rebels in the southern part of the country, most of them black Africans who had adopted Christianity or held to local animist beliefs. More than 2 million people had died in the current stage of that war, which began in 1983.

At the urging of religious groups in the United States, Bush sent former Republican senator John Danforth of Missouri to Sudan as his personal representative. Diplomacy by Danforth and United Nations officials helped lead to a cease-fire in 2003 and a formal peace agreement in January 2005.

No sooner had that conflict begun to wind down, however, than another one arose in Sudan, this time in the western region known as Darfur. There, militias aligned with and armed by the government used violence and terror tactics to suppress another rebellion. The fighting quickly drove hundreds of thousands of people from their homes and raised international fears about a death toll of gigantic proportions. After an investigation by U.S. diplomats, Secretary of State Powell in September 2004 declared that the killing represented a "genocide"; it was the first time any major government had issued such a finding while a conflict was under way. Powell's statement stood in sharp contrast to the Clinton administration's unwillingness to take a forthright stand during the 1994 genocide in Rwanda. Despite Powell's dramatic pronouncement, the United States limited its action to rhetoric, providing relief aid to the victims, and sending money for a limited peacekeeping force manned by African nations.

The Bush administration's other notable intervention in Africa came in July 2003, when a grisly civil war in Liberia reached a crisis point. Under pressure from the United Nations and religious leaders in the United States, Bush sent Navy ships carrying about 2,000 U.S. Marines to the coast of Liberia. That show of force was enough to cause Liberian leader Charles Taylor—who had fomented conflicts in several neighboring countries as well as his own—to flee into exile in Nigeria, thus creating at least a possibility for peace.

Closer to home, the Bush administration intervened only occasionally in the affairs of other countries in the Western Hemisphere. Cuba was the one persistent exception to the rule, as Bush acted repeatedly to tighten the economic sanctions that had failed for four decades to unseat Fidel Castro. In this case, Bush clearly was motivated by domestic politics: anti-Castro Cuban-Americans had been among Bush's strongest supporters in 2000, and it was widely assumed that their support would be necessary again for Bush to carry Florida in the 2004 presidential election. In February 2004 Bush also joined with France and other countries in pressuring Haiti's president, Jean-Bertrand Aristide, to give up power. The Clinton administration had restored Aristide to office a decade earlier following a military coup, but Haiti continued a slide into anarchy and even deeper poverty. A new U.S.-backed government, protected by a United Nations peacekeeping force, made little progress toward restoring order during the rest of 2004.

The Bush administration had more trouble deciding on a clear-cut course of action for dealing with an even pricklier leftist Latin American leader: Hugo Chavez of Venezuela. A former Army colonel, Chavez had won the presidency in 1999 and embarked on program of social spending to improve the lives of the country's desperately poor majority. Chavez also consolidated political power in his own hands, effectively marginalizing the business community and anyone else who questioned his goals or methods. He also criticized the United States in harsh terms and threatened to export what he called his "Bolivarian revolution" to other countries in the region. A handful of business and military leaders staged a coup against Chavez in April 2002; apparently relieved to be rid of Chavez, the White House issued statements widely interpreted as endorsing the coup. Two days later, Chavez clawed his way back to power. A superb political tactician, Chavez also used stalling tactics later in 2002 and all through 2003 to delay an opposition-sponsored referendum that sought to oust him from office via the ballot box. By the time the referendum finally was held, in August 2004, Venezuelans had lost patience with the disorganized opposition and instead handed Chavez a convincing victory—one that left the Bush administration with no leverage over events in a country that was a major source of oil for the United States.

If any Latin American leader could have expected to benefit from the Bush presidency, it was Vicente Fox, who had been elected president of Mexico in July 2000, breaking a seven-decade monopoly on power by the center-left Institutional Revolutionary Party. Bush and Fox, both conservative former businessmen, appeared to have much in common, and early in 2001 they pledged to work to resolve the long-festering dispute over Mexican immigration into the United States. After the Sept. 11 terrorist attacks, however, any talk of immigration reform became politically risky in the United States. Bush put the initiative in the deep freeze—leaving an embarrassed Fox with nothing to show for his friendship with the American president. For that and other domestic reasons Fox continued to falter politically, and by 2003 opposition parties had blocked nearly all elements of his taxation and economic stimulus agenda.

ADMINISTRATION DIVISIONS

More than any other administration in recent decades, the Bush administration appeared to be divided into two distinct camps when it came to foreign policy and national security matters. On the one hand were a few high-level pragmatists, led by Secretary of State Powell, who favored old-fashioned diplomacy and working through multilateral institutions, including the United Nations. A retired Army general (and chair of the Joint Chiefs of Staff under the first president Bush and then Clinton), Powell often appeared skeptical that either diplomacy or military action, by themselves, could solve major problems, and so he advocated a broad approach that sought to gain support for U.S. positions from key international allies. Powell and his like-minded colleagues in the administration were outnumbered, and in most cases outmaneuvered, by officials in the White House and Pentagon who routinely favored a more muscular approach to policy making, generally by setting out U.S. positions and demanding that other countries toe the line. The White House went to great lengths to keep Bush above this fray, and both he and his national security advisor, Condoleezza Rice, rarely intervened to settle internal policy disputes, some of which lingered for months.

Homeland Security

In the aftermath of the terrorist attacks on the World Trade Center and the Pentagon, Bush moved quickly not only to go after the al Qaeda network in Afghanistan but to heighten homeland security. Brushing aside concerns about a diminution of civil liberties, the administration sought, and Congress quickly provided, expanded powers to track down, arrest, and prosecute suspected terrorists. The law (PL 107-56), formally titled the USA Patriot Act, was cleared six weeks after the attacks. Among is dozens of provisions, it permitted law enforcement agencies to obtain nationwide search warrants and permission to conduct "roving wiretaps," made it easier for investigators to monitor Internet communications, permitted searches of suspects' property without advance notice, allowed the indefinite detention of immigrants viewed as national security threats, authorized disclosures of grand jury information to law enforcement agencies, tightened banking regulations in a bid to curtail money laundering, and lifted the statute of limitations on some terrorist crimes. In the only significant concession to legislators' concerns, the administration agreed that many surveillance provisions would expire in 2005 unless Congress reauthorized them.

In November 2001 Bush signed sweeping airport security legislation (PL 107-71) that within a year had replaced the thousands of airport contract workers who screened baggage and passengers with federal employees hired and trained by the Transportation Department. The president initially opposed such an expansion of the federal workforce, but he backed down after polling showed that the public strongly favored putting federal workers in charge of airport security.

Bush also initially opposed creation of the new Department of Homeland Security, which combined all or parts of twenty-two federal agencies responsible for counterterrorism in a single entity. It was the largest reorganization of the federal bureaucracy since the start of the Cold War. Bush had set up an office of homeland security within the White House immediately after Sept. 11, and he insisted that it was capable of providing the needed security. The office was headed by former Pennsylvania governor Tom Ridge, who frustrated lawmakers by repeatedly refusing to testify on the administration's plans for protecting the nation against another terrorist act.

Amid increased congressional scrutiny of pre–Sept. 11 intelligence lapses and declining public approval ratings, the Bush administration reversed its position in June 2002 and offered a proposal to create a Homeland Security Department. The House quickly approved a measure closely tracking the president's proposal, but the Democratic Senate sought to ensure the department's employees retained their rights to union representation. Bush had asked for "significant flexibility" in hiring, pay, and personnel management and threatened to veto the bill if he did not get it. Debate stalled until after the midterm election. When Republicans won Senate control—after arguing on the campaign trail that Democrats who opposed the president on the homeland security bill were unpatriotic—they quickly pushed through the measure, which allowed the new department to write its own personnel rules.

In other action following Sept. 11, Congress appropriated $40 billion for the response and recovery, an amount that dwarfed the size of any previous supplemental spending package. The president was given unprecedented leeway to spend half the money as he saw fit so long as he told Congress how he planned to use the funds; the remainder was divided between recovery efforts in New York, Pennsylvania, and Virginia and homeland defense efforts. Congress also cleared a $15 billion package to help the nation's airline industry, which was hobbled by the economic downturn in general and a fear of flying in particular.

Bush's ability to bob and weave in response to political necessity also was illustrated by his handling of calls for a high-level investigation of the government's failure to prevent the Sept. 11 attacks. Bush at first opposed such an investigation, apparently fearing Democrats would use its findings to attack him and his administration. But families of the victims of the Sept. 11 attacks mounted unstoppable political pressure for an investigation, and Bush relented in late 2002. A high-level commission headed by former New Jersey governor Thomas H. Kean (a Republican) and former U.S. representative Lee H. Hamilton (an Indiana Democrat) began its work in 2003 but had to fight for access to administration documents. The commission held several widely publicized hearings that demonstrated—more graphically than two previous congressional reports—how the CIA, the FBI, and other government agencies missed or misread evidence that Islamist terrorists were planning a major attack on U.S. soil. The most riveting testimony came on March 24, 2004, from Richard Clarke, who had been President Clinton's chief counterterrorism advisor and had served in that capacity during the early months of Bush's presidency. Clarke said the new Bush administration had given fighting terrorism a low priority—until the Sept. 11 attacks.

The Sept. 11 commission, as it was known, issued its report on July 22, 2004. In deliberately understated but nevertheless powerful prose it described how U.S. intelligence agencies and policymakers had failed to imagine the possibility that terrorists would fly airplanes into buildings. As was *de rigueur* in such a report, the commission laid out dozens of recommendations for bureaucratic and policy changes, starting with appointment of a single official with broad authority to coordinate the nation's fifteen intelligence agencies. Sen. John F. Kerry, the presumed Democratic presidential candidate, immediately embraced most of the panel's findings and recommendations. Bush hesitated, however, saying his administration needed to study the report, even though the broad nature of its conclusions had been known for months. Facing election-year pressure to act, Bush eventually embraced the recommendations and urged Congress to adopt legislation putting the key ones into law. Political maneuvering held up final action until after the November elections, when Bush was called upon to nudge reluctant Republicans. Bush on Dec. 17 signed into law (PL 108-458) the resulting legislation that implemented many—but not all—of the Sept. 11 commission recommendations. Rarely had Congress acted so quickly—in a matter of just a few months—to adopt the recommendations of such a commission. Even so, commission members vowed to keep up the political pressure to ensure that the administration and Congress did not backtrack and that its other recommendations were acted on as well.

The Economy

In addition to potential threats to the homeland from another terrorist attack, the president also had to deal with a desultory economy. Bush had the misfortune of entering office just as the longest economic expansion in modern American was coming to an end. The economic slowdown tipped into mild recession in the aftermath of the 2001 terrorist attacks. The economy began to grow again at the end of the year, and interest and inflation rates remained low throughout Bush's first term. But growth was fitful, and businesses added comparatively few new jobs. Bush just narrowly escaped becoming the first president since Herbert Hoover (1929–1933) to register a net job loss during his term.

The economic slowdown—combined with massive tax cuts, spending on the wars in Iraq and Afghanistan, and funding for domestic priorities—also helped turn the budget surplus Bush inherited into record budget shortfalls—$374 billion in fiscal 2003 and $412 billion in fiscal 2004. Those deficits were likely to greatly hamper, and probably block, legislation calling for significant new spending.

But when Bush took office in 2001, surpluses were still soaring, and the president won quick approval for his chief domestic policy priority—the deepest tax cut since reductions President Ronald Reagan (1981–1989) pushed to enactment in 1981, the first year of his presidency. The measure, which carried out the centerpiece of Bush's 2000 election campaign, reduced personal income taxes by $1.4 trillion through fiscal 2005. Its central features were a reduction in income tax rates, alleviation of the so-called marriage penalty, a phase-out of the estate tax, and expansion of the child tax credit. To win support, particularly in the evenly divided Senate, the benefits in the bill were focused more on low-income taxpayers than Bush had originally proposed, and the total was about three-fourths of what he had originally sought.

Two years later, in 2003, with both the budget deficit and the sluggish job creation increasingly controversial, Bush pushed through a second major tax cut of $330 billion over eleven years. Bush said the tax cut was needed to put the post–Sept. 11 economy back on sure footing. Although lawmakers reduced and reworked Bush's initial proposal, the measure still closely followed top Republican fiscal priorities, including accelerating the reductions in individual rates that were part of the 2001 tax law, allowing faster write-offs for business investment, and reducing individual taxes on corporate dividends and capital gains. To gain the support of Senate moderates, it also contained additional federal aid to help states cope with severe fiscal problems. The moderate support proved crucial: The bill cleared only because of Vice President Cheney's tie-breaking vote in the Senate.

In 2004 Congress cleared a $146 billion package of tax break extensions for individuals and families. The measure, passed just six weeks before the election, won broad bipartisan support. But Congress did not even take up Bush's request to make the 2001 and 2003 tax cuts permanent, given mounting concern about the widening budget deficit.

After the economy faltered in 2001, Bush consistently portrayed the tax cuts as the best way to stimulate investment, economic growth, and job creation. Democrats derided the tax reductions, saying their main intent was to benefit the rich at the expense of the poor and the middle class. In somewhat of a role reversal from earlier quarrels over budget deficits, Democrats also argued that the tax cuts adopted after 2001 were fiscally irresponsible in the face of mounting deficits. The Bush administration contended that although the dollar amount of the deficit had reached record highs in 2003 and 2004, the budget deficit was still well within the normal range when measured as a share of the entire economy.

Nonetheless, Bush promised in his fiscal 2005 budget to cut the deficit in half within five years. Democrats and some Republicans immediately challenged the president, pointing out that he was not counting in the budget some potentially expensive programs, including the costs of the ongoing military operations in Afghanistan and Iraq. They also said that anticipated spending cuts in the Bush budget were unrealistic.

Democrats and some Republicans also complained that Bush's policies did not do enough to create jobs more quickly, particularly in the states that were losing manufacturing jobs. One administration effort to boost manufacturing jobs backfired. In 2002 Bush imposed high tariffs on steel imports only to withdraw them in 2003 after the World Trade Organization ruled they were illegal and automakers and other users of steel in the United States complained that the tariffs were making their products uncompetitive and thus costing more jobs than they were creating.

Domestic Issues

After Sept. 11, most domestic issues unrelated to homeland security or the economy and federal spending receded into the background. Still, the Bush administration was highly effective in winning congressional approval for some of its top priorities, killing legislation it did not want, and using a handful of congressional losses to good benefit on the campaign trail. Bush accomplished all this without vetoing a single bill passed by Congress.

EDUCATION AND HEALTH

Although Republicans traditionally promoted a reduced role and size for government, two of Bush's top priorities represented major extensions of the federal government into American life. The first was the president's proposal to tie federal education aid to improvement in test scores, a move that required schools to follow federal rules and regulations to a greater extent than ever before if they wanted to receive federal aid. Dubbed the No Child Left Behind Act, the measure, passed by Congress in December 2001, was the most ambitious overhaul to date of the 1965 Elementary and Secondary Education Act (PL 89-10). Although Congress declined to go along with Bush's plan for government vouchers that could be spent on private school tuition, the measure contained the thrust of Bush's education policy proposals, requiring annual student testing and school improvements aimed at helping disadvantaged students catch up with their peers and creating consequences for schools with chronically low test scores.

At Democratic insistence the bill also authorized substantial increases in federal aid to education, which neither the president nor Congress followed through on with actual money. Moreover, after two years of struggling with what were said to be confusing and costly rules and regulations imposed by the Department of Education, a growing number of educators and officials were raising objections to federal implementation of the law and in some cases to the law itself. By 2004 nearly one-third of the nation's schools had been labeled low-performing under the standards, and critics in both political parties were beginning to say the law was unworkable.

The second priority was a prescription drug benefit program, under Medicare, for the nation's senior citizens. The measure, which the president signed into law in December 2003, represented the largest entitlement program enacted since Medicare itself was passed in the 1960s. Although many Republicans generally opposed entitlement programs because of the difficulty of controlling spending (benefits had to be paid to anyone who met the eligibility criteria of an entitlement program), Republicans, and their Democratic colleagues, were responding to promises both parties had made to help the elderly cope with the rising costs of prescription drugs. Republicans found the law palatable because it expanded the role played by private insurers and created tax-free health saving accounts to cover the costs of unreimbursed medical expenses. The law also included billions of dollars for hospitals, physicians, and other providers in rural areas—money that helped attract bipartisan support for the overhaul.

Democrats, however, were angered that the final bill did not allow seniors to import prescription drugs from Canada, where prices tended to be lower than in the United States, and that it prohibited the federal government from negotiating with the pharmaceutical companies for discounts on prescription drugs for the elderly. Democrats said these aspects of the bill showed that the administration's real interest was in helping the drug industry rather than aiding senior citizens. Democrats and some Republicans were even more irate when it was revealed early in 2004 that administration officials had known for several months, but not told Congress, that the projected cost of the new prescription drug program was likely to be well over $500 billion in its first ten years; the figure Congress had worked with during debate on the bill was $400 billion.

ENERGY AND ENVIRONMENT

Bush's policies on energy and environmental protection were controversial from the outset. A former oil industry executive, Bush had long advocated relaxing government regulations and instead allowing what he called "market forces" to set the pace on protecting the environment. He made no secret of his intention to ease or reverse many of the environmental protection regulations put in place by the Clinton administration. An energy plan, drafted by a task forced headed by Vice President Cheney and made public just four months after Bush took office, touched off heated controversy because it heavily emphasized energy production and called for reducing environmental regulations that were opposed by energy companies. Bush said the energy plan struck a balance between meeting energy needs and protecting the environment.

Environmental groups and their supporters, however, called the plan an energy industry "wish list." In addition to noting Bush's oil industry background, they also pointed out that Cheney had been chair of the board of Halliburton Inc., an oil service company, for several years before becoming vice president. Environmentalists, who had largely been excluded from participation in the task force, also observed that several of the industry executives who had attended a meeting in which many of the task force recommendations originated were appointed to senior positions within the Bush administration—the better to promote their policies, the environmentalists contended.

Few of the task force recommendations required congressional action. Several of those that did were packaged into a bill that supporters said would reduce America's dependence on foreign oil and create thousands of jobs to bolster the economy in the process. One of the more controversial features of that plan was a proposal to permit oil exploration and drilling in the Arctic National Wildlife Refuge, the country's largest and ecologically most important remaining wilderness. The House and Senate approved versions of the energy bill in the 107th Congress, but were unable to reconcile their differences. In 2003 after both chambers again approved differing versions, Republican leaders wrote a final bill in secret, but were then unable to overcome a Senate filibuster against the measure.

Bush was able to undertake most of the other task force recommendations on his own authority, either by issuing an executive order or by sending directives to federal agencies. During Bush's first term, the administration rolled back Clinton administration rules protecting nearly 60 million acres of national forests from development and took steps to pare back regulations on clean water, endangered species, wilderness protection, and other matters.

One of the president's most controversial moves—a new rule reducing requirements for electric utilities and other smokestack industries to install updated pollution-control equipment at existing plants—remained tied up in a court challenge from several states.

The administration committed one major political blunder when it reversed a Clinton policy reducing permissible levels of arsenic in the nation's drinking water. That move led to widespread protests that the administration was putting business interests ahead of public health. A chastened administration eventually reversed itself and stuck by the Clinton policy.

Bush also backed away from his own campaign promise to require power plants to reduce carbon dioxide emissions, which were a main component of the so-called greenhouse gases generally believed to be the main cause of global warming. About six weeks after taking office, Bush said that he had decided to reverse his position and would not impose mandatory emissions reductions on carbon dioxide. According to press reports, Bush had come under intense pressure from congressional Republicans and representatives of the oil and gas industries. The policy reversal was the first of two important steps the president took on global warming issues. In June 2001 Bush stopped U.S. participation in the 1997 Kyoto Protocol, which was intended to reduce greenhouse gas emissions by the industrialized countries.

SOCIAL ISSUES

Bush's views on many social issues of the day coincided with those of the conservative and religious groups that formed the most solid part of his base constituency. But on at least two key issues—gay marriage and stem cell research—the president's position differed, if only marginally, from that of his base. Bush's key initiative in this area was his faith-based initiative, in which he called for making federal money available to several new categories of faith-based social services. After legislation to implement the initiative died in the 107th Congress, the administration issued an executive order allowing church-sponsored groups to retain their religious identity when managing federally funded social programs.

The Bush administration also won passage of a ban on a procedure that opponents called "partial birth" abortion. Enacted in November 2003, it was the first federal statute to restrict an abortion procedure since the Supreme Court legalized abortions in the 1973 case of *Roe v. Wade.* The ban, which had long been sought by pro-life forces, was immediately challenged in three separate federal district courts; those cases were still pending at the end of 2004. Supporters of abortion rights who saw the ban as an attempt to undermine the *Roe* decision were further distressed in 2004 when Congress cleared legislation making it a separate offense to harm a fetus during the commission of a federal crime against a pregnant woman. It was the first time federal legal status was given to a fetus.

The Bush administration also pleased its conservative supporters when it sought to refocus federal programs dealing with sex education and reproductive health on sexual abstinence. One of the more controversial policies was a requirement that a portion of federal funds used to fight HIV/AIDS overseas be used on abstinence programs. Detractors said it was unrealistic to expect abstinence programs to have much effect on a sexually transmitted disease in cultures where sexual norms were different from those in the United States.

Bush surprised observers in August 2001 when he announced that he would permit limited federal funding of scientific research on human embryonic stem cells. Scientists hoped such research would lead to new cures and treatment for many debilitating conditions such as Parkinson's disease, diabetes, and spinal cord injuries. But social conservatives opposed the research because the stem cells were extracted from human embryos that died in the process. Bush's endorsement of limited funding was a reversal of his campaign pronouncements that he was flatly opposed to such research, and he was taken to task by many social conservatives who equated killing human embryos with abortion.

The issue arose again during the 2004 election campaign, when Nancy Reagan, among others, called on Bush to further loosen federal restrictions on funding the research. Her husband, former President Reagan, who died in June, suffered from Alzheimer's disease—one of the conditions that some medical researchers thought might be treatable some day with stem cell therapies.

In the eyes of many social conservatives, Bush was also slow in calling for a constitutional amendment banning gay marriage. Bush had long professed his belief in marriage as a union between a man and a woman but after the Massachusetts Supreme Judicial Court struck down the state's ban on gay marriage in November 2003, the president came under intense pressure to support an amendment to the federal Constitution barring same-sex marriage. Bush resisted endorsing such an amendment for several months. But after the Massachusetts court confirmed its earlier ruling and San Francisco's mayor authorized gay marriages in that city, Bush could no longer ignore the clamor from conservatives. On Feb. 24, 2004, he announced his support for a constitutional amendment defining marriage as a union between a man and a woman.

Neither chamber of Congress, however, mustered the two-thirds vote required to pass a constitutional amendment. That may have reflected the ambivalence of the American public about tinkering with the Constitution. But the votes also allowed Bush campaign to energize social conservatives upset by court rulings in favor of gay marriage while expending little political capital on the doomed amendments. Eleven states put referendums barring gay marriage on their November 2004 ballots, and many political observers said conservatives who might otherwise have stayed away from the polls turned out to support the bans and stayed on to vote for Bush. Conservative turnout in favor of Ohio's gay marriage referendum was widely credited with giving Bush the win in that crucial state over Massachusetts senator John Kerry. Bush's victory in Ohio gave him enough electoral votes to win a second term in office.

NOMINATIONS

The majority of President Bush's nominees for his cabinet and the federal judiciary met with little or no opposition. Two cabinet appointees ran into significant opposition, but were confirmed. Most contentious were a handful of judicial nominations from the more conservative ranks of the GOP base. Those choices touched off a rancorous debate that had not been resolved by the end of 2004 and still threatened to deeply divide the Senate.

Environmental groups tried to defeat the nomination of Gale A. Norton to be Interior secretary. Norton, the former attorney general of Colorado, was a protégé of Reagan administration Interior secretary James G. Watt, a controversial figure abhorred by environmentalists for policies he advocated and tried to put into effect. Environmentalist groups, who spent more than $1 million on an advertising campaign to defeat the nomination, warned that Norton was likely to support efforts to open public lands to drilling, mining, and other resource development. Despite the organized opposition, Norton easily won confirmation, 75–24.

A much closer vote came on Bush's nomination of John Ashcroft, a former senator from Missouri, to be attorney general. Ashcroft's conservative stands on issues such as abortion and civil rights, and the role he played in thwarting some of President Clinton's judicial nominees, made him a lightning rod for criticism from congressional Democrats, as well as from pro-choice and civil liberties organizations. After weeks of acrimonious debate and intense lobbying by outside groups, the Senate confirmed Ashcroft on a vote or 58–42. Eight Democrats joined all fifty Republicans in support of Ashcroft.

Opposition Democrats said the forty-two votes cast against Ashcroft—the most ever cast against a nominee for attorney general—sent a message to the White House not to choose nominees for the federal bench, especially the Supreme Court, from the GOP's most conservative wing. It was a message that the White House chose to ignore, and the fight over President Bush's selections for federal judgeships became one of the harshest partisan disputes of the first term.

Senate Republicans made a priority of trying to help Bush reshape the federal judiciary in a more conservative vein, while the Democratic majority and its allies in liberal advocacy groups were intent on setting boundaries for that effort. Both parties viewed the fight, which focused on a handful of appellate court seats and on the pace of Senate action on Bush's nominees, as a proxy war for the next Supreme Court nominee. There had not been a vacancy on the high court since 1994, and a number of the justices by the end of 2004 were in their eighties and at least two were known to have health problems.

During the 107th Congress, the Senate confirmed 100 nominees to the federal appellate and district courts. In 2002, with Democrats in control of the Senate, the Judiciary Committee rejected two of Bush's more conservative picks on party-line votes. Democrats objected to Charles W. Pickering Sr., a federal judge from Mississippi, and to Priscilla Owen, a Texas Supreme Court justice, both nominated to a seat on the Fifth Circuit Court of Appeals, largely because of their opposition to abortion. The committee did not take a vote on twenty-eight other judicial nominees.

The standoff over judicial appointments escalated in 2003 when Senate Democrats—now in the minority—mounted the first coordinated filibusters against judicial nominations in more than a quarter century, blocking six of President's Bush's choices from taking appeals courts seats. It was the first time filibusters had succeeded against judicial nominees since 1968, when Republicans blocked the elevation of Supreme Court Justice Abe Fortas to be chief justice.

At the beginning of 2004, Bush exercised his constitutional authority to make appointments during congressional recesses to fill temporarily two appeals court vacancies with two nominees whose appointments had been blocked in 2003. The recess appointments enraged Senate Democrats, who blocked all judicial nominees until May, when Bush promised to make no more recess appointments for the rest of his first term. At that point, Democrats permitted votes to confirm twenty-five of Bush's less controversial nominees. But for various reasons they continued to block eleven others.

Although no further action was taken on these nominees, Senate majority leader Bill Frist, R-Tenn., continued to hint that he might resort to the "nuclear option" in 2005, particularly if the Democrats threatened to filibuster a Supreme Court nominee. With Chief Justice William H. Rehnquist suffering from thyroid cancer, a high court vacancy appeared increasingly likely. The nuclear option—so-called because of the profoundly polarizing effect it would have on partisan Senate relations—would effectively eliminate the filibuster as a tool for thwarting judicial nominees, allowing nominations to be approved by a simple, fifty-one vote majority. The continuing argument over the eleven justices tended to obscure the fact that the Senate confirmed 203 of Bush's nominees to

the federal judiciary during his first term. That represented nearly a quarter of all federal judges.

Bush and the Executive Branch

At the same time that Bush was trying to shape the federal judiciary he also moved to strengthen the presidency. Both he and Vice President Cheney spoke frequently of the need to restore the power of the presidency to it pre-Watergate strength. For example, Bush used his power to make appointments during congressional recesses to put a pair of his more controversial choices on the federal appeals courts—thereby trumping, at least temporarily, the filibuster powers that the minority Senate Democrats had been using to block those nominations.

Bush also made forceful use of "signing statements," the documents that a president often issued when he signed legislation outlining how his administration planned to implement, or not implement, the new law. Although these statements rarely provoked a strong reaction, political scientists and others observed that they could tilt the balance of lawmaking power toward the executive branch by allowing the president to go unchallenged in deciding how, if at all, to carry out his constitutional requirement to "take care that the laws be faithfully executed."

In November 2003 for example, as Bush signed a law (PL 108-106) providing $87.5 billion in supplemental spending for the occupation and reconstruction of Iraq and Afghanistan, he angered lawmakers by putting a short leash on a watchdog that Congress created to keep track of the billions of dollars being spent on rebuilding Iraq. He ordered that the occupant of the inspector general position written into the law by Senate Appropriations Committee Chair Ted Stevens, R-Alaska, "shall refrain from initiating, carrying out or completing and audit or investigation . . . the disclosure of which would constitute a serious threat to national security."

On another front, the White House actively resisted congressional efforts to pry information loose from the executive branch. Bush, for example, refused to testify publicly before the independent commission investigating the Sept. 11 terrorist attacks and initially imposed strict conditions on his private meeting with the commission. The White House also initially refused to release documents related to an intelligence briefing given to the president on Aug. 6, 2001, warning that al Qaeda was planning terrorist attacks against the United States. After the commission issued a subpoena, the White House relented, apparently concerned about the negative political consequences of the president appearing to be hiding something.

One instance where the White House held its ground came in 2002, when Cheney won a lawsuit that sought to force him to tell Congress the names of everyone who had participated in the task force that established the administration's energy policy. The suit was brought by the General Ac-

BUSH'S TOP WHITE HOUSE ADVISERS

Like all presidents, George W. Bush received policy and political advice from many people both inside and outside the White House. In addition to Vice President Dick Cheney, four of Bush's closest advisers were notable for their loyalty and skill.

Karl Rove, who began working with Bush when he first ran for governor of Texas in 1993, was Bush's top political strategist, the man Bush called "The Architect" and the "Boy Genius." A secretive man and an aggressive campaigner, Rove was widely admired—even by his many detractors—for his political acumen.

Rove began his political career with the College Republicans, which he chaired in 1973–1974 and where he met the current president's father. In the late 1970s he worked on the successful campaigns of Texas governor William P. Clements (1979–1983, 1987–1991), a Republican, and of Texas representative Phil Gramm, then a Democrat. In 1981 Rove set up an Austin-based public affairs firm, which he ran until 1999, when he joined Bush's presidential campaign.

Rove served as a senior adviser in the Bush White House during the first term, counseling the president on the political ramifications of policy issues as well as on his reelection campaign. Rove was widely credited with turning out the conservative religious vote in 2004, which was a key factor in Bush's victory over Massachusetts senator John Kerry. In February 2005 Bush elevated Rove to the position of deputy chief of staff.

Bush's other key political strategist was Karen Hughes, a former television news reporter who started in politics as the Texas coordinator for the Reagan-Bush campaign in 1984. Hughes served as Bush's director of communications when he was governor, and then as a special advisor to the president in 2001–2002, where she oversaw the offices of the press secretary, media affairs, speechwriting, and communications. It was Hughes who was responsible for shaping the public's image of the president and his policies. Bush once remarked that he wanted Hughes in the room whenever a major decision was made.

Midway through Bush's first term, Hughes left the White House to return to her family in Texas. But she remained in daily contact with the Bush campaign operation and spoke with Bush by telephone several times each week.

In August 2004 she rejoined the campaign full-time. In March 2005 Bush made Hughes the undersecretary of state for public diplomacy. Bush defined Hughes' job as an "aggressive effort to share and communicate America's fundamental values while respecting the cultures and traditions of other nations"—an assignment that many considered one of the toughest in Washington.

While some pundits called Hughes the most powerful woman in the White House, others gave that honor to Condoleezza Rice, Bush's top foreign policy adviser who served as chair of the National Security Council. Rice had planned on a career as a concert pianist but changed her mind after taking a course in international affairs (taught by Joseph Korbel, father of President Bill Clinton's secretary of state Madeleine Albright). Rice became a tenured professor at Stanford University with a deep interest in Russia and Eastern Europe. She served as the National Security Council director of Soviet and Eastern European Affairs in the first President Bush's National Security Council.

Rice returned to Stanford, where she served as provost, but took a leave of absence to be Bush's foreign policy adviser during the 2000 presidential campaign. She resigned her Stanford position in December 2000 when Bush named her chair of the National Security Council. In November 2005 Bush named Rice to succeed Colin Powell as secretary of state.

An outspoken defender of the administration's decision to invade Iraq, Rice was sometimes criticized for what some opponents saw as her misrepresentation of prewar intelligence on Iraq. During her confirmation hearings in early 2005 some Democrats also questioned whether her personal closeness to the president would make it less likely that she would offer an independent assessment on foreign policy issues. Most Republicans said such criticism was unwarranted. Rice was frequently mentioned as a possible Republican candidate for president in the future. She claimed no interest in the presidency, but said, only partly in jest, that she would some day love to be commissioner of the National Football League.

The fourth member of the quartet of advisers was Andrew H. Card, Jr., the president's chief of staff, who managed the day-to-day operations of the White House. Card served in the Reagan White House in several positions, including director of intergovernmental affairs, and he was deputy chief of staff under George H. W. Bush, until mid-1992, when Bush named him transportation secretary. From 1993 until he joined the transition staff for President-elect George W. Bush, Card served as General Motors vice president for governmental relations. Known in the White House as "The Chief," Card had a reputation for being low-key and unflappable.

counting Office (since renamed the General Accountability Office), the investigative arm of Congress. Environmentalists had charged that the controversial plan was written largely by energy industry executives and lobbyists with little input from environmentalists, academics, or other stakeholders.

In an administration that prided itself on shaping the public perception of events as well as the events themselves, the Sept. 11 attacks, and the Bush administration's response to them, may have indirectly aided Bush in his efforts to establish the executive branch as the "first among equals."

While Bush did not exercise any new powers in his role as commander in chief, the public perception of Bush as a strong and unbending war president lent an aura of strength to the presidency that it might otherwise not have had.

By speaking with an unusually unified voice, the Bush administration also added to the perception of a strong presidency. Unlike any other White House within recent memory, the Bush team did a remarkable job of staying "on message." As a consequence, the administration was able to shape the news about its policies and activities, presenting administration achievements in the most positive and best political light possible and downplaying, or even ignoring, matters that could tarnish the president's image.

Bush himself became adept at presenting the message and then reinforcing it at every possible turn. On the failure of the economy to put people back to work, for example, Bush said repeatedly that he would not be satisfied with the economic recovery until every American who wanted a job had one. He then insisted that the best way to create jobs was through the massive tax reductions that he had proposed and Congress had enacted. Repetition of this single message, coupled with gradual improvement in the job market, tended to blunt the Democratic claim that Bush was not doing enough to get Americans back to work.

The Bush administration was also adept at deflecting blame when something went wrong that might reflect badly on the president. After revelations of accounting fraud and other misdeeds led to the bankruptcy of several major American corporations—including the Texas energy giant Enron, which had been an important contributor to the Bush campaign—the administration insisted that the problem was limited to a handful of unscrupulous individuals and companies. Later allegations of pervasive misdeeds in the mutual fund and insurance industries raised little public comment from administration officials.

Similarly, in the wake of the Abu Ghraib prisoner abuse scandal, the administration insisted that the misdeeds had been committed by "just a handful" of soldiers and were not sanctioned by any top officials. Democrats and human rights organizations disputed those claims, which were further undermined in June 2004 with the publication of a Justice Department legal opinion appearing to condone torture of terrorist suspects. The Justice Department later rewrote the opinion to prohibit torture, but critics said the original language demonstrated that the administration had lowered the standards of acceptable behavior, thus creating the atmosphere that made the abuses at Abu Ghraib and other detention centers possible. Although several lower-level military personnel were court-martialed or other otherwise disciplined, no action was taken against any senior military or civilian defense officials in Washington.

Bush's Relations with Congress

Despite his reputation for stubbornness and a Congress closely divided between the two political parties, especially in the Senate, Bush had the highest presidential support score (81 percent) of any president since Lyndon B. Johnson (1963–1969) and the third highest since Congressional Quarterly began measuring congressional support of the president's positions in 1953. Bush was aided by wartime patriotism. But the president also benefited from his style for dealing with Congress—a blend of compromise, careful selection of battles, and tactical shifts to avoid defeat.

Perhaps most significantly, Bush reaped the benefits of a like-minded congressional leadership bent on avoiding presidential vetoes and willing to twist arms so that the president could score wins and conserve his political capital for essential battles. Although Bush threatened numerous vetoes to help shape legislation to his liking, he was the first president since John Quincy Adams in the 1820s not to issue a single veto during an entire four-year term.

Reprising a formula he developed with the state legislature during his six years as governor of Texas, Bush's signature strategy on Capitol Hill was to begin by outlining his desires in broad terms, rather than detailed legislative language. Then, after concluding that he had achieved the best outcome possible given the will of Congress, Bush often chose to declare the final compromise a victory—even when some of the principles he set out were scrapped or some of his requests were ignored.

For example, he embraced the $1.4 trillion tax cut bill Congress passed in June 2001, even though it was $290 billion short of the mark he initially said was "just right." On education reform, Congress kept Bush's proposals for annual testing and holding schools accountable for their student's performance, but spurned his campaign call for school vouchers. Nonetheless, when Bush signed the measure, he hailed it as a "great symbol of what is possible in Washington, when good people come together to do what's right."

Second, Bush selected a rather narrow universe of issues on which to take a stand. While many disagreements played out behind the scenes, especially during conference negotiations, Bush pronounced an unambiguous up-or-down preference in advance on relatively few votes, compared with his predecessor Bill Clinton. When he did take a firm stand, it usually was in favor of legislation Congress had drafted and therefore was likely to approve.

When Congress did appear on the edge of approving something Bush opposed, he often worked with the GOP leadership in both houses to eliminate the offending provision in conference. For example, in 2003, the Senate voted to block his administration's proposed changes to overtime rules, and it joined the House in voting for a rider on a spending bill that would have effectively ended the ban on travel to Cuba. At the insistence of White House aides, congressional negotiators on the final spending package jettisoned both riders.

At other times, Bush stayed away from the legislative fray for as long as possible. In 2004, for example, he stayed on the periphery of House-Senate negotiations on the controversial measure to overhaul the nation's intelligence community.

Only in the final weeks did he take a firm stance and intervene with recalcitrant lawmakers in his own party, and then only after success looked attainable and Republican leaders told him his support was necessary.

Finally, Bush showed a flexibility that initially surprised some observers, changing course from week to week, lobbying hard on points, then backing away from them to nudge legislators along. Like a tacking sailboat he would typically first push the right for a strongly conservative measure in the House, where GOP numbers and party discipline could help him achieve what he wanted. Later, he would move back to the center, lobbying for a compromise that often was different from his original desire. For example, in 2001 Bush initially opposed the federalization of airport security workers, helping the GOP win a hard-fought victory in the House, yet he later embraced the final version of the aviation security measure even though it included the very federalization he opposed.

Occasionally, Bush was able to capitalize on his losses, using them to help reinforce his message or solidify his electoral base. On the campaign trail in 2004, for example, Bush frequently criticized Senate Democrats for filibustering a measure that would cap some medical malpractice awards. Bush claimed that the failure to limit such awards was a key factor driving up the costs of health insurance. The criticism was also a dig at the Democratic vice presidential contender, North Carolina senator John Edwards, who had a highly lucrative practice as a trial lawyer representing patients in medical malpractice cases.

In addition, Bush's defeats in 2004 on judicial nominations, a constitutional amendment to ban same-sex marriages, and a highway bill limiting spending played to his political advantage with conservatives, helping to increase his voter turnout in November.

Bush Reelection

That turnout may have been crucial to Bush's election to a second term in office. For much of 2004, it appeared possible that Bush would join his father in the ranks of single-term presidents. The younger Bush was buffeted by so many problems that he was widely seen as politically vulnerable, just as his father had proved to be in 1992. Indeed, on election night, John Kerry, the Democratic challenger, went to bed believing he would be the next president.

In historical terms, Democrats had every reason to believe Bush could be defeated. The Bush administration had succeeded brilliantly in overturning the despotic regime of Saddam Hussein in Iraq. But its plan for quickly stabilizing the country failed, and its unsuccessful efforts to quell a growing insurgency led some critics to compare the situation in Iraq to the "quagmire" of the Vietnam War more than three decades earlier.

At home, the administration was able to produce statistics and technical evidence showing that the economy was recovering nicely from its brief recession in 2001. But many

President George W. Bush and First Lady Laura Bush in Washington, D.C., on Nov. 2, 2004, basking in the afterglow of his victory over Democrat John Kerry a day earlier. *Source: AP Wide World Photos/Pablo Martinez Monsivais*

ordinary Americans remained nervous about their personal economic prospects. They pointed in particular to the slow pace of job creation and the fact that many new jobs were in low-paying service industries, to the steadily rising number of poor and middle-class Americans who could not afford health insurance, to termination of pension plans by many companies, and to many other economic challenges that fell most heavily on middle- and low-income Americans.

Moreover, Bush himself sparked strong feelings. Some voters never forgave him for "stealing" the presidency in 2000. In that election, Democrat Al Gore won the popular vote, but Bush won the all-important electoral college vote when Florida's contested electoral votes were awarded to him on a 5–4 vote of the Supreme Court. After four years in office, Bush had become a deeply polarizing figure, admired by his supporters as a determined and righteous leader and derided by his critics as a demagogue.

For their part, Democrats—seeing an opportunity to oust a sitting Republican president—avoided the self-destructive internal conflicts that had split them in the past. After Kerry took a commanding lead in the early Democratic primaries, the party closed ranks behind the Massachusetts senator and his running mate, North Carolina senator John Edwards, backed the ticket with record amounts of fund-raising, and mounted a sophisticated drive to register and turn out Democratic voters.

Republicans and their supporters matched both the Democratic fund-raising and voter turnout drives—and then some. Moreover, under the brilliant tutelage of his political mentor, Karl Rove, Bush ran an exceptionally focused campaign in which he portrayed his actions as president in the best light possible, reciting over and over again his main messages in simple and declarative terms. On potentially damaging issues such as the prison abuse at Abu Ghraib or the failure to find any weapons of mass destruction in Iraq, Bush showed himself adept at deflecting blame, downplaying the importance of the criticism, or denouncing the critics.

The Bush campaign was also effective in keeping Kerry off balance by raising questions about his character and leadership ability that the Massachusetts Democrat was never able to overcome. Although polls showed that a majority of voters preferred Kerry on domestic issues such as jobs, education, and health and that he had bested Bush in the three presidential debates, Kerry could never shake the image that he "flip-flopped" on the issues or that he had misrepresented his heroism during the Vietnam War. In an election that ultimately turned on which candidate would be the stronger leader against outside threats to the United States, a majority of voters appeared to place their trust in the sitting Republican president.

Exit polling showed that about one-fifth of the voters cited "terrorism" as the most important issue, and 86 percent of those voters cast their ballots for Bush. In contrast, 15 percent of those polled said that Iraq was the most important issue, and 74 percent of those voters backed Kerry.

Much was also made on the political talk shows of exit polling showing that more than a fifth of the voters cited "moral values" as the issue of most importance to them, and nearly 80 percent of those voters cast their ballots for Bush. Although the term was never defined, it was clear that many religious conservatives were motivated to go to the polls to register their opposition to same-sex marriage. Referendums barring gay marriage were on the ballots in eleven states, and they all passed with at least 60 percent of the vote. One of those states was Ohio, where voters who turned out to back the referendum and stayed to vote for Bush were widely credited with giving the president the victory in that state and in the Electoral College. Bush won the state with 118,601 votes, enough for Kerry to decide that a recount was unlikely to change the outcome. Kerry, who had gone to bed early in the morning of Nov. 3 thinking that he had won the election, conceded to Bush the following afternoon.

The president won the popular vote by just over 3 million votes in record turnout of 122.3 million ballots cast; he won 286 electoral college votes to Kerry's 251. Together with a net gain of four seats in the Senate and three seats in the House, Republicans viewed the election as a smashing victory for the party that portended Republican control of the political landscape for some time to come. Others were more cautious, noting that while the pendulum seemed to be swinging toward the Republican side of the electorate, it still had not moved far from the center. And, they warned, a centrist electorate could balk if the Republican leadership tried to advance a conservative agenda too far too soon.

Appendix

Glossary of Congressional Terms

AA—(*See Administrative Assistant.*)

Absence of a Quorum—Absence of the required number of members to conduct business in a house or a committee. When a quorum call or roll-call vote in a house establishes that a quorum is not present, no debate or other business is permitted except a motion to adjourn or motions to request or compel the attendance of absent members, if necessary by arresting them.

Absolute Majority—A vote requiring approval by a majority of all members of a house rather than a majority of members present and voting. Also referred to as constitutional majority.

Account—Organizational units used in the federal budget primarily for recording spending and revenue transactions.

Act—(1) A bill passed in identical form by both houses of Congress and signed into law by the president or enacted over the president's veto. A bill also becomes an act without the president's signature if he does not return it to Congress within ten days (Sundays excepted) and if Congress has not adjourned within that period. (2) Also, the technical term for a bill passed by at least one house and engrossed.

Ad Hoc Select Committee—A temporary committee formed for a special purpose or to deal with a specific subject. Conference committees are ad hoc joint committees. A House rule adopted in 1975 authorizes the Speaker to refer measures to special ad hoc committees, appointed by the Speaker with the approval of the House.

Adjourn—A motion to adjourn is a formal motion to end a day's session or meeting of a house or a committee. A motion to adjourn usually has no conditions attached to it, but it sometimes may specify the day or time for reconvening or make reconvening subject to the call of the chamber's presiding officer or the committee's chairman. In both houses, a motion to adjourn is of the highest privilege, takes precedence over all other motions, is not debatable, and must be put to an immediate vote. Adjournment of a house ends its legislative day. For this reason, the House or Senate sometimes adjourns for only one minute, or some other brief period of time, during the course of a day's session. The House does not permit a motion to adjourn after it has resolved into Committee of the Whole or when the previous question has been ordered on a measure to final passage without an intervening motion.

Adjourn for More Than Three Days—Under Article I, Section 5 of the Constitution, neither house may adjourn for more than three days without the approval of the other. The necessary approval is given in a concurrent resolution to which both houses have agreed.

Adjournment *Sine Die*—Final adjournment of an annual or two-year session of Congress; literally, adjournment without a day. The two houses must agree to a privileged concurrent resolution for such an adjournment. A *sine die* adjournment precludes Congress from meeting again until the next constitutionally fixed date of a session (Jan. 3 of the following year) unless Congress determines otherwise by law or the president calls it into special session. Article II, Section 3 of the Constitution authorizes the president to adjourn both houses until such time as the president thinks proper when the two houses cannot agree to a time of adjournment. No president, however, has ever exercised this authority.

Adjournment to a Day (and Time) Certain—An adjournment that fixes the next date and time of meeting for one or both houses. It does not end an annual session of Congress.

Administration Bill—A bill drafted in the executive office of the president or in an executive department or agency to implement part of the president's program. An administration bill is introduced in Congress by a member who supports it or as a courtesy to the administration.

Administrative Assistant (AA)—The title usually given to a member's chief aide, political advisor, and head of office staff. The administrative assistant often represents the member at meetings with visitors or officials when the member is unable (or unwilling) to attend.

Adoption—The usual parliamentary term for approval of a conference report. It is also commonly applied to amendments.

Advance Appropriation—In an appropriation act for a particular fiscal year, an appropriation that does not become available for spending or obligation until a subsequent fiscal year. The amount of the advance appropriation is counted as part of the budget for the fiscal year in which it becomes available for obligation.

Advance Funding—A mechanism whereby statutory language may allow budget authority for a fiscal year to be increased, and obligations to be incurred, with an offsetting decrease in the budget authority available in the succeeding fiscal year. If not used, the budget authority remains available for obligation in the succeeding fiscal year. Advance funding is sometimes used to provide contingency funding of a few benefit programs.

Adverse Report—A committee report recommending against approval of a measure or some other matter. Committees usually pigeonhole measures they oppose instead of reporting them adversely, but they may be required to report them by a statutory rule or an instruction from their parent body.

Advice and Consent—The Senate's constitutional role in consenting to or rejecting the president's nominations to executive branch and judicial offices and treaties with other nations. Confirmation of nominees requires a simple majority vote of senators present and voting. Treaties must be approved by a two-thirds majority of those present and voting.

Aisle—The center aisle of each chamber. When facing the presiding officer, Republicans usually sit to the right of the aisle, Democrats to the left. When members speak of "my side of the aisle" or "this side," they are referring to their party.

Amendment—A formal proposal to alter the text of a bill, resolution, amendment, motion, treaty, or some other text. Technically, it is a motion. An amendment may strike out (eliminate) part of a text, insert new text, or strike out and insert—that is, replace all or part of the text with new text. The texts of amendments considered on the floor are printed in full in the *Congressional Record.*

Amendments Between the Houses This is a method for reconciling differences between the House and Senate versions of a measure by passing the measure back and forth between the two chambers until both have agreed to identical language.

Amendment in the Nature of a Substitute—Usually, an amendment to replace the entire text of a measure. It strikes out everything after the enacting clause and inserts a version that may be somewhat, substantially, or entirely different. When a committee adopts extensive amendments to a measure, it often incorporates them into such an amendment. Occasionally, the term is applied to an amendment that replaces a major portion of a measure's text.

Amendment Tree—A diagram showing the number and types of amendments that the rules and practices of a house permit to be offered to a measure before any of the amendments is voted on. It shows the relationship of one amendment to the others, and it may also indicate the degree of each amendment, whether it is a perfecting or substitute amendment, the order in which amendments may be offered, and the order in which they are put to a vote. The same type of diagram can be used to display an actual amendment situation.

Annual Authorization—Legislation that authorizes appropriations for a single fiscal year and usually for a specific amount. Under the rules of the authorization-appropriation process, an annually authorized agency or program must be reauthorized each year if it is to receive appropriations for that year. Sometimes Congress fails to enact the reauthorization (or authorization) but nevertheless provides appropriations to continue (or fund) the program, circumventing the rules by one means or another.

Appeal—A member's formal challenge of a ruling or decision by the presiding officer or committee chair. On appeal, a house or a committee may overturn the ruling by majority vote. The right of appeal ensures the body against arbitrary control by the chair. Appeals are rarely made in the House and are even more rarely successful. Rulings are more frequently appealed in the Senate and occasionally overturned, in part because its presiding officer is not the majority party's leader, as in the House.

Apportionment—The action, after each decennial census, of allocating the number of members in the House of Representatives to each state. By law, the total number of House members (not counting delegates and a resident commissioner) is fixed at 435. The number allotted to each state is based approximately on its proportion of the nation's total population. Because the Constitution guarantees each state one representative no matter how small its population, exact proportional distribution is virtually impossible. The mathematical formula currently used to determine the apportionment is called the Method of Equal Proportions. *(See Method of Equal Proportions.)*

Appropriated Entitlement—An entitlement program, such as veterans' pensions, that is funded through annual appropriations rather than by a permanent appropriation. Because such an entitlement law requires the government to provide eligible recipients the benefits to which they are entitled, whatever the cost, Congress must appropriate the necessary funds.

Appropriation—(1) Legislative language that permits a federal agency to incur obligations and make payments from the Treasury for specified purposes, usually during a specified period of time. (2) The specific amount of money made available by such language. The Constitution prohibits payments from the Treasury except "in Consequence of Appropriations made by Law." With some exceptions, the rules of both houses forbid consideration of appropriations for purposes that are unauthorized in law or of appropriation amounts larger than those authorized in law. The House of Representatives claims the exclusive right to originate appropriation bills—a claim the Senate denies in theory but accepts in practice.

At-Large—Elected by and representing an entire state instead of a district within a state. The term usually refers to a representative rather than to a senator. *(See Apportionment; Congressional District; Redistricting.)*

August Adjournment—A congressional adjournment during the month of August in odd-numbered years, required by the Legislative Reorganization Act of 1970. The law instructs the two houses to adjourn for a period of at least thirty days before the second day after Labor Day, unless Congress provides otherwise or if, on July 31, a state of war exists by congressional declaration.

Authorization—(1) A statutory provision that establishes or continues a federal agency, activity, or program for a fixed or indefinite period of time. It may also establish policies and restrictions and deal with organizational and administrative matters. (2) A statutory provision, as described in (1), may also, explicitly or implicitly, authorize congressional action to provide appropriations for an agency, activity, or program. The appropriations may be authorized for one year, several years, or an indefinite period of time, and the authorization may be for a specific amount of money or an indefinite amount ("such sums as may be necessary"). Authorizations of specific amounts are construed as ceilings on the amounts that subsequently may be appropriated in an appropriation bill, but not as minimums; either house may appropriate lesser amounts or nothing at all.

Authorization-Appropriation Process—The two-stage procedural system that the rules of each house require for establishing and funding federal agencies and programs: first, enactment of authorizing legislation that creates or continues an agency or program; second, enactment of appropriations legislation that provides funds for the authorized agency or program.

Automatic Roll Call—Under a House rule, the automatic ordering of the yeas and nays when a quorum is not present on a voice or division vote and a member objects to the vote on that ground. It is not permitted in the Committee of the Whole.

Backdoor Spending Authority—Authority to incur obligations that evades the normal congressional appropriations process because it is provided in legislation other than appropriation acts. The most common forms are borrowing authority, contract authority, and entitlement authority.

Baseline—A projection of the levels of federal spending, revenues, and the resulting budgetary surpluses or deficits for the upcoming and subsequent fiscal years, taking into account laws enacted to date and assuming no new policy decisions. It provides a benchmark for measuring the budgetary effects of proposed changes in federal revenues or spending, assuming certain economic conditions.

Bells—A system of electric signals and lights that informs members of activities in each chamber. The type of activity taking place is indicated by the number of signals and the interval between them. When the signals are sounded, a corresponding number of lights are lit around the perimeter of many clocks in House or Senate offices.

Bicameral—Consisting of two houses or chambers. Congress is a bicameral legislature whose two houses have an equal role in enacting legislation. In most other national bicameral legislatures, one house is significantly more powerful than the other.

Bigger Bite Amendment—An amendment that substantively changes a portion of a text including language that had previously been amended. Normally, language that has been amended may not be amended again. However, a part of a sentence that has been changed by amendment, for example, may be changed again by an amendment that amends a "bigger bite" of the text—that is, by an amendment that also substantively changes the unamended parts of the sentence or the entire section or title in which the previously amended language appears. The biggest possible bite is an amendment in the nature of a substitute that amends the entire text of a measure. Once adopted, therefore, such an amendment ends the amending process.

Bill—The term for the chief vehicle Congress uses for enacting laws. Bills that originate in the House of Representatives are designated as HR, those in the Senate as S, followed by a number assigned in the order in which they are introduced during a two-year Congress. A bill becomes a law if passed in identical language by both houses and signed by the president, or passed over the president's veto, or if the president fails to sign it within ten days after receiving it while Congress is in session.

Bill of Attainder—An act of a legislature finding a person guilty of treason or a felony. The Constitution prohibits the passage of such a bill by the U.S. Congress or any state legislature.

Bills and Resolutions Introduced—Members formally present measures to their respective houses by delivering them to a clerk in the chamber when their house is in session. Both houses permit any number of members to join in introducing a bill or resolution. The first member listed on the measure is the sponsor; the other members listed are its cosponsors.

Bills and Resolutions Referred—After a bill or resolution is introduced, it is normally sent to one or more committees that have jurisdiction over its subject, as defined by House and Senate rules and precedents. A Senate measure is usually referred to the committee with jurisdiction over the predominant subject of its text, but it may be sent to two or more committees by unanimous consent or on a motion offered jointly by the majority and minority leaders. In the House, a rule requires the Speaker to refer a measure to the committee that has primary jurisdiction. The Speaker is also authorized to refer measures sequentially to additional committees and to impose time limits on such referrals.

Bipartisan Committee—A committee with an equal number of members from each political party. The House Committee on Standards of Official Conduct and the Senate Select Committee on Ethics are the only bipartisan, permanent full committees.

Borrowing Authority—Statutory authority permitting a federal agency, such as the Export-Import Bank, to borrow money from the public or the Treasury to finance its operations. It is a form of backdoor spending. To bring such spending under the control of the congressional appropriation process, the Congressional Budget Act requires that new borrowing authority shall be effective only to the extent and in such amounts as are provided in appropriations acts.

Budget—A detailed statement of actual or anticipated revenues and expenditures during an accounting period. For the national government, the period is the federal fiscal year (Oct. 1 to Sept. 30). The budget usually refers to the president's budget submission to Congress early each calendar year. The president's budget estimates federal government income and spending for the upcoming fiscal year and contains detailed recommendations for appropriation, revenue, and other legislation. Congress is not required to accept or even vote directly on the president's proposals, and it often revises the president's budget extensively. *(See Fiscal Year.)*

Budget Act—Common name for the Congressional Budget and Impoundment Control Act of 1974, which established the basic procedures of the current congressional budget process; created the House and Senate Budget Committees; and enacted procedures for reconciliation, deferrals, and rescissions. *(See Budget Process; Deferral; Impoundment; Reconciliation; Rescission. See also Gramm-Rudman-Hollings Act of 1985.)*

Budget and Accounting Act of 1921—The law that, for the first time, authorized the president to submit to Congress an annual budget for the entire federal government. Before passage of the act, most federal agencies sent their budget requests to the appropriate congressional committees without review by the president.

Budget Authority—Generally, the amount of money that may be spent or obligated by a government agency or for a government program or activity. Technically, it is statutory authority to enter into obligations that normally result in outlays. The main forms of budget authority are appropriations, borrowing authority, and contract authority. It also includes authority to obligate and expend the proceeds of offsetting receipts and collections. Congress may make budget authority available for only one year, several years, or an indefinite period, and it may specify definite or indefinite amounts.

Budget Enforcement Act of 1990—An act that revised the sequestration process established by the Gramm-Rudman-Hollings Act of 1985, replaced the earlier act's fixed deficit targets with adjustable ones, established discretionary spending limits for fiscal years 1991 through 1995, instituted pay-as-you-go rules to enforce deficit neutrality on revenue and mandatory spending legislation, and reformed the budget and accounting rules for federal credit activities. Unlike the Gramm-Rudman-Hollings Act, the 1990 act emphasized restraints on legislated changes in taxes and spending instead of fixed deficit limits.

Budget Enforcement Act of 1997—An act that revised and updated the provisions of the Budget Enforcement Act of 1990, including by extending the discretionary spending caps and pay-as-you-go rules through 2002.

Budget Process—(1) In Congress, the procedural system it uses (a) to approve an annual concurrent resolution on the budget that sets goals for aggregate and functional categories of federal expenditures, revenues, and the surplus or deficit for an upcoming fiscal year; and (b) to implement those goals in spending, revenue, and, if necessary, reconciliation and debt-limit legislation. (2) In the executive branch, the process of formulating the president's annual budget, submitting it to Congress, defending it before congressional committees, implementing subsequent budget-related legislation, impounding or sequestering expenditures as permitted by law, auditing and evaluating programs, and compiling final budget data. The Budget and Accounting Act of 1921 and the Congressional Budget and Impoundment Control Act of 1974 established the basic elements of the current budget process. Major revisions were enacted in the Gramm-Rudman-Hollings Act of 1985, the Budget Enforcement Act of 1990, and the Budget Enforcement Act of 1997.

Budget Resolution—A concurrent resolution in which Congress establishes or revises its version of the federal budget's broad financial features for the upcoming fiscal year and several additional fiscal years. As with other concurrent resolutions, it does not have the force of law, but it provides the framework within which Congress subsequently considers revenue, spending, and other budget-implementing legislation. The framework consists of two basic elements: (1) aggregate budget amounts (total revenues, new budget authority, outlays, loan obligations and loan guarantee commitments, deficit or surplus, and debt limit); and (2) subdivisions of the relevant aggregate amounts among the functional categories of the budget. Although it does not allocate funds to specific programs or accounts, the budget committees' reports accompanying the resolution often discuss the major program assumptions underlying its functional amounts. Unlike those amounts, however, the assumptions are not binding on Congress.

By Request—A designation indicating that a member has introduced a measure on behalf of the president, an executive agency, or a private individual or organization. Members often introduce such measures as a courtesy because neither the president nor any person other than a member of Congress can do so. The term, which appears next to the sponsor's name, implies that the member who introduced the measure does not necessarily endorse it. A House rule dealing with by-request introductions dates from 1888, but the practice goes back to the earliest history of Congress.

Byrd Rule—The popular name of an amendment to the Congressional Budget Act that bars the inclusion of extraneous matter in any reconciliation legislation considered in the Senate. The ban is enforced by points of order that the presiding officer sustains. The provision defines different categories of extraneous matter, but it also permits certain exceptions. Its chief sponsor was Sen. Robert C. Byrd, D-W.Va.

Calendar—A list of measures or other matters (most of them favorably reported by committees) that are eligible for floor consideration. The House has four calendars; the Senate has two. A place on a calendar does not guarantee consideration. Each house decides which measures and matters it will take up, when, and in what order, in accordance with its rules and practices.

Calendar Wednesday—A House procedure that on Wednesdays permits its committees to bring up for floor consideration nonprivi-leged measures they have reported. The procedure is so cumbersome and susceptible to dilatory tactics, however, that it is rarely used.

Call Up—To bring a measure or report to the floor for immediate consideration.

Casework—Assistance to constituents who seek assistance in dealing with federal and local government agencies. Constituent service is a high priority in most members' offices.

Caucus—(1) A common term for the official organization of each party in each house. (2) The official title of the organization of House Democrats. House and Senate Republicans and Senate Democrats call their organizations "conferences." (3) A term for an informal group of members who share legislative interests, such as the Black Caucus, Hispanic Caucus, and Children's Caucus.

Censure—The strongest formal condemnation of a member for misconduct short of expulsion. A house usually adopts a resolution of censure to express its condemnation, after which the presiding officer reads its rebuke aloud to the member in the presence of his or her colleagues.

Chairman—The presiding officer of a committee, a subcommittee, or a task force. At meetings, the chairman preserves order, enforces the rules, recognizes members to speak or offer motions, and puts questions to a vote. The chairman of a committee or subcommittee usually appoints its staff and sets its agenda, subject to the panel's veto.

Chamber—The Capitol room in which a house of Congress normally holds its sessions. The chamber of the House of Representatives, officially called the Hall of the House, is considerably larger than that of the Senate because it must accommodate 435 representatives, four delegates, and one resident commissioner. Unlike the Senate chamber, members have no desks or assigned seats. In both chambers, the floor slopes downward to the well in front of the presiding officer's raised desk. A chamber is often referred to as "the floor," as when members are said to be on or going to the floor. Those expressions usually imply that the member's house is in session.

Christmas Tree Bill—Jargon for a bill adorned with amendments, many of them unrelated to the bill's subject, that provide benefits for interest groups, specific states, congressional districts, companies, and individuals.

Classes of Senators—A class consists of the thirty-three or thirty-four senators elected to a six-year term in the same general election. Because the terms of approximately one-third of the senators expire every two years, there are three classes.

Clean Bill—After a House committee extensively amends a bill, it often assembles its amendments and what is left of the bill into a new measure that one or more of its members introduces as a "clean bill." The revised measure is assigned a new number.

Clerk of the House—An officer of the House of Representatives responsible principally for administrative support of the legislative process in the House. The clerk is invariably the candidate of the majority party.

Cloakrooms—Two rooms with access to the rear of each chamber's floor, one for each party's members, where members may confer privately, sit quietly, or have a snack. The presiding officer sometimes urges members who are conversing too loudly on the floor to retire to their cloakrooms.

Closed Hearing—A hearing closed to the public and the media. A House committee may close a hearing only if it determines that disclosure of the testimony to be taken would endanger national security, violate any law, or tend to defame, degrade, or incriminate any person. The Senate has a similar rule. Both houses require roll-call votes in open session to close a hearing.

Closed Rule—A special rule reported from the House Rules Committee that prohibits amendments to a measure or that only permits amendments offered by the reporting committee.

Cloture—A Senate procedure that limits further consideration of a pending proposal to thirty hours to end a filibuster. Sixteen senators must first sign and submit a cloture motion to the presiding officer. One hour after the Senate meets on the second calendar day thereafter, the chair puts the motion to a yea-and-nay vote following a live quorum call. If three-fifths of all senators (sixty if there are no vacancies) vote for the motion, the Senate must take final action on the cloture proposal by the end of the thirty hours of consideration and may consider no other business until it takes that action. Cloture on a proposal to amend the Senate's standing rules requires approval by two-thirds of the senators present and voting.

Code of Official Conduct—A House rule that bans certain actions by House members, officers, and employees; requires them to conduct themselves in ways that "reflect creditably" on the House; and orders them to adhere to the spirit and the letter of House rules and those of its committees. The code's provisions govern the receipt of outside compensation, gifts, and honoraria, and the use of campaign funds; prohibit members from using their clerk-hire allowance to pay anyone who does not perform duties commensurate with that pay; forbids discrimination in members' hiring or treatment of employees on the grounds of race, color, religion, sex, handicap, age, or national origin; orders members convicted of a crime who might be punished by imprisonment of two or more years not to participate in committee business or vote on the floor until exonerated or reelected; and restricts employees' contact with federal agencies on matters in which they have a significant financial interest. The Senate's rules contain some similar prohibitions.

College of Cardinals—A popular term for the subcommittee chairmen of the appropriations committees, reflecting their influence over appropriation measures. The chairmen of the full appropriations committees are sometimes referred to as popes.

Colloquy—A discussion between members to put a mutual understanding about the intent of a measure or amendment on the record. The discussion usually is scripted in advance.

Comity—The practice of maintaining mutual courtesy and civility between the two houses in their dealings with each other and in members' speeches on the floor. Although the practice is largely governed by long-established customs, a House rule explicitly cautions its members not to characterize any Senate action or inaction, refer to individual senators except under certain circumstances, or quote from Senate proceedings except to make legislative history on a measure. The Senate has no rule on the subject but references to the House have been held out of order on several occasions. Generally the houses do not interfere with each other's appropriations although minor conflicts sometimes occur. A refusal to receive a message from the other house has also been held to violate the practice of comity.

Committee—A panel of members elected or appointed to perform some service or function for its parent body. Congress has four types of committees: standing, special or select, joint, and, in the House, a Committee of the Whole. Committees conduct investigations, make studies, issue reports and recommendations, and, in the case of standing committees, review and prepare measures on their assigned subjects for action by their respective houses. Most committees divide their work among several subcommittees. With rare exceptions, the majority party in a house holds a majority of the seats on its committees, and their chairmen are also from that party.

Committee Jurisdiction—The legislative subjects and other functions assigned to a committee by rule, precedent, resolution, or statute. A committee's title usually indicates the general scope of its jurisdiction but often fails to mention other significant subjects assigned to it.

Committee of the Whole—Common name of the Committee of the Whole House on the State of the Union, a committee consisting of all members of the House of Representatives. Measures from the union calendar must be considered in the Committee of the Whole before the House officially completes action on them; the committee often considers other major bills as well. A quorum of the committee is 100, and it meets in the House chamber under a chairman appointed by the Speaker. Procedures in the Committee of the Whole expedite consideration of legislation because of its smaller quorum requirement, its ban on certain motions, and its five-minute rule for debate on amendments. Those procedures usually permit more members to offer amendments and participate in the debate on a measure than is normally possible. The Senate no longer uses a Committee of the Whole.

Committee Ratios—The ratios of majority to minority party members on committees. By custom, the ratios of most committees reflect party strength in their respective houses as closely as possible.

Committee Report on a Measure—A document submitted by a committee to report a measure to its parent chamber. Customarily, the report explains the measure's purpose, describes provisions and any amendments recommended by the committee, and presents arguments for its approval.

Committee Veto—A procedure that requires an executive department or agency to submit certain proposed policies, programs, or action to designated committees for review before implementing them. Before 1983, when the Supreme Court declared that a legislative veto was unconstitutional, these provisions permitted committees to veto the proposals. Committees no longer conduct this type of policy review, and the term is now something of a misnomer. Nevertheless, agencies usually take the pragmatic approach of trying to reach a consensus with the committees before carrying out their proposals, especially when an appropriations committee is involved.

Concur—To agree to an amendment of the other house, either by adopting a motion to concur in that amendment or a motion to concur with an amendment to that amendment. After both houses have agreed to the same version of an amendment, neither house may amend it further, nor may any subsequent conference change it or delete it from the measure. Concurrence by one house in all amendments of the other house completes action on the measure; no vote is then necessary on the measure as a whole because both houses previously passed it.

Concurrent Resolution—A resolution that requires approval by both houses but does not need the president's signature and therefore cannot have the force of law. Concurrent resolutions deal with the prerogatives or internal affairs of Congress as a whole. Designated H Con Res in the House and S Con Res in the Senate, they are numbered consecutively in each house in their order of introduction during a two-year Congress.

Conferees—A common title for managers, the members from each house appointed to a conference committee. The Senate usually authorizes its presiding officer to appoint its conferees. The Speaker appoints House conferees, and under a rule adopted in 1993, can remove conferees "at any time after an original appointment" and also appoint additional conferees at any time. Conferees are expected to support the positions of their houses despite their personal views, but in practice this is not always the case. The party ratios of conferees generally reflect the ratios in their houses. Each house may appoint as many conferees as it pleases. House conferees often outnumber their Senate colleagues; however, each house has only one vote in a conference, so the size of its delegation is immaterial.

Conference—(1) A formal meeting or series of meetings between members representing each house to reconcile House and Senate differences on a measure (occasionally several measures). Because one house cannot require the other to agree to its proposals, the conference usually reaches agreement by compromise. When a conference completes action on a measure, or as much action as appears possible, it sends its recommendations to both houses in the form of a conference report, accompanied by an explanatory statement. (2) The official title of the organization of all Democrats or Republicans in the Senate and of all Republicans in the House of Representatives. (*See Party Caucus.*)

Conference Committee—A temporary joint committee formed for the purpose of resolving differences between the houses on a measure. Major and controversial legislation usually requires conference committee action. Voting in a conference committee is not by individuals but within the House and Senate delegations. Consequently, a conference committee report requires the support of a majority of the conferees from each house. Both houses require that conference committees open their meetings to the public. The Senate's rule permits the committee to close its meetings if a majority of conferees in each delegation agree by a roll-call vote. The House rule permits closed meetings only if the House authorizes them to do so on a roll-call vote. Otherwise, there are no congressional rules governing the organization of, or procedure in, a conference committee. The committee chooses its chairman, but on measures that go to conference annually, such as general appropriation bills, the chairmanship traditionally rotates between the houses.

Conference Report—A document submitted to both houses that contains a conference committee's agreements for resolving their differences on a measure. It must be signed by a majority of the conferees from each house separately and must be accompanied by an explanatory statement. Both houses prohibit amendments to a conference report and require it to be accepted or rejected in its entirety.

Congress—(1) The national legislature of the United States, consisting of the House of Representatives and the Senate. (2) The national legislature in office during a two-year period. Congresses are numbered sequentially; thus, the 1st Congress of 1789–1791 and the 106th Congress of 1999–2001. Before 1935, the two-year period began on the first Monday in December of odd-numbered years. Since then it has extended from January of an odd-numbered year through noon on Jan. 3 of the next odd-numbered year. A Congress usually holds two annual sessions, but some have had three sessions and the 67th Congress had four. When a Congress expires, measures die if they have not yet been enacted.

Congressional Accountability Act of 1995 (CAA)—An act applying eleven labor, workplace, and civil rights laws to the legislative branch and establishing procedures and remedies for legislative branch employees with grievances in violation of these laws. The following laws are covered by the CAA: the Fair Labor Standards Act of 1938; Title VII of the Civil Rights Act of 1964; Americans with Disabilities Act of 1990; Age Discrimination in Employment Act of 1967; Family and Medical Leave Act of 1993; Occupational Safety and Health Act of 1970; Chapter 71 of Title 5, *U.S. Code* (relating to federal service labor-management relations); Employee Polygraph Protection Act of 1988; Worker Adjustment and Retraining Notification Act; Rehabilitation Act of 1973; and Chapter 43 of Title 38, *U.S. Code* (relating to veterans' employment and reemployment).

Congressional Budget and Impoundment Control Act of 1974—The law that established the basic elements of the congressional budget process, the House and Senate budget committees, the Congressional Budget Office, and the procedures for congressional review of impoundments in the form of rescissions and deferrals proposed by the president. The budget process consists of procedures for coordinating congressional revenue and spending decisions made in separate tax, appropriations, and legislative measures. The impoundment provisions were intended to give Congress greater control over executive branch actions that delay or prevent the spending of funds provided by Congress.

Congressional Budget Office (CBO)—A congressional support agency created by the Congressional Budget and Impoundment Control Act of 1974 to provide nonpartisan budgetary information and analysis to Congress and its committees. CBO acts as a scorekeeper when Congress is voting on the federal budget, tracking bills to ensure they comply with overall budget goals. The agency also estimates what proposed legislation would cost over a five-year period. CBO works most closely with the House and Senate Budget committees.

Congressional Directory—The official who's who of Congress, usually published during the first session of a two-year Congress.

Congressional District—The geographical area represented by a single member of the House of Representatives. For states with only one representative, the entire state is a congressional district. After the reapportionment from the 2000 census, seven states had only one representative each: Alaska, Delaware, Montana, North Dakota, South Dakota, Vermont and Wyoming.

Congressional Record—The daily, printed, and substantially verbatim account of proceedings in both the House and Senate chambers. Extraneous materials submitted by members appear in a section titled "Extensions of Remarks." A "Daily Digest" appendix contains highlights of the day's floor and committee action plus a list of committee meetings and floor agendas for the next day's session.

Although the official reporters of each house take down every word spoken during the proceedings, members are permitted to edit and "revise and extend" their remarks before they are printed. In the Senate section, all speeches, articles, and other material submitted by senators but not actually spoken or read on the floor are set off by large black dots, called bullets. However, bullets do not appear when a senator reads part of a speech and inserts the rest. In the House section, undelivered speeches and materials are printed in a distinctive typeface. The term "permanent *Record*" refers to the bound volumes of the daily *Records* of an entire session of Congress.

Congressional Research Service (CRS)—Established in 1917, a department of the Library of Congress whose staff provide nonpartisan, objective analysis, and information on virtually any subject to committees, members, and staff of Congress. Originally the Legislative Reference Service, it is the oldest congressional support agency.

Congressional Support Agencies—A term often applied to three agencies in the legislative branch that provide nonpartisan information and analysis to committees and members of Congress: the Congressional Budget Office, the Congressional Research Service of the Library of Congress, and the Government Accountability Office (previously called the General Accounting Office).

Congressional Terms of Office—A term normally begins on Jan. 3 of the year following a general election and runs two years for representatives and six years for senators. A representatives chosen in a special election to fill a vacancy is sworn in for the remainder of the predecessor's term. An individual appointed to fill a Senate vacancy usually serves until the next general election or until the end of the predecessor's term, whichever comes first. Some states, however, require their governors to call a special election to fill a Senate vacancy shortly after an appointment has been made.

Constitutional Option—*(See Nuclear Option.)*

Constitutional Rules—Constitutional provisions that prescribe procedures for Congress. In addition to certain types of votes required in particular situations, these provisions include the following: (1) the House chooses its Speaker, the Senate its president pro tempore, and both houses their officers; (2) each house requires a majority quorum to conduct business; (3) less than a majority may adjourn from day to day and compel the attendance of absent members; (4) neither house may adjourn for more than three days without the consent of the other; (5) each house must keep a journal; (6) the yeas and nays are ordered when supported by one-fifth of the members present; (7) all revenue-raising bills must originate in the House, but the Senate may propose amendments to them. The Constitution also sets out the procedure in the House for electing a president, the procedure in the Senate for electing a vice president, the procedure for filling a vacancy in the office of vice president, and the procedure for overriding a presidential veto.

Constitutional Votes—Constitutional provisions that require certain votes or voting methods in specific situations. They include (1) the yeas and nays at the desire of one-fifth of the members present; (2) a two-thirds vote by the yeas and nays to override a veto; (3) a two-thirds vote by one house to expel one of its members and by both houses to propose a constitutional amendment; (4) a two-thirds vote of senators present to convict someone whom the House has impeached and to consent to ratification of treaties; (5) a two-thirds vote in each house to remove political disabilities from persons who have engaged in insurrection or rebellion or given aid or comfort to the enemies of the United States; (6) a majority vote in each house to fill a vacancy in the office of vice president; (7) a majority vote of all states to elect a president in the House of Representatives when no candidate receives a majority of the electoral votes; (8) a majority vote of all senators when the Senate elects a vice president under the same circumstances; and (9) the casting vote of the vice president in case of tie votes in the Senate.

Contempt of Congress—Willful obstruction of the proper functions of Congress. Most frequently, it is a refusal to obey a subpoena to appear and testify before a committee or to produce documents demanded by it. Such obstruction is a misdemeanor and persons cited for contempt are subject to prosecution in federal courts. A house cites an individual for contempt by agreeing to a privileged resolution to that effect reported by a committee. The presiding officer then refers the matter to a U.S. attorney for prosecution.

Continuing Body—A characterization of the Senate on the theory that it continues from Congress to Congress and has existed continuously since it first convened in 1789. The rationale for the theory is that under the system of staggered six-year terms for senators, the terms of only about one-third of them expire after each Congress and, therefore, a quorum of the Senate is always in office. Consequently, under this theory, the Senate, unlike the House, does not have to adopt its rules at the beginning of each Congress because those rules continue from one Congress to the next. This makes it extremely difficult for the Senate to change its rules against the opposition of a determined minority because those rules require a two-thirds vote of the senators present and voting to invoke cloture on a proposed rules change.

Continuing Resolution (CR)—A joint resolution that provides funds to continue the operation of federal agencies and programs at the beginning of a new fiscal year if their annual appropriation bills have not yet been enacted; also called continuing appropriations. Continuing resolutions are enacted shortly before or after the new fiscal year begins and usually make funds available for a specified period. Additional resolutions are often needed after the first expires. Some continuing resolutions have provided appropriations for an entire fiscal year. Continuing resolutions for specific periods customarily fix a rate at which agencies may incur obligations based either on the previous year's appropriations, the president's budget request, or the amount as specified in the agency's regular annual appropriation bill if that bill has already been passed by one or both houses. In the House, continuing resolutions are privileged after Sept. 15.

Contract Authority—Statutory authority permitting an agency to enter into contracts or incur other obligations even though it has not received an appropriation to pay for them. Congress must eventually fund them because the government is legally liable for such payments. The Congressional Budget Act of 1974 requires that new contract authority may not be used unless provided for in advance by an appropriation act, but it permits a few exceptions.

Cordon Rule—A Senate rule that requires a committee report to show changes the reported measure would make in current law. The rule is named after its sponsor, Sen. Guy Cordon, R-Ore. The House's analogous rule is called the Ramseyer rule. *(See Ramseyer Rule.)*

Correcting Recorded Votes—The rules of both houses prohibit members from changing their votes after a vote result has been announced. Nevertheless, the Senate permits its members to withdraw or change their votes, by unanimous consent, immediately after the announcement. In rare instances, senators have been granted unanimous consent to change their votes several days or weeks after the announcement. Votes tallied by the electronic voting system in the House may not be changed. But when a vote actually given is not recorded during an oral call of the roll, a member may demand a correction as a matter of right. On all other alleged errors in a recorded vote, the Speaker determines whether the circumstances justify a change. Occasionally, members merely announce that they were incorrectly recorded; announcements can occur hours, days, or even months after the vote and appear in the *Congressional Record.*

Cosponsor—A member who has joined one or more other members to sponsor a measure. Joining on the day of introduction qualifies the member as an original sponsor.

Credit Authority—Authority granted to an agency to incur direct loan obligations or to make loan guarantee commitments. The Congressional Budget Act of 1974 bans congressional consideration of credit authority legislation unless the extent of that authority is made subject to provisions in appropriation acts.

C-SPAN—Cable-Satellite Public Affairs Network, which provides live, gavel-to-gavel coverage of Senate floor proceedings on one cable television channel and coverage of House floor proceedings on another channel. C-SPAN also televises important committee hearings in both houses. Each house also transmits its televised proceedings directly to congressional offices.

Current Services Estimates—Executive branch estimates of the anticipated costs of federal programs and operations for the next and future fiscal years at existing levels of service and assuming no new initiatives or changes in existing law. The president submits these estimates to Congress with the annual budget and includes an explanation of the underlying economic and policy assumptions on which they are based, such as anticipated rates of inflation, real economic growth, and unemployment, plus program caseloads and pay increases.

Custody of the Papers—Possession of an engrossed measure and certain related basic documents that the two houses produce as they try to resolve their differences over the measure.

Dance of the Swans and the Ducks—A whimsical description of the gestures some members use in connection with a request for a recorded vote, especially in the House. When members wants their colleagues to stand in support of the request, they move their hands and arms in a gentle upward motion resembling the beginning flight of a graceful swan. When they want their colleagues to remain seated to avoid such a vote, they move their hands and arms in a vigorous downward motion resembling a diving duck.

Dean—Within a state's delegation in the House of Representatives, the member with the longest continuous service; also the longest-serving members of the House.

Debate—In congressional parlance, speeches delivered during consideration of a measure, motion, or other matter, as distinguished from speeches in other parliamentary situations, such as one-minute and special order speeches when no business is pending. Virtually all debate in the House of Representatives is under some kind of time limitation. Most debate in the Senate is unlimited; that is, a senator, once recognized, may speak for as long as he or she chooses, unless the Senate invokes cloture.

Debt Limit—The maximum amount of outstanding federal public debt permitted by law. The limit (or ceiling) covers virtually all debt incurred by the government except agency debt. Each congressional budget resolution sets forth the new debt limit that may be required under its provisions.

Deferral—An impoundment of funds for a specific period of time that may not extend beyond the fiscal year in which it is proposed. Under the Impoundment Control Act of 1974, the president must notify Congress that he is deferring the spending or obligation of funds provided by law for a project or activity. Congress can disapprove the deferral by legislation.

Deficit—The amount by which the government's outlays exceed its budget receipts for a given fiscal year. Both the president's budget and the annual congressional budget resolution provide estimates of the deficit or surplus for the upcoming and several future fiscal years.

Degrees of Amendment—Designations that indicate the relationships of amendments to the text of a measure and to each other. In general, an amendment offered directly to the text of a measure is an amendment in the first degree, and an amendment to that amendment is an amendment in the second degree. Both houses normally prohibit amendments in the third degree—that is, an amendment to an amendment to an amendment.

Delegate—A nonvoting member of the House of Representatives elected to a two-year term from the District of Columbia, the territory of Guam, the territory of the Virgin Islands, or the territory of American Samoa. By law, delegates may not vote in the full House but they may participate in debate, offer motions (except to reconsider), and serve and vote on standing and select committees. On their committees, delegates possess the same powers and privileges as other members and the Speaker may appoint them to appropriate conference committees and select committees.

Denounce—A formal action that condemns a member for misbehavior; considered by some experts to be equivalent to censure. *(See Censure.)*

Dilatory Tactics—Procedural actions intended to delay or prevent action by a house or a committee. They include, among others, offering numerous motions, demanding quorum calls and recorded votes at every opportunity, making numerous points of order and parliamentary inquiries, and speaking as long as the applicable rules permit. The Senate rules permit a battery of dilatory tactics, especially lengthy speeches, except under cloture. In the House, possible dilatory tactics are more limited. Speeches are always subject to time limits and debate-ending motions. Moreover, a House rule instructs the Speaker not to entertain dilatory motions and lets the Speaker decide whether a motion is dilatory. However, the Speaker may not override the constitutional right of a member to demand the yeas and nays, and in practice usually waits for a point of order before exercising that authority. *(See Cloture.)*

Discharge a Committee—Remove a measure from a committee to which it has been referred in order to make it available for floor consideration. Noncontroversial measures are often discharged by unanimous consent. However, because congressional committees have no obligation to report measures referred to them, each house has procedures to extract controversial measures from recalcitrant committees.

District Office—Representatives maintain one or more offices in their districts for the purpose of assisting and communicating with constituents. The costs of maintaining these offices are paid from members' official allowances. Senators can use the official expense allowance to rent offices in their home state, subject to a funding formula based on their state's population and other factors.

District Work Period—The House term for a scheduled congressional recess during which members may visit their districts and conduct constituency business.

Division Vote—A vote in which the chair first counts those in favor of a proposition and then those opposed to it, with no record made of how each member votes. In the Senate, the chair may count raised hands or ask senators to stand, whereas the House requires members to stand; hence, often called a standing vote. Committees in both houses ordinarily use a show of hands. A division usually occurs after a voice vote and may be demanded by any member or ordered by the chair if there is any doubt about the outcome of the voice vote. The demand for a division can also come before a voice vote. In the Senate, the demand must come before the result of a voice vote is announced. It may be made after a voice vote announcement in the House, but only if no intervening business has transpired and only if the member was standing and seeking recognition at the time of the announcement. A demand for the yeas and nays or, in the House, for a recorded vote, takes precedence over a division vote.

Earmark—A set-aside within an appropriations measure for a specific purpose.

Effective Dates—Provisions of an act that specify when the entire act or individual provisions in it become effective as law. Most acts become effective on the date of enactment, but it is sometimes necessary or prudent to delay the effective dates of some provisions.

Electronic Voting—Since 1973 the House has used an electronic voting system to record the yeas and nays and to conduct recorded votes. Members vote by inserting their voting cards in one of the boxes at several locations in the chamber. They are given at least fifteen minutes to vote. When several votes occur immediately after each other, the Speaker may reduce the voting time to five minutes on the second and subsequent votes. The Speaker may allow additional time on each vote but may also close a vote at any time after the minimum time has expired. Members can change their votes at any time before the Speaker announces the result. The House also uses the electronic system for quorum calls. While a vote is in progress, a large panel above the Speaker's desk displays how each member has voted. Smaller panels on either side of the chamber display running totals of the votes and the time remaining. The Senate does not have electronic voting.

Enacting Clause—The opening language of each bill, beginning "Be it enacted by the Senate and House of Representatives of the United States of America in Congress assembled . . ." This language gives legal force to measures approved by Congress and signed by the president or enacted over the president's veto. A successful motion to strike it from a bill kills the entire measure.

Engrossed Bill—The official copy of a bill or joint resolution as passed by one chamber, including the text as amended by floor action, and certified by the clerk of the House or the secretary of the Senate (as appropriate). Amendments by one house to a measure or amendments of the other also are engrossed. House engrossed documents are printed on blue paper; the Senate's are printed on white paper.

Enrolled Bill—The final official copy of a bill or joint resolution passed in identical form by both houses. An enrolled bill usually is printed on parchment. After it is certified by the chief officer of the house in which it originated and signed by the House Speaker and the Senate president pro tempore, the measure is sent to the White House for the president's signature.

Entitlement Program—A federal program under which individuals, businesses, or units of government that meet the requirements or qualifications established by law are entitled to receive certain payments if they seek such payments. Major examples include Social Security, Medicare, Medicaid, unemployment insurance, and military and federal civilian pensions. Congress cannot control their expenditures by refusing to appropriate the sums necessary to fund them because the government is legally obligated to pay eligible recipients the amounts to which the law entitles them.

Equality of the Houses—A component of the Constitution's emphasis on checks and balances under which each house is given essentially equal status in the enactment of legislation and in the relations and negotiations between the two houses. Although the House of Representatives initiates revenue and appropriation measures, the Senate has the right to amend them. Either house may initiate any other type of legislation, and neither can force the other to agree to, or even act on, its measures. Moreover, each house has a potential veto over the other because legislation requires agreement by both. Similarly, in a conference to resolve their differences on a measure, each house casts one vote, as determined by a majority of its conferees. In most other national bicameral legislatures, the powers of one house are markedly greater than those of the other.

Ethics Rules—Several rules or standing orders in each house that mandate certain standards of conduct for members and congressional employees in finance, employment, franking, and other areas. The Senate Permanent Select Committee on Ethics and the House Committee on Standards of Official Conduct investigate alleged violations of conduct and recommend appropriate actions to their respective houses.

Exclusive Committee—(1) Under the rules of the Republican Conference and House Democratic Caucus, a standing committee whose members usually cannot serve on any other standing committee. As of 2005 the Appropriations, Energy and Commerce (for Democrats beginning in the 105th Congress), Financial Services (for Democrats beginning in the 109th Congress), Ways and Means, and Rules Committees were designated as exclusive committees. (2) Under the rules of the two-party conferences in the Senate, a standing committee whose members may not simultaneously serve on any other exclusive committee.

Executive Calendar—The Senate's calendar for committee reports on its executive business, namely treaties and nominations. The calendar numbers indicate the order in which items were referred to the calendar but have no bearing on when or if the Senate will consider them. The Senate, by motion or unanimous consent, resolves itself into executive session to consider them

Executive Document—A document, usually a treaty, sent by the president to the Senate for approval. It is referred to a committee in the same manner as other measures. Resolutions to ratify treaties have their own "treaty document" numbers. For example, the first treaty submitted in the 106th Congress would be "Treaty Doc 106-1."

Executive Order—A unilateral proclamation by the president that has a policy-making or legislative impact. Members of Congress have challenged some executive orders on the grounds that they usurped the authority of the legislative branch. Although the Supreme Court has ruled that a particular order exceeded the president's authority, it has upheld others as falling within the president's general constitutional powers.

Executive Privilege—The assertion that presidents have the right to withhold certain information from Congress. Presidents have based their claim on (1) the constitutional separation of powers; (2) the need for secrecy in military and diplomatic affairs; (3) the need to protect individuals from unfavorable publicity; (4) the need to safeguard the confidential exchange of ideas in the executive branch; and (5) the need to protect individuals who provide confidential advice to the president.

Executive Session—(1) A Senate meeting devoted to the consideration of treaties or nominations. Normally, the Senate meets in legislative session; it resolves itself into executive session, by motion or by unanimous consent, to deal with its executive business. It also keeps a separate *Journal* for executive sessions. Executive sessions are usually open to the public, but the Senate may choose to close them.

Expulsion—A member's removal from office by a two-thirds vote of his or her house; the supermajority is required by the Constitution. It is the most severe and most rarely used sanction a house can invoke against a member. Although the Constitution provides no explicit grounds for expulsion, the courts have ruled that it may be applied only for misconduct during a member's term of office, not for conduct before the member's election. Generally, neither house will consider expulsion of a member convicted of a crime until the judicial processes have been exhausted. At that stage, members sometimes resign rather than face expulsion. In 1977 the House adopted a rule urging members convicted of certain crimes to voluntarily abstain from voting or participating in other legislative business.

Extensions of Remarks—An appendix to the daily *Congressional Record* that consists primarily of miscellaneous extraneous material submitted by members. It often includes members' statements not delivered on the floor, newspaper articles and editorials, praise for a member's constituents, and noteworthy letters received by a member, among other material. Representatives supply the bulk of this material; senators submit little. "Extensions of Remarks" pages are separately numbered, and each number is preceded by the letter "E." Materials may be placed in the Extensions of Remarks section only by

unanimous consent. Usually, one member of each party makes the request each day on behalf of his or her party colleagues after the House has completed its legislative business of the day.

Fast Track—This is a procedure that circumvents or speeds up all or part of the legislative process. Some rulemaking statutes prescribe expedited procedures for certain measures, such as trade agreements.

Federal Debt—The total amount of monies borrowed and not yet repaid by the federal government. Federal debt consists of public debt and agency debt. Public debt is the portion of the federal debt borrowed by the Treasury or the Federal Financing Bank directly from the public or from another federal fund or account. For example, the Treasury regularly borrows money from the Social Security trust fund. Public debt accounts for about 99 percent of the federal debt. Agency debt refers to the debt incurred by federal agencies such as the Export-Import Bank but excluding the Treasury and the Federal Financing Bank, which are authorized by law to borrow funds from the public or from another government fund or account.

Filibuster—The use of time-consuming parliamentary tactics by one member or a minority of members to delay, modify, or defeat proposed legislation or rules changes. Filibusters are also sometimes used to delay urgently needed measures to force the body to accept other legislation. The Senate's rules permitting unlimited debate and the extraordinary majority it requires to impose cloture make filibustering particularly effective in that chamber. Under the stricter rules of the House, filibusters in that body are short-lived and therefore ineffective and rarely attempted

Fiscal Year—The federal government's annual accounting period. It begins Oct. 1 and ends on the following Sept. 30. A fiscal year is designated by the calendar year in which it ends and is often referred to as FY. Thus, fiscal year 2005 began Oct. 1, 2004, ended Sept. 30, 2005, and is called FY05. In theory, Congress is supposed to complete action on all budgetary measures applying to a fiscal year before that year begins. It rarely does so.

Five-Minute Rule—(1) A House rule that limits debate on an amendment offered in Committee of the Whole to five minutes for its sponsor and five minutes for an opponent. In practice, the committee routinely permits longer debate by three devices: offering pro forma amendments, each debatable for five minutes; unanimous consent for a member to speak longer than five minutes; and special rule. Consequently, debate on an amendment sometimes continues for hours. At any time after the first ten minutes, however, the committee may shut off debate immediately or by a specified time, either by unanimous consent or by majority vote on a nondebatable motion. The motion, which dates from 1847, is also used in the House as in Committee of the Whole, where debate also may be shut off by a motion for the previous question.

Floor—The ground level of the House or Senate chamber where members sit and the houses conduct their business. When members are attending a meeting of their house they are said to be on the floor. Floor action refers to the procedural actions taken during floor consideration such as deciding on motions, taking up measures, amending them, and voting.

Floor Manager—A majority party member responsible for guiding a measure through its floor consideration in a house and for devising the political and procedural strategies that might be required to get it passed. The presiding officer gives the floor manager priority recognition to debate, offer amendments, oppose amendments, and make crucial procedural motions. The minority party member is referred to as the minority floor manager.

Frank—Informally, members' legal right to send official mail postage free under their signatures; often called the franking privilege. Technically, it is the autographic or facsimile signature used on envelopes instead of stamps that permits members and certain congressional officers to send their official mail free of charge. The franking privilege has been authorized by law since the first Congress, except for a few months in 1873. Congress reimburses the U.S. Postal Service for the franked mail it handles.

Function or Functional Category—A broad category of national need and spending of budgetary significance. A category provides an accounting method for allocating and keeping track of budgetary resources and expenditures for that function because it includes all budget accounts related to the function's subject or purpose such as agriculture, administration of justice, commerce and housing and energy. Functions do not necessarily correspond with appropriations acts or with the budgets of individual agencies. As of 2005 there were twenty functional categories, each divided into a number of subfunctions.

Gag Rule—A pejorative term for any type of special rule reported by the House Rules Committee that proposes to prohibit amendments to a measure or only permits amendments offered by the reporting committee.

Galleries—The balconies overlooking each chamber from which the public, news media, staff, and others may observe floor proceedings.

General Appropriation Bill—A term applied to each of the annual bills that provide funds for most federal agencies and programs and also to the supplemental appropriation bills that contain appropriations for more than one agency or program.

Germaneness—The requirement that an amendment be closely related—in terms of subject or purpose, for example—to the text it proposes to amend. A House rule requires that all amendments be germane. In the Senate, only amendments offered to general appropriation bills and budget measures or proposed under cloture must be germane. Germaneness rules can be waived by suspension of the rules in both houses, by unanimous consent agreements in the Senate, and by special rules from the Rules Committee in the House. Moreover, presiding officers usually do not enforce germaneness rules on their own initiative; therefore, a nongermane amendment can be adopted if no member raises a point of order against it. Under cloture in the Senate, however, the chair may take the initiative to rule amendments out of order as not being germane, without a point of order being made. All House debate must be germane except during general debate in the Committee of the Whole, but special rules invariably require that such debate be "confined to the bill." The Senate requires germane debate only during the first three hours of each daily session. Under the precedents of both houses, an amendment can be relevant but not necessarily germane. A crucial factor in determining germaneness in the House is how the subject of a measure or matter is defined. For example, the subject of a measure authorizing construction of a naval vessel is defined as being the construction of a single vessel; therefore, an amendment to authorize an additional vessel is not germane.

Gerrymandering—The manipulation of legislative district boundaries to benefit a particular party, politician, or minority group. The term originated in 1812 when the Massachusetts legislature redrew the lines of state legislative districts to favor the party of Gov. Elbridge Gerry, and some critics said one district resembled a salamander. *(See also Congressional District; Redistricting.)*

Government Accountability Office (GAO)—A congressional support agency, often referred to as the investigative arm of Congress. It evaluates and audits federal agencies and programs in the United States and abroad on its initiative or at the request of congressional committees or members. The office, created in 1921, was called the General Accounting Office until 2004.

Gramm-Rudman-Hollings Act of 1985—Common name for the Balanced Budget and Emergency Deficit Control Act of 1985, which established new budget procedures intended to balance the federal budget by fiscal year 1991. (The timetable subsequently was extended and then deleted.) The act's chief sponsors were senators Phil Gramm, R-Texas, Warren Rudman, R-N.H., and Ernest Hollings, D-S.C.

Grandfather Clause—A provision in a measure, law, or rule that exempts an individual, entity, or a defined category of individuals or entities from complying with a new policy or restriction. For example, a bill that would raise taxes on persons who reach the age of sixty-five after a certain date inherently grandfathers out those who are sixty-five before that date. Similarly, a Senate rule limiting senators to two major committee assignments also grandfathers some senators who were sitting on a third major committee before a specified date.

Grants-in-Aid—Payments by the federal government to state and local governments to help provide for assistance programs or public services.

Hearing—Committee or subcommittee meetings to receive testimony on proposed legislation during investigations or for oversight purposes. Relatively few bills are important enough to justify formal hearings. Witnesses often include experts, government officials, spokespersons for interested groups, officials of the Government Accountability Office, and members of Congress.

Hold—A senator's request that his or her party leaders delay or halt floor consideration of certain legislation or presidential nominations. The majority leader usually honors a hold for a reasonable period of time, especially if its purpose is to assure the senator that the matter will not be called up during his or her absence or to give the senator time to gather necessary information.

Hold (or Have) the Floor—A member's right to speak without interruption, unless he or she violates a rule, after recognition by the presiding officer. At the member's discretion, he or she may yield to another member for a question in the Senate or for a question or statement in the House, but may reclaim the floor at any time.

Hold-Harmless Clause—In legislation providing a new formula for allocating federal funds, a clause to ensure that recipients of those funds do not receive less in a future year than they did in the current year if the new formula would result in a reduction for them. Similar to a grandfather clause, it has been used most frequently to soften the impact of sudden reductions in federal grants. *(See Grandfather Clause.)*

Hopper—A box on the clerk's desk in the House chamber into which members deposit bills and resolutions to introduce them. In House jargon, to drop a bill in the hopper is to introduce it.

Hour Rule—A House rule that permits members, when recognized, to hold the floor in debate for no more than one hour each. The majority party member customarily yields one-half the time to a minority member. Although the hour rule applies to general debate in Committee of the Whole as well as in the House, special rules routinely vary the length of time for such debate and its control to fit the circumstances of particular measures.

House as in Committee of the Whole—A hybrid combination of procedures from the general rules of the House and from the rules of the Committee of the Whole, sometimes used to expedite consideration of a measure on the floor.

House Calendar—The calendar reserved for all public bills and resolutions that do not raise revenue or directly or indirectly appropriate money or property when they are favorably reported by House committees.

House Manual—A commonly used title for the handbook of the rules of the House of Representatives, published in each Congress. Its official title is *Constitution, Jefferson's Manual, and Rules of the House of Representatives.*

House of Representatives—The house of Congress in which states are represented roughly in proportion to their populations, but every state is guaranteed at least one representative. By law, the number of voting representatives is fixed at 435. Four delegates and one resident commissioner also serve in the House; they may vote in their committees but not on the House floor. Although the House and Senate have equal legislative power, the Constitution gives the House sole authority to originate revenue measures. The House also claims the right to originate appropriation measures, a claim the Senate disputes in theory but concedes in practice. The House has the sole power to impeach (only the Senate convicts, however), and it elects the president when no candidate has received a majority of the electoral votes. It is sometimes referred to as the lower body.

Immunity—(1) Members' constitutional protection from lawsuits and arrest in connection with their legislative duties. They may not be tried for libel or slander for anything they say on the floor of a house or in committee. Nor may they be arrested while attending sessions of their houses or when traveling to or from sessions of Congress, except when charged with treason, a felony, or a breach of the peace. (2) In the case of a witness before a committee, a grant of protection from prosecution based on that person's testimony to the committee. It is used to compel witnesses to testify who would otherwise refuse to do so on the constitutional ground of possible self-incrimination. Under such a grant, none of a witness's testimony may be used against him or her in a court proceeding except in a prosecution for perjury or for giving a false statement to Congress. *(See also Contempt of Congress.)*

Impeachment—The first step to remove the president, vice president, or other federal civil officers from office and to disqualify them from any future federal office "of honor, Trust or Profit." An impeachment is a formal charge of treason, bribery, or "other high Crimes and Misdemeanors." The House has the sole power of impeachment and the Senate the sole power of trying the charges and convicting.

The House impeaches by a simple majority vote; conviction requires a two-thirds vote of all senators present.

Impeachment Trial, Removal, and Disqualification—The Senate conducts an impeachment trial under a separate set of twenty-six rules that appears in the *Senate Manual.* Under the Constitution, the chief justice of the Supreme Court presides over trials of the president, but the vice president, the president pro tempore, or any other senator may preside over the impeachment trial of another official.

The Constitution requires senators to take an oath for an impeachment trial. During the trial, senators may not engage in colloquies or participate in arguments, but they may submit questions in writing to House managers or defense counsel. After the trial concludes, the Senate votes separately on each article of impeachment without debate unless the Senate orders the doors closed for private discussions. During deliberations senators may speak no more than once on a question, not for more than ten minutes on an interlocutory question and not more than fifteen minutes on the final question. These rules may be set aside by unanimous consent or suspended on motion by a two-thirds vote.

The Senate's impeachment trial of President Bill Clinton in 1999 was only the second such trial involving a president. It continued for five weeks, with the Senate voting not to convict on the two impeachment articles.

Senate impeachment rules allow the Senate, at its discretion, to name a committee to hear evidence and conduct the trial, with all senators thereafter voting on the charges. The impeachment trials of three federal judges were conducted this way, and the Supreme Court upheld the validity of these rules in *Nixon v. United States,* 506 U.S. 224, 1993.

An official convicted on impeachment charges is removed from office immediately. However, the convicted official is not barred from holding a federal office in the future unless the Senate, after its conviction vote, also approves a resolution disqualifying the convicted official from future office. For example, federal judge Alcee L. Hastings was impeached and convicted in 1989, but the Senate did not vote to bar him from office in the future. In 1992 Hastings was elected to the House of Representatives, and no challenge was raised against seating him when he took the oath of office in 1993.

Impoundment—An executive branch action or inaction that delays or withholds the expenditure or obligation of budget authority provided by law. The Impoundment Control Act of 1974 classifies impoundments as either deferrals or rescissions, requires the president to notify Congress about all such actions, and gives Congress authority to approve or reject them.

Inspector General in the House of Representatives—A position established with the passage of the House Administrative Reform Resolution of 1992. The duties of the office have been revised several times and are now contained in House Rule II. The inspector general (IG), who is subject to the policy direction and oversight of the Committee on House Administration, is appointed for a Congress jointly by the Speaker and the majority and minority leaders of the House. The IG communicates the results of audits to the House officers or officials who were the subjects of the audits and suggests appropriate corrective measures. The IG submits a report of each audit to the Speaker, the majority and minority leaders, and the chairman and ranking minority member of the House Administration Committee; notifies these five members in the case of any financial irregularity discovered; and reports to the Committee on Standards of Official Conduct on possible violations of House rules or any applicable law by any House member, officer, or employee. The IG's office also has certain duties to audit various financial operations of the House that had previously been performed by the Government Accountability Office.

Instruct Conferees—A formal action by a house urging its conferees to uphold a particular position on a measure in conference. The instruction may be to insist on certain provisions in the measure as passed by that house or to accept a provision in the version passed by the other house. Instructions to conferees are not binding because the primary responsibility of conferees is to reach agreement on a measure and neither house can compel the other to accept particular provisions or positions.

Investigative Power—The authority of Congress and its committees to pursue investigations, upheld by the Supreme Court but limited to matters related to, and in furtherance of, a legitimate task of the Congress. Standing committees in both houses are permanently authorized to investigate matters within their jurisdictions. Major investigations are sometimes conducted by temporary select, special, or joint committees established by resolutions for that purpose.

Some rules of the House provide certain safeguards for witnesses and others during investigative hearings. These permit counsel to accompany witnesses, require that each witness receive a copy of the committee's rules, and order the committee to go into closed session if it believes the testimony to be heard might defame, degrade, or incriminate any person. The committee may subsequently decide to hear such testimony in open session. The Senate has no rules of this kind.

Item Veto—Item veto authority, which is available to most state governors, allows governors to eliminate or reduce items in legislative measures presented for their signature without vetoing the entire measure, and sign the rest into law. A similar authority was briefly granted to the U.S. president under the Line Item Veto Act of 1996. According to the majority opinion of the Supreme Court in its 1998 decision overturning that law, a constitutional amendment would be necessary to give the president item such veto authority.

Jefferson's Manual—Short title of *Jefferson's Manual of Parliamentary Practice,* prepared by Thomas Jefferson for his guidance when he was president of the Senate from 1797 to 1801. Although it reflects English parliamentary practice in his day, many procedures in both houses of Congress are still rooted in its basic precepts. Under a House rule adopted in 1837, the manual's provisions govern House procedures when applicable and when they are not inconsistent with its standing rules and orders. The Senate, however, has never officially acknowledged it as a direct authority for its legislative procedure.

Johnson Rule—A policy instituted in 1953 under which all Democratic senators are assigned to one major committee before any Democrat is assigned to two. The Johnson Rule is named after its author, Sen. Lyndon B. Johnson, D-Texas, then the Senate's Democratic leader. Senate Republicans adopted a similar policy soon thereafter.

Joint Committee—A committee composed of members selected from each house. The functions of most joint committees involve investigation, research, or oversight of agencies closely related to Congress. Permanent joint committees, created by statute, are sometimes called standing joint committees. Once quite numerous, only four joint committees remained as of 2005: Joint Economic, Joint Taxation, Joint Library, and Joint Printing. None has authority to report legislation.

Joint Explanatory Statement—This is a statement appended to a conference report that explains in plain English the conference agreement and the intent of the conferees.

Joint Resolution—A legislative measure that Congress uses for purposes other than general legislation. Similar to a bill, it has the force of law when passed by both houses and either approved by the president or passed over the president's veto. Unlike a bill, a joint resolution enacted into law is not called an act; it retains its original title. Most often, joint resolutions deal with such relatively limited matters as the correction of errors in existing law, continuing appropriations, a single appropriation, or the establishment of permanent joint committees. Unlike bills, however, joint resolutions also are used to propose constitutional amendments; these do not require the president's signature and become effective only when ratified by three-fourths of the states. The House designates joint resolutions as H J Res, the Senate as S J Res. Each house numbers its joint resolutions consecutively in the order of introduction during a two-year Congress.

Joint Session—Informally, any combined meeting of the Senate and the House. Technically, a joint session is a combined meeting to count the electoral votes for president and vice president or to hear a presidential address, such as the State of the Union message; any other formal combined gathering of both houses is a joint meeting. Joint sessions are authorized by concurrent resolutions and are held in the House chamber, because of its larger seating capacity. Although the president of the Senate and the Speaker sit side by side at the Speaker's desk during combined meetings, the former presides over the electoral count and the latter presides on all other occasions and introduces the president or other guest speaker. The president and other guests may address a joint session or meeting only by invitation.

Joint Sponsorship—Two or more members sponsoring the same measure.

Journal—The official record of House or Senate actions, including every motion offered, every vote cast, amendments agreed to, quorum calls, and so forth. Unlike the *Congressional Record,* it does not provide reports of speeches, debates, statements, and other items. The Constitution requires each house to maintain a *Journal* and to publish it periodically.

Junket—A member's trip at government expense, especially abroad, ostensibly on official business but, it is often alleged, for pleasure.

Killer Amendment—An amendment that, if agreed to, might lead to the defeat of the measure it amends, either in the house in which the amendment is offered or at some later stage of the legislative process. Members sometimes deliberately offer or vote for such an amendment in the expectation that it will undermine support for the measure in Congress or increase the likelihood that the president will veto it.

King of the Mountain (or Hill Rule)—*(See Queen of the Hill Rule.)*

LA—*(See Legislative Assistant.)*

Lame Duck—Jargon for a member who has not been reelected, or did not seek reelection, and is serving the balance of his or her term.

Lame Duck Session—A session of a Congress held after the election for the succeeding Congress, so-called after the lame duck members still serving.

Last Train Out—Colloquial name for last must-pass bill of a session of Congress.

Law—An act of Congress that has been signed by the president, passed over the president's veto, or allowed to become law without the president's signature.

Lay on the Table—A motion to dispose of a pending proposition immediately, finally, and adversely; that is, to kill it without a direct vote on its substance. Often simply called a motion to table, it is not debatable and is adopted by majority vote or without objection. It is a highly privileged motion, taking precedence over all others except the motion to adjourn in the House and all but three additional motions in the Senate. It can kill a bill or resolution, an amendment, another motion, an appeal, or virtually any other matter.

Tabling an amendment also tables the measure to which the amendment is pending in the House, but not in the Senate. The House does not allow the motion against the motion to recommit, in Committee of the Whole, and in some other situations. In the Senate it is the only permissible motion that immediately ends debate on a proposition, but only to kill it.

(The) Leadership—Usually, a reference to the majority and minority leaders of the Senate or to the Speaker and minority leader of the House. The term sometimes includes the majority leader in the House and the majority and minority whips in each house and, at other times, other party officials as well.

Legislation—(1) A synonym for legislative measures: bills and joint resolutions. (2) Provisions in such measures or in substantive amendments offered to them. (3) In some contexts, provisions that change existing substantive or authorizing law, rather than provisions that make appropriations.

Legislation on an Appropriation Bill—A common reference to provisions changing existing law that appear in, or are offered as amendments to, a general appropriation bill. A House rule prohibits the inclusion of such provisions in general appropriation bills unless they retrench expenditures. An analogous Senate rule permits points of order against amendments to a general appropriation bill that propose general legislation.

Legislative Assistant (LA)—A member's staff person responsible for monitoring and preparing legislation on particular subjects and for advising the member on them; commonly referred to as an LA.

Legislative Day—The day that begins when a house meets after an adjournment and ends when it next adjourns. Because the House of Representatives normally adjourns at the end of a daily session, its legislative and calendar days usually coincide. The Senate, however, frequently recesses at the end of a daily session, and its legislative day may extend over several calendar days, weeks, or months. Among other uses, this technicality permits the Senate to save time by circumventing its morning hour, a procedure required at the beginning of every legislative day.

Legislative History—(1) A chronological list of actions taken on a measure during its progress through the legislative process. (2) The

official documents relating to a measure, the entries in the *Journals* of the two houses on that measure, and the *Congressional Record* text of its consideration in both houses. The documents include all committee reports and the conference report and joint explanatory statement, if any. Courts and affected federal agencies study a measure's legislative history for congressional intent about its purpose and interpretation.

Legislative Process—(1) Narrowly, the stages in the enactment of a law from introduction to final disposition. An introduced measure that becomes law typically travels through reference to committee; committee and subcommittee consideration; report to the chamber; floor consideration; amendment; passage; engrossment; messaging to the other house; similar steps in that house, including floor amendment of the measure; return of the measure to the first house; consideration of amendments between the houses or a conference to resolve their differences; approval of the conference report by both houses; enrollment; approval by the president or override of the president's veto; and deposit with the Archivist of the United States. (2) Broadly, the political, lobbying, and other factors that affect or influence the process of enacting laws.

Legislative Veto—A procedure, declared unconstitutional in 1983, that allowed Congress or one of its houses to nullify certain actions of the president, executive branch agencies, or independent agencies. Sometimes called congressional vetoes or congressional disapprovals. Following the Supreme Court's 1983 decision, Congress amended several legislative veto statutes to require enactment of joint resolutions, which are subject to presidential veto, for nullifying executive branch actions.

Limitation on a General Appropriation Bill—Language that prohibits expenditures for part of an authorized purpose from funds provided in a general appropriation bill. Precedents require that the language be phrased in the negative: that none of the funds provided in a pending appropriation bill shall be used for a specified authorized activity. Limitations in general appropriation bills are permitted on the grounds that Congress can refuse to fund authorized programs and, therefore, can refuse to fund any part of them as long as the prohibition does not change existing law. House precedents have established that a limitation does not change existing law if it does not impose additional duties or burdens on executive branch officials, interfere with their discretionary authority, or require them to make judgments or determinations not required by existing law. The proliferation of limitation amendments in the 1970s and early 1980s prompted the House to adopt a rule in 1983 making it more difficult for members to offer them. The rule bans such amendments during the reading of an appropriation bill for amendments, unless they are specifically authorized in existing law. Other limitations may be offered after the reading, but the Committee of the Whole can foreclose them by adopting a motion to rise and report the bill back to the House. In 1995 the rule was amended to allow the motion to rise and report to be made only by the majority leader or his or her designee. The House Appropriations Committee, however, can include limitation provisions in the bills it reports.

Line Item—An amount in an appropriation measure. It can refer to a single appropriation account or to separate amounts within the account. In the congressional budget process, the term usually refers to assumptions about the funding of particular programs or accounts that underlie the broad functional amounts in a budget resolution.

These assumptions are discussed in the reports accompanying each resolution and are not binding.

Line-Item Veto—*(See Item Veto; Line Item Veto Act of 1996.)*

Line Item Veto Act of 1996—A law, in effect only from January 1997 until June 1998, that granted the president authority intended to be functionally equivalent to an item veto, by amending the Impoundment Control Act to incorporate an approach known as enhanced rescission. Key provisions established a new procedure that permitted the president to cancel amounts of new discretionary appropriations (budget authority), new items of direct spending (entitlements), or certain limited tax benefits. It also required the president to notify Congress of the cancellation in a special message within five calendar days after signing the measure. The cancellation would become permanent unless legislation disapproving it was enacted within thirty days. On June 25, 1998, in *Clinton v. City of New York* the Supreme Court held the Line Item Veto Act unconstitutional, on the grounds that its cancellation provisions violated the presentment clause in Article I, clause 7, of the Constitution.

Live Pair—A voluntary and informal agreement between two members on opposite sides of an issue, one of whom is absent for a recorded vote, under which the member who is present withholds or withdraws his or her vote to offset the failure to vote by the member who is absent. Usually the member in attendance announces that he or she has a live pair, states how each would have voted, and votes "present." In the House, under a rules change enacted in the 106th Congress, a live pair is only permitted on the rare occasions when electronic voting is not used.

Live Quorum—In the Senate, a quorum call to which senators are expected to respond. Senators usually suggest the absence of a quorum, not to force a quorum to appear, but to provide a pause in the proceedings during which senators can engage in private discussions or wait for a senator to come to the floor. A senator desiring a live quorum usually announces his or her intention, giving fair warning that there will be an objection to any unanimous consent request that the quorum call be dispensed with before it is completed.

Loan Guarantee—A statutory commitment by the federal government to pay part or all of a loan's principal and interest to a lender or the holder of a security in case the borrower defaults.

Lobby—To try to persuade members of Congress to propose, pass, modify, or defeat proposed legislation or to change or repeal existing laws. Lobbyists attempt to promote their preferences or those of a group, organization, or industry. Originally the term referred to persons frequenting the lobbies or corridors of legislative chambers in order to speak to lawmakers. In a general sense, lobbying includes not only direct contact with members but also indirect attempts to influence them, such as writing to them or persuading others to write or visit them, attempting to mold public opinion toward a desired legislative goal by various means, and contributing or arranging for contributions to members election campaigns. The right to lobby stems from the First Amendment to the Constitution, which bans laws that abridge the right of the people to petition the government for a redress of grievances.

Lobbying Disclosure Act of 1995—The principal statute requiring disclosure of—and also, to a degree, circumscribing—the activities of lobbyists. In general, it requires lobbyists who spend more than 20 percent of their time on lobbying activities to register and make semiannual reports of their activities to the clerk of the House and the secretary of the Senate, although the law provides for a number of exemptions. Among the statute's prohibitions, lobbyists are not allowed to make contributions to the legal defense fund of a member or high government official or to reimburse for official travel. Civil penalties for failure to comply may include fines of up to $50,000. The act does not include grassroots lobbying in its definition of lobbying activities.

The act amended several other lobby laws, notably the Foreign Agents Registration (FARA), so that lobbyists can submit a single filing. Since the measure was enacted, the number of lobby registrations has risen from about 12,000 to more than 20,000. In 1998 expenditures on federal lobbying, as disclosed under the Lobbying Disclosure Act, totaled $1.42 billion. The 1995 act supersedes the 1946 Federal Regulation of Lobbying Act, which was repealed in Section 11 of the 1995 Act.

Logrolling—Jargon for a legislative tactic or bargaining strategy in which members try to build support for their legislation by promising to support legislation desired by other members or by accepting amendments they hope will induce their colleagues to vote for their bill.

Lower Body—A way to refer to the House of Representatives, which is considered pejorative by House members.

Mace—The symbol of the office of the House sergeant at arms. Under the direction of the Speaker, the sergeant at arms is responsible for preserving order on the House floor by holding up the mace in front of an unruly member, or by carrying the mace up and down the aisles to quell boisterous behavior. When the House is in session, the mace sits on a pedestal at the Speaker's right; when the House is in Committee of the Whole, it is moved to a lower pedestal. The mace is forty-six inches high and consists of thirteen ebony rods bound in silver and topped by a silver globe with a silver eagle, wings outstretched, perched on it.

Majority Leader—The majority party's chief floor spokesperson, elected by that party's caucus—sometimes called floor leader. In the Senate, the majority leader also develops the party's political and procedural strategy, usually in collaboration with other party officials and committee chairmen. The majority leader negotiates the Senate's agenda and committee ratios with the minority leader and usually calls up measures for floor action. The chamber traditionally concedes to the majority leader the right to determine the days on which it will meet and the hours at which it will convene and adjourn. In the House, the majority leader is the Speaker's deputy and heir apparent and helps plan the floor agenda and the party's legislative strategy and often speaks for the party leadership in debate.

Managers—(1) The official title of members appointed to a conference committee, commonly called conferees. The ranking majority and minority managers for each house also manage floor consideration of the committee's conference report. (2) The members who manage the initial floor consideration of a measure. (3) The official title of House members appointed to present impeachment articles to the Senate and to act as prosecutors on behalf of the House during the Senate trial of the impeached person.

Mandatory Appropriations—Amounts that Congress must appropriate annually because it has no discretion over them unless it first amends existing substantive law. Certain entitlement programs, for example, require annual appropriations.

Markup—A meeting or series of meetings by a committee or subcommittee during which members mark up a measure by offering, debating, and voting on amendments to it.

Means-Tested Programs—Programs that provide benefits or services to low-income individuals who meet a test of need. Most are entitlement programs, such as Medicaid, food stamps, and Supplementary Security Income. A few—for example, subsidized housing and various social services—are funded through discretionary appropriations.

Members' Allowances—Official expenses that are paid for or for which members are reimbursed by their houses. Among these are the costs of office space in congressional buildings and in their home states or districts; office equipment and supplies; postage-free mailings (the franking privilege); a set number of trips to and from home states or districts, as well as travel elsewhere on official business; telephone and other telecommunications services; and staff salaries.

Member's Staff—The personal staff to which a member is entitled. The House sets a maximum number of staff and a monetary allowance for each member. The Senate does not set a maximum staff level, but it does set a monetary allowance for each member. In each house, the staff allowance is included with office expenses allowances and official mail allowances in a consolidated allowance. Representatives and senators can spend as much money in their consolidated allowances for staff, office expenses, or official mail, as long as they do not exceed the monetary value of the three allowances combined. This provides members with flexibility in operating their offices.

Method of Equal Proportions—The mathematical formula used since 1950 to determine how the 435 seats in the House of Representatives should be distributed among the fifty states in the apportionment following each decennial census. It minimizes as much as possible the proportional difference between the average district population in any two states. Because the Constitution guarantees each state at least one representative, fifty seats are automatically apportioned. The formula calculates priority numbers for each state, assigns the first of the 385 remaining seats to the state with the highest priority number, the second to the state with the next highest number, and so on until all seats are distributed. *(See Apportionment.)*

Midterm Election—The general election for members of Congress that occurs in November of the second year in a presidential term.

Minority Leader—The minority party's leader and chief floor spokesperson, elected by the party caucus; sometimes called minority floor leader. With the assistance of other party officials and the ranking minority members of committees, the minority leader devises the party's political and procedural strategy.

Minority Staff—Employees who assist the minority party members of a committee. Most committees hire separate majority and minority party staffs but they also may hire nonpartisan staff. Senate rules state that a committee's staff must reflect the relative number of its majority and minority party committee members, and the rules guarantee the minority at least one-third of the funds available for hiring partisan staff. In the House, each committee is authorized thirty professional staff, and the minority members of most committees may select up to ten of these staff (subject to full committee approval). Under House rules, the minority party is to be "treated fairly" in the apportionment of additional staff resources. Each House committee determines the portion of its additional staff it allocates to the minority; some committees allocate one-third; and others allot less.

Modified Rule—A special rule from the House Rules Committee that permits only certain amendments to be offered to a measure during its floor consideration or that bans certain specified amendments or amendments on certain subjects.

Morning Business—In the Senate, routine business that is to be transacted at the beginning of the morning hour. The business consists, first, of laying before the Senate, and referring to committees, matters such as messages from the president and the House, federal agency reports, and unreferred petitions, memorials, bills, and joint resolutions. Next, senators may present additional petitions and memorials. Then committees may present their reports, after which senators may introduce bills and resolutions. Finally, resolutions coming over from a previous day are taken up for consideration. In practice, the Senate adopts standing orders that permit senators to introduce measures and file reports at any time, but only if there has been a morning business period on that day. Because the Senate often remains in the same legislative day for several days, weeks, or months at a time, it orders a morning business period almost every calendar day for the convenience of senators who wish to introduce measures or make reports.

Morning Hour—A two-hour period at the beginning of a new legislative day during which the Senate is supposed to conduct routine business, call the calendar on Mondays, and deal with other matters described in a Senate rule. In practice, the morning hour rarely, if ever, occurs, in part because the Senate frequently recesses, rather than adjourns, at the end of a daily session. Therefore the rule does not apply when the senate next meets. The Senate's rules reserve the first hour of the morning for morning business. After the completion of morning business, or at the end of the first hour, the rules permit a motion to proceed to the consideration of a measure on the calendar out of its regular order (except on Mondays). Because that normally debatable motion is not debatable if offered during the morning hour, the majority leader may, but rarely does, use this procedure in anticipating a filibuster on the motion to proceed. If the Senate agrees to the motion, it can consider the measure until the end of the morning hour, and if there is no unfinished business from the previous day it can continue considering it after the morning hour. But if there is unfinished business, a motion to continue consideration is necessary, and that motion is debatable.

Motion—A formal proposal for a procedural action, such as to consider, to amend, to lay on the table, to reconsider, to recess, or to adjourn. It has been estimated that at least eighty-five motions are possible under various circumstances in the House of Representatives, somewhat fewer in the Senate. Not all motions are created equal; some are privileged or preferential and enjoy priority over others. Some motions are debatable, amendable, or divisible, while others are not.

Multiple and Sequential Referrals—The practice of referring a measure to two or more committees for concurrent consideration (multiple referral) or successively to several committees in sequence (sequential referral). A measure may also be divided into several parts, with each referred to a different committee or to several committees sequentially (split referral). In theory this gives all committees that have jurisdiction over parts of a measure the opportunity to consider and report on them.

Before 1975, House precedents banned such referrals. A 1975 rule required the Speaker to make concurrent and sequential referrals "to the maximum extent feasible." On sequential referrals, the Speaker could set deadlines for reporting the measure. The Speaker ruled that this provision authorized him to discharge a committee from further consideration of a measure and place it on the appropriate calendar of the House if the committee fails to meet the Speaker's deadline. The Speaker also used combinations of concurrent and sequential referrals. In 1995 joint referrals were prohibited. Measures are referred to a primary committee and also may be referred, either concurrently or sequentially, to one or more other committees, but usually only for consideration of portions of the measure that fall within the jurisdiction of each of those other committees. In 2003 the Speaker was authorized to not designate a primary committee under "extraordinary circumstances."

In the Senate, before 1977 concurrent and sequential referrals were permitted only by unanimous consent. In that year, a rule authorized a privileged motion for such a referral if offered jointly by the majority and minority leaders. Debate on the motion and all amendments to it is limited to two hours. The motion may set deadlines for reporting and provide for discharging the committees involved if they fail to meet the deadlines. To date, this procedure has never been invoked; multiple referrals in the Senate continue to be made by unanimous consent.

Multiyear Appropriation—An appropriation that remains available for spending or obligation for more than one fiscal year; the exact period of time is specified in the act making the appropriation.

Multiyear Authorization—(1) Legislation that authorizes the existence or continuation of an agency, program, or activity for more than one fiscal year. (2) Legislation that authorizes appropriations for an agency, program, or activity for more than one fiscal year.

Nomination—A proposed presidential appointment to a federal office submitted to the Senate for confirmation. Approval is by majority vote. The Constitution explicitly requires confirmation for ambassadors, consuls, "public Ministers" (department heads), and Supreme Court justices. By law, other federal judges, all military promotions of officers, and many high-level civilian officials must be confirmed.

Nuclear Option—A common name for a parliamentary maneuver that changes Senate rules to prevent filibusters on judicial nominations to force a floor vote. Also referred to as the constitutional option.

Oath of Office—On taking office, members of Congress must swear or affirm that they will "support and defend the Constitution . . . against all enemies, foreign and domestic," that they will "bear true faith and allegiance" to the Constitution, that they take the obligation "freely, without any mental reservation or purpose of evasion," and that they will "well and faithfully discharge the duties" of their office. The oath is required by the Constitution, and the wording is prescribed by a statute. All House members must take the oath at the beginning of each new Congress. Usually, the member with the longest continuous service in the House swears in the Speaker, who then swears in the other members. The president of the Senate or a surrogate administers the oath to newly elected or reelected senators.

Obligation—A binding agreement by a government agency to pay for goods, products, services, studies, and so on, either immediately or in the future. When an agency enters into such an agreement, it incurs an obligation. As the agency makes the required payments, it liquidates the obligation. Appropriation laws usually make funds available for obligation for one or more fiscal years but do not require agencies to spend their funds during those specific years. The actual outlays can occur years after the appropriation is obligated, as with a contract for construction of a submarine may provide for payment to be made when it is delivered in the future. Such obligated funds are often said to be "in the pipeline." Under these circumstances, an agency's outlays in a particular year can come from appropriations obligated in previous years as well as from its current-year appropriation. Consequently, the money Congress appropriates for a fiscal year does not equal the total amount of appropriated money the government will actually spend in that year.

Off-Budget Entities—Specific federal entities whose budget authority, outlays, and receipts are excluded by law from the calculation of budget totals, although they are part of government spending and income. As of 2005 these included the Social Security trust funds (Federal Old-Age and Survivors Insurance Fund and the Federal Disability Insurance Trust Fund) and the Postal Service. Government-sponsored enterprises are also excluded from the budget because they are considered private rather than public organizations.

Office of Management and Budget (OMB)—A unit in the Executive Office of the President, reconstituted in 1990 from the former Bureau of the Budget. The Office of Management and Budget (OMB) assists the president in preparing the budget and in formulating the government's fiscal program. The OMB also plays a central role in supervising and controlling implementation of the budget, pursuant to provisions in appropriations laws, the Budget Enforcement Act, and other statutes. In addition to these budgetary functions, the OMB has various management duties, including those performed through its three statutory offices: Federal Financial Management, Federal Procurement Policy, and Information and Regulatory Affairs.

Officers of Congress—The Constitution refers to the Speaker of the House and the president of the Senate as officers and declares that each house "shall chuse" its "other Officers," but it does not name them or indicate how they should be selected. A House rule refers to its clerk, sergeant at arms, and chaplain as officers. Officers are not named in the Senate's rules, but *Riddick's Senate Procedure* lists the president pro tempore, secretary of the Senate, sergeant at arms, chaplain, and the secretaries for the majority and minority parties as officers. A few appointed officials are sometimes referred to as officers, including the parliamentarians and the legislative counsels. The House elects its officers by resolution at the beginning of each Congress. The Senate also elects its officers, but once elected Senate officers serve from Congress to Congress until their successors are chosen.

Official Objectors—House members who screen measures on the Private Calendar and decide whether or not to object to the consideration of any one or more of them.

Omnibus Bill—A measure that combines the provisions of several disparate subjects into a single and often lengthy bill.

One-Minute Speeches—Addresses by House members that can be on any subject but are limited to one minute. They are usually permitted at the beginning of a daily session after the chaplain's prayer, the pledge of allegiance, and approval of the *Journal*. They are a customary practice, not a right granted by rule. Consequently, recognition for one-minute speeches requires unanimous consent and is entirely within the Speaker's discretion. The Speaker sometimes refuses to permit them when the House has a heavy legislative schedule or limits or postpones them until a later time of the day.

Open Rule—A special rule from the House Rules Committee that permits members to offer as many floor amendments as they wish as long as the amendments are germane and do not violate other House rules.

Order of Business (House)—The sequence of events prescribed by a House rule during the meeting of the House on a new legislative day that is supposed to take place, also called the general order of business. The sequence consists of (1) the chaplain's prayer; (2) reading and approval of the *Journal;* (3) the pledge of allegiance; (4) correction of the reference of public bills to committee; (5) disposal of business on the Speaker's table; (6) unfinished business; (7) the morning hour call of committees and consideration of their bills; (8) motions to go into Committee of the Whole; and (9) orders of the day. In practice, the House never fully complies with this rule. Instead, the items of business that follow the pledge of allegiance are supplanted by any special orders of business that are in order on that day (for example, conference reports; the corrections, discharge, or private calendars; or motions to suspend the rules) and by other privileged business (for example, general appropriation bills and special rules) or measures made in order by special rules or unanimous consent. The regular order of business is also modified by unanimous consent practices and orders that govern recognition for one-minute speeches (which date from 1937) and for morning-hour debates, begun in 1994. By this combination of an order of business with privileged interruptions, the House gives precedence to certain categories of important legislation, brings to the floor other major legislation from its calendars in any order it chooses, and provides expeditious processing for minor and noncontroversial measures.

Order of Business (Senate)—The sequence of events at the beginning of a new legislative day, as prescribed by Senate rules and standing orders. The sequence consists of (1) the chaplain's prayer; (2) the pledge of allegiance; (3) the designation of a temporary presiding officer if any; (4) *Journal* reading and approval; (5) recognition of the majority and minority leaders or their designees under the standing order; (6) morning business in the morning hour; (7) call of the calendar during the morning hour (largely obsolete); and (8) unfinished business from the previous session day.

Organization of Congress—The actions each house takes at the beginning of a Congress that are necessary to its operations. These include swearing in newly elected members, notifying the president that a quorum of each house is present, making committee assignments, and fixing the hour for daily meetings. Because the House of Representatives is not a continuing body, it must also elect its Speaker and other officers and adopt its rules.

Original Bill—(1) A measure drafted by a committee and introduced by its chairman or another designated member when the committee reports the measure to its house. Unlike a clean bill, it is not referred back to the committee after introduction. The Senate permits all its legislative committees to report original bills. In the House, this authority is referred to in the rules as the "right to report at any time," and five committees (Appropriations, Budget, House Administration, Rules, and Standards of Official Conduct) have such authority under circumstances specified in House Rule XIII, clause 5.

(2) In the House, special rules reported by the Rules Committee often propose that an amendment in the nature of a substitute be considered as an original bill for purposes of amendment, meaning that the substitute, as with a bill, may be amended in two degrees. Without that requirement, the substitute may only be amended in one further degree. In the Senate, an amendment in the nature of a substitute automatically is open to two degrees of amendment, as is the original text of the bill, if the substitute is offered when no other amendment is pending.

Original Jurisdiction—The authority of certain committees to originate a measure and report it to the chamber. For example, general appropriation bills reported by the House Appropriations Committee are original bills, and special rules reported by the House Rules Committee are original resolutions.

Other Body—A commonly used reference to a house by a member of the other house. Congressional comity discourages members from directly naming the other house during debate.

Outlays—Amounts of government spending. They consist of payments, usually by check or in cash, to liquidate obligations incurred in prior fiscal years as well as in the current year, including the net lending of funds under budget authority. In federal budget accounting, net outlays are calculated by subtracting the amounts of refunds and various kinds of reimbursements to the government from actual spending.

Override a Veto—Congressional enactment of a measure over the president's veto. A veto override requires a recorded two-thirds vote of those voting in each house, a quorum being present. Because the president must return the vetoed measure to its house of origin, that house votes first, but neither house is required to attempt an override, whether immediately or at all. If an override attempt fails in the house of origin, the veto stands and the measure dies.

Oversight—Congressional review of the way in which federal agencies implement laws to ensure that they are carrying out the intent of Congress and to inquire into the efficiency of the implementation and the effectiveness of the law. The Legislative Reorganization Act of 1946 defined oversight as the function of exercising continuous watchfulness over the execution of the laws by the executive branch.

Oxford-Style Debate—The House held three Oxford-style debates in 1994, modeled after the famous debating format favored by the Oxford Union in Great Britain. Neither chamber has held Oxford-style debates since then. The Oxford-style debates aired nationally over C-SPAN television and National Public Radio. The organized event featured eight participants divided evenly into two teams, one team representing the Democrats (then holding the majority in the chamber) and the other the Republicans. Both teams argued a single question chosen well ahead of the event. A moderator regulated the debate, and began it by stating the resolution at issue. The order of the speakers alternated by team, with a debater for the affirmative speaking first and a debater for the opposing team offering a rebuttal. The rest of the speakers alternated in kind until all gained the chance to speak.

Parliamentarian—The official advisor to the presiding officer in each house on questions of procedure. The parliamentarian and his or her assistants also answer procedural questions from members and congressional staff, refer measures to committees on behalf of the presiding officer, and maintain compilations of the precedents. The House parliamentarian revises the House Manual at the beginning of every Congress and usually reviews special rules before the Rules Committee reports them to the House. Either a parliamentarian or an assistant is always present and near the podium during sessions of each house.

Party Caucus—Generic term for each party's official organization in each house. Only House Democrats officially call their organization a caucus. House and Senate Republicans and Senate Democrats call their organizations conferences. The party caucuses elect their leaders, approve committee assignments and chairmanships (or ranking minority members, if the party is in the minority), establish party committees and study groups, and discuss party and legislative policies. On rare occasions, they have stripped members of committee seniority or expelled them from the caucus for party disloyalty.

Pay-as-You-Go (PAYGO)—A provision first instituted under the Budget Enforcement Act of 1990 that applies to legislation enacted before Oct. 1, 2002. It requires that the cumulative effect of legislation concerning either revenues or direct spending should not result in a net negative impact on the budget. If legislation does provide for an increase in spending or decrease in revenues, that effect is supposed to be offset by legislated spending reductions or revenue increases. If Congress fails to enact the appropriate offsets, the act requires presidential sequestration of sufficient offsetting amounts in specific direct spending accounts. Congress and the president can circumvent this requirement if both agree that an emergency requires a particular action or if a law is enacted declaring that deteriorated economic circumstances make it necessary to suspend the requirement.

Permanent Appropriation—An appropriation that remains continuously available, without current action or renewal by Congress, under the terms of a previously enacted authorization or appropriation law. One such appropriation provides for payment of interest on the public debt and another the salaries of members of Congress.

Permanent Authorization—An authorization without a time limit. It usually does not specify any limit on the funds that may be appropriated for the agency, program, or activity that it authorizes, leaving such amounts to the discretion of the appropriations committees and the two houses.

Permanent Staff—Term used formerly for committee staff authorized by law, who were funded through a permanent authorization and also called statutory staff. Most committees were authorized thirty permanent staff members. Most committees also were permitted additional staff, often called investigative staff, who were authorized by annual or biennial funding resolutions. The Senate eliminated the primary distinction between statutory and investigative staff in 1981. The House eliminated the distinction in 1995 by requiring that funding resolutions authorize money to hire both types of staff.

Personally Obnoxious (or Objectionable)—A characterization a senator sometimes applies to a president's nominee for a federal office in that senator's state to justify his or her opposition to the nomination.

Pocket Veto—The indirect veto of a bill as a result of the president withholding approval of it until after Congress has adjourned *sine die*. A bill the president does not sign but does not formally veto while Congress is in session automatically becomes a law ten days (excluding Sundays) after it is received. But if Congress adjourns its annual session during that ten-day period the measure dies even if the president does not formally veto it.

Point of Order—A parliamentary term used in committee and on the floor to object to an alleged violation of a rule and to demand that the chair enforce the rule. The point of order immediately halts the proceedings until the chair decides whether the contention is valid.

Pork or Pork Barrel Legislation—Pejorative terms for federal appropriations, bills, or policies that provide funds to benefit a legislator's district or state, with the implication that the legislator presses for enactment of such benefits to ingratiate himself or herself with constituents rather than on the basis of an impartial, objective assessment of need or merit. The terms are often applied to such benefits as new parks, federal offices, dams, canals, bridges, roads, water projects, sewage treatment plants, and public works of any kind, as well as demonstration projects, research grants, and relocation of government facilities. Funds released by the president for various kinds of benefits or government contracts approved by him allegedly for political purposes are also sometimes referred to as pork.

Postcloture Filibuster—A filibuster conducted after the Senate invokes cloture. It employs an array of procedural tactics rather than lengthy speeches to delay final action. The Senate curtailed the postcloture filibusters effectiveness by closing a variety of loopholes in the cloture rule in 1979 and 1986.

Power of the Purse—A reference to the constitutional power Congress has over legislation to raise revenue and appropriate monies from the Treasury. Article I, Section 8 states that Congress "shall have Power To lay and collect Taxes, Duties, Imposts and Excises, [and] to pay the Debts." Section 9 declares: "No Money shall be drawn from the Treasury, but in Consequence of Appropriations made by Law."

Preamble—Introductory language describing the reasons for and intent of a measure, sometimes called a whereas clause. It occasionally appears in joint, concurrent, and simple resolutions but rarely in bills.

Precedent—A previous ruling on a parliamentary matter or a long-standing practice or custom of a house. Precedents serve to control arbitrary rulings and serve as the common law of a house.

President of the Senate—One constitutional role of the vice president is serving as the presiding officer of the Senate, or president of the Senate. The Constitution permits the vice president to cast a vote in the Senate only to break a tie, but the vice president is not required to do so.

President Pro Tempore—Under the Constitution, an officer elected by the Senate to preside over it during the absence of the vice president of the United States. Often referred to as the "pro tem," this senator is usually a member of the majority party with the longest continuous service in the chamber and also, by virtue of seniority, a committee chairman. When attending to committee and other duties the president pro tempore appoints other senators to preside.

Presiding Officer—In a formal meeting, the individual authorized to maintain order and decorum, recognize members to speak or offer motions, and apply and interpret the chamber's rules, precedents, and practices. The Speaker of the House and the president of the Senate are the chief presiding officers in their respective houses.

Previous Question—A nondebatable motion that, when agreed to by majority vote, usually cuts off further debate, prevents the offering of additional amendments, and brings the pending matter to an immediate vote. It is a major debate-limiting device in the House; it is not permitted in Committee of the Whole in the House or in the Senate.

Private Bill—A bill that applies to one or more specified persons, corporations, institutions, or other entities, usually to grant relief when no other legal remedy is available to them. Many private bills deal with claims against the federal government, immigration and naturalization cases, and land titles.

Private Calendar—Commonly used title for a calendar in the House reserved for private bills and resolutions favorably reported by committees. The private calendar is officially called the Calendar of the Committee of the Whole House.

Private Law—A private bill enacted into law. Private laws are numbered in the same fashion as public laws.

Privilege—An attribute of a motion, measure, report, question, or proposition that gives it priority status for consideration. Privileged motions and motions to bring up privileged questions are not debatable.

Privilege of the Floor—In addition to the members of a house, certain individuals are admitted to its floor while it is in session. The rules of the two houses differ somewhat but both extend the privilege to the president and vice president, Supreme Court justices, cabinet members, state governors, former members of that house, members of the other house, certain officers and officials of Congress, certain staff of that house in the discharge of official duties, and the chamber's former parliamentarians. They also allow access to a limited number of committee and members' staff when their presence is necessary.

Pro Forma Amendment—In the House, an amendment that ostensibly proposes to change a measure or another amendment by moving "to strike the last word" or "to strike the requisite number of words." A member offers it not to make any actual change in the measure or amendment but only to obtain time for debate.

Pro Tem—A common reference to the president pro tempore of the Senate or, occasionally, to a Speaker pro tempore. *(See President Pro Tempore; Speaker Pro Tempore.)*

Procedures—The methods of conducting business in a deliberative body. The procedures of each house are governed first by applicable provisions of the Constitution, and then by its standing rules and orders, precedents, traditional practices, and any statutory rules that apply to it. The authority of the houses to adopt rules in addition to those specified in the Constitution is derived from Article I, Section 5, clause 2, of the Constitution, which states: "Each House may determine the Rules of its Proceedings. . . ." By rule, the House of Representatives also follows the procedures in *Jefferson's Manual* that are not inconsistent with its standing rules and orders. Many Senate procedures also conform with Jefferson's provisions, but by practice rather than by rule. At the beginning of each Congress, the House uses procedures in general parliamentary law until it adopts its standing rules.

Proxy Voting—The practice of permitting a member to cast the vote of an absent colleague in addition to his or her own vote. Proxy voting is prohibited on the floors of the House and Senate, but the Senate permits its committees to authorize proxy voting, and most do. In 1995, House rules were changed to prohibit proxy voting in committee.

Public Bill—A bill dealing with general legislative matters having national applicability or applying to the federal government or to a class of persons, groups, or organizations.

Public Debt—Federal government debt incurred by the Treasury or the Federal Financing Bank by the sale of securities to the public or borrowings from a federal fund or account.

Public Law—A public bill or joint resolution enacted into law. It is cited by the letters "PL" followed by a hyphenated number. The digits before the hyphen indicate the number of the Congress in which it was enacted; the digits after the hyphen indicate its position in the numerical sequence of public measures that became law during that Congress. For example, the Budget Enforcement Act of 1990 became PL 101-508 because it was the 508th measure in that sequence for the 101st Congress. *(See also Private Law.)*

Qualification (of Members)—The Constitution requires members of the House of Representatives to be twenty-five years of age at the time their terms begin. They must have been citizens of the United States for seven years before that date and, when elected, must be "Inhabitant[s]" of the state from which they were elected. There is no constitutional requirement that they reside in the districts they represent. Senators are required to be thirty years of age at the time their terms begin. They must have been citizens of the United States for nine years before that date and, when elected, must be "Inhabitant[s]" of the states in which they were elected. The "Inhabitant" qualification is broadly interpreted, and in modern times a candidate's declaration of state residence has generally been accepted as meeting the constitutional requirement.

Queen of the Hill Rule—A special rule from the House Rules Committee that permits votes on a series of amendments, especially complete substitutes for a measure, in a specified order, but directs that the amendment receiving the greatest number of votes shall be the winning one. This kind of rule permits the House to vote directly on a variety of alternatives to a measure. In doing so, it sets aside the precedent that once an amendment has been adopted, no further amendments may be offered to the text it has amended. Under an earlier practice, the Rules Committee reported "king of the hill" rules under which there also could be votes on a series of amendments, again in a specified order. If more than one of the amendments was adopted under this kind of rule, it was the last amendment to receive a majority vote that was considered as having been finally adopted, whether or not it had received the greatest number of votes.

Quorum—The minimum number of members required to be present for the transaction of business. Under the Constitution, a quorum in each house is a majority of its members: 218 in the House and 51 in the Senate when there are no vacancies. By House rule, a quorum in Committee of the Whole is 100. In practice, both houses usually assume a quorum is present even if it is not, unless a member makes a point of no quorum in the House or suggests the absence of a quorum in the Senate. Consequently, each house transacts much of its business, and even passes bills, when only a few members are present. For House and Senate committees, chamber rules allow a minimum quorum of one-third of a committee's members to conduct most types of business.

Quorum Call—A procedure for determining whether a quorum is present in a chamber. In the Senate, a clerk calls the roll (roster) of senators. The House usually employs its electronic voting system.

Ramseyer Rule—A House rule that requires a committee's report on a bill or joint resolution to show the changes the measure, and any committee amendments to it, would make in existing law. The rule requires the report to present the text of any statutory provision that would be repealed and a comparative print showing, through typographical devices such as stricken-through type or italics, other changes that would be made in existing law. The rule, adopted in 1929, is named after its sponsor, Rep. Christian W. Ramseyer, R-Iowa. The Senate's analogous rule is called the Cordon Rule. *(See Cordon Rule.)*

Rank or Ranking—A member's position on the list of his or her party's members on a committee or subcommittee. When first assigned to a committee, a member is usually placed at the bottom of the list, then moves up as those above leave the committee. On subcommittees, however, a member's rank may not have anything to do with the length of his or her service on it.

Ranking Member—(1) Most often a reference to the minority member with the highest ranking on a committee or subcommittee. (2) A reference to the majority member next in rank to the chairman or to the highest ranking majority member present at a committee or subcommittee meeting.

Ratification—(1) The president's formal act of promulgating a treaty after the Senate has approved it. The resolution of ratification agreed to by the Senate is the procedural vehicle by which the Senate gives its consent to ratification. (2) A state legislature's act in approving a proposed constitutional amendment. Such an amendment becomes effective when ratified by three-fourths of the states.

Reapportionment—*(See Apportionment.)*

Recess—(1) A temporary interruption or suspension of a meeting of a chamber or committee. Unlike an adjournment, a recess does not end a legislative day. Because the Senate often recesses from one calendar day to another, its legislative day may extend over several calendar days, weeks, or even months. (2) A period of adjournment for more than three days to a day certain, especially over a holiday or in August during odd-numbered years.

Recess Appointment—A presidential appointment to a vacant federal position made after the Senate has adjourned *sine die* or has adjourned or recessed for more than thirty days. If the president submits the recess appointee's nomination during the next session of the Senate, that individual can continue to serve until the end of the session even though the Senate might have rejected the nomination. When appointed to a vacancy that existed thirty days before the end of the last Senate session, a recess appointee is not paid until confirmed.

Recommit—To send a measure back to the committee that reported it; sometimes called a straight motion to recommit to distinguish it from a motion to recommit with instructions. A successful motion to recommit kills the measure unless it is accompanied by instructions.

Recommit a Conference Report—To return a conference report to the conference committee for renegotiation of some or all of its agreements. A motion to recommit may be offered with or without instructions.

Recommit with Instructions—To send a measure back to a committee with instructions to take some action on it. Invariably in the House and often in the Senate, when the motion recommits to a standing committee, the instructions require the committee to report the measure "forthwith" with specified amendments.

Reconsider—A practice that gives a chamber an opportunity to review its action on any proposition. Any member who voted on the prevailing side can ask to reconsider the vote, creating, in effect, another vote on the same proposition. Usually this procedures creates the anomalous situation of an opponent of a measure changing his or her "no" vote to a "yea" vote to force a new vote.

Reconciliation—A procedure for changing existing revenue and spending laws to bring total federal revenues and spending within the limits established in a budget resolution. Congress has applied reconciliation chiefly to revenues and mandatory spending programs, especially entitlements. Discretionary spending is controlled through annual appropriation bills.

Recorded Vote—(1) Generally, any vote in which members are recorded by name for or against a measure; also called a record vote or roll-call vote. The only recorded vote in the Senate is a vote by the yeas and nays and is commonly called a roll-call vote. (2) Technically, a recorded vote is one demanded in the House of Representatives and supported by at least one-fifth of a quorum (forty-four members) in the House sitting as the House or at least twenty-five members in Committee of the Whole.

Recorded Vote by Clerks—A voting procedure in the House where members pass through the appropriate "aye" or "no" aisle in the chamber and cast their votes by depositing a signed green (yea) or red (no) card in a ballot box. These votes are tabulated by clerks and reported to the chair. The electronic voting system is much more convenient and has largely supplanted this procedure. *(See Committee of the Whole; Recorded Vote; Teller Vote.)*

Redistricting—The redrawing of congressional district boundaries within a state after a decennial census. Redistricting may be required to equalize district populations or to accommodate an increase or decrease in the number of a state's House seats that might have resulted from the decennial apportionment. The state governments determine the district lines. *(See Apportionment; Congressional District; Gerrymandering.)*

Referral—The assignment of a measure to committee for consideration. Under a House rule, the Speaker can refuse to refer a measure if the Speaker believes it is "of an obscene or insulting character."

Report—(1) As a verb, a committee is said to report when it submits a measure or other document to its parent chamber. (2) A clerk is said to report when he or she reads a measure's title, text, or the text of an amendment to the body at the direction of the. (3) As a noun, a committee document that accompanies a reported measure. It describes the measure, the committee's views on it, its costs, and the changes it proposes to make in existing law; it also includes certain impact statements. (4) A committee document submitted to its parent chamber that describes the results of an investigation or other study or provides information it is required to provide by rule or law.

Representative—An elected and duly sworn member of the House of Representatives who is entitled to vote in the chamber. The Constitution requires that a representative be at least twenty-five years old, a citizen of the United States for at least seven years, and an inhabitant of the state from which he or she is elected. Customarily, the member resides in the district he or she represents. Representatives are elected in even-numbered years to two-year terms that begin the following January.

Reprimand—A formal condemnation of a member for misbehavior, considered a milder reproof than censure. The House of Representatives first used it in 1976. The Senate first used in 1991. *(See also Censure; Code of Official Conduct; Denounce; Ethics Rules; Expulsion; Seniority Loss.)*

Rescission—A provision of law that repeals previously enacted budget authority in whole or in part. Under the Impoundment Control Act of 1974, the president can impound such funds by sending a message to Congress requesting one or more rescissions and the reasons for doing so. If Congress does not pass a rescission bill for the programs requested by the president within forty-five days of continuous session after receiving the message, the president must make the funds available for obligation and expenditure. If the president does not, the comptroller general of the United States is authorized to bring suit to compel the release of those funds. A rescission bill may rescind all, part, or none of an amount proposed by the president, and may rescind funds the president has not impounded.

Reserving the Right to Object—Members' declaration that at some indefinite future time they may object to a unanimous consent request. It is an attempt to circumvent the requirement that members may prevent such an action only by objecting immediately after it is proposed.

Resident Commissioner from Puerto Rico—A nonvoting member of the House of Representatives, elected to a four-year term. The resident commissioner has the same status and privileges as delegates. As with the delegates, the resident commissioner may not vote in the House or Committee of the Whole.

Resolution—(1) A simple resolution; that is, a nonlegislative measure effective only in the house in which it is proposed and not requiring concurrence by the other chamber or approval by the president. Simple resolutions are designated H Res in the House and S Res in the Senate. Simple resolutions express nonbinding opinions on policies or issues or deal with the internal affairs or prerogatives of a house. (2) Any type of resolution: simple, concurrent, or joint. *(See Concurrent Resolution; Joint Resolution.)*

Resolution of Inquiry—A resolution usually simple rather than concurrent calling on the president or the head of an executive agency to provide specific information or papers to one or both houses.

Resolution of Ratification—The Senate vehicle for agreeing to a treaty. The constitutionally mandated vote of two-thirds of the senators present and voting applies to the adoption of this resolution. However, it may also contain amendments, reservations, declarations, or understandings that the Senate had previously added to it by majority vote.

Revenue Legislation—Measures that levy new taxes or tariffs or change existing ones. Under Article I, Section 7, clause 1 of the Constitution, the House of Representatives originates federal revenue measures, but the Senate can propose amendments to them. The House Ways and Means Committee and the Senate Finance Committee have jurisdiction over such measures, with a few minor exceptions.

Revise and Extend One's Remarks—A unanimous consent request to publish in the *Congressional Record* a statement a member did not deliver on the floor, a longer statement than the one made on the floor, or miscellaneous extraneous material.

Revolving Fund—A trust fund or account whose income remains available to finance its continuing operations without any fiscal year limitation.

Rider—Congressional slang for an amendment unrelated or extraneous to the subject matter of the measure to which it is attached. Riders often contain proposals that are less likely to become law on their own merits as separate bills, either because of opposition in the committee of jurisdiction, resistance in the other house, or the probability of a presidential veto. Riders are more common in the Senate.

Roll Call—A call of the roll to determine whether a quorum is present, to establish a quorum, or to vote on a question. Usually, the House uses its electronic voting system for a roll call. The Senate does not have an electronic voting system; its roll is always called by a clerk.

Rule—(1) A permanent regulation that a house adopts to govern its conduct of business, its procedures, its internal organization, behavior of its members, regulation of its facilities, duties of an officer, or some other subject it chooses to govern in that form. (2) In the House, a privileged simple resolution reported by the Rules Committee that provides methods and conditions for floor consideration of a measure or, rarely, several measures.

Rule Twenty-Two—A common reference to the Senate's cloture rule. *(See Cloture.)*

Second-Degree Amendment—An amendment to an amendment in the first degree. It is usually a perfecting amendment.

Section—A subdivision of a bill or statute. By law, a section must be numbered and, as nearly as possible, contain "a single proposition of enactment."

Select or Special Committee—A committee established by a resolution in either house for a special purpose and, usually, for a limited time. Most select and special committees are assigned specific investigations or studies but are not authorized to report measures to their chambers.

Secretary of the Senate—The chief financial, administrative, and legislative officer of the Senate. Elected by resolution or order of the Senate, the secretary is invariably the candidate of the majority party and usually chosen by the majority leader. In the absence of the vice president and pending the election of a president pro tempore, the secretary presides over the Senate. The secretary is subject to policy direction and oversight by the Senate Committee on Rules and Administration. The secretary manages a wide range of functions that support the administrative operations of the Senate as an organization as well as those functions necessary to its legislative process, including record keeping, document management, certifications, housekeeping services, administration of oaths, and lobbyist registrations. The secretary is responsible for accounting for all funds appropriated to the Senate and conducts audits of Senate financial activities. On a semiannual basis the secretary issues the Report of the Secretary of the Senate, a compilation of Senate expenditures.

Senate—The house of Congress in which each state is represented by two senators; each senator has one vote. Article V of the Constitution declares that "No State, without its Consent, shall be deprived of its equal Suffrage in the Senate." The Constitution also gives the Senate equal legislative power with the House of Representatives. Although the Senate is prohibited from originating revenue measures, and as a matter of practice it does not originate appropriation measures, it can amend both. Only the Senate can give or withhold consent to treaties and nominations from the president. It also acts as a court to try impeachments by the House and elects the vice president when no candidate receives a majority of the electoral votes. It is often referred to as "the upper body," but not by members of the House.

Senate Manual—The handbook of the Senate's standing rules and orders and the laws and other regulations that apply to the Senate, usually published once each Congress.

Senator—A duly sworn elected or appointed member of the Senate. The Constitution requires that a senator be at least thirty years old, a citizen of the United States for at least nine years, and an inhabitant of the state from which he or she is elected. Senators are usually elected in even-numbered years to six-year terms that begin the following January. When a vacancy occurs before the end of a term, the state governor can appoint a replacement to fill the position until a successor is chosen at the state's next general election or, if specified under state law, the next feasible date for such an election, to serve the remainder of the term. Until the Seventeenth Amendment was ratified in 1913, senators were chosen by their state legislatures.

Senatorial Courtesy—The Senate's practice of declining to confirm a presidential nominee for an office in the state of a senator of the president's party unless that senator approves.

Seniority—The priority, precedence, or status accorded members according to the length of their continuous service in a house or on a committee.

Seniority Loss—A type of punishment that reduces a member's seniority on his or her committees, including the loss of chairmanships. Party caucuses in both houses have occasionally imposed such punishment on their members, for example, for publicly supporting candidates of the other party.

Seniority Rule—The customary practice, rather than a rule, of assigning the chairmanship of a committee to the majority party member who has served on the committee for the longest continuous period of time.

Seniority System—A collection of long-standing customary practices under which members with longer continuous service than their colleagues in their house or on their committees receive various kinds of preferential treatment. Although some of the practices are no longer as rigidly observed as in the past, they still pervade the organization and procedures of Congress.

Sequestration—A procedure for canceling budgetary resources—that is, money available for obligation or spending—to enforce budget limitations established in law. Sequestered funds are no longer available for obligation or expenditure.

Sergeant at Arms—The officer in each house responsible for maintaining order, security, and decorum in its wing of the Capitol, including the chamber and its galleries. Although elected by their respective houses, both sergeants at arms are invariably the candidates of the majority party.

Session—(1) The annual series of meetings of a Congress. Under the Constitution, Congress must assemble at least once a year at noon on Jan. 3 unless it appoints a different day by law. (2) The special meetings of Congress or of one house convened by the president, called a special session. (3) A house is said to be in session during the period of a day when it is meeting.

Severability (or Separability) Clause—Language stating that if any particular provisions of a measure are declared invalid by the courts the remaining provisions shall remain in effect.

Sine Die—Without fixing a day for a future meeting. An adjournment *sine die* signifies the end of an annual or special session of Congress.

Slip Law—The first official publication of a measure that has become law. It is published separately in unbound, single-sheet form or pamphlet form. A slip law usually is available two or three days after the date of the law's enactment.

Speaker—The presiding officer of the House of Representatives and the leader of its majority party. The Speaker is selected by the majority party and formally elected by the House at the beginning of each Congress. Although the Constitution does not require the Speaker to be a member of the House, in fact, all Speakers have been members.

Speaker Pro Tempore—A member of the House who is designated as the temporary presiding officer by the Speaker or elected by the House to that position during the Speaker's absence.

Speaker's Vote—The Speaker is not required to vote, and the Speaker's name is not called on a roll-call vote unless so requested. Usually, the Speaker votes either to create a tie vote, and thereby defeat a proposal, or to break a tie in favor of a proposal. Occasionally, the Speaker also votes to emphasize the importance of a matter.

Special Session—A session of Congress convened by the president, under his constitutional authority, after Congress has adjourned *sine die* at the end of a regular session. *(See Adjournment Sine Die; Session.)*

Spending Authority—The technical term for backdoor spending. The Congressional Budget Act of 1974 defines it as borrowing authority, contract authority, and entitlement authority for which appropriation acts do not provide budget authority in advance. Under the Budget Act, legislation that provides new spending authority may not be considered unless it provides that the authority shall be effective only to the extent or in such amounts as provided in an appropriation act.

Spending Cap—The statutory limit for a fiscal year on the amount of new budget authority and outlays allowed for discretionary spending. The Budget Enforcement Act of 1997 requires a sequester if the cap is exceeded.

Split Referral—A measure divided into two or more parts, with each part referred to a different committee.

Sponsor—The principal proponent and introducer of a measure or an amendment.

Staff Director—The most frequently used title for the head of staff of a committee or subcommittee. On some committees, that person is called chief of staff, clerk, chief clerk, chief counsel, general counsel, or executive director. The head of a committee's minority staff is usually called minority staff director.

Standing Committee—A permanent committee established by a House or Senate standing rule or standing order. The rule also describes the subject areas on which the committee may report bills and resolutions and conduct oversight. Most introduced measures must be referred to one or more standing committees according to their jurisdictions.

Standing Order—A continuing regulation or directive that has the force and effect of a rule, but is not incorporated into the standing rules. The Senate's numerous standing orders, such as its standing rules, continue from Congress to Congress unless changed or the order states otherwise. The House uses relatively few standing orders, and those it adopts expire at the end of a session of Congress.

Standing Rules—The rules of the Senate that continue from one Congress to the next and the rules of the House of Representatives that it adopts at the beginning of each new Congress.

Standing Vote—An alternative and informal term for a division vote, during which members in favor of a proposal and then members opposed stand and are counted by the chair.

Star Print—A reprint of a bill, resolution, amendment, or committee report correcting technical or substantive errors in a previous printing; so called because of the small black star that appears on the front page or cover.

State of the Union Message—A presidential message to Congress under the constitutional directive that the president shall "from time to time give to the Congress Information of the State of the Union, and recommend to their Consideration such Measures as he shall judge necessary and expedient." Customarily, the president sends an annual State of the Union message to Congress, usually late in January.

Statutes at Large—A chronological arrangement of the laws enacted in each session of Congress. Though indexed, the laws are not arranged by subject matter nor is there an indication of how they affect or change previously enacted laws. The volumes are numbered by Congress, and the laws are cited by their volume and page number. The Gramm-Rudman-Hollings Act, for example, appears as 99 Stat. 1037.

Straw Vote Prohibition—Under a House precedent, a member who has the floor during debate may not conduct a straw vote or otherwise ask for a show of support for a proposition. Only the chair may put a question to a vote.

Strike from the *Record*—Expunge objectionable remarks from the *Congressional Record,* after a member's words have been taken down on a point of order.

Strike the Last Word—*(See Pro Forma Amendment.)*

Subcommittee—A panel of committee members assigned a portion of the committee's jurisdiction or other functions. On legislative committees, subcommittees hold hearings, mark up legislation, and report measures to their full committee for further action; they cannot report directly to the chamber. A subcommittee's party composition usually reflects the ratio on its parent committee.

Subpoena Power The authority granted to committees by the rules of their respective houses to issue legal orders requiring individuals to appear and testify, or to produce documents pertinent to the committee's functions, or both. Persons who do not comply with subpoenas can be cited for contempt of Congress and prosecuted.

Subsidy—Generally, a payment or benefit made by the federal government for which no current repayment is required. Subsidy payments may be designed to support the conduct of an economic enterprise or activity, such as ship operations, or to support certain market prices, as in the case of farm subsidies.

Sunset Legislation—A term sometimes applied to laws authorizing the existence of agencies or programs that expire annually or at the end of some other specified period of time. One of the purposes of setting specific expiration dates for agencies and programs is to encourage the committees with jurisdiction over them to determine whether they should be continued or terminated.

Sunshine Rules—Rules requiring open committee hearings and business meetings, including markup sessions, in both houses, and also open conference committee meetings. However, all may be closed under certain circumstances and using certain procedures required by the rules.

Supermajority—A term sometimes used for a vote on a matter that requires approval by more than a simple majority of those members present and voting; also referred to as extraordinary majority.

Supplemental Appropriation Bill—A measure providing appropriations for use in the current fiscal year, in addition to those already provided in annual general appropriation bills. Supplemental appropriations are often for unforeseen emergencies.

Suspension of the Rules (House)—An expeditious procedure for passing relatively noncontroversial or emergency measures by a two-thirds vote of those members voting, a quorum being present.

Suspension of the Rules (Senate)—A procedure to set aside one or more of the Senate's rules; it is used infrequently, and then most often to suspend the rule banning legislative amendments to appropriation bills.

Task Force—A title sometimes given to a panel of members assigned to a special project, study, or investigation. Ordinarily, these groups do not have authority to report measures to their respective houses.

Tax Expenditure—Loosely, a tax exemption or advantage, sometimes called an incentive or loophole; technically, a loss of governmental tax revenue attributable to some provision of federal tax laws that allows a special exclusion, exemption, or deduction from gross income or that provides a special credit, preferential tax rate, or deferral of tax liability.

Televised Proceedings—Television and radio coverage of the floor proceedings of the House of Representatives have been available since 1979 and of the Senate since 1986. They are broadcast over a coaxial cable system to all congressional offices and to some congressional agencies on channels reserved for that purpose. Coverage is also available free of charge to commercial and public television and radio broadcasters. The Cable-Satellite Public Affairs Network (C-SPAN) carries gavel-to-gavel coverage of both houses.

Teller Vote—A voting procedure, formerly used in the House, in which members cast their votes by passing through the center aisle to be counted, but not recorded by name, by a member from each party appointed by the chair. The House deleted the procedure from its rules in 1993, but during floor discussion of the deletion a leading member stated that a teller vote would still be available in the event of a breakdown of the electronic voting system.

Third-Degree Amendment—An amendment to a second-degree amendment. Both houses prohibit such amendments.

Third Reading—A required reading to a chamber of a bill or joint resolution by title only before the vote on passage. In modern practice, it has merely become a pro forma step.

Three-Day Rule—(1) In the House, a measure cannot be considered until the third calendar day on which the committee report has been available. (2) In the House, a conference report cannot be considered until the third calendar day on which its text has been available in the *Congressional Record*. (3) In the House, a general appropriation bill cannot be considered until the third calendar day on which printed hearings on the bill have been available. (4) In the Senate, when a committee votes to report a measure, a committee member is entitled to three calendar days within which to submit separate views for inclusion in the committee report. (In House committees, a member is entitled to two calendar days for this purpose, after the day on which the committee votes to report.) (5) In both houses, a majority of a committee's members may call a special meeting of the committee if its chairman fails to do so within three calendar days after three or more of the members, acting jointly, formally request such a meeting.

In calculating such periods, the House omits holiday and weekend days on which it does not meet. The Senate makes no such exclusion.

Tie Vote—When the votes for and against a proposition are equal, it loses. The president of the Senate may cast a vote only to break a tie. Because the Speaker is invariably a member of the House, the Speaker is entitled to vote but usually does not. The Speaker may choose to do so to break, or create, a tie vote.

Title—(1) A major subdivision of a bill or act, designated by a roman numeral and usually containing legislative provisions on the same general subject. Titles are sometimes divided into subtitles as well as sections. (2) The official name of a bill or act, also called a caption or long title. (3) Some bills also have short titles that appear in the sentence immediately following the enacting clause. (4) Popular titles are the unofficial names given to some bills or acts by common

usage. For example, the Balanced Budget and Emergency Deficit Control Act of 1985 (short title) is almost invariably referred to as Gramm-Rudman (popular title). In other cases, significant legislation is popularly referred to by its title number (see definition (1) above). For example, the federal legislation that requires equality of funding for women's and men's sports in educational institutions that receive federal funds is popularly called Title IX.

Track System—An occasional Senate practice that expedites legislation by dividing a day's session into two or more specific time periods, commonly called tracks, each reserved for consideration of a different measure.

Transfer Payment—A federal government payment to which individuals or organizations are entitled under law and for which no goods or services are required in return. Payments include welfare and Social Security benefits, unemployment insurance, government pensions, and veterans benefits.

Treaty—A formal document containing an agreement between two or more sovereign nations. The Constitution authorizes the president to make treaties, but the president must submit them to the Senate for its approval by a two-thirds vote of the senators present. Under the Senate's rules, that vote actually occurs on a resolution of ratification. Although the Constitution does not give the House a direct role in approving treaties, that body has sometimes insisted that a revenue treaty is an invasion of its prerogatives. In any case, the House may significantly affect the application of a treaty by its equal role in enacting legislation to implement the treaty.

Trust Funds—Special accounts in the Treasury that receive earmarked taxes or other kinds of revenue collections, such as user fees, and from which payments are made for special purposes or to recipients who meet the requirements of the trust funds as established by law. Of the more than 150 federal government trust funds, several finance major entitlement programs, such as Social Security, Medicare, and retired federal employees' pensions. Others fund infrastructure construction and improvements, such as highways and airports.

Unanimous Consent—Without an objection by any member. A unanimous consent request asks permission, explicitly or implicitly, to set aside one or more rules. Both houses and their committees frequently use such requests to expedite their proceedings.

Uncontrollable Expenditures—A frequently used term for federal expenditures that are mandatory under existing law and therefore cannot be controlled by the president or Congress without a change in the existing law. Uncontrollable expenditures include spending required under entitlement programs and also fixed costs, such as interest on the public debt and outlays to pay for prior-year obligations. In recent years, uncontrollables have accounted for approximately three-quarters of federal spending in each fiscal year.

Unfunded Mandate—Generally, any provision in federal law or regulation that imposes a duty or obligation on a state or local government or private sector entity without providing the necessary funds to comply. The Unfunded Mandates Reform Act of 1995 amended the Congressional Budget Act of 1974 to provide a mechanism for the control of new unfunded mandates.

Union Calendar—A calendar of the House of Representatives for bills and resolutions favorably reported by committees that raise revenue or directly or indirectly appropriate money or property. In addition to appropriation bills, measures that authorize expenditures are also placed on this calendar. The calendar's full title is the Calendar of the Committee of the Whole House on the State of the Union.

Upper Body—A common reference to the Senate, but not used by members of the House.

U.S. Code—Popular title for the *United States Code: Containing the General and Permanent Laws of the United States in Force on . . .* It is a consolidation and partial codification of the general and permanent laws of the United States arranged by subject under 50 titles. The first six titles deal with general or political subjects, the other forty-four with subjects ranging from agriculture to war, alphabetically arranged. A supplement is published after each session of Congress, and the entire Code is revised every six years.

User Fee—A fee charged to users of goods or services provided by the federal government. When Congress levies or authorizes such fees, it determines whether the revenues should go into the general collections of the Treasury or be available for expenditure by the agency that provides the goods or services.

Veto—The president's disapproval of a legislative measure passed by Congress. The president returns the measure to the house in which it originated without his signature but with a veto message stating his objections to it. When Congress is in session, the president must veto a bill within ten days, excluding Sundays, after the president has received it; otherwise it becomes law without his signature. The ten-day clock begins to run at midnight following his receipt of the bill. *(See also Committee Veto; Item Veto; Line Item Veto Act of 1996; Override a Veto; Pocket Veto.)*

Voice Vote—A method of voting in which members who favor a question answer aye in chorus, after which those opposed answer no in chorus, and the chair decides which position prevails.

Voting—Members vote in three ways on the floor: (1) by shouting "aye" or "no" on voice votes; (2) by standing for or against on division votes; and (3) on recorded votes (including the yeas and nays), by answering "aye" or "no" when their names are called or, in the House, by recording their votes through the electronic voting system.

War Powers Resolution of 1973—An act that requires the president "in every possible instance" to consult Congress before committing U.S. forces to ongoing or imminent hostilities. If the president commits them to a combat situation without congressional consultation, the president must notify Congress within forty-eight hours. Unless Congress declares war or otherwise authorizes the operation to continue, the forces must be withdrawn within sixty or ninety days, depending on certain conditions. No president has ever acknowledged the constitutionality of the resolution.

Well—The sunken, level, open space between members' seats and the podium at the front of each chamber. House members usually address their chamber from their party's lectern in the well on its side of the aisle. Senators usually speak at their assigned desks.

Whip—The majority or minority party member in each house who acts as assistant leader, helps plan and marshal support for party strategies, encourages party discipline, and advises his or her leader on how colleagues intend to vote on the floor.

Yeas and Nays—A vote in which members usually respond "aye" or "no" (despite the official title of the vote) on a question when their names are called in alphabetical order. The Constitution requires the yeas and nays when a demand for it is supported by one-fifth of the members present, and it also requires an automatic yea-and-nay vote on overriding a veto. Senate precedents require the support of at least one-fifth of a quorum, a minimum of eleven members with the present membership of 100.

The Legislative Process in Brief

Note: *Parliamentary terms used below are defined in the glossary.*

INTRODUCTION OF BILLS

A House member (including the resident commissioner of Puerto Rico and nonvoting delegates of the District of Columbia, Guam, the Virgin Islands, and American Samoa) may introduce any one of several types of bills and resolutions any time the House is in session by handing it to the clerk of the House or placing it in a box called the hopper. A senator usually introduces a measure by presenting it, along with a formal statement, to a clerk at the presiding officer's desk.

As the usual next step in either the House or Senate, the bill is numbered, referred to the appropriate committee, labeled with the sponsor's name, and sent to the Government Printing Office so that copies can be made for subsequent study and action. House and Senate bills may be jointly sponsored and carry several lawmakers' names. Print and electronic versions of the bill are available to the public. A bill written in the executive branch and proposed as an administration measure usually is introduced by the chairman of the congressional committee that has jurisdiction, as a courtesy to the White House.

Bills—Prefixed with HR in the House, S in the Senate, followed by a number. Used as the form for most legislation, whether general or special, public, or private.

Joint Resolutions—Designated H J Res or S J Res. Subject to the same procedure as bills, with the exception of a joint resolution proposing an amendment to the Constitution. The latter must be approved by two-thirds of both houses and then sent directly to the administrator of general services for submission to the states for ratification instead of being presented to the president for his approval.

Concurrent Resolutions—Designated H Con Res or S Con Res. Used for matters affecting the operations of both houses. These resolutions do not become law.

Resolutions—Designated H Res. or S Res. Used for a matter concerning the operation of either house alone and adopted only by the chamber in which it originates.

COMMITTEE ACTION

With few exceptions, bills are referred to the appropriate standing committees. The job of referral formally is the responsibility of the Speaker of the House and the presiding officer of the Senate, but this task usually is carried out on their behalf by the parliamentarians of the House and Senate. Precedent, statute, and the jurisdictional mandates of the committees as set forth in the rules of the House and Senate determine which committees receive what kinds of bills. Bills are technically considered "read for the first time" when referred to House committees.

When a bill reaches a committee it is placed on the committee's calendar. Failure of a committee to act on a bill is equivalent to killing it and most fall by the legislative roadside. The measure can be withdrawn from the committee's purview by a discharge petition signed by a majority of the House membership on House bills, or, for example, by adoption of a special resolution in the Senate. Discharge attempts rarely succeed and the Senate procedure is rarely used.

The first committee action taken on a bill may be a request for comment on it by interested agencies of the government. The committee chairman may assign the bill to a subcommittee for study and hearings, or it may be considered by the full committee. Hearings may be public, closed (executive session) or both. A subcommittee, after considering a bill, reports to the full committee its recommendations for action and any proposed amendments.

The full committee then votes on its recommendation to the House or Senate. This procedure is called "ordering a bill reported." Occasionally a committee may order a bill reported unfavorably; most of the time a report, submitted by the chairman of the committee to the House or Senate, calls for favorable action on the measure since the committee can effectively "kill" a bill by simply failing to take any action.

After the bill is reported, the committee chairman instructs the staff to prepare a written report. The report describes the purposes and scope of the bill, explains the committee revisions, notes proposed changes in existing law and, usually, includes the views of the executive branch agencies consulted. Often committee members opposing a measure issue dissenting minority statements that are included in the report.

Usually, the committee "marks up" or proposes amendments to the bill. If they are substantial and the measure is complicated, the committee may order a "clean bill" introduced, which will embody the proposed amendments. The original bill then is put aside and the clean bill, with a new number, is reported to the floor.

The chamber must approve, alter, or reject the committee amendments before the bill itself can be put to a vote.

FLOOR ACTION

After a bill is reported back to the house where it originated, it is placed on the calendar.

There are four legislative calendars in the House, issued in one cumulative calendar titled *Calendars of the United States House of Representatives and History of Legislation.* The House calendars are:

The Union Calendar to which are referred bills raising revenues, general appropriations bills, and any measures directly or indirectly appropriating money or property. It is the Calendar of the Committee of the Whole House on the state of the Union.

The House Calendar to which are referred bills of public character not raising revenue or appropriating money.

The Private Calendar to which are referred bills for relief in the nature of claims against the United States or private immigration bills that are passed without debate when the Private Calendar is called the first and third Tuesdays of each month.

The Discharge Calendar to which are referred motions to discharge committees when the necessary signatures are signed to a discharge petition.

There is only one legislative calendar in the Senate and one "executive calendar" for treaties and nominations submitted to the Senate.

Debate

A bill is brought to debate by varying procedures. In the Senate the majority leader, in consultation with the minority leader and others, schedules the bills that will be taken up for debate. If it is urgent or important it can be taken up in the Senate either by unanimous consent or by a motion agreed to by majority vote.

In the House, precedence is granted if a special rule is obtained from the Rules Committee. A request for a special rule usually is made by the chairman of the committee that favorably reported the bill. The request is considered by the Rules Committee in the same fashion that other committees consider legislative measures. The committee proposes a resolution providing for the consideration of the bill. The Rules Committee reports the resolution to the House where it is debated and voted on in the same fashion as regular bills.

The resolutions providing special rules are important because they specify how long the bill may be debated and whether it may be amended from the floor. If floor amendments are banned, the bill is considered under a "closed rule."

When a bill is debated under an "open rule," germane amendments may be offered from the floor. Committee amendments always are taken up first but may be changed, as may all amendments up to the second degree; that is, an amendment to an amendment to an amendment is not in order.

Duration of debate in the House depends on whether the bill is under discussion by the House proper or before the House when it is sitting as the Committee of the Whole House on the state of the Union. In the former, the amount of time for debate occurs under the one-hour rule, which allows members to hold the floor for one hour each. In practice, the members first recognized to speak moves the previous question after an hour, which the House almost always approves and which ends further debate. In the Committee of the Whole the amount of time specified in the special rule for general debate is equally divided between proponents and opponents. At the end of general debate, the bill is often read section by section for amendment if it is considered under an open rule. Debate on an amendment is limited to five minutes for each side; this is called the "five-minute rule." In practice, amendments regularly are debated more than ten minutes, with members gaining the floor by offering pro forma amendments or obtaining unanimous consent to speak longer than five minutes.

Senate debate usually is unlimited. It can be halted or limited only by unanimous consent, by certain laws, by adoption of a motion to table, or by "cloture," which requires a three-fifths majority of the entire Senate except for proposed changes in the Senate rules. The latter requires a two-thirds vote.

The House considers almost all important bills within a parliamentary framework known as the Committee of the Whole. It is not a committee as the word usually is understood; it is the full House meeting under another name for the purpose of speeding action on legislation. Technically, the House sits as the Committee of the Whole when it considers any tax measure or bill dealing with public appropriations. After adoption of a special rule, the Speaker declares the House resolved into the Committee of the Whole and appoints a member of the majority party to serve as the chairman. Instead of the required quorum of 218 for the House, the rules of that chamber permit the Committee of the Whole to meet when a quorum of 100 members is present on the floor and to amend and act on bills. When the Committee of the Whole has concluded consideration of a bill for amendment, it "rises," the Speaker returns as the presiding officer of the House and the member appointed chairman of the Committee of the Whole reports the action of the committee and its recommendations. The Committee of the Whole cannot pass a bill; instead it reports the measure to the full House with whatever amendment it has adopted. The full House then may pass or reject the bill—or, on occasion, recommit the bill to committee. Amendments adopted in the Committee of the Whole may be put to a second vote in the full House.

Votes

Voting on bills may occur repeatedly before they are finally approved or rejected. The House votes on the rule for the bill and on various amendments to the bill. Voting on amendments often is a more illuminating test of a bill's support than is the final tally. Sometimes members approve final passage of bills after vigorously supporting amendments that, if adopted, would have scuttled the legislation.

The Senate has three different methods of voting: an untabulated voice vote, a standing vote (called a division), and a recorded roll call to which members answer "yea" or "nay" when their names are called. The House also employs voice and standing votes, but since January 1973 yeas and nays have been recorded by an electronic voting device, eliminating the need for time-consuming roll calls.

After amendments to a bill have been voted upon it is "read for the third time." Then a vote may be taken on a motion to recommit the bill or joint resolution to committee. If carried, which rarely occurs, this vote is usually a death blow to the bill. Rejection of the motion to recommit is followed by a vote on final passage of the bill. The final vote is followed by a pro forma motion to reconsider, which is automatically laid on the table. With that, the bill has been formally passed by the chamber.

ACTION IN SECOND CHAMBER

After a bill is passed it is sent to the other chamber. This body may then take one of several steps. It may pass the bill as is—accepting the other chamber's language. It may send the bill to committee for scrutiny or alteration, or reject the entire bill, advising the other house of its actions. Or it simply may ignore the bill submitted while it continues work on its version of the proposed legislation. Frequently, one chamber may approve a version of a bill that is greatly at variance with the version already passed by the other house and then substitute its contents for the language of the other, retaining only the latter's bill number.

Often the second chamber makes only minor changes. If these are readily agreed to by the other house, the bill then is routed to the president. However, if the opposite chamber significantly alters the bill submitted to it, the measure usually is "sent to conference." The chamber that has possession of the "papers" (engrossed bill, engrossed amendments, messages of transmittal) requests a conference and the other chamber may agree to it. If the second chamber does not agree, the bill dies. Unless other parliamentary actions take place. For example, a senator could reoffer the rejected bill as a nonrelevant amendment to another measure. If both chambers agreed to the nonrelevant amendment, the president could sign the legislative package into law.

CONFERENCE ACTION

A conference works out conflicting House and Senate versions of a legislative bill. The conferees usually are senior members from the committees that managed the legislation who are appointed by the presiding officers of the two houses. Under this arrangement the conferees of one house have the duty of trying to maintain their chamber's position in the face of amending actions by the conferees (also referred to as "managers") of the other house.

The number of conferees from each chamber may vary, from single to double or even triple digits depending on the length or complexity of the bill and the number of committees involved. But a majority vote controls the action of each group so that a large representation does

How a Bill Becomes Law

This graphic shows the most typical way in which proposed legislation is enacted into law. There are more complicated, as well as simpler, routes, and most bills never become law. The process is illustrated with two hypothetical bills, House bill No. 1 (HR 1) and Senate bill No. 2 (S 2). Bills must be passed by both houses in identical form before they can be sent to the president. The path of HR 1 is traced by a black line, that of S 2 by a gray line. In practice, most bills begin as similar proposals in both houses.

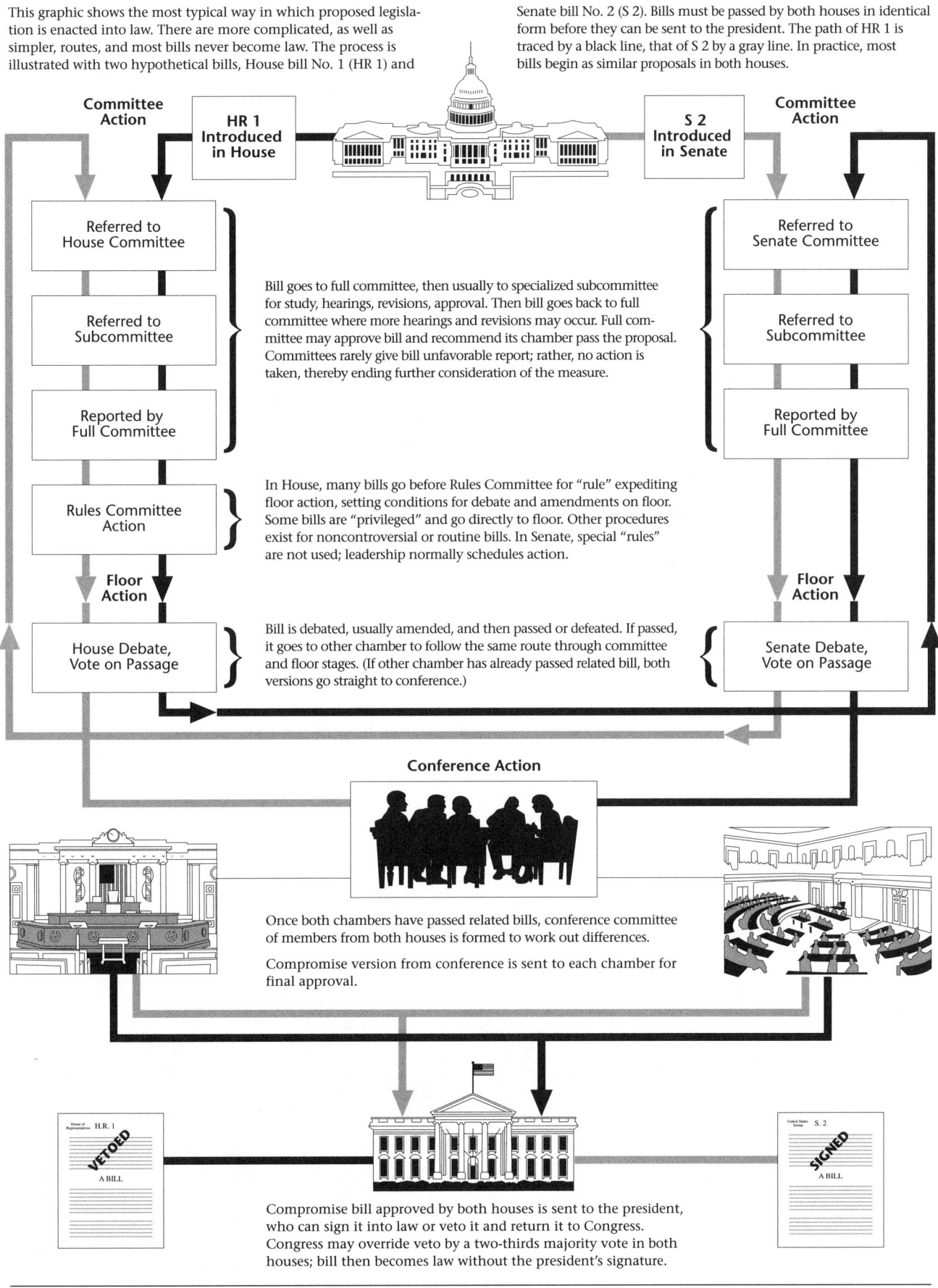

Committee Action

HR 1 Introduced in House

S 2 Introduced in Senate

Committee Action

Referred to House Committee

Referred to Senate Committee

Referred to Subcommittee

Referred to Subcommittee

Reported by Full Committee

Reported by Full Committee

Bill goes to full committee, then usually to specialized subcommittee for study, hearings, revisions, approval. Then bill goes back to full committee where more hearings and revisions may occur. Full committee may approve bill and recommend its chamber pass the proposal. Committees rarely give bill unfavorable report; rather, no action is taken, thereby ending further consideration of the measure.

Rules Committee Action

In House, many bills go before Rules Committee for "rule" expediting floor action, setting conditions for debate and amendments on floor. Some bills are "privileged" and go directly to floor. Other procedures exist for noncontroversial or routine bills. In Senate, special "rules" are not used; leadership normally schedules action.

Floor Action

Floor Action

House Debate, Vote on Passage

Bill is debated, usually amended, and then passed or defeated. If passed, it goes to other chamber to follow the same route through committee and floor stages. (If other chamber has already passed related bill, both versions go straight to conference.)

Senate Debate, Vote on Passage

Conference Action

Once both chambers have passed related bills, conference committee of members from both houses is formed to work out differences.

Compromise version from conference is sent to each chamber for final approval.

H.R. 1 — VETOED — A BILL

S. 2 — SIGNED — A BILL

Compromise bill approved by both houses is sent to the president, who can sign it into law or veto it and return it to Congress. Congress may override veto by a two-thirds majority vote in both houses; bill then becomes law without the president's signature.

Examples of Legislative Documents

not give one chamber a voting advantage over the other chamber's conferees.

Theoretically, conferees are not allowed to write new legislation in reconciling the two versions before them, but this curb sometimes is bypassed. Many bills have been put into acceptable compromise form only after new language was provided by the conferees. Frequently the ironing out of difficulties takes days or even weeks. Conferences on complex and controversial bills sometimes are particularly drawn out.

As a conference proceeds, conferees reconcile differences between the versions, but generally they grant concessions only insofar as they remain sure that the chamber they represent will accept the compromises. Occasionally, uncertainty over how either house will react, or the positive refusal of a chamber to back down on a disputed amendment, results in an impasse, and the bills die in conference even though each was approved by its sponsoring chamber.

When the conferees have reached agreement, they prepare a conference report embodying their recommendations (compromises) and a joint explanatory statement. The report, in document form, must be submitted to each house. The conference report must be approved by each house. Consequently, approval of the report is approval of the compromise bill. In the order of voting on conference reports, the chamber that asked for a conference yields to the other chamber the opportunity to vote first.

FINAL ACTION

After a bill has been passed by both the House and Senate in identical form, all of the original papers are sent to the enrolling clerk of the chamber in which the bill originated. The clerk then prepares an enrolled bill, which is printed on parchment paper.

When this bill has been certified as correct by the secretary of the Senate or the clerk of the House, depending on which chamber originated the bill, it is signed first (no matter whether it originated in the Senate or House) by the Speaker of the House and then by the president of the Senate. It is next sent to the White House to await action.

If approving of the bill, the president signs it, dates it, and usually writes the word "approved" on the document. If the president does not sign it within ten days (Sundays excepted) and Congress is in session, the bill becomes law without his signature.

If Congress adjourns *sine die* at the end of the second session, the president can pocket veto a bill and it dies without Congress having the opportunity to override.

A president vetoes a bill by refusing to sign it and, before the ten-day period expires, returning it to Congress with a message stating his reasons. The message is sent to the chamber that originated the bill. If no action is taken on the message, the bill dies. Congress, however, can attempt to override the president's veto and enact the bill, "the objections of the president to the contrary notwithstanding." Overriding a veto requires a two-thirds vote of those present in each chamber, who must number a quorum and vote by roll call.

If the president's veto is overridden by a two-thirds vote in both houses, the bill becomes law. Otherwise it is dead.

When bills are passed finally and signed, or passed over a veto, they are given law numbers in numerical order as they become law. There are two series of numbers, one for public and one for private laws, starting at the number "1" for each two-year term of Congress. They are then identified by law number and by Congress—for example, Private Law 10, 109th Congress; Public Law 33, 109th Congress (or PL 109-33).

Key Votes

Each year Congressional Quarterly selects a series of key votes on major issues. An issue is judged by the extent to which it represents one or more of the following:
- A matter of major controversy.
- A test of presidential or political power.
- A decision of potentially great impact on the nation and lives of Americans.

For each series of related votes on an issue only one key vote is usually chosen. This vote is the roll call in the House or Senate that in the opinion of Congressional Quarterly was the most important in determining the outcome.

Senate

1. ASHCROFT NOMINATION

Within hours of his nomination, Attorney General John Ashcroft emerged as the most controversial pick for President George W. Bush's cabinet. Opponents and supporters waged a vigorous and sometimes nasty debate for a month over whether Ashcroft was too deeply ideological to be the nation's top law enforcement official, leading to the closest vote of any successful cabinet nomination in decades. Liberal interest groups, including People for the American Way and the Leadership Conference on Civil Rights, mobilized against him, hoping to recreate their 1987 defeat of the Supreme Court nomination of Robert Bork. Conservative groups, such as the American Conservative Union, joined forces to defend Ashcroft and others. *(Action on nomination, p. 759)*

The divisiveness of the debate provided an early challenge to the Bush administration's pledge to "change the tone in Washington" but the implications of the vote went beyond political symbolism. Bush was seeking to assert his authority after winning a controversial election and Democrats were eager to demonstrate their power to shape the national agenda, particularly in a Senate divided equally between fifty Republicans and fifty Democrats. Ashcroft had served one term as a senator from Missouri and was defeated for reelection in 2000. During his time in the Senate, he established himself as a strong voice for the conservative movement, introducing legislation to ban most abortions and voting against gun control, for example. He briefly toyed with running for president.

Opponents also tried to make much of a 1998 interview Ashcroft granted to *Southern Partisan*, published by the League of the South, a group that supported southern independence and that some accused of promoting racist views. A quote from the article made it appear Ashcroft endorsed the group's agenda but he said he had no knowledge of the League's activities. Ashcroft's opponents also questioned his opposition to President Bill Clinton's judicial nominations, focusing in particular on his efforts as a U.S. senator in 1999 to block the nomination of Ronnie L. White, a Missouri Supreme Court Justice whom Clinton had chosen for a federal judgeship. White had written dissents in several capital cases, which Ashcroft said made him unfit to be a federal judge because he "voted to give clearly guilty murders new trials." White's supporters argued that Ashcroft only opposed White leading up to his close reelection bid, when the death penalty and prosecuting murderers could be a useful political tool.

During two days of questioning by his former colleagues on the Senate Judiciary Committee, Ashcroft was repeatedly asked if he could set aside his personal views, including abortion, and enforce laws such as one protecting abortion providers from violent protesters. "I think it's fair to say that I know the difference between an enactment role and an enforcement role," he said. Despite such assurances, Democrats on the committee were not convinced. "It's very hard to change your stripes or change your spots," said Dianne Feinstein, D-Calif.

But Republicans held their members and picked up a few Democrats. In committee voting only one Democrat, Russell D. Feingold of Wisconsin, voted for Ashcroft's nomination. He said he wanted to give Ashcroft the benefit of the doubt on questions of his character and the intentions behind his actions as a senator.

The Senate on Feb. 1 confirmed Ashcroft as attorney general by a vote of 58–42: R 50–0; D 8–42. Although eight Democrats voted for him, as a party they had made an important point about their ability to hang together against enormous political pressure to let the president choose his cabinet. By keeping the nomination from getting sixty votes—a threshold majority that Senate procedures require to end debate on contentious legislation and force a vote—Democrats proved they would be a force in future debates, including the shaping of the Bush tax plan in the spring. *(Vote, p. 812)*

2. ERGONOMICS RULES

Republicans and the business community had long opposed the idea of workplace rules on ergonomics and the Clinton administration's attempt, late in the president's term, to implement new regulations. When the proposed rules changes were published in fall 2000, business lobbyists set a top priority on blocking implementation. But it was only through a stealth campaign in the first months of the Bush administration and the use of a little-noticed 1996 congressional review law that GOP leaders were able to overturn the regulation before Democrats had time to marshal a defense. *(Legislative details, p. 565)*

The ergonomics regulation had taken effect Jan. 16, 2001, and enforcement would have begun Oct. 14. It required employers to educate their workers about ways to prevent injuries from repetitive motion such as typing, sorting, or lifting heavy loads. If a worker reported an injury, the rule required employers to reconfigure their workplaces in order to prevent a recurrence. Workers who reported injuries lasting seven days or longer would have been able to receive compensation of up to 90 percent of their salary for as long as ninety days if they were unable to work.

Organized labor had sought such rules for more than a decade but business groups said the Clinton regulation would cost U.S. companies more than $100 billion a year. In the fall of 2000 Republicans tried to include language in the fiscal 2001 Labor–Health and Human Services–Education spending bill (PL 106-554) barring the Occupational Safety and Health Administration (OSHA) from finalizing the ergonomics policy. But the Democratic White House outmatched Republicans by allowing OSHA to publish the final rule while the labor spending bill was still mired in negotiations.

The behind-the-scenes campaign to defeat the rule in January and February of 2001 was orchestrated by Don Nickles, R-Okla., who was the assistant majority leader of the Senate at the time, in concert with a coalition of business groups. Nickles' weapon was a 1996 law, the Congressional Review Act, which he had written with Harry Reid, D-Nev., and tucked into a broader regulatory overhaul measure that was enacted as part of a bill raising the debt limit (PL 104-121). The law allowed Congress to overturn a major regulation within a certain time limit if both houses passed a joint resolution of disapproval by a simple majority vote. The law limited debate and amendments and further prohibited the administration from writing a new rule in "substantially the same form" as one that Congress rejected.

Nickles and the business groups concentrated on winning over centrist Democrats, such as John B. Breaux of Louisiana, with a pitch that the ergonomics rule would be onerous for business, particularly for small business. Eventually, six Democrats crossed over, five of them from the South, enabling Republicans to pass a resolution of disapproval (S J Res 6—PL 107-5), 56–44: R 50–0; D 6–44. The

House sealed the fate of the ergonomics rule by passing the resolution the following day. Democrats were thunderstruck. "I'm still trying to figure out what the hell happened," said one Democratic aide after the Senate vote. *(Vote, p. 812)*

3. CAMPAIGN FINANCE

The Senate embarked March 19, 2001, on the first wide-open debate of campaign finance laws in almost a decade. That the debate happened at all was a testament to the determination and political skills of John McCain, R-Ariz., and Russell D. Feingold, D-Wis., who had long labored to bring their campaign finance bill (S 27) to a vote. The arrival of a Senate debate on campaign finance ended years of stalling tactics by opponents of the legislation, who had succeeded in keeping the matter off the floor through a mix of filibusters and threats. The House had twice passed a bill similar to the one McCain and Feingold proposed, so it was widely believed Senate passage would ensure that campaign finance laws would be rewritten for the first time in nearly 30 years. *(Legislative details, p. 731)*

As floor debate began, the question was whether McCain and Feingold could hold together the fragile bipartisan coalition that had allowed them to force the extraordinary two-week debate in the first place. The Senate's Republican leadership had long opposed the legislation, as had powerful outside interests on the left and the right. But as the battle neared, the Democrats, who had always been the chief proponents of a McCain-Feingold bill, suddenly got nervous. In particular, Democrats were preparing to bolt and bring down the bill over amendments related to the issue of "hard money," the contributions to individual political candidates. The primary goal of the McCain-Feingold legislation was to ban the large and unregulated "soft money" contributions to political parties that the two sponsors viewed as corrupting the political system. But to attain support for closing off that pipeline of cash, McCain and Feingold knew they would have to address demands from some in Congress to raise the limits on hard money. The limits on direct-to-candidate contributions had stood at $1,000 per candidate per election since 1974, and Republicans, who had long raised more hard money than Democrats, demanded it be raised.

Democrats balked. The Democratic Party had come to rely on soft money to make up for the GOP's hard-money advantage, and Democrats were increasingly worried that banning it would put them at a financial disadvantage. Raising the limits on hard money at the same time, in their view, would make matters even worse. "Raising hard money [limits] will split our caucus big time," said Tom Daschle, D-S.D., who was then minority leader. "It's so anti-reform, and secondly, it so greatly advantages Republicans." Daschle reluctantly voted for a compromise, hammered out by Fred Thompson, R-Tenn., and Dianne Feinstein, D-Calif., to double the limit on contributions to candidates to $2,000 per election and raise the limit on contributions to national parties to $25,000 per year. But sixteen members of his caucus said no, and some continued to complain about the deal.

Republicans accused Democrats of hypocrisy, of looking for an excuse to vote against a soft-money ban now that it seemed likely to become law. "It sounds like people who are looking for the exit sign in the tall grass," Thompson said. That accusation stung, and it ultimately helped save the bill. Even with elements of their base opposed to the bill and their own careers perhaps at stake, Democrats found they had painted themselves into a corner. Saying no to McCain-Feingold was no longer an option. "We've taken so strong a position as a party in favor of this bill and against soft money that we've got to stay the course," said Joseph I. Lieberman, D-Conn.

On April 2, the Senate passed the bill, believing at the time that the House already had the votes to endorse the Senate action. Only three Democrats voted no, but twelve Republicans crossed over to support the legislation. The vote was 59–41: R 12–38; D 47–3. McCain and Feingold had won the first round. *(Vote, p. 812)*

4. BUDGET RESOLUTION/EDUCATION SPENDING

That the House would pass President Bush's $1.6 trillion ten-year tax cut was never in doubt but the Senate's 50–50 split between the two parties put the bill's fate in that chamber in the hands of a few moderates of both parties who preferred a smaller figure. The fiscal 2002 congressional budget resolution (H Con Res 83), which set the parameters for the size of the tax cut and provided filibuster protection in the Senate for the subsequent tax cut legislation, became a key battleground. The tax cut was Bush's campaign centerpiece and the first crucial test of his Capitol Hill clout following a bitterly contested electoral victory. His hopes for securing all of the tax cut he sought were dashed when a handful of Republicans defected on an amendment to the budget resolution offered by Tom Harkin, D-Iowa, to reduce the tax cut by $448 billion—with the amount to be divided evenly between education funding and additional reduction of the national debt. The budget that ultimately emerged from the Senate called for a tax cut of $1.3 trillion. The Senate adopted Harkin's amendment April 4 on a key vote of 53–47: R 4–46; D 49–1. *(Vote, p. 812)*

Senate Budget Committee Chairman Pete V. Domenici, R-N.M., had been unable to move a budget resolution through a panel divided 11–11, forcing the GOP to use special budget rules allowing the measure to go directly before the Senate after April 1. In the weeks leading to the floor debate, Bush tried to pressure Senate Democrats by appearing in campaign-style rallies for the tax cut in states such as Louisiana, Georgia, South Dakota, and Montana. Those states, all easily carried by Bush, were represented respectively by Democrats Mary L. Landrieu, Max Cleland, Tim Johnson, and Max Baucus—all of whom faced reelection in 2002.

The drama continued through the start of the Senate debate, during which there was more action behind the scenes than on the floor. Vice President Richard B. Cheney, White House budget director Mitchell E. Daniels Jr., and other White House officials descended on the Capitol to hunt for Democratic defections and to press Republican moderates to commit to Bush's plan. John B. Breaux, D-La., who had been the subject of intense personal lobbying by Bush, took the lead among Senate moderates in trying to limit the size of Bush's tax cut. While floor debate continued, he held a news conference to unveil his $1.3 trillion tax cut proposal as a starting point for negotiation. Breaux promised that at least one Republican would join him at the press event. He knew Lincoln Chafee, R-R.I., was on board but because Georgia Democrat Zell Miller had pledged his support for Bush's plan, Breaux needed one more Republican to turn the tide.

In the moments leading up to the news conference, moderate Republican James M. Jeffords of Vermont had been in another room of the Capitol, in the end stages of several days of talks with Senate GOP leaders and White House negotiators. Jeffords was pressing for a deal to increase special education funding, a pet cause of his, but his fellow Republicans declined to meet his demands. Jeffords' dramatic arrival at Breaux's side after the conference was under way signaled the demise of Bush's hopes for getting all of his tax cut into the budget resolution. (A few weeks later, Jeffords would leave the GOP, handing control of the Senate to the Democrats.)

Breaux's amendment was never put to a vote. Instead, senators left the conference to vote on the Harkin amendment, which was adopted with the help of Republicans Chafee, Jeffords, and Arlen Specter of Pennsylvania. When it was clear the amendment would be adopted, Majority Leader Trent Lott, R-Miss., switched from a "no" to a "yes" for a procedural reason: It allowed him to move to reconsider the vote later in the debate if he could find enough people to switch. But that never happened. With the size of the tax cut reduced, moderate Democrats joined the bandwagon and the budget resolution passed, 65–35.

In the wake of the Senate's action, news media accounts tended to portray it as a loss for Bush and an episode mishandled by White House strategists. In the end, the conference report on the budget called for a $1.4 trillion tax cut—more than three-quarters of what initially came before the Senate.

5. TAX CUTS

Nowhere did the vagaries of the 50–50 Senate, which lasted from January through May, create more of a high-stakes balancing act than in the writing of the 2001 tax cut law. With the economy already showing signs of weakness as the year began, a broad majority existed in Congress for devoting some of the surplus to a potentially stimulative tax cut. But there the agreement ended—not only between the two parties but also, especially in the Senate, within the Republican as well as Democratic caucuses. The multifaceted dynamic guaranteed that a bipartisan compromise, written to appeal to moderate senators in each party, was the only way to assure that President Bush would win the broad tax cut that was the top priority for his first year in office. *(Legislative details, pp. 86–87, 89)*

The first threshold question—how deep to cut—was settled in the fiscal 2002 budget resolution. Effectively written by the centrists, it set a limit of $1.4 trillion through fiscal 2011 by saying anything above that would have to muster the support of sixty senators, a political impossibility at the time. At that point, Republican leaders considered advancing a bill designed to reflect Bush's wishes as closely as possible given the budget restraint, in the hope it could be pushed to passage with almost exclusively GOP votes. At the same time, Democratic leaders considered mounting a campaign to stop the drive for tax legislation outright, principally by refusing to cooperate with the GOP. Instead, a package designed to win over moderates in both parties was cobbled together by the leaders of the Finance Committee, Charles E. Grassley, R-Iowa, and Max Baucus, D-Mont. While following the outline of Bush's plan, it was modified to stay within the confines of the budget. (The rate cuts, for example, were not as deep as the president wanted.) Room was made for additional provisions designed to appeal to the more liberal Republicans, such as allowing poorer parents to claim part of the child tax credit, and more conservative Democrats, primarily an expansion of tax breaks for education.

The key moment came May 23, when the Senate passed the bill by a vote of 62–38: R 50–0; D 12–38. The vote showed that Grassley and Baucus had found the formula for a tax package that could claim to have "broad bipartisan support." Not only did their trade-offs succeed in sustaining the support of all Republicans, it also reflected the year's apogee of prominence for the centrist Democrats, a dozen of whom (24 percent of all Democratic senators) voted for the legislation. *(Vote, p. 812)*

The tally also signaled that the deepest tax cut in a generation would happen, and that Bush would score his first big legislative triumph, sooner than almost anyone had predicted. Only twenty-four days elapsed between when the ceiling for the tax cut was set and when the Senate cleared the legislation (PL 107-16)—unusually fast for such wide-ranging, expensive, and politically precarious legislation.

The same dozen Democrats who voted for the original bill voted for the final version as well, a reflection of how closely the latter resembled the former. To make sure of that, two of the four lawmakers who cut the deal with the White House were Baucus and John B. Breaux of Louisiana, a leader of centrist Senate Democrats. Baucus

and five other Democrats who backed the bill were up for reelection in 2002, and all of them expected competitive races. Only two Democrats seen as vulnerable in 2002, Iowa's Tom Harkin and Minnesota's Paul Wellstone, voted "no" May 23.

Two Republicans who embraced the initial bill spurned the final deal, however: John McCain of Arizona, who opposed deep tax cuts when he ran against Bush for the party's 2000 presidential nomination, and fiscal moderate Lincoln Chafee of Rhode Island. But another pivotal moderate, James M. Jeffords of Vermont, supported the package—his vote for initial Senate passage coming before he announced he was abandoning the GOP to become an Independent, thereby giving Senate control to the Democrats. As a result, the climactic vote for the tax cut also stands as a high-water mark for the short-lived period—the first since 1954—of unilateral Republican control of the legislative and executive branches.

6. PATIENTS' RIGHTS

Immediately after becoming Senate majority leader in June, Tom Daschle, D-S.D., said a patients' bill of rights, left on the back burner by Republicans during the first part of the year, would be the first major piece of legislation he would bring to the floor. On June 19 Democrats began debate on a broad managed-care overhaul bill (S 1052) drafted by Edward M. Kennedy, D-Mass., John McCain, R-Ariz., and John Edwards, D-N.C. To ensure a vote on final passage, Daschle threatened to keep the Senate in session through the July 4 recess, if necessary, to finish. The Kennedy-McCain-Edwards measure was designed with all the provisions that patients' rights advocates had been pushing for years, including requirements that plans cover visits to specialists and emergency rooms, as well as a stipulation that insurers be prohibited from imposing restrictions on what doctors could tell their patients about treatment options. *(Legislative details, p. 475)*

The biggest controversy, as always, was over liability. The bill proposed, for the first time, to allow patients to sue their health plans in federal court for damages if harmed or injured by a health plan's coverage decision. The bill capped civil damages at $5 million in federal court but economic and non-economic damages were unlimited. The debate, and resulting vote, put Republicans in a tough position. Polls had shown that a managed-care overhaul was popular with voters but businesses and the insurance industry lobbied heavily against it. A Republican version encompassing broad "principles" laid out by the Bush administration clearly did not have the votes to pass. But Democrats also faced a complex strategic calculation in bringing the bill to a vote. They knew Bush would oppose their version, and, indeed, the White House issued a veto threat during the first week of debate. That meant a choice for Daschle and his party. They had to decide whether to call Bush's bluff and pass a bill anyway, or try to work it out in advance to ensure his signature. They chose the former course, partly because they figured that the bill they passed would be their opening bid in a conference to reconcile it with whatever was produced by the GOP-controlled House.

During the two weeks of Senate debate, Republicans proposed amendment after amendment designed to change the bill's liability provisions. Most of them failed. However, GOP moderates were successful in attaching amendments designed to make the bill more acceptable to business, especially large employers. One such amendment, sponsored by Olympia J. Snowe, R-Maine, would allow employers who appointed a "designated decision maker" for medical decisions to be shielded from lawsuits. Big business groups and their Republican allies had seized on the issue, painting the bill as one that would make large employers—not just less-popular insurance companies—vulnerable to higher costs. As Minority Whip Don Nickles, R-Okla., said: "Employers beware. There's language in this bill that will bankrupt you." The Snowe amendment gave some cover to Republicans who were concerned about the bill's potential effect on employers. Along with three Republicans, Democrat Ernest F. Hollings of South Carolina opposed her amendment.

But on final passage Daschle—in his first big test as majority leader—held his caucus together, with no Democrats opposing the bill. It passed June 29 by a vote of 59–36: R 9–35; D 50–0; I 0-1. In addition to McCain, eight Republicans voted for the final product, including three who were up for reelection in 2002: Susan Collins of Maine, Gordon H. Smith of Oregon, and John W. Warner of Virginia. Republican-turned-Independent James M. Jeffords of Vermont—the senator whose party switch enabled Democrats to bring the measure to the floor in the first place—was not among the supporters. *(Vote, p. 812)*

7. FARM BILL

As its opening foray into rewriting what both parties viewed as a badly flawed farm law, the Senate engaged in a surprisingly partisan fight over how much short-term relief to provide producers—transforming the debate into one that was at least as much about fiscal discipline as about agriculture policy. Farm bill differences are usually regional in nature but an uncertain surplus picture, combined with the political pressure of drafting a new law heading into an election year, led Republican and Democratic leaders to stake out different positions on the question of how much to boost direct government payments to farmers beyond the subsidies they were already due. *(Legislative details, p. 449)*

Democrats, newly in control of the Senate, wanted to spend $7.4 billion, painting themselves as the better advocates for the nation's farmers. Republicans, backed by a veto threat from President Bush, cloaked themselves in the mantle of fiscal restraint as they fought successfully to keep the bill within the confines of the fiscal 2002 budget resolution (H Con Res 83), which set aside $5.5 billion for the supplemental farm package. The turning point came as Congress was pressing to clear a path to its month-long August recess. Agriculture Committee Chairman Tom Harkin, D-Iowa, called up his $7.4 billion version of the bill and—when it became clear Republican leaders were intent on stopping the additional $1.9 billion in funding—moved to invoke cloture, thereby curtailing the debate and limiting amendments. Harkin needed sixty votes to get his way but came up eleven short on the key vote Aug. 3. Only two Republicans took his side in favor of the more generous package, and they were offset by two Democrats who voted with the GOP. The tally was 49–48: R 2–46; D 46–2; I 1–0. *(Vote, p. 812)*

By showing that the Democrats could not muster the three-fifths majority needed to get their way, the vote signaled that Republicans, although in the minority, had sufficient muscle to help Bush hold the line on spending. In the end, however, the outcome was dictated by bureaucratic deadline as much as political will. Under the budget resolution, the Department of Agriculture had only until Sept. 30 to provide whatever extra aid Congress authorized during fiscal 2001, and newly authorized government checks can take weeks to process and deliver. As a result, many believed that the opportunity to provide supplemental assistance would be lost if Congress did not act before its August break.

Harkin and Majority Leader Tom Daschle, D-S.D., initially saw the time constraint as leverage that would help persuade Bush and Republicans to drop their resistance to the more generous package. Republicans saw the same deadline as a way to compel the Democrats to drop a proposal that—in the face of a veto threat and clear opposition from the House, which had given voice vote approval to the less costly plan—could not quickly become law. Once it became evident

to Democrats that their pressure tactics were not working, they suggested they might wait and continue their fight in September. But hours after their bid to limit debate failed, they gave up and allowed the Senate to clear the House-passed measure (HR 2213) by voice vote. Still, the midyear farm aid law (PL 107-25) marked the fourth time in as many years that Congress had stepped in to provide direct payments to farmers—a total of $31.5 billion since 1997—on top of federal support they received under the 1996 farm law (PL 104-127), which had been geared toward weaning farmers from federal subsidies and providing them instead with fixed payments to help them adjust to a more free market system.

8. USE OF FORCE RESOLUTION

Unified in its anger over the Sept. 11 terrorist attacks at the World Trade Center and Pentagon, the Senate acted swiftly in unanimously approving a resolution (S J Res 23) giving President Bush the power to pursue and punish the perpetrators. The resolution authorized the president to "use all necessary and appropriate force against those nations, organizations or persons he determined planned, authorized, committed or aided" the attacks or against the nations that harbored the terrorists. The Senate adopted the resolution by a vote of 98–0: R 47–0; D 50–0; I 1–0. *(Vote, p. 812)*

Congress gave Bush free rein to pursue his subsequent military campaign against alleged mastermind Osama bin Laden and his al Qaeda terrorist network, as well as the Taliban regime in Afghanistan that sheltered the group. But the resolution blurred the lines separating the president's and Congress' respective constitutional roles in initiating military hostilities.

Lawmakers also put off a debate over whether Bush's plan to conduct a global war against terrorism extended to countries beyond Afghanistan, particularly Iraq. Conservatives, such as Republican Policy Committee Chairman Larry E. Craig of Idaho, argued for passing a declaration of war or a broad resolution to give Bush unfettered power to prosecute terrorism around the world. "I'm not for putting a lot of strings on it," said Republican Jon Kyl of Arizona, a member of the Senate Intelligence Committee. "Are we going to be able to give the president enough flexibility to act if we put a lot of restrictions in legislation?" That view was shared by the White House, which initially proposed that it also be granted "all necessary and appropriate force" to "deter and pre-empt any future acts of terrorism or aggression against the United States." But many lawmakers, especially Democrats, believed that would go too far and would infringe on congressional authority. They feared that an open-ended commitment would come back to haunt them, much as an earlier generation came to lament its support for the 1964 Gulf of Tonkin resolution (PL 88-408). That resolution was cited by the Johnson and Nixon administrations as congressional authorization for waging the Vietnam War.

Senate Foreign Relations Committee Chairman Joseph R. Biden Jr., D-Del., said lawmakers had struck an appropriate balance between the two branches of government while ensuring congressional prerogative. "We gave the president all the authority he needed without giving up our constitutional right to decide whether force should be used," Biden said.

9. BASE CLOSINGS

The Senate approved President Bush's proposal to close surplus military bases after repeatedly rejecting requests by President Clinton for nearly identical legislation. But in a bid to ease House concerns, the Senate delayed the start of the process until 2005. Lawmakers repeatedly had fought efforts to shutter bases, fearing that installations economically important to their states might be targeted. But in September, fourteen senators made an about-face on the issue, supporting Bush where they had opposed Clinton either for political reasons or in the belief that their bases would be on the hit list. *(Legislative details, p. 315)*

Clinton and Bush made the same argument for closing more bases: the Pentagon was wasting billions of dollars trying to maintain unnecessary facilities. But a new argument was offered during debate on the fiscal 2002 defense authorization bill (S 1438). Base-closing proponents said the savings were even more important as the military waged war against terrorism and faced new duties in homeland defense after the Sept. 11 terrorist attacks. Base-closing opponents, led by Jim Bunning, R-Ky., challenged the Pentagon's statement that previous closings had yielded significant savings. They said another round would be ill-timed amid a recession and as the services were deciding what deployments might be needed to fight terrorism. The key vote occurred on an amendment by Bunning to delete the base-closing provision from the defense bill. It was tabled (killed) by a vote of 53–47: R 21–28; D 31–19; I 1–0. *(Vote, p. 812)*

Although Democrats provided the majority of the support for an initiative by a Republican president, the difference between this vote and the Senate's 63–35 rejection of a similar proposal in June 2000 was the number of members—eight Republicans and six Democrats—who switched from opposition to support. John W. Warner of Virginia, ranking Republican on the Senate Armed Services Committee, had voted against Clinton's plans although he acknowledged that additional bases needed to be closed. He argued that Clinton had politicized the process in 1995 by ordering the Air Force to have private contractors take over aircraft overhaul depots in vote-rich California and Texas, even though the base-closing commission had recommended they be shut down.

Other lawmakers switched because bases that once looked vulnerable now appeared safe. Majority Leader Tom Daschle, whose state of South Dakota was home to Ellsworth Air Force Base, voted against closure in 2000 amid talk that Ellsworth might be a target. But the base's future seemed more certain when the Air Force announced in June that it was one of two at which B-1 bomber operations would be consolidated. This time, Daschle voted for base closings.

10. ANTITERRORISM

In the Senate, all the real debate on the antiterrorism package proposed by Attorney General John Ashcroft took place behind closed doors. Some members privately expressed concern about the breadth of the bill but the power of a popular president and public fears of more terrorist attacks helped push it to passage with very few changes and only one senator voting no. The debate over the Bush administration's tactics in the home-front war on terrorism would continue on Capitol Hill but the lopsided vote in the Senate sent an important signal early on that Congress would give wide latitude to the White House in dealing with the crisis. *(Legislative action, p. 187)*

On Sept. 19 Ashcroft asked Congress to give him broader powers to investigate acts of terrorism and other crimes. He argued that limitations in existing law tied his hands and made it far too difficult to track the persons responsible for Sept. 11 attack. He wanted to update the laws to make it easier to track Internet communications, get nationwide search warrants for terrorism investigations, authorize more secret searches of a suspect's residence, and indefinitely detain aliens he believed were national security risks. He also wanted investigators to be able to give information to intelligence agents and receive information in turn.

Almost as soon as the request arrived on Capitol Hill, senators began closed-door discussions on the provisions. The talks, led by Judiciary Committee Chairman Patrick J. Leahy, D-Vt., and the panel's ranking Republican, Orrin G. Hatch of Utah, included administration representatives nearly from the start. That was in contrast to the House, where Judiciary Committee Chairman F. James Sensenbrenner Jr., R-Wis., negotiated largely among committee members to come up with a bill. Although the House Judiciary Committee produced a bipartisan bill, it was never brought to the floor. Members instead voted on a bill much closer to the measure finally agreed on by the Senate negotiators.

After weeks of negotiations, and several breakdowns, Leahy and others announced Oct. 4 that they had reached a deal. The agreement gave the administration most of what it sought, although senators did delete a provision that would have allowed U.S. government officials to use the results of unconstitutional wiretaps by foreign governments. The bill incorporating the deal (S 1510) was introduced by Majority Leader Tom Daschle, D-S.D., on Oct. 4. It skipped committee and went straight to the floor, where it passed 96–1 on Oct. 11 with less than three hours of actual debate. Daschle told his colleagues to vote against amendments offered by Russell D. Feingold, D-Wis., not because he opposed the substance of the amendments but in order to preserve the carefully negotiated compromise with the administration. Feingold was the only dissenting vote.

After the House passed its version Oct. 12, members spent about a week working out a compromise. The final bill (HR 3162) included much of the Senate bill but also contained a key House-passed end to the authorization for many of the most contentious parts of the bill after four years. The Senate took up the final bill Oct. 25, the day after the House passed it. The Senate cleared the bill for the president 98–1: R 49–0; D 48–1; I 1–0. The president signed it the next day. Feingold again was the only no vote; Mary L. Landrieu, D-La., did not vote. *(Vote, p. 812)*

House

1. ERGONOMICS RULES

House Republican leaders were eager to follow their Senate counterparts in 2001 in overturning a controversial Clinton administration regulation on workplace ergonomics. After weeks of careful groundwork, Republicans had sprung their trap in the Senate on March 6 before Democrats could respond with a procedural defense. They had an easier time in the House the next day, where the GOP controlled the rules more tightly.

The debate over ergonomics and repetitive motion injuries in factories and offices had been going on for more than a decade. Democrats, with their staunch support of organized labor, generally favored new rules; Republicans generally opposed the idea, since it could cost business dearly. The Clinton administration published a final ergonomics rule in fall 2000, preempting a Republican effort to block the rule in the fiscal 2001 Labor–Health and Human Services–Education spending bill (PL 106-554). House Republicans were eager to push through a repeal as one of the first acts of the session. *(Legislative details, p. 565)*

The ergonomics regulation had taken effect Jan. 16 and enforcement would have begun Oct. 14, 2001. It required employers to educate workers about ways to prevent injuries from repetitive motion such as typing, sorting, or lifting heavy loads. It required employers to make changes in their workplaces if a worker reported a repetitive motion injury. Business groups, which said the requirement would have cost U.S. companies more than $100 billion a year, made it a top goal to overturn the rule before it took effect.

Working behind the scenes, House Republicans and business groups persuaded some centrist Democrats to support overturning the regulation using a little-noticed 1996 law, the Congressional Review Act, which was enacted as part of a debt-limit extension (PL 104-121). When the House took up the bill March 7, sixteen Democrats, fourteen of them from the South, supported overturning the ergonomics regulation, more than offsetting the thirteen Republicans, many of them from the Northeast and upper Midwest, who sided with labor and voted to keep the regulation. The vote was 223–206: R 206–13; D 16–192; I 1–1. *(Vote, p. 814)*

Some centrist Democrats justified their votes in 2001 against the Clinton-era regulation by saying they would push for legislation that would require the Labor Department to issue narrower ergonomics policies. However, those bills did not move through either chamber. Democrats were particularly frustrated that Republicans used the Congressional Review Act because it also banned the administration from writing another regulation that had "substantially the same form." Later in the year, Labor Secretary Elaine L. Chao held hearings on the ergonomics issue, but the agency did not issue a new round of worker safety regulations that employers would have to implement.

2. TAX CUTS

With Republicans simultaneously controlling the Capitol and the White House for the first time in five decades, and with evidence of an economic downturn already apparent, a tax cut in 2001 seemed to be a certainty as the year began. Its potential scope and speed remained largely unknown, however, until the narrow but united majority of Republicans won a vote that displayed the House's ability to deliver to President George W. Bush the type of tax cut that was the centerpiece of his campaign.

Because the Constitution stipulates that revenue bills must originate in the House, it was certain the debate on the Bush tax plan would start in the more receptive of the two congressional chambers. It was left to House GOP leaders—and in particular Bill Thomas, R-Calif., the new chairman of the Ways and Means Committee—to decide how best to leverage a bipartisan willingness to cut taxes. As the year began, Democratic leaders had lined up behind a $900 million plan—signaling they were willing to go more than halfway toward Bush's $1.6 trillion package of cuts over ten years. *(Legislative details, pp. 86–87, 89)*

But rather than easing into the tax cut issue with negotiations on a broad package or an easy vote on a minimally controversial tax cut—or simply waiting until the administration had settled its macro disputes over fiscal policy—the GOP took a decidedly different tack: it arranged to make the year's most politically difficult vote on taxes the first vote on taxes. By vaulting past the most difficult hurdle first, party leaders believed, they would help build a sense of inevitability for the deepest tax cut in a generation.

The day after the president sent his first budget outline to Congress, and without any consultation with Democrats, the House GOP started moving its version of Bush's most contentious and costly tax proposal: the first across-the-board reduction of personal income tax rates in fifteen years, with the sharpest reduction for those with the highest incomes. The Republican legislation (HR 3) would have reduced revenues by $958 billion through fiscal 2011, three-fifths the total of Bush's entire proposal. The bill presented the House not only with its first vote on the new president's platform but also with a vote on the central element of his economic program. The vote March 8 to pass the measure was 230–198: R 219–0; D 10–197; I 1–1. *(Vote, p. 814)*

The vote demonstrated not only the outcome of the Bush tax package but also the nature of partisanship in the House and the continued differences between the House and Senate. House GOP leaders learned that their caucus was united behind the Bush tax cut.

They learned that, even with the narrowest majority since the 83rd Congress, they could push through one of the most contentious bills of the year without even pretending to collaborate with Democrats—and that more than a handful of Democrats would vote with them anyway. (Most of the ten who did so had just been reelected in politically competitive districts; the House votes on other central elements of the Bush plan—tax relief for parents and ending the estate tax—drew many more Democratic votes; twenty-eight Democrats eventually voted for the reconciliation package that became law in June.)

The rate cut vote also showed House GOP leaders that their main argument, that quick action was needed to deliver a boost to a sagging economy, could triumph over the two most politically potent counterarguments. Liberals maintained that the Bush tax cut, especially the personal income rate cut, was inappropriately tilted to the rich. Most of the party's conservatives argued that it was wrong to cut taxes before setting an overall budget framework that could balance the demands on what was, at the time, a robust federal surplus.

Business lobbyists and others hoping to include their special interests in the tax bill also took a lesson from the vote: their priorities would have to wait because the House GOP was only interested in writing its own version of the president's program. Finally, the clarity of the vote allowed House leaders early in the year to pass off to the Senate the job of balancing all the debate's competing pressures. The Senate's 50–50 split at the time, combined with rules that essentially require any proposal of controversy to win sixty supporters, always meant it would be a more difficult ground for the tax cut fight.

3. EDUCATION

President Bush's education overhaul plan turned almost entirely on an idea that had enemies in both parties: annual testing in reading and math for children in grades three through eight. As a result the White House knew it had a fight on its hand when Reps. Peter Hoekstra, R-Mich., and Barney Frank, D-Mass., teamed up in May to try to delete that element from the House education overhaul bill (HR 1). *(Legislative details, p. 540)*

There would have been little point to the overhaul bill without the annual testing. The idea was to hold states, school districts, and schools accountable for how much students learn, with rewards for the best schools and penalties for the worst. To do that, there had to be a yardstick for measuring students' progress. Annual tests were the best available yardstick, supporters of the Bush plan said, and they were essential to allow the bill's multilayered "accountability" system to work.

It quickly became clear, however, that the annual testing offered something for everyone to hate. Conservatives thought it was a backdoor way to establish the national test they all feared, just four years after they defeated President Bill Clinton's plans for voluntary national tests in reading and math. Liberals argued that children were being forced to take too many tests already, and warned that standardized tests were unfair to poor and minority students. It was a powerful undercurrent of opposition, and even though the education bill had been approved by the House Education and the Workforce Committee by a strong bipartisan vote of 41–7, members remained nervous over the issue. When Hoekstra and Frank announced they would offer an amendment on the House floor to remove the testing requirement, administration officials feared the opposing bipartisan forces would join together.

The alliance of Hoekstra, a conservative, and Frank, a liberal, captured the wide spectrum of opposition to the annual tests. Both argued that the tests would impose an unfair mandate on the states and that they would represent a heavy-handed federal role in education, which traditionally was a state and local responsibility. All along, the

Bush administration and the House bill's main authors—Education and the Workforce Chairman John A. Boehner, R-Ohio, and top Democrat George Miller of California—had to negotiate with Republicans and Democrats to keep them from offering divisive amendments that could destroy the bill's fragile bipartisan support. They swung into action to make sure Hoekstra and Frank did not attract enough support to cut out the bill's centerpiece.

White House Chief of Staff Andrew H. Card Jr. and presidential adviser Karl Rove discouraged conservatives from voting for the amendment. Boehner and Miller spoke passionately on behalf of the testing provision. The Business Roundtable sent out an e-mail alert asking its members to urge lawmakers to oppose the amendment, warning that it would "take the teeth out of the bill." Ultimately, the vote was not as close as the bill's supporters had feared. The Hoekstra-Frank amendment was rejected May 22 by a vote of 173–255: R 52–166; D 119–89; I 2–0. *(Vote, p. 814)*

However, the amendment did draw the support of 119 Democrats, including some of the most powerful ones in the House: Minority Leader Richard A. Gephardt of Missouri, Minority Whip David E. Bonior of Michigan, and David R. Obey of Wisconsin, the ranking member of the Appropriations Committee. Still, the fact that the testing survived the onslaught of so many opponents was a defining moment for the education bill. At that moment, it became clear that nothing could stand in the bill's way—because even the most unpopular provision was not fatal.

4. CAMPAIGN FINANCE

Plenty of members, Republicans and Democrats alike, had qualms about the campaign finance legislation that reached the House floor July 12. But when the bill (HR 2356) came crashing down, tangled in a dispute over the rule (H Res 188) for debate, each side blamed the other for the failure. There was room for both parties to portray events in the light that best suited them. In the end, there were no votes for or against the bill in the House, nothing to put members clearly on record. The vote on the rule was open to interpretation. *(Legislative details, p. 733)*

In the weeks leading up to the debate, the sponsors of the campaign finance bill—Democrat Martin T. Meehan of Massachusetts and Republican Christopher Shays of Connecticut—had worked to fine-tune their bill so that it closely matched the Senate-passed version (S 27) sponsored by John McCain, R-Ariz., and Russell D. Feingold, D-Wis. The goal was to avoid a conference committee, where supporters of the bill feared hostile Republican leaders would have another chance to kill it.

But from the start a critical Senate compromise dogged Democrats in the House. In exchange for banning "soft money," the unregulated contributions to political parties, McCain and Feingold had agreed to raise the limits on "hard money," or direct-to-candidate contributions. Democrats already were having second thoughts about banning soft money as the 2002 midterm elections approached. Raising the limits on hard money, where the GOP has long had the edge, gave them one more reason to say no to the bill. The fractures were most visible in the Congressional Black Caucus, whose thirty-six members said soft money was crucial to get-out-the-vote and voter registration efforts in minority communities. Republican leaders, who opposed Shays-Meehan, unveiled a rival bill aimed at those fears, driving another wedge into the Democratic caucus. The bill (HR 2360) would have capped, rather than banned, soft money.

Meanwhile, House Minority Leader Richard A. Gephardt, D-Mo., who had taken flak for not fighting visibly enough for Shays-Meehan, lobbied his caucus to stay behind the bill. He was still working to secure votes when the dispute over the rule for debate came to a head

July 12. Shays and Meehan had asked the House Rules Committee to bundle fourteen last-minute changes to their bill—aimed mostly at bringing it in line with the Senate version—into a single "manager's amendment." The Rules Committee refused and said each of the changes would be voted on separately on the floor. Shays, Meehan, and their supporters angrily accused the Republican leadership of trying to bring down the bill with a complicated, obstacle-strewn rule. Republicans countered that Democrats were looking for a face-saving way to scuttle the bill because they did not have the votes to pass it.

Speaker J. Dennis Hastert, R-Ill., offered to compromise on the rule but he withdrew after conservatives in his caucus demanded that the original rule go forward. In the end, the rule for debating campaign finance legislation in the House was rejected 203–228: R 201–19; D 1–208; I 1–1. It was the first time Hastert lost a vote on a rule, which is typically seen as a matter of party loyalty from which members have little room to deviate. *(Vote, p. 814)*

With the defeat of the rule, campaign finance dropped from the House agenda; Hastert promptly said he had no intention of giving the debate another chance. Shays-Meehan supporters quickly began collecting signatures on a "discharge petition" to force the bill back to the floor under rules more to their liking, and by Sept. 11, they were just nine names short of the 218 they needed. Then the terrorist attacks put it all on hold. The petition was good for the duration of the 107th Congress, so Shays and Meehan had time for another push in 2002 but that would be an election year, which could further complicate their efforts.

5. ARSENIC STANDARDS

Early in spring 2001 when President Bush was coming under fire from environmental lobbyists for his industry-favoring policies, there was one decision that became a rallying cry—Environmental Protection Agency (EPA) Administrator Christine Todd Whitman's announcement that stricter standards for arsenic in drinking water would be delayed.

Arsenic occurred naturally in the soil and water, but it also was released by some industrial processes. Studies had linked long-term exposure to arsenic in drinking water to cancer of the bladder, lungs, skin, kidney, liver, and prostate. Polls showed that most people roundly supported a Clinton administration regulation that would have lowered the allowable standard from fifty parts per billion—the level that had been permitted for decades—to ten parts per billion. The lower standard had been recommended by the European Union and the World Health Organization. The dangers of arsenic were not a new topic for Congress. Five years earlier, lawmakers had directed the administration to study the health risks associated with arsenic as part of its safe drinking water amendments (PL 104-182).

Mining and chemical companies opposed the more stringent Clinton regulations. They had argued that science did not support such a tough policy. The regulation also was opposed by officials from many of the 3,000 towns that would have to update their water systems. When Whitman insisted that the regulation be put on hold, she said the EPA should take the time to make sure the policy, which was not slated to take effect until 2006, was founded in science, though she herself supported the more stringent standard. Environmentalists pounced on her announcement as a sign that the White House was abandoning the policy and, as many lobbyists put it, trying to allow more cancer-causing chemicals in the public's water.

The Bush administration had delayed or reversed several orders and regulations that Clinton had issued in the waning days of his term, but none of Bush's decisions resonated as the one on arsenic did. Amid a flood of news stories and polls, it was clear that the new administration had miscalculated. Congress was not long in making the point that Bush had gone too far. On July 27 House Democrats succeeded in attaching an amendment to the fiscal 2002 appropriations bill (HR 2620) for the departments of Veterans Affairs and Housing and Urban Development (HUD) to prohibit the EPA from weakening the Clinton standards for arsenic in drinking water. With nineteen Republicans crossing party lines, the amendment, offered by Minority Whip David E. Bonior, D-Mich., was adopted 218–189: R 19–182; D 198–6; I 1–1. *(Vote, p. 814)*

The administration did not admit defeat but it retreated in the following months. At the EPA's request, the National Academy of Sciences studied the issue and its report, completed in September, found that arsenic in drinking water was more harmful to humans than previous studies had indicated. The report suggested that the government consider arsenic limits even more restrictive than those proposed by Clinton. Following this report, Whitman announced Oct. 31 that the EPA would, after all, adopt the Clinton standard.

6. HUMAN CLONING

The House drew a new line on how far it was willing to go in restricting biomedical research July 31, passing a comprehensive ban on cloning human embryos either for reproductive purposes or to develop medical treatments. The 265–162 vote for the ban (HR 2505), sponsored by Dave Weldon, R-Fla., reflected the growing discomfort many lawmakers felt with the prospect of scientists creating human embryos so their cells could be harvested for medical purposes. *(Legislative details, p. 493)*

But the precise extent of the discomfort was evident just before the vote on the Weldon measure when the House in a key vote rejected a substitute amendment by James C. Greenwood, R-Pa., that would have outlawed cloning for the purpose of starting a pregnancy but allowed it to create tissue for medical research. The amendment was defeated 178–249: R 25–194; D 153–53; I 0–2. *(Vote, p. 814)*

The cloning votes were intertwined with the separate but related issue of whether the government should fund stem cell research. Researchers in 1998 had announced the ability to isolate primitive human stem cells from days-old embryos. The so-called master cells were capable of evolving into bone, muscle, and virtually every kind of human tissue, giving researchers hope they might be able to develop healthy replacement cells to cure such afflictions as juvenile diabetes, spinal cord injuries, and Parkinson's disease.

However, the field was controversial because extracting stem cells involved destroying embryos—an act that antiabortion forces equated with taking a life. Stem cells currently were extracted from leftover embryos developed through in vitro fertilization. Research opponents maintained that human embryos soon could be cloned solely for the purpose of supplying stem cells, pointing to plans by the Worcester, Mass., biotechnology company Advanced Cell Technologies to conduct such "therapeutic cloning."

The Greenwood substitute served as a referendum on that procedure. Supporters suggested that the extraction of stem cells offered a high-resolution view of early human development that might force Congress to change its position on when life begins. During an often emotional four hours of debate, some noted that the act of making cells divide in a petri dish alone would not ensure that they developed into an embryo unless they were implanted in a womb. They urged members not to impose what they considered onerous new regulations, such as the Weldon ban, on a still-developing field.

The substitute lost by an unexpectedly large margin thanks to intense lobbying by antiabortion groups, which dubbed the Greenwood provision a "clone to kill" bill. Some skeptics also questioned how one could practically enforce the Greenwood provision and en-

sure that an embryo created for research purposes was not later implanted in a surrogate mother without violating doctor-patient confidentiality agreements.

The cloning debate did not break precisely along the lines of past abortion votes. Fifty-three Democrats joined with 194 Republicans and two Independents to reject the Greenwood measure. Some lawmakers on both sides of the debate expressed discomfort afterward at having to assimilate complicated technical information and parse the differences between what the Weldon and Greenwood measures would do. Greenwood and biotechnology industry officials suggested the outcome ironically would give lawmakers more leeway to support embryonic stem cell research, allowing conservatives to support the medical promise of using stem cells from leftover embryos in fertility clinics and still appear to be taking a firm line against human cloning. The separate congressional debate over funding stem cell research was settled in August, when President Bush endorsed limited federal funding for the work.

7. DRILLING IN ARCTIC NATIONAL WILDLIFE REFUGE

The issue of whether to open the coast of Alaska's Arctic National Wildlife Refuge (ANWR) to oil and natural gas exploration had divided lawmakers and pitted environmentalists against oil companies and Alaska officials for more than forty years. Despite the West Coast's electricity shortage earlier in 2001 environmentalists were confident they had the upper hand, pointing to polls showing that a majority of Americans opposed drilling in the distant refuge because of the potential ecological harm. However, the House defeat of a proposal to ban drilling showed how the combined lobbying of the White House, House Republican leaders, energy industries, and labor unions could outmaneuver and overwhelm environmental groups. *(Legislative details, p. 414)*

Environmentalists described the coastal plain as an important birthing place for caribou, a feeding ground for snow geese, and a den site for polar bears. They also noted it would take as long as ten years to begin piping oil from the refuge, and that even then, it would be of little help to California and other states that got less than 1 percent of their power from oil-fired plants. However, Bush decided earlier in his administration to talk up the benefits of ANWR as a way to help wean the United States from its dependence on foreign oil. He appointed Vice President Richard B. Cheney to head an energy task force that recommended in May that a portion of the refuge be opened for exploration.

The House Resources Committee subsequently included the ANWR language in a bill that was combined with three other measures to form an omnibus energy package (HR 4) developed in response to the Cheney task force's report. Environmentalists and their allies in Congress promised to remove the language on ANWR, arguing that opening the refuge would permanently alter it no matter how carefully the work was done. But proponents of drilling framed the debate in economic rather than environmental terms. The International Brotherhood of Teamsters ran a series of radio advertisements claiming that opening the refuge would create as many as 750,000 jobs.

Environmentalists disputed the figures but the idea of stimulating employment through increased domestic energy production as unemployment began creeping higher for the first time in years resonated with some undecided lawmakers. "I was moved by the prospects . . . for some jobs," said Jack Quinn, R-N.Y., a moderate with close ties to organized labor. To win over other lawmakers concerned about the possible environmental damage, House Republican leaders encouraged them to support two amendments that critics said were intended to provide political cover. One would split future oil and gas royalties evenly between the state of Alaska and the federal government, instead of giving Alaska 90 percent. The other would limit the ground that could be covered by oil production facilities in the refuge to 2,000 acres. Both amendments were adopted.

However, the decisive amendment by Edward J. Markey, D-Mass., to remove the ANWR language from the bill was rejected by a vote of 206–223: R 34–186; D 171–36; I 1–1. After the vote, opponents of drilling were consoled by its dim prospects in the Senate where Democrats held the majority and put off energy legislation for the year. But ANWR supporters in the House lamented that their intensive lobbying did not register. "It was a tough coalition to beat," Markey said after the vote, "the oil and gas industry, the building trades, the president of the United States, and millions of dollars of lobbying." *(Vote, p. 814)*

8. PATIENTS' RIGHTS

One of the most intriguing parts of the managed-care story in 2001 was how the bill came to the House floor in the first place. After the Senate passed its bill in June House leaders promised to bring patients' rights legislation to a vote before the August recess. Beyond that, they were stuck. The White House, House Speaker J. Dennis Hastert, R-Ill., and other GOP leaders liked a bill (HR 2315) produced by Ernie Fletcher, R-Ky. However, the Republicans did not have enough support for House passage.

The more popular measure was one (HR 2563) sponsored by Republicans Charlie Norwood of Georgia and Greg Ganske of Iowa and Democrat John D. Dingell of Michigan. It would expand Americans' ability to sue health maintenance organizations (HMOs) in federal courts and allow plaintiffs to collect civil damages of up to $5 million and unlimited economic and noneconomic damages. Patients also could sue insurers in state courts, with damage caps set by individual states. For years, federal employee benefits law had limited such suits to federal courts, and damages were limited to the cost of denied care. *(Legislative details, p. 475)*

Republican House leaders were never happy that Norwood, a dentist, and Ganske, a surgeon, were in the other camp, but the GOP leadership had come to accept it as a fact of managed-care politics. On Aug. 1, Norwood appeared in the White House briefing room with the president and announced a "compromise." Dingell and Ganske were furious. House leaders were jubilant: the measure produced by Norwood and the president was one they could support. The key provision concerned liability. The deal would allow suits in state courts over HMO medical decisions and cap liability at $1.5 million for noneconomic damages and $1.5 million for punitive damages, which would be allowed only if a HMO had ignored the decision of an independent review panel.

Hastert quickly brought the Ganske-Dingell bill to the floor the next day with the intention of having the Norwood-Bush deal offered as an amendment. But the House burst into a fiercely partisan and sometimes personal debate, with Ganske accusing Norwood of "free-lancing" and Norwood defending himself by saying his deal with Bush was the only way to get a managed-care bill enacted. The tension was palpable when the Norwood amendment itself came up. Said Ganske: "This is the nitty-gritty of the debate. We have sort of been fooling around until we get to the Norwood amendment." Both sides worked furiously to win votes. The White House and insurance companies lobbied for adoption of the amendment; the American Medical Association and some state officials, who feared the Norwood-Bush deal would preempt state laws, worked against it. Dingell, Ganske and their supporters argued that the Norwood-Bush deal was more beneficial to insurance companies than to consumers.

The Norwood-Bush deal was criticized by all sides—conservatives, moderates, and Democrats. Many who voted for it said they did so just to get a bill to conference. Ultimately, the amendment was successful because it did one thing no patients' rights legislation had done: It gave much-needed cover to Republicans who wanted to vote for a patients' rights bill while also supporting their president. The amendment was adopted Aug. 2, 218–213: R 214–6; D 3–206; I 1–1. *(Vote, p. 814)*

Three GOP members who had cosponsored the original Norwood-Dingell-Ganske bill followed Norwood: Bob Barr of Georgia, Benjamin A. Gilman of New York, and Steve Horn of California. The bill, as amended, passed the House 226–203 shortly after. For his part, Norwood insisted the deal he cut with Bush was not the final word, and suggested changes could be made in conference. "I know this isn't the final bill, and so do you," he told his colleagues. "I know there are words that need to be changed."

9. USE OF FORCE AGAINST TERRORISTS

Intent on pursuing Osama bin Laden and rooting out terrorism after the Sept. 11 attacks on New York City and Washington, D.C., the House overwhelmingly approved a resolution (H J Res 64) giving President Bush the authority to punish those behind the assaults—with one lone voice of dissent. The vote, which reflected the strong bipartisan anger stemming from the attacks, was 420–1: R 214–0; D 204–1; I 2–0. *(Legislative details, p. 187; Vote, p. 814)*

Following the vote, the House passed an identical Senate resolution (S J Res 23) by voice vote, clearing it for the president. The resolution authorized the president to "use all necessary and appropriate force against those nations, organizations or persons he determined planned, authorized, committed or aided" the attacks or the nations that harbored them. In clearing the measure, Congress gave Bush the power to launch the subsequent military campaign against the Taliban regime in Afghanistan, suspected of protecting bin Laden and the al Qaeda terrorist network. Left unclear were answers to the long-time questions about the constitutional roles of the president and Congress in initiating military operations.

Rep. Barbara Lee, D-Calif., voted against the resolution after attending a prayer service at the Washington National Cathedral. Lee cited the words of the Rev. Nathan D. Baxter, an Episcopal priest and the Cathedral dean, who counseled, "Let us also pray for divine wisdom as our leaders consider the necessary actions for national security, that despite our grief we may not become the evil we deplore." Lee, whose district included Berkeley, with its long-standing antiwar perspective added, "Somebody has to say this in the U.S. Congress. And if we all vote in one way, no one does that."

Lawmakers put off debate over whether Bush's global war against terrorism extended beyond Afghanistan to countries such as Iraq. Conservatives, such as Bob Barr, R-Ga., had argued for passing a declaration of war or a broad resolution to give the president unlimited power to prosecute terrorism around the world. That view was shared by the White House, which initially proposed that it also be granted "all necessary and appropriate force" to "deter and preempt any future acts of terrorism or aggression against the United States." But many lawmakers, particularly Democrats, believed that went too far. They feared that an open-ended commitment would come back to haunt them, much as an earlier generation came to regret its support for the 1964 Gulf of Tonkin resolution (PL 88-408). That resolution was cited by the Johnson and Nixon administrations as congressional authorization for waging the Vietnam War. "We need to tread very cautiously," said Alcee L. Hastings, D-Fla. "We shouldn't cave in and say 'fire at will.' "

10. FARM BILL

The debate over how to rebuild the federal safety net under the farm economy while it was in the middle of a devastating downturn led to one of the clearer choices in the House in 2001 between taking an "old" or a "new" approach. Farm-state lawmakers and commodity groups sought to enhance the array of subsidies available to those who grew grains and oilseeds. But urban and suburban members, who typically stayed in the background during farm bill debates, joined with conservation and sportsmen's groups to mount a serious challenge to that system by proposing conservation programs from which all farmers could benefit. (*Legislative details, p. 812*)

The debate occurred on a farm bill (HR 2646) being written to update the 1996 farm law (PL 104-127), enacted by a new Republican congressional majority eager to implement an agenda that the GOP said brought them to power in the 1994 elections. The aim in that legislation was to wean farmers from the federal subsidies that were among the longest lasting legacies of the New Deal, but that goal went largely unmet as falling crop prices worldwide compelled Congress to provide supplementary aid almost every year since.

Republican House Agriculture Committee Chairman Larry Combest and ranking Democrat Charles W. Stenholm, both Texans, proposed abandoning the 1996 law and providing an additional $73.5 billion over the next ten years for farm programs, three-fifths of it to subsidize farmers of the nation's major export commodities: corn, wheat, soybeans, other grains and oilseeds, rice, and cotton. The benefits of doing so would be concentrated mostly on the large, profitable farms of the Great Plains, Upper Midwest, and deep South.

The alternative was to expand the reach, rather than the generosity, of federal farm aid by increasing the spending on conservation programs—such as those that paid farmers to idle environmentally sensitive land and to protect wildlife and wetlands—which were not confined to any particular region or type of farm. This drew the support of environmentalists, antisprawl groups, and other groups. Wisconsin Democrat Ron Kind, a member of the Agriculture panel, teamed up with two leading environmentalists among House Republicans, Sherwood Boehlert of New York and Wayne T. Gilchrest of Maryland, as well as Michigan Democrat John D. Dingell, arguably the most powerful advocate of gun owners' rights in the House, to propose taking $19 billion of the subsidy payments in the Combest-Stenholm bill and spending it instead on conservation.

As the vote approached, the White House signaled sympathy with the environmentalist approach, releasing a report that emphasized the importance of conservation programs and issuing a harsh critique of the commodity-centric Agriculture Committee measure. With the new approach gaining momentum, Combest threatened to scuttle the entire bill if the Kind-Boehlert-Dingell amendment were adopted. Although their plan drew bipartisan support—one-quarter of the Republicans voted for it, as did seven out of ten Democrats—it was narrowly rejected the night of Oct. 4. The key vote was 200–226: R 54–161; D 145–64; I 1–1. (*Vote, p. 814*)

With the alternative swept aside, the House voted overwhelmingly the next day to pass the more traditional, subsidy-focused farm bill. But the closeness of the vote helped shape the Senate debate later in the year and seemed destined to influence the outcome when a compromise was written in 2002. Even in failure, the amendment's proponents "changed American farm politics forever," said Mike Casey of the Environmental Working Group, which lobbied hard for the plan. "They basically said suburban America and Northeast coastal areas have a stake in what farm policy looks like, and never again are farm-state legislators going to be able to say, 'We are the committee; we know what we're doing; shut up and sit down.' "

11. ANTITERRORISM

Overwhelming votes of support in the House for antiterrorism legislation in October belied the measure's troubled path. A group of Democrats and Republicans voiced misgivings that the legislation sought by the Bush administration sacrificed civil liberties for greater police powers, and the group even drew up a bipartisan alternative, though it went nowhere. In the end, the vast majority of House members supported the drive to give the Bush administration greater powers to track, investigate and prosecute those accused of terrorism and other crimes. (*Legislative details, p. 187*)

Attorney General John Ashcroft first went to Congress just eight days after the Sept. 11 attacks with a request for a package of broad new authorities that would allow his investigators to track communications over the Internet, secretly search a suspect's home, and obtain a nationwide warrant for searches in terrorism investigations. Liberal groups immediately denounced the move as a power grab, noting that much of the enhanced authority had been requested by previous administrations—and rejected by Congress—well before the terrorist attacks. Some conservatives also said they were worried the administration was reaching too far. Ashcroft and others defended the request, saying the new dangers that terrorism posed required new tools for law enforcement.

House Judiciary Committee Chairman F. James Sensenbrenner Jr., R-Wis., staked his committee's claim on the Ashcroft proposal, arguing that it should proceed through the regular legislative process. He won approval from the GOP House leadership to take the bill through committee, so long as it moved quickly to the floor. Sensenbrenner began negotiations with his committee's ranking Democrat, John Conyers Jr. of Michigan, and others. They came up with a compromise bill that dropped some of the most controversial proposals in the administration's package, such as provisions to broaden the circumstances under which secret searches of suspects' property and the indefinite detention of aliens would be allowed. The Judiciary Committee then met and approved the bill (HR 2975) unanimously, a rare occurrence for the normally fractious committee.

In the meantime, top members of the Senate Judiciary Committee were negotiating their own version of the bill, this time with Justice Department and White House participation. These negotiations produced a bill much more to the administration's liking, a bill the Senate passed after little real debate. As the House prepared to debate the Judiciary Committee's version, the White House began to pressure the GOP leadership and Sensenbrenner to bring to the floor a package closer to Ashcroft's proposal. In the wake of the strong Senate vote, House leaders complied, scuttling the committee provisions in favor of language closer to the Senate bill.

They did retain one key provision from the committee to end the authority for certain sections of the bill. The "sunset" was set at five years. After the rule to bring the substitute bill to the floor was narrowly adopted, 214–208, the House passed the revised bill (HR 2975), 337–79. At that point, it was clear the administration would get what it wanted. On Oct. 24, after negotiations with the Senate, the House brought a final version of the bill (HR 3162) to the floor. It gave the administration broader authority to do secret searches, for example, but it retained the House-passed sunsets, shortened to four years. The House passed it 357–66: R 211–3; D 145–62; I 1–1. (*Vote, p. 814*)

12. AVIATION SECURITY

After the Sept. 11 terrorist attacks, it seemed only a matter of time before Congress would remove the low-paid private security personnel who screened passengers and baggage at the nation's airports and put federal workers in charge—something airlines had resisted for decades, citing higher costs. While many members of Congress were ready to let the federal government assume the responsibility and cost in the wake of the attacks, a group of House conservatives stood in the way, led by Texas Republicans Richard Armey, the majority leader, and Tom DeLay, the majority whip. Creating as many as 28,000 new federal jobs would not guarantee better security, they argued, but it would increase the size of the federal government and the membership of federal employee unions largely loyal to Democrats.

The debate tied up House action on a broad aviation security package for more than six weeks as Armey and DeLay refused to budge. A bill (HR 3150) eventually drafted by the Transportation and Infrastructure Committee would have given the president the option of having private or government screeners. *(Legislative details, p. 199)*

When the Senate passed an aviation security bill of its own (S 1447) on Oct. 11 to make all screeners federal employees, it appeared the House Republican effort was doomed. The Senate bill passed 100–0, showing the broad support for federalization. President Bush, though he said he preferred having a choice on airport security, indicated he would sign the Senate bill if the House passed it. Facing a big loss, and amid intensive lobbying for federalization by airline pilots and organized labor, Armey and DeLay persuaded the White House to support their effort. Bush, along with Transportation Secretary Norman Y. Mineta and Rep. John L. Mica, R-Fla., chairman of the House Transportation Subcommittee on Aviation, lobbied intensively. They targeted members who had not announced their support for the Republican bill, including conservative Southern "Blue Dog" Democrats and undecided New Yorkers who wanted additional help for New York City.

DeLay and Armey persuaded the Rules Committee to design a floor procedure that allowed a vote on the Senate bill first, which Democrats wanted. But it also allowed the Republicans to offer a manager's amendment that they could alter at the last minute to include whatever deals they reached with wavering members for their support. When the amendment finally was offered, it included liability limits for several organizations affected by the attacks, including Boeing Co., the Port Authority of New York and New Jersey, which built and operated the World Trade Center, and jet engine manufacturers General Electric Co. and Pratt & Whitney. It included security waivers for passengers carrying musical instruments and even a provision that would have required airlines to carry live animals, such as baby chicks, in their freight. In the end, the strategy worked. The House voted on Nov. 1 to reject the Senate bill 214–218: R 8–211; D 205–6; I 1–1. *(Vote, p. 814)*

Three of the six dissenting Democrats—Luis V. Gutierrez and Rod R. Blagojevich of Illinois and Solomon P. Ortiz of Texas—represented districts with large immigrant populations. They said they voted against the Senate bill because of a requirement that screeners be U.S. citizens for five years. The vote showed the tactical skill of DeLay and Armey and their ability to persuade the administration to back their play. But Bush's support was as short-lived as the House victory. In conference with the Senate, Republicans agreed to make all airport screeners federal employees, and Bush signed the bill Nov. 19, three days after Congress cleared it.

13. FAST-TRACK TRADE AUTHORITY

Securing fast-track trade negotiating authority from Congress was one of President Bush's top priorities but convincing lawmakers to go

along was expected to be a challenge. The decades-old authority, which had been granted to presidents beginning with Gerald Ford but was withheld from President Bill Clinton in 1994, allowed the executive branch to negotiate trade agreements and then bring them to Congress for an up-or-down vote without amendments and under mandatory deadlines. Opposition to the legislation (HR 3005), which the Bush White House renamed trade promotion authority, cut across regional lines. Democrats had become the main obstacle to its passage. They feared that free trade agreements with less-developed countries could weaken labor standards and environmental protection in the United States and its trading partners. Democrats were joined in this view by a small but significant group of Republicans who primarily represent industrial districts. *(Legislative details, p. 150)*

Republican leaders in the House began their fast-track campaign for the year in June. In an effort to firm up votes, Speaker J. Dennis Hastert, R-Ill., called for a vote before the August recess but the vote was canceled when it became clear the measure would not pass. The issue returned in late September as the White House portrayed free trade as an important part of the war on terrorism but that backfired as a public relations gambit and Democrats easily blocked a fast-track markup. In November GOP leaders tentatively scheduled another floor vote but again put it off.

Both sides dug in for a showdown in early December. House Ways and Means Committee Chairman Bill Thomas, R-Calif., had marked up a fast-track bill Oct. 9 with the help of three protrade Democrats—Cal Dooley of California, William J. Jefferson of Louisiana, and John Tanner of Tennessee. That was enough for Thomas to call it a bipartisan measure. It also included some labor and environmental protection as negotiating goals in trade agreements, a provision that many Democrats sought. But most protrade Democrats, who were members of the New Democratic Coalition, still did not like the bill because they said it was out of date. They said it was too focused on manufacturing and agriculture trade when other issues, such as antitrust and intellectual property, had become just as important.

In the week leading up to the House vote, GOP leaders decided to focus their lobbying on wavering Republicans rather than trying to attract more Democrats, which had been a failed strategy of the past. The shift proved to be pivotal. The lobbying was intense. Select Republicans were invited to travel with Bush on *Air Force One* and were promised projects and provisions in the trade bill and other measures. Republican Reps. Jim DeMint of South Carolina and Robin Hayes of North Carolina changed their positions and supported the bill after party leaders pledged to try changing the sub-Saharan African and Caribbean Basin trade preference law (PL 106-200) enacted in 2001, to help protect textile dyeing and finishing industries in their districts. The promise also extended to the Andean nations trade bill (HR 3009), which had been passed by the House but was pending in the Senate.

As tough as the lobbying got, the debate kept pace. On the floor Dec. 6, Republican leaders infuriated Democrats by saying that rejecting fast-track would undermine Bush's standing in the global community in the midst of a war. Some Democrats, including protraders from high-tech districts suffering from increased unemployment, said they could not support the bill without an economic stimulus measure (HR 3090) to help workers laid off after Sept. 11, a measure that had stalled. The vote ran extremely close and was held open while final deals were struck with Republicans from the textile South. The moment the yeas edged past the nays, the vote was closed and victory was declared 215–214: R 194–23; D 21–189; I 0–2. *(Vote, p. 814)*

1. Ashcroft Nomination/Confirmation. Confirmation of President Bush's nomination of John Ashcroft of Missouri to be attorney general. Confirmed 58–42: R 50–0; D 8–42 (ND 6–35, SD 2–7), Feb. 1, 2001. A "yea" was a vote in support of the president's position.

2. S J Res 6. Ergonomics Rule Disapproval/Passage. Passage of the joint resolution disapproving the ergonomics rule promulgated in 2000 by the Labor Department during the Clinton administration, stating the rule would have no force or effect. Passed 56–44: R 50–0; D 6–44 (ND 1–40, SD 5–4), March 6, 2001.

3. S 27. Campaign Finance Overhaul/Passage. Passage of the bill to ban "soft-money" donations to political parties, prohibit corporate and union general treasury funds from being spent on issue ads, and require disclosure of individuals who pay for issue ads that run within sixty days of a general election or thirty days of a primary. It also prevented certain issue ads from targeting specific candidates within the sixty-day and thirty-day periods. The bill, as amended, increased the individual contribution limit per candidate to $2,000 per election, the individual limit to national parties to $25,000 per year and the individual aggregate limit to $37,500 per year. Passed 59–41: R 12–38; D 47–3 (ND 40–1, SD 7–2), April 2, 2001.

4. H Con Res 83. Fiscal 2002 Budget Resolution/Education Spending. Harkin, D-Iowa, amendment to the Domenici, R-N.M., substitute amendment. The Harkin amendment reduced the size of the tax cut by $448 billion and increased education spending by $224 billion over ten years. It also provided an increase of approximately $224 billion for debt reduction over ten years. Adopted 53–47: R 4–46; D 49–1 (ND 41–0, SD 8–1), April 4, 2001. A "nay" was a vote in support of the president's position.

5. HR 1836. Tax Cut Reconciliation/Passage. Passage of the bill to reduce income tax rates and make other tax cuts totaling $1.4 trillion over eleven years. The bill reduced rates in the top four income tax brackets, retained the 15 percent bracket and created a new 10 percent bracket. It set the standard deduction for married couples and the income eligible for the 15 percent rate bracket at double that of singles beginning in 2005, gradually repealed the estate tax, doubled the $500 per child tax credit by 2011, and made the research and development credit permanent. Annual limits on contributions to Individual Retirement Accounts (IRAs) were increased to $5,000 by 2011. Passed 62–38: R 50–0; D 12–38 (ND 7–34, SD 5–4), May 23, 2001. A "yea" was a vote in support of the president's position.

6. S 1052. Patients' Rights/Passage. Passage of the bill to provide federal protections, such as access to specialty and emergency room care, and allow patients to appeal a health plan organization's decision on coverage and treatment. It also permitted patients to sue health insurers in state courts over quality-of-care claims and at the federal level over administrative or nonmedical coverage disputes. Federal-level economic and non-economic damages could not be capped, and punitive damages were capped at $5 million. State damages were to be determined by state law. Passed 59–36: R 9–35; D 50–0 (ND 41–0, SD 9–0); I 0–1, June 29, 2001. A "nay" was a vote in support of the president's position.

7. S 1246. Fiscal 2001 Supplemental Agriculture Assistance/Cloture. Motion to invoke cloture (thus limiting debate) on the bill to authorize $7.4 billion in additional economic assistance to farmers in fiscal 2001. Motion rejected 49–48: R 2–46; D 46–2 (ND 37–2, SD 9–0); I 1–0, Aug. 3, 2001. Three-fifths of the total Senate (sixty) is required to invoke cloture.

8. S J Res 23. Use of Force Authorization/Passage. Passage of the joint resolution to authorize the president to use all necessary and appropriate force against the nations, organizations, or people he determines planned, authorized, committed or aided the terrorist attacks that occurred Sept. 11, 2001, or that harbored such organizations or people, to prevent future acts of terrorism against the United States. Passed 98–0: R 47–0; D 50–0 (ND 41–0, SD 9–0); I 1–0, Sept. 14, 2001. A "yea" was a vote in support of the president's position.

9. S 1438. Fiscal 2002 Defense Authorization/Base Closures. Warner, R-Va., motion to table (kill) the Bunning, R-Ky., amendment that eliminated the provision in the bill authorizing an additional round of base realignment and closures in 2003. Motion agreed to 53–47: R 21–28; D 31–19 (ND 25–16, SD 6–3); I 1–0, Sept. 25, 2001.

10. HR 3162. Anti-Terrorism Authority/Passage. Passage of the bill to expand law enforcement authority to investigate suspected terrorists. The bill allowed disclosure of wiretap information among certain government officials, authorized limited disclosure of secret grand jury information to certain government officials, and allowed the detention of foreigners suspected of having ties to terrorism. It also made it easier for law enforcement to track voice and Internet communications using surveillance techniques and strengthened laws to combat money laundering. Most of the bill's intelligence-gathering provisions were to end, or "sunset," after four years. Passed (thus cleared for the president) 98–1: R 49–0; D 48–1 (ND 40–1, SD 8–0); I 1–0, Oct. 25, 2001. A "yea" was a vote in support of the president's position.

KEY			
	Democrats	*Republicans*	**Independent**
Y Voted for ("yea")			– Announced against
N Voted against ("nay")			P Voted "present"
+ Announced for			C Voted "present" to avoid possible conflict of interest
# Paired for			? Did not vote or otherwise make a position known
X Paired against			

ND   Northern Democrats
SD   Southern Democrats
Southern states – Ala., Ark., Fla., Ga., Ky., La., Miss., N.C., Okla., S.C., Tenn., Texas, Va.

Senate Key Votes	1	2	3	4	5	6	7	8	9	10
ALABAMA										
Shelby	Y	Y	N	N	Y	N	N	Y	Y	Y
Sessions	Y	Y	N	N	Y	N	N	Y	N	Y
ALASKA										
Stevens	Y	Y	Y	N	Y	N	N	Y	Y	Y
Murkowski	Y	Y	N	N	Y	?	?	Y	Y	Y
ARIZONA										
McCain	Y	Y	Y	N	Y	Y	N	N	Y	N
Kyl	Y	Y	N	N	Y	N	N	Y	N	Y
ARKANSAS										
Hutchinson	Y	Y	N	N	Y	N	Y	Y	N	Y
Lincoln	N	Y	Y	Y	Y	N	Y	Y	Y	Y
CALIFORNIA										
Feinstein	N	N	Y	Y	Y	Y	Y	Y	Y	Y
Boxer	N	N	Y	Y	N	Y	Y	Y	Y	Y
COLORADO										
Campbell	Y	Y	Y	N	Y	N	N	Y	N	Y
Allard	Y	Y	N	N	Y	N	N	N	N	Y
CONNECTICUT										
Dodd	Y	N	Y	Y	N	Y	Y	Y	Y	Y
Lieberman	N	N	Y	Y	N	Y	Y	Y	Y	Y
DELAWARE										
Carper	N	N	Y	Y	N	Y	Y	Y	Y	Y
Biden	N	N	Y	Y	N	Y	Y	Y	Y	Y
FLORIDA										
Graham	N	N	Y	Y	N	Y	Y	Y	Y	Y
Nelson	N	N	Y	Y	N	Y	Y	Y	Y	Y
GEORGIA										
Miller	Y	Y	Y	N	Y	Y	Y	Y	Y	Y
Cleland	N	N	Y	Y	Y	Y	Y	Y	Y	Y
HAWAII										
Inouye	N	N	Y	Y	N	Y	Y	Y	Y	Y
Akaka	N	N	Y	Y	N	?	?	?	?	?
IDAHO										
Craig	Y	Y	N	N	Y	N	N	Y	N	Y
Crapo	Y	Y	N	N	Y	N	N	Y	N	Y
ILLINOIS										
Durbin	N	N	Y	Y	N	Y	Y	Y	Y	Y
Fitzgerald	Y	Y	Y	N	Y	N	N	N	Y	Y
INDIANA										
Lugar	Y	Y	Y	N	Y	Y	Y	Y	N	Y
Bayh	N	N	Y	Y	N	Y	Y	Y	N	Y
IOWA										
Grassley	Y	Y	N	N	Y	N	N	Y	N	Y
Harkin	N	N	Y	Y	N	Y	Y	Y	Y	Y
KANSAS										
Brownback	Y	Y	N	N	Y	N	N	Y	N	Y
Roberts	Y	Y	N	N	Y	N	N	Y	?	Y
KENTUCKY										
McConnell	Y	Y	N	N	Y	N	N	Y	N	Y
Bunning	Y	Y	N	N	Y	N	N	Y	Y	Y
LOUISIANA										
Breaux	Y	Y	N	Y	Y	Y	Y	Y	Y	Y
Landrieu	N	Y	Y	Y	Y	Y	Y	Y	Y	Y
MAINE										
Snowe	Y	Y	Y	N	Y	Y	Y	Y	N	Y
Collins	Y	Y	Y	N	Y	Y	Y	Y	N	Y
MARYLAND										
Sarbanes	N	N	Y	Y	N	Y	Y	Y	Y	Y
Mikulski	N	N	Y	Y	N	Y	Y	Y	Y	Y
MASSACHUSETTS										
Kennedy	N	N	Y	Y	N	Y	Y	Y	Y	Y
Kerry	N	N	Y	Y	N	Y	Y	Y	Y	Y
MICHIGAN										
Levin	N	N	Y	Y	N	Y	Y	Y	Y	Y
Stabenow	N	N	Y	Y	N	Y	Y	Y	Y	Y
MINNESOTA										
Wellstone	N	N	Y	Y	N	Y	Y	Y	Y	Y
Dayton	N	N	Y	Y	N	Y	Y	Y	N	Y
MISSISSIPPI										
Cochran	Y	Y	Y	N	Y	N	N	Y	Y	Y
Lott	Y	Y	N	Y	Y	N	N	Y	N	Y
MISSOURI										
Bond	Y	Y	N	N	Y	N	N	Y	N	?
Carnahan	N	N	Y	Y	Y	Y	Y	Y	Y	Y

Senate Key Votes	1	2	3	4	5	6	7	8	9	10
MONTANA										
Baucus	N	Y	Y	Y	Y	Y	Y	Y	Y	Y
Burns	Y	Y	N	N	Y	N	N	Y	N	Y
NEBRASKA										
Nelson	Y	N	Y	Y	Y	Y	Y	Y	Y	Y
Hagel	Y	Y	N	N	Y	Y	N	Y	Y	Y
NEVADA										
Reid	N	N	Y	Y	N	Y	Y	Y	Y	Y
Ensign	Y	Y	N	N	Y	N	N	?	?	?
NEW HAMPSHIRE										
Smith	Y	Y	Y	N	Y	Y	N	N	N	Y
Gregg	Y	Y	Y	N	Y	Y	N	Y	N	Y
NEW JERSEY										
Corzine	N	N	Y	Y	N	Y	Y	Y	Y	Y
Torricelli	N	N	Y	Y	Y	Y	Y	Y	Y	Y
NEW MEXICO										
Domenici	Y	Y	Y	N	Y	N	N	Y	N	Y
Bingaman	N	N	Y	Y	N	Y	Y	Y	Y	Y
NEW YORK										
Clinton	N	N	Y	Y	N	Y	Y	Y	N	Y
Schumer	N	N	Y	Y	N	Y	Y	Y	N	Y
NORTH CAROLINA										
Helms	Y	Y	N	N	Y	–	?	?	?	?
Edwards	N	N	Y	Y	N	N	Y	Y	Y	Y
NORTH DAKOTA										
Conrad	Y	N	Y	Y	N	Y	Y	Y	N	Y
Dorgan	Y	N	Y	Y	N	Y	Y	Y	N	Y
OHIO										
DeWine	Y	Y	N	N	Y	N	N	Y	N	Y
Voinovich	Y	Y	N	N	Y	Y	N	N	N	Y
OKLAHOMA										
Nickles	Y	Y	N	N	Y	N	N	N	N	Y
Inhofe	Y	Y	N	N	Y	N	N	Y	N	Y
OREGON										
Wyden	N	N	Y	Y	N	Y	Y	Y	Y	Y
Smith	Y	Y	N	N	Y	Y	Y	Y	N	Y
PENNSYLVANIA										
Specter	Y	Y	Y	Y	Y	Y	Y	Y	N	Y
Santorum	Y	Y	N	N	Y	N	N	Y	N	Y
RHODE ISLAND										
Reed	N	N	Y	Y	N	Y	Y	Y	Y	Y
Chafee	Y	Y	Y	Y	Y	Y	Y	Y	Y	Y
SOUTH CAROLINA										
Thurmond	Y	Y	N	N	Y	N	N	Y	N	Y
Hollings	N	Y	N	Y	N	Y	Y	Y	Y	Y
SOUTH DAKOTA										
Daschle	N	N	Y	Y	N	Y	Y	Y	Y	Y
Johnson	N	N	Y	Y	N	Y	Y	Y	Y	Y
TENNESSEE										
Thompson	Y	Y	N	N	Y	N	N	Y	N	Y
Frist	Y	Y	N	N	Y	N	N	Y	N	Y
TEXAS										
Gramm	Y	Y	N	N	Y	N	N	Y	Y	N
Hutchison	Y	Y	N	N	Y	N	N	Y	N	Y
UTAH										
Hatch	Y	Y	N	N	Y	N	N	Y	N	Y
Bennett	Y	Y	N	N	Y	N	N	Y	Y	Y
VERMONT										
Leahy	N	N	Y	Y	N	Y	Y	Y	Y	Y
Jeffords[1]	Y	Y	Y	Y	Y	Y	Y	Y	Y	Y
VIRGINIA										
Warner	Y	Y	N	N	Y	N	N	Y	N	Y
Allen	Y	Y	N	N	Y	N	N	Y	N	Y
WASHINGTON										
Cantwell	N	N	Y	Y	N	Y	Y	Y	Y	Y
Murray	N	N	Y	Y	N	Y	Y	Y	Y	Y
WEST VIRGINIA										
Byrd	Y	N	Y	Y	N	Y	Y	Y	Y	Y
Rockefeller	N	N	Y	Y	N	Y	Y	Y	Y	Y
WISCONSIN										
Kohl	N	N	Y	Y	Y	Y	Y	Y	Y	Y
Feingold	Y	N	Y	Y	N	Y	Y	N	Y	Y
WYOMING										
Thomas	Y	Y	N	N	Y	N	N	Y	N	Y
Enzi	Y	Y	N	N	Y	N	N	Y	N	Y

[1] Sen. James M. Jeffords of Vermont left the Republican Party to become an Independent, effective at the close of business June 5, 2001. The first vote for which he was eligible as an Independent was vote 5.

1. S J Res 6. Ergonomics Rule Disapproval/Passage. Passage of the joint resolution to provide for congressional disapproval of the ergonomics rule submitted by the Labor Department during the Clinton administration, stating the rule would have no force or effect. Passed 223–206: R 206–13; D 16–192 (ND 2–152, SD 14–40); I 1–1, March 7, 2001.

2. HR 3. Income Tax Reduction/Passage. Passage of the bill to lower federal income taxes by restructuring the five existing tax brackets into four: 10 percent, 15 percent, 25 percent, and 33 percent. Passed 230–198: R 219–0; D 10–197 (ND 3–150, SD 7–47); I 1–1, March 8, 2001. A "yea" was a vote in support of the president's position.

3. HR 1. ESEA Reauthorization/Testing Requirement. Hoekstra, R-Mich., amendment to strike provisions mandating state reading and math tests for students in grades three through eight. The amendment retained existing law requiring states to test students in all subjects in which the states had developed standards. Rejected 173–255: R 52–166; D 119–89 (ND 91–63, SD 28–26); I 2–0, May 22, 2001. A "nay" was a vote in support of the president's position.

4. HR 2356. Campaign Finance Overhaul/Rule. Adoption of the rule (H Res 188) to provide for House floor consideration of the bill to ban "soft-money" donations to national political parties but allow up to $10,000 in soft-money donations to state and local parties for voter registration and get-out-the-vote activity. The bill prevented issue ads from targeting specific candidates within sixty days of a general election or thirty days of a primary. The bill maintained the existing individual contribution limit of $1,000 per election for House candidates but raised it to $2,000 for Senate candidates. Both limits were indexed for inflation. Rejected 203–228: R 201–19; D 1–208 (ND 1–154, SD 0–54); I 1–1, July 12, 2001.

5. HR 2620. Fiscal 2002 VA–HUD Appropriations/Arsenic Standards. Bonior, D-Mich., amendment to ban use of funds in the bill to delay national drinking water regulations for arsenic or to further a rule to raise arsenic levels under those regulations. Adopted 218–189: R 19–182; D 198–6 (ND 151–2, SD 47–4); I 1–1, July 27, 2001. A "nay" was a vote in support of the president's position.

6. HR 2505. Human Cloning Ban/Substitute. Greenwood, R-Pa., substitute amendment to ban human cloning to begin a pregnancy but allow the cloning of embryos for medical research as long as a researcher registers with the Department of Health and Human Services. The bill made it illegal to receive or transport the products of cloning if they would be used to begin a pregnancy. The ban on reproductive cloning was to expire in ten years. Rejected 178–249: R 25–194; D 153–53 (ND 118–35, SD 35–18); I 0–2, July 31, 2001. A "nay" was a vote in support of the president's position.

7. HR 4. Energy Plan/Alaskan Refuge Drilling Ban. Markey, D-Mass., amendment to maintain the existing prohibition on oil drilling in the Arctic National Wildlife Refuge by striking language opening the reserve up to development. Rejected 206–223: R 34–186; D 171–36 (ND 141–13, SD 30–23); I 1–1, Aug. 1, 2001. A "nay" was a vote in support of the president's position.

8. HR 2563. Patients' Rights/Provider Liability. Norwood, R-Ga., amendment to limit liability and damage awards when a patient is harmed by denial of health care. It allowed a patient to sue a health maintenance organization (HMO) in state court but specified that federal, not state, law would govern. An employer could remove cases to federal court. It limited noneconomic damages to $1.5 million. Punitive damages were limited to the same amount and only allowed when a decision maker failed to abide by a grant of benefits by an independent medical reviewer. Patients were authorized to seek court reviews when an independent reviewer found against them, but the patients were required to produce clear and convincing evidence to overturn the decision. Adopted 218–213: R 214–6; D 3–206 (ND 2–153, SD 1–53); I 1–1, Aug. 2, 2001. A "yea" was a vote in support of the president's position.

9. H J Res 64. Use of Force Authorization/Passage. Passage of the joint resolution to authorize the president to use all necessary and appropriate force against the nations, organizations, or people he determines planned, authorized, committed or aided the terrorist attacks that occurred Sept. 11, 2001, or that harbored such organizations or people, to prevent future acts of terrorism against the United States. Passed 420–1: R 214–0; D 204–1 (ND 150–1, SD 54–0); I 2–0, Sept. 14, 2001. (Under a unanimous consent agreement, the House subsequently passed an identical Senate resolution (S J Res 23), clearing the measure for the president.) A "yea" was a vote in support of the president's position.

10. HR 2646. Farm Bill/Conservation. Boehlert, R-N.Y., amendment that would shift $1.9 billion from the bill's fixed and countercyclical payments to farm and undeveloped land conservation programs, including the Farm and Ranchland Protection Program and the Wildlife Habitat Incentives Program. The measure also would increase the amount of land that could be included in various preservation programs. Rejected 200–226: R 54–161; D 145–64 (ND 132–23, SD 13–41); I 1–1, Oct. 4, 2001.

11. HR 3162. Antiterrorism Authority/Passage. Sensenbrenner, R-Wis., motion to suspend the rules and pass the bill to expand law enforcement's power to investigate suspected terrorists. The bill allowed disclosure of wiretap information among certain government officials, authorized limited disclosure of secret grand jury information to certain government officials, and authorized the detention of foreigners with suspected ties to terrorism. It also made it easier for law enforcement to track voice and Internet communications using surveillance techniques and strengthened laws to combat money laundering. Most of the bill's intelligence-gathering provisions were to end after four years. Motion agreed to 357–66: R 211–3; D 145–62 (ND 103–50, SD 42–12); I 1–1, Oct. 24, 2001. A two-thirds majority of those present and voting (282 in this case) was required for passage under suspension of the rules. A "yea" was a vote in support of the president's position.

12. HR 3150. Aviation Security/Democratic Substitute. Oberstar, D-Minn., amendment to federalize passenger and baggage screeners at the country's 140 largest airports and give the Justice Department responsibility for airport and airline security. HR 3150 included additional security provisions similar to those in the underlying bill but did not broaden liability caps. Rejected 214–218: R 8–211; D 205–6 (ND 154–3, SD 51–3); I 1–1, Nov. 1, 2001. A "nay" was a vote in support of the president's position.

13. HR 3005. Trade Promotion Authority/Passage. Passage of the bill to allow expedited negotiation and implementation of trade agreements between the executive branch and foreign countries. The bill included provisions requiring increased consultations with Congress on any proposed changes of tariffs for imports of sensitive agriculture products and on trade disparities for textile products. Passed 215–214: R 194–23; D 21–189 (ND 7–150, SD 14–39); I 0–2, Dec. 6, 2001. A "yea" was a vote in support of the president's position.

KEY

	Democrats	*Republicans*	Independent

Y Voted for ("yea")
N Voted against ("nay")
+ Announced for
# Paired for
X Paired against

– Announced against
P Voted "present"
C Voted "present" to avoid possible conflict of interest
? Did not vote or otherwise make a position known

ND Northern Democrats
SD Southern Democrats
Southern states – Ala., Ark., Fla., Ga., Ky., La., Miss., N.C., Okla., S.C., Tenn., Texas, Va.

House Key Votes	1	2	3	4	5	6	7	8	9	10	11	12	13
ALABAMA													
1 *Callahan*	Y	Y	N	Y	?	N	N	Y	Y	N	Y	N	Y
2 *Everett*	Y	Y	N	Y	N	N	N	Y	Y	N	Y	N	Y
3 *Riley*	Y	Y	Y	Y	N	N	N	Y	Y	N	Y	N	Y
4 *Aderholt*	Y	Y	N	Y	N	N	N	Y	Y	N	Y	N	N
5 Cramer	Y	Y	N	N	Y	N	N	N	Y	N	Y	N	N
6 *Bachus*	Y	Y	N	Y	N	N	N	Y	Y	N	Y	N	Y
7 Hilliard	N	N	Y	N	Y	Y	N	N	Y	N	N	Y	N
ALASKA													
AL *Young*	Y	Y	N	Y	?	N	N	Y	Y	N	?	N	?
ARIZONA													
1 *Flake*	Y	Y	Y	Y	N	N	N	Y	Y	N	N	N	Y
2 Pastor	N	N	Y	N	Y	Y	Y	N	Y	Y	N	Y	N
3 *Stump*	Y	Y	Y	Y	N	N	N	Y	Y	N	Y	N	Y
4 *Shadegg*	Y	Y	Y	Y	N	N	N	Y	Y	N	N	N	Y
5 *Kolbe*	Y	Y	N	Y	N	Y	N	Y	Y	Y	Y	N	Y
6 *Hayworth*	Y	Y	N	Y	N	N	N	Y	Y	N	Y	N	Y
ARKANSAS													
1 Berry	N	N	Y	N	Y	N	N	N	Y	N	Y	Y	N
2 Snyder	N	N	N	N	Y	Y	Y	N	Y	N	Y	Y	Y
3 *Hutchinson/ Boozman*[1]	Y	Y	N	Y	N	–	?	N					Y
4 Ross	N	N	Y	N	Y	Y	N	N	Y	N	Y	Y	N
CALIFORNIA													
1 Thompson	N	N	Y	N	Y	Y	Y	N	Y	Y	Y	Y	N
2 *Herger*	Y	Y	N	Y	N	N	N	Y	Y	N	Y	N	Y
3 *Ose*	Y	Y	N	Y	N	Y	N	Y	Y	N	Y	N	Y
4 *Doolittle*	Y	Y	Y	Y	N	N	N	Y	Y	N	Y	N	Y
5 Matsui	N	N	Y	N	Y	Y	Y	N	Y	Y	Y	Y	N
6 Woolsey	N	N	Y	N	Y	Y	Y	N	Y	Y	N	Y	N
7 Miller, George	N	N	Y	N	Y	Y	Y	N	Y	Y	N	Y	N
8 Pelosi	N	N	Y	N	Y	Y	Y	N	Y	Y	Y	Y	N
9 Lee	N	N	Y	N	Y	Y	Y	N	N	Y	N	Y	N
10 Tauscher	N	N	Y	N	Y	Y	Y	N	Y	Y	Y	Y	N
11 *Pombo*	Y	Y	Y	Y	N	N	N	Y	Y	N	Y	N	Y
12 Lantos	N	N	Y	N	Y	Y	Y	N	Y	Y	Y	Y	N
13 Stark	N	N	N	N	Y	?	?	N	Y	Y	N	Y	N
14 Eshoo	N	N	Y	N	Y	Y	Y	N	Y	Y	Y	Y	N
15 Honda	N	N	Y	N	Y	Y	Y	N	Y	Y	Y	Y	N
16 Lofgren	N	N	Y	N	Y	Y	Y	N	Y	Y	Y	Y	N
17 Farr	N	N	Y	N	Y	Y	Y	N	?	Y	N	Y	N
18 Condit	N	Y	N	N	Y	Y	Y	N	Y	N	Y	Y	N
19 *Radanovich*	Y	Y	N	Y	N	N	N	Y	Y	N	Y	N	Y
20 Dooley	Y	N	Y	N	N	Y	Y	N	Y	N	Y	Y	Y
21 *Thomas*	Y	Y	N	Y	–	Y	N	Y	Y	N	Y	N	Y
22 Capps	N	N	Y	N	Y	Y	Y	N	Y	Y	Y	Y	N
23 *Gallegly*	Y	Y	N	Y	N	N	N	Y	Y	N	N	N	Y
24 Sherman	N	N	Y	N	Y	Y	Y	N	Y	Y	Y	Y	N
25 *McKeon*	Y	Y	N	Y	N	N	N	Y	Y	N	Y	N	Y
26 Berman	N	N	Y	N	Y	Y	Y	N	Y	Y	Y	Y	N
27 Schiff	N	N	Y	N	Y	Y	Y	N	Y	Y	Y	Y	N
28 *Dreier*	Y	Y	N	Y	N	N	N	Y	Y	N	Y	N	Y
29 Waxman	N	N	Y	N	Y	Y	Y	N	Y	Y	Y	Y	N
30 Becerra	–	N	Y	N	Y	Y	Y	N	Y	Y	Y	Y	N
31 Solis	N	N	Y	N	Y	Y	Y	N	Y	Y	Y	Y	N
32 Watson[2]				N	Y	Y	Y	N	Y	Y	N	Y	N
33 Roybal-Allard	N	N	Y	N	Y	Y	Y	N	Y	Y	Y	Y	N
34 Napolitano	N	N	Y	N	Y	Y	Y	N	Y	Y	Y	Y	N
35 Waters	N	N	Y	N	Y	Y	Y	N	Y	Y	N	Y	N
36 Harman	N	N	Y	N	Y	Y	Y	N	Y	Y	Y	Y	N
37 Millender-McD.	N	N	Y	N	Y	Y	Y	N	Y	Y	Y	Y	N
38 *Horn*	N	Y	N	Y	N	Y	Y	N	Y	N	N	N	Y
39 *Royce*	Y	Y	N	Y	N	N	N	Y	Y	N	N	N	Y
40 *Lewis*	Y	Y	N	+	N	N	N	Y	Y	N	Y	N	Y
41 *Miller, Gary*	Y	Y	N	Y	N	N	N	Y	Y	N	Y	N	Y
42 Baca	N	N	Y	N	Y	Y	Y	N	Y	Y	Y	Y	N
43 *Calvert*	Y	Y	N	Y	N	N	N	Y	Y	N	Y	N	Y
44 *Bono*	Y	Y	N	Y	N	N	Y	N	Y	N	Y	N	Y
45 *Rohrabacher*	Y	Y	N	Y	N	N	N	Y	Y	Y	Y	N	Y
46 Sanchez	N	N	Y	N	Y	Y	Y	N	?	Y	N	Y	N
47 *Cox*	Y	Y	N	Y	N	N	N	Y	Y	N	Y	N	Y
48 *Issa*	Y	Y	N	Y	N	N	N	Y	Y	N	Y	N	Y
49 Davis	N	N	Y	N	Y	Y	Y	N	Y	Y	Y	Y	N
50 Filner	N	N	Y	N	Y	Y	Y	N	Y	Y	N	Y	N
51 *Cunningham*	Y	Y	N	Y	N	N	N	Y	Y	N	Y	N	Y
52 *Hunter*	Y	Y	N	Y	N	N	N	Y	Y	N	Y	N	Y
COLORADO													
1 DeGette	N	N	N	N	Y	Y	Y	N	Y	Y	N	Y	N
2 Udall	N	N	N	N	Y	Y	Y	N	Y	Y	N	Y	N
3 *McInnis*	Y	Y	N	Y	?	N	N	Y	Y	N	Y	N	Y
4 *Schaffer*	Y	Y	Y	Y	N	N	N	Y	Y	N	N	N	Y
5 *Hefley*	Y	Y	Y	Y	N	N	N	Y	Y	N	Y	N	Y
6 *Tancredo*	Y	Y	Y	Y	N	N	N	Y	Y	N	N	N	Y
CONNECTICUT													
1 Larson	N	N	Y	N	Y	Y	Y	N	Y	Y	N	Y	N
2 *Simmons*	Y	Y	N	N	Y	Y	Y	N	Y	Y	Y	Y	N
3 DeLauro	N	N	Y	N	Y	Y	Y	N	Y	Y	N	Y	N
4 *Shays*	Y	Y	N	N	Y	Y	Y	Y	Y	Y	Y	Y	Y
5 Maloney	N	N	N	N	Y	Y	Y	N	Y	Y	Y	Y	N
6 *Johnson*	Y	Y	N	N	Y	Y	Y	Y	Y	N	Y	N	Y
DELAWARE													
AL *Castle*	Y	Y	N	N	Y	Y	Y	Y	Y	N	Y	N	Y
FLORIDA													
1 *Scarborough/ Miller, J.*[3]	Y	Y	Y	Y	N	N	N	Y			Y	N	Y
2 Boyd	Y	N	Y	N	Y	Y	Y	N	Y	N	Y	Y	N
3 Brown	N	N	Y	N	Y	Y	Y	N	Y	Y	Y	Y	N
4 *Crenshaw*	Y	Y	N	Y	N	N	N	Y	Y	N	Y	N	Y
5 Thurman	N	N	Y	N	Y	Y	Y	N	Y	Y	Y	Y	N
6 *Stearns*	Y	Y	Y	Y	N	N	N	Y	Y	N	Y	N	Y
7 *Mica*	Y	Y	N	Y	N	N	N	Y	Y	N	Y	N	Y
8 *Keller*	Y	Y	N	Y	?	N	N	Y	Y	N	Y	N	Y
9 *Bilirakis*	Y	Y	Y	Y	N	N	N	Y	Y	Y	?	N	Y
10 *Young*	Y	Y	N	Y	N	N	N	Y	Y	N	Y	N	Y
11 Davis	N	N	Y	N	Y	Y	Y	N	Y	Y	Y	Y	Y
12 *Putnam*	Y	Y	N	Y	N	N	N	Y	Y	N	Y	N	N
13 *Miller, D.*	Y	Y	N	Y	?	N	N	Y	Y	N	Y	N	Y
14 *Goss*	Y	Y	N	Y	N	N	N	Y	Y	N	Y	N	Y
15 *Weldon*	Y	Y	Y	Y	N	N	N	Y	Y	N	Y	N	Y
16 *Foley*	Y	Y	N	Y	N	N	N	Y	Y	N	Y	N	Y
17 Meek	N	N	Y	N	Y	Y	Y	N	Y	Y	N	N	?
18 *Ros-Lehtinen*	Y	Y	N	Y	?	N	N	Y	Y	N	Y	N	Y
19 Wexler	N	N	Y	N	Y	Y	Y	N	Y	Y	N	Y	N
20 Deutsch	N	N	N	N	Y	Y	Y	N	Y	Y	Y	Y	N
21 *Diaz-Balart*	Y	Y	N	Y	N	N	N	Y	Y	N	Y	N	Y
22 *Shaw*	Y	Y	N	Y	N	N	N	Y	Y	Y	Y	Y	Y
23 Hastings	N	N	Y	N	Y	?	Y	N	Y	Y	N	N	Y
GEORGIA													
1 *Kingston*	Y	Y	N	Y	N	N	N	Y	Y	N	Y	N	Y
2 Bishop	N	Y	N	N	Y	N	N	N	Y	N	N	Y	N
3 *Collins*	Y	Y	N	Y	?	N	N	Y	Y	N	?	Y	N
4 McKinney	N	N	Y	N	Y	Y	Y	N	Y	Y	N	Y	N
5 Lewis	N	N	Y	N	Y	Y	Y	N	Y	Y	N	Y	N
6 *Isakson*	Y	Y	N	Y	N	N	N	Y	Y	N	Y	N	Y
7 *Barr*	Y	Y	N	Y	N	N	N	Y	Y	N	N	N	Y
8 *Chambliss*	Y	Y	N	Y	N	N	N	Y	Y	N	Y	N	Y
9 *Deal*	Y	Y	N	Y	N	N	N	Y	Y	N	Y	N	Y
10 *Norwood*	Y	Y	N	Y	N	N	N	Y	Y	N	Y	N	Y
11 *Linder*	Y	Y	N	Y	?	N	N	Y	Y	N	N	N	Y
HAWAII													
1 Abercrombie	N	N	+	N	Y	N	N	Y	Y	Y	?	Y	N
2 Mink	N	N	Y	N	Y	N	Y	N	Y	N	N	Y	N
IDAHO													
1 *Otter*	Y	Y	N	Y	N	N	N	Y	N	N	N	N	Y
2 *Simpson*	Y	Y	N	Y	N	N	N	Y	Y	N	N	N	Y
ILLINOIS													
1 Rush	N	N	N	N	Y	Y	Y	N	Y	Y	N	Y	N
2 Jackson	N	N	Y	N	Y	Y	Y	N	Y	Y	N	Y	N
3 Lipinski	N	N	N	?	?	?	?	?	Y	N	Y	Y	N
4 Gutierrez	N	N	Y	N	Y	Y	Y	N	Y	Y	Y	Y	N
5 Blagojevich	N	N	Y	N	Y	Y	Y	N	Y	Y	Y	Y	N

[1] Rep. Asa Hutchinson, R, resigned Aug. 6. The last vote for which Hutchinson was eligible was vote 8. He was succeeded by Rep. John Boozman, R, who was sworn in Nov. 29. The first vote for which Boozman was eligible was vote 13.

[2] Rep. Diane Watson, D, was sworn in June 7. The first vote for which she was eligible was vote 4.

[3] Rep. Joe Scarborough, R, resigned Sept. 6. The last vote for which Scarborough was eligible was vote 8. He was succeeded by Rep. Jeff Miller, R, who was sworn in Oct. 23. The first vote for which Miller was eligible was vote 11.

KEY

	Democrats	*Republicans*	**Independent**	
Y	Voted for ("yea")		–	Announced against
N	Voted against ("nay")		P	Voted "present"
+	Announced for		C	Voted "present" to avoid possible conflict of interest
#	Paired for			
X	Paired against		?	Did not vote or otherwise make a position known

ND Northern Democrats
SD Southern Democrats
Southern states – Ala., Ark., Fla., Ga., Ky., La., Miss., N.C., Okla., S.C., Tenn., Texas, Va.

House Key Votes	1	2	3	4	5	6	7	8	9	10	11	12	13
6 *Hyde*	Y	Y	Y	Y	N	N	N	N	Y	N	Y	N	Y
7 Davis	N	N	N	N	Y	Y	Y	N	Y	Y	N	Y	N
8 *Crane*	Y	Y	N	Y	N	N	N	Y	N	N	Y	N	Y
9 Schakowsky	N	N	Y	N	Y	Y	Y	N	Y	Y	N	Y	N
10 *Kirk*	Y	Y	N	Y	Y	Y	Y	Y	Y	Y	Y	N	Y
11 *Weller*	Y	Y	N	Y	N	N	N	Y	N	N	Y	N	Y
12 Costello	N	N	Y	N	Y	N	N	Y	N	N	Y	Y	N
13 *Biggert*	Y	Y	N	Y	N	Y	N	Y	N	Y	Y	N	Y
14 *Hastert*[4]	Y	Y	N	Y			N	Y	N	N	Y		Y
15 *Johnson*	Y	Y	N	Y	N	N	N	Y	N	N	Y	N	Y
16 *Manzullo*	Y	Y	Y	Y	N	N	N	N	Y	N	Y	N	Y
17 Evans	N	N	Y	N	Y	Y	Y	N	Y	N	Y	Y	N
18 *LaHood*	Y	Y	N	Y	N	N	Y	N	Y	N	Y	N	Y
19 Phelps	Y	Y	N	N	Y	N	N	N	Y	N	Y	Y	N
20 *Shimkus*	Y	Y	N	Y	N	N	N	Y	N	N	Y	N	Y
INDIANA													
1 Visclosky	N	N	N	N	Y	Y	Y	N	Y	?	N	Y	N
2 *Pence*	Y	Y	Y	Y	N	N	N	Y	N	N	Y	N	Y
3 Roemer	N	N	N	N	Y	N	Y	N	Y	Y	Y	Y	N
4 *Souder*	Y	Y	Y	N	N	N	N	Y	N	N	Y	N	Y
5 *Buyer*	Y	Y	N	Y	N	N	N	Y	N	N	Y	N	Y
6 *Burton*	Y	Y	N	Y	N	N	N	Y	N	–	?	N	Y
7 *Kerns*	Y	Y	Y	Y	N	N	N	Y	N	N	Y	N	Y
8 *Hostettler*	Y	Y	Y	Y	N	N	N	Y	N	N	Y	N	?
9 Hill	N	N	Y	N	Y	N	Y	N	Y	N	?	Y	Y
10 Carson	N	N	N	N	Y	Y	Y	N	Y	Y	Y	Y	N
IOWA													
1 *Leach*	Y	Y	N	N	Y	Y	Y	N	Y	N	Y	N	Y
2 *Nussle*	Y	Y	N	Y	N	N	N	Y	N	N	Y	N	Y
3 Boswell	N	N	Y	N	Y	Y	N	Y	N	N	Y	Y	N
4 *Ganske*	Y	Y	Y	N	Y	N	N	N	Y	N	Y	N	Y
5 *Latham*	Y	Y	N	Y	N	N	N	Y	N	N	Y	N	Y
KANSAS													
1 *Moran*	Y	Y	Y	Y	N	N	N	Y	N	N	Y	N	Y
2 *Ryun*	Y	Y	Y	Y	N	N	N	Y	N	N	Y	N	Y
3 Moore	N	N	N	–	Y	Y	Y	N	Y	N	Y	Y	Y
4 *Tiahrt*	Y	Y	N	Y	N	N	N	Y	N	N	Y	N	Y
KENTUCKY													
1 *Whitfield*	Y	Y	N	Y	N	N	N	Y	N	N	Y	N	Y
2 *Lewis*	Y	Y	N	Y	N	N	N	Y	N	N	Y	N	Y
3 *Northup*	Y	Y	N	Y	N	N	N	Y	N	N	Y	N	Y
4 Lucas	N	Y	N	N	N	N	N	Y	N	N	Y	Y	Y
5 *Rogers*	Y	Y	–	Y	N	N	N	Y	N	N	Y	N	N
6 *Fletcher*	Y	Y	N	Y	N	N	N	Y	N	N	Y	N	Y
LOUISIANA													
1 *Vitter*	Y	Y	Y	Y	N	N	N	Y	N	N	Y	N	Y
2 Jefferson	N	N	N	N	Y	N	N	N	N	Y	Y	Y	Y
3 *Tauzin*	Y	Y	N	Y	N	N	N	Y	N	N	Y	N	Y
4 *McCrery*	Y	Y	N	Y	?	N	N	Y	N	N	Y	N	Y
5 *Cooksey*	Y	Y	N	Y	N	N	N	Y	N	N	Y	N	Y
6 *Baker*	Y	Y	N	Y	N	N	N	Y	N	N	Y	N	Y
7 John	Y	Y	N	N	Y	N	N	Y	N	N	Y	Y	Y
MAINE													
1 Allen	N	N	N	N	Y	Y	Y	N	Y	Y	Y	Y	N
2 Baldacci	N	N	N	N	Y	Y	Y	N	Y	Y	Y	Y	N
MARYLAND													
1 *Gilchrest*	Y	Y	Y	Y	N	Y	Y	Y	Y	Y	Y	N	Y
2 *Ehrlich*	Y	Y	N	Y	N	N	N	Y	N	Y	Y	N	Y
3 Cardin	N	N	N	N	Y	Y	Y	N	Y	Y	Y	Y	N
4 Wynn	N	N	N	N	Y	Y	Y	N	Y	Y	Y	Y	N
5 Hoyer	N	N	N	N	Y	Y	Y	N	Y	Y	Y	Y	N
6 *Bartlett*	Y	Y	N	Y	N	N	N	Y	N	N	Y	N	Y
7 Cummings	N	N	N	N	Y	Y	Y	N	Y	Y	Y	Y	N
8 *Morella*	Y	Y	N	N	Y	Y	Y	N	Y	Y	Y	N	Y
MASSACHUSETTS													
1 Olver	N	N	Y	N	Y	Y	Y	N	Y	Y	N	Y	N
2 Neal	N	N	Y	N	Y	Y	Y	N	Y	Y	Y	Y	N
3 McGovern	N	N	Y	N	Y	Y	Y	N	Y	Y	N	Y	N
4 Frank	N	N	Y	N	Y	Y	Y	N	Y	Y	Y	Y	N
5 Meehan	N	N	N	N	Y	Y	Y	N	Y	Y	Y	Y	N
6 Tierney	N	N	Y	N	Y	Y	Y	N	Y	Y	Y	Y	N
7 Markey	N	N	Y	N	Y	Y	Y	N	Y	Y	Y	Y	N
8 Capuano	N	N	Y	N	Y	Y	Y	N	Y	Y	Y	Y	N
9 Moakley/Lynch[5]	N	N	?							Y	Y	Y	N
10 Delahunt	N	N	Y	N	Y	N	Y	N	Y	Y	Y	Y	N
MICHIGAN													
1 Stupak	?	?	Y	N	Y	N	Y	N	Y	Y	Y	Y	N
2 *Hoekstra*	Y	Y	N	Y	N	N	N	Y	N	Y	Y	N	Y
3 *Ehlers*	Y	Y	N	Y	N	N	Y	Y	Y	N	Y	N	Y
4 *Camp*	Y	Y	N	Y	N	N	N	Y	N	N	Y	N	Y
5 Barcia	N	N	Y	N	N	N	N	Y	N	N	Y	Y	Y
6 *Upton*	Y	Y	N	N	N	N	N	Y	Y	N	Y	N	Y
7 *Smith*	Y	Y	Y	Y	N	N	N	Y	N	N	Y	N	Y
8 *Rogers*	Y	Y	N	Y	N	N	N	Y	N	N	Y	N	Y
9 Kildee	N	N	N	N	Y	N	Y	N	Y	N	Y	Y	N
10 Bonior	N	N	Y	N	Y	Y	Y	N	Y	N	Y	Y	N
11 *Knollenberg*	Y	Y	N	Y	N	N	N	Y	N	N	Y	N	Y
12 Levin	N	N	N	N	Y	Y	Y	N	Y	N	Y	Y	N
13 Rivers	N	N	Y	N	Y	Y	Y	N	Y	N	Y	Y	N
14 Conyers	N	N	Y	N	Y	Y	Y	N	Y	?	N	Y	N
15 Kilpatrick	N	N	Y	N	Y	Y	Y	N	?	Y	?	Y	N
16 Dingell	N	N	N	N	Y	Y	Y	N	Y	N	Y	Y	N
MINNESOTA													
1 *Gutknecht*	Y	Y	Y	Y	N	N	N	Y	Y	N	Y	N	Y
2 *Kennedy*	Y	Y	Y	Y	N	N	Y	Y	Y	N	Y	N	Y
3 *Ramstad*	Y	Y	Y	Y	Y	Y	Y	Y	Y	Y	Y	Y	Y
4 McCollum	N	N	Y	N	Y	Y	Y	N	Y	N	Y	Y	N
5 Sabo	N	N	Y	N	Y	Y	Y	N	Y	N	Y	Y	N
6 Luther	N	N	Y	N	Y	Y	Y	N	Y	Y	Y	Y	N
7 Peterson	N	Y	Y	N	Y	N	N	Y	N	N	Y	Y	Y
8 Oberstar	N	N	Y	N	Y	N	N	Y	N	N	Y	Y	N
MISSISSIPPI													
1 *Wicker*	Y	Y	N	Y	N	N	N	Y	N	N	Y	N	Y
2 Thompson	N	N	Y	N	Y	Y	Y	N	Y	N	Y	Y	N
3 *Pickering*	Y	Y	Y	Y	N	N	N	Y	N	N	Y	N	Y
4 Shows	+	+	N	N	N	N	N	N	N	N	Y	Y	N
5 Taylor	Y	Y	N	N	N	N	N	Y	N	N	Y	Y	N
MISSOURI													
1 Clay	N	N	Y	N	Y	Y	Y	N	Y	Y	?	Y	N
2 *Akin*	Y	Y	Y	Y	N	N	N	Y	N	N	Y	N	Y
3 Gephardt	N	N	Y	N	N	N	N	Y	N	N	Y	Y	N
4 Skelton	Y	?	N	N	N	N	N	Y	N	N	Y	Y	Y
5 McCarthy	N	N	Y	N	Y	Y	Y	N	Y	N	Y	Y	N
6 *Graves*	Y	Y	N	Y	N	N	N	Y	N	N	Y	N	Y
7 *Blunt*	Y	Y	N	Y	N	N	N	Y	N	N	Y	N	Y
8 *Emerson*	Y	Y	N	Y	N	N	N	Y	N	N	Y	N	Y
9 *Hulshof*	Y	Y	N	Y	N	N	N	Y	N	N	Y	N	Y
MONTANA													
AL *Rehberg*	Y	Y	N	Y	N	N	N	Y	N	N	Y	N	Y
NEBRASKA													
1 *Bereuter*	Y	Y	Y	Y	N	N	N	Y	N	N	Y	N	Y
2 *Terry*	Y	Y	Y	Y	N	N	N	Y	N	N	Y	N	Y
3 *Osborne*	Y	Y	N	Y	N	N	N	Y	N	N	Y	N	Y
NEVADA													
1 Berkley	N	N	N	N	Y	Y	Y	N	Y	N	Y	Y	N
2 *Gibbons*	Y	Y	N	Y	N	N	N	Y	N	?	Y	N	Y
NEW HAMPSHIRE													
1 *Sununu*	Y	Y	N	Y	?	N	N	Y	N	Y	Y	N	Y
2 *Bass*	Y	Y	N	N	N	Y	Y	Y	Y	Y	Y	N	Y
NEW JERSEY													
1 Andrews	N	N	N	N	Y	Y	Y	N	Y	Y	Y	Y	N
2 *LoBiondo*	N	Y	N	N	Y	N	Y	Y	Y	Y	Y	N	Y
3 *Saxton*	N	Y	N	Y	Y	N	Y	N	?	Y	Y	N	Y
4 *Smith*	N	N	Y	N	Y	N	Y	Y	Y	Y	Y	N	Y
5 *Roukema*	Y	Y	N	N	N	N	Y	N	Y	Y	Y	Y	?
6 Pallone	N	N	N	N	Y	Y	Y	N	Y	Y	Y	Y	N
7 *Ferguson*	N	Y	N	Y	Y	N	Y	Y	Y	Y	Y	N	Y
8 Pascrell	N	N	Y	N	Y	Y	Y	N	Y	Y	Y	Y	N
9 Rothman	N	N	N	N	Y	Y	Y	N	Y	Y	Y	Y	N
10 Payne	N	N	N	N	Y	Y	Y	N	Y	Y	Y	N	N
11 *Frelinghuysen*	Y	Y	N	Y	Y	N	Y	N	Y	Y	Y	N	Y
12 Holt	N	N	N	N	Y	Y	Y	N	Y	Y	Y	Y	N
13 Menendez	N	N	N	N	Y	Y	Y	N	Y	Y	Y	Y	N
NEW MEXICO													
1 *Wilson*	Y	Y	N	Y	Y	N	N	Y	?	N	N	N	Y
2 *Skeen*	Y	Y	N	Y	N	N	Y	Y	Y	N	Y	N	Y
3 Udall	N	N	N	N	Y	Y	Y	N	Y	N	Y	N	Y

House Key Votes	1	2	3	4	5	6	7	8	9	10	11	12	13
NEW YORK													
1 *Grucci*	N	Y	N	Y	N	N	N	Y	Y	Y	Y	N	Y
2 Israel	N	N	N	N	Y	Y	Y	N	Y	Y	Y	Y	N
3 *King*	N	Y	N	Y	N	N	N	Y	?	Y	Y	Y	N
4 McCarthy	N	N	N	N	Y	N	Y	N	Y	Y	Y	Y	N
5 Ackerman	N	?	Y	N	Y	Y	Y	N	Y	Y	Y	Y	N
6 Meeks	N	N	Y	N	Y	Y	Y	N	Y	Y	Y	Y	N
7 Crowley	N	N	N	N	Y	Y	Y	N	Y	Y	Y	Y	N
8 Nadler	N	N	N	N	Y	Y	Y	N	Y	Y	N	Y	N
9 Weiner	N	N	N	N	Y	Y	Y	N	Y	Y	Y	Y	N
10 Towns	N	N	Y	N	Y	Y	Y	N	Y	Y	Y	Y	N
11 Owens	N	N	Y	N	Y	Y	Y	N	Y	Y	N	Y	N
12 Velázquez	N	N	Y	N	Y	Y	Y	N	Y	Y	N	Y	N
13 *Fossella*	Y	Y	N	Y	N	N	N	Y	Y	Y	Y	N	Y
14 Maloney	N	N	N	N	Y	Y	Y	N	Y	Y	Y	Y	N
15 Rangel	N	N	Y	N	Y	Y	Y	N	Y	Y	Y	Y	N
16 Serrano	N	N	N	N	Y	Y	Y	N	Y	Y	N	Y	N
17 Engel	N	N	N	N	Y	Y	Y	N	Y	Y	Y	Y	N
18 Lowey	N	N	Y	N	Y	Y	Y	N	Y	Y	Y	Y	N
19 *Kelly*	Y	Y	N	Y	Y	Y	Y	Y	Y	Y	Y	N	Y
20 *Gilman*	N	Y	Y	Y	Y	Y	Y	Y	Y	Y	Y	N	N
21 McNulty	N	N	N	N	Y	N	Y	N	Y	Y	Y	Y	N
22 *Sweeney*	Y	Y	N	Y	N	N	Y	Y	Y	Y	Y	N	Y
23 *Boehlert*	N	Y	N	N	N	Y	Y	Y	Y	Y	Y	N	Y
24 *McHugh*	N	Y	N	Y	N	N	N	Y	Y	Y	Y	N	N
25 *Walsh*	Y	Y	N	Y	N	N	Y	Y	Y	Y	Y	N	N
26 Hinchey	N	N	N	N	Y	Y	Y	N	Y	Y	Y	Y	N
27 *Reynolds*	Y	Y	N	Y	N	N	N	Y	Y	Y	Y	N	Y
28 Slaughter	N	N	N	N	+	Y	Y	Y	Y	Y	Y	Y	N
29 LaFalce	N	N	Y	N	Y	N	Y	Y	Y	Y	Y	Y	N
30 *Quinn*	N	Y	N	Y	?	N	N	Y	Y	Y	Y	N	?
31 *Houghton*	Y	Y	N	N	N	Y	Y	Y	Y	?	Y	N	Y
NORTH CAROLINA													
1 Clayton	N	N	Y	N	Y	Y	Y	N	Y	N	N	Y	N
2 Etheridge	N	N	N	N	Y	Y	Y	N	Y	N	Y	Y	Y
3 *Jones*	Y	Y	Y	Y	N	N	N	Y	N	N	Y	N	N
4 Price	N	N	N	N	Y	Y	Y	N	Y	Y	Y	Y	N
5 *Burr*	Y	Y	N	Y	N	N	N	Y	N	N	Y	N	Y
6 *Coble*	Y	Y	Y	Y	N	N	N	Y	N	N	Y	N	N
7 McIntyre	Y	Y	N	N	Y	N	N	Y	N	N	Y	Y	N
8 *Hayes*	Y	Y	N	Y	N	N	N	Y	N	N	Y	N	Y
9 *Myrick*	Y	Y	Y	Y	N	N	N	Y	N	N	Y	N	Y
10 *Ballenger*	Y	+	N	Y	N	N	N	Y	?	N	N	Y	Y
11 *Taylor*	Y	Y	N	Y	?	N	N	Y	N	N	Y	N	N
12 Watt	N	N	N	N	?	Y	Y	N	Y	N	N	Y	N
NORTH DAKOTA													
AL Pomeroy	N	N	N	N	Y	N	Y	N	Y	N	Y	Y	N
OHIO													
1 *Chabot*	Y	Y	Y	Y	N	N	N	Y	N	N	Y	N	Y
2 *Portman*	Y	Y	N	Y	N	N	N	Y	N	N	Y	N	Y
3 Hall	N	N	N	Y	N	N	N	Y	N	Y	Y	Y	N
4 *Oxley*	+	Y	N	Y	N	N	N	Y	N	N	Y	N	Y
5 *Gillmor*	Y	Y	N	Y	N	N	N	Y	N	N	Y	N	Y
6 Strickland	N	N	Y	N	Y	Y	Y	N	Y	Y	Y	Y	N
7 *Hobson*	Y	Y	N	Y	N	N	N	Y	N	N	Y	N	Y
8 *Boehner*	Y	Y	N	Y	N	N	N	Y	N	N	Y	N	Y
9 Kaptur	N	N	Y	N	Y	N	N	Y	N	Y	Y	Y	N
10 Kucinich	N	N	Y	N	Y	N	Y	N	Y	Y	N	Y	N
11 Jones	N	N	Y	N	Y	+	Y	N	Y	Y	N	Y	N
12 *Tiberi*	Y	Y	N	Y	N	N	N	Y	N	N	Y	N	Y
13 Brown	N	N	Y	N	Y	Y	Y	N	Y	Y	N	Y	N
14 Sawyer	N	N	Y	N	Y	Y	Y	N	Y	Y	Y	Y	N
15 *Pryce*	Y	Y	N	Y	N	N	N	Y	N	N	Y	N	Y
16 *Regula*	Y	Y	N	Y	N	N	N	Y	N	N	Y	N	Y
17 Traficant	N	N	Y	N	Y	N	N	Y	N	N	Y	N	Y
18 *Ney*	Y	Y	N	Y	N	N	N	Y	N	N	Y	N	Y
19 *LaTourette*	Y	Y	N	Y	N	N	N	Y	N	N	Y	Y	N
OKLAHOMA													
1 *Largent*	Y	Y	N	Y	?	N	N	Y	Y	N	N	Y	N
2 Carson	Y	N	N	N	Y	N	N	Y	N	N	Y	Y	Y
3 *Watkins*	Y	Y	N	Y	N	N	N	Y	N	N	Y	N	Y
4 *Watts*	Y	Y	N	Y	N	N	N	Y	N	N	Y	N	Y
5 *Istook*	Y	Y	Y	Y	N	N	N	Y	N	N	Y	N	Y
6 *Lucas*	Y	Y	Y	Y	N	N	N	Y	N	N	Y	N	Y
OREGON													
1 Wu	N	N	Y	N	Y	N	Y	N	Y	N	Y	Y	N
2 *Walden*	Y	Y	N	Y	N	N	N	Y	Y	N	Y	N	Y
3 Blumenauer	N	N	Y	N	+	Y	Y	N	Y	Y	N	Y	N
4 DeFazio	N	N	N	N	Y	N	Y	N	Y	Y	N	Y	N
5 Hooley	N	N	N	N	Y	Y	Y	N	Y	Y	Y	Y	N
PENNSYLVANIA													
1 Brady	N	N	Y	N	Y	Y	Y	N	Y	Y	Y	Y	N
2 Fattah	N	N	Y	N	Y	Y	Y	N	Y	Y	Y	Y	N

House Key Votes	1	2	3	4	5	6	7	8	9	10	11	12	13
3 Borski	N	N	Y	N	Y	N	Y	N	Y	Y	Y	Y	N
4 Hart	Y	Y	N	Y	N	N	N	Y	Y	Y	Y	N	Y
5 Peterson	Y	Y	N	Y	N	N	N	Y	Y	N	Y	N	Y
6 Holden	N	N	N	N	Y	N	N	Y	N	Y	Y	Y	N
7 Weldon	N	Y	N	Y	N	N	N	Y	Y	Y	Y	N	Y
8 Greenwood	Y	Y	N	Y	N	Y	Y	Y	Y	Y	Y	N	Y
9 *Shuster, Bud/*													
Shuster, Bill[6]		N	Y	N	Y	N	N	N	Y	Y	Y	Y	N	Y
10 *Sherwood*	Y	Y	N	Y	N	N	N	Y	Y	Y	Y	N	Y
11 Kanjorski	N	N	N	N	Y	N	N	Y	N	Y	Y	Y	N
12 Murtha	N	N	Y	N	Y	N	N	Y	N	Y	Y	Y	N
13 Hoeffel	N	N	N	N	Y	Y	Y	N	Y	Y	Y	Y	N
14 Coyne	N	N	Y	N	Y	Y	Y	N	Y	Y	N	Y	N
15 *Toomey*	Y	Y	Y	Y	N	N	N	Y	N	Y	Y	N	Y
16 *Pitts*	Y	Y	Y	Y	N	N	N	Y	N	Y	Y	N	Y
17 *Gekas*	Y	Y	N	Y	N	N	N	Y	N	Y	Y	N	Y
18 Doyle	N	N	N	N	Y	N	N	Y	N	Y	Y	Y	N
19 *Platts*	Y	Y	N	Y	N	N	N	Y	N	N	Y	N	Y
20 Mascara	N	N	N	N	Y	N	N	Y	N	Y	Y	Y	N
21 *English*	Y	Y	N	Y	Y	N	N	Y	N	Y	Y	N	Y
RHODE ISLAND													
1 Kennedy	N	N	N	N	Y	Y	Y	N	Y	Y	Y	Y	N
2 Langevin	N	N	Y	N	Y	N	Y	N	Y	Y	Y	Y	N
SOUTH CAROLINA													
1 *Brown*	Y	Y	N	Y	N	N	N	Y	N	Y	N	Y	N
2 *Spence[7]*	Y	Y	N	Y	?	?	?	?	?				
3 *Graham*	Y	Y	Y	N	N	N	N	Y	N	Y	N	Y	N
4 *DeMint*	Y	Y	N	Y	N	N	N	Y	N	Y	N	Y	Y
5 Spratt	Y	N	N	N	Y	Y	+	N	Y	N	Y	Y	N
6 Clyburn	Y	N	Y	N	Y	Y	Y	N	N	Y	N	Y	N
SOUTH DAKOTA													
AL *Thune*	Y	Y	N	Y	N	N	N	Y	N	N	Y	N	Y
TENNESSEE													
1 *Jenkins*	Y	Y	N	Y	N	N	N	Y	N	Y	N	Y	Y
2 *Duncan*	Y	Y	Y	N	N	N	N	Y	N	Y	N	Y	Y
3 *Wamp*	Y	Y	N	N	N	N	N	Y	N	Y	N	Y	Y
4 *Hilleary*	Y	Y	N	Y	N	N	N	Y	N	Y	N	Y	N
5 Clement	Y	Y	N	N	Y	N	Y	N	Y	N	Y	Y	N
6 Gordon	N	Y	N	N	Y	N	Y	N	Y	N	Y	Y	N
7 *Bryant*	Y	Y	N	Y	N	N	N	Y	N	Y	N	Y	Y
8 Tanner	Y	N	N	N	Y	N	N	Y	N	N	Y	Y	Y
9 Ford	N	N	N	N	Y	Y	Y	N	Y	N	Y	Y	N
TEXAS													
1 Sandlin	N	N	N	N	Y	Y	N	N	N	N	Y	Y	N
2 Turner	N	N	N	N	Y	N	N	Y	N	N	Y	Y	N
3 *Johnson, S.*	Y	Y	Y	N	N	N	N	Y	N	N	Y	N	Y
4 *Hall*	Y	Y	N	Y	N	N	N	Y	N	N	Y	N	Y
5 *Sessions*	Y	Y	Y	Y	N	N	N	Y	N	N	Y	N	Y
6 *Barton*	Y	Y	Y	Y	N	N	N	Y	N	N	Y	N	Y
7 *Culberson*	Y	Y	N	Y	N	N	N	Y	N	N	Y	N	Y
8 *Brady*	Y	Y	N	Y	N	N	N	Y	N	N	Y	N	Y
9 Lampson	N	N	N	N	Y	Y	Y	N	Y	N	Y	Y	N
10 Doggett	N	N	N	N	Y	Y	Y	N	Y	Y	Y	Y	N
11 Edwards	N	N	N	N	Y	N	N	Y	N	N	Y	Y	N
12 *Granger*	Y	Y	N	Y	N	Y	N	Y	N	N	Y	N	Y
13 *Thornberry*	Y	Y	N	Y	N	N	N	Y	N	N	Y	N	Y
14 *Paul*	Y	Y	Y	?	N	N	N	?	N	N	Y	N	Y
15 Hinojosa	N	N	Y	N	?	Y	Y	N	Y	Y	Y	Y	Y
16 Reyes	N	N	Y	N	Y	N	Y	N	Y	Y	Y	Y	N
17 Stenholm	Y	N	N	N	Y	N	N	Y	N	N	Y	Y	N
18 Jackson-Lee	N	N	N	N	Y	Y	Y	N	Y	N	Y	Y	N
19 *Combest*	Y	Y	N	Y	N	N	N	Y	N	N	Y	N	Y
20 Gonzalez	N	N	N	N	Y	Y	N	Y	N	Y	Y	Y	N
21 *Smith*	Y	Y	N	Y	?	N	N	Y	N	N	Y	N	Y
22 *DeLay*	Y	Y	N	Y	N	N	N	Y	N	N	Y	N	Y
23 *Bonilla*	Y	Y	N	Y	N	N	N	Y	N	N	Y	N	Y
24 Frost	N	N	N	N	?	Y	Y	N	Y	Y	Y	Y	Y
25 Bentsen	N	N	N	N	Y	Y	Y	N	Y	N	Y	Y	Y
26 *Armey*	Y	Y	N	Y	N	N	N	Y	N	N	Y	N	Y
27 Ortiz	N	N	N	N	Y	N	N	Y	N	N	Y	Y	N
28 Rodriguez	N	N	Y	N	Y	Y	N	Y	N	Y	Y	Y	N
29 Green	N	N	N	N	Y	N	Y	N	Y	Y	Y	Y	N
30 Johnson, E.	N	N	Y	N	Y	Y	Y	N	Y	N	Y	Y	N

[4] The Speaker votes only at his discretion, usually to break a tie or to emphasize the importance of a matter.

[5] Rep. Joe Moakley, D, died May 28. The last key vote he cast was vote 3. He was succeeded by Rep. Stephen F. Lynch, D, who was sworn in Oct. 23. The first vote for which Lynch was eligible was vote 11.

[6] Rep. Bill Shuster, R, was sworn in May 17. The first vote for which he was eligible was vote 3. He replaced Rep. Bud Shuster, R, who resigned Feb. 3.

[7] Rep. Floyd D. Spence, R, died Aug. 16. The last key vote he cast was vote 8.

KEY

	Democrats	*Republicans*	**Independent**	
Y	Voted for ("yea")		–	Announced against
N	Voted against ("nay")		P	Voted "present"
+	Announced for		C	Voted "present" to avoid
#	Paired for			possible conflict of interest
X	Paired against		?	Did not vote or otherwise
				make a position known

ND Northern Democrats
SD Southern Democrats
Southern states – Ala., Ark., Fla., Ga., Ky., La., Miss., N.C., Okla., S.C., Tenn., Texas, Va.

House Key Votes	1	2	3	4	5	6	7	8	9	10	11	12	13
UTAH													
1 *Hansen*	Y	Y	?	Y	?	N	N	Y	Y	N	+	N	Y
2 Matheson	N	N	N	N	Y	N	Y	N	Y	N	Y	Y	Y
3 *Cannon*	Y	Y	N	Y	N	N	N	Y	Y	N	Y	N	Y
VERMONT													
AL **Sanders**	N	N	Y	N	Y	N	Y	N	Y	Y	N	Y	N
VIRGINIA													
1 *Davis, J.*	Y	Y	Y	Y	N	N	N	Y	Y	N	Y	N	Y
2 *Schrock*	Y	Y	N	Y	N	N	N	Y	Y	N	Y	N	Y
3 Scott	N	N	Y	N	Y	Y	Y	N	Y	N	N	Y	N
4 Sisisky/*Forbes*[8]	Y	N		Y	N	N	N	Y	Y	N	Y	N	N
5 **Goode**	Y	Y	Y	Y	N	N	N	Y	Y	N	Y	N	N
6 *Goodlatte*	Y	Y	N	Y	N	N	N	Y	Y	N	Y	N	Y
7 *Cantor*	Y	Y	Y	Y	N	N	N	Y	Y	N	Y	N	Y
8 Moran	N	N	N	N	Y	Y	Y	N	Y	Y	Y	Y	Y
9 Boucher	N	N	Y	N	Y	Y	Y	N	Y	Y	Y	N	Y
10 *Wolf*	Y	Y	N	N	?	N	N	Y	Y	Y	Y	Y	Y
11 *Davis, T.*	Y	Y	N	Y	N	N	Y	Y	Y	Y	Y	N	Y

House Key Votes	1	2	3	4	5	6	7	8	9	10	11	12	13
WASHINGTON													
1 Inslee	N	N	N	N	Y	Y	Y	N	Y	Y	Y	Y	N
2 Larsen	N	N	N	N	Y	Y	Y	N	Y	Y	Y	Y	N
3 Baird	N	N	Y	N	Y	Y	Y	N	Y	Y	Y	Y	N
4 *Hastings*	Y	Y	N	Y	N	N	N	Y	Y	N	N	N	Y
5 *Nethercutt*	Y	Y	N	Y	N	N	N	Y	Y	N	Y	N	Y
6 Dicks	N	N	N	N	Y	Y	Y	N	Y	Y	Y	Y	Y
7 McDermott	N	N	Y	N	Y	Y	Y	N	Y	Y	N	Y	N
8 *Dunn*	Y	Y	N	Y	–	N	Y	Y	Y	N	Y	–	Y
9 Smith	N	N	N	N	Y	Y	Y	N	Y	Y	Y	Y	N
WEST VIRGINIA													
1 Mollohan	N	N	Y	N	Y	N	N	N	Y	Y	N	Y	N
2 *Capito*	Y	Y	N	Y	N	N	N	Y	Y	Y	Y	N	N
3 Rahall	N	N	N	N	Y	N	Y	N	Y	Y	N	Y	N
WISCONSIN													
1 *Ryan*	Y	Y	Y	Y	N	N	N	Y	Y	Y	Y	N	Y
2 Baldwin	N	N	Y	N	Y	Y	Y	N	Y	Y	N	Y	N
3 Kind	N	N	N	N	Y	Y	Y	N	Y	Y	Y	Y	N
4 Kleczka	N	N	N	N	Y	Y	Y	N	Y	Y	Y	Y	N
5 Barrett	N	N	N	N	Y	Y	Y	N	Y	Y	N	Y	N
6 *Petri*	N	Y	N	N	N	N	Y	Y	+	Y	Y	N	Y
7 Obey	N	N	Y	N	Y	Y	Y	N	Y	Y	Y	Y	N
8 *Green*	Y	Y	N	Y	N	N	N	Y	Y	Y	Y	N	Y
9 *Sensenbrenner*	Y	Y	Y	Y	N	N	N	Y	Y	Y	Y	N	Y
WYOMING													
AL *Cubin*	Y	Y	?	Y	?	N	N	Y	Y	N	?	N	Y

[8] Rep. Norman Sisisky, D, died March 29. The last key vote he cast was vote 2. He was succeeded by Rep. Randy Forbes, R, who was sworn in June 26. The first vote for which he was eligible was vote 4.

Senate

1. FARM BILL

A basic tenet of the politics of agriculture in Congress is that the fault lines are always regional and hardly ever ideological. The most notable exception came in 1996 when the newly ascendant Republicans won enactment of a law (PL 104-127) designed to wean farmers from a federal subsidy system. But in the 107th Congress, there was never much doubt that the 1996 law would be repudiated. The big questions were how much more to spend and—reviving the regional battles of old—which commodities to treat a bit better than others. The first question was answered in 2001. In October, the House passed a farm, conservation, nutrition, and rural development package promising a double-digit increase in spending for the new decade. The Senate took up the bill (HR 2646) and by year's end signaled it would seek to spend even more. The question became what else the Senate would need to do to advance the bill, especially in an election year in which some of the most competitive Senate races were in farming or ranching states. *(Legislative details, p. 449)*

Republican senators from farm states sharply criticized the farm bill that two Midwest Democrats—Majority Leader Tom Daschle of South Dakota and Agriculture Committee Chairman Tom Harkin of Iowa—had written. The bill was pushed to relatively easy passage Feb. 13 but only after it was altered to get the support of more senators. That was the key agriculture policy vote of the year—because it set the stage for negotiations during the next two months on a six-year farm bill (PL 107-171) that generally maintained the regional deals embodied in the Senate measure. The vote was 58–40: R 9–38; D 48–2; I 1–0. *(Vote, p. 830)*

A $2 billion support program for small dairy farmers persuaded Maine's two Republican senators, Susan Collins and Olympia J. Snowe, as well as Pennsylvania Republican Arlen Specter to support the bill. The hefty dairy program also won over James M. Jeffords, I-Vt. Similarly, a $4.4 billion program for peanut farmers brought the Republican Senate delegations from Alabama and Virginia, while also guaranteeing the support of Georgia's two Democratic senators, Zell Miller and Max Cleland.

Daschle and Harkin were able to keep almost all of the remaining Democratic senators in line by warning that if their bill did not pass quickly, under the congressional budget rules, the $73.5 billion in additional spending that had been earmarked by Congress in 2001 was at strong risk of evaporating. Democratic senators who were not from states with large agricultural sectors were warned that a vote against the bill could cost Democrats control of the Senate. Only two Democrats voted against the Senate bill: Jon Corzine of New Jersey, who viewed the package as too expensive; and Blanche Lincoln of Arkansas, who did not find the benefits for the rice and cotton farmers of her state sufficiently generous.

2. FUEL ECONOMY STANDARDS

Senate debate on an omnibus energy bill (HR 4) in 2002 mirrored a seeming contradiction in the national psyche: Americans believed it more important to protect the environment than to drill for more oil but were unwilling to give up their big, fuel-guzzling vehicles in order to reduce demand. Mindful of voter ambivalence, Congress had done little to force the issue. Corporate average fuel economy (CAFE) standards adopted in 1975 had been largely unchanged since 1985. Between 1995 and 1999, House Republicans added language to annual transportation spending laws blocking even a study of new standards.

As President George W. Bush took office, however, the situation appeared to be changing. Faced with growing political pressure to emphasize conservation, leading Republicans said they were willing to consider higher CAFE standards. In the House-passed energy bill, this translated into a modest increase: a requirement that automakers implement changes to save 5 billion gallons of oil over the next six years. In the Senate, plans were being laid for a more ambitious CAFE goal. Democrat John Kerry of Massachusetts and Republican John McCain of Arizona drafted a proposal to require all classes of cars and light trucks to average 36 miles per gallon (mpg) by 2015, a jump of between 5 mpg and 10 mpg across the fleets. Proponents contended that automakers had or were developing the technology to make such a figure attainable. *(Legislative details, p. 414)*

As the Senate debate approached, the auto industry lobbied hard for more flexibility, similar to the approach in the House bill. Opponents of the Kerry-McCain plan argued that higher fuel efficiency would mean smaller, lighter, and more dangerous cars—and fewer jobs for autoworkers. Left unsaid was that expensive sport utility vehicles, with their high-profit margins, had become crucial to automakers' finances. The opponents of higher CAFE standards decided their best approach was to offer an alternative. The amendment—by Carl Levin, D-Mich., and Christopher S. Bond, R-Mo.—would have required the National Highway Traffic Safety Administration (NHTSA) to increase mileage standards for light trucks, including sports utility vehicles (SUVs), within fifteen months and for cars within two years.

Industry officials said the Levin amendment ensured that some increase would occur, but not under the "aggressive" timetable envisioned by Kerry and McCain. The choice was cast as between a mandate that would be imposed by Congress, at the cost of jobs and vehicle safety, and a more considered decision by an agency that would have to take economics into consideration. A phalanx of interests, including the auto industry, unions, rural and suburban minivan and truck drivers, and business lobbyists, converged on Capitol Hill to lobby—and on March 13 the amendment by Levin and Bond was adopted, 62–38: R 43–6; D 19–31; I 0–1. *(Vote, p. 830)*

3. CAMPAIGN FINANCE

The battle over whether to rewrite the campaign finance law on the books since the Watergate scandal in the 1970s had stretched over more than a decade, through one veto and hundreds of votes. Even after the measure (HR 2356) was passed by the House on Feb. 14 and came roaring into the Senate, most lawmakers expected one last fight on the floor. Mitch McConnell, R-Ky., long the bill's leading opponent who had filibustered earlier campaign finance measures, was reticent about his plans. Majority Leader Tom Daschle, D-S.D., prepared to muscle it through the chamber with a complicated series of procedural votes designed to break a filibuster. *(Legislative details, p. 734)*

McConnell managed to delay action on the bill for more than a month and forced its supporters to prove they had the sixty votes required to overcome a filibuster. But he had conceded defeat even before the bill reached the floor. The March 20 vote to clear the legislation was 60–40: R 11–38; D 48–2; I 1–0, as one in five Republicans broke from their leadership to support enactment. President Bush signed the bill into law (PL 107-155) on March 27. *(Vote, p. 830)*

As examples of questionable fundraising practices on both sides piled up, supporters of an overhaul shaped and reshaped their legislation, making compromises and dropping some proposals as politically unpalatable. Abandoned, for example, was a provision that would have banned contributions from political action committees, which was included in the first campaign finance bill introduced in 1995 by Sens. John McCain, R-Ariz., and Russell D. Feingold, D-Wis.

The center of the final bill—the ban on soft money and restrictions on political advertising funded with those unregulated contributions—took shape gradually. The final pieces began coming together during the 2000 elections. McCain made campaign finance the foundation of his presidential race, boosting him and the cause to national prominence. His popularity and tenacity helped keep the bill moving forward. When the 107th Congress began, turnover in the Senate, where McCain and Feingold had been blocked for years by filibusters, shifted the balance of power. Seven senators who voted to block the 1999 campaign finance bill were replaced by supporters of McCain and Feingold. Another five Republicans who had opposed the measure in the past switched their votes. The first to announce a change of heart was Thad Cochran of Mississippi, who said he had watched his colleagues struggle against a tide of opposition money and concluded that McCain had been right.

4. FEDERAL ELECTION STANDARDS

Before the terrorism of Sept. 11, 2001, and the anthrax attacks later that year, perhaps the most immediate crisis the 107th Congress promised to address were the defects in election procedures seen in the 2000 president race, which had cast doubt on the outcome of the presidential contest and deepened voter skepticism about the reliability and fairness of the entire electoral process. But it was not until seventeen months after that election—when the Senate in April passed an election overhaul bill embodying a set of carefully balanced trade-offs—that Republicans and Democrats cemented a pact that would carry the legislation through a summer of negotiations to President Bush's desk. *(Legislative details, p. 727)*

To ensure that eligible voters would not again be denied the right to vote, Democrats wanted to set the first federal standards for conducting elections and provide money to help carry out those requirements. They likened the effort to a revival of the civil rights legislative campaigns of the 1960s. After fits and starts, the House passed a bipartisan bill (HR 3295) at the end of 2001 that set broad minimum standards while giving states considerable flexibility in deciding how to meet them. And at the same time, it appeared that a similar bridging of the breach had been accomplished in the Senate. The key was a willingness by Democrats to include antifraud protections as a condition of winning Republican support. Sen. Christopher S. Bond, R-Mo., blamed fraud for defeats of Republican colleagues in both the Senate and gubernatorial races in Missouri the year before, so the only election bill that he and many other Republicans would support was one that would make it "easier to vote and harder to cheat."

As soon as the compromise (S 565) came to the Senate floor in February, however, the antifraud provisions ran into trouble. Democrats Charles E. Schumer of New York and Ron Wyden of Oregon argued that the language—to require voters who had registered by mail to produce proof of identity and residency when they voted for the first time—would have disenfranchised poor and minority voters. Civil rights and voting rights group took their side. Schumer and Wyden tried to replace the language they disliked with language allowing new voters to vouch for their identities with a signature. The Senate, by 46–51, rejected a move that would have tabled, and thereby killed, the Democrats' alternative. That was the moment that almost caused the fragile deal to unravel. Republicans refused to continue work on the bill unless the amendment was withdrawn, and the legislation was pulled from the floor for a month.

Ultimately, however, Democrats decided they had to leave the antifraud provisions in the bill for it to pass. The best Schumer and Wyden could get was an exception allowing voters in Oregon and Washington—where most voting was conducted by mail—to submit their driver's license numbers or part of their Social Security numbers to prove their identities. When the bill returned to the floor in April, the nearly unanimous support for the package's basic bargain—easier access to the polls in return for tougher rules to restrict fraud—was made clear. The vote for passage was 99–1: R 48–1; D 50–0; I 1–0. *(Vote, p. 830)*

The vote would not be the last hurdle for the bill. Conference negotiations almost fell apart several times but the trade-off that had been finalized by the Senate proved to be enough to keep Democrats and Republicans talking. Ultimately, it was the trade-off at the core of the measure (PL 107-252) that Bush signed Oct. 29—almost two years after the disputed election that moved election issues high onto the public agenda.

5. ARCTIC NATIONAL WILDLIFE REFUGE

The promise of oil beneath the coastal plain of Alaska's Arctic National Wildlife Refuge (ANWR) was a centerpiece of President Bush's energy strategy and the focus of nearly two years of debate in the 107th Congress. In 2001 the oil industry, the administration, its congressional allies, and the Teamsters Union framed the debate in economic terms—energy independence and jobs—and were able to win House passage of an energy bill (HR 4) that would allow oil and gas exploration on ANWR's coast, with actual development limited to 2,000 acres. *(Legislative details, p. 416)*

Shaken by the House vote, environmental groups poured resources into stopping the proposal in the Senate. They recruited officials from other unions to fight the plan and aired pleas from celebrities not to allow drilling in ANWR. Environmental groups—citing polls showing that a majority of Americans feared that drilling would pose ecological harm—made it clear that senators who voted for drilling would be held accountable in November. Those who favored drilling also had lost some momentum by the time of the debate in the spring. Bush did not publicly insist that he would veto an energy bill without an ANWR drilling provision. Concerns about an electricity shortage on the West Coast had subsided and gasoline prices were down, easing the pressure for more energy resources.

Through weeks of Senate debate, the parties maneuvered for advantage. Republicans repeatedly demanded Senate action while avoiding a vote by failing to submit an ANWR amendment because they lacked the sixty votes required to shut off a promised Democratic filibuster. After threatening to file for cloture on the entire energy bill, which would have precluded an ANWR amendment, Majority Leader Tom Daschle, D-S.D., finally brought the issue to a head April 18, arranging a vote on whether to bring the debate on the ANWR question to a close. Sixty votes were required, and proponents of the drilling came up fourteen short. The defection of eight Republicans denied the amendment sponsors even the simple majority they might have cited in conference as evidence of Senate support for drilling. The vote on invoking cloture was 46–54: R 41–8; D 5–45; I 0–1. *(Vote, p. 830)*

6. FAST-TRACK TRADE PROCEDURES

Since fast-track trade authority lapsed in 1994, deep congressional divisions over the impact of free trade on U.S. industry and the environment prevented the White House from regaining broad latitude to negotiate trade deals. Fast-track authority required Congress to vote for or against a trade agreement within ninety days of its receipt from the president but prohibited amendments.

Soon after entering office in 2001 President Bush made renewing fast track one of his top international policy objectives. Dubbing it "trade promotion authority," Bush said he needed to assure trading partners that Congress would not tinker with deals after they had been negotiated. Most Democrats and some Republicans feared that the U.S. would lose manufacturing jobs to overseas competitors paying lower wages and operating under weaker environmental standards. But House Republican leaders managed to pass their fast-track bill (HR 3005) by a single vote in December 2001. (Legislative details, p. 150)

While the Senate normally was more inclined to support trade liberalization, Democratic leaders had to consider the concerns of their political base in the labor and environmental communities. Majority Leader Tom Daschle of South Dakota and Finance Committee Chairman Max Baucus of Montana decided that the best way to appease those groups was to compel Bush and the GOP to accept—as a condition of reviving fast track—a substantial expansion of Trade Adjustment Assistance (TAA) programs, which provided financial assistance and job training to workers who were laid off as a consequence of foreign competition.

The White House expressed support for a generous TAA package but not the most conservative Republicans in the Senate, who described an expansion as essentially a government handout for industries that were dying because they could no longer stay competitive in their markets. Particularly troublesome for those senators was a proposed subsidy for trade-displaced workers to help them cover the cost of medical insurance. Negotiations among Baucus, Finance Committee ranking Republican Charles E. Grassley of Iowa, and Phil Gramm, R-Texas, dragged on until the White House persuaded Gramm to accept a compromise. It called for a $12 billion TAA expansion over ten years that included a tax credit—but not a direct subsidy—for health care.

But the legislation before the Senate (HR 3009) faced other hurdles. Mark Dayton, D-Minn., and Larry E. Craig, R-Idaho, won solid backing for an amendment that would allow the Senate to strip trade pacts, by a simple majority vote, of any language that would undercut U.S. antidumping laws. The vote came even though business groups turned out en masse to oppose the amendment, pledging campaign retribution against supporters. Bush said he would veto the entire trade package if the Dayton-Craig language were retained. The year's most important trade vote in the Senate, therefore, came May 23 on passage of trade legislation written with the policy objectives of both parties in mind. With the Democrats split almost evenly and the Republicans breaking eight-to-one in favor, the vote was 66–30: R 41–5; D 24–25; I 1–0. (Vote, p. 830)

The tally gave Bush's trade agenda substantial momentum but it also demonstrated the resolve of Senate Democrats to influence U.S. trade policy—and the willingness of the Republicans to go along. The Senate-passed bill became the framework for the measure ultimately enacted (PL 107-210). Much of the TAA expansion was retained at Democratic insistence and the Dayton-Craig provision was removed. The Senate vote to clear the bill was nearly the same as its vote for initial passage, 64–34.

7. TAX CUT EXTENSION: ESTATE TAX

Since the day in June 2001 that President Bush put his signature on the deepest tax reduction in a generation, its sunset provision—the ended all the reductions at the end of the decade—had been labeled by the statute's Republican proponents as its most noteworthy blemish. While efforts to extend all or parts of the law (PL 107-16) came up short in 2002, the Senate did cast one ballot that buoyed advocates' hope of someday making the year's cut "permanent." Neither the president, nor his allies at the Capitol, ever intended to confine the duration of the tax reductions. But budget rules and the limits of Republican power in the 107th Congress forced the GOP to agree that the package would expire altogether on Dec. 31, 2010. The $1.4 trillion total was set by a congressional budget resolution, meaning that all of the revenue had to be forgone within the ten-year time frame of that budget—unless, as a practical matter, three-fifths of the entire Senate was willing to create an exception. (Legislative details, p. 93)

No such Senate supermajority existed in 2001, which is why the sunset provision was part of the law. Moreover, in light of the return of federal budget deficits and the polarizing effect of the tax debate in an election year, the votes to extend the cuts were still lacking in 2002. Although House Republicans pushed through such a bill (HR 586) along party lines in April, any similar measure was doomed in the Senate. Political pragmatists in the GOP were willing to settle for something less: a Senate test vote on indefinitely extending one broadly popular provision. Although the chance of winning even that was low, the GOP viewed such a vote as an opportunity to draw a clear distinction in the minds of voters between themselves and most Democrats.

For their campaign, the GOP chose the repeal of the estate tax, which had a broad and bipartisan base of support but also the shortest life span under the law. After a gradual reduction in the top rate from 55 percent to 46 percent by 2007, the tax would be wiped off the books altogether—but only for heirs of people who died in 2010. Only a few thousand people annually would be affected by the tax's resurrection the following year, because the great majority of estates (those valued at less than $675,000) were exempt from taxation before the 2001 law and because a majority of the tax was paid on inherited stocks, bonds, real estate or other nonbusiness assets. Still, Republicans successfully painted the debate as a fight to preserve family farms and family-controlled small businesses, which drew support from Democrats who represented farm country or large numbers of small businesses.

The test vote, in the GOP view, allowed the party to win no matter the outcome: either enough politically vulnerable Democrats would be pressed to vote "yes" to create an upset victory, or the Republicans would have an issue to use against those senators in the midterm elections. Majority Leader Tom Daschle, D-S.D., promised to allow the year's key Senate vote on tax policy in return for a loosening of Senate Republican objections to the year's energy legislation (HR 4). On June 12 senators voted to waive the budgetary restrictions preventing an extension of the estate tax repeal. The vote was 54–44: R 45–2; D 9–41; I 0–1. (Vote, p. 830)

Although insufficient to advance the tax cutters' quest—sixty votes were required to prevail—the vote allowed Republicans to boast that a solid Senate majority favored the idea. At the same time, Democrats claimed some success at resisting the GOP maneuver. Only three of the fourteen Democratic senators then seeking reelection—Finance Committee Chairman Max Baucus of Montana, Max Cleland of Georgia, and Mary L. Landrieu of Louisiana—voted with the Republicans. Six of the twelve Democrats who had voted to enact the tax law in 2001 voted against allowing an extension of the estate tax repeal.

8. TERRORISM INSURANCE

In the wake of the terrorist attacks of Sept. 11, 2001, which resulted in an estimated $40 billion in insurance claims, commercial property and casualty insurers said that—absent a federal backstop—they would no longer routinely insure businesses, sports stadiums, and skyscrapers against the risk of such catastrophic terrorism. The House passed a bill (HR 3210) in November 2001 to make the federal government the insurer of last resort, but the Senate remained hamstrung over the question of whether to ban punitive damages in civil lawsuits arising from terrorist acts. Such a ban, which was included in the House bill, was unacceptable to Senate Majority Leader Tom Daschle, D-S.D. He stopped a Senate Banking Committee compromise that would have barred such awards. But Senate Republicans, such as Phil Gramm of Texas and Mitch McConnell of Kentucky, said a ban was necessary to prevent trial lawyers from profiting from terrorism. *(Legislative details, p. 204)*

For months, Republicans thwarted Daschle's attempts to bring a bill without a punitive damages ban to the floor. They finally relented in June after senior Bush administration officials sent a letter to Minority Leader Trent Lott, R-Miss., saying they would recommend that Bush not sign a bill that "leaves the American economy and victims of terrorist acts subject to predatory lawsuits and punitive damages." Republicans took the letter as a sign that Bush would not abandon them during House-Senate conference negotiations. They allowed Daschle to bring a bill (S 2600) to the floor that did not ban punitive damages but stipulated that such awards would not be insured losses subject to government aid. But the key vote—because it displayed the united resolve of Senate Democrats to stick to their position in subsequent conference negotiations—came on June 18 when the Senate voted to pass the bill. The vote was 84–14: R 34–14; D 49–0; I 1–0. *(Vote, p. 830)*

That overwhelming show of support for the bill demonstrated that most Senate Republicans cared more about establishing a federal terrorism insurance program than about setting new ground rules for tort law. The vote also reflected that Senate Democrats were prepared to steadfastly oppose the addition of a punitive damages ban during negotiations with the White House, which was eager to complete the bill as a means of helping stimulate the economy. The White House relented on the issue of punitive damages when it became clear that Senate Democrats would not agree to language specifying that federal legislation would not necessarily infringe on state legal standards. That was important because a handful of states already banned punitive damages awards. Bush then successfully lobbied congressional Republicans, especially the House GOP leaders who strongly supported a punitive damages ban, to swallow their misgivings and adopt the conference report. The president signed the bill (PL 107-297) on Nov. 26.

9. CORPORATE REGULATION

The year 2002 began with indignant lawmakers lining up to castigate current and former executives of the bankrupt Enron Corp. Numerous congressional investigations and legislative proposals were not far behind as Congress responded to a series of corporate scandals. But by early summer, momentum for legislative action had dissipated. In April the House had passed a Bush administration-backed bill (HR 3763) that was dismissed by critics as a tepid response to a debilitating crisis in investor confidence. The administration's push for creation of a Department of Homeland Security, along with a burgeoning Middle East crisis, diverted attention from the corporate accounting issue, and from an effort by Senate Banking Committee Chairman Paul S. Sarbanes, D-Md., to move a more stringent bill. Some Democrats fretted that Sarbanes had squandered the corporate accountability mandate by waiting until May to unveil his bill and until June to begin a markup. *(Legislative details, p. 130)*

Then came the June 25 revelation that telecommunications giant WorldCom Inc. improperly counted $3.9 billion in expenses as capital costs. Literally overnight, corporate fraud legislation went from a sidetracked casualty of gridlock to must-pass legislation that practically no one on Capitol Hill or in the administration dared to oppose. By the time Sarbanes' bill reached the Senate floor after the July 4th recess, a crackdown on corporate cheating had become unstoppable. Several amendments were adopted during a week of debate, including one offered by Judiciary Committee Chairman Patrick J. Leahy, D-Vt., that mandated prison terms for shareholder fraud and obstruction of justice involving document shredding. Across the Capitol, House Financial Services Committee Chairman Michael G. Oxley, R-Ohio, dryly observed that at that moment "summary execution would get about eight-five votes."

When the vote came not a single senator voted against the most sweeping corporate regulatory measure since the Depression—a clear signal that the Senate's approach would be very nearly the package that became law. That vote July 15 to pass the bill was 97–0: R 46–0; D 50–0; I 1–0. *(Vote, p. 830)*

Senate Democrats rode that wave of support through a quick conference with the House. The absence of dissent in the Senate, combined with President Bush's insistence that Congress send him a bill before it left town for its August recess, allowed Senate Democrats to largely dictate to Republicans the terms of the conference report. Just two weeks after the vote, Bush signed a law (PL 107-204) closely tracking the Senate's bill, with creation of an oversight board to set standards for audits and oversee the accounting industry, and a prohibition on auditors providing other services to the publicly traded companies they audit.

10. MEDICARE PRESCRIPTION COVERAGE

After the House passed a bill June 28 to create a Medicare prescription drug benefit, the pressure was on the Democrats who led the Senate to respond in kind. In the middle of July, Majority Leader Tom Daschle, D-S.D., called up a bill (S 812) designed to speed government approval of less expensive generic drugs, using it as a vehicle for a floor fight over a Medicare prescription drug benefit. *(Legislative details, p. 486)*

All year Daschle had blocked the Finance Committee from considering a Medicare drug bill because he knew centrists John B. Breaux, D-La., and James M. Jeffords, I-Vt., would side with panel Republicans to report a version similar to the House bill (HR 4954)—an approach opposed by a majority of Senate Democrats. But he also knew, well before the floor debate began, that his own side lacked the sixty votes needed to overcome procedural hurdles. As the floor debate unfolded, it was clear there was still a "fundamental divide," as Daschle called it, over whether private insurance companies or the government-run Medicare program should deliver a drug benefit to senior citizens. Off the floor, sponsors of competing plans worked to develop a compromise—just as they had earlier in the year. But one by one, alternative proposals, including fallback plans seeking to bridge the partisan divide, were rejected. Neither side could muster the sixty votes necessary to waive budget points of order that were raised because most plans exceeded the $300 billion, ten-year cost that had been sanctioned in the fiscal 2002 budget resolution.

A proposal by Democrats Bob Graham of Florida, Zell Miller of Georgia and Edward M. Kennedy of Massachusetts failed to surmount the point of order, 52–47. A competing amendment—known as the "tripartisan plan" because it was sponsored by Republican Charles E. Grassley of Iowa along with Breaux and Jeffords—was defeated by a vote of 48–51. A far more limited plan by Chuck Hagel, R-Neb., and John Ensign, R-Nev., failed on a different procedural challenge, 51–48. It offered a discount card to help low-income Medicare beneficiaries buy drugs and capped out-of-pocket costs based on a sliding income scale.

By the end of the week both sides voiced frustration at the stalemate and the atmosphere appeared good for a compromise. Graham, working with Republican Gordon H. Smith of Oregon, attempted to build on the Hagel proposal with a $400 billion, ten-year plan that would cover all Medicare recipients who earned up to double the poverty level and those with annual drug bills in excess of $3,300. The proposal was endorsed by AARP, the biggest lobbying group for senior citizens and those nearing retirement. While AARP preferred a more comprehensive program, with four days left before the August recess, the Graham-Smith amendment was seen as the last best chance for a Medicare prescription drug benefit to pass the Senate in the 107th Congress. The vote on this plan—technically another vote on whether to waive a budget point of order—would be key.

Sponsors believed that members' fear of going home emptyhanded would outweigh their objections to this particular proposal. But it also failed by a vote of 49–50: R 4–44; D 45–5; 0–1. The closeness of the vote again showed the philosophical divide on Medicare, though a handful of senators on both sides voted against the majority of their party. The vote was a setback for Daschle and the Democrats, who believed they had moved as far as they could to win GOP support. But opponents, most of them Republicans, continued to insist that the issue should be returned to the Finance Committee where they knew they could prevail on their preferred version. *(Vote, p. 830)*

11. INDEPENDENT SEPT. 11 COMMISSION

By the time they were called on to decide whether to launch an independent investigation of government lapses before the Sept. 11, 2001, terrorist attacks, senators were more than ready to take up another tool to force additional answers out of the Bush administration. At the time of the vote, Sept. 24, 2002, the House and Senate Intelligence committees had been at work for almost four months on their joint inquiry into government intelligence failures before the attacks, and they were receiving few answers they viewed as credible. Lawmakers such as Richard C. Shelby of Alabama, the ranking Republican on Senate Intelligence, had begun to accuse the Central Intelligence Agency (CIA) and other covert agencies of stonewalling and blocking the release of information in hopes of waiting out the inquiry, scheduled to close early in 2003. *(Investigation details, p. 180)*

Slowly senators began reexamining legislation (S 1867) originally put forward by Joseph I. Lieberman, D-Conn., and John McCain, R-Ariz., in December 2001. The bill proposed an independent commission with subpoena powers and the power to investigate all branches of the government to see what, if anything, could have been done to prevent the four hijackings that resulted in the worst terrorist attack ever on the United States. Lieberman, chairman of the Governmental Affairs Committee, had won his panel's backing for the proposal in March. But the measure languished as Lieberman failed to secure any promises from the Senate leadership to bring it to the floor.

Momentum started to build in July, and in the House as well. Tim Roemer, D-Ind., a member of the House Intelligence Committee, also had grown dissatisfied with the pace of the congressional probe.

Blocked by the Republican leadership from winning a vote on broad language similar to Lieberman's, Roemer nonetheless was able to secure adoption in the House of a proposal to create an independent commission with the narrow mandate of reviewing the intelligence agencies' implementation of recommendations from the joint House-Senate inquiry and from other investigations.

Within weeks it became clear the sentiment existed in Congress to go beyond that. By the time Congress left for its August recess several Republican senators, including Fred Thompson of Tennessee and Pat Roberts of Kansas, indicated that they would support an independent investigation similar to Lieberman's original proposal. Four days before the vote took place, the White House publicly reversed course to signal it would support the idea. As a result, the Senate majority was overwhelming. With only eight of the president's most loyal allies in dissent, the Senate voted to make the creation of an independent commission with a broad mandate part of a larger bill (HR 5005) to establish a Homeland Security Department. The vote was 90–8: R 41–8; D 48–0; I 1–0. *(Vote, p. 830)*

But the homeland security bill quickly became tied up in a partisan dispute about workers' rights and did not move further until after the election. In the interim proponents of a broadly constituted commission—prodded by families of the victims of Sept. 11—learned that White House support for an independent panel did not necessarily mean the president supported the kind of commission envisioned by Congress. The level of support in the Senate vote Sept. 24 served as crucial leverage in getting the administration to compromise on some of its demands about the scope and powers of the probe. The pressure ultimately yielded an agreement in the lame-duck session under the fiscal 2003 intelligence authorization law (PL 107-306), which President Bush signed Nov. 27, to create an eighteen-month probe with a chairman appointed by the president and a majority of its members appointed by supporters of an aggressive investigation.

12. HOMELAND SECURITY

The most divisive issue blocking the creation of a new Homeland Security Department pitted federal employees' unions against the White House over "management flexibility" that gave the department authority to write its own personnel rules. As the midterm election neared the debate escalated from a philosophical difference into an increasingly acerbic and entrenched political fight. The venue was the Senate floor, where the bill (HR 5005) had languished since the House passed its version in July. *(Legislative details, p. 182)*

In the weeks before Election Day moderates tried to broker a compromise over the president's powers to remove employees from their collective bargaining agreements on national security grounds. Bush wanted to preserve authority the president possessed since 1962 to prevent the unionization of intelligence and national security workers. Unions, fearful the president would use the powers to eliminate them from the new department, wanted to narrow the exemption to employees who were given substantially new jobs as part of the reorganization. The pleas by moderates to step up negotiations were drowned out by the rhetoric of Republicans and Democrats, each blaming the other for stalling the bill. GOP leaders said Democrats were more interested in protecting the power of their top union contributors than in protecting national security. Democratic leaders charged that Republicans only wanted an election issue, not a compromise.

Majority Leader Tom Daschle, D-S.D., resorted to a tactic he rarely used—and had chastised Republicans for employing extensively in the past. He "filled the amendment tree," a parliamentary maneuver in the Senate that allows one side to shut down a debate by preventing any additional motions or amendments from being offered. Reflecting the partisan tenor of the moment the Senate voted along nearly precise party lines Sept. 26 to reject a bid to push the debate toward a conclusive action. The key vote came on a bid to invoke cloture, and thereby restrict debate, on the Democratic version of the homeland measure, by Governmental Affairs Committee Chairman Joseph I. Lieberman of Connecticut. The vote was 50–49: R 1–48; D 48–1; I 1–0. The majority was ten short of the sixty votes required for cloture. *(Vote, p. 830)*

The vote was pivotal because it heralded the high-water mark for whatever momentum the Democrats had built for fundamentally reshaping the homeland bill—and especially its labor provisions—to their liking. Because the Democrats were unable to draw any more GOP votes to their cause, the outcome made it clear that the decisive issue in the debate would not be resolved before the election. Republicans refused to allow further action unless promised that their version of the employment language, the one Bush insisted on, would not be altered. Democratic leaders hoped that on Election Day the voters might revive the momentum in their direction. In fact, the opposite happened. The Democrats lost control of the Senate for the 108th Congress, in part because swing voters in some close races signaled that they did not like the party's prounion emphasis. Soon after, Republicans were able to leverage substantial victories on the measure (PL 107-296) that Bush signed Nov. 25.

13. IRAQ USE-OF-FORCE RESOLUTION

Little disagreement existed between President Bush and his civilian leaders in the Pentagon over the president's desire to confront Iraq. But throughout August and September there were reports hints that Secretary of State Colin L. Powell, the Vietnam war veteran who rose to the rank of chairman of the Joint Chiefs of Staff, had misgivings about another Persian Gulf conflict. In the Senate, senior members of the Foreign Relations Committee reflected Powell's cautionary view, in part because of the good relations the top diplomat had cultivated in Congress since taking over at State. Powell's Democratic and Republican allies were looking out for his interests even if he was unwilling to express his doubts publicly.

Faced with Bush's request for far-reaching authority to challenge Iraq and embodied by the initial resolution (H J Res 45) the White House sent to Congress on Sept. 19, Foreign Relations Committee Chairman Joseph R. Biden Jr., D-Del., and Richard G. Lugar, R-Ind., joined forces in writing a narrower measure. It would have limited the war authorization to efforts to uncover and disarm Iraq's nuclear, chemical, and biological weapons. It also would have required the president, before using force, to either win backing of the U.N. Security Council or state that the threat was "so grave" that immediate action was warranted—an approach that emphasized the need for diplomacy. Separately, Senate Armed Services Committee Chairman Carl Levin, D-Mich., wrote a proposal that would condition U.S. action against Iraq on U.N. support. *(Legislative details, p. 238)*

Bush sought to reach a compromise with Senate Democratic leaders in order to quash any public opposition and to strengthen his hand in negotiations about Iraq at the U.N. Security Council, with Powell and National Security Adviser Condoleezza Rice negotiating with the senators. When that failed, Bush turned to House Minority Leader Richard A. Gephardt, D-Mo., a possible presidential rival in 2004 who had taken a hard line toward Iraq earlier in the year. Gephardt and Bush compromised on a resolution that would give the president the broadest latitude on deciding if and when to go to war against Iraq. Once the two reached agreement Oct. 1 all momentum for the Biden-Lugar and Levin alternatives was gone, and passage of the Bush-Gephardt resolution was assured. Sen. Robert C. Byrd, D-W.Va., was one of the few to muster a voice in opposition, saying

expediency had won in a "fateful decision. It involves the treasure of this country. It involves the blood of our fighting men and women."

But hours after the Senate on Oct. 10 overwhelmingly rejected Byrd amendments to limit the authorization the chamber voted resoundingly to clear the measure (PL 107-243) that gave the president the authority he sought. The vote was 77–23: R 48–1; D 29–21; I 0–1. *(Vote, p. 830)*

House

1. CAMPAIGN FINANCE

After the Senate passed its version of the campaign finance bill in March 2001, supporters of the companion legislation in the House (HR 2356) faced uncertainty and restlessness among Democrats. House Democrats had provided most of the votes for passage of similar bills twice before, in 1998 and 1999. But with the Senate hurdle overcome and the legislation closer to becoming law, some Democrats were uneasy with key provisions: a ban on unregulated "soft money" contributions from businesses, unions, and wealthy individual to the political parties. Another concern of some Democrats was the bill's increased limits on "hard money" contributions—regulated donations given directly to candidates—that Republicans were better at obtaining. *(Legislative details, p. 734)*

The measure stalled in the House in July 2001 when Democrats and a few Republicans voted down a rule for floor consideration that was drafted by GOP leaders. The rule made it difficult for sponsors Christopher Shays, R-Conn., and Martin T. Meehan, D-Mass., to alter their bill on the floor to bring it in line with the Senate-passed measure, which they were eager to do to avoid sending it back to the Senate for another debate. On Jan. 24, 2002, after months of effort, Shays and Meehan gathered the last of the 218 signatures they needed on a "discharge petition" to bring their bill to the floor under debate rules more to their liking. The sponsors also had the benefit of momentum created by the collapse of Enron Corp., a giant energy-trading company, and revelations about the company's network of political giving and legislative influence.

GOP leaders were preparing a series of amendments they hoped would sink the bill. Their goal was to attach amendments that the Senate would never accept, while also providing political cover for lawmakers who wanted to say they had voted for a change in the system. In the end, the momentum for the campaign finance overhaul designed by Meehan and Shays—and their Senate counterparts, John McCain, R-Ariz., and Russell D. Feingold, D-Wis.—proved unstoppable. The Shays-Meehan coalition largely held in the House, while mixed signals from the White House undercut efforts to unify House Republicans against the legislation. Speaker J. Dennis Hastert, R-Ill., asked President George W. Bush for help before the debate began but Bush chose to keep his distance. Just as the battle on the House floor was beginning Feb. 13, White House spokesperson Ari Fleischer signaled that Bush would sign any bill that would improve the campaign finance system.

Not long after, the president himself said he was endorsing nothing but would look closely at whatever Congress sent him. By then, supporters of the bill were on their way to victory. Despite the intense pressure Republican leaders put on their caucus and more than fourteen hours of maneuvering on the floor aimed at bringing down the bill, the House rejected every amendment that bill supporters feared would force a conference with the Senate. The climax—and key vote—came in the early morning hours of Feb. 14, 2002, when forty-one Republicans joined the solid majority in the House to pass the bill. Only twelve

Democrats voted no. The vote was 240–189: R 41–176; D 198–12; I: 1–1. The campaign finance bill was on its way back to the Senate, which cleared it on March 20. Bush called the measure "flawed" but signed it (PL 107-155) a week later. *(Vote, p. 832)*

2. BROADBAND/INTERNET SERVICE

Telecommunications legislation was among the most technically intricate and heavily lobbied measures in Congress. When legislation came to the floor, the parliamentary maneuvering was just as intense. A single major telecommunications bill was considered by Congress in 2002. It was sponsored by House Energy and Commerce Committee Chairman Billy Tauzin, R-La., and ranking panel Democrat John D. Dingell of Michigan. It attracted considerable attention and lobbing from the telecommunications industry and consumer groups. Nevertheless, in spite of the importance to public policy and the complex issues involved, the key vote came on an obscure procedural question without precedent in ninety-two years.

The Tauzin-Dingell bill (HR 1542) deregulated interstate high-speed Internet services provided over telephone lines by the four regional Bell companies—Verizon, SBC Communications, BellSouth, and Qwest Communications—and allowed them to offer the services without opening their local telephone markets to competitors, which was a requirement under a sweeping 1996 telecommunications policy law (PL 104-104). *(Legislative details, p. 373)*

As the bill was readied for floor action, a complex strategy evolved. Christopher B. Cannon, R-Utah, and John Conyers Jr. of Michigan, the senior Democrat on the House Judiciary Committee, wanted to offer an amendment to restore the state and federal regulatory authority that the legislation would remove. Steve Buyer, R-Ind., and Edolphus Towns, D-N.Y., countered with an amendment to restore some of the Federal Communications Commission's regulatory authority but still keep the deregulatory-friendly spirit of the bill. The pivotal decision was for Buyer and Towns to ask that their amendment be considered as a second-degree amendment to Cannon-Conyers, meaning that Buyer-Towns would be voted on first, and if it were adopted, the Cannon-Conyers language would not be voted on at all.

As the debate proceeded in the House, everyone waited for the expected sequence to take place. But Cannon did not offer his amendment during the time allocated. There was much puzzlement on the floor until Cannon's ally, Edward J. Markey, D-Mass., offered a motion to recommit, or send, the bill back to committee with instructions to add the Cannon-Conyers language. His reasoning, Markey said, was that Cannon-Conyers deserved an up-or-down vote, and this was the only way to accomplish that. Buyer was upset because his move to block Cannon-Conyers had been countered. A recommittal motion is typically a tool used by lawmakers in the minority party. But this bill was hardly typical—members of both parties were on each side of the bill.

The showdown commenced when the presiding officer, Ray La-Hood, R-Ill., ordered a vote on the "previous question," essentially moving to stop debate on the Markey recommittal motion. If approved, the vote on the Markey motion could proceed. But it failed, 173–256: R 62–157; D 109–99; I 2–0. The Congressional Research Service (CRS) called the episode "an unusual parliamentary process," marking the first time since 1910 that a motion on the previous question on a motion to recommit was defeated. *(Vote, p. 832)*

More immediately, the vote was a harbinger that Markey—the leading opponent of the regional Bells' efforts—did not have nearly enough votes to derail the Tauzin-Dingell bill. Soon after another rare occurrence came into play. Buyer and Towns were allowed to add

their amendment to Markey's recommittal motion and to the bill itself without need for a separate recorded vote on their measure. Some protested that the recommittal process was being abused but in the end the underlying bill passed, 273–157, a tally that closely mirrored the outcome of the key vote on Markey's parliamentary maneuver.

3. DEFENSE AUTHORIZATION

The usual partisan divide in Congress over defense spending had been muddled since the presidency of Bill Clinton when vigorous economic activity provided ample tax revenues for government spending. Democrats, traditionally suspicious of big increases in the military, went along with larger defense authorizations as long as there was enough money to fund domestic programs. But that political equation changed in 2001 when the large tax cuts that were President Bush's top priority and a stalled economy slashed projected federal budget surpluses. Bush insisted that domestic spending be kept tight at the same time that he proposed a $30 billion increase over the fiscal 2001 budget for defense—the last Clinton defense plan.

The 2001 House vote on the fiscal 2002 defense authorization bill may not have reflected members' fundamental policy views because it came two weeks after the Sept. 11 terrorist attacks. Rather, the vote on the fiscal 2003 defense authorization bill was a better test of House Democrats' resolve for challenging the size of the defense budget. Although the House version of the bill amounted to $13 billion less than Bush requested, that difference reflected some technical bookkeeping decisions. Essentially, the bill endorsed Bush's request for a $45 billion increase in defense spending—the largest since the Vietnam war in the 1960s and early 1970s. More than two-thirds of the Democrats voted for it. *(Legislative details, p. 320)*

The House GOP leadership barred consideration of several floor amendments, including one that would have cut $1.8 billion from the F-22 fighter program and another that would have eliminated $475 million authorized for the Army's Crusader cannon, which Defense Secretary Donald H. Rumsfeld had decided to cancel but which the House version of the defense authorization bill (HR 4546) approved. But the Democrats made their stand on a narrow collection of issues. They presented a series of amendments designed to restrict the administration's study of the use of tactical nuclear weapons in wartime. They also proposed several amendments that would have restrained Bush's missile defense program, though none that would have reduced the $7.8 billion antimissile budget for fiscal 2003.

The House, splitting largely along party lines, rejected all of these amendments. In the end, in a vote that ensured the Bush administration an unimpeded road to an enormous military build-up, the House passed the bill May 10 by a vote of 359–58: R 212–1; D 146–56; I 1–1. *(Vote, p. 832)*

4. WELFARE REAUTHORIZATION

The 104th Congress ended more than sixty years of unfettered public assistance by writing a landmark welfare law (PL 104-193) in 1996 that tied payments to tough new work requirements. It was the most sweeping social policy change won by the Republicans who had won congressional majorities in the 1994 elections. Many Democrats, who thought the terms of the overhaul were too tough, predicted that a future Congress would regret the harshness of the changes and face revisions.

But in 2002, most members of the 107th Congress, in both parties, demonstrated that they were generally satisfied with the basics of the measure, mindful that welfare caseloads had declined by more than half since its enactment. Instead, they debated whether work or education and training would best lead welfare recipients out of poverty, and how much flexibility states should be given to run the programs. *(Legislative details, p. 521)*

With major provisions slated to end Sept. 30, Congress needed to reauthorize the law or let it expire. President Bush made reauthorization a 2002 priority, calling for even tougher work rules for adult recipients and significant funding for programs that promote marriage. House Republicans wrote a bill (HR 4737) that tracked Bush's priorities and—they knew—would serve as the most conservative possible counterweight to what they expected would be a much softer welfare bill coming out of the Democratic-controlled Senate.

The GOP proposed requiring recipients to work forty hours a week, up from thirty in existing law. States would be required to have at least 70 percent of their recipients employed by 2007, up from 50 percent required under the 1996 law. House Democrats said that while recipients should be required to work, they should also be given more opportunities to take vocational training or attend adult education classes. They argued that many adults still on welfare were the toughest cases—drug-addicted, mentally ill, or illiterate—who could not easily find employment.

By the time the debate reached the House floor May 16, any hope that the House might find a middle ground had been abandoned. Instead, the debate broke along party lines, and featured well-used partisan disagreements over social policy. Only fourteen conservative Democrats voted for the GOP bill and only four Republicans voted against it. The vote was 229–197: R 214–4; D 14–192; I 1–1. *(Vote, p. 832)*

Despite the partisan character of the debate and of the vote, the bill's passage demonstrated a recognition on Capitol Hill, even among some Democrats, that there would be no retreat from the 1996 decision to require work of welfare recipients. The Senate Finance Committee later amended the House bill to retain the thirty-hour work requirement and provide for $5.5 billion in child care funding but the measure died anyway, forcing lawmakers to pass a temporary extension into 2003.

5. DISCRETIONARY SPENDING LIMIT

A single House procedural vote on a spring evening heralded one of the most bruising annual fights over discretionary spending in modern times. The outcome was set in such intractable divisions—between Republican factions in Congress, between the House and the Senate, and between Congress and President Bush—that the year ended with none of the domestic spending bills enacted for fiscal 2003.

The vote came after the House Republican majority had adopted a budget resolution (H Con Res 353) that endorsed Bush's budget proposal, with an overall limit on discretionary spending of $759 billion. That figure included Bush's request for a $10 billion defense reserve fund to be spent at the administration's discretion, an idea Congress quickly rejected. *(Legislative details, p. 63)*

Bush had proposed a big increase in defense spending but not even an inflationary increase for the rest of government. Republicans on the Appropriations Committee reluctantly supported the budget resolution, expecting to be able to exceed the spending limit later in the process or to negotiate a higher level with the Senate. Senate Budget Committee Democrats marked up a budget (S Con Res 100) calling for about $9 billion more in nondefense spending than the House. Their plan had little chance of adoption on the floor, however, lacking any Republican support and facing the threat of Democratic defections. Majority Leader Tom Daschle, D-S.D., never brought a budget up for debate but the Senate Appropriations Committee pressed ahead, marking up bills with the Senate Budget Committee's $768 billion grand total as their target.

With no prospect that a final budget would be written, Republican House appropriators sought to ignore their version. They began talking openly about producing spending bills with a total roughly equivalent to the Senate's more expensive bottom line. House leaders soon came under pressure, from the White House as well as from fiscal conservatives in their ranks, to hold the appropriators in check. To that end, Republican leaders called on the House to cast another vote committing itself to living under the spending ceiling in its budget. Although by itself the language they proposed would have imposed no enforceable restraint on spending, appropriators from both parties were furious. It was an unusual move, and the appropriators feared that the provision's adoption would doom them to a year of frustration—unable to win passage of domestic spending bills written under the ceiling.

The key vote came May 22 on a procedural measure setting the rules for floor debate on the fiscal 2002 supplemental appropriations bill (PL 107-206). Republican leaders had drafted the rule so that, if adopted, it would automatically attach the spending limit language to the popular appropriations bill. The only option that GOP appropriators had was to defeat the rule for consideration of the supplemental bill. Such procedural matters are normally considered party loyalty votes but in this case GOP leaders were stung by a handful of defections. Appropriations subcommittee chairmen Sonny Callahan of Alabama and Jim Kolbe of Arizona went against their party, as did fellow GOP appropriator Roger Wicker of Mississippi. Three other Republican appropriators registered their protest by voting "present": Zach Wamp of Tennessee, George Nethercutt of Washington, and Henry Bonilla of Texas, another subcommittee chairman. Several other GOP appropriators waited until late in the roll call to vote, forcing party leaders to work hard to head off other defections. But in the end, the rule was adopted, 216–209: R 214–3; D 1–205; I 1–1. *(Vote, p. 832)*

While its Senate counterparts, operating under a higher spending ceiling, approved all thirteen of their fiscal 2003 spending bills on unanimous votes, the House committee never tried to mark up two of the largest domestic spending bills, one covering the Commerce, Justice, and State departments and the other for the Labor, Health and Human Services, and Education departments. The House passed only five of the thirteen bills, and the 107th Congress adjourned with only two measures enacted: defense and military construction.

6. MEDICARE PRESCRIPTION COVERAGE

Congressional Republicans, especially the more conservative ones who ran the House, had long espoused a limited role for government in health care. To the extent that they had in the past supported a prescription drug benefit for Medicare, it had been a modest offering. A House-passed plan in 2000 would have cost $40 billion over five years.

In this context it was significant when Republican leaders decided in summer 2002 that it was imperative for the House to pass a Medicare drug benefit with a cost estimated at $350 billion over ten years. Taking action would send the powerful message that the GOP-led House could deliver a Medicare drug bill before the Democratic-led Senate on one of the Democrats' core campaign issues. If the Senate did act, the House would be ready with its conference position. *(Legislative details, p. 486)*

But it turned out that the Republican plan (HR 4954), cosponsored by Ways and Means Chairman Bill Thomas of California and Energy and Commerce Chairman Billy Tauzin of Louisiana, was not the easy election-year sell that House leaders thought it would be. First, they had to wrestle with demands from rural Republicans and others in the rank and file that the bill include $30 billion over ten years for health care providers. There was pressure to spare doctors and other health care professionals from more payment cuts scheduled under the Balanced Budget Act of 1997 (PL 105-33).

Next, leaders had to squelch a group of about three dozen Republican dissidents who had joined with Democrats in seeking provisions that would lower drug costs by directly restricting how the pharmaceutical industry does business. Those provisions included one to allow the wholesale importation of drugs sold more cheaply in Canada, and another to tighten patent laws to make it more difficult for manufacturers of brand-name drugs to impede low cost generic competition.

The legislation would have allowed Medicare enrollees to purchase private insurance policies covering prescription drugs, beginning in 2005, with a monthly premium estimated at $33. Patients would pay the first $250 of their drug costs each year, 20 percent of costs from $251 to $1,000, and 50 percent of the next $1,000. The patient would have to pay all drug costs from $2,001 to $3,700, after which insurers would pay the entire cost. The bill offered subsidies for low-income seniors to reduce or eliminate their insurance premiums and limit their copayments.

AARP, the nation's largest advocacy group for Americans age fifty and older, criticized the plan as a poor deal for Medicare enrollees. Democrats denounced it as a sellout to the insurance industry. Negotiations among Republicans over provider payments, drug pricing, and other issues of contention continued right up to the point when the rule for debate came to the House floor. Thomas, Tauzin, and Speaker J. Dennis Hastert of Illinois led a two-hour GOP conference meeting to try to sell members on the bill. More than two dozen Republicans expressed concerns about the bill.

GOP leaders tried to "educate" the dissidents into supporting the bill and, when necessary, leaned a little harder. Policy aides from the White House visited members' offices. At one point during the week, Hastert threatened to hold the House in session into the weekend, delaying the start of the Fourth of July recess if necessary, to act on the bill. To maintain control and force Democrats into an up-or-down vote, the Rules Committee barred amendments on the floor. The 218–213 vote to adopt that closed rule for floor debate gave GOP leaders confidence they had the votes to pass the bill. It also allowed Hastert to declare victory as the House voted 221–208 on June 28 to pass the bill: R 212–8; D 8–199; I 1–1. *(Vote, p. 832)*

The measure never became law but it demonstrated that House Republicans were willing to expand the scope of benefits under the 1965 Medicare program to meet demands of seniors, provided they could do so through private insurers rather than the government.

7. INDEPENDENT SEPTEMBER 11 COMMISSION

Hopes seemed dim for much of the year for those persons—most vocally the families of people who died in the Sept. 11 terrorist attacks—who wanted an independent commission to conduct a broad inquiry into government actions that not only failed to prevent those. Such a panel, in their view, would have looked at everything from immigration policy to federal construction standards.

Although a joint inquiry into the attacks by the House and Senate Intelligence committees was well under way by summer, some members of the House panel, led by Democrat Tim Roemer of Indiana, believed a broader investigation was necessary. They had come to this conclusion because the congressional inquiry was limited to the actions of covert agencies and because some panel members were not convinced they were receiving candid answers from the intelligence community. *(Attack investigations, p. 181)*

Roemer, backed by lawmakers in both parties, threatened to amend the fiscal 2003 intelligence authorization legislation (HR 4628) to include authorization for an independent panel with the power to investigate any government policy or program that might have contributed to the ability of the terrorists' to carry out the attacks on Sept. 11, 2001. Roemer's proposal was based on legislation (S 1867) first put forward in the Senate in late 2001 by Joseph I. Lieberman, D-Conn., and John McCain, R-Ariz. As chairman of the Governmental Affairs Committee, Lieberman had managed to get the measure through his panel in March 2002 but he was unable to secure a promise from the Senate leadership to bring the bill to the floor.

Momentum for their cause did not grow after revelations in May that FBI headquarters had ignored warnings—received in the summer of 2001 from an agent in Phoenix—hinting that terrorists were taking flight lessons with the intention of piloting jets into buildings. In addition, the White House opposed an independent investigation, especially while Congress was conducting its inquiry. Under pressure from the White House, the GOP leadership wrote a rule for debate on the House's intelligence bill that allowed only a narrow amendment. Roemer responded with an amendment proposing a commission to review intelligence agency efforts to implement recommendations by the joint House-Senate inquiry and other investigative panels. It also provided for the commission to review resource allocation, recommend organizational changes, and determine technological needs in the intelligence community.

Roemer and his supporters saw the amendment as an opening for authorizing a broader independent inquiry later, and that is what happened. On July 25 the House adopted the amendment with twenty-five Republicans—many of whom had not indicated support for a probe in the past—opposing the president and the GOP leadership and voting for the idea of an independent commission. The vote was 219–188: R 25–183; D 193–4; I 1–1. *(Vote, p. 832)*

The vote demonstrated that Congress did not want its inquiry to be the final word on the matter. By the time lawmakers returned from their August recess, the White House was preparing to reverse its position by expressing willingness to work out a deal with them on some sort of independent commission. On Sept. 24 the Senate applied more pressure, voting 90–8 to create a panel with a broad mandate as part of its version of the homeland security bill (HR 5005). Negotiations stretched into November as probe backers and the White House bickered about the details of the new commission's scope and makeup. A compromise was finally reached under which the president would name the chairman of the panel but members of Congress who backed the commission would name most of its members. The president signed the provision into law as part of the intelligence authorization bill Nov. 27.

8. HOMELAND SECURITY

The debate over creating a Homeland Security Department evolved into a bitter political fight over a issue not directly related to the national security: the rights of federal workers. The administration insisted on authority to write personnel rules for the new department that eliminated standard civil service protections. Democrats, longtime allies of federal workers' unions, ardently disagreed.

In particular, the two sides were at odds over the administration's view that in designing a new personnel system, it should have the broad power to fire and transfer workers and exempt some department employees from union representation on national security grounds. Organized labor argued that the administration was using homeland security as a smoke screen to gut collective bargaining protections. The administration tried to give assurances that existing protections, such as fair labor standards and civil rights rules, would apply in the new department. But labor groups and their Democratic friends were not mollified, and it was becoming increasingly clear that the question of workers' rights would be central to the outcome of the legislation creating the new security department. *(Legislative details, p. 176)*

After a nine-member Select Committee on Homeland Security in the Republican-controlled House reported out a bill (HR 5005) that accommodated most of the administration's wishes, Constance A. Morella, R-Md., offered an amendment during floor debate that would have stipulated that workers transferred to the new department would retain their collective bargaining rights, unless their job descriptions were significantly changed. The White House branded the language a nonstarter, saying it would diminish powers that presidents had enjoyed since 1962, when John F. Kennedy asserted his authority to exclude unions from agencies primarily concerned with intelligence, investigations or security. The authority was codified by the 1978 Civil Service Reform Act (PL 95-454).

Faced with the prospect of moderate Republicans siding with Morella's amendment on worker rights, House Republican leaders sought to give wavering lawmakers an alternative. They arranged for Christopher Shays, R-Conn., to offer an amendment before Morella's that similarly would affirm union members' rights but would allow the president a waiver to set aside collective bargaining agreements that could have an "adverse impact" on the department's ability to keep the nation secure. All but two Republicans voted for the language, while eleven conservative Democrats crossed over to vote for it as well, and it was adopted 229–201.

Morella then offered her amendment. The eight-term congresswoman faced a tough reelection fight in a predominantly Democratic district that is home to thousands of federal workers. She proposed effectively nullifying the waiver that would have been created under the Shays amendment. Morella raised the possibility of an "arbitrary" application of the national security waiver of collective bargaining rights, saying federal workers needed more ironclad assurances they would retain their rights.

With the Shays amendment adopted, the vote on Morella's proposal offered a clear indication of the depth of House support for taking the union point of view—and rebuffing the president—in resolving the workers' rights dispute. But on the key vote, Morella persuaded only four moderate Republicans to join her, while seven Democrats voted against her language. As a result it was rejected on July 26 by a vote of 208–222: R 5–214; D 202–7; I 1–1. *(Vote, p. 832)*

Senate Democrats included language virtually identical to Morella's in the homeland security bill approved by the Governmental Affairs Committee but it was dropped in negotiations over the final version of the legislation. Morella lost her bid for a ninth term in November in a district that had been reconfigured by Democrats in Maryland to favor a Democratic candidate.

9. FAST-TRACK TRADE PROCEDURES

After the Senate in May joined the House in passing legislation to revive fast-track procedures for congressional action on trade deals, the stage was set for a summer of contentious conference negotiations. The main stumbling block to an easy deal was the Senate bill (HR 3009), which included a ten-year, $12 billion expansion of Trade Adjustment Assistance (TAA) programs for those who lost their jobs as a consequence of expanded trade. Many Republicans viewed TAA as an overly generous entitlement for workers in outdated industries. *(Legislative details, p. 150)*

Even after House Ways and Means Committee Chairman Bill Thomas, R-Calif., and Senate Finance Committee Chairman Max Baucus, D-Mont., settled a bizarre public spat over which of them would chair the conference (Thomas prevailed), disagreements over the worker provisions continued to impede progress. Though supportive of the bill's central purpose—giving the president the power to reach trade agreements with other nations that Congress could reject or endorse but not tinker with—GOP fiscal conservatives were reluctant to embrace the TAA expansion as a price for their support.

Democrats in both chambers threatened to oppose any bill that did not include something as generous as the Senate TAA package. In addition, as the midterm elections approached, labor and environmental groups were becoming increasingly vocal in their opposition to the fast-track bill. With Democrats newly emboldened by the backlash against corporate accounting scandals, GOP leaders were talking about delaying the final vote on the trade bill until a postelection, lame-duck session.

At that point the White House ratcheted up the pressure for a compromise, pushing hard to get a bill on President Bush's desk before the congressional August recess. A frenzied week of conference negotiations followed, culminating in a three-hour, closed-door session late the evening of July 25 between Thomas and Baucus. The House chairman agreed to accept most of the Senate TAA package. The Senate chairman agreed to a revision of Senate language that would have allowed the Senate to amend trade deals if they affected U.S. anti-dumping laws.

Still, the conference report fate was by no means assured. Administration officials showed up to lobby probusiness Democrats. Bush himself came to the Capitol to rally the House Republican rank and file to support the top trade objective of his presidency. +Textile state lawmakers, who proved vital in the original House vote, were not convinced the conference report protected their industries adequately. House appropriators were angry that the package, which did not go through their committee, would expand federal spending in a way they could not control.

But Bush's persistence—and some last-minute deals—paid off. The president telephoned to assuage Appropriations Committee Chairman C. W. Bill Young, R-Fla. Five probusiness Democrats—Adam Smith and Rick Larsen of Washington, Ellen O. Tauscher and Jane Harman of California, and Harold E. Ford Jr. of Tennessee—resisted pressure from their party leadership and voted for the conference agreement after having opposed the initial House bill in December. Amid all the narrow but potentially decisive crosscurrents the GOP leadership navigated the fragile deal to a bare embrace. After an overnight debate that started the Friday that the chamber's summer recess was to begin, the House adopted the conference report with essentially one vote to spare. The final tally shortly after 3 a.m. on Saturday, July 27, was 215–212: R 190–27; D 25–183; I 0–2. *(Vote, p. 832)*

10. IRAQ USE-OF-FORCE RESOLUTION

One of President Bush's central themes after he took office was the threat he said was posed to U.S. national security by Iraq's attempts to develop chemical, biological, and nuclear weapons. In his 2002 State of the Union address, Bush included Iraq as part of an "axis of evil"—a trio of nations including Iran and North Korea, all of which were trying to acquire unconventional weapons. Bush warned that the United States had no choice but to confront this threat. The president went much further in a speech he delivered in June at the U.S. Military Academy at West Point. There, Bush explained that his administration would confront unconventional threats with a policy of military preemption. This new policy—unprecedented in U.S. history—meant that Bush was prepared to wage war against countries to prevent them from developing and using weapons of mass destruction against the United States.

Congress worried that Bush was leading the country to war without its approval, and lawmakers insisted that he submit a war resolution to Congress. At first White House officials said Bush did not need congressional approval to defend the country. However, in early September, he agreed to submit a resolution. Once Bush made it clear he would respect Congress' role in the decision to use force against Iraq, he was assured a victorious vote. Despite deep reservations about Bush's policy toward Iraq, many lawmakers—Democrats and Republicans—were reluctant to vote against the popular president on a matter of national security on the eve of midterm elections. *(Legislative details, p. 238)*

For Bush, however, the issue was his margin of victory on Capitol Hill. He did not want a repeat of the 1991 Persian Gulf War resolution (PL 102-1), in which Congress narrowly gave his father, President George Bush, approval to end Iraq's occupation of Kuwait. He also wanted strong bipartisan support to strengthen his hand in negotiations with the United Nations, which had yet to vote on its own resolution to deal with Iraq.

As the White House and lawmakers negotiated for mutually acceptable wording, Bush was unable to reach a compromise with Senate Majority Leader Tom Daschle, D-S.D. As a result, Bush struck a deal with House Minority Leader Richard A. Gephardt, D-Mo., that gave him broad authority for launching a war against Iraq and a free hand to act without approval from the United Nations. With Gephardt on the president's side and Daschle politically isolated, the House easily passed a measure (H J Res 114) authorizing military action against Iraq by a vote of 296–133: R 215–6; D 81–126; I 0–1. *(Vote, p. 832)*

11. ABORTION OPPONENTS' RIGHTS

A single provision in a comprehensive overhaul of the nation's bankruptcy code provided abortion opponents with their most significant victory of the year. On a late-session procedural move to bring a conference report to the House floor, antiabortion forces showed they held at least as much influence over Republicans as did financial services lobbyists. But their action also guaranteed that another year would pass without the enactment of a bankruptcy bill under discussion since 1997. *(Legislative details, p. 481)*

The provision that caught their attention was aimed at preventing abortion protesters from filing for bankruptcy to avoid paying court-ordered judgments. It resulted from painstaking negotiations between Sen. Charles E. Schumer, D-N.Y., who wanted a strict crackdown on such practices, and Rep. Henry J. Hyde, R-Ill., who was more sympathetic to abortion foes. The language provoked enough concern among Hyde's antiabortion colleagues that they stalled consideration of the conference agreement on the bill (HR 333) in August. But in November, with the election recently behind them, Republican leaders thought it was a good bet they could win a majority for the measure. A "yes" vote in the House was sure to be matched by a vote to clear the bill by the Senate.

To protect the conference agreement from parliamentary attacks, House GOP leaders wrote a resolution to set the rules for floor debate Nov. 14. Votes in favor of the rule were slow in coming, and many that showed up on the electronic tally in the "aye" column soon switched to "nay." In the well of the House, Republicans were caught in a tug of war between their leadership, which was trying to make good on a promise to their financial services industry backers, and their conservative colleagues, who were never willing to stray too far from the antiabortion forces that made up their base of political support. In the end, the antiabortion side won the votes of two-fifths of the Republicans that day, more than enough to counterbalance the one-quarter of the Democrats who voted with the rest of the GOP to keep the bill alive. The rejection of the rule killed the bankruptcy bill for the 107th Congress. The vote was 172–243: R 124–87; D 48–155; I 0–1. *(Vote, p. 832)*

1. HR 2646. Farm Bill. Passage of the bill to reauthorize federal agriculture programs for five years, including $2 billion in direct federal subsidies to milk producers, and to reestablish programs that supply payments to farmers when commodity prices fall below a specified level. Passed 58–40: R 9–38; D 48–2 (ND 40–1; SD 8–1); I 1–0, Feb. 13, 2002.. A "nay" was a vote in support of the president's position

2. S 517. Fuel Economy Standards. Levin, D-Mich., amendment to the Daschle, D-S.D., substitute amendment to strike the CAFE standard in the substitute and replace it with language directing the National Highway Traffic Safety Administration (NHTSA) to set a new standard in fifteen months. Adopted 62–38: R 43–6; D 19–31 (ND 14–27, SD 5–4); I 0–1, March 13, 2002.

3. HR 2356. Campaign Finance Overhaul. Passage of the bill to ban "soft money" donations to national political parties but allow up to $10,000 in soft money donations to state and local parties for voter registration and get-out-the-vote activity, to increase the individual contribution limit from $1,000 to $2,000 per election for House and Senate candidates, and to index future contributions for inflation. Passed (thus cleared for the president) 60–40: R 11–38; D 48–2 (ND 40–1, SD 8–1); I 1–0, March 20, 2002.

4. S 565. Federal Election Standards. Passage of the bill to impose detailed voting-procedure requirements on states including requiring states to let voters verify their votes before casting ballots, allowing voters to change their ballots before submitting their votes, and notifying voters if they vote for more than one candidate for an office. Passed 99–1: R 48–1; D 50–0 (ND 41–0, SD 9–0); I 1–0, April 11, 2002.

5. S 517. Artic National Wildlife Refuge. Motion to invoke cloture (thus limiting debate) on Murkowski, R-Alaska, amendment to allow oil and gas development in a portion of the Arctic National Wildlife Refuge if the president certified to Congress that production in the area is in the nation's economic and security interests. Limited the amount of surface disturbances to 2,000 acres, imposed an export ban on oil produced from the refuge, and designated an additional 1.5 million acres as wilderness in exchange for opening to drilling approximately 1.5 million acres of nonwilderness in the coastal plain region of the refuge. Motion rejected 46–54: R 41–8; D 5–45 (ND 2–39, SD 3–6); I 0–1, April 18, 2002. Three-fifths of the total Senate (sixty) was required to invoke cloture.

6. HR 3009. Fast-Track Trade Procedures. Passage of the bill to extend duty-free status to certain products from Bolivia, Colombia, Ecuador, and Peru; renew the president's fast-track trade negotiation authority; and reauthorize and expand a program to provide retraining and relocation assistance to U.S. workers hurt by trade agreements. Passed 66–30: R 41–5; D 24–25 (ND 16–24, SD 8–1); I 1–0, May 23, 2002. A "yea" was a vote in support of the president's position.

7. HR 8. Tax Cut Extension: Estate Tax. Gramm, R-Texas, motion to waive the Budget Act with respect to the Conrad, D-N.D., point of order against the Gramm amendment that would permanently extend the repeal of the estate tax contained in the $1.4 trillion tax cut enacted in 2001. Motion rejected 54–44: R 45–2; D 9–41 (ND 4–37, SD 5–4); I 0–1, June 12, 2002. A three-fifths majority vote (sixty) of the total Senate was required to waive the Budget Act. A "yea" was a vote in support of the president's position. (Subsequently the point of order was sustained and the Gramm amendment fell.).

8. S 2600. Terrorism Insurance. Passage of the bill to require the federal government to reimburse insurance companies for 90 percent of catastrophic losses related to terrorism between $10 billion and $100 billion in 2002, with an option to renew the program the following year to cover 90 percent of claims between $15 billion and $100 billion. Passed 84–14: R 34–14; D 49–0 (ND 40–0, SD 9–0); I 1–0, June 18, 2002.

9. S 2673. Corporate Regulation, Accounting. Passage of the bill to require more complete disclosure of corporate finances and overhaul regulation of the accounting industry, establish a new oversight board to police accounting firms, and forbid firms from providing investment banking, management consulting and other services for publicly traded companies. S 2673 created new criminal penalties for shareholder fraud and obstruction of justice involving document shredding and required chief executive officers and chief financial officers to attest to the accuracy of financial statements included in SEC filings. Passed 97–0: R 46–0; D 50–0 (ND 41–0, SD 9–0); I 1–0, July 15, 2002.

10. S 812. Medicare Prescription Coverage. Graham, D-Fla., motion to waive the Budget Act on legislation to provide prescription drug coverage for Medicare recipients, provide coverage for drug costs above a certain expense amount, make all recipients eligible for a discount of 5 percent or more on prescription drugs, and allow individuals to import prescription drugs from Canada under certain conditions. Motion rejected 49–50: R 4–44; D 45–5 (ND 38–3, SD 7–2); I 0–1, July 31, 2002. A three-fifths majority vote (sixty) of the total Senate was required to waive the Budget Act.

11. HR 5005. Commission to Investigate Sept. 11 Attacks. Lieberman, D-Conn., amendment to establish the National Commission on Terrorist Attacks Upon the United States to investigate the facts and circumstances relating to the Sept. 11 terrorist attacks with an initial report in six months and a final report within one year. Adopted 90–8: R 41–8; D 48–0 (ND 39–0, SD 9–0); I 1–0, Sept. 24, 2002.

12. HR 5005. Homeland Security Department. Motion to invoke cloture (thus limiting debate) on the Lieberman, D-Conn., amendment to create a cabinet-level Homeland Security Department charged with protecting domestic security. Motion rejected 50–49: R 1–48; D 48–1 (ND 41–0, SD 7–1); I 1–0, Sept. 26, 2002. Three-fifths of the total Senate (sixty) was required to invoke cloture.

13. H J Res 114. Iraq Use of Force Resolution. Passage of the joint resolution to authorize the use of force against Iraq. Passed 77–23: R 48–1; D 29–21 (ND 21–20, SD 8–1); I 0–1, Oct. 11, 2002 (in the session that began and the *Congressional Record* dated Oct. 10, 2002). A "yea" was a vote in support of the president's position.

KEY

	Democrats	Republicans	
Y	Voted for ("yea")	–	Announced against
N	Voted against ("nay")	P	Voted "present"
+	Announced for	C	Voted "present" to avoid possible conflict of interest
#	Paired for	?	Did not vote or otherwise make a position known
X	Paired against		

ND   Northern Democrats
SD   Southern Democrats
Southern states – Ala., Ark., Fla., Ga., Ky., La., Miss., N.C., Okla., S.C., Tenn., Texas, Va.

Senate Key Votes	1	2	3	4	5	6	7	8	9	10	11	12	13
ALABAMA													
Shelby	Y	Y	N	Y	Y	?	Y	Y	Y	N	Y	N	Y
Sessions	Y	Y	N	Y	Y	N	Y	N	Y	N	Y	N	Y
ALASKA													
Stevens	N	Y	N	Y	Y	Y	Y	Y	Y	N	Y	N	Y
Murkowski	N	Y	N	Y	Y	Y	Y	Y	Y	N	Y	N	Y
ARIZONA													
McCain	N	N	Y	Y	N	Y	N	Y	Y	N	Y	N	Y
Kyl	N	Y	N	Y	Y	Y	Y	N	Y	N	Y	N	Y
ARKANSAS													
Hutchinson	N	Y	N	Y	Y	Y	Y	Y	Y	Y	Y	N	Y
Lincoln	N	Y	Y	Y	N	Y	Y	Y	Y	Y	Y	Y	Y
CALIFORNIA													
Feinstein	Y	N	Y	Y	N	Y	N	Y	Y	Y	Y	Y	Y
Boxer	Y	N	Y	Y	N	N	N	Y	Y	Y	Y	Y	N
COLORADO													
Campbell	N	Y	N	Y	Y	Y	Y	N	Y	N	Y	N	Y
Allard	N	Y	N	Y	Y	Y	Y	Y	Y	N	Y	N	Y
CONNECTICUT													
Dodd	Y	N	Y	Y	N	N	N	Y	Y	Y	Y	Y	Y
Lieberman	Y	N	Y	Y	N	Y	N	Y	Y	Y	Y	Y	Y
DELAWARE													
Carper	Y	Y	Y	Y	N	Y	N	Y	Y	Y	Y	Y	Y
Biden	Y	N	Y	Y	N	Y	N	Y	Y	Y	Y	Y	Y
FLORIDA													
Graham	Y	N	Y	Y	N	Y	N	Y	Y	Y	Y	Y	N
Nelson	Y	N	Y	Y	N	Y	Y	Y	Y	Y	Y	Y	Y
GEORGIA													
Miller	Y	Y	Y	Y	Y	Y	Y	Y	Y	Y	Y	N	Y
Cleland	Y	Y	Y	Y	N	Y	Y	Y	Y	Y	Y	Y	Y
HAWAII													
Inouye	Y	N	Y	Y	Y	?	N	N	Y	Y	?	Y	N
Akaka	Y	N	Y	Y	Y	N	N	Y	Y	Y	Y	Y	N
IDAHO													
Craig	N	Y	N	Y	Y	Y	Y	N	+	N	Y	N	Y
Crapo	N	Y	N	Y	Y	Y	?	Y	+	N	Y	N	Y
ILLINOIS													
Durbin	Y	N	Y	Y	N	N	N	Y	Y	Y	Y	Y	N
Fitzgerald	Y	Y	Y	Y	N	Y	Y	Y	Y	N	Y	N	Y
INDIANA													
Lugar	N	Y	Y	Y	Y	Y	Y	Y	Y	N	N	N	Y
Bayh	Y	Y	Y	Y	N	Y	Y	Y	Y	Y	Y	Y	Y
IOWA													
Grassley	Y	Y	N	Y	Y	Y	Y	Y	Y	N	Y	N	Y
Harkin	Y	N	Y	Y	N	Y	N	Y	Y	N	Y	Y	Y
KANSAS													
Brownback	N	Y	N	Y	Y	?	Y	Y	Y	N	Y	N	Y
Roberts	N	Y	N	Y	Y	Y	Y	Y	Y	N	Y	N	Y
KENTUCKY													
McConnell	N	Y	N	Y	Y	Y	Y	Y	Y	N	Y	N	Y
Bunning	N	Y	N	Y	Y	Y	Y	Y	Y	N	Y	N	Y
LOUISIANA													
Breaux	Y	Y	N	Y	Y	Y	N	Y	Y	N	Y	Y	Y
Landrieu	Y	Y	Y	Y	Y	Y	Y	Y	Y	Y	Y	?	Y
MAINE													
Snowe	Y	N	Y	Y	N	Y	Y	Y	Y	N	Y	N	Y
Collins	Y	N	Y	Y	N	Y	Y	Y	Y	Y	Y	N	Y
MARYLAND													
Sarbanes	Y	N	Y	Y	N	N	N	Y	Y	Y	Y	Y	N
Mikulski	Y	Y	Y	Y	N	N	N	Y	Y	Y	Y	Y	N
MASSACHUSETTS													
Kennedy	Y	N	Y	Y	N	N	N	Y	Y	Y	Y	Y	N
Kerry	Y	N	Y	Y	N	Y	N	+	Y	Y	Y	Y	Y
MICHIGAN													
Levin	Y	Y	Y	Y	N	N	N	Y	Y	Y	Y	Y	N
Stabenow	Y	Y	Y	Y	N	N	N	Y	Y	Y	Y	Y	N
MINNESOTA													
Wellstone	Y	N	Y	Y	N	N	N	Y	Y	Y	Y	Y	N
Dayton	Y	N	Y	Y	N	Y	N	Y	Y	Y	Y	Y	N
MISSISSIPPI													
Cochran	N	Y	Y	Y	Y	Y	Y	Y	Y	N	N	N	Y
Lott	N	Y	N	Y	Y	Y	Y	Y	Y	N	N	N	Y
MISSOURI													
Bond	N	Y	N	Y	Y	Y	Y	Y	Y	N	N	N	Y
Carnahan	Y	Y	Y	Y	N	N	N	Y	Y	Y	Y	Y	Y

Senate Key Votes	1	2	3	4	5	6	7	8	9	10	11	12	13
MONTANA													
Baucus	Y	Y	Y	Y	N	Y	Y	Y	Y	Y	?	Y	Y
Burns	N	Y	N	N	Y	Y	Y	N	Y	N	Y	N	Y
NEBRASKA													
Nelson	Y	Y	N	Y	N	Y	Y	Y	Y	N	Y	N	Y
Hagel	N	Y	N	Y	Y	Y	Y	Y	Y	N	Y	N	Y
NEVADA													
Reid	Y	N	Y	Y	N	N	N	Y	Y	Y	Y	Y	Y
Ensign	N	Y	N	Y	Y	N	Y	Y	Y	N	Y	N	Y
NEW HAMPSHIRE													
Smith	N	Y	N	Y	N	Y	Y	Y	Y	N	Y	N	Y
Gregg	N	N	N	Y	Y	N	Y	Y	Y	N	N	N	Y
NEW JERSEY													
Corzine	N	N	Y	Y	N	N	N	Y	Y	Y	Y	Y	N
Torricelli	Y	N	Y	Y	N	N	N	Y	Y	Y	Y	Y	Y
NEW MEXICO													
Domenici	?	Y	Y	Y	Y	Y	Y	Y	Y	N	N	N	Y
Bingaman	Y	N	Y	Y	N	Y	N	Y	Y	Y	Y	Y	N
NEW YORK													
Clinton	Y	N	Y	Y	N	N	N	Y	Y	Y	Y	Y	Y
Schumer	Y	N	Y	Y	N	N	N	Y	Y	Y	Y	Y	Y
NORTH CAROLINA													
Helms	N	Y	N	Y	Y	?	+	?	+	–	Y	N	Y
Edwards	Y	N	Y	Y	N	Y	N	Y	Y	Y	Y	Y	Y
NORTH DAKOTA													
Conrad	Y	Y	Y	Y	N	Y	N	Y	Y	Y	Y	Y	N
Dorgan	Y	Y	Y	Y	N	Y	N	Y	Y	Y	Y	Y	Y
OHIO													
DeWine	N	Y	N	Y	Y	Y	Y	Y	Y	N	Y	N	Y
Voinovich	N	Y	N	Y	Y	Y	Y	Y	Y	N	N	N	Y
OKLAHOMA													
Nickles	N	Y	N	Y	Y	Y	Y	Y	Y	N	Y	N	Y
Inhofe	N	Y	N	Y	Y	Y	Y	Y	Y	N	Y	N	Y
OREGON													
Wyden	Y	N	Y	Y	N	Y	N	Y	Y	Y	Y	Y	N
Smith	N	N	N	Y	Y	N	Y	Y	Y	Y	Y	Y	Y
PENNSYLVANIA													
Specter	Y	Y	Y	Y	N	Y	Y	Y	Y	Y	Y	N	Y
Santorum	N	Y	N	Y	Y	Y	Y	Y	Y	N	Y	N	Y
RHODE ISLAND													
Reed	Y	N	Y	Y	N	N	N	Y	Y	Y	Y	Y	N
Chafee	N	N	Y	Y	N	Y	N	Y	Y	N	Y	Y	N
SOUTH CAROLINA													
Thurmond	N	Y	N	Y	Y	N	Y	Y	Y	N	Y	N	Y
Hollings	Y	N	Y	Y	N	N	N	Y	Y	N	Y	Y	Y
SOUTH DAKOTA													
Daschle	Y	Y	Y	Y	N	Y	N	Y	Y	Y	Y	Y	Y
Johnson	Y	Y	Y	Y	N	N	N	Y	Y	Y	Y	Y	Y
TENNESSEE													
Thompson	N	Y	N	Y	Y	Y	Y	Y	Y	N	Y	N	Y
Frist	N	Y	N	Y	Y	Y	Y	Y	Y	N	Y	N	Y
TEXAS													
Gramm	N	Y	N	Y	Y	Y	Y	Y	Y	N	N	N	Y
Hutchison	N	Y	N	Y	Y	Y	Y	Y	Y	N	Y	N	Y
UTAH													
Hatch	N	Y	N	Y	Y	Y	Y	Y	Y	N	Y	N	Y
Bennett	?	Y	N	Y	Y	Y	Y	Y	Y	N	Y	N	Y
VERMONT													
Leahy	Y	N	Y	Y	N	N	N	Y	Y	Y	Y	Y	N
Jeffords	Y	N	Y	Y	N	N	N	Y	Y	N	Y	Y	N
VIRGINIA													
Warner	Y	Y	Y	Y	Y	Y	Y	Y	Y	N	Y	N	Y
Allen	Y	Y	N	Y	Y	Y	Y	Y	Y	N	Y	N	Y
WASHINGTON													
Cantwell	Y	N	Y	Y	N	N	N	Y	Y	Y	Y	Y	Y
Murray	Y	N	Y	Y	N	N	N	Y	Y	Y	Y	Y	N
WEST VIRGINIA													
Byrd	Y	Y	Y	Y	N	N	N	Y	Y	Y	Y	Y	N
Rockefeller	Y	N	Y	Y	N	N	N	Y	Y	Y	Y	Y	Y
WISCONSIN													
Kohl	Y	Y	Y	Y	N	N	N	Y	Y	Y	Y	Y	Y
Feingold	Y	Y	Y	Y	N	N	N	Y	Y	N	Y	Y	N
WYOMING													
Thomas	N	Y	N	Y	Y	Y	Y	Y	N	N	N	N	Y
Enzi	N	Y	N	Y	Y	Y	Y	N	Y	N	Y	N	Y

1. HR 2356. Campaign Finance Overhaul. Passage of the bill to ban "soft money" donations to national political parties but allow up to $10,000 in soft money donations to state and local parties for voter registration and get-out-the-vote activities. The bill barred issue ads from targeting specific candidates within sixty days of a general election or thirty days of a primary. The bill also increased the individual contribution limit from $1,000 to $2,000 per election for House and Senate candidates, both of were indexed for inflation thereafter. Passed 240–189: R 41–176; D 198–12 (ND 150–6, SD 48–6); I 1–1, Feb. 14, 2002 (in the session that began and the *Congressional Record* dated Feb. 13, 2002).

2. HR 1542. High-Speed Internet Access. Motion to order the previous question (thus ending debate and possibility of amendment) on the Markey, D-Mass., motion to recommit the bill to the House Energy and Commerce Committee with instructions to add language that would maintain the ability of the states and the Federal Communications Commission to enforce current telecommunications law regulations over the entry of regional telephone companies (the so-called Baby Bells) into the high-speed Internet access market. Motion rejected 173–256: R 62–157; D 109–99 (ND 98–56, SD 11–43); I 2–0, Feb. 27, 2002.

3. HR 4546. Fiscal 2003 Defense Authorization. Passage of the bill to authorize $383.4 billion for defense programs for fiscal 2003, including the president's request of $7.8 billion for missile defense systems and $7.3 billion for counterterrorism programs. It provided $475 million for the Crusader artillery system, exempted military activities from certain environmental regulations, and included an average 4.7 percent pay increase for military personnel. Passed 359–58: R 212–1; D 146–56 (ND 100–51, SD 46–5); I 1–1, May 10, 2002 (in the session that began and the *Congressional Record* dated May 9, 2002).

4. HR 4737. Welfare Reauthorization. Passage of the bill that to authorize $16.5 billion to renew the Temporary Assistance for Needy Families block grant program through fiscal 2007 and require new welfare aid conditions. The bill required individuals to work forty hours per week (up from thirty in existing law) to be eligible for assistance and require states to have 70 percent or more of their families working by 2007. It authorized additional funding for child care and marriage promotion activities and allowed states to combine different types of block grants but barred them from using a waiver to transfer funds from one welfare account to another. Motion agreed to 229–197: R 214–4; D 14–192 (ND 7–147, SD 7–45); I 1–1, May 16, 2002. A two-thirds majority of those present and voting (282 in this case) was required for passage under suspension of the rules. A "yea" was a vote in support of the president's position.

5. HR 4775. Fiscal 2002 Supplemental Appropriations. Adoption of the rule (H Res 428) to permit House floor consideration of the bill to provide $28.8 billion in supplemental appropriations for fiscal 2002, more than half of which was intended for military operations. Adopted 216–209: R 214–3; D 1–205 (ND 1–153, SD 0–52); I 1–1, May 22, 2002.

6. HR 4954. Prescription Drug Coverage. Passage of the bill covering prescription drug costs for Medicare recipients through private insurance policies beginning in 2005 at an estimated cost of $350 billion over ten years. Patients were to pay a $33 monthly premium, with a $250 annual deductible. HR 4954 specified that patients would pay 20 percent of drug costs from $251 to $1,000 and 50 percent of the next $1,000, all costs from $2,001 to $3,700; after reaching that level insurers would pay the entire cost. Subsidies were provided to reduce premiums and co-payments for low-income patients. Passed 221–208: R 212–8; D 8–199 (ND 6–148, SD 2–51); I 1–1, June 28, 2002 (in the session that began and the *Congressional Record* dated June 27, 2002).

7. HR 4628. Establish Commission on Sept. 11 Attacks. Roemer, D-Ind., amendment to establish a National Commission on Terrorist Attacks Upon the United States to investigate the terrorist attacks that occurred on Sept. 11, 2001. Adopted 219–188: R 25–183; D 193–4 (ND 145–1, SD 48–3); I 1–1, July 25, 2002 (in the session that began and the *Congressional Record* that was dated July 24, 2002). A "nay" was a vote in support of the president's position.

8. HR 5005. Homeland Security/Union Membership. Morella, R-Md., amendment to give federal employees who transferred into the Homeland Security Department the right to join a union if they were under union protection before the transfer. Allowed the president to exempt employees from union membership when duties were directly related to the war on terrorism.

Rejected 208–222: R 5–214; D 202–7 (ND 153–2, SD 49–5); I 1–1, July 26, 2002. A "nay" was a vote in support of the president's position.

9. HR 3009. Trade Promotion Authority. Adoption of the conference report on the bill to allow special trade promotion authority for congressional consideration of trade agreements reached before June 1, 2005, and extend duty-free status to certain products from Bolivia, Colombia, Ecuador, and Peru. The bill reauthorized and expanded a program to provide retraining assistance to U.S. workers hurt by trade agreements, created a 65 percent tax credit for health insurance costs for displaced workers, and authorized a five-year extension of the Generalized System of Preferences. Adopted 215–212: R 190–27; D 25–183 (ND 11–143, SD 14–40); I 0–2, July 27, 2002 (in the session that began and the *Congressional Record* dated July 26, 2002). A "yea" was a vote in support of the president's position.

10. H J Res 114. Use of Force. Passage of the joint resolution to authorize the use of force against Iraq and require the administration to report to Congress that diplomatic options had been exhausted no later than forty-eight hours after military action began. Passed 296–133: R 215–6; D 81–126 (ND 49–105, SD 32–21); I 0–1, Oct. 10, 2002. A "yea" was a vote in support of the president's position.

11. HR 333. Bankruptcy Overhaul/Abortion. Adoption of the rule (H Res 606) to provide for House floor consideration of the conference report on the bill requiring debtors able to repay $10,000 or 25 percent of their debts over five years, to file under Chapter 13 of the bankruptcy statute, which required a reorganization of debts under a repayment plan, instead of seeking to discharge debts under the more consumer-friendly Chapter 7. HR 333 also prevented persons protesting abortion and other issues from declaring bankruptcy to avoid paying court-ordered fines and judgments. Rejected 172–243: R 124–87; D 48–155 (ND 24–127, SD 24–28); I 0–1, Nov. 14, 2002.

KEY

Democrats	*Republicans*	**Independent**

Y Voted for ("yea")
N Voted against ("nay")
+ Announced for
\# Paired for
X Paired against

– Announced against
P Voted "present"
C Voted "present" to avoid possible conflict of interest
? Did not vote or otherwise make a position known

ND Northern Democrats
SD Southern Democrats
Southern states – Ala., Ark., Fla., Ga., Ky., La., Miss., N.C., Okla., S.C., Tenn., Texas, Va.

House Key Votes	1	2	3	4	5	6	7	8	9	10	11
ALABAMA											
1 Callahan	N	N	Y	Y	N	Y	?	N	Y	Y	?
2 Everett	N	N	Y	Y	Y	Y	N	N	Y	Y	N
3 Riley	–	N	+	Y	Y	Y	N	N	Y	Y	Y
4 Aderholt	N	N	Y	Y	Y	Y	N	N	Y	Y	N
5 Cramer	Y	N	Y	Y	N	N	Y	Y	N	Y	Y
6 Bachus	N	N	Y	Y	Y	Y	N	N	Y	Y	Y
7 Hilliard	N	N	Y	N	N	N	Y	Y	N	N	N
ALASKA											
AL Young	N	N	Y	Y	Y	Y	?	N	N	Y	Y
ARIZONA											
1 Flake	N	Y	Y	Y	Y	N	N	N	Y	Y	N
2 Pastor	Y	N	Y	N	N	N	Y	Y	N	N	N
3 Stump	N	N	Y	Y	Y	Y	?	N	?	?	?
4 Shadegg	N	Y	Y	Y	Y	Y	N	N	Y	Y	N
5 Kolbe	N	Y	Y	Y	Y	Y	N	N	Y	Y	Y
6 Hayworth	N	Y	Y	Y	Y	Y	N	N	Y	Y	N
ARKANSAS											
1 Berry	Y	N	Y	N	N	N	Y	Y	N	Y	Y
2 Snyder	Y	N	Y	N	N	N	Y	Y	Y	N	Y
3 Boozman	N	N	Y	Y	Y	Y	N	N	Y	Y	N
4 Ross	Y	N	Y	N	N	N	Y	Y	N	Y	Y
CALIFORNIA											
1 Thompson	Y	Y	Y	N	N	N	Y	Y	N	N	Y
2 Herger	N	N	Y	Y	Y	Y	N	N	Y	Y	Y
3 Ose	Y	N	+	Y	Y	Y	N	N	Y	Y	Y
4 Doolittle	N	N	Y	Y	Y	Y	N	N	Y	Y	?
5 Matsui	Y	N	Y	N	N	N	Y	Y	N	N	N
6 Woolsey	Y	Y	N	N	N	N	Y	Y	N	N	N
7 Miller, George	Y	Y	N	N	N	N	Y	Y	N	N	N
8 Pelosi	Y	Y	Y	N	N	N	Y	Y	N	N	N
9 Lee	Y	Y	N	N	N	N	Y	Y	N	N	N
10 Tauscher	Y	N	Y	N	N	N	Y	Y	Y	Y	Y
11 Pombo	N	Y	Y	?	Y	Y	N	N	Y	Y	N
12 Lantos	Y	Y	Y	N	N	N	Y	Y	N	N	N
13 Stark	Y	Y	N	N	N	N	Y	Y	N	N	N
14 Eshoo	Y	Y	Y	N	N	N	Y	Y	N	N	N
15 Honda	Y	Y	N	N	N	N	Y	Y	N	N	N
16 Lofgren	Y	Y	N	N	N	N	Y	Y	N	N	N
17 Farr	Y	Y	N	N	N	N	Y	Y	N	N	N
18 Condit	Y	Y	Y	N	N	Y	?	Y	N	N	?
19 Radanovich	N	N	Y	Y	Y	Y	N	N	Y	Y	Y
20 Dooley	Y	Y	Y	N	N	N	Y	Y	Y	Y	Y
21 Thomas	N	N	Y	Y	Y	Y	N	N	Y	Y	Y
22 Capps	Y	Y	Y	N	N	N	Y	Y	N	N	N
23 Gallegly	N	N	Y	Y	Y	Y	N	N	Y	Y	Y
24 Sherman	Y	Y	Y	N	N	N	Y	Y	N	Y	N
25 McKeon	N	N	Y	Y	Y	Y	N	N	Y	Y	N
26 Berman	Y	Y	Y	N	N	N	Y	Y	N	N	N
27 Schiff	Y	N	Y	N	N	N	Y	Y	N	N	N
28 Dreier	N	N	Y	Y	Y	Y	N	N	Y	Y	Y
29 Waxman	Y	Y	?	N	N	N	Y	Y	N	N	N
30 Becerra	Y	Y	N	N	N	N	Y	Y	N	N	N
31 Solis	Y	Y	Y	N	N	N	Y	Y	N	N	N
32 Watson	Y	Y	?	N	N	N	Y	Y	N	N	N
33 Roybal-Allard	Y	Y	Y	N	N	N	Y	Y	N	N	N
34 Napolitano	Y	Y	Y	N	N	N	Y	Y	N	N	N
35 Waters	Y	Y	Y	N	N	N	Y	Y	N	N	N
36 Harman	Y	Y	Y	N	N	N	Y	Y	Y	N	N
37 Millender-McD.	Y	Y	?	N	N	N	Y	Y	N	N	N
38 Horn	Y	N	Y	Y	Y	Y	N	N	Y	Y	Y
39 Royce	N	Y	Y	Y	Y	Y	N	N	Y	Y	Y
40 Lewis	N	N	Y	Y	Y	Y	N	N	Y	Y	Y
41 Miller, Gary	N	N	Y	Y	Y	Y	N	N	Y	Y	Y
42 Baca	Y	N	Y	N	N	N	Y	Y	N	N	N
43 Calvert	N	N	Y	Y	Y	Y	N	N	Y	Y	Y
44 Bono	Y	N	Y	Y	Y	Y	N	N	Y	Y	Y

House Key Votes	1	2	3	4	5	6	7	8	9	10	11
45 Rohrabacher	N	Y	Y	Y	Y	Y	Y	N	N	Y	Y
46 Sanchez	Y	N	Y	N	N	N	Y	Y	N	N	N
47 Cox	N	Y	Y	Y	Y	Y	?	N	Y	Y	Y
48 Issa	N	N	Y	Y	Y	Y	?	N	Y	Y	Y
49 Davis	Y	Y	Y	N	N	N	Y	Y	N	N	N
50 Filner	Y	N	N	N	N	N	Y	Y	N	N	N
51 Cunningham	N	N	Y	Y	Y	Y	N	N	Y	Y	N
52 Hunter	N	N	Y	Y	Y	Y	N	N	Y	Y	N
COLORADO											
1 DeGette	Y	Y	N	N	N	N	Y	Y	N	N	N
2 Udall	Y	Y	N	N	N	N	Y	Y	N	N	N
3 McInnis	N	Y	Y	Y	Y	Y	N	N	Y	Y	Y
4 Schaffer	N	Y	Y	Y	Y	Y	N	N	Y	Y	N
5 Hefley	?	Y	Y	Y	Y	Y	N	N	Y	Y	N
6 Tancredo	N	N	Y	Y	Y	Y	Y	N	Y	Y	N
CONNECTICUT											
1 Larson	Y	N	Y	N	N	N	Y	Y	N	N	N
2 Simmons	Y	N	Y	Y	Y	Y	N	Y	N	Y	Y
3 DeLauro	Y	Y	Y	N	N	N	Y	Y	N	N	N
4 Shays	Y	Y	Y	Y	Y	Y	N	N	Y	Y	Y
5 Maloney	Y	N	Y	N	N	Y	N	Y	N	N	Y
6 Johnson	Y	N	Y	Y	Y	Y	N	Y	Y	Y	Y
DELAWARE											
AL Castle	Y	Y	Y	Y	Y	Y	N	Y	Y	Y	Y
FLORIDA											
1 Miller, J.	N	N	Y	Y	Y	Y	N	N	Y	Y	N
2 Boyd	Y	N	Y	Y	N	N	N	N	N	Y	?
3 Brown	Y	N	Y	N	N	N	Y	Y	N	N	N
4 Crenshaw	N	Y	Y	Y	Y	Y	N	N	Y	Y	Y
5 Thurman	Y	Y	Y	N	N	N	Y	Y	N	N	N
6 Stearns	N	N	Y	Y	Y	Y	–	N	N	N	N
7 Mica	N	N	Y	Y	Y	Y	N	N	Y	Y	N
8 Keller	N	N	Y	Y	Y	Y	N	N	Y	Y	N
9 Bilirakis	N	N	Y	Y	Y	Y	N	N	Y	Y	N
10 Young	N	Y	Y	Y	Y	Y	N	N	Y	Y	N
11 Davis	Y	Y	Y	N	N	N	Y	Y	Y	Y	Y
12 Putnam	N	N	Y	Y	Y	Y	N	N	Y	Y	N
13 Miller, D.	N	N	Y	Y	Y	Y	N	N	Y	Y	Y
14 Goss	N	N	Y	Y	Y	Y	N	N	Y	Y	Y
15 Weldon	N	N	Y	Y	Y	Y	N	N	Y	Y	N
16 Foley	Y	N	Y	Y	Y	Y	N	Y	Y	Y	Y
17 Meek	Y	N	Y	N	N	N	Y	Y	N	N	N
18 Ros-Lehtinen	Y	N	Y	Y	Y	Y	N	N	Y	Y	Y
19 Wexler	Y	N	Y	N	?	N	Y	Y	N	Y	N
20 Deutsch	Y	Y	Y	N	?	Y	N	Y	N	Y	N
21 Diaz-Balart	N	N	Y	Y	Y	Y	N	N	Y	Y	?
22 Shaw	N	N	Y	Y	Y	Y	N	N	Y	Y	N
23 Hastings	Y	N	Y	N	N	N	Y	Y	N	N	N
GEORGIA											
1 Kingston	N	Y	Y	Y	Y	Y	N	N	Y	Y	Y
2 Bishop	Y	N	Y	N	N	N	Y	Y	N	N	N
3 Collins	N	N	Y	Y	Y	N	N	?	Y	Y	Y
4 McKinney	Y	Y	N	N	N	N	Y	Y	N	N	?
5 Lewis	Y	N	?	N	N	N	Y	Y	N	N	N
6 Isakson	N	N	Y	Y	Y	Y	N	N	Y	Y	Y
7 Barr	N	N	Y	Y	Y	Y	N	N	Y	Y	N
8 Chambliss	N	N	Y	Y	Y	Y	N	N	Y	Y	N
9 Deal	N	N	Y	Y	Y	Y	N	N	Y	Y	N
10 Norwood	N	N	Y	Y	Y	Y	N	N	Y	Y	N
11 Linder	N	Y	Y	Y	Y	Y	N	N	Y	Y	Y
HAWAII											
1 Abercrombie	Y	Y	Y	N	N	N	Y	Y	N	N	N
2 Mink[1]	Y	Y	Y	N	N	N	Y	Y	N		
IDAHO											
1 Otter	N	N	Y	Y	Y	Y	?	N	Y	Y	N
2 Simpson	N	N	Y	Y	Y	Y	N	N	Y	Y	Y
ILLINOIS											
1 Rush	Y	N	Y	N	N	N	Y	Y	N	N	N
2 Jackson	Y	N	Y	N	N	N	Y	Y	N	N	N
3 Lipinski	N	Y	Y	N	?	N	Y	Y	?	N	N
4 Gutierrez	Y	N	Y	N	N	N	+	Y	N	N	N
5 Blagojevich	Y	N	Y	N	N	N	Y	Y	N	Y	?
6 Hyde	N	N	Y	Y	Y	Y	N	N	Y	Y	Y
7 Davis	Y	N	Y	N	N	N	Y	Y	N	N	N
8 Crane	N	N	?	Y	Y	Y	N	N	Y	Y	N
9 Schakowsky	Y	Y	N	N	N	N	Y	Y	N	N	N
10 Kirk	Y	N	Y	Y	Y	Y	N	Y	Y	Y	Y
11 Weller	N	N	Y	Y	Y	Y	N	N	Y	Y	N
12 Costello	N	N	Y	Y	Y	N	Y	N	N	Y	Y
13 Biggert	N	Y	Y	Y	Y	Y	N	N	Y	Y	Y

[1] Rep. Patsy T. Mink, D, died Sept. 28, 2002. The last vote she cast was vote 9.

KEY

	Democrats	*Republicans*	**Independent**	
Y	Voted for ("yea")		–	Announced against
N	Voted against ("nay")		P	Voted "present"
+	Announced for		C	Voted "present" to avoid
#	Paired for			possible conflict of interest
X	Paired against		?	Did not vote or otherwise
				make a position known

ND Northern Democrats
SD Southern Democrats
Southern states – Ala., Ark., Fla., Ga., Ky., La., Miss., N.C., Okla., S.C., Tenn., Texas, Va.

House Key Votes	1	2	3	4	5	6	7	8	9	10	11
14 Hastert[2]	N		Y	Y	Y	Y	N		Y	Y	Y
15 Johnson	Y	N	Y	Y	Y	Y	N	N	Y	Y	N
16 Manzullo	N	N	Y	Y	Y	N	N	N	Y	Y	N
17 Evans	Y	?	Y	N	N	N	Y	Y	N	N	N
18 LaHood	N	N	Y	Y	Y	Y	N	N	Y	Y	N
19 Phelps	Y	Y	Y	Y	N	N	Y	Y	N	N	N
20 Shimkus	N	N	Y	Y	Y	Y	N	N	Y	Y	N
INDIANA											
1 Visclosky	Y	N	Y	N	N	N	Y	Y	N	N	N
2 Pence	N	N	Y	Y	Y	Y	N	N	Y	Y	N
3 Roemer	Y	Y	Y	N	N	N	Y	Y	N	N	N
4 Souder	N	N	Y	Y	Y	Y	N	N	Y	Y	N
5 Buyer	N	N	Y	?	Y	Y	N	N	Y	Y	Y
6 Burton	N	N	+	Y	+	Y	N	N	Y	Y	N
7 Kerns	N	N	Y	Y	Y	Y	N	N	Y	Y	N
8 Hostettler	N	N	Y	Y	N	N	N	N	N	N	N
9 Hill	Y	N	N	N	N	N	Y	Y	Y	Y	N
10 Carson	Y	Y	Y	N	N	N	Y	Y	N	N	N
IOWA											
1 Leach	Y	Y	Y	Y	Y	Y	Y	N	Y	N	Y
2 Nussle	N	N	Y	Y	Y	Y	N	N	Y	Y	Y
3 Boswell	Y	Y	Y	Y	N	N	Y	Y	N	Y	Y
4 Ganske	Y	N	Y	Y	Y	Y	Y	N	Y	Y	Y
5 Latham	N	Y	Y	Y	Y	Y	N	N	Y	Y	Y
KANSAS											
1 Moran	N	Y	Y	Y	Y	Y	N	N	Y	Y	N
2 Ryun	N	Y	Y	Y	Y	Y	N	N	Y	Y	N
3 Moore	Y	Y	Y	N	N	N	Y	Y	N	Y	Y
4 Tiahrt	N	N	Y	Y	Y	Y	N	N	Y	Y	N
KENTUCKY											
1 Whitfield	N	N	Y	Y	Y	Y	N	N	Y	Y	N
2 Lewis	N	N	Y	Y	Y	Y	N	N	Y	Y	N
3 Northup	N	N	Y	Y	Y	Y	N	N	Y	Y	Y
4 Lucas	Y	N	Y	Y	N	Y	Y	N	Y	Y	Y
5 Rogers	N	N	Y	Y	Y	Y	N	N	Y	Y	Y
6 Fletcher	N	N	Y	Y	Y	Y	N	N	Y	Y	Y
LOUISIANA											
1 Vitter	N	N	Y	Y	Y	Y	N	N	Y	Y	N
2 Jefferson	Y	N	Y	N	N	?	Y	Y	Y	Y	N
3 Tauzin	N	N	Y	Y	Y	Y	N	N	Y	Y	N
4 McCrery	N	N	Y	Y	Y	Y	N	N	Y	Y	Y
5 Cooksey	N	N	Y	Y	Y	N	N	Y	Y	Y	?
6 Baker	N	N	Y	Y	Y	Y	N	N	Y	Y	Y
7 John	Y	N	?	N	N	N	Y	Y	Y	Y	N
MAINE											
1 Allen	Y	N	Y	N	N	N	Y	Y	N	N	N
2 Baldacci	Y	?	Y	N	N	N	Y	Y	N	N	N
MARYLAND											
1 Gilchrest	Y	Y	Y	Y	Y	Y	Y	N	Y	Y	Y
2 Ehrlich	N	Y	Y	Y	Y	Y	Y	N	Y	Y	?
3 Cardin	Y	N	Y	N	N	N	Y	Y	N	N	N
4 Wynn	Y	N	Y	N	N	N	Y	Y	N	Y	Y
5 Hoyer	Y	N	Y	N	N	N	Y	Y	N	Y	N
6 Bartlett	N	Y	Y	Y	Y	Y	Y	N	Y	N	N
7 Cummings	Y	N	Y	N	N	N	Y	Y	N	N	N
8 Morella	Y	N	Y	N	N	Y	Y	Y	Y	N	Y
MASSACHUSETTS											
1 Olver	Y	Y	N	N	N	N	Y	Y	N	N	N
2 Neal	Y	N	Y	N	N	N	Y	Y	N	N	N
3 McGovern	Y	N	N	N	N	N	Y	Y	N	N	N
4 Frank	Y	Y	N	N	N	N	Y	Y	N	N	N
5 Meehan	Y	Y	Y	N	N	N	Y	?	?	N	N
6 Tierney	Y	Y	N	N	N	N	Y	Y	N	N	N
7 Markey	Y	Y	Y	N	N	N	Y	Y	N	N	N
8 Capuano	Y	Y	N	N	N	N	Y	Y	N	N	N
9 Lynch	Y	Y	N	N	N	N	Y	Y	N	N	N
10 Delahunt	Y	Y	N	N	N	N	Y	Y	N	N	N

House Key Votes	1	2	3	4	5	6	7	8	9	10	11
MICHIGAN											
1 Stupak	Y	Y	Y	N	N	N	Y	Y	N	N	N
2 Hoekstra	N	Y	Y	Y	Y	Y	N	N	Y	Y	Y
3 Ehlers	N	N	Y	Y	Y	Y	Y	N	Y	Y	Y
4 Camp	N	N	Y	Y	Y	Y	N	N	Y	Y	Y
5 Barcia	N	N	Y	Y	N	N	Y	Y	N	N	N
6 Upton	Y	N	Y	Y	Y	Y	Y	N	Y	Y	Y
7 Smith	Y	N	Y	Y	Y	N	N	N	Y	Y	Y
8 Rogers	N	Y	Y	Y	Y	Y	N	N	Y	Y	Y
9 Kildee	Y	N	Y	N	N	N	Y	Y	N	N	N
10 Bonior	Y	N	N	N	N	N	?	Y	N	N	N
11 Knollenberg	N	N	Y	Y	Y	Y	–	N	Y	Y	Y
12 Levin	Y	N	Y	N	N	N	Y	Y	N	N	N
13 Rivers	Y	Y	N	N	N	N	Y	Y	N	N	Y
14 Conyers	Y	Y	N	N	N	N	Y	Y	N	N	N
15 Kilpatrick	Y	Y	N	N	N	N	Y	Y	N	N	N
16 Dingell	Y	Y	Y	N	N	N	Y	Y	N	N	N
MINNESOTA											
1 Gutknecht	N	N	Y	Y	Y	Y	N	Y	Y	Y	N
2 Kennedy	N	N	+	Y	Y	Y	N	N	Y	Y	N
3 Ramstad	Y	Y	Y	Y	Y	Y	N	N	Y	Y	Y
4 McCollum	Y	Y	Y	N	N	N	Y	Y	N	N	N
5 Sabo	Y	Y	Y	N	N	N	Y	Y	N	N	N
6 Luther	Y	Y	Y	N	N	N	Y	Y	N	N	N
7 Peterson	N	Y	Y	Y	N	Y	Y	Y	N	Y	N
8 Oberstar	Y	Y	N	N	N	N	Y	Y	N	N	N
MISSISSIPPI											
1 Wicker	N	Y	Y	Y	N	Y	N	N	Y	Y	N
2 Thompson	N	N	N	N	N	N	Y	Y	N	N	N
3 Pickering	N	N	Y	Y	Y	Y	N	N	Y	Y	N
4 Shows	N	N	Y	N	N	N	Y	Y	N	Y	N
5 Taylor	Y	N	Y	N	N	N	Y	Y	N	N	N
MISSOURI											
1 Clay	Y	N	?	N	N	?	?	Y	N	N	N
2 Akin	N	N	Y	Y	Y	Y	N	N	Y	Y	N
3 Gephardt	Y	Y	Y	N	N	N	Y	Y	N	N	N
4 Skelton	Y	Y	Y	N	N	N	Y	Y	Y	Y	Y
5 McCarthy	Y	Y	Y	N	N	N	+	Y	N	N	N
6 Graves	N	N	Y	Y	Y	Y	N	N	Y	Y	Y
7 Blunt	N	N	Y	Y	Y	Y	?	?	?	Y	Y
8 Emerson	N	N	Y	Y	+	N	Y	Y	Y	Y	Y
9 Hulshof	N	N	Y	Y	Y	Y	N	N	Y	Y	Y
MONTANA											
AL Rehberg	N	N	Y	Y	Y	Y	N	N	Y	Y	N
NEBRASKA											
1 Bereuter	Y	Y	Y	Y	Y	Y	N	N	Y	Y	Y
2 Terry	N	N	Y	Y	Y	Y	N	N	Y	Y	Y
3 Osborne	Y	N	Y	Y	Y	Y	N	N	Y	Y	N
NEVADA											
1 Berkley	Y	Y	Y	N	N	N	Y	Y	N	N	N
2 Gibbons	N	N	Y	Y	Y	Y	N	N	Y	Y	Y
NEW HAMPSHIRE											
1 Sununu	N	Y	Y	Y	Y	Y	N	N	Y	Y	Y
2 Bass	Y	N	Y	Y	Y	Y	N	N	Y	Y	Y
NEW JERSEY											
1 Andrews	Y	Y	Y	N	N	N	Y	Y	N	N	N
2 LoBiondo	Y	N	Y	Y	Y	Y	Y	N	N	Y	N
3 Saxton	N	N	Y	Y	Y	Y	Y	N	Y	Y	N
4 Smith	N	N	Y	Y	Y	Y	Y	N	N	Y	N
5 Roukema	?	Y	?	Y	Y	?	?	N	?	?	?
6 Pallone	Y	Y	Y	N	N	N	Y	Y	N	N	N
7 Ferguson	N	N	Y	Y	Y	Y	Y	N	Y	Y	N
8 Pascrell	Y	N	Y	N	N	N	Y	Y	N	N	N
9 Rothman	Y	Y	Y	N	N	N	Y	Y	N	N	Y
10 Payne	Y	Y	Y	N	N	N	Y	Y	N	N	N
11 Frelinghuysen	Y	Y	Y	Y	Y	Y	Y	N	Y	Y	Y
12 Holt	Y	Y	Y	N	N	N	Y	Y	N	N	N
13 Menendez	Y	N	Y	N	N	N	Y	Y	N	N	N
NEW MEXICO											
1 Wilson	N	Y	Y	Y	Y	Y	N	N	Y	Y	Y
2 Skeen	N	Y	Y	Y	Y	Y	N	N	Y	Y	Y
3 Udall	Y	Y	Y	N	N	N	Y	Y	N	N	N
NEW YORK											
1 Grucci	Y	N	Y	Y	Y	Y	N	N	Y	Y	+
2 Israel	Y	Y	Y	N	N	Y	Y	Y	N	Y	Y
3 King	N	N	Y	?	Y	Y	N	N	Y	Y	Y
4 McCarthy	Y	N	Y	N	N	N	Y	Y	N	Y	Y
5 Ackerman	Y	N	Y	N	N	N	Y	Y	N	N	N
6 Meeks	Y	N	Y	N	N	N	Y	Y	N	N	N
7 Crowley	Y	Y	Y	N	N	N	Y	Y	N	N	N
8 Nadler	Y	Y	N	N	N	N	Y	Y	N	N	N

House Key Votes	1	2	3	4	5	6	7	8	9	10	11
9 Weiner	Y	Y	N	N	N	N	Y	Y	N	Y	N
10 Towns	Y	N	N	N	N	?	Y	Y	N	N	N
11 Owens	Y	Y	N	N	N	N	Y	Y	N	N	N
12 Velázquez	Y	Y	N	N	N	N	Y	Y	N	N	N
13 *Fossella*	N	N	Y	Y	Y	Y	N	N	Y	Y	Y
14 Maloney	Y	Y	Y	N	N	N	Y	Y	N	Y	Y
15 Rangel	Y	Y	N	N	N	N	Y	Y	N	N	N
16 Serrano	Y	N	N	N	N	N	Y	Y	N	N	N
17 Engel	Y	N	Y	N	N	N	Y	Y	N	N	N
18 Lowey	Y	Y	Y	N	N	N	Y	Y	N	N	N
19 *Kelly*	N	N	Y	Y	Y	Y	N	N	Y	Y	Y
20 *Gilman*	Y	–	Y	Y	Y	Y	N	Y	N	Y	Y
21 McNulty	Y	Y	N	N	N	N	Y	Y	N	N	N
22 *Sweeney*	N	N	Y	Y	Y	Y	N	Y	N	Y	Y
23 *Boehlert*	Y	N	Y	Y	Y	Y	N	Y	N	Y	Y
24 *McHugh*	Y	N	Y	Y	Y	Y	N	N	N	Y	Y
25 *Walsh*	Y	N	Y	Y	Y	Y	N	N	N	Y	Y
26 Hinchey	Y	Y	N	N	N	N	Y	Y	N	N	N
27 *Reynolds*	N	N	Y	Y	Y	Y	N	Y	N	Y	Y
28 Slaughter	Y	Y	Y	N	N	N	?	Y	N	N	N
29 LaFalce	Y	Y	Y	N	N	N	?	Y	N	N	N
30 *Quinn*	Y	N	Y	Y	Y	Y	N	N	N	Y	Y
31 *Houghton*	Y	N	Y	Y	Y	Y	N	N	Y	N	?
NORTH CAROLINA											
1 Clayton	Y	N	N	N	N	N	Y	Y	N	N	N
2 Etheridge	Y	Y	Y	N	N	N	Y	Y	Y	Y	Y
3 *Jones*	N	Y	Y	Y	Y	Y	Y	N	N	Y	N
4 Price	Y	N	Y	N	N	N	Y	Y	N	N	Y
5 *Burr*	N	N	Y	Y	Y	Y	N	N	Y	Y	Y
6 *Coble*	N	N	Y	Y	Y	Y	N	N	Y	Y	Y
7 McIntyre	Y	N	Y	N	N	N	Y	Y	N	N	N
8 *Hayes*	N	N	Y	Y	Y	Y	N	N	N	Y	N
9 *Myrick*	N	N	Y	Y	Y	Y	N	N	Y	Y	Y
10 *Ballenger*	N	N	Y	Y	Y	Y	N	N	N	Y	Y
11 *Taylor*	N	N	Y	Y	Y	Y	N	N	N	Y	Y
12 Watt	Y	Y	N	N	N	N	Y	Y	N	N	N
NORTH DAKOTA											
AL Pomeroy	Y	Y	Y	Y	N	N	N	Y	N	Y	N
OHIO											
1 *Chabot*	N	Y	Y	Y	Y	Y	N	N	Y	Y	Y
2 *Portman*	N	N	Y	Y	Y	Y	N	N	Y	Y	N
3 Hall[3]	Y	N	?	N	N	N	?	Y	N		
4 *Oxley*	N	N	Y	Y	Y	Y	N	N	Y	Y	Y
5 *Gillmor*	N	N	Y	Y	Y	Y	N	N	Y	Y	Y
6 Strickland	Y	N	N	N	N	N	Y	Y	N	N	N
7 *Hobson*	N	Y	Y	Y	Y	Y	N	N	Y	Y	Y
8 *Boehner*	N	N	Y	Y	Y	Y	?	N	Y	Y	Y
9 Kaptur	Y	Y	Y	N	N	N	Y	Y	N	N	N
10 Kucinich	Y	Y	N	N	N	N	Y	Y	N	N	N
11 Jones	Y	Y	Y	N	N	N	Y	Y	N	N	N
12 *Tiberi*	N	N	Y	Y	Y	Y	N	N	Y	Y	Y
13 Brown	Y	Y	N	N	N	N	Y	Y	N	N	N
14 Sawyer	Y	N	Y	N	N	N	Y	Y	N	N	N
15 *Pryce*	N	N	Y	Y	Y	Y	N	N	Y	Y	Y
16 *Regula*	N	N	Y	Y	Y	Y	N	N	N	Y	Y
17 Traficant[4]	?	?	?	?	?	?					
18 *Ney*	N	N	Y	Y	Y	Y	N	N	Y	Y	Y
19 *LaTourette*	Y	N	Y	Y	Y	Y	Y	N	N	Y	Y
OKLAHOMA											
1 *Largent/Sullivan*[5]	N	N	Y	Y	Y	Y	N	N	Y	Y	N
2 Carson	Y	Y	Y	N	N	N	Y	Y	Y	Y	Y
3 *Watkins*	N	N	Y	Y	Y	Y	N	N	Y	Y	Y
4 *Watts*	N	Y	Y	Y	Y	Y	N	N	Y	Y	Y
5 *Istook*	N	N	Y	Y	N	Y	N	N	Y	Y	N
6 *Lucas*	N	N	Y	Y	Y	Y	N	N	Y	Y	Y
OREGON											
1 Wu	Y	Y	N	Y	N	N	Y	Y	N	N	Y
2 *Walden*	N	N	Y	Y	Y	Y	N	N	Y	Y	Y
3 Blumenauer	Y	Y	N	N	N	N	Y	Y	N	N	N
4 DeFazio	Y	Y	N	N	N	N	Y	Y	N	N	N
5 Hooley	Y	Y	Y	N	N	N	Y	Y	N	N	?
PENNSYLVANIA											
1 Brady	Y	N	Y	N	N	N	Y	Y	N	N	N
2 Fattah	Y	Y	Y	N	N	N	Y	Y	N	N	N
3 Borski	Y	Y	Y	N	N	N	Y	Y	N	Y	N
4 *Hart*	N	N	Y	Y	Y	Y	N	N	Y	Y	Y
5 *Peterson*	N	Y	Y	Y	Y	Y	N	N	Y	Y	Y
6 Holden	Y	Y	Y	N	N	N	Y	Y	N	Y	N
7 *Weldon*	Y	Y	Y	Y	Y	Y	N	N	Y	Y	Y
8 *Greenwood*	N	Y	Y	Y	Y	Y	N	N	Y	Y	Y
9 *Shuster, Bill*	N	N	Y	Y	Y	Y	N	N	Y	Y	Y
10 *Sherwood*	N	N	Y	Y	Y	Y	N	N	Y	Y	Y

House Key Votes	1	2	3	4	5	6	7	8	9	10	11
11 Kanjorski	Y	Y	Y	N	Y	N	Y	Y	N	Y	N
12 Murtha	N	N	Y	?	N	N	?	Y	N	Y	N
13 Hoeffel	Y	Y	Y	N	N	N	Y	Y	N	Y	N
14 Coyne	Y	Y	N	N	N	N	Y	Y	N	N	N
15 *Toomey*	N	N	Y	Y	Y	Y	N	N	Y	Y	?
16 *Pitts*	N	Y	Y	Y	Y	Y	N	N	Y	Y	N
17 *Gekas*	N	N	Y	Y	Y	Y	N	N	Y	Y	Y
18 Doyle	Y	Y	Y	N	N	N	Y	Y	N	N	N
19 *Platts*	Y	Y	Y	Y	Y	Y	N	N	Y	Y	Y
20 Mascara	Y	Y	Y	–	?	N	Y	Y	N	Y	N
21 *English*	N	N	Y	Y	Y	Y	N	N	Y	Y	Y
RHODE ISLAND											
1 Kennedy	Y	N	Y	N	N	N	Y	Y	N	Y	N
2 Langevin	Y	N	Y	N	N	N	Y	Y	N	N	N
SOUTH CAROLINA											
1 *Brown*	N	N	Y	Y	Y	Y	N	N	Y	Y	Y
2 *Wilson*	N	N	Y	Y	Y	Y	N	N	Y	Y	N
3 *Graham*	Y	N	Y	Y	Y	Y	N	N	Y	Y	N
4 *DeMint*	N	Y	Y	Y	Y	Y	N	N	Y	Y	N
5 Spratt	Y	N	Y	N	N	N	Y	Y	N	Y	Y
6 Clyburn	Y	N	Y	N	N	N	Y	Y	N	N	N
SOUTH DAKOTA											
AL *Thune*	Y	Y	Y	Y	Y	Y	N	N	Y	Y	N
TENNESSEE											
1 *Jenkins*	N	Y	Y	Y	Y	Y	N	N	Y	Y	Y
2 *Duncan*	N	Y	Y	Y	Y	Y	N	N	N	N	Y
3 *Wamp*	Y	Y	Y	Y	P	Y	N	N	Y	Y	N
4 *Hilleary*	N	N	Y	Y	Y	Y	N	N	Y	Y	N
5 Clement	Y	N	Y	N	N	N	Y	Y	N	Y	N
6 *Gordon*	Y	N	Y	N	N	N	?	Y	N	Y	Y
7 *Bryant*	N	N	Y	Y	Y	Y	N	N	Y	Y	N
8 Tanner	Y	N	Y	?	N	N	Y	Y	Y	Y	Y
9 Ford	Y	N	Y	N	N	N	Y	Y	N	N	N
TEXAS											
1 Sandlin	Y	N	Y	N	N	N	Y	Y	N	Y	N
2 Turner	Y	N	Y	N	N	N	?	Y	N	Y	Y
3 *Johnson, Sam*	N	Y	Y	Y	Y	Y	N	N	Y	Y	N
4 Hall	N	N	Y	Y	Y	Y	N	N	Y	Y	N
5 *Sessions*	N	N	Y	Y	Y	Y	N	N	Y	Y	Y
6 *Barton*	N	N	Y	Y	Y	Y	N	N	Y	Y	Y
7 *Culberson*	N	N	Y	Y	Y	Y	N	N	Y	Y	Y
8 *Brady*	?	N	Y	Y	Y	Y	N	N	Y	Y	Y
9 Lampson	Y	N	Y	?	N	N	Y	Y	N	Y	Y
10 Doggett	Y	Y	N	N	N	N	Y	Y	N	N	N
11 Edwards	Y	N	Y	N	N	N	Y	Y	N	Y	Y
12 *Granger*	N	N	Y	Y	Y	Y	N	N	Y	Y	Y
13 *Thornberry*	N	N	Y	Y	Y	Y	N	N	Y	Y	Y
14 *Paul*	N	Y	N	N	Y	?	N	N	N	N	N
15 Hinojosa	Y	N	Y	N	N	N	Y	Y	N	N	N
16 Reyes	Y	N	?	N	N	N	Y	Y	N	Y	N
17 Stenholm	Y	N	Y	N	N	N	Y	Y	Y	Y	Y
18 Jackson-Lee	Y	N	Y	N	N	N	Y	Y	N	N	N
19 *Combest*	N	Y	?	?	Y	Y	?	N	?	Y	?
20 Gonzalez	Y	N	Y	N	N	N	Y	Y	N	Y	N
21 *Smith*	N	N	Y	Y	Y	Y	N	N	Y	Y	Y
22 *DeLay*	N	N	Y	Y	Y	Y	N	N	Y	Y	Y
23 *Bonilla*	N	N	Y	Y	P	Y	N	N	Y	Y	Y
24 Frost	Y	N	Y	N	N	N	Y	Y	N	Y	Y
25 Bentsen	Y	N	Y	N	N	N	Y	Y	N	Y	Y
26 *Armey*	N	N	Y	Y	Y	Y	N	N	Y	Y	Y
27 Ortiz	Y	N	Y	N	N	N	Y	Y	N	+	N
28 Rodriguez	Y	N	Y	N	N	N	Y	Y	N	N	N
29 Green	Y	N	Y	N	N	N	Y	Y	N	Y	N
30 Johnson, E.B.	Y	Y	Y	N	N	N	Y	Y	N	N	Y
UTAH											
1 *Hansen*	N	Y	Y	Y	Y	Y	?	N	?	Y	Y
2 *Matheson*	Y	N	Y	N	N	Y	Y	Y	Y	Y	Y
3 *Cannon*	N	Y	?	Y	Y	Y	N	N	Y	Y	Y

[2] The Speaker votes only at his discretion, usually to break a tie or to emphasize the importance of a matter.

[3] Rep. Tony P. Hall, D, resigned effective Sept. 9, 2002. The last vote for which he was eligible was vote 9. No election was held for a replacement during the 107th Congress.

[4] Rep. James A. Traficant Jr., D, was expelled from the House of Representatives July 24, 2002. The last vote for which he was eligible was vote 6. No election was held for a replacement during the 107th Congress.

[5] Steve Largent, R, resigned effective Feb. 15, 2002, to run for governor of Oklahoma. The last vote for which Largent was eligible was vote 1. He was succeeded by Rep. John Sullivan, R, who was sworn Feb. 27, 2002. The first vote for which Sullivan was eligible was vote 2.

	KEY		
	Democrats	*Republicans*	**Independent**
Y	Voted for ("yea")	–	Announced against
N	Voted against ("nay")	P	Voted "present"
+	Announced for	C	Voted "present" to avoid possible conflict of interest
#	Paired for	?	Did not vote or otherwise make a position known
X	Paired against		

ND Northern Democrats
SD Southern Democrats
Southern states – Ala., Ark., Fla., Ga., Ky., La., Miss., N.C., Okla., S.C., Tenn., Texas, Va.

House Key Votes	1	2	3	4	5	6	7	8	9	10	11
VERMONT											
AL **Sanders**	Y	Y	N	N	N	N	Y	Y	N	N	N
VIRGINIA											
1 *Davis, J.*	N	N	Y	Y	Y	Y	N	N	N	Y	N
2 *Schrock*	N	N	Y	Y	Y	Y	N	N	Y	Y	Y
3 Scott	N	Y	Y	N	N	N	Y	Y	N	N	N
4 *Forbes*	N	Y	Y	Y	Y	Y	N	N	Y	Y	N
5 *Goode*[6]	N	Y	Y	Y	Y	Y	N	N	N	Y	N
6 *Goodlatte*	N	N	Y	Y	Y	Y	N	N	Y	Y	N
7 *Cantor*	N	Y	Y	Y	Y	Y	N	N	Y	Y	Y
8 Moran	Y	Y	Y	N	N	N	Y	Y	Y	N	Y
9 Boucher	N	N	Y	N	N	N	?	Y	N	Y	Y
10 *Wolf*	Y	Y	Y	Y	Y	Y	Y	N	Y	Y	N
11 *Davis, T.*	N	Y	Y	Y	Y	Y	?	N	Y	Y	?

House Key Votes	1	2	3	4	5	6	7	8	9	10	11
WASHINGTON											
1 Inslee	Y	Y	Y	N	N	N	Y	Y	N	N	N
2 Larsen	Y	N	Y	N	N	N	Y	Y	Y	N	Y
3 Baird	Y	Y	Y	N	N	N	Y	Y	N	N	Y
4 *Hastings*	N	Y	Y	Y	Y	Y	N	N	Y	Y	Y
5 *Nethercutt*	N	N	+	Y	P	Y	Y	N	Y	Y	Y
6 Dicks	Y	N	Y	N	N	N	Y	Y	Y	Y	Y
7 McDermott	Y	Y	N	N	N	N	Y	Y	N	N	N
8 *Dunn*	N	Y	Y	Y	Y	Y	N	N	Y	Y	Y
9 Smith	Y	N	Y	N	N	N	?	Y	Y	Y	Y
WEST VIRGINIA											
1 Mollohan	N	N	Y	N	N	N	Y	Y	N	N	N
2 *Capito*	Y	N	Y	Y	Y	Y	Y	Y	N	Y	Y
3 Rahall	N	N	Y	N	N	N	Y	Y	N	N	N
WISCONSIN											
1 *Ryan*	N	N	Y	Y	Y	Y	N	N	Y	Y	Y
2 Baldwin	Y	N	N	N	N	N	Y	Y	N	N	N
3 Kind	Y	N	N	N	N	N	Y	Y	N	Y	Y
4 Kleczka	Y	Y	N	N	N	N	Y	Y	N	N	N
5 Barrett	Y	Y	N	N	N	N	Y	Y	N	N	N
6 *Petri*	Y	N	Y	Y	Y	Y	N	Y	Y	Y	Y
7 Obey	Y	Y	N	N	N	N	Y	Y	N	N	N
8 *Green*	N	N	Y	Y	Y	Y	N	N	Y	Y	Y
9 *Sensenbrenner*	N	Y	Y	Y	Y	Y	N	N	Y	Y	Y
WYOMING											
AL *Cubin*	?	?	Y	Y	Y	Y	N	N	Y	Y	N

[6] Rep. Virgil H. Goode Jr. of Virginia switched his party affiliation from independent to Republican, effective Aug. 1, 2002.

Senate

1. CLEAN AIR ACT

The administration of George W. Bush proposed in December 2002 a regulatory change to reinterpret a provision of the 1990 Clean Air Act (PL 101-549) that required some new or expanded power plants and factories to install updated antipollution equipment. The administration's plan allowed power plants and factories greater leeway to make changes under "routine maintenance," which did not require federal review or new pollution control equipment.

An amendment to a fiscal 2003 omnibus appropriations bill (H J Res 2—PL 108-7), offered by John Edwards, D-N.C., would have delayed the proposed pollution control regulations for six months. It also would have required a National Academy of Sciences study "to determine the effects of the final rule on air pollution and human health." Critics—including Northeastern Republican senators who would prove pivotal on a number of environmental issues throughout the year—said the rule would allow power plants to pollute more, costing states more for environmental cleanup. The administration disputed that and said power plants were now discouraged from performing routine maintenance because of the burdensome regulations. (Legislative details, p. 437)

Christine Todd Whitman, administrator of the Environmental Protection Agency (EPA) at the time, lobbied undecided members on Jan. 21, the night before the Senate vote. Her biggest challenge was to persuade northeastern Republicans. The coal-burning factories and power plants targeted by the pollution controls were concentrated in the Midwest and parts of the South but their emissions often were carried by easterly winds to the Northeast and fell to the ground as acid rain. She did not succeed: all five northeastern Republicans and independent James M. Jeffords of Vermont voted for the amendment. However the administration brought a handful of southern Democrats to its side: the four senators from Louisiana and Arkansas, and Zell Miller of Georgia. The final vote against the Edwards amendment was 46–50: R 6–45; D 39–5; I 1–0. (Vote, p. 847)

The regional breakdown of New England Republicans opposing the president and some southern Democrats backing him reflected Senate sentiment on environmental issues in 2003, a division that later would be repeated on omnibus energy legislation, global warming, and an air pollution proposal from the president. Before the Edwards amendment was defeated, the Senate adopted, 51–45, an alternative offered by James M. Inhofe, R-Okla., chairman of the Environment and Public Works Committee, calling for the same study but allowing the new rules to take effect in March. Democrats claimed they were pleased with the closeness of the vote. They expected to return to the issue during 2004, and they gained a partial victory when implementation of the rule was blocked by a federal court on Christmas Eve.

2. FIRST ESTRADA CLOTURE VOTE

The use of the filibuster in the Senate had historically been focused on legislation; it was only rarely employed on nominations from the president. Only one judicial nomination had been successfully filibustered: the proposed elevation of Supreme Court Justice Abe Fortas to chief justice of the United States was blocked in 1968 when a motion to stop debate and bring his nomination to a vote was defeated. Fortas then withdrew his candidacy. Before 2003 judicial candidates were rejected on occasion but no lower-court nomination had been blocked by a filibuster. Senators had tried to conduct filibusters against nominees to the U.S. Courts of Appeals but eventually votes were held on each of the nominees.

Senate Democrats knew this history as they mulled in early 2003 trying to block a vote on Miguel A. Estrada, a lawyer in private practice nominated for a seat on the influential Court of Appeals for the District of Columbia Circuit. To do so successfully, Democrats needed forty-one votes against invoking cloture. Senate rules require sixty votes to end prolonged debate and bring an issue or nomination to a vote. Many Democrats argued that Estrada might be too conservative and, unlike most appellate nominees, he had not built a dossier of opinions that set out his legal philosophy. The Bush administration had rebuffed Democratic requests for access to some of Estrada's memos and work papers from the time he served in the solicitor general's office during the Clinton administration. (Nomination details, p. 623)

GOP leaders began debate on Estrada's nomination Feb. 4 but did not schedule a vote immediately. For weeks, the nomination was the main business on the Senate floor as Republican leaders weighed how to go forward. Many in the GOP caucus were reluctant to vote on—and risk losing—a motion to invoke cloture. Some Democrats were concerned that a filibuster would someday haunt the party when it was once again in control of the presidency. But others argued that Estrada's confirmation would encourage the Bush administration to send similar conservative judicial nominations as vacancies occurred. Democrats by Feb. 11 had secured more than the necessary forty-one votes to continue the filibuster but Republican leaders did not schedule a vote until March 6 and then fell five votes short in invoking cloture: 55–44: R 51–0; D 4–43; I 0–1. (Vote, p. 847)

The vote showed that even as the minority party Democrats could exert some control over who was seated on the federal bench. It also raised the stakes in the already rancorous struggle over the shape of the judiciary. Democrats used the same strategy to block five other nominations in 2003. Republicans sought to invoke cloture to force a vote on those candidates and Estrada a total of fifteen more times over the year but they never got any closer to the sixty votes they needed. On Sept. 4 Bush withdrew Estrada's nomination at the candidate's request after seven attempts to bring his name to a vote were defeated.

Use of filibusters to block judicial nominations added to already existing tensions in the usually civilized Senate. Twice during the year an angry and frustrated Majority Leader Bill Frist, R-Tenn., scheduled a series of back-to-back cloture votes on contentious nominees. He also proposed a plan to change Senate rules that would make it more difficult to sustain a filibuster of a presidential nominee. (Details, p. 625)

3. ARCTIC NATIONAL WILDLIFE REFUGEE

President Bush's energy plan, first released in 2001, focused largely on increasing domestic production of oil, gas, and coal to reduce the nation's dependence on foreign oil. A main element of Bush's plan was oil drilling in the Arctic National Wildlife Refuge (ANWR), a remote area on Alaska's northern coast. But efforts in the 107th

Congress to authorize drilling in ANWR were blocked in the Senate by environmentalists, who argued that it would harm wildlife in the refuge. Supporters of the plan countered that it would provide a new source of energy and create hundreds of thousands of jobs. (*Legislative details, p. 432*)

After an attempt to break a Democratic filibuster mustered just forty-six votes in 2002, Republican leaders tried a new approach in the 108th Congress. They sought to sidestep a filibuster by including a provision in the Senate version of the budget resolution (S Con Res 23) to provide de facto authority for oil drilling in ANWR by assuming there would be $2.1 billion in revenue in fiscal 2004 from federal royalties from energy leases in the refuge. Revenue and spending provisions in the budget resolution were protected from filibusters.

GOP leaders then set about winning the simple majority needed to keep the language from being stripped from the resolution. They targeted four senators they thought might be wavering—Arkansas Democrats Mark Pryor and Blanche Lincoln, and Republicans Gordon H. Smith of Oregon and Norm Coleman of Minnesota. But all four later voted against allowing ANWR drilling. On March 19, 2003, the Senate voted to adopt an amendment by Barbara Boxer, D-Calif., stripping the ANWR language from the budget resolution. The vote was 52–48: R 8–43; D 43–5 ; I 1–0. (*Vote, p. 847*)

4. TAX CUT LIMITATIONS

Bush began the fiscal 2004 budget cycle with a politically ambitious proposal—$1.5 trillion in tax cuts over the next decade including an eleven-year, $726 billion "economic growth" package. Released amid dire predictions about a soaring federal budget deficit and less than two years after the 2001 tax cut (PL 107-16), the plan immediately drew fire from Democrats and skepticism from some Republicans. Bush's plan called for accelerating implementation of the 2001 tax law and eliminating taxes on stock dividends. House and Senate Republican budget writers agreed to put the recommendations in a budget "reconciliation" package. By doing so they would give the tax cut package protection against Democratic-led filibusters in the closely divided Senate. (*Legislative details, p. 105*)

But in early March, as Senate Budget Chairman Don Nickles, R-Okla., and his conservative-dominated panel constructed a procedural blueprint (S Con Res 23) for Bush's plan, Senate centrists began to formulate an alternative proposal. They supported some tax cuts to invigorate the economy but concluded that a plan as expensive as Bush's was inappropriate given the deficit and the costs of the looming war in Iraq. The group, led by Democrat John B. Breaux of Louisiana with Republicans George V. Voinovich of Ohio and Olympia J. Snowe of Maine, decided the tax cut package should be pared down by more than half, to $350 billion.

Doubt existed that the group would stay unified and bring other Democrats and a few Republicans to their plan. Some Democrats were opposed to any tax cut but many nonetheless backed the moderates' smaller reduction as an acceptable alternative to Bush's plan. But when one of them—Ernest F. Hollings of South Carolina—refused to sign on it was clear the plan would be just short of fifty-one votes. Several Democrats then withdrew their support and the amendment was defeated, 38–62.

Republican leaders were anxious to complete a budget resolution quickly but Democrats, angry that GOP leaders were pushing for a final budget vote before the Bush administration released the cost of its expected Iraq war spending supplemental, forced Majority Leader Bill Frist, R-Tenn., to suspend debate until the following week. The delay, as it turned out, breathed new life into Breaux's proposal. Over the weekend, the administration announced that its supplemental re-

quest would be for $74.7 billion, a staggering figure that came just as U.S. troops began to encounter strong resistance in Iraq.

When the Senate returned to the budget debate, Breaux decided to try again. He knew that despite the lopsided setback of the previous week, he was really only one or two votes short, and that most Democrats opposed to any tax cuts would support his $350 billion ceiling if they were certain it would be adopted. Hollings did not rule out switching his vote, and Republican moderate Lincoln Chafee of Rhode Island said that while he opposed new tax cuts, he would provide the winning vote if needed to help shrink the package.

Breaux tweaked his amendment, adding nonbinding language that would earmark the revenue saved by reducing the tax cuts for Social Security. On March 25 Breaux brought his new amendment to the floor and surprised Senate Republican leaders. Hollings, Chafee, and another holdout, Tom Harkin, D-Iowa, voted for the amendment, prompting other Democrats to follow suit. The vote to adopt the amendment was 51–48: R 3–48; D 47–0; I 1–0. (*Vote, p. 847*)

5. PRESCRIPTION DRUGS THROUGH MEDICARE

In two previous Congresses, the Senate had been the graveyard for Medicare prescription drug bills passed by the House. In both 2000 and 2002 the House passed bills under which private companies would develop drug plans for seniors but the Senate never considered them. Democrats and Republicans could not get past their fundamental differences over how to structure a Medicare prescription drug program. Democrats thought it should be an addition to the Medicare program, available to all; Republicans preferred a private-sector approach.

That stalemate was broken in 2003 when Finance Chairman Charles E. Grassley, R-Iowa, and ranking Democrat Max Baucus of Montana drafted their bill (S 1) that split their differences. Among the provisions in their bill was one that would guarantee that a government-run "fallback" plan would be available to seniors who did not have a choice of at least two private drug plans in their area. (*Legislative details, p. 497*)

Senators from both parties had reasons to oppose the bill. Conservative Republicans disliked the idea of creating a new $400 billion entitlement for prescription drug coverage—particularly without a larger role for the private sector and stronger measures to control costs. Democrats saw gaping holes in the bill's coverage: under the Finance Committee measure, beneficiaries would have to pay all of their prescription drug costs between $4,500 and $5,813 a year because Medicare would not have enough money available to pay those costs. They warned that premiums would vary across the country, meaning some seniors might have to pay well above the national average of $35 a month. Democrats also knew that the passage of a bill while Republicans held the White House and majorities in the House and Senate would deprive Democrats of the chance to do it their way—even though a Medicare prescription drug benefit was originally their idea.

But it was the backing of one Democrat—Sen. Edward M. Kennedy of Massachusetts—that made it possible for leaders to sustain any rebellion against the bill. Kennedy, who has exercised a leadership role on health care in the Democratic caucus for many years, believed that it would be a mistake to miss the chance to put a program in place, which he contended could be improved later. When the measure reached the Senate floor Republican and Democratic leaders did their best to maintain the bipartisan balance. Democrats offered amendments to provide more generous benefits in the bill but they did not raise serious objections when the amendments were defeated. Majority Leader Bill Frist, R-Tenn., said he hoped for a bigger private-sector role but he also urged his GOP colleagues to avoid changes that would jeopardize strong Democratic support.

As the Senate moved toward final passage late the night of June 26, a last-minute threat to the bill developed in the form of an amendment by Dianne Feinstein, D-Calif., and Don Nickles, R-Okla., to tie Medicare premiums to beneficiaries' incomes. Kennedy, who said he believed Medicare's broad public support would be jeopardized if wealthy seniors had to pay more than others, opposed the amendment. In a shouting match on the floor with Feinstein and Rick Santorum, R-Pa., he threatened to hold the bill hostage unless the amendment was defeated. To appease Kennedy, senators engineered a defeat of the amendment by voice vote, in which Democrats prevailed by yelling "no" at the top of their lungs. Only a handful of liberal Democrats and conservative Republicans did not to back the legislation on the final vote. The Grassley-Baucus bill won strong bipartisan support when the Senate voted in the early morning hours of June 27, 76–21: R 40–10; D 35–11; I 1–0. *(Vote, p. 847)*

The bipartisan approach did not last beyond the passage of the Senate bill. In drafting the final measure with the House Republican negotiators excluded all Democrats except two centrists: Baucus and John B. Breaux, D-La. That allowed them to write a conference report more acceptable to conservative Republicans. But it lost the support of most Democrats, including Kennedy. By that time, however, the Medicare bill had risen from the Senate graveyard—and in doing so, it had picked up the momentum it needed to survive final negotiations and become law.

6. OVERTIME RULES

Democratic Sen. Tom Harkin of Iowa had a hunch that he could defeat Bush administration efforts to streamline the nation's labor laws. Harkin knew that organized labor had spent the August recess lobbying intensely against a proposed Labor Department rule that would change the eligibility for overtime pay but he needed a little scheduling help to ensure victory. The proposed rule would make 1.3 million low-income workers eligible for overtime pay for the first time. But it also would strip about 650,000 white-collar workers of their eligibility for overtime pay, according to the department. Opponents argued that as many as 8 million workers would lose their overtime rights under the proposal. *(Legislative details, p. 574)*

The AFL-CIO launched a grassroots effort targeting vulnerable incumbents and senators from states with a large union membership. The union ran ads in support of an amendment Harkin planned to offer to the Labor–Health and Human Services (HHS)–Education spending bill (HR 2660), which would ban funding for any rule that would take away overtime pay eligibility. The commercials aired in Maine, Ohio, Missouri, and nationally on CNN. The House had narrowly defeated a similar measure by three votes in July.

Holding up a vote on the amendment, the Republican leadership was miffed that Democrats wanted to dictate the timing of the vote to ensure that all four Senate Democratic presidential aspirants could attend. The four—Joseph I. Lieberman of Connecticut, John Kerry of Massachusetts, John Edwards of North Carolina, and Bob Graham of Florida—missed votes during 2003 while campaigning in early primary states. But given the importance of the vote to organized labor all four said they would be there when a time was set for the vote.

Under pressure to move appropriations measures through the Senate, Majority Leader Bill Frist, R-Tenn., finally agreed to set the vote for Sept. 10. Democrats were united, with only Zell Miller of Georgia voting against the amendment. Meanwhile, six Republicans defected. Of that number, three—Lisa Murkowski of Alaska, Ben Nighthorse

Campbell of Colorado, and Arlen Specter of Pennsylvania—were up for reelection in 2004 in states where organized labor was a powerful political force. The amendment was adopted 54–45: R 6–44, D 47–1; 1–0. *(Vote, p. 847)*

The vote was a major rebuke for the administration, as key GOP lawmakers voted with Democrats. They included Specter, who was sponsor of the Senate's version of the Labor-HHS-Education bill (S 1356), and Senate Appropriations Chairman Ted Stevens of Alaska. Moderate Republicans Lincoln Chafee of Rhode Island and Olympia J. Snowe of Maine also voted with Harkin. Frist's decision to go ahead with the vote was made with the assurances that the White House would veto the bill if the Harkin amendment were included in a final House-Senate conference report on the spending bill. He felt confident that the Harkin amendment could not survive with Republicans in charge of the conference negotiations. Despite months of campaigning by Specter to keep the rider in the bill, Frist's gambit paid off as Republicans stripped the Harkin amendment in an omnibus spending package (HR 2673) that included the Labor-HHS-Education bill.

7. MEDIA OWNERSHIP

When the Federal Communications Commission (FCC) decided June 2, 2003, to allow media conglomerates to own more television stations and newspapers, complaints flooded congressional offices after critics said the changes could allow a handful of corporations to gain control over most of the nation's media outlets. Efforts in Congress to overturn the new rules initially were given little chance of success. GOP leaders supported the FCC changes, and the Bush administration threatened to veto such legislation if it were passed. But in the Senate, a bipartisan coalition of opponents to the FCC's changes led by Byron L. Dorgan, D-N.D., and Trent Lott, R-Miss., resorted to a rarely used legislative maneuver to force a roll-call vote in their chamber. *(Legislative details, p. 389)*

On July 15 Dorgan introduced a joint resolution of disapproval (S J Res 17) to reverse the FCC ruling. The resolution was permitted under the 1996 Congressional Review Act (PL 104-121), which allowed Congress to overturn new federal regulations with a simple majority vote of both houses and the president's signature. It had been successfully used only once, when a Republican Congress repealed workplace ergonomics regulations put in place at the end of the Clinton administration. The law contained a provision to allow expedited consideration of the resolution in the Senate—but not the House. Dorgan easily obtained the thirty signatures needed under the law to discharge the resolution from committee and bring it directly to the Senate floor. The law limited debate to ten hours and prohibited amendments. *(Details, p. 389)*

Sen. George Allen, R-Va., and other supporters of the FCC's changes argued that they were needed to update outmoded regulations written before the advent of the Internet and 500-channel cable television systems. But it was clear from the start of the debate they were outnumbered. In a rebuke to FCC Chairman Michael K. Powell, the Senate passed the resolution Sept. 16 by a vote of 55–40: R 12–38; D 42–2; I 1–0. The combination of twelve GOP senators joining forty-two Democrats and the Senate's single independent was widely seen as a strong message to the White House that the FCC's rule was not going to stand with Congress. While the resolution did not pass the House it did lay the groundwork for a compromise approved later that reversed part of the FCC's actions. *(Vote, p. 847)*.

8. IRAQ RECONSTRUCTION

The White House enjoyed strong support on its Iraq policy from the Republican majorities in both chambers in 2003, despite rising U.S. casualties, mounting criticism over postwar planning from Democrats, and two ongoing congressional inquiries into the quality of prewar intelligence on Iraq. But the Bush administration received an unwelcome surprise when it tried to sell to Congress its $87 billion supplemental budget request for Iraq and Afghanistan. Growing concern in both parties over the higher-than-expected price tag became apparent Oct. 16 when the Senate narrowly voted to convert $10 billion out of the measure's $20.3 billion slice for reconstruction into a loan. It was the first major setback for the administration on Iraq, made more significant by the defections of eight GOP senators. (*Legislative details, p. 291*)

The White House vigorously opposed the proposal, arguing that it would be unfair to saddle Iraq with even more obligations on top of its external debt, which was estimated to be about $125 billion. But the amendment's sponsors, centrist Democrats Evan Bayh of Indiana and Ben Nelson of Nebraska, included a provision that many senators saw as a "win-win" sweetener: if Iraq's lenders forgave 90 percent of the country's bilateral debt, the $10 billion loan would be converted into a grant. That measure drew praise from those Democrats who wanted to ease Iraq's debt burden, while the loan component attracted several fiscal conservatives in the GOP who faced constituent opposition to the bill's cost.

Before the vote, the White House lobbied undecided senators, some of whom were invited to the White House to meet with Bush. But several of those lawmakers later said those tactics backfired. Indeed, when the amendment finally came to the floor, it won the support of eight Republicans, including close White House allies such as Lindsey Graham of South Carolina and Saxby Chambliss of Georgia. Only four Democrats opposed it. The vote was 51–47: R 8–43; D 42–4; I 1–0. (*Vote, p. 847*)

9. 'PARTIAL BIRTH' ABORTION

For eight years, social conservatives pushed for a federal law criminalizing a procedure they called "partial birth" abortion. But until 2003 the effort always ended short of success: abortion foes twice succeeded in pushing a partial-birth ban through Congress but were never able to muster an override of President Bill Clinton's vetoes of the legislation. With Republicans controlling both chambers of Congress and the White House in 2003, supporters of the ban were confident of victory, with passage in the House all but guaranteed and a promise from President Bush to sign the bill into law. The only potential obstacles lay in the Senate, where abortion rights advocate Barbara Boxer, D-Calif., insisted on a full debate on the issue before every vote—including procedural tallies. Supporters of legal abortion tried to limit the scope of the ban through a handful of amendments. (*Legislative details, p. 510*)

The effort to enact the ban in the 108th Congress also was the first time the bill had come before the Senate since the Supreme Court's decision in 2000 to strike down a similar law in Nebraska. But with Bush's endorsement, opponents of the ban lost some of the cover they had during the Clinton administration. In the past, those members could vote for the measure—avoiding the ire of the antiabortion lobby—even though they disagreed with it because they knew Clinton would veto it.

Although the 2003 debate and votes on the bill (S 3) had the potential to put some senators—particularly Republicans and the chamber's newest members—in the tricky spot of having to weigh when life begins and how far to curtail a woman's legal right to an abortion, the Senate passed the bill with relative ease March 13 by a vote of 64–33, sending it on to the House. The House on June 4 passed its version of the legislation (HR 760) by a vote of 282–139. When the conference agreement came before the Senate in October, supporters and opponents acknowledged the bill would be approved. The House already had adopted the conference report 281–142 on Oct. 2. The Senate cleared for the president on Oct. 21 by a vote of 64–34: R 47–3; D 17–30; I 0–1. (*Vote, p. 847*)

10. CLASS ACTION LAWSUITS

Conservative lawmakers and business lobbyists spent much of 2003 trying to round up a filibuster-proof sixty-vote Senate majority for a measure to make it easier to remove class action lawsuits from state courts and send them to federal courts. Supporters of the legislation (S 1751) pushed it as a needed reform for the civil tort system, which backers of the bill portrayed as badly abused by trial lawyers who filed specious cases in plaintiff-friendly state courts. Opponents countered that the bill would make it more difficult, and more expensive, for wronged parties to seek legal redress. (*Legislative details, p. 608*)

The House passed its version of the bill (HR 1115) 253–170 on June 12 and Senate Majority Leader Bill Frist, R-Tenn., repeatedly promised to bring the measure to a vote in 2003. For months, business lobbyists publicly counted fifty-seven votes in the Senate for the bill. Privately, they said that while several more senators were prepared to vote for it, those lawmakers would not publicly declare their intentions for fear of criticism from opponents.

The Senate showdown came Oct. 22, when Frist decided to test the math by forcing a vote to end a filibuster on a procedural motion to take up the legislation, the one item on the GOP's so-called tort reform agenda that has the best chance of being enacted. Months earlier, on July 9, the Senate rejected a motion to invoke cloture on another lawsuit-related bill that would cap noneconomic damages for pain and suffering and punitive damages in medical malpractice lawsuits.

The October class action vote was enmeshed in end-of-session partisanship. Senate Democrats complained about being mostly shut out of conference negotiations on Medicare prescription drug legislation (PL 108-173) and a major energy bill (HR 6). They buttressed their claim of heavy-handedness by the GOP by pointing to the fact that the class action bill Frist brought to the floor was not the one (S 274) approved in April by the Judiciary Committee. The new version incorporated a change made at the behest of Arlen Specter, R-Pa., regarding "mass action" lawsuits.

As a result the outcome was uncertain when Frist called for a vote on the cloture motion. As lobbyists paced outside the Senate chamber, Mary L. Landrieu, D-La.—whom supporters of the bill long had counted as an ally—approached Frist with a list of changes she wanted made. When Frist would not promise Landrieu that she could get what she wanted, she voted against limiting debate. Landrieu's vote proved decisive when the roll call was one short of the sixty needed. The vote was 59–39: R 50–1; D 8–38; I 1–0. (*Vote, p. 847*)

11. CUBA TRAVEL BAN

When the Senate last voted in 1999 to lift the ban on traveling to Cuba, the amendment was tabled 55–43. In 2003, however, the Senate for the first time voted to lift the ban by including a provision in the fiscal 2004 Transportation-Treasury spending bill (HR 2989). The amendment was offered by Byron L. Dorgan, D-N.D., whose fellow Farm Belt senators were among the most vehement foes of the travel ban. Twenty of them voted against tabling the amendment, while just four of those voting to kill it—all of them Republicans—were from the same region—Norm Coleman of Minnesota, Peter G. Fitzgerald of Illinois, Charles E. Grassley of Iowa, and Richard G. Lugar of Indiana. (*Legislative details, p. 299*)

Agricultural interests saw an untapped market in Cuba and made the case that economic engagement—rather than isolation—was the way to change the behavior of Fidel Castro's government. Supporters of the travel ban in Congress and administration officials argued that easing sanctions on the island nation would do little to alter Castro's behavior but would provide him with currency he otherwise could not get. The Bush administration took a strong stand against lifting sanctions on the communist regime, particularly heading into an election year when Florida's electoral votes were considered central to a presidential victory. Even so, for the fourth straight year the House also voted to lift the travel ban.

The motion to table the Dorgan amendment was rejected Oct. 23 by 36–59: R 30–19; D 6–39; I 0–1. Subsequently, the amendment was adopted by voice vote. Support for easing sanctions from majorities in both chambers was not enough to overcome a veto threat, and the GOP leadership stood with the administration. The provision lifting the travel ban was stripped out in the conference committee on legislation. (*Vote, p. 847*)

12. 'HEALTHY FORESTS' INITIATIVE

Many observers were skeptical that Congress could pass forest-thinning legislation, a White House environmental priority that President Bush highlighted in his State of the Union speech in January 2003. Bush's "Healthy Forests" initiative was intended to restrict environmental reviews and legal challenges for projects designed to thin forests and remove the debris that fuels wildfires. The House passed a bill based on Bush's plan without difficulty in May but environmental groups disliked the measure; their influence in the Senate was thought strong enough to scuttle the measure.

Senate Democrats voiced significant discontent with the House-passed bill, saying it would permit clear-cutting of older, larger trees deep in the nation's forests and would not provide enough protections for communities with the highest risks for wildfire. The stand-off looked like a repeat of 2002, when GOP attempts to add elements of Bush's forest plan to the fiscal 2003 Interior appropriations bill bogged down in the Senate. Democrats had countered with a proposal to limit logging to areas near communities. Neither side was able to win the sixty votes necessary to avoid the other's filibuster, and the measure died. This time, however, two Democrats—Sens. Dianne Feinstein of California and Ron Wyden of Oregon—joined with Republicans who were determined to avoid a stalemate. In a series of meetings that included Forest Service officials, the bipartisan group wrote a new version of the bill. (*Legislative details, p. 433*)

The revised Senate measure, released at the end of September, authorized $760 million a year for thinning—the House had not specified an amount—and proposed that at least 50 percent of the money be spent in areas within a half mile of communities at risk for wildfires. It also required protection of old-growth trees. It proposed a limit of three environmental reviews for thinning projects, instead of the one recommended by the House. Preliminary court injunctions would be limited to sixty days rather than forty-five days as in the House bill.

Initially, it was not clear whether the compromise was enough to appease environmentalists. Democrats Jeff Bingaman of New Mexico and Tom Harkin of Iowa placed holds on the measure, blocking the unanimous consent needed to bring it up. Both said they needed more time to review the language. With a busy schedule near the end of the session, the measure appeared to be stalled. But raging wild-

fires in Southern California began to capture headlines just a few days later, putting opponents on the defensive. Bingaman and Harkin dropped their objections, and the measure was passed Oct. 30 in a rare show of environmental bipartisanship. The vote was 80–14: R 50–0; D 30–13; I 0–1. The final bill, which was easily cleared Nov. 21, retained almost all of the Senate compromise. (*Vote, p. 847*)

13. FAA REAUTHORIZATION

The Bush administration's campaign to privatize thousands of federal government jobs became a major point of conflict in Congress, leading even some Republicans to challenge the White House. The issue of contracting out air traffic control jobs within the Federal Aviation Administration (FAA) was particularly sensitive because of its implications—real or imagined—for aviation safety. The administration touched off congressional action with a decision early in the year to reclassify air traffic control as a commercial rather than an inherently governmental function—even though it did not plan to immediately privatize any of the jobs. The House included language in its version of the FAA reauthorization bill (HR 2115) to ban further privatization of air traffic controllers. The Senate version would have banned privatizing controllers or support staff. (*Legislative details, p. 382*)

However, with the White House threatening to veto any bill that restricted its ability to privatize the air traffic control system, Republican conferees met hastily July 24 and agreed to replace the proposed ban. Instead, the conference agreement allowed for the privatization of sixty-nine airport control towers, most of them at secondary airports or in small cities, with further privatization to be allowed after Oct. 1, 2007. Following a revolt in the House, the conference report was rewritten to delete any mention of privatization and was finally adopted by the House. But Senate Democrats threatened a filibuster, noting that the bill's silence on privatization would allow the FAA to privatize all or part of the air traffic control system at its discretion.

In an effort to end the threat to the bill, FAA Administrator Marion C. Blakey wrote a letter promising that the administration "has no plans to privatize the national air traffic control system" for a year. The guarantee, which arrived Nov. 17 even as the Senate was voting on whether or not to cut off the debate, applied only to air traffic controllers, not to support staff at control towers and flight service stations as the Senate wanted. It did not satisfy opponents of privatization, and the motion to invoke cloture was rejected, 45–43: R 42–3; D 3–39; I 0–1. (*Vote, p. 847*)

Finally, the administration sent a letter Nov. 21 that met lawmakers' demands for a one-year moratorium on any new privatization of air traffic control personnel. Just minutes later, the Senate cleared the conference report by voice vote. The issue was settled for a year although labor unions and their Democratic supporters vowed to try to get a permanent prohibition on privatization written into law in 2004.

14. ENERGY POLICY

Almost three years after President Bush proposed a new national energy policy, weeks of sometimes bitter negotiations finally yielded in November what Republican leaders described as a saleable compromise: a package designed to stimulate domestic production of oil, gas, and ethanol; improve management of the nation's electricity grid in the aftermath of a crippling summertime blackout; and create thousands of jobs to bolster the economy. But less than a week after a deal was struck, the measure had been consigned to indefinite legislative limbo—sunk, probably for the rest of the 108th Congress, mainly by a provision that took up just twenty-four lines in the 571-page conference report embodying the deal (HR 6—H Rept 108-375). *(Legislative details, p. 425)*

That wording shielded producers of methyl tertiary butyl ether (MTBE) from defective product lawsuits, including some already in the courts. MTBE was used to make fuel burn more cleanly but had been found to contaminate groundwater when it leaks from pipes or storage tanks. Senate negotiators had agreed to the liability limitations at the insistence of Republican House Majority Leader Tom De-Lay, who represented a district in Texas, home to many of the nation's MTBE producers.

Sen. Charles E. Schumer, D-N.Y., had been threatening for more than a month to lead a filibuster against any bill with such a liability waiver, which he maintained would transfer billions of dollars in MTBE cleanup costs from the industry to consumers. But GOP leaders believed they could pull together the sixty votes needed to invoke cloture and shut down a filibuster by loading the bill with special-interest provisions—from ethanol subsidies to earmarks for spending on parochial energy initiatives. They also sought to defuse opposition by deleting the most contentious provisions under consideration: to permit oil and gas drilling in Alaska's Arctic National Wildlife Refuge, for example, or to inventory oil reserves in the Outer Continental Shelf off the nation's coasts, where drilling was prohibited.

The conference report went through the House on Nov. 18 even as Schumer's filibuster campaign gained momentum. Judd Gregg of New Hampshire led a coalition of Republicans who took to the Senate floor to support the filibuster. Majority Leader Bill Frist, R-Tenn., was able to muster fifty-eight votes—more than sufficient to pass the bill, but two shy of the sixty required to end a filibuster. Thirteen Democrats, mostly from oil- or ethanol-producing states, voted for cloture, but that was not enough to overcome the defection of six Republicans, all but one from the Northeast. The final vote Nov. 21 was 57–40: R 44–7; D 13–32; I 0–1. *(Vote, p. 847)*

House

1. FISCAL 2004 BUDGET RESOLUTION

The most pressing business for the reassembled GOP majority at the start of the 108th Congress was to pass the second major tax cut of George W. Bush's presidency in an attempt to stimulate the slumping national economy. The House Republican's fiscal 2004 budget resolution (H Con Res 95) was an important part of the plan. It called for initiating a fast-track budget reconciliation process to allow the Senate—under Republican control after the 2002 elections—to pass the tax measure by a simple majority vote instead of facing the usual sixty-vote margin required in budget matters.

While the primary objective was passage of the tax plan, the measure sparked an internal GOP debate over cutting spending. That debate came as the White House issued a forecast for a record federal budget deficit—even before knowing the costs of a war in Iraq. Jim Nussle, R-Iowa, chairman of the House Budget Committee, drafted a budget plan that would force a 1 percent cut in virtually all mandatory spending programs, including Medicare and Medicaid, the federal-state health care plans for the elderly and the poor. *(Legislative details, p. 66)*

The savings in entitlement programs, which would have required a separate reconciliation bill, were to total $467 billion over ten years but would have reduced the allocation available for a prescription drug benefit—a priority Bush objective—to only $28 billion. The Nussle draft also included the full $726 billion over eleven years for the Bush tax plan. Nussle's plan was met with a rebellion by Republi-

can moderates that forced House leaders to rewrite the measure before bringing it to the floor. As modified for floor debate, most of the cuts for Medicare and popular veterans' programs were dropped. Even so, it took considerable pressure by GOP leaders to advance the measure, which was adopted by a vote of 215–212: R 214–12; D 1–199; I 0–1. *(Vote, p. 849)*

2. TAX REDUCTIONS

House Republicans won final approval May 23 for a $330 billion tax cut, the third largest in U.S. history. Though many Republicans were angry that the final bill was less than half the size of the $726 billion tax cut originally sought by President Bush, they closed ranks to adopt the conference report in the face of almost unanimous Democratic opposition. *(Legislative details, p. 105)*

The House initially endorsed a $726 billion tax cut package as part of the fiscal 2004 budget resolution, but Senate moderates succeeded in reducing the cost to $350 billion including revenue-raising offsets. House and Senate negotiators compromised on a $550 billion plan, which the House reluctantly accepted. But as the Senate was about to vote on the final budget resolution, Finance Chairman Charles E. Grassley, R-Iowa, announced that to get the support of Senate centrists, he had promised—with the support of Senate Majority Leader Bill Frist, R-Tenn.—that any tax reconciliation package would cost no more than $350 billion.

House Republicans were furious about the deal and pressed ahead with a $550 billion tax cut bill (HR 2), while the Senate approved a $350 billion version. In conference, Thomas agreed to accept a $350 billion cap but insisted that in return the House deserved a stronger role in determining the content of the tax cut. He won agreement for a plan to reduce the tax rate on both dividends and capital gains to 15 percent for most taxpayers, in lieu of Bush's original proposal to end dividend taxes. Under existing law, dividends were taxed as regular income at a top rate of 38.6 percent, and certain capital gains were taxed at 20 percent.

Most Democrats strongly opposed the plan, citing its tilt toward taxpayers who are better off and its impact on the deficit at a time when the war in Iraq was already requiring billions in deficit spending. On the final vote only seven Democrats backed the conference report and just one Republican opposed it. That vote was 231–200: R 224–1; D 7–198; I 0–1. *(Vote, p. 849)*

3. OVERTIME PAY

The Bush administration in 2003 moved into the contentious area of labor relations by issuing a preliminary rule in March to change overtime pay rules that critics said were outdated and confusing. The proposed rule allowed 1.3 million low-income workers who were exempt under existing law from overtime pay to be eligible for such premium compensation. But the Labor Department said that under the rule about 650,000 white-collar workers would lose their eligibility for overtime pay. Opponents said as many as 8 million workers, mostly white-collar professionals such as paralegals, engineers, and dental hygienists, would lose their right to overtime pay.

Democrats, traditionally sympathetic to the interests of organized labor, moved to block the change. Democratic Rep. David R. Obey of Wisconsin on July 10 offered an amendment to the fiscal 2004 Labor–Health and Human Services (HHS)–Education appropriations bill (HR 2660) that would bar funding to implement the rule. On the roll call on Obey's amendment, Democrats lost only three "no" votes. Meanwhile, fourteen labor-friendly Republicans voted with the Democrats. *(Legislative details, p. 574)*

House Republican leaders exerted pressure on wavering members to avoid an embarrassing defeat. GOP leaders noted that the regulations had not been thoroughly updated in more than twenty-five years and that the change would help workers who earned less than $22,100, a majority of whom were women and minorities. The GOP leaders held the vote open for several minutes until they gained a few extra votes for victory. They told undecided lawmakers that the White House had threatened to veto the bill if it included the Obey amendment, thus putting at risk money in the bill for education and medical research. The final vote was 210–213: R 14–210; D 195–3; I 1–0. (Vote, p. 849)

Lawmakers representing hard-hit manufacturing areas remained upset about the rule. The House Oct. 2 voted 221–203 to instruct its conferees on the Labor-HHS-Education spending conference to accept a Senate amendment that would ban funding to implement the rule. This time twenty-one Republicans voted for the measure, including eight who voted with GOP leadership in July. Ultimately, however, the Senate amendment was removed from the conference report on the bill.

4. PATRIOT ACT SEARCH WARRANTS

The broad antiterrorism law (PL 107-56) enacted in 2001, weeks after the Sept. 11 terrorist attacks, came under increasing scrutiny in 2003, both on Capitol Hill and across the United States. House and Senate lawmakers from both parties introduced several bills to scale back parts of the law, known as the Patriot Act. The most tangible sign of congressional misgivings about the scope of the act came in July, when the House voted on an amendment to the fiscal 2004 spending bill for the Commerce, Justice, and State departments and the judiciary (HR 2799). (Legislative details, p. 219)

The amendment, by C. L. "Butch" Otter, R-Idaho, barred the Justice Department from spending fiscal 2004 funds to seek and execute search warrants without first notifying the targets, as allowed under the law. Otter who was one of only three Republicans to vote against the Patriot Act in 2001. The amendment aimed at Section 213 of the law, often called the "sneak and peek" provision. That section allowed judges to give federal agents the power to conduct searches under court order and inform the targets of such searches "within a reasonable period." Previously, agents were required to tell targets of search warrants either at the beginning of the search or soon thereafter. Critics said the delayed notification was a violation of the Fourth Amendment, which protects people against unreasonable searches and seizures.

The vote on July 22 was the first taken regarding the Patriot Act since its enactment. Even though most did not expect the amendment to survive conference negotiations, it still allowed lawmakers to record their position on the scope of the law, specifically on one of its most controversial provisions, two years after Sept. 11. Almost all of the chamber's Democrats and roughly half of its Republicans supported the Otter amendment, which the House adopted 309–118: R 113–114; D 195–4; I 1–0. In November, the Commerce, Justice, and State departments bill was folded into an omnibus appropriations measure (HR 2673). During conference negotiations on that bill, Republican congressional leaders removed Otter's language from the Commerce, Justice, and State portion of the bill. (Vote, p. 849)

5. HEAD START REAUTHORIZATION

House Republican leaders tried in early the morning of July 25 to pass a Head Start reauthorization bill that allowed eight states to manage the early childhood development program in tandem with local activities. The leadership won by a single vote but it was a fleeting victory. The hard-fought vote, combined with strong opposition in the Senate, indicated that President Bush's plan for more local control of Head Start would proceed no further in the 108th Congress.

Bush had proposed restructuring Head Start as part of his February budget, including a plan to turn significant control over to the states. The administration argued that change was critical because low-income children in the program were lagging behind their peers in math and literacy skills when they enter elementary school. House sponsor Michael N. Castle, R-Del., had to rewrite the controversial proposal twice, reducing it to a small pilot program in order to mollify GOP moderates who faced intense pressure from a grassroots coalition of groups that opposed the bill. (Legislative details, p. 000)

The opposition was led by the National Head Start Association, which represented Head Start workers and parents with children in the program. They were joined by other family advocacy and education groups including the American Civil Liberties Union and Catholic Charities USA. Opponents argued the bill was the first step in converting Head Start into a block grant program that no longer had federal standards. With Democrats united in opposition, the GOP whip operation had a fight on its hands. Slowly, they pulled wavering members back into the fold. To help ensure victory, Majority Leader Tom DeLay, R-Texas, dispatched an aide to get John Sullivan, R-Okla., who was under doctor's orders for bed rest after a car accident damaged his eyesight July 23. Sullivan was pushed into the chamber in a wheelchair shortly before 1 a.m. and helped to stand so he could vote.

Sullivan's vote—combined with the absences of Democrats Richard A. Gephardt of Missouri, who was seeking his party's nomination for president, and Ed Pastor of Arizona—provided a one-vote victory for the Castle bill. The final tally was 217–216: R 217–12; D 0–203; I 0–1. A more bipartisan Senate bill won approval from the Health, Education, Labor and Pensions Committee in October. At the insistence of key committee Republicans, the pilot project was left out. (Vote, p. 849)

6. DRUG REIMPORTATION

Mounting complaints about prescription drug prices put many lawmakers in the uncomfortable position of wanting to address an important consumer issue without imposing price controls. One widely discussed proposal would allow consumers, pharmacists, and drug wholesalers to import drugs from countries where prices often were less than in the United States. In exchange for her support of a House Republican Medicare drug bill (HR 1) that passed by one vote, Rep. Jo Ann Emerson, R-Mo., struck a deal with GOP leaders to hold a vote on a drug importation measure (HR 2427) and give lawmakers an opportunity to demonstrate they were doing something about high drug costs. The vote also allowed bill supporters to align themselves with a growing number of states and localities that are considering importation as a means to curb the costs of public health programs. (Legislative details, p. 508)

The bill permitted importation of FDA-approved drugs from FDA-approved facilities in twenty-five industrialized countries. It was strenuously opposed by a bipartisan majority of senators and the Bush administration, which said it could bring counterfeit, ineffective, or adulterated medicines into the U.S. that would endanger consumers. An unusual mix of coalitions formed for and against the bill. Conservative Republicans such as Dan Burton of Indiana and Jeff Flake of Arizona sided with many Democrats who said it is not fair for U.S. taxpayers to finance drug research and then pay more than consumers in other countries to buy those drugs. But liberal Democrats, such as John D. Dingell of Michigan and Robert Menendez of New Jersey, the party's conference chairman, joined with the FDA and drug companies to oppose the bill. The FDA maintained it could not verify that imported medicines were safe.

A variety of factors worked in the bill's favor. Wavering members did not want to go home for the August recess empty-handed on the issue. Many from border states knew constituents and relatives who traveled to Canada or other countries to save on drug expenses. Some Republicans also were miffed that GOP leaders, such as House Majority Leader Tom DeLay, R-Texas, actively worked against the bill after promising Emerson her vote. The showdown came early the morning of July 25. Emerson and allies Gil Gutknecht, R-Minn., and Rahm Emanuel, D-Ill., argued that a vote for the legislation was a vote for consumers and against the drug industry. They prevailed by a wide margin. The bill passed by a vote of 243–186: R 87–141; D 155–45; I 1–0. (*Vote, p. 849*)

But just hours later, fifty-three senators signed a letter opposing the bill, repeating concerns it would lead to unsafe drugs. The issue was later addressed in the Medicare drug bill by allowing importation from Canada if the Secretary of Health and Human Services (HHS) said the practice was safe and saved consumers money. Bush's HHS secretary, Tommy G. Thompson, had already said he could not guarantee the safety of imported drugs. The Medicare bill also called for a study on safety and trade issues surrounding importation.

7. DISTRICT OF COLUMBIA SCHOOL VOUCHERS

Conservatives for many years had advocated using tax dollars to help students escape substandard public education systems by transferring to private schools but only once had Congress passed a measure that would have created vouchers to start such an effort. That bill, limited solely to the District of Columbia, was vetoed by President Bill Clinton in 1998.

With Republicans controlling the White House and both chambers of Congress, voucher supporters saw 2003 as a new opportunity to enact the first federally funded school voucher program in the country. President Bush's fiscal 2004 budget sought $75 million for voucher pilot programs in several cities. But that broad plan was set aside by his GOP congressional allies, who chose to focus their energies only on a $10 million experiment in Washington. The shift came a month after Anthony Williams, the city's Democrat mayor, said he would back vouchers if equal infusions of money for the city's public and charter schools were provided through the annual appropriations bill for the city. (*Legislative details, p. 549*)

The mayor's support allowed Republicans to neutralize the argument that they would be imposing vouchers on an unwilling city, although Democrats continued to point out that many city officials opposed the plan and that the local government could implement a voucher program at any time. Proponents sold vouchers as a means of giving underprivileged children, particularly minorities, the same educational opportunities as their wealthier counterparts. The plan had the backing of Cardinal Theodore E. McCarrick, the Roman Catholic archbishop of Washington. Most of the voucher recipients would be expected to attend Catholic schools.

Teacher unions, school administrators, most Democrats, and a cadre of moderate Republicans remained adamantly opposed to spending public money on private schools. Some argued that sending tax dollars to religiously affiliated schools would violate the constitutional separation of church and state; others complained that sending public money out of the education system was tantamount to giving up on public schools just when strict and expensive new standards had been put in place by the 2001 education overhaul law.

Instead of writing voucher provisions into the D.C. spending bill (HR 2765), GOP leaders opted to hold a floor vote on an amendment incorporating the plan into the bill—a move that, if successful, would make clear the House's position in favor of vouchers. Such a vote would be particularly important because of the level of opposition in the Senate, where sixty supporters would be needed to cut off a filibuster.

On the House floor, the voucher amendment, by Government Reform Chairman Thomas M. Davis III, R-Va.—whose panel has jurisdiction over policies for the nation's capital—appeared headed for defeat the afternoon of Sept. 5. But as was the case on several close votes during the year, at least one Republican flipped from "no" to "yes" in the closing minutes of the roll call, securing a razor-thin 205–203 victory for GOP leaders: R 201–14; D 4–188; I 0–1. (*Vote, p. 849*)

A subsequent vote to strip the program died on a tie vote. The next week, Democrats were able to demand a revote on the Davis amendment and it proved just as dramatic. John Linder, R-Ga., had to be retrieved from a party for his sixty-first birthday to cast a tie-breaking vote reaffirming the amendment's adoption. But the initial House vote remained the bellwether moment for the voucher campaign. After maneuvering around a Democratic filibuster in the Senate, the language survived for inclusion in the legislation combining the D.C. measure and six other fiscal 2004 appropriations bills into an omnibus conference report. The House adopted the conference report on the omnibus Dec. 8.

8. FEDERAL JOB OUTSOURCING

Declining to back down in the face of a veto threat, the House voted to block White House plans to contract out thousands of federal jobs to private workers. The vote came on an amendment to the fiscal 2004 appropriations bill for the Transportation and Treasury departments. The White House's Office of Management and Budget (OMB) announced May 29 that it was revising the regulation, known as Circular A-76, governing the outsourcing of government work. OMB said the purpose was to encourage federal agencies to expand competitive bidding for more than 800,000 federal jobs. Members made several attempts to scuttle the outsourcing plan, each time meeting with a veto threat. (*Legislative details, p. 690*)

An attempt to amend the Interior appropriations bill in July was reduced to a provision blocking studies on privatizing two small projects. In another effort, the House-passed bill to reauthorize the Federal Aviation Administration included a ban on privatizing air traffic controllers. The most direct attack was undertaken by Chris Van Hollen, a freshman Democrat whose Maryland district was home to thousands of federal employees. His amendment to the Transportation-Treasury appropriations bill (HR 2989) specified simply that "none of the funds made available by this act may be used to implement the revision to Office of Management and Budget Circular A-76 made on May 29, 2003."

Ernest Istook, R-Okla., chairman of the Appropriations panel that wrote the bill, warned members against supporting the amendment. "If you want to try to kill the bill and all that it does for transportation in the U.S., go ahead and vote," he said. "This bill is too important for that. If this bill were to be vetoed . . . bulldozers across the country would stop." But twenty-six Republicans, most with large constituencies of federal workers in their districts, joined Van Hollen, giving him enough votes to prevail Sept. 9 on a vote of 220–198: R 26–195; D 193–3); I 1–0. (*Vote, p. 849*)

Language similar to the Van Hollen amendment was offered on the Transportation-Treasury bill in the Senate but was rejected, 47–48. The amendment was dropped in conference but the fight over limiting the administration's privatization plans was one of the last issues settled in negotiations on the year-end omnibus appropriations package, which included the Transportation-Treasury bill. At White House insistence, most of the privatization language was dropped. However, two significant provisions survived: federal jobs would no longer automatically be considered for privatization every five years, and jobs could not be privatized if those jobs would then be sent overseas.

9. 'DO NOT CALL' REGISTRY

In a legislative body not known for quick action, House passage of a bill authorizing the Federal Trade Commission (FTC) to create and enforce a do-not-call list for telemarketers was as remarkable as it was sudden. Less than forty-eight hours after a federal judge issued a decision stopping the FTC from launching the registry, the House passed a bill (HR 3161) rescuing the list and lending it explicit statutory authority. *(Legislative details, p. 391)*

The FTC list allowed people to register telephone numbers they do not want telemarketers to call. The FTC was authorized to punish violators with fines of $11,000 per call. The program generated widespread interest as soon as the FTC began allowing people to register phone numbers in late June. By September, 50 million phone numbers had already been registered. The service was scheduled to take effect Oct. 1, but several telemarketing companies and industry trade groups opposed it, saying the barrier to calls would violate their free speech rights and eliminate millions of telemarketing jobs. On Sept. 23, a district court judge in Oklahoma answered their concerns, ruling the FTC had overstepped its authority in creating the list.

The public outcry, swift and loud. resonated with lawmakers across the political spectrum because the idea of banning unwanted phone calls was widely popular across the country. On Sept. 24, the day after the court ruling, Billy Tauzin, R-La., chairman of the House Energy and Commerce Committee, met with aides at noon and ordered them to draw up legislation explicitly authorizing the FTC to launch the registry. Getting the bill to the floor was another matter. House leaders opposed inserting language into a continuing resolution aimed at keeping the government funded after Oct. 1. To draw immediate attention to the issue, Tauzin turned to the news media. He called a 3 p.m. press conference to attack the decision by the Oklahoma court.

That set off a flurry of press releases and statements from lawmakers expressing outrage at the decision. By 5:30 p.m., House leaders agreed to take up the legislation the following day on the floor. At 6:25 p.m., Tauzin signed off on the legislation, which was handed to him by an aide while he was doing a live interview on CNN. The next day, Sept. 25, the House passed the bill on a vote of 412–8: R 219–5; D 192–3; I 1–0. *(Vote, p. 849)*

The Senate followed suit, clearing the measure 95–0 later in the day. However, within minutes after the House passed the bill, a federal judge in Denver put the do-not-call registry again on hold, ruling that it violated the free speech rights of telemarketers because it exempted charitable organizations. Bush signed the bill anyway on Sept. 29, and a federal appeals court ruled Oct. 7 that the FTC could begin enforcing the list while the case was argued.

10. 'PARTIAL BIRTH' ABORTION

After the 2002 elections, which placed the Senate, House and White House in Republican hands, abortion foes confidently predicted they would soon see enactment of a federal ban on a procedure they called "partial birth" abortion. The House had backed the legislation for some time. In the 104th and 105th Congresses, the

House not only had passed legislation outlawing the procedure but then mustered the necessary two-thirds supermajority to override President Clinton's vetoes of the measure. The Senate failed to override those vetoes. In June the House easily passed the legislation (HR 760) by a vote of 282–139 after supporters fended off an amendment to rewrite the bill so it applied only to abortions done after a fetus would be viable outside the womb. *(Legislative details, p. 510)*

The House took up the measure again in October, when it considered the conference report on the bill. What made this vote historic was that both opponents and supporters acknowledged the measure would soon become law. In floor speeches and news conferences, lawmakers on both sides of the issue focused more on the court battles to come than on trying to change the outcome on the House floor. The House on Oct. 2 adopted the conference report by a vote of 281–142: R 218–4; D 63–137; I 0–1. *(Vote, p. 849)*

With that action, the House sent the conference report to the Senate, which cleared the measure by a vote of 64–34. Although Bush signed the bill into law (PL 108-105) on Nov. 5, several court challenges immediately blocked its enforcement.

11. IRAQI RECONSTRUCTION LOANS

With the U.S. economy faltering and concern about the cost of the Iraq conflict escalating, a number of Democrats and Republicans argued for converting some U.S. military and reconstruction aid to that country into loans. The House became the main battlefield—and the burial ground—for a proposal to turn part of the $18.6 billion in reconstruction aid into loans. President Bush and House Republican leaders led the opposition to the measure, which was defeated in the House. *(Legislative details, p. 291)*

While there was support in the Senate for the loan idea, the House showed it would back the president despite bipartisan concerns about the rapidly increasing cost of the war. The House vote strengthened the president's hand as House and Senate negotiators went into conference. And when the House's position ultimately prevailed, it helped secure an even stronger position for Bush to conduct the war. For many members, the political stakes involved in the vote were considerable. Loan supporters said it made no sense to them or their constituents to increase deficit spending when oil-rich Iraq would soon be an economic power, thanks to U.S. help. But Bush insisted on providing all the money as a grant, saying Iraq already faced too much debt. He argued that his efforts to persuade other countries to forgive Iraqi debt would ring hollow if the United States added to Iraq's debt burden.

To push that view, Bush pressured members, especially Republican loyalists who were leaning in favor of the loan idea, to stay with him. As a result, several House Republicans dropped plans to offer loan amendments to their version of the supplemental (HR 3289) despite grassroots appeal of the idea. Only one loan amendment received Rules Committee permission for a floor vote. That amendment, which came up for a vote Oct. 16, was sponsored by David R. Obey of Wisconsin, ranking Democrat on the Appropriations Committee, and Tom Lantos of California, ranking Democrat on the International Relations Committee. The House rejected it, with many Republicans who had praised the loan idea voting against the amendment under intense pressure from the GOP leadership. The vote was 200–226: R 18–208; D 181–18; I 1–0. *(Vote, p. 849)*

The House action also gave Republican senators a chance to vote for the loan idea, assured that the proposal would be dropped in conference. On Oct. 16 eight Republican senators joined forty-two Democrats and one independent in a 51–47 vote to attach a loan amendment to their version of the supplemental (S 1689). But as expected, the House position prevailed in conference.

12. MEDICARE PRESCRIPTION DRUG BENEFIT

When Congress set aside $400 billion for a Medicare prescription drug bill in the fiscal 2004 budget (H Con Res 95), many lawmakers saw it as an opportunity that could not be passed up. The 2004 elections would make it difficult to put the issue off for another year, and passage of the bill would give President Bush a domestic victory and hand a traditionally Democratic issue to the Republicans. The House and Senate passed differing versions of Medicare drug legislation within hours of each other on June 27. The House passed HR 1 by just one vote, 216–215, while the Senate measure (S 1) had far more bipartisan support and passed by 76–21. (*Legislative details, p. 497*)

A conference agreement, reached Nov. 15, after weeks of late-night and weekend meetings, scaled back some of the most contentious proposals urged by conservatives, including one known as "premium support" to require the traditional Medicare program to compete with private health plans on price. Instead, conferees opted for a limited pilot program starting in 2010. An endorsement from the AARP, the nation's largest advocacy group for older Americans, helped send some wavering lawmakers over to the side of the bill's supporters. The measure also included billions of dollars for health care providers in rural areas, money that helped the measure attract bipartisan support from rural states.

Nevertheless, the outcome was in doubt. With the House voting first on the conference agreement, the result in that chamber would be decisive and free up Senate moderates to vote for the bill. Speaker J. Dennis Hastert, R-Ill., decided to schedule a vote the night of Friday, Nov. 21. Thus began perhaps the most remarkable and controversial—Democrats called it infamous—voting exercise of the 108th Congress, an event that carried on through the night and required many extensions of the time normally allowed for a roll call. As late as that evening, Hastert called the bill's chances only "tenuous." GOP conservatives were holding firm against the huge new entitlement expansion, and the leadership could count on only about ten defections from the Democratic side—making victory in the narrowly divided House far from assured.

Rep. Doc Hastings, R-Wash., presiding over the House, finally called for a fifteen-minute vote on the bill at 3 a.m. on Nov. 22. Shortly before 4 a.m., 215 "yes" votes had been recorded and the tally in the "no" column had ticked up to 219. Democrats, however, were concerned that any outward signs of mirth might spur some GOP members to change their votes and erase the fragile lead. By 5 a.m., the board had changed only once more when Rep. Ernest Istook, R-Okla., changed his vote to "yes." The tally then remained unchanged for nearly an hour, while the Republican whip operation—aided by Bush on the phone and Health and Human Services Secretary Tommy G. Thompson on the floor—continued to press its case. For at least a half hour, Hastert and Thompson flanked conservative Nick Smith, R-Mich., and Bush called him on his cell phone. But Smith, who was retiring after the 108th Congress, refused to change his "no" vote. Rep. Jo Ann Emerson, R-Mo., voted quickly and left the floor to avoid a repeat of the June vote on the House version of the Medicare bill, when leaders persuaded a tearful Emerson to change her vote to "yes" despite her opposition to the portion of the bill that essentially banned the importation of prescription drugs from foreign countries, where they are often cheaper. Emerson later returned to the floor to watch the proceedings but hid behind a banister on the Democratic side to avoid having to discuss her vote with the leadership.

With the vote stalled at 216–218, Republican Reps. Charles W. "Chip" Pickering Jr. of Mississippi and Barbara Cubin of Wyoming, two conservatives who supported the bill, began to spread word to fellow conservatives that if the measure were not adopted, Democrats would force a House vote on a more moderate version of Medicare legislation. Rep. C. L. "Butch" Otter of Idaho and six other Republicans who voted against the bill gathered in a room off the floor. Pickering told the group that the Democrats would be able to gather 218 signatures on a discharge petition to force their version of a drug bill to the floor. Otter was also being lobbied on his cell phone by the president.

At 5:51 a.m., Otter switched his vote from no to yes. Then Republican Trent Franks of Arizona did the same. Their decisions put the "yes" votes at 218 and transferred victory from the Democrats to the Republicans. Democrat David Wu of Oregon, who had held back because he did not want to decide the issue, then voted "yes." When the victory became obvious, others switched sides and the report was adopted two hours and fifty-one minutes after the vote had started. The final tally: 220–215: R 204–25; D 16–189; I 0–1. The bill weathered a filibuster attempt in the Senate and was cleared 54–44 on Nov. 25. Bush signed the measure into law Dec. 8. (*Vote, p. 849*)

1. H J Res 2. Clean Air. Edwards, D-N.C., amendment to authorize a National Academy of Sciences study of new rules regarding the New Source Review (NSR) section of the Clean Air Act and delay implementation of those rules for six months. Rejected 46–50: R 6–45; D 39–5 (ND 36–0, SD 3–5); I 1–0, Jan. 22, 2003. A "nay" was a vote in support of the president's position.

2. Estrada Nomination. Motion to invoke cloture (thus limiting debate) on the motion to proceed to a vote on President Bush's nomination of Miguel A. Estrada of Virginia to be a judge for the U.S. Circuit Court of Appeals for the District of Columbia. Motion rejected 55–44: R 51–0; D 4–43 (ND 1–38, SD 3–5); I 0–1, March 6, 2003. Three-fifths of the total Senate (sixty) is required to invoke cloture. A "yea" was a vote in support of the president's position.

3. S Con Res 23. Arctic National Wildlife Refugee. Boxer, D-Calif., amendment to strike language in the concurrent resolution to give procedural protection to legislation authorizing oil drilling in part of the Arctic National Wildlife Refuge in Alaska. Adopted 52–48: R 8–43; D 43–5 (ND 37–2, SD 6–3); I 1–0, March 19, 2003. A "nay" was a vote in support of the president's position.

4. S Con Res 23. Tax Cut limitations. Breaux, D-La., amendment to reduce tax cuts protected by reconciliation instructions to $350 billion and create a $396 billion Social Security reserve account for use in implementing future legislation to strengthen Social Security. Adopted 51–48: R 3–48; D 47–0 (ND 39–0, SD 8–0); I 1–0, March 25, 2003. A "nay" was a vote in support of the president's position.

5. S 1. Prescription Drug Benefit. Passage of the bill to authorize $400 billion over ten years to create a prescription drug benefit for Medicare recipients beginning in 2006. Passed 76–21: R 40–10; D 35–11 (ND 29–8, SD 6–3); I 1–0, June 27, 2003 (in the session that began and the *Congressional Record* dated June 26, 2003).

6. HR 2660. Overtime Pay Regulations. Harkin, D-Iowa, amendment to prohibit funds in the bill from being used to promulgate or implement any regulation that would take away eligibility for overtime for any worker. Adopted 54–45: R 6–44; D 47–1 (ND 39–0, SD 8–1); I 1–0, Sept. 10, 2003. A "nay" was a vote in support of the president's position.

7. S J Res 17. Media Ownership Rule. Passage of the joint resolution to provide for congressional disapproval of the Federal Communications Commission broadcast media ownership rule that would allow media conglomerates to own more television stations, stating the rule would have no force or effect. Passed 55–40: R 12–38; D 42–2 (ND 37–0, SD 5–2); I 1–0, Sept. 16, 2003. A "nay" was a vote in support of the president's position.

8. S 1689. Iraq Reconstruction Loans. Bayh, D-Ind., amendment to provide $10.3 billion as a grant to rebuild Iraq and structure an additional $10 billion as a loan that would be converted to a grant if 90 percent of all bilateral debt incurred by the former Iraqi regime of Saddam Hussein has been forgiven by other countries. Adopted 51–47: R 8–43; D 42–4 (ND 34–3, SD 8–1); I 1–0, Oct. 16, 2003. A "nay" was a vote in support of the president's position.

9. S 3. "Partial Birth" Abortion Ban. Adoption of the conference report on the bill to ban a medical procedure opponents called "partial birth" abortion. The procedure would be allowed only if it is necessary to save a woman's life. Those who unlawfully performed the procedure would face fines and up to two years in prison. Adopted (thus cleared for the president) 64–34: R 47–3; D 17–30 (ND 11–28, SD 6–2); I 0–1, Oct. 21, 2003. A "yea" was a vote in support of the president's position.

10. S 1751. Class Action Lawsuits. Motion to invoke cloture (thus limiting debate) on the motion to proceed to the bill to overhaul class action litigation rules by allowing class actions with at least 100 plaintiffs to be removed to federal courts from state courts when at least $5 million was at stake and when fewer than two-thirds of class members, as well as the primary defendants, were citizens of the state in which the case was filed. Motion rejected 59–39: R 50–1; D 8–38 (ND 6–32, SD 2–6); I 1–0, Oct. 22, 2003. Three-fifths of the total Senate (sixty) was required to invoke cloture.

11. HR 2989. Cuba Travel Ban. Stevens, R-Alaska, motion to table (kill) the Dorgan, D-N.D., amendment to prohibit any funds in the bill from being used to enforce a ban on U.S. citizens traveling to Cuba. Motion rejected 36–59: R 30–19; D 6–39 (ND 4–33, SD 2–6); I 0–1, Oct. 23, 2003. A "yea" was a vote in support of the president's position. Subsequently, the amendment was adopted by voice vote.

12. HR 1904. Forest Thinning/Passage. Passage of the bill to authorize $760 million for thinning dense forests on up to 20 million acres of federal land at high risk of catastrophic wildfire. The legislation limited preliminary court injunctions against logging projects to sixty days, subject to renewal once the court had reviewed them; required federal agencies to fully maintain or contribute to the restoration of old-growth trees; and reduced the number of reviews required by the National Environmental Policy Act. Passed 80–14: R 50–0; D 30–13 (ND 23–13, SD 7–0); I 0–1, Oct. 30, 2003. A "yea" was a vote in support of the president's position.

13. HR 2115. FAA Reauthorization. Motion to invoke cloture (thus limiting debate) on the conference report on the bill to reauthorize the Federal Aviation Administration for fiscal 2004–2007. The legislation authorized $62 billion over four years for aviation programs and extended for the same period the requirement that all revenue credited to the Aviation Trust Fund each year must be spent on aviation programs. Motion rejected 45–43: R 42–3; D 3–39 (ND 2–33, SD 1–6); I 0–1, Nov. 17, 2003. Three-fifths of the total Senate (sixty) was required to invoke cloture.

14. HR 6. Energy Policy. Motion to invoke cloture (thus limiting debate) on the conference report on the bill to implement a comprehensive national policy for energy conservation, research, and development. The legislation authorized $25.7 billion in tax breaks over ten years and authorized $18 billion in loan guarantees for a natural gas pipeline from Alaska. Ethanol producers were required to more than double output by 2012. Makers of the gasoline additive MTBE were protected from liability but had to cease production of the additive by 2015. The legislation also imposed reliability standards for electricity transmission networks and eased restrictions on utility ownership and mergers. Motion rejected 57–40: R 44–7; D 13–32 (ND 8–30, SD 5–2); I 0–1, Nov. 21, 2003. Three-fifths of the total Senate (sixty) was required to invoke cloture. A "yea" was a vote in support of the president's position.

KEY		
	Democrats *Republicans*	Independent
Y Voted for ("yea")		– Announced against
N Voted against ("nay")		P Voted "present"
+ Announced for		C Voted "present" to avoid possible conflict of interest
# Paired for		? Did not vote or otherwise
X Paired against		make a position known

ND Northern Democrats
SD Southern Democrats
Southern states – Ala., Ark., Fla., Ga., Ky., La., Miss., N.C., Okla., S.C., Tenn., Texas, Va.

Senate Key Votes	1	2	3	4	5	6	7	8	9	10	11	12	13	14
ALABAMA														
Shelby	N	Y	N	N	Y	N	Y	N	Y	N	Y	?	Y	Y
Sessions	N	Y	N	N	Y	N	N	N	Y	Y	Y	Y	Y	Y
ALASKA														
Stevens	N	Y	N	N	Y	Y	N	N	Y	Y	Y	Y	Y	Y
Murkowski, L.	N	Y	N	N	Y	Y	N	Y	Y	Y	Y	Y	Y	Y
ARIZONA														
McCain	Y	Y	Y	N	N	N	N	N	Y	Y	Y	Y	Y	N
Kyl	N	Y	N	N	Y	N	N	N	Y	Y	Y	Y	Y	Y
ARKANSAS														
Pryor	N	N	Y	Y	Y	Y	Y	Y	Y	N	N	Y	N	Y
Lincoln	N	N	Y	Y	Y	Y	Y	Y	Y	Y	N	Y	N	Y
CALIFORNIA														
Feinstein	?	N	Y	Y	Y	Y	Y	Y	Y	N	N	Y	N	N
Boxer	Y	N	Y	Y	Y	Y	Y	Y	N	N	–	Y	N	N
COLORADO														
Campbell	N	Y	N	N	Y	Y	N	Y	Y	Y	N	Y	Y	Y
Allard	N	Y	N	N	N	N	Y	N	Y	Y	N	Y	Y	Y
CONNECTICUT														
Dodd	Y	N	Y	Y	Y	Y	Y	Y	N	N	N	N	?	N
Lieberman	Y	N	Y	Y	?	Y	Y	?	N	Y	Y	?	?	N
DELAWARE														
Carper	Y	N	Y	Y	Y	Y	Y	Y	Y	N	N	N	N	N
Biden	Y	N	Y	Y	Y	Y	Y	N	Y	N	N	N	N	N
FLORIDA														
Graham	Y	?	Y	Y	N	Y	?	Y	N	N	Y	Y	?	N
Nelson	Y	Y	Y	Y	Y	Y	Y	N	Y	N	Y	N	N	N
GEORGIA														
Miller	N	Y	N	?	Y	N	N	N	Y	Y	N	Y	Y	Y
Chambliss	N	Y	N	N	Y	N	N	Y	Y	Y	Y	Y	Y	Y
HAWAII														
Inouye	?	N	N	Y	Y	Y	Y	N	N	N	N	Y	N	N
Akaka	Y	N	N	Y	Y	Y	Y	N	N	N	N	Y	N	N
IDAHO														
Craig	N	Y	N	N	Y	N	N	N	Y	Y	N	Y	Y	Y
Crapo	N	Y	N	N	Y	N	N	N	Y	Y	N	Y	Y	Y
ILLINOIS														
Durbin	Y	N	Y	Y	Y	Y	Y	Y	N	N	N	N	N	N
Fitzgerald	N	Y	Y	N	Y	N	N	N	Y	Y	Y	Y	Y	Y
INDIANA														
Lugar	N	Y	N	N	N	N	N	N	Y	Y	N	Y	Y	Y
Bayh	Y	N	Y	Y	Y	Y	Y	Y	Y	N	N	N	N	N
IOWA														
Grassley	N	Y	N	N	Y	N	N	N	Y	Y	Y	Y	Y	Y
Harkin	?	N	Y	Y	N	Y	Y	N	N	N	N	N	N	Y
KANSAS														
Brownback	N	Y	N	N	Y	N	N	Y	Y	Y	N	Y	?	Y
Roberts	N	Y	N	N	Y	N	N	N	Y	Y	N	Y	Y	Y
KENTUCKY														
McConnell	N	Y	N	N	Y	N	N	N	Y	Y	Y	Y	Y	Y
Bunning	N	Y	N	N	Y	N	N	N	Y	Y	Y	Y	+	Y
LOUISIANA														
Breaux	N	Y	N	Y	Y	Y	Y	N	Y	N	N	Y	N	Y
Landrieu	N	N	N	Y	Y	Y	Y	Y	Y	N	N	Y	N	Y
MAINE														
Snowe	Y	Y	Y	Y	Y	Y	Y	N	Y	Y	Y	Y	Y	N
Collins	Y	Y	Y	N	Y	N	Y	N	Y	Y	N	Y	Y	N
MARYLAND														
Sarbanes	Y	N	Y	Y	N	Y	Y	N	Y	N	N	Y	N	N
Mikulski	Y	N	Y	Y	Y	Y	Y	N	Y	N	N	Y	N	N
MASSACHUSETTS														
Kennedy	Y	N	Y	Y	Y	Y	Y	N	Y	N	N	N	N	N
Kerry	Y	N	Y	Y	?	Y	?	Y	N	–	–	?	–	–
MICHIGAN														
Levin	Y	N	Y	Y	N	Y	Y	N	Y	N	N	N	N	N
Stabenow	Y	N	Y	Y	Y	Y	Y	N	Y	N	N	Y	N	N
MINNESOTA														
Coleman	N	Y	N	N	Y	N	N	N	Y	Y	Y	Y	Y	Y
Dayton	Y	N	Y	Y	Y	Y	Y	N	Y	N	N	N	Y	N
MISSISSIPPI														
Cochran	N	Y	N	N	Y	N	N	N	Y	Y	Y	Y	Y	Y
Lott	N	Y	N	N	N	N	Y	N	Y	Y	Y	Y	Y	Y
MISSOURI														
Bond	N	Y	N	N	Y	N	N	N	Y	Y	?	Y	N	Y
Talent	N	Y	N	N	Y	N	N	N	Y	Y	Y	Y	Y	Y

Senate Key Votes	1	2	3	4	5	6	7	8	9	10	11	12	13	14
MONTANA														
Baucus	Y	N	Y	Y	Y	Y	Y	N	Y	N	N	Y	Y	Y
Burns	N	Y	N	N	Y	N	N	N	Y	Y	?	Y	Y	Y
NEBRASKA														
Nelson	Y	Y	Y	Y	Y	Y	Y	N	Y	Y	N	?	Y	Y
Hagel	N	Y	N	N	Y	N	N	N	Y	Y	N	Y	Y	Y
NEVADA														
Reid	Y	N	Y	Y	Y	Y	Y	N	Y	N	N	Y	N	N
Ensign	N	Y	N	N	N	N	N	Y	Y	Y	Y	Y	Y	Y
NEW HAMPSHIRE														
Sununu	Y	Y	N	N	N	N	N	N	Y	Y	N	Y	?	N
Gregg	Y	Y	N	N	N	N	N	N	Y	Y	Y	Y	?	N
NEW JERSEY														
Corzine	Y	N	Y	Y	Y	Y	Y	N	Y	N	N	Y	?	N
Lautenberg	Y	N	Y	Y	Y	Y	Y	N	N	N	N	Y	N	N
NEW MEXICO														
Domenici	N	Y	N	N	Y	N	N	N	Y	Y	Y	Y	Y	Y
Bingaman	Y	N	Y	Y	Y	Y	Y	N	N	N	N	Y	N	N
NEW YORK														
Clinton	Y	N	Y	Y	N	Y	Y	N	Y	N	N	N	N	N
Schumer	Y	N	Y	Y	Y	Y	Y	N	Y	N	N	N	N	N
NORTH CAROLINA														
Dole	N	Y	N	N	Y	N	N	Y	N	Y	Y	Y	Y	Y
Edwards	Y	N	Y	Y	N	Y	?	Y	?	?	?	?	?	?
NORTH DAKOTA														
Conrad	Y	N	Y	Y	Y	Y	Y	N	Y	N	N	Y	N	Y
Dorgan	Y	N	Y	Y	Y	Y	Y	N	Y	N	N	Y	N	Y
OHIO														
DeWine	N	Y	N	N	Y	N	N	N	Y	Y	N	Y	Y	Y
Voinovich	N	Y	N	N	Y	N	Y	N	Y	Y	N	Y	Y	Y
OKLAHOMA														
Nickles	N	Y	N	N	N	N	N	N	Y	Y	Y	Y	Y	Y
Inhofe	N	Y	N	N	?	N	N	N	Y	Y	Y	Y	Y	Y
OREGON														
Wyden	Y	N	Y	Y	Y	Y	Y	N	Y	N	N	N	N	N
Smith	N	Y	Y	N	Y	?	?	N	Y	Y	Y	Y	Y	Y
PENNSYLVANIA														
Specter	N	Y	N	N	Y	Y	N	N	Y	Y	N	Y	N	Y
Santorum	N	Y	N	N	N	N	N	N	Y	Y	Y	Y	Y	Y
RHODE ISLAND														
Reed	Y	N	Y	Y	Y	Y	Y	N	Y	N	N	N	N	N
Chafee	Y	Y	Y	Y	Y	Y	Y	N	N	Y	N	Y	N	N
SOUTH CAROLINA														
Graham	N	Y	N	N	N	N	N	Y	Y	Y	Y	Y	?	Y
Hollings	?	N	Y	Y	N	Y	Y	Y	Y	N	N	?	N	?
SOUTH DAKOTA														
Daschle	Y	N	Y	Y	Y	Y	Y	Y	Y	N	N	N	N	Y
Johnson	Y	N	Y	Y	Y	Y	Y	Y	Y	N	N	Y	N	Y
TENNESSEE														
Alexander	N	Y	N	N	Y	N	N	N	Y	Y	Y	Y	Y	Y
Frist	N	Y	N	N	Y	N	N	N	Y	Y	Y	Y	N	N
TEXAS														
Cornyn	N	Y	N	N	N	N	N	N	Y	Y	Y	Y	Y	Y
Hutchison	N	Y	N	N	N	N	Y	N	?	Y	Y	Y	Y	Y
UTAH														
Hatch	N	Y	N	N	Y	N	N	N	Y	Y	Y	Y	Y	Y
Bennett	N	Y	N	N	Y	N	N	N	Y	Y	N	Y	?	Y
VERMONT														
Leahy	Y	N	Y	Y	Y	Y	?	Y	Y	N	N	N	N	N
Jeffords	Y	N	Y	Y	Y	Y	Y	N	Y	N	N	N	N	N
VIRGINIA														
Warner	N	Y	N	N	Y	N	N	N	Y	Y	Y	Y	Y	Y
Allen	N	Y	N	N	Y	N	N	N	Y	Y	Y	Y	Y	Y
WASHINGTON														
Cantwell	Y	N	Y	Y	Y	Y	Y	N	N	N	N	N	N	N
Murray	Y	N	Y	Y	Y	Y	Y	N	N	N	N	Y	N	N
WEST VIRGINIA														
Byrd	Y	N	Y	Y	N	Y	Y	?	Y	N	N	N	N	N
Rockefeller	Y	N	Y	Y	Y	Y	Y	N	Y	N	N	N	N	N
WISCONSIN														
Kohl	Y	N	Y	Y	Y	Y	Y	N	Y	N	N	N	N	N
Feingold	Y	N	Y	Y	Y	Y	Y	N	Y	N	N	N	N	N
WYOMING														
Thomas	N	Y	N	N	Y	N	N	N	Y	Y	Y	Y	Y	Y
Enzi	N	Y	N	N	Y	N	N	N	Y	Y	N	Y	Y	Y

1. H Con Res 95. Fiscal 2004 Budget Resolution. Adoption of the concurrent resolution to set broad spending and revenue targets for the following ten years including: $1.3 trillion in tax cuts; $265 billion in mandatory spending reductions; $775.4 billion in discretionary spending for fiscal 2004; a reduction of 1 percent from the existing level in discretionary funding unrelated to defense and homeland security; a $400 billion, ten-year reserve fund for Medicare overhaul; and a prescription drug benefit. Adopted 215–212: R 214–12; D 1–199 (ND 0–145, SD 1–54); I 0–1, March 21, 2003 (in the session that began and the Congressional Record dated March 20, 2003).

2. HR 2. Tax Reductions. Adoption of the conference report on the bill to provide $350 billion in tax reductions over eleven years, including: $20 billion in state aid that consisted of $10 billion for Medicaid and $10 billion to be used at states' discretion; a new top tax rate of 15 percent on capital gains and dividends through 2008 (5 percent for lower-income taxpayers through 2007 and no tax in 2008); acceleration of income tax cuts enacted in 2001 and scheduled to take effect in 2006; an increase in the child tax credit to $1,000 through 2004, establishing the standard deduction for married couples at a level double that for a single filer through 2004; and business tax breaks increasing the deduction that small businesses may take on investments to $100,000 through 2005. Adopted 231–200: R 224–1; D 7–198 (ND 1–147, SD 6–51); I 0–1, May 23, 2003 (in the session that began and the *Congressional Record* dated May 22, 2003). A "yea" was a vote in support of the president's position.

3. HR 2660. Overtime Pay. Obey, D-Wis., amendment to block the use of funds for the Labor Department to implement a department proposal to allow employers to more easily reclassify some workers as "executive, administrative or professional employees," exempt from overtime pay. Rejected 210–213: R 14–210; D 195–3 (ND 141–1, SD 54–2); I 1–0, July 10, 2003. A "nay" was a vote in support of the president's position.

4. HR 2799. Patriot Act Search Warrants. Otter, R-Idaho, amendment to bar the use of funds to implement a provision of the 2001 antiterrorism act that allowed the government to delay giving notice to an individual that a search warrant had been obtained to search that person's premises. Adopted 309–118: R 113–114; D 195–4 (ND 143–2, SD 52–2); I 1–0, July 22, 2003.

5. HR 2210. Head Start Reauthorization. Passage of the bill to reauthorize the Head Start program through fiscal 2008 including $6.9 billion in fiscal 2004, establish a pilot program to allow eight states to coordinate their state preschool programs with Head Start centers, and allow religious organizations operating Head Start programs to consider religion as a factor in hiring teachers. Passed 217–216: R 217–12; D 0–203 (ND 0–146, SD 0–57); I 0–1, July 25, 2003 (in the session that began and the *Congressional Record* dated July 24, 2003). A "yea" was a vote in support of the president's position.

6. HR 2427. Importation of Prescription Drugs. Passage of the bill to require the Food and Drug Administration (FDA) to establish a program for the importation of FDA-approved prescription drugs from FDA-approved facilities in twenty-five countries. Passed 243–186: R 87–141; D 155–45 (ND 115–30, SD 40–15); I 1–0, July 25, 2003 (in the session that began and the *Congressional Record* dated July 24, 2003). A "nay" was a vote in support of the president's position.

7. HR 2765. District of Columbia School Vouchers. Tom Davis, R-Va., amendment to authorize a school voucher program in the District of Columbia making students who were residents of the District and whose family income was under 185 percent of the federal poverty level eligible for up to $7,500 in funds to attend a private elementary or high school in the District. Adopted 205–203: R 201–14; D 4–188 (ND 1–136, SD 3–52); I 0–1, Sept. 5, 2003.

8. HR 2989. Federal Job Outsourcing. Van Hollen, D-Md., amendment to prohibit funds in the Transportation and Treasury appropriations bill from being used to implement an Office of Management and Budget rule allowing an agency to determine whether tasks performed by federal workers should be contracted to private companies. Adopted 220–198: R 26–195; D 193–3 (ND 138–1, SD 55–2); I 1–0, Sept. 9, 2003. A "nay" was a vote in support of the president's position.

9. HR 3161. "Do Not Call" Registry. Passage of the bill to give the Federal Trade Commission explicit authority to create a "do not call" list, begin enforcing it Oct. 1, 2003, and impose fines on violators. Passed 412–8: R 219–5; D 192–3 (ND 140–2, SD 52–1); I 1–0, Sept. 25, 2003.

10. S 3. "Partial Birth" Abortion Ban Report. Adoption of the conference report on the bill to ban a medical procedure opponents referred to as "partial birth" abortion, allowing the procedure only when it was necessary to save a woman's life, and imposing fines and up to two years in prison. Adopted 281–142: R 218–4; D 63–137 (ND 32–111, SD 31–26); I 0–1, Oct. 2, 2003. A "yea" was a vote in support of the president's position.

11. HR 3289. Iraqi Reconstruction Loans. Obey, D-Wis., amendment to require half of all reconstruction aid to Iraq to be in the form of loans. Rejected 200–226: R 18–208; D 181–18 (ND 129–15, SD 52–3); I 1–0, Oct. 16, 2003. A "nay" was a vote in support of the president's position.

12. HR 1. Medicare Prescription Drug Benefit. Adoption of the conference report on the bill to create a prescription drug benefit for Medicare recipients beginning in 2006 and make structural changes to the program allowing beneficiaries to obtain coverage through traditional Medicare or a private health plan. Adopted 220–215: R 204–25; D 16–189 (ND 5–143, SD 11–46); I 0–1, Nov. 22, 2003 (in the session that began and the *Congressional Record* dated Nov. 21, 2003). A "yea" was a vote in support of the president's position.

KEY

	Democrats	Republicans	Independent
Y	Voted for ("yea")		
N	Voted against ("nay")		
+	Announced for		
#	Paired for		
X	Paired against		

–	Announced against
P	Voted "present"
C	Voted "present" to avoid possible conflict of interest
?	Did not vote or otherwise make a position known

ND Northern Democrats
SD Southern Democrats
Southern states – Ala., Ark., Fla., Ga., Ky., La., Miss., N.C., Okla., S.C., Tenn., Texas, Va.

House Key Votes	1	2	3	4	5	6	7	8	9	10	11	12
ALABAMA												
1 Bonner	Y	Y	N	Y	Y	N	Y	N	Y	Y	N	Y
2 Everett	Y	Y	N	Y	Y	Y	Y	N	Y	Y	N	Y
3 Rogers	Y	Y	N	Y	Y	N	?	N	Y	Y	N	Y
4 Aderholt	Y	Y	N	N	Y	Y	Y	N	Y	Y	N	Y
5 Cramer	N	Y	?	Y	N	Y	N	Y	Y	Y	N	Y
6 Bachus	Y	Y	N	Y	Y	N	Y	N	Y	Y	N	Y
7 Davis	N	N	Y	Y	N	Y	N	Y	Y	Y	Y	N
ALASKA												
AL Young	Y	Y	N	Y	Y	N	?	N	Y	Y	N	Y
ARIZONA												
1 Renzi	Y	Y	N	N	Y	Y	Y	N	Y	Y	N	Y
2 Franks	Y	Y	N	Y	Y	Y	Y	N	Y	Y	N	Y
3 Shadegg	Y	Y	N	N	Y	Y	Y	N	Y	Y	N	N
4 Pastor	N	N	Y	Y	?	?	N	Y	?	N	Y	N
5 Hayworth	Y	Y	N	Y	Y	Y	Y	N	Y	Y	N	Y
6 Flake	Y	Y	N	Y	Y	Y	Y	N	N	N	N	N
7 Grijalva	N	N	Y	Y	N	Y	N	Y	Y	N	Y	N
8 Kolbe	Y	Y	N	Y	Y	Y	Y	N	Y	N	N	Y
ARKANSAS												
1 Berry	N	N	Y	Y	N	Y	N	Y	Y	Y	Y	N
2 Snyder	?	N	Y	Y	N	Y	N	Y	Y	N	N	N
3 Boozman	Y	Y	N	Y	Y	Y	Y	N	Y	Y	N	Y
4 Ross	N	N	Y	Y	N	Y	N	Y	Y	Y	Y	N
CALIFORNIA												
1 Thompson	N	N	Y	Y	N	N	N	Y	Y	N	Y	N
2 Herger	Y	Y	N	N	Y	N	Y	N	Y	Y	N	Y
3 Ose	Y	Y	N	Y	Y	N	Y	N	Y	Y	Y	Y
4 Doolittle	Y	Y	N	N	Y	N	Y	?	Y	Y	N	Y
5 Matsui	N	N	Y	Y	N	N	N	Y	Y	N	Y	N
6 Woolsey	N	N	Y	Y	N	Y	?	+	Y	N	Y	N
7 Miller, George	N	N	Y	Y	N	Y	N	Y	Y	N	Y	N
8 Pelosi	N	N	Y	Y	N	Y	N	Y	Y	N	Y	N
9 Lee	N	N	Y	Y	N	Y	N	Y	Y	N	Y	N
10 Tauscher	N	N	Y	Y	N	N	N	Y	Y	N	Y	N
11 Pombo	Y	Y	N	Y	Y	N	Y	N	?	Y	N	Y
12 Lantos	N	N	Y	Y	N	Y	N	Y	Y	N	Y	N
13 Stark	N	N	Y	Y	N	Y	N	Y	Y	N	N	N
14 Eshoo	N	N	Y	Y	N	N	N	Y	Y	–	Y	N
15 Honda	N	N	Y	Y	N	N	N	Y	Y	N	Y	N
16 Lofgren	N	N	Y	Y	N	N	?	Y	Y	N	Y	N
17 Farr	N	N	Y	Y	N	Y	N	Y	Y	N	Y	N
18 Cardoza	N	N	Y	Y	N	Y	N	Y	Y	N	Y	N
19 Radanovich	Y	Y	N	Y	Y	N	Y	N	Y	Y	N	Y
20 Dooley	N	N	N	Y	N	N	N	Y	Y	N	Y	N
21 Nunes	Y	Y	N	N	Y	N	Y	N	Y	Y	N	Y
22 Thomas	Y	Y	N	N	Y	N	Y	N	Y	Y	N	Y
23 Capps	N	N	Y	Y	N	Y	N	Y	Y	N	Y	N
24 Gallegly	Y	Y	N	N	Y	N	Y	N	Y	Y	N	Y
25 McKeon	Y	Y	N	N	Y	N	Y	N	Y	Y	?	Y
26 Dreier	Y	Y	N	N	Y	N	Y	N	Y	?	N	Y
27 Sherman	N	N	Y	Y	N	N	N	Y	Y	N	Y	N
28 Berman	N	N	Y	Y	N	N	N	Y	Y	N	Y	N
29 Schiff	N	N	Y	Y	N	N	N	Y	Y	N	Y	N
30 Waxman	N	N	Y	Y	N	N	?	Y	Y	N	Y	N
31 Becerra	N	N	Y	Y	N	Y	N	Y	Y	N	Y	N
32 Solis	N	N	Y	Y	N	Y	N	Y	Y	N	Y	N
33 Watson	N	N	Y	Y	N	Y	N	Y	Y	N	Y	N
34 Roybal-Allard	N	N	Y	Y	N	Y	–	Y	Y	N	Y	N
35 Waters	N	N	Y	Y	N	Y	N	Y	Y	N	Y	N
36 Harman	N	N	?	N	N	Y	N	Y	Y	N	Y	N
37 Millender-McD.	N	N	?	Y	N	Y	N	Y	Y	N	Y	N
38 Napolitano	N	N	Y	Y	N	Y	N	Y	Y	N	Y	N
39 Sanchez, Linda	N	N	Y	Y	N	Y	N	Y	Y	N	Y	N
40 Royce	Y	Y	N	N	Y	N	Y	N	Y	Y	N	Y
41 Lewis	Y	Y	N	N	Y	N	Y	N	Y	Y	N	Y
42 Miller, Gary	Y	Y	N	N	Y	N	Y	N	Y	Y	N	Y

House Key Votes	1	2	3	4	5	6	7	8	9	10	11	12
43 Baca	N	N	Y	Y	N	Y	N	Y	Y	N	Y	N
44 Calvert	Y	Y	N	Y	Y	N	Y	N	Y	Y	N	Y
45 Bono	Y	Y	N	Y	Y	Y	Y	N	Y	Y	N	Y
46 Rohrabacher	Y	Y	N	Y	Y	Y	Y	N	Y	Y	Y	Y
47 Sanchez, Loretta	N	N	+	Y	N	Y	N	Y	Y	N	Y	N
48 Cox	Y	Y	N	N	Y	N	Y	N	Y	Y	N	Y
49 Issa	Y	Y	N	Y	Y	N	Y	N	Y	?	N	Y
50 Cunningham	Y	Y	N	N	Y	N	Y	N	Y	Y	N	Y
51 Filner	N	N	Y	Y	N	Y	N	Y	Y	N	Y	N
52 Hunter	Y	Y	N	N	Y	Y	Y	N	Y	Y	N	Y
53 Davis	N	N	Y	Y	N	Y	N	Y	Y	N	Y	N
COLORADO												
1 DeGette	N	N	Y	Y	N	N	?	N	Y	N	N	N
2 Udall	–	N	Y	Y	N	N	N	?	Y	N	N	N
3 McInnis	Y	Y	N	Y	Y	N	Y	N	Y	Y	N	Y
4 Musgrave	Y	Y	N	Y	Y	Y	Y	N	Y	Y	N	Y
5 Hefley	N	Y	N	Y	Y	N	Y	N	Y	Y	N	Y
6 Tancredo	Y	Y	N	Y	Y	Y	Y	N	Y	Y	N	Y
7 Beauprez	Y	Y	N	Y	N	Y	Y	N	Y	Y	N	Y
CONNECTICUT												
1 Larson	N	N	Y	Y	N	Y	N	Y	+	N	Y	N
2 Simmons	Y	Y	N	N	N	N	–	Y	Y	N	N	Y
3 DeLauro	N	N	Y	Y	N	Y	N	Y	Y	N	Y	N
4 Shays	Y	Y	N	N	N	Y	Y	N	?	Y	N	Y
5 Johnson	N	Y	N	N	N	Y	Y	N	Y	N	N	Y
DELAWARE												
AL Castle	N	Y	N	Y	Y	Y	Y	N	Y	Y	N	Y
FLORIDA												
1 Miller, J.	Y	Y	N	Y	Y	N	Y	N	Y	Y	N	N
2 Boyd	N	N	Y	Y	N	N	N	Y	Y	Y	Y	Y
3 Brown	N	N	Y	Y	N	N	N	Y	Y	N	N	N
4 Crenshaw	Y	Y	N	Y	Y	N	Y	N	Y	Y	N	Y
5 Brown-Waite	Y	Y	N	N	Y	N	Y	N	Y	Y	N	Y
6 Stearns	Y	Y	N	Y	Y	Y	Y	N	Y	Y	Y	Y
7 Mica	Y	Y	N	Y	Y	Y	Y	N	Y	Y	N	Y
8 Keller	Y	Y	N	Y	N	N	Y	?	Y	Y	N	Y
9 Bilirakis	Y	Y	N	Y	Y	N	Y	N	Y	Y	N	Y
10 Young	Y	Y	N	Y	Y	Y	Y	N	Y	Y	N	Y
11 Davis	N	N	Y	Y	N	N	N	Y	Y	Y	N	N
12 Putnam	Y	Y	N	Y	Y	N	Y	N	Y	Y	?	Y
13 Harris	Y	Y	N	Y	Y	N	Y	N	Y	Y	N	Y
14 Goss	Y	Y	?	N	Y	N	Y	N	Y	Y	N	Y
15 Weldon	Y	Y	N	Y	Y	N	Y	N	Y	Y	N	Y
16 Foley	Y	Y	N	Y	Y	N	?	N	Y	Y	N	Y
17 Meek	N	N	Y	?	N	N	N	Y	N	N	Y	N
18 Ros-Lehtinen	Y	Y	N	Y	Y	N	Y	N	Y	Y	N	Y
19 Wexler	N	N	Y	Y	N	Y	N	Y	Y	N	Y	N
20 Deutsch	N	N	Y	Y	N	Y	N	Y	Y	N	Y	N
21 Diaz-Balart, L.	Y	Y	N	Y	Y	N	Y	N	Y	Y	N	Y
22 Shaw	Y	Y	N	Y	Y	Y	Y	N	Y	Y	N	Y
23 Hastings	N	N	Y	Y	N	Y	N	Y	Y	N	Y	N
24 Feeney	Y	Y	N	Y	Y	N	Y	N	Y	Y	N	Y
25 Diaz-Balart, M.	Y	Y	N	Y	Y	N	Y	N	Y	Y	N	Y
GEORGIA												
1 Kingston	Y	Y	N	Y	Y	Y	Y	N	Y	Y	N	Y
2 Bishop	N	N	Y	Y	N	Y	N	Y	?	Y	Y	N
3 Marshall	N	N	Y	Y	N	N	N	Y	Y	Y	?	Y
4 Majette	N	N	Y	Y	N	Y	N	Y	Y	N	N	N
5 Lewis	N	N	Y	Y	N	Y	N	Y	?	N	Y	N
6 Isakson	Y	Y	N	N	Y	N	Y	N	Y	Y	N	Y
7 Linder	Y	Y	N	N	Y	N	Y	N	Y	Y	N	Y
8 Collins	Y	Y	N	N	Y	N	Y	N	Y	Y	N	Y
9 Norwood	Y	Y	N	N	Y	N	Y	N	Y	Y	N	Y
10 Deal	Y	Y	N	N	Y	N	Y	N	Y	Y	N	Y
11 Gingrey	Y	Y	N	N	Y	N	Y	N	Y	Y	N	Y
12 Burns	Y	Y	N	Y	Y	N	Y	N	Y	Y	N	Y
13 Scott	N	N	Y	Y	N	N	N	Y	Y	N	Y	N
HAWAII												
1 Abercrombie	N	N	Y	N	N	N	N	Y	Y	N	Y	N
2 Case	N	N	Y	Y	N	Y	N	Y	Y	N	N	N
IDAHO												
1 Otter	Y	Y	N	Y	Y	Y	Y	N	Y	Y	N	Y
2 Simpson	Y	Y	N	Y	Y	Y	Y	N	Y	Y	N	Y
ILLINOIS												
1 Rush	N	N	Y	Y	N	N	N	Y	Y	N	Y	N
2 Jackson	N	N	Y	Y	N	N	N	Y	Y	N	Y	N
3 Lipinski	?	N	Y	Y	N	Y	N	Y	Y	Y	Y	N
4 Gutierrez	N	N	Y	Y	N	?	N	Y	Y	N	Y	N
5 Emanuel	N	N	Y	Y	N	N	N	Y	Y	N	Y	N
6 Hyde	Y	Y	N	N	Y	N	Y	N	Y	Y	?	N
7 Davis	N	N	Y	Y	N	N	N	Y	Y	N	Y	N

House Key Votes	1	2	3	4	5	6	7	8	9	10	11	12
8 Crane	Y	Y	N	Y	Y	N	Y	N	Y	Y	N	Y
9 Schakowsky	N	N	Y	Y	N	Y	N	Y	Y	N	Y	N
10 Kirk	Y	Y	N	Y	Y	N	Y	N	Y	?	N	Y
11 Weller	Y	Y	N	N	Y	N	Y	N	Y	Y	N	Y
12 Costello	N	N	Y	Y	N	Y	N	Y	Y	Y	Y	N
13 Biggert	Y	Y	N	Y	Y	N	N	N	Y	Y	N	Y
14 Hastert[1]	Y	Y	N		Y	N				Y	N	Y
15 Johnson	Y	Y	Y	Y	N	N	N	Y	Y	Y	N	Y
16 Manzullo	Y	Y	N	N	Y	N	Y	N	Y	Y	N	Y
17 Evans	N	N	Y	Y	N	Y	N	Y	Y	?	Y	N
18 LaHood	Y	Y	N	Y	Y	Y	?	N	Y	Y	N	Y
19 Shimkus	Y	Y	N	Y	Y	N	Y	Y	Y	Y	N	Y
INDIANA												
1 Visclosky	N	N	Y	Y	N	N	N	Y	Y	Y	Y	N
2 Chocola	Y	Y	N	N	Y	N	Y	N	Y	Y	N	Y
3 Souder	Y	Y	N	N	Y	N	Y	N	Y	Y	?	Y
4 Buyer	?	Y	N	N	Y	N	Y	N	Y	Y	N	Y
5 Burton	Y	Y	N	N	Y	N	Y	N	Y	Y	Y	N
6 Pence	Y	Y	N	N	Y	N	Y	N	Y	Y	N	N
7 Carson	N	N	Y	Y	N	Y	N	Y	Y	N	Y	N
8 Hostettler	N	Y	N	N	Y	N	Y	Y	Y	Y	N	N
9 Hill	N	N	Y	Y	N	N	N	Y	Y	Y	Y	N
IOWA												
1 Nussle	Y	Y	Y	Y	Y	N	Y	N	Y	Y	N	Y
2 Leach	Y	N	Y	Y	N	Y	?	Y	Y	Y	N	Y
3 Boswell	N	N	Y	Y	N	Y	N	Y	Y	?	Y	N
4 Latham	Y	Y	N	Y	Y	N	Y	Y	Y	Y	N	Y
5 King	Y	Y	N	Y	Y	Y	N	Y	Y	Y	N	Y
KANSAS												
1 Moran	N	Y	N	Y	Y	Y	Y	N	Y	Y	N	N
2 Ryun	Y	Y	N	N	Y	N	Y	N	Y	Y	N	N
3 Moore	N	N	Y	Y	N	Y	N	Y	Y	N	Y	N
4 Tiahrt	Y	Y	N	N	Y	N	Y	N	Y	Y	N	Y
KENTUCKY												
1 Whitfield	N	Y	N	Y	Y	N	?	N	Y	Y	N	Y
2 Lewis	Y	Y	N	Y	Y	N	Y	Y	Y	Y	N	Y
3 Northup	Y	Y	N	N	Y	Y	Y	N	Y	Y	N	Y
4 Lucas	N	Y	Y	Y	N	Y	N	Y	Y	Y	Y	N
5 Rogers	Y	Y	N	N	Y	N	Y	N	Y	Y	N	Y
6 Fletcher	Y	Y	–	Y	Y	N	N	Y	Y	Y	N	Y
LOUISIANA												
1 Vitter	Y	Y	N	N	Y	Y	Y	N	Y	Y	N	Y
2 Jefferson	N	N	Y	Y	N	–	N	Y	Y	Y	N	N
3 Tauzin	Y	Y	N	N	Y	N	Y	N	Y	Y	N	Y
4 McCrery	Y	Y	N	Y	Y	N	Y	N	Y	Y	N	Y
5 Alexander	N	Y	Y	Y	N	N	N	Y	Y	Y	Y	Y
6 Baker	Y	Y	N	Y	Y	N	Y	N	Y	Y	N	Y
7 John	N	N	Y	Y	N	N	?	N	Y	Y	Y	N
MAINE												
1 Allen	N	N	Y	Y	N	Y	N	Y	Y	N	N	N
2 Michaud	N	N	Y	Y	N	Y	N	Y	Y	Y	Y	N
MARYLAND												
1 Gilchrest	Y	Y	N	N	Y	Y	Y	N	Y	Y	N	Y
2 Ruppersberger	N	N	Y	Y	N	Y	N	Y	Y	Y	Y	N
3 Cardin	N	N	Y	Y	N	N	N	Y	Y	N	Y	N
4 Wynn	N	N	Y	Y	N	Y	N	Y	Y	N	Y	N
5 Hoyer	N	N	Y	Y	N	Y	N	Y	Y	N	N	N
6 Bartlett	N	Y	N	Y	Y	Y	Y	N	Y	Y	N	Y
7 Cummings	N	N	Y	Y	N	Y	N	?	Y	N	Y	N
8 Van Hollen	N	N	Y	Y	N	Y	N	Y	Y	N	N	N
MASSACHUSETTS												
1 Olver	N	N	Y	Y	N	Y	N	Y	Y	Y	Y	N
2 Neal	N	N	Y	Y	N	Y	N	Y	Y	N	Y	N
3 McGovern	N	N	Y	Y	N	Y	N	Y	Y	N	Y	N
4 Frank	N	N	Y	Y	N	Y	?	Y	Y	N	Y	N
5 Meehan	N	N	Y	Y	N	Y	N	Y	Y	N	Y	N
6 Tierney	N	N	Y	Y	N	Y	N	Y	Y	N	Y	N
7 Markey	N	N	Y	Y	N	Y	N	Y	Y	N	Y	N
8 Capuano	N	N	Y	Y	N	Y	N	Y	Y	N	Y	N
9 Lynch	N	N	Y	Y	N	Y	N	Y	Y	Y	Y	N
10 Delahunt	N	N	Y	Y	N	Y	N	Y	Y	N	Y	N
MICHIGAN												
1 Stupak	N	N	Y	Y	N	Y	N	Y	Y	Y	Y	N
2 Hoekstra	Y	Y	N	N	Y	Y	Y	?	Y	Y	N	Y
3 Ehlers	Y	Y	N	Y	Y	Y	Y	N	Y	Y	N	Y
4 Camp	Y	Y	N	N	Y	N	Y	N	Y	Y	N	Y
5 Kildee	N	N	Y	Y	N	Y	N	Y	Y	Y	Y	N
6 Upton	Y	Y	N	Y	Y	Y	Y	N	Y	Y	N	Y
7 Smith	Y	Y	N	N	Y	N	Y	N	Y	Y	N	Y
8 Rogers	Y	Y	N	N	Y	N	Y	N	Y	Y	N	Y
9 Knollenberg	Y	Y	N	N	Y	N	Y	–	Y	Y	N	Y
10 Miller	Y	Y	N	N	Y	Y	Y	N	Y	Y	N	Y
11 McCotter	Y	Y	N	Y	Y	N	Y	N	Y	Y	N	Y
12 Levin	N	N	Y	Y	N	Y	N	Y	Y	N	Y	N
13 Kilpatrick	N	N	Y	Y	N	Y	N	Y	Y	N	Y	N
14 Conyers	N	N	Y	?	N	Y	N	Y	Y	N	Y	N
15 Dingell	N	N	Y	Y	N	N	N	Y	Y	Y	Y	N
MINNESOTA												
1 Gutknecht	Y	Y	N	Y	Y	Y	Y	N	Y	Y	N	N
2 Kline	Y	Y	N	N	Y	N	Y	N	Y	Y	N	Y
3 Ramstad	Y	Y	N	N	Y	N	N	N	Y	Y	Y	Y
4 McCollum	N	N	Y	Y	N	Y	N	Y	Y	N	N	N
5 Sabo	N	N	Y	Y	N	Y	N	Y	Y	?	Y	N
6 Kennedy	Y	Y	N	N	Y	N	Y	N	Y	Y	N	Y
7 Peterson	N	N	Y	Y	N	Y	N	Y	Y	Y	N	Y
8 Oberstar	N	N	Y	Y	N	Y	N	Y	Y	Y	?	N
MISSISSIPPI												
1 Wicker	Y	Y	N	Y	Y	Y	Y	N	Y	Y	N	Y
2 Thompson	N	N	Y	Y	N	N	N	Y	Y	N	Y	N
3 Pickering	Y	Y	N	Y	Y	N	?	N	Y	+	N	Y
4 Taylor	N	N	Y	Y	N	Y	Y	Y	Y	Y	Y	N
MISSOURI												
1 Clay	N	N	Y	Y	N	Y	N	Y	Y	N	?	N
2 Akin	Y	Y	N	Y	Y	N	Y	N	Y	Y	N	N
3 Gephardt	N	N	?	?	?	?	N	?	?	?	?	N
4 Skelton	N	N	Y	Y	N	Y	N	Y	Y	N	Y	N
5 McCarthy	–	N	Y	Y	N	Y	N	Y	Y	N	Y	N
6 Graves	Y	Y	N	Y	Y	N	Y	N	Y	Y	N	Y
7 Blunt	Y	Y	N	Y	Y	N	Y	N	Y	Y	N	Y
8 Emerson	Y	?	N	Y	Y	Y	Y	?	Y	Y	N	Y
9 Hulshof	Y	Y	N	N	Y	N	Y	N	Y	Y	Y	Y
MONTANA												
AL Rehberg	Y	Y	N	Y	Y	Y	Y	N	Y	Y	N	Y
NEBRASKA												
1 Bereuter	Y	Y	N	Y	Y	N	Y	N	Y	Y	N	Y
2 Terry	Y	Y	N	Y	Y	N	Y	N	N	Y	N	Y
3 Osborne	Y	Y	N	Y	Y	Y	Y	N	Y	Y	N	Y
NEVADA												
1 Berkley	N	N	Y	?	N	Y	N	Y	Y	N	Y	N
2 Gibbons	Y	Y	N	Y	N		Y	N	+	Y	N	Y
3 Porter	Y	Y	N	Y	Y	N	Y	N	Y	Y	N	Y
NEW HAMPSHIRE												
1 Bradley	Y	Y	N	N	Y	N	Y	N	Y	Y	N	Y
2 Bass	Y	Y	N	N	Y	Y	Y	N	Y	Y	N	Y
NEW JERSEY												
1 Andrews	N	N	Y	N	Y	N	N	Y	Y	N	Y	N
2 LoBiondo	Y	Y	N	N	Y	N	N	Y	Y	Y	N	Y
3 Saxton	?	Y	N	N	Y	N	N	Y	Y	Y	N	Y
4 Smith	Y	Y	N	Y	Y	Y	Y	Y	Y	Y	N	Y
5 Garrett	Y	Y	N	N	Y	Y	Y	N	Y	Y	N	N
6 Pallone	N	N	Y	Y	N	Y	N	Y	Y	N	Y	N
7 Ferguson	Y	Y	N	?	Y	N	Y	N	Y	Y	N	Y
8 Pascrell	N	N	Y	Y	N	Y	N	Y	Y	Y	Y	N
9 Rothman	N	N	Y	Y	N	Y	N	Y	Y	N	Y	N
10 Payne	N	N	?	Y	N	Y	N	Y	Y	N	Y	N
11 Frelinghuysen	Y	Y	N	N	Y	N	Y	N	Y	Y	N	Y
12 Holt	N	N	Y	Y	N	Y	N	Y	Y	N	Y	N
13 Menendez	N	N	Y	Y	N	Y	N	Y	Y	N	Y	N
NEW MEXICO												
1 Wilson	Y	Y	N	N	Y	N	Y	N	Y	Y	N	Y
2 Pearce	Y	Y	N	N	Y	N	Y	N	Y	Y	N	Y
3 Udall	N	N	Y	Y	N	Y	N	Y	Y	N	Y	N
NEW YORK												
1 Bishop	N	N	Y	Y	N	Y	N	Y	Y	N	Y	N
2 Israel	N	N	Y	Y	N	Y	N	Y	Y	N	Y	N
3 King	Y	Y	N	Y	N	Y	Y	N	Y	Y	N	Y
4 McCarthy	N	N	Y	Y	N	Y	N	Y	Y	N	Y	N
5 Ackerman	N	N	Y	Y	N	Y	?	Y	Y	N	Y	N
6 Meeks	N	N	Y	Y	N	N	N	Y	Y	Y	Y	N
7 Crowley	N	N	Y	Y	N	Y	N	Y	Y	Y	Y	N
8 Nadler	N	N	Y	Y	N	Y	N	Y	?	N	Y	N
9 Weiner	N	N	Y	Y	N	Y	N	Y	Y	N	Y	N
10 Towns	N	N	Y	Y	N	Y	N	Y	N	?	Y	N
11 Owens	N	N	+	Y	N	Y	N	Y	Y	N	Y	N
12 Velázquez	N	N	Y	Y	N	Y	N	Y	Y	?	Y	N
13 Fossella	Y	Y	?	N	Y	N	Y	?	Y	Y	N	Y
14 Maloney	N	N	Y	Y	N	Y	N	Y	Y	N	Y	N
15 Rangel	N	N	Y	Y	N	Y	?	?	Y	Y	N	N
16 Serrano	N	N	Y	Y	N	Y	N	?	Y	N	Y	N

[1] The Speaker votes only at his discretion, usually to break a tie or to emphasize the importance of a matter.

KEY

	Democrats	*Republicans*	**Independent**

Y Voted for ("yea")
N Voted against ("nay")
+ Announced for
# Paired for
X Paired against

– Announced against
P Voted "present"
C Voted "present" to avoid possible conflict of interest
? Did not vote or otherwise make a position known

ND Northern Democrats
SD Southern Democrats
Southern states – Ala., Ark., Fla., Ga., Ky., La., Miss., N.C., Okla., S.C., Tenn., Texas, Va.

House Key Votes	1	2	3	4	5	6	7	8	9	10	11	12
17 Engel	N	N	Y	Y	N	Y	N	Y	Y	N	Y	N
18 Lowey	N	N	Y	Y	N	Y	N	Y	Y	N	Y	N
19 *Kelly*	Y	Y	Y	N	Y	N	Y	Y	Y	Y	N	Y
20 *Sweeney*	Y	Y	Y	N	Y	N	Y	Y	Y	Y	N	Y
21 McNulty	N	N	Y	Y	N	Y	N	Y	Y	Y	Y	N
22 Hinchey	N	N	Y	Y	N	Y	N	Y	Y	N	Y	N
23 *McHugh*	N	Y	Y	Y	Y	Y	N	Y	Y	Y	N	Y
24 *Boehlert*	Y	Y	Y	N	N	Y	N	Y	N	Y	N	Y
25 *Walsh*	Y	Y	N	N	N	Y	Y	N	Y	?	N	Y
26 *Reynolds*	Y	Y	N	Y	N	Y	Y	N	Y	Y	N	Y
27 *Quinn*	N	Y	Y	Y	N	Y	N	Y	Y	Y	N	Y
28 Slaughter	N	N	Y	Y	N	Y	N	Y	Y	N	Y	N
29 *Houghton*	N	Y	?	N	Y	N	Y	N	Y	Y	N	Y
NORTH CAROLINA												
1 Ballance	N	N	Y	Y	N	Y	N	Y	Y	N	Y	N
2 Etheridge	N	N	Y	Y	N	N	N	Y	Y	Y	Y	N
3 *Jones*	Y	Y	N	Y	Y	Y	Y	Y	Y	Y	Y	N
4 Price	N	N	Y	Y	N	N	N	Y	Y	N	Y	N
5 *Burr*	Y	Y	N	Y	Y	N	?	Y	Y	Y	N	Y
6 *Coble*	Y	Y	N	N	Y	N	Y	Y	Y	Y	Y	Y
7 McIntyre	N	N	Y	N	N	Y	N	Y	Y	Y	N	Y
8 *Hayes*	Y	Y	N	N	Y	N	Y	N	Y	Y	N	Y
9 *Myrick*	Y	Y	N	Y	Y	Y	+	N	Y	Y	N	Y
10 *Ballenger*	Y	Y	N	Y	Y	N	?	N	Y	Y	N	Y
11 *Taylor*	Y	Y	N	Y	Y	Y	Y	Y	Y	Y	N	Y
12 Watt	N	N	Y	Y	N	Y	N	Y	?	N	Y	N
13 Miller	N	N	Y	N	N	Y	N	Y	Y	N	Y	N
NORTH DAKOTA												
AL Pomeroy	N	N	Y	Y	N	Y	N	Y	Y	Y	Y	Y
OHIO												
1 *Chabot*	Y	Y	N	N	Y	N	Y	N	Y	Y	Y	N
2 *Portman*	Y	Y	N	Y	Y	N	Y	N	Y	Y	N	Y
3 *Turner*	Y	Y	N	N	Y	N	Y	N	Y	Y	N	Y
4 *Oxley*	Y	Y	N	Y	Y	N	Y	N	Y	Y	N	Y
5 *Gillmor*	Y	Y	N	N	Y	N	Y	N	Y	Y	N	Y
6 Strickland	N	N	Y	Y	N	Y	N	Y	N	N	Y	N
7 *Hobson*	Y	Y	N	N	Y	N	Y	N	Y	Y	N	Y
8 *Boehner*	Y	?	N	N	Y	N	Y	N	Y	Y	N	Y
9 Kaptur	N	N	Y	Y	Y	Y	Y	Y	Y	Y	N	N
10 Kucinich	N	N	Y	Y	N	Y	?	?	?	N	N	N
11 Jones	N	N	Y	Y	P	Y	N	Y	?	N	?	N
12 *Tiberi*	Y	Y	N	Y	Y	N	Y	N	Y	Y	Y	Y
13 Brown	N	N	Y	Y	N	Y	N	Y	Y	N	Y	N
14 *LaTourette*	N	Y	Y	Y	Y	Y	N	Y	Y	Y	N	Y
15 *Pryce*	Y	Y	N	Y	Y	N	Y	N	Y	Y	N	Y
16 *Regula*	Y	Y	N	N	Y	N	Y	N	Y	Y	N	Y
17 Ryan	N	N	Y	Y	N	Y	N	Y	N	Y	Y	N
18 *Ney*	Y	Y	N	N	Y	N	N	N	Y	Y	N	Y
OKLAHOMA												
1 *Sullivan*	Y	Y	N	Y	Y	N	?	Y	Y	Y	N	Y
2 Carson	N	N	Y	N	Y	N	N	Y	Y	Y	Y	Y
3 *Lucas*	Y	Y	N	N	N	N	Y	N	Y	Y	N	Y
4 *Cole*	Y	Y	N	Y	Y	N	Y	N	Y	Y	N	Y
5 *Istook*	Y	Y	N	Y	Y	Y	Y	N	Y	Y	Y	Y
OREGON												
1 Wu	N	N	Y	Y	N	Y	N	Y	Y	N	Y	Y
2 *Walden*	Y	Y	N	Y	Y	N	Y	N	Y	Y	N	Y
3 Blumenauer	N	N	Y	Y	N	Y	N	Y	Y	N	Y	N
4 DeFazio	N	N	Y	Y	N	Y	N	Y	Y	N	Y	N
5 Hooley	N	N	Y	Y	N	Y	N	Y	Y	N	Y	N
PENNSYLVANIA												
1 Brady	N	N	Y	Y	N	Y	N	Y	Y	N	Y	N
2 Fattah	N	N	Y	Y	N	Y	N	Y	Y	N	Y	N
3 *English*	Y	Y	N	Y	N	Y	N	Y	Y	Y	N	Y
4 *Hart*	Y	Y	N	N	Y	N	Y	N	Y	Y	N	Y
5 *Peterson*	Y	Y	N	Y	N	Y	N	Y	Y	Y	N	Y
6 *Gerlach*	Y	Y	N	N	Y	N	Y	N	Y	Y	N	Y

House Key Votes	1	2	3	4	5	6	7	8	9	10	11	12
7 *Weldon*	Y	Y	N	Y	Y	?	Y	N	?	Y	N	Y
8 *Greenwood*	Y	Y	N	N	Y	N	Y	N	Y	N	N	Y
9 *Shuster, Bill*	Y	Y	N	Y	Y	Y	Y	Y	Y	Y	N	Y
10 *Sherwood*	Y	Y	N	N	Y	Y	Y	N	Y	Y	N	Y
11 Kanjorski	N	N	Y	Y	N	Y	N	Y	Y	Y	Y	N
12 Murtha	N	N	Y	Y	N	Y	?	Y	Y	Y	Y	N
13 Hoeffel	N	N	Y	Y	N	Y	N	Y	Y	N	Y	N
14 Doyle	N	N	Y	Y	N	Y	N	Y	Y	Y	Y	N
15 *Toomey*	Y	Y	N	Y	Y	Y	Y	N	Y	Y	N	Y
16 *Pitts*	Y	Y	N	N	Y	N	Y	N	Y	Y	N	Y
17 Holden	N	N	Y	Y	N	Y	N	Y	Y	Y	Y	N
18 *Murphy*	Y	Y	N	N	Y	N	Y	N	Y	Y	N	Y
19 *Platts*	N	Y	N	N	Y	Y	N	Y	Y	Y	Y	Y
RHODE ISLAND												
1 Kennedy	N	N	Y	Y	N	Y	N	Y	Y	Y	Y	N
2 Langevin	N	N	Y	Y	N	Y	N	Y	Y	Y	Y	N
SOUTH CAROLINA												
1 *Brown*	Y	Y	N	N	Y	N	Y	N	Y	Y	N	Y
2 *Wilson*	Y	Y	N	Y	Y	N	Y	N	Y	Y	N	Y
3 *Barrett*	Y	Y	N	Y	Y	N	Y	N	Y	Y	N	Y
4 *DeMint*	Y	Y	N	N	Y	Y	Y	N	Y	Y	N	Y
5 Spratt	N	N	Y	Y	N	Y	N	Y	Y	N	Y	N
6 Clyburn	N	N	Y	Y	N	Y	N	Y	Y	Y	Y	Y
SOUTH DAKOTA												
AL *Janklow*	Y	Y	N	Y	Y	Y	?	?	Y	Y	N	Y
TENNESSEE												
1 *Jenkins*	Y	Y	N	Y	Y	Y	Y	Y	Y	Y	N	Y
2 *Duncan*	Y	Y	N	Y	N	Y	Y	N	Y	Y	Y	Y
3 *Wamp*	Y	Y	N	Y	Y	Y	Y	N	Y	Y	N	Y
4 Davis	N	N	Y	?	N	Y	N	Y	Y	Y	Y	Y
5 Cooper	N	N	Y	Y	N	Y	N	Y	Y	Y	Y	N
6 Gordon	?	N	Y	Y	N	Y	N	Y	Y	Y	Y	N
7 *Blackburn*	Y	Y	N	N	Y	N	Y	N	Y	Y	N	Y
8 Tanner	N	N	Y	Y	N	N	N	Y	Y	Y	Y	Y
9 Ford	N	N	Y	?	N	?	Y	Y	Y	Y	Y	N
TEXAS												
1 Sandlin	N	N	Y	Y	N	Y	N	N	Y	Y	Y	N
2 Turner	N	N	Y	Y	N	Y	N	Y	Y	Y	Y	N
3 *Johnson, Sam*	Y	Y	N	N	Y	N	Y	N	Y	Y	N	Y
4 *Hall*	Y	Y	N	Y	N	Y	N	Y	Y	Y	Y	Y
5 *Hensarling*	Y	Y	N	Y	Y	Y	Y	N	Y	Y	N	Y
6 *Barton*	Y	Y	N	Y	N	Y	Y	N	Y	Y	N	Y
7 *Culberson*	Y	Y	N	Y	Y	Y	Y	N	Y	Y	N	Y
8 *Brady*	Y	Y	N	N	Y	N	Y	N	Y	+	N	Y
9 Lampson	N	N	Y	Y	N	Y	N	Y	Y	Y	Y	N
10 Doggett	N	N	Y	Y	N	Y	N	Y	Y	N	Y	N
11 Edwards	N	N	Y	Y	N	Y	N	Y	Y	N	Y	N
12 *Granger*	Y	Y	N	N	Y	N	Y	N	Y	Y	N	Y
13 *Thornberry*	+	Y	N	N	Y	N	Y	N	Y	Y	N	Y
14 *Paul*	N	N	Y	N	Y	N	N	N	Y	Y	N	Y
15 Hinojosa	N	N	Y	Y	N	Y	N	Y	Y	N	Y	N
16 Reyes	N	N	Y	Y	N	Y	N	Y	?	Y	Y	N
17 Stenholm	N	N	Y	N	N	Y	N	Y	?	Y	Y	Y
18 Jackson-Lee	N	N	Y	Y	N	Y	N	Y	Y	N	Y	N
19 *Combest/ Neugebauer*[2]	Y	?	N	Y	Y	N	Y	N	Y	Y	N	Y
20 Gonzalez	N	N	Y	Y	N	Y	N	Y	Y	N	Y	N
21 *Smith*	Y	Y	N	N	Y	N	Y	N	Y	Y	N	Y
22 *DeLay*	Y	Y	N	N	Y	N	Y	N	Y	Y	N	Y
23 *Bonilla*	Y	?	N	N	Y	N	Y	N	Y	Y	N	Y
24 Frost	N	Y	Y	Y	N	Y	N	Y	Y	N	Y	N
25 Bell	N	N	Y	Y	N	Y	N	Y	Y	N	Y	N
26 *Burgess*	Y	Y	N	Y	Y	N	Y	N	Y	Y	N	Y
27 Ortiz	N	N	Y	Y	N	Y	N	N	Y	Y	N	Y
28 Rodriguez	N	N	Y	Y	N	Y	–	Y	Y	N	Y	N
29 Green	N	N	Y	Y	N	Y	N	Y	Y	N	Y	N
30 Johnson, E.B.	N	N	Y	Y	N	Y	N	Y	Y	N	Y	N
31 *Carter*	Y	Y	N	N	Y	N	Y	N	Y	Y	N	Y
32 *Sessions*	Y	Y	N	N	Y	N	Y	N	Y	Y	N	Y
UTAH												
1 *Bishop*	Y	Y	N	Y	Y	N	Y	N	Y	Y	N	Y
2 Matheson	N	Y	Y	Y	N	N	N	Y	Y	Y	Y	Y
3 *Cannon*	Y	Y	N	N	Y	N	Y	N	Y	Y	N	Y
VERMONT												
AL **Sanders**	N	N	Y	Y	N	Y	N	Y	Y	N	Y	N
VIRGINIA												
1 *Davis, J.*	Y	Y	N	Y	Y	Y	Y	Y	Y	Y	N	Y
2 *Schrock*	Y	Y	N	Y	Y	Y	Y	N	Y	Y	N	Y
3 Scott	N	N	Y	Y	N	Y	N	Y	Y	N	Y	N
4 *Forbes*	Y	Y	N	N	Y	N	Y	N	Y	Y	N	Y
5 *Goode*	Y	Y	N	N	Y	N	Y	N	Y	Y	N	Y
6 *Goodlatte*	Y	Y	N	N	Y	Y	Y	N	Y	Y	N	Y

House Key Votes	1	2	3	4	5	6	7	8	9	10	11	12
7 *Cantor*	Y	Y	N	N	Y	N	Y	N	Y	Y	N	Y
8 *Moran*	N	N	Y	Y	N	Y	N	Y	Y	N	+	N
9 *Boucher*	N	N	Y	Y	N	Y	N	Y	Y	N	Y	Y
10 *Wolf*	Y	Y	N	N	Y	Y	Y	Y	Y	Y	N	Y
11 *Davis, T.*	Y	Y	N	Y	Y	N	Y	N	Y	Y	N	Y
WASHINGTON												
1 Inslee	N	N	Y	Y	N	Y	N	Y	Y	N	Y	N
2 Larsen	N	N	Y	Y	N	Y	N	Y	Y	N	N	N
3 Baird	N	N	Y	Y	N	Y	N	Y	Y	N	N	N
4 *Hastings*	Y	Y	N	Y	Y	Y	Y	N	Y	Y	N	Y
5 *Nethercutt*	Y	Y	N	Y	Y	N	Y	N	Y	Y	N	Y
6 Dicks	N	N	Y	Y	N	Y	N	Y	Y	N	N	N
7 McDermott	N	N	Y	Y	N	Y	N	Y	Y	N	N	N
8 *Dunn*	Y	Y	N	Y	Y	N	Y	N	Y	Y	N	Y
9 Smith	N	N	Y	Y	N	N	N	N	Y	N	N	N
WEST VIRGINIA												
1 Mollohan	N	N	Y	Y	N	Y	?	Y	Y	Y	N	N
2 *Capito*	Y	Y	N	N	Y	Y	Y	Y	Y	Y	N	Y
3 Rahall	N	N	Y	Y	N	Y	N	Y	Y	Y	Y	N

House Key Votes	1	2	3	4	5	6	7	8	9	10	11	12
WISCONSIN												
1 *Ryan*	Y	Y	N	N	Y	Y	Y	N	Y	Y	N	Y
2 Baldwin	N	N	Y	Y	N	Y	N	Y	Y	N	Y	N
3 Kind	N	N	Y	Y	N	Y	N	Y	Y	N	Y	N
4 Kleczka	N	N	Y	Y	N	Y	N	Y	Y	Y	Y	N
5 *Sensenbrenner*	Y	Y	N	N	Y	Y	Y	N	Y	Y	Y	Y
6 *Petri*	Y	Y	N	Y	Y	Y	Y	N	Y	Y	Y	Y
7 Obey	N	N	Y	Y	N	Y	N	Y	Y	Y	Y	N
8 *Green*	Y	Y	N	N	Y	Y	Y	N	Y	Y	N	Y
WYOMING												
AL *Cubin*	Y	Y	N	Y	Y	N	Y	N	Y	Y	N	Y

[2] Rep. Larry Combest, R, resigned effective May 31, 2003. The last vote for which Combest was eligible was vote 2. He was succeeded by Rep. Randy Neugebauer, R, who was sworn in June 5, 2003. The first vote for which Neugebauer was eligible was vote 3.

Senate

1. SURFACE TRANSPORTATION SPENDING

An election-year debate over federal highway and public transit spending demonstrated how local political interests often trump party alliances. In a rare affront to President George W. Bush, Senate Republicans voted by a 2-to-1 margin in February 2004 to return a generous amount of federal transportation dollars to the states despite administration entreaties to hold to a much harder line on spending.

The degree of overwhelming bipartisan support for the highway measure (S 1072) appeared more than sufficient to override a threatened presidential veto. But it never came to that; nettlesome policy disputes with the House meant the president never had to even consider a veto. That was because the $256 billion administration proposal sent to Capitol Hill in early February was not going to pass in any event. Politically influential states in the fast-growing South and Southwest—including Florida, South Carolina, Texas, Arizona, and Nevada—were developing a voracious appetite for transportation funds and wanted at least 95 cents back from each gasoline tax dollar they send to Washington. Currently, they got a minimum of 90.5 cents to the dollar. (*Legislative details, p. 387*)

But under the White House plan these "donor" states would get more money only if billions of dollars were shifted away from a number of Northeastern and northern Plains states that already used more highway dollars than they put into the Highway Trust Fund. Although typically seen as a solid Republican fiscal conservative, James M. Inhofe of Oklahoma, the chairman of the Senate Environment and Public Works Committee, sided with prohighway spenders, saying more infrastructure financing paid important dividends later because it boosted safety, created jobs, and helped the economy stay strong. Bush administration officials said they did not disagree with Inhofe's premise but argued the federal budget deficit and a still tentative economy meant that the transportation bill had to meet three tests to win enactment: it could not increase the deficit; it could not raise taxes, including the federal excise tax on gasoline; and it could not use borrowing.

Supporting the administration in the Senate was a small group of fiscal conservatives including Oklahoma's other senator, Republican Budget Chairman Don Nickles. But the fiscal conservatives were in the minority. Majority Leader Bill Frist, R-Tenn., sympathetic to the arguments of the dissenters but anxious to get a bill passed, brought the measure to a vote the evening of Feb. 12. It passed by a lopsided 76–21; R 34–17; D 41–4; I 1–0. By the end of the year, however, the Senate's fiscal conservatives got their way when the legislation stalled in a House-Senate conference committee; lawmakers could not find a way to overcome the White House objections over the spending level or the concerns of lawmakers from the donor states. (*Vote, p. 864*)

2. MEDICAL MALPRACTICE LIABILITY

Bill Frist of Tennessee, a heart and lung transplant surgeon for most of his professional life, wanted to make improving the health care system the signature achievement of his first term as the Senate's Republican majority leader. After shepherding the creation of a Medicare prescription drug benefit into law (PL 108-173) in 2003, he made limitations on medical malpractice liability his top health care priority for 2004. (*Legislative details, p. 517*)

But Frist's campaign went nowhere, even after he narrowed his objective to shielding some of the most politically sympathetic medical specialists—obstetricians, gynecologists, and nurse midwives—from multimillion-dollar punitive damages and framed his campaign as an effort to improve medical care for women. Despite Frist's efforts, the bill stalled mostly on party lines.

Frist sought to cap noneconomic damage awards in all medical malpractice lawsuits at $250,000, arguing that would achieve two objectives: help slow increases in doctors' insurance premiums, which have driven some of them into early retirement, and hold down health costs by limiting the practice of "defensive medicine" that involved ordering tests or procedures with marginal benefit because of the fear of future lawsuits. The House passed a comprehensive bill shielding all doctors in 2003; it came to a halt in the Senate when Frist's bid to limit debate on that narrow bill (S 2061) came up a dozen votes short of the sixty required for invoking cloture. The vote was 48–45; R 47–3; D 1–41; I 0–1. Only one Democrat, Robert C. Byrd of West Virginia, stood with him, while three Republicans went against him: Michael D. Crapo of Idaho, Richard C. Shelby of Alabama, and Lindsey Graham of South Carolina. (*Vote, p. 864*)

After his narrow proposal stalled, Frist sought to revive his campaign one more time by pressing a bill (S 2207) that would have limited punitive damages against emergency room doctors and trauma center personnel as well as obstetricians and gynecologists. But that legislation died in April as another cloture vote once again came up far short of success. That vote was 49–48.

3. EXTENSION OF ASSAULT WEAPONS BAN

Gun rights advocates believed they were in position to win at least one significant success in Congress during the year. Their primary goal was enactment of legislation to bar, with some exceptions, lawsuits against the manufacturers, distributors, dealers, and importers of firearms and ammunition. The purpose was to limit attempts at making the gun industry financially liable for the consequences of gun violence—cases that usually failed but nevertheless required defendants to spend large sums on legal expenses.

The House passed its version of the legislation (HR 1036) with ease in April 2003. As the Republican leaders prepared to put the companion measure (S 1805) on the Senate floor eleven months later, the National Rifle Association (NRA) pressed its senatorial allies to vote against a series of expected "killer" amendments. The White House, for its part, issued a statement of administration policy encouraging the Senate to pass the bill essentially untouched. (*Legislative details, p. 615*)

But that effort failed almost from the outset. On the first amendment offered, senators voted overwhelmingly to buck the gun lobby's wishes and require the sale of a child safety lock with every handgun transaction. When the debate resumed March 2, the Senate delivered the final blow to the bill, voting to renew prohibitions against a collection of semiautomatic assault weapons that was enacted in 1994 but due to expire in six months. The vote to add the assault weapons ban to the bill was 52–47: R 10–41; D 41–6; I 1–0. *(Vote, p. 864)*

Gun control advocates were able to build support for the amendment, eventually winning the votes of ten Republicans, by capitalizing on the electorate's heightened concerns about terrorism in an election year. But even a few hours before the vote, the proposal's principal sponsors—Democrats Dianne Feinstein of California and Charles E. Schumer of New York—predicted they would not prevail. Mindful that the vote would be close, they worked to ensure that everyone in their caucus was on hand—including John Kerry of Massachusetts, who by then had all-but-formally secured his party's presidential nomination, and John Edwards of North Carolina, the eventual vice-presidential nominee, who abandoned his presidential bid later that night after a final series of primary and caucus losses.

On two fronts, the ballot was a high-water mark in the 108th Congress for the advocates of gun control—and their first substantive legislative success at the Capitol in five years. Soon after the language was added, the sponsors of the underlying bill turned against the measure and engineered its defeat.

4. 'PAY AS YOU GO' BUDGET RULES

From the beginning of 2004 top Republicans warned that a fiscal 2005 budget resolution might never be finished, in large part because of disagreements between the party's moderates and conservatives over tax policy. In an election year when the Congressional Budget Office at the start of the year was projecting a record federal deficit of $477 billion, the stage was set for a particularly bumpy budget debate. *(Legislative details, p. 61)*

Senate GOP leaders said that President Bush's most ambitious tax cut plans had no chance until he won a second term. Instead, leaders sought to focus their efforts on extending a trio of popular tax breaks set to expire at the end of 2004—a $1,000 per child tax credit, an expanded 10 percent tax bracket, and tax relief for married couples. Senate Budget Chairman Don Nickles, R-Okla., proposed a budget blueprint (S Con Res 95) that would have provided procedural "reconciliation" protections for $82.6 billion in tax cuts, enough to cover extending those three breaks and little more.

Even this modest plan met with skepticism from several GOP moderates and deficit hawks who said that the deepening deficit would make it difficult for them to support the proposal. Instead, the moderates lined up behind an amendment by Wisconsin Democrat Russell D. Feingold to reinstate pay-as-you-go language requiring that any new tax cuts or new entitlement spending program be offset by accompanying tax increases or spending cuts—or face being struck down on the Senate floor, at least during the five-year period covered by the budget resolution, by a point of order that could be overcome only with the support of sixty or more senators. Nickles's included a less-stringent version of the pay-as-you-go requirement in his budget resolution. It required that new entitlement spending be offset unless sixty senators in effect voted otherwise. It did not subjected the tax cuts called for within the budget blueprint to the same rule.

But that was not enough to win over fellow Republicans Olympia J. Snowe and Susan Collins of Maine, Lincoln Chafee of Rhode Island, and John McCain of Arizona. When the Senate voted on the Feingold amendment March 10, those four joined forty-six Democrats and Independent James M. Jeffords of Vermont in voting for it. In a defeat that momentarily stunned GOP leaders, the amendment was adopted, 51–48: R 4–47; D 46–1; I 1–0. Zell Miller of Georgia was the only Democrat to vote against it. *(Vote, p. 864)*

The vote sealed the fiscal policy impasse for the year. For only the third time in the three decades of modern budget law, no annual congressional budget resolution was adopted by Congress in 2004. House conservatives made clear they were adamantly opposed to placing any restrictions on tax cuts in a compromise budget document. Weeks of tortured conference negotiations followed before Senate and House GOP leaders settled on a one-year budget deal that would exempt the three proposed tax cut extensions from pay-as-you-go rules. When all four of the pivotal Senate GOP moderates spurned that language as well, the talks collapsed.

5. CRIMINALIZATION OF HARM TO A FETUS

Social conservatives in Congress had tried without success since 1999 to create a new category of crimes against a fetus. Proponents described the effort as a law-and-order campaign but opponents of abortion rights quietly hoped that their cause would be strengthened if the fetus were recognized under federal law as an entity distinct from the pregnant woman. The House passed such a bill twice by comfortable margins, in 1999 and 2001, but the Senate never took up the legislation. The cause gained momentum in April 2003 when the bodies of Laci Peterson and the fetus she had carried nearly to term washed ashore near San Francisco. Peterson's husband, Scott, was eventually charged under state law with two counts of murder because California is one of thirty states with fetal homicide laws.

The extensive coverage of the case made a federal version of such a law politically attractive but timing was an issue. Because other pressing items were on their agenda in 2003—including the enactment of the law (PL 108-105) that criminalized a procedure described as "partial birth" abortion—social conservatives decided to wait until the election year. The House passed the legislation (HR 1997) Feb. 26, 2004, with 254 votes, essentially the same number that had backed the measure in the House the previous two times. *(Legislative details, p. 513)*

Some abortion rights advocates wanted an aggressive effort to again stop the bill in the Senate. However, mindful that the Peterson case was giving support for the measure, Democrats who generally aligned themselves with abortion rights decided they did not want to erect too many procedural roadblocks. After just one day of substantive debate the Senate March 25 cleared the legislation by a comfortable margin, 61–38: R 48–2; D 13–35; I 0–1. *(Vote, p. 864)*

Only two abortion rights Republicans, Lincoln Chafee of Rhode Island and Olympia J. Snowe of Maine, voted against the bill. Democrats joined them by a ratio of 2-to-1; among those voting "no" were John Kerry of Massachusetts and John Edwards of North Carolina, who later in the year became the party's national ticket. Among the thirteen Democrats voting for it, however, where Minority Leader Tom Daschle of South Dakota and Minority Whip Harry Reid of Nevada.

The bill defined an "unborn child" as "a member of the species homo sapiens, at any stage of development, who is carried in the womb." Opponents said that was a clear attempt to lay the legal groundwork for neutralizing *Roe v. Wade*, the 1973 Supreme Court decision that legalized abortion. In that landmark case, Supreme Court Justice Harry A. Blackmun, writing for the majority, concluded that "the unborn have never been recognized in the law as persons in the whole sense" and that the court was not ruling on "the difficult question of when life begins."

6. CHILD CARE FOR WELFARE RECIPIENTS

Eight years after the enactment of the legislation revising federal welfare programs, lawmakers continue to argue over the proper formula to assist the nation's remaining 2 million welfare families escape poverty. They reached no resolution in 2004 but a lopsided Senate vote in March reflected the balancing of "carrots" and "sticks" that was needed to get a welfare policy rewrite through the Republican-run Congress. Most lawmakers characterized the 1996 law (PL 104-193) as a success. That legislation ended more than sixty years of guaranteed cash assistance for recipients and ushered in new work requirements and a five-year limit on benefits. Caseloads fell by more than half after enactment, although some skeptics of the law believed the decline had as much to do with prosperous economic times during that decade as with the changes in the welfare system.

President Bush and his congressional GOP allies argued that work was the most important ingredient to help people move from a handout to a paycheck. This view was reflected in the version of the welfare reauthorization (HR 4) passed by the House in 2003; it increased the work requirement for adult participants to a full forty hours a week, up from thirty hours in existing law. The House measure also contained $1 billion in additional child care funding and a $200 million White House initiative to promote healthy marriages to the poor. *(Legislative details, p. 525)*

But in the Senate, Democrats and some moderate Republicans contended that increasing the length of the required workweek by one-third would hamper the ability of welfare recipients to keep in order other aspects of their lives such as child care, transportation, and education that were considered essential to employment. Finance Committee Chairman Charles E. Grassley, R-Iowa, who believe that a forty-hour workweek requirement could not pass the Senate, moved a bill through his panel that raised the threshold to thirty-four hours.

To win committee approval, Grassley promised moderate Republican Olympia J. Snowe of Maine that she could offer an first amendment to provide $6 billion in additional mandatory child care funding over the next five years. Snowe maintained that current spending was only enough to serve one in seven families eligible for that type of assistance. The White House opposed Snowe's proposal on the ground that the extra money could go not to welfare families but to families who had left the welfare rolls but continued to have incomes low enough to make them eligible for the subsidies. The Senate, however, sided overwhelmingly with Snowe. Her amendment was adopted 78–20: R 31–19; D 46–1; I 1–0. *(Vote, p. 864)*

Three out of every five Republicans from across the GOP ideological spectrum broke with the White House and voted for the language, including Grassley, Majority Leader Bill Frist of Tennessee, and nearly all Republicans facing tough reelection campaigns. Grassley hoped the Snowe amendment would be the sweetener to win Democrats' support for the underlying bill. But Democrats refused to allow a final vote unless they were given an opportunity to vote on an amendment to raise the minimum wage. When GOP leaders rebuffed that request, the bill fell into limbo for the rest of the year.

7. OVERTIME REGULATIONS

Supporters of a Bush administration plan to change overtime pay rules for millions of workers were aware that they faced a heated battle in Congress. The White House had been on the defensive on the issue since March 2003 when it first proposed a comprehensive rewrite of overtime pay rules, including a reordering of the job descriptions that would be eligible for premium pay. It was the first overhaul of the overtime provisions in the Fair Labor Standards Act in more than fifty years. That law established the forty-hour workweek. *(Legislative details, p. 574)*

Senate Democrats were aided by the support of a few Republicans sympathetic to labor unions to hand the Bush administration a politically embarrassing defeat on the workplace issue in May. The victory was short-lived. Congress later allowed the new regulations to take effect but the effort to highlight the issue was helpful to the Democrats in several ways. Sen. John Kerry of Massachusetts, the party's presidential nominee, was able to use it to solidify his support among labor union members and to portray President Bush as insensitive to the concerns of working Americans. The party's Senate candidates also were given ammunition for attacking Republicans from high-unemployment states.

It was also the second time in six months that Democrats won a Senate vote on the issue but were unable to alter the underlying policy. In September 2003 senators voted to block implementation of any Labor Department rule that would take away existing overtime eligibility from any worker. But that language—which had been added to the fiscal 2004 spending package for the department—was dropped at the last minute at the insistence of the White House.

Sensing congressional uneasiness, the Labor Department revised its proposed regulations in April, declaring that more workers would retain overtime eligibility than would have under the initial rules. But the alterations did not satisfy the labor unions. They claimed that the altered rule would take overtime eligibility away from as many as 6 million workers—a figure the administration said was wildly exaggerated. As a condition of allowing a rewrite of the corporate tax code (S 1637) to move through the Senate, Democrats won the right to offer an amendment, by Iowa's Tom Harkin, nearly identical to the one adopted the previous fall.

Fearing a vote against the president, Republican leaders offered a competing amendment. Judd Gregg of New Hampshire, chairman of the Health, Education, Labor and Pensions Committee, said his proposal would protect overtime pay eligibility for employees in fifty-five professions who were not expressly protected in the final rule. The Gregg amendment was meant to siphon the support of the six Republicans who voted for the Harkin amendment in 2003—and, in fact, it was adopted without a single dissenting vote. But senators nonetheless voted on May 4 to adopt Harkin's amendment as well. The vote was 52–47: R 5–46; D 46–1; I 1–0. *(Vote, p. 864)*

Republicans Lisa Murkowski of Alaska, Ben Nighthorse Campbell of Colorado, Lincoln Chafee of Rhode Island, Olympia J. Snowe of Maine, and Arlen Specter of Pennsylvania crossed party lines to vote with all the Democrats except Zell Miller of Georgia. Senate Appropriations Chairman Ted Stevens of Alaska was the only Republican who voted with Harkin in 2003 but returned to the GOP fold this year. Conferees later dropped the language from the final version of the corporate tax bill and the overtime rules took effect Aug. 23.

8. BASE CLOSURE DELAY

Congress agreed in 2001 to President Bush's request for another round of military base closings and realignments but only if the changes were delayed until 2005, thereby requiring Bush to win reelection if he wanted to control the process. In the intervening period a group of lawmakers from both parties fought doggedly to modify or delay the process further. But their campaign began to collapse after they narrowly lost a pivotal Senate vote in the spring. As happened four other times since the process was created in 1988, the commissions would review a Pentagon plan for proposed closures and draw up a final list, which would take effect unless Congress voted to reject it entirely. That never happened with previous base closing plans.

Opposition to additional base closures was generally been stronger in the House where many lawmakers stand for reelection every two years in districts with economies dominated by the presence of military installations. But because plenty of senators, in both parties, had similar concerns the Senate, votes on the topic were close and the debates heated. In the House, the Armed Services Committee wrote a fiscal 2005 defense authorization bill in May that delayed all base closings for two years, until 2007. The next week, the Senate was called on to decide whether to go along with the House or side with the president, who was insisting on proceeding with base closures in 2005. By the narrowest of margins, they sided with Bush.

The vote came May 18 on an amendment to the Senate's defense authorization bill (S 2400) by Trent Lott, R-Miss. It limited the 2005 round to U.S. overseas bases and permitted no domestic closures before 2007, and then only under a new series of requirements. In a vote during which partisanship was replaced almost entirely by parochialism the amendment was rejected, 47–49: R 21–29; D 26–19; I 0–1. *(Vote, p. 864)*

The following day the White House threatened to veto any defense authorization bill that delayed or blocked the 2005 round. The House emphatically ignored that warning however, when 259 lawmakers voted against an amendment that would have scratched the delaying language from the defense authorization bill and kept the base closing schedule on course. The Senate considered its defense bill off and on for another five weeks before passing it June 23 but no further effort was made to challenge the 2005 base closures.

9. CLASS ACTION LAWSUITS

Republicans lost their best chance to enact business-backed legislation to overhaul the civil litigation system when a cloture vote that would have sped passage of the bill (S 2062) failed. The vote was the pivotal test of each party's ability to use Senate rules to advance its election-year legislative agenda. By stalling the bill the minority Democrats demonstrated that they would not be steamrolled, even though many of them supported the bill, and the majority Republicans subsequently arranged for the Democrats to offer some of their amendments as a price for moving high-profile legislation. The bill would have shifted more class action lawsuits from state to federal courts, which advocates said would reduce the number of suits moved to jurisdictions where large financial judgments were commonplace. *(Legislative details, p. 608)*

By the time the measure reached the Senate floor it had the support of all fifty-one Republicans and a dozen Democrats, together more than enough senators to invoke cloture and limit debate. But the bill's wide support made it attractive for unrelated amendments as the legislative year neared conclusion. Majority Leader Bill Frist, R-Tenn., insisted that adding provisions that were not germane to the bill would consume too much of the Senate's limited time and make it more difficult to push the bill through a conference with the House. Minority Leader Tom Daschle, D-S.D., saw matters entirely differently. He and other Democrats wanted to use the debate on the bill to highlight their election-year priorities, proposing amendments to raise the minimum wage, extend federal unemployment insurance, and block administration-backed Labor Department rules on overtime pay.

Rather than permit votes on the Democratic amendments, Frist used his prerogative as majority leader to "fill the amendment tree, " which meant introducing enough amendments of his own to preclude any others from being offered. The maneuver drew protests from some Republicans as well as the Democrats. Frist's last hope was

a motion to invoke cloture, thereby limiting the debate to amendments germane to civil litigation. Frist pulled the bill off the floor altogether when his cloture motion fell sixteen votes short of the supermajority required. The vote was 44–43: R 42–3; D 2–39; I 0–1. *(Vote, p. 864)*

Ten of the twelve Democratic supporters of the bill stuck with their party leader on this test of wills: Evan Bayh of Indiana, Jeff Bingaman of New Mexico, Maria Cantwell of Washington, Thomas R. Carper of Delaware, Christopher J. Dodd of Connecticut, Dianne Feinstein of California, Herb Kohl of Wisconsin, Mary L. Landrieu of Louisiana, Blanche Lincoln of Arkansas, and Charles E. Schumer of New York. The only Democrats who broke with Daschle were Ben Nelson of Nebraska and the perpetually iconoclastic Zell Miller of Georgia. At the same time, three Republicans who wanted to amend the bill with election-year priorities of their own broke with Frist: Larry E. Craig of Idaho, Richard C. Shelby of Alabama, and John McCain of Arizona.

10. GAY MARRIAGE PROHIBITION

A pair of judicial rulings in 2003 convinced social conservatives that the Supreme Court would overturn a 1996 statute (PL 104-199) that defined marriage under federal law as "the union of a man and a woman." Their efforts to make gay marriage a defining political issues led to Senate and House votes on a constitutional amendment to prohibit marriage of homosexual couples, the first taken by Congress. But the initial test vote on the proposal, in the Senate in July, showed that the conservatives were far short of the support they need to get approval of an amendment.

In June 2003 the Supreme Court declared unconstitutional a Texas law outlawing sodomy. Five months later the Massachusetts Supreme Judicial Court ruled that gay people had the same right to be married under that state's constitution as straight people. The rulings revived what had been a moribund campaign to make the definition of marriage part of the Constitution. Under strong pressure from social conservatives to make the issue a defining election-year theme Republican leaders agreed to put it at the top of the crowded summertime legislative agenda.

On July 12, shortly before the opening of the Democratic National Convention in Boston, Majority Leader Bill Frist, R-Tenn., tried to call up a resolution (S J Res 40) by Wayne Allard, R-Colo., proposing a constitutional amendment defining marriage as the union of a man and a woman and specifying that neither the U.S. Constitution nor any state constitution sanctions marriages that do not comply with that definition. *(Legislative details, p. 613)*

Supporters cast themselves as defenders of marriage—and, by extension, allies of children and families—not as opponents of gay rights. They argued that without a constitutional amendment judges would legalize gay marriage everywhere. Opponents said the institution of marriage was not threatened, that the Constitution was the wrong place to have the debate over the definition of marriage, and that the debate was an unnecessary diversion from more immediate domestic and foreign policy matters.

When Republicans could not agree among themselves on the ideal language, Frist proposed votes on two versions: the one by Allard and another without the language barring judges from ruling that gays have the right to marry. When Democrats resisted, Frist moved to invoke cloture limiting debate on his motion to consider the measure. The debate was set aside after his motion was rejected, 48–50: R 45–6; D 3–43; I 0–1. *(Vote, p. 864)*

The forty-eight votes were a dozen short of the sixty needed to overcome a filibuster and nineteen short of the two-thirds majority needed to approve a constitutional amendment for the states to consider. Six moderate Republicans voted against Frist; only three Democrats voted with him. The two missing senators were the party's 2004 national ticket: John Kerry of Massachusetts and John Edwards of North Carolina. In September the House fell forty-nine votes short of adopting a companion resolution.

11. PRIVATIZATION OF FEDERAL JOBS

One of President Bush's few policies that ran into significant opposition from his party in Congress was his proposal to turn over to private enterprise more work now performed by federal employees. When Republicans with large numbers of government workers as constituents once again sided with Democrats to oppose such privatization, the administration quietly backed away from one narrow but symbolically important aspect of its plan.

In December 2003 the Homeland Security Department set in motion a competition that could have led to the privatization of more than 1,100 immigration services jobs, a relatively small slice of the estimated 23,000 positions that the administration was considering for privatization at the time. Before long, though, the struggle between the employees of the department's Citizenship and Immigration Services bureau and the companies that might bid for their jobs spilled over into debate on the fiscal 2005 Homeland Security funding measure (HR 4567). In June the House voted by a wide margin, 242–163, to adopt an amendment to the bill preventing the department from carrying out its plans to contract-out the jobs. Some of the forty-nine Republicans in the majority had immigration services workers as constituents; others represented districts where labor unions were a potent political force. (Legislative details, p. 690)

The Office of Management and Budget warned the Senate against following the House lead, saying the president's advisers would recommend he veto the spending bill if it restricted the administration's competitive sourcing efforts, which it said could save $1 billion over time. But Patrick J. Leahy, D-Vt., argued that the work, which included citizenship application processing, was too sensitive to be left to the private sector. He offered an amendment later that day similar to the House language that the Senate narrowly adopted 49–47: R 5–46; D 43–1; I 1–0. (Vote, p. 864)

With the support of Pennsylvania's Arlen Specter, one of the most prolabor Republicans in the Senate, the language was retained in the conference agreement on the bill. But, almost simultaneously, Homeland Security Secretary Tom Ridge had a letter delivered to the conferees announcing that he was canceling the jobs competition on his own authority, making the Bush veto threat moot. The president signed the bill (PL 108-334) on Oct. 18.

12. EXTENDING MIDDLE-CLASS TAX CUTS

Republicans began 2004 committed to extending many of the tax breaks recently enacted as part of a package protected under special budgetary rules limiting Senate debate. Members in both parties wanted those tax cut extensions scaled back in order to reduce their cost to the government. These so-called deficit hawks were more concerned about limiting the rapidly widening gap between federal revenues and expenditures. But some of the Bush tax cuts enjoyed a broad appeal in Congress despite a record federal budget deficit. A lopsided Senate vote in September demonstrated conclusively the attraction of voting for lower taxes in an election year.

But hopes for significant tax cuts collapsed when the annual budget resolution died early in the year over disputes about spending and revenue. Republicans then began considering a campaign strategy to benefit the GOP while creating a predicament for the Democrats, particularly their presidential candidate, John Kerry. To pay for some of his campaign initiatives, the Massachusetts senator advocated the repeal of many of the 2001 and 2003 tax cuts for families annually earning more than $200,000. The Republicans' strategy also promised to test the resolve of their own deficit hawks, especially in the Senate, who had worked with the Democrats to block tax cuts they regarded as overly generous budget-busters. (Legislative details, p. 111)

At the start of summer, the White House urged senior Republicans to move ahead on an extension of popular tax cuts in July. A midsummer vote would have forced Kerry, vice presidential candidate John Edwards of North Carolina, and other Democrats to choose whether to support or oppose tax breaks right before the party's national convention.

Just before the summer recess in August the White House spurned a deal on a $75 billion short-term extension of tax breaks nearly worked out by Senate Finance Committee Chairman Charles E. Grassley, R-Iowa. The deal had the backing of Minority Leader Tom Daschle, who was eager to bend on taxes while he waged his intense, and ultimately unsuccessful, bid for election to a fourth Senate term from South Dakota. The addition of language accelerating a scheduled increase in the refundable child tax credit helped win the support of some wavering Democratic moderates. But as the vote on the final measure (HR 1308) approached, just weeks before members were headed home to campaign, Democratic opposition collapsed altogether. Just before the roll was called Sept. 23, Kerry was on the campaign trail in Pennsylvania, where he announced his endorsement of the package as a means to help families "squeezed by the weak Bush economy."

On the vote the only dissent came from a trio of deficit hawks who objected to the measure's cost, $146 billion over ten years, and criticized the lack of offsets to pay for it. The Senate cleared the bill by a vote of 92–3: R 49–2; D 42–1; I 1–0. (Vote, p. 864)

Signed into law Oct. 4 (PL 108-311), the measure extended the $1,000 per-child tax credit through 2009, the upper limit for the 10 percent income tax bracket through 2010, and tax breaks for married couples through 2008. It also extended for one year the existing income exemptions from the alternative minimum tax and extended the research and development tax credit through 2005.

13. INTELLIGENCE-GATHERING OVERHAUL

In a rare display of bipartisan cooperation just one month before a strongly contested presidential election, the Senate voted overwhelmingly for legislation to reorganize the nation's intelligence system along the lines proposed by an independent commission that investigated government failings in advance of the Sept. 11 terrorist attacks. The Pentagon did not like the bill, House Republican leaders pushed for a different approach, and President Bush appeared ambivalent about the entire plan until late in the fall. But during the ensuing two months, the nearly unanimous support for the initial Senate measure would dictate the terms for the most important law enacted during the year. (Legislative details, p. 263)

Many senators had reservations about the measure (S 2845) when it came to the floor. Two Senate moderates were the bill's main sponsors—Republican Susan Collins of Maine and Democrat Joseph I. Lieberman of Connecticut. Collins, who chaired the Governmental Affairs Committee, and Lieberman, the ranking Democrat, accepted the need for a powerful national intelligence director and a national counterterrorism center that were recommended by the Sept. 11 commission, which Congress had created a year after the attacks. The two worked together to overcome concerns of Armed Services and

Appropriations committee members who feared they would lose control over the fifteen-agency, $40 billion intelligence system.

In spite of sharp criticism from some of the most powerful figures in the Senate, among them Appropriations Chairman Ted Stevens, R-Alaska, Armed Services Chairman John W. Warner, R-Va., and Robert C. Byrd, D-W.Va., the ranking minority party member on Appropriations, most senators were ready to stick close to the commission's recommendations. Collins and Lieberman did not lose a single roll call on proposed amendments to their bill; either they engineered the defeat of the proposals they opposed, or they worked to modify amendments before accepting them. The bill passed on Oct 6 by 96–2: R 51–0; D 44–2; I 1–0. (*Vote, p. 864*)

14. CORPORATE TAX OVERHAUL

Business groups had watched and waited through the first three years of the Bush administration while the president won $1.7 trillion in tax cuts targeted mainly to individuals. Republican leaders repeatedly assured them that they would get their turn. It came late on the last day of the regular session in 2004, when, after a weekend of filibusters and side deals, the Senate cleared the corporate tax bill. The measure (HR 4520—PL 108-357), which was expected to reduce business taxes by $137 billion over ten years, the biggest corporate tax overhaul since 1986.

The Senate had enthusiastically embraced its own version of the legislation, passing it 92–5 in May. That bill included the repeal of the $5 billion-a-year export subsidy; the need to end international sanctions against U.S. goods triggered by the subsidy created the need for the bill in the first place. That subsidy was replaced with $167 billion in business tax breaks. But to get it through the Senate, GOP leaders also included enough revenue-raising provisions and accounting maneuvers to declare that the entire cost had been offset.

In assembling the final version of the bill, House Ways and Means Committee Chairman Bill Thomas, R-Calif., worked with lawmakers in both chambers to see what they would need to support the final product. He also managed to find ways to offset the cost—including shifting some expensive tax cuts to the middle-class tax bill also moving toward enactment—without losing House conservatives who viewed such provisions as tax increases.

The final package also included a $10 billion buyout of tobacco farmers needed to secure the votes of southerners in the House but did not include federal regulation of tobacco products. The Senate in July paired the buyout with tobacco regulation but the latter was unacceptable to many House members including key leaders. Thomas calculated that he could leave regulation out and use the billions of dollars in sweeteners added to the legislation to move it through the House and then win at least the sixty votes needed to overcome any Senate filibuster. That gamble paid off with ease in the House, which adopted the conference report overwhelmingly. It worked in the Senate as well, although not before a weekend session of lengthy floor speeches during which disgruntled senators extracted even a few more symbolic concessions, all of which died at the end of the session. With all the haggling done, the Senate cleared the bill on a bipartisan a vote of 69–17: R 43–3; D 25–14; I 1–0. (*Vote, p. 864*)

The centerpiece was a $77 billion tax break on manufacturing income. The legislation also provided $43 billion in tax cuts on the overseas profits of U.S. multinationals, aimed at enhancing their competitive position against foreign rivals. About $14 billion in tax breaks went to a long list of beneficiaries, from fishermen to bow and arrow makers.

House

1. UNEMPLOYMENT BENEFITS EXTENSION

Democrats in 2004 expected that they could develop a potent campaign issue at the start of the year after the Republican-run Congress declined to renew a supplemental unemployment insurance program (PL 108-26) that expired at the end of 2003. Uneasiness about the state of the economic recovery was not confined to Democrats. Some Republicans from the industrial Midwest worried about the decline of manufacturing for their constituents. House GOP leaders, however, would not permit a vote on a bill to continue the federal benefits, fearing that the measure would pass and send a skeptical message about the economy while President George W. Bush was preparing his reelection campaign. The expired program, begun when the Sept. 11, 2001, terrorist attacks contributed to a sharp economic downturn, provided thirteen extra weeks of benefits for persons who had exhausted their twenty-six weeks of state benefits. (*Legislative details, p. 573*)

But George Miller of California, the ranking Democrat on the Education and the Workforce Committee, saw opportunity in early February when a bill to reauthorize the Community Services Block Grant program (HR 3030) came to the floor under procedures that allowed amendments. Miller offered an amendment to extend the federal unemployment benefits for six months; this tactic of forcing Republicans to vote on proposals of principal benefit to the working class individuals and families became a theme of Democratic legislative strategies the rest of the year.

Republican leaders opposed the proposal, arguing that it was more about scoring political points than helping the unemployed. John A. Boehner, R-Ohio, chairman of the Education and the Workforce Committee, argued that the amendment would authorize the program without appropriate any money for it. But a majority of lawmakers—every Democrat on the House floor Feb. 4 and one-sixth of the Republican caucus—decided that it was unwise to vote against federal unemployment aid at the outset of an election year. Thirty-nine Republicans broke ranks with the GOP leadership. In an important embarrassment for the GOP leadership Miller's amendment was adopted easily by a vote of 227–179: R 39–179; D 187–0; I 1–0. (*Vote, p. 866*)

The underlying bill passed by voice vote. The Senate passed its version of the community services bill later in February but the measure went no further. Most Republicans who supported the Miller amendment represented states that had lost manufacturing jobs. Others were moderates or the holders of politically competitive seats.

2. SUCCESS OF WAR IN IRAQ

One year after the U.S.-led military coalition toppled Saddam Hussein from power in Iraq, Republicans commemorated the anniversary by writing a resolution—without any Democratic input—and using its adoption by the House as a powerful campaign document. At a time when the Democratic presidential candidate, Sen. John Kerry of Massachusetts, appeared ambivalent about the war in Iraq, Republicans worded the resolution (H Res 557) in such a way that House Democrats, by a narrow majority, concluded they had to support it. The vote highlighted the party's mixed feelings and messages about the war, making it all the more difficult for Democrats to use the conduct of the campaign as a defining issue against President Bush and congressional Republicans. To that extent, the vote helped to neutralize the war as an issue for the remaining eight months of the election year. *(Legislative details, p. 283)*

The resolution was brought to the floor March 17, the first anniversary of Bush's ultimatum to Hussein to leave Iraq or face invasion. At the resolution's core was a series of statements about Saddam's regime that amounted to a human rights argument that had been only tangential to the president's rationale for invading Iraq. The resolution said nothing about the weapons of mass destruction that had been a central argument in the administration's case for war.

The resolution affirmed that "the United States and the world have been made safer with the removal of Saddam Hussein and his regime from power in Iraq," and acclaimed the military performance that accomplished it. It also commended the Iraqi people for their courage during Saddam's reign and their adoption of an interim constitution.

The deftly written set of statements prompted many Democrats to conclude that supporting the language was a wiser political move than opposing it. The House adopted the resolution by a resounding 327–93: R 222–2 D 105–90; I 0–1. Thirty-six of the Democrats who in 2002 voted against the law (PL 107-243) authorizing the use of force against Iraq voted in favor of the congratulatory resolution. Nine went the other way. *(Vote, p. 866)*

3. SURFACE TRANSPORTATION SPENDING

The vote in the House in spring 2004 to reauthorize surface transportation programs at generous levels marked a collision of three potent and ultimately irreconcilable political forces. There was the White House, which had a strong desire to hold down federal spending as President Bush campaigned for a second term as a fiscal conservative. There was the House GOP leadership, which had hopes of shielding the president from an embarrassing campaign season showdown with rank-and-file members of his party. There also were those very Republican lawmakers, in reelection races of their own, who wanted to bring home as much spending as possible for local highway and public transit projects before the November voting.

There were no clear winners in that clash. The chairman of the House Transportation and Infrastructure Committee, Alaska Republican Don Young, led an overwhelming majority of House members April 2 in defying a strongly worded White House veto threat and passing a reauthorization bill (HR 3550) that far exceeded the bottom line set by the president. The vote was a bipartisan 357–65: R 162–59; D 194–6; I 1–0. *(Legislative details, p. 387; Vote, p. 866)*

The huge majority showed that a presidential veto almost certainly would be overridden by Congress, especially because seven weeks earlier the Senate had voted by an even wider margin to pass a highway bill (S 1072) that was more expensive than the House bill.

Rather than force Bush to issue the first veto of his presidency, however, the House and Senate votes signaled the end for a long-term surface transportation policy bill in the 108th Congress. Negotiators never came close to agreeing on a funding formula or spending level, and as a consequence thousands of road projects that lawmakers had hoped to see started during the summer of 2004 were delayed.

4. LIMITATIONS ON FEDERAL SPENDING

It was not the House Republican leadership's intention to permit debates on reviving expired statutory caps on appropriations or increasing entitlement programs. To do so would highlight internal party divisions or requiring scheduling legislation that was likely to be defeated. But that is exactly what happened during a floor debate on legislation (HR 4663) to impose a two-year appropriations cap on

discretionary spending and institute a "pay-as-you-go" requirement on new mandatory spending. *(Legislative details, p. 61)*

The measure came to the floor because a small band of GOP fiscal conservatives, led by Gil Gutknecht of Minnesota, demanded the debate as their price for supporting the fiscal 2005 congressional budget resolution (S Con Res 95). The debate was intended to highlight Republicans' commitment to hold down spending and to be a forum for votes on a variety of plans to "reform" the much criticized congressional budget process. The legislation was intended to require Congress to stick to its budget or risk across-the-board spending cuts. It would have revived statutory limits on appropriations and a pay-as-you-go law requiring offsetting spending cuts or new revenue in any legislation to increase mandatory spending.

C. W. Bill Young, R-Fla., chairman of Appropriations, led critics against the bill, describing the proposed spending caps as an encroachment on Congress' power of the purse because the president would have a say in setting the limits. Congress had endorsed statutory spending caps on three separate occasions—in 1990, 1993, and 1997—which led some lawmakers to question why appropriators were so dead set against them now. For their part, Democrats unified against the bill for two reasons. They criticized the idea of not reviving pay-as-you-go requirements for tax cuts, and they considered the proposed lid on appropriations too tight.

Instead, the eight-hour debate on the measure—followed by its clear defeat—was a reminder of the power of the Appropriations Committee and the lasting strength of its allies in both parties in battles against GOP spending conservatives. When the bill finally came to a vote shortly after midnight June 25, one out of three Republicans voted against it, as did every Democrat. The vote defeating the bill was 146–268: R 146–72; D 0–195; I 0–1. *(Vote, p. 866)*

5. LIMITS ON FEDERAL SEARCH POWERS

Members of Congress sensitive to the protection of civil liberties expressed increasing concern about many of the provisions of the three-year-old counterterrorism law known as the USA PATRIOT Act. One of the provisions they particularly disliked permitted federal law enforcement officers conducting terrorism investigations to obtain search warrants for "any tangible thing" without having to offer a detailed rationale for the search. During summer 2004 the House came close to repealing that power altogether. Although the effort did not quite succeed the vote showed that the libertarian wing of the Republican Party could combine with Democrats to reshape the Patriot Act when it was scheduled for reauthorization in the 109th Congress.

The opportunity to limit the provision came on July 8 when the House took up the fiscal 2005 appropriations package (HR 4754) for the Justice Department. Bernard Sanders of Vermont, the one Independent in the House, proposed an amendment to prohibit the use of funds authorized by the Foreign Intelligence Surveillance Act (PL 95-511) to acquire library circulation records, library or bookstore patron lists, Internet records, or records of book purchases. As the roll-call vote began, the number of votes in the "yea" column steadily moved upward. Before the electronic voting system's timing clock had gone to zero the tally briefly stood at 219–200 in favor of the amendment.

But then the Republican leadership, sensing an unexpected election-year embarrassment for President Bush in the making, stepped up its efforts to defeat the proposal. As angry Democrats demanded "regular order" and chanted "shame, shame, shame," Republicans held the vote open for thirty minutes—double the customary time for a House floor vote and long enough to convince eight Republicans and one Democrat to switch their votes to "nay." As soon as the tally became a tie, the presiding officer, Doc Hastings, R-Wash., gaveled the voting to an end; under the rules the Sanders's amendment was rejected on the tie vote of 210–210: R 18–206; D 191–4; I 1–0. *(Vote, p. 866)*

Several lawmakers who changed their votes said they were swayed not by leadership threats or promises but by a letter from a Justice Department official that Frank R. Wolf, R-Va., circulated on the floor while the voting was under way. The letter, to Judiciary Committee Chairman F. James Sensenbrenner Jr., R-Wis., the sponsor of the Patriot Act, declared that the provision Sanders had targeted was essential. No information was offered on how often library or book sales information has been used or whether it has played a role in successful prosecutions. Bush had threatened to veto the legislation if it repealed any part of the Patriot Act. Nonetheless, the Sanders amendment vote was an important gauge of Republican unease with some Patriot Act provisions. Eighteen GOP lawmakers, or 8 percent of those voting that day, went against the president's position.

6. MEXICAN IDENTIFICATION CARDS

The divisive issue of immigration policy within the Republican Party was on display during a House debate in September 2004 over federal government position on identity cards that the Mexican government issued to its citizens living in the United States. President Bush and some members of his party supported a liberalization of immigration laws to help promote domestic economic growth, a position long advocated by many Democrats. At the start 2004, the president proposed giving millions of undocumented workers in the United States a chance to legalize their status temporarily with guest worker visas. But the proposal went nowhere, thwarted by other Republicans including influential members of Congress from border states such as such as Tom DeLay of Texas, the House majority leader. In their view, short-term security risks and the uncertain long-term economic effects of illegal immigration far outweighed any benefits to relaxing the borders. *(Legislative details, p. 621)*

The "matricula consular"—or consular registration—cards issued by Mexico to its citizens living in the United States were increasingly accepted by banks and other businesses as well as by federal government agencies as a valid form of identification. The cards included the holder's name, date and place of birth, U.S. address, and photograph. Critics said that making the cards valid for so many purposes effectively condones and perhaps encourages illegal immigration—partly, they argued, because the document could be readily forged by a Mexican who is in the United States illegally.

In July the House Appropriations Committee approved language in its fiscal 2005 Treasury Department spending bill (HR 5025) to reverse Bush administration policy and prohibit banks from accepting the matricula cards as identification by individuals hoping to open a bank account or obtain a mortgage or other financial services. Texas Republican John Culberson, who wrote the provision, said that state law enforcement agencies as well as officials of the Justice and Homeland Security departments had described the identification cards to him as an unjustified security risk. DeLay backed his argument. Many security-conscious Republicans bought that argument but there were not enough of them willing to go against the White House and the banking industry, both of which lobbied intensely to leave the policy alone.

Bankers, who saw immigrants as a lucrative market—Latin American immigrants send billions of dollars in remittances to families back home each year, in addition to their other banking in the United States—argued that the Culberson provision would force many con-

sumers to use underground, unregulated financial services. The Treasury contended that the identification cards actually enhance homeland security because they allow banks and law enforcement agents to keep an accurate watch on where money is flowing. The combination of Bush administration and bank support proved too strong for the opponents of the cards. Ohio Republican Michael G. Oxley, chairman of the Financial Services Committee, pushed an amendment to delete Culberson's provision, and it was adopted on a bipartisan vote of 222–177: R 49–161; D 172–16; I 1–0. *(Vote, p. 866)*

7. EXTENDING TAX CUTS FOR THE MIDDLE CLASS

By spring 2004 disagreement within the Republican ranks over fiscal policy blocked preparation of a budget resolution this year, which meant there could be no tax cut enacted under the expedited rules of the budget process. As their second choice, House GOP leaders decided to make election-year political life more difficult for the Democrats by daring them to oppose a series of bills to extend—without revenue-raising offsets—several of this decade's more popular tax cuts beyond their scheduled expirations at the end of the year.

As it turned out, the repeated votes quickly became a divisive issue within Democratic ranks. Democratic leaders were against the legislation, deriding the absence of offsets as a recipe for a long-term deficit disaster. But many rank-and-file members of the party, fearing constituent wrath, questioned whether Democrats should focus attention on the deficit issue. Instead, they said, their party should be joining the cause of tax relief as long as it was confined to those of low and modest incomes—part of the Democratic Party's base of electoral support. *(Legislative details, p. 111)*

Republicans recognized that they could exploit the split in order to extend three expiring tax breaks for families: the $1,000-per-child tax credit, tax breaks for married couples, and the expanded 10 percent tax bracket. At the insistence of President Bush, they wrote a bill to preserve those breaks for four to six years, more than twice as long as congressional Republicans initially sought.

To help guarantee solid bipartisan support the package was expanded to incorporate some items on the Democratic wish list, including an acceleration of the scheduled expansion of the refundable version of the child tax credit and a more generous version of that tax break for families of soldiers in combat. Including those provisions prompted two of the most senior Democrats on the Ways and Means Committee, Charles B. Rangel of New York and Sander M. Levin of Michigan, to break with their leadership and back the bill.

The Democratic leaders continued to argue that the bill, by deepening the deficit, would do more harm than good to middle-class families in the long run. But they also made clear that rank-and-file members were free to support it if doing so would help their campaigns. Given that choice six weeks before election day, Democrats backed the bill by a ratio of nearly 2-to-1, and the vote Sept. 23 to adopt the conference agreement was a overwhelming 339–65: R 213–0; D 125–65; I 1–0. *(Vote, p. 866)*

8. GAY MARRIAGE PROHIBITION

Pushed aggressively by social and religious conservatives and with the presidential election a month away, Republican leaders decided to take a vote on a constitutional amendment to prohibit gay marriage—knowing full well that the proposal would receive nothing close to the two-thirds House majority required. Nonetheless, GOP leaders took some satisfaction when the measure drew the support of a solid 55 percent of those voting. Conservative activists said they were pleased to highlight their new marquee issue close to election day and to have the tally as a baseline from which to begin the next step in their campaign.

When President Bush called on Congress in February to send such an amendment to the states for ratification, House Republican leaders reacted cautiously. "We don't want to do this in haste," Majority Leader Tom DeLay of Texas said at the time. That stance reflected both the difficulty DeLay knew he faced in trying to pass such a measure and the reluctance of many conservative Republicans to alter the Constitution. But social conservatives kept up a steady drumbeat of demands for a House vote. They were eager for Congress to act—and for the issue to gain prominence in the 2004 campaign—after the Massachusetts Supreme Judicial Court ruled in 2003 that homosexuals have a right to marry under the state constitution and after Mayor Gavin Newsom permitted same-sex marriages in San Francisco. Nevertheless, the campaign ended in July when the Senate voted to keep alive a filibuster against a gay marriage constitutional amendment (S J Res 40). *(Legislative details, p. 613)*

But in the House, with the presidential general election campaign in full swing, DeLay had a change of heart. He scheduled a House vote on a resolution (H J Res 106) by Marilyn Musgrave, R-Colo., that would constitutionally define marriage as "the union of a man and a woman." To do so DeLay circumvented the Judiciary Committee, whose chairman, F. James Sensenbrenner Jr., R-Wis., was cool to the proposal and had declined to hold a markup. With twenty-seven Republicans voting against the idea and thirty-six Democrats voting for it, the Sept. 30 House ballot on the resolution came up forty-nine votes short of the two-thirds of lawmakers present and voting necessary for passage. The tally was 227–186: R 191–27; D 36–158; I 0–1, *(Vote, p. 866)*

Still, the vote demonstrated substantial support in the House for such an amendment. It also put emphasis on the issue of gay marriage just weeks before voters in eleven states cast ballots on whether to allow gays to wed in their state. Supporters said the amendment was needed to protect the institutions of marriage and family against homosexual couples who wished to wed, and against courts inclined to allow them to do so. Opponents derided the amendment as constitutional overkill.

9. CORPORATE TAX OVERHAUL

It took more than two years of planning on Capitol Hill and in corporate lobbying offices to get the House vote in October 2004 on the biggest business tax policy change in almost two decades. Lawmakers and businesses strongly disagreed on the types of tax cuts that should replace an export tax break other countries considered unfair. Congress was under pressure to act in 2004 because the European Union had imposed retaliatory sanctions against U.S. products for keeping the prohibited export subsidy in effect.

House Ways and Means Chairman Bill Thomas, R-Calif., who drafted the final bill (HR 4520—PL 108-357), assembled an assortment of tax cuts that largely rewarded domestic manufacturers and the overseas operations of multinational corporations. But few lawmakers supported tax breaks for both groups of businesses or thought they were good economic policy. *(Legislative details, p. 115)*

Many House Democrats and Republicans from manufacturing districts complained that the overseas tax breaks, which Thomas insisted were necessary to help U.S. multinationals compete against foreign-owned rivals, would encourage more U.S. companies to move jobs overseas. The White House, the Internal Revenue Service (IRS) and the Congressional Budget Office all criticized the bill's $77 billion in tax cuts over a decade for manufacturing, saying that lost revenue would not help revive the ailing manufacturing sector but

would encourage new tax avoidance practices while proving impossible to administer.

Furthermore, to accommodate senators who wanted to reduce the budget deficit the bill included language designed to crack down on tax avoidance practices in an effort to raise billions of dollars needed to offset expensive tax cuts. That drew the ire of House conservatives who considered these offsets tantamount to tax increases. The remainder of the tax cuts were offset by a bit of budget legerdemain—moving some effective dates to lower costs—and by extending existing Customs user fees.

To attract more than enough votes to guarantee enactment, Thomas added a host of sweeteners that appealed to lawmakers seeking reelection. Some of them were extraordinarily narrow and parochial, including special tax breaks for native Alaskan whalers and the owners of NASCAR race tracks. But by far the most politically compelling, and expensive, was a $10 billion buyout of tobacco farmers. That provision drew votes across party lines throughout the South, particularly in the Carolinas and Kentucky.

Another lure was partial restoration of the federal income tax deduction for state sales taxes that was eliminated in 1986. Under this legislation, taxpayers could deduct sales taxes in lieu of local income taxes through 2005. Lawmakers of both parties from Texas, Florida, South Dakota, and Tennessee were particularly drawn to this provision because these states did not levy state income taxes. Some members criticized the "Christmas tree" approach to winning votes. "This is a blatant example of corporate welfare, full of pork for the special interests," Minority Leader Nancy Pelosi, D-Calif., said during the final House debate Oct. 7. "The oinking is so loud, the Republicans can't even think straight."

Yet the vote on the measure was the most bipartisan endorsement of a tax bill during President Bush's first term. The House adopted the conference report with the support of seventy-three Democrats, many from the South, and despite the opposition of sixteen Republicans. The tally was 280–141: R 207–16; D 73–124; I 0–1. *(Vote, p. 866)*

10. INTELLIGENCE-GATHERING OVERHAUL

House Republican leaders found the limits of their political independence as the year came to an end when they bowed to White House pressure and accepted a face-saving compromise on legislation to restructure the nation's intelligence system. They had held out for two months against the Senate version of the plan, which they argued might harm military intelligence and would not do enough to slow illegal immigration. Their resistance was stiffened by the support of the chairman of the Joint Chiefs of Staff, Air Force Gen. Richard B. Myers, and the apparent ambivalence of President Bush, who had endorsed the Senate version of the legislation but spent almost none of his political capital pushing for the enactment of a compromise bill before he stood for reelection in November. *(Legislative details, p. 263)*

Initial, strong differences between House and Senate Republicans were apparent soon after the independent Sept. 11 commission—which Congress had created two years ago with a broad mandate to probe all government failings that may have precipitated the al Qaeda attacks—recommended creation of a cabinet-level office of national intelligence to oversee the nation's fifteen spy agencies and creation of a national counterterrorism center, among dozens of other steps. By October the Senate had passed a bill along the lines the commission recommended. But House GOP leaders went a different way, writing a bill that would have given a new national intelligence director more limited powers than the Senate had endorsed and included tough measures designed to reduce illegal immigration and increase law enforcement powers.

For a time, those changes came close to transforming the House debate into another partisan spat. On Oct. 8 eight Republicans split with their party and voted with the Democrats to substitute the Senate version of the bill for the House measure. The amendment narrowly failed, 203–213. By late November, House and Senate conferees had reached an uneasy agreement on the bill but two House committee chairman remained adamantly opposed. Armed Services Chairman Duncan Hunter, R-Calif., said the new structure might interfere with military intelligence and Judiciary Chairman F. James Sensenbrenner Jr. R-Wis., complained that his immigration provisions were being dropped.

Unable to gain the support of a sufficient number of Republicans, even though there were enough GOP and Democratic votes to adopt the conference report, Speaker J. Dennis Hastert, R-Ill., refused to bring the measure to the floor. The White House responded by shifting its lobbying into high gear. The president made public appeals, and Vice President Richard B. Cheney lobbied recalcitrant GOP lawmakers in private. Myers announced he had backed off his initial opposition to the measure—in what appeared to be a coordinated effort by the administration to weaken Hunter's position.

House GOP leaders agreed to allow a vote on a final version of the bill (S 2845) that was written largely along the lines of the Senate measure. That compromise, however, proved far more popular on the floor than the initial version of the bill that the House had passed two months before. The vote Dec. 7 to adopt the conference report was a lopsided 336–75: R 152–67; D 183–8; I 1–0. Solid majorities in both parties backed the deal; only the most conservative one-third of Republicans and the most liberal handful of Democrats opposed it. *(Vote table, p. 866)*

1. S 1072. Surface Transportation Spending. Passage of the bill to authorize $318.9 billion in federal aid for highways, highway safety programs, and transit programs over six years including $255 billion for highways, $56.5 billion for transit, and $6 billion for safety programs, and to guarantee that states receive a 95 percent return on their Highway Trust Fund contributions by 2009. Passed 76–21: R 34–17; D 41–4 (ND 35–2, SD 6–2); I 1– 0, Feb. 12, 2004. A "nay" was a vote in support of the president's position.

2. S 2061. Medical Malpractice Liability. Motion to invoke cloture (thus limiting debate) on the motion to proceed to consideration of the bill that would place caps on damage awards in medical malpractice lawsuits against obstetricians and gynecologists. Motion rejected 48–45: R 47–3; D 1–41 (ND 1–34, SD 0–7); I 0–1, Feb. 24, 2004. Three-fifths of the total Senate (sixty) was required to invoke cloture. A "yea" was a vote in support of the president's position.

3. S 1805. Assault Weapons Ban. Feinstein, D-Calif., amendment to provide a ten-year reauthorization of the assault weapons ban that was to expire in September 2004. Adopted 52–47: R 10–41; D 41–6 (ND 34–4, SD 7–2); I 1–0, March 2, 2004.

4. S Con Res 95. 'Pay As you Go' Budget Rules. Feingold, D-Wis., amendment to restore pay-as-you-go (PAYGO) rules, which required a sixty-vote margin to overcome a point of order against direct spending or revenue legislation that increased the on-budget deficit or cause an on-budget deficit, thereby requiring tax cuts and new entitlement spending to off-set with revenue increases or spending cuts. Adopted 51–48: R 4–47; D 46–1 (ND 38–0, SD 8–1); I 1–0, March 10, 2004.

5. HR 1997. Criminalization of Harm to a Fetus. Passage of the bill to make it a criminal offense to injure or kill a fetus during the commission of a violent crime, and to establish criminal penalties equal to those that would apply if the injury or death occurred to the pregnant woman for those who harm a fetus regardless of the perpetrator's knowledge of the pregnancy or intent to harm the fetus. Passed 61–38: R 48–2; D 13–35 (ND 9–30, SD 4–5); I 0–1, March 25, 2004. A "yea" was a vote in support of the president's position.

6. HR 4. Child Care for Welfare Recipients. Snowe, R-Maine, amendment to increase mandatory child care funding by $6 billion over the following five years. Adopted 78–20: R 31–19; D 46–1 (ND 38–0, SD 8– 1); I 1–0, March 30, 2004. A "nay" was a vote in support of the president's position.

7. S 1637. Overtime Pay Rules. Harkin, D-Iowa, amendment to block implementation of language in a new Labor Department rule that would cause some workers to lose their eligibility for overtime pay. Adopted 52–47: R 5–46; D 46–1 (ND 38–0, SD 8–1); I 1– 0, May 4, 2004. A "nay" was a vote in support of the president's position.

8. S 2400. Base Closure Delay. Lott, R-Miss., amendment to require the 2005 base realignment and closure round to apply only to U.S. military installations located overseas, delaying new U.S. domestic base closings until 2007. Rejected 47–49: R 21–29; D 26–19 (ND 20–16, SD 6–3); I 0–1, May 18, 2004. A "nay" was a vote in support of the president's position.

9. S 2062. Class Action Lawsuits. Motion to invoke cloture (thus limiting debate) on the bill to allow class action cases involving at least 100 plaintiffs to be sent to federal court if at least $5 million was at stake and fewer than two-thirds of the plaintiffs live in the same state as the defendant. Motion rejected 44–43: R 42–3; D 2–39 (ND 1–32, SD 1–7); I 0–1, July 8, 2004. Three-fifths of the total Senate (sixty) was required to invoke cloture. A "yea" was a vote in support of the president's position.

10. S J Res 40. Gay Marriage Prohibition. Motion to invoke cloture (thus limiting debate) on the motion to proceed to consideration of a constitutional amendment that would define marriage as consisting only of the union of a man and a woman, and to provide that the U.S. Constitution or any state's constitution could not be construed to require that marriage or any other constructs of marriage be conferred to any other union. Motion rejected 48–50: R 45–6; D 3–43 (ND 2–36, SD 1–7); I 0–1, July 14, 2004. Three-fifths of the total Senate (sixty) was required to invoke cloture. A "yea" was a vote in support of the president's position.

11. HR 4567. Privatization of Federal Jobs. Leahy, D-Vt., amendment to prohibit the use of funds to privatize or contract out services provided by the Bureau of Citizenship and Immigration Services. Adopted 49–47: R 5–46; D 43–1 (ND 36–0, SD 7–1); I 1–0, Sept. 8, 2004. A "nay" was a vote in support of the president's position.

12. HR 1308. Extending Middle Class Tax Cuts. Adoption of the conference report on the bill to extend the $1,000 per child tax credit through 2009, the upper limit for the current 10 percent bracket through 2010, and tax breaks for married couples through 2008, and to provide a one-year extension of existing income exemptions from the alternative minimum tax and extend the expiring research and development tax credit through 2005. Adopted 92–3: R 49– 2; D 42–1 (ND 35–0, SD 7–1); I 1–0, Sept. 23, 2004. A "yea" was a vote in support of the president's position.

13. S 2845. Intelligence Overhaul. Passage of the bill to reorganize fifteen U.S. intelligence agencies and create a national intelligence director with the power to freely transfer money among the CIA, National Security Agency and other defense and civilian agencies. It also would created a counterterrorism center with operational planning capabilities and a Privacy and Civil Liberties Oversight Board to investigate use of intelligence powers and act as a watchdog for civil liberties concerns. Passed 96–2: R 51–0; D 44–2 (ND 37–1, SD 7–1); I 1–0, Oct. 6, 2004.

14. HR 4520. Corporate Tax Overhaul. Adoption of the conference report on the bill to repeal an export provision in the U.S. tax code that had been ruled an unfair subsidy by the World Trade Organization and to provide for $137 billion in new tax cuts for corporations over ten years. It also included a $10 billion buyout of tobacco farmers. Adopted 69–17: R 43–3; D 25–14 (ND 20–14, SD 5–0); I 1–0, Oct. 11, 2004.

KEY				
		Democrats	*Republicans*	**Independent**
Y	Voted for ("yea")		–	Announced against
N	Voted against ("nay")		P	Voted "present"
+	Announced for		C	Voted "present" to avoid possible conflict of interest
#	Paired for		?	Did not vote or otherwise
X	Paired against			make a position known

ND Northern Democrats
SD Southern Democrats
Southern states – Ala., Ark., Fla., Ga., Ky., La., Miss., N.C., Okla., S.C., Tenn., Texas, Va.

Senate Key Votes	1	2	3	4	5	6	7	8	9	10	11	12	13	14
ALABAMA														
Shelby	Y	N	N	N	Y	Y	N	N	N	Y	N	Y	Y	Y
Sessions	N	Y	N	N	Y	N	N	N	Y	Y	N	Y	Y	Y
ALASKA														
Stevens	Y	Y	N	N	Y	Y	N	Y	Y	Y	N	Y	Y	Y
Murkowski, L.	Y	Y	N	N	Y	Y	Y	Y	Y	Y	N	Y	Y	Y
ARIZONA														
McCain	N	Y	N	Y	Y	Y	N	N	N	N	N	Y	Y	?
Kyl	N	Y	N	N	Y	N	N	N	Y	Y	N	Y	Y	Y
ARKANSAS														
Lincoln	Y	N	Y	Y	N	Y	Y	N	N	N	Y	Y	Y	Y
Pryor	Y	N	Y	Y	Y	Y	Y	Y	N	N	Y	Y	Y	Y
CALIFORNIA														
Feinstein	Y	N	Y	Y	N	Y	Y	Y	Y	N	Y	Y	Y	N
Boxer	Y	?	Y	Y	N	Y	Y	Y	?	N	Y	Y	Y	N
COLORADO														
Campbell	Y	Y	N	N	Y	Y	Y	Y	?	N	N	Y	Y	?
Allard	Y	Y	N	N	Y	N	N	N	Y	Y	N	Y	Y	Y
CONNECTICUT														
Dodd	Y	N	Y	Y	N	Y	Y	Y	N	N	Y	Y	Y	N
Lieberman	Y	N	Y	Y	N	Y	Y	N	N	N	Y	Y	Y	Y
DELAWARE														
Biden	Y	N	Y	Y	N	Y	Y	N	?	N	Y	Y	Y	N
Carper	Y	N	Y	Y	Y	Y	Y	N	N	N	Y	Y	Y	N
FLORIDA														
Graham	N	N	Y	Y	N	Y	Y	N	N	N	Y	Y	Y	?
Nelson	Y	N	Y	Y	N	Y	Y	N	N	N	Y	Y	Y	Y
GEORGIA														
Miller	N	?	N	N	Y	N	N	N	Y	Y	N	Y	Y	?
Chambliss	N	Y	N	N	Y	N	N	N	Y	Y	N	Y	Y	?
HAWAII														
Inouye	Y	N	Y	Y	N	Y	Y	?	N	N	Y	?	Y	Y
Akaka	Y	N	Y	Y	N	Y	Y	N	N	N	?	?	Y	N
IDAHO														
Craig	N	Y	N	N	Y	N	N	Y	N	Y	N	Y	Y	Y
Crapo	Y	N	N	N	Y	N	N	Y	Y	Y	N	Y	Y	Y
ILLINOIS														
Fitzgerald	Y	Y	Y	N	Y	Y	N	Y	?	Y	N	Y	Y	Y
Durbin	Y	N	Y	Y	N	Y	Y	Y	Y	N	Y	Y	Y	N
INDIANA														
Lugar	Y	Y	Y	N	Y	Y	N	N	Y	Y	N	Y	Y	Y
Bayh	Y	N	Y	Y	N	Y	Y	Y	Y	N	Y	Y	Y	Y
IOWA														
Grassley	Y	Y	N	N	Y	Y	N	N	Y	Y	N	Y	Y	Y
Harkin	Y	N	Y	Y	N	Y	Y	N	Y	N	Y	Y	Y	Y
KANSAS														
Brownback	N	Y	N	N	Y	Y	N	N	Y	Y	N	Y	Y	Y
Roberts	Y	Y	N	N	Y	Y	N	N	Y	Y	N	Y	Y	Y
KENTUCKY														
McConnell	N	Y	N	N	Y	N	N	N	Y	Y	N	Y	Y	Y
Bunning	Y	Y	N	N	Y	Y	N	+	Y	Y	N	Y	Y	Y
LOUISIANA														
Breaux	Y	N	Y	Y	Y	Y	Y	Y	N	N	Y	Y	Y	Y
Landrieu	Y	N	N	Y	Y	Y	Y	Y	N	N	Y	Y	Y	Y
MAINE														
Snowe	Y	Y	Y	Y	N	Y	Y	Y	Y	N	Y	N	Y	Y
Collins	Y	Y	Y	Y	Y	Y	N	Y	Y	N	Y	Y	Y	N
MARYLAND														
Sarbanes	Y	N	Y	Y	N	Y	Y	Y	N	N	Y	Y	Y	N
Mikulski	Y	N	Y	Y	N	Y	Y	Y	?	N	Y	Y	Y	Y
MASSACHUSETTS														
Kennedy	Y	N	Y	Y	N	Y	Y	N	Y	N	Y	?	Y	N
Kerry	+	–	Y	Y	N	+	?	?	?	?	?	?	?	?
MICHIGAN														
Levin	Y	N	Y	Y	N	Y	Y	N	N	N	Y	Y	Y	N
Stabenow	Y	N	Y	Y	N	Y	Y	N	N	N	Y	Y	Y	Y
MINNESOTA														
Dayton	Y	N	Y	Y	Y	Y	Y	N	N	N	Y	Y	Y	Y
Coleman	Y	Y	N	N	Y	Y	N	N	Y	Y	N	Y	Y	Y
MISSISSIPPI														
Cochran	Y	Y	N	N	Y	Y	N	Y	Y	Y	N	Y	Y	Y
Lott	Y	Y	N	N	Y	N	N	Y	Y	Y	N	Y	Y	Y
MISSOURI														
Bond	Y	Y	N	N	Y	Y	N	N	Y	Y	Y	Y	Y	Y
Talent	Y	Y	N	N	Y	Y	N	N	Y	Y	N	Y	Y	Y

Senate Key Votes	1	2	3	4	5	6	7	8	9	10	11	12	13	14
MONTANA														
Burns	Y	Y	N	N	Y	N	N	Y	Y	Y	N	Y	Y	Y
Baucus	Y	N	N	Y	N	Y	Y	Y	N	N	Y	Y	Y	Y
NEBRASKA														
Hagel	N	Y	N	N	Y	Y	N	N	?	Y	N	Y	Y	Y
Nelson	+	N	N	Y	Y	Y	Y	Y	Y	Y	Y	Y	Y	Y
NEVADA														
Reid	Y	N	N	Y	Y	Y	Y	N	N	N	Y	Y	Y	Y
Ensign	N	Y	N	N	Y	N	N	N	?	Y	N	Y	Y	Y
NEW HAMPSHIRE														
Gregg	N	Y	Y	N	?	N	N	Y	Y	Y	N	Y	Y	N
Sununu	N	Y	N	N	Y	N	N	Y	Y	N	N	Y	Y	?
NEW JERSEY														
Lautenberg	Y	N	Y	Y	N	Y	Y	?	Y	N	Y	Y	Y	?
Corzine	Y	?	Y	Y	N	Y	Y	Y	Y	N	Y	Y	Y	N
NEW MEXICO														
Domenici	Y	Y	N	N	Y	?	N	Y	Y	Y	N	Y	Y	Y
Bingaman	Y	N	Y	Y	Y	Y	Y	Y	N	N	Y	Y	Y	Y
NEW YORK														
Schumer	Y	N	Y	Y	N	Y	Y	Y	N	N	Y	Y	Y	Y
Clinton	Y	N	Y	Y	N	Y	Y	Y	?	N	?	Y	Y	Y
NORTH CAROLINA														
Edwards	?	?	Y	Y	N	Y	Y	Y	?	?	?	?	?	?
Dole	Y	Y	N	N	Y	Y	N	N	Y	Y	N	Y	Y	Y
NORTH DAKOTA														
Conrad	Y	N	Y	Y	Y	Y	Y	N	N	N	Y	Y	Y	Y
Dorgan	Y	N	Y	Y	Y	Y	Y	Y	N	N	Y	Y	Y	?
OHIO														
DeWine	Y	Y	Y	N	Y	N	N	N	Y	Y	N	Y	Y	N
Voinovich	Y	Y	Y	N	Y	N	N	N	Y	Y	N	Y	Y	Y
OKLAHOMA														
Nickles	N	Y	N	N	Y	N	N	N	Y	Y	N	Y	Y	Y
Inhofe	Y	Y	N	N	Y	N	N	Y	Y	Y	N	Y	Y	Y
OREGON														
Wyden	Y	N	Y	Y	N	Y	Y	N	N	N	Y	Y	Y	Y
Smith	Y	Y	Y	N	Y	Y	N	N	Y	Y	N	Y	Y	Y
PENNSYLVANIA														
Specter	N	Y	N	N	Y	Y	Y	Y	Y	N	Y	Y	Y	?
Santorum	N	Y	N	N	Y	N	N	N	?	Y	N	Y	Y	Y
RHODE ISLAND														
Reed	Y	N	Y	Y	N	Y	Y	N	N	N	Y	Y	Y	N
Chafee	Y	Y	Y	Y	N	Y	Y	Y	Y	N	Y	N	Y	Y
SOUTH CAROLINA														
Hollings	Y	N	Y	Y	N	Y	Y	Y	N	N	Y	N	N	?
Graham	N	N	N	N	Y	Y	N	Y	Y	Y	N	Y	Y	Y
SOUTH DAKOTA														
Daschle	Y	N	Y	Y	Y	Y	Y	Y	N	N	Y	Y	Y	Y
Johnson	Y	–	?	?	N	Y	Y	Y	N	N	Y	Y	Y	Y
TENNESSEE														
Frist	Y	Y	N	N	Y	Y	N	Y	Y	Y	N	Y	Y	Y
Alexander	N	Y	N	N	Y	Y	N	N	Y	Y	N	Y	Y	Y
TEXAS														
Hutchison	N	Y	N	N	Y	Y	N	N	Y	Y	N	Y	Y	Y
Cornyn	Y	Y	N	N	Y	N	N	N	Y	Y	N	Y	Y	Y
UTAH														
Hatch	Y	Y	N	N	Y	Y	N	N	Y	Y	N	Y	Y	Y
Bennett	Y	?	N	N	Y	Y	N	Y	Y	Y	N	Y	Y	Y
VERMONT														
Leahy	Y	N	Y	Y	N	Y	Y	N	N	N	Y	Y	Y	?
Jeffords	Y	N	Y	Y	N	Y	Y	N	N	N	Y	Y	Y	Y
VIRGINIA														
Warner	Y	Y	Y	N	Y	N	N	N	Y	Y	N	Y	Y	Y
Allen	Y	Y	N	N	Y	N	N	N	Y	Y	N	Y	Y	Y
WASHINGTON														
Murray	Y	N	Y	Y	N	Y	Y	N	N	N	Y	Y	Y	Y
Cantwell	Y	N	Y	Y	N	Y	Y	N	N	N	Y	Y	Y	Y
WEST VIRGINIA														
Byrd	Y	Y	Y	Y	N	Y	Y	N	?	Y	Y	Y	N	N
Rockefeller	Y	N	Y	Y	Y	Y	Y	N	N	N	Y	Y	Y	N
WISCONSIN														
Kohl	N	N	Y	Y	N	Y	Y	N	N	N	Y	Y	Y	P
Feingold	N	N	N	Y	N	Y	Y	N	N	N	Y	Y	Y	Y
WYOMING														
Thomas	Y	Y	N	N	Y	N	N	N	Y	Y	N	Y	Y	Y
Enzi	Y	Y	N	N	Y	N	N	N	?	Y	N	Y	Y	Y

1. HR 3030. Unemployment Benefits. Miller, D-Calif., amendment to authorize such sums as necessary under the Community Services Block Grants program for a six-month federal program providing an additional thirteen weeks of unemployment benefits for people who had exhausted their state jobless benefits. Adopted 227–179: R 39–179; D 187–0 (ND 132–0, SD 55–0); I 1–0, Feb. 4, 2004.

2. H Res 557. War in Iraq and U.S. Troops. Adoption of the resolution to affirm the United States and the world are safer with the removal of Saddam Hussein and his regime from power in Iraq, to commend U.S. and coalition forces for liberating Iraq, and commend the Iraqi people on the adoption of Iraq's new interim constitution. Adopted 327–93: R 222–2; D 105–90 (ND 64–76, SD 41–14); I 0–1, March 17, 2004. A "yea" was a vote in support of the president's position.

3. HR 3550. Surface Transportation. Passage of the bill to authorize $283.2 billion for federal highway, mass transit, safety, and research programs from fiscal 2004 to 2009. The funding total included $217 billion in guaranteed spending for highways, $51.5 billion for mass transit and other public transportation programs, and $11.1 billion for members' projects. It also froze funding in fiscal 2006 and beyond unless legislation were enacted to ensure that states get back at least 95 percent of the dollars their motorists send to the Highway Trust Fund by fiscal 2009. Passed 357–65: R 162–59; D 194–6 (ND 144–1, SD 50–5); I 1–0, April 2, 2004. A "nay" was a vote in support of the president's position.

4. HR 4663. Budget Enforcement. Passage of the bill to set statutory caps on discretionary spending for fiscal 2005 and 2006, and institute pay-as-you-go rules to require any mandatory spending increases be offset by new revenue or other spending reductions. Rejected 146–268: R 146–72; D 0–195 (ND 0–142, SD 0–53); I 0–1, June 25, 2004 (in the session that began and the Congressional Record dated June 24, 2004). A "yea" was a vote in support of the president's position.

5. HR 4754. Limits on Federal Search Powers. Sanders, I-Vt., amendment to prohibit funds from being used to make an application under the Foreign Intelligence Surveillance Act to acquire library circulation records, library patron lists, library Internet records, bookseller sales records, or bookseller customer lists. Rejected 210–210: R 18–206; D 191–4 (ND 142–2, SD 49–2); I 1–0, July 8, 2004. A "nay" was a vote in support of the president's position.

6. HR 5025. Mexican Identification Cards. Oxley, R-Ohio, amendment to strike language that would prohibit the Treasury Department from using funds in the bill to implement regulations allowing financial institutions to accept Mexican "matricula consular" identification documents. Adopted 222–177: R 49–161; D 172–16 (ND 128–7, SD 44–9); I 1–0, Sept. 14, 2004. A "yea" was a vote in support of the president's position.

7. HR 1308. Family and Corporate Tax Breaks. Adoption of the conference report on the bill to extend the $1,000 per child tax credit through 2009, the upper limit for the current 10 percent bracket through 2010, and tax breaks for married couples through 2008, and to provide a one-year extension of current income exemptions from the alternative minimum tax and extend the expiring research and development tax credit through 2005. Adopted (thus sent to the Senate) 339–65: R 213–0; D 125–65 (ND 83–57, SD 42–8); I 1–0, Sept. 23, 2004. A "yea" was a vote in support of the president's position.

8. H J Res 106. Same-Sex Marriage Ban Constitutional Amendment. Passage of the joint resolution to propose a constitutional amendment to define marriage as consisting only of the union of a man and a woman. Rejected 227–186: R 191–27; D 36–158 (ND 7–135, SD 29–23); I 0–1, Sept. 30, 2004. A two-thirds majority vote of those present and voting (276 in this case) is required to pass a joint resolution proposing an amendment to the Constitution. A "yea" was a vote in support of the president's position.

9. HR 4520. Corporate Tax Overhaul. Adoption of the conference report on the bill to repeal an export provision in the U.S. tax code that has been ruled an unfair subsidy by the World Trade Organization, and to provide $137 billion in new tax cuts for corporations over ten years and a $10 billion buyout of tobacco farmers. Adopted (thus sent to the Senate) 280–141: R 207–16; D 73–124 (ND 25–118, SD 48– 6); I 0–1, Oct. 7, 2004.

10. S 2845. Intelligence Overhaul. Adoption of the conference report on the bill to reorganize fifteen U.S. intelligence agencies and create a new director of national intelligence to oversee all U.S. intelligence activities and determine the intelligence budget. Adopted (thus sent to the Senate) 336–75: R 152–67; D 183–8 (ND 133–7, SD 50–1); I 1–0, Dec. 7, 2004. A "yea" was a vote in support of the president's position.

KEY

	Democrats	*Republicans*	Independent

Y Voted for ("yea") — Announced against
N Voted against ("nay") P Voted "present"
+ Announced for C Voted "present" to avoid possible conflict of interest
# Paired for ? Did not vote or otherwise make a position known
X Paired against

ND Northern Democrats
SD Southern Democrats
Southern states – Ala., Ark., Fla., Ga., Ky., La., Miss., N.C., Okla., S.C., Tenn., Texas, Va.

House Key Votes	1	2	3	4	5	6	7	8	9	10
ALABAMA										
1 Bonner	N	Y	Y	N	N	?	?	Y	Y	Y
2 Everett	N	Y	Y	N	N	?	Y	Y	Y	N
3 Rogers	N	Y	Y	N	N	N	Y	Y	Y	N
4 Aderholt	N	Y	Y	N	N	N	Y	Y	Y	N
5 Cramer	Y	Y	Y	N	Y	N	Y	Y	Y	Y
6 Bachus	Y	Y	Y	N	?	Y	Y	Y	Y	N
7 Davis	Y	P	Y	N	Y	?	Y	Y	Y	?
ALASKA										
AL Young	N	Y	Y	Y	Y	?	Y	Y	Y	?
ARIZONA										
1 Renzi	N	Y	Y	N	Y	N	Y	Y	Y	Y
2 Franks	N	Y	N	Y	N	N	Y	Y	Y	Y
3 Shadegg	N	Y	N	Y	N	N	Y	Y	Y	Y
4 Pastor	Y	N	Y	N	Y	Y	N	N	N	Y
5 Hayworth	N	Y	Y	Y	N	N	Y	Y	Y	N
6 Flake	N	Y	N	Y	N	Y	Y	Y	Y	N
7 Grijalva	Y	N	Y	N	Y	Y	Y	N	N	Y
8 Kolbe	N	Y	N	N	N	Y	Y	N	Y	Y
ARKANSAS										
1 Berry	Y	Y	Y	N	?	Y	N	Y	Y	Y
2 Snyder	Y	Y	Y	N	Y	Y	Y	N	N	Y
3 Boozman	N	Y	Y	Y	N	Y	Y	Y	Y	N
4 Ross	Y	Y	Y	N	Y	Y	Y	Y	Y	Y
CALIFORNIA										
1 Thompson	Y	N	Y	N	Y	Y	N	N	Y	Y
2 Herger	N	Y	Y	Y	N	N	Y	Y	Y	N
3 Ose	N	Y	Y	Y	N	Y	Y	N	N	N
4 Doolittle	N	Y	Y	Y	N	N	Y	Y	Y	N
5 Matsui	Y	N	Y	N	Y	Y	Y	N	N	Y
6 Woolsey	Y	N	Y	N	Y	Y	N	N	N	Y
7 Miller, George	Y	N	?	N	Y	Y	N	N	N	Y
8 Pelosi	Y	N	Y	N	Y	Y	N	N	N	Y
9 Lee	Y	N	Y	N	Y	Y	N	N	N	Y
10 Tauscher	Y	N	Y	N	Y	Y	Y	N	N	Y
11 Pombo	N	Y	Y	Y	N	N	Y	Y	Y	N
12 Lantos	Y	P	Y	N	Y	Y	Y	N	N	Y
13 Stark	Y	N	+	N	Y	Y	N	N	N	Y
14 Eshoo	Y	N	Y	N	Y	Y	Y	N	N	Y
15 Honda	Y	N	Y	N	Y	Y	N	N	N	Y
16 Lofgren	Y	N	Y	N	P	Y	Y	N	N	Y
17 Farr	Y	N	Y	N	Y	Y	Y	N	N	Y
18 Cardoza	Y	Y	Y	N	Y	Y	Y	N	N	Y
19 Radanovich	N	Y	Y	Y	N	N	Y	Y	Y	N
20 Dooley	Y	Y	Y	N	Y	Y	Y	N	Y	?
21 Nunes	N	Y	Y	Y	N	N	+	Y	Y	Y
22 Thomas	N	Y	Y	Y	N	N	Y	Y	Y	Y
23 Capps	Y	N	Y	N	Y	Y	N	N	N	Y
24 Gallegly	N	Y	Y	Y	N	Y	Y	Y	Y	N
25 McKeon	N	Y	Y	Y	N	N	Y	Y	Y	Y
26 Dreier	N	Y	Y	Y	N	Y	N	Y	Y	Y
27 Sherman	Y	Y	Y	N	Y	Y	Y	N	N	Y
28 Berman	Y	Y	Y	?	Y	Y	Y	N	N	Y
29 Schiff	Y	Y	Y	N	Y	Y	Y	N	N	Y
30 Waxman	Y	P	?	N	Y	Y	N	N	N	Y
31 Becerra	Y	N	Y	N	Y	Y	N	N	N	Y
32 Solis	Y	N	Y	N	Y	Y	N	N	N	Y
33 Watson	?	N	Y	N	Y	Y	N	N	N	Y
34 Roybal-Allard	Y	N	Y	N	Y	Y	N	N	N	Y
35 Waters	Y	N	Y	N	Y	Y	N	N	N	Y
36 Harman	Y	Y	Y	N	Y	Y	N	?	N	Y
37 Millender-McD.	?	N	Y	N	Y	Y	N	N	?	Y
38 Napolitano	?	N	Y	N	Y	Y	N	N	N	Y
39 Sánchez, Linda	Y	N	Y	N	Y	Y	N	N	N	Y
40 Royce	N	Y	Y	Y	N	Y	Y	Y	Y	N
41 Lewis	N	Y	Y	Y	N	Y	Y	Y	Y	Y
42 Miller, Gary	N	Y	Y	Y	N	N	Y	Y	Y	N

House Key Votes	1	2	3	4	5	6	7	8	9	10
43 Baca	Y	Y	Y	N	Y	Y	Y	N	N	Y
44 Calvert	?	Y	Y	N	N	N	Y	Y	Y	N
45 Bono	N	Y	Y	N	N	N	Y	N	Y	N
46 Rohrabacher	N	Y	Y	Y	N	N	Y	Y	N	N
47 Sanchez, Loretta	Y	N	Y	N	Y	Y	Y	N	N	Y
48 Cox	N	Y	Y	Y	N	N	Y	N	Y	Y
49 Issa	N	Y	Y	Y	N	N	Y	Y	Y	N
50 Cunningham	N	Y	Y	N	N	N	Y	Y	Y	Y
51 Filner	Y	N	Y	N	Y	Y	Y	N	?	Y
52 Hunter	N	Y	?	N	N	N	Y	?	Y	Y
53 Davis	Y	P	Y	N	Y	Y	Y	N	N	Y
COLORADO										
1 DeGette	?	N	Y	N	Y	Y	N	N	N	Y
2 Udall	Y	Y	Y	N	Y	?	?	Y	Y	Y
3 McInnis	?	Y	Y	Y	Y	?	?	N	Y	N
4 Musgrave	N	Y	Y	Y	N	N	Y	Y	Y	Y
5 Hefley	N	Y	Y	Y	N	N	Y	Y	Y	N
6 Tancredo	N	Y	N	Y	N	N	Y	Y	Y	Y
7 Beauprez	N	Y	Y	Y	N	Y	Y	Y	Y	Y
CONNECTICUT										
1 Larson	Y	N	Y	N	Y	Y	N	N	N	Y
2 Simmons	Y	?	Y	N	N	Y	N	Y	Y	Y
3 DeLauro	Y	Y	Y	N	Y	Y	N	N	N	Y
4 Shays	Y	N	Y	Y	N	Y	N	N	Y	Y
5 Johnson	N	Y	Y	Y	N	Y	N	N	Y	Y
DELAWARE										
AL Castle	N	Y	N	Y	Y	Y	Y	N	N	Y
FLORIDA										
1 Miller, J.	N	Y	N	N	N	?	?	Y	Y	Y
2 Boyd	Y	Y	N	Y	N	Y	Y	Y	Y	Y
3 Brown	Y	N	Y	N	Y	Y	N	?	Y	Y
4 Crenshaw	N	Y	N	N	N	Y	Y	Y	Y	Y
5 Brown-Waite	?	Y	N	Y	N	N	Y	Y	Y	N
6 Stearns	N	Y	Y	N	N	N	Y	Y	Y	Y
7 Mica	N	Y	Y	N	N	N	Y	Y	Y	Y
8 Keller	N	Y	N	Y	N	N	Y	Y	Y	Y
9 Bilirakis	N	Y	N	N	N	N	Y	Y	Y	Y
10 Young	N	Y	N	N	N	N	Y	Y	N	Y
11 Davis	Y	N	Y	N	Y	N	Y	N	?	?
12 Putnam	N	Y	Y	N	N	Y	Y	Y	Y	Y
13 Harris	N	Y	N	N	N	N	Y	Y	Y	Y
14 Goss[1]	—	Y	N	N	N	?	?			
15 Weldon	N	Y	N	N	N	N	Y	Y	Y	N
16 Foley	N	Y	Y	N	N	N	Y	N	Y	Y
17 Meek	Y	N	Y	N	Y	Y	Y	?	N	Y
18 Ros-Lehtinen	N	Y	N	Y	N	Y	Y	?	N	Y
19 Wexler	Y	N	Y	N	Y	Y	Y	N	N	Y
20 Deutsch	Y	Y	Y	?	?	Y	Y	N	N	Y
21 Diaz-Balart, L.	N	Y	Y	N	Y	N	Y	?	N	Y
22 Shaw	N	Y	N	N	N	N	Y	Y	Y	Y
23 Hastings	Y	N	Y	?	?	Y	N	?	Y	?
24 Feeney	N	Y	Y	N	N	N	Y	Y	Y	N
25 Diaz-Balart, M.	N	Y	N	Y	N	Y	Y	?	N	Y
GEORGIA										
1 Kingston	N	Y	N	N	N	Y	Y	Y	Y	N
2 Bishop	Y	Y	Y	N	?	Y	+	Y	Y	Y
3 Marshall	Y	Y	Y	N	Y	Y	Y	Y	Y	Y
4 Majette	Y	N	Y	N	Y	Y	Y	N	?	Y
5 Lewis	Y	N	Y	N	Y	Y	Y	N	N	Y
6 Isakson	N	Y	N	N	N	N	Y	Y	Y	Y
7 Linder	?	Y	N	Y	N	N	Y	Y	Y	Y
8 Collins	N	Y	Y	?	?	N	?	Y	Y	N
9 Norwood	N	Y	N	N	N	N	Y	Y	?	?
10 Deal	N	Y	N	N	N	N	Y	Y	Y	Y
11 Gingrey	N	Y	N	N	N	N	Y	Y	Y	Y
12 Burns	Y	Y	N	N	N	N	Y	Y	Y	Y
13 Scott	Y	Y	Y	N	Y	Y	Y	Y	Y	Y
HAWAII										
1 Abercrombie	Y	N	Y	N	Y	Y	N	N	N	?
2 Case	Y	Y	Y	N	Y	N	Y	N	N	?
IDAHO										
1 Otter	N	Y	N	Y	N	N	Y	Y	Y	N
2 Simpson	N	Y	N	N	N	N	Y	Y	Y	N
ILLINOIS										
1 Rush	Y	N	Y	N	Y	Y	N	N	N	Y
2 Jackson	Y	N	Y	N	Y	Y	N	N	N	Y
3 Lipinski	?	Y	Y	N	Y	N	?	N	?	?
4 Gutierrez	?	N	Y	N	Y	Y	N	N	N	Y
5 Emanuel	Y	Y	Y	N	Y	Y	N	N	N	Y

[1] Rep. Porter J. Goss, R, resigned effective Sept. 23, 2004. The last vote for which he was eligible was vote 7.

KEY

	Democrats	*Republicans*	**Independent**
Y	Voted for ("yea")		– Announced against
N	Voted against ("nay")		P Voted "present"
+	Announced for		C Voted "present" to avoid possible conflict of interest
#	Paired for		? Did not vote or otherwise make a position known
X	Paired against		

ND Northern Democrats
SD Southern Democrats
Southern states – Ala., Ark., Fla., Ga., Ky., La., Miss., N.C., Okla., S.C., Tenn., Texas, Va.

House Key Votes	1	2	3	4	5	6	7	8	9	10
6 Hyde	N	Y	Y	N	N	N	Y	Y	Y	Y
7 Davis	Y	N	Y	N	Y	Y	N	?	Y	Y
8 Crane	N	Y	Y	Y	N	N	Y	Y	Y	N
9 Schakowsky	Y	N	Y	N	Y	Y	N	N	N	Y
10 Kirk	N	Y	Y	Y	Y	N	Y	N	N	Y
11 Weller	N	Y	Y	N	N	Y	Y	Y	Y	Y
12 Costello	Y	Y	Y	N	Y	Y	Y	Y	N	Y
13 Biggert²	N	Y	Y	Y	N	Y	Y	N	Y	Y
14 Hastert²	N	Y	N			Y	Y	Y	Y	
15 Johnson	Y	Y	Y	Y	Y	N	Y	Y	Y	Y
16 Manzullo	N	Y	Y	Y	N	N	Y	Y	Y	N
17 Evans	Y	N	Y	N	Y	Y	Y	N	N	Y
18 LaHood	N	Y	Y	N	?	Y	Y	Y	N	N
19 Shimkus	Y	Y	Y	Y	N	N	Y	Y	Y	Y
INDIANA										
1 Visclosky	Y	N	Y	N	Y	N	N	N	N	Y
2 Chocola	N	Y	Y	Y	N	N	Y	Y	Y	Y
3 Souder	N	Y	N	N	N	N	Y	Y	Y	Y
4 Buyer	N	Y	Y	Y	N	N	Y	Y	Y	Y
5 Burton	N	Y	Y	Y	N	N	Y	Y	Y	Y
6 Pence	N	Y	N	Y	N	N	Y	Y	Y	Y
7 Carson	Y	P	Y	?	?	Y	Y	N	N	Y
8 Hostettler	N	Y	Y	Y	N	N	Y	N	Y	N
9 Hill	Y	Y	N	N	Y	Y	N	N	Y	Y
IOWA										
1 Nussle	N	Y	Y	Y	N	Y	Y	Y	Y	Y
2 Leach	Y	N	Y	N	Y	Y	Y	N	Y	Y
3 Boswell	Y	Y	Y	N	Y	Y	Y	N	Y	?
4 Latham	N	Y	Y	N	N	Y	Y	Y	Y	Y
5 King	N	Y	Y	Y	N	N	Y	Y	Y	N
KANSAS										
1 Moran	N	Y	Y	Y	Y	N	Y	Y	Y	Y
2 Ryun	N	Y	Y	Y	N	N	Y	Y	Y	Y
3 Moore	Y	Y	Y	N	Y	Y	Y	N	Y	Y
4 Tiahrt	N	Y	Y	N	N	N	Y	Y	Y	Y
KENTUCKY										
1 Whitfield	N	Y	Y	N	N	N	Y	Y	Y	Y
2 Lewis	N	Y	Y	N	N	N	Y	Y	Y	N
3 Northup	N	Y	Y	N	N	N	Y	Y	Y	Y
4 Lucas	Y	Y	Y	N	Y	Y	?	Y	Y	?
5 Rogers	N	Y	Y	N	N	N	Y	Y	Y	Y
6 Chandler³		Y	Y	C	Y	Y	Y	Y	Y	Y
LOUISIANA										
1 Vitter	N	Y	Y	Y	N	N	?	Y	Y	Y
2 Jefferson	Y	N	Y	N	Y	Y	Y	Y	Y	Y
3 Tauzin	N	?	?	?	?	?	?	?	?	Y
4 McCrery	?	Y	Y	Y	N	Y	Y	Y	Y	Y
5 Alexander⁴	Y	Y	Y	N	Y	N	Y	Y	Y	Y
6 Baker	N	Y	Y	Y	N	?	?	Y	Y	Y
7 John	Y	Y	Y	N	Y	?	Y	Y	Y	Y
MAINE										
1 Allen	Y	Y	Y	N	Y	Y	Y	N	N	Y
2 Michaud	Y	Y	Y	N	Y	Y	Y	N	N	Y
MARYLAND										
1 Gilchrest	N	Y	Y	Y	N	Y	Y	N	Y	Y
2 Ruppersberger	?	Y	Y	N	Y	Y	Y	N	Y	Y
3 Cardin	Y	Y	Y	N	Y	Y	Y	N	N	Y
4 Wynn	Y	Y	Y	N	Y	Y	Y	N	N	Y
5 Hoyer	Y	Y	Y	N	Y	Y	N	N	N	Y
6 Bartlett	N	Y	Y	Y	Y	N	Y	Y	Y	N
7 Cummings	Y	N	Y	N	Y	Y	Y	N	N	Y
8 Van Hollen	Y	N	Y	N	Y	Y	Y	N	N	Y
MASSACHUSETTS										
1 Olver	Y	N	Y	N	Y	Y	N	N	N	Y
2 Neal	Y	Y	Y	N	Y	Y	N	N	N	Y
3 McGovern	Y	N	Y	N	Y	Y	N	N	N	Y
4 Frank	Y	N	Y	N	Y	Y	N	N	N	Y

House Key Votes	1	2	3	4	5	6	7	8	9	10
5 Meehan	Y	P	Y	N	Y	Y	N	N	N	Y
6 Tierney	Y	N	Y	N	Y	Y	N	N	N	Y
7 Markey	Y	N	Y	N	Y	Y	N	N	N	Y
8 Capuano	Y	Y	Y	N	Y	Y	N	N	N	Y
9 Lynch	Y	Y	Y	N	Y	Y	Y	N	N	Y
10 Delahunt	Y	N	Y	N	Y	Y	?	N	N	Y
MICHIGAN										
1 Stupak	Y	Y	Y	N	Y	Y	Y	N	N	Y
2 Hoekstra	N	Y	Y	N	N	N	Y	Y	Y	Y
3 Ehlers	N	Y	Y	Y	N	Y	Y	Y	Y	Y
4 Camp	Y	Y	Y	Y	N	Y	Y	Y	Y	N
5 Kildee	Y	Y	Y	N	Y	Y	Y	N	N	Y
6 Upton	Y	Y	Y	Y	N	Y	Y	Y	N	Y
7 Smith	N	Y	N	?	N	N	Y	Y	Y	?
8 Rogers	Y	Y	N	Y	N	+	Y	Y	Y	Y
9 Knollenberg	N	Y	Y	N	N	N	Y	Y	Y	Y
10 Miller	Y	Y	Y	N	N	N	Y	Y	Y	Y
11 McCotter	Y	Y	Y	Y	N	N	Y	Y	Y	Y
12 Levin	Y	N	Y	N	Y	Y	Y	N	N	Y
13 Kilpatrick	Y	N	Y	N	Y	Y	N	N	N	Y
14 Conyers	?	N	Y	N	Y	?	N	N	N	Y
15 Dingell	Y	Y	Y	N	Y	Y	Y	N	N	Y
MINNESOTA										
1 Gutknecht	N	Y	N	N	N	N	Y	Y	Y	N
2 Kline	N	Y	N	Y	N	N	Y	Y	Y	Y
3 Ramstad	N	Y	Y	Y	N	N	Y	Y	Y	Y
4 McCollum	Y	N	Y	N	Y	Y	N	N	N	Y
5 Sabo	Y	N	Y	N	Y	Y	N	N	N	N
6 Kennedy	N	Y	Y	N	N	Y	Y	Y	Y	Y
7 Peterson	Y	Y	Y	N	Y	N	Y	Y	Y	Y
8 Oberstar	Y	N	Y	N	Y	Y	N	?	N	N
MISSISSIPPI										
1 Wicker	N	Y	Y	N	N	N	Y	Y	Y	Y
2 Thompson	Y	Y	Y	N	Y	Y	?	Y	Y	Y
3 Pickering	N	Y	Y	Y	N	Y	Y	Y	Y	Y
4 Taylor	Y	Y	Y	N	Y	?	N	Y	Y	Y
MISSOURI										
1 Clay	Y	N	Y	N	Y	?	N	N	N	Y
2 Akin	N	Y	N	Y	N	N	Y	Y	Y	Y
3 Gephardt	?	Y	Y	?	?	?	Y	N	?	Y
4 Skelton	Y	Y	Y	N	Y	Y	Y	N	Y	Y
5 McCarthy	+	N	Y	N	Y	Y	+	N	N	Y
6 Graves	N	Y	Y	Y	N	N	+	Y	Y	Y
7 Blunt	N	Y	N	Y	N	Y	Y	Y	Y	Y
8 Emerson	Y	Y	Y	N	N	N	Y	Y	Y	Y
9 Hulshof	N	Y	?	Y	N	Y	Y	Y	Y	Y
MONTANA										
AL Rehberg	N	Y	Y	Y	N	N	Y	Y	Y	N
NEBRASKA										
1 Bereuter⁵	N	Y	Y	?	N					
2 Terry	N	Y	Y	N	N	Y	Y	Y	Y	Y
3 Osborne	N	Y	Y	N	N	Y	?	Y	Y	Y
NEVADA										
1 Berkley	Y	Y	Y	N	Y	Y	Y	N	N	Y
2 Gibbons	N	Y	Y	Y	N	N	Y	N	Y	Y
3 Porter	N	Y	Y	N	Y	Y	Y	N	Y	Y
NEW HAMPSHIRE										
1 Bradley	N	Y	Y	N	N	Y	Y	Y	N	Y
2 Bass	N	Y	Y	Y	N	N	Y	N	N	Y
NEW JERSEY										
1 Andrews	Y	Y	Y	N	Y	Y	N	N	N	Y
2 LoBiondo	Y	Y	Y	N	N	N	Y	Y	Y	Y
3 Saxton	Y	Y	?	N	N	N	Y	Y	Y	Y
4 Smith	Y	Y	Y	N	N	Y	Y	Y	Y	Y
5 Garrett	N	Y	Y	Y	N	N	?	Y	Y	Y
6 Pallone	Y	N	Y	N	Y	Y	N	N	N	Y
7 Ferguson	N	Y	Y	N	N	N	Y	Y	Y	Y
8 Pascrell	+	Y	Y	N	Y	Y	Y	N	N	Y
9 Rothman	Y	N	Y	?	Y	Y	Y	N	N	Y
10 Payne	Y	N	Y	N	Y	Y	N	N	N	+
11 Frelinghuysen	N	Y	Y	N	N	N	Y	Y	N	Y
12 Holt	Y	Y	Y	N	Y	Y	N	N	N	Y
13 Menendez	Y	Y	Y	N	Y	Y	Y	?	N	Y
NEW MEXICO										
1 Wilson	Y	Y	Y	N	N	Y	Y	Y	N	N
2 Pearce	N	Y	Y	Y	N	N	Y	Y	Y	Y
3 Udall	Y	N	Y	N	Y	Y	N	N	N	Y
NEW YORK										
1 Bishop	Y	Y	Y	N	Y	Y	Y	N	N	Y
2 Israel	Y	Y	Y	N	Y	Y	Y	N	N	Y
3 King	Y	Y	Y	N	N	Y	Y	Y	Y	Y

House Key Votes	1	2	3	4	5	6	7	8	9	10
4 McCarthy	Y	Y	Y	N	Y	Y	Y	N	N	Y
5 Ackerman	Y	N	Y	N	Y	?	Y	N	N	Y
6 Meeks	Y	N	Y	N	Y	Y	Y	?	Y	Y
7 Crowley	Y	Y	Y	N	Y	?	Y	N	Y	Y
8 Nadler	Y	N	Y	N	Y	Y	Y	N	N	Y
9 Weiner	Y	N	Y	N	Y	?	Y	N	N	Y
10 Towns	Y	N	Y	N	Y	?	N	N	?	Y
11 Owens	Y	N	Y	N	Y	?	N	N	N	Y
12 Velázquez	Y	N	Y	N	Y	?	Y	N	N	Y
13 Fossella	Y	Y	Y	Y	N	N	Y	Y	Y	Y
14 Maloney	Y	N	Y	N	Y	Y	+	N	N	Y
15 Rangel	Y	N	Y	N	Y	Y	Y	?	N	Y
16 Serrano	Y	N	Y	N	Y	?	Y	N	N	Y
17 Engel	Y	Y	Y	N	Y	?	Y	N	N	Y
18 Lowey	Y	Y	Y	N	Y	Y	Y	N	N	Y
19 Kelly	Y	Y	Y	Y	N	N	Y	Y	Y	Y
20 Sweeney	Y	Y	Y	N	N	N	Y	N	Y	N
21 McNulty	Y	Y	Y	N	Y	Y	Y	N	N	Y
22 Hinchey	Y	N	Y	N	?	Y	Y	N	N	Y
23 McHugh	+	Y	Y	N	N	N	Y	Y	Y	Y
24 Boehlert	Y	Y	Y	Y	N	?	Y	?	?	?
25 Walsh	Y	Y	Y	N	N	Y	Y	Y	Y	Y
26 Reynolds	N	Y	Y	Y	N	N	Y	Y	Y	Y
27 Quinn	Y	Y	Y	N	?	Y	?	Y	Y	Y
28 Slaughter	Y	Y	Y	N	Y	+	Y	N	?	Y
29 Houghton	N	Y	Y	?	N	?	Y	N	Y	?
NORTH CAROLINA										
1 Ballance/Butterfield[6]	Y	N	Y			Y	Y	N	Y	Y
2 Etheridge	Y	Y	Y	N	Y	Y	Y	Y	Y	Y
3 Jones	Y	Y	N	Y	N	N	Y	Y	Y	N
4 Price	Y	Y	Y	N	Y	Y	Y	N	N	Y
5 Burr	Y	Y	Y	Y	N	N	Y	Y	Y	?
6 Coble	N	Y	Y	N	N	N	Y	Y	Y	N
7 McIntyre	Y	Y	Y	N	Y	N	Y	Y	Y	Y
8 Hayes	Y	Y	Y	N	N	N	Y	Y	Y	Y
9 Myrick	N	Y	N	Y	N	N	?	Y	Y	N
10 Ballenger	N	Y	Y	?	N	?	Y	Y	Y	?
11 Taylor	Y	Y	Y	N	N	N	Y	Y	Y	N
12 Watt	Y	N	Y	N	Y	Y	Y	N	N	Y
13 Miller	Y	Y	Y	N	Y	Y	Y	N	Y	Y
NORTH DAKOTA										
AL Pomeroy	Y	Y	Y	N	Y	Y	Y	N	Y	Y
OHIO										
1 Chabot	N	Y	Y	Y	N	N	Y	Y	Y	N
2 Portman	N	Y	Y	Y	N	Y	Y	Y	Y	Y
3 Turner	Y	Y	Y	Y	N	Y	N	Y	Y	Y
4 Oxley	N	Y	Y	Y	N	Y	Y	Y	Y	Y
5 Gillmor	N	Y	Y	Y	N	Y	Y	Y	Y	Y
6 Strickland	Y	Y	Y	N	Y	Y	Y	N	N	Y
7 Hobson	N	Y	Y	N	N	Y	N	Y	Y	Y
8 Boehner	N	Y	N	Y	N	Y	Y	Y	Y	Y
9 Kaptur	Y	Y	Y	N	Y	Y	Y	N	Y	Y
10 Kucinich	?	?	Y	N	Y	Y	Y	N	N	N
11 Jones	Y	Y	Y	?	Y	Y	Y	N	N	?
12 Tiberi	N	Y	Y	Y	N	Y	Y	Y	Y	Y
13 Brown	Y	Y	Y	N	Y	Y	Y	N	N	Y
14 LaTourette	Y	Y	Y	N	N	Y	Y	Y	Y	Y
15 Pryce	N	Y	Y	N	N	Y	Y	N	Y	Y
16 Regula	N	Y	Y	N	N	N	Y	Y	Y	Y
17 Ryan	Y	Y	Y	N	Y	N	Y	N	N	Y
18 Ney	Y	Y	Y	Y	Y	Y	Y	Y	Y	Y
OKLAHOMA										
1 Sullivan	N	Y	N	Y	N	N	Y	Y	Y	N
2 Carson	Y	Y	Y	N	Y	N	Y	Y	Y	Y
3 Lucas	?	Y	N	Y	N	Y	Y	Y	Y	N
4 Cole	N	Y	N	Y	N	N	Y	Y	Y	N
5 Istook	N	Y	N	N	N	N	+	Y	Y	N
OREGON										
1 Wu	Y	Y	Y	N	Y	Y	Y	N	Y	Y
2 Walden	Y	Y	Y	N	N	N	Y	Y	Y	Y
3 Blumenauer	Y	N	Y	N	?	Y	N	N	N	Y
4 DeFazio	Y	Y	Y	N	Y	Y	Y	N	N	Y
5 Hooley	Y	Y	Y	N	Y	Y	Y	N	Y	Y
PENNSYLVANIA										
1 Brady	Y	N	Y	N	Y	Y	N	N	N	Y
2 Fattah	Y	N	Y	N	Y	Y	?	N	N	?
3 English	Y	Y	Y	N	N	Y	Y	Y	Y	Y
4 Hart	N	Y	Y	Y	N	Y	Y	Y	Y	Y
5 Peterson	Y	Y	Y	N	N	N	Y	Y	Y	Y
6 Gerlach	N	Y	Y	N	N	N	Y	Y	Y	Y
7 Weldon	Y	?	Y	Y	Y	Y	Y	Y	Y	Y
8 Greenwood	N	Y	Y	Y	N	N	Y	Y	N	Y
9 Shuster, Bill	N	Y	Y	Y	N	N	Y	Y	Y	Y

House Key Votes	1	2	3	4	5	6	7	8	9	10
10 Sherwood	N	?	Y	N	N	?	Y	Y	Y	Y
11 Kanjorski	Y	N	Y	N	Y	Y	N	N	N	Y
12 Murtha	Y	N	Y	N	Y	?	N	?	N	N
13 Hoeffel	Y	?	Y	N	Y	Y	Y	N	N	Y
14 Doyle	Y	N	Y	N	Y	Y	N	N	N	Y
15 Toomey	N	Y	N	Y	N	Y	Y	Y	Y	Y
16 Pitts	N	Y	Y	Y	N	N	Y	Y	Y	N
17 Holden	Y	Y	Y	N	N	N	Y	Y	N	Y
18 Murphy	Y	Y	Y	N	Y	Y	Y	Y	Y	Y
19 Platts	N	Y	Y	Y	N	N	Y	Y	Y	Y
RHODE ISLAND										
1 Kennedy	Y	Y	Y	N	Y	Y	Y	N	N	Y
2 Langevin	?	Y	Y	N	Y	?	Y	N	N	Y
SOUTH CAROLINA										
1 Brown	N	Y	Y	Y	N	N	Y	Y	Y	Y
2 Wilson	N	Y	Y	Y	N	Y	Y	Y	Y	Y
3 Barrett	N	Y	N	Y	N	N	Y	Y	Y	N
4 DeMint	N	Y	?	Y	N	N	Y	Y	Y	Y
5 Spratt	Y	Y	Y	N	Y	Y	Y	Y	Y	Y
6 Clyburn	Y	N	Y	N	Y	Y	Y	N	Y	Y
SOUTH DAKOTA										
AL Herseth[7]				N	Y	Y	?	Y	Y	Y
TENNESSEE										
1 Jenkins	N	Y	Y	N	N	N	Y	Y	Y	N
2 Duncan	N	Y	Y	Y	Y	N	Y	Y	Y	N
3 Wamp	N	Y	Y	N	N	N	Y	Y	Y	N
4 Davis	Y	Y	Y	N	Y	Y	Y	Y	Y	Y
5 Cooper	Y	Y	Y	N	N	Y	Y	N	Y	Y
6 Gordon	Y	Y	Y	?	N	Y	Y	Y	Y	N
7 Blackburn	N	Y	Y	Y	N	N	Y	Y	Y	Y
8 Tanner	Y	Y	?	N	Y	N	N	Y	Y	Y
9 Ford	Y	Y	Y	N	Y	Y	Y	Y	Y	Y
TEXAS										
1 Sandlin	Y	Y	Y	N	Y	Y	Y	N	Y	Y
2 Turner	Y	Y	Y	N	Y	Y	Y	N	Y	Y
3 Johnson, Sam	N	Y	N	Y	N	N	Y	Y	Y	N
4 Hall[8]	N	Y	Y	N	N	N	Y	Y	Y	Y
5 Hensarling	N	Y	Y	Y	N	N	Y	Y	Y	N
6 Barton	N	Y	N	?	N	N	Y	Y	Y	Y
7 Culberson	?	Y	?	N	N	N	Y	Y	Y	N
8 Brady	N	Y	N	Y	N	N	Y	Y	Y	Y
9 Lampson	Y	Y	Y	N	Y	Y	Y	N	Y	Y
10 Doggett	Y	Y	Y	N	Y	Y	?	N	N	Y
11 Edwards	Y	Y	Y	N	N	Y	Y	Y	Y	Y
12 Granger	?	Y	Y	?	N	?	Y	Y	Y	Y
13 Thornberry	N	Y	Y	N	N	N	Y	Y	Y	Y
14 Paul	N	N	N	Y	N	N	Y	N	?	N
15 Hinojosa	Y	Y	Y	N	Y	Y	Y	N	Y	Y
16 Reyes	Y	Y	?	N	N	Y	Y	?	Y	Y
17 Stenholm	Y	Y	Y	N	N	N	Y	Y	Y	Y
18 Jackson-Lee	Y	N	Y	N	Y	Y	Y	N	Y	Y
19 Neugebauer	N	Y	Y	Y	N	N	Y	Y	Y	N
20 Gonzalez	Y	Y	Y	N	N	Y	Y	N	Y	Y
21 Smith	N	Y	Y	Y	N	N	Y	Y	Y	Y
22 DeLay	N	Y	Y	Y	N	N	Y	Y	Y	Y
23 Bonilla	Y	Y	Y	N	N	N	Y	Y	Y	Y
24 Frost	Y	Y	Y	N	Y	Y	Y	N	Y	Y
25 Bell	N	Y	Y	N	?	Y	Y	N	Y	?
26 Burgess	N	Y	Y	Y	N	N	Y	Y	Y	N
27 Ortiz	?	Y	Y	N	Y	Y	Y	N	?	Y
28 Rodriguez	Y	Y	Y	N	Y	Y	?	N	Y	Y
29 Green	Y	Y	Y	N	Y	Y	?	N	Y	Y
30 Johnson, E.B.	Y	P	Y	N	Y	?	Y	N	Y	Y
31 Carter	N	Y	Y	Y	N	N	Y	Y	Y	Y
32 Sessions	N	Y	Y	Y	N	N	Y	Y	Y	Y

[2] The Speaker votes only at his discretion, usually to break a tie or to emphasize the importance of a matter.

[3] Rep. Ben Chandler, D, was sworn in Feb. 24, 2004. The first vote for which he was eligible was vote 2. He replaced Rep. Ernest Fletcher, R, who resigned Dec. 8, 2003, after being elected Kentucky governor

[4] Rep. Rodney Alexander switched parties from Democrat to Republican effective Sept. 7, 2004.

[5] Rep. Doug Bereuter, R, resigned effective Aug. 31, 2004. The last vote for which he was eligible was vote 5.

[6] Rep. Frank W. Ballance Jr., D, resigned effective June 11, 2004. The last vote for which Ballance was eligible was vote 3. He was succeeded by Rep. G. K. Butterfield, D, who was sworn in July 21, 2004. The first vote for which Butterfield was eligible was vote 6.

[7] Rep. Stephanie Herseth, D, was sworn in June 3, 2004, to fill the At Large seat vacated when Rep. Bill Janklow, R, resigned Jan. 20, 2004. The first vote for which Herseth was eligible was vote 4.

[8] Rep. Ralph M. Hall, switched parties from Democrat to Republican effective Jan. 5, 2004.

KEY

	Democrats	*Republicans*	**Independent**

Y Voted for ("yea")
N Voted against ("nay")
+ Announced for
# Paired for
X Paired against

– Announced against
P Voted "present"
C Voted "present" to avoid possible conflict of interest
? Did not vote or otherwise make a position known

ND Northern Democrats
SD Southern Democrats
Southern states – Ala., Ark., Fla., Ga., Ky., La., Miss., N.C., Okla., S.C., Tenn., Texas, Va.

House Key Votes	1	2	3	4	5	6	7	8	9	10
UTAH										
1 *Bishop*	N	Y	Y	Y	N	N	Y	Y	Y	N
2 Matheson	Y	Y	Y	N	Y	Y	Y	Y	Y	Y
3 *Cannon*	N	Y	Y	Y	N	?	?	?	Y	?
VERMONT										
AL **Sanders**	Y	N	Y	N	Y	Y	Y	N	N	Y
VIRGINIA										
1 *Davis, J.*	N	Y	Y	N	N	N	Y	Y	Y	N
2 *Schrock*	N	Y	Y	Y	N	?	Y	Y	Y	Y
3 Scott	Y	N	N	N	Y	Y	N	N	N	Y
4 *Forbes*	N	Y	Y	Y	N	N	Y	Y	Y	N
5 *Goode*	Y	Y	Y	Y	N	N	Y	Y	Y	N
6 *Goodlatte*	N	Y	Y	Y	N	N	Y	Y	Y	Y
7 *Cantor*	N	Y	N	Y	N	Y	Y	Y	Y	Y

House Key Votes	1	2	3	4	5	6	7	8	9	10
8 Moran	Y	N	Y	N	Y	Y	Y	N	N	Y
9 Boucher	Y	Y	Y	N	Y	N	Y	Y	Y	Y
10 *Wolf*	N	Y	Y	N	N	N	Y	Y	N	Y
11 *Davis, T.*	N	Y	Y	N	N	Y	Y	Y	Y	Y
WASHINGTON										
1 Inslee	Y	Y	Y	N	Y	Y	N	N	Y	Y
2 Larsen	Y	Y	Y	N	Y	Y	N	N	Y	Y
3 Baird	Y	Y	Y	N	Y	Y	Y	N	Y	Y
4 *Hastings*	N	Y	Y	?	N	Y	Y	Y	Y	Y
5 *Nethercutt*	Y	Y	Y	N	N	?	Y	?	Y	Y
6 Dicks	?	Y	Y	N	Y	Y	N	N	Y	Y
7 McDermott	Y	N	Y	?	Y	Y	N	N	N	N
8 *Dunn*	N	Y	Y	Y	N	?	Y	?	Y	Y
9 Smith	?	?	Y	N	N	Y	?	N	Y	Y
WEST VIRGINIA										
1 Mollohan	Y	N	Y	?	Y	Y	N	N	N	N
2 *Capito*	Y	Y	Y	Y	N	N	Y	Y	Y	Y
3 Rahall	?	N	Y	N	Y	Y	Y	Y	N	?
WISCONSIN										
1 *Ryan*	N	Y	N	Y	N	N	Y	Y	Y	Y
2 Baldwin	Y	N	Y	N	Y	Y	Y	N	N	Y
3 Kind	Y	Y	Y	N	Y	Y	Y	N	N	Y
4 Kleczka	Y	N	Y	N	Y	?	?	N	N	Y
5 *Sensenbrenner*	N	Y	N	Y	N	N	Y	Y	N	N
6 *Petri*	N	Y	Y	Y	Y	N	Y	Y	Y	N
7 Obey	Y	N	Y	N	Y	Y	N	N	N	N
8 *Green*	Y	Y	N	Y	N	N	Y	Y	Y	N
WYOMING										
AL *Cubin*	N	Y	Y	Y	N	N	Y	Y	Y	N

Congress and Its Members

Senate Membership in the 107th Congress

Lineup as of Jan. 3, 2001: Republicans 50, Democrats 50

Alabama
Richard C. Shelby (R)
Jeff Sessions (R)

Alaska
Ted Stevens (R)
Frank H. Murkowski (R)[1]

Arizona
John McCain (R)
Jon Kyl (R)

Arkansas
Tim Hutchinson (R)
Blanche Lincoln (D)

California
Dianne Feinstein (D)
Barbara Boxer (D)

Colorado
Ben Nighthorse Campbell (R)
Wayne Allard (R)

Connecticut
Christopher J. Dodd (D)
Joseph I. Lieberman (D)

Delaware
Joseph R. Biden Jr. (D)
Thomas R. Carper (D)

Florida
Bob Graham (D)
Bill Nelson (D)

Georgia
Max Cleland (D)
Zell Miller (D)

Hawaii
Daniel K. Inouye (D)
Daniel K. Akaka (D)

Idaho
Larry E. Craig (R)
Michael D. Crapo (R)

Illinois
Richard J. Durbin (D)
Peter Fitzgerald (R)

Indiana
Richard G. Lugar (R)
Evan Bayh (D)

Iowa
Charles E. Grassley (R)
Tom Harkin (D)

Kansas
Sam Brownback (R)
Pat Roberts (R)

Kentucky
Mitch McConnell (R)
Jim Bunning (R)

Louisiana
John B. Breaux (D)
Mary L. Landrieu (D)

Maine
Olympia J. Snowe (R)
Susan Collins (R)

Maryland
Paul S. Sarbanes (D)
Barbara A. Mikulski (D)

Massachusetts
Edward M. Kennedy (D)
John F. Kerry (D)

Michigan
Carl Levin (D)
Debbie Stabenow (D)

Minnesota
Paul D. Wellstone (D)[2]
Mark Dayton (D)

Mississippi
Thad Cochran (R)
Trent Lott (R)

Missouri
Christopher S. Bond (R)
Jean Carnahan (D)

Montana
Max Baucus (D)
Conrad Burns (R)

Nebraska
Chuck Hagel (R)
Ben Nelson (D)

Nevada
Harry Reid (D)
John Ensign (R)

New Hampshire
Robert C. Smith (R)
Judd Gregg (R)

New Jersey
Robert G. Torricelli (D)
Jon Corzine (D)

New Mexico
Pete V. Domenici (R)
Jeff Bingaman (D)

New York
Charles E. Schumer (D)
Hillary Rodham Clinton (D)

North Carolina
Jesse Helms (R)
John Edwards (D)

North Dakota
Kent Conrad (D)
Byron L. Dorgan (D)

Ohio
Mike DeWine (R)
George V. Voinovich (R)

Oklahoma
Don Nickles (R)
James M. Inhofe (R)

Oregon
Ron Wyden (D)
Gordon H. Smith (R)

Pennsylvania
Arlen Specter (R)
Rick Santorum (R)

Rhode Island
Jack Reed (D)
Lincoln Chafee (R)

South Carolina
Strom Thurmond (R)
Ernest F. Hollings (D)

South Dakota
Tom Daschle (D)
Tim Johnson (D)

Tennessee
Fred Thompson (R)
Bill Frist (R)

Texas
Phil Gramm (R)
Kay Bailey Hutchison (R)

Utah
Orrin G. Hatch (R)
Robert F. Bennett (R)

Vermont
Patrick J. Leahy (D)
James M. Jeffords (R)[3]

Virginia
John W. Warner (R)
George F. Allen (R)

Washington
Patty Murray (D)
Maria Cantwell (D)

West Virginia
Robert C. Byrd (D)
John D. Rockefeller IV (D)

Wisconsin
Herb Kohl (D)
Russell D. Feingold (D)

Wyoming
Craig Thomas (R)
Michael B. Enzi (R)

1. Murkowski resigned Dec. 2, 2002, after being elected governor of Alaska. On Dec. 20, 2002, he appointed his daughter, Lisa Murkowski (R) to fill the final two years of his Senate term. She began service on Dec. 20, 2002.
2. Wellstone died in a place crash Oct. 25, 2002, while campaigning for reelection. Dean Barkley (Independence Party) was appointed Nov. 4, 2002, to fill the Senate seat for the remaining weeks of Wellstone's term.
3. Jeffords switched from Republican to Independent effective June 5, 2001, and caucused with the Democrats. This gave Democrats a 51–49 majority and allowed them to take control of the Senate, including committee chairmanships.

House Membership in the 107th Congress

Lineup as of Jan. 3, 2001: Republicans 221, Democrats 211, Independent 2; Vacancy 1

Alabama
1. Sonny Callahan (R)
2. Terry Everett (R)
3. Bob Riley (R)
4. Robert Aderholt (R)
5. Robert E. "Bud" Cramer (D)
6. Spencer Bachus (R)
7. Earl F. Hilliard (D)

Alaska
AL Don Young (R)

Arizona
1. Jeff Flake (R)
2. Ed Pastor (D)
3. Bob Stump (R)
4. John Shadegg (R)
5. Jim Kolbe (R)
6. J. D. Hayworth (R)

Arkansas
1. Marion Berry (D)
2. Vic Snyder (D)
3. Asa Hutchinson (R)
   (resigned Aug. 6, 2001)
   John Boozman (R)
   (sworn in Nov. 29, 2001)
4. Mike Ross (D)

California
1. Mike Thompson (D)
2. Wally Herger (R)
3. Doug Ose (R)
4. John T. Doolittle (R)
5. Robert T. Matsui (D)
6. Lynn Woolsey (D)
7. George Miller (D)
8. Nancy Pelosi (D)
9. Barbara Lee (D)
10. Ellen O. Tauscher (D)
11. Richard W. Pombo (R)
12. Tom Lantos (D)
13. Pete Stark (D)
14. Anna G. Eshoo (D)
15. Michael M. Honda (D)
16. Zoe Lofgren (D)
17. Sam Farr (D)
18. Gary A. Condit (D)
19. George P. Radanovich (R)
20. Cal Dooley (D)
21. Bill Thomas (R)
22. Lois Capps (D)
23. Elton Gallegly (R)
24. Brad Sherman (D)
25. Howard P. "Buck" McKeon (R)
26. Howard L. Berman (D)
27. Adam B. Schiff (D)
28. David Dreier (R)
29. Henry A. Waxman (D)
30. Xavier Becerra (D)
31. Hilda L. Solis (D)
32. Diane Watson (D)
33. Lucille Roybal-Allard (D)
34. Grace F. Napolitano (D)
35. Maxine Waters (D)
36. Jane Harman (D)
37. Juanita Millender-McDonald (D)
38. Steve Horn (R)
39. Ed Royce (R)
40. Jerry Lewis (R)
41. Gary G. Miller (R)
42. Joe Baca (D)
43. Ken Calvert (R)
44. Mary Bono (R)
45. Dana Rohrabacher (R)
46. Loretta Sanchez (D)
47. Christopher Cox (R)
48. Darrell Issa (R)
49. Susan A. Davis (D)
50. Bob Filner (D)
51. Randy "Duke" Cunningham (R)
52. Duncan Hunter (R)

Colorado
1. Diana DeGette (D
2. Mark Udall (D)
3. Scott McInnis (R)
4. Bob Schaffer (R)
5. Joel Hefley (R)
6. Tom Tancredo (R)

Connecticut
1. John B. Larson (D)
2. Rob Simmons (R)
3. Rosa DeLauro (D)
4. Christopher Shays (R)
5. Jim Maloney (D)
6. Nancy L. Johnson (R)

Delaware
AL Michael Castle (R)

Florida
1. Joe Scarborough (R)
   (resigned Sept. 6, 2001)
   Jeff Miller (R)
   (sworn in Oct. 23, 2001)
2. Allen Boyd (D)
3. Corrine Brown (D)
4. Ander Crenshaw (R)
5. Karen L. Thurman (D)
6. Clifford B. Stearns (R)
7. John L. Mica (R)
8. Richard "Ric" Keller (R)
9. Michael Bilirakis (R)
10. C. W. Bill Young (R)
11. Jim Davis (D)
12. Adam H. Putnam (R)
13. Dan Miller (R)
14. Porter J. Goss (R)
15. Dave Weldon (R)
16. Mark Foley (R)
17. Carrie P. Meek (D)
18. Ileana Ros-Lehtinen (R)
19. Robert Wexler (D)
20. Peter Deutsch (D)
21. Lincoln Diaz-Balart (R)
22. E. Clay Shaw Jr. (R)
23. Alcee L. Hastings (D)

Georgia
1. Jack Kingston (R)
2. Sanford D. Bishop Jr. (D)
3. Mac Collins (R)
4. Cynthia A. McKinney (D)
5. John Lewis (D)
6. Johnny Isakson (R)
7. Bob Barr (R)
8. Saxby Chambliss (R)
9. Nathan Deal (R)
10. Charlie Norwood (R)
11. John Linder (R)

Hawaii
1. Neil Abercrombie (D)
2. Patsy T. Mink (D)
   (died Sept. 28, 2002)

Idaho
1. C. L. "Butch" Otter (R)
2. Mike Simpson (R)

Illinois
1. Bobby L. Rush (D)
2. Jesse L. Jackson Jr. (D)
3. William O. Lipinski (D)
4. Luis V. Gutierrez (D)
5. Rod R. Blagojevich (D)
6. Henry J. Hyde (R)
7. Danny K. Davis (D)
8. Philip M. Crane (R)
9. Jan Schakowsky (D)
10. Mark Steven Kirk (R)
11. Jerry Weller (R)
12. Jerry F. Costello (D)
13. Judy Biggert (R)
14. J. Dennis Hastert (R)
15. Timothy V. Johnson (R)
16. Donald Manzullo (R)
17. Lane Evans (D)
18. Ray LaHood (R)
19. David Phelps (D)
20. John Shimkus (R)

Indiana
1. Peter J. Visclosky (D)
2. Mike Pence (R)
3. Tim Roemer (D)
4. Mark Souder (R)
5. Steve Buyer (R)
6. Dan Burton (R)
7. Brian Kerns (R)
8. John Hostettler (R)
9. Baron P. Hill (D)
10. Julia Carson (D)

Iowa
1. Jim Leach (R)
2. Jim Nussle (R)
3. Leonard L. Boswell (D)
4. Greg Ganske (R)
5. Tom Latham (R)

Kansas
1. Jerry Moran (R)
2. Jim Ryun (R)
3. Dennis Moore (D)
4. Todd Tiahrt (R)

Kentucky
1. Edward Whitfield (R)
2. Ron Lewis (R)
3. Anne M. Northup (R)
4. Ken Lucas (D)
5. Harold Rogers (R)
6. Ernie Fletcher (R)

Louisiana
1. David Vitter (R)
2. William J. Jefferson (D)
3. W. J. "Billy" Tauzin (R)
4. Jim McCrery (R)
5. John Cooksey (R)
6. Richard H. Baker (R)
7. Chris John (D)

Maine
1. Tom Allen (D)
2. John Baldacci (D)

Maryland
1. Wayne T. Gilchrest (R)
2. Robert L. Ehrlich Jr. (R)
3. Benjamin L. Cardin (D)
4. Albert R. Wynn (D)
5. Steny H. Hoyer (D)
6. Roscoe G. Bartlett (R)
7. Elijah E. Cummings (D)
8. Constance A. Morella (R)

Massachusetts
1. John W. Olver (D)
2. Richard E. Neal (D)
3. Jim McGovern (D)
4. Barney Frank (D)
5. Martin T. Meehan (D)
6. John F. Tierney (D)
7. Edward J. Markey (D)
8. Michael E. Capuano (D)
9. Joe Moakley (D)
   (died May 28, 2001)
   Stephen F. Lynch (D)
   (sworn in Oct. 23, 2001)
10. William Delahunt (D)

Michigan
1. Bart Stupak (D)
2. Peter Hoekstra (R)
3. Vernon J. Ehlers (R)
4. Dave Camp (R)
5. James A. Barcia (D)
6. Fred Upton (R)
7. Nick Smith (R)
8. Mike Rogers (R)

9. Dale E. Kildee (D)
10. David E. Bonior (D)
11. Joe Knollenberg (R)
12. Sander M. Levin (D)
13. Lynn Rivers (D)
14. John Conyers Jr. (D)
15. Carolyn Cheeks Kilpatrick (D)
16. John D. Dingell (D)

Minnesota
1. Gil Gutknecht (R)
2. Mark Kennedy (R)
3. Jim Ramstad (R)
4. Betty McCollum (D)
5. Martin Olav Sabo (D)
6. William P. "Bill" Luther (D)
7. Collin C. Peterson (D)
8. James L. Oberstar (D)

Mississippi
1. Roger Wicker (R)
2. Bennie Thompson (D)
3. Charles W. "Chip" Pickering Jr. (R)
4. Ronnie Shows (D)
5. Gene Taylor (D)

Missouri
1. William Lacy Clay (D)
2. Todd Akin (R)
3. Richard A. Gephardt (D)
4. Ike Skelton (D)
5. Karen McCarthy (D)
6. Sam Graves (R)
7. Roy Blunt (R)
8. Jo Ann Emerson (R)
9. Kenny Hulshof (R)

Montana
AL Denny Rehberg (R)

Nebraska
1. Doug Bereuter (R)
2. Lee Terry (R)
3. Tom Osborne (R)

Nevada
1. Shelley Berkley (D)
2. Jim Gibbons (R)

New Hampshire
1. John E. Sununu (R)
2. Charles Bass (R)

New Jersey
1. Robert E. Andrews (D)
2. Frank A. LoBiondo (R)
3. H. James Saxton (R)
4. Christopher H. Smith (R)
5. Marge Roukema (R)
6. Frank Pallone Jr. (D)
7. Mike Ferguson (R)
8. Bill Pascrell Jr. (D)
9. Steven R. Rothman (D)
10. Donald M. Payne (D)
11. Rodney Frelinghuysen (R)
12. Rush D. Holt (D)
13. Robert Menendez (D)

New Mexico
1. Heather A. Wilson (R)

2. Joseph R. Skeen (R)
3. Tom Udall (D)

New York
1. Felix J. Grucci Jr. (R)
2. Steve Israel (D)
3. Peter T. King (R)
4. Carolyn McCarthy (D)
5. Gary L. Ackerman (D)
6. Gregory W. Meeks (D)
7. Joseph Crowley (D)
8. Jerrold Nadler (D)
9. Anthony Weiner (D)
10. Edolphus Towns (D)
11. Major R. Owens (D)
12. Nydia M. Velázquez (D)
13. Vito J. Fossella (R)
14. Carolyn B. Maloney (D)
15. Charles B. Rangel (D)
16. Jose E. Serrano (D)
17. Eliot L. Engel (D)
18. Nita M. Lowey (D)
19. Sue W. Kelly (R)
20. Benjamin A. Gilman (R)
21. Michael R. McNulty (D)
22. John E. Sweeney (R)
23. Sherwood Boehlert (R)
24. John M. McHugh (R)
25. James T. Walsh (R)
26. Maurice D. Hinchey (D)
27. Thomas M. Reynolds (R)
28. Louise M. Slaughter (D)
29. John J. LaFalce (D)
30. Jack Quinn (R)
31. Amo Houghton (R)

North Carolina
1. Eva Clayton (D)
2. Bob Etheridge (D)
3. Walter B. Jones (R)
4. David E. Price (D)
5. Richard M. Burr (R)
6. Howard Coble (R)
7. Mike McIntyre (D)
8. Robin Hayes (R)
9. Sue Myrick (R)
10. Cass Ballenger (R)
11. Charles H. Taylor (R)
12. Melvin Watt (D)

North Dakota
AL Earl Pomeroy (D)

Ohio
1. Steve Chabot (R)
2. Rob Portman (R)
3. Tony P. Hall (D)
   (resigned Sept. 9, 2002)
4. Michael G. Oxley (R)
5. Paul E. Gillmor (R)
6. Ted Strickland (D)
7. David L. Hobson (R)
8. John A. Boehner (R)
9. Marcy Kaptur (D)
10. Dennis J. Kucinich (D)
11. Stephanie Tubbs Jones (D)
12. Pat Tiberi (R)
13. Sherrod Brown (D)
14. Tom Sawyer (D)

15. Deborah Pryce (R)
16. Ralph Regula (R)
17. James A. Traficant Jr. (D)
   (expelled July 24, 2002)
18. Bob Ney (R)
19. Steven C. LaTourette (R)

Oklahoma
1. Steve Largent (R)
   (resigned Feb. 15, 2002)
   John Sullivan (R)
   (sworn in Feb. 27, 2002)
2. Brad Carson (D)
3. Wes Watkins (R)
4. J. C. Watts Jr. (R)
5. Ernest Istook (R)
6. Frank D. Lucas (R)

Oregon
1. David Wu (D)
2. Greg Walden (R)
3. Earl Blumenauer (D)
4. Peter A. DeFazio (D)
5. Darlene Hooley (D)

Pennsylvania
1. Robert A. Brady (D)
2. Chaka Fattah (D)
3. Robert A. Borski (D)
4. Melissa A. Hart (R)
5. John E. Peterson (R)
6. Tim Holden (D)
7. Curt Weldon (R)
8. James C. Greenwood (R)
9. E. G. "Bud" Shuster (R)
   (resigned Feb. 13, 2001)
   Bill Shuster (R)
   (sworn in May 17, 2001)
10. Donald L. Sherwood (R)
11. Paul E. Kanjorski (D)
12. John P. Murtha (D)
13. Joseph M. Hoeffel (D)
14. William J. Coyne (D)
15. Patrick J. Toomey (R)
16. Joseph R. Pitts (R)
17. George W. Gekas (R)
18. Mike Doyle (D)
19. Todd R. Platts (R)
20. Frank R. Mascara (D)
21. Phil English (R)

Rhode Island
1. Patrick J. Kennedy (D)
2. Jim Langevin (D)

South Carolina
1. Henry E. Brown Jr. (R)
2. Floyd Spence (R)
   (died Aug. 16, 2001)
   Joe Wilson (R)
   (sworn in Dec. 19, 2001)
3. Lindsey Graham (R)
4. Jim DeMint (R)
5. John M. Spratt Jr. (D)
6. James E. Clyburn (D)

South Dakota
AL John Thune (R)

Tennessee
1. William L. Jenkins (R)
2. John J. "Jimmy" Duncan Jr. (R)
3. Zach Wamp (R)
4. Van Hilleary (R)
5. Bob Clement (D)
6. Bart Gordon (D)
7. Ed Bryant (R)
8. John Tanner (D)
9. Harold E. Ford Jr. (D)

Texas
1. Max Sandlin (D)
2. James Turner (D)
3. Sam Johnson (R)
4. Ralph M. Hall (D)
5. Pete Sessions (R)
6. Joe L. Barton (R)
7. John Culberson (R)
8. Kevin Brady (R)
9. Nick Lampson (D)
10. Lloyd Doggett (D)
11. Chet Edwards (D)
12. Kay Granger (R)
13. William M. "Mac" Thornberry (R)
14. Ron Paul (R)
15. Rub Hinojosa (D)
16. Silvestre Reyes (D)
17. Charles W. Stenholm (D)
18. Sheila Jackson-Lee (D)
19. Larry Combest (R)
20. Charlie Gonzalez (D)
21. Lamar Smith (R)
22. Tom DeLay (R)
23. Henry Bonilla (R)
24. Martin Frost (D)
25. Ken Bentsen (D)
26. Richard Armey (R)
27. Solomon P. Ortiz (D)
28. Ciro D. Rodriguez (D)
29. Gene Green (D)
30. Eddie Bernice Johnson (D)

Utah
1. James V. Hansen (R)
2. Jim Matheson (D)
3. Christopher B. Cannon (R)

Vermont
AL Bernard Sanders (I)

Virginia
1. Jo Ann Davis (R)
2. Ed Schrock (R)
3. Robert C. Scott (D)
4. Norman Sisisky (D)
   (died March 29, 2001)
   J. Randy Forbes (R)
   (sworn in June 26, 2001)
5. Virgil H. Goode Jr. (I)[1]
6. Robert W. Goodlatte (R)
7. Eric Cantor (R)
8. James P. Moran (D)
9. Rick C. Boucher (D)
10. Frank R. Wolf (R)
11. Thomas M. Davis III (R)

Washington

1. Jay Inslee (D)
2. Rick Larsen (D)
3. Brian Baird (D)
4. Richard "Doc" Hastings (R)
5. George Nethercutt (R)
6. Norm Dicks (D)
7. Jim McDermott (D)
8. Jennifer Dunn (R)
9. Adam Smith (D)

West Virginia

1. Alan B. Mollohan (D)
2. Shelley Moore Capito (R)
3. Nick J. Rahall II (D)

Wisconsin

1. Paul D. Ryan (R)
2. Tammy Baldwin (D)
3. Ron Kind (D)
4. Gerald D. Kleczka (D)
5. Thomas M. Barrett (D)
6. Thomas E. Petri (R)
7. David R. Obey (D)
8. Mark Green (R)
9. F. James Sensenbrenner Jr. (R)

Wyoming

AL   Cubin Barbara (R)

NOTE: Changes that occurred during 2001 and 2002 are noted following the names of individuals who did not serve out their full terms. Members of the 107th Congress also included delegates Eni F. H. Faleomavaega, D-American Samoa; Eleanor Holmes Norton, D-District of Columbia; Robert Underwood, D-Guam; Donna M. C. Christian, D-Virgin Islands; and resident commissioner Anibal Acevedo-Vilá, D-Puerto Rico.

1. Goode switched from Independent to Republican on Aug. 1, 2002.

Membership Changes, 107th and 108th Congresses

107th Congress

Member/Party	Died	Resigned	Switched party	Successor/Party	Elected	Sworn in
Senate						
James M. Jeffords, R-Vt.[1]			I, 6/5/01			
Frank H. Murkowski, R-Ak.[2]		12/2/02		Lisa Murkowski, R-Ak.		
Paul Wellstone, D-Minn.[3]	10/25/02					
House						
Julian C. Dixon, D-Calif.[4]	12/8/00			Diane E. Watson, D	6/5/01	6/7/01
E. G. "Bud" Shuster, R-Pa.[5]		2/3/01		Bill Shuster, R	5/15/01	5/17/01
Norman Sisisky, D-Va.	3/29/01			J. Randy Forbes, R	6/19/01	6/2601
Joe Moakley, D-Mass.	5/28/01			Stephen F. Lynch, D	10/16/01	10/23/01
James A. Traficant Jr., D-Ohio[6]		7/24/02				
Asa Hutchinson, R-Ark.[7]		8/6/01		John Boozman, R	11/20/01	11/29/01
Floyd D. Spence, R-S.C.	8/16/01			Joe Wilson, R	12/18/01	12/19/01
Joe Scarborough, R-Fla.		9/6/01		Jeff Miller, R	10/16/01	10/23/01
Tony P. Hall, D-Ohio[8]		9/9/02				
Patsy T. Mink, D-Hawaii[9]	9/28/02			Ed Case, D	11/30/02	11/30/02
Steve Largent, R-Okla.[10]		2/15/02		John Sullivan, R	1/8/02	2/27/02
Virgil H. Goode Jr., I-Va.			R, 8/1/02			

108th Congress

Member/Party	Died	Resigned	Switched party	Successor/Party	Elected	Sworn in
Senate						
None						
House						
Larry Combest, R-Texas		5/31/03		Randy Neugebauer, R	6/3/03	6/5/03
Ernest Fletcher, R-Ky.[11]		12/8/03		Ben Chandler, D	2/17/04	2/24/04
Ralph Moody Hall, D-Texas			R, 1/5/04			
William J. Janklow, R-S.D.[12]		1/20/04		Stephanie Herseth, D	6/1/04	6/3/04
Frank W. Ballance Jr., D-N.C.[13]		6/11/04		G. K. Butterfield, D	7/20/04	7/21/04
Doug Bereuter, R-Neb.[14]		8/31/04				
Rodney Alexander, D-La.			R, 8/9/04			
Porter Goss, R-Fla.[15]		9/23/04				
Robert T. Matsui, D-Calif.[16]	1/1/05			Doris Matsui, D	3/9/05	3/11/05

1. Jeffords switched from Republican to Independent effective June 5, 2001; he then caucused with the Democrats, giving them a 51–49 majority. This allowed the Democrats to take organizational control of the Senate, including committee chairmanships.
2. Murkowski resigned after being elected Alaska governor in November. On Dec. 20, 2002, he appointed his daughter, Lisa Murkowski (R) to fill the final two years of his Senate term. She began service in 2003.
3. Wellstone died in a plane crash while campaigning for reelection. Dean Barkley (Independence Party) was appointed Nov. 4, 2002, to fill the Senate seat for the remaining weeks of Wellstone's term.
4. Dixon died after the 2000 election. Watson was elected in 2001 to fill the remainder of his term in the 107th Congress.
5. Shuster resigned for health reasons. His son was elected to fill the remainder of his term in the 107th Congress.
6. Traficant was expelled from the House July 24, 2002, after his conviction on bribery, tax evasion, and fraud changes. No special election was held to fill the remainder of his term.
7. Hutchinson resigned to become head of the federal Drug Enforcement Administration.
8. Hall resigned to become U.S. ambassador to the United Nations. No special election was held to fill the seat.
9. Mink was posthumously elected in November 2002 to a seat in the 108th Congress. Case was elected in November to fill the rest of her term in the 107th Congress and elected in January 2003 to succeed her in the 108th Congress.
10. Largent resigned to seek the Oklahoma's governor's office, an election he lost in November.
11. Fletcher resigned after being elected Kentucky governor.
12. Janklow resigned after being convicted of second-degree manslaughter Dec. 8, 2003. Janklow had driven his car at high speed through a stop sign and collided with a motorcyclist, who died instantly.
13. Ballance resigned, citing health reasons. However, on Nov. 9, 2004, Balance pleaded guilty to a federal conspiracy charge related to mishandling money by his charitable foundation. He pleaded guilty to one charge of conspiracy to commit mail fraud and money laundering.
14. Bereuter resigned to become president of the Asia Foundation. No special election was held to fill the seat.
15. Goss resigned to become director of the Central Intelligence Agency. No special election was held to fill the seat.
16. Matsui's death came three days before 109th Congress was to begin. His wife, Doris Matsui, was elected to fill his seat in the new Congress beginning in 2005.

Senate Membership in the 108th Congress

Lineup as of Jan. 3, 2003: Republicans 51, Democrats 48; Independent 1

Alabama
Richard C. Shelby (R)
Jeff Sessions (R)

Alaska
Ted Stevens (R)
Lisa Murkowski (R)

Arizona
John McCain (R)
Jon Kyl (R)

Arkansas
Blanche Lincoln (D)
Mark Pryor (D)

California
Dianne Feinstein (D)
Barbara Boxer (D)

Colorado
Ben Nighthorse Campbell (R)
Wayne Allard (R)

Connecticut
Christopher J. Dodd (D)
Joseph I. Lieberman (D)

Delaware
Joseph R. Biden Jr. (D)
Thomas R. Carper (D)

Florida
Bob Graham (D)
Bill Nelson (D)

Georgia
Zell Miller (D)
Saxby Chambliss (R)

Hawaii
Daniel K. Inouye (D)
Daniel K. Akaka (D)

Idaho
Larry E. Craig (R)
Michael D. Crapo (R)

Illinois
Richard J. Durbin (D)
Peter Fitzgerald (R)

Indiana
Richard G. Lugar (R)
Evan Bayh (D)

Iowa
Charles E. Grassley (R)
Tom Harkin (D)

Kansas
Sam Brownback (R)
Pat Roberts (R)

Kentucky
Mitch McConnell (R)
Jim Bunning (R)

Louisiana
John B. Breaux (D)
Mary L. Landrieu (D)

Maine
Olympia J. Snowe (R)
Susan Collins (R)

Maryland
Paul S. Sarbanes (D)
Barbara A. Mikulski (D)

Massachusetts
Edward M. Kennedy (D)
John F. Kerry (D)

Michigan
Carl Levin (D)
Debbie Stabenow (D)

Minnesota
Mark Dayton (D)
Norm Coleman (R)

Mississippi
Thad Cochran (R)
Trent Lott (R)

Missouri
Christopher S. Bond (R)
Jim Talent (R)

Montana
Max Baucus (D)
Conrad Burns (R)

Nebraska
Chuck Hagel (R)
Ben Nelson (D)

Nevada
Harry Reid (D)
John Ensign (R)

New Hampshire
Judd Gregg (R)
John E. Sununu (R)

New Jersey
Jon Corzine (D)
Frank R. Lautenberg (D)

New Mexico
Pete V. Domenici (R)
Jeff Bingaman (D)

New York
Charles E. Schumer (D)
Hillary Rodham Clinton (D)

North Carolina
John Edwards (D)
Elizabeth Dole (R)

North Dakota
Kent Conrad (D)
Byron L. Dorgan (D)

Ohio
Mike DeWine (R)
George V. Voinovich (R)

Oklahoma
Don Nickles (R)
James M. Inhofe (R)

Oregon
Ron Wyden (D)
Gordon H. Smith (R)

Pennsylvania
Arlen Specter (R)
Rick Santorum (R)

Rhode Island
Jack Reed (D)
Lincoln Chafee (R)

South Carolina
Ernest F. Hollings (D)
Lindsey Graham (R)

South Dakota
Tom Daschle (D)
Tim Johnson (D)

Tennessee
Bill Frist (R)
Lamar Alexander (R)

Texas
Kay Bailey Hutchison (R)
John Cornyn (R)

Utah
Orrin G. Hatch (R)
Robert F. Bennett (R)

Vermont
Patrick J. Leahy (D)
James M. Jeffords (I)

Virginia
John W. Warner (R)
George F. Allen (R)

Washington
Patty Murray (D)
Maria Cantwell (D)

West Virginia
Robert C. Byrd (D)
John D. Rockefeller IV (D)

Wisconsin
Herb Kohl (D)
Russell D. Feingold (D)

Wyoming
Craig Thomas (R)
Michael B. Enzi (R)

House Membership in the 108th Congress

Lineup as of Jan. 3, 2003: Republicans 229, Democrats 205, Independent 1

Alabama
1. Jo Bonner (R)
2. Terry Everett (R)
3. Mike D. Rogers (R)
4. Robert B. Aderholt (R)
5. Robert E. "Bud" Cramer (D)
6. Spencer Bachus (R)
7. Artur Davis (D)

Alaska
AL Don Young (R)

Arizona
1. Rick Renzi (R)
2. Trent Franks (R)
3. John Shadegg (R)
4. Ed Pastor (D)
5. J. D. Hayworth (R)
6. Jeff Flake (R)
7. Raul M. Grijalva (D)
8. Jim Kolbe (R)

Arkansas
1. Marion Berry (D)
2. Vic Snyder (D)
3. John Boozman (R)
4. Mike Ross (D)

California
1. Mike Thompson (D)
2. Wally Herger (R)
3. Doug Ose (R)
4. John T. Doolittle (R)
5. Robert T. Matsui (D)
6. Lynn Woolsey (D)
7. George Miller (D)
8. Nancy Pelosi (D)
9. Barbara Lee (D)
10. Ellen O. Tauscher (D)
11. Richard W. Pombo (R)
12. Tom Lantos (D)
13. Pete Stark (D)
14. Anna G. Eshoo (D)
15. Michael M. Honda (D)
16. Zoe Lofgren (D)
17. Sam Farr (D)
18. Dennis Cardoza (D)
19. George P. Radanovich (R)
20. Cal Dooley (D)
21. Devin Nunes (R)
22. Bill Thomas (R)
23. Lois Capps (D)
24. Elton Gallegly (R)
25. Howard P. "Buck" McKeon (R)
26. David Dreier (R)
27. Brad Sherman (D)
28. Howard L. Berman (D)
29. Adam B. Schiff (D)
30. Henry A. Waxman (D)
31. Xavier Becerra (D)
32. Hilda L. Solis (D)
33. Diane Watson (D)
34. Lucille Roybal-Allard (D)
35. Maxine Waters (D)
36. Jane Harman (D)
37. Juanita Millender-McDonald (D)
38. Grace F. Napolitano (D)
39. Linda T. Sanchez (D)
40. Ed Royce (R)
41. Jerry Lewis (R)
42. Gary G. Miller (R)
43. Joe Baca (D)
44. Ken Calvert (R)
45. Mary Bono (R)
46. Dana Rohrabacher (R)
47. Loretta Sanchez (D)
48. Christopher Cox (R)
49. Darrell Issa (R)
50. Randy "Duke" Cunningham (R)
51. Bob Filner (D)
52. Duncan Hunter (R)
53. Susan A. Davis (D)

Colorado
1. Diana DeGette (D)
2. Mark Udall (D)
3. Scott McInnis (R)
4. Marilyn Musgrave (R)
5. Joel Hefley (R)
6. Tom Tancredo (R)
7. Bob Beauprez (R)

Connecticut
1. John B. Larson (D)
2. Rob Simmons (R)
3. Rosa DeLauro (D)
4. Christopher Shays (R)
5. Nancy L. Johnson (R)

Delaware
AL Michael Castle (R)

Florida
1. Jeff Miller (R)
2. Allen Boyd (D)
3. Corrine Brown (D)
4. Ander Crenshaw (R)
5. Ginny Brown-Waite (R)
6. Clifford B. Stearns (R)
7. John L. Mica (R)
8. Ric Keller (R)
9. Michael Bilirakis (R)
10. C. W. Bill Young (R)
11. Jim Davis (D)
12. Adam H. Putnam (R)
13. Katherine Harris (R)
14. Porter Goss (R)
    (resigned Sept. 23, 2004)
15. Dave Weldon (R)
16. Mark Foley (R)
17. Kendrick B. Meek (D)
18. Ileana Ros-Lehtinen (R)
19. Robert Wexler (D)
20. Peter Deutsch (D)
21. Lincoln Diaz-Balart (R)
22. E. Clay Shaw Jr. (R)
23. Alcee L. Hastings (D)
24. Tom Feeney (R)
25. Mario Diaz-Balart (R)

Georgia
1. Jack Kingston (R)
2. Sanford D. Bishop Jr. (D)
3. Jim Marshall (D)
4. Denise L. Majette (D)
5. John Lewis (D)
6. Johnny Isakson (R)
7. John Linder (R)
8. Mac Collins (R)
9. Charlie Norwood (R)
10. Nathan Deal (R)
11. Phil Gingrey (R)
12. Max Burns (R)
13. David Scott (D)

Hawaii
1. Neil Abercrombie (D)
2. Ed Case (D)

Idaho
1. C. L. "Butch" Otter (R)
2. Mike Simpson (R)

Illinois
1. Bobby L. Rush (D)
2. Jesse L. Jackson Jr. (D)
3. William O. Lipinski (D)
4. Luis V. Gutierrez (D)
5. Rahm Emanuel (D)
6. Henry J. Hyde (R)
7. Danny K. Davis (D)
8. Philip M. Crane (R)
9. Jan Schakowsky (D)
10. Mark Steven Kirk (R)
11. Jerry Weller (R)
12. Jerry F. Costello (D)
13. Judy Biggert (R)
14. J. Dennis Hastert (R)
15. Timothy V. Johnson (R)
16. Donald Manzullo (R)
17. Lane Evans (D)
18. Ray LaHood (R)
19. John Shimkus (R)

Indiana
1. Peter J. Visclosky (D)
2. Chris Chocola (R)
3. Mark Souder (R)
4. Steve Buyer (R)
5. Dan Burton (R)
6. Mike Pence (R)
7. Julia Carson (D)
8. John Hostettler (R)
9. Baron P. Hill (D)

Iowa
1. Jim Nussle (R)
2. Jim Leach (R)
3. Leonard L. Boswell (D)
4. Tom Latham (R)
5. Steve King (R)

Kansas
1. Jerry Moran (R)
2. Jim Ryun (R)
3. Dennis Moore (D)
4. Todd Tiahrt (R)

Kentucky
1. Edward Whitfield (R)
2. Ron Lewis (R)
3. Anne M. Northup (R)
4. Ken Lucas (D)
5. Harold Rogers (R)
6. Ernest Fletcher (R)
   (resigned Dec. 8, 2003)
   Ben Chandler (D)
   (sworn in Feb. 24, 2004)

Louisiana
1. David Vitter (R)
2. William J. Jefferson (D)
3. W. J. "Billy" Tauzin (R)
4. Jim McCrery (R)
5. Rodney Alexander (D)[1]
6. Richard H. Baker (R)
7. Chris John (D)

Maine
1. Tom Allen (D)
2. Michael H. Michaud (D)

Maryland
1. Wayne T. Gilchrest (R)
2. C. A. Dutch Ruppersberger (D)
3. Benjamin L. Cardin (D)
4. Albert R. Wynn (D)
5. Steny H. Hoyer (D)
6. Roscoe G. Bartlett (R)
7. Elijah E. Cummings (D)
8. Chris Van Hollen (D)

Massachusetts
1. John W. Olver (D)
2. Richard E. Neal (D)
3. Jim McGovern (D)
4. Barney Frank (D)
5. Martin T. Meehan (D)
6. John F. Tierney (D)
7. Edward J. Markey (D)
8. Michael E. Capuano (D)
9. Stephen L. Lynch (D)
10. William Delahunt (D)

Michigan
1. Bart Stupak (D)
2. Peter Hoekstra (R)
3. Vernon J. Ehlers (R)
4. Dave Camp (R)
5. Dale E. Kildee (D)
6. Fred Upton (R)

7. Nick Smith (R)
8. Mike Rogers (R)
9. Joe Knollenberg (R)
10. Candice S. Miller (R)
11. Thaddeus McCotter (R)
12. Sander M. Levin (D)
13. Carolyn Cheeks Kilpatrick (D)
14. John Conyers Jr. (D)
15. John D. Dingell (D)

Minnesota
1. Gil Gutknecht (R)
2. John Kline (R)
3. Jim Ramstad (R)
4. Betty McCollum (D)
5. Martin Olav Sabo (D)
6. Mark Kennedy (R)
7. Collin C. Peterson (D)
8. James L. Oberstar (D)

Mississippi
1. Roger Wicker (R)
2. Bennie Thompson (D)
3. Charles W. "Chip" Pickering Jr. (R)
4. Gene Taylor (D)

Missouri
1. William Lacy Clay (D)
2. Todd Akin (R)
3. Richard A. Gephardt (D)
4. Ike Skelton (D)
5. Karen McCarthy (D)
6. Sam Graves (R)
7. Roy Blunt (R)
8. Jo Ann Emerson (R)
9. Kenny Hulshof (R)

Montana
AL   Denny Rehberg (R)

Nebraska
1. Doug Bereuter (R)
   (resigned Aug. 31, 2004)
2. Lee Terry (R)
3. Tom Osborne (R)

Nevada
1. Shelley Berkley (D)
2. Jim Gibbons (R)
3. Jon Porter (R)

New Hampshire
1. Jeb Bradley (R)
2. Charles Bass (R)

New Jersey
1. Robert E. Andrews (D)
2. Frank A. LoBiondo (R)
3. H. James Saxton (R)
4. Christopher H. Smith (R)
5. Scott Garrett (R)
6. Frank Pallone Jr. (D)
7. Mike Ferguson (R)
8. Bill Pascrell Jr. (D)
9. Steven R. Rothman (D)
10. Donald M. Payne (D)
11. Rodney Frelinghuysen (R)
12. Rush D. Holt (D)
13. Robert Menendez (D)

New Mexico
1. Heather A. Wilson (R)
2. Steve Pearce (R)
3. Tom Udall (D)

New York
1. Timothy H. Bishop (D)
2. Steve Israel (D)
3. Peter T. King (R)
4. Carolyn McCarthy (D)
5. Gary L. Ackerman (D)
6. Gregory W. Meeks (D)
7. Joseph Crowley (D)
8. Jerrold Nadler (D)
9. Anthony Weiner (D)
10. Edolphus Towns (D)
11. Major R. Owens (D)
12. Nydia M. Velázquez (D)
13. Vito J. Fossella (R)
14. Carolyn B. Maloney (D)
15. Charles B. Rangel (D)
16. Jose E. Serrano (D)
17. Eliot L. Engel (D)
18. Nita M. Lowey (D)
19. Sue W. Kelly (R)
20. John E. Sweeney (R)
21. Michael R. McNulty (D)
22. Maurice D. Hinchey (D)
23. John M. McHugh (R)
24. Sherwood Boehlert (R)
25. James T. Walsh (R)
26. Thomas M. Reynolds (R)
27. Jack Quinn (R)
28. Louise M. Slaughter (D)
29. Amo Houghton (R)

North Carolina
1. Frank W. Ballance Jr. (D)
   (resigned June 11, 2004)
   G. K. Butterfield (D)
   (sworn in July 21, 2004)
2. Bob Etheridge (D)
3. Walter B. Jones (R)
4. David E. Price (D)
5. Richard M. Burr (R)
6. Howard Coble (R)
7. Mike McIntyre (D)
8. Robin Hayes (R)
9. Sue Myrick (R)
10. Cass Ballenger (R)
11. Charles H. Taylor (R)
12. Melvin Watt (D)
13. Brad Miller (D)

North Dakota
AL   Earl Pomeroy (D)

Ohio
1. Steve Chabot (R)
2. Rob Portman (R)
3. Michael R. Turner (R)
4. Michael G. Oxley (R)
5. Paul E. Gillmor (R)
6. Ted Strickland (D)
7. David L. Hobson (R)
8. John A. Boehner (R)
9. Marcy Kaptur (D)
10. Dennis J. Kucinich (D)
11. Stephanie Tubbs Jones (D)
12. Pat Tiberi (R)

13. Sherrod Brown (D)
14. Steven C. LaTourette (R)
15. Deborah Pryce (R)
16. Ralph Regula (R)
17. Tim Ryan (D)
18. Bob Ney (R)

Oklahoma
1. John Sullivan (R)
2. Brad Carson (D)
3. Frank D. Lucas (R)
4. Tom Cole (R)
5. Ernest Istook (R)

Oregon
1. David Wu (D)
2. Greg Walden (R)
3. Earl Blumenauer (D)
4. Peter A. DeFazio (D)
5. Darlene Hooley (D)

Pennsylvania
1. Robert A. Brady (D)
2. Chaka Fattah (D)
3. Phil English (R)
4. Melissa A. Hart (R)
5. John E. Peterson (R)
6. Jim Gerlach (R)
7. Curt Weldon (R)
8. James C. Greenwood (R)
9. Bill Shuster (R)
10. Don Sherwood (R)
11. Paul E. Kanjorski (D)
12. John P. Murtha (D)
13. Joseph M. Hoeffel (D)
14. Mike Doyle (D)
15. Patrick J. Toomey (R)
16. Joe Pitts (R)
17. Tim Holden (D)
18. Tim Murphy (R)
19. Todd R. Platts (R)

Rhode Island
1. Patrick J. Kennedy (D)
2. Jim Langevin (D)

South Carolina
1. Henry E. Brown Jr. (R)
2. Joe Wilson (R)
3. J. Gresham Barrett (R)
4. Jim DeMint (R)
5. John M. Spratt Jr. (D)
6. James E. Clyburn (D)

South Dakota
AL   William J. Janklow (R)
   (resigned Jan. 20, 2004)
   Stephanie Herseth (D)
   (sworn in June 3, 2004)

Tennessee
1. William L. Jenkins (R)
2. John J. "Jimmy" Duncan Jr. (R)
3. Zach Wamp (R)
4. Lincoln Davis (D)
5. Jim Cooper (D)
6. Bart Gordon (D)
7. Marsha Blackburn (R)
8. John Tanner (D)
9. Harold E. Ford Jr. (D)

Texas
1. Max Sandlin (D)
2. Jim Turner (D)
3. Sam Johnson (R)
4. Ralph M. Hall (R)[2]
5. Jeb Hensarling (R)
6. Joe L. Barton (R)
7. John Culberson (R)
8. Kevin Brady (R)
9. Nick Lampson (D)
10. Lloyd Doggett (D)
11. Chet Edwards (D)
12. Kay Granger (R)
13. William M. "Mac" Thornberry (R)
14. Ron Paul (R)
15. Ruben Hinojosa (D)
16. Silvestre Reyes (D)
17. Charles W. Stenholm (D)
18. Sheila Jackson-Lee (D)
19. Larry Combest (R)
   (resigned May 31, 2003)
   Randy Neugebauer (R)
   (sworn in June 5, 2003)
20. Charlie Gonzalez (D)
21. Lamar Smith (R)
22. Tom DeLay (R)
23. Henry Bonilla (R)
24. Martin Frost (D)
25. Chris Bell (D)
26. Michael C. Burgess (R)
27. Solomon P. Ortiz (D)
28. Ciro D. Rodriguez (D)
29. Gene Green (D)
30. Eddie Bernice Johnson (D)
31. John Carter (R)
32. Pete Sessions (R)

Utah
1. Rob Bishop (R)
2. Jim Matheson (D)
3. Christopher B. Cannon (R)

Vermont
AL   Bernard Sanders (I)

Virginia
1. Jo Ann Davis (R)
2. Ed Schrock (R)
3. Robert C. Scott (D)
4. J. Randy Forbes (R)
5. Virgil H. Goode Jr. (R)
6. Robert W. Goodlatte (R)
7. Eric Cantor (R)
8. James P. Moran (D)
9. Rick C. Boucher (D)
10. Frank R. Wolf (R)
11. Thomas M. Davis III (R)

Washington
1. Jay Inslee (D)
2. Rick Larsen (D)
3. Brian Baird (D)
4. Richard "Doc" Hastings (R)
5. George Nethercutt (R)
6. Norm Dicks (D)
7. Jim McDermott (D)
8. Jennifer Dunn (R)
9. Adam Smith (D)

West Virginia
1. Alan B. Mollohan (D)
2. Shelley Moore Capito (R)
3. Nick J. Rahall II (D)

Wisconsin
1. Paul D. Ryan (R)
2. Tammy Baldwin (D)
3. Ron Kind (D)

4. Gerald D. Kleczka (D)
5. F. James Sensenbrenner Jr. (R)
6. Tom Petri (R)

7. David R. Obey (D)
8. Mark Green (R)

Wyoming
AL Cubin Barbara (R)

NOTE: Changes that occurred during 2003 and 2004 are noted following the names of individuals who did not serve out their full terms. Members of the 108th Congress also included delegates Eni F. H. Faleomavaega, D-American Samoa; Eleanor Holmes Norton, D-District of Columbia; Madeleine Z. Bordallo, D-Guam; Donna M. C. Christian, D-Virgin Islands; and resident commissioner Anibal Acevedo-Vilá, D-Puerto Rico.
1. Alexander switched from Democrat to Republican on Aug. 6, 2004.
2. Hall switched from Democrat to Republican on Jan. 5, 2004.

Members of Congress, 2001–2005

The names in this list include, alphabetically, all senators, representatives, resident commissioners and territorial delegates who served in the 107th and 108th Congresses—from Jan. 3, 2001 to Jan. 3, 2005.

The material is organized as follows: name; relationship to other members and presidents and vice presidents; party, state (of service); date of birth; date of death (if applicable); congressional service; service as president, vice president, member of the cabinet or Supreme Court, governor, Speaker of the House, president pro tempore of the Senate, majority leader, minority leader and chairman of the Democratic or Republican National Committee.

If the member changed parties during his or her congressional service, the party designation appearing after the member's name is that which applied at the end of such service and further information is included in the entry. Where the service date is left open, the member continued to serve in the 109th Congress (as of January 4, 2005).

Dates of service are inclusive, starting in year of service and ending when service ends. Under the Constitution, terms of service since 1934 have been from Jan. 3 to Jan. 3. In actual practice, members have been sworn in on other dates at the beginning of a Congress. The exact date is shown (where available) if a member began or ended his or her service in midterm.

The major sources for the following list were Congressional Quarterly's *Biographical Directory of the American Congress 1774–1996*; *America Votes* series; the *CQ Almanac*; *American Political Leaders 1789–2000*; *CQ Weekly* magazine and online database.

In the list, D stands for Democrat; R, Republican, and I, Independent.

A

Abercrombie, Neil (D-Hawaii) June 26, 1938– ; House Sept. 23, 1986–1987, 1991– .

Acevedo-Vilá, Anibal (D-P.R.) Feb. 13, 1962– ; House (Resident Commissioner) 2001– .

Ackerman, Gary L. (D-N.Y.) Nov. 19, 1942– ; House March 1, 1983– .

Aderholt, Robert (R-Ala.) July 22, 1965– ; House 1997– .

Akaka, Daniel K. (D-Hawaii) Sept. 11, 1924– ; House 1977–May 16, 1990; Senate May 16, 1990– .

Akin, Todd (R-Mo.) July 5, 1947– ; House 2001– .

Allard, Wayne (R-Colo.) Dec. 2, 1943– ; House 1991–1997; Senate 1997– .

Allen, George F. (R-Va.) March 18, 1952– ; House 1991–1993; Senate 2001– ; Gov. 1994–1998.

Allen, Thomas H. (D-Maine) April 18, 1945– ; House 1997– .

Alexander, Lamar (R-Tenn.) July 3, 1940– ; Senate 2003– ; Gov. 1979–1987.

Alexander, Rodney (R-La.) Dec. 5, 1946– ; House 2003– (2003–Aug. 9, 2004 Democrat).

Andrews, Robert E. (D-N.J.) Aug. 4, 1957– ; House 1990– .

Armey, Richard (R-Texas) July 7, 1940– ; House 1985–2003 ; House majority leader 1995–2003.

B

Baca, Joe (D-Calif.) Jan. 23, 1947– ; House Nov. 16, 1999– .

Bachus, Spencer (R-Ala.) Dec. 28, 1947– ; House 1993– .

Baird, Brian (D-Wash.) March 7, 1956– ; House 1999– .

Baker, Richard H. (R-La.) May 22, 1948– ; House 1987– .

Baldacci, John (D-Maine) Jan. 30, 1955– ; House 1995–2003.

Baldwin, Tammy (D-Wis.) Feb. 11, 1962– ; House 1999– .

Ballance, Frank W. Jr. (D-N.C.) Feb. 15, 1942– ; House 2003–June 11, 2004.

Ballenger, Cass (great-great grandson of Lewis Cass) (R-N.C.) Dec. 6, 1926– ; House 1986–2005.

Barcia, James A. (D-Mich.) Feb. 25, 1952– ; House 1993–2003.

Barkley, Dean (I-Minn.) Aug. 31, 1950– ; Senate Nov. 12, 2002–2003.

Barr, Bob (R-Ga.) Nov. 5, 1948– ; House 1995–2003.

Barrett, J. Gresham (R-S.C.) Feb. 14, 1961– ; House 2003– .

Barrett, Thomas M. (D-Wis.) Dec. 8, 1953– ; House 1993–2003.

Bartlett, Roscoe G. (R-Md.) June 3, 1926– ; House 1993– .

Barton, Joe L. (R-Texas) Sept. 15, 1949– ; House 1985– .

Bass, Charles (son of Perkins Bass) (R-N.H.) Jan. 8, 1952– ; House 1995– .

Baucus, Max (D-Mont.) Dec. 11, 1941– ; House 1975–Dec. 14, 1978; Senate Dec. 15, 1978– .

Bayh, Evan (son of Birch Bayh) (D-Ind.) Dec. 26, 1955– ; Senate 1999– ; Gov. 1989–1997.

Beauprez, Bob (R-Colo.) Sept. 22, 1948– ; House 2003– .

Becerra, Xavier (D-Calif.) Jan. 26, 1958– ; House 1993– .

Bell, Chris (D-Texas) Nov. 23, 1959– ; House 2003–2005.

Bennett, Robert F. (R-Utah) Sept. 18, 1933– ; Senate 1993– .

Bentsen, Ken (nephew of Lloyd Bentsen) (D-Texas) June 3, 1959– ; House 1995–2003.

Bereuter, Doug (R-Neb.) Oct. 6, 1939– ; House 1979–Aug. 31, 2004.

Berkley, Shelley (D-Nev.) Jan. 21, 1951– ; House 1999– .

Berman, Howard L. (D-Calif.) April 15, 1941– ; House 1983– .

Berry, Marion (D-Ark.) Aug. 27, 1942– ; House 1997– .

Biden, Joseph R. Jr. (D-Del.) Nov. 20, 1942– ; Senate 1973– .

Biggert, Judy (R-Ill.) Aug. 15, 1937– ; House 1999– .

Bilirakis, Michael (R-Fla.) July 16, 1930– ; House 1983– .

Bingaman, Jeff (D-N.M.) Oct. 3, 1943– ; Senate 1983– .

Bishop, Rob (R-Utah) July 13, 1951– ; House 2003– .

Bishop, Sanford D. Jr. (D-Ga.) Feb. 4, 1947– ; House 1993– .

Bishop, Timothy H. (D-N.Y.) June 1, 1950– ; House 2003– .

Blackburn, Marsha (R-Tenn.) June 6, 1952–; House 2003– .

Blagojevich, Rod R. (D-Ill.) Dec. 10, 1956–; House 1997–2003.

Blumenauer, Earl (D-Ore.) Aug. 16, 1949– ; House May 30, 1996– .

Blunt, Roy (R-Mo.) Jan. 10, 1950– ; House 1997– .

Boehlert, Sherwood (R-N.Y.) Sept. 28, 1936– ; House 1983– .

Boehner, John A. (R-Ohio) Nov. 17, 1949– ; House 1991– .

Bond, Christopher S. (R-Mo.) March 6, 1939– ; Senate 1987– .

Bonilla, Henry (R-Texas) Jan. 2, 1954– ; House 1993– .

Bonior, David E. (D-Mich.) June 6, 1945– ; House 1977–2003.

Bonner, Jo (R-Ala.) Nov. 19, 1959– ; House 2003– .

Bono, Mary (R-Calif.) Oct. 24, 1961; House April 21, 1998– .

Boozman, John (R-Ark.) Dec. 10, 1950– ; House Nov. 29, 2001– .

Bordallo, Madeleine Z. (D-Guam) May 31, 1933– ; House (Delegate) 2003– .

Borski, Robert A. (D-Pa.) Oct. 20, 1948– ; House 1983–2003.

Boswell, Leonard L. (D-Iowa) Jan. 10, 1934– ; House 1997– .

Boucher, Rick (D-Va.) Aug. 1, 1946– ; House 1983– .

Boxer, Barbara (D-Calif.) Nov. 11, 1940– ; House 1983–1993; Senate 1993– .

Boyd, Allen (D-Fla.) June 6, 1945– ; House 1997– .

Bradley, Jeb (R-N.H.) Oct. 20, 1952– ; House 2003– .

Brady, Kevin (R-Texas) April 11, 1955– ; House 1997– .

Brady, Robert A. (D-Pa.) April 7, 1945– ; House May 28, 1998– .

Breaux, John B. (D-La.) March 1, 1944– ; House Sept. 30, 1972–1987; Senate 1987–2005.

Brown, Corrine (D-Fla.) Nov. 11, 1946– ; House 1993– .

Brown, Henry E. Jr. (R-S.C.) Dec. 20, 1935– ; House 2001– .

Brown, Sherrod (D-Ohio) Nov. 9, 1952– ; House 1993– .

Brownback, Sam (R-Kan.) Sept. 12, 1956– ; House 1995–Nov. 6, 1996; Senate Nov. 27, 1996– .

Brown-Waite, Ginny (R-Fla.) Oct. 5, 1943– ; House 2003– .

Bryant, Ed (R-Tenn.) Sept. 7, 1948– ; House 1995–2003.

Bunning, Jim (R-Ky.) Oct. 23, 1931– ; House 1987–1999; Senate 1999– .

Burgess, Michael (R-Texas) Dec. 23, 1950– ; House 2003– .

Burns, Conrad (R-Mont.) Jan. 25, 1935– ; Senate 1989– .

Burns, Max (R-Ga.) Nov. 8, 1948– ; House 2003–2005.

Burr, Richard M. (R-N.C.) Nov. 30, 1955– ; House 1995–2005; Senate 2005– .

Burton, Dan (R-Ind.) June 21, 1938– ; House 1983– .

Butterfield, G. K. (D-N.C.) April 27, 1947– ; House July 21, 2004– .

Buyer, Steve (R-Ind.) Nov. 26, 1958– ; House 1993– ; Gov. 1971–1975.

Byrd, Robert C. (D-W.Va.) Nov. 20, 1917– ; House 1953–1959; Senate 1959– ; Senate minority leader, 1981–1987; Senate majority leader 1977–1981, 1987–1989; pres. pro tempore 1989–1995.

C

Callahan, Sonny (R-Ala.) Sept. 11, 1932– ; House 1985–2003.

Calvert, Ken (R-Calif.) June 8, 1953– ; House 1993– .

Camp, Dave (R-Mich.) July 9, 1953– ; House 1991– .

Campbell, Ben Nighthorse (R-Colo.) April 13, 1933– ; House 1987–1993; Senate 1993–2005 (1987–March 3, 1995, Democrat).

Cannon, Christopher B. (R-Utah) Oct. 20, 1950– ; House 1997– .

Cantor, Eric I. (R-Va.) June 6, 1963– ; House 2001– .

Cantwell, Maria (D-Wash.) Oct. 13, 1958– ; House 1993–1994; Senate 2001– .

Capito, Shelley Moore (R-W.Va.) Nov. 26, 1953– ; Houses 2001– .

Capps, Lois D. (D-Calif.) Jan. 10, 1938– ; House March 17, 1998– .

Capuano, Michael D. (D-Mass.) Jan. 9, 1952– ; House 1999– .

Cardin, Benjamin L. (D-Md.) Oct. 5, 1943– ; House 1987– .

Cardoza, Dennis (D-Calif.) March 31, 1959– ; House 2003– .

Carnahan, Jean (D-Mo.) Dec. 20, 1933– ; Senate 2001–2003.

Carper, Thomas R. (D-Del.) Jan. 23, 1947– ; House 1983–1993; Senate 2001– ; Gov. 1993–2001.

Carson, Brad (D-Okla.) March 11, 1967– ; House 2001–2005.

Carson, Julia M. (D-Ind.) July 8, 1938– ; House 1997– .

Carter, John (R-Texas) Nov. 6, 1941– ; House 2003– .

Case, Ed (D-Hawaii) Sept. 27, 1952– ; House Nov. 30, 2002–

Castle, Michael N. (R-Del.) July 2, 1939– ; House 1993– .

Chabot, Steve (R-Ohio) Jan. 22, 1953– ; House 1995– .

Chafee, Lincoln (R-R.I.) (son of John H. Chafee) March 26, 1953– ; Senate Nov. 4, 1999– .

Chambliss, Saxby (R-Ga.) Nov. 10, 1943– ; House 1995–2003; Senate 2003– .

Chandler, Ben (D-Ky.) Sept. 12, 1959– ; House Feb. 24, 2004– .

Chocola, Chris (R-Ind.) Feb. 24, 1962– ; House 2003– .

Christensen, Donna M. C. (D-Virgin Is.) Sept. 19, 1945– ; House (Delegate) 1997– .

Clay, William Lacy Jr. (son of William L. Clay) (D-Mo.) July 27, 1956– ; House 2001– .

Clayton, Eva (D-N.C.) Sept. 16, 1934– ; House Nov. 4, 1992–2003.

Cleland, Max (D-Ga.) Aug. 24, 1942– ; Senate 1997–2003.

Clement, Bob (D-Tenn.) Sept. 23, 1943– ; House 1988–2003.

Clinton, Hillary Rodham (D-N.Y.) Oct. 26, 1947– ; Senate 2001– ; wife of President Bill Clinton; first lady 1993–2001.

Clyburn, James E. (D-S.C.) July 21, 1940– ; House 1993– .

Coble, Howard (R-N.C.) March 18, 1931– ; House 1985– .

Cochran, Thad (R-Miss.) Dec. 7, 1937– ; House 1973–Dec. 26, 1978; Senate Dec. 27, 1978– .

Cole, Tom (R-Okla.) April 28, 1949– ; House 2003– .

Coleman, Norm (R-Minn.) Aug. 17, 1949– ; Senate 2003– .

Collins, Mac (R-Ga.) Oct. 15, 1944– ; House 1993–2005.

Collins, Susan (R-Maine) Dec. 7, 1952– ; Senate 1997– .

Combest, Larry (R-Texas) March 20, 1945– ; House 1985–May 31, 2003.

Condit, Gary A. (D-Calif.) April 21, 1948– ; House Sept. 20, 1989–2003.

Conrad, Kent (D-N.D.) March 12, 1948– ; Senate 1987–Dec. 14, 1992, Dec. 14, 1992– .

Conyers, John Jr. (D-Mich.) May 16, 1929– ; House 1965– .

Cooksey, Jim (R-La.) Aug. 20, 1941– ; House 1997–2003.

Cooper, Jim (D-Tenn.) June 19, 1954– ; House 1983–1995; 2003– .

Cornyn, John (R-Texas) Feb. 2, 1952– ; Senate Dec. 2, 2002– .

Corzine, Jon (D-N.J.) Jan. 1, 1947– ; Senate 2001– .

Costello, Jerry F. (D-Ill.) Sept. 25, 1949– ; House Aug. 11, 1988– .

Cox, Christopher (R-Calif.) Oct. 16, 1952– ; House 1989– .

Coyne, William J. (D-Pa.) Aug. 24, 1936– ; House 1981–2003.

Craig, Larry E. (R-Idaho) July 20, 1945– ; House 1981–1991; Senate 1991– .

Cramer, Robert E. "Bud" (D-Ala.) Aug. 22, 1947– ; House 1991– .

Crane, Philip M. (brother of Daniel Bever Crane) (R-Ill.) Nov. 3, 1930– ; House 1969–2005.

Crapo, Michael D. (R-Idaho) May 20, 1951– ; House 1993–1999; Senate 1999– .

Crenshaw, Ander (R-Fla.) Sept. 1, 1944– ; House 2001– .

Crowley, Joseph (D-N.Y.) March 16, 1962– ; House 1999– .

Cubin, Barbara (R-Wyo.) Nov. 30, 1946– ; House 1995– .

Culberson, John (R-Texas) Aug. 24, 1956– ; House 2001– .

Cummings, Elijah E. (D-Md.) Jan. 18, 1951– ; House April 25, 1996– .

Cunningham, Randy "Duke" (R-Calif.) Dec. 8, 1941– ; House 1991–2005.

D

Daschle, Tom (D-S.D.) Dec. 9, 1947– ; House 1979–1987; Senate 1987–2005; Senate minority leader 1995–June 6, 2001; majority leader June 6, 2001–2003; minority leader 2003–2005.

Davis, Artur (D-Ala.) Oct, 9, 1957– ; House 2003– .

Davis, Danny K. (D-Ill.) Sept. 6, 1941– ; House 1997– .

Davis, Jim (D-Fla.) Oct. 11, 1957– ; House 1997– .

Davis, Jo Ann (R-Va.) June 29, 1950– ; House 2001– .

Davis, Lincoln (D-Tenn.) Sept. 13, 1943– ; House 2003– .

Davis, Susan A. (D-Calif.) April 13, 1944– ; House 2001– .

Davis, Thomas M. III (R-Va.) Jan. 5, 1949– ; House 1995– .

Dayton, Mark (D-Minn.) Jan. 26, 1947– ; Senate 2001– .

Deal, Nathan (R-Ga.) Aug. 25, 1942– ; House 1993– (1993–April 10, 1995, Democrat).

DeFazio, Peter A. (D-Ore.) May 27, 1947– ; House 1987– .

DeGette, Diana (D-Colo.) July 29, 1957– ; House 1997– .

Delahunt, William (D-Mass.) July 18, 1941– ; House 1997– .

DeLauro, Rosa (D-Conn.) March 2, 1943– ; House 1991– .

DeLay, Tom (R-Texas) April 8, 1947– ; House 1985– .

DeMint, Jim (R-S.C.) Sept. 2, 1951– ; House 1999–2005; Senate 2005– .

Deutsch, Peter (D-Fla.) April 1, 1957– ; House 1993–2005.

DeWine, Mike (R-Ohio) Jan. 5, 1947– ; House 1983–1991; Senate 1995– .

Diaz-Balart, Lincoln (brother of Mario Diaz-Balart) (R-Fla.) Aug. 13, 1954– ; House 1993– .

Diaz-Balart, Mario (brother of Lincoln Diaz-Balart) (R-Fla.) Sept. 25, 1961– ; House 2003– .

Dicks, Norm (D-Wash.) Dec. 16, 1940– ; House 1977– .

Dingell, John D. (son of John David Dingell) (D-Mich.) July 8, 1926– ; House Dec. 13, 1955– .

Dodd, Christopher J. (son of Thomas Joseph Dodd) (D-Conn.) May 27, 1944– ; House 1975–1981; Senate 1981– .

Doggett, Lloyd (D-Texas) Oct. 6, 1946– ; House 1995– .

Dole, Elizabeth (wife of Robert J. Dole) (R-N.C.) July 29, 1936– ; Senate 2003– .

Domenici, Pete V. (R-N.M.) May 7, 1932– ; Senate 1973– .

Dooley, Cal (D-Calif.) Jan. 11, 1954– ; House 1991–2005.

Doolittle, John T. (R-Calif.) Oct. 30, 1950– ; House 1991– .

Dorgan, Byron L. (D-N.D.) May 14, 1942– ; House 1981–Dec. 14, 1992; Senate Dec. 15, 1992– .

Doyle, Mike (D-Pa.) Aug. 5, 1953– ; House 1995– .

Dreier, David (R-Calif.) July 5, 1952– ; House 1981– .

Duncan, John J. "Jimmy" Jr. (son of John J. Duncan) (R-Tenn.) July 21, 1947– ; House 1988– .

Dunn, Jennifer (R-Wash.) July 29, 1941– ; House 1993–2005.

Durbin, Richard J. (D-Ill.) Nov. 21, 1944– ; House 1983–1997; Senate 1997– .

E

Edwards, Chet (D-Texas) Nov. 24, 1951– ; House 1991– .

Edwards, John (D-N.C.) June 10, 1953– ; Senate 1999–2005.

Ehlers, Vernon J. (R-Mich.) Feb. 6, 1934– ; House Jan. 25, 1994– .

Ehrlich, Robert Jr. (R-Md.) Nov. 25, 1957– ; House 1995–2003.

Emanuel, Rahm (D-Ill.) Nov. 29, 1959– ; House 2003– .

Emerson, Jo Ann (R-Mo.) Sept. 16, 1950– ; House Nov. 5, 1996– . (Elected as an Independent in a 1996 special election following the death of her husband, Bill Emerson, because the filing date had passed but ran as a Republican in the general election and thereafter.)

Engel, Eliot L. (D-N.Y.) Feb. 18, 1947– ; House 1989– .

English, Phil (R-Pa.) June 20, 1956– ; House 1995– .

Ensign, John (R-Nev.) March 25, 1958– ; House 1995–1999; Senate 2001– .

Enzi, Michael B. (R-Wyo.) Feb. 1, 1944– ; Senate 1997– .

Eshoo, Anna G. (D-Calif.) Dec. 13, 1942– ; House 1993– .

Etheridge, Bob (D-N.C.) Aug. 7, 1941– ; House 1997– .

Evans, Lane (D-Ill.) Aug. 4, 1951– ; House 1983– .

Everett, Terry (R-Ala.) Feb. 15, 1937– ; House 1993– .

F

Faleomavaega, Eni F. H. (D-Am. Samoa) Aug. 15, 1943– ; House (Delegate) 1989– .

Farr, Sam (D-Calif.) July 4, 1941– ; House June 16, 1993– .

Fattah, Chaka (D-Pa.) Nov. 21, 1956– ; House 1995– .

Feeney, Tom (R-Fla.) May 21, 1958– ; House 2003– .

Feingold, Russell D. (D-Wis.) March 2, 1953– ; Senate 1993– .

Feinstein, Dianne (D-Calif.) June 22, 1933– ; Senate Nov. 10, 1992– .

Ferguson, Mike (R-N.J.) July 22, 1970– ; House 2001– .

Filner, Bob (D-Calif.) Sept. 4, 1942– ; House 1993– .

Fitzgerald, Peter G. (R-Ill.) Oct. 20, 1960– ; Senate 1999–2005.

Flake, Jeff (R-Ariz.) Dec. 31, 1962– ; House 2001– .

Fletcher, Ernest (R-Ky.) Nov. 12, 1952– ; House 1999–Dec. 8, 2003. Gov. 2004– .

Foley, Mark (R-Fla.) Sept. 8, 1954– ; House 1995– .

Forbes, J. Randy (R-Va.) Feb. 17, 1952– ; House June 26, 2001– .

Ford, Harold E. Jr. (D-Tenn.) May 11, 1970– ; House 1997–

Fossella, Vito J. (R-N.Y.) March 9, 1965– ; House Nov. 5, 1997– .

Frank, Barney (D-Mass.) March 31, 1940– ; House 1981– .

Franks, Trent (R-Ariz.) June 19, 1957– ; House 2003– .

Frelinghuysen, Rodney (son of Peter Hood Ballentine Frelinghuysen) (R-N.J.) April 29, 1946– ; House 1995– .

Frist, Bill (R-Tenn.) Feb. 22, 1952– ; Senate 1995– ; Senate majority leader 2003– .

Frost, Martin (D-Texas) Jan. 1, 1942– ; House 1979–2005.

G

Gallegly, Elton (R-Calif.) March 7, 1944– ; House 1987– .

Ganske, Greg (R-Iowa) March 31, 1949– ; House 1995–2003.

Garrett, Scott (R-N.J.) July 9, 1959– ; House 2003– .

Gekas, George W. (R-Pa.) April 14, 1930– ; House 1983–2003.

Gephardt, Richard A. (D-Mo.) Jan. 31, 1941– ; House 1976–2005.

Gerlach, Jim (R-Pa.) Feb. 25, 1955– ; House 2003– .

Gibbons, Jim (R-Nev.) Dec. 16, 1944– ; House 1997– .

Gilchrest, Wayne T. (R-Md.) April 15, 1946– ; House 1991– .

Gillmor, Paul E. (R-Ohio) Feb. 1, 1939– ; House 1989– .

Gilman, Benjamin A. (R-N.Y.) Dec. 6, 1922– ; House 1973–2003.

Gingrey, Phil (R-Ga.) July 10, 1942– ; House 2003– .

Gonzalez, Charlie (son of Henry B. Gonzalez) (D-Texas) May 5, 1945– ; House 1999– .

Goode, Virgil H. Jr. (R-Va.) (Elected 1997 as a Democrat; announced in January 2000 he would seek reelection as an Independent; changed affiliation from Independent to Republican on Aug. 1, 2002) Oct. 17, 1946– ; House 1997– .

Goodlatte, Robert W. (R-Va.) Sept. 22, 1952– ; House 1993– .

Gordon, Bart (D-Tenn.) Jan. 24, 1949– ; House 1985– .

Goss, Porter J. (R-Fla.) Nov. 26, 1938– ; House 1981–1987, 1989–Sept. 23, 2004.

Graham, Bob (D-Fla.) Nov. 9, 1936– ; Senate 1987–2005.

Graham, Lindsey (R-S.C.) July 9, 1955– ; House 1995–2003; Senate 2003– .

Gramm, Phil (R-Texas) July 8, 1942– ; House 1979–Jan. 5, 1983, Feb. 22, 1983–1985 (1979–Jan. 5, 1983, Democrat); Senate 1985–2003.

Granger, Kay (R-Texas) Jan. 18, 1943– ; House 1997– .

Grassley, Charles E. (R-Iowa) Sept. 17, 1933– ; House 1975–1981; Senate 1981– .

Graves, Sam (R-Mo.) Nov. 7, 1963– ; House 2001– .

Green, Gene (D-Texas) Oct. 17, 1947– ; House 1993– .

Green, Mark (R-Wis.) June 1, 1960– ; House 1999– .

Greenwood, James C. (R-Pa.) May 4, 1951– ; House 1993–2005.

Gregg, Judd (R-N.H.) Feb. 14, 1947– ; Senate 1993– .

Grijalva, Raúl M. (D-Ariz.) Feb. 19, 1948– ; House 2003– .

Grucci, Felix J. Jr. (R-N.Y.) Nov. 25, 1951– ; House 2001–2003.

Gutierrez, Luis V. (D-Ill.) Dec. 10, 1954– ; House 1993– .

Gutknecht, Gil (R-Minn.) March 20, 1951– ; House 1995– .

H

Hagel, Chuck (R-Neb.) Oct. 4, 1946– ; Senate 1997– .

Hall, Ralph M. (R-Texas) May 3, 1923– ; House 1981– (1981–Jan. 5, 2004 Democrat).

Hall, Tony P. (D-Ohio) Jan. 16, 1942– ; House 1979–Sept. 9, 2002.

Hansen, James V. (R-Utah) Aug. 14, 1932– ; House 1981–2003.

Harkin, Tom (D-Iowa) Nov. 19, 1939– ; House 1975–1985; Senate 1985– .

Harman, Jane (D-Calif.) June 28, 1945– ; House 1993–1999; 2001– .

Harris, Katherine (R-Fla.) April 5, 1957– ; House 2003– .

Hart, Melissa (R-Pa.) April 4, 1962– ; House 2001– .

Hastert, J. Dennis (R-Ill.) Jan. 2, 1942– ; House 1987– ; Speaker 1999– .

Hastings, Alcee L. (D-Fla.) Sept. 5, 1936– ; House 1993– .

Hastings, Richard "Doc" (R-Wash.) Feb. 7, 1941– ; House 1995– .

Hatch, Orrin G. (R-Utah) March 22, 1934– ; Senate 1977– .

Hayes, Robin (R-N.C.) Aug. 14, 1945– ; House 1999– .

Hayworth, J. D. (R-Ariz.) July 12, 1958– ; House 1995–

Hefley, Joel (R-Colo.) April 18, 1935– ; House 1987– .

Helms, Jesse (R-N.C.) Oct. 18, 1921– ; Senate 1973–2003.

Hensarling, Jeb (R-Texas) May 29, 1957– ; House 2003– .

Herger, Wally (R-Calif.) May 20, 1945– ; House 1987– .

Herseth, Stephanie (D-S.D.) Dec. 3, 1970– ; House June 3, 2004– .

Hill, Baron P. (D-Ind.) June 23, 1953– ; House 1999–2005.

Hilleary, Van (R-Tenn.) June 20, 1959– ; House 1995–2003.

Hilliard, Earl F. (D-Ala.) April 9, 1942– ; House 1993–2003.

Hinchey, Maurice D. (D-N.Y.) Oct. 27, 1938– ; House 1993– .

Hinojosa, Ruben (D-Texas) Aug. 20, 1940– ; House 1997– .

Hobson, David L. (R-Ohio) Oct. 17, 1936– ; House 1991– .

Hoeffel, Joseph M. (D-PA.) Sept. 3, 1950– ; House 1999–2005.

Hoekstra, Peter (R-Mich.) Oct. 30, 1953– ; House 1993– .

Holden, Tim (D-Pa.) March 5, 1957– ; House 1993– .

Hollings, Ernest F. (D-S.C.) Jan. 21, 1922– ; Nov. 9. 1966–2005; Gov. 1959–1963.

Holt, Rush D. (D-N.J.) Oct. 15, 1948– ; House 1999– .

Honda, Mike (D-Calif.) June 27, 1941– ; House 2001– .

Hooley, Darlene (D-Ore.) April 4, 1939– ; House 1997– .

Horn, Steve (R-Calif.) May 31, 1931– ; House 1993–2003.

Hostettler, John (R-Ind.) July 19, 1961– ; House 1995– .

Houghton, Amo (grandson of Alanson Bigelow Houghton) (R-N.Y.) Aug. 7, 1926– ; House 1987–2005.

Hoyer, Steny H. (D-Md.) June 14, 1939– ; House June 3, 1981– .

Hulshof, Kenny (R-Mo.) May 22, 1958– ; House 1997– .

Hunter, Duncan L. (R-Calif.) May 31, 1948– ; House 1981– .

Hutchinson, Asa (brother of Tim Hutchinson) (R-Ark.) Dec. 3, 1950– ; House 1997–Aug. 6, 2001.

Hutchinson, Tim (brother of Asa Hutchinson) (R-Ark.) Aug. 11, 1949– ; House 1993–1997; Senate 1997–2003.

Hutchison, Kay Bailey (R-Texas) July 22, 1943– ; Senate June 14, 1993– .

Hyde, Henry J. (R-Ill.) April 18, 1924– ; House 1975– .

I

Inhofe, James M. (R-Okla.) Nov. 17, 1934– ; House 1987– Nov. 15, 1994; Senate Nov. 17, 1994– .

Inouye, Daniel K. (D-Hawaii) Sept. 7, 1924– ; House Aug. 21, 1959–1963; Senate 1963– .

Inslee, Jay (D-Wash.) Feb. 9, 1951– ; House 1993–1995; 1999– .

Isakson, Johnny (R-Ga.) Dec. 28, 1944– ; House Feb. 25, 1999–2005; Senate 2005– .

Israel, Steven (D-N.Y.) May 30, 1958– ; House 2001– .

Issa, Darrell (R-Calif.) Nov. 1, 1953– ; House 2001– .

Istook, Ernest (R-Okla.) Feb. 11, 1950– ; House 1993– .

J

Jackson, Jesse Jr. (D-Ill.) March 11, 1965– ; House Dec. 14, 1995– .

Jackson-Lee, Sheila (D-Texas) Jan. 12, 1950– ; House 1995– .

Janklow, William J. (R-S.D.) Sept. 13, 1939– ; House 2003–Jan. 20, 2004.

Jefferson, William J. (D-La.) March 14, 1947– ; House 1991– .

Jeffords, James M. (I-Vt.) May 11, 1934– ; House 1975–1989 (Republican); Senate 1989– (1989–June 5, 2001 Republican).

Jenkins, William L. (R-Tenn.) Nov. 29, 1936– ; House 1997– .

John, Chris (D-La.) Jan. 5, 1960– ; House 1997–2005.

Johnson, Eddie Bernice (D-Texas) Dec. 3, 1935– ; House 1993– .

Johnson, Nancy L. (R-Conn.) Jan. 5, 1935– ; House 1983– .

Johnson, Sam (R-Texas) Oct. 11, 1930– ; House May 22, 1991– .

Johnson, Tim (D-S.D.) Dec. 28, 1946– ; House 1987–1997; Senate 1997– .

Johnson, Timothy V. (R-Ill.) July 23, 1946– ; House 2001– .

Jones, Stephanie Tubbs (R-Ohio) Sept. 10, 1949– ; House 1999– .

Jones, Walter B. Jr. (son of Walter Beaman Jones) (R-N.C.) Feb. 10, 1943– ; House 1995– .

K

Kanjorski, Paul E. (D-Pa.) April 2, 1937– ; House 1985– .

Kaptur, Marcy (D-Ohio) June 17, 1946– ; House 1983– .

Keller, Richard "Ric" (R-Fla.) Sept. 5, 1964– ; House 2001– .

Kelly, Sue W. (R-N.Y.) Sept. 26, 1936– ; House 1995– .

Kennedy, Edward M. (father of Patrick J. Kennedy, brother of John Fitzgerald Kennedy and Robert Francis Kennedy, grandson of John Francis Fitzgerald, uncle of Joseph P. Kennedy II) (D-Mass.) Feb. 22, 1932– ; Senate Nov. 7, 1962– .

Kennedy, Mark (R-Minn.) April 11, 1957– ; House 2001– .

Kennedy, Patrick J. (son of Edward M. Kennedy, nephew of John Fitzgerald Kennedy and Robert Francis Kennedy, cousin of Joseph P. Kennedy, great grandson of John Francis Fitzgerald) (D-R.I.) July 14, 1967– ; House 1995– .

Kerns, Brian (R-Ind.) May 22, 1957– ; House 2001–2003.

Kerry, John (D-Mass.) Dec. 11, 1943– ; Senate 1985– .

Kildee, Dale E. (D-Mich.) Sept. 16, 1929– ; House 1977– .

Kilpatrick, Carolyn Cheeks (D-Mich.) June 25, 1945– ; House 1997– .

King, Peter T. (R-N.Y.) April 5, 1944– ; House 1993– .

King, Steve (R-Iowa) May 28, 1949– ; House 2003– .

Kingston, Jack (R-Ga.) April 24, 1955– ; House 1993– .

Kirk, Mark Steven (R-Ill.) Sept. 15, 1959– ; House 2001– .

Kleczka, Gerald D. (D-Wis.) Nov. 26, 1943– ; House April 10, 1984–2005.

Kline, John (R-Minn.) Sept. 6, 1947– ; House 2003– .

Knollenberg, Joe (R-Mich.) Nov. 28, 1933– ; House 1993– .

Kohl, Herb (D-Wis.) Feb. 7, 1935– ; Senate 1989– .

Kolbe, Jim (R-Ariz.) June 28, 1942– ; House 1985– .

Kucinich, Dennis J. (D-Ohio) Oct. 8, 1946– ; House 1997– .

Kyl, Jon (son of John Henry Kyl) (R-Ariz.) April 25, 1942– ; House 1987–1995; Senate 1995– .

L

LaFalce, John J. (D-N.Y.) Oct. 6, 1939– ; House 1975–2003.

LaHood, Ray (R-Ill.) Dec. 6, 1945– ; House 1995–

Lampson, Nick (D-Texas) Feb. 14, 1945– ; House 1997–2005.

Landrieu, Mary L. (D-La.) Nov. 23, 1955– ; Senate 1997– .

Langevin, Jim (D-R.I.) April 22, 1964– ; House 2001– .

Lantos, Tom (father-in-law of Dick Swett) (D-Calif.) Feb. 1, 1928– ; House 1981– .

Largent, Steve (R-Okla.) Sept. 28, 1955– ; House Nov. 29, 1994–Feb. 15, 2002.

Larsen, Rick (D-Wash.) June 15, 1965– ; House 2001– .

Larson, John B. (D-Conn.) July 22, 1948– ; House 1999– .

Latham, Tom (R-Iowa) July 14, 1948– ; House 1995– .

LaTourette, Steven C. (R-Ohio) July 22, 1954– ; House 1995– .

Lautenberg, Frank R. (D-N.J.) Jan. 23, 1924– ; Senate Dec. 27, 1982–2001; 2003– .

Leach, Jim (R-Iowa) Oct. 15, 1942– ; House 1977– .

Leahy, Patrick J. (D-Vt.) March 31, 1940– ; Senate 1975– .

Lee, Barbara (D-Calif.) July 16, 1946– ; House April 21, 1998– .

Levin, Carl (brother of Sander M. Levin) (D-Mich.) June 28, 1934– ; Senate 1979– .

Levin, Sander M. (brother of Carl Levin) (D-Mich.) Sept. 6, 1931– ; House 1983– .

Lewis, Jerry (R-Calif.) Oct. 21, 1934– ; House 1979– .

Lewis, John (D-Ga.) Feb. 21, 1940– ; House 1987– .

Lewis, Ron (R-Ky.) Sept. 14, 1946– ; House May 26, 1994– .

Lieberman, Joseph I. (D-Conn.) Feb. 24, 1942– ; Senate 1989– .

Lincoln, Blanche Lambert (D-Ark.) Sept. 30, 1960– ; House 1993–1997; Senate 1999– .

Linder, John (R-Ga.) Sept. 9, 1942– ; House 1993– .

Lipinski, William O. (D-Ill.) Dec. 22, 1937– ; House 1983–2005.

LoBiondo, Frank A. (R-N.J.) May 12, 1946– ; House 1995– .

Lofgren, Zoe (D-Calif.) Dec. 21, 1947– ; House 1995– .

Lott, Trent (R-Miss.) Oct. 9, 1941– ; House 1973–1989; Senate 1989– ; Senate majority leader June 12, 1996–2003.

Lowey, Nita M. (D-N.Y.) July 5, 1937– ; House 1989– .

Lucas, Frank D. (R-Okla.) Jan. 6, 1960– ; House May 17, 1994– .

Lucas, Ken (D-Ky.) Aug. 22, 1933– ; House 1999–2005.

Lugar, Richard G. (R-Ind.) April 4, 1932– ; Senate 1977– .

Luther, William P. "Bill" (D-Minn.) June 27, 1945– ; House 1995–2003.

Lynch, Stephen F. (D-Mass.) March 31, 1955– ; House Oct. 23, 2001– .

M

Majette, Denise L. (D-Ga.) May 18, 1955– ; House 2003–2005.

Maloney, Carolyn B. (D-N.Y.) Feb. 19, 1948– ; House 1993– .

Maloney, James H. (D-Conn.) Sept. 17, 1948– ; House 1997–2003.

Manzullo, Donald (R-Ill.) March 24, 1944– ; House 1993– .

Markey, Edward J. (D-Mass.) July 11, 1946– ; House Nov. 2, 1976– .

Mascara, Frank R. (D-Pa.) Jan. 19, 1930– ; House 1995–2003.

Marshall, Jim (R-Ga.) March 31, 1948– ; House 2003– .

Matheson, Jim (D-Utah) March 21, 1960– ; House 2001– .

Matsui, Robert T. (D-Calif.) Sept. 17, 1941–Jan. 1, 2005; House 1979–Jan. 1, 2005.

McCain, John (R-Ariz.) Aug. 29, 1936– ; House 1983–1987; Senate 1987– .

McCarthy, Carolyn (D-N.Y.) Jan. 5, 1944– ; House 1997– .

McCarthy, Karen (D-Mo.) March 18, 1947– ; House 1995–2005.

McCollum, Betty (D-Minn.) July 12, 1954– ; House 2001– .

McConnell, Mitch (R-Ky.) Feb. 20, 1942– ; Senate 1985– .

McCotter, Thaddeus (R-Mich.) Aug. 22, 1965– ; House 2003– .

McCrery, Jim (R-La.) Sept. 18, 1949– ; House 1988– .

McDermott, Jim (D-Wash.) Dec. 28, 1936– ; House 1989– .

McGovern, James (D-Mass.) Nov. 20, 1959– ; House 1997– .

McHugh, John M. (R-N.Y.) Sept. 29, 1948– ; House 1993– .

McInnis, Scott (R-Colo.) May 9, 1953– ; House 1993–2005.

McIntyre, Mike (D-N.C.) Aug. 6, 1956– ; House 1997– .

McKeon, Howard P. "Buck" (R-Calif.) Sept. 9, 1939– ; House 1993– .

McKinney, Cynthia A. (D-Ga.) March 17, 1955– ; House 1993–2003.

McNulty, Michael R. (D-N.Y.) Sept. 16, 1947– ; House 1989– .

Meehan, Martin T. (D-Mass.) Dec. 30, 1956– ; House 1993– .

Meek, Carrie P. (D-Fla.) April 29, 1926– ; House 1993–2003.

Meek, Kendrick (son of Carrie P. Meek) (D-Fla.) Sept. 6, 1966– ; House 2003– .

Meeks, Gregory W. (D-N.Y.) Sept. 25, 1953– ; House Feb. 5, 1998– .

Menendez, Robert (D-N.J.) Jan. 1, 1954– ; House 1993– .

Mica, John L. (R-Fla.) Jan. 27, 1943– ; House 1993– .

Michaud, Michael H. (D-Maine) Jan. 18, 1955– ; House 2003– .

Mikulski, Barbara A. (D-Md.) July 20, 1936– ; House 1977–1987; Senate 1987– .

Millender-McDonald, Juanita (D-Calif.) Sept. 7, 1938– ; House April 16, 1996– .

Miller, Brad (D-N.C.) May 19, 1953– ; House 2003– .

Miller, Candice S. (R-Mich.) May 7, 1954– ; House 2003– .

Miller, Dan (R-Fla.) May 30, 1942– ; House 1993–2003.

Miller, Jeff (R-Fla.) June 27, 1959– ; House Oct. 23, 2001– .

Miller, Gary (R-Calif.) Oct. 16, 1948– ; House 1999– .

Miller, George (D-Calif.) May 17, 1945– ; House 1975– .

Miller, Zell (D-Ga.) Feb. 24, 1932– ; Senate July 27, 2000–2005; Gov. 1991–1999.

Mink, Patsy T. (D-Hawaii) Dec. 6, 1927–Sept. 28, 2002; House 1965–1977, Sept. 27, 1990–Sept. 28, 2002.

Moakley, Joe (D-Mass.) April 27, 1927–May 28, 2001; House 1973–May 28, 2001 (elected as an Independent Democrat; changed affiliation to Democrat Jan. 2, 1973).

Mollohan, Alan B. (son of Robert Homer Mollohan) (D-W.Va.) May 14, 1943– ; House 1983– .

Moore, Dennis (D-Kan.) Nov. 8, 1945– ; House 1999– .

Moran, James P. (D-Va.) May 16, 1945– ; House 1991– .

Moran, Jerry (R-Kan.) May 29, 1954– ; House 1997– .

Morella, Constance A. (R-Md.) Feb. 12, 1931– ; House 1987–2003.

Murkowski, Frank H. (father of Lisa Murkowski) (R-Alaska) March 28, 1933– ; Senate 1981–Dec. 2, 2002.

Murkowski, Lisa (daughter of Frank Murkowski who appointed her to complete his term after he won election as Alaska governor in 2002) (R-Alaska) May 22, 1957– ; Senate Jan. 7, 2003– .

Murphy, Tim (R-Pa.) Sept. 11, 1952– ; House 2003– .

Murray, Patty (D-Wash.) Oct. 11, 1950– ; Senate 1993– .

Murtha, John P. (D-Pa.) June 17, 1932– ; House Feb. 5, 1974– .

Musgrave, Marilyn (R-Colo.) Jan. 27, 1949– ; House 2003– .

Myrick, Sue (R-N.C.) Aug. 1, 1941– ; House 1995– .

N

Nadler, Jerrold (D-N.Y.) June 13, 1947– ; House Nov. 4, 1992– .

Napolitano, Grace Flores (D-Calif.) Dec. 4, 1936– ; House 1999– .

Neal, Richard E. (D-Mass.) Feb. 14, 1949– ; House 1989– .

Nelson, Ben (D-Neb.) May 17, 1941– ; Senate 2001– ; Gov. 1991–1999.

Nelson, Bill (D-Fla.) Sept. 29, 1942– ; House 1979–1991; Senate 2001– .

Nethercutt, George (R-Wash.) Oct. 7, 1944– ; House 1995–2005.

Neugebauer, Randy (R-Texas) Dec. 24, 1949– ; House June 5, 2003– .

Ney, Bob (R-Ohio) July 5, 1954– ; House 1995– .

Nickles, Don (R-Okla.) Dec. 6, 1948– ; Senate 1981–2005.

Northup, Anne E. (R-Ky.) July 22, 1948– ; House 1997– .

Norton, Eleanor Holmes (D-D.C.) June 13, 1937– ; House (Delegate) 1991– .

Norwood, Charlie (R-Ga.) July 27, 1941– ; House 1995– .

Nunes, Devin (R-Calif.) Oct. 1, 1973– ; House 2003– .

Nussle, Jim (R-Iowa) June 27, 1960– ; House 1991– .

O

Oberstar, James L. (D-Minn.) Sept. 10, 1934– ; House 1975– .

Obey, David R. (D-Wis.) Oct. 3, 1938– ; House April 1, 1969– .

Olver, John W. (D-Mass.) Sept. 3, 1936– ; House June 18, 1991– .

Ortiz, Solomon P. (D-Texas) June 3, 1937– ; House 1983– .

Osborne, Tom (R-Neb.) Feb. 23, 1937– ; House 2001– .

Ose, Doug (R-Calif.) June 27, 1955– ; House 1999–2005.

Otter, C. L. 'Butch' (R-Idaho) May 3, 1942– ; House 2001– .

Owens, Major R. (D-N.Y.) June 28, 1936– ; House 1983– .

Oxley, Michael G. (R-Ohio) Feb. 11, 1944– ; House June 25, 1981– .

P

Pallone, Frank Jr. (D-N.J.) Oct. 30, 1951– ; House Nov. 8, 1988– .

Pascrell, Bill Jr. (D-N.J.) Jan. 25, 1937– ; House 1997– .

Pastor, Ed (D-Ariz.) June 28, 1943– ; House Oct. 3, 1991– .

Paul, Ron (R-Texas) Aug. 20, 1935– ; House 1976–1977; 1979–1985; 1997– .

Payne, Donald M. (D-N.J.) July 16, 1934– ; House 1989– .

Pearce, Steve (R-N.M.) Aug. 23, 1947– ; House 2003– .

Pelosi, Nancy (daughter of Thomas D'Allesandro Jr.) (D-Calif.) March 26, 1940– ; House June 9, 1987– .

Pence, Mike (R-Ind.) June 7, 1959– ; House 2001– .

Peterson, Collin C. (D-Minn.) June 29, 1944– ; House 1991– .

Peterson, John E. (R-Pa.) Dec. 25, 1938– ; House 1997– .

Petri, Thomas E. (R-Wis.) May 28, 1940– ; House April 3, 1979– .

Phelps, David D. (D-Ill.) Oct. 26, 1947– ; House 1999–2003.

Pickering, Charles W. (R-Miss.) Aug. 10, 1963– ; House 1997– .

Pitts, Joseph R. (R-Pa.) Oct. 10, 1939– ; House 1997– .

Platts, Todd (R-Pa.) March 5, 1962– ; House 2001– .

Pombo, Richard W. (R-Calif.) Jan. 8, 1961– ; House 1993– .

Pomeroy, Earl (D-N.D.) Sept. 2, 1952– ; House 1993– .

Porter, Jon (R-Nev.) May 16, 1955– ; House 2003– .

Portman, Rob (R-Ohio) Dec. 19, 1955– ; House May 5, 1993– .

Price, David (D-N.C.) Aug. 17, 1940– ; House 1987–1995, 1997– .

Pryce, Deborah (R-Ohio) July 29, 1951– ; House 1993– .

Pryor, Mark (D-Ark.) Jan. 10, 1963– ; Senate 2003– .

Putnam, Adam (R-Fla.) July 31, 1974– ; House 2001– .

Q

Quinn, Jack (R-N.Y.) April 13, 1951– ; House 1993–2005.

R

Radanovich, George P. (R-Calif.) June 20, 1955– ; House 1995– .

Rahall, Nick J. II (D-W.Va.) May 20, 1949– ; House 1977– .

Ramstad, Jim (R-Minn.) May 6, 1946– ; House 1991– .

Rangel, Charles B. (D-N.Y.) June 11, 1930– ; House 1971– .

Reed, Jack (D-R.I.) Nov. 12, 1949– ; House 1991–1997; Senate 1997– .

Regula, Ralph (R-Ohio) Dec. 3, 1924– ; House 1973– .

Rehberg, Denny (R-Mont.) Oct. 5, 1955– ; House 2001– .

Reid, Harry (D-Nev.) Dec. 2, 1939– ; House 1983–1987; Senate 1987– .

Renzi, Rick (R-Ariz.) June 11, 1958– ; House 2003– .

Reyes, Silvestre (D-Texas) Nov. 10, 1944– ; House 1997– .

Reynolds, Thomas M. (R-N.Y.) Sept. 3, 1950– ; House 1999– .

Riley, Bob (R-Ala.) Oct. 3, 1944– ; House 1997–2003.

Rivers, Lynn (D-Mich.) Dec. 19, 1956– ; House 1995–2003.

Roberts, Pat (R-Kan.) April 20, 1936– ; House 1981–1997; Senate 1997– .

Rockefeller, John D. IV (nephew of Nelson Aldrich Rockefeller and great grandson of Nelson Aldrich) (D-W.Va.) June 18, 1937– ; Senate Jan. 15, 1985– ; Gov. 1977–1985.

Rodriguez, Ciro D. (D-Texas) Dec. 9, 1946– ; House April 17, 1997–2005.

Roemer, Tim (son-in-law of J. Bennett Johnston) (D-Ind.) Oct. 30, 1956– ; House 1991–2003.

Rogers, Harold (R-Ky.) Dec. 31, 1937– ; House 1981– .

Rogers, Mike (R-Mich.) June 2, 1963– ; House 2001– .

Rogers, Mike D. (R-Ala.) July 16, 1958– ; House 2003– .

Rohrabacher, Dana (R-Calif.) June 21, 1947– ; House 1989– .

Ros-Lehtinen, Ileana (R-Fla.) July 15, 1952– ; House 1989– .

Ross, Mike (D-Ark.) Aug. 2, 1961– ; House 2001– .

Rothman, Steven R. (D-N.J.) Oct. 14, 1952– ; House 1997– .

Roukema, Marge (R-N.J.) Sept. 19, 1929– ; House 1981–2003.

Roybal-Allard, Lucille (D-Calif.) June 12, 1941– ; House 1993– .

Royce, Ed (R-Calif.) Oct. 12, 1951– ; House 1993– .

Ruppersberger, C. A. Dutch (D-Md.) Jan. 31, 1946– ; House 2003– .

Rush, Bobby L. (D-Ill.) Nov. 23, 1946– ; House 1993– .

Ryan, Paul D. (R-Wis.) Jan. 29, 1970– ; House 1999– .

Ryan, Tim (D-Ohio) July 16, 1973– ; House 2003– .

Ryun, Jim (R-Kan.) April 29, 1947– ; House Nov. 27, 1996– .

S

Sabo, Martin Olav (D-Minn.) Feb. 28, 1938– ; House 1979– .

Sanchez, Linda T. (sister of Loretta Sanchez) (D-Calif.) Jan. 28, 1969– ; House 2003– .

Sanchez, Loretta (sister of Linda Sanchez) (D-Calif.) Jan. 7, 1960– ; House 1997– .

Sanders, Bernard (I-Vt.) Sept. 8, 1941– ; House 1991– .

Sandlin, Max (D-Texas) Sept. 29, 1952– ; House 1997–2005.

Santorum, Rick (R-Pa.) May 10, 1958– ; House 1991–1995; Senate 1995– .

Sarbanes, Paul S. (D-Md.) Feb. 3, 1933– ; House 1971–1977; Senate 1977– .

Sawyer, Thomas C. (D-Ohio) Aug. 15, 1945– ; House 1987–2003.

Saxton, H. James (R-N.J.) Jan. 22, 1943– ; House 1984– .

Scarborough, Joe (R-Fla.) April 9, 1963– ; House 1995–Sept. 6, 2001.

Schaffer, Bob (R-Colo.) July 24, 1962– ; House 1997–2003.

Schakowsky, Janice D. "Jan" (D-Ill.) May 26, 1944– ; House 1999– .

Schiff, Adam (D-Calif.) June 22, 1960– ; House 2001– .

Schrock, Edward L. (R-Va.) April 6, 1941– ; House 2001–2005.

Schumer, Charles E. (D-N.Y.) Nov. 23, 1950– ; House 1981–1999; Senate 1999– .

Scott, David (D-Ga.) June 27, 1946– ; House 2003– .

Scott, Robert C. (D-Va.) April 30, 1947– ; House 1993– .

Sensenbrenner, F. James Jr. (R-Wis.) June 14, 1943– ; House 1979– .

Serrano, Jose E. (D-N.Y.) Oct. 24, 1943– ; House March 28, 1990– .

Sessions, Jeff (R-Ala.) Dec. 24, 1946– ; Senate 1997– .

Sessions, Pete (R-Texas) March 22, 1955– ; House 1997– .

Shadegg, John (R-Ariz.) Oct. 22, 1949– ; House 1995– .

Shaw, E. Clay Jr. (R-Fla.) April 19, 1939– ; House 1981– .

Shays, Christopher (R-Conn.) Oct. 18, 1945– ; House Sept. 9, 1987– .

Shelby, Richard C. (R-Ala.) May 6, 1934– ; House 1979–1987; Senate 1987– (1979–Nov. 19, 1994, Democrat).

Sherman, Brad (D-Calif.) Oct. 24, 1954– ; House 1997– .

Sherwood, Donald L. (R-Pa.) March 5, 1941– ; House 1999– .

Shimkus, John M. (R-Ill.) Feb. 21, 1958– ; House 1997– .

Shows, Ronnie (D-Miss.) Jan. 26, 1947– ; House 1999–2003.

Shuster, E. G. "Bud" (R-Pa.) Jan. 23, 1932– ; House 1973–Feb. 3, 2001.

Shuster, Bill (son of E. G. "Bud" Shuster) (R-Pa.) Jan. 10, 1961– ; House May 17, 2001– .

Simmons, Rob (R-Conn.) Feb. 11, 1943– ; House 2001– .

Simpson, Mike (R-Idaho) Sept. 8, 1950– ; House 1999– .

Sisisky, Norman (D-Va.) June 9, 1927–March 29, 2001; House 1983–March 29, 2001.

Skeen, Joseph R. (R-N.M.) June 30, 1927–Dec. 7, 2003 ; House 1981–2003.

Skelton, Ike (D-Mo.) Dec. 20, 1931– ; House 1977– .

Slaughter, Louise M. (D-N.Y.) Aug. 14, 1929– ; House 1987– .

Smith, Adam (D-Wash.) June 15, 1965– ; House 1997– .

Smith, Christopher H. (R-N.J.) March 4, 1953– ; House 1981– .

Smith, Gordon H. (R-Ore.) Mary 25, 1952– ; Senate 1997– .

Smith, Lamar (R-Texas) Nov. 19, 1947– ; House 1987– .

Smith, Nick (R-Mich.) Nov. 5, 1934– ; House 1993–2005.

Smith, Robert C. (R-N.H.) March 30, 1941– ; House 1985–Dec. 7, 1990; Senate Dec. 7, 1990–2003.

Snowe, Olympia J. (wife of John R. McKernan Jr.) (R-Maine) Feb. 21, 1947– ; House 1979–1995; Senate 1995– .

Snyder, Vic (D-Ark.) Sept. 27, 1947– ; House 1997– .

Solis, Hilda (D-Calif.) Oct. 20, 1957– ; House 2001– .

Souder, Mark (R-Ind.) July 18, 1950– ; House 1995– .

Specter, Arlen (R-Pa.) Feb. 12, 1930– ; Senate 1981– .

Spence, Floyd D. (R-S.C.) April 9, 1928–Aug. 16, 2001; House 1971–Aug. 16, 2001.

Spratt, John M. Jr. (D-S.C.) Nov. 1, 1942– ; House 1983– .

Stabenow, Debbie (D-Mich.) April 29, 1950– ; House 1997–2001; Senate 2001– .

Stark, Fortney "Pete" (D-Calif.) Nov. 11, 1931– ; House 1973– .

Stearns, Clifford B. (R-Fla.) April 16, 1941– ; House 1989– .

Stenholm, Charles W. (D-Texas) Oct. 26, 1938– ; House 1979–2005.

Stevens, Ted (R-Alaska) Nov. 18, 1923– ; Senate Dec. 24, 1968– .

Strickland, Ted (D-Ohio) Aug. 4, 1941– ; House 1993–1995, 1997– .

Stump, Bob (R-Ariz.) April 4, 1927–June 20, 2003; House 1977–June 20, 2003 (1977–June 11, 1982, Democrat).

Stupak, Bart (D-Mich.) Feb. 29, 1952– ; House 1993– .

Sullivan, John (R-Okla.) Jan. 1, 1965– ; House Feb. 27, 2002– .

Sununu, John E. (R-N.H.) Sept. 10, 1964– ; House 1997–2003; Senate 2003– .

Sweeney, John R. (R-N.Y.) Aug. 9, 1955– ; House 1999– .

T

Talent, James M. (R-Mo.) Oct. 18, 1956– ; House 1993–2001; Senate Nov. 25, 2002– .

Tancredo, Tom (R-Colo.) Dec. 20, 1945– ; House 1999– .

Tanner, John (D-Tenn.) Sept. 22, 1944– ; House 1989– .

Tauscher, Ellen O. (D-Calif.) Nov. 15, 1951– ; House 1997– .

Tauzin, W. J. "Billy" (R-La.) June 14, 1943– ; House May 17, 1980–2005 (1980–Aug. 6, 1995, Democrat).

Taylor, Charles H. (R-N.C.) Jan. 23, 1941– ; House 1991– .

Taylor, Gene (D-Miss.) Sept. 17, 1953– ; House Oct. 24, 1989– .

Terry, Lee (R-Neb.) Jan. 29, 1962– ; House 1999– .

Thomas, William (R-Calif.) Dec. 6, 1941– ; House 1979– .

Thomas, Craig (R-Wyo.) Feb. 17, 1933– ; House May 2, 1989–1995; Senate 1995– .

Thompson, Bennie (D-Miss.) Jan. 28, 1948– ; House April 20, 1993– .

Thompson, Fred (R-Tenn.) Aug. 19, 1942– ; Senate Dec. 9, 1994–2003.

Thompson, Mike (D-Calif.) Jan. 24, 1951– ; House 1999– .

Thornberry, William M. "Mac" (R-Texas) July 15, 1958– ; House 1995– .

Thune, John (R-S.D.) Jan. 7, 1961– ; House 1997–2003.

Thurman, Karen L. (D-Fla.) Jan. 12, 1951– ; House 1993–2003.

Thurmond, Strom (R-S.C.) Dec. 5, 1902–June 26, 2003; Senate Dec. 24, 1954–April 4, 1956, Nov. 1956–2003 (1947–Sept. 16, 1964, Democrat); pres. pro tempore 1981–1987, 1995–1997; Gov. 1947–1951.

Tiahrt, Todd (R-Kan.) June 15, 1951– ; House 1995– .

Tiberi, Pat (R-Ohio) Oct. 21, 1962– ; House 2001– .

Tierney, John F. (D-Mass.) Sept. 18, 1951– ; House 1997– .

Toomey, Patrick J. (R-Pa.) Nov. 17, 1961– ; House 1999–2005.

Torricelli, Robert G. (D-N.J.) Aug. 26, 1951– ; House 1983–1997; Senate 1997–2003.

Towns, Edolphus (D-N.Y.) July 21, 1934– ; House 1983– .

Traficant, James A. Jr. (D-Ohio) May 8, 1941– ; House 1985–July 24, 2002.

Turner, James (D-Texas) Feb. 6, 1946– ; House 1997–2005.

Turner, Michael R. (R-Ohio) Jan. 11, 1960– ; House 2003– .

U

Udall, Mark (son of Morris K. Udall, House 1961–1991; cousin of Tom Udall) (D-Colo.) July 18, 1950– ; House 1999– .

Udall, Tom (son of Steward Udall House 1955–1961; cousin of Mark Udall House 1999–) (D-N.M.) May 18, 1948– ; House 1999– .

Underwood, Robert A. (D-Guam) July 13, 1948– ; House (Delegate) 1993–2003.

Upton, Fred (R-Mich.) April 23, 1953– ; House 1987– .

V

Van Hollen, Chris (D-Md.) Jan. 10, 1959– ; House 2003– .

Velázquez, Nydia M. (D-N.Y.) March 22, 1953– ; House 1993– .

Visclosky, Peter J. (D-Ind.) Aug. 13, 1949– ; House 1985– .

Vitter, David (R-La.) May 3, 1961– ; House June 8, 1999–2005; Senate 2005– .

Voinovich, George V. (R-Ohio) July 15, 1936– ; Senate 1999– ; Gov. 1991–1998.

W

Walden, Greg (R-Ore.) Jan. 10, 1957– ; House 1999– .

Walsh, James T. (R-N.Y.) June 19, 1947– ; House 1989– .

Wamp, Zach (R-Tenn.) Oct. 28, 1957– ; House 1995– .

Warner, John W. (R-Va.) Feb. 18, 1927– ; Senate Jan. 2, 1979– .

Waters, Maxine (D-Calif.) Aug. 15, 1938– ; House 1991– .

Watkins, Wes (R-Okla.) Dec. 15, 1938– ; House 1997–2003 (1977–1991 Democrat).

Watson, Diane (D-Calif.) Nov. 12, 1933– ; House June 7, 2001– .

Watt, Melvin (D-N.C.) Aug. 26, 1945– ; House 1993– .

Watts, J. C. Jr. (R-Okla.) Nov. 18, 1957– ; House 1995–2003.

Waxman, Henry A. (D-Calif.) Sept. 12, 1939– ; House 1975– .

Weiner, Anthony (D-N.Y.) Sept. 4, 1964– ; House 1999– .

Weldon, Curt (R-Pa.) July 22, 1947– ; House 1987– .

Weldon, Dave (R-Fla.) Aug. 31, 1953– ; House 1995– .

Weller, Gerald C. (R-Ill.) July 7, 1957– ; House 1995– .

Wellstone, Paul (D-Minn.) July 21, 1944–Oct. 25, 2002; Senate 1991–Oct. 25, 2002.

Wexler, Robert (D-Fla.) Jan. 2, 1961– ; House 1997– .

Whitfield, Edward (R-Ky.) May 25, 1943– ; House 1995– .

Wicker, Roger (R-Miss.) July 5, 1951– ; House 1995– .

Wilson, Heather (R-N.M.) Dec. 30, 1960– ; House June 25, 1998– .

Wilson, Joe (R-S.C.) July 31, 1947– ; House Dec. 19, 2001– .

Wolf, Frank R. (R-Va.) Jan. 30, 1939– ; House 1981– .

Woolsey, Lynn (D-Calif.) Nov. 3, 1937– ; House 1993– .

Wu, David (R-Ore.) April 8, 1955– ; House 1999– .

Wyden, Ron (D-Ore.) May 3, 1949– ; House 1981–Feb. 5, 1996; Senate Feb. 6, 1996– .

Wynn, Albert R. (D-Md.) Sept. 10, 1951– ; House 1993– .

Y

Young, C. W. "Bill" (R-Fla.) Dec. 16, 1930– ; House 1971– .

Young, Don (R-Alaska) June 9, 1933– ; House March 6, 1973– .

Following is a list of congressional committees and subcommittees for the 107th and 108th Congresses. The House committee listings are as of the beginning of both congresses, in 2001 and 2003. The Senate listings for the 107th Congress are divided between the first half of 2001 and the remainder of the year and through 2002 because of a change in control of that chamber (*see below*).

Committee jurisdictions, party ratios, committee chairmen and the dates of their service in that capacity, ranking minority members (in italics), and subcommittee chairmen are included. Political and joint committees also are listed.

In both the 107th and 108th Congresses the House committees and subcommittee chairmen are Republicans and ranking minority members are Democrats. In the Senate, party control in the 107th Congress changed from Republican to Democratic in June 2001. Party ratios for House committees do not include delegates or the resident commissioner.

Senate Committees

The 2000 elections resulted in an even split in the Senate with fifty Democrats and fifty Republicans. Democrats held committee chairmanships for a brief period between the 107th Congress convening on Jan. 3, 2001, when Democratic Vice President Al Gore could cast a tie-breaking vote, and Jan. 20, when Republican Richard B. Cheney was sworn in and took over Gore's position. With Cheney's tie-breaking vote the Republicans became the majority party and controlled the chairmanships (although the two parties worked out a power-sharing arrangement on the committees). However, in the spring Republican senator James M. Jeffords of Vermont left the GOP to become an Independent but to caucus with the Democrats, effective June 6, 2001. When his switch occurred in June the Democrats became the majority party and took over control of the Senate, including the committee chairmanships. The information that follows shows the Republican chairmen of the Senate committees from January 20 to June followed by the Democratic chairmen from June through the remainder of the 107th Congress, which ended in January 2003.

AGRICULTURE, NUTRITION, AND FORESTRY

Agriculture in general; animal industry and diseases; crop insurance and soil conservation; farm credit and farm security; food from fresh waters; food stamp programs; forestry in general; home economics; human nutrition; inspection of livestock, meat, and agricultural products; pests and pesticides; plant industry, soils, and agricultural engineering; rural development, rural electrification, and watersheds; school nutrition programs.

R 10–D 10 (*107th Congress January–June 2001*)

Richard G. Lugar, Ind.
Tom Harkin, Iowa

Forestry, Conservation and Rural Revitalization—Michael D. Crapo, Idaho.

Marketing, Inspection and Product Promotion—Peter G. Fitzgerald, Ill.
Production and Price Competitiveness—Pat Roberts, Kan.
Research, Nutrition and General Legislation—Mitch McConnell, Ky.

D 11–R 10 (*107th Congress, June 2001–January 2003*)

Tom Harkin, Iowa
Richard G. Lugar, Ind.

Forestry, Conservation and Rural Revitalization—Blanche Lincoln, Ark.
Marketing, Inspection and Product Promotion—Max Baucus, Mont.
Production and Price Competitiveness—Kent Conrad, N.D.
Research, Nutrition and General Legislation—Patrick J. Leahy, Vt.

R 11–D 10 (*108th Congress*)

Thad Cochran, Miss.
Tom Harkin, Iowa

Forestry, Conservation and Rural Revitalization—Michael D. Crapo, Idaho
Marketing, Inspection and Product Promotion—Jim Talent, Mo.
Production and Price Competitiveness—Elizabeth Dole, N.C.
Research, Nutrition and General Legislation—Peter G. Fitzgerald, Ill.

APPROPRIATIONS

Appropriation of revenue; rescission of appropriations; new spending authority under the Congressional Budget Act.

R 14–D 14 (*107th Congress January–June 2001*)

Ted Stevens, Alaska
Robert C. Byrd, W.Va.

Agriculture, Rural Development and Related Agencies—Thad Cochran, Miss.
Commerce, Justice, State and Judiciary—Judd Gregg, N.H.
Defense—Ted Stevens, Alaska
District of Columbia—Mike DeWine, Ohio
Energy and Water Development—Pete V. Domenici, N.M.
Foreign Operations—Mitch McConnell, Ky.
Interior—Conrad Burns, Mont.
Labor, Health and Human Services and Education—Arlen Specter, Pa.
Legislative Branch—Robert F. Bennett, Utah
Military Construction—Kay Bailey Hutchison, Texas
Transportation—Richard C. Shelby, Ala.

Treasury and General Government—Ben Nighthorse Campbell, Colo.
VA, HUD and Independent Agencies—Christopher S. Bond, Mo.

D 15–R 14 *(107th Congress June 2001–January 2003)*

Robert C. Byrd, W.Va.
Ted Stevens, Alaska

Agriculture, Rural Development and Related Agencies—Herb Kohl, Wis.
Commerce, Justice, State and Judiciary—Ernest F. Hollings, S.C.
Defense—Daniel K. Inouye, Hawaii
District of Columbia—Mary L. Landrieu, La.
Energy and Water Development—Harry Reid, Nev.
Foreign Operations—Patrick J. Leahy, Vt.
Interior—Robert C. Byrd, W.Va.
Labor, Health and Human Services and Education—Tom Harkin, Iowa
Legislative Branch—Richard J. Durbin, Ill.
Military Construction—Dianne Feinstein, Calif.
Transportation—Patty Murray, Wash.
Treasury and General Government—Byron L. Dorgan, N.D.
VA, HUD and Independent Agencies—Barbara A. Mikulski, Md.

R 15–D 14 *(108th Congress)*

Ted Stevens, Alaska
Robert C. Byrd, W.Va.

Agriculture, Rural Development and Related Agencies—Robert F. Bennett, Utah
Commerce, Justice, State and Judiciary—Judd Gregg, N.H.
Defense—Ted Stevens, Alaska
District of Columbia—Mike DeWine, Ohio
Energy and Water Development—Pete V. Domenici, N.M.
Foreign Operations—Mitch McConnell, Ky.
Homeland Security—Thad Cochran, Miss.
Interior—Conrad Burns, Mont.
Labor, Health and Human Services and Education—Arlen Specter, Pa.
Legislative Branch—Ben Nighthorse Campbell, Colo.
Military Construction—Kay Bailey Hutchinson, Texas
Transportation—Richard C. Shelby, Ala.
VA, HUD and Independent Agencies—Christopher S. Bond, Mo.

ARMED SERVICES

Defense and defense policy generally; aeronautical and space activities peculiar to or primarily associated with the development of weapons systems or military operations; maintenance and operation of the Panama Canal, including the Canal Zone; military research and development; national security aspects of nuclear energy; naval petroleum reserves (except Alaska); armed forces generally; Selective Service System; strategic and critical materials.

R 12–D 12 *(107th Congress January–June 2001)*

John W. Warner, Va.
Carl Levin, Mich.

Airland Forces—Rick Santorum, Pa.
Emerging Threats and Capabilities—Pat Roberts, Kan.
Personnel—Tim Hutchinson, Ark.
Readiness—James M. Inhofe, Okla.
Seapower—Jeff Sessions, Ala.
Strategic Forces—Wayne Allard, Colo.

D 13–R 12 *(107th Congress June 2001–January 2003)*

Carl Levin, Mich.
John W. Warner, Va.

Airland Forces—Joseph I. Lieberman, Conn.
Emerging Threats and Capabilities—Mary L. Landrieu, La.
Personnel—Max Cleland, Ga.
Readiness and Management Support—Daniel K. Akaka, Hawaii
Seapower—Edward M. Kennedy, Mass.
Strategic Forces—Jack Reed, R.I.

R 13–D 12 *(108th Congress)*

John W. Warner, Va.
Carl Levin, Mich.

Airland Forces—Jeff Sessions, Ala.
Emerging Threats and Capabilities—Pat Roberts, Kan.
Personnel—Saxby Chambliss, Ga.
Readiness and Management Support—John Ensign, Nev.
Seapower—Jim Talent, Mo.
Strategic Forces—Wayne Allard, Colo.

BANKING, HOUSING, AND URBAN AFFAIRS

Banks, banking, and financial institutions; price controls; deposit insurance; economic stabilization and growth; defense production; export and foreign trade promotion; export controls; federal monetary policy, including Federal Reserve System; financial aid to commerce and industry; issuance and redemption of notes; money and credit, including currency and coinage; nursing home construction; public and private housing, including veterans' housing; renegotiation of government contracts; urban development and mass transit; international economic policy.

R 10–D 10 *(107th Congress January–June 2001)*

Phil Gramm, Texas
Paul S. Sarbanes, Md.

Economic Policy—Jim Bunning, Ky.
Financial Institutions—Robert F. Bennett, Utah
Housing and Transportation—Wayne Allard, Colo.
International Trade and Finance—Chuck Hagel, Neb.
Securities and Investment—Michael B. Enzi, Wyo.

D 11–R 10 *(107th Congress June 2001–January 2003)*

Paul S. Sarbanes, Md.
Phil Gramm, Texas

Economic Policy—Charles E. Schumer, N.Y.
Financial Institutions—Tim Johnson, S.D.

Housing and Transportation—Jack Reed, R.I.
International Trade and Finance—Evan Bayh, Ind.
Securities and Investment—Christopher J. Dodd, Conn.

R 11–D 10 (108th Congress)

Richard C. Shelby, Ala.
Paul S. Sarbanes, Md.

Economic Policy—Jim Bunning, Ky.
Financial Institutions—Robert F. Bennett, Utah
Housing and Transportation—Wayne Allard, Colo.
International Trade and Finance—Chuck Hagel, Neb.
Securities and Investment—Michael B. Enzi, Wyo.

BUDGET

Federal budget generally; concurrent budget resolutions; Congressional Budget Office.

R 11–D 11 (107th Congress January–June 2001)

Pete V. Domenici, N.M.
Kent Conrad, N.D.

D 12–R 11 (107th Congress June 2001–January 2003)

Kent Conrad, N.D.
Pete V. Domenici, N.M.

R 12–D 11 (108th Congress)

Don Nickles, Okla.
Kent Conrad, N.D.

No standing subcommittees.

COMMERCE, SCIENCE, AND TRANSPORTATION

Interstate commerce and transportation generally; Coast Guard; coastal zone management; communications; highway safety; inland waterways, except construction; marine fisheries; Merchant Marine and navigation; nonmilitary aeronautical and space sciences; oceans, weather, and atmospheric activities; interoceanic canals generally; regulation of consumer products and services; science, engineering, and technology research, development and policy; sports; standards and measurement; transportation and commerce aspects of outer continental shelf lands.

R 11–D 11 (107th Congress January–June 2001)

John McCain, Ariz.
Ernest F. Hollings, S.C.

Aviation—Kay Bailey Hutchinson, Texas
Communications—Conrad Burns, Mont.
Consumer Affairs, Foreign Commerce and Tourism—Peter G. Fitzgerald, Ill.
Manufacturing and Competitiveness—John Ensign, Nev.
Oceans and Fisheries—Olympia J. Snowe, Maine
Science, Technology and Space—George F. Allen, Va.

Surface Transportation and Merchant Marine—Gordon H. Smith, Ore.

D 12–R 11 (107th Congress June 2001–January 2003)

Ernest F. Hollings, S.C.
John McCain, Ariz.

Aviation—John D. Rockefeller IV, W.Va.
Communications—Daniel K. Inouye, Hawaii
Consumer Affairs, Foreign Commerce and Tourism—Byron L. Dorgan, N.D. (subcommittee was dissolved after June takeover)
Oceans, Atmosphere, and Fisheries—John Kerry, Mass.
Science, Technology and Space—Ron Wyden, Ore.
Surface Transportation and Merchant Marine—John Breaux, La.

R 12–D 11 (108th Congress)

John McCain, Ariz.
Ernest F. Hollings, S.C.

Aviation—Trent Lott, Miss.
Communications—Conrad Burns, Mont.
Competition, Foreign Commerce and Infrastructure—Gordon H. Smith, Ore.
Consumer Affairs and Product Safety—Peter G. Fitzgerald, Ill.
Oceans, Fisheries and Coast Guard—Olympia J. Snowe, Maine
Science, Technology and Space—Sam Brownback, Kan.
Surface Transportation and Merchant Marine—Kay Bailey Hutchinson, Texas

ENERGY AND NATURAL RESOURCES

Energy policy, regulation, conservation, research, and development; coal; energy-related aspects of deep-water ports; hydroelectric power, irrigation, and reclamation; mines, mining, and minerals generally; national parks, recreation areas, wilderness areas, wild and scenic rivers, historic sites, military parks, and battlefields; naval petroleum reserves in Alaska; nonmilitary development of nuclear energy; oil and gas production and distribution; public lands and forests; solar energy systems; territorial possessions of the United States.

R 11–D 11 (107th Congress January–June 2001)

Frank H. Murkowski, Alaska
Jeff Bingaman, NW.

Energy Research, Development, Production and Regulation—Don Nickles, Okla.
Forests and Public Land Management—Larry E. Craig, Idaho
National Parks, Historic Preservation and Recreation—Craig Thomas, Wyo.
Water and Power—Gordon H. Smith, Ore.

D 12–R 11 (107th Congress June 2001–January 2003)

Jeff Bingaman, N.M.
Frank H. Murkowski, Alaska

Energy—Bob Graham, Fla.
National Parks—Daniel K. Akaka, Hawaii

Public Lands and Forests—Ron Wyden, Ore.
Water and Power—Bryon L. Dorgan, N.D.

R 12–D 11 *(108th Congress)*

Pete V. Domenici, N.M.
Jeff Bingaman, N.M.

Energy—Lamar Alexander, Tenn.
National Parks—Craig Thomas, Wyo.
Public Lands and Forests—Larry E. Craig, Idaho
Water and Power—Lisa Murkowski, Alaska

ENVIRONMENT AND PUBLIC WORKS

Environmental policy, research, and development; air, water, and noise pollution; construction and maintenance of highways; environmental aspects of outer continental shelf lands; environmental effects of toxic substances other than pesticides; fisheries and wildlife; flood control and improvements of rivers and harbors; nonmilitary environmental regulation and control of nuclear energy; ocean dumping; public buildings and grounds; public works, bridges, and dams; regional economic development; solid waste disposal and recycling; water resources.

R 9–D 9 *(107th Congress January–June 2001)*

Robert C. Smith, N.H.
Harry Reid, Nev.

Clean Air, Wetlands, Private Property and Nuclear Safety—George V. Voinovich, Ohio
Fisheries, Wildlife, and Water—Michael D. Crapo, Idaho
Superfund, Waste Control, and Risk Assessment—Lincoln Chafee, R.I.
Transportation and Infrastructure—James M. Inhofe, Okla.

D 10–R 9 *(107th Congress June 2001–January 2003)*

James M. Jeffords, Vt.
Robert C. Smith, N.H.

Clean Air, Wetlands, and Climate Change—Joseph L. Lieberman, Conn.
Fisheries, Wildlife, and Water—Bob Graham, Fla.
Superfund, Toxics, Risk, and Waste Management—Barbara Boxer, Calif.
Transportation, Infrastructure, and Nuclear Safety—Harry Reid, Nev.

R 10–D 9 *(108th Congress)*

James M. Inhofe, Okla.
James M. Jeffords, Vt.

Clean Air, Climate Change, and Nuclear Safety—George V. Voinovich, Ohio
Fisheries, Wildlife, and Water—Michael D. Crapo, Idaho
Superfund and Waste Management—Lincoln Chafee, R.I.
Transportation and Infrastructure—Christopher S. Bond, Mo.

FINANCE

Revenue measures generally; taxes; tariffs and import quotas; reciprocal trade agreements; customs; revenue sharing; federal debt limit; Social Security; health programs financed by taxes or trust funds.

R 10–D 10 *(107th Congress January–June 2001)*

Charles E. Grassley, Iowa
Max Baucus, Mont..

Health Care—Olympia J. Snowe, Maine
International Trade—Orrin G. Hatch, Utah
Long-Term Growth, Debt and Deficit Reduction—Frank H. Murkowski, Alaska
Social Security and Family Policy—Jon Kyl, Ariz.
Taxation and IRS Oversight—Don Nickles, Okla.

D 11–R 10 *(107th Congress June 2001–January 2003)*

Max Baucus, Mont.
Charles E. Grassley, Iowa.

Health Care—John D. Rockefeller IV, W.Va.
International Trade—Max Baucus, Mont.
Long-Term Growth and Debt Reduction—Bob Graham, Fla.
Social Security and Family Policy—John B. Breaux, La.
Taxation and IRS Oversight—Kent Conrad, N.D.

R 11–D 10 *(108th Congress)*

Charles E. Grassley, Iowa
Max Baucus, Mont.

Health Care—Jon Kyl, Ariz.
International Trade—Craig Thomas, Wyo.
Long-Term Growth and Debt Reduction—Gordon H. Smith, Ore.
Social Security and Family Policy—Rick Santorum, Pa.
Taxation and IRS Oversight—Don Nickles, Okla.

FOREIGN RELATIONS

Relations of the United States with foreign nations generally; treaties; foreign economic, military, technical, and humanitarian assistance; foreign loans; diplomatic service; International Red Cross; international aspects of nuclear energy; International Monetary Fund; intervention abroad and declarations of war; foreign trade; national security; oceans and international environmental and scientific affairs; protection of U.S. citizens abroad; United Nations; World Bank and other development assistance organizations.

R 9–D 9 *(107th Congress January–June 2001)*

Jesse Helms, N.C.
Joseph R. Biden Jr., Del.

African Affairs—Bill Frist, Tenn.
East Asian and Pacific Affairs—Craig Thomas, Wyo.
European Affairs—Gordon H. Smith, Ore.
International Economic Policy, Export and Trade Promotion—Chuck Hagel, Neb.

International Operations and Terrorism—George F. Allen, Va.
Near Eastern and South Asian Affairs—Sam Brownback, Kan.
Western Hemisphere, Peace Corps, Narcotics, and Terrorism—Lincoln Chafee, R.I.

D 10–R 9 (*107th Congress June 2001–January 2003*)

Joseph R. Biden Jr., Del.
Jesse Helms, N.C.

African Affairs—Russell D. Feingold, Wis.
Central Asia and the South Caucasus—Robert G. Torricelli, N.J.
East Asian and Pacific Affairs—John F. Kerry, Mass.
European Affairs—Joseph R. Biden Jr., Del.
International Economic Policy, Export and Trade Promotion—Paul S. Sarbanes, Md.
International Operations and Terrorism—Barbara Boxer, Calif.
Near Eastern and South Asian Affairs—Paul Wellstone, Minn.
Western Hemisphere, Peace Corps, Narcotics Affairs—Christopher J. Dodd, Conn.

R 11–D 10 (*108th Congress*)

Richard G. Lugar, Ind.
Joseph R. Biden Jr., Del.

African Affairs—Lamar Alexander, Tenn.
East Asian and Pacific Affairs—Sam Brownback, Kan.
European Affairs—George Allen, Va.
International Economic Policy, Export and Trade Promotion—Chuck Hagel, Neb.
International Operations and Terrorism—John E. Sununu, N.H.
Near Eastern and South Asian Affairs—Lincoln Chafee, R.I.
Western Hemisphere, Peace Corps, Narcotics Affairs—Norm Coleman, Minn.

GOVERNMENTAL AFFAIRS[1]

Archives of the United States; budget and accounting measures; census and statistics; federal civil service; congressional organization; intergovernmental relations; government information; District of Columbia; organization and management of nuclear export policy; executive branch organization and reorganization; Postal Service; efficiency, economy, and effectiveness of government.

R 8–D 8 (*107th Congress January–June 2001*)

Fred Thompson, Tenn.
Joseph I. Lieberman, Conn.

International Security, Proliferation, and Federal Services—Thad Cochran, Miss.
Investigations—Susan Collins, Maine
Oversight of Government Management, Restructuring, and the District of Columbia—George V. Voinovich, Ohio

D 9–R 8 (*107th Congress June 2001–January 2003*)

Joseph I. Lieberman, Conn.
Fred Thompson, Tenn.

International Security, Proliferation, and Federal Services—Daniel K. Akaka, Hawaii
Investigations—Carl Levin, Mich.
Oversight of Government Management, Restructuring, and the District of Columbia—Richard J. Durbin, Ill.

R 9–D 8 (*108th Congress*)

Susan Collins, Maine
Joseph I. Lieberman, Conn.

Financial Management, Budget, and International Security—Peter G. Fitzgerald, Ill.
Government Management, Federal Workforce, and the District of Columbia—George V. Voinovich, Ohio
Investigations—Norm Coleman, Minn.

HEALTH, EDUCATION, LABOR, AND PENSIONS

Education, labor, health, and public welfare in general; aging; arts and humanities; biomedical research and development; child labor; convict labor; domestic activities of the Red Cross; equal employment opportunity; handicapped people; labor standards and statistics; mediation and arbitration of labor disputes; occupational safety and health; private pensions; public health; railway labor and retirement; regulation of foreign laborers; student loans; wages and hours; agricultural colleges; Gallaudet University; Howard University; St. Elizabeth's Hospital in Washington, D.C.

R 10–D 10 (*107th Congress January–June 2001*)

James M. Jeffords, Vt.
Edward M. Kennedy, Mass.

Aging—Tim Hutchinson, Ark.
Children and Families—Judd Gregg, N.H.
Employment, Safety and Training—Michael B. Enzi, Wyo.
Public Health—Bill Frist, Tenn.

D 11–R 10 (*107th Congress June 2001–January 2003*)

Edward M. Kennedy, Mass.
Judd Gregg, N.H.

Aging—Barbara Mikulski, Md.
Children and Families—Christopher J. Dodd, Conn.
Employment, Safety, and Training—Paul Wellstone, Minn.
Public Health—Edward M. Kennedy, Mass.

R 11–D 10 (*108th Congress*)

Judd Gregg, N.H.
Edward M. Kennedy, Mass.

Aging—Christopher S. Bond, Mo.
Children and Families—Lamar Alexander, Tenn.
Employment, Safety and Training—Michael B. Enzi, Wyo.
Substance Abuse and Mental Health Services—Mike DeWine, Ohio

INDIAN AFFAIRS

Problems and opportunities of Native Americans, including Native American land management and trust responsibilities, education, health, special services, loan programs, and claims against the United States.

R 7–D 7 *(107th Congress January–June 2001)*

Ben Nighthorse Campbell, Colo.
Daniel K. Inouye, Hawaii

D 8–R 7 *(107th Congress June 2001–January 2003)*

Ben Nighthorse Campbell, Colo.
Daniel K. Inouye, Hawaii

R 8–D 7 *(108th Congress)*

Daniel K. Inouye, Hawaii
Ben Nighthorse Campbell, Colo.

No standing subcommittees.

JUDICIARY

Civil and criminal judicial proceedings in general; national penitentiaries; bankruptcy, mutiny, espionage, and counterfeiting; civil liberties; constitutional amendments; apportionment of representatives; government information; immigration and naturalization; interstate compacts in general; claims against the United States; patents, copyrights, and trademarks; monopolies and unlawful restraints of trade; holidays and celebrations; revision and codification of the statutes of the United States; state and territorial boundary lines.

R 9–D 9 *(107th Congress January–June 2001)*

Orrin G. Hatch, Utah
Patrick J. Leahy, Vt.

Administrative Oversight and the Courts—Charles E. Grassley, Iowa
Antitrust, Business Rights, and Competition—Mike DeWine, Ohio
Constitution, Federalism, and Property Rights—Strom Thurmond, S.C.
Criminal Justice Oversight—Strom Thurmond, S.C.
Immigration—Sam Brownback, Kan.
Technology, Terrorism, and Government Information—Jon Kyl, Ariz.
Youth Violence—Jeff Sessions, Ala.

D 10–R 9 *(107th Congress June 2001–January 2003)*

Orrin G. Hatch, Utah
Patrick J. Leahy, Vt.

Administrative Oversight and the Courts—Charles E. Schumer, N.Y.

Antitrust, Competition, and Business and Consumer Rights—Herb Kohl, Wis.
The Constitution—Russell Feingold, Wis.
Crime and Drugs—Joseph R. Biden, Del.
Immigration—Edward. M. Kennedy, Mass.
Technology, Terrorism, and Government Information—Dianne Feinstein, Calif.

R 10–D 9 *(108th Congress)*

Orrin G. Hatch, Utah
Patrick J. Leahy, Vt.

Administrative Oversight and the Courts—Jeff Sessions, Ala.
Antitrust, Competition Policy, and Consumer Rights—Mike DeWine, Ohio
Constitution, Civil Rights, and Property Rights—John Cornyn, Texas
Crime, Corrections, and Victims' Rights—Lindsey Graham, S.C.
Immigration, Border Security, and Citizenship—Saxby Chambliss, Ga.
Terrorism, Technology, and Homeland Security—Jon Kyl, Ariz.

RULES AND ADMINISTRATION

Senate rules and regulations; Senate administration in general; corrupt practices; qualifications of senators; contested elections; federal elections in general; Government Printing Office; *Congressional Record*; meetings of Congress and attendance of members; presidential succession; the Capitol, congressional office buildings, the Library of Congress, the Smithsonian Institution, and the Botanic Garden; purchase of books and manuscripts and erection of monuments to the memory of individuals.

R 9–D 9 *(107th Congress January–June 2001)*

Mitch McConnell, Ky.
Christopher J. Dodd, Conn.

D 10–R 9 *(107th Congress June 2001–January 2003)*

Christopher J. Dodd, Conn.
Mitch McConnell, Ky.

R 10–D 9 *(108th Congress)*

Trent Lott, Miss.
Christopher J. Dodd, Conn.

No standing subcommittees.

SELECT ETHICS

Studies and investigates standards and conduct of Senate members and employees and may recommend remedial action.

R 3–D 3 *(107th Congress January–June 2001)*

Pat Roberts, Kan.
Harry Reid, Nev. (vice chairman)

D 3–R 3 *(107th Congress June 2001–January 2003)*

Harry Reid, Nev.
Pat Roberts, Kan. (vice chairman)

R 3–D 3 *(108th Congress)*

George V. Voinovich, Ohio
Harry Reid, Nev. (vice chairman)

No standing subcommittees.

SELECT INTELLIGENCE

Legislative and budgetary authority over the Central Intelligence Agency, the Defense Intelligence Agency, the National Security Agency, and intelligence activities of the Federal Bureau of Investigation and other components of the federal intelligence community.

R 8–D 8 *(107th Congress January–June 2001)*

Richard C. Shelby, Ala.
Bob Graham, Fla.

D 9–R 8 *(107th Congress June 2001–January 2003)*

Bob Graham, Fla.
Richard C. Shelby, Ala.

R 9–D 8 *(108th Congress)*

Pat Roberts, Kan.
John D. Rockefeller IV, W.Va.

No standing subcommittees.

SMALL BUSINESS AND ENTREPRENEURSHIP

Problems of small business; Small Business Administration.

R 9–D 9 *(107th Congress January–June 2001)*

Christopher S. Bond, Mo.
John Kerry, Mass.

D 10–R 9 *(107th Congress June 2001–January 2003)*

John Kerry, Mass.
Christopher S. Bond, Mo.

R 10–D 9 *(108th Congress)*

Olympia J. Snowe, Maine
John Kerry, Mass.

No standing subcommittees.

SPECIAL AGING

Problems and opportunities of older people including health, income, employment, housing, and care and assistance. Reports findings and makes recommendations to the Senate but cannot report legislation.

R 10–D 10 *(107th Congress January–June 2001)*

Larry E. Craig, Idaho
John B. Breaux, La.

D 11–R 10 *(107th Congress June 2001–January 2003)*

John B. Breaux, La.
Larry E. Craig, Idaho

R 11–D 10 *(108th Congress)*

Larry E. Craig, Idaho
John B. Breaux, La.

No standing subcommittees.

VETERANS' AFFAIRS

Veterans' measures in general; compensation; life insurance issued by the government on account of service in the armed forces; national cemeteries; pensions; readjustment benefits; veterans' hospitals, medical care and treatment; vocational rehabilitation and education; soldiers' and sailors' civil relief.

R 7–D 7 *(107th Congress January–June 2001)*

Arlen Specter, Pa.
John D. Rockefeller IV, W.Va.

D 8–R 7 *(107th Congress June 2001–January 2003)*

John D. Rockefeller IV, W.Va.
Arlen Specter, Pa.

R 8–D 7 *(108th Congress)*

Arlen Specter, Pa.
Bob Graham, Fla.

POLITICAL COMMITTEES

Democratic Policy Committee (an arm of the Democratic Caucus that advises on legislative priorities)—Byron L. Dorgan, N.D., chairman (107th and 108th Congresses)

Democratic Senatorial Campaign Committee (campaign support committee for Democratic senatorial candidates)—Patty Murray, Wash., chairman (107th Congress); Jon Corzine, N.J., chairman (108th Congress)

Democratic Steering and Coordination Committee (makes Democratic committee assignments)—John Kerry, Mass., chairman (107th Congress); Hillary Rodham Clinton, N.Y., chairman (108th Congress)

Democratic Technology and Communications Committee (seeks to improve communications with the public about the Democratic Party and its policies)—John D. Rockefeller IV, W.Va., chairman (107th and 108th Congresses)

National Republican Senatorial Committee (campaign support committee for Republican senatorial candidates)—Bill Frist, Tenn., chairman (107th Congress); George Allen, Va., chairman (108th Congress)

Republican Committee on Committees (makes Republican committee assignments)—John Kyl, Ariz., chairman (107th Congress); Larry E. Craig, Idaho, chairman (108th Congress)

Republican Policy Committee (advises on party action and policy)—Larry E. Craig, Idaho, chairman (107th Congress); Jon Kyl, Ariz., chairman (108th Congress)

House Committees

AGRICULTURE

Agriculture generally; forestry in general, and forest reserves other than those created from the public domain; adulteration of seeds, insect pests, and protection of birds and animals in forest reserves; agricultural and industrial chemistry; agricultural colleges and experiment stations; agricultural economics and research; agricultural education extension services; agricultural production and marketing and stabilization of prices of agricultural products, and commodities (not including distribution outside the United States); animal industry and diseases of animals; commodities exchanges; crop insurance and soil conservation; dairy industry; entomology and plant quarantine; extension of farm credit and farm security; inspection of livestock, poultry, meat products, seafood and seafood products; human nutrition and home economics; plant industry, soils, and agricultural engineering; rural electrification; rural development; water conservation related to activities of the Department of Agriculture.

R 27–D 24 *(107th Congress)*

Larry Combest, Texas
Charles W. Stenholm, Texas

Conservation, Credit, Rural Development, and Research—Frank D. Lucas, Okla.
Department Operations, Nutrition and Foreign Agriculture—Robert W. Goodlatte, Va.
General Farm Commodities and Risk Management—Saxby Chambliss, Ga.
Livestock and Horticulture—Richard W. Pombo, Calif.
Specialty Crops and Foreign Agriculture Programs—Terry Everett, Ala.

R 27–D 24 *(108th Congress)*

Robert W. Goodlatte, Va.
Charles W. Stenholm, Texas

Conservation, Credit, Rural Development, and Research—Frank D. Lucas, Okla.
Department Operations, Oversight, Nutrition and Forestry—Gil Gutknecht, Minn.
General Farm Commodities and Risk Management—Jerry Moran, Kan.

Livestock and Horticulture—Robin Hayes, N.C.
Specialty Crops and Foreign Agriculture Programs—Bill Jenkins, Tenn.

APPROPRIATIONS

Appropriation of the revenue for the support of the government; rescissions of appropriations contained in appropriation acts; transfers of unexpended balances; new spending authority under the Congressional Budget Act.

R 35–D 29; I 1 *(107th Congress)*

C. W. Bill Young, Fla.
David R. Obey, Wis.

Agriculture, Rural Development, FDA and Related Agencies—Henry Bonilla, Texas
Commerce, Justice, State, and Judiciary—Frank R. Wolf, Va.
Defense—Jerry Lewis, Calif.
District of Columbia—Joe Knollenberg, Mich.
Energy and Water Development—Sonny Callahan, Ala.
Foreign Operations, Export Financing and Related Agencies—Jim Kolbe, Ariz.
Interior—Joe Skeen, N.M.
Labor, Health and Human Services and Education—Ralph Regula, Ohio
Legislative—Charles H. Taylor, N.C.
Military Construction—David L. Hobson, Ohio
Transportation—Harold Rogers, Ky.
Treasury, Postal Service and General Government—Ernest Istook, Okla.
Veterans Affairs, Housing and Urban Development and Independent Agencies—James T. Walsh, N.Y.

R 27–D 24 *(108th Congress)*

C. W. Bill Young, Fla.
David R. Obey, Wis.

Agriculture, Rural Development, FDA and Related Agencies—Henry Bonilla, Texas
Commerce, Justice, State, and Judiciary—Frank R. Wolf, Va.
Defense—Jerry Lewis, Calif.
District of Columbia—Rodney Frelinghuysen, N.J.
Energy and Water Development—David L. Hobson, Ohio
Foreign Operations, Export Financing and Related Programs—Jim Kolbe, Ariz.
Homeland Security—Harold Rogers, Ky.
Interior—Charles H. Taylor, N.C.
Labor, Health and Human Services and Education—Ralph Regula, Ohio
Legislative—Jack Kingston, Ga.
Military Construction—Joe Knollenberg, Mich.
Transportation and Treasury—Ernest Istook, Okla.
Veterans Affairs, Housing and Urban Development and Independent Agencies—James T. Walsh, N.Y.

ARMED SERVICES

Ammunition depots; forts; arsenals; Army, Navy, and Air Force reservations and establishments; common defense generally; conservation, development, and use of naval petroleum and oil shale reserves; Department of Defense generally, including the Departments of the Army, Navy, and Air Force generally; interoceanic canals generally; including measures relating to the maintenance, operation, and administration of interoceanic canals; Merchant Marine Academy, and state maritime academies; military applications of nuclear energy; tactical intelligence and intelligence related activities of the Department of Defense; national security aspects of merchant marine, including financial assistance for the construction and operation of vessels, the maintenance of the U.S. shipbuilding and ship repair industrial base, cabotage, cargo preference, and merchant marine officers and seamen as these matters relate to the national security; pay, promotion, retirement, and other benefits and privileges of members of the armed forces; scientific research and development in support of the armed services; selective service; size and composition of the Army, Navy, Marine Corps, and Air Force; soldiers' and sailors' homes; strategic and critical materials necessary for the common defense.

R 32–D 28 *(107th Congress)*

Bob Stump, Ariz.
Ike Skelton, Mo.

Military Installations and Facilities—H. James Saxton, N.J.
Military Personnel—John M. McHugh, N.Y.
Military Procurement—Floyd D. Spence, S.C.
Military Readiness—Curt Weldon, Pa.
Military Research and Development—Duncan Hunter, Calif.

R 33–D 28 *(108th Congress)*

Duncan Hunter, Calif.
Ike Skelton, Mo.

Projection Forces—Roscoe G. Bartlett, Md.
Readiness—Joel Hefley, Colo.
Strategic Forces—Terry Everett, Ala.
Tactical Air and Land Forces—Curt Weldon, Pa.
Terrorism, Unconventional Threats and Capabilities—H. James Saxton, N.J.
Total Forces—John M. McHugh, N.Y.

BUDGET

Congressional budget process generally; concurrent budget resolutions; measures relating to special controls over the federal budget; Congressional Budget Office.

R 24–D 19 *(107th Congress)*

Jim Nussle, Iowa
John M. Spratt Jr., S.C.

R 24–D 19 *(108th Congress)*

Jim Nussle, Iowa
John M. Spratt Jr., S.C.

No standing subcommittees.

EDUCATION AND THE WORKFORCE

Measures relating to education or labor generally; child labor; Columbia Institution for the Deaf, Dumb, and Blind; Howard University; Freedmen's Hospital; convict labor and the entry of goods made by convicts into interstate commerce; food programs for children in schools; labor standards and statistics; mediation and arbitration of labor disputes; regulation or prevention of importation of foreign laborers under contract; U.S. Employees' Compensation Commission; vocational rehabilitation; wages and hours of labor; welfare of miners; work incentive programs.

R 27–D 22 *(107th Congress)*

John A. Boehner, Ohio
George Miller, Calif.

21st Century Competitiveness—Howard P. "Buck" McKeon, Calif.
Education Reform—Michael N. Castle, Del.
Employer-Employee Relations—Sam Johnson, Texas
Select Education—Peter Hoekstra, Mich.
Workforce Protections—Charlie Norwood, Ga.

R 27–D 22 *(108th Congress)*

John A. Boehner, Ohio
George Miller, Calif.

21st Century Competitiveness—Howard P. "Buck" McKeon, Calif.
Education Reform—Michael N. Castle, Del.
Employer-Employee Relations—Sam Johnson, Texas
Select Education—Peter Hoekstra, Mich.
Workforce Protections—Charlie Norwood, Ga.

ENERGY AND COMMERCE

Interstate and foreign commerce generally; biomedical research and development; consumer affairs and consumer protection; health and health facilities, except health care supported by payroll deductions; interstate energy compacts; measures relating to the exploration, production, storage, supply, marketing, pricing, and regulation of energy resources, including all fossil fuels, solar energy, and other unconventional or renewable energy resources; measures relating to the conservation of energy resources; measures relating to energy information generally; measures relating to (1) the generation and marketing of power (except by federally chartered or federal regional power marketing authorities), (2) the reliability and interstate transmission of, and ratemaking for, all power, and (3) the siting of generation facilities, except the installation of interconnections between government water power projects; measures relating to general management of the Department of Energy, and the management and all functions of the Federal Energy Regulatory Commission; national energy policy generally; public health and quarantine; regulation of the domestic nuclear energy industry, including regulation of research and development reactors and nuclear regulatory research; regulation of interstate and foreign communications; travel and tourism; nuclear and other energy.

R 31–D 26 *(107th Congress)*

Billy Tauzin, La.
John D. Dingell, Mich.

Commerce, Trade, and Consumer Protection—Cliff Stearns, Fla.
Energy and Air Quality—Joe L. Barton, Texas
Environment and Hazardous Materials—Paul E. Gillmor, Ohio
Health—Michael Bilirakis, Fla.
Oversight and Investigations—James C. Greenwood, Pa.
Telecommunications and the Internet—Fred Upton, Mich.

R 31–D 26 *(108th Congress)*

Joe L. Barton, Texas
John D. Dingell, Mich.

Commerce, Trade, and Consumer Protection—Cliff Stearns, Fla.
Energy and Air Quality—Joe L. Barton, Texas
Environment and Hazardous Materials—Paul E. Gillmor, Ohio
Health—Michael Bilirakis, Fla.
Oversight and Investigations—James C. Greenwood, Pa.
Telecommunications and the Internet—Fred Upton, Mich.

FINANCIAL SERVICES

Banks and banking, including deposit insurance and federal monetary policy; economic stabilization, defense production, renegotiation, and control of the price of commodities, rents, and services; financial aid to commerce and industry (other than transportation); insurance generally; international finance; international financial and monetary organizations; money and credit, including currency and the issuance of notes and redemption thereof; gold and silver, including the coinage thereof; valuation and revaluation of the dollar; public and private housing; securities and exchanges; and urban development

R 37–D 32 *(107th Congress)*

Michael G. Oxley, Ohio
John J. LaFalce, N.Y.

Capital Markets, Securities and Government-Sponsored Enterprises— Richard H. Baker, La.
Domestic Monetary Policy, Technology, and Economic Growth— Peter T. King, N.Y.
Financial Institutions and Consumer Credit—Spencer Bachus, Ala.
Housing and Community Opportunity—Marge Roukema, N.J.
International Monetary Policy and Trade—Doug Bereuter, Neb.
Oversight and Investigations—Sue W. Kelly, N.Y.

R 37–D 33 *(108th Congress)*

Michael G. Oxley, Ohio
Barney Frank, Mass.

Capital Markets, Insurance, and Government-Sponsored Enterprises—Richard H. Baker, La.
Domestic and International Monetary Policy, Trade, and Technology—Peter T. King, N.Y.

Financial Institutions and Consumer Credit—Spencer Bachus, Ala.
Housing and Community Opportunity—Bob New, Ohio
Oversight and Investigations—Sue W. Kelly, N.Y.

GOVERNMENT REFORM

Civil service, including intergovernmental personnel; the status of officers and employees of the United States, including their compensation, classification, and retirement; measures relating to the municipal affairs of the District of Columbia in general, other than appropriations; federal paperwork reduction; budget and accounting measures, generally; holidays and celebrations; overall economy, efficiency, and management of government operations and activities, including federal procurement; National Archives; population and demography generally, including the census; Postal Service generally, including the transportation of mail; public information and records; relationship of the federal government to the states and municipalities generally; reorganizations in the executive branch of the government.

R 24–D 19–I 1 *(107th Congress)*

Dan Burton, Ind.
Henry A. Waxman, Calif.

Census—Dan Miller, Fla.
Civil Service and Agency Organization—Joe Scarborough, Fla.
Criminal Justice, Drug Policy, and Human Resources—Mark Souder, Ind.
District of Columbia—Constance A. Morella, Md.
Energy Policy, Natural Resources, and Regulatory Affairs— Doug Ose, Calif.
Government Efficiency, Financial Management, and Intergovernmental Relations—Steve Horn, Calif.
National Security, Veterans Affairs, and International Relations— Christopher Shays, Conn.
Technology and Procurement Policy—Thomas M. Davis III, Va.

R 24–D 20 *(106th Congress)*

Thomas M. Davis III, Va.
Henry A. Waxman, Calif.

Civil Service and Agency Organization—Jo Ann Davis, Va.
Criminal Justice, Drug Policy, and Human Resources—Mark Souder, Ind.
Energy Policy, Natural Resources, and Regulatory Affairs— Doug Ose, Calif.
Government Efficiency and Financial Management—Todd R. Platts, Pa.
National Security, Emerging Threats, and International Relations—Christopher Shays, Conn.
Technology, Information Policy, Intergovernmental Relations, and the Census—Adam H. Putnam, Fla.
Wellness and Human Rights—Dan Burton, Ind.

HOUSE ADMINISTRATION

Accounts of the House generally; assignment of office space for members and committees; disposition of useless executive papers;

matters relating to the election of the president, vice president, or members of Congress; corrupt practices; contested elections; credentials and qualifications; federal elections generally; appropriations from accounts for committee salaries and expenses (except for the Committee on Appropriations), House Information Systems, and allowances and expenses of members, House officers, and administrative offices of the House; auditing and settling of all such accounts; expenditure of such accounts; employment of persons by the House, including clerks for members and committees, and reporters of debates; Library of Congress and the House Library; statuary and pictures; acceptance or purchase of works of art for the Capitol; the Botanic Garden; management of the Library of Congress; purchase of books and manuscripts; Smithsonian Institution and the incorporation of similar institutions; Franking Commission; printing and correction of the *Congressional Record*; services to the House, including the House restaurant, parking facilities, and administration of the House office buildings and of the House wing of the Capitol; travel of members of the House; raising, reporting, and use of campaign contributions for candidates for office of representative in the House of Representatives, of delegate, and of resident commissioner to the United States from Puerto Rico; compensation, retirement and other benefits of the members, officers, and employees of the Congress.

R 6–D 3 *(107th Congress)*

Bob Ney, Ohio
Steny H. Hoyer, Md.

R 6–D 3 *(108th Congress)*

Bob Ney, Ohio
John B. Larson, Conn.

No standing subcommittees.

INTERNATIONAL RELATIONS

Relations of the United States with foreign nations generally; acquisition of land and buildings for embassies and legations in foreign countries; establishment of boundary lines between the United States and foreign nations; export controls, including nonproliferation of nuclear technology and nuclear hardware; foreign loans; international commodity agreements (other than those involving sugar), including all agreements for cooperation in the export of nuclear technology and nuclear hardware; international conferences and congresses; international education; intervention abroad and declarations of war; measures relating to the diplomatic service; measures to foster comme4rcial intercourse with foreign nations and to safeguard American business interests abroad; measures relating to international economic policy; neutrality; protection of American citizens abroad and expatriation; American National Red Cross; trading with the enemy; U.N. organizations.

R 26–D 23 *(107th Congress)*

Henry J. Hyde, Ill.
Tom Lantos, Calif.

Africa—Ed Royce, Calif.
Asia and the Pacific—Jim Leach, Iowa
Europe—Elton Gallegly, Calif.

International Operations and Human Rights—Ileana Ros-Lehtinen, Fla.
Middle East and South Asia—Benjamin A. Gilman, N.Y.
Western Hemisphere—Cass Ballenger, N.C.

R 26–D 23 *(108th Congress)*

Henry J. Hyde, Ill.
Tom Lantos, Calif.

Africa—Ed Royce, Calif.
Asia and the Pacific—Jim Leach, Iowa
Europe—Doug Bereuter, Neb.
International Terrorism, Nonproliferation, and Human Rights—Elton Gallegly, Calif.
Middle East and Central Asia—Ileana Ros-Lehtinen, Fla.
Western Hemisphere—Cass Ballenger, N.C.

JUDICIARY

The judiciary and judicial proceedings, civil and criminal; administrative practice and procedure; apportionment of representatives; bankruptcy, mutiny, espionage, and counterfeiting; civil liberties; constitutional amendments; federal courts and judges, and local courts in the territories and possessions; immigration and naturalization; interstate compacts, generally; measures relating to claims against the United States; meetings of Congress, attendance of members and their acceptance of incompatible offices; national penitentiaries; patents, the Patent Office, copyrights, and trademarks; presidential succession; protection of trade and commerce against unlawful restraints and monopolies; revision and codification of the Statutes of the United States; state and territorial boundaries; subversive activities affecting the internal security of the United States.

R 21–D 16 *(107th Congress)*

F. James Sensenbrenner Jr., Wis.
John Conyers Jr., Mich.

Commercial and Administrative Law—Bob Barr, Ga.
Constitution—Steve Chabot, Ohio
Courts, the Internet, and Intellectual Property—Howard Coble, N.C.
Crime—Lamar Smith, Texas
Immigration and Claims—George W. Gekas, Pa.

R 21–D 16 *(108th Congress)*

F. James Sensenbrenner Jr., Wis.
John Conyers Jr., Mich.

Commercial and Administrative Law—Chris Cannon, Utah
Constitution—Steve Chabot, Ohio
Courts, the Internet, and Intellectual Property—Lamar Smith, Texas
Crime, Terrorism, and Homeland Security—Howard Coble, N.C.
Immigration, Border Security, and Claims—John Hostettler, Ind.

RESOURCES

Public lands generally, including entry, easements, and grazing; mining interests generally; fisheries and wildlife, including research, restoration, refuges, and conservation; forest reserves and national parks created from the public domain; forfeiture of land grants and alien ownership, including alien ownership of mineral lands; Geological Survey; international fishing agreements; interstate compacts relating to apportionment of waters for irrigation purposes; irrigation and reclamation, including water supply for reclamation projects, and easements of public lands for irrigation projects, and acquisition of private lands when necessary to complete irrigation projects; measures relating to the care and management of Indians, including the care and allotment of Native American lands and general and special measures relating to claims which are paid out of Native American funds; measures relating generally to the insular possessions of the United States, except those affecting the revenue and appropriations; military parks and battlefields, national cemeteries administered by the secretary of the interior, parks within the District of Columbia, and the erection of monuments to the memory of individuals; mineral land laws and claims and entries thereunder; mineral resources of the public lands; mining schools and experimental stations; marine affairs (including coastal zone management), except for measures relating to oil and other pollution of navigable waters; oceanography; petroleum conservation on the public lands and conservation of the radium supply in the United States; preservation of prehistoric ruins and objects of interest on the public domain; relations of the United States with the Native Americans and the Native American tribes; disposition of oil transported by the Trans-Alaska Oil Pipeline.

R 28–D 24 *(107th Congress)*

James V. Hansen, Utah
Nick J. Rahall II, W.Va

Energy and Mineral Resources—Barbara Cubin, Wyo.
Fisheries Conservation, Wildlife, and Oceans—Wayne T. Gilchrest, Md.
Forests and Forest Health—Scott McInnis, Colo.
National Parks and Public Lands—Joel Hefley, Colo.
Water and Power—Ken Calvert, Calif.

R 28–D 24 *(108th Congress)*

Richard W. Pombo, Calif.
Nick J. Rahall II, W.Va.

Energy and Mineral Resources—Barbara Cubin, Wyo.
Fisheries Conservation, Wildlife, and Oceans—Wayne T. Gilchrest, Md.
Forests and Forest Health—Scott McInnis, Colo.
National Parks, Recreation, and Public Lands—George P. Radanovich, Calif.
Water and Power—Ken Calvert, Calif.

RULES

Rules and joint rules (other than rules or joint rules relating to the Code of Official Conduct), and order of business of the House; recesses and final adjournments of Congress.

R 9–D 4 *(107th Congress)*

David Dreier, Calif.
Joe Moakley, Mass.

Legislative and Budget Process—Deborah Pryce, Ohio
Technology and the House—John Linder, Ga.

R 9–D 4 *(108th Congress)*

David Dreier, Calif.
Martin Frost, Texas

Legislative and Budget Process—Deborah Pryce, Ohio
Technology and the House—John Linder, Ga.

SCIENCE

All energy research, development, and demonstration, and projects thereof, and all federally owned or operated nonmilitary energy laboratories; astronautical research and development, including resources, personnel, equipment, and facilities; civil aviation research and development; environmental research and development; marine research; measures relating to the commercial application of energy technology; National Institute of Standards and Technology, standardization of weights and measures and the metric system; National Aeronautics and Space Administration; National Space Council; National Science Foundation; National Weather Service; outer space, including exploration and control thereof; science scholarships; scientific research, development, and demonstration, and projects thereof.

R 25–D 22 *(107th Congress)*

Sherwood Boehlert, N.Y.
Ralph M. Hall, Texas

Energy—Roscoe G. Bartlett, Md.
Environment, Technology, and Standards—Vernon J. Ehlers, Mich.
Research—Nick Smith, Mich.
Space and Aeronautics—Dana Rohrabacher, Calif.

R 25–D 22 *(108th Congress)*

Sherwood Boehlert, N.Y.
Ralph M. Hall, Texas

Energy—Judy Biggert, Ill.
Environment, Technology, and Standards—Vernon J. Ehlers, Mich.
Research—Nick Smith, Mich.
Space and Aeronautics—Dana Rohrabacher, Calif.

SELECT HOMELAND SECURITY[2]

Overall homeland security policy; organization and administration of the Department of Homeland Security; functions of the Department of Homeland Security; border and port security (except immigration policy and non-border enforcement); customs (except customs revenue); integration, analysis, and dissemination of homeland security information; domestic preparedness for and collective response to terrorism; research and development; transportation security.

R 27–D 23 (*108th Congress*)

Christopher Cox, Calif.
Jim Turner, Texas

Cybersecurity, Science, and Research and Development—William M. Thornberry, Texas
Emergency Preparedness and Response—John Shadegg, Ariz.
Infrastructure and Border Security—Dave Camp, Mich.
Intelligence and Counterterrorism—Jim Gibbons, Nev.
Rules—Lincoln Diaz-Balart, Fla.

SELECT INTELLIGENCE

Legislative and budgetary authority over the National Security Agency and the director of central intelligence, the Defense Intelligence Agency, the National Security Agency, intelligence activities of the Federal Bureau of Investigation and other components of the federal intelligence community.

R 11–D 9 (*107th Congress*)

Porter J. Goss, Fla.
Nancy Pelosi, Calif.

Human Intelligence, Analysis and Counterintelligence—Jim Gibbons, Nev.
Intelligence Policy and National Security—Michael N. Castle, Del.
Technical and Tactical Intelligence—Doug Bereuter, Neb.

R 11–D 9 (*108th Congress*)

Porter J. Goss, Fla.
Jane Harman, Calif.

Human Intelligence, Analysis and Counterintelligence—Jim Gibbons, Nev.
Intelligence Policy and National Security—Doug Bereuter, Neb.
Technical and Tactical Intelligence—Peter Hoekstra, Mich.
Terrorism and Homeland Security—Ray LaHood, Ill.

SMALL BUSINESS

Assistance to and protection of small business, including financial aid, regulatory flexibility, and paperwork reduction; participation of small business enterprises in federal procurement and government contracts.

R 19–D 17 (*107th Congress*)

Donald Manzullo, Ill.
Nydia M. Velazquez, N.Y.

Regulatory Reform and Oversight—Mike Pence, Ind.
Rural Enterprises and Agricultural Policy—John Thune, S.D.
Tax, Finance, and Exports—Patrick J. Toomey, Pa.
Workforce, Empowerment, and Government Programs—Jim DeMint, S.C.

R 19–D 17 (*108th Congress*)

Donald Manzullo, Ill.
Nydia M. Velazquez, N.Y.

Regulatory Reform and Oversight—Ed Schrock, Va.
Rural Enterprises, Agricultural Policy, and Technology—Sam Graves, Mo.
Tax, Finance, and Exports—Patrick J. Toomey, Pa.
Workforce, Empowerment, and Government Programs—Todd Akin, Mo.

STANDARDS OF OFFICIAL CONDUCT

Measures relating to the Code of Official Conduct.

R 5–D 5 (*107th Congress*)

Joel Hefley, Colo.
Howard L. Berman, Calif.

R 5–D 5 (*108th Congress*)

Joel Hefley, Colo.
Alan B. Mollohan, W.Va.

TRANSPORTATION AND INFRASTRUCTURE

Transportation, including civil aviation, railroads, water transportation, transportation safety (except automobile safety), transportation infrastructure, transportation labor, and railroad retirement and unemployment (except revenue measures); water power; the Coast Guard; federal management of emergencies and natural disasters; flood control and improvement of waterways; inspection of merchant marine vessels; navigation and related laws; rules and international arrangements to prevent collisions at sea; measures, other than appropriations, that relate to construction, maintenance and safety of roads; buildings and grounds of the Botanic Gardens, the Library of Congress and the Smithsonian Institution and other government buildings within the District of Columbia; post offices, customhouses, Federal courthouses, and merchant marine, except for national security aspects; pollution of navigable waters; and bridges and dams and related transportation regulatory agencies.

R 41–D 34 (*107th Congress*)

Don Young, Alaska
James L. Oberstar, Minn.

Aviation—John L. Mica, Fla.
Coast Guard and Maritime Transportation—Frank A. LoBiondo, N.J.
Economic Development, Public Buildings, and Emergency Management—Steven C. LaTourette, Ohio

Highways and Transit—Tom Petri, Wis.
Railroads—Jack Quinn, N.Y.
Water Resources and Environment—John J. "Jimmy" Duncan Jr., Tenn.

R 41–D 34 (108th Congress)

Don Young, Alaska
James L. Oberstar, Minn.

Aviation—John L. Mica, Fla.
Coast Guard and Maritime Transportation—Frank A. LoBiondo, N.J.
Economic Development, Public Buildings, and Emergency Management—Steven C. LaTourette, Ohio
Highways, Transit, and Pipelines—Tom Petri, Wis.
Railroads—Jack Quinn, N.Y.
Water Resources and Environment—John J. "Jimmy" Duncan Jr., Tenn.

VETERANS' AFFAIRS

Veterans' measures generally; cemeteries of the United States in which veterans of any war or conflict are or may be buried, whether in the United States or abroad, except cemeteries administered by the secretary of the Interior; compensation, vocational rehabilitation, and education of veterans; life insurance issued by the government on account of service in the armed forces; pensions of all the wars of the United States, readjustment of service personnel to civil life; soldiers' and sailors, civil relief; veterans' hospitals, medical care, and treatment of veterans.

R 17–D 14 (107th Congress)

Christopher H. Smith, N.J.
Lane Evans, Ill.

Benefits—J. D. Hayworth, Ariz.
Health—Jerry Moran, Kan.
Oversight and Investigations—Steve Buyer, Ind.

R 17–D 14 (108th Congress)

Christopher H. Smith, N.J.
Lane Evans, Ill.

Benefits—Henry E. Brown Jr., S.C.
Health—Rob Simmons, Conn.
Oversight and Investigations—Steve Buyer, Ind.

WAYS AND MEANS

Revenue measures generally; reciprocal trade agreements; customs, collection districts, and ports of entry and delivery; revenue measures relating to the insular possessions; bonded debt of the United States; deposit of public moneys; transportation of dutiable goods; tax-exempt foundations and charitable trusts; national Social Security, except (1) health care and facilities programs that are supported from general revenues as opposed to payroll deductions and (2) work incentive programs.

R 24–D 17 (107th Congress)

Bill Thomas, Calif.
Charles B. Rangel, N.Y.

Health—Nancy L. Johnson, Conn.
Human Resources—Wally Herger, Calif.
Oversight—Amo Houghton, N.Y.
Social Security—E. Clay Shaw Jr., Fla.
Trade—Philip M. Crane, Ill.

R 24–D 27 (108th Congress)

Bill Thomas, Calif.
Charles B. Rangel, N.Y.

Health—Nancy L. Johnson, Conn.
Human Resources—Wally Herger, Calif.
Oversight—Amo Houghton, N.Y.
Select Revenue Measures—Jim McCrery, La.
Social Security—E. Clay Shaw Jr., Fla.
Trade—Philip M. Crane, Ill.

POLITICAL COMMITTEES

Democratic Congressional Campaign Committee (provides campaign support for Democratic House candidates)—Nita M. Lowery, N.Y., chairman (107th Congress); Robert T. Matsui, Calif., chairman (108th Congress)

Democratic Steering Committee (makes Democratic committee assignments)—Richard A. Gephardt, Mo., and Steny H. Hoyer, Md., cochairs (107th Congress); Nancy Pelosi, Calif., and Rosa DeLauro, cochairs (108th Congress)

National Republican Congressional Committee (provides campaign support for Republican House candidates)—Thomas M. Davis III, Va., chairman (107th Congress); Thomas M. Reynolds, N.Y., chairman (108th Congress)

Republican Policy Committee (advises on party action and policy)—Christopher Cox, Calif., chairman (107th and 108th Congresses)

Republican Steering Committee (makes Republican committee assignments)—J. Dennis Hastert, Ill., chairman (107th and 108th Congresses)

Joint Committees

Joint committees are set up to examine specific questions and are established by public law. Membership is drawn from both chambers and both parties. When a senator serves as chairman, the vice chairman usually is a representative, and vice versa. The chairmanship traditionally rotates from one chamber to the other at the beginning of each Congress (except for the Committee on Taxation chairmanship, which rotates at the start of each session).

ECONOMIC

Studies and investigates all recommendations in the president's annual *Economic Report to Congress*. Reports findings and recommendations to the House and Senate.

Rep. H. James Saxton, R-N.J., chairman (107th Congress)

*Sen. Robert F. Bennett, R-Utah., vice chairman
(107th Congress January–June 2001)*

Rep. H. James Saxton, R-N.J., chairman
(107th Congress June 2001–January 2003)

*Sen. Jack Reed, D-R.I., vice chairman
(107th Congress June 2001–January 2003)*

Sen. Robert F. Bennett, R-Utah, chairman (108th Congress)

H. James Saxton, R-N.J., vice chairman (108th Congress)

No standing subcommittees.

LIBRARY

Management and expansion of the Library of Congress; receipt of gifts for the benefit of the library; development and maintenance of the Botanic Garden; placement of statues and other works of art in the Capitol.

Rep. Ted Stevens, R-Alaska, chairman
(107th Congress January–June 2001)

*Rep. Bill Thomas, R-Calif., vice chairman
(107th Congress January–June 2001)*

Rep. Vernon J. Ehlers, R-Mich., chairman
(107th Congress June 2001–January 2003)

*Sen. Christopher Dodd, D-Conn., vice chairman
(107th Congress June 2001–January 2003)*

Sen. Ted Stevens, R-Alaska, chairman (108th Congress)

Rep. Vernon J. Ehlers, R-Mich., vice chairman (108th Congress)

No standing subcommittees.

PRINTING

Probes inefficiency and waste in the printing, binding and distribution of federal government publications. Oversees arrangement and style of the *Congressional Record.*

Rep. Bill Thomas, R-Calif., chairman (107th Congress)

*Sen. Mitch McConnell, R-Ky, vice chairman
(107th Congress January–June 2001)*

Sen. Mark Dayton, D-Minn., chairman
(107th Congress June 2001–January 2003)

*Rep. Robert W. Ney, R-Ohio, vice chairman
(107th Congress June 2001–January 2003)*

Rep. Robert W. Ney, R-Ohio, chairman (108th Congress)

Sen. Thad Cochran, R-Miss, vice chairman (108th Congress)

Sen. Saxby Chambliss, R-Miss, vice chairman (108th Congress)

No standing subcommittees.

TAXATION

Operation, effects, and administration of the federal system of internal revenue taxes; measures and methods for simplification of taxes.

Rep. Bill Thomas, R-Texas, chairman (2002, 2003)

Sen. Max Baucus, D-Mont., vice chairman (2002)

Sen. Charles E. Grassley, R-Iowa, vice chairman (2003)

Sen. Charles E. Grassley, R-Iowa, chairman (2003)

Rep. Bill Thomas, R-Texas, vice chairman (2004)

No standing subcommittees.

1. Committee was renamed Homeland Security and Governmental Affairs in Senate action late in 2004, effective at the beginning of the 109th Congress in 2005.
2. Committee did not exist in the 107th Congress.

Postelection Sessions

A postelection session of Congress often is labeled a lame duck session. It takes place after an election for the next Congress but before the official end of the current Congress. As a result members who participate in the lame duck session are from the existing, or current, Congress, not from the Congress that will convene as a result of the just-held elections.

Lame duck sessions in the modern sense began in 1935 after the Twentieth Amendment to the Constitution was ratified in 1933. This amendment specified that regular congressional sessions would begin on Jan. 3 of each year unless Congress passed a law designating a different date. Also, terms of members of Congress begin and end on Jan. 3 of odd-numbered years, regardless of the date that a Congress officially ends its session. Originally the Constitution specified much later starting dates in recognition of the difficulty of travel in the early years of the nation, but those dates meant that lame duck sessions occurred in the second session of every Congress. In the modern sense, post-1935, a lame duck session is any meeting of Congress after election day in even-numbered years but before the following Jan. 3.

Congress held fifteen postelection sessions between 1935 and the end of 2004.

1941. The 76th Congress actually had adjourned in 1939 but President Franklin D. Roosevelt called the legislators into special session—technically, the third session of that Congress—to deal with the threat of war in Europe. However, little of substance was accomplished during the lame duck session.

1942. By this year the United States was at war with Germany, Japan, and Italy but little was done during the period as legislators decided to leave many major decisions to the next Congress. Congress did approve bills on overtime pay for government workers and to provide for the military draft of eighteen- and nineteen-year-old men.

1944. World War II was well along by this time, which meant Congress faced a host of exceptionally important issues including postwar universal military training, continuing the war effort, Social Security taxes, a rivers and harbors bill, and various postwar reconstruction matters. But, like the previous several lame duck sessions, legislators decided to postpone most actions until the new Congress convened in 1945.

1948. The 1948 postelection session of the 80th Congress lasted only two hours. Both chambers swore in new members, approved several minor resolutions and received last-minute reports from committees. In addition to final floor action, several committees resumed work. The most active was the House Un-American Activities Committee, which continued its investigation of alleged communist espionage in the federal government.

1950. After the 1950 elections, President Harry S. Truman sent a "must" agenda to the lame duck session of the 81st Congress. The president's list included supplemental defense appropriations, an excess profits tax, aid to Yugoslavia, a three-month extension of federal rent controls and statehood for Hawaii and Alaska. During a marathon session that lasted until only a few hours before its successor took over, the 81st Congress acted on all of the president's legislative items except the statehood bills, which were blocked by a Senate filibuster.

1954. Only one chamber of the 83rd Congress convened after the 1954 elections. The Senate returned Nov. 8 to hold what has been called a "censure session," a continuing investigation into the conduct of Sen. Joseph R. McCarthy, R-Wis. (1947–1957). By a 67–22 roll call, the Senate Dec. 2 voted to "condemn" McCarthy for his behavior. In

Recent Lame-Duck Sessions

Year	Congress	Dates
1941	76th	Adjourned Jan. 3, 1941*
1942	77th	Adjourned Dec. 16, 1942*
1944	78th	Nov. 14, 1944—Dec. 19, 1944
1948	80th	Dec. 31, 1948 (two-hour session)
1950	81st	Nov. 27, 1950—Jan. 2, 1951
1954	83rd	Nov. 8, 1954—Dec. 2, 1954
1970	91st	Nov. 16, 1970—Jan. 2, 1971 (Senate)
1974	93rd	Nov. 18, 1974—Dec. 20, 1974
1980	96th	Nov. 12, 1980—Dec. 16, 1980
1982	97th	Nov. 29, 1982—Dec. 23, 1982 (Senate)
		Nov. 29, 1982—Dec. 21, 1982 (House)
1994	103rd	Nov. 29, 1994 (House)
		Nov. 30, 1994—Dec. 1, 1994 (Senate)
1998	105th	Dec. 17, 1998—Dec. 19, 1998 (House)
2000	106th	Nov. 13, 2000—Dec. 15, 2000 (House)
		Nov. 14, 2000—Dec. 15, 2000 (Senate)
2002	107th	Adjourned Nov. 20, 2002 (Senate)*
		Adjourned Nov. 22, 2002 (House)*
2004	108th	Nov. 16, 2004—Dec. 7, 2004 (House)
		Nov. 16, 2004—Dec. 8, 2004 (Senate)

*Congress stayed in session.

other postelection floor action, the Senate passed a series of miscellaneous and administrative resolutions and swore in new members.

1970. President Richard Nixon criticized the lame duck Congress as one that had "seemingly lost the capacity to decide and the will to act." Filibusters and intense controversy contributed to inaction on the president's request for trade legislation and welfare reform. Congress nevertheless claimed some substantive results during the session, which ended Jan. 2, 1971. Several major appropriations bills were cleared for presidential signature. Congress also approved foreign aid to Cambodia, provided interim funding for the supersonic transport (SST) plane and repealed the Tonkin Gulf Resolution that had been used as a basis for American military involvement in Vietnam.

1974. In a session that ran from Nov. 18 to Dec. 20, 1974, the 93rd Congress cleared several important bills for presidential signature, including a mass transit bill, a Labor–Health, Education and Welfare appropriations bill and a foreign assistance package. A House-Senate conference committee reached agreement on a major strip-mining bill but President Gerald R. Ford vetoed it. Congress approved the nomination of Nelson A. Rockefeller as vice president. It also overrode presidential vetoes of two bills—one broadening the Freedom of Information Act, a second authorizing educational benefits for Korean War and Vietnam-era veterans.

1980. The lame duck session of the 96th Congress was productive, at least until Dec. 5, the original adjournment date set by congressional leaders. By that date a budget had been approved, along with a budget reconciliation measure. Ten regular appropriations bills had cleared, though one subsequently was vetoed. Congress had approved two major environmental measures—an Alaskan lands bill and toxic waste "superfund" legislation—as well as a three-year extension of general revenue sharing.

After Dec. 5, however, the legislative pace slowed noticeably. Action on a continuing appropriations resolution for those departments and agencies whose regular funding had not been cleared was delayed, first by a filibuster on a fair housing bill and later by more than 100 "Christmas tree" amendments, including a $10,000-a-year pay raise for members. After the conference report failed in the Senate and twice was rewritten, the bill was shorn of virtually all its "ornaments" and finally cleared by both chambers on Dec. 16.

1982. Despite the reluctance of congressional leaders, President Ronald Reagan urged the convening of a postelection session at the end of the 97th Congress, principally to pass remaining appropriations bills. Rising unemployment—and Democratic election gains in the House—made job creation efforts the focus of the lame duck Congress, however. Overriding the objections of Republican conservatives, Congress passed Reagan-backed legislation raising the federal gasoline tax from 4 cents to 9 cents a gallon to pay for highway repairs and mass transit. Supporters said the legislation would help alleviate unemployment by creating 300,000 jobs.

Congress eventually cleared four additional appropriations bills, packaging the remaining six in a continuing appropriations resolution that also included a pay raise for House members. Conferees dropped funding for emergency jobs programs to avert a threatened veto of the resolution. The lame duck session also was highlighted by Congress's refusal to fund production and procurement of the first five MX intercontinental missiles. This was the first time in recent history that either house of Congress had denied a president's request to fund production of a strategic weapon.

1994. Congress reconvened to reconsider, and ultimately approve, the Uruguay Round pact strengthening the General Agreement on Tariffs and Trade (GATT). The bill had been submitted Sept. 27, 1994, by President Bill Clinton under fast-track rules for trade legislation, which allowed each chamber only an up-or-down vote on the bill without amendments. But the rules also allowed every chairman with jurisdiction to take up to forty-five days to review the bill. Sen. Ernest F. Hollings, D-S.C., demanded his forty-five days, forcing the Senate leadership to schedule a two-day lame duck session. Clinton asked the House to approve the bill before the October adjournment but the Democratic leadership delayed consideration. The House reconvened for a one-day session Nov. 29 and passed the GATT bill by a wide margin. Following a twenty-hour debate Nov. 30 and Dec. 1, the Senate gave overwhelming approval to the bill.

1998. The House reconvened in December for a remarkable and historic event: to vote on the impeachment of a president. After a tumultuous political year, House Republicans pushed through articles of impeachment for what they believed was President Clinton's lying under oath. The event was characterized by a year-long political chasm between House Republicans, who led the effort for impeachment, and Democrats in both chambers. It also was characterized by charges of sexual misconduct involving Clinton and release of a controversial and in places graphic report about the sexual conduct of the president that Republicans defended as necessary to prove their case. The report was prepared by an independent prosecutor. In the short time the House was in session it voted—largely along party lines—in favor of impeachment charges, which would be tried—and rejected— by the Senate early in the following year.

2000. Congress returned after the 2000 elections largely to complete action of appropriations measures that had remained unfinished as President Clinton continued to wrestle with his Republican adversaries in Congress over spending priorities. Partisan fighting over spending and taxes had been one of the principal matters that divided the White House and Capitol Hill during the latter years of Clinton's presidency. The year 2000 was no exception as Congress was unable to avert its annual pileup of appropriations bills at the end of the session. The pileup was exacerbated in 2000 because of the controversial presidential elections that were not decided until a Supreme Court decision in December awarding contested Florida electoral votes to Republican George W. Bush. With the GOP about to reclaim the White House, party members in Congress suddenly had new leverage in the final bargaining over appropriations. The lame duck session lumbered into mid-December when an omnibus package was used to close the books on four spending bills and move other unrelated legislation.

2004. Congress came back after Republicans scored impressive gains in the fall elections that returned George W. Bush to the White House and increased GOP control of both chambers of Congress. The additional votes meant the GOP was strongly positioned to push Bush's legislative program in the 109th Congress. However, important legislative matters still remained undecided for the 108th Congress. The most important was a sweeping overhaul of the U.S. intelligence community, Congress's last major act of the year. It came only at the prodding of the independent, bipartisan National Commission on Terrorist Attacks Upon the United States—better known as the 9/11 commission—and the powerful lobbying of some of the victims' families. In addition, all but four of the appropriations bills had been left hanging when Congress went out of the elections break. Congress bundled the other nine into an omnibus bill during the lame duck session and cleared it on Nov. 20.

Senate Cloture Votes, 1917–2004

The filibuster, identified by the public primarily as nonstop speech, has been an enshrined Senate tradition throughout the chamber's history but became a focus of increasing criticism in the twentieth century as a device to thwart majority decisions. It was not until 1917 that the Senate adopted a rule, known as cloture, that allowed a majority—albeit a supermajority—to end a filibuster and bring a measure to a vote. The number of votes required to invoke cloture has varied over the years, standing at sixty in 2005 if there are no Senate vacancies. (The actual rules required a three-fifths majority of members to invoke cloture; the Senate has 100 members.)

Even with the rule in place, however, the number of filibusters and attempts to invoke cloture were limited until the 92nd Congress in 1971–1973. From that time on, and especially during the 1990s, cloture attempts expanded greatly as the character of the Senate changed from what one scholar called "communitarian" and deliberative to individualistic, increasingly partisan, and media-driven. In the ten Congresses during the twenty years from 1971 to 1991 cloture was attempted no less than thirteen times in each two-year period, and on the average twenty-five times each Congress. As dramatic as that growth was, it paled against the expansion in the following seven Congresses from 1991 to 2005. In that fifteen-year period cloture attempts averaged 51.4 a Congress. (*Table, p. 913*)

During President Bill Clinton's second term, a particularly partisan period from 1997 to 2001, a substantial number of cloture votes—more than 35 percent—were decided by a majority of 70 to 100 votes in favor. This higher success rate (than in previous decades) suggested that cloture was used less in connection with debates on far-reaching national issues—as was often the case in the past—and more for political and legislative maneuvering. The pattern in Clinton's second term was seen again in President George W. Bush's first term, from 2001 to 2005. Of the 109 cloture roll calls in his four years, 32 percent were by margins of 70 to 100 votes. A fifth of the cloture votes during 2001–2005 were on nominations of appeals court judges, reflecting the highly contentious judicial nomination controversies that were a hallmark of the president's first term. Only three of the judicial nomination clotures were successful.

CHANGES IN THE RULE

The Senate's ultimate check on the filibuster is the provision for cloture, or limitation of debate, contained in Rule 22 of its Standing Rules. The original Rule 22 was adopted in 1917 following a furor over the "talking to death" of a proposal by President Woodrow Wilson for arming American merchant ships before the United States entered World War I. The new cloture rule required the votes of two-thirds of all the senators present and voting to invoke cloture. In 1949, during a parliamentary skirmish preceding scheduled consideration of a Fair Employment Practices Commission bill, the requirement was raised to two-thirds of the entire Senate membership.

A revision of the rule in 1959 provided for limitation of debate by a vote of two-thirds of the senators present and voting, two days after a cloture petition was submitted by sixteen senators. If cloture was adopted by the Senate, further debate was limited to one hour for each senator on the bill itself and on all amendments affecting it. No new amendments could be offered except by unanimous consent. amendments that were not germane to the pending business and dilatory motions were out of order. The rule applied both to regular legislation and to motions to change the Standing Rules.

Rule 22 was revised significantly in 1975 by lowering the vote needed for cloture to three-fifths of the Senate membership (sixty if there were no vacancies). That revision applied to any matter except proposed rules changes, for which the old requirement of a two-thirds majority of senators present and voting still applied.

In a further revision of the rule, the Senate in 1979 limited post-cloture delaying tactics by providing that once cloture was invoked, a final vote had to be taken after no more than 100 hours of debate. All time spent on quorum calls, roll-call votes, and other parliamentary procedures was to be included in the 100-hour limit.

When the Senate decided to televise its floor proceedings in 1986, it further tightened up the time on postcloture debate. Rule 22 was revised to reduce to thirty hours, from 100, the time allowed for debate, procedural moves, and roll-call votes after the Senate had invoked cloture to end a filibuster.

Following is a list of the 654 cloture votes taken between 1917, when Senate Rule 22 was adopted, and the end of 2004; 240 of the votes (in **bold type**) were successful.

Issue	Date	Vote	Yeas needed
Versailles Treaty	Nov. 15, 1919	78–16	63
Emergency tariff	Feb. 2, 1921	36–35	48
Tariff bill	July 7, 1922	45–35	54
World Court	Jan. 25, 1926	68–26	63
Migratory birds	June 1, 1926	46–33	53
Branch banking	Feb. 15, 1927	65–18	56
Disabled officers	Feb. 26, 1927	51–36	58
Colorado River	Feb. 26, 1927	32–59	61
D.C. buildings	Feb. 28, 1927	52–31	56
Prohibition Bureau	Feb. 28, 1927	55–27	55
Banking Act	Jan. 19, 1933	58–30	59
Antilynching	Jan. 27, 1938	37–51	59
Antilynching	Feb. 16, 1938	42–46	59
Anti–poll tax	Nov. 23, 1942	37–41	52
Anti–poll tax	May 15, 1944	36–44	54
Fair Employment Practices Commission	Feb. 9, 1946	48–36	56
British loan	May 7, 1946	41–41	55
Labor disputes	May 25, 1946	3–77	54
Antipoll tax	July 31, 1946	39–33	48
Fair employment	May 19, 1950	52–32	64
Fair employment	July 12, 1950	55–33	64

Issue	Date	Vote	Yeas needed
Atomic Energy Act	July 26, 1954	44–42	64
Civil Rights Act	March 10, 1960	42–53	64
Amend Rule 22	Sept. 19, 1961	37–43	54
Literacy tests	May 9, 1962	43–53	64
Literacy tests	May 14, 1962	42–52	63
Comsat Act	Aug. 14, 1962	63–27	60
Amend Rule 22	Feb. 7, 1963	54–42	64
Civil Rights Act	June 10, 1964	71–29	67
Legislative reapportionment	Sept. 10, 1964	30–63	62
Voting Rights Act	May 25, 1965	70–30	67
Right-to-work repeal	Oct. 11, 1965	45–47	62
Right-to-work repeal	Feb. 8, 1966	51–48	66
Right-to-work repeal	Feb. 10, 1966	50–49	66
Civil Rights Act	Sept. 14, 1966	54–42	64
Civil Rights Act	Sept. 19, 1966	52–41	62
D.C. Home Rule	Oct. 10, 1966	41–37	52
Amend Rule 22	Jan. 24, 1967	53–46	66
Open housing	Feb. 20, 1968	55–37	62
Open housing	Feb. 26, 1968	56–36	62
Open housing	March 1, 1968	59–35	63
Open Housing	March 4, 1968	65–32	65

Issue	Date	Vote	Yeas needed
Fortas nomination	Oct. 1, 1968	45–43	59
Amend Rule 22	Jan. 16, 1969	51–47	66
Amend Rule 22	Jan. 28, 1969	50–42	62
Electoral college	Sept. 17, 1970	54–36	60
Electoral college	Sept. 29, 1970	53–34	58
Supersonic transport	Dec. 19, 1970	43–48	61
Supersonic transport	Dec. 22, 1970	42–44	58
Amend Rule 22	Feb. 18, 1971	48–37	57
Amend Rule 22	Feb. 23, 1971	50–36	58
Amend Rule 22	March 2, 1971	48–36	56
Amend Rule 22	March 9, 1971	55–39	63
Military draft	June 23, 1971	65–27	62
Lockheed loan	July 26, 1971	42–47	60
Lockheed loan	July 28, 1971	59–39	66
Lockheed loan	July 30, 1971	53–37	60
Military draft	Sept. 21, 1971	61–30	61
Rehnquist nomination	Dec. 10, 1971	52–42	63
Equal job opportunity	Feb. 1, 1972	48–37	57
Equal job opportunity	Feb. 3, 1972	53–35	59
Equal job opportunity	Feb. 22, 1972	71–23	63
U.S.-Soviet arms pact	Sept. 14, 1972	76–15	61
Consumer agency	Sept. 29, 1972	47–29	51
Consumer agency	Oct. 3, 1972	55–32	58
Consumer agency	Oct. 5, 1972	52–30	55
School busing	Oct. 10, 1972	45–37	55
School busing	Oct. 11, 1972	49–39	59
School busing	Oct. 12, 1972	49–38	58
Voter registration	April 30, 1973	56–31	58
Voter registration	May 3, 1973	60–34	63
Voter registration	May 9, 1973	67–32	66
Public campaign financing	Dec. 2, 1973	47–33	54
Public campaign financing	Dec. 3, 1973	49–39	59
Rhodesian chrome ore	Dec. 11, 1973	59–35	63
Rhodesian chrome ore	Dec. 13, 1973	62–33	64
Legal services program	Dec. 13, 1973	60–36	64
Legal services program	Dec. 14, 1973	56–29	57
Rhodesian chrome ore	Dec. 18, 1973	63–26	60
Legal services program	Jan. 30, 1974	68–29	65
Genocide Treaty	Feb. 5, 1974	55–36	61
Genocide Treaty	Feb. 6, 1974	55–38	62
Government pay raise	March 6, 1974	67–31	66
Public campaign financing	April 4, 1974	60–36	64
Public campaign financing	April 9, 1974	64–30	63
Public debt ceiling	June 19, 1974	50–43	62
Public debt ceiling	June 19, 1974	45–48	62
Public debt ceiling	June 26, 1974	48–50	66
Consumer agency	July 30, 1974	56–42	66
Consumer agency	Aug. 1, 1974	59–39	66
Consumer agency	Aug. 20, 1974	59–35	63
Consumer agency	Sept. 19, 1974	64–34	66
Export-Import Bank	Dec. 3, 1974	51–39	60
Export-Import Bank	Dec. 4, 1974	48–44	62
Trade reform	Dec. 13, 1974	71–19	60
Fiscal 1975 supplemental funds	Dec. 14, 1974	56–27	56
Export-Import Bank	Dec. 14, 1974	49–35	56
Export-Import Bank	Dec. 16, 1974	54–34	59
Social services programs	Dec. 17, 1974	70–23	62
Tax law changes	Dec. 17, 1974	67–25	62
Rail Reorganization Act	Feb. 26, 1975	86–8	63
Amend Rule 22	March 5, 1975	73–21	63
Amend Rule 22	March 7, 1975	73–21	63
Tax reduction	March 20, 1975	59–38	60
Tax reduction	March 21, 1975	83–13	60
Consumer advocacy agency	May 13, 1975	71–27	60
Senate staffing	June 11, 1975	77–19	64
New Hampshire Senate seat	June 24, 1975	57–39	60
New Hampshire Senate seat	June 25, 1975	56–41	60
New Hampshire Senate seat	June 26, 1975	54–40	60
New Hampshire Senate seat	July 8, 1975	57–38	60
New Hampshire Senate seat	July 9, 1975	57–38	60
New Hampshire Senate seat	July 10, 1975	54–38	60
Voting Rights Act	July 21, 1975	72–19	60
Voting Rights Act	July 23, 1975	76–20	60
Oil price decontrol	July 30, 1975	54–38	60
Anti–school busing amendments	Sept. 23, 1975	46–48	60
Anti–school busing amendments	Sept. 24, 1975	64–33	60
Common-site picketing	Nov. 11, 1975	66–30	60
Common-site picketing	Nov. 14, 1975	58–31	60
Common-site picketing	Nov. 18, 1975	62–37	60
Rail reorganization	Dec. 4, 1975	61–27	60
New York City aid	Dec. 5, 1975	70–27	60
Rice Production Act	Feb. 3, 1976	70–19	60

Issue	Date	Vote	Yeas needed
Antitrust amendments	June 3, 1976	67–22	60
Antitrust amendments	Aug. 31, 1976	63–27	60
Civil rights attorneys' fees	Sept. 23, 1976	63–26	60
Draft resisters pardons	Jan. 24, 1977	53–43	60
Campaign financing	July 29, 1977	49–45	60
Campaign financing	Aug. 1, 1977	47–46	60
Campaign financing	Aug. 2, 1977	52–46	60
Natural gas pricing	Sept. 26, 1977	77–17	60
Labor law revision	June 7, 1978	42–47	60
Labor law revision	June 8, 1978	49–41	60
Labor law revision	June 13, 1978	54–43	60
Labor law revision	June 14, 1978	58–41	60
Labor law revision	June 15, 1978	58–39	60
Labor law revision	June 22, 1978	53–45	60
Revenue Act of 1978	Oct. 9, 1978	62–28	60
Energy taxes	Oct. 14, 1978	71–13	60
Windfall profits tax	Dec. 12, 1979	53–46	60
Windfall profits tax	Dec. 13, 1979	56–40	60
Windfall profits tax	Dec. 14, 1979	56–39	60
Windfall profits tax	Dec. 17, 1979	84–14	60
Lubbers nomination	April 21, 1980	46–60	60
Lubbers nomination	April 22, 1980	62–34	60
Rights of institutionalized	April 28, 1980	44–39	60
Rights of institutionalized	April 29, 1980	56–34	60
Rights of institutionalized	April 30, 1980	53–35	60
Rights of institutionalized	May 1, 1980	60–34	60
Bottlers' antitrust immunity	May 15, 1980	86–6	60
Draft registration funding	June 10, 1980	62–32	60
Zimmerman nomination	Aug. 1, 1980	51–35	60
Zimmerman nomination	Aug. 4, 1980	45–31	60
Zimmerman nomination	Aug. 5, 1980	63–31	60
Alaska lands	Aug. 18, 1980	63–25	60
Vessel tonnage/strip mining	Aug. 21, 1980	61–32	60
Fair Housing amendments	Dec. 3, 1980	51–39	60
Fair Housing amendments	Dec. 4, 1980	62–32	60
Fair Housing amendments	Dec. 9, 1980	54–43	60
Breyer nomination	Dec. 9, 1980	68–28	60
Justice Department authorization	July 10, 1981	38–48	60
Justice Department authorization	July 13, 1981	54–32	60
Justice Department authorization	July 29, 1981	59–37	60
Justice Department authorization	Sept. 10, 1981	57–33	60
Justice Department authorization	Sept. 16, 1981	61–36	60
Justice Department authorization	Dec. 10, 1981	64–35	60
State, Justice, Commerce, Judiciary funds	Dec. 11, 1981	59–35	60
Justice Department authorization	Feb. 9, 1982	63–33	60
Broadcast Senate proceedings	April 20, 1982	47–51	60
Criminal Code Reform Act	April 27, 1982	45–46	60
1982 supplemental funds	May 27, 1982	95–2	60
Voting Rights Act	June 15, 1982	86–8	60
Debt limit increase	Sept. 9, 1982	41–47	60
Debt limit increase	Sept. 13, 1982	45–35	60
Debt limit increase	Sept. 15, 1982	50–44	60
Debt limit increase	Sept. 20, 1982	50–39	60
Debt limit increase	Sept. 21, 1982	53–47	60
Debt limit increase	Sept. 22, 1982	54–46	60
Debt limit increase	Sept. 23, 1982	53–45	60
Antitrust Equal Enforcement Act	Dec. 2, 1982	38–58	60
Antitrust Equal Enforcement Act	Dec. 2, 1982	44–51	60
Transportation Assistance Act	Dec. 13, 1982	75–13	60
Transportation Assistance Act	Dec. 16, 1982	48–50	60
Transportation Assistance Act	Dec. 16, 1982	5–93	60
Transportation Assistance Act	Dec. 19, 1982	89–5	60
Transportation Assistance Act	Dec. 20, 1982	87–8	60
Transportation Assistance Act	Dec. 23, 1982	81–5	60
Jobs funding/interest withholding	March 16, 1983	50–48	60
Jobs funding/interest withholding	March 16, 1983	59–39	60
International trade/interest withholding	April 19, 1983	34–53	60
International trade /interest withholding	April 19, 1983	39–59	60
Defense authorizations, 1984	July 21, 1983	55–41	60
Radio broadcasting to Cuba	Aug. 3, 1983	62–33	60
National Gas Policy Act	Nov. 3, 1983	86–7	60
Capital punishment	Feb. 9, 1984	65–26	60
Hydroelectric power plants	July 30, 1984	60–28	60
Wilkinson nomination	July 31, 1984	57–39	60
Agriculture funds, fiscal 1985	Aug. 6, 1984	54–31	60
Agriculture funds, fiscal 1985	Aug. 8, 1984	68–30	60
Wilkinson nomination	Aug. 9, 1984	65–32	60
Financial Services Act	Sept. 10, 1984	89–3	60
Financial Services Act	Sept. 13, 1984	92–6	60
Broadcasting of Senate proceedings	Sept. 18, 1984	73–26	60
Broadcasting Senate proceedings	Sept. 21, 1984	37–44	60
Surface Transportation Act	Sept. 24, 1984	70–12	60

Issue	Date	Vote	Yeas needed	Issue	Date	Vote	Yeas needed
Continuing funds	Sept. 29, 1984	92–4	60	Omnibus crime package	June 5, 1990	54–37	60
Anti-apartheid	July 10, 1985	88–8	60	Omnibus crime package	June 7, 1990	57–37	60
Line-item veto	July 18, 1985	57–42	60	Air travel rights for the blind	June 12, 1990	56–44	60
Line-item veto	July 23, 1985	57–41	60	**Civil Rights Act of 1990**	July 17, 1990	62–38	60
Line-item veto	July 24, 1985	58–40	60	Defense authorization, fiscal 1991	Aug. 3, 1990	58–41	60
Anti-apartheid	Sept. 9, 1985	53–34	60	**Motor Vehicle Fuel Efficiency Act**	Sept. 14, 1990	68–28	60
Anti-apartheid	Sept. 11, 1985	57–41	60	Motor Vehicle Fuel Efficiency Act	Sept. 25, 1990	57–42	60
Anti-apartheid	Sept. 12, 1985	11–88	60	Title X family planning amendments	Sept. 26, 1990	50–46	60
Debt limit/balanced budget	Oct. 6, 1985	57–38	64	National motor-voter registration	Sept. 26, 1990	55–42	60
Debt limit/balanced budget	Oct. 9, 1985[1]	53–39	62	Foreign operations funds, fiscal 1991	Oct. 12, 1990	51–38	60
Conrail sale	Jan. 23, 1986	90–7	60	**Vertical price fixing**	May 7, 1991	61–37	60
Conrail sale	Jan. 30, 1986	70–27	60	**Vertical price fixing**	May 8, 1991	63–35	60
Fitzwater nomination	March 18, 1986	64–33	60	Crime bill	June 28, 1991	41–58	60
Washington airports transfer	March 21, 1986	50–39	60	Crime bill	July 10, 1991	56–43	60
Washington airports transfer	March 25, 1986	66–32	60	**Crime bill**	July 10, 1991	71–27	60
Hobbs Act amendments	April 16, 1986	44–54	60	National motor-voter registration	July 18, 1991	57–41	60
Defense authorization, fiscal 1987	Aug. 6, 1986	53–46	60	VA-HUD funds, fiscal 1992	July 18, 1991	57–40	60
Aid to Nicaraguan contras	Aug. 13, 1986	59–40	60	National motor-voter registration	July 18, 1991	59–40	60
South Africa sanctions	Aug. 13, 1986	89–11	60	**Foreign aid authorization**	July 24, 1991	87–10	60
Aid to Nicaraguan contras	Aug. 13, 1986	62–37	60	Foreign aid authorization	July 25, 1991	52–44	60
Rehnquist nomination	Sept. 17, 1986	68–31	60	**Foreign aid authorization**	July 25, 1991	63–33	60
Product liability reform	Sept. 25, 1986	97–1	60	**Extended unemployment benefits**	July 29, 1991	96–1	60
Omnibus drug bill	Oct. 15, 1986	58–38	60	Defense authorization, fiscal 1992	Aug. 2, 1991	58–40	60
Immigration reform	Oct. 17, 1986	69–21	60	Interior funds, fiscal 1992	Sept. 19, 1991	55–41	60
Contra aid moratorium	March 23, 1987	46–45	60	**Federal Facility Compliance Act**	Oct. 17, 1991	85–14	60
Contra aid moratorium	March 24, 1987	50–50	60	**Civil Rights Act**	Oct. 22, 1991	93–4	60
Contra aid moratorium	March 25, 1987	54–46	60	National energy policy	Nov. 1, 1991	50–44	60
Relief for the homeless	April 9, 1987	68–29	60	**Banking reform**	Nov. 13, 1991	76–19	60
Defense authorization, fiscal 1988	May 15, 1987	52–36	60	Iranian hostage release investigation	Nov. 22, 1991	51–43	60
Defense authorization, fiscal 1988	May 19, 1987	58–41	60	Crime conference report	Nov. 27, 1991	49–38	60
Defense authorization, fiscal 1988	May 20, 1987	59–39	60	**School improvement bill**	Jan. 21, 1992	93–0	60
Campaign finance	June 9, 1987	52–47	60	**National energy strategy**	Feb. 4, 1992	90–5	60
Campaign finance	June 16, 1987	49–46	60	**Joint ventures antitrust**	Feb. 25, 1992	98–0	60
Campaign finance	June 17, 1987	51–47	60	Lumbee Tribe recognition	Feb. 27, 1992	58–39	60
Campaign finance	June 18, 1987	50–47	60	**Public Broadcasting Corp.**	March 3, 1992	87–7	60
Campaign finance	June 19, 1987	45–43	60	Crime bill	March 19, 1992	54–43	60
Kuwaiti tanker reflagging	July 9, 1987	57–42	60	Defense/domestic spending walls	March 26, 1992	50–48	60
Kuwaiti tanker reflagging	July 14, 1987	53–40	60	**Fetal tissue research**	March 31, 1992	98–2	60
Kuwaiti tanker reflagging	July 15, 1987	54–44	60	**Motor-voter registration**	May 7, 1992	61–38	60
Wells nomination	Sept. 9, 1987	65–24	60	Motor-voter registration	May 12, 1992	58–40	60
Campaign finance	Sept. 10, 1987	53–42	60	**Drug abuse mental health**	June 9, 1992	84–9	60
Campaign finance	Sept. 15, 1987	51–44	60	Striker replacement	June 11, 1992	55–41	60
Kuwaiti tanker escort	Oct. 1, 1987	54–45	60	Striker replacement	June 16, 1992	57–42	60
Defense authorization, fiscal 1988	Oct. 1, 1987	41–58	60	Balanced budget amendment	June 30, 1992	56–39	60
Verity nomination	Oct. 13, 1987	85–8	60	Balanced budget amendment	July 1, 1992	56–39	60
War powers compliance	Oct. 20, 1987	67–28	60	National energy strategy	July 23, 1992	58–33	60
Nuclear waste depository	Nov. 10, 1987	87–0	60	**National energy strategy**	July 28, 1992	93–3	60
Campaign finance	Feb. 26, 1988	53–41	60	**Carnes nomination**	Sept. 9, 1992	66–30	60
Polygraph protection	March 3, 1988	77–19	60	Product liability	Sept. 10, 1992	57–39	60
Intelligence oversight	March 15, 1988	73–18	60	Product liability	Sept. 10, 1992	58–38	60
Risk notification	March 23, 1988	33–59	60	**School improvement bill**	Sept. 15, 1992	85–6	60
Risk notification	March 24, 1988	2–93	60	Labor, HHS, Education funds	Sept. 16, 1992	56–38	60
Risk notification	March 28, 1988	41–44	60	**START treaty**	Sept. 29, 1992	87–6	60
Risk notification	March 29, 1988	42–52	60	School improvement bill	Oct. 2, 1992	59–40	60
Campaign spending limitations	April 21, 1988	52–42	60	Crime bill	Oct. 2, 1992	55–43	60
Campaign spending limitations	April 22, 1988	53–37	60	**Fetal tissue research**	Oct. 2, 1992	85–12	60
Immigration legalization program extension	April 28, 1988	40–56	60	**National energy strategy**	Oct. 8, 1992	84–8	60
Drug-related killings death penalty	June 9, 1988	70–26	60	**Tax bill**	Oct. 8, 1992	80–10	60
Great Smoky Mountain Wilderness Act	June 20, 1988	49–35	60	Motor-voter registration	March 5, 1993	52–36	60
Great Smoky Mountain Wilderness Act	June 21, 1988	54–42	60	**Motor-voter registration**	March 9, 1993	62–38	60
Plant-closing notification	June 29, 1988	58–39	60	Motor-voter registration	March 16, 1993	59–41	60
Plant closing notification	July 6, 1988	88–5	60	Stimulus package	April 2, 1993	55–43	60
Textile import quotas	Sept. 7, 1988	68–29	60	Stimulus package	April 3, 1993	52–37	60
Minimum wage restoration	Sept. 22, 1988	53–43	60	Stimulus package	April 5, 1993	49–29	60
Minimum wage restoration	Sept. 23, 1988	56–35	60	Stimulus package	April 21, 1993	56–43	60
Parental and medical leave	Oct. 3, 1988	85–6	60	**Motor-voter registration**	May 11, 1993	63–37	60
Parental and medical leave	Oct. 7, 1988	50–46	60	Campaign finance	June 10, 1993	53–41	60
Defense authorization, fiscal 1990	Aug. 2, 1989	84–13	60	Campaign finance	June 15, 1993	52–45	60
Airline smoking ban	Sept. 14, 1989	77–21	60	**Campaign finance**	June 16, 1993	62–37	60
Eastern Airlines strike commission	Oct. 3, 1989	61–36	60	National service	July 29, 1993	59–41	60
Nicaraguan election aid	Oct. 13, 1989	52–42	60	Dellinger nomination	Oct. 7, 1993	59–39	60
Nicaraguan election aid	Oct. 17, 1989	74–25	60	Interior funds	Oct. 21, 1993	53–41	60
Eastern Airlines strike commission	Oct. 26, 1989	62–38	60	Interior funds	Oct. 26, 1993	51–45	60
Capital gains tax cut	Nov. 14, 1989	51–47	60	Interior funds	Oct. 28, 1993	54–44	60
Capital gains tax cut	Nov. 15, 1989	51–47	60	State Department nominations	Nov. 3, 1993	58–42	60
Government pay-and-ethics package	Nov. 17, 1989	90–9	60	Brady bill (gun controls)	Nov. 19, 1993	57–42	60
Armenian genocide day	Feb. 22, 1990	49–49	60	**Napolitano nomination**	Nov. 19, 1993	72–26	60
Armenian genocide day	Feb. 27, 1990	48–51	60	Brady bill (gun controls)	Nov. 19, 1993	57–41	60
Hatch Act revisions	May 1, 1990	70–28	60	Competitiveness bill	March 15, 1994	56–42	60
AIDS emergency relief	May 15, 1990	95–3	60	Federal worker retirement buyout	March 24, 1994	58–41	60
Chemical weapons sanctions	May 17, 1990	87–4	60	**Federal worker retirement buyout**	March 24, 1994	63–36	60

Issue	Date	Vote	Yeas needed
Education Goals 2000	March 26, 1994	62–23	60
Shearer nomination	May 24, 1994	63–35	60
Brown nomination	May 24, 1994	54–44	60
Brown nomination	May 25, 1994	56–42	60
Product liability	June 28, 1994	54–44	60
Product liability	June 29, 1994	57–41	60
Striker replacement	July 12, 1994	53–47	60
Striker replacement	July 13, 1994	53–46	60
Crime bill	Aug. 25, 1994	61–38	60
Campaign finance	Sept. 22, 1994	96–2	60
California desert protection	Sept. 23, 1994	73–20	60
Campaign finance	Sept. 27, 1994	57–43	60
Campaign finance	Sept. 30, 1994	52–46	66[2]
Tigert nomination	Oct. 3, 1994	63–32	65[3]
Sarokin nomination	Oct. 4, 1994	85–12	60
Elementary and secondary education	Oct. 5, 1994	75–24	60
Lobbying disclosure/gift ban	Oct. 6, 1994	52–46	60
Lobbying disclosure/gift ban	Oct. 7, 1994	55–42	60
California desert protection	Oct. 8, 1994	68–23	60
Unfunded mandates	Jan. 19, 1995	54–44	60
Balanced-budget amendment	Feb. 16, 1995	57–42	60
Striker replacement	March 15, 1995	58–39	60
Health insurance tax deduction	April 3, 1995	83–0	60
Supplemental funds and rescissions	April 6, 1995	56–44	60
Product liability	May 4, 1995	46–53	60
Product liability	May 4, 1995	47–52	60
Product liability	May 8, 1995	43–49	60
Product liability	May 9, 1995	60–38	60
Interstate waste	May 11, 1995	50–47	60
Telecommunications	June 14, 1995	89–11	60
Foster nomination	June 21, 1995	57–43	60
Foster nomination	June 22, 1995	57–43	60
Regulatory overhaul	July 17, 1995	48–46	60
Regulatory overhaul	July 18, 1995	53–47	60
Regulatory overhaul	July 20, 1995	58–40	60
State Department authorization	Aug. 1, 1995	55–45	60
State Department authorization	Aug. 1, 1995	55–45	60
Cuba sanctions	Oct. 12, 1995	56–37	60
Cuba sanctions	Oct. 17, 1995	59–36	60
Cuba sanctions	Oct. 18, 1995	98–0	60
Farm bill	Feb. 1, 1996	53–45	60
Farm bill	Feb. 6, 1996	59–34	60
District of Columbia funds	Feb. 27, 1996	54–44	60
District of Columbia funds	Feb. 29, 1996	52–42	60
District of Columbia funds	March 5, 1996	53–43	60
District of Columbia funds	March 12, 1996	56–44	60
Whitewater committee extension	March 12, 1996	53–47	60
Whitewater committee extension	March 13, 1996	53–47	60
Whitewater committee extension	March 14, 1996	51–46	60
Product liability	March 20, 1996	60–40	60
Whitewater committee extension	March 20, 1996	53–47	60
Whitewater committee extension	March 21, 1996	52–46	60
Presidio Park management	March 27, 1996	51–49	60
Presidio Park management	March 28, 1996	55–45	60
Whitewater committee extension	April 16, 1996	51–46	60
Term limits constitutional amendment	April 23, 1996	58–42	60
Immigration revision	April 29, 1996	91–0	60
Immigration revision	May 2, 1996	100–0	60
White House Travel Office reimbursement	May 7, 1996	52–44	60
White House Travel Office reimbursement	May 8, 1996	53–45	60
White House Travel Office reimbursement	May 9, 1996	52–44	60
White House Travel Office reimbursement	May 14, 1996	54–43	60
Missile defense	June 4, 1996	53–46	60
Campaign finance overhaul	June 25, 1996	54–46	60
Defense authorization	June 26, 1996	52–46	60
Defense authorization	June 28, 1996	53–43	60
Right-to-work legislation	July 10, 1996	31–68	60
Nuclear waste storage	July 16, 1996	65–34	60
FAA reauthorization	Oct. 3, 1996	66–31	60
Volunteer liability limitation	April 29, 1997	53–46	60
Volunteer liability limitation	April 30, 1997	55–44	60
Supplemental funds	May 7, 1997	100–0	60
Compensatory time, flexible credit	May 15, 1997	53–47	60
Compensatory time, flexible credit	June 4, 1997	51–47	60
Defense authorization, fiscal 1998	July 8, 1997	46–45	60
Klein nomination	July 14, 1997	78–11	60
FDA overhaul	Sept. 5, 1997	89–5	60
FDA overhaul	Sept. 16, 1997	94–4	60
District of Columbia funds, fiscal 1998	Sept. 30, 1997	58–41	60
Campaign finance reform	Oct. 7, 1997	52–48	60
Campaign finance reform	Oct. 7, 1997	53–47	60
District of Columbia funds	Oct. 7, 1997	99–1	60
Campaign finance reform	Oct. 8, 1997	52–47	60
Campaign finance reform	Oct. 9, 1997	52–47	60
Campaign finance reform	Oct. 9, 1997	51–48	60
Highway and transit reauthorization	Oct. 23, 1997	48–52	60
Highway and transit reauthorization	Oct. 23, 1997	48–50	60
Highway and transit reauthorization	Oct. 24, 1997	43–49	60
Highway and transit reauthorization	Oct. 28, 1997	52–48	60
Education savings accounts	Oct. 31, 1997	56–41	60
Defense authorization, fiscal 1998	Oct. 31, 1997	93–2	60
Education savings accounts	Nov. 4, 1997	56–44	60
Fast-track trade procedures	Nov. 4, 1997	69–31	60
Satcher confirmation	Feb. 10, 1998	75–23	60
Human cloning research ban	Feb. 11, 1998	42–54	60
Restrict political use of union dues	Feb. 26, 1998	51–48	60
Restrict political use of union dues	Feb. 26, 1998	45–54	60
Highway and mass transit programs	March 11, 1998	96–3	60
Education savings accounts	March 17, 1998	74–24	60
Expand education savings accounts	March 19, 1998	55–44	60
Expand education savings accounts	March 26, 1998	58–42	60
U.S. antimissile defense policy	May 13, 1998	59–41	60
Create nuclear waste storage in Nevada	June 2, 1998	56–39	60
Set federal policies to curb smoking	June 9, 1998	42–56	62
Set federal policies to curb smoking	June 10, 1998	43–55	60
Set federal policies to curb smoking	June 11, 1998	43–56	60
Set federal policies to curb smoking	June 17, 1998	57–42	60
Limit product liability suits	July 7, 1998	71–24	60
Limit product liability punitive damages	July 9, 1998	51–47	60
U.S. court review, local zoning decisions	July 13, 1998	52–42	60
Legislative branch funds, fiscal 1999	July 21, 1998	83–16	60
U.S. missile defense policy	Sept. 9, 1998	59–41	60
Consumer bankruptcy laws	Sept. 9, 1998	99–1	60
Campaign finance reform	Sept. 10, 1998	52–48	60
Parental consent abortion bill	Sept. 11, 1998	97–0	60
Limit union organizing	Sept. 14, 1998	52–42	60
Evading parental consent abortion laws	Sept. 22, 1998	54–45	60
Limit presidential appointment powers	Sept. 24, 1998	96–1	60
Limit presidential appointment powers	Sept. 28, 1998	53–38	60
Ban Internet sales taxes	Sept. 29, 1998	89–6	60
Banking regulation revision	Oct. 5, 1998	93–0	60
Ban Internet sales taxes for two years	Oct. 7, 1998	94–4	60
Waive federal education spending rules	March 8, 1999	54–41	60
Waive federal education spending rules	March 9, 1999	55–39	60
Authorize $11.4 billion for new teacher hires	March 10, 1999	44–55	60
Special education funding	March 10, 1999	55–44	60
U.S. troops in Kosovo	March 23, 1999	55–44	60
Social Security "lockbox," debt limit	April 22, 1999	54–45	60
Y2K liability limits	April 26, 1999	94–0	60
Y2K liability limits	April 29, 1999	52–47	60
Social Security "lockbox," debt limit	April 30, 1999	49–44	60
Y2K liability limits	May 18, 1999	53–45	60
Social Security "lockbox," debt limit	June 15, 1999	53–46	60
Steel, oil, gas loan guarantee	June 15, 1999	70–29	60
Social Security "lockbox"	June 16, 1999	55–44	60
Steel import quotas	June 22, 1999	42–57	60
Agriculture funds, fiscal 2000	June 28, 1999	50–37	60
Transportation funds, fiscal 2000	June 28, 1999	49–40	60
Commerce, State, Justice funds, fiscal 2000	June 28, 1999	49–39	60
Foreign operations funds, fiscal 2000	June 28, 1999	49–41	60
Budget procedures	July 1, 1999	99–1	60
Social Security "lockbox," debt limit	July 16, 1999	52–43	60
Intelligence authorization, fiscal 2000	July 20, 1999	99–0	60
Juvenile justice programs	July 28, 1999	77–22	60
Agriculture funds/milk marketing, fiscal 2000	Aug. 4, 1999	53–47	60
Transportation funds, fiscal 2000	Sept. 9, 1999	49–49	60
Puerto Rican nationalists clemency	Sept. 13, 1999	93–0	60
Oil royalty valuation system	Sept. 13, 1999	54–40	60
Bankruptcy law revision	Sept. 21, 1999	53–45	60
Stewart nomination	Sept. 21, 1999	55–44	60
Oil royalty valuation system	Sept. 23, 1999	62–39	60
Agriculture funds, fiscal 2000	Oct. 12, 1999	79–20	60
Campaign finance soft money ban	Oct. 19, 1999	52–48	60
Campaign finance soft money, union dues	Oct. 19, 1999	53–47	60
Trade with Sub-Saharan Africa	Oct. 26, 1999	91–8	60
Sub-Saharan African, Caribbean trade	Oct. 29, 1999	45–46	60
Sub-Saharan African, Caribbean trade	Nov. 2, 1999	74–23	60
Omnibus funds, fiscal 2000	Nov. 19, 1999	87–9	60
Nuclear waste storage	Feb. 2, 2000	94–3	60
Berzon nomination	March 8, 2000	86–13	60

Issue	Date	Vote	Yeas needed	Issue	Date	Vote	Yeas needed
Paez nomination	March 8, 2000	85–14	60	Drug patents	July 31, 2002	66–33	60
Flag desecration constitutional amendment	March 29, 2000	100–0	60	Trade promotion authority	Aug. 1, 2002	64–32	60
Federal gas tax suspension	March 30, 2000	86–11	60	Interior funds, fiscal 2002/farm disaster aid	Sept. 17, 2002	50–49	60
Federal gas tax suspension	April 11, 2000	43–56	60	Homeland security department	Sept. 19, 2002	50–49	60
Marriage penalty tax	April 13, 2000	53–45	60	Interior funds, fiscal 2002/farm disaster aid	Sept. 23, 2002	49–46	60
Marriage penalty tax	April 13, 2000	53–45	60	Interior funds, fiscal 2002/farm disaster aid	Sept. 25, 2002	51–47	60
Victims rights	April 25, 2000	82–12	60	Homeland Security Department	Sept. 25, 2002	49–49	60
Marriage penalty tax	April 27, 2000	51–44	60	Homeland Security Department	Sept. 26, 2002	50–49	60
African trade agreement	May 11, 2000	76–18	60	Homeland security/worker union rights	Sept. 26, 2002	44–53	60
Estate tax repeal	July 11, 2000	99–1	60	Homeland security/worker union rights	Oct. 1, 2002	45–52	60
Treasury funds, fiscal 2001	July 26, 2000	97–0	60	Justice department reauthorization	Oct. 3, 2002	93–5	60
Intelligence authorization, fiscal 2001	July 26, 2000	96–1	60	Use of force against Iraq	Oct. 3, 2002	95–1	60
Energy, water funds, fiscal 2001	July 27, 2000	100–0	60	Use of force against Iraq	Oct. 10, 2002	75–25	60
Trade with China	July 27, 2000	86–12	60	Homeland security/worker union rights	Nov. 13, 2002	89–8	60
High technology visas	Sept. 19, 2000	97–1	60	Homeland Security Department	Nov. 15, 2002	65–29	60
High technology visas	Sept. 26, 2000	94–3	60	Homeland Security Department	Nov. 19, 2002	83–16	60
High technology visas	Sept. 28, 2000	92–3	60	Terrorism insurance	Nov. 19, 2002	85–12	60
Interior funds, fiscal 2001	Oct. 5, 2000	89–8	60	Estrada appeals court nomination	March 6, 2003	55–44	60
Bankruptcy law revision	Nov. 1, 2000	53–30	60	Estrada appeals court nomination	March 13, 2003	55–42	60
Bankruptcy law revision	Dec. 5, 2000	67–31	60	Estrada appeals court nomination	March 18, 2003	55–45	60
Bankruptcy law revision	March 14, 2001	80–19	60	Estrada appeals court nomination	April 2, 2003	55–44	60
ESEA reauthorization	May 1, 2001	96–3	60	Owen appeals court nomination	May 1, 2003	52–44	60
Bankruptcy law revision	July 12, 2001	88–10	60	Estrada appeals court nomination	May 5, 2003	52–39	60
Bankruptcy law revision	July 17, 2001	88–10	60	Estrada appeals court nomination	May 8, 2003	54–43	60
Mexican trucks access to U.S.	July 26, 2001	70–30	60	Owen appeals court nomination	May 8, 2003	52–45	60
Transportation funds/Mexican trucks in U.S.	July 27, 2001	57–27	60	Medical malpractice award caps	July 9, 2003	49–48	60
Supplemental farm funds	July 30, 2001	95–2	60	Owen appeals court nomination	July 29, 2003	53–43	60
Transportation/Mexican trucks in U.S.	Aug. 2, 2001	100–0	60	Estrada appeals court nomination	July 30, 2003	55–43	60
Supplemental farm funds	Aug. 3, 2001	49–48	60	Pryor appeals court nomination	July 31, 2003	53–44	60
Defense/energy funds authorization	Oct. 2, 2001	100–0	60	Class action lawsuits	Oct. 22, 2003	59–39	60
Federal airport security	Oct. 9, 2001	97–0	60	Pickering appeals court nomination	Oct. 30, 2003	54–43	60
Aviation workers assistance	Oct. 11, 2001	56–44	60	Pryor appeals court nomination	Nov. 6, 2003	51–43	60
Foreign operations funds	Oct. 15, 2001	50–46	60	Owen appeals court nomination	Nov. 14, 2003	53–42	60
Foreign operations funds	Oct. 23, 2001	50–47	60	Kuhl appeals court nomination	Nov. 14, 2003	53–43	60
Safety officers collective bargaining rights	Nov. 6, 2001	56–44	60	Brown appeals court nomination	Nov. 14, 2003	53–43	60
Pension contribution limits	Nov. 29, 2001	96–4	60	Dorr agriculture undersecretary nomination	Nov. 18, 2003	57–39	60
Energy policies/human cloning	Dec. 3, 2001	1–94	60	Dorr Commodity Credit Corp. nomination	Nov. 18, 2003	57–39	60
Railroad retirement pension board	Dec. 3, 2001	81–15	60	Energy policy bill conference report	Nov. 21, 2003	57–40	60
Farm policy revisions	Dec. 5, 2001	73–26	60	Medicare prescription drug bill	Nov. 24, 2003	70–29	60
Farm policy revisions	Dec. 13, 2001	53–45	60	Omnibus appropriations, fiscal 2004	Jan. 20, 2004	48–45	60
Farm policy revisions	Dec. 18, 2001	54–43	60	Omnibus appropriations, fiscal 2004	Jan. 22, 2004	61–32	60
Farm policy revisions	Dec. 19. 2001	54–43	60	Highway funding	Feb. 2, 2004	75–11	60
Tax bill/unemployment benefits	Feb. 6, 2002	56–39	60	Highway funding	Feb. 12, 2004	86–11	60
Business tax cut/unemployment benefits	Feb. 6, 2002	48–47	60	Medical malpractice lawsuit caps	Feb. 24, 2004	48–45	60
Election procedures requirements	March 1, 2002	49–39	60	Gun liability lawsuits	Feb. 25, 2004	75–22	60
Election procedures requirements	March 4, 2002	51–44	60	Corporate tax changes	March 24, 2004	51–47	60
Campaign finance revisions	March 20, 2002	68–32	60	Welfare reauthorization	April 1, 2004	51–47	60
Energy policy bill	April 10, 2002	48–50	60	Medical malpractice lawsuit caps	April 7, 2004	49–48	60
Energy bill/ANWR drilling	April 18, 2002	36–64	60	Corporate tax changes	April 7, 2004	50–47	60
Energy bill/ANWR drilling	April 18, 2002	46–54	60	Asbestos claims fund	April 22, 2004	50–47	60
Energy policy bill	April 23, 2002	86–13	60	Internet tax moratorium	April 26, 2004	74–11	60
Andean duty-free trade	April 29, 2002	69–21	60	Internet tax/ethanol	April 29, 2004	40–59	60
Andean trade/steelworkers health insurance	May 21, 2002	56–40	60	Internet tax/energy policy	April 29, 2004	55–43	60
Andean duty-free trade	May 22, 2002	68–29	60	Internet tax moratorium	April 29, 2004	64–34	60
Supplemental funds, fiscal 2002	June 6, 2002	87–10	60	Corporate tax changes	May 11, 2004	90–8	60
Hate crimes definitions	June 11, 2002	54–43	60	Class action lawsuits	July 8, 2004	44–43	60
Terrorism insurance	June 18, 2002	65–31	60	Same-sex marriage amendment	July 14, 2004	48–50	60
Defense authorization, fiscal 2003	June 26, 2002	98–0	60	Myers appeals court nomination	July 20, 2004	53–44	60
Accounting industry reform	July 12, 2002	91–2	60	Saad appeals court nomination	July 22, 2004	52–46	60
Smith appeals court nomination	July 15, 2002	94–3	60	Griffin appeals court nomination	Jul 22, 2004	54–44	60
Drug patents	July 17, 2002	99–0	60	McKeague appeals court nomination	July 22, 2004	53–44	60
Clifton appeals court nomination	July 18, 2002	97–1	60	Intelligence operations overhaul	Oct. 5, 2004	85–10	60
Carmona surgeon general nomination	July 23, 2002	98–0	60	Senate intelligence oversight	Oct. 8, 2004	88–3	60
Gibbons appeals court nomination	July 26, 2002	89–0	60	Corporate tax changes	Oct. 10, 2004	66–14	60
				Tariffs and trade bill	Nov. 19, 2004	88–5	60

1. Vote was taken after midnight in the session that began Oct. 8, 1985.

2. Because the bill would have changed Senate rules, two-thirds of those present and voting were required to invoke cloture: 66 in this case instead of the usual 60.

3. Because the bill would have changed Senate rules, two-thirds of those present and voting were required to invoke cloture: 65 in this case instead of the usual 60.

Attempted and Successful Cloture Votes, 1919–2005

Congress		Attempted cloture votes	Successful cloture votes	Congress		Attempted cloture votes	Successful cloture votes
66th	(1919–1921)	1	1	92nd	(1971–1973)	20	4
67th	(1921–1923)	1	0	93rd	(1973–1975)	31	9
68th	(1923–1925)	0	0	94th	(1975–1977)	27	17
69th	(1925–1927)	5	2	95th	(1977–1979)	13	3
70th	(1927–1929)	0	0	96th	(1979–1981)	21	10
71st	(1929–1931)	0	0	97th	(1981–1983)	27	9
72nd	(1931–1933)	1	0	98th	(1983–1985)	19	11
73rd	(1933–1935)	0	0	99th	(1985–1987)	23	10
74th	(1935–1937)	2	0	100th	(1987–1989)	43	11
75th	(1937–1939)	0	0	101st	(1989–1991)	24	11
76th	(1939–1941)	0	0	102nd	(1991–1993)	48	23
77th	(1941–1943)	1	0	103rd	(1993–1995)	42	13
78th	(1943–1945)	1	0	104th	(1995–1997)	50	9
79th	(1945–1947)	4	0	105th	(1997–1999)	53	18
80th	(1947–1949)	0	0	106th	(1999–2001)	58	28
81st	(1949–1951)	2	0	107th	(2001–2003)	61	33
82nd	(1951–1953)	0	0	108th	(2003–2005)	48	12
83rd	(1953–1955)	1	0	TOTALS		654	238
84th	(1955–1957)	0	0				
85th	(1957–1959)	0	0				
86th	(1959–1961)	1	0				
87th	(1961–1963)	4	1				
88th	(1963–1965)	3	1				
89th	(1965–1967)	7	1				
90th	(1967–1969)	6	1				
91st	(1969–1971)	6	0				

NOTE: The number of votes required to invoke cloture was changed March 7, 1975, from two-thirds of those present and voting, to three-fifths of the total Senate membership, as Rule xxii of the standing rules of the Senate was amended.

SOURCES: *Congress and the Nation*, selected volumes (Washington, D.C.: CQ Press, selected years); *CQ Almanac*, selected volumes (Washington, D.C.: Congressional Quarterly, selected years); Richard S. Beth, Congressional Research Service, Library of Congress.

House Discharge Petitions since 1931

The discharge petition is a little-used but dramatic House device that enables a majority of representatives to bring to the floor legislation blocked in committee. The following table shows the frequency with which the discharge petition has been used since the present discharge procedure was adopted in 1931 through 2004.

Although the procedure is rarely used and even more rarely successful, it may on occasion indirectly succeed by prompting a legislative committee, the Rules Committee, or the leadership to act on a measure and thereby avoid the discharge.

Congress		Discharge petitions filed	Discharge motion		Committee discharged	Underlying measure[3]	
			Entered[1]	Called up[2]		Passed House	Received final approval[4]
72nd	(1931–1933)	12	5	5	1	1	–
73rd	(1933–1935)	31	6	1	1	1	–
74th	(1935–1937)	33	3	2	2	–	–
75th	(1937–1939)	43	4	4	3[5]	2	1
76th	(1939–1941)	37[5]	2	2	2	2	–
77th	(1941–1943)	15	1	1	1	1	–
78th	(1943–1945)	21	3	3	3	3	1[6]
79th	(1945–1947)	35	3	1	1	1	–
80th	(1947–1949)	20	1	1	1	1	–
81st	(1949–1951)	34	3[7]	1	1	1	–
82nd	(1951–1953)	14	–	–	–	–	–
83rd	(1953–1955)	10	1	1	1	1	–
84th	(1955–1957)	6	–	–	–	–	–
85th	(1957–1959)	7	1	1	1	1	–
86th	(1959–1961)	7	1	1	1	1	1
87th	(1961–1963)	6	–	–	–	–	–
88th	(1963–1965)	5	–	–	–	–	–
89th	(1965–1967)	6	1	1	1	1	–
90th	(1967–1969)	4	–	–	–	–	–
91st	(1969–1971)	12	1	1	1	1	–
92nd	(1971–1973)	15	1	1	1	–	–
93rd	(1973–1975)	10	–	–	–	–	–
94th	(1975–1977)	15	–	–	–	–	–
95th	(1977–1979)	11	–	–	–	–	–
96th	(1979–1981)	14	2	1	1	–	–
97th	(1981–1983)	24	1	–	–	–	–
98th	(1983–1985)	13	1	–	–	–	–
99th	(1985–1987)	10	1	–	–	–	–
100th	(1987–1989)	5[8]	–	–	–	–	–
101st	(1989–1991)	8	1	–	–	–	–
102nd	(1991–1993)	8	1[9]	1[9]	1[9]	–	–
103rd	(1993–1995)	26	2[9]	2[9]	2[9]	1	1[6]
104th	(1995–1997)	15	–	–	–	–	–
105th	(1997–1999)	8	–	–	–	–	–
106th	(1999–2001)	11	–	–	–	–	–
107th	(2001–2003)	12	1	–	–	–	–
108th	(2003–2005)	16	–	–	–	–	–
	TOTALS	579	47	31	26	19	4

NOTE: As of end of 2005.

1. A discharge motion is "entered" when the petition receives sufficient signatures for it to be entered on the Calendar of Motions to Discharge Committees. This number was 145 in the 72nd and 73rd Congresses, 219 in the 86th and 87th Congresses, and 218 for all other Congresses in the table.

2. A discharge motion may be offered on the floor on any second or fourth Monday falling at least seven legislative days after the discharge petition is entered. Each day on which the House convenes is usually a legislative day.

3. A discharge petition may be filed to bring to the floor either a substantive measure in committee or a "special rule" from the Committee on Rules providing for House consideration of such a measure that is either in committee or previously reported. The last two columns of this table reflect action on the underlying, substantive measure, not on the special rule, if any, on which discharge was directly sought.

4. Includes bills and joint resolutions becoming law; constitutional amendments submitted to the states for ratification; resolutions agreed to by the House; and concurrent resolutions finally agreed to by both chambers.

5. During this Congress, the Rules Committee was discharged from a special rule for consideration of one measure, and the measure was taken up but then recommitted. Subsequently, the Rules Committee was discharged from a second special rule for consideration of the measure. This measure accordingly appears twice under "Committee discharged" and earlier columns, but only once under "Passed House" and subsequently.

6. Resolution attempting to change House Rules.

7. Includes one petition entered with respect to a special rule on a measure and another on the same measure directly.

8. Includes one petition filed on a special rule for considering two measures.

9. Includes one measure in the 102nd Congress and two in the 103rd from which the committee was discharged, and which were brought to the floor, by unanimous consent after the discharge petition was entered.

SOURCE: Richard S. Beth, "The Discharge Rule in the House: Recent Use in Historical Context," Congressional Research Service (CRS), Library of Congress, Sept. 15, 1997; update provided by CRS, Sept. 1999, April 2000, Dec. 2005.

Congressional Apportionment, 1789–2004

	Constitution (1789)[2]	1790	1800	1810	1820	1830	1840	1850	1860	1870	1880	1890	1900	1910	1930[3]	1940	1950	1960	1970	1980	1990	2000
		Year of census[1]																				
Alabama				1[4]	3	5	7	7	6	8	8	9	9	10	9	9	9	8	7	7	7	7
Alaska																	1[4]	1	1	1	1	1
Arizona														1[4]	1	2	2	3	4	5	6	8
Arkansas						1[4]	1	2	3	4	5	6	7	7	7	7	6	4	4	4	4	4
California							2[4]	2	3	4	6	7	8	11	20	23	30	38	43	45	52	53
Colorado										1[4]	1	2	3	4	4	4	4	4	5	6	6	7
Conn.	5	7	7	7	6	6	4	4	4	4	4	4	5	5	6	6	6	6	6	6	6	5
Delaware	1	1	1	2	1	1	1	1	1	1	1	1	1	1	1	1	1	1	1	1	1	1
Florida							1[4]	1	1	2	2	2	3	4	5	6	8	12	15	19	23	25
Georgia	3	2	4	6	7	9	8	8	7	9	10	11	11	12	10	10	10	10	10	10	11	13
Hawaii																	1[4]	2	2	2	2	2
Idaho											1[4]	1	1	2	2	2	2	2	2	2	2	2
Illinois				1[4]	1	3	7	9	14	19	20	22	25	27	27	26	25	24	24	22	20	19
Indiana				1[4]	3	7	10	11	11	13	13	13	13	13	12	11	11	11	11	10	10	9
Iowa							2[4]	2	6	9	11	11	11	11	9	8	8	7	6	6	5	5
Kansas									1	3	7	8	8	8	7	6	6	5	5	5	4	4
Kentucky		2	6	10	12	13	10	10	9	10	11	11	11	11	9	9	8	7	7	7	6	6
Louisiana				1[4]	3	3	4	4	5	6	6	6	7	8	8	8	8	8	8	8	7	7
Maine				7[4]	7	8	7	6	5	5	4	4	4	4	3	3	3	2	2	2	2	2
Maryland	6	8	9	9	9	8	6	6	5	6	6	6	6	6	6	6	7	8	8	8	8	8
Massachusetts	8	14	17	13[5]	13	12	10	11	10	11	12	13	14	16	15	14	14	12	12	11	10	10
Michigan							1[4]	3	4	6	9	11	12	13	17	17	18	19	19	18	16	15
Minnesota								2[4]	2	3	5	7	9	10	9	9	9	8	8	8	8	8
Mississippi				1[4]	1	2	4	5	5	6	7	7	8	8	7	7	6	5	5	5	5	4
Missouri					1	2	5	7	9	13	14	15	16	16	13	13	11	10	10	9	9	9
Montana											1[4]	1	1	2	2	2	2	2	2	2	1	1
Nebraska									1[4]	1	3	6	6	6	5	4	4	3	3	3	3	3
Nevada									1[4]	1	1	1	1	1	1	1	1	1	1	2	2	3
New Hampshire	3	4	5	6	6	5	4	3	3	3	2	2	2	2	2	2	2	2	2	2	2	2
New Jersey	4	5	6	6	6	6	5	5	5	7	7	8	10	12	14	14	14	15	15	14	13	13
New Mexico														1[4]	1	2	2	2	2	3	3	3
New York	6	10	17	27	34	40	34	33	31	33	34	34	37	43	45	45	43	41	39	34	31	29
North Carolina	5	10	12	13	13	13	9	8	7	8	9	9	10	10	11	12	12	11	11	11	12	13
North Dakota											1[4]	1	2	3	2	2	2	2	1	1	1	1
Ohio			1[4]	6	14	19	21	21	19	20	21	21	21	22	24	23	23	24	23	21	19	18
Oklahoma													5[4]	8	9	8	6	6	6	6	6	5
Oregon				-				1[4]	1	1	1	2	2	3	3	4	4	4	4	5	5	5
Pennsylvania	8	13	18	23	26	28	24	25	24	27	28	30	32	36	34	33	30	27	25	23	21	19
Rhode Island	1	2	2	2	2	2	2	2	2	2	2	2	2	3	2	2	2	2	2	2	2	2
South Carolina	5	6	8	9	9	9	7	6	4	5	7	7	7	7	6	6	6	6	6	6	6	6
South Dakota											2[4]	2	2	3	2	2	2	2	2	1	1	1
Tennessee		1[4]	3	6	9	13	11	10	8	10	10	10	10	10	9	10	9	9	8	9	9	9
Texas							2[4]	2	4	6	11	13	16	18	21	21	22	23	24	27	30	32
Utah												1[4]	1	2	2	2	2	2	2	3	3	3
Vermont		2	4	6	5	5	4	3	3	3	2	2	2	2	1	1	1	1	1	1	1	1
Virginia	10	19	22	23	22	21	15	13	11	9	10	10	10	10	9	9	10	10	10	10	11	11
Washington											1[4]	2	3	5	6	6	7	7	7	8	9	9
West Virginia										3	4	4	5	6	6	6	6	5	4	4	3	3
Wisconsin							2[4]	3	6	8	9	10	11	11	10	10	10	10	9	9	9	8
Wyoming											1[4]	1	1	1	1	1	1	1	1	1	1	1
TOTAL	65	106	142	186	213	242	232	237	243	293	332	357	391	435	435	435	437[6]	435	435	435	435	435

1. Apportionment effective with congressional election two years after census.
2. Original apportionment made in Constitution, pending first census.
3. No apportionment was made in 1920.
4. These figures are not based on any census, but indicate the provisional representation accorded newly admitted states by Congress, pending the next census.
5. Twenty members were assigned to Massachusetts, but seven of these were credited to Maine when that area became a state.
6. Normally 435, but temporarily increased two seats by Congress when Alaska and Hawaii became states.

SOURCES: *Biographical Directory of the American Congress* and Bureau of the Census.

The Presidency

President George W. Bush, the first Republican to occupy the White House in eight years, selected a cabinet that remained largely intact throughout his first term, with only one major departure. After winning reelection in 2004, however, a number of the cabinet heads left as the White House reorganized for a second term.

Bush's nominations in 2001 included well-known individuals with experience in Washington or in high positions in state capitals. Nevertheless, a number of the appointments were controversial, although all but one were confirmed by the Senate, generally by comfortable margins.

But events—primarily the Sept. 11, 2001, terrorist attacks and the later invasion of Iraq—focused most of the public attention throughout the period on two departments: state and defense. For defense Bush chose Donald H. Rumsfeld, who had held the post under President Gerald R. Ford in the 1970s and had other extensive Washington experience. For state Bush named Colin L. Powell, the highly respected military general and one-time head of the joint chiefs. These two top officials became rallying points for opposing sides in the controversial decision to invade Iraq and topple the regime of Saddam Hussein who was believed to hold weapons of mass destruction. Rumsfeld, and a collection of high defense officials often associated with neoconservative thinking in the United States, were strong advocates of the war and of a robust American military presence in the world, and dismissive of nations that opposed use of force in Iraq. Powell was seen as representing and advocating a more multilateral approach, including involvement of the United Nations. He was though to harbor reservations about the war, although in public he forcefully supported the administration's actions.

Rumsfeld was controversial for other reasons, as well. One was his efforts to recast the entire military in a different way than it had existed for decades, with much larger reliance on smaller and more mobile forces and use of high technology to maintain a military advantage. These changes were unpopular with many military veterans, although top echelon members of the uniformed services supported them, at least in public. But Rumsfeld had the opportunity, in Iraq, to try out his theories by using a smaller force to conduct the war. While successful in toppling Saddam, the relatively small numbers of soldiers was later seen as an obstacle to fully pacifying the country. The debate had not been settled at the end of Bush's term, but Rumsfeld stayed on in the second term while Powell left the administration.

The most controversial appointment was that of former senator John Ashcroft as attorney general. He had served one term from Missouri and was one of the most conservative members of the Senate. He had taken conservative positions on abortion and civil rights, and was a leader in blocking judicial nominations by President Bill Clinton. He also was opposed by civil libertarians who were concerned after the 2001 terrorist attacks about his promotion of new legislation to greatly increase the government's powers to combat terrorism. Ashcroft resigned at the end of the term but was replaced by an equally controversial individual, Alberto Gonzales, who was identified by opponents as being an architect of what they considered oppressive tactics in dealing with individuals thought to be involved with terrorism.

The single major—and the most embarrassing—casualty for the Bush administration was Paul O'Neill, who was named Treasury secretary. He resigned, at the request of the White House, at the end of 2002, after repeated clashes with Bush officials over economic policies. A principal sore point was his penchant to publicly express his doubts about the economic wisdom of a number of major administration policies, especially large tax cuts.

Other controversial nominations included Gale A. Norton as interior secretary and Elaine L. Chao at labor. Environmentalists said Norton's record in the states showed she would push business interests over environmental concerns. Organized labor was critical of Chao but mainly used her as a foil to criticize Republican policies on such issues as the minimum wage, workplace safety, and job security. Both, however, stayed on for Bush's second term. Bush's first choice for labor secretary, Linda Chavez, was the only one officially nominated who never made it to congressional hearings. She withdrew from consideration a few days after her nomination when it became known that she did not pay taxes for domestic help.

Outside the immediate cabinet, the most controversial official may have been George Tenet, who headed the Central Intelligence Agency. Tenet was a holdover from the Clinton administration and was well respected for serving presidents of both parties. However, the devastating attacks on Sept. 11, 2001, which the intelligence community missed, and the incorrect intelligence reports that Saddam Hussein possessed weapons of mass destruction, were believed to play a key factor in his resignation in June 2004. This came just weeks before the anticipated release of a Senate Select Intelligence Committee report on prewar intelligence on Iraq's weapons of mass destruction, the principal argument for the preemptive war. The report was expected to castigate the CIA for out-dated information, sloppy analysis, and unreliable sources.

Cabinet 2001–2005

AGRICULTURE

Ann M. Veneman, a California lawyer, was President George W. Bush's choice as his first secretary of agriculture. She was confirmed by the Senate Jan. 20, 2001, by voice vote, and remained in office through most of Bush's first term. Following Bush's reelection she announced on Nov. 12, 2004, that she would leave her position; she officially left on Jan. 20, 2005.

Veneman, the first woman to head the agriculture department, had served as deputy secretary in the agency from 1991 to 1993 and as secretary of the California Department of Food and Agriculture from 1995 to 1999. In a cordial Senate confirmation hearing on her nomination she pledged to help farmers and ranchers through difficult times, to end trade barriers to U.S. farm products, and work on new marketing opportunities for farmers. But she came into office amidst declining farm income and a new farm law that sought to push American agriculture toward market-based decisions and away from government subsidies. Her background in California, where agriculture was less dominated by subsidies than in the Midwest, was an additional burden on her acceptance as the chief representative for farmers and ranchers in all regions. Her tenure was buffeted by a scare over mad cow disease, a series of natural disasters including drought and excessive rainfall, and enactment of a major farm bill that reversed the recent law on market-based decisions.

BUSH ADMINISTRATION CABINET

Following is a list of cabinet officers who served in the administration of President George W. Bush during his four years in office between Jan. 20, 2001, and Jan. 20, 2005. A few listings include individuals sworn in after Bush's inauguration for his second term. The list does not include acting secretaries. It includes two positions that Bush elevated to cabinet status: the U.S. trade representative and director of the Office of Management and Budget.

Dates given are for actual service in office, beginning with the cabinet officers' swearing-in date, which may vary from date of confirmation by the Senate.

	Dates of Service
Secretary of State	
Colin L. Powell	Jan. 20, 2001–Jan. 26, 2005
Condoleezza Rice	Jan. 26, 2005–
Secretary of the Treasury	
Paul H. O'Neill	Jan. 20, 2001–Dec. 31, 2002
John W. Snow	Feb. 3, 2003–
Secretary of Defense	
Donald H. Rumsfeld	Jan. 20, 2001–
Attorney General	
John Ashcroft	Feb. 1, 2001–Feb. 3, 2005
Alberto R. Gonzales	Feb. 3, 2005–
Secretary of the Interior	
Gale A. Norton	Jan. 31, 2001–
Secretary of Agriculture	
Ann M. Veneman	Jan. 20, 2001–Jan. 20, 2005
Mike Johannas	Jan. 21, 2005–
Secretary of Commerce	
Donald L. Evans	Jan. 20, 2001–Feb. 7, 2005
Carlos M. Gutierrez	Feb. 7, 2005–
Secretary of Labor	
Elaine L. Chao	Jan. 31, 2001–
Secretary of Health and Human Services	
Tommy G. Thompson	Feb. 2, 2001–Jan. 26, 2005
Michael O. Leavitt	Jan. 26, 2005–

	Dates of Service
Secretary of Education	
Rod Paige	Jan. 24, 2001–Jan. 20, 2005
Margaret Spellings	Jan. 20, 2005–
Secretary of Housing and Urban Development	
Mel Martinez	Jan. 24, 2001–Dec. 9, 2003
Alphonso R. Jackson	April 1, 2004–
Secretary of Transportation	
Norman Y. Mineta	Jan. 25, 2001–
Secretary of Energy	
Spencer Abraham	Jan. 20, 2001–Feb. 1, 2005
Samuel W. Bodman	Feb. 1, 2005–
Secretary of Veterans Affairs	
Anthony J. Principi	Jan. 24, 2001–Jan. 24, 2005
Jim Nicholson	Jan. 26, 2005–
Secretary of Homeland Security	
Thomas J. Ridge	Jan. 24, 2003–Feb. 1, 2005
Michael Chertoff	March 3, 2005–
U.S. Trade Representative	
Robert B. Zoellick	Feb. 7, 2001–Feb. 22, 2005
Director of Office of Management and Budget	
Mitch Daniels	Jan. 23, 2001–June 6, 2003
Joshua Bolton	June 26, 2003–

"She probably had more challenges than any secretary of Agriculture in recent memory," said Bob Stallman, president of the American Farm Bureau Federation. When she resigned, some farm lobbyists said Veneman failed to connect with farmers in the Midwest and South, at least partly because her California background made her less familiar with their concerns. She also backed the president on some decisions that were unpopular with many small farmers. The administration sometimes opposed efforts by lawmakers to provide additional disaster assistance for drought-stricken farmers.

Veneman did not advocate mandatory country-of-origin labeling for meats and other foods, putting her at odds with the view of ranchers in the Upper Midwest who worried about competition from Canada. A leading critic of the Bush administration's farm policies said he "naturally disagreed" with Veneman on many issues but blamed the White House for the differences. "Most of those disagreements were over unnecessary obstacles to carrying out the farm bill thrown up by the White House and its Office of Management and Budget," said Sen. Tom Harkin, D-Iowa, who was chairman of the Agriculture Committee during the 2002 farm bill negotiations.

One lobbyist on agriculture issues, noting that Veneman failed to play an aggressive role in developing the 2002 farm law (PL 107-171), said there was a public perception that no one was standing up for farmers. Other agriculture lobbyists defended Veneman, saying she presided over many difficult issues, including the discovery of mad cow disease in a Washington state Holstein in December 2003 and the threat of foot and mouth disease from overseas. She also oversaw a quick implementation of the 2002 farm law, signed after the crop year had already started, and difficult international trade negotiations.

As her replacement, Bush chose Nebraska governor Mike Johanns, who was confirmed by the Senate in early 2005 and sworn in on Jan. 21. Johanns, 54, was first elected governor in 1998. He grew up on an Iowa dairy farm, an experience he said that made everything else in life seem easy. He took the agriculture department leadership at a time when the nation's farm programs faced scrutiny from Congress and the international community. A major challenge was expected in negotiations with Congress on the next farm law. The existing version (PL 107-171), signed in 2002, was scheduled to expire in 2007. The international community also viewed many U.S. farm programs with skepticism. The World Trade Organization (WTO), in response to a complaint from Brazil, had ruled that U.S. cotton subsidies distorted global prices, although the government was appealing the action as Johanns took office. The United States also struggled as some countries banned imports of U.S. beef after mad cow disease was discovered in Washington state.

Johanns also had aggressively campaigned for drought relief for Midwestern farmers to relieve economic damage from a severe lack of rainfall. Farm-state members of Congress battled with the administration during Veneman's term over emergency relief funding. National Farmers Union president Dave Frederickson praised the selection of Johanns, saying he was "encouraged that he has had leadership experience in a state with so much of its economy dependent on agriculture." As governor, Johanns also supported increased rural development and ethanol production in Nebraska.

ATTORNEY GENERAL

Of President Bush's many nominations during his first term, the most controversial unquestionably was for the post of attorney general. John Ashcroft's conservative stands on issues such as abortion and civil rights, and the role he played in thwarting President Bill Clinton's judicial nominations, made him a lightening rod for criticism from congressional Democrats, as well as from pro-choice and civil liberties organizations. Moreover, his nomination for the post in his second term, Alberto Gonzales, who was serving as White House counsel, proved exceptionally controversial also.

Nevertheless, after five weeks of impassioned and polarizing debate, the Senate on Feb. 1, 2001, confirmed Ashcroft to be attorney general. The 58–42 vote broke largely along party lines, with eight Democrats joining all fifty Republicans to support the nominee. The Judiciary Committee had confirmed him on a 10–8 vote on Jan. 30 with just one Democrat—Russell D. Feingold of Wisconsin—joining all nine Republicans in support.

Ashcroft was a one-term senator (1995–2001) from Missouri who lost his reelection bid by a narrow margin in 2000. He was just a few weeks out of a job when Bush tapped him as attorney general to head the Justice Department. A staunch conservative and deeply religious man, Ashcroft during a successful political career in Missouri, including attorney general and two terms as governor, continually worked to tug Republicans to the right with unyielding insistence on tax cuts and a steady support of Christian fundamentalist positions. Legislative efforts to shrink government and rely on church-based organizations to solve welfare-related problems were mixed successes.

In the Senate, Ashcroft had been among the most conservative members of the chamber before losing his reelection bid in 2000, and his conservative ideology drew much criticism from liberal groups. Ashcroft had sponsored legislation that would outlaw all abortions except to save the life of the woman, and opposed adding new restrictions to purchases of firearms at gun shows. He also advocated ex-

panding the federal definition of hate crimes to cover acts motivated by the victim's sexual identity. Critics questioned whether he would actively enforce laws he had opposed, such as those intended to protect abortion clinics from violence.

"In the case of Senator Ashcroft, his thirty-year record of intense opposition on so many critical issues involving civil rights, women's rights, gun control, and nominations speak volumes and demonstrate—clearly and convincingly—that he is the wrong person to be attorney general of the United States," said Sen. Edward M. Kennedy, D-Mass.

Opponents also said Ashcroft's 1998 interview with a neo-Confederate magazine and a 1999 appearance at Bob Jones University showed an insensitivity to racial issues that would handicap an attorney general. While outside groups concentrated their criticism on Ashcroft's conservative positions, many Senate Democrats were most angered over his aggressive tactics in opposing President Bill Clinton's nominations, particularly that of Ronnie L. White to be a federal judge in Missouri. Ashcroft, however, repeatedly pledged to uphold the nation's laws. Conservative groups mobilized to support the nomination, and Republican senators angrily defended him, saying his record was being distorted.

"A sophisticated group came together and created a caricature of who John is," said Jeff Sessions, R-Ala. "Now they want us to vote against" that caricature. In the end, Ashcroft won with fewer votes than any successful cabinet nominee in decades. His was the most contested nomination for attorney general since the battle over Edwin Meese III in 1984–1985.

Ashcroft announced his resignation after Bush won reelection in 2004. The nomination of his successor, White House Counsel Alberto Gonzales, on Nov. 10, 2004, sparked almost as much controversy as the Ashcroft nomination. Many Democrats objected to the role Gonzales played in crafting Bush administration policies on the treatment of prisoners. The Senate confirmed him on Feb. 3, 2005, by a vote of 60–36. He took office on Feb. 3, 2005.

COMMERCE

President Bush nominated Donald L. Evans, of Texas, to head the Department of Commerce. Evans won broad praise at his confirmation hearings with senators of both parties commending his background in business and as chair of the governing board of the University of Texas college system.

Evans was chair and chief executive officer of Tom Brown Inc., a large firm in the oil and gas business, where he had worked since 1975 as a "roughneck" on oil rigs and later in the executive suites. Perhaps more pertinent to his appointment was a long association with Bush. Earlier he raised funds for Bush's Texas gubernatorial campaigns and then raised about $100 million for his presidential race.

Fundraising was not at issue in his hearings, however. Trade was, with Democrats focusing on their continuing criticism of trade practices they claimed were costing American jobs. Evans acknowledged he was an advocate of free trade but added that it "must never be a one-way street."

He also said he would continue a policy of Bush's predecessor, Bill Clinton, to have agency employees, not political appointees, arrange trade trips to ensure that they are not linked to fundraising. He endorsed continued research into global climate change, from which the Bush administration later was to disassociate itself, and efforts to nurture the growth of high-tech industry.

Evans, who was confirmed by the Senate without dissent, stayed on through most of Bush's first term but submitted his resignation on Nov. 9, 2005, immediately following the election, as part of a wider cabinet shakeup for Bush's second four years. He was succeeded by Carlos M. Gutierrez, the Cuban-born head of Kellogg cereal company, who took office on Feb. 7, 2005.

DEFENSE

Donald H. Rumsfeld, a veteran Washington participant in Congress and administrations for more than forty years, was President Bush's choice as secretary of defense. He was confirmed in that post by the Senate just hours after Bush's inauguration on Jan. 20, 2001. It was not a first for Rumsfeld, who had headed the Pentagon in 1975–1977 during the administration of President Gerald R. Ford (1974–1977).

However, over the course of Bush's first term Rumsfeld became—along with Attorney General John Ashcroft—one of the most controversial cabinet members in recent years. Still, Bush defended him throughout the period and retained him as defense secretary after the president's reelection in 2004.

Rumsfeld had won widespread praise for his managerial experience, familiarity with key defense issues, and personal stature. In addition to his previous tour at the Pentagon, his credentials included service as a member of the House (1963–1969), NATO ambassador under President Richard Nixon (1969–1974), White House chief of staff for President Ford, and chair of a congressionally mandated bipartisan commission on missile defense in 1998. Rumsfeld also had been the chief executive officer of two corporations.

Rumsfeld's confirmation hearings focused on the missile defense issue because of his background in the subject and Bush's support for deployment of such a system. The nominee stressed the importance of protecting the United States and its allies from at least a small number of missiles. He told the committee that the new administration would try to secure Russia's agreement for deploying a missile defense, which would require changes in the 1972 Anti-Ballistic Missile (ABM) Treaty, but he made it clear that he considered the treaty to be "ancient history."

Although missile defense continued to be a concern during Bush's term, it was soon overshadowed by defense challenges that first arose from the Sept. 11, 2001, terrorists attacks in New York City and outside Washington, D.C., and then more directly from the invasion of Iraq in 2003. The Iraq war was launched to topple the regime of Saddam Hussein who was believed, according to Bush, to harbor weapons of mass destruction. The invasion was an immediate success, with military forces capturing Baghdad in sixteen days, but the aftermath was not. No weapons of mass destruction were found, and the initial success gave way to a continuing insurgency that U.S. forces still were battling, with mixed success, in 2005.

Blame for this unexpected turnaround was laid at Rumsfeld's office doorstep, and was compounded by later revelations of mistreatment of prisoners in Iraq. Along with the difficulty of securing Iraq—and critics said a part of that problem—was Rumsfeld's determination to remake the U.S. military, and the army in particular, into forces that he claimed were needed in the twenty-first century. He argued that military needs had to be focused on countering terrorism and smaller military actions than the massive armed conflicts of past wars.

This envisioned smaller and lighter units able to maneuver more quickly, more infantry and special-operations forces, and significantly increased reliance on technology and less on traditional massive, heavily armored military forces of past wars. Rumsfeld in fact canceled several high-profile weapons systems that were dear to the hearts of many military officers, most conceived at least a decade earlier. Rumsfeld and his allies also opposed any permanent increase in the size of the army, which was advocated by many military officers—both active and retired.

The frustrations of the Iraq occupation and Rumsfeld's far-reaching proposals for change—the most sweeping, one military expert said, since the 1930s—made the secretary controversial both within the military and among the civilians who were increasingly critical of the Iraqi invasion from the beginning.

EDUCATION

President Bush selected Rod Paige as secretary of education. He was confirmed by voice vote of the Senate and served throughout Bush's first term but announced his resignation on Nov. 15, 2004, following Bush's reelection. News reports indicated Paige wanted to stay on but was not asked to do so by the administration. He left office on Jan. 20, 2005, and was immediately succeeded by Margaret Spellings, a close ally of Bush. She had been Bush's education adviser when he was governor of Texas and was the top domestic policy adviser in the Bush White House.

Paige, who ran Houston's school system at the time of his selection, was the first person to jump directly from a superintendent position to the helm of the Department of Education. He was lauded by conservative groups and teachers' unions alike as an innovative thinker with important, ground-level experience in improving public education.

As superintendent he allowed Houston students to transfer from underperforming public schools to private schools at the state's expense. Although some observers saw this as a form of vouchers, a highly contentious issue in education, local teachers' union officials said the Houston program fell short of an all-out voucher program. Participating private schools had to accept a fixed amount of state money and follow the state's accountability rules, they said, and religious schools were not eligible.

In a Nov. 8, 2000, column in *Education Week,* Paige described his Houston policies as "a holistic approach to school improvement." He was credited with tying principals' jobs to improvements in student performance and contracting most nonacademic services out to private companies. He also helped Houston establish twenty charter schools, which received a waiver from most state and local regulations in exchange for better student performance.

Paige's background fit well with Bush's commitment to education legislation, which he had pledged as a candidate for the White House. The focus of his proposal was on accountability. He called for states to design and administer annual tests to measure student performance as a condition for receiving federal education money. Schools that repeatedly fell short of state-set standards would be subject to sanctions, such as being forced to divert a share of their federal funds to vouchers to pay for private schooling or tutoring for needy children.

This was reflected in the No Child Left Behind Act, a reauthorization of the Elementary and Secondary Education Act, in 2002. The controversial law imposed far-reaching and strict requirements on states for student performance. Critics said the law was an inappropriate federal intrusion into education policy that had traditionally been a state and local matter. By the time Paige left office, the assessment of the law remained mixed.

On occasion, controversy followed Paige over statements and actions as secretary. One of the most notable was his comment on Feb. 23, 2004, when meeting at the White House with the nation's governors, that the National Education Association was "a terrorist organization" for criticizing and, he argued, obstructing the No Child Left Behind Act. Later that day he apologized and said the comment "was an inappropriate choice of words." But he contended that the teachers' organization used "obstructionist scare tactics" against the legislation.

In January 2005 he defended his department's payment of $250,000 to a conservative black television commentator to plug the No Child Left Behind Act. Paige said the controversy about the payments was "certainly not the legacy I wish to leave behind."

ENERGY

Spencer Abraham was one of two former senators—along with Attorney General John Ashcroft—that President Bush selected to be in his cabinet during his first term. Abraham, like Ashcroft, was a one-term Republican senator who had lost his reelection in Michigan bid in 2000. He was confirmed by voice vote Jan. 20, 2001, and served until Feb. 1, 2005. On Nov. 15, 2004, following Bush's reelection, Abraham announced that he would resign his position, one of a number of cabinet members who left in the transition between Bush's terms.

Abraham, a lawyer whose grandparents were Lebanese immigrants, had been deputy chief of staff to Vice President Dan Quayle from 1990 into 1991. Earlier he was chair of the Michigan Republican party (1983–1990). From 1991 to 1993 he served as co-chair of the National Republican Congressional Committee.

Abraham's familiarity with the Senate and with Republican politics worked in his favor. His lack of experience on energy matters was a significant weakness, in the opinion of some observers, when he was named to head the energy department. He had not served on any committees that dealt with energy issues. He was also criticized for sponsoring legislation as a senator to abolish the department. In confirmation hearings Abraham told senators that the changing U.S. energy situation and improvement in the department's management structure led him to change his mind about abolishing it.

Abraham said he would seek an energy policy "that includes increasing domestic production of energy in an environmentally responsible manner, increasing our use of renewable energy, decreasing our reliance on imported oil and developing new technologies that conserve fossil fuels and reduce energy-related pollution."

His nomination came at a difficult time with the price of oil and natural gas moving upward rapidly and California in the midst of a crisis over electricity availability and cost. His term also coincided with the administration's inability to get major energy legislation through Congress, which had been one of President Bush's top agenda goals. In addition, related administration proposals—especially involving air pollution regulations and global warming—were so controversial that they diminished the department's overall record even though other agencies were involved in these policies.

After Abraham announced that he would resign the position, Bush on Dec. 10, 2004, said he would nominate Samuel W. Bodman who was serving at the time as deputy Treasury secretary. From 2001 to 2004 he was deputy commerce secretary.

Bodman, like Abraham, came to the energy job with little background in the subject. Trained as a chemical engineer, a subject he taught as a college professor for a period, he spent much of his career before Washington in the corporate business world. His lack of energy experience prompted most observers to believe he would carefully promote the administration's positions on energy development that characterized Bush's first term. He was confirmed by voice vote of the Senate on Jan. 31, 2005. He came into office as enlarged Republican majorities in the 109th Congress greatly improved prospects for enactment of Bush's energy package. By late summer, the legislation— similar but not identical to bills Congress considered during Abraham's tenure—had become law.

HEALTH AND HUMAN SERVICES

The vast Department of Health and Human Services was headed by two popular governors brought to Washington by President Bush. He nominated, and the Senate easily confirmed, Tommy Thompson as his first HHS secretary. Thompson, who became the department's nineteenth secretary, had won four terms as Wisconsin's governor. When Thompson resigned the position after the 2004 elections, Bush turned to Mike Leavitt, who had been elected Utah's governor three times but at the time of his HHS appointment was serving as administrator of the U.S. Environmental Protection Agency, a position he took on in 2003. The Senate approved him for his new post on Jan. 26, 2005.

Thompson had won recognition as a welfare reformer, initiating programs in his state that served as a model for sweeping federal legislation that became law in 1996. He came to Washington primarily to oversee reauthorization of that law, although that did not happen during his four-year tenure. Instead, Thompson helped transform the agency after the Sept. 11 terrorist attacks, creating a state-of-the-art command post outside his office and successfully pushing through Congress a series of bills to better prepare the nation for any future attack. Thompson also became active in international health issues, including becoming chairman of the board of the Global Fund to fight AIDS, tuberculosis, and malaria.

HOMELAND SECURITY

Homeland security was not a topic on the minds of most Americans much less an official federal agency when George W. Bush took office in January 2001. That changed dramatically on Sept. 11 of that year when terrorists flew airplanes into the Twin Trade Towers in New York and the Pentagon outside Washington, D.C. Those attacks led a year later to the new department, which brought together dozens of existing agencies from other areas of the government in an effort to centralize the federal efforts in the fight against terrorist activity.

Two persons were named to the position by Bush. The first was Tom Ridge, who was confirmed by a 94–0 vote of the Senate on Jan. 22, 2003. The second was Michael Chertoff, a federal judge born Nov. 28, 1953, who took over on March 3, 2005, after Ridge stepped down on Feb. 1. He had announced his plan to leave the position late in 2004. Ridge, a Vietnam veteran who had been Bush's director of homeland security, was sworn in Jan. 24, 2003, for what Sen. Arlen Specter, R-Pa., called "the toughest job in Washington today."

Members of the Senate Governmental Affairs Committee widely praised the former Pennsylvania governor and seven-term House member during a confirmation hearing in January. But it was clear that as Ridge's relationship evolved with the Senate committee that had primary oversight of the Department of Homeland Security, he would have to answer regularly for everything from bioterrorism preparedness to Coast Guard readiness to labor relations.

After Bush's reelection Ridge announced he would leave the department. Bush at first turned to former New York police commissioner Bernard Kerik, who had won national praise as head of the New York City Police Department in the aftermath of the Sept. 11 terrorist attacks. But in a stinging embarrassment to the administration, Kerik withdrew his name from consideration one week later. He said he had discovered that a former housekeeper and nanny had a questionable immigration status. He also faced questions over possible conflicts of interest and past business dealings.

Bush then nominated Chertoff, who at the time was a judge on the Court of Appeals for the Third Circuit. Bush had named him to the position in March 2003. He also was a former federal prosecutor and served as a counsel to a Senate committee that was looking into allegations against President Bill Clinton and First Lady Hillary Clinton concerning land sales in Arkansas, a probe that went by the name of "Whitewater." In 2000 Chertoff was a special counsel to a New Jersey state senate judiciary committee that was investigating racial profiling in that state. After graduating from Harvard law school in 1978 he became a clerk to Supreme Court justice William J. Brennan Jr. from 1979 to 1980. He also was in private law practices in the 1980s and 1990s. He headed the criminal division of the U.S. Department of Justice from 2001 to 2003. In that role he became deeply involved in developing the administration's legal approach in combating terrorists, including detainment of persons of Middle Eastern origin. Civil libertarians also raised concerns about his roles in the writing of the 2001 antiterrorism law known as the PATRIOT Act. His appointment as homeland secretary was approved by the Senate on a 97–0 vote on Feb. 15, 2005. He was sworn in the same day.

HOUSING AND URBAN DEVELOPMENT

President Bush named Mel Martinez of Florida as his first secretary of housing and urban development. He was confirmed by the Senate on a 100–0 vote and served until Dec. 9, 2003, when he left to run for the Senate from Florida. He was elected in an exceptionally close race the following fall.

Martinez became the first Cuban-American cabinet secretary. He came to the United States in 1962 at age fifteen as part of an airlift in which Cubans sent their children out of the country to escape the communist government. He lived with a foster family until being reunited with his parents four years later. He entered public life after a successful career as a personal injury lawyer, and in 1998 was elected chairman of Orange County—which encompasses Orlando—a position similar to mayor or executive. He sought to create more affordable housing for his constituents but his fight for property tax cuts took priority. He also has chaired a commission studying how Florida should manage its explosive growth. He followed a growth-management policy that tied the approval of new homes to school construction.

Martinez was once a trustee of the anti-Castro Cuban American National Foundation. In 2000 he was co-chair of Bush's presidential election campaign in Florida, and was a prodigious fund raiser. He also played a key role in attracting Hispanics to the GOP in Florida where animosity toward Castro remained high. "The cold war has not ended between Mr. Castro and the rest of the free world," he told the Senate Judiciary Committee in 2000 in testifying against the Clinton administration's effort to return the boy refugee Elián González to Cuba. (Details, Congress and the Nation Vol. X, p. 225)

On his appointment, we was described as one of the most obscure of the Bush cabinet designees. Democrats tried, with little success, to elicit a clear understanding about the agenda of the new president, who did not make housing a centerpiece of his campaign. Once in office, Martinez launched a HUD Center for Faith-Based and Community Services, an office intended to help religious-oriented organizations compete for federal funds. He also was an outspoken advocate for home ownership and a highly visible administration liaison on Hispanic issues.

But his effort to simplify the purchasing process for would-be homebuyers received little attention in Congress, and critics faulted him for failing to focus on issues such as increasing rental housing for poor people. Martinez also was blamed for keeping under wraps a study that showed evidence of mortgage discrimination during his tenure at HUD.

He left the cabinet to run—at Bush's urging—for an open Senate seat in the important battle-ground state of Florida. He won by a margin of slightly over 82,000 votes out of 7.4 million cast. He also survived a tough and at times nasty primary campaign in which he had to apologize to his GOP opponent, former representative Bill McCollum, for calling him "antifamily" and for saying in ads that McCollum sided with the "radical homosexual lobby."

He was succeeded by Alphonso R. Jackson, who was confirmed by a Senate voice vote on March 31, 2004. He stayed in the position in Bush's second term. He had been deputy secretary since June 2001 and became the first person in that position to later become HUD secretary. Jackson was born in Texas in a family of twelve children. He later earned political science and education degrees and a law degree from Washington University. He was public safety director in St. Louis where he also was executive director of the St. Louis Housing Authority. He also headed the Dallas housing authority and was director of public and assisted housing in Washington, D.C.

INTERIOR

Gale A. Norton, President Bush's choice for interior secretary, was one of the more controversial selections for a cabinet position. She quickly drew the wrath of environmental advocates and was viewed skeptically by a number of Democratic senators. Nevertheless, the Senate voted 75–24 on Jan. 30, 2001, to confirm her, with Democrats dividing almost evenly, 25–24, in favor. She was sworn in Jan. 31, 2001, and remained in office throughout Bush's first term and into his second term after his reelection in 2004.

For someone who was little known outside the West before her nomination to a national post, Norton quickly become a lightning rod for national environmental groups, which charged she would allow corporate polluters to police themselves and open up public lands to more mining, logging, and other resource development.

Her career included close ties to conservative groups that challenged many environmental protection laws and regulations but she also had considerable exposure to the federal government. She was an attorney for the Mountain States Legal Foundation from 1979 to 1983. Norton became assistant to the deputy secretary of agriculture in 1984 and 1985, associate solicitor at the Interior Department 1985 to 1990; Colorado attorney general from 1991 to 1999, and then senior counsel in a Denver law firm. Norton ran unsuccessfully in 1996 for the Republican Senate nomination in Colorado.

Part of the focus on Norton was because of her association with President Ronald Reagan's controversial Interior Secretary James G. Watt (1981–1983), who earlier hired Norton out of law school in 1978 to work at the conservative Mountain States Legal Foundation. In 1985, she joined the Interior Department solicitor's office where she worked on issues that included opening up the Arctic National Wildlife Refuge to oil exploration.

Norton continued to support drilling in the refuge, a contentious issue that still had not been resolved in early 2005. She also was criticized for her advocacy of changing federal laws to allow polluters to avoid prolonged litigation if they turned themselves in and paid for cleanup costs.

The Sierra Club and the Natural Resources Defense Council urged the Senate to reject Norton, but without success. The criticism of Norton began in the two days of Senate confirmation hearings. Brent Blackwelder, president of Friends of the Earth, an environmental lobbying group, was typical in his comments: "[President] Bush deliberately made a very provocative choice in [Norton's] nomination. . . . I'd like to think we could find a way to work with them, but it won't be easy." Environmental groups were reported to have spent almost a million dollars on an ad campaign to defeat her nomination.

She lobbied senators actively for confirmation. At her confirmation hearings she distanced herself from some of her earlier positions. She retreated from skepticism about the value of the Endangered Species Act by vowing to enforce the law as written. And she backed away from her 1997 statement that there was no scientific consensus that pollution was slowly causing the earth's climate to warm. "There is beginning to be more of a consensus that global warming is occurring," she said. Nevertheless, the Bush administration's official position throughout the four years consistently remained skeptical of the scientific proof of global warming.

LABOR

The cabinet post of labor secretary was one of the few embarrassments the carefully scripted Bush administration suffered during the president's first term. The president's first choice was Linda Chavez, an outspoken conservative commentator. She was quickly pilloried by labor unions and minority groups for her vocal opposition to affirmative action and the minimum wage. But the critics were spared the task of a full-scale effort to defeat her when reports emerged that she had paid an illegal immigrant to do household chores. She withdrew from consideration on Jan. 9, 2001.

In her place, Bush named Elaine L. Chao, who was a fellow at the conservative Heritage Foundation think tank and the wife of Sen. Mitch McConnell, R-Ky. She was received with less controversy than surrounded Chavez but the nomination allowed senators and outside groups to debate a variety of disagreement over the nation's workplace policies.

Key issues included workers' health insurance, pension benefits, family leave policies, child labor laws, and job training. Two primary issues that emerged in debate on her nomination were an increase in the minimum wage and workplace ergonomics rules. Democrats and the allies in organized labor were pushing for a large increase in the $5.15-per-hour minimum wage; the Bush administration proposed a $1-per-hour increase while allowing states to maintain the existing rate.

Also contentious were Clinton administration rules, promulgated late in his term, to require businesses to educate workers about repetitive-work injuries and establish programs to deal with them. Business groups adamantly opposed the new rules and had lobbied aggressively to have them overturned. Chao declined to say how she would deal with the regulations, which were scheduled to take effect in October 2004. As it turned out, GOP leaders early in 2001 pushed through legislation that revoked the new rules. Chao was confirmed by voice vote of the Senate and served throughout Bush's first term. She was invited to stay on after his reelection, and did so.

STATE

President Bush selected the much decorated and admired Colin L. Powell as secretary of state. Powell, and his colleague at the defense department, Donald H. Rumsfeld, became the two defining members of the Bush cabinet during the president's first term. The two were cast, by observers and in the media, as opposite poles of a balancing act between defense department advocates of use of U.S. military might to advance American interest and State Department officials who argued for diplomatic engagement with allies to handle international issues. Whether the differences were as stark as publicly projected was less clear but the two individuals at least served as useful proxies for critics and supporters of the president's decision to invade Iraq in 2003, the administration's most controversial action in the four years.

Powell had previously served as national security adviser to President Ronald Reagan and as chairman of the Joint Chiefs of Staff during the George H. W. Bush administration and for eight months of the Bill Clinton administration. Powell was enormously popular and his confirmation hearing before the Senate Foreign Relations Committee was described by one senator as a "lovefest." Powell was a veteran of the army for thirty-five years, eventually becoming Joint Chiefs chair. He served in the Vietnam war, an experience that associates said convinced him that any significant military action had to be supported by American public opinion and that U.S. combat forces must have overwhelming power.

During his confirmation hearing, Powell adroitly handled questions from committee chair Jesse Helms, R-N.C. In one exchange—a preview of a policy debate that would soon consume Washington—Powell challenged Helms's advocacy of efforts to overthrow Iraqi president Saddam Hussein, suggesting that maintaining and tightening UN sanctions would be a wiser course. Other later reports by journalists said that Powell remained an important but lonely voice in the administration advocating restraint, diplomacy, and international cooperation as planning for the Iraq war moved swiftly ahead.

In the lead-up to that war, Powell would win out over administration hardliners in arguing for the United States to go to the United Nations to seek international support. But when the war came Powell remained a staunch defender of the U.S. course of action.

Powell continued as a counter-balance to conservatives during policy debates throughout Bush's first term. Conservatives repeatedly criticized Powell for his reluctance to embrace and promote some Bush policies, such as those in Iraq and the Middle East, and his tolerance for State Department officials who went their own way.

Powell announced his resignation on Nov. 12, 2004. He said it had always been his intention to serve a single term in office.

Bush nominated his national security advisor, Condoleezza Rice, to the position, much to the delight of conservatives who saw her term as an opportunity to replace independent-minded career bureaucrats at the State Department with people more in tune with Bush's views. Earlier, from 1988 through March 1991 she served as director of Soviet and East European Affairs in the National Security Council and as special assistant to the president for National Security Affairs. She was confirmed by the Senate on a vote of 85–13 on Jan. 26, 2005.

TRANSPORTATION

For transportation secretary President Bush selected a Democrat to serve in his cabinet: Norman Y. Mineta. A widely respected former member of the House from 1975 to 1995, Mineta served as commerce secretary in the last year's of Clinton's administration. He was the single Democrat named to the cabinet but in a job that most observers said was the least political of all.

Other than his political affiliation, Mineta was a natural selection for the job. Transportation policy is one of the more bipartisan areas in the government and a subject Mineta learned thoroughly during his years in Congress and for a short time after leaving as a vice president at Lockheed Martin Corp. working on development of "smart" transportation technologies. (Clinton had tried to interest Mineta in the transportation secretary's job when he won the White House.) Mineta had represented the California Bay Area with its heavy concentration of high technology companies, which showed in his interest in using technology to improve the nation's transportation system.

The four years proved more challenging than he expected starting with the terrorists attacks on Sept. 11, 2001, that threw the airline industry, already suffering economic woes, into turmoil and threatened the existence of some carriers. The department already faced issues of an antiquated air traffic control system and travel congestion. Airline mergers and cost cutting contributed to consumer complaints. On the ground, Congress was unable during the entire four years to pass a reauthorization of the basic surface transportation that was a central part of the department's mission. The dispute, largely between Republicans in Congress and Bush in the White House, boiled down to cost: members, including Democrats, wanted to authorize highway and mass transit spending significantly larger than the White House was willing to accept. Nevertheless, Mineta stayed on as secretary after the 2004 elections returned Bush to the presidency.

TREASURY

Paul O'Neill, President Bush's choice as Treasury secretary, was the single major cabinet casualty during the president's first term. He resigned his position, at the White House's request, in December 2002 after a long series of clashes with administration officials about economic policy. Many observers thought his particular error was speaking about these differences in public.

O'Neill was a former chair and CEO of Alcoa, the giant metals company, who was widely credited with turning around the fortunes of that business. But he was not a novice in the ways of Washington. He started his career in government in 1961 in the Veterans Administration and later became a high official in the Office of Management and Budget from 1967 to 1977 under presidents Richard M. Nixon and Gerald R. Ford.

But O'Neill was better at speaking his mind than in cheerleading for administration policies. O'Neill ran into trouble early in 2001 when he publicly questioned the economic benefits of Bush's proposed tax cuts. O'Neill was criticized for gaffes that shook the markets, for not being around at crucial times, and for insulting important legislators and corporate executives.

With the president and Republican leaders in Congress planning to push more tax cuts in 2003 as the cure-all for both the slow economy and the budget deficit, the White House in December 2002 decided it was time for O'Neill to be replaced with someone who was better able to pitch the president's economic policies on Capitol Hill and to the public. The new Treasury secretary was John W. Snow, chairman of the railroad company CSX Corp., who was nominated by the president Jan. 13, 2003, confirmed by voice vote of the Senate Jan. 30, and sworn in on Feb. 3.

One of Snow's toughest tasks was selling reluctant Republican legislators on the central feature of Bush's proposed 2003 tax cut—making dividend income tax free. Critics denounced that proposal as a favor for wealthy investors. Bush ended up with half the tax cut he wanted, largely as a result of congressional deficit concerns. A lower tax rate was set for dividends and capital gains. Snow, a once outspoken deficit hawk, also found himself the leading spokesman for the White House view that deficits were tolerable because they amounted to only a small percentage of the economy. During the 2004 election campaign, Snow had the task of helping fend off Democratic attacks on Bush's fiscal policy and what they said was a dismal record on job creation. Snow was also the administration official called upon to calm fears that the declining dollar was destabilizing the economy.

VETERANS AFFAIRS

The Veterans Administration, one of the most specialized departments in government, went to Anthony Principi, a highly respected former aide on two Senate panels dealing with veterans' issues and chair of a bipartisan federal commission that studied veterans' benefits. He was confirmed without opposition and sworn in Jan. 24,

2001, but during hearings on the nomination several senators on the Veterans Affairs Committee warned that he was taking on an agency with significant problems. These included a benefit claims processing system that Tim Hutchinson, R-Ark., said had caused many veterans "to lose faith" in the agency.

His primary goal, he told senators, was to make the agency—which ran 139 hospitals—operate more efficiently. He said that in some instances the VA still used paper files instead of computers. Principi, however, came to the job with considerable knowledge of the agency in which he served from March 1989 to September 1992 as deputy secretary during the presidency of George H. W. Bush. He became the agency's acting secretary in the last four months of Bush's term.

Under Principi's leadership, the congressionally appointed Commission on Service Members and Veterans Transition Assistance issued a report in January 1999 urging broad expansion of military and veterans' benefits, including a new GI Bill guaranteeing a full college scholarship in exchange for four years of active duty. That report served as Principi's blueprint for running the Department of Veterans Affairs. He also prompted proposals to make it easier for veterans to qualify for home loans by eliminating down payments.

When Bush nominated Principi, the president-elect said he wanted the decorated veteran, who served as California chair of Veterans for Bush during the 2000 campaign, to take "the lead in modernizing our veterans' health care system." Principi, who was a decorated Vietnam veteran, was praised by both members of Congress and outside veterans groups. Frank H. Murkowski, R-Alaska, who chaired the Senate Committee on Veterans Affairs in the mid-1980s, said that Principi was an outstanding staff director. "He was a tremendous asset to me, and he'll be a tremendous asset to the nation as a member of the president's Cabinet and as an advocate for America's veterans," Murkowski said. Veterans groups, including the American Legion and Veterans of Foreign Wars, also hailed Principi's nomination. The Paralyzed Veterans of America said that Principi had "demonstrated throughout his career a deep concern for the needs of his fellow veterans and has marshaled his talents to address those needs."

After Bush's reelection in 2004 Principi announced he would leave the position; he officially stepped down Jan. 24, 2005. In his place Bush nominated, and the Senate confirmed without dispute, Jim Nicholson. Like Principi, Nicholson, a West Point graduate, served in Vietnam for an eight year period. He retired from the army as a colonel after a thirty year career. He had not held elective office but was active for many years in the Republican Party and was chair of the Republican National Committee from 1997 to 2000. He also served as U.S. ambassador to the Vatican.

Other Major Positions

DIRECTOR OF NATIONAL INTELLIGENCE, UN REPRESENTATIVE

President Bush's pick to head the newly created post of director of national intelligence was John D. Negroponte. He was named by Bush on Feb. 17, 2005, and was confirmed by the Senate by a 98–2 vote on April 21, 2005. He was sworn in on May 18. The DNI was created in 2004 as part of an intelligence overhaul law. Bush named Lt. General Michael V. Hayden, who was serving as director of the super-secret National Security Agency, to be Negroponte's top deputy.

Negroponte, a veteran diplomat, had a long record in government service but was controversial, nevertheless. He was selected by Bush soon after the 2000 elections to be the U.S. permanent representative to the United Nations. He was confirmed by the voice vote of the Senate on Sept. 14, 2001, but the confirmation had been delayed because of controversy over his tenure as U.S. ambassador to Honduras in the early 1980s. After the White House submitted Negroponte's nomination to the Senate in May, Senate Foreign Relations Committee Democrats had poured over hundreds of documents to trace what he had known about human rights violations by the Honduran military and whether embassy officials fully and accurately reported to Congress and the State Department on alleged ties between the Honduran military and death squads. But in the aftermath of the Sept. 11 terrorist attacks, members recognized the importance of having the U.S. representative in place at the United Nations instead of an interim figure and quickly moved the nomination through the Senate. Negroponte served in the U.N. post until June 22, 2004, when he left to become the first U.S. ambassador to post-war Iraq. His nomination at DNI, however, revived criticism of his role in Latin America.

When Negroponte moved from the post of U.S. representative to the United Nations, President Bush nominated John C. Danforth, a former Republican senator from Missouri (1976–1995) and an heir to the Ralston Purina fortune, as his successor. Danforth was confirmed by voice vote on June 24, 2004, ten days after Bush submitted his nomination. The president had been eager to have Danforth in place at the United Nations prior to the June 30 U.S. turnover of political sovereignty to Iraq and before the United States was to help preside over the annual U.N. General Assembly session in September.

In addition to his eighteen years in the Senate, Danforth's diverse career had included practicing law, serving as a Missouri prosecutor, and being ordained an Episcopal priest. He officiated at the funeral services for former president Ronald Reagan in 2004 at the Washington National Cathedral and, at the same location, for legendary *Washington Post* publisher Katherine Graham in 2001.

At the behest of the Clinton administration, in 1999 he had conducted a probe of allegations of wrong-doing by the FBI during a raid at Waco, Texas, and since 2001 he had been serving as Bush's special envoy for peace in Sudan. Bush announced his plan to nominate Danforth for the U.N. post just days after Danforth had helped usher through agreements aimed at ending the twenty-one-year-old civil war in Sudan.

But Danforth did not remain long in the position. He submitted his resignation on Nov. 22, 2004, effective the following Jan. 20. The resignation surprised members of Congress and other observers who thought Danforth would be the U.S. representative for some period to come.

To replace Danforth, Bush on March 7, 2005, picked one of the more controversial officials in the Washington bureaucracy: John R. Bolton. Bolton served as undersecretary of state for arms control since May 2001 and was a strong advocate for the U.S. invasion of Iraq. He earlier served in State Department positions and the Justice Department during the presidency of George H. W. Bush. Bolton was strongly opposed by many Democrats, and his nomination remained unconfirmed at the end of July 2005. The Senate twice rejected cutting off a Democratic-led filibuster that prevented a vote on the nomination. Some Republicans, also, were troubled by Bolton. Foreign Relations Committee senator George V. Voinovich, R-Ohio, decided to oppose Bolton, which meant that the nomination went from the committee to the full Senate without a recommendation.

However, on Aug. 1, 2005, President Bush gave him a recess appointment to the job after Congress left for its summer break, which meant he could serve until the next Congress convened in 2007. The unprecedented action was sharply criticized by Democrats who said a person representing the United States to the United Nations should have Senate approval. Bolton drew the criticism partly for his outspoken and critical assessment of the United Nations. Democrats said his demeanor, and his attitudes toward the United Nations, made him a poor candidate to represent the United States. Some State Department officials said he berated career officials and analysts who challenged his opinions. Other critics said he chose intelligence information selectively to support his views on foreign policy issues.

His supporters, however, said his bluntness was exactly what was needed at the United Nations, and his opinions about required changes at the institution clearly reflected the attitude of the Bush administration. He had advocated U.S. recognition of Taiwan as an independent state, an action that would likely inflame relations with China, which considered the island state as a renegade Chinese province. He also was a blunt critic of Iran and North Korea for developing nuclear weapons.

CENTRAL INTELLIGENCE AGENCY

The CIA, more than any other agency, was buffeted from nearly every angle in the aftermath of the terrorists attacks of Sept. 11, 2001, and the claims, proven incorrect, that Iraq was developing weapons of mass destruction, which had been an under-pinning for the invasion of that country in 2003. The director, George J. Tenet, however, remained in office during most of Bush's first term.

He became CIA director in 1997 during the Clinton administration and remained in the job until July 11, 2004, his seventh anniversary in that post. Only Allen W. Dulles in the Eisenhower administration in the 1950s served longer. Clinton named Tenet to the job after another candidate, Anthony Lake, withdrew when the nomination became entangled in partisan controversy over foreign policy and political fund-raising practices. *(Congress and the Nation Vol. X, p. 983)*

Tenet had been acting director of central intelligence, following the resignation of John M. Deutch in December 1996 and served under Lake on the National Security Council before becoming deputy CIA director in 1995.

Although his background in intelligence, serving administrations of both political parties, gave him a strong claim to be CIA director, the traumatic events after Bush's inauguration eventually caught up with him. Tenet submitted his resignation on June 3, 2004, just weeks before the anticipated release of a Senate Select Intelligence Committee report on prewar intelligence on Iraq's weapons of mass destruction. The report was expected to castigate the CIA for out-dated information, sloppy analysis, and unreliable sources, and some on Capitol Hill linked the timing of Tenet's resignation to it. A second scathing assessment of the intelligence community—the report of the independent commission on the Sept. 11 attacks—was expected later that summer. Tenet's departure set the stage for a broad debate on restructuring the intelligence community. His deputy, John McLaughlin, became the acting CIA director after he stepped down. President Bush awarded Tenet the Presidential Medal of Freedom, the nation's highest civilian award, at a White House ceremony on Dec. 14, 2004. *(Intelligence reports, pp. 274, 275)*

In August 2004, Bush nominated Rep. Porter J. Goss, R-Fla., to be the new director. Republicans on Capitol Hill lauded the selection of Goss, who had been a CIA agent for a decade, a member of Congress since 1989, and chair of the House Select Intelligence Committee since 1997. But Democrats warned that the selection of a politician instead of a career intelligence operative could lead to the politicization of intelligence and, during Senate Intelligence Committee confirmation hearings, they grilled Goss on his votes and statements. Democrats provided all the dissenting votes when the full Senate approved the Goss nomination by a vote of 77–17 on Sept. 22, 2004. They continued their criticism of the new director after Goss took several Capitol Hill staffers with him to the CIA and began reorganizations, moves that led to the resignations of several top officials in the CIA's clandestine services division.

ENVIRONMENTAL PROTECTION AGENCY

The Environmental Protection Agency, a cabinet-rank agency, was one of the more controversial in the government, reflecting sharp disagreements in the country between environmental advocates and business and other groups. The EPA administrator position was widely seen as one of the more thankless in the government's bureaucratic hierarchy. Unlike many government agencies, the EPA did not have a single, uniform clientele with a largely uniform agenda.

It was charged with enforcing a variety of environmental laws, many of which dated from earlier decades when support for cleaning up air and water pollution, protecting endangered species, reversing land contamination, and similar activities had wider public and congressional support. In more recent years, under prodding from business interests and after Republicans took control of the House in 1995, the agency came under increasing fire from conservatives for heavy-handed regulation, poor science, and unwillingness to balance economic costs against environmental goals.

President Bush named Christine Todd Whitman, a moderate Republican who had served as governor of New Jersey. Like previous administrators, she and the agency were caught between bitterly opposed environmental groups on the one hand and corporate interests, particularly energy producers, and the White House on the other. Her job was made more difficult because she served in a Republican administration that was expected to be favorable to business interests and to view the environmental groups' agenda with skepticism. She stayed in the job only two years and was followed by Utah governor Michael O. Leavitt, who himself moved on at the end of Bush's first term to become Secretary of Health and Human Services.

Whitman served as New Jersey governor from 1993 to 2001 and built an often-praised record of environmental policy and actions in the state including fighting urban sprawl and preserving open spaces. However, in the increasingly conservative GOP Whitman, who supported many women's rights issues, was sometimes suspect and was seen as lacking the influence of higher profile conservatives in the administration.

Her relatively short two-year term (only one other top position, the Treasury secretary, changed hands in so short a time) reflected the underlying difficulties. She was approved without dissent by the Environment and Public Works Committee and confirmed by a 99–0 vote of the Senate on Jan. 31, 2001. It was a difficult two years. Although she denied it, many reports circulated that she was routinely overruled by the administration on policy issues. The reports suggested that the ongoing fights left her exhausted and eager to depart Washington. She all but confirmed these suspicions when she commented to reporters at her May 2003 resignation announcement: "Halfway through last December [2002], I was . . . saying, 'Do I really want to live this lifestyle for another two and a half years?' It was pretty apparent I didn't." She departed on June 27.

Leavitt, whom Bush nominated in the fall, was confirmed by the Senate on Oct. 28, 2003, by an 88–8 vote and sworn in Nov. 6. Although he won praise from many quarters, not all environmentalists were enthused and some used the confirmation process to denounce the Bush administration's environmental policies. A typical comment was from Carl Pope, Sierra Club executive director, who said Leavitt's Utah record "suggests that he will be a good fit for the Bush administration but a disappointing choice for Americans concerned with environmental protection." Greg Wetstone of the Natural Resources Defense Council, agreed, saying Leavitt's record "does not give us confidence that he has the desire or the capability to stem this administration's anti-environmental agenda."

Environmentalists noted that Leavitt would join other westerners in key administration roles in environment and energy affairs, including the secretary of interior, Gale Norton, and Kathleen Clarke, head of the Bureau of Land Management. His brief tenure reflected that of other administrators, with critics pointing to what they claim was a dismal record of environmental protection when he served as governor of Utah.

He was replaced by Stephen Johnson, a long-time EPA employee and the first career scientist to hold the position. Bush named him on March 4, 2005; he was confirmed without opposition in the Senate on April 29, and sworn in May 2.

FEDERAL RESERVE

Alan Greenspan continued in his position as chair of the Federal Reserve, a post he assumed in 1987 when Ronald Reagan was president. He was appointed to a second term by President George H. W. Bush and then to two more terms by President Bill Clinton. George W. Bush appointed Greenspan to a fifth term in 2004. He was required by law to leave the Fed in January 2006.

He was one of the most powerful and yet enigmatic figures in Washington. Economists and politicians alike hung on his notoriously complex and equivocal public statements which often were delivered in convoluted, dense prose that called out for deciphering, an art few observers mastered.

When he became chair of the Federal Reserve in 1987, Greenspan was viewed as likely to stay above the political fray and focus on monetary policy, the Fed's principal activity. But Greenspan defied expectations and frequently spoke out strongly on fiscal issues facing Congress. On occasion he stunned lawmakers by endorsing specific policy choices.

In 1993 Greenspan backed tax increases as part of the deficit-reduction package pushed by President Bill Clinton. In 2001, when enormous surpluses were expected over the next decade, he advocated cutting taxes to avoid a scenario in which the nation paid off its debt too quickly and was faced with the troubling prospect of investing excess tax revenue in the stock market. On both occasions, Greenspan's nod helped ensure enactment of contentious White House fiscal initiatives.

The terrorist attacks and the slumping economy in 2001 ensured that the nation would not have to worry for years to come about what to do with surplus revenue. As the value of the dollar relative to other currencies began to slide, raising the possibility of increased inflation and interest rates, Greenspan warned of the dangers of long-term deficits, and he called upon Congress to revive the pay-as-you-go rules that until 2002 required that tax cuts or extensions of entitlement programs be offset by revenue increases or other spending cuts.

SECURITIES AND EXCHANGE COMMISSION

The Securities and Exchange Commission was not expected to be a place of turmoil in a Republican administration widely expected to project, and protect, interests of the business community, Wall Street, and investors. All the more surprising then when the two commissioners named by President Bush during his first term proved as contentious as any in the vast federal regulatory armada.

Bush first named Harvey L. Pitt, on Aug. 3, 2001, who was a staff attorney on the SEC from 1968 to 1978 and for three years prior to his appointment was the agency's general counsel. A lawyer specializing in securities issues, Pitt was in private practice for many years and taught at various law schools.

But his chairmanship fell apart from gaffs that brought turmoil and embarrassing publicity to the agency. In October 2002 Pitt named former FBI director William H. Webster as the first head of the Public Company Accounting Oversight Board, which had been created in legislation enacted in response to a number of huge corporate accounting scandals. Pitt failed to tell the SEC commission before it confirmed Webster as chair that Webster had served as chair of the audit committee for financially troubled U.S. Technologies Inc. Webster, a former head of both the Central Intelligence Agency and the Federal Bureau of Investigation, later resigned. Earlier in the year Pitt had opened himself to ridicule when he tried, unsuccessfully, to get a provision in the corporate accounting bill to raise his pay and elevate his position to cabinet level. These developments only reinforced the criticism of investor advocates who thought Pitt was too cozy with the financial community as a result of his long years in private practice. Pitt resigned on Nov. 5, 2002.

On Dec. 10, 2002, Bush picked William H. Donaldson to replace Pitt. Donaldson, who cofounded the investment firm Donaldson, Lufkin & Jenrette, was a former chair and CEO of Aetna Inc., and a former chair of the New York Stock Exchange, positions that did not position him as significantly different than Pitt.

But Donaldson created a different kind of controversy for the agency: tough regulation of business and a mandate from the president to crack down on corporate wrongdoing and restore confidence in financial markets. Donaldson came to office as the reputation of business was plummeting in the wake of scandals at some of the nations largest companies, including Enron, WorldCom, Adelphia cable, and Arthur-Anderson. *(Details of scandals, p. 124)*

The SEC under his leadership went after management practices of mutual fund companies, imposed regulations on hedge funds, and forced changes in operations of securities markets in the electronic age. He did not, however, get approval for two other controversial proposals: a rule to permit certain minority shareholders access to corporate proxy ballots in order to nominate director candidates (a proposal that was anathema to corporate officials who saw it as a way for unions and other special interest groups to get seats on company boards), and a requirement that companies be more complete in reporting about the amount and type of compensation given to top executives.

Donaldson also persuaded Congress to increase its budget and in the process hired more than 1,000 new employees, mostly lawyers and accountants—about a 33 percent increase. These and other aggressive activity by the SEC brought down the wrath of the securities industry as well as—unexpectedly—representatives of main street businesses, principally the U.S. Chamber of Commerce. Criticism centered on the cost of adhering to many of the new requirements and regulations from the SEC. But in more general terms critics charged that the SEC's more aggressive approach was inappropriate—and usually unnecessary—in U.S. markets.

To almost everyone's surprise, Donaldson on June 1, 2005, announced he would leave the SEC on June 30, even though his five-year term ran until 2007. He gave no detailed reasons but SEC followers speculated that the pressure of the job and the criticism had taken a toll on the seventy-four-year-old chair.

To replace him Bush name a House member, Christopher Cox, R-Calif., who was confirmed without difficulty by the Senate and sworn into office on Aug. 3, 2005. A one-time securities lawyer who had been in the House for seventeen years, and chaired the important homeland security committee, Cox was seen as a booster of unfettered capital markets. He helped push a bill in 1995, enacted over a veto by President Clinton, that barred class action lawsuits by investors against companies whose share prices fell. He strongly opposed a rule, scheduled to take effect in June 2005, requiring companies to account for stock options as expenses, a rule vigorously opposed by many small start-up and technological companies.

OFFICE OF MANAGEMENT AND BUDGET

Bush's first director of the Office of Management and Budget (OMB) was Mitchell E. Daniels Jr., who had served in President Ronald Reagan's administration in the 1980s and was a former executive with the pharmaceutical company Eli Lilly. President Bush called Daniels "the Blade" for his willingness to take on legislators for what he considered their excessive spending. Daniels once said that a more apt nickname might be "the Piñata," because "some folks think if they can knock my head off all the goodies in town will fall out."

When Daniels left the OMB in mid-2003 to run, successfully, for governor of Indiana, his home state, Bush named his deputy White House chief of staff, Joshua B. Bolten, to the post. Bolten had a hand in most of Bush's early domestic issues, and his more temperate personality made him a welcome successor to Daniels to many on Capitol Hill. Bolten kept a relatively low profile in his first year until he engaged appropriators over a package of domestic spending add-ons. In the end, the White House agreed to a series of offsets and budgetary maneuvers that allowed Congress to extract more spending but that let Bush claim victory on his budgetary top line. In 2004 Bolten and the White House were even more successful, holding increases in discretionary domestic spending to less than 1 percent.

NATIONAL ECONOMIC COUNCIL

The National Economic Council had been created in 1993 by President Bill Clinton. The council was to coordinate economic policy within the administration, as a counterpart to the National Security Council, which coordinated defense and foreign policy. Bush's first director was Larry B. Lindsey, who had been Bush's economic tutor during the 2000 presidential campaign and was a key architect of the 2001 tax cut. But Lindsey's overly optimistic economic forecasts and his political advice to the president made him seem out of touch with reality. Lindsey was said, for example, to have advised Bush to stop the corporate accountability legislation being considered in the Senate in 2002 even though the measure eventually passed unanimously. Lindsey was also criticized for publicly predicting that the cost of a war with Iraq could reach $200 billion, which was much higher than other administration officials were saying at the time but which turned out to be closer to actual spending.

Lindsey was forced out and was replaced by Stephen Friedman, a former chair of Goldman-Sachs. Friedman had also served as a vice chair of the Concord Coalition, a group that opposed budget deficits, and some Republicans were concerned that he might oppose tax cuts. Those concerns were unfounded; Friedman supported Bush's economic policy for the two years he held the post, which he resigned late in 2004.

COUNCIL OF ECONOMIC ADVISERS

The Council of Economic Advisers, the agency responsible for preparing the annual economic report of the president, had two chairs during Bush's first term. The first was R. Glenn Hubbard, widely credited as a chief architect of Bush's tax cut packages in 2001 and 2003. Hubbard was also the chief advocate in 2003 of eliminating taxes on stock dividends. Congress cut those dividends, along with capital gains, but did not end them. Hubbard left early in 2003 to become dean of Columbia University's School of Business.

Hubbard was succeeded by N. Gregory Mankiw, an economics professor on leave from Harvard and the author of two popular economic textbooks. Mankiw touched off a major controversy during a February 2004 news conference when he described outsourcing of American jobs to workers overseas as "just a new way of doing international trade." Although most economists would agree with Mankiw that the expansion of free trade in goods and services benefited all participating countries over the long run, Democrats immediately seized on Mankiw's remarks as confirming that Bush was insensitive to the plight of American workers.

U.S. TRADE REPRESENTATIVE

President George W. Bush's chief trade representative during his first term was Robert B. Zoellick, a pragmatic promoter of free trade known for his ability to put together deals. The U.S. trade representative was a cabinet-level office.

Those skills were greatly needed during Zoellick's tenure, as he completed negotiations on bringing China into the World Trade Organization, pushed fast-track authority for the president through a dubious Congress, and negotiated several bilateral and regional trade agreements with countries in the Middle East, Asia, and Latin America. Zoellick was also instrumental in launching a new round of multilateral trade talks known as the Doha Round, and then rescuing those talks from near-collapse.

Secretary of State Condoleezza Rice in early 2005 chose Zoellick to be deputy secretary of state, the number two person in the department. Zoellick had an extensive background in government. He had served from Feb. 7, 2001, to Feb. 22, 2005. Earlier Zoellick had worked in the Treasury department from 1985 to 1988 and as under secretary of state for economic and agricultural affairs in the administration of George H. W. Bush (1989–1993). In 1992 he moved to the White House as deputy chief of staff and assistant to the president.

Following Zoellick's move to the state department the president quickly picked Ohio representative Rob Portman to take the lead in advancing the administration's trade liberalization policies through Congress. Portman had not made trade his primary policy focus in Congress and was not well-known in global trade circles. But unlike Zoellick, whose sometimes acerbic style made for strained relations in Congress, Portman appeared to be well-liked on Capitol Hill. His nomination drew enthusiastic reactions from members of both parties as well as from many business and agricultural groups. He was confirmed by the Senate on April 29, 2005.

FEDERAL COMMUNICATIONS COMMISSION

President Bush's nomination on Jan. 22, 2001, of Michael K. Powell as chair of the FCC was later seen as one of the more controversial appointments. Powell, who was the son of secretary of state Colin Powell, served three years on the five-member commission where he was considered a reliable if occasionally independent conservative. He was appointed to the agency by President Bill Clinton on Nov. 3, 1997. Earlier he had worked in the antitrust division of the Justice Department.

Powell was well known for his enthusiasm for the operation of the market in consumer and business decisions. One critic said he was "enamored by the philosophy of the marketplace." During his tenure he became an outspoken advocate of telecommunications deregulation including allowing media companies to grow in size through acquisitions. This view, which was reflected in an important set of new rules promulgated by the FCC, set off a firestorm of controversy led by critics who said it would put control of the nation's television and other media in the hands of a few giant corporations, thereby stifling diversity and local control of broadcasting. An unlikely coalition of conservatives and liberals, in and out of Congress, forced a retreat on the rules. In addition, a federal court said the FCC had not fully justified its decision on the rules. The end result was a stinging rebuke to Powell's approach on the commission. Powell stayed through the four years of Bush's term but announced he would step down from the post in early 2005. His resignation was effective Jan. 21, 2005.

On March 17, 2005, Bush named Kevin J. Martin to replace Powell as chair. He already was serving on the commission therefore did not require Senate confirmation. Martin was best known for his strong advocacy for more stringent penalties against broadcasters for indecency on the airwaves.

SOLICITOR GENERAL

President Bush selected Theodore Olson as solicitor general. He was confirmed by a 51–47 vote on May 24, 2001, and took office on June 12. The solicitor general represents the United States before the Supreme Court when the federal government is party of a case.

The confirmation came despite accusations that he gave misleading testimony about his role in efforts to smear President Clinton. Ben Nelson of Nebraska and Zell Miller of Georgia were the only Democrats to vote for the nomination, which was supported by all Republicans who were present.

The nomination came to the floor after Majority Leader Trent Lott, R-Miss., exercised his option under the Senate's power-sharing agreement to discharge nominations that got a tie vote in committee. The Judiciary Committee had split 9–9 on May 17 over whether to send Olson's nomination to the floor.

Democrats said Olson's testimony before the Judiciary Committee was evasive, primarily about the extent of his involvement in a project by the conservative magazine *The American Spectator* to uncover damaging information about then-president Clinton and first lady Hillary Rodham Clinton.

Olson, a lawyer in private practice, had argued the Supreme Court case, *Bush v. Gore,* that resolved the presidential election and made his client, George W. Bush, president. Olson stepped down in July 2004. Bush named Paul D. Clement acting solicitor general. He served in that position until he was confirmed by the Senate, by unanimous consent, on June 8, 2005. Earlier is his career Clement was chief counsel for the Senate Judiciary Subcommittee on the Constitution, Federalism, and Property Rights.

Presidential Vetoes, 2001–2005

President George W. Bush did not veto any legislation during his first four years in office, from 2001 to 2005. He was the first president since John Quincy Adams in the 1820s to go through a full term without issuing a veto. Bush was able to do this in part because his party controlled both houses throughout the 108th Congress and the first six months of the 107th before a disaffected Republican, James Jeffords of Vermont, became an independent and gave control of the Senate to the Democrats. The GOP, however, remained in firm control of the House. The Republican leadership was intent on avoiding presidential vetoes and willing to twist arms so that the president could score wins and conserve his political capital for essential battles. Bush threatened numerous vetoes to help shape legislation to his liking, a technique he used to considerable success to get legislation that he was able to sign.

By contrast, all presidents from Dwight D. Eisenhower in 1953 issued many vetoes. Eisenhower, faced with a Democratic Congress throughout his eight years in the White House, issued many more than any of his successors. But only two were overridden.

Bush's predecessor, Bill Clinton, vetoed a total of seventeen bills (all public measures) during his first term in office. In his second four years, he vetoed twenty (also all public bills), for a total thirty-seven during his two terms in office. The number is relatively low compared to veto totals of other presidents since 1953 who faced a Congress in the control of the opposition party. Democrats controlled Congress only during the first two years of Clinton's presidency. He did not cast any vetoes during that two-year period, making him the first president since 1853 to go an entire Congress without vetoing a single bill. The last president to do that was Millard Fillmore during the 32nd Congress (1851–1853).

Grover Cleveland issued the most vetoes in one term, 414. Franklin Roosevelt, who served as president for three full terms and into a fourth, vetoed the most measures, 635. Seven presidents before Bush vetoed no bills.

Vetoes, 1953–2005

President (Congresses)	Regular Vetoes	Pocket Vetoes	Total Vetoes	Overridden
Dwight D. Eisenhower (83rd–86th)	73	108	181	2
John F. Kennedy (87th–88th)	12	9	21	0
Lyndon B. Johnson (88th–90th)	16	14	30	0
Richard M. Nixon (91st–93rd)	26	17	43	7
Gerald R. Ford (93rd–94th)	48	18	66	12
Jimmy Carter (95th–96th)	13	18	31	2
Ronald Reagan (97th–100th)	39	39	78	9

President (Congresses)	Regular Vetoes	Pocket Vetoes	Total Vetoes	Overridden
George Bush[1] (101st–102nd)	29	15	44	1
Bill Clinton[2] (103rd–106th)	36	1	37	2
George W. Bush (107th–108th)	0	0	0	–

1. President George H. W. Bush attempted to pocket-veto two bills during recess periods. Congress considered the two bills enacted into law because of the President's failure to return the legislation. The bills are not counted as pocket vetoes in this table.
2. Does not include line-item vetoes, which were permitted under a 1996 law that was struck down by the Supreme Court.

Selected Texts, 2001–2004

President Bush's Inaugural Address

Following is the inaugural address of George W. Bush, the nation's forty-third president, delivered on Jan. 20, 2001.

Chief Justice [William H.] Rehnquist, President [Jimmy] Carter, President [George] Bush, President [Bill] Clinton, distinguished guests and my fellow citizens: The peaceful transfer of authority is rare in history, yet common in our country. With a simple oath, we affirm old traditions and make new beginnings.

As I begin, I thank President Clinton for his service to our nation. And I thank Vice President [Al] Gore for a contest conducted with spirit and ended with grace.

I am honored and humbled to stand here, where so many of America's leaders have come before me, and so many will follow.

We have a place, all of us, in a long story—a story we continue, but whose end we will not see. It is the story of a new world that became a friend and liberator of the old; a story of a slave-holding society that became a servant of freedom; the story of a power that went into the world to protect but not possess, to defend but not to conquer.

It is the American story—a story of flawed and fallible people, united across the generations by grand and enduring ideals.

The grandest of these ideals is an unfolding American promise that everyone belongs, that everyone deserves a chance, that no insignificant person was ever born.

Americans are called to enact this promise in our lives and in our laws. And though our nation has sometimes halted, and sometimes delayed, we must follow no other course.

Through much of the last century, America's faith in freedom and democracy was a rock in a raging sea. Now it is a seed upon the wind, taking root in many nations.

Our democratic faith is more than the creed of our country, it is the inborn hope of our humanity, an ideal we carry but do not own, a trust we bear and pass along. And even after nearly 225 years, we have a long way yet to travel.

While many of our citizens prosper, others doubt the promise, even the justice, of our own country. The ambitions of some Americans are limited by failing schools and hidden prejudice and the circumstances of their birth. And sometimes our differences run so deep, it seems we share a continent, but not a country.

We do not accept this, and we will not allow it. Our unity, our union, is the serious work of leaders and citizens in every generation. And this is my solemn pledge: I will work to build a single nation of justice and opportunity.

I know this is in our reach because we are guided by a power larger than ourselves who creates us equal in His image. And we are confident in principles that unite and lead us onward.

America has never been united by blood or birth or soil. We are bound by ideals that move us beyond our backgrounds, lift us above our interests and teach us what it means to be citizens. Every child must be taught these principles. Every citizen must uphold them. And every immigrant, by embracing these ideals, makes our country more, not less, American.

Today, we affirm a new commitment to live out our nation's promise through civility, courage, compassion and character.

America, at its best, matches a commitment to principle with a concern for civility. A civil society demands from each of us good will and respect, fair dealing and forgiveness.

Some seem to believe that our politics can afford to be petty because, in a time of peace, the stakes of our debates appear small.

But the stakes for America are never small. If our country does not lead the cause of freedom, it will not be led. If we do not turn the hearts of children toward knowledge and character, we will lose their gifts and undermine their idealism. If we permit our economy to drift and decline, the vulnerable will suffer most.

We must live up to the calling we share. Civility is not a tactic or a sentiment. It is the determined choice of trust over cynicism, of community over chaos. And this commitment, if we keep it, is a way to shared accomplishment.

America, at its best, is also courageous.

Our national courage has been clear in times of depression and war, when defending common dangers defined our common good. Now we must choose if the example of our fathers and mothers will inspire us or condemn us. We must show courage in a time of blessing by confronting problems instead of passing them on to future generations.

Together, we will reclaim America's schools, before ignorance and apathy claim more young lives.

We will reform Social Security and Medicare, sparing our children from struggles we have the power to prevent. And we will reduce taxes, to recover the momentum of our economy and reward the effort and enterprise of working Americans.

We will build our defenses beyond challenge, lest weakness invite challenge.

We will confront weapons of mass destruction, so that a new century is spared new horrors.

The enemies of liberty and our country should make no mistake: America remains engaged in the world by history and by choice, shaping a balance of power that favors freedom. We will defend our allies and our interests. We will show purpose without arrogance. We will meet aggression and bad faith with resolve and strength. And to all nations, we will speak for the values that gave our nation birth.

America, at its best, is compassionate. In the quiet of American conscience, we know that deep, persistent poverty is unworthy of our nation's promise.

And whatever our views of its cause, we can agree that children at risk are not at fault. Abandonment and abuse are not acts of God, they are failures of love.

And the proliferation of prisons, however necessary, is no substitute for hope and order in our souls.

Where there is suffering, there is duty. Americans in need are not strangers, they are citizens; not problems, but priorities. And all of us are diminished when any are hopeless.

Government has great responsibilities for public safety and public health, for civil rights and common schools. Yet compassion is the work of a nation, not just a government.

And some needs and hurts are so deep they will only respond to a mentor's touch or a pastor's prayer. Church and charity, synagogue and mosque lend our communities their humanity, and they will have an honored place in our plans and in our laws.

Many in our country do not know the pain of poverty, but we can listen to those who do.

And I can pledge our nation to a goal: When we see that wounded traveler on the road to Jericho, we will not pass to the other side.

America, at its best, is a place where personal responsibility is valued and expected.

Encouraging responsibility is not a search for scapegoats, it is a call to conscience. And though it requires sacrifice, it brings a deeper fulfillment. We find the fullness of life not only in options, but in commitments. And we find that children and community are the commitments that set us free.

Our public interest depends on private character, on civic duty and family bonds and basic fairness, on uncounted, unhonored acts of decency which give direction to our freedom.

Sometimes in life we are called to do great things. But as a saint of our times has said, every day we are called to do small things with great love. The most important tasks of a democracy are done by everyone.

I will live and lead by these principles: to advance my convictions with civility; to pursue the public interest with courage; to speak for greater justice and compassion; to call for responsibility and try to live it as well.

In all these ways, I will bring the values of our history to the care of our times.

What you do is as important as anything government does. I ask you to seek a common good beyond your comfort; to defend needed reforms against easy attacks; to serve your nation, beginning with your neighbor. I ask you to be citizens: citizens, not spectators; citizens, not subjects; responsible citizens, building communities of service and a nation of character.

Americans are generous and strong and decent, not because we believe in ourselves, but because we hold beliefs beyond ourselves. When this spirit of citizenship is missing, no government program can replace it. When this spirit is present, no wrong can stand against it.

After the Declaration of Independence was signed, Virginia statesman John Page wrote to Thomas Jefferson: "We know the race is not to the swift nor the battle to the strong. Do you not think an angel rides in the whirlwind and directs this storm?"

Much time has passed since Jefferson arrived for his inauguration. The years and changes accumulate. But the themes of this day he would know: our nation's grand story of courage and its simple dream of dignity.

We are not this story's author, who fills time and eternity with his purpose. Yet his purpose is achieved in our duty, and our duty is fulfilled in service to one another.

Never tiring, never yielding, never finishing, we renew that purpose today, to make our country more just and generous, to affirm the dignity of our lives and every life.

This work continues. This story goes on. And an angel still rides in the whirlwind and directs this storm.

God bless you all, and God bless America.

President Bush's 2002 State of the Union Address

Following is President Bush's first State of the Union address, delivered to a joint session of Congress on Jan. 29, 2002.

Mr. Speaker, Vice President Cheney, members of Congress, distinguished guests, fellow citizens: As we gather tonight, our nation is at war, our economy is in recession and the civilized world faces unprecedented dangers. Yet the state of our union has never been stronger.

We last met in an hour of shock and suffering. In four short months, our nation has comforted the victims, begun to rebuild New York and the Pentagon, rallied a great coalition, captured, arrested and rid the world of thousands of terrorists, destroyed Afghanistan's terrorist training camps, saved a people from starvation and freed a country from brutal oppression.

The American flag flies again over our embassy in Kabul. Terrorists who once occupied Afghanistan now occupy cells at Guantanamo Bay. And terrorist leaders who urged followers to sacrifice their lives are running for their own.

America and Afghanistan are now allies against terror. We will be partners in rebuilding that country. And this evening we welcome the distinguished interim leader of a liberated Afghanistan: Chairman Hamid Karzai.

The last time we met in this chamber, the mothers and daughters of Afghanistan were captives in their own homes, forbidden from working or going to school. Today, women are free, and are part of Afghanistan's new government. And we welcome the new minister of women's affairs, Dr. Sima Samar.

Our progress is a tribute to the spirit of the Afghan people, to the resolve of our coalition and to the might of the United States military.

When I called our troops into action, I did so with complete confidence in their courage and skill. And tonight, thanks to them, we are winning the war on terror. The men and women of our armed forces have delivered a message now clear to every enemy of the United States: Even 7,000 miles away, across oceans and continents, on mountaintops and in caves you will not escape the justice of this nation.

For many Americans, these four months have brought sorrow and pain that will never completely go away. Every day, a retired firefighter returns to ground zero to feel closer to his two sons who died there. At a memorial in New York, a little boy left his football with a note for his lost father: "Dear Daddy, please take this to Heaven. I don't want to play football until I can play with you again someday." Last month, at the grave of her husband, Michael, a CIA officer and Marine who died in Mazar-e-Sharif, Shannon Spann said these words of farewell: "Semper fi, my love."

'OUR CAUSE IS JUST'

Shannon is with us tonight. Shannon, I assure you and all who have lost a loved one that our cause is just, and our country will never forget the debt we owe Michael and all who gave their lives for freedom.

Our cause is just, and it continues. Our discoveries in Afghanistan confirmed our worst fears and showed us the true scope of the task ahead. We have seen the depth of our enemies' hatred in videos where they laugh about the loss of innocent life. And the depth of their hatred is equaled by the madness of the destruction they design. We have found diagrams of American nuclear power plants and public water facilities, detailed instructions for making chemical weapons, surveillance maps of American cities, and thorough descriptions of landmarks in America and throughout the world.

What we have found in Afghanistan confirms that, far from ending there, our war against terror is only beginning. Most of the 19 men who hijacked planes on September the 11th were trained in Afghanistan's camps. And so were tens of thousands of others. Thousands of dangerous killers, schooled in the methods of murder, often supported by outlaw regimes, are now spread throughout the world like ticking time bombs, set to go off without warning.

Thanks to the work of our law enforcement officials and coalition partners, hundreds of terrorists have been arrested, yet tens of thousands of trained terrorists are still at large. These enemies view the entire world as a battlefield, and we must pursue them wherever they are. So long as training camps operate, so long as nations harbor terrorists, freedom is at risk, and America and our allies must not, and will not, allow it.

Our nation will continue to be steadfast, and patient and persistent in the pursuit of two great objectives. First, we will shut down terrorist camps, disrupt terrorist plans and bring terrorists to justice. And second, we must prevent the terrorists and regimes who seek chemical, biological or nuclear weapons from threatening the United States and the world.

Our military has put the terror training camps of Afghanistan out of business, yet camps still exist in at least a dozen countries. A terrorist underworld—including groups like Hamas, Hezbollah, Islamic Jihad and Jaish-i-Mohammed—operates in remote jungles and deserts, and hides in the centers of large cities.

While the most visible military action is in Afghanistan, America is acting elsewhere. We now have troops in the Philippines helping to train that country's armed forces to go after terrorist cells that have executed an American and still hold hostages. Our soldiers, working with the Bosnian government, seized terrorists who were plotting to bomb our embassy. Our Navy is patrolling the coast of Africa to block the shipment of weapons and the establishment of terrorist camps in Somalia.

My hope is that all nations will heed our call and eliminate the terrorist parasites who threaten their countries and our own. Many nations are acting forcefully. Pakistan is now cracking down on terror, and I admire the strong leadership of President Musharraf. But some governments will be timid in the face of terror. And make no mistake about it: If they do not act, America will.

'AXIS OF EVIL'

Our second goal is to prevent regimes that sponsor terror from threatening America or our friends and allies with weapons of mass destruction. Some of these regimes have been pretty quiet since Sept. 11, but we know their true nature.

North Korea is a regime arming with missiles and weapons of mass destruction, while starving its citizens.

Iran aggressively pursues these weapons and exports terror, while an unelected few repress the Iranian people's hope for freedom.

Iraq continues to flaunt its hostility toward America and to support terror. The Iraqi regime has plotted to develop anthrax and nerve gas and nuclear weapons for over a decade. This is a regime that has already used poison gas to murder thousands of its own citizens, leaving the bodies of mothers huddled over their dead children. This is a regime that agreed to international inspections then kicked out the inspectors. This is a regime that has something to hide from the civilized world.

States like these, and their terrorist allies, constitute an axis of evil, arming to threaten the peace of the world. By seeking weapons of mass destruction, these regimes pose a grave and growing danger. They could provide these arms to terrorists, giving them the means to match their hatred. They could attack our allies or attempt to blackmail the United States. In any of these cases, the price of indifference would be catastrophic.

We will work closely with our coalition to deny terrorists and their state sponsors the materials, technology and expertise to make and deliver weapons of mass destruction. We will develop and deploy effective missile defenses to protect America and our allies from sudden attack. And all nations should know: America will do what is necessary to ensure our nation's security.

We'll be deliberate, yet time is not on our side. I will not wait on events while dangers gather. I will not stand by as peril draws closer and closer. The United States of America will not permit the world's most dangerous regimes to threaten us with the world's most destructive weapons.

Our war on terror is well begun, but it is only begun. This campaign may not be finished on our watch, yet it must be and it will be waged on our watch.

We can't stop short. If we stopped now, leaving terror camps intact and terror states unchecked, our sense of security would be false and temporary. History has called America and our allies to action, and it is both our responsibility and our privilege to fight freedom's fight.

BUDGET PRIORITIES

Our first priority must always be the security of our nation, and that will be reflected in the budget I send to Congress. My budget supports three great goals for America: We will win this war, we will protect our homeland, and we will revive our economy.

Sept. 11 brought out the best in America and the best in this Congress, and I join the American people in applauding your unity and resolve.

Now Americans deserve to have this same spirit directed toward addressing problems here at home. I am a proud member of my Party. Yet as we act to win the war, protect our people and create jobs in America, we must act first and foremost not as Republicans, not as Democrats, but as Americans.

It costs a lot to fight this war. We have spent more than a billion dollars a month—over $30 million a day—and we must be prepared for future operations. Afghanistan proved that expensive precision weapons defeat the enemy and spare innocent lives, and we need more of them. We need to replace aging aircraft and make our military more agile to put our troops anywhere in the world quickly and safely.

Our men and women in uniform deserve the best weapons, the best equipment and the best training, and they also deserve another pay raise.

My budget includes the largest increase in defense spending in two decades, because while the price of freedom and security is high, it is never too high. Whatever it costs to defend our country, we will pay.

The next priority of my budget is to do everything possible to protect our citizens and strengthen our nation against the ongoing threat of another attack.

Time and distance from the events of September the 11th will not make us safer unless we act on its lessons. America is no longer protected by vast oceans. We are protected from attack only by vigorous action abroad and increased vigilance at home.

My budget nearly doubles funding for a sustained strategy of homeland security, focused on four key areas: bioterrorism, emergency response, airport and border security, and improved intelligence.

We will develop vaccines to fight anthrax and other deadly diseases. We'll increase funding to help states and communities train and equip our heroic police and firefighters. We will improve intelligence collection and sharing, expand patrols at our borders, strengthen the security of air travel, and use technology to track the arrivals and departures of visitors to the United States.

Homeland security will make America not only stronger but in many ways better. Knowledge gained from bioterrorism research will improve public health. Stronger police and fire departments will mean safer neighborhoods. Stricter border enforcement will help combat illegal drugs.

And as government works to better secure our homeland, America will continue to depend on the eyes and ears of alert citizens. A few days before Christmas, an airline flight attendant spotted a passenger lighting a match. The crew and passengers quickly subdued the man, who had been trained by al Qaeda and was armed with explosives. The people on that airplane were alert, and as a result likely saved nearly 200 lives. And tonight we welcome and thank flight attendants Hermis Moutardier and Christina Jones.

ANTICIPATING A 'SHORT-TERM' DEFICIT

Once we have funded our national security and our homeland security, the final great priority of my budget is economic security for the American people.

To achieve these great national objectives—to win the war, protect the homeland and revitalize our economy—our budget will run a deficit that will be small and short term so long as Congress restrains spending and acts in a fiscally responsible way.

We have clear priorities, and we must act at home with the same purpose and resolve we have shown overseas. We will prevail in the war, and we will defeat this recession.

Americans who have lost their jobs need our help, and I support extending unemployment benefits and direct assistance for health care coverage. Yet American workers want more than unemployment checks. They want a steady paycheck. When America works, America prospers, so my economic security plan can be summed up in one word: jobs.

Good jobs begin with good schools, and here we've made a fine start. Republicans and Democrats worked together to achieve historic education reform so that no child is left behind. I was proud to work with members of both parties, [House Education Committee] Chairman John Boehner [R-Ohio] and Congressman George Miller [of California, the panel's ranking Democrat], Senator Judd Gregg [of New Hampshire, ranking Republican on the Senate Health, Education, Labor and Pensions (HELP) Committee].

And I was so proud of our work, I even had nice things to say about my friend Ted Kennedy [Edward M. Kennedy, D-Mass., the HELP Committee's chairman]. I know the folks at the Crawford coffee shop couldn't believe I'd say such a thing. But our work on this bill shows what is possible if we set aside posturing and focus on results.

A CALL FOR PERMANENT TAX CUTS

There's more to do. We need to prepare our children to read and succeed in school with improved Head Start and early childhood development programs. We must upgrade our teacher colleges and teacher training and launch a major recruiting drive with a great goal for America: a quality teacher in every classroom.

Good jobs also depend on reliable and affordable energy. This Congress must act to encourage conservation, promote technology, build infrastructure, and it must act to increase energy production at home so America is less dependent on foreign oil.

Good jobs depend on expanded trade. Selling into new markets creates new jobs, so I ask Congress to finally approve trade promotion authority.

On these two key issues, trade and energy, the House of Representatives has acted to create jobs, and I urge the Senate to pass this legislation.

Good jobs depend on sound tax policy. Last year, some in this hall thought my tax relief plan was too small, some thought it was too big. But when those checks arrived in the mail, most Americans thought tax relief was just about right. Congress listened to the people and responded by reducing tax rates, doubling the child credit and ending the death tax. For the sake of long-term growth, and to help Americans plan for the future, let's make these tax cuts permanent.

The way out of this recession, the way to create jobs, is to grow the economy by encouraging investment in factories and equipment, and by speeding up tax relief so people have more money to spend. For the sake of American workers, let's pass a stimulus package.

ENSURING RETIREMENT SECURITY

Good jobs must be the aim of welfare reform. As we reauthorize these important reforms, we must always remember: The goal is to reduce dependency on government and offer every American the dignity of a job. Americans know economic security can vanish in an instant without health security. I ask Congress to join me this year to enact a patients' bill of rights, to give uninsured workers credits to help buy health coverage, to approve an historic increase in spending for veterans' health and to give seniors a sound and modern Medicare system that includes coverage for prescription drugs.

A good job should lead to security in retirement. I ask Congress to enact new safeguards for 401(k) and pension plans. Employees who have worked hard and saved all their lives should not have to risk losing everything if their company fails. Through stricter accounting standards and tougher disclosure requirements, corporate America must be made more accountable to employees and shareholders and held to the highest standards of conduct.

Retirement security also depends upon keeping the commitments of Social Security, and we will. We must make Social Security financially stable and allow personal retirement accounts for younger workers who choose them.

Members, you and I will work together in the months ahead on other issues: productive farm policy, a cleaner environment, broader home ownership—especially among minorities—and ways to encourage the good work of charities and faith-based groups.

I ask you to join me on these important domestic issues in the same spirit of cooperation we have applied to our war against terrorism.

During these last few months, I've been humbled and privileged to see the true character of this country in a time of testing. Our enemies believed America was weak and materialistic, that we would splinter in fear and selfishness. They were as wrong as they are evil.

The American people have responded magnificently, with courage and compassion, strength and resolve. As I have met the heroes, hugged the families and looked into the tired faces of rescuers, I have stood in awe of the American people.

And I hope you will join me in expressing thanks to one American for the strength and calm and comfort she brings to our nation in crisis: our first lady, Laura Bush.

CREATING A 'FREEDOM CORPS'

None of us would ever wish the evil that was done on September the 11th, yet after America was attacked, it was as if our entire country looked into a mirror and saw our better selves. We were reminded that we are citizens with obligations to each other, to our country, and to history. We began to think less of the goods we can accumulate and more about the good we can do.

For too long our culture has said, "If it feels good, do it." Now America is embracing a new ethic and a new creed: "Let's roll."

In the sacrifice of soldiers, the fierce brotherhood of firefighters, and the bravery and generosity of ordinary citizens, we have glimpsed what a new culture of responsibility could look like. We want to be a nation that serves goals larger than self. We have been offered a unique opportunity, and we must not let this moment pass. My call tonight is for every American to commit at least two years—4,000 hours—over the rest of your lifetime to the service of your neighbors and your nation.

Many are already serving, and I thank you. If you aren't sure how to help, I've got a good place to start. To sustain and extend the best that has emerged in America, I invite you to join the new USA Freedom Corps. The Freedom Corps will focus on three areas of need: responding in case of crisis at home, rebuilding our communities and extending American compassion throughout the world.

One purpose of the USA Freedom Corps will be homeland security. America needs retired doctors and nurses who can be mobilized in major emergencies, volunteers to help police and fire departments, transportation and utility workers well trained in spotting danger. Our country also needs citizens working to rebuild our communities. We need mentors to love children, especially children whose parents are in prison. And we need more talented teachers in troubled schools.

USA Freedom Corps will expand and improve the good efforts of AmeriCorps and Senior Corps to recruit more than 200,000 new volunteers.

And America needs citizens to extend the compassion of our country to every part of the world, so we will renew the promise of the Peace Corps, double its volunteers over the next five years and ask it to join a new effort to encourage development and education and opportunity in the Islamic world.

This time of adversity offers a unique moment of opportunity, a moment we must seize to change our culture. Through the gathering momentum of millions of acts of service and decency and kindness, I know we can overcome evil with greater good.

And we have a great opportunity during this time of war to lead the world toward the values that will bring lasting peace. All fathers and mothers, in all societies, want their children to be educated and live free from poverty and violence. No people on Earth yearn to be oppressed or aspire to servitude or eagerly await the midnight knock of the secret police.

If anyone doubts this, let them look to Afghanistan, where the Islamic "street" greeted the fall of tyranny with song and celebration. Let the skeptics look to Islam's own rich history, with its centuries of learning and tolerance and progress.

DEFENSE OF 'HUMAN DIGNITY'

America will lead by defending liberty and justice because they are right and true and unchanging for all people everywhere. No nation owns these aspirations, and no nation is exempt from them. We have no intention of imposing our culture, but America will always stand firm for the non-negotiable demands of human dignity: the rule of law, limits on the power of the state, respect for women, private property, free speech, equal justice and religious tolerance.

America will take the side of brave men and women who advocate these values around the world—including the Islamic world—because we have a greater objective than eliminating threats and containing resentment. We seek a just and peaceful world beyond the war on terror.

In this moment of opportunity, a common danger is erasing old rivalries. America is working with Russia and China and India in ways we never have before to achieve peace and prosperity. In every region, free markets and free trade and free societies are proving their power to lift lives. Together with friends and allies from Europe to Asia, and Africa to Latin America, we will demonstrate that the forces of terror cannot stop the momentum of freedom.

The last time I spoke here, I expressed the hope that life would return to normal. In some ways it has. In others it never will. Those of us who have lived through these challenging times have been changed by them. We've come to know truths that we will never question: Evil is real, and it must be opposed.

Beyond all differences of race or creed, we are one country, mourning together and facing danger together. Deep in the American character there is honor, and it is stronger than cynicism. And many have discovered again that even in tragedy—especially in tragedy—God is near.

In a single instant, we realized that this will be a decisive decade in the history of liberty, that we have been called to a unique role in human events. Rarely has the world faced a choice more clear or consequential.

Our enemies send other people's children on missions of suicide and murder. They embrace tyranny and death as a cause and a creed. We stand for a different choice, made long ago, on the day of our founding. We affirm it again today. We choose freedom and the dignity of every life.

Steadfast in our purpose, we now press on. We have known freedom's price. We have shown freedom's power. And in this great conflict, my fellow Americans, we will see freedom's victory. Thank you all, and may God bless.

President Bush's 2003 State of the Union Address

Following President Bush's second State of the Union address, delivered to a joint session of Congress on Jan. 28, 2003.

Mr. Speaker, Vice President Cheney, members of Congress, distinguished citizens and fellow citizens, every year, by law and by custom, we meet here to consider the state of the union. This year, we gather in this chamber deeply aware of decisive days that lie ahead.

You and I serve our country in a time of great consequence. During this session of Congress, we have the duty to reform domestic programs vital to our country, we have the opportunity to save millions of lives abroad from a terrible disease. We will work for a prosperity that is broadly shared, and we will answer every danger and every enemy that threatens the American people.

In all these days of promise and days of reckoning, we can be confident.

In a whirlwind of change, and hope, and peril, our faith is sure, our resolve is firm, and our union is strong.

This country has many challenges. We will not deny, we will not ignore, we will not pass along our problems to other Congresses, to other presidents, and other generations.

We will confront them with focus, and clarity, and courage.

During the last two years we have seen what can be accomplished when we work together.

To lift the standards of our public schools, we achieved historic education reform, which must now be carried out in every school and in every classroom so that every child in America can read and learn and succeed in life.

To protect our country, we reorganized our government and created the Department of Homeland Security, which is mobilizing against the threats of a new era.

To bring our economy out of recession, we delivered the largest tax relief in a generation.

To insist on integrity in American business, we passed tough reforms, and we are holding corporate criminals to account.

Some might call this a good record. I call it a good start. Tonight, I ask the House and the Senate to join me in the next bold steps to serve our fellow citizens.

BOOSTING THE ECONOMY

Our first goal is clear: We must have an economy that grows fast enough to employ every man and woman who seeks a job.

After recession, terrorist attacks, corporate scandals and stock market declines, our economy is recovering. Yet it is not growing fast enough, or strongly enough.

With unemployment rising, our nation needs more small businesses to open, more companies to invest and expand, more employers to put up the sign that says, "Help Wanted."

Jobs are created when the economy grows; the economy grows when Americans have more money to spend and invest; and the best and fairest way to make sure Americans have that money is not to tax it away in the first place.

I am proposing that all the income tax reductions set for 2004 and 2006 be made permanent and effective this year.

And under my plan, as soon as I've signed the bill, this extra money will start showing up in workers' paychecks.

Instead of gradually reducing the marriage penalty, we should do it now.

Instead of slowly raising the child credit to $1,000, we should send the checks to American families now.

This tax relief is for everyone who pays income taxes, and it will help our economy immediately. Ninety-two million Americans will keep this year an average of almost $1,100 more of their own money. A family of four with an income of $40,000 would see their federal income taxes fall from $1,178 to $45 per year.

And our plan will improve the bottom line for more than 23 million small businesses.

You, the Congress, have already passed all these reductions, and promised them for future years.

If this tax relief is good for Americans three or five or seven years from now, it is even better for Americans today.

We should also strengthen the economy by treating investors equally in our tax laws. It's fair to tax a company's profits. It is not fair to again tax the shareholder on the same profits.

To boost investor confidence, and to help the nearly 10 million seniors who receive dividend income, I ask you to end the unfair double taxation of dividends.

Lower taxes and greater investment will help this economy expand. More jobs mean more taxpayers and higher revenues to our government.

The best way to address the deficit and move toward a balanced budget is to encourage economic growth and to show some spending discipline in Washington, D.C.

We must work together to fund only our most important priorities. I will send you a budget that increases discretionary spending by 4 percent next year, about as much as the average family's income is expected to grow. And that is a good benchmark for us: Federal spending should not rise any faster than the paychecks of American families.

A growing economy and a focus on essential priorities will be crucial to the future of Social Security. As we continue to work together to keep Social Security sound and reliable, we must offer younger workers a chance to invest in retirement accounts that they will control and they will own.

HEALTH CARE FOR EVERYONE

Our second goal is high quality, affordable health for all Americans.

The American system of medicine is a model of skill and innovation, with a pace of discovery that is adding good years to our lives. Yet for many people, medical care costs too much, and many have no coverage at all.

These problems will not be solved with a nationalized health care system that dictates coverage and rations care.

Instead, we must work toward a system in which all Americans have a good insurance policy, choose their own doctors, and seniors and low-income Americans receive the help they need.

Instead of bureaucrats and trial lawyers and HMOs, we must put doctors and nurses and patients back in charge of American medicine.

Health care reform must begin with Medicare; Medicare is the binding commitment of a caring society.

We must renew that commitment by giving seniors access to the preventive medicine and new drugs that are transforming health care in America.

Seniors happy with the current Medicare system should be able to keep their coverage just the way it is.

And just like you, the members of Congress, and your staffs and other federal employees, all seniors should have the choice of a health care plan that provides prescription drugs.

My budget will commit an additional $400 billion over the next decade to reform and strengthen Medicare. Leaders of both political parties have talked for years about strengthening Medicare. I urge the members of this new Congress to act this year.

To improve our health care system, we must address one of the prime causes of higher cost: the constant threat that physicians and hospitals will be unfairly sued.

Because of excessive litigation, everybody pays more for health care, and many parts of America are losing fine doctors. No one has ever been healed by a frivolous lawsuit; I urge the Congress to pass medical liability reform.

ENERGY AND THE ENVIRONMENT

Our third goal is to promote energy independence for our country, while dramatically improving the environment.

I have sent you a comprehensive energy plan to promote energy efficiency and conservation, to develop cleaner technology, and to produce more energy at home.

I have sent you clear skies legislation that mandates a 70 percent cut in air pollution from power plants over the next 15 years.

I have sent you a healthy forest initiative to help prevent the catastrophic fires that devastate communities, kill wildlife and burn away millions of acres of treasured forests.

I urge you to pass these measures for the good of both our environment and our economy.

Even more, I ask you to take a crucial step and protect our environment in ways that generations before us could not have imagined.

In this century, the greatest environmental progress will come about not through endless lawsuits or command-and-control regulations, but through technology and innovation.

Tonight I'm proposing $1.2 billion in research funding so that America can lead the world in developing clean, hydrogen-powered automobiles.

A simple chemical reaction between hydrogen and oxygen generates energy, which can be used to power a car, producing only water, not exhaust fumes.

With a new national commitment, our scientists and engineers will overcome obstacles to taking these cars from laboratory to showroom, so that the first car driven by a child born today could be powered by hydrogen, and pollution-free.

Join me in this important innovation to make our air significantly cleaner, and our country much less dependent on foreign sources of energy.

EMPOWERING AMERICANS

Our fourth goal is to apply the compassion of America to the deepest problems of America. For so many in our country—the homeless, and the fatherless, the addicted—the need is great. Yet there is power—wonder-working power—in the goodness and idealism and faith of the American people.

Americans are doing the work of compassion every day: visiting prisoners, providing shelter for battered women, bringing companionship to lonely seniors. These good works deserve our praise, they deserve our personal support and, when appropriate, they deserve the assistance of the federal government.

I urge you to pass both my faith-based initiative and the Citizen Service Act to encourage acts of compassion that can transform America one heart and one soul at a time.

Last year, I called on my fellow citizens to participate in the USA Freedom Corps, which is enlisting tens of thousands of new volunteers across America.

Tonight, I ask Congress and the American people to focus the spirit of service and the resources of government on the needs of some of our most vulnerable citizens: boys and girls trying to grow up without guidance and attention, and children who have to go through a prison gate to be hugged by their mom or dad.

I propose a $450 million initiative to bring mentors to more than a million disadvantaged junior high students and children of prisoners.

Government will support the training and recruiting of mentors, yet it is the men and women of America who will fill the need. One mentor, one person, can change a life forever, and I urge you to be that one person.

THE FIGHT AGAINST DRUGS

Another cause of hopelessness is addiction to drugs. Addiction crowds out friendship, ambition, moral conviction, and reduces all the richness of life to a single destructive desire.

As a government, we are fighting illegal drugs by cutting off supplies and reducing demand through anti-drug education programs. Yet for those already addicted, the fight against drugs is a fight for their own lives.

Too many Americans in search of treatment cannot get it. So tonight I propose a new $600 million program to help an additional 300,000 Americans receive treatment over the next three years.

Our nation is blessed with recovery programs that do amazing work. One of them is found at the Healing Place Church in Baton Rouge, La. A man in the program said, "God does miracles in people's lives, and you never think it could be you."

Tonight, let us bring to all Americans who struggle with drug addiction this message of hope: The miracle of recovery is possible, and it could be you.

By caring for children who need mentors, and for addicted men and women who need treatment, we are building a more welcoming society, a culture that values every life.

And in this work we must not overlook the weakest among us. I ask you to protect infants at the very hour of their birth and end the practice of "partial birth" abortion.

And because no human life should be started or ended as the object of an experiment, I ask you to set a high standard for humanity and pass a law against all human cloning.

OVERSEAS PEACE AND AID

The qualities of courage and compassion that we strive for in America also determine our conduct abroad. The American flag stands for more than our power and our interests. Our founders dedicated this country to the cause of human dignity, the rights of every person and the possibilities of every life.

This conviction leads us into the world to help the afflicted, and defend the peace, and confound the designs of evil men.

In Afghanistan, we helped to liberate an oppressed people, and we will continue helping them secure their country, rebuild their society and educate all their children, boys and girls.

In the Middle East, we will continue to seek peace between a secure Israel and a democratic Palestine.

Across the earth, America is feeding the hungry. More than 60 percent of international food aid comes as a gift from the people of the United States.

As our nation moves troops and builds alliances to make our world safer, we must also remember our calling, as a blessed country, is to make the world better.

Today, on the continent of Africa, nearly 30 million people have the AIDS virus, including 3 million children under the age of 15. There are whole countries in Africa where more than one-third of the adult population carries the infection. More than 4 million require immediate drug treatment. Yet across that continent, only 50,000 AIDS victims—only 50,000—are receiving the medicine they need.

Because the AIDS diagnosis is considered a death sentence, many do not seek treatment. Almost all who do are turned away.

A doctor in rural South Africa describes his frustration. He says, "We have no medicines, many hospitals tell people, 'You've got AIDS. We can't help you. Go home and die.' "

In an age of miraculous medicines, no person should have to hear those words.

AIDS can be prevented. Anti-retroviral drugs can extend life for many years. And the cost of those drugs has dropped from $12,000 a year to under $300 a year, which places a tremendous possibility within our grasp.

Ladies and gentlemen, seldom has history offered a greater opportunity to do so much for so many.

We have confronted, and will continue to confront, HIV/AIDS in our own country. And to meet a severe and urgent crisis abroad, tonight I propose the Emergency Plan for AIDS Relief, a work of mercy beyond all current international efforts to help the people of Africa.

This comprehensive plan will prevent 7 million new AIDS infections, treat at least 2 million people with life-extending drugs and provide humane care for millions of people suffering from AIDS and for children orphaned by AIDS.

I ask the Congress to commit $15 billion over the next five years, including nearly $10 billion in new money, to turn the tide against AIDS in the most afflicted nations of Africa and the Caribbean.

This nation can lead the world in sparing innocent people from a plague of nature.

DEFEATING TERRORISM

And this nation is leading the world in confronting and defeating the man-made evil of international terrorism.

There are days when our fellow citizens do not hear news about the war on terror. There's never a day when I do not learn of another threat, or receive reports of operations in progress, or give an order in this global war against a scattered network of killers.

The war goes on, and we are winning.

To date, we have arrested or otherwise dealt with many key commanders of al Qaeda. They include a man who directed logistics and funding for the September the 11th attacks; the chief of al Qaeda operations in the Persian Gulf who planned the bombings of our embassies in East Africa and the USS *Cole;* an al Qaeda operations chief from Southeast Asia; a former director of al Qaeda's training camps in Afghanistan; a key al Qaeda operative in Europe; a major al Qaeda leader in Yemen.

All told, more than 3,000 suspected terrorists have been arrested in many countries.

And many others have met a different fate. Let's put it this way: They are no longer a problem to the United States and our friends and allies.

We are working closely with other nations to prevent further attacks. America and coalition countries have uncovered and stopped terrorist conspiracies targeting the embassy in Yemen, the American embassy in Singapore, a Saudi military base, ships in the Straits of Hormuz and the Straits of Gibraltar. We've broken al Qaeda cells in Hamburg and Milan and Madrid and London and Paris—as well as Buffalo, N.Y.

We've got the terrorists on the run. We're keeping them on the run. One by one, the terrorists are learning the meaning of American justice.

SECURITY AT HOME

As we fight this war, we will remember where it began: here, in our own country. This government is taking unprecedented measures to protect our people and defend our homeland.

We've intensified security at the borders and ports of entry, posted more than 50,000 newly trained federal screeners in airports, begun inoculating troops and first responders against smallpox, and are deploying the nation's first early warning network of sensors to detect biological attack.

And this year, for the first time, we are beginning to field a defense to protect this nation against ballistic missiles.

I thank the Congress for supporting these measures. I ask you tonight to add to our future security with a major research and production effort to guard our people against bioterrorism, called Project Bioshield.

The budget I send you will propose almost $6 billion to quickly make available effective vaccines and treatments against agents like anthrax, botulinum toxin, ebola and plague. We must assume that our enemies would use these diseases as weapons, and we must act before the dangers are upon us.

Since September the 11th, our intelligence and law enforcement agencies have worked more closely than ever to track and disrupt the terrorists. The FBI is improving its ability to analyze intelligence, and is transforming itself to meet new threats.

Tonight, I am instructing the leaders of the FBI, the CIA, the Homeland Security and the Department of Defense to develop a Terrorist Threat Integration Center, to merge and analyze all threat information in a single location.

Our government must have the very best information possible, and we will use it to make sure the right people are in the right places to protect our citizens.

Our war against terror is a contest of will in which perseverance is power. In the ruins of two towers, at the western wall of the Pentagon, on a field in Pennsylvania, this nation made a pledge, and we renew that pledge tonight: Whatever the duration of this struggle and whatever the difficulties, we will not permit the triumph of violence in the affairs of men; free people will set the course of history.

Today, the gravest danger in the war on terror, the gravest danger facing America and the world, is outlaw regimes that seek and possess nuclear, chemical and biological weapons.

These regimes could use such weapons for blackmail, terror and mass murder. They could also give or sell those weapons to terrorist allies, who would use them without the least hesitation.

This threat is new; America's duty is familiar.

Throughout the 20th century, small groups of men seized control of great nations, built armies and arsenals, and set out to dominate the weak and intimidate the world.

In each case, their ambitions of cruelty and murder had no limit. In each case, the ambitions of Hitlerism, militarism and communism were defeated by the will of free peoples, by the strength of great alliances and by the might of the United States of America.

Now, in this century, the ideology of power and domination has appeared again and seeks to gain the ultimate weapons of terror.

U.N. SUPPORT

Once again, this nation and our friends are all that stand between a world at peace, and a world of chaos and constant alarm. Once again, we are called to defend the safety of our people and the hopes of all mankind. And we accept this responsibility.

America is making a broad and determined effort to confront these dangers.

We have called on the United Nations to fulfill its charter and stand by its demand that Iraq disarm. We are strongly supporting the International Atomic Energy Agency in its mission to track and control nuclear materials around the world. We are working with other governments to secure nuclear materials in the former Soviet Union and to strengthen global treaties banning the production and shipment of missile technologies and weapons of mass destruction.

In all of these efforts, however, America's purpose is more than to follow a process. It is to achieve a result: the end of terrible threats to the civilized world.

All free nations have a stake in preventing sudden and catastrophic attacks, and we're asking them to join us, and many are doing so.

Yet, the course of this nation does not depend on the decisions of others.

Whatever action is required, whenever action is necessary, I will defend the freedom and security of the American people.

Different threats require different strategies. In Iran, we continue to see a government that represses its people, pursues weapons of mass destruction and supports terror.

We also see Iranian citizens risking intimidation and death as they speak out for liberty and human rights and democracy. Iranians, like all people, have a right to choose their own government and determine their own destiny, and the United States supports their aspirations to live in freedom.

NORTH KOREA'S DECEIT

On the Korean Peninsula, an oppressive regime rules a people living in fear and starvation. Throughout the 1990s, the United States relied on a negotiated framework to keep North Korea from gaining nuclear weapons. We now know that that regime was deceiving the world and developing those weapons all along.

And today the North Korean regime is using its nuclear program to incite fear and seek concessions.

America and the world will not be blackmailed.

America is working with the countries of the region—South Korea, Japan, China and Russia—to find a peaceful solution and to show the North Korean government that nuclear weapons will bring only isolation, economic stagnation and continued hardship.

The North Korean regime will find respect in the world and revival for its people only when it turns away from its nuclear ambitions.

Our nation and the world must learn the lessons of the Korean Peninsula and not allow an even greater threat to rise up in Iraq. A brutal dictator, with a history of reckless aggression, with ties to terrorism, with great potential wealth will not be permitted to dominate a vital region and threaten the United States.

IRAQI THREATS

Twelve years ago, Saddam Hussein faced the prospect of being the last casualty in a war he had started and lost. To spare himself, he agreed to disarm of all weapons of mass destruction.

For the next 12 years, he systematically violated that agreement. He pursued chemical, biological and nuclear weapons even while inspectors were in his country.

Nothing to date has restrained him from his pursuit of these weapons: not economic sanctions, not isolation from the civilized world, not even cruise missile strikes on his military facilities.

Almost three months ago, the United Nations Security Council gave Saddam Hussein his final chance to disarm. He has shown instead utter contempt for the United Nations and for the opinion of the world.

The 108 U.N. inspectors were not sent to conduct a scavenger hunt for hidden materials across a country the size of California. The job of the inspectors is to verify that Iraq's regime is disarming.

It is up to Iraq to show exactly where it is hiding its banned weapons, lay those weapons out for the world to see and destroy them as directed. Nothing like this has happened.

GERM WARFARE

The United Nations concluded in 1999 that Saddam Hussein had biological weapons materials sufficient to produce over 25,000 liters of anthrax; enough doses to kill several million people. He hasn't accounted for that material. He has given no evidence that he has destroyed it.

The United Nations concluded that Saddam Hussein had materials sufficient to produce more than 38,000 liters of botulinum toxin; enough to subject millions of people to death by respiratory failure. He hasn't accounted for that material. He's given no evidence that he has destroyed it.

Our intelligence officials estimate that Saddam Hussein had the materials to produce as much as 500 tons of sarin, mustard and VX nerve agent. In such quantities, these chemical agents could also kill untold thousands. He's not accounted for these materials. He has given no evidence that he has destroyed them.

U.S. intelligence indicates that Saddam Hussein had upwards of 30,000 munitions capable of delivering chemical agents. Inspectors recently turned up 16 of them, despite Iraq's recent declaration denying their existence. Saddam Hussein has not accounted for the remaining 29,984 of these prohibited munitions. He has given no evidence that he has destroyed them.

From three Iraqi defectors, we know that Iraq, in the late 1990s, had several mobile biological weapons labs. These are designed to produce germ warfare agents and can be moved from place to place to evade inspectors. Saddam Hussein has not disclosed these facilities. He has given no evidence that he has destroyed them.

The International Atomic Energy Agency confirmed in the 1990s that Saddam Hussein had an advanced nuclear weapons development program, had a design for a nuclear weapon and was working on five different methods of enriching uranium for a bomb.

The British government has learned that Saddam Hussein recently sought significant quantities of uranium from Africa.

Our intelligence sources tell us that he has attempted to purchase high-strength aluminum tubes suitable for nuclear weapons production.

Saddam Hussein has not credibly explained these activities. He clearly has much to hide.

The dictator of Iraq is not disarming. To the contrary, he is deceiving.

From intelligence sources, we know, for instance, that thousands of Iraqi security personnel are at work hiding documents and materials from the U.N. inspectors, sanitizing inspection sites and monitoring the inspectors themselves.

Iraqi officials accompany the inspectors in order to intimidate witnesses. Iraq is blocking U-2 surveillance flights requested by the United Nations.

Iraqi intelligence officers are posing as the scientists inspectors are supposed to interview. Real scientists have been coached by Iraqi officials on what to say.

Intelligence sources indicate that Saddam Hussein has ordered that scientists who cooperate with U.N. inspectors in disarming Iraq will be killed, along with their families.

Year after year, Saddam Hussein has gone to elaborate lengths, spent enormous sums, taken great risks to build and keep weapons of mass destruction. But why?

The only possible explanation, the only possible use he could have for those weapons, is to dominate, intimidate or attack.

AIDING AL QAEDA

With nuclear arms or a full arsenal of chemical and biological weapons, Saddam Hussein could resume his ambitions of conquest in the Middle East and create deadly havoc in that region.

And this Congress and the American people must recognize another threat. Evidence from intelligence sources, secret communications and statements by people now in custody reveal that Saddam Hussein aids and protects terrorists, including members of al Qaeda. Secretly, and without fingerprints, he could provide one of his hidden weapons to terrorists, or help them develop their own.

Before September the 11th, many in the world believed that Saddam Hussein could be contained. But chemical agents, lethal viruses and shadowy terrorist networks are not easily contained.

Imagine those 19 hijackers with other weapons and other plans, this time armed by Saddam Hussein. It would take one vial, one canister, one crate slipped into this country to bring a day of horror like none we have ever known.

We will do everything in our power to make sure that that day never comes.

Some have said we must not act until the threat is imminent. Since when have terrorists and tyrants announced their intentions, politely putting us on notice before they strike?

If this threat is permitted to fully and suddenly emerge, all actions, all words and all recriminations would come too late. Trusting in the sanity and restraint of Saddam Hussein is not a strategy, and it is not an option.

The dictator who is assembling the world's most dangerous weapons has already used them on whole villages, leaving thousands of his own citizens dead, blind or disfigured.

Iraqi refugees tell us how forced confessions are obtained: by torturing children while their parents are made to watch. International human rights groups have catalogued other methods used in the torture chambers of Iraq: electric shock, burning with hot irons, dripping acid on the skin, mutilation with electric drills, cutting out tongues, and rape.

If this is not evil, then evil has no meaning.

And tonight I have a message for the brave and oppressed people of Iraq: Your enemy is not surrounding your country, your enemy is ruling your country.

And the day he and his regime are removed from power will be the day of your liberation.

A PLEA TO THE UNITED NATIONS

The world has waited 12 years for Iraq to disarm. America will not accept a serious and mounting threat to our country and our friends and our allies.

The United States will ask the U.N. Security Council to convene on February the 5th to consider the facts of Iraq's ongoing defiance of the world. Secretary of State [Colin L.] Powell will present information and intelligence about Iraq's illegal weapons programs, its attempts to hide those weapons from inspectors and its links to terrorist groups.

We will consult, but let there be no misunderstanding: If Saddam Hussein does not fully disarm for the safety of our people, and for the peace of the world, we will lead a coalition to disarm him.

Tonight I have a message for the men and women who will keep the peace, members of the American armed forces. Many of you are assembling in or near the Middle East, and some crucial hours may lay ahead.

In those hours, the success of our cause will depend on you. Your training has prepared you. Your honor will guide you. You believe in America, and America believes in you.

Sending Americans into battle is the most profound decision a president can make. The technologies of war have changed. The risks and suffering of war have not.

For the brave Americans who bear the risk, no victory is free from sorrow.

This nation fights reluctantly, because we know the cost, and we dread the days of mourning that always come.

We seek peace. We strive for peace. And sometimes peace must be defended. A future lived at the mercy of terrible threats is no peace at all.

If war is forced upon us, we will fight in a just cause and by just means, sparing, in every way we can, the innocent.

And if war is forced upon us, we will fight with the full force and might of the United States military, and we will prevail.

'GOD'S GIFT TO HUMANITY'

And as we and our coalition partners are doing in Afghanistan, we will bring to the Iraqi people food and medicines and supplies and freedom.

Many challenges, abroad and at home, have arrived in a single season. In two years, America has gone from a sense of invulnerability to an awareness of peril, from bitter division in small matters to calm unity in great causes.

And we go forward with confidence, because this call of history has come to the right country.

Americans are a resolute people, who have risen to every test of our time. Adversity has revealed the character of our country, to the world, and to ourselves.

America is a strong nation and honorable in the use of our strength. We exercise power without conquest, and we sacrifice for the liberty of strangers.

Americans are a free people, who know that freedom is the right of every person and the future of every nation. The liberty we prize is not America's gift to the world; it is God's gift to humanity.

We Americans have faith in ourselves, but not in ourselves alone. We do not claim to know all the ways of Providence, yet we can trust in them, placing our confidence in the loving God behind all of life and all of history.

May He guide us now, and may God continue to bless the United States of America.

Thank you.

President Bush's 2004 State of the Union Address

Following is President Bush's third State of the Union address, delivered to a joint session of Congress on Jan. 20, 2004.

Mr. Speaker, Vice President [Dick] Cheney, Members of Congress, distinguished guests, and fellow citizens:

America this evening is a Nation called to great responsibilities. And we are rising to meet them.

As we gather tonight, hundreds of thousands of American service men and women are deployed across the world in the war on terror. By bringing hope to the oppressed, and delivering justice to the violent, they are making America more secure.

Each day, law enforcement personnel and intelligence officers are tracking terrorist threats; analysts are examining airline passenger lists; the men and women of our new Homeland Security Department are patrolling our coasts and borders. And their vigilance is protecting America.

Americans are proving once again to be the hardest working people in the world. The American economy is growing stronger. The tax relief you passed is working.

Tonight, Members of Congress can take pride in great works of compassion and reform that skeptics had thought impossible. You are raising the standards of our public schools; and you are giving our senior citizens prescription drug coverage under Medicare.

We have faced serious challenges together—and now we face a choice. We can go forward with confidence and resolve—or we can turn back to the dangerous illusion that terrorists are not plotting and outlaw regimes are no threat to us. We can press on with economic growth, and reforms in education and Medicare—or we can turn back to the old policies and old divisions.

We have not come all this way—through tragedy, and trial, and war—only to falter and leave our work unfinished. Americans are rising to the tasks of history, and they expect the same of us. In their efforts, their enterprise, and their character, the American people are showing that the state of our Union is confident and strong.

HOMELAND SECURITY

Our greatest responsibility is the active defense of the American people. Twenty-eight months have passed since September 11, 2001—over 2 years without an attack on American soil—and it is tempting to believe that the danger is behind us. That hope is understandable, comforting—and false. The killing has continued in Bali, Jakarta, Casablanca, Riyadh, Mombassa, Jerusalem, Istanbul, and Baghdad. The terrorists continue to plot against America and the civilized world. And by our will and courage, this danger will be defeated.

Inside the United States, where the war began, we must continue to give homeland security and law enforcement personnel every tool they need to defend us. And one of those essential tools is the Patriot Act, which allows Federal law enforcement to better share information, to track terrorists, to disrupt their cells, and to seize their assets. For years, we have used similar provisions to catch embezzlers and drug traffickers. If these methods are good for hunting criminals, they are even more important for hunting terrorists. Key provisions of the Patriot Act are set to expire next year. The terrorist threat will not expire on that schedule. Our law enforcement needs this vital legislation to protect our citizens—you need to renew the Patriot Act.

America is on the offensive against the terrorists who started this war. Last March, Khalid Shaikh Mohammed, a mastermind of September 11th, awoke to find himself in the custody of U.S. and Pakistani authorities. Last August 11th brought the capture of the terrorist Hambali, who was a key player in the attack in Indonesia that killed over 200 people. We are tracking al Qaeda around the world—and nearly two-thirds of their known leaders have now been captured or killed. Thousands of very skilled and determined military personnel are on a manhunt, going after the remaining killers who hide in cities and caves—and, one by one, we will bring the terrorists to justice.

As part of the offensive against terror, we are also confronting the regimes that harbor and support terrorists, and could supply them with nuclear, chemical, or biological weapons. The United States and our allies are determined: We refuse to live in the shadow of this ultimate danger.

AFGHANISTAN AND IRAQ

The first to see our determination were the Taliban, who made Afghanistan the primary training base of al Qaeda killers. As of this month, that country has a new constitution, guaranteeing free elections and full participation by women. Businesses are opening, health care centers are being established, and the boys and girls of Afghanistan are back in school. With help from the new Afghan Army, our coalition is leading aggressive raids against surviving members of the Taliban and al Qaeda. The men and women of Afghanistan are building a nation that is free, and proud, and fighting terror—and America is honored to be their friend.

Since we last met in this chamber, combat forces of the United States, Great Britain, Australia, Poland, and other countries enforced the demands of the United Nations, ended the rule of Saddam Hussein—and the people of Iraq are free. Having broken the Baathist regime, we face a remnant of violent Saddam supporters. Men who ran away from our troops in battle are now dispersed and attack from the shadows.

These killers, joined by foreign terrorists, are a serious, continuing danger. Yet we are making progress against them. The once all-powerful ruler of Iraq was found in a hole, and now sits in a prison cell. Of the top 55 officials of the former regime, we have captured or killed 45. Our forces are on the offensive, leading over 1,600 patrols a day, and conducting an average of 180 raids every week. We are dealing with these thugs in Iraq, just as surely as we dealt with Saddam Hussein's evil regime.

The work of building a new Iraq is hard, and it is right. And America has always been willing to do what it takes for what is right. Last January, Iraq's only law was the whim of one brutal man. Today our coalition is working with the Iraqi Governing Council to draft a basic law, with a bill of rights. We are working with Iraqis and the United Nations to prepare for a transition to full Iraqi sovereignty by the end of June. As democracy takes hold in Iraq, the enemies of freedom will do all in their power to spread violence and fear. They are trying to shake the will of our country and our friends—but the United States of America will never be intimidated by thugs and assassins. The killers will fail, and the Iraqi people will live in freedom.

Month by month, Iraqis are assuming more responsibility for their own security and their own future. And tonight we are honored to welcome one of Iraq's most respected leaders: the current President of the Iraqi Governing Council, Adnan Pachachi. Sir, America stands with you and the Iraqi people as you build a free and peaceful nation.

Because of American leadership and resolve, the world is changing for the better. Last month, the leader of Libya voluntarily pledged to disclose and dismantle all of his regime's weapons of mass destruction programs, including a uranium enrichment project for nuclear weapons. Colonel Qadhafi correctly judged that his country would be better off, and far more secure, without weapons of mass murder. Nine months of intense negotiations involving the United States and Great Britain succeeded with Libya, while 12 years of diplomacy with Iraq did not. And one reason is clear: for diplomacy to be effective, words must be credible—and no one can now doubt the word of America.

Different threats require different strategies. Along with nations in the region, we are insisting that North Korea eliminate its nuclear program. America and the international community are demanding that Iran meet its commitments and not develop nuclear weapons. America is committed to keeping the world's most dangerous weapons out of the hands of the world's most dangerous regimes.

When I came to this rostrum on September 20, 2001, I brought the police shield of a fallen officer, my reminder of lives that ended, and a task that does not end. I gave to you and to all Americans my complete commitment to securing our country and defeating our enemies. And this pledge, given by one, has been kept by many. You in the Congress have provided the resources for our defense, and cast the difficult votes of war and peace. Our closest allies have been unwavering. America's intelligence personnel and diplomats have been skilled and tireless.

And the men and women of the American military—they have taken the hardest duty. We have seen their skill and courage in armored charges, and midnight raids, and lonely hours on faithful watch. We have seen the joy when they return, and felt the sorrow when one is lost. I have had the honor of meeting our service men and women at many posts, from the deck of a carrier in the Pacific, to a mess hall in Baghdad. Many of our troops are listening tonight. And I want you and your families to know: America is proud of you. And my Administration, and this Congress, will give you the resources you need to fight and win the war on terror.

I know that some people question if America is really in a war at all. They view terrorism more as a crime—a problem to be solved mainly with law enforcement and indictments. After the World Trade Center was first attacked in 1993, some of the guilty were indicted, tried, convicted, and sent to prison. But the matter was not settled. The terrorists were still training and plotting in other nations, and drawing up more ambitious plans. After the chaos and carnage of September 11th, it is not enough to serve our enemies with legal papers. The terrorists and their supporters declared war on the United States—and war is what they got.

Some in this chamber, and in our country, did not support the liberation of Iraq. Objections to war often come from principled motives. But let us be candid about the consequences of leaving Saddam Hussein in power. We are seeking all the facts—already the Kay Report identified dozens of weapons of mass destruction-related program activities and significant amounts of equipment that Iraq concealed from the United Nations. Had we failed to act, the dictator's weapons of mass destruction programs would continue to this day. Had we failed to act, Security Council resolutions on Iraq would have been revealed as empty threats, weakening the United Nations and encouraging defiance by dictators around the world. Iraq's torture chambers would still be filled with victims—terrified and innocent. The killing fields of Iraq—where hundreds of thousands of men, women, and children vanished into the sands—would still be known only to the killers. For all who love freedom and peace, the world without Saddam Hussein's regime is a better and safer place.

Some critics have said our duties in Iraq must be internationalized. This particular criticism is hard to explain to our partners in Britain, Australia, Japan, South Korea, the Philippines, Thailand, Italy, Spain, Poland, Denmark, Hungary, Bulgaria, Ukraine, Romania, the Netherlands, Norway, El Salvador, and the 17 other countries that have committed troops to Iraq. As we debate at home, we must never ignore the vital contributions of our international partners, or dismiss their sacrifices. From the beginning, America has sought international support for operations in Afghanistan and Iraq, and we have gained much support. There is a difference, however, between leading a coalition of many nations, and submitting to the objections of a few. America will never seek a permission slip to defend the security of our people.

We also hear doubts that democracy is a realistic goal for the greater Middle East, where freedom is rare. yet it is mistaken, and condescending, to assume that whole cultures and great religions are incompatible with liberty and self-government. I believe that God has planted in every heart the desire to live in freedom. And even when that desire is crushed by tyranny for decades, it will rise again.

As long as the Middle East remains a place of tyranny, despair, and anger, it will continue to produce men and movements that threaten the safety of America and our friends. So America is pursuing a forward strategy of freedom in the greater Middle East. We will challenge the enemies of reform, confront the allies of terror, and expect a higher standard from our friends. To cut through the barriers of hateful propaganda, the Voice of America and other broadcast services are expanding their programming in Arabic and Persian—and soon, a new television service will begin providing reliable news and information across the region. I will send you a proposal to double the budget of the National Endowment for Democracy, and to focus its new work on the development of free elections, free markets, free press, and free labor unions in the Middle East. And above all, we will finish the historic work of democracy in Afghanistan and Iraq, so those nations can light the way for others, and help transform a troubled part of the world.

America is a Nation with a mission—and that mission comes from our most basic beliefs. We have no desire to dominate, no ambitions of empire. Our aim is a democratic peace—a peace founded upon the dignity and rights of every man and woman. America acts in this cause with friends and allies at our side, yet we understand our special calling: This great Republic will lead the cause of freedom.

DOMESTIC PRIORITIES

In these last 3 years, adversity has also revealed the fundamental strengths of the American economy. We have come through recession, and terrorist attack, and corporate scandals, and the uncertainties of war. And because you acted to stimulate our economy with tax relief, this economy is strong, and growing stronger.

You have doubled the child tax credit from $500 to $1,000, reduced the marriage penalty, begun to phase out the death tax, reduced taxes on capital gains and stock dividends, cut taxes on small businesses, and you have lowered taxes for every American who pays income taxes.

Americans took those dollars and put them to work, driving this economy forward. The pace of economic growth in the third quarter of 2003 was the fastest in nearly 20 years. New home construction: the highest in almost 20 years. Home ownership rates: the higher ever. Manufacturing activity is increasing. Inflation is low. Interest rates are low. Exports are growing. Productivity is high. And jobs are on the rise.

These numbers confirm that the American people are using their money far better than Government would have—and you were right to return it.

America's growing economy is also a changing economy. As technology transforms the way almost every job is done, America becomes more productive, and workers need new skills. Much of our job growth will be found in high-skilled fields like health care and biotechnology. So we must respond by helping more Americans gain the skills to find good jobs in our new economy.

All skills begin with the basics of reading and math, which are supposed to be learned in the early grades of our schools. Yet for too long, for too many children, those skills were never mastered. By passing the No Child Left Behind Act, you have made the expectation of literacy the law of our country. We are providing more funding for our schools—a 36 percent increase since 2001. We are requiring higher standards. We are regularly testing every child on the fundamentals. We are reporting results to parents, and making sure they have better options when schools are not performing. We are making progress toward excellence for every child.

But the status quo always has defenders. Some want to undermine the No Child Left Behind Act by weakening standards and accountability. Yet the results we require are really a matter of common sense: We expect third graders to read and do math at third grade level—and that is not asking to much. Testing is the only way to identify and help students who are falling behind.

This Nation will not go back to the days of simply shuffling children along from grade to grade without them learning the basics. I refuse to give up on any child—and the No Child Left Behind Act is opening the door of opportunity to all of America's children.

At the same time, we must ensure that older students and adults can gain the skills they need to find work now. Many of the fastest growing occupations require strong math and science preparation, and training beyond the high school level. So tonight I propose a series of measures called Jobs for the 21st Century. This program will provide extra help to middle- and high school students who fall behind in reading and math, expand Advanced Placement programs in low-income schools, and invite math and science professionals from the private sector to teach part-time in our high schools. I propose larger Pell Grants for students who prepare for college with demanding courses in high school. I propose increasing our support for America's fine community colleges, so they can train workers for the industries that are creating the most new jobs. By all these actions, we will help more and more Americans to join in the growing prosperity of our country.

Job training is important, and so is job creation. We must continue to pursue and aggressive, pro-growth economic agenda.

Congress has some unfinished business on the issue of taxes. The tax reductions you passed are set to expire. Unless you act, the unfair tax on marriage will go back up. Unless you act, millions of families will be charged $300 more in Federal taxes for every child. Unless you act, small businesses will pay higher taxes. Unless you act, the death tax will eventually come back to life. Unless you act, Americans face a tax increase. What the Congress has given, the Congress should not take away: For the sake of job growth, the tax cuts you passed should be permanent.

Our agenda for jobs and growth must help small business owners and employees with relief from needless Federal regulation, and protect them from junk and frivolous lawsuits. Consumers and businesses need reliable supplies of energy to make our economy run—so I urge you to pass legislation to modernize our electricity system, promote conservation, and make America less dependent on foreign sources of energy. My Administration is promoting free and fair trade, to open up new markets for America's entrepreneurs, and manufacturers, and farmers, and to create jobs for America's workers. Younger workers should have the opportunity to build a nest egg by saving part of their Social Security taxes in a personal retirement account. We should make the Social Security system a source of ownership for the American people.

And we should limit the burden of Government on this economy by acting as good stewards of taxpayer dollars. In 2 weeks, I will send you a budget that funds the war, protects the homeland, and meets important domestic needs, while limiting the growth in discretionary spending to less than 4 percent. This will require that Congress focus on priorities, cut wasteful spending, and be wise with the people's money. By doing so, we can cut the deficit in half over the next 5 years.

Tonight I also ask you to reform our immigration laws, so they reflect our values and benefit our economy. I propose a new temporary worker program to match willing foreign workers with willing employers, when no Americans can be found to fill the job. This reform will be good for our economy—because employers will find needed workers in an honest and orderly system. A temporary worker program will help protect our homeland—allowing border patrol and law enforcement to focus on true threats to our national security. I oppose amnesty, because it would encourage further illegal immigration, and unfairly reward those who break our laws. My temporary worker program will preserve the citizenship path for those who respect the law, while bringing millions of hardworking men and women out from the shadows of American life.

HEALTH CARE REFORM

Our Nation's health care system, like our economy, is also in a time of change. Amazing medical technologies are improving and saving lives. This dramatic progress has brought its own challenge, in the rising costs of medical care and health insurance. Members of Congress, we must work together to help control those costs and extend the benefits of modern medicine throughout our country.

Meeting these goals requires bipartisan effort—and 2 months ago, you showed the way. By strengthening Medicare and adding a prescription drug benefit, you kept a basic commitment to our seniors: You are giving them the modern medicine they deserve.

Starting this year, under the law you passed, seniors can choose to receive a drug discount card, saving them 10 to 25 percent off the retail price of most prescription drugs—and millions of low-income seniors can get an additional $600 to buy medicine. Beginning next year, seniors will have new coverage for preventive screenings against diabetes and heart disease, and seniors just entering Medicare can receive wellness exams.

In January of 2006, seniors can get prescription drug coverage under Medicare. For a monthly premium of about $35, most seniors who do not have that coverage today can expect to see their drug bills cut roughly in half. Under this reform, senior citizens will be able to keep their Medicare just as it is, or they can choose a Medicare plan that fits them best—just as you, as Members of Congress, can choose an insurance plan that meets your needs. And starting this year, millions of Americans will be able to save money tax-free for their medical expenses, in a health savings account.

I signed this measure proudly, and any attempt to limit the choices of our seniors, or to take away their prescription drug coverage under Medicare, will meet my veto.

On the critical issue of health care, our goal is to ensure that Americans can choose and afford private health care coverage that best fits their individual needs. To make insurance more affordable, Congress must act to address rapidly rising health care costs. Small businesses should be able to band together and negotiate for lower insurance rates, so they can cover more workers with health insurance—I urge you to pass Association Health Plans. I ask you to give lower-income Americans a refundable tax credit that would allow millions to buy their own basic health insurance. By computerizing health records, we can avoid dangerous medical mistakes, reduce costs, and improve care. To protect the doctor-patient relationship, and keep good doctors doing good work, we must eliminate wasteful and frivolous medical lawsuits. And tonight I propose that individuals who buy catastrophic health care coverage, as part of our new health savings accounts, be allowed to deduct 100 percent of the premiums from their taxes.

A Government-run health care system is the wrong prescription. By keeping costs under control, expanding access, and helping more Americans afford coverage, we will preserve the system of private medicine that makes America's health care the best in the world.

AMERICAN VALUES

We are living in a time of great change—in our world, in our economy, and in science and medicine. Yet some things endure—courage and compassion, reverence and integrity, respect for differences of faith and race. The values we try to live by never change. And they are instilled in us by fundamental institutions, such as families, and schools, and religious congregations. These institutions—the unseen pillars of civilization—must remain strong in America, and we will defend them.

We must stand with our families to help them raise healthy, responsible children. And when it comes to helping children make right choices, there is work for all of us to do.

One of the worst decisions our children can make is to gamble their lives and futures on drugs. Our Government is helping parents confront this problem, with aggressive education, treatment, and law enforcement. Drug use in high school has declined by 11 percent over the past 2 years. Four hundred thousand fewer young people are using illegal drugs than in the year 2001. In my budget, I have proposed new funding to continue our aggressive, community-based strategy to reduce demand for illegal drugs. Drug testing in our schools has proven to be an effective part of this effort. So tonight I propose an additional $23 million for schools that want to use drug testing as a tool to save children's lives. The aim here is not to punish children, but to send them this message: We love you, and we don't want to lose you.

To help children make right choices, they need good examples. Athletics play such an important role in our society, but, unfortunately, some in professional sports are not setting much of an example. The use of performance-enhancing drugs like steroids in baseball, football, and other sports is dangerous, and it sends the wrong message—that there are shortcuts to accomplishment, and that performance is more important than character. So tonight I call on team owners, union representatives, coaches, and players to take the lead, to send the right signal, to get tough, and to get rid of steroids now.

To encourage right choices, we must be willing to confront the dangers young people face—even when they are difficult to talk about. Each year, about three million teenagers contract sexually transmitted diseases that can harm them, or kill them, or prevent them from ever becoming parents. In my budget, I propose a grassroots campaign to help inform families about these medical risks. We will double Federal funding for abstinence programs, so schools can teach this fact of life: Abstinence for young people is the only certain way to avoid sexually transmitted diseases. Decisions children make now can affect their health and character for the rest of their lives. All of us—parents, schools, government—must work together to counter the negative influence of the culture, and to send the right messages to our children.

A strong America must also value the institution of marriage. I believe we should respect individuals as we take a principled stand for one of the most fundamental, enduring institutions of our civilization. Congress has already taken a stand on this issue by passing the Defense of Marriage Act, signed in 1996 by President Clinton. That statute protects marriage under Federal law as the union of a man and a woman, and declares that one State may not redefine marriage for other States. Activist judges, however, have begun redefining marriage by court order, without regard for the will of the people and their elected representatives. On an issue of such great consequence, the people's voice must be heard. If judges insist on forcing their arbitrary will upon the people, the only alternative left to the people would be the constitutional process. Our Nation must defend the sanctity of marriage.

The outcome of this debate is important—and so is the way we conduct it. The same moral tradition that defines marriage also teaches that each individual has dignity and value in God's sight.

It is also important to strengthen our communities by unleashing the compassion of America's religious institutions. Religious charities of every creed are doing some of the most vital work in our country—mentoring children, feeding the hungry, taking the hand of the lonely. Yet government has often denied social service grants and contracts to these groups, just because they have a cross or Star of David or crescent on the wall. By Executive Order, I have opened billions of dollars in grant money to competition that includes faith-based charities. Tonight I ask you to codify this into law, so people of faith can know that the law will never discriminate against them again.

In the past, we have worked together to bring mentors to the children of prisoners, and provide treatment for the addicted, and help for the homeless. Tonight I ask you to consider another group of Americans in need of help. This year, some 600,000 inmates will be released from prison back into society. We know from long experience that if they can't find work, or a home, or help, they are much more likely to commit more crimes and return to prison. So tonight, I propose a 4-year, $300 million Prisoner Re-Entry Initiative to expand job training and placement services, to provide transitional housing, and to help newly released prisoners get mentoring, including from faith-based groups. America is the land of the second chance—and when the gates of the prison open, the path ahead should lead to a better life.

For all Americans, the last 3 years have brought tests we did not ask for, and achievements shared by all. By our actions, we have shown what kind of Nation we are. In grief, we found the grace to go on. In challenge, we rediscovered the courage and daring of a free people. In victory, we have shown the noble aims and good heart of America. And having come this far, we sense that we live in a time set apart.

I have been a witness to the character of the American people, who have shown calm in times of danger, compassion for one another, and toughness for the long haul. All of us have been partners in a great enterprise. And even some of the youngest understand that we are living in historic times. Last month a girl in Lincoln, Rhode Island, sent me a letter. It began, "Dear George W. Bush." "If there is anything you know, I Ashley Pearson age 10 can do to help anyone, please send me a letter and tell me what I can do to save our country." She added this P.S.: "If you can send a letter to the troops please put, 'Ashley Pearson believes in you.'"

Tonight, Ashley, your message to our troops has just been conveyed. And yes, you have some duties yourself. Study hard in school, listen to your mom and dad, help someone in need, and when you and your friends see a man or woman in uniform, say "thank you." And while you do your part, all of us here in this great chamber will do our best to keep you and the rest of America safe and free.

My fellow citizens, we now move forward, with confidence and faith. Our Nation is strong and steadfast. The cause we serve is right, because it is the cause of all mankind. The momentum of freedom in our world is unmistakable—and it is not carried forward by our power alone. We can trust in that greater power Who guides the unfolding of the years. And in all that is to come, we can know that His purposes are just and true. May God bless the United States of America. Thank you.

Selected Texts on Iraq

President Bush's Speech to the United Nations on Iraq

Following is the address President George W. Bush delivered on Sept. 12, 2002, in an appearance before the General Assembly of the United Nations. In the speech Bush argued that Iraq was a direct and urgent threat to the United States and the rest of the world.

Mr. Secretary General, Mr. President, distinguished delegates and ladies and gentlemen. We meet one year and one day after a terrorist attack brought grief to my country and brought grief to many citizens of our world.

Yesterday we remembered the innocent lives taken that terrible morning. Today we turn to the urgent duty of protecting other lives without illusion and without fear.

We've accomplished much in the last year in Afghanistan and beyond. We have much yet to do in Afghanistan and beyond. Many nations represented here have joined in the fight against global terror and the people of the United States are grateful.

The United Nations was born in the hope that survived a world war, the hope of a world moving toward justice, escaping old patterns of conflict and fear. The founding members resolved that the peace of the world must never again be destroyed by the will and wickedness of any man.

We created a United Nations Security Council so that, unlike the League of Nations, our deliberations would be more than talk, our resolutions would be more than wishes. After generations of deceitful dictators and broken treaties and squandered lives, we've dedicated ourselves to standards of human dignity shared by all and to a system of security defended by all.

Today, these standards and this security are challenged.

Our commitment to human dignity is challenged by persistent poverty and raging disease. The suffering is great. And our responsibilities are clear. The United States is joining with the world to supply aid where it reaches people and lifts up lives, to extend trade and the prosperity it brings, and to bring medical care where it is desperately needed. As a symbol of our commitment to human dignity, the United States will return to UNESCO.

This organization has been reformed, and America will participate fully in its mission to advance human rights and tolerance and learning. Our common security is challenged by regional conflicts, ethnic and religious strife that is ancient, but not inevitable.

PEACE IN THE MIDDLE EAST

In the Middle East there can be no peace for either side without freedom for both sides.

America stands committed to an independent and democratic Palestine, living side by side with Israel in peace and security. Like all other people, Palestinians deserve a government that serves their interests and listens to their voices. My nation will continue to encourage all parties to step up to their responsibilities as we seek a just and comprehensive settlement to the conflict.

Above all, our principles and our security are challenged today by outlaw groups and regimes that accept no law of morality and have no limit to their violent ambitions. In the attacks on America a year ago, we saw the destructive intentions of our enemies. This threat hides within many nations, including my own.

In cells, in camps, terrorists are plotting further destruction and building new bases for their war against civilization. And our greatest fear is that terrorists will find a shortcut to their mad ambitions when an outlaw regime supplies them with the technologies to kill on a massive scale. In one place and one regime, we find all these dangers in their most lethal and aggressive forms, exactly the kind of aggressive threat the United Nations was born to confront.

Twelve years ago, Iraq invaded Kuwait without provocation. And the regime's forces were poised to continue their march to seize other countries and their resources. Had Saddam Hussein been appeased instead of stopped, he would have endangered the peace and stability of the world. Yet this aggression was stopped by the might of coalition forces and the will of the United Nations.

IRAQ'S BROKEN PROMISES

To suspend hostilities, to spare himself, Iraq's dictator accepted a series of commitments. The terms were clear to him and to all, and he agreed to prove he is complying with every one of those obligations. He has proven instead only his contempt for the United Nations and for all his pledges. By breaking every pledge, by his deceptions and by his cruelties, Saddam Hussein has made the case against himself.

In 1991, Security Council Resolution 688 demanded that the Iraqi regime cease at once the repression of its own people, including the systematic repression of minorities, which the council said threatened international peace and security in the region. This demand goes ignored.

Last year, the U.N. Commission on Human Rights found that Iraq continues to commit extremely grave violations of human rights and that the regime's repression is all-pervasive.

Tens of thousands of political opponents and ordinary citizens have been subjected to arbitrary arrest and imprisonment, summary execution and torture by beating and burning, electric shock, starvation, mutilation and rape.

Wives are tortured in front of their husbands; children in the presence of their parents; and all of these horrors concealed from the world by the apparatus of a totalitarian state.

In 1991, the U.N. Security Council, through Resolutions 686 and 687, demanded that Iraq return all prisoners from Kuwait and other lands. Iraq's regime agreed. It broke this promise.

Last year, the secretary general's high-level coordinator for this issue reported that Kuwaiti, Saudi, Indian, Syrian, Lebanese, Iranian, Egyptian, Bahraini and Omani nationals remain unaccounted for; more than 600 people. One American pilot is among them.

In 1991, the U.N. Security Council, through Resolution 687, demanded that Iraq renounce all involvement with terrorism and permit no terrorist organizations to operate in Iraq.

Iraq's regime agreed. It broke this promise.

In violation of Security Council Resolution 1373, Iraq continues to shelter and support terrorist organizations that direct violence against Iran, Israel and Western governments. Iraqi dissidents abroad are targeted for murder.

In 1993, Iraq attempted to assassinate the emir of Kuwait and a former American president. Iraq's government openly praised the attacks of Sept. 11. And al Qaeda terrorists escaped from Afghanistan and are known to be in Iraq.

In 1991, the Iraqi regime agreed to destroy and stop developing all weapons of mass destruction and long-range missiles and to prove to the world it has done so by complying with rigorous inspections.

Iraq has broken every aspect of this fundamental pledge.

From 1991 to 1995, the Iraqi regime said it had no biological weapons. After a senior official in its weapons program defected and exposed this lie, the regime admitted to producing tens of thousands of liters of anthrax and other deadly biological agents for use with Scud warheads, aerial bombs and aircraft spray tanks.

U.N. inspectors believe Iraq has produced two to four times the amount of biological agents it declared and has failed to account for more than three metric tons of material that could be used to produce biological weapons. Right now, Iraq is expanding and improving facilities that were used for the production of biological weapons.

United Nations' inspections also revealed that Iraq likely maintains stockpiles of VX, mustard and other chemical agents, and that the regime is rebuilding and expanding facilities capable of producing chemical weapons.

And in 1995, after four years of deception, Iraq finally admitted it had a crash nuclear weapons program prior to the Gulf War.

We know now, were it not for that war, the regime in Iraq would likely have possessed a nuclear weapon no later than 1993.

CONTINUED OFFENSES

Today, Iraq continues to withhold important information about its nuclear program, weapons design, procurement logs, experiment data, and accounting of nuclear materials and documentation of foreign assistance. Iraq employs capable nuclear scientists and technicians. It retains physical infrastructure needed to build a nuclear weapon.

Iraq has made several attempts to buy high-strength aluminum tubes used to enrich uranium for a nuclear weapon. Should Iraq acquire fissile material, it would be able to build a nuclear weapon within a year.

And Iraq's state-controlled media has reported numerous meetings between Saddam Hussein and his nuclear scientists, leaving little doubt about his continued appetite for these weapons.

Iraq also possesses a force of Scud-type missiles with ranges beyond the 150 kilometers permitted by the U.N. Work at testing and production facilities shows that Iraq is building more long-range missiles that can inflict mass death throughout the region.

In 1990, after Iraq's invasion of Kuwait, the world imposed economic sanctions on Iraq. Those sanctions were maintained after the war to compel the regime's compliance with Security Council Resolutions.

In time, Iraq was allowed to use oil revenues to buy food. Saddam Hussein has subverted this program, working around the sanctions to buy missile technology and military materials. He blames the suffering of Iraq's people on the United Nations, even as he uses his oil wealth to build lavish palaces for himself and to buy arms for his country.

By refusing to comply with his own agreements, he bears full guilt for the hunger and misery of innocent Iraqi citizens. In 1991, Iraq promised U.N. inspectors immediate and unrestricted access to verify Iraq's commitment to rid itself of weapons of mass destruction and long-range missiles. Iraq broke this promise, spending seven years deceiving, evading and harassing U.N. inspectors before ceasing cooperation entirely.

Just months after the 1991 cease-fire, the Security Council twice renewed its demand that the Iraqi regime cooperate fully with inspectors, condemning Iraq's serious violations of its obligation.

The Security Council again renewed that demand in 1994, and twice more in 1996, deploring Iraq's clear violations of its obligation. The Security Council renewed its demand three more times in 1997, citing flagrant violations, and three more times in 1998, calling Iraq's behavior totally unacceptable. And in 1999, the demand was renewed yet again.

As we meet today, it's been almost four years since the last U.N. inspector set foot in Iraq—four years for the Iraqi regime to plan and to build and to test behind the cloak of secrecy. We know that Saddam Hussein pursued weapons of mass murder even when inspectors were in his country. Are we to assume that he stopped when they left?

A 'GATHERING DANGER'

The history, the logic and the facts lead to one conclusion: Saddam Hussein's regime is a grave and gathering danger.

To suggest otherwise is to hope against the evidence. To assume this regime's good faith is to bet the lives of millions and the peace of the world in a reckless gamble, and this is a risk we must not take.

Delegates to the General Assembly, we have been more than patient. We've tried sanctions. We've tried the carrot of oil for food and the stick of coalition military strikes. But Saddam Hussein has defied all these efforts and continues to develop weapons of mass destruction.

The first time we may be completely certain he has nuclear weapons is when, God forbid, he uses one. We owe it to all our citizens to do everything in our power to prevent that day from coming.

The conduct of the Iraqi regime is a threat to the authority of the United Nations and a threat to peace. Iraq has answered a decade of U.N. demands with a decade of defiance. All the world now faces a test, and the United Nations a difficult and defining moment.

Are Security Council resolutions to be honored and enforced, or cast aside without consequence?

Will the United Nations serve the purpose of its founding or will it be irrelevant?

The United States helped found the United Nations. We want the United Nations to be effective and respectful and successful. We want the resolutions of the world's most important multilateral body to be enforced. And right now those resolutions are being unilaterally subverted by the Iraqi regime.

Our partnership of nations can meet the test before us by making clear what we now expect of the Iraqi regime.

IRAQ MUST TAKE STEPS

If the Iraqi regime wishes peace, it will immediately and unconditionally forswear, disclose, and remove or destroy all weapons of mass destruction, long-range missiles and all related material.

If the Iraqi regime wishes peace, it will immediately end all support for terrorism and act to suppress it—as all states are required to do by U.N. Security Council resolutions.

If the Iraqi regime wishes peace, it will cease persecution of its civilian population, including Shi'a, Sunnis, Kurds, Turkomans and others again, as required by Security Council resolutions.

If the Iraqi regime wishes peace, it will release or account for all Gulf War personnel whose fate is still unknown.

It will return the remains of any who are deceased, return stolen property, accept liability for losses resulting from the invasion of Kuwait and fully cooperate with international efforts to resolve these issues as required by Security Council resolutions.

If the Iraqi regime wishes peace, it will immediately end all illicit trade outside the oil-for-food program. It will accept U.N. administration of funds from that program to ensure that the money is used fairly and promptly for the benefit of the Iraqi people.

If all these steps are taken, it will signal a new openness and accountability in Iraq and it could open the prospect of the United Nations helping to build a government that represents all Iraqis, a government based on respect for human rights, economic liberty and internationally supervised elections.

The United States has no quarrel with the Iraqi people. They've suffered too long in silent captivity. Liberty for the Iraqi people is a great moral cause and a great strategic goal.

The people of Iraq deserve it. The security of all nations requires it. Free societies do not intimidate through cruelty and conquest. And open societies do not threaten the world with mass murder. The United States supports political and economic liberty in a unified Iraq.

We can harbor no illusions, and that's important today to remember. Saddam Hussein attacked Iran in 1980 and Kuwait in 1990. He's fired ballistic missiles at Iran and Saudi Arabia, Bahrain and Israel. His regime once ordered the killing of every person between the ages of 15 and 70 in certain Kurdish villages in northern Iraq. He has gassed many Iranians and 40 Iraqi villages.

UNITED STATES' INVOLVEMENT

My nation will work with the U.N. Security Council to meet our common challenge. If Iraq's regime defies us again, the world must move deliberately, decisively to hold Iraq to account. We will work with the U.N. Security Council for the necessary resolutions.

But the purposes of the United States should not be doubted. The Security Council resolutions will be enforced, the just demands of peace and security will be met or action will be unavoidable, and a regime that has lost its legitimacy will also lose its power.

Events can turn in one of two ways. If we fail to act in the face of danger, the people of Iraq will continue to live in brutal submission. The regime will have new power to bully and dominate and conquer its neighbors, condemning the Middle East to more years of bloodshed and fear. The regime will remain unstable the region will remain unstable, with little hope of freedom and isolated from the progress of our times.

With every step the Iraqi regime takes toward gaining and deploying the most terrible weapons, our own options to confront that regime will narrow. And if an emboldened regime were to supply these weapons to terrorist allies, then the attacks of Sept. 11 would be a prelude to far greater horrors.

If we meet our responsibilities, if we overcome this danger, we can arrive at a very different future. The people of Iraq can shake off their captivity. They can one day join a democratic Afghanistan and a democratic Palestine, inspiring reforms throughout the Muslim world. These nations can show by their example that honest government and respect for women and the great Islamic tradition of learning can triumph in the Middle East and beyond. And we will show that the promise of the United Nations can be fulfilled in our time.

Neither of these outcomes is certain. Both have been set before us. We must choose between a world of fear and a world of progress. We cannot stand by and do nothing while dangers gather. We must stand up for our security and for the permanent rights and the hopes of mankind.

By heritage and by choice, the United States of America will make that stand. And, delegates to the United Nations, you have the power to make that stand, as well.

Thank you very much.

Joint Resolution to Authorize Use of Military Force Against Iraq

The following is the text of the legislation (H J Res 114—107-243) authorizing President George W. Bush to use military force in Iraq. After debate that stretched over three days, the House voted 296–133 to pass the joint resolution on Oct. 10, 2003. The Senate, which had opened debate on its version (S J Res 45) on Oct. 3, voted 77–23 to clear the House measure ten hours later, at 1:17 a.m. on Oct. 11.

JOINT RESOLUTION to authorize the use of United States Armed Forces against Iraq:

Whereas in 1990 in response to Iraq's war of aggression against and illegal occupation of Kuwait, the United States forged a coalition of nations to liberate Kuwait and its people in order to defend the national security of the United States and enforce United Nations Security Council resolutions relating to Iraq;

Whereas after the liberation of Kuwait in 1991, Iraq entered into a United Nations sponsored cease-fire agreement pursuant to which Iraq unequivocally agreed, among other things, to eliminate its nuclear, biological, and chemical weapons programs and the means to deliver and develop them, and to end its support for international terrorism;

Whereas the efforts of international weapons inspectors, United States intelligence agencies, and Iraqi defectors led to the discovery that Iraq had large stockpiles of chemical weapons and a large scale biological weapons program, and that Iraq had an advanced nuclear weapons development program that was much closer to producing a nuclear weapon than intelligence reporting had previously indicated;

Whereas Iraq, in direct and flagrant violation of the cease-fire, attempted to thwart the efforts of weapons inspectors to identify and destroy Iraq's weapons of mass destruction stockpiles and development capabilities, which finally resulted in the withdrawal of inspectors from Iraq on Oct. 31, 1998;

Whereas in PL 105-235 (Aug. 14, 1998), Congress concluded that Iraq's continuing weapons of mass destruction programs threatened vital United States interests and international peace and security, declared Iraq to be in "material and unacceptable breach of its international obligations" and urged the President "to take appropriate action, in accordance with the Constitution and relevant laws of the United States, to bring Iraq into compliance with its international obligations";

Whereas Iraq both poses a continuing threat to the national security of the United States and international peace and security in the Persian Gulf region and remains in material and unacceptable breach of its international obligations by, among other things, continuing to possess and develop a significant chemical and biological weapons capability, actively seeking a nuclear weapons capability, and supporting and harboring terrorist organizations;

Whereas Iraq persists in violating resolution of the United Nations Security Council by continuing to engage in brutal repression of its civilian population thereby threatening international peace and security in the region, by refusing to release, repatriate, or account for non-Iraqi citizens wrongfully detained by Iraq, including an American serviceman, and by failing to return property wrongfully seized by Iraq from Kuwait;

Whereas the current Iraqi regime has demonstrated its capability and willingness to use weapons of mass destruction against other nations and its own people;

Whereas the current Iraqi regime has demonstrated its continuing hostility toward, and willingness to attack, the United States, including by attempting in 1993 to assassinate former President Bush and by firing on many thousands of occasions on United States and Coalition Armed Forces engaged in enforcing the resolutions of the United Nations Security Council;

Whereas members of al Qaeda, an organization bearing responsibility for attacks on the United States, its citizens, and interests, including the attacks that occurred on Sept. 11, 2001, are known to be in Iraq;

Whereas Iraq continues to aid and harbor other international terrorist organizations, including organizations that threaten the lives and safety of United States citizens;

Whereas the attacks on the United States of Sept. 11, 2001, underscored the gravity of the threat posed by the acquisition of weapons of mass destruction by international terrorist organizations;

Whereas Iraq's demonstrated capability and willingness to use weapons of mass destruction, the risk that the current Iraqi regime swill either employ those weapons to launch a surprise attack against the United States or its Armed Forces or provide them to international terrorists who would do so, and the extreme magnitude of harm that would result to the United States and its citizens from such an attack, combine to justify action by the United States to defend itself;

Whereas United Nations Security Council Resolution 678 (1990) authorizes the use of all necessary means to enforce United Nations Security Council Resolution 660 (1990) and subsequent relevant resolutions and to compel Iraq to cease certain activities that threaten international peace and security, including the development of weapons of mass destruction and refusal or obstruction of United Nations weapons inspections in violation of United Nations Security Council Resolution 687 (1991), repression of its civilian population in violation of United Nations Security Council Resolution 688 (1991), and threatening its neighbors or United Nations operations in Iraq in violation of United Nations Security Council Resolution 949 (1994);

Whereas in the Authorization for Use of Military Force Against Iraq Resolution (PL 102-1), Congress has authorized the President "to use United States Armed Forces pursuant to United Nations Security Council Resolution 678 (1990) in order to achieve implementation of Security Council Resolution 660, 661, 662, 664, 665, 666, 667, 669, 670, 674, and 677";

Whereas in December 1991, Congress expressed its sense that it "supports the use of all necessary means to achieve the goals of United Nations Security Council Resolution 687 as being consistent with the Authorization of Use of Military Force Against Iraq Resolution (PL 102-1)," that Iraq's repression of its civilian population violates United Nations Security Council Resolution 688 and "constitutes a continuing threat to the peace, security, and stability of the Persian Gulf region," and that Congress, "supports the use of all necessary means to achieve the goals of United Nations Security Council Resolution 688";

Whereas the Iraq Liberation Act of 1998 (PL 105-338) expressed the sense of Congress that it should be the policy of the United States to support efforts to remove from power the current Iraqi regime and promote the emergence of a democratic government to replace that regime;

Whereas on Sept. 12, 2002, President Bush committed the United States to "work with the United Nations Security Council to meet our common challenge" posed by Iraq and to "work for the necessary resolutions," while also making clear that "the Security Council resolutions will be enforced, and the just demands of peace and security will be met, or action will be unavoidable";

Whereas the United States is determined to prosecute the war on terrorism and Iraq's ongoing support for international terrorist groups combined with its development of weapons of mass destruction in direct violation of its obligations under the 1991 cease-fire and other United Nations Security Council resolutions make clear that it is in the national security interests of the United States and in furtherance of the war on terrorism that all relevant United Nations Security Council resolutions be enforced, including through the use of force if necessary;

Whereas Congress has taken steps to pursue vigorously the war on terrorism through the provision of authorities and funding requested by the President to take the necessary actions against international terrorists and terrorist organizations, including those nations, organizations, or persons who planned, authorized, committed, or aided the terrorist attacks that occurred on Sept. 11, 2001, or harbored such persons or organizations;

Whereas the President and Congress are determined to continue to take all appropriate actions against international terrorists and terrorist organizations, including those nations, organizations, or persons who planned, authorized, committed, or aided the terrorist attacks that occurred on Sept. 11, 2001, or harbored such persons or organizations;

Whereas the President has authority under the Constitution to take action in order to deter and prevent acts of international terrorism against the United States, as Congress recognized in the joint resolution on Authorization for Use of Military Force (PL 107-40); and

Whereas it is in the national security interests of the United States to restore international peace and security to the Persian Gulf region:

Now, therefore, be it resolved by the Senate and House of Representatives of the United States of America in Congress assembled,

SECTION 1—SHORT TITLE

This joint resolution may be cited as the "Authorization for Use of Military Force Against Iraq Resolution of 2002."

SECTION 2—SUPPORT FOR UNITED STATES DIPLOMATIC EFFORTS

The Congress of the United States supports the efforts by the President to —

(1) strictly enforce through the United Nations Security Council all relevant Security Council resolutions regarding Iraq and encourages him in those efforts; and

(2) obtain prompt and decisive action by the Security Council to ensure that Iraq abandons its strategy of delay, evasion and noncompliance and promptly and strictly complies with all relevant Security Council resolutions regarding Iraq.

SECTION 3—AUTHORIZATION FOR USE OF UNITED STATES ARMED FORCES

(a) Authorization—The President is authorized to use the Armed Forces of the United States as he determines to be necessary and appropriate in order to —

(1) defend the national security of the United States against the continuing threat posed by Iraq; and

(2) enforce all relevant United Nations Security Council resolutions regarding Iraq.

(b) Presidential determination—In connection with the exercise of the authority granted in subsection (a) to use force the President shall, prior to such exercise or as soon thereafter as may be feasible, but no later than 48 hours after exercising such authority, make available to the Speaker of the House of Representatives and the President pro tempore of the Senate his determination that —

(1) reliance by the United States on further diplomatic or other peaceful means alone either (A) will not adequately protect the national security of the United States against the continuing threat posed by Iraq or (B) is not likely to lead to enforcement of all relevant United Nations Security Council resolutions regarding Iraq; and

(2) acting pursuant to this joint resolution is consistent with the United States and other countries continuing to take the necessary actions against international terrorist and terrorist organizations, including those nations, organizations, or persons who planned, authorized, committed or aided the terrorist attacks that occurred on Sept. 11, 2001.

(c) War Powers Resolution Requirements —

(1) Specific statutory authorization—Consistent with section 8(a)(1) of the War Powers Resolution, the Congress declares that this ection is intended to constitute specific statutory authorization within the meaning of section 5(b) of the War Powers Resolution.

(2) Applicability of other requirements—Nothing in this joint resolution supersedes any requirement of the War Powers Resolution.

SECTION 4—REPORTS TO CONGRESS

(a) Reports—The President shall, at least once every 60 days, submit to the Congress a report on matters relevant to this joint resolution, including actions taken pursuant to the exercise of authority granted in section 3 and the status of planning for efforts that are expected to be required after such actions are completed, including those actions described in section 7 of the Iraq Liberation Act of 1998 (PL 105-338).

(b) Single consolidated report—To the extent that the submission of any report described in subsection (a) coincides with the submission of any other report on matters relevant to this joint resolution otherwise required to be submitted to Congress pursuant to the reporting requirements of the War Powers Resolution (PL 93-148), all such reports may be submitted as a single consolidated report to the Congress.

(c) Rule of construction—To the extent that the information required by section 3 of the Authorization for Use of Military Force Against Iraq Resolution (PL 102-1) is included in the report required by this section, such report shall be considered as meeting the requirements of section 3 of such resolution.

President Bush on War with Iraq

Following are the texts of two speeches George W. Bush delivered from the White House: the first one on March 17, 2003, setting an ultimatum for Iraqi leader Saddam Hussein and his sons to leave the country within forty-eight hours; the second one on March 19, 2003, announcing that U.S. and British forces had begun attacking Iraq.

PRESIDENT BUSH'S ADDRESS TO THE NATION ON IRAQ, MARCH 17, 2003

My fellow citizens, events in Iraq have now reached the final days of decision. For more than a decade, the United States and other nations have pursued patient and honorable efforts to disarm the Iraqi regime without war. That regime pledged to reveal and destroy all its weapons of mass destruction as a condition for ending the Persian Gulf war in 1991.

Since then, the world has engaged in 12 years of diplomacy. We have passed more than a dozen resolutions in the United Nations Security Council. We have sent hundreds of weapons inspectors to oversee the disarmament of Iraq. Our good faith has not been returned.

The Iraqi regime has used diplomacy as a ploy to gain time and advantage. It has uniformly defied Security Council resolutions demanding full disarmament. Over the years, U.N. weapon inspectors have been threatened by Iraqi officials, electronically bugged, and systematically deceived. Peaceful efforts to disarm the Iraqi regime have failed again and again because we are not dealing with peaceful men.

Intelligence gathered by this and other governments leaves no doubt that the Iraq regime continues to possess and conceal some of the most lethal weapons ever devised. This regime has already used weapons of mass destruction against Iraq's neighbors and against Iraq's people.

The regime has a history of reckless aggression in the Middle East. It has a deep hatred of America and our friends. And it has aided, trained, and harbored terrorists, including operatives of Al Qaida.

The danger is clear: Using chemical, biological or, one day, nuclear weapons obtained with the help of Iraq, the terrorists could fulfill their stated ambitions and kill thousands or hundreds of thousands of innocent people in our country or any other.

The United States and other nations did nothing to deserve or invite this threat. But we will do everything to defeat it. Instead of drifting along toward tragedy, we will set a course toward safety. Before the day of horror can come, before it is too late to act, this danger will be removed.

The United States of America has the sovereign authority to use force in assuring its own national security. That duty falls to me as Commander in Chief, by the oath I have sworn, by the oath I will keep.

Recognizing the threat to our country, the United States Congress voted overwhelmingly last year to support the use of force against Iraq. America tried to work with the United Nations to address this threat because we wanted to resolve the issue peacefully. We believe in the mission of the United Nations. One reason the U.N. was founded after the Second World War was to confront aggressive dictators actively and early, before they can attack the innocent and destroy the peace.

In the case of Iraq, the Security Council did act in the early 1990s. Under Resolutions 678 and 687, both still in effect, the United States and our allies are authorized to use force in ridding Iraq of weapons of mass destruction. This is not a question of authority. It is a question of will.

Last September, I went to the U.N. General Assembly and urged the nations of the world to unite and bring an end to this danger. On November 8th, the Security Council unanimously passed Resolution 1441, finding Iraq in material breach of its obligations and vowing serious consequences if Iraq did not fully and immediately disarm.

Today, no nation can possibly claim that Iraq has disarmed, and it will not disarm so long as Saddam Hussein holds power. For the last 4 1/2 months, the United States and our allies have worked within the Security Council to enforce that Council's longstanding demands.

Yet, some permanent members of the Security Council have publicly announced they will veto any resolution that compels the disarmament of Iraq. These governments share our assessment of the danger but not our resolve to meet it.

Many nations, however, do have the resolve and fortitude to act against this threat to peace, and a broad coalition is now gathering to enforce the just demands of the world. The United Nations Security Council has not lived up to its responsibilities, so we will rise to ours.

In recent days, some governments in the Middle East have been doing their part. They have delivered public and private messages urging the dictator to leave Iraq, so that disarmament can proceed peacefully. He has thus far refused.

All the decades of deceit and cruelty have now reached an end. Saddam Hussein and his sons must leave Iraq within 48 hours. Their refusal to do so will result in military conflict, commenced at a time of our choosing. For their own safety, all foreign nationals, including journalists and inspectors, should leave Iraq immediately.

Many Iraqis can hear me tonight in a translated radio broadcast, and I have a message for them: If we must begin a military campaign, it will be directed against the lawless men who rule your country and not against you. As our coalition takes away their power, we will deliver the food and medicine you need. We will tear down the apparatus of terror, and we will help you to build a new Iraq that is prosperous and free. In a free Iraq, there will be no more wars of aggression against your neighbors, no more poison factories, no more executions of dissidents, no more torture chambers and rape rooms. The tyrant will soon be gone. The day of your liberation is near.

It is too late for Saddam Hussein to remain in power. It is not too late for the Iraqi military to act with honor and protect your country by permitting the peaceful entry of coalition forces to eliminate weapons of mass destruction. Our forces will give Iraqi military units clear instructions on actions they can take to avoid being attacked and destroyed. I urge every member of the Iraqi military and intelligence services: If war comes, do not fight for a dying regime that is not worth your own life.

And all Iraqi military and civilian personnel should listen carefully to this warning: In any conflict, your fate will depend on your actions. Do not destroy oil wells, a source of wealth that belongs to the Iraqi people. Do not obey any command to use weapons of mass destruction against anyone, including the Iraqi people. War crimes will be prosecuted. War criminals will be punished. And it will be no defense to say, "I was just following orders."

Should Saddam Hussein choose confrontation, the American people can know that every measure has been taken to avoid war and every measure will be taken to win it. Americans understand the costs of conflict because we have paid them in the past. War has no certainty, except the certainty of sacrifice. Yet, the only way to reduce the harm and duration of war is to apply the full force and might of our military, and we are prepared to do so.

If Saddam Hussein attempts to cling to power, he will remain a deadly foe until the end. In desperation, he and terrorist groups might try to conduct terrorist operations against the American people and our friends. These attacks are not inevitable. They are, however, possible. And this very fact underscores the reason we cannot live under the threat of blackmail. The terrorist threat to America and the world will be diminished the moment that Saddam Hussein is disarmed.

Our Government is on heightened watch against these dangers. Just as we are preparing to ensure victory in Iraq, we are taking further actions to protect our homeland. In recent days, American authorities have expelled from the country certain individuals with ties to Iraqi intelligence services. Among other measures, I have directed additional security of our airports and increased Coast Guard patrols of major seaports. The Department of Homeland Security is working closely with the Nation's Governors to increase armed security at critical facilities across America.

Should enemies strike our country, they would be attempting to shift our attention with panic and weaken our morale with fear. In this, they would fail. No act of theirs can alter the course or shake the resolve of this country. We are a peaceful people. Yet we're not a fragile people, and we will not be intimidated by thugs and killers. If our enemies dare to strike us, they and all who have aided them will face fearful consequences.

We are now acting because the risks of inaction would be far greater. In 1 year, or 5 years, the power of Iraq to inflict harm on all free nations would be multiplied many times over. With these capabilities, Saddam Hussein and his terrorist allies could choose the moment of deadly conflict when they are strongest. We choose to meet that threat now, where it arises, before it can appear suddenly in our skies and cities.

The cause of peace requires all free nations to recognize new and undeniable realities. In the 20th century, some chose to appease murderous dictators, whose threats were allowed to grow into genocide and global war. In this century, when evil men plot chemical, biological, and nuclear terror, a policy of appeasement could bring destruction of a kind never before seen on this Earth.

Terrorists and terror states do not reveal these threats with fair notice, in formal declarations, and responding to such enemies only after they have struck first is not self-defense; it is suicide. The security of the world requires disarming Saddam Hussein now.

As we enforce the just demands of the world, we will also honor the deepest commitments of our country. Unlike Saddam Hussein, we believe the Iraqi people are deserving and capable of human liberty. And when the dictator has departed, they can set an example to all the Middle East of a vital and peaceful and self-governing nation.

The United States, with other countries, will work to advance liberty and peace in that region. Our goal will not be achieved overnight, but it can come over time. The power and appeal of human liberty is felt in every life and every land. And the greatest power of freedom is to overcome hatred and violence and turn the creative gifts of men and women to the pursuits of peace.

That is the future we choose. Free nations have a duty to defend our people by uniting against the violent. And tonight, as we have done before, America and our allies accept that responsibility.

Good night, and may God continue to bless America.

PRESIDENT BUSH'S ADDRESS TO THE NATION ON IRAQ, MARCH 19, 2003

My fellow citizens, at this hour, American and coalition forces are in the early stages of military operations to disarm Iraq, to free its people, and to defend the world from grave danger.

On my orders, coalition forces have begun striking selected targets of military importance to undermine Saddam Hussein's ability to wage war. These are opening stages of what will be a broad and concerted campaign. More than 35 countries are giving crucial support, from the use of naval and air bases, to help with intelligence and logistics, to the deployment of combat units. Every nation in this coalition has chosen to bear the duty and share the honor of serving in our common defense.

To all the men and women of the United States Armed Forces now in the Middle East, the peace of a troubled world and the hopes of an oppressed people now depend on you. That trust is well placed. The enemies you confront will come to know your skill and bravery. The people you liberate will witness the honorable and decent spirit of the American military.

In this conflict, America faces an enemy who has no regard for conventions of war or rules of morality. Saddam Hussein has placed Iraqi troops and equipment in civilian areas, attempting to use innocent men, women, and children as shields for his own military, a final atrocity against his people.

I want Americans and all the world to know that coalition forces will make every effort to spare innocent civilians from harm. A campaign on the harsh terrain of a nation as large as California could be longer and more difficult than some predict. And helping Iraqis achieve a united, stable, and free country will require our sustained commitment.

We come to Iraq with respect for its citizens, for their great civilization, and for the religious faiths they practice. We have no ambition in Iraq, except to remove a threat and restore control of that country to its own people.

I know that the families of our military are praying that all those who serve will return safely and soon. Millions of Americans are praying with you for the safety of your loved ones and for the protection of the innocent. For your sacrifice, you have the gratitude and respect of the America people. And you can know that our forces will be coming home as soon as their work is done.

Our Nation enters this conflict reluctantly. Yet our purpose is sure. The people of the United States and our friends and allies will not live at the mercy of an outlaw regime that threatens the peace with weapons of mass murder. We will meet that threat now, with our Army, Air Force, Navy, Coast Guard and Marines, so that we do not have to meet it later with armies of firefighters and police and doctors on the streets of our cities.

Now that conflict has come, the only way to limit its duration is to apply decisive force. And I assure you, this will not be a campaign of half measures, and we will accept no outcome but victory.

My fellow citizens, the dangers to our country and the world will be overcome. We will pass through this time of peril and carry on the work of peace. We will defend our freedom. We will bring freedom to others, and we will prevail.

May God bless our country and all who defend her.

Sen. James M. Jeffords' Statement on Leaving the Republican Party

Following is a transcript of Sen. James M. Jeffords' announcement in Burlington, Vt., on May 24, 2001, of his leaving the Republican Party to become an Independent; questions and answers from listeners follows. At the beginning of the 107th Congress, the chamber was evenly divided, with fifty Republicans and fifty Democrats. With Republican vice president Dick Cheney available to cast a tie-breaking vote in his constitutional role as president of the Senate, Republicans held nominal control. When Jeffords left the GOP to become an Independent and chose to caucus with the Democrats, the Republicans lost their advantage. As a result Democrats took control of the Senate and its agenda and all of its committee chairmanships. The change occurred on June 6, 2001, and lasted for the remainder of the 107th Congress. (Jeffords switch, pp. 5, 708)

Jeffords: Good morning, everyone.

Anyone that knows me knows I love Vermont. Vermont has always been known for its independence and social conscience. It was the first state to outlaw slavery in its constitution. It proudly elected Matthew Lyon to Congress, notwithstanding his flouting of the Sedition Act.

It sacrificed a higher share of its sons in the Civil War than perhaps any other state in the Union. And I recall Vermont Sen. Ralph Flanders' dramatic statement 50 years ago, helping to bring the close on the McCarthy hearings—a sorry chapter in our history.

Today's chapter is of much smaller consequence. But I think it appropriate that I share my thoughts with my fellow Vermonters.

For the past several weeks, I have been struggling with a very difficult decision. It's difficult on a personal level, but even more difficult because of the larger impact in the Senate and also the nation. I have been talking with my family and a few close advisers about whether or not I should remain a Republican.

I do not approach this question lightly. I have spent a lifetime in the Republican Party and served 12 years in what I believe is the longest continuously held Republican seat in history. I ran for reelection as a Republican just this past fall, and had no thoughts whatsoever, then, about changing parties.

The party I grew up in was the party of George Aiken, Ernest Gibson, Ralph Flanders, Winston Prouty and Bob Stafford. These names may not mean much today outside Vermont, but each served Vermont as a Republican senator in the 20th century.

I became a Republican, not because I was born into the party, but because of the kind of fundamental principles that these and many Republicans stood for: moderation, tolerance, fiscal responsibility. Their party—our party—was the party of Lincoln.

To be sure, we had our differences in the Vermont Republican Party, but even our more conservative leaders were in many ways progressive.

Our former governor, Dean Davis, championed Act 250, which preserved our environmental heritage.

And Vermont's Calvin Coolidge, our nation's 30th president, could point with pride to his state's willingness to sacrifice in the service of others. Aiken and Gibson and Flanders and Prouty and Bob Stafford were all Republicans, but they were Vermonters first. They spoke their minds, often to the dismay of their party leaders, and did their best to guide the party in the direction of those fundamental principles they believed in.

For 26 years in Washington, first in the House of Representatives and now in the Senate, I have tried to do the same, but I can no longer do so as a Republican. Increasingly, I find myself in disagreement with my party.

I understand that many people are more conservative than I am, and they form the Republican Party. Given the changing nature of the national party, it has become a struggle for our leaders to deal with me and for me to deal with them. Indeed, the party's electoral success has underscored the dilemma that I face within the party.

In the past, without the presidency, the various wings of the Republican Party in Congress have had some freedom to argue and influence and ultimately to shape the party's agenda. The election of President Bush changed that dramatically.

We don't live in a parliamentary system, but it is only natural to expect that people like myself, who have been honored with positions of leadership, will largely support the president's agenda.

And yet, more and more, I find I cannot. Those who don't know me may have thought I took pleasure in resisting the president's budget or that I enjoyed the limelight. Nothing could be further from the truth. I had serious substantive reservations about that budget, as you all know, and the decisions it set in place for the future.

Looking ahead, I can see more and more instances where I'll disagree with the president on very fundamental issues—the issues of choice, the direction of the judiciary, tax and spending decisions, missile defense, energy and the environment, and a host of other issues, large and small.

The largest for me is education. I come from the state of Justin Smith Morrill, a U.S. senator from Vermont who gave America its land grant college system. His Republican Party stood for opportunity for all, for opening the doors of public school education to every American child.

Now, for some, success seems to be measured by the number of students moved out of the public schools.

In order to best represent my state of Vermont, my own conscience and principles I have stood for my whole life, I will leave the Republican Party and become an Independent.

(Applause.)

Control of the Senate will be changed by my decision.

Audience: *Thank you, Jeff. Thank you, Jeff. Thank you, Jeff.*

Jeffords: I'm sorry for that interruption, but I understand it.

I will make this change and will caucus with the Democrats for organizational purposes once the conference report on the tax bill is sent to the president. I gave my word to the president that I would not intercept or try to intervene in the signing of that bill.

My colleagues, many of them my friends for years, may find it difficult in their hearts to befriend me any longer. Many of my supporters will be disappointed, and some of my staffers will see their lives upended. I regret this very much.

Having made my decision, the weight that has been lifted from my shoulders now hangs heavy on my heart, but I was not elected to this office to be something that I am not. This comes as no surprise to Vermonters, because independence is the Vermont way.

My friends back home have supported and encouraged my independence. I appreciate the support they have shown when they have agreed with me, and their patience when they have not. I will ask their support and patience again, which I understand will be very difficult for a number of my close friends.

I have informed President Bush, Vice President [Dick] Cheney and Sen. [Trent] Lott [R-Miss.] of my decision.

They are good people with whom I disagree. They have been fair and decent to me, and I have informed Sen. [Tom] Daschle [D-S.D.] also of my decision. Three of these four men disagree with my decision, but I hope each understood my reasons. And it's quite entirely possible that the fourth one, with my independence, may have second thoughts down the road. But anyway, that's the way it is.

I have changed my party label, but I have not changed my beliefs. Indeed, my decision is about affirming the principles that have shaped my career. I hope that the people of Vermont will understand it. I hope in time that my colleagues will as well. I am confident that it is the right decision.

Yes?

Question: *Sen. Jeffords, what do you say to those people who, only six months ago, voted for you as a Republican?*

Jeffords: Right. I understand, and I'm sorry that I had no expectation of it.

Question: *(Off mike) . . . you were his campaign chairman, obviously?*

Jeffords: I was not the campaign chairman, but that's a small point. I believed at the time and had hoped at the time that those of us that are the moderates of the party, not just myself—and I speak, I'm sure, for many moderates in the party who had high hopes when the president spoke of education and when he gave his dedication to education—that we would be able to follow him, and I praise the president for his education package.

And that's the problem that I have with it. Because there are terrible problems out there that will have to be solved, and that is why in the budget process, I stood up and said, no, we can't give all this money back. We have too many high priorities—education, number one.

We have got to provide the resources for the president's plan. If the resources are not there, it's going to be misery in the school systems. And I told this to the president personally. So it's no secret that I have these feelings.

But I could not, after that, see the direction of the budgetary process—and you know I stood up against that, and we succeeded in getting some $300 billion extra to spend. But it's not being directed under the budget process to education.

Question: *Do you feel the president has not lived up to his campaign promises?*

Jeffords: Well, I don't know—I don't ever remember specifically a promise to fund. He gave us a promise to get us new direction in education. But new direction without funding is really no useful direction at all.

Question: *Senator, much has been made of the way the Bush White House and the Republican leadership in Congress have treated you. Has their treatment—personal treatment of you had anything to do with your decision?*

Jeffords: Oh, nothing whatsoever. It gets laughable at times, and you get upset with it—like Vermont, the national school teacher, those kind of things. But that had nothing to do with it. Nothing at all.

Question: *When did you make your decision?*

Jeffords: I'm sorry?

Question: *When did you make your decision?*

Jeffords: I made my decision yesterday on the way down, really. And I'll tell you why—"Why did you wait that long?" I promised my moderates. I met with the moderates yesterday, and it was the most emotional time that I have ever had in my life, with my closest friends urging me not to do what I was going to do because it affected their lives very substantially.

I know, for instance, the chairman of the Finance Committee has dreamed all his life of being chairman. He's chairman a couple of weeks, and now he will be no longer the chairman.

All the way down the line, I could see the anguish and the disappointment as I talked. So I told them I would not make my final decision until I had time on the way to Vermont to decide, and I did leave it open. But I could not justify not going forward.

Staff: *Last question.*

Question: *Senator, last week, the chairman of the Vermont Republican Party said he'd be terribly surprised if the idea of leaving the party had even crossed your mind. What have you done today to Republican leaders. . . ?*

Jeffords: I've communicated with them, either I or my staff have. I've had conversations with them on the phone to make sure they understood what I was doing and why I was doing it.

Staff: *Thank you very much. Thank you very much.*

2004 Presidential Conventions

DEMOCRATS

The 2004 Democratic and Republican conventions, the first after the terrorist attacks of 2001, convened under an umbrella of unprecedented security. The federal government alone allocated up to $50 million for protection at each meeting. In late July, the Democrats gathered at the FleetCenter in Boston—the first time either major party had met in that city. By chance it was also the home town of the party's presidential nominee, John F. Kerry.

The Democrats, as has become the norm for recent conventions, put on a unified display throughout the four-day event as the 4,964 delegates and alternates were hopeful of unseating incumbent president George W. Bush. Many convention attendees were angry at the Bush administration for its rationale, later discredited, for going to war with Iraq, for its inadequate preparation for the war's aftermath, and for the mounting toil in U.S. casualties and deaths. Some Democrats still refused to accept the legitimacy of Bush's presidency after the bitterly controversial 2000 election.

One of the first speakers on July 26 was former president Jimmy Carter, who said that "recent policies have cost our nation its reputation as the world's most admired champion of freedom and justice. What a difference these few months of extremism have made. . . . With our allies disunited, the world resenting us, and the Middle East ablaze, we need John Kerry to restore life to the global war against terrorism."

Also speaking on the first night was former president Bill Clinton and his wife, Sen. Hillary Clinton of New York. In his remarks the former president, who received a draft deferment during the Vietnam War, contrasted Kerry with himself, President Bush, and Vice President Richard B. Cheney. Clinton said that "many young men, including the current president, the vice president, and me, could have gone to Vietnam and didn't. John Kerry came from a privileged background. He could have avoided going too, but instead, he said: Send me." Now it was time, Clinton said, "to say to him what he has always said to America: Send me."

One surprising speaker for the Democrats on the first night was a Reagan, Ron Reagan, son of former Republican president Ronald Reagan, who had recently died. Reagan spoke in support of medical research using embryonic stem cells to help find cures for spinal cord injuries and diseases such as Alzheimer's, which had afflicted his father after he left the presidency. His mother, Nancy Reagan, also had publicly opposed the Bush administration's strict limitations on funding for stem cell research. The Democratic platform supported limited research.

On July 27 Senate candidate Barack Obama of Illinois, the son of an African American farmer from Kenya, gave the convention's keynote speech. The self-described "skinny kid with a funny name," said, "The audacity of hope! That is God's greatest gift to us, the bedrock of this nation, the belief in things not seen, the belief that there are better days ahead." Obama's electrifying speech prompted television network commentators to predict a bright future for the forty-three-year-old keynoter, including possibly an eventual presidential candidacy.

The word "hope" also was threaded through John Edwards's vice-presidential acceptance speech on July 28. The North Carolina senator urged the delegates to say "hope is on the way" to people at home who are despondent for a number of reasons, such as having a loved one fighting in Iraq. The presidential nomination roll call of the states was a foregone conclusion as most of Kerry's primary opponents, including Edwards, had released their delegates before the convention, giving the nominee a near unanimous tally. *(Table, p. 1001.)*

On the convention's final night Kerry, saluting crisply at the beginning of his acceptance speech, said that he was "reporting for duty" as the party's candidate to unseat President Bush. Kerry's words touched off an immense cheer as the delegates seemed ready to support Kerry in challenging the adage that "you don't switch horses in midstream," especially in wartime.

The Massachusetts senator sought to counter Republican criticism that he might be weak on defense in light of his opposition to the Vietnam War after serving in it as a patrol boat commander. "I defended this country as a young man and I will defend it as president," he said. "Let there be no mistake: I will never hesitate to use force when it is required. Any attack will be met with a swift and certain response. I will never give any nation or international institution a veto over our national security. And I will build a stronger American military. I will fight a smarter, more effective war on terror."

Kerry was joined on the platform by what he called "my band of brothers," men who served with him in Vietnam and were now supporting his candidacy. Among them was Jim Rassman, who credited Kerry with saving his life by pulling him from the river after he fell off the patrol boat. Former Georgia senator Max Cleland, who lost both legs and an arm in Vietnam, introduced Kerry.

The Democratic platform ran about 18,000 words and focused on national security and policies that benefited the middle class. Besides stem cell research, the platform also voiced support for preserving Social Security, maintaining abortion rights, and leaving the issue of same-sex marriage up to the states.

Following are excerpts from the Democratic platform of 2004.

Defeating Terrorism. . . . Today, the Bush Administration is waging a war against a global terrorist movement committed to our destruction with insufficient understanding of our enemy or effort to address the underlying factors that can give rise to new recruits. This war isn't just a manhunt. We cannot rest until Osama bin Laden is captured or killed, but that day will mark only a victory in the war on terror, not its end. Terrorists like al Qaeda and its affiliates are unlike any adversary our nation has ever known. We face a global terrorist movement of many groups, funded from different sources with separate agendas, but all committed to assaulting the United States and free and open societies around the globe. Despite his tough talk, President Bush's actions against terrorism have fallen far short. He still has no comprehensive strategy for victory. After allowing bin Laden to escape from our grasp at Tora Bora, he diverted crucial resources from the effort to destroy al Qaeda in Afghanistan. His doctrine of unilateral preemption has driven away our allies and cost us the support of other nations.

We must put in place a strategy to win—an approach that recognizes and addresses the many facets of this mortal challenge, from the terrorists themselves to the root causes that give rise to new recruits, and uses all the tools at our disposal. Agents of terrorism work in the shadows of more than 60 nations, on every continent. The only possible path to victory will be found in the company of others, not walking alone. With John Kerry as Commander-in-Chief, we will never wait for a green light from abroad when our safety is at stake, but we must enlist those whose support we need for ultimate victory.

Iraq. . . . More than a year ago, President Bush stood on an aircraft carrier under a banner that proclaimed "mission accomplished." But today we know that the mission is not finished, hostilities have not ended, and our men and women in uniform fight almost alone with the target squarely on their backs.

People of good will disagree about whether America should have gone to war in Iraq, but this much is clear: this Administration badly exaggerated its case, particularly with respect to weapons of mass destruction and the connection between Saddam's government and al Qaeda. This Administration did not build a true international coalition. This Administration disdained the United Nations weapons inspection process and rushed to war without exhausting diplomatic alternatives. Ignoring the advice of military leaders, this Administration did not send sufficient forces into Iraq to accomplish the mission. And this Administration went into Iraq without a plan to win the peace.

Now this Administration has been forced to change course in order to correct this fundamental mistake. They are now taking up the suggestions that many Democrats have been making for over a year. And they must—because having gone to war, we cannot afford to fail at peace. We cannot allow a failed state in Iraq that inevitably would become a haven for terrorists and a destabilizing force in the Middle East. And we must secure more help from an international community that shares a huge stake in helping Iraq become a responsible member of that community, not a breeding ground for terror and intolerance.

Strengthening the Military. . . . The Bush Administration was right to call for the "transformation" of the military. But their version of transformation neglected to consider that the dangers we face have also been transformed. The Administration was concerned with fighting classic conventional wars, instead of the asymmetrical threats we now face in Iraq, Afghanistan, and the war against al Qaeda. To rise to those challenges, we must strengthen our military, including our Special Forces, improve our technology, and task our National Guard with homeland security. . . .

We will add 40,000 new soldiers—not to increase the number of soldiers in Iraq, but to sustain our overseas deployments and prevent and prepare for other possible conflicts. This will help relieve the strain on our troops and bring back more of our soldiers, guardsmen and reservists. We are dedicated to keeping our military operating on a volunteer basis. We are committed to management reform both to ensure that our defense funding is spent effectively and to help pay for these new forces. . . .

Homeland Security. The first and foremost responsibility of government is to protect its citizens from harm. Unfortunately, Washington today is not doing enough to make America safe.

We have made some progress since the terrible attacks of September 11th. We have taken steps to secure our airports. After resisting Democratic efforts for months, the Administration finally agreed to create the Department of Homeland Security.

But we have not done nearly enough. Our intelligence services remain fragmented and lack coordination. Millions of massive shipping containers arrive at American ports every year without being searched and without even a reliable list of their contents. Our borders are full of holes. Our chemical plants are vulnerable to attack. Across America, police officers, firefighters, and other first responders still lack the information, protective gear, and communications equipment to do their jobs safely and successfully. . . .

Protecting Retirement Security. . . . We are absolutely committed to preserving Social Security. It is a compact across the generations that has helped tens of millions of Americans live their retirement years in dignity instead of poverty. Democrats believe in the progressive, guaranteed benefit that has ensured that seniors and people with disabilities receive a benefit not subject to the whims of the market or the economy. We oppose privatizing Social Security or raising the retirement age. We oppose reducing the benefits earned by workers just because they have also earned a benefit from certain public retirement plans. We will repeal discriminatory laws that penalize some retired workers and their families while allowing others to receive full benefits. Because the massive deficits under the Bush Administration have raided hundreds of billions of dollars from Social Security, the most important step we can take to strengthen Social Security is to restore fiscal responsibility. Social Security matters to all Americans, Democrats and Republicans, and strengthening Social Security should be a common cause.

Standing Up for the Middle Class. . . . President Bush and the Republicans in Congress have ignored the middle class since day one of this Administration. They have catered to the wealth of the richest instead of honoring the work of the rest of us. They have promised almost everything and paid for almost nothing. And the middle class is shouldering more taxes, earning less money, and bearing higher costs. The bottom line for the middle class under President Bush and the Republican Party is this: Instead of working hard to get ahead, the middle class is working hard just to get by. . . .

First, we must restore our values to our tax code. We want a tax code that rewards work and creates wealth for more people, not a tax code that hoards wealth for those who already have it. With the middle class under assault like never before, we simply cannot afford the massive Bush tax cuts for the very wealthiest. We should set taxes for families making more than $200,000 a year at the same level as in the late 1990s, a period of great prosperity when the wealthiest Americans thrived without special treatment. We will cut taxes for 98 percent of Americans and help families meet the economic challenges of their everyday lives. And we will oppose tax increases on middle class families, including those living abroad.

Reforming Health Care. . . . We oppose privatizing Medicare. We will not allow Republicans to destroy a commitment that has done so much good for so many seniors and people with disabilities over the past 39 years. Instead, we want to strengthen Medicare and make it more efficient.

We will ensure that seniors across the country, particularly in small-town and rural America, no longer suffer from geographic discrimination.

We will end the disgrace of seniors being forced to choose between meals and medication. Today, our seniors are paying too much for prescription drugs, while options abroad are far cheaper and just as safe. We will allow the safe reimportation of drugs from other countries.

Stem Cell Research. President Bush has rejected the calls from Nancy Reagan, Christopher Reeve and Americans across the land for assistance with embryonic stem cell research. We will reverse his wrongheaded policy. Stem cell therapy offers hope to more than 100 million Americans who have serious illnesses—from Alzheimer's to heart disease to juvenile diabetes to Parkinson's. We will pursue this research under the strictest ethical guidelines, but we will not walk away from the chance to save lives and reduce human suffering.

Voting Rights. Voting is the foundation of democracy, a central act of civic engagement, and an expression of equal citizenship. Voting rights are important precisely because they are protective of all other rights. We will call for legislative action that will fully protect and enforce the fundamental Constitutional right of every American to vote—to ensure that the Constitution's promise is fully realized and that, in disputed elections, every vote is counted fully and fairly.

To advance these goals, and to guarantee the integrity of our elections and to increase voter confidence, we will seek action to ensure that voting systems are accessible, independently auditable, accurate, and secure. We will support the full funding of programs to realize this goal. Finally, it is the priority of the Democratic Party to fulfill the promise of election reform, reauthorize the expiring provisions of the Voting Rights Act, and vigorously enforce all our voting rights laws.

A Strong American Community. We will extend the promise of citizenship to those still struggling for freedom. Today's immigration laws do not reflect our values or serve our security, and we will work for real reform. The solution is not to establish a massive new status of second-class workers; that betrays our values and hurts all working people. Undocumented immigrants within our borders who clear a background check, work hard and pay taxes should have a path to earn full participation in America. We will hasten family reunification for parents and children, husbands and wives, and offer more English-language and civic education classes so immigrants can assume all the rights and responsibilities of citizenship. As we undertake these steps, we will work with our neighbors to strengthen our security so we are safer from those who would come here to harm us. We are a nation of immigrants, and from Arab-Americans in California to Latinos in Florida, we share the dream of a better life in the country we love.

We will defend the dignity of all Americans against those who would undermine it. Because we believe in the privacy and equality of women, we stand proudly for a woman's right to choose, consistent with Roe v. Wade, and regardless of her ability to pay. We stand firmly against Republican efforts to undermine that right. At the same time, we strongly support family planning and adoption incentives. Abortion should be safe, legal, and rare.

We support full inclusion of gay and lesbian families in the life of our nation and seek equal responsibilities, benefits, and protections for these families. In our country, marriage has been defined at the state level for 200 years, and we believe it should continue to be defined there. We repudiate President Bush's divisive effort to politicize the Constitution by pursuing a "Federal Marriage Amendment." Our goal is to bring Americans together, not drive them apart. . . .

Diversity. . . . We pledge to stand up for our beliefs and rally Americans to our cause. But we recognize that disagreements will remain, and we believe disagreement should not mean disrespect. Members of our party have deeply held and differing views on some matters of conscience and faith. We view diversity of views as a source of strength, and we welcome into our ranks all Americans who seek to build a stronger America. We are committed to resolving our differences in a spirit of civility, hope and mutual respect.

That's the America we believe in.

REPUBLICANS

For their convention held August 30 to September 2, the Republicans strategically chose New York, the city that lost the most lives and property in the 2001 terrorist attacks on the United States. The heavily secured convention site's proximity to lower Manhattan, where the World Trade Center towers fell, provided the delegates a constant reminder of President Bush's finest hour: his calming leadership when the nation needed it most.

Even the Democratic nominee Kerry had given grudging praise to the president in his nomination acceptance speech in Boston a month earlier. "I am proud that after September 11th all our people rallied to President Bush's call for unity to meet the danger," Kerry said. "There were no Democrats. There were no Republicans. There were only Americans. How we wish it had stayed that way."

Clearly, the Republicans, in choosing New York City as their convention site for the first time, hoped to recapture the post–September 11 spirit and show that the feeling of unity had indeed "stayed that way." They wanted the public to remember it was a Republican president who had taken the nation safely past that dreadful day. They also sought to show that their party was best suited to protect Americans from future attacks.

One of the first speakers to address the Madison Square Garden convention in television prime time was former New York City mayor Rudolph Giuliani, who himself had won widespread praise for the city's response to the terrorist attack. He noted that shortly after September 11, 2001, the president had gone before Congress and "announced the Bush doctrine when he said: 'Our war on terror begins with Al Qaeda, but it doesn't end there. It will not end until every terrorist group of global reach has been found, stopped and defeated. Either you are with us or you are with the terrorists.'"

Another speaker on opening night was Sen. John McCain of Arizona, who had sought the party's presidential nomination in 2000. Defending his former rival's decision to invade Iraq, he said the choice "wasn't between a benign status quo and the bloodshed of war. It was between war and a graver threat." McCain singled out Michael Moore as a "disingenuous filmmaker" who had opposed that decision. Moore, sitting in the press section, had made *Fahrenheit 9/11*, a documentary sharply critical of the Iraq war. At the mention of Moore, the delegates booed and chanted, "Four More Years!"

Many of the 2,509 delegates and 2,344 alternates wore on their faces Band-Aids depicting the Purple Heart medal. They were mocking Kerry's three Purple Hearts for being wounded in Vietnam War action. After the Democratic convention in July, a group called Swift Boat Veterans for Truth began airing television ads accusing Kerry of lying to obtain medals for what they claimed were superficial wounds. McCain denounced the ads as "dishonest and dishonorable."

Addressing the convention on August 31, film actor and California governor Arnold Schwarzenegger told of listening to presidential candidates Richard Nixon and Hubert H. Humphrey, shortly after his arrival from Austria in 1968. Impressed with Nixon's views, he asked a friend who was translating for him whether Nixon was Republican or Democrat. When the friend replied "Republican," Schwarzenegger said, " 'Then I'm a Republican,' and I've been one ever since. And, trust me, in my wife's family that is no small achievement." The delegates laughed, knowing his wife is Maria Shriver, a member of the Kennedy family of stalwart Democrats.

The Republicans scored a victory when they signed up conservative Democratic senator Zell Miller of Georgia to give the keynote address on September 1. "Motivated more by partisan politics than by national security, today's Democratic leaders see America as an occupier, not a liberator. Nothing makes this Marine madder than someone calling American troops invaders rather than liberators," Miller said. Angry with his party, he fumed that the "nation is being torn apart and made weaker because of the Democrats' manic obsession to bring down our commander in chief." Miller, a keynoter at the 1992 Democratic convention, was leaving the Senate in 2005.

Conspicuously missing from the speakers' rostrum was Nancy Reagan, widow of former president Ronald Reagan, who died two months earlier. She reportedly had declined several invitations to speak because she objected to the party's use of her husband's quotes and images. She also disagreed with the administration's limits on funding for embryonic stem cell research to find cures for diseases such as Alzheimer's, which afflicted her husband.

As they did in 2000, the Republicans used a "rolling roll call" of the state delegations spanning three days for the formal renomination of President Bush. In the final tally Bush received 2,508 votes with one abstention. Vice President Cheney was renominated by acclamation. (*Table, p. 1000.*)

In his acceptance speech on September 1, Cheney praised Bush's steady, determined leadership in time of war and doubted whether Kerry was up to the task. He pointed to the various defense measures that Kerry had opposed during his lengthy Senate career as a weakness in the critical area of national security. "A senator can be wrong for 20 years, without consequence to the nation. But a president—a president—always casts the deciding vote. And in this time of challenge, America needs—and America has—a president we can count on to get it right."

On September 2 President Bush delivered his nomination acceptance speech to enthusiastic convention crowd. He defended the administration's decision to invade Iraq: "We must, and we will, confront threats to America before it is too late. In Saddam Hussein, we saw a threat." According to Bush, the decision to go to war was in keeping with what he called "the most solemn duty of the American president . . . to protect the American people." For his domestic agenda, he promised to promote "an ownership society," where citizens "own their health care plans, and have the confidence of owning a piece of their retirement."

The Republican platform ran 42,000 words long and focused greatly on national security. The word "terror" or a variant, such as "terrorist," appeared almost 200 times. The platform also supported the tax cuts initiated during the president's first term, advocated drilling in the Arctic National Wildlife Refuge, and opposed abortion rights and same-sex marriage.

Following are excerpts from the Republican platform of 2004.

Iraq. As Republicans, we do not equivocate, as others have done, about whether America should have gone to war in Iraq. The best intelligence available at the time indicated that Saddam Hussein was a threat. On that point, President Bush, members of both parties in Congress, and the United Nations agreed. While the stockpiles of weapons of mass destruction we expected to find in Iraq have not yet materialized, we have confirmed that Saddam Hussein had the capability to reconstitute his weapons programs and the desire to do so. Our nation did the right thing, and the American people are now safer because we and our allies ended the brutal dictatorship of Saddam Hussein, halting his decades-long pursuit of chemical, biological, and nuclear weapons. President Bush had a choice to make: Trust a madman or defend America. He chose defending America.

War on Terror. We applaud President Bush for his success in mobilizing such international cooperation in the War on Terror, which the 9/11 Commission judges to be "on a vastly enlarged scale" and to have expanded dramatically since September 11, 2001. We also question the credibility of our opponents, who claim to support global alliances while nominating a candidate who has insulted our allies by calling the nations fighting in Iraq "window-dressing" and referring to them as a "coalition of the coerced and the bribed." Directing ugly rhetoric at America's allies in a time of war is irresponsible. It does not represent the gratitude and respect the vast majority of Americans have for the men and women from other nations who are risking their lives to make the world safer.

Private Retirement Accounts. Individual ownership of voluntary personal retirement accounts for today's workers will make Social Security more equitable, but, just as importantly, will put the system on sure financial footing. Fifty years ago there were 16 workers to support every one beneficiary of Social Security. Today there are just 3.3 workers for each beneficiary. By the time young men and women who are entering the workforce today turn 65, there will be only two workers for each beneficiary. Doing nothing is not an option. We must keep faith with both the past and the future by strengthening and enhancing Social Security. . . .

An Ownership Era. Ownership gives citizens a vital stake in their communities and their country. By expanding ownership, we will help turn economic growth into lasting prosperity. As Republicans, we trust people to make decisions about how to spend, save, and invest their own money. We want individuals to own and control their income. We want people to have a tangible asset that they can build and rely on, making their own choices and directing their own future. Ownership should not be the preserve of the wealthy or the privileged. As Republicans who believe in the power of ownership to create better lives, we want more people to own a home. We want more people to own and build small businesses. We want more people to own and control their health care. We want more people to own personal retirement accounts. . . .

Lower Taxes and Economic Growth. In 2001, President Bush and the Republican Congress worked together to pass the most sweeping tax relief in a generation. By letting families, workers, and small business owners keep more of the money they earn, they helped bring America from recession to a steadily expanding economy. Despite enduring the aftereffects of the stock market's irrational exuberance in the late 1990s, terrorist attacks on our nation, and corporate scandals that bubbled to the surface after years of inattention, the U.S. economy has now grown for 33 straight months. And unlike four years ago, there are no signs of an end to the current economic growth.

Fiscal Discipline and Government Reform. It is important to view the size of the [federal] deficit in relation to the size of the nation's economy. By that measure, today's deficit, although unwelcome, is well within historical ranges. A deficit that is 3.8 percent of GDP [gross domestic product], as is now projected for this year, would be smaller than the deficits in nine of the last 25 years, and far below the peak deficit figure of 6 percent of GDP reached in 1983. This deficit is also in line with what other industrialized nations are facing today. The U.S. deficit matches the average deficit within the Organization for Economic Cooperation and Development, and is below the levels of France, Germany, and Japan.

Much more importantly, because the President and Congress enacted pro-growth economic policies, the deficit is headed strongly in the right direction. Next year's projected deficit, at 2.7 percent of GDP, would be smaller than those in 14 of the last 25 years. As Republicans in Congress work with the President to restrain spending and strengthen economic growth, the federal deficit will fall to 1.5 percent of the nation's economic output in 2009—well below the 2.2 percent average of the last 40 years.

Corporate Responsibility. After fraudulent corporate practices rooted in the irrational exuberance of the late 1990s began to surface in the closing months of 2001, President Bush worked with the Congress to take decisive action to restore honesty and integrity to America's corporate boardrooms. In July 2002, President Bush signed the Sarbanes-Oxley Act, the most far-reaching reform of American business practices since the 1940s. Under this new law, CEOs and Chief Financial Officers are required to personally vouch for the truth and fairness of their companies' disclosures; for the first time, an independent board has been established to oversee the accounting profession; investigators have been given new tools to root out corporate fraud; and enhanced penalties are ensuring that dishonest corporate officials do hard time.

Reforming the Litigation System. America's litigation system is broken. Junk and frivolous lawsuits are driving up the cost of doing business in America by forcing companies to pay excessive legal expenses to fight off or settle often baseless lawsuits. Those costs are being paid by small business owners, manufacturers, their employees, and consumers. A typical small business with $10 million in annual revenue pays about $150,000

a year in tort liability costs. That is money that could be used to invest and hire new employees. Inefficiency and waste in the legal system is costing the average American family of four $1,800 every year, equivalent to an extra 3 percent tax on wages. And the bulk of jury awards to plaintiffs don't even go to the people who deserve it. Injured persons on average collect less than 50 cents of every dollar that the legal system costs. Trial lawyers get rich from the misfortune of others. If small business is America's economic engine, trial lawyers are the brakes: They cost hundreds of thousands of good jobs, drive honest employers out of business, deprive women of critical medical care—then skip out with fat wallets and nary a thought for the economic havoc and human misery they leave in their wake.

Developing U.S. Oil Resources. Using the most sophisticated technologies, we can explore and develop oil resources here at home with minimal environmental impact. Our Party continues to support energy development in the coastal plain of the Arctic National Wildlife Refuge (ANWR), which, according to the U.S. Geological Survey, holds as much as 16 billion barrels of oil—enough to replace oil imports from Saudi Arabia for nearly 20 years. The drilling footprint can be confined to just 2,000 acres (the entire refuge contains 19 million acres), about the size of Washington's Dulles Airport, on ice roads that melt away in the summer, leaving little trace of human intervention. We have already wasted precious time. If the previous Administration had not vetoed the ANWR proposal passed by the Republican Congress in 1995, at this moment ANWR would be producing up to one million barrels of oil a day.

Reforming the Medical Liability System. The medical liability system is harming our medical delivery system. Doctors are afraid to practice medicine. Frequent, unwarranted, lawsuits force doctors out of certain specialty areas and geographic regions. The most dangerous result of this is the declining availability of emergency trauma care and women's health services. In many cases, costs are so prohibitive that many obstetrics/gynecology practices are scaling back service or choosing not to practice altogether. Junk lawsuits add at least $60 billion to health care costs in America because doctors are forced to practice defensive medicine, ordering extensive, unnecessary, and expensive tests and procedures to keep trial lawyers at bay.

The President has proposed, and the Republican House of Representatives has passed, reforms that would speed compensation to injured patients, reduce health care costs, and improve Americans' access to quality health care. Shamefully driven by the powerful trial lawyer lobby, Democrat Senators have repeatedly thwarted the efforts of the Republican majority to deliver meaningful medical liability reform. They have employed their obstructionist tactics three times in the current Congress alone. The Republican Party reaffirms its commitment to putting patients and doctors ahead of trial lawyers. We will continue to battle for litigation reforms that help keep doctors in practice, adopt reasonable caps on non-economic awards in medical malpractice suits, and ensure that Americans have access to quality affordable health care.

Faith-Based and Community Services. We applaud President Bush's efforts to promote the generous and compassionate work of America's faith-based and neighborhood charities. The President established the Office of Faith-Based and Community Initiatives in the White House to coordinate federal, state, and local efforts to tear down barriers that have prevented religiously affiliated groups from applying for government grants on an equal footing with secular organizations. While the federal government must not promote religious activity, advocate on behalf of any religion, or fund any organization that discriminates on the basis of religion when providing taxpayer-funded services, no organization should be disqualified from receiving federal funds simply because it displays religious symbols, has a statement of faith in its mission statement, or has a religious leader on its board.

Voting Rights. The foundation of our democratic republic is our commitment to conducting free and fair elections. Unfortunately, in November 2000, too many people believed they were denied the right to vote. Many African Americans, Hispanics, and others fear they may lose the right to vote because of inaccurate or insecure technology or because of a rolling back in the gains made by the passage of civil rights legislation. Our national commitment to a voting process that has integrity was underscored in 2002 when the Congress passed and the President signed the Help America Vote Act (HAVA). We will continue to do all we can to ensure that every lawful vote counts for all Americans.

Judiciary. In the federal courts, scores of judges with activist backgrounds in the hard-left now have lifetime tenure. Recent events have made it clear that these judges threaten America's dearest institutions and our very way of life. In some states, activist judges are redefining the institution of marriage. The Pledge of Allegiance has already been invalidated by the courts once, and the Supreme Court's ruling has left the Pledge in danger of being struck down again—not because the American people have rejected it and the values that it embodies, but because a handful of activist judges threaten to overturn commonsense and tradition. And while the vast majority of Americans support a ban on partial birth abortion, this brutal and violent practice will likely continue by judicial fiat. We believe that the self-proclaimed supremacy of these judicial activists is antithetical to the democratic ideals on which our nation was founded. President Bush has established a solid record of nominating only judges who have demonstrated respect for the Constitution and the democratic processes of our republic, and Republicans in the Senate have strongly supported those nominees. We call upon obstructionist Democrats in the Senate to abandon their unprecedented and highly irresponsible filibuster of President Bush's highly qualified judicial nominees, and to allow the Republican Party to restore respect for the law to America's courts.

Protecting Marriage. After more than two centuries of American jurisprudence, and millennia of human experience, a few judges and local authorities are presuming to change the most fundamental institution of civilization, the union of a man and a woman in marriage. Attempts to redefine marriage in a single state or city could have serious consequences throughout the country, and anything less than a Constitutional amendment, passed by the Congress and ratified by the states, is vulnerable to being overturned by activist judges. On a matter of such importance, the voice of the people must be heard. The Constitutional amendment process guarantees that the final decision will rest with the American people and their elected representatives. President Bush will also vigorously defend the Defense of Marriage Act, which was supported by both parties and passed by 85 votes in the Senate. This common sense law reaffirms the right of states not to recognize same-sex marriages licensed in other states.

Defense of Life. We praise the President for his bold leadership in defense of life. We praise him for signing the Born Alive Infants Protection Act. This important legislation ensures that every infant born alive—including an infant who survives an abortion procedure—is considered a person under federal law.

We praise Republicans in Congress for passing, with strong bipartisan support, a ban on the inhumane procedure known as partial birth abortion. And we applaud President Bush for signing legislation outlawing partial birth abortion and for vigorously defending it in the courts.

In signing the partial birth abortion ban, President Bush reminded us that "the most basic duty of government is to defend the life of the innocent. Every person, however frail or vulnerable, has a place and a purpose in this world." We affirm the inherent dignity and worth of all people. We oppose the non-consensual withholding of care or treatment because of disability, age, or infirmity, just as we oppose euthanasia and assisted suicide, which especially endanger the poor and those on the margins of society.

Selected Texts on the 2001 Terrorist Attacks

President Bush's Statements Following the 2001 Terrorist Attacks

Following are President George W. Bush's remarks in Sarasota, Fla., on Sept. 11, 2001, following that morning's terrorist attacks in New York City.

Ladies and gentlemen, this is a difficult moment for America. I, unfortunately, will be going back to Washington after my remarks. Secretary Rod Paige and the lieutenant governor will take the podium and discuss education.

I do want to thank the folks here at the Booker Elementary School for their hospitality.

Today we've had a national tragedy. Two airplanes have crashed into the World Trade Center in an apparent terrorist attack on our country. I have spoken to the vice president, to the governor of New York, to the director of the FBI, and I've ordered that the full resources of the federal government go to help the victims and their families, and to conduct a full-scale investigation to hunt down and to find those folks who committed this act.

Terrorism against our nation will not stand.

And now if you join me in a moment of silence.

May God bless the victims, their families and America. Thank you very much.

Following are President George W. Bush's remarks on arriving at Barksdale Air Force Base in Louisiana on Sept. 11, 2001.

Freedom itself was attacked this morning by a faceless coward. And freedom will be defended.

I want to reassure the American people that the full resources of the federal government are working to assist local authorities to save lives and to help the victims of these attacks.

Make no mistake: The United States will hunt down and punish those responsible for these cowardly acts.

I've been in regular contact with the vice president, the secretary of Defense, the national security team and my Cabinet. We have taken all appropriate security precautions to protect the American people. Our military at home and around the world is on high alert status, and we have taken the necessary security precautions to continue the functions of your government.

We have been in touch with the leaders of Congress and with world leaders to assure them that we will do whatever is necessary to protect America and Americans.

I ask the American people to join me in saying a thanks for all the folks who have been fighting hard to rescue our fellow citizens and to join me in saying a prayer for the victims and their families.

The resolve of our great nation is being tested. But make no mistake, we will show the world that we will pass this test.

God bless.

Following is President George W. Bush's address to the nation from the White House on Sept. 11, 2001.

Good evening.

Today, our fellow citizens, our way of life, our very freedom came under attack in a series of deliberate and deadly terrorist acts. The victims were in airplanes or in their offices: secretaries, businessmen and women, military and federal workers, moms and dads, friends and neighbors.

Thousands of lives were suddenly ended by evil, despicable acts of terror. The pictures of airplanes flying into buildings, fires burning, huge structures collapsing have filled us with disbelief, terrible sadness and a quiet, unyielding anger.

These acts of mass murder were intended to frighten our nation into chaos and retreat. But they have failed. Our country is strong. A great people has been moved to defend a great nation.

Terrorist attacks can shake the foundations of our biggest buildings, but they cannot touch the foundation of America. These acts shatter steel, but they cannot dent the steel of American resolve.

America was targeted for attack because we're the brightest beacon for freedom and opportunity in the world. And no one will keep that light from shining.

Today, our nation saw evil, the very worst of human nature, and we responded with the best of America, with the daring of our rescue workers, with the caring for strangers and neighbors who came to give blood and help in any way they could.

Immediately following the first attack, I implemented our government's emergency response plans. Our military is powerful, and it's prepared.

Our emergency teams are working in New York City and Washington, D.C., to help with local rescue efforts. Our first priority is to get help to those who have been injured and to take every precaution to protect our citizens at home and around the world from further attacks.

The functions of our government continue without interruption. Federal agencies in Washington which had to be evacuated today are reopening for essential personnel tonight and will be open for business tomorrow.

Our financial institutions remain strong, and the American economy will be open for business as well.

The search is under way for those who are behind these evil acts. I've directed the full resources for our intelligence and law enforcement communities to find those responsible and bring them to justice. We will make no distinction between the terrorists who committed these acts and those who harbor them.

I appreciate so very much the members of Congress who have joined me in strongly condemning these attacks. And on behalf of the American people, I thank the many world leaders who have called to offer their condolences and assistance.

America and our friends and allies join with all those who want peace and security in the world and we stand together to win the war against terrorism.

Tonight I ask for your prayers for all those who grieve, for the children whose worlds have been shattered, for all whose sense of safety and security has been threatened. And I pray they will be comforted by a power greater than any of us spoken through the ages in Psalm 23: "Even though I walk through the valley of the shadow of death, I fear no evil for you are with me."

This is a day when all Americans from every walk of life unite in our resolve for justice and peace. America has stood down enemies before, and we will do so this time.

None of us will ever forget this day, yet we go forward to defend freedom and all that is good and just in our world.

Thank you. Good night and God bless America.

Following are remarks by President George W. Bush after a meeting in the Cabinet Room with his national security team on Sept. 12, 2001.

I just completed a meeting with our national security team, and we've received the latest intelligence updates.

The deliberate and deadly attacks which were carried out yesterday against our country were more than acts of terror. They were acts of war. This will require our country to unite in steadfast determination and resolve. Freedom and democracy are under attack.

The American people need to know we're facing a different enemy than we have ever faced. This enemy hides in shadows and has no regard for human life. This is an enemy who preys on innocent and unsuspecting people, then runs for cover, but it won't be able to run for cover forever. This is an enemy that tries to hide, but it won't be able to hide forever. This is an enemy that thinks its harbors are safe, but they won't be safe forever. This enemy attacked not just our people but all freedom-loving people everywhere in the world.

The United States of America will use all our resources to conquer this enemy. We will rally the world. We will be patient. We'll be focused, and we will be steadfast in our determination. This battle will take time and resolve, but make no mistake about it, we will win.

The federal government and all our agencies are conducting business, but it is not business as usual. We are operating on heightened security alert. America is going forward, and as we do so, we must remain keenly aware of the threats to our country.

Those in authority should take appropriate precautions to protect our citizens. But we will not allow this enemy to win the war by changing our way of life or restricting our freedoms.

This morning, I am sending to Congress a request for emergency funding authority so that we are prepared to spend whatever it takes to rescue victims, to help the citizens of New York City and Washington, D.C., respond to this tragedy, and to protect our national security.

I want to thank the members of Congress for their unity and support. America is united. The freedom-loving nations of the world stand by our side. This will be a monumental struggle of good versus evil, but good will prevail.

Thank you very much.

Following are President George W. Bush's remarks while inspecting the damage at the Pentagon on Sept. 12, 2001.

I am so grateful to the people who are working here.

We're here to say thanks to not only the workers on this site, but the workers who are doing the same work in New York City. I want to say thanks to the folks who have given blood to the Red Cross. I want to say thanks for the hundreds of thousands of Americans who pray for the victims and their families.

[Defense] Secretary [Donald] Rumsfeld told me, when I talked to him, that he felt the blast shake the Pentagon—even though he was on the other side of the building, the building rocked. And now I know why.

Coming here makes me sad, on the one hand; it also makes me angry. Our country will, however, not be cowed by terrorists, by people who don't share the same values we share, by people who are willing to destroy people's lives because we embrace freedom. The nation mourns, but our government will go on, the country will function. We are on high alert for possible activity.

But coming here confirms what the Secretary and I both know: that this is a great nation. People here working hard prove it, people out here working their hearts out to answer families' questions, to remove the rubble and debris from this office. I want to thank everybody not only on this site, but all across America, for responding so generously, so kindly, in their prayers, in their contributions of love and their willingness to help in any way they can.

Following are remarks by President George W. Bush at the Washington National Cathedral on Sept. 14, 2001.

We are here in the middle hour of our grief. So many have suffered so great a loss, and today we express our nation's sorrow. We come before God to pray for the missing and the dead, and for those who love them.

On Tuesday, our country was attacked with deliberate and massive cruelty. We have seen the images of fire and ashes, and bent steel.

Now come the names, the list of casualties we are only beginning to read. They are the names of men and women who began their day at a desk or in an airport, busy with life. They are the names of people who faced death, and in their last moments called home to say: Be brave, and I love you.

They are the names of passengers who defied their murderers, and prevented the murder of others on the ground. They are the names of men and women who wore the uniform of the United States, and died at their posts.

They are the names of rescuers, the ones whom death found running up the stairs and into the fires to help others. We will read all these names. We will linger over them, and learn their stories, and many Americans will weep.

To the children and parents and spouses and families and friends of the lost, we offer the deepest sympathy of the nation. And I assure you, you are not alone.

Just three days removed from these events, Americans do not yet have the distance of history. But our responsibility to history is already clear: to answer these attacks and rid the world of evil.

War has been waged against us by stealth and deceit and murder. This nation is peaceful, but fierce when stirred to anger. This conflict was begun on the timing and terms of others. It will end in a way, and at an hour, of our choosing.

Our purpose as a nation is firm. Yet our wounds as a people are recent and unhealed, and lead us to pray. In many of our prayers this week, there is a searching, and an honesty. At St. Patrick's Cathedral in New York on Tuesday, a woman said, "I prayed to God to give us a sign that He is still here." Others have prayed for the same, searching hospital to hospital, carrying pictures of those still missing.

God's signs are not always the ones we look for. We learn in tragedy that his purposes are not always our own. Yet the prayers of private suffering, whether in our homes or in this great cathedral, are known and heard, and understood.

There are prayers that help us last through the day, or endure the night. There are prayers of friends and strangers that give us strength for the journey. And there are prayers that yield our will to a will greater than our own.

This world He created is of moral design. Grief and tragedy and hatred are only for a time. Goodness, remembrance and love have no end.

And the Lord of life holds all who die, and all who mourn.

It is said that adversity introduces us to ourselves. This is true of a nation as well. In this trial, we have been reminded, and the world has seen, that our fellow Americans are generous and kind, resourceful and brave. We see our national character in rescuers working past exhaustion; in long lines of blood donors; in thousands of citizens who have asked to work and serve in any way possible.

And we have seen our national character in eloquent acts of sacrifice. Inside the World Trade Center, one man who could have saved himself stayed until the end at the side of his quadriplegic friend. A beloved priest died giving the last rites to a firefighter. Two office workers, finding a disabled stranger, carried her down 68 floors to safety. A group of men drove through the night from Dallas to Washington to bring skin grafts for burn victims.

In these acts, and in many others, Americans showed a deep commitment to one another, and an abiding love for our country. Today, we feel what Franklin Roosevelt called the warm courage of national unity. This is a unity of every faith, and every background.

It has joined together political parties in both houses of Congress. It is evident in services of prayer and candlelight vigils, and American flags, which are displayed in pride and wave in defiance.

Our unity is a kinship of grief, and a steadfast resolve to prevail against our enemies. And this unity against terror is now extending across the world.

America is a nation full of good fortune, with so much to be grateful for. But we are not spared from suffering. In every generation, the world has produced enemies of human freedom. They have attacked America, because we are freedom's home and defender. And the commitment of our fathers is now the calling of our time.

On this national day of prayer and remembrance, we ask almighty God to watch over our nation, and grant us patience and resolve in all that is to come. We pray that He will comfort and console those who now walk in sorrow. We thank Him for each life we now must mourn, and the promise of a life to come.

As we have been assured, neither death nor life, nor angels nor principalities nor powers, nor things present nor things to come, nor height nor depth, can separate us from God's love. May He bless the souls of the departed. May He comfort our own. And may He always guide our country.

God bless America.

President Bush's Address to Congress on the 2001 Terrorist Attacks

Following is President George W. Bush's speech on Sept. 20, 2001, to a joint session of Congress on the Sept. 11, 2001, attacks and in which he delivered an ultimatum to the Taliban in Afghanistan.

Mr. Speaker, Mr. President Pro Tempore, members of Congress, and fellow Americans:

In the normal course of events, Presidents come to this chamber to report on the state of the Union. Tonight, no such report is needed. It has already been delivered by the American people.

We have seen it in the courage of passengers, who rushed terrorists to save others on the ground—passengers like an exceptional man named Todd Beamer. And would you please help me to welcome his wife, Lisa Beamer, here tonight.

We have seen the state of our Union in the endurance of rescuers, working past exhaustion. We have seen the unfurling of flags, the lighting of candles, the giving of blood, the saying of prayers—in English, Hebrew, and Arabic.

We have seen the decency of a loving and giving people who have made the grief of strangers their own.

My fellow citizens, for the last nine days, the entire world has seen for itself the state of our Union—and it is strong.

Tonight we are a country awakened to danger and called to defend freedom. Our grief has turned to anger, and anger to resolution. Whether we bring our enemies to justice, or bring justice to our enemies, justice will be done.

I thank the Congress for its leadership at such an important time. All of America was touched on the evening of the tragedy to see Republicans and Democrats joined together on the steps of this Capitol, singing "God Bless America." And you did more than sing; you acted, by delivering $40 billion to rebuild our communities and meet the needs of our military.

Speaker [J. Dennis] Hastert [R-Ill.], Minority Leader [Richard A.] Gephardt [D-Mo.], Majority Leader [Tom] Daschle [D-S.D.] and Senator [Trent] Lott [R-Miss.], I thank you for your friendship, for your leadership and for your service to our country. And on behalf of the American people, I thank the world for its outpouring of support. America will never forget the sounds of our National Anthem playing at Buckingham Palace, on the streets of Paris, and at Berlin's Brandenburg Gate.

We will not forget South Korean children gathering to pray outside our embassy in Seoul, or the prayers of sympathy offered at a mosque in Cairo. We will not forget moments of silence and days of mourning in Australia and Africa and Latin America.

Nor will we forget the citizens of 80 other nations who died with our own: dozens of Pakistanis; more than 130 Israelis; more than 250 citizens of India; men and women from El Salvador, Iran, Mexico and Japan; and hundreds of British citizens. America has no truer friend than Great Britain.

Once again, we are joined together in a great cause—so honored the British prime minister has crossed an ocean to show his unity of purpose with America. Thank you for coming, friend.

On Sept. 11, enemies of freedom committed an act of war against our country. Americans have known wars—but for the past 136 years, they have been wars on foreign soil, except for one Sunday in 1941. Americans have known the casualties of war—but not at the center of a great city on a peaceful morning. Americans have known surprise attacks—but never before on thousands of civilians. All of this was brought upon us in a single day—and night fell on a different world, a world where freedom itself is under attack.

Americans have many questions tonight. Americans are asking: Who attacked our country? The evidence we have gathered all points to a collection of loosely affiliated terrorist organizations known as al Qaeda. They are the same murderers indicted for bombing American embassies in Tanzania and Kenya, and responsible for bombing the USS *Cole*.

Al Qaeda is to terror what the Mafia is to crime. But its goal is not making money; its goal is remaking the world—and imposing its radical beliefs on people everywhere.

The terrorists practice a fringe form of Islamic extremism that has been rejected by Muslim scholars and the vast majority of Muslim clerics—a fringe movement that perverts the peaceful teachings of Islam. The terrorists' directive commands them to kill Christians and Jews, to kill all Americans, and make no distinction among military and civilians, including women and children.

This group and its leader—a person named Osama bin Laden—are linked to many other organizations in different countries, including the Egyptian Islamic Jihad and the Islamic Movement of Uzbekistan. There are thousands of these terrorists in more than 60 countries. They are recruited from their own nations and neighborhoods and brought to camps in places like Afghanistan, where they are trained in the tactics of terror. They are sent back to their homes or sent to hide in countries around the world to plot evil and destruction.

The leadership of al Qaeda has great influence in Afghanistan and supports the Taliban regime in controlling most of that country. In Afghanistan, we see al Qaeda's vision for the world. Afghanistan's people have been brutalized—many are starving and many have fled. Women are not allowed to attend school. You can be jailed for owning a television. Religion can be practiced only as their leaders dictate. A man can be jailed in Afghanistan if his beard is not long enough.

The United States respects the people of Afghanistan—after all, we are currently its largest source of humanitarian aid—but we condemn the Taliban regime. It is not only repressing its own people, it is threatening people everywhere by sponsoring and sheltering and supplying terrorists. By aiding and abetting murder, the Taliban regime is committing murder.

And tonight, the United States of America makes the following demands on the Taliban: Deliver to United States authorities all the leaders of al Qaeda who hide in your land. Release all foreign nationals, including American citizens, you have unjustly imprisoned. Protect foreign journalists, diplomats and aid workers in your country. Close immediately and permanently every terrorist training camp in Afghanistan, and hand over every terrorist, and every person in their support structure, to appropriate authorities. Give the United States full access to terrorist training camps, so we can make sure they are no longer operating.

These demands are not open to negotiation or discussion. The Taliban must act, and act immediately. They will hand over the terrorists, or they will share in their fate. I also want to speak tonight directly to Muslims throughout the world. We respect your faith. It's practiced freely by many millions of Americans, and by millions more in countries that America counts as friends. Its teachings are good and peaceful, and those who commit evil in the name of Allah blaspheme the name of Allah. The terrorists are traitors to their own faith, trying, in effect, to hijack Islam itself. The enemy of America is not our many Muslim friends; it is not our many Arab friends. Our enemy is a radical network of terrorists and every government that supports them.

Our war on terror begins with al Qaeda, but it does not end there. It will not end until every terrorist group of global reach has been found, stopped and defeated.

Americans are asking, why do they hate us? They hate what we see right here in this chamber—a democratically elected government. Their leaders are self-appointed. They hate our freedoms—our freedom of religion, our freedom of speech, our freedom to vote and assemble and disagree with each other. They want to overthrow existing governments in many Muslim countries, such as Egypt, Saudi Arabia and Jordan. They want to drive Israel out of the Middle East. They want to drive Christians and Jews out of vast regions of Asia and Africa.

These terrorists kill not merely to end lives, but to disrupt and end a way of life. With every atrocity, they hope that America grows fearful, retreating from the world and forsaking our friends. They stand against us, because we stand in their way.

We are not deceived by their pretenses to piety. We have seen their kind before. They are the heirs of all the murderous ideologies of the 20th century. By sacrificing human life to serve their radical visions—by abandoning every value except the will to power—they follow in the path of fascism, and Nazism, and totalitarianism. And they will follow that path all the way, to where it ends: in history's unmarked grave of discarded lies.

A LENGTHY CAMPAIGN

Americans are asking: How will we fight and win this war? We will direct every resource at our command—every means of diplomacy, every tool of intelligence, every instrument of law enforcement, every financial influence and every necessary weapon of war—to the disruption and to the defeat of the global terror network.

This war will not be like the war against Iraq a decade ago, with a decisive liberation of territory and a swift conclusion. It will not look like the air war above Kosovo two years ago, where no ground troops were used and not a single American was lost in combat.

Our response involves far more than instant retaliation and isolated strikes. Americans should not expect one battle, but a lengthy campaign, unlike any other we have ever seen. It may include dramatic strikes, visible on TV, and covert operations, secret even in success. We will starve terrorists of funding, turn them one against another, drive them from place to place, until there is no refuge or no rest. And we will pursue nations that provide aid or safe haven to terrorism. Every nation, in every region, now has a decision to make. Either you are with us, or you are with the terrorists. From this day forward, any nation that continues to harbor or support terrorism will be regarded by the United States as a hostile regime.

Our nation has been put on notice: We are not immune from attack. We will take defensive measures against terrorism to protect Americans. Today, dozens of federal departments and agencies, as well as state and local governments, have responsibilities affecting homeland security. These efforts must be coordinated at the highest level. So tonight I announce the creation of a Cabinet-level position reporting directly to me—the Office of Homeland Security.

And tonight I also announce a distinguished American to lead this effort, to strengthen American security: a military veteran, an effective governor, a true patriot, a trusted friend—Pennsylvania's Tom Ridge. He will lead, oversee and coordinate a comprehensive national strategy to safeguard our country against terrorism and respond to any attacks that may come.

These measures are essential. But the only way to defeat terrorism as a threat to our way of life is to stop it, eliminate it, and destroy it where it grows.

Many will be involved in this effort, from FBI agents to intelligence operatives to the reservists we have called to active duty. All deserve our thanks, and all have our prayers. And tonight, a few miles from the damaged Pentagon, I have a message for our military: Be ready. I've called the Armed Forces to alert, and there is a reason. The hour is coming when America will act, and you will make us proud.

This is not, however, just America's fight. And what is at stake is not just America's freedom. This is the world's fight. This is civilization's fight. This is the fight of all who believe in progress and pluralism, tolerance and freedom.

We ask every nation to join us. We will ask, and we will need, the help of police forces, intelligence services and banking systems around the world. The United States is grateful that many nations and many international organizations have already responded—with sympathy and with support. Nations from Latin America, to Asia, to Africa, to Europe, to the Islamic world. Perhaps the NATO Charter reflects best the attitude of the world: An attack on one is an attack on all. The civilized world is rallying to America's side. They understand that if this terror goes unpunished, their own cities, their own citizens may be next.

Terror, unanswered, can not only bring down buildings, it can threaten the stability of legitimate governments. And you know what—we're not going to allow it.

Americans are asking: What is expected of us? I ask you to live your lives, and hug your children. I know many citizens have fears tonight, and I ask you to be calm and resolute, even in the face of a continuing threat. I ask you to uphold the values of America, and remember why so many have come here. We are in a fight for our principles, and our first responsibility is to live by them. No one should be singled out for unfair treatment or unkind words because of their ethnic background or religious faith.

I ask you to continue to support the victims of this tragedy with your contributions. Those who want to give can go to a central source of information, libertyunites.org, to find the names of groups providing direct help in New York, Pennsylvania, and Virginia.

The thousands of FBI agents who are now at work in this investigation may need your cooperation, and I ask you to give it.

I ask for your patience, with the delays and inconveniences that may accompany tighter security; and for your patience in what will be a long struggle.

I ask your continued participation and confidence in the American economy. Terrorists attacked a symbol of American prosperity. They did not touch its source. America is successful because of the hard work, and creativity, and enterprise of our people. These were the true strengths of our economy before Sept. 11th, and they are our strengths today.

And finally, please continue praying for the victims of terror and their families, for those in uniform and for our great country. Prayer has comforted us in sorrow, and will help strengthen us for the journey ahead.

Tonight I thank my fellow Americans for what you have already done and for what you will do. And ladies and gentlemen of the Congress, I thank you, their representatives, for what you have already done and for what we will do together.

Tonight, we face new and sudden national challenges. We will come together to improve air safety, to dramatically expand the number of air marshals on domestic flights, and take new measures to prevent hijacking. We will come together to promote stability and keep our airlines flying, with direct assistance during this emergency.

We will come together to give law enforcement the additional tools it needs to track down terror here at home. We will come together to strengthen our intelligence capabilities to know the plans of terrorists before they act, and find them before they strike. We will come together to take active steps that strengthen America's economy, and put our people back to work.

Tonight we welcome two leaders who embody the extraordinary spirit of all New Yorkers: Governor George Pataki and Mayor Rudolph Giuliani. As a symbol of America's resolve, my administration will work with Congress, and these two leaders, to show the world that we will rebuild New York City.

After all that has just passed—all the lives taken and all the possibilities and hopes that died with them—it is natural to wonder if America's future is one of fear. Some speak of an age of terror. I know there are struggles ahead, and dangers to face. But this country will define our times, not be defined by them. As long as the United States of America is determined and strong, this will not be an age of terror; this will be an age of liberty, here and across the world.

Great harm has been done to us. We have suffered great loss. And in our grief and anger we have found our mission and our moment. Freedom and fear are at war. The advance of human freedom—the great achievement of our time and the great hope of every time—now depends on us. Our nation—this generation—will lift a dark threat of violence from our people and our future. We will rally the world to this cause by our efforts, by our courage.

We will not tire, we will not falter and we will not fail. It is my hope that in the months and years ahead, life will return almost to normal. We'll go back to our lives and routines, and that is good. Even grief recedes with time and grace. But our resolve must not pass. Each of us will remember what happened that day, and to whom it happened. We'll remember the moment the news came—where we were and what we were doing. Some will remember an image of a fire, or a story of rescue. Some will carry memories of a face and a voice gone forever.

And I will carry this: It is the police shield of a man named George Howard, who died at the World Trade Center trying to save others. It was given to me by his mom, Arlene, as a proud memorial to her son. This is my reminder of lives that ended, and a task that does not end.

I will not forget this wound to our country or those who inflicted it. I will not yield; I will not rest; I will not relent in waging this struggle for freedom and security for the American people.

The course of this conflict is not known, yet its outcome is certain. Freedom and fear, justice and cruelty, have always been at war, and we know that God is not neutral between them.

Fellow citizens, we'll meet violence with patient justice—assured of the rightness of our cause, and confident of the victories to come. In all that lies before us, may God grant us wisdom, and may He watch over the United States of America. Thank you.

Congressional Resolutions Following 2001 Terrorist Attacks

Following is the joint resolution (S J Res 23—PL 107-40) passed by the Senate and House on Sept. 14, 2001, in response to the terrorist attacks on Sept. 11.

To authorize the use of United States Armed Forces against those responsible for the recent attacks launched against the United States.

Whereas, on September 11, 2001, acts of despicable violence were committed against the United States and its citizens; and

Whereas, such acts render it both necessary and appropriate that the United States exercise its rights to self-defense and to protect United States citizens both at home and abroad; and

Whereas, in light of the threat to the national security and foreign policy of the United States posed by these grave acts of violence; and

Whereas, such acts continue to pose an unusual and extraordinary threat to the national security and foreign policy of the United States,

Whereas the President has authority under the Constitution to take action to deter and prevent acts of international terrorism against the United States.

Resolved by the Senate and the House of Representatives of the United States of America in Congress assembled,

SECTION 1. SHORT TITLE

This joint resolution may be cited as the "Authorization for Use of Military Force."

SECTION 2. AUTHORIZATION FOR USE OF UNITED STATES ARMED FORCES

(a) That the President is authorized to use all necessary and appropriate force against those nations, organizations, or persons he determines planned, authorized, committed, or aided the terrorist attacks that occurred on September 11, 2001, or harbored such organizations or persons, in order to prevent any future acts of international terrorism against the United States by such nations, organizations or persons.

(b) War Powers Resolution Requirements

(1) Specific Statutory Authorization—Consistent with section 8(a)(1) of the War Powers Resolution, the Congress declares that this section is intended to constitute specific statutory authorization within the meaning of section 5(b) of the War Powers Resolution.

(2) Applicability of Other Requirements—Nothing in this resolution supersedes any requirement of the War Powers Resolution.

Following is the joint resolution (H J Res 61, S J Res 22) passed by both chambers on Sept. 12, 2001.

Expressing the sense of the Senate and House of Representatives regarding the terrorist attacks launched against the United States on September 11, 2001.

Whereas on September 11, 2001, terrorists hijacked and destroyed four civilian aircraft, crashing two of them into the towers of the World Trade Center in New York City, and a third into the Pentagon outside Washington, D.C.;

Whereas thousands of innocent Americans were killed and injured as a result of these attacks, including the passengers and crew of the four aircraft, workers in the World Trade Center and in the Pentagon, rescue workers, and bystanders;

Whereas these attacks destroyed both towers of the World Trade Center, as well as adjacent buildings, and seriously damaged the Pentagon; and

Whereas these attacks were by far the deadliest terrorist attacks ever launched against the United States, and, by targeting symbols of American strength and success, clearly were intended to intimidate our nation and weaken its resolve: Now, therefore, be it resolved by the Senate and House of Representatives of the United States of America in Congress assembled, that Congress:

(1) condemns in the strongest possible terms the terrorists who planned and carried out the September 11, 2001, attacks against the United States, as well as their sponsors;

(2) extends its deepest condolences to the victims of these heinous and cowardly attacks, as well as to their families, friends, and loved ones;

(3) is certain that the people of the United States will stand united as our Nation begins the process of recovering and rebuilding in the aftermath of these tragic acts;

(4) commends the heroic actions of the rescue workers, volunteers, and state and local officials who responded to these tragic events with courage, determination, and skill;

(5) declares that these premeditated attacks struck not only at the people of America, but also at the symbols and structures of our economic and military strength, and that the United States is entitled to respond under international law;

(6) thanks those foreign leaders and individuals who have expressed solidarity with the United States in the aftermath of the attacks, and asks them to continue to stand with the United States in the war against international terrorism;

(7) commits to support increased resources in the war to eradicate terrorism;

(8) supports the determination of the President, in close consultation with Congress, to bring to justice and punish the perpetrators of these attacks as well as their sponsors; and

(9) declares that September 12, 2001, shall be a National Day of Unity and Mourning, and that when Congress adjourns today, it stands adjourned out of respect to the victims of the terrorist attacks.

President Bush's Statement Announcing Military Action in Afghanistan

Following is President Bush's statement on Oct. 7, 2001, announcing the beginning of military operations in Afghanistan.

Good afternoon. On my orders, the United States military has begun strikes against al Qaeda terrorist training camps and military installations of the Taliban regime in Afghanistan. These carefully targeted actions are designed to disrupt the use of Afghanistan as a terrorist base of operations, and to attack the military capability of the Taliban regime.

We are joined in this operation by our staunch friend, Great Britain. Other close friends, including Canada, Australia, Germany and France, have pledged forces as the operation unfolds. More than 40 countries in the Middle East, Africa, Europe and across Asia have granted air transit or landing rights. Many more have shared intelligence. We are supported by the collective will of the world.

More than two weeks ago, I gave Taliban leaders a series of clear and specific demands: Close terrorist training camps; hand over leaders of the al Qaeda network; and return all foreign nationals, including American citizens, unjustly detained in your country. None of these demands were met. And now the Taliban will pay a price. By destroying camps and disrupting communications, we will make it more difficult for the terror network to train new recruits and coordinate their evil plans.

Initially, the terrorists may burrow deeper into caves and other entrenched hiding places. Our military action is also designed to clear the way for sustained, comprehensive and relentless operations to drive them out and bring them to justice.

At the same time, the oppressed people of Afghanistan will know the generosity of America and our allies. As we strike military targets, we'll also drop food, medicine and supplies to the starving and suffering men and women and children of Afghanistan.

The United States of America is a friend to the Afghan people, and we are the friends of almost a billion worldwide who practice the Islamic faith. The United States of America is an enemy of those who aid terrorists and of the barbaric criminals who profane a great religion by committing murder in its name.

This military action is a part of our campaign against terrorism, another front in a war that has already been joined through diplomacy, intelligence, the freezing of financial assets and the arrests of known terrorists by law enforcement agents in 38 countries. Given the nature and reach of our enemies, we will win this conflict by the patient accumulation of successes, by meeting a series of challenges with determination and will and purpose.

Today we focus on Afghanistan, but the battle is broader. Every nation has a choice to make. In this conflict, there is no neutral ground. If any government sponsors the outlaws and killers of innocents, they have become outlaws and murderers, themselves. And they will take that lonely path at their own peril.

I'm speaking to you today from the Treaty Room of the White House, a place where American presidents have worked for peace. We're a peaceful nation. Yet, as we have learned, so suddenly and so tragically, there can be no peace in a world of sudden terror. In the face of today's new threat, the only way to pursue peace is to pursue those who threaten it.

We did not ask for this mission, but we will fulfill it. The name of today's military operation is Enduring Freedom. We defend not only our precious freedoms, but also the freedom of people everywhere to live and raise their children free from fear.

I know many Americans feel fear today. And our government is taking strong precautions. All law enforcement and intelligence agencies are working aggressively around America, around the world and around the clock. At my request, many governors have activated the National Guard to strengthen airport security. We have called up Reserves to reinforce our military capability and strengthen the protection of our homeland.

In the months ahead, our patience will be one of our strengths—patience with the long waits that will result from tighter security; patience and understanding that it will take time to achieve our goals; patience in all the sacrifices that may come.

Today, those sacrifices are being made by members of our Armed Forces who now defend us so far from home, and by their proud and worried families. A commander in chief sends America's sons and daughters into a battle in a foreign land only after the greatest care and a lot of prayer. We ask a lot of those who wear our uniform. We ask them to leave their loved ones, to travel great distances, to risk injury, even to be prepared to make the ultimate sacrifice of their lives. They are dedicated, they are honorable; they represent the best of our country. And we are grateful.

To all the men and women in our military—every sailor, every soldier, every airman, every Coast Guardsman, every Marine—I say this: Your mission is defined; your objectives are clear; your goal is just. You have my full confidence, and you will have every tool you need to carry out your duty.

I recently received a touching letter that says a lot about the state of America in these difficult times—a letter from a fourth-grade girl, with a father in the military: "As much as I don't want my Dad to fight," she wrote, "I'm willing to give him to you."

This is a precious gift, the greatest she could give. This young girl knows what America is all about. Since Sept. 11, an entire generation of young Americans has gained new understanding of the value of freedom, and its cost in duty and in sacrifice. The battle is now joined on many fronts. We will not waver; we will not tire; we will not falter; and we will not fail. Peace and freedom will prevail.

Thank you. May God continue to bless America.

Report of the Commission on the Sept. 11, 2001, Attacks on the United States

The September 11, 2001, terrorist attacks against the United States were made possible by the government's failure to comprehend the true danger of Islamist radicalism and an institutional inability to take effective action to counter it. These were the main conclusions of a landmark report released July 22, 2004, by a federal commission that devoted nearly two years to studying all aspects of the terrorist attacks, which killed nearly 3,000 people, damaged the U.S. economy, and led to major U.S. wars in Afghanistan and Iraq. The commission recommended a revamping of the government's intelligence-gathering agencies and a broad series of programs to defeat terrorists and make the United States more secure against their attacks.

Following is the text of the executive summary of The 9/11 Commission Report: The Final Report of the National Commission on Terrorist Attacks upon the United States, *released July 22, 2004. The commission was composed of Thomas H. Kean, chairman; Lee H. Hamilton, vice chairman; and Richard Ben-Veniste, Fred F. Fielding, Jamie S. Gorelick, Slade Gorton, Bob Kerrey, John F. Lehman, Timothy J. Roemer, and James R. Thompson.*

We present the narrative of this report and the recommendations that flow from it to the President of the United States, the United States Congress, and the American people for their consideration. Ten Commissioners—five Republicans and five Democrats chosen by elected leaders from our nation's capital at a time of great partisan division—have come together to present this report without dissent.

We have come together with a unity of purpose because our nation demands it. September 11, 2001, was a day of unprecedented shock and suffering in the history of the United States. The nation was unprepared.

A NATION TRANSFORMED

At 8:46 on the morning of September 11, 2001, the United States became a nation transformed.

An airliner traveling at hundreds of miles per hour and carrying some 10,000 gallons of jet fuel plowed into the North Tower of the World Trade Center in Lower Manhattan. At 9:03, a second airliner hit the South Tower. Fire and smoke billowed upward. Steel, glass, ash, and bodies fell below. The Twin Towers, where up to 50,000 people worked each day, both collapsed less than 90 minutes later.

At 9:37 that same morning, a third airliner slammed into the western face of the Pentagon. At 10:03, a fourth airliner crashed in a field in southern Pennsylvania. It had been aimed at the United States Capitol or the White House, and was forced down by heroic passengers armed with the knowledge that America was under attack.

More than 2,600 people died at the World Trade Center; 125 died at the Pentagon; 256 died on the four planes. The death toll surpassed that at Pearl Harbor in December 1941.

This immeasurable pain was inflicted by 19 young Arabs acting at the behest of Islamist extremists headquartered in distant Afghanistan. Some had been in the United States for more than a year, mixing with the rest of the population. Though four had training as pilots, most were not well-educated. Most spoke English poorly, some hardly at all. In groups of four or five, carrying with them only small knives, box cutters, and cans of Mace or pepper spray, they had hijacked the four planes and turned them into deadly guided missiles.

Why did they do this? How was the attack planned and conceived? How did the U.S. government fail to anticipate and prevent it? What can we do in the future to prevent similar acts of terrorism?

A SHOCK, NOT A SURPRISE

The 9/11 attacks were a shock, but they should not have come as a surprise. Islamist extremists had given plenty of warning that they meant to kill Americans indiscriminately and in large numbers. Although Osama Bin Laden himself would not emerge as a signal threat until the late 1990s, the threat of Islamist terrorism grew over the decade.

In February 1993, a group led by Ramzi Yousef tried to bring down the World Trade Center with a truck bomb. They killed six and wounded a thousand. Plans by Omar Abdel Rahman and others to blow up the Holland and Lincoln tunnels and other New York City landmarks were frustrated when the plotters were arrested. In October 1993, Somali tribesmen shot down U.S. helicopters, killing 18 and wounding 73 in an incident that came to be known as "Black Hawk down." Years later it would be learned that those Somali tribes-men had received help from al Qaeda.

In early 1995, police in Manila uncovered a plot by Ramzi Yousef to blow up a dozen U.S. airliners while they were flying over the Pacific. In November 1995, a car bomb exploded outside the office of the U.S. program manager for the Saudi National Guard in Riyadh, killing five Americans and two others. In June 1996, a truck bomb demolished the Khobar Towers apartment complex in Dhahran, Saudi Arabia, killing 19 U.S. servicemen and wounding hundreds. The attack was carried out primarily by Saudi Hezbollah, an organization that had received help from the government of Iran.

Until 1997, the U.S. intelligence community viewed Bin Laden as a financier of terrorism, not as a terrorist leader. In February 1998, Osama Bin Laden and four others issued a self-styled fatwa, publicly declaring that it was God's decree that every Muslim should try his utmost to kill any American, military or civilian, anywhere in the world, because of American "occupation" of Islam's holy places and aggression against Muslims.

In August 1998, Bin Laden's group, al Qaeda, carried out near-simultaneous truck bomb attacks on the U.S. embassies in Nairobi, Kenya, and Dar es Salaam, Tanzania. The attacks killed 224 people, including 12 Americans, and wounded thousands more. In December 1999, Jordanian police foiled a plot to bomb hotels and other sites frequented by American tourists, and a U.S. Customs agent arrested Ahmed Ressam at the U.S. Canadian border as he was smuggling in explosives intended for an attack on Los Angeles International Airport.

In October 2000, an al Qaeda team in Aden, Yemen, used a motorboat filled with explosives to blow a hole in the side of a destroyer, the USS *Cole*, almost sinking the vessel and killing 17 American sailors.

The 9/11 attacks on the World Trade Center and the Pentagon were far more elaborate, precise, and destructive than any of these earlier assaults. But by September 2001, the executive branch of the U.S. government, the Congress, the news media, and the American public had received clear warning that Islamist terrorists meant to kill Americans in high numbers.

WHO IS THE ENEMY?

Who is this enemy that created an organization capable of inflicting such horrific damage on the United States? We now know that these attacks were carried out by various groups of Islamist extremists. The 9/11 attack was driven by Osama Bin Laden.

In the 1980s, young Muslims from around the world went to Afghanistan to join as volunteers in a jihad (or holy struggle) against the Soviet Union. A wealthy Saudi, Osama Bin Laden, was one of them. Following the defeat of the Soviets in the late 1980s, Bin Laden and others formed al Qaeda to mobilize jihads elsewhere.

The history, culture, and body of beliefs from which Bin Laden shapes and spreads his message are largely unknown to many Americans. Seizing on symbols of Islam's past greatness, he promises to restore pride to people who consider themselves the victims of successive foreign masters. He uses cultural and religious allusions to the holy Quran and some of its interpreters. He appeals to people disoriented by cyclonic change as they confront modernity and globalization. His rhetoric selectively draws from multiple sources—Islam, history, and the region's political and economic malaise. Bin Laden also stresses grievances against the United States widely shared in the Muslim world. He inveighed against the presence of U.S. troops in Saudi Arabia, which is the home of Islam's holiest sites, and against other U.S. policies in the Middle East.

Upon this political and ideological foundation, Bin Laden built over the course of a decade a dynamic and lethal organization. He built an infrastructure and organization in Afghanistan that could attract, train, and use recruits against ever more ambitious targets. He rallied new zealots and new money with each demonstration of al Qaeda's capability. He had forged a close alliance with the Taliban, a regime providing sanctuary for al Qaeda.

By September 11, 2001, al Qaeda possessed:

• leaders able to evaluate, approve, and supervise the planning and direction of a major operation;

• a personnel system that could recruit candidates, indoctrinate them, vet them, and give them the necessary training;

• communications sufficient to enable planning and direction of operatives and those who would be helping them;

• an intelligence effort to gather required information and form assessments of enemy strengths and weaknesses;

• the ability to move people great distances; and

• the ability to raise and move the money necessary to finance an attack.

1998 TO SEPTEMBER 11, 2001

The August 1998 bombings of U.S. embassies in Kenya and Tanzania established al Qaeda as a potent adversary of the United States.

After launching cruise missile strikes against al Qaeda targets in Afghanistan and Sudan in retaliation for the embassy bombings, the Clinton administration applied diplomatic pressure to try to persuade the Taliban regime in Afghanistan to expel Bin Laden. The administration also devised covert operations to use CIA-paid foreign agents to capture or kill Bin Laden and his chief lieutenants. These actions did not stop Bin Laden or dislodge al Qaeda from its sanctuary.

By late 1998 or early 1999, Bin Laden and his advisers had agreed on an idea brought to them by Khalid Sheikh Mohammed (KSM) called the "planes operation." It would eventually culminate in the 9/11 attacks. Bin Laden and his chief of operations, Mohammed Atef, occupied undisputed leadership positions atop al Qaeda. Within al Qaeda, they relied heavily on the ideas and enterprise of strong-willed field commanders, such as KSM, to carry out worldwide terrorist operations.

KSM claims that his original plot was even grander than those carried out on 9/11—ten planes would attack targets on both the East and West coasts of the United States. This plan was modified by Bin Laden, KSM said, owing to its scale and complexity. Bin Laden provided KSM with four initial operatives for suicide plane attacks within the United States, and in the fall of 1999 training for the attacks began. New recruits included four from a cell of expatriate Muslim extremists who had clustered together in Hamburg, Germany. One became the tactical commander of the operation in the United States: Mohamed Atta.

U.S. intelligence frequently picked up reports of attacks planned by al Qaeda. Working with foreign security services, the CIA broke up some al Qaeda cells. The core of Bin Laden's organization nevertheless remained intact. In December 1999, news about the arrests of the terrorist cell in Jordan and the arrest of a terrorist at the U.S.-Canadian border became part of a "millennium alert." The government was galvanized, and the public was on alert for any possible attack.

In January 2000, the intense intelligence effort glimpsed and then lost sight of two operatives destined for the "planes operation." Spotted in Kuala Lumpur, the pair were lost passing through Bangkok. On January 15, 2000, they arrived in Los Angeles. Because these two al Qaeda operatives had spent little time in the West and spoke little, if any, English, it is plausible that they or KSM would have tried to identify, in advance, a friendly contact in the United States. We explored suspicions about whether these two operatives had a support network of accomplices in the United States. The evidence is thin—simply not there for some cases, more worrisome in others.

We do know that soon after arriving in California, the two al Qaeda operatives sought out and found a group of ideologically like-minded Muslims with roots in Yemen and Saudi Arabia, individuals mainly associated with a young Yemeni and others who attended a mosque in San Diego. After a brief stay in Los Angeles about which we know little, the al Qaeda operatives lived openly in San Diego under their true names. They managed to avoid attracting much attention.

By the summer of 2000, three of the four Hamburg cell members had arrived on the East Coast of the United States and had begun pilot training. In early 2001, a fourth future hijacker pilot, Hani Hanjour, journeyed to Arizona with another operative, Nawaf al Hazmi, and conducted his refresher pilot training there. A number of al Qaeda operatives had spent time in Arizona during the 1980s and early 1990s.

During 2000, President Bill Clinton and his advisers renewed diplomatic efforts to get Bin Laden expelled from Afghanistan. They also renewed secret efforts with some of the Taliban's opponents—the Northern Alliance—to get enough intelligence to attack Bin Laden directly. Diplomatic efforts centered on the new military government in Pakistan, and they did not succeed. The efforts with the Northern Alliance revived an inconclusive and secret debate about whether the United States should take sides in Afghanistan's civil war and support the Taliban's enemies. The CIA also produced a plan to improve intelligence collection on al Qaeda, including the use of a small, unmanned airplane with a video camera, known as the Predator.

After the October 2000 attack on the USS *Cole*, evidence accumulated that it had been launched by al Qaeda operatives, but without confirmation that Bin Laden had given the order. The Taliban had earlier been warned that it would be held responsible for another Bin Laden attack on the United States. The CIA described its findings as a "preliminary judgment"; President Clinton and his chief advisers told us they were waiting for a conclusion before deciding whether to take military action. The military alternatives remained unappealing to them.

The transition to the new Bush administration in late 2000 and early 2001 took place with the *Cole* issue still pending. President George W. Bush and his chief advisers accepted that al Qaeda was responsible for the attack on the Cole, but did not like the options available for a response.

Bin Laden's inference may well have been that attacks, at least at the level of the *Cole,* were risk free.

The Bush administration began developing a new strategy with the stated goal of eliminating the al Qaeda threat within three to five years.

During the spring and summer of 2001, U.S. intelligence agencies received a stream of warnings that al Qaeda planned, as one report put it, "something very, very, very big." Director of Central Intelligence George Tenet told us, "The system was blinking red."

Although Bin Laden was determined to strike in the United States, as President Clinton had been told and President Bush was reminded in a Presidential Daily Brief article briefed to him in August 2001, the specific threat information pointed overseas. Numerous precautions were taken overseas. Domestic agencies were not effectively mobilized. The threat did not receive national media attention comparable to the millennium alert.

While the United States continued disruption efforts around the world, its emerging strategy to eliminate the al Qaeda threat was to include an enlarged covert action program in Afghanistan, as well as diplomatic strategies for Afghanistan and Pakistan. The process culminated during the summer of 2001 in a draft presidential directive and arguments about the Predator aircraft, which was soon to be deployed with a missile of its own, so that it might be used to attempt to kill Bin Laden or his chief lieutenants. At a September 4 meeting, President Bush's chief advisers approved the draft directive of the strategy and endorsed the concept of arming the Predator. This directive on the al Qaeda strategy was awaiting President Bush's signature on September 11, 2001.

Though the "planes operation" was progressing, the plotters had problems of their own in 2001. Several possible participants dropped out; others could not gain entry into the United States (including one denial at a port of entry and visa denials not related to terrorism). One of the eventual pilots may have considered abandoning the planes operation. Zacarias Moussaoui, who showed up at a flight training school in Minnesota, may have been a candidate to replace him.

Some of the vulnerabilities of the plotters become clear in retrospect. Moussaoui aroused suspicion for seeking fast-track training on how to pilot large jet airliners. He was arrested on August 16, 2001, for violations of immigration regulations. In late August, officials in the intelligence community realized that the terrorists spotted in Southeast Asia in January 2000 had arrived in the United States.

These cases did not prompt urgent action. No one working on these late leads in the summer of 2001 connected them to the high level of threat reporting. In the words of one official, no analytic work foresaw the lightning that could connect the thundercloud to the ground.

As final preparations were under way during the summer of 2001, dissent emerged among al Qaeda leaders in Afghanistan over whether to proceed. The Taliban's chief, Mullah Omar, opposed attacking the United States. Although facing opposition from many of his senior lieutenants, Bin Laden effectively overruled their objections, and the attacks went forward.

SEPTEMBER 11, 2001

The day began with the 19 hijackers getting through a security checkpoint system that they had evidently analyzed and knew how to defeat. Their success rate in penetrating the system was 19 for 19. They took over the four flights, taking advantage of air crews and cockpits that were not prepared for the contingency of a suicide hijacking.

On 9/11, the defense of U.S. air space depended on close interaction between two federal agencies: the Federal Aviation Administration (FAA) and North American Aerospace Defense Command (NORAD). Existing protocols on 9/11 were unsuited in every respect for an attack in which hijacked planes were used as weapons. What ensued was a hurried attempt to improvise a defense by civilians who had never handled a hijacked aircraft that attempted to disappear, and by a military unprepared for the transformation of commercial aircraft into weapons of mass destruction.

A shootdown authorization was not communicated to the NORAD air defense sector until 28 minutes after United 93 had crashed in Pennsylvania. Planes were scrambled, but ineffectively, as they did not know where to go or what targets they were to intercept. And once the shootdown order was given, it was not communicated to the pilots. In short, while leaders in Washington believed that the fighters circling above them had been instructed to "take out" hostile aircraft, the only orders actually conveyed to the pilots were to "ID type and tail."

Like the national defense, the emergency response on 9/11 was necessarily improvised.

In New York City, the Fire Department of New York, the New York Police Department, the Port Authority of New York and New Jersey, the building employees, and the occupants of the buildings did their best to cope with the effects of almost unimaginable events—unfolding furiously over 102 minutes. Casualties were nearly 100 percent at and above the impact zones and were very high among first responders who stayed in danger as they tried to save lives. Despite weaknesses in preparations for disaster, failure to achieve unified incident command, and inadequate communications among responding agencies, all but approximately one hundred of the thousands of civilians who worked below the impact zone escaped, often with help from the emergency responders.

At the Pentagon, while there were also problems of command and control, the emergency response was generally effective. The Incident

Command System, a formalized management structure for emergency response in place in the National Capital Region, overcame the inherent complications of a response across local, state, and federal jurisdictions.

OPERATIONAL OPPORTUNITIES

We write with the benefit and handicap of hindsight. We are mindful of the danger of being unjust to men and women who made choices in conditions of uncertainty and in circumstances over which they often had little control.

Nonetheless, there were specific points of vulnerability in the plot and opportunities to disrupt it. Operational failures—opportunities that were not or could not be exploited by the organizations and systems of that time—included:

• not watchlisting future hijackers Hazmi and Mihdhar, not trailing them after they traveled to Bangkok, and not informing the FBI about one future hijacker's U.S. visa or his companion's travel to the United States;

• not sharing information linking individuals in the *Cole* attack to Mihdhar;

• not taking adequate steps in time to find Mihdhar or Hazmi in the United States;

• not linking the arrest of Zacarias Moussaoui, described as interested in flight training for the purpose of using an airplane in a terrorist act, to the heightened indications of attack;

• not discovering false statements on visa applications;

• not recognizing passports manipulated in a fraudulent manner;

• not expanding no-fly lists to include names from terrorist watchlists;

• not searching airline passengers identified by the computer-based CAPPS screening system; and

• not hardening aircraft cockpit doors or taking other measures to pre-pare for the possibility of suicide hijackings.

GENERAL FINDINGS

Since the plotters were flexible and resourceful, we cannot know whether any single step or series of steps would have defeated them. What we can say with confidence is that none of the measures adopted by the U.S. government from 1998 to 2001 disturbed or even delayed the progress of the al Qaeda plot. Across the government, there were failures of imagination, policy, capabilities, and management.

Imagination

The most important failure was one of imagination. We do not believe leaders understood the gravity of the threat. The terrorist danger from Bin Laden and al Qaeda was not a major topic for policy debate among the public, the media, or in the Congress. Indeed, it barely came up during the 2000 presidential campaign.

Al Qaeda's new brand of terrorism presented challenges to U.S. governmental institutions that they were not well-designed to meet. Though top officials all told us that they understood the danger, we believe there was uncertainty among them as to whether this was just a new and especially venomous version of the ordinary terrorist threat the United States had lived with for decades, or it was indeed radically new, posing a threat beyond any yet experienced.

As late as September 4, 2001, Richard Clarke, the White House staffer long responsible for counterterrorism policy coordination, asserted that the government had not yet made up its mind how to answer the question: "Is al Qaeda a big deal?"

A week later came the answer.

Policy

Terrorism was not the overriding national security concern for the U.S. government under either the Clinton or the pre-9/11 Bush administration. The policy challenges were linked to this failure of imagination. Officials in both the Clinton and Bush administrations regarded a full U.S. invasion of Afghanistan as practically inconceivable before 9/11.

Capabilities

Before 9/11, the United States tried to solve the al Qaeda problem with the capabilities it had used in the last stages of the Cold War and its immediate aftermath. These capabilities were insufficient. Little was done to expand or reform them.

The CIA had minimal capacity to conduct paramilitary operations with its own personnel, and it did not seek a large-scale expansion of these capabilities before 9/11. The CIA also needed to improve its capability to collect intelligence from human agents. At no point before 9/11 was the Department of Defense fully engaged in the mission of countering al Qaeda, even though this was perhaps the most dangerous foreign enemy threatening the United States.

America's homeland defenders faced outward. NORAD itself was barely able to retain any alert bases at all. Its planning scenarios occasionally considered the danger of hijacked aircraft being guided to American targets, but only aircraft that were coming from overseas.

The most serious weaknesses in agency capabilities were in the domestic arena. The FBI did not have the capability to link the collective knowledge of agents in the field to national priorities. Other domestic agencies deferred to the FBI.

FAA capabilities were weak. Any serious examination of the possibility of a suicide hijacking could have suggested changes to fix glaring vulnerabilities—expanding no-fly lists, searching passengers identified by the CAPPS screening system, deploying federal air marshals domestically, hardening cockpit doors, alerting air crews to a different kind of hijacking possibility than they had been trained to expect. Yet the FAA did not adjust either its own training or training with NORAD to take account of threats other than those experienced in the past.

Management

The missed opportunities to thwart the 9/11 plot were also symptoms of a broader inability to adapt the way government manages problems to the new challenges of the twenty-first century. Action officers should have been able to draw on all available knowledge about al Qaeda in the government. Management should have ensured that information was shared and duties were clearly assigned across agencies, and across the foreign-domestic divide.

There were also broader management issues with respect to how top leaders set priorities and allocated resources. For instance, on December 4, 1998, DCI Tenet issued a directive to several CIA officials and the DDCI for Community Management, stating: "We are at war. I want no resources or people spared in this effort, either inside CIA or the Community." The memorandum had little overall effect on mobilizing the CIA or the intelligence community. This episode indicates the limitations of the DCI's authority over the direction of the intelligence community, including agencies within the Department of Defense.

The U.S. government did not find a way of pooling intelligence and using it to guide the planning and assignment of responsibilities for joint operations involving entities as disparate as the CIA, the FBI, the State Department, the military, and the agencies involved in homeland security.

SPECIFIC FINDINGS

Unsuccessful Diplomacy

Beginning in February 1997, and through September 11, 2001, the U.S. government tried to use diplomatic pressure to persuade the Taliban regime in Afghanistan to stop being a sanctuary for al Qaeda, and to expel Bin Laden to a country where he could face justice. These efforts included warnings and sanctions, but they all failed.

The U.S. government also pressed two successive Pakistani governments to demand that the Taliban cease providing a sanctuary for Bin Laden and his organization and, failing that, to cut off their support for the Taliban. Before 9/11, the United States could not find a mix of incentives and pressure that would persuade Pakistan to reconsider its fundamental relationship with the Taliban.

From 1999 through early 2001, the United States pressed the United Arab Emirates, one of the Taliban's only travel and financial outlets to the outside world, to break off ties and enforce sanctions, especially those related to air travel to Afghanistan. These efforts achieved little before 9/11.

Saudi Arabia has been a problematically in combating Islamic extremism. Before 9/11, the Saudi and U.S. governments did not fully share intelligence information or develop an adequate joint effort to track and disrupt the finances of the al Qaeda organization. On the other hand, government officials of Saudi Arabia at the highest levels worked closely with top U.S. officials in major initiatives to solve the Bin Laden problem with diplomacy.

Lack of Military Options

In response to the request of policymakers, the military prepared an array of limited strike options for attacking Bin Laden and his organization from May 1998 onward. When they briefed policymakers, the military presented both the pros and cons of those strike options and the associated risks. Policymakers expressed frustration with the range of options presented.

Following the August 20, 1998, missile strikes on al Qaeda targets in Afghanistan and Sudan, both senior military officials and policymakers placed great emphasis on actionable intelligence as the key factor in recommending or deciding to launch military action against Bin Laden and his organization. They did not want to risk significant collateral damage, and they did not want to miss Bin Laden and thus make the United States look weak while making Bin Laden look strong. On three specific occasions in 1998–1999, intelligence was deemed credible enough to warrant planning for possible strikes to kill Bin Laden. But in each case the strikes did not go forward, because senior policymakers did not regard the intelligence as sufficiently actionable to offset their assessment of the risks.

The Director of Central Intelligence, policymakers, and military officials expressed frustration with the lack of actionable intelligence. Some officials inside the Pentagon, including those in the special forces and the counterterrorism policy office, also expressed frustration with the lack of military action. The Bush administration began to develop new policies toward al Qaeda in 2001, but military plans did not change until after 9/11.

Problems within the Intelligence Community

The intelligence community struggled throughout the 1990s and up to 9/11 to collect intelligence on and analyze the phenomenon of transnational terrorism. The combination of an overwhelming number of priorities, flat budgets, an outmoded structure, and bureaucratic rivalries resulted in an insufficient response to this new challenge.

Many dedicated officers worked day and night for years to piece together the growing body of evidence on al Qaeda and to understand the threats. Yet, while there were many reports on Bin Laden and his growing al Qaeda organization, there was no comprehensive review of what the intelligence community knew and what it did not know, and what that meant. There was no National Intelligence Estimate on terrorism between 1995 and 9/11.

Before 9/11, no agency did more to attack al Qaeda than the CIA. But there were limits to what the CIA was able to achieve by disrupting terrorist activities abroad and by using proxies to try to capture Bin Laden and his lieutenants in Afghanistan. CIA officers were aware of those limitations.

To put it simply, covert action was not a silver bullet. It was important to engage proxies in Afghanistan and to build various capabilities so that if an opportunity presented itself, the CIA could act on it. But for more than three years, through both the late Clinton and early Bush administrations, the CIA relied on proxy forces, and there was growing frustration within the CIA's Counterterrorist Center and in the National Security Council staff with the lack of results. The development of the Predator and the push to aid the Northern Alliance were products of this frustration.

Problems in the FBI

From the time of the first World Trade Center attack in 1993, FBI and Department of Justice leadership in Washington and New York became increasingly concerned about the terrorist threat from Islamist extremists to U.S. interests, both at home and abroad. Throughout the 1990s, the FBI's counterterrorism efforts against international terrorist organizations included both intelligence and criminal investigations. The FBI's approach to investigations was case-specific, decentralized, and geared toward prosecution. Significant FBI resources were devoted to after-the-fact investigations of major terrorist attacks, resulting in several prosecutions.

The FBI attempted several reform efforts aimed at strengthening its ability to prevent such attacks, but these reform efforts failed to implement organization-wide institutional change. On September 11, 2001, the FBI was limited in several areas critical to an effective preventive counterterrorism strategy. Those working counterterrorism matters did so despite limited intelligence collection and strategic analysis capabilities, a limited capacity to share information both internally and externally, insufficient training, perceived legal barriers to sharing information, and inadequate resources.

Permeable Borders and Immigration Controls

There were opportunities for intelligence and law enforcement to exploit al Qaeda's travel vulnerabilities. Considered collectively, the 9/11 hijackers:

• included known al Qaeda operatives who could have been watchlisted;
• presented passports manipulated in a fraudulent manner;
• presented passports with suspicious indicators of extremism;
• made detectable false statements on visa applications;
• made false statements to border officials to gain entry into the United States; and
• violated immigration laws while in the United States.

Neither the State Department's consular officers nor the Immigration and Naturalization Service's inspectors and agents were ever considered full partners in a national counterterrorism effort. Protecting borders was not a national security issue before 9/11.

Permeable Aviation Security

Hijackers studied publicly available materials on the aviation security system and used items that had less metal content than a handgun and were most likely permissible. Though two of the hijackers were on the U.S. TIPOFF terrorist watchlist, the FAA did not use TIPOFF data. The hijackers had to beat only one layer of security—the security checkpoint process. Even though several hijackers were selected for extra screening by the CAPPS system, this led only to greater scrutiny of their checked baggage. Once on board, the hijackers were faced with aircraft personnel who were trained to be non-confrontational in the event of a hijacking.

Financing

The 9/11 attacks cost somewhere between $400,000 and $500,000 to execute. The operatives spent more than $270,000 in the United States. Additional expenses included travel to obtain passports and visas, travel to the United States, expenses incurred by the plot leader and facilitators outside the United States, and expenses incurred by the people selected to be hijackers who ultimately did not participate.

The conspiracy made extensive use of banks in the United States. The hijackers opened accounts in their own names, using passports and other identification documents. Their transactions were unremarkable and essentially invisible amid the billions of dollars flowing around the world every day.

To date, we have not been able to determine the origin of the money used for the 9/11 attacks. Al Qaeda had many sources of funding and a pre-9/11 annual budget estimated at $30 million. If a particular source of funds had dried up, al Qaeda could easily have found enough money elsewhere to fund the attack.

An Improvised Homeland Defense

The civilian and military defenders of the nation's airspace—FAA and NORAD—were unprepared for the attacks launched against them. Given that lack of preparedness, they attempted and failed to improvise an effective home-land defense against an unprecedented challenge.

The events of that morning do not reflect discredit on operational personnel. NORAD's Northeast Air Defense Sector personnel reached out for information and made the best judgments they could based on the information they received. Individual FAA controllers, facility managers, and command center managers were creative and agile in recommending a nationwide alert, ground-stopping local traffic, ordering all aircraft nationwide to land, and executing that unprecedented order flawlessly.

At more senior levels, communication was poor. Senior military and FAA leaders had no effective communication with each other. The chain of command did not function well. The President could not reach some senior officials. The Secretary of Defense did not enter the chain of command until the morning's key events were over. Air National Guard units with different rules of engagement were scrambled without the knowledge of the President, NORAD, or the National Military Command Center.

Emergency Response

The civilians, firefighters, police officers, emergency medical technicians, and emergency management professionals exhibited steady determination and resolve under horrifying, overwhelming conditions on 9/11. Their actions saved lives and inspired a nation.

Effective decision-making in New York was hampered by problems in command and control and in internal communications. Within the Fire Department of New York, this was true for several reasons: the magnitude of the incident was unforeseen; commanders had difficulty communicating with their units; more units were actually dispatched than were ordered by the chiefs; some units self-dispatched; and once units arrived at the World Trade Center, they were neither comprehensively accounted for nor coordinated. The Port Authority's response was hampered by the lack both of standard operating procedures and of radios capable of enabling multiple commands to respond to an incident in unified fashion. The New York Police Department, because of its history of mobilizing thousands of officers for major events requiring crowd control, had a technical radio capability and protocols more easily adapted to an incident of the magnitude of 9/11.

Congress

The Congress, like the executive branch, responded slowly to the rise of transnational terrorism as a threat to national security. The legislative branch adjusted little and did not restructure itself to address changing threats. Its attention to terrorism was episodic and splintered across several committees. The Congress gave little guidance to executive branch agencies on terrorism, did not reform them in any significant way to meet the threat, and did not systematically perform robust oversight to identify, address, and attempt to resolve the many problems in national security and domestic agencies that became apparent in the aftermath of 9/11.

So long as oversight is undermined by current congressional rules and resolutions, we believe the American people will not get the security they want and need. The United States needs a strong, stable, and capable congressional committee structure to give America's national intelligence agencies oversight, sup-port, and leadership.

Are We Safer?

Since 9/11, the United States and its allies have killed or captured a majority of al Qaeda's leadership; toppled the Taliban, which gave al Qaeda sanctuary in Afghanistan; and severely damaged the organization. Yet terrorist attacks continue. Even as we have thwarted attacks, nearly everyone expects they will come. How can this be?

The problem is that al Qaeda represents an ideological movement, not a finite group of people. It initiates and inspires, even if it no longer directs. In this way it has transformed itself into a decentralized force. Bin Laden may be limited in his ability to organize major attacks from his hideouts. Yet killing or capturing him, while extremely important, would not end terror. His message of inspiration to a new generation of terrorists would continue.

Because of offensive actions against al Qaeda since 9/11, and defensive actions to improve homeland security, we believe we are safer today. But we are not safe. We therefore make the following recommendations that we believe can make America safer and more secure.

RECOMMENDATIONS

Three years after 9/11, the national debate continues about how to protect our nation in this new era. We divide our recommendations into two basic parts: What to do, and how to do it.

What to Do? A Global Strategy

The enemy is not just "terrorism." It is the threat posed specifically by Islamist terrorism, by Bin Laden and others who draw on a long tradition of extreme intolerance within a minority strain of Islam that does not distinguish politics from religion, and distorts both.

The enemy is not Islam, the great world faith, but a perversion of Islam. The enemy goes beyond al Qaeda to include the radical ideological movement, inspired in part by al Qaeda, that has spawned other terrorist groups and violence. Thus our strategy must match our means to two ends: dismantling the al Qaeda network and, in the long term, prevailing over the ideology that contributes to Islamist terrorism.

The first phase of our post-9/11 efforts rightly included military action to topple the Taliban and pursue al Qaeda. This work continues. But long-term success demands the use of all elements of national power: diplomacy, intelligence, covert action, law enforcement, economic policy, foreign aid, public diplomacy, and homeland defense. If we favor one tool while neglecting others, we leave ourselves vulnerable and weaken our national effort.

What should Americans expect from their government? The goal seems unlimited: Defeat terrorism anywhere in the world. But Americans have also been told to expect the worst: An attack is probably coming; it may be more devastating still.

Vague goals match an amorphous picture of the enemy. Al Qaeda and other groups are popularly described as being all over the world, adaptable, resilient, needing little higher-level organization, and capable of anything. It is an image of an omnipotent hydra of destruction. That image lowers expectations of government effectiveness.

It lowers them too far. Our report shows a determined and capable group of plotters. Yet the group was fragile and occasionally left vulnerable by the marginal, unstable people often attracted to such causes. The enemy made mistakes. The U.S. government was not able to capitalize on them.

No president can promise that a catastrophic attack like that of 9/11 will not happen again. But the American people are entitled to expect that officials will have realistic objectives, clear guidance, and effective organization. They are entitled to see standards for performance so they can judge, with the help of their elected representatives, whether the objectives are being met.

We propose a strategy with three dimensions: (1) attack terrorists and their organizations, (2) prevent the continued growth of Islamist terrorism, and (3) protect against and prepare for terrorist attacks.

Attack Terrorists and Their Organizations

• Root out sanctuaries. The U.S. government should identify and prioritize actual or potential terrorist sanctuaries and have realistic country or regional strategies for each, utilizing every element of national power and reaching out to countries that can help us.

• Strengthen long-term U.S. and international commitments to the future of Pakistan and Afghanistan.

• Confront problems with Saudi Arabia in the open and build a relation-ship beyond oil, a relationship that both sides can defend to their citizens and includes a shared commitment to reform.

Prevent the Continued Growth of Islamist Terrorism

In October 2003, Secretary of Defense Donald Rumsfeld asked if enough was being done "to fashion a broad integrated plan to stop the next generation of terrorists." As part of such a plan, the U.S. government should:

• Define the message and stand as an example of moral leadership in the world. To Muslim parents, terrorists like Bin Laden have nothing to offer their children but visions of violence and death. America and its friends have the advantage—our vision can offer a better future.

• Where Muslim governments, even those who are friends, do not offer opportunity, respect the rule of law, or tolerate differences, then the United States needs to stand for a better future.

• Communicate and defend American ideals in the Islamic world, through much stronger public diplomacy to reach more people, including students and leaders outside of government. Our efforts here should be as strong as they were in combating closed societies during the Cold War.

• Offer an agenda of opportunity that includes support for public education and economic openness.

• Develop a comprehensive coalition strategy against Islamist terrorism, using a flexible contact group of leading coalition governments and fashioning a common coalition approach on issues like the treatment of captured terrorists.

• Devote a maximum effort to the parallel task of countering the proliferation of weapons of mass destruction.

• Expect less from trying to dry up terrorist money and more from following the money for intelligence, as a tool to hunt terrorists, understand their networks, and disrupt their operations.

Protect against and Prepare for Terrorist Attacks

• Target terrorist travel, an intelligence and security strategy that the 9/11 story showed could be at least as powerful as the effort devoted to terrorist finance.

• Address problems of screening people with biometric identifiers across agencies and governments, including our border and transportation systems, by designing a comprehensive screening system that addresses common problems and sets common standards. As standards spread, this necessary and ambitious effort could dramatically strengthen the world's ability to intercept individuals who could pose catastrophic threats.

• Quickly complete a biometric entry-exit screening system, one that also speeds qualified travelers.

• Set standards for the issuance of birth certificates and sources of identification, such as driver's licenses.

• Develop strategies for neglected parts of our transportation security system. Since 9/11, about 90 percent of the nation's $5 billion annual investment in transportation security has gone to aviation, to fight the last war.

• In aviation, prevent arguments about a new computerized profiling system from delaying vital improvements in the "no-fly" and "automatic selectee" lists. Also, give priority to the improvement of check-point screening.

• Determine, with leadership from the President, guidelines for gathering and sharing information in the new security systems that are needed, guidelines that integrate safeguards for privacy and other essential liberties.

• Underscore that as government power necessarily expands in certain ways, the burden of retaining such powers remains on the executive to demonstrate the value of such powers and ensure adequate supervision of how they are used, including a new board to oversee the implementation of the guidelines needed for gathering and sharing information in these new security systems.

• Base federal funding for emergency preparedness solely on risks and vulnerabilities, putting New York City and Washington, D.C., at the top of the current list. Such assistance should not remain a program for general revenue sharing or pork-barrel spending.

• Make homeland security funding contingent on the adoption of an incident command system to strengthen teamwork in a crisis, including a regional approach. Allocate more radio spectrum and improve connectivity for public safety communications, and encourage wide-spread adoption of newly developed standards for private-sector emergency preparedness—since the private sector controls 85 percent of the nation's critical infrastructure.

How to Do It? A Different Way of Organizing Government

The strategy we have recommended is elaborate, even as presented here very briefly. To implement it will require a government better organized than the one that exists today, with its national security institutions designed half a century ago to win the Cold War. Americans should not settle for incremental, ad hoc adjustments to a system created a generation ago for a world that no longer exists.

Our detailed recommendations are designed to fit together. Their purpose is clear: to build unity of effort across the U.S. government. As one official now serving on the front lines overseas put it to us: "One fight, one team." We call for unity of effort in five areas, beginning with unity of effort on the challenge of counterterrorism itself:

• unifying strategic intelligence and operational planning against Islamist terrorists across the foreign-domestic divide with a National Counterterrorism Center;

• unifying the intelligence community with a new National Intelligence Director;

• unifying the many participants in the counterterrorism effort and their knowledge in a network-based information sharing system that transcends traditional governmental boundaries;

• unifying and strengthening congressional oversight to improve quality and accountability; and

• strengthening the FBI and homeland defenders.

Unity of Effort: A National Counterterrorism Center

The 9/11 story teaches the value of integrating strategic intelligence from all sources into joint operational planning—with *both* dimensions spanning the foreign-domestic divide.

In some ways, since 9/11, joint work has gotten better. The effort of fighting terrorism has flooded over many of the usual agency boundaries because of its sheer quantity and energy. Attitudes have changed. But the problems of coordination have multiplied. The Defense Department alone has three unified commands (SOCOM, CENTCOM, and NORTHCOM) [the three regional commands, Southern Command, Central Command, and Northern Command] that deal with terrorism as one of their principal concerns.

Much of the public commentary about the 9/11 attacks has focused on "lost opportunities." Though characterized as problems of "watch-listing," "information sharing," or "connecting the dots," each of these labels is too narrow. They describe the symptoms, not the disease.

Breaking the older mold of organization stovepiped purely in executive agencies, we propose a National Counterterrorism Center (NCTC) that would borrow the joint, unified command concept adopted in the 1980s by the American military in a civilian agency, combining the joint intelligence function alongside the operations work.

The NCTC would build on the existing Terrorist Threat Integration Center and would replace it and other terrorism "fusion centers" within the government. The NCTC would become the authoritative knowledge bank, bringing information to bear on common plans. It should task collection requirements both inside and outside the United States.

The NCTC should perform joint operational planning, assigning lead responsibilities to existing agencies and letting them direct the actual execution of the plans.

Placed in the Executive Office of the President, headed by a Senate-confirmed official (with rank equal to the deputy head of a cabinet department) who reports to the National Intelligence Director, the NCTC would track implementation of plans. It would be able to influence the leadership and the budgets of the counterterrorism operating arms of the CIA, the FBI, and the departments of Defense and Homeland Security.

The NCTC should *not* be a policymaking body. Its operations and planning should follow the policy direction of the president and the National Security Council.

Unity of Effort: A National Intelligence Director

Since long before 9/11—and continuing to this day—the intelligence community is not organized well for joint intelligence work. It does not employ common standards and practices in reporting intelligence or in training experts overseas and at home. The expensive national capabilities for collecting intelligence have divided management. The structures are too complex and too secret.

The community's head—the Director of Central Intelligence—has at least three jobs: running the CIA, coordinating a 15-agency confederation, and being the intelligence analyst-in-chief to the president. No one person can do all these things.

A new National Intelligence Director should be established with two main jobs: (1) to oversee national intelligence centers that combine experts from all the collection disciplines against common targets—like counterterrorism or nuclear proliferation; and (2) to oversee the agencies that contribute to the national intelligence program, a task that includes setting common standards for personnel and information technology.

The national intelligence centers would be the unified commands of the intelligence world—a long-overdue reform for intelligence comparable to the 1986 Goldwater-Nichols law that reformed the organization of national defense. The home services—such as the CIA, DIA [Defense Intelligence Agency], NSA [National Security Agency], and FBI—would organize, train, and equip the best intelligence professionals in the world, and would handle the execution of intelligence operations in the field.

This National Intelligence Director (NID) should be located in the Executive Office of the President and report directly to the president, yet be confirmed by the Senate. In addition to overseeing the National Counterterrorism Center described above (which will include both the national intelligence center for terrorism and the joint operations planning effort), the NID should have three deputies:

• For foreign intelligence (a deputy who also would be the head of the CIA);

• For defense intelligence (also the under secretary of defense for intelligence);

• For homeland intelligence (also the executive assistant director for intelligence at the FBI or the under secretary of homeland security for information analysis and infrastructure protection).

The NID should receive a public appropriation for national intelligence, should have authority to hire and fire his or her intelligence deputies, and should be able to set common personnel and information technology policies across the intelligence community.

The CIA should concentrate on strengthening the collection capabilities of its clandestine service and the talents of its analysts, building pride in its core expertise.

Secrecy stifles oversight, accountability, and information sharing. Unfortunately, all the current organizational incentives encourage overclassification. This balance should change; and as a start, open information should be provided about the overall size of agency intelligence budgets.

Unity of Effort: Sharing Information

The U.S. government has access to a vast amount of information. But it has a weak system for processing and using what it has. The system of "need to know" should be replaced by a system of "need to share."

The President should lead a government-wide effort to bring the major national security institutions into the information revolution, turning a mainframe system into a decentralized network. The obstacles are not technological. Official after official has urged us to call attention to problems with the unglamorous "back office" side of government operations.

But no agency can solve the problems on its own—to build the net-work requires an effort that transcends old divides, solving common legal and policy issues in ways that can help officials know what they can and cannot do. Again, in tackling information issues, America needs unity of effort.

Unity of Effort: Congress

Congress took too little action to adjust itself or to restructure the executive branch to address the emerging terrorist threat. Congressional oversight for intelligence—and counterterrorism—is dysfunctional. Both Congress and the executive need to do more to minimize national security risks during transitions between administrations.

For intelligence oversight, we propose two options: either a joint committee on the old model of the Joint Committee on Atomic Energy or a single committee in each house combining authorizing and appropriating committees. Our central message is the same: the intelligence committees cannot carry out their oversight function unless they are made stronger, and thereby have both clear responsibility and accountability for that oversight.

Congress should create a single, principal point of oversight and review for homeland security. There should be one permanent standing committee for homeland security in each chamber.

We propose reforms to speed up the nomination, financial reporting, security clearance, and confirmation process for national security officials at the start of an administration, and suggest steps to make sure that incoming administrations have the information they need.

Unity of Effort: Organizing America's Defenses in the United States

We have considered several proposals relating to the future of the domestic intelligence and counterterrorism mission. Adding a new domestic intelligence agency will not solve America's problems in collecting and analyzing intelligence within the United States. We do not recommend creating one.

We propose the establishment of a specialized and integrated national security workforce at the FBI, consisting of agents, analysts, linguists, and surveillance specialists who are recruited, trained, rewarded, and retained to ensure the development of an institutional culture imbued with a deep expertise in intelligence and national security. At several points we asked: Who has the responsibility for defending us at home? Responsibility for America's national defense is shared by the Department of Defense, with its new Northern Command, and by the Department of Homeland Security. They must have a clear delineation of roles, missions, and authority.

The Department of Defense and its oversight committees should regularly assess the adequacy of Northern Command's strategies and planning to defend against military threats to the homeland.

The Department of Homeland Security and its oversight committees should regularly assess the types of threats the country faces, in order to determine the adequacy of the government's plans and the readiness of the government to respond to those threats.

* * *

We call on the American people to remember how we all felt on 9/11, to remember not only the unspeakable horror but how we came together as a nation—one nation. Unity of purpose and unity of effort are the way we will defeat this enemy and make America safer for our children and grandchildren. We look forward to a national debate on the merits of what we have recommended, and we will participate vigorously in that debate.

Congressional Intelligence Committees Report on the Sept. 11, 2001, Attacks

A special congressional panel investigating the Sept. 11, 2001, terrorist attacks against the United States found that U.S. intelligence and law enforcement agencies had collected bits of information ahead of time that might have alerted them that a major attack was imminent. The report said the information had not been examined in such a way to give decision makers an adequate warning. The congressional report was the result of a joint inquiry by the House and Senate intelligence committees. The panels held hearings during 2002 and issued what they called a final report on Dec. 11, 2002. An expanded version was released the following July.

The inquiry was the first major investigation into the government's failure to detect plans by four teams of men from Arab countries to hijack airplanes and fly them into the World Trade Center towers in New York City, the Pentagon near Washington, and another building in Washington, probably the White House. (The latter plane crashed in rural Pennsylvania.) The joint investigating committee was cochaired by the chairmen of the House and Senate intelligence committees: Rep. Porter J. Goss, R-Fla., a former CIA agent, and Sen. Bob Graham, a Democrat who previously was governor of Florida. (Investigation details, p. 276)

The report released in December 2002 contained the panel's recommendations and many details of findings from its hearings and its review of government documents. That document argued that bureaucratic failures were largely responsible for numerous lapses by U.S. agencies, notably the FBI. The panel concluded that bureaucratic obstacles, misunderstandings, lack of follow-through, and simple human errors had prevented the agencies from assembling bits of information that had been collected into a coherent analysis. No single piece of information could have alerted the government to the conspiracy in time to prevent the attacks, the panel said. "The joint inquiry did not uncover a smoking gun."

The panel recommended nineteen specific changes in U.S. counterterrorism operations, the most controversial of which was requiring all intelligence agencies to report to a single director.

Much of the 800-page report was withheld at that time, however, pending the Bush administration's review of the classified information contained in it. That review reportedly resulted in numerous disputes between the congressional panel and the administration over what information could be made public. The process was completed by mid-July 2003, and on July 24 the panel published what it again called its "final" report that included some of the information that had been deleted seven months earlier. The final version offered new details of the attacks but even then the Bush administration withheld numerous pieces of information from the public, including a twenty-eight-page section that reportedly discussed possible support for the hijackers by people with ties to the government of Saudi Arabia.

Following are excerpts from the "Joint Inquiry into Intelligence Community Activities Before and After the Terrorist Attacks of Sept. 11, 2001," a report by the Senate Select Committee on Intelligence and the House Permanent Select Committee on Intelligence. The excerpts are from the version released by the committee on July 24, 2003. Brackets followed by the word "deleted" indicate classified material that was removed before public release. Paragraphs that begin and end with brackets identify sections that were rewritten in whole or in part before public release to remove classified information. Double sets of brackets indicate material added by CQ Press editors for clarity. Some spellings of names and groups have been changed from those used in the report to spellings commonly used in news reports and elsewhere in this volume.

INTELLIGENCE COMMUNITY ACTIVITIES BEFORE AND AFTER SEPT. 11, 2001

I. The Joint Inquiry

In February 2002, the Senate Select Committee on Intelligence and the House Permanent Select Committee on Intelligence agreed to conduct a Joint Inquiry into the activities of the U.S. Intelligence Community in connection with the terrorist attacks perpetrated against our nation on Sept. 11, 2001. Reflecting the magnitude of the events of that day, the Committees' decision was unprecedented in Congressional history: for the first time, two permanent committees, one from the House and one from the Senate, would join together to conduct a single, unified inquiry.

The three principal goals of this Joint Inquiry were to:

• conduct a factual review of what the Intelligence Community knew or should have known prior to Sept. 11, 2001, regarding the international terrorist threat to the United States, to include the scope and nature of any possible international terrorist attacks against the United States and its interests;

• identify and examine any systemic problems that may have impeded the Intelligence Community in learning of or preventing these attacks in advance; and

• make recommendations to improve the Intelligence Community's ability to identify and prevent future international terrorist attacks. . . .

II. The Context

Sept. 11, 2001, while indelible in our collective memory, was by no means America's first confrontation with international terrorism. Although the nature of the threat had evolved considerably over time, the United States and its interests have long been prime terrorist targets. For example, the bombings of the Marine barracks and the U.S. Embassy in Beirut, Lebanon in 1983 should have served as a clear warning that terrorist groups were not reluctant to attack U.S. interests when they believed such attacks would further their ends.

The Intelligence Community also had considerable evidence before Sept. 11 that international terrorists were capable of, and had planned, major terrorist strikes within the United States. The 1993 attack on the World Trade Center confirmed this point, as did the 1993 plots to bomb New York City landmarks and the 1999 arrest at the U.S.-Canadian border of Ahmad Ressam, who intended to bomb the Los Angeles International Airport.

Osama bin Laden's role in international terrorism had also been well known for some time before Sept. 11. He initially came to the attention of the Intelligence Community in the early 1990s as a financier of terrorism. However, bin Laden's own words soon provided evidence of the steadily escalating threat to the United States he and his organization posed. In August 1996, he issued a fatwa—or religious decree—authorizing attacks on Western military targets in the Arabian Peninsula. In February 1998, bin Laden issued a second fatwa authorizing attacks on U.S. civilians and military personnel anywhere in the world. bin Laden's fatwas cited the U.S. military presence in Saudi Arabia and the Persian Gulf, the Palestinian issue, and U.S. support for Israel as justification for ordering these attacks.

The gradual emergence of bin Laden and others like him marked a change from the type of terrorist threat that had traditionally confronted the Intelligence Community. Throughout the Cold War, radical left and ethno-nationalist groups had carried out most terrorist acts. Many of these groups were state-sponsored. The first bombing

of the World Trade Center in February 1993, however, led to a growing recognition in the Intelligence Community of a new type of terrorism that did not conform to the Cold War model: violent radical Islamic cells, not linked to any specific country, but united in anti-American zeal. A July 1995 National Intelligence Estimate noted the danger of this "new breed". By 1996, agencies within the Intelligence Community were aware that bin Laden was organizing these kinds of cells, and they began to collect intelligence on him actively. . . .

The August 1998 bombing of two American embassies in East Africa definitively put the U.S. Intelligence Community on notice of the danger that bin Laden and his network, al Qaeda, posed. The attacks showed that bin Laden's network was capable of carrying out very bloody, simultaneous attacks and inflicting mass casualties. In December 1998, George Tenet, the Director of Central Intelligence, gave a chilling direction to his deputies at the CIA:

"We must now enter a new phase in our effort against bin Laden. . . . We are at war. . . . I want no resources or people spared in this effort, either inside the CIA or the [[Intelligence]] Community."

Discovering and disrupting al Qaeda's plans proved exceptionally difficult, however. Details of major terrorist plots were not widely shared within the al Qaeda organization, making it hard to develop the intelligence necessary to preempt or disrupt attacks. Senior al Qaeda officials were sensitive to operational security, and many al Qaeda members enjoyed sanctuary in Afghanistan, where they could safely plan and train for their missions. Finally, senior members of al Qaeda were skilled and purposeful: they learned from their mistakes and were flexible in organization and planning.

Nonetheless, particularly after the bombings in East Africa, the Intelligence Community amassed a body of information detailing bin Laden's ties to terrorist activities against U.S. interests around the world. Armed with that information, prior to Sept. 11, 2001, U.S. Government counterterrorist efforts to identify and disrupt terrorist operations focused to a substantial degree on bin Laden and his network. The Intelligence Community achieved some successes—in some cases, major successes—in these operations. In other cases, little came of the Intelligence Community's efforts.

By late 2000 and 2001, the Intelligence Community was engaged in an extensive, shadowy struggle against al Qaeda. Despite such efforts, bin Laden carried out successful and devastating attacks against Americans and citizens of other nations, including the bombing of USS Cole in Yemen in October 2000 and the attacks on the World Trade Center and the Pentagon on Sept. 11, 2001.

III. Findings and Conclusions

In reviewing the documents, interview reports, and witness testimony gathered during this Inquiry, the Joint Inquiry has sought to determine what information was available to the Intelligence Community prior to Sept. 11, 2001 that was relevant to the attacks that occurred on that day. The record that has been established through this Inquiry leads to the following factual findings and conclusions.

1. Finding: While the Intelligence Community had amassed a great deal of valuable intelligence regarding Osama bin Laden and his terrorist activities, none of it identified the time, place, and specific nature of the attacks that were planned for Sept. 11, 2001. Nonetheless, the Community did have information that was clearly relevant to the Sept. 11 attacks, particularly when considered for its collective significance.

Discussion: This Inquiry has uncovered no intelligence information in the possession of the Intelligence Community prior to the attacks of Sept. 11 that, if fully considered, would have provided specific, advance warning of the details of those attacks. The task of the Inquiry was not, however, limited to a search for the legendary, and often absent, "smoking gun." The facts surrounding the Sept. 11 attacks demonstrate the importance of strengthening the Intelligence Community's ability to detect and prevent terrorist attacks in what appears to be the more common, but also far more difficult, scenario. Within the huge volume of intelligence reporting that was available prior to Sept. 11, there were various threads and pieces of information that, at least in retrospect, are both relevant and significant. The degree to which the Community was or was not able to build on that information to discern the bigger picture successfully is a critical part of the context for the Sept. 11 attacks and is addressed in the findings that follow.

2. Finding: During the spring and summer of 2001, the Intelligence Community experienced a significant increase in information indicating that bin Laden and al Qaeda intended to strike against U.S. interests in the very near future.

Discussion: The National Security Agency (NSA), for example, reported at least 33 communications indicating a possible, imminent terrorist attack in 2001. Senior U.S. Government officials were advised by the Intelligence Community on June 28 and July 10, 2001, that the attacks were expected, among other things, to "have dramatic consequences on governments or cause major casualties" and that "[a]ttack preparations have been made. Attack will occur with little or no warning."

Some Community personnel described the increase in threat reporting as unprecedented, at least in their own experience. The Intelligence Community advised senior policymakers of the likelihood of an attack but, given the non-specific nature of the reporting, could not identify when, where, and how an attack would take place. Deputy Secretary of State Richard Armitage, in his testimony, described his recollection of the threat and the U.S. Government's response:

"We issued between January and September nine warnings, five of them global, because of the threat information we were receiving from the intelligence agencies in the summer, when [DCI] George Tenet was around town literally pounding on desks saying, something is happening, this is an unprecedented level of threat information. He didn't know where it was going to happen, but he knew that it was coming."

3. Finding: Beginning in 1998 and continuing into the summer of 2001, the Intelligence Community received a modest, but relatively steady, stream of intelligence reporting that indicated the possibility of terrorist attacks within the United States. Nonetheless, testimony and interviews confirm that it was the general view of the Intelligence Community, in the spring and summer of 2001, that the threatened bin Laden attacks would most likely occur against U.S. interests overseas, despite indications of plans and intentions to attack in the domestic United States.

Discussion: Communications intercepts, the arrests of suspected terrorists in the Middle East and Europe, and a credible report of a plan to attack a U.S. Embassy in the Middle East shaped the Community's thinking about where an attack was likely to occur. While former FBI Director Louis Freeh testified that the FBI was "intensely focused" on terrorist targets within the United States, the FBI's Executive Assistant Director for Counterterrorism testified that in 2001 he thought there was a high probability—"98 percent"—that the attack would be overseas. The latter was the clear majority view, despite the fact that the Intelligence Community had information suggesting that bin Laden had planned, and was capable of, conducting attacks within the domestic United States.

This stream of reporting began as early as 1998 and continued during the time of heightened threat levels in 2001. For example, the Community received reporting in May 2001 that bin Laden support-ers were planning to infiltrate the United States to conduct terrorist operations and, in late summer 2001, that an al Qaeda associate was considering mounting terrorist attacks within the United States.

[Of particular interest to the Joint Inquiry was whether and to what extent the President received threat-specific warnings during this period. The Joint Inquiry was advised by a representative of the Intelligence Community that, in August 2001, a closely held intelligence report for senior government officials included information that bin Laden had wanted to conduct attacks in the United States since 1997. The information included discussion of the arrest of Ahmed Ressam in December 1999 at the U.S.-Canadian border and the 1998 bombings of U.S. embassies in Kenya and Tanzania. It mentioned that members of al Qaeda, including some U.S. citizens, had resided in or traveled to the United States for years and that the group apparently maintained a support structure here. The report cited uncorroborated information obtained and disseminated in 1998 that bin Laden wanted to hijack airplanes to gain the release of U.S.-held extremists; FBI judgments about patterns of activity consistent with preparations for hijackings or other types of attacks; as well as information acquired in May 2001 that indicated a group of bin Laden supporters was planning attacks in the United States with explosives].

4. Finding: From at least 1994, and continuing into the summer of 2001, the Intelligence Community received information indicating that terrorists were contemplating, among other means of attack, the use of aircraft as weapons. This information did not stimulate any specific Intelligence Community assessment of, or collective U.S. Government reaction to, this form of threat.

Discussion: [While the credibility of the sources was sometimes questionable and the information often sketchy, the Inquiry confirmed that the Intelligence Community did receive intelligence reporting concerning the potential use of aircraft as weapons. For example, the Community received information in 1998 about a bin Laden operation that would involve flying an explosive-laden aircraft into a U.S. airport and, in summer 2001, about a plot to bomb a U.S. embassy from an airplane or crash an airplane into it. The FBI and CIA were also aware that convicted terrorist Abdul Hakim Murad and several others had discussed the possibility of crashing an airplane into CIA Headquarters as part of "the Bojinka Plot" in the Philippines, discussed later in this report. Some, but apparently not all, of these reports were disseminated within the Intelligence Community and to other agencies].

The Transportation Security Administration, for example, advised the Committees that the Federal Aviation Administration (FAA) had not received three of these reports, that two others were received by the FAA but through State Department cables, and that one report was received by the FAA, but only after Sept. 11, 2001. Many policymakers and U.S. Government officials apparently remained unaware of this kind of potential threat and the Intelligence Community did not produce any specific assessments of the likelihood that terrorists would in fact use airplanes as weapons. For example, former National Security Advisor Sandy Berger testified before these Committees that:

"I don't recall being presented with any specific threat information about an attack of this nature [the use of aircraft as weapons] or any alert highlighting this threat or indicating it was any more likely than any other."

That testimony is consistent with the views publicly expressed by the current National Security Advisor, Condoleezza Rice, shortly after the Sept. 11 attacks. Similarly, Deputy Under Secretary of Defense Paul Wolfowitz testified that he had not been made aware of this type of potential threat:

"I don't recall any warning of the possibility of a mass casualty attack using civilian airliners or any information that would have led us to contemplate the possibility of our shooting down a civilian airliner."

Even within the Intelligence Community, the possibility of using aircraft as weapons was apparently not widely known. At the FBI, for instance, the FBI Phoenix field office agent who wrote the so-called "Phoenix memo" testified that he was aware of the plot to crash a plane into CIA Headquarters, but not the other reports of terrorist groups considering the use of aircraft as weapons. The Chief of the Radical Fundamentalist Unit in the FBI's Counterterrorism Division also confirmed, in an Joint Inquiry interview, that he was not aware of such reports.

5. Finding: Although relevant information that is significant in retrospect regarding the attacks was available to the Intelligence Community prior to Sept. 11, 2001, the Community too often failed to focus on that information and consider and appreciate its collective significance in terms of a probable terrorist attack. Neither did the Intelligence Community demonstrate sufficient initiative in coming to grips with the new transnational threats. Some significant pieces of information in the vast stream of data being collected were overlooked, some were not recognized as potentially significant at the time and therefore not disseminated, and some required additional action on the part of foreign governments before a direct connection to the hijackers could have been established. For all those reasons, the Intelligence Community failed to capitalize fully on available, and potentially important, information. The sub-findings below identify each category of this information.

[Terrorist Communications in 1999]

5.a. [During 1999, the National Security Agency obtained a number of communications—none of which included specific detail regarding the time, place or nature of the Sept. 11 attacks—connecting individuals to terrorism who were identified, after Sept. 11, 2001, as participants in the attacks that occurred on that day].

Discussion: [In early 1999, the National Security Agency (NSA) analyzed communications involving a suspected terrorist facility in the Middle East that had previously been linked to al Qaeda activities directed against U.S. interests. Information obtained [deleted] included, among other things, the full name of future hijacker Nawaf al-Hazmi. Beyond the fact that the communications involved a suspected terrorist facility in the Middle East, the communications did not, in NSA's view at the time, feature any other terrorist-related information. The information was not published because the individuals mentioned in the communications were unknown to NSA, and, according to NSA, the information did not meet NSA's reporting thresholds. NSA has explained that these thresholds are flexible, sometimes changing daily, and consist of several factors, including: the priority of the intelligence requirement; the apparent intelligence value of the information; the level of customer interest in the topic; the current situation; and the volume of intercept to be analyzed and reported].

[During the summer of 1999, NSA analyzed additional communications involving a suspected terrorist facility in the Middle East that included the name of Khaled. At about the same time, the name Khallad also came to NSA's attention. This information did not meet NSA's reporting thresholds and thus was not disseminated]. [In late 1999, NSA analyzed communications involving a suspected terrorist facility in the Middle East that included the names of Khaled and Nawaf. At this time, NSA did not associate the latter individual with the Nawaf al-Hazmi it had learned about in early 1999. Later, the two individuals [deleted] were determined to be Khalid al-Mihdhar and Nawaf al-Hazmi, now known to be two of the Sept. 11 hijackers. [deleted]. This information was passed to the CIA as well as the FBI in late 1999. In early 2000, NSA also [deleted] passed additional information about Khalid to the CIA, FBI, FAA, the Departments of State, Treasury, Transportation, and Justice, and others in the U.S. Government].

Malaysia Meeting and Travel of al Qaeda Operatives to the United States

5.b. The Intelligence Community acquired additional, and highly significant, information regarding Khalid al-Mihdhar and Nawaf al-Hazmi in early 2000. Critical parts of the information concerning al-Mihdhar and al-Hazmi lay dormant within the Intelligence Community for as long as eighteen months, at the very time when plans for the Sept. 11 attacks were proceeding. The CIA missed repeated opportunities to act based on the information in its possession that these two bin Laden-associated terrorists were traveling to the United States, and to add their names to watchlists.

Discussion: [By early January 2000, CIA knew al-Mihdhar's full name and that it was likely Nawaf's last name was al-Hazmi, knew that they had attended what was believed to be a gathering of al Qaeda associates in Malaysia, was aware that they had been traveling together, and had documents indicating that al-Mihdhar held a U.S. B-1B-2 multiple entry visa that would allow him to travel to and from the United States until April 6, 2000. CIA arranged surveillance of the meeting and the DCI was kept informed as the operation progressed].

Despite having all this information, and despite the republication of CTC guidance regarding watchlisting procedures in December 1999 (see Appendix, "CTC Watchlisting Guidance—December 1999"), CIA did not add the names of these two individuals to the State Department, INS, and U.S. Customs Service watchlists that are used to deny individuals entry into the United States. The weight of the record also suggests that, despite providing the FBI with other, less critical, information about the Malaysia meeting, the CIA did not advise the FBI about al-Mihdhar's U.S. visa and the very real possibility that he would travel to the United States. The CIA stated its belief that the visa information was sent to the FBI and produced a cable indicating that this had been done.

The FBI, for its part, had no record the visa information was received. Although the facts of the Malaysia meeting were included in several briefings for senior FBI officials, including FBI Director Louis Freeh, no record could be found that the visa information was part of these briefings.

[On March 5, 2000, CIA Headquarters received a cable from an overseas CIA station indicating that Nawaf al-Hazmi had traveled to Los Angeles, California on Jan. 15, 2000. The following day, March 6, CIA Headquarters received a message from another CIA station noting its "interest" in the first cable's "information that a member of this group had traveled to the U.S." The CIA did not act on either message, again did not watchlist al-Hazmi or al-Mihdhar, and, again, did not advise the FBI of their possible presence in the United States. In 2000, these same two individuals had numerous contacts with an active FBI counterterrorism informant while they were living in San Diego, California].

On Jan. 4, 2001, CIA acquired information that Khallad, a principal planner in the bombing of USS Cole, had, along with al-Mihdhar and al-Hazmi, attended the January 2000 meeting in Malaysia. Again, the CIA did not watchlist these two individuals. At the time, al-Mihdhar was abroad, but al-Hazmi was still in the United States. FBI Director Robert Mueller testified to the Joint Inquiry that: "al-Mihdhar's role in the Sept. 11 plot . . . before his re-entry into the United States may well have been that of the coordinator and organizer of . . . the non-pilot hijackers."

In May 2001, the CIA provided FBI Headquarters with photographs taken in Malaysia, including one of al-Mihdhar, for purposes of identifying another Cole bombing suspect. Although the CIA told FBI Headquarters about the Malaysia meeting and about al-Mihdhar's travel in Southeast Asia at that time, the CIA did not advise the FBI about al-Mihdhar's or al-Hazmi's possible travel to the United States. Again, the CIA did not watchlist the two individuals. While CIA personnel were working closely with the FBI in support of the USS Cole bombing investigation, the importance and urgency of information tying suspected terrorists to the domestic United States apparently never registered with them. CIA Director Tenet testified that CIA personnel:

"... in their focus on the [USS Cole] investigation, did not recognize the implications of the information about al-Hazmi and al-Mihdhar that they had in their files."

On June 11, 2001, FBI Headquarters and CIA personnel met with the New York FBI field office agents who were handling the USS Cole investigation. The New York agents were shown the Malaysia photographs, but were not given copies. Although al-Mihdhar's name was mentioned, the New York agents' requests for more information about al-Mihdhar and the circumstances surrounding the photographs were refused, according to one of the field office agents. The FBI Headquarters analyst recalls that she said at the meeting that she would try to get the information the agents had requested. . . .

Again, in that meeting, the CIA had missed yet another opportunity to advise the FBI about al-Mihdhar's visa and possible travel to the United States and, again, the CIA took no action to watchlist these individuals. Just two days later, al-Mihdhar obtained a new U.S. visa and, on July 4, 2001, he re-entered the United States.

It was not until mid July 2001, that a concerned CIA officer assigned to the FBI triggered a CIA review of its cables regarding the Malaysia meeting, a task that, ironically, fell to an FBI analyst assigned to the CTC. Working with the Immigration and Naturalization Service (INS), the FBI analyst determined that both al-Mihdhar and al-Hazmi had entered the United States. As a result of that effort, on Aug. 23, 2001, the CIA finally notified the FBI and requested of the State Department that the two individuals should be watchlisted.

Even then, there was less than an all-out effort to locate what amounted to two bin Laden-associated terrorists in the United States during a period when the terrorist threat level had escalated to a peak level. For example, neither CIA, FBI, nor State Department informed the FAA. On Aug. 21, 2001, coincidentally, FAA had issued a Security Directive, entitled "Threat to U.S. Aircraft Operators." That Directive alerted commercial airlines that nine named terrorism-associated individuals—none of whom were connected to the 19 hijackers—were planning commercial air travel and should receive additional security scrutiny if they attempted to board an aircraft. The Directive was updated on Aug. 24 and Aug. 28, 2001. Had FAA been advised of the presence of al-Hazmi and al-Mihdhar in the United States, a similar directive could have been issued, subjecting the two, their luggage and any carry-on items to detailed, FAA-directed searches.

Further, only the FBI's New York field office received a request from FBI Headquarters to conduct a search for the two prior to Sept. 11, 2001. The Headquarters written instruction to the New York field office only identified al-Mihdhar in its subject line. Nawaf al-Hazmi was mentioned in the text, and it is not clear whether it was intended that he be a subject of the search as well. It was not until Sept. 11, 2001 that the Los Angeles FBI field office was asked to conduct a search. Other FBI offices with potentially useful informants, such as San Diego, were not notified prior to Sept. 11.

A New York FBI field office agent testified that he urged FBI Headquarters on Aug. 28, 2001 to allow New York field office criminal agents to participate in the search with FBI intelligence agents, given the limited resources that are often applied to intelligence investigations. The request was refused by FBI Headquarters because of concerns about the perceived "wall" between criminal and intelligence matters. . . .

Joint Inquiry witnesses testified that other federal agencies with potentially valuable information databases were never asked to assist in FBI's search.

[Terrorist Communications in Spring 2000]

5.c. [In January 2000, after the meeting of al Qaeda operatives in Malaysia, Khalid al-Mihdhar and Nawaf al-Hazmi entered the United States [deleted]. Thereafter, the Intelligence Community obtained information indicating that an individual named "Khaled" at an unknown location had contacted a suspected terrorist facility in the Middle East. The Intelligence Community reported some of this information, but did not report all of it. Some of it was not reported because it was deemed not terrorist-related. It was not until after Sept. 11, 2001 that the Intelligence Community determined that these contacts had been made from future hijacker Khalid al-Mihdhar while he was living within the domestic United States].

Discussion: [While the Intelligence Community had information regarding these communications, it did not determine the location from which they had been made [deleted] [deleted]. After Sept. 11, the FBI determined from domestic toll records that it was in fact the hijacker Khalid al-Mihdhar who had made these communications and that he had done so from within the United States. The Intelligence Community did not identify what was critically important information in terms of the domestic threat to the United States: the fact that the communications were between individuals within the United States and suspected terrorist facilities overseas. That kind of information could have provided crucial investigative leads to law enforcement agencies engaged in domestic counterterrorist efforts].

[Two Hijackers Had Numerous Contacts with an Active FBI Informant]

5.d. [This Joint Inquiry confirmed that these same two future hijackers, Khalid al-Mihdhar and Nawaf al-Hazmi, had numerous contacts with a long time FBI counterterrorism informant in California and that a third future hijacker, Hani Hanjour, apparently had more limited contact with the same informant. In mid- to late-2000, the CIA already had information indicating that al-Mihdhar had a multiple entry U.S. visa and that al-Hazmi had in fact traveled to Los Angeles, but the two had not been watchlisted and information suggesting that two suspected terrorists could well be in the United States had not yet been given to the FBI. The San Diego FBI field office, which handled the informant in question, did not receive that information or any of the other intelligence information pertaining to al-Mihdhar and al-Hazmi, prior to Sept. 11, 2001. As a result, the FBI missed the opportunity to task a uniquely well-positioned informant—who denies having any advance knowledge of the plot—to collect information about the hijackers and their plans within the United States.]

Discussion: [Nawaf al-Hazmi and Khalid al-Mihdhar had numerous contacts with a long-time FBI counterterrorism informant while they were living in San Diego, California. There are several indications that hijacker Hani Hanjour may have had more limited contact with the same informant in December 2000.]

[During the summer of 2000, the informant advised the FBI handling agent that the informant had contacts with two individuals named "Nawaf" and "Khalid". The informant described meeting these individuals. The informant described the two to the FBI agent as Saudi Muslim youths who were legally in the United States to visit and attend school. The FBI agent did not, at the time, consider these individuals to be of interest to the FBI. While the agent says he asked the informant for the individuals' last names, the informant never provided that information and the FBI agent did not press for the names because he had no reason to think they were significant until after Sept. 11, 2001.]

[deleted][During one of their last contacts, al-Hazmi advised the informant that he was moving to Arizona to attend flight training, but the informant did not advise the FBI of this information until after the Sept. 11 attacks].

[When the FBI's San Diego field office determined after the attacks that a longtime FBI counterterrorism informant had had numerous contacts in 2000 with two of the Sept. 11 hijackers, personnel there were immediately suspicious about whether the informant was involved in the plot. Subsequently, however, all of the field office personnel, including senior managers and various case agents, concluded that the informant was unwitting of, and had no role in, the Sept. 11 plot].

[Several questions remain, however, with regard to the informant's credibility. First, while there are several indications suggesting that future hijacker Hani Hanjour had contact with the informant in December 2000, the informant has repeatedly advised the FBI that the informant does not recognize photos of Hanjour. Second, the informant told the FBI that the hijackers did nothing to arouse the informant's suspicion, but the informant also acknowledged that al-Hazmi had contacts with at least four individuals the informant knew were of interest to the FBI and about whom the informant had previously reported to the FBI. Third, the informant has made numerous inconsistent statements to the FBI during the course of interviews after Sept. 11, 2001. Fourth, the informant's responses during an FBI polygraph examination to very specific questions about the informant's advance knowledge of the Sept. 11 plot were judged by the FBI to be "inconclusive," although the FBI asserts that this type of result is not unusual for such individuals in such circumstances].

[Finally, there is also information which conflicts with the information provided by the informant concerning the dates of contacts with the hijackers. The Joint Inquiry, for example, brought to the FBI's attention information that is inconsistent with the date of initial contact as provided by the informant. In its Nov. 18, 2002, written response to the Joint Inquiry, the FBI has acknowledged that there are "significant inconsistencies" in the informant's statements about these contacts. The FBI investigation regarding this issue is continuing].

[The Administration has to date objected to the Inquiry's efforts to interview the informant in order to attempt to resolve those inconsistencies. The Administration also would not agree to allow the FBI to serve a Committee subpoena and deposition notice on the informant. Instead, written interrogatories from the Joint Inquiry were, at the suggestion of the FBI, provided to the informant. Through an attorney, the informant has declined to respond to those interrogatories and has indicated that, if subpoenaed, the informant would request a grant of immunity prior to testifying].

[The FBI agent who was responsible for the informant testified before the Joint Inquiry that, had he had access to the intelligence information on al-Mihdhar's and al-Hazmi's significance at the time they were in San Diego:

"It would have made a huge difference. We would have immediately opened [deleted] investigations. We had the predicate for a [deleted] investigation if we had that information. . . .

[W]e would immediately go out and canvas the sources and try to find out where these people were. If we locate them, which we probably would have since they were very close—they were nearby—we would have initiated investigations immediately. . . . We would have done everything. We would have used all available investigative techniques. We would have given them the full court press. We would . . . have done everything—physical surveillance, technical surveillance and other assets."

[Whether, as the agent testified he believes, that kind of investigative work would have occurred and would have then uncovered the hijackers' future plans will necessarily remain speculation. What is clear, however, is that the informant's contacts with the hijackers, had they been capitalized on, would have given the San Diego FBI field office perhaps the Intelligence Community's best chance to unravel the Sept. 11 plot. Given the CIA's failure to disseminate, in a timely manner, intelligence information on the significance and location of al-Mihdhar and al-Hazmi, that chance, unfortunately, never materialized].

The Phoenix Electronic Communication

5.e. On July 10, 2001, an FBI Phoenix field office agent sent an "Electronic Communication" to four individuals in the Radical Fundamentalist Unit (RFU) and two individuals in the Osama bin Laden Unit (UBLU) at FBI Headquarters, and to two agents on International Terrorism squads in the FBI New York field office. In the communication, the agent expressed his concerns, based on his first-hand knowledge, that there was a coordinated effort underway by bin Laden to send students to the United States for civil aviation-related training. He noted that there was an "inordinate number of individuals of investigative interest" in this type of training in Arizona and expressed his suspicion that this was an effort to establish a cadre of individuals in civil aviation who would conduct future terrorist activity. The Phoenix agent's communication requested that FBI Headquarters consider implementing four recommendations:

• accumulate a list of civil aviation universities/colleges around the country;
• establish liaison with these schools;
• discuss the theories contained in the Phoenix EC with the Intelligence Community; and
• consider seeking authority to obtain visa information concerning individuals seeking to attend flight schools.

However, the FBI Headquarters personnel did not take the action requested by the Phoenix field office agent prior to Sept. 11, 2001. The Phoenix communication generated little or no interest at either FBI Headquarters or the FBI's New York field office. . . .

The FBI Investigation of Zacarias Moussaoui

5.f. In August 2001, the FBI's Minneapolis field office, in conjunction with the INS, detained Zacarias Moussaoui, a French national who had enrolled in flight training in Minnesota. FBI agents there also suspected that Moussaoui was involved in a hijacking plot. FBI Headquarters attorneys determined that there was not probable cause to obtain a court order to search Moussaoui's belongings under the Foreign Intelligence Surveillance Act (FISA). However, personnel at FBI Headquarters, including the Radical Fundamentalist Unit and the National Security Law Unit, as well as agents in the Minneapolis field office, misunderstood the legal standard for obtaining an order under FISA. As a result, FBI Minneapolis field office personnel wasted valuable investigative resources trying to connect the Chechen rebels to al Qaeda. Finally, no one at the FBI apparently connected the Moussaoui investigation with the heightened threat environment in the summer of 2001, the Phoenix communication, or the entry of al-Mihdhar and al-Hazmi into the United States. . . .

Hijackers in Contact with Persons of FBI Investigative Interest in the United States

5.g. The Joint Inquiry confirmed that at least some of the hijackers were not as isolated during their time in the United States as has been previously suggested. Rather, they maintained a number of contacts both in the United States and abroad during this time period. Some of those contacts were with individuals who were known to the FBI, through either past or, at the time, ongoing FBI inquiries and investigations. Although it is not known to what extent any of these contacts in the United States were aware of the plot, it is now clear that they did provide at least some of the hijackers with substantial assistance while they were living in this country. . . .

Hijackers' Associates in Germany

5.h. [Since 1995, the CIA had been aware of a radical Islamic presence in Germany, including individuals with connections to Osama bin Laden. Prior to Sept. 11, 2001, the CIA had unsuccessfully sought additional information on individuals who have now been identified as associates of some of the hijackers]. . . .

Khalid Shaykh Mohammad

5.i. Prior to Sept. 11, the Intelligence Community had information linking Khalid Shaykh Mohammed (KSM), now recognized by the Intelligence Community as the mastermind of the attacks, to bin Laden, to terrorist plans to use aircraft as weapons, and to terrorist activity in the United States. The Intelligence Community, however, relegated KSM to rendition target status following his 1996 indictment in connection with the Bojinka Plot and, as a result, focused primarily on his location, rather than his activities and place in the al Qaeda hierarchy. The Community also did not recognize the significance of reporting in June 2001 concerning KSM's active role in sending terrorists to the United States, or the facilitation of their activities upon arriving in the United States. Collection efforts were not targeted on information about KSM that might have helped better understand al Qaeda's plans and intentions, and KSM's role in the Sept. 11 attacks was a surprise to the Intelligence Community.

Discussion: [According to information obtained by the Intelligence Community from several sources after Sept. 11, 2001, Khalid Shaykh Mohammed (KSM)—also known as "Mukhtar" (Arabic for "The Brain")—masterminded the Sept. 11 attacks. The information indicates that KSM presented a plan to Osama bin Laden to mount an attack using small rental aircraft filled with explosives. Osama bin Laden reportedly suggested using even larger planes. Thus, the idea of hijacking commercial airliners took hold. Thereafter, KSM reportedly instructed and trained the hijackers for their mission, including directing them to undergo pilot training].

KSM came to the attention of the Intelligence Community as a terrorist in early 1995 when he was linked to Ramzi Yousef's "Bojinka Plot" in the Philippines. One portion of that plot involved the idea of crashing an airplane into CIA Headquarters. Through additional intelligence and investigative efforts in 1995, KSM was also connected to the first World Trade Center bombing. He was indicted by a U.S. grand jury in January 1996. The indictment was kept under seal until 1998 while the FBI and CIA attempted to locate him and arrange to take him into custody. Subsequently, indications were received that he might have been involved in the East Africa U.S. Embassy bombings.

[In June 2001, [deleted] disseminated a report to all Intelligence Community agencies, [deleted], military commanders, and components in the Treasury and Justice Departments emphasizing KSM's ties to bin Laden as well as his continuing travel to the United States. The report explained that KSM appears to be one of bin Laden's most trusted lieutenants and was active in recruiting people to travel outside Afghanistan, including to the United States, on behalf of bin Laden. According to the report, he traveled frequently to the United States, including as recently as May 2001, and routinely told others that he could arrange their entry into the United States as well. Reportedly, these individuals were expected to establish contact with colleagues already there. The clear implication of his comments, according to the report, was that they would be engaged in planning terrorist related activities].

Although this particular report was sent from the CIA to the FBI, neither agency apparently recognized the significance of a bin Laden lieutenant sending terrorists to the United States and asking them to establish contacts with colleagues already there. CTC questioned this report at the time and commented: "We doubt the real [KSM] would do this . . . because if it is [KSM], we have both a significant threat and an opportunity to pick him up." Neither the CIA nor the FBI has been able to confirm whether KSM had in fact been traveling to the United States or sending recruits here prior to Sept. 11. . . .

B. CONCLUSION—FACTUAL FINDINGS

In short, for a variety of reasons, the Intelligence Community failed to capitalize on both the individual and collective significance of available information that appears relevant to the events of Sept. 11. As a result, the Community missed opportunities to disrupt the Sept. 11 plot by denying entry to or detaining would-be hijackers; to at least try to unravel the plot through surveillance and other investigative work within the United States; and, finally, to generate a heightened state of alert and thus harden the homeland against attack.

No one will ever know what might have happened had more connections been drawn between these disparate pieces of information. We will never definitively know to what extent the Community would have been able and willing to exploit fully all the opportunities that may have emerged. The important point is that the Intelligence Community, for a variety of reasons, did not bring together and fully appreciate a range of information that could have greatly enhanced its chances of uncovering and preventing Osama bin Laden's plan to attack the United States on Sept. 11, 2001.

C. SYSTEMIC FINDINGS

Our review of the events surrounding Sept. 11 has revealed a number of systemic weaknesses that hindered the Intelligence Community's counterterrorism efforts before Sept. 11. If not addressed, these weaknesses will continue to undercut U.S. counterterrorist efforts. In order to minimize the possibility of attacks like Sept. 11 in the future, effective solutions to those problems need to be developed and fully implemented as soon as possible.

1. Finding: Prior to Sept. 11, the Intelligence Community was neither well organized nor equipped, and did not adequately adapt, to meet the challenge posed by global terrorists focused on targets within the domestic United States. Serious gaps existed between the collection coverage provided by U.S. foreign and U.S. domestic intelligence capabilities. The U.S. foreign intelligence agencies paid inadequate attention to the potential for a domestic attack. The CIA's failure to watchlist suspected terrorists aggressively reflected a lack of emphasis on a process designed to protect the homeland from the terrorist threat. As a result, CIA employees failed to watchlist al-Mihdhar and al-Hazmi. At home, the counterterrorism effort suffered from the lack of an effective domestic intelligence capability. The FBI was unable to identify and monitor effectively the extent of activity by al Qaeda and other international terrorist groups operat-

ing in the United States. Taken together, these problems greatly exacerbated the nation's vulnerability to an increasingly dangerous and immediate international terrorist threat inside the United States.

Discussion: The United States has a long history of defining internal threats as either foreign or domestic and assigning responsibility to the intelligence and law enforcement agencies accordingly. This division reflects a fundamental policy choice and is codified in law. For example, the National Security Act of 1947 precludes CIA from exercising any internal security or law enforcement powers. The Congressional investigations of the 1970's into the activities of the intelligence agencies, including their efforts to collect information regarding anti-Vietnam War activists and other "radicals," reinforced the importance of this division in the minds of the Congress, the American public, and the agencies.

The emergence, in the 1990s, of a threat posed by international terrorists who operate across national borders demanded huge changes in focus and approach from intelligence agencies traditionally organized and trained to operate primarily in either the United States or abroad. The legal authorities, operational policies and cultures that had molded agencies like CIA, NSA and the FBI for years had not responded to the "globalization" of terrorism that culminated in the Sept. 11 attacks in the United States. While some efforts, such as the creation of the CTC at CIA in 1986, were made to increase collaboration between these agencies, the agencies focused primarily on what remained essentially separate spheres of operations. In the absence of any collective national strategy, they retained significant autonomy in deciding how to attack and array their resources against Osama bin Laden and al Qaeda. Efforts to develop such a strategy might have exposed the significant counterterrorism gaps that existed between the agencies as well as the increasingly urgent need to compensate for those gaps in the absence of more fundamental changes in organization and legal authority.

Prior to Sept. 11, CIA and NSA continued to focus the bulk of their efforts on the foreign operations of terrorists. While intelligence reporting indicated that al Qaeda intended to strike in the United States, these agencies believed that defending against this threat was primarily the responsibility of the FBI. This Joint Inquiry found that both agencies routinely passed a large volume of intelligence to the FBI, but that neither agency followed up to determine what the FBI learned from or did with that information. Neither did the FBI keep NSA and CIA adequately informed of developments within its areas of responsibility.

As noted earlier, the record confirms instances where, despite numerous opportunities, information that was directly relevant to the domestic threat was simply overlooked and not disseminated in a timely manner to the FBI. For example, the CIA analyst who neglected to raise the information concerning al-Mihdhar and al-Hazmi's U.S. travel in a June 2001 meeting with the FBI in New York said in a Joint Inquiry interview that the information he had learned concerning the pair's travel to Los Angeles "did not mean anything to him." He also explained to the Joint Inquiry that the information was operational in nature and he would have needed permission before disclosing it.

The CIA's inconsistent performance regarding the watchlisting of suspected terrorists prior to Sept. 11 also suggests a lack of attention to the domestic threat. Watchlists are a vital link in denying entry to the United States by terrorists and others who threaten the national security, and CTC had reminded personnel of the importance of watchlisting in December 1999. . . . Yet, some CIA officers in CTC indicated they did not put much emphasis on watchlists. The Joint Inquiry confirmed that there was no formal process in place at the CTC prior to Sept. 11 for watchlisting suspected terrorists, even where, as

was the case with al-Hazmi and al-Mihdhar, there were indications of travel to the United States.

Other CIA personnel reported that they received no training on watchlisting and that names were added on an ad hoc basis. In the days and weeks following the Sept. 11 attacks, more focused CIA review of over 1,500 Classified Intelligence Reports that had not previously been provided to the State Department for watchlist purposes resulted in the identification of 150 suspected terrorists and the addition of 58 suspected terrorist names to the watchlist. DCI Tenet acknowledged in his testimony before the Joint Inquiry that CIA's watchlisting training had been deficient and that a mistake had been made in the failure to watchlist both al-Mihdhar and al-Hazmi promptly.

[There were also gaps between NSA's coverage of foreign communications and the FBI's coverage of domestic communications that suggest a lack of sufficient attention to the domestic threat. Prior to Sept. 11, neither agency focused on the importance of identifying and then ensuring coverage of communications between the United States and suspected terrorist-associated facilities abroad [deleted]. Consistent with its focus on communications abroad, NSA adopted a policy that avoided intercepting the communications between individuals in the United States and foreign countries].

NSA adopted this policy even though the collection of such communications is within its mission and it would have been possible for NSA to obtain FISA Court authorization for such collection. NSA Director Hayden testified to the Joint Inquiry that NSA did not want to be perceived as targeting individuals in the United States and believed that the FBI was instead responsible for conducting such surveillance. NSA did not, however, develop a plan with the FBI to collect and to ensure the dissemination of any relevant foreign intelligence to appropriate domestic agencies. This further evidences the slow response of the Intelligence Community to the developing transnational threat.

[The Joint Inquiry has learned that one of the future hijackers communicated with a known terrorist facility in the Middle East while he was living in the United States. The Intelligence Community did not identify the domestic origin of those communications prior to Sept. 11, 2001 so that additional FBI investigative efforts could be coordinated. Despite this country's substantial advantages, there was insufficient focus on what many would have thought was among the most critically important kinds of terrorist-related communications, at least in terms of protecting the Homeland].

While most of the Intelligence Community focused on the collection of foreign intelligence, the Joint Inquiry was told repeatedly that the nation lacked an effective domestic intelligence capability prior to Sept. 11. . . .

While the FBI's counterterrorist program had produced successful investigations and major prosecutions of both domestic and international terrorists, numerous witnesses told the Joint Inquiry that the program was, at least prior to Sept. 11, incapable of producing significant intelligence products. The FBI's traditional reliance on an aggressive, case-oriented, law enforcement approach did not encourage the broader collection and analysis efforts that are critical to the intelligence mission. Lacking appropriate personnel, training, and information systems, the FBI primarily gathered intelligence to support specific investigations, not to conduct all-source analysis for dissemination to other intelligence agencies. . . .

Numerous individuals told this Inquiry that the FBI's 56 field offices enjoy a great deal of latitude in managing their work, consistent with the dynamic and reactive nature of its traditional law enforcement mission. In counterterrorism efforts, however, that flexibility apparently served to dilute the FBI's national focus on bin Laden and al Qaeda. Although the FBI made counterterrorism a "Tier One" priority, not all of its field offices responded consistently to this FBI Headquarters decision. The New York Field Office did make terrorism a high priority and was given substantial responsibility for the al Qaeda target following the first attack on the World Trade Center in 1993. However, many other FBI offices were not focused on al Qaeda and had little understanding of the extent of the threat it posed within this country prior to Sept. 11.

The combination of these factors seriously handicapped efforts to identify and defend against the foreign terrorist threat to the domestic United States. It is not surprising, in the absence of more focused intelligence, that senior policymakers told this Inquiry that, prior to Sept. 11, they believed the terrorist threat was focused on U.S. interests overseas. Deputy Secretary of State Armitage, for example, testified that "... I don't think we really had made the leap in our mind that we are no longer safe behind these two great oceans...." Former Deputy Secretary of Defense John Hamre said in a Joint Inquiry interview that he could not remember ever seeing an intelligence report on the existence of terrorist sleeper cells in the United States. In retrospect, he recalled: "... we thought we were dealing in important things, but we missed the domestic threat from international terrorism."

2. Finding: Prior to Sept. 11, 2001, neither the U.S. Government as a whole nor the Intelligence Community had a comprehensive counterterrorist strategy for combating the threat posed by Osama bin Laden. Furthermore, the Director of Central Intelligence (DCI) was either unwilling or unable to marshal the full range of Intelligence Community resources necessary to combat the growing threat to the United States.

Discussion: The Intelligence Community is a large distributed organism. It encompasses 14 agencies and tens of thousands of employees. The number of people employed exclusively in the effort against Osama bin Laden and al Qaeda was relatively small. In addition, these people were operating in geographically dispersed locations, often not connected by secure information technologies, and within established bureaucracies that were not culturally or organizationally attuned to one another's requirements. Many of them had limited experience against the target, and did not know one another. To achieve success in such an environment, leadership is a critical factor. The Joint Inquiry found that the Intelligence Community's structure made leadership difficult.

Osama bin Laden first came to the attention of the Intelligence Community in the early 1990s, initially as a financier of terrorist activities. In 1996, as bin Laden's direct involvement in planning and directing terrorist acts became more evident, the DCI's Counterterrorist Center (CTC) created a special unit to focus specifically on him and the threat he posed to the interests of the United States. Personnel within CTC recognized as early as 1996 and 1997 that Osama bin Laden posed a grave danger to the United States.

Following the August 1998 bombings of two U.S. embassies in East Africa, the DCI made combating the threat posed by Osama bin Laden one of the Intelligence Community's highest priorities, establishing it as a "Tier 0 priority." The DCI raised the status of the bin Laden threat still further when he announced in writing in December 1998 regarding bin Laden: "We are at war.... I want no resources or people spared in this effort, either inside the CIA or the [Intelligence] Community." This declaration appeared in a memorandum from the DCI to CIA senior managers, the Deputy DCI for Community Management and the Assistant DCI for Military Support.

The Intelligence Community as a whole, however, had only a limited awareness of this declaration. For example, some senior managers in the National Security Agency and the Defense Intelligence Agency say they were aware of the declaration. However, it was apparently not well known within the Federal Bureau of Investigation. In fact, the Assistant Director of the FBI's Counterterrorism Division testified to the Joint Inquiry that he "was not specifically aware of that declaration of war."

Furthermore, and even more disturbing, Joint Inquiry interviews of FBI field office personnel indicated that they were not aware of the DCI's declaration, and some had only a passing familiarity with the very existence of Osama bin Laden and al Qaeda prior to Sept. 11. Neither were the Deputy Secretary of Defense or the Chairman of the Joint Chiefs of Staff aware of the DCI's declaration. This suggests a fragmented Intelligence Community that was operating without a comprehensive strategy for combating the threat posed by bin Laden, and a DCI without the ability to enforce consistent priorities at all levels throughout the Community....

The inability to realign Intelligence Community resources to combat the threat posed by Osama bin Laden is a relatively direct consequence of the limited authority of the DCI over major portions of the Intelligence Community. As former Senator Warren Rudman noted on October 8, 2002 in his testimony before the Joint Inquiry: "You have a Director of Central Intelligence who is also the Director of CIA; eighty-five percent of [the Intelligence Community's budget] is controlled by the Department of Defense."...

While the FBI devoted considerable resources to the criminal investigations of the terrorist attacks overseas, substantial efforts to prevent similar attacks at home were lacking. Former National Security Advisor Sandy Berger told the Joint Inquiry: "... if there was a flood of intelligence information [on terrorism] from the CIA, there was hardly a trickle from the FBI." In some FBI field offices, there was little focus on, or awareness of, Osama bin Laden and al Qaeda. This included the San Diego field office where FBI agents would discover, after Sept. 11, that there had been numerous local connections to at least two of the hijackers....

3. Finding: Between the end of the Cold War and Sept. 11, 2001, overall Intelligence Community funding fell or remained even in constant dollars, while funding for the Community's counterterrorism efforts increased considerably. Despite those increases, the accumulation of intelligence priorities, a burdensome requirements process, the overall decline in Intelligence Community funding, and reliance on supplemental appropriations made it difficult to allocate Community resources effectively against an evolving terrorist threat. Inefficiencies in the resource and requirements process were compounded by problems in Intelligence Community budgeting practices and procedures....

4. Finding: While technology remains one of this nation's greatest advantages, it has not been fully and most effectively applied in support of U.S. counterterrorism efforts. Persistent problems in this area included a lack of collaboration between Intelligence Community agencies, a reluctance to develop and implement new technical capabilities aggressively, the FBI's reliance on outdated and insufficient technical systems, and the absence of a central counterterrorism database....

5. Finding: Prior to Sept. 11, the Intelligence Community's understanding of al Qaeda was hampered by insufficient analytic focus and quality, particularly in terms of strategic analysis. Analysis and analysts were not always used effectively because of the perception in some quarters of the Intelligence Community that they were less important to agency counterterrorism missions than were operations personnel. The quality of counterterrorism analysis was inconsistent, and many analysts were inexperienced, unqualified, under-trained, and without access to critical information. As a result, there was a dearth of creative, aggressive analysis targeting bin Laden and a persistent inability to comprehend the collective significance of individual pieces of intelligence. These analytic deficiencies seriously under-

cut the ability of U.S. policymakers to understand the full nature of the threat, and to make fully informed decisions. . . .

6. Finding: Prior to Sept. 11, The Intelligence Community was not prepared to handle the challenge it faced in translating the volumes of foreign language counterterrorism intelligence it collected. Agencies within the Intelligence Community experienced backlogs in material awaiting translation, a shortage of language specialists and language-qualified field officers, and a readiness level of only 30% in the most critical terrorism-related languages. . . .

7. Finding: [Prior to Sept. 11, the Intelligence Community's ability to produce significant and timely signals intelligence on counterterrorism was limited by NSA's failure to address modern communications technology aggressively, continuing conflict between Intelligence Community agencies, NSA's cautious approach to any collection of intelligence relating to activities in the United States, and insufficient collaboration between NSA and the FBI regarding the potential for terrorist attacks within the United States]. . . .

8. Finding: The continuing erosion of NSA's program management expertise and experience has hindered its contribution to the fight against terrorism. NSA continues to have mixed results in providing timely technical solutions to modern intelligence collection, analysis, and information sharing problems. . . .

9. Finding: The U.S. Government does not presently bring together in one place all terrorism-related information from all sources. While CTC does manage overseas operations and has access to most Intelligence Community information, it does not collect terrorism-related information from all sources, domestic and foreign. Within the Intelligence Community, agencies did not adequately share relevant counterterrorism information, prior to Sept. 11. This breakdown in communications was the result of a number of factors, including differences in the agencies' missions, legal authorities and cultures. Information was not sufficiently shared, not only between different Intelligence Community agencies, but also within individual agencies, and between the intelligence and the law enforcement agencies. . . .

10. Finding: Serious problems in information sharing also persisted, prior to Sept. 11, between the Intelligence Community and relevant non-Intelligence Community agencies. This included other federal agencies as well as state and local authorities. This lack of communication and collaboration deprived those other entities, as well as the Intelligence Community, of access to potentially valuable information in the "war" against bin Laden. The Inquiry's focus on the Intelligence Community limited the extent to which it explored these issues, and this is an area that should be reviewed further.

Discussion: This Inquiry confirmed that, prior to Sept. 11, problems in information sharing reached beyond the boundaries of the Intelligence Community to encumber the flow of information to and from various other entities. At each level, communications with potentially valuable partners in the war against terrorism—other federal agencies, state and local authorities—were restricted. Witnesses testified that these restrictions on information flow occurred at great cost to the counterterrorism effort.

Officials in the Departments of Treasury, Transportation, and State told the Joint Inquiry that, although they receive threat information from the Intelligence Community, they do not always receive the information that adds context to the threat warnings. In many instances, officials told the Joint Inquiry, this lack of context prevents them from properly estimating the value of the threat information and taking preventive actions. The Joint Inquiry was also told that not all threat information in the possession of the Intelligence Community is shared with non-Intelligence Community entities that need it the most in order to counter the threats. . . .

11. Finding: Prior to Sept. 11, 2001, the Intelligence Community did not effectively develop and use human sources to penetrate the al Qaeda inner circle. This lack of reliable and knowledgeable human sources significantly limited the Community's ability to acquire intelligence that could be acted upon before the Sept. 11 attacks. In part, at least, the lack of unilateral (i.e., U.S.-recruited) counterterrorism sources was a product of an excessive reliance on foreign liaison services. . . .

12. Finding: During the summer of 2001, when the Intelligence Community was bracing for an imminent al Qaeda attack, difficulties with FBI applications for Foreign Intelligence Surveillance Act (FISA) surveillance and the FISA process led to a diminished level of coverage of suspected al Qaeda operatives in the United States. The effect of these difficulties was compounded by the perception that spread among FBI personnel at Headquarters and the field offices that the FISA process was lengthy and fraught with peril. . . .

14. Finding: [Senior U.S. military officials were reluctant to use U.S. military assets to conduct offensive counterterrorism efforts in Afghanistan, or to support or participate in CIA operations directed against al Qaeda prior to Sept. 11. At least part of this reluctance was driven by the military's view that the Intelligence Community was unable to provide the intelligence needed to support military operations. Although the U.S. military did participate in [deleted] counterterrorism efforts to counter Osama bin Laden's terrorist network prior to Sept. 11, 2001, most of the military's focus was on force protection]. . . .

15. Finding: The Intelligence Community depended heavily on foreign intelligence and law enforcement services for the collection of counterterrorism intelligence and the conduct of other counterterrorism activities. The results were mixed in terms of productive intelligence, reflecting vast differences in the ability and willingness of the various foreign services to target the bin Laden and al Qaeda network. Intelligence Community agencies sometimes failed to coordinate their relationships with foreign services adequately, either within the Intelligence Community or with broader U.S. Government liaison and foreign policy efforts. This reliance on foreign liaison services also resulted in a lack of focus on the development of unilateral human sources. . . .

16. Finding: [The activities of the Sept. 11 hijackers in the United States appear to have been financed, in large part, from monies sent to them from abroad and also brought in on their persons. Prior to Sept. 11, there was no coordinated U.S. Government-wide strategy to track terrorist funding and close down their financial support networks. There was also a reluctance in some parts of the U.S. Government to track terrorist funding and close down their financial support networks. As a result, the U.S. Government was unable to disrupt financial support for Osama bin Laden's terrorist activities effectively].

Discussion: [Tracking terrorist funds can be an especially effective means of identifying terrorists and terrorist organizations, unraveling and disrupting terrorist plots, and targeting terrorist financial assets for sanctions, seizures, and account closures. As with organized criminal activity, financial support is critically important to terrorist networks like al Qaeda. Prior to Sept. 11, 2001, however, no single U.S. Government agency was responsible for tracking terrorist funds, prioritizing and coordinating government-wide efforts, and seeking international collaboration in that effort. Some tracking of terrorist funds was undertaken before Sept. 11. For the most part, however, these efforts were unorganized and ad-hoc, and there was a reluctance to take actions such as seizures of assets and bank accounts and arrests of those involved in the funding. A U.S. Government official testified before the Joint Inquiry, for example, that this reluctance hindered counterterrorist efforts against bin Laden: "Treasury was concerned about any activity that could adversely affect the international financial system. . . .]"

D. RELATED FINDINGS

During the course of this Joint Inquiry, testimony and information were received that pertained to several issues involving broader, policy questions that reach beyond the boundaries of the Intelligence Community. In the three areas described below, the Inquiry finds that policy issues were relevant to our examination of the events of Sept. 11.

17. Finding: Despite intelligence reporting from 1998 through the summer of 2001 indicating that Osama bin Laden's terrorist network intended to strike inside the United States, the United States Government did not undertake a comprehensive effort to implement defensive measures in the United States.

Discussion: As noted earlier, the Joint Inquiry has established that the Intelligence Community acquired and disseminated from 1998 through the summer of 2001 intelligence reports indicating in broad terms that Osama bin Laden's network intended to carry out terrorist attacks inside the United States. This information encompassed, for example, indications of plots for attacks within the United States that would include:

- attacks on civil aviation;
- assassinations of U.S. public officials;
- use of high explosives;
- attacks on Washington, D.C., New York City, and cities on the West Coast;
- crashing aircraft into buildings as weapons; and
- using weapons of mass destruction.

The intelligence that was acquired and shared by the Intelligence Community was not specific as to time and place, but should have been sufficient to prompt action to insure a heightened sense of alert and implementation of additional defensive measures. Such actions could have included: strengthened civil aviation security measures; increased attention to watchlisting suspected terrorists so as to keep them out of the United States; greater collaboration with state and local law enforcement authorities concerning the scope and nature of the potential threat; a sustained national effort to inform and alert the American public to the growing danger; and improved capabilities to deal with the consequences of attacks involving mass destruction and casualties. The U.S. Government did take some steps in regard to detecting and preventing the use of weapons of mass destruction, but did not pursue a broad program of additional domestic defensive measures or public awareness. . . .

18. Finding: Between 1996 and September 2001, the counterterrorism strategy adopted by the U. S. Government did not succeed in eliminating Afghanistan as a sanctuary and training ground for Osama bin Laden's terrorist network. A range of instruments was used to counter al Qaeda, with law enforcement often emerging as a leading tool because other means were deemed not to be feasible or failed to produce results. Although numerous successful prosecutions were generated, law enforcement efforts were not adequate by themselves to target or eliminate bin Laden's sanctuary. While the United States persisted in observing the rule of law and accepted norms of international behavior, bin Laden and al Qaeda recognized no rules and thrived in the safehaven provided by Afghanistan. . . .

19. Finding: Prior to Sept. 11, the Intelligence Community and the U.S. Government labored to prevent attacks by Osama bin Laden and his terrorist network against the United States, but largely without the benefit of an alert, mobilized and committed American public. Despite intelligence information on the immediacy of the threat level in the spring and summer of 2001, the assumption prevailed in the U.S. Government that attacks of the magnitude of Sept. 11 could not happen here. As a result, there was insufficient effort to alert the American public to the reality and gravity of the threat.

Discussion: The record of this Joint Inquiry indicates that, prior to Sept. 11, 2001, the U.S. Intelligence Community was involved in fighting a "war" against bin Laden largely without the benefit of what some would call its most potent weapon in that effort: an alert and committed American public. Senior levels of the Intelligence Community, as well as senior U.S. Government policymakers, were aware of the danger posed by bin Laden. Information that was shared with senior U.S. Government officials, but was not made available to the American public because of its national security classification, was explicit about the gravity and immediacy of the threat posed by bin Laden. . . .

Political Charts

Summary of Presidential Elections, 1789–2004

Year	No. of states	Candidates	Party	Electoral vote	Popular vote
1789[1]	10	**George Washington**	**Fed.**	**69**	—[2]
		John Adams	Fed.	34	
1792[1]	15	**George Washington**	**Fed.**	**132**	—[2]
		John Adams	Fed.	77	
1796[1]	16	**John Adams**	**Fed.**	**71**	—[2]
		Thomas Jefferson	Dem.-Rep.	68	
1800[1]	16	**Thomas Jefferson**	**Dem.-Rep.**	**73**	—[2]
		Aaron Burr	Dem.-Rep.	73	
		John Adams	Fed.	65	
		Charles Cotesworth Pinckney	Fed.	64	
1804	17	**Thomas Jefferson**	**Dem.-Rep.**	**162**	—[2]
		George Clinton			
		Charles Cotesworth Pinckney	Fed.	64	
		Rufus King			
1808	17	**James Madison**	**Dem.-Rep.**	**122**	—[2]
		George Clinton			
		Charles Cotesworth Pinckney	Fed.	64	
		Rufus King			
1812	18	**James Madison**	**Dem.-Rep.**	**128**	—[2]
		Elbridge Gerry			
		George Clinton	Fed.	89	
		Jared Ingersoll			
1816	19	**James Monroe**	**Dem.-Rep.**	**183**	—[2]
		Daniel D. Tompkins			
		Rufus King	Fed.	34	
		John Howard			
1820	24	**James Monroe**	**Dem.-Rep.**	**231**[3]	—[2]
		Daniel D. Tompkins			
1824[4]	24	**John Quincy Adams**	**Dem.-Rep.**	**99**	**113,122 (30.9%)**
		John C. Calhoun			
		Andrew Jackson	Dem.-Rep.	84	151,271 (41.3%)
		Nathan Sanford			
1828	24	**Andrew Jackson**	**Dem.-Rep.**	**178**	**642,553 (56.0%)**
		John C. Calhoun			
		John Quincy Adams	Nat.-Rep.	83	500,897 (43.6%)
		Richard Rush			
1832[5]	24	**Andrew Jackson**	**Dem.**	**219**	**701,780 (54.2%)**
		Martin Van Buren			
		Henry Clay	Nat.-Rep.	49	484,205 (37.4%)
		John Sergeant			
1836[6]	26	**Martin Van Buren**	**Dem.**	**170**	**764,176 (50.8%)**
		Richard M. Johnson			
		William Henry Harrison	Whig	73	550,816 (36.6%)
		Francis Granger			

Year	No. of states	Candidates	Party	Electoral vote	Popular vote
1840	26	**William Henry Harrison**	Whig	234	1,275,390 (52.9%)
		John Tyler			
		Martin Van Buren	Dem.	60	1,128,854 (46.8%)
		Richard M. Johnson			
1844	26	**James K. Polk**	**Dem.**	**170**	**1,339,494 (49.5%)**
		George M. Dallas			
		Henry Clay	Whig	105	1,300,004 (48.1%)
		Theodore Frelinghuysen			
1848	30	**Zachary Taylor**	**Whig**	**163**	**1,361,393 (47.3%)**
		Millard Fillmore			
		Lewis Cass	Dem.	127	1,223,460 (42.5%)
		William O. Butler			
1852	31	**Franklin Pierce**	**Dem.**	**254**	**1,607,510 (50.8%)**
		William R. King			
		Winfield Scott	Whig	42	1,386,942 (43.9%)
		William A. Graham			
1856[7]	31	**James Buchanan**	**Dem.**	**174**	**1,836,072 (45.3%)**
		John C. Breckinridge			
		John C. Fremont	Rep.	114	1,342,345 (33.1%)
		William L. Dayton			
1860[8]	33	**Abraham Lincoln**	**Rep.**	**180**	**1,865,908 (39.8%)**
		Hannibal Hamlin			
		Stephen A. Douglas	Dem.	12	1,380,202 (29.5%)
		Herschel V. Johnson			
1864[9]	36	**Abraham Lincoln**	**Rep.**	**212**	**2,218,388 (55.0%)**
		Andrew Johnson			
		George B. McClellan	Dem.	21	1,812,807 (45.0%)
		George H. Pendleton			
1868[10]	37	**Ulysses S. Grant**	**Rep.**	**214**	**3,013,650 (52.7%)**
		Schuyler Colfax			
		Horatio Seymour	Dem.	80	2,708,744 (47.3%)
		Francis P. Blair Jr.			
1872	37	**Ulysses S. Grant**	**Rep.**	**286**	**3,598,235 (55.6%)**
		Henry Wilson			
		Horace Greeley	Dem.	—[11]	2,834,761 (43.8%)
		Benjamin Gratz Brown			
1876	38	**Rutherford B. Hayes**	**Rep.**	**185**	**4,034,311 (47.9%)**
		William A. Wheeler			
		Samuel J. Tilden	Dem.	184	4,288,546 (51.0%)
		Thomas A. Hendricks			
1880	38	**James A. Garfield**	**Rep.**	**214**	**4,446,158 (48.3%)**
		Chester A. Arthur			
		Winfield S. Hancock	Dem.	155	4,444,260 (48.2%)
		William H. English			
1884	38	**Grover Cleveland**	**Dem.**	**219**	**4,874,621 (48.5%)**
		Thomas A. Hendricks			
		James G. Blaine	Rep.	182	4,848,936 (48.2%)
		John A. Logan			

(table continues)

Year	No. of states	Candidates	Party	Electoral vote	Popular vote
1888	38	**Benjamin Harrison** *Levi P. Morton*	**Rep.**	233	**5,443,892 (47.8%)**
		Grover Cleveland *Allen G. Thurman*	Dem.	168	5,534,488 (48.6%)
1892[12]	44	**Grover Cleveland** *Adlai E. Stevenson*	**Dem.**	277	**5,551,883 (46.1%)**
		Benjamin Harrison *Whitelaw Reid*	Rep.	145	5,179,244 (43.0%)
1896	45	**William McKinley** *Garret A. Hobart*	**Rep.**	271	**7,108,480 (51.0%)**
		William J. Bryan *Arthur Sewall*	Dem.	176	6,511,495 (46.7%)
1900	45	**William McKinley** *Theodore Roosevelt*	**Rep.**	292	**7,218,039 (51.7%)**
		William J. Bryan *Adlai E. Stevenson*	Dem.	155	6,358,345 (45.5%)
1904	45	**Theodore Roosevelt** *Charles W. Fairbanks*	**Rep.**	336	**7,626,593 (56.4%)**
		Alton B. Parker *Henry G. Davis*	Dem.	140	5,028,898 (37.6%)
1908	46	**William Howard Taft** *James S. Sherman*	**Rep.**	321	**7,676,258 (51.6%)**
		William J. Bryan *John W. Kern*	Dem.	162	6,406,801 (43.0%)
1912[13]	48	**Woodrow Wilson** *Thomas R. Marshall*	**Dem.**	435	**6,293,152 (41.8%)**
		William Howard Taft *James S. Sherman*	Rep.	8	3,486,333 (23.2%)
1916	48	**Woodrow Wilson** *Thomas R. Marshall*	**Dem.**	277	**9,126,300 (49.2%)**
		Charles E. Hughes *Charles W. Fairbanks*	Rep.	254	8,546,789 (46.1%)
1920	48	**Warren G. Harding** *Calvin Coolidge*	**Rep.**	404	**16,133,314 (60.3%)**
		James M. Cox *Franklin D. Roosevelt*	Dem.	127	9,140,884 (34.2%)
1924[14]	48	**Calvin Coolidge** *Charles G. Dawes*	**Rep.**	382	**15,717,553 (54.1%)**
		John W. Davis *Charles W. Bryan*	Dem.	136	8,386,169 (28.8%)
1928	48	**Herbert C. Hoover** *Charles Curtis*	**Rep.**	444	**21,411,991 (58.2%)**
		Alfred E. Smith *Joseph T. Robinson*	Dem.	87	15,000,185 (40.8%)
1932	48	**Franklin D. Roosevelt** *John N. Garner*	**Dem.**	472	**22,825,016 (57.4%)**
		Herbert C. Hoover *Charles Curtis*	Rep.	59	15,758,397 (39.6%)
1936	48	**Franklin D. Roosevelt** *John N. Garner*	**Dem.**	523	**27,747,636 (60.8%)**
		Alfred M. Landon *Frank Knox*	Rep.	8	16,679,543 (36.5%)
1940	48	**Franklin D. Roosevelt** *Henry A. Wallace*	**Dem.**	449	**27,263,448 (54.7%)**
		Wendell L. Willkie *Charles L. McNary*	Rep.	82	22,336,260 (44.8%)
1944	48	**Franklin D. Roosevelt** *Harry S. Truman*	**Dem.**	432	**25,611,936 (53.4%)**
		Thomas E. Dewey *John W. Bricker*	Rep.	99	22,013,372 (45.9%)
1948[15]	48	**Harry S. Truman** *Alben W. Barkley*	**Dem.**	303	**24,105,587 (49.5%)**
		Thomas E. Dewey *Earl Warren*	Rep.	198	21,970,017 (45.1%)
1952	48	**Dwight D. Eisenhower** *Richard M. Nixon*	**Rep.**	442	**33,936,137 (55.1%)**
		Adlai E. Stevenson II *John J. Sparkman*	Dem.	89	27,314,649 (44.4%)
1956[16]	48	**Dwight D. Eisenhower** *Richard M. Nixon*	**Rep.**	457	**35,585,245 (57.4%)**
		Adlai E. Stevenson II *Estes Kefauver*	Dem.	73	26,030,172 (42.0%)
1960[17]	50	**John F. Kennedy** *Lyndon B. Johnson*	**Dem.**	303	**34,221,344 (49.7%)**
		Richard Nixon *Henry Cabot Lodge*	Rep.	219	34,106,671 (49.5%)
1964	50*	**Lyndon B. Johnson** *Hubert H. Humphrey*	**Dem.**	486	**43,126,584 (61.1%)**
		Barry Goldwater *William E. Miller*	Rep.	52	27,177,838 (38.5%)
1968[18]	50*	**Richard Nixon** *Spiro T. Agnew*	**Rep.**	301	**31,785,148 (43.4%)**
		Hubert H. Humphrey *Edmund S. Muskie*	Dem.	191	31,274,503 (42.7%)
1972[19]	50*	**Richard Nixon** *Spiro T. Agnew*	**Rep.**	520	**47,170,179 (60.7%)**
		George McGovern *Sargent Shriver*	Dem.	17	29,171,791 (37.5%)
1976[20]	50*	**Jimmy Carter** *Walter F. Mondale*	**Dem.**	297	**40,830,763 (50.1%)**
		Gerald R. Ford *Robert Dole*	Rep.	240	39,147,793 (48.0%)
1980	50*	**Ronald Reagan** *George Bush*	**Rep.**	489	**43,904,153 (50.7%)**
		Jimmy Carter *Walter F. Mondale*	Dem.	49	35,483,883 (41.0%)
1984	50*	**Ronald Reagan** *George Bush*	**Rep.**	525	**54,455,074(58.8%)**
		Walter F. Mondale *Geraldine Ferraro*	Dem.	13	37,577,137 (40.6%)
1988[21]	50*	**George Bush** *Dan Quayle*	**Rep.**	426	**48,881,278 (53.4%)**
		Michael S. Dukakis *Lloyd Bentsen*	Dem.	111	41,805,374 (45.6%)

Year	No. of states	Candidates	Party	Electoral vote	Popular vote	Year	No. of states	Candidates	Party	Electoral vote	Popular vote
1992	50*	**Bill Clinton** *Al Gore*	**Dem.**	**370**	**44,908,233 (43.0%)**	2000[22]	50*	**George W. Bush** *Richard B. Cheney*	**Rep.**	**271**	**50,455,156 (47.9%)**
		George Bush *Dan Quayle*	Rep.	168	39,102,282 (37.4%)			Al Gore *Joseph I. Lieberman*	Dem.	266	50,992,335 (48.4%)
1996	50*	**Bill Clinton** *Al Gore*	**Dem.**	**379**	**47,402,357 (49.2%)**	2004[23]	50*	**George W. Bush** *Richard B. Cheney*	**Rep.**	**286**	**62,040,610 (50.7%)**
		Bob Dole *Jack Kemp*	Rep.	159	39,198,755 (40.7%)			John Kerry *John Edwards*	Dem.	251	59,028,439 (48.3%)

SOURCES: Harold W. Stanley and Richard G. Niemi, *Vital Statistics on American Politics,* 5th ed. (Washington, D.C.: CQ Press, 1995), table 3-13; Richard M. Scammon, Alice V. McGillivray, and Rhodes Cook, *America Votes 24* (Washington, D.C.: CQ Press, 2001), 9, 13.

NOTES: Bold indicates victors. In the elections of 1789, 1792, 1796, and 1800, each candidate ran for the office of president. The candidate with the second highest number of electoral votes became vice president. For elections after 1800, italic indicates vice-presidential candidates. Dem.-Rep.—Democratic-Republican; Fed.—Federalist; Nat.-Rep.—National-Republican; Dem.—Democratic; Rep.—Republican.   1. Elections of 1789–1800 were held under rules that did not allow separate voting for president and vice president.   2. Popular vote returns are not shown before 1824 because consistent, reliable data are not available.   3. Monroe ran unopposed. One electoral vote was cast for John Adams and Richard Stockton, who were not candidates.   4. 1824: All four candidates represented Democratic-Republican factions. William H. Craw-ford received 41 electoral votes, and Henry Clay received 37 votes. Since no candidate received a majority, the election was decided (in Adams's favor) by the House of Representatives.   5. 1832: Two electoral votes were not cast.   6. 1836: Other Whig candidates receiving electoral votes were Hugh L. White, who received 26 votes, and Daniel Webster, who received 14 votes.   7. 1856: Millard Fillmore, Whig-American, received 8 electoral votes.   8. 1860: John C. Breckinridge, Southern Democrat, re-ceived 72 electoral votes. John Bell, Constitutional Union, received 39 electoral votes.   9. 1864: Eighty-one electoral votes were not cast.   10. 1868: Twenty-three elec-toral votes were not cast.   11. 1872: Horace Greeley, Democrat, died after the election. In the electoral college, Democratic electoral votes went to Thomas Hendricks, 42 votes; Benjamin Gratz Brown, 18 votes; Charles J. Jenkins, 2 votes; and David Davis, 1 vote. Seventeen electoral votes were not cast.   12. 1892: James B. Weaver, People's Party, received 22 electoral votes.   13. 1912: Theodore Roosevelt, Progressive Party, received 86 electoral votes.   14. 1924: Robert M. La Follette, Progressive Party, re-ceived 13 electoral votes.   15. 1948: J. Strom Thurmond, States' Rights Party, received 39 electoral votes.   16. 1956: Walter B. Jones, Democrat, received 1 electoral vote. 17. 1960: Harry Flood Byrd, Democrat, received 15 electoral votes.   18. 1968: George C. Wallace, American Independent Party, received 46 electoral votes.   19. 1972: John Hospers, Libertarian Party, received 1 electoral vote.   20. 1976: Ronald Reagan, Republican, received 1 electoral vote.   21. 1988: Lloyd Bentsen, the Democratic vice-presidential nominee, received 1 electoral vote for president.   22. 2000: One District of Columbia elector did not vote.   23. 2004: A Democratic elector in Minnesota cast a vote for Edwards rather than Kerry.   *Fifty states plus the District of Columbia.

Victorious Party in Presidential Races, 1860–2004

State	1860	1864	1868	1872	1876	1880	1884	1888	1892	1896	1900	1904	1908	1912	1916	1920	1924	1928
Alabama	SD	[2]	R	R	D	D	D	D	D	D	D	D	D	D	D	D	D	D
Alaska																		
Arizona														D	D	R	R	R
Arkansas	SD	[2]	R	[4]	D	D	D	D	D	D	D	D	D	D	D	D	D	D
California	R	R	R	R	R	D[6]	R	R	D[7]	R[12]	R	R	R	PR	D	R	R	R
Colorado					R	R	R	R	PP	D	D	R	D	D	D	R	R	R
Connecticut	R	R	R	R	D	R	D	D	D	R	R	R	R	D	R	R	R	R
Delaware	SD	D	D	R	D	D	D	D	D	R	R	R	R	D	R	R	R	R
Dist. of Columbia																		
Florida	SD	[2]	R	R	R	D	D	D	D	D	D	D	D	D	D	D	D	R
Georgia	SD	[2]	D	D[5]	D	D	D	D	D	D	D	D	D	D	D	D	D	D
Hawaii																		
Idaho									PP	D	D	R	R	D	D	R	R	R
Illinois	R	R	R	R	R	R	R	R	D	R	R	R	R	D	R	R	R	R
Indiana	R	R	R	R	D	R	D	R	D	R	R	R	R	D	R	R	R	R
Iowa	R	R	R	R	R	R	R	R	R	R	R	R	R	D	R	R	R	R
Kansas		R	R	R	R	R	R	R	PP	D	R	R	R	D	D	R	R	R
Kentucky	CU	D	D	D	D	D	D	D	D	R[13]	D	D	D	D	D	D	R	R
Louisiana	SD	[2]	D	[4]	R	D	D	D	D	D	D	D	D	D	D	D	D	D
Maine	R	R	R	R	R	R	R	R	R	R	R	R	R	D	R	R	R	R
Maryland	SD	R	D	D	D	D	D	D	D	R	R	D[14]	D[15]	D	D	R	R	R
Massachusetts	R	R	R	R	R	R	R	R	R	R	R	R	R	D	R	R	R	D
Michigan	R	R	R	R	R	R	R	R	R[8]	R	R	R	R	PR	R	R	R	R
Minnesota	R	R	R	R	R	R	R	R	R	R	R	R	R	PR	R	R	R	R
Mississippi	SD	[2]	[3]	R	D	D	D	D	D	D	D	D	D	D	D	D	D	D
Missouri	D	R	R	D	D	D	D	D	D	D	D	R	R	D	R	R	R	R
Montana									R	D	D	R	R	D	D	R	R	R
Nebraska			R	R	R	R	R	R	R	D	R	R	D	D	D	R	R	R
Nevada		R	R	R	R	R	D	R	PP	D	D	R	D	D	D	R	R	R
New Hampshire	R	R	R	R	R	R	R	R	R	R	R	R	R	D	R	R	R	R
New Jersey	R[1]	D	D	R	D	D	D	D	D	R	R	R	R	D	R	R	R	R
New Mexico														D	D	R	R	R
New York	R	R	D	R	D	R	D	R	D	R	R	R	R	D	R	R	R	R
North Carolina	SD	[2]	R	R	D	D	D	D	D	D	D	D	D	D	D	D	D	R
North Dakota									[9]	R	R	R	R	D	D	R	R	R
Ohio	R	R	R	R	R	R	R	R	R[10]	R	R	R	R	D	R	R	R	R
Oklahoma													D	D	D	R	D	R
Oregon	R	R	D	R	R	R	R	R	R[11]	R	R	R	R	D	R	R	R	R
Pennsylvania	R	R	R	R	R	R	R	R	R	R	R	R	R	PR	R	R	R	R
Rhode Island	R	R	R	R	R	R	R	R	R	R	R	R	R	D	R	R	R	D
South Carolina	SD	[2]	R	R	D	D	D	D	D	D	D	D	D	D	D	D	D	D
South Dakota									R	D	R	R	R	PR	R	R	R	R
Tennessee	CU	[2]	R	D	D	D	D	D	D	D	D	D	D	D	D	R	D	R
Texas	SD	[2]	[3]	D	D	D	D	D	D	D	D	D					D	R
Utah										D	D	R	R	R	D	R	R	R
Vermont	R	R	R	R	R	R	R	R	R	R	R	R	R	R	R	R	R	R
Virginia	CU	[2]	[3]	R	D	D	D	D	D	D	D	D	D	D	D	D	D	R
Washington									R	D	R	R	R	PR	D	R	R	R
West Virginia		R	R	R	D	D	D	D	D	R	R	R	R	D	R[16]	R	R	R
Wisconsin	R	R	R	R	R	R	R	R	D	R	R	R	R	D	R	R	PR	R
Wyoming									R	D	R	R	R	D	D	R	R	R
Winning Party	R	R	R	R	R	R	D	R	D	R	R	R	R	D	D	R	R	R

Note: With the exception of the District of Columbia, blanks indicate states not yet admitted to the Union. The District of Columbia received the presidential vote in 1961.

Key: AI-American Independent Party; CU-Constitutional Union Party; D-Democratic Party; PP-People's Party; PR-Progressive (Bull Moose) Party; R-Republican Party; SD-Southern Democratic Party; SR-States' Rights Democratic Party.

1. Four electors voted Republican; three, Democratic.
2. Confederate states did not vote in 1864.
3. Did not vote in 1868.
4. Votes were not counted.
5. Three votes for Greeley not counted.
6. Five electors voted Democratic; one, Republican.
7. Eight electors voted Democratic; one, Republican.
8. Nine electors voted Republican; five, Democratic.
9. One vote each for Democratic, Republican and People's parties.
10. Twenty-two electors voted Republican; one, Democratic.
11. Three electors voted Republican; one, People's Party.

| | | | | | | | | | | | | | | | | | | | Number of times parties won | | |
| | | | | | | | | | | | | | | | | | | | | | |
1932	1936	1940	1944	1948	1952	1956	1960	1964	1968	1972	1976	1980	1984	1988	1992	1996	2000	2004	Dems.	Reps.	Other
D	D	D	D	SR	D	D[18]	D[19]	R	AI	R	D	R	R	R	R	R	R	R	22	11	3
							R	D	R	R	R	R	R	R	R	R	R	R	1	11	0
D	D	D	D	D	R	R	R	R	R	R	R	R	R	R	D	R	R	R	8	16	0
D	D	D	D	D	D	D	D	D	AI	R	R	R	R	R	D	R	R	R	26	7	2
D	D	D	D	D	R	R	R	D	D	R	R	R	R	R	D	D	D	D	13	23	1
D	D	R	R	D	R	R	R	D	R	R	R	R	R	R	D	R	R	R	10	22	1
R	D	D	D	R	R	D	D	D	D	R	R	R	R	R	D	D	D	D	15	22	0
R	D	D	D	R	R	R	D	D	R	R	D	R	R	R	D	D	D	D	18	18	1
							D	D	D	D	D	D	D	D	D	D	D[26]	D	11	0	0
D	D	D	D	D	R	R	R	D	R	R	D	R	R	R	D	R	R	R	20	15	1
D	D	D	D	D	D	D	D	R	AI	R	D	R	R	R	D	R	R	R	27	7	2
							D	D	D	R	D	D	R	D	D	D	D	D	10	2	0
D	D	D	D	D	R	R	R	D	R	R	R	R	R	R	R	R	R	R	10	18	1
D	D	D	D	D	R	R	D	D	R	R	R	R	R	R	D	D	D	D	13	24	0
D	D	R	R	R	R	R	R	D	R	R	R	R	R	R	R	R	R	R	7	30	0
D	D	R	R	D	R	R	R	D	R	R	R	R	D	D	D	D	D	D	9	28	0
R	R	R	R	R	R	R	R	D	R	R	R	R	R	R	R	R	R	R	6	29	1
D	D	D	D	D	D	R	R	D	R	R	D	R	R	D	R	D	R	R	24	12	1
D	D	D	D	SR	D	R	D	R	AI	R	D	R	R	R	D	R	R	R	23	9	3
R	R	R	R	R	R	R	R	D	D	R	R	R	R	D	D	D	D	D	7	30	0
D	D	D	D	R	R	R	D	D	D	R	D	D	R	D	D	D	D	D	24	12	1
D	D	D	D	D	R	R	D	D	D	D	D	R	R	D	D	D	D	D	17	20	1
D	D	R	D	R	R	R	D	D	D	R	R	R	R	D	D	D	D	D	10	26	1
D	D	D	D	D	R	R	D	D	D	R	D	D	D	D	D	D	D[27]	D	16	20	1
D	D	D	D	SR	D	D	[20]	R	AI	R	D	R	R	R	R	R	R	R	21	10	4
D	D	D	D	D	R	R	D	D	R	R	D	R	R	R	R	R	R	R	22	15	0
D	D	D	D	D	R	R	R	D	R	R	R	R	R	R	R	R	R	R	11	18	0
D	D	R	R	R	R	R	D	R	R	R	R	R	R	R	R	R	R	R	7	28	0
D	D	D	D	D	R	R	D	D	R	R	R	R	R	D	R	R	R	R	15	20	1
R	D	D	D	R	R	R	R	D	R	R	R	R	R	D	D	R	R	D	9	28	0
D	D	D	D	R	R	R	D	D	R	R	R	R	R	D	D	D	D	D	18	19	0
D	D	D	D	D	R	R	D	D	R	R	R	R	R	D	D	D	D	R	12	12	0
D	D	D	D	R	R	R	D	D	R	D	R	R	R	D	D	D	D	D	18	19	0
D	D	D	D	D	D	D	D	R[22]	R	D	R	R	R	R	R	R	R	R	23	12	1
D	D	R	R	R	R	R	R	D	R	R	R	R	R	R	R	R	R	R	5	23	1
D	D	D	R	D	R	R	R	D	R	R	D	R	R	R	R	R	R	R	10	27	0
D	D	D	D	D	R	R	R[21]	D	R	R	R	R	R	R	R	R	R	R	10	15	0
D	D	D	D	R	R	R	R	D	R	R	R	R	D	D	D	D	D	D	12	25	0
R	D	D	D	R	R	R	D	D	D	R	D	R	R	R	D	D	D	D	11	25	1
D	D	D	D	D	R	R	D	D	D	R	D	D	R	D	D	D	D	D	17	20	0
D	D	D	D	SR	D	D	D	R	R	R	D	R	R	R	R	R	R	R	21	13	2
D	D	R	R	R	R	R	R	D	R	R	R	R	R	R	R	R	R	R	4	24	1
D	D	D	D	D[17]	R	R	R	D	R	D	R	R	R	D	R	R	R	R	22	13	1
D	D	D	D	D	R	R	D	D	R	R	D	R	R	R	R	R	R	R	23	11	1
D	D	D	D	D	R	R	R	D	R	R	R	R	R	R	R	R	R	R	8	20	0
R	R	R	R	R	R	R	R	D	R	R	R	R	R	D	D	D	D	D	5	32	0
D	D	D	D	D	R	D	D	D	D	R[23]	R	R	R	R	R	R	R	R	19	15	1
D	D	D	D	D	R	R	R	D	D	R	R[24]	R	R	D	D	D	D	D	14	14	1
D	D	D	D	D	D	R	D	D	D	R	D	D	R	D[25]	D	D	R	R	20	16	0
D	D	D	R	D	R	R	R	D	R	D	R	R	D	D	D	D	D	D	13	23	1
D	D	D	R	D	R	R	R	D	R	R	R	R	R	R	R	R	R	R	8	21	0
D	D	D	D	D	R	R	D	D	R	R	D	R	R	R	D	D	R	R	14	23	0

12. Eight electors voted Republican; one, Democratic.
13. Twelve electors voted Republican; one, Democratic.
14. Seven electors voted Democratic; one, Republican.
15. Six electors voted Democratic; two, Republican.
16. Seven electors voted Republican; one, Democratic.
17. Eleven electors voted Democratic; one, States' Rights.
18. One elector voted for Walter B. Jones.
19. Six of eleven electors voted for Harry F. Byrd.

20. Eight independent electors voted for Byrd.
21. One vote cast for Byrd.
22. Twelve electors voted Republican; one, American Independent.
23. One elector voted Libertarian.
24. One elector voted for Ronald Reagan.
25. One elector voted for Lloyd Bentsen.
26. One elector did not vote.
27. A Democratic elector cast a vote for John Edwards rather than John Kerry.

2000 Presidential Election

State	Total vote	George W. Bush (Republican) Votes	%	Al Gore (Democrat) Votes	%	Ralph Nader (Green) Votes	%	Patrick J. Buchanan (Reform) Votes	%	Other Votes	%	Plurality	
Alabama	1,666,272	941,173	56.5	692,611	41.6	18,323	1.1	6,351	0.4	7,814	0.5	248,562	R
Alaska	285,560	167,398	58.6	79,004	27.7	28,747	10.1	5,192	1.8	5,219	1.8	88,394	R
Arizona	1,532,016	781,652	51.0	685,341	44.7	45,645	3.0	12,373	0.8	7,005	0.5	96,311	R
Arkansas	921,781	472,940	51.3	422,768	45.9	13,421	1.5	7,358	0.8	5,294	0.6	50,172	R
California	10,965,856	4,567,429	41.7	5,861,203	53.4	418,707	3.8	44,987	0.4	75,530	0.7	1,293,774	D
Colorado	1,741,368	883,748	50.8	738,227	42.4	91,434	5.3	10,465	0.6	17,494	1.0	145,521	R
Connecticut	1,459,525	561,094	38.4	816,015	55.9	64,452	4.4	4,731	0.3	13,233	0.9	254,921	D
Delaware	327,622	137,288	41.9	180,068	55.0	8,307	2.5	777	0.2	1,182	0.4	42,780	D
Florida	5,963,110	2,912,790	48.8	2,912,253	48.8	97,488	1.6	17,484	0.3	23,095	0.4	537	R
Georgia	2,596,645	1,419,720	54.7	1,116,230	43.0	13,273	0.5	10,926	0.4	36,496	1.4	303,490	R
Hawaii	367,951	137,845	37.5	205,286	55.8	21,623	5.9	1,071	0.3	2,126	0.6	67,441	D
Idaho	501,621	336,937	67.2	138,637	27.6	12,292	2.5	7,615	1.5	6,140	1.2	198,300	R
Illinois	4,742,123	2,019,421	42.6	2,589,026	54.6	103,759	2.2	16,106	0.3	13,811	0.3	569,605	D
Indiana	2,199,302	1,245,836	56.6	901,980	41.0	18,531	0.8	16,959	0.8	15,996	0.7	343,856	R
Iowa	1,315,563	634,373	48.2	638,517	48.5	29,374	2.2	5,731	0.4	7,568	0.6	4,144	D
Kansas	1,072,218	622,332	58.0	399,276	37.2	36,086	3.4	7,370	0.7	7,154	0.7	223,056	R
Kentucky	1,544,187	872,492	56.5	638,898	41.4	23,192	1.5	4,173	0.3	5,432	0.4	233,594	R
Louisiana	1,765,656	927,871	52.6	792,344	44.9	20,473	1.2	14,356	0.8	10,612	0.6	135,527	R
Maine	651,817	286,616	44.0	319,951	49.1	37,127	5.7	4,443	0.7	3,680	0.6	33,335	D
Maryland	2,020,480	813,797	40.3	1,140,782	56.5	53,768	2.7	4,248	0.2	7,885	0.4	326,985	D
Massachusetts	2,702,984	878,502	32.5	1,616,487	59.8	173,564	6.4	11,149	0.4	23,282	0.9	737,985	D
Michigan	4,232,711	1,953,139	46.1	2,170,418	51.3	84,165	2.0	2,061	0.0	22,928	0.5	217,279	D
Minnesota	2,438,685	1,109,659	45.5	1,168,266	47.9	126,696	5.2	22,166	0.9	11,898	0.5	58,607	D
Mississippi	994,184	572,844	57.6	404,614	40.7	8,122	0.8	2,265	0.2	6,339	0.6	168,230	R
Missouri	2,359,892	1,189,924	50.4	1,111,138	47.1	38,515	1.6	9,818	0.4	10,497	0.4	78,786	R
Montana	410,997	240,178	58.4	137,126	33.4	24,437	5.9	5,697	1.4	3,559	0.9	103,052	R
Nebraska	697,019	433,862	62.2	231,780	33.3	24,540	3.5	3,646	0.5	3,191	0.5	202,082	R
Nevada	608,970	301,575	49.5	279,978	46.0	15,008	2.5	4,747	0.8	7,662	1.3	21,597	R
New Hampshire	569,081	273,559	48.1	266,348	46.8	22,198	3.9	2,615	0.5	4,361	0.8	7,211	R
New Jersey	3,187,226	1,284,173	40.3	1,788,850	56.1	94,554	3.0	6,989	0.2	12,660	0.4	504,677	D
New Mexico	598,605	286,417	47.8	286,783	47.9	21,251	3.6	1,392	0.2	2,762	0.5	366	D
New York	6,821,999	2,403,374	35.2	4,107,697	60.2	244,030	3.6	31,599	0.5	35,299	0.5	1,704,323	D
North Carolina	2,911,262	1,631,163	56.0	1,257,692	43.2	—	0.0	8,874	0.3	13,533	0.5	373,471	R
North Dakota	288,256	174,852	60.7	95,284	33.1	9,486	3.3	7,288	2.5	1,346	0.5	79,568	R
Ohio	4,701,998	2,350,363	50.0	2,183,628	46.4	117,799	2.5	26,721	0.6	23,484	0.5	166,735	R
Oklahoma	1,234,229	744,337	60.3	474,276	38.4	—	0.0	9,014	0.7	6,602	0.5	270,061	R
Oregon	1,533,968	713,577	46.5	720,342	47.0	77,357	5.0	7,063	0.5	15,629	1.0	6,765	D
Pennsylvania	4,913,119	2,281,127	46.4	2,485,967	50.6	103,392	2.1	16,023	0.3	26,610	0.5	204,840	D
Rhode Island	409,047	130,555	31.9	249,508	61.0	25,052	6.1	2,273	0.6	1,659	0.4	118,953	D
South Carolina	1,382,717	785,937	56.8	565,561	40.9	20,200	1.5	3,519	0.3	7,500	0.5	220,376	R
South Dakota	316,269	190,700	60.3	118,804	37.6	—	0.0	3,322	1.1	3,443	1.1	71,896	R
Tennessee	2,076,181	1,061,949	51.1	981,720	47.3	19,781	1.0	4,250	0.2	8,481	0.4	80,229	R
Texas	6,407,637	3,799,639	59.3	2,433,746	38.0	137,994	2.2	12,394	0.2	23,864	0.4	1,365,893	R
Utah	770,754	515,096	66.8	203,053	26.3	35,850	4.7	9,319	1.2	7,436	1.0	312,043	R
Vermont	294,308	119,775	40.7	149,022	50.6	20,374	6.9	2,192	0.7	2,945	1.0	29,247	D
Virginia	2,739,447	1,437,490	52.5	1,217,290	44.4	59,398	2.2	5,455	0.2	19,814	0.7	220,200	R
Washington	2,487,433	1,108,864	44.6	1,247,652	50.2	103,002	4.1	7,171	0.3	20,744	0.8	138,788	D
West Virginia	648,124	336,475	51.9	295,497	45.6	10,680	1.6	3,169	0.5	2,303	0.4	40,978	R
Wisconsin	2,598,607	1,237,279	47.6	1,242,987	47.8	94,070	3.6	11,446	0.4	12,825	0.5	5,708	D
Wyoming	218,351	147,947	67.8	60,481	27.7	4,625	2.1	2,724	1.2	2,574	1.2	87,466	R
Dist. of Col.	201,894	18,073	9.0	171,923	85.2	10,576	5.2	—	0.0	1,322	0.7	153,850	D
Total	105,396,627	50,455,156	47.9	50,992,335	48.4	2,882,738	2.7	449,077	0.4	617,321	0.6	537,179	D

2000 Electoral Votes

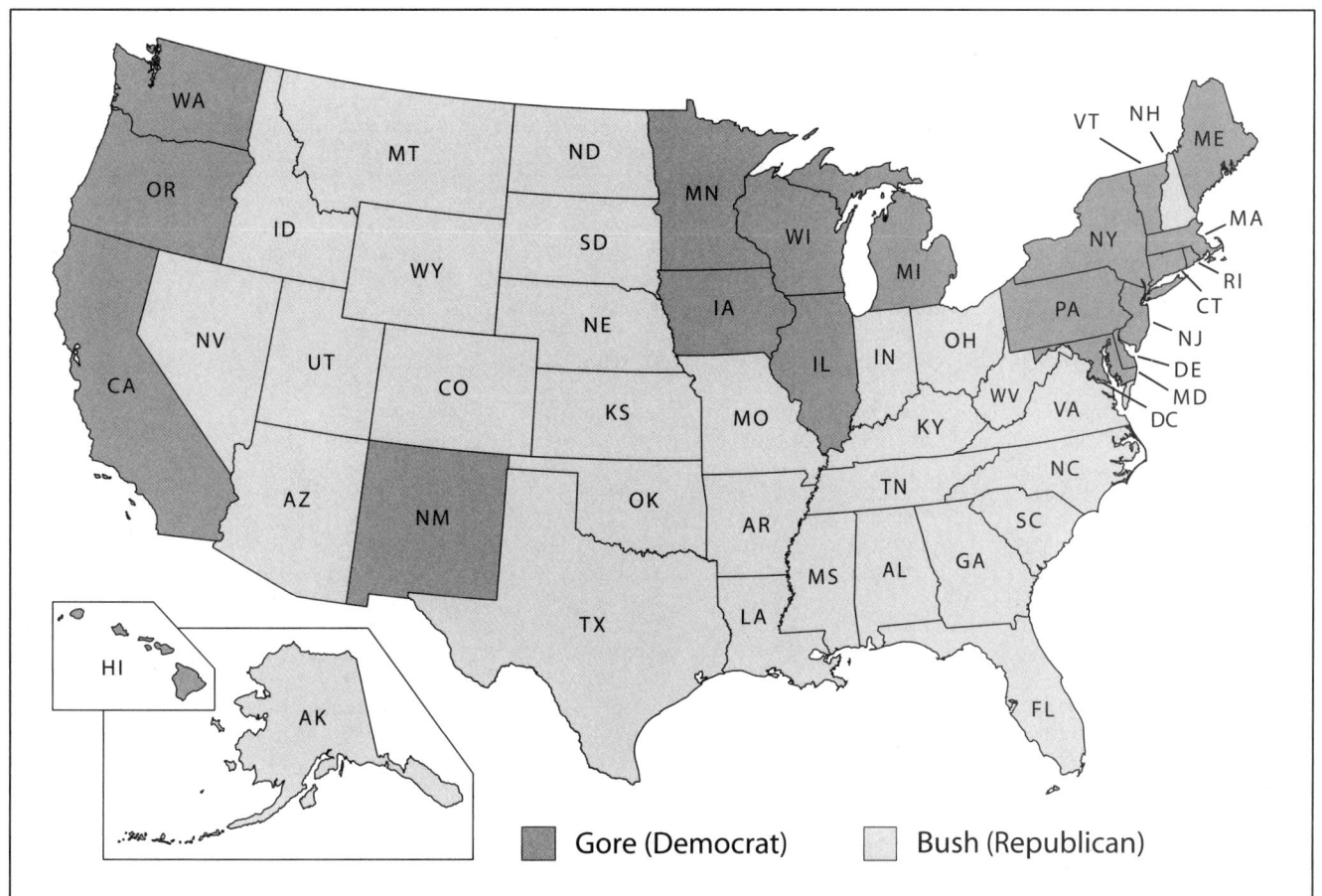

Gore (Democrat)   Bush (Republican)

States	Electoral votes	Bush	Gore	States	Electoral votes	Bush	Gore
Alabama	(9)	9	–	Nebraska	(5)	5	–
Alaska	(3)	3	–	Nevada	(4)	4	–
Arizona	(8)	8	–	New Hampshire	(4)	4	–
Arkansas	(6)	6	–	New Jersey	(15)	–	15
California	(54)	–	54	New Mexico	(5)	–	5
Colorado	(8)	8	–	New York	(33)	–	33
Connecticut	(8)	–	8	North Carolina	(14)	14	–
Delaware	(3)	–	3	North Dakota	(3)	3	–
District of Columbia[1]	(3)	–	2	Ohio	(21)	21	–
Florida	(25)	25	–	Oklahoma	(8)	8	–
Georgia	(13)	13	–	Oregon	(7)	–	7
Hawaii	(4)	–	4	Pennsylvania	(23)	–	23
Idaho	(4)	4	–	Rhode Island	(4)	–	4
Illinois	(22)	–	22	South Carolina	(8)	8	–
Indiana	(12)	12	–	South Dakota	(3)	3	–
Iowa	(7)	–	7	Tennessee	(11)	11	–
Kansas	(6)	6	–	Texas	(32)	32	–
Kentucky	(8)	8	–	Utah	(5)	5	–
Louisiana	(9)	9	–	Vermont	(3)	–	3
Maine	(4)	–	4	Virginia	(13)	13	–
Maryland	(10)	–	10	Washington	(11)	–	11
Massachusetts	(12)	–	12	West Virginia	(5)	5	–
Michigan	(18)	–	18	Wisconsin	(11)	–	11
Minnesota	(10)	–	10	Wyoming	(3)	3	–
Mississippi	(7)	7	–				
Missouri	(11)	11	–	Totals	(538)	271	266
Montana	(3)	3	–				

1. Barbara Lett-Simmons, a Gore elector in Washington, D.C., withheld her vote from Gore as a symbolic protest over the political status of the district.

2004 Presidential Election

State	Total vote	George W. Bush (Republican) Votes	%	John Kerry (Democrat) Votes	%	Other Votes	%	Plurality	
Alabama	1,883,449	1,176,394	62.5	693,933	36.8	13,122	0.7	482,461	R
Alaska	312,598	190,889	61.1	111,025	35.5	10,684	3.4	79,864	R
Arizona	2,012,585	1,104,294	54.9	893,524	44.4	14,767	0.7	210,770	R
Arkansas	1,054,945	572,898	54.3	469,953	44.5	12,094	1.2	102,945	R
California	12,421,852	5,509,826	44.4	6,745,485	54.3	166,541	1.3	1,235,659	D
Colorado	2,130,330	1,101,255	51.7	1,001,732	47.0	27,343	1.3	99,523	R
Connecticut	1,578,769	693,826	43.9	857,488	54.3	27,455	1.8	163,662	D
Delaware	375,190	171,660	45.8	200,152	53.3	3,378	0.9	28,492	D
Florida	7,609,810	3,964,522	52.1	3,583,544	47.1	61,744	0.8	380,978	R
Georgia	3,301,875	1,914,254	58.0	1,366,149	41.4	21,472	0.6	548,105	R
Hawaii	429,013	194,191	45.3	231,708	54.0	3,114	0.7	37,517	D
Idaho	598,447	409,235	68.4	181,098	30.3	8,114	1.3	228,137	R
Illinois	5,274,322	2,345,946	44.5	2,891,550	54.8	36,826	0.7	545,604	D
Indiana	2,468,002	1,479,438	59.9	969,011	39.3	19,553	0.8	510,427	R
Iowa	1,506,908	751,957	49.9	741,898	49.2	13,053	0.9	10,059	R
Kansas	1,187,756	736,456	62.0	434,993	36.6	16,307	1.4	301,463	R
Kentucky	1,795,860	1,069,439	59.6	712,733	39.7	13,688	0.7	356,706	R
Louisiana	1,943,106	1,102,169	56.7	820,299	42.2	20,638	1.1	281,870	R
Maine	740,752	330,201	44.6	396,842	53.6	13,709	1.8	66,641	D
Maryland	2,386,678	1,024,703	42.9	1,334,493	55.9	27,482	1.2	309,790	D
Massachusetts	2,912,388	1,071,109	36.8	1,803,800	61.9	37,479	1.3	732,691	D
Michigan	4,839,252	2,313,746	47.8	2,479,183	51.2	46,323	1.0	165,437	D
Minnesota	2,828,387	1,346,695	47.6	1,445,014	51.1	36,678	1.3	98,319	D
Mississippi	1,152,145	684,981	59.5	458,094	39.8	9,070	0.7	226,887	R
Missouri	2,731,364	1,455,713	53.3	1,259,171	46.1	16,480	0.6	196,542	R
Montana	450,445	266,063	59.1	173,710	38.6	10,672	2.3	92,353	R
Nebraska	778,186	512,814	65.9	254,328	32.7	11,044	1.4	258,486	R
Nevada	829,587	418,690	50.5	397,190	47.9	13,707	1.6	21,500	R
New Hampshire	677,738	331,237	48.9	340,511	50.2	5,990	0.9	9,274	D
New Jersey	3,611,691	1,670,003	46.2	1,911,430	52.9	30,258	0.9	241,427	D
New Mexico	756,304	376,930	49.8	370,942	49.0	8,432	1.2	5,988	R
New York	7,391,036	2,962,567	40.1	4,314,280	58.4	114,189	1.5	1,351,713	D
North Carolina	3,501,007	1,961,166	56.0	1,525,849	43.6	13,992	0.4	435,317	R
North Dakota	312,833	196,651	62.9	111,052	35.5	5,130	1.6	85,599	R
Ohio	5,627,903	2,859,764	50.8	2,741,165	48.7	26,974	0.5	118,599	R
Oklahoma	1,463,758	959,792	65.6	503,966	34.4		0.0	455,826	R
Oregon	1,836,782	866,831	47.2	943,163	51.3	26,788	1.5	76,332	D
Pennsylvania	5,769,590	2,793,847	48.4	2,938,095	50.9	37,648	0.7	144,248	D
Rhode Island	437,134	169,046	38.7	259,760	59.4	8,328	1.9	90,714	D
South Carolina	1,617,730	937,974	58.0	661,699	40.9	18,057	1.1	276,275	R
South Dakota	388,215	232,584	59.9	149,244	38.4	6,387	1.7	83,340	R
Tennessee	2,437,319	1,384,375	56.8	1,036,477	42.5	16,467	0.7	347,898	R
Texas	7,410,765	4,526,917	61.1	2,832,704	38.2	51,144	0.7	1,694,213	R
Utah	927,844	663,742	71.5	241,199	26.0	22,903	2.5	422,543	R
Vermont	312,309	121,180	38.8	184,067	58.9	7,062	2.3	62,887	D
Virginia	3,198,367	1,716,959	53.7	1,454,742	45.5	26,666	0.8	262,217	R
Washington	2,859,084	1,304,894	45.6	1,510,201	52.8	43,989	1.6	205,307	D
West Virginia	755,887	423,778	56.1	326,541	43.2	5,568	0.7	97,237	R
Wisconsin	2,997,007	1,478,120	49.3	1,489,504	49.7	29,383	1.0	11,384	D
Wyoming	243,428	167,629	68.9	70,776	29.1	5,023	2.0	96,853	R
District of Columbia	227,586	21,256	9.3	202,970	89.2	3,360	1.5	181,714	D
Totals	122,295,345	62,040,610	50.7	59,028,439	48.3	1,226,296	1.0	3,012,171	R

2004 Electoral Votes

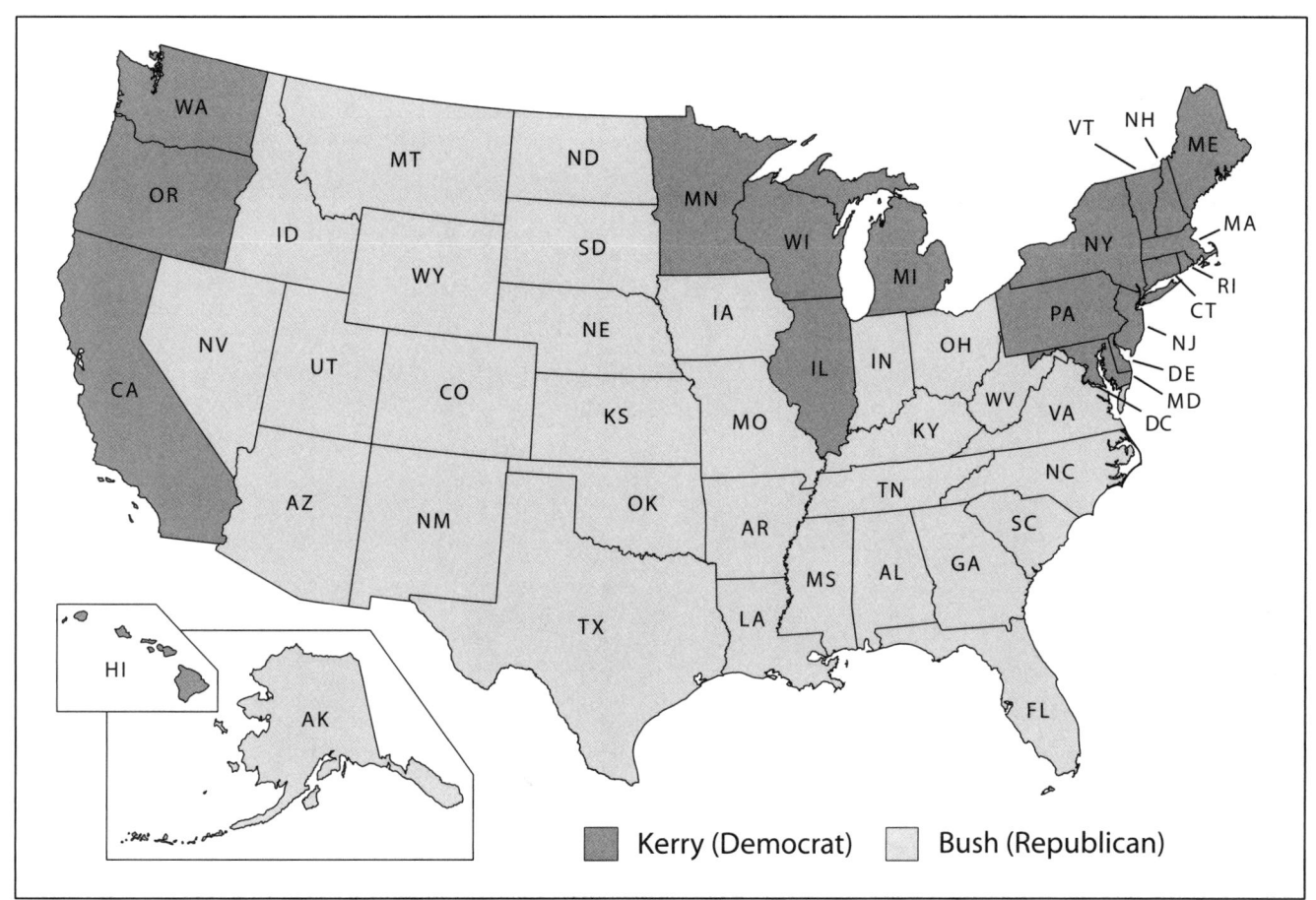

Kerry (Democrat) | Bush (Republican)

States	Electoral votes	Bush	Kerry	Edwards	States	Electoral votes	Bush	Kerry	Edwards
Alabama	(9)	9	–	–	Nebraska	(5)	5	–	–
Alaska	(3)	3	–	–	Nevada	(5)	5	–	–
Arizona	(10)	10	–	–	New Hampshire	(4)	–	4	–
Arkansas	(6)	6	–	–	New Jersey	(15)	–	15	–
California	(55)	–	55	–	New Mexico	(5)	5	–	–
Colorado	(9)	9	–	–	New York	(31)	–	31	–
Connecticut	(7)	–	7	–	North Carolina	(15)	15	–	–
Delaware	(3)	–	3	–	North Dakota	(3)	3	–	–
District of Columbia	(3)	–	3	–	Ohio	(20)	20	–	–
Florida	(27)	27	–	–	Oklahoma	(7)	7	–	–
Georgia	(15)	15	–	–	Oregon	(7)	–	7	–
Hawaii	(4)	–	4	–	Pennsylvania	(21)	–	21	–
Idaho	(4)	4	–	–	Rhode Island	(4)	–	4	–
Illinois	(21)	–	21	–	South Carolina	(8)	8	–	–
Indiana	(11)	11	–	–	South Dakota	(3)	3	–	–
Iowa	(7)	7	–	–	Tennessee	(11)	11	–	–
Kansas	(6)	6	–	–	Texas	(34)	34	–	–
Kentucky	(8)	8	–	–	Utah	(5)	5	–	–
Louisiana	(9)	9	–	–	Vermont	(3)	–	3	–
Maine	(4)	–	4	–	Virginia	(13)	13	–	–
Maryland	(10)	–	10	–	Washington	(11)	–	11	–
Massachusetts	(12)	–	12	–	West Virginia	(5)	5	–	–
Michigan	(17)	–	17	–	Wisconsin	(10)	–	10	–
Minnesota[1]	(10)	–	9	1	Wyoming	(3)	3	–	–
Mississippi	(6)	6	–	–					
Missouri	(11)	11	–	–	Totals	(538)	286	251	1
Montana	(3)	3	–	–					

1. A Democratic elector cast a vote for John Edwards rather than John Kerry.

2004 Republican Convention Balloting

State	Total votes	George W. Bush	Not Voting
Alabama	48	48	
Alaska	29	29	
American Samoa	9	9	
Arizona	52	52	
Arkansas	35	35	
California	173	173	
Colorado	50	50	
Connecticut	30	30	
Delaware	18	18	
District of Columbia	19	19	
Florida	112	112	
Georgia	69	69	
Guam	9	9	
Hawaii	20	20	
Idaho	32	32	
Illinois	73	73	
Indiana	55	55	
Iowa	32	31	1
Kansas	39	39	
Kentucky	46	46	
Louisiana	45	45	
Maine	21	21	
Maryland	39	39	
Massachusetts	44	44	
Michigan	61	61	
Minnesota	41	41	
Mississippi	38	38	
Missouri	57	57	
Montana	28	28	
Nebraska	35	35	
Nevada	33	33	
New Hampshire	32	32	
New Jersey	52	52	
New Mexico	24	24	
New York	102	102	
North Carolina	67	67	
North Dakota	26	26	
Ohio	91	91	
Oklahoma	41	41	
Oregon	31	31	
Pennsylvania	75	75	
Puerto Rico	23	23	
Rhode Island	21	21	
South Carolina	46	46	
South Dakota	27	27	
Tennessee	55	55	
Texas	138	138	
Utah	36	36	
Vermont	18	18	
Virgin Islands	9	9	
Virginia	64	64	
Washington	41	41	
West Virginia	30	30	
Wisconsin	40	40	
Wyoming	28	28	
Total	2,509	2,508	1

2004 Democratic Convention Balloting

State	Total votes	John Kerry	Present	Abstain
Alabama	62	62		
Alaska	18	17	1	
Arkansas	47	47		
Arizona	64	64		
California	441	441		
Colorado	63	50	13	
Connecticut	62	62		
Delaware	23	23		
Florida	201	201		
Georgia	101	98		3
Hawaii	29	17	8	4
Iowa	57	57		
Idaho	23	23		
Illinois	186	186		
Indiana	81	81		
Kansas	41	41		
Kentucky	57	57		
Louisiana	72	71		1
Massachusetts	121	121		
Maryland	99	99		
Maine	35	28	6	1
Michigan	155	155		
Minnesota	86	85	1	
Missouri	88	88		
Mississippi	41	40		1
Montana	21	21		
North Carolina	107	102	4	1
North Dakota	22	22		
Nebraska	31	31		
New Hampshire	27	26		1
New Jersey	128	116		12
New Mexico	37	37		
Nevada	32	32		
New York	284	284		
Ohio	159	159		
Oklahoma	47	47		
Oregon	59	56	3	
Pennsylvania	178	178		
Rhode Island	32	32		
South Carolina	55	55		
South Dakota	22	22		
Tennessee	85	85		
Texas	232	232		
Utah	29	28		1
Virginia	98	98		
Vermont	22	22		
Washington	95	88	7	
Wisconsin	87	87		
West Virginia	39	39		
Wyoming	19	19		
District of Columbia	39	39		
Puerto Rico	57	56		1
Virgin Islands	6	6		
American Samoa	6	6		
Guam	5	5		
Democrats Abroad	9	9		
Totals	4,322	4,253	43	26

Distribution of House Seats, 1963–2013, and Electoral Votes, 1952–2008

State	U.S. House Seats									Electoral Votes					
	1963–1973	1970 Census Changes	1973–1983	1980 Census Changes	1983–1993	1990 Census Changes	1993–2003	2000 Census Changes	2003–2013	1952, 1956, 1960	1964, 1968	1972, 1976, 1980	1984, 1988	1992, 1996, 2000	2004, 2008
Alabama	8	−1	7	—	7	—	7	—	7	11	10	9	9	9	9
Alaska	1	—	1	—	1	—	1	—	1	3	3	3	3	3	3
Arizona	3	+1	4	+1	5	+1	6	+2	8	4	5	6	7	8	10
Arkansas	4	—	4	—	4	—	4	—	4	8	6	6	6	6	6
California	38	+5	43	+2	45	+7	52	+1	53	32	40	45	47	54	55
Colorado	4	+1	5	+1	6	—	6	+1	7	6	6	7	8	8	9
Connecticut	6	—	6	—	6	—	6	−1	5	8	8	8	8	8	7
Delaware	1	—	1	—	1	—	1	—	1	3	3	3	3	3	3
Dist. of Col.	—	—	—	—	—	—	—	—	—	—	3	3	3	3	3
Florida	12	+3	15	+4	19	+4	23	+2	25	10	14	17	21	25	27
Georgia	10	—	10	—	10	+1	11	+2	13	12	12	12	12	13	15
Hawaii	2	—	2	—	2	—	2	—	2	3	4	4	4	4	4
Idaho	2	—	2	—	2	—	2	—	2	4	4	4	4	4	4
Illinois	24	—	24	−2	22	−2	20	−1	19	27	26	26	24	22	21
Indiana	11	—	11	−1	10	—	10	−1	9	13	13	13	12	12	11
Iowa	7	−1	6	—	6	−1	5	—	5	10	9	8	8	7	7
Kansas	5	—	5	—	5	−1	4	—	4	8	7	7	7	6	6
Kentucky	7	—	7	—	7	−1	6	—	6	10	9	9	9	8	8
Louisiana	8	—	8	—	8	−1	7	—	7	10	10	10	10	9	9
Maine	2	—	2	—	2	—	2	—	2	5	4	4	4	4	4
Maryland	8	—	8	—	8	—	8	—	8	9	10	10	10	10	10
Massachusetts	12	—	12	−1	11	−1	10	—	10	16	14	14	13	12	12
Michigan	19	—	19	−1	18	−2	16	−1	15	20	21	21	20	18	17
Minnesota	8	—	8	—	8	—	8	—	8	11	10	10	10	10	10
Mississippi	5	—	5	—	5	—	5	−1	4	8	7	7	7	7	6
Missouri	10	—	10	−1	9	—	9	—	9	13	12	12	11	11	11
Montana	2	—	2	—	2	−1	1	—	1	4	4	4	4	3	3
Nebraska	3	—	3	—	3	—	3	—	3	6	5	5	5	5	5
Nevada	1	—	1	+1	2	—	2	+1	3	3	3	3	4	4	5
New Hampshire	2	—	2	—	2	—	2	—	2	4	4	4	4	4	4
New Jersey	15	—	15	−1	14	−1	13	—	13	16	17	17	16	15	15
New Mexico	2	—	2	+1	3	—	3	—	3	4	4	4	5	5	5
New York	41	−2	39	−5	34	−3	31	−2	29	45	43	41	36	33	31
North Carolina	11	—	11	—	11	+1	12	+1	13	14	13	13	13	14	15
North Dakota	2	−1	1	—	1	—	1	—	1	4	4	3	3	3	3
Ohio	24	−1	23	−2	21	−2	19	−1	18	25	26	25	23	21	20
Oklahoma	6	—	6	—	6	—	6	−1	5	8	8	8	8	8	7
Oregon	4	—	4	+1	5	—	5	—	5	6	6	6	7	7	7
Pennsylvania	27	−2	25	−2	23	−2	21	−2	19	32	29	27	25	23	21
Rhode Island	2	—	2	—	2	—	2	—	2	4	4	4	4	4	4
South Carolina	6	—	6	—	6	—	6	—	6	8	8	8	8	8	8
South Dakota	2	—	2	−1	1	—	1	—	1	4	4	4	3	3	3
Tennessee	9	−1	8	+1	9	—	9	—	9	11	11	10	11	11	11
Texas	23	+1	24	+3	27	+3	30	+2	32	24	25	26	29	32	34
Utah	2	—	2	+1	3	—	3	—	3	4	4	4	5	5	5
Vermont	1	—	1	—	1	—	1	—	1	3	3	3	3	3	3
Virginia	10	—	10	—	10	+1	11	—	11	12	12	12	12	13	13
Washington	7	—	7	+1	8	+1	9	—	9	9	9	9	10	11	11
West Virginia	5	−1	4	—	4	−1	3	—	3	8	7	6	6	5	5
Wisconsin	10	−1	9	—	9	—	9	−1	8	12	12	11	11	11	10
Wyoming	1	—	1	—	1	—	1	—	1	3	3	3	3	3	3

NOTE: Table is based on the censuses of 1950, 1960, 1970, 1980, 1990, and 2000.

Party Affiliations in Congress and the Presidency, 1789–2007

Year	Congress	House Majority party	House Principal minority party	Senate Majority party	Senate Principal minority party	President
1789–1791	1st	AD-38	Op-26	AD-17	Op-9	F (Washington)
1791–1793	2nd	F-37	DR-33	F-16	DR-13	F (Washington)
1793–1795	3rd	DR-57	F-48	F-17	DR-13	F (Washington)
1795–1797	4th	F-54	DR-52	F-19	DR-13	F (Washington)
1797–1799	5th	F-58	DR-48	F-20	DR-12	F (J. Adams)
1799–1801	6th	F-64	DR-42	F-19	DR-13	F (J. Adams)
1801–1803	7th	DR-69	F-36	DR-18	F-13	DR (Jefferson)
1803–1805	8th	DR-102	F-39	DR-25	F-9	DR (Jefferson)
1805–1807	9th	DR-116	F-25	DR-27	F-7	DR (Jefferson)
1807–1809	10th	DR-118	F-24	DR-28	F-6	DR (Jefferson)
1809–1811	11th	DR-94	F-48	DR-28	F-6	DR (Madison)
1811–1813	12th	DR-108	F-36	DR-30	F-6	DR (Madison)
1813–1815	13th	DR-112	F-68	DR-27	F-9	DR (Madison)
1815–1817	14th	DR-117	F-65	DR-25	F-11	DR (Madison)
1817–1819	15th	DR-141	F-42	DR-34	F-10	DR (Monroe)
1819–1821	16th	DR-156	F-27	DR-35	F-7	DR (Monroe)
1821–1823	17th	DR-158	F-25	DR-44	F-4	DR (Monroe)
1823–1825	18th	DR-187	F-26	DR-44	F-4	DR (Monroe)
1825–1827	19th	AD-105	J-97	AD-26	J-20	DR (J.Q. Adams)
1827–1829	20th	J-119	AD-94	J-28	AD-20	DR (J.Q. Adams)
1829–1831	21st	D-139	NR-74	D-26	NR-22	DR (Jackson)
1831–1833	22nd	D-141	NR-58	D-25	NR-21	D (Jackson)
1833–1835	23rd	D-147	AM-53	D-20	NR-20	D (Jackson)
1835–1837	24th	D-145	W-98	D-27	W-25	D (Jackson)
1837–1839	25th	D-108	W-107	D-30	W-18	D (Van Buren)
1839–1841	26th	D-124	W-118	D-28	W-22	D (Van Buren)
1841–1843	27th	W-133	D-102	W-28	D-22	W (W. Harrison); W (Tyler)
1843–1845	28th	D-142	W-79	W-28	D-25	W (Tyler)
1845–1847	29th	D-143	W-77	D-31	W-25	D (Polk)
1847–1849	30th	W-115	D-108	D-36	W-21	D (Polk)
1849–1851	31st	D-112	W-109	D-35	W-25	W (Taylor); W (Fillmore)
1851–1853	32nd	D-140	W-88	D-35	W-24	W (Fillmore)
1853–1855	33rd	D-159	W-71	D-38	W-22	D (Pierce)
1855–1857	34th	R-108	D-83	D-40	R-15	D (Pierce)
1857–1859	35th	D-118	R-92	D-36	R-20	D (Buchanan)
1859–1861	36th	R-114	D-92	D-36	R-26	D (Buchanan)
1861–1863	37th	R-105	D-43	R-31	D-10	R (Lincoln)
1863–1865	38th	R-102	D-75	R-36	D-9	R (Lincoln)
1865–1867	39th	U-149	D-42	U-42	D-10	R (Lincoln); R (A. Johnson)
1867–1869	40th	R-143	D-49	R-42	D-11	R (A. Johnson)
1869–1871	41st	R-149	D-63	R-56	D-11	R (Grant)
1871–1873	42nd	R-134	D-104	R-52	D-17	R (Grant)
1873–1875	43rd	R-194	D-92	R-49	D-19	R (Grant)
1875–1877	44th	D-169	R-109	R-45	D-29	R (Grant)
1877–1879	45th	D-153	R-140	R-39	D-36	R (Hayes)
1879–1881	46th	D-149	R-130	D-42	R-33	R (Hayes)
1881–1883	47th	R-147	D-135	R-37	D-37	R (Garfield); R (Arthur)
1883–1885	48th	D-197	R-118	R-38	D-36	R (Arthur)
1885–1887	49th	D-183	R-140	R-43	D-34	D (Cleveland)
1887–1889	50th	D-169	R-152	R-39	D-37	D (Cleveland)
1889–1891	51st	R-166	D-159	R-39	D-37	R (B. Harrison)
1891–1893	52nd	D-235	R-88	R-47	D-39	R (B. Harrison)
1893–1895	53rd	D-218	R-127	D-44	R-38	D (Cleveland)
1895–1897	54th	R-244	D-105	R-43	D-39	D (Cleveland)
1897–1899	55th	R-204	D-113	R-47	D-34	R (McKinley)
1899–1901	56th	R-185	D-163	R-53	D-26	R (McKinley)

(table continues)

Year	Congress	House		Senate		President
		Majority party	Principal minority party	Majority party	Principal minority party	
1901–1903	57th	R-197	D-151	R-55	D-31	R (McKinley); R (T. Roosevelt)
1903–1905	58th	R-208	D-178	R-57	D-33	R (T. Roosevelt)
1905–1907	59th	R-250	D-136	R-57	D-33	R (T. Roosevelt)
1907–1909	60th	R-222	D-164	R-61	D-31	R (T. Roosevelt)
1909–1911	61st	R-219	D-172	R-61	D-32	R (Taft)
1911–1913	62nd	D-228	R-161	R-51	D-41	R (Taft)
1913–1915	63rd	D-291	R-127	D-51	R-44	D (Wilson)
1915–1917	64th	D-230	R-196	D-56	R-40	D (Wilson)
1917–1919	65th	D-216	R-210	D-53	R-42	D (Wilson)
1919–1921	66th	R-240	D-190	R-49	D-47	D (Wilson)
1921–1923	67th	R-301	D-131	R-59	D-37	R (Harding)
1923–1925	68th	R-225	D-205	R-51	D-43	R (Coolidge)
1925–1927	69th	R-247	D-183	R-56	D-39	R (Coolidge)
1927–1929	70th	R-237	D-195	R-49	D-46	R (Coolidge)
1929–1931	71st	R-267	D-167	R-56	D-39	R (Hoover)
1931–1933	72nd	D-220	R-214	R-48	D-47	R (Hoover)
1933–1935	73rd	D-310	R-117	D-60	R-35	D (F. Roosevelt)
1935–1937	74th	D-319	R-103	D-69	R-25	D (F. Roosevelt)
1937–1939	75th	D-331	R-89	D-76	R-16	D (F. Roosevelt)
1939–1941	76th	D-261	R-164	D-69	R-23	D (F. Roosevelt)
1941–1943	77th	D-268	R-162	D-66	R-28	D (F. Roosevelt)
1943–1945	78th	D-218	R-208	D-58	R-37	D (F. Roosevelt)
1945–1947	79th	D-242	R-190	D-56	R-38	D (F. Roosevelt); D (Truman)
1947–1949	80th	R-245	D-188	R-51	D-45	D (Truman)
1949–1951	81st	D-263	R-171	D-54	R-42	D (Truman)
1951–1953	82nd	D-234	R-199	D-49	R-47	D (Truman)
1953–1955	83rd	R-221	D-211	R-48	D-47	R (Eisenhower)
1955–1957	84th	D-232	R-203	D-48	R-47	R (Eisenhower)
1957–1959	85th	D-233	R-200	D-49	R-47	R (Eisenhower)
1959–1961	86th	D-283	R-153	D-64	R-34	R (Eisenhower)
1961–1963	87th	D-263	R-174	D-65	R-35	D (Kennedy)
1963–1965	88th	D-258	R-177	D-67	R-33	D (Kennedy); D (L. Johnson)
1965–1967	89th	D-295	R-140	D-68	R-32	D (L. Johnson)
1967–1969	90th	D-247	R-187	D-64	R-36	D (L. Johnson)
1969–1971	91st	D-243	R-192	D-57	R-43	R (Nixon)
1971–1973	92nd	D-254	R-180	D-54	R-44	R (Nixon)
1973–1975	93rd	D-239	R-192	D-56	R-42	R (Nixon); R (Ford)
1975–1977	94th	D-291	R-144	D-60	R-37	R (Ford)
1977–1979	95th	D-292	R-143	D-61	R-38	D (Carter)
1979–1981	96th	D-276	R-157	D-58	R-41	D (Carter)
1981–1983	97th	D-243	R-192	R-53	D-46	R (Reagan)
1983–1985	98th	D-269	R-165	R-54	D-46	R (Reagan)
1985–1987	99th	D-252	R-182	R-53	D-47	R (Reagan)
1987–1989	100th	D-258	R-177	D-55	R-45	R (Reagan)
1989–1991	101st	D-259	R-174	D-55	R-45	R (G. Bush)
1991–1993	102nd	D-267	R-167	D-56	R-44	R (G. Bush)
1993–1995	103rd	D-258	R-176	D-57	R-43	D (Clinton)
1995–1997	104th	R-230	D-204	R-53	D-47	D (Clinton)
1997–1999	105th	R-227	D-207	R-55	D-45	D (Clinton)
1999–2001	106th	R-222	D-211	R-55	D-45	D (Clinton)
2001–2003	107th	R-221	D-212	R-50	D-50	R (G.W. Bush)
2003–2005	108th	R-229	D-205	R-51	D-48	R (G.W. Bush)
2005–2007	109th	R-232	D-202	R-55	D-44	R (G.W. Bush)

SOURCES: U.S. Bureau of the Census, *Historical Statistics of the United States, Colonial Times to 1970* (Washington, D.C.: Government Printing Office, 1975); and U.S. Congress, Joint Committee on Printing, *Official Congressional Directory* (Washington, D.C.: Government Printing Office, 1967–); and *CQ Weekly,* selected issues.

NOTE: Figures are for the beginning of the first session of each Congress. Key to abbreviations: AD—Administration; AM—Anti-Masonic; D—Democratic; DR—Democratic-Republican; F—Federalist; J—Jacksonian; NR—National Republican; Op—Opposition; R—Republican; U—Unionist; W—Whig.

Special House Elections, 107th Congress

	Vote total	Percent		Vote total	Percent
Arkansas 3rd CD –Nov. 20, 2001			**Oklahoma 1st CD–Jan. 8, 2002**		
John Boozman (R)	53,308	57.2	John Sullivan (R)	61,694	53.8
Mike Hathorn (D)	40,237	42.0	Doug Dodd (D)	50,850	44.3
California 32nd CD–June 5, 2001			**Pennsylvania 9th CD–May 15, 2001**		
Diane Watson (D)	75,584	74.8	Bill Shuster (R)	55,670	51.7
Noel Irwin Hentschel (R)	20,008	19.8	H. Scott Conklin (D)	47,220	43.9
Florida 1st CD–Oct. 16, 2001			**South Carolina 2nd CD–Dec. 18, 2001**		
Jeff Miller (R)	53,247	65.7	Joe Wilson (R)	40,355	73.0
Steve Briese (D)	22,695	28.0	Brent Weaver (D)	14,034	24.4
John G. Ralls Jr. (no party)	5,115	5.1	**Virginia 4th CD–June 19, 2001**		
Hawaii 2nd CD–Nov. 30, 2002			J. Randy Forbes (R)	70,917	52.0
Ed Case (D)	23,576	51.4	L. Louise Lucas (D)	65,190	47.8
John F. Mink (R)	16,624	36.3			
Massachusetts 9th CD– Oct. 16, 2001					
Stephen F. Lynch (D)	44,943	65.0			
Jo Ann Sprague (R)	22,645	32.7			

Special Senate Elections, 107th Congress

None

2001 Gubernatorial Elections

New Jersey			**Virginia**		
James E. McGreevey (D)	1,256,853	56.4	Mark Warner (D)	984,177	52.2
Bret Schundler (R)	928,174	41.7	Mark L. Earley (R)	887,234	47.0

NOTE: Vote totals are included for all candidates listed on the ballot who received 5 percent or more of the total vote. For candidates who received under 5 percent, consult *America Votes 25* (Washington, D.C.: CQ Press, 2003).

2002 Elections Returns for Governor, Senate, and House

Following are the official vote returns for the gubernatorial, Senate, and House races compiled by Congressional Quarterly from figures supplied by the fifty state election boards.

Vote totals are included for all candidates listed on the ballot who received 5 percent or more of the total vote. For candidates who received under 5 percent, consult *America Votes 25* (Washington, D.C.: CQ Press, 2003). The percent column shows the percentage of the total vote cast.

An asterisk (*) indicates an incumbent.

An "X" denotes candidates without major part opposition; no votes were tallied.

An "AL" indicates an at-large member of Congress in a state with a single congressional district.

		Vote total	Per- cent
Alabama			
Governor			
	Bob Riley (R)	672,225	49.2
	Donald Siegelman (D)*	669,105	48.9
Senate			
	Jeff Sessions (R)*	792,561	58.6
	Susan Parker (D)	538,878	39.8
House			
1	Jo Bonner (R)	108,102	60.5
	Judy McCain Belk (D)	67,507	37.8
2	Terry Everett (R)*	129,233	68.8
	Charles Woods (D)	55,495	29.5
3	Mike D. Rogers (R)	91,169	50.3
	Joe Turnham (D)	87,351	48.2
4	Robert B. Aderholt (R)*	139,705	86.7
	Tony Hughes McLendon (LIBERT)	20,858	13.0
5	Robert E. "Bud" Cramer (D)*	143,029	73.3
	Stephen P. Engel (R)	48,226	24.7
6	Spencer Bachus (R)*	178,171	89.8
	J. Holden McAllister (LIBERT)	19,639	9.9
7	Artur Davis (D)	153,735	92.4
	Lauren Orth McCay (LIBERT)	12,100	7.3
Alaska			
Governor			
	Frank H. Murkowski (R)	129,279	55.8
	Fran Ulmer (D)	94,216	40.7
Senate			
	Ted Stevens (R)*	179,438	78.2
	Frank Vondersaar (D)	24,133	10.5
	Jim Sykes (GREEN)	16,608	7.2
House			
AL	Don Young (R)*	169,685	74.5

		Vote total	Per- cent
	Clifford Mark Greene (D)	39,357	17.3
	Russell deForest (GREEN)	14,435	6.3
Arizona			
Governor			
	Janet Napolitano (D)	566,284	46.2
	Matt Salmon (R)	554,465	45.2
	Richard Mahoney (I)	84,947	6.9
House			
1	Rick Renzi (R)	85,967	49.2
	George Cordova (D)	79,730	45.6
2	Trent Franks (R)	100,359	59.9
	Randy Camacho (D)	61,217	36.6
3	John Shadegg (R)*	104,847	67.3
	Charles Hill (D)	47,173	30.3
4	Ed Pastor (D)*	44,517	67.4
	Jonathan Barnert (R)	18,381	27.8
5	J. D. Hayworth (R)*	103,870	61.2
	Craig Columbus (D)	61,559	36.3
6	Jeff Flake (R)*	103,094	65.9
	Deborah Thomas (D)	49,355	31.6
7	Raul M. Grijalva (D)	61,256	59.0
	Ross Hieb (R)	38,474	37.1
8	Jim Kolbe (R)*	126,930	63.3
	Mary Judge Ryan (D)	67,328	33.6
Arkansas			
Governor			
	Mike Huckabee (R)*	427,082	53.0
	Jimmie Lou Fisher (D)	378,250	46.9
Senate			
	Mark Pryor (D)	433,306	53.9
	Tim Hutchinson (R)*	370,653	46.1
House			
1	Marion Berry (D)*	129,701	66.8
	Tommy F. Robinson (R)	64,357	33.2
2	Vic Snyder (D)*	142,752	92.9
	Ed Garner (write-in)	10,874	7.1

		Vote total	Per- cent
3	John Boozman (R)*	141,478	98.9
4	Mike Ross (D)*	119,633	60.6
	Jay Dickey (R)	77,904	39.4
California			
Governor			
	Gray Davis (D)*	3,533,490	47.3
	Bill Simon (R)	3,169,801	42.4
	Peter Miguel Camejo (GR)	393,036	5.3
House			
1	Mike Thompson (D)*	118,669	64.1
	Lawrence Wiesner (R)	60,013	32.4
2	Wally Herger (R)*	117,747	65.8
	Mike Johnson (D)	52,455	29.3
3	Doug Ose (R)*	121,732	62.5
	Howard Beeman (D)	67,136	34.4
4	John T. Doolittle (R)*	147,997	64.8
	Mark Norberg (D)	72,860	31.9
5	Robert T. Matsui (D)*	92,726	70.5
	Richard Frankhuizen (R)	34,749	26.4
6	Lynn Woolsey (D)*	139,750	66.7
	Paul L. Erickson (R)	62,052	29.6
7	George Miller (D)*	97,849	70.7
	Charles R. Hargrave (R)	36,584	26.4
8	Nancy Pelosi (D)*	127,684	79.6
	G. Michael German (R)	20,063	12.5
	Jay Pond (GREEN)	10,033	6.3
9	Barbara Lee (D)*	135,893	81.4
	Jerald Udinsky (R)	25,333	15.2
10	Ellen O. Tauscher (D)*	126,390	75.6
	Sonia E. Alonso Harden (LIBERT)	40,807	24.4
11	Richard W. Pombo (R)*	104,921	60.3
	Elaine Dugger Shaw (D)	69,035	39.7
12	Tom Lantos (D)*	105,597	68.1
	Michael Moloney (R)	38,381	24.8
	Maad Abu-Ghazalah (LIBERT)	11,006	7.1
13	Pete Stark (D)*	86,495	71.1
	Syed R. Mahmood (R)	26,852	22.1
14	Anna G. Eshoo (D)*	117,055	68.2
	Joseph H. Nixon (R)	48,346	28.2
15	Michael M. Honda (D)*	87,482	65.8
	Linda Rae Hermann (R)	41,251	31.0
16	Zoe Lofgren (D)*	72,370	67.0
	Douglas Adams McNea (R)	32,182	29.8
17	Sam Farr (D)*	101,632	68.1
	Clint Engler (R)	40,334	27.0
18	Dennis Cardoza (D)	56,181	51.3
	Dick Monteith (R)	47,528	43.4
19	George P. Radanovich (R)*	106,209	67.3
	John Veen (D)	47,403	30.0

		Vote total	Percent
20	Cal Dooley (D)*	47,627	63.7
	Andre Minuth (R)	25,628	34.3
21	Devin Nunes (R)	87,544	70.5
	David G. LaPere (D)	32,584	26.2
22	Bill Thomas (R)*	120,473	73.3
	Jaime A. Corvera (D)	38,988	23.7
23	Lois Capps (D)*	95,752	59.0
	Beth Rogers (R)	62,604	38.6
24	Elton Gallegly (R)*	120,585	65.2
	Fern Rudin (D)	58,755	31.8
25	Howard P. "Buck" McKeon (R)*	80,775	65.0
	Robert "Bob" Conaway (D)	38,674	31.1
26	David Dreier (R)*	95,360	63.8
	Marjorie Musser Mikels (D)	50,081	33.5
27	Brad Sherman (D)*	79,815	62.0
	Robert M. Levy (R)	48,996	38.0
28	Howard L. Berman (D)*	73,771	71.4
	David R. Hernandez Jr. (R)	23,926	23.2
	Kelley L. Ross (LIBERT)	5,629	5.5
29	Adam B. Schiff (D)*	76,036	62.6
	Jim Scileppi (R)	40,616	33.4
30	Henry A. Waxman (D)*	130,604	70.4
	Tony D. Goss (R)	54,989	29.6
31	Xavier Becerra (D)*	54,569	81.2
	Luis Vega (R)	12,674	18.8
32	Hilda L. Solis (D)*	58,530	68.8
	Emma E. Fischbeck (R)	23,366	27.5
33	Diane Watson (D)*	97,779	82.5
	Andrew Kim (R)	16,699	14.1
34	Lucille Roybal-Allard (D)*	48,734	74.0
	Wayne Miller (R)	17,090	26.0
35	Maxine Waters (D)*	72,401	77.5
	Ross Moen (R)	18,094	19.4
36	Jane Harman (D)*	88,198	61.4
	Stuart Johnson (R)	50,328	35.0
37	Juanita Millender-McDonald (D)*	63,445	72.9
	Oscar A. Velasco (R)	20,154	23.2
38	Grace F. Napolitano (D)*	62,600	71.1
	Alex A. Burrola (R)	23,126	26.3
39	Linda T. Sanchez (D)	52,256	54.8
	Tim Escobar (R)	38,925	40.8
40	Ed Royce (R)*	92,422	67.6
	Christina Avalos (D)	40,265	29.5
41	Jerry Lewis (R)*	91,326	67.4
	Keith A. Johnson (D)	40,155	29.6
42	Gary G. Miller (R)*	98,476	67.8
	Richard Waldron (D)	42,090	29.0
43	Joe Baca (D)*	45,374	66.4
	Wendy C. Neighbor (R)	20,821	30.5
44	Ken Calvert (R)*	76,686	63.7
	Louis Vandenberg (D)	38,021	31.6
45	Mary Bono (R)*	87,101	65.2
	Elle K. Kurpiewski (D)	43,692	32.7
46	Dana Rohrabacher (R)*	108,807	61.7
	Gerrie Schipske (D)	60,890	34.5
47	Loretta Sanchez (D)*	42,501	60.6
	Jeff Chavez (R)	24,346	34.7
48	Christopher Cox (R)*	122,884	68.4
	John L. Graham (D)	51,058	28.4
49	Darrell Issa (R)*	94,594	77.2
	Karl W. Dietrich (LIBERT)	26,891	21.9
50	Randy "Duke" Cunningham (R)*	111,095	64.3
	Del G. Stewart (D)	55,855	32.3
51	Bob Filner (D)*	59,541	57.9
	Maria Guadalupe Garcia (R)	40,430	39.3
52	Duncan Hunter (R)*	118,561	70.2
	Peter Moore-Kochlacs (D)	43,526	25.8

		Vote total	Percent
53	Susan A. Davis (D)*	72,252	62.2
	Bill Van DeWeghe (R)	43,891	37.8

Colorado

Governor

	Vote total	Percent
Bill Owens (R)*	884,583	62.6
Rollie Heath (D)	475,373	33.7

Senate

	Vote total	Percent
Wayne Allard (R)*	717,892	50.7
Tom Strickland (D)	648,129	45.8

House

		Vote total	Percent
1	Diana DeGette (D)*	111,718	66.3
	Ken Chlouber (R)	49,884	29.6
2	Mark Udall (D)*	123,504	60.1
	Sandy Hume (R)	75,564	36.8
3	Scott McInnis (R)*	143,433	65.8
	Denis Berckefeldt (D)	68,160	31.3
4	Marilyn Musgrave (R)	115,359	54.9
	Stan Matsunaka (D)	87,499	41.7
5	Joel Hefley (R)*	128,118	69.4
	Curtis Imrie (D)	45,587	24.7
	Biff Baker (LIBERT)	10,972	5.9
6	Tom Tancredo (R)*	158,851	66.9
	Lance Wright (D)	71,327	30.0
7	Bob Beauprez (R)	81,789	47.3
	Mike Feeley (D)	81,668	47.2

Connecticut

Governor

	Vote total	Percent
John G. Rowland (R)*	573,958	56.1
Bill Curry (D)	448,984	43.9

House

		Vote total	Percent
1	John B. Larson (D)*	134,698	66.8
	Phil Steele (R)	66,968	33.2
2	Rob Simmons (R)*	117,434	54.1
	Joseph D. Courtney (D)	99,674	45.9
3	Rosa DeLauro (D)*	121,557	65.6
	Richter Elser (R)	54,757	29.5
4	Christopher Shays (R)*	113,197	64.4
	Stephanie Sanchez (D)	62,491	35.6
5	Nancy L. Johnson (R)*	113,626	54.2
	Jim Maloney (D)*	90,616	43.3

Delaware

Senate

	Vote total	Percent
Joseph R. Biden Jr. (D)*	135,253	58.2
Raymond J. Clatworthy (R)	94,793	40.8

House

		Vote total	Percent
AL	Michael N. Castle (R)*	164,605	72.1
	Micheal C. Miller Sr. (D)	61,011	26.7

Florida

Governor

	Vote total	Percent
Jeb Bush (R)*	2,856,845	56.0
Bill McBride (D)	2,201,427	43.2

House

		Vote total	Percent
1	Jeff Miller (R)*	152,635	74.6
	Bert Oram (D)	51,972	25.4
2	Allen Boyd (D)*	152,164	66.9
	Tom McGurk (R)	75,275	33.1
3	Corrine Brown (D)*	88,462	59.3
	Jennifer Carroll (R)	60,747	40.7
4	Ander Crenshaw (R)*	171,152	99.7
5	Ginny Brown-Waite (R)	121,998	47.9
	Karen L. Thurman (D)*	117,758	46.2
6	Cliff Stearns (R)*	141,570	65.4
	David E. Bruderly (D)	75,046	34.6
7	John L. Mica (R)*	142,147	59.6
	Wayne Hogan (D)	96,444	40.4

		Vote total	Percent
8	Ric Keller (R)*	123,497	65.1
	Eddie Diaz (D)	66,099	34.9
9	Michael Bilirakis (R)*	169,369	71.5
	Chuck Kalogianis (D)	67,623	28.5
10	C. W. Bill Young (R)	X	X
11	Jim Davis (D)*	X	X
12	Adam H. Putnam (R)*	X	X
13	Katherine Harris (R)	139,048	54.8
	Jan Schneider (D)	114,739	45.2
14	Porter J. Goss (R)*	X	X
15	Dave Weldon (R)*	146,414	63.1
	Jim Tso (D)	85,433	36.8
16	Mark Foley (R)*	176,171	78.9
	Jack McLain (CNSTP)	47,169	21.1
17	Kendrick B. Meek (D)	113,749	99.9
18	Ileana Ros-Lehtinen (R)*	103,512	69.1
	Ray Chote (D)	42,852	28.6
19	Robert Wexler (D)*	156,747	72.2
	Jack Merkl (R)	60,477	27.8
20	Peter Deutsch (D)*	X	X
21	Lincoln Diaz-Balart (R)*	X	X
22	E. Clay Shaw Jr. (R)*	131,930	60.8
	Carol Roberts (D)	83,265	38.4
23	Alcee L. Hastings (D)*	96,347	77.5
	Charles Laurie (R)	27,986	22.5
24	Tom Feeney (R)	135,576	61.7
	Harry Jacobs (D)	83,667	38.2
25	Mario Diaz-Balart (R)	81,845	64.7
	Annie Betancourt (D)	44,757	35.4

Georgia

Governor

	Vote total	Percent
Sonny Perdue (R)	1,042,700	51.4
Roy Barnes (D)*	937,070	46.2

Senate

	Vote total	Percent
Saxby Chambliss (R)	1,071,467	52.8
Max Cleland (D)*	932,156	45.9

House

		Vote total	Percent
1	Jack Kingston (R)*	103,661	72.1
	Don Smart (D)	40,026	27.9
2	Sanford D. Bishop Jr. (D)*	102,925	100.0
3	Jim Marshall (D)	75,394	50.5
	Calder Clay (R)	73,866	49.5
4	Denise L. Majette (D)	118,045	77.0
	Cynthia Van Auken (R)	35,202	23.0
5	John Lewis (D)*	116,230	100.0
6	Johnny Isakson (R)*	163,252	79.9
	Jeff Weisberger (D)	41,043	20.1
7	John Linder (R)*	138,997	78.9
	Michael R. Berlon (D)	37,127	21.1
8	Mac Collins (R)*	142,505	78.3
	Angelos Petrakopoulos (D)	39,422	21.7
9	Charlie Norwood (R)*	123,313	72.8
	Barry Gordon Irwin (D)	45,974	27.2
10	Nathan Deal (R)*	129,242	100.0
11	Phil Gingrey (R)	69,261	51.6
	Roger Kahn (D)	64,007	48.4
12	Max Burns (R)	77,479	55.2
	Charles "Champ" Walker Jr. (D)	62,904	44.8
13	David Scott (D)	70,011	59.6
	Clay Cox (R)	47,405	40.4

Hawaii

Governor

	Vote total	Percent
Linda Lingle (R)	197,009	51.6
Mazie Hirono (D)	179,647	47.0

House

		Vote total	Percent
1	Neil Abercrombie (D)*	131,673	72.9
	Mark Terry (R)	45,032	24.9

	Vote total	Percent
2 Patsy T. Mink (D)*	100,671	56.2
Bob McDermott (R)	71,661	40.0

Idaho

Governor

	Vote total	Percent
Dirk Kempthorne (R)*	231,566	56.3
Jerry M. Brady (D)	171,711	41.7

Senate

	Vote total	Percent
Larry E. Craig (R)*	266,215	65.2
Alan Blinken (D)	132,975	32.5

House

	Vote total	Percent
1 C. L. "Butch" Otter (R)*	120,743	58.6
Betty Richardson (D)	80,269	38.9
2 Mike Simpson (R)*	135,605	68.2
Edward W. Kinghorn (D)	57,769	29.0

Illinois

Governor

	Vote total	Percent
Rod R. Blagojevich (D)	1,847,040	52.2
Jim Ryan (R)	1,594,960	45.1

Senate

	Vote total	Percent
Richard J. Durbin (D)*	2,103,766	60.3
Jim Durkin (R)	1,325,703	38.0

House

	Vote total	Percent
1 Bobby L. Rush (D)*	149,068	81.2
Raymond G. Wardingley (R)	29,776	16.2
2 Jesse L. Jackson Jr. (D)*	151,443	82.3
Doug Nelson (R)	32,567	17.7
3 William O. Lipinski (D)*	156,042	100.0
4 Luis V. Gutierrez (D)*	67,339	79.7
Anthony J. "Tony" Lopez-Cisneros (R)	12,778	15.1
Marjorie Kohls (LIBERT)	4,396	5.2
5 Rahm Emanuel (D)	106,514	66.8
Mark A. Augusti (R)	46,008	28.9
6 Henry J. Hyde (R)*	113,174	65.1
Tom Berry (D)	60,698	34.9
7 Danny K. Davis (D)*	137,933	83.2
Mark Tunney (R)	25,280	15.3
8 Philip M. Crane (R)*	95,275	57.4
Melissa L. Bean (D)	70,626	42.6
9 Jan Schakowsky (D)*	118,642	70.3
Nicholas M. Duric (R)	45,307	26.8
10 Mark Steven Kirk (R)*	128,611	68.8
Henry H. "Hank" Perritt Jr. (D)	58,300	31.2
11 Jerry Weller (R)*	124,192	64.3
Keith S. Van Duyne (D)	68,893	35.7
12 Jerry F. Costello (D)*	131,580	69.3
David Sadler (R)	58,440	30.8
13 Judy Biggert (R)*	139,546	70.3
Thomas Mason (D)	59,069	29.7
14 J. Dennis Hastert (R)*	135,198	74.1
Laurence J. Quick (D)	47,165	25.9
15 Timothy V. Johnson (R)*	134,650	65.2
Joshua T. Hartke (D)	64,131	31.0
16 Donald Manzullo (R)*	133,339	70.6
John Kutsch (D)	55,488	29.4
17 Lane Evans (D)*	127,093	62.4
Peter Calderone (R)	76,519	37.6
18 Ray LaHood (R)*	192,567	100.0
19 John Shimkus (R)*	133,956	54.8
David Phelps (D)*	110,517	45.2

Indiana

House

	Vote total	Percent
1 Peter J. Visclosky (D)*	90,443	66.9
Mark J. Leyva (R)	41,909	31.0
2 Chris Chocola (R)	95,081	50.5
Jill Long Thompson (D)	86,253	45.8
3 Mark Souder (R)*	92,566	63.1
Jay Rigdon (D)	50,509	34.5
4 Steve Buyer (R)*	112,760	71.4
Bill Abbott (D)	41,314	26.1
5 Dan Burton (R)*	129,442	72.0
Katherine Fox Carr (D)	45,283	25.2
6 Mike Pence (R)*	118,436	63.8
Ann Melina Fox (D)	63,871	34.4
7 Julia Carson (D)*	77,478	53.1
Brose McVey (R)	64,379	44.1
8 John Hostettler (R)*	98,952	51.3
Bryan L. Hartke (D)	88,763	46.0
9 Baron P. Hill (D)*	96,654	51.2
Mike Sodrel (R)	87,169	46.1

Iowa

Governor

	Vote total	Percent
Tom Vilsack (D)*	540,449	52.7
Doug Gross (R)	456,612	44.5

Senate

	Vote total	Percent
Tom Harkin (D)*	554,278	54.2
Greg Ganske (R)	447,892	43.8

House

	Vote total	Percent
1 Jim Nussle (R)*	112,280	57.2
Ann Hutchinson (D)	83,779	42.6
2 Jim Leach (R)*	108,130	52.2
Julie Thomas (D)	94,767	45.7
3 Leonard L. Boswell (D)*	115,367	53.4
Sam Thompson (R)	97,285	45.0
4 Tom Latham (R)*	115,430	54.8
John Norris (D)	90,784	43.1
5 Steve King (R)*	113,257	62.1
Paul Shomshor (D)	68,853	37.8

Kansas

Governor

	Vote total	Percent
Kathleen Sebelius (D)	441,858	52.9
Tim Shallenburger (R)	376,830	45.1

Senate

	Vote total	Percent
Pat Roberts (R)*	641,075	82.5
Steven A. Rosile (LIBERT)	70,725	9.1
George Cook (REF)	65,050	8.4

House

	Vote total	Percent
1 Jerry Moran (R)*	189,976	91.1
Jack W. Warner (LIBERT)	18,585	8.9
2 Jim Ryun (R)*	127,477	60.4
Dan Lykins (D)	79,160	37.5
3 Dennis Moore (D)*	110,095	50.2
Adam Taff (R)	102,882	46.9
4 Todd Tiahrt (R)*	115,691	60.6
Carlos Nolla (D)	70,656	37.0

Kentucky

Senate

	Vote total	Percent
Mitch McConnell (R)*	731,679	64.7
Lois Combs Weinberg (D)	399,634	35.3

House

	Vote total	Percent
1 Edward Whitfield (R)*	117,600	65.3
Klint Alexander (D)	62,617	34.7
2 Ron Lewis (R)*	122,773	69.6
David L. Williams (D)	51,431	29.2
3 Anne M. Northup (R)*	118,228	51.6
Jack Conway (D)	110,846	48.4
4 Ken Lucas (D)*	87,776	51.1
Geoff Davis (R)	81,651	47.6
5 Harold Rogers (R)*	137,986	78.3
Sidney "Jane" Bailey-Bamer (D)	38,254	21.7
6 Ernie Fletcher (R)*	115,622	72.0
Gatewood Galbraith (I)	41,753	26.0

Louisiana

Senate

	Vote total	Percent
Mary L. Landrieu (D)*	573,347	46.0
Suzanne Haik Terrell (R)	339,506	27.2
(Dec. 7 runoff)[1]		
Mary L. Landrieu (D)*	638,654	51.7
Suzanne Haik Terrell (R)	596,642	48.3

House

	Vote total	Percent
1 David Vitter (R)*	147,117	81.5
Monica L. Monica (R)	20,268	11.2
2 William J. Jefferson (D)*	90,310	63.5
Irma Muse Dixon (D)	28,480	20.0
Silky Sullivan (R)	15,440	10.9
3 Billy Tauzin (R)*	130,323	86.7
William Beier (I)	12,964	8.6
David Iwanico (I)	7,055	4.7
4 Jim McCrery (R)*	114,649	71.6
John Milkovich (D)	42,340	26.4
5[1] Rodney Alexander (D)	52,952	28.7
Lee Fletcher (R)	45,278	24.5
Clyde C. Holloway (R)	42,573	23.1
Robert J. Barham (R)	34,533	18.7
Dec. 7 runoff[1]		
Rodney Alexander (D)	86,718	50.3
Lee Fletcher (R)	85,744	49.7
6 Richard H. Baker (R)*	146,932	84.0
Rick Moscatello (I)	27,898	16.0
7 Chris John (D)*	138,659	86.8
Roberto Valletta (I)	21,051	13.2

Maine

Governor

	Vote total	Percent
John Baldacci (D)	238,179	47.1
Peter E. Cianchette (R)	209,496	41.5
Jonathan K. Carter (GI)	46,903	9.3

Senate

	Vote total	Percent
Susan Collins (R)*	295,041	58.4
Chellie Pingree (D)	209,858	41.6

House

	Vote total	Percent
1 Tom Allen (D)*	172,646	63.8
Steven Joyce (R)	97,931	36.2
2 Michael H. Michaud (D)	116,868	52.0
Kevin L. Raye (R)	107,849	48.0

Maryland

Governor

	Vote total	Percent
Robert L. Ehrlich Jr. (R)	879,592	51.6
Kathleen Kennedy Townsend (D)	813,422	47.7

House

	Vote total	Percent
1 Wayne T. Gilchrest (R)*	192,004	76.7
Ann D. Tamlyn (D)	57,986	23.2
2 C. A. Dutch Ruppersberger (D)	105,718	54.2
Helen Delich Bentley (R)	88,954	45.7
3 Benjamin L. Cardin (D)*	145,589	65.7
Scott Alan Conwell (R)	75,721	34.2
4 Albert R. Wynn (D)*	131,644	78.6
John B. Kimble (R)	34,890	20.8
5 Steny H. Hoyer (D)*	137,903	69.3
Joseph T. Crawford (R)	60,758	30.5
6 Roscoe G. Bartlett (R)*	147,825	66.1
Donald M. DeArmon (D)	75,575	33.8

		Vote total	Per cent
7	Elijah E. Cummings (D)*	137,047	73.5
	Joseph E. Ward (R)	49,172	26.4
8	Chris Van Hollen (D)	112,788	51.7
	Constance A. Morella (R)*	103,587	47.5

Massachusetts

Governor

	Vote total	Per cent
Mitt Romney (R)	1,091,988	49.8
Shannon P. O'Brien (D)	985,981	44.9

Senate

	Vote total	Per cent
John Kerry (D)*	1,605,976	80.0
Michael E. Cloud (LIBERT)	369,807	18.4

House

		Vote total	Per cent
1	John W. Olver (D)*	137,841	67.6
	Matthew W. Kinnaman (R)	66,061	32.4
2	Richard E. Neal (D)*	153,387	99.1
3	Jim McGovern (D)*	155,697	98.8
4	Barney Frank (D)*	166,125	99.0
5	Martin T. Meehan (D)*	122,562	60.1
	Charles McCarthy (R)	69,337	34.0
	Ilana Freedman (LIBERT)	11,729	5.8
6	John F. Tierney (D)*	162,900	68.3
	Mark C. Smith (R)	75,462	31.6
7	Edward J. Markey (D)*	170,968	98.2
8	Michael E. Capuano (D)*	111,861	99.6
9	Stephen F. Lynch (D)*	168,055	99.5
10	Bill Delahunt (D)*	179,238	69.2
	Luiz Gonzaga (R)	79,624	30.8

Michigan

Governor

	Vote total	Per cent
Jennifer M. Granholm (D)	1,633,796	51.4
Dick Posthumus (R)	1,506,104	47.4

Senate

	Vote total	Per cent
Carl Levin (D)*	1,896,614	60.6
Andrew Raczkowski (R)	1,185,545	37.9

House

		Vote total	Per cent
1	Bart Stupak (D)*	150,701	67.7
	Don Hooper (R)	69,254	31.1
2	Peter Hoekstra (R)*	156,937	70.4
	Jeffrey A. Wrisley (D)	61,749	27.7
3	Vernon J. Ehlers (R)*	153,131	70.0
	Kathryn D. Lynnes (D)	61,987	28.3
4	Dave Camp (R)*	149,090	68.2
	Lawrence D. Hollenbeck (D)	65,950	30.2
5	Dale E. Kildee (D)*	158,709	91.6
	Clint Foster (LIBERT)	9,344	5.4
6	Fred Upton (R)*	126,936	69.2
	Gary C. Giguere Jr. (D)	53,793	29.3
7	Nick Smith (R)*	121,142	59.7
	Mike Simpson (D)	78,412	38.6
8	Mike Rogers (R)*	156,525	67.9
	Frank McAlpine (D)	70,920	30.8
9	Joe Knollenberg (R)*	141,102	58.1
	David Fink (D)	96,856	39.9
10	Candice S. Miller (R)	137,339	63.3
	Carl J. Marlinga (D)	77,053	35.5
11	Thaddeus McCotter (R)	126,050	57.2
	Kevin Kelley (D)	87,402	39.7
12	Sander M. Levin (D)*	140,970	68.3
	Harvey R. Dean (R)	61,502	29.8
13	Carolyn Cheeks Kilpatrick (D)*	120,869	91.6
	Raymond H. Warner (LIBERT)	11,072	8.4
14	John Conyers Jr. (D)*	145,285	83.2
	Dave Stone (R)	26,544	15.2
15	John D. Dingell (D)*	136,518	72.2
	Martin Kaltenbach (R)	48,626	25.7

Minnesota

Governor

	Vote total	Per cent
Tim Pawlenty (R)	999,473	44.4
Roger Moe (D)	821,268	36.5
Timothy J. Penny (INDC)	364,534	16.2

Senate

	Vote total	Per cent
Norm Coleman (R)	1,116,697	49.5
Walter F. Mondale (D)	1,067,246	47.3

House

		Vote total	Per cent
1	Gil Gutknecht (R)*	163,570	61.5
	Steve Andreasen (D)	92,165	34.7
2	John Kline (R)	152,970	53.3
	Bill Luther (D)*	121,121	42.2
3	Jim Ramstad (R)*	213,334	72.0
	Darryl Tyree Stanton (D)	82,575	27.9
4	Betty McCollum (D)*	164,597	62.2
	Clyde Billington (R)	89,705	33.9
5	Martin Olav Sabo (D)*	171,572	67.0
	Daniel Nielsen Mathias (R)	66,271	25.9
	Tim Davis (GR)	17,825	7.0
6	Mark Kennedy (R)*	164,747	57.3
	Janet Robert (D)	100,738	35.1
	Dan Becker (INDC)	21,484	7.5
7	Collin C. Peterson (D)*	170,234	65.3
	Dan Stevens (R)	90,342	34.6
8	James L. Oberstar (D)	194,909	68.7
	Robert Lemen (R)	88,673	31.2

Mississippi

Senate

	Vote total	Per cent
Thad Cochran (R)*	533,269	84.6
Shawn O'Hara (REF)	97,226	15.4

House

		Vote total	Per cent
1	Roger Wicker (R)*	95,404	71.4
	Rex N. Weathers (D)	32,318	24.2
2	Bennie Thompson (D)*	89,913	55.1
	Clinton B. LeSueur (R)	69,711	42.8
3	Charles W. "Chip" Pickering Jr. (R)*	139,329	63.6
	Ronnie Shows (D)*	76,184	34.8
4	Gene Taylor (D)*	121,742	75.2
	Karl Mertz (R)	34,373	21.2

Missouri

Senate

	Vote total	Per cent
Jim Talent (R)	935,032	49.8
Jean Carnahan (D)*	913,778	48.7

House

		Vote total	Per cent
1	William Lacy Clay (D)*	133,946	70.1
	Richard Schwadron (R)	51,755	27.1
2	Todd Akin (R)*	167,057	67.1
	John Hogan (D)	77,223	31.0
3	Richard A. Gephardt (D)*	122,181	59.1
	Catherine S. Enz (R)	80,551	38.9
4	Ike Skelton (D)*	142,204	67.6
	James A. Noland Jr. (R)	64,451	30.7
5	Karen McCarthy (D)*	122,645	65.9
	Steve Gordon (R)	60,245	32.4
6	Sam Graves (R)*	131,151	63.0
	Cathy Rinehart (D)	73,202	35.2
7	Roy Blunt (R)*	149,519	74.8
	Ron Lapham (D)	45,964	23.0
8	Jo Ann Emerson (R)*	135,144	71.8
	Gene Curtis (D)	50,686	26.9
9	Kenny Hulshof (R)*	146,032	68.2
	Donald M. "Don" Deichman (D)	61,126	28.6

Montana

Senate

	Vote total	Per cent
Max Baucus (D)*	204,853	62.7
Mike Taylor (R)	103,611	31.7

House

		Vote total	Per cent
AL	Denny Rehberg (R)*	214,100	64.6
	Steve Kelly (D)	108,233	32.7

Nebraska

Governor

	Vote total	Per cent
Mike Johanns (R)*	330,349	68.7
Stormy Dean (D)	132,348	27.5

Senate

	Vote total	Per cent
Chuck Hagel (R)*	397,438	82.8
Charlie A. Matulka (D)	70,290	14.6

House

		Vote total	Per cent
1	Doug Bereuter (R)*	133,013	85.4
	Robert Eckerson (LIBERT)	22,831	14.7
2	Lee Terry (R)*	89,917	63.3
	Jim Simon (D)	46,843	33.0
3	Tom Osborne (R)*	163,939	93.2
	Jerry Hickman (LIBERT)	12,017	6.8

Nevada

Governor

	Vote total	Per cent
Kenny Guinn (R)*	344,001	68.2
Joe Neal (D)	110,935	22.0

House

		Vote total	Per cent
1	Shelley Berkley (D)*	64,312	53.7
	Lynette Maria Boggs-McDonald (R)	51,148	42.7
2	Jim Gibbons (R)*	149,574	74.3
	Travis O. Souza (D)	40,189	20.0
3	Jon Porter (R)	100,378	56.1
	Dario Herrera (D)	66,659	37.2

New Hampshire

Governor

	Vote total	Per cent
Craig Benson (R)	259,663	58.6
Mark Fernald (D)	169,277	38.2

Senate

	Vote total	Per cent
John E. Sununu (R)	227,229	50.8
Jeanne Shaheen (D)	207,478	46.4

House

		Vote total	Per cent
1	Jeb Bradley (R)	128,993	58.1
	Martha Fuller Clark (D)	85,426	38.5
2	Charles Bass (R)*	125,804	56.8
	Katrina Swett (D)	90,479	40.9

New Jersey

Senate

	Vote total	Per cent
Frank R. Lautenberg (D)	1,138,193	53.9
Doug Forrester (R)	928,439	43.9

House

		Vote total	Per cent
1	Robert E. Andrews (D)*	121,846	92.7
	Timothy Haas (LIBERT)	9,543	7.3
2	Frank A. LoBiondo (R)*	116,834	69.2
	Steven A. Farkas (D)	47,735	28.3
3	H. James Saxton (R)*	123,375	65.0
	Richard Strada (D)	64,364	33.9
4	Christopher H. Smith (R)*	115,293	66.2
	Mary Brennan (D)	55,967	32.1
5	Scott Garrett (R)	118,881	59.5
	Anne Sumers (D)	76,504	38.3
6	Frank Pallone Jr. (D)*	91,379	66.5
	Ric Medrow (R)	42,479	30.9
7	Mike Ferguson (R)*	106,055	58.0
	Tim Carden (D)	74,879	40.9

	Vote total	Per-cent
8 Bill Pascrell Jr. (D)*	88,101	66.8
Jared Silverman (R)	40,318	30.6
9 Steven R. Rothman (D)*	97,108	69.8
Joseph Glass (R)	42,088	30.2
10 Donald M. Payne (D)*	86,433	84.5
Andrew Wirtz (R)	15,913	15.6
11 Rodney Frelinghuysen (R)*	132,938	72.4
Vij Pawar (D)	48,477	26.4
12 Rush D. Holt (D)*	104,806	61.0
DeForest "Buster" Soaries (R)	62,938	36.6
13 Robert Menendez (D)*	72,605	78.3
James Geron (R)	16,852	18.2

New Mexico

Governor

	Vote total	Per-cent
Bill Richardson (D)	268,693	55.5
John A. Sanchez (R)	189,074	39.0
David E. Bacon (GREEN)	26,466	5.5

Senate

	Vote total	Per-cent
Pete V. Domenici (R)*	314,301	65.0
Gloria Tristani (D)	168,039	35.0

House

	Vote total	Per-cent
1 Heather A. Wilson (R)*	95,711	55.3
Richard Romero (D)	77,234	44.7
2 Steve Pearce (R)	79,631	56.2
John Arthur Smith (D)	61,916	43.7
3 Tom Udall (D)*	122,921	100.0

New York

Governor

	Vote total	Per-cent
George E. Pataki (R, C)*	2,262,255	49.4
H. Carl McCall (D, WFM)	1,534,064	33.5
Blase Tom Golisano (INDC)	654,016	14.3

House

	Vote total	Per-cent
1 Timothy H. Bishop (D, WFM)	84,276	50.2
Felix J. Grucci Jr. (R, C, INDC, RTL)*	81,524	48.6
2 Steve Israel (D, INDC, WFM)*	85,451	58.5
Joseph P. Finley (R, C, RTL)	59,117	40.5
3 Peter T. King (R, C, INDC, RTL)*	121,537	71.9
Stuart L. Finz (D)	46,022	27.2
4 Carolyn McCarthy (D, INDC, WFM)*	94,806	56.3
Marilyn F. O'Grady (R, C, RTL)	72,882	43.2
5 Gary L. Ackerman (D, INDC, L, WFM)*	68,773	92.3
Perry S. Reich (C)	5,718	7.7
6 Gregory W. Meeks (D, L, WFM)*	72,799	96.5
7 Joseph Crowley (D, WFM)*	50,967	73.3
Kevin Brawley (R, C)	18,572	26.7
8 Jerrold Nadler (D, L, WFM)*	81,002	76.1
Jim Farrin (R, INDC)	19,674	18.5
9 Anthony Weiner (D, L, WFM)*	60,737	65.7
Alfred F. Donohue (R, C)	31,698	34.3
10 Edolphus Towns (D, L)*	73,859	97.8
11 Major R. Owens (D, WFM)*	76,917	86.6
Susan Cleary (R, INDC)	11,149	12.5
12 Nydia M. Velazquez (D, WFM)*	48,408	95.8
13 Vito J. Fossella (R, C, RTL)*	72,204	69.6
Arne M. Mattsson (D, L, WFM)	29,366	28.3
14 Carolyn B. Maloney (D, INDC, L, WFM)*	95,931	75.3
Anton Srdanovic (R, C)	31,548	24.7
15 Charles B. Rangel (D, WFM)*	84,367	88.5
Jessie Fields (R, INDC)	11,008	11.5
16 Jose E. Serrano (D, WFM)*	50,716	92.1
Frank Dellavalle (R, C)	4,366	7.9
17 Eliot L. Engel (D, L, WFM)*	77,535	62.6
C. Scott Vanderhoef (R, C, INDC)	42,634	34.4
18 Nita M. Lowey (D, WFM)*	98,957	92.0
Michael J. Reynolds (RTL)	8,558	8.0
19 Sue W. Kelly (R, C, INDC)*	121,129	70.0
Janine M. H. Selendy (D)	44,967	26.0
20 John E. Sweeney (R, C)*	140,238	73.3
Frank Stoppenbach (D)	45,878	24.0
21 Michael R. McNulty (D, C, INDC, WFM)*	161,329	75.1
Charles B. Rosenstein (R)	53,525	24.9
22 Maurice D. Hinchey (D, INDC, L, WFM)	113,280	64.2
Eric Hall (R, C)	58,008	32.9
23 John M. McHugh (R, C)*	124,682	100.0
24 Sherwood Boehlert (R)*	108,017	70.7
David L. Walrath (C)	32,991	21.6
25 James T. Walsh (R, C, INDC)*	144,610	72.3
Stephanie Aldersley (D)	53,290	26.6
26 Thomas M. Reynolds (R, C, INDC)*	135,089	73.6
Ayesha F. Nariman (D)	41,140	22.4
27 Jack Quinn (R, C)*	120,117	69.1
Peter Crotty (D, WFM)	47,811	27.5
28 Louise M. Slaughter (D, WFM)*	99,057	62.5
Henry F. Wojtaszek (R, C, INDC)	59,547	37.5
29 Amo Houghton (R, C)*	127,657	73.1
Kisun J. Peters (D)	37,128	21.3

North Carolina

Senate

	Vote total	Per-cent
Elizabeth Dole (R)	1,248,664	53.6
Erskine B. Bowles (D)	1,047,983	45.0

House

	Vote total	Per-cent
1 Frank W. Ballance Jr. (D)	93,157	63.7
Greg Dority (R)	50,907	34.8
2 Bob Etheridge (D)*	100,121	65.4
Joseph L. Ellen (R)	50,965	33.3
3 Walter B. Jones (R)*	131,448	90.7
Gary Goodson (LIBERT)	13,486	9.3
4 David E. Price (D)*	132,185	61.2
Tuan A. Nguyen (R)	78,095	36.1
5 Richard M. Burr (R)*	137,879	70.2
David Crawford (D)	58,558	29.8
6 Howard Coble (R)*	151,430	90.4
Tara Grubb (LIBERT)	16,067	9.6
7 Mike McIntyre (D)*	118,543	71.1
James Adams (R)	45,537	27.3
8 Robin Hayes (R)*	80,298	53.6
Chris Kouri (D)	66,819	44.6
9 Sue Myrick (R)*	140,095	72.4
Ed McGuire (D)	49,974	25.8
10 Cass Ballenger (R)*	102,768	59.3
Ron Daugherty (D)	65,587	37.8
11 Charles H. Taylor (R)*	112,335	55.5
Sam Neill (D)	86,664	42.8
12 Melvin Watt (D)*	98,821	65.3
Jeff Kish (R)	49,588	32.8
13 Brad Miller (D)	100,287	54.7
Carolyn W. Grant (R)	77,688	42.4

North Dakota

	Vote total	Per-cent
AL Earl Pomeroy (D)*	121,073	52.4
Rick Clayburgh (R)	109,957	47.6

Ohio

Governor

	Vote total	Per-cent
Bob Taft (R)*	1,865,007	57.8
Tim Hagan (D)	1,236,924	38.3

House

	Vote total	Per-cent
1 Steve Chabot (R)*	110,760	64.8
Greg Harris (D)	60,168	35.2
2 Rob Portman (R)*	139,218	74.0
Charles W. Sanders (D)	48,785	25.9
3 Michael R. Turner (R)	111,630	58.8
Rick Carne (D)	78,307	41.2
4 Michael G. Oxley (R)*	120,001	67.5
Jim Clark (D)	57,726	32.5
5 Paul E. Gillmor (R)*	126,286	67.1
Roger Anderson (D)	51,872	27.6
John F. Green (LIBERT)	10,096	5.4
6 Ted Strickland (D)*	113,972	59.5
Mike Halleck (R)	77,643	40.5
7 David L. Hobson (R)*	113,252	67.6
Kara Anastasio (D)	45,568	27.2
Frank A. Doden (I)	8,812	5.3
8 John A. Boehner (R)*	119,947	70.8
Jeff Hardenbrook (D)	49,444	29.2
9 Marcy Kaptur (D)*	132,236	74.0
Edward Emery (R)	46,481	26.0
10 Dennis J. Kucinich (D)*	129,997	74.1
Jon A. Heben (R)	41,778	23.8
11 Stephanie Tubbs Jones (D)*	116,590	76.3
Patrick A. Pappano (R)	36,146	23.7
12 Pat Tiberi (R)*	116,982	64.4
Edward S. Brown (D)	64,707	35.6
13 Sherrod Brown (D)*	123,025	69.0
Ed Oliveros (R)	55,357	31.0
14 Steven C. LaTourette (R)*	134,413	72.1
Dale Virgil Blanchard (D)	51,846	27.8
15 Deborah Pryce (R)*	108,193	66.6
Mark P. Brown (D)	54,286	33.4
16 Ralph Regula (R)*	129,734	68.9
Jim Rice (D)	58,644	31.1
17 Tim Ryan (D)	94,441	51.1
Ann Womer Benjamin (R)	62,188	33.7
James A. Traficant Jr. (I)	28,045	15.2
18 Bob Ney (R)*	125,546	100.0

Oklahoma

Governor

	Vote total	Per-cent
Brad Henry (D)	448,143	43.3
Steve Largent (R)	441,277	42.6
Gary L. Richardson (I)	146,200	14.1

Senate

	Vote total	Per-cent
James M. Inhofe (R)*	583,579	57.3
David L. Walters (D)	369,789	36.3
James Germalic (I)	65,056	6.4

House

	Vote total	Per-cent
1 John Sullivan (R)*	119,566	55.6
Doug Dodd (D)	90,649	42.2
2 Brad Carson (D)*	146,748	74.1
Kent Pharaoh (R)	51,234	25.9
3 Frank D. Lucas (R)*	148,206	75.6
Robert T. Murphy (LIBERT)	47,884	24.4
4 Tom Cole (R)	106,452	53.8
Darryl Roberts (D)	91,322	46.2

	Vote total	Percent
5 Ernest Istook (R)*	121,374	62.2
Lou Barlow (D)	63,208	32.4
Donna Davis (I)	10,469	5.4

Oregon

Governor

Theodore R. Kulongoski (D)	618,004	49.0
Kevin L. Mannix (R)	581,785	46.2

Senate

Gordon H. Smith (R)*	712,287	56.2
Bill Bradbury (D)	501,898	39.6

House

1 David Wu (D)*	149,215	62.7
Jim Greenfield (R)	80,917	34.0
2 Greg Walden (R)*	181,295	71.9
Peter Buckley (D)	64,991	25.8
Mike Wood (LIBERT)	5,681	2.3
3 Earl Blumenauer (D)*	156,851	66.8
Sarah Seale (R)	62,821	26.7
4 Peter A. DeFazio (D)*	168,150	63.8
Liz Van Leeuwen (R)	90,523	34.4
5 Darlene Hooley (D)*	137,713	54.7
Brian Boquist (R)	113,441	45.1

Pennsylvania

Governor

Edward G. Rendell (D)	1,913,235	53.4
Mike Fisher (R)	1,589,408	44.4

House

1 Robert A. Brady (D)*	121,076	86.4
Marie G. Delany (R)	17,444	12.5
2 Chaka Fattah (D)*	150,623	87.8
Thomas G. Dougherty (R)	20,988	12.2
3 Phil English (R)*	116,763	77.7
Andrea M. Benson (GREEN)	33,554	22.3
4 Melissa A. Hart (R)*	130,534	64.6
Stevan Drobac Jr. (D)	71,674	35.4
5 John E. Peterson (R)*	124,942	87.4
Thomas A. Martin (LIBERT)	18,078	12.6
6 Jim Gerlach (R)	103,648	51.4
Dan Wofford (D)	98,128	48.6
7 Curt Weldon (R)*	146,296	66.1
Peter A. Lennon (D)	75,055	33.9
8 James C. Greenwood (R)*	127,475	62.6
Timothy T. Reece (D)	76,178	37.4
9 Bill Shuster (R)*	124,184	71.0
John R. Henry (D)	50,558	28.9
10 Don Sherwood (R)*	152,017	92.9
Kurt J. Shotko (GREEN)	11,613	7.1
11 Paul E. Kanjorski (D)*	93,758	55.6
Louis J. Barletta (R)	71,543	42.4
12 John P. Murtha (D)*	124,201	73.5
Bill Choby (R)	44,818	26.5
13 Joseph M. Hoeffel (D)*	107,945	50.9
Melissa Brown (R)	100,295	47.3
14 Mike Doyle (D)*	123,323	100.0
15 Patrick J. Toomey (R)*	98,493	57.4
Edward J. O'Brien (D)	73,212	42.6
16 Joe Pitts (R)*	119,046	88.4
Will Todd (GREEN)	8,720	6.5
Kenneth C. Brenneman (CNSTP)	6,766	5.0
17 Tim Holden (D)*	103,483	51.4
George W. Gekas (R)*	97,802	48.6
18 Tim Murphy (R)	119,885	60.1
Jack M. Machek (D)	79,451	39.9
19 Todd R. Platts (R)*	143,097	91.1
Ben G. Price (GREEN)	7,900	5.0

	Vote total	Percent

Rhode Island

Governor

Donald L. Carcieri (R)	181,827	54.7
Myrth York (D)	150,229	45.2

Senate

Jack Reed (D)*	253,922	78.4
Robert G. Tingle (R)	69,881	21.6

House

1 Patrick J. Kennedy (D)*	95,286	59.9
David W. Rogers (R)	59,370	37.3
2 Jim Langevin (D)*	129,390	76.3
John O. Matson (R)	37,767	22.3

South Carolina

Governor

Mark Sanford (R)	585,422	52.8
Jim Hodges (D)*	521,140	47.1

Senate

Lindsey Graham (R)	600,010	54.4
Alex Sanders (D)	487,359	44.2

House

1 Henry E. Brown Jr. (R)*	127,562	89.6
James E. Dunn (UC)	9,560	6.9
2 Joe Wilson (R)*	144,149	84.1
Mark Whittington (UC)	17,189	10.0
James R. "Jim" Legg (LIBERT)	9,650	5.6
3 J. Gresham Barrett (R)	119,644	67.1
George Brightharp (D)	55,743	31.3
4 Jim DeMint (R)*	122,422	69.0
Peter J. Ashy (D, UC)	52,635	29.7
5 John M. Spratt Jr. (D)*	121,912	85.9
Doug Kendall (LIBERT)	11,013	7.8
Steve Lefemine (CNSTP)	8,930	6.3
6 James E. Clyburn (D)*	115,855	67.0
Gary McLeod (R)	55,490	32.1

South Dakota

Governor

Michael Rounds (R)	189,920	56.8
Jim Abbott (D)	140,263	41.9

Senate

Tim Johnson (D)*	167,481	49.6
John Thune (R)	166,957	49.5

House

AL Bill Janklow (R)	180,023	53.5
Stephanie Herseth (D)	153,656	45.6

Tennessee

Governor

Phil Bredesen (D)	837,284	50.6
Van Hilleary (R)	786,803	47.6

Senate

Lamar Alexander (R)	891,420	54.3
Bob Clement (D)	728,295	44.3

House

1 Bill Jenkins (R)*	127,300	98.8
2 John J. "Jimmy" Duncan Jr. (R)*	146,887	79.0
John Greene (D)	37,035	19.9
3 Zach Wamp (R)*	112,254	64.5
John Wolfe Jr. (D)	58,824	33.8
4 Lincoln Davis (D)	95,989	52.1
Janice H. Bowling (R)	85,680	46.5
5 Jim Cooper (D)	108,903	63.7
Robert Duvall (R)	56,825	33.3
6 Bart Gordon (D)*	117,034	65.9
Robert L. Garrison (R)	57,401	32.3

	Vote total	Percent
7 Marsha Blackburn (R)	138,314	70.7
Tim Barron (D)	51,790	26.5
8 John Tanner (D)*	117,811	70.1
Mat McClain (R)	45,853	27.3
9 Harold E. Ford Jr. (D)*	120,904	83.8
Tony Rush (I)	23,208	16.1

Texas

Governor

Rick Perry (R)*	2,632,591	57.8
Tony Sanchez (D)	1,819,798	40.0

Senate

John Cornyn (R)	2,496,243	55.3
Ron Kirk (D)	1,955,758	43.3

House

1 Max Sandlin (D)*	86,384	56.4
John Lawrence (R)	66,654	43.6
2 Jim Turner (D)*	85,492	60.8
Van Brookshire (R)	53,656	38.2
3 Sam Johnson (R)*	113,974	73.9
Manny Molera (D)	37,503	24.3
4 Ralph M. Hall (D)*	97,304	57.8
John Graves (R)	67,939	40.4
5 Jeb Hensarling (R)	81,439	58.2
Ron Chapman (D)	56,330	40.3
6 Joe L. Barton (R)*	115,396	70.3
Felix Alvarado (D)	45,404	27.7
7 John Culberson (R)*	96,795	89.2
Drew Parks (LIBERT)	11,674	10.8
8 Kevin Brady (R)*	140,575	93.1
Gil Guillory (LIBERT)	10,351	6.9
9 Nick Lampson (D)*	86,710	58.6
Paul Williams (R)	59,635	40.3
10 Lloyd Doggett (D)*	114,428	84.4
Michele Messina (LIBERT)	21,196	15.6
11 Chet Edwards (D)*	74,678	51.6
Ramsey W. Farley (R)	68,236	47.1
12 Kay Granger (R)*	121,208	91.9
Edward A. Hanson (LIBERT)	10,723	8.1
13 William M. "Mac" Thornberry (R)*	119,401	79.3
Zane Reese (D)	31,218	20.7
14 Ron Paul (R)*	102,905	68.1
Corby Windham (D)	48,224	31.9
15 Ruben Hinojosa (D)*	66,311	100.0
16 Silvestre Reyes (D)*	72,383	100.0
17 Charles W. Stenholm (D)*	84,136	51.4
Rob Beckham (R)	77,622	47.4
18 Sheila Jackson-Lee (D)*	99,161	76.9
Phillip J. Abbott (R)	27,980	21.7
19 Larry Combest (R)*	117,092	91.6
Larry Johnson (LIBERT)	10,684	8.4
20 Charlie Gonzalez (D)*	68,685	100.0
21 Lamar Smith (R)*	161,836	72.9
John Courage (D)	56,206	25.3
22 Tom DeLay (R)*	100,499	63.2
Tim Riley (D)	55,716	35.0
23 Henry Bonilla (R)*	77,573	51.5
Henry Cuellar (D)	71,067	47.2
24 Martin Frost (D)*	73,002	64.7
Mike Rivera Ortega (R)	38,332	34.0
25 Chris Bell (D)	63,590	54.8
Tom Reiser (R)	50,041	43.1
26 Michael C. Burgess (R)	123,195	74.8
Paul William Lebon (D)	37,485	22.8
27 Solomon P. Ortiz (D)*	68,559	61.1
Pat Ahumada (R)	41,004	36.5
28 Ciro D. Rodriguez (D)*	71,393	71.1
Gabriel Perales Jr. (R)	26,973	26.9

		Vote total	Per-cent
29	Gene Green (D)*	55,760	95.2
30	Eddie Bernice Johnson (D)*	88,980	74.3
	Ron Bush (R)	28,981	24.2
31	John Carter (R)	111,556	69.1
	David Bagley (D)	44,183	27.4
32	Pete Sessions (R)*	100,226	67.8
	Pauline K. Dixon (D)	44,886	30.3

Utah

House

1	Rob Bishop (R)	109,265	60.9
	Dave Thomas (D)	66,104	36.9
2	Jim Matheson (D)*	110,764	49.4
	John Swallow (R)	109,123	48.7
3	Chris Cannon (R)*	103,598	67.4
	Nancy Jane Woodside (D)	44,533	29.0

Vermont

Governor

	Jim Douglas (R)	103,436	44.9
	Doug Racine (D)	97,565	42.4
	Cornelius "Con" Hogan (I)	22,353	9.7

House

AL	Bernard Sanders (I)*	144,880	64.3
	William Meub (R)	72,813	32.3

Virginia

Senate

	John W. Warner (R)*	1,229,894	82.6
	Nancy Spannaus (I)	145,102	9.7
	Jacob G. Hornberger Jr. (I)	106,055	7.1

House

1	Jo Ann Davis (R)*	113,168	95.9
2	Ed Schrock (R)*	103,807	83.1
	D. C. Amarasinghe (GREEN)	20,589	16.5
3	Robert C. Scott (D)*	87,521	96.1
4	J. Randy Forbes (R)*	108,733	97.9
5	Virgil H. Goode Jr. (R)*	95,360	63.5
	Meredith Richards (D)	54,805	36.5

		Vote total	Per-cent
6	Robert W. Goodlatte (R)*	105,530	97.1
7	Eric Cantor (R)*	113,658	69.5
	Ben L. "Cooter" Jones (D)	49,854	30.5
8	James P. Moran (D)*	102,759	59.8
	Scott C. Tate (R)	64,121	37.3
9	Rick Boucher (D)*	100,075	65.8
	Jay Katzen (R)	52,076	34.2
10	Frank R. Wolf (R)*	115,917	71.7
	John B. Stevens Jr. (D)	45,464	28.1
11	Thomas M. Davis III (R)*	135,379	82.9
	Frank W. Creel (CNSTP)	26,892	16.5

Washington

House

1	Jay Inslee (D)*	114,087	55.6
	Joe Marine (R)	84,696	41.3
2	Rick Larsen (D)*	101,219	50.1
	Norma Smith (R)	92,528	45.8
3	Brian Baird (D)*	119,264	61.7
	Joseph Zarelli (R)	74,065	38.3
4	Doc Hastings (R)*	108,257	66.9
	Craig Mason (D)	53,572	33.3
5	George Nethercutt (R)*	126,757	62.7
	Bart Haggin (D)	65,146	32.2
	Rob Chase (LIBERT)	10,379	5.1
6	Norm Dicks (D)*	126,116	64.2
	Bob Lawrence (R)	61,584	31.4
7	Jim McDermott (D)*	156,300	74.1
	Carol Thorne Cassady (R)	46,256	21.9
8	Jennifer Dunn (R)*	121,633	59.8
	Heidi Behrens-Benedict (D)	75,931	37.3
9	Adam Smith (D)*	95,805	58.5
	Sarah Casada (R)	63,146	38.6

West Virginia

Senate

	John D. Rockefeller IV (D)*	275,281	63.1
	Jay Wolfe (R)	160,902	36.9

House

1	Alan B. Mollohan (D)*	110,941	99.7

		Vote total	Per-cent
2	Shelley Moore Capito (R)*	98,276	60.0
	Jim Humphreys (D)	65,400	40.0
3	Nick J. Rahall II (D)*	87,783	70.2
	Paul E. Chapman (R)	37,229	29.8

Wisconsin

Governor

	James E. Doyle (D)	800,515	45.1
	Scott McCallum (R)*	734,779	41.4
	Ed Thompson (LIBERT)	185,455	10.5

House

1	Paul D. Ryan (R)*	140,176	67.2
	Jeff Thomas (D)	63,895	30.6
2	Tammy Baldwin (D)*	163,313	66.0
	Ron Greer (R)	83,694	33.8
3	Ron Kind (D)*	131,038	62.8
	Bill Arndt (R)	69,955	33.5
4	Gerald D. Kleczka (D)*	122,031	86.3
	Brian Verdin (WG)	18,324	13.0
5	F. James Sensenbrenner Jr. (R)*	191,224	86.1
	Robert R. Raymond (I)	29,567	13.3
6	Tom Petri (R)*	169,834	99.2
7	David R. Obey (D)*	146,364	64.2
	Joe Rothbauer (R)	81,518	35.8
8	Mark Green (R)*	152,745	72.6
	Andrew M. Becker (D)	50,284	23.9

Wyoming

Governor

	Dave Freudenthal (D)	92,662	50.0
	Eli Bebout (R)	88,873	47.9

Senate

	Michael B. Enzi (R)*	133,710	73.0
	Joyce Jansa Corcoran (D)	49,570	27.1

House

AL	Barbara Cubin (R)*	110,229	60.5
	Ron Akin (D)	65,961	36.2

1. Runoff elections for senator and in Congressional District 5 were required because no candidate received a majority vote in the Nov. 5 general election.

108th Congress Special Elections, 2003 Gubernatorial Elections

Special House Elections, 108th Congress

	Vote total	Percent		Vote total	Percent
Hawaii 2nd–Jan. 4, 2003			**South Dakota At Large–June 1, 2004**		
Ed Chase (D)	33,002	43.7	Stephanie Herseth (D)	132,420	50.6
Matt Matsunaqa (D)	23,050	30.5	Larry Diedrich (R)	129,415	49.4
Kentucky 6th CD–Feb. 17, 2004			**Texas 19th CD–June 3, 2003[1]**		
Ben Chandler (D)	84,168	55.2	Randy Neugebauer (R)	28,546	50.5
Alice Forgy Kerr (R)	65,474	42.9	Mike Conaway (R)	27,959	49.5
North Carolina 1st CD–July 20, 2004					
G.K. Butterfield (D)	48,567	71.2			
Greg Dority (R)	18,491	27.1			

Special Senate Elections, 108th Congress

None

2003 Gubernatorial Elections

California Recall Vote[2]			**Louisiana[3]**		
Yes	4,976,274	55.4	Kathleen B. Blanco (D)	731,358	51.9
No	4,007,783	44.6	Bobby Jindal (R)	676,484	48.1
California Governor			**Mississippi**		
Arnold Schwarzenegger (R)	4,206,284	48.6	Haley Barbour (R)	470,404	52.6
Cruz Bustamante (D)	2,724,874	31.5	Ronnie Musgrove (D)	409,787	45.8
Kentucky					
Ernie Fletcher (R)	596,284	55.0			
Ben Chandler (D)	487,159	45.0			

NOTE: Vote totals are included for all candidates listed on the ballot who received 5 percent or more of the total vote. For candidates who received under 5 percent, consult *America Votes 26* (Washington, D.C.: CQ Press, 2005).

1. The Texas election was a special runoff between the two candidates who received the most votes in a regular special election held on May 3, 2003.

2. California in 2003 held a special election with a two-part ballot. The first part was on the question of whether Democratic governor Gray Davis should be recalled. A plurality of 968,491 voted for Davis's recall. The second part of the ballot chose his successor. All candidates ran together regardless of party affiliation. The table above first gives the votes for recall and second gives the votes for the leading Republican and Democratic candidates on the second part of the ballot.

3. Louisiana results are for a runoff election between the two candidates with the highest vote totals in the primary election in which no candidate received a majority. Under Louisiana's system a candidate receiving a majority in the primary is elected governor and no runoff is held.

2004 Elections Returns for Governor, Senate, and House

Following are the official vote returns for the gubernatorial, Senate, and House races compiled by Congressional Quarterly from figures supplied by the fifty state election boards.

Vote totals are included for all candidates listed on the ballot who received 5 percent or more of the total vote. For candidates who received under 5 percent, consult *America Votes 26* (Washington, D.C.: CQ Press, 2005). The percent column shows the percentage of the total vote cast.

An asterisk (*) indicates an incumbent.

An "X" denotes candidates without major part opposition; no votes were tallied.

An "AL" indicates an at-large member of Congress in a state with a single congressional district.

		Vote total	Per-cent
Alabama			
Senate			
	Richard C. Shelby (R)*	1,242,200	67.5
	Wayne Sowell (D)	595,018	32.4
House			
1	Jo Bonner (R)*	161,067	63.1
	Judy McCain Belk (D)	93,938	36.8
2	Terry Everett (R)*	177,086	71.4
	Charles D "Chuck" James (D)	70,562	28.5
3	Mike D. Rogers (R)*	150,411	61.2
	Bill Fuller (D)	95,240	38.7
4	Robert B. Aderholt (R)*	191,110	74.7
	Carl Cole (D)	64,278	25.1
5	Robert E. "Bud" Cramer (D)*	200,999	73.0
	Gerald "Gerry" Wallace (R)	74,145	26.9
6	Spencer Bachus (R)*	264,819	98.8
7	Artur Davis (D)*	183,408	75.0
	Steve F. Cameron (R)	61,019	24.9
Alaska			
Senate			
	Lisa Murkowski (R)*	149,773	48.6
	Tony Knowles (D)	140,424	45.5
House			
AL	Don Young (R)*	213,216	71.1
	Thomas M. Higgins (D)	67,074	22.4
Arizona			
Senate			
	John McCain (R)*	1,505,372	76.7
	Stuart Starky (D)	404,507	20.6
House			
1	Rick Renzi (R)*	148,315	58.5
	Paul Babbitt (D)	91,776	36.2
	John Crockett (LIBERT)	13,260	5.2
2	Trent Franks (R)*	165,260	59.2
	Randy Camacho (D)	107,406	38.5
3	John Shadegg (R)*	181,012	80.1
	Mark J. Yannone (LIBERT)	44,962	19.9

		Vote total	Per-cent
4	Ed Pastor (D)*	77,150	70.1
	Don Karg (R)	28,238	25.7
5	J. D. Hayworth (R)*	159,455	59.5
	Elizabeth Rogers (D)	102,363	38.2
6	Jeff Flake (R)*	202,822	79.4
	Craig Stritar (LIBERT)	52,695	20.6
7	Raúl M. Grijalva (D)*	108,868	62.1
	Joseph "Joe" Sweeney (R)	59,066	33.7
8	Jim Kolbe (R)*	183,363	60.4
	Eva Bacal (D)	109,963	36.2
Arkansas			
Senate			
	Blanche Lincoln (D)*	580,973	55.9
	Jim Holt (R)	458,036	44.1
House			
1	Marion Berry (D)*	162,388	66.6
	Vernon Humphrey (R)	81,556	33.4
2	Vic Snyder (D)*	160,834	58.2
	Marvin Parks (R)	115,655	41.8
3	John Boozman (R)*	160,629	59.3
	Jan Judy (D)	103,158	38.1
4	Mike Ross (D)*	X	X
California			
Senate			
	Barbara Boxer (D)*	6,955,728	57.7
	Bill Jones (R)	4,555,922	37.8
House			
1	Mike Thompson (D)*	189,366	66.9
	Lawrence Wiesner (R)	79,970	28.3
2	Wally Herger (R)*	182,119	66.9
	Mike Johnson (D)	90,310	33.1
3	Dan Lungren (R)*	177,738	61.9
	Gabe Castillo (D)	100,025	34.8
4	John T. Doolittle (R)*	221,926	65.4
	David L. Winters (D)	117,443	34.6
5	Robert T. Matsui (D)*	138,004	71.4
	Mike Dugas (R)	45,120	23.3

		Vote total	Per-cent
6	Lynn Woolsey (D)*	226,423	72.6
	Paul L. Erickson (R)	85,244	27.4
7	George Miller (D)*	166,831	76.1
	Charles R. Hargrave (R)	52,446	23.9
8	Nancy Pelosi (D)*	224,017	82.9
	Jennifer Depalma (R)	31,074	11.5
9	Barbara Lee (D)*	215,630	84.5
	Claudia Bermudez (R)	31,278	12.3
10	Ellen O. Tauscher (D)*	182,750	65.7
	Jeff Ketelson (R)	95,349	34.3
11	Richard W. Pombo (R)*	163,582	61.2
	Gerald M. "Jerry" McNerney (D)	103,587	38.8
12	Tom Lantos (D)*	171,852	68.0
	Mike Garza (R)	52,593	20.8
	Pat Gray (GREEN)	23,038	9.1
13	Pete Stark (D)*	144,605	71.6
	George I. Bruno (R)	48,439	24.0
14	Anna G. Eshoo (D)*	182,712	69.8
	John C. "Chris" Haugen (R)	69,564	26.6
15	Michael M. Honda (D)*	154,385	72.0
	Raymond L. Chukwu (R)	59,953	28.0
16	Zoe Lofgren (D)*	129,222	70.9
	Douglas Adams McNea (R)	47,992	26.3
17	Sam Farr (D)*	148,958	66.7
	Mark Risley (R)	65,117	29.2
18	Dennis Cardoza (D)*	103,732	67.5
	Charles F. Pringle Sr. (R)	49,973	32.5
19	George P. Radanovich (R)*	155,354	66.0
	James Lex Bufford (D)	64,047	27.2
20	Jim Costa (D)	61,005	53.4
	Roy Ashburn (R)	53,231	46.6
21	Devin Nunes (R)*	140,721	73.2
	Fred B. Davis (D)	51,594	26.8
22	Bill Thomas (R)*	209,384	100.0
23	Lois Capps (D)*	153,980	63.0
	Donald E. Regan (R)	83,926	34.4
24	Elton Gallegly (R)*	178,660	62.8
	Brett Wagner (D)	96,397	33.9
25	Howard P. "Buck" McKeon (R)*	145,575	64.4
	Fred "Tim" Willoughby (D)	80,395	35.6
26	David Dreier (R)*	134,596	53.6
	Cynthia M. Matthews (D)	107,522	42.8
27	Brad Sherman (D)*	125,296	62.3
	Robert M. Levy (R)	66,946	33.3
28	Howard L. Berman (D)*	115,303	71.0
	David R. Hernandez Jr. (R)	37,868	23.3
29	Adam B. Schiff (D)*	133,670	64.6
	Harry Frank Scolinos (R)	62,871	30.4
30	Henry A. Waxman (D)*	216,682	71.2
	Victor Elizalde (R)	87,465	28.8

ABBREVIATIONS FOR PARTY DESIGNATIONS

C	Conservative	LIBERT	Libertarian
CNSTP	Constitution	PRO	Progressive
D	Democratic	R	Republican
GREEN	Green	REF	Reform
I	Independent	WFM	Working Families
INDC	Independence	WG	Wisconsin Greens

		Vote total	Percent
31	Xavier Becerra (D)*	89,363	80.2
	Luis Vega (R)	22,048	19.8
32	Hilda L. Solis (D)*	119,144	85.0
	Leland Faegre (LIBERT)	21,002	15.0
33	Diane Watson (D)*	166,801	88.6
	Robert G. Weber Jr. (LIBERT)	21,513	11.4
34	Lucille Roybal-Allard (D)*	82,282	74.5
	Wayne Miller (R)	28,175	25.5
35	Maxine Waters (D)*	125,949	80.5
	Ross Moen (R)	23,591	15.1
36	Jane Harman (D)*	151,208	62.0
	Paul Whitehead (R)	81,666	33.5
37	Juanita Millender-McDonald (D)*	118,823	75.1
	Vernon Van (R)	31,960	20.2
38	Grace F. Napolitano (D)*	116,851	100.0
39	Linda T. Sánchez (D)*	100,132	60.7
	Tim Escobar (R)	64,832	39.3
40	Ed Royce (R)*	147,617	67.9
	J. Tilman Williams (D)	69,684	32.1
41	Jerry Lewis (R)*	181,605	82.9
	Peymon Mottahedek (LIBERT)	37,332	17.1
42	Gary G. Miller (R)*	167,632	68.1
	Lewis Myers (D)	78,393	31.9
43	Joe Baca (D)*	86,830	66.4
	Ed Laning (R)	44,004	33.6
44	Ken Calvert (R)*	138,768	61.6
	Louis Vandenberg (D)	78,796	35.0
45	Mary Bono (R)*	153,523	66.6
	Richard J. Meyer (D)	76,967	33.4
46	Dana Rohrabacher (R)*	171,318	61.9
	Jim Brandt (D)	90,129	32.6
47	Loretta Sanchez (D)*	65,684	60.4
	Alexandria A. "Alex" Coronado (R)	43,099	39.6
48	Christopher Cox (R)*	189,004	65.0
	John L. Graham (D)	93,525	32.2
49	Darrell Issa (R)*	141,658	62.6
	Mike Byron (D)	79,057	34.9
50	Randy "Duke" Cunningham (R)*	169,025	58.4
	Francine P. Busby (D)	105,590	36.5
51	Bob Filner (D)*	111,441	61.6
	Michael Giorgino (R)	63,526	35.1
52	Duncan Hunter (R)*	187,799	69.2
	Brian S. Keliher (D)	74,857	27.6
53	Susan A. Davis (D)*	146,449	66.1
	Darin Hunzeker (R)	63,897	28.9

Colorado

Senate

	Vote total	Percent
Ken Salazar (D)	1,081,188	51.3
Pete Coors (R)	980,668	46.5

House

		Vote total	Percent
1	Diana DeGette (D)*	177,077	73.5
	Roland Chicas (R)	58,659	24.3
2	Mark Udall (D)*	207,900	67.2
	Stephen M. Hackman (R)	94,160	30.4
3	John Salazar (D)*	153,500	50.6
	Greg Walcher (R)	141,376	46.6
4	Marilyn Musgrave (R)*	155,958	51.1
	Stan Matsunaka (D)	136,812	44.8
5	Joel Hefley (R)*	193,333	70.5
	Fred Hardee (D)	74,098	27.0
6	Tom Tancredo (R)*	212,778	59.5
	Joanna L. Conti (D)	139,870	39.1
7	Bob Beauprez (R)*	135,571	54.7
	Dave Thomas (D)	106,026	42.8

Connecticut

Senate

	Vote total	Percent
Christopher J. Dodd (D)*	945,347	66.4
Jack Orchulli (R)	457,749	32.1

House

		Vote total	Percent
1	John B. Larson (D)*	198,802	73.0
	John M. Halstead (R)	73,601	27.0
2	Rob Simmons (R)*	166,412	54.2
	Jim Sullivan (D)	140,536	45.8
3	Rosa DeLauro (D)*	200,638	72.4
	Richter Elser (R)	69,160	25.0
4	Christopher Shays (R)*	152,493	52.4
	Diane Farrell (D)	138,333	47.6
5	Nancy L. Johnson (R)*	168,268	59.8
	Theresa B. Gerratana (D)	107,438	38.2

Delaware

Governor

	Vote total	Percent
Ruth Ann Minner (D)*	185,687	50.9
William Swain Lee (R)	167,115	45.8

House

		Vote total	Percent
AL	Michael N. Castle (R)*	245,978	69.1
	Paul Donnelly (D)	105,716	29.7

Florida

Senate

	Vote total	Percent
Mel Martinez (R)	3,672,864	49.4
Betty Castor (D)	3,590,201	48.3

House

		Vote total	Percent
1	Jeff Miller (R)*	236,604	76.5
	Mark S. Coutu (D)	72,506	23.5
2	Allen Boyd (D)*	201,577	61.6
	Bev Kilmer (R)	125,399	38.3
3	Corrine Brown (D)*	172,833	99.2
4	Ander Crenshaw (R)*	256,157	99.5
5	Ginny Brown-Waite (R)*	240,315	65.9
	Robert G. Whittel (D)	124,140	34.1
6	Cliff Stearns (R)*	211,137	64.4
	David E. Bruderly (D)	116,680	35.6
7	John L. Mica (R)*	X	X
8	Ric Keller (R)*	172,232	60.5
	Stephen Murray (D)	112,343	39.5
9	Michael Bilirakis (R)*	284,035	99.9
10	C.W. Bill Young (R)*	207,175	69.3
	Robert D. "Bob" Derry (D)	91,658	30.7
11	Jim Davis (D)*	191,780	85.8
	Robert Edward Johnson (LIBERT)	31,579	14.1
12	Adam H. Putnam (R)*	179,204	64.9
	Bob Hagenmaier (D)	96,965	35.1
13	Katherine Harris (R)*	190,477	55.3
	Jan Schneider (D)	153,961	44.7
14	Connie Mack (R)	226,662	67.6
	Robert M. Neeld (D)	108,672	32.4
15	Dave Weldon (R)*	210,388	65.4
	Simon Pristoop (D)	111,538	34.6
16	Mark Foley (R)*	215,563	68.0
	Jeff Fisher (D)	101,247	32.0
17	Kendrick B. Meek (D)*	178,690	99.6
18	Ileana Ros-Lehtinen (R)*	143,647	64.7
	Sam Sheldon (D)	78,281	35.3
19	Robert Wexler (D)*	X	X
20	Debbie Wasserman-Schultz (D)	191,195	70.2
	Margaret Hostetter (R)	81,213	29.8
21	Lincoln Diaz-Balart (R)*	146,507	72.8
	Frank J. Gonzalez (LIBERT)	54,736	27.2
22	E. Clay Shaw Jr. (R)*	192,581	62.8
	Robin Rorapaugh (D)	108,258	35.3

		Vote total	Percent
23	Alcee L. Hastings (D)*	X	X
24	Tom Feeney (R)*	X	X
25	Mario Diaz-Balart (R)	X	X

Georgia

Senate

	Vote total	Percent
Johnny Isakson (R)	1,864,202	57.9
Denise L. Majette (D)	1,287,690	40.0

House

		Vote total	Percent
1	Jack Kingston (R)*	188,347	100.0
2	Sanford D. Bishop Jr. (D)*	129,984	66.8
	Dave Eversman (R)	64,645	33.2
3	Jim Marshall (D)*	136,273	62.9
	Calder Clay (R)	80,453	37.1
4	Cynthia A. McKinney (D)	157,461	63.8
	Catherine Davis (R)	89,509	36.2
5	John Lewis (D)*	201,773	100.0
6	Tom Price (R)	267,542	100.0
7	John Linder (R)*	258,982	100.0
8	Lynn Westmoreland (R)	227,524	75.6
	Silvia Delamar (D)	73,632	24.4
9	Charlie Norwood (R)*	197,869	74.3
	Bob Ellis (D)	68,462	25.7
10	Nathan Deal (R)*	219,136	100.0
11	Phil Gingrey (R)*	120,696	57.4
	Rick Crawford (R)	89,591	42.6
12	John Barrow (D)	113,036	51.8
	Max Burns (R)*	105,132	48.2
13	David Scott (D)*	170,657	100.0

Hawaii

Senate

	Vote total	Percent
Daniel K. Inouye (D)*	313,629	75.5
Cam Cavasso (R)	87,172	21.0

House

		Vote total	Percent
1	Neil Abercrombie (D)*	128,567	63.0
	Dalton Tanonaka (R)	69,371	34.0
2	Ed Case (D)*	133,317	62.8
	Mike Gabbard (R)	79,072	37.2

Idaho

Senate

	Vote total	Percent
Michael D. Crapo (R)*	499,796	99.2

House

		Vote total	Percent
1	C. L. "Butch" Otter (R)*	207,662	69.5
	Naomi Preston (D)	90,927	30.5
2	Mike Simpson (R)*	193,704	70.7
	Lin Whitworth (D)	80,133	29.3

Illinois

Senate

	Vote total	Percent
Barack Obama (D)	3,597,456	70.0
Alan L. Keyes (R)	1,390,690	27.1

House

		Vote total	Percent
1	Bobby L. Rush (D)*	212,109	84.9
	Raymond G. Wardingley (R)	37,840	15.1
2	Jesse L. Jackson Jr. (D)*	207,535	88.5
	Stephanie Sailor (LIBERT)	26,990	11.5
3	Daniel Lipinski (D)	167,034	72.6
	Ryan Chlada (R)	57,845	25.2
4	Luis V. Gutierrez (D)*	104,761	83.7
	Tony Cisneros (R)	15,536	12.4
5	Rahm Emanuel (D)*	158,400	76.2
	Bruce Best (R)	49,530	23.8
6	Henry J. Hyde (R)*	139,627	55.8
	Christine Cegelis (D)	110,470	44.2
7	Danny K. Davis (D)*	221,133	86.1
	Antonio Davis-Fairman (R)	35,603	13.9

	Vote total	Percent
8 Melissa Bean (D)	139,792	51.7
Philip M. Crane (R)*	130,601	48.3
9 Jan Schakowsky (D)*	175,282	75.7
Kurt J. Eckhardt (R)	56,135	24.3
10 Mark Steven Kirk (R)*	177,493	64.1
Lee Goodman (D)	99,218	35.9
11 Jerry Weller (R)*	173,057	58.7
Tari Renner (D)	121,903	41.3
12 Jerry F. Costello (D)*	198,962	69.5
Erin R. Zweigart (R)	82,677	28.9
13 Judy Biggert (R)*	200,472	65.0
Gloria Schor Andersen (D)	107,836	35.0
14 J. Dennis Hastert (R)*	191,618	68.6
Ruben K. Zamora (D)	87,590	31.4
15 Timothy V. Johnson (R)*	178,114	61.1
David Gill (D)	113,625	38.9
16 Donald Manzullo (R)*	204,350	69.1
John Kutsch (D)	91,452	30.9
17 Lane Evans (D)*	172,320	60.7
Andrea Lane Zinga (R)	111,680	39.3
18 Ray LaHood (R)*	216,047	70.2
Steve Waterworth (D)	91,548	29.8
19 John Shimkus (R)*	213,451	69.4
Tim Bagwell (D)	94,303	30.6

Indiana

Governor

	Vote total	Percent
Mitch Daniels (R)*	1,302,912	53.2
Joseph E. Kernan (D)*	1,113,900	45.5

Senate

	Vote total	Percent
Evan Bayh (D)*	1,496,976	61.6
Marvin B. Scott (R)	903,913	37.2

House

	Vote total	Percent
1 Peter J. Visclosky (D)*	178,406	68.3
Mark J. Leyva (R)	82,858	31.7
2 Chris Chocola (R)*	140,496	54.2
Joe Donnelly (D)	115,513	44.5
3 Mark Souder (R)*	171,389	69.2
Maria M. Parra (D)	76,232	30.8
4 Steve Buyer (R)*	190,445	69.5
David Sanders (D)	77,574	28.3
5 Dan Burton (R)*	228,718	71.8
Katherine Fox Carr (D)	82,637	26.0
6 Mike Pence (R)*	182,529	67.1
Melina Ann "Mel" Fox (D)	85,123	31.3
7 Julia Carson (D)*	121,303	54.4
Andrew "Andy" Horning (R)	97,491	43.7
8 John Hostettler (R)*	145,576	53.4
Jon P. Jennings (D)	121,522	44.5
9 Mike Sodrel (R)	142,197	49.5
Baron P. Hill (D)*	140,772	49.0

Iowa

Senate

	Vote total	Percent
Charles E. Grassley (R)*	1,038,175	70.2
Arthur Small (D)	412,365	27.9

House

	Vote total	Percent
1 Jim Nussle (R)*	159,993	55.2
Bill Gluba (D)	125,490	43.3
2 Jim Leach (R)*	176,684	58.9
Dave Franker (D)	117,405	39.2
3 Leonard L. Boswell (D)*	168,007	55.2
Stan Thompson (R)	136,099	44.7
4 Tom Latham (R)*	181,294	60.9
Paul W. Johnson (D)	116,121	39.0
5 Steve King (R)*	168,583	63.3
E. Joyce Schulte (D)	97,597	36.6

Kansas

Senate

	Vote total	Percent
Sam Brownback (R)*	780,863	69.2
Lee Jones (D)	310,337	27.5

House

	Vote total	Percent
1 Jerry Moran (R)*	239,776	90.7
Jack W. Warner (LIBERT)	24,517	9.3
2 Jim Ryun (R)*	165,325	56.1
Nancy Boyda (D)	121,532	41.3
3 Dennis Moore (D)*	184,050	54.8
Kris Kobach (R)	145,542	43.3
4 Todd Tiahrt (R)*	173,151	66.1
Michael R. Kinard (D)	81,388	31.1

Kentucky

Senate

	Vote total	Percent
Jim Bunning (R)*	873,507	50.7
Daniel Mongiardo (D)	850,855	49.3

House

	Vote total	Percent
1 Edward Whitfield (R)*	175,972	67.3
Billy R. Cartwright (D)	85,229	32.6
2 Ron Lewis (R)*	185,394	67.9
Adam Smith (D)	87,585	32.1
3 Anne M. Northup (R)*	197,736	60.3
Tony Miller (D)	124,040	37.8
4 Geoff Davis (R)	160,982	54.4
Nick Clooney (D)	129,876	43.9
5 Harold Rogers (R)*	177,579	100.0
6 Ben Chandler (D)*	175,355	58.6
Tom Buford (R)	119,716	40.0

Louisiana

Senate

	Vote total	Percent
David Vitter (R)	943,014	51.0
Chris John (D)	542,150	29.3
John Kennedy (D)	275,821	14.9

House

	Vote total	Percent
1 Bobby Jindal (R)	225,708	78.4
Roy Armstrong (D)	19,266	6.7
2 William J. Jefferson (D)*	173,510	79.0
Arthur L. "Art" Schwertz (R)	46,097	21.0
3 Billy Tauzin III (R)	84,680	32.0
Charlie Melancon (D)	63,328	23.9
Craig Romero (R)	61,132	23.1
Damon J. Baldone (D)	25,783	9.7
Charmaine Caccioppi (D)	19,347	7.3
Dec. 4 runoff[1]		
Charlie Melancon (D)	57,611	50.2
Billy Tauzin III (R)	57,042	49.8
4 Jim McCrery (R)*	X	X
5 Rodney Alexander (R)*	141,845	59.4
Zelma "Tisa" Blakes (D)	58,591	24.6
John W. "Jock" Scott (R)	37,971	16.0
6 Richard H. Baker (R)*	189,106	72.2
Rufus Holt Craig Jr. (D)	50,732	19.4
Edward Anthony "Scott" Galmon (D)	22,031	8.4
7 Charles Boustany Jr. (R)	105,761	38.6
Willie Landry Mount (D)	69,079	25.2
Don Cravins (D)	67,389	24.6
David Thibodaux (R)	26,526	9.7
Dec. 4 runoff[1]		
Charles Boustany Jr. (R)	75,039	55.0
Willie Landry Mount (D)	61,493	45.0

Maine

House

	Vote total	Percent
1 Tom Allen (D)*	219,077	59.7
Charles E. Summers Jr. (R)	147,663	40.3
2 Michael H. Michaud (D)*	199,303	58.0
Brian N. Hamel (R)	135,547	39.5

Maryland

Senate

	Vote total	Percent
Barbara A. Mikulski (D)*	1,504,691	64.8
E.J. Pipkin (R)	783,055	33.7

House

	Vote total	Percent
1 Wayne T. Gilchrest (R)*	245,149	75.8
Kostas Alexakis (D)	77,872	24.1
2 C.A. Dutch Ruppersberger (D)*	164,751	66.6
Jane Brooks (R)	75,812	30.7
3 Benjamin L. Cardin (D)*	182,066	63.4
Robert P. Duckworth (R)	97,008	33.8
4 Albert R. Wynn (D)*	196,809	75.2
John McKinnis (R)	52,907	20.2
5 Steny H. Hoyer (D)*	204,867	68.7
Brad Jewitt (R)	87,189	29.2
6 Roscoe G. Bartlett (R)*	206,076	67.4
Kenneth T. Bosley (D)	90,108	29.5
7 Elijah E. Cummings (D)*	179,189	73.4
Tony Salazar (R)	60,102	24.6
8 Chris Van Hollen (D)*	215,129	74.8
Chuck Floyd (R)	71,989	25.0

Massachusetts

House

	Vote total	Percent
1 John W. Olver (D)*	229,465	99.0
2 Richard E. Neal (D)*	217,682	98.7
3 Jim McGovern (D)*	192,036	70.5
Ronald A. Crews (R)	80,197	29.4
4 Barney Frank (D)*	219,260	77.7
Charles A. Morse (I)	62,293	22.1
5 Martin T. Meehan (D)*	179,652	67.0
Thomas P. Tierney (R)	88,232	32.9
6 John F. Tierney (D)*	213,458	69.9
Steven P. O'Malley Jr. (R)	91,597	30.0
7 Edward J. Markey (D)*	202,399	73.6
Kenneth G. Chase (R)	60,334	21.9
8 Michael E. Capuano (D)*	165,852	98.7
9 Stephen F. Lynch (D)*	218,167	99.0
10 Bill Delahunt (D)*	222,013	65.9
Michael J. Jones (R)	114,879	34.1

Michigan

House

	Vote total	Percent
1 Bart Stupak (D)*	211,571	65.6
Don Hooper (R)	105,706	32.8
2 Peter Hoekstra (R)*	225,343	69.3
Kimon Kotos (D)	94,040	28.9
3 Vernon J. Ehlers (R)*	214,465	66.6
Peter H. Hickey (D)	101,395	31.5
4 Dave Camp (R)*	205,274	64.4
Mike Huckleberry (D)	110,885	34.8
5 Dale E. Kildee (D)*	208,163	67.2
Myrah Kirkwood (R)	96,934	31.3
6 Fred Upton (R)*	197,425	65.3
Scott Elliot (D)	97,978	32.4
7 Joe Schwarz (R)	176,053	58.4
Sharon Renier (D)	109,527	36.3
8 Mike Rogers (R)*	207,925	61.1
Robert Alexander (D)	125,619	36.9
9 Joe Knollenberg (R)*	199,210	58.5
Steven Reifman (D)	134,764	39.5
10 Candice S. Miller (R)*	227,720	68.6
Rob Casey (D)	98,029	29.5
11 Thaddeus McCotter (R)*	186,431	57.0
Phillip Truran (D)	134,301	41.0

		Vote total	Percent
12	Sander M. Levin (D)*	210,827	69.3
	Randell J. Shafer (R)	88,256	29.0
13	Carolyn Cheeks Kilpatrick (D)*	173,246	78.2
	Cynthia Cassell (R)	40,935	18.5
14	John Conyers Jr. (D)*	213,681	83.9
	Veronica Pedraza (R)	35,089	13.8
15	John D. Dingell (D)*	218,409	70.9
	Dawn Anne Reamer (R)	81,828	26.6

Minnesota

House

1	Gil Gutknecht (R)*	193,132	59.6
	Leigh Pomeroy (D)	115,088	35.5
2	John Kline (R)*	206,313	56.4
	Teresa Daly (D)	147,527	40.3
3	Jim Ramstad (R)*	231,871	64.6
	Deborah Watts (D)	126,665	35.3
4	Betty McCollum (D)*	182,387	57.5
	Patrice Bataglia (R)	105,467	33.2
	Peter F. Vento (INDC)	29,099	9.2
5	Martin Olav Sabo (D)*	218,434	69.7
	Daniel Nielsen Mathias (R)	76,600	24.4
	Jay Pond (GREEN)	17,984	5.7
6	Mark Kennedy (R)*	203,669	54.0
	Patty Wetterling (D)	173,309	45.9
7	Collin C. Peterson (D)*	207,628	66.1
	David E. Sturrock (R)	106,349	33.8
8	James L. Oberstar (D)*	228,586	65.2
	Mark Groettum (R)	112,693	32.2

Mississippi

House

1	Roger Wicker (R)*	219,328	79.0
	Barbara Dale Washer (REF)	58,256	21.1
2	Bennie Thompson (D)*	154,626	58.4
	Clinton B. LeSueur (R)	107,647	40.6
3	Charles W. "Chip" Pickering Jr. (R)*	234,874	80.1
	Jim Giles (I)	40,426	13.8
	Lamonica L. Magee (REF)	18,068	6.2
4	Gene Taylor (D)*	181,614	64.8
	Michael Lott (R)	96,740	34.5

Missouri

Governor

	Matt Blunt (R)	1,382,419	50.8
	Claire McCaskill (D)	1,301,442	47.9

Senate

	Christopher S. Bond (R)*	1,518,089	56.1
	Nancy Farmer (D)	1,158,261	42.8

House

1	William Lacy Clay (D)*	213,658	75.3
	Leslie L. Farr II (R)	64,791	22.8
2	Todd Akin (R)*	228,725	65.4
	George D. "Boots" Weber (D)	115,366	33.0
3	Russ Carnahan (D)	146,894	52.9
	Bill Federer (R)	125,422	45.1
4	Ike Skelton (D)*	190,800	66.2
	James A. "Jim" Noland Jr. (R)	93,334	32.4
5	Emanuel Cleaver II (D)	161,727	55.2
	Jeanne Patterson (R)	123,431	42.1
6	Sam Graves (R)*	196,516	63.8
	Charles S. Broomfield (D)	106,987	34.8
7	Roy Blunt (R)*	210,080	70.4
	Jim Newberry (D)	84,356	28.3
8	Jo Ann Emerson (R)*	194,039	72.2
	Dean Henderson (D)	71,543	26.6

		Vote total	Percent
9	Kenny Hulshof (R)*	193,429	64.6
	Linda Jacobsen (D)	101,343	33.8

Montana

Governor

	Brian Schweitzer (D)	225,016	50.4
	Bob Brown (R)	205,313	46.0

House

AL	Denny Rehberg (R)*	286,076	64.4
	Tracy Velazquez (D)	145,606	32.8

Nebraska

House

1	Jeff Fortenberry (R)	143,756	54.2
	Matt Connealy (D)	113,971	43.0
2	Lee Terry (R)*	152,608	61.1
	Nancy Thompson (D)	90,292	36.2
3	Tom Osborne (R)*	218,751	87.5
	Donna J. Anderson (D)	26,434	10.6

Nevada

Senate

	Harry Reid (D)*	494,805	61.1
	Richard Ziser (R)	284,640	35.1

House

1	Shelley Berkley (D)*	133,569	66.0
	Russ Mickelson (R)	63,005	31.1
2	Jim Gibbons (R)*	195,466	67.2
	Angie G. Cochran (D)	79,978	27.5
3	Jon Porter (R)*	162,240	54.5
	Tom Gallagher (D)	120,365	40.4

New Hampshire

Governor

	John Lynch (D)	340,299	51.0
	Craig Benson (R)*	325,981	48.9

Senate

	Judd Gregg (R)*	434,847	66.2
	Doris "Granny D" Haddock (D)	221,549	33.7

House

1	Jeb Bradley (R)*	204,836	63.3
	Justin Nadeau (D)	118,226	36.6
2	Charles Bass (R)*	191,188	58.3
	Paul Hodes (D)	125,280	38.2

New Jersey

House

1	Robert E. Andrews (D)*	201,163	75.0
	S. Daniel Hutchison (R)	66,109	24.6
2	Frank A. LoBiondo (R)*	172,779	65.1
	Timothy J. Robb (D)	86,792	32.7
3	H. James Saxton (R)*	195,938	63.4
	Herb Conaway (D)	107,034	34.7
4	Christopher H. Smith (R)*	192,671	67.0
	Amy Vasquez (D)	92,826	32.3
5	Scott Garrett (R)*	171,220	57.6
	Dorothea Anne Wolfe (D)	122,259	41.1
6	Frank Pallone Jr. (D)*	153,981	66.9
	Sylvester Fernandez (R)	70,942	30.8
7	Mike Ferguson (R)*	162,597	56.9
	Steve Brozak (D)	119,081	41.7
8	Bill Pascrell Jr. (D)*	152,001	69.5
	George Ajjan (R)	62,747	28.7
9	Steven R. Rothman (D)*	146,038	67.5
	Edward Trawinski (R)	68,564	31.7
10	Donald M. Payne (D)*	155,697	96.9
11	Rodney Frelinghuysen (R)*	200,915	67.9
	James W. Buell (D)	91,811	31.0

		Vote total	Percent
12	Rush D. Holt (D)*	171,691	59.2
	Bill Spadea (R)	115,014	39.7
13	Robert Menendez (D)*	121,018	75.9
	Richard W. Piatkowski (R)	35,288	22.1

New Mexico

House

1	Heather A. Wilson (R)*	147,372	54.4
	Richard Romero (D)	123,339	45.5
2	Steve Pearce (R)*	130,498	60.2
	Gary King (D)	86,292	39.8
3	Tom Udall (D)*	175,269	68.7
	Gregory M. Tucker (R)	79,935	31.3

New York

Senate

	Charles E. Schumer (D, INDC, WFM)*	4,769,824	71.2
	Howard Mills (R)	1,625,069	24.2

House

1	Timothy H. Bishop (D, INDC, WFM)*	156,354	56.2
	Bill Manger (R, C)	121,855	43.8
2	Steve Israel (D, INDC, WFM)*	161,593	66.6
	Richard Hoffmann (R, C)	80,950	33.4
3	Peter T. King (R, INDC, C)*	171,259	63.0
	Blair H. Mathies Jr. (D)	100,737	37.0
4	Carolyn McCarthy (D, INDC, WFM)*	159,969	63.0
	James A. Garner (R, C)	94,141	37.0
5	Gary L. Ackerman (D, INDC, WFM)*	119,726	71.3
	Stephen Graves (R, C)	46,867	27.9
6	Gregory W. Meeks (D, WFM)*	129,688	100.0
7	Joseph Crowley (D, WFM)*	104,275	80.9
	Joseph Cinquemain (R, C)	24,548	19.1
8	Jerrold Nadler (D, WFM)*	162,082	80.5
	Peter Hort (R,C,INDC)	39,240	19.5
9	Anthony Weiner (D, WFM)*	113,025	71.3
	Gerard J. Cronin (R, C, INDC)	45,451	28.7
10	Edolphus Towns (D, WFM)*	136,113	91.5
	Harvey R. Clarke (R)	11,099	7.5
11	Major R. Owens (D, WFM)*	144,999	94.0
12	Nydia M. Velazquez (D, WFM)*	107,796	86.3
	Paul A. Rodriguez (R, C)	17,166	13.7
13	Vito J. Fossella (R, C)*	112,934	59.0
	Frank J. Barbaro (D, INDC, WFM)	78,500	41.0
14	Carolyn B. Maloney (D, INDC, WFM)*	186,688	81.1
	Anton Srdanovic (R, C)	43,623	18.9
15	Charles B. Rangel (D, WFM)*	161,351	91.1
	Kenneth P. Jefferson Jr. (R)	12,355	7.0
16	José E. Serrano (D, WFM)*	111,638	95.2
17	Eliot L. Engel (D, WFM)*	140,530	76.2
	Matthew I. Brennan (R)	40,524	22.0
18	Nita M. Lowey (D, INDC, WFM)*	170,715	69.8
	Richard A. Hoffman (R)	73,975	30.2
19	Sue W. Kelly (R, INDC, C)*	175,401	66.7
	Michael Jaliman (D)	87,429	33.3
20	John E. Sweeney (R, INDC, C)*	188,753	65.8
	Doris F. Kelly (D)	96,630	33.7

	Vote total	Per-cent
21 Michael R. McNulty (D, C, INDC, WFM)*	194,033	70.8
Warren Redlich (R)	80,121	29.2
22 Maurice D. Hinchey (D, C, INDC, WFM)*	167,489	67.2
William A. Brenner (R)	81,881	32.8
23 John M. McHugh (R, C, INDC, WFM)*	160,079	70.7
Robert J. Johnson (D)	66,448	29.3
24 Sherwood Boehlert (R, INDC)*	143,000	56.9
Jeffrey A. Miller (D)	85,140	33.9
David L. Walrath (C)	23,228	9.2
25 James T. Walsh (R, INDC, C)*	189,063	90.4
Howie Hawkins (GREEN)	20,106	9.6
26 Thomas M. Reynolds (R, INDC, C)*	157,466	55.6
Jack Davis (D, WFM)	125,613	44.4
27 Brian Higgins (D, INDC, WFM)	143,332	50.7
Nancy Naples (R, C)	139,558	49.3
28 Louise M. Slaughter (D, WFM)*	159,655	72.6
Michael D. Laba (R, C)	54,543	24.8
29 John R. "Randy" Kuhl Jr. (R)	136,883	50.7
Samara Barend (D, WFM)	110,241	40.8
Mark W. Assini (C)	17,272	6.4

North Carolina

Governor

	Vote total	Per-cent
Michael F. Easley (D)*	1,939,154	55.6
Patrick J. Ballantine (R)	1,495,021	42.9

Senate

Richard M. Burr (R)	1,791,450	51.6
Erskine Bowles (D)	1,632,527	47.0

House

1 G.K. Butterfield (D)*	137,667	64.0
Greg Dority (R)	77,508	36.0
2 Bob Etheridge (D)*	145,079	62.3
Billy J. Creech (R)	87,811	37.7
3 Walter B. Jones (R)*	171,863	70.7
Roger A. Eaton (D)	71,227	29.3
4 David E. Price (D)*	217,441	64.1
Todd A. Batchelor (R)	121,717	35.9
5 Virginia Foxx (R)	167,546	58.8
Jim A. Harrell Jr. (D)	117,271	41.2
6 Howard Coble (R)*	207,470	73.1
William W. Jordan (D)	76,153	26.9
7 Mike McIntyre (D)*	180,382	73.2
Ken Plonk (R)	66,084	26.8
8 Robin Hayes (R)*	125,070	55.5
Beth Troutman (D)	100,101	44.5
9 Sue Myrick (R)*	210,783	70.2
Jack Flynn (D)	89,318	29.8
10 Patrick T. McHenry (R)	157,884	64.1
Anne N. Fischer (D)	88,233	35.9
11 Charles H. Taylor (R)*	159,709	54.9
Patsy Keever (D)	131,188	45.1
12 Melvin Watt (D)*	154,908	66.8
Ada M. Fisher (R)	76,898	33.2
13 Brad Miller (D)*	160,896	58.8
Virginia Johnson (R)	112,788	41.2

North Dakota

Governor

John Hoeven (R)*	220,803	71.3
Joseph A. Satrom (D)	84,877	27.4

Senate

Byron L. Dorgan (D)*	212,143	68.3
Mike Liffrig (R)	98,553	31.7

House

AL Earl Pomeroy (D)*	185,130	59.6
Duane Sand (R)	125,684	40.4

Ohio

Senate

George V. Voinovich (R)*	3,464,356	63.9
Eric D. Fingerhut (D)	1,961,249	36.1

House

1 Steve Chabot (R)*	173,430	59.8
Greg Harris (D)	116,235	40.1
2 Rob Portman (R)*	227,102	71.7
Charles W. Sanders (D)	89,598	28.3
3 Michael R. Turner (R)*	197,290	62.3
Jane Mitakides (D)	119,448	37.7
4 Michael G. Oxley (R)*	167,807	58.6
Ben Konop (D)	118,538	41.4
5 Paul E. Gillmor (R)*	196,649	67.0
Robin Weirauch (D)	96,656	33.0
6 Ted Strickland (D)*	223,844	99.9
7 David L. Hobson (R)*	186,534	65.0
Kara Anastasio (D)	100,617	35.0
8 John A. Boehner (R)*	201,675	69.0
Jeff Hardenbrook (D)	90,574	31.0
9 Marcy Kaptur (D)*	205,149	68.1
Larry A. Kaczala (R)	95,983	31.9
10 Dennis J. Kucinich (D)*	172,406	60.0
Edward Fitzpatrick Herman (R)	96,463	33.6
Barbara Ann Ferris (I)	18,343	6.4
11 Stephanie Tubbs Jones (D)*	222,371	100.0
12 Pat Tiberi (R)*	198,912	62.0
Edward S. Brown (D)	122,109	38.0
13 Sherrod Brown (D)*	201,004	67.4
Robert Lucas (R)	97,090	32.6
14 Steven C. LaTourette (R)*	201,652	62.7
Capri S. Cafaro (D)	119,714	37.3
15 Deborah Pryce (R)*	166,520	60.0
Mark P. Brown (D)	110,915	40.0
16 Ralph Regula (R)*	202,544	66.5
Jeff Seemann (D)	101,817	33.5
17 Tim Ryan (D)*	212,800	77.2
Frank V. Cusimano (R)	62,871	22.8
18 Bob Ney (R)*	177,600	66.2
Brian R. Thomas (D)	90,820	33.8

Oklahoma

Senate

Tom Coburn (R)	763,433	52.8
Brad Carson (D)	596,750	41.2
Sheila Bilyeu (I)	86,663	6.0

House

1 John Sullivan (R)*	187,145	60.2
Doug Dodd (D)	116,731	37.5
2 Dan Boren (D)	179,579	65.9
Wayland Smalley (R)	92,963	34.1
3 Frank D. Lucas (R)*	215,510	82.2
Gregory M. Wilson (I)	46,621	17.8
4 Tom Cole (R)*	198,985	77.8
Charlene K. Bradshaw (I)	56,869	22.2
5 Ernest Istook (R)*	180,430	66.1
Bert Smith (D)	92,719	33.9

Oregon

Senate

Ron Wyden (D)*	1,128,728	63.4
Al King (R)	565,254	31.7

House

1 David Wu (D)*	203,771	57.5
Goli Ameri (R)	135,164	38.1
2 Greg Walden (R)*	248,461	71.6
John C. McColgan (D)	88,914	25.6
3 Earl Blumenauer (D)*	245,559	70.9
Tami Mars (R)	82,045	23.7
4 Peter A. DeFazio (D)*	228,611	61.0
Jim Feldkamp (R)	140,882	37.6
5 Darlene Hooley (D)*	184,833	52.9
Jim Zupancic (R)	154,993	44.3

Pennsylvania

Senate

Arlen Specter (R)*	2,925,080	52.6
Joseph M. Hoeffel (D)	2,334,126	42.0

House

1 Robert A. Brady (D)*	214,462	86.3
Deborah L. Williams (R)	33,266	13.4
2 Chaka Fattah (D)*	253,226	88.0
Stewart Bolno (R)	34,411	12.0
3 Phil English (R)*	166,580	60.1
Steven Porter (D)	110,684	39.9
4 Melissa A. Hart (R)*	204,329	63.1
Stevan Drobac Jr. (D)	116,303	35.9
5 John E. Peterson (R)*	192,852	88.0
Thomas A. Martin (LIBERT)	26,239	12.0
6 Jim Gerlach (R)*	160,348	51.0
Lois Murphy (D)	153,977	49.0
7 Curt Weldon (R)*	196,556	58.8
Paul Scoles (D)	134,932	40.3
8 Michael G. Fitzpatrick (R)	183,229	55.3
Virginia Waters Schrader (D)	143,427	43.3
9 Bill Shuster (R)*	184,320	69.5
Paul I. Politis (D)	80,787	30.5
10 Don Sherwood (R)	191,967	92.8
Veronica A. Hannevig (CNSTP)	14,805	7.2
11 Paul E. Kanjorski (D)*	171,147	94.4
Kenneth C. Brenneman (CNSTP)	10,105	5.6
12 John P. Murtha (D)*	204,504	100.0
13 Allyson Y. Schwartz (D)	171,763	55.7
Melissa Brown (R)	127,205	41.3
14 Mike Doyle (D)*	220,139	100.0
15 Charlie Dent (R)	170,634	58.6
Joe Driscoll (D)	114,646	39.4
16 Joe Pitts (R)*	183,620	64.4
Lois K. Herr (D)	98,410	34.5
17 Tim Holden (D)*	172,412	59.1
Scott Paterno (R)	113,592	38.9
18 Tim Murphy (R)*	197,894	62.8
Mark G. Boles (D)	117,420	37.2
19 Todd R. Platts (R)*	224,274	91.4

Rhode Island

House

1 Patrick J. Kennedy (D)*	124,923	64.1
David W. Rogers (R)	69,819	35.9
2 Jim Langevin (D)*	154,392	74.5
Arthur "Chuck" Barton III (R)	43,139	20.8

	Vote total	Percent

South Carolina

Senate

| Jim DeMint (R) | 857,167 | 53.7 |
| Inez Tenenbaum (D) | 704,384 | 44.1 |

House

1 Henry E. Brown Jr. (R)*	186,448	87.8
James E. Dunn (GREEN)	25,674	12.1
2 Joe Wilson (R)*	181,862	65.0
Michael Ray Ellisor (D)	93,249	33.3
3 J. Gresham Barrett (R)*	191,052	99.5
4 Bob Inglis (R)	188,795	69.8
Brandon P. Brown (D)	78,376	29.0
5 John M. Spratt Jr. (D)*	152,867	63.0
Albert F. Spencer (R)	89,568	36.9
6 James E. Clyburn (D)*	161,987	67.0
Gary McLeod (R, C)	79,600	32.9

South Dakota

Senate

| John Thune (R) | 197,848 | 50.6 |
| Tom Daschle (D)* | 193,340 | 49.4 |

House

| AL Stephanie Herseth (D) | 207,837 | 53.4 |
| Larry Diedrich (R) | 178,823 | 45.9 |

Tennessee

House

1 Bill Jenkins (R)*	172,543	73.9
Graham Leonard (D)	56,361	24.1
2 John J. "Jimmy" Duncan Jr. (R)*	215,575	79.1
John Greene (D)	52,155	19.1
3 Zach Wamp (R)*	166,154	64.7
John Wolfe Jr. (D)	84,295	32.8
4 Lincoln Davis (D)*	138,459	54.8
Janice H. Bowling (R)	109,993	43.5
5 Jim Cooper (D)*	168,970	69.3
Scott Knapp (R)	74,978	30.7
6 Bart Gordon (D)*	167,448	64.2
Nick Demas (R)	87,523	33.6
7 Marsha Blackburn (R)*	232,404	100.0
8 John Tanner (D)*	173,623	74.3
James L. Hart (R)	59,853	25.6
9 Harold E. Ford Jr. (D)*	190,648	82.0
Ruben M. Fort (R)	41,578	17.9

Texas

House

1 Louie Gohmert (R)	157,068	61.5
Max Sandlin (D)*	96,281	37.7
2 Ted Poe (R)	139,951	55.5
Nick Lampson (D)*	108,156	42.9
3 Sam Johnson (R)*	180,099	85.6
Paul Jenkins (I)	16,966	8.1
James Vessels (LIBERT)	13,287	6.3
4 Ralph M. Hall (R)*	182,866	68.2
Jim Nickerson (D)	81,585	30.4
5 Jeb Hensarling (R)*	148,816	64.5
Bill Bernstein (D)	75,911	32.9
6 Joe L. Barton (R)*	168,767	66.0
Morris Meyer (D)	83,609	32.7
7 John Culberson (R)*	175,440	64.1
John Martinez (D)	91,126	33.3
8 Kevin Brady (R)*	179,599	68.9
James "Jim" Wright (D)	77,324	29.7
9 Al Green (D)	114,462	72.2
Arlette Molina (R)	42,132	26.6

	Vote total	Percent

10 Michael McCaul (R)	182,113	78.6
Robert Fritsche (LIBERT)	35,569	15.4
Lorenzo Sadun (I) (write-in)	13,961	6.0
11 K. Michael Conaway (R)	177,291	76.8
Wayne Raasch (D)	50,339	21.8
12 Kay Granger (R)*	173,222	72.3
Felix Alvarado (D)	66,316	27.7
13 William M. "Mac" Thornberry (R)*	189,448	92.3
M.J. "Smitty" Smith (LIBERT)	15,793	7.7
14 Ron Paul (R)*	173,668	100.0
15 Rubén Hinojosa (D)*	96,089	57.8
Michael D. Thamm (R)	67,917	40.8
16 Silvestre Reyes (D)*	108,577	67.5
David Brigham (R)*	49,972	31.1
17 Chet Edwards (D)*	125,309	51.2
Arlene Wohlgemuth (R)	116,049	47.4
18 Sheila Jackson-Lee (D)*	136,018	88.9
Tom Bazan (I)	9,787	6.4
19 Randy Neugebauer (R)*	136,459	58.4
Charles W. Stenholm (D)*	93,531	40.1
20 Charlie Gonzalez (D)*	112,480	65.5
Roger Scott (R)	54,976	32.0
21 Lamar Smith (R)*	209,774	61.5
Rhett R. Smith (D)	121,129	35.5
22 Tom DeLay (R)*	150,386	55.2
Richard R. Morrison (D)	112,034	41.1
23 Henry Bonilla (R)	170,716	69.3
Joseph P. "Joe" Sullivan (D)	72,480	29.4
24 Kenny Marchant (R)	154,435	64.0
Gary R. Page (D)	82,599	34.2
25 Lloyd Doggett (D)*	108,309	67.6
Rebecca Armendariz Klein (R)	49,252	30.7
26 Michael C. Burgess (R)*	180,519	65.8
Lico Reyes (D)	89,809	32.7
27 Solomon P. Ortiz (D)*	112,081	63.1
William "Willie" Vaden (R)	61,955	34.9
28 Henry Cuellar (D)	106,323	59.0
James F. "Jim" Hopson (R)	69,538	38.6
29 Gene Green (D)*	78,256	94.1
Clifford Lee Messina (LIBERT)	4,868	5.9
30 Eddie Bernice Johnson (D)*	144,513	93.0
John Davis (LIBERT)	10,821	7.0
31 John Carter (R)*	160,247	64.8
Jon Porter (D)	80,292	32.5
32 Pete Sessions (R)*	109,859	54.3
Martin Frost (D)*	89,030	44.0

Utah

Governor

| Jon Huntsman Jr. (R) | 531,190 | 57.7 |
| Scott M. Matheson Jr. (D) | 380,359 | 41.3 |

Senate

| Robert F. Bennett (R)* | 626,640 | 68.7 |
| R. Paul Van Dam (D) | 258,955 | 28.4 |

House

1 Rob Bishop (R)*	199,615	67.9
Steve Thompson (D)	85,630	29.1
2 Jim Matheson (D)*	187,250	54.8
John Swallow (R)	147,778	43.2
3 Chris Cannon (R)*	173,010	63.4
Beau Babka (D)	88,748	32.5

	Vote total	Percent

Vermont

Governor

| Jim Douglas (R)* | 181,540 | 58.7 |
| Peter Clavelle (D) | 117,327 | 37.9 |

Senate

| Patrick J. Leahy (D)* | 216,972 | 70.6 |
| John "Jack" McMullen (R) | 75,398 | 24.5 |

House

AL Bernard Sanders (I, PRO)*	205,774	67.5
Greg Parke (R)	74,271	24.4
Larry Drown (D)	21,684	7.1

Virginia

House

1 Jo Ann Davis (R)*	225,071	78.5
William A. Lee (I)	57,434	20.0
2 Thelma Drake (R)	132,946	55.1
David Ashe (D)	108,180	44.8
3 Robert C. Scott (D)*	159,373	69.3
Winsome Sears (R)	70,194	30.5
4 J. Randy Forbes (R)*	182,444	64.5
Jonathan Menefee (D)	100,413	35.5
5 Virgil H. Goode Jr. (R)*	172,431	63.7
Al Weed (D)	98,237	36.3
6 Robert W. Goodlatte (R)*	206,560	96.7
7 Eric Cantor (R)*	230,765	75.5
W. Brad Blanton (I)	74,325	24.3
8 James P. Moran (D)*	171,986	59.7
Lisa Marie Cheney (R)	106,231	36.9
9 Rick Boucher (D)*	150,039	59.3
Kevin Triplett (R)	98,499	38.9
10 Frank R. Wolf (R)*	205,982	63.8
James Socas (D)	116,654	36.1
11 Thomas M. Davis III (R)*	186,299	60.2
Ken Longmyer (D)	118,305	38.3

Washington

Governor

| Christine Gregoire (D) | 1,373,361 | 48.9 |
| Dino Rossi (R) | 1,373,232 | 48.9 |

Senate

| Patty Murray (D)* | 1,549,708 | 55.0 |
| George Nethercutt (R) | 1,204,584 | 42.7 |

House

1 Jay Inslee (D)*	204,121	62.3
Randy Eastwood (R)	117,850	36.0
2 Rick Larsen (D)*	202,383	63.9
Suzanne Sinclair (R)	106,333	33.6
3 Brian Baird (D)*	193,626	61.9
Thomas Crowson (R)	119,027	38.1
4 Doc Hastings (R)*	154,627	62.6
Sandy Matheson (D)	92,486	37.4
5 Cathy McMorris (R)	179,600	59.7
Don Barbieri (D)	121,333	40.3
6 Norm Dicks (D)*	202,919	69.0
Doug Cloud (R)	91,228	31.0
7 Jim McDermott (D)*	272,302	80.7
Carol Thorne Cassady (R)	65,226	19.3
8 Dave Reichert (R)	173,298	51.5
Dave Ross (D)	157,148	46.7
9 Adam Smith (D)*	162,433	63.3
Paul J. Lord (R)	88,304	34.4

West Virginia

Governor

| Joe Manchin III (D) | 472,758 | 63.5 |
| Monty Warner (R) | 253,131 | 34.0 |

		Vote total	Percent
House			
1	Alan B. Mollohan (D)*	166,583	67.8
	Alan Lee Parks (R)	79,196	32.2
2	Shelley Moore Capito (R)*	147,676	57.5
	Erik Wells (D)	106,131	41.3
3	Nick J. Rahall II (D)*	142,682	65.2
	Rick Snuffer (R)	76,170	34.8

Wisconsin

		Vote total	Percent
Senate			
	Russell D. Feingold (D)*	1,632,697	55.4
	Tim Michels (R)	1,301,183	44.1

		Vote total	Percent
House			
1	Paul D. Ryan (R)*	233,372	65.4
	Jeffery Chapman Thomas (D)	116,250	32.6
2	Tammy Baldwin (D)*	251,637	63.3
	David Magnum (R)	145,810	36.7
3	Ron Kind (D)*	204,856	56.4
	Dale W. Schultz (R)	157,866	43.5
4	Gwen Moore (D)	212,382	69.6
	Gerald H. Boyle (R)	85,928	28.2
5	F. James Sensenbrenner Jr. (R)*	271,153	66.6
	Bryan Kennedy (D)	129,384	31.8

		Vote total	Percent
6	Tom Petri (R)*	238,620	67.0
	Jef Hall (D)	107,209	30.1
7	David R. Obey (D)*	241,306	85.6
	Mike Miles (WG)	26,518	9.4
8	Mark Green (R)*	248,070	70.2
	Dottie Le Clair (D)	105,513	29.8

Wyoming

		Vote total	Percent
House			
AL	Barbara Cubin (R)*	132,107	55.3
	Ted Ladd (D)	99,989	41.8

1. Runoff elections for Congressional Districts 3 and 7 were required because no candidate received a majority vote in the general election.

Results of House Elections, 1928–2004

	1928	1930	1932	1934	1936	1938	1940	1942	1944	1946	1948	1950	1952	1954	1956	1958	1960	1962	1964
Totals																			
Democrats	165	217	313	322	334	262	268	222	242	188	263	235	213	232	234	283	263	259	295
Republicans	269	217	117	103	88	169	162	209	191	246	171	199	221	203	201	153	174	176	140
Alabama																			
Democrats	10	10	9[1]	9	9	9	9	9	9	9	9	9	9	9	9	9	9	8[1]	3
Republicans	0	0	0	0	0	0	0	0	0	0	0	0	0	0	0	0	0	0	5
Alaska																			
Democrats	—	—	—	—	—	—	—	—	—	—	—	—	—	—	—	1	1	1	1
Republicans	—	—	—	—	—	—	—	—	—	—	—	—	—	—	—	0	0	0	0
Arizona																			
Democrats	1	1	1	1	1	1	1	2[2]	2	2	2	2	1	1	1	1	1	2[2]	2
Republicans	0	0	0	0	0	0	0	0	0	0	0	0	1	1	1	1	1	1	1
Arkansas																			
Democrats	7	7	7	7	7	7	7	7	7	7	7	7	6[1]	6	6	6	6	4[1]	4
Republicans	0	0	0	0	0	0	0	0	0	0	0	0	0	0	0	0	0	0	0
California																			
Democrats	1	1	11[2]	13	15	12	11	12[2]	16	9	10	10	11[2]	11	13	16	16	25[2,3]	23
Republicans	10	10	9	7	4	8	9	11	7	14	13	13	19	19	17	14	14	13	15
Colorado																			
Democrats	1	1	4	4	4	4	2	1	0	1	3	2	2	2	2	3	2	2	4
Republicans	3	3	0	0	0	0	2	3	4	3	1	2	2	2	2	1	2	2	0
Connecticut																			
Democrats	0	2	2[2]	4	6	2	6	0	4	0	3	2	1	1	0	6	4	5	6
Republicans	5	3	4	2	0	4	0	6	2	6	3	4	5	5	6	0	2	1	0
Delaware																			
Democrats	0	0	1	0	1	0	1	0	1	0	0	0	0	1	0	1	1	1	1
Republicans	1	1	0	1	0	1	0	1	0	1	1	0	1	0	0	0	0	0	0
Florida																			
Democrats	4	4	5[2]	5	5	5	5	6[2]	6	6	6	6	8[2]	7	7	7	7	10[2]	10
Republicans	0	0	0	0	0	0	0	0	0	0	0	0	0	1	1	1	1	2	2
Georgia																			
Democrats	12	12	10[1]	10	10	10	10	10	10	10	10	10	10	10	10	10	10	10	9
Republicans	0	0	0	0	0	0	0	0	0	0	0	0	0	0	0	0	0	0	1
Hawaii																			
Democrats	—	—	—	—	—	—	—	—	—	—	—	—	—	—	—	—	1	2[2]	2
Republicans	—	—	—	—	—	—	—	—	—	—	—	—	—	—	—	—	0	0	0
Idaho																			
Democrats	0	0	2	2	2	1	1	1	1	0	1	0	1	1	1	1	2	2	1
Republicans	2	2	0	0	0	1	1	1	1	2	1	2	1	1	1	1	0	0	1
Illinois																			
Democrats	6	13[4]	19	21	21	17	11	7[1]	11	6	12	8	9[1]	12	11	14	14	12[1]	13
Republicans	21	14	8	6	6	10	16	19	15	20	14	18	16	13	14	11	11	12	11
Indiana																			
Democrats	3	9	12[1]	11	11	5	4	2[1]	2	2	7	2	1	2	2	8	4[4]	4	6
Republicans	10	4	0	1	1	7	8	9	9	9	4	9	10	9	9	3	7	7	5
Iowa																			
Democrats	0	1	6[1]	6	5	2	2	0[1]	0	0	0	0	0	0	1	4	2	1[1]	6
Republicans	11	10	3	3	4	7	7	8	8	8	8	8	8	8	7	4	6	6	1
Kansas																			
Democrats	1	1	3[1]	3	2	1	1	0[1]	0	0	0	0	1	0	1	3	1	0[1]	0
Republicans	7	7	4	4	5	6	6	6	6	6	6	6	5	6	5	3	5	5	5
Kentucky																			
Democrats	2	9	9[1]	8	8	8	8	8	8	6	7	7	6[1]	6	6	7	7	5[1]	6
Republicans	9	2	0	1	1	1	1	1	1	3	2	2	2	2	2	1	1	2	1
Louisiana																			
Democrats	8	8	8	8	8	8	8	8	8	8	8	8	8	8	8	8	8	8	8
Republicans	0	0	0	0	0	0	0	0	0	0	0	0	0	0	0	0	0	0	0
Maine																			
Democrats	0	0	2[1]	2	0	0	0	0	0	0	0	0	0	0	1	2	0	0[1]	1
Republicans	4	4	1	1	3	3	3	3	3	3	3	3	3	3	2	1	3	2	1
Maryland																			
Democrats	4	6	6	6	6	6	6	4	5	4	4	3	3[2]	4	4	7	6	6[2]	6
Republicans	2	0	0	0	0	0	0	2	1	2	2	3	4	3	3	0	1	2	2
Massachusetts																			
Democrats	3	4	5[1]	7	5	5	6	4[1]	4	5	4	6	6	7	7	8	8	7[1]	7
Republicans	13	12	10	8	10	10	9	10	10	9	8	8	8	7	7	6	6	5	5
Michigan																			
Democrats	0	0	10[2]	6	8	5	6	5	6	3	5	5	5[2]	7	6	7	7	8[2]	12
Republicans	13	13	7	11	9	12	11	12	11	14	12	12	13	11	12	11	11	11	7
Minnesota																			
Democrats	0	0	1[1]	1	1	1	0	0	2	1	4	4	4	5	5	4	3	4[1]	4
Republicans	9	9	3	5	3	7	8	8	7	8	5	5	5	4	4	5	6	4	4
Mississippi																			
Democrats	8	8	7[1]	7	7	7	7	7	7	7	7	7	6[1]	6	6	6	6	5[1]	4
Republicans	0	0	0	0	0	0	0	0	0	0	0	0	0	0	0	0	0	0	1
Missouri																			
Democrats	6	12	13[1]	12	12	12	10	5	7	4	12	10	7	9	10	10	9	8[1]	8
Republicans	10	4	0	1	1	1	3	8	6	9	1	3	4	2	1	1	2	2	2

1. State lost seats due to reapportionment.
2. State gained seats due to reapportionment.
3. Alaska 1972, California 1962, and Louisiana 1972: national and state totals reflect the reelection of a Democrat who died before the election but whose name remained on the ballot.
4. Illinois 1930, Indiana 1960 and 1984, and New Hampshire 1936: national and state totals reflect the final outcome of a contested election in which a Republican was first certified the winner, but the House decided to seat the Democrat.

	1966	1968	1970	1972	1974	1976	1978	1980	1982	1984	1986	1988	1990	1992	1994	1996	1998	2000	2002	2004
Totals																				
Democrats	248	243	255	243	291	292	277	243	269	253	258	260	267	258	204	207	211	212	205	202
Republicans	187	192	180	192	144	143	158	192	166	182	177	175	167	176	230	227	223	221	229	232
Alabama																				
Democrats	5	5	5	4[1]	4	4	4	4	5	5	5	5	5	4	4	2	2	2	2	2
Republicans	3	3	3	3	3	3	3	3	2	2	2	2	2	3	3	5	5	5	5	5
Alaska																				
Democrats	0	0	1	1[3]	0	0	0	0	0	0	0	0	0	0	0	0	0	0	0	0
Republicans	1	1	0	0	1	1	1	1	1	1	1	1	1	1	1	1	1	1	1	1
Arizona																				
Democrats	1	1	1	1[2]	1	2	2	2	2[2]	1	1	1	1	3[2]	1	1	1	1	2	2
Republicans	2	2	2	3	3	2	2	2	3	4	4	4	4	3	5	5	5	5	6	6
Arkansas																				
Democrats	3	3	3	3	3	3	2	2	2	3	3	3	3	2	2	2	2	3	3	3
Republicans	1	1	1	1	1	1	2	2	2	1	1	1	1	2	2	2	2	1	1	1
California																				
Democrats	21	21	20	23[2]	28	29	26	22	28[2]	27	27	27	26	30[2]	27	29	28	32	33	33
Republicans	17	17	18	20	15	14	17	21	17	18	18	18	19	22	25	23	24	20	20	20
Colorado																				
Democrats	3	3	2	2[2]	3	3	3	3	3[2]	2	3	3	3	2	2	2	2	2	2	3
Republicans	1	1	2	3	2	2	2	2	3	4	3	3	3	4	4	4	4	4	5	4
Connecticut																				
Democrats	5	4	3	3	4	4	5	4	4	3	3	3	3	3	3	4	4	3	2	2
Republicans	1	2	2	3	2	2	1	2	2	3	3	3	3	3	3	2	2	3	3	3
Delaware																				
Democrats	0	0	0	0	0	0	0	0	1	1	1	1	1	0	0	0	0	0	0	0
Republicans	1	1	1	1	1	1	1	1	0	0	0	0	0	1	1	1	1	1	1	1
Florida																				
Democrats	9	9	9	11[2]	10	10	12	11	13[2]	12	12	10	9	10[2]	8	8	8	8	7	7
Republicans	3	3	3	4	5	5	3	4	6	7	7	9	10	13	15	15	15	15	18	18
Georgia																				
Democrats	8	8	8	9	10	10	9	9	9	8	8	9	9	7[2]	4	3	3	3	5	6
Republicans	2	2	2	1	0	0	1	1	1	2	2	1	1	4	7	8	8	8	8	7
Hawaii																				
Democrats	2	2	2	2	2	2	2	2	2	2	1	1	2	2	2	2	2	2	2	2
Republicans	0	0	0	0	0	0	0	0	0	0	1	1	0	0	0	0	0	0	0	0
Idaho																				
Democrats	0	0	0	0	0	0	0	0	0	1	1	1	2	1	0	0	0	0	0	0
Republicans	2	2	2	2	2	2	2	2	2	1	1	1	0	1	2	2	2	2	2	2
Illinois																				
Democrats	12	12	12	10	13	12	11	10	12[1]	13	13	14	15	12[1]	10	10	10	10	9	10
Republicans	12	12	12	14	11	12	13	14	10	9	9	8	7	8	10	10	10	10	10	9
Indiana																				
Democrats	5	4	5	4	9	8	7	6	5[1]	5[4]	6	6	8	7	4	4	4	4	3	2
Republicans	6	7	6	7	2	3	4	5	5	5	4	4	2	3	6	6	6	6	6	7
Iowa																				
Democrats	2	2	2	3[1]	5	4	3	3	3	2	2	2	2	1[1]	0	1	1	1	1	1
Republicans	5	5	5	3	1	2	3	3	3	4	4	4	4	4	5	4	4	4	4	4
Kansas																				
Democrats	0	0	1	1	1	2	1	1	2	2	2	2	2	2[1]	0	0	1	1	1	1
Republicans	5	5	4	4	4	3	4	4	3	3	3	3	3	2	4	4	3	3	3	3
Kentucky																				
Democrats	4	4	5	5	5	5	4	4	4	4	4	4	4	4[1]	2	1	1	1	1	1
Republicans	3	3	2	2	2	2	3	3	3	3	3	3	3	2	4	5	5	5	5	5
Louisiana																				
Democrats	8	8	8	7[3]	6[5]	6	5	6	6	6	5	4	4	4[1]	4	2	2	2	3	2
Republicans	0	0	0	1	2	2	3	2	2	2	3	4	4	3	3	5	5	5	4	5
Maine																				
Democrats	2	2	2	1	0	0	0	0	0	0	1	1	1	1	1	2	2	2	2	2
Republicans	0	0	0	1	2	2	2	2	2	2	1	1	1	1	1	0	0	0	0	0
Maryland																				
Democrats	5	4	5	4	5	5	6	7	7	6	6	6	5	4	4	4	4	4	6	6
Republicans	3	4	3	4	3	3	2	1	1	2	2	2	3	4	4	4	4	4	2	2
Massachusetts																				
Democrats	7	7	8	9[6]	10	10	10	10	10[1]	10	10	10	10	8[1]	8	10	10	10	10	10
Republicans	5	5	4	3	2	2	2	2	1	1	1	1	1	2	2	0	0	0	0	0
Michigan																				
Democrats	7	7	7	7	12	11	13	12	12[1]	11	11	11	11	10[1]	9	10	10	9	6	6
Republicans	12	12	12	12	7	8	6	7	6	7	7	7	7	6	7	6	6	7	9	9
Minnesota																				
Democrats	3	3	4	4	5	5	4	3	5	5	5	5	6	6	6	6	6	5	4	4
Republicans	5	5	4	4	3	3	4	5	3	3	3	3	2	2	2	2	2	3	4	4
Mississippi																				
Democrats	5	5	5	3	3	3	3	3	3	3	4	4	5	5	4	2	3	3	2	2
Republicans	0	0	0	2	2	2	2	2	2	2	1	1	0	0	1	3	2	2	2	2
Missouri																				
Democrats	8	9	9	9	9	8	8	6	6[1]	6	6	5	5	6	6	6	5	5	4	4
Republicans	2	1	1	1	1	2	2	4	3	3	4	4	3	3	3	3	4	4	5	5

5. Louisiana 1974: national and state totals reflect the final outcome of a contested election in which no winner was declared, followed by a special election won by the Republican.
6. Massachusetts 1972 and Pennsylvania 1980: national and state Democratic totals reflect the election of an Independent candidate who previously announced he would serve as a Democrats.

	1928	1930	1932	1934	1936	1938	1940	1942	1944	1946	1948	1950	1952	1954	1956	1958	1960	1962	1964
Montana																			
Democrats	1	1	2	2	2	1	1	2	1	1	1	1	1	1	2	2	1	1	1
Republicans	1	1	0	0	0	1	1	0	1	1	1	1	1	1	0	0	1	1	1
Nebraska																			
Democrats	2	4	5[1]	4	4	2	2	0[1]	0	0	1	0	0	0	0	2	0	0[1]	1
Republicans	4	2	0	1	1	3	3	4	4	4	3	4	4	4	4	2	4	3	2
Nevada																			
Democrats	0	0	1	1	1	1	1	1	1	0	1	1	0	0	1	1	1	1	1
Republicans	1	1	0	0	0	0	0	0	0	1	0	0	1	1	0	0	0	0	0
New Hampshire																			
Democrats	0	0	1	1	1[4]	0	0	0	0	0	0	0	0	0	0	0	0	0	1
Republicans	2	2	1	1	1	2	2	2	2	2	2	2	2	2	2	2	2	2	1
New Jersey																			
Democrats	2	3	4[2]	4	7	3	4	3	2	2	5	5	5	6	4	5	6	7[2]	11
Republicans	10	9	10	10	7	11	10	11	12	12	9	9	9	8	10	9	8	8	4
New Mexico																			
Democrats	0	1	1	1	1	1	1	2[2]	2	2	2	2	2	2	2	2	2	2	2
Republicans	1	0	0	0	0	0	0	0	0	0	0	0	0	0	0	0	0	0	0
New York																			
Democrats	23	23	29[2]	29	29	25	25	23	22	16	24	23	16[1]	17	17	19	22	20[1]	27
Republicans	20	20	16	16	16	19	19	21	22	28	20	22	27	26	26	24	21	21	14
North Carolina																			
Democrats	8	10	11[2]	11	11	11	11	12[2]	12	12	12	12	11	11	11	11	11	9[1]	9
Republicans	2	0	0	0	0	0	0	0	0	0	0	0	1	1	1	1	1	2	2
North Dakota																			
Democrats	0	0	0[1]	0	0	0	0	0	0	0	0	0	0	0	0	1	0	0	1
Republicans	3	3	2	2	2	2	2	2	2	2	2	2	2	2	2	1	2	2	1
Ohio																			
Democrats	3	9	18[2]	18	22	9	12	3[1]	6	4	12	7	6	6	6	9	7	6[2]	10
Republicans	19	13	6	6	2	15	12	20	17	19	11	15	16	17	17	14	16	18	14
Oklahoma																			
Democrats	5	7	9[2]	9	9	9	8	7[1]	6	6	8	6	5[1]	5	5	5	5	5	5
Republicans	3	1	0	0	0	0	1	1	2	2	0	2	1	1	1	1	1	1	1
Oregon																			
Democrats	0	1	2	1	2	1	1	0[2]	0	0	0	0	0	1	3	3	2	3	3
Republicans	3	2	1	2	1	2	2	4	4	4	4	4	4	3	1	1	2	1	1
Pennsylvania																			
Democrats	1	3	11[1]	23	27	15	19	14[1]	15	5	16	13	11[1]	14	13	16	14	13[1]	15
Republicans	35	33	23	11	7	9	15	19	18	28	19	20	19	16	17	14	16	14	12
Rhode Island																			
Democrats	1	1	2[1]	2	2	0	2	2	2	2	2	2	2	2	2	2	2	2	2
Republicans	2	2	0	0	0	2	0	0	0	0	0	0	0	0	0	0	0	0	0
South Carolina																			
Democrats	7	7	6[1]	6	6	6	6	6	6	6	6	6	6	6	6	6	6	6	6
Republicans	0	0	0	0	0	0	0	0	0	0	0	0	0	0	0	0	0	0	0
South Dakota																			
Democrats	0	0	2[1]	2	1	0	0	0	0	0	0	0	0	0	1	1	0	0	0
Republicans	3	3	0	0	1	2	2	2	2	2	2	2	2	2	1	1	2	2	2
Tennessee																			
Democrats	8	8	7[1]	7	7	7	7	8[2]	8	8	8	8	7[1]	7	7	7	7	6	6
Republicans	2	2	2	2	2	2	2	2	2	2	2	2	2	2	2	2	2	3	3
Texas																			
Democrats	17	17	21[2]	21	21	21	21	21	21	21	21	21	22[2]	21	21	21	21	21[2]	23
Republicans	1[7]	1	0	0	0	0	0	0	0	0	0	0	0	0	1	1	1	2	0
Utah																			
Democrats	0	0	2	2	2	2	2	2	2	1	2	2	0	0	0	1	2	0	1
Republicans	2	2	0	0	0	0	0	0	0	1	0	0	2	2	2	1	0	2	1
Vermont																			
Democrats	0	0	0[1]	0	0	0	0	0	0	0	0	0	0	0	0	1	0	0	0
Republicans	2	2	1	1	1	1	1	1	1	1	1	1	1	1	1	0	1	1	1
Virginia																			
Democrats	8	9	9[1]	9	9	9	9	9	9	9	9	9	7[2]	8	8	8	8	8	8
Republicans	2	1	0	0	0	0	0	0	0	0	0	0	3	2	2	2	2	2	2
Washington																			
Democrats	1	1	6[2]	6	6	6	6	3	4	1	2	2	1[2]	1	1	1	2	1	5
Republicans	4	4	0	0	0	0	0	3	2	5	4	4	6	6	6	6	5	6	2
West Virginia																			
Democrats	1	2	6	6	6	5	6	3	5	2	6	6	5	6	4	5	5	4[1]	4
Republicans	5	4	0	0	0	1	0	3	1	4	0	0	1	0	2	1	1	1	1
Wisconsin																			
Democrats	0	1	5[1]	3	3	0	1	3	2	0	2	1	1	3	3	5	4	4	5
Republicans	11	10	5	0	0	8	6	5	7	10	8	9	9	7	7	5	6	6	5
Wyoming																			
Democrats	0	0	0	1	1	0	1	0	0	0	0	0	0	0	0	0	0	1	0
Republicans	1	1	1	0	0	1	0	1	1	1	1	1	1	1	1	1	1	1	0

Notes: State totals reflect the number of Democrats and Republicans in each House delegation at the start of each Congress. The above totals do not include "other" representatives elected as independent or third-party candidates. Those numbers are California: Progressive 1936 (1). (No formal party. The representative became a Democrat in 1938.) Minnesota: Farmer-Labor 1928– 1930 (1), 1932 (5), 1934 (3), 1936 (5), 1938–1942 (1). (Merged with D in 1944.) New York: American Labor 1938–1948 (1). (Party disbanded after 1954.) Ohio: Independent 1950–1952 (1). (Defeated by Democrat in 1954.) Wisconsin: Progressive 1934 (7), 1936–1938 (2), 1940 (3), 1942 (2) and 1944 (1). (Disbanded after 1944. The last Progressive became a Republican in 1946.) Vermont: Independent 1990–2004 (1). Virginia: Independent 2000 (1). National totals: 1928–1930 (1), 1932 (5), 1934 (10), 1936 (13), 1938 (4), 1940 (5), 1942 (4), 1944 (2), 1946–1952 (1), 1990–1998 (1), 2000 (2), and 2002–2004 (1).

	1966	1968	1970	1972	1974	1976	1978	1980	1982	1984	1986	1988	1990	1992	1994	1996	1998	2000	2002	2004
Montana																				
Democrats	1	1	1	1	2	1	1	1	1	1	1	1	1	1[1]	1	1	0	0	0	0
Republicans	1	1	1	1	0	1	1	1	1	1	1	1	1	0	0	0	1	1	1	1
Nebraska																				
Democrats	0	0	0	0	0	1	1	0	0	0	0	1	1	1	0	0	0	0	0	0
Republicans	3	3	3	3	3	2	2	3	3	3	3	2	2	2	3	3	3	3	3	3
Nevada																				
Democrats	1	1	1	0	1	1	1	1	1[2]	1	1	1	1	1	0	0	1	1	1	1
Republicans	0	0	0	1	0	0	0	0	1	1	1	1	1	1	2	2	1	1	2	2
New Hampshire																				
Democrats	0	0	0	0	1	1	1	1	1	0	0	0	1	1	0	0	0	0	0	0
Republicans	2	2	2	2	1	1	1	1	1	2	2	2	1	1	2	2	2	2	2	2
New Jersey																				
Democrats	9	9	9	8	12	11	10	8	9[1]	8	8	8	8	7[1]	5	6	7	7	7	7
Republicans	6	6	6	7	3	4	5	7	5	6	6	6	6	6	8	7	6	6	6	6
New Mexico																				
Democrats	2	0	1	1	1	1	1	0	1[2]	1	1	1	1	1	1	1	1	1	1	1
Republicans	0	2	1	1	1	1	1	2	2	2	2	2	2	2	2	2	2	2	2	2
New York																				
Democrats	26	26	24	22[1]	27	28	26	22	20[1]	19	20	21	21	18[1]	17	18	18	19	19	20
Republicans	15	15	17	17	12	11	13	17	14	15	14	13	13	13	14	13	13	12	10	9
North Carolina																				
Democrats	8	7	7	7	9	9	9	7	9	6	8	8	7	8[2]	4	6	5	5	6	6
Republicans	3	4	4	4	2	2	2	4	2	5	3	3	4	4	8	6	7	7	7	7
North Dakota																				
Democrats	0	0	1	0[1]	0	0	0	1	1	1	1	1	1	1	1	1	1	1	1	1
Republicans	2	2	1	1	1	1	1	0	0	0	0	0	0	0	0	0	0	0	0	0
Ohio																				
Democrats	5	6	7	7[1]	8	10	10	11	10[1]	11	11	11	11	10[1]	6	8	8	8	6	6
Republicans	19	18	17	16	15	13	13	12	11	10	10	10	10	9	13	11	11	11	12	12
Oklahoma																				
Democrats	4	4	4	5	6	5	5	5	5	5	4	4	4	4	1	0	0	1	1	1
Republicans	2	2	2	1	0	1	1	1	1	1	2	2	2	2	5	6	6	5	4	4
Oregon																				
Democrats	2	2	2	2	4	4	4	3	3[2]	3	3	3	4	4	3	4	4	4	4	4
Republicans	2	2	2	2	0	0	0	1	2	2	2	2	1	1	2	1	1	1	1	1
Pennsylvania																				
Democrats	14	14	14	13[1]	14	17	15	13[6]	13[1]	13	12	12	11	11[1]	11	11	11	10	7	7
Republicans	13	13	13	12	11	8	10	12	10	10	11	11	12	10	10	10	10	11	12	12
Rhode Island																				
Democrats	2	2	2	2	2	2	2	1	1	1	1	0	1	1	2	2	2	2	2	2
Republicans	0	0	0	0	0	0	0	1	1	1	1	2	1	1	0	0	0	0	0	0
South Carolina																				
Democrats	5	5	5	4	5	5	4	2	3	3	4	4	4	3	2	2	2	2	2	2
Republicans	1	1	1	2	1	1	2	4	3	3	2	2	2	3	4	4	4	4	4	4
South Dakota																				
Democrats	0	0	2	1	0	0	1	1	1[1]	1	1	1	1	1	0	0	0	0	0	1
Republicans	2	2	0	1	2	2	1	1	0	0	0	0	0	0	0	1	1	1	1	0
Tennessee																				
Democrats	5	5	5	3[1]	5	5	5	5	6[2]	6	6	6	6	6	4	4	4	4	5	5
Republicans	4	4	4	5	3	3	3	3	3	3	3	3	3	3	5	5	5	5	4	4
Texas																				
Democrats	21	20	20	20[2]	21	22	20	19	22[2]	17	17	19	19	21[2]	19	17	17	17	17	11
Republicans	2	3	3	4	3	2	4	5	5	10	10	8	8	9	11	13	13	13	15	21
Utah																				
Democrats	0	0	1	2	2	1	1	0	0[2]	0	1	1	2	2	1	0	0	1	1	1
Republicans	2	2	1	0	0	1	1	2	3	3	2	2	1	1	2	3	3	2	2	2
Vermont																				
Democrats	0	0	0	0	0	0	0	0	0	0	0	0	0	0	0	0	0	0	0	0
Republicans	1	1	1	1	1	1	1	1	1	1	1	1	0	0	0	0	0	0	0	0
Virginia																				
Democrats	6	5	4	3	5	4	4	1	4	4	5	5	6	7[2]	6	6	6	4	3	3
Republicans	4	5	6	7	5	6	6	9	6	6	5	5	4	4	5	5	5	6	8	8
Washington																				
Democrats	5	5	6	6	6	6	6	5	5[2]	5	5	5	5	8[2]	2	3	5	6	6	6
Republicans	2	2	1	1	1	1	1	2	3	3	3	3	3	1	7	6	4	3	3	3
West Virginia																				
Democrats	4	5	5	4[1]	4	4	4	2	4	4	4	4	4	3[1]	3	3	3	2	2	2
Republicans	1	0	0	0	0	0	0	2	0	0	0	0	0	0	0	0	0	1	1	1
Wisconsin																				
Democrats	3	3	5	5[1]	7	7	6	5	5	5	5	5	4	4	3	5	4	5	4	4
Republicans	7	7	5	4	2	2	3	4	4	4	4	4	5	5	6	4	5	4	4	4
Wyoming																				
Democrats	0	1	1	1	1	0	0	0	0	0	0	0	0	0	0	0	0	0	0	0
Republicans	1	1	0	0	0	0	1	1	1	1	1	1	1	1	1	1	1	1	1	1

7. Texas 1928: national and state totals reflect the final outcome of a contested election in which a Democrats was at first certified the winner, but the House decided to seat the Republican.

Governors, 2001–2005

Following is a list of governors who served during the period of President George W. Bush's first term, 2001–2005. All governors serve four-year terms except those representing New Hampshire and Vermont; they serve two-year terms. Party designations appear in parentheses following the governor's name. The following abbreviations were used: (D) Democrat; (I) Independent; (R) Republican; (REF) Reform. (*Governors, 1985–1988, Congress and the Nation Vol. VII, p. 1143; 1989–1992, Congress and the Nation Vol. VIII, p. 1259; 1993–1996, Congress and the Nation Vol. IX, p. 1211; 1997–2001, Congress and the Nation Vol. X, p. 1094.*)

	Dates of service
Alabama	
Don Siegelman (D)	Jan. 18, 1999–Jan. 21, 2003
Bob Riley (R)	Jan. 21, 2003–
Alaska	
Tony Knowles (D)	Dec. 5, 1994–Dec. 2, 2002
Frank H. Murkowski (R)	Dec. 2, 2002–
Arizona	
Jane D. Hull (R)	Sept. 5, 1997–Jan. 6, 2003
Janet Napolitano (D)	Jan. 6, 2003–
Arkansas	
Mike Huckabee (R)	July 15, 1996–
California	
Gray Davis (D)	Jan. 4, 1999–Nov. 17, 2003
Arnold Schwarzenegger (R)	Nov. 17, 2003–
Colorado	
Bill Owens (R)	Jan. 12, 1999–
Connecticut	
John G. Rowland (R)	Jan. 4, 1995–July 1, 2004
M. Jodi Rell (R)	July 1, 2004–
Delaware	
Thomas R. Carper (D)	Jan. 19, 1993–Jan. 3, 2001
Ruth Ann Miner (D)	Jan. 3, 2001–
Florida	
Jeb Bush (R)	Jan. 5, 1999–
Georgia	
Roy E. Barnes (D)	Jan. 11, 1999–Jan. 13, 2003
Sonny Perdue (R)	Jan. 13, 2003–
Hawaii	
Benjamin J. Cayetano (D)	Dec. 5, 1994–Dec. 2, 2002
Linda Lingle (R)	Dec. 2, 2002–
Idaho	
Dirk Kempthorne (R)	Jan. 8, 1999–

	Dates of service
Illinois	
George H. Ryan (R)	Jan. 11, 1999–Jan. 13, 2003
Rod R. Blagojevich (D)	Jan. 13, 2003–
Indiana	
Frank L. O'Bannon (D)	Jan. 13, 1997–Sept. 13, 2003
Joseph E. Kernan (D)	Sept. 13, 2003–Jan. 10, 2005
Mitchell E. Daniels Jr. (R)	Jan. 10, 2005–
Iowa	
Tom Vilsack (D)	Jan. 15, 1999–
Kansas	
Bill Graves (R)	Jan. 9, 1995–Jan. 13, 2003
Kathleen Sebelius (D)	Jan. 13, 2003–
Kentucky	
Paul E. Patton (D)	Dec. 12, 1995–Dec. 9, 2003
Ernest L. Fletcher (R)	Dec. 9, 2003–
Louisiana	
Mike Foster (R)	Jan. 8, 1996–Jan. 12, 2004
Kathleen B. Blanco (D)	Jan. 12, 2004–
Maine	
Angus S. King Jr. (I)	Jan. 5, 1995–Jan. 8, 2003
John E. Baldacci (D)	Jan. 8, 2003–
Maryland	
Parris N. Glendening (D)	Jan. 18, 1995–Jan. 15, 2003
Robert L. Ehrlich Jr. (R)	Jan. 15, 2003–
Massachusetts	
Argeo "Paul" Cellucci (R)	July 29, 1997–April 10, 2001
Jane Swift (R)	April 10, 2001–Jan. 2, 2003
Mitt Romney (R)	Jan. 2, 2003–
Michigan	
John Engler (R)	Jan. 1, 1991–Jan. 1, 2003
Jennifer Granholm (D)	Jan. 1, 2003–
Minnesota	
Jesse Ventura (REF)	Jan. 5, 1999–Jan. 6, 2003
Tim Pawlenty (R)	Jan. 6, 2003–

	Dates of service
Mississippi	
Ronnie Musgrove (D)	Jan. 11, 2000–Jan. 13, 2004
Haley Barbour (D)	Jan. 13, 2004–
Missouri	
Bob Holden (D)	Jan. 8, 2001–Jan. 10, 2005
Matt Blunt (R)	Jan. 10, 2004–
Montana	
Judy Martz (R)	Jan. 2, 1993–Jan. 3, 2005
Brian Schweitzer (D)	Jan. 3, 2005–
Nebraska	
Mike Johanns (R)	Jan. 7, 1999–Jan. 20, 2005
Dave Heineman (R)	Jan. 21, 2005–
Nevada	
Kenny Guinn (R)	Jan. 4, 1999–
New Hampshire	
Jeanne Shaheen (D)	Jan. 9, 1997–Jan. 9, 2003
Craig Benson (R)	Jan. 9, 2003–Jan. 6, 2005
John Lynch (D)	Jan. 6, 2005–
New Jersey	
Christine Todd Whitman (R)	Jan. 18, 1994–Feb. 1, 2001
Donald T. DiFrancesco (R)	Feb. 1, 2001–Jan. 8, 2002
John O. Bennett III (R)	Jan. 8, 2002–Jan. 12, 2002
Richard J. Codey (D)	Jan. 12, 2002–Jan. 15, 2002
James E. McGreevey (D)	Jan. 15, 2002–Nov. 15, 2004
Richard J. Codey (D)	Nov. 15, 2004–
New Mexico	
Gary E. Johnson (R)	Jan. 1, 1995–Jan. 1, 2003
William "Bill" Richardson (D)	Jan. 1, 2003–
New York	
George E. Pataki (R)	Jan. 1, 1995–
North Carolina	
James B. Hunt Jr. (D)	Jan. 9, 1993–Jan. 6, 2001
Michael Easley (D)	Jan. 6, 2001–
North Dakota	
John Hoeven (R)	Dec. 15, 2000–
Ohio	
Robert A. Taft II (R)	Jan. 11, 1999–
Oklahoma	
Frank Keating (R)	Jan. 9, 1995–Jan. 13, 2003
Brad Henry (D)	Jan. 13, 2003–
Oregon	
John Kitzhaber (D)	Jan. 9, 1995–Jan. 8, 2003
Ted Kulongoski (D)	Jan. 8, 2003–

	Dates of service
Pennsylvania	
Tom Ridge (R)	Jan. 17, 1995–Oct. 5, 2001
Mark S. Schweiker (R)	Oct. 5, 2001–Jan. 21, 2003
Edward G. Rendell (D)	Jan. 21, 2003–
Rhode Island	
Lincoln C. Almond (R)	Jan. 3, 1995–Jan. 7, 2003
Donald L. Carcieri (R)	Jan. 7, 2003–
South Carolina	
Jim Hodges (D)	Jan. 13, 1999–Jan. 15, 2003
Mark Sanford (R)	Jan. 15, 2003–
South Dakota	
William J. Janklow (R)	Jan. 4, 1995–Jan. 7, 2003
M. Michael Rounds (R)	Jan. 7, 2003–
Tennessee	
Don Sundquist (R)	Jan. 21, 1995–Jan. 18, 2003
Phil Bredesen (D)	Jan. 18, 2003–
Texas	
Rick Perry (R)	Dec. 21, 2000–
Utah	
Mike O. Leavitt (R)	Jan. 3, 1993–Nov. 5, 2003
Olene S. Walker (R)	Nov. 5, 2003–Jan. 3, 2005
Jon M. Huntsman Jr. (R)	Jan. 3, 2005–
Vermont	
Howard Dean (D)	Aug. 14, 1991–Jan. 9, 2003
James H. Douglas (R)	Jan. 9, 2003–
Virginia	
James S. Gilmore (R)	Jan. 17, 1999–Jan. 12, 2002
Mark R. Warner (D)	Jan. 12, 2002–
Washington	
Gary Locke (D)	Jan. 15, 1997–Jan. 12, 2005
Christine Gregoire (D)	Jan. 12, 2005–
West Virginia	
Bob Wise (D)	Jan. 15, 2001–Jan. 17, 2005
Joe Manchin III (D)	Jan. 17, 2005–
Wisconsin	
Tommy G. Thompson (R)	Jan. 5, 1987–Feb. 1, 2001
Scott McCallum (R)	Feb. 1, 2001–Jan. 6, 2003
James Doyle (D)	Jan. 6, 2003–
Wyoming	
Jim Geringer (R)	Jan. 2, 1995–Jan. 6, 2003
David Freudenthal (D)	Jan. 6, 2003–

Public Laws 2001–2005

Public Laws 2001–2005

Following are the public laws passed by Congress and signed by President George W. Bush from 2001 through 2004. The list is divided by *year of congressional enactment even though the president signed some of the bills in January of the following year.*

107th Congress–2001

PL 107-1 (H J Res 7) Recognize the 90th birthday of Ronald Reagan. Introduced by Cox, R-Calif., on Jan. 31, 2001. House passed, under suspension of the rules, Feb. 6. Senate passed Feb. 6. President signed Feb. 15, 2001.

PL 107-2 (HR 559) Designate the U.S. courthouse located at 1 Courthouse Way in Boston, Mass., as the "John Joseph Moakley United States Courthouse." Introduced by McGovern, D-Mass., on Feb. 13, 2001. House passed Feb. 14. Senate passed Feb. 15. President signed March 13, 2001.

PL 107-3 (S 279) Affect the representation of the Senate majority and minority membership of the Joint Economic Committee. Introduced by Lott, R-Miss., on Feb. 7, 2001. Senate passed Feb. 7. House passed Feb. 14. President signed, March 13, 2001.

PL 107-4 (H J Res 19) Provide for the appointment of Walter E. Massey as a citizen regent of the Board of Regents of the Smithsonian Institution. Introduced by Johnson, R-Texas, on Feb. 13, 2001. House Administration discharged. House passed Feb. 28. Senate passed March 1. President signed March 16, 2001.

PL 107-5 (S J Res 6) Provide for congressional disapproval of the rule submitted by the Department of Labor under Chapter 8, Title 5, U.S. Code, relating to ergonomics. Introduced by Nickles, R-Okla., on March 1, 2001. Senate Health, Education, Labor and Pensions discharged March 5. Senate passed March 6. House passed March 7. President signed March 20, 2001.

PL 107-6 (HR 132) Designate the facility of the U.S. Postal Service at 620 Jacaranda St., Lanai City, Hawaii, as the "Goro Hokama Post Office Building." Introduced by Mink, D-Hawaii, on Jan. 3, 2001. House passed, under suspension of the rules, Feb. 7. Senate passed March 21, 2001. President signed April 12, 2001.

PL 107-7 (HR 395) Designate the facility of the U.S. Postal Service located at 2305 Minton Road in West Melbourne, Florida, as the "Ronald W. Reagan Post Office of West Melbourne, Florida." Introduced by Weldon, R-Fla., on Feb. 6, 2001. House passed, under suspension of the rules, Feb. 6. Senate passed March 21. President signed April 12, 2001.

PL 107-8 (HR 256) Extend for 11 additional months the period for which Chapter 12, Title 11 of the U.S. Code is reenacted. Introduced by Smith, R-Mich., on Jan. 30, 2001. House Judiciary reported Feb. 26 (H Rept 107-2). House passed, under suspension of the rules, Feb. 28. Senate passed April 26. President signed May 11, 2001.

PL 107-9 (S 700) Establish a federal interagency task force for the purpose of coordinating actions to prevent the outbreak of bovine spongiform encephalopathy (commonly known as "Mad Cow disease") and foot-and-mouth disease in the United States. Introduced by Campbell, R-Colo., on April 4, 2001. Senate passed, amended, April 5. House passed May 9. President signed May 24, 2001.

PL 107-10 (HR 428) Authorize the secretary of State to endorse and obtain observer status for Taiwan at the annual summit of the World Health Organization. Introduced by Brown, D-Ohio, on Feb. 6, 2001. House passed, amended, under suspension of the rules, April 24. Senate Foreign Relations discharged. Senate passed, with amendment, May 9. House agreed to Senate amendment, under suspension of the rules, May 15. President signed May 28, 2001.

PL 107-11 (HR 1696) Expedite the construction of the World War II memorial in the District of Columbia. Introduced by Stump, R-Ariz., on May 3, 2001. House passed, under suspension of the rules, May 15. Senate Energy and Natural Resources discharged. Senate passed, with amendment, May 21. House agreed to Senate amendment, under suspension of the rules, May 22. President signed May 28, 2001.

PL 107-12 (HR 802) Authorize the Public Safety Officer Medal of Valor. Introduced by Smith, R-Texas, on Feb. 28, 2001. House Judiciary reported March 12 (H Rept 107-15). House passed, under suspension of the rules, March 22. Senate Judiciary reported May 10 (no written report). Senate passed May 14. President signed May 30, 2001.

PL 107-13 (HR 581) Authorize the secretaries of Agriculture and the Interior to use funds appropriated for wildland fire management in the Department of the Interior and Related Agencies Fiscal 2001 Appropriations Act, to reimburse the U.S. Fish and Wildlife Service and the National Marine Fisheries Service to facilitate the interagency cooperation required under the Endangered Species Act of 1973 in connection with wildland fire management. Introduced by Hefley, R-Colo., on Feb. 13, 2001. House Resources reported April 3 (H Rept 107-35). House passed, amended, May 9. Senate Environment and Public Works reported May 23 (no written report.) Senate passed May 24. President signed June 3, 2001.

PL 107-14 (HR 801) Amend Title 38, U.S. Code, to expand eligibility for Champva, and to provide for family coverage and retroactive expansion of the increase in maximum benefits under Servicemembers' Group Life Insurance. Introduced by Smith, R-N.J., on Feb. 28, 2001. House Veterans' Affairs reported, amended, March 26 (H Rept 107-27). House passed, amended, under suspension of the rules, March 27. Senate Veterans' Affairs discharged. Senate passed, with amendments, May 24. House agreed to Senate amendments May 24. President signed June 5, 2001.

PL 107-15 (HR 1727) Amend the Taxpayer Relief Act of 1997 to provide for consistent treatment of survivor benefits for public safety officers killed in the line of duty. Introduced by Ramstad, R-Minn., on May 3, 2001. House Ways and Means reported, amended, May 15

(H Rept 107-65). House passed, amended, May 15. Senate passed May 22. President signed June 5, 2001.

PL 107-16 (HR 1836) Provide for reconciliation pursuant to Section 104 of the concurrent resolution on the budget for fiscal 2002. Introduced by Thomas, R-Calif., on May 15, 2001. House Rules reported May 15 (H Rept 107-68). House passed May 16. Senate passed, with amendment, May 23. Conference report filed in the House on May 26 (H Rept 107-84). House agreed to conference report May 26. Senate agreed to conference report May 26. President signed June 7, 2001.

PL 107-17 (HR 1914) Extend for four additional months the period for which Chapter 12, Title 11 of the U.S. Code is reenacted. Introduced by Smith, R-Mich., on May 17, 2001. House passed, under suspension of the rules, June 6. Senate passed June 8. President signed June 26, 2001.

PL 107-18 (S 1029) Clarify the authority of the Department of Housing and Urban Development with respect to the use of fees during fiscal 2001 for the manufactured housing program. Introduced by Sarbanes, D-Md., on June 13, 2001. Senate passed June 13. House passed, under suspension of the rules, June 20. President signed July 5, 2001.

PL 107-19 (S 657) Authorize funding for the National 4-H Program Centennial Initiative. Introduced by Lugar, R-Ind., on March, 29, 2001. Senate Agriculture, Nutrition and Forestry discharged. Senate passed, amended, June 19. House passed, under suspension of the rules, June 25. President signed July 10, 2001.

PL 107-20 (HR 2216) Make supplemental appropriations for the fiscal year ending Sept. 30, 2001. Introduced by Young, R-Fla., on June 19, 2001. House Appropriations reported June 19 (H Rept 107-102). House passed, amended, June 20. Senate passed, with amendment, July 10. Conference report filed in the House on July 19 (H Rept 107-148). House agreed to conference report July 20. Senate agreed to conference report July 20. President signed July 24, 2001.

PL 107-21 (S 360) Honor Paul D. Coverdell. Introduced by Lott, R-Miss., on Feb. 15, 2001. Senate passed Feb. 15. House passed, under suspension of the rules, July 17. President signed July 26, 2001.

PL 107-22 (S 1190) Amend the Internal Revenue Code of 1986 to rename the education individual retirement accounts as the "Coverdell Education Savings Account." Introduced by Lott, R-Miss., on July 18, 2001. Senate passed July 18. House Ways and Means discharged. House passed July 23. President signed July 26, 2001.

PL 107-23 (S 468) Designate the federal building at 6230 Van Nuys Blvd., Van Nuys, Calif., as the "James C. Corman Federal Building." Introduced by Feinstein, D-Calif., on March 6, 2001. Senate Environment and Public Works reported May 23 (no written report). Senate passed May 24. House passed, under suspension of the rules, July 23. President signed Aug. 3, 2001.

PL 107-24 (HR 1954) Extend the authorities of the Iran and Libya Sanctions Act of 1996 until Aug. 5, 2006. Introduced by Gilman, R-N.Y., on May 23, 2001. House International Relations reported, amended, June 22 (H Rept 107-107, Pt. 1). House Ways and Means reported, amended, July 16 (H Rept 107-107, Pt. 2). House Financial Services and House Government Reform discharged. House passed, amended, under suspension of the rules, July 26. Senate passed July 27. President signed Aug. 3, 2001.

PL 107-25 (HR 2213) Respond to the continuing economic crisis adversely affecting U.S. agricultural producers. Introduced by Combest, R-Texas, on June 19, 2001. House Agriculture reported, amended, June 26 (H Rept 107-111). House passed, amended, under suspension of the rules, June 26. Senate Agriculture, Nutrition, and Forestry discharged. Senate passed Aug. 3. President signed Aug. 13, 2001.

PL 107-26 (HR 2131) Reauthorize the Tropical Forest Conservation Act of 1998 through fiscal 2004. Introduced by Portman, R-Ohio, on June 12, 2001. House International Relations reported, amended, June 28 (H Rept 107-119). House passed, amended, under suspension of the rules, July 10. Senate Foreign Relations discharged. Senate passed July 23. President signed Aug. 17, 2001.

PL 107-27 (HR 93) Amend Title 5, U.S. Code, to provide that the mandatory separation age for federal firefighters be made the same as the age that applies with respect to federal law enforcement officers. Introduced by Gallegly, R-Calif., on Jan. 3, 2001. House passed, amended, under suspension of the rules, Jan. 30. Senate Governmental Affairs reported Aug. 2 (no written report). Senate passed Aug. 3. President signed Aug. 20, 2001.

PL 107-28 (HR 271) Direct the secretary of the Interior to convey a former Bureau of Land Management administrative site to the city of Carson City, Nev., for use as a senior center. Introduced by Gibbons, R-Nev., on Jan. 30, 2001. House Resources reported July 10 (H Rept 107-122). House passed, under suspension of the rules, July 23. Senate passed Aug. 3. President signed Aug. 20, 2001.

PL 107-29 (HR 364) Designate the facility of the U.S. Postal Service located at 5927 S.W. 70th St. in Miami, Fla., as the "Marjory Williams Scrivens Post Office." Introduced by Meeks, D-Fla., on Jan. 31, 2001. House passed, under suspension of the rules, March 14. Senate Governmental Affairs reported Aug. 2 (no written report). Senate passed Aug. 3. President signed Aug. 20, 2001.

PL 107-30 (HR 427) Provide further protections for the watershed of the Little Sandy River as part of the Bull Run Watershed Management Unit, Ore. Introduced by Blumenauer, D-Ore., on Feb. 6, 200l. House Resources reported July 23 (H Rept 107-151, Pt. 1). House Agriculture discharged. House passed, under suspension of the rules, July 23. Senate passed Aug. 3. President signed Aug. 20, 2001.

PL 107-31 (HR 558) Designate the federal building and U.S. courthouse located at 504 W. Hamilton St. in Allentown, Pa., as the "Edward N. Cahn Federal Building and U.S. Courthouse." Introduced by Toomey, R-Pa., on Feb. 12, 2001. House passed, under suspension of the rules, Feb. 28. Senate Environment and Public Works discharged. Senate passed Aug. 3. President signed Aug. 20, 2001.

PL 107-32 (HR 821) Designate the facility of the U.S. Postal Service located at 1030 S. Church St., Asheboro, N.C., as the "W. Joe Trogdon Post Office Building." Introduced by Coble, R-N.C., on March 1, 2001. House passed, under suspension of the rules, March 14. Senate Governmental Affairs reported Aug. 2 (no written report). Senate passed Aug. 3. President signed Aug. 20, 2001.

PL 107-33 (HR 988) Designate the U.S. courthouse located at 40 Centre St., New York, N.Y., as the "Thurgood Marshall U.S. Courthouse." Introduced by Engel, D-N.Y., on March 13, 2001. House Transportation and Infrastructure reported July 26 (H Rept 107-166). House passed Aug. 2. Senate passed Aug. 3. President signed Aug. 20, 2001.

PL 107-34 (HR 1183) Designate the facility of the U.S. Postal Service located at 113 S. Main St., Sylvania, Ga., as the "G. Elliot Hagan Post Office Building." Introduced by Kingston, R-Ga., on March 22, 2001. House passed, under suspension of the rules, June 5. Senate Governmental Affairs reported Aug. 2 (no written report). Senate passed Aug. 3. President signed Aug. 20, 2001.

PL 107-35 (HR 1753) Designate the facility of the U.S. Postal Service located at 419 Rutherford Ave., N.E., Roanoke, Va., as the "M. Caldwell Butler Post Office Building." Introduced by Goodlatte, R-Va., on May 8, 2001. House passed, under suspension of the rules, June 20. Senate Governmental Affairs reported Aug. 2 (no written report). Senate passed Aug. 3. President signed Aug. 20, 2001.

PL 107-36 (HR 2043) Designate the facility of the U.S. Postal Service located at 2719 South Webster St., Kokomo, Ind., as the "Elwood Haynes 'Bud' Hillis Post Office Building." Introduced by Buyer, R-Ind., on May 26, 2001. House passed, under suspension of the rules, June 5. Senate Governmental Affairs reported Aug. 2 (no written report). Senate passed Aug. 3. President signed Aug. 20, 2001.

PL 107-37 (HR 2882) Provide for the expedited payments of certain benefits for a public safety officer who was killed or suffered a catastrophic injury as a direct and proximate result of a personal injury sustained in the line of duty in connection with the terrorist attacks of Sept. 11, 2001. Introduced by Nadler, D-N.Y., on Sept. 13. House Judiciary discharged. House passed Sept. 13. Senate passed Sept. 13. President signed Sept. 18, 2001.

PL 107-38 (HR 2888) Make emergency supplemental appropriations for fiscal 2001 for additional disaster assistance, for antiterrorism initiatives, and for assistance in the recovery from the tragedy that occurred Sept. 11, 2001. Introduced by Young, R-Fla., on Sept. 14, 2001. House passed Sept. 14. Senate passed Sept. 14. President signed Sept. 18, 2001.

PL 107-39 (S J Res 22) Express the sense of the Senate and House of Representatives regarding the terrorist attacks launched against the United States on Sept. 11, 2001. Introduced by Daschle, D-S.D., on Sept. 12, 2001. Senate passed Sept. 12. House passed Sept. 13. President signed Sept. 18, 2001.

PL 107-40 (S J Res 23) Authorize the use of United States armed forces against those responsible for the recent attacks launched against the United States. Introduced by Daschle, D-S.D., on Sept. 14, 2001. Senate passed Sept. 14. House passed Sept. 14. President signed Sept. 18, 2001.

PL 107-41 (HR 2133) Establish a commission for the purpose of encouraging and providing for the commemoration of the 50th anniversary of the Supreme Court decision in Brown v. Board of Education. Introduced by Ryun, R-Kan., on June 12, 2001. House passed, amended, under suspension of the rules, June 27. Senate Judiciary reported, with amendments (no written report) Aug. 2. Senate passed, with amendments, Aug. 3. House agreed to Senate amendments, under suspension of the rules, Sept. 10. President signed Sept. 18, 2001.

PL 107-42 (HR 2926) Preserve the continued viability of the United States air transportation system. Introduced by Young, R-Alaska, on Sept. 21, 2001. Senate passed Sept. 21. House passed Sept. 21. President signed Sept. 22, 2001.

PL 107-43 (HR 2603) Implement the agreement establishing a United States-Jordan free trade area. Introduced by Thomas, R-Calif., on July 24, 2001. House Ways and Means reported, amended July 31 (H Rept 107-176, Pt. 1). House Judiciary discharged. House passed, amended, under suspension of the rules, July 31. Senate Finance discharged. Senate passed Sept. 24. President signed Sept. 28, 2001.

PL 107-44 (H J Res 65) Make continuing appropriations for fiscal 2002. Introduced by Young, R-Fla., on Sept. 24, 2001. House passed Sept. 24. Senate passed Sept. 25. President signed Sept. 28, 2001.

PL 107-45 (S 1424) Amend the Immigration and Nationality Act to provide permanent authority for the admission of "S" visa nonimmigrants. Introduced by Kennedy, D-Mass., on Sept. 13, 2001. Senate passed Sept. 13. House passed Sept. 15. President signed Oct. 1, 2001.

PL 107-46 (S 248) Amend the Admiral James W. Nance and Meg Donovan Foreign Relations Authorization Act, Fiscal Years 2000 and 2001, to adjust a condition on the payment of arrearages to the United Nations that sets the maximum share of any United Nations peacekeeping operation's budget that may be assessed of any country. Introduced by Helms, R-N.C., on Feb. 6, 2001. Senate Foreign Relations reported Feb. 7 (no written report). Senate passed Feb. 7. House passed, under suspension of the rules, Sept. 24. President signed Oct. 5, 2001.

PL 107-47 (HR 2510) Extend the expiration date of the Defense Production Act of 1950. Introduced by King, R-N.Y., on July 17, 2001. House Financial Services reported July 30 (H Rept 107-173). House passed, under suspension of the rules, Sept. 5. Senate Banking, Housing, and Urban Affairs discharged. Senate passed, with amendment, Sept. 21. House agreed to Senate amendment, with amendments, Sept. 25. Senate agreed to House amendments Sept. 26. President signed Oct. 5, 2001.

PL 107-48 (H J Res 68) Make further continuing appropriations for fiscal 2002. Introduced by Young, R-Fla., on Oct. 11, 2001. House Appropriations discharged. House passed Oct. 11. Senate passed Oct. 12. President signed Oct. 12, 2001.

PL 107-49 (HR 1583) Designate the federal building and United States courthouse located at 121 West Spring St., New Albany, Ind., as the "Lee H. Hamilton Federal Building and United States Courthouse." Introduced by Hill, D-Ind., on April 25, 2001. House passed, under suspension of the rules, Sept. 24. Senate passed Sept. 25. President signed Oct. 15, 2001.

PL 107-50 (HR 1860) Reauthorize the Small Business Technology Transfer Program. Introduced by Ehlers, R-Mich., on May 16, 2001. House Small Business reported, amended, on Sept. 21 (H Rept 107-213, Pt. 1). House Science discharged. House passed, under suspension of the rules, Sept. 24. Senate passed Sept. 26. President signed Oct. 15, 2001.

PL 107-51 (H J Res 42) Memorialize fallen firefighters by lowering the American flag to half-staff in honor of the National Fallen Firefighters Memorial Service in Emittsburg, Md. Introduced by Castle, R-Del., on March 29, 2001. House passed, amended, under suspension of the rules, Oct. 2. Senate passed Oct. 4. President signed Oct. 16, 2001.

PL 107-52 (H J Res 51) Approve the extension of nondiscriminatory treatment with respect to the products of the Socialist Republic of Vietnam. Introduced by Armey, R-Texas, on June 12, 2001. House Ways and Means reported Sept. 5 (H Rept 107-198). House passed Sept. 6. Senate passed Oct. 3. President signed Oct. 16, 2001.

PL 107-53 (H J Res 69) Make further continuing appropriations for fiscal 2002. Introduced by Young, R-Fla., on Oct. 17, 2001. House Appropriations discharged. House passed Oct. 17. Senate passed Oct. 17. President signed Oct. 22, 2001.

PL 107-54 (S J Res 19) Provide for the reappointment of Anne d'Harnoncourt as a citizen regent of the Board of Regents of the Smithsonian Institution. Introduced by Cochran, R-Miss., on July 12, 2001. Senate Rules and Administration reported Aug. 2 (no written report). Senate passed Sept. 13. House passed, under suspension of the rules, Oct. 9. President signed Oct. 24, 2001.

PL 107-55 (S J Res 20) Provide for the appointment of Roger W. Sant as a citizen regent of the Board of Regents of the Smithsonian Institution. Introduced by Cochran, R-Miss., on July 12, 2001. Senate Rules and Administration reported Aug. 2 (no written report). Senate passed Sept. 13. House passed, under suspension of the rules, Oct. 9. President signed Oct. 24, 2001.

PL 107-56 (HR 3162) Deter and punish terrorist acts in the United States and around the world and enhance law enforcement investigatory tools. Introduced by Sensenbrenner, R-Wis., on Oct. 23, 2001. House passed, under suspension of the rules, Oct. 24. Senate passed Oct. 25. President signed Oct. 26, 2001.

PL 107-57 (S 1465) Authorize the president to exercise waivers of foreign assistance restrictions with respect to Pakistan through Sept. 30, 2003. Introduced by Brownback, R-Kan., on Sept. 25, 2001. Senate Foreign Relations reported, amended, Oct. 4 (no written report). Senate passed, amended, Oct. 4. House passed, under suspension of the rules, Oct. 16. President signed Oct. 27, 2001.

PL 107-58 (H J Res 70) Make further continuing appropriations for fiscal 2002. Introduced by Young, R-Fla., on Oct. 24, 2001. House passed Oct. 25. Senate passed Oct. 25. President signed Oct. 31, 2001.

PL 107-59 (HR 146) Authorize the secretary of the Interior to study the suitability and feasibility of designating the Great Falls Historic District in Paterson, N.J., as a unit of the National Park System. Introduced by Pascrell, D-N.J., on Jan. 3, 2001. House Resources reported April 24 (H Rept 107-47). House passed May 9. Senate Energy and Natural Resources reported Oct. 1 (S Rept 107-74). Senate passed Oct. 17. President signed Nov. 5, 2001.

PL 107-60 (HR 1000) Adjust the boundary of the William Howard Taft National Historic Site in Ohio and authorize an exchange of land in connection with the site. Introduced by Portman, R-Ohio, on March 13, 2001. House Resources reported, amended, June 6 (H Rept 107-88). House passed, under suspension of the rules, June 6. Senate Energy and Natural Resources reported Oct. 1 (S Rept 107-76). Senate passed Oct. 17. President signed Nov. 5, 2001.

PL 107-61 (HR 1161) Authorize the American Friends of the Czech Republic to establish a memorial to honor Tomas G. Masaryk in the District of Columbia. Introduced by Gilman, R-N.Y., on March 22, 2001. House Resources reported, amended, Sept. 28 (H Rept 107-221). House passed, under suspension of the rules, Oct. 2. Senate passed Oct. 17. President signed Nov. 5, 2001.

PL 107-62 (HR 1668) Authorize the Adams Memorial Foundation to establish a commemorative work on federal land in the District of Columbia and its environs to honor former President John Adams and his family. Introduced by Roemer, D-Ind., on May 1, 2001. House passed, amended, under suspension of the rules, June 25. Senate En-

ergy and Natural Resources reported Oct. 1 (S Rept 107-77). Senate passed Oct.17. President signed Nov. 5, 2001.

PL 107-63 (HR 2217) Make appropriations for the Department of the Interior and related agencies for the fiscal year ending Sept. 30, 2002. Introduced by Skeen, R-N.M., on June 19, 2001. House Appropriations reported June 19 (H Rept 107-103). House passed, with amendments, June 21. Senate Appropriations reported, with amendments, June 29 (S Rept 107-36). Senate passed, with amendments, July 12. Conference report filed in the House, on Oct. 11 (H Rept 107-234). House agreed to conference report Oct. 17. Senate agreed to conference report Oct. 17. President signed Nov. 5, 2001.

PL 107-64 (HR 2904) Make appropriations for military construction, family housing and base realignment and closure for the Department of Defense for the fiscal year ending Sept. 30, 2002. Introduced by Hobson, R-Ohio, on Sept. 20, 2001. House Appropriations reported Sept. 20 (H Rept 107-207). House passed Sept. 21. Senate Appropriations discharged. Senate passed, amended, Sept. 26. Conference report filed in the House on Oct. 16 (H Rept 107-246). House agreed to conference report Oct. 17. Senate agreed to conference report Oct. 18. President signed Nov. 5, 2001.

PL 107-65 (HR 182) Amend the Wild and Scenic Rivers Act to designate a segment of the Eight Mile River in Connecticut for study for potential addition to the National Wild and Scenic Rivers System. Introduced by Simmons, R-Conn., Jan. 3, 2001. House Resources reported, amended, April 3 (H Rept 107-36). House passed, amended, under suspension of the rules, May 1. Senate Energy and Natural Resources reported Oct. 1 (S Rept 107-75). Senate passed Oct. 17. President signed Nov. 6, 2001.

PL 107-66 (HR 2311) Make appropriations for energy and water development for the fiscal year ending Sept. 30, 2002. Introduced by Callahan, R-Ala., on June 26, 2001. House Appropriations reported June 26, (H Rept 107-112). House passed, amended, June 28. Senate Appropriations Committee discharged. Senate passed, with amendments, July 19. Conference report filed in the House on Oct. 30 (H Rept 107-258). House agreed to conference report Nov. 1. Senate agreed to conference report Nov. 1. President signed Nov. 12, 2001.

PL 107-67 (HR 2590) Make appropriations for the Treasury Department, the U.S. Postal Service, the Executive Office of the President, and certain Independent Agencies, for the fiscal year ending Sept. 30, 2002. Introduced by Istook, R-Okla., on July 23, 2001. House Appropriations reported July 23 (H Rept 107-152). House passed, with amendments, July 25. Senate Appropriations discharged. Senate passed, amended, Sept. 19. Conference report filed in the House on Oct. 26 (H Rept 107-253). House agreed to conference report Oct. 31. Senate agreed to conference report Nov. 1. President signed Nov. 12, 2001.

PL 107-68 (HR 2647) Make appropriations for the legislative branch for the fiscal year ending Sept. 30, 2002. Introduced by Taylor, R-N.C., on July 26, 2001. House Appropriations reported July 26 (H Rept 107-169). House passed, with amendments, July 31. Senate passed, with amendments, July 31. Conference report filed in the House on Oct. 30 (H Rept 107-259). House agreed to conference report Nov. 1. Senate agreed to conference report Nov. 1. President signed Nov. 12, 2001.

PL 107-69 (HR 2925) Amend the Reclamation Recreation Management Act of 1992 to provide for the security of dams, facilities and resources under the jurisdiction of the Bureau of Reclamation. Introduced by Calvert, R-Calif., on Sept. 21, 2001. House Resources reported, amended, Oct. 3 (no written report). House passed, amended, under suspension of the rules, Oct. 23. Senate passed Oct. 30. President signed Nov. 12, 2001.

PL 107-70 (H J Res 74) Make further continuing appropriations for fiscal 2002. Introduced by Young, R-Fla., on Nov. 15, 2001. House Appropriations discharged. House passed Nov. 15. Senate passed Nov. 15. President signed Nov. 17, 2001.

PL 107-71 (S 1447) Improve aviation security. Introduced by Hollings, D-S.C., on Sept. 21, 2001. Senate passed, amended, Oct. 11. House passed, amended, Nov. 6. Conference report filed in the House on Nov. 16 (H Rept 107-296). Senate agreed to conference report Nov. 16. House agreed to conference report Nov. 16. President signed Nov. 19, 2001.

PL 107-72 (HR 768) Amend the Improving America's Schools Act of 1994 to extend the favorable treatment of need-based education aid under the antitrust laws. Introduced by Smith, R-Texas, on Feb. 28, 2001. House Judiciary reported April 3 (H Rept 107-32). House passed, under suspension of the rules, April 3. Senate Health, Education, Labor, and Pensions discharged. Senate Judiciary discharged. Senate passed, amended, Oct. 3. House agreed to Senate amendments, under suspension of the rules, Nov. 6. President signed Nov. 20, 2001.

PL 107-73 (HR 2620) Make appropriations for the departments of Veterans Affairs and Housing and Urban Development, and for independent agencies, boards, commissions, corporations and offices for the fiscal year ending Sept. 30, 2002. Introduced by Walsh, R-N.Y., on July 25, 2001. House Appropriations reported July 25 (H Rept 107-159). House passed, amended, July 31. Senate passed, with amendment, Aug. 2. Conference report filed in the House on Nov. 6 (H Rept 107-272). House agreed to conference report Nov. 8. Senate agreed to conference report Nov. 8. President signed Nov. 26, 2001.

PL 107-74 (HR 1042) Prevent the elimination of certain reports. Introduced by Grucci, R-N.Y., on March 15, 2001. House passed, amended, under suspension of the rules, March 21. Senate Governmental Affairs reported Oct. 31 (S Rept 107-90). Senate passed Nov. 15. President signed Nov. 28, 2001.

PL 107-75 (HR 1552) Extend the moratorium enacted by the Internet Tax Freedom Act through Nov. 1, 2003. Introduced by Cox, R-Calif., on April 24, 2001. House Judiciary reported, amended, Oct. 16 (H Rept 107-240). House passed, amended, under suspension of the rules, Oct. 16. Senate passed Nov. 15. President signed Nov. 28, 2001.

PL 107-76 (HR 2330) Make appropriations for agriculture, rural development, Food and Drug Administration, and related agencies' programs for the fiscal year ending Sept. 30, 2002. Introduced by Bonilla, R-Texas, on June 27, 2001. House Appropriations reported June 27 (H Rept 107-116). House passed, amended, July 11. Senate Appropriations discharged. Senate passed, with amendment, Oct. 25. Conference report filed in the House on Nov. 9 (H Rept 107-275). House agreed to conference report Nov. 13. Senate agreed to conference report Nov. 15. President signed Nov. 28, 2001.

PL 107-77 (HR 2500) Make appropriations for the departments of Commerce, Justice, State, and the Judiciary, and related agencies for the fiscal year ending Sept. 30, 2002. Introduced by Wolf, R-Va.,

on July 13, 2001. House Appropriations reported July 13 (H Rept 107-139). House passed, amended, July 18. Senate passed, with amendments, Sept. 13. Senate amended its amendment Sept. 21. Conference report filed in the House on Nov. 9 (H Rept 107-278). House agreed to conference report Nov. 14. Senate agreed to conference report Nov. 15. President signed Nov. 28, 2001.

PL 107-78 (HR 2924) Provide authority to the Federal Power Marketing Administrations to reduce vandalism and destruction of property. Introduced by Calvert, R-Calif., on Sept. 21, 2001. House Resources reported Oct. 3 (no written report). House passed, amended, under suspension of the rules, Oct. 23. Senate passed Nov. 15. President signed Nov. 28, 2001.

PL 107-79 (H J Res 76) Make further continuing appropriations for fiscal 2002. Introduced by Young, R-Fla., on Dec. 5, 2001. House Appropriations discharged. House passed Dec. 5. Senate passed Dec. 5. President signed Dec. 7, 2001.

PL 107-80 (S 1459) Designate the federal building and U.S. courthouse located at 550 West Fort St., Boise, Idaho, as the "James A. McClure Federal Building and U.S. Courthouse." Introduced by Crapo, R-Idaho, on Sept. 25, 2001. Senate Environment and Public Works reported Nov. 8 (no written report). Senate passed Nov. 15. House passed, under suspension of the rules, Nov. 27. President signed Dec. 12, 2001.

PL 107-81 (S 1573) Authorize provision of education and health assistance to the women and children of Afghanistan. Introduced by Hutchison, R-Texas, on Oct. 25, 2001. Senate passed, amended, Nov. 15. House passed, under suspension of the rules, Nov. 27. President signed Dec. 12, 2001.

PL 107-82 (HR 2291) Extend the authorization of the Drug-Free Communities Support Program for an additional five years and authorize a National Community Antidrug Coalition Institute. Introduced by Portman, R-Ohio, on June 21, 2001. House Government Reform reported July 30 (H Rept 107-175, Pt. 1). House Energy and Commerce discharged. House passed under suspension of the rules, Sept. 5. Senate passed Nov. 29. President signed Dec. 14, 2001.

PL 107-83 (H J Res 78) Make further continuing appropriations for fiscal 2002. Introduced by Young, R-Fla., on Dec. 12, 2001. House Appropriations discharged. House passed Dec. 13. Senate passed Dec. 14. President signed Dec. 15, 2001.

PL 107-84 (HR 717) Amend the Public Health Service Act to provide for research and services with respect to Duchenne muscular dystrophy. Introduced by Wicker, R-Miss., on Feb. 14, 2001. House Energy and Commerce reported, amended, Sept. 5 (H Rept 107-195). House passed, under suspension of the rules, Sept. 24. Senate Health, Education, Labor, and Pensions reported, amended, Oct. 30 (no written report). Senate passed, Nov. 15. House agreed to Senate amendment Nov. 29. President signed Dec. 18, 2001.

PL 107-85 (HR 1766) Designate the facility of the U.S. Postal Service at 4270 John Marr Drive, Annandale, Va., as the "Stan Parris Post Office Building." Introduced by Wolf, R-Va., on May 8, 2001. House passed, under suspension of the rules, Sept. 10. Senate Governmental Affairs reported Nov. 16 (no written report). Senate passed Nov. 30. President signed Dec. 18, 2001.

PL 107-86 (HR 2261) Designate the facility of the U.S. Postal Service at 2853 Candler Road, Decatur, Ga., as the "Earl T. Shinhoster

Post Office." Introduced by McKinney, D-Ga., on June 20, 2001. House passed, under suspension of the rules, Oct. 16. Senate Governmental Affairs reported Nov. 16 (no written report). Senate passed Nov. 30. President signed Dec. 18, 2001.

PL 107-87 (HR 2299) Make appropriations for the Department of Transportation and related agencies for the fiscal year ending Sept. 30, 2002. Introduced by Rogers, R-Ky., on June 22, 2001. House Appropriations reported June 22 (H Rept 107-108). House passed, amended, June 26. Senate Appropriations discharged. Senate passed, with amendment, Aug. 1. Conference report filed in the House on Nov. 30 (H Rept 107-308). House agreed to conference report Nov. 30. Senate agreed to conference report Dec. 4. President signed Dec. 18, 2001.

PL 107-88 (HR 2454) Designate the facility of the U.S. Postal Service at 5472 Crenshaw Blvd. in Los Angeles as the "Congressman Julian C. Dixon Post Office Building." Introduced by Watson, D-Calif., on July 10, 2001. House passed, amended, under suspension of the rules, Oct. 16. Senate Governmental Affairs reported Nov. 16 (no written report). Senate passed Nov. 30. President signed Dec. 18, 2001.

PL 107-89 (H J Res 71) Amend Title 36, U.S. Code, to designate Sept. 11 as Patriot Day. Introduced by Fossella, R-N.Y., on Oct. 25, 2001. House passed Oct. 25. Senate Judiciary discharged. Senate passed Nov. 30. President signed Dec. 18, 2001.

PL 107-90 (HR 10) Provide for pension reform. Introduced by Portman, R-Ohio, on March 14, 2001. House Ways and Means reported, amended, May 1 (H Rept 107-51, Pt. 1). House Education and the Workforce reported, amended, May 1 (H Rept 107-51, Pt. 2). House passed, amended, May 2. Senate passed, with amendments, Dec. 5. House agreed to Senate amendments, under suspension of the rules, Dec. 11. President signed Dec. 21, 2001.

PL 107-91 (HR 1230) Provide for the establishment of the Detroit River International Wildlife Refuge in Michigan. Introduced by Dingell, D-Mich., on March 27, 2001. House Resources reported, amended, Nov. 5 (H Rept 107-270). House passed, under suspensions of the rules, Nov. 27. Senate Environment and Public Works discharged. Senate passed Dec. 8. President signed Dec. 21, 2001.

PL 107-92 (HR 1761) Designate the facility of the U.S. Postal Service at 8588 Richmond Highway, Alexandria, Va., as the "Herb Harris Post Office Building." Introduced by Moran, D-Va., on May 8, 2001. House passed, amended, under suspension of the rules, Sept. 10. Senate Governmental Affairs discharged. Senate passed Dec. 6. President signed Dec. 21, 2001.

PL 107-93 (HR 2061) Amend the charter of Southeastern University of the District of Columbia. Introduced by Norton, D-D.C., on June 5, 2001. House passed, under suspension of the rules, Sept. 20. Senate Governmental Affairs reported Nov. 29 (S Rept 107-102). Senate passed Dec. 6. President signed Dec. 21, 2001.

PL 107-94 (HR 2540) Amend Title 38, U.S. Code, to provide a cost of living adjustment in the rates of disability compensation for veterans with service-related disabilities and in the rates of dependency and indemnity compensation for survivors of such veterans. Introduced by Smith, R-N.J., on July 18, 2001. House Veterans' Affairs reported, amended, July 24 (H Rept 107-156). House passed, amended, under suspension of the rules, July 31. Senate Veterans' Affairs discharged. Senate passed, with amendments, Nov. 15. House agreed to Senate amendments Dec. 11. President signed Dec. 21, 2001.

PL 107-95 (HR 2716) Amend Title 38, U.S. Code, to revise, improve and consolidate provisions of law providing benefits and services for homeless veterans. Introduced by Smith, R-N.J., on Aug. 2, 2001. House Veterans' Affairs reported, amended, Oct. 16 (H Rept 107-241, Pt. 1). House Financial Services discharged. House passed, amended, under suspension of the rules, Oct. 16. Senate passed, with amendment, Dec. 6, 2001. House agreed to Senate amendment Dec. 11. President signed Dec. 21, 2001.

PL 107-96 (HR 2944) Make appropriations for the government of the District of Columbia and other activities chargeable in whole or in part against the revenues of the District for the fiscal year ending Sept. 30, 2002. Introduced by Knollenberg, R-Mich., on Sept. 24, 2001. House Appropriations reported Sept. 24 (H Rept 107-216). House passed, amended, Sept. 25. Senate Appropriations discharged. Senate passed, with amendment, Nov. 7. Conference report filed in the House on Dec. 5 (H Rept 107-321). House agreed to conference report Dec. 6. Senate agreed to conference report Dec. 7. President signed Dec. 21, 2001.

PL 107-97 (H J Res 79) Make further continuing appropriations for fiscal 2002. Introduced by Young, R-Fla., on Dec. 19, 2001. House passed Dec. 20. Senate passed Dec. 20. President signed Dec. 21, 2001.

PL 107-98 (H J Res 80) Appoint the day for convening the second session of the 107th Congress. Introduced by Armey, R-Texas, on Dec. 20, 2001. House passed Dec. 20. Senate passed Dec. 20. President signed Dec. 21, 2001.

PL 107-99 (S 494) Provide for a transition to democracy and promote economic recovery in Zimbabwe. Introduced by Frist, R-Tenn., on March 8, 2001. Senate Foreign Relations reported, amended, July 16 (no written report). Senate passed, amended, Aug. 1. House International Relations reported, with amendment, Dec. 4 (H Rept 107-312, Pt. 1). House Financial Services discharged. House passed, with amendment, under suspension of the rules, Dec. 4. Senate agreed to House amendment Dec. 11. President signed Dec. 21, 2001.

PL 107-100 (S 1196) Amend the Small Business Investment Act of 1958. Introduced by Bond, R-Mo., on July 18, 2001. Senate Small Business reported Aug. 28 (S Rept 107-55). Senate passed, amended, Nov. 15. House passed, with amendment, Nov. 16. Senate agreed to House amendment with amendment Dec. 8. House agreed to Senate amendment, Dec. 11. President signed Dec. 21, 2001.

PL 107-101 (S J Res 26) Provide for the appointment of Patricia Q. Stonesifer as a citizen regent of the Board of Regents of the Smithsonian Institution. Introduced by Cochran, R-Miss., on Oct. 17, 2001. Senate Rules and Administration discharge. Senate passed Nov. 29. House passed, under suspension of the rules, Dec. 11. President signed Dec. 21, 2001.

PL 107-102 (HR 483) Modify the use of the trust land and resources of the Confederated Tribes of the Warm Springs Reservation of Oregon. Introduced by Walden, R-Ore., on Feb. 6, 2001. House Resources reported, amended, Oct. 30 (H Rept 107-257). House passed, amended, under suspension of the rules, Oct. 30. Senate Indian Affairs discharged. Senate passed Dec. 13. President signed Dec. 27, 2001.

PL 107-103 (HR 1291) Amend Title 38, U.S. Code, to increase the amount of education benefits for veterans under the Montgomery GI Bill. Introduced by Smith, R-N.J., on March 29, 2001. House passed, under suspension of the rules, June 19. Senate Veterans' Affairs discharged. Senate passed, with amendments, Dec. 8. House agreed to

Senate amendments with an amendment, Dec. 11. Senate agreed to House amendment Dec. 13. President signed Dec. 27, 2001.

PL 107-104 (HR 2559) Amend Chapter 90 of Title 5, U.S. Code, relating to federal long-term care insurance. Introduced by Scarborough, R-Fla., on July 18, 2001. House Judiciary reported Oct. 11 (H Rept 107-235, Pt. 1). House passed, under suspension of the rules, Oct. 30. Senate Governmental Affairs reported Nov. 27 (S Rept 107-128). Senate passed Dec. 17. President signed Dec. 27, 2001.

PL 107-105 (HR 3323) Ensure that covered entities comply with standards for electronic health care transactions and code sets adopted under Part C of Title XI of the Social Security Act. Introduced by Hobson, R-Ohio, Nov. 16, 2001. House passed, amended, under suspension of the rules, Dec. 4. Senate passed Dec. 12. President signed Dec. 27, 2001.

PL 107-106 (HR 3442) Establish the National Museum of African American History and Culture Plan for Action Presidential Commission to develop a plan of action for establishing and maintaining the National Museum of African American History and Culture in Washington, D.C. Introduced by Lewis, D-Ga., on Dec. 11, 2001. House passed, under suspension of the rules, Dec. 11. Senate passed Dec. 17. President signed Dec. 28, 2001.

PL 107-107 (S 1438) Authorize appropriations for fiscal 2002 for military activities of the Department of Defense, military constructions, and defense activities of the Department of Energy, and prescribe personnel strengths for the armed forces. Introduced by Levin, D-Mich., on Sept. 19, 2001. Senate passed, amended, Oct. 2. House passed, with an amendment, Oct. 17. Conference report filed in the House on Dec. 12 (H Rept 107-333). House agreed to conference report Dec. 13. Senate agreed to conference report Dec. 13. President signed Dec. 28, 2001.

PL 107-108 (HR 2883) Authorize appropriations for fiscal 2002 for intelligence and intelligence-related activities of the U.S. government, the Community Management Account, and the Central Intelligence Agency Retirement and Disability System. Introduced by Goss, R-Fla., on Sept. 13, 2001. House Intelligence reported, amended, Sept. 26 (H Rept 107-219). House passed, amended, Oct. 5. Senate passed, with an amendment, Nov. 8. Conference report filed in the House on Dec. 6 (H Rept 107-328). House agreed to conference report Dec. 12. Senate agreed to conference report Dec. 13. President signed Dec. 28, 2001.

PL 107-109 (S 1789) Amend the Federal Food, Drug and Cosmetic Act to improve the safety and efficacy of pharmaceuticals for children. Introduced by Dodd, D-Conn., on Dec. 8, 2001. Senate passed Dec. 12. House passed, under suspension of the rules, Dec. 18. President signed Jan. 4, 2002.

PL 107-110 (HR 1) Amend the Elementary and Secondary Education Act of 1965 (ESEA) to revise, reauthorize and consolidate various programs, and authorize appropriations for ESEA programs through fiscal 2007. Introduced by Boehner, R-Ohio, on March 22, 2001. House Education and the Workforce reported, amended, May 14 (H Rept 107-63, Pt. I). House Judiciary discharged May 15. House passed, amended, May 23. Senate passed, with amendments, June 14. Conference report filed in the House on Dec. 13 (H Rept 107-334). House agreed to conference report Dec. 13. Senate agreed to conference report Dec. 18. President signed Jan. 8, 2002.

PL 107-111 (HR 643) Reauthorize the African Elephant Conservation Act of 1997. Introduced by Gilchrest, R-Md., on Feb. 14, 2001. House Resources reported, amended, June 12 (H Rept 107-93). House passed, under suspension of the rules, June 12. Senate Environment and Public Works reported Nov. 30 (S Rept 107-104). Senate passed Dec. 18. President signed Jan. 8, 2002.

PL 107-112 (HR 645) Reauthorize the Rhinoceros and Tiger Conservation Act of 1994. Introduced by Gilchrest, R-Md., on Feb. 14, 2001. House Resources reported, amended, June 25 (H Rept 107-109). House passed, under suspension of the rules, June 25. Senate Environment and Public Works reported Nov. 30 (S Rept 107-105). Senate passed Dec. 18. President signed Jan. 8, 2002.

PL 107-113 (HR 2199) Amend the National Capital Revitalization and Self-Government Improvement Act of 1997 to permit any federal law enforcement agency to enter into a cooperative agreement with the Metropolitan Police Department of the District of Columbia to assist the department in carrying out crime prevention and law enforcement activities in the District if deemed appropriate by the chief of the department and the U.S. Attorney for the District of Columbia. Introduced by Norton, D-D.C., on June 14, 2001. House Government Reform reported July 25 (no written report). House passed, under suspension of the rules, Sept. 25. Senate Governmental Affairs reported Nov. 29 (S Rept 107-103). Senate passed, with an amendment, Dec. 11. House agreed to Senate amendment, under suspension of the rules, Dec. 19. President signed Jan. 8, 2002.

PL 107-114 (HR 2657) Amend Title 11, District of Columbia Code, to redesignate the Family Division of the Superior Court of the District of Columbia as the Family Court of the Superior Court, to recruit and retain trained and experienced judges to serve in the family court, and to promote consistency and efficiency in the assignment of judges to the family court and in the actions and proceedings of the court. Introduced by DeLay, R-Texas, on July 26, 2001. House passed, under suspension of the rules, Sept. 20. Senate Governmental Affairs reported, amended, Dec. 5 (S Rept 107-108). Senate passed, with an amendment, Dec. 14. House agreed to Senate amendment, under suspension of the rules, Dec. 19. President signed Jan. 8, 2002.

PL 107-115 (HR 2506) Make appropriations for foreign operations, export financing, and related programs for the fiscal year ending Sept. 30, 2002. Introduced by Kolbe, R-Ariz., on July 17, 2001. House Appropriations reported July 17 (H Rept 107-142). House passed, amended, July 24. Senate Appropriations reported, with amendment, Sept. 4 (S Rept 107-58). Senate passed, with amendments, Oct. 24. Conference report filed in the House on Dec. 19 (H Rept 107-345). House agreed to conference report Dec. 19. Senate agreed to conference report Dec. 20. President signed Jan. 10, 2002.

PL 107-116 (HR 3061) Make appropriations for the Departments of Labor, Health and Human Services, and Education, and related agencies for the fiscal year ending Sept. 30, 2002. Introduced by Regula, R-Ohio, on Oct. 9, 2001. House Appropriations reported Oct. 9 (H Rept 107-229). House passed, amended, Oct. 11. Senate passed, with amendment, Nov. 6. Conference report filed in the House on Dec. 19 (H Rept 107-342). House agreed to conference report Dec. 19. Senate agreed to conference report Dec. 20. President signed Jan. 10, 2002.

PL 107-117 (HR 3338) Make appropriations for the Department of Defense for the fiscal year ending Sept. 30, 2002. Introduced by Lewis, R-Calif., on Nov. 19, 2001. House Appropriations reported

Nov. 19 (H Rept 107-298). House passed, amended, Nov. 28. Senate Appropriations reported, with amendment, Dec. 5 (S Rept 107-109). Senate passed, with amendment, Dec. 7. Conference report filed in the House Dec. 19 (H Rept 107-350). House agreed to conference report Dec. 20. Senate agreed to conference report Dec. 20. President signed Jan. 10, 2002.

PL 107-118 (HR 2869) Provide certain relief for small businesses from liability under the Comprehension Environmental Response, Compensation, and Liability Act of 1980, and amend the act to promote the cleanup and reuse of brownfields, provide financial assistance for brownfields revitalization, and enhance state response programs. Introduced by Gillmor, R-Ohio, on Sept. 10, 2001. House passed, amended, under suspension of the rules, Dec. 20. Senate passed Dec. 20. President signed Jan. 11, 2002.

PL 107-119 (S 1202) Amend the Ethics in Government Act of 1978 to extend the authorization of appropriations for the Office of Government Ethics through fiscal 2006. Introduced by Lieberman, D-Conn., on July 19, 2001. Senate Governmental Affairs reported Oct. 30 (S Rept 107-88). Senate passed Nov. 15. House passed, under suspension of the rules, Dec. 20. President signed Jan. 15, 2002.

PL 107-120 (S 1714) Provide for the installation of a plaque to honor Dr. James Harvey Early in the Williamsburg, Ky., Post Office Building. Introduced by McConnell, R-Ky., on Nov. 15, 2001. Senate Governmental Affairs discharged Dec. 6. Senate passed Dec. 6. House passed, under suspension of the rules, Dec. 20. President signed Jan. 15, 2002.

PL 107-121 (S 1741) Amend Title XIX of the Social Security Act to clarify that Indian women with breast or cervical cancer who are eligible for health services provided under a medical care program of the Indian Health Service or of a tribal organization are included in the optional Medicaid eligibility category of breast or cervical cancer patients added by the Breast and Cervical Prevention and Treatment Act of 2000. Introduced by Bingaman, D-N.M., on Nov. 28, 2001. Senate passed Nov. 28. House passed, under suspension of the rules, Dec. 20. President signed Jan. 15, 2002.

PL 107-122 (S 1793) Provide the secretary of education with specific waiver authority to respond to conditions in the national emergency declared by the president on Sept. 14, 2001. Introduced by Collins, R-Maine, on Dec. 10, 2001. Senate Health, Education, Labor and Pensions reported Dec. 12 (no written report). Senate passed Dec. 14. House passed, under suspension of the rules, Dec. 20. President signed Jan. 15, 2002.

PL 107-123 (HR 1088) Amend the Securities Exchange Act of 1934 to reduce fees collected by the Securities and Exchange Commission. Introduced by Fossella, R-N.Y., on March 19, 2001. House Financial Services reported, amended, May 1 (H Rept 107-52, Pt. 1). House Government Reform discharged May 25. House passed June 14. Senate passed Dec. 20. President signed Jan. 16, 2002.

PL 107-124 (HR 2277) Provide for work authorization for nonimmigrant spouses of treaty traders and treaty investors. Introduced by Gekas, R-Pa., on June 21, 2001. House Judiciary reported Aug. 2 (H Rept 107-187). House passed, under suspension of the rules, Sept. 5. Senate Judiciary reported Dec. 13 (no written report). Senate passed Dec. 20. President signed Jan. 16, 2002.

PL 107-125 (HR 2278) Provide for work authorization for nonimmigrant spouses of intracompany transferees, and reduce the period of time during which certain intracompany transferees have to be continuously employed before applying for admission to the United States. Introduced by Gekas, R-Pa., on June 21, 2001. House Judiciary reported Aug. 2 (H Rept 107-188). House passed, under suspension of the rules, Sept. 5. Senate Judiciary reported Dec. 13 (no written report). Senate passed Dec. 20. President signed Jan. 16, 2002.

PL 107-126 (HR 2336) Make permanent the authority to redact financial disclosure statements of judicial employees and judicial officers. Introduced by Coble, R-N.C., on June 27, 2001. House Judiciary reported Oct. 12 (H Rept 107-239). House passed, under suspension of the rules, Oct. 16. Senate Governmental Affairs reported Dec. 7 (S Rept 107-111). Senate passed, with amendments, Dec. 11. House agreed to Senate amendments, under suspension of the rules, Dec. 20. President signed Jan. 16, 2002.

PL 107-127 (HR 2751) Authorize the president to award a gold medal on behalf of the Congress to Gen. Henry H. Shelton and provide for the production of bronze duplicates of such medal for sale to the public. Introduced by Etheridge, D-N.C., on Aug. 2, 2001. House passed, amended, under suspension of the rules, Dec. 19. Senate passed Dec. 20. President signed Jan. 16, 2002.

PL 107-128 (HR 3030) Extend the "Basic Pilot" employment verification system. Introduced by Latham, R-Iowa, on Oct. 4, 2001. House Judiciary reported, amended, Nov. 30 (H Rept 107-310, Pt. 1). House Education and the Workforce discharged Nov. 30. House passed, under suspension of the rules, Dec. 11. Senate passed Dec. 20. President signed Jan. 16, 2002.

PL 107-129 (HR 3248) Designate the facility of the U.S. Postal Service located at 65 North Main St., Cranbury, N.J., as the "Todd Beamer Post Office Building." Introduced by Holt, D-N.J., on Nov. 7, 2001. House passed, under suspension of the rules, Dec. 5. Senate Governmental Affairs discharged Dec. 20. Senate passed Dec. 20. President signed Jan. 16, 2002.

PL 107-130 (HR 3334) Designate the Richard J. Guadagno Headquarters and Visitors Center at Humboldt Bay National Wildlife Refuge, Calif. Introduced by Thompson, D-Calif., on Nov. 16, 2001. House Resources reported Dec. 5 (H Rept 107-319). House passed, under suspension of the rules, Dec. 18. Senate passed Dec. 20. President signed Jan. 16, 2002.

PL 107-131 (HR 3346) Amend the Internal Revenue Code of 1986 to simplify reporting requirements relating to higher education tuition and related expenses. Introduced by Manzullo, R-Ill., on Nov. 27, 2001. House passed, under suspension of the rules, Dec. 4. Senate passed Dec. 20. President signed Jan. 16, 2002.

PL 107-132 (HR 3348) Designate the National Foreign Affairs Training Center as the George P. Shultz National Foreign Affairs Training Center. Introduced by Hyde, R-Ill., on Nov. 27, 2001. House passed, under suspension of the rules, Dec. 5. Senate Foreign Relations discharged Dec. 20. Senate passed Dec. 20. President signed Jan. 16, 2002.

PL 107-133 (HR 2873) Extend and amend the Promoting Safe and Stable Families program under Title IV-B, Subpart 2 of the Social Security Act, and provide new authority to support programs for mentoring children of incarcerated parents; amend the Foster Care Independent Living program under Title IV-E of the act to provide for education and training vouchers for youths aging out of foster care. Introduced by Herger, R-Calif., on Sept. 10, 2001. House Ways and Means reported, amended Nov. 13 (H Rept 107-281). House passed, under suspension of the rules, Nov. 13. Senate passed Dec. 13. President signed Jan. 17, 2002.

PL 107-134 (HR 2884) Amend the Internal Revenue Code of 1986 to provide tax relief for victims of the Sept. 11 terrorist attacks. Introduced by Thomas, R-Calif., on Sept. 13, 2001. House Ways and Means discharged Sept. 13. House passed, Sept. 13. Senate Finance discharged Nov. 16. Senate passed, with amendments, Nov. 16. House agreed to Senate amendments with amendment Dec. 13. Senate agreed to House amendment with amendment Dec. 20. House agreed to Senate amendment Dec. 20. President signed, Jan. 23, 2002.

PL 107-135 (HR 3447) Amend Title 38, U.S. Code, to enhance the authority of the secretary of Veterans Affairs (VA) to recruit and retain qualified nurses for the Veterans Health Administration, provide an additional basis for establishing the inability of veterans to defray expenses of necessary medical care, and enhance certain VA health care programs. Introduced by Smith, R-N.J., on Dec. 11, 2001. House passed, under suspension of the rules, Dec. 11. Senate passed Dec. 20. President signed Jan. 23, 2002.

PL 107-136 (HR 3392) Name the national cemetery in Saratoga, N.Y., the Gerald B. H. Solomon Saratoga National Cemetery. Introduced by Hastert, R-Ill., on Dec. 4, 2001. House passed, under suspension of the rules, Dec. 4. Senate Veterans' Affairs discharged Dec. 20. Senate passed Dec. 20. President signed Jan. 24, 2002.

107th Congress–2002

PL 107-137 (HR 400) Authorize the secretary of the Interior to establish the Ronald Reagan Boyhood Home National Historic Site. Introduced by Hastert, R-Ill., on Feb. 6, 2001. House Resources reported Nov. 5 (H Rept 107-268). House passed, under suspension of the rules, Nov. 13. Senate passed Jan. 29, 2002. President signed Feb. 6, 2002.

PL 107-138 (HR 1913) Require the valuation of nontribal interest ownership of subsurface rights within the boundaries of the Acoma Indian Reservation. Introduced by Skeen, R-N.M., on May 17, 2001. House Resources reported, amended, Nov. 13 (H Rept 107-285). House passed, under suspension of the rules, Nov. 27. Senate Indian Affairs discharged Jan. 28, 2002. Senate passed Jan. 28. President signed Feb. 6, 2002.

PL 107-139 (S 1762) Amend the Higher Education Act of 1965 to establish fixed interest rates for student and parent borrowers and extend current law with respect to special allowances for lenders. Introduced by Johnson, D-S.D., on Dec. 4, 2001. Senate Health, Education, Labor, and Pensions reported Dec. 12 (no written report). Senate passed Dec. 14. House passed Jan. 24, 2002. President signed Feb. 8, 2002.

PL 107-140 (S 1888) Amend Title 18 of the U.S. Code to correct a technical error in the codification of Title 36 of the U.S. Code. Introduced by Stevens, R-Alaska, on Dec. 20, 2001. Senate passed Dec. 20. House passed, under suspension of the rules, Feb. 6, 2002. President signed Feb. 8, 2002.

PL 107-141 (HR 700) Reauthorize the Asian Elephant Conservation Act of 1997. Introduced by Saxton, R-N.J., on Feb. 14, 2001. House Resources reported, amended, June 12 (H Rept 107-94).

House passed, under suspension of the rules, June 12. Senate Environment and Public Works reported, amended, Dec. 7 (S Rept 107-113). Senate passed, with amendment, Dec. 18. House agreed to Senate amendment, under suspension of the rules, Jan. 23, 2002. President signed Feb. 12, 2002.

PL 107-142 (HR 1937) Authorize the secretary of the Interior to engage in certain feasibility studies of water resource projects in the state of Washington. Introduced by Larsen, D-Wash., on May 22, 2001. House Resources reported, amended, July 24 (H Rept 107-155). House passed, under suspension of the rules, Sept. 10. Senate Indian Affairs discharged Jan. 28, 2002. Senate passed Jan. 28. President signed Feb. 12, 2002.

PL 107-143 (H J Res 82) Recognize the 91st birthday of Ronald Reagan. Introduced by Cox, R-Calif., on Feb. 5, 2002. House passed, under suspension of the rules, Feb. 6. Senate passed Feb. 6. President signed Feb. 14, 2002.

PL 107-144 (S 737) Designate the facility of the U.S. Postal Service located at 811 South Main St., Yerington, Nev., as the "Joseph E. Dini, Jr. Post Office." Introduced by Reid, D-Nev., on April 6, 2001. Senate Governmental Affairs reported Aug. 2 (no written report). Senate passed Aug. 3. House passed, under suspension of the rules, Feb. 5, 2002. President signed Feb. 14, 2002.

PL 107-145 (S 970) Designate the facility of the U.S. Postal Service located at 39 Tremont St., Paris Hill, Maine, as the Horatio King Post Office Building. Introduced by Collins, R-Maine, on May 25, 2001. Senate Governmental Affairs reported Aug. 2 (no written report). Senate passed Aug. 3. House passed, under suspension of the rules, Feb. 5, 2002. President signed Feb. 14, 2002.

PL 107-146 (S 1026) Designate the U.S. Post Office located at 60 Third Ave., Long Branch, N.J., as the "Pat King Post Office Building." Introduced by Torricelli, D-N.J., on June 13, 2001. Senate Governmental Affairs reported Aug. 2 (no written report). Senate passed Aug. 3. House Government Reform discharged Feb. 6, 2002. House passed Feb. 6. President signed Feb. 14, 2002.

PL 107-147 (HR 3090) Provide tax incentives for economic recovery. Introduced by Thomas, R-Calif., on Oct. 11, 2001. House Ways and Means reported, amended, Oct. 17 (H Rept 107-251). House passed Oct. 24. Senate Finance reported, with amendments, Nov. 9 (no written report). Senate passed, with amendment, Feb. 14, 2002. House agreed to Senate amendment, with an amendment, March 7. Senate agreed to House amendment March 8. President signed March 9, 2002.

PL 107-148 (HR 2998) Authorize the establishment of Radio Free Afghanistan. Introduced by Royce, R-Calif., on Oct. 2, 2001. House International Relations reported, amended, Nov. 1 (no written report). House passed, under suspension of the rules, Nov. 7. Senate passed, with amendment, Feb. 7, 2002. House agreed to Senate amendment, under suspension of the rules, Feb. 12. President signed March 11, 2002.

PL 107-149 (S 1206) Reauthorize the Appalachian Regional Development Act of 1965. Introduced by Voinovich, R-Ohio, on July 19, 2001. Senate Environment and Public Works reported, amended, Dec. 20 (S Rept 107-132). Senate passed, amended, Feb. 8, 2002. House passed, under suspension of the rules, Feb. 26. President signed March 12, 2002.

PL 107-150 (HR 1892) Amend the Immigration and Nationality Act to provide for the acceptance of an affidavit of support from another eligible sponsor if the original sponsor has died and the attorney general has determined for humanitarian reasons that the original sponsor's classification petition should not be revoked. Introduced by Calvert, R-Calif., on May 17, 2001. House Judiciary reported, amended, July 10 (H Rept 107-127). House passed, under suspension of the rules, July 23. Senate Judiciary reported, with amendment, Dec. 13 (no written report). Senate passed, with amendment, Dec. 20. House agreed to Senate amendment, under suspension of the rules, Feb. 26, 2002. President signed March 13, 2002.

PL 107-151 (HR 3699) Revise certain grants for continuum of care assistance for homeless individuals and families. Introduced by Crenshaw, R-Fla., on Feb. 7, 2002. House passed, under suspension of the rules, Feb. 12. Senate Banking, Housing, and Urban Affairs discharged Feb. 25. Senate passed Feb. 25. President signed March 13, 2002.

PL 107-152 (S J Res 32) Congratulate the U.S. Military Academy at West Point on its bicentennial anniversary and commend its outstanding contributions to the nation. Introduced by Reed, D-R.I., on Feb. 25, 2002. Senate passed Feb. 25. House passed, under suspension of the rules, March 6. President signed March 14, 2002.

PL 107-153 (S 1857) Encourage the negotiated settlement of tribal claims. Introduced by Campbell, R-Colo, on Dec. 19, 2001. Senate Indian Affairs reported, amended, Feb. 13, 2002 (H Rept 107-138). Senate passed, amended, Feb. 26. House passed, under suspension of the rules, March 6. President signed March 19, 2002.

PL 107-154 (HR 3986) Extend the period of availability of unemployment assistance under the Robert T. Stafford Disaster Relief and Emergency Assistance Act in the case of victims of the terrorist attacks of Sept. 11, 2001. Introduced by Quinn, R-N.Y., on March 18, 2002. House passed, under suspension of the rules, March 19. Senate passed March 20. President signed March 25, 2002.

PL 107-155 (HR 2356) Amend the Federal Election Campaign Act of 1971 to provide bipartisan campaign reform. Introduced by Shays, R-Conn., on June 28, 2001. House Administration reported July 10 (H Rept 107-131, Pt. 1). House Energy and Commerce, Judiciary discharged July 10. House passed, amended, Feb. 14, 2002. Senate passed March 20. President signed March 27, 2002.

PL 107-156 (S 2019) Extend the authority of the Export-Import Bank until April 30, 2002. Introduced by Sarbanes, D-Md., on March 14, 2002. Senate passed March 14. House passed, under suspension of the rules, March 19. President signed March 31, 2002.

PL 107-157 (HR 1499) Amend the District of Columbia College Access Act of 1999 to permit individuals who enroll in an institution of higher education more than three years after graduating from a secondary school and individuals who attend private historically black colleges and universities nationwide to participate in the tuition assistance programs under the act. Introduced by Norton, D-D.C., on April 4, 2001. House passed, under suspension of the rules, July 30. Senate Governmental Affairs reported, with amendments, Nov. 29 (S Rept 107-101). Senate passed, with amendments, Dec.12. House agreed to Senate amendments, with an amendment pursuant to H Res 364, on March 12, 2002. Senate agreed to House amendment March 14. President signed April 4, 2002.

PL 107-158 (HR 2739) Amend Public Law 107-10 to require a U.S. plan to endorse and obtain observer status for Taiwan at the annual summit of the World Health Assembly in May 2002 in Geneva, Switzerland. Introduced by Brown, D-Ohio, on Aug. 2, 2001. House passed, amended, under suspension of the rules, Dec. 19. Senate Foreign Relations reported March 19, 2002 (no written report). Senate passed March 19. President signed April 4, 2002.

PL 107-159 (HR 3985) Amend a 1955 act that authorizes the leasing of restricted Indian lands for public, religious, educational, recreational, residential, business and other purposes requiring the grant of long-term leases, to provide for binding arbitration clauses in leases and contracts related to reservation lands of the Gila River Indian Community. Introduced by Hayworth, R-Ariz., on March 18, 2002. House passed, under suspension of the rules, March 19. Senate passed March 21. President signed April 4, 2002.

PL 107-160 (HR 1432) Designate the facility of the U.S. Postal Service located at 3698 Inner Perimeter Rd. in Valdosta, Ga., as the "Major Lyn McIntosh Post Office Building." Introduced by Bishop, D-Ga., on April 4, 2001. House passed, under suspension of the rules, Dec. 20. Senate passed March 22, 2002. President signed April 18, 2002.

PL 107-161 (HR 1748) Designate the facility of the U.S. Postal Service located at 805 Glen Burnie Rd. in Richmond, Va., as the "Tom Bliley Post Office Building." Introduced by Cantor, R-Va., on May 8, 2001. House passed, under suspension of the rules, Feb. 12, 2002. Senate Governmental Affairs reported March 21 (no written report). Senate passed March 22. President signed April 18, 2002.

PL 107-162 (HR 1749) Designate the facility of the U.S. Postal Service located at 685 Turnberry Rd. in Newport News, Va., as the "Herbert H. Bateman Post Office Building." Introduced by Davis, R-Va., on May 8, 2001. House passed, under suspension of the rules, Oct. 9. Senate Governmental Affairs reported March 21, 2002 (no written report). Senate passed March 22. President signed April 18, 2002.

PL 107-163 (HR 2577) Designate the facility of the U.S. Postal Service located at 310 South State St. in St. Ignace, Mich., as the "Bob Davis Post Office Building." Introduced by Stupak, D-Mich., on July 19, 2001. House passed, under suspension of the rules, Feb. 12, 2002. Senate Governmental Affairs reported March 21 (no written report). Senate passed March 22. President signed April 18, 2002.

PL 107-164 (HR 2876) Designate the facility of the U.S. Postal Service located in Harlem, Mont., as the "Francis Bardanouve United States Post Office Building." Introduced by Rehberg, R-Mont., on Sept. 10, 2001. House passed, under suspension of the rules, Oct. 16. Senate Governmental Affairs reported March 21, 2002 (no written report). Senate passed March 22. President signed April 18, 2002.

PL 107-165 (HR 2910) Designate the facility of the U.S. Postal Service located at 3131 South Crater Rd. in Petersburg, Va., as the "Norman Sisisky Post Office Building." Introduced by Forbes, R-Va., on Sept. 20, 2001. House passed, under suspension of the rules, Oct. 30. Senate Governmental Affairs reported March 21, 2002 (no written report). Senate passed March 22. President signed April 18, 2002.

PL 107-166 (HR 3072) Designate the facility of the U.S. Postal Service located at 125 Main St. in Forest City, N.C., as the "Vernon Tarlton Post Office Building." Introduced by Taylor, R-N.C., on Oct. 9, 2001. House passed, under suspension of the rules, Dec. 18. Senate

Governmental Affairs reported March 21, 2002 (no written report). Senate passed March 22. President signed April 18, 2002.

PL 107-167 (HR 3379) Designate the facility of the U.S. Postal Service located at 375 Carlls Path in Deer Park, N.Y., as the "Raymond M. Downey Post Office Building." Introduced by Israel, D-N.Y., on Nov. 29, 2001. House passed, under suspension of the rules, Dec. 18. Senate Governmental Affairs reported March 21, 2002 (no written report). Senate passed March 22. President signed April 18, 2002.

PL 107-168 (S 2248) Extend the authority of the Export-Import Bank until May 31, 2002. Introduced by Sarbanes, D-Md., on April 24, 2002. Senate passed April 24. House passed, under suspension of the rules, April 30. President signed May 1, 2002.

PL 107-169 (HR 861) Make technical amendments to section 10 of Title 9, U.S. Code. Introduced by Gekas, R-Pa., on March 6, 2001. House Judiciary reported March 12 (H Rept 107-16). House passed, under suspension of the rules, March 14. Senate Judiciary reported Dec. 13 (no written report). Senate passed April 18, 2002. President signed May 7, 2002.

PL 107-170 (HR 4167) Extend for eight additional months the period for which Chapter 12 of Title 11, U.S. Code is reenacted. Introduced by Sensenbrenner, R-Wis., on April 11, 2002. House passed, under suspension of the rules, April 16, 2002. Senate passed April 23. President signed May 7, 2002.

PL 107-171 (HR 2646) Provide for the continuation of agricultural programs through fiscal 2007. Introduced by Combest, R-Texas, on July 26, 2001. House Agriculture reported, amended Aug. 2 (H Rept 107-191, Pt. 1). House Agriculture filed supplemental report Aug. 31 (Part 2). House International Relations reported, amended, Sept. 10 (Part 3). House passed, amended, Oct. 5. Senate passed, with amendment, Feb. 13, 2002. Conference report filed in the House May 1 (H Rept 107-424). House agreed to conference report May 2. Senate agreed to conference report May 8. President signed May 13, 2002.

PL 107-172 (S 1094) Amend the Public Health Service Act to provide for research, information and education with respect to blood cancer. Introduced by Hutchison, R-Texas, on June 22, 2001. Senate Health, Education, Labor and Pensions reported, amended, Nov. 8 (no written report). Senate passed, amended, Nov. 16. House passed, under suspension of the rules, April 30, 2002. President signed May 14, 2002.

PL 107-173 (HR 3525) Enhance the border security of the United States. Introduced by Sensenbrenner, R-Wis., on Dec. 19, 2001. House passed, amended, under suspension of the rules, Dec. 19. Senate Judiciary discharged. Senate passed, with amendments, April 18, 2002. House agreed to Senate amendments, under suspension of the rules, May 8. President signed May 14, 2002.

PL 107-174 (HR 169) Require that federal agencies be accountable for violations of anti-discrimination and whistleblower protection laws. Introduced by Sensenbrenner, R-Wis., on Jan. 3, 2001. House Judiciary reported, amended, June 14 (H Rept 107-101, Pt. 1). House passed, amended, under suspension of the rules, Oct. 2. Senate Governmental Affairs reported, with amendments, April 15, 2002 (S Rept 107-143). Senate passed, amended, April 23. House agreed to Senate amendments, under suspension of the rules, April 30. President signed May 15, 2002.

PL 107-175 (HR 495) Designate the federal building located in Charlotte Amalie, St. Thomas, U.S. Virgin Is., as the "Ron de Lugo Federal Building." Introduced by Christensen, D-Virgin Is., on Feb. 7, 2001. House Transportation and Infrastructure reported May 21 (H Rept 107-71). House passed, under suspension of the rules, May 21. Senate Environment and Public Works reported April 25, 2002 (no written report). Senate passed April 30. President signed May 17, 2002.

PL 107-176 (HR 819) Designate the federal building located at 143 West Liberty St., in Medina, Ohio, as the "Donald J. Pease Federal Building." Introduced by Brown, D-Ohio, on March 1, 2001. House Transportation and Infrastructure reported May 23 (H Rept 107-75). House passed, under suspension of the rules, June 20. Senate Environment and Public Works reported April 25, 2002 (no written report). Senate passed April 30. President signed May 17, 2002.

PL 107-177 (HR 3093) Designate the federal building and U.S. courthouse located at 501 Bell St. in Alton, Ill., as the "William L. Beatty Federal Building and United States Courthouse." Introduced by Costello, D-Ill., on Oct. 11, 2001. House Transportation and Infrastructure Committee discharged. House passed Nov. 16. Senate Environment and Public Works reported April 25, 2002 (no written report). Senate passed April 30. President signed May 17, 2002.

PL 107-178 (HR 3282) Designate the federal building and U.S. courthouse located at 400 North Main St. in Butte, Mont., as the "Mike Mansfield Federal Building and United States Courthouse." Introduced by Rehberg, R-Mont., on Nov. 13, 2001. House passed, under suspension of the rules, Dec. 11. Senate Environment and Public Works reported April 25, 2002 (no written report). Senate passed April 30. President signed May 17, 2002.

PL 107-179 (HR 2048) Require a report on the operations of the State Justice Institute. Introduced by Coble, R-N.C., on June 5, 2001. House Judiciary reported Aug. 2 (H Rept 107-189). House passed, under suspension of the rules, Sept. 5, 2001. Senate Judiciary reported Dec. 13 (no written report). Senate passed May 7, 2002. President signed May 20, 2002.

PL 107-180 (HR 2305) Require certain federal officials with responsibility for the administration of the criminal justice system of the District of Columbia to serve on and participate in the activities of the District of Columbia Criminal Justice Coordinating Council. Introduced by Morella, R-Md., on June 25, 2001. House passed, amended, under suspension of the rules, Dec. 4. Senate Governmental Affairs reported April 29, 2002 (S Rept 107-145). Senate passed May 7. President signed May 20, 2002.

PL 107-181 (HR 4156) Amend the Internal Revenue Code of 1986 to clarify that the parsonage allowance exclusion is limited to the fair rental value of the property. Introduced by Ramstad, R-Minn., on April 10, 2002. House passed, amended, under suspension of the rules, April 16. Senate Finance discharged. Senate passed May 2. President signed May 20, 2002.

PL 107-182 (S 378) Redesignate the federal building located at 3348 South Kedzie Ave., in Chicago, Ill., as the "Paul Simon Chicago Job Corps Center." Introduced by Durbin, D-Ill., on Feb. 15, 2001. Senate Environment and Public Works reported May 23 (no written report). Senate passed May 24. House Transportation and Infrastructure reported May 7, 2002 (H Rept 107-438). House passed, under suspension of the rules, May 7. President signed May 21, 2002.

PL 107-183 (HR 4592) Name the chapel located in the national cemetery in Los Angeles, Calif., as the "Bob Hope Veterans Chapel." Introduced by Cox, R-Calif., on April 25, 2002. House passed, under suspension of the rules, May 21. Senate passed May 22. President signed May 29, 2002.

PL 107-184 (HR 4608) Name the Department of Veterans' Affairs medical center in Wichita, Kan., as the "Robert J. Dole Department of Veterans Affairs Medical and Regional Office Center." Introduced by Moran, R-Kan., on April 25, 2002. House Veterans Affairs reported, amended, May 16 (H Rept 107-474). House passed, amended, under suspension of the rules, May 20. Senate passed May 22. President signed May 29, 2002.

PL 107-185 (HR 1840) Extend eligibility for refugee status of unmarried sons and daughters of certain Vietnamese refugees. Introduced by Davis, R-Va., on May 15, 2001. House Judiciary reported, amended, Oct. 29 (H Rept 107-254). House passed, amended, under suspension of the rules, Oct. 30. Senate Judiciary reported Dec. 13 (no written report). Senate passed May 10, 2002. President signed May 30, 2002.

PL 107-186 (HR 4782) Extend the authority of the Export-Import Bank until June 14, 2002. Introduced by Oxley, R-Ohio, on May 21, 2002. House passed, under suspension of the rules, May 21. Senate passed May 22. President signed May 30, 2002.

PL 107-187 (HR 3167) Endorse the vision of further enlargement of the NATO Alliance articulated by President George W. Bush on June 15, 2001, and by former President Bill Clinton on Oct. 22, 1996. Introduced by Bereuter, R-Neb., on Oct. 24, 2001. House International Relations reported, amended, Nov. 5 (H Rept 107-266). House passed, amended, Nov. 7. Senate Foreign Relations reported Dec. 12 (no written report). Senate passed May 17, 2002. President signed June 10, 2002.

PL 107-188 (HR 3448) Improve the ability of the United States to prevent, prepare for, and respond to bioterrorism and other public health emergencies. Introduced by Tauzin, R-La., on Dec. 11, 2001. House passed, under suspension of the rules, Dec. 12. Senate passed, with amendment, Dec. 20. Conference report filed in the House on May 21, 2002 (H Rept 107-481). House agreed to conference report May 22. Senate agreed to conference report May 23. President signed June 12, 2002.

PL 107-189 (S 1372) Reauthorize the Export-Import Bank of the United States. Introduced by Sarbanes, D-Md., Aug. 3, 2001. Senate Banking, Housing, and Urban Affairs reported Aug. 3 (S Rept 107-52). Senate passed, amended, March 14, 2002. House passed, with amendment, May 1. Conference report filed in the House on May 24 (H Rept 107-487). House agreed to conference report June 5. Senate agreed to conference report June 6. President signed June 14, 2002.

PL 107-190 (HR 1366) Designate the U.S. Post Office building located at 3101 West Sunflower Ave. in Santa Ana, Calif., as the "Hector G. Godinez Post Office Building." Introduced by Sanchez, D-Calif., on April 3, 2001. House Government Reform discharged. House passed April 10, 2002. Senate Governmental Affairs reported May 23 (no written report). Senate passed June 3. President signed June 18, 2002.

PL 107-191 (HR 1374) Designate the facility of the U.S. Postal Service located at 600 Calumet St. in Lake Linden, Mich., as the "Philip E. Ruppe Post Office Building." Introduced by Stupak, D-Mich., on April 3, 2001. House passed, under suspension of the rules, April 16, 2002. Senate Governmental Affairs reported May 23 (no written report). Senate passed June 3. President signed June 18, 2002.

PL 107-192 (HR 3789) Designate the facility of the U.S. Postal Service located at 2829 Commercial Way in Rock Springs, Wyo., as the "Teno Roncalio Post Office Building." Introduced by Cubin, R-Wyo., on Feb. 26, 2002. House passed, under suspension of the rules, March 5. Senate Governmental Affairs reported May 23 (no written report). Senate passed June 3. President signed June 18, 2002.

PL 107-193 (HR 3960) Designate the facility of the U.S. Postal Service located at 3719 Highway 4 in Jay, Fla., as the "Joseph W. Westmoreland Post Office Building." Introduced by Miller, R-Fla., on March 13, 2002. House passed, under suspension of the rules, April 16. Senate Governmental Affairs reported May 23 (no written report). Senate passed June 3. President signed June 18, 2002.

PL 107-194 (HR 4486) Designate the facility of the U.S. Postal Service located at 1590 East Joyce Blvd. in Fayetteville, Ark., as the "Clarence B. Craft Post Office Building." Introduced by Boozman, R-Ark., on April 18, 2002. House passed, under suspension of the rules, May 7. Senate Governmental Affairs reported May 23 (no written report). Senate passed June 3. President signed June 18, 2002.

PL 107-195 (HR 4560) Eliminate the deadlines for spectrum auctions of spectrum previously allocated to television broadcasting. Introduced by Tauzin, R-La., on April 24, 2002. House Energy and Commerce reported May 7 (H Rept 107-443). House passed, amended, under suspension of the rules, May 7. Senate passed, with amendment, June 18. House agreed to Senate amendment June 18. President signed June 19, 2002.

PL 107-196 (S 2431) Amend the Omnibus Crime Control and Safe Streets Act of 1968 to ensure that chaplains killed in the line of duty receive public safety officer death benefits. Introduced by Leahy, D-Vt., on May 1, 2002. Senate Judiciary reported, amended, May 2 (no written report). Senate passed, amended, May 7. House passed June 11. President signed June 24, 2002.

PL 107-197 (HR 3275) Implement the International Convention for the Suppression of Terrorist Bombings to strengthen criminal laws relating to attacks on places of public use, and implement the International Convention of the Suppression of the Financing of Terrorism to combat terrorism and defend the nation against terrorist acts. Introduced by Smith, R-Texas, on Nov. 9, 2001. House Judiciary reported, amended, Nov. 29 (H Rept 107-307). House passed, amended, under suspension of the rules, Dec. 19. Senate Judiciary discharged. Senate passed, with amendment, June 14, 2002. House agreed to Senate amendment June 18. President signed June 25, 2002.

PL 107-198 (HR 327) Amend Chapter 35 of Title 44, U.S. Code, for the purpose of facilitating compliance by small businesses with certain federal paperwork requirements, and establish a task force to examine information collection and dissemination. Introduced by Burton, R-Ind., on Jan. 31, 2001. House passed, amended, March 15. Senate Governmental Affairs discharged. Senate passed, with amendments, May 22, 2002. House agreed to Senate amendments June 18. President signed June 28, 2002.

PL 107-199 (S 2578) Amend Title 31 of the U.S. Code to increase the public debt limit. Introduced by Daschle, D-S.D., on June 4, 2002. Senate passed June 11. House passed June 27. President signed June 28, 2002.

PL 107-200 (H J Res 87) Approve the site at Yucca Mountain, Nev., for the development of a repository for the disposal of high-level radioactive waste and spent nuclear fuel, pursuant to the Nuclear Waste Policy Act of 1982. Introduced by Barton, R-Texas, on April 11, 2002. House Energy and Commerce reported May 1 (H Rept 107-425). House passed May 8. Senate passed July 9. President signed July 23, 2002.

PL 107-201 (S 2594) Authorize the secretary of the Treasury to purchase silver on the open market to mint coins when the silver stockpile is depleted. Introduced by Reid, D-Nev., on June 6, 2002. Senate Banking, Housing and Urban Affairs discharged June 21. Senate passed June 21. House Financial Services discharged June 28. House passed June 28. President signed July 23, 2002.

PL 107-202 (HR 2362) Establish the Benjamin Franklin Tercentenary Commission. Introduced by Borski, D-Pa., on June 28, 2001. House passed, amended, under suspension of the rules, Oct. 30. Senate passed July 9, 2002. President signed July 24, 2002.

PL 107-203 (HR 3971) Provide for an independent investigation of Forest Service firefighter deaths caused by wildfire entrapment or burnover. Introduced by Hastings, R-Wash., on March 14, 2002. House passed, under suspension of the rules, June 24. Senate passed July 10. President signed July 24, 2002.

PL 107-204 (HR 3763) Protect investors by improving the accuracy and reliability of corporate disclosures made pursuant to the securities laws. Introduced by Oxley, R-Ohio, on Feb. 14, 2002. House Financial Services reported, amended, April 22 (H Rept 107-414). House passed, amended, April 24. Senate Banking, Housing and Urban Affairs discharged July 15. Senate passed, with amendment, July 15. Conference report filed in the House on July 24 (H Rept 107-610). House agreed to conference report July 25. Senate agreed to conference report July 25. President signed July 30, 2002.

PL 107-205 (HR 3487) Amend the Public Health Service Act with respect to health professions programs in the field of nursing. Introduced by Bilirakis, R-Fla., on Dec. 13, 2001. House passed, under suspension of the rules, Dec. 20. Senate passed, with amendment, July 22, 2002. House agreed to Senate amendment, under suspension of the rules, July 22. President signed Aug. 1, 2002.

PL 107-206 (HR 4775) Make supplemental appropriations for the fiscal year ending Sept. 30, 2002. Introduced by Young, R-Fla., on May 20, 2002. House Appropriations reported May 20 (H Rept 107-480). House passed, amended, May 24. Senate passed, with amendment, June 7. Conference report filed in the House on July 19 (H Rept 107-593). House agreed to conference report July 23. Senate agreed to conference report July 24. President signed Aug. 2, 2002.

PL 107-207 (HR 2175) Protect infants who are born alive. Introduced by Chabot, R-Ohio, on June 14, 2001. House Judiciary reported Aug. 2 (H Rept 107-186). House passed, under suspension of the rules, March 12, 2002. Senate passed July 18. President signed Aug. 5, 2002.

PL 107-208 (HR 1209) Amend the Immigration and Nationality Act to determine whether an alien is a child, for purposes of classification as an immediate relative, based on the age of the alien on the date the classification petition with respect to the alien is filed. Introduced by Gekas, R-Pa., on March 26, 2001. House Judiciary reported April 20 (H Rept 107-45). House passed, amended, under suspension of the rules, June 6. Senate Judiciary reported, with amendment, May

16, 2002 (no written report). Senate passed, with amendment, June 13. House agreed to Senate amendment, under suspension of the rules, July 22. President signed Aug. 6, 2002.

PL 107-209 (S J Res 13) Confer honorary U.S. citizenship on Paul Yves Roch Gilbert du Motier, also known as the Marquis de Lafayette. Introduced by Warner, R-Va., on April 24, 2001. Senate Judiciary reported Dec. 13 (no written report). Senate passed Dec. 18. House Judiciary reported, with amendments, July 19, 2002 (H Rept 107-595). House passed, with amendments, under suspension of the rules, July 22. Senate agreed to House amendments July 24. President signed Aug. 6, 2002.

PL 107-210 (HR 3009) Extend the Andean Trade Preference Act, grant the president trade promotion authority and expand the Trade Adjustment Assistance program. Introduced by Crane, R-Ill., on Oct. 3, 2001. House Ways and Means reported, amended, Nov. 14 (H Rept 107-290). House passed, amended, Nov. 16. Senate Finance reported, with amendment, Dec. 14 (S Rept 107-126). Senate passed, with amendment, May 23, 2002. House agreed to Senate amendment with amendment pursuant to H Res 450 on June 26. Conference report filed in the House on July 26 (H Rept 107-624). House agreed to conference report July 27. Senate agreed to conference report Aug. 1. President signed Aug. 6, 2002.

PL 107-211 (HR 223) Amend the Clear Creek County, Colo., Public Lands Transfer Act of 1993 to provide additional time for Clear Creek County to dispose of certain lands transferred to the county under the act. Introduced by Udall, D-Colo., on Jan. 3, 2001. House passed, under suspension of the rules, March 13. Senate Energy and Natural Resources reported June 28, 2002 (S Rept 107-198). Senate passed Aug. 1. President signed Aug. 21, 2002.

PL 107-212 (HR 309) Allow Guam to tax earnings of foreign investors at the same rates as those applied by the 50 states under U.S. tax treaties with foreign nations. Introduced by Underwood, D-Guam, on Jan. 30, 2001. House Resources reported April 24 (H Rept 107-48). House passed, under suspension of the rules, May 1. Senate Energy and Natural Resources reported June 24, 2002 (S Rept 107-173). Senate passed Aug. 1. President signed Aug. 21, 2002.

PL 107-213 (HR 601) To redesignate certain lands within the Craters of the Moon National Monument in Idaho pursuant to Presidential Proclamation 7373 of Nov. 9, 2000. Introduced by Simpson, R-Idaho, on Feb. 13, 2001. House Resources reported, amended, April 3 (H Rept 107-34). House passed, amended, under suspension of the rules, May 1. Senate Energy and Natural Resources reported June 26, 2002 (S Rept 107-181). Senate passed Aug. 1. President signed Aug. 21, 2002.

PL 107-214 (HR 1384) Designate the route in Arizona and New Mexico on which the Navajo and Mescalero Indian tribes were forced to walk in 1863 and 1864 for possible inclusion in the national trail system. Introduced by Udall, D- N.M., on April 3, 2001. House Resources reported, amended, Sept. 28 (H Rept 107-222). House passed, amended, under suspension of the rules, Oct. 2. Senate Energy and Natural Resources reported June 27, 2002 (S Rept 107-184). Senate passed Aug. 1. President signed Aug. 21, 2002.

PL 107-215 (HR 1456) Expand the boundary of the Booker T. Washington National Monument. Introduced by Goode, R-Va., on April 4, 2001. House Resources reported Sept. 28 (H Rept 107-223). House passed, under suspension of the rules, Oct. 2. Senate Energy and Natural Resources reported June 28, 2002 (S Rept 107-199). Senate passed Aug. 1. President signed Aug. 21, 2002.

PL 107-216 (HR 1576) Designate certain lands in the Arapaho and Roosevelt National Forests in Colorado as the James Peak Wilderness and Protection Area. Introduced by Udall, D-Colo., on April 24, 2001. House Resources reported, amended, Dec. 5 (H Rept 107-316). House passed, amended, under suspension of the rules, Dec. 11. Senate Energy and Resources reported June 28, 2002 (S Rept 107-200). Senate passed Aug. 1. President signed Aug. 21, 2002.

PL 107-217 (HR 2068) Revise, codify and enact without substantive change certain general and permanent laws related to public buildings, property and works, as Title 40, U.S. Code, "Public Buildings, Property, and Works." Introduced by Sensenbrenner, R-Wis., on June 6, 2001. House Judiciary reported, amended, May 20, 2002 (H Rept 107-479). House passed, under suspension of the rules, June 11. Senate Judiciary reported June 21 (no written report). Senate passed Aug. 1. President signed Aug. 21, 2002.

PL 107-218 (HR 2234) Revise the boundary of the Tumacacori National Historical Park in Arizona. Introduced by Pastor, D-Ariz., on June 19, 2001. House Resources reported, amended, Dec. 6 (H Rept 107-327). House passed, under suspension of the rules, Jan. 23, 2002. Senate Energy and Natural Resources reported June 27 (S Rept 107-185). Senate passed Aug. 1. President signed Aug. 21, 2002.

PL 107-219 (HR 2440) Rename Wolf Trap Farm Park as "Wolf Trap National Park for the Performing Arts." Introduced by Davis, R-Va., on July 10, 2001. House Resources reported, amended, Dec. 11 (H Rept 107-330). House passed, under suspension of the rules, Dec. 11. Senate Energy and Natural Resources reported June 26, 2002 (S Rept 107-182). Senate passed Aug. 1. President signed Aug. 21, 2002.

PL 107-220 (HR 2441) Amend the Public Health Service Act to redesignate a facility as the National Hansen's Disease Programs Center. Introduced by Baker, R-La., on July 10, 2001. House Energy and Commerce reported July 30 (H Rept 107-174). House passed, under suspension of the rules, Dec. 4. Senate Health, Education, Labor and Pensions discharged Aug. 1, 2002. Senate passed Aug. 1. President signed Aug. 21, 2002.

PL 107-221 (HR 2643) Authorize the acquisition of additional lands for inclusion in the Fort Clatsop National Memorial in Oregon. Introduced by Wu, D-Ore., on July 25, 2001. House Resources reported, amended, May 14, 2002 (H Rept 107-456). House passed, under suspension of the rules, July 8. Senate passed Aug. 1. President signed Aug. 21, 2002.

PL 107-222 (HR 3343) Amend Title X of the Energy Policy Act of 1992. Introduced by Shimkus, R-Ill., on Nov. 19, 2001. House Energy and Commerce reported, amended, Dec. 18 (H Rept 107-341). House passed, amended, under suspension of the rules, Dec. 18. Senate passed Aug. 1, 2002. President signed Aug. 21, 2002.

PL 107-223 (HR 3380) Authorize the secretary of the Interior to issue right-of-way permits for natural gas pipelines within the boundary of Great Smoky Mountains National Park. Introduced by Jenkins, R-Tenn., on Nov. 29, 2001. House Resources reported June 5, 2002 (H Rept 107-491). House passed, under suspension of the rules, July 8. Senate passed Aug. 1. President signed Aug. 21, 2002.

PL 107-224 (HR 5012) Amend the John F. Kennedy Center Act to authorize the secretary of Transportation to carry out a project for construction of a plaza adjacent to the John F. Kennedy Center for the Performing Arts. Introduced by Young, R-Alaska, on June 25, 2002. House Transportation and Infrastructure reported July 26 (H Rept 107-622). House passed, under suspension of the rules, Sept. 4. Senate passed Sept. 5. President signed Sept. 18, 2002.

PL 107-225 (HR 3287) Redesignate the facility of the U.S. Postal Service located at 900 Brentwood Road, N.E., in Washington, D.C., as the "Joseph Curseen, Jr. and Thomas Morris, Jr. Processing and Distribution Center." Introduced by Wynn, D-Md., on Nov. 13, 2001. House passed, under suspension of the rules, Sept. 4, 2002. Senate passed Sept. 5. President signed Sept. 24, 2002.

PL 107-226 (HR 3917) Authorize a national memorial to commemorate the passengers and crew of Flight 93 who gave their lives Sept. 11, 2001, thereby thwarting a planned attack on the nation's capital. Introduced by Murtha, D-Pa., on March 7, 2002. House Resources reported, amended, July 22 (H Rept 107-597). House passed, amended, under suspension of the rules, July 22. Senate Energy and Natural Resources discharged Sept. 10. Senate passed Sept. 10. President signed Sept. 24, 2002.

PL 107-227 (HR 5207) Designate the facility of the U.S. Postal Service located at 6101 West Old Shakopee Road in Bloomington, Minn., as the "Thomas E. Burnett, Jr. Post Office Building." Introduced by Ramstad, R-Minn., on July 24, 2002. House passed, under suspension of the rules, Sept. 4. Senate passed Sept. 5. President signed Sept. 24, 2002.

PL 107-228 (HR 1646) Authorize appropriations for the Department of State for fiscal years 2002 and 2003. Introduced by Hyde, R-Ill., on April 27, 2001. House International Relations reported amended May 4 (H Rept 107-57). House passed, amended, May 16. Senate Foreign Relations discharged May 1, 2002. Senate passed, with amendment, May 1. Conference report filed in the House on Sept. 23 (H Rept 107-671). House agreed to conference report Sept. 25. Senate agreed to conference report Sept. 26. President signed Sept. 30, 2002.

PL 107-229 (H J Res 111) Make continuing appropriations for fiscal 2003. Introduced by Young, R-Fla., on Sept. 25, 2002. House passed Sept. 26. Senate passed Sept. 26. President signed Sept. 30, 2002.

PL 107-230 (HR 3880) Provide a temporary waiver from certain transportation conformity requirements and metropolitan transportation planning requirements under the Clean Air Act and other laws for certain areas in New York where the planning offices and resources have been destroyed by acts of terrorism. Introduced by Fossella, R-N.Y., on March 6, 2002. House Energy and Commerce reported, amended, Sept. 9 (H Rept 107-649, Pt. 1). House Transportation and Infrastructure discharged Sept. 9. House passed, amended, under suspension of the rules, Sept. 10. Senate passed Sept. 12. President signed Oct. 1, 2002.

PL 107-231 (HR 4687) Provide for the establishment of investigative teams to assess building performance and emergency response and evacuation procedures in the wake of any building failure that has resulted in substantial loss of life or that posed significant potential of substantial loss of life. Introduced by Boehlert, R-N.Y., on May 9, 2002. House Science reported, amended, June 25 (H Rept 107-530). House passed, amended, July 12. Senate passed, with amendment, Sept. 9. House agreed to Senate amendment, under suspension of the rules, Sept. 17. President signed Oct. 1, 2002.

PL 107-232 (HR 5157) Amend Section 5307 of Title 49, U.S. Code, to allow transit systems in urbanized areas that exceeded 200,000 in population for the first time in the 2000 census to retain flexibility in using federal transit formula grants in fiscal 2003. Introduced by Young, R-Alaska, on July 18, 2002. House Transportation and Infrastructure reported Sept. 5 (H Rept 107-644). House passed, under suspension of the rules, Sept. 9. Senate passed Sept. 13. President signed Oct. 1, 2002.

PL 107-233 (S 2810) Amend the Communications Satellite Act of 1962 to extend the deadline for the INTELSAT initial public offering. Introduced by Hollings, D-S.C., on July 26, 2002. Senate passed July 26. House passed, under suspension of the rules, Sept. 10. President signed Oct. 1, 2002.

PL 107-234 (HR 4558) Extend the Irish Peace Process Cultural and Training Program. Introduced by Walsh, R-N.Y., on April 23, 2002. House Judiciary reported July 22 (H Rept 107-596, Pt. 1). House International Relations discharged July 22. House passed, under suspension of the rules, July 22. Senate Foreign Relations reported Aug. 1 (no written report). Senate passed Sept. 18. President signed Oct. 4, 2002.

PL 107-235 (H J Res 112) Make further continuing appropriations for fiscal 2003. Introduced by Young, R-Fla., on Oct. 1, 2002. House passed Oct. 3. Senate passed Oct. 3. President signed Oct. 4, 2002.

PL 107-236 (HR 640) Adjust the boundaries of Santa Monica Mountains National Recreation Area. Introduced by Gallegly, R-Calif., on Feb. 14, 2001. House Resources reported, amended, June 6 (H Rept 107-90). House passed, amended, under suspension of the rules, June 6. Senate Energy and Natural Resources reported, with amendment, July 3, 2002 (S Rept 107-204). Senate passed, with amendment, Aug. 1. House agreed to Senate amendment, under suspension of the rules Sept. 24. President signed Oct. 9, 2002.

PL 107-237 (S 238) Authorize the secretary of the Interior to conduct feasibility studies on water optimization in the Burnt River basin, Malheur River basin, Owyhee River basin and Powder River basin in Oregon. Introduced by Wyden, D-Ore., on Feb. 1, 2001. Senate Energy and Natural Resources reported June 5 (S Rept 107-22). Senate passed Aug. 3. House Resources reported Sept. 4, 2002 (H Rept 107-638). House passed, under suspension of the rules, Sept. 24. President signed Oct. 11, 2002.

PL 107-238 (S 1175) Modify the boundary of Vicksburg National Military Park to include the property known as Pemberton's Headquarters. Introduced by Lott, R-Miss., on July 12, 2001. Senate Energy and Natural Resources reported, amended, June 27, 2002 (S Rept 107-183). Senate passed, with amendment, July 24. House passed, under suspension of the rules, Sept. 24. President signed Oct. 11, 2002.

PL 107-239 (S 1325) Ratify an agreement between the Aleut Corporation and the United States to exchange land rights received under the Alaska Native Claims Settlement Act for certain land interests on Adak Island. Introduced by Murkowski, R-Alaska, on Aug. 2, 2001. Senate Energy and Natural Resources reported, amended, June 26, 2002 (S Rept 107-180). Senate passed, with amendment, Aug. 1. House passed, under suspension of the rules, Sept. 24. President signed Oct. 11, 2002.

PL 107-240 (H J Res 122) Make further continuing appropriations for fiscal 2003. Introduced by Young, R-Fla., on Oct. 10, 2002. House passed Oct. 10. Senate passed Oct. 11. President signed Oct. 11, 2002.

PL 107-241 (HR 3214) Amend the charter of the AMVETS organization. Introduced by Bilirakis, R-Fla., on Nov. 1, 2001. House Judiciary reported July 12, 2002 (H Rept 107-569). House passed, under suspension of the rules, July 15. Senate Judiciary reported Sept. 5 (no written report). Senate passed Oct. 2. President signed Oct. 16, 2002.

PL 107-242 (HR 3838) Amend the charter of the Veterans of Foreign Wars of the United States organization to make members of the armed forces who receive special pay for duty subject to hostile fire or imminent danger eligible for membership. Introduced by Smith, R-N.J., on March 4, 2002. House Judiciary reported July 12 (H Rept 107-570). House passed, under suspension of the rules, July 15. Senate Judiciary reported Sept. 5 (no written report). Senate passed Oct. 2. President signed Oct. 16, 2002.

PL 107-243 (H J Res 114) Authorize the use of U.S. Armed Forces against Iraq. Introduced by Hastert, R-Ill., on Oct. 2, 2002. House International Relations reported amended Oct. 7 (H Rept 107-721). House passed, with amendment, Oct. 10. Senate passed Oct. 11. President signed Oct. 16, 2002.

PL 107-244 (H J Res 123) Make further continuing appropriations for fiscal 2003. Introduced by Young, R-Fla., on Oct. 15, 2002. House passed Oct. 16. Senate passed Oct. 16. President signed Oct. 18, 2002.

PL 107-245 (HR 5531) Facilitate famine relief efforts and a comprehensive solution to the war in Sudan. Introduced by Tancredo, R-Colo., on Oct. 2, 2002. House passed, amended, under suspension of the rules, Oct. 7. Senate passed Oct. 9, 2002. President signed Oct. 21, 2002.

PL 107-246 (HR 2121) Make available funds under the Foreign Assistance Act of 1961 to expand democracy, good governance and anti-corruption programs in the Russian Federation. Introduced by Lantos, D-Calif., on June 12, 2001. House passed, amended, under suspension of the rules, Dec. 11. Senate Foreign Relations reported, with amendment, Aug. 1, 2002 (no written report). Senate passed, with amendments, Sept. 20. House agreed to Senate amendments, under suspension of the rules, Oct. 7. President signed Oct. 23, 2002.

PL 107-247 (HR 4085) Increase, effective Dec. 1, 2002, rates of compensation for veterans with service-connected disabilities and rates of dependency and indemnity compensation for survivors of certain service-connected disabled veterans. Introduced by Smith, R-N.J. on April 9, 2002. House Veterans' Affairs reported, amended, May 16 (H Rept 107-472). House passed, amended, under suspension of the rules, May 21. Senate Veterans' Affairs discharged Sept. 26. Senate passed, with amendments, Sept. 26. House agreed to Senate amendments, under suspension of the rules, Oct. 7, 2002. President signed Oct. 23, 2002.

PL 107-248 (HR 5010) Make appropriations for the Department of Defense for the fiscal year ending Sept. 30, 2003. Introduced by Lewis, R-Calif., on June 25, 2002. House Appropriations reported June 25 (H Rept 107-532). House passed, amended, June 27. Senate Appropriations reported, with amendment, July 18 (S Rept 107-213). Senate passed, with amendment, Aug. 1. Conference report filed in the House Oct. 9 (H Rept 107-732). House agreed to conference report Oct. 10. Senate agreed to conference report Oct. 16. President signed Oct. 23, 2002.

PL 107-249 (HR 5011) Make appropriations for military construction, family housing and base realignment and closure for the Department of Defense for the fiscal year ending Sept. 30, 2003. Introduced by Hobson, R-Ohio, on June 25, 2002. House Appropriations reported June 25 (H Rept 107-533). House passed, amended, June 27. Senate passed, with amendment, July 18. Conference report filed in the House Oct. 9 (H Rept 107-731). House agreed to conference report Oct. 10. Senate agreed to conference report Oct. 11. President signed Oct. 23, 2002.

PL 107-250 (HR 5651) Amend the Federal Food, Drug and Cosmetic Act to make improvements in the regulation of medical devices. Introduced by Greenwood, R-Pa., on Oct. 16, 2002. House Energy and Commerce discharged. House passed Oct. 16. Senate passed Oct. 17. President signed Oct. 26, 2002.

PL 107-251 (S 1533) Amend the Public Health Service Act to reauthorize and strengthen the health centers program and the National Health Service Corps, and to establish the Healthy Communities Access Program to help coordinate services for the uninsured and underinsured. Introduced by Kennedy, D-Mass., on Oct. 11, 2001. Senate Health, Education, Labor and Pensions reported Oct. 11 (H Rept 107-83). Senate passed, amended, April 16, 2002. House passed with amendment, under suspension of the rules, Oct. 16. Senate agreed to House amendment Oct. 17. President signed Oct. 26, 2002.

PL 107-252 (HR 3295) Require states and localities to meet uniform and nondiscriminatory requirements for federal elections; establish grant programs to assist states and localities in meeting those requirements; improve election technology and the administration of federal elections, and establish the Election Administration Commission. Introduced by Ney, R-Ohio, on Nov. 14, 2001. House Administration reported, amended, Dec. 10 (H Rept 107-329, Pt. 1). House Judiciary, Science, Government Reform and Armed Services discharged. House passed, amended, Dec. 12. Senate Rules and Administration discharged. Senate passed, with amendments, April 11, 2002. Conference report filed in the House Oct. 8 (H Rept 107-730). House agreed to conference report Oct. 10. Senate agreed to conference report Oct. 16. President signed Oct. 29, 2002.

PL 107-253 (HR 2486) Authorize the National Oceanic and Atmospheric Administration, through the U.S. Weather Service, to conduct research and development, training and outreach activities to improve tropical cyclone inland forecasting. Introduced by Etheridge, D-N.C., on July 12, 2001. House Science reported, amended, June 5, 2002 (H Rept 107-495). House passed, amended, July 11. Senate Commerce, Science and Transportation reported Oct. 10 (S Rept 107-310). Senate passed Oct. 16. President signed Oct. 29, 2002.

PL 107-254 (HR 5647) Authorize the duration of the base Navy-Marine Corps Intranet contract to be more than five years but not more than seven years. Introduced by Davis, R-Va., on Oct. 16, 2002. House Armed Services discharged. House passed Oct. 16. Senate passed Oct. 17. President signed Oct. 29, 2002.

PL 107-255 (H J Res 113) Recognize the contributions of Patsy T. Mink. Introduced by Miller, D-Calif., on Oct. 2, 2002. House passed, amended, under suspension of the rules, Oct. 9. Senate passed Oct. 11. President signed Oct. 29, 2002.

PL 107-256 (S 1227) Authorize the secretary of the Interior to conduct a study of the suitability and feasibility of establishing the Niagara Falls National Heritage Area in the state of New York. Introduced by Schumer, D-N.Y., on July 24, 2001. Senate Energy and Natural Resources reported, amended, June 26, 2002 (S Rept 107-179). Senate passed, amended, Aug. 1. House Resources reported Sept. 23 (H Rept 107-668). House passed Oct. 16. President signed Oct. 29, 2002.

PL 107-257 (S 1270) Designate the U.S. courthouse to be constructed at 8th Ave. and Mill St. in Eugene, Ore., as the "Wayne Lyman Morse United States Courthouse." Introduced by Wyden, D-Ore., on July 30, 2001. Senate Environment and Public Works reported Sept. 25 (no written report). Senate passed Nov. 15. House Transportation and Infrastructure discharged. House passed Oct. 16, 2002. President signed Oct. 29, 2002.

PL 107-258 (S 1339) Amend the Bring Them Home Alive Act of 2000 to provide an asylum program with regard to American Persian Gulf War POW/MIAs. Introduced by Campbell, R-Colo., on Aug. 2, 2001. Senate Judiciary reported, amended, June 27, 2002 (no written report). Senate passed, amended, July 29. House Judiciary reported Oct. 15 (H Rept 107-749, Pt. 1). House passed, under suspension of the rules, Oct. 15. President signed Oct. 29, 2002.

PL 107-259 (S 1646) Identify certain routes in the states of Texas, Oklahoma, Colorado, and New Mexico as part of the Ports-to-Plains Corridor, a high-priority corridor on the National Highway System. Introduced by Bingaman, D-N.M., on Nov. 7, 2001. Senate Environment and Public Works reported June 19, 2002 (S Rept 107-165). Senate passed June 26. House Transportation and Infrastructure discharged. House passed Oct. 16. President signed Oct. 29, 2002.

PL 107-260 (S 2558) Amend the Public Health Service Act to provide for the collection of data on benign brain-related tumors through the national program of cancer registries. Introduced by Reed, D-R.I., on May 23, 2002. Senate Health, Education, Labor and Pensions discharged. Senate passed Aug. 1. House Energy and Commerce discharged. House passed Oct. 10. President signed Oct. 29, 2002.

PL 107-261 (HR 669) Designate the facility of the U.S. Postal Service located at 127 Social St. in Woonsocket, R.I., as the "Alphonse F. Auclair Post Office Building." Introduced by Kennedy, D-R.I., on Feb. 14, 2001. House Government Reform discharged. House passed Oct. 10, 2002. Senate passed Oct. 17. President signed Oct. 30, 2002.

PL 107-262 (HR 670) Designate the facility of the U.S. Postal Service located at 7 Commercial St. in Newport, R.I., as the "Bruce F. Cotta Post Office Building." Introduced by Kennedy, D-R.I., on Feb. 14, 2001. House Government Reform discharged. House passed Oct. 10, 2002. Senate passed Oct. 17. President signed Oct. 30, 2002.

PL 107-263 (HR 3034) Redesignate the facility of the U.S. Postal Service located at 89 River St. in Hoboken, N.J., as the "Frank Sinatra Post Office Building." Introduced by Menendez, D-N.J., on Oct. 4, 2001. House passed, under suspension of the rules, June 27, 2002. Senate Governmental Affairs reported Oct. 15 (no written report). Senate passed Oct. 17. President signed Oct. 30, 2002.

PL 107-264 (HR 3738) Designate the facility of the U.S. Postal Service located at 1299 North 7th St. in Philadelphia as the "Herbert Arlene Post Office Building." Introduced by Brady, D-Pa., on Feb. 13, 2002. House passed, under suspension of the rules, June 11. Senate Governmental Affairs reported Oct. 15 (no written report). Senate passed Oct. 17. President signed Oct. 30, 2002.

PL 107-265 (HR 3739) Designate the facility of the U.S. Postal Service located at 6150 North Broad St. in Philadelphia as the "Rev. Leon Sullivan Post Office Building." Introduced by Brady, D-Pa., on Feb. 13, 2002. House passed, under suspension of the rules, June 11.

Senate Governmental Affairs reported Oct. 15 (no written report). Senate passed Oct. 17. President signed Oct. 30, 2002.

PL 107-266 (HR 3740) Designate the facility of the U.S. Postal Service located at 925 Dickinson St. in Philadelphia as the "William V. Cibotti Post Office Building." Introduced by Brady, D-Pa., on Feb. 13, 2002. House passed, amended, under suspension of the rules, June 11. Senate Governmental Affairs reported Oct. 15 (no written report). Senate passed Oct. 17. President signed Oct. 30, 2002.

PL 107-267 (HR 4102) Designate the facility of the U.S. Postal Service located at 120 North Maine St. in Fallon, Nev., as the "Rollan D. Melton Post Office Building." Introduced by Gibbons, R-Nev., on April 9, 2002. House passed, under suspension of the rules, Sept. 17. Senate Governmental Affairs reported Oct. 15 (no written report). Senate passed Oct. 17. President signed Oct. 30, 2002.

PL 107-268 (HR 4717) Designate the facility of the U.S. Postal Service located at 1199 Pasadena Boulevard in Pasadena, Texas, as the "Jim Fonteno Post Office Building." Introduced by Bentsen, D-Texas, on May 14, 2002. House passed, under suspension of the rules, June 18. Senate Governmental Affairs reported Oct. 15 (no written report). Senate passed Oct. 17. President signed Oct. 30, 2002.

PL 107-269 (HR 4755) Designate the facility of the U.S. Postal Service located at 204 South Broad St. in Lancaster, Ohio, as the "Clarence Miller Post Office Building." Introduced by Hobson, R-Ohio, on May 16, 2002. House passed, under suspension of the rules, July 15. Senate Governmental Affairs reported Oct. 15 (no written report). Senate passed Oct. 17. President signed Oct. 30, 2002.

PL 107-270 (HR 4794) Designate the facility of the U.S. Postal Service located at 1895 Avenida Del Oro in Oceanside, Calif., as the "Ronald C. Packard Post Office Building." Introduced by Issa, R-Calif., on May 22, 2002. House passed, under suspension of the rules, June 18. Senate Governmental Affairs reported Oct. 15 (no written report). Senate passed Oct. 17. President signed Oct. 30, 2002.

PL 107-271 (HR 4797) Redesignate the facility of the U.S. Postal Service located at 265 South Western Ave., Los Angeles, as the "Nat King Cole Post Office." Introduced by Becerra, D-Calif., on May 22, 2002. House passed, under suspension of the rules, Sept. 9, 2002. Senate Governmental Affairs reported Oct. 15 (no written report). Senate passed Oct. 17. President signed Oct. 30, 2002.

PL 107-272 (HR 4851) Redesignate the facility of the U.S. Postal Service located at 6910 South Yorktown Ave. in Tulsa, Okla., as the "Robert Wayne Jenkins Station." Introduced by Sullivan, R-Okla., on May 23, 2002. House passed, under suspension of the rules, Oct. 1. Senate passed Oct. 17. President signed Oct. 30, 2002.

PL 107-273 (HR 2215) Authorize appropriations for the Department of Justice for fiscal 2002-2003. Introduced by Sensenbrenner, R-Wis., on June 19, 2001. House Judiciary reported, amended, July 10 (H Rept 107-125). House passed, amended, under suspension of the rules, July 23. Senate Judiciary reported, with amendment, Oct. 30 (no written report). Senate passed, with amendment, Dec. 20. Conference report filed in the House Sept. 25, 2002 (H Rept 107-685). House agreed to conference report Sept. 26. Senate agreed to conference report Oct. 3. President signed Nov. 2, 2002.

PL 107-274 (HR 4967) Establish new nonimmigrant classes for border commuter students. Introduced by Kolbe, R-Ariz., on June 19, 2002. House Judiciary reported Oct. 15 (H Rept 107-753). House passed, under suspension of the rules, Oct. 15. Senate passed Oct. 16. President signed Nov. 2, 2002.

PL 107-275 (HR 5542) Consolidate all black lung benefit responsibility under a single official. Introduced by Hart, R-Pa., on Oct. 3, 2002. House passed, amended, under suspension of the rules, Oct. 9. Senate passed Oct. 16. President signed Nov. 2, 2002.

PL 107-276 (HR 5596) Amend Section 527 of the Internal Revenue Code of 1986 to eliminate notification and return requirements for state and local party committees and candidate committees, and avoid duplicate reporting by certain state and local political committees of information required to be reported and made publicly available under state law. Introduced by Brady, R-Texas, on Oct. 10, 2002. House Ways and Means discharged. House passed Oct. 16. Senate passed Oct. 17. President signed Nov. 2, 2002.

PL 107-277 (HR 2733) Authorize the National Institute of Standards and Technology to work with major manufacturing industries on an initiative to develop and implement standards for electronic enterprise integration. Introduced by Barcia, D-Mich., on Aug. 2, 2001. House Science reported, amended, June 20, 2002 (H Rept 107-520). House passed, amended, July 11. Senate Commerce, Science and Transportation reported Oct. 16 (S Rept 107-319). Senate passed Oct. 17. President signed Nov. 5, 2002.

PL 107-278 (HR 3656) Amend the International Organizations Immunities Act to make it applicable to the European Central Bank. Introduced by Leach, R-Iowa, on Jan. 29, 2002. House passed, under suspension of the rules, Sept. 24. Senate Foreign Relations reported Oct. 8 (no written report). Senate passed Oct. 17. President signed Nov. 5, 2002.

PL 107-279 (HR 3801) Provide for improvement of federal education research, statistics, evaluation, information and dissemination. Introduced by Castle, R-Del., on Feb. 27, 2002. House Education and the Workforce reported, amended, April 11 (H Rept 107-404). House passed, amended, under suspension of the rules, April 30. Senate Health, Education, Labor and Pensions discharged. Senate passed, with amendment, Oct. 15. House agreed to Senate amendment Oct. 16. President signed Nov. 5, 2002.

PL 107-280 (HR 4013) Amend the Public Health Service Act to establish an Office of Rare Diseases at the National Institutes of Health. Introduced by Shimkus, R-Ill., on March 20, 2002. House Energy and Commerce reported June 26 (H Rept 107-543). House passed, under suspension of the rules, Oct. 1. Senate passed Oct. 17. President signed Nov. 6, 2002.

PL 107-281 (HR 4014) Amend the Federal Food, Drug, and Cosmetic Act to authorize appropriations for fiscal 2002 through 2006 for grants and contracts for the development of drugs for rare diseases and conditions. Introduced by Foley, R-Fla., on March 20, 2002. House Energy and Commerce reported Oct. 1 (H Rept 107-702). House passed, under suspension of the rules, Oct. 1. Senate passed Oct. 17. President signed Nov. 6, 2002.

PL 107-282 (HR 5200) Establish wilderness areas, promote conservation, improve public land and provide for high quality development in Clark County, Nev. Introduced by Gibbons, R-Nev., on July 24, 2002. House Resources reported, amended, Oct. 15 (H Rept 107-750). House passed, amended, Oct. 16. Senate passed Oct. 17. President signed Nov. 6, 2002.

PL 107-283 (HR 5308) Designate the facility of the U.S. Postal Service located at 301 South Howes St. in Fort Collins, Colo., as the "Barney Apodaca Post Office." Introduced by Schaffer, R-Colo., on July 26, 2002. House passed, under suspension of the rules, Sept. 4. Senate Governmental Affairs reported Oct. 15 (no written report). Senate passed Oct. 17. President signed Nov. 6, 2002.

PL 107-284 (HR 5333) Designate the facility of the U.S. Postal Service located at 4 East Central St. in Worcester, Mass., as the "Joseph D. Early Post Office Building." Introduced by McGovern, D-Mass., on Sept. 4, 2002. House passed, under suspension of the rules, Sept. 17. Senate Governmental Affairs reported Oct. 15 (no written report). Senate passed Oct. 17. President signed Nov. 6, 2002.

PL 107-285 (HR 5336) Designate the facility of the U.S. Postal Service located at 380 Main St. in Farmingdale, N.Y., as the "Peter J. Ganci Jr. Post Office Building." Introduced by King, R-N.Y., on Sept. 5, 2002. House passed, under suspension of the rules, Sept. 9. Senate Governmental Affairs reported Oct. 15 (no written report). Senate passed Oct. 17. President signed Nov. 6, 2002.

PL 107-286 (HR 5340) Designate the facility of the U.S. Postal Service located at 5805 White Oak Ave. in Encino, Calif., as the "Francis Dayle 'Chick' Hearn Post Office." Introduced by Sherman, D-Calif., on Sept. 5, 2002. House passed, under suspension of the rules, Oct. 7. Senate passed Oct. 17. President signed Nov. 6, 2002.

PL 107-287 (HR 3253) Amend Title 38, U.S. Code, to provide for the establishment of emergency medical preparedness centers in the Department of Veterans Affairs. Introduced by Smith, R-N.J., on Nov. 8, 2001. House Veterans' Affairs reported, amended, May 16, 2002 (H Rept 107-471). House passed, amended, under suspension of the rules, May 20. Senate Veterans' Affairs discharged. Senate passed, with amendments, Aug. 1. House agreed to Senate amendments with amendment, Sept. 17. Senate agreed to House amendment, with amendment, Oct. 15. House agreed to Senate amendment Oct. 16. President signed Nov. 7, 2002.

PL 107-288 (HR 4015) Amend Title 38, U.S. Code, to revise and improve employment, training and placement services furnished to veterans. Introduced by Simpson, R-Idaho, on March 20, 2002. House Veterans' Affairs reported, amended, May 20 (H Rept 107-476). House passed, amended, under suspension of the rules, May 21. Senate Veterans' Affairs discharged. Senate passed, with amendment, Oct. 15. House agreed to Senate amendment Oct. 16. President signed Nov. 7, 2002.

PL 107-289 (HR 4685) Amend Title 31, U.S. Code, to expand the types of federal agencies that are required to prepare audited financial statements. Introduced by Toomey, R-Pa., on May 8, 2002. House passed, amended, under suspension of the rules, Oct. 7. Senate passed Oct. 17. President signed Nov. 7, 2002.

PL 107-290 (HR 5205) Amend the District of Columbia Retirement Protection Act of 1997 to permit the secretary of the Treasury to use estimated amounts in determining the service longevity component of the federal benefit payment to certain retirees of the Metropolitan Police Department. Introduced by Morella, R-Md., on July 24, 2002. House Government Reform discharged. House passed Oct. 10. Senate passed Oct. 17. President signed Nov. 7, 2002.

PL 107-291 (HR 5574) Designate the facility of the U.S. Postal Service located at 206 South Main St. in Glennville, Ga., as the "Michael Lee Woodcock Post Office." Introduced by Kingston, R-Ga.,

on Oct. 8, 2002. House Government Reform discharged. House passed Oct. 10. Senate passed Oct. 17. President signed Nov. 7, 2002.

PL 107-292 (S 1210) Reauthorize the Native American Housing Assistance and Self-Determination Act of 1996. Introduced by Campbell, R-Colo., on July 20, 2001. Senate Indian Affairs reported, amended, Aug. 28, 2002 (S Rept 107-246). Senate Banking, Housing and Urban Affairs reported amended Sept. 17 (no written report). Senate passed, amended, Oct. 4. House Financial Services discharged. House passed Oct. 16. President signed Nov. 13, 2002.

PL 107-293 (S 2690) Reaffirm the reference to one nation under God in the Pledge of Allegiance. Introduced by Hutchinson, R-Ark., on June 27, 2002. Senate passed June 27. House Judiciary reported, with amendment, Sept. 17 (H Rept 107-659). House passed, with amendment, under suspension of the rules, Oct. 8. Senate agreed to House amendment Oct. 17. President signed Nov. 13, 2002.

PL 107-294 (H J Res 124) Make further continuing appropriations for fiscal 2003. Introduced by Young, R-Fla., on Nov. 12, 2002. House passed Nov. 13. Senate passed Nov. 19. President signed Nov. 23, 2002.

PL 107-295 (S 1214) Amend the Merchant Marine Act, 1936, to establish a program to ensure greater security for U.S. seaports. Introduced by Hollings, D-S.C., on July 20, 2001. Senate Commerce, Science and Transportation reported Sept. 14 (S Rept 107-64). Senate passed, amended, Dec. 20. House passed, with amendment, June 4, 2002. Conference report filed in the House on Nov. 13 (H Rept 107-777). Senate agreed to conference report Nov. 14. House agreed to conference report Nov. 14. President signed Nov. 25, 2002.

PL 107-296 (HR 5005) Establish the Department of Homeland Security. Introduced by Armey, R-Texas, on June 24, 2002. House Agriculture, Appropriations, Armed Services, Energy and Commerce, Financial Services, Government Reform, Intelligence, International Relations, Judiciary, Science, Transportation and Infrastructure, and Ways and Means discharge. House Select Homeland Security reported, amended, July 24 (H Rept 107-609, Pt. 1). House passed, amended, July 26. Senate passed, with amendment, Nov. 19. House agreed to Senate amendment Nov. 22. President signed Nov. 25, 2002.

PL 107-297 (HR 3210) Establish a federal terrorism insurance program to serve as a backstop for commercial property and casualty insurers in the event of cataclysmic terrorist acts. Introduced by Oxley, R-Ohio, on Nov. 1, 2001. House Financial Services reported, amended, Nov. 19 (H Rept 107-300, Pt. 1). House Ways and Means reported, amended, Nov. 19 (H Rept 107-300, Pt. 2). House Budget and Judiciary discharged. House passed, amended, Nov. 29. Senate passed, with amendment, July 25, 2002. Conference report filed in the House on Nov. 13 (H Rept 107-779). House agreed to conference report Nov. 14. Senate agreed to conference report Nov. 19. President signed Nov. 26, 2002.

PL 107-298 (HR 2546) Amend Title 49, U.S. Code, to prohibit states from requiring a license or fee for a motor vehicle that is providing prearranged interstate ground transportation service. Introduced by Blunt, R-Mo., on July 18, 2001. House Transportation and Infrastructure reported, amended, Nov. 13 (H Rept 107-282). House passed, amended, under suspension of the rules, Nov. 13. Senate Commerce, Science and Transportation reported, with amendments, Aug. 1, 2002 (S Rept 107-237). Senate passed, with amendments, Oct. 17. House agreed to Senate amendments, under suspension of the rules, Nov. 12. President signed Nov. 26, 2002.

PL 107-299 (HR 3389) Reauthorize the National Sea Grant College Program Act. Introduced by Gilchrest, R-Md., on Nov. 30, 2001. House Resources reported, amended, March 7, 2002 (H Rept 107-369, Pt. 1). House Science reported, amended, April 15 (H Rept 107-369, Pt. 2). House passed, amended, June 19. Senate passed, with amendment, Oct. 11. House agreed to Senate amendment, under suspension of the rules, Nov. 12. President signed Nov. 26, 2002.

PL 107-300 (HR 4878) Provide for reduction of improper payments by federal agencies. Introduced by Horn, R-Calif., on June 6, 2002. House passed, amended, under suspension of the rules, July 9. Senate Governmental Affairs reported Oct. 15 (S Rept 107-333). Senate passed, with amendment, Oct. 17. House agreed to Senate amendment, under suspension of the rules, Nov. 12. President signed Nov. 26, 2002.

PL 107-301 (HR 5349) Facilitate the use of a portion of the former O'Reilly General Hospital in Springfield, Mo., by the local Boys and Girls Club through the release of the interests retained by the United States in 1955 when the land was conveyed to the state of Missouri. Introduced by Blunt, R-Mo., on Sept. 9, 2002. House Government Reform discharged. House passed Oct. 10. Senate passed Nov. 13. President signed Nov. 26, 2002.

PL 107-302 (S 3044) Authorize the Court Services and Offender Supervision Agency of the District of Columbia to provide for the interstate supervision of offenders on parole, probation and supervised release. Introduced by Durbin, D-Ill., on Oct. 3, 2002. Senate Governmental Affairs reported Oct. 15 (S Rept 107-332). Senate passed Nov. 13. House passed Nov. 15. President signed Nov. 26, 2002.

PL 107-303 (HR 1070) Authorize the EPA to make grants for remediation of sediment contamination and authorize assistance for research and development of innovative technologies for such purposes; and modify provisions in the Federal Water Pollution Control Act and the Water Resources Development Act of 2000 relating to the Lake Champlain basin. Introduced by Ehlers, R-Mich., on March 15, 2001. House Transportation and Infrastructure reported July 18, 2002 (H Rept 107-587, Pt. 1). House Science discharged. House passed, amended, under suspension of the rules, Sept. 4. Senate Environment and Public Works reported, with amendment, Oct. 15 (S Rept 107-312). Senate passed, with amendment, Oct. 17. House agreed to Senate amendment, under suspension of the rules, Nov. 12. President signed Nov. 27, 2002.

PL 107-304 (HR 3340) Amend Title 5, U.S. Code, to allow participants age 50 and over to make certain catch-up contributions to the Thrift Savings Plan. Introduced by Morella, R-Md., on Nov. 19, 2001. House Government Reform reported Sept. 25, 2002 (H Rept 107-686). Passed House passed, amended, under suspension of the rules, Oct. 7. Senate passed Nov. 13. President signed Nov. 27, 2002.

PL 107-305 (HR 3394) Authorize funding for computer and network security research and for development and research fellowship programs. Introduced by Boehlert, R-N.Y., on Dec. 4, 2001. House Science reported Feb. 4, 2002 (H Rept 107-355, Pt. 1). House Education and the Workforce discharged. House passed Feb. 7. Senate Commerce, Science and Transportation discharged. Senate passed, with amendment, Oct. 16. House agreed to Senate amendment, under suspension of the rules, Nov. 12. President signed Nov. 27, 2002.

PL 107-306 (HR 4628) Authorize appropriations for fiscal 2003 for intelligence and intelligence-related activities of the U.S. government, the Community Management Account, and the Central Intelligence Agency Retirement and Disability System. Introduced by Goss, R-Fla., on May 1, 2002. House Intelligence reported, amended, July 18 (H Rept 107-592). House passed, amended, July 25. Senate Intelligence discharged. Senate passed, with amendment, Sept. 25. Conference report filed in the House on Nov. 14 (H Rept 107-789). House agreed to conference report Nov. 15. Senate agreed to conference report Nov. 15. President signed Nov. 27, 2002.

PL 107-307 (HR 2621) Amend Title 18, U.S. Code, to increase consumer product protection against tampering. Introduced by Hart, R-Pa., on July 25, 2001. House Judiciary reported, amended, May 23, 2002 (H Rept 107-485). House passed, amended, under suspension of the rules, June 11. Senate passed, with amendment, Oct. 16. House agreed to Senate amendment Nov. 15. President signed Dec. 2, 2002.

PL 107-308 (HR 3908) Reauthorize the North American Wetlands Conservation Act. Introduced by Hansen, R-Utah, on March 7, 2002. House Resources reported, amended, April 29 (H Rept 107-421). House passed, amended, under suspension of the rules, May 7. Senate Environment and Public Works reported, with amendments, Oct. 8 (H Rept 107-304). Senate passed, with amendments, Nov. 14. House agreed to Senate amendments Nov. 15. President signed Dec. 2, 2002.

PL 107-309 (HR 3988) Amend Title 36, U.S. Code, to clarify the requirements for eligibility in the American Legion. Introduced by Gekas, R-Pa., on March 18, 2002. House Judiciary reported July 12 (H Rept 107-571). House passed, under suspension of the rules, July 15. Senate Judiciary reported Nov. 14 (no written report). Senate passed Nov. 14. President signed Dec. 2, 2002.

PL 107-310 (HR 4727) Reauthorize the national dam safety program. Introduced by Shuster, R-Pa., on May 14, 2002. House Transportation and Infrastructure reported, amended, Sept. 4 (H Rept 107-626). House passed, amended, Sept. 5. Senate Environment and Public Works reported Sept. 26 (no written report). Senate passed Nov. 14. President signed Dec. 2, 2002.

PL 107-311 (HR 5590) Amend Title 10, U.S. Code, to provide for the enforcement and effectiveness of civilian court orders of protection on military installations. Introduced by Hayes, R-N.C., on Oct. 9, 2002. House passed, under suspension of the rules, Oct. 15. Senate passed Nov. 14. President signed Dec. 2, 2002.

PL 107-312 (HR 5708) Reduce existing PAYGO balances. Introduced by Nussle, R-Iowa, on Nov. 12, 2002. House passed Nov. 14. Senate passed Nov. 15. President signed Dec. 2, 2002.

PL 107-313 (HR 5716) Amend the Employee Retirement Income Security Act of 1974 and the Public Health Service Act to extend the mental health benefits parity provisions for an additional year. Introduced by Boehner, R-Ohio, on Nov. 13, 2002. House Energy and Commerce, and House Education and the Workforce discharged. House passed Nov. 15. Senate passed Nov. 15. President signed Dec. 2, 2002.

PL 107-314 (HR 4546) Authorize appropriations for fiscal 2003 for military activities of the Department of Defense, for military construction, for defense activities of the Department of Energy and to prescribe military personnel strengths for fiscal 2003. Introduced by Stump, R-Ariz., on April 23, 2002. House Armed Services reported, amended, May 3 (H Rept 107-436). House Armed Services filed supplemental report May 6 (H Rept 107-436, Pt. 2). House passed, amended, May 10. Senate passed, with amendment, June 27. House agreed to Senate amendment, with amendment, July 25. Conference report filed in the House on Nov. 12 (H Rept 107-772). House agreed to conference report, under suspension of the rules, Nov. 12. Senate agreed to conference report Nov. 13. President signed Dec. 2, 2002.

PL 107-315 (H J Res 117) Approve the location of the commemorative work in the District of Columbia honoring former President John Adams. Introduced by Roemer, D-Ind., on Oct. 7, 2002. House Resources discharged. House passed Nov. 15. Senate passed Nov. 20. President signed Dec. 2, 2002.

PL 107-316 (S 3156) Provide a grant for the construction of a new community center in St. Paul, Minn., in honor of the late Sen. Paul Wellstone and his wife, Sheila. Introduced by Barkley, I-Minn., on Nov. 14, 2002. Senate passed Nov. 14. House passed Nov. 15. President signed Dec. 2, 2002.

PL 107-317 (HR 3833) Facilitate the creation of a new, second-level Internet domain within the U.S. country code domain for material that promotes positive experiences for children and families using the Internet, provides a safe online environment for children and helps to prevent children from being exposed to harmful material on the Internet. Introduced by Shimkus, R-Ill., on March 4, 2002. House Energy and Commerce reported, amended, May 8 (H Rept 107-449). House passed, amended, under suspension of the rules, May 21. Senate Commerce, Science and Transportation discharged. Senate passed, with amendment, Nov. 13. House agreed to Senate amendment Nov. 15. President signed Dec. 4, 2002.

PL 107-318 (HR 5504) Provide for the improvement of the safety of child restraints in passenger motor vehicles. Introduced by Shimkus, R-Ill., on Oct. 1, 2002. House Energy and Commerce reported, amended, Oct. 7 (H Rept 107-726). House passed, amended, Nov. 15. Senate passed Nov. 18. President signed Dec. 4, 2002.

PL 107-319 (HR 727) Amend the Consumer Product Safety Act to provide that low-speed electric bicycles are consumer products subject to the act. Introduced by Stearns, R-Fla., on Feb. 27, 2001. House Energy and Commerce reported March 5 (H Rept 107-5). House passed, under suspension of the rules, March 6. Senate Commerce, Science and Transportation discharged. Senate passed Nov. 18, 2002. President signed Dec. 4, 2002.

PL 107-320 (HR 2595) Direct the secretary of the Army to convey a parcel of land to Chatham County, Ga. Introduced by Kingston, R-Ga., on July 23, 2001. House passed, amended, under suspension of the rules, Dec. 11. Senate Armed Services discharged. Senate Environment and Public Works reported Sept. 26, 2002 (no written report). Senate passed Nov. 18. President signed Dec. 4, 2002.

PL 107-321 (HR 5469) Suspend for six months the determination of the Librarian of Congress of July 8, 2002, on rates and terms for the digital performance of sound recordings and ephemeral recordings. Introduced by Sensenbrenner, R-Wis., on Sept. 26, 2002. House passed, amended, under suspension of the rules, Oct. 7. Senate passed, with amendment, Nov. 14. House agreed to Senate amendment Nov. 15. President signed Dec. 4, 2002.

PL 107-322 (S 1010) Extend the deadline for start of construction of a hydroelectric project in North Carolina. Introduced by Helms, R-N.C., on June 11, 2001. Senate Energy and Natural Resources reported, June 28, 2002 (S Rept 107-192). Senate passed Aug. 1. House Energy and Commerce discharged. House passed, Nov. 15. President signed Dec. 4, 2002.

PL 107-323 (S 1226) Require the display of the POW/MIA flag at the World War II memorial, the Korean War Veterans Memorial and the Vietnam Veterans Memorial. Introduced by Campbell, R-Colo., on July 24, 2001. Senate Judiciary discharged. Senate passed, Oct. 2, 2002. House Resources discharged. House passed Nov. 15. President signed Dec. 4, 2002.

PL 107-324 (S 1907) Direct the secretary of the Interior to convey certain land to the city of Haines, Ore. Introduced by Smith, R-Ore., on Jan. 29, 2002. Senate Energy and Natural Resources reported, amended, June 28 (S Rept 107-197). Senate passed, amended, Aug. 1. House Resources reported Sept. 24 (H Rept 107-680). House passed Nov. 15. President signed Dec. 4, 2002.

PL 107-325 (S 1946) Amend the National Trails System Act to designate the Old Spanish Trail as a national historic trail. Introduced by Campbell, R-Colo., on Feb. 14, 2002. Senate Energy and Natural Resources reported, amended, July 3 (S Rept 107-203). Senate passed, amended, Aug. 1. House Resources reported Sept. 23 (H Rept 107-670). House passed Nov. 15. President signed Dec. 4, 2002.

PL 107-326 (S 2239) Amend the National Housing Act to simplify the down payment requirements for FHA mortgage insurance for single-family home buyers. Introduced by Sarbanes, D-Md., on April 24, 2002. Senate Banking, Housing and Urban Affairs reported, amended, Oct. 15 (no written report). Senate passed, amended, Oct. 17. House Financial Services discharged. House passed Nov. 15. President signed Dec. 4, 2002.

PL 107-327 (S 2712) Authorize economic and democratic development assistance for Afghanistan, and authorize military assistance for Afghanistan and certain other foreign countries. Introduced by Hagel, R-Neb., on July 9, 2002. Senate Foreign Relations reported, amended, Sept. 12 (S Rept 107-278). Senate passed, amended, Nov. 14. House passed Nov. 15. President signed Dec. 4, 2002.

PL 107-328 (S J Res 53) Resolve that the first session of the 108th Congress will convene at noon on Jan. 7, 2003. Introduced by Daschle, D-S.D., on Nov. 14, 2002. Senate passed Nov. 14. House passed Nov. 15. President signed Dec. 4, 2002.

PL 107-329 (S 1240) Provide for the acquisition of land and construction of an interagency administrative and visitor facility at the entrance to American Fork Canyon, Utah. Introduced by Bennett, R-Utah, on July 25, 2001. Senate Energy and Natural Resources reported, amended, June 25, 2002 (S Rept 107-178). Senate passed, amended, Aug. 1. House Resources reported, Sept. 23 (H Rept 107-669). House passed, with amendment, under suspension of the rules, Sept. 24. Senate agreed to House amendment Nov. 20. President signed Dec. 6, 2002.

PL 107-330 (S 2237) Amend Title 38, U.S. Code, to improve veterans' benefits related to compensation, dependency and indemnity compensation, pensions, education, housing, memorial affairs, life insurance and certain other benefits, and to improve the administration of benefits and the procedures relating to judicial review of veterans' claims. Introduced by Rockefeller, D-W.Va., on April 24, 2002. Senate Veterans' Affairs reported, amended, Aug. 1 (S Rept 107-234). Senate passed, amended, Sept. 26. House passed, with amendments, Nov. 15. Senate agreed to House amendments Nov. 18. President signed Dec. 6, 2002.

PL 107-331 (S 2017) Amend the Indian Financing Act of 1974 to improve the effectiveness of the Native American loan guarantee and insurance program. Introduced by Campbell, R-Colo., on March 14, 2002. Senate Indian Affairs reported, amended, Aug. 28 (S Rept 107-249). Senate passed, amended, Sept. 17. House passed, with amendment, Nov. 15. Senate agreed to House amendment Nov. 20. President signed Dec. 13, 2002.

PL 107-332 (HR 38) Provide for additional lands to be included within the boundaries of the Homestead National Monument of America in Nebraska. Introduced by Bereuter, R-Neb., on Jan. 3, 2001. House Resources reported, amended, Dec. 6 (H Rept 107-325). House passed, amended, under suspension of the rules, Dec. 11. Senate Energy and Natural Resources reported Sept. 9, 2002 (S Rept 107-260). Senate passed Nov. 20. President signed Dec. 16, 2002.

PL 107-333 (HR 308) Establish the Guam War Claims Review Commission. Introduced by Underwood, D-Guam, on Jan. 30, 2001. House passed, amended, under suspension of the rules, March 13. Senate Energy and Natural Resources reported June 24, 2002 (S Rept 107-172). Senate passed Nov. 20. President signed Dec. 16, 2002.

PL 107-334 (HR 451) Make certain adjustments to the boundaries of the Mount Nebo Wilderness Area in Utah. Introduced by Hansen, R-Utah, on Feb. 6, 2001. House Resources reported, amended, July 23 (H Rept 107-150). House passed, amended, under suspension of the rules, July 23. Senate Energy and Natural Resources reported Oct. 8, 2002 (no written report). Senate passed Nov. 20. President signed Dec. 16, 2002.

PL 107-335 (HR 706) Direct the secretary of the Interior to convey certain properties in the vicinity of the Elephant Butte Reservoir and the Caballo Reservoir in New Mexico. Introduced by Skeen, R-N.M., on Feb. 14, 2001. House Resources reported, amended, March 7, 2002 (H Rept 107-368). House passed, amended, under suspension of the rules, March 19. Senate Energy and Natural Resources reported Sept. 17 (S Rept 107-287). Senate passed Nov. 20. President signed Dec. 16, 2002.

PL 107-336 (HR 1712) Authorize the secretary of the Interior to make adjustments to the boundary of the National Park of American Samoa to include certain portions of the islands of Ofu and Olosega within the park. Introduced by Faleomavaega, D-Am. Samoa, on May 3, 2001. House Resources reported, amended, March 12, 2002 (H Rept 107-372). House passed, amended, under suspension of the rules, March 19. Senate Energy and Natural Resources reported Sept. 11 (S Rept 107-270). Senate passed Nov. 20. President signed Dec. 16, 2002.

PL 107-337 (HR 1776) Authorize the secretary of the Interior to study the suitability and feasibility of establishing the Buffalo Bayou National Heritage Area in west Houston, Texas. Introduced by Green, D-Texas, on May 9, 2001. House Resources reported, amended, Oct. 30 (H Rept 107-256). House passed, amended, under suspension of the rules, Oct. 30. Senate Energy and Natural Resources reported Sept. 9, 2002 (S Rept 107-262). Senate passed Nov. 20. President signed Dec. 16, 2002.

PL 107-338 (HR 1814) Amend the National Trails System Act to designate the Metacomet-Monadnock-Mattabesett Trail extending through western Massachusetts and central Connecticut for study for potential addition to the National Trails System. Introduced by Olver, D-Mass., on May 10, 2001. House Resources reported, amended, Sept. 28 (H Rept 107-224). House passed, amended, under suspension of the rules, Oct. 23. Senate Energy and Natural Resources reported Sept. 9, 2002 (S Rept 107-263). Senate passed Nov. 20. President signed Dec. 16, 2002.

PL 107-339 (HR 1870) Provide for the sale of certain real estate property within the Newlands Project to the city of Fallon, Nev. Introduced by Gibbons, R-Nev., on May 16, 2001. House Resources reported, amended, March 6, 2002 (H Rept 107-366). House passed, amended, under suspension of the rules, March 6. Senate Energy and Natural Resources reported Sept. 11 (S Rept 107-271). Senate passed Nov. 20. President signed Dec. 16, 2002.

PL 107-340 (HR 1906) Amend the act that established the Pu'uhonua O Honaunau National Historical Park to expand the boundaries of that park. Introduced by Mink, D-Hawaii, on May 17, 2001. House Resources reported, amended, May 3, 2002 (H Rept 107-435). House passed, amended, under suspension of the rules, June 17. Senate Energy and Natural Resources reported Sept. 11 (S Rept 107-272). Senate passed Nov. 20. President signed Dec. 16, 2002.

PL 107-341 (HR 1925) Direct the secretary of the Interior to study the suitability and feasibility of designating the Waco Mammoth Site Area in Waco, Texas, as a unit of the National Park System. Introduced by Edwards, D-Texas, on May 21, 2001. House Resources reported, amended, Dec. 5 (H Rept 107-317). House passed, amended, under suspension of the rules, May 14, 2002. Senate Energy and Natural Resources reported Sept. 9 (S Rept 107-264). Senate passed Nov. 20. President signed Dec. 16, 2002.

PL 107-342 (HR 2099) Amend the Omnibus Parks and Public Lands Management Act of 1996 to provide adequate funding authorization for the Vancouver National Historic Reserve. Introduced by Baird, D-Wash., on June 7, 2001. House Resources reported, amended, Sept. 4, 2002 (H Rept 107-627). House passed, amended, under suspension of the rules, Sept. 24. Senate passed Nov. 20. President signed Dec. 17, 2002.

PL 107-343 (HR 2109) Authorize the secretary of the Interior to conduct a special resource study of Virginia Key Beach Park in Biscayne Bay, Fla., for possible inclusion in the National Park System. Introduced by Meek, D-Fla., on June 7, 2001. House Resources reported, amended, April 9, 2002 (H Rept 107-390). House passed, amended, under suspension of the rules, April 30. Senate Energy and Natural Resources reported, Sept. 11 (S Rept 107-273). Senate passed, Nov. 20. President signed Dec. 17, 2002.

PL 107-344 (HR 2115) Authorize the secretary of the Interior to participate in the design, planning and construction of a project to reclaim and reuse wastewater within and outside of the service area of the Lakehaven Utility District, Wash. Introduced by Smith, D-Wash., on June 7, 2001. House Resources reported Nov. 27 (H Rept 107-302). House passed, under suspension of the rules, Dec. 5. Senate Energy and Natural Resources reported Sept. 17, 2002 (S Rept 107-288). Senate passed Nov. 20. President signed Dec. 17, 2002.

PL 107-345 (HR 2187) Amend Title 10, U.S. Code, to make receipts collected from mineral leasing activities on certain naval oil shale reserves available to cover government environmental restoration, waste management and environmental compliance costs incurred with respect to the reserves. Introduced by Hefley, R-Colo., on June 14, 2001. House Resources reported, amended, Sept. 10 (H Rept 107-202, Pt. 1). House Energy and Commerce discharged. House passed, amended, under suspension of the rules, Dec. 18. Senate

Armed Services discharged. Senate passed Nov. 20, 2002. President signed Dec. 17, 2002.

PL 107-346 (HR 2385) Convey certain property to the city of St. George, Utah, in order to provide for the protection and preservation of certain rare paleontological resources. Introduced by Hansen, R-Utah, on June 28, 2001. House Resources reported, amended, Sept. 24 (H Rept 107-215). House passed, amended, under suspension of the rules, Oct. 2. Senate Energy and Natural Resources reported, amended, Sept. 11, 2002 (S Rept 107-274). Senate passed, amended, Nov. 20. President signed Dec. 17, 2002.

PL 107-347 (HR 2458) Establish a federal chief information officer within the Office of Management and Budget, and establish a broad framework of measures that require using Internet-based information technology to enhance citizen access to government information and services. Introduced by Turner, D-Texas, July 11, 2001. House Government Reform reported, amended, Nov. 14, 2002 (H Rept 107-787, Pt. 1). House Judiciary discharged. House passed, amended, Nov. 15. Senate passed Nov. 15. President signed Dec. 17, 2002.

PL 107-348 (HR 2628) Direct the secretary of the Interior to conduct a study of the suitability and feasibility of establishing the Muscle Shoals National Heritage Area in Alabama. Introduced by Cramer, D-Ala., on July 25, 2001. House Resources reported April 11, 2002 (H Rept 107-398). House passed, under suspension of the rules, April 30. Senate Energy and Natural Resources reported Oct. 8 (no written report). Senate passed Nov. 20. President signed Dec. 17, 2002.

PL 107-349 (H 2828) Authorize refunds to qualified Klamath Project entities and individual contractors for amounts assessed to them for operation and maintenance of the Klamath Project for 2001. Introduced by Walden, R-Ore., on Aug. 2, 2001. House Resources reported, amended, Nov. 13 (H Rept 107-284). House passed, amended, under suspension of the rules, Nov. 13. Senate Energy and Natural Resources reported Sept. 17, 2002 (S Rept 107-289). Senate passed Nov. 20. President signed Dec. 17, 2002.

PL 107-350 (HR 2937) Provide for the conveyance of certain public land in Clark County, Nev., for use as a shooting range. Introduced by Gibbons, R-Nev., on Sept. 21, 2001. House Resources reported, amended, April 9, 2002 (H Rept 107-387). House passed, amended, under suspension of the rules, April 9. Senate Energy and Natural Resources discharged. Senate passed Nov. 20. President signed Dec. 17, 2002.

PL 107-351 (HR 2990) Amend the Lower Rio Grande Valley Water Resources Conservation and Improvement Act of 2000 to authorize additional projects. Introduced by Hinojosa, D-Texas, on Oct. 2, 2001. House Resources reported, amended, July 16, 2002 (H Rept 107-580). House passed, amended, under suspension of the rules, July 22. Senate Energy and Natural Resources reported Oct. 8 (no written report). Senate passed Nov. 20. President signed Dec. 17, 2002.

PL 107-352 (HR 3180) Consent to certain amendments to the New Hampshire-Vermont Interstate School Compact. Introduced by Bass, R-N.H., on Oct. 30, 2001. House Judiciary reported May 20, 2002 (H Rept 107-478). House passed, under suspension of the rules, June 26. Senate Judiciary reported Nov. 14 (no written report). Senate passed Nov. 20. President signed Dec. 17, 2002.

PL 107-353 (HR 3401) Provide for the conveyance of Forest Service facilities and lands that make up the Five Mile Regional Learning Center in California to the Clovis Unified School District, and authorize a new special use permit regarding the continued use of unconveyed lands used by the Center. Introduced by Radanovich, R-Calif., on Dec. 4, 2001. House Resources reported, amended, July 15, 2002 (H Rept 107-574). House passed, amended, under suspension of the rules, July 22. Senate Energy and Natural Resources reported Oct. 8 (no written report). Senate passed Nov. 20. President signed Dec. 17, 2002.

PL 107-354 (HR 3449) Revise the boundaries of the George Washington Birthplace National Monument. Introduced by Davis, R-Va., on Dec. 11, 2001. House Resources reported Sept. 4, 2002 (H Rept 107-631). House passed, under suspension of the rules, Sept. 24. Senate passed Nov. 20. President signed Dec. 17, 2002.

PL 107-355 (HR 3609) Amend Title 49, U.S. Code, to enhance the security and safety of pipelines. Introduced by Young, R-Alaska, on Dec. 20, 2001. House Transportation and Infrastructure reported, amended, July 23, 2002 (H Rept 107-605, Pt. 1). House Energy and Commerce reported, amended, July 23 (H Rept 107-605, Pt. 2). House passed, amended, under suspension of the rules, July 23. Senate Commerce, Science and Transportation discharged. Senate passed, with amendment, Nov. 13. House agreed to Senate amendment Nov. 15. President signed Dec. 17, 2002.

PL 107-356 (HR 3858) Modify the boundaries of the New River Gorge National River, W.Va. Introduced by Rahall, D-W.Va., on March 6, 2002. House Resources reported June 17 (H Rept 107-509). House passed, under suspension of the rules, June 24. Senate Energy and Natural Resources reported Oct. 8 (no written report). Senate passed Nov. 20. President signed Dec. 17, 2002.

PL 107-357 (HR 4692) Amend the act authorizing the establishment of the Andersonville National Historic Site in Georgia to provide for the addition of certain donated lands to the site. Introduced by Bishop, D-Ga., on May 9, 2002. House Resources reported Oct. 1 (H Rept 107-712). House passed, under suspension of the rules, Oct. 1. Senate passed Nov. 20. President signed Dec. 17, 2002.

PL 107-358 (HR 4823) Repeal the sunset of the Economic Growth and Tax Relief Reconciliation Act of 2001 with respect to the exclusion from federal income tax for restitution received by victims of the Nazi regime. Introduced by Shaw, R-Fla., on May 22, 2002. House passed, under suspension of the rules, June 4. Senate passed Nov. 20. President signed Dec. 17, 2002.

PL 107-359 (HR 5125) Amend the American Battlefield Protection Act of 1996 to authorize the secretary of the Interior to establish a battlefield acquisition grant program. Introduced by Miller, R-Calif., on July 15, 2002. House Resources reported, amended, Oct. 1 (H Rept 107-710). House passed, amended, under suspension of the rules, Oct. 1. Senate Energy and Natural Resources reported Oct. 8 (no written report). Senate passed Nov. 20. President signed Dec. 17, 2002.

PL 107-360 (HR 5738) Amend the Public Health Service Act with respect to special diabetes programs for Type I diabetes and for Indians. Introduced by Shimkus, R-Ill., on Nov. 14, 2002. House Energy and Commerce discharged. House passed Nov. 15. Senate passed Nov. 20. President signed Dec. 17, 2002.

PL 107-361 (HR 2818) Authorize the secretary of the Interior to convey certain public land within the Sand Mountain Wilderness Study Area in Idaho to resolve an occupancy encroachment dating back to 1971. Introduced by Simpson, R-Idaho, on Aug. 2, 2001. House Resources reported May 7, 2002 (H Rept 107-440). House passed, under suspension of the rules, May 7. Senate Energy and Natural Resources reported Oct. 8 (no written report). Senate passed Nov. 20. President signed Dec. 17, 2002.

PL 107-362 (HR 3048) Resolve the claims of Cook Inlet Region, Inc., to lands adjacent to the Russian River in Alaska. Introduced by Young, R-Alaska, on Oct. 4, 2001. House Resources reported, amended, July 15, 2002 (H Rept 107-573). House passed, under suspension of the rules, July 22. Senate Energy and Natural Resources reported Sept. 11 (S Rept 107-275). Senate passed Nov. 20. President signed Dec. 19, 2002.

PL 107-363 (HR 3747) Direct the secretary of the Interior to conduct a study of the site commonly known as Eagledale Ferry Dock at Taylor Avenue in Washington for potential inclusion in the National Park System. Introduced by Inslee, D-Wash., on Feb. 13, 2002. House Resources reported Sept. 25 (H Rept 107-690). House passed Nov. 15. Senate passed Nov. 20. President signed Dec. 19, 2002.

PL 107-364 (HR 3909) Designate certain federal lands in Utah as the Gunn McKay Nature Preserve. Introduced by Hansen, R-Utah, on March 7, 2002. House Resources reported April 9 (H Rept 107-392). House passed, under suspension of the rules, April 30. Senate Energy and Natural Resources reported Oct. 8 (no written report). Senate passed Nov. 20. President signed Dec. 19, 2002.

PL 107-365 (HR 3954) Designate certain waterways in the Caribbean National Forest in the Commonwealth of Puerto Rico as components of the National Wild and Scenic Rivers System. Introduced by Acevedo-Vilá, D-P.R., on March 13, 2002. House Resources reported, amended, May 7 (H Rept 107-441). House passed, under suspension of the rules, May 7. Senate Energy and Natural Resources reported Oct. 8 (no written report). Senate passed Nov. 20. President signed Dec. 19, 2002.

PL 107-366 (HR 4129) Amend the Central Utah Project Completion Act to clarify the responsibilities of the secretary of the Interior with respect to the Central Utah Project, to redirect unexpended budget authority for wastewater treatment and reuse, to provide for prepayment of repayment contracts for municipal and industrial water delivery facilities and to eliminate a deadline for such prepayment. Introduced by Cannon, R-Utah, on April 10, 2002. House Resources reported, amended, July 8 (H Rept 107-554). House passed, amended, under suspension of the rules, Oct. 1. Senate passed Nov. 20. President signed Dec. 19, 2002.

PL 107-367 (HR 4638) Reauthorize the Mni Wiconi Rural Water Supply Project in South Dakota. Introduced by Thune, R-S.D., on May 1, 2002. House Resources reported Sept. 4 (H Rept 107-633). House passed, under suspension of the rules, Sept. 24. Senate passed Nov. 20. President signed Dec. 19, 2002.

PL 107-368 (HR 4664) Authorize appropriations for fiscal years 2003 through 2007 for the National Science Foundation. Introduced by Smith, R-Mich., on May 7, 2002. House Science reported, amended, June 4 (H Rept 107-488). House passed, amended, June 5. Senate Health, Labor and Pensions discharged. Senate passed, with amendments, Nov. 14. House agreed to Senate amendments Nov. 15. President signed Dec. 19, 2002.

PL 107-369 (HR 4682) Revise the boundary of the Allegheny Portage Railroad National Historic Site. Introduced by Murtha, D-Pa., on May 8, 2002. House Resources reported Sept. 4 (H Rept 107-634). House passed, amended, under suspension of the rules, Sept. 24. Senate Energy and Natural Resources reported Oct. 8 (no written report). Senate passed Nov. 20. President signed Dec. 19, 2002.

PL 107-370 (HR 4750) Designate certain lands in California as components of the National Wilderness Preservation System. Introduced by Farr, D-Calif., on May 16, 2002. House Resources discharged. House passed Nov. 15. Senate passed Nov. 20. President signed Dec. 19, 2002.

PL 107-371 (HR 4874) Direct the secretary of the Interior to disclaim any federal interest in lands adjacent to Spirit Lake and Twin Lakes in Idaho resulting from possible omission of lands from an 1880 survey. Introduced by Otter, R-Idaho, on June 5, 2002. House Resources reported Sept. 24 (H Rept 107-676). House passed, under suspension of the rules, Oct. 1. Senate passed Nov. 20. President signed Dec. 19, 2002.

PL 107-372 (HR 4883) Reauthorize the Hydrographic Services Improvement Act of 1998. Introduced by Young, R-Alaska, on June 6, 2002. House Resources reported, amended, July 26 (H Rept 107-621). House passed, amended, Nov. 15. Senate passed Nov. 20. President signed Dec. 19, 2002.

PL 107-373 (HR 4944) Designate the Cedar Creek and Belle Grove National Historical Park in Virginia as a unit of the National Park System. Introduced by Wolf, R-Va., on June 13, 2002. House Resources reported, amended, Oct. 1 (H Rept 107-713). House passed, amended, under suspension of the rules, Oct. 1. Senate passed Nov. 20. President signed Dec. 19, 2002.

PL 107-374 (HR 4953) Direct the secretary of the Interior to grant to the counties of Deschutes and Crook in Oregon a right-of-way to West Butte Road. Introduced by Walden, R-Ore., on June 17, 2002. House Resources reported, amended, Sept. 4 (H Rept 107-637). House passed, amended, under suspension of the rules, Sept. 24. Senate passed Nov. 20. President signed Dec. 19, 2002.

PL 107-375 (HR 5099) Extend the periods of authorization for the secretary of the Interior to implement capital construction projects associated with the endangered fish recovery implementation programs for the Upper Colorado and San Juan River Basins. Introduced by Hansen, R-Utah, on July 11, 2002. House Resources reported Sept. 24 (H Rept 107-672). House passed, under suspension of the rules, Sept. 24. Senate Energy and Natural Resources reported Oct. 8 (no written report). Senate passed Nov. 20. President signed Dec. 19, 2002.

PL 107-376 (HR 5436) Extend the deadline for commencement of construction of a hydroelectric project in Oregon. Introduced by DeFazio, D-Ore., on Sept. 24, 2002. House Energy and Commerce discharged. House passed Nov. 15. Senate passed Nov. 20. President signed Dec. 19, 2002.

PL 107-377 (HR 5472) Extend for six months the period for which Chapter 12 of Title 11, U.S. Code providing bankruptcy relief for family farmers is reenacted. Introduced by Sensenbrenner, R-Wis., on Sept. 26, 2002. House passed, under suspension of the rules, Oct. 1. Senate passed Nov. 20. President signed Dec. 19, 2002.

108th Congress–2003

PL 108-1 (S 23) Provide for an extension of the Temporary Extended Unemployment Compensation Act of 2002 and for a transition period for individuals receiving compensation when the program under the act ends. Introduced by Fitzgerald, R-Ill., on Jan. 7, 2003. Senate passed Jan. 7. House passed Jan. 8. President signed Jan. 8, 2003.

PL 108-2 (H J Res 1) Make further continuing appropriations for fiscal 2003. Introduced by Young, R-Fla., on Jan. 7, 2003. House passed Jan. 8. Senate passed Jan. 9. President signed Jan. 10, 2003.

PL 108-3 (HR 11) Extend the national flood insurance program. Introduced by Oxley, R-Ohio, on Jan. 7, 2003. House passed, under suspension of the rules, Jan. 8. Senate passed Jan. 9. President signed Jan. 13, 2003.

PL 108-4 (H J Res 13) Make further continuing appropriations for fiscal 2003. Introduced by Young, R-Fla., on Jan. 27, 2003. House passed Jan. 28. Senate passed Jan. 29. President signed Jan. 31, 2003.

PL 108-5 (H J Res 18) Make further continuing appropriations for fiscal 2003. Introduced by Young, R-Fla., on Feb. 4, 2003. House passed Feb. 5. Senate passed Feb. 5. President signed Feb. 7, 2003.

PL 108-6 (HR 16) Authorize salary adjustments for U.S. justices and judges for fiscal 2003. Introduced by Sensenbrenner, R-Wis., Jan. 7, 2003. House passed, under suspension of the rules, Jan. 8. Senate passed Jan. 30. President signed Feb. 13, 2003.

PL 108-7 (H J Res 2) Make consolidated appropriations for the fiscal year ending Sept. 30, 2003. Introduced by Young, R-Fla., on Jan. 7, 2003. House passed Jan. 8. Senate passed, with amendment, Jan. 23. Conference report filed in the House on Feb. 13 (H Rept 108-10). House agreed to conference report Feb. 13. Senate agreed to conference report Feb. 13. President signed Feb. 20, 2003.

PL 108-8 (S 141) Improve the calculation of the federal subsidy rate with respect to small-business loans. Introduced by Snowe, R-Maine, on Jan. 10, 2003. Senate passed Jan. 10. House passed, under suspension of the rules, Feb. 11. President signed Feb. 25, 2003.

PL 108-9 (H J Res 19) Recognize the 92nd birthday of Ronald Reagan. Introduced by Cox, R-Calif., on Feb. 4, 2003. House passed, under suspension of the rules, Feb. 11. Senate passed Feb. 13. President signed March 6, 2003.

PL 108-10 (HR 395) Authorize the Federal Trade Commission to collect fees for the implementation and enforcement of a "do-not-call" registry. Introduced by Tauzin, R-La., on Jan. 28, 2003. House Energy and Commerce reported Feb. 11 (H Rept 108-8). House passed Feb. 12. Senate passed Feb. 13. President signed March 11, 2003.

PL 108-11 (HR 1559) Make emergency wartime supplemental appropriations for the fiscal year ending Sept. 30, 2003. Introduced by Young, R-Fla., on April 2, 2003. House Appropriations reported April 2 (H Rept 108-55). House passed, amended, April 3. Senate passed, with amendment, April 7. Conference report filed in the House on April 12 (H Rept 108-76). House agreed to conference report April 12. Senate agreed to conference report April 12. President signed April 16, 2003.

PL 108-12 (HR 397) Reinstate and extend the deadline for beginning construction of a hydroelectric project in Illinois. Introduced by Shimkus, R-Ill., on Jan. 28, 2003. House Energy and Commerce reported Feb. 4 (H Rept 108-6). House passed, under suspension of the rules, Feb. 11. Senate Energy and Natural Resources reported March 19 (S Rept 108-27). Senate passed April 7. President signed April 22, 2003.

PL 108-13 (HR 672) Rename the Guam South Elementary/Middle School of the Department of Defense Domestic Dependents Elementary and Secondary Schools System in honor of Navy Commander William "Willie" McCool, who was the pilot of the Space Shuttle *Columbia* when it was lost Feb. 1, 2003. Introduced by Bordallo, D-Guam, on Feb. 11, 2003. House passed, amended, under suspension of the rules, Feb. 26. Senate Armed Services discharged. Senate passed April 7. President signed April 22, 2003.

PL 108-14 (HR 145) Designate the federal building located at 290 Broadway in New York, N.Y., as the "Ted Weiss Federal Building." Introduced by Nadler, D-N.Y., on Jan. 7, 2003. House Transportation and Infrastructure reported March 10 (H Rept 108-30). House passed, under suspension of the rules, March 18. Senate Environment and Public Works reported April 9 (no written report). Senate passed April 11. President signed April 23, 2003.

PL 108-15 (HR 258) Ensure continuity for the design of the 5-cent coin and establish the Citizens Coinage Advisory Committee. Introduced by Cantor, R-Va., on Jan. 8, 2003. House Financial Services reported, amended, Feb. 26 (H Rept 108-20). House passed, amended, under suspension of the rules, Feb. 26. Senate Banking, Housing and Urban Affairs discharged April 11. Senate passed April 11. President signed April 23, 2003.

PL 108-16 (HR 273) Provide for the eradication and control of nutria in Maryland and Louisiana. Introduced by Gilchrest, R-Md., on Jan. 8, 2003. House passed, under suspension of the rules, April 8. Senate passed April 9. President signed April 23, 2003.

PL 108-17 (HR 1505) Designate the facility of the U.S. Postal Service located at 2127 Beatties Ford Rd., Charlotte, N.C., as the "Jim Richardson Post Office." Introduced by Watt, D-N.C., on March 27, 2003. House passed, under suspension of the rules, March 31. Senate Governmental Affairs discharged April 10. Senate passed April 10. President signed April 23, 2003.

PL 108-18 (S 380) Amend Chapter 83 of Title 5, U.S. Code, to reform the funding of benefits under the Civil Service Retirement System for employees of the U.S. Postal Service. Introduced by Collins, R-Maine, on Feb. 12, 2003. Senate Governmental Affairs reported, amended, April 1 (S Rept 108-35, filed April 18). Senate passed, amended, April 2. House passed April 8. President signed April 23, 2003.

PL 108-19 (HR 1584) Implement effective measures to stop trade in conflict diamonds. Introduced by Houghton, R-N.Y., on April 3, 2003. House passed, amended, under suspension of the rules, April 8. Senate passed, with amendment, April 10. House agreed to Senate amendment April 11. President signed April 25, 2003.

PL 108-20 (HR 1770) Provide benefits and other compensation for certain individuals with injuries resulting from administration of smallpox countermeasures. Introduced by Burr, R-N.C., on April 11, 2003. House Energy and Commerce, Education and the Workforce, and Judiciary discharged. House passed April 11. Senate passed April 11. President signed April 30, 2003.

PL 108-21 (S 151) Prevent child abduction and the sexual exploitation of children. Introduced by Hatch, R-Utah, on Jan. 13, 2003. Senate Judiciary reported, amended, Jan. 30 (S Rept 108-2). Senate passed, amended, Feb. 24. House Judiciary discharged. House passed, with amendment, March 27. Conference report filed in the House on April 9 (H Rept 108-66). House agreed to the conference report April 10. Senate agreed to the conference report April 10. President signed April 30, 2003.

PL 108-22 (S 162) Provide for the distribution of certain funds awarded to the Gila River Pima-Maricopa Indian Community. Introduced by McCain, R-Ariz., on Jan. 15, 2003. Senate Indian Affairs reported March 10 (S Rept 108-17). Senate passed March 13. House passed, under suspension of the rules, April 29. President signed May 14, 2003.

PL 108-23 (HR 289) Expand the boundaries of the Ottawa National Wildlife Refuge Complex and the Detroit River International Wildlife Refuge. Introduced by Kaptur, D-Ohio, on Jan. 8, 2003. House passed, amended, under suspension of the rules, April 1. Senate Environment and Public Works reported April 9 (no written report). Senate passed May 1. President signed May 19, 2003.

PL 108-24 (H J Res 51) Increase the statutory limit on the public debt. Introduced on April 11, 2003. House passed April 11. Senate passed May 23. President signed May 27, 2003.

PL 108-25 (HR 1298) Authorize assistance to foreign countries to combat HIV/AIDS, tuberculosis and malaria. Introduced by Hyde, R-Ill., on March 17, 2003. House International Relations reported, amended, April 7. House passed, amended, May 1. Senate passed, with amendments, May 16. House agreed to Senate amendments May 21. President signed May 27, 2003.

PL 108-26 (HR 2185) Extend the Temporary Extended Unemployment Compensation Act of 2002. Introduced by Dunn, R-Wash., on May 21, 2003. House passed May 22. Senate passed May 23. President signed May 28, 2003.

PL 108-27 (HR 2) Provide for reconciliation pursuant to section 201 of the concurrent resolution on the budget for fiscal year 2004. Introduced by Thomas, R-Calif., on Feb. 27, 2003. House Ways and Means reported, amended, May 8 (H Rept 108-94). House passed May 9. Senate passed, with amendment, May 15. Conference report filed in the House on May 22 (H Rept 108-126). House agreed to the conference report May 23. Senate agreed to the conference report May 23. President signed May 28, 2003.

PL 108-28 (S 243) Authorize the secretary of State to obtain observer status for Taiwan at a World Health Organization session. Introduced by Allen, R-Va., on Jan. 29, 2003. Senate Foreign Relations reported April 9 (no written report). Senate passed May 1. House International Relations discharged. House passed May 14. President signed May 29, 2003.

PL 108-29 (S 330) Further the protection and recognition of veterans' memorials. Introduced by Campbell, R-Colo., on Feb. 6, 2003. Senate Judiciary reported March 20 (no written report). Senate passed March 27. House Judiciary reported May 19 (H Rept 108-112, Pt. 1). House Transportation discharged. House passed, under suspension of the rules, May 20. President signed May 29, 2003.

PL 108-30 (S 870) Amend the Richard B. Russell National School Lunch Act to extend the availability of funds to carry out the fruit and vegetable pilot program. Introduced by Harkin, D-Iowa, on April 10, 2003. Senate passed April 10. House passed, under suspension of the rules, May 14. President signed May 29, 2003.

PL 108-31 (HR 192) Amend the Microenterprise for Self-Reliance Act of 2000 and the Foreign Assistance Act of 1961 to increase assistance for the poorest people in developing countries under microenterprise assistance programs. Introduced by Smith, R-N.J., on Jan. 7, 2003. House passed, under suspension of the rules, May 14. Senate Foreign Relations reported May 21 (no written report). Senate passed May 23. President signed June 17, 2003.

PL 108-32 (S 273) Provide for the expeditious completion of the acquisition of land owned by the State of Wyoming within the boundaries of Grand Teton National Park. Introduced by Thomas, R-Wyo., on Feb. 4, 2003. Senate Energy and Natural Resources reported March 5 (S Rept 108-14). Senate passed April 3. House passed June 5. President signed June 17, 2003.

PL 108-33 (HR 1625) Designate the facility of the U.S. Postal Service located at 1114 Main Ave. in Clifton, N.J., as the "Robert P. Hammer Post Office Building." Introduced by Pascrell, D-N.J., on April 3, 2003. House passed, under suspension of the rules, May 6. Senate Governmental Affairs discharged. Senate passed June 10. President signed June 23, 2003.

PL 108-34 (S 222) Approve the settlement of the water rights claims of the Zuni Indian Tribe in Apache County, Ariz. Introduced by Kyl, R-Ariz., on Jan. 28, 2003. Senate Indian Affairs reported March 10 (S Rept 108-18). Senate passed March 13. House defeated, under suspension of the rules, June 3. House passed June 5. President signed June 23, 2003.

PL 108-35 (S 763) Designate the federal building and U.S. courthouse located at 46 Ohio St. in Indianapolis, Ind., as the "Birch Bayh Federal Building and United States Courthouse." Introduced by Lugar, R-Ind., on April 2, 2003. Senate Environment and Public Works reported April 9 (no written report). Senate passed April 11. House passed, under suspension of the rules, June 9. President signed June 23, 2003.

PL 108-36 (S 342) Amend the Child Abuse Prevention and Treatment Act to reauthorize and revise programs under the act. Introduced by Gregg, R-N.H., on Feb. 11, 2003. Senate Health, Education, Labor and Pensions reported March 4 (S Rept 108-12). Senate passed March 19. House passed, with amendment, March 26. Conference report filed in the House on June 12 (H Rept 108-150). House agreed to the conference report June 17. Senate agreed to the conference report June 19. President signed June 25, 2003.

PL 108-37 (S 703) Designate the regional headquarters building for the National Park Service under construction in Omaha, Neb., as the "Carl T. Curtis National Park Service Midwest Regional Headquarters Building." Introduced by Hagel, R-Neb., on March 25, 2003. Senate Environment and Public Works reported April 10 (no written report). Senate passed April 11. House Transportation reported June 2 (H Rept 108-135). House passed, under suspension of the rules, June 16. President signed June 26, 2003.

PL 108-38 (S J Res 8) Express the sense of Congress with respect to raising awareness and encouraging prevention of sexual assault in the United States and supporting the goals and ideals of National Sexual Assault Awareness and Prevention Month. Introduced by Brownback, R-Kan., on March 11, 2003. Senate Judiciary reported

April 11 (no written report). Senate passed April 11. House Judiciary reported May 19 (H Rept 108-113). House passed, under suspension of the rules, June 10. President signed June 26, 2003.

PL 108-39 (HR 2312) Amend the Communications Satellite Act of 1962 to provide for the orderly dilution of the ownership interest in Inmarsat by former signatories to the Inmarsat Operating Agreement. Introduced by Shimkus, R-Ill., on June 3, 2003. House Energy and Commerce discharged. House passed June 12. Senate passed June 20. President signed June 30, 2003.

PL 108-40 (HR 2350) Reauthorize the Temporary Assistance for Needy Families block grant program through fiscal 2003. Introduced by Herger, R-Calif., on June 5, 2003. House passed, under suspension of the rules, June 11. Senate passed June 27. President signed June 30, 2003.

PL 108-41 (HR 389) Authorize the use of certain grant funds to establish an information clearinghouse to increase public access to defibrillation in schools. Introduced by Shimkus, R-Ill., on Jan. 27, 2003. House Energy and Commerce reported Feb. 13 (H Rept 108-13). House passed, under suspension of the rules, March 12. Senate Health, Education, Labor and Pensions discharged. Senate passed June 17. President signed July 1, 2003.

PL 108-42 (HR 519) Authorize the secretary of the Interior to conduct a study of the San Gabriel River Watershed. Introduced by Solis, D-Calif., on Jan. 31, 2003. House passed, under suspension of the rules, March 19. Senate Energy and Natural Resources reported June 9 (S Rept 108-65). Senate passed June 16. President signed July 1, 2003.

PL 108-43 (HR 788) Revise the boundary of the Glen Canyon National Recreation Area in Utah and Arizona. Introduced by Cannon, R-Utah, on Feb. 13, 2003. House passed, under suspension of the rules, March 25. Senate Energy and Natural Resources reported June 9 (S Rept 108-67). Senate passed June 16. President signed July 1, 2003.

PL 108-44 (HR 658) Provide for the protection of investors, increase confidence in the capital markets system, and fully implement the Sarbanes-Oxley Act of 2002 by streamlining the hiring process for certain employment positions in the Securities and Exchange Commission. Introduced by Baker, R-La., on Feb. 11, 2003. House Financial Services reported, amended, April 8 (H Rept 108-63, Pt. 1). House Government Reform discharged. House passed, amended, under suspension of the rules, June 17. Senate passed June 19. President signed July 3, 2003.

PL 108-45 (S 1276) Improve the manner in which the Corporation for National and Community Service approves, and records obligations relating to, national service positions. Introduced by Bond, R-Mo., on June 18, 2003. Senate passed June 18. House passed June 19. President signed July 3, 2003.

PL 108-46 (HR 825) Redesignate the facility of the U.S. Postal Service located at 7401 West 100th Place in Bridgeview, Ill., as the "Michael J. Healy Post Office Building." Introduced by Lipinski, D-Ill., on Feb. 13, 2003. House passed, under suspension of the rules, March 26. Senate Governmental Affairs reported June 20 (no written report). Senate passed June 25. President signed July 14, 2003.

PL 108-47 (HR 917) Designate the facility of the U.S. Postal Service located at 1830 South Lake Drive in Lexington, S.C., as the "Floyd Spence Post Office Building." Introduced by Wilson, R-S.C., on Feb. 25, 2003. House passed, under suspension of the rules,

March 26. Senate Governmental Affairs reported June 20 (no written report). Senate passed June 25. President signed July 14, 2003.

PL 108-48 (HR 925) Redesignate the facility of the U.S. Postal Service located at 1859 South Ashland Ave. in Chicago, Ill., as the "Cesar Chavez Post Office." Introduced by Gutierrez, D-Ill., on Feb. 26, 2003. House passed, under suspension of the rules, June 10. Senate Governmental Affairs reported June 20 (no written report). Senate passed June 25. President signed July 14, 2003.

PL 108-49 (HR 981) Designate the facility of the U.S. Postal Service located at 141 Erie St. in Linesville, Pa., as the "James R. Merry Post Office." Introduced by English, R-Pa., on Feb. 27, 2003. House passed, under suspension of the rules, March 26. Senate Governmental Affairs reported June 20 (no written report). Senate passed June 25. President signed July 14, 2003.

PL 108-50 (HR 985) Designate the facility of the U.S. Postal Service located at 111 West Washington St. in Bowling Green, Ohio, as the "Delbert L. Latta Post Office Building." Introduced by Gillmor, R-Ohio, on Feb. 27, 2003. House passed, under suspension of the rules, May 13. Senate Governmental Affairs reported June 20 (no written report). Senate passed June 25. President signed July 14, 2003.

PL 108-51 (HR 1055) Designate the facility of the U.S. Postal Service located at 1901 West Evans St. in Florence, S.C., as the "Dr. Roswell N. Beck Post Office Building." Introduced by Clyburn, D-S.C., on March 4, 2003. House passed, under suspension of the rules, April 7. Senate Governmental Affairs reported June 20 (no written report). Senate passed June 25. President signed July 14, 2003.

PL 108-52 (HR 1368) Designate the facility of the U.S. Postal Service located at 7554 Pacific Ave. in Stockton, Calif., as the "Norman D. Shumway Post Office Building." Introduced by Pombo, R-Calif., on March 19, 2003. House passed, amended, under suspension of the rules, April 7. Senate Governmental Affairs reported June 20 (no written report). Senate passed June 25. President signed July 14, 2003.

PL 108-53 (HR 1465) Designate the facility of the U.S. Postal Service located at 4832 East Highway 27 in Iron Station, N.C., as the "General Charles Gabriel Post Office." Introduced by Ballenger, R-N.C., on March 27, 2003. House passed, under suspension of the rules, June 2. Senate Governmental Affairs reported June 20 (no written report). Senate passed June 25. President signed July 14, 2003.

PL 108-54 (HR 1596) Designate the facility of the U.S. Postal Service located at 2318 Woodson Rd. in St. Louis, Mo., as the "Timothy Michael Gaffney Post Office Building." Introduced by Clay, D-Mo., on April 3, 2003. House passed, under suspension of the rules, May 6. Senate Governmental Affairs reported June 20 (no written report). Senate passed June 25. President signed July 14, 2003.

PL 108-55 (HR 1609) Redesignate the facility of the U.S. Postal Service located at 201 West Boston St. in Brookfield, Mo., as the "Admiral Donald Davis Post Office Building." Introduced by Graves, R-Mo., on April 3, 2003. House passed, under suspension of the rules, May 7. Senate Governmental Affairs reported June 20 (no written report). Senate passed June 25. President signed July 14, 2003.

PL 108-56 (HR 1740) Designate the facility of the U.S. Postal Service located at 1502 East Kiest Blvd. in Dallas, Texas, as the "Dr. Caesar A. W. Clark Sr. Post Office Building." Introduced by Johnson, D-Texas, on April 10, 2003. House passed, under suspension of the rules, May 6. Senate Governmental Affairs reported June 20 (no written report). Senate passed June 25. President signed June 14, 2003.

PL 108-57 (HR 2030) Designate the facility of the U.S. Postal Service located at 120 Baldwin Ave. in Paia, Maui, Hawaii, as the "Patsy Takemoto Mink Post Office Building." Introduced by Case, D-Hawaii, on May 8, 2003. House passed, under suspension of the rules, June 10. Senate Governmental Affairs reported June 20 (no written report). Senate passed June 25. President signed July 14, 2003.

PL 108-58 (HR 2474) Authorize the Congressional Hunger Center to award Bill Emerson and Mickey Leland Hunger Fellowships for fiscal years 2003 and 2004. Introduced by Emerson, R-Mo., on June 16, 2003. House passed, amended, under suspension of the rules, June 25. Senate passed June 27. President signed July 14, 2003.

PL 108-59 (S 858) Extend the Abraham Lincoln Bicentennial Commission. Introduced by Durbin, D-Ill., on April 10, 2003. Senate Judiciary reported May 22 (no written report). Senate passed May 23. House passed, under suspension of the rules, June 25. President signed July 14, 2003.

PL 108-60 (S 709) Award a congressional gold medal to British Prime Minister Tony Blair. Introduced by Dole, R-N.C., on March 26, 2003. Senate Banking, Housing, and Urban Affairs reported May 9 (no written report). Senate passed May 15. House Financial Services discharged. House passed July 14. President signed July 17, 2003.

PL 108-61 (HR 2330) Sanction the ruling Burmese military junta, strengthen Burma's democratic forces and support and recognize the National League of Democracy as the legitimate representative of the Burmese people. Introduced by Lantos, D-Calif., on June 4, 2003. House International Relations reported, amended, June 17 (H Rept 108-159, Pt. 1). House Judiciary reported, amended, July 11 (H Rept 108-159, Pt. 2). House Ways and Means discharged. House Financial Services discharged. House passed, under suspension of the rules, July 15. Senate passed July 16. President signed July 28, 2003.

PL 108-62 (HR 255) Authorize the secretary of the Interior to grant an easement to facilitate access to the Lewis and Clark Interpretative Center in Nebraska City, Neb. Introduced by Bereuter, R-Neb., on Jan. 8, 2003. House passed, amended, under suspension of the rules, May 14. Senate Energy and Natural Resources reported July 11 (S Rept 108-99). Senate passed July 17. President signed July 29, 2003.

PL 108-63 (HR 733) Authorize the secretary of the Interior to acquire the McLoughlin House in Oregon City, Ore., for inclusion in the Fort Vancouver Historic Site. Introduced by Hooley, D-Ore., on Feb. 12, 2003. House passed, under suspension of the rules, April 8. Senate Energy and Natural Resources reported, with amendment, June 9 (S Rept 108-66). Senate passed, with amendment, June 16. House passed, under suspension of the rules, July 16. President signed July 29, 2003.

PL 108-64 (HR 1577) Designate the visitor center in Organ Pipe National Monument in Arizona as the "Kris Eggle Visitor Center." Introduced by Tancredo, R-Colo., on April 2, 2003. House passed, amended, under suspension of the rules, May 14. Senate Energy and Natural Resources reported July 11 (S Rept 108-100). Senate passed July 17. President signed July 29, 2003.

PL 108-65 (S 1399) Redesignate the facility of the U.S. Postal Service located at 101 South Vine St. in Glenwood, Iowa, as the "William J. Scherle Post Office Building." Introduced by Harkin, D-Iowa, on

July 14, 2003. Senate Governmental Affairs discharged. Senate passed July 17. House passed, under suspension of the rules, July 21. President signed July 29, 2003.

PL 108-66 (S 246) Provide that certain Bureau of Land Management land shall be held in trust for the Pueblo of Santa Clara and the Pueblo of San Ildefonso in New Mexico. Introduced by Domenici, R-N.M., on Jan. 29, 2003. Senate Energy and Natural Resources reported, with amendments, June 9 (S Rept 108-60). Senate passed, with amendments, June 16. House passed, under suspension of the rules, July 16. President signed July 30, 2003.

PL 108-67 (HR 74) Direct the secretary of Agriculture to convey certain land in the Lake Tahoe Basin Management Unit in Nevada, to the secretary of the Interior, in trust for the Washoe Indian Tribe of Nevada and California. Introduced by Gibbons, R-Nev., on Jan. 7, 2003. House Resources reported June 26 (H Rept 108-185). House passed, under suspension of the rules, July 16. Senate passed July 17. President signed Aug. 1, 2003.

PL 108-68 (S 1280) Limit the liability of the National Center for Missing and Exploited Children for certain actions by volunteers. Introduced by Hatch, R-Utah, on June 18, 2003. Senate Judiciary reported, with amendment, July 10 (no written report). Senate passed, with amendment, July 14. House passed, under suspension of the rules, July 21. President signed Aug. 1, 2003.

PL 108-69 (HR 2859) Make emergency supplemental appropriations for the fiscal year ending Sept. 30, 2003. Introduced by Young, R-Fla., on July 24, 2003. House passed July 25. Senate passed July 31. President signed Aug. 8, 2003.

PL 108-70 (HR 1018) Designate the building located at 1 Federal Plaza in New York as the "James L. Watson United States Court of International Trade Building." Introduced by Rangel, D-N.Y., on Feb. 27, 2003. House Transportation reported May 1 (H Rept 108-85). House passed, under suspension of the rules, May 19. Senate Environment and Public Works discharged. Senate passed July 31. President signed Aug. 14, 2003.

PL 108-71 (HR 1761) Designate the facility of the U.S. Postal Service located at 9350 East Corporate Hill Drive in Wichita, Kan., as the "Garner E. Shriver Post Office Building." Introduced by Tiahrt, R-Kan., on April 10, 2003. House passed, under suspension of rules, July 8. Senate Governmental Affairs discharged. Senate passed July 31. President signed Aug. 14, 2003.

PL 108-72 (HR 2195) Authorize additional space and resources for national collections held by the Smithsonian Institution. Introduced by Regula, R-Ohio, on May 21, 2003. House passed, under suspension of rules, July 15. Senate passed July 31. President signed Aug. 15, 2003.

PL 108-73 (HR 2465) Extend Chapter 12 bankruptcy protection for family farmers for six months to Jan. 1, 2004. Introduced by Sensenbrenner, R-Wis., on June 12, 2003. House passed, under suspension of rules, June 23. Senate passed July 31. President signed Aug. 15, 2003.

PL 108-74 (HR 2854) Amend title XXI of the Social Security Act to extend the availability of allotments for fiscal years 1998 through 2001 under the State Children's Health Insurance Program. Introduced by Tauzin, R-La., on July 24, 2003. House Energy and Commerce discharged. House passed July 25. Senate passed July 31. President signed Aug. 15, 2003.

PL 108-75 (S 1015) Authorize grants through the Centers for Disease Control and Prevention for mosquito control programs to prevent mosquito-borne diseases. Introduced by Gregg, R-N.H., on May 7, 2003. Senate Health, Education, Labor and Pensions reported June 12 (H Rept 108-69). Senate passed June 16. House passed July 25. President signed Aug. 15, 2003.

PL 108-76 (HR 1412) Authorize the secretary of Education to waive or modify any statutory or regulatory provision applicable to federal student financial aid programs in order to assist students whose lives are disrupted by being called to serve in the U.S. armed forces. Introduced by Kline, R-Minn., on March 25, 2003. House passed, under suspension of rules, April 1. Senate Health, Education, Labor and Pensions discharged. Senate passed July 31. President signed Aug. 18, 2003.

PL 108-77 (HR 2738) Implement the United States-Chile Free Trade Agreement. Introduced by DeLay on July 15, 2003. House Ways and Means reported July 21 (H Rept 108-224, Pt. 1). House Judiciary reported July 22 (H Rept 108-224, Pt. 2). House passed July 24. Senate passed July 31. President signed Sept. 3, 2003.

PL 108-78 (HR 2739) Implement the United States-Singapore Free Trade Agreement. Introduced by DeLay on July 15, 2003. Ways and Means reported July 21 (H Rept 108-225, Pt. 1). House Judiciary reported July 22 (H Rept 108-225, Pt. 2). House passed July 24. Senate passed July 31. President signed Sept. 3, 2003.

PL 108-79 (S 1435) Provide for an analysis of the incidence and effects of prison rape in federal, state, and local institutions and provide information, resources, recommendations, and funding to protect individuals from prison rape. Introduced by Sessions on July 21, 2003. Senate passed July 21. House passed July 25. President signed Sept. 4, 2003.

PL 108-80 (HR 1668) Designate the building located at 101 North Fifth St. in Muskogee, Okla., as the "Ed Edmondson United States Courthouse." Introduced by CARSON, D-Okla., on April 8, 2003. House Transportation reported July 17 (H Rept 108-217). House passed, under suspension of the rules, Sept. 3. Senate passed Sept. 9. President signed Sept. 17, 2003.

PL 108-81 (HR 13) Reauthorize the Museum and Library Services Act. Introduced by Hoekstra, R-Mich., on Jan. 7, 2003. House Education and the Workforce Committee reported Feb. 25 (H Rept 108-16). House passed March 6. Senate passed, with amendment, Aug. 1. House agreed to Senate amendments, under suspension of the rules, Sept. 16. President signed Sept. 25, 2003.

PL 108-82 (HR 3161) Ratify the authority of the Federal Trade Commission to establish a "do not call" registry. Introduced by Tauzin, R-La., on Sept. 24, 2003. House passed Sept. 25. Senate passed Sept. 25. President signed Sept. 29, 2003.

PL 108-83 (HR 2657) Make appropriations for the legislative branch for the fiscal year ending Sept. 30, 2004. Introduced by Kingston, R-Ga., on July 1, 2003. House Appropriations reported July 1 (H Rept 108-186). House passed July 9. Senate passed, with amendments, July 11. Conference report filed in the House on Sept. 18 (H Rept 108-279). House agreed to conference report Sept. 24. Senate agreed to conference report Sept. 24. President signed Sept. 30, 2003.

PL 108-84 (H J Res 69) Make continuing appropriations for fiscal 2004. Introduced by Young, R-Fla., on Sept. 24, 2003. House passed Sept. 25. Senate passed Sept. 25. President signed Sept. 30, 2003.

PL 108-85 (S 520) Authorize the secretary of the Interior to convey certain facilities to the Fremont-Madison Irrigation District in Idaho. Introduced by Crapo, R-Idaho, on March 5, 2003. Senate Energy and Natural Resources reported June 9 (S Rept 108-62). Senate passed June 16. House passed, under suspension of the rules, Sept. 16. President signed Sept. 30, 2003.

PL 108-86 (S 678) Require postmasters and postmasters' organizations to be included in the process for the development and planning of certain U.S. Postal Service policies, schedules and programs. Introduced by Akaka, D-Hawaii, on March 20, 2003. Senate Governmental Affairs reported July 25 (S Rept 108-112). Senate passed, with amendment, July 29. House passed, under suspension of the rules, Sept. 16. President signed Sept. 30, 2003.

PL 108-87 (HR 2658) Make appropriations for the Department of Defense for the fiscal year ending Sept. 30, 2004. Introduced by Lewis, R-Calif., on July 2, 2003. House Appropriations reported July 2 (H Rept 108-187). House passed, with amendment, July 8. Senate passed, with amendments, July 17. Conference report filed in the House on Sept. 24 (H Rept 108-283). House agreed to the conference report Sept. 24. Senate agreed to the conference report Sept. 25. President signed Sept. 30, 2003.

PL 108-88 (HR 3087) Provide an extension of highway, highway safety, motor carrier safety, transit and other programs funded out of the Highway Trust Fund pending enactment of a law reauthorizing the Transportation Equity Act for the 21st Century. Introduced by Young, R-Alaska, on Sept. 16, 2003. House passed, amended, under suspension of the rules, Sept. 24. Senate passed Sept. 26. President signed Sept. 30, 2003.

PL 108-89 (HR 3146) Extend the Temporary Assistance for Needy Families block grant program and certain tax and trade programs. Introduced by Thomas, R-Calif., on Sept. 23, 2003. House passed, amended, under suspension of the rules, Sept. 24. Senate passed, with amendment, Sept. 30. House agreed to Senate amendment, Sept. 30. President signed Oct. 1, 2003.

PL 108-90 (HR 2555) Make appropriations for the Department of Homeland Security for the fiscal year ending Sept. 30, 2004. Introduced by Rogers, R-Ky., on June 23, 2003. House Appropriations reported June 23 (H Rept 108-169). House passed, with amendments, June 24. Senate Appropriations reported, amended, July 10 (S Rept 108-86). Senate passed, with amendments, July 24. Conference report filed in the House on Sept. 23 (H Rept 108-280). House agreed to the conference report Sept. 24. Senate agreed to the conference report Sept. 24. President signed Oct. 1, 2003.

PL 108-91 (HR 659) Amend Section 242 of the National Housing Act regarding the requirements for mortgage insurance for hospitals. Introduced by Ney, R-Ohio, on Feb. 11, 2003. House Financial Services reported March 6 (H Rept 108-27). House passed, amended, under suspension of the rules, March 12. Senate Banking, Housing and Urban Affairs discharged. Senate passed, with an amendment, Sept. 2. House agreed to Senate amendments, under suspension of the rules, Sept. 17. President signed Oct. 3, 2003.

PL 108-92 (HR 978) Amend Chapter 84, Title 5 of the U.S. Code to provide that certain federal annuity computations are adjusted by

1 percentage point for periods during which the employee received disability payments. Introduced by J. Davis, R-Va., on Feb. 27, 2003. House passed, under suspension of the rules, Sept. 10. Senate passed Sept. 11. President signed Oct. 3, 2003.

PL 108-93 (S 111) Direct the secretary of the Interior to conduct a special resource study to determine the national significance of the Miami Circle site in Florida as well as the suitability and feasibility of its inclusion in the National Park System as part of Biscayne National Park. Introduced by Graham, D-Fla., on Jan. 9, 2003. Senate Energy and Natural Resources reported, amended, Feb. 11 (S Rept 108-4). Senate passed, with an amendment, March 4. House Resources reported Sept. 11 (H Rept 108-268). House passed, under suspension of the rules, Sept. 23. President signed Oct. 3, 2003.

PL 108-94 (S 233) Direct the secretary of the Interior to conduct a study of Coltsville in Connecticut for potential inclusion in the National Park System. Introduced by Dodd, D-Conn., on Jan. 29, 2003. Senate Energy and Natural Resources reported Feb. 11 (S Rept 108-9). Senate passed March 4. House Resources reported Sept. 3 (H Rept. 108-252). House passed, under suspension of the rules, Sept. 23. President signed Oct. 3, 2003.

PL 108-95 (S 278) Make certain adjustments to the boundaries of the Mount Naomi Wilderness Area. Introduced by Bennett, R-Utah, on Feb. 4, 2003. Senate Energy and Natural Resources reported March 19 (S Rept 108-23). Senate passed April 7. House Resources reported Sept. 3 (H Rept 108-253). House passed, under suspension of the rules, Sept. 23. President signed Oct. 3, 2003.

PL 108-96 (HR 1925) Reauthorize programs under the Runaway and Homeless Youth Act and the Missing Children's Assistance Act. Introduced by Gingrey, R-Ga., on May 1, 2003. House Education and the Workforce reported May 20 (H Rept 108-118). House passed, amended, under suspension of the rules, May 20. Senate Judiciary discharged. Senate passed Sept. 30. President signed Oct. 10, 2003.

PL 108-97 (HR 2826) Designate the facility of the U.S. Postal Service located at 1000 Avenida Sanchez Osorio in Carolina, Puerto Rico, as the "Roberto Clemente Walker Post Office Building." Introduced by Acevedo-Vilá, D-P.R., on July 23, 2003. House passed, under suspension of the rules, Sept. 23. Senate Governmental Affairs discharged. Senate passed Oct. 1. President signed Oct. 10, 2003.

PL 108-98 (S 570) Amend the Higher Education Act of 1965 with respect to the qualifications of foreign schools. Introduced by Ensign, R-Nev., on March 6, 2003. Senate Health, Education, Labor and Pensions discharged. Senate passed July 16. House passed, under suspension of the rules, Sept. 30. President signed Oct. 10, 2003.

PL 108-99 (HR 2152) Amend the Immigration and Nationality Act to extend for an additional five years the special immigrant religious worker program. Introduced by Frank, D-Mass., on May 19, 2003. House Judiciary reported Sept. 16 (H Rept 108-271). House passed, under suspension of the rules, Sept. 17. Senate Judiciary discharged. Senate passed Oct. 3. President signed Oct. 15, 2003.

PL 108-100 (HR 1474) Improve check clearing by use of electronic transactions. Introduced by Hart, R-Pa., on March 27, 2003. House Financial Services Committee reported June 2 (H Rept 108-132). House passed June 5. Senate Banking, Housing and Urban Affairs discharged. Senate passed, amended, June 27. Conference report filed in the House on Oct. 1. House agreed to conference report Oct. 8. Senate agreed to conference report Oct.15. President signed Oct. 28, 2003.

PL 108-101 (HR 1900) Award a congressional gold medal to Jackie Robinson. Introduced by Neal, D-Mass., on April 30, 2003. House passed, under suspension of the rules, Oct. 7. Senate passed Oct. 17. President signed Oct. 29, 2003.

PL 108-102 (HR 3229) Transfer to the Public Printer authority over the individuals responsible for preparing indexes of the Congressional Record. Introduced by Ney, R-Ohio, on Oct. 2, 2003. House passed, under suspension of the rules, Oct. 7. Senate passed Oct. 15. President signed Oct. 29, 2003.

PL 108-103 (S 1591) Redesignate the facility of the U.S. Postal Service located at 48 South Broadway, Nyack, N.Y., as the "Edward O'Grady, Waverly Brown, Peter Paige Post Office Building." Introduced by Schumer, D-N.Y., on Sept. 8, 2003. Senate passed Sept. 25. House passed, under the suspension of the rules, Oct. 20. President signed Oct. 29, 2003.

PL 108-104 (H J Res 75) Make further continuing appropriations for fiscal 2004. Introduced by Young, R-Fla., on Oct. 28, 2003. House passed Oct. 30. Senate passed Oct. 30. President signed Oct. 31, 2003.

PL 108-105 (S 3) Ban the procedure opponents call "partial birth" abortion. Introduced by Santorum, R-Pa., on Feb. 14, 2003. Senate passed, amended, March 13. House passed, with amendments, June 4. Conference report filed in the House Sept. 30 (H Rept 108-288). House agreed to conference report Oct. 2. Senate agreed to conference report Oct. 21. President signed Nov. 5, 2003.

PL 108-106 (HR 3289) Make emergency appropriations for the defense and reconstruction of Iraq and Afghanistan. Introduced by Young, R-Fla., on Oct. 14, 2003. House Appropriations reported Oct. 14 (H Rept 108-312). House passed, with amendments, Oct. 17. Senate passed, with amendments, Oct. 17. Conference report filed in the House on Oct. 30 (H Rept 108-337). House agreed to the conference report Oct. 30. Senate agreed to the conference report Nov. 3. President signed Nov. 6, 2003.

PL 108-107 (H J Res 76) Make further continuing appropriations for fiscal 2004. Introduced by Young, R-Fla., on Nov. 4, 2003. House passed Nov. 5. Senate passed Nov. 7. President signed Nov. 7, 2003.

PL 108-108 (HR 2691) Make appropriations for the Department of the Interior and related agencies for the fiscal year ending Sept. 30, 2004. Introduced by Taylor, R-N.C., on July 10, 2003. House Appropriations reported July 10 (H Rept 108-195). House passed, with amendment, July 17. Senate passed, with amendments, Sept. 23. Conference report filed in the House on Oct. 28 (H Rept 108-330). House agreed to the conference report Oct. 30. Senate agreed to the conference report Nov. 3. President signed Nov. 10, 2003.

PL 108-109 (HR 1516) Provide for the expansion of the national cemetery system. Introduced by Gerlach, R-Pa., on March 31, 2003. House Veterans' Affairs reported, amended, July 10 (H Rept 108-199). House passed, under suspension of the rules, July 21. Senate Veterans Affairs reported, amended, Oct. 14 (S Rept 108-164). Senate passed, with amendments, Oct. 17. House agreed to Senate amendments, under suspension of the rules, Oct. 29. President signed Nov. 11, 2003.

PL 108-110 (HR 1610) Redesignate the facility of the U.S. Postal Service located at 120 East Ritchie Ave. in Marceline, Mo., as the "Walt Disney Post Office Building." Introduced by Graves, R-Mo., on April 3, 2003. House passed, under suspension of the rules, June 9.

Senate Governmental Affairs reported Oct. 27 (no written report). Senate passed Oct. 29. President signed Nov. 11, 2003.

PL 108-111 (HR 1882) Designate the facility of the U.S. Postal Service located at 440 South Orange Blossom Trail in Orlando, Fla., as the "Arthur 'Pappy' Kennedy Post Office." Introduced by Brown, D-Fla., on April 30, 2003. House passed, under suspension of the rules, Sept. 30. Senate Governmental Affairs reported Oct. 27 (no written report). Senate passed Oct. 29. President signed Nov. 11, 2003.

PL 108-112 (HR 2075) Designate the facility of the U.S. Postal Service located at 1905 West Blue Heron Blvd. in West Palm Beach, Fla., as the "Judge Edward Rogers Post Office Building." Introduced by Hastings, D-Fla., on May 13, 2003. House passed, under suspension of the rules, Sept. 30. Senate Governmental Affairs reported Oct. 27 (no written report). Senate passed Oct. 29. President signed Nov. 11, 2003.

PL 108-113 (HR 2254) Designate the facility of the U.S. Postal Service located at 1101 Colorado St. in Boulder City, Nev., as the "Bruce Woodbury Post Office Building." Introduced by Porter, R-Nev., on May 22, 2003. House passed, under suspension of the rules, June 16. Senate Governmental Affairs reported Oct. 27 (no written report). Senate passed Oct. 29. President signed Nov. 11, 2003.

PL 108-114 (HR 2309) Designate the facility of the U.S. Postal Service located at 2300 Redondo Ave. in Long Beach, Calif., as the "Stephen Horn Post Office Building." Introduced by Millender-McDonald, D-Calif., on June 3, 2003. House passed, amended, under suspension of the rules, Sept. 3. Senate Governmental Affairs reported Oct. 27 (no written report). Senate passed Oct. 29. President signed Nov. 11, 2003.

PL 108-115 (HR 2328) Designate the facility of the U.S. Postal Service located at 2001 East Willard St. in Philadelphia as the "Robert A. Borski Post Office Building." Introduced by Hoeffel, D-Pa., on June 4, 2003. House passed, under suspension of the rules, July 21. Senate Governmental Affairs reported Oct. 27 (no written report). Senate passed Oct. 29. President signed Nov. 11, 2003.

PL 108-116 (HR 2396) Designate the facility of the U.S. Postal Service located at 1210 Highland Ave. in Duarte, Calif., as the "Francisco A. Martinez Flores Post Office." Introduced by Solis, D-Calif., on June 9, 2003. House passed, under suspension of the rules, July 8. Senate Governmental Affairs reported Oct. 27 (no written report). Senate passed Oct. 29. President signed Nov. 11, 2003.

PL 108-117 (HR 2452) Designate the facility of the U.S. Postal Service located at 339 Hicksville Road in Bethpage, N.Y., as the "Brian C. Hickey Post Office Building." Introduced by King, R-N.Y., on June 12, 2003. House passed, under suspension of the rules, Oct. 8. Senate Governmental Affairs reported Oct. 27 (no written report). Senate passed Oct. 29. President signed Nov. 11, 2003.

PL 108-118 (HR 2533) Designate the facility of the U.S. Postal Service located at 10701 Abercorn St. in Savannah, Ga., as the "J.C. Lewis Jr. Post Office Building." Introduced by Kingston, R-Ga., on June 19, 2003. House passed, under suspension of the rules, Sept. 23. Senate Governmental Affairs reported Oct. 27 (no written report). Senate passed Oct. 29. President signed Nov. 11, 2003.

PL 108-119 (HR 2746) Designate the facility of the U.S. Postal Service located at 141 Weston St. in Hartford, Conn., as the "Barbara B. Kennelly Post Office Building." Introduced by Larson, D-Conn., on July 15, 2003. House Government Reform discharged. House

passed July 25. Senate Governmental Affairs reported Oct. 27 (no written report). Senate passed Oct. 29. President signed Nov. 11, 2003.

PL 108-120 (HR 3011) Designate the facility of the U.S. Postal Service located at 135 East Olive Ave. in Burbank, Calif., as the "Bob Hope Post Office Building." Introduced by Schiff, D-Calif., on Sept. 4, 2003. House passed, under suspension of the rules, Sept. 30. Senate Governmental Affairs reported Oct. 27 (no written report). Senate passed Oct. 29. President signed Nov. 11, 2003.

PL 108-121 (HR 3365) Increase the death gratuity payable with respect to deceased members of the armed forces and provide additional tax relief for members of the armed forces and their families. Introduced by Renzi, R-Ariz., on Oct. 21, 2003. House passed, under suspension of the rules, Oct. 29. Senate passed, with amendments, Nov. 3, and amended further Nov. 4. House agreed to Senate amendments, under suspension of the rules, Nov. 5. President signed Nov. 11, 2003.

PL 108-122 (H J Res 52) Recognize the Dr. Samuel D. Harris National Museum as the official national museum of dentistry in the United States. Introduced by Cummings, D-Md., on April 11, 2003. House passed, under suspension of the rules, Oct. 7. Senate passed Oct. 23. President signed Nov. 11, 2003.

PL 108-123 (S 926) Increase the annual and aggregate limits on student loan repayments by federal agencies. Introduced by Voinovich, R-Ohio, on April 28, 2003. Senate Governmental Affairs reported July 21 (S Rept 108-109). Senate passed July 30. House passed, under suspension of the rules, Oct. 28. President signed Nov. 11, 2003.

PL 108-124 (HR 1883) Designate the facility of the U.S. Postal Service located at 1601-1 Main St. in Jacksonville, Fla., as the "Eddie Mae Steward Post Office." Introduced by Brown, D-Fla., on April 30, 2003. House passed, under suspension of the rules, Oct. 15. Senate Governmental Affairs reported Oct. 27 (no written report). Senate passed Oct. 29. President signed Nov. 11, 2003.

PL 108-125 (S 470) Extend the authority for the construction of a memorial to Martin Luther King Jr. Introduced by Sarbanes, D-Md., on Feb. 27, 2003. Senate Energy and Natural Resources reported, amended, July 11 (S Rept 108-90). Senate passed July 17. House passed, under suspension of the rules, Oct. 28. President signed Nov. 11, 2003.

PL 108-126 (HR 1442) Authorize the design and construction of a visitor center for the Vietnam Veterans Memorial. Introduced by Pombo, R-Calif., on March 26, 2003. House Resources reported, amended, Oct. 2 (H Rept 108-295). House passed, under suspension of the rules, Oct. 15. Senate passed, with amendments, Nov. 5. House agreed to Senate amendments, under suspension of the rules, Nov. 6. President signed Nov. 17, 2003.

PL 108-127 (HR 3288) Make technical corrections to Title XXI of the Social Security Act with respect to the definition of qualifying state. Introduced by Tauzin, R-La., on Oct. 14, 2003. House passed, under suspension of the rules, Oct. 20. Senate passed Oct. 31. President signed Nov. 17, 2003.

PL 108-128 (S 677) Revise the boundary of the Black Canyon of the Gunnison National Park and Gunnison Gorge National Conservation Area in Colorado. Introduced by Campbell, R-Colo., on March 20, 2003. Senate Energy and Natural Resources reported, amended, July 11 (S Rept 108-96). Senate passed, amended, July 17. House Resources reported Nov. 4 (H Rept 108-344). House passed, under suspension of the rules, Nov. 4. President signed Nov. 17, 2003.

PL 108-129 (S 924) Authorize the exchange of lands between an Alaska Native Village Corporation and the Department of the Interior. Introduced by Murkowski, R-Alaska, on April 11, 2003. Senate Energy and Natural Resources reported, amended, July 11 (S Rept 108-97). Senate passed, amended, July 17. House Resources reported Nov. 4 (H Rept 108-345). House passed, under suspension of the rules, Nov. 4. President signed Nov. 17, 2003.

PL 108-130 (S 313) Amend the Federal Food, Drug, and Cosmetic Act to establish a program of fees relating to animal drugs. Introduced by Ensign, R-Nev., on Feb. 5, 2003. Senate Health, Education, Labor and Pensions reported, amended, May 21 (S Rept 108-51). Senate passed, with an amendment, June 3. House passed, with amendment, under suspension of the rules, Nov. 4. Senate agreed to House amendment Nov. 7. President signed Nov. 18, 2003.

PL 108-131 (HR 274) Authorize the secretary of the Interior to acquire the property in Cecil County, Md., known as Garrett Island for inclusion in the Blackwater National Wildlife Refuge. Introduced by Gilchrest, R-Md., on Jan. 8, 2003. House passed, under suspension of the rules, April 29. Senate Environment and Public Works reported Oct. 30 (S Rept 108-180). Senate passed Nov. 7. President signed Nov. 22, 2003.

PL 108-132 (HR 2559) Make appropriations for military construction, family housing and base realignment and closure for the Department of Defense for the fiscal year ending Sept. 30, 2004. Introduced by Knollenberg, R-Mich., on June 23, 2003. House Appropriations reported June 23 (H Rept 108-173). House passed June 26. Senate passed, with an amendment, July 11. Conference report filed in the House on Nov. 4 (H Rept 108-342). House agreed to the conference report Nov. 5. Senate agreed to the conference report Nov. 12. President signed Nov. 22, 2003.

PL 108-133 (HR 3054) Permit military service previously performed by members and former members of the Metropolitan Police Department of the District of Columbia, the Fire Department of the District of Columbia, the United States Park Police and the United States Secret Service to count as creditable service for purposes of calculating retirement annuities. Introduced by T. Davis, R-Va., on Sept. 10, 2003. House passed, amended, under suspension of the rules, Oct. 8. Senate Governmental Affairs discharged. Senate passed Nov. 11. President signed Nov. 22, 2003.

PL 108-134 (HR 3232) Reauthorize certain school lunch and child nutrition programs through March 31, 2004. Introduced by Castle, R-Del., on Oct. 2, 2003. House passed, amended, under suspension of the rules, Oct. 28. Senate Agriculture, Nutrition and Forestry discharged. Senate passed Nov. 6. President signed Nov. 22, 2003.

PL 108-135 (H J Res 79) Make further continuing appropriations for fiscal 2004. Introduced by Young, R-Fla., on Nov. 21, 2003. House Appropriations discharged. House passed Nov. 21. Senate passed Nov. 21. President signed Nov. 22, 2003.

PL 108-136 (HR 1588) Authorize appropriations for the fiscal year ending Sept. 30, 2004, for military activities of the Department of Defense, for military construction, and for defense activities of the Department of Energy and prescribe military personnel strengths for fiscal 2004. Introduced by Hunter, R-Calif., on April 3, 2003. House Armed Services reported, amended, May 16 (H Rept 108-106). House

passed, with amendments, May 22. Senate passed, amended, June 4. Conference report filed in the House on Nov. 7 (H Rept 108-354). House agreed to the conference report Nov. 7. Senate agreed to the conference report Nov. 12. President signed Nov. 24, 2003.

PL 108-137 (HR 2754) Make appropriations for energy and water development for the fiscal year ending Sept. 30, 2004. Introduced by Hobson, R-Ohio, on July 16, 2003. House Appropriations reported July 16 (H Rept 108-212). House passed, amended, July 18. Senate passed, amended, Sept. 16. Conference report filed Nov. 7 (H Rept 108-357). House agreed to the conference report Nov. 18. Senate agreed to the conference report Nov. 18. President signed Dec. 1, 2003.

PL 108-138 (S 1066) Correct a technical error from Unit T-07 of the John H. Chafee Coastal Barrier Resources System. Introduced by Hutchison, R-Texas, on May 14, 2003. Senate Environment and Public Works reported, amended, Oct. 29 (S Rept 108-177). Senate passed, amended, Nov. 7. House passed, under suspension of the rules, Nov. 17. President signed Dec. 1, 2003.

PL 108-139 (S J Res 18) Commend the Inspectors General for their efforts to prevent and detect waste, fraud, abuse and mismanagement, and to promote economy, efficiency and effectiveness in the federal government during the past 25 years. Introduced by Collins, R-Maine, on Sept. 29, 2003. Senate Governmental Affairs discharged. Senate passed Oct. 14. House passed, under suspension of the rules, Nov. 17. President signed Dec. 1, 2003.

PL 108-140 (S J Res 22) Recognize the Agricultural Research Service of the Department of Agriculture for 50 years of outstanding service to the nation. Introduced by Cochran, R-Miss., on Nov. 3. Senate passed Nov. 3. House passed, under suspension of the rules, Nov. 17. President signed Dec. 1, 2003.

PL 108-141 (S 1590) Redesignate the facility of the U.S. Postal Service located at 315 Empire Blvd. in Crown Heights, Brooklyn, N.Y., as the "James E. Davis Post Office Building." Introduced by Schumer, D-N.Y., on Sept. 8, 2003. Senate Governmental Affairs reported Oct. 27 (no written report). Senate passed Oct. 29. House passed, under suspension of the rules, Nov. 19. President signed Dec. 1, 2003.

PL 108-142 (S 254) Revise the boundary of the Kaloko-Honokohau National Historical Park in Hawaii. Introduced by Akaka, D-Hawaii, on Jan. 30, 2003. Senate Energy and Natural Resources reported Feb. 10 (S Rept 108-10). Senate passed March 4. House Resources reported Oct. 2 (H Rept 108-296). House passed, under suspension of the rules, Nov. 18. President signed Dec. 2, 2003.

PL 108-143 (S 867) Designate the facility of the U.S. Postal Service located at 710 Wicks Lane in Billings, Mont., as the "Ronald Reagan Post Office Building." Introduced by Burns, R-Mont., on April 10, 2003. Senate Governmental Affairs reported June 20 (no written report). Senate passed June 25. House passed, under suspension of the rules, Nov. 18. President signed Dec. 2, 2003.

PL 108-144 (S 1718) Designate the facility of the U.S. Postal Service located at 3710 West 73rd Terrace in Prairie Village, Kan., as the "Senator James B. Pearson Post Office." Introduced by Roberts, R-Kan., on Oct. 14, 2003. Senate Governmental Affairs reported Oct. 27 (no written report). Senate passed Oct. 29. House passed, under suspension of the rules, Nov. 18. President signed Dec. 2, 2003.

PL 108-145 (HR 3182) Reauthorize the adoption incentive payments program under Part E of Title IV of the Social Security Act. Introduced by Camp, R-Mich,. on Sept. 25, 2003. House passed, under suspension of the rules, Oct. 8. Senate Finance discharged. Senate passed Nov. 14. President signed Dec. 2, 2003.

PL 108-146 (HR 23) Amend the Housing and Community Development Act of 1974 to authorize communities to use community development block grant funds for construction of tornado-safe shelters in mobile home parks. Introduced by Bachus, R-Ala., on Jan. 7, 2003. House Financial Services reported, amended, June 12 (H Rept 108-151). House passed, amended, under suspension of the rules, July 21. Senate Banking, Housing and Urban Affairs discharged. Senate passed Nov. 18. President signed Dec. 3, 2003.

PL 108-147 (HR 1683) Increase, effective Dec. 1, 2003, the rates of disability compensation for veterans with service-connected disabilities and the rates of dependency and indemnity compensation for survivors of certain service-connected disabled veterans. Introduced by C. Smith, R-N.J., on April 9, 2003. House Veterans' Affairs reported May 19 (H Rept 108-108). House passed, under suspension of the rules, May 22. Senate Veterans' Affairs discharged. Senate passed Nov. 21. President signed Dec. 3, 2003.

PL 108-148 (HR 1904) Reduce the number of forest fires through the application of various methods of proper hazardous fuel burning in order to protect watersheds and other types of lands. Introduced by McInnis, R-Colo., on May 1, 2003. House Agriculture reported May 9 (H Rept 108-96, Pt. 1). House Resources discharged. House Judiciary reported May 16 (H Rept 108-96, Pt. 2). House passed May 20. Senate Agriculture, Nutrition and Forestry reported, amended, July 31 (S Rept 108-121). Senate passed, with amendments, Oct. 30. Conference report filed in the House on Nov. 20 (H Rept 108-386). House agreed to the conference report Nov. 21. Senate agreed to the conference report Nov. 21. President signed Dec. 3, 2003.

PL 108-149 (HR 2744) Designate the facility of the U.S. Postal Service located at 514 17th St. in Moline, Ill., as the "David Bybee Post Office Building." Introduced by Evans, D-Ill., on July 15, 2003. House passed, under suspension of the rules, Oct. 28. Senate Governmental Affairs discharged. Senate passed Nov. 18. President signed Dec. 3, 2003.

PL 108-150 (HR 3175) Designate the facility of the U.S. Postal Service located at 2650 Cleveland Ave., NW, in Canton, Ohio, as the "Richard D. Watkins Post Office Building." Introduced by Regula, R-Ohio, on Sept. 24, 2003. House passed, under suspension of the rules, Oct. 28. Senate Governmental Affairs discharged. Senate passed Nov. 18. President signed Dec. 3, 2003.

PL 108-151 (HR 3379) Designate the facility of the U.S. Postal Service located at 3210 East 10th St. in Bloomington, Ind., as the "Francis X. McCloskey Post Office Building." Introduced by Hill, D-Ind., on Oct. 28, 2003. House passed, under suspension of the rules, Nov. 5. Senate Governmental Affairs discharged. Senate passed Nov. 18. President signed Dec. 3, 2003.

PL 108-152 (S 117) Authorize the secretary of Agriculture to sell or exchange certain land in Florida as it relates to national forests. Introduced by Graham, D-Fla., on Jan. 9, 2003. Senate Energy and Natural Resources reported Feb. 11 (S Rept 108-5). Senate passed March 4. House passed, under suspension of the rules, Nov. 19. President signed Dec. 3, 2003.

PL 108-153 (S 189) Authorize appropriations for nanoscience, nanoengineering, and nanotechnology research. Introduced by Wyden,

D-Ore., on Jan. 16, 2003. Senate Commerce, Science and Transportation reported, amended, Sept. 15 (S Rept 108-147). Senate passed, with amendments, Nov. 18. House passed, under suspension of the rules, Nov. 20. President signed Dec. 3, 2003.

PL 108-154 (S 286) Revise and extend the Birth Defects Prevention Act of 1998. Introduced by Bond, R-Mo., on Feb. 4, 2003. Senate Health, Education, Labor and Pensions Committee reported, amended, Nov. 6 (S Rept 108-188). Senate passed, with an amendment, Nov. 11. House passed, under suspension of the rules, Nov. 20. President signed Dec. 3, 2003.

PL 108-155 (S 650) Amend the Federal Food, Drug, and Cosmetic Act to authorize the Food and Drug Administration to require that license applications for new drugs assess the use of the drug for pediatric patients. Introduced by DeWine, R-Ohio, on March 18, 2003. Senate Health, Education, Labor and Pensions reported, amended, June 27 (S Rept 108-84). Senate passed, with amendments, July 23. House passed, under suspension of the rules, Nov. 19. President signed Dec. 3, 2003.

PL 108-156 (S 1685) Extend and expand the basic pilot program for employment eligibility verification. Introduced by Grassley, R-Iowa, on Sept. 30, 2003. Senate Judiciary reported, amended, Nov. 6 (no written report). Senate passed, with an amendment, Nov. 12. House passed, under suspension of the rules, Nov. 19. President signed Dec. 3, 2003.

PL 108-157 (S 1720) Provide for federal court proceedings in Plano, Texas. Introduced by Cornyn, R-Texas, on Oct. 14, 2003. Senate Judiciary reported, amended, Oct. 30 (no written report). Senate passed, with an amendment, Nov. 4. House passed, under suspension of the rules, Nov. 19. President signed Dec. 3, 2003.

PL 108-158 (S 1824) Amend the Foreign Assistance Act of 1961 to reauthorize the Overseas Private Investment Corporation. Introduced by Lugar, R-Ind., on Nov. 5, 2003. Senate Foreign Relations reported Nov. 11 (S Rept 108-194). Senate passed Nov. 14. House passed, under suspension of the rules, Nov. 19. President signed Dec. 3, 2003.

PL 108-159 (HR 2622) Amend the Fair Credit Reporting Act to prevent identity theft, improve resolution of consumer disputes, improve the accuracy of consumer records, and make improvements in the use of, and consumer access to, credit information. Introduced by Bachus, R-Ala., on June 26, 2003. House Financial Services reported, amended, Sept. 4 (H Rept 108-263). Supplementary report filed Sept. 9 (H Rept 108-263, Pt. 2). House passed, with amendments, Sept. 10. Senate Banking, Housing and Urban Affairs discharged. Senate passed, with an amendment, Nov. 5. Conference report filed in the House on Nov. 21 (H Rept 108-396). House agreed to conference report Nov. 21. Senate agreed to conference report Nov. 22. President signed Dec. 4, 2003.

PL 108-160 (HR 421) Reauthorize the U.S. Institute for Environmental Conflict Resolution. Introduced by Kolbe, R-Ariz., on Jan. 28, 2003. House Resources reported Nov. 17 (H Rept 108-371, Pt. 1). House passed, under suspension of the rules, Nov. 19. Senate passed Nov. 21. President signed Dec. 6, 2003.

PL 108-161 (HR 1367) Authorize the secretary of Agriculture to assist veterinarians with educational loan repayments if they agree to practice in areas where there is a shortage of veterinary services. Introduced by Pickering, R-Miss., on March 19, 2003. House passed, amended, under suspension of the rules, Nov. 17. Senate Committee on Agriculture, Nutrition and Forestry discharged. Senate passed Nov. 24. President signed Dec. 6, 2003.

PL 108-162 (HR 1821) Award a congressional gold medal to Dr. Dorothy Height in recognition of her many contributions to the nation. Introduced by Watson, D-Calif., on April 11, 2003. House passed, under suspension of the rules, Oct. 15. Senate Banking, Housing and Urban Affairs discharged. Senate passed Nov. 21. President signed Dec. 6, 2003.

PL 108-163 (HR 3038) Make technical and conforming amendments to correct the Health Care Safety Net Amendments of 2002. Introduced by Bilirakis, R-Fla., on Sept. 9, 2003. House Energy and Commerce reported Sept. 17 (H Rept 108-275). House passed, under suspension of the rules, Oct. 1. Senate Health, Education, Labor and Pensions discharged. Senate passed Nov. 20. President signed Dec. 6, 2003.

PL 108-164 (HR 3140) Provide for the availability of contact lens prescriptions. Introduced by Burr, R-N.C., on Sept. 23, 2003. House Energy and Commerce reported, amended, Oct. 15 (H Rept 108-318). House passed, under suspension of the rules, Nov. 19. Senate passed Nov. 20. President signed Dec. 6, 2003.

PL 108-165 (HR 3166) Designate the facility of the U.S. Postal Service located at 57 Old Tappan Road in Tappan, N.Y., as the "John G. Dow Post Office Building." Introduced by Engel, D-N.Y., on Sept. 24, 2003. House passed, under suspension of the rules, Nov. 4. Senate passed Nov. 20. President signed Dec. 6, 2003.

PL 108-166 (HR 3185) Designate the facility of the U.S. Postal Service located at 38 Spring St. in Nashua, N.H., as the "Hugh Gregg Post Office Building." Introduced by Bass, R-N.H., on Sept. 25, 2003. House passed, under suspension of the rules, Nov. 17. Senate passed Nov. 20. President signed Dec. 6, 2003.

PL 108-167 (HR 3349) Authorize salary adjustments for United States justices and judges for fiscal 2004. Introduced by Sensenbrenner, R-Wis., on Oct. 20, 2003. House passed, under suspension of the rules, Nov. 5. Senate passed Nov. 21. President signed Dec. 6, 2003.

PL 108-168 (S 579) Reauthorize the National Transportation Safety Board. Introduced by McCain, R-Ariz., on March 7, 2003. Senate Commerce, Science and Transportation reported May 22 (S Rept 108-53). Senate passed, with amendments, Nov. 21. House passed Nov. 22. President signed Dec. 6, 2003.

PL 108-169 (S 1152) Reauthorize the United States Fire Administration. Introduced by McCain, R-Ariz., on May 23, 2003. Senate Commerce, Science and Transportation reported, amended, Aug. 26 (S Rept 108-126). Senate passed, with amendments, Nov. 20. House passed, under suspension of the rules, Nov. 21. President signed Dec. 6, 2003.

PL 108-170 (S 1156) Improve and enhance the provision of health care for veterans and authorize major construction projects for the Department of Veterans Affairs. Introduced by Specter, R-Pa., on May 23, 2003. Senate Veterans' Affairs reported, amended, Nov. 10 (S Rept 108-193). Senate passed, with amendments, Nov. 19. House passed, under suspension of the rules, Nov. 21. President signed Dec. 6, 2003.

PL 108-171 (S 1768) Extend the national flood insurance program. Introduced by Bunning, R-Ky., on Oct. 21, 2003. Senate Bank-

ing, Housing and Urban Affairs discharged. Senate passed Oct. 27. House Financial Services discharged. House passed, with an amendment, Nov. 21. Senate agreed to House amendment, Nov. 24. President signed Dec. 6, 2003.

PL 108-172 (S 1895) Extend temporarily the programs under the Small Business Act and the Small Business Investment Act of 1958 through March 15, 2004. Introduced by Snowe, R-Maine, on Nov. 19, 2003. Senate passed Nov. 19. House passed Nov. 20. President signed Dec. 6, 2003.

PL 108-173 (HR 1) Amend Title XVIII of the Social Security Act to provide for a voluntary prescription drug benefit under the Medicare program and to strengthen and improve the Medicare program. Introduced by Hastert, R-Ill., on June 25, 2003. House passed, with amendments, June 27. Senate passed, with amendments, July 7. Conference report filed in the House on Nov. 21 (H Rept 108-391). House agreed to conference report Nov. 22. Senate agreed to conference report Nov. 25. President signed Dec. 8, 2003.

PL 108-174 (HR 3348) Reauthorize a ban on undetectable firearms. Introduced by Sensenbrenner, R-Wis., on Oct. 20, 2003. House passed, amended, under suspension of the rules, Nov. 5. Senate passed Nov. 25. President signed Dec. 9, 2003.

PL 108-175 (HR 1828) Require the imposition of sanctions against Syria unless the president certifies that Syria is abiding by certain conditions or waives the requirements in the interest of national security. Introduced by Engel, D-N.Y., on April 12, 2003. House International Relations reported, amended, Oct. 15 (H Rept 108-314). House passed, under suspension of the rules, Oct. 15. Senate passed, with an amendment, Nov. 11. House agreed to Senate amendments, under suspension of the rules, Nov. 20. President signed Dec. 12, 2003.

PL 108-176 (HR 2115) Reauthorize programs for the Federal Aviation Administration. Introduced by Young, R-Alaska, on May 15, 2003. House Transportation and Infrastructure reported, amended, June 6 (H Rept 108-143). House passed, with amendments, June 11. Senate passed, with an amendment, June 12. Conference report filed in the House on July 25 (H Rept 108-240). House recommitted the conference report to the conference committee, Oct. 28. New conference report filed in the House on Oct. 29 (H Rept 108-334). House agreed to the conference report Oct. 30. Senate agreed to the conference report Nov. 21. President signed Dec. 12, 2003.

PL 108-177 (HR 2417) Authorize appropriations for fiscal 2004 for intelligence and intelligence-related activities of the U.S. government, the Community Management Account, and the Central Intelligence Agency Retirement and Disability System. Introduced by Goss, R-Fla., on June 11, 2003. House Intelligence reported, amended, June 18 (H Rept 108-163). House passed, with amendments, June 27. Senate passed, with an amendment, July 31. Conference report filed in the House on Nov. 19 (H Rept 108-381). House agreed to the conference report Nov. 20. Senate agreed to the conference report Nov. 21. President signed Dec. 13, 2003.

PL 108-178 (HR 1437) Make technical changes in the U.S. Code in relation to public buildings, property and works. Introduced by Sensenbrenner, R-Wis., on March 25, 2003. House Judiciary reported May 15 (H Rept 108-103). House passed, under suspension of the rules, July 21. Senate Judiciary discharged. Senate passed Nov. 25. President signed Dec. 15, 2003.

PL 108-179 (HR 1813) Amend the Torture Victims Relief Act of 1998 to authorize appropriations to assist domestic and foreign centers and programs for the treatment of victims of torture. Introduced by C. Smith, R-N.J., on April 11, 2003. House International Relations reported Sept. 4 (H Rept 108-261, Pt. 1). House Energy and Commerce reported Sept. 17 (H Rept 108-261, Pt. 2). House passed, under suspension of the rules, Nov. 19. Senate passed Nov. 25. President signed Dec. 15, 2003.

PL 108-180 (HR 3287) Award congressional gold medals posthumously in behalf of Rev. Joseph A. DeLaine, Harry and Eliza Briggs, and Levi Pearson in recognition of their contributions to the nation as pioneers in the effort to desegregate public schools that led directly to the landmark desegregation case of *Brown v. the Board of Education*. Introduced by Clyburn, D-S.C., on Oct. 10, 2003. House passed, under suspension of the rules, Nov. 18. Senate passed Nov. 25. President signed Dec. 15, 2003.

PL 108-181 (H J Res 80) Appoint the day for the convening of the second session of the 108th Congress. Introduced by DeLay, R-Texas, on Nov. 21, 2003. House passed Nov. 22. Senate passed Nov. 25. President signed Dec. 15, 2003.

PL 108-182 (S 459) Ensure that a public safety officer who suffers a fatal heart attack or stroke while on duty will be presumed to have died in the line of duty for purposes of public safety officer survivor benefits. Introduced by Leahy, D-Vt., on Feb. 26, 2003. Senate Judiciary discharged. Senate passed May 16. House passed, with an amendment, Nov. 22. Senate agreed to House amendment, Nov. 25. President signed Dec. 15, 2003.

PL 108-183 (HR 2297) Amend Title 38, U.S. Code, to improve benefits under laws administered by the secretary of Veterans Affairs. Introduced by C. Smith, R-N.J., on June 2, 2003. House Veterans' Affairs reported, amended, July 15 (H Rept 108-211). House passed, amended, under suspension of the rules, Oct. 8. Senate Veterans' Affairs discharged. Senate passed, with an amendment, Nov. 19. House agreed to Senate amendments, under suspension of the rules, Nov. 20. President signed Dec. 16, 2003.

PL 108-184 (HR 3491) Establish within the Smithsonian Institution the National Museum of African American History and Culture. Introduced by Lewis, D-Ga., on Nov. 17, 2003. House passed Nov. 19. Senate passed Nov. 20. President signed Dec. 16, 2003.

PL 108-185 (H J Res 82) Make further continuing appropriations for fiscal 2004. Introduced by Young, R-Fla., on Dec. 8, 2003. House Appropriations discharged. House passed Dec. 8. Senate passed Dec. 9. President signed Dec. 16, 2003.

PL 108-186 (S 811) Support certain housing proposals in the fiscal 2003 budget for the federal government, including the down payment assistance initiative under the Home Investment Partnership Act. Introduced by Allard, R-Colo., on April 8, 2003. Senate Banking, Housing and Urban Affairs discharged. Senate passed, with an amendment, Nov. 24. House passed Dec. 8. President signed Dec. 16, 2003.

PL 108-187 (S 877) Regulate interstate commerce by imposing limitations and penalties on the transmission of unsolicited commercial electronic mail via the Internet. Introduced by Burns, R-Mont., on April 10, 2003. Senate Commerce, Science and Transportation reported, amended, July 16 (S Rept 108-102). Senate passed, with amendments, Oct. 22. House passed, with additional amendment,

under suspension of the rules, Nov. 22. Senate agreed to House amendments, with an amendment, Nov. 25. House agreed to the Senate amendment Dec. 8. President signed Dec. 16, 2003.

PL 108-188 (H J Res 63) Approve the Compact of Free Association, as amended, between the U.S. government and the government of Micronesia, and the Compact of Free Association, as amended, between the U.S. government and the government of the Republic of the Marshall Islands, and appropriate funds to carry out the amended compacts. Introduced by Leach, R-Iowa, on July 8, 2003. House International Relations reported, amended, Sept. 4 (H Rept 108-262, Pt. 1). House Resources reported, amended, Sept. 15 (H Rept 108-262, Pt. 2). House Judiciary reported, amended, Sept. 15 (H Rept 108-262, Pt. 3). House passed, amended, under suspension of the rules, Oct. 28. Senate passed, with an amendment, Nov. 6. House agreed to Senate amendment, under suspension of the rules, Nov. 20. President signed Dec. 17, 2003.

PL 108-189 (HR 100) Revise the Soldiers' and Sailors' Civil Relief Act of 1940 and improve the benefits and protections for regular and reserve members of the armed forces deployed or mobilized in the interest of national security. Introduced by Smith, R-N.J., on Jan. 7, 2003. House Veterans' Affairs reported, amended, April 30 (H Rept 108-81). House passed, amended, under suspension of the rules, May 7. Senate Veterans' Affairs discharged. Senate passed, with an amendment, Nov. 21. House agreed to Senate amendment, Dec. 8. President signed Dec. 19, 2003.

PL 108-190 (HR 622) Provide for the exchange of certain lands in the Coconino and Tonto National Forests in Arizona. Introduced by Renzi, R-Ariz., on Feb. 5, 2003. House passed, under suspension of the rules, April 1. Senate Energy and Natural Resources reported Aug. 26 (S Rept 108-137). Senate passed, with amendments, Nov. 24. House agreed to Senate amendments, Dec. 8. President signed Dec. 19, 2003.

PL 108-191 (HR 1006) Amend the Lacey Act Amendments of 1981 to further the conservation of certain wildlife species. Introduced by McKeon, R-Calif., on Feb. 27, 2003. House Resources Committee reported, amended, Sept. 11 (H Rept 108-269). House passed, under suspension of the rules, Nov. 19. Senate passed, with amendments, Nov. 24. House agreed to Senate amendments, Dec. 8. President signed Dec. 19, 2003.

PL 108-192 (HR 1012) Establish the Carter G. Woodson Home National Historic Site in the District of Columbia. Introduced by Norton, D-D.C., on Feb. 27, 2003. House passed, under suspension of the rules, May 14. Senate Energy and Natural Resources reported, amended, Aug. 26 (S Rept 108-138). Senate passed, with an amendment, Nov. 24. House agreed to Senate amendment, Dec. 8. President signed Dec. 19, 2003.

PL 108-193 (HR 2620) Authorize appropriations for fiscal years 2004 and 2005 for the Trafficking Victims Protection Act of 2000. Introduced by Smith, R-N.J., on June 26, 2003. House International Relations reported, amended, Sept. 5 (H Rept 108-264, Pt. 1). House Judiciary reported, amended, Sept. 29 (H Rept 108-264, Pt. 2). House passed, under suspension of the rules, Nov. 5. Senate passed Dec. 9. President signed Dec. 19, 2003.

PL 108-194 (S 686) Provide assistance for poison prevention and stabilize the funding of regional poison control centers. Introduced by DeWine, R-Ohio, on March 21, 2003. Senate Health, Education,

Labor and Pensions reported, amended, June 11 (S Rept 108-68). Senate passed, amended, June 20. House passed, under suspension of the rules, Nov. 20. Senate agreed to House amendment, Dec. 9. President signed Dec. 19, 2003.

PL 108-195 (S 1680) Reauthorize the Defense Production Act of 1950. Introduced by Shelby, R-Ala., on Sept. 30, 2003. Senate Banking, Housing and Urban Affairs reported Sept. 30 (S Rept 108-156). Senate passed, with an amendment, Sept. 30. House passed, with an amendment, under suspension of the rules, Oct. 15. Senate agreed to House amendment, with an amendment, Nov. 21. House agreed to the Senate amendment Dec. 8. President signed Dec. 19, 2003.

PL 108-196 (S 1683) Provide for a report on the parity of pay and benefits among federal law enforcement officers and establish an exchange program between federal law enforcement employees and state and local law enforcement employees. Introduced by Voinovich, R-Ohio, on Sept. 30, 2003. Senate Governmental Affairs reported Nov. 22 (S Rept 108-207). Senate passed Nov. 25. House Government Reform discharged. House passed Dec. 8. President signed Dec. 19, 2003.

PL 108-197 (S 1929) Amend the Employee Retirement Income Security Act of 1974 and the Public Health Service Act to extend the mental health benefits parity provisions for an additional year. Introduced by Gregg, R-N.H., on Nov. 21, 2003. Senate passed Nov. 21. House passed Dec. 8. President signed Dec. 19, 2003.

PL 108-198 (S 1947) Prohibit financial institutions from offering credit to a financial institution examiner. Introduced by Leahy, D-Vt., on Nov. 24, 2003. Senate passed Nov. 24. House Judiciary discharged. House passed Dec. 8. President signed Dec. 19, 2003.

108th Congress–2004

PL 108-199 (HR 2673) Make consolidated appropriations for the fiscal year ending Sept. 30, 2004. Introduced by Bonilla, R-Texas, on July 9, 2003. House Appropriations reported July 9 (H Rept 108-193). House passed, amended, July 14. Senate passed, with amendments, Nov. 6. Conference report filed in the House Nov. 25 (H Rept 108-401). House agreed to the conference report Dec. 8. Senate agreed to the conference report Jan. 22, 2004. President signed Jan. 23, 2004.

PL 108-200 (HR 2264) Authorize appropriations for fiscal 2004 to carry out the Congo Basin Forest Partnership program. Introduced by Shaw, R-Fla., on May 22, 2003. House passed, under suspension of the rules, Oct. 7. Senate Foreign Relations discharged. Senate passed, with amendments, Dec. 9. House agreed to Senate amendments, under suspension of the rules, Feb. 3, 2004. President signed Feb. 13, 2004.

PL 108-201 (S 610) Amend the provisions of Title 5, U.S. Code, to provide for workforce flexibilities and certain federal personnel provisions relating to the National Aeronautics and Space Administration. Introduced by Voinovich, R-Ohio, on March 13, 2003. Senate Governmental Affairs reported, amended, July 28 (S Rept 108-113). Senate passed, amended, Nov. 24. House passed Jan. 28, 2004. President signed Feb. 24, 2004.

PL 108-202 (HR 3850) Provide an extension of highway, highway safety, motor carrier safety, transit and other programs funded out of the Highway Trust Fund, pending enactment of a law reauthorizing

the Transportation Equity Act for the 21st Century (TEA-21). Introduced by Young, R-Alaska, on Feb. 26, 2004. House Resources, Science, Transportation and Infrastructure, and Ways and Means discharged. House passed Feb. 26. Senate passed Feb. 27. President signed Feb. 29, 2004.

PL 108-203 (HR 743) Amend the Social Security Act and the Internal Revenue Code of 1986 to provide additional safeguards for Social Security and Supplemental Security Income beneficiaries with representative payees. Introduced by Shaw, R-Fla., on Feb. 12, 2003. House defeated, under suspension of the rules, March 5. House Ways and Means reported, amended, March 24 (H Rept 108-46). House passed April 2. Senate Finance reported, with amendment, Oct. 29 (S Rept 108-176). Senate passed, with amendment, Dec. 9. House agreed to Senate amendment Feb. 11, 2004. President signed March 2, 2004.

PL 108-204 (S 523) Make technical corrections to law relating to Native Americans. Introduced by Campbell, R-Colo., on March 5, 2003. Senate Indian Affairs reported, amended, May 15 (S Rept 108-49). Senate passed, amended, July 30. House Resources reported Nov. 17 (H Rept 108-374, Pt. 1). House Agriculture discharged. House passed, under suspension of the rules, Feb. 11, 2004. President signed March 2, 2004.

PL 108-205 (HR 3915) Provide for an additional temporary extension of programs under the Small Business Act and the Small Business Investment Act of 1958. Introduced by Manzullo, R-Ill., on March 9, 2004. House passed, amended, under suspension of the rules, March 10. Senate passed March 12. President signed March 15, 2004.

PL 108-206 (S 714) Provide for the conveyance of a small parcel of Bureau of Land Management land in Douglas County, Ore., to the county to improve management of and recreational access to the Oregon Dunes National Recreation Area. Introduced by Wyden, D-Ore., on March 26, 2003. Senate Energy and Natural Resources reported, amended, Aug. 26 (S Rept 108-135). Senate passed, with amendments, Nov. 24. House passed, under suspension of the rules, Feb. 24, 2004. President signed March 15, 2004.

PL 108-207 (S 2136) Extend the final report and termination date of the National Commission on Terrorist Attacks Upon the United States and provide additional funding for the commission. Introduced by Roberts, R-Kan., on Feb. 26, 2004. Senate Intelligence reported Feb. 26 (no written report). Senate passed Feb. 27. House passed March 3. President signed March 16, 2004.

PL 108-208 (HR 506) Provide for the protection of archaeological sites in the Galisteo Basin in New Mexico. Introduced by Udall, D-N.M., on Jan. 29, 2003. House Resources reported, amended, Nov. 4 (H Rept 108-346). House passed, amended, under suspension of the rules, Nov. 4. Senate passed March 4, 2004. President signed March 19, 2004.

PL 108-209 (HR 2059) Designate Fort Bayard Historic District in New Mexico as a National Historic Landmark. Introduced by Pearce, R-N.M., on May 9, 2003. House Resources reported Sept. 3 (H Rept 108-257). House passed, under suspension of the rules, Sept. 23. Senate passed March 4, 2004. President signed March 19, 2004.

PL 108-210 (S 2231) Reauthorize the Temporary Assistance for Needy Families block grant program through June 30, 2004. Introduced by Grassley, R-Iowa, on March 25, 2004. Senate passed

March 25. House passed, under suspension of the rules, March 30. President signed March 31, 2004.

PL 108-211 (S 2241) Reauthorize certain school lunch and child nutrition programs through June 30, 2004. Introduced by Cochran, R-Miss., on March 26, 2004. Senate passed March 26. House passed, under suspension of the rules, March 30. President signed March 31, 2004.

PL 108-212 (HR 1997) Amend Title 18, U.S. Code, and the Uniform Code of Military Justice to create a separate federal offense for harming a fetus during the commission of a federal crime. Introduced by Hart, R-Pa., on May 7, 2003. House Judiciary reported, amended, Feb. 11, 2004 (H Rept 108-420, Pt. 1). House Armed Services discharged. House passed, amended, Feb. 26. Senate passed March 25. President signed April 1, 2004.

PL 108-213 (HR 3724) Amend the National Housing Act to make a technical correction to restore allowable increases in the maximum mortgage limits for FHA-insured mortgages for multifamily housing projects to cover increased costs of installing a solar energy system or residential energy conservation measures. Introduced by Shays, R-Conn., on Jan. 21, 2004. House passed, under suspension of the rules, Feb. 3. Senate Banking, Housing, and Urban Affairs discharged. Senate passed March 12. President signed April 1, 2004.

PL 108-214 (S 1881) Amend the Federal Food, Drug, and Cosmetic Act to make technical corrections relating to amendments made by the Medical Device User Fee and Modernization Act of 2002. Introduced by Alexander, R-Tenn., on Nov. 18, 2003. Senate Health, Education, Labor and Pensions reported, amended, Nov. 24 (no written report). Senate passed, with an amendment, Nov. 25. House Energy and Commerce reported, amended, March 9, 2004 (H Rept 108-433). House passed, with an amendment, under suspension of the rules, March 10. Senate agreed to House amendment March 12. President signed April 1, 2004.

PL 108-215 (HR 254) Authorize the president to agree to certain amendments to a U.S.-Mexico agreement concerning the establishment of a Border Environment Cooperation Commission and a North American Development Bank. Introduced by Bereuter, R-Neb., on Jan. 8, 2003. House Financial Services reported Feb. 25 (H Rept 108-17). House passed, under suspension of the rules, Feb. 26. Senate Foreign Relations discharged. Senate passed, with amendment, March 12, 2004. House agreed to Senate amendment, under suspension of the rules, March 25. President signed April 5, 2004.

PL 108-216 (HR 3926) Amend the Public Health Service Act to promote organ donation. Introduced by Bilirakis, R-Fla., on March 10, 2004. House passed, under suspension of the rules, March 24. Senate passed March 25. President signed April 5, 2004.

PL 108-217 (HR 4026) Provide for an additional temporary extension of programs under the Small Business Act and the Small Business Investment Act of 1958 through June 4, 2004. Introduced by Manzullo, R-Ill., on March 30, 2004. House passed, under suspension of the rules, March 30. Senate passed April 1. President signed April 5, 2004.

PL 108-218 (HR 3108) Amend the Employee Retirement Income Security Act of 1974 and the Internal Revenue Code of 1986 to temporarily replace the rate on the 30-year Treasury bond with a rate based on long-term corporate bonds for certain pension plan funding requirements and other provisions. Introduced by Boehner, R-Ohio, on Sept. 17, 2003. House passed, amended, Oct. 8. Senate Finance discharged. Senate passed, with amendment, Jan. 28, 2004. Conference report filed in the House April 1 (H Rept 108-457). House agreed to the conference report April 2. Senate agreed to the conference report April 8. President signed April 10, 2004.

PL 108-219 (HR 2584) Provide for the conveyance to the Utrok Atoll local government of a decommissioned National Oceanic and Atmospheric Administration ship. Introduced by Faleomavaega, D-Am. Samoa, on June 24, 2003. House Resources reported Nov. 18 (H Rept 108-378). House passed, amended, under suspension of the rules, Nov. 21. Senate Energy and Natural Resources discharged. Senate Commerce, Science and Transportation discharged. Senate passed, with amendments, March 24, 2004. House agreed to Senate amendments, under suspension of the rules, March 29. President signed April 13, 2004.

PL 108-220 (S 2057) Require the secretary of Defense to reimburse members of the Armed Forces for domestic travel expenses incurred as part of the rest and recuperation program, retroactive, to the expansion of the program. Introduced by Coleman, R-Minn., on Feb. 9, 2004. Senate Armed Services discharged. Senate passed March 3. House passed, under suspension of the rules, March 30. President signed April 22, 2004.

PL 108-221 (HR 1274) Direct the administrator of the General Services Administration to convey to Fresno County, Calif., the existing federal courthouse. Introduced by Dooley, D-Calif., on March 13, 2003. House Transportation and Infrastructure reported, amended, Nov. 4 (H Rept 108-341). House passed, under suspension of the rules, Nov. 18. Senate passed April 20, 2004. President signed April 30, 2004.

PL 108-222 (HR 2489) Provide for the distribution of judgment funds to the Cowlitz Indian Tribe in the state of Washington. Introduced by Baird, D-Wash., on June 17, 2003. House Resources reported, amended, Nov. 17 (H Rept 108-368). House passed, under suspension of the rules, March 23, 2004. Senate passed April 20. President signed April 30, 2004.

PL 108-223 (HR 3118) Designate the Orville Wright Federal Building and the Wilbur Wright Federal Building in Washington, D.C. Introduced by Hayes, R-N.C., on Sept. 17, 2003. House Transportation and Infrastructure reported Oct. 15 (H Rept 108-317). House passed, under suspension of the rules, Nov. 4. Senate Environment and Public Works discharged. Senate passed April 20, 2004. President signed April 30, 2004.

PL 108-224 (HR 4219) Provide an extension of highway, highway safety, motor carrier safety, transit and other programs funded out of the Highway Trust Fund pending enactment of a law reauthorizing the Transportation Equity Act for the 21st Century through June 30, 2004. Introduced by Petri, R-Wis. on April 27, 2004. House passed, under suspension of the rules, April 28. Senate passed April 29. President signed April 30, 2004.

PL 108-225 (S 1904) Designate the U.S. courthouse at 400 North Miami Ave. in Miami, Fla., as the "Wilkie D. Ferguson Jr. United States Courthouse." Introduced by Graham, D-Fla., on Nov. 20, 2003. Senate Environment and Public Works reported on March 10, 2004 (no written report). Senate passed March 12. House passed, under suspension of the rules, April 28. President signed May 7, 2004.

PL 108-226 (S 2022) Designate the federal building located at 250 West Cherry St. in Carbondale, Ill., the "Senator Paul Simon Federal Building." Introduced by Durbin, D-Ill., on Jan. 22, 2004. Senate Environment and Public Works reported March 10 (no written report). Senate passed March 12. House passed, under suspension of the rules, April 21. President signed May 7, 2004.

PL 108-227 (S 2043) Designate a federal building in Harrisburg, Pa., as the "Ronald Reagan Federal Building." Introduced by Specter, R-Pa., on Feb. 2, 2004. Senate Environment and Public Works reported March 10 (no written report). Senate passed March 12. House passed, under suspension of the rules, April 28. President signed May 7, 2004.

PL 108-228 (S 2315) Amend the Communications Satellite Act of 1962 to extend the deadline for the INTELSAT initial public offering. Introduced by Burns, R-Mont., on April 8, 2004. Senate Commerce, Science and Transportation discharged. Senate passed April 27. House Energy and Commerce discharged. House passed May 5. President signed May 18, 2004.

PL 108-229 (HR 408) Provide for expansion of Sleeping Bear Dunes National Lakeshore in Michigan. Introduced by Camp, R-Mich., on Jan. 28, 2003. House Resources reported, amended, Oct. 2 (H Rept 108-292). House passed, under suspension of the rules, Oct. 8. Senate Energy and Natural Resources reported March 9, 2004 (S Rept 108-240). Senate passed May 19. President signed May 28, 2004.

PL 108-230 (HR 708) Require the conveyance of certain National Forest System lands in Mendocino National Forest, Calif., and provide for the use of the proceeds for National Forest purposes. Introduced by Thompson, D-Calif., on Feb. 11, 2003. House Resources reported, Oct. 2 (H Rept 108-293). House passed, under suspension of the rules, Oct. 8. Senate Energy and Natural Resources reported March 9, 2004 (S Rept 108-242). Senate passed May 19. President signed May 28, 2004.

PL 108-231 (HR 856) Authorize the secretary of the Interior to revise a repayment contract with the Tom Green County Water Control and Improvement District No. 1, San Angelo project, Texas. Introduced by Stenholm, D-Texas, on Feb. 13, 2003. House passed, under suspension of the rules, May 14. Senate Energy and Natural Resources reported March 9, 2004 (S Rept 108-243). Senate passed May 19. President signed May 28, 2004.

PL 108-232 (HR 923) Amend the Small Business Investment Act of 1958 to allow certain premier certified lenders to elect to maintain an alternative loss reserve. Introduced by Doolittle, R-Calif., on Feb. 26, 2003. House Small Business reported, amended, June 12 (H Rept 108-153). House passed, under suspension of the rules, June 24. Senate Small Business and Entrepreneurship discharged. Senate passed May 18, 2004. President signed May 28, 2004.

PL 108-233 (HR 1598) Amend the Reclamation Wastewater and Groundwater Study and Facilities Act to authorize the secretary of the Interior to participate in projects within the San Diego Creek Watershed, Calif. Introduced by Cox, R-Calif., on April 3, 2003. House Resources reported, Oct. 8 (H Rept 108-306). House passed, under suspension of the rules, Oct. 15. Senate Energy and Natural Resources reported March 9, 2004 (S Rept 108-244). Senate passed May 19. President signed May 28, 2004.

PL 108-234 (HR 3104) Provide for the establishment of separate campaign medals to be awarded to members of the uniformed services who participate in Operation Enduring Freedom and in Operation Iraqi Freedom. Introduced by Snyder, D-Ark., on Sept. 16, 2003. House passed, amended, under suspension of the rules, March 30, 2004. Senate Armed Services reported May 11 (no written report). Senate passed May 18. President signed May 28, 2004.

PL 108-235 (S 2092) address the participation of Taiwan in the World Health Organization. Introduced by Allen, R-Va., on Feb. 12, 2004. Senate Foreign Relations reported, amended, April 29 (no written report). Senate passed May 6. House passed May 20. President signed June 14, 2004.

PL 108-236 (S J Res 28) Recognize the 60th anniversary of the Allied landing at Normandy during World War II. Introduced by Campbell, R-Colo., on Feb. 25, 2004. Senate Judiciary discharged. Senate passed April 1. House passed, under suspension of the rules, June 2. President signed June 15, 2004.

PL 108-237 (HR 1086) Encourage the development and promulgation of voluntary consensus standards for industry and various levels of government by providing relief under the antitrust laws to organizations that develop the standards. Introduced by Sensenbrenner, R-Wis., on March 5, 2003. House Judiciary reported May 22 (H Rept 108-125, Pt. 1). House Judiciary supplemental report filed June 4 (H Rept 108-125, Pt. 2). House passed, under suspension of the rules, June 10. Senate Judiciary reported, amended, Nov. 6 (no written report). Senate passed, with an amendment, April 2, 2004. House agreed to Senate amendment, under suspension of the rules, June 2. President signed June 22, 2004.

PL 108-238 (S 1233) Authorize assistance for the National Great Blacks in Wax Museum and Justice Learning Center in Baltimore, Md. Introduced by Mikulski, D-Md., on June 11, 2003. Senate Judiciary reported June 19 (no written report). Senate passed July 14. House Resources reported, Nov. 17 (H Rept 108-372, Pt. 1). House Judiciary discharged. House passed, with an amendment, under suspension of the rules, June 1, 2004. Senate agreed to House amendment, June 3. President signed June 22, 2004.

PL 108-239 (HR 1822) Designate the facility of the U.S. Postal Service located at 3751 West 6th St., Los Angeles, Calif., as the "Dosan Ahn Chang Ho Post Office." Introduced by Watson, D-Calif., on April 11, 2003. House passed, under suspension of the rules, April 20, 2004. Senate Governmental Affairs reported June 7 (no written report). Senate passed June 9. President signed June 25, 2004.

PL 108-240 (HR 2130) Redesignate the facility of the U.S. Postal Service located at 121 Kinderkamack Road in River Edge, N.J., as the "New Bridge Landing Post Office." Introduced by Garrett, R-N.J., on May 15, 2003. House passed, amended, under suspension of the rules, Nov. 18. Senate Governmental Affairs reported June 7, 2004 (no written report). Senate passed June 9. President signed June 25, 2004.

PL 108-241 (HR 2438) Designate the facility of the U.S. Postal Service located at 115 West Pine St. in Hattiesburg, Miss., as the "Major Henry A. Commiskey Sr. Post Office Building." Introduced by Taylor, D-Miss., on June 11, 2003. House passed, under suspension of the rules, Nov. 4. Senate Governmental Affairs reported June 7, 2004 (no written report). Senate passed June 9. President signed June 25, 2004.

PL 108-242 (HR 3029) Designate the facility of the U.S. Postal Service located at 255 North Main St. in Jonesboro, Ga, as the "S. Truett Cathy Post Office Building." Introduced by Scott, D-Ga. on

Sept. 5, 2003. House passed, under suspension of the rules, Nov. 4. Senate Governmental Affairs reported June 7, 2004 (no written report). Senate passed June 9. President signed June 25, 2004.

PL 108-243 (HR 3059) Designate the facility of the U.S. Postal Service located at 304 West Michigan St. in Stuttgart, Ark., as the "Lloyd L. Burke Post Office." Introduced by Berry, D-Ark., on Sept. 10, 2003. House passed, under suspension of the rules, March 24, 2004. Senate Governmental Affairs reported June 7 (no written report). Senate passed June 9. President signed June 25, 2004.

PL 108-244 (HR 3068) Designate the facility of the U.S. Postal Service located at 2055 Siesta Drive in Sarasota, Fla., as the "Brigadier General (AUS-Ret.) John H. McLain Post Office." Introduced by Harris, R-Fla., on Sept. 10, 2003. House passed, under suspension of the rules, Oct. 20. Senate Governmental Affairs reported June 7, 2004 (no written report). Senate passed June 9. President signed June 25, 2004.

PL 108-245 (HR 3234) Designate the facility of the U.S. Postal Service located at 14 Chestnut St. in Liberty, N.Y., as the "Ben R. Gerow Post Office Building." Introduced by Hinchey, D-N.Y., on Oct. 2, 2003. House passed, under suspension of the rules, Oct. 28. Senate Governmental Affairs reported June 7, 2004 (no written report). Senate passed June 9. President signed June 25, 2004.

PL 108-246 (HR 3300) Designate the facility of the U.S. Postal Service located at 15500 Pearl Road in Strongsville, Ohio, as the "Walter F. Ehrnfelt Jr. Post Office Building." Introduced by LaTourette, R-Ohio, on Oct. 15, 2003. House passed, under suspension of the rules, Nov. 18. Senate Governmental Affairs reported June 7, 2004 (no written report). Senate passed June 9. President signed June 25, 2004.

PL 108-247 (HR 3353) Designate the facility of the U.S. Postal Service located at 525 Main St. in Tarboro, N.C., as the "George Henry White Post Office Building." Introduced by Ballance, D-N.C., on Oct. 21, 2003. House passed, under suspension of the rules, Nov. 17. Senate Governmental Affairs reported June 7, 2004 (no written report). Senate passed June 9. President signed June 25, 2004.

PL 108-248 (HR 3536) Designate the facility of the U.S. Postal Service located at 210 Main St. in Malden, Ill., as the "Army Staff Sgt. Lincoln Hollinsaid Malden Post Office." Introduced by Weller, R-Ill., on Nov. 19, 2003. House passed, under suspension of the rules, March 9, 2004. Senate Governmental Affairs reported June 7 (no written report). Senate passed June 9. President signed June 25, 2004.

PL 108-249 (HR 3537) Designate the facility of the U.S. Postal Service located at 185 State St. in Manhattan, Ill., as the "Army Pvt. Shawn Pahnke Manhattan Post Office." Introduced by Weller, R-Ill., on Nov. 19, 2003. House passed, under suspension of the rules, March 9, 2004. Senate Governmental Affairs reported June 7 (no written report). Senate passed June 9. President signed June 25, 2004.

PL 108-250 (HR 3538) Designate the facility of the U.S. Postal Service located at 201 South Chicago Ave. in Saint Anne, Ill., as the "Marine Capt. Ryan Beaupre Saint Anne Post Office." Introduced by Weller, R-Ill., on Nov. 19, 2003. House passed, under suspension of the rules, March 9, 2004. Senate Governmental Affairs reported June 7 (no written report). Senate passed June 9. President signed June 25, 2004.

PL 108-251 (HR 3690) Designate the facility of the U.S. Postal Service located at 2 West Main St. in Batavia, N.Y., as the "Barber Conable Post Office Building." Introduced by Reynolds, R-N.Y., on

Dec. 8, 2003. House passed, under suspension of the rules, Feb. 25, 2004. Senate Governmental Affairs reported June 7 (no written report). Senate passed June 9. President signed June 25, 2004.

PL 108-252 (HR 3733) Designate the facility of the U.S. Postal Service located at 410 Huston St. in Altamont, Kan., as the "Myron V. George Post Office." Introduced by Ryun, R-Kan., on Jan. 27, 2004. House passed, under suspension of the rules, March 16. Senate Governmental Affairs reported June 7 (no written report). Senate passed June 9. President signed June 25, 2004.

PL 108-253 (HR 3740) Designate the facility of the U.S. Postal Service located at 223 South Main St. in Roxboro, N.C., as the "Oscar Scott Woody Post Office Building." Introduced by Miller, D-N.C., on Jan. 28, 2004. House passed, under suspension of the rules, May 18. Senate Governmental Affairs reported June 7 (no written report). Senate passed June 9. President signed June 25, 2004.

PL 108-254 (HR 3769) Designate the facility of the U.S. Postal Service located at 137 East Young High Pike in Knoxville, Tenn., as the "Ben Atchley Post Office Building." Introduced by Duncan, R-Tenn., on Feb. 4, 2004. House passed, under suspension of the rules, March 2. Senate Governmental Affairs reported June 7 (no written report). Senate passed June 9. President signed June 25, 2004.

PL 108-255 (HR 3855) Designate the facility of the U.S. Postal Service located at 607 Pershing Drive in Laclede, Mo., as the "General John J. Pershing Post Office." Introduced by Graves, R-Mo., on Feb. 26, 2004. House passed, under suspension of the rules, April 20. Senate Governmental Affairs reported June 7 (no written report). Senate passed June 9. President signed June 25, 2004.

PL 108-256 (HR 3917) Designate the facility of the U.S. Postal Service located at 695 Marconi Blvd. in Copiague, N.Y., as the "Maxine S. Postal United States Post Office." Introduced by Israel, D-N.Y, on March 9, 2004. House passed, under suspension of the rules, March 29. Senate Governmental Affairs reported June 7 (no written report). Senate passed June 9. President signed June 25, 2004.

PL 108-257 (HR 3939) Redesignate the facility of the U.S. Postal Service located at 14-24 Abbott Road in Fair Lawn, N.J., as the "Mary Ann Collura Post Office Building." Introduced by Rothman, D-N.J., on March 11, 2004. House passed, under suspension of the rules, May 11. Senate Governmental Affairs reported June 7 (no written report). Senate passed June 9. President signed June 25, 2004.

PL 108-258 (HR 3942) Redesignate the facility of the U.S. Postal Service located at 7 Commercial Blvd. in Middletown, R.I., as the "Rhode Island Veterans Post Office Building." Introduced by Kennedy, D-R.I., on March 11, 2004. House passed, under suspension of the rules, April 27. Senate Governmental Affairs reported June 7 (no written report). Senate passed June 9. President signed June 25, 2004.

PL 108-259 (HR 4037) Designate the facility of the U.S. Postal Service located at 475 Kell Farm Drive in Cape Girardeau, Mo., as the "Richard G. Wilson Processing and Distribution Facility." Introduced by Emerson, R-Mo., on March 25, 2004. House passed, under suspension of the rules, April 20. Senate Governmental Affairs reported June 7 (no written report). Senate passed June 9. President signed June 25, 2004.

PL 108-260 (HR 4176) Designate the facility of the U.S. Postal Service located at 122 West Elwood Ave. in Raeford, N.C., as the "Bobby Marshall Gentry Post Office Building." Introduced by Hayes,

R-N.C., on April 20, 2004. House passed, under suspension of the rules, May 18. Senate Governmental Affairs reported June 7 (no written report). Senate passed June 9. President signed June 25, 2004.

PL 108-261 (HR 4299) Designate the facility of the U.S. Postal Service located at 410 South Jackson Road in Edinburg, Texas, as the "Dr. Miguel A. Nevarez Post Office Building." Introduced by Hinojosa, D-Texas, on May 6, 2004. House passed, under suspension of the rules, May 11. Senate Governmental Affairs reported June 7 (no written report). Senate passed June 9. President signed June 25, 2004

PL 108-262 (HR 4589) Reauthorize the Temporary Assistance for Needy Families block grant program through Sept. 30, 2004. Introduced by Herger, R-Calif., on June 16, 2004. House passed, under suspension of the rules, June 22. Senate passed June 22. President signed June 30, 2004.

PL 108-263 (HR 4635) Provide an extension through July 31, 2004, of highway, highway safety, motor carrier safety, transit and other programs funded out of the Highway Trust Fund pending enactment of a law reauthorizing the Transportation Equity Act for the 21st Century. Introduced by Young, R-Alaska, on June 22, 2004. House passed, under suspension of the rules, June 23. Senate passed June 23. President signed June 30, 2004.

PL 108-264 (S 2238) Amend the National Flood Insurance Act of 1968 to reduce losses to properties for which repetitive flood insurance claim payments have been made. Introduced by Bunning, R-Ky., on March 25, 2004. Senate Banking, Housing and Urban Affairs reported May 13 (S Rept 108-262). Senate passed, amended, June 15. House passed, under suspension of the rules, June 21. President signed June 30, 2004.

PL 108-265 (S 2507) Amend the Richard B. Russell National School Lunch Act and the Child Nutrition Act of 1966 to provide children with increased access to food and nutrition assistance, to simplify program operations and improve program management and to reauthorize child nutrition programs. Introduced by Cochran, R-Miss., on June 7, 2004. Senate Agriculture, Nutrition and Forestry reported June 7 (S Rept 108-279). Senate passed, amended, June 23. House passed June 24. President signed June 30, 2004.

PL 108-266 (HR 3378) Assist in the conservation of marine turtles and the nesting habitats of marine turtles in foreign countries. Introduced by Gilchrest, R-Md., on Oct. 28, 2003. House Resources reported, amended, May 20, 2004 (H Rept 108-507). House passed, under suspension of the rules, June 14. Senate passed June 18. President signed July 2, 2004.

PL 108-267 (HR 3504) Amend the Indian Self-Determination and Education Assistance Act to redesignate the American Indian Education Foundation as the National Fund for Excellence in American Indian Education. Introduced by Renzi, R-Ariz., on Nov. 17, 2003. House Resources reported May 20, 2004 (H Rept 108-510, Pt. 1). House passed, under suspension of the rules, June 14. Senate passed June 18. President signed July 2, 2004.

PL 108-268 (HR 4322) Provide for the transfer of the Nebraska Ave. Naval Complex in the District of Columbia to facilitate the establishment of the headquarters for the Department of Homeland Security and provide for the acquisition by the Department of the Navy of suitable replacement facilities. Introduced by Hunter, R-Calif., on May 11, 2004. House Armed Services reported, amended,

May 13 (no written report). House passed, under suspension of the rules, June 14. Senate passed June 21. President signed July 2, 2004.

PL 108-269 (S 1848) Amend the Bend Pine Nursery Land Conveyance Act to direct the secretary of Agriculture to sell the Bend Pine Nursery Administration Site in the state of Oregon. Introduced by Wyden, D-Ore., on Nov. 11, 2003. Senate Energy and Natural Resources reported, amended, March 9, 2004 (S Rept 108-238). Senate passed, with amendment, May 19. House passed, under suspension of the rules, June 21. President signed July 2, 2004.

PL 108-270 (HR 884) Provide for the use and distribution of the funds awarded to the Western Shoshone identifiable group under Indian Claims Commission Docket Numbers 326-A-1, 326-A-3, and 326-K. Introduced by Gibbons, R-Nev., on Feb. 25, 2003. House Resources reported, amended, Oct. 7 (H Rept 108-299). House passed, under suspension of the rules, June 21, 2004. Senate passed June 24. President signed July 7, 2004.

PL 108-271 (HR 2751) Change the name of the General Accounting Office to the General Accountability Office and alter the agency's personnel rules. Introduced by J. Davis, R-Va., on July 16, 2003. House Government Reform reported, amended, Nov. 19 (H Rept 108-380). House passed, amended, Feb. 25, 2004. Senate Governmental Affairs discharged. Senate passed June 24. President signed July 7, 2004.

PL 108-272 (H J Res 97) Approve the renewal of import restrictions contained in the Burmese Freedom and Democracy Act of 2003. Introduced by Lantos, D-Calif., on June 3, 2004. House passed, under suspension of the rules, June 14. Senate passed June 24. President signed July 7, 2004.

PL 108-273 (S 2017) Designate the U.S. courthouse and post office building located at 93 Atocha St. in Ponce, Puerto Rico, as the "Luis A. Ferre United States Courthouse and Post Office Building." Introduced by Santorum, R-Pa., on Jan. 22, 2004. Senate Governmental Affairs reported June 7 (no written report). Senate passed June 9. House passed, under suspension of the rules, June 22. President signed July 7, 2004.

PL 108-274 (HR 4103) Extend and modify trade benefits under the African Growth and Opportunity Act. Introduced by Thomas, R-Calif., on April 1, 2004. House Ways and Means reported, amended, May 19 (H Rept 108-501). House passed, under suspension of the rules, June 14. Senate passed June 24. President signed July 13, 2004.

PL 108-275 (HR 1731) Amend Title 18, U.S. Code, to establish penalties for aggravated identity theft. Introduced by Carter, R-Texas, on April 10, 2003. House Judiciary reported, amended, June 8, 2004 (H Rept 108-528). House passed, under suspension of the rules, June 23. Senate passed June 25. President signed July 15, 2004.

PL 108-276 (S 15) Amend the Public Health Service Act to provide protections and countermeasures against chemical, radiological, or nuclear agents that may be used in a terrorist attack against the United States by giving the National Institutes of Health contracting flexibility, infrastructure improvements, and expedited scientific peer review procedures, and by streamlining the Food and Drug Administration approval process for countermeasures. Introduced by Gregg, R-N.H., on March 11, 2003. Senate Health, Education, Labor and Pensions reported, amended, March 25 (no written report). Senate passed, amended, May 19, 2004. House passed July 14. President signed July 21, 2004.

PL 108-277 (HR 218) Amend Title 18, U.S. Code, to exempt qualified current and former law enforcement officers from state laws prohibiting the carrying of concealed handguns. Introduced by Cunningham, R-Calif., on Jan. 7, 2003. House Judiciary reported, amended, June 22, 2004 (H Rept 108-560). House passed, under suspension of the rules, June 23. Senate passed July 7. President signed July 22, 2004.

PL 108-278 (HR 3846) Authorize the secretary of Agriculture and the secretary of the Interior to enter into an agreement or contract with Indian tribes meeting certain criteria to carry out projects to protect Indian forest land. Introduced by Pombo, R-Calif., on Feb. 26, 2004. House Resources reported, amended, May 20, 2004 (H Rept 108-509, Pt. 1). House Agriculture discharged. House passed, under suspension of the rules, June 21. Senate passed June 25. President signed July 22, 2004.

PL 108-279 (S 1167) Resolve the boundary conflicts in Barry and Stone counties in the state of Missouri. Introduced by Bond, R-Mo., on June 2, 2003. Senate Energy and Natural Resources reported, amended, March 9, 2004 (S Rept 108-234). Senate passed, amended, May 19. House passed, under suspension of the rules, July 12. President signed July 22, 2004.

PL 108-280 (HR 4916) Provide an extension of highway, highway safety, motor carrier safety, transit, and other programs funded out of the Highway Trust Fund pending enactment of a law reauthorizing the Transportation Equity Act for the 21st Century. The extension goes through Sept. 24 for highways and through Sept. 30 for transit and other activities. Introduced by Young, R-Alaska, on July 22, 2004. House Resources, House Science, House Transportation and Infrastructure, and House Ways and Means discharged. House passed July 22. Senate passed July 22. President signed July 30, 2004.

PL 108-281 (HR 1303) Amend the E-Government Act of 2002 with respect to rulemaking authority of the Judicial Conference. Introduced by Smith, R-Texas, on March 18, 2003. House Judiciary reported, amended, July 25 (H Rept 108-239). House passed, under suspension of the rules, Oct. 7. Senate Governmental Affairs reported July 7, 2004 (no written report). Senate passed July 9. Senate vitiated reporting of HR 1303, July 14. Senate vitiated passage of HR 1303, July 14. Senate Governmental Affairs discharged. Senate passed July 15. President signed Aug. 2, 2004.

PL 108-282 (S 741) Amend the Federal Food, Drug and Cosmetic Act with regard to new animal drugs. Introduced by Sessions, R-Ala., on March 27, 2003. Senate Health, Education, Labor and Pensions reported, amended, Feb. 18, 2004 (S Rept 108-226). Senate passed, amended, March 8. House Energy and Commerce reported July 15 (H Rept 108-608). House passed, under suspension of the rules, July 20. President signed Aug. 2, 2004.

PL 108-283 (S 2264) Require a report on the conflict in Uganda. Introduced by Feingold, D-Wis., on March 31, 2004. Senate Foreign Relations reported April 29 (no written report). Senate passed May 7. House passed, under suspension of the rules, July 19. President signed Aug. 2, 2004.

PL 108-284 (S J Res 38) Provide for the appointment of Eli Broad as a citizen regent of the Board of Regents of the Smithsonian Institution. Introduced by Cochran, R-Miss., on June 3, 2004. Senate Rules and Administration discharged. Senate passed June 9. House passed, under suspension of the rules, July 20. President signed Aug. 2, 2004.

PL 108-285 (HR 4363) Facilitate self-help housing homeownership opportunities. Introduced by Green, R-Wis., on May 13, 2004. House Financial Services reported, amended, June 16 (H Rept 108-546). House passed, under suspension of the rules, June 21. Senate Banking, Housing and Urban Affairs discharged. Senate passed July 14. President signed Aug. 2, 2004.

PL 108-286 (HR 4759) Implement the United States-Australia Free Trade Agreement. Introduced by DeLay, R-Texas, on July 6, 2004. House Ways and Means reported July 12 (H Rept 108-597). House passed July 14. Senate passed July 15. President signed Aug. 3, 2004.

PL 108-287 (HR 4613) Make appropriations for the Department of Defense for the fiscal year ending Sept. 30, 2005. Introduced by Lewis, R-Calif., on June 18, 2004. House Appropriations reported June 18 (H Rept 108-553). House passed, amended, June 22. Senate passed, amended, June 24. Conference report filed in the House on July 20 (H Rept 108-622). House agreed to the conference report July 22. Senate agreed to the conference report July 22. President signed Aug. 5, 2004.

PL 108-288 (HR 1572) Designate the U.S. courthouse located at 100 North Palafox St. in Pensacola, Fla., as the "Winston E. Arnow United States Courthouse." Introduced by Miller, R-Fla., on April 2, 2003. House Transportation and Infrastructure reported, amended, July 17, 2003 (H Rept 108-216). House passed, under suspension of the rules, Sept. 3. Senate Environment and Public Works reported June 24, 2004 (no written report). Senate passed July 19. President signed Aug. 6, 2004.

PL 108-289 (HR 1914) Provide for the issuance of a coin to commemorate the 400th anniversary of the Jamestown settlement. Introduced by Davis, J., R-Va., on May 1, 2003. House Financial Services reported April 27, 2004 (H Rept 108-472, Pt. 1). House Ways and Means reported, amended, July 6 (H Rept 108-472, Pt. 2). House passed, under suspension of the rules, July 14. Senate passed July 20. President signed Aug. 6, 2004.

PL 108-290 (HR 2768) Require the secretary of the Treasury to mint coins in commemoration of Chief Justice John Marshall. Introduced by Bachus, R-Ala., on July 17, 2003. House Financial Services reported April 27, 2004 (H Rept 108-473, Pt. 1). House Ways and Means reported, amended, July 6 (H Rept 108-473, Pt. 2). House passed, under suspension of the rules, July 14. Senate passed July 20. President signed Aug. 6, 2004.

PL 108-291 (HR 3277) Require the secretary of the Treasury to mint coins in commemoration of the 230th anniversary of the U.S. Marine Corps and to support construction of the Marine Corps Heritage Center. Introduced by Murtha, D-Pa., on Oct. 8, 2003. House Financial Services reported April 27, 2004 (H Rept 108-474, Pt. 1). House Ways and Means reported, amended, July 6 (H Rept 108-474, Pt. 2). House passed, under suspension of the rules, July 14. Senate passed July 20. President signed Aug. 6, 2004.

PL 108-292 (HR 4380) Designate the facility of the U.S. Postal Service located at 4737 Mile Stretch Drive in Holiday, Fla., as the "Sergeant First Class Paul Ray Smith Post Office Building." Introduced by Bilirakis, R-Fla., on May 18, 2004. House passed, under suspension of the rules, July 12. Senate Governmental Affairs discharged. Senate passed July 19. President signed Aug. 6, 2004.

PL 108-293 (HR 2443) Authorize appropriations for fiscal 2004 and 2005 for the U.S. Coast Guard. Introduced by Young, R-Alaska, on June 12, 2003. House Transportation and Infrastructure reported, amended, July 24 (H Rept 108-233). House passed Nov. 5. Senate Commerce, Science and Transportation discharged. Senate passed with an amendment March 30, 2004. Conference report filed in the House on July 20 (H Rept 108-617). House agreed to the conference report July 21. Senate agreed to the conference report July 22. President signed Aug. 9, 2004.

PL 108-294 (HR 3340) Redesignate the facilities of the U.S. Postal Service located at 7715 and 7748 S. Cottage Grove Ave. in Chicago, Ill., as the "James E. Worsham Post Office" and the "James E. Worsham Carrier Annex Building," respectively. Introduced by Rush, D-Ill., on Oct. 20. 2003. House passed, under suspension of the rules, July 6, 2004. Senate Governmental Affairs reported July 22 (no written report). Senate passed July 22. President signed Aug. 9, 2004.

PL 108-295 (HR 3463) Amend titles III and IV of the Social Security Act to improve the administration of unemployment taxes and benefits. Introduced by Herger, R-Calif., on Nov. 16, 2003. House passed, under suspension of the rules, July 14, 2004. Senate passed July 22. President signed Aug. 9, 2004.

PL 108-296 (HR 4222) Designate the facility of the U.S. Postal Service located at 550 Nebraska Ave. in Kansas City, Kan., as the "Newell George Post Office Building." Introduced by Moore, D-Kan., on April 27, 2004. House passed, under suspension of the rules, June 21. Senate Governmental Affairs reported July 22 (no written report). Senate passed July 22. President signed Aug. 9, 2004.

PL 108-297 (HR 4226) Make conforming changes to provisions governing the registration of aircraft and the recordation of instruments in order to implement the Cape Town Treaty. Introduced by Young, R-Alaska, on April 28, 2004. House Transportation and Infrastructure reported, amended, June 8 (H Rept 108-526). House passed, under suspension of the rules, June 22. Senate Commerce, Science and Transportation discharged. Senate passed July 21. President signed Aug. 9, 2004.

PL 108-298 (HR 4327) Designate the facility of the U.S. Postal Service located at 7450 Natural Bridge Road in St. Louis, Mo., as the "Vitilas 'Veto' Reid Post Office Building." Introduced by Clay, D-Mo., on May 11, 2004. House passed, under suspension of the rules, July 6. Senate Governmental Affairs reported July 22 (no written report). Senate passed July 22. President signed Aug. 9, 2004.

PL 108-299 (HR 4417) Modify certain deadlines pertaining to machine-readable, tamper-resistant entry and exit documents and passports that contain biometric identifiers. Introduced by Sensenbrenner, R-Wis., on May 20, 2004. House passed, under suspension of the rules, June 14. Senate Judiciary discharged. Senate passed July 22. President signed Aug. 9, 2004.

PL 108-300 (HR 4427) Designate the facility of the U.S. Postal Service located at 73 South Euclid Ave. in Montauk, N.Y., as the "Perry B. Duryea Jr. Post Office." Introduced by Bishop, D-N.Y., on May 20, 2004. House passed, under suspension of the rules, July 6. Senate Governmental Affairs reported July 22 (no written report). Senate passed July 22. President signed Aug. 9, 2004.

PL 108-301 (S 2712) Preserve the ability of the Federal Housing Administration to insure mortgages under sections 238 and 519 of the National Housing Act. Introduced by Reed, D-R.I., on July 21, 2004. Senate Banking, Housing and Urban Affairs discharged. Senate passed July 22. House passed July 22. President signed Aug. 9, 2004.

PL 108-302 (HR 4842) Implement the U.S.-Morocco Free Trade Agreement. Introduced by DeLay, R-Texas, on July 15, 2004. House Ways and Means reported, July 21 (H Rept 108-627). House passed July 22. Senate passed July 22. President signed Aug. 17, 2004.

PL 108-303 (HR 5005) Make emergency supplemental appropriations for the fiscal year ending Sept. 30, 2004. Introduced by Young, R-Fla., on Sept. 7, 2004. House passed, under suspension of the rules, Sept. 7. Senate passed Sept. 7. President signed Sept. 8, 2004.

PL 108-304 (HR 361) Designate certain conduct by sports agents relating to the signing of contracts with student athletes as unfair and deceptive acts or practices to be regulated by the Federal Trade Commission. Introduced by Gordon, D-Tenn., on Jan. 27, 2003. House Energy and Commerce reported March 5 (H Rept 108-24, Pt. 1). House Judiciary reported, amended, June 2 (H Rept 108-24, Pt. 2). House passed, under suspension of the rules, June 4. Senate Commerce, Science and Transportation discharged. Senate passed Sept. 9, 2004. President signed Sept. 24, 2004.

PL 108-305 (HR 3908) Provide for the conveyance of the real property located at 1081 West Main St. in Ravenna, Ohio. Introduced by Ryan, D-Ohio, on March 4, 2004. House passed, under suspension of the rules, June 2. Senate Health, Education, Labor and Pensions discharged. Senate passed Sept. 10. President signed Sept. 24, 2004.

PL 108-306 (HR 5008) Provide an additional temporary extension through Sept. 30, 2004, of programs under the Small Business Act and the Small Business Investment Act of 1958. Introduced by Manzullo, R-Ill., on Sept. 7, 2004. House passed, under suspension of the rules, Sept. 13. Senate passed Sept. 14. President signed Sept. 24, 2004.

PL 108-307 (S 1576) Revise the boundary of Harpers Ferry National Historical Park. Introduced by Byrd, D-W.Va., on Sept. 3, 2003. Senate Energy and Natural Resources reported March 9, 2004 (S Rept 108-236). Senate passed May 19. House Resources reported Sept. 7 (H Rept 108-655). House passed, under suspension of the rules, Sept. 13. President signed Sept. 24, 2004.

PL 108-308 (HR 5149) Reauthorize the Temporary Assistance for Needy Families block grant program through March 31, 2005. Introduced by Herger, R-Calif., on Sept. 24, 2004. House passed, under suspension of the rules, Sept. 30. Senate passed Sept. 30. President signed Sept. 30, 2004.

PL 108-309 (H J Res 107) Make continuing appropriations for fiscal 2005. Introduced by Young, R-Fla., on Sept. 28, 2004. House passed Sept. 29. Senate passed Sept. 29. President signed Sept. 30, 2004.

PL 108-310 (HR 5183) Extend highway, highway safety, motor carrier safety, transit and other programs funded out of the Highway Trust Fund through May 31, 2005, pending enactment of a law reauthorizing the Transportation Equity Act for the 21st Century. Introduced by Young, R-Alaska, on Sept. 29, 2004. House passed Sept. 30. Senate passed Sept. 30. President signed Sept. 30, 2004.

PL 108-311 (HR 1308) Amend the Internal Revenue Code to provide tax relief for working families. Introduced by Thomas, R-Calif., on March 18, 2003. House passed March 19. Senate passed, with an amendment, June 5. Conference report filed in the House on Sept. 23, 2004 (H Rept 108-696). House agreed to the conference report Sept. 23. Senate agreed to the conference report Sept. 23. President signed Oct. 4, 2004.

PL 108-312 (HR 265) Provide for an adjustment of the boundaries of Mount Rainier National Park. Introduced by Dunn, R-Wash., on Jan. 8, 2003. House Resources reported, amended, May 17, 2004 (H Rept 108-495). House passed, under suspension of the rules, June 1. Senate Energy and Natural Resources reported Aug. 25 (S Rept 108-330). Senate passed Sept. 15. President signed Oct. 5, 2004.

PL 108-313 (HR 1521) Provide for additional lands to be included within the boundary of the Johnstown Flood National Memorial in Pennsylvania. Introduced by Murtha, D-Pa., on March 31, 2003. House Resources reported, amended, Oct. 7 (H Rept 108-301). House passed, under suspension of the rules, Oct. 15. Senate Energy and Natural Resources reported May 20 (S Rept 108-276). Senate passed Sept. 15. President signed Oct. 5, 2004.

PL 108-314 (HR 1616) Authorize the exchange of certain lands within the Martin Luther King Jr. National Historic Site for lands owned by the City of Atlanta, Ga. Introduced by Lewis, D-Ga., on April 3, 2003. House Resources reported Sept. 3 (H Rept 108-255). House passed, under suspension of the rules, Oct. 28. Senate Energy and Natural Resources reported Aug. 25, 2004 (S Rept 108-332). Senate passed Sept. 15. President signed Oct. 5, 2004.

PL 108-315 (HR 1648) Authorize the secretary of the Interior to convey certain water distribution systems of the Cachuma Project in California, to the Carpinteria Valley Water District and the Montecito Water District. Introduced by Capps, D-Calif., on April 7, 2003. House Resources reported Nov. 17 (H Rept 108-363). House passed, under suspension of the rules, Nov. 17. Senate Energy and Natural Resources reported June 25, 2004 (S Rept 108-287). Senate passed Sept. 15. President signed Oct. 5, 2004.

PL 108-316 (HR 1732) Amend the Reclamation Wastewater and Groundwater Study and Facilities Act to authorize the secretary of the Interior to participate in the Williamson County, Texas, Water Recycling and Reuse Project. Introduced by Carter, R-Texas, on April 10, 2003. House Resources reported Nov. 17 (H Rept 108-364). House passed, under suspension of the rules, Nov. 17. Senate Energy and Natural Resources reported June 25, 2004 (S Rept 108-288). Senate passed Sept. 15. President signed Oct. 5, 2004.

PL 108-317 (HR 2696) Establish institutes to demonstrate and promote the use of adaptive ecosystem management to reduce the risk of wildfires, and to restore the health of fire-adapted forest and woodland ecosystems of the interior West. Introduced by Renzi, R-Ariz., on July 10, 2003. House Resources reported, amended, Nov. 21 (H Rept 108-397, Pt. 1). House Agriculture discharged. House passed, under suspension of the rules, Feb. 24, 2004. Senate Energy and Natural Resources reported March 29 (S Rept 108-252). Senate passed Sept. 15. President signed Oct. 5, 2004.

PL 108-318 (HR 3209) Amend the Reclamation Project Authorization Act of 1972 to clarify the acreage for which the North Loup division is authorized to provide irrigation water under the Missouri River Basin project. Introduced by Osborne, R-Neb., on Sept. 30, 2003. House Resources reported Nov. 7 (H Rept 108-356). House passed, under suspension of the rules, Nov. 17. Senate Energy and Natural Resources reported June 25, 2004 (S Rept 108-289). Senate passed Sept. 15. President signed Oct. 5, 2004.

PL 108-319 (HR 3249) Extend the term of the Forest Counties Payments Committee. Introduced by Walden, R-Ore., on Oct. 3, 2003. House passed, under suspension of the rules, Oct. 28. Senate Energy and Natural Resources reported May 20, 2004 (S Rept 108-277). Senate passed Sept. 15. President signed Oct. 5, 2004.

PL 108-320 (HR 3389) Amend the Stevenson-Wydler Technology Innovation Act of 1980 to permit Malcolm Baldrige National Quality Awards to be made to nonprofit organizations. Introduced by Miller, D-N.C., on Oct. 29, 2003. House Science reported, Feb. 11, 2004 (H Rept 108-419). House passed, under suspension of the rules, March 3. Senate Commerce, Science and Transportation discharged. Senate passed Sept. 23. President signed Oct. 5, 2004.

PL 108-321 (HR 3768) Expand the Timucuan Ecological and Historic Preserve in St. Johns River Valley, Jacksonville, Fla. Introduced by Crenshaw, R-Fla., on Feb. 4, 2004. House Resources reported, amended, May 17 (H Rept 108-493). House passed, under suspension of the rules, May 17. Senate Energy and Natural Resources reported Aug. 25 (S Rept 108-333). Senate passed Sept. 15. President signed Oct. 5, 2004.

PL 108-322 (S J Res 41) Commemorate the opening of the National Museum of the American Indian. Introduced by Campbell, R-Colo., on July 7, 2004. Senate Indian Affairs reported, amended, July 16 (no written report). Senate passed July 22. House passed, under suspension of the rules, Sept. 21. President signed Oct. 5, 2004.

PL 108-323 (HR 4654) Reauthorize the Tropical Forest Conservation Act of 1998 through fiscal 2007. Introduced by Portman, R-Ohio, on June 23, 2004. House International Relations reported July 14 (H Rept 108-603). House passed, under suspension of the rules, Sept. 7. Senate Foreign Relations discharged. Senate passed Sept. 28. President signed Oct. 6, 2004.

PL 108-324 (HR 4837) Make appropriations for military construction, family housing, and base realignment and closure for the Department of Defense for the fiscal year ending Sept. 30, 2005. Introduced by Knollenberg, R-Mich., on July 15, 2004. House Appropriations reported July 15 (H Rept 108-607). House passed July 22. Senate passed, amended, Sept. 20. Conference report filed in the House Oct. 9 (H Rept 108-773). House agreed to the conference report Oct. 9. Senate agreed to the conference report Oct. 11. President signed Oct. 13, 2004.

PL 108-325 (S 1778) Authorize a land conveyance between the United States and the City of Craig, Alaska. Introduced by Murkowski, R-Alaska, on Oct. 23, 2003. Senate Energy and Natural Resources reported, amended, May 20, 2004 (S Rept 108-271). Senate passed Sept. 15. House passed, under suspension of the rules, Sept. 28. President signed Oct. 13, 2004.

PL 108-326 (HR 982) Clarify the tax treatment of bonds and other obligations issued by the government of American Samoa. Introduced by Faleomavaega, D-Am. Samoa, on Feb. 27, 2003. House Judiciary reported May 15 (H Rept 108-102, Pt. 1). House Resources reported Oct. 7 (H Rept 108-102, Pt. 2). House passed, under suspension of the rules, Nov. 4. Senate Finance reported July 20, 2004 (no written report). Senate passed Sept. 29. President signed Oct. 16, 2004.

PL 108-327 (HR 2408) Amend the Fish and Wildlife Act of 1956 to reauthorize volunteer programs and community partnerships for national wildlife refuges. Introduced by Saxton, R-N.J., on June 10, 2003. House Resources reported, amended, Nov. 20 (H Rept 108-385). House passed, under suspension of the rules, March 23, 2004. Senate Environment and Public Works reported Aug. 25 (S Rept 108-315). Senate passed Sept. 30. President signed Oct. 16, 2004.

PL 108-328 (HR 2771) Amend the Safe Drinking Water Act to reauthorize the New York City Watershed Protection Program. Introduced by Fossella, R-N.Y., on July 17, 2003. House Energy and Commerce reported April 28, 2004 (H Rept 108-476). House passed, under suspension of the rules, May 5. Senate passed Sept. 30. President signed Oct. 16, 2004.

PL 108-329 (HR 4115) Amend federal law to allow binding arbitration clauses to be included in all contracts affecting the land within the Salt River Pima-Maricopa Indian Reservation. Introduced by Hayworth, R-Ariz., on April 1, 2004. House Resources reported June 9 (H Rept 108-535). House passed, under suspension of the rules, July 19. Senate passed Sept. 29. President signed Oct. 16, 2004.

PL 108-330 (HR 4259) Improve the financial accountability requirements applicable to the Department of Homeland Security and establish requirements for the department's Future Years Homeland Security Program. Introduced by Platts, R-Pa., on May 4, 2004. House Government Reform reported June 9 (H Rept 108-533, Pt. 1). House Select Homeland Security discharged. House passed, under suspension of the rules, July 20. Senate Governmental Affairs discharged. Senate passed Sept. 29. President signed Oct. 16, 2004.

PL 108-331 (HR 5105) Authorize the Board of Regents of the Smithsonian Institution to carry out construction and related activities in support of the collaborative Very Energetic Radiation Imaging Telescope Array System (VERITAS) project on Kitt Peak near Tucson, Ariz. Introduced by Ney, R-Ohio, on Sept. 17, 2004. House passed, under suspension of the rules, Sept. 29. Senate passed Oct. 1. President signed Oct. 16, 2004.

PL 108-332 (S 2292) Require a report on acts of anti-Semitism around the world. Introduced by Voinovich, R-Ohio, on April 7, 2004. Senate Foreign Relations reported, amended, April 29 (no written report). Senate passed May 7. House International Relations discharged. House passed, amended, Oct. 8. Senate agreed to House amendments, Oct. 10. President signed Oct. 16, 2004.

PL 108-333 (HR 4011) Promote human rights and freedom in the Democratic People's Republic of Korea. Introduced by Leach, R-Iowa, on March 23, 2004. House International Relations reported, amended, May 4 (H Rept 108-478, Pt. 1). House Judiciary discharged. House passed, under suspension of the rules, July 21. Senate Foreign Relations discharged. Senate passed, amended, Sept. 28. House agreed to Senate amendments, under suspension of the rules, Oct. 4. President signed Oct. 18, 2004.

PL 108-334 (HR 4567) Make appropriations for the Department of Homeland Security for the fiscal year ending Sept. 30, 2005. Introduced by Rogers, R-Ky., on June 15, 2004. House Appropriations reported June 15 (H Rept 108-541). House passed, amended, June 18. Senate passed, amended, Sept. 14. Conference report filed in the House Oct. 9 (H Rept 108-774). House agreed to the conference report Oct. 9. Senate agreed to the conference report Oct. 11. President signed Oct. 18, 2004.

PL 108-335 (HR 4850) Make appropriations for the government of the District of Columbia and other activities chargeable in whole or in part against the revenues of the District for the fiscal year ending Sept. 30, 2005. Introduced by Frelinghuysen, R-N.J., on July 19, 2004. House Appropriations reported July 19 (H Rept 108-610). House passed July 20. Senate Appropriations discharged. Senate passed, amended, Sept. 22. Conference report filed in the House Oct. 5 (H Rept

108-734). House agreed to the conference report Oct. 6. Senate agreed to the conference report Oct. 6. President signed Oct. 18, 2004.

PL 108-336 (S 551) Provide for the implementation of air quality programs developed in accordance with an intergovernmental agreement between the Southern Ute Indian Tribe and the State of Colorado concerning air quality control on the Southern Ute Indian Reservation. Introduced by Campbell, R-Colo., on March 16, 2003. Senate Environment and Public Works reported, amended, Nov. 19 (S Rept 108-201). Senate passed Nov. 21. House Resources reported Sept. 30, 2004 (H Rept 108-712, Pt. 1). House Energy and Commerce reported Oct. 4 (H Rept 108-712, Pt. 2). House passed, under suspension of the rules, Oct. 4. President signed Oct. 18, 2004.

PL 108-337 (S 1421) Authorize the subdivision and dedication of restricted land owned by Alaska Natives. Introduced by Murkowski, R-Alaska, on July 16, 2003. Senate Energy and Natural Resources reported, amended, March 29, 2004 (S Rept 108-251). Senate passed Sept. 15. House passed, under suspension of the rules, Oct. 4. President signed Oct. 18, 2004.

PL 108-338 (S 1537) Direct the secretary of Agriculture to convey to the New Hope Cemetery Association certain land in Arkansas for use as a cemetery. Introduced by Lincoln, D-Ark., on July 31, 2003. Senate Agriculture, Nutrition and Forestry discharged. Senate passed Nov. 24. House Resources reported Sept. 7, 2004 (H Rept 108-654). House passed, under suspension of the rules, Sept. 28. President signed Oct. 18, 2004.

PL 108-339 (S 1663) Replace certain Coastal Barrier Resources System maps. Introduced by Dole, R-N.C., on Sept. 25, 2003. Senate Environment and Public Works reported Oct. 30 (S Rept 108-179). Senate passed Nov. 6. House passed, amended, under suspension of the rules, June 14, 2004. Senate agreed to House amendments Sept. 28. President signed Oct. 18, 2004.

PL 108-340 (S 1687) Direct the secretary of the Interior to conduct a study on the preservation and interpretation of the historic sites of the Manhattan Project for potential inclusion in the National Park System. Introduced by Bingaman, D-N.M., on Sept. 30, 2003. Senate Energy and Natural Resources reported, amended, May 20, 2004 (S Rept 108-270). Senate passed Sept. 15. House passed, under suspension of the rules, Sept. 28. President signed Oct. 18, 2004.

PL 108-341 (S 1814) Transfer control of the Mingo Job Corps Center in southern Missouri from the secretary of Interior to the secretary of Agriculture. Introduced by bond, R-Mo., on Nov. 3, 2003. Senate Environment and Public Works discharged. Senate passed April 20, 2004. House Resources reported Oct. 4 (H Rept 108-716, Pt. 1). House Agriculture discharged. House Education and the Workforce discharged. House passed, under suspension of the rules, Oct. 4. President signed Oct. 18, 2004.

PL 108-342 (S 2052) Amend the National Trails System Act to designate El Camino Real de los Tejas as a National Historic Trail. Introduced by Hutchison, R-Texas, on Feb. 5, 2004. Senate Energy and Natural Resources reported, amended, Aug. 25 (S Rept 108-321). Senate passed Sept. 15. House passed, under suspension of the rules, Sept. 28. President signed Oct. 18, 2004.

PL 108-343 (S 2319) Authorize and facilitate hydroelectric power licensing of the Tapoco Project. Introduced by Alexander, R-Tenn., on April 19, 2004. Senate Energy and Natural Resources reported, amended, July 7 (S Rept 108-299). Senate passed Sept. 15. House passed, under suspension of the rules, Oct. 4. President signed Oct. 18, 2004.

PL 108-344 (S 2363) Revise and extend the Boys and Girls Clubs of America. Introduced by Hatch, R-Utah, on April 29, 2004. Senate Judiciary reported June 3 (no written report). Senate passed June 3. House Judiciary reported July 13 (H Rept 108-601). House passed, under suspension of the rules, Sept. 28. President signed Oct. 18, 2004.

PL 108-345 (S 2508) Redesignate the Ridges Basin Reservoir, Colo., as Lake Nighthorse. Introduced by Domenici, R-N.M., on June 7, 2004. Senate Energy and Natural Resources reported, amended, Aug. 25 (S Rept 108-327). Senate passed Sept. 15. House passed, under suspension of the rules, Sept. 28. President signed Oct. 18, 2004.

PL 108-346 (S 2180) Direct the secretary of Agriculture to exchange certain lands in the Arapaho and Roosevelt national forests in Colorado. Introduced by Campbell, R-Colo., on March 9, 2004. Senate Energy and Natural Resources reported, amended, June 25 (S Rept 108-285). Senate passed Sept. 15. House passed, under suspension of the rules, Sept. 28. President signed Oct. 18, 2004.

PL 108-347 (HR 854) Provide for the promotion of democracy, human rights and rule of law in the Republic of Belarus and for the consolidation and strengthening of Belarus sovereignty and independence. Introduced by Smith, R-N.J., on Feb. 13, 2003. House passed, amended, under suspension of the rules, Oct. 4, 2004. Senate passed Oct. 6. President signed Oct. 20, 2004.

PL 108-348 (S 2895) Authorize the Gateway Arch in St. Louis, Mo., to be illuminated by pink lights in honor of breast cancer awareness month. Introduced by Talent, R-Mo., on Oct. 5, 2004. Senate passed Oct. 5. House passed Oct. 8. President signed Oct. 20, 2004.

PL 108-349 (HR 5122) Amend the Congressional Accountability Act of 1995 to permit members of the board of directors of the Office of Compliance to serve for two terms. Introduced by Ney, R-Ohio, on Sept. 22, 2004. House Administration discharged. House passed Sept. 28. Senate passed, with an amendment, Oct. 4. House agreed to Senate amendment Oct. 7. President signed Oct. 21, 2004.

PL 108-350 (S 33) Authorize the secretary of Agriculture to sell or exchange all or part of certain administrative sites and other land in the Ozark-St. Francis and Ouachita National Forests and to use funds derived from the sale or exchange to acquire, construct or improve administrative sites. Introduced by Lincoln, D-Ark., on Jan. 7, 2003. Senate passed Nov. 24. House passed, under suspension of the rules, Oct. 5, 2004. President signed Oct. 21 2004.

PL 108-351 (S 1791) Amend the Lease Lot Conveyance Act of 2002 to provide that the amounts received by the United States under that act be deposited in the reclamation fund. Introduced by Domenici, R-N.M., on Oct. 28, 2003. Senate Energy and Natural Resources reported May 20, 2004 (S Rept 108-272). Senate passed Sept. 15. House passed, under suspension of the rules, Oct. 7. President signed Oct. 21, 2004.

PL 108-352 (S 2178) Make technical corrections to laws relating to certain units of the National Park System and to National Park programs. Introduced by Domenici, R-N.M., on March 9, 2004. Senate Energy and Natural Resources reported March 9, 2004 (S Rept 108-239). Senate passed May 19. House passed, under suspension of the rules, Oct. 7. President signed Oct. 21, 2004.

PL 108-353 (S 2415) Designate the facility of the U.S. Postal Service located at 4141 Postmark Drive, Anchorage, Alaska, as the "Robert J. Opinsky Post Office Building." Introduced by Stevens, R-Alaska, on May 13, 2004. Senate Governmental Affairs reported June 7 (no written report). Senate passed June 9. House passed, under suspension of the rules, Oct. 6. President signed Oct. 21, 2004.

PL 108-354 (S 2511) Direct the secretary of the Interior to conduct a feasibility study of a Chimayo water supply system and to provide for the planning, design and construction of a water supply, reclamation and filtration facility for Espanola, N.M. Introduced by Domenici, R-N.M., on June 8, 2004. Senate Energy and Natural Resources reported, amended, Aug. 25 (S Rept 108-328). Senate passed Sept. 15. House passed, under suspension of the rules, Oct. 7. President signed Oct. 21, 2004.

PL 108-355 (S 2634) Amend the Public Health Service Act to support the planning, implementation and evaluation of organized activities involving statewide youth suicide early intervention and prevention strategies, and authorize grants to institutions of higher education to reduce student mental and behavioral health problems. Introduced by Dodd, D-Conn., on July 8, 2004. Senate passed July 8. House passed, amended, under suspension of the rules, Sept. 8. Senate agreed to House amendments Sept. 9. President signed Oct. 21, 2004.

PL 108-356 (S 2742) Extend certain authority of the Supreme Court Police, modify the venue of prosecutions relating to the Supreme Court building and grounds, and authorize the acceptance of gifts to the U.S. Supreme Court. Introduced by Hatch, R-Utah, on July 22, 2004. Senate Judiciary reported Sept. 21 (no written report). Senate passed, with an amendment, Sept. 28. House passed, under suspension of the rules, Oct. 6. President signed Oct. 21, 2004.

PL 108-357 (HR 4520) Amend the Internal Revenue Code to repeal the tax exclusion for extraterritorial income and reduce corporate taxes. Introduced by Thomas, R-Calif., on June 4, 2004. House Ways and Means reported, amended, June 16 (H Rept 108-548, Pt. 1). House Agriculture discharged. House passed June 17. Senate passed, with amendments, July 15. Conference report filed in the House on Oct. 7 (H Rept 108-755). House agreed to the conference report Oct. 7. Senate agreed to the conference report Oct. 11. President signed Oct. 22, 2004.

PL 108-358 (S 2195) Amend the Controlled Substances Act to clarify the definition of anabolic steroids and to provide for research and education activities relating to steroids and steroid precursors. Introduced by Biden, D-Del., on March 11, 2004. Senate Judiciary reported Sept. 30 (no written report). Senate passed, with an amendment, Oct. 6. House passed Oct. 8. President signed Oct. 22, 2004.

PL 108-359 (HR 1533) Amend securities law to permit church pension plans to be invested in collective trusts. Introduced by Biggert, R-Ill., on April 1, 2003. House Financial Services reported Sept. 3 (H Rept 108-248). House passed, amended, under suspension of the rules, Sept. 3. Senate Banking, Housing and Urban Affairs discharged. Senate passed, with an amendment, Oct. 1, 2004. House agreed to Senate amendment, Oct. 8. President signed Oct. 25, 2004.

PL 108-360 (HR 2608) Reauthorize the National Earthquake Hazards Reduction Program. Introduced by Smith, R-Mich., on June 26, 2003. House Science reported, amended, Aug. 14 (H Rept 108-246, Pt. 1). House Resources discharged. House passed, under suspension of the rules, Oct. 1. Senate Commerce, Science and Transportation reported Oct. 5, 2004 (H Rept 108-385). Senate passed, with an amendment, Oct. 6. House agreed to Senate amendment, Oct. 8. President signed Oct. 25, 2004.

PL 108-361 (HR 2828) Authorize the secretary of the Interior to implement water supply technology and infrastructure programs aimed at increasing and diversifying domestic water resources, primarily in California. Introduced by Calvert, R-Calif., on July 23, 2003. House Resources reported June 25, 2004 (H Rept 108-573, Pt. 1). House Transportation and Infrastructure discharged. House passed, amended, July 9. Senate passed, with an amendment, Sept. 15. House agreed to Senate amendment, under suspension of the rules, Oct. 6. President signed Oct. 25, 2004.

PL 108-362 (HR 3858) Amend the Public Health Service Act to increase the supply of pancreatic islet cells for research, and to provide for better coordination of federal efforts and information on islet cell transplantation. Introduced by Nethercutt, R-Wash., on Feb. 26, 2004. House Energy and Commerce reported Oct. 5 (H Rept 108-726). House passed, under suspension of the rules, Oct. 5. Senate passed Oct. 8. President signed Oct. 25, 2004.

PL 108-363 (HR 4175) Increase, effective Dec. 1, 2004, the rates of disability compensation for veterans with service-connected disabilities and the rates of dependency and indemnity compensation for survivors of certain veterans with service-connected disabilities. Introduced by Smith, R-N.J., on April 20, 2004. House Veterans' Affairs reported, amended, June 3 (H Rept 108-524). House passed, amended, under suspension of the rules, July 22. Senate Veterans' Affairs discharged. Senate passed, with an amendment, Oct. 5. House agreed to Senate amendment, Oct. 8. President signed Oct. 25, 2004.

PL 108-364 (HR 4278) Amend the Assistive Technology Act of 1998 to support grants to states to address the assistive technology needs of individuals with disabilities. Introduced by McKeon, R-Calif., on May 5, 2004. House Education and the Workforce reported, amended, June 1 (H Rept 108-514). House passed, amended, under suspension of the rules, June 14. Senate passed, with an amendment, Sept. 30. House agreed to Senate amendment Oct. 8. President signed Oct. 25, 2004.

PL 108-365 (HR 4555) Amend the Public Health Service Act to revise and extend provisions relating to mammography quality standards. Introduced by Dingell, D-Mich., on June 14, 2004. House Energy and Commerce reported, amended, Sept. 22 (H Rept 108-694). House passed, amended, under suspension of the rules, Oct. 5. Senate passed Oct. 9. President signed Oct. 25, 2004.

PL 108-366 (HR 5185) Temporarily extend the programs under the Higher Education Act of 1965. Introduced by Boehner, R-Ohio, on Sept. 30, 2004. House passed, amended, under suspension of the rules, Oct. 6. Senate passed Oct. 9. President signed Oct. 25, 2004.

PL 108-367 (S 524) Expand the boundaries of the Fort Donelson National Battlefield to authorize the acquisition and interpretation of lands associated with the campaign that resulted in the capture of the fort in 1862. Introduced by Bunning, R-Ky., on March 5, 2003. Senate Energy and Natural Resources, reported, amended, March 9, 2004 (S Rept 108-230). Senate passed May 19. House Resources discharged. House passed Oct. 8. President signed Oct. 25, 2004.

PL 108-368 (S 1368) Authorize the president to award a gold medal on behalf of the Congress to Rev. Dr. Martin Luther King Jr.

and his widow Coretta Scott King in recognition of their contributions to the nation on behalf of the civil rights movement. Introduced by Levin, D-Mich., on June 27, 2003. Senate Banking, Housing and Urban Affairs discharged. Senate passed Sept. 9, 2004. House Financial Services discharged. House passed Oct. 8. President signed Oct. 25, 2004.

PL 108-369 (S 2864) Extend family farmer bankruptcy protection through June 30, 2005. Introduced by Grassley, R-Iowa, on Sept. 29, 2004. Senate Judiciary discharged. Senate passed Oct. 6. House Judiciary discharged. House passed Oct. 8. President signed Oct. 25, 2004.

PL 108-370 (S 2883) Amend the International Child Abduction Remedies Act to limit the tort liability of private entities or organizations that carry out responsibilities of United States Central Authority under the act. Introduced by Hatch, R-Utah, on Oct. 1, 2004. Senate passed Oct. 1. House passed Oct. 8. President signed Oct. 25, 2004.

PL 108-371 (S 2896) Modify and extend certain privatization requirements of the Communications Satellite Act of 1962. Introduced by Burns, R-Mont. on Oct. 5, 2004. Senate passed Oct. 5. House passed Oct. 8. President signed Oct. 25, 2004.

PL 108-372 (HR 2714) Reauthorize the State Justice Institute. Introduced by Smith, R-Texas, on July 14, 2003. House Judiciary reported Sept. 25 (H Rept 108-285). House passed, amended, under suspension of the rules, March 10, 2004. Senate Judiciary discharged. Senate passed with an amendment Sept. 30. House agreed to Senate amendment Oct. 8. President signed Oct. 25, 2004.

PL 108-373 (S 1134) Reauthorize and improve the programs authorized by the Public Works and Economic Development Act of 1965. Introduced by Bond, R-Mo., on May 22, 2003. Senate Environment and Public Works, reported, amended, Oct. 1, 2004 (S Rept 108-382). Senate passed, with an amendment, Oct. 6. House passed, under suspension of the rules, Oct. 7. President signed Oct. 27, 2004.

PL 108-374 (S 1721) Amend the Indian Land Consolidation Act to improve provisions relating to probate of trust and restricted land. Introduced by Campbell, R-Colo., on Oct. 14, 2003. Senate Indian Affairs, reported, amended, May 13, 2004 (S Rept 108-264). Senate passed, June 2. House Resources reported Sept. 7 (H Rept 108-656). House passed, under suspension of the rules, Oct. 7. President signed Oct. 27, 2004.

PL 108-375 (HR 4200) Authorize appropriations for fiscal 2005 for military activities of the Department of Defense, for military construction and for defense activities of the Department of Energy, and prescribe personnel strengths for the Armed Forces. Introduced by Hunter, R-Calif., on April 22, 2004. House Armed Services, reported, amended, May 14 (H Rept 108-491). House passed, amended, May 20. Senate passed, with an amendment, June 23. Conference report filed in the House, Oct. 8 (H Rept 108-767). House agreed to conference report, Oct. 9. Senate agreed to conference report, Oct. 9. President signed Oct. 28, 2004.

PL 108-376 (HR 2010) Protect the voting rights of members of the Armed Services in elections for the delegate representing American Samoa in the U.S. House of Representatives. Introduced by Faleomavaega, D-Am. Samoa, on May 7, 2003. House Resources reported, amended, June 1, 2004 (H Rept 108-515). House passed, amended, under suspension of the rules, June 14. Senate Energy and Natural Resources reported, Sept. 28 (S Rept 108-377). Senate passed Oct. 10. President signed Oct. 30, 2004.

PL 108-377 (HR 2023) Give a preference regarding states that require schools to allow students to self-administer medication to treat their asthma or anaphylaxis. Introduced by Stearns, R-Fla., on May 7, 2003. House Energy and Commerce reported, amended, July 14, 2004 (H Rept 108-606, Pt. 1). House Education and the Workforce discharged. House passed, amended, under suspension of the rules, Oct. 5. Senate passed Oct. 11. President signed Oct. 30, 2004.

PL 108-378 (HR 2400) Amend the Organic Act of Guam for the purposes of clarifying the local judicial structure of Guam. Introduced by Bordallo, D-Guam, on June 10, 2003. House Resources reported, amended, Sept. 7, 2004 (H Rept 108-638). House passed, under suspension of the rules, Sept. 13. Senate Energy and Natural Resources discharged. Senate passed Oct. 10. President signed Oct. 30, 2004.

PL 108-379 (HR 2984) Amend the Agricultural Adjustment Act to remove the requirement that processors be members of an agency administering a marketing order applicable to pears. Introduced by Walden, R-Ore., on July 25, 2003. House passed, under suspension of the rules, Oct. 5, 2004. Senate passed Oct. 11. President signed Oct. 30, 2004.

PL 108-380 (HR 3056) Clarify the boundaries of the John H. Chafee Coast Barrier Resources System Cedar Keys Unit P25 on Otherwise Protected Area P25P. Introduced by Brown-Waite, R-Fla., on Sept. 10, 2003. House Resources reported, amended, Sept. 7, 2004 (H Rept 108-641). House passed, amended, under suspension of the rules, Sept. 13. Senate Environment and Public Works discharged. Senate passed Oct. 11. President signed Oct. 30, 2004.

PL 108-381 (HR 3217) Provide for the conveyance of several small parcels of National Forest System land in the Apalachicola National Forest in Florida, to resolve boundary discrepancies involving the Mt. Trial Primitive Baptist Church of Wakulla County, Fla. Introduced by Boyd, D-Fla., on Oct. 1, 2003. House passed, under suspension of the rules, Nov. 17. Senate Agriculture, Nutrition and Forestry discharged. Senate passed Oct. 11, 2004. President signed Oct. 30, 2004.

PL 108-382 (HR 3391) Authorize the secretary of the Interior to convey certain lands and facilities of the Provo River Project. Introduced by Cannon, R-Utah, on Oct. 29, 2003. House Resources reported, amended, Oct. 4, 2004 (H Rept 108-719). House passed, amended, under suspension of the rules, Oct. 4. Senate passed Oct. 10. President signed Oct. 30, 2004.

PL 108-383 (HR 3478) Amend Title 44, U.S. Code, to improve the efficiency of operations by the National Archives and Records Administration and to reauthorize the National Historical Publications and Records Commission. Introduced by Putnam, R-Fla., on Nov. 7, 2003. House Government Reform reported Dec. 8 (H Rept 108-403). House passed, amended, under suspension of the rules, Sept. 13, 2004. Senate Governmental Affairs discharged. Senate passed Oct. 11. President signed Oct. 30, 2004.

PL 108-384 (HR 3479) Provide for the control and eradication of the brown tree snake on the island of Guam and the prevention of the introduction of the brown tree snake to other areas of the United States. Introduced by Bordallo, D-Guam, on Nov. 7, 2003. House Resources reported, amended, Sept. 15, 2004 (H Rept 108-687, Pt. 1). House Agriculture discharged. House passed, amended, under suspension of the rules, Sept. 28. Senate passed Oct. 10. President signed Oct. 30, 2004.

PL 108-385 (HR 3706) Adjust the boundary of the John Muir National Historic Site. Introduced by Miller, D-Calif. on Jan. 20, 2004. House Resources reported June 18 (H Rept 108-555). House passed, under suspension of the rules, June 21. Senate Energy and Natural Resources reported Sept. 28 (S Rept 108-378). Senate passed Oct. 10. President signed Oct. 30, 2004.

PL 108-386 (HR 3797) Authorize improvements in the operations of the government of the District of Columbia. Introduced by Davis, Thomas, R-Va., on Feb. 11, 2004. House Government Reform reported June 17 (H Rept 108-551, Pt. 1). House Education and the Workforce discharged. House Financial Services discharged. House passed, under suspension of the rules, June 21. Senate Governmental Affairs discharged. Senate passed Oct. 11. President signed Oct. 30, 2004.

PL 108-387 (HR 3819) Redesignate Fort Clatsop National Memorial as the Lewis and Clark National Historical Park and include in the park sites in the state of Washington and Oregon. Introduced by Baird, D-Wash., on Feb. 24, 2004. House Resources reported, amended, June 25 (H Rept 108-570). House passed, amended, under suspension of the rules, July 19. Senate Energy and Natural Resources discharged. Senate passed Oct. 10. President signed Oct. 30, 2004.

PL 108-388 (HR 4046) Designate the facility of the U.S. Postal Service located at 555 West 180th St. in New York as the "Sergeant Riayan A. Tejeda Post Office." Introduced by Rangel, D-N.Y., on March 25, 2004. House passed, amended, under suspension of the rules, Sept. 28. Senate passed Oct. 10. President signed Oct. 30, 2004.

PL 108-389 (HR 4066) Provide for the conveyance of certain land to the United States and revise the boundary of Chickasaw National Recreation Area in Oklahoma. Introduced by Cole, R-Okla., on March 30, 2004. House Resources reported, amended, Sept. 28 (H Rept 108-702). House passed, amended, under suspension of the rules, Sept. 28. Senate passed Oct. 10. President signed Oct. 30, 2004.

PL 108-390 (HR 4306) Amend Section 274A of the Immigration and Nationality Act to improve the process for verifying an individual's eligibility for employment. Introduced by Cannon, R-Utah, on May 6, 2004. House Judiciary reported, amended, Oct. 5 (H Rept 108-731). House passed, amended, under suspension of the rules, Oct. 6. Senate passed Oct. 11. President signed Oct. 30, 2004.

PL 108-391 (H J Res 57) Express the sense of the Congress in recognition of the contributions of the seven Columbia astronauts by supporting establishment of a Columbia Memorial Space Science Learning Center. Introduced by Roybal-Allard, D-Calif., on May 22, 2003. House passed, amended, under suspension of the rules, Oct. 5, 2004. Senate passed Oct. 10. President signed Oct. 30, 2004.

PL 108-392 (HR 4381) Designate the facility of the U.S. Postal Service located at 2811 Springdale Ave., Springdale, Ark., as the "Harvey and Bernice Jones Post Office Building." Introduced by Boozman, R-Ark., on May 18, 2004. House passed, under suspension of the rules, Sept. 7. Senate Governmental Affairs discharged. Senate passed Oct. 10. President signed Oct. 30, 2004.

PL 108-393 (HR 4471) Clarify the loan guarantee authority under Title VI of the Native American Housing Assistance and Self-Determination Act of 1996. Introduced by Renzi, R-Ariz., on June 1, 2004. House Financial Services reported June 17 (H Rept 108-550). House passed, under suspension of the rules, June 21. Senate Indian Affairs discharged. Senate passed Oct. 11. President signed Oct. 30, 2004.

PL 108-394 (HR 4481) Amend Public Law 86-434 establishing Wilson's Creek National Battlefield in the state of Missouri to expand the boundaries of the park. Introduced by Blunt, R-Mo., on June 2, 2004. House Resources reported, amended, Sept. 7 (H Rept 108-651). House passed, amended, under suspension of the rules, Sept. 13. Senate Energy and Natural Resources discharged. Senate passed Oct. 10. President signed Oct. 30, 2004.

PL 108-395 (HR 4556) Designate the facility of the U.S. Postal Service located at 1115 South Clinton Ave. in Dunn, N.C., as the "Gen. William Carey Lee Post Office Building." Introduced by Etheridge, D-N.C., on June 14, 2004. House passed, under suspension of the rules, Sept. 7. Senate Governmental Affairs discharged. Senate passed Oct. 10. President signed Oct. 30, 2004.

PL 108-396 (HR 4579) Modify the boundary of the Harry S Truman National Historic Site in the state of Missouri. Introduced by McCarthy, D-Mo., on June 15, 2004. House Resources reported Sept. 28 (H Rept 108-703). House passed, under suspension of the rules, Sept. 28. Senate passed Oct. 10. President signed Oct. 30, 2004.

PL 108-397 (HR 4618) Designate the facility of the U.S. Postal Service located at 10 West Prospect St., Nanuet, N.Y., as the "Anthony I. Lombardi Memorial Post Office Building." Introduced by Engel, D-N.Y., on June 18, 2004. House passed, under suspension of the rules, Sept. 7. Senate Governmental Affairs discharged. Senate passed Oct. 10. President signed Oct. 30, 2004.

PL 108-398 (HR 4632) Designate the facility of the U.S. Postal Service located at 19504 Linden Blvd., St. Albans, N.Y., as the "Archie Spigner Post Office Building." Introduced by Meeks, D-N.Y., on June 21, 2004. House passed, under suspension of the rules, Sept. 13. Senate Governmental Affairs discharged. Senate passed Oct. 10. President signed Oct. 30, 2004.

PL 108-399 (HR 4731) Amend the Federal Water Pollution Control Act to reauthorize the National Estuary Program. Introduced by Gerlach, R-Pa., on June 25, 2004. House Transportation and Infrastructure reported Sept. 13 (H Rept 108-678). House passed, under suspension of the rules, Sept. 29. Senate passed Oct. 11. President signed Oct. 30, 2004.

PL 108-400 (HR 4827) Amend the Colorado Canyons National Conservation Area and Black Ridge Canyons Wilderness Act of 2000 to rename the Colorado Canyons National Conservation Area as the McInnis Canyons National Conservation Area. Introduced by Walden, R-Ore., on July 13, 2004. House passed, under suspension of the rules, Sept. 28. Senate passed Oct. 10. President signed Oct. 30, 2004.

PL 108-401 (HR 4917) Amend Title 5, U.S. Code, to authorize appropriations for the Administrative Conference of the United States for fiscal years 2005, 2006 and 2007. Introduced by Cannon, R-Utah, on July 22, 2004. House Judiciary discharged. House passed Oct. 8. Senate passed Oct. 11. President signed Oct. 30, 2004.

PL 108-402 (HR 5027) Designate the facility of the U.S. Postal Service located at 411 Midway Ave., Mascotte, Fla., as the "Specialist Eric Ramirez Post Office." Introduced by Brown-Waite, R-Fla., on Sept. 8, 2004. House passed, under suspension of the rules, Sept. 28. Senate passed Oct. 10. President signed Oct. 30, 2004.

PL 108-403 (HR 5039) Designate the facility of the U.S. Postal Service located at U.S. Route 1 in Ridgeway, N.C., as the "Eva Holtz-

man Post Office." Introduced by Butterfield, D-N.C., on Sept. 9, 2004. House passed, under suspension of the rules, Sept. 22. Senate Governmental Affairs discharged. Senate passed Oct. 10. President signed Oct. 30, 2004.

PL 108-404 (HR 5051) Designate the facility of the U.S. Postal Service located at 1001 Williams St., Ignacio, Colo., as the "Leonard C. Burch Post Office Building." Introduced by McInnis, R-Colo., on Sept. 9, 2004. House passed, under suspension of the rules, Oct. 6. Senate passed Oct. 10. President signed Oct. 30, 2004.

PL 108-405 (HR 5107) Protect crime victims' rights; eliminate the substantial backlog of DNA samples collected from crime scenes and convicted offenders; improve and expand the DNA testing capacity of federal, state and local crime laboratories; increase research and development of new DNA testing technologies; develop new training programs regarding the collection and use of DNA evidence; provide post-conviction testing of DNA evidence to exonerate the innocent; and improve the performance of counsel in state capital cases. Introduced by Sensenbrenner, R-Wis., on Sept. 21, 2004. House Judiciary reported Sept. 30 (H Rept 108-711). House passed, amended, Oct. 6. Senate passed Oct. 9. President signed Oct. 30, 2004.

PL 108-406 (HR 5131) Provide assistance to support expansion of Special Olympics and development of education programs and a Healthy Athletes Program. Introduced by Blunt, R-Mo., on Sept. 23, 2004. House passed, under suspension of the rules, Oct. 6. Senate passed Oct. 10. President signed Oct. 30, 2004.

PL 108-407 (HR 5133) Designate the facility of the U.S. Postal Service located at 11110 Sunset Hills Rd., Reston, Va., as the "Martha Pennino Post Office Building." Introduced by Moran, D-Va., on Sept. 23, 2004. House passed, under suspension of the rules, Sept. 28. Senate passed Oct. 10. President signed Oct. 30, 2004.

PL 108-408 (HR 5147) Designate the facility of the U.S. Postal Service located at 23055 Sherman Way, West Hills, Calif., as the "Evan Asa Ashcraft Post Office Building." Introduced by Waxman, D-Calif., on Sept. 24, 2004. House passed, under suspension of the rules, Sept. 28. Senate passed Oct. 10. President signed Oct. 30, 2004.

PL 108-409 (HR 5186) Reduce certain special allowance payments and provide additional teacher loan forgiveness on federal student loans. Introduced by Boehner, R-Ohio, on Sept. 30, 2004. House passed, amended, under suspension of the rules, Oct. 7. Senate passed Oct. 9. President signed Oct. 30, 2004.

PL 108-410 (HR 5294) Amend the John F. Kennedy Center Act to authorize appropriations for the John F. Kennedy Center for the Performing Arts. Introduced by Young, R-Alaska, on Oct. 8, 2004. House Transportation and Infrastructure discharged. House passed Oct. 8. Senate passed Oct. 11. President signed Oct. 30, 2004.

PL 108-411 (S 129) Provide for reform relating to federal employment. Introduced by Voinovich, R-Ohio, on Jan. 9, 2003. Senate Governmental Affairs reported, amended, Jan. 27, 2004 (S Rept 108-223). Senate passed, with an amendment, April 8. House Government Reform reported, amended, Oct. 5 (H Rept 108-733). House passed, amended, under suspension of the rules, Oct. 6. Senate agreed to House amendment, Oct. 11. President signed Oct. 30, 2004.

PL 108-412 (S 144) Require the secretary of Agriculture to establish a program to assist eligible weed management entities to control or eradicate noxious weeds on public and private land. Introduced by

Craig, R-Idaho, on Jan. 13, 2003. Senate Energy and Natural Resources reported, amended, Feb. 11 (S Rept 108-6). Senate passed, with an amendment, March 4. House Resources reported, amended, June 1, 2004 (H Rept 108-517, Pt. 1). House Agriculture discharged. House passed, amended, under suspension of the rules, Oct. 4. Senate agreed to House amendment, Oct. 10. President signed Oct. 30, 2004.

PL 108-413 (S 643) Authorize the secretary of the Interior, in cooperation with the University of New Mexico, to construct and occupy a portion of the Hibben Center for Archaeological Research at the University of New Mexico. Introduced by Domenici, R-N.M. on March 18, 2003. Senate Energy and Natural Resources reported, amended, July 11 (S Rept 108-94). Senate passed, with an amendment, July 17. House passed, amended, under suspension of the rules, Sept. 28. Senate agreed to House amendment, Oct. 10. President signed Oct. 30, 2004.

PL 108-414 (S 1194) Foster local collaborations to ensure that resources are effectively and efficiently used within the criminal and juvenile justice systems. Introduced by DeWine, R-Ohio, on June 5, 2003. Senate Judiciary reported, amended, Oct. 23 (no written report). Senate passed, with an amendment, Oct. 27. House Judiciary reported, amended, Oct. 5, 2004 (H Rept 108-732). House passed, amended, under suspension of the rules, Oct. 6. Senate agreed to House amendment, Oct. 11. President signed Oct. 30, 2004.

PL 108-415 (S 2986) Amend Title 31 of the U.S. Code to increase the public debt limit. Introduced by Frist, R-Tenn., on Nov. 16, 2004. Senate passed Nov. 17. House passed Nov. 18. President signed Nov. 19, 2004.

PL 108-416 (H J Res 114) Make further continuing appropriations for fiscal 2005. Introduced by Young, R-Fla., on Nov. 19, 2004. House passed Nov. 20. Senate passed Nov. 20. President signed Nov. 21, 2004.

PL 108-417 (HR 1113) Authorize an exchange of land at Fort Frederica National Monument. Introduced by Kingston, R-Ga., on March 6, 2003. House Resources reported, amended, July 14 (H Rept 108-201). House passed, amended, under suspension of the rules, Sept. 23. Senate Energy and Natural Resources reported, amended, Sept. 28, 2004 (S Rept 108-374). Senate passed, amended, Oct. 10. House agreed to Senate amendment, under suspension of the rules, Nov. 17. President signed Nov. 30, 2004.

PL 108-418 (HR 1284) Amend the Reclamation Projects Authorization and Adjustment Act of 1992 to increase the federal share of the costs of the San Gabriel Basin demonstration project. Introduced by Napolitano, D-Calif., on March 13, 2003. House Resources reported July 14 (H Rept 108-204). House passed, under suspension of the rules, Sept. 16. Senate Energy and Natural Resources reported, amended, July 22, 2004 (S Rept 108-331). Senate passed, amended, Sept. 15. House agreed to Senate amendment, under suspension of the rules, Nov. 17. President signed Nov. 30, 2004.

PL 108-419 (HR 1417) Amend Title 17, U.S. Code, to replace copyright arbitration royalty panels with copyright royalty judges. Introduced by Smith, R-Texas, on March 25, 2003. House Judiciary reported, amended, Jan. 30, 2004 (H Rept 108-408). House passed, under suspension of the rules, March 3. Senate Judiciary reported, amended, Sept. 29 (no written report). Senate passed with an amendment, Oct. 6. House agreed to Senate amendment, under suspension of the rules, Nov. 17. President signed Nov. 30, 2004.

PL 108-420 (HR 1446) Support the efforts of the California Missions Foundation to restore and repair the Spanish colonial and mission-era missions in California and to preserve the artwork and artifacts of these missions. Introduced by Farr, D-Calif., on March 26, 2003. House passed, under suspension of the rules, Oct. 20. Senate Energy and Natural Resources reported, amended, Sept. 28, 2004 (S Rept 108-375). Senate passed, amended, Oct. 10. House agreed to Senate amendment, under suspension of the rules, Nov. 17. President signed Nov. 30, 2004.

PL 108-421 (HR 1964) Assist Connecticut, New Jersey, New York and Pennsylvania in conserving priority lands and natural resources in the Highlands region. Introduced by Frelinghuysen, R-N.J., on May 6, 2003. House Resources reported, amended, Nov. 17 (H Rept 108-373, Pt. 1). House passed, under suspension of the rules, Nov. 21. Senate Energy and Natural Resources reported, amended, Sept. 28, 2004 (S Rept 108-376). Senate passed, amended, Oct. 10. House agreed to Senate amendment, under suspension of the rules, Nov. 17. President signed Nov. 30, 2004.

PL 108-422 (HR 3936) Amend Title 38, U.S. Code, to increase the authorization for grants to benefit homeless veterans and improve management and administration of veterans' facilities and health care programs. Introduced by Smith, R-N.J., on March 11, 2004. House Veterans' Affairs reported June 25 (H Rept 108-574, Pt. 1). House Armed Services discharged. House passed, under suspension of the rules, July 20. Senate Veterans' Affairs discharged. Senate passed with an amendment Oct. 9. House agreed to Senate amendment, under suspension of the rules, Nov. 17. President signed Nov. 30, 2004.

PL 108-423 (HR 4516) Require the secretary of Energy to carry out a program of research and development to advance high-end computing. Introduced by Biggert, R-Ill., on June 4, 2004. House Science reported, amended, July 1 (H Rept 108-578). House passed, amended, under suspension of the rules, July 7. Senate Energy and Natural Resources reported, amended, Sept. 28 (S Rept 108-379). Senate passed with an amendment, Oct. 10. House agreed to Senate amendment, under suspension of the rules, Nov. 17. President signed Nov. 30, 2004.

PL 108-424 (HR 4593) Establish wilderness areas, promote conservation, improve public land and provide for development in Lincoln County, Nev. Introduced by Gibbons, R-Nev., on June 16, 2004. House Resources reported, amended, Oct. 4 (H Rept 108-720). House passed, under suspension of the rules, Oct. 4. Senate passed with an amendment, Oct. 10. House agreed to Senate amendment, under suspension of the rules, Nov. 17. President signed Nov. 30, 2004.

PL 108-425 (HR 4794) Amend the Tijuana River Valley Estuary and Beach Sewage Cleanup Act of 2000 to extend the authorization. Introduced by Hunter, R-Calif., on July 9, 2004. House Transportation and Infrastructure reported Sept. 15 (H Rept 108-688, Pt. 1). House passed, under suspension of the rules, Oct. 7. Senate passed Nov. 16. President signed Nov. 30, 2004.

PL 108-426 (HR 5163) Amend Title 49, U.S. Code, to reorganize Department of Transportation research activities. Introduced by Young, R-Alaska, on Sept. 29, 2004. House Transportation and Infrastructure reported Oct. 6 (H Rept 108-749, Pt. 1). House Energy and Commerce, and House Science discharged. House passed, amended, under suspension of the rules, Oct. 7. Senate passed Nov. 16. President signed Nov. 30, 2004.

PL 108-427 (HR 5213) Expand research information regarding multidisciplinary research projects and epidemiological studies. Introduced by Bilirakis, R-Fla., on Oct. 5, 2004. House passed, amended, under suspension of the rules, Oct. 7. Senate passed Nov. 16. President signed Nov. 30, 2004.

PL 108-428 (HR 5245) Extend the liability indemnification regime for the commercial space transportation industry. Introduced by Boehlert, R-N.Y., on Oct. 7, 2004. House Science discharged. House passed Oct. 8. Senate passed Nov. 16. President signed Nov. 30, 2004.

PL 108-429 (HR 1047) Amend the U.S. Harmonized Tariff Schedule to modify temporarily certain rates of duty and to make other technical changes to trade laws. Introduced by Crane, R-Ill., on March 4, 2003. House passed, under suspension of the rules, March 5. Senate passed, with an amendment, March 4, 2004. Conference report filed in the House Oct. 8 (H Rept 108-771). House agreed to conference report Oct. 8. Senate agreed to conference report Nov. 19. President signed Dec. 3, 2004.

PL 108-430 (HR 1630) Revise the boundary of the Petrified Forest National Park in Arizona. Introduced by Renzi, R-Ariz., on April 3, 2003. House Resources reported, amended, Sept. 30, 2004 (H Rept 108-713). House passed, under suspension of the rules, Oct. 4. Senate passed, with an amendment, Oct. 10. House agreed to Senate amendment Nov. 19. President signed Dec. 3, 2004.

PL 108-431 (HR 2912) Reaffirm the inherent sovereign rights of the Osage Tribe to determine its membership and form of government. Introduced by Lucas, R-Okla., on July 25, 2003. House Resources reported May 19, 2004 (H Rept 108-502). House passed, under suspension of the rules, June 1. Senate Indian Affairs reported Sept. 15 (S Rept 108-343). Senate passed Nov. 19. President signed Dec. 3, 2004.

PL 108-432 (H J Res 110) Recognize the 60th anniversary of the Battle of the Bulge during World War II. Introduced by Hastert, R-Ill., on Oct. 8, 2004. House passed, under suspension of the rules, Nov. 16. Senate passed Nov. 19. President signed Dec. 3, 2004.

PL 108-433 (H J Res 111) Appoint the day for convening of the first session of the 109th Congress. Introduced by Boehner, R-Ohio, on Nov. 17, 2004. House passed Nov. 17. Senate passed Nov. 19. President signed Dec. 3, 2004.

PL 108-434 (H J Res 115) Make further continuing appropriations for fiscal 2005 through Dec. 8, 2004. Introduced by Wolf, R-Va., on Nov. 24, 2004. House Appropriations discharged. House passed Nov. 24. Senate passed Nov. 24. President signed Dec. 3, 2004.

PL 108-435 (S 150) Amend the Internet Tax Freedom Act to extend for four years the moratorium on taxes on Internet access and multiple and discriminatory taxes on electronic commerce. Introduced by Allen, R-Va., on Jan. 13, 2003. Senate Commerce, Science and Transportation reported, amended, Sept. 29 (S Rept 108-155). Senate Finance discharged. Senate passed, with amendments, April 29, 2004. House passed, under suspension of the rules, Nov. 19. President signed Dec. 3, 2004.

PL 108-436 (S 434) Authorize the secretary of Agriculture to sell or exchange all or part of certain parcels of National Forest System land in Idaho and use the proceeds derived from the sale or exchange for National Forest System purposes. Introduced by Craig, R-Idaho,

on Feb. 25, 2003. Senate Energy and Natural Resources reported, amended, July 21 (S Rept 108-132). Senate passed, with an amendment, Nov. 24. House Resources reported Oct. 6, 2004 (H Rept 108-740). House passed, under suspension of the rules, Nov. 17. President signed Dec. 3, 2004.

PL 108-437 (S 1146) Implement the recommendations of the Garrison Unit Joint Tribal Advisory Committee by authorizing the construction of a rural health care facility on the Fort Berthold Indian Reservation, N.D. Introduced by Conrad, D-N.D., on May 23, 2003. Senate Indian Affairs reported, amended, Oct. 15 (S Rept 108-165). Senate passed, amended, Oct. 27. House Resources reported June 3, 2004 (H Rept 108-523, Pt. 1). House Energy and Commerce discharged. House passed, under suspension of the rules, Nov. 17. President signed Dec. 3, 2004.

PL 108-438 (S 1241) Establish the Kate Mullany National Historic Site in New York. Introduced by Clinton, D-N.Y., on June 11, 2003. Senate Energy and Natural Resources reported, amended, July 7, 2004 (S Rept 108-295). Senate passed, amended, Sept. 15. House passed, under suspension of the rules, Nov. 17. President signed Dec. 3, 2004.

PL 108-439 (S 1727) Authorize additional appropriations for the Reclamation Safety of Dams Act of 1978. Introduced by Domenici, R-N.M., on Oct. 14, 2003. Senate Energy and Natural Resources reported, amended, July 7, 2004 (S Rept 108-296). Senate passed, amended, Sept. 15. House passed, under suspension of the rules, Nov. 17. President signed Dec. 3, 2004.

PL 108-440 (S 2214) Designate the facility of the U.S. Postal Service located at 3150 Great Northern Ave. in Missoula, Mont., the "Mike Mansfield Post Office." Introduced by Burns, R-Mont., on March 12, 2004. Senate Governmental Affairs reported June 7 (no written report). Senate passed June 9. House passed, under suspension of the rules, Nov. 16. President signed Dec. 3, 2004.

PL 108-441 (S 2302) Improve access to physicians in medically underserved areas. Introduced by Conrad, D-N.D., on April 7, 2004. Senate Judiciary reported, amended, Oct. 7 (no written report). Senate passed, amended, Oct. 11. House passed, under suspension of the rules, Nov. 17. President signed Dec. 3, 2004.

PL 108-442 (S 2640) Designate the facility of the U.S. Postal Service located at 1050 North Hills Blvd. in Reno, Nev., the "Guardians of Freedom Memorial Post Office Building" and to authorize the installation of a plaque at such site. Introduced by ENSIGN, R-Nev., on July 13, 2004. Senate Governmental Affairs reported July 22 (no written report). Senate passed July 22. House passed, under suspension of the rules, Nov. 16. President signed Dec. 3, 2004.

PL 108-443 (S 2693) Designate the facility of the U.S. Postal Service located at 1475 Western Ave., Suite 45, in Albany, N.Y., the "Lieutenant John F. Finn Post Office." Introduced by Schumer, D-N.Y., on July 20, 2004. Senate Governmental Affairs discharged. Senate passed Oct. 10. House passed, under suspension of the rules, Nov. 16. President signed Dec. 3, 2004.

PL 108-444 (S 2965) Amend the Livestock Mandatory Price Reporting Act of 1999 to modify the termination date for mandatory price reporting. Introduced by Cochran, R-Miss., on Oct. 8, 2004. Senate passed Oct. 8. House passed, under suspension of the rules, Nov. 17. President signed Dec. 3, 2004.

PL 108-445 (S 2484) Amend Title 38, U.S. Code, to simplify and improve pay provisions for physicians and dentists in VA facilities and to authorize alternate work schedules and executive pay for nurses. Introduced by Specter, R-Pa., on June 1, 2004. Senate Veterans' Affairs reported, amended, Sept. 23 (S Rept 108-357). Senate passed, with an amendment, Oct. 5. House passed, under suspension of the rules, Nov. 17. President signed Dec. 3, 2004.

PL 108-446 (HR 1350) Reauthorize the Individuals with Disabilities Education Act. Introduced by Castle, R-Del., on March 19, 2003. House Education and the Workforce reported, amended, April 29 (H Rept 108-77). House passed, with amendments, April 30. Senate Health, Education, Labor and Pensions discharged. Senate passed, amended, May 13, 2004. Conference report filed Nov. 17 (H Rept 108-779). House agreed to conference report Nov. 19. Senate agreed to conference report Nov. 19. President signed Dec. 3, 2004.

PL 108-447 (HR 4818) Make appropriations for foreign operations, export financing and related programs for the fiscal year ending Sept. 30, 2005. (The conference report also incorporated eight other fiscal 2005 appropriations bills.) Introduced by Kolbe, R-Ariz., on July 13, 2004. House Appropriations reported July 13 (H Rept 108-599). House passed, with amendments, July 15. Senate Appropriations discharged. Senate passed, with amendments, Sept. 23. Conference report filed in the House Nov. 20 (H Rept 108-792). House agreed to the conference report Nov. 20. Senate agreed to the conference report Nov. 20. President signed Dec. 8, 2004.

PL 108-448 (S 2618) Amend Title XIX of the Social Security Act to extend Medicare cost-sharing for the Medicare part B premium for qualifying individuals through September 2005. Introduced by Grassley, R-Iowa, on July 7, 2004. Senate Finance discharged. Senate passed Nov. 16, 2004. House passed, under suspension of the rules, Nov. 19. President signed Dec. 8, 2004.

PL 108-449 (HR 2655) Amend and extend the Irish Peace Process Cultural and Training Program Act of 1998. Introduced by Walsh, R-N.Y., on June 26, 2003. House Judiciary reported Sept. 4 (H Rept 108-260, Pt. 1). House International Relations discharged. House passed, amended, under suspension of the rules, Oct. 7. Senate Foreign Relations discharged. Senate passed, with an amendment, Nov. 19, 2004. House agreed to Senate amendment, Nov. 20. President signed Dec. 10, 2004.

PL 108-450 (HR 4302) Amend Title 21, District of Columbia Official Code, to enact the provisions of the Mental Health Civil Commitment Act of 2002 that affect the Commission on Mental Health and require action by Congress in order to take effect. Introduced by T. Davis, R-Va., on May 6, 2004. House Government Reform reported Oct. 5 (H Rept 108-729). House passed, amended, under suspension of the rules, Oct. 6. Senate passed Nov. 20. President signed Dec. 10, 2004.

PL 108-451 (S 437) Provide for adjustments to the Central Arizona Project, authorize the Gila River Indian Community water rights settlement, and reauthorize and amend the Southern Arizona Water Rights Settlement Act of 1982. Introduced by Kyl, R-Ariz., on Feb. 25, 2003. Senate Energy and Natural Resources reported, amended, Sept. 28, 2004 (S Rept 108-360). Senate passed, with an amendment, Oct. 10. House passed, under suspension of the rules, Nov. 17. President signed Dec. 10, 2004.

PL 108-452 (S 1466) Facilitate the transfer of land in the state of Alaska. Introduced by Murkowski, R-Alaska, on July 25, 2003. Senate Energy and Natural Resources discharged. Senate passed, with an amendment, Oct. 10, 2004. House passed, under suspension of the rules, Nov. 17. President signed Dec. 10, 2004.

PL 108-453 (S 2192) Amend Title 35, U.S. Code, to promote co-operative research involving universities, the public sector, and private enterprises. Introduced by Hatch, R-Utah, on March 10, 2004. Senate Judiciary reported April 29 (no written report). Senate passed June 25. House passed Nov. 20. President signed Dec. 10, 2004.

PL 108-454 (S 2486) Amend Title 38, U.S. Code, to improve and enhance housing, education and other benefits under the laws administered by the secretary of Veterans Affairs. Introduced by Specter, R-Pa., on June 1, 2004. Senate Veterans' Affairs reported, amended, Sept. 20 (S Rept 108-352). Senate passed, with an amendment, Oct. 8. House passed, under suspension of the rules, Nov. 17. President signed Dec. 10, 2004.

PL 108-455 (S 2873) Extend the authority of the U.S. District Court for the Southern District of Iowa to hold court in Rock Island, Ill. Introduced by Grassley, R-Iowa, on Sept. 30, 2004. Senate Judiciary discharged. Senate passed, with an amendment, Nov. 19. House passed Nov. 20. President signed Dec. 10, 2004.

PL 108-456 (S 3014) Reauthorize the Harmful Algal Bloom and Hypoxia Research and Control Act of 1998. Introduced by Snowe, R-Maine, on Nov. 19, 2004. Senate passed Nov. 19. House passed Nov. 20. President signed Dec. 10, 2004.

PL 108-457 (HR 4012) Amend the District of Columbia College Access Act of 1999 to reauthorize for two additional years the public school and private school tuition assistance programs established under the act. Introduced by T. Davis, R-Va., on March 23, 2004. House Government Reform reported June 8 (H Rept 108-527). House passed, amended, under suspension of the rules, July 14. Senate Governmental Affairs reported July 22 (no written report). Senate passed with amendments, Nov. 24. House agreed to Senate amendments, under suspension of the rules, Dec. 6. President signed Dec. 17, 2004.

PL 108-458 (S 2845) Reform the intelligence community and the intelligence and intelligence-related activities of the United States government. Introduced by Collins, R-Maine, on Sept. 23, 2004. Senate passed with amendments, Oct. 6. House passed, amended, Oct. 16. Conference report filed in the House Dec. 7 (H Rept 108-796). House agreed to the conference report Dec. 7. Senate agreed to the conference report Dec. 8. President signed Dec. 17, 2004.

PL 108-459 (HR 480) Redesignate the facility of the United States Postal Service located at 747 Broadway in Albany, N.Y., the "United States Postal Service Henry Johnson Annex." Introduced by McNulty, D-N.Y., on Jan. 29, 2003. House passed, under suspension of the rules, Sept. 22, 2004. Senate passed Dec. 7. President signed Dec. 21, 2004.

PL 108-460 (HR 2119) Provide for the conveyance of Federal lands, improvements, equipment and resource materials at the Oxford Research Station in Granville County, N.C., to the State of North Carolina. Introduced by Ballance, D-N.C., on May 15, 2003. House passed, amended, under suspension of the rules, Oct. 5, 2004. Senate passed Dec. 7. President signed Dec. 21, 2004.

PL 108-461 (HR 2523) Designate the United States courthouse located at 125 Bull Street in Savannah, Ga., the "Tomochichi United States Courthouse." Introduced by Burns, R-Ga., on June 19, 2003. House Transportation and Infrastructure reported March 25, 2004 (H Rept 108-447). House passed, under suspension of the rules, May 11. Senate Environment and Public Works discharged. Senate passed Dec. 7. President signed Dec. 21, 2004.

PL 108-462 (HR 3124) Designate the facility of the United States Geological Survey and the United States Bureau of Reclamation located at 230 Collins Road, Boise, Idaho, the "F.H. Newell Building." Introduced by Otter, R-Idaho, on Sept. 17, 2003. House passed, under suspension of the rules, Sept. 29, 2004. Senate passed Dec. 7. President signed Dec. 21, 2004.

PL 108-463 (HR 3147) Designate the federal building located at 324 Twenty-Fifth Street in Ogden, Utah, the "James V. Hansen Federal Building." Introduced by Cannon, R-Utah, on Sept. 23, 2003. House Transportation and Infrastructure reported, amended, March 25, 2004 (H Rept 108-449). House passed, amended, under suspension of the rules, April 21. Senate Environment and Public Works discharged. Senate passed Dec. 7. President signed Dec. 21, 2004.

PL 108-464 (HR 3204) Require the secretary of the Treasury to mint coins in commemoration of the tercentenary of the birth of Benjamin Franklin. Introduced by Castle, R-Del., on Sept. 30, 2003. House Financial Services discharged. House passed Nov. 17, 2004. Senate passed Dec. 7. President signed Dec. 21, 2004.

PL 108-465 (HR 3242) Ensure an abundant and affordable supply of highly nutritious fruits, vegetables and other specialty crops for American consumers and international markets by enhancing the competitiveness of U.S.-grown specialty crops. Introduced by Ose, R-Calif., on Oct. 2, 2003. House Agriculture reported, amended, Oct. 6, 2004 (H Rept 108-750, Pt. 1). House Ways and Means discharged. House passed, amended, under suspension of the rules, Oct. 7. Senate passed Dec. 7. President signed Dec. 21, 2004.

PL 108-466 (HR 3734) Designate the federal building located at Fifth and Richardson Avenues in Roswell, N.M., the "Joe Skeen Federal Building." Introduced by Wilson, R-N.M., on Jan. 27, 2004. House Transportation and Infrastructure reported July 12 (H Rept 108-596). House passed, under suspension of the rules, Sept. 22. Senate passed Dec. 7. President signed Dec. 21, 2004.

PL 108-467 (HR 3884) Designate the Federal building and United States courthouse located at 615 East Houston Street in San Antonio the "Hipolito F. Garcia Federal Building and United States Courthouse." Introduced by Gonzalez, D-Texas, on March 3, 2004. House Transportation and Infrastructure reported June 21 (H Rept 108-557). House passed, under suspension of the rules, July 21. Senate Environment and Public Works discharged. Senate passed Dec. 7. President signed Dec. 21, 2004.

PL 108-468 (HR 4232) Redesignate the facility of the United States Postal Service located at 4025 Feather Lakes Way in Kingwood, Texas, the "Congressman Jack Fields Post Office." Introduced by Brady, R-Texas, on April 28, 2004. House passed, under suspension of the rules, Oct. 6. Senate passed Dec. 7. President signed Dec. 21, 2004.

PL 108-469 (HR 4324) Amend chapter 84 of title 5, U.S. Code, to provide for federal employees to make elections to make, modify and terminate contributions to the Thrift Savings Fund at any time. Introduced by T. Davis, R-Va., on May 11, 2004. House passed, under

suspension of the rules, amended, Nov. 19. Senate passed Dec. 7. President signed Dec. 21, 2004.

PL 108-470 (HR 4620) Confirm the authority of the secretary of Agriculture to collect approved state commodity assessments on behalf of the state from the proceeds of marketing assistance loans. Introduced by Nethercutt, R-Wash., on June 18, 2004. House passed, under suspension of the rules, amended, Oct. 5. Senate passed Dec. 7. President signed Dec. 21, 2004.

PL 108-471 (HR 4807) Designate the facility of the United States Postal Service located at 140 Sacramento Street in Rio Vista, Calif., the "Adam G. Kinser Post Office Building." Introduced by Ose, R-Calif., on July 9, 2004. House passed, under suspension of the rules, Oct. 6. Senate passed Dec. 7. President signed Dec. 21, 2004.

PL 108-472 (HR 4847) Designate the facility of the United States Postal Service located at 560 Bay Isles Road in Longboat Key, Fla., the "Lieutenant General James V. Edmundson Post Office Building." Introduced by Harris, R-Fla., on July 15, 2004. House passed, under suspension of the rules, Oct. 6. Senate passed Dec. 7. President signed Dec. 21, 2004.

PL 108-473 (HR 4968) Designate the facility of the United States Postal Service located at 25 McHenry Street in Rosine, Ky., the "Bill Monroe Post Office." Introduced by Lewis, R-Ky., on July 22, 2004. House passed, under suspension of the rules, Oct. 6. Senate passed Dec. 7. President signed Dec. 21, 2004.

PL 108-474 (HR 5360) Authorize grants to establish academies for teachers and students of American history and civics. Introduced by Wicker, R-Miss., on Nov. 16, 2004. House passed, under suspension of the rules, amended, Nov. 19. Senate passed Dec. 7. President signed Dec. 21, 2004.

PL 108-475 (HR 5364) Designate the facility of the United States Postal Service located at 5505 Stevens Way in San Diego the "Earl B. Gilliam/Imperial Avenue Post Office Building." Introduced by Filner, D-Calif., on Nov. 16, 2004. House passed, under suspension of the rules, Nov. 17. Senate passed Dec. 7. President signed Dec. 21, 2004.

PL 108-476 (HR 5365) Treat certain arrangements maintained by the YMCA Retirement Fund as church plans for the purposes of certain provisions of the Internal Revenue Code of 1986. Introduced by English, R-Pa., on Nov. 16, 2004. House passed, under suspension of the rules, Nov. 19. Senate passed Dec. 7. President signed Dec. 21, 2004.

PL 108-477 (HR 5370) Designate the facility of the United States Postal Service located at 4985 Moorhead Avenue in Boulder, Colo., the "Donald G. Brotzman Post Office Building." Introduced by Udall, D-Colo., on Nov. 16, 2004. House Government Reform discharged. House passed Nov. 19. Senate passed Dec. 7. President signed Dec. 21, 2004.

PL 108-478 (HR 4829) Designate the facility of the United States Postal Service located at 103 East Kleberg in Kingsville, Texas, the "Irma Rangel Post Office Building." Introduced by Hinojosa, D-Texas, on July 14, 2004. House passed, under suspension of the rules, Oct. 6. Senate passed Dec. 7. President signed Dec. 21, 2004.

PL 108-479 (H J Res 102) Recognize the 60th anniversary of the Battle of Peleliu and the end of Imperial Japanese control of Palau during World War II and urging the Secretary of the Interior to work to protect the historic sites of the Peleliu Battlefield National Historic Landmark and to establish commemorative programs honoring the Americans who fought there. Introduced by Flake, R-Ariz., on Sept. 9, 2004. House passed, under suspension of the rules, Sept. 28. Senate passed Dec. 7. President signed Dec. 21, 2004.

PL 108-480 (HR 2457) Authorize funds for an educational center for the Castillo de San Marcos National Monument. Introduced by MICA, R-Fla., on June 12, 2003. House Resources reported, amended, Sept. 7, 2004 (H Rept 108-639). House passed, under suspension of the rules, Sept. 13. Senate Energy and Natural Resources discharged. Senate passed Dec. 8. President signed Dec. 23, 2004.

PL 108-481 (HR 2619) Provide for the expansion of Kilauea Point National Wildlife Refuge. Introduced by Case, D-Hawaii, on June 26, 2003. House Resources reported, amended, June 3, 2004 (H Rept 108-522). House passed, under suspension of the rules, July 19. Senate Environment and Public Works discharged. Senate passed Dec. 8. President signed Dec. 23, 2004

PL 108-482 (HR 3632) Prevent and punish counterfeiting of copyrighted copies and records. Introduced by Smith, R-Texas, on Nov. 21, 2003. House Judiciary reported, amended, July 13, 2004 (H Rept 108-600). House passed, under suspension of the rules, Sept. 21. Senate Judiciary discharged. Senate passed Dec. 8. President signed Dec. 23, 2004.

PL 108-483 (HR 3785) Authorize the exchange of certain land in the Everglades National Park. Introduced by Diaz-Balart, M., R-Fla., on Feb. 10, 2004. House Resources reported, amended, June 1 (H Rept 108-516). House passed, under suspension of the rules, July 19. Senate passed Dec. 8. President signed Dec. 23, 2004.

PL 108-484 (HR 3818) Amend the Foreign Assistance Act of 1961 to improve the results and accountability of microenterprise development assistance programs. Introduced by Smith, R-N.J., on Feb. 24, 2004. House International Relations reported, amended, April 2 (H Rept 108-459). House passed, amended, Nov. 20. Senate passed Dec. 8. President signed Dec. 23, 2004.

PL 108-485 (HR 4027) Authorize the secretary of Commerce to make available to the University of Miami property under the administrative jurisdiction of the National Oceanic and Atmospheric Administration on Virginia Key, Fla., for use as a Marine Life Science Center. Introduced by Ros-Lehtinen, R-Fla., on March 24, 2004. House Resources reported, amended, Sept. 8 (H Rept 108-665). House passed, under suspension of the rules, Sept. 13. Senate Commerce, Science and Transportation discharged. Senate passed Dec. 8. President signed Dec. 23, 2004.

PL 108-486 (HR 4116) Require the secretary of the Treasury to mint coins celebrating the recovery and restoration of the American bald eagle. Introduced by Jenkins, R-Tenn., on April 1, 2004. House Financial Services discharged. House passed, amended, Dec. 7. Senate passed Dec. 8. President signed Dec. 23, 2004.

PL 108-487 (HR 4548) Authorize appropriations for fiscal 2005 for U.S. intelligence and intelligence-related activities, and for the CIA Retirement and Disability System. Introduced by Goss, R-Fla., on June 14, 2004. House Intelligence reported, amended, June 21 (H Rept 108-558). House passed, amended, June 23. Senate Intelligence discharged. Senate passed, with an amendment, Oct. 11. Conference report filed in the House Dec. 7 (H Rept 108-798). House agreed to

the conference report Dec. 7. Senate agreed to the conference report Dec. 8. President signed Dec. 23, 2004.

PL 108-488 (HR 4569) Provide for the development of a national plan for the control and management of Sudden Oak Death, a tree disease caused by the fungus-like pathogen Phytophthora ramorum. Introduced by Burns, R-Ga., on June 15, 2004. House passed, under suspension of the rules, Oct. 5. Senate passed Dec. 8. President signed Dec. 23, 2004.

PL 108-489 (HR 4657) Amend the Balanced Budget Act of 1997 to improve the administration of federal pension benefit payments for District of Columbia teachers, police officers and fire fighters. Introduced by Davis, T., R-Va., on June 23, 2004. House passed, amended, under suspension of the rules, Sept. 28. Senate passed Dec. 8. President signed Dec. 23, 2004.

PL 108-490 (HR 5204) Amend the Public Health Service Act to modify provisions regarding the determination of the amount of payments for indirect expenses associated with operating approved graduate medical residency training programs. Introduced by Eshoo, D-Calif., on Oct. 4, 2004. House passed, under suspension of the rules, Oct. 6. Senate passed Dec. 8. President signed Dec. 23, 2004.

PL 108-491 (HR 5363) Authorize salary adjustments for justices and judges of the United States for fiscal 2005. Introduced by Sensenbrenner, R-Wis., on Nov. 16, 2004. House passed, under suspension of the rules, Nov. 17. Senate passed Dec. 8. President signed Dec. 23, 2004.

PL 108-492 (HR 5382) Promote the development of the emerging commercial human space flight industry. Introduced by Rohrabacher, R-Calif., on Nov. 18, 2004. House passed, under suspension of the rules, Nov. 20. Senate passed Dec. 8. President signed Dec. 23, 2004.

PL 108-493 (HR 5394) Amend the Internal Revenue Code to modify the taxation of arrow components. Introduced by Ryan, R-Wis., on Nov. 19, 2004. House passed, under suspension of the rules, Dec. 6. Senate passed Dec. 8. President signed Dec. 23, 2004.

PL 108-494 (HR 5419) Facilitate the reallocation of spectrum from government to commercial users, and improve the nation's homeland security, public safety and citizen activated emergency response capabilities through the use of enhanced 911 services. Introduced by Upton, R-Mich., on Nov. 20, 2004. House Energy and Commerce discharged. House passed Nov. 20. Senate passed Dec. 8. President signed Dec. 23, 2004.

PL 108-495 (S 1301) Prohibit video voyeurism at locations under federal jurisdiction. Introduced by DeWine, R-Ohio, on June 19, 2003. Senate Judiciary reported, amended, July 24 (no written report). Senate passed Sept. 25. House Judiciary reported, amended, May 20, 2004 (H Rept 108-504). House passed, under suspension of the rules, Sept. 21. Senate agreed to House amendment, Dec. 7. President signed Dec. 23, 2004.

PL 108-496 (S 2657) Establish programs under which supplemental dental and vision benefits are made available to federal employees, retirees, and their dependents and expand the contracting authority of the Office of Personnel Management. Introduced by Collins, R-Maine, on July 14, 2004. Senate Governmental Affairs reported, amended, Oct. 8 (S Rept 108-393). Senate passed, with an amendment, Nov. 20. House passed, under suspension of the rules, Dec. 6. President signed Dec. 23, 2004.

PL 108-497 (S 2781) Express the sense of Congress regarding the conflict in Darfur, Sudan and authorize assistance to Sudanese refugees in Darfur and eastern Chad. Introduced by Lugar, R-Ind., on Sept. 9, 2004. Senate Foreign Relations discharged. Senate passed, amended, Sept. 23. House passed, with an amendment, under sus-

pension of the rules, Nov. 19. Senate agreed to House amendment, Dec. 7. President signed Dec. 23, 2004.

PL 108-498 (S 2856) Limit the transfer of certain Commodity Credit Corporation funds between conservation programs for technical assistance. Introduced by Cochran, R-Miss., on Sept. 28, 2004. Senate Agriculture, Nutrition and Forestry discharged. Senate passed Oct. 11. House passed, under suspension of the rules, Dec. 6. President signed Dec. 23, 2004.

Index

Index

Boxes, figures, and tables are indicated by b, f, and t after the page number.